1 MONTH OF
FREE
READING

at
www.ForgottenBooks.com

By purchasing this book you are eligible for one month membership to ForgottenBooks.com, giving you unlimited access to our entire collection of over 1,000,000 titles via our web site and mobile apps.

To claim your free month visit:

www.forgottenbooks.com/free918140

ISBN 978-0-265-97548-0
PIBN 10918140

The

Musical Standard,

A NEWSPAPER FOR MUSICIANS,

· PROFESSIONAL AND AMATEUR.

———

VOL. XXIV. NEW SERIES.

JANUARY TO JUNE, 1883.

———

"The powers of music are felt or known by all men."—SIR W. TEMPLE.

———

LONDON:

WILLIAM REEVES: "MUSICAL STANDARD" OFFICE, 185, FLEET STREET.

Price Nine Shillings, bound in cloth.

INDEX TO VOL. XXIV. NEW SERIES.

THE MUSICAL STANDARD

A NEWSPAPER FOR MUSICIANS PROFESSIONAL AND AMATEUR

No. 962. VOL. XXIV. FOURTH SERIES.   SATURDAY, JANUARY 6, 1883.   WEEKLY: PRICE 3D.

Musical Intelligence.

"THE MESSIAH" ON NEW YEAR'S DAY.

Mr. Barnby, conductor of the Royal Albert Hall Choral Society, gave a performance of "The Messiah," on the evening of Monday. The principal soloists were Miss Anna Williams, Mdme. Fassett, Mr. E. Lloyd, and Mr. Santley. Some of the choruses were encored, but only one was repeated : "Unto us a child is born." Mr. Santley declined a *bis* of "Why do the nations," and Miss Williams for the air of Part III., "I know that my Redeemer liveth," where Handel, as in "Let the bright Seraphim," modulates so effectively into his subdominant key. The audience, for a New Year's night, was numerous.

MR. AGUILAR'S PIANOFORTE RECITALS.

The second of these agreeable recitals was held on Wednesday afternoon, before a select and laudably reticent audience. Mr. Aguilar began well, with Beethoven's Sonata in G, Op. 31, No. 1, a remarkably beautiful inspiration of the great master, who is supposed by some *quidnunes* to have "taken off" conventionalities of the modern Italian opera in the *adagio*, where, to speak truthfully, *fioriture* seems to flourish at the expense of idea. The Romeo Finale, so exquisite an inspiration in itself, might force admiration from auditors half asleep, or detain "fashionable females" from their carriages, if only for the beautiful imitation of the leading *motif* in the relative (E) minor.

Mr. Aguilar (to speak for the present of *past* masters") afterwards played a Prelude and Fugue of old Sebastian Bach in G minor, which the ladies much liked.

Thalberg's Sonata in C minor, "Op. 56," requires more than one hearing, if one has not heard it before. With all due respect for the great Austrian pianist, so famous in London between the years 1840 and 1851, I must avow a dislike and a certain dread of him as a *composer*. When he borrows other men's ideas (as in opera), he does little more than show off what is called the "genius" of his own adopted instrument, after the old and effete "semiquaver splitting" fashion. This Sonata in C minor fails to create a craving for more of Thalberg's original composition, but Mr. Aguilar merits many thanks from the musical world for unshelving the dormant text, not necessarily dry, but dusty. The first movement of the sonata, seasoned with some national air, must be further studied, with a view to comprehension. The Scherzo Pastorale, in G minor and major, was admired by the audience. The andante Cantabile in A flat, an agreeable though not striking strain of genuine vocal music, is diluted by the treatment, far too extensive for so slender a subject. The finale, one of Thalberg's fire-eating *bravuras*, relieved by a tuneful "second theme," in B minor, is well worked up, with tremendous *tours de force*, and was thought by "outsiders" with whom I concur, to be the best of all the movements. All said and done, however, let it be admitted that Thalberg's *forte* was not invention. He lived on the hackneyed *motif* of modern Italian opera ; and at a concert of the Philharmonic Society in 1842, his reception, however flattering on the whole, was "under protest."

Mr. Aguilar, at all events, must be thanked for thus ably illustrating a sonata that ought not to be forgotten, even if too difficult for ordinary pianists. The extraordinary ones may not condescend to take it up, and I don't think they will.

Mr. Aguilar played, in the course of the recital, several fugitive pieces, which were much admired. His own "Cheristana," a romantic and dramatic piece in F sharp minor and major, strikes one as a well-told story of tragical horrors, relieved by sunshiny glimpses of fairyland. The "Overture Scherzo" in E flat has been recently appraised.

The two short solos, "Contented" in A, and "Esmeralda" in D flat, always at these agreeable receptions flutter the gentle and somewhat *too passive* "doves of Corioli." The scheme was completed with two excerpts from the 5th Book of the "Lieder ohne Worte" (Nos. 1 and 2 in G and B flat) ; and Mr. Aguilar's own *esquisses*, short but sweet, viz., "Warning Day" in F, and "Away," a contradictory melodie in C, seeing that the audience decline to go *away*, and always want a *repetition*.

WATFORD.

During the evening service at St. Matthew's Church on St. John's Day, the first part of the "Messiah" was given by the Church Oratorio Society, which is comprised of the leading amateurs of Watford, Bushey, Rickmansworth, Harrow, Pinner, The Langleys, and other places in the vicinity. There was a very large congregation, who must have enjoyed the excellent performance of Handel's greatest work.

The soprano solos were safe in the hands of Miss Alice Brooks, who possesses all the qualities of voice and style which oratorio requires. Thus the manner in which the recitatives following the pastoral symphony were declaimed, and the devotional feeling imparted to "Come unto Him," were alike commendable, while "Rejoice greatly" was distinguished for its fervour and brilliant vocalization. Miss Barker, of Rickmansworth, was entrusted with the airs "O thou that tellest" and "He shall feed his flock," which were given with much sweetness. The recitative "Comfort ye" and the air "Every Valley" were carefully rendered by an amateur, and Mr. Charles Healey (one of the most successful students at the School of Music) gave the recitative "Thus saith the Lord," and the air "But who may abide," with great power and finish. The Rev. T. M. Everett, who also conducted, in the absence of Mr. J. Farmer, sang "The people that walked in darkness" with effect. With so fine a body of vocalists, most of whom were perfectly at home in their work, the choruses could not fail to receive justice. All the parts came out well, especially the alto. The rendering of "For unto us a child is born," and "Hallelujah," which terminated the selection, was particularly meritorious. Mr. James Turpin presided at the organ with his usual ability, his playing of the overture and the Pastoral Symphony being most impressive.—*The Watford Observer.*

NEWCASTLE-ON-TYNE.

(From our Own Correspondent.)

Christmas, with its social festivities and enjoyments, has brought a welcome lull in the great activity of our musical season. The time-honoured and indispensable performance of "The Messiah" took place in the Town Hall, on December the 26th, and the usual invitation concerts were given by our Local Amateur Vocal Societies shortly before Christmas.

Mr. Henry Holmes will lead the string quartets at the next Chamber Concert, on January 16th, at the Assembly Rooms ; and, for the last concert of the series, engagements are pending with Herr Joachim, Signor Piatti, and Miss Agnes Zimmermann.

Mr. Rea's second Subscription Concert will take place on January 23rd. The programme is a miscellaneous one. Mdme. Trebelli, Mons. Musin, Herr Ganz (pianoforte), etc., will appear as soloists. Mr. Rea's choir will perform part-songs under Mr. Rea's conductorship.

At Mr. Charles Hallé's third Orchestral Concert, in February, the following instrumental items will be performed :—Overture, "Der Freischütz" (Weber) ; "The Unfinished," Symphony B minor (Schubert) ; overture, "Leonora" (Beethoven) ; overture, "Ruy Blas" (Mendelssohn) ; and Entr'act and Ballet (Schubert). Mr. Hallé will appear as pianist in Beethoven's pianoforte Concerto, in G major, "Nocturne" in G, and "Polonaise" in A flat, by Chopin.

Dr. Armes's oratorio, "St. John the Evangelist," was excellently performed at a concert in the Town Hall, on December 22nd. The talented composer wielded the bâton, and Mr. Albion Alderson presided at the organ. The choruses were performed by amateur singers, the soloists being Mdmes. Watford and Lewis, Mr. Welch and Mr. John Nutton. A collection was made in aid of the Royal College was taken during the interval. The second part of the programme contained Macfarren's "Christmas," which was also well performed on all hands.

Miss F. Hipwell, Mr. Harper Kearton, and Mr. Grice were the soloists at the people's concert, on December 30th. As the programmes for these concerts have in general contained too many ballads and royalty songs, I am pleased to note that "The Messiah" will be given at the concert this week.

At present the pantomimes reign supremely at our two theatres. As being an unusual thing, I ought to mention that "Blue Beard," performed at the Tyne Theatre, has been wedded to exceptional good and suitable music, by Mr. Leggatt, the musical director of the establishment.

H. W.

OSWESTRY.

The Oswestry annual musical and literary festival was held at the Powis Hall, Oswestry, on January 1st. The morning proceedings opened with an address from the President, Major Barnes, after which the programme was gone through, in which several competitions took place. Among those of interest were the choral competitions of juvenile choirs of not more than twenty voices, the prize being won by Oswestry. The choral competition "Then round about the starry throne" was won by the Oswestry Harmonic Society. At night the second programme was gone through. Mr. Henry Leslie presided. Several competitions were given, among the principal being "The Reapers' Chorus," won by the Lodge Choir. The event of the day was a great choral competition for a prize of £25 and a silver medal to the conductor. The piece was "Thanks be to God," from "Elijah," for choirs of not less than forty voices, and was won by the Lodge and Brony-garth Choir, conducted by H. M. Hughes, Oswestry.

HERR POZNANSKI AND MR. WM. CARTER'S CHAMBER CONCERTS.

The third and last concert was held in Kensington Gardens Square, at the Blüthner Rooms on December 20th. The programme included a sonata of Haydn for piano and violin and a duet of Rubinstein for the same instruments, in A minor. Mr. Carter played some of the "Lieder ohne Worte." Mr. Pomanski's tour in the provinces seems to have been brilliantly successful. At Oxford a short time ago, when interpreting the violin part of the "Kreutzer" sonata, the first string broke a few bars from the end, when Mr. Poznanski, instead of "leading" in the lower octave, pluckily played the notes (as written) on the second, or A string, which of course he had to "stop" accordingly. The "Rhapsodie Hongroise" of Hanser made a great sensation. The local press of Oxford, Cambridge, Liverpool, Birmingham, Plymouth, Norwich, and Edinburgh are loud in unqualified praise of M. Poznanski. A Huddersfield paper appreciates his avoidance of "gymnastic flights," and the faithful, or strictly objective reproduction of his composers' texts. His bowing is eulogized as smooth and easy, at the same time powerful, and the tone produced is rich and full.

DR. SULLIVAN'S "IOLANTHE."

The first number of a new series of *The Theatre*, edited by Mr. Clement Scott, contains admirable photographs of Mrs. Beatty-Beere and Mr. Wilson Barrett, and some interesting articles, including an appreciative criticism on "Iolanthe" by Mr. Bentley-Kingston, in which he thus speaks of the music :—"I do not hesitate to say that the music of 'Iolanthe' is Dr. Sullivan's *chef-d'œuvre*. The quality throughout is more even, and maintained at a higher standard, than in any of his earlier works, each one of which has successively exhibited a marked advance upon its precursor. In fitting notes to words so exactly that the 'book' and its setting appears to be one and indivisible, our gifted countryman is without a rival in Europe, now that Offenbach is no more. His vein of melody seems inexhaustible, and in constructive skill he can hold his own with any contemporary composer. Increase of years has brought him augmented geniality of humour and grace of expression. His musical quips and cranks are every whit as effective as Mr. Gilbert's literary jests ; and to be instrumentally funny, without lapsing into vulgarity, is one of the most difficult feats in composition. 'Iolanthe' has manifestly been a labour of love. From beginning to end it does not contain one ugly or even wearisome musical number. The overture epitomises the opera very agreeably, and is orchestrated with remarkable ability. As a work 'Iolanthe' is of greater musical importance than 'Patience.' Its tunes, however, are fewer in number, and perhaps a thought less catching in character than those of 'Bunthorne's Bride'; but in every respect it sustains Dr. Sullivan's reputation as the most spontaneous, fertile and scholarly composer of comic opera this country has ever produced."

On New Year's Day two young and deservedly recognised artists, Miss Julia Gayford and Mr. Packard were married. They are leading members of the Carl Rosa Company.

LEEDS.

The Leeds Choral Society gave a performance of the "Messiah" in Leeds Town Hall on Tuesday evening, Dec. 26th, this being the third in the same building within the space of one week, but the fact that it was Boxing Day, and that the price of admission was reduced, brought together a very large audience. Miss Bessie Holt, who was, we believe, new to Leeds, sang the soprano music with great taste and refinement. She possesses a fine voice of excellent quality, and her rendering of the recit. "There were Shepherds" at once produced a favourable impression, which was fully sustained throughout. In the lovely air, "I know that my Redeemer liveth," she was also very successful. The contralto music was allotted to Miss A. Clarke, of whom we have had occasion lately to speak in terms of high praise, and her delivery of the recit. "Behold a Virgin," and the air "O Thou that tellest" was marked by true feeling and expression. Mr. R. Sutchliffe, tenor, late of the York Cathedral, was successful in the music that fell to his share. Mr. E. Jackson, bass, Lincoln Cathedral, sang in splendid style, some of his airs being loudly applauded. The careful training of the chorus under their energetic conductor, Dr. Creser, was shown in the admirable manner in which the various choral numbers were rendered, and special mention must be made of the fine choruses, "For unto us," "Lift up your Heads," the sublime "Hallelujah Chorus," and the impressive "Worthy is the Lamb." Mr. Acomb was leader of the band, Mr. A. Benton rendered valuable assistance at the organ, and Dr. Creser conducted in his usual efficient style.

Dr. Spark's organ recitals in the Town Hall are now resumed on Tuesday afternoons and Saturday evenings.

LIVERPOOL.

(From our Own Correspondent.)

JAN. 2.

The Carl Rosa Opera Company opened their season at the Court Theatre, on Christmas Day, by a sacred concert, the first part of which comprised Rossini's "Stabat Mater," the second part being miscellaneous. The principal artists in Rossini's work were Mdme. Marie Roze, Miss Josephine Yorke, Mr. Barton McGuckin, Mr. Ludwig, and Mr. Pope. In the second part appeared in addition to the above, Miss Perry, Mr. Ben Davies, Mr. Turner, Mr. Harley, and Mr. Crotty. Mr. Goosens conducted the "Stabat Mater," and Mr. Pew the second, miscellaneous part. Mr. James J. Monk presided at the harmonium, and the band and chorus were the ordinary opera orchestral players and singers. The only novelty during the week was the production in English of Verdi's "Rigoletto," a very good performance. The other operas given have really nothing new, particularly in the casts, to commend them. Old favourites are greatly missed, and those replacing them are not altogether suitable. The "Bohemian Girl," "Mignon," "La Dame Blanche," "Maritana," "Lucrezia Borgia," and "Fidelio," have filled up the intervening nights. The performances have been well attended, and success has attended each representation. There have been several performances of Handel's "Messiah," but, really, what can one say about these performances? Would it not be an advantage if the "Messiah" could shelved for a time? Why cannot we have a chance of hearing other oratorios not so well known? There are oratorios lying by which it would be for the good and interest of art to bring before the public. Why are not these works produced? There are works by living English musicians well worthy of being performed ; works of which no country would be ashamed to own the composers, and yet we never hear of these works being performed. Is there anything wrong with English musical art? Who is to blame? Perhaps the £ s. d. is the arbitrator of these matters! A great deal is talked about English musical art, but very little is done. Is there no Englishman able to write a sacred musical drama, or are we so fettered to German work that English music will not go down? I leave the elucidation of these queries and remarks to abler hands, and candidly hope that some lucid explanations will be given by men capable of grasping the subject, and at the same time fearlessly attack the evil.   J. J. M.

WOLVERHAMPTON.

The second of the Wolverhampton Choral Society's fifteenth series of concerts took place at the Agricultural Hall recently, when a performance of Handel's "Messiah" was given. The principal artists engaged were Miss Clara Samuel, soprano ; Miss Emilie Lloyd, contralto ; Mr. Harper-Kearton, tenor ; and Signor Foli, bass ; solo trumpet, Mr. F. H. McGrath. The chorus and band numbered 300, under the *bâton* of Dr. C. S. Heap. The room, was densely packed in every part. The choruses throughout were given with great precision and accuracy, and showed that the choir were well versed in their work. The voices were evenly balanced, and the general effect was excellent. The three choruses most noticeable were "All we like sheep," "Hallelujah," and and the final chorus and fugue, "Worthy is the Lamb, Amen." The band, under the leadership of Mr. Abbott, played with great judgment and skill, and in no part was it unduly prominent. Great praise is due to Dr. C. S. Heap for his tact and skill as conductor.

GLASGOW.

The re-appearance of Herr Joseph Joachim at the third Subscription Concert of the Choral Union, after a prolonged absence, was marked by a most cordial reception. His magnificent performance was intently listened to, and the broad, massive, and technically perfect style of his playing was highly appreciated. He played Beethoven's Concerto in D, Op. 61 ; Romance from the "Hungarian" Concerto (Joachim) ; Preludium and Gavotte in E (Bach) ; and a Capriccio in E (Paganini). The orchestra under Mr. Manns performed a number of works by Cherubini, Schubert, Sullivan, and Mendelssohn, the symphony being Mozart's G minor.

The annual performance of the "Messiah" was given on January 1, the principal vocalists being Miss Carlotta Elliot, Mdme. Patey, Mr. Harper Kearton, and Mr. Egbert Roberts. The whole work was rendered with every degree of taste. The next concert will be given on Jan. 4.
J. B.

foreign Musical Intelligence.

The Teatro Regio of Turin opened with Wagner's "Rienzi," the Italian version being by Boito.

The inauguration of Spohr's monument at Cassel, is announced for April 25th.

Godefroid, the well known harpist, has written a new opera, in five acts, called "The Daughter of Saul."

A comic opera, in three acts, called "Joli Gille" has been written by M. Poise for the Paris Opéra Comique.

The St. Louis U.S. papers say good things of the organ playing of Mr. E. M. Bowman, A.C.O., of that town.

One of the novelties in the way of speculative companies is a "Voice Insurance Company" in Paris.

M. Jules Vieuxtemps, youngest brother of the distinguished violinist, died suddenly the other day in Paris.

A new buffo opera, "La Mille et deuxième Nuit," music by M. Poujade, is to be produced shortly at Rheims.

The Criterion (St. Louis, U. S.) says that the philanthropist Mr. Reuben Spring, has recently given another munificent gift to the College of Music, Cincinnati, an institution already well supported.

Schumann's opera, "Genevieve," was somewhat coldly received on its first production in Rotterdam recently, notwithstanding the undoubted beauties of the score. "Genevieve" is the only opera Schumann ever wrote.

Contrary to general anticipation, there will be no Italian opera at Nice this season. Signor Vianesi, who had organised his company, has renounced the project, and set out for Barcelona.

Some interesting concerts have been given in Florence, which included performances of some of Mozart's and Beethoven's chamber music, and Rubinstein's Sonata in D for violoncello and pianoforte, Schumann's Symphony in B flat, Bazzini's "Saul," and Beethoven's "Coriolanus" overture.

Délibes' "Jean di Nivelles" has not it appears been a great success in Brussels, chiefly through the fault of a heavy libretto. The music is indeed described as graceful and elegant, and at times is effectively orchestrated.

The Italian papers speak well of a new five act opera entitled "Flora Macdonald," which was recently produced in Bologna. The composer, John Urich, a nephew of Karl Vogt, is a native of Trinidad in the West Indies.

The *Gazetta Provinciale* notes at length the assumption of the office of Chapel Master at the Basilica of S. Maria Maggiore by Ponchielli, who it is believed will maintain "the splendid musical traditions" of that church.

It is stated that Michot, the tenor who created the part of Vasco da Gama in Verdi's "Africaine," in Paris, and sang with success in London, is now reduced to singing at a second-rate café-concert on the Boulevards. *Sic transit !*

Mr. Cowen's "Scandinavian" symphony has been given with success at Aix-la-Chapelle, on December 21st. The same work has been also performed by Dr. Damrosch's orchestra at Toronto, creating an impression of a most favourable kind.

The annual Advent service, including the singing of the "Messiah" at St. John's, Ealing Dean, took place on December 20th. The vicar, the Rev. Julius Summerhayes, conducted. Mr. E. H. Turpin was the organist. Among the soloists were Miss Jessie Jones and Mr. Forrington.

The long and spirited contest between Mr. Gye and Mr. Abbey to secure the management of the new Opera House, New York, ended, the other day, in the victory of Mr. Abbey, who signed the contract for a year's lease of the house, to be opened on October 22nd with Nilsson, Valleria, Campanini, Del Puente, and other artists not yet secured. The stage of the new house will be the largest in America. Mr. Gye and Mr. Mapleson claim Mdme. Nilsson under her contract to sing with them. Signor Campanini's contract binds him to sing for ten nights per month for seven months, at a thousand dollars a night.

GREAT SINGERS AND GREAT SONGS.

In an article in *Musical People,* by C. W. Sykes, on "The Golden Age of Song," the writer points out that the great songs have been greatly sung, and will ever continue to be the study of the finest singers. In giving his operatic experience as an American, Mr. Sykes says :—

No singer ever approached Jenny Lind in "I know that my Redeemer!" but she could not compare with Sontag in the Prayer from "Freischütz." Sontag was the best Amina ever heard; but Albani's singing of "Ah non credea" and "Ah non giunge" was infinitely more soulful and brilliant. Sontag's "Roberto, toi qui j'aime" was never approached by any other singer. Parodi could sing "Casta Diva" as well as Jenny Lind, and Lind never could sing Malibran's "Rataplan" as Parodi did, nor "Jerusalem, thou that'stonest the prophets" ("St. Paul"). Three great singers have sung for us, "O luce di quest anima" —Lind, Sontag, and Parepa—but Parepa was greatest in that song. Gerster, Cary, Vietti, Proch, and Albani have sung "It is better to laugh than be sighing," but after Vietti only Albani is to be thought of. It was with her the most unctuous piece of vocalization ever heard in America. The most tremendous effect ever seen on the American opera stage was Grisi's curse of Pollio in "Norma," and next to that, Adelaide Phillips as Azucena in "Trovatore" has perhaps made people's blood run cold more than any other singer. Between Bosio and Nilsson lies the palm for "Lucia." Bosio was the most refined, but Nilsson the most pathetic, perhaps. Kellogg has shone in "L'Etoile du Nord" with unequalled excellence, and in "Mignon" as Philena has never been surpassed. Of male singers, Salvi, Mario, and Campanini are the three great tenors. Salvi was the superior of Mario in physique, power, and manliness, and could sing "Fra pico a me" ("Lucia "), and "Spirito Gentil" better than Mario, but the latter could occasionally do a delicate thing incomparably, and was unapproachable in tender scenes. Campanini is more like Salvi than like Mario, but not as great a singer as either. Bodiali, Amodio, and Del Puente are the three best baritones we have ever heard here. Carl Formes, Marini, and Lusini were great bassos ; Formes having the greatest volume ever known, and Lusini with a grand voice having phenomenal executive facility.

Organ News.

LIVERPOOL.

Subjoined are the programmes of organ recitals given by Mr. W. T. Best, in St. George's Hall, on the undermentioned dates :—

THURSDAY EVENING, DEC. 28th.

Concerto in F major	Handel.
Serenade, " Mira la bianca Luna "	Rossini.
March in F sharp minor (Third Symphony)	Widor.
Prelude and Fugue in C major	Bach.
Pastoral Chorus, " L'Adieu des Bergers " (" L'Enfance du Christ ")	Berlioz.
Largo e Allegro maestoso in G major	Best.

SATURDAY AFTERNOON, DEC. 30th.

Festal March	Best.
Air in D (Overture to " Ariadne,") Final chorus (" Scipione ")	Handel.
Choral Song and Fugue on a Theme by Travers	Wesley.
Allegretto Villereccio	Fumagalli.
Marcia Religiosa	Perelli.
Overture (" L'Ombra ")	Flotow.

SATURDAY EVENING, DEC. 30th.

Overture (" Henry VIIIth ")	Hatton.
Air, " On wings of music "	Mendelssohn.
Introduction and Fugue in D major	Mozart.
Marche Religieuse (" Procession du S. Sacrement ")	Chauvet.
Concert Fantasia on Rode's air	Best.
The Norwegian National Hymn	Hofmann.

WARE.

Annexed is the programme of an organ recital given in the parish church, by Mr. James L. Gregory, A.Mus., A.C.O., on Sunday, Dec. 24th :—

Pastoral Symphony (" Messiah ")	Handel.
" Gloria in Excelsis " (" Twelfth Mass ")	Mozart.
" Quem vidistis pastores ! "	Best.
Offertoire sur deux Noëls	Guilmant.
Air, " My heart ever faithful "	Bach.
Christmas March	Merkel.

Mr. Gregory gave the following selection after evensong on Sunday, Dec. 31st :—

" Evening Prayer "	Smart.
Romanza with chorale	Stark.
Melody in A flat	Guilmant.
Festal March	Calkin.

BOLTON.

An organ recital was given in the Albert Hall, by Mr. Wm. Mullineux, F.C.O., on Saturday, Dec. 30th. The following was the programme :—

Overture in F minor	Morandi.
Andante Cantabile in E major	Dearle.
Glee, " Chough and Crow "	Bishop.
Fantasia in F major	Best.
Gavotte in E minor, " Le Tambourin "	Rameau.
Gavotte in F major	Martini.
Old French Gavotte in C minor	
" Ave Maria "	Schubert.
Marche Solennelle, Op. 204	Ketterer.

At the opening of the new organ (erected by Messrs. Forster & Andrews) in St. George the Martyr Church, Daubhill, on Thursday, Dec. 21st, Mr. William Mullineux, F.C.O., performed :—

Coronation March (" Le Prophète ")	Meyerbeer.
Offertoire sur deux Noëls, No. 1	Guilmant.
Paraphrase on " Gloria Giel "	Be-t.
Wienachtspastorale, Op. 56	Merkel.
Toccata con Fuga in D minor	Bach.
Air with variations	Wély.
Choruses, " For unto us," " Hallelujah "	Handel.

PRESTON.

Subjoined are the programmes of organ recitals given in the new Public Hall, by Mr. James Tomlinson, on Saturday, Dec. 30th :—

AFTERNOON PROGRAMME.

Overture in F minor	Morandi.
Adagio in E	Merkel.
March	Wély.
Andante (Sonata in B flat)	Mendelssohn.
Chorus, " I will sing " (" Israel in Egypt ")	Handel.
Overture (" Othello ")	Rossini.

EVENING PROGRAMME.

Overture (" Samson ")	Handel.
Prelude and Fugue in C major	Bach.
Air (" Faust ")	Gounod.
Minuetto	Calkin.
Marche Nuptiale	Gounod.
Overture (" La Gazza Ladra ")	Rossini.

YORKSHIRE.

Mr. W. Clough gave a recital in the Wesleyan Chapel, Dunholme, on Thursday, Dec. 28. His programme included :—

Concerto in B flat major, No. 2	Handel.
Andante maestoso—Allegro—Adagio—Allegro ma non presto.	
Toccata et Fuga in D minor	Bach.
Overture (" Jubilee ")	Weber.

The choir of the chapel sang several anthems very effectively.

WATERLOO ROAD.

Subjoined is the programme of an organ recital given on Thursday, Dec. 21st, at St. John's Church, by Mr. George E. Blunden :—

Sonata	Gladstone.
Andante (Symphony in E flat)	Haydn.
Prelude and Fugue in A minor	Bach.
Caprice in B flat	Guilmant.
March (" Ahab ")	Arnold.
Air with variations	Best.
Con moto moderato, en forme d'Ouverture	Smart.

BRISTOL.

An organ recital was given by Mr. J. W. Lawson, in the Grammar School, on Saturday, Dec. 16th, when he played the following :—

Overture (" Occasional ")	Handel.
Air and variations	Hesse.
Adagio (Quartet in G minor)	Spohr.
Grand Chorus	Guilmant.
Bourrée in B minor	Bach.
Meditation (arr. by J. W. Lawson)	Raff.
Allegretto (" Lobgesang ")	Mendelssohn.
Gavotte	Reh.
Allegro Pomposo	Smart.

PEEBLES.

The following is the specification of an organ erected by Messrs. Brindley & Foster, of Sheffield, in S. Peter's (Episcopal) Church :—

GREAT ORGAN. CC TO G.

1. Open Diapason	8 ft.	4. Harmonic Flute	8 ft.
2. Hohl Flöte	8 „	5. Spare slide.	
3. Dulciana	8 „		

SWELL ORGAN. CC TO G.

6. Violin Diapason	8 ft.	9. Oboe	8 ft.
7. Lieblich Gedact	8 „	10. Spare slide.	
8. Salicet	4 „		

PEDAL ORGAN. CCC TO F.

11. Sub Bass	16 ft.	12. Flute Bass	8 ft.

COUPLERS.

13. Swell Super Octave.	15. Swell to Pedal.
14. Swell to Great.	15. Great to Pedal.

Two Composition Pedals.

WINDSOR.

The old organ of St. George's Chapel, which included choir, swell, and great organ arrangements, is being remodelled and altered from an F to a C instrument. The new arrangement, which is being carried out by Messrs. Gray & Davison, will comprise choir, swell, great, and solo organ. The pipes and old action have been removed from the case in the gallery, and some time must necessarily elapse before the instrument will be ready for use. This welcome advance may be hailed as the result of Mr. Walter Parratt's recent appointment as organist of St. George's Chapel Royal. That gentleman spoke of the new organ scheme at a recent meeting of highly interested members of the College of Organists. A model of the stops, etc., was exhibited upon the same occasion, and a lecture given by Mr. Bosanquet, of Oxford. The rebuilding of the instrument is in good and skilled hands, and the Royal Chapel will at last have a worthy organ.

Mr. William Charles Box, organist of St. John's Church, Worcester, and Associate of the College of Organists, London, has been elected honorary organist to the Worcester Musical Society.

AN AMUSING ORGAN SPECIFICATION.

Though far-fetched and not very brilliant as a specimen of acute American wit, the following, obligingly placed in our hands, may amuse, as a satire on the schemes of monster organs :—

1776   E—PLURIBUS—ORGANUS.   1876

GRAND ORGAN
FOR THE
ENHARMONIC TEMPLE, SIAM.
MANUFACTURED ESPECIALLY FOR THIS OCCASION BY THE
Great North American Organ and Accordian Co. (Limited).

And which can now be seen and heard (by the aid of a smoked glass) in its position, OVER THE LEFT *of the Grand Gallery of the other side of the Great Hall, of the*
CENTENNIAL BUILDINGS.
(SEE GUIDE BOOK.)

Height of Case, with flag pole, 210 feet. Height of Case, without flag pole, something less.
Width of Case, from the front to the back door, 18 feet 6 inches.
Manual Compass, 7 by 9. Pedal Compass, 9 by 7. Latitude 7 octaves. Longitude, once a month.

Motors :—Steam, Gas, Windmill, Hydropathy.

The key boards are numerously supplied with extra sharps and flats, for the sake of the music of the future and the noise to come.

GREAT ORGAN.

Open Diapason (front pipes)	2 feet.
Shut Diapason (back pipes)	2 feet and a half.
Gamboge (metal)	6 ft.
Bella-Donna	5 ft. 10.
Double-Header	10 ft. 5.
Whistle (pure tin)	32 ft.
Octave and a half	16 ft.
Harts Horn (very strong)	18 inches.
Twelfth (Tweedle-dum)	2 ft.
Fifteenth (Tweedle-dee)	4 ft.
Nineteenth (Something new)	3 ft.
Cough Mixture	Rank poison.
Jews' Harp	5 ranks.
Fish Horn	2 ranks.
Penny Trumpet	2 ft.
Calliope	16 ft.
Blunderbuss (" Mine ancient Pistol ")	12 o'clock.
Free Lunch	

* Wagner's Centennial March and Drawing Room Cars attached to every train, and each Manual supplied with hot and cold water and all modern improvements.

A most ingenious bit of electric machinery is Roostervelt's arrangement for fugue playing ; by a very simple contrivance (which is applied to all the levers, and which is always in order), any organist of proper calibre can play any fugue by any composer, at any time. (Sundays excepted.) Further explanation impossible.

SWELL. (English.)

Bourbon (very old)	2 gallons.
Open Sesame (Sheet Iron)	7 ft.
Saleratus	2 ft.
Quinine (gelatine coated)	3 grains.
Tea Pot	3 ranks.
Flue Angelique (Stovepipe on the chimney)	
Flute Spasmodique (Each pipe speaks its other octave)	3 ft.
Flute (another kind)	2 or 3 ft.
Fiddle-de-dee	on a string.
Kangaroo	fore feet and hind legs.
Vial di Laudanum..	15 cts.
Old Boy	2 ft.
Cornocopia	3 ft.
Rooster	4 ft.
Awfulclide	32 ft.
*Nux Vomica de Friedbugs	

* Copied from the Original Jacob's by a man who was there. (Humanity itself could not produce such an unearthly tone as this truly remarkable stop—not even a goat.)

N.B.—This Swell is most remarkable, having window-blinds, three sets of shades, and a Mansard roof, also a tin spout.

CHOIR ORGAN.

Soprano (brass)	2 ft.
Contralto (wooden)	3 ft.
Tenoroon (metal)	4 ft.
Bassoon (very heavy)	8 ft.
Raw Flute (hard pan)	5 ft.
Wild Flute (papier mache)	7 ft.
Flute (by way of variety)..	8 ft.
Catarrh	2 ft.
Squint	4 ranks.
Pickerel (large scale)	3 pounds.

SOLO ORGAN.

Melodian (Mediæval and squeaky)	2 ft.
Bagpipe (Scotch Scale)	16 ft.
Cat-a-waul (Maltese)	4 ft.
Triangle	3 ft.
Fish Harmonica (free Reed)	4 ft.
Vox Angelica	2 ft.
Brass Band (extra wind—Gilmore)	5 ranks.
Nightmare	1 A.M.
Grand Centennial Tuba Miraculous (Nitro-glycerine)	
Bells-ze-bub (brass)	

(*A Crinoline with capacity for 58 Belles*).
This wonderful Solo Organ is all on extra wind (too much) and is connected to the bellows blower by a new Centennial ashmatic action. (Patent applied for 1976).

PEDAL ORGAN.

Seven League Boots (pegged)	2 ft.
Steam Elevator	32 ft.
Organist	16 ft.
Kaleidoscope	17 ft.
Monitor	21 ft.
Flute (pure zinc)	2 ft.
Earthquake	40 ranks.
Overshoes (and umbrella)	for T 2 ft.
Flute (one more)	2 ranks.
Pipes (mixed)	2 ranks.

MECHANICAL STOPS.

Crank—Boy to turn it — Boiler—Burglar Alarm—Mousetrap—Spittoon (electric)—Swell to Great—Balance Swell on Tightrope—Great Swell (English)—Four in Hand—Pedals and Organist.

COMBINATION PEDALS.

No. 1.—Draws full Organ.	No. 3.—Draws the Salaries.
No. 2.—Rehearses the Choir.	No. 4.—Anything you like.

Total Number of Pipes	2,000,000.
Total Number of Stops	2,000,000.
Total Cost	2,000,000.

The Roostervelt Rheumatic Action is applied to all the levers, and all the levers are applied to the Roostervelt Rheumatic Action. (Patent applied for 1976.)

☞   ADMISSION, TWENTY-FIVE CENTS.   ☜

MUSIC IN JAPAN.

The report of Mr. Luther Mason's experiences in Japan as recorded in *Tonic Sol-Fa Reporter* is of interest, as the following extracts will show. Mr. Mason was for three years director of the imperial conservatory of music at Tokio :—

In Japan, Mr. Mason's work has been most interesting. He has been judicious in his reforms, saying nothing against the Japanese scale and instruments. The Japanese scale has no 4th and 7th, and the 3rd and 6th are sung and played sharp, as if partly to fill up the gap left. There is also a great deal of portamento in both playing and singing. The flutes have large holes, and the player can raise or lower a note by his finger. Thus the whole effect is indecisive. The Japanese have no notion of harmony, except some slight idea of accompanying in 5ths and and 4ths, and as a natural consequence they have no tonality or key. Some of their music is minor, the 2nd and 6th of the minor scale being omitted. As to singing, this is chiefly a kind of recitative used by players, who sing about what they are going to play. There is also another kind, in which men and women join, singing in (absolute) unison.

In this sort of singing the aim of the women is to sing as low as possible, and of the men to sing as high as possible. The way the women are trained is this. An old hag will take a company of young girls out on a damp and cold night. They sit on a bridge, or by a roadside, until they have caught cold. Then, when they are sufficiently hoarse, perhaps next day, the training begins, the younger ones imitating the croak of their preceptress. They sing violently—after the fashion recommended by the Rev. Mr Sandilands—and it is considered a good sign if they spit blood. This process—getting hoarse and singing loudly—is repeated until the necessary depth of voice is attained ; the women then can reach C on the second space of the bass clef. The men work in the opposite direction and strain their chest registers up to G and A. The united result is not lovely.

Mr. Mason, when he got to Japan, began in the kindergarten school, attended by the children of noblemen. He introduced " Bonny Doon," " Auld lang syne," " There is a happy land, " and other pentatonic melodies, which of course the Japanese children readily sang. The 4th and 7th had afterwards to be taught. The 7th gave special trouble, as there was a strong tendency to sing it half a tone flat. When it was sung rightly, then the *doh* above was often given half a tone too sharp.

The Court musicians had meanwhile watched Mr. Mason's doings and they came to him enquiring for the reason of the difference between their scale and that of Europe. They asked Mr. Mason which was the best scale. He declined to express an opinion, but advised them to get the Professor of Physics at the University (a German) to give them a lecture on the ratios and general structure of the European scale, so that they might draw their own conclusions. The lecture duly came off, and it fully satisfied the Court musicians. Two military bands, under European bandmasters (a Frenchman and a Russian) were already in existence, and a full orchestra was at once established. This is under Mr. Mason's charge, and he has compiled elementary manuals for the violin, viola, 'cello, and double bass for its use. Mr. Mason does not know more than a few words of the language, and works always through interpreters.

Mr. Mason has also compiled an elementary singing manual for the primary schools, but has not encouraged its circulation, because he sees that teachers, not books, are the first requisite in Japan. If this book were circulated it would be misused ; its use is to stimulate, instead of preceding trained teachers. Mr. Mason has concentrated his efforts upon the Normal School for teachers, at Tokio, and hopes, in a few years, to send large numbers of qualified teachers to all parts of the land. His method of working shows him to be a true educationist.

Reviews.

Welcome to Our Festival. By E. J. Hopkins. (Stanley Lucas, Weber & Co.).—A beautiful and artistic contribution to the stores of part music for ladies or boys' voices, set in three parts, and sure to find much favour.

The Better World, song. By Michael Bergson. (Stanley Lucas, Weber & Co.).—An artistic production with accompaniments, admirably written for violin, harmonium, and pianoforte.

Not Once or Twice, song. By F. Neale. (Duncan Davison).—A taking melody well laid out.

In the Haven, song. By H. Croft Hiller. (Duncan Davison).—Has a graceful, though at times almost too ornate, melody. Will make an effective concert song.

The Awakening, song. By H. J. Stark. (A. Cox).—An original and very artistic song.

The Wood Nymphs' Revel. By R. A. Klitz. (Ashdown).—A clever and very effective pianoforte solo, with brilliant and well laid out sentences.

Mazurka. By Gordon Saunders. (Novello & Co.).—A charming and brilliant pianoforte piece, with fresh ideas well treated.

The Sergeant-Drummer's March. By Michael Watson. (B. Williams).—A cleverly written and very effective piece of the military order for pianoforte.

Welcome, valse fantastique. By G. Tartaglione. (A. Hays, Bond Street).—A showy and effective pianoforte solo, with original and tuneful themes.

There is one I can't forget. By Mrs. H. Scobell ; and, *Fading Flowers*, by same composer. (Weekes & Co).—Two songs, having graceful thoughts ; the first, which is the less ambitious, is the better and more singable of the two.

Cynthia. By G. H. Smith. (Banks, York).—Called a dance measure by the composer ; an effective and musicianly piece of the gavotte kind.

Au Printemps. By Emile Waldteufel. (Metzler and Co.).—A graceful and attractive set of waltzes by a well-known writer.

Valse Vénitienne. By Waldteufel. (Metzler & Co.).—An effective set, admirably laid out for dancing and artistically illustrated.

Air de Danse. By D. R. Munro. (Duncan Davison and Co.).—A fairly written, and, on the whole, graceful piece of the gavotte type.

Evening Bells. By Oliver Cramer. (Weekes & Co.).—A pretty and effectively written reverie for pianoforte.

Sonata in A major. By Mozart. (Willey & Co.).—One of the series edited by Lindsay Sloper. The sonata is the well-known one commencing with the beautiful air with variations. It is admirably edited and very clearly printed.

The Moonlight March. By Crosby Smith. (A. Bertini).—A march of not much originality but yet tuneful on the whole.

After the Rain. By H. J. Stark. (A. Cox, King Street, Regent Street).—A musicianly and effective concert song, with an artistic accompaniment.

Gavotte and Musette. By Sydney Smith. (E. Ashdown).—Clever specimens of the use of old forms in a modern style. The ideas have breadth and individuality, and are well treated.

The Minster Tower. By Sydney Smith. (E. Ashdown).—A clever piece, in which the effect of serious harmony, combined with bell ringing descending scale is neatly realised on the pianoforte.

Rigaudon. By Boyton Smith. (Edwin Ashdown).—A capital piece for pianoforte, with much character, and with a well-sustained interest throughout.

Romeo and Juliet. By Sydney Smith. (Edwin Ashdown).—A fantasia upon melodies from Bellini's opera, written with that facility and aptitude for display of player and instrument which has popularised Mr. S. Smith's pianoforte pieces.

La Tristesse. By Sydney Smith. (E. Ashdown).—An effective melody, showily treated for pianoforte.

Derwent Water, No. 2 of "Lakeland." By Michael Watson. (B. Williams).—An easy and melodious pianoforte duet, well laid out for the player's hands.

Kissing Little Maidens. By A. D. Duvivier. (Stanley Lucas, Weber & Co.).—A lively, pert, yet artistically written song.

Haymaking. By Sir F. W. Brady, Bart. (Duncan Davison & Co.).—The melody of this song, for voices of medium pitch, has grace and some character.

Musical Bijou, No. 50 and 51. (Metzler & Co.).—A collection of dance tunes, written for dancing purposes by knowing hands.

Pauline Waltz. By H. Klein. (E. S. Lane, Holborn Viaduct).—Has graceful figures, and will please those who admire this type of music.

Glover's Galop di Bravura. (Duncan Davison).—A spirited piece, though one or two passages are not adapted quite for galop pace.

Br'er Rabbit Polka. By A. Tindal. (Metzler & Co.).—A well-marked, spirited dance tune.

Springtide Revels. By Edward Harper. (Metzler and Co.).—A taking, piquant movement of the "Pas Redouble" type, set for the pianoforte.

Danse des Fées. By Hugh Clendon. (Metzler & Co.).—A spirited and piquant specimen of the gavotte tribe.

Old-fashioned Friends. By Michael Watson. (Ashdown & Parry).—A ballad, with a graceful, singable melody.

Sea Breezes, sketch. By D. R. Munro. (Duncan Davison & Co.).—A pianoforte piece of some merit, though having several progressions which show a slight want of writing experience. The melody has in it something of Mendelssohn's manner.

Transcription of Mendelssohn's Song of Love. By S. Kahlenberg. (B. Williams).—A clear and effective pianoforte rendering of one of the master's well-known melodies.

Gertrude, polka mazurka. By S. Kahlenberg. (B. Williams).—An unusually piquant, yet withal simple dance tune, admirably laid out for dancing.

The Flower that Smiles, song. By J. Storer. (Ashdown).—A musicianly and very nice song.

Only a Year, song. By C. S. Hartog. (Ashdown).—A ballad with an expressive and rather taking melody.

"PARSIFAL."

The following words are quoted by *Musical Critic* from an article on "Parsifal," by Dr. Edward Hanslick of Vienna :—

The Wagner cultus has at present reached, if not already passed, its culminating point. Reason and experience teach us that after such unparalleled inebriation people gradually sober down extremely. Many with us in Bayreuth thought they had already perceived and remarked signs of this, and even warm adherents of Wagner became impatient over the trying game of catching the guiding-motives. Beneath the strongly dazzling charm of novelty, we see more and more plainly the falseness of this one-sided method. The fit of sobriety to which I have referred will probably become downright seediness directly men of small talent shall begin composing in the false operatic style which Wagner's great talent created and alone can wield. At present, the greatest, or at any rate the most sensitive and most grateful part of the public : young persons, women, painters, dilettanteising poetico-musicians and music-poets, belong to Wagner. We, who demand of music that it shall fashion plastically and not merely flow crepuscularly along, and who consider the music of "Don Juan," "Fidelio," and "Der Freischütz," as not alone musically finer, but also more full of life *dramatically* than the uniformly declamatory music of Wagner, are in the minority. This minority will not, however, die out, but sooner or later, grow up into a majority against the tyranny of the Wagner cultus. If the assertion that posterity alone will estimate him correctly applies to any composer, it applies to Richard Wagner. Not because, like Mozart and Beethoven, not enough, but because too much was made of him during his life.

"Two Loves and a Life" is the title of a story by "Cherubino" in the Christmas number of *Figaro*, having reference to certain incidents connected with the Parisian life of Chopin and Liszt.

Academical Intelligence.

UNIVERSITY OF LONDON.

The following are lists of the candidates who have passed the recent examinations :—

INTERMEDIATE EXAMINATION IN MUSIC.

PASS LIST.

First Division.

Curtis, Joseph (Trinity College and private study).
Foulds, William, B.A. (Private study).
Ierson, Frank Henry, B.A. (Private study).

Second Division.

Barnicott, Olinthus Roberts (St. John's College, Cambridge).
Handley, Samuel Bennett (Private study).
Murphy, Joseph John (Private study).

B.MUS. EXAMINATION.

PASS LIST.

First Division.

Hall, Charles John (Private study).

Second Division.

Foxell, William James, B.A. (Private study).

TRINITY COLLEGE, LONDON.
UNIVERSITY LECTURES.

Arrangements have been made for establishing a Centre, in connection with the University Extension Scheme, at Trinity College, London, at which place a course of lectures will be commenced, immediately after the Christmas vacation, on the "Theory of Sound with especial reference to Music."

The College Lecturer on Acoustics, Dr. W. H. Stone, M.A., M.B., F.R.C.P., Balliol, Oxford, has been appointed the Lecturer, and, at the conclusion of his course of twelve lectures, an examination will be held by an Examiner specially commissioned by the Joint Board of the Universites of Oxford, Cambridge, and London, and Certificates will be awarded to meritorious students, signed on behalf of the Universities' Board. A committee for carrying out the local details has been nominated by Trinity College, the Honorary Secretary being the Rev. R. Gwynne, B.A., to whom all applications for particulars of admission to the course should be addressed, at Trinity College.

The London Society for the Extension of University Teaching, in whose hands the arrangements for the Metropolis have been placed by the Universities, will give all necessary powers to the committee thus formed, and it is hoped that other courses of lectures will be organized for the benefit of musical students in the more popular subjects of study. The lectures will be open to all comers, and the prescribed payment for the course will include the fee for the examination, which is optional.

The University Lectures will in no way clash with or supersede the ordinary curriculum and examinations of the College, which will remain entirely distinct and independent of external control.

The silver medal offered by the Academical Board of Trinity College, London, for the best student in the class for musical acoustics has been awarded, on the recommendation of the lecturer, Dr. W. H. Stone, M.A., M.B., to Joseph Curtis.

On Tuesday evening, December 28th, a very good performance of "The Messiah" was given by the Kew Road Musical Society, Richmond. The solo vocalists were Mdme. Clara West, Mrs. J. Pocock, Mr. Herbert, and Mr. Forington. Mr. J. F. Goodban, R.A.M., presided at the organ ; and Mr. F. A. Crew was conductor. Mdme. West was enthusiastically applauded for her efficient rendering of "Rejoice greatly" and "I know that my Redeemer liveth," as was also Mr. Forington for "Why do the Nations," and the choruses were mostly very well rendered.

NEW ORGAN PIECE, by M. GUILMANT.—
SPOHR'S 24th PSALM (English words), 9d. and 2s. Ditto
arranged for Organ Solo by M. GUILMANT, 1s. 6d.
London : NOVELLO, EWER & CO.

LONDON : SATURDAY, JANUARY 6, 1883.

MUSIC IN THE NEW YEAR.

THE marked progress music has made of late years will, according to many signs, be continued doubtless in the new year now on the threshold of its career. This progress has been not only a notable feature of our English art-life, but has been an equally characteristic growth in the midst of other advanced nationalities. The chief features of this growing artistic power here, have been naturally manifested in the three directions of composition, executive skill, and advanced educational resources. Our English composers have indeed, one is proud to chronicle the fact, again built up an undeniable reputation for this country as a music-producing nation, and further, *mirabile dictu*, have succeeded to a great extent in convincing our own people that they possess composers of real merit of their own. Among the tokens of this general advance and increased appreciation are the continued success of sundry English specimens of dramatic music, the actual bestowal of commissions to write English operas on the part of a spirited and far-sighted manager, and the timely, though somewhat timid, advance made by our oldest musical society, in the offer of a prize for an overture. As to the progress of our executants, it is to be noted that our singers and players are multiplying and gaining strength in all directions. But the most significant and marked advance is shewn in way of increased educational power, as in the development of such established institutions as the Royal Academy of Music, the College of Organists, Trinity College, and the Guildhall School of Music, to proceed chronologically, and in the energetic efforts, aided by the highest in the land, now being made to establish the Royal College of Music. Nor can the well directed efforts of the Tonic Sol-fa College be unrecorded, or the high and valuable work done by the Musical Association and Musical Artists' Society and the earnest action in the North of the Society of Professional Musicians, be overlooked. Then, again, our strong enthusiastic army of volunteer musicians, who are non-professional in the sense of not being dependent upon their artistic work, have gained ground distinctly in their practical skill, and consequently in their appreciation of good art and conscientious professional artists, and are lending earnest and valuable support to every undertaking which is calculated to advance the best interests of music and its professors. There are signs too of increased activity and growing power in our musical journalism and verbal literature. With such an outlook, with such growing accessions of artistic sunlight and warm enthusiasm, surely the musical prospects of the new year are more than encouraging; they give promise indeed of a full, ripe harvest, well calculated to gladden the hearts of all earnest lovers of music, and to extend far and wide the joys and blessings which ever follow in the footsteps of pure and earnestly cultivated art.　　E. H. TURPIN.

A TRIBUTE TO THE MEMORY OF HENRY SMART.

THE authorities of Trinity College, London, have taken no step which will meet with more sincere public approval than the foundation of a scholarship, to be called the "Henry Smart Scholarship," in memory of the late distinguished musician, who was a member of the College Council, and an Examiner to the Board up to the date of his death. The scholarship, it is announced, will be open to all comers of either sex under conditions of competition, which the Secretary of the College is ready to furnish to applicants, and will entitle the holder to a three years' course of training on the organ, pianoforte, and in the higher branches of musicianship, preparatory to examination, in view of the complete building up of the successful student's artistic career. HENRY SMART took an earnest and active interest in the work being done by Trinity College, and his attendance and assistance at the meetings, examinations, and composition classes of "Form and Orchestration," were among the last acts of his professional duties, so his memory is held as specially dear to the workers, both teachers and students, of the institution. But higher than such local recollections is the consideration that the memory of a great, honest Englishman, and a true artist of rare powers, has been recognised by the erection of one of the best of monumental structures, a lasting benefit to the art the man honoured thus loved and served so well—a monument which not only helps to keep his memory green, but holds up at the same time his solid work and sturdy artistic honesty by the simple force of his good name, as an example for good, earnest students to follow. There are similar memorials in the Royal Academy of Music; this step is however notable as the first of the kind taken by the authorities of Trinity College, and as the first scholarship bearing the name of our eminent composer. The authorities of our musical institutions cannot do more wisely than multiply scholarships dedicated to the memories of English musical worthies, both as honouring English art and as offering a dignified encouragement for students of mark.　　E. H. TURPIN.

ORCHESTRAL EFFECTS AND KEY-BOARD MANNERISMS.

I.

THE more or less successful transference of those most eloquent and picturesque of musical idioms we speak of technically as. orchestral effects to the less powerfully suggestive mediums of the key-board instruments, forms a subject of much interest, not only as regards the simple transcription of precious thoughts from one medium to another, but as helping to inculcate useful habits of thought as, to the creation of eloquent effects upon the key-board instruments themselves. For instance, much of the power found in Beethoven's pianoforte sonatas arises from orchestral habits of thought; they are, indeed, key-board symphonies, and the student of orchestration can find no better practice than would be furnished by scoring these masterpieces for the orchestra, a practice Auber is said to have found much artistic pleasure in practically carrying out. Again, there are many organ effects which are reflections from the orchestra; doubtless students have noticed that the College of Organists' examination papers constantly give aptly selected passages from the stores of classical organ writers, as furnishing happy instances of orchestral effects from the candidate's own key-board as it were. Just as human thought is based in all verbal languages alike upon the same aspirations and motive powers, so in music, the trained thoughts of the musician have their origin in those mental springs which lie beyond all the mediums of expression, though to some extent musical inspirations are necessarily affected by the habits of thought contracted through the different powers of the mediums to which ideas are assigned. So it is important that the student of composition and the producer of the generalised effects peculiar to key-board instruments should gain by contemplation and practical experience a thorough understanding of the parallelisms and approachable points of resemblance, to be noticed and realised, as existing between combinations of single toned instruments and instruments destined to serve the art as producers of generalised and embodied effects.
　　E. H. TURPIN.

The fifth annual concert in aid of the Choir-boys' Fund, St. Luke's, Lower Norwood, was successfully given at the Institute, Lower Norwood, on the 29th December. The Christmas carols—always a feature at these concerts —were admirably sung by the choir-boys, and Mdme. Jarratt, Miss Minnie Gwynne, and several members of the congregation afforded great pleasure by their appropriate songs and excellent pianoforte playing. Miss Plowright, a pupil of Dr. Sloman, was very successful in one of Weber's Rondo. The concert-room was well filled, the proceeds amounting to £30. Dr. Sloman organised and conducted the concert.

MIDSUMMER NIGHT'S DREAM MUSIC OF MENDELSSOHN.

"Midsummer Night's Dream," one of his earliest productions, must be regarded as his most characteristic work. It is a most marvellous result of inspiration and capability of genius and study. It opens at once a new world to our admiring gaze, although we are well accustomed to dream of the original drama and dwell upon its delicious fancies. Shakespeare had led painters and other illustrators of his text to exercise their art in the attempt to realize his imaginings, had occupied critics of the most painstaking kind to unfold the beauties of his creation; but when he inspired Mendelssohn, it became doubly evident that as yet the subject of this dream was not exhausted.

It is really strange that the composer Mendelssohn, who was so devoted a disciple of John Sebastian Bach, and wrote in the contrapuntal style with such great earnestness of purpose, and in true sympathy with the spirit of the old masters, should excel so markedly in fantastic subjects. For counterpoint seems to demand first of all a solid part for the bass and a certain dignity of style that is apparently foreign in nature to this fairy-like music, and to the particular form of *scherzo* that Mendelssohn inserted. Some of these *scherzi* are "worked out" in an orderly and thoroughly musician-like style, showing wonderful skill and consistency; and yet, notwithstanding this consistency and regularity, they are extremely excited, feverish, fitful and flurried, and suffused as with a hectic flush.

With reference to a fantastical, airy subject for musical composition, Mendelssohn himself says it is difficult to hit the right medium. If you grasp it too firmly it is apt to become prosaic and formal; and if too delicately, it dissolves and does not become a well-defined form. Facts should not become too dry nor fancies too misty. A comparison of the score of "Midsummer Night's Dream" overture with that of "Queen Mab," by Berlioz, will show how markedly different are the ways in which these two great composers have treated a kindred subject.

It is most remarkable also that musicians (one might suppose, would be glad of a subject giving them so good an excuse for revelling at will in fairy-land, indulging in unrestrained fancies) waited for Mendelssohn to open this new region for exploration before venturing into it.

In the second place, it must be allowed that he succeeded well in this his first essay. Thirdly, and stranger still, it must be noted that he accomplished his ends by employing the old forms so exclusively and with such (almost religious) reverence as to give his detractors an excuse for ridiculing him as a pedantic. But by his thorough scholarship he compelled his seniors to acknowledge him as a master, although still very young (which Berlioz could not accomplish); and by this acquired knowledge, which he employed in the development of musical ideas, he gained for his productions a unity of organic structure which greatly raised their immediate value as art-products and yet did not injure their fantastical character. In addition to all this he proved that the old forms had capabilities yet unknown, which was tantamount to inventing new ones.

If Mendelssohn had not acquired the art of adhering to a certain unity of plan his works might have become too incoherent, shapeless, and unsymmetrical to be accounted beautiful as wholes, whatever may have been the charms of various details, or however true the music might be to the nature of the subject. This "Midsummer Night's Dream" overture is as regular in its plan as the most commonplace allegro or first movement of a symphony, being also in the so-called "sonata form." But beyond and above all this, it deserves to be pointed out that although this work may be regarded as "program music," yet it may be most thoroughly enjoyed simply as music, irrespective of all the dramatic intentions of the composer. No doubt thousands of persons hear it and play it in the form of an arrangement for the pianoforte with great gratification, and yet remain in ignorance of the fact that almost every phrase has its strongly-marked characterization. The frolics of the knavish sprite Puck, of Peablossom, Mustard-seed, Cobweb, and of the lightsome throng of their nameless compatriots—as well as the roar of Bottom, etc., etc.—are all idealized herein; yet the music, simply as music, is good. The expressions of Bottom are such original and beautiful phrases that one hardly suspects the composer's intentions.—*S. Austen Pearce in the Home Journal, U. S.*

PECULIARITIES OF MEYERBEER.

Meyerbeer, it now leaks out, used to bribe the press awfully. A scandalous gossiper on the peculiarities of the *maestro*, says that "before Meyerbeer brought out a new opera, or revived an old one, which had been some months off the bills, he invited all the leading musical critics to dine with him at the Trois Frères, where he gave them the most sumptuous entertainment the head-cook could imagine. How can a fellow of decent feeling write harshly of a man who has been pouring the choicest vintages of France, and the most delicate tit-bits of sea, air, forest, orchard and garden down one's throat? Try it. You will find the thing impossible. This custom is deplorable, for it militates against the independence and truth of the press. But this was not the worst of Meyerbeer. There were few musical critics in Paris who were not in receipt of annual pensions from Meyerbeer! These pensions of no trifling gratuities, but solid pensions of several hundred dollars, and in one or two instances they exceeded a thousand dollars annually. There were Paris critics who had been in receipt of large pensions from 1831 to 1865. Meyerbeer did not content himself with paying them pensions and good dinners; he also made it a point of duty to give them costly presents on their name-days and on New Year's Day. Meyerbeer used to defend this custom by saying that he did not lay these gentlemen under obligations, *he* was the person obliged, and he could not see any objection to his giving evidence of his gratitude to them for the substantial service they had rendered him. The habit was unpardonable, and was solely due to what Carl von Weber called the accursed desire of success.

"Meyerbeer could not bear the sight of a musk-melon; he fainted when one came near him. Scribe ordered an artist to decorate his dining-room; the unlucky painter placed a musk-melon among the fruit which adorned the room. Scribe was out of town; upon his return he discovered the melon, and ordered its immediate removal, solely because he never could get Meyerbeer to dine with him if that fruit was visible."—*American Art Journal.*

PANTOMIME MUSIC.

Art may be "long," but art advances, and notably the art with which this journal is particularly concerned. One instance of progress may be cited, to wit, the case of pantomime music. Forty, aye, even twenty years ago, the so-called "Overture" to the "New Grand Comic Christmas Pantomime" consisted of common barrel-organ tunes strung together like onions on a rope; and one point was the delivery of some popular ditty by the House, as an "episode" in the "overture." The writer remembers to have heard the air, "My lodging is the cold, cold ground" thus treated at Drury Lane Theatre, when Wieland, the famous clown, took part in a pantomime called "Harlequin and Jack Frost." Then, during the harlequinade, the band played, with tedious reiteration, a set of vulgar tunes, such as might be heard at the old fairs in the country. In short, the music of the pantomime was simply an infliction.

Nous avons changé tout cela! To speak only of Drury Lane Theatre, where the new Pantomime is admitted by all to be a triumph of *spectacle*, the episodical music equally delights the ear, and its association with the kindred art of Terpsichore invests the entertainment with a spirit of elegance. The writer, at a morning performance last Saturday, heard several really pretty tunes, light and effervescent, yet quite free from music-hall vulgarity. Amongst familiar programmes of harmony, the—at ordinary theatres—not very common modulation into the relative minor of the *dominant* was gladly recognised; also the more hackneyed, but always effective, harmonisation of the mediant note of the scale with the dominant (common chord) of the relative minor. A Mozartean suspension of the cadence on the strong accent of the bar did not escape notice. The old complaint of alternate "tonic and dominant" cannot justly be made against the *chef d'orchestre* of Old Drury. At other theatres the same gratifying improvement of taste may doubtless be observed.

Of course, when the harlequinade begins, a descent to the bathos is inevitable; but the harlequinade at Drury Lane, poor and stupid enough, only endures for three scenes, where the old jokes of calling policemen, and making artificial slides are ruthlessly repeated. In former days, the harlequinade was usually the salient feature of the pantomime, and lasted at least as long as the introduction. "Transformation" scenes were then unknown in the present grand spectacular sense of the term ; the climax of scene-painting was reserved for the end. The harlequin, columbine, clown and pantaloon did not, as now, slip in, ready dressed, from the wings ; but at the command of a fairy, doffed the integuments in which they had previously acted as special "characters" of the introduction, and revealed the welcome costumes of the pantomime. "Here we are !" cried clown and pantaloon. Tom Matthews, famous in his day, generally engaged a friend in the gallery to interrupt him with a "gag" word at the end of each stanza in "Hot Codlins," and affected to resent the interruption by crying out : "I'll tell your mother of you," and "One fool's enough at a time." On one occasion, the gallery friend suggested an obvious rhyme—the word "drunk"—to which Matthews retorted, "nothing so vulgar"; thereby exciting roars of laughter. "Hot Codlins" and "Tippetywitchet" have given place to the more elegant strains of the orchestra, and the most inveterate Conservative will hardly protest against the reform.   A. M.

WIND PRESSURE.

In one of a series of articles—"On the Organ and In the Organ"—Mr. Hermann Smith contributed to *Musical Opinion*, the following passage occurs:—

The ordinary organ pressure is three inches, and, referring to the table, you will see that when the gauge records three inches the pressure per square foot is 15lb. 9oz.; therefore, whatever the superficial area of the bellows may be, that will be the ratio per foot ; the wood-top of bellows will of course be reckoned in the weight. So also every inch more of water supported tells that there has been 5lb. 3oz. added for each square foot. The reservoir supplying the reed-stops is very commonly weighted to six inches. Notice how largely the amount of the pounds must be made up on the bellows. Then, again, in large organs the wind frequently, for reservoirs supplying certain reed stops, is fixed at nine inches, and we are required to place the enormous amount of 46lb. 12oz. for every square foot of surface. In some organs this even is doubled. Further, notice what for any given pressure must be the initial velocity of the stream entering at the foot of the pipe, and think of all that is implied in a fact having that significance. More astonishing still is the following table, which we owe to Dr. W. H. Stone. Nothing of the kind had been done previously, and this is due to the rarity of the combination of conversance with the higher branches of science, and practical skill and knowlege of wind instruments. I have witnessed Dr. Stone's experiments, and give you his own words describing the method for obtaining the data. "The wind-chest in this case is invariably the human thorax ; the experiments were made for the purpose of determining what the pressures within the thorax actually were. A water-gauge was connected with a small curved piece of tube by means of a long flexible india-rubber pipe. The curved tube, being inserted in the angle of the mouth, did not, after a little practice, interfere with the ordinary playing of the instrument. The various notes were then sounded successively, and the height at which the column stood was noted. The following table was obtained as an average of many experiments :—

TABLE OF PRESSURES.

			From lowest notes to highest.
Oboe	...	...	9in. to 17in.
Clarinet	...	...	15in. to 8in.
Bassoon	...	...	12in. to 24in.
Horn	...	...	5in. to 27in.
Cornet	...	...	10in. to 34in.
Trumpet	...	...	12in. to 33in.
Euphonium	...	...	3in. to 40in.
Bombardon	...	...	3in. to 36in."

Among orchestral instruments, the clarinet displays a remarkable peculiarity. The order of pressure is reversed ; the lowest notes demand the greatest pressure, and the highest the least, whilst, as will be seen, all the other instruments begin with low pressure, and need powerful wind to evoke the high notes. And what pressures they are ! The organ is weak, indeed, in comparison. Multiply 40in. at 5lb. 3oz. per square foot per inch. The value of such a tabulated record cannot be thoroughly recognized until you place the former table of velocities, weights, and pressures side by side with this, and consider them together : then these figures will acquire a fuller emphasis, and will sufficiently explain the cause of the superior intensity characterising the orchestral wind instruments. If a corresponding record of the power of the human voice could be obtained, no doubt the index would reach a high figure. It has been estimated that an ordinary effort of the voice as in calling, is equal to 8in. pressure.

THE FRENCH GOVERNMENT GRANT TO CATHEDRALS.

The French Government, which gives the Opéra the handsome annual subsidy of £32,000, has suppressed the grant for £12,000 hitherto allowed the French cathedrals for the organ and choir. M. Charles Gounod has written an eloquent protest against the step, which he describes as a heavy blow to the cause of solid musical education. Cathedral choirs have always, he says, been the nursery of great musicians, and he instances Palestrina in Italy, Orlando di Lasso in France, and Tallis in England to illustrate his statement. Later on Sebastian Bach, "the colossus on whose shoulders all modern music rests, and Handel, the giant of the oratorio in England," had the same training. Of the same school, too, were Marcello and Pergolesi, Porpora, Haydn's master, and, in our own day the Abbé Vogler, who taught Weber and Meyerbeer. Plain chant he considers the noblest introduction to the science of harmony, and he knows no work of any master which can "challenge comparison with the redoubtable majesty of these sublime chants we hear every day in our temples at funeral services, the 'Dies Iræ' and the 'De Profundis.'" The church choir, he says in conclusion, is the only place where music is studied without pernicious striving after effect, "an aim born of vanity, which cannot produce servants of truth. The cause of the cathedral choirs is the cause of musical probity."

All musical people will sympathise with M. Gounod in his appeal, although he is somewhat astray in claiming Bach and Handel as children of the cathedral choir, and might have included Haydn, Mozart, and even, to some extent, Beethoven, in his list, not to add our own Purcell and other great composers. The step taken by the French Republic is simply a move in obedience to public opinion, and may be indicative of an overstrained relationship between the church and certain political sections ; it may indicate too an approach to the possible ultimate separation of the church from State patronage and control. The policy thus inaugurated, putting aside other considerations not here to be discussed, will be regretted as likely to check the progress of church music, which, in France, calls for careful nurture from the too persistent employment of plain song, pure and simple. Further, it will throw the support of one of the most valuable of all the artistic classes, the church musician, upon the general resources of the cathedral establishments, or upon extraneous aid. Though it is to be hoped that the French national authorities will yet reconsider their proposals and not leave the inference that the nation is more solicitous about the support of the opera, than anxious to foster church music, it is not necessary to take too gloomy a view of the matter. In truth, the French State-helped opera is by no means a healthy institution and the State subsidy does little more than protect the opera from wholesome criticism and healthy public opinion. The opera, indeed, should stand or fall upon its own merits now, for the State protection has failed to secure even artistic success. Then surely that institution, which is built upon a rock, and will live on regardless of the world and worldly help, cannot and will not fail to support those charged with the duty of maintaining the sacred song of the church. In spite of much that is said to the contrary, the church in France is strong, and holds a high place in the affections of a large portion of the people, and the musical requirements of the time-honoured cathedrals will neither be forgotten nor overlooked.

The fifth season of the London Amateur Society has commenced, and the members of the choir have begun the rehearsals of two new works, viz., a "Stabat Mater' by Anton Dvorak, and a "Messe Solenelle de Paques" by Gounod, in addition to Schumann's "Manfred," and other important works. The society has taken up a new position, and appeals to the sympathy of the general public on the ground of the fact that the performances of the society having hitherto been only of a *quasi*-public character, tended to narrow the influence the society might otherwise have exercised; and it was "obvious that sooner or later these restrictions would have to be broken through, and the performances of the society brought more prominently forward." The great difficulty will be to ensure sufficient rehearsals, without which no choral society can succeed.—*Sporting and Dramatic News.*

ACCENTUATION IN ORGAN PLAYING.

The remark is frequently made that no *accent* can be given upon the organ, and hence the effect produced must in a large degree be monotonous. Writes Mr. H. Clarence Eddy in the *Indicator* :—This to a certain extent is true, for, unlike the pianoforte, which responds to the various qualities of *touch*, and produces a tone in accordance with the power of attack, the organ tone is not intensified by a pressure stronger than that sufficient to hold the keys fully down, and therefore sharp accents are against the very nature of the organ. Nevertheless, it has been observed that under certain conditions, or perhaps more tersely expressed, under certain *fingers*, the effects have been wonderfully vigorous, crisp and brilliant, even to such an extent that former theories have been exploded in the minds of connoisseurs, as may be seen from the following extract, written by Boston's eminent musical critic, Mr. John S. Dwight, concerning an organ concert given in that city :—"In all his performances we were impressed by two qualities, which we have rarely found possessed in so high a degree by any of our organists. The first was a certain art of *phrasing*, which in the nature of things would seem to be almost impossible upon the organ ; and yet, by some clever management, he did give us the effect of phrasing, even without accent. The other was his perfectly firm and even time in fugue playing," etc. The secret of this "art of phrasing" which surprised the venerable critic, Mr. Dwight, lies mainly in the manner of removing the hands or the fingers from the keys, and here it may be remarked that the method of producing good effects upon the organ is to be found quite as much in the manner of *leaving the keys*, as in the mode of *pressing them down*.

Promptness of attack is indispensable, the keys (both pedal and manual) should never be *struck* with a sharp blow, as is too frequently the case, even in piano playing, but *pressed* down *firmly* and *quickly*, thus imparting ease and grace to the performance. The action of the fingers in leaving the keys should likewise be *prompt* and *quick*, thereby insuring well-defined harmonies and a clearness of execution otherwise not attainable.

By means of the *legato* touch, groups of two or more notes are joined together into phrases, and the proper method of connecting these notes constitutes the *art of phrasing*.

The playing of that veteran organist August. Haupt, of Berlin, was remarkable for its force, vigour, animation, and brilliancy, although at all times it was perfectly *clear* and *steady*. Upon analyzing his performance, it was found that the secret of his power consisted not only in his perfect mastery of phrasing, but in a peculiar emphasis, which he invariably placed upon the *first* note of each melodic phrase, which, however, was not exaggerated to such an extent that the note seemed to be dotted, or that the phrase was uneven, but by judiciously prolonging the introductory note of each phrase, and the primary part of each measure, the result gave a perfect sense of *accentuation*, and therefore an unmistakable *life* and *meaning*. Haupt possessed this art of *phrasing* in such a high degree that everything he played was imbued with a peculiar magnetism, and the great preludes and fugues of Johann Sebastian Bach, especially, seemed to possess a new life and individuality under his masterly touch. Throughout all his playing, which was unusually animated and vigorous, there remained always a perfect sense of *dignity* and *repose*, the tempo being kept perfectly even and steady. Such a mastery of the enormous difficulties presented required indeed a highly developed *technique* and extraordinary facility of execution, but without that inborn sense of rhythm, accentuation and phrasing, the playing would be dry and uninteresting ; the form might be preserved, but the spirit would be wanting.

Unfortunately, we have too many examples of feverish, unsteady, superficial and meaningless playing, which, to say the least, is inartistic and thoroughly unsatisfactory. The value of playing *in time* is totally disregarded by the majority of students, and even professional musicians. While this may, perhaps, be regarded as a digression from the subject under consideration, yet it is a vastly important element in a satisfactory performance upon any instrument, and especially upon the organ. The general lack of appreciation for most music of a *strict* character, such as fugues, toccatas, canons, sonatas and suites is due mainly to the indifferent, lackadaisical, and even slovenly manner in which they are usually ground out. The theme and the counterpoint are all alike to the would-be artist, and quite naturally the audience is suffered to remain in ignorance of their distinguishing characteristics. In all polyphonic music, where one or more themes are developed according to scientific principles, this is especially true, and it is just here that the value of *accentuation* and *phrasing* is untold, and to a great extent *unknown*. The principal themes should be pronounced in a manner to indicate a definite character ; they may always be easily recognised whenever they occur throughout the composition. The counterpoint should be smooth and flowing, like the undercurrent of a mighty river, but at the same time, the rhythmical form should be ever felt in its onward course, and this may be secured by dwelling slightly upon the primary part of each measure, or more properly upon the first note of every well-defined phrase. If organists generally would consider these principles and study more carefully the *contents* of the pieces which they perform, the result would be a far better appreciation of those works by the executant and a more positive sense of enjoyment on the part of his listeners.

Without enlarging unnecessarily upon this subject, it seems desirable to indicate some of the mistaken notions which prevail in regard to the *termination* of a musical phrase. In the first place, the analysis of a composition is to many players what syntax and prosody are to the average elocutionist—a sealed book, the key to which they are unable to find, and are content with a few marks of punctuation, without investigating the various forms of periods and sentences. It is therefore to be expected that these signs of expression and phrasing will often be applied without intelligence, and the result will be a false interpretation.

The *slur*, when placed over a group of two or more notes of equal length, is understood to signify that the notes are to be played in a smooth and connected manner. It is also employed as a sign for phrasing whereby not only the first note of each phrase is to receive an accent, but the last note is to be shortened. This rule is sometimes explained as invariable, which is undeniably incorrect. Nearly all examples of groups containing only two notes of equal value are to be played as indicated above, exception to the notes being taken when the notes are too long in slow tempo, in which case the second note is connected closely to the first, and held its full length, the slur signifying merely that the first of the two notes is to receive an accent, likewise when the second note is of greater value than the first. On the contrary, groups containing three or more notes of equal length are, as a rule, to be played in a smooth and connected manner, without detaching one group from another, except in cases of melodic phrasing complete in themselves. The first note of each group, however, should receive a slight accent unless especial marks of emphasis are written. The various other means of expression do not come under the subject of this article, but organ-playing would become more characteristic and potent if the study of *touch* alone were more earnestly regarded.—*Musical Record* (Boston).

THE GRESHAM LECTURES.

The lectures founded by Sir Thomas Gresham will be read to the public on the following days in the months of January, February, and March, 1883, in English, at six o'clock p.m., in the theatre of Gresham College, Basinghall Street in the following order :—Geometry—The Very Rev. B. M. Cowie, B.D., Dean of Manchester, Tuesday, January 16 ; Wednesday, 17 ; Thursday, 18 ; and Friday, 19. Law—Mr. J. T. Abdy, LL.D., Tuesday, January 23 ; Wednesday, 24 ; Thursday, 25 ; and Friday, 26. Rhetoric—Mr. J. E. Nixon, M.A., Tuesday, January 30 ; Wednesday, 31 ; Thursday, February 1 ; and Friday, 2. Physic—Mr. Symes Thompson, M.D., Monday, February 5 ; Tuesday, 6 ; Thursday, 8 ; and Friday, 9. *Music—Mr. Henry Wylde, Mus.D., Tuesday, February 13 ; Wednesday, 14 ; Thursday, 15 ; and Friday, 16.* Divinity—The Very Rev. J. W. Burgon, B.D., Dean of Chichester, Tuesday, February 20 ; Wednesday, 21 ; Thursday, 22 ; and Friday, 23. Astronomy—Rev. E. Ledger, M.A., F.R.A.S., Tuesday, February 27 ; Wednesday, 28 ; Thursday, March 1 ; and Friday, 2.

OUR NATIONAL ANTHEM AS A CANTO FERMO.

As a supplement to the interesting notes on this subject sent to you in May last (*Mus. Stand.*, May 27th), by Dr. E. J. Hopkins, the following extract from the *Harmonium*, 1824, may perhaps find a place. Describing the "Concerts Spirituels" given at the King's Theatre during Lent of that year, the writer, mentioning the instrumental part of these concerts, goes on to say : "The most successful effort of this fine orchestra was made in the performance of a movement in a new 'National Symphony' by Mr. Clementi, in which he introduces 'God Save the King' in an uncommonly scientific and ingenious manner, and with the happiest result. The same thing, however, had been done by Mr. Attwood, in his anthem performed at the coronation ; the merit, therefore, of originating the thought, is due to the latter."

Clementi being so little known as a writer for the orchestra—even so well informed a musician as Herr Pauer stating that he "concentrated his talent as a composer entirely on the pianoforte" ("Beethoven's Earlier Sonatas," *Mus. Stand.* Dec. 9th, 1882),—I may mention that a symphony of his was performed by the Philharmonic Society, April 21st 1823. The notice in the *Quarterly Musical Magazine* says : "The symphony of Clementi was a noble composition, conducted with consummate art, wrought with great judgment, and replete with fine and novel effects. It demonstrated that this justly admired veteran is still in possession of the fulness of his powers, and displayed a vigour of imagination and conception more correspondent with a genius in the plenitude of youthful strength, than that of a man who had passed the limit by which human life is ordinarily bounded." (Clementi was then 71 years of age).

The following year, 1824, the Philharmonic Society produced a MS. overture by Clementi, the performance taking place on March 22nd. It is described as a work full of vigour and learning, and containing power and brilliancy of orchestral effect. At the farewell concert given by Ferd. Ries, April 8th, 1824, "Mr. Clementi conducted a new overture, composed by himself, in person." This may have been the one just mentioned.

None of these works have been published, and because they are never heard now it does not follow that they are worthless, and must die. Concert directors should bring forth from the treasures of art "things new and old." It would be most interesting to hear some works by writers of the last century and the beginning of this ; for by such means we could better measure progress in orchestral writing, than by listening always to works by those still "head and shoulders" above all successors.

STEPHEN S. STRATTON.

PROF. MACFARREN'S MUSIC TO "AJAX."

The following extracts are from an appreciative description in the *Athenæum* of the setting as recently given in Cambridge with much success. The music consists of "An orchestral prelude, four unison choruses with instrumental accompaniment, and an interlude introducing the second scene. The work is full of charming melody, and the unison choruses are so tastefully accompanied by the orchestra as never to become monotonous. A serious difficulty which presented itself to the composer has been overcome with consummate skill—we refer to the setting of the original text in place of an English translation. The Greek verses are so different in metre and accent from those of our own language that no small amount of ingenuity is required to adapt to musical forms which shall be acceptable to our ears without at the same time being so modern in spirit as to be at variance with the general feeling of the drama. Little attempt has been made to introduce ancient modes, beyond the occasional use of the scale without the leading note, as in the chorus in E minor. Prof. Macfarren has unquestionably shown sound judgment in speaking to his audience in a musical idiom familiar to their ears rather than endeavouring to reproduce faithfully the art of a past age. What is required in such a case is that the music should produce upon the hearers of to-day an approximation to the mental effect of that which two thousand years ago accompanied the first performance of the drama. The conditions of art have so changed that were it possible to secure and perform the original choruses of the work it is morally certain that the impression produced by them would be at the least unsatisfying. In the chorus of 'Ajax' we find the spirit and feeling required, though the means by which the effect is obtained differ very widely from those employed by the Greeks. Such choruses as the first, and the hymn to Pan which precedes the entry of the messenger, leave nothing to desire, either from the point of view of absolute music or as the appropriate illustration of the dramatic situation. The gem of the whole work is perhaps the final chorus, preceded by a short funeral march, while the body of Ajax is carried off. Following the example of Handel, Prof. Macfarren has written his 'Dead March' in a major key, and the experiment has been completely successful, great effect being obtained by means of the utmost simplicity. There is only one number in the whole of the work which (at least on a first hearing), appears unsatisfactory. The orchestral interlude which occurs at the change of scene has rather too lively a character for its surroundings. Considered simply as music, it is excellent, but in its position here it appears to us out of place. On the whole, the music of 'Ajax' is likely to increase the fame of its composer, though probably the fact of its being written to a Greek text will prevent its being so often heard as it deserves.

A MODERN OPERA PLOT.

ACT I.

A lady (very high soprano)
  Is buried in the depths of woe ;
The deeper grows her vocal sorrow,
  The higher up her head tones go.

Beloved by an awkward tenor,
  She clings to him with faithful heart ;
Her brother (very heavy basso),
  However, tears the pair apart.

The tenor, after singing falsely,
  Decamps and goes to parts unknown ;
The lady proves that this afflicts her
  By flatting almost half a tone.

She tells her troubles to her servant,
  A very faithful (alto) maid,
Who listens without much emotion,
  As if she felt quite underpaid.

ACT II.

A marriage follows with another,
  (A tenor of the second class) ;
Her brother seals the fatal nuptials,
  And things come to a frightful pass.

Her lover had a round-trip ticket
  When he went off to parts afar ;
He comes back just too late to stop it,
  The wedding's done—and here we are.

The lady faints to heavy brasses,
  The lover curses with the strings ;
A tumult follows in orchestra.
  Then all the crowd together sing.

ACT III.

The lady, after long cadenzas,
  Plunges a dagger in her breast :
The lover doesn't seem to like it,
  And draws a high C from his chest.

The brother stabs the awkward tenor,
  Who doesn't know which way to fall,
But finally becomes recumbent,
  With an enormous caterwaul.

The brother, lonely and forsaken,
  Upon the dead soprano calls ;
The chorus, looking apathetic,
  Sing on until the curtain falls.

—*Music and Drama.*

It is related that Rev. Dr. Samuel West, of New Bedford, U.S., once reduced a refractory choir in the following way :—It having been rumoured that they would not sing a note on the next Sabbath, he commenced the morning service by giving out the hymn,

"Come ye that love the Lord."

After reading it through, he looked up very emphatically at the choir, and said, "You will begin at the second verse—

  'Let those refuse to sing
  Who never knew our Lord.'"

Passing Events.

Mr. E. J. Breakspeare read an admirable and thoughtful paper on "Musical Æsthetics," his second on this subject, before the "Musical Association," on January 1st.

Prof. G. A. Macfarren, whose great gifts and untiring industry have done so much for English art, is said to be busily engaged upon his new oratorio, "King David," for the Leeds Festival of October next.

Gounod's oratorio "The Redemption," it is understood, will be rendered, with full orchestra, in Westminster Abbey, some time before Easter, the day being not yet fixed.

At the Christmas service at Dr. Allon's church at Islington, Mr. Robert Kennedy, of the well-known family of Scottish vocalists, gave "Comfort ye my people" and and "Every valley" with much expression.

The Christmas music from the "Messiah" was rendered to the accompaniment of a small but efficient orchestra at a special service by the choir of St. Paul's, Knightsbridge, on Sunday last, and was conducted by the Precentor, the Rev. J. Baden Powell.

A soirée of London Tonic Sol-fa-ists and friends, as Falcon Square Lecture Hall (close to the General Post Office) which is to be held on the evening of Monday, the 8th inst., will, it is expected, be attended by a large number of influential supporters of the movement.

The Welcome, a well-conducted illustrated magazine published by Partridge & Co., does not overlook music. In the current number, under the title of "The New Year," a fine old English melody of 1650 is given, as judiciously harmonized by T. Crampton. The general contents of The Welcome are good and well varied.

Under the direction of Mr. F. A. W. Docker, a new association has been formed which promises a high artistic usefulness. The works now in preparation are Handel's "Belshazzar," "Utrecht Jubilate," Funeral Anthem, the "Ways of Zion," and "Water Music," together with compositions by Gluck, Brahms, and Raff.

The Musical World says that the original copy of the pianoforte score of Mendelssohn's "Elijah," which Mrs. Mounsey Bartholomew gave to the Sacred Harmonic Society with a reservation, that if the Society were ever dissolved, the MS. should revert to her, has been returned by the Committee to Mrs. Bartholomew. There are 43 numbers. "O rest in the Lord," was taken from it for presentation to the Guildhall Library, and has been lost or mislaid ever since.

The Musical Review, published by Novello & Co., is not the only new paper of its class issued for the first time at the beginning of the new year; another publishing firm, Messrs. Patey and Willis, have started a paper called The Lyre, to be edited by that learned and experienced writer Mr. J. Bennett. Earnest good wishes for the success of these new instruments for the advancement of the art are offered.

A new field for musical tuition will be gained in the City of London College, the new building of which will open in a few weeks, when music classes under Mr. W. G. McNaught (elementary and choral), and Mr. Geo. Oakey, Mus.Bac. (harmony and counterpoint), will be formed. The new college, which has been built at a cost of £16,000, and will accommodate 4,000 students, will, no doubt, open most prosperously. Violin and pianoforte classes are also to be held.

Speaking of "Colomba," Mr. Carl Rosa's leading novelty for next season, the musical editor of Figaro, who is ubiquitous and astute enough to be accounted the "Ariel" of musical criticism, says the composer, Mr. McKenzie, has made considerable use of the "leitmotif," and has given great importance to the orchestration, although otherwise the opera, it is said, is debtor but slightly to the teachings of Richard Wagner and his followers.

Miss Alice Roselli held a grand concert at the Music Hall, Chester, on the evening of December 19th. She sang Rossini's "Una voce," Roeckel's "Lord Mayor Whittington," and M. Welling's song "Forget, forgive." Concerted pieces, led by Miss Roselli, equally displayed her brilliant execution and fine style. Mr. W. H. Cummings, Mdme. Patey, and Sig. Villa sang in turn.

The Querist.

REPLY.

THE KALLIFFTHONGON.—This instrument (by a M. Fiebig, and stated to be an improvement upon one of the same kind by Mr. Hawkins), was exhibited in London in 1829, and is thus described :—"The effect it produces is that of a violin quartet, and it is played in the same manner as the pianoforte. A bow is attached to each string, and is drawn to and fro by means of a pedal, which the performer keeps in motion ; the keys bringing those strings that are required in contact with the bows. The instrument possesses considerable power, while its tone may be diminished to a pianissimo." The inventor gave performances upon it, and played pieces of his own composition, evincing considerable talent. The upper tones of the instrument were described as harsh, and the touch heavy enough to ruin the finger of any pianist.—S. S. S.

Service Lists.

FIRST SUNDAY AFTER EPIPHANY,

JANUARY 7th.

London.

ST. PAUL'S CATHEDRAL.—Morn.: Service, Te Deum and Benedictus, Best ; Introit, From the rising of the sun (Ouseley) ; Communion Service, Eyre in E flat. Even.: Service, Magnificat and Nunc Dimittis, Stanford in A ; Anthem, I desired wisdom (Stainer).

TEMPLE CHURCH.—Morn.: Service, Te Deum and Jubilate, Nares in F ; Apostles' Creed, Harmonized Monotone ; Anthem, When Jesus, our Lord (Mendelssohn) ; Kyrie Eleison, Massey in E flat. Even.: Service, Magnificat and Nunc Dimittis, Nares in F ; Apostles' Creed, Harmonized Monotone ; Anthem, Let us now go even unto Bethlehem (Hopkins).

LINCOLN'S INN HALL.—Morn.: Service, Rogers in D ; Kyrie, Rogers ; Anthems, Thus saith the Lord, and, And He shall purify (Handel). Even.: Service, Rogers in D ; Anthem, O clap your hands (Greene).

ST. AUGUSTINE AND ST. FAITH, WATLING STREET.—Morn.: Service, Calkin in B flat (throughout) ; Offertory, shine (Elvey). Even.: Service, Smart in F ; Anthem, I desired wisdom (Stainer).

ST. BARNABAS, MARYLEBONE.—Morn.: Service, Te Deum and Benedictus, Turle in D ; Anthem, Rejoice in the Lord (Purcell) ; Kyrie and Nicene Creed, Cooke in G. Even.: Service, Magnificat and Nunc Dimittis, Turle in D ; Anthems, Rejoice greatly, and, His yoke is easy (Handel).

FOUNDLING CHAPEL.—Morn.: Service, Nares in F ; Anthem, Sing we merrily (Mozart). Aft.: Service, Nares in F ; Anthem, There shall a star (" Christus," Mendelssohn).

ST. JAMES'S PRIVATE EPISCOPAL CHAPEL, SOUTHWARK.—Morn.: Service, Introit, As with gladness (Hymn 79) ; Communion Service, Bach in B minor (curtailed). Even.: Service, Stanford in B flat ; Anthem, Lo, star-led chiefs, and, Be peace (Crotch) ; Carols.

ST. MAGNUS, LONDON BRIDGE.—Morn.: Service, Opening Anthem, If we say (Calkin) ; Te Deum and Jubilate, Boyce in C ; Kyrie, Bach. Even.: Service, Cantate and Deus Misereatur, Prendergast in F ; Anthem, Arise, shine (Elvey).

ST. MARGARET PATTENS, ROOD LANE, FENCHURCH STREET.—Morn.: Service, Te Deum, Sullivan in D ; Benedictus, Dykes in F ; Communion Service, Offertory Anthem, Lo, star-led chiefs (Crotch) ; Kyrie, Credo, Sanctus, Benedictus, Agnus Dei, and Gloria in excelsis, Schubert in B flat. Even.: Service, Magnificat and Nunc Dimittis, Oakeley in E flat ; a performance of Christmas and Epiphany music after evensong.

ST. MARY ABCHURCH, E.C.—Morn.: Service, Boyce in C ; Communion Service, Garrett in E flat. Even.: Service, Turle in D.

ST. MARY BOLTONS, WEST BROMPTON, S.W.—Morn.: Service, Te Deum, Smart in F ; Benedictus, Chant. Even.: Service, Magnificat and Nunc Dimittis, Smart in F ; Anthem, Arise, shine, for thy light is come (Elvey) ; Carol, "The First Nowell."

ST. PAUL'S, AVENUE ROAD, SOUTH HAMPSTEAD.—Morn.: Service, Te Deum, Dykes in F ; Benedictus, J. W. Bennett ; Kyrie, Arnold in A ; Offertory, Barnby. Even.: Service, Magnificat and Nunc Dimittis, Calkin in B flat ; Anthem, Arise, shine (Elvey).

ST. PAUL'S, BOW COMMON, E. — Morn.: Service, Te Deum and Benedictus, Chants ; Communion Service, Kyrie, Credo, Sanctus, Offertory, and Gloria in excelsis, Stainer in A and D ; Benedictus and Agnus Dei, Vernham in F. Even.: Service, Magnificat and Nunc Dimittis, Stainer in A ; Anthem, When Jesus, our Lord (Mendelssohn) ; Carol, "The First Nowell."

ST. PETER'S, VERE STREET, W.—Even.: Service, Magnifica tand Nunc Dimittis, Tuckerman in F ; Anthem, O give thanks (Goss).

Country.

ST. ASAPH CATHEDRAL.—Morn.: Service, Roberts in D ; Anthem, When Jesus our Lord (Mendelssohn). Even.: Service, The Litany ; Anthem, Ascribe unto the Lord (Travers).

ASHBURNE CHURCH, DERBYSHIRE. — Morn.: Service, Kempton in B flat ; Kyrie, Credo, and Gloria in excelsis, Field in D. Even.: Service, Arnold in A ; Anthem, O taste and see (Goss).

BATH (ST. MARY'S, BATHWICK). — Morn.: Service, Te Deum, Goss in A ; Communion Service, Kyrie, Credo, Sanctus, Benedictus, Agnus Dei, O Salutaris Hostia, and Gloria in excelsis, Brown in C ; Offertory Anthem, Say, where is He born (Mendelssohn). Even.: Service, Magnificat and Nunc Dimittis, Tours in F.

BEDDINGTON CHURCH, SURREY.—Morn.: Service, Bunnett in F ; Introit, As with gladness men of old (Hymn 79) ; Communion Service, Garrett. Even.: Service, Bunnett in F ; Anthem, O thou that tellest (Handel).

BIRMINGHAM (ST. CYPRIAN'S, HAY MILLS).—Morn.: Service, Kent in C ; Anthem, When Jesus our Lord (Mendelssohn). Even.: Service, Clark Whitfeld in D ; Anthem, Ascribe unto the Lord (Travers).

CANTERBURY CATHEDRAL. — Morn.: Service, Te Deum, Goss in F ; Jubilate, Oakeley in F ; Anthem, O God, our refuge (Oakeley). Even.: Service, King in A ; Anthem, Thus saith the Lord (Ouseley).

CARLISLE CATHEDRAL.—Morn.: Service, Walmisley in F ; Introit, The Gentiles shall come (Reay) ; Kyrie, Walmisley in F ; Nicene Creed, Harmonized Monotone. Even.: Service, Hopkins in E flat ; Anthem, Lead, kindly light (Stainer).

DUBLIN, ST. PATRICK'S (NATIONAL) CATHEDRAL.—Morn.: Service, Te Deum and Jubilate, Aldrich in G ; Anthem, O God, Lord God (Mozart). Even.: Service, Cantate and Deus Misereatur, Hayes in E flat ; Anthems, The Lord gave the word (Handel), and, Ascribe unto the Lord (Travers).

ELY CATHEDRAL.—Morn.: Service, Hopkins in F ; Kyrie and Credo, Best in G ; Gloria, "Ely ;" Anthem, Arise, shine (Elvey). Even.: Service, Hopkins in F ; Anthem, I desired wisdom (Stainer).

EXETER CATHEDRAL.—Morn.: Service, Walmisley in C ; Communion Service, Wesley and Travers in F ; Introit, God so loved the world (Wood). Even.: Service, Walmisley in C ; Anthem, I will love thee (Clark).

GLASGOW (BLYTHSWOOD PARISH CHURCH).—Aft.: Service, O thou that tellest (Handel).

LEEDS PARISH CHURCH.—Morn.: Service, Tours in F ; Anthem, Lo, star-led chiefs (Crotch) ; Communion Service, Tours in F. Even.: Service, Tours in F ; Anthem, Ascribe unto the Lord (Wesley).

LICHFIELD CATHEDRAL. — Morn.: Service, Garrett in D ; Anthem, Rejoice, O ye people (Mendelssohn). Aft.: Service, Garrett in D ; Anthem, O sing unto the Lord (Purcell).

LIVERPOOL CATHEDRAL. — Aft.: Service, Turle in D ; Anthem, O thou that tellest (Handel).

MANCHESTER CATHEDRAL.—Morn.: Service, Smart in F (throughout) ; Anthem, From the rising of the sun (Ouseley). Aft.: Service, Smart in F ; Anthem, Lo, star-led chiefs (Crotch).

MANCHESTER (ST. BENEDICT'S).—Morn.: Service, Kyrie, Elvey ; Credo, Sanctus, Benedictus, Agnus Dei, and Gloria in excelsis, Farmer in B flat. Even.: Service, Magnificat and Nunc Dimittis, Wesley.

MANCHESTER (ST. JOHN BAPTIST, HULME).—Morn.: Service, Kyrie, Credo, Sanctus, Benedictus, Agnus Dei, and Gloria in excelsis, Tours in F. Even.: Service, Magnificat and Nunc Dimittis, Bunnett in F ; Anthem, From the rising of the sun (Ouseley).

ROCHESTER CATHEDRAL. — Morn.: Service, Goss in A ; Kyrie and Creed, Armes in A ; Anthem, The Lord is my light (Macfarren). Even.: Service, Goss in C ; Anthems, For behold, darkness, The people that walked, and, And the glory (Handel).

SHEFFIELD PARISH CHURCH. — Morn.: Service, Kyrie, Gounod in G. Even.: Service, Magnificat and Nunc Dimittis, Hopkins in F ; Anthem, Sing and rejoice (Barnby).

SOUTHWELL COLLEGIATE CHURCH, NOTTS.—Morn.: Service, Goss in A ; Kyrie, Elvey in A ; Creed, Goss in D. Even.: Service, Arnold in F ; Anthem, Lo, star-led chiefs (Crotch).

WORCESTER CATHEDRAL.—Morn.: Service, Turle in D ; Anthem, All kings shall fall down before Him (Boyce). Even.: Service, Turle in D ; Anthem, Ascribe unto the Lord (Travers).

[The attention of the several Organists is called to the favour they confer upon their brother musicians by forwarding their notices regularly : this column of the paper is much valued as an index to what is going on in the choice of cathedral music, so much so that intermissions constantly give rise to remonstrance. Lists should be sent in a week in advance if possible.—ED. *Mus. Stand.*]

NOTICES TO CORRESPONDENTS.

NEWSPAPERS sent should have *distinct marks* opposite to the matter to which attention is required.

NOTICE.—*All communications intended for the Editor are to be sent to his private address. Business communications to be addressed to 185, Fleet Street, E.C.*

"W. VINCENT WALLACE FUND."

	£	s.	d.
Collected by Mrs Wyatt-Smith	5	6	0
E. H. Turpin, Esq.	I	I	0
Chas. E. Stephens, Esq.	I	I	0
"A. O. T. N. S." (Streatham)	I	0	0
Collected by Mrs. Ede (Guildford)	I	13	6
"Instead of a Christmas Card"	0	5	0
Charles Volkert, Esq. (Messrs. Schott & Co.)	I	I	0
Per Wilton Road Post Office	0	5	0

ERRATUM.—By a mistake the name of the talented composer of the Cantata "The Healing of the Canaanite's Daughter" was omitted on page 426 of last issue. The gentleman in question Mr. John E. West.

Printed for the Proprietor by BOWDEN, HUDSON & CO., at 23, Red Lion Street, Holborn, London, W.C.; and Published by WILLIAM REEVES, at
the Office, 185, Fleet Street, E.C. West End Agents.—WEEKES & CO., 14, Hanover Street, Regent Street, W. Subscriptions and Advertisements are
received either by the Publisher or West End Agents.—Communications for the Editor are to be forwarded to his private address, 6, Argyle Square, W.C
SATURDAY, JAN. 6, 1883.—Entered at the General Post Office as a Newspaper.

The Musical Standard

A NEWSPAPER FOR MUSICIANS PROFESSIONAL AND AMATEUR

No. 963. VOL. XXIV. FOURTH SERIES. SATURDAY, JANUARY 13, 1883. WEEKLY: PRICE 3D.

TRIADS: THEIR RELATIONSHIP AND TREATMENT.*

By FRANCIS EDWARD GLADSTONE, MUS.DOC.

THE subject upon which I have undertaken to speak this evening is one which may well occupy the attention of every student of harmony or counterpoint. The many books which have been written upon modern harmony are chiefly intended to illustrate and to explain the use of discords; while the comparatively few modern treatises on counterpoint generally deal more with the movements of combined parts than with the chords which are the result of those movements. It would, of course, be foolish to assert that the question of the relationship of triads has never been fully discussed. Those of you who have read the admirable and profoundly learned work by Professor Helmholtz on the "Sensations of Tone" would at once contradict such a statement. But, inasmuch as the average student of harmony or counterpoint gains from his books little beyond a knowledge of the generally-accepted rules of the musical art, and since an appeal to our sense of hearing is insufficient of itself to explain these rules (although it will certainly corroborate them), I trust that the remarks which I have to offer may not be thought altogether useless, although they will cover but a small portion of the wide field for research which lies before us.

The basis of music is the diatonic scale. The derivation of the scale will be considered later. For the present I will ask you to let the scale of C major be assumed, and to call to mind the triads which may be built upon its several notes. Purposely omitting the triad upon the seventh of the scale, because of its imperfect fifth, I will play to you a series of chords formed from the other six triads, adding a cadence to complete the phrase. Next, I will play the same chords in exactly reversed order; and then you shall hear a few bars in which, without transgressing the well-known law against consecutive fifths and octaves, I have nevertheless intermingled the same six chords in such a way as to produce a very ugly result:—

Ex. 1. A.

Ex. 1. B.

Ex. 1. C.

Having heard these three examples, you will probably agree with me that the first is good, the second is awkward, and the third is *worse* than awkward. It would be premature if I were at once to analyze any of the progressions which you have just heard. My object in drawing your attention to them now is merely

* A paper read before the College of Organists.

to point out the direction which our enquiries are to take. We have, in short, to endeavour to ascertain—(1) what progressions from one triad to another are agreeable to the ear, and (2) why they are so.

Our modern major scale is formed from three triads thus: Taking C as the starting point, add to it a major 3rd (E) and perfect 5th (G); next, take the G thus found as the basis of a second triad, G, B, D; lastly, take C as the highest note of another, F, A, C:—

Ex. 2.

Now, if these intervals are tuned accurately, *i.e.*, if G and F are perfect 5ths respectively above and below C, if D is a perfect 5th above G, and if the 3rds are true major 3rds above F, C, and G, we obtain seven sounds, which, arranged scale-wise (with the octave to C added), stand at the following distances from one another: D is a major tone above C, E is a minor tone above D, F is a major semitone above E, G is a major tone above F, A is a minor tone above G, B is a major tone above A, and C is a major semitone above B:—

Ex. 3.

Major tone   Minor tone   Major semitone   Major tone   Minor tone   Major tone   Major semitone

But there may be some among you who are more familiar with the scale of equal temperament, now generally adopted for the tuning of organs as well as pianofortes, than with the theoretically-accurate scale formed in the manner which I have described. For the sake of clearness and completeness, therefore, I will remind you that, whereas our pianoforte key-board gives us (or, at all events, professes to give us) equal tones and equal semitones throughout its compass, the true diatonic major scale has two distinct intervals in addition to the semitone. It is very important to our present purpose that we should clearly recognize this fact, because, although we are accustomed to intervals slightly out of tune, there can be little doubt that in progressions from note to note, or from chord to chord, our ears accept the notes for what they should be rather than for what they are. I hope to illustrate this presently. In the meanwhile I will return to our scale of C major, and ask you to examine its various intervals with a view to testing the accuracy of my list. We all know that a perfect fourth is obtained by inverting the notes forming the interval of a perfect 5th, and mathematicians have given the name "major tone" to that interval by which a 5th overlaps a 4th. Thus, from C to G, in the true scale of C, is a perfect 5th, and from G to D downwards is a perfect 4th—therefore the interval from C to D is a major tone; similarly, it may be shown that the interval from F to G is a major tone. But A and B are at the distance of a major 3rd from F and G respectively, therefore A and B must also be separated by the interval of a major tone. The term "minor tone" has been applied to the interval by which a major 3rd exceeds a major tone. Thus, the interval from C to E being a major 3rd, and that from C to D a major tone, the distance from D to E will be a minor tone; similarly, it may be shown that the distance from G to A is a minor tone. I will ask you further to notice that the interval of a true minor 3rd exceeds that of a major tone by the shortest interval found in our diatonic scale, viz., a major semitone; this last interval is also the difference between a perfect 4th and major 3rd. Now, if we proceed to analyze the scale itself, we shall find that we must at once dismiss the loose teaching of our childhood, viz., that the modern major scale is formed of two equal portions separated by the distance of a tone. For, whereas, in ascending the lower half, the major tone comes first, in ascending the upper half, the minor tone precedes the major. The true divisions of the scale are, I believe, the following:—

Ex. 4.

The first three notes form one section, the next three form another section exactly corresponding to the first, and the 7th and 8th form an independent section completing the scale, independent, that is to say, of the section immediately preceding it, although, as I hope to show, closely connected in reality with the first group of three notes. This method of dividing the scale was adopted by Logier in his "System of Music," and it appears to me to be justified by the discoveries of scientific men in regard to the phenomena of acoustics. These discoveries teach us that nearly all musical sounds are of a compound nature, and that a stretched string (such as that of a pianoforte or violin) when properly set in motion, not only vibrates throughout its whole length, but also divides and subdivides itself, producing higher and higher sounds, known as harmonics, overtones, or upper partial tones. It will be convenient to employ one only of these terms. I will therefore speak of the first, second, third, &c., *harmonic*, counting the prime tone or generator as number one. This may not be scientifically accurate, but it is sufficiently so for our purpose. These harmonics rise in regular arithmetical proportions, and by ever-decreasing intervals, but there is a continual recurrence of the original sound in higher and higher octaves. Let me put this in another way. The 2nd harmonic is an octave above the 1st; the 4th harmonic is an octave above the 2nd, with one sound intervening; the 8th harmonic is an octave above the 4th, with three sounds intervening; the 16th harmonic is an octave above the 8th, with seven sounds intervening, and so on. Thus, if we rise from a note to its octave, either at once, or touching on our way in regular succession the various sounds occurring in any one of the higher octaves of the harmonic series, we are but copying what nature does, and the effect consequently is satisfactory. Now, although our major scale does not contain all, or nearly all, the harmonics of any one sound, it is a significant fact that all its notes but two may be derived from one generator. To illustrate this I will direct your attention to the 4th octave of the harmonic series rising from C below the bass staff

I have written the sounds belonging to our scale as minims, and those which are foreign to it as crotchets:—

Ex. 5.

The numbers refer to the places of the notes in the harmonic series, and they also show the proportionate speed of their vibrations. Mathematicians have proved that when two sounds stand at the distance of a major tone apart, the ratio of their vibrations is as 8 to 9; that is to say, if the lower one makes 8 vibrations in a given time, the higher one will make 9. But they have also proved the very important fact that the number of any sound in the harmonic series determines the speed of its vibrations in relation to every other sound derived from the same prime tone or generator.

Thus the 9th harmonic stands at the interval of a major tone above the 8th, and consequently the first two notes in the 4th octave above

correspond exactly with the first two notes of our scale of C major; similarly, it is proved that the distance between the 9th and 10th harmonics is identical with the interval of a minor tone, that the 8th and 12th harmonics are a perfect fifth apart, and that the 12th and 15th are separated by the interval of a major third. So far, then, our scale agrees with what may be called the scale of nature. The 1st, 2nd, 3rd, 5th, 7th, and 8th degrees are all copied exactly from the 8th, 9th, 10th, 12th, 15th, and 16th harmonics. But if we attempt to ascend our scale of C major, the imitation of the natural scale ceases at the 4th note: our F is flatter than the 11th harmonic. You will remember that, in order to obtain the 4th and 6th degrees of our scale, we took C as the 5th (not the root) of a triad, and C stands towards F in the same relationship that G does towards C; in other words, G is the 3rd harmonic in the series starting from C, and C is the 3rd harmonic in the series starting from F. If, therefore, we continue our ascent of the major scale of C, we shall, on arriving at F, change from one series of harmonics, having

for its starting point, to another whose generator is

Now, the next note (G) belongs equally to the series of sounds beginning on C, and to that beginning on F: in one case it is the 12th, in the other it is the 9th, harmonic. But the sixth note of our scale can only be derived from F, and we have thus three sounds in succession, F, G, A, which bear the same relationship to

hat our first three notes, C, D, E, bore to

Proceeding upwards, we re-enter the harmonic series of C. The seventh and eighth degrees of our scale agree exactly with the 15th and 16th harmonics arising from the prime tone

But the step by which we ascend is the wide interval of a major tone, and thus the return from the harmonic series of F to that of C is more abrupt than was the departure. In the latter case we not only copied nature in ascending by a smaller interval than the preceding one, but that interval (*i.e.*, from E to F), although not the next in order, corresponded with the 15th and 16th harmonics arising from F, and so the step was an easy one. In passing from A to B, however, we take a wider instead of a narrower step than the preceding one (viz., that from G to A), and thus the new note B has no direct connection with the preceding note A. It is this fact, no doubt, which gives to the 7th of the sale that peculiar upward tendency which is recognized by modern composers. Having commenced the scale by three notes derived from C and followed these by three notes derived from F, we make a sudden leap into the original harmonic series ; but the note to which this leap is made is inconclusive by itself, and so our craving for a re-establishment of the first totality carries us up to C.

I will now play to you Example 4, making a slight pause at the end of each section, when, even with our tempered scale, I believe that your sense of hearing will support my views.

If, however, we proceed to add chords to the scale, the relationship, or otherwise, between note and note is still more evident.

(*To be continued.*)

Musical Intelligence.

MONDAY POPULAR CONCERTS.

These Concerts, after a brief interval of vacation, were resumed on Monday evening.

PROGRAMME.

PART I.

Quartet in A major, Op. 93, for two violins, viola,
  and violoncello .... Spohr.
Mdme. Norman-Néruda, MM. L. Ries, Holländer, and Piatti.
Pianoforte solos—
Polonaise in F sharp minor, Op. 44 }
Three Studies, Op. 25, Nos. 6, 8, 9, } .... Chopin.
        Herr Pachmann.

PART II.

Sonata in A major, for violoncello, with pianoforte
  'accompaniment......................... Boccherini.
        Signor Piatti.
Sonata in G major, Op. 30, No. 3, for pianoforte and
  violin .... Beethoven.
  Herr Pachmann and Mdme. Norman-Néruda.

Accompanist · · · Mr. Zerbini.

The quartet of Spohr, in three movements, re-introduced Madame Norman-Néruda to the subscribers ; and her fine performance excited a sensation throughout the *séance*. Among salient features should be specially noted the delivery of the second theme (E major), of the first movement ; the full tone of the 4th string in the same part of the larghetto (where the key changes from F to C), and the spirited delivery of the sparkling rondo finale, the only movement in simple common time. Signor Piatti, who admirably supported the three upper strings in the quartet, enjoyed his own particular triumphal entry at the beginning of the second part. The annotator, or the printer, has made a blunder in the date of the first production of this Sonata ("the *fourth* season, Feb. 1882.")

Herr Pachmann made his last appearance. With the exception of the Polonaise, he played the same "Studies" as on Dec. 18, and "by desire"—no wonder. A repetition of previous eulogies is therefore unnecessary ; the audience, if that were possible, applauded more enthusiastically than on the first occasion, and the young pianist, on a "recall" played Chopin's familiar Nocturne in D flat. The Polonaise in F sharp minor is an elaborate affair, as it comprises a mazurka movement in A major, and thus agreeably varies the piece with a change of rhythmical accent. The "tributaries" to this Mazurka strike the ear as exquisitely tuneful ; and the modulations, chromatic and enharmonic, impart much variety of colour. Herr Pachmann's *finesse* of style, and nicety of *nuances*, not to speak of his *tours de force* and effective climax at the close, must be imagined by unfortunate absentees, for pen and ink are inadequate to tell the tale. The "Studies" are really what they profess to be, and enormously difficult. No. 6 has double notes in thirds, for the right hand, with double *sharps* into the bargain. In No. 8, there are also double notes for the right hand, but here in sixths ; whilst in the bass, a similar doubling occurs above the "fundamentals," a few fifths alternating with the sixth. In No. 9, the melodious Study in G flat, the wrist is severely exercised by groups of four notes, two to be played legato and two staccato ; the double notes for right hand consist of thirds, octaves, fourths, and a second.

Madame Menter will play this afternoon, and again on Monday.

The complaints of your "Saturday Afternoon" contributor are only too well founded. On Monday a solemn pause ensued before the second movement of Spohr's quartet could be begun, a long file of "late entries" quite blocked the way ; even before this, those who sat in the recesses were grievously annoyed by passers-by, sometimes moving on, but often halting in front !   A. M.

DERBY.

Recently Mendelssohn's "Elijah" was given by the Choral Union, under the painstaking conductorship of Mr. T. Tallis Trimnell, Mus.Bac. Miss M. Davies, Mdme. Patey, Mrs. Gardener, Mr. Dunkerton and Mr. F. King, were the chief singers. The orchestra and chorus were well up to their work, some of the choruses being highly effective. The orchestra included Messrs. Lazarus, Twinn, Avison, etc. Mr. Cox was the organist.

DENBIGH.

The Philharmonic Society gave a performance of Dr. Stainer's "Daughter of Jairus" and Mendelssohn's Hymn of Praise at the Town Hall on Friday Jan. 5th, 1883. The vocalists engaged were Miss Kate Hardy, R.A.M., and Mr. Levison Wyatt (Chester Cathedral) Mr. Stephenson led the orchestra. Master Myrick Robert presided at the piano and Major Casson at the harmonium, and Mr. Felix C. Watkins conducted. During the interval the Mayor of Denbigh presented to the conductor, Mr. Felix C. Watkins, a gold mounted ivory bâton and an illuminated address subscribed for by the members of the National Eisteddfod Choir 1882.

MDME. MENTER.

At Mr. Boosey's first "Ballad" concert, last Saturday afternoon, a number of popular airs and some part-songs were well rendered by various artists, inclusive of Miss M. Davies, Miss A. Larkcom, Miss Damian, Mrs. Hutchinson, Mr. E. Lloyd, Mr. Santley, &c. The chief attraction to *connoisseurs* was the first appearance this season of Mdme. Sophie Menter, whose splendid performances last year, when she held several "recitals," were highly eulogised at the time in these columns.

On Saturday, this gifted pupil of the Abbé Liszt played only a few fugitive pieces, all, however, of sterling merit. A favourite Etude of Chopin in the mazurka form excited an outburst of enthusiastic applause hardly to be expected at a miscellaneous "Ballad" concert, where vocal music usually bears the palm. In her next piece, the so-called Spinnlied in C, from Book VI. of Mendelssohn's "Lieder ohne Worte," the reading was thought to be rather too restless for the style, which obviously requires a smooth and even exposition of the text. In "Les Patineurs" of Liszt, a clever though rhapsodical "Transcription" of the beautiful ballet scene in "La Prophète" of Meyerbeer, Mdme. Menter found herself absolutely in her own element, and achieved a glorious success. The delivery of the graphic *glissando* passages, were not only delicious, but quite appropriate to the "situation," commanding the admiration of all, the uninitiated as well as the knowing ones. The delicate and playful humouring of this long *asquisse* could not be clearly described. Mdme. Menter's ineffable charm of style, fine touch, and intellectual intuition, have before been noticed ; an alleged wanting of "sensibility," as already hinted, must be looked for in the *auditors* who may be unable, from some "twist" in "the things they call their minds"—as Lord Westbury would have said—to appreciate excellence so general, so remarkable. Mdme. Menter was re-called with honour. She is engaged to play "Le Carnaval" of Schumann to-day (Saturday) at the Popular Concert, and again on Monday night, when Chopin's "Polonaise" in A flat and Schumann's pianoforte Quartet in E flat are on the list of numbers. It is a privilege to hear two such pianists as Mdme. Menter and Herr Pachmann within the space of a short month. Mr. Arthur Chappell ought to be warmly thanked for the opportunity thus afforded. Mr. Chappell, as an "opportunist," approaches the late lamented Gambetta.

LEEDS.

The Leeds Parish Church Choir gave their annual concert in the Church Institute on Thursday evening, Dec. 4. The first part of the programme consisted of Sterndale Bennett's cantata, "the Woman of Samaria," which was gone through in a highly creditable manner. The soloists were Masters Parkinson and Hardaker, sopranos; Master Bramham, contralto; Mr. Verney Binns, tenor; and Mr. W. Morton, bass. The performance throughout was excellent, but special mention must be made of the lovely unaccompanied quartet "God is a Spirit," which was rendered in a most impressive manner. The second part of the programme included the opening chorus "Come from the woods," from Dr. Creser's new work "Eudora," which was sung in capital style, and the whole concluded with the chorus from "Tannhäuser," "Hall, bright abode." Dr. Creser played the pianoforte accompaniments.

EDINBURGH.

(From our Own Correspondent.)

Jan. 9, 1883.

While the Choral Union deserve the thanks of all musicians for their bold attempt to give a first-class popular concert in the Waverley Market on December 30th, it was to be deplored greatly that, owing chiefly to the unsuitability of the hall, the performance could not be said to have been successful. It really seems "hard lines" that the masses in our city cannot possibly ever have a chance of properly hearing good music well performed. Nevertheless, the trial was in the right direction, and if it in any way furthers the chance, through making evident our present want, that of obtaining some time or other a new hall of proper dimensions for orchestral concerts; then our thanks will be doubly due to the committee of the Choral Union for the concert on the 30th.

"Familiarity," it is well known, "breeds contempt," which wise old saw found ample support from the performance of the "Messiah" on Tuesday, 2nd January. Who was to blame it is difficult to say, but let it be who it may, many of the choruses were most carelessly sung, so much so that, once or twice, had it not been for the orchestra and Mr. Hartley at the organ it would be difficult to say what might have happened. The organ, by the way, was in a worse condition than usual, and evidently handicapped Mr. Hartley to some extent. Every cloud, though, has a silver lining, Mdme. Patey on this occasion being the brighter side of the picture. Her performance—like that of how few, alas!—was quite above criticism and must ever remain with her hearers as a most pleasant recollection. Miss Carlotta Elliott was successful in several of the soprano airs, and Mr. Harper Kearton, if he had infused a little more life into his singing, would have made a feature of the tenor music, but by what accident Mr. Roberts was selected to take the bass part it is difficult to imagine.

The fifth orchestral concert was given on Wednesday, 3rd January, when the chief items of interest were Spohr's Symphony No. 4, "the consecration of sound," overture and garden scene from "The Veiled Prophet," by C. Villiers Stanford, and overture "Les Francs Juges," by Berlioz. M. Victor Buziau on this occasion showed his large musicianly skill as a violinist, and Miss Carlotta Elliot sang several numbers with great acceptance.

Of minor concerts it is impossible to even mention all; one or two, however, deserve passing notice. Mr. Magnus Peterson gave a most ambitious programme lately at the Queen Street Hall. Indeed, although Mr. Peterson's purpose of popularizing the music of the future is to be admired, it is questionable policy to do so through the medium of an amateur choir. The singing, on this occasion, of Miss Middleton, who bids fair to be, ere long, one of our best local sopranos, was a most enjoyable feature, her taste in executing even the most difficult passages being characterised by great breadth of treatment.

The St. Giles Choral Society, which is a promising body of singers, gave a pleasant Christmas recital, consisting of selections from the "Messiah" and Mendelssohn's "Fest Gesang." Miss Mackenzie sung the soprano soli with a sympathetic feeling and musical ability which called for all praise. Mr. J. O. Sinclair conducted and Mr. John Hartley at the "vocalion" accompanied.

J. C. D.

LIVERPOOL.

(From our Own Correspondent.)

Mr. Max Bruch has resigned the conductorship of the Philharmonic Society, and will vacate the appointment at the end of the present season, in April. He has accepted the position of conductor of the concerts in Breslau, the capital of Silesia, and the largest provincial town in Germany. In addressing the committee of the Philharmonic Society, Mr. Max Bruch wrote :—"I intend and hope to visit England frequently in the future, and I trust it may be my good fortune to keep up those friendly relations with the Liverpool Philharmonic Society which I value so highly." A strong wish is expressed that Mr. Fred. Cowen will be appointed to the post.

The Carl Rosa Opera season is running along successfully at the Royal Court Theatre. On Monday evening, Donizetti's "La Favorita" was produced for the first time in English, and with a success that reflects additional lustre upon the enterprise of the impresario and the members of the company. The cast was as follows :—

Leonora	Mdme. Marie Roze.
Alfonso	Mr. Ludwig.
Baldassare	Mr. Henry Pope.
Don Gaspare	Mr. Esmond.
Ines	Miss Clara Perry.
Fernando	Mr. Barton McGuckin.

In the character of Leonora, Mdme. Roze had a part in which she appeared to greater advantage than in anything she has so far undertaken in English opera. The music suits her voice, and she fully enters into the spirit of the character. Her rendering of the Cavatina, "Dearest Fernando," was full of intense expression and feeling, and, withal, a thoroughly artistic performance. Mr. Barton McGuckin as Fernando eclipsed his former efforts in other parts. Donizetti's hero is completely suited to Mr. McGuckin's capacities, and with the improvement he has made (both vocally and as an actor) lately, it was a pleasure to be assisting at a creation in which he appeared to such pre-eminent advantage. Of Mr. Ludwig one can only say that in the part of the king he has added another to the long list of triumphs, of which he has reason to be proud. The smaller parts were creditably filled; the dresses were superb, the staging excellent; the orchestration, notwithstanding a few slips, was enjoyable, and the whole performance, under the conductorship of Mr. Goosens, was heartily enjoyed and warmly applauded by the large audience assembled. There were calls before the curtain after each act.

The Philharmonic Society gave their seventh concert of the present season last evening, the principal artists being Mdme. Norman-Néruda and Mdme. Patey. The programme included Viotti's Violin Concerto in A minor; Villiers Standford's Orchestra Serenade, composed from the last Birmingham Festival; and the overtures "Iphigenie en Aulide" (Gluck); "William Tell" (Rossini); "L'Etoile du Nord" (Meyerbeer). Amongst the vocal items was Gounod's song, "The golden thread," also produced at the festival above mentioned, and sung by Mdme. Patey. Mr. Max Bruch conducted, and Mr. Branscombe acted as accompanist.

At Mr. Halle's Orchestral Concert, on Tuesday next, the same two artists who were the attraction at the Philharmonic Concert last evening, are to appear, together with Signor Piatti.

The Karl Meyder Orchestral Concerts have come to an abrupt ending. They did not pay. The following was the programme of the Fortnightly Tuesday Afternoon Concert, given by the pupils of the School for the Blind, yesterday, under the direction of Mr. W. D. Hall :—

Anthem, "Behold I bring you"	Goss.
Recit., "When Jesus our Lord"	
Trio, "Say, where is He born"	Mendelssohn.
Chorus, "There shall a Star from Jacob"	
Anthem, "Let us now go even unto Bethlehem"	Hopkins.
Chorus, "Hallelujah"	Handel.
Song, "Bethlehem"	Gounod.
Part-song, "Who shall win my lady fair"	Pearsall.
Song, "Rags, thou angry storm"	Benedict.
Duet, "Why listen to the carols"	Mendelssohn.
Song, "Entreat me not to leave thee"	Gounod.
Part-song, "Good night, good night, beloved"	Pinsuti.

J. J. M.

Herr Louis Roth, of Vienna, has just completed an operetta called "Der Marquis von Rivoli." Goldmark's "Hönigin von Saba" was lately given for the first time in Brunswick with well deserved success.

Foreign Musical Intelligence.

Wagner's " Rienzi " has been heard at Turin recently.

Brahms's Symphony in D has been given in Naples recently with much success.

A. Thomas's " Mignon " has been successfully given in Venice lately.

Wagner's " Nibelungen Ring," and Boïto's " Mephistofele " are to be given soon in Brussels.

It is proposed to erect a statue of Méhul in his native town, Givet.

The German Academy of Singing celebrated on November 9th, the 90th anniversary of its existence.

A society for the cultivation of instruments of the guitar and mandoline tribe has been formed at Bologna.

It is said that Conrad Kreuzer, the composer, celebrated his 100th birthday at Vienna, on November 22nd.

A quartet in E, by Karl Dittersdorf, and a pianoforte trio in A flat (Op. 65) by Herr Kiel, were lately heard at Cassel.

The remains of John Howard Payne, the author of " Home sweet Home," are to be removed from Tunis to America.

Johann Baptist André, well known abroad as a pianist and composer of considerable repute, died at Offenbach-on-the-Main on the 9th inst., in the 60th year of his age.

L'Union de la Sarthe notices a new Mass of merit by Madame de Grandval, produced at Christmas at the Cathedral of Mans.

Under the title of " The Queens of Song," Le Menestrel is giving appreciative notices of sundry great singers. On January 7th, Madame Carvalho is the subject of the article.

Messrs. Breikopf and Härtel have recently issued their gigantic catalogue in a regular and alphabetical shape. It names some 16,000 works, and covers nearly 1,000 pages.

La Gasetta Provinciale di Bergamo gives a glowing account of Signor Ponchielli's new Mass in that city, and tells of the profound impression produced by what is evidently a work of much thought and musical power.

Saint-Saëns's opera " Samson and Delila " is promised as one of the novelties of the present season in Munich. The chief parts are to be taken by Herr and Frau Vogl.

It is stated that a younger sister of Madame Sophie Menter has lately appeared in Vienna as a pianist. She is reported to be not only a clever executant, but to possess much musical feeling.

The Musikalisches Wochenblatt gives an account of Herr Wilhelm Fischer's new instrument, the Adiaphon. Tuning-forks are struck by hammers, as in the ordinary pianoforte. The tone is spoken of as very fascinating.

The entire collection of violins and bows belonging to Vieuxtemps has been purchased by the Duke of Campo-Medinæ, for the sum of fifty thousand francs. The Duke owns one of the finest collections of instruments in existence.

It is announced that the committee of the International Exhibition to be held next year in Amsterdam have decided for financial reasons to do nothing in connection with music beyond the performance of a cantata to be composed for the opening ceremony by Herr Verhulst.

Liszt, it seems, has, as a matter of self-protection, addressed an appeal to the German musical papers, deprecating the habit common amongst young aspiring composers, of sending him their scores for inspection. " All contributions to collections of autographs," Liszt adds, " I have modestly declined for many years."

M. Eugène D'Albert, son of Mr. Charles D'Albert, has recently played with great éclat at Berlin and at Weimar, before the Emperor of Germany. His success at the Popular Concerts, two years ago, is a matter of history. This promising pianist is now thoroughly "accepted" in æsthetical Germany, and his studies in that country will tend to increase his reputation.

A prize has been offered at Palermo for the best original composition for the pianoforte.

Signor Disconzi is announced as engaged upon the composition of an opera-ballo " La Cortigiana."

A new opera, the " Wilde Jager " by Nessler, has had a triumphant production at Strasburg.

A kind of secular oratorio, " Alrico," has been performed at Darmstadt. The work is by Herr Vierling.

Joseph Wieniawski is now settled in Brussels, where he is highly esteemed as a teacher.

Gounod's " Philemon et Baucis " is being rehearsed at the Vienna Court Opera House. His " Tribut de Zamora " will be performed for the first time in Vienna on the 20th inst.

The French Quartet Society gave an interesting concert in Paris the other week. The programme included a quartet by Lalo, a trio by Boisdeffre, and a quintet of Félicien David.

Herr August Klughardt's new symphony, lately produced in Dresden, has been very favourably criticised by the German press. A 'Swedish Rhapsody," by Herr Hallen, was performed recently in Berlin, under the direction of Herr Bilse, and well received.

The " Association Artistique " of Angers recently gave a festival in honour of Litolff, who conducted several of his own compositions. Two of these, " Les Chant des Guelfes " and an overture, " Les Girondins," were received with marked favour.

The nature of Hans von Bülow's illness is now stated to be not so dangerous as was believed at first. He is said to be suffering from a nervous complaint, which although serious enough has not in any way affected the brain. In order to pursue the course of treatment thought necessary by his physicians, the celebrated pianist has retired to a hydropathic establishment.

The climate of Verviers, the native town of Vieuxtemps, seems to be favourable to the production of violinists. The son of M. Nicolas Herman, a professor of music in Verviers, was a successful one of 53 candidates who competed for 19 vacancies in the Liege Conservatoire lately. The young violinist is only six years of age.

The following is a list from La Gassetta Musicale of the new operas produced in Italian in 1882 : " Mitridate " (serious opera), by E. Serrano, first performed at Madrid, Jan. 14th ; " Ivan " (buffo), A. Lucidi, Bologna, Feb. 6th ; " Bianca da Cervia " (serious), A. Smareglia, Milan, Feb. 7th : " Il Progettista " (farcical), A. Scontrino, Rome, Feb. 8th ; " Il Conte Chatillon " (serious), N. Massa, Reggio Emilia, Feb. 11th ; " Erodiade " (serious), G. Massenet, Milan, Feb. 23rd ; " Il tributo di Zamora " (serious), C. Gounod, Turin, March 5th ; " Margherita " (serious), C. Pinsuti, Venice, March 8th ; " Il Duca d'Alba " (serious), G. Donizetti, Rome, March 22nd ; " Rabagas " (serious), N. De Giosa, Rome, March 23rd ; " Il Dottor Cosmos " (operetta), E. De Champs, Florence, March 27th ; " Alceste " (serious), A Gambaro, Leghorn, March 27th ; " Maria di Vasco " (serious), C. Brizi, Bologna, March 29th ; " Beatrice " (serious), Guimaraes, Lisbon, March 29th ; " Il Violino di Cremona " (semi-serious), G. Litta, Milan, April 18th ; " La corona d'ora " (semi-serious), Maglioni, Florence, April 18th ; " Cesiro d'Aragona " (serious), Bianchedi, Corinaldo, April 18th ; " Carlotta Clepier " (serious), P. Floridia, Naples, May 7th, " Masine Spinola " (serious) ; A. Joctean Turin, May 11th ; " Il Bacio al Diavolo " (serious), A. Sauvage, Trieste, May 11th : " Amelia " (operetta), Walter Graziani, Florence, May 14th ; " Nella " (semi-serious), A. Disconzi, Parma, May 28th ; " La Modella " (serious), O. Bimboni, Berlin, May 30th ; " Fayel " (serious) F. Caronna, Rome, June 11th ; " Il Sortilegio " (buffo), A. Scontrino, Turin, June 21st ; " Regina e Contadina " (comic), E. Sarria, Naples, June 21st ; " La Stella d'Oriente " (operetta), F. Curci, Naples, June 21st ; " Velleda " (serious), Lenepveu, London, July 4th ; " Ersilia " (buffo), C. Pascucci, Rome, July 4th ; " Manfredi di Svevia " (serious) ; T. Giribaldi, Montevideo, July 18th ; " Adina " (comic), T. Bruti, Cupramontana, Aug. 9th ; " Partita a scacchi " (farcical), Delitala, Cagliari, Nov. 25th ; " Nella " (serious), Ettore Ricci, Ravenna, Nov. 27th ; " Flora Mac-Donald " (serious), John Urich, Bologna, December 6th.

In 1875, Sight Singing Classes were established in the Academy, through which every pupil is required to pass ; this was a revival truly, but of a matter which had been so long in disuse that the revival had the air of a novelty. In the same year the Public Choral and Orchestral Concerts by the pupils, which previously had never been given in an arena larger than the Hanover Square Rooms, were transferred to St. James's Hall, where they are now attended by audiences of from 1500 to 2000 in number, and are thus the means of affording experience of performing in public to the executants, and of making the public acquainted with the working of the Institution. In 1876, because the growing number of the pupils could no longer be accommodated in the space occupied by the Academy, the new Concert-room was built at the cost of from 4000*l*. to 5000*l*., wherein the Weekly Choral and Orchestral practices are held, as are also the Yearly Examinations and the Monthly Concerts of Chamber Music. In this year were instituted fortnightly meetings of professors and pupils, whereat the less advanced learners make first essay of their powers between the maturer performances of their elders. A Quartet Class for the Practice of Concerted Instrumental Music was likewise established in 1876, and the Operatic Class was then first opened for the study of the Lyrical Drama, and this Class gives performances, at least once in every term, that have included the whole or portions of operas by the best masters, and occasional productions of the pupils. The formation of Classes for Modern Languages, the appointment of a Professor of Acoustics, and the occasional delivery of Lectures on this and other subjects connected with Music, are all incidental to the period in question.

The foregoing may perhaps be accepted as proofs of the internal activity of the Academy. As an influence on the musical culture of the nation, separately from its own teaching, the institution has sought to be useful by means of the Local Examinations of students held at every important centre, wherein the ability of teachers is tested through the practical evidence of their pupils. The scheme has been two years in operation, and though its details may, and doubtless will, be improved, its efficacy thus far is widely acknowledged. Yet graver in its possible results is the Metropolitan Examination of artists and teachers, which is designed to apply to all branches of practical musicianship such inspection as the universities make of theoretical attainments, and the diploma granted to every successful candidate is a testimony of ability that may in time receive such respect as is paid to a university degree. These two may perhaps be admitted be the best means, because the long roll of names of eminent musicians that have been nurslings of the academy is an incentive to students in the school to emulate the distinction of their predecessors. The academy may be the best means, because those of its former scholars who, like yourself, my dear Sir, have received the title of member or associate are jealous of the honour of the kind mother under whose wings their own talent was fostered, and therefore do all they can to advance the interests and secure the permanence of their early home.

Many well-wishers of the Royal Academy are inconsiderate enough to say that there is room in England for two great musical seminaries ; inconsiderate, I must believe, because the opinion seems not to have been duly balanced. The supposition might have ground were the operations of the academy circumscribed either by the terms of its royal charter or by the policy of its managing body. On the contrary, however, the charter is so elastic in its nature that it allows of the expansion of the academy's doings in any and every direction that may advance the art of music. The committee are anxious to avail themselves of this elasticity in every possible manner, and they have officially signified such wish to his Royal Highness the Prince of Wales and previously to the Lords of the Privy Council. One establishment holding the confidence of the musical profession is likelier to labour with good effect than two which would contend for public support, and might spend those energies in factious opposition which should be concentrated on internal duties. It was once said that there was room in the ocean for two North Americas, and much noble blood was gloriously shed in support of the hypothesis ; but the world seems now to be convinced that the Federal Union is for the true welfare of the Continent.

Everything that is wanted, everything that is possible for musical culture is within the scope of the academy, which needs but fiscal resources to accomplish its purposes. The plan I offered in March to your notice waits but for such means to be fulfilled—the plan, namely, of opening branch schools in principal centres under academy auspices. The Royal Academy of Music does not reject the offerings of those lovers of art who trust in its power for good, and prove their trust by financial testimony. You are one of these, and were your example followed of setting aside a sum towards the establishment of a branch School in Manchester, I cannot doubt that one would speedily be organised wherein the teaching powers of the local professors would be valuably utilised, and the budding musicianship of the neighbourhood would be worthily trained.

The centralising tendency which draws artists of every denomination to the metropolis is not yet so universal as to drain the great provincial centres of all the truly admirable ability of their residents. This ability ought to be appropriated to its great moral and intellectual purposes of education in the several localities where it remains, and the wish of the Academy management is that such powers should be made of avail until that period in a student's career when the example of London performances is needed to illustrate the teaching of the most highly approved instructors. The executive musical talent of all the world is yearly displayed in London, and professors from all parts of Europe make that city their home ; hence, it would be no slight of the merits of provincial musicians to invite them to act in association with a long-tried metropolitan body, to whose final charge and approbation the results of local teaching might be confided.—I am, dear Mr. Wrigley, faithfully yours, G. A. MACFARREN.

The Covent Garden Promenade Concerts are being continued with a frequent change of programme calculated to suit all tastes. At the first classical night of the new series was given Mendelssohn's overture to "Ruy Blas," Mozart's "Jupiter" symphony, and other smaller works, when the excellence of the orchestra, directed by Mr. A. Gwyllym Crowe was specially manifested. In portions of Beethoven's Septet, the following solo instrumentalists were heard to advantage :—Mr. Carrodus (violin), Mr. Hann (viola), Mr. Mann (horn), Mr. Clinton (clarinet), Mr. Hutchins (bassoon), Mr. E. Howell (violoncello) ; and Mr. E. Ould (double bass). Mdlle. D. Badia and Mr. Maas contributed vocal pieces with marked success. During the past week or so a national night and a Balfe night were among the attractions.

Second Edition, Revised and Enlarged, cloth, 3s. 6d.

BEETHOVEN'S PIANOFORTE SONATAS, explained by ERNST von ELTERLEIN, translated by E. Hill. Preface by E. Pauer.

W. REEVES, 185, FLEET STREET, LONDON.

PRINCIPAL CONTENTS OF THIS NUMBER.

LONDON : SATURDAY, JANUARY 13, 1883.

INDIA AND THE NATIONAL ANTHEM.

 COMMITTEE has recently been formed with the object of supplying our Indian subjects with a version of the British National Anthem fitted for their use. Such a design is worthy of the support of all loyal people. Now that the QUEEN of ENGLAND has become EMPRESS of HINDOSTAN, the dusky millions who own her sway ought certainly to be afforded similar opportunities of displaying their loyalty, to those enjoyed by the other branches of our far-spreading empire. Space need not be wasted in commenting on the great importance that is rightly attached to the songs of a nation. Indeed, the *dictum* of ANDREW FLETCHER of Saltoun to the effect, that the national songs of a people are of greater importance than the laws manufactured for them, is to a certain extent true. The student of history will doubtless remember the important part that such songs have frequently played at certain crises in the history of nations. Whether the *locale* be Scotland, England, France, Germany, Russia, or Italy, it will be found that such songs have often not only greatly aided in preparing the minds of the people for changes that have affected the constitution of their country, but they have further nerved the arms of those fighting, and, when war was over, have also served to consolidate together a newly formed nation. The aim therefore of the "Committee of the National Anthem "for India" is both important and laudable. We occupy there a position altogether unique. About one hundred-and-twenty thousand Englishmen govern people numbering two hundred and seventy millions. Such a task requires the genius, intelligence and devotion, that are happily some of the characteristics of our fighting and colonizing race. And now that the various nations which inhabit this vast peninsula, whatever may be their diverse type or semi-independent status, have to acknowledge the supreme headship of the British Government, the attempt to unite them to us in closer bonds of loyalty becomes a matter of national utility.

But having admitted so much, it becomes our duty as practical people to look at the question in all its aspects, and see if the desire expressed is capable of realization. There are obstacles in the way, and moreover they are no slight ones. A person of ordinary intelligence, who has not specially thought on this subject, may wonderingly ask : What is the difficulty ! is not music an universal language common to all civilized people, and do we not daily see words in connection with it, specially written for one nation, quickly and easily adapted to the speech and idioms of another ? The answer to this query must necessarily be in the affirmative, but it should be observed that the general conditions which exist in Europe do not obtain in far away India. It may be remarked that, with the exception of those who have a practical acquaintance with the country, few of us have a correct idea of India. We are too apt to consider it as a sort of over-grown semi-civilized land, mainly inhabited by people of a similar type, and presenting in its general features more uniformity than is to be found in dis-united Europe. Almost the converse of this is the case. The area of the country nearly equals that of Europe proper, while its population is but little under that with which this entire continent is credited. Independently of the small native states owning the suzerainty of Her Im-PERIAL MAJESTY, in the eight provinces into which India is divided there are several more languages spoken than are to be found in Europe entire ; these languages differ from one another more than does English from French. Without dwelling on the divergence which exist between the feelings and ideas of its various peoples, it may suffice to point out, that whereas throughout Europe (even including Turkey) but one Supreme Being is acknowledged as GOD, in India each racial division has its particular gods, mutually abominating the divinities worshipped by the others. Finally, the musical tonality which prevails throughout Europe is as unintelligible to the Indians as is their peculiar mode to us.

From the above remarks it will be seen that there are two main impediments connected with the scheme proposed ; the first has to do with the question of translation, while the second relates to the music proper. With regard to the linguistic difficulty, but little need be said here. It is evident that if the various nations of India are to sing the National Anthem, their version must contain sentiments that they can appreciate, and must be written in a language that they can understand. It will, therefore, be necessary to make as many translations as there are dialects. This can no doubt be done ; but the difficulty of finding a precise equivalent for "GOD" seems likely to afford a bone of endless contention to the amateur theologists connected with the enterprise. The two divisions of Mohammedans would probably be satisfied with the name "ALLAH ;" but to select from polytheistic concourse, worshipped by the various sects of Buddhists and Brahmins, the name of the particular deity to be invoked is indeed a formidable undertaking. Some of these sub-divisions utterly reject the favourite divinities of the others. It has been proposed to employ the Sanskrit word "DEVA," which, according to the authority of philologists, is the root of the Greek "Theos" and the Latin "Deus ;" but though this word is used by the missionaries working in India, it is said to be practically unknown to the vast mass of the people. The creed of the Parsees being monotheistic, the task is an easier one. There appears to be yet another linguistic anxiety, viz., that of correctly translating the new title of "EMPRESS. There may probably be some little trouble over the versification of Kaiser-i-Hind, but this is a matter which ought not to stop the way.

We now approach the consideration of the purely musical aspect of the question, and the obstacle here appears to be insuperable. The seven intervals, together with the chromatic semitones, into which the European octave has been divided, constitute the materials from which all our music is built up. No doubt this system has been gradually, perhaps arbitrarily, developed from the ancient pentatonic scale, but the science of acoustics has proved that our division is true to nature's laws. Having heard only these intervals from our childhood, we can appreciate no music except that constructed according to this scale. The Hindoos sub-divide their octave into twenty-two notes ; thus, our music, founded on a scale divided into twelve sounds only, is as unintelligible to them as theirs proves to be to us. It is useless to dogmatise on this divergence, and assert that our method is alone right, or to say that Hindoo, Chinese, Japanese, Arab and all music differing from it must necessarily be mere uncouth noise. The fact that nations so ancient, so civilised, so distinguished for their literature and beautiful art productions, have for ages enjoyed their national music, proves that there are systems and systems. Indeed, according to the evidence of the learned Orientalist Sir William Jones, there is gratification to be obtained from Hindoo music. In view, then, of the great distinction that exists between Indian music and our own, one is anxious to know what the National Anthem Committee propose to do. Is an attempt to be made to engraft the hymn on the ancient *raginees* stem, or will the Committee boldly and simply supply the air and its attendant harmonies as we use it ? Here is, indeed, a dilemma, and it appears impossible to avoid impalement on either horn. If the first supposition be adopted, then the Indian "God Save the Queen" will not be identical with our version ; while, if the second course be followed, the untrained voices of the natives will be unable to sing sounds their ears cannot appreciate. A popular national hymn must be the true representative of the people's desires ; it is not likely to be successful if manufactured for them extraneously. We know the old proverb as to the difficulty of making the horse drink the water to which he was led, and it is quite probable that a similar want of success will attend the well meant efforts of those who have entered upon this movement. It ought to cause some misgiving in their minds to reflect, that though the domiciled English people and our regimental bands have been singing and playing the National Anthem and other music for the last hundred years in the country, not a single melody has been retained, or any portion of our musical system adopted by the Hindoos. Despite the onward march of Western civilisation, in the case of so peculiar a conservatism as India exhibits, the time seems far distant when its natives will be qualified to adopt European music.

A word as to the version to be followed. We ought to know what is to be the precise text of the music selected, and hear whether it is true that a supposed improved edition of the words by a Rev. F. K. HARFORD is to be employed. This gentleman has eliminated what may be termed the damnatory clauses, and has turned their rough terseness into Christianity of another type. History shows that from time to time such improvements have been made. But whether they have been suggested by an outbreak of war-fever, the birth of a new prince, or a providential escape from the assassin, the improvements have survived their occasion but a brief period. If the Rev. Mr. HARFORD will but refer to the Bible, especially the Psalms, he will there find employed most of the expressions he has presumed to reject. If India is to be supplied with a new arrangement both of the words and music, she will certainly not possess the British National Anthem as we know it. Like the Irishman's oft mended coat, the original will have well-nigh disappeared under the patchings to which it has been subjected.

One is curious to know to whom the Committee is going to ascribe the authorship of the music. Will they follow the blunders of CLARK with his exploded fables about Dr. J. BULL, or adopt the theory now generally conceded that CAREY gave us the hymn in its present form?   T. L. SOUTHGATE.

THE LOGIC OF COUNTERPOINT.

THIRD SERIES.

I.

THE consideration of the construction of counterpoint in four parts involves, in the very presence of a fourth part, something of a new problem in the building up of the contrapuntal harmony, the constant handling of an overplus voice so to speak, seeing that as a general rule three parts may be made to express complete five-three chords and their six-three inversions. It may be here noted, however, that in consequence of enforced melodic progressions and resolutions of a more peremptory character in the movement of the external voices than in the action of the internal part, complete five-three or six-three harmony is frequently unattainable in three-part harmony; consequently one great use of harmony in four or more parts, is the power it possesses of securing completely formed chords. Sometimes, indeed, as in cadence points in which a two-fold obligation carries both the fifth of the dominant and its third, the leading-note, to the tonic, an important chord is shorn of one of its essential elements, either its fifth or its third; the ancients often preferred, perhaps, with an instinct for real strength, to sacrifice the third to the retention of the

fifth, while modern writers almost invariably elect to give up the fifth and retain the weaker but sweeter sound of the third. So even four parts are not always sufficient to secure complete harmony in chords having only three elements, although as a general rule, four-part writing is found the best, as the clearest and most evenly balanced method of building up successive harmonies in their generally complete forms. Four part counterpoint may be said also to open another question for the student's consideration, the comparative immunity of the part actions from the law forbidding the hidden, covered or enclosed consecution of perfect concords, save as regards the relationship between the two outside parts. Even in the conduct of three-part counterpoint a few exceptions to the rule in question are not only found to be advisable, but now and then become absolutely necessary, as often between the two last bars when the *canto fermo* is not in the lowest part. Naturally the multiplication of parts, by crowding and restricting the movement of the different voices compels a leniency in this respect, which must become more and more elastic as the number of the employed parts increases. In short, this leniency with regard to covered consecutive perfect concords is more or less necessary in all examples in which the number of parts in action, exceeds the very limited number of directions in which part movements are possible. The student anxious to secure contrapuntal strength and independence, will do well, however, to appeal as little as possible to the relaxation of the rule concerning the presence of hidden consecutives. An unwise tendency to consider the rule as practically done away in four-part counterpoint as regards all part actions save the movements between the external voices, will inevitably lead to a weakness in the writing, and to a loss of time, for a given number of exercises written under notions of such wholesale relaxation will not impart half the clearness and strength to the writer's mind which may be secured by the more severe aspect of the question which will only permit such indulgent ease when absolutely inevitable. The wiser course for the student is a complete obedience to the spirit of the rule, which seeks as far as possible to enforce a power of independence in the part actions, without which faculty indeed counterpoint has little character or strength.

    E. H. TURPIN.

THE ROYAL COLLEGE OF MUSIC.

The following has been addressed by Mr. Gladstone to a leading musician:—

Sir,—The time has at last arrived when the affairs of the proposed Royal College of Music should be taken from the sphere of private endeavour to that of a State-supported institution. When I appeared on the platform at St. James's Palace, in company with the leader of her Majesty's Opposition, I was fully aware of the expectations that would naturally be roused by such a step. The only condition on which, in my mind, I made the grant of Government support dependent, was that sufficient interest should be shown by the public in the enterprise, and that that interest should take the practical form of subscriptions. Both conditions have been complied with to an unexpected degree, and in a manner not always as dignified as the character of the institution would have made desirable. Trade enterprise has connected itself with the movement, and the hope that the sun of royalty would shine on aldermanic autographs has been held out as a stimulus. It is time, Sir that this should cease, and before finally abandoning the control of the public purse strings, I am determined to unloose them once more in so excellent and harmonious a cause.

EXPERIENCES OF AN ORGANIST.

IV.

About this time there occurred in our church an event which, for a while, diverted attention from my delinquencies. The minister and deacons fell out. Our excitable parson preached a sermon on the doctrine of eternal punishment, and in the course of his eloquent remarks he showed so clearly the imminent danger of the sinner that I think the deacons began to feel alarmed about their own safety. Recollecting, perhaps, the many misdeeds which are a necessary part of every deacon's career, they took exception to this discourse, and found considerable fault with it. Now, if there is one thing which, more than any other, convinces me of the truth and justice of the doctrine referred to, it is the conduct of certain deacons whom I could name. Therefore it seems to me that the deacons, of all persons in the world, were the very last who should have found fault with the sermon. Nevertheless, such is the frailty of human nature that what is most for our good is often least to our liking. The deacons complained that their minister was too warm (as if anybody could be too warm on such a subject!). The minister retorted that his deacons were too cold. They said he was too sweeping in his denunciations. He replied that the church was full of spiritual cobwebs, and needed to be swept. And so they went on bandying words until at last neither he nor they could any longer be accurately described as either cold or warm, for all were decidedly hot, I think I may say piping hot.

The holy war, thus begun, was carried on with great spirit and energy on both sides, and in a few weeks the entire congregation was divided, like the House of Commons, into two hostile parties. A church-meeting was held forthwith. The proceedings were opened by the singing of a hymn :—

"Blest is the tie that binds
Our hearts in Christian love ;" etc.

The minister then made a statement : the deacons disputed its accuracy ; and a stormy discussion followed. The minister tendered his resignation: the deacons tendered theirs. He withdrew his resignation at the urgent request of his party : they, at the equally urgent request of their party, withdrew theirs. A great deal of talking ensued, but as the ordinary rules of debate were not scrupulously observed, the speakers sometimes coming forward in batches, instead of singly, as usual, it was difficult to hear, and, at this distance of time, is still more difficult to remember, what was said. I recollect, however, that somebody, who, though he had been speaking, or trying to speak, for a considerable period, had not succeeded in getting anybody to listen to him, suddenly accused somebody else's daughters of laughing at him, and referred to them contemptuously as "giggling girls." The father of these mirthful maidens rose to ask the chairman to protect his daughters from the insolence of the previous speaker. The previous speaker expressed his opinion that the "giggling girls'" father ought to be ashamed to show his face, as he had not paid his pew-rent. This accusation he shrieked out at the top of his voice. He was greeted with cries of "shame," and amid the confusion which followed, the chairman made many gallant attempts to restore order ; but the assistance he received was so overwhelming that for a long time his efforts were unavailing. An indignant lady, sitting near me, uttered the word "viper," but whether the epithet was intended for the father of the injured damsels, or for their accuser, or for the chairman, it is impossible to guess. At last, however, the tumult subsided ; the chairman announced that the discussion would be resumed next week, and the meeting was then closed with prayer.

The opposing spiritual forces were at first about equally matched, but the minister's party soon began to decrease in numbers, while the deacon's party continued to increase, and ere long the former found themselves in a small minority. The reason of this is easily explained. Our parson would persist in treating as his bitterest foes all who did not at once warmly and blindly espouse his cause, and, by this means, frightened the undecided and wavering into the camp of the enemy, and drove a good many of his friends in the same direction. The deacons, on the other hand, maintained a calm Christian bearing, which contrasted most favourably with the passion and vehemence of their "beloved but misguided pastor," as they called him, and was especially well calculated to

draw towards them the deaf old ladies, of whom there were a good many in our church, and who could plainly see their angelic faces, but could not so plainly hear their less angelic voices. Hence, when the next church-meeting came round, and the call to arms was sounded, it was evident that the deacons and their followers must eventually get the best of the affray. Nevertheless the ministerialists (to borrow a parliamentary expression) were nothing daunted by the tremendous odds which were against them, but rather urged thereby to mightier feats of arms (if it be not incorrect to speak of arms when I mean tongues). They fought long and desperately, as Christian soldiers will, especially when fighting with one another. At last, amid an indescribable scene of confusion, the parson once more tendered his resignation, in an excited speech, in which he boldly denounced friend and foe alike, and then shutting his ears to the remonstrances which greeted him on all sides, vacated the chair, and strode hastily but majestically out of the room, breaking up the meeting in disorder, and, in his anxiety to escape the maledictions which were hurled at him as he disappeared through the door, quite forgetting the benediction which it was his duty to have pronounced.

Thus we found ourselves suddenly deserted by our spiritual head, and left to our own devices. We remained in this dangerous condition for about a year and a half, during which period the leading members of the congregation were so busy quarrelling among themselves that my humble doings as organist and choirmaster fortunately escaped their notice, and I was allowed to take my own course without interference of any kind. Making the most of my opportunity, I exerted myself strenuously to improve the singing, and am happy to say that my efforts were fairly successful. That they were not more so is due to the unsolicited assistance which I received from a young lady in the congregation, whose voice was more powerful than pleasing, and whose ear was not worthy of the trust she placed in it. This fair damsel had once applied for admission into the choir, and, being refused, chose to revenge herself by singing very loudly, very harshly, and very much out of tune in the gallery. Sometimes, therefore, our delicate *pianissimo* effects were marred, and our beautiful *rallentando* cadences spoilt, by the independent operations of this harassing young woman. Still, notwithstanding this militating influence (which, indeed, was only what might have been expected in such a church militant as ours), our Sunday performances were certainly above mediocrity, and compared favourably with those of many neighbouring congregations.

At last we got a new minister. If we could have more easily agreed among ourselves, we might have got one long before, for parsons are not scarce in this highly favoured land. Indeed, I fear the market is just now rather overstocked with that commodity. But a great many scenes, similar to those already described, had to be enacted before the deacons could contrive to persuade the congregation that the man on whom they (the deacons) had all along had their eye was the man whom providence had designed for the vacant office. However, after a long and patient struggle with many obdurate hearts, their praiseworthy endeavours were ultimately crowned with success, and the new minister was duly elected. He was a man of energy, and a man of action. His energy was so abundant that it enabled him not only to attend to his own business, but to assist in that of every member of his flock, and his thirst for action was so great that he was no sooner settled among us than he began to look about for something to reform. Going round on his pastoral visits, he was speedily made acquainted, by the musical malcontents of the church, with my sins. Calling upon my former patron, the oracle, he learned that great man's candid opinion of me, which was that I was "a very obstinate young man." Here, then, was something for him to reform. What more fitting object for reformation than this obstinate organist, this stubborn sinner, who had so far forgotten his position as to assume the entire control of the music of the church. So, having now a noble purpose in view, he continued his professional peregrinations with greater zest, and by the time they were over, he had gathered together such a mass of evidence against the unsuspecting organist, as convinced him that that self-willed young man was, in his unreformed state, a dangerous enemy of religion, and that prompt and decisive action was absolutely necessary in order to save the church from impending ruin.

He took an opportunity of paying me a visit, or perhaps I should call it a visitation, and proceeded to favour me with his views on music in general and church music in particular. As he knew nothing whatever about music of any kind, it may be imagined that his discourse on this occasion was more amusing than instructive. He talked enthusiastically of the great masters, among whom he included Mr. Sankey, of the firm of Moody and Sankey, the American Revivalists, who were then performing at the Agricultural Hall. He strongly recommended me to go and hear that "sweet singer of Israel," as a means of improving my taste, which he rather broadly hinted was much in need of improvement. I promised to go, for I saw that he would not be satisfied unless I did. Then, after he had kindly pointed out all my defects as an organist, and as a leader of congregational psalmody (and, looked at from his musicianly point of view, they were by no means insignificant), he took his leave, apparently under the pleasing impression that he had discharged a very delicate duty in a very delicate manner.

DUAL TEMPERAMENT.

A correspondent writes thus :—

SIR,—In order to improve our harmony, I suggest the use of duplicate flutes, hautboys, bassoons, etc., like the clarionets. For pianos and organs, a slide from right to left might shift one note in each octave, leaving room for a total of five or six duplicate strings or pipes. The finger keys would not be altered or moved, but only the five or six swivel or jointed levers. After much thought and experience, I freely present this idea to all who may work it out, and I name it the dual temperament. My theory is, that if you add one note to each octave, and divide the diluted "wolf" or discord into two parts, you practically conquer it. A 24th part of the "wolf" is very different from a 12th part. *Slightly* imperfect fifths *will* yearn and yield to perfect neighbours, but with the present scale they refuse to accommodate us. The rule would be—humour most the sharp keys, to suit strings in C, G, D, A, and E, and drive the very small discord to the extra note provided. Moral :—Attend to the fifths, and leave the thirds and accidentals to take care of themselves. Odd sharps or flats are but passing notes, and even they would be better than at present. Thirds, we know, may be variable without offending us, but fifths—oh ! murder !— listen to prolonged fifths on wolfish flutes and hautboys ! The simple chords opening the "Midsummer" overture are rarely endurable. The twofold clarionets seldom annoy us. Then, as to bassoons, Chopin foolishly wrote a unison passage (in a piano concerto) for bassoon and piano. The scale was B minor, ascending, and it was not a little, but shockingly out of tune. I thought, does anyone notice this, or am I a hair-splitting maniac ? Fortunately the eminent pianist stopped. "Cannot you play that better in tune ? it makes one quite nervous." "No, Monsieur ;" and on went the rehearsal. The bassoonist was a first-rate solo player, but he required a duplicate bassoon. If you provide *two* wind instruments, you must greatly improve matters ; just as a brass band, using a few flat keys, *can be* better in tune than a present mixed orchestra. I know that in bands where all are "professors" and *musicians*, the notes are often raised and depressed, but this art is confined to a few. We want to raise *all* music in the scale of excellence. Remember, also, the outer world. *A fine ear is no artist's monopoly.* I have known outsiders with most acute perceptions of discord, and wincing when the *best performers* were playing a piano trio. The late masterly flautist, Richardson, could "whine" up a passage like sliding a finger on a violin ; but it is impossible to know the wants of every chord without looking at a score. Therefore, I say, raise the whole platform of music and simplify where possible. Expense is nothing for such an object. As to 'cellists and violinists, they screw this, and unscrew that, yet they can never enjoy repose or comfort ; so that all tends to swell the chorus of—Reform it altogether. Let us hope for a speedy release.   Yours truly,
Jan. 6th, 1883.   ANTI-WOLF.

P.S.—In time we may arrive at triple temperament with two D sharps, or two E naturals. There is room for fourteen notes where now are twelve. In any case, we are on the right road. Directions : Shave part of C lever ; bend B flat lever close to C, leaving room for a swivel on B flat lever, to act on B flat (No. 1), and B flat (No. 2). The *visible* finger keys would remain exactly as at present. Of course a perfectly tuned "'cello" gives out a C *painfully different* from that of the pianoforte. This should be altered. One of the world's greatest organ builders writes :— "If a couple more notes could be introduced into the scale, we might have more satisfaction in listening to a tempered organ ; ' one note would be a good step.'" A learned maker says :— "The bassoon is lamentably deficient." Another :—"No escape but by *separate* instruments."

GOSSIP ABOUT ROSSINI.

Rossini lived then in the Rue Basse du Rempart, a street which has nearly disappeared now, but he soon settled down in those larger apartments at the corner of the Boulevard des Italiens and the Rue de la Chaussée d'Antin.

I must, for the clear understanding of what follows, give a slight description of these apartments. From the ante-room you enter the dining-room, a moderate-sized oblong table to seat fourteen people filling it nearly wholly. To the right of it was the drawing-room where on Saturday nights the famous soirées were given which brought together celebrities of every class or section of politics, art, science, or financial position ; to the left was his studio—in fact, his bedroom—a square little place, containing a bed, a writing table, a Pleyel piano, and a wardrobe full of perishable linen and his imperishable manuscripts. On the little table in his bedroom he wrote them—on the big dining-room table the copyist copied them, because he never allowed a manuscript to go out of his house.

It is certainly incredible that he should have written the "Barber of Seville" in fifteen days, not that there can be the slightest doubt about the spontaneity of the melodies streaming quicker into his pen than out of it, but precisely because, although writing very fast, he had a way of rounding the head of the notes which took time, and writing a whole operatic score in a fortnight does not allow of many wasted minutes.

Donizetti wrote quickly, to such an extent that when I saw him write for the first time I did not think he was writing music. He had a knack of covering the pages with dots like a telegraph strip, and when he had done so he added the tails and lines. Rossini used to set to work at ten o'clock in the morning, having got up at nine. From ten to twelve, while he wrote, numbers of people came— some with letters of introduction, or old friends, and so on. He was very glad to make the acquaintance of talented young artists ; and received them with immense kindness, giving them advice, and sometimes letters. But what he absolutely hated was to be stared at as one of the sights of Paris.

Once his old friend Caraffa came and told him :— "There is a Russian Princess on the boulevard who waited two hours yesterday to see you pass. She wants so much to make your acquaintance. What shall I tell her ?" "Tell her," said Rossini, "that I am excessively fond of asparagus. She need only go to Potel et Chabot and buy the finest bunch she can get and bring it here. I shall then get up, and, after she has well inspected me in front, I shall turn round, and she can complete her inspection by taking the other view, too ; and then she may go."

He was rather fond, not only of asparagus, but of anything good to eat, and whenever he was sent some delicacy in that line he enjoyed it in advance by unpacking it himself, and then he used to say with delighted looks :—"Viola a quio la gloire est bonne." His visitors gone or not at twelve, he put on his wig, which until then lay quietly on the table, his big bald head being covered with a towel for the time being ; then he dresses, and by one o'clock every day he went. He took the first cab he met and asked :—"Est-ce que vos chevaux sont fatigues ?" When the unfortunate driver says "Non, Monsieur," he never took him, he never would trust himself to other than tired horses, and during all his life never had he entered a railway carriage.

Then he usually drove to the Palais Royal, in the latter days to the Passage de l'Opera, and walked up and down in the shaded galleries, meeting a number of friends and hearing with great interest all the newest gossip about singers, composers, and operatic chat in general.—*Temple Bar.*

A special correspondent of the *Daily News*, in a recent account of Arabi's past political position, tells how the people applauded Arabi Pacha's contemptuous remarks on the State subsidy of £9,000 to the Cairo Opera House, a "wretched imitation," as he described it, of Paris and Vienna, which "corrupted the morals of our youth." The speaker delared he would much prefer that the money should be paid for keeping the Opera House closed. But he would be still better pleased if the money were spent upon village schools, for lack of which the people must necessarily remain in their immemorial ignorance.

Academical Intelligence.

TRINITY COLLEGE, LONDON

The authorities of Trinity College, London, have. just completed the details of the " Henry Smart Scholarship." The following are some of the regulations :—

Candidates must be British subjects by birth, and at the date of examination must not be over eighteen years of age.

Candidates must produce a satisfactory certificate of moral character from a clergyman, magistrate, or other responsible person.

The Examination for the Scholarship will be held shortly before the commencement of the academical year, in September, 1883.

Candidates may offer as the principal subject of examination either the Organ or the Pianoforte, to which they may add such other practical or theoretical subjects as they may desire for the purposes of the Competition, subject to the approval of the Board.

In the subjects of Organ or Pianoforte playing candidates must submit for performance before the Examiners any one or more compositions from Section D of the Official List of the College, Pianoforte or Organ (*Senior Division*), of the Regulations for the Local Examinations in Instrumental and Vocal Music, which also may be had of the Secretary. In the optional subjects, candidates desiring to offer them must clearly state the pieces or standard of work in which they ask to be examined.

Conspicuous merit in at least one of the principal subjects will be essential to success, and artistic appreciation no less than technical skill will be requisite.

The successful candidate will receive the value of the Scholarship in the form of free instruction during a period of three consecutive academical years in three subjects, having his own choice thereof, with the proviso that the Organ shall in any case be one of the prescribed subjects during the entire course of the Scholarship. The Scholar shall also attend upon any additional classes, lectures, practice, College performances or rehearsals, free of College fees, which the Board or Chief Director of Studies may deem desirable ; and the said Scholar shall be expected to pass the Public Examinations of the College, in due course, but no examination fee will in such cases be required.

DONIZETTI.

The *Corriere di San Remo* publishes the following interesting letters by John Ruffini, who while in Paris composed the libretto of *Don Pasquale* for Donizetti, describing the state of that master towards the close of his life :—

Paris, March 29, 1847.

I have just returned from a long and sad visit. For some time I had felt a lively desire to see poor Donizetti once more before he left this world. He is in the Maison de Santé, about an hour's distance from Paris. I was there to-day with Accursi. I have never seen a more pitiable spectacle : a man with scarcely the form of man ; an inhert machine which has outlasted its extinguished intelligence and soul. He occupies at Ivry, in a house destined for lunatics, a small apartment on the ground floor, consisting of a small parlour and bedroom. He has the use of a little garden, in which we found him walking. When I say walking I only use a mode of speech, for he was strongly supported by a servant on each side, and scarcely helped himself, generally allowing his legs to drag. His neck was bent on his left shoulder generally, as was the case all to-day ; his eyes are closed. For the rest, he showed neither pleasure at our visit nor regret at our departure. His left hand is closed convulsively, so that the nails wound the palm. He rarely plants his whole foot on the ground, but stands on the heel or the toes. His whole body is periodically agitated by nervous jerks. In short he gave me exactly the impression of a man struck by the hand of God, and changed into a beast. Such must have been Nebuchadnezzar. . . . JOHN RUFFINI.—" Paris April 19, 1847. You exaggerate, my dear, the effect produced on me by the miserable state of poor Donizetti. Apart from the first sad impression, to tell the truth, the sight only left an intense feeling of compassion, and natural reflections on the nothingness and misery of men and of human things. Provident nature, who watches over the preservation both of the individual and the species, has furnished us with a kind of philosophical indifference to evils which have no remedy and, so to speak, exceed the limits of our capabilities of suffering. The evils of this world are so many hat if we could feel them all with the intensity claimed by every special case we should be so many Jobs, doing nothing but complain, stretched on our beds and strewing ashes on our heads, and God knows how the world would run. Nature therefore, outside of a small circle whose sorrows are our own, has given us a safety-valve in a kind of egoism ; the evils without the bounds of this small circle have only the rights to draw from us a limited quantity of sensibility almost subject to our will. Such is my case with regard to Donizetti. I deplore in him the genius so precipitated to the abyss, the magnificent star extinguished before its setting. I suffer for him, so to say, by reflection ; but my heart is very little interested in the question, at least far less than you seem to imagine. He never valued me otherwise, and I believe he never really liked any one in the world. He found his account in making use of me, as I found mine in being of use to him. There were cordial relations between us, but it was a friendship and plastic cordiality that never penetrated below the skin. . . . .—JOHN RUFFINI."

Passing Events.

Mr. Poznanski was engaged to play some violin solos at Swindon on Wednesday night.

Mr. F. Kingsbury has been appointed to the professorship of singing at the Blackheath Conservatoire of Music.

Signor Villa, a baritone of great merit, has recently sung in the provinces with success. At Bedford he sustained the part of " Elijah " so efficiently as to receive the thanks of Mr. Diemer, the conductor.

Under the will of the late Richard Ellison, Esq., of Sudbrooke Holme, Lincolnshire, a legacy of £500 has been left to the Choir Benevolent Fund Society, which is established for the benefit of the widows and orphans of the lay clerks in cathedrals and collegiate churches.

On Thursday, January 4th, the Choral Society of St. Asaph, gave a performance of Van Bree's " St. Cecilia's Day," and a miscellaneous selection. Miss Florence Norman and Mr. Levison Wyatt were the vocalists engaged. Master Myrick Roberts presided at the piano, and Mr. Felix C. Watkins conducted.

The Academical Board of Trinity College, London, has lately awarded the following Medals :—Silver Medal for Diligence and Regularity to Francis Poyson ; Bronze Medal for Diligence and Regularity to Edith G. Collet ; Silver Medal to Joseph Curtis, as the best student in the class for Musical Acoustics.

A highly interesting feature in the programme of the ensuing season of the Philharmonic Society, says the *Musical World*, will be a MS. motet by Cherubini. The MS. had been for many years in the Royal Library at Buckingham Palace, and Her Majesty the Queen has graciously given her consent to the performance of it by the Philharmonic Society. The work has never yet been heard in public.

The current number of Mr. Walford's *Antiquarian Magazine and Bibliographer* contains, *inter alia*, an interesting article on " An Unique MS. Collection of Ancient Church Music " contained in the library of the College of Peterhouse, Cambridge. It illustrates the choral service of the Church of England during the period immediately preceding the great rebellion.

Mr. Algernon Ashton announces that he will give a concert on the 20th, at which a selection from his compositions of chamber music will be performed at the request of Mr. and Mrs. Holiday and other friends. The scheme includes :—Trio in E flat for pianoforte, violin, and violoncello ; sonata in D for pianoforte and violin ; and quartet in F sharp minor for pianoforte, violin, viola, and violoncello.

The Athenæum says :—" The compositions of Theodore Kirchner are but little known in this country, and some interest attached to the performance of eight numbers of his ' Novelletten,' Op. 59, for piano, violin, and violoncello, at Mr. Dannreuther's concert on Thursday week. The comparatively few master-minds of music inevitably influence a number of more modestly gifted workers in the art, and Kirchner may in this way be deemed a disciple of Schumann. His works are mostly for the pianoforte and are nearly all of small calibre. In the ' Novelletten ' the keyed instrument is far more effectively treated than are the strings ; but on the whole these little pieces are extremely pleasing and some of them really charming."

It is announced that " Olivette " will be revived at the Avenue Theatre this evening.

Arrangements for a season of Richter Concerts are completed. Herr Richter will direct nine concerts to be given at St. James's Hall during May and June. To Herr Frantzen will again be confided the responsibility of rehearsing the chorus.

It is stated that Messrs. Spiers and Pond (Limited) are in negotiation for the purchase or hiring of the Alexandra Palace and Park. If the negotiations succeed the Palace will probably re-open on Easter Monday, under their control and management.

The first of a series of ballad concerts at Stratford Town-hall, was given on Monday evening by the Popular Ballad Concert Committee, in aid of the funds for the establishment of a Sea-side Convalescent Home for Working men. Among the artists announced were Mdme. Edith Wynne, Miss Agnes Larkcom, and Mr. John Radcliffe (flute). The Sea-side Home will be worked in connection with the Hospital Saturday Fund, and will be rendered, it is hoped, self-supporting. The president is Mr. Samuel Morley, and the treasurer Mr. H. N. Hamilton Hoare.

A contemporary says the increasing importance of comic opera seems likely to attract the attention of leading writers for the stage besides Mr. Gilbert. The libretto of the forthcoming opera, " Nell Gwynne," to which M. Planquette is now composing the music, is from the pen of Mr. Dion Boucicault. The new work has, we believe, been secured by Mr. Henderson. Mr. G. R. Sims has likewise written the libretto of a new operetta, which is being set to music by Mr. Frederic Clay, composer of " Princess Toto." It will, we believe, be produced by Miss Kate Santley at the Royalty about Easter time.

The Sacred Harmonic Society announces a series of four concerts, to be given on Friday evenings, at St. James's Hall, under the direction of Mr. Charles Hallé. " The Redemption " will be given on February 23rd, " Elijah " on April 6th, Schubert's Mass in E flat and the " Lobgesang " on April 27th, and " The Messiah " on May 11th. The scheme is acknowledged to be mainly experimental, but the Council declare their intention of issuing " a much more comprehensive prospectus for the season 1883-84." The performances will be looked forward to with much interest, and the good wishes of all will be with the rejuvenescent society.

At the meeting of the Musical Association, on January 1st, Mr. C. A. Barry occupied the chair. Mr. E. J. Breakspeare read a paper on " Musical Æsthetics," being a continuation of a paper on the same important subject with which Mr. Breakspeare has thoughfully identified himself, contributed by him two years since. The lecturer admitted the difficulties surrounding a practical treatment of the subject, but advocated the formation of a more definite system of criticism of musical works in their æsthetic aspect, as gone apart from their scientific aspect. Alluding to the loose phraseology and rough-and-ready manner usually adopted by journalistic critics, Mr. Breakspeare acknowledged the comparative poverty of the English language in terms conveying slight but significant variations of meaning. A brief discussion followed, in which Mr. F. Praeger, Mr. Bannister, and Mr. J. S. Shedlock took part. On February 5; a paper will be read by Mr. Baillie Hamilton, the inventor of the Vocalion.

M. Alfred Talandier, a deputy, lately submitted an influentially signed bill to the Chamber of Deputies with the view of reorganizing the regimental bands in the French army, the existence of which he declares is threatened. In the preamble, he states that in 1867 Marshal Niel suppressed the bands in the cavalry, and with regard to those in the infantry, M. Félix Germain, in a work called the " Dictionnaire du Budget," expresses a widely prevalent opinion when he says that the millions of francs which are expended annually upon musicians and instruments are simply a waste of money. M. Talandier proposes therefore to add to the utility of the bandsmen. He would enact that in every regiment there should be a separate company trained to perform a double service— in time of peace playing in the band and attending ambulance-drill, and in time of war acting as auxiliaries to the hospital corps. It is to be hoped that a more liberal spirit will prevail with regard to the preservation and development of the many excellent military orchestras possessed by France.

The Querist.

QUERIES.

ORGAN CONCERTOS.—Can any subscriber kindly say who is the publisher, and where these can be obtained :—Concerto No. 2, in G minor, by Camidge, and Concerto in E minor, by Goetz, both for organ ?—W. B. G.

CHRISTMAS ANTHEM.—Where can a copy be obtained of a Christmas Anthem by Edward Sturges, formerly Organist of the Foundling Hospital, to the words " I know their sorrows and I am come down to deliver them " ; also in what year was the composer born, and when did he die ?—JAS. B. SHAW.

Service Lists.

SECOND SUNDAY AFTER EPIPHANY,
JANUARY 14th.

London.

ST. PAUL'S CATHEDRAL.—Morn.: Service, Te Deum and Benedictus, Stainer in E flat ; Introit, Songs of thankfulness (Hymn 81) ; Communion Service, Monk in C. Even.: Service, Magnificat and Nunc Dimittis, Gounod ; Anthem, When Jesus our Lord (Mendelssohn).

WESTMINSTER ABBEY. — Morn.: Service, Garrett in F ; Communion Service, Gibbons. Aft.: Service, Garrett in F ; Anthem, Arise, shine (Greene).

TEMPLE CHURCH.—Morn.: Service, Te Deum and Jubilate, Barrow in F ; Apostles' Creed, Harmonized Monotone ; Anthem, In the days of Herod the King (Handel). Even.: Service, Magnificat and Nunc Dimittis, Barrow in F ; Apostles' Creed, Harmonized Monotone ; Anthem, Lo, star-led chiefs (Crotch).

LINCOLN'S INN HALL.—Morn.: Service, Steggall in C ; Kyrie, Steggall ; Anthem, Sing unto God, O ye kingdoms (Croft). Even.: Service, Steggall in G ; Anthem, The Lord gave the word (Handel).

ALL SAINTS, MARGARET STREET. — Morn.: Service, Te Deum, Smart in F ; Benedictus, Simcox ; Communion Service, Silas in C ; Offertory Anthem, Brightest and best (Smart). Even.: Service, Stainer in B flat ; Anthem, Deus tibi laus et honor ; Motet, No. 3 (Mozart).

ST. BARNABAS, MARYLEBONE.—Morn.: Service, Te Deum and Jubilate, Aldrich in G ; Anthem, Lord, who shall dwell (Rogers) ; Kyrie and Nicene Creed, Aldrich in G. Even.: Service, Magnificat and Nunc Dimittis, Aldrich in G ; Anthem, God is gone up (Croft).

CHRIST CHURCH, CLAPHAM.—Morn.: Service, Te Deum, Plain-song ; Kyrie and Credo, Gounod (Messe Solennelle) ; Offertory Anthem, From the rising of the sun (Ouseley) ; Sanctus, Benedictus, Agnus Dei, and Gloria in excelsis, Gounod. Even.: Service, Magnificat and Nunc Dimittis, Martin in A ; Anthem, my prayer (Mendelssohn).

FOUNDLING CHAPEL.—Morn.: Service, Te Deum and Jubilate, Garrett in D ; Anthem, O thou that tellest (" Messiah," Handel). Aft.: Service, Magnificat and Nunc Dimittis, Garrett in D ; Anthem, Arise, shine (Elvey).

HOLY TRINITY, TULSE HILL. — Morn.: Chant Service ; Kyrie and Gloria, Agutter in B flat. Even.: Service, Hopkins in F ; Anthems, In His hands, and, For His is the sea (Mendelssohn).

ST. JAMES'S PRIVATE EPISCOPAL CHAPEL, SOUTHWARK. —Morn.: Service, Introit, Farmer in B flat. Even.: Service, Gadsby in C ; Anthem, But the Lord from the North (Mendelssohn).

ST. MAGNUS, LONDON BRIDGE.—Morn.: Service, Opening Anthem, To the Lord our God (Calkin) ; Te Deum and Jubilate, Boyce in C ; Kyrie, Reay. Even.: Service, Magnificat and Nunc Dimittis, Walmisley in D minor ; Anthem, From the rising of the sun (Ouseley).

ST. MARGARET PATTENS, ROOD LANE, FENCHURCH STREET.—Morn.: Service, Te Deum, Smart in F ; Benedictus, Stainer ; Communion Service, Offertory Anthem, How beautiful are the feet (Handel) ; Kyrie, Credo, Sanctus, Benedictus, Agnus Dei, and Gloria in excelsis, Schubert in C. Even.: Service, Magnificat and Nunc Dimittis, Gadsby in C ; Anthem, Lovely appear (" Redemption," Gounod).

ST. MARY ABCHURCH, E.C. — Morn.: Service, Wesley in F; Communion Service, Garrett in D. Even.: Service, Chants.

ST. MARY BOLTONS, WEST BROMPTON, S.W.—Morn.: Service, Te Deum, Smart in F; Benedictus, Smart in F; Communion Service, Kyrie, Credo, Sanctus, Benedictus, Agnus Dei, and Gloria in excelsis, Eyre in E flat. Even.: Service, Magnificat and Nunc Dimittis, Smart in F; Anthem, From the rising of the sun (Ouseley).

ST. MICHAEL'S, CORNHILL.—Morn.: Service, Te Deum and Jubilate, Attwood in C; Anthem, O praise the Lord (Croft); Kyrie and Creed, Marbecke. Even.: Service, Magnificat and Nunc Dimittis, Ouseley in B flat; Anthem, O sing unto the Lord (Purcell).

ST. PAUL'S, AVENUE ROAD, SOUTH HAMPSTEAD.—Morn.: Service, Te Deum, Tilleard in F; Benedictus, Lawes; Kyrie, Stainer in E flat. Even.: Service, Magnificat and Nunc Dimittis, Gounod in D; Anthem, Send out Thy light (Gounod).

ST. PAUL'S, BOW COMMON, E. — Morn.: Service, Te Deum and Benedictus, Garrett in D. Even.: Service, Magnificat and Nunc Dimittis, Tours in D; Anthem, Arise, shine for thy light is come (Elvey).

ST. PETER'S (EATON SQUARE). — Morn.: Service, Te Deum, Boyce in A. Even.: Service, Turle in D; Anthem, O God, Lord God (Mozart).

ST. PETER'S, VERE STREET, W.—Even.: Service, Magnificat and Nunc Dimittis, Tours in F; Anthem, The Lord is with thee (G. A. Osborne).

Country.

ST. ASAPH CATHEDRAL. — Morn.: Service, Stainer in E flat; Anthem, Lo! star-led chiefs (Crotch). Even.: Service, Stainer in E flat; Anthem, O worship the Lord (Hayes).

ASHBURNE CHURCH, DERBYSHIRE. — Morn.: Service, Hopkins in C, to end of Benedictus; Continuation, Lloyd in E flat; Anthem, Thus speaketh the Lord of Hosts (Stainer).

BEDDINGTON CHURCH, SURREY. — Morn.: Service, Tours in F; Introit, Songs of thankfulness and praise (Hymn 81); Communion Service, Tours in F. Even.: Service, Ebdon in C; Anthem, O Lord our Governor (Marcello).

BIRMINGHAM (ST. CYPRIAN'S, HAY MILLS).—Morn.: Service, Kent in C; Anthem, Sing, O heavens (Kent). Even.: Service, Clark Whitfeld in D; Anthem, Give the King thy judgments (Boyce).

CANTERBURY CATHEDRAL.—Morn.: Service, Porter in D; Anthem, In my Father's house (Callcott); Communion Service, Porter in D. Even.: Service, Porter in D; Anthem, The Lord is my light (Boyce).

CARLISLE CATHEDRAL.—Morn.: Service, Calkin in B flat; Introit, Blessed be the God (Ouseley); Kyrie, Cooke in G; Nicene Creed, Stainer in G. Even.: Service, Metcalfe in F; Anthem, O give thanks (Purcell).

CHESTER (ST. MARY'S CHURCH).— Morn.: Service, Turle in D; Communion Service, Lee in G. Even.: Service, Goss in E; Anthem, Awake, awake, put on thy strength, O Zion (Stainer).

DUBLIN, ST. PATRICK'S (NATIONAL) CATHEDRAL.—Morn.: Service, Te Deum and Jubilate, King in D; Anthem, Why rage fiercely the heathen (Mendelssohn). Even.: Service, Magnificat and Nunc Dimittis, Rev. C. Dickinson in G; Anthems, Cast thy burden (Meyerbeer), and, He that under the shield (Meyerbeer).

ELY CATHEDRAL.—Morn.: Service, Te Deum, Boyce in C; Benedictus, Plain-song; Kyrie and Credo, Arnold in B minor; Gloria, Tours; Anthem, Blessing and glory (Boyce). Even.: Service, Arnold in F; Anthem, O where shall wisdom (Boyce).

GLASGOW (BLYTHSWOOD PARISH CHURCH).—Aft.: Service, Anthem, Send out thy light (Gounod).

LEEDS PARISH CHURCH.—Morn.: Service, Boyce in A; Anthem, Seek ye the Lord (Roberts); Kyrie and Creed, Turle in D. Even.: Service, Turle in D; Anthem, When Jesus our Lord (Mendelssohn).

LICHFIELD CATHEDRAL. — Morn.: Service, Cooke in G; Anthem, Why rage fiercely (Mendelssohn). Aft.: Service, Cooke in G; Anthem, Plead Thou my cause (Mozart).

LIVERPOOL CATHEDRAL. — Aft.: Service, Smart in G; Anthem, Awake, awake, put on strength (Stainer).

MANCHESTER CATHEDRAL. — Morn.: Service, Stainer in E flat; Anthem, Arise, shine (Elvey). Aft.: Service, Stainer in E flat; Anthem, When Jesus our Lord (Mendelssohn).

MANCHESTER (ST. BENEDICT'S). — Morn.: Service, Te Deum, Sullivan in D; Kyrie, Elvey; Credo, Sanctus, Benedictus, Agnus Dei, and Gloria in excelsis, Farmer in B flat. Even.: Service, Magnificat and Nunc Dimittis, Jordan.

MANCHESTER (ST. JOHN BAPTIST, HULME).—Morn.: Service, Kyrie, Credo, Sanctus, Benedictus, Agnus Dei, and Gloria in excelsis, Monk in C. Even.: Service, Magnificat and Nunc Dimittis, Stainer.

ROCHESTER CATHEDRAL.—Morn.:Service, Attwood in C; Anthem, Brightest and best (Hopkins). Even.: Service, Attwood in C; Anthem, Arise, shine (Elvey).

SHEFFIELD PARISH CHURCH. — Morn.: Service, Kyrie, Gounod in G. Even.: Service, Cantate and Deus Misereatur, Chants; Anthem, O Lord our Governor (Marcello).

SOUTHAMPTON (ST. MARY'S CHURCH).—Morn.: Service, Te Deum and Benedictus, Stainer in E flat; Introit, Jesus said (Stainer); Communion Service, Stainer in E flat; Offertory, Not every one, and, While we have time (Stainer); Benedictus and Agnus Dei, Agutter in B flat; Paternoster, Hoyte. Even.: Service, Magnificat and Nunc Dimittis, Stainer in E flat; Apostles' Creed, Harmonized Monotone (Hopkins).

WELLS CATHEDRAL.—Morn.: Service, Rogers in G; Introit, The Lord hath been mindful (Macfarren); Kyrie, Ouseley in G. Even.: Service, Gilbert in E; Anthem, With angels and archangels (Pring).

WORCESTER CATHEDRAL.—Morn.: Service, Dykes in F; Anthem, Blessed are they (Wesley). Even.: Service, Dykes in F; Anthem, O come, let us worship (Mendelssohn).

[The attention of the several Organists is called to the favour they confer upon their brother musicians by forwarding their notices regularly: this column of the paper is much valued as an index to what is going on in the choice of cathedral music, so much so that intermissions constantly give rise to remonstrance. Lists should be sent in a week in advance if possible.—ED. *Mus. Stand.*]

⁎⁎ Post-cards must be sent to the Editor, 6, Argyle Square, W.C., by Wednesday. Lists are frequently omitted in consequence of not being received in time.

NOTICES TO CORRESPONDENTS.

NEWSPAPERS sent should have *distinct marks* opposite to the matter to which attention is required.

NOTICE.—*All communications intended for the Editor are to be sent to his private address. Business communications to be addressed to 185, Fleet Street, E.C.*

APPOINTMENT.

MR. ERNEST A. THOMPSON, formerly of St. Cuthbert's Church, Birmingham, Organist and Choirmaster to Holy Trinity Church, Hartlepool.

ERRATUM.—In "Passing Events" last week, the name of a new musical journal, given as the *Lyre*, should have been the *Lute*.

Printed for the Proprietor by BOWDEN, HUDSON & Co., at 23, Red Lion Street, Holborn, London, W.C. ; and Published by WILLIAM REEVES, at
the Office, 185, Fleet Street, E.C. West End Agents :—WEEKES & CO., 14, Hanover Street, Regent Street, W. Subscriptions and Advertisements are
received either by the Publisher or West End Agents.—Communications for the EDITOR are to be forwarded to his private address, 6, Argyle Square, W.C
SATURDAY, JAN. 13, 1883.—Entered at the General Post Office as a Newspaper.

MUSICAL STANDARD

A NEWSPAPER FOR MUSICIANS PROFESSIONAL AND AMATEUR

No. 964. Vol. XXIV. FOURTH SERIES.   SATURDAY, JANUARY 20, 1883.   WEEKLY: PRICE 3D.

TRIADS: THEIR RELATIONSHIP AND TREATMENT.

By Francis Edward Gladstone, Mus.Doc.

(Continued from page 20.)

You will remember that we formed our scale from three triads, each consisting of a major 3rd and perfect 5th placed above a given note. The idea of such a combination of sounds is obviously suggested by nature's chord, to which reference has been already made in connection with the scale. Further, the idea of making the 5th of one chord the connecting link between it and another one similarly composed as to intervals, is also derived from the harmonic series.

The harmonic chord contains three sounds which, because of their more frequent repetition, are more prominent than others. These three sounds are the root or generator, the perfect 5th, and the major 3rd. Taking the series up to the 32nd harmonic from

we find six C's, four G's and three E's. Here is the chord thus arising :—

Ex. 6. A.

But if we take the 3rd harmonic as a fresh starting point we shall find that the addition to it of the 6th, 9th, 12th, 15th, 18th, 24th, and 30th harmonics gives us the following chord,—all the intervals in which are, like those of the former, in perfect tune :—

Ex. 6. B.

From this it may be fairly argued that the progression from one major chord to another a 5th above it is in accordance with the suggestions of nature. Now, if we accompany the first three notes of the ascending scale of C with, to use the ordinary technical terms, "tonic" and "dominant" harmony, we obtain a result perfectly satisfactory so far as it goes, and we might leave off at this point without any feeling of disturbance :—

Ex. 7. A.

If, however, we proceed to the next chord,

Ex. 7. B.

we feel that we have entered another harmonic region, and there is a slight sense of unrest until after passing through the new country,

Ex. 7. C.

the sudden re-appearance of the "dominant" harmony of C, followed by the "tonic" chord,

Ex. 7. D.

brings us back to the same land whence we took our departure.

Of course I am aware that it is the custom of musicians to speak of the chord upon the 4th degree of the scale as the "subdominant" chord. No doubt this is a convenient term, but that it is somewhat misleading, and that its influence in the scale is rather disturbing than governing, I will now further endeavour to shew.

Let us begin to descend our scale. The first two chords stand in the same relationship towards one another as that of the first two chords in the ascending scale, and we might return to C with perfectly good effect :—

Ex. 8. A.

But in attempting to descend another step our way is blocked. There is a clear gap between the two chords, for they have not a note in common :—

Ex. 8. B.

You may ask why this want of connection was not noticed in ascending. I reply, that it *was* felt to some extent. There is always something like a wrench experienced in passing, with similar motion between Soprano and Bass, from the common chord on the subdominant to that on the dominant, but this twist is not unwelcome when it leads us *towards* our key note, whereas it is very much so when it takes us from it.

I am anxious not to be misunderstood in this matter. I hold that the charm of all musical progressions lies in the fact that when, a given tonality having been established, we wander away through chords or keys more or less related to one another, we can by similar means always return to our starting point. Musicians are divided as to what constitutes an actual modulation, or change of key, but there can be no serious difference of opinion as to what produces a change of HARMONIC relationship. The note C as a generator can only produce two major chords, viz. :—that of C (the tonic) and that of G (the dominant), but the chord of C is also generated by the note F in the scale of C; and it thus has a dual relationship of the most intimate kind : it is the tonic of G, but the dominant of F. The use by Church composers of what is known as the "plagal cadence" affords an *apparent*, but not, I think, a *real* contradiction to this view. When, after a series of passages in any key, the concluding chords are built upon the subdominant and tonic of that key, I always feel that a mental reference is made to the dominant harmony, and that in a passage like the following :—

Ex. 9. A.

used as a cadence, the following intervening chord,

Ex. 9. B.]

is as it were, understood, the complete phrase standing thus :—

Ex. 9. C.

On this point I may quote with advantage a paragraph from Mr. Banister's excellent treatise on Music. He says with reference to the plagal cadence : "This cadence is not used as a *substitute* for the perfect cadence, not being nearly so indicative of key, but as an *appendix* to it." It is, in fact, only effective when the key has already been thoroughly re-established. But if in our movements from chord to chord we were restricted to tonic and dominant harmonies, and if we had no concords but those with major 3rds above the root, our music would soon become tedious : we should be satiated with its unvarying sweetness. As a matter of fact, we know that, in progressions from chord to chord, a due intermingling of minor with major chords produces the most satisfactory result. Let us then proceed to consider the nature and origin of the minor triad and scale. Helmholtz's theory of consonance shews us why the interval of a minor 3rd produces a satisfactory effect to the ear, but musicians are not unanimous in their opinions as to the proper derivation and scientific construction of the modern minor scale. It must I think be admitted that the minor scale is more artificial than the major, but, although I am treading on debatable ground, I will venture to offer you a method of construction which commends itself to me. Turning again to the harmonic range extending upwards from the octave below

we shall find in addition to the two major chords

Ex. 10. A.

a series of sounds which may be united to form a minor chord

Ex. 10. B.

the intervals which it comprises being perfectly in tune ; that is to say, G is a true minor 3rd, and B is a perfect 5th above E.

(*To be continued.*)

Musical Intelligence.

SATURDAY POPULAR CONCERTS.

These concerts were resumed last Saturday with the following programme :—

Quartet in A minor, Op. 13, for two violins, viola, and violoncello .... Mendelssohn.
    MM. Straus, L. Ries, Hollander, and Piatti.
Air, "Nasce al bosco" .... Handel.
    Mr. Santley.
"Carnaval" ("Scènes Mignonnes"), Op. 9, for pianoforte alone .... Schumann.
    Mdme. Sophie Menter.
Saltarella, Op. 55, for violin, with pianoforte accompaniment .... Molique.
    Herr Straus.
Song, "Le Nom de Marie" .... Gounod.
    Mr. Santley.
Trio in C minor, Op. 1, No. 3, for pianoforte, violin, and violoncello .... Beethoven.
    Mdme. Sophie Menter, MM. Straus and Piatti.
        Accompanist - - - Mr. Zerbini.

Herr Straus's earnest and musicianly leadership is always productive of satisfying results. His solo by the graceful writer Bernhard Molique, whom our programme compares, not unjustly, to Spohr, was received with enthusiastic appreciation. The great charm in Herr Straus is his perfect simplicity—his entire absence of affectation and struggle for effect. If his mantle of simplicity could fall on Mdme. Menter's shoulders she would have a greater charm—at least, to me. Anything more restless, *rubato* and ranting, than her interpretation of the Carnival Scenes could scarcely be imagined. If some one word of direction to the player could be affixed to each of these scenes, it would be the one word *semplice*, which is attached to the "Valse Allemande." If they do not captivate the hearer by their natural grace and quaint humour, no amount of affectation in the performance can render them captivating, though it may—for a fearful power is in the hands of the interpreter—render them something only a degree removed from vulgar. Where was the beauty and where was the sense of taking the "Valse Allemande" quite slowly instead of molto vivace, as directed, and hurrying the last four bars most ungracefully to a close ? What was the meaning of "Coquette" being begun three times as fast as it was continued ? What satisfactory result arose from the odd liberties taken with the time in "Arlequin," and the forced expression given to the second part of "Reconnaissance"?

Alas, poor Schumann ! Though he has himself written concerning this Opus 9 of his : "One piece after another was completed during the carnival season of 1835, in a serious mood, and under peculiar circumstances. I afterwards gave titles to the numbers, and named the entire collection 'The Carnival'"; the programmist still contends (and very likely he may be right) that they were begun in "1834 and finished in 1835." It really would not matter which way it was, if he did not continue to tell us that "Beethoven or Mendelssohn would have done it in a couple of days." If this speech did not call to mind the lady who said that her daughter *must* play better than her teacher, for when they were playing a duet the daughter always reached the bottom of the page first, it would have to be accepted as a reflection on Schumann's genius. But how senseless an one ! Beethoven wrote 12 bagatelles for piano, beginning in 1820 and ending in 1822, and published them as

Op. 119. Schumann wrote 21 bagatelles for piano in a shorter space of time, and published them as Op. 9. Wherein, then does Schumann differ from his great forerunner? Next time the Carnival Scenes are played a stronger argument or none at all had better be put forth.

Mr. Santley was in magnificent voice, and sang the song whose fame he has made, as well as that by Handel, in his own perfect manner.

B. F. WYATT-SMITH.

MONDAY POPULAR CONCERTS.

The concert on Monday evening was well attended in spite of execrable weather.

PROGRAMME.

PART I.

Quartet in E major, No. 8, for two violins, viola,
　and violoncello .... Mozart.
　Mdme. Norman-Néruda, MM. L. Ries, Hollander, and Piatti.
Serenade.................................... Schubert.
　Mr. Henderson.
Study, and Polonaise in A flat, for pianoforte alone　Chopin.
　Mdme. Sophie Menter.

PART II.

Sonata in D major, for violin, and pianoforte accom-
　paniment.................................. Corelli
　Mdme. Norman-Néruda.
Song, "Love in her eyes" .... Handel.
　Mr. Henderson.
Quartet in E flat, Op. 47, for pianoforte, violin,
　viola, and violoncello .... Schumann.
Mesdames Sophie-Menter and Norman-Néruda, MM. Hollander
　and Piatti.

Accompanist · · · · Mr. Zerbini.

Well may "praisers of past times" expatiate on the inexhaustible beauty of Mozart's compositions! The programme book of Monday used by the writer might be compared with the edition of Racine's dramas, every page whereof was figuratively marked by Voltaire with the words "fine, pathetic, harmonious, sublime." This eighth quartet, written a year before Mozart's death, is pregnant with grace and refinement throughout, apart from the ideas in the abstract, and only to speak of their treatment. A vein of purest melody, and the use of counterpoint without a tinge of pedantry. The allegretto (second movement) in C reminds one of Haydn's humorous style. The trio of the Minuet, with its passages of thirds and distant intervals of thirteenth, fifteenth, and tenth in the upper part, was applauded to the echo. The allegro finale, played quasi presto, is a specimen of a spirit "touched to finest issues;" and the violoncello part reveals most of the quaint fun so frequently found in the texts of "Papa" (Haydn). Schumann's Quartet, by the Germans unaccountably preferred to the earlier Quintet in the same key, naturally checked any premature exodus from the Hall, except in the case of the incorrigibles, who have not even the decency to depart between the movements, but skulk out during the performance.

Mdme. Menter, whose fine and forcible execution in the Quartet could not efface the impression always made by Mdme. Schumann, to whom the interpretation of her husband's works was a labour of love, and love's labour not lost, made a good choice of Chopin's Polonaise, the sixth and the most popular. Great power, manifest in the delivery of the main subject, was blended with exquisite grace and delicacy in the episodical portions; the sotto voce subject in E major, with octaves in the bass, sempre staccato, may be specially noted. On a rapturous encore, Mdme. Menter played the "Study" (of black keys) in G flat; she used a Erard grand.

Your other contributor will speak of the Saturday afternoon performance, and the grand execution of Schumann's "Le Carnaval," which attracted all the critics.

Corelli's interesting Violin Sonata gave great satisfaction; fine music, and not too old-fashioned for us moderns of catholic and cultivated taste. The tone of the fourth string, the finesse of the scale passages, and the abandon of the style in the quick movements, secured for Mdme. Norman-Néruda a vociferous recall. Mr. Henderson, the vocalist, excelled more in Schubert's "Ständchen" than in the excerpt from "Acis and Galatea," of which the reading struck me as tame and passionless. How admirably it was rendered at Drury Lane Theatre in 1842, by Mrs. German Reed (then Miss Priscilla Horton), when Mr. Macready so splendidly "mounted" the Cantata, will not be forgotten by one at least. Schubert's charming lied is said by Herr Doppler to have been improvised at a village inn, on the back of the

bill of fare, for want of proper paper, amidst a clatter of plates and glasses, the noise of skittles, the playing of fiddles, and the rush of waiters! So Pestal, the Polish captive, scratched his valse on the wall of his dismal dungeon.

On Monday next Mr. Charles Hallé is to conduct Brahms's Pianoforte Trio in C, Op. 87 (first time of performance).

A. M.

MR. AGUILAR'S PIANOFORTE RECITALS.

Of these agreeable and edifying réunions the third and last (of the present Christmas series) was held at Mr. Aguilar's own house on Wednesday afternoon. His first pièce de résistance on the occasion—"a dainty dish" indeed to set before the assembled queens—was Beethoven's Sonata in D minor, "Op. 31, No. 2." It may be remembered that the first of this fine triad, the one in G major, was played at the recital of January 3rd. The Sonata in D minor is known to be a favourite with classical pianists of both sexes. The text cannot be interpreted, even if tolerably played, by ordinary amateurs. The alternation, at the outset, of the "recitative" subject (largo) with the allegro requires of itself something more than a "'prentice hand"; whilst the adagio (second movement) in B flat, which opens with that charming and most effective change from the treble to the bass clef, can only be entrusted, so to speak, to a patte de velours encased in white kid glove. The delicately accentuated rhythm of the final allegretto (proportionately larger than the other movements), with its chromatic runs and arpeggio accompaniment, would be simply assassinated by feebleness and school-girl treatment. Mr. Aguilar's reading of the sonata may be commended as scrupulously reverent, with an intellectual observance of all lights and shades—in the sonata as numerous as the colours of a sun-lit wood in the latter days of autumn.

Mr. Aguilar's own (MS.) sonata of three movements in E major was played by him later on, and suffered no eclipse by comparisons. The first allegro is charmingly playful in style, and with some fiery passages of passionate remonstrance, a certain tuneful theme very often recurrent, may be called bewitching. The Andante in G, an air varié, has many traits of excellence, and a sort of stately chorale at the close dignifies the movement. The finale, allegretto scherzando, is what the title imports—gay, spirited, and full of espièglerie. Here a powerful left hand thunders out a bass, which the right relieves with poetical passages in the upper part of the instrument; the movement is admirably worked up. One of Mr. Aguilar's shorter compositions, the "Ophelia" in D flat, is a clever combination of the sweet girl's gentleness and piety (according to the Shaksperean theory) with an episodical agitato strikingly suggestive of the more tragical features in the play; a second theme in the subordinate key characterises the piece in "tone" language. The transcription from Mr. Aguilar's cantata, "Summer Night," and a melody, "At Last," in A major, very sweet, and with the tune well "picked out" in the upper register, evoked much applause; the melody, in fact, was encored, but Mr. Aguilar, too unobtrusive, modestly declined to repeat the piece. Effective transcriptions of a sarabande, from Bach's violin sonatas, and a gigue from the "Orchestral Suite," served to show how the old masters could move the world, even through the medium of dance music. The graceful "Dream Dance" in A, and the "Couleur de Rose" in A flat, always regale the ear as sprightly "motives," likely to stir up people disposed to dance, and most daintily dealt with by their accomplished composer. A fugue of Scarlatti in D minor; Liszt's 9th Hungarian Rhapsody in E flat; Sir W. Sterndale Bennett's beautiful "Allegro grazioso" in A major, a long piece, marked "Opus 18"; and two "Lieder ohne Worte" completed a choice scheme. Mr. Aguilar, in the case of Mendelssohn's "Lieder," chose Nos. 1 and 4 from Book II., in E flat and B minor, known as "Contemplation," and "L'Egaré." Poor Lubeck played the first-named "lied" at the Musical Union one day—A.D. 1869 or 1870.

Easter, this year, falls very early, so that the Spring recitals of Mr. Aguilar will not long "loom in the distance."

Mr. J. F. Barnett is said to be getting well forward with his delicate task of completing the score of an unfinished symphony by Schubert.

SWINDON.

The committee of the Mechanics' Institution, New Swindon, Wilts, held a grand concert on the evening of January 10th, under the able direction of Mr. P. E. Van Noorden. The conductor opened the concert with the pretty overture to Nicolai's opera, "The Merry Wives of Windsor," arranged as a duet for the pianoforte ; the *primo* part was played by Miss Nellie Sykes, and the *secondo* by Mr. Van Noorden. Herr Poznanski played two violin solos with signal success, namely, Signor Hauser's "Rhapsodie Hongroise" and De Beriot's "Tremolo." Miss Nellie Sykes played à grand fantasia for the pianoforte on American airs, by Sivrai, and Mr. J. A. Brouail some pleasing violoncello pieces by Reber, Dunkler, and Servais. Mdme. Dukas sang Gounod's "Ave Maria" with great taste and expression to the accompaniment of Herr Poznanski on the violin, and Mr. Van Noorden on the harmonium. Some of the London artists were obliged to return to Paddington by the late, or rather the early train, which leaves Swindon at about 2 o'clock, a.m.

ST. ALBANS.

A good amateur concert was given in the Town Hall, St. Albans, on Friday, the 12th inst., under the patronage of several influential ladies in the county. The proceeds were devoted to building a village-room at Colney Heath, a hamlet near St. Albans. The platform was beautifully decorated with palms and other exotics. Among the items in the programme that are worthy of notice were the songs of Mrs. Pagden (*née* Miss Ferrari), who kindly consented to appear and sing "Clover Blooms" (F. Moir), and Gounod's "Serenade" (violin obbligato, M. Romer), in the latter of which this lady's charming voice was heard at its best, and as an encore she gave "My heart is sair for somebody." The pianoforte duet "Tancredi" was played in a most finished style by Mrs. Marten and Miss Andrews. The violin solo by Mr. Romer, and his duet with Mrs. Marten, fantasia from "Guillaume Tell," were heartily appreciated by the audience. Mr. Dundas Gardiner gave "Rochester Bells" and "I fear no foe." The programme concluded with a trio, very well sung by Mrs. Pagden, Mr. Thorley, and Mr. Dundas Gardiner, "I Naviganti" (A. Randegger). Miss Ferrari acted as accompanist. Unfortunately very few people were present, and this is to be wondered at, as it is so seldom the inhabitants of St. Albans get a chance of hearing good music in their own town.

BRIGHTON.

A series of organ recitals, under the management of Mr. Alfred King, Mus. Bac. (Honorary Organist to the Corporation) was commenced in the Dome. The series just inaugurated promises to prove unusually attractive, several of the eminent organists of the town having kindly promised their services in giving recitals. The programme was carried out by Mr. King, and it was gratifying to notice that the room, though not crowded, was better filled than at any of the previous recitals given on the Dome organ. Mr. King was in his best form, and the various selections rendered by him were thoroughly appreciated. The recital opened with Smart's "Overture in D," a composition worthy of the great English composer. The overture was given in masterly style, and elicited warm applause, even at that early stage of the evening's performance. A "Pastorale" by Kullak was also much admired, while Bach's fine Toccata and Fugue in D proved, from an artistic point of view, one of the most successful during the evening. Guilmant's "Marche Funébre et Chant Séraphique" (played for the first time at these recitals), however, carried off the palm, and, appealing to the popular tastes, proved so admirably suited to the audience, and proved so attractive that its repetition was redemanded. Mr. King did not grant the encore, but, proceeding with his recital, gave Mozart's Larghetto from Clarinet Quintet. The following number—Guilmant's Fantasia on two English airs ("Home, sweet home," and "Rule Britannia")—which Mr. King has given with such marked success at previous recitals, was also well received. A most successful recital concluded with Lemmen's Marche Triomphale ; the brilliant composition being finely rendered. The organist, who was heartily applauded, will be followed at the next recital by Mr. F. J. Sawyer, Mus. Bac,

LIVERPOOL.

(*From our Own Correspondent.*)

JAN. 17.

Rumours regarding the conductorship of the Philharmonic Society are various, and, it is to be presumed, cannot be relied upon.

A report that Mr. Hallé is to be appointed to the vacant post is going about ; another, that Mr. Karl Meyder is to receive the coveted appointment. It is to be earnestly hoped that the Committee will not blunder over the matter this time.

Talking of the Liverpool Philharmonic Society, just reminds me that Mr. George Hirst, who was at one time the organist to this society, has just died at Silverdale. He was a man of great musical talent, and while in Liverpool he was much esteemed and looked up to as a member of the musical profession. He gave up music and went into partnership with his brother as a woollen manufacturer ; it was a better paying concern, I suppose. The deceased was also for some years organist at Great George Street Chapel, and was at one time, also, music-master at the School for the Blind.

The English opera season at the Royal Court Theatre runs merrily along, and is one of the most successful seasons Mr. Carl Rosa has had in this city. "Mignon" and the "Bohemian Girl" are the greatest draws. The first-named opera was given once last week, and is set down for two performances this. Mdme. Marie Roze assumes the title part, and is very successful. This artist also appeared in Verdi's "Il Trovatore," given on Saturday evening last, and was warmly received by an audience which filled the theatre. Miss Yorke's Azucena deserves particular mention, the delineation of the character being a veritable triumph.

"Colomba," by A. C. Mackenzie, and "Esmeralda," by Goring Thomas, are in rehearsal for the London season. Mr. Mackenzie's opera is very difficult, and, it is thought, not sufficiently melodious to become popular ; while, on the other hand, Mr. Thomas's work is very melodious, and at the same time musicianly.

At Mr. Hallé's orchestral concert, given last evening, the chief items were :—Beethoven's triple Concerto for piano, violin, and violoncello, Raff's "Leonore" Symphony, Gade's "Hamlet" Overture, Mendelssohn's Tema con Variazioni, in D, for piano and violoncello. The performers were Mr. Hallé, Signor Piatti, and Mdme. Norman-Néruda.

There is a rumour that the Cathedral choir is in a very weak state as regards its existence, and that, but for the members of the Chapter coming forward and offering to defray the expenses during the current year, the pro-Cathedral would have been minus a choir. Heretofore, it seems, the rector has borne the expense, and that, so far, the bishop has given no encouragement to the choir which daily renders the musical part of the service in the establishment over which he presides.

Mr. John Hodgson begins on Saturday afternoon next, the 20th inst., a series of monthly organ recitals on the organ in St. Anne's Church, Aigburth, where he holds the position of organist and choirmaster. The programme of the first recital will be found in the organ news columns. Mr. Hodgson is known as an organist of great ability, and his performance on the St. George's Hall organ, while Mr. Best was absent from his post, was one the most successful of the series.

The supposed communication anent the Royal College from Mr. Gladstone would appear to have originated in somebody having indulged in a spasm of acute humour in the columns of our new and spirited contemporary the *Musical Review*. Says that paper :—" Mr. Gladstone's communication, published in our last, seems to have made quite a little sensation in the musical world, and not in the musical world alone. We have received numbers of inquiries as to the person to whom the letter—or rather the post-card had been addressed, and regarding the intentions of Government in connection with the Royal College. These persons we must refer to the heading, 'What might be, or should be,' under which the letter appeared. If they had observed that heading all their wonderment would have dissolved itself into thin Utopian air. But who now-a-days takes the trouble to read his newspaper carefully ?"

THE SATURDAY POPULAR ORGAN RECITALS at BOW will be RESUMED on SATURDAY NEXT, 27th January.

NEW ORGAN PIECE, by M. GUILMANT.— SPOHR'S 24th PSALM (English words), 9d. and 2s. Ditto arranged for Organ Solo by M. GUILMANT, 1s. 6d.
London: NOVELLO, EWER & CO.

MR. E. DAVIDSON PALMER, Mus.Bac., Oxon., author of "What is Falsetto?" "Pronunciation in Singing," etc., gives LESSONS in VOICE TRAINING and SOLO SINGING, at his residence, 19, Gladesmore-road, Stamford Hill, N.

PRINCIPAL CONTENTS OF THIS NUMBER.

LONDON: SATURDAY, JANUARY 20, 1883.

THE LATE JOHN CROWDY.

THE cause of the Art, especially as regards the department of Church music, has lost by the sudden death on the 12th of Mr. JOHN CROWDY a notable champion. No writer on musical topics in our day has evidenced greater power and fervour than was displayed by this gifted and highly cultivated *litterateur* and *dilettante*. Widely as his labours in the cause of the arts have been recognised, in many directions his influence has been felt almost unconsciously, for he had much of power and interest to say conversationally; his valuable, tersely expressed thoughts, practical observations, and sound advice on musical and literary topics were freely, kindly, and modestly tendered to those who enjoyed the privilege of being fellow-workers with him in the interests of art, and to those who had also the advantage of his personal friendship. It may been felt by some that the very earnestness of his views on art matters gave now and then to his advocacy of high art principles something of the flavour of Utopianism. Again, it was possible that his power of concentration on a given subject or department, artistic or literary, imparted at times a slightly crotchety aspect to his writings. But, how rare are the splendid qualities, earnestness of purpose and intense power of concentration upon which such hyper-criticism was really based! JOHN CROWDY's earnestness arose from a love of art, which was indeed a passion, admitting no thoughts of self-interest or temporary disloyalty; he gazed, indeed, so earnestly into the azure sky of pure art, that he had little thought for the subordination of artistic power to the business interests of a world in which art is rather an angelic sojourner than a native inhabitant,

Then, of this earnestness came his remarkable power of thought and verbal concentration; indeed, his mastery over the English language was a rare characteristic in these days of rapid writing, slip-shod criticism, and hurried, negligent reading. So assiduously did this powerful critic and keen observer cultivate his mastery over our language, that he spent many years in transposing and re-planning the polished sentences of our English classics, notably those of ADDISON, a favourite model, in order that he might acquire that nervous, terse power of expression which became a technical characteristic of his literary labours. Mr. JOHN CROWDY—working at a period when music and the sister arts may be described as in a transition state, as escaping from some of the bonds of excessive artificiality and springing into a new and more earnest existence—exercised considerable influence in the cause of art; standing in the prudential position of firmly abiding in his faith in such of the canons of art as bear the seal of natural truth and express the experience of centuries of profound thought, yet at the same time he anxiously encouraged the development of all artistic impulses stamped by the earnestness of genius and the logical reasonableness of that common sense which characterises all true art. His protestations against pretentious, self-seeking empiricism, were as instant and earnest as were his ready, frank, acknowledgment of real merit, and his unflinching advocacy of those artistic manifestations his instincts and training convinced him were good and true. Like so many of our literary men and journalists, Mr. CROWDY was in the National service, his department being that of the Admiralty, where he enjoyed the companionable friendship of another earnest and able worker in the domains of art and literature, Mr. CHARLES MACKESON. Mr. CROWDY was for many years engaged upon the *Guardian*, as sub-editor, if I remember rightly, the well-recognised musical critic, Mr. C. A. BARRY, being a fellow-worker with him.

As editor of the *Choirmaster*, afterwards the *Musician*, Mr. CROWDY laboured conscientiously for the art, and he aided the late RICHARD LIMPUS by his writings and personal influence in the establishment of the College of Organists. For some years, from 1872 to 1876, Mr. JOHN CROWDY was the able and esteemed editor of the *Musical Standard*, contributing to these columns many of his most thoughtful and earnest articles and criticisms.

Mr. T. L. SOUTHGATE, his much esteemed *collaborateur*, and for some time the able editor of this paper, writes thus :—"The deceased gentleman has "been connected with the *Musical Standard* from the "date of its birth. Indeed, he, in company with its "first editor and proprietor, the late Mr. J. W. HAM-"MOND, and two well-known musicians still working "amongst us, assisted in planning the paper and "determining the independent policy which has been "its characteristic. Mr. CROWDY's philological at-"tainments, and the journalistic experience he "brought to bear on the paper were of no small "value. An important series of articles, 'On the "Musical Illustration of the Church Services,' which "he wrote upwards of twenty years ago, showed "that he possessed a reflective and cultured mind, and

"were the means of eliciting many valuable opinions "on worship-music by some of our foremost "English musicians of the period. From time to "time Mr. CROWDY contributed many valuable articles "on various matters connected with music. All "who knew him can bear testimony to the unflagging "devotion towards his duties that he exhibited. No "amount of work that was thrown upon him seemed "to daunt him, and the watchful attention he "bestowed on every event affecting the art rendered "the journal under his editorship a complete "conspectus of all that a musician should know. "Although Mr. CROWDY's health, never robust, "began to give way under the strain of his literary "duties, he retained his interest in musical events "and frequently favoured us with his views on various "matters ripe for comment. A series of exhaustive "articles which he wrote on the 'Wagner theory,' "were remarkable for the painstaking care and critical "ability exhibited in the examination of this question "from a practical point of view. His writings were "always marked by much freshness of thought, inde-"pendence of tone, fairness of judgment, and force of "diction. It was hoped that the fresh country air, and "comparative freedom from the toilsome duties of a "literary life, would bring such health as would enable "him to do valuable work for many a year to come ; "but it has been ordered otherwise. His death will "be mourned by a wide circle of friends, and by none "more than those connected with this journal, of "which he was so able a supporter."

The proprietors and many readers of this paper duly remembering his services and consistent advocacy of the art within these pages, will, I know, join with his many friends in lamenting his loss. For many years Mr. CROWDY suffered from delicate health. At the termination of his period of service at the Admiralty, he retired to a pleasant country house which he built for himself (at Fair Oaks, Addlestone, Surrey), his connection with the art-world being preserved by one direct link, the editorship of the *Artist*, wherein he served with characteristic earnestness the painter's art, bringing to his task sympathetic thoughtfulness, a wide knowledge of artistic topics, and his epigrammatic mastery over the English language. Among his notable contributions to the verbal literature of music were his poetic and masterly analytical programmes of Handel's "Messiah," and Mendelssohn's "St. Paul," written for concert use and well deserving the honour of being constantly attached preface-fashion to those musical master-pieces. Although possessed of considerable technical knowledge of the art of composition, Mr. CROWDY did not write much music or set himself up as an executant beyond his home circle. He entertained, indeed, such high standards of artistic excellence as precluded such thoughts of pretension as incline less wise people to parade their incomplete accomplishments. He will be remembered for his noteworthy efforts to secure the simplification and reformation of the Anglican Chant in his invention of Free Chant by which the Canticles and Psalms could be enunciated in simple, natural, unfettered song. Herein the inventor displayed an instinctive recognition of the foundation of good chanting upon the principles which govern speech and a far-sighted knowledge of the angular character of our language with its obstinate fixity of accent, moving on the whole unsatisfactorily with the elastic flow of genuine Plain Chant as the best medium for the conveyance of the plastic words of the Latin language. In this direction Mr. CROWDY gained the adhesion of such thoughtful artists as Mr. JOHN C. WARD, and the approval of many such earnest Churchmen and intelligent non-professional lovers of music as his faithful friend Dr. E. T. WATKINS. The Free Chant is an undoubted fact in the history of the modern revival of ecclesiastical music. It may be that its adoption upon the lines of its inventor will not be fully realised, but it will remain as one of the engines by which the standard of good musical recitation is destined to be reformed and advanced. The indulgent reader will permit me to here record my own indebtedness to the late eminent critic. Seeing my first essays with the pen, he sought me out, and with characteristic kindness became at once my teacher, guide, and friend. His indifferent health and love of retirement had latterly led him away from the crowded scenes of a public life. The sacred ground of a pure, gentle, loving domestic life, and the irreparable loss his widow and children have sustained in his untimely death, at the early age of forty-eight, are subjects not to be encroached upon. In the quiet country he rests, where the birds will carol their MAKER'S praise in cadences as true and simple as his own Free Chant. His memory will be long cherished by loving friends and his works will still live on. *Requiescat in pace.*

E. H. TURPIN.

Foreign Musical Intelligence.

The Grand Duke of Mecklenburg-Schwerin has given a gold medal to Sarasate the violinist.

Dvorak's opera, "Der Bauerein Schelm," has been given successfully in Hamburg.

"The Poor Student" is the name of a new operetta by a Viennese composer, Herr Millöcker.

Signor Belluci has written an opera on the story of "Charlotte Corday."

A new opera is to be given at Frankfort, called "Alona," and composed by an artist bearing the decidedly English name of William Hill.

Mr. Villiers Stanford has finished an opera in three acts and a prologue, having for its story the life of Savonarola. Mr. Gilbert A'Beckett is the writer of the libretto.

It is satisfactory to hear of the improvement in Hans von Bulow's health. He has been able to conduct several orchestral rehearsals, and is announced to play Raff's Pianoforte Concerto in Meiningen, on the 23rd inst.

It is said that a new opera, written in the Roumanian language, and composed by Oreste Bimboni, will shortly be produced at Bucharest. The Government is evidently anxious to promote native art, since it has itself engaged the chorus and orchestra.

Meritorious, rather than great, is the verdict pronounced upon a new orchestral symphony in E (No. 3), by Max Bruch, which was played in New York on December 16th, at a concert of the Symphony Society, to which body it is dedicated.

One of the oldest musical journals ceased to exist in the latter end of 1882, the *Allgemeine Musikalische Zeitung*, which was founded in 1798, by Breitkopf and Härtel, but afterwards was published by Rieter-Biedermann from 1848. The last editor was Herr Chrysander.

Academical Intelligence.

UNIVERSITY OF LONDON.

During the proceedings at a meeting of convocation of the University of London, held on the 16th, at the University Building, Burlington Gardens, Dr. Storrar, the chairman, presiding, Mr. M. P. Christie, B.A., moved, "That the Senate be requested to propose terms upon which graduates in music shall be admitted to Convocation." He said he could only account for the present condition of things in regard to music by supposing that when the charter was granted, it was not foreseen that music would take the high place which it had done. The examination for the degree in music was of a very high character indeed, and required as much varied and special information as any of the other examinations. Mr. Hennell, B.A., seconded the motion, which was carried *nem. con.*

This step is one it is gratifying to chronicle, as evidencing the advancing claims of music and musicians to proper recognition, and as showing a desire on the part of the University authorities to duly respect the holders of their own musical degrees.

COLLEGE OF ORGANISTS.

At the Examinations of January 9th, 10th, and 11th, the following gentlemen obtained the diploma of Associateship :—R. C. Banks, Rochdale ; F. N. Baxter, Tetbury ; Rowland Briant, London ; T. Cox, Wolverhampton ; Michael Fairs, South Shields ; Sidney Hall, Stalybridge ; A. Hann, Ilminster ; H. H. Hoyle, Queensbury, Bradford ; W. Jones, Woodville, Burton-on-Trent ; E. H. Lemare, Ventnor ; O. A. Mansfield, Warminster ; J. H. Olding, London ; R. Yates Mander, Leamington ; C. E. Melville, Leeds ; H. W. Richards, London ; C. W. Moss, Ipswich ; G. J. Robertson, North Tawton ; S. Round, Tipton ; C. H. H. Tippel, Reading ; P. A. Strickland, Leeds ; F. W. Sykes, Selby ; R. F. Tyler, Woolwich ; J. W. Wallis, London ; J. E. W. West, London ; and H. Davan Whetton, London. The following gentlemen having previously obtained Associateship, secured the diploma of Fellowship :—F. N. Abernethy, London ; F. J. Harper, Hull ; Henry Hudson, Southport ; and Hamilton Robertson, London. The examiners were C. J. Frost, Mus.Doc. ; Henry Gadsby ; Jas. Higgs, Mus. Bac. ; E. J. Hopkins, Mus.Doc. ; E. H. Turpin, and Thomas Wingham. The examinations were attended by a very large number of candidates. A most gratifying feature was the marked advance in the artistic character of the work done. With regard to the organ playing, the pieces (almost entirely selected from Bach and Mendelssohn's organ works) were mostly rendered in excellent style and with great finish. Still more noticeable was the admirable judgment and good solid technicalities shown in the performance of the church playing tests. In the paper work tests a corresponding improvement was observable, many musicianly examples of counterpoint, orchestration, etc., coming before the examiners' notice. It is, indeed, a simple fact that the work done by the College of Organists during the past few years has made a distinctly appreciable mark upon the high and noble profession of the organist in this country. It is to be earnestly hoped that this good work will be carried forward with the same good results from year, to year to the more complete training of its followers, and to the ultimate elevation to its true place in our social strata of one of the highest executive branches of the art.

Mr. Stephen S. Stratton, of Birmingham, writes thus to the *Musical Review* : " Dr. Filippi's interesting account of ' A visit to Wagner' reminds me of a note I made while indexing *Harmonicon*. In the last volume there is a brief notice of music in Leipzig ; and mention is made of the performance of a ' symphony by Richard Wagner, scarcely twenty years of age, which was much and deservedly applauded.' The recently published *Statistik der Concerte im Saale des Gewandhauses zu Leipzig* gives the date of the performance as January 10th, 1833. It also mentions an overture, performed February 23rd, 1832."

Organ News.

WELLINGBOROUGH.

An organ recital was given in the Congregational Church on Thursday, Jan. 18th, by Mr. W. T. Best, with the following programme :—

Sonata in F minor, No. 1	Mendelssohn.
Air with variations in A major	Haydn.
Festal March	Best.
Siciliana and Fugue in G minor	Bach.
Fantaisie in E flat major	Saint-Saëns.
Andante in G major	Smart.
Selection ("Water Music")	Handel.

MANCHESTER.

Mr. J. Kendrick Pyne gave an organ recital in the Town Hall, on Saturday, Jan. 13th. Subjoined is the programme :—

Prelude and Fugue in G major	Mendelssohn.
Nocturne ("L'Adieu des Bergers à la Sainte Famille")	Berlioz.
Sonata in D minor	Guilmant.
Meditation in G major ("Ricordati")	Gottschalk.
Air ("Exhibition Ode")	Wesley.
March ("Tannhäuser")	Wagner.

PRESTON.

Subjoined are the programmes of organ recitals given in the new Public Hall, by Mr. James Tomlinson, on Saturday, Jan. 13th :—

AFTERNOON PROGRAMME.

Overture ("Jessonda")	Spohr.
Andante with variations ("Septuor")	Beethoven.
Selection ("Water Music")	Handel.
Pastorale	Widor.
Paraphrase on "Gloria Ciel"	Best.
Grand Solemn March	Smart.

EVENING PROGRAMME.

Overture ("Occasional")	Handel.
Andante Cantabile	Bennett.
Fanfare	Lemmens.
"Air du Dauphin"	Roeckel-Best.
March in C	Wely.
Overture ("Le Calif de Bagdad")	Boieldieu.

EDINBURGH.

Sir Herbert Oakeley gave an organ recital in the Music Class Room, on Thursday, Jan. 11th, when he performed the following :—

Prelude and Fugue in G	Bach.
Minuet ("Berenice,") Chorus, "Happy, happy, happy pair, None but the brave deserve the fair" ("Alexander's Feast")	Handel.
Romanza ("La Reine de France")	Haydn.
Andante religioso, Allegretto, Finale (Sonata No. 4)	Mendelssohn.
Allegretto in F minor, No. 5, Op. 94	Schubert.
Lento, and Andante, "Von seligen Geistern" ("Orpheus")	Gluck.
March in C (Suite No. 6, Op. 150)	Lachner.

LEEDS.

Dr. Spark gave a recital on the grand organ in the Town Hall, in memoriam Léon Gambetta, on Saturday, Jan. 13th. The programme included :—

Funeral March	Beethoven.
Selection ("Requiem")	Mozart.
Funeral March, Op. 43	Scharwenka.
Dead March ("Saul")	Handel.
Funeral March, composed for a Military Band	Mendelssohn.
French and English airs.	

In consequence of the large audience, this programme was repeated on Jan. 16th.

BOLTON.

An organ recital was given in the Albert Hall, by Mr. Wm. Mullineux, F.C.O., on Saturday, Jan. 6th. The following was the programme :—

Concerto in G minor, No. 1	Handel.
Andante (Fourth Symphony)	Haydn.
"Adoremus," Op. 72	Ravina.
"March des Troubadours," arr. by Lott	Roubier.
Wedding March	Mendelssohn.

And on Saturday, Jan. 13th :—

Offertoire in G major	Wely.
Theme with variations, "Carillons de Dunkerque"	E. H. Turpin.
Toccata in A flat	Hesse.
Selection ("Rigoletto")	Verdi.
Festival March in E flat	Lachner.

WATERLOO ROAD.

Subjoined is the programme of an organ recital given on Thursday, Jan. 11th, at St. John's Church, by Mr. Edwin Evans, F.C.O. :—

Toccata and Fugue in C	Bach.
Fantaisie en forme d'Offertoire	Tours.
Allegro molto—Andante con moto—Allegro Vivace.	
Suite de Pièces	Evans.
Andante and Allegro molto vivace (Violin Concerto, Op. 64)	Mendelssohn.
Marcia Villereccia, Op. 214, No. 6	Fumagalli.

BURTON-ON-TRENT.

Mr. A. B. Plant, Mus.Bac., Oxon., F.C.O., gave a recital in St. Paul's Institute, on Wednesday, Jan. 10th. The programme included :—

Overture ("Cenerentola")	Rossini.
Andante, Offertoire in D	Batiste.
Allegretto in B minor	Guilmant.
Fugue in G minor	Bach.
Andante	Mozart.
"Hallelujah" Chorus	Beethoven.

FINSBURY PARK.

On the occasion of the opening of the new organ in the Wesleyan Chapel, on Wednesday, Jan. 17th, Mr. Fountain Meen performed the following :—

Sonata in B flat	Mendelssohn.
Andante in F	Smart.
Fugue in B minor	Bach.
Fantasia, "The Storm"	Lemmens.
Air with variations	Rea.
"Hallelujah" ("Messiah")	Handel.
Grand Chœur	Guilmant.

BIRKENHEAD.

The following is the programme of an organ recital given by Mr. E. Townshend Driffield, in the Music Hall, on Saturday, Jan. 13th :—

Toccata and Fugue in D minor	Bach.
Andante in F, March in C	Wely.
Selection ("Faust")	Gounod.
"Schiller" March	Meyerbeer.
Gavotte in B flat	Driffield.
Largo and Allegro ("Cuckoo and Nightingale")	Handel.
Overture ("Tancredi")	Rossini.

EDINBURGH.

The following is the specification of an organ erected in S. Thomas's (Episcopal) Church, by Messrs. Brindley and Foster, of Sheffield :—

GREAT ORGAN. CC TO G.

1. Double Diapason	16 ft.	6. Harmonic Flute	4 ft.
2. Open Diapason	8 „	7. Harmonic Piccolo	2 „
3. Höhl Flöte	8 „	8. Mixture (3 ranks).	
4. Dulciana	8 „	9. Trumpet	8 „
5. Principal	4 „		

SWELL ORGAN. CC TO G.

10. Lieblich Bourdon	16 ft.	14. Salicet	8 ft.
11. Violin Diapason	8 „	15. Mixture (3 ranks)	
12. Gedact	8 „	16. Oboe	8 „
13. Vox Angelica	8 „	17. Cornopean	8 „

PEDAL ORGAN. CCC TO F.

18. Major Bass	16 ft.	20. Principal Bass	8 ft.
19. Sub Bass	16 „	21. Flute Bass	8 „

COUPLERS.

22. Swell to Great.	24. Great to Pedals.
23. Swell to Pedals.	

Three Composition pedals to Great organ.			
Three	„	„	to Pedal organ.
Two	„	„	to Swell organ.

Though not immediately concerning the "sons of harmony," who are usually wise enough to have little occasion for speaking in the Law Courts, and who are not likely to be called upon practically to "sooth the savage breasts" of those who delight to "bark and bite," it is not out of place to record in these columns the reported failure of the palatial rooms of the New Palace of Justice, from the acoustical point of sight. When will our architects pay that attention, which is emphatically demanded, to the question of securing certain and satisfactory acoustical results? Surely the matter is important enough, seeing that every building and room must necessarily be constructed for uses employing the sense of hearing. Our musical bodies would do well to advance in this matter by opening an investigation as to the best principles upon which to build a model concert-room.

Passing Events.

Herr Pachmann has left London for the continent, playing at Paris for M. Pasdeloup before going to St. Petersburg.

Messrs. Puttick and Simpson hold a sale on Tuesday next, when a good collection of valuable string and wind instruments, etc., will be offered for purchase.

Gounod's "Redemption," it is said, will take the place of Bach's Passion Music (" St. John ") at St. Anne's, Soho, and will be conducted by Mr. Barnby. The work will most probably be given in two parts, to be sung alternately on Friday evenings at eight.

A very excellent concert was given at Littleport, near Ely, by Dr. Chipp (organist of Ely Cathedral), and several ladies and gentlemen. Weber's "Preciosa" was exceedingly well rendered, and was followed by a very attractive selection.

Messrs. J. Cowley & Co., of Hull, are supplying direct from America several models of the American reed organ, exhibiting very high perfection as regards tone and a finished mechanism. The largest-sized instrument is effective in churches and school-rooms of good size.

The Dundee Festival of the 24th, 25th, and 26th inst., under conductorship of H. M. Henry Nägel, will include performances of Gounod's "Redemption," and orchestral concert with Beethoven's Choral Symphony (this one concert being under the direction of Mr. Manns), and Handel's "Israel in Egypt."

Mr. R. S. Burton gave a performance of Berlioz's "Faust" in the Leeds Town Hall, last week. The principals were Miss Davies, Mr. E. Lloyd, Mr. F. King, and Mr. Thornton Wood. The chorus was supplied by the Bradford Choral Society. Mr. J. T. Carrodus was leader of the orchestra, and Mr. Burton was conductor.

The Graphic judiciously points out that something more might be done for vocal music at the Monday Popular Concerts. Nothing, indeed, could be more acceptable than the systematic performance of the delicious lyrics of Schubert, Schumann, Mendelssohn, Bennett, Gounod, H. Smart, etc.

"Don Eugenio" is the title of a comic opera by Herr Mohr, which was produced at Berlin, on December 30th. Gounod's "Faust" has been heard in St. Petersburg in the Russian language ; and the same composer's "Redemption" will be performed for the first time on the continent at Brussels, in April.

Amongst the recent subscriptions in aid of the Fund for the Royal College of Music is a subscription for £5,000 from Mr. Andrew Carnegie, of New York, a native of Dunfermline (N.B.). The subscription list at Newcastle-on-Tyne is gaining strength, £400 has already been obtained, Sir William Armstrong heading the list with £100.

It is gratifying to learn that Mr. Williams, the new and esteemed organist of Gloucester Cathedral, has proved himself to be an able conductor at a recent performance given in that city, when Dr. Stainer's "Daughter of Jairus" was given. The news has special significance in view of Three Choir Festival Meetings held from time to time in Gloucester.

The Bloomsbury Church Choir Union is the title of a new association formed by the choirs of that important section of mid-London. The objects of the society are the cultivation and development of high-class church music, and the careful, earnest endeavour to secure the fitting and devotional rendering of service music in all its departments. The combined choirs meet in the different churches by turns, and propose to hold a choral festival each year, between Easter and Whitsuntide. The local clergy are the society's vice-presidents, and a strong committee of management has been formed, consisting of the different church organists and representatives from the various choirs forming the "Union." Mr. C. H. Mason, of Broad Street, W. C., is the hon. secretary of the association. Such a society deserves earnest sympathy and support, for the proposal to zealously cultivate the proper and artistic rendering of the best church music is surely one of the highest stand-points any musical body can claim as the object of its existence.

Service Lists.

SEPTUAGESIMA SUNDAY.

JANUARY 21st.

London.

ST. PAUL'S CATHEDRAL.—Morn.: Service, Te Deum and Benedictus, Hopkins in F; Introit, Thou visitest the earth (Greene) ; Communion Service, Schubert in G. Even.: Service, Magnificat and Nunc Dimittis, Hopkins in F ; Anthem, In the beginning God created, and, The heavens are telling (Haydn).

WESTMINSTER ABBEY.—Morn.: Service, Benedicite, Foster in E ; Jubilate and Continuation, Barnby in E. Aft.: Service, Wesley in E ; Anthems, In the beginning, and, The heavens are telling (Haydn).

TEMPLE CHURCH.— Morn.: Service, Jubilate, Aldrich in G; Apostles' Creed, Harmonized Monotone ; Anthems, In the beginning, and, The heavens are telling (Haydn). Even.: Service, Cantate and Deus Misereatur, Attwood in D ; Apostles' Creed, Harmonized Monotone ; Anthem, When the earth was without form (Handel).

LINCOLN'S INN HALL.—Morn.: Service, Childe in G ; Kyrie, Mendelssohn ; Anthem, Sing to the Lord a new-made song (Mendelssohn). Even.: Service, Childe in G ; Anthem, We have heard with our ears, O God (Steggall).

ST. AUGUSTINE AND ST. FAITH, WATLING STREET.—Morn.: Service, Stainer in E flat (throughout) ; Offertory, Let your light (Stainer). Even.: Service, Stainer in E flat ; Anthems, In splendour bright, and, The heavens are telling (Haydn).

ST. BARNABAS, MARYLEBONE.—Morn.: Service, Te Deum and Jubilate, Clarke-Whitfeld in E ; Anthem, I have set God (Goldwin) ; Kyrie and Nicene Creed, Harvey Löhr in A minor. Even.: Service, Magnificat and Nunc Dimittis, Clarke-Whitfeld in E ; Anthem, Lord at all times ("Lauda Sion," Mendelssohn).

CHRIST CHURCH, CLAPHAM.—Morn.: Service, Te Deum, Plain-song ; Kyrie, Credo, Sanctus, Benedictus, Agnus Dei, and Gloria in excelsis, Mozart in B flat. Even.: Service, Magnificat and Nunc Dimittis, Arnold in A ; Anthem, I was glad (Elvey).

FOUNDLING CHAPEL.—Morn.: Service, Te Deum, Dykes in F ; Jubilate, Ebdon in C ; Anthem, In splendour bright, and The heavens are telling ("Creation," Haydn). Aft.: Service, Magnificat and Nunc Dimittis, Foster in A ; Anthem, Let all men praise the Lord ("Hymn of Praise," Mendelssohn).

ST. JAMES'S PRIVATE EPISCOPAL CHAPEL, SOUTHWARK. —Morn.: Service, Introit, The earth is my possession (Gounod); Communion Service, Gounod. Even.: Service, Thorne in D ; Anthem, Hallelujah (Beethoven).

ST. MAGNUS, LONDON BRIDGE.—Morn.: Service, Opening Anthem, To the Lord our God (Calkin) ; Te Deum and Jubilate, Boyce in A ; Kyrie, Reay. Even.: Service, Magnificat and Nunc Dimittis, Walmisley Anthem, O come let us worship (Mendelssohn).

ST. MARGARET PATTENS, ROOD LANE, FENCHURCH STREET.—Morn.: Service, Te Deum, Sullivan in D ; Benedictus, Dykes in F ; Communion Service, Offertory Anthem, But the Lord is mindful (Mendelssohn) ; Kyrie, Credo, Sanctus, Benedictus, Agnus Dei, and Gloria in excelsis, Schubert in B flat. Even.: Service, Magnificat and Nunc Dimittis, Oakeley in E flat ; Anthem, The heavens are telling (Haydn).

ST. MARY ABCHURCH, E.C.—Morn.: Service, Chipp in D ; Communion Service, Nares in F. Even.: Service, Garrett in D.

ST. MARY BOLTONS, WEST BROMPTON, S.W.—Morn.: Service, Benedicite, Best in C ; Benedictus, Chant ; Kyrie, Credo, Sanctus, and Gloria in excelsis, Thorne in G ; Benedictus and Agnus Dei, Monk in C ; Offertory, Barnby. Even.: Service, Magnificat and Nunc Dimittis, Parry in D ; Anthem, Like as a father pitieth (Hatton).

ST. MICHAEL'S, CORNHILL. — Morn.: Service, Benedicite, Best ; Jubilate, Wesley in F ; Anthem, How dear are Thy counsels (Crotch) ; Kyrie, Evison ; Creed, Goss. Even.: Service, Magnificat and Nunc Dimittis, Thorne in E flat ; Anthem, Acquaint thyself with God (Greene).

ST. PAUL'S, AVENUE ROAD, SOUTH HAMPSTEAD.—Morn.: Service, Benedicite, Stainer, Turle, and Irons ; Benedictus, Barnby ; Kyrie, Merbecke ; Offertory, Barnby ; Credo, Sanctus, and Gloria in excelsis, Merbecke. Even.: Service, Magnificat and Nunc Dimittis, Walmisley in D minor ; Anthem, Behold, now praise the Lord (Calkin).

ST. PAUL'S, BOW COMMON, E.—Morn.: Service, Benedicite, Best in C ; Benedictus, Chant ; Communion Service, Kyrie, Credo, Sanctus, Benedictus, Agnus Dei, and Gloria in excelsis, Vernham in F ; Offertory, Calkin. Even.: Service, Magnificat and Nunc Dimittis, Stainer in A ; Anthem, In the beginning (Haydn).

ST. PETER'S (EATON SQUARE). — Morn.: Service, Benedicite, Best in C. Even.: Service, Hopkins in A ; Anthem, In the beginning God created (Haydn).

ST. PETER'S, VERE STREET, W.—Even.: Service, Magnificat and Nunc Dimittis, Tuckerman in F ; Anthem, Lovely appear ("Redemption," Gounod).

Country.

ST. ASAPH CATHEDRAL. — Morn.: Service, Benedicite, Chant ; Anthem, In the beginning (Haydn). Even.: Service, The Litany ; Anthem, The earth is the Lord's (Trimnell).

ASHBURNE CHURCH, DERBYSHIRE. — Morn.: Service, Baker in F ; Kyrie and Credo, Barnby in E. Even.: Service, Stainer in A ; Anthem, Doth not wisdom cry (Haking).

BEDDINGTON CHURCH, SURREY.— Morn.: Service, Benedicite, Stainer ; Benedictus, Dykes in F ; Communion Service, Dykes in F. Even.: Service, Calkin in D ; Anthem, Power and love (arranged by Gounod from "Redemption "), and, The marvellous work (Haydn).

BIRMINGHAM (ST. CYPRIAN'S, HAY MILLS).—Morn.: Service, Kent in C ; Anthem, The heavens are telling (Haydn). Even.: Service, Clark Whitfeld in D ; Anthem, The heavens declare (Boyce).

CANTERBURY CATHEDRAL. — Morn.: Service, Benedicite, Turle in A ; Jubilate, Hake in A ; Anthem, O praise God in his holiness (Weldon) ; Communion Service, Maxted in E flat. Even.: Service, Hayes in E flat ; Anthem, O praise the Lord of heaven (Elvey).

CARLISLE CATHEDRAL.—Morn.: Service, Best ; Introit, I will love thee (Macfarren) ; Kyrie, Chipp in A ; Nicene Creed, Goss. Even.: Service, Macfarren in E flat ; Anthem, O sing unto the Lord (Purcell).

DUBLIN, ST. PATRICK'S (NATIONAL) CATHEDRAL.—Morn.: Service, Te Deum and Jubilate, Stanford in B flat ; Anthem, And God saw everything ("Creation," Haydn). Even.: Service, Magnificat and Nunc Dimittis, Stanford in B flat ; Anthem, Distracted with care (Haydn), and, In the beginning (Haydn and Stevenson).

DURHAM CATHEDRAL.—Morn.: Service, Benedicite, Foster ; Anthem, O come, let us worship (Mendelssohn) ; Introit, We wait for thy loving kindness (Armes) ; Communion Service, Smart in G. Even.: Service, Smart in G ; Anthem, In the beginning (Haydn).

ELY CATHEDRAL. — Morn.: Service, Benedicite, Chants ; Benedictus, Plain-song ; Kyrie and Credo, Oakeley in E flat ; Gloria, Chipp in A flat ; Anthem, O Lord, how manifold (Barnby). Even.: Service, Oakeley in E flat ; Anthem, The eyes of all wait ("I will give ") (Barnby).

EXETER CATHEDRAL.—Morn.: Service, King in C ; Communion Service, Gilbert in F. Even.: Service, King in C ; Anthem, I will love thee (Clark).

GLASGOW (BLYTHSWOOD PARISH CHURCH).—Aft.: Service, Anthem, The Lord is my Shepherd (Macfarren).

LIVERPOOL CATHEDRAL — Aft.: Service, Collingwood. Banks in E flat ; Anthem, The heavens declare the glory of God (Boyce).

MANCHESTER CATHEDRAL. — Morn.: Service, Ouseley in G ; Anthem, All thy works (Thorne) ; Communion Service, Bridge in G. Aft.: Service, Ouseley in G ; Anthem, In the beginning (Haydn).

PETERBOROUGH CATHEDRAL. — Morn.: Service, Boyce in C ; Introit, Give ear (Mozart) ; Communion Service, Smart in F and Ross in G. Even.: Service, Turle in D ; Anthem, Lift thine eyes (Mendelssohn).

RIPON CATHEDRAL.—Morn.: Service, Tours in F ; Anthem, Seek ye the Lord (Roberts). Even.: Service, The Litany ; Anthem, Hear my prayer (Mendelssohn).

ROCHESTER CATHEDRAL. — Morn.: Service, Walmisley in E ; Anthem, O taste and see (Goss). Even.: Service, Hopkins in B flat ; Anthems, In the beginning, and, The heavens are telling (Haydn).

WELLS CATHEDRAL.— Morn.: Service, Summers in A ; Introit, Blessed are the pure in heart (Macfarren) ; Kyrie, Cooke in G. Even.: Service, Clarke in F ; Anthem, Behold, now praise the Lord (Oakeley).

WORCESTER CATHEDRAL. — Morn.: Service, Turle in D ; Anthem, Thou, Lord, our refuge (Mendelssohn). Even.: Service, Turle in D ; Anthem, In the beginning (Haydn).

ERRATA.—A correspondent desires the correction of a long overlooked error in the statement of issue of Nov. 11th (1882), anent the Thanksgiving Service at St. James's Church, Benwell, Newcastle, which should have mentioned that Mr. A. T. Atkinson, choirmaster, conducted the music upon that occasion. In No. 6 of "Passing Events" last week, read Francis Pogson.

APPOINTMENTS.

MR. E. BURRITT LANE, Organist to Holy Trinity, Twickenham.

MR. FRANK H. BRADLEY, Organist and Choir Director of S. John the Evangelist, Wilton Road, Pimlico, S.W., has been appointed to a Professorship for the Organ by the Board of Trinity College, London, in that institution.

Printed for the Proprietors by BOWDEN, HUDSON & CO., at 23, Red Lion Street, Holborn, London, W.C.; and Published by WILLIAM REEVES, at the Office, 185, Fleet Street, E.C. West End Agents:—WEEKES & CO., 14, Hanover Street, Regent Street, W. Subscriptions and Advertisements are received either by the Publisher or West End Agents.—Communications for the EDITOR are to be forwarded to his private address, 6, Argyle Square, W.C.
SATURDAY, JAN. 20, 1883.—Registered at the General Post Office as a Newspaper.

MUSICAL STANDARD

A NEWSPAPER FOR MUSICIANS PROFESSIONAL AND AMATEUR

No. 965. VOL. XXIV. FOURTH SERIES. SATURDAY, JANUARY 27, 1883. WEEKLY: PRICE 3D.

TRIADS: THEIR RELATIONSHIP AND TREATMENT.

BY FRANCIS EDWARD GLADSTONE, MUS. DOC.

(Continued from page 35.)

Now this chord has two notes in common with each of the others; nevertheless, when the 1st chord and the 3rd are played in succession, the transition sounds abrupt; whereas, if the third is preceded by the 2nd the effect is excellent. The reason for this apparent inconsistency is, like so many other difficulties, explained by Helmholtz. In passing from the chord of G major to that of E minor, we retain in the second chord the characteristic interval (viz., the major 3rd G ; B) of the former; but, in passing from the chord of C major to that of E minor, although we retain the two notes common to both chords, these notes are characteristic, not of the first but of the second, and thus the change of harmony is more forced and sudden. But if we combine the 3rd, 6th, and octave of our scale of C major, placing another A below them as a bass, we obtain a minor chord, standing in the same relationship to the chord of C major that E minor occupies towards G major; moreover, these two minor chords are connected in precisely the same way as are the major chords, *i.e.*, the 5th of one is the root of the other.

Proceeding as we did in the formation of the major scale let us place these two chords in juxtaposition:—

Ex. 11. **A.**

This of course only gives us an incomplete scale. We will however place the notes in regular order within the compass of an octave, adding the upper E:—

Ex. 11. **B.**

Dividing these notes into sections similar to those of the major scale, we find that only the middle section is complete. However, the interval from E to G in the first section corresponds exactly with the interval from A to C in the second; and it is only necessary to add F ♯, a major tone above E, to make the resemblance perfect:—

Ex. 11. **C.**

Here we are confronted with a difficulty. If D ♮ be borrowed from the scale of C major, although this will produce the earliest known form of the minor scale, the effect, to modern ears trained to appreciate the sensitive character of the leading note, will seem inconclusive and therefore unsatisfactory. If however we now continue our system of scale formation from three triads and place F ♯ above B, it will be found that these two notes form the interval of a perfect 5th (F ♯ being a major tone above E, and E a perfect 5th below B); and it only remains to add D♯, a major 3rd above B, to complete the dominant triad, and with it our modern minor scale:—

Ex. 11. **D.**

It will be seen that there is a close analogy between this scale and the major scale already formed; but there is a marked difference in regard to the intervals which separate the first group of three notes from the second group, and the second section from the third. This gives a somewhat uncouth effect to the ascending octave; and therefore it is (as we know) usual to lessen this roughness, in passages of melody, by sharpening the 6th degree in ascending, and to lower the 7th degree in descending the scale. It is interesting to observe that there is here, again, some correspondence between our artificial scale and the scale of nature.

The series of harmonics rising from

includes, between the 10th and 20th, the following sounds:—

Ex. 12.

The 11th is of course too flat for our scale; but if the 15th, 16th, 18th, and 20th harmonics are taken in succession, beginning with the highest, they agree well with the intervals of our descending melodic minor scale, and if the 15th, 17th, 19th, and 20th could be heard in ascending order they would be found to be, not (it is true) in perfect tune with the true C ♯ and D ♯ of the chromatic scale of C, but as nearly as possible (short of exactness) in tune with the scale of equal temperament. This fact, although of less consequence than others which we have been considering, seems to me not without its significance, especially when it is remembered that the exact intonation of chromatic intervals in melody is a matter of smaller importance than that of diatonic intervals.

Returning now to the major scale, we shall be in a position to make an examination of the relationship or otherwise existing between the various triads which may be formed from it.

We have found that the most natural progression in harmony is from "tonic" to "dominant" and back again, and that if we move from the "tonic" chord to that of the "subdominant," the return *viâ* the dominant is grateful:—

Ex. 13.

Supposing, however, that we desire more variety than can be obtained from the employment of major chords only, we may bring into use one of the minor chords which have helped us in forming the minor scale. It has been already shown that a minor chord based upon the sixth degree of the major scale follows the tonic harmony very agreeably, because both chords contain the characteristic interval of a major 3rd from the tonic root. But a minor chord is, for similar reasons, satisfactorily followed by the major chord situated a 3rd below it, inasmuch as the two higher sounds of the major triad are identical with the two characteristic sounds of the minor triad. We may therefore interpolate a chord of A minor between the first and second chords in the progression just quoted:—

Ex. 14.

and the result will still be good. If, however, we begin by a movement from the tonic to the dominant chord, we may take a wider excursion. Let the progression from the chord of C be followed by another from G major to E minor, and this again by a third step from E minor to A minor, the roots ascending a fourth :—

Ex. 15.

It is only necessary to add chords 3, 4, and 5 from our last example

to produce a good result.

Five out of the seven triads which may be formed from the scale of C have thus been brought into use. But there is another upon the second of the scale (D) which now claims our consideration. At first sight this is as good a minor chord as that on A or E. A moment's thought will however shew us that this is not so. Remembering that the interval from C to D is a major tone, while that from G to A is a minor tone, we find that the interval from D to A is flatter than a perfect 5th, and, as a minor 3rd is equal to the sum of a *major* tone and a major semitone, the interval from D to F must be less than a minor 3rd. It follows that the triad on D in the scale of C major is not a concord at all. It is in fact a portion of the chord of the dominant 9th, both F and A being discords. Students of harmony will however remember that the absence of the root of a discord often relaxes the rules for the resolution of the dissonant note or notes, and if the triad under notice be followed by dominant harmony, the parts progressing each to the nearest available note, the progression is quite satisfactory. We may therefore add this chord on D to the series of triads already produced :—

Ex. 16.

It is worth while to observe moreover that the 9th (A) is here regularly resolved, and that although the 7th (F) falls to D, in the first instance, it afterwards rises to E, the note of its ordinary resolution.

It will be well, before considering other combinations of chords in a major key to compare those already noticed with similar progressions in a minor key; and this comparison will be more readily made by transposing the scale already formed. Taking A as the tonic, the scale will stand thus :—

Ex 17.

At first sight, the six lowest notes correspond to a portion of the scale of C major ; but there is one important difference, viz., that the note D now stands at the interval of a perfect 5th below A, and therefore also a true minor 3rd below F. This of course displaces the order of major and minor tones. The significance of these changes will presently appear.

I may here be charged with inconsistency. It will perhaps be said that as the scale of E minor has been compared to a portion of the harmonic series of C, and inasmuch as the chord of E minor has actually been derived from that source, I ought, logically, to contend that E minor is the true relative minor key to C. I venture to point out, however, that most authorities agree in regarding the dominant chord as a second derivative of the tonic root although, taken as the basis of a scale, this chord would produce sounds foreign to the original scale; and that in going a step further and looking at the minor chord as a third derivative from the original root, I am only following out the same principle. There is an obvious relationship between the *scales* of G major and E minor, arising from the fact that the three last notes of one are identical with the three first notes of the other, and the close relationship existing between the *chords* has been already shewn.

The idea which I wish to suggest is that the chords of C major, G major, and E minor are all the direct offspring of the parent C, but that the two latter belong to a later generation than the former ; they are, as it were grandchildren (brother and sister) and thus their relationship towards C is of a different kind to their relationship towards one another.

I have only to add that the chords of C major and A minor have of course a parallel connection.

(*To be continued.*)

Musical Intelligence.

ROYAL ALBERT HALL CHORAL SOCIETY.

Mr. Barnby, on the evening of January 17th, gave a fine performance of " The Creation," at the Albert Hall. Haydn's great oratorio, which, he said, had occupied him a long time, because he intended the work to *last* a long time, may be classed, for its perennial reputation with " The Messiah " and " Elijah ;" although, certainly not quite so often brought before the public. Mr. Charles Hallé chose the oratorio for the first musical festival of Bristol, held in October, 1873, and the Sacred Harmonic Society represented it from time to time.

The vocal "principals," on January 17th, were Mdme. Marie Roze, Mr. Joseph Maas, and Mr. Santley—a goodly triad of fine and accomplished artists. Mdme. Roze excelled in the air, " With verdure clad," where ascent is made by a run to the high B flat, and the air (with chorus) "The marvellous work " was also a feature. Mr. Maas made the most of the tenor song, " In native worth," and Mr. Santley rendered some service in the duets of Part II. His most successful solos were, " Rolling in foaming billows," and he read the recitatives effectively. It may be thought odd that Haydn has made Adam, who here appears as a married lover, a basso (or baritone) instead of a tenor. The choruses went well, especially the glorious one in C, " The heavens are telling." Mr. Barnby held the *bâton*, and Dr. Stainer was organist. " The Messiah " is down for Ash Wednesday (February 7th).

SATURDAY POPULAR CONCERTS.

PROGRAMME.

Quartet in E flat, Op. 44, No. 3, for two violins,
  viola, and violoncello .... Mendelssohn.
  Mdme. Norman-Néruda, MM. L. Ries, Straus, and Piatti.
Air, "Adelaide" .... Beethoven.
        Mr. Edward Lloyd.
Impromptus, Op. 142, Nos. 1, 2, and 4, for piano-
  forte alone .... Schubert.
        Mr. Charles Hallé.
Sonata in A major, No. 2, for pianoforte and violin Bach.
  Mr. Charles Hallé and Mdme. Norman-Néruda.
Serenade, "Awake, awake" .... Piatti.
        Mr Edward Lloyd.
      Violoncello obbligato—Signor Piatti.
Serenade Trio, in D major, Op. 8, for violin, viola,
  and violoncello .... Beethoven.
  Mdme. Norman-Néruda, MM. Straus, and Piatti.

    Accompanist - - - Mr. Zerbini.

The first number on the above (last Saturday's) programme was heard for the eighteenth, and the closing
trio for the twenty-fourth, time at these concerts. Though
no fault could reasonably be found with so admirable a
selection, it is possible that a few enterprising spirits
among the audience may occasionally sigh for a little
change of diet. Rheinberger, Svendsen, Sgambati, and
others might be allowed one hearing during the season,
and it would have been a graceful act to have devoted
one programme to the honour and memory of Joachim
Raff. It is scarcely to be wished that these Popular
Concerts should degenerate into "Ancient" ones; for
though it may not be their province to introduce new and
untried works, there are many glorious compositions that
are neither absolute novelties, nor second-rate productions of first-rate men heard for the twenty-fourth
time at these concerts exclusively, and the hundred and
twenty-fourth all other concerts inclusively.

Mdme. Norman-Néruda was warmly welcomed back,
and how delightfully she led the quartet, especially the
noble adagio, will be imagined by all those who are
acquainted with her playing and Mendelssohn's work.
Herr Straus fills a secondary place as admirably as he
leads—we do not look upon his like every day.

If Mr. Charles Hallé has a particular favour for any
composer, that composer is Schubert. He played the
No. 4 Impromptu with a piquancy and grace that could
not be equalled by any other pianist. Mr. Hallé has the
true expression for Schubert.

Bach's sonata is a perfect example of pleasing and
tuneful music in strictly scientific form.

Mr. Lloyd made the most of Signor Piatti's common-
place production, the second part of which seems to
have no connection with the first. His rendering of
"Adelaide" is well known. Mr. Zerbini evidently took
much pains with his accompaniments, and the result, it is
pleasant to be able to record, was entirely satisfactory.

                    B. F. WYATT-SMITH.

MONDAY POPULAR CONCERTS.

The concert of last Monday evening was attended by
the Prince and Princess of Wales.

PROGRAMME.

PART I.

Trio in C major, Op. 87, for pianoforte, violin, and
  violoncello .... Brahms.
          (First time.)
  Mr. Charles Hallé, Mdme. Norman-Néruda, and Signor Piatti.
Air, "Lusinghe più care" .... Handel.
        Miss Thudichum.
Sonata in F sharp, Op. 78, for pianoforte alone .... Beethoven.
        Mr. Charles Hallé.

PART II.

Sonata in G major, Op. 96, for pianoforte and violin Beethoven.
  Mr. Charles Hallé and Mdme. Norman-Néruda.
Song, "Im Herbst" .... Franz.
        Miss Thudichum.
Quartet in B flat, Op. 64, No. 5, for two violins,
  viola, and violoncello .... Haydn.
  Mdme. Norman-Néruda, MM. L. Ries, Straus, and Piatti.

    Accompanist - - - Mr. Zerbini.

Brahms's trio, a very recent production, took the place
of the customary trio. A first hearing disposes
the attentive auditor to admire the work—discursive, if
not excursive, like all this master's compositions, but not
"without form, or void." The trio comprises four movements : an allegro in C, an andante con moto in A minor,
a presto (scherzo) in C minor, and a (final) allegro giocoso
in the original key. The opening movement, which includes a "free Fantasia," various "tributaries," many
reminiscences, and the usual show-off bits of contrapuntal
writing, struck me, in spite of its length, as genial and
interesting music. The andante, a national air with those

always trying "variations," here very cleverly treated, has
a pianoforte accompaniment of full chords in syncopation ;
and one of the (five) varieties is a duologue for the string
instruments. The scherzo, which follows in another minor
key (rather a mistake in point of form), has the form of a
spiritual presto, in semi-quavers, 6-8 time, quaint, but not
very new, because reminding one of the used-up "Hungarian" style. The finale struck one as more remarkable
for the ingenious use of the pianoforte, here well brought
out, and the working up treatment than for any original
ideas. Of course the trio will soon be heard again ; assuredly at one of Mr. C. Hallé's spring recitals.

Mr. Hallé played his difficult part so as to evolve all
the fine features of the work. His refined reading of
Beethoven's lovely little Sonata in F sharp major, composed in 1809, is well known. Ten minutes suffice for
the performance. A long interval of prolific productivity
elapsed between this sonata and the famous "Op. 57" in
F major. Some musicians opine that the working out of
the second movement of Op. 78 (also in F sharp) savours
a little of the "piece-writing," or "passage-writing" style.
The signature of the sonata and the necessary use of
double sharps in the modulations (as to C sharp major)
deter many amateurs from attempting to play it, and the
world is not a loser !

The duet sonata in G (at the head of Part II.), last of
the set, is recognised as a chef d'œuvre. The earlier
sonata in the same key is one of the "Emperor Alexander"
triad employed a few weeks ago, with Herr Pachmann as
pianist. Mr. Hallé executed his task with exactness, and
seemed to breathe out his soul in the cadences, especially
in the last of all. Mdme. Norman-Néruda, here an able
"second," shone afterwards brilliantly as "first fiddle," in
Haydn's 41st quartet, thought to be his finest—a great
deal to say !

Miss Thudichum's voice has much flexibility and an
extensive compass.

The Prince and Princess of Wales remained until the
end.   A. M.

LEEDS.

The Leeds Philharmonic Society gave a concert of
vocal and instrumental music in the Leeds Town Hall
last week, when the following excellent programme was
gone through :—

PART I.

Part-song, "Waken, lords and ladies gay" .... S. Reay.
Song, "For ever and for ever" .... Tosti.
Quartet in E flat, Op. 16, for pianoforte, violin,
  viola, and violoncello .... Beethoven.
Songs—
  "Preludium" }
  "Tarantelle" } .... D. Popper.
Song, "Thou'rt passing hence" .... Sullivan.
Dramatic Chorus, "Liberty" .... Eaton Faning.

PART II.

Two German Volkslieder—
  "In silent night" (harmonised by Joh. Brahms)
  "The enchanted nightingale" (harmonised by
      Otto Goldschmidt)
Violin solo, "Airs Russes" .... Wieniawski.
Song, "O swallow" .... Piatti.
      (With violoncello obbligato).
Quartet in E flat, Op. 47, for pianoforte, violin,
  viola, and violoncello .... Schumann.
Part-song, "Bird of the wilderness" .... Jas. Broughton.
Duet, "When the wind bloweth in from the sea" .. Hy. Smart.
Part-song, "New Year's Song" .... Berthold Tours.

The vocalists were Mrs. A. Broughton and Mr. F. King.
Mr. James Broughton was conductor, and Mr. Alfred
Broughton accompanied at the piano.

It is not often that pantomime music is worthy of notice
in these columns, but an exception may be made in favour
of the pantomime "Robinson Crusoe," now running at
the Grand Theatre here. Miss Fanny Leslie deserves
special praise for her charming rendering of the patriotic
song "Run up the flag," specially written for her by Mr.
Clement Scott, and this lady is also very successful in the
pretty "Dreaming Song."

Dr. Spark's organ recitals have been resumed, and
visitors to Leeds might do worse than look in at the
Leeds Town Hall some Tuesday afternoon, when they
will have the opportunity of hearing one of the finest
organs in the kingdom. A special feature of the Tuesday's
performance was Sullivan's song "The Lost Chord"
specially arranged for the organ by Dr. Spark. The programme also included Dr. Spark's "Morceau pour les
Carillons" F Major, and the "Toy Symphony" (Romberg),
and one of the organ concertos as adapted, and one may
say adopted, by J. S. Bach.

MR. VAN. NOORDEN'S CONCERTS.

Mr. P. E. Van. Noorden held his second concert at the Ladbroke Hall, on the evening of Thursday, January 18th. The room was crowded to the lobbies. The able *entrepreneur* himself did not play at all, but his son Mr. Walter Van Noorden, distinguished himself as pianist, in his father's spirited "Polka de Concert," and also in the splendid duet for two pianofortes, written by M. Saint-Säens, of Paris, on the theme of the trio (Scherzo) from Beethoven's pianoforte sonata in E flat "Op. 31." Mr. Lindsay Sloper was W. Van Noorden's able *collaborateur*, and the piece evoked loud applause. Miss Reba, a pupil of Mr. Van Noorden, sang "L'Alba" (by Signor Rotoli) with *éclat*, also Roeckel's "Of course." Mr. A. Thomas won a *bis* for a new song, "The Skipper's Flag," and Molloy's "Three merry men." Mdme. Julie Pelletier evoked much applause for Mr. Randegger's song. "Only for me," and she also took part in concerted pieces. A farce called "Chiselling" was afterwards performed under the direction of Mr. H. Murray Lane.

CITY OF LONDON CHORAL UNION.

There has been much controversy of late among a certain class of people (who imagine that they would not be fulfilling the duties of life without endeavouring to make themselves obnoxious by trying to find fault in the well-doing of their fellow men) as to the advisability or necessity of giving entertainment of a high order to inmates of our hospitals, workhouses, infirmaries, &c., and, indeed, they have gone so far as to try to advance a question as to the legality of such an admirable undertaking.

At the concert of which I am about to speak there were between 700 and 800 inmates present; and to see the beam of delight which showed itself conspicuously on the faces of these poor old people, as one by one the artists stepped upon the platform, must have at once crushed any contrary feeling, if the person or persons beholding such a pleasing sight had any heart or sympathy, however small. It has also been urged that the inmates of workhouses are, as a rule, not able to appreciate good music ; but this opinion must be taken for what it is worth, and, from my experience, I am vain enough to say that it is worth but little. If those persons who have advanced such an uncharitable rebuke could have been present at the concert given to the inmates of the City of London Union, on Thursday, the 18th inst., I feel sure they must have altered their opinion. Besides this we must remember who inhabit our workhouses, and also that they were founded for the express purpose of sheltering the old age of those who have known brighter and better days, but through adverse circumstances have come down in the world. So it is not fair to say because they are poor and dependent upon charity now, that they always were so, nor is it charitable to say that in their brighter days they had not opportunities of hearing good music as much as ourselves. Should we not take a delight in giving pleasure, however little, to these old people ? We should try to think what a monotonous life they pass as day by day they go through the workhouse routine of duty, and what pleasure it must afford them, not only to be present during these concerts, but to think that they are not forgotten by us who are fortunate enough to be "outside." Remember that they are human as ourselves, and to give them any entertainment or recreation by which their position may for a time be set aside, demands in humanity's name, that the quibbles of law, and party feeling should for once be passed over.

The concert was a complete success, the principal artists being Mdme. Cave Ashton, Misses Browning and Ryan, Messrs. H. Milward, Alfred Kenningham and Alfred Moore. There was a most efficient band and chorus under the able conductorship of Mr. R. J. Pitt, in whose hands was the entire management of the concert. Besides the above-named artists, Mr. John Jefferys presided at the organ, and Mr. Geo. F. Grover at the piano. The honours for vocal solos fell to Mdme. Ashton, Mr. Kenningham, and Mr. Moore; while Mr. John Jeffrys, for his organ solo, Mr. Arthur Payne, and Mr. Elphick, violin solos, and Mr. H. W. Hollis, for his flute solo, must each be congratulated for displaying great skill on their respective instruments. I learn that the expense of the concert was kindly borne by Mr. Alfred Lyon, who, in an admirable speech, clearly proved that he had but the interest of the inmates at heart.

GEO. F. GROVER.

CORK.

On the 16th inst. the Chevalier Antoine de Kontski gave the first of a series (to consist of three) of piano recitals at the Opera House. Here is the programme, all played from memory :—

PART I.

Adagio and Finale (Manuscript), from Sonata......	Weber.
"Spring," "Serenade," "The Hunter" (Lieder ohne Worte)	Mendelssohn.
Concert Fantasia upon "Faust"	Kontski.

PART II.

"The Awakening of the Lions" (Caprice Heroïc)..	Kontski.
Nocturne	Döhler.
"Invitation à la Valse"	Weber.
Mazurka	Chopin.
Scherzo de la Seconde Symphonie	Kontski.

His playing was characterised by great brilliancy of execution, particularly shown in his rendering of Chopin's mazurka. He was very well received, and will no doubt have a full house to-day at the second of his recitals.

F. ST. JOHN LACY.

GLASGOW.

The concerts of the Choral Union have been so far entirely successful. The number of subscribers and frequenters has not in any degree diminished, and the prevailing impression is that the present season will prove ultimately more successful than any former one. Complaints have appeared in the local papers anent the excessive amount of Wagnerian, or advanced music introduced into this season's programmes, and these have given rise to quite a controversy on the matter, other writers having appeared on the defensive side of the question. As a matter of fact, the programmes should be so selected as to give a moderate idea of what has been done in the way of composition by musicians of both the past and the present. The main purpose of the concerts, considered apart from their relation to a commercial speculation, is to give educational facilities to that portion of the Glasgow public which aspires to be considered musically inclined. To suit this section of the public it is indeed needful that the programmes be retrospective as well as progressive in character.

Notice of the various miscellaneous concerts, and the production of Gounod's "Redemption" is held over till next week.

J. B.

WIMBLEDON MUSICAL SOCIETY.

This society, which is rapidly coming to the front rank of suburban societies, gave a capital performance of Mendelssohn's "Athalie," on Wednesday, the 17th inst. The solos were well sung by Miss Alice Parry, Miss Whitehead (amateur), and Mrs. Dean, each of whom delivered their parts with great declamatory power, pure tone, and artistic style, the trio, "Hearts feel that love thee," being most enjoyable. The overture and "War March" were played with great spirit and precision, the latter being redemanded. The chorus sang as usual with crispness and good intonation, but once or twice the soprano seemed to lack decision in attack. On the whole, however, the performance was most creditable. The second part of the concert opened with Beethoven's "Prometheus" (overture), played well. Miss Alice Parry followed with "Nobil Signor," beautifully sung, in which she displayed a voice of good compass, quality, and great power, while her execution of the florid passages were remarkably good. Schubert's "Rosamunde" music was perhaps not quite as well rendered as the other items entrusted to the orchestra, a slight dragging being apparent in "Entr'acte, No. 2. "Oh, that we two were maying," was sung by Mrs. Dean in a manner that drew forth an enthusiastic encore. The part-songs, "Hunting Song" (Smart), and "Gipsy Life" (Schumann), although well sung, seemed to fall somewhat flat after the spirited choruses of "Athalie." The programme concluded with a new march, "Masonic," by Boucher, which made a marked and perhaps *novel* effect—*novel* in that it succeeded in keeping the whole of the audience seated until its close. The orchestra, a very efficient one, numbered some sixty instrumentalists, mostly residents, and the chorus about a hundred voices. Mr. Sumner, as usual, conducted. Mendelssohn's "Hymn of Praise" will be given on February 21st,

LIVERPOOL.

(*From our Own Correspondent.*)

JAN. 23rd.

The Carl Rosa opera season terminated at the Royal Court Theatre, on Saturday evening, with a very fine performance of "Mignon." The four weeks' season has been the most successful, financially and artistically, that the company has ever had in this city, and regrets, both on the part of the members of the company, and on that of the general public, have been expressed that the season was not a longer one.

The performances of the various operas given have been more finished in little matters of detail than has been the case heretofore, and the staging of the works has been much more complete and better than have been the accessories in preceding representations given in Liverpool. This of course reflects credit upon the management of the theatre, but more particularly upon Mr. H. Brooklyn, Mr. Rosa's stage manager, to whose untiring exertions great praise is justly due. Of the artists, it is impossible not to sing their praises in language that may appear devoid of criticism, but it must be remembered that all have had long experience and have for some time been singing and acting in the same operas, thereby being able to pick out weak points and develop good ones at each recurring performance. In addition to this, rehearsals are always going on ; and again, Mr. Rosa himself is always about, superintending and overlooking each representation.

Mdme. Marie Roze has much improved, and each character she has represented has been excellently pourtrayed. Miss Burns, as usual, has been brilliant ; Miss Yorke irreproachable ; Miss Perry is gaining strength in her voice, and more character in her acting.

Of the gentlemen, the two most conspicuous are of course Mr. Turner and Mr. Ludwig, both of whom have been in splendid trim during the whole of the engagement. Mr. M'Guckin's bearing on the stage is much easier than it was, and at times he sings very well, but there is occasionally a disagreeable nasal twang which detracts rather from his success.

Mr. Snazelle's "Mephistofeles" is now a very finished performance and worthy of mention. Mr. Pope has rendered good service in parts where his ponderous bass voice is in requisition. Mr. Harley, the new American tenor, has had no chance of shewing what he is made of, and Mr. Ben. Davis has not had anything great to do so far either. Both gentlemen have good voices and no doubt will be acquisitions. Mr. John Pew has had the greater part of the conducting to do, and who could do it better?

Mr. Goosens has also gained warm approbation for the admirable manner in which he has piloted his forces when sitting at the conductor's desk. The splendid success of "Favorita" is in a great measure owing to his exertions.

The company return to Liverpool in September, when the two new operas "Colomba" and "Esmeralda" are promised. The Alexandra Theatre is to be the scene of their next visit.

The first of the third series of the Ladies' Classical Chamber Concerts took place in the saloon of the Liverpool Philharmonic Hall, on Saturday afternoon. There was a large and fashionable audience. The artists, who were all well-known, were Miss Dora Schirmacher, Messrs. Schiever, Harmer, Speelman, and Völlmar. The programme contained items by Beethoven, Haydn, Handel, Scarlatti, Rheinberger and Tartini.

To-night Benedict's "Graziella" is to be given by the Philharmonic Society, the composer conducting. Mdme. Marie Roze (who, by the way, seems to work excessively hard) is to sustain the title *rôle*, which was originally written for her.

Mr. Randegger is mentioned in connection with the soon to be vacant conductorship of this society.

J. J. M.

The following was accidentally omitted last week in the advertisement on the back page ("American Organs"): "We are now allowing 25 per cent. discount off our organs until further notice, so as to thoroughly introduce them into this country."

BIRMINGHAM.

(*From our Own Correspondent.*)

The most interesting concert of the new year has been that given by Mr. Stockley, in the Town Hall, on the 18th inst. (the third of the present series). The programme cannot be said, however, to present much novelty, nor, as will be seen, were the items very artistically arranged :—

Overture, "Athalie"	Mendelssohn.
Air, "Love in her eyes sits playing "	Handel.
Quartet, "The Austrian Hymn "	Haydn.
Song, "I rejoice in my youth "	Macfarren.
Symphony No. 4, "The Italian "	Mendelssohn.
Overture, "Leonora " No. 3	Beethoven.
Air, "Walter's Prize Song " ("Meistersinger ")	Wagner.
Aria and Rondo ("Sonnambula ")	Bellini.
Suite No. 4, "Scènes Pittoresques "	Massenet.
Song, "The Garland "	Mendelssohn.
New sacred song, "Where the shadows never fall "	F. L. Moir.
Overture "Alfonso and Estrella "	Schubert.

The "Italian" symphony, the "Leonora" overture, and the rest of the orchestral pieces are familiar enough, by this time, to Birmingham concert-lovers. The band was not so satisfactory on this occasion as it generally is, one or two of the movements in the symphony being rather coarsely rendered ; the grand Beethovian prelude, was, however, finely played. Massenet's very interesting set of pieces, was, if I remember rightly, first produced here by Mr. Stockley during his season of 1881-2, when the choice little works of the French composer made a distinct and most favourable impression. Tunefulness of theme with piquantly varied orchestration seem their chief characteristics. If it were not for the instrumental charm, the pieces themselves might seem a little too "spun-out," No. 3 of the suite especially.

The characteristic titles of the four movements are—(*a*) "Marche," (*b*) "Air de Ballet," (*c*) "Angelus," (*d*) "Fête Boheme." The slow movement with variations, "God preserve the Emperor," was the only one from Haydn's famous quartet played on this occasion ; it was rendered by the entire body of strings. I do not make the objection to this sort of thing that some musical precisians do ; it all depends upon whether you can get 40 players to execute the work with the same unanimity and delicacy as four. On this occasion no fault on this score could be found with the performance ; the accord of the band was perfectly good. If this item did not excite very great interest it was because the place of its introduction was not better considered. Schubert's lively overture to the ill-fated opera "Alfonso and Estrella" was performed here (if we except its production a little time back at one of the semi-private concerts of the Midland Institute) for the first time, and "by desire." It is a work which its composer evidently "knocked-off in no time." It depends for the charm it evidently has on the little sprightly, fascinating "second subject" (one of those strains that "catch" the ear at once) ; the remaining portions of the overture consist, though, of nothing but bang and blare.

Mr. Edward Lloyd and Miss Eleanor Farnol were the vocalists engaged ; and it is gratifying to note that they did nothing in their selection of songs to disgrace the instrumental portion of the concert. If "Do not mingle" hardly seems a tasteful pendant to Wagner's transcendent lyric, neither of the vocalists could well be blamed for the inconsiderate juxtaposition of two such pieces ; and the programme-framer may justly plead the difficulty of arranging the heterogeneous items of a vocal and instrumental concert. Mr. Lloyd undoubtedly realised his very best in the incomparable "Preislied." The interest of the audience mounted to enthusiasm, and the artist was twice or thrice recalled. The graceful song by Mendelssohn as well as the ever-charming old aria from "Acis and Galatea," were likewise sung with all Mr. Lloyd's characteristic refinement of expression. Miss Farnol was most successful in Macfarren's florid soprano aria (from "St. John the Baptist") ; she considerably enhanced the good opinion already formed of her powers. In the Bellini *fiorituri* she was a little out of her element, the light *abandon*, spontaneity, and flexibility of voice necessary to the part of the heroine of "La Sonnambula" being a little wanting on this occasion to our gifted townswoman. She sang the new song of Mr. Moir in an excellent, declamatory style, but the piece (whether wrongly placed or coming too late in the concert) did not make much impression. It is too pretentiously declamatory, not having sufficient melodic pith in it, and is too heavily orchestrated. The words, supposed to express pietic sentiment of the most fervent, ecstatic degree, are of the usual artificial order, and this alone might account for anything failing in the music.

Mr. Stockley conducted his forces with his customary tact and ability. Without endeavouring to bring out any subtle *nuances* of interpretation he is always safe, sound, and musicianly. It is only a matter of abstract justice to say this ; compliments (simply as such) are thrown away on Mr. Stockley, as he is one of those wise gentlemen who make a point never to concern themselves with what is said in print about them.

I ought to mention that, at the previous concert, Spohr's Symphony, "Die Weihe der Töne" (undoubtedly that Master's instrumental *chef d'œuvre*) was produced in Birmingham for the first time, barring its preliminary trial before the Midland Institute people. This is the only great novelty as yet. On the next occasion, however (April 19th), Mr. Cowen is expected to conduct the first performance of his "Scandinavian" Symphony.

The Festival Choral Society, during the season, has brought forward Costa's "Eli," an unworthy performance ; in parts a downright *fiasco* ; and Gounod's "Redemption," insufficiently "cast" in the solo parts.

The Philharmonic Union, among other good things, have presented to us Hiller's "Song of Victory" and Mr. Stanford's orchestral "Serenade" (produced at the festival).

The Amateur Harmonic Association (under new restrictive regulations) have given a good miscellaneous concert. Among the items of the "sacred" part figured Mendelssohn's 43rd Psalm and Spohr's 8th Psalm (for double chorus and solo voices). At their next concert (March 1st) Sullivan's "Prodigal Son" will be "revived," and another performance given of Mr. Gaul's festival work, "The Holy City."

Mr. Stratton's chamber concerts have become, by this time, a firm institution. A distinctive feature about them is the production at each concert of some instrumental novelty. Mr. Stratton's *plébiscité* of last season resulted in the second production of Mr. Stanford's piano quartet (this work having gained the largest number of votes.)

Among other pieces produced this season for the first time, I note Mr. Ebenezer Prout's string quartet, and a chamber composition by the late Charles Lucas, of the Royal Academy. An interesting production yet to be made will be a chamber composition by the late Mr. Griesbach.

Of the Amateur Musical Union I have had no signs.

The Musical Association still carries on successfully its work of disseminating the knowledge of good art among the people at large. The cheap Saturday Evening Concerts are as uniformly good and largely attended as ever. During the season of 1881-2 27 concerts were given in the Town Hall, at which the total attendance was 70,990, being an average of 2,629 per concert. Among the more important works produced have been Bennett's "May Queen," Gounod's "Gallia," Costa's "Date Sonitum," Mendelssohn's "Hear my prayer," and the cantata "To the Sons of Art"; Heap's "Voice of Spring," Bridge's "Boadicea," Gaul's "Ruth," Gade's "Crusaders," Anderton's "Wreck of the Hesperus," Rossini's "Song of the Titans"; also selections from "Messiah," "Elijah," "Judas Maccabeus," "Creation," "Stabat Mater," "Faust," "William Tell," and "Il Trovatore"; and the following orchestral works :—Beethoven's Symphony No. 1, and Romance in G for violin and orchestra, Schubert's ballet music in "Rosamunde," Mozart's Piano Concerto No. 4, overtures to "Masaniello," "William Tell," etc.

An amateur band and chorus has been formed (under the conductorship of Mr. C. J. Stevens) in permanent connection with the association.   BR.

NEWCASTLE-ON-TYNE.

The eleventh concert, promoted by the Chamber Music Society, took place at the Assembly Rooms, on January 16th. The fashionable audience was larger and more enthusiastic than at any of the previous concerts of the season. Messrs. Henry Holmes, Burnett, Gibson, and Howell gave a refined and intellectual rendering of Beethoven's quartet, No. 1, Op. 18, and Spohr's quartet, No. 1, Op. 58. Mr. Holmes, as a leader in a quartet, displays the rare gift of being able to animate his coadjutors, so that one mind and one will alone seems at work. The magnificent playing of Spohr's quartet brought to my memory the remarks made by the composer himself, to one of his friends some twenty years ago, when he had heard the two brother Holmes play in Cassel: "They caused everywhere the greatest sensa-

tion by their splendid playing, and especially excited admiration by their highly finished rendering of my own compositions."

Mr. Welch, of Durham Cathedral, was the vocalist, and Mr. Leggatt officiated as accompanist.

The programme for the next concert, on March 1st, will include, among other items, Beethoven's Trio in B flat, Op. 97, performed by Miss Agnes Zimmermann, Herr Joachim, and Signor Piatti. The vocalist will be Miss Carlotta Elliot.

Mr. W. Rea's second subscription concert was given on the 23rd.

Sir William Armstrong, with his well-known generosity, has given, a few days ago, £500 towards the adornment of the Cathedral. It is expected the gift will be appropriated towards the purchase of a case for the new organ, the work of Messrs. T. C. Lewis and Co., London, which is not yet completely finished.   H. W.

VENTNOR.—The Ventnor Choral Society recently gave a concert under the conductorship of Mr. Edwin Lemare, whose zeal and ability, says a local journal, have been successfully devoted to the interests of the society since its formation, over 20 years ago. A large portion of Haydn's "Creation" was excellently given. In the miscellaneous selection, Mr. E. H. Lemare's artistic pianoforte playing was a decided feature. Mr. C. Fletcher also created a marked impression by his violin solo ; Madame Clara Suter, Messrs. Fulkerson, and Frank May were the chief singers, and Mr. Frank Cox acted as organist.

KING'S LYNN.—The Philharmonic Society gave their first concert of the season to a large and attentive audience in the Music Hall, on Friday evening, Jan. 19th, under the direction of Dr. H. Hill, when the first part of the programme was devoted to Barnett's cantata "The Ancient Mariner," accompanied by a miscellaneous second part. The rendering of the cantata fully came up to all expectations, and afforded another proof of the steady progress the society has made. The principal vocalists were Miss Ellen Lamb, Miss E. Dones, Mr. Sidney Towers, and Mr. R. De Lacy (of St. Paul's Cathedral), all of whom did ample justice to their respective parts. The band largely augmented from Norwich and the district, and led as usual by Mr. John Bray, were well up to their work, but the brass element, perhaps at times seemed rather to predominate. Credit is due to the chorus, who, were in capital form, and who with the exception of a bad start in the Bridal chorus, sustained their parts in a manner which showed at once their careful training. Mr. W. O. Jones presided at the organ, and Mr. J. H. Pratt at the piano. The second part commenced with Verdi's overture to "Nabucodonosor," which was excellently played by the band. Mr Sidney Towers gave a fine rendering of Sullivan's "Distant Shore," and in answer to repeated calls, he substituted as an encore "Good-bye, sweetheart, good-bye." Mr. Hutchinson's duet, "Tell me why you love me," was given by Miss Lamb and Mr. De Lacy, the last part being repeated. Miss Dones followed with a good performance of Blumenthal's "Sunshine and Rain," continually but unsuccessfully redemanded. Mr. J. Flint (formerly a resident) contributed a charming flute solo in the shape of a fantasia from "Lucia di Lammermoor." An attractive new song entitled "Trust not," from the pen of Dr. Hill was given, and was admirably sung by Miss Lamb, accompanied by the composer, both of whom were recalled at its conclusion. Mendelssohn's splendid part song, "The Hunters," followed, in which the basses showed themselves rather afraid of an E sharp towards the end. Next came Pinsuti's quartet "In this hour of softened splendour," which was sung to perfection by the principal vocalists unaccompanied, and fairly brought the house down ; when seeing nothing short of an encore would suffice, Molloy's "Three Merry Men" was given in capital style. Balfe's favourite duet "The sailor sighs," was finely interpreted by Miss Dones and Mr. Tower. "Elijah" will now be put in rehearsal.—H. E. D.

The Cincinnati College of Music, under the presidency of G. Ward Nichols, seems to be a well-managed and prosperous institution. There are two departments in its scheme—an Academic Department and a General Music School—the Academic Department, for those who desire to become professionals, or amateurs who enter for graduation, all of whom will be required to pursue a definite course of study for a period of time ; the General Music School, for general or special instruction, where any one may enter for a number of terms, receiving the valuable instruction which is afforded by the presence of a large number of excellent teachers (with the advantage of free admission to sixty other lessons, embracing a complete musical education, "lectures," "concerts," "recitals," "chorus," and other classes), with the best methods, exercises, text books, and the discipline of a well-appointed school.

Foreign Musical Intelligence.

MUSIC IN PARIS.
(From our Own Correspondent.)

JAN. 23, 1883.

The programmes at last Sunday's concerts were extremely interesting, though few novelties were presented in them.

At the Châtelet M. Colonne gave us another opportunity of hearing the ever welcome and delightful "Désert" of Félicien David, which was played with the usual thoroughness and brilliancy of the Châtelet orchestra, and duly appreciated.

M. Lamoureux treated us, at the Chateau d'Eau, to a well-nigh faultless execution of the glorious "Choral Symphony," and some charming selections from Gluck's "Armide" (to which I hope to return next week), together with such minor items as the "Hebrides" overture, and a selection from M. Lalo's "Namouna."

At the Cirque M. Pasdeloup gave us the appended :—

Symphonie Romaine	Mendelssohn.
Allegro—Andante—Scherzo—Saltarelle.	
Ouverture Dramatique (1re audition).............	B. Godard.
(Sous la direction de l'auteur).	
Concerto en ré mineur, pour piano	Mozart.
Allegro—Andante—Rondo.	
Par M. Pachmann.	
Sérénade pour violon, alto, et violoncelle (Thème et variations)............................	Beethoven.
Par tous les premiers violons, altos, et violoncelles.	
Air des Saisons	V. Massé.
Par Mdme. Masson.	
Polonaise de Struensée	Meyerbeer.
Directeur de l'Orchestre - - - M. J. PASDELOUP.	

C. HARRY MELTZER.

The French pianist Planté has been playing in Madrid.

Boïto's "Mefistofele" has been played at the Brussels Théâtre de la Monnaie.

Franz Liszt has left Berlin with the intention of spending the next three months at Budapest.

Max Bruch is the newly appointed director of the Orchestral Union, Breslau, in place of Bernard Scholz.

A choral society in Buenos Ayres celebrated the nineteenth anniversary of its foundation some two months since.

The Neue Zeitschrift für Musik, founded by Schumann, will this year celebrate the fiftieth anniversary of its first publication.

Herr Benno Walter, a violinist of Munchen, recently concluded a very satisfactory tour through the principal towns in Holland.

After an oblivion of 30 years, Boïeldieu's opera, "La Fête au Village Voisin" has been most successfully revived in Brussels.

Rubinstein's "Maccabäer" was given in Dresden on the 19th inst., and was also announced for performance in Moscow during the present month.

The proprietors of Music and the Drama (New York) have taken a notable and spirited step in the history of musical journalism by issuing a daily number.

M. César Franck has written a symphonic poem for orchestra, called "La Chasse Fantastique," which is shortly to be heard at one of the concerts to be given by the National Society.

Le Guide Musical has an appreciative article on Edouard Lassen, a well-known musician, who has for the last 25 years been musical director at the Grand Ducal Theatre of Weimar.

The Municipal Council of St. Raphael has given the name of Gounod to one of the streets of that town. The composer is said to have written his "Romeo and Juliet" during a stay at St. Raphael.

Lecocq's charming operetta, "Le Petit Duc," has been revived at the Renaissance Theatre, Paris. An unpublished opera has been brought out with success at the Grand-Théâtre of Marseilles. "Lauriane," the work in question, is in four acts, and the work of M. Oliveiro Machado, a Lisbon amateur composer, who has already written several comic operas.

SATURDAY POPULAR ORGAN RECITALS, BOW, E.—TO-NIGHT at 8.0, "DAUGHTER OF JAIRUS"; Mr. W. HODGE.—Next Saturday, Mr. W. T. BEST.

PRINCIPAL CONTENTS OF THIS NUMBER.

LONDON : SATURDAY, JANUARY 27, 1883.

MONOTONIC READING IN CHURCH.

THAT wide-spread disease, that masterpiece of subtle malice we often dignify in its different manifestations as the odium theologicum, meets us in unexpected forms at times, and in Puritanical quarters directs its venom too often against "heaven-born music." Strangely enough, the most simple, natural, congregational, and ancient of all musical institutions, such as Psalm-chanting and the musical rendering of the versicles are almost invariably the chief objects of attack. Happily, Psalm-chanting has securely passed to an all but universally recognised position in Divine Service, although it is still an institution requiring consideration and cultivation as to the best methods of its practical presentation. Then, again, the singing of Responses is rapidly gaining ground and is destined soon to be regarded as an essential as well as a most eloquent and venerable feature of Public Worship, as distinguished from private prayer. The artillery of those whose judgment being embittered by the poison of the odium theologicum are striving still to stay the musical bonds of unity in the Universal Church from attaining their full fruition and power for good, though becoming feebler and more uncertain from day to day, is not yet quite silenced; and the last engagements between those who love to see all the arts adorning the Service of the Most High, and those who more or less selfishly or ignorantly wish the one art, that of pulpit eloquence to retain its Puritanical monopoly, will possibly be fought out in connection with the questions concerning the use of a musical rendering of the responsive sentences and the monotone reading of the Prayers with their musical inflections. Doubtless until our clergy receive that musical training which must in the end be regarded as an indispensible feature of their scholastic preparations, we shall have to listen to the non-musical clergymen doing violence to general good judgment, perplexing their choirs and trying the growing musical perceptions of their congregations by reading exactly as they did in the by-gone days when they enjoyed as an accompaniment the droning voice of the parish clerk. Truly it is strange to find still in our midst, worthy clergymen who are credited with duly noting the signs of the times, but who yet deliberately persist in reading the prayers as Mr. HENRY IRVING reads Shakespeare, rather than render them as St. Ambrose would eloquently intone them. The inconsistency of the human mind when warped by prejudice never finds a more curious illustration than in connection with this subject. The good clergyman who will be horrified at the mere notion of the use of those beautiful old inflections the Church has ever cherished, will not hesitate to make any number of irrelevant, not to say unconsciously irreverent, inflections in his ordinary reading tone, and has perhaps even received his instructions from an actor, whose stage practice the clergyman would feel it derogatory to his calling and position to listen to. The object of these words is not the condemnation of good emphatic reading in its right place, but the assertion that the use of the monotone and the employment of certain time-honoured inflections should be regarded as essentially characteristic of the services of the Church. The construction of the interchangeable sentences of minister, choir, and people involve some simple form of musical recitation for their distinct and fitting enunciation; and the use of the monotone, with occasional restful inflections, must surely be the most effectual means whereby the avoidance of personal display, possible affectations of style, together with ill-regulated inflections of the reader's voice, may be judiciously and fully secured.

E. H. TURPIN.

ORCHESTRAL EFFECTS AND KEY-BOARD MANNERISMS.

II.

IT is well, in order to realise the nature of the task of reproduction or transcription from the musical forces we speak of collectively as the orchestra to the two great key-board instruments, the pianoforte and organ, to clearly set before our minds the broad distinctions of utterance, methods, phrasing, and tone-qualities existing between the two great instrumental divisions. There are, on the one hand, the vast accumulation of mental and physical power and never-ending shades of force and intermingled expressions in the orchestra, and on the other side the calmer fixed wind pressures of the organ with its set lines of demarcation by tone variations as produced by adding or deducting tiers of coldly speaking pipes, and as differing from the comparatively weak and fading—though wonderfully sensitive through touch—sounds of the pianoforte. Again, in methods of tone production the orchestra has the

bowed instruments, a powerful army in themselves, the pipe-speaking flutes, the single reed clarinets, the double reed oboes and bassoons, the variously modelled open mouthpieces of the trumpets, horns, and trombones, and rhythm-marking instruments of percussion,—as distinguished from the less forcible and less sympathetic key actions of the organ and pianoforte. As regards phrasing powers, the orchestra possesses that magic force which arises from the close passage from note to note of the players' fingers and lips upon strings and tubes in a continuous vibratory condition, as differing from the distinctly formed sounds brought separately into existence by the intervening key mechanisms of the organ and pianoforte. Even with respect to tone-qualities, the orchestra is wonderfully rich in the purest, strongest sympathetic and living tone colours, and the rich store is possessed with a power of intermingling the distinct qualities and varying the lights and shades with a promptitude, character, and power entirely unapproachable, as distinguished from the calm, cold set-tone outlines of the organ and the but small powers of change—even possible with a remarkably developed sense of touch—of the pianoforte. In short, on the side of the orchestra are apparently endless tone riches; while the resources of the key-board instruments are much more limited in their nature, and are set out upon such fixed and definite lines as tend to the requirement of a pretty large exercise of the "art which hides art"; at the same time, these instruments possess the glorious faculty of embodying complete ideas and harmonies, and at least succeed in imitating, if not always realising those effects, which only attain their full glory through the multiform influences and kaleidoscope power of the orchestra. Of course it will be remembered that in dealing with the consideration of transference of musical ideas, one is not calling into question the peculiarly characteristic functions, the organic effects and pianisms which individualise the organ and pianoforte, as the medium of classical music of their own, even though so much of the thought power of such music essentially springs from the orchestra, as the very sun of the musical system and the great source of all tone colour effects.

E. H. TURPIN.

THE PHILHARMONIC SOCIETY.

The following has been recently published :—

St. James's Hall, London,
January, 1883.

The Directors of the Philharmonic Society have great pleasure in announcing that, at a special general meeting of the members it has been unanimously resolved that a limited number (100) of ladies and gentlemen interested, as amateurs, in cultivation of musical taste by means of high-class performances of standard works, combined with due recognition of contemporary talent, be invited to join the Society as "*Fellows*" (F. P. S.) on the following terms ;—

Entrance Fee   .   .   *Five Guineas.*

Fellows will be entitled, on payment (optional) of half-a-guinea at the commencement of any season, to admission for themselves or their nominees to the full rehearsals immediately preceding the concerts of that season.

Ladies and gentlemen desirous of election as *Fellows* must be recommended by three members or associates of the Society, a list of whose names can be obtained on application by letter to the Honorary Treasurer, Mr. Charles E. Stephens, 37, Howley Place, Maida Hill, W., or the Honorary Secretary, St. James's Hall, W.

(By Order)
HENRY HERSEE,
Honorary Secretary.

Organ News.

FINSBURY PARK.

Many of the Nonconformist places of worship are alive to the necessity of sparing neither pains nor expense to make their musical services as attractive and elevating as possible, and foremost among them may be mentioned the Finsbury Park Wesleyan Chapel, which is now in possession of a very fine organ, built by the eminent firm, Messrs. Brindley & Foster, of Sheffield. The opening service took place on Wednesday evening, the 17th inst., when a selection of music was artistically performed by Mr. Fountain Meen, who abundantly displayed the capabilities of the instrument. The congregation also attentively listened to a fine rendering of vocal music by an augmented choir. During the evening the resident minister (the Rev. G. Stringer Rowe), announced that, chiefly owing to the exertions of the choir, who were fired by the enthusiasm and zeal of their able conductor and organist, Mr. C. J. Dale, the contributions received and promised were sufficient to discharge all liability in respect to the organ, but that a debt larger than the cost of the instrument had been incurred in the building of a suitable chamber. The opening services were continued on Sunday last, the organist for the morning being Mr. Ernest Squire (Stoke Newington Chapel), and for the evening Mr. Alfred Rhodes, R.A.M. (Rev. Baldwin Brown's church). The organist for to-morrow morning and evening will be Mr. J. P. Harding, of the Finsbury Choral Association. Appended is a description of the organ :—

GREAT ORGAN. CC TO G.

1. Double Stopt Diapason	16 ft.	7. Harmonic Flute	4 ft.
2. Open Diapason	8 „	8. Dulcet Twelfth	2⅔„
3. Viol di Gamba	8 „	9. Fifteenth (Harmonic)	2 „
4. Höhl Flote	8 „	10. Mixture (3 ranks).	
5. Dulciana	8 „	11. Clarinet	8 „
6. Principal	4 „	12. Trumpet	8 „

SWELL ORGAN. CC TO G.

13. Lieblich Bourdon	16 ft.	18. Salicet	4 ft
14. Violin Diapason	8 „	19. Mixture (3 ranks)	
15. Lieblich Gedact	8 „	20. Oboe	8 „
16. Vox Angelica	8 „	21. Horn	8 „
17.*Voix Celestes	8 „		

* Undulating with No. 14.

CHOIR ORGAN.

(Prepared for).

PEDAL ORGAN. CCC TO F.

22. Major Bass	16 ft.	25. Flute Bass	8 ft.
23. Sub Bass	16 „	26. Trombone Bass	16 „
24. Principal Bass	8 „	27. Trumpet Bass	8 „

COUPLERS.

28. Swell to Great.	31. Swell Super Octave to
29. Swell to Pedal.	Great.
30. Great to Pedal.	

Three Composition pedals to Great and Pedal organ.
Two   „   „   to Swell organ.

SUMMARY.—Great, 12 stops, 772 pipes ; Swell, 9 stops, 592 pipes ; Choir, 6 stops prepared ; Pedal, 6 stops, 180 Notes ; Couplers, 6. Total, 39 stops, 1490 pipes (at present).

LIVERPOOL.

Mr. W. T. Best gave two organ recitals in St. George's Hall, on Saturday, Jan. 20th :—

AFTERNOON RECITAL.

Overture ("Alcina ")	Handel.
Pomposo—Allegro fugato—Musette—Minuetto.	
Andante in E flat major	Wesley.
Prelude and Fugue in C major (Vol. IV, No. 1).	Bach.
Hymn, "Il Sol, la Luna, e le Stelle "	Bellini.
Sarabande (" Dorothea ")	Parker.
Marche Hongroise, " Rakoczy"	Liszt.

EVENING RECITAL.

Overture (" La Barcarolle ")	Auber.
Duet, "Della Mosa " (" Il Profeta ")	Meyerbeer.
Minuetto (" Clarissa ")	Parker.
Fugue in C minor	Bach.
Polonaise (Third Concerto)	Handel.
March (" Il Pirata ")	Bellini.

NOTTING HILL.

The new organ in Christ Church, Notting Hill, was used for the first time on Sunday, Jan. 7th. It was built by Messrs. Forster & Andrews, of Hull, and contains the following stops :—

GREAT ORGAN. CC TO G.

1. Open Diapason	8 ft.	5. Harmonic Flute	8 ft.
2. Stopped Diapason	8 „	6. Fifteenth	2 „
3. Dulciana	8 „	7. Mixture (3 ranks)	
4. Principal	4 „	8. Trumpet	8 „

SWELL ORGAN. CC TO G.

9. Geigen Principal	8 ft.	13. Piccolo	2 ft
10. Salicional	8 „	14. Cornopean	8 „
11. Voix Celeste	8 „	15. Orchestral Oboe	8 „
12. Gemshorn	4 „		

PEDAL ORGAN. CCC TO F.

16. Open Diapason	16 ft.	17. Bourdon	16 ft.

COUPLERS.

18. Swell to Great.	20. Swell to Pedals.
19. Swell Sub Octave.	21. Great to Pedals.

Two Composition Pedals to Great organ.
Two   „   „   to Swell organ.

The case is pitch pine, varnished, and the front pipes are decorated.

WATERLOO ROAD.

Subjoined is the programme of an organ recital given on Thursday, Jan. 25th, at the church of St. John the Evangelist, by Mr. Henry J. B. Dart :—

Sonata No. 3	Mendelssohn.
Con moto maestoso—Andante.	
Andante (Quartet in F)	Haydn.
Adagio and Finale (Quartet in E major, Op. 4)	Spohr.
Pastorale in A	Merkel.
Fantasie in C minor, Op. 25	Beresa.

BOLTON.

An organ recital was given in the Albert Hall, by Mr. Wm. Mullineux, F.C.O., on Saturday, Jan. 20th. The following was the programme :—

Concerto in B flat, No. 2	Handel.
Andante in A flat	Chinner.
March in D major	Best.
Air à la Bourrée	Silvia.
Air, "Pro Peccatis " (" Stabat Mater ")	Rossini.
Overture (" Le Cheval de Bronze ")	Auber.

PRESTON.

Subjoined are the programmes of organ recitals given in the new Public Hall, by Mr. James Tomlinson, on Saturday, Jan. 20th :—

AFTERNOON PROGRAMME.

Adagio and Finale (Flute Concerto)	Rink.
Air varie	Wesley.
Tema con variazioni (Serenade Trio)	Beethoven.
Overture (" A Midsummer Night's Dream ")	Mendelssohn.
Serenade	Schubert.
Triumphal March, " Vom Fels zum Meer"	Liszt.

EVENING PROGRAMME.

Premiere Sonata	Guilmant.
Largo—Allegro—Pastorale—Allegro.	
Andante (Quartet in F)	Haydn.
Air, " Arm, arm ye brave," and chorus, " We come in bright array " (" Judas Maccabæus ")	Handel.
Overture (" Gustavus ")	Auber.
Allegretto Villereccio	Fumagalli.
Hungarian March	Berlioz.

BRIGHTON.

Mr. Alfred King, Mus.Bac., gave an organ recital in the Dome, Royal Pavilion, on Monday, Jan. 15th, with the following programme :—

Overture in D	Smart.
Pastorale	Kullak.
Toccata and Fugue in D	Bach.
Marche Funèbre et Chant Séraphique	Guilmant.
Larghetto (Clarinet Quintet)	Mozart.
Fantasia on two English airs	Guilmant.
Andante in E, Andante in G	Batiste.
" Funeral March of a Marionette "	Gounod.
Marche Triomphale	Lemmens.

And on Monday last :—

" Cuckoo and Nightingale " Concerto	Handel.
Andante (Violin Concerto)	Mendelssohn.
Prelude and Fugue in C major	Bach.
Voluntary in D	Stanley.
" The Pilgrimage "	Mendelssohn.
Flute Concerto	Rinck.
Air and variations	Hesse.
" Ave Maria d'Arcadelt "	Liszt.
March	Silas.

MANCHESTER.

Mr. J. Kendrick Pyne gave an organ recital in the Town Hall, on Saturday, Jan. 20th. Subjoined is the programme :—

Marziale in D minor, for piano....................	Schumann.
Andantino (" Rosamunde ")	Schubert.
Prelude and Fugue in E minor	Bach.
Overture (" Semiramide ")	Rossini.
Larghetto in F major, from a Concerto............	Handel.
March (" Egmont ")	Beethoven.

EAST FINCHLEY.

An organ recital was given by Dr. C. J. Frost in the Congregational Church on Monday, Jan. 22nd. Subjoined is the programme :—

Concerto in B flat..............................	Handel.
March in C minor	Spindler.
Tema con variazioni in D major	Beethoven.
Sonata in F, No. 1	Mendelssohn.
Andante with variations in F	Spohr.
Weihnachtspastorale	Merkel.
March in C	Frost.

AIGBURTH.

An organ recital was given in St. Anne's Church by Mr. J. Hodgson on Saturday, Jan. 20th, when the programme comprised :—

Overture (" The Last Judgment ")..................	Spohr.
Pastorale in F	Kullak.
Prelude and Fugue in D major	Bach.
Fantasia, " O Sanctissima "	Lux.
Air, " Ave Maria "	Schubert.
Christmas March................................	Merkel.

BURNLEY.

On the occasion of the opening of the new organ (built by Messrs. Jardine & Co.) in St. Andrew's Church, on Wednesday, Jan. 17th, Mr. W. T. Best performed the following :—

Solemn Processional March, and air, " O had I Jubal's lyre " (" Joshua ")	Handel.
Sonata in F minor, No. 1	Mendelssohn.
Allegro moderato—Adagio—Andante recitando—Allegro vivace.	
Fugue in C minor................................	Bach.
Air with variations in A major....................	Haydn.
Festal March	Best.
Christmas Pastorale.............................	Moriconi.
Andante in G major..............................	Smart.
The Norwegian National Hymn....................	Hofmann.

EXPERIENCES OF AN ORGANIST.

V.

Encouraged by the attitude of Christian hostility assumed by the new parson towards the organist, the adverse critics of that unfortunate official gathered fresh strength and courage, and expressed their dissatisfaction freely, if not discriminatingly. The concluding voluntaries were too loud. Bach's fugues were not devotional. Batiste's Andante in G was better, but that was not played often enough. The hymns were sung too fast ; the tunes were not judiciously selected. These and similar complaints reached the ears of " our dear pastor," who retailed them to me, and week after week I was tormented with various remedial suggestions, often of a conflicting nature, until I began seriously to consider whether thirty pounds a year was a sufficient remuneration for the annoyance which I experienced.

I had now been organist at this church for three years. During the latter half of that period I had been diligently studying music, both practically and theoretically, under one of the best masters in England. I was preparing for a university degree, and had already passed the preliminary examination. It will, therefore, be seen that I must have been much better fitted for my position at the end of these three years than I was at the beginning. And yet no one in the congregation appeared to be at all aware that I had improved in the least. When I first came I was pronounced to be excellent ; my playing and conducting met with general approval, and I seemed to give satisfaction to everybody. Now, however, although I had, in the meantime, been working hard to make myself a better musician, I met with nothing but hostile criticism, and seemed to give satisfaction to nobody. Disheartening as such an experience must be to any one, it was particularly so to me, because, in my youthful ignorance,

I did not then know that it was a common experience of organists, but thought my case a singular one, and was puzzled to understand my failure. There is a proverb which every organist, and indeed every other public man, would do well to bear in mind—" New brooms sweep clean." My dear young reader, you whose feet and fingers are just beginning to run the musical race which is set before you, when you get your first appointment, do not be too elated by the encomiums which your doubtless very remarkable abilities will receive, but think of your unfortunate predecessor, who at first met with a similar reception, but who is now considered of no account in comparison with you, and has been got rid of without compunction. Remember the proverb above quoted, and reflect that in two or three years' time you, too, may fail to give satisfaction, and be cast aside like a worn-out broom. Do not flatter yourself that your superior talents will prevent such a catastrophe. That those talents are of a superior order I have not the slightest doubt, otherwise you would hardly care to read such writings as mine. But your talents will not avail you. The religious public is a fickle one, quite as fickle as the political public, and a good deal more wily. Deacons are like domestic servants in one respect, they are rather fond of a change ; and the flocks which they lead have the nomadic instinct strongly developed, and are continually on the look out for fresh pasturage in the form of a new minister or a new organist, each of whom they consider as so much green stuff to be either swallowed up or mowed down in due course.

The tide having, at length, so decidedly turned against me, I was not greatly surprised when, one evening, I received a letter from one of the diaconate, informing me that, at a meeting of the minister and deacons, it had been decided that in future the minister should select the tunes, and that I was to be forbidden to play any other than soft voluntaries at the conclusion of the services, as the loud ones were calculated to destroy the effect of the sermon. (We had beautiful sermons from our new parson, and it certainly was a pity to destroy their effect.) These restrictions, however, seemed to me to be unwarrantable, and I felt that I could not submit to them. If the minister selected the tunes, why should not the organist select the hymns ? If he chose my voluntaries, why should not I choose his texts ? If he objected to my playing Bach's fugues, why should he be allowed to make use of Barnes's Commentaries ? This is the way I, in my presumption, reasoned to myself, and the conclusion to which I came was that I was an ill-used person, and that, rather than my privileges should be curtailed in the manner proposed, it would be better for me to resign my position, notwithstanding the enormous pecuniary sacrifice which such a course would entail. I therefore sent in my resignation. Not many weeks afterwards, having taken an affecting leave of my two particular friends, the organ and the organ-blower, not to mention one other even more particular friend, who chanced to come into the church to " look for her hymn-book " (so she said), I disappeared from the vineyard in which I had been labouring, and left the sour grapes to be sucked by my successor.

The sense of freedom which I experienced was at first a delicious one. To see my brother-organists working away on their several treadmills Sunday after Sunday, while it awakened my compassion, was not calculated to lessen my happiness. I felt like a bird that had escaped out of the snare of the fowler. In a short time, however, my feelings changed. I grew discontented with my liberty, and longed for bondage again, like the Israelites in the Wilderness. Then I began to answer advertisements, and attend organ-competitions. I do not know what may be the opinion of other organists regarding organ-competitions, but, for my own part, I cannot say that I like these trials of skill. To me they are trials in more senses than one. On such occasions, when my turn comes, and I walk up to the organ-seat, I experience a sensation somewhat similar, I suppose, to that of the soldier who walks up to the mouth of a loaded cannon. In the one case, as in the other, an unusual amount of courage is requisite, but the military hero has this advantage, that, if he be successful, he may expect to be rewarded with the Victoria Cross, while the musical hero, however successful he may be, cannot hope to be similarly honoured. But why not ? " Peace hath her victories, no less renown'd than war ; " and if Her Majesty only knew what deeds of heroism are daily performed by organists in the battle of life, I feel convinced that even these much despised beings would sometimes obtain a decoration from Her gracious hands—a cross, a star, or perhaps (if the squeamish reader will excuse my mentioning it), a garter! Of course, the amount of courage needed by the musical competitor depends a good deal upon the nature of the competition in which he is called upon to take part. To display one's musical skill before a miscellaneous church or chapel committee is not a very serious matter. With these committees a little impudence goes a long way, and is often mistaken for genius. The self-satisfied but ill-taught organist who works the swell-pedal up and down as though he were at a sewing-machine, and who moves his head and body from side to side like the lions in the Zoological Gardens, is almost sure to make a profound impression. But to perform before a professional umpire of established reputation is quite a different thing, and is, I think, as trying an ordeal as the most penance-loving sinner could wish to pass through. What more terrible predicament can be imagined than that of the nervous candidate who, touching the pedals with trembling toes, discovers, too late, that he has drawn the trombone instead of the bourdon, or who, putting his unready hands on the wrong keyboard, hears his intended soft chords coming out fortissimo on the trumpet stop? Yet such mishaps will sometimes occur when the player loses his presence of mind. However, after taking part, with more or less trepidation, in several of these musical conflicts, I had, at last, the good fortune to be successful in one of them, and so obtained a new appointment.

This time I found myself among Scotchmen, the church to which I was appointed organist being a Presbyterian church. Hitherto the music in this church had been without instrumental accompaniment, the use of the organ having until quite recently been prohibited by the Presbyterian Synod. The organ, therefore, was a new one, having only just been erected when I came. It was a large, three-manual instrument, with forty stops, and was a considerable improvement upon the organ at which I had previously presided. The salary, too, was much larger than that which I had formerly received, being fifty pounds a year. A good deal of attention had always been paid to the musical portion of the services, and I found the singing to be much above the average of congregational singing. A somewhat unusual, and, to my mind, highly advantageous plan was adopted in the formation of the choir. Every musical member of the congregation was urged to enrol himself or herself a member of the choir, and to attend the practices, and thus a large choir of sixty or seventy voices was obtained. This was divided into two equal parts, each of which occupied the choir-seats alternately month by month, those who were off duty being scattered about the congregation. Hence it will be seen that the organist, while he was surrounded by a complete and sufficiently numerous choir, was, at the same time, enabled to rely upon the assistance of individual members of that body in all parts of the building. By this means the tendency to drag and to sing flat, which is so characteristic of congregational singing, was to a great extent obviated.

The organ, being an innovation, had its enemies, of course, though they were fortunately few. Some of them, however, when they found it no longer possible to exclude the instrument, made a strenuous effort to prevent the use of the usual opening and concluding voluntaries, and to confine the organist to the playing of hymn-tunes, hoping, thus, no doubt, to restrain within narrower limits the evil influence which they expected the newly-imported musical monster to exercise. Failing in this attempt, the indignation of these fervent souls (the faithful few who would not bow the knee to Baal) knew no bounds, and was a sight which angels might have witnessed with pleasure, if angels have any sense of the ridiculous. On the Sunday on which the organ was first used they listened with horror to the strains of Mendelssohn's "How lovely are the messengers," with which the morning service concluded, and declared that the performance was a desecration both of the sanctuary and of the Sabbath; and when, in the evening, the "Hallelujah Chorus" was played, by the special desire of some heterodox Scotchman, one female saint, whose ideas concerning music, either secular or sacred, must have been somewhat vague, was heard to remark, as she walked haughtily out of the church, that "such profanity was terrible to witness," and that it was "as bad as being in a theatre!"

TRINITY COLLEGE, LONDON.

A correspondence much too lengthy for these columns, between Messrs. Lennox Browne and Llewelyn Thomas and the Secretary of Trinity College, has been forwarded by the two gentlemen first named. Reluctantly compelled from want of space to give only the chief points of the matter contained in the letters, I will endeavour—trying to take as my guide the motto *Recté et suaviter*—to give the leading points of the correspondence. In the first letter Messrs. Lennox Browne and Thomas, as lecturers on "Vocal and Aural Physiology," note that "an examination paper was set in vocal and aural physiology, by Mr. James Keene, to the pupils of Trinity College. We should like to know on what course of lectures that examination was based."

In reply the College Secretary writes that the examination paper in question set by Mr. Keene was "not based upon any course of lectures, as no lectures have been delivered here on the subject since January-April, 1881. May I venture to say that I do not see the object of your enquiry, as I assume that your knowledge of the working of the College is sufficiently intimate for you to know that the examinations are open to all comers, not only College students, and that vocal and aural physiology is but a part of the examination scheme." It is difficult to see why an institution which has always selected its examiners from the leading professors of each scientific or artistic department, regardless of the question of immediate connection with the institution, and so fairly claimed public confidence in its examinations, should not continue to pursue a course which, as regards the public at least, can only be spoken of as highly honourable. However, Messrs. Lennox Browne and Llewelyn Thomas do not take this view, and write that they "do not desire to be a party to a scheme which, while publishing the names of lecturers, and an elaborate prospectus of a school for the study of vocal and aural physiology, takes no trouble to consult the appointed lecturers and teachers in the school, but at the same time leads the public to understand that these special advantages are employed." And they add: —"We should have resigned some time ago, when Mr. Keene was appointed an examiner on these subjects, without consultation with either of us, though one is an original member of your Council, had it not been from a desire not to do anything which might appear inimical to your interests."

Next Mr. Lennox Browne writes singly to the College secretary thus:—"Some years ago, without any consultation with me, or indeed without any communication whatever, I found my name printed in your Calendar as 'Lecturer on Public Health.' I spoke on the subject to your predecessor, but consented, at his request, to allow it so to remain. Since, however, I have never been asked to give a single lecture on the subject, and as probably not a single pupil has ever asked for a course." The question why Mr. Lennox Browne waited for a grievance, real or imaginary, before setting himself right in this matter, may or may not have arisen from a natural feeling of kindly forbearance, though it is somewhat unfortunate that he has thought fit to revive here what he must surely have noticed long ago, and which may be explainable in the formation of young institutions, as arising from the desire of individual promoters to strengthen their scheme by informally, and perhaps only verbally, asking for the co-operation of the most eminent living authorities on given subjects. Next the secretary of "The Central Throat Hospital" informs the corresponding official of Trinity College of the to be expected expiration of the privileged connection of the students of the last-named with the former institution in these words, which form a resolution it was intended to move before the Hospital Committee: "That any association of this hospital as a school for lectures on vocal and aural physiology with Trinity College, London, be dissolved." A corresponding resolution of the Academical Board of Trinity College closes the correspondence forwarded, in these words: "As no advantage appears to have been gained by the College students of Vocal and Aural Physiology by the connection existing between the London Throat and Ear Hospital and Trinity College, it is hereby decided to resign the connection with that institution."—ED. *Mus. Stand.*

Dr. G. Grove's admirable descriptions of Beethoven's Symphonies are being printed in pamphlet form in America.

Correspondence.

ORGAN RECITALS.

TO THE EDITOR OF THE "MUSICAL STANDARD."

SIR,—Some time since attention was called in your columns to the lack of judgment frequently displayed by organists in the incongruity of the various pieces selected for performance at recitals in churches.

An evil of the same nature, but in my estimation of far greater magnitude, is that of the unseemly choice of music sometimes made for church voluntaries. These should, I think, in every case, at least be free from secular associations, and also of a dignified nature, in order to correspond with the services to which they form a commencement and an end. Unfortunately, these conditions are not infrequently violated, " The Funeral March of a Marionette" having very lately done duty as a concluding voluntary at an important church in the north of London, and selections from the "May Queen" at another church in the same district.

It cannot be too strongly impressed upon such organists how much they detract from the dignity of the position they occupy by such a choice of music, and how much violence they must do to the good taste and reverent feelings of the congregation.

I am, dear Sir, yours very truly,　　J. B.
January 22nd, 1883.

A SUGGESTION.

At a meeting under the presidency of H.R.H. the Prince of Wales, convened in order to carry out the project of erecting memorials to the memory of the late Archbishop Tait, it was decided to carry out the following objects :—(1) To place a monument in Canterbury Cathedral ; (2) To erect memorials in Westminster Abbey and St. Paul's Cathedral ; (3) And to undertake the completion and restoration of Lambeth Palace Chapel ; and it was further settled "That while this committee resolves that any surplus which may remain shall be devoted to some purpose of public usefulness, and is disposed to view favourably the resolution first proposed, it is of opinion that the determination upon the matter should be adjourned to a future day."

Now, surely no memorial could be in better taste or equal in practical usefulness than a new organ for Canterbury Cathedral. The late Archbishop, it is true, was not what in these days may be called a "musical man," but officially he was connected with music and musical institutions, and personally he wisely regarded the advancement of good, sound, well rendered church music as an important essential to the well-being and healthy progress of the Church. Then, look at the present state of affairs in our chief cathedral. The great metropolitan church at Canterbury is musically furnished with a miserable instrument of inadequate resources and in a chronic condition of unplayableness, if one may coin a word. Such an instrument would not be tolerated in any ordinary church with a congregation having any claims to self-respect, or possessing any desire to see the home of Divine worship decently and properly furnished. The worthy organist of Canterbury Cathedral, it is true, patiently continues his trying work upon a worn-out, worthless, and utterly inadequate instrument, upon which no properly written organ music can be said to be playable, year after year ; and in the grand old church even the present miserable organ rolls through the vaulted aisles with an effect to some extent misleading, as tending to leave the easy-going people of the sleepy, quiet city satisfied with the skilfully-handled and yet very unworthy machine. But this question is at once a national as well as a local one ; and there is now an opportunity for both national and local action which should not be lost. One monumental proposal has been the fitting preparation of the new Archbishop's palaces, but surely the seemly furnishing of the house of God would be a far more worthy undertaking. It is to be hoped that earnest and immediate action will be taken in this matter. The attention of the Cathedral authorities, of the memorial committee, and all interested, if not prompted by the obvious necessity and absolute propriety of the course pointed out, should be aroused by a vigorous expression of local and general public opinion.—ED. *Musical Standard.*

Passing Events.

The Richter Concerts will take place at St. James's Hall on May 7th, 10th, 21st, 28th ; June 4th, 11th, 18th, 25th, and July 2nd. Rehearsals for the choir will be held every Friday evening at the Royal Academy of Music.

Mr. Gye was travelling from Philadelphia to New York to meet Mdme. Albani, when, during a slight detention of the train, he left the car for a moment, and on returning he missed a satchel containing property worth fifty thousand dollars. A solitaire and a pair of earrings which the late Czar gave to Madame Albani are the chief items of loss. The other property consisted of jewellery and cash.—*Globe.*

Mr. Eustace J. Breakspeare has been authorised by Professor Heinrich Ehlich, of Berlin, to undertake the English translation of his recent work entitled "Die Musik-Æsthik," and Mr. Breakspeare is at the present time engaged upon a translation of Dr. Edward Hanslick's "Vom Musikalisch Schonen." No more competent writer could have been found to undertake these congenial tasks.

All readers will regret to learn that Mr. C. Warwick Jordan, the well-known and much esteemed organist, is suffering from ill-health, brought on by overwork. His physician, Dr. Hughlings Jackson, has ordered him to take a rest of at least six weeks, and to proceed at once upon a voyage to America. It is to be earnestly hoped that Mr. C. Warwick Jordan will soon be able to resume his professional duties with completely restored health and strength.

Mr. Maurice Strakosch, who is Miss Thursby's impresario, is carrying out during the present month an original scheme, known as a "Historical Concert Cyclus," consisting of five concerts, given at Chickering Hall, New York. This "Cyclus" included the performance of about one hundred compositions, dating from Palestrina, 1524, to the latest and most modern composers. The "Cyclus" was interpreted by Miss Emma Thursby, assisted at each concert by distinguished artists.

The *Musical Courier* has the following sensible words :—" A public *début* is a serious matter for a young student, and it is to be regretted that its importance is not more generally felt. In that event we should not have the frequent spectacle of immature players showing off their unfitness to appear before a critical tribunal. It is a great mistake for those who should be studying thus to injure themselves at the outset, and teachers who permit and urge scholars to make too early a *début* do a wrong all round."

Mr. Thomas Hopkinson, of Hull, whose writings and suggestions are known and duly appreciated by the readers of this paper, has spent some thought upon a proposal to form a "Board of Musical Commissioners," to use his own words, for the inspection of new musical works, and to initiate steps for the due recognition of works of merit. Such a board, if properly constituted and fully recognised, would indeed do useful work, and greatly forward the interests of English art. Mr. Hopkinson thinks that the first steps in this direction might be well taken by some one of our well established educational institutions.

The kind attention and interest of the many musical Freemasons is hereby solicited in behalf of Ernest Arthur Steed, who is a candidate for the April election at the Royal Masonic Institution for Boys. This little fellow is the son of the late Mr. A. Orlando Steed, who died suddenly of typhoid fever at the age of 42 only, leaving a widow and seven children under 13, without adequate means of support. Mr. A. Orlando Steed was greatly esteemed as a gifted, thoughtful, painstaking musician, and some of his writings have been duly appreciated by the readers of this paper. Votes may be sent to the Rev. C. J. Martyn, Long Melford Rectory, Suffolk ; W. H. Cummings, Esq., Thurlow Park Road, Dulwich, S.E. ; J. H. Jewell, Esq., Westerham, Kent ; William Cook, Esq., St. John's, Penge, S.E. As an expression of respect for the departed musician, and as a real exercise of kindly charity, it is to be hoped that all possible help will be given.

Church Bells has a short but appreciative notice of the late John Crowdy, who contributed an admirable series of papers on church music to that weekly publication.

"Iolanthe," although somewhat sharply criticised at first, continues to do very well at the Standard, New York, says the *Musical Critic*, and thus far duplicates the success of "Patience."

Verdi has written a letter of condolence to M. Gambetta, the elder, on the death of his illustrious son. The Italian representative composer has himself attained considerable experience in the political world.

The closing Promenade Concerts at Covent Garden Theatre have included some excellent selections. One night furnished " Faust " music from the various settings of that inexhaustible legend.

On Sunday last, special services were given at St James's, Stepney, and collections made in aid of the funds of the Self-Help-Mission for poor girls of that parish. After the evening service an organ recital was given to a large congregation by Dr. R. Sloman.

The Leicester Amateur Harmonic Society gave Mr. J. Farmer's " Christ and his Soldiers " on the 15th, under the conductorship of Mr. D. T. Jackson. Mr. W. J. Bunney was the organist. The chief singers were Mrs. Kirby, Miss Blackwell, Mr. M. Roline, and Mr. Ford.

Miss Annie Glen gave her first concert at Steinway Hall on Thursday, January 25th. The artists were : Miss Annie Glen, Madame Enriquez, Mr. Redfern Hollins, Mr. Bicknell Young, Mr. Frank L. Moir ; violoncello, Mr. W. E. Whitehouse ; pianoforte, Miss Thomas, Miss Adelaide Thomas, and Mdlle. Mazzucato ; conductors, Signor Visetti, Mr. Eaton Faning, and Mr. Harvey Lohr.

Herr Max Bruch, says the *Athenæum*, having accepted an appointment as Capellmeister at Breslau, is resigning his post as conductor of the Liverpool Philharmonic Society. Judging from past experience, it is probably too much to hope that the directors of the society will show sufficient respect for native art to elect an Englishman as successor to Herr Bruch.

Mozart's music to " King Thamos " was performed for the first time in England last Monday evening by the Borough of Hackney Choral Association, at Shoreditch Town Hall, under the direction of Mr. E. Prout. This interesting work includes the original version of two of the composer's motets, as they are called in their Latin adaptation.

The popular Bow and Bromley organ recitals are to be resumed to-night, when Dr. J. Stainer's " Daughter of Jairus " will be repeated, and amongst early engagements to be noted are those of Mr. Best and Mons. Guilmant. An opportunity of hearing those favourite players which should not be missed. Mr. W. T. Best, of Liverpool, will give the recitals of Feb. 3rd and 10th.

On Friday evening the 12th inst. a handsome silver salver was presented to Mr. James Partridge, formerly organist of St. Andrew's, Hammersmith, on his retirement from that office, after holding it nearly six years. The salver bore the following inscription : " Presented to Mr. James Partridge, A.R.A.M., by Members of the Choir and Choral Society of St. Andrew's, Hammersmith, Christmas, 1882."

A very successful concert took place in the Corn Exchange, Ely, on Wednesday, January 10th, organised by Mr. H. Martin Cooke, in which the following artists assisted :—The Misses Constance and Eva Layton (soprano and mezzo-soprano), Mr. Taylor (bass), Miss Edith Greenop (pianoforte), Herr J. Ludwig (1st) and Mr. R. B. Creak (2nd violin), Mr. Blagrove (viola and solo concertina), and Mons. B. Albert (solo violoncello).

The authorities of the College of Organists have arranged for some of their lecture meetings to be held at the Holborn Town Hall : one by Mr. E. Prout on Feb. 6th on the " Orchestra in Combination with the Organ, especially in Church Music," and a course of four lectures by Professor G. A. Macfarren on " Twenty-four Preludes and Fugues by J. S. Bach," a work issued after the wonderful forty-eight preludes and fugues, these lectures being given on Feb. 20th, 27th, March 6th and 13th. The remaining lectures of the season, it is understood, will be given at the Neumeyer Hall. Members of the College are invited to attend, and their friends are also welcomed.

The Querist.

QUERY.

FRENCH MUSICAL PAPER.—Can any of your readers give me the name of a good monthly musical paper in the French language ; also the price, and where it may be obtained in England ?—H. B.

REPLY.

CHRISTMAS ANTHEM.—Referring to the query of Jas. B. Shaw in *Musical Standard* of 13th inst., I do not know if the anthem, " I know their sorrows," by Edward Sturges, is published, but in the service lists for Christmas Day, 1875, published in *Concordia* of that date, I find the anthem in question was sung at St. Peter's Church, Manchester ; in all probability it is in the church books in MS., I never having seen a copy of it. Mr. Shaw would doubtless get the desired information by applying to the above-mentioned church. Mr. Sturges my father) was born Feb. 25th, 1808, and died Feb. 16th, 1848, being within a few days of 40 when he died.—EDWD. J. STURGES.—The anthem " I know their sorrows," by Edward Sturges, was published by Shepherd & Jones, 40, Warwick Lane, Newgate Street, and it was sold in Edinburgh by Wood and Co., Waterloo Place.—BILLINIE PORTER.

Service Lists.

SEXAGESIMA SUNDAY.
JANUARY 28th.

London.

ST. PAUL'S CATHEDRAL.—Morn.: Service, Te Deum Wesley in E ; Benedictus, Barnby in E ; Introit, How goodly are thy tents (Ouseley) ; Communion Service, Wesley in E and Barnby in E. Even.: Service, Magnificat and Nunc Dimittis, Wesley in E ; Anthem, He in tears that soweth (Hiller).

WESTMINSTER ABBEY.—Morn.: Service, Walmisley in C ; Communion, Bridge in G. Aft.: Service, Hopkins in F ; Anthem, We have heard (Sullivan).

TEMPLE CHURCH.—Morn.: Service, Te Deum and Jubilate, Cooke in G ; Apostles' Creed, Harmonized Monotone ; Anthems, Heaven and the earth display (Mendelssohn). Even.: Service, Magnificat and Nunc Dimittis, Goss in E ; Apostles' Creed, Harmonized Monotone ; Anthem, Praise the Lord (Goss).

LINCOLN'S INN HALL.—Morn.: Service, Boyce in C ; Kyrie, Distin ; Anthem, O God, thou art my God (Purcell). Even.: Service, Cooke in G ; Anthem, I will love Thee, O Lord (Clark).

ALL SAINTS, MARGARET STREET.—Morn.: Service, Te Deum and Benedictus, Stainer ; Communion Service, Weber in G ; Offertory Anthem, God is a spirit (Bennett). Even.: Service, Smart in F ; Anthem, Hear my prayer (Mendelssohn).

ST. AUGUSTINE AND ST. FAITH, WATLING STREET.—Morn.: Service, Stainer in A (throughout) ; Offertory, Stainer. Even.: Service, Martin in B flat ; Anthem, Praise the Lord (Goss).

ST. BARNABAS, MARYLEBONE.—Morn.: Service, Te Deum and Jubilate, Wesley's Chant Service in F ; Anthems, If with all your hearts, and, Cast thy burden (Mendelssohn) ; Kyrie and Nicene Creed, Merbecke. Even.: Service, Magnificat and Nunc Dimittis, Walmisley in D minor ; Anthem, O that I knew (S. Bennett).

CHILDREN'S HOME CHAPEL, BONNER ROAD, E.—Morn.: Service, Anthems, Grant, O Lord (Mozart), and, In Jewry (Whitfield). Aft.: Service, Anthems, Sweet is thy mercy (Barnby), and, Lo ! my shepherd's hand (Haydn).

CHRIST CHURCH, CLAPHAM.—Morn.: Service, Benedicite, Stainer ; Kyrie, Credo, Sanctus, Benedictus, and Agnus Dei, Tours in F ; Communio, Jesu, Word of God (Ave Verum, Mozart) ; Gloria in excelsis, Tours in F. Even.: Service, Magnificat and Nunc Dimittis, Tuckerman in F ; Anthems, Now we are ambassadors, and, How lovely are the messengers (" St. Paul," Mendelssohn).

HOLY TRINITY, TULSE HILL.—Morn.: Chant Service. Even.: Service, Agutter in D ; Anthem, Wherewithal shall a young man (Elvey).

ST. JAMES'S PRIVATE EPISCOPAL CHAPEL, SOUTHWARK. —Morn.: Service, Introit, Communion Service, and Offertory, Silas in C. Even.: Service, Gibbons ; Anthem, Come, my Saviour, and, My spirit was in heaviness (Bach).

St. Magnus, London Bridge.—Morn.: Service, Opening Anthem, To the Lord our God (Ouseley) ; Te Deum and Jubilate, Boyce in A ; Kyrie, Reay. Even.: Service, Magnificat and Nunc Dimittis, Walmisley in D minor ; Anthem, Come and let us return (Goss).

St. Margaret Pattens, Rood Lane, Fenchurch Street.—Morn.: Service, Benedicite and Benedictus, Gregorian ; Communion Service, Offertory Anthem, Cast thy burden (Mendelssohn) ; Kyrie, Credo, Sanctus, Benedictus, Agnus Dei, and Gloria in excelsis, Hummel in B flat. Even.: Service, Magnificat and Nunc Dimittis, Tuckerman in F ; Anthem, Lead, kindly light (Stainer).

St. Mary Abchurch, E.C.—Morn.: Service, Garrett in D ; Communion Service, Armes in A. Even.: Service, Chants.

St. Mary Boltons, West Brompton, S.W.—Morn.: Service, Te Deum and Benedictus, Dykes in F ; Holy Communion, Kyrie, Credo, Sanctus, and Gloria in excelsis, Thorne in G ; Benedictus and Agnus Dei, Monk in C ; Offertory, Barnby. Even.: Service, Magnificat and Nunc Dimittis, Dykes in F ; Anthem, Give peace in our time (Callcott).

St. Michael's, Cornhill. — Morn.: Service, Te Deum and Jubilate, Nares in F ; Anthem, In thee, O Lord (Weldon) ; Kyrie, Thorne in G ; Creed, Stainer in G. Even.: Service, Magnificat and Nunc Dimittis, Nares in F ; Anthem, O where shall wisdom (Boyce).

St. Paul's, Avenue Road, South Hampstead.—Morn.: Service, Te Deum, Hopkins in G ; Benedictus, Stainer in E flat ; Anthems, Now we are ambassadors, and, How lovely are the messengers (Mendelssohn) ; Kyrie, Tours in F ; Offertory, Barnby ; Credo, Sanctus, and Gloria in excelsis, Tours in F. Even.: Service, Magnificat and Nunc Dimittis, Bridge in C ; Anthem, Ascribe unto the Lord (Wesley).

St. Paul's, Bow Common, E.—Morn.: Service, Te Deum and Benedictus, Garrett in D. Even.: Service, Magnificat and Nunc Dimittis, Tours in F ; Anthem, As the hart pants (Mendelssohn).

St. Peter's (Eaton Square).—Morn.: Service, Te Deum, Goss in A. Even.: Service, Bridge in G ; Anthem, I waited for the Lord (Mendelssohn).

St. Peter's, Vere Street, W.—Morn.: Service, Magnificat and Nunc Dimittis, Wood in F ; Anthem, I waited for the Lord (Mendelssohn).

Country.

St. Asaph Cathedral.—Morn.: Service, Colborne in C ; Anthem, Doth not wisdom cry (Haking). Even.: Service, Ebdon in C ; Anthem, The radiant morn (Woodward).

Ashburne Church, Derbyshire. — Morn.: Service, Garrett in F (throughout). Even.: Service, Garrett in F; Anthem, Send out thy light (Gounod).

Birmingham (St. Cyprian's, Hay Mills).—Morn.: Service, Kent in C ; Anthem, Wherewithal shall a young man cleanse his way (Elvey). Even.: Service, Clark Whitfeld in D ; Anthem, My song shall be of mercy and judgment (Kent).

Canterbury Cathedral.—Morn.: Service, Calkin in B flat ; Anthem, O Lord, give Thy holy spirit (Buck) ; Communion Service, Calkin in B flat. Even.: Service, Calkin in B flat; Anthem, The glory of the Lord (Goss).

Carlisle Cathedral.—Morn.: Service, Steggall in G ; Introit, Up, Lord, why sleepest Thou ! (Reay); Kyrie, and Nicene Creed, Steggall in G. Even.: Service, Attwood in F ; Anthem, Praise the Lord (Mozart).

Doncaster (Parish Church). — Morn.: Service, Boyce in A. Even.: Service, Calkin in B flat ; Anthem; Blow ye the trumpet (Taylor).

Dublin, St. Patrick's (National) Cathedral.—Morn.: Service, Te Deum and Jubilate, Smart in F ; Anthem, And as he journeyed ("St. Paul," Mendelssohn). Even.: Service, Magnificat and Nunc Dimittis, Smart in F ; Anthems, Doth not wisdom cry? (Haking), and, O where shall wisdom ? (Boyce).

Ely Cathedral. — Morn.: Service, Roberts in D; Kyrie and Credo, Roberts in D, Gloria, " Ely " ; Anthem, Ponder my words (Zingarelli). Even.: Service, In the beginning ("Creation," Haydn).

Exeter Cathedral.—Morn.: Service, Boyce in C ; Communion Service, Wesley in C. Even. Service, Attwood in C; Anthem, I will love Thee (Clark).

Glasgow (Blythswood Parish Church).—Aft.: Service, Anthem, How dear are Thy counsels (Crotch)

Leeds Parish Church. — Morn.: Service, Chants ; Anthem, O Lord, Thou has searched (Bennett) ; Kyrie and Creed, Dykes in F. Even.: Service, Hopkins in F; Anthem, Saviour of sinners (Mendelssohn).

Lichfield Cathedral.—Morn.: Service, Hopkins in F ; Anthem, O come let us worship (Mendelssohn). Aft.: Service, Hopkins in F ; Anthem, By the waters of Babylon (Boyce).

Liverpool Cathedral. — Aft.: Service, Hopkins in F ; Anthem, O come before His presence (Martin).

Manchester Cathedral. — Morn.: Service, Hopkins in F ; Anthem, How dear are thy counsels (Crotch). Aft.: Service, Hopkins in F ; Anthem, Teach me, O Lord (Attwood).

Manchester (St. Benedict's). — Morn.: Service, Kyrie, Hoyte ; Credo, Sanctus, Benedictus, Agnus Dei, and Gloria in excelsis, De la Hache in B flat. Even.: Service, Magnificat and Nunc Dimittis, Stainer.

Manchester (St. John Baptist, Hulme).—Morn.: Service, Kyrie, Credo, Sanctus, Benedictus, Agnus Dei, and Gloria in excelsis, Sutton in F. Even.: Service, Magnificat and Nunc Dimittis, Jordan.

Musselburgh (Loretto School). — Morn.: Introit, Give peace in our time (Callcott) ; Service, Stainer in E flat ; Anthem, There is none like unto the God of Jeshurun (Goss and Sullivan). Even.: Service, Anthem, O Lord our Governor (Marcello).

Peterborough Cathedral. — Morn.: Service, Tours in F ; Introit, Teach me, O Lord (Attwood) ; Communion Service, Tours in F and Goss in D. Even.: Service, Tours in F ; Anthem, Be thou faithful (Mendelssohn).

Ripon Cathedral.—Morn.: Service, Chants ; Anthem, On Thee each living soul awaits (Haydn), Even.: Sevice, Stainer in E ; Anthems, O rest, and, For He shall give (Mendelssohn).

Rochester Cathedral.—Morn.: Service, Nares in F; Anthem, O come every one (Mendelssohn). Even.: Service, Cooke in C ; Anthem, O where shall wisdom (Boyce).

Sheffield Parish Church. — Morn.: Service, Kyrie, Schubert in F. Even.: Service, Magnificat and Nunc Dimittis, Stainer in D ; Anthem, The earth is the Lord's (Trimnell).

Southwell Collegiate Church, Notts.—Morn.: Service, Smart in F ; Kyrie, Barnby in E ; Creed, Hopkins in G. Even.: Service, Smart in F ; Anthem, O where shall wisdom be found (Boyce).

Wells Cathedral.—Morn.: Service, Arnold in D ; Introit, Behold, to obey (Macfarren) ; Kyrie, Attwood in G. Even.: Service, Arnold in D ; Anthem, Praise the Lord (Croft).

Worcester Cathedral.—Morn.: Service, Jackman in D ; Anthem, O taste and see (Sullivan) ; Credo, &c., Wesley in E. Even.: Service, Jackman in D ; Anthem, Wherewithal shall a young man (Elvey).

[The attention of the several Organists is called to the favour they confer upon their brother musicians by forwarding their notices regularly: this column of the paper is much valued as an index to what is going on in the choice of cathedral music, so much so that intermissions constantly give rise to remonstrance. Lists should be sent in a week in advance if possible.—Ed. *Mus. Stand.*]

⁂ *Post-cards must be sent to the Editor, 6, Argyle Square, W.C., by Wednesday. Lists are frequently omitted in consequence of not being received in time.*

NOTICES TO CORRESPONDENTS.

Wanted the address of S. J. Rowton, who, some years ago, contributed words for music to the *Choir* or *Musical Standard.* —A. H. F.

Newspapers sent should have *distinct marks* opposite to the matter to which attention is required.

Notice.—*All communications intended for the Editor are to be sent to his private address. Business communications to be addressed to* 185, *Fleet Street, E.C.*

APPOINTMENTS.

Mr. P. Strickland, A.C.O., to be Organist and Choirmaster of the Parish Church, Pudsey, and Conductor of the Pudsey Choral Union.

Mr. F. Treverton has been appointed Organist and Choirmaster to the General Baptist Church, Bethnal Green Road.

Printed for the Proprietor by BOWDEN, HUDSON & CO., at 23, Red Lion Street, Holborn, London, W.C.; and Published by WILLIAM REEVES, at the Office, 185, Fleet Street, E.C. West End Agents:—WEEKES & CO., 14, Hanover Street, Regent Street, W. Subscriptions and Advertisements are received either by the Publisher or West End Agents.—*Communications for the EDITOR are to be forwarded to his private address, 6, Argyle Square, W.C.*
SATURDAY, JAN. 27, 1883.—*Entered at the General Post Office as a Newspaper.*

The MUSICAL STANDARD

A NEWSPAPER FOR MUSICIANS PROFESSIONAL AND AMATEUR

No. 966. VOL. XXIV. FOURTH SERIES. SATURDAY, FEBRUARY 3, 1883. WEEKLY: PRICE 3D.

TRIADS: THEIR RELATIONSHIP AND TREATMENT.

By FRANCIS EDWARD GLADSTONE, MUS. DOC.

(Continued from page 47.)

I will now put before you some ordinary progressions in the key of A minor.

The first and most obvious progression is, as in the major key, from tonic to dominant and back again. Next, we may proceed from the tonic to the minor chord on the fourth of the scale, which, like the major key, has a bond of union with the tonic, because the 5th of one is the root of the other. If this is followed by the dominant harmony, we are at once led back to our tonic. (N.B.—It must be remembered that the so-called "sub-dominant" chord has a true minor 3rd and perfect 5th, and so differs from the chord on D in the scale of C major).

Ex. 18.

We have seen, however, that there is a close relationship between two chords whose roots are a third apart, and, as the scale of A minor contains a triad upon F, the intervals of which are a true major 3rd and a perfect 5th from the root, we may insert this major concord between the first two chords of the last example :—

Ex. 19.

Thus far the successions of chords in the minor scale correspond exactly to the first few quotations of chords based upon the major scale. We may even go further, and may admit, to make the correspondence more complete, the dissonant triad on the 2nd degree of the scale, provided that this is followed by dominant harmony :—

Ex. 20.

You will recollect that the triad on the 2nd degree of the major scale has been referred to a dominant root. I here regard the triad on B in a similar light. D and F are respectively the dominant 7th and minor 9th to the root E. Here, however, the resemblance between the major and minor key for the present ceases. In the major key we were able to use a minor triad on the 3rd of the scale, following upon the dominant chord, and followed by the minor chord on the 6th of the scale. In the minor key no similar concord is available, because the interval from C to G ♯ is an augmented 5th.

Having now noticed the triads which are commonly used in the minor key, we shall be able to account for some further progressions which may occur in the major key. Let me play two :—

Ex. 21. A.

Ex. 21. B.

In both of these examples the 3rd chord is that which we have discovered to be not a true concord in the scale of C, and yet it is not followed as before by dominant harmony. Two explanations of its good effect may be offered. One is that A, the major 9th above the dominant, is retained for two chords, and eventually resolved, while F, the 7th, is resolved at once upon E. The other possible explanation is that the chord in question is followed, and, in one case, also, preceded, by the chord of A minor, so that it may be regarded as a true minor triad borrowed for the moment from the scale of A minor.

I have before spoken of the slight element of disturbance in the tonality felt, by myself at all events, whenever the "sub-dominant" chord occurs. I must now add my opinion that it is only when we use tonic and dominant harmony alternately that we can be said to be literally and exactly in any one key. If I play to you the following :—

Ex. 22. A.

the passage is clearly, I think, in F, although the first chord is the chord of C; but if I play the first four chords of a recent example :—

Ex. 22. B.

and rest there, we receive no decided impression as to the key. The fact appears to be, that in every piece of music passages occur in which it would be difficult to say at certain moments what the key really is. It is this view which, to my mind (as I have already said), gives to music its charm, and composers are thus able, by lingering on certain chords, or progressions of chords, not strictly belonging to the key to which they are going or returning, to keep the hearers in a state of expectation and interest until a cadence is reached.

It is far from my intention or wish to recommend to you for general purposes that vagueness or confusion of tonality which may be sometimes met with, more especially in the writings of those whose minds are imbued with a flavour of old church modes, derived from constant association with the Gregorian tones. But even this amount of indecision in regard to the key may have its proper place; and the composer, whose judgment is sound and experience mature, may sometimes venture to express a feeling of restlessness by wavering between two keys, or for some special effect to bring about a startling surprise by a leap into some remote tonality. Such considerations are, however, beside my present purpose, which is to consider the relationship of chords to a key note and to one another. My next step will be to endeavour to find a reason for the ill-effect of what is known as the "false relation of tritone," or, as the old authorities had it, "Mi contra fa."

Hitherto, with one exception, the only progressions spoken of have been those in which both chords have had one or more notes in common. The exception has been in the progression from the "sub-dominant" of a key to the dominant. We have seen that this succession of chords may be grateful to the ear in spite of the apparent "false relation of tritone"; but if we reverse the chords the result is not satisfactory :—

Ex. 23.

To explain this we must again make experiments with the scale harmonized as a melody. Although, in attempting to harmonize the descending scale with the three triads from which it was produced, we were stopped at the third note, we may, by beginning at this note, harmonize all the remaining notes of the scale with its fundamental chords only :—

Ex. 24.

Now, there is no doubt that in all chord progressions when the parts move in notes of equal value, and with equal strength and quality, the highest part is that which most strongly arrests attention. When, therefore, we move thus—

Ex. 25.

the effect is unexpected and disagreeable, for when the melody proceeds from the leading note to the keynote it is simply the concluding progression of the ascending scale, and this points to dominant and tonic harmony as the most natural accompaniment. But if we alter the position of the parts thus—

Ex. 26.

the effect is wholly different. The melody now consists of two fragments of the *descending* scale with the skip of a 3rd intervening, and the chords are those which have been already employed in harmonizing similar progressions.

But, you may ask, is there no way of accompanying the upper half of the descending scale satisfactorily with three common chords? Strictly speaking, there is not. Still, if we modulate to the scale of G, we obtain a result very like the upper portion of the scale of C :—

Ex. 27.

although the sharper A (the perfect 5th above D) does not belong to the latter scale. The whole difficulty arises from the fact that between the 4th and 5th, and between the 6th and 7th degrees of the major scale the interval of a major tone occurs, so that when these notes stand a major 3rd apart in the relation of treble and bass to each other, both parts proceed by a major tone. This was found objectionable by the old contrapuntists. It is still considered bad in two-part writing, and it is peculiarly offensive in descending unless the resources of modern harmony are brought to our aid ; thus—

Ex. 28.

Here the 2nd and 3rd chords are of course traced to the same root by modern theorists.

Let me now call your attention to a very familiar progression from one chord to another having no note in common with it :—

Ex. 29. A.

and to the same progression reversed :—

Ex. 29. B.

Both these are of common occurrence, and their justification no doubt lies in the fact already noticed, that the chord of A minor is most intimately connected with that of C major, containing, as it does, its essential and characteristic notes—C and E. In each case the minor chord forms a satisfactory substitute for that which is commonly, and, as I believe, correctly, called its "relative major" chord. Similar considerations will shew that the following progressions are not only agreeable but also justifiable :—

Ex. 30. A.

Ex. 30. B.

The chord of A minor, if my view is correct, owes its origin to the harmonic series, having F for its root, and from this cause it possesses its two characteristic notes, A and C, in common with the chord of F. The latter, therefore, serves as excellent deputy for the former.

It should be observed in the foregoing examples that the doubling of the keynote to avoid consecutive 5ths strengthens our feeling that the chord on the 6th of the scale is a near relative of the tonic chord.

Reference has already been made to the anomalous position of the triad upon the 2nd degree of the major scale. I will now endeavour to show that this is not merely a fanciful theory, but that an appeal to the ear will prove the accuracy of my statement that a true minor triad on D has no place in the scale of C major. Let me however first remind you of a belief, which I have already expressed, and for which I am indebted to Professor Macfarren's interesting "Lectures on Harmony," that, in spite of equal temperament, we all of us unconsciously accept the divisions of the scale, not for what they actually are, but for what they should be.

Now, when the chord in question is played, it gives us one or the other of two possible impressions. We listen to it either as a true minor concord, or as a dissonant combination. Whatever view you take of the following progression :—

Ex. 31. A.

I think you will admit at all events a want of connection between the 2nd and 3rd chords ; whereas, if I play the two following :—

Ex. 31. B.

Ex. 31. C.

the effect is satisfactory. The explanation I offer is that in the 1st example either the A and F are discords, and should be resolved, or else the D is a note which does not belong to the scale of C. In the 2nd example the discords are sooner or later resolved, and in the 3rd the chord is treated as a true concord belonging to the scale of A minor.

One other proof I will advance. If I play the chord of C and then that of D minor, with consecutive 5ths between the treble and bass,

Ex. 32. A.

the effect is undeniably bad. If, however, you will listen to an apparently similar succession of 5ths, with an alteration of one of the inner parts, I think you will

feel with me that the impression is much altered, and that, although the objectionable effect may not be entirely mitigated, it is certainly somewhat softened :—

Ex. 32. B.

The explanation of this change will now, I think, suggest itself to your minds. In the former case we received the impression that the highest and lowest part were proceeding by parallel movement in two different scales ; in the latter case the B ♮ added to the tenor part refers us to G as the root, and to A and F, not as true concords above D, but as the dominant 9th and 7th in the key of C.

(*To be continued.*)

Musical Intelligence.

SATURDAY POPULAR CONCERTS.

PROGRAMME.

Quintet in A major, for two violins, clarionet, viola,
  and violoncello .... Mozart.
  Mdme. Norman-Néruda, MM. L. Ries, Lazarus, Hollänaer,
  and Piatti.
Song, "Pupille amate" .... Mozart.
  Miss Santley.
Fantasia in C minor } for pianoforte alone .... Mozart.
Sonata in C minor }
  Mr. Charles Hallé.
Sonata in D major, for pianoforte and violin.. .... Mozart.
  Mr. Charles Hallé and Mdme. Norman-Néruda.
Air, "Voi che sapete" ("Le Nozze di Figaro")..... Mozart.
  Miss Santley.
Quartet in D minor, Op. 10, No. 2, for two violins,
  viola, and violoncello .... Mozart.
  Mdme. Norman-Néruda, MM. L. Ries, Holländer, and Piatti.
  Accompanist - - - Mr. Zerbini.

It will be seen that last Saturday, to commemorate Mozart's birthday, the programme was devoted entirely to his works. The quintet, introduced at these concerts by Mr. Lazarus twenty-three years ago, was rendered in an entirely perfect manner ; though, of course, the lion's share of the glory belongs to the clarionetist, or, as the programme somewhat fancifully puts it—" The Quintet in A major may be regarded as a musical drama, in which the clarionet supports the character of the hero (a lover, most likely, Mozart being the author), the other personages, represented by the four stringed instruments, being grouped around the chief figure, and, as in respect and duty bound, uttering 'no more than is set down for them' —so that no 'necessary question' of the musical design may be disturbed or interrupted." Surely the variations that composed the finale of this work were never surpassed, even by Beethoven, for ingenuity and interest, until Schumann came and gave a new life to this most time-honoured form ! The rest of the programme is too well known to call for special mention, and it is not necessary to say that complete justice was done to each and all of the works in the performance.

"Look at all those disagreeable people going out !" a lady was heard to remark, during the quartet. (There certainly was a longer stream even than usual leaving the Hall). How the lady in question came to know that all these people whose time is so precious are "disagreeable," it is not for us to decide ; nevertheless, it cannot do any harm to let them know that they are placed on that category unhesitatingly by perhaps a large number of their fellow auditors.

Miss Santley's songs were not suited to her ; but she was in this instance bound down to one composer and one style. "Pupille amate" especially she must have found trying ; but she hid her want of ease with the skill of a thorough artist, and Mr. Zerbini's accompaniments were in every respect excellent.

B. F. WYATT-SMITH.

MONDAY POPULAR CONCERTS.

Wet weather again vexed the subscribers on Monday evening,

PROGRAMME.

PART I.

Quartet in B flat, No. 9, for two violins, viola,
　and violoncello .... Mozart.
　Mdme Norman-Néruda, MM. L. Ries, Holländer, and Piatti.
Song, "O swallow, swallow" .... Piatti.
　Mr. Santley.
　Violoncello obbligato—Signor Piatti.
Faschingschwank, for pianoforte alone .... Schumann.
　Mdme. Frickenhaus.

PART II.

Sonata in D minor, for violin, and pianoforte accom-
　paniment .... Rust.
　Mdme. Norman-Néruda.
Songs—
　"Tröstung" .... Mendelssohn.
　"Ho messo nuove corde" .... Gounod.
　Mr. Santley.
Quartet in E flat, Op. 38, for pianoforte, violin,
　viola, and violoncello .... Rheinberger.
　Mesdames. Frickenhaus and Norman-Néruda, MM. Holländer
　and Piatti.

Accompanist　·　·　·　Mr. Zerbini.

It will be seen that Mozart again figured conspicuously, although not exclusively in the scheme ; but this quartet was the penultimate of all, written seven years after the one in D minor, performed on the previous Saturday. The larghetto in E flat, where the first violin is silent at the opening, would stamp the composer's individuality in any part of the world ; not only the melody, but the "decomposition" of the rhythm are unmistakable, and the subject may be called sublime. The minuet, with its piquant divisions of semiquavers in the first and fifth bars, is no less thoroughly characteristic, and its trio regales the eye as a specimen of neatest counterpoint, illustrative of heaven's first law, order—never by true musicians to be violated.

Rheinberger's pianoforte quartet, introduced in 1874 by Dr. Hans von Bülow, should be eulogised for the same observance of canonical construction, whilst the themes, especially in the first movement, sound positively refreshing after the dry and laboured works of certain erudite but not always inspired writers. The two inner movements (adagio and minuet) are in G major and minor. Mdme. Frickenhaus, the pianist of the evening, conducted the work in admirable style, and played Schumann's "Faschingschwank," not only with fine taste, but after a manner that recalled to mind the interpretation by the composer's gifted wife. An encore ensued, and Mdme. Frickenhaus volunteered one of the "Lieder ohne worte," nicknamed "The Bee's Wedding." Mdme. Norman-Néruda had a double recall after Rust's sonata ; and Mr. Santley was honoured in the same way. The audience were enthusiastic. Reverting to Schumann's pianoforte works, his partiality for flat keys is remarkable. In this case, as in the "Carnaval," the "Humoreske," and the "Kreisleriana," he adheres to the tonalities of B flat, D minor, G minor, E flat, and their cognates. Mr. Charles Hallé, on Monday next, will introduce two valses of Chopin for the first time, marked as "Op. 64," in C sharp minor and D flat.

[In a recent notice the printer made the key of Beethoven's "Sonata Appassionata" F major instead of F minor.] A. M.

MISS ANNIE GLEN'S CONCERT.

A few details of Miss Glen's first concert (briefly reported last week, as a matter of fact) will be interesting. The young lady may be congratulated on a fair success, to which no doubt her pleasing physiognomy and winning manner contributed almost as much as her fine vocalization. Miss Glen sang Schubert's "Ständchen" and Meyerbeer's "Fisher-Maiden" with a range from C to F and G ; she won a bis for Robandi's florid Italian song in F, "Alla Stella Confidente," where high A has to be attacked and taken, to use the phraseology of military tactics. Miss Glen certainly captured, or captivated, her audience.

The dramatic duet of Félicien David in E flat, "La nuit déployant ses ailes," interpreted by Miss Glen and Mr. Redfern Hollins made an adequate impression ; the more so, as sung for the first time in London. In the absence of another lady, Miss Glen played on the harmonium Chopin's Nocturne in E flat, and Mozart's "Deh Vieni olla finestra" from "Don Giovanni." Her rendering

of the ballad "My heart is sair" won another encore. The assistant vocalists included Messrs. R. Hollins, B. Young, and F. L. Moir. Pianoforte pieces were played by Miss Adelaide Thomas, Mr. Eaton Faning, and Mr. Harvey Löhr. One of these pieces (chosen by Miss Thomas) deserves notice.

The pre-eminent composer and first pianist in Europe, Rubinstein, has given to the world what he calls an "Etude sur les fausses notes," a peculiar title, seeing that false notes must, of necessity, offend every sensitive ear. Musicians who ought to know better sometimes speak of "false fifths" (such as the skip from G to C sharp, downwards, in the overture to Auber's opera "Haydée," produced at the Opéra Comique in 1848, and subsequently represented, in motley English dress, at the Royal Italian Opera during the recess, a year afterwards, when Mrs. Sims Reeves made her début on the stage in the title-part).

To revert to the pianoforte piece of Rubinstein. The "Study" of Rubinstein is in C major, and appears well adapted to show off the "genius" of a grand pianoforte, if not remarkable as music. The principal feature of the piece consists in arpeggio runs of demisemiquavers, with constant crossing of the hands, a favourite device of this composer. The episode in C minor, where intervals of thirds and sixths are used, with a rapid flight of octaves, will hardly be thought so pleasing as the arpeggios. A queer arpeggio chord at the outset, where a C natural is added to the intervals of the dominant of the relative A minor, rather grates on the ear, and other crudities might possibly be noticed by microscopic eyes.

THE BURNS FESTIVAL AT THE ALBERT HALL.

The anniversary of Burns's birth was commemorated on Thursday, January 25th, both at St. James's and the Royal Albert Halls. At South Kensington, as may be supposed à priori, Scottish airs and part-songs were the staple of the entertainment ; but in the second part of the concert the "Garden Scene" of Gounod's "Faust" was acted in costume on the platform, with Mdme. Marie Roze as Margherita, Mr. Vernon Rigby as Faust, and Mr. Barrington Foote as Mephistopheles. The music was well executed, and Mdme. Marie Roze sang with her usual brilliancy ; but the hall, long before the termination of the concert, presented the appearance, not of an audience in session, intent and interested, but a processional "stampede" of women, young, old, and mediæval, heedless of the gross slight that they offered to the artists by turning their backs upon the stage, and only anxious to block up the doorways outside until their vehicles drew up. This nuisance is complained of everywhere, and surely it might be abated if the managers would do their duty. English audiences, as a rule, behave worse than savages ; they not only insult the performers, but annoy attentive and well-bred visitors. Selfishness is predominant.

The miscellaneous part of the concert, in Part I afforded scope for the vocal display of Mr. W. Carter's Choir, with the Misses Badia, P. Winter, and Le Brun, Mdme. Enriquez, Mdme. Antoinette Sterling, Mr. Rigby, Mr. Sauvage, and Mr. B. Foote. An interesting item of this part to musicians was the violin fantasia (on Scottish airs) of Mr. Poznanski, whose full, rich, and round tone asserted the value of every note—and notes not a few—in the furthest corner of the hall. The mechanism, too, was wonderful, and the "harmonics" worthy of Paganini himself. Mr. Poznanski's success may be reported as decisive.

MISS MEYNELL'S CONCERT.

Miss Ida Meynell, a young lady with a pleasing mezzo-soprano voice, held a soirée on Tuesday at the Athenæum, Shepherd's Bush. Miss Meynell introduced a new and pretty song by Mr. George Asch, called "Hide and Seek," accompanied by the composer, which won, and is safe in the future to win, public favour. A second success was achieved in "A Wayside Posy" by Mr. Watson. Mdme. Isabella Powers distinguished herself in Jackman's "At Vespers," and the same composer's "Now or Never." Miss Alice Kean sang Hutchison's "Ehren on the Rhine," and "Lilla's a Lady." Herr Schuberth, the conductor of the concert, gratified the audience with his own violoncello solo "Ave Maria," and pieces by Tours and Berenger.

THE "PEOPLE'S" ENTERTAINMENT SOCIETY.

At a concert held last Saturday evening at the Drill Hall, Bermondsey, by Mdme. Julie Pelletier and Mr. Thorman's Concert Company, this lady sang Mr. Van Noorden's "Yet" and "The Old Folks" of Foster, which won a *bis*, whereupon "Home, sweet home" was substituted. Mdme. Pelletier also took part in duets and quartets with invariable success. To Miss Alice Parry is due the re-introduction of C. E. Horn's beautiful, but neglected, setting of Herrick's old song "Cherry ripe" in E flat, which was streperously encored. Mr. Manton and Mr. Thorman assisted, and Mr. Harvey Löhr was at the pianoforte.

GLASGOW.

The production of Gounod's "Redemption," on Jan. 23, was successfully effected, the vocalists being Mrs. Hutchinson, Miss H. Wilson, Mr. Maas, and Mr. Santley, with members of the Choral Union. The manner in which the work was rendered was highly creditable to all parties concerned, but the impression made by the work itself was meagre enough. Portions of it are pretty, and other parts rise to a considerable pitch of power, but of real sublimity, as exhibited in Mendelssohn and Handel, etc., there was a disappointing deficiency. The conclusion arrived at by most of the critics who noticed its original production seems to hold good, for no one need doubt that "Faust" will survive when the "Redemption" is forgotten.

Concerts have recently been given by "The Glasgow Select Choir," Mr. Lambeth's Choir, and the "Govanhill Musical Association," while many others are in prospect. The Govanhill Musical Association concert, under the conductorship of Mr. William Stobs, was moderately successful. The programme consisted of sacred and secular pieces by good composers, but the singing generally was commonplace, if not vulgar. Of the vocalists, the soprano who sang "With verdure clad" was most enjoyable: she has a peculiarly brilliant, if somewhat uncultivated voice. A tenor also sang with much taste, though his style is open to objection on the score of want of culture. The society is new, and improvement will probably come in time.

J. B.

ASHFORD.

The Ashford Choral Society gave their first concert on January 25th. The works performed were, Mendelssohn's "Lauda Sion" and Bennett's "May Queen," intersected by a group of four solos by the principal singers—Miss Kate Hardy, R.A.M., Mrs. Brooks, Mr. Sidney Tower, and Mr. Musgrove Tufnail, R.A.M. The accompaniments were rendered upon the pianoforte and harmonium in combination; but it is to be hoped that so notable a start as this concert proved to be, will end in the establishment of an orchestra. The pianoforte accompaniments of Miss Weldon, a non-professional lady, were indeed most excellent, displaying much artistic judgment, a sensitive touch, and very delicate tact. Miss Kate Hardy sang her parts with great artistic power and much charm; and her solo, Weber's scena "Softly sighs," created a marked sensation. Mrs. Brooks, a local singer, was an efficient mezzo and contralto, singing Sullivan's "Guinevere" with much taste and in good style. Messrs. Sidney Tower and Musgrove Tufnail were in every way artistic and effective. It would be difficult to name a more efficient rendering of the solo parts of the "May Queen" than the performance of this occasion. The chorus acquitted themselves most creditably, showing special care in matters of light and shade, producing some effective *crescendo* passages, and singing generally with such care, enthusiasm, and good attack as not only evidenced painstaking training, but gave much promise of future excellence in whatever the society may undertake. It should be added that a large and discriminating audience found good reason for encoring all the solo singers by turns, and duly recognised the earnest efforts of the choral force. Mr. Alfred Legg, the parish church organist, conducted with much care and zeal, and displayed such good qualities of leadership as will doubtless be advantageously employed in the future career of the society. It was gratifying to note in Ashford the presence of so much musical intelligence and enthusiasm, both of performers and listeners.

FINSBURY CHORAL ASSOCIATION.

On Thursday, the 25th ult., the Finsbury Choral Association gave a performance of Dr. Stainer's "Daughter of Jairus" and selections from the "Elijah" in the Wesleyan Chapel, Old Kent-road. The soprano solos were sung by Miss Fusselle, a pupil of Madame Sainton-Dolby. This young lady possesses a voice of great purity and freshness; she sings with the refinement and taste of an intelligent artist, and may expect a prosperous future. Miss Jennie Rosse sang the contralto music. Mr. Newth, as an amateur, sang the tenor solos with much care and effect; he has a pleasing though not a powerful voice.

Mr. Vaughan Edwardes is to be congratulated upon his successful appearance before a London audience. This gentleman, we understand, is a student at the Royal Academy of Music; he already gives evidence of the advantages of artistic training, and is the fortunate owner of a rich baritone voice. His rendering of the air, "Lord God of Abraham," created a marked impression. With perseverance and care, Mr. Edwardes has the clear prospect of a successful career.

The choruses were, on the whole, rendered with the precision and effect for which this association has established its character. Mr. J. P. Harding accompanied on the organ with judgment and skill; and Mr. C. J. Dale conducted with his usual ability.

We notice that on the 8th February the "Daughter of Jairus" and "Stabat Mater" are to be given in the Holloway Hall by the association. Particulars will be found in our advertising columns.

SUTTON, SURREY.—Mr. G. C. Burry's second concert of the season was given in the Public Hall, on Monday last, and drew together the *élite* of the neighbourhood. The scheme consisted of Mendelssohn's "Hymn of Praise," and an operatic selection for second part of concert. The vocalists were Miss Mary Davies, Miss Hilda Coward, and Mr. Hanson. The orchestra consisted of about 30 members. Mr. G. C. Burry's choir did justice to the choral part of the programme. The inhabitants of the locality may be congratulated on being enabled to hear such performances.

SALISBURY.—The Salisbury Vocal Union gave their first concert of the season on Monday, the 29th January, in the Hamilton Hall, when A. R. Gaul's sacred cantata "Ruth" was given. The soloists were Miss Julia Jones, Misses Sutton, Wheeler, and Mr. Charles Kelsey. The work was exceedingly well performed by all concerned, and well received. The second part of the programme was devoted to a miscellaneous selection, the soloists being Miss Jones, Mrs. Hayden, and Mr. Kelsey. A special feature of the concert was a harp solo, finely played by Mr. Goslett. Miss Harding and Mr. Luxton ably presided at the pianoforte and organ, and Mr. John M. Hayden conducted. There was a large audience, and the concert was a great success.

Organ News.

PRESTON.

Subjoined is the programme of an organ recital given in the new Public Hall, by Mr. James Tomlinson, on Thursday, Jan. 25th:—

Sonata in F minor	Mendelssohn.
Fantasie on the Prayer ("Der Freischütz")	Lux.
Andante ("Rosamunde")	Schubert.
"Invitation pour la Valse"	Weber.
Allegro Cantabile (Fifth Symphony)	Widor.
Overture ("Il Barbiere di Seviglia")	Rossini.

Mr. James Tomlinson also gave two recitals in the new Public Hall, on Saturday, Jan. 27th:—

AFTERNOON PROGRAMME.

Variations on a Theme by Beethoven	Markel.
Largo (String Quartet)	Bishop.
Andante in G minor	Mozart.
Overture ("Egmont")	Beethoven.
Communion	Saint-Saëns.
Pastorale	Widor.
Marche Triomphale	Archer.

EVENING PROGRAMME.

Symphony in C	Haydn.
Elegie	Silas.
Toccata and Fugue in D minor	Bach.
Airs ("Nabucco")	Verdi.
Pastorale in G	Markel.
Overture ("Stradella")	Flotow.

SHEFFIELD.

Mr. W. T. Best gave two organ recitals in the Albert Hall on Tuesday, Jan. 30th.

Afternoon Recital.

Sonata in B flat, No. 4	Mendelssohn.
Christmas Pastorale	Moriconi.
Fugue in C minor	Bach.
Adagio in E flat major	Spohr.
Rigaudon de Louis XIV.	Lulli.
Fantasia Cromatica in A minor	Thiele.
Andante Tranquillo in D flat major, Offertoire	
Funèbre in F minor	Wély.
Festal March	Best.

Evening Recital.

Marche du Couronnement	Meyerbeer.
Allegro Cantabile in F minor	Widor.
Selection ("Water Music")	Handel.
Andante Cantabile in A flat major	Guiraud.
Siciliana and Fugue in G minor	Bach.
Andante in A major	Smart.
Introduction and Fugue on a Trumpet Fanfare	Best.
Fantaisie in E flat major	Saint-Saëns.

The audiences were small, as they are unfortunately too often here, at high-class performances.

CASTLE HOWARD.

An organ recital was given in the private chapel, by Mr. J. R. Brooke, on Sunday, Jan. 28th, when he performed the following programme :—

"Cujus Animam"	Rossini.
Fifth Concerto	Handel.
"The Lost Chord"	Sullivan.
Fanfare	Lemmens.
"Holsworthy Church Bells"	Wesley.
Procession March	Batiste.

UPPER EDMONTON.

An organ recital was given in St. James's Church on Wednesday afternoon, Jan. 31st, by Mr. James Langran, when he performed :—

Reminiscence ("Lobgesang")	Mendelssohn.
Adagio (Quartet in G minor)	Spohr.
Andante	Mozart.
Fugue in D minor ("The Giant")	Bach.
Romanza	Haydn.
March ("Notturno")	Spohr.
Adagio (Symphony in G)	Haydn.
Chorus, "Hallelujah"	Beethoven.

Annexed is the programme of a recital given in the evening, by Mr. Humphrey J. Stark, Mus.Bac., Oxon. :—

Overture ("Athalia")	Handel.
Adagio in D major, Op. 2	Beethoven.
Prelude and Fugue in D minor	Hesse.
Aria in E major	Paradies.
March ("Egmont")	Beethoven.
Andante	Bodly.
Sarabande	Lott.
Cantilène et Grand Chœur	Salomé.

BRIGHTON.

Mr. J. Crapps, F.C.O., gave an organ recital in the Dome, Royal Pavilion, on Monday, Jan. 29th, with the following programme :—

Offertoire in E, No. 44	Batiste.
Choral Song and Fugue in C	Wesley.
Andante con moto in E flat	Driffield.
Sonata in F minor, No. 1	Mendelssohn.
Andante with variations in G	Lemmens.
Prelude and Fugue in G minor	Bach.
Dead March ("Saul")	Handel.
Fantasia in E minor	Lemmens.
Adagio in C (String Quartet)	Beethoven.
Grand Chœur in D	Guilmant.

EDINBURGH.

Sir Herbert Oakeley gave an organ recital in the Music Class Room of the University, before a crowded audience, on Thursday, Jan. 25th, when he performed the following :—

Chorale, "Sleepers wake" ("Wachet auf," A.D. 1600), air, "Be thou faithful" ("St. Paul")	Mendelssohn.
March ("Scipio"), Bourrée (Concerto No. 7)	Handel.
Adagio (Sextet)	Beethoven.
Allegretto in G ("Rosamunde")	Schubert.
Ballad, "Le Parlate d'Amor"; Canzona, "Il re di Thule" ("Faust")	Gounod.
Andante and Allegro	Bache.

LEEDS.

Dr. Spark gave a recital on the grand organ in the Town Hall, on Saturday, Jan. 27th. The programme ran thus :—

Marche Romaine	Gounod.
Song, "The Lost Chord"	Sullivan.
Andante in G major	Batiste.
Concerto in G major	Bach.
Morceau pour les Carillons in F major	Spark.
Gavotte in G minor and major	Rameau.
Gavotte in F major (Temps de Louis XIV.)	
Ballad, "When other lips" ("Bohemian Girl")	Balfe.
"Toy" Symphony	Romberg.

CALNE, WILTS.

The following is the specification of an organ in course of construction at Mr. Eustace Ingram's organ factory, Holloway, for the parish church :—

Great Organ.　CC to G.

1. Large Open Diapsn.	8 ft.		7. Principal		4 ft.
2. Open Diapason	8 „		8. Fifteenth		2 „
3. Stopped Diapason	8 „		9. Sesquialtra (3 ranks)		
4. Clarabella	8 „		10. Trumpet		8 „
5. Gamba	8 „		11. Clarion		4 „
6. Harmonic Flute	4 „				

Swell Organ.　CC to G.

12. Contra Gamba	16 ft.		17. Geigen Principal		4 ft.
13. Open Diapason	8 „		18. Mixture (3 ranks).		
14. Höhl Flöte	8 „		19. Cornopean		8 „
15. Vox Angelica	8 „		20. Oboe		8 „
16. Voix Celeste	8 „		21. Clarion		4 „

Choir Organ.　CC to G.

22. Open Diapason	8 ft.		26. Gemshorn		4 ft.
23. Dulciana	8 „		27. Wald Flute		8 „
24. Viol d'Amore	8 „		28. Piccolo Harmonique		2 „
25. Lieblich Gedact	8 „		29. Cremona		8 „

Pedal Organ.　CCC to F.

30. Grand Open Diap.	16 ft.		33. Principal		8 ft.
31. Bourdon	16 „		34. Trombone		16 „
32. Bass Flute	8 „				

Couplers.

35. Swell to Great.	38. Swell to Choir.
36. Swell to Pedals.	39. Choir to Pedals.
37. Swell Super Octave.	40. Great to Pedal.

Four Composition pedals to Great organ.
Three 　„　　„　to Swell organ.
One to act on Great to Pedal coupler.

Improved noiseless pedal valves; handsome oak case, designed by J. L. Pearson, Esq., R.A.; playable in factory during two last weeks in February. The builders invite inspection.

NEWRY.

The fine new organ lately erected in the Dominican Church, by Messrs. P. Conacher & Co., of Huddersfield, was opened on Sunday, the 14th inst. Mr. McDonnell presided at the instrument during the celebration of high mass, and afterwards gave an organ recital. The following is the specification :—

Great Organ.　CC to G.

1. Open Diapsn. (large)	8 ft.		6. Fifteenth		2 ft.
2. Violin Diapason	8 „		7. Mixture (3 ranks)		
3. Flute à Cheminée	8 „		8. Trumpet Harmonique		8 „
4. Harmonic Flute	4 „		9. Clarion (prepared for)		
5. Principal	4 „				

Swell Organ.　CC to G.

10. Lieblich Gedact	8 ft.		17. Mixture (3 ranks)		
11. Violone	8 „		18. Horn		8 ft.
12. Rohr Gedact	8 „		19. Oboe		8 „
13. Salicional	8 „		20. Vox Humana		8 „
14. Voix Celeste	8 „		21. Clarion		4 „
15. Gemshorn (conical)	4 „		22. Tremulant.		
16. Piccolo	2 „				

Choir Organ.

23. Viol d'Amour	8 ft.		27. Piccolo Harmonique		2 ft.
24. Dulciana	8 „		28. Contra Fagotto		16 „
25. Gedact	8 „		29. Clarionette		8 „
26. Flute Harmonique	4 „				

Pedal Organ.　CCC to F.

30. Double Open Diap.	16 ft.		32.*Violoncello		8 ft.
31. Bourdon	16 „		33.*Flute Bass		8 „

* By octave coupler.

Couplers.

34. Swell to Great.	37. Swell to Pedals.
35. Swell Super Octave.	38. Great to Pedals.
36. Swell to Choir.	39. Choir to Pedals.

Seven Composition Pedals.

All the pipes are made of bright spotted metal. The Swell organ is voiced by 4½-inch pressure; the Great, Choir, and Pedal organs are on 4-inch pressure. The wind is supplied by one of Duncan's patent hydraulic engines. Handsome case of Gothic design, to harmonize with the church.

ST. JAMES'S HALL.

Mr. Willing's Choir gave Mendelssohn's "Elijah" at their second concert on Jan. 30th. The chief singers were Miss Anna Williams, Miss Hilda Coward, Miss J. Rosse, Mdme. Patey, Messrs. E. Lloyd, A. James, Chaplin Henry, and F. King. The band was of the best quality and well balanced ; and the chorus showed many signs of enthusiasm as well as tokens of good training. Mr. Willing was, of course, the conductor.

THE MUSIC OF NATURE.

There is something inexpressibly sad in the bare aspect of the trees that stand like mammoth harps, upon whose strings of branch and twig the wind plays dirges to its victims—the fallen leaves, which lie about in heaps of brown unhappiness, emitting a doleful crackle as I pass over them. To draw again from the well of figurative language, how like untuned instruments are the trees! Tuned were they by April and May ; the summer months produced from them a rich melody of green ; but it was not until touched by October's skilful hand that the responsive leaf-keys brought forth their exquisite harmonies of color, each modulation of which was attended with some new and striking beauty. Now the foliage key-board is destroyed, and nothing but the framework that contained it remains ; let us console ourselves, however, by the reflections that a new key-board will be provided, and that the process of re-tuning the trees is delayed only till the arrival of the tuner Spring, under whose influence shall they, in company with the grass and flowers, shoot bud and blossom into tune, preparatory to giving forth their hymn of loveliness, beneath the control of another summer and autumn.

How closely allied are color and tone ! the spectrum from red to violet corresponds to the scale, from its lowest to highest sounds, in that various tints and shades coincide with whole and semi-tones; we are constantly borrowing phrases from each to apply to the other, and indeed so interdependent are they, that with many persons the letters of the musical alphabet are mentally colored, so that their hues become incorporated with the tones they represent to such a degree that when listening to a composition the combination of letters suggested by moving harmonies present to their individuals a fabric of mingled dyes, that form with the music a double panorama, adding greatly to their enjoyment. Whether this matter of coloring a tone is exclusively dependent upon its letter, the writer, owing to limited investigations, is unable to determine. There may be those to whom musical sounds, independent of letters, convey color, but in any case a development of the subject would no doubt show many curious phases and prove of no small interest.

Yes, the days of melancholy music are come. The great music-caterer, Nature, has nothing but sadness to offer. Her prima-donnas have flown to fulfil engagements made by their concert-manager, the South, while her insect violinists that have charmed us through the summer with delightful *matinées* and *soirées*, have ceased to draw the bow, and even her mighty thunder-drum is silent.

Is the northern portion of her choir and orchestra, then, disbanded ? By no means. New and different performers are being introduced upon the stage of Time to supply the places of those withdrawn, and another movement in a minor key of her wondrous symphony has begun ; warblers of less note appear, to take less prominent parts, and piccolos and whistles are added to the wind-instruments, for which snow-accompaniments are speedily promised.

The music of Nature is gradually assuming a colder character, becoming more strict and rigid in harmonic treatment and less lcome still. We should ever be content to lis-rovides, for only by so doing can we appreciate those attributes o Master Composer, presented by the music of his interpreter.

What lessons teachers of Art may learn from this grand interpretation of God, in which expression and technique are so beautifully and sublimely blended as to thrill the soul with awed delight ! Here is no preponderance of the one over the other, as is so often the case in man's vocal and instrumental performances. Whatever of this melodious knowledge is borne into consciousness breathes of the coalition of divinity and its technical presentation. Let all musicians follow the glorious example thus afforded, and seek in performing to combine soul and executive ability, for it is only the right blending of these qualities that electrifies an audience and wins a shrine in the temple of Fame.—HENRY W. STRATTON, in the *Musical Record*, U.S.A.

A lady has given a donation of five hundred pounds to the Chelsea Hospital for Women, for the wards in the New Building, which is situated in the Fulham Road. There are now but three out of the seventeen wards remaining to be furnished. Those desiring a good object for charitable concerts could not be engaged in better work than that of aiding the above-named scheme.

THE ORGAN.—INFLUENCE OF THE ORGAN ON HISTORY, by DUDLEY BUCK (the foremost Composer, &c., of the United States).—Price One Shilling. W. REEVES, 185, Fleet-street, London.

SATURDAY POPULAR ORGAN RECITALS, BOW, E.—TO-NIGHT, Mr. W. T. BEST. Vocalist, Miss Marian Burton.

PRINCIPAL CONTENTS OF THIS NUMBER.

LONDON : SATURDAY, FEBRUARY 3, 1883.

FRIEDRICH FREIKERR VON FLOTOW.

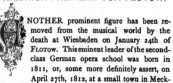

NOTHER prominent figure has been removed from the musical world by the death at Wiesbaden on January 24th of FLOTOW. This eminent leader of the second-class German opera school was born in 1811, or, some more definitely assert, on April 27th, 1812, at a small town in Mecklenburgh-Schwerin. As a member of a noble family, he studied and practised music as a lover, rather than as a professional follower of the art. In pursuance of his father's wish that he should prepare himself for the diplomatic service, he proceeded to Paris to complete his education and to attain experience in the chief seat of the political world. However, he soon commenced the study of music under REICHA, and subsequently spent much of his time in the French capital, where indeed a good many of his works were first heard. FLOTOW's first essay on the lyric stage was "Pierre et Colombine," produced in 1832. This was followed by "Rob Roy" and "La Duchesse de "Guise." His first solid success as an operatic composer appears to have been secured by "Noufrage de la Méduse," written for the Théatre de la Renaissance (1839) ; "L'Esclave de Camoens (Paris, 1843), and "L'Ombre," produced at the Opéra Comique in 1869, were also received with great applause. His most popular work, "Martha," was given for the first time at Vienna in 1847, and soon made its composer famous all the world over. An Italian version was brought out at Covent Garden in 1858. In Germany, says the *Times*, its popularity continues unabated, and only a few days ago HERR BOTEL, a tenor, and, like WACHTEL, a former coachman, made a sensational *début* as " Lionel" at Hamburg. The work which stands second in popularity if not in merit to " Martha" is " Allessandro Stradella," originally an operetta written for the Palais Royal, in 1837, and re-modelled as an opera in 1844, when it was produced at Hamburg and received with the most rapturous applause. " Stradella" was given in English at Drury Lane (1846), and in Italian at Covent Garden (1864), but it failed here to secure the success generally accorded to it on the Continent. Of his other works must be mentioned " Indra," " Rubezahl," " Marie Katerina," " Le Forestier" (1840); " L'Ame en Peine" (in 1846), played in English at the Princess's Theatre as " Leoline" in 1848; " Die Matrosen," about 1859; " Albin," 1856; and " Le Veuve Grossier," produced at the Bouffes Parisiens in the autumn of 1852. In 1854 FLOTOW accepted office as Intendant of the Court Theatre in Schwerin ; continuing to hold this appointment until 1863. The incidental music to Dinglestedt's version of " A Winter's Tale," an opéra-bouffe in one act, " La Veuve Grapin," written for the theatre of his friend Offenbach, " Zilda," 1866 ; and a few occasional compositions were the comparatively small results of the seven years he spent at Scherwin. In 1864 FLOTOW was elected corresponding member of the Institut de France.

It has been the fashion to treat FLOTOW's talents and acquirements with much less consideration than they deserve. As a melodist, and melody is now too often all but absent from even works of large pretensions, FLOTOW had abundant powers, combining the pure vocalisms of the Italian school with the vivacity and piquancy of the French opera. The *Daily Telegraph* critic, who speaks decidedly with regard to the advanced school says : " Musical innovators are ad-" dicted to saying that the fountain of tune is dried " up. They show us that the notes of our scale con-" tain only a certain number of permutations now " practically exhausted, and go on to contend that " reliance must be placed on other sources opened up " by modern development. The man who cannot " discover the fountain, and comes before the world " with an empty pitcher, proclaims that the waters " have run dry, in order to cover his confusion. Let " us not listen to him, at any rate when looking on " FLOTOW's grave. The stream is running still for " those who have the grace to find it, and when some " great singer arises—a singer like MOZART or MEN-" DELSSOHN—whose pure strains well forth from a " natural source—

'As effortless as woodland nooks
Send violets up and paint them blue,'

" an end will be put to all the fantastic notions that " now, under various high-sounding names, try to dis-" tract attention from the rents and rags of artistic " poverty. Meanwhile, the danger is that our young " musicians in whom a gift of melody may develop " itself will be drawn aside from its proper cultivation " in order to become 'tone-painters' and so forth. " It is so cheap to fall in with tendencies that have an " imposing terminology, that are vaunted as based " upon philosophy, and talked about rapturously, if " understood dimly, in the circles of the 'advanced.'"

It was the mission of FLOTOW to show the healthy, refreshing power of tune, and his memory will not be overlooked, even though he aspired not to revolution and mysticism. His work, indeed, was characterised by the general absence of pretension and effort, and by the presence of naturalness and spontaneity. Though FLOTOW composed a fair amount of chamber music of various kinds, he did not succeed in what may be called the severer forms of the art, perhaps in part because he did not find cause to work with sufficient intensity, viewing the art with something of the ease of the distinguished amateur, even though he really loved its pursuit after his own fashion and in pleasant places. The now old-fashioned feature of an opera, a regularly constructed overture, FLOTOW succeeded in writing with some success, the overture in this direction being, perhaps, the overture to " Stradella," which, however, is not without weak points, though the beauty of its introductory movement is undeniable ; again, his overture to " Martha," with its intermingled graceful, and vivacious sentences, is worthy of the pen of AUBER. FLOTOW made no pretensions to contrapuntal skill, but his harmonies are well chosen, judicious, and effective. His orchestration is clear, bright, and appropriate, with now and then artistic touches of no ordinary power. His *chef d'œuvre*, in popular estimation, " Martha," will live, and it is not impossible that " Stradella," and some other specimens from his genial pen, will again be tried, and perhaps will once more meet with a measure of success.   E. H. TURPIN.

THE LOGIC OF COUNTERPOINT.

THIRD SERIES.

II.

CHERUBINI commences his observations on Four-part Counterpoint by briefly setting forth the abatement of the severity of the laws governing the composition of counterpoint as the number of the employed parts is increased. He points out that the classical composers particularly PALESTRINA, indulged in such relaxations from the rules as seem at first sight to reveal actual faults, or at least to indicate a tendency in the direction of too much license. Now, though it is unnecessary to again enter the question as to the power of the composer to supplement " strength" by that wise " freedom" which is indeed a second strength, it may be well to remark that the greatest of practical contrapuntists, as such typical writers as PALESTRINA and BACH, did wisely elect to accept the spirit rather than the letter of the law, and chose to regard rules as merely means to an end—that of pure, strong writing. At the same time let the student remember that such freedom does not belong to any preparatory stage of his contrapuntal career when it is his business to train his musical thoughts, but to his artistic manhood, when he applies his scholastic attainments without pedantic restraint to the real life-work of the composer. It is fitting here to repeat a regret more than once expressed—that CHERUBINI's examples do not always illustrate or even observe the rules he sets forth so logically ; and it is further to be regretted that the different standard works on Counterpoint, ancient and modern, present many examples in which

" freedom " prevails to the prejudice of such law-abiding principles as would best train the ear and eye of the student in the art of building up accurately grammatical progressions. This, be it understood, is not said from any love of pedantry, but from an earnest belief that the best and shortest road to the attainment of contrapuntal strength and independence is by the seemingly narrow, but safe pathway of law-abiding conscientiousness, by which the student can alone fortify his mind with the experience of centuries of theoretical knowledge and practical skill. An exhortation to prefer laws to licenses should meet the student's eye as a balance to the statement of the privileged abatement of the severity of the rules by reason of the increased difficulties of movement to be encountered in the throng of an increasingly crowded score. The Florentine theorist now explains in accordance with the remarks made in the article pre-

$$\begin{matrix} & 5 & 6 \\ & 1 & 1 \end{matrix}$$

ceding the present one, that the chords 3 and 3, being composed of three harmonic elements only, it is necessary to double one of these elements in four-part

$$\begin{matrix} 5 \\ 1 \end{matrix}$$

counterpoint. In the chords 3, he continues, all its harmonic members may be doubled alternately, according to the position and proximity of the different parts to the different elements of the chord. In the words "the octave and the third should be "doubled more frequently than the unison or fifth," CHERUBINI expresses an opinion which has more force than seems evident at first sight. With regard to the unison, its absorbing effect is a manifest reason against its frequent doubling. With regard to the fifth, it should be noted that its firm, not to say assertive character, should as a rule forbid its being doubled until the root note of the chord has been also doubled; and as the two elements cannot be doubled at once in the same chord in four parts without the entire loss of the third, it is clear that the fifth cannot well be doubled, save exceptionally in four parts. On the whole, too, doubled thirds should be "few and far between," if contrapuntal strength is

$$\begin{matrix} 5 \\ 3 \\ 1 \end{matrix}$$

duly valued; and when doubled in the chord 3 should be duplicated, if possible, in the second and third octaves above the bass note and fundamental sound of the chord, so as to endorse the natural scheme of the harmonic range. The theorist adds,

$$\begin{matrix} 5 & 6 \\ 3 & 3 \\ 1 & 1 \end{matrix}$$

"If one or other of the chords 3 or 3 be employed

" in an incomplete form which is occasionally permitted, "and which is often indispensably necessary—it is then "requisite to double two of their harmonic elements, or "even to triple one of them, an expedient to which "recourse should be had only in perplexing situations." The student should strive to avoid using two or more incomplete chords in succession, and endeavour as a rule to present concordant combinations in such way as to secure not only complete but well distributed harmonies. E. H. TURPIN.

THE NATIONAL ANTHEM FOR INDIA.

The subject of the translation of the National Anthem into the languages of India has lately evoked much interesting criticism in the English journals. A number of obstacles to be surmounted by the committee which has undertaken the work have been paraded before the British public, and many a dilemma created, on either horn of which impalement has been prophesied. To one well acquainted with the character and genius of the Indian people, and the aims of the committee in question, these fears and apprehensions are as much a subject of amusement as the terrors inspired by giants and monsters inhabiting that terra incognita which imaginative nurses have the privilege of describing to their juvenile charges.

A brief *resumé* of these objections and obstacles may be instructive. It has been observed, "that, whereas throughout Europe one Supreme Being is acknowledged as GOD, in India each racial division has its particular gods, abominating the divinities worshipped by the others." Now, the leading sects of India deriving their doctrines from the Vedas (and they are by far the greater portion of the Indian people) are the Smarthas, Sivas, and Vaishnavas. There are sub-divisions of each of them with trivial differences. These sects all acknowledge the one thousand and eight names of GOD, which form simply an amplified list of the names of the three-fold division of the GODHEAD : BRAHMA, VISHNU, and SIVA. A careful study of these names will prove that they mean but *one* Supreme Being. The Vedas distinctly say, " GOD is Brahma, Siva, Indra, The Immutable, The Supreme, The Self-Existent Sovereign of the Universe." But it may be contended that these are truths realised and appreciated only by the learned, and that the people have no distinct idea of the unity of GOD.

Let us examine the folk-lore of India, or more especially of Southern India.

Thayumanavar, whose poems, though mainly of a spiritual character, are yet as popular among the Tamils as those of Burns are among the British people, says : " Adoration be to GOD—of whom it is impossible to say He is there or here—who is the perfection of beatitude and mercy, who is above all doctrinal differences, about whom the innumerable sects of the world contend in the words ' He is *our* GOD, and not yours.' " The Avivotha Voonthyan, which is a very popular Tamil lyric, says : " We don't care what sect it is ; every sect that reveals the GODHEAD is a true sect." The writings of the well-known Telugu poet Vemana, whose verses are quoted by thousands every day in the country, abound in similar sentiments. These three are but a few out of a great body of eminent writers on the religious folk-lore of the country ; and need it be pointed out that the folk-lore of a country is but a mirror that reflects the leading ideas and principles of the people?

In brief, the Indian people are cognizant of simple and sublime truths about the GODHEAD, irrespective of the sectarian differences and theological hostilities that abound in their country, as in every other part of the world, where intellectual ability has been a co-existent factor of religious faith.

The most ordinary term in Tamil for GOD is " DEVAN," a form of the Sanskrit word " DEVA," which, according to the authority of philologists, is the root of the Greek " Theos " and the Latin " Deus." The Telugu form of the word is " DEVUDU." To say that though the word DEVA is used by the missionaries working in India it is practically unknown to the vast mass of the people, is an opinion evidently based upon incorrect information.

These terms are in common use among the people of Southern India, as the word " ISVARA " is in the North ; and all these terms convey exactly the same meaning as the English words " GOD " or " THE LORD."

Next comes the question of the adaptation of the music of the Anthem. All comparative knowledge of music apart, it may be asked : " Suppose an air is played or sung to a foreign people, and they like it and express their delight in unreserved terms, will it not recommend itself to them if the words to which it is sung should be translated into their own language or dialect?" The people in the Southern part of India, of whom we may speak from personal experience, already appreciate the air of the Anthem ; and why should it not be popular among them if the words are given in their own language?

Some have gone to the length of suggesting that the ideas in the Anthem are foreign to the people of India. In reply, it may be averred that for almost every idea or sentiment in it, a corresponding one may be cited in the literature of the Indian people.

Another oft-repeated query has been, "Will an anthem manufactured for the people of India by the British public recommend itself to them?" This query loses sight of the very peculiar relations at present subsisting between India and England. The two nations, or, as some would put it, the nationalities inhabiting India, and the people of Britain, form one empire under one sovereign; and there are many things, whether social, or political, or literary, in which they may with mutual advantage help each other. The propounders of the query have only to abide the event; for, if the enthusiasm with which the movement has already been greeted in the Indian Empire is not counted sufficient evidence, the actual reception of the Anthem when it shall have been translated into the Indian languages, will, we may rest assured, dispel any doubts yet lingering in their minds as to the ultimate success of the endeavours of the Anthem Committee.

It has been urged " that though the domiciled English people and our regimental bands have been singing and playing the National Anthem and other music for the last hundred years in the country, not a single melody has been retained, nor any portion of our musical system adopted by the Hindoos." But, as a matter of fact, the people of India have adopted more of the music of England than people in England are aware of. At almost every procession in leading cities of Southern India, people who can afford it employ bands of Eurasians who play English music. These bands have become so much in vogue that now it would be counted as detracting from the importance of the event not to employ them. It need hardly be pointed out that these bands often conclude with " God Save the Queen." The fiddle, which is so popular in India at present, is purely an English or European instrument; and the English tunes which Indian fiddlers play, and often so admirably, are applauded by enthusiastic audiences in a manner which speaks volumes for the appreciation of European music by the people of India. It must further be added, that this taste for European music has been and is steadily growing.

These remarks sufficiently show that the ground in India for the reception of the National Anthem is fully prepared.

P. V. RAMASWAMI RAJU, B.A.
Formerly Head Master of Conjeveram High School, and late Inspector of Customs, Madras.

MUSICAL OBITUARY FOR 1882.

From the scattered notices in periodical literature, of deceased musicians, few people would form any idea of the annual "bill of mortality" in this profession; but when anything like a complete list is made out, the total assumes alarming proportions. Having, during the past year, noted all the deaths advertised or referred to in the English and some foreign publications, I think the following table will possess some interest (of a mournful nature) for the readers of the *Musical Standard.* The list does not, of course, pretend to anything like absolute completeness or correctness, but it is the nearest attempt at such yet made. In many cases conflicting dates have been given, and such instances have, wherever possible, been corrected by reference to advertisements; in other cases it has been quite impossible to ascertain the day, while even the month is sometimes matter of conjecture. In addition to the following, deaths have occurred of relatives; but, without evidence of such belonging to the profession, I have not thought it advisable or proper to insert their names.

[*Where no dates are put, they could not be ascertained*].

January　5...SCHNEIDER, CARL, Professor of Singing; at Cologne, aged 59.
　　,,　6...MARCK, EDUARD L., known in America as Pierre Latour; at Philadelphia, aged 56.
　　,,　8...VERA-LORINA, SOPHIA, at Leghorn.
　　,,　8...FISCHER, MARIE (sister of the violoncellist, Adolphe Fischer), vocalist; at Saint Joose-ten-Noode.
　　,,　8...DAY, T. G., Medallist, R.A.M.; at Nice, aged 23.
　　,,　9...JOURDAIN, FERDINAND, baritone; at Paris.
　　,,　21...TITL, ANTON EMIL; at Vienna, aged 73.
　　,,　25...SINGER, PETER, Franciscan Monk, writer on music, and inventor of the Pansymphonicon; aged 71.

January　31...VASCHETTI, CESARE; in London, aged 55.
　　SELIGMANN, HIPPOLYTE PROSPER, violoncellist; aged 64.
　　TAGLIONI, Mdme. PAUL, danseuse; at Berlin, aged 78.
　　THUNDER, H. G.; at Philadelphia, aged 50.
　　NIEMANN, G. ADOLPH, violinist; at Helsingfors, aged 41.
　　KOBATEK, R. A., zither virtuoso; aged 46.
February　2...CAMPANA, FABIO; in London, aged 67.
　　,,　2...BRAND, WILLEM, musical director; at Antwerp, aged 29.
　　,,　3...ENGEL, F., violinist; at Oldenburg, from apoplexy during a concert rehearsal.
　　,,　3...QUARENGHI, GUGLIELMO, violoncellist; aged 55.
　　,,　4...HILES, JOHN; in London, aged 72.
　　,,　5...SARMENTIO Y VERDEJO, DON PEDRO, flautist and professor at the Madrid Conservatoire; at Madrid, aged 64.
　　,,　6...COGNIARD, Hippolyte; at Paris, aged 74.
　　,,　8...STRINI, Mdme. PAULINE (née Maurel), contralto; at Boston, U.S., aged 25.
　　,,　9...ERL, JOSEPH, royal opera singer; from a fall down stairs in his own house at Dresden, aged 71.
　　,,　11...SCHMIDT, GUSTAV; at Darmstadt, aged 65.
　　,,　12...CELESTE, Mdme.; at Paris, aged 70.
　　,,　12...TUCKER, Henry, song composer; at New York.
　　,,　16...CALLCOTT, J. (father of J· G. Callcott); at Richmond, aged 81.
　　,,　20...KINNS, ALFRED GEORGE, organist; London, aged 27.
　　,,　22...STEPHENS, CATHERINE (Dowager Countess of Essex); London, aged 88.
　　,,　24...PERRY, GEORGE (son of George Perry, of Norwich); London, aged 63.
　　,,　26...RUDERSDORFF, ERMINIA; at Boston (or Philadelphia), U.S., aged 59.
　　,,　28...JAELL, ALFRED; at Paris, aged 49.
　　BILLAUT-VAUCHELET, horn player; at Paris, aged 55.
　　EGHARDT, —, buffo-basso; Prague.
　　FOURNIER, EMILE, horn player; at Lyons, aged 44.
　　ARMANDI, —, tenor; at Toulon.
　　HOFFMANN, CHRISTIAN; New Jersey.
　　CERRUTI, CALISTO; at Turin.
　　ROSSI, ITALO, violinist; at Parma.
　　ALVAREZ, DON JOSÉ MARIA, maestro di cappella, cathedral, Tuy, Spain.
March　1...SZARVADY, FREDERIC (husband of Wilhelmine Clauss); at Paris, aged 60.
　　,,　1...KULLAK, Dr. THEODOR; at Berlin, aged 63.
　　,,　2...KUFFERATH, LOUIS; at Saint Joose-ten-Noode, aged 70.
　　,,　6...KELLY, JOHN, of Her Majesty's Theatre Orchestra; London, aged 62.
　　,,　6...WICARD, CHARLES MARIE, tenor; at Brussels, aged 55.
　　,,　7...WERNER, ANNA (née Schmidt); at Bückeburg.
　　,,　7...FAVALE, PASQUALE; who bequeathed to Her Majesty Queen Victoria his opera "Alviza," to be performed for the benefit of the poor of London.
　　,,　19...HARTEL, LOUISE (née Haufe), pianist; wife of Raymond Härtel, of the firm of Breitkoff and Härtel.
　　,,　19...BEALE, CHARLES JAMES, chorus-master at Her Majesty's Theatre; in London, aged 63.
　　,,　24...BORST, FRAU (née Hoggenbrouwers), vocalist; at The Hague.
　　,,　26...LEBACQZ, EDMOND, clarinetist; at Roubaix.
　　,,　30...GARDONI, ITALO; at Paris, aged 62.
　　STEFFENS, JULIUS, violoncellist; at Wiesbaden, aged 51.
　　SCHULZE, FRANZ, Director of the Cathedral Choir, Naumburg.
　　TOBOADO, FREDERICO, Military Music Director, Saragossa.
April　3...KUCKEN, FRIEDRICH WILHELM; at Schwerin (struck with apoplexy while in a tram-car), aged 71.
　　,,　10...LOTT, GEORGE HERMANN; in London, aged 19.

April 12...BOWMAKER, Charles ; at Tottenham, aged
        54.
  „   13...RIES, Peter Joseph ; in London, aged 91.
  „   16...BOWLING, John ; at Leeds, aged 64.
  „   20...SCHORNSTEIN, C. Hermann (pupil of Hum-
        mel) ; at Elberfeld, aged 71.
  „   20...HARDING, Edward, vocalist ; at New York.
  „   25...HIPKINS, James, aged 82.
  „   25...BRADLEY, James ; at Birkenhead, aged 57.
  „   28...BERTHOLD, Karl Friedrich Theodor,
        Court organist at Dresden, aged 66.
        COVON, Emile, bassoonist ; at Paris, aged 52.
        BAUR, Jacques, pianist and composer ; at Paris.
        CORONARO, Giovanni, young composer ; at
        Bologna.
        DELABARRE, Albert, organist ; at Brussels,
        aged 36.
        CASAMITJANA, Don Juan ; at Valencia, aged
        76.
        PRAWIT, Adolf, vocalist ; at Breslau.
        CICERCHIA-ROSSI, Pietro, vocalist ; at Rome.
        LEONI, Leono, professor of the bassoon ; at Pisa.
May   9...WIGAND, Emilie, vocalist ; at Leipzig.
  „   11...RAINEV, Archibald Edward, organist ; at
        Spilsby, aged 21.
  „   15...ZSASSKOVSKI, Andreas, organist of Cathe-
        dral, Erlau, aged 58.
  „   16...WHISH, Henry, Mus.Bac. ; at Hamilton,
        Canada.
  „   21...ZUNDEL, Johann, organist and composer ; at
        Cannstadt, aged 67.
  „   23...GRIMM, Karl Constantin Louis ; at Berlin,
        aged 62.
  „   25...CONLY, George A., bass. } Members of
  „   25...RIETZEL, Hermann, pianist. } the Kellogg
        Concert Company, drowned at Brattleboro',
        Vermont, U.S.
  „   26...MAGI (MAGGIO), Fortunato, Professor at the
        Liceo Marcello, Venice, aged 42.
  „   26...KURZ, Louis, music director at Neuenberg, aged
        71.
  „   29...STADE, Heinrich Bernhard, Stadt cantor,
        and restorer of the "Bach organ," Arnstadt,
        aged 66.
  „   31...PACCINI, Pietro Giorgi, baritone ; at Lisbon.
        DEVRIENT, Therese, widow of Eduard
        Devrient.
        GIPPA, Maestro Giovanni ; at Milan, aged 73.
        BOLGORSCHEK, Franz, professor at the Music
        School, The Hague, aged 70.
        KASTNER, Frederico, inventor of the pyro-
        phone ; at Strasburg, aged 30.
        REEVES, Edwin (brother of Sims Reeves) ; at
        Liverpool.
        BOWDEN, James B. ; at Liverpool, aged 91.
June   3...VANHAUTE, Pierre Eugen ; London, aged 59.
  „   14...QUIN, Francis Stainstreet ; at Dublin, aged
        54.
  „   17...MURPHY, William, Mus.Bac. ; at Dublin.
  „   17...DEADMAN, George Francis, A.C.O. ; at
        Tunbridge Wells, aged 30.
  „   18...NORMANN, Rudolf von, director of the Court
        Theatre, Dresden, aged 76.
  „   20...COMPTA, Don Eduardo, professor at National
        School of Music, Madrid.
  „   24...ESPIN Y GUILLEN, Joaquin ; at Madrid,
        aged 70.
  „   25...RAFF, Joseph Joachim (night of 24th and
        25th) ; at Frankfort-on-the-Maine, aged 60.
  „   28...TURLE, James ; in London, aged 81.
        LABRO, Nicolas Charles ; at Paris, aged 71.
        FLORES, Maestro Luigi ; at Naples, aged 56.
        TARUFFI, Vincenzo ; at Florence. .
July   2...DAUBERT, Hugo, violoncellist ; London, aged
        48.
  „   4...SCARSBROOK, Thomas, aged 80.
  „   13...PEASE, Alfred H., dropped dead in a street at
        St. Louis, U.S., aged 40.
  „   13...GRASSONI, Giuseppe ; at Ancona, aged 68.
  „   29...ALBERINI, Nicola ; at Rome.
  „   31...PERONI, Giuseppe, violinist ; at Milan, aged
        70.

July   FANTONI, Antonio ; at Piacenza, aged 43.
        LAMPERTI, Amalia (née Conta), vocalist ; at
        Monza.
        BRANDT, Carl, pianist and composer ; at
        Strasburg.
        GUERREAU, Auguste, violinist ; at Paris,
        aged 59.
        BONNE, Louis de ; at Castres, aged 69.
        BISCOTTINI, Casimiro ; at Naples, aged 76.
        HOFFMANN, Francisco, composer ; at Fiume,
        aged 68.
        SALVIETTI, —, professor of the flute ; at
        Naples.
August   1...FICHTNER-SPOHR, Frau Auguste, at Co-
        burg.
  „   3...KOLBE, D., violinist ; at Hanover.
  „   4...WOODWARD, William Wolfgang ; at Derby,
        aged 60.
  „   5...CALLCOTT, William Hutchins ; at Ken-
        sington, aged 74.
  „   6...VANDERSYPEN, Charles ; at Etterbeek, near
        Brussels, aged 63.
  „   7...COVENTRY, Madame Gerard (daughter of Dr.
        Prytherck) ; at Southend, aged 33.
  „   7...MANSTADT, Frida, harpist ; at Dresden ; aged
        19.
  „   7...LABORY, Henri Joseph ; at Velaine-sur-
        Sambre, aged 39.
  „   12...SIGL, Edward, basso-buffo ; at Munich, aged 72.
  „   12...WARTEL, Pierre François ; at Paris, aged 76.
  „   21...DEMEUR, Jules Antoine ; at Paris, aged 67.
  „   22...ROSENTHAL, Elizabeth, wife of Sigismund
        Rosenthal, aged 64.
  „   28...GODFREY, Adolphus Frederick ; aged 45.
  „   29...VOSS, Carl ; at Vienna, aged 66.
        TERRY, Edward ; at Liège, aged 66.
        GRAU, Maurice, reported death from yellow
        fever at Havannah.
        STAMATY, Madeline ; at Paris.
        VANZETTI, — tenor ; at Vanilla.
        PINELLI, Elena ; at Manilla.
Sept.   1...SANTLEY, Gertrude (née Kemble) ; in London,
        aged 45.
  „   3...ARNOUTS, Franz, violoncellist ; at Port St.
        Louis, Mauritius, aged 25.
  „   4...ALBERT, Max, zither virtuoso ; at Berlin, aged
        49.
  „   4...EISFELD, Theodor ; at Wiesbaden, aged 66.
  „   5...MASSEN, Gustav, baritone ; at Wiesbaden.
  „   7...LINDRIDGE, George, organist ; at St. Leonard's.
  „   9...DECKER, Pauline (née Schätzell) ; aged 70.
  „   11...MEMBREE, Edmond, of an aneurism while seated
        at table with his family ; at Domont, aged 61.
  „   12...HARTKAS, Friedrich Wilhelm ; at Berlin,
        aged 77.
  „   16...SCHOBER, Franz von ; at Dresden, aged 84.
  „   20...SCHUBERT, Maschinka (née Schneider) ; aged
        67.
  „   26...PERNAU, Alexander Eugen Josef ; at Ant-
        werp, aged 46.
  „   30...WEISSENBORN, A., in Texas, U.S, aged 34.
        DEMARANS, — murdered by his native servants
        at Cairo.
        SCHUBERT, Theresia, widow of Ferdinand
        Schubert.
        SCHWAB, François Marie Louis ; at Stras-
        burg, aged 53.
        DORN, Adele, sister of Heinrich Dorn ; at
        Berlin.
        BIANCHI, Eliodoro ; at Bucharest, aged 43.
        GIACOMETTI, Paolo, dramatic author ; at Rome.
        MICHEUZ, Georges ; at Villeroy, aged 79.
        FEYGHINE, Mdlle., cousin of M. Servais, violon-
        cellist.
        FERRARI, Bernardino, violinist ; at Vercelli,
        aged 72.
        HERTZ, Ch. A., dramatic author ; at Copen-
        hagen, aged 58.
        PARSINA, Don Ulisse ; at Bologna, aged 54.
        RIBERI, Alessandro ; at Turin, aged 28.
        MULLER, Wilhelm ; at Agram, aged 82.
        CASAMORATA, Louis Ferdinand, President
        of the Musical Institute, Florence, aged 75.

Oct. 9...MARCONI - SCHONBERGER, MARIANNE ; at Darmstadt; aged 97.

„ 11...SIMPSON, JAMES F. ; London, aged 37.

„ 16...KUNKEL, JAMES ; at St. Louis, U.S., aged 36.

„ 19...DIELMAN, JOHN C. H., at Emmettsburg, U.S., aged 72.

„ 25...ESCHMANN, JULIUS CARL ; at Zurich, aged 57.

„ 26...MOLIQUE, MARIE ; at Cannstadt, aged 76.

„ 27...GUTMAN, ADOLPH ; at Spezzia, aged 63.

„ 28...HOWELL, FRANCIS ; aged 48.

„ 28...RONGE, JEAN BAPTISTE ; at Liège. aged 57.

„ 28...GOETZ, EDWARD L. ; at Ramsgate, aged 60.

„ 31...NOTTEBOHM, MARTIN GUSTAV (night of October, 30-31) ; at Graz, aged 64.

ATKINS, JOHN (died in a railway carriage, during a journey from Lewisham to London), aged 60.

GAIBA, ALESSANDRO, violinist ; at Bologna, aged 69.

WITT, — Choir Inspector, Berlin Opera.

KOLDERUPP, Fräulein, prima donna of the Court Theatre, Cassel ; in Norway.

VIGIER, Le Comte CHARLES, husband of Sophie Cruvelli ; at Paris.

VIZENTINI, JULES ; aged 72.

TINTI, ERCOLE, operatic manager ; at Florence, aged 69.

MASSART, WALTHERE LOUIS ; at St. Quentin, aged 82.

CASTRI, PAULINE, prima donna ; at Paris.

BONNISSEAU, J. A., late bandmaster of the Scots Greys.

Nov. 1...MERELLI, EUGENIO ; at Milan, aged 56.

„ 2...EDLER, JOSEPH ; at Vienna.

„ 8...EGERTON, WILLIAM ; in London, aged 47.

„ 14...CLAUSS, CARL ; at St. Petersburg.

„ 15...SCHELLE, Prof. EDUARD ; at Vienna, aged 66.

„ 17...ENGEL, CARL., suicide ; in London, aged 64.

„ 20...KELER, BELA (Albert von Keler); at Wiesbaden, aged 62.

„ 20...DOTSCH, AUG., violoncellist ; at Wiesbaden.

„ 21...ROLANDO, FEDELE ; at Milan, aged 52.

BOSENDORFER, CŒLESTINE ; at Vienna.

GIORDANI, SEBASTIANO, baritone ; at Naples.

CIZOS, VICTOR (Chéri), found dead in his house at Paris, aged 52.

DUMAS, JEAN, tenor ; at Paris, aged 42.

LANDOWSKY, JULIE (née Vieuxtemps) ; at Algiers. Her husband, Dr. Landowsky, died a few days afterwards.

Dec. 3...PALMERINI, RAFFAELLO (of Florence) ; in London, aged 58.

„ 9...ANDRE, JOHANN BAPTIST ; at Offenbach, on the Maine, aged 59.

„ 11...PETTIT, WALTER, violoncellist ; in London, aged 46.

„ 20...FREELAND, ERNEST, organist ; suicide, London, aged 28.

„ 21...TAMBORINI, ODOARDO; at Milan.

„ 24...BLOCKLEY, JOHN ; in London, aged 81.

KELLY, MISS FRANCIS, celebrated as singer and actress, niece of Michael Kelly, aged 92.

MARZINI, ——, at Vercelli.

VIEUXTEMPS, JULES JOSEPH ERNEST, violoncellist ; at Paris.

JATHO, ——, Court music director ; at Darmstadt, aged 57.

PERPIPNAN, FAUSTIN ANSELME STANISLAS, clarinetist, at Avignon, aged 26.

PUCCINI, GIOVANNI, violinist ; at Pisa.

WENZEL, ENRICO ; at Naples, aged 66.

TOMBETTI, AGOSTINO, director of the School of Music, Verona.

To this list we may add the names of some amateurs of note, and others connected with music :—Ferdinand Herold, at Paris (January) ; M. Rouzaud, husband of Christine Nilsson, February 23 ; Marquis de Pontécoulant, writer on musical history, etc. (February) ; the Earl of Wilton, at Melton Mowbray, aged 82, March 7 ; Louis Désiré Lejeune, amateur violinist, whose house at Antwerp was the resort of the greatest artists, aged 83 (March); Sir Henry Cole, at South Kensington, aged 73 (April) ; Lady Charles Bertie Percy, at Guy's Cliff, Warwick, June 11, aged 77, known as the Hon. Mrs. Bertie Percy, as a song com-

poser ; Cecil G. Lawson, the painter (June) ; Ernest Boieldieu, nephew of the great composer (June); Richard B. Barton, barrister, and well known as a musical amateur.

Among the trades connected with music organ building occupies an important position. The following organ builders have died during the year :—George Jardine, at New York, February 10, aged 82 ; Pietro Barchetto, at Turin (April) ; S. R. Warren, at Toronto, Canada, July 30 ; Luigi Lingiardi, of Padua (Sept.), aged 68. Pianoforte makers ; Raffaele Federico, of Naples (January), aged 28 ; G. A. Challenger, London, February 4, aged 53 ; John Allison, London, February 9, aged 51 ; Haydn Collard, London, March 9, aged 75 ; William Porter Dreaper, Liverpool, April 13 ; John Marr, Aberdeen, November 10. Makers of musical instruments, and prominent members of the music trade, publishers, etc. ; Antoine Courtois, Paris (Jan.) ; Marcus Moses, Dublin, April 21, aged 81 ; Theodore Reid, of the firm of Reid Brothers (April) ; Mary Ann Williams, widow of B. Williams, May 12, aged 73 ; Barnett, Samuel, head of the firm of Barnett Samuel & Sons, June 13, aged 62 ; John Hyam, London, June 23 ; Otto Herold, bell founder, Komotau, Bohemia (September) ; Paolo Maisco, Milan (October), aged 79 ; Alex. Guthell, publisher, at Moscow (December) ; and Pierre Louis Gauthrot, Paris (December).

In the above I have, when it could be ascertained, added the age (always counting completed years), and some instruction might be deduced from the varying figures—19 to 97 ! What promising careers have been cut off ! And in how many instances the idea that musicians are short-lived is proved fallacious. Leaving all further speculations to such of your readers as may have the leisure and inclination to indulge in them, I will only express the hope that this compilation may be useful for reference, as well as interesting for the lessons that may be drawn therefrom.

STEPHEN S. STRATTON.

Birmingham, January 19, 1883.

Correspondence.

"THE CREATION."

TO THE EDITOR OF THE "MUSICAL STANDARD."

SIR,—In the notice of "The Creation," in your last issue, the writer remarks, "It may be thought odd that Haydn has made Adam, who here appears as a married lover, a basso (or baritone) instead of a tenor." There is a statement on the authority of Signora Storace, that when Haydn was engaged in the composition of "The Creation," he was on terms of friendship with a bass singer of great excellence, for whom he wrote the part—this owing chiefly to the fact that there was no tenor of any eminence in Vienna at the time.

Yours faithfully,
STEPHEN S. STRATTON.

Birmingham.

REFRESHMENT BARS AND THE HANDEL FESTIVAL.

TO THE EDITOR OF THE "MUSICAL STANDARD."

SIR,—As the Crystal Palace Company takes upon itself the sole management of the forthcoming Handel Festival, the directors will naturally wish to mark the new departure by perfecting the arrangements. Hitherto there has been one terrible annoyance. I refer to the barriers or screens at the transept end of each of the refreshment bars under the orchestra front. In past years they served the admirable purpose of cutting off a large part of the orchestra from the view and hearing of thousands down the nave each way. It would be a trifling matter to remove them, if only temporarily, and the gain would be enormous.

Then, as "refreshments," after all, are not the sole object of life, would it be too presumptuous to suggest that these two particular bars might be closed during the performances on festival days, so that the audience, as well as the band and chorus, might be spared the clatter of spoons, cups, saucers, etc., which, on previous occasions, has formed an "additional accompaniment" not to be found in any score ?

Whether it might not be another improvement to depend more on the voices, and less on the brass, is perhaps too delicate a question.

Yours faithfully,
EXCELSIOR.

Jan. 27, 1883.

The Musical Review is doing good by calling attention to the generally inferior music of our theatres. It is to be hoped that a reformation, of which signs are not wanting, is at hand in this direction.

Passing Events.

A new oratorio by Richard Hol, called "David," has been heard and favourably criticised in Amsterdam.

The Queen has been graciously pleased to accept the position of Patroness of the Leeds Musical Festival.

Miss Annie Glen gave her first evening concert on January 25th, at the Steinway Hall.

Le Guide Musical has a word to say about the late John Crowdy.

The Emperor of Germany has bestowed the Red Order of the Eagle on the composer Barziel.

L'Avenir Musicale (the organ of the Gallin-Paris-Chevé system) is translating Mr. J. S. Curwen's " Musical Notes in Paris."

Hand and Heart for February contains an appreciative account of Mr. W. H. Jude, with a portrait of that talented Liverpool organist.

A French journal, *Le Parnasse*, has opened a competition for the best libretto of a comic opera in three or more acts.

At the Vienna Court Opera during the past year 74 operas, by 33 composers, were given, representing the performances of 219 evenings.

A "Sportsman's Exhibition" is being held, until February 10th, at the Agricultural Hall. The music of the chase will probably not be overlooked in the scheme.

Household Words for February contains an article " On the Composition of an Orchestra," which gives, in a familiar, simple style, a brief description of the different instruments, with some of their leading effects.

A new musical society, called the Eccles District Vocal Union, has just been established in Eccles for the encouragement of part-singing in that locality. Mr. R. Froude Coules, organist to the Earl of Mulgrave, has been appointed musical director.

The Brixton Choral and Orchestral Society will give, on Monday next, Henry Gasby's "The Lord of the Isles." The leader of the band will be Mr. F. Decker, the organist Mr. W. E. Stark, and the conductor Mr. William Lemare.

An important selection from Mendelssohn's "St. Paul" was given at St. Paul's Cathedral on January 25th (Conversion of St. Paul), in accordance with an excellent annual custom. The employment of the orchestra is a happy characteristic from year to year of this notable service.

Mr. Richard Ling, for many years the respected organist of St. Alphage, London Wall, died recently. Mr. Ling was a well-known amateur musician, the friend of many artists, and an earnest lover of organ music and good organs, having sound judgment upon matters musical.

A concert was given on Monday evening at the Shoreditch Town Hall under the patronage of the Baroness Burdett-Coutts in aid of the organ fund for St. Peter's, Hoxton Square. The vocalists included Mdme. Edith Wynne and Mr. Vernon Rigby; Mr. John Thomas was the harpist.

On Jan. 27th, Dr. Stainer's "Daughter of Jairus" was well given, under the conductorship of Mr. W. McNaught, at the Bow and Bromley Institute. Mr. W. Hodge was the very able organist, displaying in his solos of the miscellaneous part much artistic power and skill. A very large audience attended the performance.

At Mr. Henry Holmes's "musical evening" of the 24th, at the R.A.M. Rooms, Brahms's Quintet for strings Op. 88, was performed. A pretty general verdict was that the work, like other compositions by the same hand, is overwrought, and some say wanting in genuine inspiration and freshness of thought. The quintet consists of three divisions—an allegro non troppo, ma con brio; a following movement, with changes of tempo and rhythm and of the mixed character of a slow movement and a scherzo ; and a final allegro energico, culminating in a presto. Beethoven's "Kreutzer's Sonata" and Mozart's Quartet in D (No. 10) were also performed upon this occasion.

The Querist.

BEETHOVEN'S SYMPHONIES.—Can anyone inform me where I could obtain the description of Beethoven's Symphonies by Dr. George Grove (mentioned on page 56 of the *Musical Standard*), also the title of the pamphlet ? May I also ask if the final parts of Dr. Hand's "Musical Æsthetics" are in course of publication ?—AN ENQUIRER.

FUNDAMENTAL CHORDS AND DISCORDS.—Will any of your readers kindly tell me what are meant by fundamental chords and fundamental discords, what chords these two classes include, and name any text-book that thoroughly explains the above ?—STUDENT.

Service Lists.

QUINQUAGESIMA SUNDAY.

FEBRUARY 4th.

London.

ST. PAUL'S CATHEDRAL.—Morn.: Service, Garrett in F ; Introit, Gracious Spirit ; Communion Service, Garrett in F. Even.: Service, Garrett in F; Anthem, Awake my heart (Villiers Stanford).

WESTMINSTER ABBEY. — Morn.: Service, Smart in F (throughout). Aft.: Service, Smart in F ; Anthem, Blessed be the God and Father (Wesley).

ALL SAINTS, MARGARET STREET. — Morn.: Service, Te Deum, Benedictus, Monk in F. Holy Communion Service in B flat (Hummel) ; Offertory Anthem, As pants the hart (Spohr). Even.: Service, in B flat (Hoyte) ; Anthem, The wilderness (Wesley).

TEMPLE CHURCH.—Morn.: Service, Te Deum and Jubilate, King in C ; Apostles' Creed, Harmonised Monotone ; Anthems, Blessed be the God (Wesley) ; Kyrie Eleison, Young in B flat. Even.: Service, Magnificat and Nunc Dimittis, King in C ; Apostles' Creed, Harmonised Monotone ; Anthem, O give thanks (Purcell).

ST. ANDREW'S (WELLS STREET, ST. MARYLEBONE.—Morn.: Service, Te Deum and Benedictus, Tours in F; Anthem, Lord most holy (Haydn) ; Kyrie, Creed, Sanctus, and Gloria, Gounod (Messe Solennelle). Even.: Service, Magnificat and Nunc Dimittis, Hatton in E ; Anthem, The world is very evil (Schubert).

ST. AUGUSTINE AND ST. FAITH, WATLING STREET.—Morn.: Service, Tours in F ; Offertory, Barnby. Even.: Service, Martin in C ; Anthem, I will wash my hands in innocency (Hopkins).

ST. BARNABAS, MARYLEBONE.—Morn.: Service, Te Deum and Benedictus, Stainer in E flat ; Anthem, Stand up and bless (Goss) ; Kyrie and Nicene Creed, Smart in F. Even.: Service, Magnificat and Nunc Dimittis, Eaton Faning in C ; Anthem, O where shall wisdom (Boyce).

CHILDREN'S HOME CHAPEL, BONNER ROAD, E.—Morn.: Service, Anthems, There is a river (Novello), and, I was glad (Callcott). Aft.: Service, Anthems, Hear my prayer (Kent), and, O Saviour of the world (Goss).

CHRIST CHURCH, CLAPHAM.—Morn.: Service, Benedicite, Stainer ; Kyrie and Credo, Weber in E flat ; Offertory Anthem, Cast thy burden (Mendelssohn) ; Sanctus, Benedictus, Agnus Dei, and Gloria in excelsis, Weber. Even.: Service, Magnificat and Nunc Dimittis, Tours in F ; Anthem, O taste and see (Goss).

FOUNDLING CHAPEL.—Morn.: Service, Te Deum and Jubilate, Smart in F ; Anthem, Blessed be the God and Father (Wesley). Aft.: Service, Magnificat and Nunc Dimittis, Cooke in G ; Anthem, O taste and see (Goss).

HOLY TRINITY, TULSE HILL. — Morn.: Chant Service. Even.: Service, Tours in F ; Anthem, O rest in the Lord, and, He that shall endure (Mendelssohn).

ST. JAMES'S PRIVATE EPISCOPAL CHAPEL, SOUTHWARK. —Morn.: Service, Introit, Lord for Thy tender mercies' sake (Farrant) ; Communion Service, Haydn in C (No. 2). Even.: Service, Tours in F ; Anthem, He in tears (Hiller).

ST. MAGNUS, LONDON BRIDGE.—Morn.: Service, Opening Anthem, To the Lord our God (Ouseley) ; Te Deum and Jubilate, Boyce in A ; Kyrie, Reay. Even.: Service, Magnificat and Nunc Dimittis, Walmisley in D minor ; Anthem, be glad, O ye righteous (Smart).

ST. MARY ABCHURCH, E.C.—Morn.: Service, Nares in F ; Communion Service, Armes in A. Even.: Service, Nares in F.

ST. MARY BOLTONS, WEST BROMPTON, S.W.—Morn.: Service, Te Deum and Benedictus, Dykes in F. Even.: Service, Magnificat and Nunc Dimittis, Dykes in F; Anthem, Come and let us return (Goss).

ST. MICHAEL'S, CORNHILL. — Morn.: Service, Te Deum and Jubilate, Boyce in A; Anthem, Blessed be the God and Father (Wesley); Kyrie and Creed, Nares in F. Even.: Service, Magnificat and Nunc Dimittis, Garrett in F; Anthem, Teach me, O Lord (Attwood).

ST. PAUL'S, BOW COMMON, E.—Morn.: Service, Te Deum and Benedictus, Chants; Communion Service, Kyrie, Credo, Sanctus, Benedictus, Agnus Dei, and Gloria in excelsis, Vernham in F; Offertory, Stainer. Even.: Service, Magnificat and Nunc Dimittis, Hopkins in F; Anthem, Here by Babylon's wave (Gounod).

Country.

ST. ASAPH CATHEDRAL.—Morn.: Service, Boyce in C; Anthem, Behold how good and joyful (Whitfield). Even.: Service, The Litany; Anthem, It is a good thing (Bridge).

ASHBURNE CHURCH, DERBYSHIRE. — Morn.: Service, Smart in F; Kyrie, Credo, and Gloria, Eyre in E flat. Even.: Service, Hopkins in F; Anthem, O come, let us worship (Mendelssohn).

BEDDINGTON CHURCH, SURREY.—Morn.: Service, Garrett in F; Introit, Come, gracious Spirit (Hymn 210); Communion Service, Garrett in F. Even.: Service, Garrett in F; Anthem, Whoso dwelleth under the defence (Martin).

BIRMINGHAM (ST. CYPRIAN'S, HAY MILLS).—Morn.: Service, Kent in C; Anthem, Ascribe unto the Lord (Wesley). Even.: Service, Clarke Whitfield in D; Anthem, Blessed be the God and Father (Wesley).

BIRMINGHAM (S. PHILIP'S CHURCH). — Morn.: Service, Barnby in E; Communion Service, Barnby in E. Even.: Service, Barnby in E; Anthem, Praise the Lord (Goss).

CANTERBURY CATHEDRAL.—Morn.: Service, Smart in F; Anthem, O Lord, we trust alone in Thee (Handel); Communion Service, Smart in F. Even.: Service, Smart in F; Anthem, The wilderness (Goss).

CARLISLE CATHEDRAL.—Morn.: Service, Best in D; Introit, I will love thee (Macfarren); Kyrie and Nicene Creed, Goss. Even.: Service, Cooke in C; Anthem, Stand up and bless the Lord (Goss).

CHESTER (ST. MARY'S CHURCH).—Morn.: Service, Tearne in A; Communion Service, Tuckerman in F. Even.: Service, Tearne in A; Anthem, Plead Thou my cause (Mozart).

DEWSBURY PARISH CHURCH.—Morn.: Service, Benedicite, Best in C; Kyrie and Creed, Garrett in F; Offertory Sentences, Barnby. Even.: Service, Anthem, How excellent is Thy name, O Lord (Handel).

ELY CATHEDRAL. — Morn.: Service, Benedicite, Chants; Benedictus, Plain-song; Kyrie, Credo, and Gloria, Cambridge in C; Anthem, The Lord is loving (Garrett). Even.: Service, Stainer in A; Anthem, Praise the Lord (Garrett).

FOLKESTONE (ST. MICHAEL'S). — Morn.: Service, Introit, Cast thy burden (Mendelssohn); Kyrie, Credo, Sanctus, Gloria, etc., Ouseley in G. Even.: Service, Magnificat and Nunc Dimittis, Clarke-Whitfield in E; Anthem, I waited for the Lord (Mendelssohn).

GLASGOW (BLYTHSWOOD PARISH CHURCH).—Aft.: Service, Anthem, What are these (Stainer). Even.: Service, Anthem, Send out thy light (Gounod), and, God is gone up (Croft).

LEEDS PARISH CHURCH. — Morn.: Service, Stanford in B flat; Anthem, Zadoc the Priest (Handel); Kyrie, Creed, Ter Sanctus, and Gloria, Wesley in E. Even.: Service, Calkin in B flat; Anthem, The wilderness (Wesley).

LICHFIELD CATHEDRAL.—Morn.: Service, Hopkins in C; Communion Service, Barnby in E; Anthem, Jesu, Word of God (Mozart). Aft.: Service, Walmisley in D minor; Anthem, The Lord is very great and terrible (Beckwith).

LIVERPOOL CATHEDRAL.—Aft.: Service, Hatton in E flat; Anthem, Praise the Lord, O my soul (Mozart).

MANCHESTER CATHEDRAL.—Morn.: Service, Kempton in B flat; Anthem, As the hart pants (Gounod). Aft.: Service, Kempton in B flat; Anthem, Judge me, O God (Mendelssohn).

MANCHESTER (ST. BENEDICT'S).— Morn.: Service, Kyrie, Elvey; Credo, Sanctus, Benedictus, Agnus Dei, and Gloria in excelsis, Farmer in B flat. Even.: Service, Magnificat and Nunc Dimittis, Stainer.

MANCHESTER (ST. JOHN BAPTIST, HULME).—Morn.: Service, Kyrie, Credo, Sanctus, Benedictus, Agnus Dei, and Gloria in excelsis, Agutter in B flat. Even.: Service, Magnificat and Nunc Dimittis, Wesley.

MUSSELBURGH (LORETTO SCHOOL). — Morn.: Introit, Incline thine ear (Himmel); Service, Clarke-Whitfield in E; Anthem, All we like sheep ("Messiah," Handel). Even.: Service, Anthem, Bless the Lord, O my soul (Mozart).

NORTH BERWICK, N.B. (S. BALDRED'S).—Morn.: Service, Te Deum, Steggall in G; Introit, O God unseen (Hymn 320); Kyrie, Nares. Even.: Service, Chants; Anthem, O Lord, who hast taught us (Marsh).

PETERBOROUGH CATHEDRAL.—Morn.: Service, Boyce in C; Introit, To Father, Son, and Holy Ghost (Bach); Communion Service, Smart in F and Ross in G. Even.: Service, Tours in F; Anthem, Blessed be the God (Wesley).

RIPON CATHEDRAL. — Morn.: Service, Chants; Anthem, Come unto Him (Gounod). Even.: Sevice, The Litany; Anthem, My God, my God (Mendelssohn).

ROCHESTER CATHEDRAL.—Morn.: Service, Barnby in B; Kyrie and Creed, Hopkins in G; Anthem, Turn Thee again (Attwood). Even.: Service, Elvey in A; Anthem, Thus saith the Lord, But who may abide, and, And He shall purify (Handel).

SHEFFIELD PARISH CHURCH. — Morn.: Service, Kyrie, Ouseley in C. Even.: Service, Cantate and Deus Misereatur, Chants; Anthem, O Lord my God (Nares).

SOUTHAMPTON (ST. MARY'S CHURCH).—Morn.: Service, Te Deum and Jubilate, Clarke-Whitfeld in E; Communion Service, Introit, I will love Thee (Macfarren); Service, Agutter in B flat; Offertory, Not every one (Barnby); Paternoster, Field. Even.: Service, Magnificat and Nunc Dimittis, Clarke-Whitfeld in E; Apostles' Creed, Harmonized Monotone.

WELLS CATHEDRAL.—Morn.: Service, Travers in F; Introit, I know whom (Macfarren). Even.: Service, Kent in D; Anthem, O come hither (Crotch).

WORCESTER CATHEDRAL. — Morn.: Service, Mendelssohn in A; Anthem, Behold, how good and joyful (Whitfield). Even.: Service, Stewart in G; Anthem, Great is the Lord (Ouseley).

———

[The attention of the several Organists is called to the favour they confer upon their brother musicians by forwarding their notices regularly: this column of the paper is much valued as an index to what is going on in the choice of cathedral music, so much so that intermissions constantly give rise to remonstrance. Lists should be sent in a week in advance if possible.—ED. *Mus. Stand.*]

⁎ *Post-cards must be sent to the Editor, 6, Argyle Square, IV.C., by Wednesday. Lists are frequently omitted in consequence of not being received in time.*

NOTICES TO CORRESPONDENTS.

NEWSPAPERS sent should have *distinct marks* opposite to the matter to which attention is required.

NOTICE.—*All communications intended for the Editor are to be sent to his private address. Business communications to be addressed to* 185, *Fleet Street, E.C.*

APPOINTMENT.

MR. C. F. THOMPSON to be Assistant Organist, S. Luke's, West Holloway.

ERRATUM.—In paragraph, page 52 of last issue, on Buenos Ayres Choral Society, read *ninetieth* anniversary.

The Musical Standard

A NEWSPAPER FOR MUSICIANS PROFESSIONAL AND AMATEUR

No. 967. VOL. XXIV. FOURTH SERIES. SATURDAY, FEBRUARY 10, 1883. WEEKLY: PRICE 3D.

TRIADS: THEIR RELATIONSHIP AND TREATMENT.

By Francis Edward Gladstone, Mus.Doc.

(*Continued from page* 64.)

It has been seen that the most natural, and therefore the smoothest, progressions from triad to triad are those in which the root of one is a fifth, or a fourth, above or below the other, and those in which the roots descend a third:—

Ex. 33.

The progression from one chord to another having its root a third *above* has, however, a good effect when the second chord is made the stepping-stone to a new key:—

Ex. 34. A.

Ex. 34. B.

Ex. 34. C.

Ex. 34. D.

In fact, it may be stated as a rule that, if we move from one chord to another whose root is a third lower, we shall find it easy to re-establish the tonality from which for the moment we are straying, whilst in the opposite case, *i.e.*, when the root of the 2nd chord is a third above the 1st, we shall obtain a better result by modulating to some scale in which it appears as the tonic or "sub-dominant."

It will doubtless have been observed that in the choice of chords we are more restricted in the minor than in the major key, and from this cause many of the difficulties which beset the student of harmony and counterpoint arise. The similarity in appearance between most of the intervals of relative major and minor scales frequently leads to confusion between the chords properly belonging to each. If we would avoid vague and indefinite tonality, it will always be well not to introduce into the minor key a chord peculiar to the relative major scale, unless it is our intention to make a modulation to the latter key, in which case the intruding chord should be followed by some chord or chords derived from the major scale. Herein lies a noteworthy difference between the major and minor modes. We have seen that it is possible to use two minor chords in succession in the major key without material disturbance of the tonality. In the minor key, however, it appears to be a fact that two major chords in succession produce an effect inconsistent with the sombre character of the scale, and that the sounding of the tonic or dominant harmony of the relative major scale begets an instant craving for the establishment of that key:—

Ex. 35. A.

Ex. 35. B.

In both of these examples there is a laxity in the choice of chords which gives indecision to the effect, and which reminds us of the vague tonality of the old Church modes. In the following examples a transient but clear modulation is made to the relative major:—

Ex. 36. A.

Ex. 36. B.

and the return to the minor key, if less welcome than the departure, is at all events unmistakable. Many irregularities in this and other respects are however justifiable when the parts progress sequentially.

Ex. 37. A.

Ex. 37. B.

Ex. 37. C.

Observe the falling leading note and the good effect of the usually abrupt progression from the chord of E minor to that of F major in the example in the key of C major, the intrusion of the chord of C major into the minor key in the second of the last quoted examples, and the false relation in the third. All these irregularities are introduced in order to carry out the sequences, and although such progressions would be open to criticism if taken separately, in this form they are not only tolerable, but even beautiful.

Hitherto I have discussed only various combinations of triads (or, more properly speaking, of triads having one sound doubled) with the "root," as it is usually called, in the Bass. I must now proceed to the consideration of the inversion of triads. In doing so I must call your attention to a very curious and remarkable acoustical phenomenon, which was first discovered more than a century ago, although Professor Helmholtz seems to have been the first investigator who observed the full importance of its bearing upon practical harmony. I refer to what are known as combinational or resultant tones. No doubt most of you are aware of the fact that, when two adjacent sounds of the harmonic series are sounded together, their combination produces a third sound which has for its vibrational number the difference between the respective vibrational numbers of the primary sounds. Thus, for example, if the two combined sounds make 200 and 300 vibrations respectively in a given time, the resultant sound will make 100 vibrations in the same time. If any one who is not familiar with the fact cares to satisfy himself in regard to it, a very simple experiment will suffice. The tones of a harmonium, or the stopped diapason of an organ, are well adapted for the purpose. Let the two sounds C and F

(on the 3rd space and 5th line of the treble staff) be sustained for a moment, and then let G

be substituted for F, the C being still retained. A sort of ghost-like bass will be distinctly audible. The first of these additional notes will be the double octave below the F, the second will be the octave below the C. It may be necessary to repeat the experiment several times in the case of an unpractised ear, but when the attention has been properly directed for a little time, the clearness with which these combinational, or resultant, tones come out is astonishing.

We have seen that any note as a generator of harmonics produces first its octave, then its 12th, then its double octave, then the major 3rd above this double octave, and then the octave above its 12th, these six sounds producing a very satisfactory major chord. It must now be noticed that the prominent resultant tone formed by the combination of the first six harmonics will be the generator itself. In fact, the generator produces the harmonics, the harmonics in combination reproduce the generator. The interest attaching to this discovery increases when we observe the effect of the union of three sounds. If the triad on C is sounded in its closest position

the resultant tones are respectively one and two octaves below C;

the upper note is produced by the union of C and G; the lower one is doubly caused, first by the union of C with E, next by the union of E with G. Now, if these observations are carried yet further, we find that the first inversion of the same triad produces the same combinational tones as the triad itself with the addition of the 12th above the generator, and that the 2nd inversion produces three repetitions of C, the root: the following example will show this clearly. The triads are written as minims, the resultant tones as crotchets :—

Ex. 38.

These facts seem to point to the conclusion, which is certainly borne out by our hearing faculties, that a major chord retains its essential characteristics even when its intervals are inverted. Nature's bass (if the expression may be allowed) is still present, although unpractised ears do not readily separate its sounds from the louder notes of the chord with which it mingles. When, however, we turn to examine the combinational tones of a minor triad we find different results. Let me yet once more ask your attention to the harmonic series of sounds arising from C.

You will remember that the minor triad on E was formed by uniting the 10th, 12th, and 15th harmonics. Now, by the law which has been already mentioned, the 10th and 12th harmonics in combination will give us the 2nd harmonic as a resultant tone; that is to say, E and G will produce C.

Ex. 39. A.

Ex. 39. B.

Again, the combination of the 12th with the 15th harmonic will give us the 3rd harmonic, the difference between their numbers being 3.

Thus the major 3rd, G, B,

Ex. 39. C.

will produce the double octave below the G, i.e.

Ex. 39. D.

But the union of E and B,

Ex. 39. E.

qualities, together with such powers of prolonged breathing and sustentation of linked sounds as are rarely found in these days, are among the qualities necessary for the development of the rich yet reserved spirituality of the Palestrina school. Such music rebukes the presumption of the dramatic readers of sacred text, and in awe-struck reverential streams of evenly expressed contrapuntal figures, tells us that the task of adequately setting such words may after all be best attained in the devotional forgetfulness of personality and in unpretentious yet strongly built up counterpoint, rather than in the transparent theatrical devices of over-vaulting musical ambition. The reading of Palestrina by the Bach Choir was solid and largely sympathetic, though naturally somewhat wanting in that contemplative power which is largely absent from our modern choirs, trained chiefly under instrumental influences, and which is a large essential in the just rendering of Palestrina's saintly, heaven-born music. The presence of a number of boys' voices lent some sonority and solidity to the upper parts. The chorus singing was of a very high order indeed, tune and general style being alike excellent. Such good qualities were admirably displayed in Wilbye's "Stay, Corydon," and T. Attwood Walmisley's "Sweete Floweres." A recitative¦and trio from Mr. Otto Goldschmidt's "Ruth" for soprano, contralto and tenor, proved very acceptable, and it might be well to reproduce the entire work. Gade's part-song "Upon the deep blue water," the Swedish volkslied, "How splendid is crystal" (harmonised by Otto Goldschmidt), and Mendelssohn's "The Nightingale" (encored) were capitally rendered. Mdme. Norman-Néruda played two solos of the old world of violin music, a "Larghetto" by Nardini, and a "Tambourin" by Léclair, with pianoforte accompaniment arranged from figured bass by Ferdinand David. A "Sanctus" in C (J. S. Bach), for the first time by this choir, closed the concert. This dignified and masterly piece "formed," said the programme, "an integral part of the Lutheran service at Leipzig, in which it closed the preface to the Communion at the three great annual festivals. Four specimens have been published in full score by the German Bach Society in the volume for the year 1861 (vol. xi) ; and the first of these is the Sanctus in C, selected for performance this evening ; the remaining three being the Sanctus in D major, already performed by the Bach Choir, and two others in D minor and G major respectively. The editor of the German score states that the authenticity of the first and second of these compositions, as by J. S. Bach, is clearly established ; but he evidently entertains some doubt with regard to the authorship of the third and fourth." It was given upon this occasion with organ, and it was rendered with much character and power. The conductor was Dr. J. Stainer (in the unavoidable absence of Mr. Otto Goldschmidt), who performed his responsible duties with all the requisite tact and judgment. The principal vocalists were Miss Robertson and Mdme. Isabel Fassett, whose singing was very artistic ; Messrs. Frost, Kenningham, Tremere, and Thomas Kempton, and their parts were excellently rendered. The accompaniments were given at the pianoforte by Mr. Stephen Kemp, and the organist was Mr. Thomas Pettit. These gentlemen did their work with artistic skill and musicianly judgment.

At the second grand concert, on March 8th, "Odysseus" (scenes from the "Odyssey") for chorus, solo, voices, and orchestra, by Max Bruch, will be performed. This performance, the first in London of the entire work, will be conducted by the composer. There will be a complete professional orchestra.

MDME. VIARD-LOUIS'S LECTURES.

At the meeting of January 31st (held in lieu of January 22nd), Mdms. Viard-Louis delivered, through the medium of her (English) reader, Mrs. Warrington Smyth, a most interesting lecture in continuation of her present suggestive subject—the literature of the pianoforte—and illustrated the text with a programme of sterling music. The lectures comprised the composers who flourished at the beginning of the 19th century. It is contended by Mdme. Viard-Louis that the masters in the art have always been the interpreters of the popular feeling of their own time, and not in advance of their time. At the close of the 18th century two currents were flowing side by side. The upper ranks of society (the "Rose" tribe) wanted pleasure and repose, after the long civil and religious wars of Europe, but the "Third Estate" demanded liberty, and the storm of revolution broke out with fury. Thus the last works of Mozart were separated by a few years only from the maturity of Beethoven, and these two masters may be considered as types of the two currents above mentioned. Mozart had been spoken of in a previous discourse as the unrivalled songster of the privileged classes ; and in Beethoven it is all humanity that sings or weeps. "And here we may stop, for the art of music has nothing more to desire. It has its Homer, its Dante, its Michael Angelo, Virgil, and Raffaelle ; and yet more, for we must ascend to the Sacred Prophets themselves to find again expression of truth and feeling so divine and yet so human."

But if this second Ezekiel dominates over his epoch, there is a powerful army about him, preceding and accompanying their leader and general. Handel had written his oratorios ; Gluck had raised lyrical tragedy to an altitude until then unknown ; and vocal music of greatest excellence had prepared the way for the advent of *symphony*, of a far higher order than had yet appeared. Beethoven came, after Haydn and Mozart, to make of the symphony Jacob's ladder, the summit of which should reach to heaven and the infinite. And under the pressure brought about by the development of thought, instruments were invented more adequate to the aspirations of the art. The "Hammer-Clavier," or modern pianoforte, now appeared, although very inferior to the magnificent instruments manufactured in the present day. After remarking how imperfectly great men like Beethoven were understood in their own life-time, and how few eminent geniuses spring from the higher class of society—as if poverty and suffering braced and strengthened the soul—the lecturer said that whatever she might hope she was unable to understand how the art of music could advance higher still. An opinion was also expressed that Beethoven, Weber, and Mendelssohn, lofty geniuses, and men of "wonderful talents," such as Hummel and Schubert, had never been surpassed.

Mdme. Viard-Louis proceeded to speak of writers for the modern pianoforte, who, although not stars of the first magnitude have yet rendered good service to the art. Daniel Steibelt, famous for his "Storm" rondo (which she afterwards played), had a great reputation in his day (1765—1823). The reporter remembers that 57 years ago this piece was in the portfolio of every lady amateur that could play at all, and all the artists throughout Europe produced it. Steibelt created the (terribly absurd) "genre" of "Variations." J. P. Hummel (1778—1837) was spoken of at length, and his biography carefully epitomised. Hummel's style was a mixed one ; as a composer, he is certainly great ; a "power" in music, with plentitude of means and richness of combination, his relative inferiority is caused by Beethoven's immense poetic power. Hummel never rises to the point of making the pianoforte *speak*. The "Fantaisie," Op. 18 (played by the lecturer) cannot be considered a "tone-poem." There are to be found in it dramatic power, exquisite grace, passionate agitation, and well-defined improvisation ; but all stops short of perfection ; one never forgets the piano, the performer, and the composer. Hummel's inferiority to his gigantic contemporary is radical. Weber had already been extolled. Mdme. Viard-Louis, like most learned musicians, considers this master's genius essentially operatic and orchestral ; it is clearly typified by "Der Freischütz." The 3rd sonata in D minor, Op. 49 (played in illustration), reminds Mdme. Viard-Louis of the opera-house and orchestral combinations.

Schubert recalls, in his music, the remembrance of some past emotion. The lecturer, making Schubert much below Beethoven and Weber, nevertheless esteems all his works as of a high order. Mdme. Viard-Louis played a "Moment Musical" in A flat.

Beethoven's life and career had been fully described in a previous lecture. His Sonatas, said by Hector Berlioz to be his "tone legacy" to posterity, were naturally dwelt upon as the more immediate subject matter. The great master made the orchestra tell the tale of human life in trumpet tongues, but the pianoforte was ever his *confidante*, the friend of his heart—yet more, his *voice*, when he could not utter a syllable. His marvellous improvisations on the instrument have been recorded, and an anecdote supplied by Pleyel attested this power. The great variety to be found in the sonatas is surprising ; in later life, Beethoven became more metaphysical and mysterious, and to ascend with him to these sublime heights is beyond the capacity of ordinary mortals. The Sonata in D minor, Op. 31, No. 2, was played as a specimen and thoroughly analysed in the text of the lecture itself.

Mendelssohn's works for the pianoforte always (said the lecturer) display the lightness, agitation, and hurry of the fairy world. The Capriccio, Op. 23, was played. George Onslow (1784—1853), was born in France, of a French mother by an English father. His musical vocation was late to declare itself. Unfortunately for the development of his talents, Onslow led too calm and peaceful a life ; he lived in the country, enjoyed a large fortune, and was, so to speak, too happy. Adversity squeezes out the quintessence of choice spirits. Onslow's music shows "an estimable talent," and nothing more. The lecturer played the Sonata for pianoforte and violin (Herr Henkel), No. 7, Op. 16, in A by way of illustrating Onslow's style.

MUSIC AT READING.

(*From our Own Correspondent.*)

Writing musically, little of interest has occurred here during the last month, which seems to have been given up by tacit consent to the private social gatherings of the season.

On Tuesday evening, January 30th, the Annual Concert of the Temperance Choir was given in the Town Hall, and attracted a large audience of the working classes. Miss Agnes Larckom, Miss Susie Fenn, and Mr. Harper Kearton were, as usual, the solo vocalists engaged ; and Miss Marie Schumann (violin), and Mr. F. J. Read (organ), contributed the instrumental items of the programme. The Temperance Choir also sang choruses and part songs ; but I am sorry that I cannot yet report any improvement in the style of singing. Why do ordinary "Tonic Sol-fa" classes always seem to be so rough ? Perhaps the real reason is the raw material of which they are composed.

Miss Marie Schumann, whom I have previously mentioned as one of the most promising students at the Guildhall School of Music, has of late been made much of at popular concerts at Reading, and I would express the hope that her frequent appearances here may not be to her disadvantage. As a young player, she evinces talent which may be successfully developed ; but her playing at present needs very much more cultivation in every way, and I question if it be wise to encourage (?) her public performances with too much flattery and applause.

On Friday, February 2nd, morning and evening Recitals were given in the Old Town Hall, by Mdme. Norman-Néruda and Mr. Charles Hallé. The few real music lovers in the neighbourhood assembled in all their force (though that, unfortunately, but a small one), at the *matinée*, despite the discouragement of a thoroughly wet day, and no doubt all thoroughly enjoyed the classical programme provided. Mdme. Néruda played the Adagio and Rondo from Spohr's 9th Concerto, Ballade in G minor (Néruda), and "Le Mouvement Perpétuel" (Paganini), as the violin solos, and, with Mr. Hallé, Schumann's Fantasie Stücke (Op. 73) for violin and piano, and Brahms's Grand Sonata in G, Op. 78. Mr. Hallé's solos were the "Moonlight" Sonata, and two of Schubert's impromptus. Of the playing of Mdme. Néruda I cannot help writing enthusiastically as ever. All the most delicate *nuances* and difficult executive passages were alike charmingly interpreted with that refined artistic feeling which Mdme. Néruda always evinces.

The programme of the evening recital included works by Bach, Handel, Corelli, Dussek, Viextemps, and Beethoven (the "Appassionata," Sonata, and Sonata in G for piano and violin); but, although it seemed to appeal to the more popular taste, the audience, even in the old and small Town Hall, looked very meagre, and I am afraid we cannot wonder if concert-givers are discouraged from providing *good* music for the Reading public.

I hear that the Philharmonic Society will perform the "Elijah" early in April, and two or three weeks later the County Society will give the "Martyr of Antioch." The latter performance, I believe, will be in aid of the Royal College of Music, for which a fund has already been sub-

scribed in the county to the amount of £1,500. A local committee has been formed, of which the Mayor is chairman, and he has lately expressed his intention of inviting subscriptions from the townspeople, and obtaining the assistance of the Philharmonic Society in organising a concert in aid of the fund.

--

EDINBURGH.

Few performances here have caused so much expectation and quiet excitement as that of Gounod's "Redemption," the week before last. It is well known that of anything of which we expect much, disappointment is pretty sure to be the final result, and in music this is very true. The more a piece is lauded before being heard the more is expected from it, and, as a natural result, the performance falls short of our expectations. Of the vast audience collected to hear Gounod's "magnum opus," many no doubt went expecting another "Elijah." It would be interesting to know how many came away under the impression that they had heard such a work. By the way, why cannot, or rather, why *is* not, the plan adopted of making audiences at first performances record their opinions in some simple way ? The trouble would be *nil*, and the result decidedly interesting. Supposing, for instance, a paper was handed to each one on entering, with one or two simple questions printed, which could be answered in monosyllables, the papers to be given up on leaving the hall. This plan if once adopted would be sure to recommend itself as the only one to correctly determine the degree of favour with which a new work was received. In amateur and band contests the results would be even more valuable and conclusive.

To return to the "Redemption." One thing greatly in its favour here was an exceptionally good performance : a better performance, of anything, our Choral Union has seldom given. Mr. Adam Hamilton, the choral master, who conducted, must be congratulated on the successful result of what must have been great labour and skill in training the choir, which sang, considering the composition, with great taste and considerable precision. The orchestra, led by M. Victor Buziau, played splendidly, and Mr. H. Hartley at the organ did admirable service. The ninth concert of the series included Haydn's Symphony, No. 7 (Saloman Series), concerto for piano and orchestra, No. 4 (Beethoven) and a pretty intermezzo by Leo Delibes. Mr. W. Townsend, a local pianist, acquitted himself very creditably in the concerto and some pieces for piano and orchestra by Raff. Mr. Townsend's only shortcoming is that his playing is too mathematical, if such a term may be used. It is not, in the modern æsthetic phraseology, by any means "intense."

Sir Herbert Oakeley gave one of his delightful organ recitals to the students on the 25th Janv., when several numbers, including ballet music from "Rosamunde" (arranged for organ by Sir Herbert), Andante and Allegro for organ by F. Bache, and part of Handel's Organ Concerto No. 7, were given with great effect by the professor. During the recital a student sang with much acceptance "Lascio ch'io pianga," by Handel and a pleasing ballad by Abt.   J. C. P.

WOLVERHAMPTON CLASSICAL CONCERTS.

The second concert of the series took place on the evening of the 25th inst., when the following artists were engaged : violins, Mr. H. Hayward and Mr. F. C. Hayward ; violas, Mr. Geo. Roberts and Mr. H. Hayward, junr. ; violoncello, Mr. Jos. Owen ; pianoforte, Miss Edith Yonge ; vocalist, Miss Annie Guest.

The following programme was gone through :—

Quintet in C, for strings	Mozart.
Song, "With verdure clad"	Haydn.
Piano Solo, "Walstein" Sonata	Beethoven.
Violoncello Solo, "Nocturne"	Golterman.
Quartet in C minor, for piano and strings	Mendelssohn.
Song, "Softly sighs"	Weber.
Violin Solo, Concerto	Guhrs.
Song, "Rode's Air and Variations"	
Quartet, "God preserve the Emperor"	Haydn.

The Quintet of Mozart and Haydn's Quartet was very ably played ; but the gem of the evening was certainly Mendelssohn's beautiful work. The piano part, which has the lion's share of the work was played by Miss Yonge, in a manner that shewed she is gifted with musical powers of a very high order, and doubtless she has a very great future before her. The scherzo and allegro moderato were exceptionally well played by the whole of the artists engaged. Mr. Owen's solo was given in his usual happy style, and greatly pleased the audience. Miss Yonge in the difficult sonata set down for her again shewed her exceptional musical powers. Mr. Hayward met with a very warm reception on his reappearance after a long illness, and his rendering of the concerto set down for him, which is a work that can only be played by artists of the highest order, shewed that he has not lost any of his power, the whole being an exhibition of remarkable tone and finish. Miss Guest in the three difficult songs set down for her, exhibited her sweet voice with much effect, her execution in Rode's Air being particularly good. The accompaniments were very ably played by Miss Haywood and Mr. W. A. Guest. The next and last concert is announced for Feb. 22nd.

OLDHAM.—The Monday recitals organized by Mr. Houghton still continue to be well patronised, the executant (Mr. J. Greaves) being warmly received. The programmes put forth are classical, and include some good MS. works heard for the first time. At intervals Master D. M. Greaves executed solos on the violin, and songs by Messrs. Lloyd and Hilton, the former rendering a new baritone Egyptian war song in a fine style. On Ash Wednesday a selection from the "Messiah," &c., was given in the Congregational Church, under the direction of Mr. R. Jackson, R.A.M.

THE OWENS COLLEGE, MANCHESTER.—At a meeting of the Debating Society, on Friday night, Dr. Hiles lectured upon the importance of music as a part of a liberal education. He spoke of the growing recognition of music as a highly educational discipline, of its admission at Cambridge into the curriculum, and the admission of its graduates into the Convocation of the London University. The following resolution was passed:— "That the study of music has an educational influence of so high and exacting a character as to entitle it to full recognition as an essential part of collegiate training."

LEEDS.—At the recent Church Mission in Leeds, the singing of hymns formed an important feature, and at some of the services for men only the hymn-singing was particularly fine. At the men's meeting in the Town Hall, which was presided over by the Archbishop of York, the effect of so many male voices in unison was remarkably grand and impressive. On Saturday Dr. Spark gave a recital of sacred music on the Town Hall organ prior to an address by the Rev. W. Aitken in connection with the Church Mission. The singing was led by the Blue Ribbon Army Choir, consisting of nearly 200 male and female voices.

CORK.—On the 29th ult. the choral class of the Cork School of Music gave the annual recital, consisting, this year, of Spohr's "Last Judgment," and a second part miscellaneous. The oratorio was excellently rendered, and reflected great credit on the conductor, Mr. T. J. Sullivan, and, indeed, on all parties concerned in its production. The solos were given by Mrs. O'Connell, Mrs. Murphy, Mr. Fitzgibbon, and Mr. Paul. The school, which is now in its fifth session, has shown in this recital that it is doing good work, and is in every way a great success, owing to the tuition being of the best, while the charges are very moderate.

EALING.—The Ealing Orchestral Society played a selection of pieces at the usual Monday popular entertainment at the Lyric Hall, on the 29th ult. This was the first public appearance of the orchestra, and the performances reflected great credit upon the conductor, Mr. Harold E. Stidolph, and the members. Amongst the pieces were the overture to "The Poet and Peasant" (Suppe); Haydn's Third Symphony; and a Gavotte ("Louis XV.") by Maurice Lee. The vocalists were Miss Annie Larratt and Miss Alice Davies, both of whom were eminently successful in their efforts. These popular entertainments have met with great success, the hall being well filled every week.

GRESHAM HALL, BRIXTON.—A performance of Henry Gadsby's dramatic cantata, "The Lord of the Isles," was given on Monday, the 5th inst., by the members of the Brixton Choral and Orchestral Society, under the able direction of Mr. W. Lemare. The soloists were Mdme. Worrell (Edith), Mdme. Raymond (Isabel), Mr. Henry Yates (Ronald and Allaster), Mr. Bell (The Abbot), and Mr. Frederick Bevan (Robert Bruce). The music allotted to the character of Ronald was to have been taken by Mr. H. Taylor, but, in his absence, Mr. Henry Yates (an amateur) very creditably sustained the part, although the endeavour to sing both the parts of Ronald and Allaster proved nearly too much for his vocal powers. A word of praise is due to Mdme. Worrell for her finished singing in the scena, "Tears, bitter tears," and also to Mdme. Raymond and Mr. Bevan in their respective solos, "Hear, Holy Virgin," and "Oh, holy man." The chorus sang with much more fervour and attack than usual. The orchestra also, although at times slightly at variance, was a great improvement upon the last concert.

PRINCIPAL CONTENTS OF THIS NUMBER.

LONDON: SATURDAY, FEBRUARY 10, 1883.

CHURCH ORATORIOS BY CHURCH MUSICIANS.

ALTHOUGH it is most important to beware of the too rigid adoption of mannerisms and styles in art, there is undoubtedly such a thing as propriety. Of late it has been pointed out by leading musical critics that our excellent living Church composers have in their acceptable contributions to our oratorio school shown a somewhat too pronounced leaning towards the ecclesiastical style. Now, from the eclectic point of sight, it may be fairly asked, Why should a Church composer be denied the right of selecting, within proper limits as regards the just expression of the words, that style for oratorio composition in which his habits of thought will best prompt his musical eloquence? Church art has its own traditions in all its several departments; and the contemplative position of the listener in Church is a distinct attitude, as compared with the more dramatic but less spiritual function of the concert-room auditor. Then the different available means of production at the disposal of the composer of Church music should naturally incline him to the realisation of the passive, reflective effects peculiar to ecclesiastical musical idioms, rather than to the attempt to secure the more vivid and brilliant results of the concert-room. Mendelssohn in his "St. Paul" and "Elijah" may be said to have illustrated the two types of oratorio in good taste and without any narrowness of local feeling, "St. Paul" being written under the influence of the great cantor of Leipzig, and "Elijah" being planned for the adopted country of the great composer of the "Messiah." Indeed, now the oratorio is travelling home again to the shelter of the Church, it should be a matter of congratulation to find our ecclesiastical musicians turning their attention to the compositions of oratorios, in some instances to be primarily heard at our great cathedral festivals. And the development of the Anthem into the Oratorio is by no means an unnatural or unwelcome feature of that great musical movement which is carrying the "musical sermon" back to its real and original home —the Church. It is to be earnestly desired that those of our composers who write with Church-like instincts and yet without too much servility to mere mannerisms, will build up for us a school of English Church oratorios. The works of such men as ARMES, J. BARNBY, J. F. BRIDGE, G. GARRATT, F. E. GLADSTONE, OUSELEY, STAINER, etc., have already laid the foundations for such a structure. E. H. TURPIN.

ORCHESTRAL EFFECTS AND KEY-BOARD MANNERISMS.

III.

THE intelligent transcription from the original to a new tone medium should be made subject to one leading condition—the suitability of at least a large portion of the original to the expressions and powers of the new executive medium. If this condition be seriously kept in view, there can be little impropriety in the proposed musical translation. Thus it may happen, as a rare case in point, that a given piece originally intended for the violin, may be justifiably re-arranged for the organ. Bach has himself shown to us the practical testimony of approval in this direction. On the other hand, the want of sound judgment in this matter is only too often displayed, and movements which rely entirely upon the special tone colour or mechanical peculiarities of their original mediums, are ruthlessly dragged again into publicity in some new shape or other by which the original flavour of the music is completely sacrificed or destroyed. It may be a fact that the prevailing universality of the pianoforte actually compels the transcription, sooner or later, of every piece, vocal or instrumental, which has attained popularity in some other primary condition; but such a necessity is surely to be deplored. However, it is time to attempt to deal practically with this matter of musical transference. The question may be viewed pictorially with some gain, perhaps. Save in full and generalised effects, orchestral passages usually present prominent or foreground figures, with more or less subordinate background filling in or harmonic support; and there is to complete the animation of the picture, an inevitable amount of activity, sometimes to be found in the prominent foreground figures, but quite as often to be noted as present in the more subordinate filling in or background of the scene. Now, in approaching the task of re-arrangement or transcription, the arranger

must take care to present all the leading or front melodic figures if possible, even if at times the exigencies of the key-board instrument compel the alteration or reduction of some of the idioms into some one compass or other which will bring the conjointly moving chief figures within the player's manual grip. Or at other times it may be found necessary to give up some such melodic figures as stand out clearly in the orchestra, but which on the key-board cannot be well brought within the mechanism of the instrument, or expressed without too much interference with the prominence of the absolutely chief present figure of melody. Then the transcriber must secure the presence of enough of the background and filling in harmonies as will support the leading objects on the musical canvas, so to speak. And, lastly, he must take care to represent the subordinate activity, which, running in an undercurrent, is nevertheless an essential feature of the musical scheme, as forming a musical atmosphere, in which the chief figures live, and which lends to the general effect the particular sense of pace and time proportion, without which the piece has but little definite meaning or purpose.

E. H. TURPIN.

NEW ENGLISH OPERA MUSIC.

A NEW comic opera entitled "Cymbia, or the Magic Thimble," will shortly be produced at the Strand Theatre. The libretto of the work has been written by Mr. H. PAULTON, and the music is composed by FLORIAN PASCAL. So far as one can judge from an examination of the words and music, the opera contains the necessary elements of success. It is bright, tuneful, and, while presenting many examples of the strong rhythmic features which seem generally to underlie what is accepted as "popular music," it is at the same time devoid of that taint of vulgarity that is so offensive to the cultured musical ear. The scoring is clear and the orchestral colouring ingeniously contrived; the interest of the work is maintained up to its close, the third act—usually the weakest in comic opera—being probably the best.

There are not wanting signs for those who can read them, that English musical art in all its phases is gradually throwing off the foreign leading strings which have done so much to hamper and indeed well nigh obliterate, native talent. Besides orchestral works by some of our modern English composers that are finding acceptance abroad, Mr. VILLIERS STANFORD'S opera, "The Veiled Prophet," has recently been produced at Hanover, where it seems to have met with distinct success. Native composers are evidently beginning to assert their individuality, and all who are interested in the now perceptible renaissance of English musical art must rejoice at the indications of the growing, vigorous life which it is exhibiting. Opera, both in its serious and comic forms, has for many years past been freely, indeed, almost entirely, supplied by foreign writers. If only our English composers, with eyes observant of the advance of art, will show that they can supply works alike free from French inanities and German dulness, but possessing tune, together with the higher attributes of musicianly treatment and dramatic fitness, they will certainly find audiences ready both to appreciate and support their efforts.

As there are already two operas, one by Mr. MAC-KENZIE and the other by Mr. THOMAS, announced for immediate production, "Cymbia," will make the third new work from English pens to be given in London during the forthcoming season. The freshness and originality of FLORIAN PASCAL's songs and pianoforte works have already attracted considerable attention ; one can but wish that his essay in the new field of operatic music may display equal ability, and meet with public approval.

♪oreign Musical Intelligence.

MUSIC IN PARIS.

(From our Own Correspondent.)

JAN. 31, 1883.

This would not be an ill-chosen moment for casting a backward glance at the doings of the musical season, now more than half way on the road to its close. For M. Pasdeloup has come to the end of two of his three series of concerts already. Easter will soon be upon us, and then—farewell to classical music again for another six months or so.

All things considered, the season has not been a very remarkable one. The directors of all the concert enterprises have relied almost wholly upon the attraction of old established favourites like the Beethoven symphonies, the "Damnation of Faust," and the like. MM. Hille-macher's "Loreley," M. Duvernoy's "Sardanapale," and M. Godard's "Dramatic Overture" have indeed been almost the only important novelties we have heard. The preludes to "Parsifal" and "Tristan and Isolde" have been the chief Wagnerian features in the programmes. Félicien David's "Désert" has been given with great success at the Châtelet, and Liszt's "Faust" music with less success at the Cirque ; while M. Lamoureux has given us an opportunity, too rare, unhappily, of hearing a few fragments of that "Armide" which, in the days when he was only a candidate for the managership of the opera, M. Vaucorbeil was always promising to revive for our delectation. And this is almost all in the concert programmes which needs recalling except the magnificent execution of the Choral Symphony, under M. Lamoureux's direction, and the appearance of Mdme. Essipoff, who played Chopin's Concerto in E minor at the Théâtre du Chateau d'Eau last Sunday, and was received with heartier demonstrations of enthusiasm than, perhaps, Rubinstein himself has ever been greeted with here. And well the gifted artist deserved the applause she got. She has the four great qualities all pianists should have to be perfect. Oddly enough they all begin with a p—power, poetry, piquancy, and precision.

I append the full programme given at the Chateau d'Eau on the occasion :—

"Michael Angelo" (Concert Overture)..........	Niels Gade.
"Choral Symphony" (600 executants)............	Beethoven.
Soli by Mdlles. Anne Soubre and Rocher, MM. Bosquin and Augues.	
Concerto in E minor, for piano .... Mdme. Essipoff.	Chopin.
Prelude to "Tristan and Iseult"...................	Wagner.
Overture to "Athalie"	Mendelssohn.
Conductor . . : M. LAMOUREUX.	

M. Pasdeloup's programme—a remarkably full one—comprised the "Pastoral" Symphony, an air from M. Saint-Saëns' Cantata "La Lyre et la Harpe" (which, by-the-bye, was performed not long ago at the Conservatoire), and a Larghetto of Mozart's, and the whole of the opening act of "Lohengrin," with soli by MM. Bolly (Lohengrin), Lauwers (Frederick), Claverie (the king), Mdme. Caron (Elsa), and Mdlle. Barre (Ortrud).

I have said nothing so far, I believe, of the opening of the new Eden Theatre, which has been one of the theatrical events of the month in Paris. Music plays a great part in the programmes of the management, and a band which would do no discredit to the Opéra or to any of the

concert halls has been gathered together under the able direction of the two conductors, Signor Pantaleoni, who conducts the execution of the ballet music to "Excelsior," and M. Félix Pardon, the conductor of the occasional and bal masqué music. Signor Pantaleoni is better known in Italy than in Paris. He conducts somewhat à la Verdi, but with less spirit. M. Félix Pardon was for some time director of the band at the Brussels Eden, and is well known as the composer of several operettas, and other works.

MM. Pantaleoni and Pardon have, roughly, seventy instruments in their orchestra, amongst them fifteen first violins, ten second violins, eight altos, six or eight 'celle, eight contrabasses, four cornets-à-piston, two bassoons, two clarinets, two oboes, two flutes, a nouvelle basse, saxhorn contrebasse, etc.

A capital band of Tziganes also plays at irregular intervals in the promenade upstairs, and altogether the musical arrangements of the Eden are as satisfactory as the most critical could desire them to be.

C. HARRY MELTZER.

"La Befana" is the name of a new fantastic operetta by Signor Canti, of Rome.

At Namur a new Quartet Society has been founded. Concerts will be given in March and April.

News from Madrid tells of the great success of Ambroise Thomas's "Hamlet," with the new Ophelia, Bianca Donadio.

The Allgemeine Deutsche Musik-Zeitung notes with admiration the custom common both in England and America of using analytical programmes at classical concerts.

M. Michaelis, the Parisian music publisher, is still adding to the "Chefs d'Œuvre de l'Opera Francais," the last contribution being "Ernelinde, Princesse de Norvège," words by Poinsinet, music by Philidor.

After spending some days at Venice with his son-in-law, Richard Wagner, the Abbé Liszt has arrived in Pesth, where he will remain until the spring. According to custom, he will make Weimar his summer residence.

The Theatre Royal de la Monnaie, Brussels, has lately been concerned with the production of the "Nibelungen," which met with more than ordinary success. A Wagner concert was afterwards given in Brussels by the members of Herr Angelo Neumann's company.

The indefatigable composer Suppé has written a new operetta, "Le Voyage en Afrique," to a libretto by MM. West and Genée. The first performance will take place towards the end of this month or the beginning of next at the "Ander Wien" Theatre, Vienna.

Herr Albert Cohn, of Berlin, announces the publication of a "Biography of the Musical Composers up to the year 1700, which are preserved in the Town Library, the Library of the Academic Institute for Church Music, the Royal and University Libraries of Breslau. A contribution to the History of Music in the XV., XVI., and XVII. centuries, by Emil Bohn. Price 14 marks."

TOTTENHAM.—On Wednesday, January 31, a successful concert was given by the Tottenham Wesleyan Musical Society, the conductor of which is Mr. R. J. Pitt, who is to be congratulated on raising the choir to such proficiency. Only two seasons back this society was performing but simple part-songs and glees, but, owing to the untiring efforts of Mr. R. J. Pitt, the society was able to bring forward at this concert Spohr's "Last Judgment," and in such a way that we may say with safety that no local choral society could possibly have performed it better. The choruses were rendered very carefully. All members of the choir appeared to take an individual interest in the work before them, and this is the surest and only way of working successfully. The principal soloists were Miss Jessie Royd, Mr. George F. Grover, Mr. Hanson, and Alfred Moore. There was also a most efficient band of Academy students and others. Mr. John Jefferys presided at the organ, and Mr. George F. Grover at the piano. The second part of the programme was of a miscellaneous character, the chief feature in which was a violin solo, Andante and Allegro (concerto), by Mendelssohn, performed by Mr. Arthur Payne, R.A.M.

Organ News.

PRESTON.

Subjoined are the programmes of organ recitals given in the new Public Hall, by Mr. James Tomlinson, on Saturday, Feb. 3rd :—

AFTERNOON PROGRAMME.

Overture (" Semele ")	Handel.
Andante (Sonata in E minor)	Weber.
Gigue	Bach.
Marche Solennelle	Gounod.
" On every tree " (" Ungeduld "), Barcarolle	Schubert.
Overture in C	Mendelssohn.

EVENING PROGRAMME.

Offertoire in G	Wély.
Adagio (Fourth Symphony)	Beethoven.
Solemn March in A minor	Best.
Overture (" La Dame Blanche ")	Boieldieu.
Largo (" Serse ")	Handel.
Overture (" Guy Mannering ")	Bishop.

MANCHESTER.

Mr. J. Kendrick Pyne gave an organ recital in the Town Hall, on Saturday, Jan. 27th. Subjoined is the programme :—

Funeral March (Pianoforte Sonata, Op. 35)	Chopin.
Romance in B minor, for pianoforte	Henselt.
Concerto in F major	Handel.
Pastoral (" Fatto per la Notte di Natale ")	Corelli.
Air varied in A major (Symphony in D)	Haydn.
Marche Militaire, for brass orchestra	Gounod.

And on Saturday, Feb. 3rd :—

Overture (" Otho ")	Handel.
Romance, for bassoon and piano	Spohr.
Sonata in C minor	Merkel.
Adagio Cantabile (" Sonata Pathetique ")	Beethoven.
Nocturne (" Magnus Dominus ")	Carmusel.
Hero's March, for pianoforte (Op. 92)	Mendelssohn.

BOLTON.

An organ recital was given in the Albert Hall, by Mr. Wm. Mullineux, F.C.O., on Saturday, Feb. 3rd. The following was the programme :—

Concerto in G, No. 3	Handel.
" Chant du Paysan "	Rendano.
Introduction, variations, and Fugue (" Jerusalem the Golden ")	Dearnaley.
Sonata in F minor, No. 1	Mendelssohn.
Meditation	Gottschalk.
" March of the Israelites "	Costa.

NORWICH.

Annexed is the programme of an organ recital given in St. Andrew's Hall, by Dr. Bunnett, F.C.O., on Saturday, Feb. 3rd :—

Overture (" Occasional ")	Handel.
Andante in E	Smart.
Overture (" Midsummer Night's Dream "), Adagio in A flat (from a Quartet), Sonata in B flat, No. 4, Andante in C	Mendelssohn.
" Chapel by the Sea "	Barnett.
Andante (" Reformation " Symphony); Duet, " Lieder ohne worte "; Nocturne (" Midsummer Night's Dream "; Adagio (" Hymn of Praise ")	Mendelssohn.

Feb. 3rd being the anniversary of Mendelssohn's birth, selections chiefly from his works were performed.

EDINBURGH.

Mr. William Blakeley, A.C.O., gave an organ recital in the United Presbyterian Church, Morningside, on Thursday, Jan. 18th. Subjoined is the programme :—

Overture (" Occasional ")	Handel.
Air with variations (Sept)	Beethoven.
Prelude and Fugue in D major	Bach.
Sonata in A major, No. 3	Mendelssohn.
Cantilène Pastorale	Guilmant.
March in C minor	Spindler.

BRISTOL.

Annexed is the programme of the organ recital given by Mr. George Riseley in the Colston Hall on Saturday, Feb. 3rd :—

Overture (" Julius Cæsar ")	Handel.
Adagio (Violin Concerto, Op. 47)	Spohr.
Prelude and Fugue in A minor	Bach.
Largo	Handel.
Bourrée in B minor, Gavotte in E	Bach.
" La Carita "	Rossini.
" Les Huguenots "	Meyerbeer.

HINDLEY, NEAR WIGAN.

Subjoined is the programme of the sixth organ recital given in St. Peter's Church, by Mr. Chas. D. Mortimer, on Sunday, Feb. 4th :—

" Ave Maria "	Schubert.
Offertoire in D, No. 5	Batiste.
Adagio (Quartet in G minor)	Spohr.
" Zadock the Priest," " And all the people rejoiced " (" God save the King," Coronation anthem)	Handel.
March in E flat, Vol. 2	Salomé.

HOCKERILL.

An organ recital was given in All Saints' Church, on Tuesday, Jan. 30th, by Mr. Phillip Sharpe. The programme included :—

Offertoire in G	Wély.
Andante in A	Smart.
Prelude and Fugue in D	A. W. Bach.
Andante in G	Batiste.
Pastorale (First Sonata)	Guilmant.
Andante Piacevole	Hopkins.
March (" Eli ")	Costa.

HALSTEAD, ESSEX.

The following is the programme of an organ recital given in Holy Trinity Church by Mr. George Leake, A.C.O., on Sunday, Jan. 28th :—

Sonata No. 4	Mendelssohn.
" Cujus Animam "	Rossini.
" The horse and his rider " (" Israel in Egypt ")	Handel.
Barcarolle (Fourth Concerto)	Bennett.
Fugue in G minor	Bach.
Grand Chœur (à la Handel)	Guilmant.

HULL

An organ recital was given in Holy Trinity Church, by Mr. T. Craddock, Mus.Bac., Oxon., on Monday, Jan. 29, when the programme comprised :—

Choral Song and Fugue	Wesley.
Meditation on Bach's First Prelude	Gounod.
Marche Funèbre	Chopin.
Præludium and Fuga in E minor	Bach.
Rhapsodie (" Cantique Breton ")	Saint-Saëns.
Sonata in D, No. 5	Mendelssohn.
" Carillons de Dunkerque "	Cæter.
Allegro Cantabile in F minor	Widor.
Overture in E	Morandi.

CRICKHOWEL.

On the occasion of opening the new organ in the church of St. Edmund the Martyr, on Wednesday, Jan. 31st, Mr. T. Davies, A.Mus., T.C.L., gave a recital. The following was the programme :—

Sonata No. 1	Mendelssohn.
Andante in G	Batiste.
Coronation anthem, " God save the King "	Handel.
Offertoire in G	Wély.
Fugue in D minor	Bach.
" Hallelujah " chorus	Handel.

The church was crowded with an attentive congregation. A local paper says —" The Crickhowel people are to be congratulated on possessing the finest organ in Breconshire, and an organist worthy of the instrument."

DEWSBURY.

The following is the programme of an organ recital given by Mr. S. W. Pilling, in the Centenary Chapel, on Friday, Jan. 26th :—

Overture in C minor	Merkel.
Andante con moto	Archer.
Præludium and Fuga in C	Bach.
Pastorale, Caprice in B flat	Guilmant.
Fanfare	Lemmens.
March (with Hymn of Priests)	Chauvet.
Minuetto and Trio	Bennett.
Introduction, Air, and variations	Wrigley.
Elevation and Finale	Saint-Saëns.

WATERLOO ROAD.

Subjoined is the programme of an organ recital given on Thursday, Feb. 6th, at the church of St. John the Evangelist, by Mr. J. Tunstall :—

Overture (" Occasional ")	Handel.
Andante in F	Smart.
Fantasia on a Russian Church Melody	Freyer.
Andante, Op. 25	Guilmant.
March	Schumann.
Prière in E major	Lemmens.
Andante in F major	Wély.
Allegretto (from an Overture)	Handel.
Andantino	Chauvet.
Finale in D major	Lemmens.

UPPER BARNSBURY STREET.

Appended is the programme of an organ recital (No. 9 of the series) given on Tuesday, Jan. 30th, by Mr. Edwin Evans, F.C.O., at Rozel House :—

Prelude and Fugue in E flat, "St. Ann's"	Bach.
Concertstück	Spark.
Andante in A	Smart.
Sonata No. 6	Mendelssohn.
Barcarolle (Fourth Concerto)	Bennett.
Concert Fantasia "March of the Men of Harlech"	Best.

PORTSMOUTH.

An organ recital was given in St. Mark's Church, by Mr. A. Blissett, on Monday, Jan. 29th, when the programme included :—

Russian National Anthem, with variations	Freyer.
Offertoire in A	Wély.
Barcarolle in F	Bennett.
Christmas Offertoire	Lemmens.
Air in E, with variations	Handel.
Fugue in D major	Bach.

EDINBURGH.

The specification of an organ in St. Thomas's Church, Edinburgh, erected by Messrs. Brindley & Foster, of Sheffield, is herewith given in a corrected form :—

GREAT ORGAN.   CC TO G.

1.	Open Diapason	8 ft.	5.	Harmonic Flute ...	4 ft.
2.	Höhl Flote	8 „	6.	Dulcet Twelfth	3 „
3.	Viola	8 „	7.	Harmonic Piccolo...	2 „
4.	Principal	4 „	8.	Trumpet	8 „

SWELL ORGAN.   CC TO G.

9.	Lieblich Bourdon...	16 ft.	13.	Salicet	4 ft.
10.	Violin Diapason	8 „	14.	Mixture (3 ranks)	
11.	Vox Angelica	8 „	15.	Oboe	8 „
12.	Stopped Diapason	8 „	16.	Cornopean	8 „

CHOIR ORGAN.   CC TO G.

17.	Dulciana	8 ft.	19.	Lieblich Flute	4 ft.
18.	Lieblich Gedact	8 „	20.	Clarionet	8 „

PEDAL ORGAN.   CCC TO F.

21.	Open Diapason	16 ft.	23.	Bass Flute	8 ft.
22.	Bourdon	16 „			

COUPLERS.

24. Swell to Great.	27. Swell to Choir.
25. Swell to Pedal.	28. Choir to Pedal.
26. Great to Pedal.	29. Great Sub Octave.

Three Composition pedals to Great organ.
Two   „   „ to Swell organ.

BOW AND BROMLEY INSTITUTE.

Mr. W. T. Best's recital of Saturday drew a large and admiring audience. The first piece was a Festival Prelude by G. A. Thomas on "Ein Feste Burg." This, in the hands of Mr. Best, proved to be very fine and effective. A Christmas Pastorale, by Moriconi, proved to be ear-tickling enough to win an encore. The composer is now organist at St. Peter's, Rome. The piece is neither particularly interesting, original, or valuable ; and had it been written by a native of any portion of the United Kingdom, would not have secured the smallest consideration from the Liverpool organist. Handel's cheery, fine Water Music met with great applause. Rossini's "William Tell" overture was finely played, and only escaped an encore probably owing to the lateness of the hour. Liszt's Marche Hongroise, "Racokzy," made a capital finale to an interesting recital. Miss Marian Burton was the vocalist, and was encored in Sullivan's "The Lost Chord." Mr. W. G. Wood accompanied. Mr. Best will again be the solo organist this evening.

COLLEGE OF ORGANISTS.

On Tuesday last Mr. E. Prout, B.A., gave a lecture of very remarkable interest on the "Combination of the Orchestra and Organ, especially in Church Music," at the Holborn Town Hall. The subject is one of large and growing importance ; for in these days of large musical effects and combinations, the two musical giants are being brought more and more into mutual relationship, and the Church is once more welcoming back to her aid the orchestra, after much misapprehension and foolish neglect, almost amounting at one period to banishment. An exceptionally large audience of members and friends of the College of Organists awaited with serious attention Mr. Prout's thoughtful words and weighty opinions. The lecture opened with an extensive and singularly per-

spicuous historical survey of the scores of the great masters in which the organ is employed, from Bach to Mendelssohn. The use of the organ by Haydn and Mozart was a very interesting branch of Mr. Prout's paper. This valuable historical survey was followed by some very artistic and judicious hints as to the use of the organ by the organist as well as by the composer. Dr. J. F. Bridge occupied, in an able manner, the position of chairman. Mr. James Higgs and Dr. Gladstone also addressed the meeting.

The next lectures of the College of Organists will be a course of four by Prof. G. A. Macfarren, on Bach's "24 Preludes and Fugues," a work of later date than the immortal "48." Mr. Windyer Clarke will play the pianoforte illustrations. The course will be delivered on four successive Tuesdays, beginning with February 20th, at the Holborn Town Hall.

EASTBOURNE.

At the St. Saviour's recent Parochial Festival the Rev. Sir F. A. Gore Ouseley, Bart., Mus. Doc., gave a short lecture on "The main principles of musical services in the Church of England."

The lecturer said he had thought it would be well to divide the subject into two parts—first of all to say a few words on the rise and progress historically of English Church music from the time of the Reformation ; and secondly to offer a few remarks on what were the special characteristics of the true choral services. He thought on both points there might be some who would not be sorry to have a few facts laid before them with which they were probably unacquainted at present. At the time of the Reformation—the schools of France and Germany, having for centuries been the central and rallying point of music —great changes were caused by more than one circumstance. In the first place there was the translation from Latin into English, and there followed an important change in the general style of church music. One of the great features of the Reformation was that the great rage for metrical Psalm singing sprang up, causing more elaborate choral services to be kept up in the cathedrals. Then originated the English National School of Church Music, which he had always said there was every reason to be proud of. He thought so as an Englishman, and having heard the best music of the Roman Catholics abroad—in Rome, Germany and France—he said deliberately that on the whole the English School of Church Music was by far the best for the services of the sanctuary. He was not alone in that opinion. He remembered being in Rome in 1851, and meeting a Roman priest doing duty under a cardinal, who had one of the largest libraries of music in the city, and the priest told him that he had no hesitation in saying that in some respects the English Church music was superior to that in the Vatican Library. And to whom did they owe this ! The first composer of choral services was Marbeck, and when they met with persons not well informed upon this matter, who told them his works were a relic of Popery or something of that sort, they should be prepared to refute the assertion, because it was a stern fact that Marbeck very nearly suffered death for his strong Reformation principles. He then went on to notice Tallis, Bird, Bence, Batten, Morley, Gibbons and other composers of choral services of the fifteenth century, remarking that Gibbons's music was the most pure counterpoint ever produced and would compare favourably with the Italian writers, and they were indebted to him as the great standard. The madrigals died out with Gibbons, but exercised a great influence on church music. Troublous times then came on, and during the time of Oliver Cromwell nothing but metrical Psalms were used, and the English school was not revived until Charles II. came to the throne, when the organs were restored and the choirs re-endowed. The first distinguished composers of the choral church music of that day were Hopkins, Turner, Blow, Rogers and Crichton, who was more of the old school. There was at that time a great demand for new music, and the two greatest writers were Blow and Purcell, the last-named being the greatest genius of his time, from 1658 to 1695, and composed a prodigious quantity of music. Then there were Weldon, Clark and Croft, but none of these came on the same level as Purcell, who would have produced a school of his own, except for the advent of Handel, who was taken up and almost worshipped by all lovers of music, and who checked the indigenous choral style. He did not know whether the influence of Handel on English church music was on the whole good. Then followed Sir John Travers, Lord Chandos and Lord Mornington, who had the choral services kept up, but it was still experimental and was only kept up in the colleges and cathedrals. Battishill Dr. Crotch, Charles and Samuel Wesley, Sir John Goss and the junior Dr. Wesley were then instanced as composers of church music, and there were a great many other talented men who contributed to the repertoire of church music. They had reason to think in the present day that a great time was coming for English church music. Passing to the second part of his subject, the

Doctor remarked that one great characteristic in church music should be variety. The different parts of the services required different treatment. If the whole of the service was treated in the same way it became tedious, and people were unable to keep up their attention. In many small parish churches they must be satisfied without much variety, but at St. Saviour's they could do anything, and he congratulated them upon having such an organ and choir. The first part of the service he would notice was the reading, which was the music of eloquence. There was the monotone in which the prayers were read. Then the inflections of plain song and the Psalm chants, which should be without hurry, and in regular and strict time, and with the accents and pointing so as not to destroy the grammar. He thought they best all that at St. Saviour's. He then noticed the Canticles, which were not quite an anthem—the words should not be repeated too frequently. Last of all they came to the great development of anthems, which they had come to look upon as a sort of choir voluntary—which the congregation did not take part in, but listened to. The object of anthems was to dispose the mind to devotion and to relieve from fatigue, and had become an important factor in church services. Then there were the metrical Psalms and hymn tunes, which were not a part of cathedral music, which he might term hymnody, if he might use such a word. He should like to hear more of the congregations join in it as much as they could. He had not made up his mind whether it was best to have all the hymns sung in harmony, or whether it would not be better to have some of them in unison. The great point which the congregations ought to bear in mind was that the hymns were what they ought to sing lustily and with a good courage. The advantages of variety were many. If they had all the services in a monotone, could they stand it? Or if they had all anthems could they keep up their attention? That would be simply a concert in church. He concluded by remarking that he had been rather longer than he anticipated, but it was a difficult matter to condense so many different matters into one short speech.

Dr. Sangster (organist at St. Saviour's) next gave a brief address relative to the new organ. In the course of his remarks he said :—In addressing you about the organ at St. Saviour's I feel that we have arrived at that point when the organ may be said to speak for itself, which it does in tones of a most religious and noble quality. I reasoned thus in preparing the specification : St. Saviour's is an important church in an important town on the South coast—a church remarkable for its architectural beauties and for the crowds of worshippers that assemble there—therefore the organ should be no ordinary instrument, but one of the best we could get, and in this I consider we have succeeded. It has tones diverse, refined and grand, and some of the highest authorities pronounce it to be one of the finest organs ever turned out by the eminent firm of Walker and Sons. There is an idea abroad that it is too large for the church. I have heard this said of many good church organs. You cannot get all these varieties of tone without building a large instrument. After the admirable recital given this afternoon upon the organ by Sir Frederick Ouseley, I am more than ever convinced that we have done a good thing in adding such a splendid piece of art-work to St. Saviour's.

PROFESSIONAL MUSICIANS AND MUSICAL DIRECTORIES.

At a meeting of the Society of Professional Musicians, held in the Old Town Hall, Manchester, on Saturday evening, Dr. R. W. Crowe, of Liverpool, presiding, a paper was read by Mr. James J. Monk, of Liverpool, on "The Compilation of Musical Directories."

Mr. Monk complained of the erratic manner in which musical directories are compiled, remarking that the absence of a trustworthy directory of the profession seemed to be explained by the fact that there was no system of registration for teachers of music. At present it was quite competent for amateurs or "semi-professionals" to have their names inserted in a directory called "musical," thereby putting themselves on a par as musicians with men who had made music their life-study and the sole means of their existence. By this means "semi-professionals," as they styled themselves, were enabled to get trade and professional quotations, to the injury of the teacher of the art and the dealer in music and musical instruments; and also, by the same false representative publicity, to secure engagements as professional singers or players, thereby earning fees which rightly belonged to professional musicians. One great reason why the musical directories were so untrustworthy was the present lack of any central source of authoritative information ; but surely this might be overcome by appointing in each town a musician of good standing, whose trustworthiness and impartiality could be thoroughly relied upon for local compilation. This system appeared to be feasible until such a time as a local registry should be formulated under the proposed Registration Act.—In the discussion which ensued on the paper, Dr. Hiles said that

as a society they ought to decline to subscribe to any directory published on the present system.—Mr. Edward Hilton and the chairman said that the real cure for the evil complained of could only come with a system of legal registration.—Mr. Monk said that that society might do something in the way of bringing out a trustworthy directory.—Mr. W. D. Hall (Liverpool) said there could be no doubt of the need of a trustworthy directory. It was a work which, in his opinion, could only be satisfactorily done through a society like that, with the co-operation of professional musicians throughout the country.—The secretary said that in the present state of affairs it would be better to try to purge the existing directories than to initiate a new work. In the absence of a system of registration, they would find themselves in a difficulty as to knowing who were really professional men and who were not. If a Registration Bill was passed, the society could start a directory if no one else would do it.—Mr. Monk said that it would not be of the slightest avail to try to influence the present publishers.—The Chairman said he could not see that there would be any great difficulty in getting the names of men who actually made their livelihood by teaching music. That would be enough for the purposes of a directory.—Dr. Marsden and Mr. John Wrigley also took part in the discussion. It was ultimately unanimously resolved, on the motion of Mr. Hall, seconded by Mr. W. J. Young, "That the members of this society, being aware of the defects of existing musical directories, desire the council to take into consideration the feasibility of compiling a musical directory to be issued under this society's auspices, soliciting for that purpose, in the first instance, the co-operation of well-known musicians throughout the country."

The Liverpool Evening Express has a leader on Mr. Monk's paper, endorsing his views on the subject matter of his lecture :—

'From the paper on "Musical Directories" which Mr. James J. Monk read at Manchester on Saturday before the associated musicians, it is evident that he is very much in earnest in his protest against amateurs being described as "professors of music." No doubt those who devote themselves to music and depend upon it for a livelihood have some ground for feeling aggrieved at the position assumed by persons who only use music to fill up their leisure, or to eke out incomes derived from other sources. But it is easier to acknowledge the evil of the present system than to discover a remedy. Mr. Monk suggests that the musical directories should be made directories of *bond fide* professionals whose income is derived solely from the practice of the art, and to secure the exclusion of the non-professional or semi-professional musician he would submit all names to local censors. It is obvious if this were done the names excluded would exceed those entered, and would tend largely to diminish the sale and circulation of the books, which are points of consideration to the publishers, even if the professional musicians think them beneath notice. Mr. Monk's only hope will lie in the power of the new association to bring out a directory of their own. Do they feel strong enough for this enterprise ?

The Liverpool Courier remarks, in the course of a leading article :—

The fact that a person is "only an amateur" does not prove incompetence for the position assumed. Even if a standard registry is obtained it will be difficult to exclude many amateurs, though the list might with advantage be freed from names which are obviously out of place there.

Anecdote of Rossini.—The first time the *Barbiere di Seviglia* was produced (at the Theatre Argentino in Rome) a singular combination of comic circumstances, which in Naples would be considered as the result of the evil eye, "jettatura," aided in causing a fiasco. The theatre was unusually full of priests, and a great prejudice existed against the bold young composer who had dared to set to new music the opera of "Paisiello." To add to this prejudice, Rossini unfortunately wore a greenish-coloured coat, which excited a storm of laughter as soon as he appeared in the orchestra. No sooner did Almaviva (played by Garcia) commence the serenade beneath Rosina's window than all the cords of his guitar snapped with a loud twang, calling forth another burst of ominous laughter. The same thing happened to Figaro's mandolin as soon as the jolly barber attempted to touch a string. Then appeared Don Basilio, who, under the influence of the fatal "jettatura," stumbled and fell, knocking his nose against the side scene, so that on rising his white bands were stained with blood. In his pain and confusion he wiped his nose on the hem of his soutane, and now whistles, calls, and shouts of laughter drowned the voices of the singers and the din of the orchestra, and poor Rossini, covered with shame, fled to hide in his own house. It is well known that the second representation of the opera was a triumph. Rossini was in bed, and was aroused by loud acclamations below his window. He was forced to rise, dress in haste, and descend into the street, and was accompanied by a festive supper by crowds of enthusiastic people carrying torches.

Passing Events.

Mr. Geaussent's Choir gave a concert at St. James's Hall on February 6th. The programme included Mendelssohn's psalm, "Sing to the Lord."

Berlioz's "Harold in Italy," and Bach's Double Concerto in C, for two pianos, formed portions of one of Mr. C. Hallé's recent Manchester concerts.

A new opera, entitled "Mam'zelle Nitouche," by Hervé, was produced at the Théâtre des Variétés, Paris, on the 26th of January. The work is described as being completely successful.

The *Brightonian* of February 3rd contains a cartoon portrait of Mr. J. Sawyer, Mus.Bac., F.C.O., as a well recognised local member of the profession, writer on theoretical and antiquarian musical topics, and organist at one of the leading Brighton churches.

Handel's "Samson" was well performed on January 31st at Canterbury by the local Philharmonic Society, under the excellent direction of Dr. Longhurst. The chief singers were the Misses Ellen Horne and Winthrop, Messrs. A. Kenningham and R. Rhodes.

Two lectures, given under the auspices of the Philological Society on the 2nd and 16th, are of interest to the musician. The first was on the "History of English Sounds," by Mr. Henry Sweet, M.A., and the second, by the same gentleman, "On the Intonation of spoken English."

The Toronto Philharmonic Society will, under the direction of Mr. F. H. Torrington, perform Gounod's "Redemption" this season. The same work was recently given in Boston, U.S., but, in consequence of legal difficulties, with the accompaniments on pianofortes and American organ.

The Crystal Palace Company have decided to manage the details of the approaching Handel Festival themselves. Many of the leading artists will be the same as before, no doubt, including M. Sainton as leading first violin, and Sir M. Costa as conductor. The band will consist of 425 players, and the chorus will be composed of both town and country singers.

The public trial of a new chemical fire-engine on the Thames Embankment on February 7th was a matter of interest to owners and managers of concert-rooms, musical instrument manufactories, etc. A feature of the invention is the use of chemicalised water charged with carbonic acid gas, a sure antidote to fire. The utility and economy of the invention are undeniable.

The Academical Board of Trinity College, London, has awarded the gold medal annually offered for an essay on a musical subject to Miss Melloney Stephens, of St. Leonard's-on-Sea, for her essay on "The Value to the Musician of a Knowledge of Modern Languages"; and the prize of two guineas to Miss H. L. Elmes, of Addlestone, for her essay on "Early Writers for the Pianoforte."

It will be noticed that Dr. C. J. Frost will give a recital on the very fine and interesting organ at Christ Church, Newgate Street, on February 12th. This is the first recital in the church most probably which has been given since Mendelssohn played there. It is to be hoped that Dr. C. J. Frost will meet with such encouragement as will lead to his continuing to give similar performances. The possession by Christ Church of such an organ, and the presence of so accomplished an organist, fully justify this hope.

On February 1st a most interesting lecture was given at the London Institution on "The Anthem," by the Rev. W. Sparrow Simpson, D.D., F.S.A., sub-dean, succentor, and librarian of St. Paul's Cathedral. The illustrations were sung by Messrs. S. Barry, T. W. Hanson, H. J. Dutton, E. Dalsell, E. Wharton, Charles Tinney, and some of the chorister boys of St. Paul's Cathedral. Mr. G. C. Martin, Mus.Bac., sub-organist of St. Paul's, played the accompaniments on the pianoforte. The anthems sung included specimens by John Redford (organist of St. Paul's Cathedral between 1530 and 1540), Farrant, A. Gibbons, H. Purcell, Haydn, Thomas Attwood (organist of St. Paul's Cathedral), Mendelssohn, S. S. Wesley, C. Gounod, J. Barnby, and J. Stainer.

The St. George's Glee Union held their 169th monthly concert at the Pimlico Rooms on the 2nd inst. The programme was a miscellaneous one, vocal solos being contributed by Miss N. Watts and Miss Matbilde Prague, Mr. H. Schartan, and Mr. R. F. Roberts. Herr von Joel and Mr. George J. Sumpter played selections for the pianoforte. Owing to the bad weather there were only about fifty members in the choir, but the part-songs were unusually well sung. They included "The dawn of day" (Reay), "Come, live with me" (S. Bennett), "My bonnie lass, she smileth" (Morley), etc. Mr. Joseph Monday conducted.

A Correspondent writes :—"The advantage of committing the musical department of a leading London paper to a foreigner is amusingly exemplified by a statement made in a brief obituary of the late Flotow, in which the writer inferred that the opera composer had himself written the air known as the "Last Rose of Summer," and that its popularity in England dated only from the success of the opera "Martha," in which it appeared. The same writer, in treating of the piracy of Americans who steal our musical works, and then serve them afresh for their orchestra, remarks :—"Even experienced artists can never fully realize the living power of a great musical creation from the dead symbols inserted in the staff of five lines." This must surely raise a smile even from the tyro of score reading. As well might one say that we can only fully understand books by hearing them read, and denounce the dead letters which form but the symbols of silent words.

Service Lists.

FIRST SUNDAY IN LENT,
FEBRUARY 11th.

London.

WESTMINSTER ABBEY.—Morn.: Service, Benedicite, Turle in A; Jubilate and Communion, Turle in D. Aft.: Service, Turle in D; Anthem, By the waters (Boyce).

TEMPLE CHURCH.—Morn.: Service, Te Deum and Jubilate, Smart in F; Apostles' Creed, Harmonized Monotone; Anthem, O Lord, have mercy (Pergolesi). Even.: Service, Magnificat and Nunc Dimittis, Smart in F; Apostles' Creed, Harmonised Monotone; Anthem, In Thee, O Lord (Weldon).

LINCOLN'S INN HALL.—Morn.: Service, Steggall in G; Kyrie, Steggall; Anthem, Out of the deep have I called (Hatton). Even.: Service, Steggall in G; Anthem, Bow thine ear, O Lord (Bird).

ALL SAINTS, MARGARET STREET.—Morn.: Service, Benedicite, Irons; Benedictus, Stainer; Communion Service, Barnby in E; Offertory Anthem, Turn Thy face from my sins (Attwood). Even.: Service, Orlando di Lasso in C; Anthem, By Babylon's wave (Gounod); Miserere, Allegri.

ST. AUGUSTINE AND ST. FAITH, WATLING STREET.—Morn.: Service, Benedictus, Hopkins in F; Communion Service, Smart in G; Offertory, Lord for Thy tender mercies' sake (Farrant). Even.: Service, Barnby in E; Anthem, Lead, kindly light (Stainer).

ST. BARNABAS, MARYLEBONE.—Morn.: Service, Te Deum and Jubilate, Boyce in C; Anthem, Turn Thy face (Attwood); Kyrie and Nicene Creed, Cooke in G. Even.: Service, Magnificat and Nunc Dimittis, Walmisley in D minor; Anthem, O Saviour of the world (Goss).

CHILDREN'S HOME CHAPEL, BONNER ROAD, E.—Morn.: Service, Anthems, Holy, Holy (Vogler), and, Lo I my shepherd (Haydn). Aft.: Service, Anthems, Evening prayer ("Eli," Costa), and, My God, look upon me (Reynolds).

CHRIST CHURCH, CLAPHAM.—Morn.: Service, Benedicite, Stainer; Kyrie and Credo, Dykes in F; Offertory Anthem, Turn Thy face from my sins (Attwood); Sanctus, Dykes; Benedictus and Agnus Dei, Monk in C; Gloria in excelsis, Dykes. Even.: Service, Magnificat and Nunc Dimittis, Hoyte in B flat; Anthem, As the hart pants (Mendelssohn); Miserere, Helmore.

FOUNDLING CHAPEL. — Morn.: Service, Sullivan in D; Anthems, Ye people rend your hearts, and, Cast thy burden (Mendelssohn). Aft.: Service, King in F; Anthem, Come unto Him (Gounod).

HOLY TRINITY, TULSE HILL. — Morn.: Chant Service. Even.: Service, Garrett in D; Anthem, Ye people, rend your hearts (Mendelssohn).

ST. JAMES'S PRIVATE EPISCOPAL CHAPEL, SOUTHWARK. —Morn.: Service, Introit, O Lamb of God (Weber) ; Communion Service, Mozart (No. 7). Even.: Service, King in F ; Anthem, Lord, Jesus Christ ("Requiem," Cherubini).

ST. MAGNUS, LONDON BRIDGE.—Morn.: Service, Opening Anthem, I will arise (Clarke Whitfield) ; Te Deum and Jubilate, Boyce in A ; Kyrie, Purcell. Even.: Service, Cantate and Deus Misereatur, Hayes in E flat ; Anthem, By the waters of Babylon (Boyce).

ST. MARY BOLTONS, WEST BROMPTON, S.W.—Morn.: Service, Benedicite, Best ; Benedictus, Chants ; Communion Service, Kyrie, Creed, Sanctus, and Gloria in excelsis, Thorne in G ; Offertory, Barnby ; Benedictus and Agnus Dei, Monk. Even.: Service, Magnificat and Nunc Dimittis, Stainer's Third Series of Tones ; Anthem, Come unto Him (Gounod).

ST. MICHAEL'S, CORNHILL. — Morn.: Service, Te Deum and Benedictus, Thorne in C ; Anthem, Turn Thy face (Attwood) ; Kyrie and Creed, Marbecke. Even.: Service, Magnificat and Nunc Dimittis, Walmisley in D minor ; Anthem, By the waters of Babylon (Boyce).

ST. PAUL'S, BOW COMMON, E. — Morn.: Service, Benedicite, Best ; Benedictus, Dykes. Even.: Service, Magnificat and Nunc Dimittis, Garrett in F ; Anthem (unaccompanied), Judge me, O God (Mendelssohn).

Country.

ST. ASAPH CATHEDRAL —Morn.: Service, Rogers in D ; Anthem, Ye people, rend your hearts (Mendelssohn). Even.: Service, Rogers in D ; Anthem, All ye who weep (Gounod).

ASHBURNE CHURCH, DERBYSHIRE. — Morn.: Service, Benedicite, Best ; Continuation, Dykes in F. Even.: Service, Goss in E ; Anthem, Come and let us return (Goss).

BEDDINGTON CHURCH, SURREY.—Morn.: Service, Benedicite and Benedictus, Dykes ; Introit, Weary of earth (Hymn 252) ; Communion Service, Marbecke. Even.: Service, King in F ; Anthem, Jesu, Word of God Incarnate (Gounod).

BIRMINGHAM (ST. CYPRIAN'S, HAY MILLS).—Morn.: Service, Benedicite, Simms ; Benedictus, Field in D ; Anthem, Put me not to rebuke (Greene). Even.: Service, Kent in C ; Anthem, Hear my prayer (Kent).

CANTERBURY CATHEDRAL. — Morn.: Service, Richardson in F ; Anthem, O taste and see (Rogers) ; Communion Service, Richardson in F. Even.: Service, Richardson in F ; Anthem, Thou, O God, art praised in Zion (Greene).

CARLISLE CATHEDRAL. — Morn.: Service, Sullivan in D ; Introit, Remember, Lord (Verrinder) ; Kyrie and Nicene Creed, Turle in D. Even.: Service, Selby in A ; Anthem, Hear my crying (Hummel).

CHARDSTOCK COLLEGE. — Even.: Service, Tours in F ; Anthem, Come and let us return (Goss).

DONCASTER (PARISH CHURCH).—Morn.: Service, Wesley in F. Even.: Service, Stainer in B flat ; Anthem, Come and let us return (Goss).

DUBLIN, ST. PATRICK'S (NATIONAL) CATHEDRAL—Morn.: Service, Te Deum and Jubilate, Boyce in A ; Anthem, The heavens declare (Boyce). Even.: Service, Magnificat and Nunc Dimittis, Smith in B flat ; Anthems, All we like sheep (Handel). and, Give the king thy judgments (Boyce).

DURHAM CATHEDRAL.—Morn.: Service, Hopkins in B flat ; Anthem, Lord, before Thy footstool bending (Spohr) ; Introit, O taste and see (Rogers) ; Communion Service, Armes in B flat. Even.: Service, Hopkins in B flat ; Anthem, I will cry unto God (Mozart).

ELY CATHEDRAL. — Morn.: Service, Benedicite, Chants ; Benedictus, Plain-song ; Kyrie and Creed, Steggall in G ; Gloria, "Ely ;" Anthem, O Saviour of the world (Goss). Even.: Service, Steggall in G ; Anthem, Come and let us return (Goss).

EXETER CATHEDRAL.—Morn.: Service, Rogers in F ; Communion Service, Rogers in F. Even.: Service, Ouseley in B minor ; Anthem, O Lord, rebuke me not (Haydn).

FOLKESTONE (ST. MICHAEL'S).—Morn.: Service, Benedicite, Husband in F ; Benedictus, Chant (Turle) ; Communion Service, Introit, For our offences, Jesus (Mendelssohn) ; Kyrie, Credo, Sanctus, &c., Bordese in C. Even.: Service, Magnificat and Nunc Dimittis, Nares in F ; Anthem, All ye who weep (Faure).

GLASGOW (BLYTHSWOOD PARISH CHURCH).—Aft.: Service, Anthem, Thou knowest, Lord (Purcell).

LEEDS PARISH CHURCH. — Morn.: Service, Turle and Stainer ; Anthem, Come unto Him (Gounod) ; Kyrie and Creed, Smart in F. Even.: Service, Walmisley in D minor ; Anthem, Behold the Lamb (Handel).

LICHFIELD CATHEDRAL.—Morn.: Service, Benedicite, Martin in F ; Jubilate, Smart in F ; Anthem, In Thee, O Lord (Weldon). Aft.: Service, Goss in E ; Anthem, These are they (Dykes).

LIVERPOOL CATHEDRAL. — Aft.: Service, Walmisley in D minor ; Anthem, Come and let us return (Goss).

MANCHESTER CATHEDRAL. — Morn.: Service, Gibbons in F ; Anthem, Come unto Him (Gounod). Aft.: Service, Gibbons in F ; Anthem, Withdraw not Thou Thy mercy (Attwood).

MANCHESTER (ST. BENEDICT'S). - Morn.: Service, Kyrie, and Credo, Nares in F ; Sanctus, Benedictus, and Agnus Dei, Palestrina (Æterna Christi Munera). Even.: Service, Magnificat and Nunc Dimittis, Jordan.

MANCHESTER (ST. JOHN BAPTIST, HULME).—Morn.: Service, Kyrie, Glover ; Credo and Sanctus, Garrett in D ; Benedictus and Agnus Dei, De la Hache. Even.: Service, Magnificat and Nunc Dimittis, Gregorian ; Miserere, Redhead.

MUSSELBURGH (LORETTO SCHOOL). — Morn.: Introit, Lord, for Thy tender mercies' sake (Farrant) ; Service, Stainer in E flat ; Anthems, I know that my Redeemer liveth, and, Since by man ("Messiah," Handel). Even.: Service, Anthem, Blessed be the God and Father (Wesley).

PETERBOROUGH CATHEDRAL. — Morn.: Service, Gibbons in F ; Introit, Turn ye to me (Jackson) ; Communion Service, Barnby (Monotone) and Stainer in A. Even.: Service, Keeton in B flat (Chant Service) ; Anthem, Out of the deep (Gounod).

RIPON CATHEDRAL. — Morn.: Service, Chants ; Anthem, Unto Thee (Elvey). Even.: Sevice, Parry in D ; Anthem, As pants the hart (Spohr).

ROCHESTER CATHEDRAL.—Morn.: Service, Aldrich in G ; Anthem, Lord, for Thy tender (Farrant). Even.: Service, Aldrich in G ; Anthem, Here by Babylon's wave (Gounod).

SHEFFIELD PARISH CHURCH. — Even.: Service, Cantate and Deus Misereatur, Chants ; Anthem, Turn Thy face from my sins (Attwood).

SOUTHAMPTON (ST. MARY'S CHURCH).—Morn.: Service, Benedicite, Best in C ; Benedictus, Turle ; Communion Service, Introit, O Saviour of the world (Macfarren) ; Service, Woodward in E flat ; Offertory, He that soweth (Barnby) ; Paternoster, Helmore. Even.: Service, Stainer's Parisian Tones ; Apostles' Creed, Harmonized Monotone.

SOUTHWELL COLLEGIATE CHURCH, NOTTS.—Morn.: Service, Barnby in E ; Anthem, Far from my heavenly home (A. Page) ; Kyrie, Marriott in F ; Creed, Hopkins in G. Even.: Service, Barnby in E ; Anthem, Come, and let us return (Goss).

WELLS CATHEDRAL.—Morn.: Service, Benedicite, Pascoe ; Benedictus, Steggall in G ; Introit, Blessed are they (Macfarren) ; Kyrie, King in A. Even.: Service, Bennett in G ; Anthem, Hear my crying (Turle).

WORCESTER CATHEDRAL.—Morn.: Service, Lloyd in E flat ; Anthem, Wash me thoroughly (Wesley). Even.: Service, Lloyd in E flat ; Anthem, Call to remembrance (Battishill).

APPOINTMENT.

MASTER J. F. BREWER has been appointed Organist of the Catholic church, Farm Street, Berkeley Square. J. Lemmens and F. Archer were among the former organists of the Farm Street Chapel.

ERRATA.—In issue of Jan. 20th, page 40, list of the successful candidates, Coll. of Organists, line 6 from commencement, for " H. H. Hoyle" read " W. H. Hoyle." In issue of Feb. 3, the second word of title of leader, page 68, for " Friekerr " read " Freiherr ;" lines 22 and 23 of same article, for " Noufrage " read " Naufrage." In last issue, page 74, col. 1, line 10 from top, for " Barziel " read " Bargiel "; line 37, same column, read " Gadsby."

Printed for the Proprietor by BOWDEN, HUDSON & Co., at 23, Red Lion Street, Holborn, London, W.C.; and Published by WILLIAM REEVES, at
the Office, 185, Fleet Street, E.C. West End Agents:—WEEKES & CO., 14, Hanover Street, Regent Street, W. Subscriptions and Advertisements are
received either by the Publisher or West End Agents.—*Communications for the Editor are to be forwarded to his private address, 6, Argyle Square, W.C.*
SATURDAY, FEB. 10, 1883.—*Entered at the General Post Office as a Newspaper.*

The MUSICAL STANDARD

A NEWSPAPER FOR MUSICIANS PROFESSIONAL AND AMATEUR

No. 968. VOL. XXIV. FOURTH SERIES. SATURDAY, FEBRUARY 17, 1883. WEEKLY: PRICE 3D.

TRIADS: THEIR RELATIONSHIP AND TREATMENT.

BY FRANCIS EDWARD GLADSTONE, MUS.DOC.

(Continued from page 80.)

The following extracts from Helmholtz may here be quoted with advantage. He says (p. 326, of Mr. Ellis's translation): "The minor triad is very decidedly less harmonious than the major triad, in consequence of the combinational tones." And again (p. 328) speaking of the combinational tones, he says, "the foreign element thus introduced into the minor chord is not sufficiently distinct to destroy the harmony, but it is enough to give a mysterious, obscure effect to the musical character and meaning of these chords, an effect for which the hearer is unable to account, because the weak combinational tones on which it depends are concealed by other louder tones, and are audible only to a practised ear " (*i.e., separately* audible.)

But, in connection with this fact, another one of equal, if not greater, importance must be mentioned, viz., that whereas the inversions of a major triad retain their character as part of a major chord, the 1st inversion of a minor triad does not possess quite the same serious or gloomy character as that which marked the chord in its original position.

This is because, in the first place, the interval of a minor 3rd is less consonant than its inversion, a major 6th (and the only intervals present in the inverted chord are the major 3rd, the major 6th, and the perfect fourth); and in the second place the combinational tones resulting from this inverted chord are the double octave below the lowest note, the 12th below the middle note, and the 5th below the lowest :—.

Ex. 40.

It thus happens that, whereas in the original position of the minor triad, the note C, as the lowest combinational tone, makes its influence felt, in the 1st inversion the lowest resultant sound is G, and there is therefore a strengthening of the existing bass, rather than the suggestion of another.

No doubt, it is to this indeterminate character of an inverted minor triad that the good effect of a succession of first inversions, up or down the scale, may be traced.

Ex. 41.

If the minor triad on E is succeeded by the major triad on F, both being in their original position,

Ex. 42. A.

the transition is very abrupt, because the former triad suggests a scale with F ♯ in it, while the root of the latter is F ♮. Whereas the 1st inversion of the 1st chord is not sufficiently indicative of any scale to make its progression to the 1st inversion of the 2nd chord in any degree harsh.

Ex. 42. B.

All the notes of the major scale may be taken as the bass of a triad in its first inversion. Even the imperfect triads on the 2nd and 7th degrees lose to some extent their dissonant character when they are inverted.

In dealing with the minor key, however, more care is needful. The 5th of the scale cannot, strictly speaking, be taken as the bass of a 1st inversion, because the interval from the leading note to the 3rd of the scale is a diminished 4th, and therefore is a harsh dissonance. It has, however, been the constant practice of the great composers to write an inverted triad upon the lowered 7th of the scale when the bass descends by the step of a second :—

Ex. 43. A.

and examples are not wanting of the exceptional use also of a chord of the 6th on the 2nd of the scale with a lowered 7th in the highest part, and of a 1st inversion having the 5th of the scale for its bass, again with the 7th lowered. But the examples which I have found invariably occur in a chain of descending 6ths, thus:

Ex. 43. B.

Any student who is desirous to verify this statement will find illustrations in Beethoven's Sonatas, Op. 10, No. 1, and Op. 27, No. 2 (in the first movement of one, and the last of the other), also in the slow movement of Mendelssohn's first organ Sonata, and, if these are not sufficient, in Bach's great Toccata in F.

I had intended to make my remarks more complete by adding a few words in regard to the 2nd inversion of triads, but this paper has already reached so immoderate a length that I refrain. Before concluding, however, I trust you will pardon me if I direct your attention to two chords which were formerly used more frequently than they are at the present time. I allude to a major chord on the 4th and a minor chord on the 2nd degree of the minor scale. These chords both contain the chromatically raised 6th degree of the scale, and they are only used with good effect when the part which contains this note is proceeding by conjunct degrees from the 5th to the leading note of the scale :—

Ex. 44. A.

Ex. 44. B.

Ex. 44. C.

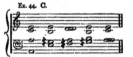

These must be regarded as exceptional progressions, arising from the desire of contrapuntists to avoid, in purely vocal passages, the step of an augmented 2nd, but I venture to think that such chords, when properly introduced, have a really beautiful effect, quaint though it may be ; and I would argue from this that, although in making ordinary combinations of chords the suggestions of Nature will. be our safest guide, Art will sometimes discover other methods. It is possible to copy nature so closely that some element of beauty is hidden. For example, the painter who wishes to pourtray a butterfly in actual flight must give to the wings that filmy appearance which is produced by their rapid movement, but in doing so the exquisite markings on those wings are lost to the eye, and it is therefore a question for consideration whether the representation of a butterfly poised in the air, apparently motionless, might not be truer art, although it would be a less faithful copy of Nature. The illustration is perhaps rather far-fetched, but it may serve to elucidate my meaning.

My main endeavour in following out this enquiry has, however, been to ascertain what musical progressions are the most natural. The subject has expanded to an extent that I never dreamed of when I first took it in hand, and now that I relinquish it I feel that it has been very inadequately treated. Nevertheless, if my observations should suggest to any student of harmony only one idea which may prove useful to him in the pursuit of our art, I shall feel that neither his time nor mine has been wasted.

Musical Intelligence.

CRYSTAL PALACE CONCERTS.

PROGRAMME.

Overture, " Benvenuto Cellini "	Berlioz.
Song, "The Golden Thread "	Gounod.
	Mdme. Patey.
Concerto Symphonique for pianoforte and orchestra	Litolff.
M. Louis Breitner.	
(His first appearance at these Concerts.)	
Song, " Peacefully slumber"	A. Randegger.
	Mdme. Patey.
Gavotte from " Idomeneo "	Mozart.
Pianoforte solos—	
Barcarolle	Rubinstein.
Etude	Chopin.
Impromptu	Chopin.
Marche Turque	Beethoven.
M. Louis Breitner.	
Symphony No 5. in C minor	Beethoven.
Conductor - - - AUGUST MANNS.	

The Crystal Palace concerts were resumed on Saturday last, the audience being a fairly good one, notwithstanding the unfavourable state of the weather. The chief attraction was Beethoven's Symphony No. 5, in C minor, which is so great a favourite that when the last *plébiscite* was taken for the performance of a particular symphony, the C minor was second on the list, the Pastoral coming first by only a few votes. There was no appreciable falling off in the far-famed Crystal Palace orchestra, which is rather surprising, seeing that for the last seven weeks it has been doing duty at the pantomime, playing music-hall songs, and imparting animation to the acro-batic feats of clown and pantaloon. No wonder that we too often hear of the resignation of some of the best performers, whilst they are compelled to undergo this annual infliction. Mr. Manns was warmly received on his re-appearance after an absence of eight weeks in Scotland, and the concert commenced with Berlioz's charming overture, " Benvenuto Cellini."

The only novelty in the programme was No. 5 Concerto, by Litolff, not No. 3, which was described in the book of words. As the name of Litolff is known chiefly as one of the great German publishers, it may be well to state that Mr. Henry Litolff is on his mother's side an Englishman, and was born in London in 1818. He was for three years a pupil of Moscheles, who, encountering the boy when only ten years old, at Collard's pianoforte warehouse, and finding him to be in extreme poverty, with his usual kindness gave him lessons for nothing. He afterwards settled in Germany, and brought out many compositions, especially pianoforte concertos. If we are to judge of his works by the one performed on Saturday last it will be better that we should look upon him as an eminent publisher than a composer, for a more uninteresting thing than this concerto has not been heard for a long time at the Crystal Palace. During the performance a general drowsiness came over the audience ; but as one has heard before now of exemplary people going to sleep in church, a few winks during an. unattractive piece of music may be very excusable.

M. Louis Breitner, who made his first appearance at these concerts, was, no doubt, unfortunate in his choice of this concerto, but, with due allowance for this, his touch was at times hard and unsympathetic. He was, however, more successful in the shorter pieces by Rubinstein, Chopin, and Beethoven.

Mdme. Patey needs no need of praise, as she is generally happy in her choice and successful in her interpretation.   R. S.

Another contributor writes :—

I am not afraid that Dr. Sloman will dissent from my own humble opinion about the " Concerto Symphonique " of Litolff in C minor, No. 5, vexatiously substituted at the very last moment for the *announced* one in E flat. Why remove from the dusty shelf this dreary specimen of *non-*inspiration? The very title sounds conceited, but is justified to a certain extent I for the orchestral score quite overbears the pianoforte, here too often reduced to the lowly condition of an *obbligato* instrument, only allowed to speak at intervals, as it were, on sufferance. Mr. Litolff has extended his heavy work to four movements. I could find but little to admire except in the slow one, a rather sweet cantabile, but too rudely broken by an agitato after the manner, but not the *style*, of Schubert in his 10th Sonata (A major) and the unfinished symphony, No. 8. Both the allegros sound wild, uncouth, unsymmetrical, and boisterous ; the scherzo, a sort of "tarantella," with pointed accentuation, might be thought quaint, but is hardly original. The composer reminds one of the aphorism about good intentions not carried out. Mr. Breitner's unsympathetic touch and rather monotonous style could do nothing to promote the success of the work, received with chilling indifference by a rather thin audience. The pianoforte solos seemed to please the public. The gavotte of Mozart made no impression ; why not have chosen, instead, the pretty little March in F from the same opera ? The symphony, unhappily placed last on the list of numbers, might surely be allowed an interval of repose. This and the " Eroica " (not to speak of the " Pastoral ") are worked to death by our grand orchestras, whilst other works, by various masters, equally fine, are only reproduced after long intervals. I heard Berlioz's fiery overture in Paris, fifteen months ago, at one of Colonne's Sunday afternoon concerts at the Châtelet Theatre, Paris, where it evoked more applause than at the Crystal Palace.   A. M.

The above remarks on Litolff's concerto are partly corroborated by the learned critic of the *Times*, who writes :—

"This concerto is an example of how much can be done in art by one who, although not gifted with supreme *genius*, cultivates with care and zeal such *talents* as nature has granted him. . . . . . The title "Symphonic Concerto," invented by Litolff, is not *altogether* inappropriate. For the pianoforte appears in the light of *an orchestral component* rather than of a *solo instrument*, and the number of movements is four. It is earnest in character and broadly designed, and although the actual power of the composer is not always equal to the high purpose he evidently aims at, his *intention* at least should be acknowledged. . . . . . The chief materials of the first movement have been announced and even partially developed *before the solo instrument is heard.* . . . . . The slow movement is, as far as may be judged by a first hearing, the most successful portion of the work. A *tender* first theme is *interrupted* by a loud flourish of the *brass*. . . . . The 3rd movement, although more *conventional* than its predecessor, is not without the delicate humour beseeming a scherzo. It is bright and joyful, the triangle marking the lively rhythm. The last movement, although the most effective from the *virtuoso's* point, is, perhaps partly for that reason the least interesting as an artistic conception ; its structure is somewhat incoherent. Mr. Breitner's *touch* seemed somewhat loud and wanting in flexibility. . . . ." etc. [The italics are our own].

MONDAY POPULAR CONCERTS.

Another fearful precipitation from the clouds preceded and partly accompanied the concert of Monday night, as a supplement to the flood of Saturday afternoon.

PROGRAMME.

PART I.

Quartet in D minor, Op. 161, for strings	Schubert.
Messrs. H. Holmes, L. Ries, Holländer, and Piatti.	
Air, " Lenio il pie "	Mozart.
Miss Cravino.	
Prelude and Fugue à la Tarantelle, for pianoforte alone	Bach.
Mdlle. Marie Krebs.	

PART II.

Ballade in B flat	A. Holmes.
Scherzo in D, Op. 135, for violin, with pianoforte accompaniment....................	Spohr.
Mr. H. Holmes.	
Song, "Cangiò d' aspetto	Handel.
Miss Cravino.	
Trio in F, Op. 80, for pianoforte, violin, and violoncello........................	Schumann.
Mdlle. Krebs, Mr. H. Holmes, and Signor Piatti.	
Accompanist - - - Mr. Zerbini.	

The performance of this scheme requires but brief notice, as the works are all familiar to the subscribers. Mr. Henry Holmes, a pupil of Spohr, is recognised as a very superior violinist of the *virtuoso* school ; more remarkable for exact execution, "regular" reading, and objective style, than for impulsive feeling, or the passion that proceeds from souls set on fire by their texts. Mr. Holmes led Schubert's quartet with the skill and *savoir faire* of a veteran, and was twice recalled after his solos. The "Ballade" of the late Alfred Holmes, a self-taught musician, is worthy of the artist's elder brother ; this greatly to be respected musician, after doing much good work for his art, died in Paris about seven years ago. Spohr highly esteemed both brothers, and was never slack to express his friendly sentiments towards them. The Scherzo in D major, a graceful trifle, was first introduced by Herr Joachim in 1866.

Mdlle. Krebs won the encore of the evening, after her intelligent reading of Bach's piece, said, by the annotator of the book, to be "one of the most remarkable, individual, and difficult pieces ever composed for a keyed instrument." I hope that the majority of the audience were able to follow this elaborately analytical review of the work ; but I am, perhaps, morbidly sceptical ! Mdme. Goddard—be it never forgotten—first played this fugue at the beginning of 1861. The vocal music calls for no comment ; the artists were recalled, as usual.   A.M.

SATURDAY POPULAR CONCERTS.

PROGRAMME.

Quartet in B flat, Op. 55, No. 3, for two violins, viola, and violoncello	Haydn.
MM. Henry Holmes, L. Ries, Holländer, and Piatti.	
Song, "The Valley "	Gounod.
Mr. Santley.	
Sonata in D minor, Op. 31, No. 2, for pianoforte alone	Beethoven.
Mdme. Frickenhaus.	
Allemande, Largo, and Allegro, for violoncello, with pianoforte accompaniment	Veracini.
Signor Piatti.	
Songs—	
"An die Leyer "	Schubert.
"Widmung"	Schumann.
Mr. Santley.	
Trio in E flat, Op. 70, No. 2, for pianoforte, violin, and violoncello	Beethoven.
Mdme. Frickenhaus, Mr. Henry Holmes, and Signor Piatti.	
Accompanist - - - Mr. Zerbini.	

It was a strange chance that placed the two "Erdödy" trios on the programme of successive Saturdays, as they were not the choice of the same pianist or violinist ; but it was a chance not to be quarrelled with, for they rank among the most genial and individual, though not among the grandest, of Beethoven's works.

No disrespect to Haydn is intended, but it was decidedly disappointing to find that one of his quartets had been substituted at the eleventh hour for the promised movements by Schubert. Mr. Henry Holmes is an effective leader, and the rendering of both quartet and trio was satisfactory, though Mdme. Frickenhaus might have made more of her part in the latter work. Her reading of the sonata, too, was tame and uninteresting ; but the piece she selected as an "encore" went far more spiritedly : it was the novelette from Schumann's Op. 99—not one of the grander set of eight, which is Op. 21, dedicated to Henselt.

The honour of encores was fairly distributed. Signor Piatti gave with much taste and feeling a transcription of Schubert's "Litany," and Mr. Santley repeated Schumann's "Widmung," at the request of a portion of the audience. This insatiableness sometimes overreaches itself. It did in this instance, for Mr. Santley had thrown his whole soul into his delivery of this passionate inspiration, and what could follow but an anti-climax, though Mr. Santley is a genuine artist of the highest rank ? Byron has said "I cannot get people to understand . . . that there is no such thing as a life of passion any more than there is a continuous earthquake or an eternal fire" ; and Byron was right, though he might not have been able to make a popular concert audience "understand" it.   B. F. WYATT-SMITH.

BIRMINGHAM.

(From our Own Correspondent.)

The programme of the fourth concert of Mr. Stratton's chamber series, given on the 29th ult. in the Masonic Hall, was most interesting and well-devised. As customary at these concerts, a work novel to Birmingham audiences was brought forward, the selection on the occasion being an early work by the now famous Norwegian composer, J. Svendsen. The programme in its entirety was as follows :—

Sonata in A minor, Op. 19, for pianoforte and violin	Rubinstein.
Variations Serieuses, for pianoforte	Mendelssohn.
Octet in A major, for strings	Svendsen.
Ballade in G minor, for pianoforte ,..............	Chopin.
Quintet in G minor, Op. 17, for strings	Onslow

The Rubinstein sonata is fully characteristic of its author, but altogether is hardly so perfect a work of its class as others by the same hand. The two opening movements seem the most successful, the impassioned character of the allegro, with its by-themes of tender, yearning melody marking unmistakably the individuality of the composer. The subject upon which the adagio is based, however, seems a trifle commonplace, as far as this quality can well be attached to Rubinstein's work ; and the ornamental embroidery of the *piano* passages, if sparkling, is not of the most original style. The concluding movement is of most intense and vigorous expression throughout, and the closing passages are highly effective. The work was very finely rendered by Dr. Heap and Mr. Ward, the style of the latter being eminently suited to work of this kind. Dr. Heap's performance of Mendelssohn's superb variations was most masterly, though the pianist at the opening seemed to run risk of endangering his climax by hastening the tempo, and playing with a little too much fire. The interest of this work should be gradually intensified. I liked Dr. Heap better in the second of his solo performances. It was played with the same mastery over the extreme and peculiar technical difficulties of the piece, and in the same refined and truly Chopinesque spirit, which characterised his rendering of the same work on a previous occasion. The opening movement of the octet of Svendsen presents for its first subject a suave, flowing theme, and the movement throughout is distinguished by a flow of pure cantible strain. The structure of the work is very clear, and there is no such eccentricity remarkable in the themes themselves, or their treatment, as in the case of the composer Grieg, with whom it is, perhaps, natural that Svendsen should be brought up in comparison. The Scandinavian element pervades the work, but there is little decidedly *outré* about the composition—no barbaric rhythms or tedious confinement to a range of minor keys. It is the spirit of the Northern *volksliedei* and *tänse* that one remarks in the work rather than the actual adoption, as with Grieg, of such subjects in their entirety. These remarks of course apply to the whole of the movements. The scherzo opens with a weird theme of somewhat melo-dramatic character, fantastically instrumented, capriciously changing its sentiment in the alternating trios. The melody of the andante is like that of the opening movement, clear, lyrical, and flowing. A noticeable feature is its beautiful calando passages at the close. The charm of the entire composition, in short, centres in this simple lyrical force of expression rather than in any elaboration of structure or development. What may be lacking in this latter way is more than atoned for by the beauty and originality of what may be termed its essentially vocal character. As·regards the workmanship of the piece, the composer either presents his strains in a broad flowing style by the whole force of strings, or the melody is delivered by a portion of the strings with simple accompaniment of the remainder, in which the pizzicato is noticeably a favourite feature. I did not detect much novelty in the way of harmonisation; but the figuration of the different instruments is originally and cleverly treated. The finale is based upon a subject of extreme joviality—one can imagine a rustic merry-making *à la Teniers*. A remarkable point is a vigorously-worked crescendo passage at the coda. The work was listened to with extreme interest, and the applause justly accorded the performers at the close was in proportion. The mosaic-like musical structure of the composer Onslow —peculiarly a favourite of players themselves—agreeably concluded the concert.

At the next concert Miss Constance Bache (sister of Mr. Walter Bache) will appear as pianist. A M.S. composition of the lamented F. E. Bache will be introduced, and a novelty (for Birmingham, at least) in the sonata for pianoforte and violin of Grieg (op. 8). Schubert's String Quintet (Op. 163) will also be performed.

The third concert of Messrs. Harrison's series was given in the Town Hall on the 5th inst. Engaging only artists *de premier ordre*, the directors enjoy a support which seems not to be shaken by the fault-finding of critics. There is, undoubtedly, a requirement·always existing for musical entertainments of a lighter, more *recherché* kind than that afforded by "educational" concerts, to employ a doubtful term lately devised; and where the artistry is of the superior quality as that exhibited at these concerts under notice, the success which for so many past has rewarded the enterprise of Messrs. Harrison cannot be regarded as unmerited. It would be unfair, though, to infer that the policy of the Messrs. Harrison is based altogether on the star-system; till very recently it was only on the occasions when Mr. Charles Hallé appeared at these concerts with his orchestral company that we had an opportunity of hearing a symphony or any other important class·of orchestral composition produced in a respectable manner. This period I am reviewing, if not quite antecedent to the formation of Mr. Stockley's society, was before this worthy townsman had succeeded in gaining that support which now so justly favours him. So, taking these concerts all round, there is something more to be noted than mere ballad-singing by heavily-paid vocalists, or instrumental performances which are simple displays of virtuosity. Messrs. Harrison appeal to all tastes; and, in so doing, they succeed in filling the Town Hall, which is certainly better than to present ambitious programmes, with scratch performers to execute them, and so get only an array of empty benches in the place of listeners In this so-called "educational" movement it is to be feared that we sometimes overshoot the mark, and press amateur audiences with advanced work before the popular taste has been rightly formed to appreciate it; the consequence being that we make musical hypocrites instead of musical connoisseurs. It is with the growth of popular taste as, according to Goethe's saying, it is with that of trees— Providence having well seen to it that their tops do not quite shoot themselves up into the high heavens. These remarks are made in view of the frequent disparaging criticism of these concerts—as to their programmes not invariably presenting a sufficient amount of "classic" work—most often by those who themselves have no critical appreciation of classical music when they do hear it —having some stereotyped "text-book" acquaintance with names of composers and compositions, and, on the strength of this, assume a taste they do not possess.

On the present occasion the artists engaged were Mesdames Marie Roze, Trebelli, de Fonblanque, Messrs. F. Boyle and Ghilberti (vocalists); Mdme. Sophie Menter appearing as solo pianist, and Mons. Musin as solo violinist. Marie Roze was, of course, the bright particular star of the evening. After the remarks already

made it will be understood that a very detailed account of the pieces produced is hardly necessitated, the *how* being the attractive thing rather than the *what*. Mdme. Roze sang, "Tacea la notte," from "Il Trovatore," and "Lovers' vows" from Benedict's festival cantata "Graziella." The singer's splendid powers (though hardly showing at their best on the concert platform) were fully exhibited in these selections. Mdme. Trebelli revived successfully the *aria* from "l'Italiana in Algieri" "Pensa alla patron" (sung in her usual impressive style), the "Brindisi" from "Lucretia Borgia," and with M. Musin's violin obbligato Gounod's "Quand tu chantes." Miss de Fonblanque pleased greatly by her expressive rendering of Cowen's "I think of all thou art to me," and Dr. Arne's charming "Cuckoo song"; she also took part with Mdme. Trebelli and the two gentlemen vocalists in a very welcome extract from Méhul's little heard-of opera "L'Emporté," "Oh! ciel, que faire"; and, again, with the Messrs. Ghilberti and Boyle in Bishop's light, pleasing trio "Maiden fair." Mr. Ghilberti possesses a very fine bass voice, and he was very effective in his selections. Pinsuti's "Minute gun," and Mr. F. L. Moir's "Gold," a song evidently intended for the popular taste, and recalling a song from Gounod's "Le Médecin malgré lui," known in England as "O wander through the world so wide." Mr. Frank Boyle has a very agreeable light tenor voice, and a most pleasing distinctness of enunciation. He sang C. Dick's "Voice of her I love," but was most praiseworthy in his most sympathetic rendering of the old Irish song "Snowy-breasted pearl." I should advise him to cultivate as a "specialty" this class of song. Mons. Musin obtained his usual hearty reception, playing with even more than his usual beautiful freedom and graceful transcendency over technical difficulties His pieces were Leonard's "Souvenir de Baden-Baden," Paganini's "Monochord" fantasy on the prayer from "Mosé in Egitto," besides joining Mr. Ganz in the adagio and rondo from Dussek's pianoforte and violin sonato (Op. 69, No. 1). There only remains to mention the incomparable playing of Mdme. Sophie Menter in the pieces chosen on this occasion. An etude of Chopin, a "lied ohne worte" of Mendelssohn (that known as "La Fileuse," or more popularly as "The Bee's Wedding"), and the more astounding than charming virtuosi transcript of Liszt's "Les Patineurs" (based on themes from the skating scene in "Le Prophète.") It is needless to comment upon the superb delivery of these items of the programme. Messrs. Harrison announce an engagement entered into with Mdme. Menter for a recital in Birmingham on the 22nd of this month; at the same time the announcement of their last concert of the series, March 8th, when Mr. Hallé and his band will form the prime attraction; Miss Orridge and Mr. Santley vocalists.

The Festival Choral Society gave recently another performance of Berlioz's "Faust," with Mr. Lloyd and Miss Davis principal vocalists (as on the former occa-sion, when I noticed the performance at length).

At the last concert of the Musical Section of the Midland Institute the instrumental portion of the programme was "educationally" representative of the composer John Sebastian Bach.   Br.

ROYAL ALBERT HALL CHORAL SOCIETY.

On Ash Wednesday evening Mr. Brnaby, conductor of this society, gave a performance of "The Messiah" at the at the Albert Hall, which was fully attended. The principal vocalists were Mdme. Lemmens-Sherrington, Mdme. Patey, Mr. Maas, and W. J· Williams (*vice* Mr. King). The chorus in G, "Unto us a child is born" induced the customary encore. Dr. Stainer was at the organ.

With the approval of Sir Frederick A. Gore Ouseley, Bart., and of Professor G. A. Macfarren, Mr. Ridley Prentice is preparing a work which aims at imparting to pianoforte students a knowledge of musical form. It is entitled "The Musician, a Guide for Pianoforte Students: Helps towards the better understanding and enjoyment of beautiful music"; and its plan is that combining the study of musical form with the ordinary pianoforte practice. The first grade, now on the eve of publication by Messrs. Swan, Sonnenschein and Co., accompanies the student through a course of study calculated to last from one to two years, the work analysed being extremely easy, and suited for beginners. Five other grades are to follow, of which the second, now complete in MS., is in the printer's hands.

HIGH WYCOMBE.

On Monday evening, the 5th inst., the Choral Association gave their second subscription concert of the season, in the Town Hall, before a numerous assembly. The following formed the programme :—

"The Daughter of Jairus "	Dr. Stainer.
Part-song, "Come, live with me "	Bennett.
Song, "The Children's Home "	Cowen.
Pianoforte solo, Polonaise in C sharp minor	Chopin.
Serenade, "Wake, in all thy beauty "	Cowen.
Part-song, "Night "	Blumenthal.
Song, "The Worker "	Gounod.
Pianoforte Solos—	
Impromptu No. 2, Op. 142	Schubert.
Grand Étude, "La Fontaine "	Mayer.
Glee, "Thy voice, O Harmony "	Webbe.

The chief interest was centered in Dr. Stainer's cantata, which was now performed in its entirety for the first time in Wycombe ; portions, however, have been frequently sung in our parish church. The work made a most favourable impression, several numbers being most warmly applauded. I think there is very little doubt that in time it will become a stock-piece with country societies, and it is to be hoped that the talented Doctor will give us another work of such unvarying excellency. The execution was excellent, the chorus quite maintaining their reputation, nor were the soloists—all members of the society—less unsuccessful. The unaccompanied part-singing in the second part was very good and much appreciated ; several of the vocal solos were encored, and a like compliment was paid to the conductor, Mr. J. G. Wrigley, Mus.Bac., Oxon, for his performance of Schubert's "Impromptu," and Mayer's "Étude."

LEEDS.—The annual masonic concert took place in the Albert Hall last week. The principal vocalists were Miss Annie Street (soprano), Miss Amelia Clarke (contralto), and Mr. G. H. Welch, of Durham Cathedral (tenor). The programme was an excellent one, and a glee party sang a number of glees and part-songs in capital style. Mr. W. B. Townsend was accompanist.

MEDICAL UNION SOCIETY.—At the *conversazione* recently held, an excellent selection of vocal music was given under the direction of Signor D'Havet Zuccardi ; and some capital instrumental pieces were played by the West London Orchestral Society, under the conductorship of Mr. W. R. Cave, including Haydn's 2nd Symphony in D, and an artistic performance by Mr. Viotti Collins of Vieuxtemps's "Reverie " for violin.—*The Medical News.*

PEMBERTON, NEAR WIGAN.—Mr. James Gaskell, organist of the parish church, gave his annual concert on Monday the 6th February in the Mechanic's Institution when Gaul's sacred cantata "The Holy City" and a miscellaneous selection were performed. Miss Bessie Holt, R.A.M., and Mr. Fred. Gordon were the principal vocalists, and there was an orchestra and chorus of 70 performers, Mr. Gaskell conducting. There was a crowded audience and the performance was in every way successful.

SWANSEA GLEE AND MADRIGAL SOCIETY.—This society held its first invitation concert under the conductorship of Mr. J. Matthews, organist of St. James's Church, on the 6th, in the Albert Minor Hall, which was well filled with a select and appreciative audience. Gade's "Spring's Message" was one of the chief features of the evening, the Swansea Orchestral Society rendering good service in the picturesque score of this charming little work. Solos, including the conductor's "Song of the Streamlet," were sustained by ladies and gentlemen of the class, and the part-songs, more especially Leslie's "Lullaby of Life," and Macfarren's "Sands of Dee" appeared to give much satisfaction. Desorme's pizzicato piece, "Serenade des Mandolines," was also received with much favour.

S. PETER'S, EATON SQUARE.—A well-chosen selection from Mendelssohn's "S. Paul" was given in this church at even-song, on the 25th ult. The ordinary choir (50 in number) was supplemented by a few additional voices. The performance from first to last left nothing to be desired. The solos alloted to the boys were marked by feeling, and in some instances showed a dramatic perception scarcely to be looked for; those taken by the men received full justice, and the choruses were always crisp and brilliant, not a point being missed. The service was Barnby in E flat, and went so admirably as to suggest the wish that the distinguished composer, formerly choirmaster of S. Peter's, could have been present. Why, by the way, in the Nunc Dimittis, is the verse "To be a light" separated from its legitimate context by the interpolated repetition, "Lord, now lettest thou thy servant depart in peace," to the damage of the sense? It would be unpardonable to pass over unnoticed Mr. Sergison's judicious and masterly accompaniments, and his fine rendering, with much orchestral colouring, of the difficult overture to the oratorio.

OLDHAM.—The Carl Rosa Opera Company have visited the Theatre Royal, and given "Fidelio," "Maritana," "Bohemian Girl," "Faust," "Mignon," &c., the principals being Mdme. M. Roze, Messrs. Davies, McGuckin, Snazelle, &c. The chorus and band have worked well, and the operas have been well put on the stage. Mr. Houghton's recitals still continue, Mr. J. Greaves playing with success several of his own MS. works. He has been assisted by Mr. Smith Warburton, a baritone vocalist possessing a rare organ, who was excellent in Watson's "Powder Monkey." Mr. Tom Upton is a good tenor, and Master D. M. Greaves plays some good violin solos in capital style.

HONITON.—On the evening of Feb. 1st, the committee of the Honiton Cricket Club gave an excellent and high-class concert at the Dolphin Assembly Rooms. The weather was rough, but nevertheless a large audience assembled. The chief feature of the evening was the singing of Mdlle. Roselli ; her voice is of extensive compass and remarkably flexible. In each of her songs she was much admired, as was also Mrs. McLees, who, with the aid of her accomplished daughter, Miss McLees, as pianist and accompanist, ensured the success of the evening. Messrs. Stilliard, Tozer, Hawker, and Dison (from the Exeter Cathedral choir) sang some part-songs, which were greatly enjoyed by the audience.

SOUTH LONDON MUSICAL CLUB.—The annual dinner of this club, whose *locale* is the Angell Town Institution, Brixton, took place at the Holborn Restaurant on Saturday evening last, with H. Gadsby, Esq., in the chair. About 120 members and their friends sat down to a most excellent *déjeuner*, to which full justice was done. After dinner the usual loyal toast of " The Queen" having been given, the chairman gave that of the club, associating with it the names of Mr. Charles Stevens, the conductor, and Mr. E. G. Richardson, the hon. secretary. This was received with enthusiasm and was responded to at some length by the two gentlemen whose names were associated with the toast. Mr. Davies, F.R.A.S., then proposed in a somewhat racy and telling speech the chairman and the visitors, and these were in due course responded to by Mr. Gadsby, and Dr. Frost respectively. During the course of the evening a selection of glees and part-songs, embracing Lachner's "Battle Song," Coward's "Peaceful, slumb'ring," Mellon's "Crowned with clusters"; Horsley's "Nymphs of the forest ; Storch's "Drowsy woods"; Macfarren's "King Canute " ; and Otto's "Chinese March " were sung by the active members of the society, and solos were also well given by three members, Mr. C. Pompe, Mr. E. G. Richardson and Mr. Cranch.

DUNDEE.—On Jan. 29th a meeting was held in the Hall of the Dundee Young Men's Christian Association to present Mr. Henry Nagel with a cheque for £1000, a valuable gold watch, and a handsome silver jug, on the occasion of his retirement from the leadership of the Dundee Amateur Choral Union, a position he has held for twenty-five years. There was a large attendance of ladies and gentlemen. Provost Moncur presided, and among those on the platform were—Colonel Walker, Mr. J. J. Weinberg, Mr. V. Fraenkl, Mr. James Brebner, Mr. George S. Lamb, and Mr. R. A. Miller, Mr. Henry Durlac, Mr. Montague Cannon, Dr. Greig, Mr. William Kerr, Mr A. O. Parker, Mr. James Johnston, etc. The number of contributors to this well-deserved testimonial numbered no less than 306, and the total sum subscribed came to £1,116 3s. 6d. After defraying the cost of the above valuable articles, it is the intention of the committee to invest the remaining £30 in some remembrance for Mrs. Nagel. The names of the subscribers, alphabetically arranged, are to be written on vellum, with the following inscription, which appears also on the watch and jug :—"Presented to Mr. Henry Nagel, with a gold watch, silver jug, and one thousand pounds, by the following subscribers, as a recognition of his long and arduous services to the cause of music in Dundee, and more particularly of his valuable work as conductor of the Dundee Amateur Choral Union, which position he filled gratuitously for the long period of twenty-five years. Dundee, 29th January, 1883."

While learned societies are exerting themselves to procure a version of our National Anthem suited to the people of India, a native poet and composer in Calcutta, Mr. Bowmanjee Cursetjee Bandoopwalla, has come forward with an entirely new patriotic and loyal song, consisting of five stanzas set to original music. They commence with the following curious lines—

India's land and India's shore
Had some latent in store ;
Now the happy event to aggrandize
When all our hopes be realized
Has at length arrived.
God bless the Empress !

In referring to this well-meant effort of loyalty, the Calcutta *Englishman* observes that while the time is eccentric, according to European notions, the tune is less unintelligible than the words, and in parts sounds very like a plagiarism of one of our most beautiful hymn-tunes,

Foreign Musical Intelligence.

Signor Ponchielli's "I Promessi Sposi" has had a successful hearing in Venice.

The death of Signor G. G. Guidi at Florence is announced. He was much esteemed as an editor and writer on musical topics, and founded the paper *Boccherini*.

Some days since the death was announced of Signor Tamberlik at Cadiz. This report has now been contradicted by the eminent tenor himself, who says that he was never in better health.

The first performance of "Henry VIII." at the Paris Opéra will take place on the 20th or 28th of this month. The following was last week's programme at the Opéra:—"Aida," "Le Prophète," "Guillaume Tell," "Faust," and "Hamlet." At the Opéra Comique these works were given: "Les Noces de Figaro," "Giralda," "Battez Philidor," "Le Chalét," "Les Dragons de Villars," "L'Amour Médecin," "Fra Diavolo," "Le Maçon," "Pré aux Clercs," "Richard," "La Dame Blanche," "La Fille du Régiment." Three morning performances were given at the Opéra Comique, which accounts for the unusual number of works performed.

HAYDN'S "OX MINUET."

Translated from the *Neue Musiker Zeitung* by Miss E. E. SOUTHGATE.

In the year 1787, when Haydn was Music Director to Prince Esterhazy, he was sitting at the piano in his comfortable dwelling engaged in the composition of one of his finest symphonies. Shortly previous to the event narrated, he had received a flattering invitation from Prague, viz.: to compose an opera for the theatre there. Haydn, with much modesty and tact, declined the honour, declaring, in a decided manner, that he did not consider himself important enough to contend for a prize against the great Mozart. Haydn was interrupted in his work by a loud knocking at his door; as the visitor received an invitation to enter, there appeared in the room a broad-shouldered stout man, in the dress of a well-to-do Hungarian farmer. He greeted Haydn politely, and strengthened his greeting by so forcible a shake of the hand, that the grip gave some pain to the soft palm of the genial Kapellmeister. "Beg pardon, your honour, if I disturb," said the new-comer, "but I want to ask you to grant me a favour. Your honour composes such splendid music that it sounds quite different to the fiddling and scraping of our gipsy musicians: as for example, 'The Seven Last Words,' which I heard last Sunday in our church (for I am always the first at church when the oratorio, or any little song from your beautiful Masses is given.)" The frank bearing of the man touched Haydn; he invited him to take a seat, and state his request. "Because your honour is kind hearted," said the man, "I hope that you would willingly write a little bit of music for me." The Kapellmeister could not forbear smiling. It is true he had received many important commissions for works for churches and concert-rooms, but as yet no one had spoken to him from so homely a side. However, he was far from being offended; on the contrary, he was rather pleased about it. "Now let us hear," said Haydn kindly, "for what purpose you want your music—something for your church, or for a funeral?" "Oh, bother your funeral! Your honour, I want the little piece for a much gayer occasion. The fact is, my daughter —I have only this one—is shortly to be married to Herr Fichtelhaimer, who is a merchant in Oldenburg, and is a very respectable person. As you have composed so many pretty things, which sound so merry that one's heart always laughs for pleasure, I should like therefore for this wedding a good humorous minuet—I mean just such a one as will make the feet dance the same as after hearing the pipe of the Rat-catcher of Magdalenengrunde in Könenberg. It is truly glorious, your honour, to hear an oratorio or a Mass with sweet angel voices; but I prefer a pretty minuet, so I beg for that, please." Haydn had a difficulty in hiding his amusement over the naïve comparison of his guest; but he was always willing to oblige, and declared himself ready to accede to the request. "A thousand thanks," said the music-lover, "My name is Zapolya—just the same as the great Zapolya, only his name was Stephen; but my nobility is quite as

good as his, and I deal in oxen and swine, you know. I am a man that has wherewith to live, and that is certainly a good thing." The dealer in cattle promised to call again in a few days, and took his departure.

Haydn wrote the minuet at once in order to be rid of the thing, and put the trifle on one side. After a few days the noble Herr von Zapolya came again. He was delighted with the piece, which Haydn played to him once, and took it away with thanks. The Kapellmeister could hardly refrain from muttering to himself something about cheap gratitude.

About a fortnight passed. Suddenly, one day, Haydn heard music under his window, distinguishing, amidst more false than right notes, the theme of his own minuet. Curious to know what it meant, he went to the window and looked below. He there saw an uncommon sight: an ox decorated with leaves and flowers was led along, accompanied with music, and in the midst of the comical scene was the figure of Zapolya. The cattle dealer advanced towards the house, and soon after appeared in Haydn's room. "God greet your honour," he began, "I dare say that you wondered at the beginning of our acquaintance, and remember that as yet I have only thanked you with words for your beautiful minuet. Now that the wedding festivities of my daughter have passed over joyfully, and the minuet has set the legs of the old as well as the young in quick movement, I cannot fail to repay your kindness with my best ox. When you please to allow, I will lead him into the stall, for he is now your property. So now, God protect your honour's health, and may you enjoy the ox." The donor then disappeared. The ox was conducted to the stall, the melody of Haydn's minuet accompanying him. Haydn sold the animal to the Esterhazy Agency, and in after life rejoiced as much over the singular thanks he had received for the Minuet as over the fame accruing from his master-pieces "The Seasons" and "The Creation." The minuet of the tale has since borne the whimsical title of "Das Ochsen-Minuet."

MUSICAL DIRECTORIES.

By a mistake the passage quoted last week as from the *Liverpool Evening Express* should have been given as from the *Liverpool Courier*. In connection with this subject, the *Express* says:—

Professors of music—and by the term "professor" we do not mean everybody who chooses to dub himself by the name—have long had a special grievance to complain of in the absence of any definite standard of qualification for the exercise of their profession. It may, indeed, almost be said of the musical profession that, like that of ordinary teaching, it is a last refuge of those who have failed at everything else. If this description does not exactly apply, it is at least true that hundreds, nay, thousands, of persons assume the title of "professor" of music whose qualifications, if subjected to any adequate test, would be found utterly incapable of justifying the designation, and by their incapacity an honourable profession is brought into disrepute, the general standard of musical teaching is appreciably lowered, and the pecuniary interests of competent musicians are seriously interfered with. This disorganised state of the musical profession is ministered to, and in some sense fostered by two publications which should exercise their influence in the precisely opposite direction—the musical directories which contain the names not merely of men who have made music the study and pursuit of their lives, but of every butcher and baker and candlestick-maker who, after the regular labours of his day are ended, earns a few shillings by teaching or singing at concerts, or who on Sunday officiates as organist or part leader in some local church or chapel. The directories consequently lose whatever value they might otherwise possess as indices of the recognised members of the musical profession, and become mere registers of "amateur" vanity and incompetence. The cause of this confusion, however, is not far to seek. As the knowledge of music does not, like the practice of medicine or law, involve loss or injury to life or property, its profession has not been hedged round by the Legislature with restrictions that at once ensure the proficiency and define the status of its professors. For some time past there has been a movement in professional circles in favour of legal registration of musical practitioners as a necessary preliminary to undertaking the duties of musical tuition. There are many difficulties in the way of such a reform, not the least of which is the question of exclusion or admission of competent amateurs, who, with a limited amount of tuition, combine other means of earning a livelihood, but many musicians feel, and rightly, that until some such system is compulsorily adopted, the musical profession must continue to suffer both socially and pecuniarily in a way that is in the highest degree detrimental to the progress of musical culture throughout the country.

PRINCIPAL CONTENTS OF THIS NUMBER.

NOTICE TO SUBSCRIBERS. — All Subscriptions due for the current year which have not already been sent in should be forwarded at once.

LONDON: SATURDAY, FEBRUARY 17, 1883.

RICHARD WAGNER.

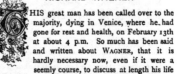

THIS great man has been called over to the majority, dying in Venice, where he had gone for rest and health, on February 13th at about 4 p.m. So much has been said and written about WAGNER, that it is hardly necessary now, even if it were a seemly course, to discuss at length his life work. It cannot be said that the principles he has forcibly and eloquently enunciated have so far produced such a healthy glow of conviction as will, according to present vision, produce a great school; for though his mannerisms have been to a small extent imitated, he has no successors. His death, it may be, will stand out as an extinguishing darkness warning us of the approaching close of the great musical cycle, just as other arts have closed their brilliant periods of productive power, to be followed by a wide-spread and intelligent mediocrity. His neglect, amounting almost to contempt, of the canons of the art, will now tell more against his fame as a genius of much power than it has yet done even in the heat of much prejudiced controversy; for the man of genius must live in the future to no small extent by his power of eloquence through the universally received impressions of order and mental prescience, through which the spirit of beauty is transmitted from one generation to another. The reputation of the man who feels called upon to violate the principles of the language he speaks, usually suffers when his personal influence and the power of his immediate followers are no longer present to ensure the seeming justification of such departures from the use of established idioms. In the end no man is strong enough to stand by his own eloquence, and the power of a great departed genius depends to no small extent upon the strength of solid, good workmanship, and the most precious thoughts are inevitably those which have been most carefully built up. Certainly the future fame of RICHARD WAGNER will have to undergo a sharper test in this direction than has yet fallen upon the work of any other kindred genius. His career offers a splendid and most instructive exemplification of the rich and varied powers possessed, but not always so widely cultivated by men of exceptional intellectual power. WAGNER was a philosopher in his own peculiar way, seeing in the arts a united sisterhood, whose different mediums of expression through the distinct organs of sight and hearing, were to be concentrated upon the setting up of one complete poetical realisation. Though in the burning pursuit of his great conception of the universality and unbroken sympathy of the sister arts, he often neglected to strengthen himself with the requisite technical power, his memory will ever live as that of the first great expositor of the cosmopolitan character of art in its own domains. The large, wide mind of the distinguished poet, composer, literate, and artist in the widest sense of the word, scanned the vast horizon of the art-world with a power of vision exceeding its actual powers of flight; WAGNER, indeed, dreamt of and pointed to greater glories than he even realized. Is there now vitality and originality enough in the world of music to advance upon this wide art-pathway combined with such judgment as will avoid the technical weaknesses and vain ebullition of eccentricity as so often marred the work of the aspiring author of the "Nibelungen Ring"? Naturally so large, reflective, and widely artistic a mind as that of WAGNER was one of slow development, and his works illustrate this growth with clearness. It might furnish matter for curious speculation, to trace out the general concensus of public opinion upon the different operas representing the several periods of his mental development.

WAGNER was born in Leipzig on May 22nd, 1813. From an early age his musical, poetic, and dramatic instincts displayed themselves. He commenced his career practically as the conductor of a small operatic troupe at Magdeburg, and in 1839 he was similarly engaged with another company at Riga. Late in the same year he proceeded to Paris with introductions from MEYERBEER, but Paris was not a rightly chosen home for WAGNER. His genius and courage sustained him now through years of misery and disappointment; whilst he continued to develop his varied mental powers. His real life of prominence began with the success of "Rienzi" in Dresden in 1842, "Der Fliegende Holländer," showing a notable advance in the composer's method, was produced in Dresden in 1843, only to be heard in England in 1870; "Tannhäuser" also came out at Dresden; "Lohengrin," at Weimar, in 1850; "Tristan und Isolde" at Munich in 1865; "Die Meistersinger von Nurnberg" also at Munich in 1868; "Der Ring des Nibelungen" at different dates for its different divisions during 1869 and 1870, the entire work being given at Bayreuth for the first time in 1876; and "Parsifal" at Bayreuth in 1882. In addition to these great operas, he wrote several choral and orchestral works, and a few pianoforte pieces, including one sonata and several songs. His literary labours included a large number of essays bearing upon art-topics. He is destined, however, to be judged and remembered by his remarkable operas, in which he illustrated so unique a union of large and varied powers, and in which, if he did not prove himself the founder of a school, he at least led the way to an operatic reformation, displayed a genius of a high order, and has shown himself to be the greatest master of orchestration the world has yet known.

OUR MUSICAL DIRECTORIES.

A LIVERPOOL Professor, Mr. J. J. MONK, who is well known for his earnest and consistent efforts in the direction of securing a better *status* for the English professional musician, has spoken out frankly about the present position of our Musical Directories, properly describing them as being unsatisfactory as to the reliability of the information they profess to furnish, and as tending to maintain the present disorganised condition of the musical profession. Mr. MONK is not alone by any means in his opinion; still, it seems only fair to balance considerations and difficulties from two points of sight, and it is possible to prove that not only is the compilation of a Musical Directory a difficult matter, but that its compilers are not altogether to be blamed for the erratic character of their work. In the first place, although something needs to be done in order to secure a stronger, more definite, and compact professional *status* for the benefit of the public at large, as well as for the elevation of our professional artists, the movement is one requiring serious forethought and much common-sense moderation. The clerical, legal, and medical professions are often pointed to as strong, well built-up, and definite organisations. Still, it may be asked, are there no amateurs, in the best sense of the word, to be found within their respective ranks, and whose names are included in their official registers? What should prevent men from the exercise of acquired skill? surely not any motive in connection with money merely, or the left-handed selfishness of some protective scheme or other. One might as well say that friendly hospitality must henceforth cease to exist, because the exercise of such a virtue militates against the interests of the properly licensed hotel proprietors. So long as a clergyman may rightly preach the Gospel without thought of gain, so long as the friendly doctor shall exercise his benevolent skill without thought of profit, and the barrister who does or does not practise, warn his friends to beware of the pitfalls of the law, so long will the musical amateur, with good motives and a real love of music hold an honoured and useful place in the annals of the art. Does anyone read Lord BYRON's poems, CHARLES LAMB's "Essays," or ANTHONY TROLLOPE's stories with less enjoyment because they were originally written from the amateur point of sight? Or, to turn to music, are the compositions of MENDELSSOHN, FLOTOW, and KUCKEN of less value because their authors were practically non-professional artists? As I have before pointed out, it would be impossible to get the art-work of any nation done without the aid of amateurs; to take the organist class alone, an army of non-professional players are absolutely necessary, for there could be neither means nor teaching enough to support an exclusively professional body of organ players. Then, again, our non-professional brethren are often to be ranked as our best and most appreciative friends. By all means let us register the profession, or take such steps as will effectually stamp out rampant quackery and empiricism—nearly as dangerous as quackery itself. But let us view the question from a large point of sight, and not regard shortsightedly or ungratefully the often unselfish and frequently valuable, not to say distinguished labours, of our non-professional brethren. The question must be placed indeed upon such a broad basis as will enlist the interest and support of professional and non-professional artists alike; for, in truth, both sections of the artistic world are concerned in the development of real and fully attested artistic power. Until such a condition of affairs is secured, it is difficult to see how our Musical Directories are to be free from anomalies. If their publishers only announced the names of artists holding accredited diplomas and certificates, a large number even of our deservedly established professors would be excluded, and a goodly number of thoroughly competent amateurs would have their names enrolled on the given lists. To the Rev. H. G. BONAVIA HUNT, Mus.Bac., the musical world is not only indebted for taking leading action in the foundation of Trinity College, London, but also for taking the initiative step in the direction of the legal registration of musicians. Surely no one could object to the presence of the names of such men as the founders of HENRY LESLIE's Choir, and Trinity College, London, to mention only two distinguished amateurs, who have rendered signal service to the art, in a Musical Directory; and surely one is glad to know that the interest taken in music by H.R.H. the Duke of EDINBURGH is genuine enough to take a practical shape, and the name of a Royal musician would surely be a gain to the roll-call of the artistic world. One finds with sincere pleasure the names of a goodly number of musical clergymen in one of our Musical Directories; nay, it must surely be a sign of the increased respect in which the noble calling of the musician is now being held, to find the name of the Dean of one of our cathedrals given in the same list; and be it remembered, that to our musically competent clergymen is assigned much of the task of elevating Church music and the position of its avowed servants, our organists and choristers. There is, though, undoubtedly a dark side to the picture, which Mr. J. J. MONK may well endeavour to expose to the daylight of public opinion. Undoubtedly, many who have no claims to such distinction are allowed to register their names in our Musical Directories upon the basis of such unworthy motives as the vanity of being considered members of the profession, and, worse still, from the mean desire to get music at reduced price, to get the commissions allowed to professionals on the sale of musical instruments, and, in short, to pander to that snobbish and despicable wish to cheapen, barter, and to unfairly gain advantages, which largely characterizes the too prevalent upstart mushroom pretensions of a struggling and competitive society. In this direction something

should be done, though the evils of such a condition of affairs may only be uprooted by the general uplifting of professional interests, and the development of mutual respect between the professional and amateur sections of the artistic world. If commissions, etc., are to exist for the benefit of the profession, then our musicsellers and musical instrument dealers should be called upon to resist all temptations to allow such advantages to any save fully accredited and duly registered musicians, even though it may seem hard to some to send custom from their doors in these days of sharp competition. To this end, the first movement should be the proper registration of all qualified artists based entirely upon the ground of a proper qualification in each case, as are the other professional registers. Again, the public at large, should be urged to decidedly prefer the teaching of duly qualified musicians only. Then the publishers of the Musical Directories may be fairly called upon to make their works reliable representations of the legally registered list of qualified artists. Even now, our professional musicians might take decided steps in view of the more careful compilation of the offending directories, and they would find the publishers not unwilling to meet their reasonable wishes. At the same time, let us bear in mind that art must be served purely and loyally, and that money motives must be held as subordinate in the consideration of the advancement of the musical world. The chief concern is, therefore, the educational aspect of the question; only let our musicians fully prepare and equip themselves for their life-work, then they will certainly secure the loyal help and good-will of the large and indispensable army of volunteer artists, and the two sections of the art-world will then surely work together, to their mutual gain, and to the securing of the common good of all.   E. H. TURPIN.

ÆSTHETICISM.[*]

It is strongly characteristic of the English people that when they are not altogether impassive and indifferent with respect to any new development or manifestation in arts, science, or literature, they are inclined to run to an extreme degree of infatuation in their enthusiastic worship or condemnation (just as it happens to be), of the thing attracting their attention. If this theory stands in need of illustration, we have only to refer to the unflattering attention which of late has been bestowed upon what has been dubbed "the æsthetic craze." Like most things having to pass under popular criticism, the æsthetic school has had to bear up under a deal of ignorant prejudice on the part of the public at large, and not a little wilful perversion of facts on the part of those who have undertaken to criticise its principles. The word "prejudice" is not to be taken as denoting any active or ill-natured attitude as far as concerns the public; it simply marks the readiness with which the British Philistine will accept any gross caricature of an art-movement, if put before it skilfully and persistently, as a truthful representation of the actual thing, while not caring—so long as it is amused —to investigate for itself, and so discover the veritable nature of the subject.

It would be absurd to become angry with those who have only derived their notions from Du Maurier's caricatures in Punch, or from witnessing Messrs. Gilbert and Sullivan's entertaining "Patience," because they may see nothing more in the æsthetic cultus but a passing phase of fashionable tomfoolery, lending itself, if not to actual ridicule, to amusing persiflage and parody. Nothing is so likely to kill any novel artistic endeavour as satirical

---

* The Æsthetic Movement in England. By Walter Hamilton. London: Reeves & Turner (third edition).

laughter raised against it ; and it is certain that if nothing more serious lay at the bottom of the æsthetic movement than what is generally represented, it would be in a dangerous way by this time.

The author of the little work under notice seeks to lay clear the deeper springs of the movement, while predicting for the æsthetic school ultimate recognition as a distinct typical growth of nineteenth-century art, just as in literature the " Lake School" of poetry marks the opening period of the present century.

The main tenets of the new school are those respecting —in the first place, the *correlation of arts*, the endeavour to effect a closer intimacy in art-practice between poetry and painting on the one hand, and again between poetry and music ; and, secondly, the establishment of *authority on matters of taste*—as Mr. Hamilton says, "they even go so far as to decide what shall be considered beautiful, and those who do not accept their ruling are termed Philistines, and there is no hope for them." There are, no doubt, many who will put in a declaimer against the institution of any class arrogating to itself the right of pronouncing judgment without appeal on all questions concerning art, gifting itself with the sole privilege of stamping any art-work, as it were, with the hall-mark of its approval ; but if it is reflected how long—from the time of the first professed æsthetician, Baumgarten—we have been in trying to arrive at the positive determination of the beautiful, of defining the nature and limits of each art (in which little result has been arrived at) such a solution of the difficulty appears the easiest, readiest, and, perhaps, after all, the most philosophical. The old maxim *Vox populi, vox Dei*, has, at any rate, been found to have no ground at all in the settlement of questions concerning art and taste in general. Mr. Hamilton has, certainly, in his interesting sketch of the rise and development of this movement, kept in view particularly the doings of the leaders of the modern school in the arts of poetry and painting, touching upon the sister-art of music, as affected by, or affecting, æsthetic culture, but very briefly. If no more extended notice is given to the later development of the musical spirit than a simple passing reference to Liszt, Rubinstein, and Wagner, this cannot proceed so much from any lack of representation on the part of music in this new art-development, as, perhaps, from a want on the part of the author, of a closer insight into musical matters which would enable him to pick up the threads of affinity, and follow out in the music, along with the other arts, its parallel course of esoteric development. And, again, though it would not be hard to demonstrate the like corresponding movement in our own artistic sphere, and refer the modern tendencies of each art to the same underlying principle which has influenced of late years all departments of art in equally the same degree, the outward manifestation of the same has not, in musical art, become so defined and *prononcé* as it has in the departments of poetry and the decorative arts. So, although Mr. Hamilton has little to say upon the part music takes in this new art-development (while not pretending to elaborate any profound philosophical theories in his light and agreeable discussion of the subject), for those who can supply the deficiency in the way remarked this book can be recommended here as a most charming, enlightening work on a generally misunderstood subject. It will be seen that æsthetic culture is no forced and artificial thing confined to a handful of charlatan posers, but arises out of the grand spirit of modern art, whose aim, as before said, it is to amalgamate perfectly the hitherto distinct forms. This, as well understood, is the underlying principle of the Wagnerian Drama. The whole tendency of modern musical art is in this direction. Even with purely instrumental music—and such without any decided " programme "—this striving after a more decided poetical motive is to be recognised as the distinctive sign of modern musical art. The consequential revolution in matters of musical taste has not been slow. Only comparatively recently has the music of Chopin been brought into vogue ; while only twelve months or so back did we get to make full acquaintance with the transcendental orchestral compositions of Berlioz. It is useless to contest the fact that the " absolute " principle in musical art has had its day ; the musician *pur et simple* is an anachronism. Of course (it is perhaps needful to say) we are not necessitated to shelve Mozart, Mendelssohn, or Haydn in following a new evolution of art. It is the contemporary artist we regard ; if he is to " march with the times " there must be something else evident in his work than simple musical display,

however ingeniously artistic the arrangement of the specific "materials." As far, too, as writers on art are concerned the ultra-conservatists would be wiser to conform at once. The Wagnerian Idea is pretty well a *fait accompli* : they may as well subscribe to it at first graciously as be left consigned in the end to the region of old-fogeydom. In song-composition it is natural that we look most particularly for signs of this more elevated artistic spirit. And it is gratifying to find that a more refined class of song-literature is becoming approved, in which endeavour is made to more intimately unite music with the higher order of poetical compositions. This inter-permeation of the arts being recognised as the grand feature of Æstheticism, the artist, whatever his special department, cannot neglect to take notice of whatever movements may be taking place in any other departments than his own, or any question affecting the progress of general artistic culture. On this ground (although, as I have intimated, our author does not sufficiently treat with music in this light) I have deemed it not inconsistent with the profession of this journal to bring under notice here this most artistic little work, and make it the text of these remarks, which might else seem altogether irrelevant. It will not be needful however to discuss the matter of the book in detail. The author, while showing himself an enthusiastic apologist, does not sacrifice critical impartiality ; and so those musicians, " professional and amateur," who will not deem it utterly lost time in giving attention to a book not strictly academical and technical, or even directly bearing on musical art, may take Mr. Hamilton as a safe guide in a closer study of the æsthetic movement. Very many so doing are likely to have their opinions on this subject greatly modified. Mr. Hamilton deals in the first place with the pre-Raphaelite brethren, and gives an interesting account of their paper, " The Germ." He discusses next Mr. Ruskin, as critic, and the artists of the Grosvenor Gallery—the late Dante Gabriel Rossetti and Mr. E. Burne-Jones, among the foremost ; and then treats severally with the poets of the Æsthetic school—D. G. Rossetti, W. M. Rossetti, Thomas Woolner, William Morris, Algernon C. Swinburne, and Arthur O'Shaughnessy. Mr. Hamilton keenly recriminates upon *Punch* for its over-done caricaturing of the Æsthetes. Mr. Oscar Wilde, who is generally regarded as the personification of the movement by those who cannot discern its wider bearings, is presented in a very favourable light ; the sketch of his career is very interesting, and the poetical extracts show Mr. Wilde to be, undoubtedly, a literary artist of no mean order. No less interesting is the account of a pilgrimage made by the author to the "Home for the Æsthetes," at Bedford Park. Mr. Hamilton is successful in demonstrating the good that has been wrought so far by the movement in improving taste, not only in arts, but in matters of common life, such as dress, furniture, and house-decoration. Careful distinction is drawn between false and true Æstheticism. " Let it be borne in mind," the author says, " that that higher Æstheticism has nothing in common with the affected and superficial Æstheticism which has been forced into a hot-house existence by caricaturists, and fostered by those who mistake artistic slang and stained-glass attitudes for culture and high art. For herein lies the essence of it all : Real culture is a hardy plant ; it will thrive where it has once taken root. *Pseudo-Æstheticism* may for a time be confounded with it by those who have learnt all they know of it from *Punch* or " Patience," but by no others, and it will fade away as rapidly as it sprang into existence, with all the more speed now that as a theme for comic writers it is nearly exhausted." It will remain for those herein interested to draw the parallel before claimed between the arts here discussed and music. But although Mr. Hamilton leaves us to do this ourselves, the underlying spirit of Æstheticism, as here exhibited, will be found easily discoverable in the musical tendency of the present day, although, as before pointed out, not assuming perhaps any such marked character as in the directions of poetry and painting, being broader and more general in its manifestation. Nevertheless, the distinctive features of what (for want of a better term) may be styled the Æsthetic *cultus*, namely, a superior decision in art-criticism, and the tendency to an esoteric and subtle form of musico-poetical expression will be remarked in our own department of art. The higher development of pianoforte playing may be adduced in additional illustration, to what has been already said, with respect to the tendency of modern song-composition—the most perfect representative of the latter department of superior musical culture being the German Franz. Mr. H. F. Myers, in a recent article on this subject (*Cornhill*), in discussing the merits of the artist Rossetti, speaks of him as "a member of that new aristocracy—that optimacy of passion and genius." A like optimacy makes its influence correspondingly felt in the world of Musical Art ; and it is such an aristocratic spirit as this, it may in conclusion be remarked, which is neither breathed nor cherished in schools and academies, nor determined nor arrested by the popular taste.

EUSTACE J. BREAKSPEARE.

Organ News.

PRESTON.

Subjoined are the programmes of organ recitals given in the new Public Hall, by Mr. James Tomlinson, on Saturday, Feb. 10th :—

AFTERNOON PROGRAMME.

Grande Fantasie	Callaerts.
Adagio	Morandi.
Rigaudon	Silas.
Pastorale	Wély.
Overture ("Preciosa ")	Weber.
Andante	Mailly.
Marcia	Bargiel.

EVENING PROGRAMME.

Overture ("Zauberflöte ")	Mozart.
Air varied	Hiles.
Cantique de Noel	Adam.
Marche Funèbre et Chant Séraphique	Guilmant.
Gavotte de Louis XV.	Lee.
Airs ("Tannhäuser ")	Wagner.

MANCHESTER.

Mr. J. Kendrick Pyne gave an organ recital in the Town Hall, on Saturday, Feb. 10th. Subjoined is the programme :—

Overture ("Seven Last Words ")	Haydn.
Andante Solennelle ("Evening Prayer ")	Smart.
Sonata in D minor	Topfer.
Lamentation in D minor	Guilmant.
March for a Church Festival, in G major	Best.

BOLTON.

At the opening of the new organ (built by Messrs. T. C. Lewis & Co.), in the Wesleyan Chapel, Park Street, on Wednesday, Feb. 14th, Mr. W. T. Best performed the following :—

AFTERNOON RECITAL.

Allegretto in C major, Moderato in F major	Gade.
Fugue in C minor	Bach.
Christmas Pastorale	Moriconi.
Festal March	Best.
Andante Tranquillo in D flat major, Offertoire Funèbre in F minor	Wély.
Andante Cantabile in G major, No. 2	Wesley.
"Swell the full chorus " ("Solomon ")	Handel.

EVENING RECITAL.

Sonata in F minor, No. 1	Mendelssohn.
Andante in G major	Smart.
Toccata and Fugue in the Dorian mode	Bach.
Andante in B flat major	Widor.
Marcia Religiosa	Perelli.
Allegretto Villereccio	Fumagalli.
Introduction and Fugue on a Trumpet Fanfare	Best.
"Joys in gentle train appearing" ("Athalia ")	Handel.

An organ recital was given in the Albert Hall, by Mr. Wm. Mullineux, F.C.O., on Saturday, Feb. 10th. The following was the programme :—

Concertstück in C minor	Topfer.
Adagio (Trio for two oboes and English horn	Beethoven.
Elevation	Batiste.
Scherzo Symphonique	Lemmens.
Cantilène Pastorale	Guilmant.
Military March in C major	Dutton.

NORWICH.

Annexed is the programme of an organ recital given in St. Andrew's Hall, by Dr. Bunnett, F.C.O., on Saturday, Feb. 10th :—

Overture ("Alcina ")	Handel.
Russian air in G with variations	Bunnett.
"Ave Maria "	D'Arcadelt.
Chaconne (Air with variations)	Bach.
Offertoire in F	Batiste.
Sonata, "O Filii "	Lemmens.
Sketch (Descriptive)	Bunnett.
Study (Allegretto)	Chipp.
Marche Religieuse	Gigout.
"Nazareth "	Gounod.

BRISTOL.

Annexed is the programme of the organ recital given by Mr. George Riseley in the Colston Hall on Saturday, Feb. 10th :—

Overture ("Sosarmes ")	Handel.
Andante (Symphony No. 4)	Mendelssohn.
Prelude and Fugue in G minor	Bach.
Funeral March	Chopin.
"The horse and his rider," " But the waters "	Handel.
Pastorale	Wély.
Overture ("Zanetta ")	Auber.

CRYSTAL PALACE.

Mr. Eyre's programmes after the first Saturday concert included the following :—

Choral and March ("Meistersinger ")	Wagner.
" La Berceuse "	Gounod.
Prelude and Fugue in G	Mendelssohn.
Minuet and Trio	Bridge.
Air, "My heart ever faithful "	Bach.
Fantasia on a Lenten hymn	Stephens.
Andante in F	Smart.
Selection ("St. Paul ")	Mendelssohn.
March in D	Moscheles.

WATERLOO ROAD.

Subjoined is the programme of an organ recital given on Thursday, Feb. 15th, at the church of St. John the Evangelist, by Mr. C. E. Miller :—

Overture in C	Adams.
Slow movement (Third Quartet)	Onslow.
Andante (MS.)	Lloyd.
Air and variations, and Finale with Fugue	O姜ley.
Minuet and Trio	Bennett.
Fantasia and Fugue in C minor	Bach.
Overture ("Ruy Blas ")	Mendelssohn.

This recital was remarkable, not only for a programme containing works of special interest, but for the artistic playing of an organist not previously heard in London as a recitalist, though already known as a musician of excellent attainments.

EAST HILL.

The first organ recital of a series was given by Mr. J. E. Bowcher, in Wandsworth Congregational Church, on Tuesday, Feb. 6th, when the programme comprised :—

Sonata in C minor	Rheinberger.
Andante in G, Allegretto in D, Allegro in G	Bowcher.
Barcarolle in F	Bennett.
Toccata et Fuga in D minor	Bach.
Andante, from Symphony	Haydn.
Offertoire in C minor	Wély.
Selection ("Water Music ")	Handel.

The programme of the second recital on Tuesday, Feb. 13th, was as follows : —

Choral Song and Fugue	Wesley.
Larghetto in E flat	Mozart.
Festival March in B flat	Bowcher.
Andante in C	Smart.
March, from Orchestral Suite	Lachner.
Cantilène et Grand Chœur	Salomé.

SUTTON.

The following is the programme of an organ recital given by Dr. Charles Joseph Frost on the new organ (built by Messrs. Bevington & Son) in Christ Church, on Tuesday, Feb. 6th :—

Fugue in G major	Krebs.
Andante in A major	Smart.
Marche Religieuse	Gigout.
Adagio non Troppo in F minor, Andante Pastorale in F major	Stephens.
Rhapsodie in E major	Saint-Saëns.
" Austrian Hymn," with variations	Chipp.
Pastorale and Finale (Sonata in D minor)	Guilmant.
Chorus, "Hallelujah "	Handel.

BOW AND BROMLEY INSTITUTE.

The audience had again the advantage of hearing Mr. W. T. Best, of Liverpool, on Saturday last. The first piece was a ' Marche du Couronnement" by Meyerbeer, a fine piece of pageantry music. An Andante in E flat, by S. S. Wesley, and a stately old-fashioned " Rigaudon," by Tulli, formed a group of interest. Bach's C minor Fugue, Vol. 4, No. 9, was finely rendered, and received with great applause ; as was an artistic and effective "Fantasia Pastorale " by Mr. Best himself. Donizetti's overture " Gemmà di Vergy," made a good and spirited finale to an admirable recital. Miss Agnes Larkcom sang charmingly, and was received with great favour, being encored and recalled. Her performance of Bellini's " Casta Diva," and Haydn's "On mighty pens," greatly pleased musical critics. Mr. W. G. Wood was the accompanist. To-night Mons. A. Guilmant will be the organist, and Mr. Arthur Thompson the vocalist.

NEWGATE STREET.

The following is the programme of an organ recital given in Christ Church, by Dr. Charles Joseph Frost, on February 12th :—

Grand Chœur Dialogue	Gigout.
Pilgrims' March ("Italian" symphony)	Mendelssohn.
Sonata in A minor, No. 4	Rheinberger.
Fantasia, "The Storm"	Lemmens.
Christmas Offertoire in F	Wély.
Fantasia in E flat major	Haydn.
Allegretto in B flat major	Guilmant.
Toccata and Fugue in C major	Bach.

The event of a recital in Christ Church, Newgate Street, is one of unusual interest. It was upon the organ of this church that Mendelssohn was heard, indeed, he gave what may fairly have been called the last recital preceding Dr. Frost's performance of the other evening—save the performance of Mr. J. T. Cooper, as mentioned by an esteemed correspondent. It was here, about 40 years ago, that the great composer of " Elijah " revealed, in his own incomparable manner, the majesty and beauty of Bach's organ music, being listened to by Samuel Wesley, the first English disciple of the illustrious cantor of Leipzig, and many other eminent musicians. Then, again, the organ at Christ Church has itself occupied an important position in the history of English organ building and organ music. As originally built by Elliot & Hill, the organ was one of exceptional value and interest ; but as rebuilt by William Hill it became one of the chief and earliest examples of the adoption in England—under the intelligent advocacy of Dr. Gauntlett, and by the foresight of the distinguished organ builder· just named—of the German compass of manuals and pedals, and of the presence of a pedal organ of the exceptional capacity, in this country, of 10 stops. The success of Dr. C. J· Frost's very admirable recital of Monday last, before an appreciative congregation, encourages the hope that it was, indeed, only the first of a long series of similar performances upon this most interesting instrument.

DUNDEE.

The following is the specification of a chamber organ recently erected for J· Martin White, Esq., of Balruddery, by Messrs. Forster & Andrews, of Hull :—

GREAT ORGAN. CC TO G.

1. Open Diapason	8 ft.	7. Flauto Traverso	4 ft.
2. Gedact	8 ,,	6. Fifteenth	2 ,,
3. Dulciana	8 ,,	7. Corno di Bassetto ..	8 ,,
4. Principal	4 ,,		

SWELL ORGAN. CC TO G.

8. Violin Diapason	8 ft.	11. Gemshorn	4 ft.
9. Salicional	8 ,,	12. Oboe	8 ,,
10. Voix Celestes	8 ,,		

PEDAL ORGAN. CCC TO F.

13. Bourdon	16 ft.	14. Violoncello	8 ft.

COUPLERS.

15. Swell to Great.	17. Swell to Pedals.
16. Swell Octave.	18. Great to Pedals.

Four Composition Pedals to Great organ.
· Two   ,,   ,, to Swell organ.

Pedal-board concave and radiating ; hydraulic engine and feeders.

THE DATES OF WAGNER'S WORKS.

I leave to our author the mournful task of delivering a "funeral oration" in print over the great man whom the world has just lost. I only write to correct a (supposed) error of dates, as regards Wagner's operas, in the rather vague " obituary " notice of the *Times* (Wednesday, Feb. 14). According to Mr. Edward Dannreuther, in his interesting *brochure* on Wagner and his works, "Lohengrin" was *not* first performed in Switzerland, A.D. 1853, but (under Liszt) at *Weimar*, A.D. 1850. The dates of the *production* of Wagner's operas, supplied by my esteemed friend Mr. Dannreuther, are as follow, viz. :—" Rienzi," 1842, at Dresden ; " Der Fliegende Holländer," 1843, at Dresden ; " Tannhäuser," 1845, at Dresden ; " Lohengrin," " first performed under Liszt, 1850, at *Weimar* " ; "Tristan und Isolde," in 1865, at Munich, under Dr. von Bülow ; " Die Meistersinger von Nürnberg," in 1868, at Munich (also under Dr. Von Bülow) ; " Der Ring des Nibelungen," in 1876, at Bayreuth (the first two sections or divisions of the work were *attempted* at Munich, in 1869 and 1870) ; lastly, " Parsifal," in 1882, at Bayreuth. The introduction to " Parsifal" was performed on Thursday, at the first concert of the old Philharmonic Society.   A. M.

𝔓𝔞𝔰𝔰𝔦𝔫𝔤 𝔈𝔳𝔢𝔫𝔱𝔰.

There are now fifteen Parisian papers devoted to musical topics.

The Kyrle Society gave Handel's " Samson" under the excellent direction of Mr. M. L. Lawson, at Trinity Chapel, Poplar. The organ was in the hands of Mr. E. H. Turpin.

A student's concert takes place this evening at the Royal Academy of Music. It will be seen that the public have the privilege of attending these very interesting performances by payment at the doors.

Mr. F. Dewberry, organist of Caius College, Cambridge, obtained the diploma of Licentiateship at the recent examinations at the Royal Academy of Music, the organ examiners being Dr. C. Steggall, Dr. G. Stainer, and Mr. E. H. Turpin.

Handel's " Messiah " was well rendered at St. Mary's Bryanstone Square, on Feb. 13th, by efficient soloists and a large choral force, under the conductorship of Mr. A. H. D. Prendergast. The organist was Mr. E. H. Turpin.

The Kensington Orchestral and Choral Society will give a concert at the Academy Rooms, Tenterden Street, under the conductorship of Mr. Wm. Buels, on the 20th inst., the programme to include Mendelssohn's "95th Psalm " and Gade's " Spring's Message."

On the 4th inst. Sir Michael Costa entertained a party of friends at dinner to celebrate his 73rd natal day. The company included the Rev. J· E. Cox, D.D., Mr. Husk, Professor Ella, and Signor Perugini. I am happy to say that the state of the maestro's health continues to be satisfactory.

Mrs. Meadows-White (Alice Mary Smith) has set Kingsley's Ballad of the " Little Baltung " as a piece for chorus and soli (male voices). The Lombard Amateur Musical Society will bring it out under the conductorship of Mr. A. H. D. Prendergast at the Cannon Street Hotel, at their next smoking concert, on Thursday, March 1st.

Mr. Eustace Ingram, Eden Grove, Holloway, London, invites those interested in the introduction of organs into their churches to visit his factory during the present month, where an opportunity will be afforded for the inspection of a three manual and pedal organ constructed for the Parish Church, Calne, Wilts. The case is of oak, the design being from the pencil of J. L. Pearson, R.A.

A musical agent, named Schlesinger, the other day sued Mr. Hart, proprietor of the Star and Garter Music Hall, in Bermondsey, for £100 commission on the purchase of that establishment. Although Mr. Justice Stephen expressed a doubt whether the plaintiff could, as represented, be in a position to say that he could get the place for five or six hundred pounds less than anybody else, the jury gave a verdict in his favour.

Some items of interest to the musician appear in data to be found in a special number of the *Gazzetta dei Teatri*, relating to artistic life in Italy and abroad. In the year 1882 there were represented in Italy 45 new operas and 54 abroad. There were nine new ballets in Italy and only five abroad. The same year there died in Italy three Italian opera singers, and 38 musical composers. Of foreign artists there died 20 singers and 48 composers.

The very valuable and lucid lecture by Dr. F. E. Gladstone, on " Triads : their Relationship and Treatment," now being printed in these columns, by kind permission of the author, is being published by Messrs. Weekes and Co. in pamphlet form. The work will, in that form, be of much use to students for reference. Editors who may wish to reprint are referred to the author for permission to do so.

Mr. John Owen (Owain Alaw), a musical composer, who was well-known throughout both North and South Wales, died on Jan. 30, at Chester, in his sixty-third year. For many years he has taken an active part in the furtherance of Welsh musical education, and has been chosen an adjudicator at nearly all the Eisteddfodau held in the Principality. He was also a favourite conductor at other choral gatherings. His musical compositions were received with great favour in Wales.

Mr. G. Jacobi desires to contradict a report that he is engaging a band from abroad for Mr. Leader's season at Her Majesty's Theatre.

Among the large number of candidates examined recently by the College of Preceptors, the subject of music was not overlooked. In this department the examiners were Dr. W. Westbrook and Mr. E. H. Turpin.

Legal steps have been properly taken in America to prevent Gounod's "Redemption" from being re-scored by another hand for the benefit of too enterprising concert managers.

One of the features of opera in America lately has been the combined performances of Mdmes. Patti and Scalchi. The two ladies played together in "Semiramide" at Chicago with the greatest success.

The Bloomsbury Choral Association gave a concert on Feb. 10th, under the painstaking direction of Mr. W. G. Goodworth at the Richmond Street School-room. The programme opened with a musicianly anthem "Rejoice to-day," by Mr. Goodworth.

Miss Adelaide Thomas (pupil of Herr Pauer, and Prince of Wales Scholar, late National Training School for Music), gave an artistic pianoforte recital, at the Marlborough Rooms, Regent Street, assisted by Miss Mary Thomas and Mr. Clifford Harrison. The performance included an admirable selection of modern pianoforte music.

A valuable and interesting paper on "The Position of Choirs and Organs in Churches" was read by Mr. H. W. Brewer, before the Architectural Association, on the 2nd. The *Builder* of Feb. 10th reports the lecture and discussion at length, and gives a large and admirable design for an organ placed at the entrance of the chancel on an open archway. It is hoped that the paper will be duly presented to our readers.

On Monday, February 12th, an organ recital was given by Mr. John E. West, A.C.O., at the Memorial Church, Hackney Road. The works performed were selections from Bach, Smart, Wesley, Salome, Gade, John E. West, &c.; the "St. Ann's Fugue" (Bach) and "Air," with variations (West), especially pleasing the audience. Some vocal music was also admirably rendered by Mdme. Clara West, Miss Lottie West, Mr. C. J. Murton, and Mr. Bernard Fountain.

Sterndale Bennett's motet for double choir, "In Thee, O Lord," and an unpublished work of the same kind by Gounod, are the most important features of the four subscription concerts to be given by the Henry Leslie Choir under its new conductor, Signor Randegger. New part-songs by Henry Leslie, A. R. Gaul, Caldicott, and Ciro Pinsuti are also promised. The dates of the concerts are stated as fixed for Thursday, February 22nd, evening; Saturday, April 14, afternoon; and on the evenings of Thursdays, May 31 and June 28.

At a general meeting of the Bristol Musical Festival Society on Jan. 30th, it was resolved to hold a festival in 1885, and a hope was expressed that the Committee would be able to secure for the performance some great work by an English composer. The Mayor read a communication from the secretary of the Royal College of Music, intimating that the Prince of Wales hoped to open the College in May, and throw fifty scholarships open for competition; and the Prince's suggestion of local examinations for testing the competitors was referred to the Executive Committee.

St. Cecilia Magazine has a stirring paragraph. "The question of instrumental music in the Church is no longer to be confined to the organ. Dr. Gordon, of St. Andrew's Episcopal Church, Glasgow, lecturing on the subject a few weeks ago, ventured to say that 'if the Psalms of David were meant to be sung at all in the Church now, they were meant to be sung or chanted as they were of old—that was, with instrumental accompaniments, with the cornet, the flute, the psaltery, and harp, and last, though not least, the melodious fiddle.' After all, it does seem strange that the theatre should enjoy a monopoly of the orchestra while the Church must go a-begging for a harmonium or an organ." We must look out lest Scotland will gain upon us after all in the matter of church music.

Ξħℇ Ɋuℇɽⁱˢͭ.

COMPOSER OF TRIO.—What is the name of composer of trio for A. T. B. "As a rosy wreath I bound," and where can it be obtained?—ORPHEUS.

REPLY.

FUNDAMENTAL CHORDS AND DISCORDS. — In answer to "Student," Fundamental Chords are those chords in the key which contain a major third to the root, thus: the chords of the tonic, subdominant, and dominant are Fundamental Chords. Fundamental Discords are chords containing a discord which needs *no preparation*, thus: the chord of the dominant seventh, and the chord of the added sixth, are Fundamental Discords. In the former the seventh needs *no preparation*, while in the latter the fifth and sixth likewise need none. In Fundamental Discords the third to the root must be major.—J. JACKSON.

Service Lists.

SECOND SUNDAY IN LENT,
FEBRUARY 18th.

London.

ST. PAUL'S CATHEDRAL.—Morn.: Service, Benedicite, Best; Benedictus, Best in F; Introit, Saviour, when in dust to Thee (Hymn 251); Communion Service, Alwyn in C. Even.: Service, Magnificat and Nunc Dimittis, Barnby in E flat; Anthem, Remember, Lord, and, Lord before Thy footstool bending (Spohr).

WESTMINSTER ABBEY.—Morn.: Service, Benedicite, Keeton in E flat; Jubilate, Calkin in B flat; Communion, Service, Garrett in E flat. Aft.: Service, Walmisley in D major; Anthem, Unto Thee (Elvey).

TEMPLE CHURCH.—Morn.: Service, Te Deum and Jubilate, Apostles' Creed, Harmonized Monotone; Anthem, Sing ye praise (Mendelssohn); Kyrie, Calah in C. Even.: Service, Magnificat and Nunc Dimittis, Arnold in A; Apostles' Creed, Harmonized Monotone; Anthem, Call to remembrance (Battishill).

LINCOLN'S INN HALL.—Morn.: Service, Smart in F; Kyrie, Gibbs; Anthem, Turn Thee unto me, O Lord (Boyce). Even.: Service, Tours in F; Anthem, Hear my crying, O God (Weldon).

ALL SAINTS, MARGARET STREET.—Morn.: Service, Benedictus, Herbert; Communion Service, Stanford in B flat; Benedictus and Agnus Dei, Niedermeyer; Offertory Anthem, Come unto Him (Gounod). Even.: Service, Palestrina in B flat; Anthem, Daughters of Zion (Mendelssohn); Miserere, Novello.

ST. ANDREW'S (WELLS STREET, ST. MARYLEBONE.—Morn.: Service, Benedicite and Benedictus, Docker; Anthem, Is it nothing unto you (Gounod); Introit, Hymn 216; Kyrie, Creed, Sanctus, and Gloria, Silas in C. Even.: Service, Magnificat and Nunc Dimittis, Goss in E; Anthem, From the deep (Gounod).

ST. AUGUSTINE AND ST. FAITH, WATLING STREET.—Morn.: Service, Benedicite, Stainer, Turle, and Irons; Benedictus, Gounod in G; Communion Service, Armes in A; Offertory, The sacrifices of God (Calkin). Even.: Service, Smart in G; Anthem, O God, have mercy (Mendelssohn).

ST. BARNABAS, MARYLEBONE.—Morn.: Service, Te Deum and Jubilate, Rogers in D; Anthem, For our offences (Mendelssohn); Kyrie and Nicene Creed, Rogers. Even.: Service, Magnificat and Nunc Dimittis, Rogers in D; Anthem, Abide with me (Bennett).

CHILDREN'S HOME CHAPEL, BONNER ROAD, E.—Morn.: Service, Anthems, If ye love Me (Monk), and, What are these (Stainer). Aft.: Service, Anthems, Turn Thy face (Attwood), and, By the waters of Babylon (Allen).

CHRIST CHURCH, CLAPHAM.—Morn.: Service, Benedicite, Stainer; Kyrie and Credo, Monk in C; Offertory Anthem, O Saviour of the world (Goss); Sanctus, Monk; Benedictus and Agnus Dei, Sewell in E flat; Communion, O saving victim (Gounod, Messe des Orphéonistes); Gloria in excelsis, Monk. Even.: Service, Magnificat and Nunc Dimittis, Stainer in A; Anthem, Call to remembrance (Novello); Miserere, Helmore.

FOUNDLING CHAPEL.—Morn.: Service, Tours in F; Anthem, Hear my crying (Hummel). Aft.: Service, Ebdon in C; Anthem, Lord, for Thy tender mercies' sake (Farrant).

HOLY TRINITY, TULSE HILL.—Morn.: Chant Service. Even.: Service, Hopkins in F; Anthem, Love not the world (Sullivan).

HOLY TRINITY (BESSBOROUGH GARDENS), WESTMINSTER.—Morn.: Service, Benedicite in C (Best); Benedictus (Wesley); Communion Service, Readhead (throughout). Offertory Sentences (Monk). Even.: Service, Magnificat and Nunc Dimittis, Turle in D; Anthem, Hear my prayer (Mendelssohn).

ST. JAMES'S PRIVATE EPISCOPAL CHAPEL, SOUTHWARK.—Morn.: Service, Introit, For us, the Christ (Gounod); Communion Service, Schubert in B flat. Even.: Service, Garrett in D; Anthem, Hear my prayer (Mendelssohn).

ST. MAGNUS, LONDON BRIDGE.—Morn.: Service, Opening Anthem, I will arise (Clarke Whitfield); Te Deum and Jubilate, Stainer in E flat; Kyrie, Purcell. Even.: Service, Cantate and Deus Misereatur, Hayes in E flat; Anthem, Rejoice in the Lord (Purcell).

ST. MARY ABCHURCH, E.C.—Morn.: Service, Boyce in C; Communion Service, Garrett in E flat. Even.: Service, Turle in D.

ST. MARY MAGDALENE, WEST BROMPTON, S.W.—Morn.: Service, Benedicite, Stainer, Winn, and Walker; Benedictus, Stainer; Third Series of Tones; Communion Service, Kyrie, Credo, Sanctus, and Gloria in excelsis, Thorne in G; Benedictus and Agnus Dei, Monk; Offertory, Barnby. Even.: Service, Magnificat and Nunc Dimittis, Stainer's Third Series of Tones; Anthem, O Saviour of the world (Goss).

ST. MICHAEL'S, CORNHILL. — Morn.: Service, Te Deum and Benedictus, Stainer in E flat; Anthem, Wash me thoroughly (Wesley); Kyrie, Sullivan; Creed, Goss. Even.: Service, Magnificat and Nunc Dimittis, Wesley in F; Anthem, I will love thee (Clarke).

ST. PAUL'S, BOW COMMON, E. — Morn.: Service, Benedicite, Stainer, Winn, and Walker; Benedictus, Chant; Communion Service, Kyrie, Credo, Sanctus, Benedictus, Agnus Dei, and Gloria in excelsis, Calkin in B flat; Offertory, Stainer. Even.: Service, Magnificat and Nunc Dimittis, Goss in A; Anthem (unaccompanied), I wrestle and pray (Bach).

Country.

ST. ASAPH CATHEDRAL.—Morn.: Service, Baker in F; Anthem, Turn Thy face (Sullivan). Even.: Service, The Litany; Anthem, O Lord have mercy (Pergolesi).

ASHBURNE CHURCH, DERBYSHIRE. — Morn.: Service, Steggall in G; Kyrie and Credo, Barnby in E. Even.: Service, Walmisley in D minor; Anthem, O Saviour of the world (Goss).

BEDDINGTON CHURCH, SURREY.—Morn.: Service, Benedicite, South; Benedictus, Tuckerman in F; Introit, Christian dost thou see them (Hymn 91); Communion Service, Smee in E. Even.: Service, Martin; Anthem, O Lord have mercy upon me (Leslie).

BIRMINGHAM (ST. CYPRIAN'S, HAY MILLS).—Morn.: Service, Benedicite, Simms in B flat; Benedictus, Field in D; Anthem, If with all your hearts, and, Cast thy burden (Mendelssohn). Even.: Service, Kent in C; Anthems, All ye that cried, and, I waited for the Lord (Mendelssohn).

CANTERBURY CATHEDRAL. — Morn.: Service, Te Deum, Barnby in B flat; Jubilate, Hopkins in B flat; Anthem, O praise the Lord (Goss). Even.: Service, Havergal in A; Anthem, O give thanks (Boyce).

CARLISLE CATHEDRAL. — Morn.: Service, Wesley in E; Introit, Behold, God is my helper (Stainer); Kyrie, Wesley in E; Nicene Creed, Harmonized Monotone. Even.: Service, Stainer in B flat; Anthem, O where shall wisdom (Boyce).

DONCASTER (PARISH CHURCH). — Morn.: Service, Tours in F. Even.: Service, Hopkins in B flat; Anthem, The sorrows (Mendelssohn).

DUBLIN, ST. PATRICK'S (NATIONAL) CATHEDRAL.—Morn.: Service, Te Deum and Jubilate, Stainer in A; Anthem, I looked, and lo! a Lamb (Stevenson). Even.: Service, Magnificat and Nunc Dimittis, Stevenson in E flat; Anthems, Come unto Him (Gounod), and, Lord, how are they increased (Stevenson).

ELY CATHEDRAL. — Morn.: Service, Benedicite, Chants; Jubilate, Plain-song; Kyrie, Credo, and Gloria, Jackman in D; Anthem, Turn Thee again (Attwood). Even.: Service, Frobisher in F; Anthem, Plead Thou my cause (Mozart).

EXETER CATHEDRAL.—Morn.: Service, Leslie in D; Communion Service, Hopkins in F; Anthem, Their sound is gone out (Handel). Even.: Service, Kelway in B minor; Anthem, By the waters (Boyce).

FOLKESTONE (ST. MICHAEL'S). — Morn.: Communion Service, Introit, Heal us, Emmanuel (Husband); Kyrie, Credo, Sanctus, &c., Ouseley in C. Even.: Service, Magnificat and Nunc Dimittis, Clarke-Whitfeld in E; Anthem, Selection from Gounod's "Redemption."

GLASGOW (BLYTHSWOOD PARISH CHURCH).—Aft.: Service, Anthem, My God, look upon me (Reynolds).

LEEDS PARISH CHURCH. — Morn.: Service, Boyce in A; Anthem, He counteth all your sorrows (Mendelssohn); Kyrie and Creed, Garrett in D. Even.: Service, Elvey in A; Anthem, In that day (Elvey).

LICHFIELD CATHEDRAL.—Morn.: Ordination Service, Veni Creator, Palestrina; Litany and Communion Service, Dykes in F. Aft.: Service, Stainer in E flat; Anthem, Hear my prayer (Mendelssohn).

LIVERPOOL CATHEDRAL. — Aft.: Service, Turle in D; Anthem, I cried unto the Lord (Heap).

MANCHESTER CATHEDRAL. — Morn.: Service, Benedicite, Barnby; Benedictus, Gibbons in F; Anthem, Lord, pour Thy spirit (Thorne). Aft.: Service, Gibbons in F; Anthem, By the waters of Babylon (Boyce).

MANCHESTER (ST. BENEDICT'S). — Morn.: Service, Kyrie, and Credo, Nares in F; Sanctus, Benedictus, and Agnus Dei, Palestrina (Æterna Christi Munera). Even.: Service, Magnificat and Nunc Dimittis, Jordan.

MANCHESTER (ST. JOHN BAPTIST, HULME).—Morn.: Service, Benedicite, Marbeck; Kyrie, Meyerbeer; Credo and Sanctus, Garrett in D; Benedictus and Agnus Dei, De la Hache. Even.: Service, Magnificat and Nunc Dimittis, Gregorian.

MUSSELBURGH (LORETTO SCHOOL). — Morn.: Introit, Enter not into judgment (Attwood); Service, Stainer in E flat; Anthem, O God Thou art my God (Purcell). Even.: Service, Anthem, Judge me, O God (Mendelssohn).

RIPON CATHEDRAL.—Morn.: Ordination Service. Even.: Sevice, Armes in G; Anthems, Ye people, and, Cast thy burden (Mendelssohn).

ROCHESTER CATHEDRAL. — Morn.: Service, Walmisley in E; Anthem, Come, Holy Ghost (Hopkins). Even.: Service, Goss in E; Anthem, O Lord, Thou hast searched (Croft).

SHEFFIELD PARISH CHURCH. — Morn.: Service, Kyrie, Gounod in G. Even.: Service, Magnificat and Nunc Dimittis, Trimnell in D; Anthem, Then shall the righteous (Mendelssohn).

SHERBORNE ABBEY.—Morn.: Service, Chant; Kyrie, Mendelssohn in G; Offertories, (Gaul). Even.: Service, Anthem, O Saviour of the world (Goss).

SOUTHAMPTON (ST. MARY'S CHURCH).—Morn.: Service, Benedicite, Best in C; Benedictus, Harris; Communion Service, Introit, O Saviour of the world (Macfarren); Service, Dykes in F; Agnus Dei and Benedictus, Gray in F; Offertory,, While we have time and Godliness is great (Barnby); Paternoster, Helmore. Even.: Service, Magnificat and Nunc Dimittis, Wesley in F; Anthem, Lord for thy tender mercies', Farrant; Apostles' Creed, Harmonized Monotone (Hopkins).

SOUTHWELL COLLEGIATE CHURCH, NOTTS.—Morn.: Service, Benedicite (Turle); Benedictus (Barnby); Kyrie and Creed, Marriott in F; Gloria in Excelsis (Elvey); Sanctus (Maurice); E. Hopkins in F; Anthem, I wrestle and pray (Bach).

WELLS CATHEDRAL.—Morn.: Service, Boyce and Hayes in G; Introit, Remember me, O Lord (Macfarren); Kyrie, Mendelssohn in G. Even.: Service, Ebdon in C; Anthem, By the Waters of Babylon (Boyce).

WORCESTER CATHEDRAL.—Morn.: Service, Smart in G. Even.: Service, Smart in G; Anthem, Hear, O Thou Shepherd of Israel (Walmisley).

[The attention of the several Organists is called to the favour they confer upon their brother musicians by forwarding their notices regularly: this column of the paper is much valued as an index to what is going on in the choice of cathedral music, so much so that intermissions constantly give rise to remonstrance. Lists should be sent in a week in advance if possible.—EDI Mus. Stand.]

NOTICES TO CORRESPONDENTS.

NEWSPAPERS sent should have distinct marks opposite to the matter to which attention is required.

NOTICE.—All communications intended for the Editor are to be sent to his private address. Business communications to be addressed to 185, Fleet Street, E.C.

"W. VINCENT WALLACE FUND."—C. Hubert H, Parry, £4.

ERRATA.—In last week's issue, page 81, line 18 from bottom should be "the pure elevation of a soul strengthened spiritually, with."—In article "Eastbourne," page 83, lines 32, 21, and 9 from bottom of the page, read "Bevin, Humphreys, and the Duke of Chandos."

Printed for the Proprietor by BOWDEN, HUDSON & Co., at 23, Red Lion Street, Holborn, London, W.C.; and Published by WILLIAM REEVES, at the Office, 185, Fleet Street, E.C. West End Agents:—WEEKES & CO., 14, Hanover Street, Regent Street, W. Subscriptions and Advertisements are received either by the Publisher or West End Agents.—*Communications for the EDITOR are to be forwarded to his private address, 6, Argyle Square, W.C.*
SATURDAY, FEB. 17, 1883.—*Entered at the General Post Office as a Newspaper.*

THE MUSICAL STANDARD

A NEWSPAPER FOR MUSICIANS PROFESSIONAL AND AMATEUR

No. 969. VOL. XXIV. FOURTH SERIES. SATURDAY, FEBRUARY 24, 1883. WEEKLY: PRICE 3D.

THE EXPRESSION AND DEVELOPMENT OF MUSICAL THOUGHT IN COMPOSITION.*

By E. H. TURPIN, Esq.

PERMIT me to explain the reasons for my present attack upon your kindness and patience. It has struck me that students find their progress in composition considerably impeded by a want of systematic and methodised knowledge of the treatment of available ideas; and by a similar want of ready acquaintance with the appropriate requirements, and suitable adjuncts given types of ideas call for in order to secure their most advantageous presentation and development. And although I cordially applaud such remarkable and valuable additions to our musical literature as the works lately given to us by thoughtful and eminent writers, I am anxious to call forth the observations of those who are so well qualified by their abilities and experience to assist us in an earnest examination of the general principles and motive power, so to speak, of the art of composition. By way of further preface, I should add that my present remarks are simply intended for students, and will not trench upon technical ground. I must also claim your indulgence in another direction; I shall venture to call attention to certain topics which I have already spoken about. Our scientific men are apparently reducing their search after the sources of power at work in the universe to the contemplation of one great mainspring of activity, Electricity; there are signs in the world of art of a similar character, for the operations and impulses of all the arts are being traced by degrees to one common philosophical platform, and the government of artistic power, whatever may be the medium of its communication, is being demonstrated more clearly day by day to be based upon those simple laws of evolution and gravitation which have been erected by the All-wise Creator for the control of all things.

Permit me to add the explanation, that I have nothing of technical value to impart; my wish is merely to encourage my young student friends by very simple, and, I hope, common sense, words.

We are all practically familiar with the fact that even a fair knowledge of the grammar of any spoken language will not enable us to speak that language, although we know at the same time how greatly grammatical laws will direct and strengthen speech. These grammatical rules support, but do not prompt, the mental formation of thought; and similarly, the laws of harmony, invaluable as they are, do not compass in their operations the thought-creating processes of the musical composer. These mental operations are indeed as subtle and mysterious as are the wonderful brain processes which govern the exercise of will and its power over our physical and mechanical means of putting mental decisions into practical action and effect. Undoubtedly there are few, if any, who do not possess musical ideas, but only the trained musician has at hand the workman's skill of shaping and utilising such ideas to the full extent of their possible fruition.

Let me endeavour, however imperfectly, to trace some of the active principles of musical composition. The first motive power it is impossible perhaps to analyse. A direction may, in the first instance, be given to the composer's thought by an assigned task; he may be called upon to compose a work of a given type, he may be prompted by enthusiastic impressions derived from the hearing or contemplation of some masterpiece; or his mental promptings may arise from emotions having their origin in the affections, in the act of self-communing, and in the contemplation of the spiritual, mental, and natural wonders of the

great universe and its Maker; the very thought of such contemplation indeed exalts this human life of ours. Such promptings last mentioned as arising from emotions of the affections, and from personal, spiritual, and mental power, are of course the highest felt by the composer, and the most powerful in their influence over his work. Granting a primary cause, the result may be described as primary impulse. The mood of the composer's mind will be tinged and coloured by human feelings, either joyful, sorrowful, expectant, or regretful. Then the tangible result or primary musical impulse will be in keeping, germs of tune expressive of a given state of feeling coming into something like a definite existence. Now, the musician's work is first brought to bear upon the material so far created. The evolutionary process commences in the power of the composer to select musical initials and fragments which by habit of mind are quickly and instinctively shaped into musical feet, having the life-giving power of palpable accentuation. The law of gravitation sets its mark at once upon the embryo thought. The idea is joyful, or expectant, and hopeful, then the tune particles arise from and return to some centre tone or other, upon major intervals of the scale ladder or harmonic range, which are most frank, palpable, springing, and healthy in their character. Or the idea is sorrowful, or regretful and reflective, then the melodic particles rise and return to a pivot note, upon minor intervals, with closely clinging semitones here and there—for the chromatic genus is the very mainspring of sensitive, sympathetic, melodic action—which are the most expressive and timid in their impulses. Now the composer begins his work in earnest, and looks round for his available machinery and tools; his rhythmical forms, time measurements, appropriate key and mediums of performance, his plane, hammer, screws and nails, so to speak. With an innate knowledge of the nature of the primary impulse of his work, he finds a suitable key, or the idea, most likely, has already formed itself in his practical mind upon some scale map or other, which in most cases, after reflection, he will not see fit to change. The evolutionary process is continued, the leaves of the musical tree begin to expand themselves into corresponding forms, musical feet of the same kind get welded together, their accents point their formation and division, bar lines rise up as the patterns are developed, and a phrase is definitely formed. Now the progress of the idea calls for a decision as to its more complete gravitation, the writer's mind seizes for the first time the extent of ground required for the building up of his thought; he requires so much length of scale, then a centre is fixed upon, his tune is authentic or plagal, or begins in accordance with the strong natural principle of tone-gravitation to adopt more or less elastic externals and to accept some mid-way pivot note or other. Now the sense of proportion, partly acting through rhythmical impulses, comes fairly into action: one figure or phrase will extend in either direction from the centre, to be drawn back to the magnetic pivot sound; then to sweep through another figure or phrase, again to return towards the mentally chosen centretone; so lines of melodic power and beauty, stretched over the still hidden though felt treasures of harmonic combination, are formed in obedience to the great universal laws of evolution and gravitation, and partly shaped by that sense of proportion which is the immediate outcome of these two great powers. Another immediate result of the operation of these natural laws is the entrance of logical influence—a musical sentence becomes a tone syllogism, distinct premises are formed by the action of the melodic figures in different directions, a musical thesis is to be followed by its anti-thesis, and the cadence points the conclusion, as it were. By the time the first sentence

* A Paper read before the College of Organists.

is completed, the general mood or complexion of the piece is disclosed ; for every musical piece has its single or complex state of mind or mood ; which may be indicative of given emotion or emotions, or may be descriptive of some natural and external influences. Look, for instance, at the two quick movements of Beethoven's "Sonata Pathetique," as expressions of impulsive, passionate haste ; at the slow movement of the same work as a picture of self-contained pathos and sorrowful calmness ; again, take the same composer's opening movement of the "Pastoral" Symphony, in which, by skilful reiteration of simple figures, the composer takes us into the drowsy, humming, brain-resting, sunlit fields ; or, once more, contemplate the gigantic wilfulness and pungent humour of such a movement as the scherzo of the "Choral" Symphony. As a general rule, the expression and development of musical types of passion of an energetic or active type are assigned to quickly moving times, and calm, passive, or reflective ideas will find their natural expression in slowly moving measures. The varied rhythmical types, too, are employed with deliberation, in view of the particular kind of thought to be enunciated. Thus the usual 2, 4, and 8 bar sentences are employed, as I have had occasion to point out before, for music expressing vigorous health, frank and genial thoughts ; contracted rhythm, as in the allegro of Beethoven's "Sonata Pathetique," has its special use in aiding the expression of impulsive and passionate ideas ; and extended rhythmical forms add greatly to the enunciation of calm, large, and patient thoughts —witness the first movement of the so-called "Moonlight Sonata." Whatever the character of ideas expressed, the composer is pledged to the maintenance of various types of activity by which the life and circulation of his material is sustained. These are, apparently, of three kinds. There is the deep, underlying movement of the harmonic foundations or chord roots, proceeding in a procession of impulses somewhat slower than the pulsatory beats, which the composer must carefully regulate at a comparatively slow rate of movement, whatever may be the artificial speed of the music, lest the brain of the listener should become fatigued in the effort of realising the widely extended elements of the harmonies employed. Here one may note the extreme value of the modern forms of broken harmony, which enable the composer to sustain great amount of activity without calling for any strain upon the mind of the listener. Another thought connected with the subject of a comparatively slow rate of root progress is the selection of appropriate harmonies. When the melody to be harmonised is frank, natural, and marked by an absence of constrained or acute types of thought, the composer should carefully abstain from the use of chromatic, augmented, or dimished harmonies, as contradictory in effect, and should rely upon the more natural harmonic conbinations. He will do well, indeed, to regard exceptional harmonies as they were regarded by the theorist who proclaimed discordant elements to be chiefly contractions and extensions of natural harmonies, compressed downwards or extended upwards for the better expression of intensified sympathies and emotions. And, like a wary workman, he should be careful in the economy of his materials ; and further should avoid the contraction of habits in the use of extravagant harmonies, which may become tokens of eccentricity rather than signs of eloquence. The next, and perhaps the most vital of the musical activities, is the preservation of the pulsatory beat. It might be shown that throughout the history of music the count-beat has never been greatly disturbed in its regular pace, and an examination of all music, from the simple plain-song to the most elaborate modern score will, I think, prove this, whether the count-beat

be taken as the breve as of old, or the minim as in the Church music of the sixteenth century, or as the crotchet and quaver in our modern time measurements. The pulsation of a healthy man is about seventy-two per minute, and strangely enough the musical pulsatory beat varies similarly, with a comparatively small range, from about sixty to a hundred per minute, and deviations, either slower or quicker, are more artificial than real, for whatever the pace may be at which the music proceeds, the mind clings to some landmarks or other which represent a substantial and moderate rate of progress. The composer must, therefore, I take it, be fully aware of the importance of the proper regulation and maintenance of the pulsatory beat—which should be made to be quietly though firmly felt throughout somewhere in the harmonic strata, only to be stayed in the enunciation of ideas typical of surprise, fear, doubt or expectancy. It will not be necessary to enlarge upon this topic, for all will readily recognise the power the composer gains by the studied employment of properly adjusted pulsations. As the pulsatory beats must as a rule be somewhat more active than the procession of chord roots, in the general proportion of 2 to 1, or 3 to 2, or 3 to 1, in accordance with the varying impetuosity or calmness of the ideas to be presented, so the composer will have to resort frequently to the exchanging of chord positions, and inversions, and other devices by which harmonies may, as it were, be moved without being disturbed. The third kind of activity to be maintained is found in those groups of notes which, being shorter than the pulsatory beats, shelter as it were their recurrent throbbings, remove the laboured stiffness which would result from the too prominent enunciation of pulsatory power, lend grace to the melodic figures, and furnish a sort of useful background to the musical picture. The composer must select the details of this form of musical activity in keeping with the general tone of his ideas ; thus the division of the pulsations into broken harmonies or underlying melodic figures of twos, will furnish a suitable background for ideas of dignity, majesty, or calmness ; triplets will add gracefulness, amiability, and easy action to the expression of a given idea ; and groups of fours to each pulsation will be available for impulsive, brilliant thoughts. Modern composers, in order to present the figure of melodic isolation, absence, contemplation or studied neglect, have pitted triplets against groups of twos and fours, and have so secured such positions by the apparent absence of the melody from the work going on and the general machinery in action around the central figure of the musical picture. Irregular and spasmodic grouping in this form of activity will produce a sense of sharp surprise, or even grotesqueness of thought ; a too long continued irregularity will, on the other hand, invite weariness through its monotony ; although some modern composers have fascinated by the dexterity with which they have produced a sort of perpetual motion by the use of rapid figures sufficiently varied and thin in outline to avoid the usual results of monotonous action. In writing rapid music, the artificial action must be chiefly diatonic, built up in natural and not unfamiliar details, and spread out in thin, transparent tone lines. If the student will go to the piano and play a number of separate chords in rapid succession, he will experience, through the sense of hearing, the same brain oppression which is communicated by the too rapidly moving objects of a panoramic picture. The proper distribution of definite pictorial objects not only seems to correspond with the judicious placing of the themes, but bears comparison with the judicious and never too rapidly moving or overloaded harmony.

(To be continued.)

Musical Intelligence.

CRYSTAL PALACE CONCERTS.

PROGRAMME.

"Siegfried's Death" ("Götterdämmerüng") ...... Wagner.
New Dramatic Cantata, "Alfred", ... E. Prout.
(First time at the Crystal Palace).
Alswitha (Betrothed to Alfred).......... Miss Annie Marriott.
Alfred (King of the West Saxons) .... Mr. Vernon Rigby.
Guthrum (King of the Danes) .... Mr. Bridson.
Chorus of Saxons and Danes, by
The Borough of Hackney Choral Association.
A Selection from the Music to "Thamos, King of
Egypt" .... Mozart.
(First time at these Concerts.)

Conductor   -   -   -   EBENEZER PROUT.

Nowhere in England did the death of Wagner produce so great an impression as in the neighbourhood of Sydenham, for at the Crystal Palace his music has been for many years constantly heard. At other places in our own country conductors have been more or less chary of his music ; but Mr. Manns, with his well-known cosmopolitan taste, has never hesitated to give the Crystal Palace audience the benefit of hearing his overtures and selections from his various works. It was therefore to be expected that on the first opportunity after the death of this great musician, something of his should be performed as a small tribute to his memory, and nothing more fitting could have been chosen than the magnificent march from Siegfried's death-scene.

The libretto of "Alfred" has been ably supplied by Mr. Grist, and first sets before us Alfred as a fugitive from the Danes. After a long love-scene with Alswitha, his promised bride, follows the well-known incident of his appearing in the Danish camp, disguised as a minstrel, when he proves himself as superior to the Danish leader in song as he does afterwards on the battle-field. The last scene describes the surrender of Guthrum, and his pardon by the generous Alfred, on condition that he and his host become Christian. It will thus be seen that the libretto is by no means ill-adapted for varied and effective treatment. Mr. Prout has not failed to avail himself of the opportunities afforded by the libretto ; his well-known knowledge of instrumentation is patent throughout the work ; his artistic and varied groupings of strings, wood, and brass are all highly effective, and his 'celli passages are now and again full of charm. The alternate groupings of wood and corni with harp obbligato are especially felt in Alfred's plaintive song, "Wail, my harp, in saddened strain." Upon the whole, the choruses are bold and well defined, but no attempt at contrapuntal skill, whilst the songs are those of a musician, but lacking in freshness and spontaneity. In his recitatives Mr. Prout follows the old models ; so much so that I remarked to a friend at the time, "Why, that is quite Handelian." The march near the end of the work was extremely well played and well received, and Mr. Prout, at the end of the performance, was much cheered by the audience.

The work was noticed in detail on its production by the Borough of Hackney Choral Association in the *Musical Standard* of May 6th, 1882.

The soloists, Miss Annie Marriott, Mr. Vernon Rigby, and Mr. Bridson, were one and all very successful in their respective parts, and the Hackney Choral Society—which has been carefully trained by Mr. Prout—acquitted itself with great credit. A selection from Mozart's "Thamos King of Egypt," brought the concert to a close.   R. S.

Another contributor writes :—

The success obtained by Mr. E. Prout's cantata, "Alfred," at the Shoreditch Town Hall, in May, 1882, was confirmed last Saturday at Sydenham. Mr. Southgate's admirable analysis of the work (which appeared on May 6th) may be referred to, and his general tone of eulogy will be not feebly echoed. Miss Marriott, however, did much to mar the effect of the soprano music by her lack of fervour, and want of dramatic intelligence. Mr. Prout has made an advance on his former cantata, "Hereward." I agree with a learned member of your staff in thinking the music of Mozart's "King Thamos" very interesting ; so full of beauty, and carefully scored.

The "Dead March," from "Die Götterdämmerung," was played in Wagner's honour. It ought to have been played at the Philharmonic Concert, on February 15th, but the requisite tubas were not forthcoming ! The "Dead March," from "Saul," does duty on parochial organs for every respectable tradesman or local nobody who happens to be officially connected with the church. It is no compliment now-a-days.   A. M.

SATURDAY POPULAR CONCERTS.

PROGRAMME.

Quartet in E flat, Op. 58, No. 1, for two violins,
viola, and violoncello .... Spohr.
Mdme. Norman-Néruda, MM. L. Ries, Hollander, and Piatti.
Song, "Spiagge amate" .... Glück.
Miss Santley.
Two Studies, in B flat minor and F major, for
pianoforte alone .... Mendelssohn.
Mdlle. Marie Krebs.
Sonata in B flat, No. 10, for pianoforte and violin.. Mozart.
Mdlle. Marie Krebs and Mdme. Norman-Néruda.
Song, "Children" .... Arthur Cecil.
Miss Santley.
Quartet in G minor, Op. 25, for pianoforte, violin,
viola, and violoncello .... Brahms.
Mdlle. Marie Krebs, Mdme. Norman-Néruda, MM. Hollander
and Piatti.

Accompanist   -   -   -   Mr. Zerbini.

Spohr's Quartet, introduced for the first time at these concerts within the last few weeks on a Monday, and repeated for the benefit of the Saturday audience in the above programme, is an important addition to the repertory of the Popular Concerts. How fresh, how genial and unaffected is Spohr when he is at his best ; or, indeed when he is himself at all ! This quartet is in the usual four movements and strictly in sonata form. The first allegro starts without introduction, with one of those simple outpourings of melody so characteristic of its composer—melody that flows without a break. On the other hand the striking effect of the accompaniment to the second theme commands attention by its originality. The slow movement contains a beautiful melody and an important episode, which has one of those rare enharmonic changes, "not made, but born," that once heard is never forgotten. The scherzo and trio is equal in interest to the other movements, delicate and graceful ; while the finale—a true rondo, with a pleasing and tuneful rondo subject—brings one of the most equal, unpretentious, and pleasing of all string quartets to a close.

Mdlle. Marie Krebs was very successful in her rendering of the Studies, and obtained the usual encore. In the duet sonata—one of the most interesting Mozart has left us—her touch was occasionally unsympathetic, especially when her part was simply accompaniment.

If a performance at these concerts ever falls short of absolute perfection, the fault lies invariably with the pianist. Brahms's Quartet suffered somewhat from Mdlle. Kreb's failure to blend with the other parts. Her lamentable want of sympathy was positively irritating in the intermezzo, which the muted strings began so delicately without the piano ; but there was an end of all delicacy when the pianoforte part entered and asserted its rights. This shortcoming was the more to be regretted as the movement is one of the most original and effective in the whole range of chamber music. Who can wonder that Schumann wrote enthusiastically of the author of this quartet and the Op. 26 in A major ! It is vain to conjecture what he would have written of their author's later works, if he had lived to trace what followed the rich promises of youth.

Miss Santley introduced a musicianly setting of Longfellow's well-known lines "Come to me, O ye children," by Arthur Cecil, which deserves to be popular. In response to the double recal she repeated the last verse.

B. F. WYATT-SMITH.

M. von Zastrow's agreeable drawing-room concerts have been resumed at Glendower Mansions, South Kensington. One held last Saturday afternoon merits a passing notice. Mr. Bond-Andrews, one of M. von Zastrow's most accomplished pianists, played the first movement of Schubert's Sonata in A minor, Op. 47 (No. 1 on the list), also a Polonaise and Valse of Chopin, and (by desire) his own "Grotesque and Pastoral." The success was decisive. M. de Wolff sang with taste and forcible expession Balfe's fine song in G, "Good night."

MONDAY POPULAR CONCERTS.

Last Monday evening another favourite pianist was engaged by the active director.

PROGRAMME.

PART I.

Quartet in E minor, Op. 45. No. 2, for two violins,
viola, and violoncello .... Spohr.
Mdme. Norman-Néruda, MM, L. Ries, Holländer, and Piatti.
Song, "Gretchen am Spinnrade " .... Schubert.
Miss Thudichum.
Three Musical Sketches ("The Lake, the Mill-
stream, and the Fountain") for pianoforte alone S. Bennett.
Miss Agnes Zimmermann.

PART II.

Sonata in D minor, Op. 12, for pianoforte and
violoncello .... Gernsheim.
(First time).
Miss Agnes Zimmermann and Signor Piatti.
Songs—
"It was a dream" .... Lassen.
"Qual ruscelletto " .... Paradies.
Miss Thudichum.
Trio in D minor, Op. 49, for pianoforte, violin,
and violoncello .... Mendelssohn.
Miss Agnes Zimmermann, Mdme. Norman-Néruda, and
Signor Piatti.

Accompanist · · · Mr. Zerbini.

For once, the weather was not wet! *Cretâ nox notanda!* Spohr's quartet pleased me quite as much as the latest one in E flat, twice performed at these concerts within a fortnight or three weeks. The second theme of the first allegro in G minor is "sweet" indeed, and quite redolent of the master. The larghetto, in C major, melodious, but hardly "unstudied," would seem to have been inspired by a pious meditation of Holy Writ, so *religioso* is the theme. The minuet and trio, full of grace and elegance, remind one of "Papa Haydn," and the finale, where the second subject is again given out—(*pace* Mr. Walter Macfarren)—in the "relative" major, may be cited as a fine specimen of spontaneous effusion, a gem of genius, bright, lively, and finely accentuated. I was glad to hail Mdme. Norman-Néruda again as the leader of the strings.

The director may, as a wag once said, reverence age, but he decidedly favours the young folk. Miss Agnes Zimmermann, a pupil of our own Academy, is really naturalised in England, and is not only a classical pianist, but a prolific composer of finest concerted music for the chamber. Her choice of the three pastoral pieces dedicated by the esteemed composer to his old friend Mr. Jas. W. Davison (how sadly missed in the hall), indicated excellent taste, both in a moral and musical sense. The few idiots who sneer at Sir Sterndale as a mild writer and a cold performer may be left, like Æsop's viper, to gnaw the file and break their own teeth. Would that we could hear the lovely sonata in A flat, "The Maid of Orleans," now and then. Miss Zimmermann played her sketches with unaffected grace, and on a recal—now the inevitable result—resumed her seat at the grand Broadwood to play a canon by Jaddssohn.

I like Gernsheim's duet sonata, which, of course, received the best of treatment at the hands of the accomplished artists. The work comprises an andante with moto in D minor, an allegretto in F major, and an allegro con brio in D major. The annotator rightly approves the piece "as agreeable to listen to, easily followed and understood from beginning to end, and happily not spun out to inordinate length." The composer threatens a fugue, but cuts the matter short. The "laying-out" for the instruments is admirable work; the violoncello expresses the very soul of the music, whilst the keyed instrument embroiders the canto so enunciated with affection and elegant accomplishments. Mr. Hallé and Mr. Arthur Chappell have introduced another of Gernsheim's concerted works (a pianoforte trio in F) at the Spring recitals and the popular concerts. The composer, a Hebrew, is a native of Worms, and 43 years of age.

Miss Thudichum continues to please the subscribers, and she chose a charming specimen of Schubert's vocal style, not to mention the air of Paradies.

Herr Joachim will reappear on Monday next to lead the second Rasoumoski quartet in E minor, and to play a chaconne of Bach.   A. M.

P.S.—I am always glad to quote the observations of writers whom I respect, especially when they do not positively contradict my own views. There are no Popes in *this* world, theological, political, literary, or musical, and those who arrogate to themselves the title must be left to the stern rebuke of Mr. Pickwick, who, on a cer-

tain Christmas Day at Dingley Hall, denounced his friend Mr. Winkle as " a humbug and an impostor." The critic of the *Daily Telegraph* gives the following account of Gernsheim's sonata, the one novelty of this concert, and a work that must and will be repeated. The writer says :—

On one or two previous occasions Mr. Chappell has given amateurs an opportunity of forming an opinion as to Herr Gernsheim's talents. The decision arrived at was most favourable, and we may safely believe that it gained strength from the further experience of Monday night. In the work then presented we find a happy illustration of the fact, often proved, yet in many quarters doubted, that observance of classic form is compatible with the requirements of novelty, just as a Gothic cathedral may be, in general plan, like all other Gothic cathedrals, while in detail so differing from each as to give variety and afford scope for the architect's original ideas. Herr Gernsheim's sonata is of classic design, and at the same time a reproduction of no model. That it contains but three movements merely shows regard for the earliest sonata form, but the refusal of a " working out " section in the opening allegro is a decidedly independent stroke, worthy of observation though interfering little with the logical structure of the movement. While otherwise mindful of established rule, the allegro is treated according to the freedom of modern practice. Thanks, however, to its order and symmetry, it never becomes vague or degenerates into diffuseness. The second movement, an allegretto corresponding to the *minuet* (or scherzo) and trio of more strict form, offers a contrast to its predecessor by a distinct approach towards those earlier models which combine joyous and and unrestrained expression with scholastic language. Herr Gernsheim has fairly succeeded in a task of acknowledged difficulty, and one that becomes more arduous as scholasticism goes increasingly out of fashion. His music is good in structure and charming in effect—revealing a mastery of which we take pleased and careful note. The finale is much more modern, notwithstanding the feint of a fugue with which it begins. As regards that feint, Herr Gernsheim resembles the hero in " Cox and Box," who made solemn preparations for throwing himself over the cliff, took a run to the brink, stopped, and went home. This is a favourite trick now-a-days, and shows, perhaps, a saving discretion. No doubt it may be said that the great masters showed the way; but it is also true that they sometimes took the leap. Apart from its dallying with fugue, the finale belongs entirely to the modern free style, and here and there continues discoursing without having anything particular to say. Nevertheless, taking the sonata as a whole, we are glad to see it in Mr. Chappell's repertory, and ready to welcome it again and again. The performers did full justice to their theme. Indeed, the sonata could not have been, from an interpretive point of view, more perfectly laid before the audience ; who, we may add, received it with instant appreciation.

PHILHARMONIC SOCIETY.

The first concert of the seventy-first series was given at St. James's Hall on the evening of the 15th inst. One is glad to learn that the season promises to be a successful one, so far as pecuniary matters are affected. The Subscriptions show an increase over those of any previous year, while the Guarantee Fund already amounts to sixteen hundred pounds. This fund forms some sort of test as to the estimation in which our old society is held in London. Among the names of the guarantors will be found most of those of our best known professional musicians and amateurs. There is little doubt that if the Directors were to take the trouble of making this feature more widely known, such a hearty response would be given to any appeal put forth, that so far as the sinews of war at least are concerned, the institution would be placed in a position thoroughly satisfactory. The long list of important, indeed immortal, works that have been produced during its time-honoured history, as well as the roll of its distinguished conductors, show that its aims have always been directed towards true æstheticism, and that the Philharmonic Society has established enduring claims on the gratitude of the world of music. It has seen younger rivals, whether under native or foreign management, die out, despite much trumpeting and high-sounding protestations. There are, however, some persons who maintain that the society exhibits signs of fossilization ; while others contend that its Directors show a decided negligence respecting the works of Englishmen. There are not wanting indications but that there is a certain amount of truth in the latter accusation. Though art belongs to no country, the cultured music followers of London require that the best works of all contemporaneous schools shall be presented to them, yet it cannot be denied that compositions by our own countrymen naturally present the first claim to our attention. The only important provision they should exhibit is, to be up to the standard of the highest art requirements of the age. If, then, this necessity be only complied with, the Directors of the society should boldly produce such works, fearing neither the attacks of foreign, nor the sneers of unfriendly English, newspaper critics. There is too much competition, and there are more than sufficient active advisers to allow the Philharmonic to become fossilized ; but those who move in musical circles know that complaints are at times heard to the effect that the society is too indifferent to English authors. It is said that the works already in their library are ignored, and that important novelties are often produced elsewhere, or meet with neglect at their hands. The request addressed to Mr. A. C. Mackenzie to write a symphony for the society, and the invitation lately issued to write a competitive overture, is a step in the right direction ; but experience shows that commissioned works are rarely successful.

The programme of the concert was as follows :—

Overture, "The Naïads"		S. Bennett.
Chorus of Dervishes		
Turkish March	} "The Ruins of Athens"....	Beethoven.
March and Chorus		
Romance, "Le Vallon"		Gounod.
	Mr. Frederic King.	
Introduction to "Parsifal"		Wagner.
Choral Fantasia		Beethoven.
	The Philharmonic Choir.	
	Solo pianoforte— Mdme. Sophie Menter.	
Symphony in A minor (The "Scotch")		Mendelssohn.
Aria, "Zeffiretti lusinghieri" ("Idomeneo")		Mozart.
	Miss Santley.	
Pianoforte solos—		
Andante Spianato and Polonaise		Chopin.
Etude in D flat		Liszt.
	Mdme. Sophie Menter.	
"L'Invitation à la Valse" (arranged for orchestra		
by Berlioz)		Weber.

Sir Sterndale Bennett's poetical overture was written n 1836, at a time when its gifted composer was yet a youth at the Royal Academy of Music. It was given in London at the beginning of the following year, and a few days afterwards it was played under Mendelssohn's auspices, at the Gewandhaus concerts, obtaining the admiration of all the listeners. This lovely work, with its haunting, graceful melodies, refined thoughts, and delicate orchestration, is so well-known and appreciated, that it is needless to dilate on its manifold beauties. The incidental music to the "Ruins of Athens" is a remarkable instance of the great composer's power of adaptation to local tone. Not that (according to the statement of competent authorities) the Turks possess any music of their own worth hearing, but still Beethoven's music, with its strongly marked rhythms and *bruyant* accents, pictures to one's mind coarse Eastern music, with its semi-barbaric features. In the case of the March, the marked effect produced by the emphasized accents is singularly effective. The choir sang the music well, but the chorus of Dervishes would have been improved by a little more vigour and fervour.

The death of Wagner, who was an Hon. Member of the society, was appropriately commemorated by a performance of Handel's "Dead March," the audience standing as a mark of respect. The prelude to "Parsifal," the deceased master's latest dramatic work, which was given for the second time in England (having been previously heard at the Crystal Palace) may possibly be effective in its proper place, as an introduction to the "Bühnenweihfestspiel" on the stage, but viewed as a piece of absolute music it cannot be pronounced successful. Of the drama itself, which has been described as exhibiting its materialistic composer's contempt for a religion he had no sympathy with, no remarks need here be made ; but the brief description of the opera and its aims given in the programme-book of the evening, and the introduction of its prelude, are not without significance. It seems as if the way is to be gradually prepared for the production on the stage of this travesty of holy mysteries. Whether the thick and thin devotees of the eccentric Bayreuth master will succeed in their desire, remains to be seen. They should reflect that, though the English public laughed over pink-steam-vomiting dragons, magic swords, giants, mermaids, and other fantastic devices, of which Wagner's operas contain plenty of examples ; yet the same public would probably view a stage treatment of "The Lord's Supper" with feelings altogether different. The prelude itself is but a poor specimen of Wagner's genius ; it is of a sombre cast throughout, and its dulness is not relieved by any variety in the colouring of its orchestral tone. Mere chord-excursions oined together by jerky unmelodious fragments are not

yet accepted as proper examples of seriously constructed music, nor does fertility in orchestral devices make up for poverty in artistic invention.

Mdme. Sophie Menter gave a superb rendering of Beethoven's Choral Fantasia, a work in which the great tone-poet was evidently preparing himself for the gigantic Choral Symphony. Its brightness and regularity presented a startling contrast to the gloom of the preceding piece. The choral portions of the work were admirably rendered. Mendelssohn's highly imaginative Scotch Symphony (No. 3) was the most attractive item of the programme. It was indeed splendidly played, and the picture presented of Scottish scenery, character, and sounds, was indeed a treat to view. The symphony is probably its gifted composer's most original and poetical work, redolent alike of musical beauty, inventiveness, and picturesque instrumentation. Why Mr. Cusins disobeyed the directions Mendelssohn himself attached to the score, to the effect that "the separate movements must follow one another immediately, and not be divided by the elsewhere customary interruptions," one is at a loss to know. No gain ensued from this, but it rather breaks in the current of thoughts.

In Chopin's charming "Andante and Polonaise," Mdme. Menter was heard at her best ; tone, *technique*, and feeling being alike most enjoyable ; not so, however, in the study of Liszt. The composition may be all very well as a vehicle for exhibiting her extraordinary mechanical powers, but it contains no real music, and frequently led the pianiste to force from the pianoforte harsh, wiry tones, through the terrible blows to which the keys were subjected. Weber's "Invitation" is not a fit piece for a Philharmonic concert, and the suggestion made as to its novel freshness is amusing to those who have heard and admired Berlioz's ingenious scoring for the last quarter of a century.

"Gounod's "Le Vallon" proved a dull, heavy song, and Mr. King was unable to awaken much interest in it, in spite of his careful singing. Mozart's delicate song from "Idomeneo" suited Miss Santley's sweet voice well ; her refined tone and tasteful execution gave general satisfaction.

Sarasate plays at the next concert, and a performance of Raff's "Im Walde" symphony is announced.

T. L. SOUTHGATE.

LIVERPOOL.

(From our Own Correspondent.)

FEB. 21, 1883.

There has been nothing of any importance musically here lately, except the stormy meeting of the proprietors of the Liverpool Philharmonic Society held some few days ago. It seems that the meeting and its objects were illegal, but a kind of compromise was come to, and the committee of the society agreed to meet some eight of the proprietors and consult them as to the future of the society's working and the choice of a new director. I believe the real object the forty proprietors who summoned the meeting had in view, was the appointment of a conductor, which appointment will have to be finally settled at the meeting in May. There are very decided rumours that Mr. Charles Hallé is to be appointed to the vacant post, but I believe that, as yet, nothing is fixed or finally resolved upon. Englishmen would seem to be at a discount with the Liverpool Philharmonic Society, committee and proprietors alike.

There has been a large amount of correspondence in the local newspapers regarding the society, but a great deal of it has been chaff aimed at the forty proprietors who called the meeting of their brother proprietors, and then found that the meeting was not a legal one.

The Charles Hallé orchestral concerts came to an end last evening, when several items from the Wagner repertoire were included in the programme in memory of the great composer.

Mr. John Hodgson gave his second organ recital at St. Ann's, Aigburth, on Saturday afternoon last ; the programme will be found in the proper column.

I am delighted to find that Mr. Best's salary as corporation organist is to be increased by £100 a year. Even with this increase the salary is much too small.

Mdme. Marie Roze is selected to sing at Mr. Lee's concert at the Philharmonic Hall, to be held early next month.   J. J. M.

LEEDS.

Another chamber concert was given in the Albert Hall last week, when the following was the programme :—

Trio in E minor	Spohr.
Song, "Orpheus with his lute"	Sullivan.
Violin Solos—	
Romance	Raff.
Tarantella	Moszkowski.
Pianoforte Solo, Sonata	Scarlatti.
Sonata in E flat, Op. 12, for violin and piano	Beethoven.
Songs—	
"Solveigslied"	Grieg.
"Wiegenlied"	Brahms.
Pianoforte Solos—	
Ballo and Bourrée	Gluck.
Polonaise, Op. 89	Beethoven.
Trio in A major	Haydn.

The artists were Mdlle. Marie Krebs (pianoforte), Herr Otto Peininger (violin), Mr. Chas. Ould (violoncello), and Mrs. Hutchinson was the vocalist. Mr. C. Wilkinson accompanied on the piano. The next of these interesting concerts will take place on Tuesday, March 13.

ROYAL ACADEMY OF MUSIC.

At the Student's Concert of February 17th, before a crowded audience, the "Dead March" in "Saul" was played by Mr. G. J. Bennett, on the organ, in memory of Wilhelm Richard Wagner, at the commencement of the programme. The choir then gave a "Gloria in Excelsis Deo," by Hauptman. Amongst the pieces were Mendelssohn's 3rd organ Sonata well played by Mr. H. C. Tonking ; two sketches for pianoforte, charmingly given by the composer, Miss Annie Cantelo ; a Serenade with horn obbligato, by Mr. C. S. Macpherson, a student ; Miss Kate Hardy sang artistically solos by Rubinstein and Schumann ; Mr. Frank Arnold played, in good style, a violin solo ; several other solos, vocal and pianoforte, were excellently given ; and the choir sang Professor Macfarren's charming setting of Shakespeare's " Orpheus with his lute," and two artistic and graceful choral trios by Mr. G. J. Bennett, for female voices. The concert at once attested the excellency of the work done at this institution and its strong hold upon public favour.

UNIVERSITY OF DUBLIN CHORAL SOCIETY.

On Saturday last the College Choral Society inaugurated the season 1883 with Carissimi's cantata "Jonah." Sir Robert Stewart replaced the obsolete score by a more modern orchestration expressly written for this performance. The manner in which the band performed its part deserves particular mention, because the material which Sir Robert Stewart supplied it with helped the audience considerably in appreciating Carissimi's composition as it deserves. Mr. Walter Bapty's recitative singing also gave the cantata an advantage.

The following particulars respecting the composer are taken from the book of the concert, and may not be without interest for our readers :—

Giacomo Carissimi was born in 1580, and lived to the advanced age of ninety, greatly honoured and respected by his contemporaries. Kircher in his "Musurgia," mentions him as a master then living (in 1650) who had long filled, with great reputation, the place of Composer to the "Collegio Appolinare" at Rome, and the Pontifical Chapel. Carissimi exercised a most important influence in the progress of music by his development of recitative, which Caccini had originated. Other composers of the time also wrote in this form, but to Carissimi belongs the merit of having matured it. He was the first who wrote cantatas on sacred subjects, and introduced accompaniments of stringed instruments, thus laying the foundation of the present form of oratorios. It was from Carissimi's oratorio, "Jephtha," that Handel appropiated the chorus, "Plorati, filiæ Israel," setting it to the English text, "Hear, Jacob's God," in his oratorio "Samson." It is quite probable that Carissimi never heard his double choruses sung with more than one voice to a part. It will be observed that in "Jonah" there are several choruses in three-part writing, and the voice that has sung narration recitative is silent in the chorus that follows. This is a guiding principle, and can only have resulted from the absolute necessity of giving breathing time to the performers.

A selection from "Acis and Galatea," furnished the second part of the concert, which was attended by the members of the Viceregal Court. The conductor of the society may be congratulated on the brilliant auspices under which the present season has been opened.

MUSIC IN CHELTENHAM.

(From our Own Correspondent.)

Ever since the opening of the season in October last, there has been a continual flow of music. It has been asserted that Cheltenham is not a musical town, and it has been observed in high quarters that it has no resident orchestra, but is obliged, like many other opulent and crowded places, to depend on overworked musicians of London and Manchester, whenever an orchestra suitable for public performance is needed. We have lately had very favourable exhibitions of local orchestras, consisting for the most part of resident musicians. I allude to those engaged at Mr. J. A. Matthews's Choral and Orchestral Society, and Mr. A. von Holst's afternoon concerts lately instituted. We have the material in our midst for a really fine orchestra. If a little more interest were given by local musicians to rehearsals, good results would soon be manifested. The performance of Mendelssohn's oratorio "Elijah," by the choral society above mentioned, on Tuesday evening, Feb. 13th, at the Assembly Rooms, was most successful. The band and chorus numbered about 150 performers. The work was exceedingly well done throughout, and reflected great credit on all who took part in it. The solos were well rendered by Miss Julia Jones, soprano ; Miss Emily Dones, contralto ; Mr. A. Kenningham, tenor ; and Mr. Montague Worlock, bass. The latter gentleman made a good impression on this his first appearance in Cheltenham. He possesses a fine baritone voice of good power and compass, and sings in a most finished manner. The leader of the band was Mr. E. G. Woodward, and Mr. J. A. Matthews occupied the post of conductor.

Mr. A. von Holst's first afternoon concert took place at the Rotunda on Saturday week. It was well attended, and the programme, entirely instrumental, was exceedingly well rendered by our local musicians. The programme included Mozart's Trio in E flat, and Raff's Gavotte for piano and orchestra. Mr. von Holst played in a brilliant and faultless manner.

The Quartet Society will give its next subscription concert on Monday, Feb. 26th. Herr J. Ludwig, 1st violin ; Herr van Praag, 2nd violin ; Mr. Richard Blagrove, viola ; M. Albert, violoncello ; and Miss Amy Hare will preside at the piano. The programme contains Quartet in A minor (Schubert), Trio in B flat, Op. 97 (Beethoven), solo violin from Concerto (Mendelssohn), and Quartet in G minor, Op. 74, No. 3 (Haydn). This excellent society is doing good work and receives fair patronage.

The Mayor has received an invitation to hold a local examination here of candidates for the Royal College of Music. The local examiners appointed are Dr. A. Dyer, Mr. A. von Holst, and Mr. J. A. Matthews. The Ladies' College is granted for the purpose.

Mr. Joseph Maas is announced to make his first appearance here on March 8th at a ballad concert. The star system is usually very successful here, as in other places. Let us hope the programme will contain fewer *royalty* songs than we are in the habit of having at this class of concert.

I hear the Musical Society is going to honour its worthy conductor, Dr. Dyer, with a performance of his exercise, composed for his Doctor's degree, at Easter, in the Winter Gardens. This is worth noting, and I trust other native composers will receive the same kind of recognition. The work is a short oratorio ; its title is "Salvator Mundi."

In addition to these leading events, many other musical bodies have given, or announce, concerts for local charities. Amateur concerts are always very profitable here, and ofttimes the performances are very creditable.

The Choral Society takes up Gounod's oratorio "Redemption" for practice.　　CANTOR.

HAYDN's "PASSION" IN LIVERPOOL.—The English adaptation of the above splendid work was rendered on Wednesday, the 14th inst., at St. Jude's Church, by Mr. R. W. Banner's well-known choir in a most efficient manner, and will be repeated each Wednesday in Lent. This is certainly an innovation in the right direction in Liverpool, for Lenten services, as a rule, have commended themselves to but little to the sympathies of the congregations. On this occasion the superb strain of the "Seven Last Words" were listened to by an immense congregation, and seemed to make a deep impression on all present. Mr. J. L. Hughes was the leader of the choir, and Mr. S. Claude Ridley presided at the organ. It is probable that full orchestral accompaniments will be supplied for Holy Week.

GLASGOW.

The Choral Union season terminated on February 14th, and, for the present, orchestral music ceases to be performed in Glasgow. At the tenth concert, February 6th, the programme included : overture, "Oberon" (Weber) ; Symphony No. 3, "Scandinavian" (Cowen) ; Concerto for pianoforte and orchestra, in A (Schumann) ; Vorspiel to "Parsifal" (Wagner) ; overture, "Tannhäuser" (Wagner) ; some vocal pieces by Miss Julia Gaylord ; and four pianoforte pieces by M. Louis Breitner. The leading feature of the concert was M. Cowen's symphony, conducted by the composer. This noble production was listened to with much interest by the audience, and the impression it gave was one of admiration and pleasure. There can be no doubt as to the place which this work must hold in the realm of British instrumental music, and we have no hesitation in assigning it the foremost place in the class to which it belongs. The young school of British musicians is rapidly coming to the front, and it is certain that, when the educational facilities now preparing are fully in progress, the pre-eminence held by the English during the 16th and 17th centuries will experience something like a revival.

At the eleventh concert Handel's "Samson" was produced. The vocalists were Miss Annie Marriott (for Miss Williams, ill), Mdme. Bolinbroke, Mr. J. Maas, Mr. H. Blower, and Mr. J. Bridson (for Signor Foli, ill). Dr. Peace presided at the organ, and Herr Manns conducted. The choral portions of the work had been efficiently prepared, under Mr. Allan Macbeth's direction, but the effectiveness of much of the work was lost through a too protracted performance. The *cuts* were judicious, but not sufficiently numerous. It would be much more creditable to the Choral Union if an annual performance of Handel's "Messiah" was made representative of the master's claims to a hearing. There are numerous worthy British musicians with oratorios well worth performance, and it is thought these should be made known to the public through the agency of powerful societies like the Glasgow Choral Union. The effect of a general movement among our choral societies to encourage what is somewhat ambiguously termed *native talent* would be to raise the whole status of the musical art, and to do an immeasurable service to British musicians. The solo portions of "Samson" were only moderately well performed.

The concluding concert of the series was given on February 14th, the programme being appropriately prefaced by a performance of the "Dead March" in tribute to the demise of Wagner. The programme included overture, "The Merry Wives of Windsor" (Nicolai) ; intermezzo, "On the Water," from "Jason" (Mackenzie) ; symphonic poem, "Mazeppa" (Liszt) ; overture, "A Midsummer's Night's Dream" (Mendelssohn) ; variations for strings on the "Austrian Hymn" (Haydn) ; and Symphony No. 7, in A (Beethoven). Miss Marriott was the vocalist, in place of Miss Anna Williams (indisposed). Most of the items were familiar, and that which was the most pleasing novelty was Mr. Mackenzie's intermezzo. This piece is very cleverly wrought out, and gives rise to a desire to hear the whole work. The symphonic poem of Liszt it is difficult on a first hearing to judge, and one can only say that it is either a huge contemporary joke, or a work of vast genius only suited to the musical comprehension of a remote posterity. I have reason to believe that the orchestral performers were by no means delighted with it, either as a work of genius or a work for performance. A *plebiscité* was taken at this concert, as had been done at the previous Saturday Popular, and the result of the voting gave the following programme, which may be taken as a questionable specimen of the Glasgow musical taste :—Overture, "William Tell" (Rossini), 392 votes ; "Symphonie Fantastique" (Berlioz), 432 votes ; Overture, "Oberon" (Weber), 172 votes ; Intermezzo, "Vergiszmeinnicht" (Allan Macbeth), 189 votes ; Selection from "Rosamunde" (Schubert), 195 votes ; Dance from the "Tempest" (Sullivan), 330 votes ; Overture, "Tannhäuser" (Wagner), 423 votes. The voting in the symphony division of the works set apart for selection gave Berlioz 432 (as above) ; Beethoven's "Pastoral" 419, Cowen's "Scandinavian," 394, etc., while in the other departments the voting was similar in most respects to last year.

The Glasgow Select Choir will give a concert in St. Andrew's Halls, on Saturday, February 24th, the programme to consist of glees, part-songs and solos. Dr. Peace will also appear at the organ.   J. B.

PRINCIPAL CONTENTS OF THIS NUMBER.

NOTICE TO SUBSCRIBERS. — All Subscriptions due for the current year which have not already been sent in should be forwarded at once.

LONDON : SATURDAY, FEBRUARY 24, 1883.

THE PRESENT POSITION OF THE COMPOSER.

I.

THE admirable and thoughtful article on Æstheticism by Mr. EUSTACE J. BREAKSPEARE in last week's issue, should command the careful attention of composers and students. The author points out that the world has discovered and to a large extent accepted the fact that the spirit of modern art is to "amalgamate perfectly the distinct "forms," to secure the "correlation of arts," which in music has caused "a striving after a more decidedly "poetical motive" as a primary action in the composition of tone-pictures. It is hardly the time to point out here that the great composers' works show us that this is by no means an absolutely new feature in the art, seeing that such works indeed prove the "correlation of the arts," in their poetical thoughts, shapely forms, and exquisitely proportioned parts ; and, to go still further, one may assert that the spirit of beauty in each of the arts inevitably involves the expression of art canons forming the guiding principles of all art-life. However, to turn to the more immediate object of these articles. One of the most serious difficulties which meet even the well directed efforts of competent writers of music, is the obstinate reluctance of performers and audiences alike to accept compositions planned upon necessarily stereotyped forms. To take two examples, the world, broadly speaking, apparently cares for no pianoforte sonatas save those by Beethoven, and no organ fugues save those by Bach. This aptitude for conservative restriction appears to press more upon the producer of music than upon any other class of inventive artists. It may be that the great masters have supplied us with a present sufficiency of works built upon given forms, and, what is more probable, this restrictive aptitude results from a certain indolence of apprehension, and a still widely-spread ignorance as to the elasticity of established forms. Curiously enough, the poet may still successfully write sonnets, the painter may limn landscapes, and the architect build churches; undoubtedly the shortsighted restrictive attitude of the public mind as regards the musical composer is anything but true and liberal. Possibly our composers themselves have assisted such general ignorance and obstinacy with regard to this restrictive attitude in music by not aiming sufficiently towards the amplification, development, and expansion of the forms they employ. Certainly no single great composer can be named who failed in some direction or other to amplify the musical architectural schemes which formed the accepted mediums for the expression of each given personal display of thought, genius, and skill. The young composer will do wisely in giving some consideration to this special difficulty; and he should not allow himself to shrink from the task of conquering a narrow and unjust prejudice, even though he may desire to attain some present success by prudently approaching public appreciation through other form mediums than those apparently already monopolised, according to public opinion, by the great masters of the art.

E. H. TURPIN.

LENT AND EASTER MUSIC.

THE Church of England is rather conventional in its choice of Psalmody, especially for special occasions and particular seasons. Lent, by few practical persons observed in any fashion—"Seldom at church, 'tis such a busy life"—is the signal for gloomy tunes in minor keys.

Very often, especially at the week-day services, the organ is stopped, or "stopped off," entirely, in order that the contrast may be the more striking when the church-goers look up again at Easter, and jubilant music comes once more into fashion. Illogical clergymen often drop the "Te Deum" in Lent and use the "Benedicite" canticle instead; because, say they, the former hymn is too jubilant! If this be the case, surely the personification of the Creator's works, and the call upon them to glorify GOD in hearty praise, must lie open to the same objection. On Easter Day Worgan's Hymn in D, with its horrible scream on the high F sharp for the charity children (when the charity children form the "choir"), supplants the sombre tunes of Ash Wednesday and Lent; and flowers replace the sad violet drapery of the Ritualistic churches.

This year a slight difficulty of ritual occurs, already pointed out by a contemporary. For the first time in 139 years the festival of Easter falls on March 25th,

commonly called "Lady-Day." Easter is a high day, the "Annunciation" of much less signification or importance. With regard to the music, this should be exclusively of and for Easter. It is fortunate that Easter so rarely falls on March 25; other days recur with sexennial or quinquennial regularity, but, as before stated, nearly a century and a half has elapsed since this extraordinary coincidence of Easter Day and the Annunciation.

A. M.

THE LOGIC OF 'COUNTERPOINT.

THIRD SERIES.

III.

THE observation Cherubini makes with regard to the employment of the unison in four-part counterpoint of the first species calls for some remark. He says, "It "should be avoided as much as possible, especially "between the upper parts, where it is sometimes "tolerated. It is permitted between the two under "parts, provided this permission be not abused, and "that it is only employed after attempting every means "of avoiding it. The unison is open to no reproach "with regard to any of the parts in the first and last "measures." It should be noted that the unison is more objectionable in the first species, in which the parts move "note against note," than in any other kind, as under such conditions of part action the voices taking the unison do not only represent a rather prolonged weakness and stagnation in the harmony, but as moving absolutely together are less traceable and are more completely absorbed than is the case when two parts fall upon the unison together in the other species. All the same, the occasional unison of two parts for the moment sometimes not unpleasantly thins the harmony, and so affords the ear a slight sense of repose. Opinions will differ perhaps as to the preference of the unison between the two lower parts rather than between the two upper voices. The presence of two parts on the unison, and their approach to such a combination on the same sound, tends slightly to unduly strengthen that sound in performance in the mass of harmony, and it may be a question of taste as to which of the two, the lowest or highest sound, is most satisfactorily enforced in this way. Again, there is a liability when the preference—which the theorist himself inclines to—is in favour of doubling the lowest sound by taking the two under parts to the unison, that those two voices are moving too closely together for the best and most natural distribution of the harmony—an objection which does not exist when the inclination is in favour of the unison appearing between the two upper parts; indeed, the inclination of the preference for the unison being above rather than below, is in favour of the formation of the most natural and the brightest toned harmonic distribution. Anyway, the unison between two given parts should be quite exceptional in four-part counterpoint, especially in that of the first species.

E. H. TURPIN.

The Royal College of Music is to open about the end of May it is thought. The *Times* the other day gave a long list of local examiners who are to test candidates for admission. Paying pupils are to pay £40 per annum, it is said.

Organ News.

PRESTON.

The following is the programme of an organ recital given by Mr. James Tomlinson, in the new Public Hall, on Thursday, Feb. 15th :—

Fifth Concerto	Handel.
Andante con moto (Fifth Symphony)	Beethoven.
Canzone	Guilmant.
Airs ("Les Huguenots")	Meyerbeer.
Allegretto in E ("Lieder ohne Worte")	Mendelssohn.
Overture ("Le Macon")	Auber.

Subjoined are the programmes of organ recitals given in the new Public Hall, by Mr. James Tomlinson, on Saturday, Feb. 17th :—

AFTERNOON RECITAL.

Marcia Religiosa	Perelli.
Adagio for violin and organ	Merkel.
Allegretto Scherzando (Eighth Symphony)	Beethoven.
Gavotte in D	Bach.
Overture ("The Naiades")	Bennett.
Air ("Ezio")	Handel.
Postlude	Smart.

EVENING RECITAL.

First Symphony	Beethoven.
Meditation on Bach's First Prelude	Gounod.
Chaconne in D	Handel.
Overture ("Semiramide")	Rossini.
Offertoire in D	Batiste.
Marche Triomphale	Tomlinson.

BOLTON.

An organ recital was given in the Albert Hall, by Mr. Wm. Mullineux, F.C.O., on Saturday, Feb. 17th. The following was the programme :—

Fantasia and Fugue in G minor	Bach.
Mélodie Religieuse, "Adoremus," Op. 70	Ravina.
"Marche des Pompiers"	Watson.
Concerto in F major, No. 4	Handel.
Fantasia in E minor	Lemmens.
Overture ("Fra Diavolo")	Auber.

The services in connection with the inauguration of the new organ in Park Street Wesleyan Chapel (built by Messrs. T. C. Lewis & Co.), commenced on the 4th inst., were continued on Sunday last, on which occasion Mr. S. W. Pilling was the organist. The selections played at the morning and evening services included :—

Larghetto	Merkel.
Allegretto	Jordan.
Festival March	Thorne.
Andante	Archer.
Air varied	Smart.
Targetto	Rossini.
Grand Chorus	Salomé.

NORWICH.

Annexed is the programme of an organ recital given in St. Andrew's Hall, by Dr. Bunnett, F.C.O., on Saturday, Feb. 17th :—

Overture in D	Méhul.
Pastorale in G	Merkel.
Prelude and Fugue in D minor	Bach.
Adagio ("Maid of Orleans")	Bennett.
Cantilène	Salomé.
Andante in F	Beethoven.
Concertante in C	Handel.
Adagio in G, from a Sonata	Mendelssohn.
"Hymne à Ste. Cécile"	Gounod.
Marche Religieuse	Guilmant.

MANCHESTER.

Mr. J. Kendrick Pyne gave an organ recital in the Town Hall, on Saturday, Feb. 17th. Subjoined is the programme :—

Prelude and Fugue in C major	Bach.
Andantino (Pianforte Sonata in A major, Op. 164)	Schubert.
Suite en Mi majeur, Op. 26	Bernard.
Nocturne on "Gethsemane"	Bonifazio.
Entr'acte in E flat major, for pianoforte	Callier.
March in D major, from a Posthumous Work	Mozart.

CRYSTAL PALACE.

Mr. A. J. Eyre's programme on Saturday last was as follows :—

Marche Funèbre (Sonata in A flat)	Beethoven.
Barcarolle	Bennett.
Allegretto ("Lobgesang")	Mendelssohn.
Adagio non troppo	Stephens.
Fugue in D minor, "The Giant"	Bach.
Sanctus ("Messe Solennelle")	Rossini.
Minuet and Gavotte	Spark.
Overture ("Last Judgment")	Spohr.
Andante in F	Smart.
Military March	Beethoven.

LEEDS.

Dr. Spark gave a recital on the grand organ in the Town Hall, on Tuesday, Feb. 20th. The programme ran thus :—

Offertoire in G major	Batiste.
Andante in F major (Sonata in C major)	Mozart.
Recit., "Deeper and deeper still," air, "Waft her, Angels" ("Jephtha")	Handel.
Barcarolle in F major, from a Pianoforte Concerto	Bennett.
Scena, "The Death of Nelson"	Braham.
Reminiscences of "Les Huguenots"	Meyerbeer.

NOTTINGHAM.

The following is the programme of an organ recital given in the High Pavement Chapel by M. Alexandre Guilmant, on Tuesday, Feb. 13th :—

Toccata in F, with pedal solos	Bach.
Canzonet in A minor, Nuptial March	Guilmant.
Allegro (Concerto in D)	Handel.
Prelude in D minor	Clérambault.
Petite Fugue in G major	Krebs.
Sonata in D minor	Guilmant.
Andantino in D flat ; March, with Hymn of Priests	Chauvet.
Improvisation.	
Fugue in D major	Guilmant.

A local and excellent authority states that the improvisation was most masterly, displaying great command over contrapuntal resources. The subject was given by Mr. A. Page, F.C.O.

OLDHAM.

The following programme was performed in St. Stephen's Church, Lower Moor, on Wednesday, Feb. 14, by Mr. J. Greaves :—

Opening movement	Greaves.
Overture ("Samson")	Handel.
Adagio, Moderato, Allegro, and Finale Presto	Greaves.
Overture ("William Tell")	Rossini.
Lento and Andante (minor)	Greaves.
"Go, baffled coward" ("Samson")	Handel.

AIGBURTH.

The second organ recital of the series in St. Anne's Church was given by Mr. J. Hodgson, on Saturday, Feb. 17th, when he performed :—

Concerto in B flat, No. 2	Handel.
Romanza, "La Reine de France"	Haydn.
Prelude and Fugue in E major	Bach.
Andante con moto (Symphony in C minor)	Beethoven.
Serenade in A major	Spohr.
March in B flat	Smart.

TORQUAY.

An organ recital was given in Upton Church, by Mr. T. Craddock, Mus.Bac., on Wednesday, Feb. 21st, with the annexed programme :—

Sonata in C, No. 2	Mendelssohn.
Pastorale, Op. 57	Kullak.
Prelude and Fugue in C	Bach.
Rhapsodie ("Cantique Breton")	Saint-Saëns.
Funeral March, Op. 35	Chopin.
Adagio in D	Mozart.
Andante in G	Batiste.
Overture ("Occasional")	Handel.

ALDGATE.

At the 173rd anniversary service of Sir John Cass's Foundation Schools, held at the church of St. Botolph, on Tuesday last, the following selection was played by Mr. W. T. Goold :—

Sonata No. 2	Mendelssohn.
Grand March	Guilmant.
"Fixed in His everlasting seat"	Handel.
Postlude in D	Tours.

BOW AND BROMLEY INSTITUTE.

On Saturday last Mons. A. Guilmant was the organist. The programme opened with Fantasia and Fugue in C minor (J. S. Bach). The Prayer in A flat and "Scherzo Symphonique" by the player, both artistic and characteristic pieces, formed an effective group, resulting in an encore ; an Andantino by A. Chauvet, and an Andante con moto by Boëly, received the same honour, and were charmingly played. The theme selected for Mons. Guilmant's improvisation was the "Bridal Chorus" in "Lohengrin," which was handled in a very musicanly and interesting manner. Wesley's "Choral Song" formed a finale to an excellent recital. Mr. Arthur Thompson, a very promising and artistic tenor singer, made a most favourable impression by his admirable performances. Mr. Wood was the accompanist.—To-night Mr. A. Carder will be the organist. His programme includes, by desire, the "March" in Tannhäuser.

FRIZINGTON.

The following is the specification of a charming little organ erected in St. Paul's Church, by Messrs. Brindley and Foster, of Sheffield :—

GREAT ORGAN. CC TO G.

1. Open Diapason......	8 ft.		4. Harmonic Flute......	4 ft.
2. Clarabella and Stopped Bass...	8 „		5. Principal	4 „
			6. Harmonic Piccolo...	2 „
3. Dulciana	8 „		7. Clarionet	8 „

SWELL ORGAN. CC TO G.

8. Violin Diapason......	8 ft.		11. Salicet	4 ft.
9. Lieblich Gedact......	8 „		12. Oboe	8 „
10. Viola	8 „		13. Trumpet...............	8 „

PEDAL ORGAN. CCC TO F.

14. Sub Bass ...　...　...　...　...　... 16 ft.

COUPLERS.

15. Swell to Great.	17. Great to Pedal.
16. Swell to Pedal.	

Two Composition Pedals.

The organ was opened by Mr. Hamilton White, of Retford.

THE LATE RICHARD WAGNER.

The remains of the departed composer were removed from Venice on the 16th, after due honours had been offered to the memory of the great musician. At Munich the station was draped in black. The musical societies formed in line on either side, each man bearing a lighted torch. Many ladies in mourning were present. The adjutant of the King of Bavaria, in full uniform, was the bearer of his Majesty's colossal laurel wreath. As the train slowly entered the station the funeral march from "Siegfried" was played.

The funeral train arrived at Bayreuth about midnight on the 17th, and remained at the station until the afternoon of Sunday, the 18th, when the interment took place. The body was accompanied from the station to Wagner's villa by a large crowd and by many intimate friends, some being from London.

In Bayreuth numberless black flags waved from the housetops. The street lamps were covered with black crape. The shops were closed. Four black horses drew the hearse, preceded by mourners and bands of music. A procession, numbering thousands of persons, followed the coffin to the grave. All the Wagner societies sent deputations. There was some admirable singing at the grave, some of the best passages from Wagner's operas being given by the local societies of Munich.

A requiem was, it is stated, celebrated by the Hamburg Philharmonic Society, an institution quite as conservative, if not more so than its London namesake. The Hamburg Opera also had a performance in honour of the composer. Some surprise has been expressed at the reported decision of the Intendant-General of the royal theatres in Berlin not to give any performance in honour of Wagner. With regard to the fund to be raised for the deceased composer's only son, Siegfried, by special performances, the proposal of Mr. Angelo Neumann will most likely not be accepted. The King of Bavaria, the munificent patron and admirer of Wagner, will no doubt, it is thought, take upon himself to provide, if necessary, for the son's future.

Notwithstanding the not unnatural outbursts of enthusiastic and just now intensified admiration on the part of the deceased composer's personal friends and most enthusiastic admirers, the general comments of the Press have been characterised by such remarkable evidences of just discrimination and due appreciation as prove that the genius and life-work of the great musician are being carefully assessed by thoughtful writers, and that the world will be neither blind to his defects nor averse to the proper recognition of his varied and splendid powers.

MR. CHARLES OBERTHUR.—One has to note the return of this eminent harpist from Paris, where he has given a most successful concert. Mr. Oberthür, on whose shoulders it may be said the mantle of the Englishman Parish-Alvars, the greatest of all harpists of his time, has fallen, is not only a virtuosi on his instrument, but also the composer of operas and many valuable chamber-compositions. The Queen of the Belgians has presented Mr. Oberthür with a very valuable breast-pin, in the shape of a harp set in diamonds, in recognition of his talents.

Academical Intelligence.

UNIVERSITY OF OXFORD.

FIRST EXAMINATION FOR THE DEGREE OF BACHELOR IN MUSIC.

The following have satisfied the examiners :—

William Henry Eady, New College, and Bank House, Chertsey.

Leonard James Rogers, Scholar of Baliol.

William Edmund Stevenson, New College, and Croydon.

Daniel Ferguson Wilson, New College, and Ayr, N.B.

Examiners :—

Sir F. A. Gore Ouseley, M.A., Mus.Doc., Christ Church.

Professor C. W. Corfe, Mus.Doc., Christ Church, Choragus.

J. Varley Roberts, Mus.Doc., Magdalen.

EXAMINATION FOR DEGREES IN MUSIC.

EXAMINATION FOR THE DEGREE OF DOCTOR IN MUSIC.

This examination will be holden in October next.

SECOND EXAMINATION FOR THE DEGREE OF BACHELOR IN MUSIC.

This examination will be holden in October next. In addition to the usual subjects, there will be required a critical knowledge of the full scores of—

Beethoven's Symphony No. 6 ("Pastorale ").

Mozart's Motet "Misericordias Domini."

All exercises are to be sent to the Professor of Music, St. Michael's, Tenbury, as early as possible. None can be received after the end of June.

FREDERICK A. GORE OUSELEY,

February 17, 1883.   Professor of Music.

TRINITY COLLEGE, LONDON.

At the recent Higher Examinations for Diplomas and for the Higher Certificates in Music, the following satisfied the Examiners :—

LICENTIATES IN MUSIC.

(None Passed.)

ASSOCIATES IN MUSIC.

William Henry Barry, Tunbridge Wells; Ernest Burton, Bristol; William J. D. Butt, Brighton; Thomas James Chapman, Margate; Albert Leslie Draper, Southwick; William G. Eveleigh, Guildford; Alfred Furse, Trinity College, London; Clement Rowland Gale, Caterham; Emily Hagger, Trinity College, London; Davis Hunt, Brampton; Lucy E. H. Jackson, Oxford; Orlando A. Mansfield, Warminster; Florence Marshall, Loughborough; Charlotte Jane Ullett, London; Maggie Westwicke, Southampton; Arthur R. Wood, Caterham Valley.

The following satisfied the Examiners for the Studentship in Music, or preliminary examination for Associate in Music :—Frederick J. W. Crowe, Wells; Egerton B. Harding, Trinity College, London; Arthur Hibbett, Ashton-under-Lyne; Francis Pogson, Trinity College, London; Jessie Scooues, Canterbury.

The following obtained the Higher Certificates for :—

PIANOFORTE PLAYING, *Class* 1 (in order of merit) :—Claude Schneider, Trinity College, London; Mary A. E. Pistter, Trinity College, London; Edith Maud Pardy, London; Kate Hannah Frost, Colchester. *Class* 2 (in order of merit) :—Emily Jane Champion, Trinity College, London; Nessie Agnes S. Waite, Bristol; Emily Sworn, Bournemouth; Kate White, Budleigh Salterton; Esther Julia Hawkins, Witham; Florence Eva Dunn, Worcester, *and* Mary Francis Coutts Grey, London, *equal*; Lucy Hackett, St. Ives; Harriett Amelia Turner, London; Arabella Hunt, Trinity College, London; John William Bely, Galashiels.

ORGAN PLAYING, *Class* 2 :—Alfred Henry Day, Eastbourne.

VIOLIN PLAYING, *Class* 1 :—Annie Mary Holloway.

HARMONY, *Class* 1 :—Frederick Nathaniel Baxter, Tetbury; Ada Louisa Cunningham, Loughton; Harriet Agnes Strettell, Guildford; Catherine Agnes Tallant, Guilsborough. *Class* 2 : Leila Edger, Trinity College, London; Louisa Payne, Guildford; Charles Shelford, Brackley.

COUNTERPOINT, *Class* 3 :—Mary Wells, Hinckley.

The following gentlemen kindly acted as Examiners :—Sir George Elvey, E. J. Hopkins, Mus. Doc., A. H. Mann, Mus. Doc., H. A. Harding, Mus. Doc., W. H. Walshe, M.D., F.R.C.P., C. E. Stephens, L. Mus., T.C.L., Walter Parratt, G. A. Osborne, Signor Papini, and G. E. Bambridge.

OOLLEGE OF ORGANISTS.

On Tuesday last, Prof. G. A. Macfarren gave the first of a course of four lectures on "Twenty-four Preludes and Fugues, by J. S. Bach." The interest, not to add curiosity, of the many admirers of the great Cantor of Leipsic, naturally added to what is ever an attractive occasion—a thoughtful discourse by the learned and much esteemed Cambridge professor and principal of the R.A.M. The examples received very artistic illustration on the pianoforte at, or rather from, the hands of Mr. Windyer Clarke, whose playing was characterized by admirable clearness and excellent phrasing. Prof. Macfarren opened his lecture by an interesting account of the composition and compilation of the Twenty-four Preludes and Fugues, forming the accepted second volume of the immortal "48." He then lucidly described the fugal form with its different component parts, together with its origin in ancient diaphony or organum, which was, according to Prof. Macfarren's belief, not sung in successions of 5ths and 4ths but rendered antiphonally, and represented an early form of canonical scoring. Very interesting amongst many most interesting features of the lecture was the tracing out of the foreshadowing of modern forms, as in the prelude in D, with the mixed twelve-eight and ordinary duple measures. The lecturer kept his large and appreciative audience deeply engaged with him in his intellectual and instructive lecture for about two hours, and at the close was applauded with every demonstration of satisfaction and delight. Mr. James Higgs ably occupied the chair, and moved a vote of earnest thanks to the lecturer. Mr. C. E. Stephens proposed a vote of thanks to Mr. Windyer Clarke for his excellently played illustrations, and Mr. E. H. Turpin called upon the audience to acknowledge their obligations to the chairman, who reminded the audience that the course of lectures will be continued on Tuesdays Feb. 27, March 6 and 13.

MAIDENHEAD.—On Tuesday evening, the 6th instant, the Philharmonic Society gave their second concert of the season in the Town Hall. The chief choral works were Dr. Garrett's psalm, "Just Judge of Heaven"; Haydn's motet, "Insanæ et vanæ curæ," and Beethoven's "Hallelujah" chorus. The singing of the chorus was excellent and much applauded. Miss Cravino, as the soloist in the psalm, sang exceedingly well, her fine voice doing full justice to a most beautiful part. The chorus also sang several part-songs in the second part of the programme—Pearsall's "Who shall win my lady fair" had to be repeated. Vocal solos were sung by Miss Cravino (who was encored for a fine rendering of Sullivan's "Will he come," and Master Walter Luttman, a little fellow with a beautiful sweet voice, sang Dr. Bridge's beautiful air, "This is my rest for ever," with much taste and expression. Mr. J. G. Wrigley and Mr. J. S. Liddle, played the variations from Beethoven's "Kreutzer" sonata, with great success; at the close they were warmly recalled. Mr. Wrigley also played Chopin's "Nocturne in G," and Mr. Liddle a barcarolle of his own composition, and an introduction and gavotte by Ries. Mr. J. G. Wrigley, Mus.B., Oxon, conducted. The last concert of the season is announced for April 3rd, when Hiller's "Song of Victory" will be performed for the first time, with orchestral accompaniments.

THE HASTINGS AND ST. LEONARD'S ORCHESTRAL SOCIETY.—On Monday, February 5th, at the Warrior Square Rooms, St. Leonard's-on-Sea, the newly-established Hastings and St. Leonard's Orchestral Society, gave its opening concert before a numerous and select company. The principal items of the programme were Beethoven's overture to "Prometheus," and Mozart's Symphony in D. In addition to these works, two pieces of chamber-music were introduced, as well as some lighter compositions for the band. The orchestra, being but in its infancy, was necessarily deficient in some of the wind instruments, &c. The overture went with considerable vigour, and augured well for the rest of the performance. A sonata, for violin and piano (Beethoven) was played in a masterly manner by Messrs. J. P. Morris and H. C. Nixon. Mozart's symphony was fairly rendered by the small orchestra; this was followed by Reissiger's Quintet in G, for piano and strings (Messrs. Nixon, Morris, Burfield, H. Muscat, and J. Elliott), the performance of which afforded evident pleasure to the audience, and elicited from them marked signs of approval, the violoncello solo in the slow movement being particularly well rendered by Mr. Elliott. Selections from a Russian suite by Wuerst, for muted strings, with violin solo, were played by the band (principal violin, Mr. Morris); these pieces were very pleasing. The concert wound up with a march by Lachner, effectively rendered by the orchestra. For a first concert, the society and its painstaking conductor (Mr. H. Muscat) may be congratulated on the way in which the whole of the music was performed,

Correspondence.

MUSICAL DIRECTORIES.

TO THE EDITOR OF THE "MUSICAL STANDARD."

SIR,—With reference to your leading article last week, perhaps you will kindly permit me to observe that in the Directories of other recognised professions will be found the names, not only of those in actual practice, but also of those who are entitled by reason of their degrees or other qualifications to adopt the calling if they should desire to do so. An examination of the "Medical Directory" will show that several of the clergy are included in the list (although, of course, they are not in medical practice), on the ground that they hold medical or surgical qualifications.

As, in the course of that article, you have made a most generous and undeserved reference to myself, I may add that, on the same principle, I should certainly claim to be included in any authorised Register or Directory of professional musicians, not as an actual practitioner, but as the holder of certain qualifications to practise, and I feel certain that others of my brother clergymen, who, like myself, do not live by the art, would do the same.

May I take this opportunity of suggesting that the more nearly our existing Musical Directories are assimilated in method and detail to those of the sister professions (notably "Crockford," or the "Medical"), the more practically useful they will be as a means of professional reference? Not only the source, but the *date*, of any degree or certificate should be given, as some kind of indication of the professional standing of the practitioner, and as a further means of verification.

In accordance with which suggestion, I beg to append an illustration of the method, and to subscribe myself, Sir,

Your obedient Servant,
H. G. BONAVIA HUNT,
Mus. B., Ch. Ch., Oxon (*May*, 1876).
(Hon.) L. Mus. T.C.L. (*Feb.* 1877).

ORGAN RECITALS AT CHRIST CHURCH, NEWGATE STREET.

TO THE EDITOR OF THE "MUSICAL STANDARD."

SIR,—In the "Passing Events" column of your issue of the 10th inst., Dr. Frost's recital is said to be most probably the first which has been given in the Church since Mendelssohn played there.

May I be allowed to state that, at any rate, *one* recital has been given at Christ Church, since Mendelssohn's time? for I well remember hearing a very fine performance by the late Mr. J. T. Cooper (for many years organist of the church), on April 13th, 1867, just after Messrs. Hill & Son had effected important improvements to the organ, including the completion of the choir and pedal organs.

Upon referring to the *Musical Standard* for 1867, I find that a notice of the recital appears upon page 261, Vol. vi. (old series.)

I think it is only due to Mr. Cooper's memory that his fine performance should not be forgotten.

I am, Sir, yours faithfully,
Anerley, S.E.,   H. HARFORD BATTLEY.
13th Feb., 1883.

TO THE EDITOR OF THE "MUSICAL STANDARD."

SIR,—The Christ Church organ was built by Renatus Harris, in 1690, and I think Elliott and Hill repaired it, about the year 1842. Dr. Gauntlett used to play for perhaps half-an-hour at the close of the Sunday-evening services; but upon a change of vicar the performances, were, I believe, discontinued.

Yours truly,
Feb. 19.   C. H. K. F.

A WORTHY EXAMPLE.

TO THE EDITOR OF THE "MUSICAL STANDARD."

SIR,—We hear so much about the darkness which is supposed to hover over the Provinces in musical matters, that I think it may be interesting to your readers to see what is being done in Salisbury, and what a brave fight a lady is carrying on there in the good cause. I therefore send you a programme of the first concert given by Miss Aylward during the present season. This programme is noteworthy for several reasons. In the first place, vocal music, which owing to the deficient education of our vocalists, and the mercenary motives which too often animate them in their choice of songs, has become a bane, both to the classical concert-giver and the more earnest portion of his audience, is entirely eschewed. In the second place, all the executants, without any exception, are natives of England. This latter is a point which I should be the last to insist upon from any false patriotism, and I only adduce it as a curious commentary upon the statement lately promulgated by a high authority, that if we want to hear good music well done, we must either go out of England or import the performers. That this programme is good music, will, I presume, be allowed; that it is well done I will pledge by word. Miss Aylward is a member of a famous family which has produced more than one star in the musical firmament, and we-professors in the West Country look upon her with great pride, and wish her every possible success in her high enterprise.

PROGRAMME.

Quintet in E flat, Op. 16, for pianoforte, oboe, clarionet, horn, and bassoon	Beethoven.
Sonata in A minor, Op. 47 (" Kreutzer "), for pianoforte and violin	Beethoven.
Septuor in E flat, Op. 20, for violin, viola, violoncello, contra bass, clarionet, horn, and bassoon	Beethoven.

I am, yours very truly,
Sherborne, Dorset,   LOUIS N. PARKER.
Feb. 16, 1883.

THE ROYAL COLLEGE OF MUSIC.

TO THE EDITOR OF THE "MUSICAL STANDARD."

SIR,—In one of your late numbers (Dec. 30), is the following paragraph:—

"THE ROYAL COLLEGE OF MUSIC.—A letter has been received by the Mayor of Liverpool from the Secretary of the Royal College of Music, in which it is stated :—' Provision has been made for two classes of scholarships. A scholarship may be founded by the payment of £2,500, providing education in the College and maintenance for one pupil in perpetuity, obtainable by open competition among all classes of Her Majesty's subjects. The second form is founded by the payment of £3,000, providing education and maintenance, and is obtainable by competition restricted to a district or class, as may be preferred by the founder."

Permit me to ask what security there is that Parliament will never divert the said £3,000 from the district, or frustrate the intentions of the founder notwithstanding his having paid £500 to ensure them? I may be told that the Commons (who manage all money clauses) are bound in honour to respect the intentions of a donor or testator. Judging the future by the past, I say with Master Dumbleton, when he declined sending the two-and-twenty yards of satin for Sir John Falstaff's short cloak and slops,—that "I like not the security." The cautious silk-mercer required "better assurance than Bardolph's"; and so should I.   HUGH CARLETON.
Royal Colonial Institute,
15, Strand.

CONCERT AT READING.

TO THE EDITOR OF THE "MUSICAL STANDARD."

SIR,—Permit me to call attention to one or two points in the notice of our annual concert, which appeared in your issue of 10th inst.

Your "Own Correspondent" states : "The concert attracted a large audience of the working classes." As a matter of fact the audience on the occasion referred to was fairly representative, and could not strictly be said to belong to any class.

Your "Own Correspondent" regrets he cannot yet report improvement in the singing, and asks, "Why do ordinary Tonic Sol-fa classes always seem so rough?"

This is not a Tonic Sol-fa choir at all—less than 20 per cent. of its members singing from that notation, and the roughness cannot, therefore, be ascribed to its adhesion to the method referred to.

As to Tonic Sol-fa choirs generally, I beg to instance the choirs under Mr. Venables, Mr. McNaught, and Mr. Proudman, and numerous others that are well known to your readers, and do not require to be named here. I ask, are these noted for their roughness?   Yours truly,
January 30.   ROBT. J. BURROUGHS.

TO THE EDITOR OF THE "MUSICAL STANDARD."

SIR,—I cannot help thinking that Mr. Burroughs has been quick to take offence where none was intended; but I shall be glad to add a few words of explanation to the "one or two points" of my report to which he has called attention.

The very designation of the choir is sufficient to show that it is intimately connected with the "working classes"; and by its programmes and prices I have supposed that it has wished to provide entertainment for them. This would be honourable enough in itself, and I hope Mr. Burroughs is not ashamed of my noticing it. I did so on this occasion because the body of the hall was well filled, and evidently, to my mind, by respectable working people. In this respect the audience differed from that usually seen at concerts in the Reading Town Hall.

Then, Mr. Burroughs quotes my criticism of the singing of the choir, and the question, en passant, "Why do ordinary Tonic Sol-fa' classes always seem so rough?" On this occasion, as upon a previous one, I could not help noticing the roughness of the choir, but in all kindness I ascribed it, by inference, to the material or the system; and, according to my observation, ordinary Tonic Sol-fa classes are rough.

The excellent choirs conducted by Mr. Venables and Mr. McNaught are very different from the ordinary provincial specimen; and I do not think either of the well-known conductors named would appreciate an implied comparison in this instance. These well-known London choirs I should call extra-ordinary examples of Tonic Sol-fa training.

But, then, Mr. Burroughs says that any roughness in his choir could not be attributed to the Tonic Sol-fa system, as it was not generally adhered to. The method of proceeding led me to suppose that it was, especially as the conductor, Mr. T. Watte, was advertised as "Graduate, Tonic Sol-Fa College, London."

In writing for a musical paper of high standard, I did not think it necessary to be blind to all faults, and flatter with indiscriminate praise. I will only add that I wrote the offending words without the least prejudice against the Reading Temperance Choir, which, I sincerely hope, will improve in good work, and not take hasty offence, or even discouragement, from a little kindly criticism.

YOUR "OWN CORRESPONDENT."
Reading, February 19th, 1883.

THE HUMAN VOICE.

On Saturday the 17th, a lecture on singing was delivered at the Royal Institution, by Dr. W. H. Stone, who exhibited some beautiful photographs which Mr. Behnke has succeeded in obtaining of his own soft palate and vocal ligaments in the act of tone production. These photographs were thrown upon a screen by means of the electric light.

For many years scientific men have tried, but in vain, to achieve this result, which will help to settle many disputed points; and the knowledge derived therefrom will be of great value to all teachers of singing and of elocution. These photographs are the first result of the joint enterprise of Mr. Lennox Browne and Mr. Behnke, who are actively engaged in embodying in a new and comprehensive book their respective experiences of vocal surgeon and of voice trainer.

ENGLISH MUSIC IN MANCHESTER.

It is remarked, now and then, that Mr. C. Hallé does not display anxiety as regards the presentation of National music before his English audiences. The following letter addressed to the Editor of the Manchester Guardian explains itself—

"SIR,—I should like to express to your critic the gratitude which all musicians must feel for his outspoken remarks respecting the difficulties against which English music and its authors still have to struggle. His opinion of the melodic fertility of much of the German music to which we are condemned to listen, and for the sake of which English strains are thrust aside, is entirely in consonance with the remarks with which Dr. Hiles concluded the paper he read at the opening meeting of the Society of Professional Musicians, a paper that ought to be studied by all who could help on the cause of musical education. The Gentlemen's Concerts seem to be now at a discount. Is it not because the directors have been content feebly to agree to plans ready made for them? Let them exert themselves earnestly on behalf of English music, strike out a path for themselves that shall atone for past shortcomings, and they will not appeal in vain for support.—I am, &c., JAS. DAWBER, Mus.B."

OLDHAM.—The Carl Rosa Opera Company have visited the Theatre Royal, commencing Monday, Feb. 12th, and have given some well-known operas, foremost of which were Beethoven's "Fidelio," produced on the opening night, and Donizetti's "Lucrezia Borgia" on Friday. Mdme. Marie Roze appeared in the principal parts of the same, and received able support from the members of the company, including : Misses Burns, Yorke, and Berry, Messrs. J· W. Turner, M'Guckin, Snazelle, Ludwig, etc. The chorus showed signs of careful training, and the orchestra were well up to the work. "Maritana," "The Bohemian Girl," "Mignon," "Lucrezia Borgia," and "Faust," have been given before large audiences. The pianoforte recitals are still continued by Mr. Houghton assisted by Mr. J· Greaves. The programme of Monday contained Beethoven's "Moonlight" Sonata in C sharp minor, and various other classical selections, all of which were well played. Mr. Smith Warburton contributed Diehl's "The Desert" and Watson's popular "Powder Monkey Joe" and Master D. M. Greaves contributed some violin solos.

A morning performance of Mr. Sullivan's "Iolanthe" was given on the 15th, at which all the leading professionals connected with the London stage were invited to be present.

Passing Events.

Suppe's "Boccaccio" has been the latest attraction in Rio de Janeiro.

"La Belle Lurette," Offenbach's posthumous opera, will shortly be produced at the Avenue Theatre.

Spohr's "Jessonda" has been given very successfully at the Berlin Opera House.

Gounod's "Redemption" will be performed in Vienna on March 1st, under the personal direction of the composer.

Gounod's "Redemption" is to be given at Milan, the profits of the performance being destined to aid the fund for the sufferers from the recent inundations in Italy.

The *Brightonian* for the 10th has an excellent cartoon portrait of Mr. Alfred King, Mus.Bac., the corporation organist, and a highly esteemed Brighton professor of music.

The new opéra bouffe entitled "Le Droit d'Ainesse," which is now being played at the Theatre des Nouveautes in Paris, will be produced at the Strand Theatre next month. The music is by M. Chassaigue.

The Strolling Players' Amateur Orchestral Society, conducted by Mr. Norfolk Megone, gave an interesting concert (instrumental and vocal), on Feb. 22nd, at St. Andrew's Hall, Newman Street. The orchestra consisted of 70 performers.

Mr. F. Archer is just now giving a series of six organ recitals at the Chickering Hall, New York. The papers seem to agree that his most remarkable successes as a player are in the lighter and more brilliant pieces. Organ recitals are fast obtaining recognition in America; and the United States can show a goodly array of competent organ players.

M. Poznanski played some of his effective violin solos at the Town Hall, Shoreditch, on Feb. 13th, and was to play at Stratford, Essex, on Thursday evening. These solos were De Beriot's "Tremolo," and Hansen's Fantasie on Scottish Airs. Mr. W. Ganz, at this concert, played with *éclat* his own "Galop de Concert," and took part with M. Poznanski in a grand duet of Thalberg and De Beriot on "Les Huguenots." Mdme. Patey sang the "Creation's Hymn" of Beethoven in superb style.

The Rev. Henry Macnamara, Incumbent of St. Paul's, Dundee, writes to the *Musical Review* that an Italian friend of his possesses the score of a "melodrama," entitled the "Mamertine Prison," by Giovanni Paccini, the once famous composer of "Sappho" and other operas. The scene of the action is laid in that famous prison where SS. Peter and Paul were incarcerated by Nero. The score is in the possession of the author of the libretto, the father of Mr. Macnamara's Italian friend, who is willing to part with the manuscript "for a consideration."

For the Edinburgh Orchestral Festival (the development through the exertions of Sir Herbert Oakeley of the annual concert in commemoration of General Reid, the founder of the Edinburgh Chair of Music, into a three days' festival), Mr. C. Hallé's orchestra was engaged, with Mdme. Norman-Néruda, Miss M. Davies, and Mr. Edward Lloyd as soloists. Admirable selections were given from the works of Handel, Haydn, Mozart, Beethoven, Schubert, Weber, Spohr, Mendelssohn, Schumann, Wagner, Cherubini, Rossini, Berlioz, Gounod, Raff, Sterndale Bennett, Gen. Reid, and Sir Herbert Oakeley.

The Western Madrigal Society met on Wednesday, Feb. 14th, under the conductorship of Dr. Bridge, and performed the following :—Madrigals : "Now morn awaketh" (Anerio) ; "Hope of my heart" (Ward) ; "Queen of the world" (Marenzio) ; "What then is love" (Ford) ; "When Cloris heard" (Wilbye) ; "My lady fair" (Ferretti) ; "In the golden sunset" (T. Distin) ; "Let me careless" (Linley) ; "Cold winter's ice" (Weelkes) ; "The Shepherd's pipes" (Marenzio) ; "O fly not love" (Bateson) ; "Soon as the silver moonbeams" (Gastoldi) ; "Phillis, go take thy pleasure" (Weelkes) ; "In going to my lonely bed" (Edwardes) ; Anthem, "O Lord, turn Thy wrath" (Bird) : Motet, "Jehovah reigns" (Palestrina).

Dr. Stainer has lost no time in proving the earnestness of his endeavour to do justice to the Tonic Sol-fa system in his new position as Inspector of Music in Training Colleges and Schools. The advantage of having a practical Sol-faist associated with him in the work is obvious, and we are glad that Dr. Stainer has recognised it. On New Year's Day the appointment of Mr. W. G. McNaught as an assistant inspector was made by the Education Department. Mr. W. A. Barrett, Mus.B., will continue to act, and it may naturally be anticipated that they will divide the visiting of the Training Colleges between them. The setting of papers is, however, a far more important matter than the visiting, and we hope that Mr. McNaught's appointment will work a revolution as regards the Tonic Sol-fa questions. For the moment, the whole attention of the new officials must have been concentrated upon the scheme for examining schools in singing by note. Our readers will, one and all, join in congratulating Mr. McNaught upon his appointment. From a financial point of view neither he nor Dr. Stainer are gainers ; they are rather to be commiserated. But the possibilities of national work that lie before them are enough to stir the least generous mind. To do this work with tact and firmness, with a skilful, practical wisdom, and yet with a resolution that cannot be shaken, will tax all their energies and all their judgment. We assure Dr. Stainer of the hearty sympathy and best wishes of Tonic-Sol-faists for the new *régime.—Tonic Sol-fa Reporter.*

Service Lists.

THIRD SUNDAY IN LENT,

FEBRUARY 25th.

London.

St. Paul's Cathedral.—Morn.: Service, Benedicite, Martin (No. 1) ; Benedictus, Smart in F ; Introit, O Lord, turn not Thy face from me (Hymn 93) ; Communion Service, Smart in F. Even.: Service, Magnificat and Nunc Dimittis, Walmisley in D minor ; Anthem, Here by Babylon's wave (Gounod).

Temple Church.—Morn.: Service, Te Deum and Jubilate, Aldrich in G ; Apostles' Creed, Harmonized Monotone ; Anthem, Hear my prayer (Mendelssohn), Even.: Service, Magnificat and Nunc Dimittis, Aldrich in G ; Apostles' Creed, Harmonized Monotone ; Anthem, Turn Thee unto me (Boyce).

Lincoln's Inn Hall. — Morn.: Service, Hatton in E ; Kyrie, Steggall ; Anthem, Judge me, O God (Mendelssohn). Even.: Service, Goss in A ; Anthem, Lord, thou hast been our refugue (Hayes).

All Saints, Margaret Street.—Morn.: Service, Benedicite, South; Benedictas, Stainer; Communion Service, Thorne in E flat ; Offertory Anthem, Turn Thy face (Attwood) ; Benedictus and Agnus Dei, Mozart. Even.: Service, Orlando di Lasso in G minor ; Anthem, My God, why hast Thou forsaken me (Mendelssohn) ; Miserere, Allegri.

St. Augustine and St. Faith, Watling Street.—Morn.: Service, Benedicite, Martin (No. 2) ; Benedictus in D ; Communion Service, Martin in C ; Offertory, If we say that we have no sin (Calkin). Even.: Service, Gounod ; Anthem, Remember, Lord (Spohr).

St. Barnabas, Marylebone.—Morn.: Service, Te Deum and Jubilate, Wesley's Chant Service in F ; Anthem, If we believe (Goss) ; Kyrie and Nicene Creed, Merbecke. Even.: Service, Magnificat and Nunc Dimittis, Walmisley in D minor ; Anthem, O rest in the Lord, and, He that shall endure (Mendelssohn).

St. Botolph, Aldgate.—Morn.: Service, Te Deum, Hopkins in B flat ; Jubilate, Goss. Even.: Service, Magnificat and Nunc Dimittis, Stainer in A ; Anthem, He was despised, and, Surely He hath borne ("Messiah," Handel).

Children's Home Chapel, Bonner Road, E.—Morn.: Service, Anthems, There is a green hill (Lord Somerset), and, Arise, shine (Elvey). Aft.: Service, Anthems, As pants the hart (Spohr), and, My God, look upon me (Reynolds).

Christ Church, Clapham.—Morn.: Service, Benedicite, Stainer ; Kyrie and Credo, Weber in E flat ; Offertory Anthem, Lord, for Thy tender mercies' sake (Farrant) ; Sanctus, Benedictus, Agnus Dei, and Gloria in excelsis, Weber. Even.: Service, Magnificat and Nunc Dimittis, Bunnett in F ; Anthem, By the waters of Babylon (Allen) ; Miserere, Helmore.

FOUNDLING CHAPEL.—Morn.: Service, Te Deum, Barnby in E; Benedictus, Smart in F; Anthem, Hear my prayer (Mendelssohn). Aft.: Service, Dykes in F; Anthem, In Thee, O Lord (Weldon).

HOLY TRINITY, TULSE HILL.—Morn.: Chant Service. Even.: Service, Gadsby in C; Anthem, Hear my prayer (Mendelssohn).

ST. JAMES'S PRIVATE EPISCOPAL CHAPEL, SOUTHWARK. —Morn.: Service, Introit, Soul of Jesus (Ancient Hymn); Communion Service, Hummel in D. Even.; Service, Barnby in E; Anthem, Through the darkness (Rossini).

ST. MAGNUS, LONDON BRIDGE.—Morn.: Service, Opening Anthem, I will arise (Clarke Whitfield); Te Deum and Jubilate, Stainer in E flat; Kyrie, Purcell. Even.: Service, Cantate and Deus Misereatur, Hayes in E flat; Anthem, Hear my prayer (Stroud).

ST. MARY ABCHURCH, E.C.—Morn.: Service, Benedicite, Bishop; Communion Service, Garrett in D. Even.: Service, Chants.

ST. MARY BOLTONS, WEST BROMPTON, S.W.—Morn.: Service, Benedicite, Turle in D; Benedictus, Turle; Communion Service, Kyrie, Credo, Sanctus, and Gloria in excelsis, Dykes in F; Offertory, Barnby; Benedictus and Agnus Dei, Redhead in F. Even.: Service, Magnificat and Nunc Dimittis, Stainer's Third Series of Tones; Anthem, Jesu, Word of God Incarnate (Gounod).

ST. MICHAEL'S, CORNHILL.—Morn.: Service, Te Deum, Wesley in F; Benedictus, Dykes in F; Anthem, O Saviour of world (Goss); Kyrie and Creed, Thorne in G; Offertory Sentences, Stainer. Even.: Service, Magnificat and Nunc Dimittis, Ouseley in B flat; Anthem, Withdraw not Thou Thy mercy (Attwood).

ST. PAUL'S, BOW COMMON, E.—Morn.: Service, Benedicite, Best in C; Benedictus, Dykes in F. Even.: Service, Magnificat and Nunc Dimittis, Garrett in F; Anthem (unaccompanied), Come unto Him, all ye who labour (Gounod).

Country.

ARDINGLY COLLEGE, SUSSEX.—Morn.: Communion Service, Hatton in E; Gloria, Wesley in C. Even.: Service, Hatton in E; Anthem, Distracted with care (Haydn).

ST. ASAPH CATHEDRAL.—Morn.: Service, Gilholy in B flat; Anthem, O Lord God of my salvation (Whitfeld). Even.: Service, Roberts in D; Anthem, Unto Thee have I cried (Elvey).

ASHBURNE CHURCH, DERBYSHIRE.—Morn.: Service, Benedicite, Best; Continuation, Dykes in F. Even.: Service, Thackwray in C; Anthem, Turn Thee again (Attwood).

BEDDINGTON CHURCH, SURREY.—Morn.: Service, Benedicite and Benedictus, Turle; Introit, When at Thy footstool, Lord (Hymn 245); Communion Service, Marbecke. Even.: Service, Bunnett in F; Anthem, Come unto Him (Gounod).

CANTERBURY CATHEDRAL.—Morn.: Service, Smart in G; Introit, Praise the Lord (Child); Communion Service, Smart in G. Even.: Service, Smart in G; Anthem, The wilderness (Wesley).

CARLISLE CATHEDRAL.—Morn.: Service, Barnby in E; Introit, Blessed is the man (Stainer); Kyrie and Nicene Creed, Ouseley in A. Even.: Service, Barnby in E; Anthem, Praise the Lord (Wesley).

DONCASTER (PARISH CHURCH).—Morn.: Service, Tours in F. Even.: Service, Tours in F; Anthems, O Lord, Thou hast searched, and, God is a spirit (Bennett).

DUBLIN, ST. PATRICK'S (NATIONAL) CATHEDRAL.—Morn.: Service, Te Deum and Jubilate, Stewart in E flat; Anthem, We have heard with our ears (Sullivan). Even.: Service, Magnificat and Nunc Dimittis, Smart in B flat; Anthems, Distracted with care (Haydn), and, In the Lord put I my trust (Stewart).

DURHAM CATHEDRAL.—Morn.: Service, Boyce in A; Anthem, For He shall give His angels (Mendelssohn); Introit, To the Lord our God (Calkin); Communion Service, Arnold in A. Even.: Service, Arnold in A; Anthem, Think, good Jesu (Mozart).

ELY CATHEDRAL.—Morn.: Service, Benedicite, Chants; Jubilate, Plain-song; Kyrie, Credo, and Gloria, Tours in F; Anthem, Lord, on our offences (Mendelssohn). Even.: Service, Fitzgerald in B flat; Anthem, My God, my God (Mendelssohn).

FOLKESTONE (ST. MICHAEL's).—Morn.: Benedicite, Husband in F; Benedictus, Goss; Communion Service, Introit, Forty days and forty nights (Hymn 92); Kyrie, Credo, Sanctus, &c., Husband in G. Even.: Service, Magnificat and Nunc Dimittis, King in F; Anthem, The Passion Music from "Messiah," Handel).

GLASGOW (BLYTHSWOOD PARISH CHURCH).—Aft.: Service, Anthem, God be merciful (Wesley).

LEEDS PARISH CHURCH.—Morn.: Service, Benedicite, Turle and Stainer; Anthem, Rejoice in the Lord (Purcell); Kyrie and Creed, King in C. Even.: Service, Elvey in A; Anthem, O God, have mercy (Mendelssohn).

LICHFIELD CATHEDRAL.—Morn.: Service, Cooke in G; Anthem, Why rage fiercely the heathen (Mendelssohn). Aft.: Service, Oakeley in E flat; Anthem, O clap your hands (Stainer).

LIVERPOOL CATHEDRAL.—Aft.: Service, Kelway in B minor; Anthem, My soul is weary of life (Beckwith).

MANCHESTER CATHEDRAL.—Morn.: Service, Benedicite, Battishill in E flat; Benedictus, Dr. Garrett in G; Anthem, All ye who weep (Gounod);. Communion Service, Monk in A. Aft.: Service, Chipp in A; Anthem, Why rage (Mendelssohn).

MANCHESTER (ST. BENEDICT's).—Morn.: Service, Kyrie, and Credo, Nares in F; Sanctus, Benedictus, and Agnus Dei, Palestrina (Æterna Christi Munera). Even.: Service, Magnificat and Nunc Dimittis, Jordan; Miserere, Redhead.

MANCHESTER (ST. JOHN BAPTIST, HULME).—Morn.: Service, Benedicite, Marbeck; Kyrie, Credo, and Sanctus, Dykes in F; Benedictus, Thorne; Agnus Dei, Miné in F. Even.: Service, Magnificat and Nunc Dimittis, Gregorian; Miserere, Redhead.

MUSSELBURGH (LORETTO SCHOOL).—Morn.: Introit, Turn Thy face from my sins (Attwood); Service, Dykes in F; Anthem, Then round about the starry throne ("Samson," Handel). Even.: Service, Anthem, Plead Thou my cause (Mozart).

PETERBOROUGH CATHEDRAL.—Morn.: Service, Goss in A; Introit, Cast thy burden (Mendelssohn); Communion Service, Barnby's Monotone and Tours in F. Even.: Service, Tours in B flat; Anthem, De Profundis (Gounod).

RIPON CATHEDRAL.—Morn.: Service, Chants; Anthem, Seek ye the Lord (Roberts). Even.: Service, Haynes in G; Anthem, O God have mercy (Mendelssohn).

ROCHESTER CATHEDRAL.—Morn.: Service, Hopkins in G; Anthem, Rend your heart (Colborne). Even.: Service, Hopkins in G; Anthem, Hear my prayer (Mendelssohn).

SHEFFIELD PARISH CHURCH.—Morn.: Service, Kyrie, Mendelssohn. Even.: Service, Magnificat and Nunc Dimittis, Trimnell in D; Anthem, Incline Thine ear (Himmel).

SHERBORNE ABBEY.—Even.: Service, Anthems, He was despised, and, Surely He hath borne (Handel).

WELLS CATHEDRAL.—Morn.: Service, Barnby in E; Introit, Blessed is the man (Stainer). Even.: Service, Barnby in E; Anthem, I wrestle and pray (Bach).

WORCESTER CATHEDRAL.—Morn.: Service, Lloyd in E flat; Anthem, Turn Thy face (Attwood). Even.: Service, Smart in G; Anthem, Henceforth when ye hear (Mendelssohn).

NOTICES TO CORRESPONDENTS.

NEWSPAPERS sent should have *distinct marks* opposite to the matter to which attention is required.

ERRATUM.—In article "College of Organists," issue of Jan. 20, page 40, col. 2, line 19, *for* "Robertson" *read* "Robinson."

THE MUSICAL STANDARD

A NEWSPAPER FOR MUSICIANS PROFESSIONAL AND AMATEUR

No. 970. VOL. XXIV. FOURTH SERIES.   SATURDAY, MARCH 3, 1883.   WEEKLY: PRICE 3D.

THE MUSICAL STANDARD is published every Saturday, price 3d., by post, 3½d.; and may be had of any bookseller or newsagent by ordering its regular supply.

SUBSCRIPTION.—*The Musical Standard* is posted to subscribers at 15s. a year; half a year, 7s. 6d., payable in advance.

The rate is the same to France, Belgium, Germany, Italy, United States, and Canada.

Post Office Orders to be made payable to the Publisher, William Reeves, 185, Fleet Street, London, or to the West-end Agents, Messrs. Weekes & Co., 14, Hanover Street, Regent Street, W.

ADVERTISEMENTS.—The charge for ordinary advertisements in *The Musical Standard* is 2s. 6d. for three lines or less; and 6d. for each line (10 words) in addition. "Organist wanted," 3s. 6d. for 3 lines or less. A reduction is made for a series.

FRONT PAGE.—Concert and auction advertisements, &c., are inserted in the front page of *The Musical Standard*, and charged one-third in addition to the ordinary rates. Other advertisements will be inserted on the front page, or in the leader page, if desired, at the same terms.

JUST PUBLISHED.

16mo, cloth, price 1s., **CHEAP EDITION** (being the Fifteenth), of

The Psalter; or, Canticles & Psalms of David,

POINTED for CHANTING on a NEW PRINCIPLE. With Explanations and Directions. By the late STEPHEN ELVEY, Mus.Doc., Organist of New and St. John's Colleges, and Organist and Choragus to the University of Oxford. With a Memorandum on the Pointing of the "Gloria Patri" by Sir G. J. Elvey.

ALSO

II. **FCAP. 8vo. EDITION** (the Fourteenth), limp cloth, 2s. 6d.; with Proper Psalms, 3s.

III. **LARGE-TYPE EDITION** (the Eighth), for **ORGAN**, demy 8vo, cloth, 5s.

The **PROPER PSALMS** separately. Fcap. 8vo, sewed, 6d

The **CANTICLES** separately. Seventeenth Edition. Fcap. 8vo, 3d.

THIS PSALTER IS USED AT ST. GEORGE'S CHAPEL, WINDSOR, and at many Cathedrals.

PARKER & CO., Oxford; and, 6, Southampton-street, Strand, London.

CRYSTAL PALACE.—THIS DAY, at 3.0, SATURDAY CONCERT IN MEMORIAM RICHARD WAGNER. The Programme will entirely consist of selections from Wagner's Works, and will include the Funeral March, "Siegfried's Death"; Overture, "Tannhäuser"; "The Siegfried Idyll"; "Isolde Liebestod"; Selections from "Die Meistersinger"; "Charfreitages Zauber" ("Parsifal,") (first time in England); "The Ride of the Walkyries"; "Kaiser March."—Vocalist, Miss Anna Williams. Conductor, Mr. AUGUST MANNS.—Seats, 2s. 6d. and 1s. Admission to Concert Room, 6d.

COLLEGE OF ORGANISTS.

On TUESDAY NEXT, MARCH 6th, and on MARCH 13th, at 8 each Evening, Prof. G. A. MACFARREN, Mus.Doc., will continue his course of Four Lectures, with Musical Illustrations, to be played by Mr. WINDYER CLARKE, on Bach's "Twenty-Four Preludes and Fugues in all Keys," the work issued 18 years after the "Equal Tempered Clavier."—Members and Friends admitted by Cards of Membership. The above Meetings will be held at the HOLBORN TOWN HALL, Gray's Inn Road.
E. H. TURPIN, Hon. Secretary.

95, Great Russell-street, Bloomsbury, W.C.

MAKERS AND REPAIRERS.

GEORGE WITHERS & CO.

(Late of Coventry Street),

WHOLESALE IMPORTERS OF

MUSICAL STRINGS,

From Rome, Padua, and Naples.

A FINE COLLECTION OF ITALIAN INSTRUMENTS. Bows, Cases, Music Stands, &c. See Price Lists.

51, ST. MARTIN'S LANE, LONDON.

Price 3s., paper; 4s., cloth.

REEVES' MUSICAL DIRECTORY

FOR 1883.

A DIRECTORY OF

THE TRADES AND PROFESSIONS

OF THE

UNITED KINGDOM.

CORRECTED TO DECEMBER 1st.

W. REEVES, 185, Fleet-street, London.

AMERICAN ORGANS FOR THE CHURCH, CHAPEL, SUNDAY SCHOOL, Or HOME.

J. COWLEY & CO.'S FAMOUS ORGANS ARE SUPERIOR TO ALL OTHERS.

SPECIAL.—ONE AND TWO MANUAL PEDAL ORGANS. Illustrated List, with latest Press Opinions, post free.

EUROPEAN OFFICES:—21, Prince's Dock-street, Hull.

VIOLIN.—GOOD TONE VIOLIN, with 2 Bows, and Lock-up case. Price 25s.—Address, VIOLIN, 26, Poppin's Court, Fleet-street, E.C.

WANTED.—ORGANIST for SOUTHERNHAY CONGREGATIONAL CHURCH, Exeter. Only Professionals need apply. Salary £50.—JOHN W. PETHERICK, 8, Southernhay, Exeter.

JUST PUBLISHED.—Full Anthem, "BE NOT DRUNK WITH WINE, WHEREIN IS EXCESS." For Temperance Services, etc., by E. H. TURPIN. Price 4d. net.—Messrs. WEEKES & CO., 14, Hanover-street, W.

MR. C. WARWICK JORDAN, Mus.Bac., Oxon., Fell. Coll. Org., etc., will, on his return from America at Easter next have a vacancy for an ARTICLED PUPIL. Splendid Organ; Daily Services; Home Comforts.—69, Granville-park, Lewisham, S E.

A YOUNG LADY with a fairly GOOD VOICE would be glad to have further TUITION, at a moderate Fee, with a view to getting Engagements at Concerts, etc.—Address, Z. Y. X. H., care of May's Advertising Offices, 159, Piccadilly.

THE EXPRESSION AND DEVELOPMENT OF MUSICAL THOUGHT IN COMPOSITION.

By E. H. Turpin, Esq.

(Continued from page 111.)

One of the most serious duties of the composer engaged in the expression and development of his musical thoughts is the act of fully engaging the listener's mind and attention, a matter requiring much tact, observation, and experience. This difficult task must be encountered at once, for the listener is sure almost to be unprepared for the fixed attention required, and will be almost inevitably pre-occupied in thought. This act of securing attention is very frequently accomplished by a slow introductory movement, in which stately reared up harmonies, striking, detached figures, seize the listener's fancy and compel his attention. The slow introduction has been well compared in its effects to the west front of a cathedral or other great public building which strikes the beholder's mind and prepares him for the grandeur of the interior presently to be revealed. Another comparison is furnished by our ordinary habits of conversation. When friends meet, they regard each other as unprepared for the interchange of thoughts and information of real present importance; in obedience to a really artistic impulse, they proceed by talking upon general topics, until a mutual understanding and prepared state of mind has been secured which will justify the utterance of important and confidential communications. So the musician draws his listener's faculties towards himself either by the striking introduction; or, if the character of his piece be too modest to justify so pretentious a beginning, or too impulsive to brook delay, he may plunge at once into his theme. But here his tact is not left unexercised. Still recognising the unpreparedness and possible preoccupation of his listener, he takes care to present figures which shall be both natural and striking, so as to secure attention quickly, yet without alarming or overtaxing his auditor's powers. Then he has to communicate several pieces of musical intelligence: in the establishment of his accepted key, to which end he at first avoids modulatory or chromatic influences; in the indication of the general tone of his work, to express which promptly he selects decided, perhaps detached and suggestive, figures which help to strike and secure the auditor's sympathetic attention. Doubtful of this at first, the composer generally reserves his choicest and best sustained melody as a second subject. In the selection of the form or framework upon which his ideas are to be placed, the composer has a task deserving much consideration. He should primarily decide this matter in accordance with the general character of his work and their fitting ideas. The Duplex or Binary Form seems, from its scope for development and the travelling away for some time from the tonic, to be specially adapted as the medium of thoughts full of earnestness, containing fruitful germs of tune and prone to general activity. The fugal and contrapuntal forms are the best mediums for brief and firmly knit together figures which call for canonical or logical treatment. The Triplex, Ternary, or Episodical Form, with its well-defined leaning to the tonic, and not large tendency to development, invites the production of frank, calm, confiding, straightforward musical thoughts. The Rondo Form, in its older method or as now intermingled with the features of the allegro plan, with its frequent return to the tonic and simple, well-defined outlines, seems specially useful for the demonstration of happy, simple thoughts; and its frequent coming home, as it were, to the tonic, specially fits the form for use in final movements.

Just as it would be inartistic to crowd large buildings so close together that they dwarf their different proportions, or to leave them so isolated that the vacant space around deprives the beholder of the charm and force of comparison, so would it be weak on the part of the composer to present important leading themes without their necessarily adjunctive accessory thoughts, which have the further use of supplying to the listener that relief which is wanted in the contemplation of great objects and leading features. Care must be taken, therefore, to secure the presence of several accessory thoughts of sufficient piquancy to command interest and to refresh by calling attention for the time from the more prominent themes. When all the ideas are ready to hand, the composer must secure some thread of similarity, which, running more or less through the entire chain of ideas, shall be kept sufficiently in the background as not in any way to detract from the different individualities of the several chief themes.

It is not possible to suggest any universally satisfactory method as to the order of writing. Different types of mind will devise different methods of mental exposition. Some composers have carefully prepared and trimmed the several themes before commencing in earnest the task of digesting them into a complete form; some have acquired the power of rapid and prompt composition with apparently little or no premeditation, as was the case with Mozart and Mendelssohn; others have accepted a well proportioned method to be used upon almost all occasions, as did Rossini in his operatic overtures; some have attained marvellous skill in beating out to the full the golden thoughts they have selected with admirable clearness and method, as Bach, Haydn, and some other great writers have done; and others have been oppressed by either the very redundance of their ideas, as was Schubert, or found difficulties from the inflexible strangeness of their thoughts, as did Schumann. I would venture to advise the student in composition to systematically select well contrasted and apposite themes, to choose a suitable framework for their exposition, and, in short, to decide upon the general scheme and leading features of his work without tying himself too rigidly down to given conditions before setting out upon his journey as a composer.

Though the several forms have their special features of adaptability to different purpose and types of thought, the principles of musical architecture are, broadly viewed, the same in all plans. The composer presents his themes first, for they are characters or personalities, his text or proposition; he proceeds to development, to illustrate the growth of his characters, or strengthen his position by the presentation as it were of musical arguments; and he finally draws his conclusion by bringing his themes home together, having completed a circle, and crowns, if he elects to do so, his work by a coda or peroration. It is important that the different main sections of his work should carry a sense of proportion as regards the length and consequent relative importance of the different chief parts of his musical structure. A piece of music may be described as a series of extending circles, the first theme being the first of the series, and it presents a complete epitome of the three principles of structure—presentation, development, and recapitulation, which in a larger sense govern the complete form of the entire work.

It may be that extemporization is more difficult to untrained minds than composition on paper. The original Samuel Wesley, as his son, our much-esteemed treasurer tells, when applied to by a pupil anxious to learn extemporization, answered to the effect that he could not tell how he himself set about extemporizing. Schumann, again, declared the real test of musicianship was to be found in putting ideas satisfactorily on paper, and that extemporization was a matter of comparative ease. Now, I am not sure but that the student, and especially the young organist, should not try to systematise and strengthen by mental training his powers of extemporary performance, whether they be great or small. I venture to think that such attempts to acquire the power of methodically thinking, would be further a useful adjunct to the general study of composition. To this end, the student might place before himself the small form of duplex sentences of about sixteen bars, as proposed on the examination papers of this College by way of test in the art of extemporization, skeleton fashion—that is, make out a map of some sixteen bars, inserting a proposed initial in the two first measures, and at the usual point of their re-entrance at the ninth and tenth bars, the vacant measures being filled up by the player *ad libitum*. Such exercise might with advantage be preceded by mentally formed decisions as to scale structure and balance and character of the melody to be formed, with the corresponding style of the harmonies. To this form presently a tonic pedal of a few bars might be appended by way of coda, over which fragments of the initial theme might be freely imitated. Other forms could also be adopted in a similar outlined form, with possibly notes of direction written over as to the best positions for cadence points or available small modulatory excursions and other hints. Of course I neither pretend to say that music can be manufactured, or desire to induce those gifted with tone-thoughts to chain themselves to mechanical schemes. I do, though, earnestly desire the student to realise the fact that the act of successful composition involves the skilled use of idioms and methods. To compose well is to speak a language eloquently, but the musician has the special glory and difficulty of conversing in a language set apart from all other forms, impressions, and idioms. He must, therefore, work daily and earnestly in order to secure familiarity with the art he practises, and in order to promote the necessary flow of thought required in continued efforts of composition. The student should be wary of being misled by the assumed freedom of the advanced school, even though it is well he should have a manly sense of self-respect as regards the methods he may select for the enunciation of his own musical thoughts. He should be careful to avail himself of all the machinery and appliances of composition rather than to deny himself the advantage of the help they undoubtedly afford. To neglect their legitimate use will place the student in the undesirable position of being a sort of voluntary artistic Robinson Crusoe, who compels himself to make his tools, as well as to build his own house, and who suffers from the usual disadvantages attending the use of badly made appliances and ill-shaped tools.

I will further venture to advise all students to study composition, for the contemplation of its methods and appliances must at least strengthen the intellectual faculties of the executive artist, if it does not indeed lead to higher results. It is needless, and I have not proposed to myself to attempt to expatiate upon the more technical branches of my subject; indeed, I must crave pardon for having so long tried your patience as my very indulgent listeners.

A performance was given in the Sheldonian Theatre, Oxford, on Feb. 28th, of Psalm lxv., "Thou, O God, art praised in Sion," composed as an exercise for the degree of Doctor in Music, by Edward Brown, Mus.Bac., New College. The work contains a number of solos, etc., and several choral numbers, illustrating the composer's academical attainments, and was performed by soloists, chorus, and a complete orchestra.

Musical Intelligence.

CRYSTAL PALACE CONCERTS.

The programme last Saturday included the following :—

Symphony in G minor.....................	S. Bennett.
Adagio for violoncello and orchestra	Bargiel.
(First time at these concerts).	
Allegro de Concert, for violoncello and orchestra ..	Davidoff.
(First time at these concerts.)	
Selection from suite, "L'Arlésienne"	Bizet.
(First time at these concerts).	
Overture, "Leonore" No. 3....................	Beethoven.
Vocalist—Miss Edith Santley.	
Violoncello—Herr Hausmann.	
Conductor - - - AUGUST MANNS.	

Schubert's charming overture, "Alfonso and Estrella," is not so often played as one could wish. Like most of his orchestral works, it is brimming over with fanciful passages, pouring forth a rich stream of melody, now tender and emotional, and now bold and vigorous, but never overstrained and always original. Why it took the place of his better known "Rosamünde," as announced in the programme, I cannot tell, but it proved an agreeable substitute.

Bennett's Symphony in G minor·was most welcome. One often hears it at the daily concerts, but, strange to say, it has not been played on a Saturday since 1876. It is needless to say how much each movement was enjoyed and applauded, nor how perfect a, model it is of musicianly skill and poetical feeling, nor yet how much it is to be regretted that the composer's time should have been employed in the daily round of teaching, thereby leaving him so little leisure for composition. The performance of the work was as near perfection as possible. There are spots even in the sun, but it is the sun all the same ; the light overpowers the shade.

No. 3 overture to "Fidelio" is more than an overture in the ordinary sense of the word ; it is a fantasia, a complete symphonic poem. Both Beethoven and Mozart were accustomed to write or play several overtures before selecting the one most suited to the work that was to follow. Shortly before the performance of "Don Giovanni," Mozart played three splendid overtures for that opera. The first was in E flat major, the second in C minor (a fugued fantasia like that to "Die Zauberflöte," but totally different in character), and lastly the well-known one in D, which he subsequently penned so quickly. It is said that he could not be persuaded to write down the others.

Bizet's movements proved most acceptable, and Herr Hausmann's 'cello performance was as charming as ever. It seems ungracious to place the lady vocalist last of all ; but it is due to no lack of appreciation of Miss Santley's merits, whose last song was so much enjoyed by the audience that she was persuaded by Mr. Manns to favour them with a repetition of it.   R. S.

SATURDAY POPULAR CONCERTS.

PROGRAMME.

Sextet in G major, Op. 36, for two violins, two violas, and two violoncellos	Brahms.
Mdme. Norman-Néruda, MM. L. Ries, Straus, Zerbini, Pezze, and Piatti.	
Air, "Deh vieni".............................	Mozart.
Mdlle. Carlotta Badia.	
Sonata in B flat, Op. 22, for pianoforte alone	Beethoven.
Miss Agnes Zimmermann.	
Adagio in F major, for violin, with pianoforte accompaniment................................	Spohr.
Mdme. Norman-Néruda.	
A Hebrew Love Song.........................	Salaman.
Mdlle. Carlotta Badia.	
Sonata in D major, Op. 18, for pianoforte and violoncello	Rubinstein.
Miss Agnes Zimmermann and Signor Piatti.	
Accompanist - - - Mr. Zerbini.	

Brahms's sextet, the second of the two he has published, was heard for the fifth time at these concerts. For heaviness and general unpleasantness it probably has no rival, if we except the same composer's violin concerto and a few of his other later works. Herr Brahms does not seem to be aware that it is quite possible for a composition in the strictest sonata form to be essentially "without form and void." Surely there never was a more notable example of Boileau's *galimatias double*—something which neither audience nor author can understand. Most of us know that when Corneille was once asked to explain an obscure passage in his *Tite et Bérénice*, he said, after carefully examining it :

"Je ne l'entends pas très-bien non plus; mais récitez-le toujours: tel qui ne l'entendra pas l'admirera." This may be also Brahms's opinion, but the general feeling at the Saturday Popular did not seem to be one of admiration, though the inability to understand was sufficiently apparent.

Even Rubinstein's sonata sounded fresh and genial after this most laboured affair, though of that the best one can say is—

Common is the commonplace,
And vacant chaff well meant for grain.

All that I remarked when this sonata was heard at the last concert in October need not be repeated. The first movement remains as prelude-like as ever in my mind, and the finale I still consider the most agreeable portion of the work. Perhaps a little more recklessness in the performance (especially of the wild, Hungarian-like second subject of the finale) might lead to better effects, and Miss Zimmermann seemed to recognise this possibility—I preferred her reading to Mdlle. Janotha's—but Signor Piatti was not to be startled out of his truly classical decorum.

Miss Zimmermann gave a thoroughly intellectual reading of the sonata she chose as her solo, and Mdme. Norman-Néruda called forth, at the conclusion of Spohr's beautiful adagio, one of those unanimous, ringing bursts of applause that is refreshing to hear and to join in; so different is it from the conventional expressions of approbation, full of sound and fury.

Mdlle. Badia sang with a very fair amount of success; and Mr. Zerbini accompanied intelligently, as well as taking part in the sextet.

B. F. WYATT-SMITH.

MONDAY POPULAR CONCERTS.

The fine concert of last Monday evening was remarkable for the re-appearance of Herr Joachim, the prince of violinists.

PROGRAMME.

PART I.

Quartet in E minor, Op. 59, No. 2, for two violins,
   viola, and violoncello .... Beethoven.
   MM. Joachim, L. Ries, Straus, and Piatti.
Serenade, "Awake, awake" .... Piatti.
   Mr. Edward Lloyd.
   Violoncello obbligato—Signor Piatti.
Three Sonatas, for pianoforte alone .... D. Scarlatti.
   Mdlle. Marie Krebs.

PART II.

Chaconne in D minor, for violin alone .... Bach.
   Herr Joachim.
Song, "The Garland" .... Mendelssohn.
   Mr. Edward Lloyd.
Trio in E minor, Op. 119, for pianoforte, violin,
   and violoncello .... Spohr.
   Mdlle. Marie Krebs, MM. Joachim and Piatti.

Accompanist . . . Mr. Zerbini.

This season the subscribers have been favoured with the presence of Herr Joachim before as well as after Christmas; nevertheless, his reappearance on Monday night caused the hall to be crammed, and vociferous applause greeted the great Hungarian when he mounted the platform a little after eight o'clock. The second "Rasoumowski" quartet, with its other Russian melody in the third movement, is not exactly a "new thing" to our modern Athenians; nor does M. Joachim's interpretation require a special reporter after so many pleasing experiences. He was thought by the writer and by other connoisseurs to be in splendid form, and to say where he especially excelled would be difficult, if not invidious. In a word, he has never played better. The solo, Bach's Chaconne with 29 variations, played without accompaniment, has now been heard at the "Popular" 27 times. Herr Becker first introduced it in 1859, and Joachim now interprets the difficult piece in marvellous style. No slight work for either hand with the chords, double stopping, rapid scale passages, arpeggios, chromatic intervals, and other little "lions in the path," but Herr Joachim, like Jack the valiant Cornishman, if, in this case, he did not make the giants, certainly overcomes and, in one sense, kills them. The variations, 9 to 12 inclusive, evoked particular demonstrations from the audience. An encore ensued as of course, and M. Joachim then played Beethoven's rarely-heard "Romance" in G. This (Saturday) afternoon he will lead the third "Rasoumowski" quartet in C, and play the "Kreutzer" sonanta with Miss Krebs. Miss Krebs, now playing alternately with Miss Zimmermann, made a capital choice of Domenico Scarlatti's sonatas, Nos. 7, 8,

and 9, in D and A major, from the third books, but the audience were not quite up to the classical music of perennial freshness and beauty. What could exceed, for melody, the second theme (in D minor) of the sonata No. 7? or surpass, for grace and piquancy of rhythm, the one in A, No. 8, with its taking ritornelles? The one No. 9, in D, a presto alla tarantella in 12.8 time, is remarkably racy, full of life and spirit. Mdme. Krebs played in a chaste, scholastic style, suited to the subject; for once, the audience called for no encore.

Spohr's pianoforte trio was first played at the concerts, by the same three gifted artists, in February, 1879. How effective the F natural in the second theme of the first movement (G Major), and the bravura "tributary" that follows. The larghetto, in A, is a lovely air, delicately worked out, and the episode, with digression to C, not to be passed over. In the scherzo might be noted some peculiar modulations, followed up by Schubert in his sonatas. In the finale, so well seasoned by its humoursome treatment of the instruments, an incidental passage reminds one of the pretty Bridesmaids' Chorus in "Der Freischütz," the whole work worth its weight in gold.

Mr. E. Lloyd charmed his audience, but really some check should be administered to the silly people who, as on Monday, persist in their repetition of calls, or "recals," whether with a view to encore, or from a desire to flatter, one is at a loss to say. At least ten minutes must be lost at every concert by those irrational stoppages of business.   A. M.

SACRED HARMONIC SOCIETY.

It would be as foolish not to look well into the constitution and arrangements of a new musical undertaking as it would for the mariner to neglect the due inspection of the signs of the weather in setting out upon a voyage, although apparently sure of present freedom from storms. The resuscitated Sacred Harmonic Society at their first performance on Friday, Feb. 23rd, gave in many respects an excellent rendering of Gounod's "Redemption." Mr. C. Hallé, as conductor, had evidently taken pains to secure a faithful reproduction of the score, and the organ was in the competent hands of Mr. Fountain Meen. The soloists were Misses M. Davies, Santley, and Hilda Wilson, Messrs. H. Guy, Santley, and Buggon. The chorus containing, it must be assumed, many of the old, tried, and experienced choristers, displayed many of the choral effects so well as to point to the general excellence of the material and its careful training. Mr. H. Leslie's version of the National Anthem preceded the oratorio. The band comprised a goodly number of well known instrumentalists, many of whom were engaged in the production of the work at the Birmingham Festival of last year.

For some time whispered rumours have been afloat with regard to possible changes in the constitution of the orchestra. The banishment of the non-professional strings on the occasion of the first concert has been regarded as the thin end of the wedge; and the new conductor may be expected, perhaps not unnaturally, to surround himself gradually by his own people, and may not improbably decide upon re-forming the entire orchestra in process of time, as his personal power increases. No one doubts the services rendered to the art in different directions by Mr. Chas. Hallé; still thoughtful musicians have, with every desire to gratefully recognize his valued labours to music, been much exercised by his acceptance of the office of conductor to the Sacred Harmonic Society; and the first performance, it must be reluctantly allowed, has to some extent justified the fears of those who doubted the wisdom of the committee of the Sacred Harmonic Society in their anything but well advised arrangements in this direction. No man can do justice to such an organization as the Sacred Harmonic Society without the time to develop its large and varied resources, the faculty of securing the complete cohesion of its different interests, and real sympathy with its long and carefully nurtured host of non-professional executants. Certainly the lamentable weakness of the strings, the general want of tone-balance, richness of quality and at times firmness of attack evidenced on the 23rd, must be remedied. Considering the character of the music performed by the Society, its well-trained and long attached body of non-professional strings deserves more consideration than has so far been displayed by the new conductor and committee; and the directors of the Society would do wisely by carefully conserving the results of the past labours of years by developing the non-professional department of their orchestra, by watchfully guarding against needless changes in their staff of well tried professional players, and, in short, by firmly insisting upon the harmonious fusion of the different professional and non-professional elements, which was an original and strong feature of the scheme in days of old, and which secured the adhesion of their most enthusiastic and faithful supporters. It is time indeed again to protest against the appointment of foreign conductors to the direction of thoroughly English societies; unless indeed they have proved themselves to be possessed of not only great leading skill and power, but of real knowledge of our oratorio traditions and well-tried sympathy with the cause of our National art. It cannot be said the gifted pianist to whose care the artistic fortunes of the Sacred Harmonic Society have been committed, has fulfilled satisfactorily such imperative conditions as are above named.

Says another writer: The generally unfavourable impression made upon myself after three attentive hearings of "The Redemption," at the Albert Hall and the Crystal Palace, supported as it is by a studious examination of the score, remains uneffaced by last week's performance of Gounod's oratorio at St. James's Hall at the hands of the resucitated "Sacred Harmonic Society." An eminent professional musician holds the same opinion as the writer. Technically (it is rather satirically said), successions of major thirds actually appear to have been the sole raison d'etre of many a passage throughout the work. Other equally eligible sources of inspiration (?) may also be detailed.

The truth must be told, sooner or later. It is always wrong and uncharitable to impute motives, but it is believed that a respectable music-selling "interest" has not been altogether "out of the reckoning" in some highly laudatory notices that have appeared in the public press, and are repeated this week. One reporter, evidently a man of the world, kindly cautions the Society that the rush of auditors on February 23, must not be taken as an index to future incursions. The British public go in for "fashion." At the Albert Hall, for example, on Nov. 1, not a seat was vacant, but an ebb of the tide took place between the first performance of "The Redemption" and the second, on Saturday, Dec. 9, and the inundation partly subsided.

It will be seen that Mr. Manns intends to repeat the oratorio at Sydenham (by reason of its alleged success) on an early Wednesday afternoon. As regards the performance at the Sacred Harmonic Concert, it is thought that the readings of Mr. Hallé were not invariably selon les règles; that the band, an imperfectly drilled company, played coarsely but that the chorus is an improvement upon the old society.

MANCHESTER.

(From our Own Correspondent.)

Mr. Hallé's last choral concert consisted of a not particularly good performance of "Elijah." Without previous communication with Mr. Hallé, Mrs. Hutchinson took the place of Miss Anna Williams. That the work was too arduous for the former lady to undertake without rehearsal, and at the shortest possible notice, only adds to our appreciation of the kind spirit which actuated Mrs. Hutchinson in coming forward at the last moment. Mdme. Patey was not in very good voice, nor did Mr. M'Guckin seem altogether at home. Mr. Santley, however, was in great form, and his singing of "Is not his word" electrified the audience as much as it ever did in his best days. The choruses were good, but conductor and band were alike wearied out with a long journey from Scotland. The man must indeed be an ardent musician who would choose to play the whole of "Elijah" on an empty stomach.

Last week the miscellaneous programme comprised :— Beethoven's A major Symphony, and the "Moonlight" Sonata, and Weber's Concertstück, the latter grandly played by Mr. Hallé. Miss Elliott was the vocalist. She introduced a charming song from Stanford's new opera, and also sang "O bid your faithful ariel fly" to an accompaniment that was simply disgraceful.

C. J. H.

MR. ISIDORE DE LARA'S NEW OPERETTA.

Mr. Isidore De Lara, a favourite baritone vocalist, and a composer of some very effective songs, produced last Saturday night, at Major and Mrs. William Carpenter's elegant house in Astley Place, Victoria Street, an operetta in one act, called "The Royal Word." The libretto, written by Mr. Henry Hersee, one of our most accomplished littérateurs, and worthy of his pen, turns on a (fictitious) incident in the reign of Charles II. The music, scored for a regular band, is bright and sparkling, but of course does not affect profundity ; it is essentially a light opera buffa.

The four principal characters were sustained by Mr. De Lara (Charles II.), Miss Wadman (Mrs. St. Vincent St. Jervis), Mr. W. S. Rising, and Mr. Fredk. De Lara. Mr. Albert Visetti conducted the band, and Mr. Walter Scott Hersee was an efficient stage manager. The opera was regularly "mounted," and the singers appeared in proper costume. In the early part of the evening Mr. W. S. Rising (who gave the soirée) sang several times, with success, and solos on the violin and pianoforte were played by Signor Erba and M. Henri Logé.

STATE CONCERT AT DUBLIN CASTLE.

Through the courtesy of Colonel Dease, Chamberlain to the Irish Court, I had the honour of representing your paper at a State Concert in Dublin Castle on the 23rd of Feb., the anniversary of Handel's natal day. The coincidence appears to have been unnoticed by the performers, as the only reminiscence of the famous composer was the fine aria for a bass voice, which was sung by Mr. Grattan Kelly. The vocal solos included two arias, one by Mozart for soprano, the other a pathetic composition from Gluck's "Orfeo ed Euridice." Mrs. Scott Fennell sang the latter ; whilst the former, as well as a berceuse of Gounod, were sung by Miss Hanlon remarkably well. The choice of music made by this young lady, may, however, be open to objection, owing to the unusual length of the items she selects, and a studied avoidance of English subjects. Mr. Bapty elected to sing one of a set of six cantatas composed by Dr. Pepusch, when the present century was in its teens, and Mr. J. F. Jones was fairly successful in a song from the pen of the conductor, Signor Caracciolo. The concerted vocal pieces were, a quintet by Bishop, who, on the occasion of his visit to Ireland, circa 1820, received the freedom of the City of Dublin ; the madrigal "Who shall win my lady fair?" (Pearsall), a group of Italian "Rime Popolari," arranged for two female voices by Signor Caracciolo, and a quintet from "Cosi fan tutte." Miss Elsner and Herr Elsner performed a sonata for pianoforte and violoncello by Marcello (1686—1739), and the performances of the two vocalists were enhanced by the tasteful violoncello obbligato supplied by Herr Elsner. Signor Esposito was the solo pianist ; but I have already noticed his performances of the same compositions on previous occasions. The National Anthem furnished a fitting finale to this very enjoyable performance.

P. J. CONMEY.

LEEDS.—Dr. Sparks's organ recital on Saturday evening was taken entirely from the works of the late Richard Wagner. The programme included extracts from "Tannhäuser," "Lohengrin," "Gotterdämmerung," Niebelüngen Ring," "The Flying Dutchman," and the March in F Major from "Rienzi." There was a large attendance, and the programme is to be repeated next Saturday. The idea of devoting one evening to the works of a single composer seems a good one, and from an educational point of view must be specially valuable.

EALING.—At the Popular Concert on Monday at the Lyric Hall, Hummell's Third Trio for violin, violoncello, and piano, was played by Messrs. P. A. Rooke, Acraman, and H. E. Stidolph, and also Reissiger's Trio in D. Messrs. Stidolph and Rooke also played Handel's Sonata in F, for violin and piano. Madame Frances Brooke was enthusiastically applauded for her songs, "I dreamed a dream," and "Just as well," and Mr. Joseph Lynde also created a very favourable impression by his rendering of "In sheltered vale," and "Simon the Cellarer." Mr. Harold E. Stidolph conducted.

ST. JAMES'S SMALLER HALL.—On Thursday, Feb. 21st., Madame Frances gave her annual ballad concert to a crowded house. She was assisted by some well-known artists, including Miss Minnie Gwynne, Miss Rosa Kissel, Miss Ford-Drake (piano), Mr. Hilton Carter, and Mr. Lovett King, who, besides acting as conductor, contributed two songs ; Mr. J. Hilton Carter displayed the possession of a good tenor voice. Madame Frances also gained great applause by her singing. A very favourable reception was accorded to Miss Rosa Kissel (pupil of Mr. Geo. F. Grover), who possesses a fresh soprano voice. The concert altogether was a success, but though ballad concerts are much appreciated, it is a question whether they tend to raise music to its proper level among the people of England.

OLDHAM.—On Wednesday, the 28th ult., Haydn's "Creation" was performed by Mr. S. R. Platt's choir and orchestra, the principals being Mrs. Hutchinson, Mr. Joseph Maas, and Mr. Jas. Whittaker; conductor, Dr. Marsden.—Mr. Houghton's recitals still continue, Mr. J. Greaves producing fresh programmes weekly, assisted by various local artists as vocalists.—A treat was given to the inmates of the Oldham Union on the 27th inst., in shape of a concert by Mr. J. Greaves and a concert party. The excellent singing of Mr. Lloyd, a local tenor, was highly appreciated, as were also the solos on the violin by Master D. M. Greaves.

HOLBORN TOWN HALL.—A concert in aid of the "Central Ear and Throat Hospital," Gray's Inn Road, was held at this hall on the evening of Feb. 21, under the management of the "Holborn Orchestral and Choral Society." The band played Rossini's (now almost *effete*) overture to "Tancredi," an opera resuscitated at the Royal Italian in 1848, for the sake of Mdlle. Alboni, also movements from Haydn's "Surprise" Symphony. The choir sang part-songs of Purcell and Sir R. Stewart. Mdlle. Alice Barth won a *bis* for Bishop's song "Tell me, my heart," and Hudson's "In Arcady." Mr. F. Quatremayne, in good voice, pleased the audience, and eke the conductor, in Handel's air from "Samson," "Honour and arms scorn such a foe"; he was encored in Pinsuti's sensational song "The minute gun." Miss C. Myers and other vocalists sang in turn. A notable number of the scheme was Sir Julius Benedict's pianoforte quartets, arranged from texts of Chopin, and played by himself, Miss L. O'Brien, Mr. F. S. Southgate, and Mr. A. L'Estrange. Sir Julius appeared to be in good spirits, and was evidently well pleased at the success of his work. Mr. F. Sewell Southgate conducted the concert, Mr. J. M. Eunis was accompanist, and Mr. H. Hunter leader of the violins.

GIBRALTAR CHORAL SOCIETY.—This Society gave an excellent concert at the theatre on the 16th February, to a house crowded from top to bottom. A short miscellaneous first part was composed as follows :—"Montrose's Love Song," sung by Mr. Gartly, Mendelssohn's Rondo Capriccioso for piano, by Master M. Relle, Maud White's "Absent, yet Present," sung by Miss King, Beethoven's Sonata No. 5, for piano and violin, by Miss Ashton and Mr. Llambias, and the favourite "Marta" quartet, "Que vuol dir ciò," sung by Mrs. Galliano, Miss Mosley, Mr. Calamaro and Mr. Gartly. The second part consisted of Sterndale Bennett's cantata, "The May Queen," given with a full orchestra, and the conductor, Signor Ruggero Labocetta, must be considered to have accomplished something little short of a miracle in giving this work complete in every detail. Only those who took part in the performance could know of the apparently insurmountable difficulties which had to be overcome in a place situated as Gibraltar is, and the Society is to be congratulated on the pluck and perseverance which has enabled them to come triumphantly out of the ordeal. The solos in the cantata were taken by Mrs. Relle, soprano, Miss Mosley, alto, Mr. Calamaro, tenor, and Mr. Porral, bass.

BANBURY.—On Thursday, Feb. 22, the sacred cantata, by G. F. Root, entitled "Under the Palms," was given in the Exchange Hall, under the conductorship of Mr. S. Hughes. The chorus numbered upwards of 400, and included a large proportion of Sunday School scholars. The soloists were : Miss Julia Jones (London), soprano ; Miss Currall (Birmingham), contralto ; Ms. Hodgson (Magdalene College, Oxford), tenor ; and Mr. Phillips (Magdalene College, Oxford), bass. The work, which is particularly well adapted to a choir of this nature, is descriptive of the Jewish flower feast, and, if not strikingly original, contains some very pleasing numbers. On Thursday, a want of balance in the parts rather marred the effect of the choruses—noticeably one for humming—and, at times, evidence of imperfect training was perceptible, but, as a whole, the performance was satisfactory, and was well received by the very large audience. In the second part, which consisted of "Sacred solos by the Great Masters," Miss Jones sang "I know that my Redeemer liveth" with exquisite sweetness, while Miss Currall was the recipient of quite an ovation for her rendering of "O rest in the Lord." Miss Currall has a clear contralto voice of much power and melody, which, together with her youth, justifies the augury for a very successful future. The general arrangements for the concert left much to be desired.

WIMBLEDON MUSICAL SOCIETY.—This Society gave Mendelssohn's "Hymn of Praise" on February 21st—a highly creditable rendering, marred only by the evidently unprepared condition of the soprano soloist. Mr. Fredericks, of Hereford Cathedral, however, sang the tenor solo splendidly and won golden opinions for himself. The symphony was well played by the society's efficient orchestra, the trombones and trumpets being particularly good, whilst the violoncellos (eight) told out beauti-

fully in the allegretto ma poco agitato. In the second part of the programme were included Mendelssohn's "Serenade and allegro giojoso," for piano and orchestra, and De Beriot's 9th violin concerto, the solo parts of which were well sustained by Miss Rivenhall and Mr. Crowe respectively, while Miss Emily Dones sang Gounod's "There is a green hill," with orchestral accompaniments, with great pathos—a refined rendering which drew forth an irresistible encore. Later on, Miss Dones was joined in the trio, "Ti prego," which was delightfully sung, by Mr. Fredericks and Miss Whitfield, the latter appearing to be one of the conductor's main supports, playing at the first desk in the orchestra, singing secondary solo parts in the cantata, and playing the pianoforte accompaniments. Mr. Sumner conducted. The hall was crowded. Rossini's "Stabat Mater" will be given on March 8th, with Miss Alice Pany, Miss Emily Dones, Mr. Fredericks, and Mr. Orlando Christian as principals.

Foreign Musical Intelligence.

Spohr's monument at Cassel will be unveiled on April 5th.

The Madrid *Cronica de la Musica* has had its title changed to that of the *Ilustracion Musical.*

The German papers of last week came to hand with a mourning page in honour of Richard Wagner.

Professor Helmholtz, the eminent authority on acoustics, has been decorated by the German emperor.

Music to Shakespeare's "Tempest," by Franz van der Stucken, was lately heard in Antwerp, and favourably criticised.

"Noël," an oratorio by M. Saint-Saens, formed the chief attraction of a recent concert given by the National Society of Music in Paris.

The "Gesangverein" of Posen recently gave a first performance of Blumner's oratorio, "The Fall of Jerusalem" which was well received.

The committee of the Angers Popular Concerts has provided a novelty for the subscribers in the shape of an unpublished symphony by Mendelssohn, written at the early age of 13.

The Dunkerque Society for the Encouragement of Art and Science has opened a series of prize competitions. The prize for music is a gold medal valued at 300 francs, to be awarded to the composer of the best quintet for violin, clarionet, viola, bassoon and double bass.

Signor Terziani's new opera, built upon Massimo d'Azeglio's novel "The Siege of Florence," was produced at the Apollo Theatre, Rome, on the 24th of Feb. An enthusiastic audience encored several movements and called for the author seventeen times, it is said.

It was at the desire of his daughter, Mdme. Cosima Wagner, and in the interests of his health, that Liszt was not present at the funeral of his illustrious son-in-law. The venerable Abbé will remain at Buda-Pesth until Easter, when he will rejoin his daughter and grandchildren at the Villa Wahnfried.

During the Russian Coronation festivities Glinka's "The life for the Czar," followed by "Night and Day," a new Ballet, and Rubinstein's "Demon" will be represented, the Moscow opera troupe being strengthened by performers from St. Petersburgh. A body of 1000 musicians and 8000 school children will render the National Anthem ; other musical arrangements are in progress and Rubinstein is writing a coronation march which he will himself conduct.

A profound sensation has been caused in Ancona by the tragic death of an operatic tenor named Ronconi, the son of a baritone celebrated in the days of Lablache, Grisi, and Alboni. He was taking the part of Faust, and when the curtain rose on the first act was seen to be suffering from indisposition, attributed by the manager to nervousness. The curtain was rung down, and the audience entreated to be patient until the tenor had recovered himself. But this was not to be. Poor Ronconi never regained consciousness and died early the next morning, the cause being effusion on the brain, which appeared to have seized him when he was discovered in Faust's arm-chair,

Reviews.

The Redemption, a sacred Trilogy, by Chas. Gounod. (Novello, Ewer and Co.).—Though much has been said of this great work, wherein the story of the revealed scheme of man's salvation is epitomised as it were, it seems fitting that the publication of so notable a contribution to our musical literature shall not pass without some acknowledgment in these pages. At first there was a tendency to compare M. Gounod's oratorio with the great choral works we English people have long been happily familiar with. It was soon realised that such a method of judgment by comparison was not the best way of approaching an oratorio, coming from a nation practically without oratorios, and a work by a man of an undoubtedly large musical individuality. "The Redemption" is one of those poetical works which can only be fairly dealt with by an earnest effort in the direction of appreciation rather than in the way of criticism. The composer tells us that the work was first thought of in 1867, and only completed after much interruption in the course of some twelve years. This simple statement gives evidence of the serious and persistent thought the composer has devoted to his scheme ; and we have on record the author's deliberate words, that he elects to regard this oratorio as the chief work of his life. In attempting to speak of the characteristics and merits of this work, it is well to keep clearly in view the character of the composer's genius and musical tendencies. From early predilections and training, M. Gounod's talents were turned towards the direction of sacred art, and his mind became imbued with something of the quaint spirit of plain-song. His genius is of a plastic order, receiving, absorbing, and reproducing impressions, so his music is the refined embodiment of mediæval tune, in an exalted and richly adorned form ; and this power assumed historical force when he, with ripened powers, at about the age of 44, produced his setting of the legend of "Faust" in 1859. Now this last exposition of the genius of the leading French composer, is, as it were, a kind of musical miracle-play ; the "Christ's Passion" by Gregory Nazianzenus, one of the most ancient of the type, might indeed have furnished M. Gounod with the foundation of his book. It is the dramatic setting in scenes, a sort of mediæval picture of separate incidents on separate panels, of the greatest narrative the world can ever know. The music is full of picturesque, and in its way genuine religious teaching, occasional dramatic touches of rare power, and abundant tune of a quaint, old-world flavour, yet set forward with exquisite modern life and technicalities, including an orchestral colouring of the richest type. Logically and contrapuntally the work is often weak, and in some of its attempted realisations painfully inconsistent — as notably in the "March to Calvary," in which the leading gentle, suffering figure is surely musically absent, and we have little save in the serious tone of the music beyond the pompous tramp of an organized force. The whole scene is as painfully misread as it would indeed have been had it been even depicted as a procession of ecclesiastical pomp and display. It would far better illustrate a march of Knights Templar to a tournament, than it does the touching and wonderful progress—the very thought of which should make "angels fear to tread." Then the melodramatic little scraps by which certain passages of the text are instrumentally announced and ticketed, so to speak, are in some instances not sufficiently sustained to do their work, and consequently, though instinctively, dramatic, are not justified, as lacking sustained dignity and purpose. The scenes named "The Two Thieves" and "The Earthquake" are illustrations of this aptitude for vivid, yet illogical and unconsciously presumptuous, dramatic depiction. But, although no one can presume to compare M. Gounod's "Redemption" as an emanation of genius with Milton's "Paradise Lost," it must be listened to as that great poem must be read—with the desire to appreciate its many charms rather than to criticise its plan and detail. M. Gounod's tender gracefulness finds some effective exemplifications in certain solo sentences and in some of the choral numbers, as in the scenes of "The Holy Women before the Apostles," "The Pentecost," and "The Apostles in Prayer." Though the work has very few manifestations of contrapuntal power of a sustained, strong type, some of the choruses have points and situations of harmonic weight and grandeur,

as the last chorus in the work, with its characteristic harmonies, rising step by step to the dominant, to prepare for a brief coda of massive power and dignity. The future of the work will be an interesting chapter in musical history. It may lead to the formation indeed of a school of semi-ecclesiastical, semi-dramatic, and essentially Roman, oratorios, in which modern dramatic power and grace in tune will be flavoured by the quaint spirit of antique plain-song ; but it will neither displace the older oratorio types, or possibly even secure in England or Germany that enthusiastic and unchanging admiration which has been conceded to the great sacred works of Bach, Handel, and Mendelssohn, to name only three typical composers of oratorio music.

Welcome to Our Festival. By E. J. Hopkins. (Stanley Lucas, Weber & Co.).— A beautiful and artistic contribution to the stores of part music for ladies or boys' voices, set in three parts, and sure to find much favour.

The Better World, song. By Michael Bergson. (Stanley Lucas, Weber & Co.).—An artistic production with accompaniments, admirably written for violin, harmonium, and pianoforte.

Not Once or Twice, song. By F. Neale. (Duncan Davison).—A taking melody well laid out.

In the Haven, song. By H. Croft Hiller. (Duncan Davison).—Has a graceful, though at times almost too ornate, melody. Will make an effective concert song.

The Awakening, song. By H. J. Stark. (A. Cox).—An original and very artistic song.

The Wood Nymphs' Revel. By R. A. Klitz. (Ashdown).—A clever and very effective pianoforte solo, with brilliant and well laid out sentences.

Mazurka. By Gordon Saunders. (Novello & Co.).—A charming and brilliant pianoforte piece, with fresh ideas well treated.

The Sergeant-Drummer's March. By Michael Watson. (B. Williams).—A cleverly written and very effective piece of the military order for pianoforte.

Welcome, valse fantastique. By G. Tartaglione. (A. Hays, Bond Street).—A showy and effective pianoforte solo, with original and tuneful themes.

There is one I can't forget. By Mrs. H. Scobell ; and, *Fading Flowers*, by same composer. (Weekes & Co.).—Two songs, having graceful thoughts ; the first, which is the least ambitious, is the best and most singable of the two.

Cynthia. By G. H. Smith. (Banks, York).—Called a dance measure by the composer ; an effective and musicianly piece of the gavotte kind.

Au Printemps. By Emile Waldteufel. (Metzler and Co.).—A graceful and attractive set of waltzes by a well-known writer.

Valse Vénitienne. By Waldteufel. (Metzler & Co.).—An effective set, admirably laid out for dancing and artistically illustrated.

Air de Danse. By D. R. Munro. (Duncan Davison and Co.).—A fairly written, and, on the whole, graceful piece of the gavotte type.

Evening Bells. By Oliver Cramer. (Weekes & Co.).—A pretty and effectively written reverie for pianoforte.

Sonata in A major. By Mozart. (Willey & Co.).—One of the series edited by Lindsay Sloper. The sonata is the well-known one commencing with the beautiful air with variations. It is admirably edited and very clearly printed.

The Moonlight March. By Crosby Smith. (A. Bertini).—A march of not much originality, but yet tuneful.

Yet, song. Words by W. B. Ryall ; music by P. E. Van Noorden. (J. B. Cramer & Co.).—Mr. Van Noorden has written a smooth and most agreeable strain in the key of E flat, relieved by a change of rhythm from 4 — 4 to 6 — 8 time. An effective chromatic progression of the bass, at page 3, leads to a climacteric pause on the dominant of the relative (C) minor ; and, a few bars further on, the chords of G flat and C flat are introduced. The range is from E flat to E flat, or F natural (the last note optional).

Reeves' Musical Directory for 1883 shows signs of much careful preparation, and is systematically laid out. The list of professors of various instruments includes performers upon sundry inventions which one hardly expects to find likely to engage the serious study of any earnest artists. It might be well to add separate lists of pianists (concert-players), organists, concert conductors and accompanists. However, the Directory is singularly complete, carefully compiled, and answers all its purposes.

Trio, for piano, violin and violoncello. By Rachel Sassoon, Op. 3. (Howard & Co.)—This trio was recently played at Mr. Bonawitz's third chamber concert. The score displays elegant writing and refined scholarship, whilst the work for the three instruments is well "laid out" for effect. The movements are four :—An allegro in E minor ; an andante in A major ; an allegro vivace (or scherzo) in E major, and a finale in E minor.

The Streamlet (Etude de Salon), for the pianoforte. By Lillie Albrecht. (Duncan Davison & Co.)—A pretty piece in the old "water-course" form. It consists of running arpeggio passages in semiquavers, for both hands alternately—and ends with a rather bold cadence, a progression from the discotd of the "extreme sharp sixth" on D flat to the *tonic* (F major) by contrary motion. The flat ninth (A flat) or the *root* (G) has been used by Miss Albrecht, and in such a case the resolution is ordinarily on the chord of the 6 —4, stigmatised as *fade* (insipid) by Jean Jacques Rousseau, but useful at the cadence, especially where, as in concertos, a *point d'orgue* is wanted.

Dr. Stainer's Tutor for the American Organ (Metzler & Co., Great Marlborough Street).—As will be expected, a lucid and artistic book of instruction. The book is entirely devoted to the instrument, and the excellent collection of music given for it. There is one odd repetition to be noted—a little piece by Herold is given twice over in different keys. The Editor includes in his very valuable matter practical examples of the different treatment of chants and tunes, as played in pure vocal harmony, with the melody and bass doubled by turns, and with the leading part treated solo fashion. The exercises for both hands and feet, the hints for registering, and the large, fresh, ample supply of arranged music, are alike excellent from every point of sight.

The Theatre for February leads off with a very interesting article by F. Corder on "Richard Wagner as a Stage Manager." The writer says that his original opinions as to the complexity of Wagner's stage being amateurish were "knocked on the head" by his attendance on July 30th, at the performance of "Parsifal." Mr. F. Corder's account of the stage inventions and effects seems indeed to reveal the composer of "Parsifal" as a man of extraordinary talent for stage effects, and as having remarkable inventive power in suggesting their practical realisation.

RICHARD WAGNER.

(Born, May 22, 1813. Died, February 13, 1883).

In Music-World arch-revolutionist,
  Titan-assailant of its elder gods,
    For him the menace of the Jovian nods,
The thunders and the rock storm. Yet he kist
With climbing crest the empyrean's crown,
  Out-nodding old Olympus in his mood
    Of most aggressive mastery. Of the brood
Of Demiurgus militant, whose frown,
Like that of mailéd Mars amidst the boys,
  Frightens away Convention's chirrupers,
    And to wild cackle as of Goose-flights stirs
Pale Peace's pretty fluters of small joys
And fine factitious sorrows. Then what wonder
  He brought the sword into mild Music's sphere,
    And in the clangour of the hurtling spear,
The clashing mail, and the loud battle-thunder,
Missed, sometime, of the finer harmony
  The still small voice, known of the subtler ear,
    Which outlives all War's clarions? Year on year
May pass ere he is measured. Yet we see
The work of a strong shaper, one whose part
  Was with new light to show a newer way.
    He stripped the gewgaw'd shams of Opera,
Lord of two spheres, he wedded Art with Art,
And Music, sunned in brighter, larger fame,
May date its nobler dawn from WAGNER's mighty name.
                      —Punch.

SATURDAY POPULAR ORGAN RECITALS, BOW, E.—TO-NIGHT, Mr. E. H. THORNE, of St. Michael's, Cornhill. Vocalists, Miss Lizzie Evans and Mr. F. Arundel.

PRINCIPAL CONTENTS OF THIS NUMBER.

NOTICE TO SUBSCRIBERS. — All Subscriptions due for the current year should be forwarded at once to our office.

LONDON : SATURDAY, MARCH 3, 1883.

THE PRESENT POSITION OF THE COMPOSER.

II.

THE matter of approaching the public is indeed one of the most serious undertakings the composer has to encounter. It is not too much to say that the want of respect for art, the feverish desire to anticipate results by rushing before the public only to invite judgment upon premature efforts and other similar ill-advised yearnings for popularity specially rampant in a competitive age, wreck more composers than does even the want of composing skill. The results of a premature advance upon public opinion, are, in the case of almost inevitable failure, of such a serious nature as the adoption of a lower artistic standard by which the young composer may induce himself to believe that he can readily persuade the public which declined to accept a symphony to purchase copies of and use a set of valses or quadrilles. This lowering of the standard, this forgetfulness of the true watch-word of the composer, "Excelsior!" sometimes ends in such a palpable want of self-respect as the adoption of a *nom de plume* under which the misguided composer fondly believes he can securely write such music as his higher artistic instincts tell him will place him in danger of the mean, sordid guilt of art-degradation, a crime he well knows not only helps to stay the world's upward progress, but will in no way advance him in his career as the hopeful doer of good work. There are snares for the feet of the anxious young composer, such as the temptation to embark in the hateful royalty system as in vogue in too many concert-rooms. Indeed, the composer and singer alike, who respect art, will diligently avoid the foolish though tempting entanglements of this malpractice, which is degrading to both composer and executant. It may be laid down as a safe axiom by the producing artist in whatever department of art he may practise, that the only lasting success is that which the public sanction by honestly and openly sought for verdicts; and no temporary success built upon the royalty system will prove in the end of any real value. The fact is, the composer, like all other art-producing workers, must learn to regard the getting of money as a secondary matter. Art is a jealous mistress and is apt to revenge herself upon those who think to over-reach the just decrees which time will bring to all who work earnestly and sincerely. This does not imply that the composer may neglect legitimate opportunities and such friendly aid as rarely fail those who respect themselves as servitors of pure art. The pathway of usefulness must not, indeed, be neglected by the composer, for the opportunities he may surely find if he will for the compositions of such forms of music as are daily required are not only a legitimate means of gaining reputation, but form a ready school of experience. Such opportunities, however humble apparently, strengthen the composer in his knowledge of his own powers, in his acquaintance with the exigencies of art, and if made good use of surely bring to him a meed of public appreciation. The position of publishers as regards the career of the composer, at present an unsatisfactory one for the most part, must with other aspects of the subject in hand, be discussed another time.   E. H. TURPIN.

ORCHESTRAL EFFECTS AND KEY-BOARD MANNERISMS.

IV.

ONE great distinction between the presentation of orchestral idioms on the pianoforte and organ arises from the presence on the first named instrument of an exquisite sense of touch which is absent from the organ, and the power of the last named instrument of producing many distinct tone qualities which is not possessed by the pianoforte. The pianoforte tone functions correspond, as has been shown before, with the art of engraving; it possesses many shades, but all of one tinge, and wanting in real colouring power. On the other side, the organ has varied and decided tone colouring properties, with the great wind instrument faculty of sustaining the sounds at the will of the performer; but its disadvantages are found in its fixed wind pressures, which result in hard outlines lacking that nice sense of shading off and tone expression which is secured by the sense of touch in the pianoforte, even though the sounds of the keyboard stringed instrument lack the power of producing distinct qualities and the almost equally precious faculty of sustaining given sounds at will. The task of representing orchestral effects on the pianoforte is,

therefore, in a large degree dependable upon the special power of the instrument in its readily varied touch, and in a less degree in the transference of as much of orchestral activity as possible to its keyboard, as attainable partly through its executive facilities and partly by its comparatively colourless tone quality, which permits rapidity without the mental fatigue attending the excessive activity of tones of a very pronounced quality. On the other hand, the transference of orchestral sentences to the organ keyboard must be noted in two nearly opposite directions —in the adroit use of tone qualities as similar as may be to their orchestral prototypes, and in the judicious abridgment of redundant activity, as not only incompatible with fixed and more or less pronounced wind tone qualities, but as being ill-adapted for the more complex mechanisms and somewhat reluctant speaking powers of the organ.   E. H. TURPIN.

ASMODEUS IN THE MUSICAL WORLD.

CHAP. I.

" NAY, thou knowest most ingenious spirit, that the adventures of my ancestor Don Cleofas must be known unto me, wherefore, then, shouldst thou be surprised that I should seek thy help? " " Tell me, then, wherein I might serve thee," said Asmodeus. " Why, spirit," answered Don Pedro Cleofas Escolano Zambullo, the first speaker, " I have joined the brotherhood of harmony, and so would delight to see the members thereof from a point of vantage, to know them as in solitude they write their melodies divine, to see them in their social pleasures "—" Stay," interrupted Asmodeus, " I have no power with these ladies and gentlemen; truly they follow a calling which lifts you mortals away from the influence and spells of the spirits of mischief." " Still," said Don Cleofas, " the musicians of this famous city of Madrid can be but mortal." " Thou hast, indeed, hit the truth," returned the playful demon; " and I may serve thee, providing only I come not within the reach of the magic of their harmony; and fear not but that even those mortals who serve the cause of harmony, although for the most part innocent enough, have their little foibles, the contemplation of which may afford thee some little instruction, and possibly some amusement." " Agreed, then," cried Don Zambullo, I will, with thine aid, O friendly demon, penetrate some of the secrets of the world of song." " Thine ancestor only *——— generations back sought not the company of musicians; however, every one to his taste, and as thou hast sought me out, and after the manner of thine ancestor released me from the baleful influence of the malignant magician, I will not be ungrateful. Come, then, as I said to thine ancestor, my whilom friend, let us make the best of our way; take hold of the end of my cloak and fear not; in our flight I will show you some of the doings of the musical world, on a vastly different scale to such a family concert as afforded amusement to your somewhat cynical and worldly-minded, though at the bottom of his heart really worthy ancestor, in which a spinet, an oboe, and a couple of ill-assorted singers took part." Conversation now ceased, for Asmodeus found his skill in avoiding observation during a daylight journey severely taxed, and the aspiring, curious musical student was too giddy in his novel aerial flight to be inclined to talk, or even to listen. Asmodeus by his magic power permitted the student to see several notable musicians in their own homes. " But," said Don Cleofas, " I hear no music." " No," cried Asmodeus, " your celebrated musicians are rarely able quietly to enjoy the art they serve so well; albeit, even when their professional labours are over, the burden of the art's development presses sorely upon them in the way of attendance at their committee meet-

* The exact date of the MS. from which this narrative is printed it is not thought necessary to reveal; neither is it deemed advisable to announce the date of the adventures here detailed; the ingenious reader may guess if he likes with regard to the date thereof, and should he be perplexed by the likeness of the incidents to similar adventures he has heard of elsewhere, he may, if he should choose to do so, console himself with the thought that "history repeats itself."

ings and in the slavery of an endless correspondence." [This strange passage almost awakens a suspicion as to the really modern character of open discussions and postal facilities.] "However," continued the friendly demon, "thou shalt know more of some of these gentlemen by-and-bye; let us now hasten to a notable spot where your divine art is being expounded upon an imposing scale." "Señor Asmodeus," presently cried the noble young student, "we are leaving Madrid behind us, and are rapidly approaching the Palacio del Vidrio, and I know that thou wouldst enable me to learn something of the great festival of the mighty German, Wandel, whose noble strains are to be drawn forth by the potent and self-confident Don Comercio. Methinks even now that I hear a murmuring sound, as of voices engaged in a not inharmonious struggle with tones which strike me as those of a military band, from the strange preponderance of such noisy instruments as are in more musical countries deemed to be best reserved for secular purposes and out-door pleasures." [It would not appear that any investigation of the archives of Madrid has revealed documentary evidence as to the existence there of a great naturalised composer, any trace of the conducting art, the presence of an able and autocratic conductor, the accompanying incense of conductor worship, and of any aptitude for musical festivals; still the above statement certainly appears in the MS. from which this narrative is printed, and it may again be pointed out that history repeats itself; the reader must draw his own conclusions.] "Surely, friend Asmodeus," said Don Zambullo, when these worthy and strange companions had fairly perched themselves in the highest available resting place of the vast Palacio del Vidrio, "the sounds I hear cannot be the unadulterated, sweet, noble choral strains of the great Wandel!" "No, truly, Don Cleofas," returned Asmodeus, "but dost thou not know that the potent Don Comercio is the chief propounder of the new doctrine which tells that success secured by comparatively easy means is the first duty of the leader, that to this end the music must be made to go, and that it is ever more important to secure by the strong rhythmical assertive pomp of trumpets and drums, &c., credit for the leader, than it is necessary to respect the historical intentions and judgment of the composer? And so your fine leader scruples not to alter, add to, and overload, in order that the world may admire without stint the potency of his magic wand." More of this notable conversation must be reserved for another chapter, when the reader may, if he likes, resume his perusal of this delectable narrative.

AN UNIQUE MS. COLLECTION OF ANCIENT CHURCH MUSIC.

The following extracts are from a most interesting article by R. C. Hope, in the *Antiquarian Magazine*:—

There is in the Library of that most ancient College of Peterhouse, at Cambridge—once *the* University—an unique collection of music of the fullest kind as yet discovered, illustrating the Choral Service of the Church of England during the period immediately preceding the Great Rebellion, and composed of Services and Anthems.

The collection consists of two incomplete sets of part-books. The first set comprises four small folio volumes, viz., part books of the Medius, and Bassus Cantoris, Contra-Tenor, and Bassus Decani.

The second set is far more complete than its compeer, consisting of seven volumes the same size as the first, and in the same kind of binding, viz., Medius, Tenor, and Bass Cantoris, Medius, Contra-Tenor, Tenor, and Bassus Decani.

Neither the handwriting nor the musical notation is of later date than the period immediately preceding the Great Rebellion; on the other hand, some of the pieces are coeval with the Reformation. The indexes, though very systematic, are both defective and incorrect. Some of the compositions are by most distinguished men, almost unknown, and some of them have not been discovered anywhere else. The Rev. Mr. Jebb, in his index, says, after a very careful examination, he thinks "the collection was at least completed and put into shape while Dr. Cosin, the celebrated Bishop of Durham, was Master of Peterhouse, for the following reasons:—

(1) An English Litany, set to music by Molle, and a

Latin *Te Deum*, by Dr. Child, were composed at Dr. Cosin's request, as appears by the notice prefixed.

(2) Accompanying the part-books is a fine copy of the black-letter folio Prayer-book, printed by Barker, of the date 1634, the very year when Dr. Cosin entered upon his Mastership. This volume is interleaved with music-paper, in the places required by the usages of the fullest choral method, and it contains selections from the compositions in the part-books, and one of the above-mentioned notices of Dr. Cosin's request.

(3) The compositions in those volumes include contributions, not only of the principal musicians then at Cambridge and Ely (as Loosmoor, Ramsay, Molle, and Amnor), but of those connected with the Cathedrals, of which Dr. Cosin was a member, namely, Durham and Peterborough.

It is probable that a choral service had been used by the society before and after the Reformation, in the aisle of the neighbouring church of Little St. Mary's, which served for their chapel till 1632, and that some of the Latin documents, of ante-Reformation date, belonged to their choir, especially the four part-books of Latin services still preserved at Peterhouse; but whether the choir was kept up after the Reformation or not, at all events it would seem at least to have been reinforced on the building of the chapel in 1632, under the auspices of Dr. Wren, and that he and Bishop Cosin collected materials for the service from the contemporary composers at Cambridge and elsewhere.

The black-letter folio Prayer Book has the Preces set by various composers; the celebrated service of Gibbons in F throughout, including the Venite, set as a canticle, as was customary in the older services, several sets of responses, three Litanies, several Kyries, the Nicene by Gibbons, a Sanctus with the preceding versicles, probably by Amner, and a "Gloria in Excelsis" by Amner. It is to be remarked that there is a blank music leaf inserted at the offertory, which it was probably intended to fill up, as we find that an offertory sentence was sometimes set to music in old times. At the end of this volume is a Latin translation of the Morning and Evening Service (but not of the Litany, Communion Service, or Psalter), interleaved with music-paper. From this it may be inferred that the Latin service was occasionally used at Peterhouse, as it still is at Christ Church in Oxford. There are also two Latin musical Litanies by Loosemoor and Molle; the latter is expressly designated "Pro Coll. Sti. Petri." The version used for these Litanies differs both from that employed at Oxford, and from that recited at the meetings of the Convocation of the Province of Canterbury. As far as Mr. Jebb is aware, nothing of this particular version has been discovered, beyond what is preserved in these musical adaptations of the suffrages. The translation of the matins and evensong also differs, it is believed, from any now extant.

The few Latin services in the part-books consist of the *Te Deum*, the *Jubilate*, and in one instance only of the Kyrie and Creed. There are no evening services so adapted; from which it may be inferred that the Latin form was used occasionally only. The same remark is applicable to at least one of these, which was made with respect to the black-letter Prayer Book.

As to the English services, those for the evening are more numerous than for the morning. Either the choral service was then, as now at Trinity College, confined to surplice times, which are nearly twice as frequent in the evening as in the morning; or the matins on week-days were more simply performed than in the evening.

The Latin *Te Deum*, by Dr. Child, was composed, "for the Right Worshipful Dr. Cosin." If this designation points to his Vice-Chancellorship, the date is 1639. It may possibly have been intended for some solemn occasion at St. Mary's. It may be observed that as there are in the collection Latin Litanies, by Loosemoor and Ramsay, organists of King's and Trinity, and by Molle, who seems to have been connected with Peterhouse. These Litanies were probably used on certain occasions in the above-named colleges; and if so, it may be reasonably inferred that the Litanies used before the University were not less solemnly performed, but were sung in Latin, as is still the usage of Oxford towards the beginning of each term.

In some instance occurs a very singular kind of musical writing, the notes being of a rhomboidal form, very bold and distinct, often accompanied by Gothic or old-English letter. The notation of the black-letter Prayer Book is from the same hand, but the words are written cursively

In the original indexes the compositions are methodically distributed under distinct heads, thus :—

1. " Ad Domine labia," *i.e.*, the preces or versicles before the Psalms.

2. " Psalmi Festivales," or the psalms arranged like canticles, such as we find in many of the older services used on great festivals—a feature of the Church service now obsolete.

3. The *Venite Exultemus*, arranged as a canticle.

4. " Ad Dominus vobiscum," or the responses after the Creed.

5. " Litanies," English and Latin.

6. " Full Services," under the three heads of " Ad Matutines," " Ad officium Altaris " (consisting of Kyrie and Creed, including also, in a few instances, the Gloria before the Gospel and an offertory sentence), and of " Ad Vespertinas. "

7. " Verse services," with the same three-fold division.

8. " Full Anthems," in the divisions " of praise," " of prayer," " of penitence."

9. " Verse anthems," similarly classed.

10. " Ad sursum corda " and " Ad Gloria in Excelsis." There are, however, no settings of the Sursum Corda, except the black-letter Prayer Book, and but few of the Sanctus and Gloria in Excelsis.

11. " Antiphonæ Festivales," being, for the most part, the proper collects of the great festivals.

The same designations, as far as they are applicable, are observed in the black-letter Prayer Book. This distribution confirms the fact, of which, however, there is ample evidence besides, that the distinction between full and verse services and anthems has existed at least since the Reformation.

REMOVAL OF THE CHURCH SCREEN.

Under the above title appears an article in the *Musical World*, signed " Pencerdd Gwllym," and the following paragraph from it deserves special attention :—

The removal of the Cathedral screen is a sign that the age of exclusiveness is passing away ; a sign that the service and anthem of former days, written and performed for the delectation and edification of a few, are doomed to give place to something better adapted to the widened area, with its thousands of occupants. The leaders and followers of what is called the " Catholic revival " of the present generation are making demands upon the musician as well as builder and decorator ; they call for music to aid in securing the attention and interest of the people. And it must be acknowledged that our young church composers are responding with great alacrity, and some ability. Never before has there been so much written and published, and never before has music reached the multitude with such force. The sacred compositions now teeming from the press show above all things yearnings and strivings for effect. The style of the last century is discarded for what is thought more earnest and stirring. Artifices, deemed once upon a time essential to writings with any pretence to learning, are passed by in the hurry of producing themes with a grip strong enough to hold the unwilling and agitate the listless. This anxious wish for vigour is now a characteristic of the greater portion of the Church, where, happily, however, it can find expression without travestying either religion or music. Nevertheless, the younger musician is often found resorting to modes not altogether free from violence. An undue force in the musical illustration of Scriptural text, and an extreme form of emphasis and accent on certain solemn words, are errors regretted by those not inclined to overlook impropriety because zeal is the prompter. This excess is particularly noticeable in passages embodying the mysteries of our holy religion—themes of such an awful import as to bow the discomfited mind of man to the earth—in dealing with these unfathomable subjects the modern composer presumptuously tries to represent, as it were, the miracle which first accompanied and substantiated the spiritual verities. Thus, for instance, in the recital of the passion of our Lord, the musician is sometimes found labouring, by abrupt transitions, or unnatural harmonic combinations, to supply by his art the place of supernatural confirmation. Far better and wiser would it be for him to pass by such impenetrable mysteries with the modesty and self-abnegation of predecessors. Besides, does not the special effect of to-day become the discarded clap-trap of to-morrow ? The Church composer has assuredly a field before him wide enough for the exercise of the greatest genius or the vastest ambition—for, has he not the heart of man with all its emotional attributes open to his touch ? By his art, which is well called " divine," he has free entrance into, and potent sway over, that too often closely-guarded realm. At his bidding, the gentler passions troop out from their hiding-places, whilst pity and love are drawn wheresoever he wills.

Organ News.

LIVERPOOL.

Mr. W. T. Best gave two organ recitals in St. George's Hall, on Saturday, Feb. 24th :—

AFTERNOON PROGRAMME.

Sonata in B flat major, No. 4	Mendelssohn.
Andantino in D flat major	Chauvet.
Chaconne in F major	Handel.
Fantasia Cromatica	Thiele.
Pastorale	Moricone.
March (Symphony No. 3)	Widor.

EVENING PROGRAMME.

Overture (" Il Barbiere di Seviglia ")	Rossini.
Romanza	Pesca.
Festival Prelude on " Ein feste Burg "	Thomas.
Sarabande (" Dorothea ")	Parker.
Coronation March	Meyerbeer.

PRESTON.

Subjoined are the programmes of organ recitals given in the new Public Hall, by Mr. James Tomlinson, on Saturday, Feb. 24th :—

AFTERNOON RECITAL.

Sonata in C minor	Mendelssohn.
Andante Cantabile (Piano Duets)	Weber.
Pastorale	Merkel.
Overture (" Rienzi ")	Wagner.
Berceuse	Guilmant.
Marche Solennelle	Ketterer.

EVENING RECITAL.
In memoriam RICHARD WAGNER.

Marche Funèbre	Chopin.
Overture (" Tannhäuser ")	Wagner.
Cavatina	Raff.
Introduction to third act, and Bridal Chorus (" Lohengrin ")	Wagner.
" The Harmonious Blacksmith "	Handel.
March and Chorus (" Tannhäuser ")	Wagner.

BOLTON.

An organ recital was given in the Albert Hall by M. Alexandre Guilmant, on Wednesday, Feb. 21st, with the annexed programme :—

Toccata in F (with pedal solos)	Bach.
Andante con moto in G minor	Boëly.
Prelude in D minor	Clérambault.
Petite Fugue in G major	Krebs.
Sonata in D minor, No. 1	Guilmant.
Canon in B major	Schumann.
Scherzo Symphonique Concertant	Lemmens.
Concerto in D, No. 10	Handel.
Funeral March and Hymn of Seraphs	Guilmant.
Andantino in D flat ; March, with Hymn of Priests	Chauvet.
Improvisation.	
Grand Chorus in A major	Salomé.

An organ recital was given in the Albert Hall by Mr. Wm. Mullineux, F.C.O., on Saturday, Feb. 24th. The following was the programme :—

Introduction (" Seven Last Words ")	Haydn.
Larghetto (Clarionet Quintet)	Mozart.
Marche Religieuse	Adam.
Communion in E major	Saint-Saëns.
Concert Fantasia on a Welsh March	Best.
March (Sixth Suite)	Lachner.

NORWICH.

Annexed is the programme of an organ recital given in St. Andrew's Hall, by Dr. Bunnett, F.C.O., on Saturday, Feb. 24th :—

Fantasia, " The Pilgrims' Return "	Hermann.
Allegretto Tranquillamente	Jordan.
Larghetto in F	Cramer.
Siciliano and Finale, from a Concerto	Handel.
Marcia Funèbre (*in memoriam* Richard Wagner)	Beethoven.
Cavatina	Raff.
Adagio (" Scotch " Symphony)	Mendelssohn.
Marche Religieuse	Wagner.
Bourrée in B minor	Bach.
Motet, " The arm of the Lord "	Haydn.

MANCHESTER.

Mr. J. Kendrick Pyne gave an organ recital in the Town Hall, on Saturday, Feb. 24th. Subjoined is the programme :—

Prelude and Fughetta	Bach.
Minuet and Trio in E flat (Pf. Sonata, Op. 47)	Beethoven.
Suite in E major	Bernard.
Romance in B flat	Smart.
Overture (" Alessandro Stradella ")	Flotow.
Melody in G	Gladstone.
Jubilant March	Stainer.

BRISTOL.

Annexed is the programme of the organ recital given by Mr. George Riseley in the Colston Hall on Saturday, Feb. 24th :—

Offertoire No. 5	Batiste.
Andante (Symphony No. 3)	Beethoven.
Prelude and Fugue in D major	Bach.
Minuet et Trio	Bennett.
"Partant pour la Syrie"	Haynes.
Gavotte (" Mignon ")	Thomas.
Overture (" Le Brasseur de Preston ")	Adam.

EDINBURGH.

Mr. William Blakeley, A.C.O., gave an organ recital in the United Presbyterian Church, Morningside, on Monday, Feb. 19th. Subjoined is the programme :—

Military March in D major	Beethoven.
Toccata and Fugue in Dorian mode	Bach.
Andante con moto in G major	Blakeley.
Gavotte (" Mignon ")	Thomas.
Sonata in D minor, No. 6	Mendelssohn.
Barcarolle (Fourth Concerto)	Bennett.
Aria, " Cujus Animam "	Rossini.
Overture (" Oberon ")	Weber.

CASTLE HOWARD.

An organ recital was given in the private chapel, by Mr. J. R. Brooke, on Sunday, Feb. 25th, when he performed the following programme :—

Overture (" Occasional "), Slow Movement, and March	Handel.
Minuet and Trio	Mozart.
Fantasia	Bunnett.
" Ah ! Che la Morte " (" Il Trovatore ")	Verdi.
" We're the Temple " (" Jeremiah ")	Oven.
Andante in A minor	Batiste.
" Hallelujah "	Beethoven.

PERTH.

The following is the programme of an organ recital given at Kinnoult Parish Church, by Mr. R. Wood Thorpe Browne :—

Andante No. 3, in C	Smart.
Fantasia	Stephens.
Andante and Variations (Septuor)	Beethoven.
Prelude and Fugue in B flat, Prelude and Fugue in F (Book 8, Peters' Edition)	Bach.
Minuet	Calkin.
Marche Nuptiale	Guilmant.
Sonnet, " Liebes Gruhling "	Ungl.
Con moto moderato, en forme d'Ouverture	Smart.

The recital was the first of a series to be given monthly, and was attended by a large congregation.

STYAL.

The following is the programme of a recital given in Norcliffe Chapel, on Saturday, Feb. 24th, by Mr. Wm. Gouldtborp :—

Allegretto in D	Tours.
Communion in E flat	Ravina.
Slow Movement in B flat	Spohr.
Offertoire in D	Batiste.
Andante in D flat	Mozart.
Air, " Angels ever bright and fair "	Handel.
War March of the Priests (" Athalie ")	Mendelssohn.
Offertoire in G	Wély.
Organ Movement	Novello.
Minuet and Trio	Bennett.
Andantino	Batiste.
Air, " Cujus Animam "	Rossini.

SOUTHPORT.

Appended is the programme of an organ recital given by Mr. S. W. Pilling, in Chapel Street Congregational Church, on Saturday, Feb. 24th :—

Overture in C minor	Merkel.
Andante in A major	Batiste.
Caprice in B flat	Guilmant.
March, with Hymn of Priests	Chauvet.
"Adeste Fideles"	Adams.
Recit., " Deeper and deeper still," air, " Waft her, Angels " (" Jephtha ")	Handel.
Allegro movement	Deane.

CRYSTAL PALACE.

Mr. A. J. Eyre's programme on Saturday last was as follows :—

Solemn March	Mendelssohn.
Andantino (" Rosamunde ")	Schubert.
Serenade	Heller.
Concert Fugue in G	Krebs.
Pastorale	Moricool.
Variations on " Holsworthy Church Bells "	Wesley.
Minuet and Trio	Calkin.
Two Vocal Duets	Mendelssohn.
Grand Chœur	Guilmant.
Largo in G	Handel.
" Cujus Animam "	Rossini.

BOW AND BROMLEY INSTITUTE.

On Saturday last Mr. Alfred Carder was the organist. His opening solos were a selection from Rossini's " Stabat Mater" and a Toccata in F from Widor's second set of organ symphonies, in which the player was not at all points at his best. Lux's " O Sanctissima " and Wagner's " Tannhäuser " March (by desire) formed the next and popular group. Mr. Carder's selection from Gounod's " Redemption " was seriously marred by an unfortunate cyphering. A pleasing selection from "Don Giovanni" received a skilful and effective rendering, and was duly appreciated. A " Festival March," by Horner, completed the organ solos. Mdlle. Eugene Bernard proved herself to be an accomplished pianist, playing Chopin's " Ballade " in G minor, and Listr's " Rhapsodie Hongroise " with much finish and skill. The vocalist, Mr. James Sauvage, has an excellent voice, and is an artist. His rendering of Purcell's " Mad Tom " secured an encore. By-the-way, the date given on the programme, 1650, was some 40 years too early ; Purcell was born in 1658. Mr. Sauvage's other songs greatly pleased the audience. Mr. Fountain Meen was the able accompanist. On March 10th, Mr. James Higgs, the esteemed Hon. Sec. of the Musical Association, will be the organist ; Mr. T. T. Trimnell, of Sheffield, plays on March 17th, and Mr. W. de M. Sergison, on March 24th ; Prof. Macfarren and the Committee of the Royal Academy of Music have kindly consented to the appearance here of the Royal Academy of Music Operatic Class, on March 12th, under the direction of Messrs. Gustave Garcia and Fiori.

Academical Intelligence.

TRINITY COLLEGE, LONON.

PRIZE MUSICAL COMPETITIONS.

The Academical Board of Trinity College, London, offer the following prizes for 1883 :—For a Chamber Music Composition (Adjudicator, Sir Michael Costa), Ten Guineas and a Gold Medal. For an Essay on "The Use of the Orchestra in the Services of the Church " (Adjudicator, Mr. E. H. Turpin), a Gold Medal. For a " Chorale " (Adjudicator, Dr. W. H. Longhurst), Three Guineas. " Musical History " Essays (Adjudicator, Mr. W. H. Cummings), Three Guineas and Two Guineas. It is stated that the Regulations are now ready, and may be had on application to the Secretary.

COLLEGE OF ORGANISTS.

Prof. G. A. Macfarren gave the second of his course of four lectures on Bach's " Twenty-four Preludes and Fugues," on Tuesday last, the course being completed on March 6th and 13th, at the Holborn Town Hall. Mr. Windyer Clarke was again the able illustrator of the Professor's learned and deeply interesting analysis of Bach's great work. The inspection was proceeded with in detail up to the Prelude and Fugue in F Minor, terminating the first half of the work. In his opening observations Prof. Macfarren spoke of the early English editions of Preludes and Fugues, saying there seemed to be some evidence to show that that one issue anticipated by a year or so the first German print ; the Professor also alluded to the Preston, Wesley and Horn editions, the last by the combined editors being marked by much care and judgment. In the course of Prof. Macfarren's masterly analysis, he pointed out with remarkable acumen several substantial indications of modern form, as in the Prelude in E flat, 9.8 time, as a model of the " Songs without words," and the pathetic prelude in F minor, in 2.4 measure, as a distinct epitome of the dual allegro form. The lecturer's most interesting and very valuable observations were closely followed by a large audience, many having copies of the work, reference being facilitated by the number of bar in each case being announced. Mr. Windyer Clarke played the illustrations with much clearness, charm, and character. Mr. James Higgs efficiently acted as chairman, and duly reminded those present of the dates (March 6th and 13th) of the two remaining lectures.

Correspondence.

THE CHRIST CHURCH ORGAN.

TO THE EDITOR OF THE "MUSICAL STANDARD."

SIR,—Permit me to state that the date given in my letter last week referred, not to the organ, but to Dr. Gauntlett's performance thereon. It may, perhaps, interest some of your readers if I add, that attached to the case of the instrument are six brass plates, one of which, I am told, records the introduction of a double dulciana and another stop, the gift of a former rector of the parish. Over the manuals there is an embellishment presented by a gentleman who contributed largely to the reconstruction of the organ in the year 1839.

Feb. 26.

Yours truly,
C. H. K. F.

WAGNER AND GOUNOD.

However it may fare with politics and business, music is in perpetual session. London is being constantly flooded with music. At the end of the season, it simply adjourns in a mass into the provinces. From external and public appearances, it might be argued that there is no great difference between the musical past and present. Formerly, the metropolis had its operas and concerts from Easter to August. As good music was performed for the delight of the subjects of George III. as for the pleasure of the subjects of Queen Victoria. To read the diary of Thomas Moore, it would be thought the English public two thirds of a century ago was as musically enlightened as in these days. When society migrated into the country, Birmingham and the three cathedrals held their musical celebrations as now. These were as enthusiastically and almost as numerously attended. The difference is that music, until within a very brief period, was a monopoly. There was a musical public thoroughly and learnedly instructed. Outside were black pitch, ignorance, and insensibility. Dinners and balls were needed to allure popular audiences in the shires. In London, the public did not pretend to understand or sympathize. A crowded house to listen to the compositions of Herr Wagner now implies an enormous multitude as curious and as intelligent waiting for its turn and share afterward. The thousands who hung absorbed upon M. Gounod's setting of the mysteries of Christianity represented a hundred-fold the numbers which have been training themselves by musical habituation and practice to appreciate its merits. Impostors may be detected in abundance, as at all times, and in reference to all subjects, who repeat commonplaces of musical criticism, while perceiving much less of their meaning than the Cambridge pretenders to familiarity with thermo-dynamics denounced by Mr. G. H. Darwin. Enthusiasm for music is often affected, when none is felt. At present, the hypocrisy is at all events the homage rendered by the few to the musical taste of the many rather than the reverse. It is a mere accident of place and opportunity where music plants its standard and summons it votaries.

M. Gounod and Herr Wagner have very little in common. Both, however, agree in expecting from music at once more and less than their great predecessors demanded. Music was disembodied formerly. Bach, Handel, Mozart, and Beethoven might be inspired by occurrences outside them : their lofty creations were reared on no others foundation than the builder's sense of harmony and melody ; he obeyed and expressed his own mood ; the material words and plot to which he happened to attach it were the merest afterthought. The music of the present, as of the future, whether it be dramatic or epic, aims at commenting upon themes formally, and deliberately compelling or praying its assistance to illustrate them. It has consented to be a servant, that it may help to guide and govern where before it claimed to be independent, abiding by its own laws, and flowering in accordance with none beside them. The disciple of Herr Wagner as to see and read as well as hear. Hearers of M. Gounod are invited to come with minds attuned to particular emotions and ideas to which "The Redemption" will give a brighter meaning, a more gracious significance. Herr Wagner bids the world listen, and learn to think and feel as he acts the minstrel before it. M. Gounod asks his admirers to bring hearts and minds charged with pious awe, and he will surround them with the atmosphere in which they can most fitly breathe. Herr Wagner requires a surrender. M. Gounod desires to co-operate and accompany. Each exacts an attendance of thoughts and feelings beyond those in which music was content once to lap itself. Music has been brought down from the realm in which it dwelt apart to be the companion and minister of the dramatist and poet. It is to be hoped that what it loses by ceasing to be its own sole interpreter other fields of art may gain in which it agrees to serve as interpreter for them. But that for itself there is some diminution in freedom and spontaneity it would be difficult to deny.—*Musical Herald.*

THE PHILHARMONIC CONCERTS.

A contributor writes :—

Mr. Southgate's report of the first Philharmonic concert, on February 15th, was doubtless exhaustive and strictly just. A difference of opinion appears to exist amongst critics respecting the efficiency of the band. One gentleman pronounces the orchestral performance to be perfection, and the exacting writer in the *Times* has no qualifying expression of disapproval to alloy his general tone of laudation. Mr. Cusins may be credited with all skill and *savoir faire* as a conductor, and his industry I know to be untiring, but the band have not the advantage of frequent rehearsals or constant co-operations. The "Ruins of Athens" music was welcome. Lo! and behold, how a great master could write in unison for voices, as testifieth that "Chorus of Dervishes" in E minor! An old Philharmonic, I must admit, and I rejoice to admit, that the performance of the prelude to "Parsifal" was excellent ; it had been evidently studied severely. The prelude itself I do not profess to fathom at present, and naturally avoid adverse criticism (even if called for), at this mournful time. The themes may be difficult to understand ; the scoring, especially in the latter part of the piece, is recognised by musicians as transcendently grand.

Certainly the orchestra of the Philharmonic, according to another pen, stands in the sunlight of a great artistic and historical position, and must expect the cobwebs and dust to be seen and protested against by the critical world. For years the occasional want of light and shade, and now and then of general finish—notwithstanding the many excellences of its material and generally fine tone—have been topics of observation. The directors cannot do more wisely than solicit anxious and well-timed criticism. And it will be well for the critics to exercise their power with all care and judgment ; remembering that there are no perfect orchestras anywhere, and that all existing in this and in other countries are capable of being vastly improved ; avoiding foolish conductor-worship, an idiotic craze rather rampant at times ; and bearing in mind that partisanship and prejudice, so easily overbalanced, are features of, often real, musical enthusiasm, which are commonly fatal to the best interests of the art.

STRATFORD.—The opening concert of the Upton Choral Society was given in the Stratford Town Hall on Monday evening the hall being well filled, and those who were present had good reason to congratulate themselves on not having missed so good a performance. The first piece on the programme was Mendelssohn's 42nd Psalm, which was very effectively rendered throughout, the solos being taken by Miss F. A. Jones, who was well supported in the choruses by a well-trained choir of ladies and gentlemen. The concluding chorus was very spiritedly given in excellent time, and called forth much applause. The second and third parts of the programme comprised an admirable selection of songs and part-songs, in all which the vocalists showed exceptional ability ; the prominent among these were Miss Brough and Mr. Atherton Latta, who were both very warmly encored. Mr. F. C. Kitson, who presided at the pianoforte, also took part in a duet with Mr. G. B. Gilbert with signal success.

SOUTH LONDON INSTITUTE OF MUSIC.—The fifth annual concert of the season by the Camberwell Choral Association took place on Tuesday last, when Mendelssohn's "Lauda Sion," and the wedding music from Handel's "Joseph," formed the chief item in the programme. Miss Mawhinny, Miss Myers, Mr. A. Thompson, and Mr. A. Moore were the soloists, the orchestral band of the Institute supplied the accompaniments, and Mr. L. Venables conducted with his accustomed care and skill. The chorus, though very short of tenors, did its work well, especially in "Immortal pleasures" and "O Lord, we trust alone in Thee," from "Joseph," but the band was somewhat out of tune, and in the accompaniments to the soli portions was considerably louder than was needful. Mr. Moore's capital singing of the difficult bass air in "Joseph," earned an enthusiastic recal? In the second part of the programme, the principal features were the violin solo of Mr. Gatehouse and the artistic singing of Sullivan's "Distant shore," by Mr. Thomson. The ladies also contributed vocal solos, but the effect in one instance was marred by an indifferently played violin obbligato—*not* by Mr. Gatehouse. Part-songs were given by the choir, and the band was heard in a gavotte by W. S. Lambert, which was chiefly noticeable as beginning on the first beat of the bar instead of the third, as, in my opinion it should do. The hall was well filled by an appreciative audience.

Passing Events.

Mr. Russell Lochner announces a benefit concert at the Lancaster Hall, Notting Hill, on March 12th.

The Brousil family resumed their serial concerts of chamber music on Thursday afternoon, March 1, at their house in Harrow Road.

Herr Friedmann, a baritone de la premiere force, will give a grand concert in May, at Kensington, under the immediate patronage of H.R.H. the Duke of Edinburgh.

Mr. W. H. Jude, of Liverpool, contributes to Hand and Heart for March, a spirited temperance chorus having a vigorous theme, and, in good contrast, a tranquil episodical sentence.

Mr. W. A. Barrett gave his lecture on Balfe at the London Institution on March 1st. The same lecturer will address the members of the College of Organists on April 3rd.

On March 7th, at the Rooms of the Society of Arts, a lecture will be given on "The History of the Pianoforte," by Mr. A. J. Hipkins. John Stainer, M.A., Mus.Doc., will preside.

The Sherborne School Musical Society give their 71st concert on Easter Monday, March 26th, the 56th anniversary of the death of Beethoven (1827). The programme will include, Symphony in C major, Op. 21 (Beethoven); "The Messiah" (Handel); and Siegfried Idyll (Wagner). Conductor, Mr. Louis N. Parker.

Mdme. Sophie Menter gave a pianoforte recital on Feb. 20th, at the Assembly Rooms, Bath. For one hour and three quarters, without the aid of notes, and with very little rest, she took her audience through a programme which contained selections from the works of J. S. Bach, Beethoven, D. Scarlatti, Mendelssohn, Liszt, Chopin, and Rubinstein, passing from one to the other with perfect ease.

A valuable collection of musical instruments, comprising pianofortes by Erard, Broadwood, and other well-known makers, three curious old clavichords, violins, violoncellos, and double basses, wind instruments, etc., also a library of valuable musical works, including a curious collection of early printed music for the harpsichord and clavecin, some scarce manuscripts of Scarlatti, Jomelli, Pergolesi, Handel, Purcell, etc., instrumental and vocal works, etc., were recently sold by auction by Messrs. Puttick & Simpson.

Prof. G. A. Macfarren completed his 70th year on Friday, March 2nd. That the esteemed Cambridge Professor and Principal of the R.A.M. will long continue to enjoy the admiration and profound respect of the musical world will be the earnest wish not only of those who are privileged to know him personally, but also of all who are interested in the cause of English art, and gratefully remember the very remarkable services rendered thereto by the greatly honoured bearer of the name of G. A. Macfarren.

In pursuance of the political craze of all parties—the bidding too exclusively for the support of the humbler classes, the Standard puts forth an insane proposal for taxing the owners of pianofortes £5 per annum on each instrument, the effect of such proposal being the imposition of increased burdens upon our middle classes, to the immunity of the extreme classes, for the rich would not feel such an imposition. To thus check the growth of the refining cultivation of music, to practically deprive thousands of others of their most valued comfort, would be a policy as idiotic and as cruel as the reinstating of such condemned taxes upon life, health, and progress, as the window and paper taxes. Surely the income tax falls heavily enough already upon our middle classes, without further special burdens in the same direction. Figaro says upon the new proposal :—"The lower classes would not feel the tax because they would not pay it. The upper classes would pay the tax, but they would not feel it. It is time, not that the middle classes should be further taxed, but that they should have some relief from taxation. Nothing could, therefore, be more monstrously unjust than to levy a new tax the burden of which would fall almost exclusively upon their shoulders. He who pleads for a tax of five pounds a year on the musical instrument which in these days adorns the most modest drawing-room, has few sympathisers."

The Committee of the Organ Builders' Benevolent Institution announce that a ticket benefit will take place in aid of its funds, from Monday, March 5th, to Friday, March 9th, when will be acted the "Silver King." The secretary is Mr. W. Farmer, 4, Queen Street, Camden Town.

Mr. Emil Behnke gave a valuable and interesting lecture before the Society of Arts on the 22nd, on "The Human Voice as a Musical Instrument, its Mechanism and Management." Mr. Lennox Browne, a distinguished authority in throat and vocal surgery, was in the chair. It is interesting to know that Mr. Emil Behnke has succeeded in obtaining some good photographs of his own vocal cords and soft palate in the act of tone production. For 28 years this result has been tried for in different countries, but until now without success.

Service Lists.

FOURTH SUNDAY IN LENT,

MARCH 4th.

London.

ST. PAUL'S CATHEDRAL.—Morn.: Service, Benedicite, Martin (No. 3); Benedictus, Tours in F; Introit, Lord, in this Thy mercy's day (Hymn 94); Communion Service, Tours in F. Even.: Service, Magnificat and Nunc Dimittis, Steggall in C; Anthem, Hear my prayer (Mendelssohn).

WESTMINSTER ABBEY.—Morn.: Service, Benedicite, Smith in F; Jubilate and Continuation, Tours. Aft.: Service, Elvey in A; Anthem, Come and let us return (Goss).

TEMPLE CHURCH.—Morn.: Service, Te Deum and Benedictus, Hopkins in C; Apostles' Creed, Harmonized Monotone; Anthem, God is a Spirit (Bennett); Kyrie Eleison, Hopkins in C. Even.: Service, Magnificat and Nunc Dimittis, Elvey in A; Apostles' Creed, Harmonized Monotone; Anthem, The Heavens declare the glory of God (Boyce).

LINCOLN'S INN HALL.— Morn.: Service, Distin in C; Kyrie, Distin; Anthem, I will mention the loving kindnesses (Sullivan). Even.: Service, Distin in C; Anthem, Why rage fiercely the heathen (Mendelssohn).

ALL SAINTS, MARGARET STREET.—Morn.: Service, Benedicite and Benedictus, Stainer; Introit, The sorrows of death (Redhead); Communion Service, Pyne in A flat; Benedictus and Agnus Dei, Mozart; Offertory Anthem, Come unto Him (Gounod). Even.: Service, Hoyte in A; Anthem, Motet—"Ne pulvis et cinis" (Mozart); Miserere, Allegri.

ST. AUGUSTINE AND ST. FAITH, WATLING STREET.—Morn.: Service, Benedicite, Martin (No. 3); Benedictus, Barnby in E; Communion Service, Eyre in E flat; Offertory, Comfort, O Lord (Crotch). Even.: Service, Walmisley in D; Anthem, Sing ye praise (Mendelssohn).

ST. BARNABAS, MARYLEBONE.—Morn.: Service, Te Deum and Jubilate, Wesley's Chant Service in F; Anthem, If we believe (Goss); Kyrie and Nicene Creed, Merbecke. Even.: Service, Magnificat and Nunc Dimittis, Walmisley in D minor; Anthems, O rest in the Lord, and, He that shall endure (Mendelssohn).

CHILDREN'S HOME CHAPEL, BONNER ROAD, E.—Morn.: Service, Anthems, I was glad (Callcott); and, The Lord is my strength (Monk). Aft.: Service, Anthems, Incline Thine ear (Himmel), and, Lo! my Shepherd (Haydn).

CHRIST CHURCH, CLAPHAM.—Morn.: Service, Benedicite, Stainer; Kyrie and Credo, Smart in F; Offertory Anthem, As the hart pants (Mendelssohn); Sanctus, Smart; Benedictus and Agnus Dei, Sewell in E flat; Gloria in excelsis, Smart. Even.: Service, Magnificat and Nunc Dimittis, Goss in A; Miserere, Helmore; for the Anthem, the Cantata, "Out of the deep" (Bunnett).

FOUNDLING CHAPEL.—Morn.: Service, Te Deum, Garrett in D; Anthem, Hear my crying (Hummel). Aft.: Service, Cooke in G; Anthem, O Saviour of the world (Goss).

HOLY TRINITY, TULSE HILL.— Morn.: Chant Service. Even.: Service, Gadsby in C; Anthem, Plead Thou my cause (Mozart).

ST. JAMES'S PRIVATE EPISCOPAL CHAPEL, SOUTHWARK.—Morn.: Service, Introit, Glory be to Jesus (Hymn); Communion Service, Weber in E flat. Even.: Service, Walmisley in F; Anthem, Then is Jesus condemned, and, "March to Calvary" ("Redemption," Gounod).

ST. MAGNUS, LONDON BRIDGE.—Morn.: Service, Opening Anthem, I will arise (Clarke Whitfield); Te Deum and Jubilate, Attwood in F; Kyrie, Purcell. Even.: Service, Cantate and Deus Misereatur, Hayes in E flat; Anthem, The God of Jeshurun (Goss).

ST. MARY BOLTONS, WEST BROMPTON, S.W.—Morn.: Service, Benedicite and Benedictus, Foster in E. Even.: Service, Wesley in F; Magnificat and Nunc Dimittis, Wesley in F; Anthem, Here by Babylon's wave (Gounod).

ST. MICHAEL'S, CORNHILL. — Morn.: Service, Te Deum and Benedictus, Thorne in C; Anthem, Come unto Him (Gounod); Kyrie and Creed, Wesley in E. Even.: Service, Magnificat and Nunc Dimittis, Walmisley in D minor; Anthem, O God of my righteousness (Greene).

S. MILDRED'S, LEE, S.E. — Benedicite, Turle; Benedictus, Heathcote; Introit, Bread of Heaven (Barnby); Communion Service, Wesley in E. Even.: Service, Parisian Tones, Stainer; Anthem, O Saviour of the world (Goss); after sermon, Miserere, Redhead.

ST. PAUL'S, BOW COMMON, E. — Morn.: Service, Benedicite, Stainer, Turle, and Irons; Benedictus, Chant; Communion, Service, Kyrie, Credo, Offertory, Sanctus, Benedictus, Agnus Dei, and Gloria in excelsis, Calkin in B flat. Even.: Service, Magnificat and Nunc Dimittis, Rogers in D; Anthem (unaccompanied), Lord, for Thy tender mercies' sake (Farrant).

Country.

ARDINGLY COLLEGE, SUSSEX.—Morn.: Communion Service, Nares in F; Gloria, Lewington in F. Even.: Service, King in C; Anthem, All we like like sheep (Handel).

ST. ASAPH CATHEDRAL. — Morn.: Service, Goss in A; Anthem, O Lord my God (Wesley). Even.: Service, The Litany; Anthem, Hear, O Thou Shepherd (Walmisley).

ASHBURNE CHURCH, DERBYSHIRE. — Morn.: Service, Benedicite, Best; Continuation, to end of Credo, Rogers in D. Even.: Service, Turle in D; Anthem, My God, my God (Benson).

BEDDINGTON CHURCH, SURREY.—Morn.: Service, Benedicite and Benedictus, Dykes; Introit, Lord Jesus, think on me (Hymn 185); Communion Service, Dykes in F. Even.: Service, Calkin; Anthem, If with all your hearts, and, He that shall endure (Mendelssohn).

BIRMINGHAM (ST. CYPRIAN'S, HAY MILLS).—Morn.: Service, Benedicite, Simms in B flat; Benedictus, Field in D; Anthem, Hear my prayer (Mendelssohn). Even.: Service, Kent in C; Anthem, O Lord, Thou hast searched me out (Croft).

CANTERBURY CATHEDRAL.—Morn.: Service, Te Deum, Hopkins in G; Jubilate, Hake in G; Introit, Praise the Lord (Scott); Communion Service, Skeats in C. Even.: Service, Goss in A; Anthem, I saw the Lord (Stainer).

CARLISLE CATHEDRAL. — Morn.: Service, Goss in F; Introit, Remember Lord (Verrinder); Kyrie, Hopkins in F; Nicene Creed, Harmonized Monotone. Even.: Service, Garrett in F; Anthem, Unto Thee have I cried (Elvey).

DONCASTER (PARISH CHURCH).—Morn.: Service, Kempton in B flat; Introit, O Saviour of the world (Goss). Even.: Service, Calkin in B flat; Anthems, Sing ye praise ((Mendelssohn).

ELY CATHEDRAL. — Morn.: Service, Benedicite, Chants; Jubilate, Plain-song; Kyrie and Credo, Thorne in E flat; Gloria, Richardson in F; Anthem, Hear, O Lord (Goss). Even.: Service, Goss in E; Anthem, Who is this that cometh (Kent).

EXETER CATHEDRAL.—Morn.: Service, Young in G; Communion Service, Farrant in G minor; Anthem, Rend your hearts. Even.: Service, Cooke in G; Anthem, O Lord God.

FOLKESTONE (ST. MICHAEL's).—Morn.: Communion Service, Stainer in E flat. Even.: Service, Magnificat and Nunc Dimittis, Clarke-Whitfield in E; Anthem, All ye who weep (Faure).

GLASGOW (BLYTHSWOOD PARISH CHURCH).—Aft.: Service, Anthem, The wilderness (Goss). Even.: Service, Cantate and Deus Misereatur, Hopkins in B flat; Anthems, Awake up my glory (Peace), and, Blessed be the God and Father (Wesley).

HIGH WYCOMBE PARISH CHURCH. — Even.: Service, Anthem, Hear my Prayer (Mendelssohn).

LEEDS PARISH CHURCH. — Morn.: Service, Benedicite, Turle; Anthem, He shall feed (Handel); Communion Service, Dykes in F. Even.: Service, Garrett in F; Anthem, My hope is in the everlasting (Stainer).

LICHFIELD CATHEDRAL.—Morn.: Service, Porter in D; Anthem, O that I knew (Bennett). Aft.: Service, Anthem, Blessed be the God and Father (Wesley).

LIVERPOOL CATHEDRAL.—Aft.: Service, Burstall in D; Anthem, Out of the deep (Hatton).

MANCHESTER CATHEDRAL. — Morn.: Service, Benedicite, Hopkins in E flat: Benedictus, Langdon in F; Anthem, Save me, O God (Boyce); Kyrie, Creed, Sanctus, and Gloria, Richardson in F. Aft.: Service, Richardson in F; Anthem, O come near the cross (Gounod).

MANCHESTER (ST. BENEDICT's). — Morn.: Service, Kyrie, and Credo, Nares in F; Sanctus, Benedictus, and Agnus Dei, Casciolini in A minor. Even.: Service, Magnificat and Nunc Dimittis, Jordan; Miserere, Redhead.

MANCHESTER (ST. JOHN BAPTIST, HULME).—Morn.: Service, Benedicite, Marbeck; Kyrie, Credo, and Sanctus, Dykes in F; Benedictus, Thorne in E flat; Agnus Dei, Miné in F. Even.: Service, Magnificat and Nunc Dimittis, Gregorian; Miserere, Redhead.

MUSSELBURGH (LORETTO SCHOOL). — Morn.: Introit, Turn Thy face from my sins (Attwood); Service, Clarke-Whitfeld in E; Anthem, Judge me, O God (Mendelssohn). Even.: Service, Anthem, O Lord God of my salvation (Clarke-Whitfeld).

NORTH BERWICK, N.B. (S. BALDRED's).—Morn.: Service, Benedicite, De Lacey, Gibbs, etc.; Introit, (Hymn 317); Kyrie, Mendelssohn. Even.: Service, Chants; Anthem, O Saviour of the world (Goss).

RIPON CATHEDRAL. — Morn.: Service, Chants; Anthem, O Saving Victim (Gounod); Kyrie and Credo, Garrett in F. Even.: Service, The Litany; Anthem, Lord God of Heaven (Spohr).

ROCHESTER CATHEDRAL. — Morn.: Service, Goss in A; Jubilate, Hopkins in A; Anthem, Deliver us, O Lord (Battten); Communion Service, Armes in A. Even.: Service, Clarke in C; Anthem, Call to remembrance (Battishill).

SHEFFIELD PARISH CHURCH. — Morn.: Service, Kyrie, Weber in E flat. Even.: Service, Cantate and Deus Misereatur, Chants; Anthem, If with all your hharts (Mendelssohn).

SHERBORNE ABBEY.—Morn.: Service, Kyrie Smart; Offertories, Barnby. Even.: Service, Anthem, Consider and hear me (Evelyn).

SOUTHAMPTON (ST. MARY'S CHURCH).—Morn.: Service, Benedicite, Best in C; Benedictus, Turton; Communion Service, Introit, O Saviour of the world (Macfarren); Service, Custard in E flat; Offertory,, Lay not up (Barnby); Paternoster, Helmore. Even.: Service, Magnificat and Nunc Dimittis, Wesley in F; Anthem, Turn Thy face (Attwood); The Litany, Tallis's Ferial.

SOUTHWELL COLLEGIATE CHURCH, NOTTS.—Morn.: Service, Benedicite and Benedictus, Barnby; Kyrie and Creed, Marriott in F. Even.: Service, Goss in E; Anthem, Come, Holy Ghost (Elvey).

WELLS CATHEDRAL. — Morn.: Service, Porter in D; Introit, O Lord, correct me (MS.). Even.: Service, Gladstone in E; Anthem, Be merciful (Barnby).

WORCESTER CATHEDRAL. — Morn.: Service, Benedicite, Hall in F; Benedictus, Dykes in F; Anthem, Hear my prayer (Hall). Even.: Service, Smart in G (Verse); Anthem, As pants the hart (Spohr).

NOTICES TO CORRESPONDENTS.

NEWSPAPERS sent should have *distinct marks* opposite to the matter to which attention is required.

APPOINTMENT.

MR. F. BUTLER, A.C.O., has been appointed Organist of the Brighton Aquarium.

ERRATUM.—Through no fault of the compositor, but solely owing to the bad manner in which the copy was prepared, the name of Mr. Philip Sharpe, of Bishop's Stortford, was omitted from last week's list of Certificated Musical Students, Trinity College.

Printed for the Proprietor by BOWDEN, HUDSON & Co., at 23, Red Lion Street, Holborn, London, W.C. ; and Published by WILLIAM REEVES, at the Office, 185, Fleet Street, E.C. West End Agents:—WEEKES & CO., 14, Hanover Street, Regent Street, W. Subscriptions and Advertisements are received either by the Publisher or West End Agents.—Communications for the EDITOR are to be forwarded to his private address, 6, Argyle Square, W.C.
SATURDAY, MARCH 17, 1883.—Entered at the General Post Office as a Newspaper.

A NEWSPAPER FOR MUSICIANS PROFESSIONAL AND AMATEUR

No. 971. Vol. XXIV. FOURTH SERIES. SATURDAY, MARCH 10, 1883. WEEKLY: PRICE 3D.

L. VAN BEETHOVEN'S LATER SONATAS.

A Lecture delivered in the London Institution on March 22, 1883.

BY HERR ERNST PAUER.

Principal Professor of the Pianoforte at the Royal College of Music, Professor of the Pianoforte at the Guildhall School of Music, the School of Art and Science, Crystal Palace, &c., &c.

LADIES AND GENTLEMEN,—The subject of our lecture this evening is, "The Later Sonatas of Beethoven." You will recollect that on the last occasion we discussed the nature and character of Beethoven's earlier sonatas; I had also an opportunity of observing that his sonatas show an enormous progress compared with those of Haydn, Clementi, and Mozart, and that he was able to produce effects in them of which Haydn and Mozart scarcely ever dreamed. In some respects the later sonatas of Beethoven differ from his earlier works in that form. We shall find that in later years when a sad and dire calamity—deafness—had overtaken him, our great master deviated occasionally from the plain and beaten path of order, a path along which he had travelled through hard struggles and incessant toil; he himself began to think somewhat lighter of the laws of order and rule, which he had followed with wonderful faithfulness, and he, the triumphant representative of classicism in all its best and most powerful phases, became towards the end of his life slightly diffuse and less thoroughly satisfactory, somewhat cloudy, and at times even unintelligible.

Beethoven's later life became more and more solitary. He was difficult of access; his deafness made him mistrustful. He would not listen to the advice of his friends; any suggestion they good-naturedly made, was received with mistrust, and yet the man himself was thoroughly good and noble, and his soul as pure as that of a child. Beethoven was a man of intense feeling, he was moved by violent, strong passions, which influenced him the more, as owing to his deafness he was condemned to a solitary life, and was unable to impart his moral sufferings to other people. If we only make due allowance for all the eccentricities, the oddities of his character, that resulted from his deafness, we find in him a powerful nature, equally strong in love and in hate. The innermost essence of Beethoven's nature was a deep longing for love and completeness, as we find it so touchingly expressed in his letters. His innermost power exhibits itself also in a strong self-consciousness, and in a certain pride. Beethoven expresses in his works a high truly Germanic idealism. He held his art as high as possible. Music was for him " a higher revelation than wisdom and philosophy." His iron will and wonderful perseverance showed itself not only on himself, but also in his works. He did not possess that spontaneity and electric rapidity of producing that distinguished Mozart; Beethoven had to dive deeper; he required the contact with other intellects; for this reason we find that Beethoven's music is neither a mere sensuous enjoyment, only depending on the beauty of its sound, nor a symbolical, moralising, or poetically playful one—it is real *ethical* art, originating in the desire to reveal the Highest and the most Sacred, aiming at "touching the depth of man's heart," "lifting him up to a better and purer sphere from the petty troubles of this nether world." Beethoven's music does not touch us merely superficially—it moves and excites and pacifies our feelings; it makes us tremble by the might of its contrasts, and again it pacifies and tranquilises us by its iron logic and by the solemn earnestness through which these contrasts are solved.

These introductory remarks, Ladies and Gentlemen, were necessary in order to prepare the ground of our present discussion. It is indispensable to know the *reason* why there is such a vast difference between the earlier and later sonatas of Beethoven, and this reason is really and truly the effect of his unfortunate malady—deafness—upon his whole nature and feeling. No words could better apply to Beethoven's case than Schiller's lines in "Wallenstein"; this last period of Beethoven's life presents a sad contrast with—

> These first years,
> When he was making progress with great effort,
> But since that ill-starr'd day
> A gloomy, darkened and distrustful spirit,
> Unsteady and suspicious, has possess'd him.
> His quiet mind forsook him, and no longer
> Did he yield up himself in joy and faith
> To his old luck and individual power.

Much has been said about the illustrious master's aberrations, about the indistinctness and the absence of harmony and unity of his last works, when compared with those of his former years; but, after all, if we closely examine the features which have been planned in these last works, we shall find that they are merely *exaggerations of eminent qualities*. The beauties are still there, the marks of genius in their highest potency, but the just proportion is wanting, that assigned to each charm its appropriate place and measure—and the very fulness and exuberance of the various qualities produces a sense of disturbance. No composer has ever written finer melodies than Beethoven has produced over and over again; but whilst the nature of music demands that a *melody* should be surrounded, supplemented, and completed by *harmony*—which harmony consists of tones that have a secondary importance only, we find in Beethoven's last works so great a desire to *sing in his parts* that each of them actually becomes a melody in itself, and thus destroys, or at least interferes with, the indispensable balance of power. These faults are faults arising neither from ignorance, nor from negligence; they are the idiosyncrasies and peculiarities which may never be wholly disassociated from the human intelligence, when it soars away on the track of ideal enthusiasm. "The giants must live alone." They are above ordinary mortals and ordinary rules. They may be condemned before the tribunal of criticism for incorrectness or for a forbidden license; many a passage, which revealed itself to the composer's spirit during the highest flight, appeared to him combined in a unity far above the conditions of daily rule or common perception.

Now we come to the illustrations, chosen to exhibit in a practical manner the correctness of the just mentioned remarks. I have selected three sonatas, all belonging to the later period of Beethoven's life, namely the (commonly called) Characteristic Sonata: "Les Adieux, l'Absence, et le Retour," No. 26, Op. 81; the Sonata No. 30, Op. 109, in E major, and the last of Beethoven's Sonatas, No. 32, Op. 111, in C minor. I propose to read some analytical remarks before performing these works; and thus I shall have an opportunity to elucidate several points not touched upon in the introductory remarks.

With regard to the sonata "Les Adieux, l'Absence, et le Retour," I may mention that for a long time the public was under the impression that this work was the result of a poetic and affectionate feeling, and that its strains described the composer's state of mind and heart at the parting, the absence, and the return of a beloved member of the fair sex. But the sober truth soon came out, and the fact was revealed that the mysterious object of Beethoven's musical poetry was not a graceful lady, but his Imperial Highness the Archduke Rudolph, Cardinal Archbishop of Ollmütz, and pupil of Beethoven. It is well known that Beethoven had an antipathy to giving lessons; and although his Imperial Highness did everything in his power to gild the pill, although he gave the strictest orders to the members of his household to dispense in Beethoven's case with all the customary rules of etiquette, to admit him at once to his presence, indeed to treat him with the greatest possible respect and deference, Beethoven, in spite of all these favours, felt uncomfortable when giving lessons, and even went so far as to declare that "after having given one lesson he felt ill for two days." It is almost comic to read the eighty-three letters which Beethoven wrote to his Imperial Highness, and which consist (with few exceptions) of nothing but excuses for "not coming" or "not having come to give a lesson." The wonderful patience of the Imperial pupil was never exhausted by this rather capricious and whimsical behaviour of his master; he received the touchy composer at all times with unvarying kindness and urbanity, and showed his sincere respect and ardent admiration for the illustrious master on every possible occasion. It may be that Beethoven, conscience-stricken as he was at times at the consciousness of his neglect of his duties as a teacher, tried with this sonata to soften the anger—if such a feeling ever existed—of his Imperial pupil; at least, on the title page of the autograph copy is the inscription: "The farewell at the departure of his Imperial Highness the Archduke Rudolph, on the 4th of May, 1809." And the first page of the last movement shows the inscription: "The arrival of his Imperial Highness the Archduke Rudolph, 30th January, 1810." The wonderfully sincere and earnest expression of the whole sonata does not admit of the idea that Beethoven meant the work to be a joke; we must, therefore, accept it as a work planned and finished with the same care that Beethoven devoted to all his compositions. The parting and the absence are depicted with the greatest accuracy in melancholy, deeply moving, but never sentimental, tones; we may almost fancy we see the movement of the hand that waves the last farewell to a departing beloved one; whilst in the beautiful andante, the absence is described with marvellous correctness; a tone of true resignation pervades this veritable gem of a musical and psychological picture; we cannot resist sympathising with the one who is left alone and who is deeply sad. Towards the end Beethoven describes in a truly masterly way the excitement, the anxiety, the impatience of awaiting the return; with a shout of joy the returned friend rushes into the arms of the expectant one, and the excitement, almost amounting to frenzy, which is here expressed is the most correct portraiture of such a scene. How touchingly is a phrase that expresses the height of happiness repeated over and over again, both in the treble and the bass; indeed, if we think of the state of our feelings in such sad moments of parting, of our melancholy during the absence of one we love, and of our exuberant joy on the return, we shall find that Beethoven's description of these emotions is not only correct, but absolutely perfect.

Performance.—Sonata, Op. 81, "Les Adieux, l'Absence, et le Retour."

For my second illustration I have selected the beautiful Sonata No. 30, Op. 109. I may here repeat, that between the later sonatas of Beethoven and his earlier ones a great difference is to be observed. Whilst in the earlier works he is most concise and strict as to form and construction, in the later works he shows an inclination to *widen* the barriers of form, and to present a regular tone-poem, conceived by fancy and warmed by a sincerity of feeling, quite unrivalled in the history of composition. Indeed, one of the chief features of Beethoven's last works is the development of melody, the desire to make not only the principal theme as much a song as possible, but to give such singing expression also to the supple-

mentary parts that form the *harmony*. The effect thus achieved is characterised by a dreamy, a meditative expression, and no longer evinces that firmness, compactness, and strict conciseness that render Beethoven's earlier sonatas such marvels of composition. It is well known that towards the end of his life, owing to his complete deafness, Beethoven became more and more inclined to solitude. Unable—through extreme nervousness—to communicate his ideas to others, incapacitated from understanding answers to his questions, he retired at last altogether from the world, and lived a life of dreary and melancholy loneliness. Music was his only solace, his only comfort—and we cannot wonder that these last compositions express at once deep *melancholy*, a feeling *of anger*, and last, not least, a beautiful *devotion*, or rather *resignation*, to his inevitable fate. In none of the later sonatas are these various feelings more vividly expressed than in the Sonata Op. 109. The first movement expresses contemplation; the second, energy and strong will; the third, touching resignation. It is almost impossible fully to describe in words the beauties of a musical work; and, therefore, I will not waste time on mere eulogies, which no one requires less than Beethoven. The illustrious master's music speaks best for itself. But it may, perhaps, not be superfluous to draw your more particular attention to the last movement, an air with six variations. The air itself is of transcendent beauty; Beethoven indicates the way how to play it by the direction: "Singing and with the sincerest expression." Variation I. is simply an enlargement of the "singing and sincere expression." It shows, if possible, still greater warmth and a still more affectionate feeling than the theme. Variation II. is distinguished by a character of extreme lightness and airiness; in four bars only these floating passages appear in a more substantial manner, but the delightful *staccato* expression is taken up and continued to Variation III. In this, the composer alters not only the time (from 3-4 into 2-4) but also the character of the piece. Firm, energetical, this variation seems like the expression of a manly resolve, a determination not to give way to entire despondency; musically speaking, it is an excellent relief, and stands out in striking contrast to the following Variation IV., which has to be played slower than the theme; this slackening of the time is also highly favourable for the clear execution and understanding of the graceful figure with which the air is here surrounded. In Variation V. the manly feeling of the composer is again evinced, the measure changes from 3-4 into common time, and the whole is expressive of earnestness, energy, and a certain obstinacy. Variation VI. returns to the triple time, which is widened into 9-8 time. On the whole, this last variation is the least effective, and its degree of beauty is inferior to that of the preceding variations. It presents, however, a difficulty to the executant which might be compared to that which besets the helmsman of a ship when he has to avoid coming into contact with a certain dangerous rock. The dangerous *musical* rock is here the shake that is kept up throughout not less than thirty bars; if undue prominence is given to the shake, the passage sounds like the shake-study in B major by John Baptist Cramer; but, with all due respect for Cramer as an educational composer, such a reminiscence would appear as bathos at the conclusion of one of the most beautiful sonatas of Beethoven; and, I think, we may take it for granted, that the composer here imagined the shake more as a soft vibration of the atmosphere, and not as the *technical* figure, which gives brilliancy and lustre to the execution. But, take it as we will, this prolonged shake always remains a highly questionable and dangerous device of the composer.

For the momentary suspense and uncertainty thus created, we are however consoled by the re-introduction of the beautiful principal theme, which closes the whole work in the most poetical and satisfactory manner.

Performance.—Sonata in E major, Op. 109, No. 30.

For the last illustration I have selected the Sonata in C minor No. 32, Op. 111. This wonderful work appeared for the first time in April, 1823, four years before Beethoven's death. It consists of two movements only. Schindler, the so-called friend of Beethoven, mentions that when he asked the composer why he had not written a third movement, Beethoven replied, "The time was too short." I do not consider this reason a valid one, in so far as the beginning of Beethoven's autograph MS. shows the date, 13th January, 1822, and as the Sonata itself was published fifteen months later, there is no doubt that there was plenty of time to write a third movement, if the composer had deemed it necessary. But it is difficult to imagine what character this third movement would have had; both the first and second movements are eminently finished and thoroughly complete in themselves, and stand in such a striking contrast to each other, that to ordinary judges the idea of a third movement seems to suggest an anti-climax. The first movement opens with a maestoso in common time; at once we acknowledge the presence of an earnest, grand, and noble mind; we recognise the genius that 23 years earlier produced the "Sonata Pathétique;" but these 23 years had exercised a powerful influence on the feelings of the unfortunate composer; in this last sonata the feeling is deeper, the shadows are darker, the earnestness appears more intense; indeed, here we behold the veteran who has struggled through a life full of sorrow, whilst in the "Sonata Pathétique" we mark the young composer fresh in body and in mind. In this last sonata we seek in vain for those sweet strains which delight us in the slow movement of the "Sonata Pathétique," nor are we struck by that gentle tenderness which appears in so sympathetic and touching a guise in the Rondo of the earlier Sonata. The opening chords of the Maestoso prepare us for something unusual, for something far above the ordinary world of feeling; the clouds soon gather darkly, looming lower and lower across the heavens, and a fierce storm of the elements seems to break forth in the Allegro con brio ed appassionata. Instead of the customary second subject we have here only a short phrase, descriptive of a fervent prayer for pity and grace; but this woeful sentence is at once lost in the returning storm that rages again and again in terrible force. Towards the end of this wonderful first movement, the elements seem to calm themselves, their thundering force is broken, and their rolling sound is now only heard in the distance; calmness and peace return, and anxiety, fear and terror are past.

The second movement is an Arietta in C major in the unusual time of 9-16; it is followed by four variations. The character of the theme is one full of devotion; indeed, it resembles a prayer, in which a faithful congregation beseech the Almighty to grant them mercy and peace; the purity and simplicity, the naturalness and fervour, of these 16 bars are truly wonderful, only a sincere and religious man could be inspired by such an idea. Haydn called Beethoven an atheist, but Beethoven's God was not a deity of wrath and vengeance; he looked to God as to his personal Father, in whom hetrusted, and to whom he lifted up the voice of prayer in times of trouble. The star that shone bright and friendly over the dark solitude of his existence was the love of God. With regard to the variations, much has been

writen for and against them; some critics denounced them as insipid, others lauded them as the image and reflex of Heaven itself. But taking a more prosaic and practical view, we find that they are simply a splendid elaboration and enhancement of the natural beauty exemplified in the arietta. Each variation is greater than its predecessors in life, substance, and expression. Variation IV. leads into a kind of free fantasia, which brings us to the end of the whole work. My audience will observe that in this movement it is again the shake to which is entrusted a most important part, and with respect to its proper performance I may be allowed to say that in the present instance it is even more difficult to carry out the composer's intention than in the Sonata No. 30. After having heard—as it were—the theme in full chorus, in all its splendour and might, the finishing variation, which is supported by the shake, should produce a kind of ethereal effect, a sort of glorification or apotheosis of the arietta. This is one of the rare instances in which we remark the deplorable influence of Beethoven's deafness, which prevented him from clearly realising the effects of his lofty ideas, which he imagined could be rendered on the piano—which instrument, however, with all its undoubted merits, is subject to certain restrictions and imperfections caused by the nature of its construction. No single instrument could attain the effect which Beethoven expected. To do this a whole orchestra would be required.

Performance.—Sonata No. 32, Op. 111.

In summing up our remarks on Beethoven's earlier and later Sonatas, we may say that his 32 model works in this form are a complete monument of the musical art. We possess two invaluable books of musical wisdom, over which time has passed without doing them the slightest injury, and which seem to be destined to give to our successors as much joy and delight as these great works have already given to our ancestors and are now giving to ourselves. These two books of wisdom are Sebastian Bach's 48 Preludes and Fugues, and Beethoven's 32 Pianoforte Sonatas. In listening to them a feeling of awe overcomes us, similar to our sensations on entering a noble cathedral; a feeling of vastness, of majestic grandeur overpowers us, and we seem to stand in the presence of the Divine. In these works the highest mission is fulfilled that music can have, these Sonatas echo in our hearts like a divine voice calling us to soar above the cares and sorrows of this nether world. No feeling that thrills through the human heart but finds a sympathetic chord in Beethoven: grief and joy, he has an expression for each; and the more we study him the more we become impressed with the inexhaustible wealth which his music offers us. With Beethoven the intellectual, the grand and genial as exhibited in the modulations and combinations of sound, overstep the regular form, and is not the result of a passing mood of feeling, or of chance moments of inspiration; it is, in fact, the exhibition of tone-pictures, all possessing the richest fulness of power, and revelling in the inexhaustible wealth of variety, with which they strike our enraptured ear. If we devote ourselves to the study of music in its essence, scaling its heights and diving into its depths, we find in it the echo of every sudden feeling, of every striving after the sublime, that lies concealed in the recesses of the human soul. And as in such a genius as Sebastian Bach we recognise the principle of law and order, so does Beethoven appear to speak to us of that infinite revelation of charity and love that leads us onward to higher things—that seems to pour the balm of the mercy of Heaven on every heart that aches on earth. For Beethoven himself has said, and he had a right to say it: "*Art is a bond that unites all the world—and true art endures for ever!*"

Musical Intelligence.

CRYSTAL PALACE CONCERTS.

PROGRAMME.

Symphony, "Scotch"	Mendelssohn.
Recit. and Aria, "Non paventar" ("Flauto Magico")	Mozart.
Mdlle. Elly Warnots.	
Concerto for violin and orchestra	Mendelssohn.
Violin—Señor Sarasate.	
"In the olden time," Suite in D, for strings only (dedicated to the Crystal Palace orchestra)....	F. H. Cowen.
1. Air with Variations.—2. The Lute.—3. The Chase.—4. Lullaby.—5. The Dance (Tempo di Minuetto).	
(First time of performance).	
Shawl Dance, "Le Dieu et la Bayadère"	Auber.
Air with Variations	Rode.
Mdme. Elly Warnots.	
Fantasia for violin and orchestra, on Melodies from "Carmen"	Sarasate.
Violin—Señor Sarasate.	
Overture, "Zanetta"	Auber.
Conductor - - - AUGUST MANNS.	

It may not be sufficiently known, that these concerts now begin at 3.10, instead of 3 o'clock as formerly. This is a great convenience, as many passengers arrive at the low level station by the 2.50 train, and are quite unable to get tickets and reach the concert-room in ten minutes, to say nothing of the delay often occasioned by the unpunctuality of the train. I remarked some months ago that an alteration was desirable, and probably some one of greater influence was of the same opinion, and has brought about the desired change. There is now no excuse for parties coming late into the concert-room and thus annoying the conductor and those who are in time for the first piece on the programme.

Of the "Scotch" Symphony I need only say that it was splendidly played and cordially received.

Señor Sarasate, on his appearance, met with quite an ovation, and his performance of Mendelssohn's concerto roused the audience to the highest pitch of enthusiasm, as it was played with an inspiration and perfection very rarely equalled. Nothing could exceed his beautiful expression in the exquisite andante. Heine says that "perfumes are the feelings of flowers," and expression is to music what the perfume is to the flower. The fantasia from "Carmen" brought out many specialties of Sarasate's playing, especially the downward chromatic progression preparatory to the re-entrance of his theme; this is done to perfection, but he unconsciously uses it much too frequently.

Of Mr. Cowen's clever work a few words only can now be said. We may often judge from certain defects of style, which are of modern, indeed of quite recent date, that the composer is young and ambitious, hoping by spasmodic and desperate efforts to gain a reputation, but which can end in nothing but failure. Mr. Cowen is inclined to follow a more patient course, and not to forsake the only path that can lead to lasting fame. This is evident in his present work, composed entirely for strings. If it had not been intrinsically good, the ear would have tired of it long before the end, and the greatest praise that can be given is to be able to say that the interest in the suite was kept up to the end of the last number.

Mdlle. Elly Warnots sang extremely well, but one is really getting tired of Rode's Variations.

There will be no Saturday concert on the 24th of March, the next taking place on the 31st.

R. S.

Another contributor writes:—

Mr. Manns, a German, does more for "British interests," or "national talent," than the old Philharmonic. Mr. F. Cowen's "Suite," whereof I leave Dr. Sloman to give a faithful account, is dainty music skilfully written, and with a dash of old-world flavour, yet quite original. The clever construction and effective arrangement for a string band, produce, as a result, a most charming tone-picture, pleasing in outline, and in every way satisfactory, both to the musician and the amateur.

Señor Sarasate, as before, marred the last movement of the violin concerto by taking it at so terrific a speed. Miss Elly Warnots excelled in Mozart's difficult bravura air from "Die Zauberflöte," with its abnormally high range, but Rode's air should now repose in peace on the dusty shelf,

A. M.

MONDAY POPULAR CONCERTS.

The season of 1882-83 is at last over! The final programme was, as usual, a miscellany.

PROGRAMME.

PART I.

Septet in E flat, Op. 20, for clarinet, horn, bassoon, violin, viola, violoncello, and double bass......	Beethoven.
MM. Joachim, Straus, Lasserson, Wendtland, Wotton, Reynolds, and Piatti.	
Song, "Medjé"	Gounod.
Mr. Santley.	
Preludes, in B minor and D major, for pianoforte alone	Mendelssohn.
Mdlle. Marie Krebs.	
Song, "Hymn to God the Father"	Piatti.
Mr. Santley.	
Stücke im Volkston, Nos. 1, 2, and 4, Op. 102, for pianoforte and violoncello	Schumann.
Mdlle. Marie Krebs and Signor Piatti.	
PART II.	
Duo Concertante, for two violins	Spohr.
MM. Joachim and Straus.	
Arabeske and Novellette, for pianoforte alone......	Schumann.
Miss Agnes Zimmermann.	
Songs { "An die Leyer"	Schubert.
"Widmung"	Schumann.
Mr. Santley.	
Hungarian Dances, for violin and pianoforte .... }	Brahms and Joachim.
Herr Joachim and Miss Agnes Zimmermann.	
Accompanist - - - Mr. Zerbini.	

On the occasion of the director's grand night, when the Hall is always crowded by his friends, criticism, even if necessary—and it is not necessary—would be a breach of etiquette. The artists know their texts by heart, and have them, literally, at their fingers' ends.

It is needless to illuminate the works of Mr. A. Chappell's "various masters," many of them accepted as of perennial value, and all fairly respected. The long list of recalls, if enumerated, would only tire the reader. Every one was recalled, and every one would have been encored, but for the director's kindly appeal for mercy, at the end of a long and fagging season.

It is satisfactory to rest assured that the Popular Concerts, without any aid of flaming promises or appeals to a vulgar public, continue their deservedly prosperous course, and that they will be resumed early in November. A few words in season, and at the end of the season, for Mr. Willis, Mr. Saunders, and other active "scouts"—so to speak—of Messrs. Chappell and Co. They have to discharge very arduous duties, and they do their work well. A. M.

SATURDAY POPULAR CONCERTS.

The last concert of the season attracted a large and—even for a Popular Concert—unusually enthusiastic audience. The following programme was given:—

Quartet in A major, Op. 18, No. 5, for two violins, viola, and violoncello	Beethoven.
MM. Joachim, L. Ries, Straus, and Piatti.	
Air, "If with all your hearts" ("Elijah ")......	Mendelssohn.
Mr. Edward Lloyd.	
Polonaise in C major, Op. 89, for pianoforte alone..	Beethoven.
Mdlle. Marie Krebs.	
Sonata, "Il Trillo del Diavolo," for violin, with pianoforte accompaniment...................	Tartini.
Herr Joachim.	
Air, "Adelaide"	Beethoven.
Mr. Edward Lloyd.	
Accompanied by Mdlle. Marie Krebs.	
Quintet in E flat, Op. 44, for pianoforte, two violins, viola, and violoncello	Schumann.
Mdlle. Marie Krebs, MM. Joachim, L. Ries, Straus, and Piatti.	
Accompanist - - - Mr. Zerbini.	

Beethoven never created a melody more adapted for variations, more simple and graceful, than that which forms the subject of the slow movement in the above quartet. Rising and falling on successive tones and semitones of the scale—a characteristic of some of Beethoven's most beautiful melodies, as has frequently been pointed out—it has suggested one of the most interesting variations that have been left us by the great master of that form of composition. They were grandly rendered on this occasion, and evidently thoroughly enjoyed by performers and audience. The almost magical transformation which the melody undergoes in the fourth variation by the altered accompaniment—how different from the conventional and uninspired minor number that custom bids us look for among its major companions!—and the delightful arrangement of the parts in the third, will surely haunt the memory of all those whose good fortune it was to assist at this truly perfect performance. It is perhaps bold to *say*, though it is by no means bold to *think*, that the airs with variations of the Mozart-

Beethoven period are either an unbearable bore, or a sublime inspiration : the former is the rule, and this is one of the glorious and (thankfully may be added) numerous exceptions.

Mdlle. Marie Krebs won the usual encore for her brilliant rendering of Beethoven's effective Polonaise. Herr Joachim was stormily applauded after Tartini's ever-welcome sonata, and he added (not in his most perfect form) a Paganini Caprice to the programme. Mr. Zerbini's accompaniments were not so sympathetic as could be desired. Mr. Edward Lloyd, who was in good voice, rendered the songs he had chosen with his usual taste and refinement.

And now the critic's task is done for the season—having had little to blame (in the performance, whatever may be thought about the selections) and much to admire. We were dismissed with the genial melodies of Schumann's Quintet in our ears, to find their way—as such earnest outpourings of melody always must find their way, sooner or later—to every heart capable of receiving living impressions through the medium of the language of music.

B. F. WYATT-SMITH.

THE PHILHARMONIC SOCIETY.

The third concert of the season was given on the evening of the 15th inst., and again was a full audience drawn to St. James's Hall, there being hardly standing-room. A large portion consisted of Wagnerites drawn together to worship at the shrine of their deity, while the announcement that Sarasate was going to play evidently attracted a considerable number of those present. The following was the programme :—

Overture, "Die Meistersinger von Nürnberg" ..)
"Einleitung und Isolde Liebestod " ("Tristan und
Isolde ") .... |
"Der Ritt der Walküren " ("Die Walküre ") ...... } Wagner.
Charfreitags-Zauber ("Parsifal") .... |
Lied, "Traft ihr das Schiff im Meere an " ("Der
Fliegende Holländer ") .... /
              Mdme. Valleria.

Overture, "Der Fliegende Holländer" .... Wagner.
Concerto for violin, "Scotch" (first time in England) Max Bruch.
    (Conducted by the Composer).
        Señor Sarasate.

Prayer, "Elisabeth's Prayer" ("Tannhäuser ").... Wagner.
        Mdme. Valleria.

Violin Solos—
   "Romance "   }
   "Danse Espagnole " (first time) } .... Sarasate.
        Señor Sarasate.

Overture, "Ruy Blas" .... Mendelssohn.

It will be seen from the above, that the first part of the concert was entirely occupied with excerpts from the works of Wagner. The deceased composer was not only an honorary member of the society, but he had also been one of its conductors, having directed the season of 1855 —apparantly a disastrous one. It was therefore but fitting that the event of his death should be formally noticed by the Philharmonic; his connection with the society, as well as the exalted place Wagner has held in the musical world of the day, certainly entitled him to this mark of respect from the leading English musical association. The task of selecting from Wagner's works representative music fitted for concert-room use is not easy. The Bayreuth master has written but little purely orchestral music. According to the theory as laid down in his latest utterances, the art music-drama is an intimate union of poetry, music, scenery, and action. These elements and their cognates, therefore, are indissoluble, and the severance of any one of them must seriously militate against a proper representation of the author's conception. To sing or play in the concert-room extracts from Wagner's operas, is to set his cardinal principle at defiance, and to wrench strictly dramatic music from its necessary stage associations. If it succeeds in this mutilated form, then is proved false the distinct principle on which it is announced to be constructed. Success in such an event is equivalent to "hoisting the engineer with his own petard." But one cannot blame the directors of the Philharmonic for their essay ; they are but following in the steps of the inconsistent composer himself. When a few years ago Wagner conducted at the Albert Hall some special concerts of his own carefully selected music, this is the very thing he himself did. So that he has publicly violated the important principle that he and his devoted followers have asserted to be the only true and perfect method on which the music-drama can be constructed. The question

as to whether the experiment performed under these conditions is successful, is one which each auditor must determine for himself; the effect produced on the critics and many good musicians seems to have been unsatisfactory. Paradoxical as it may seem, one is unable clearly to determine whether this result is not a justification of Wagner's theories ; to succeed means to fail in a certain sense, while to fail implies the truth of the creed, so imperatively insisted on.

Now as to the music performed. The overture to the " Master-singers of Naremberg," like its kindred prelude to "Tannhäuser," is a splendid tone-picture, complete in itself, and quite adapted for concert-room use. It is impossible to give a satisfactory account of so complex a work ; but to those who know this opera, and have heard the overture performing its intended duty, as introducing that admirable delineation of German mediæval life, the performance of the prelude vividly recalled Wagner's clever comic opera. The overture does not possess the massive breadth and passionate intensity that the "Tannhäuser" boasts, but it shows its author's constructive power to have been really great. Though it is extraordinarily complicated, requiring a trained ear to distinguish and appreciate the various themes so ingeniously blended together, it is yet a grand sonorous piece of pompous music that all can appreciate. It may be objected that its materials are too overwrought, and that owing to the free employment of the brass throughout, there is felt towards the close a want of that increasingly intensified effect that is to be found in most of the overtures of the great masters. This is probably true, but we must yet acknowledge the picturesque work as one that genius alone could create. The performance was a good one, though slightly ragged in places. The " Introduction and Isolde's Death," from " Tristan und Isolde," is certainly not effective in the concert-room. Some maintain that on the stage itself, surrounded with all the accessories that the composer has deemed necessary for its perfect appreciation, it is vague and wearisome. Although long, it consists of one main theme, not in itself attractive, worked to death, and tortuously reiterated until the movement becomes excessively monotonous and tedious. Wagner is rarely content with saying a good thing once only ; he repeats it again and again, with no, or little, variation, till the diffuseness shown becomes inexpressibly tiring to the jaded ear. "The Valkyries' Ride," is one of the most extraordinary pieces of music ever written, so daringly fresh in form, and bewilderingly original. It produced an immense effect in the opera, where it illustrates and accompanies, during a terrible storm, the dead warriors borne through the clouds by the Walkyries on horseback to Walhalla. A few years ago this would have been laughed at as the frenzied dream of a maniac, and denounced as terrifically noisy pantomime music. But now it has been heard so often, that it has become well known to our concert habitués, and finds wide acceptance as a wonderful representation of natural and unnatural scenes. The "adaptation" used was made by Wagner for the concert-room, but the piece distinctly suffered from the absence of the vocal element and scenic adjuncts. The extract was not well played, the violins being too loud throughout, the remarkable bold theme enunciated on the brass not standing out with sufficient clearness ; nevertheless, an encore was demanded, and conceded.

The introduction of the orchestral piece termed "Charfreitags-Zauber" (Good Friday magic), arranged from a scene of Wagner's last work, "Parsifal," is to be condemned.

So much has been written as to the blasphemous character of this music-drama, an incongruous mixture of the legends attaching to early Christianity, sorcery, high ethics, and sensual passion, that it is needless now to comment on its offensiveness. Despite the religious mysticism running through the work, it is neither a mediæval miracle play, nor is it a sacred drama after the fashion of the Oberammergau Passion Play. The esoteric symbolism with which it deals is the most awful of those mysteries connected with the Christian faith. Even in old times, the clerical authorities who controlled plays connected with religious subjects, would never have licensed the treatment of such a theme ; certainly in this age of the world's civilisation, the Church, and not the stage, is the proper place for the commemoration of the Eucharist. As a sort of apology to the outer world, it was announced that the work would never be given outside Bayreuth. Nevertheless, there were many on-lookers who predicted that the devoted adherents of Wagner would after a time make every effort to have the opera performed in London. And unless the Lord Chamberlain's department returns an emphatic, No ! to the libretto submitted for approval, its production here is probably but a mere question of time and opportunity. Already some excerpts have found their way into our concert-rooms, and have thus paved the way for the introduction of the complete work. Perhaps when our people see the voluptuous animalism of the passionate Kundry, jumbled with a travesty of the Holy Communion on the stage, the psychological experiment presented to their gaze will cause more stir over the matter than the voices of warning critics have yet done. The Annotator of the programme book, ignoring both his practice and his duty, in the brief notice of the " Charfeitags-Zauber," said, it would not "be advisable to lable (*sic*) the melodies with fictitious names." He was wise ; but the omission can be supplied without difficulty. In the Crystal Palace Saturday Concert Programme Book of the 3rd inst. (on which date the piece was first performed) is a careful description and analysis of it from the pen of a recognised and most able Wagnerian authority. We there find the Leit motives numbered 6, 7, and 8, respectively entitled, "The Atonement," "The Sacramental Formula of the Love Feast," and "The Spear and the Saviour's Agony." After mentioning these particulars, one is not surprised to find that, commenting on the matter, one of our foremost critics writes :—

"As a specimen of the abuse of sacred things by an infidel composer, it will be sufficient to note that 'The Sacramental Formula of the Love Feast' is a parody of the Lord's Supper ; that Kundry's repentance and baptism are parodies of the scenes between our Saviour and Mary Magdalen, and that 'The Spear and the Saviour's Agony' are *leit motiven* combined in the concluding portion of this 'Parsifal' selection."

A few words will suffice as to the musical aspect of the arrangement played. It is a quiet, dreamy piece of writing, expressive in places, though at times confused, and too much spun out.

Madame Valleria is doubtless the best Senta that has been seen on the stage, and she gave a passionate rendering of the fine scena, "Yohohoe" ; but exception must be taken to her exaggeration of the accents at the beginning of the first four lines. Her delivery of "Elizabeth's Prayer" from "Tannhäuser" was admirable. This melodious Prayer is a type that Wagner has long ago abjured ; the only fault that can be found with it is the accompaniment of the wind throughout, a *continuato* which becomes monotonous, and causes one to miss the absence of the bright and sympathetic strings. The overture to "The Flying Dutchman," which concluded the Wagner selection, cannot rank high beside his other operatic preludes ; but a careful student of its orchestration will see that the composer was there trying effects that he embodied and developed with success in his subsequent works. There is an effective use of the cor anglais after the opening, but the overture is noisy at times, and it contains odd reminiscences of many composers.

What could have induced the Philharmonic Directors to accept Max Bruch's new—so-called—violin concerto was the wonderment of the *cognoscenti* present. It was unquestionably one of the weakest and most inane pieces of music that has ever graced their programmes. In the first place, its name is a misnomer ; it is no Concerto at all, but rather a formless Fantasia, with a free (indeed very "free") use of Scottish melodies. The Liverpool ex-conductor ought to know that a concerto proper must contain its proper number of movements and of subjects, and that there are certain orthodox arrangements as to construction and consecution of keys to which respect must be paid. He is either ignorant of all this, or he has boldly determined to change the entire form of the type, and give to the world an improvement on it. Great has been his failure. If he had labelled his production "Free Fantasia on Scotch airs," criticism to some extent would have been disarmed ; but to adopt the honoured title of Concerto for his flimsy and clumsily constructed piece, constitutes an act of impertinence towards English common sense. Several of the great composers have introduced a national air in their concertos, and have skilfully treated it as the main idea of the movement. If Herr Bruch had done this, no fault could have been found with his design ; but to take about a dozen Scotch airs, to chop off fragments of them, and then to alter and mutilate the well-known texts, cannot be commended, even if some fancy and scholarship were displayed over the piecing together. But these qualities are wanting in the piece. In this case, at least, it cannot be said of Herr Bruch what Dr. Johnson wrote of Goldsmith, *nihil tetigit quod non ornavit.* The music throughout is heavy, laboured, and uninteresting, and in many places it is even trivial and common-place. There are some showy variations for the violin, accompanied by the inevitable harp, very much of a pattern that one hears in the streets of Edinburgh, but invention and clever treatment of the themes may be looked for in vain. It is said that the composer has published a work on Scotch airs ; if his researches had extended to the bagpipes, and he had introduced that national instrument of torture to the Philharmonic audience, it might have created some interest, and relieved the character of his whimsical idea of a concerto. Among the airs introduced was a fragment of "Sally in our alley," written by Carey. It is, perhaps, excusable that Herr Bruch and his annotator Herr Hueffer should be unaware that the air is thoroughly English, and not Scotch. The thought crossed one's mind that Herr Bruch had mistaken his *locale*, and that the work should have been given on some Scottish festival night at the Promenade Concerts, rather than before a classical Philharmonic audience. A caustic critic has recommended that the composer of "Odysseus"—produced at the recent Bach concert—should take his work over to America on his trip, and drop it in mid-ocean. If this advice is adopted, and he will add thereto the new "Violin Concerto," the only being likely to regret the occurrence is the unfortunate fish that might swallow the MSS. The work was altogether unworthy of Sarasate's powers, though he did all for it that an able artist could do. Of his own pieces, the "Romance" was specially noteworthy, a passage he introduced in it of delicate harmonics, accompanied with *pizzicato* arpeggios, served to bring to remembrance one of Paganini's most effective devices. Spanish dances seem pretty much alike ; he was encored in his new one, and substituted the charming arrangement of Chopin's lovely Nocturne in E flat, played with the most perfect tone and exquisite taste. Mendelssohn's magnificent "Ruy Blas" overture, admirably given by the band under Mr. Cusin's painstaking direction, brought this remarkable concert to a close.

T. L. SOUTHGATE.

LEEDS.

On Friday evening, 16th inst., Bach's "Passion Music" ("St. Matthew") was sung in Leeds parish church before a large congregation. The principal vocalists were as follows : soprano, Mrs. George ; contralto, Miss A. Clarke ; tenors, Messrs. Binns and Grimshaw ; basses, Messrs. Morton and Hunter. The ordinary choir of the church was increased to about 100, including thirty female voices. The whole performance was gone through in a manner that showed very careful training, and principals and chorus did their share of the work in a thoroughly conscientious manner. The "Passion Music" has been given in this church in previous years, and, perhaps, nothing more appropriate could be found for the season of Lent. Of course it would be out of place to criticise a performance of this sort in detail. The beautiful chorales with which the work abounds were given in admirable style, and special mention may be made of the grand and impressive opening chorus, "Come, ye daughters, weep with me ; " of the unaccompanied chorales in Part II., "O Lord, who dares to smite Thee?" "Commit thy ways to Jesus," and of the final double chorus, "In tears of grief we here recline." As regards the ladies' share of the work, we may state that Mrs. George sang with much feeling the lovely air, "Jesus, Saviour, I am Thine," and was heard to advantage in the duet with Miss Clarke at the close of Part I., "My Saviour, Jesus, now is taken." Miss Clarke sang the contralto music in a refined and devotional manner, and special mention must be made of her exquisite rendering of those beautiful airs, "Have mercy upon me," "Ah ! Golgotha," and "See, the Saviour's outstretched arm." Dr. Creser presided at the organ with his usual efficiency. During the interval, a short, appropriate sermon was preached by the Rev. F. G. Hume Smith, and a collection was made to defray expenses. The "Passion Music" was repeated on Tuesday evening, the 20th inst.

MR. BONAWITZ'S CHAMBER CONCERTS.

Mr. J. B. Bonawitz resumed his serial concerts at his residence in the Marylebone Road, on the afternoon of March 14th. He conducted his own Pianoforte Trio in C minor, Op. 37, of which a good report was given on the occasion of its first performance (December 20th, 1882). Miss Cecilie Brousil and Mr. Hann held the strings. Miss C. Brousil introduced a new piece from the pen of Mr. Bonawitz, a "Concerto Dramatique" in A Minor, a dignified recitative, followed by a florid bravura, very much and deservedly admired. Mr. Bonawitz selected for his solos an air with variations of Handel, in D minor, and two movements of Mozart's Pianoforte Concerto in D minor (the second and third). As a tribute to the memory of Wagner, the pianist began the concert with Beethoven's Funeral March in A flat minor (fourth Sonata, Op. 26), and Liszt's selections from "Lohengrin," executed in a masterly style. The vocalist, Miss E. Millar, sang an air from Gounod's opera, "Cinq Mars," and Tosti's "Good-bye."

LIVERPOOL.

(From our Own Correspondent.)

MARCH 20th.

Mr. Henry Grimshaw gave his nineteenth organ recital on the fine organ in Great George Street Chapel last evening, the programme of which will be found in the proper column. Mr. Grimshaw does not neglect the works of living writers for the organ. His first piece was a Fantasia in C minor, by Dr. C. J. Frost, which was very effective. The variations from the septuor always give scope for variety of registering, and Mr. Grimshaw was very happy in his effects.

Gounod's "Redemption" is to be produced by the Liverpool Philharmonic Society this day. If we may judge by the rehearsal, the performance will not be of the best. The chorus sang very badly ; there was a want of attack, and the tone was poor and thin. In fact, the choruses (what few I heard) were given in the most listless manner, and contrasted strangely with the finished and *con amore* rendering of the Birmingham Festival Choir. The principals engaged for the performance are Miss Anna Williams, Mdme. Billinie Porter, Mdme. Isabel Fassett, Mr. Edward Lloyd, Mr. Robert Hilton, and Mr. Bridson. Mr. W. T. Best will preside at the organ, and Mr. Max Bruch will conduct.

Several concerts of a popular type are announced for Good Friday and Easter week.   J. J. M.

THE IRISH CONCERT AT THE ALBERT HALL.

Mr. Wm. Carter held an Irish Concert at the Albert Hall on Saturday evening, March 17th, in honour of St. Patrick's Day. The audience was a large one, but, as usual, behaved idiotically in that they protracted the concert by "recalling" every individual artist ! Mr. Carter's choir sang part-songs arranged from familiar Irish airs, and the Scots Guards' band played. Mdme. Trebelli sang splendidly an air from Rossini's effete opera, "L'Italiana in Algieri," and Mr. Carter's song (composed for her), "What the waves said." Mdme. Marie Roze delighted her audience with Moore's song, "Believe me, if all those endearing young charms," and "Terence's Farewell," producing the "brogue" so nicely that the fair Frenchwoman must surely have kissed the "blarney-stone" some time or other. "The minstrel boy," a clap-trap effusion at best, was encored, partly for the sake of Mdme. Trebelli, its interpreter. Mdme. Enriquez, Mr. Maas, Mr. R. Hollins, Mr. Maybrick, and other favourite vocalists, were recalled, and many of their songs encored. A welcome relief to so much Hibernian matter was a violin solo of Mr. J. B. Poznanski, the Fantasia (in A) of Vieuxtemps on "St. Patrick's Day in the morning." This is a difficult piece. It begins with an introduction, and, after due delivery of the air, occurs an elaborate *cadenza*, after a pause on the (suspended) chord of D, the subdominant. The air is then repeated, and at the close the violinist has to "double stop" two-part harmonies, with trills, and afterwards to wind up with harmonics, in octaves, tenths, twelfths, and seventeenths. The fire-eating player, on an *encore*, gave his own arrangement of "Garry Owen," a clever imitation of bag-pipe effects. The concert was so protracted that many of the audience left at eleven o'clock, in a state of musical collapse. There was to be a performance of the "Messiah" on Good Friday evening.

SATURDAY POPULAR ORGAN RECITALS, BOW, E.—TO-NIGHT, Mr. W. DE MANBY SERGISON, and Members of St. Peter's Choir, Eaton-square.

PRINCIPAL CONTENTS OF THIS NUMBER.

L. VAN BEETHOVEN'S LATER SONATAS. By Herr Ernst Pauer.

MUSICAL INTELLIGENCE :—Crystal Palace Concerts—Monday Popular Concerts—Saturday Popular Concerts—The Philharmonic Society—Leeds —Mr. Bonawitz's Chamber Concerts—Liverpool—The Irish Concert at the Albert Hall—The West London College of Music—St. Paul's Cathedral—The Brousil Chamber Concerts—Royal Academy of Music—Music in Dublin—Manchester.

EDITORIAL :—The Present Position of the Composer—IV. Orchestral Effects and Keyboard Mannerisms—V. On the Choice of Solo Vocal Music for the Concert-Room.

FOREIGN MUSICAL INTELLIGENCE.

ORGAN NEWS :—Liverpool — Bolton — Preston — Norwich—Manchester— Crystal Palace—Waterloo Road—Bristol—Leeds—Kendal—Bow and Bromley Institute.

THE CARL ROSA OPERA COMPANY.

PAGANINI REDIVIVUS.

PASSING EVENTS. Service Lists, &c.

LONDON : SATURDAY, MARCH 24, 1883.

THE PRESENT POSITION OF THE COMPOSER.

IV.

UNQUESTIONABLY the composer has more difficulties to face in his upward career than any other class of art producer is called upon to encounter. To get his works performed is even a greater difficulty than the other serious trial of getting them into print. The subject of securing adequate performance is the one difficulty which more than any other tends to prevent the proper recognition of the producer of music. Years of anxiety and disappointing trials in this direction have held back some of our best composers, until indeed they might be said to have reached that period of existence which Dante tells us is "Il mezzo del "cammin di nostra vita." And it is no injustice to our rising and eminent composers whose larger works are from time to time presented before the public, to say that they owe their opportunities as much to their social advantages as to their artistic merits. Now and then a composer, seeing no other available plan, takes upon himself the responsibility of producing some work he is prepared to stake his reputation upon. Such a step, of course, is as unwise as would be the proposal of an unknown poet to publicly recite his own verses. The truth is, the public mind must be prepared for the reception of any new musical work by a composer as yet unknown to fame. Nay, it is humiliating to remember in this age of education and liberal public patronage, how many moving springs there are apart from the desire to recognise merit, which must be met in addition before people are ready to listen to a new musical work of any pretensions from the pen of an unknown composer. It has been said that we are still in art matters much in the condition of the wild Red Indians, willing to swallow any potion prepared by a "Big Medi- "cine Man," but averse to the acceptation of any performance not sanctified by some preliminary form of recognition of the person who may claim public attention. This superstitious faith in the successful shows that we have but little sound judgment of our own to rely upon, and that we dislike to have to trust to our own unbiassed and unprepared opinions. In truth, the composer has but small hope of appreciation until he is surrounded by a friendly atmosphere. It is, therefore, quite useless for any composer to hope for genuine success until his pathway to publicity has been duly secured by friendly offices and the general estimation of a large circle. So the efforts made by a composer to secure the attention and appreciation of an unprepared, and, one may add, generally unwilling public, are nearly as futile as would be an attempt to interest the aboriginal inhabitants of Kamtchatka in the perusal of Kant's "Critical Philosophy." The young composer must not, indeed, expect to strike the world at first with a work of an ambitious character, unless he has the good fortune to have such solid, social power at his back as will secure a sufficiently friendly atmosphere. He will do much more wisely if he prepares a way for himself by building up a character which commands esteem for the man, before he attempts to claim appreciation for the productions of the artist. Most of these observations are also applicable to the case of the executive artist; but the executant has many more opportunities and is much more readily understood and appreciated by the general public than is the tone-producer. However, these considerations are not intended to deepen despondency, but to encourage prudence in the pursuit of the composer's career. *Fortes fortuna juvat* is not without an application in the case of one who, possessing heaven-born talents, is surely bound to use them to such advantage as his station and position will permit.

E. H. TURPIN.

ORCHESTRAL EFFECTS AND KEY-BOARD MANNERISMS.

V.

ONE general observation with regard to the transference of orchestral music to the key-board of the pianoforte is called for. This is, the fact that it is often deemed necessary to give fuller harmonies to the drawing-room orchestra than are involved in the expression of the same ideas by the more sonorous instruments of the band. At first sight it would seem that the chords of the orchestra by reason of its comprehensive and extensive score would be naturally fuller than their representative harmonies as rendered on the pianoforte. The reasons for this apparent discrepancy are not far to seek. The enormous power of the orchestra and its rich, vividly contrasted tone qualities, have the faculty of creating a large harmonic atmosphere, so to speak, a faculty but feebly developed on the key-board instruments, partly from the inevitable sameness of the sounds produced, especially on the pianoforte, and partly by reason of the feebleness of the accentuation of key-board instruments as compared with the strong and varied utterances of the orchestral forces. Thus it may happen that the stroke of the mass of strings in four-part, and widely distributed harmony, would have but a poor representation if re-produced in four-parts on the pianoforte. Such a passage, especially if calling for strongly marked accents, would require the full employment of both hands on the pianoforte, in order that anything like corresponding effects may be produced. The student should compare the thickly laid out chords in given passages of the arrangements, say of some of the classical symphonies, by such conscientious transcribers as HUMMEL, CZERNY, KALKBRENNER, etc., with the perspicuously scored harmonies of the original passages as laid out for the orchestra by their composers. There is no great power of harmonic concentration on the pianoforte; and massive harmonic effects must be approached by chords with largely doubled elements. Certain modern composers have failed to make us like thick harmonies in the lowest bass region of the orchestra, but such harmonies on the pianoforte key-board are not only free in occasional use from disagreeable effects, but are absolutely of great value in presenting ideas fully pronounced in a clearly scored and not overloaded orchestral passage for the instruments of tenor and bass compasses. This observation is equally applicable to the upper range of orchestral harmonies, and has its most forcible application naturally in attempts at the key-board representation of the *forte* combinations of the entire orchestra.

E. H. TURPIN.

ON THE CHOICE OF SOLO VOCAL MUSIC FOR THE CONCERT-ROOM.

THERE are two points concerning solo singers in the matter of programme-building which call for reformation. The first is in connection with the selection of songs, etc., as regards variety, and the second in the same direction bears upon the suitability of the choice made. It is no uncommon thing to find a vocal soloist living as it were for a month or two on less than half-a-dozen songs. Even the degrading obligations of the royalty system need not so limit the selection of a vocalist as to make it apparently necessary to associate an artist's name at a given period with the performance only of a slender stock of from two to four songs. In justice to themselves, our singers should take more pains to display their largely developed powers, by the execution of more extensive selections from the abundant stores of songs, forming probably the largest class of musical literature in existence. And it might be pointed out that from an artistic view, it is undesirable that a performer should be too long confined to the idioms and mannerisms of any given authors. The other matter is the judicious choice of songs with regard to proper surroundings and accompaniments. This would be secured at once by following the simple rule of · always employing the accompaniments as written by the composer. There is no reason why singers should select songs requiring orchestral adornment for performance when only a pianoforte accompaniment is available. When the orchestra is absent and the pianoforte is present, let the singer select some of the many beautiful songs by SCHUBERT, MENDELSSOHN, STERNDALE BENNETT, R. FRANZ, H. SMART, GOUNOD, etc., which have artistically written pianoforte accompaniments. Such judgment on the part of our vocalists is especially called for in the formation of the programmes intended for concerts of classical reputation and established artistic importance.

E. H. TURPIN.

THE WEST LONDON COLLEGE OF MUSIC.

Signor Casano's College of Music and Dramatic Academy, in Colville Gardens, Bayswater, is a deservedly flourishing institution. At a *soirée* held there on March 15th, some excellent music regaled the ears of a select audience. Miss H. Sasse played a chaconne of Handel, a barcarolle of Rubinstein, and a valse of Chopin with much taste, and M. Poznanski gave Hauser's "Rhapsodie Horgroise," as a violin solo ; also Vieuxtemps' fantasia on "Lucia." Several of the pupils sang in turn, and a comedietta in one act came at the end. Signor E. P. Casano conducted the concert.

ST. PAUL'S CATHEDRAL.

On the 20th, the usual Passion Week performance of Bach's "Passion Music" was given. A large congregation assembled, which included the Princess of Wales, dressed in black, and attended by Miss Knollys, Mr. W. H. Gladstone, Lord Coleridge, Lord Henry Somerset, the Bishop of London, as well as the Dean and Canons of St. Paul's. The short evening service which preceded and succeeded Bach's "Passion according to St. Matthew," was intoned by Minor Canon Kelly, and the Bishop of London pronounced the Benediction. The musical arrangements were under Dr. Stainer, the cathedral organist, who conducted ; Mr. Martin presiding at the organ. The orchestra was efficient and well-balanced. The chief vocal parts were entrusted to Messrs. Kenningham, Hanson, Winn, and Kimpton.

Although it cannot be said that the delicate texture of much of the music is adapted for exposition in St. Paul's, the vast building outlined in soft, dim light, the awe-struck listeners, and the other impressive surroundings, make up a solemn picture, which heightens the effect of the wonderful tone poem. To those whose narrow-minded prejudices would limit the functions of music in connection with worship, no more instructive and humiliating experience could be imagined than the resistless eloquence of this notable Service. The sister arts of music and painting have truly been able to illustrate the greatest tragedy and the deepest mystery the history of the world can point to, with a fervour and power no pulpit eloquence has ever yet approached. And in Bach's settings of the divine and wondrous story, we have the most powerful tone-pictures sacred art can point to, notwithstanding the presence of the mannerisms of an almost too contrapuntal habit of thought here and there. The reverent, earnest dramatic power shown, and the profound contemplative sorrow are such as inevitably touch all listeners. And those who go to hear such Services come away with no thought of being called upon to criticise, but to record an earnestly and admirably conducted musical sermon. The authorities at St. Paul's Cathedral do no truer work than that of conducting the annual service which embodies one of the noblest sermons ever preached to sinful men—Bach's "Passion Music."

THE BROUSIL CHAMBER CONCERTS.

On the afternoon of March 15th, unfortunately the "Boat Race" day, Miss Wurm and Mr. A. Brousil played Rubinstein's Sonata for pianoforte and violoncello in D with great effect ; and, reinforced by Miss Bertha Brousil and Mr. Collins, Rheinberger's Quartet in E flat. Miss Wurm's solo was Chopin's Ballade in G minor. Miss B. Brousil played, as violin solos, the " Pensées Fugitives" of Heller and Ernst, Nos. 3 and 9, in F and A major. The *matinée* was in every respect successful.

ROYAL ACADEMY OF MUSIC.

An orchestral concert, given by the students of the Royal Academy on March 16th at St. James's Hall, once more afforded practical evidence of the good work that is being carried on by this old and valued institution. Mendelssohn's " Walpurgis Night " was the chief item, and in this both band and chorus proved satisfactory, Mr. William Shakespeare being, as heretofore, the able conductor. A word of praise must be given to the excellent rendering of the soli parts by Miss Marion Burton, Mr. Hirwin Jones, and Mr. Lucas Williams. The composing faculty was represented by Mr. Herbert Smith's serenade, charmingly sung by Mr. Dyved Lewis, and two movements from Mr. G. J. Bennett's symphony, a work which evidences great skill and pronounced talents, but somewhat lacks continuity of thought. Miss Cantelo, who played Brahms's Concerto in D minor ; Miss Margaret Devey, in a movement from Sir Julius Benedict's concerto ; and Mr. Septimus Webbe, in Schumann's A minor Concerto, showed considerable ability as pianists. " Voi che sapete" was pleasingly sung by Miss Eleanor Rees. Mr. Prentice Chapman was down for a violin solo, and the overture to " Le Nozze di Figaro " ended the concert. The " Walpurgis Night " produced a marked impression, as indeed it always will, for where in the advanced school can anything be found more dramatic ? and it is remembered, that in addition to this quality, Mendelssohn's work is masterly in its plan, continuity of thought, and picturesque power.

MUSIC IN DUBLIN.

(*From our Own Correspondent.*)

Herr Elkner's annual concert was given at the Antient Concert Rooms on Saturday last. There was a very large and fashionable audience, including the Countess Spencer, who set a very desirable example, and showed her appreciation of the programme by arriving punctually and remaining to compliment Herr Elsner upon his success at the close of the concert. The programme was long, but so admirably arranged and executed, that one did not feel surfeited when the end was reached. Its length, however, precludes me from furnishing a detailed account of the various items. Miss Poole took part in a brace of duets with Mrs. Connolly, and sang two songs with considerable dramatic expression and taste. Mrs. Connolly was also applauded for " The Message" (Blumenthal) and Gounod's " Ave Maria." The instrumental items formed a prominent part in the scheme, and were performed with the thoroughness that distinguishes the performances of the members of the Dublin Chamber Music Union. The compositions performed included Raff's second Trio in G major for pianoforte (M. Billet) violin (Herr Lauer), and 'cello (Herr Elsner) ; Mendelssohn's Quartet in D major for two violins, viola, and 'cello ; and a Trio for pianoforte (Miss Elsner), violin (Dr. Smyly), and 'cello (Herr Elsner) by Hummel, whose widow, by the way, died within the past couple of weeks. Herr Elsner gave his audience a treat by playing for the " first time in Dublin " a song without words (" Friede im Herzen") by Emile Gock and an arrangement of some 17th century ballet-music by Offenbach. He also amused them by a practical illustration of the term " Musette " as produced by the 'cello. M. Billet sustained his high reputation in a study by Henselt and a valse by Chopin. Mr. W. B. Martin and Mr. Roper-Caldbeck contributed vocally, whilst several of the songs were very much enhanced by the manner of Mr. Joseph Robinson's accompaniments.

MANCHESTER.

(From our Own Correspondent.)

On the 15th inst., Mr. Hallé gave us an opportunity of hearing, for the first time in Manchester, Gounod's "Redemption," the concert being given for the benefit of the Infirmary.

To anyone who was present at the first performance of the work at Birmingham the "reading" by Mr. Hallé was especially interesting, as the forces under his command were fully capable of giving an adequate interpretation of the work. All the points in the masterly orchestration were duly taken advantage of, and the "slips" were few and trivial. The flatness of the first horn, however, more than once interfered with the general harmony. The effect of the four trumpets in the finale to the second part was also slightly marred by the insufficient elevation of the players behind the chorus. The long and laborious "March to Calvary" was rendered unduly wearisome by the slow speed at which Mr. Hallé took this number. The ordinary march tempo is hardly applicable to such an extraordinary composition. At least the composer thought otherwise when he conducted at Birmingham. The choruses were all well done. Mrs. Hutchinson sang the soprano music, and very agreeably surprised her audience. She sang with great expression and taste, and did not seem overweighted; she reached her top C admirably. In addition to the parts of our Saviour, Mr. Santley sang the whole of the bass narrator's music, and certainly he and Mr. Lloyd made more of their rather ungrateful parts than was done at Birmingham. Mdme. Patey sang the contralto music. Altogether the performance was a very successful one, and the work itself was very well received, the grand chorus "Unfold, ye Portals everlasting" working the audience to a high pitch of enthusiasm. Both the merits and demerits of the work, which have already been discussed, were brought prominently into relief.

Four days before this performance, and while his talented daughter Miss Annie Goodwin was giving a highly successful concert, Mr. J. L. Goodwin breathed his last, at the somewhat early age of 55. Coming to Manchester as a young man from the West of England, Mr. Goodwin soon made for himself a name as a violinist, organist, and teacher. His talent, though not absolutely brilliant in itself, was the cause of brilliance in his pupils, for he was thorough, painstaking, indefatigable, and conscientious. He was highly respected and well known, and some surprise seemed to be felt that his decease was in no wise noticed by Mr. Hallé, who has lost a faithful servant of twenty-five years' standing.　　C. J. H.

THE "FAUST" OF HECTOR BERLIOZ.

The Faust-Sage, a very favourite theme, has been treated, vocally and instrumentally, in all sorts of forms, by Spohr, Gounod, Berlioz, Boito, Schumann, and Liszt. "La Damnation de Faust," first produced at Paris in 1846 (or 1847), is known to be in the form of a dramatic cantata, and to end, in rather a terrible fashion, with the descent of its hero to the "naughty place," as grandmammas were wont, to emphasize the fabulous fires of Gehenna.

> Gnossias . . . . . subigitque fateri
> Quæ quis apud superos, furto lætatus inani,
> Distulit in seram commissa piacula mortem.

The "Faust" of Hector Berlioz, which proved so decided a failure at Her Majesty's Theatre, some six or seven years ago, when M. Pasdeloup came over from Paris to conduct the work, has since taken a firm hold of the British public. Mr. Arthur Chappell has found it a highly profitable enterprise; and now Mr. Barnby, of the Royal Albert Hall Choral Society, takes it up at least once every year. He repeated the cantata on the evening of March 14th, with Mdme. Valeria, Mr. E. Lloyd, Mr. H. Pyatt, and Mr. Santley in front of the orchestra. Suffice it to say, that the performance was perfectly successful, and that a large audience encored, as *de rigueur*, the "Racoczky," March in A, the Dance of Sylphs in D, and the serenade of friend "Mephisto" in B major.

The London Literary and Artistic Society are doing good work in their way. On the 14th Mr. Arthur Lilley read Shakespeare's "Hamlet" at the Egyptian Hall, Piccadilly.

BELFAST.—There was a large attendance at a miscellaneous concert given in the large hall of the Methodist College on March 13th. The proceeds will be devoted to the founding of a musical library in the college. Mr. B. Hobson Carroll, Mus.Bac. T.C.L., was conductor, and his great musical abilities contributed largely to the enjoyment of the concert. The programme was chiefly sustained by pupils of the college, and the manner in which the items were given was extremely creditable.

LANCASTER HALL.—Mr. Russell Lochner gave a concert on the 12th. The vocalists included Mdme. Adeline Paget, Miss Frances Hipwell, Messrs. Kenningham, Kempton, and Frank Quatremayne. Miss F. Bromley (a pupil of the concert giver) played pianoforte solos with much credit to herself and teacher. Mr. R. W. Buttery was the violinist, Herr Oberthür the harpist, Mr. Russell Lochner played Bach's "Toccata in C," and a movement by H. Smart, admirably upon the organ.

WIMBLEDON MUSICAL SOCIETY.—Rossini's "Stabat Mater" was the work selected for the eleventh concert of this flourishing suburban society on Thursday, 8th inst. Miss Alice Parry, Miss Emily Dones, Mr. Harper Kearton and Mr. Orlando Christian being the principals, it is needless to say that the solos were each and all well rendered, but the duet "Quis est homo" and the two quartets "Sancta Mater" and "Quando corpus" were beautifully sung. The choruses, as usual with the exception of the "Pia Mater," which was somewhat false of intonation, went well and crisply, the greatest attention being paid to light and shade. Altogether both the choir and orchestra of this society are a credit alike to the conductor and the neighbourhood. The second part of the programme opened with Méhul's overture to "Joseph," and consisted of selections from various standard works—one of the most enjoyable items of this part being Mozart's "Ave verum." The whole of the selections were given with orchestral accompaniments, Mr. Sumner, the society's conductor, occupying his usual post. Considering the bitter coldness of the night, the concert was well attended. "Elijah" will be given on April 23rd.

Foreign Musical Intelligence.

"Tripilla" is a new comic opera by Signor Luzzi.

A new opera, by Señor Reparaz, has been produced at Valencia, with the title "Il Favorito."

It is said that the young composer, Urich, has written an opera, "Il Giuramento."

Mr. Georges Boyer, of the Paris *Figaro* has won the Rossini Prize for the best lyric poem for music. The competitors numbered 169.

M. Limnander, a Belgian, has been elected the successor of Flotow as member of the Académie des Beaux Arts.

A new "Symphonie Funèbre," by M. Gustave Huberti, lately received a hearing in Brussels. The "Symphonie" is described as an interesting work by a learned and practical musician.

An unpublished opera, in four acts, called "Andolina," has been produced in Strasburg. The composer is Herr Muller-Reuter, professor of piano and harmony at the Conservatoire.

"Les Puits qui Parle," a one-act comic opera, has been successfully brought out at the Caen Theatre. M. Arthur Mancini's music is said to be bright and appropriate, and the libretto, by an anonymous writer, very amusing.

Signor Orsini, the composer of the opera of "Lola," produced at the Olympic Theatre, has died at a comparatively early age in Naples. He has left behind him some musical works, including a three-act opera, the plot of which is by Mr. Gilbert à Beckett, and the words by Orsini's former collaborator, Mr. Frank Marshall.—*Athenæum.*

The French committee, formed for the purpose of erecting a statue to Berlioz, is headed by M. Ambroise Thomas, the one in Brussels for the same purpose being presided over by M. Gevaert. It is not without interest to note that two directors of Conservatoires should head this tardy recognition of the genius of one who during his life time was excluded from all institutions of the kind. Liszt has contributed 350 francs to the movement.

The Kyrle Society gave Handel's "Messiah" at St. John's, Waterloo Road, on March 21st. Mr. M. L. Lawson conducted, and Mr. E. H. Turpin was the organist.

Organ News.

LIVERPOOL.

Subjoined are the programmes of organ recitals given by Mr. W. T. Best, in St. George's Hall, on the under-mentioned dates :—

THURSDAY EVENING, MARCH 15th.

March (Third Symphony)	Widor.
Romanza, "Arpa Genti"	Rossini.
Toccata and Fugue in the Dorian mode	Bach.
Andante (Trio in C minor)	Mendelssohn.
Funeral March (Collection of Organ Pieces, No. 35)	Best.
Overture (" Bianca e Giuseppe ")	Kittl.

SATURDAY AFTERNOON, MARCH 17th.

Festive March	Smart.
Allegro Cantabile (Fifth Symphony)	Widor.
Selection (" Le Prophète ")	Meyerbeer.
Prelude and Fugue in D major	Mendelssohn.
Norwegian National Hymn	Hofmann.

SATURDAY EVENING, MARCH 17th.

Overture (" Anna Bolena ")	Donizetti.
Romanza, "The Fisher Maiden "	Meyerbeer.
Toccata in A flat major	Hesse.
Air (" Ariadne,") March (" Judas Maccabæus ")	Handel.
Gavotte de Marie Thérèse	Neustedt.
"March of the Priests of Isis"	Rossini.

Mr. Henry Grimshaw gave his 19th organ recital in Great George Street Chapel on Monday, March 19th, with the annexed programme :—

Fantasia in C minor	Frost.
Air, " Lascia ch'io pianga "	Handel.
Sonata No. 3	Mendelssohn.
Andante with variations (Septuor)	Beethoven.
Easter Offertoire	Batiste.
Slow Movement Concertante (Quartet in G minor)	Spohr.
March and chorus (" Tannhäuser ")	Wagner.

BOLTON.

An organ recital was given in the Albert Hall, by Mr. Wm. Mullineux, F.C.O., on Saturday, March 17th. The following was the programme :—

Concerto in B flat, No. 6	Handel.
Romanza in G major	Beethoven.
Andante Grazioso in G major	Smart.
Offertoire for Easter Day	Batiste.
" Chant du Paysan "	Rendano.
Hungarian March	Berlioz.

PRESTON.

Subjoined are the programmes of organ recitals given in the new Public Hall, by Mr. James Tomlinson, on Saturday, March 17th :—

AFTERNOON RECITAL.

Overture (" Joseph ")	Méhul.
Andante Sostenuto	Batiste.
Solemn March	Best.
Offertoire in C (" L'Organiste Moderne ")	Waly.
Romanza (" La Reine de France ")	Haydn.
Marche Triomphale	Moscheles.

EVENING RECITAL.

Concerto No. 1	Handel.
Andante Cantabile (Fourth Symphony)	Mozart.
Second Movement (Duet in B flat, for piano and 'cello)	Mendelssohn.
Marche Cortège (" Reine de Saba ")	Gounod.
"Traumbilder" (" Dream Pictures ")	Lumbye.
Fantasia on Irish airs (MS.)	

NORWICH.

Annexed is the programme of an organ recital given in St. Andrew's Hall, by Dr. Bunnett, F.C.O., on Saturday, March 17th :—

Fantasia in C minor and major	Tietz.
"Ave Maria"	Cherubini.
Romanza (" La Reine de France ")	Haydn.
"Lascia ch'io pianga " (" Rinaldo ")	Handel.
Melodie in C	Silas.
Concerto	Handel.
Larghetto in F	Bunnett.
Funeral March	Mendelssohn.
Larghetto in F	Beethoven.
Prayer (" Mosè in Egitto ")	Rossini.

MANCHESTER.

Mr. J. Kendrick Pyne gave an organ recital in the Town Hall, on Saturday, March 17th. Subjoined is the programme :—

Andante con moto in G	Wesley.
Carillon de Louis XIV. (1648)	Neustedt.
Drei Tonstucke in F major	Gade.
"Brautlied," bridal song (" A Rustic Wedding, Op. 26)	Goldmark.
Air, " Lascia ch'io pianga "	Handel.
Overture (" Henry VIII.")	Sullivan.
Grand Chœur Triomphale in A major	Guilmant.

CRYSTAL PALACE.

Mr. A. J. Eyre's programme on Saturday last included the following :—

Military March	Beethoven.
Larghetto in B flat	Spohr.
Allegretto (" Lobgesang,") Prelude in D minor, Motet, (" Judge me, O God ")	Mendelssohn.
Miesst in C	Boccherini.
Fantasia on a Lenten hymn	Stephens.
Andante (" Evening Prayer ")	Smart.
Finale, from an Orchestral Suite	Schumann.
Overture (" Poet and Peasant ")	Suppé.
Largo (" Serse ")	Handel.
Musette and Entrée de Procession	Batiste.
" Tu di Grazia " (" Passion ")	Haydn.
March, from First Seige	Lachner.

WATERLOO ROAD.

Subjoined is the programme of an organ recital given on Thursday, March 15th, at the church of St. John the Evangelist, by Mr. Henry J. B. Dart :—

Sonata in B flat, No. 4	Mendelssohn.
Adagio Cantabile	Hopkins.
Toccata and Fugue in D minor	Bach.
Choral Song and Fugue	Wesley.
Impromptu in F, No. 7	Hiles.
March in E flat	Guilmant.

BRISTOL.

Annexed is the programme of the organ recital given by Mr. George Riseley in the Colston Hall on Saturday, March 17th :—

March in E flat	Ketterer.
Larghetto (Second Symphony)	Beethoven.
Sonata No. 4, in B flat	Mendelssohn.
Andante in E minor	Batiste.
Marche Funèbre et Chant Séraphique	Guilmant.
Andante with variations	Haydn.
Overture (" L'Italiana ")	Rossini.

LEEDS.

The programme of Dr. Spark's recital, the first of the series, in the Town Hall, on Saturday last, consisted of selections from Handel's works, and included :—Overture (" Occasional"); air, " Hark ! 'tis the Linnet " (" Joshua"); Coronation anthem, " Zadok the Priest "; air, " Return, O God of Hosts " (" Samson "); Concerto in G minor; " Honour and arms " (" Samson"); Gavotte in B flat major ; and chorus, " Blest be the man " (" Joseph.")

KENDAL.

Mr. S. Claude Ridley gave a recital upon the new organ in the Unitarian Chapel (built by Messrs. Wilkinson and Son), on Thursday, March 15th, with the following pro-gramme :—

Sonata in C	Mendelssohn.
Allegretto (" Chanson d'Amour ")	Hesselt.
Prelude and Fugue in F	Bach.
Air with variations in F	Waly.
Fantasia in E minor	Lemmens.
Andante with variations in E flat	Haydn.
Concert Fugue in G	Krebs.
Pageant March (" La Reine de Saba ")	Gounod.

BOW AND BROMLEY INSTITUTE.

Mr. T. Tallis Trimnell, of Sheffield parish church, was the organist on the 17th. The good impression pre-viously made by his artistic and admirable executant was more than confirmed upon this occasion. His first solo was a capital rendering of Weber's " Der Freischütz" overture. A charming work, H. Smart's Con Moto in B flat, came next. Merkel's Sonata, No. 5 in D minor, proved a real treat. The Andante was especially excellent in effect. Barth's Fantasia on a chorale was also admirably played. Balfe's overture " The Bohemian Girl " (perhaps one should add "played by permission " in these days), made a popular termination to a good programme.

Miss Helen D'Alton was in good voice and was received with enthusiasm ; she was encored in Handel's "He shall feed His flock," Roeckel's " Faithful " (singing the " Lost Chord " finely in reply), and in Balfe's " Kil-larney." Yesterday the " Messiah" was performed under Mr. W. G. MacNaught. Mr. W. De Manby Sergison, of St. Peter's, Eaton Square, will be the recitalist this evening, vocal music being given by members of his choir. Miss Theresa Beney, who is a gifted and well prepared lady organist, will give the following organ recital. This talented young lady has already been heard as a recitalist and her performances have met with much favour.

THE CARL ROSA OPERA COMPANY.

OPERA IN ENGLISH.

Mr. Carl Rosa will begin his short season of one calendar month on Easter Monday (March 26th) at Drury Lane Theatre. The opera of the opening night is to be a new one in four acts, entitled "Esmeralda," specially written for the Company by Mr. A. Goring Thomas, with Mdme. Georgina Burns in the title-part. Another specimen of "native talents" is also in preparation, namely, "Colombo," a lyrical drama in four acts, written by Dr. Francis Hueffer, and composed by Mr A. C. Mackenzie. "Fidelio" and "The Bohemian Girl" are down for Easter week.

The company of artists includes Mdme. Marie Roze, Mdme. G. Burns, Miss Josephine Yorke, Mr. Packard, Mr. J. W. Turner, Mr. Ludwig, and Mr. Snazelle. Mr. Randegger has been chosen as conductor, and it is hoped that Mr. J. D. Maclaren will continue to be acting-manager "in front."

A sneering reference to the works of Wagner appears in a contemporary journal in the form of a hope that Mr. Carl Rosa, having named none of the master's works in his *first* prospectus, will not perform them this season, or not many! *Au contraire:* let us have them again and again by all means. "Tannhäuser," "Lohengrin," "Der Fliegende Holländer," and "Tristan und Isolde," are all "mounted" at Drury Lane, and all known to the company, at least in their English form. The public have learned to appreciate these noble works; and cynics should be advised to snarl and growl, like their canine "analogues," in some remote backyard, or, as an old wag once suggested, rush into the City to "Tully's Offices," and lock themselves up there!

LINCOLN'S INN CHAPEL.

The works connected with the enlargement and partial re-construction of the chapel of Lincoln's Inn, which have been in progress during the past eighteen months, are at length completed, and the opening services are expected to take place on Sunday, April 8th. The chief features of the renovated building are an extension of 27ft. to the length, an entirely new and handsome roof, and vestries for the clergy and choir over the west entrance.

It is satisfactory to state that the excellent acoustical properties which characterised the old building have been in no way affected by the alterations, save, perhaps, in the direction of improvement.

The organ, which was partly destroyed by the fire at the builder's factory in August last, is in course of erection in its former relative position—on the screen at the west end. The opportunity has been taken to adopt, as far as practicable, the recommendations of the "Organ Conference," and several additions have been made to the scheme of the former instrument. The following is a summary of the stops it now contains :—Great Organ 10 (including a 16ft. open Diapason) ; Swell, 12 ; Choir, 7 ; pedal, 4. Each department of the organ is separate—the Great being on the south side, the Swell on the north, the Choir in front of the screen, and the longer pipes of the pedal organ lying horizontally at the back, the Console being placed behind the Choir organ. This arrangement, it will be seen, is somewhat similar to that of the organ at Westminster Abbey previous to its recent removal.

It may not be generally known that no orders are necessary for admission to the services of this chapel, special accommodation for visitors having been provided in the new portion of the building.

PAGANINI REDIVIVUS.

Although the artist rejoicing in the above title by his ill-judged advertisement anent the great violin concertos of the classical masters invoked adverse criticism, and although the too slavish imitation of a departed virtuoso is not a cause for congratulation in an artistic career which at least claims the dignity of self-respect and manly independence, it is only right and an act of simple justice to acknowledge the eccentric performer's great technical powers as a violinist. On March 20th he gave two recitals in one of the smaller rooms of St. James's Hall, without any accompaniment or extraneous support. His performance consisted of a number of studies in different styles and illustrating different mannerisms, in the execution of which he displayed an extraordinary power over the instrument. His bowing is wonderfully effective, and his double stopping shows a masterly facility and power of expressing distinct parts. His audiences are roused to enthusiasm by his remarkable dexterity, even though the tone produced is at times somewhat lacking in purity. In a notice of this really astonishing executant are the following words :—

"The violinist who is now so widely known to fame under the somewhat mysterious title of Paganini Redivivus, was first heard of at what is called a "Concours," at the Paris Conservatoire, in 1850, when he performed a most difficult solo in the presence of a committee formed of MM. Gounod, Auber, Halévy, Ambroise Thomas, Clappisson, Félicien David, and Berlioz, in addition to the violin professors, MM. Alard, Dancla, and Massart. His object was to enter some special class for the practice of the bow, for which Paris violin teachers are justly famed. After the trial performance was over, M. Massart came forward and told the violinist that the professors and the committee were of opinion that nature had evidently intended him later on to have a special style of playing of his own, and that there was no professor present who would like to risk taking it upon himself to break him of it. Shortly afterwards, he accepted the place of first violin at Muzard's concerts, at the Hôtel d'Osmond, which site is now occupied by the New Grand Opera House. There the violinists christened him by the familiar title of "Paganini No. 2." Upon one particular occasion while he was going through the rehearsal of a solo piece with the full band accompaniments, an old violin player sprang to his feet and cried out 'Messieurs, Messieurs, c'est Paganini ressuscité; c'est le même son, Messieurs.' In course of time the violinist came to London, where, at the Royal Polytechnic Institution, he drew crowds daily and nightly by a weird and clever impersonation, entitled 'Paganini's Ghost,' which he gave upwards of 200 times in that establishment. Some time afterwards, upon the occasion of Professor Pepper seceding and going to the Egyptian Hall, he took Paganini's Ghost with him, and the entertainment was continued there to delighted audiences for upwards of 300 representations. A well-known London critic commenting upon the performance at the time, observed,— 'If our mysterious virtuoso does not wish to put forward his family name, he might at least adopt a cognomen which would not frighten ladies and children. We suggest therefore that the violinist should call himself Paganini Redivivus.' From that time the name was, as it were, created, and has invariably stuck to him ever since."

During the last few years this violinist has played before varied audiences, including many notabilities, musical and otherwise.

THE NAMES OF MUSICAL INSTRUMENTS.—Mr. T. Casson writing to the editor of *Musical Opinion*, speaks thus of the odd sayings of the *American Art Journal* with regard to the nomenclature of musical instruments. The writer in the latter journal first infers that "haut-bois" (high wood) refers to the pitch of that wood instrument. I always understood that it referred to the Haut Bois, whence its use is supposed to have originated. Next he informs us that the basset horn is an instrument called a basset, improved by Horn, an instrument maker. Now, with all respect to the ability of this unknown genius, I hardly think that he could improve the *bassetta*, or *bassetti*, a diminutive double bass, into a large clarionet. The remarks as to the spelling of "violoncello" hardly call for notice The error is of a merely vulgar character, and is practically obsolete ; but one fails to understand the objection to "clarionet," or the advantage of using "clarinet." If "clarino," the diminutive of clarion, be admissible with the diminutive "etto" what is the objection to "clarino," with the well-established English diminutive "et," as found in the words "locket," "pocket," "tablet," or even "basset"? "Clarinet" is of no language, unless it be American. The term "horn," and its foreign equivalents, appears to be naturally applied to all wind instruments of tortuous form, and to be by no means especially appropriated to the "familiar *brass* instrument." The corno di bassetto was formerly known as a "cornet," and other instances immediately occur to me, such as cor Anglais, Krumm horn, Saxe horn, etc.

It is pleasant to record the first orchestral concert given at Trinity College on March 19th. The authorities deserve warm congratulations for their encouragement of the orchestral department of the institution.

Passing Events.

Ponchielli's "Gioconda" is likely to be heard at Covent Garden Theatre this season. The opera was produced in Milan in 1876, and it is stated to have received a semi-private rendering, the performance being organised by Major Wallace Carpenter.

At Mr. Van Noorden's concert on the evening of March 15, he played, with his daughter Emily, a pianoforte duet of Moskowski, "Spanish Dances," and he himself sang John Parry's comic scena " Matrimony." Miss Reba sang Spohr's " Roses softly blooming " with great taste.

At Mr. Von Zastrow's last drawing-room concert, at Glendower House, on Saturday March 17, Mr. Bond-Andrews played several texts of Beethoven, Chopin, and other masters, and Mr. De Wolfe sang classical songs. Both gentlemen distinguished themselves, and evoked much applause.

That excellent association, the Borough of Hackney Choral Society, under the direction of Mr. Ebenezer Prout, gave a performance of Schumann's most charming cantata, " Paradise and the Peri," at Shoreditch Town Hall last Monday evening. The soloists were Miss Marianne Fenna, Miss Jessie Jones, Miss Hilda Wilson, Mr. Henry Guy, and Mr. John Bridson. The chorus and band were complete and very efficient.

Miss J. R. Thomson (Licentiate, R.A.M.) gave a very interesting concert at Southgate on the 1st inst., assisted by Herr Oberthür, and other more or less distinguished artists. Miss Thomson is a pianist of much refinement and culture, and her name being thoroughly familiar as a painstaking, highly successful teacher, not only in her own immediate neighbourhood, but for some miles around, the large and appreciative audience that assembled was both a just tribute to the high order of her talent as an executant, and an agreeable proof of the thoroughly-deserved respect which her conscientious efforts among her numerous pupils have inspired.

The pupils of the Royal Irish Academy gave a choir concert on the 14th inst., when " Judas Maccabeus " was performed. The choir is making marked progress under the directorhip of the Cavalier Giuseppe Bozzelli, whose method of teaching appears to prove fruitful within a short time. The band, considering the limited number of performers, was effective, and the choruses were well given. The duet for soprano and contralto "O Lovely Peace," secured the performing pupils the success of the evening, and coming at the close of the oratorio sent the large audience away with pleasant memories of the performance.

The North-East London Choral Society gave its second concert of the season at the Morley Hall, Hackney, on Tuesday evening, March 13th. As an opening, Mendelssohn's Organ Sonata, No. 1, was played by Mr. John E. West, A.C.O., which was followed by Gade's cantata, " The Erl King's Daughter," by the choir, the solo parts being sustained by Mdme. Clara West, Miss Coyte Turner, and Mr. Charles Prickett. The second part of the programme consisted of ballads, part-songs, etc. Miss Clara Wollaston, Miss Lottie West, and Mr. Sinclair Dunn, in addition to the before-mentioned soloists, contributed, and were mostly encored. Mr. L. B. Prout and Mr. W. West were the accompanists, and Mr. John E. West was conductor. The audience was large and appreciative.

MUSICAL COPYRIGHT.—Mr. H. Lawrence Harris, secretary of the Music Publishers' Association, writes to acquaint the public of the fact that the multiplying copies, by any means whatever, of copyright music or other works, without the sanction of the owner of the copyright, is a breach of the Copyright Acts, and adds : " The Music Publishers' Association has recently been compelled to take proceedings against one lady, and to threaten proceedings against another, in respect of this very offence, and has only consented to stay further proceedings on an ample apology and payment of costs being made. In the case of similar infringements of the publishers' rights being hereafter brought to light, the offenders must expect less lenient treatment."

The Querist.

QUERY.

WORK ON CHOIR MANAGEMENT.—Is there any work published on Choir Management, suited to the needs of students preparing for the Higher Examinations of Trinity, College, London ?—LERA KUVI.

Service Lists.

EASTER SUNDAY,
MARCH 25th.
London.

ST. PAUL'S CATHEDRAL.—Morn.: Service, Te Deum and Benedictus, Stanford in B flat ; Introit, Jesus Christ is risen today (Hymn 134) ; Communion Service, Stanford in A. Even.: Service, Magnificat and Nunc Dimittis, Stanford in A ; Anthem, Awake, thou that sleepest, Love divine, and, To Him who left His throne on high (Stainer).

TEMPLE CHURCH.—Morn.: Service, Te Deum and Jubilate, Boyce in C ; Athanasian Creed, Tallis ; Anthem, Why seek ye the living (E. J. Hopkins) ; Kyrie Eleison, Arnold in A. Even.: Service, Magnificat and Nunc Dimittis, King in C ; Apostles' Creed, Harmonized Monotone ; Anthem, Behold, I shew you a mystery (Handel).

ST. AUGUSTINE AND ST. FAITH, WATLING STREET.—Morn.: Service, Garrett in E and E flat ; Offertory, Why seek ye the living (Hopkins). Even.: Service, Smart in B flat ; Anthem, But thou didst not leave, and, Hallelujah (Handel).

ST. BARNABAS, MARYLEBONE.—Morn.: Service, Te Deum and Jubilate, Smart in F ; Anthem, Since by man ("Messiah," Handel) ; Kyrie and Nicene Creed, Smart in F. Even.: Service, Magnificat and Nunc Dimittis, Smart in F ; Anthems, The trumpet shall sound, and, Worthy is the]Lamb (Handel).

CHILDREN'S HOME CHAPEL, BONNER ROAD, E.—Morn.: Service, Anthems, There is a green hill (Lord Somerset), and, Lo ! my Shepherd (Haydn). Aft.: Service, Anthems, O Saviour of the World (Goss), and, If ye love Me (Monk).

CHRIST CHURCH, CLAPHAM.—Morn.: Service, Te Deum, Plain-song ; Introit, Now is Christ risen (Allen) ; Kyrie and Credo, Schubert in F ; Offertory Anthem, But thou didst not leave (Handel) ; Sanctus, Benedictus, and Agnus Dei, Schubert ; Communio, Jesu, Word of God (Mozart) ; Gloria in excelsis, Schubert. Even.: Service, Magnificat and Nunc Dimittis, Smart in B flat ; Anthem, a selection from the "Messiah " (third part) ; during Offertory, the Hallelujah Chorus (Handel).

FOUNDLING CHAPEL.—Morn.: Service, Te Deum, Dykes in F ; Benedictus, Smith in B flat ; Anthems, The trumpet shall sound, and, But thanks (Handel). Aft.: Service, Smith in B flat ; Anthem, Hallelujah Chorus (Handel).

HOLY TRINITY, TULSE HILL.— Morn.: Chant Service. Even.: Service, Agutter in D ; Anthems, But thou didst not leave, and, Hallelujah Chorus (Handel).

ST. JAMES'S PRIVATE EPISCOPAL CHAPEL, SOUTHWARK. —Morn.: Service, Introit (processional), Jesus Christ is risen to-day (Hymn 134) ; Communion Service, Hummel in E flat. Even.: Service, Calkin in G ; Anthems, Awake, thou, Love divine, and, To Him who left (Stainer).

ST. MARY ABCHURCH, E.C.—Morn.: Service, Boyce in C ; Communion Service, Garrett in E flat. Even.: Service, Turle in D.

ST. MARY BOLTONS, WEST BROMPTON, S.W.—Morn.: Service, Te Deum, Smart in F ; Benedictus, Smart in F ; Anthem, Worthy is the Lamb (Handel) ; Communion Service, Kyrie, Credo, Sanctus, Benedictus, Agnus Dei, and Gloria in excelsis, Going in F ; Offertory, Barnby. Even.: Service, Magnificat and Nunc Dimittis, Smart in F ; Anthem, Hallelujah (Handel).

ST. PAUL'S, AVENUE ROAD, SOUTH HAMPSTEAD.—Morn.: Service, Te Deum and Benedictus, Calkin in B flat ; Anthem, Christ our Passover (Goss) ; Kyrie and Credo, Tours in F ; Offertory, Barnby ; Sanctus and Gloria in excelsis, Tours in F. Even.: Service, Magnificat and Nunc Dimittis, Gounod in D ; Anthem, Blessed be the God and Father (Wesley) ; after sermon, Easter Carols.

ST. PAUL'S, BOW COMMON, E.—Morn.: Service, Te Deum, Smart in F ; Benedictus, Chant ; Communion Service, Kyrie, Credo, Sanctus, Benedictus, Agnus Dei, and Gloria in excelsis, Eyre in E flat ; Offertory, Stainer. Even.: Service, Magnificat and Nunc Dimittis, Stainer in B flat ; Anthem, My hope is in the everlasting, and, Awake, thou that sleepest (Stainer).

ST. PETER'S (EATON SQUARE).—Morn.: Service, Te Deum, Boyce in A; Anthem, Blessed be the God (Wesley). Even.: Service, Barnby in E; Anthem, I know that my Redeemer liveth (Handel); after service, Hallelujah.

ALL SAINTS, MARGARET STREET.—Morn.: Service, Mendelssohn in A; Communion Service, Gullmant in E flat; Offertory Anthem, Worthy is the Lamb (Handel). Even.: Service, Thorne in D; Anthem, To the Paschal Victim (Nixon).

ST. PETER'S, LEIGHAM COURT ROAD, STREATHAM, S.W.—Morn.: Service, Gregorian; Communion Service (with orchestra), Schubert's Mass in G; Introit, When I wake up (Sutton); Offertory, Hymn 134. Even.: Service, Magnificat, Agutter in D; Anthem, Blessed be the God and Father (Wesley); Hallelujah Chorus ("Messiah," Handel).

Country.

ASHBURNE CHURCH, DERBYSHIRE. — Morn.: Service, Laurence in G; Kyrie, Credo, and Gloria, Martin in C. Even.: Service, Musgrave in F; Anthem, Selection from "Messiah."

BEDDINGTON CHURCH, SURREY.—Morn.: Service, Smart in F; Introit, Christ our Passover (H. Walmisley Little); Communion Service, Smart in F. Even.: Service, Stainer in B flat; Anthems, My hope is in the everlasting, and, Awake, thou that sleepest ("Daughter of Jairus," Stainer); after sermon, selection from third part of "Messiah" (Handel).

BIRMINGHAM (ST. CYPRIAN'S, HAY MILLS).—Morn.: Service, Stainer in A and D; Anthems, The trumpet shall sound, and, But thanks (Handel). Even.: Service, Smith in B flat; Anthem, O give thanks (Whitfeld).

CANTERBURY CATHEDRAL. — Morn.: Service, Calkin in B flat; Introit, Awake, thou that sleepest (Ouseley); Communion Service, Calkin in B flat. Even.: Service, Calkin in B flat; Anthem, I know that my Redeemer liveth (Handel).

CARLISLE CATHEDRAL.—Morn.: Service, Smart in F; Introit, Easter Hymn; Kyrie and Nicene Creed, Best in G. Even.: Service, Garrett in E flat; Anthems, I know that my Redeemer, Since by man, and, Hallelujah Chorus (Handel).

CHESTER (ST. MARY'S CHURCH).—Morn.: Service, Tearne in A; Anthem, Christ being raised (Elvey); Communion Service, Tearne in G and and Stewart in G. Even.: Service, Arnold in A; Anthem, He was cut off, But thou didst not leave, and, Hallelujah Chorus ("Messiah," Handel).

DEWSBURY PARISH CHURCH. — Morn.: Service, Anthem, Why seek ye (Hopkins); Kyrie, Creed, Sanctus, and Gloria in excelsis, Tours in F; Offertory Sentences, Barnby. Even.: Service, Magnificat and Nunc Dimittis, Barnby in C; Anthem, Hallelujah (Beethoven).

DONCASTER (PARISH CHURCH). — Morn.: Service, Tours in F; Introit, Christ being raised (Elvey); Anthem, Why seek ye (Hopkins). Even.: Service, Calkin in B flat; Anthems, They have taken away my Lord (Stainer), and, Hallelujah (Handel).

ELY CATHEDRAL.—Morn.: Service, Stainer in A; Kyrie, Credo, and Gloria, Stainer in A and D; Anthem, Christ being raised (Elvey). Even.: Service, Stainer in A; Anthem, Since by man (Handel).

EXETER CATHEDRAL.—Morn.: Service, Boyce in A; Communion Service, Hatton in E. Even.: Service, Hopkins in F; Anthems, He was cut off, and, Worthy is the Lamb (Handel).

GLASGOW (BLYTHSWOOD PARISH CHURCH).—Aft.: Service, Anthem, O give thanks (Goss).

HIGH WYCOMBE PARISH CHURCH. — Morn.: Service, Smart in F; Anthem, O give thanks (Goss); Offertory, Keeton. Even.: Service, Stainer in A; Anthems, I know that my Redeemer liveth, and, Hallelujah (Handel); Awake, thou that sleepest ("Jairus," Stainer).

LLANDAFF CATHEDRAL.—Morn.: Service, Stainer in E flat; Communion Service, Wesley in E. Even.: Service, The Litany; Anthem, I know that my Redeemer liveth, and, Worthy is the Lamb (Handel).

LEEDS PARISH CHURCH. — Morn.: Service, Stanford in B flat; Anthem, Hallelujah (Beethoven); Communion Service, Wesley in E. Even.: Service, Attwood in A; Anthem, I know that my Redeemer (Handel).

ST. LEONARDS-ON-SEA (ST. MARY MAGDALENE).—Morn.: Service, A. E. Tozer in C; Anthem, Christ our Passover (Goss); Kyrie, Elvey in A; Credo, Monotone; Offertory Sentences, Martin. Even.: Service, Magnificat and Nunc Dimittis, Martin in D; Anthem, They have taken away my Lord (Stainer); after sermon, Awake, thou that sleepest (Stainer).

LICHFIELD CATHEDRAL. — Morn.: Service, Le Deum and Benedictus, Barnby in E; Communion, Barnby in E; Anthem, I know that my Redeemer liveth (Handel). Aft.: Service, Cantate and Deus Misereatur, Elvey in D; Anthems, The trumpet shall sound, and, Worthy is the Lamb (Handel).

LIVERPOOL CATHEDRAL. — Aft.: Service, Oakeley in E flat; Anthem, I know that my Redeemer liveth, and, Worthy is the Lamb (Handel).

MANCHESTER CATHEDRAL. — Morn.: Service, Gounod; Anthem, Since by man (Handel). Aft.: Service, The Litany; Anthem, If we believe.

MANCHESTER (ST. BENEDICT'S).—Morn.: Service, Kyrie, Elvey; Credo, Sanctus, Benedictus, Agnus Dei, and Gloria in excelsis, Haydn in C (No. 2). Even.: Service, Magnificat and Nunc Dimittis, Bunnett in F.

MANCHESTER (ST. JOHN BAPTIST, HULME).—Morn.: Service, Te Deum and Benedictus, Stainer; Kyrie, Credo, Sanctus, and Gloria in excelsis, Stainer in A; Benedictus and Agnus Dei, De la Hache in E flat; O Salutaris, Gounod; Post Communion, I am the living Bread (Hoyte). Even.: Service, Magnificat and Nunc Dimittis, Bunnett in F; Anthem, Praise the Lord (Scott); Te Deum, Dykes in F.

MITCHAM PARISH CHURCH.—Morn.: Service, Te Deum, Smart in F; Anthem, Blessed be the God (Wesley); Kyrie, Thorne in G; Creed, Goss. Even.: Service, Magnificat and Nunc Dimittis, Hoyte in B flat; Anthem, The Lord is my strength (Smart).

NORTH BERWICK, N.B. (S. BALDRED'S).—Morn.: Service, Te Deum, Garrett in F; Anthem, Christ being raised (Elvey); Jesus Christ is risen to-day (Hymn); Kyrie, Dykes in F; Introit, Credo, Acc. Monotone. Even.: Service, Garrett in F; Anthem, Christ being raised (Elvey).

RIPON CATHEDRAL. — Morn.: Service, Chants; Anthem, Hallelujah (Beethoven); Kyrie and Credo, Merbeck. Even.: Service, Stainer in E; Anthem, He was cut off (Handel).

SHEFFIELD PARISH CHURCH.—Morn.: Service, Te Deum and Jubilate, Sullivan in D; Kyrie, Sullivan. Even.: Service, Magnificat and Nunc Dimittis, Trimnell in F; Anthem, I know that my Redeemer, and, Hallelujah (Handel).

SHERBORNE ABBEY.—Morn.: Service, Te Deum, Jackson in F; Anthem, Why do the heathen (G. Brown); Kyrie, Smallwood in F; Offertories, Barnby. Even.: Service, Anthems, But thou didst not leave, Worthy is the Lamb, and, Amen; after service, Hallelujah (Handel).

SOUTHAMPTON (ST. MARY'S CHURCH).—Morn.: Service, Te Deum and Benedictus, Garrett in D; Athanasian Creed, Helmore; Introit, This is the day (Macfarren); Communion Service, Monk in C; Offertory, Whoso hath, and, Blessed is the man (Baraby); Paternoster, Hoyte. Even.: Service, Magnificat and Nunc Dimittis, Garrett in D; Apostles' Creed, Harmonized Monotone (Hopkins); Anthem, Break forth into joy (Barnby).

WELLS CATHEDRAL.—Morn.: Service, Ring in D (throughout); Introit, I know whom I have believed (Macfarren). Even.: Service, Garrett in D; Anthem, Worthy is the Lamb, and Hallelujah (Handel).

WORCESTER CATHEDRAL.—Morn.: Service, Garrett in D; Anthem, Since by man (Handel). Even.: Service, Garrett in D; Anthems, The trumpet shall sound (Handel).

DEATH.

HAYNE.—The Rev. L. G. HAYNE, Mus.Doc., Rector of Mistley, who composed the fine tunes in Hymns Ancient and Modern, to the words "A few more years shall roll," "Thy Kingdom come, O God," and "Loving Shepherd of Thy sheep," died on the 3rd inst., aged 47 years.

Printed for the Proprietor by BOWDEN, HUDSON & Co., at 23, Red Lion Street, Holborn, London, W.C. ; and Published by WILLIAM REEVES, at the Office, 185, Fleet Street, E.C. West End Agents.—WEEKES & CO., 14, Hanover Street, Regent Street, W. Subscriptions and Advertisements are received either by the Publisher or West End Agents.—*Communications for the Editor are to be forwarded to his private address, 6, Argyle Square, W.C*

SATURDAY, MARCH 31, 1883.—*Entered at the General Post Office as a Newspaper.*

The Musical Standard

A NEWSPAPER FOR MUSICIANS PROFESSIONAL AND AMATEUR

NO. 974. VOL. XXIV. FOURTH SERIES.   SATURDAY, MARCH 31, 1883.   WEEKLY: PRICE 3D.

Musical Intelligence.

CRYSTAL PALACE CONCERTS.

PROGRAMME.

Symphony No. 2 (in C)	Schumann.
Aria, "Dove sono" ("Figaro")	Mozart.
Mdme. Rose Hersee.	
Concerto No. 2, for violin and orchestra (in D, Op. 22) ..	Wieniawski.
(First time at these concerts.)	
Violin—Señor Sarasate.	
Gavotte "Mignon"	A. Thomas.
Arietta, "If a youth" ("Freischütz")	Weber.
Mdme. Rose Hersee.	
Violin Solos—	
"Habañera " }	
"Zapateado " }	Sarasate.
Señor Sarasate.	
Concert-Overture, "Calm Sea and Prosperous Voyage" (Op. 27)	Mendelssohn.

Conductor · · · AUGUST MANNS.

Schumann was not only a great composer, but also a
man of great literary attainments, and, in order to
educate the public to a due appreciation of his works, as
well as to strike a blow at the light Italian school of
music, he, together with Wieck and others, edited the
New Musical Journal, the organ of a more poetical
school, *versus* the superficial party, whose ears were too
easily tickled with a luscious *cadenza*, a languishing
appoggiatura, or a rapid run from one end of the scale to
the other. He says, "now-a-days we must have ideas,
and those ideas well carried out. We must have poetical
conception ; everything must bear the impress of
imagination, else the effect is merely momentary." Since
his death, however, the intrinsic merit of his compositions
has done far more for their acceptance with the public
than all the literary efforts of his lifetime. His
Symphony in C was sketched during a period of great
mental and physical suffering. The date is 1846, and in
ten years from this his sufferings were ended by his
untimely death. Traces of mental conflict are evident in
this noble composition, and the hymn of thanksgiving at
the end is a touching proof that, at least for the time, the
composer had triumphed over his affliction. The work
is, of course, well known to the Crystal Palace orchestra,
and with the exception of a little unsteadiness—for a few
bars only—in the lovely scherzo, the performance was
all that could be desired.

Señor Sarasate again met with a most cordial reception, and played Wieniawski's concerto with marked
success. The work, which is full of interest, was composed especially for Señor Sarasate, and with a perfect
knowledge of his great abilities ; it may therefore be
imagined how well the great violinist availed himself of
every point, and how perfectly he acquitted himself in
every movement. We are told that Wieniawski died in
extreme poverty in one of the hospitals of Moscow, in
1880. But why one of the greatest violinists of our age,
and one who could write such a concerto as this, was
allowed to die in such a wretched manner, it is hard to
understand ; for, happily, genius and poverty are not so
closely allied as they formerly were. The other solos for
the violin were of course charmingly played, and a
double recall induced the great violinist to give the
audience one of Chopin's favourite *cantabile* pieces.

It is erroneously stated in the Crystal Palace programme that Mendelssohn's overture, "Meerestille und
Glückliche Fahrt," was last performed at the Saturday
concerts on April 5th 1879. I should not have noticed
this error did it not recall to mind the fact that, some
twelve months ago it was played here, when an awkward
accident—the flute failing to take up the tiny flourish at
the end of the adagio—compelled the conductor to begin
the overture again. An accident of this kind is so rare
at these concerts, that it can hardly fail to be remembered.

Mdme. Rose Hersee was by no means happy in her
interpretation of Mozart's song, but in Weber's Arietta
she was more successful.

R. S.

Mr. W. S. Hoyte gives a recital on the Wareham organ
at the factory of Messrs. Maley, Young and Oldknow, on
Monday next, April 9th, and Mr. E. H. Turpin will play
on the following evening, Tuesday, April 10th.

SIGNOR CASANO'S SERIAL CHAMBER CONCERTS.

At the sixth *soirée*, on March 29th, Miss E. Casano,
daughter of the Principal of the "West London College
of Music," in Colville Gardens, played Liszt's piece, "La
Regatta Veneziana" (at the outset) in excellent style.
She is a pupil of Mdme. Voarino, and does her mistress
credit. Miss K. Thompson, a young lady with a high
resonant soprano voice, sang Millard's "Waiting." In
the absence of another vocalist, Miss A. Woods, a pupil
of the institution, kindly sang Rossini's air in A, "Bel
raggio lusinghiere," from "Semiramide ; " "Le Rossignol"
of Ciardi, and the air from Auber's "L'Ambassadrice,"
in B flat, "Jusqu'a lui." Miss Wood has a high, florid,
and flexible voice. She sang up to high A and B flat,
and shook like a bird. Mrs. Turrill gave a splendid
version of "Robert, toi que j'aime." Mr. C. Oberthür
played two of his own harp solos with *éclat*, and Captain
E. Acklom gave a recitation. Mr. Probert, a professional
artist, sang airs of Sir Sterndale Bennett and Tours.
Signor Casano conducted, the concert, and afterwards
entertained his friends in hospitable fashion.

THE CARL ROSA OPERA COMPANY AT DRURY LANE.

Beethoven's "Fidelio" on Thursday, March 29th,
served to introduce a Leonora new to Londoners (only)
in the person of the charming Parisian *prima donna*,
Mdme. Marie Roze, who has recently sustained this
arduous part in the provincial towns of England with
remarkable success. It is thought, and the printed
opinions of critics might be quoted to this effect, that
Mdme. Roze's impersonation of the faithful wife, whilst
exquisitely tender, pathetic, and feminine, hardly attains
the requisite power of high tragedy. Leonora must be
gentle and loving to her husband, no doubt ; but when
she at last confronts the vile assassin, Pizarro, in the
startling pistol situation, it is almost necessary, as Shakespeare makes Richmond say in "Richard III.," to assume
the furious wrath of the tigress robbed of her whelps.
Schroeder-Devrient, and afterwards Theresa Titiens, rose
to this towering height of passion. The latter used to
rush at Pizarro like one of the gallant guards at the last
charge ("Up Guards and at 'em") on the plains of
Waterloo ; and her scream shook the theatre. This
tremendous situation—the finest known on the lyrical
stage, ought really to end the opera, for all the rest, in
comparison, seems anti-climax. Mdme. Marie. Roze's
sex, as contemporaries remark, could never have been
mistaken in real life : she is the gentle woman throughout ; but her action is always interesting, and her little
bits of by-play are instinct with genius. In the *scena* of
Act I, a lack of power was manifest. Bouquets were
freely thrown down, after the falls of the curtain. The
Duke and Duchess of Edinburgh were present.

A good all-round performance was this of March 29th,
no undue prominence of any particular feature, but the
canvas, so to speak, even and homogeneous. The general
stage movements, however, would not quite satisfy the
requirements of old Mr. Turveydrop ; a little acting
manager's drill might be advisable, and in "Esmeralda"
it has been noticed that the chorus crowd upon the
"principals" in very unseemly fashion. Mr. F. C.
Packard made a fair Florestan, and a new basso, Mr.
Franco Novaro appeared as Rocco, the Gaoler ; he has
a fine and penetrating voice. Miss C. Perry and Miss B.
Davies, filled the minor parts of Marcellina and Jaquino.
The Canon in G is now hardly ever encored.

The remarks on "Esmeralda" respecting certain Wagnerian tendencies are confirmed by contemporaries ; that
is to say, the composer rarely "pulls up" at full stop,
as in the artificially set conventional opera ; the style is
pronounced to be modern French, and the scoring very
excellent.

On Tuesday evening, "Il Trovatore," a very old and
favourite opera, once more introduced Mdme. Valleria, a
remarkably fine artist, who in addition to many other
high qualifications, has personified, to the admiration of
all *vrais connoisseurs*, the Senta of Wagner, in that
marvellous opera of marine painting, "Der Fliegende
Holländer."

As the commemorative anniversary of Washington
Irving is about to be celebrated in the United States, it

may be noticed, *en passant*, that the eminent American author in his "Bracebridge Hall," has made use of the legend in an episode entitled "The Storm Ship."

"Il Trovatore" was first heard by the British public in 1856, at the Lyceum Theatre, then the temporary refuge of the Italian Opera, after the conflagration of the large house in Bow Street, Covent Garden, in February of the same year, suspected to have been the act of an incendiary, actuated by inimical feeling against a speculative aeronaut, whom the late Mr. Gye had, most unfortunately, allowed to occupy the theatre before the regular opera season, and to give on this memorable night a *bal masqué*.

A *prima donna* of highest celebrity, Mdme. Bosio, sustained the part of Leonora at the Lyceum in 1856, and the writer has not forgotten her voice or her stage action. The performance at Drury Lane on Tuesday was excellent. Mdme. Valleria, whom the part well suits, sang and acted with much power. Miss Josephine Yorke ranted a little too much as Azucena, and so incurred a risk of crossing the line which divides deep tragedy from comic business. "Stride la vampa" was decidedly over done. Mr. Packard, a fair Manrico, would have been better if his intonation had been more precise. In the ari "desarto sulla terra," he was a little uncertain. Mr. Leslie Crotty, the Comte di Luna, excelled, and evoked much applause for "Il balen del suo sorriso." The band and chorus played and sang admirably.

On Monday, Mr. A. C. Mackenzie's lyrical drama in four acts, "Colomba," is to be produced. The libretto has been written by Dr. Francis Hueffer, the able musical reporter of *The Times*. The leading parts by Mdme. Valleria and Mr. Barton MacGuckin.

A. M.

CHELTENHAM.

At the fourth grand concert held at the Assembly Rooms of this town, Miss Alice Roselli won an *encore* for the new ballad of Milton Willing's "Forgive and forget," and evoked much applause in Roeckel's song, "Lord Mayor Whittington," the words whereof may be objected to as childish nursery twaddle, unworthy of the subject. Gounod's religious air, "Noël," was also admirably rendered by Miss Roselli. Signor Villa sang "Pro peccatis" from Rossini's "Stabat Mater," with force and dignity, and Fauré's "Les Rameaux," and he created a sensation in Churchill Sibley's song, "The Bell of St. Paul's." It is to be hoped that the great Bell in E flat will utter a more edifying sentiment than the halting verse of the poetaster, to the effect that "*Time* is King." Sad and silly moral for the *campana* of a Christian Cathedral ! Mdme. Enriquez, Mr. Vernon Rigby, Mr. Maas, and other favourite artists, sang in the course of the *soirée*. Mr. F. Cliffe and Mr. T. Lawson played Grieg's Sonata in F for pianoforte and violin ; and Mr. Cliffe pianoforte solos by Grieg and Watson.

THE HUNGARIAN CONCERT.

A concert in aid of the recent inundations in Hungary, held at St. James's Hall, on Saturday evening, March 31st, did not attract an overflowing audience, notwithstanding strong attractions. The public are too much pestered by philanthropists now-a-days ; and naturally slack to put their hard-earned pence in the too frequently presented begging-box, at church and elsewhere. Mr. J. B. Poznanski was engaged as violinist, and played Paganini's piece in D, "La Danse des Sorcières" (The Witches' Dance) with great *éclat*. A short introduction leads to a tremolo, "sul ponticello" ; a larghetto follows, with shake on A ; and then comes an andantino con variazioni, where the violin takes a wider range, with plenty of double stopping in thirds, sixths, and octaves. An elaborate cadenza closes the dance. Mr. Poznanski is a great adept at harmonics, both natural and artificial ; and whatever may be thought of this difficult accomplishment in an æsthetic, or musical sense, the feat at least serves to illustrate the mathematical principles of acoustics, as applicable to string instruments. Signor Mattei played his own pretty pianoforte solos, "L'Elégante," and "Galop de Concert." Mdme. Edith Wynne and Mdme. Liebhardt sang. Mr. W. Ganz conducted the concert.

WATFORD.

The second and third parts of Handel's "Messiah" were sung by the Church Oratorio Society at Oxhey Church on March 28th. The soloists included the Misses A. Brook and Barker, and Mr. C. Healey. Mr. J. Farmer of Harrow, conducted, and Mr. James Turpin, Mus.Bac., was the organist. The music was effectively and carefully performed.

HOLBORN TOWN HALL.

Mr. J. T. Hutchinson gave what may be called his annual concert at the Holborn Town Hall on April 5th. Mr. Hutchinson is not only widely esteemed as an artistic bass-baritone, but he has a large circle of personal friends who look forward with pleasure to his concerts. The work chosen this time was Haydn's "Creation." The chief singers were Miss Agnes Larkcom whose powers and acquirements are so well recognised, Mr. Henry Guy the well known tenor, and the concert-giver himself, whose finished singing could hardly be heard to better advantage than in the "Creation." Mr. McNaught was the experienced and excellent conductor ; the organ was in the very competent hands of Mr. Harvey Löhr, and a number of well selected strings aided in the performance. It is only to be regretted that the platform arrangements at the Holborn Town Hall are so miserably inadequate as to make a full orchestra and ample chorus impossible, for in this way Mr. Hutchinson's hands must be unfortunately tied down ; and his concerts would otherwise have doubtless assumed still larger and more interesting proportions. He is any way to be congratulated upon his efforts and upon his own excellent personal performances.

St. Peter's, Leigham Court Road, Streatham, S.W.— On Easter Day, Schubert's mass in G was sung at this church, an efficient orchestra being employed. Mr. B. Agutter, Mus.Bac., F.C.O., conducted, Mr. C. Ersfield was leader, Mr. E. J. Quance was at the organ. Mr. Agutter's Sequence "To the Paschal Victim" was scored for this occasion, a special feature being the harp obbligato.

Calderbrook.—The new, small, but sweet-toned organ built for St. James's Church by Messrs. Booth and Hepworth at the cost of £250, was recently opened by Mr. T. W. Pilling, of Bolton and Mirfield. At the conclusion of a special service that gentleman played in a masterly manner Slow movement (Merkel), Andante (G. Herman), Introduction and Offertoire (Hewlett), Pastorale (Merkel), Grand Chœur (Salomé), and andante (Boyton Smith).

Torquay.—Mr. T. Craddock, Bac.Mus., Oxon, has just completed a series of organ recitals on the very fine organ in Upton Church, Torquay, having given the six organ sonatas of Mendelssohn in rotation, besides one of Bach's fugues at each recital, and other pieces by Handel (the concertos), Saint-Saens, Kullak, Mozart, etc. The recitals having been so much appreciated, Mr. Craddock intends giving weekly performances until Whitsuntide.

Alton, Hants.—A performance of Mendelssohn's "Hymn of Praise" was given, under the able direction of Mr. C. G. Halliday, at the Assembly Rooms on the 29th ult. The soloists were Mdme. Helen M. Stark and Mr. C. E. Pillow, of Chichester Cathedral ; and Mr. H. Walmsley Little, Mus.Bac., presided at the pianoforte. The second part of the programme consisted of a selection from the "Messiah," with orchestral accompaniments, the band and chorus numbering eighty performers.

Surrey County School of Music.—At the "musical evening" on Wednesday, March 28th, an organ recital was given by Mr. Frank Bradley, who performed a selection from the works of Bach, Raff, Lemmens, Widar, Kuhmstedt, Salomé, etc., to the satisfaction of a numerous audience. The programme also included vocal music, rendered by professional students of the school, whose efforts it would perhaps be scarcely fair to criticise while they are yet *in statu pupillari*. Similar entertainments are announced for April 11th and 18th.

Bocconoc Church.—On March 27th, the new organ was opened at a special service in the evening, when a very large congregation assembled. Previous to the service Mr. John Hele, junr, of St. Peter's, Plymouth, gave a recital of classical music, much to the gratification of those present. The instrument, which was built by Messrs. Hele and Co., of Plymouth, by order of Lady Fortescue, is well suited to the church, and has been well spoken of. It contains, in the great organ—1, open diapason ; 2, stopped diapason ; 3, dulciana ; 4, flute ; 5, principal ; 6, piccolo. Swell organ—1, open diapason ; 2, gedact ; 3, violin diapason ; 4, gemshorn ; 5, cornopean. Pedal organ.— 1, bourdon. Couplers.—1, swell to great ; 2, swell to pedal ; 3, great to pedal.

ROYAL VICTORIA COFFEE HALL, S.E.—The military concert given at the above hall by Lieut.-Col. Keyser and the officers of the 7th Royal Fusiliers, on March 29th, was a great success. Colonel Keyser took the chair, and by his charming sconviviality kept the whole concert going in an exceptionally brilliant manner. He introduced Major Brook Mears as the "great gun" of the evening, and he certainly did bring down the house. Where all did their parts so efficiently it would be invidious for special praise, but one cannot pass over Lieutenant W. H. Heron Maxwell and Lieutenant H. G. Dunning, who were real "comiques," and can only be superseded by Colonel Keyser's own acting and singing. The programme for April includes a ballad concert given by Mdme. Enequist, and a miscellaneous concert in aid of the funds of the Royal College of Music, which will be attended by H.R.H. the Princess Christian.

REDRUTH.—Mr. T. J. Thuell's annual concert was given on March 27th, with an interesting selection of vocal and orchestral music, including solos for violin by Mr. Hallett, English concertina by Alsepti, an elderly blind man handling the not very tractable instrument with singular skill, cornet by Mr. T. Vincent, and clarionet by Mr. Hallett. The orchestral pieces included "The Wedding March" (Mendelssohn), and andante "Surprise Symphony" (Haydn). The vocal portions of the programme consisted of songs by Miss Lemin (organist of Redruth Church), "Dream Faces" (encored and partially repeated), and "A Mother's Story"; "The Vale of years" (composed by Mr. Thuell), by Mr. E. A. Uglow, of Falmouth; an Italian song, and another, by Signor Tito Beccarini, of Falmouth; a double quartet "The Haymakers," and a chorus from "Patience" by Sullivan.

LEEDS.—The second of the borough organist's "Hours with the Great Composers" took place on March 24th, when there was even a larger audience than on the Handel night, thus unmistakably showing to what an extent the love of John Sebastian Bach's erudite compositions has reached with the people generally. The programme was full of interest and variety, and it included the ever-welcome fugue, with an extemporaneous introduction by the executant, on St. Ana's Tune, two bourrées of the real Bach type; "The Giant" fugue in D minor, with another extemporaneous introduction, the beautiful air, "My heart ever faithful," which secured a rapturous encore; a fine concerto in three movements in G (an arrangement by Bach of one of the concertos by Vivaldi) bright and tuneful as Handel himself; and finally the famous "Toccata" in F major, in which there is a pedal solo of surpassing dignity, and withal difficult. Dr. Spark seemed to have his heart thoroughly in the work, and the whole performance was a great success.—*Yorkshire Post.*

DUBLIN GLEE CHOIR.—The large attendance at, and eulogistic notices of the inaugural concert of the second season of the above society is the best assurance of the want that was long felt having been well supplied through the exertions of Mr. Arthur Patton. I am really at a loss to select any particular item of the programme as meriting especial praise, where everything was excellently done. The part-songs, madrigals, and glees performed by the choir embraced the work of a large number of well known contemporary composers, as well as two by De Pearsall, namely the ballet madrigal "Shoot, false love," and "Allan a Dale," and a madrigal by Luca Marenzio (1570). Mrs. Hutchinson sang an Italian recitative and aria and two German songs, one by Brahms, the other by Grieg, with remarkable success. Signor Esposito, of the Royal Irish Academy of Music, justified the assertions that have been freely circulated in musical circles here respecting his exceptional ability as a pianist. He played the "Moonlight" sonata, a nocturne and allegretto of his own and Schubert-Tausig's "Marche Militaire."

CLEVEDON CHORAL SOCIETY.—This flourishing society gave a grand evening concert on March 28th, at the Public Hall, before a large audience. Valuable aid was rendered on this occasion by an efficient band, in which Mr. A. Price took the various "wind" parts with great skill upon the harmonium, Mr. Walter Somerton being equally successful with the organ parts on a second harmonium. The concert may be pronounced a success. The first work undertaken was Mendelssohn's somewhat formidable "Hymn of Praise." The opening symphony, by the band, demonstrated at once their ability, and its performance left but little to be desired. The choruses were throughout rendered in such a manner as to reflect great credit upon the class and their teacher and conductor, Mr. H. E. Marchant. The solos were taken by Miss F. Visgar, whose charming voice was heard to advantage, and Mr. A. B. Trestrail, who also sang a duet with Miss Visgar. That lady also sang with Miss Maxwell, but through an expressed desire on the programme the audience restrained their temptation to applaud during the performance of the piece. The second part comprised a work of an entirely different character—Cumming's "Fairy Ring." Many of the airs are exceedingly pretty; those rendered by Miss Maxwell and Mr. J. Hudson being particularly deserving of commendation, and the work is an artistic production well deserving a large popularity. Mr. Talbot's solos were also appreciated. The choruses again went well, with effective instrumentation by the band, and the audience was not slow to mark its approval by repeated applause.

CIRENCESTER.—The annual concert of the Cirencester Choral Society was held at the Corn Hall on March 29th, when the spacious building was well filled. The works which, after careful and studied preparation throughout the season, were selected for performance were Spohr's "Last Judgment," and Mendelssohn's "Hymn of Praise." The principal vocalists were Miss Julia Jones, Miss Lizzie Hellis, Mr. Alfred Kenningham, and Mr. Thomas Woodward. Mr. Brind, the conductor, was accorded a hearty reception, both from the members of his class (with whom he is very popular) and the audience. The first part consisted of the "Last Judgment," and from the overture to the closing chorus it went excellently. The "Hymn of Praise" was given with equal success to that which attended the former production. Perhaps one of the most admired numbers was the duet, "I waited for the Lord," by Miss Jones and Miss Hellis, which was indeed charmingly sung, and the chorus that followed, "O blessed are they that hope," was a complete success. The recitative, "We called" (Mr. Kenningham and Miss Jones), and the chorus, "The night is departing," were finely executed, and the closing choruses were sung with great spirit.

ST. ALBANS.—On Thursday, March 29th, an enjoyable amateur concert was given at the Town Hall, under the patronage of Viscountess Grimston, Mrs. Lawrence, the Mayoress of St. Albans, and other influential ladies in the city and neighbourhood. The programme opened with a pianoforte duet, "Ray Blas" (Mendelssohn), played in a finished style by Lady Harriet Grimston and Miss Mabel Williams. Miss Alice Brooks, so well known in the county by her efforts on behalf of the School of Music at the Watford Public Library, and also as a vocalist, sang "Diva" (Visetti); she also sang with exquisite taste "Although a cloud o'erspread the heaven" ("Der Freischütz"), and was encored, when she again pleased her audience by a perfect rendering of "A bird sang in a hawthorn tree." Miss Brooks and Mr. Ernest Hensley sang Marzial's pretty duet, "Friendship," with a touch of true artistic merit. Mrs. Cowper Cooper sang several times during the evening, and much pleased the audience with Cowen's beautiful song, "Regret." Mr. Ernest Hensley was heard to advantage in "The Old Brigade," and better still in the encore it called forth, viz., "My Love is come," by Theo. Marzials. Mr. Webster, who was well received, played a violin solo, Sonata in G (Handel) in a masterly style, and also sang with good effect Molloy's "Three merry men are we." The same gentleman's fine bass voice excelled itself in Rossini's "Largo al factotum." The name of Mr. J. Maude Crament (Mus.Bac., Oxon), is sufficient guarantee that the accompaniments were ably played, if at times a trifle loud. The entire arrangements for the concert were undertaken by the Viscountess Grimston and Mr. Henry Toulmin, and they are to be heartily congratulated on the results of their labours.

SHERBORNE.—The concert given by the Sherborne School Musical Society on Easter Monday, the anniversary of Beethoven's death, was highly deserving of earnest praise for (says our Sherborne correspondent) it was really the finest of the many extremely good concerts given by this society. The great school-room was filled with a discriminating audience, and the scholars were seated in a gallery raised for the occasion. The orchestra was unquestionably the finest that has been heard in this part of the country. Mr. Louis N. Parker, the society's conductor, was in his usual place. The programme opened with the Easter hymn, "Jesus Christ is risen to-day, Alleluia." This was introduced by the trumpet, and sung by the choir and audience with grand effect. Beethoven's Symphony in C major (No. 1), Op. 22, was next performed, and it was selected for this occasion in honour of Beethoven's memory. All the most popular numbers from Handel's "Messiah" (with Mozart's additional accompaniments) comprised the next part of the programme. The solos were sung by Stuart, Penny, Sayres Bennett, Lewis, and Mr. R. S. Ainslie. The choruses went admirably, notwithstanding a slight weakness noticeable in the tenors. The next and concluding number was Wagner's "Siegfried Idyll." This is a unique specimen of Wagner's music; in the first place it is, with the exception of a juvenile symphony, and two or three marches written for special occasions, the only piece of abstract orchestral music written by him; in the second place, the means employed are of the simplest nature, the orchestra only consists of one flute, one hautboy, two clarinets, one bassoon, two horns, one trumpet, and the usual complement of strings. To Mr. L. N. Parker, the able and enthusiastic conductor, and to Mr. Regan, the instructor of the amateur element of the orchestra, the highest praise is due for the great success of this the seventy-first concert of the Society.

BATH.—At St. Mary's, Bathwick, on Good Friday, a large congregation assembled, when the Passion Music of Gounod's "Redemption" was sung for the Three Hours' Service." To many possibly the work may appear in some respects crude and over-wrought, and not sufficiently relieved by flowing melodies, as in the case of other oratorios, but it must be borne in mind that the thrilling incidents are all eminently dramatic, and that the composer has throughout manifestly approached his theme with an earnest feeling for its sacred character. Instances of the realistic portions are—the Condemnation, the going to Calvary, the Crucifixion, Mary at the foot of the Cross, the episode of the two Thieves, and the death of Jesus, the music consisting principally of a very plain style of recitative, *a tempo*, accompanied by subtle harmony, of simple song, generally even measured sounds which may almost be described as earnest speech in musical effect, of purely dramatic chorus, and of independent orchestral music. Whatever objection may be taken to the treatment of these passages, praise must be given to the points where the realistic attitude gives way to the poetic in the choruses, "Forth the Royal Banners go," "The Reproaches," "Beside the Cross," with the solo "While my watch," and the chorale "Lord Jesus." All of these are compositions of that rank to which only lofty genius can attain. Clear in form, chaste in melody, graphic in harmony, and deep with moral import, "The Reproaches," and "Beside the Cross," are particularly impressive. The several solos, choruses and chorales, were rendered with a precision and finish truly surprising, when we consider the small number of executants, notably the chorus of mockers and derisive chorus of priests, wherein the taunting crowd was graphically depicted. "The Reproaches," the quartet and chorus, "Beside the Cross," and the chorales. "While her watch she is keeping"—the contralto air having been first pathetically given by one of the boy choristers—and "Lord Jesus, thou to all bringest light and salvation," which is full of deep feeling, were impressively sung. Mr. Arthur Huff adroitly sustained the solo voices, while giving ample support and effect to the full choruses. His masterly execution of the "March to Calvary," and of the graphic descriptive movement representing the darkness was intensely realistic, and both himself and choir are to be congratulated on the success which attended their efforts and crowned the labour bestowed on the preparation of the work.

NORTHAMPTON.—The Northampton Choral Society gave their third public performance this season on Thursday evening, March 29th, at the Exchange Hall, which was nearly filled by an appreciative audience. Macfarren's cantata, "The Lady of the Lake," was selected for performance, and though the venture of attempting such a comparatively unknown and difficult work was great, the success which attended its interpretation justified the choice. To say that it was perfectly rendered would not be correct, the hoarseness of Mr. Frederick King, from whom so much had been expected, and the hitch which followed FitzJames's defiance in the 17th number, being sufficient to prevent the attainment of such a desirable result, but notwithstanding these disadvantages the performance was an extremely gratifying one, and reflective of great credit on the talented and painstaking conductor (Mr. Brook Sampson), the soloists, the chorus, and orchestra. The principal artists were Miss and Miss F. Robertson, soprano and contralto; Mr. Sydney Towers, tenor; Mr. F. King and Mr. A. W. Warren, basses; Mr. J. H. Twinn, leader of the band; Mr. R. W. Strickland, pianist; Miss Annie Lea and Miss L. Gray (pupils of Mr. Brook Sampson), harpists; and Mr. Twist, principal second violin. The band and chorus comprised upwards of 200 performers, and the *tout ensemble* of the whole (occupying for the first time the new orchestra erected for the directors of the Corn Exchange Company) was striking and impressive. One of the soloists was Mr. A. W. Warren, of Northampton. He was allotted the two minor characters of James, Earl of Douglas, and John of Brent. In the music set down for the latter he was most successful, his rendering of the rollicking soldier's song—"Our Vicar still preaches that Peter and Paul laid a swinging long curse on the bonny brown bowl"—being loudly re-demanded. Of Miss Robertson, as Ellen, and Miss F. Robertson, as Malcolm Græme and Blanche of Devan, nothing but praise can be spoken. The choruses which proved the greatest favourites were, "Hail to the Chief" (essentially Scottish in character), the description of Fitzjames's pursuit of Murdock, and the funeral song, "He is gone on the mountain," which was rendered with due solemnity and impressiveness, and which the audience compelled to be repeated. The effect of the concluding chorus was considerably marred by the disturbance made by a number of persons leaving the hall. Mr. Brook Sampson must be congratulated upon the proficiency which the members of the society have acquired during the two seasons that he has been their conductor. It is gratifying to find Professor Macfarren's fine and picturesque work gaining a well-deserved public appreciation in different directions.

On Good Friday Evening "The Messiah" was given at Victoria Park Congregational Church, capable of seating two thousand persons. The performance was under the direction of Mr. W. West, who also presided at the organ. The principal soloists were Mdme. Clara West, Miss C. Wollaston, Miss Lottie West, Mr. C. J. Murton, and Mr. C. Prickett. The choir consisted of 100 voices, and there was an efficient band, led by Mr. Lewis, of the Crystal Palace. Trumpet obbligato, Mr. Davin; conductor, Mr. John E. West. There was a good attendance, and the performance was admirable throughout,

Foreign Musical Intelligence.

MUSIC IN PARIS.

(*From our Own Correspondent.*)

PARIS, March 31st, 1883.

Should Art be national or universal? The question is asked here frequently in various ways, and answered variously, as the mood of the critics or the public may dictate. At present it is being mooted again, *apropos* of the journey of M. Vaucorbeil to Italy. The Manager of the Opera (who, it may be remarked in passing, has proved a bitter disappointment as a manager) has been away in Genoa, and the rumour runs that he has undertaken his journey for the sake of getting Verdi's consent to the production of his new work, "Iago," at the Opera. This has given rise to a storm of what I fear is not altogether disinterested "patriotic" indignation, and all the critics who have works of their own, or whose friends have works, waiting for a hearing, are excitedly enquiring whether it was for *this* M. Vaucorbeil had been drawing his 800,000 francs of subsidy yearly; and profess to be greatly scandalized at the notion of the composer of "Trovatore" being preferred to M. Salvayre and to the inevitable M. Massenet. The same commotion, I remember, was caused by the revival of "Aïda" soon after M. Vaucorbeil assumed the managerial reins some years ago. The same commotion would, I doubt not, be created were "Armide," or "Iphigenie en Aulide," or "Lohengrin," to be put upon the stage, in accordance with the promises made by the present manager of the Opéra at a time when (as a Paris chroniqueur unfeelingly puts it), "having failed to make his mark as a composer," he began to hunger for the emoluments and honour attaching to the post he has since obtained. In this matter, however, M. Vaucorbeil is more enlightened than his critics, and more liberal. The Opéra was not built, at enormous expense, for a few French composers of uncertain merit, but for the whole French people. So that the public is given the best procurable music, with the best possible interpretation, no one has the slightest right to grumble; and if it so happens that M. Vaucorbeil has reason to suppose Verdi's "Iago" is likely to be more interesting than M. Massenet's "Montalto," or M. Reyer's "Sigurd," why, so much the worse for MM. Massenet and Reyer. The young composer of "Le roi de Lahore," has had the sense to see the reasonableness of this himself. He has gracefully consented to waive his turn, and make way for some other aspirant to success at the Opéra. His "Montalto" is not ready, nor will it be, I expect, for at least a year to come. In any case, it can wait far better than "Iago" could if it were ready. But "Iago," too, is far from finished, unless my Milan correspondent is much mistaken, for Verdi has been devoting great part of his time lately to the revising of "Don Carlos," and, though he had at least planned out his new Shakesperian opera three years ago, he has not been able to terminate it. Besides, when it is finished, it will be first produced—not at the Paris Opéra, but at the Scala. The wrath of the Parisians is therefore decidedly premature, nor does it seem at all fair to M. Vaucorbeil—at the very moment, too, when (yielding, it is said, to the very strong pressure put upon him) he has just put M. Saint-Säens' "Henri VIII." on the stage.

This opera, by-the-bye, "goes" much better than it did, now that it has been lightened by the excision of a whole tableau in the third act, and modified in various other ways. The oftener it is heard, the more the beauties and ingenuities of the orchestration grow upon one; and though I am still of opinion that the work does not hang together or satisfy one as a whole, dramatically or musically, I cannot deny that it has made a more favourable impression on the public than could have been anticipated from the reception given it the first night.

M. Charles Gounod contributes an interesting article on M. Saint-Säens and "Henri VIII." to the current number of *La Nouvelle Revue* (dated 1st of April). The composer of "Faust" informs us that he had always known M. Saint-Säens would grow famous. He has, according to M. Gounod, one of the most astonishing musical organisations one could meet; knows all the great masters by heart (a doubtful compliment, this!) and has a prodigious power of assimilation (a still more doubtful compliment). "He could, if he wished, write a work after the manner of Rossini, Schumann, or Wagner. He knows them all by heart—the surest way, perhaps, to avoid imitating any of them. He is not distressed by fear of failing to produce his effects (a terrible anguish for the pusillanimous). He never 'exaggerates; so he is neither tricky, nor violent, nor emphatic. (N.B.—This seems to be aimed at M. Massenet, but it might be meditated on with profit by a good many other composers). . . . . He is neither pedantic, nor solemn, nor transcendental. He has remained too childlike, and become too skilful to be either. He has no particular system; belongs to no party, no clique; does not set up for being a reformer of anything whatever; and he writes as what he *feels* and *knows* prompts him. Mozart did not reform anything; yet for all that I believe he stood at the summit of his art . . ."

The conclusion of the article is thoroughly and heartily eulogistic:—

" So now, my dear Saint-Saëns, your name is attached to one of the works which have done most honour to French art and our National Academy of Music. To those who knew you as a child (I am of the number) your destiny was certain. You had a musical childhood: unwearingly watched over by your intelligent and generous mother, you had the great masters of the art for your foster-fathers. They made you robust and strong to pursue your course. Fame had long gone before you, and prepared the way for the popularity which the stage seems exclusively privileged to bestow. All that you lacked to complete your prestige was one brilliant dramatic success; and now you have that, go on, then, dear and great musician. Your course is victorious all along the line. Inasmuch as you have been faithful to your art, the future shall be faithful to your work. God has given you light, and a master hand. May He preserve them long to you, both for your sake and for ours."

P.S.—April 1st. M. Albert Caher's mythological cantata, " Endymion," was given for the first time to-day, with fair success, at the Cirque d'Hiver, under the personal direction of the composer. I shall return to this in my next letter. At to-day's Châtelet concert, M. Colonne gave us an astounding programme, including the following works :—

"Manfred" (Poème dramatique de Lord Byron).... Schumann.
"L'Arlesienne," musique pour le drame d'Alphonse Daudet .... G. Bizet.
  1. Prélude—2. Minuetto—3 Adagietto—4. Carillon.
Marche Funèbre, pour la dernière scène "d'Hamlet." Berlioz.
"Béatrice et Bénédict" (Duo)..................... Berlioz.
"Roméo et Juliette".............. "............ Berlioz.
  (a) Scène d'amour—(b) Scherzo de la reine Mab—(c) Tristesse de Roméo—(d) Fête chez Capulet.

The Châtelet campaign will be brought to a brilliant close next Sunday with Berlioz's " Damnation of Faust."
C. HARRY MELTZER.

Gounod's Redemption " has been given in Hamburg.

Boito's " Mefistofele " has much pleased the people of Stockholm.

" Le Trésor," a new opera, music by M. Lefebure, recently scored a success at Angers.

The death is announced of Wagner's sister, Attilie, widow of Herr Hermann Brockhaus, of Leipsig.

Verdi's early opera, " La Force du Destin," is said to have entirely failed on its recent revival at Antwerp.

The Rossini prize of 3000 francs for the best opera libretto has been awarded to M. Georges Bayer, editor of the Paris *Figaro*, who was one of 169 competitors.

On Good Friday the " Société des Concerts," in connection with the Paris Conservatoire, gave a very fine performance of the " Enfance du Christ," by Berlioz. M. Guilmant presided at the organ.

An oratorio by M. Adolphe Deslandres, " Les Sept Paroles du Christ," was performed at Versailles lately, under the composer's direction, and also at Limoges, being well received in both places.

Owing to the enforced absence of Mr. Humphrey Stark, Mus.Bac., at the concert given on Friday last, at Gresham Hall, Brixton, Mr. Frank Bradley presided at the grand pianoforte, and accompanied Stainer's " Daughter of Jairus," besides playing a piano solo, Schumann's " Novelletten," and also the accompaniments to the miscellaneous selection.

THE POSITION OF THE CHOIR AND ORGANS IN CHURCHES.*

THE importance of music as an accompaniment to the service of the Almighty has been acknowledged in every age and by every form of religious worship with which history has made us acquainted ; and to realise the extraordinary attention which this branch of sacred art received at the hands of the people of old, we have only to open the Holy Scriptures and read the account given in the Second Book of Chronicles of the dedication of Solomon's Temple, in which we are told that there were present, amongst others, " the Levites which were the singers, all of them of Asaph, of Heman, of Jeduthun, with their sons and their brethren, being arrayed in white linen, having cymbals and psalteries and harps, stood at the east end of the altar, and with them an hundred and twenty priests sounding with trumpets." In the earliest days of Christianity we also read of " singing hymns," and all through the Middle Ages the same importance continued to be given to music in connexion with the services of the Church. Charlemagne, who, we should have thought, had quite enough business upon his hands to occupy all his time, yet considered it his duty to become acquainted with the discussions going on as to the correct number of the Gregorian " modes " or tones to be used in church music ; and Robert, king of France, absolutely conducted the choir of his royal chapel, arrayed in his coronation robes!

Although the Eastern Church also cultivated music, yet there was a great divergence of practice ; the Western Church admitting the use of instrumental accompaniment, and the Eastern Church strictly prohibiting it. However, it should be noted that the use of instrumental accompaniments is not, and never was, universal even in the West, and it is a well-known fact that neither organ nor orchestra has ever been admitted into the Pope's own chapel, the Sistine, nothing but pure vocal music being allowed. I believe also that the Cistercian and several other religious orders are forbidden by their rules [to have anything but vocal music in their churches. Until some twenty-five years back instrumental accompaniments were forbidden in the diocese of Lyons, and the Roman Church still prohibits the use even of the organ at high mass on the Sundays of Lent and Advent.

Long before the Reformation, most large churches in England possessed one or more organs. Durham Cathedral in the fourteenth century had as many as five. The Reformation in England does not seem to have had any perceptible effect upon church music, and in most cases the organs remained. The case was very different, however, with the Revolution. The Puritans seem to have vented their spite upon organs more than on any other article of church furniture except alone the altar, and a very lively account of their proceedings at Peterborough is given in " Mercurius Rusticus," but which is too long to quote here.

To the German Lutherans, however, must be allowed the credit of having developed the organ into the magnificent instrument which it has now become, and the immortal genius of John Sebastian Bach has given a literature to the instrument such as is possessed by no other, and is scarcely surpassed by the orchestra itself.

Ecclesiastical music had fallen into a very low condition in this country some forty years back, and those who are old enough can well recollect the state of things which then existed. The cathedral choirs were, of course, an exception, but even in cathedrals the organs were totally inadequate, few of them possessing a properly-arranged pedal-board, and all of them tempered according to the wretched old system, by which music could only be played in about three keys, and if written in any other it had to be transposed. These instruments, however, often had a fine effect of tone, from their position upon the choir-screen. The organs in parochial churches were, as a rule, dismal affairs. It is true that a few organs by Father Smith, Renatus Harris, etc., were to be found in some of the City churches ; but even these would be looked upon as totally inadequate to modern requirements, although they undoubtedly possessed a delicacy of tone that was very charming as far as it went. The choirs in parochial churches scarcely deserved the name, and in village churches the music was often ridiculous. Organs were almost unknown, and the terrific instruments of torture, the " seraphin," the barrel-organ, and the " self-acting grinder," were amongst the favourite substitutes. The shocking tricks which these instruments played often caused consternation amongst the worshippers. I knew of a " self-acting grinder " which had the disagreeable habit of occasionally treating the congregation to the whole of its twelve tunes, one after another, if by accident the man in charge did not make a rush at it and hit a certain knob or button just at the right minute. And a friend of mine related to me a very remarkable scene at which he was present, and which happened at a village church in Buckinghamshire many years ago. A hand-grinding organ was the hero in this case. The " professional " performer upon the instrument happened to be absent, and an amateur undertook to serve for him. When the hymn was given out he took hold of the

---

* A paper by Mr. H. W. Brewer, read before the Architectural Association, on the 2nd inst., and as reported in the *Builder*.

handle and ground and ground away, but nothing came of it all but a wheezing sound. In a state of intense alarm the unfortunate performer rushed to the front of the gallery and cried out, "Oh, yer reverence, this 'ere organ has gone and busted itself!"

The old village orchestras, which may possibly have been of value in earlier times had died out or dwindled away until they had become worse than useless. I recollect a very old clerk in a church near Norwich, who used to lead the singing with a cracked clarionet, and I remember his telling me that many years ago there was a band, of which he was the only survivor. As, however, he told me this nearly thirty years back, and he was then over eighty, probably the band had been given up sixty or seventy years ago.

The very remarkable revival of ecclesiastical music in this country during the past thirty or forty years, and the wonderful development of the organ during the same period, have of necessity had an effect upon our ecclesiastical architecture and the arrangement of churches and chapels; for, wonderful as has been the improvement of the musical arrangements in Anglican churches, it has been equally remarkable amongst Congregationalists and Dissenters generally. In years gone by a hymn bawled in unison was considered sufficiently artistic in places where now one will hear first-rate choral singing, accompanied by a very excellent organ. Oratorios and organ recitals are also greatly favoured by our Nonconformist fellow-countrymen, who are doing much for the development of musical taste in connexion with religious worship.

In the Roman Catholic churches of Germany a somewhat remarkable movement has taken place in connexion with ecclesiastical music. It is the abandonment of the orchestra and the orchestral style of composition, of which Mozart and Haydn were such notable masters; and the revival of the earlier and severer or vocal style which is exemplified by the magnificent compositions of Palestrina, De Lasso, and others. The disappearance of the orchestra is leading to increased importance being given to the organ. Pugin complained some thirty years back that when the choir struck up in Cologne Cathedral, with its orchestral accompaniments, the columns and arches of the building seemed to disappear, and to become replaced by the pit, boxes, and stage of the Italian Opera. He would find no cause for that complaint now, as the operatic singing is replaced by the severest church compositions, and the orchestra has been abolished, and is about to be replaced by the largest church organ ever erected. This movement has now spread so far in Germany that in addition to the cathedral of Cologne it has been adopted in those of Ratisbon, Mayence, Aix-la-Chapelle, Münster, Eichstätt, Treves, Leichtmorits, etc.

I have been obliged to dwell upon these musical facts at some length because they serve to show that the organ is every day becoming a more and more important adjunct to religious services, and during the last thirty years the progress which has been made in organ-building, and the enormous improvement which has taken place in everything connected with that instrument, is a remarkable fact in the history of music. Those who compare the organs erected half a century back with the magnificent instruments constructed by our leading English firms at the present time are simply astounded at the ingenious inventions and contrivances which have been introduced to overcome difficulties which rendered the older organs generally almost unplayable, and always most fatiguing to the performer. It must not, however, be forgotten that the more perfect the organ is the larger its bulk becomes; and the greater becomes the difficulty of the architect in finding a suitable place for it in a church or chapel.

In Mediæval times, and, in fact, as a general rule, until some thirty or forty years back, the organ gave an architect little trouble. As long as it was inclosed in a case some 10 ft. by 5 ft., and about 16 ft. high, it could be placed almost anywhere, and it did not demand consideration in planning a church; but when the same thing becomes a structure 20 ft. square and 30 ft. high, it can no longer be ignored, and provision must be made for it or it will become a serious disfigurement to the building. The difficulty must be boldly grappled with. It is simply useless for an architect to complain of the size of an organ or to suggest that it should be made smaller, so as to occupy less space; he might just as well complain of the size of a dining-table when he is designing a dining-room. The thing is wanted, and must be provided for, and the architect must discover some means of meeting the difficulty. I acknowledge that it is often a serious difficulty, but there is not the slightest chance of its vanishing or even becoming modified, as in all probability organs will get larger and larger as time goes on. All attempts at decreasing their size have hitherto proved complete failures.

There are, of course, several things to be taken into consideration in selecting the position for an organ. The first, and most important, is that the instrument should be placed where it will be heard to the best advantage. The second is that it should be in such a situation that it may be serviceable both for the choir and also for congregational singing. The third, that it should be placed where it will be secure from injury arising from damp, excessive draughts, variations of heat and cold, and, especially, leaky roofs: the gutter of a roof should never, under any circumstances, be carried over an organ; yet, in two new churches

which I have lately seen, the organ is placed under the valley between two roofs. In another church, recently restored at great expense, I noticed, a few weeks' since, that the gutter over the organ was insufficient; the consequence was that the open diapasons were receiving a regular *douche*, and the water was running out of the lips of the pipes! I pointed this out to the sexton, who was showing me over the church, and he said, "Well, sir, our organist do complain. A few Sundays back the water came down on his head during morning service; but what can be done? Our parson has spent a deal of money over that roof!" I suggested that at any rate the organ ought to be removed. Lastly, an organ must be placed in such a position that it is, if not an ornament to the building, at least no disfigurement to it.

Now, there are not many positions which a large organ can occupy in a church so as to fulfil all these conditions, and it is not surprising that it should have created a new feature in church architecture,—the organ chamber, which seems to be popular amongst Anglican Clergy, as it is to be found in very many new churches and has been added to not a few ancient ones, sometimes, I am bound to say, not to their improvement. It is, in fact, greatly to be doubted whether it is always advisable to remove an organ from the western gallery, where it has formerly stood, to place it in a kind of black-hole at the side of the chancel. This is often done under the idea that the position is more in accordance with ancient usage; but, in point of fact, while there is plenty of Mediæval authority for the western choir and organ gallery, there is none that I know of for an organ-chamber, which is an essentially modern feature in church architecture. Ancient organs in western galleries occur at Amiens Cathedral, the Cathedral of Constance, St. Mary's, Lübeck, St. Anne's, Augsburg, and St. Ulrich's, Augsburg; and although the organs have disappeared, or have been rebuilt, ancient western organ-lofts are to be seen at St. Stephen's, Vienna, Ulm, Liège, St. Mary's, Wurzburg, Ochsenfurth, the Carmelite Church at Boppard, St. Pantaleon at Cologne, &c. The last-named example, however, is so singular in its arrangement that it may have been removed from some other position. The reason for placing an organ in an organ-chamber is that it may be near the choir, who are now usually placed in the chancel. Whether a choir of laymen was, in the Middle Ages, commonly placed in the chancel seems doubtful. That the chancel was nothing like so universal a position for the singers as is generally supposed, seems proved by the arrangement of many ancient churches; for instance, in the old Abbey Church of Cornelimünster, near Aix-la-Chapelle, the choir, with its stalls and complete ritual arrangement, is to be seen in the western gallery. The same is the case in one of the earlier abbey churches, that of Seligenthal, near Landshut, where the front of the choir gallery is adorned with a series of beautiful old pictures, and the interior fitted with regular choir-stalls. The same arrangement is to be noticed at the Abbey of St. Maximin at Trèves, though unfortunately here the whole of this interesting portion of the church is much modernised. At the minster church at Roermond, the arrangement of the choir was very singular; it was divided into two parts, each of which occupied one of the triforia of the nave. Each triforium choir terminated to the east in a small apse, bracketed out into the transept, containing an altar, both of which still exist. The original high altar also exists, not in the great apse, but in a smaller apse projecting from its eastern extremity. Mr. Cuypers, who has very carefully restored this church, believes the position to be original There is a rather later western organ-gallery, but the whole is thirteenth-century work. The curious church called the Alte Pfarrkirche, at Ratisbon, contains a singularly small chancel, only about 10 ft. square, but has a very deep choir gallery at the west end. The stalls have been removed, but the marks of where they were fixed can still be traced; the date is thirteenth century. At Coburg there was evidently a western choir in a gallery, with a little apse built out over the principal doorway; the arrangement is very picturesque externally. At Limburg-on-the-Lahn, the great triforium, which is vaulted and furnished with several altars, is called "männerchor"; whether it really served the purposes of a choir is a question which it is not possible to settle, but the name would seem to suggest it.

Notwithstanding the fury which has of late years been exercised against western organs and choir galleries, there is much to be said in their favour, and it would perhaps be well to hesitate before removing them, especially in old churches. The west end of a church is an excellent situation for a large organ, both musically and as regards its appearance. The splendid examples at Lubeck and Bois-le-Duc, and St. Anne's, Augsburg, serve to show what a fine feature can be made of an organ in this position. Musically speaking, also, the western gallery is a good position for a choir, and the arrangement lends itself very well to congregational singing. Much good carving and excellent work has been destroyed by the wholesale removal of west-end organ galleries. I cannot help also regretting the destruction of the numerous fine Renaissance organ cases which have disappeared, together with the western organ-galleries.

The organs in cathedral churches in England, at any rate, were generally placed upon the chancel or rood-screen, and it is impossible to suggest a better situation for the instrument, as every single favourable condition is here complied with. The organ has plenty of space about it and it is consequently sure to sound well. It is away from any walls which could convey its sound out of the building; it is excellent for choir work, and also for congregational purposes; it is more safe from damp and draughts than in any other part of the building, and less liable to variations of temperature. The position has also the sanction of antiquity, as it is recorded that there were organs upon the rood-screens of Durham, Peterborough, York, and Winchester cathedrals, long before the Reformation. In Continental churches a few organs still exist in this position. The Cathedral of Bruges, and that of St. Gomarre at Lierre, are cases in point, though, singularly, in the latter church the organ is sunk into the screen in such a way as to be invisible from the nave of the church. The removal of organs from choir-screens has been greatly in favour of late years, but I trust to live to see them all replaced in their former position. It seems that King Charles I. inaugurated this movement by ordering the removal of the organ in York Minster because it prevented the great east window being seen from the nave. It was, however, subsequently replaced.

When the organ is placed upon the choir-screen, one of two things seem to suggest themselves: either the congregation should be excluded from the choir, or the singers should be placed in the organ gallery, The present plan of mixing up the congregation and singers in the choir-stalls of the English cathedrals has many great objections. In the first place, it is not edifying to look down the throat of a man just opposite who is singing a solo, nor is it advisable to recognise too distinctly any individual singer in a church. One may have heard him sing music of a very different character, under very different circumstances, which it is undesirable to associate with his present performance, and yet the mind cannot help making this association, to the entire destruction of all solemn thoughts and religious feelings. It is also a great advantage to every choir to have a conductor, and not to trust too implicitly to the organist. Where music in the style of Palestrina is sung unaccompanied, a conductor becomes absolutely necessary. Now a conductor is strangely out of place in the middle of a congregation.

The destruction of choir screens, both here and on the Continent, is to be regretted. Not only are these screens great ornaments to churches, but they are of considerable use for musical purposes. The magnificent rood-screens at Münster and Bois-le-Duc were, when I first recollect them, used positively as choir-screens, and the effect was remarkably fine. Both have now, unfortunately, been removed. I am told that the screens at Tournay and Bruges are threatened with the same fate, chiefly because they are not Gothic! Some years back the choir of Norwich Cathedral sang from the screen, and I fancy there must be ancient authority for this usage. In France the rood-screen is called "jubé," and I cannot help associating this name with the first word of the Complin Service,—"Jube domne benedicere." Possibly the Complin Service may have been sung from the rood-loft, and hence the name "jubé," as given to this feature of Church architecture. In Germany the rood screen is called by a different term in almost every church. At Münster it was called "Apostelgang,"—I fancy, from the statues of the Apostles which adorned it. At Halberstadt it is called "Bishofstuhl" or "ambon"; whether it really served as a bishop's throne or no, it is impossible to say. At Hildesheim it is called "Letner," a word closely akin to our word lectern,—probably because the Gospel was read from it. It should be noted that, although the rood-screen has generally been destroyed in France, yet the Gospel is always read from the place where it formerly stood. In some old descriptions of churches I have found the words 'pulpitum," "paradisus," used to signify the rood-screen.

Another position for the choir is to the rear of the altar. It is certainly the most ancient of all positions, as may be seen by the arrangement of the basilican churches. It is an excellent position from every point of view, and remarkably convenient, especially in apsidal churches. The great difficulty, however, is the organ. In French churches, where this arrangement is not uncommon, there are generally two organs,—one a small instrument for the choir, and the other placed in the nave of the church for voluntaries and congregational purposes. The disadvantage of this is, of course, its expense, as it necessitates two organs and two organists. I am aware that there is an invention by means of which the same organist can play both organs at once by the application of electricity. It would be very desirable that this invention should succeed, but owing to the expense, or some mechanical difficulties, it has not met with the success which one could wish. I trust, however, that it will not be lost sight of, for, if it could be made thoroughly practicable, it would solve many difficulties, and it may turn out to be of the greatest possible value, both from an architectural and musical point of view.

(To be continued.)

It is stated that Mr. Walter Van Noorden, the son of Mr. P. E. Van Noorden, an esteemed composer and teacher, has been awarded a scholarship at the Guildhall School of Music for pianoforte playing and general musical talents.

PRINCIPAL CONTENTS OF THIS NUMBER.

LONDON: SATURDAY, APRIL 7, 1883.

THE PROFESSIONAL STAFF OF THE ROYAL COLLEGE OF MUSIC.

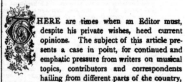

THERE are times when an Editor must, despite his private wishes, heed current opinions. The subject of this article presents a case in point, for continued and emphatic pressure from writers on musical topics, contributors and correspondents hailing from different parts of the country, demand attention on this topic; and I must, perforce, either find room separately for the expression of some of these different opinions, or speak of them collectively in one article, the course I have elected to pursue. My decision in this matter has gained strength from the fact that my esteemed contributors and correspondents have, without any want of respect for the eminent artists forming the professional staff of the Royal College of Music, thought well to criticise but not to express approval in, the general selection of the professors, as forming in their estimation an incomplete representation of our present artistic strength. It is perhaps needless to add that I only propose to quote a few typical opinions. One of our most distinguished country professors pleads disappointment on the ground that the chosen staff is not representative enough, inasmuch as a large number of our chief exponents of different departments of the art have been overlooked, including the most prominent men in certain branches of artistic skill. One contributor, holding a leading position in the metropolis, but not connected with any scholastic institutions, is anxious, while acknowledging the individual merits of many of the selected professors, to express his opinion, that the list should have been made from the very first an exceedingly strong one, even in excess of the present teaching requirements of the College, in order to have secured a large national confidence in the policy of recognising merit apart from extraneous influences, both as regards the selection of teachers and the election of scholars. He further protests that the staff ought in the departments of singing and pianoforte playing to have been made stronger in lady teachers, who are at present he considers quite inadequately represented. One writer is anxious to know why Mr. SIMS REEVES' name is not on the list, seeing that that gentleman was understood to have made the noble offer of undertaking the duties of a teacher gratuitously. It seems to me unnecessary to pursue this matter further, especially as I am anxious not to prejudice the work to be done at the Royal College, or to impede in any way the building up of an important institution, even though I know that criticism must naturally be advanced, and will rightfully claim the daylight of the press upon the proposals as well as upon the doings of those responsible for the conduct of an institution claiming national proportions. It would have been impossible for the authorities to have satisfied all sections of the musical world in their selection of assistants. At the same time, it would have been prudent to have advanced in the selection of professors a little more beyond the lines of the National Training School. However, a dispassionate examination of the list will, one rejoices to observe, convince the reader of the presence of much intellectual and practical strength. It would be unreasonable to expect the College authorities to go far afield in their selection of professors. The ramifications of social and artistic society are too complicated to admit of the selection of any body of teachers upon the simple ground of recognised merit. Social advantages, the being near at hand, and the influence of friendly impulses, are motive powers which must inevitably, and will often righteously, play their part in every scheme of this kind. Again, the selection of a small number of good instructors for a prominent institution does not in the least interfere with the usefulness of the large number of eminent artists who could not be included in any plan save of a very comprehensive character. And it cannot be expected that the Royal College will be called upon to train more than a small percentage of the rich national stores of musical talent. It must be a source of congratulation to the governing powers of the Royal Academy of Music, to note that a goodly number of their professors and students have been accepted as professors in the Royal College of Music. Now the selection is made, and it includes many notable names to justify the hope, it is the business of all to wait patiently and hopefully for good results from the labours of the distinguished artists chosen. The raison d'être of the Royal College will be proved satisfactorily to the nation through the results gained, rather than through any speculative theories, however attractive, as to the present call for the existence of such an institution.　　E. H. TURPIN.

THE PASSION PLAY AT NICE.

THE account of the performance of the Passion Play at Nice jars greatly with the feelings which obtain over such solemn subjects in England. The practice of giving at Easter a dramatic representation of the last scenes of our Saviour's life is a very ancient one, and in old times it was not without its uses. But to give a performance of these holy mysteries in a modern theatre with a grand orchestra, stage decorations, and the electric light pressed into service to illuminate the figure on the cross, seems singularly incongruous, when we remember the simplicity which surrounded the inception of Christianity. The old mysteries were played in the open air without footlights or scenery of any kind, and their simple idealism probably strengthened men's faith far more than all the realism of the modern stage-art can ever do. The behaviour of the audience, and their applause and laughter, hardly affords surprise to those who are painfully aware that most of the modern Italians are devoid of any religious sentiment whatever. But musicians, who remember that oratorio had its origin in Italy, and can recall the noble works of PALESTRINA, LEO, DURANTE, VITTORIA, and other great composers that that gifted land has produced, cannot but experience a painful shock to learn that the music played during the progress of the sacred drama, given on Good Friday last, consisted of Suppé's overture to "The Poet and Peasant," which introduced the representation, dance music being played between the tableaux, the agony in the garden of Gethsemane being preceded by the "Fleur de Noblesse" waltz.　　T. L. S.

THE LOGIC OF COUNTERPOINT.

THIRD SERIES.

V.

IN the next rule given CHERUBINI tells us that: "As "in two and in three-part counterpoint, so in "four-parts, in the first species, parts may occa- "sionally be crossed for the space of two or three "measures at the utmost." This privilege, the theorist considers. "may effect the avoidance of many "faults, and induce at times a melodic flow in the "parts." Opinions differ as to the crossing of parts ; some authorities objecting entirely to the setting up of such a privilege, and others allowing the exceptional use of such progressions in four-parts ; for the liberty of occasionally being allowed to cross the parts in counterpoint of six, seven, or eight parts must, of course, be regarded as a necessary privilege at times. Undoubtedly there are serious objections to the crossing of vocal parts ; for sympathetic vocal tones are not so distinctly traceable as are the less sympathetic and widely different sounds of distinct kinds of instruments, which may indeed be crossed for exceptional harmonic effects with decided gain now and then. Again, the voice parts suffer more than instruments from being disadvantageously placed as regards their different registers. On the whole, it is better for the student to deny himself the questionable privilege of crossing the parts in four-part counterpoint of the first species intended for voices. Next CHERUBINI repeats the unrelaxable admonition against the presence of consecutive perfect concords, whether octaves or fifths. He adds : " But two fifths " may be tolerated by contrary movement between " any two of the upper three parts, and between any " two of three lower parts. They are sometimes," he continues, " allowable between the two external " parts, but the permission for such progressions must " not be abused; and it is only available when all " other means of movement are found to be in vain." The student will not fail to notice the increase in the number of licensed progressions with the advance in the number of the parts to four. Now, if he be thoroughly in earnest in his contrapuntal work, he will regard each license as it is brought before him with watchful suspicion; inasmuch as the admission of every such license is liable to arise from weakness as well as from necessity. The permission to employ consecutive fifths by contrary motion in four parts is just one of those licenses to be regarded with wariness and circumspection. Their presence, whether between external or middle, or between one external and another internal voice part, is surely felt by a fairly keen ear to be only in a less degree objectionable than are such combinations when taken in direct motion. CHERUBINI does not seem inclined to sanction the license of octaves in contrary motion between two given parts. In truth, such a progression is, on the whole, more unsatisfactory than is the effect of two adjacent perfect fifths in contrary motion ; for the octaves are weaker in their reiterated sounds than are the fifths, and they tend to produce a colourless and inefficiently pronounced harmony.

E. H. TURPIN.

Organ News.

LIVERPOOL.

Mr. W. T. Best gave an organ recital in St. George's Hall, on Thursday, March 29th :—

Overture (" Si j'etais roi ")..................... Adam.
Siciliana in D minor, Tema con variazioni in E maj. Weber.
Fantasia in F minor............................ Mozart.
Andante Cantabile in G major, No. 2............ Wesley.
Introduction and Allegro in D major........... Bache.

And on Thursday, April 5th :—

Overture (" Giulio Cesare ").................... Handel.
Andante in F major............................ Wesley.
Introduction, Pastoral Chorus, and " L'Appel aux
    Armes" (" Le Prophète "................... Meyerbeer.
Adagio and Fugue in E major................... Best.
" Marche des Templiers " .... Benedict.

CRYSTAL PALACE.

Mr. A. J. Eyre's programmes on Saturday week comprised the following :—

Selection (" Meistersinger").................... Wagner.
Sanctus.. Rossini.
Minuet and Trio................................ Bridge.
March in C..................................... Weber.
Andante in D................................... Smart.
Marche Heroïque................................ Schubert.
Pastorale and Minuet........................... Bennett.
Intermezzo..................................... Macbeth.
Canzonet....................................... Chipp.
Elegy in F minor............................... Chipp.
    (in memoriam F. W. Clarke, Mus. Bac., obiit 22nd March).
Selection (" Messiah ").......................... Handel.

And on Saturday last :—

Concerto in B flat, No. 2...................... Handel.
Adagio in F, from a Sonata..................... Beethoven.
Bourrée and variations in B minor.............. Bach.
Serenade, from a Quartet....................... Haydn.
Concert Fugue in G............................. Krebs.
" Die Lotosblume," " Die beiden Grenadiers"..... Schumann.
Chorus of Nobles (" Belshazzar")............... Handel.
" Holzworthy Bells "........................... Wesley.
" Fixed in His everlasting seat"............... Handel.
Vocal Duets.................................... Mendelssohn.
Selection (" Faust ")........................... Gounod.

PRESTON.

Subjoined are the programmes of organ recitals given in the new Public Hall, by Mr. James Tomlinson, on Saturday, March 31st :—

AFTERNOON RECITAL.

Introduction and Allegro (Symphony in D)....... Haydn.
Andante con moto............................... Chipp.
Minuette....................................... Handel.
Overture (" Stradella ")....................... Flotow.
Adagio (Symphony in B flat).................... Beethoven.
Marche Triomphale.............................. Guilmant.

EVENING RECITAL.

Sinfonia (" Last Judgment ").................... Spohr.
Variations on " Carillons de Dunkerque "....... E. H. Turpin.
Pilgrim's March (Fourth Symphony)............. Mendelssohn.
Overture (" Il Barbiere di Sevigilia ")........ Rossini.
" Serenade," " The Rei King ".................. Schubert-Liszt.
Variations and Finale on " God save the King ". Rinck.

NORWICH.

Annexed is the programme of an organ recital given in St. Andrew's Hall, by Dr. Bunnett, F.C.O., on Saturday, March 31st :—

Easter March................................... Merkel.
Elevation (Romanze with Chorale)............... Stark.
Allegro and Fugue (Symphony in C minor)........ Haydn.
" An der Wiege " (Cradle song)................. Lange.
Concerto in G.................................. Bach.
Minuet and Trio................................ Hoyte.
Selection (" Faust ").......................... Berlioz.
" Funeral March of a Marionette "............. Gounod.
Overture (" Der Freischütz ")................. Weber.

MANCHESTER.

Mr. J. Kendrick Pyne gave an organ recital in the Town Hall, on Saturday, March 31st. Subjoined is the programme :—

Coronation anthem, " Zadok the Priest "........ Handel.
Gavotte in D major, for violoncello............ Bach.
Sonata in F sharp major........................ Rheinberger.
Andante in A major............................. Smart.
Cavatina, " Rose softly blooming "............. Spohr.
Fantasia on old English airs.

BOLTON.

An organ recital was given in the Albert Hall, by Mr. Wm. Mullineux, F.C.O., on Saturday, March 31st. The following was the programme :—

Sonata in A major, No. 3....................... Mendelssohn.
" Chant d'un Ange "............................ De Lange.
Grand Chœur Triomphale in A.................... Guilmant.
Adagio (Second Sonata)......................... Roselich.
Selection (" Faust,") Marche Cortège (" Irène ") Gounod.

BURTON-ON-TRENT.

Mr. A. B. Plant, Mus.Bac., Oxon., F.C.O., gave a recital in St. Paul's Institute, on Wednesday, March 28th. The programme included :—

Overture (" Zanetta ")......................... Auber.
Marche Religiosa............................... Perelli.
Marche Funèbre et Chant Séraphique............. Guilmant.
Gavotte (Louis Quinze)......................... Lee.
Allegretto in B flat........................... Lemmens.
" Lieder ohne Worte".......................... Mendelssohn.
March.. Gounod.

EDINBURGH.

Mr. William Blakeley, A.C.O., gave an organ recital in the United Presbyterian Church, Morningside, on Monday, March 26th. Subjoined is the programme :—

Overture (" The Chaplet ")..................... Boyce.
March, " Balmoral "............................ Linn.
Prelude and Fugue in C minor................... Bach.
Original Air with variations................... Blakeley.
Sonata in D minor, No. 2....................... Merkel.
Largo.. Handel.
Aria... Louis XIII.
Overture (" Der Freischütz ").................. Weber.

NORFOLK.

On Easter Day the new organ recently constructed in the parish church of Ingham by Messrs. Bevington and Sons was opened by Mr. J. W. Wilson. The following music was played upon the occasion :—

Andante in F................................... Smart.
Religious Fantasia............................. Wilson.
Offertoire in G minor.......................... Wély.
Andantino in E minor........................... Batiste.
March of the Priests........................... Mendelssohn.
" I know that my Redeemer".................... Handel.
Festal March................................... Riwry.
" Hallelujah " (" Messiah ")................... Handel.

WHITLEY.

An organ recital was given in Christ Church by Mr. F. J. Read, Mus.Bac., Oxon., on Wednesday, March 28th, with the annexed programme :—

Sonata No. 2	Mendelssohn.
Andante (Quartet in D)	Mozart.
Adagio and Toccata in C	Bach.
Romance (" La Reine de France ")	Haydn.
Air with variations	Smart.
Prière in F, and Grand Chorus	Guilmant.

LEEDS.

Dr. Spark gave a recital on the grand organ in the Town Hall (No. 3 of the series), on Saturday, March 31st, when the programme consisted of works by Haydn, and included :—" Kyrie Eleison" (Second Mass); Introduction and Air varied in G major; Minuet and Trio (11th Symphony); Selection ("The Seasons"); Andante in C major) "Surprise" Symphony); "God preserve the Emperor"; Selection ("The Creation.")

TUNBRIDGE WELLS.

The following selections were played on Sunday evenings in March at St. Mary's Church, Hartfield, by Mr. Wm. H. Barry, A.Mus., T.C.L. :—

Adagio (Sonata No. 1)	Mendelssohn.
Sonata No. 3	Mendelssohn.
"Albumblatt," and March in C	Wagner.
"Evening Prayer"	Smart.
Offertoire in A	Wély.
Aria, " My heart ever faithful "	Bach.
Romanza in G	Beethoven.
Air. "There is a green hill"	Gounod.
War March (" Athalie ")	Mendelssohn.
Andante in E minor	Batiste.
Marche Funèbre	Chopin.
Andante, from a Sonata	Mendelssohn.
Chorus, "Hallelujah," and aria, "I know that my Redeemer liveth" (" Messiah ")	Handel.
Overture in D	Haydn.

HEREFORDSHIRE.

The following is the specification of an organ erected in Kingsland Church, by Messrs. Brindley & Foster, of Sheffield :—

GREAT ORGAN, CC TO G.

1. Open Diapason	8 ft.	4. Harmonic Flute	8 ft.
2. Gedact	8 „	5. Flute	4 „
3. Dulciana	8 „	6. Clarionet	8 „

SWELL ORGAN, CC TO G.

7. Viol da Gamba	8 „	10. Salicet	4 ft.
8. Lieblich Gedact	8 „	11. Oboe	8 „
9. Salicional	8 „		

PEDAL ORGAN, CCC TO F.

12. Bourdon		16 ft.

COUPLERS.

13. Swell to Great.	16. Swell Sub Octave.
14. Swell to Pedal.	17. Swell Super Octave.
15. Great to Pedal.	

Two Composition Pedals.

BOW AND BROMLEY INSTITUTE.

The popular notion that ladies do not succeed entirely as organ players, would be considerably disturbed in the minds of those entertaining the idea who chanced to be present at the recital of March 31st. Although one does not like the notion of a lady struggling with a big organ and engaged in work so trying and requiring such courage and watchful power as recital playing, save in rare instances, perhaps, it must be acknowledged that ladies can play the organ, and as pedalists are exceedingly neat and sure-footed, possibly by reason of incessant practice in measuring distances by their feet without being able, as men are in walking and pedal-playing, to watch their pedal movements. On the other hand, the power and grandeur of a large organ would seem to be best handled by the sterner strength of the "lords of creation," to say nothing of questions of mental power, which the writer will not venture upon, lest his opinions bring him into "hot water." Miss Theresa Beney, A.C.O., is indeed a very gifted young lady organist, and not without some playing experience. She succeeded best in Merkel's Fantasia and Fugue in A minor, and in Bach's Toccata in F, in which the aptitude of a lady for pedal playing was admirably illustrated, and Miss Beney's special executive skill was abundantly displayed. The opening piece was Wagner's " Tannhäuser " march. An allegretto by Gade, the minuet and trio in Bennett's symphony, and Smart's Prelude in D, all nicely manipulated, were the other organ solos. Mr. E. W. Parfitt played with Miss Beney Merkel's well known Duo for violin and organ. He also played a solo cleverly, and Handel's Largo was played by violin, organ, and pianoforte, Mr Fountain Meen taking the last named instrument. Miss Eleanor Rees, R.A.M., sang remarkably well. She was recalled after Donizetti's "A mio Fernando," and encored in Gounod's characteristic song " The Worker." To-night the organ soloist will be Mr. W. G. Wood, F.C.O., whose fine playing has already been recognised at the Institute.

THE ORGAN IN BEVERLEY MINSTER.

BY ONE OF THE OLD SCHOOL.

The organ in Beverley Minster, built by Snetzler in the year 1768, has always been noted for its beauty of tone, and for its general effectiveness, prior to being removed from the screen on which it originally stood, to the floor of the north aisle of the nave, where it now stands. It contains the following :—

GREAT ORGAN, GG TO E.

1. Open Diapn. (large scale)		8. Sesquialtra (3 ranks) 4	
2. Open Diapn. (small scale)			ranks bass.
3. Stopped Diapason.		9. Fourniture (4 ranks).	
4. Principal.		10. Mixture (3 ranks).	
5. Wald Flute.		11. Trumpet.	
6. Twelfth.		12. Clarion.	
7. Fifteenth.			

CHOIR ORGAN, GG TO E.

13. Open Diapason.		18. Principal.	
14. *Dulciana.		19. Metal Flute.	
15. *Clarabel Flute.		20. Fifteenth.	
16. Stopt Diapason (bass).		21. Sesquialtra (3 ranks).	
17. Stopt Diapason (treble).		22. *Cremona.	

SWELL ORGAN, TENOR C TO E.

23. Open Diapason.		28. Fifteenth.	
24. Stopt Diapason.		29. Tierce.	
25. Principal.		30. Largot.	
26. Fifteenth.		31. Trumpet.	
27. Twelfth.		32. Hautboy.	

PEDAL ORGAN.

33. *Double Open Diapason, GGG 24ft. to E.		34. *Open Diapason, GG 12ft. to E.	

COUPLERS.

35. *Choir to Great.	39. *Swell to Choir in octaves above.
36. *Swell to Great.	
37. *Swell to Choir.	40. *Great to Pedals.
38. *Choir. to Great in octaves below.	41. *Choir to Pedals.
	42. *Pedal pipes in octaves above.

The organ was improved and enlarged by Forster and Andrews in 1848, all the stops marked with an asterisk being by them; the bass of sesquialtra on Great organ from Middle C was also added by them. In 1856 Gray and Davison put new keyboards, and substituted a fifteenth in Swell for a dulcet flute, which had been among the additions made by Forster & Andrews in 1848. In 1864 Postill, of York, put new trumpet in Great organ; with these exceptions, all the rest of the instrument is by Snetzler. In 1874 the Pedal board was converted from a G to a C. Forster and Andrews also carried down the Swell from Fiddle G to Tenor C. Some few years ago, the old screen on which the organ stood, and which was a hideous mixture of classic and Gothic, was removed, and a very handsome screen of carved oak, designed by the late Sir Gilbert Scott, and which contained iron pillars, concealed from view, for the purpose of supporting the organ, was erected in its place. It is now proposed to re-erect the organ on the screen, but it is also proposed to spend £2000 on the instrument, and, horror of horrors, it is to have no case. There is simply to be an array of bare pipes. The Archbishop of York, so I hear, has refused to allow another case to be erected at all, and it is said—with what truth I know not —that he has been instigated to this decision by the Vicar of the Minster. A design has been prepared which is simply hideous, and this in the face of a decision by Mr. J. O. Scott, who has been employed as architect to the

Minster since his father's death, not to sanction the erection of the organ on the screen without a case. But this is not the worst ;—the organ doubtless is in a dilapidated state, and requires rebuilding. Every bit of Snetzler's work is worth retaining should be retained, and treated with the most loving and reverent care, and if it be necessary, as possibly it is, to supplement this work by modern additions, they should be made to harmonise and blend with the existing diapason work of Snetzler, which cannot easily be surpassed, if equalled. I, for one, very much fear, however, that if the £2000 is spent, it will, or the bulk of it, be on work which will completely drown the mellow, rich, yet brilliant tone of the old work ; that, indeed, the identity of the old organ will be lost in the crowd of new additions. It is time to protest against the contemplated desecration : there are too few of the fine mellow-toned old organs left. Pray let us try to save the one in Beverley Minster. In the summer of last year I made a cathedral tour in the South-West of England, and I heard there a lovely old organ that I would have gone miles out of my way to listen to. I also heard a bran new monster, and the contrast was as great as first hearing Joachim on the finest Straduarius and then hearing a street musician on a shilling fiddle. Such a contrast I dread at Beverley between the old organ and the contemplated new one. The rage now-a-days seems to be for noise and not for music ; and I trust that my protest and that of others will not be in vain.

GAETANO DONIZETTI.

By Mem. Fac. Adv.

The following extracts from an article in *St. Cecilia Magazine* will be found interesting :—

Among the Elysian group of magnificent lyricists who followed the brilliant Rossini, none has obtained a more merited prominence than Gaetano Donizetti. He was born at Bergamo in 1798, under the dominance of a lucky star, for his noble exemplar preceded him by only about six years. Educated at the Conservatory of Naples under the foremost scientists of his time, he had all that artistic training could supply, and he emerged upon the arena of professional life just when the Pierian stream of melody, which rose with the Swan of Pessaro, began to overflow its banks and spread fertility around. The birds of dismal omen who had soared and croaked in the preceding twilight had drooped their wings when the sunny brightness of the joyous "Barber" proclaimed the advent of a new day. Donizetti studied and admired the score, and, despite the denunciations of his pharisaic instructors, was not faithless but believing. Continuing his research, he read and analysed every Rossirian production he could obtain, and then matured his own method and formed his own style. That they differed little from those of Rossini, is admitted on all hands. Plainly, in inspiration, arrangement, and development, the ideas of both are akin. The same voluptuous sweetness characterises the spirit of their melody, though in form the similarity is less, for in gorgeous embroidery and climatic intensification Rossini is undoubtedly supreme. Their harmonial and orchestral art are in substantial accord. They were both endowed with dramatic instinct in a high degree. They wrote with an ease which made them marvellously prolific, a clearness which made them universally intelligible, an emotional energy which secured them the sympathies of every class in every audience, depositing their gems in crystal caskets which, gleaming like diamonds on excited minds, became mirrored in delightful recollections. In the filiation of musical and poetic forms, they were pretty nearly abreast. They both belong to the priesthood of song, and are well entitled to wear the laurels and bear the mantle of genius.

For the precise line of demarcation between the artistic capacities of the two men, we should probably search in vain. How much Donizetti was indebted for his effects to the same translucent fountain of inspiration as his brilliant contemporary, how much to the study of his works, how much to his own organisation, how much to his better musical education and superior literary ability, how much the popular culture and appreciation the new developments had caused, it would be quite as futile to enquire. He was not a precocious child. He gave no preliminary indications of talent. When he began his musical career the fetters of the formalists were broken and the finest phrases of Rossini were echoing around. But though a pupil, he was neither a devotee nor an imitator of his great predecessor. Conscious, apparently, that those who attempt the experiment of Icarus are apt to meet his fate, he kept to his native vein—the specialty of his own musical organisation. Evidently he could not pour out his arias with the same dashing impetuosity as the Pessarite. While his harmonies smack of the school more and of nature less—his intervals are not so vocalistic —his modulations not so easy. Yet his melodial dialect is his own. And his operatic ideal. In the representative adaptation of sound to sentiment, situation, and sense, he was rather before than behind his master, and if he had not the Janus-like vision which regarded melody and harmony at once—which *felt* their simultaneous progression—to the same extent as Rossini, he had a breadth of understanding which kept him away from the ineffective tenuity of the old musicians on the one hand and from the labyrinthine mazes and unnatural inversions of the German potentates upon the other. With the latter he had evidently no sympathy. He believed that when harmony took the place of melody it should be upon the stage and not in the orchestra—that to conduct the motive-ideas of a piece by instrumental expression rather than by vocal, was to abandon the operatic for the symphonic; in effect, to accomplish the suicide of the art. The canon of orchestral perfection is that the instruments should aid the voices to the utmost, without overcoming, much less extinguishing, them. This canon he never violated.

A devotee of beauty and order, Donizetti never indulged in the spasmodic shrieks and discordant howls of the boaster of Bayreuth. We cannot agree with those who condemn his freer use of recitative than Rossini. Recitative is a compromise between melody and colloquy, and is, indeed, essential to the completeness of operatic art. When properly constructed, it makes the dialogue musical without diminishing either its verbal significance or naturalness. Musical intonation need neither interfere with propriety of gesture, facial expression, precision of utterance, nor dramatic action. If any of these are wanting, that is attributable to the weakness of the artist, not the incapacity of the art. It has been truly said of the recitatives of Rossini that "their eloquence is equal to that of the most beautiful airs, with which the spectator is equally charmed and surprised." The criterion of excellence in this, as in all other forms of musical expression, is that it should be appropriate to the character, sentiment, and situation. We are disposed to think that, upon the whole, Donizetti has adhered to this criterion with more rigidity than his exemplar. *Ex voluptate fides nascitur.* To us the intonation of dialogue in opera is much more agreeable than the tone of ordinary speech. And while the musical ideas of the Bergamite were symmetrical and clear, his dramatic power was great. He could direct the passions and emotions to any required situation, diminishing, suspending, or intensifying the interest with commanding skill, and exhibiting a familiarity with the phases of feeling very rarely surpassed. In one sense, indeed, he was more dramatic than Rossini, his demands upon the singer being less, on the actor more—being less floridly vocal, he admitted more histrionic force.

In the course of his long and brilliant career, Donizetti composed between fifty and sixty operas, each of them abounding in the characteristics of his style, and exhibiting the judgment "that softens all, and tempers into beauty." Though a prophet who *had* honour in his own country, he had greater profit if not greater honour elsewhere. There was a wide demand for his compositions. They delighted not only the professional and the amateur, but also the hearer of ordinary taste.

It must be admitted that the way was prepared for Donizetti by his brilliant and dauntless predecessor and contemporary. He had no professional antagonisms to overcome, no antiquated notions of indigent conservatives to detrude, no scientific errors to uproot; no novel system of improved method to discover—all was done to his hand. Beyond, the *dona nobis pacem* had been emphatically pronounced by the public, and the assaults of the elders and high priests of the old dispensation effectually suppressed. While Rossini waded so long and painfully in the troubled waters of the Stygian stream, Donizetti crossed it at once, his merits having been fully recognised upon the appearance of his first production, while his popularity increased with his assiduous culture and more daring compositional flights, till it attained its brilliant consummation with his "Lucia," "Pasquale," and "Lucrezia," the splendid fruitage of his prime. Nor has his popularity sensibly declined. He looms upon us still lofty and imposing as a Himalayan peak, bright and expansive as the milky way, his clustering beauties resplendent and sublime in the ethereal strata of the sky. It was when encrowned with a full-blown wreath of honour and blest with the conviction of an immortal renown, that the waves of care and sorrow began to roll heavily over the great Italian. A fate even worse than death befel him who had so long swayed the rod of empire over so many minds in every region of the world of art. The fiend of darkness imprisoned his soul. He ceased to know others or himself. His lucid judgment failed to maintain unequal war with his wildly vagarious fancy. Upon his splendid faculties, so exquisitely framed to inhale celestial melodies, the light of reason shone no more. His night of anguish was long. Hope, indeed, occasionally inspired his friends, but the faithless siren was false, and the fell destroyer triumphed at last. He has taken his place among the eternal stars in his own heaven of song. That his transit was not so sweetly serene as we could have wished for one who had so often cast the spell of beauty over the minds and hearts of his race, will ever be regretted by the appreciators of his art.

The Duke and Duchess of Albany will attend the Leeds Festival, and the Duke will act as president.

A MUSICAL CLUB THREE HUNDRED YEARS AGO.

When the Minnesingers of the Middle Ages, those noble singers of love and chivalry, passed away, because of the opposition of the Church, which could not bear their freedom of speech, their place was taken by the less inspired *bourgeoisie*, the merchants, the middle classes of Germany, who sought a relaxation from the cares of business in the practice of music. The rules of the societies of Meistersingers have often been published. In Germany, and even in the Netherlands, their influence, if not so elevating as that of the Minnesingers, was certainly as wide-spread. From the example set by these societies, musical clubs seem to have been the greatest delight of the better classes in those early times. We have recently come into possession of a work which strikingly illustrates the character of the lesser clubs of the sixteenth century. It is the album of a singing club of Amsterdam, which began its career in 1560 and terminated about 1590. The members of the club seem to have been of noble families, and the organisation one of especial excellence, judging by the care taken in admitting members and visitors. The work is in manuscript, written in a small blank book of very antique style. The rules of the club are in Latin, some of it of slightly inferior quality, but are richly worth translating.

RULES.

As nothing is more useful or honourable than perpetual study alternated occasionally with pleasure, it has seemed to us proper to form a society to which we will come each week at 2 o'clock,* (and remain until 4†) to recreate ourselves from the cares of labour by the modulations of music.

It seems good to us to limit the active membership to ten associates. If, however, any one is possessed of a good voice and a knowledge of music, there will be no reason to reject him as an associate.

Of the knowledge of music and the quality of voice of a candidate, the majority of the club shall judge.

Members may bring a reasonable number of friends to the meetings, if they desire.

As our object is to enjoy ourselves in a reputable and moderate manner, drunkenness is forbidden.

He who misleads any member in this respect shall also pay a fine.‡

Besides beer and new wine, nothing shall be brought to us.

Books of music and all necessary instruments shall be in readiness constantly.

In singing, this order shall be observed: only three songs or motets shall be given in succession, and, if possible, instrumental pieces shall be alternated.

He who, by chattering, laughing, or otherwise shall disturb the music, shall pay a fine of one shilling.§

He who introduces any guests must be responsible for and pay any fines they may incur.

Excuses for absence will not be taken; but one who is sick, or who is obliged to travel more than ten miles, may be excused from paying any fine.

He who comes too late must pay one shilling.

He who fails to come at all must pay six shillings.

He who misses in succession must pay eighteen shillings.

It is not the proper place for low or rude stories, and he who is accused of this shall be fined according to the vote of the members.

Scolding or brawling shall be first admonished and then fined. He who is admonished and fined, and repeats the offence at the next meeting, shall pay double the previous fine.

The treasurer shall be elected every six months. He shall warn and censure all who transgress the rules.

If any one complains of his ruling, the matter shall be laid before the club.

He himself is liable to censure by a vote of the members.

He shall have charge and care of the constitution, books, and all things belonging to the society, and must read the archives and accounts at every meeting.

He who is admitted to membership in our society must pay ten shillings, and any member who wishes to leave the society must pay the same amount.

The above rules are written in a beautiful hand, similar to that found in the old missals. In the same hand are found some Latin praises of music, partially taken from Cicero and partially (we believe) original. One of these is well worth preserving,—*Musica lætitiæ comes, Medicina Dolorum*,—"Music the companion of joy, the medicine of sorrow."

* The day is not given, but was probably Sunday.
† This part is doubtful.
‡ This is evidently aimed at the senseless custom of reciprocal drinking,—i.e., "treating."
§ The Roman *dram* is specified, but its value probably is best represented by the Dutch Shilling.

In the long list of signatures made by visitors to the club, we find ample proof that the society was held in high estimation. There are visitors from Brussels, Antwerp, Leyden, and other distant cities. There are no famous musical names, for Holland was undergoing (or had undergone) too severe a struggle to give forth great composers at this time. The Inquisition with its horrors had just been expelled. The war of "the beggars" was even yet raging in the devastated country. The Prince of Palma had not yet let loose all the rigours of war on the Southern provinces. William of Orange had not yet been assassinated. Three reminders of these painful times are found in the book of our singing club. The first is the name "Rogerino de Montmorency" written among the visitors to the club. A Montmorency could only have been in Amsterdam at that time in the character of a prisoner of war. The second instance is a page of secret writing at the close of the book. The third is contained in a page headed *Extemporaria hæc oratiuncula in Musices laudem recitatas est per puerum Joannem Gheys, Anno 1581, 7 Octobris*,—an oration delivered by a schoolboy named John Gheys, over three hundred years ago, which chance has preserved to modern times. The high character of our musical club is again proved by the fact that the oration was made before them at their invitation, and was given in Latin, and met with such success that it was copied in the album of the club. The boy's allusion to the misfortunes of that epoch is brief but unmistakable. He says, "The calamities of the present age might move us more to sighs and tears than to music and playing." Apart from this, the "little oration" is apparently a school-boy's production, and jumbles up Cicero, Seneca, Nero, Socrates, and every sage, philosopher, potentate, or what not, who had exhibited a leaning toward music, in hopeless confusion.

Altogether, the little album affords us an entertaining glimpse at the interior life of a singing club of three hundred years ago.—*Musical Herald* (U.S.A.).

COLLEGE OF ORGANISTS.

Mr. W. A. Barrett, Mus.Bac., F.C.O., gave, on April 3rd, an enjoyable lecture on "Balfe and his works" at Neumeyer Hall. The musical illustrations consisted of vocal numbers, given very artistically, by Miss Julia Jones, Mr. W. H. Brereton, and Mr. Walter Clifford, and a most interesting sonata for pianoforte and violoncello admirably rendered by Messrs. Burnham Horner and W. C. Hann. To hear the composer of the "Bohemian Girl" on the classical ground of what is known as chamber music, was indeed to many a new experience. The work in question, the Sonata in A flat, has a charming adagio written in five-four measure. In the execution of this, and indeed of the whole work, Messrs. Burnham Horner and W. C. Hann showed very high artistic attainments. Equally good was the vocal music given. Miss Jones, with a charming mezzo voice and refined manner, sang the original version of what is now called "The power of love." Mr. Walter Clifford sang "The peace of the valley" and "The green trees" with genuine expression and much power. Mr. Brereton gave the fine song "From bushy beds of silver Nile," and "We'll meet again" (a favourite of the composer) with fervour and in good style. The accompaniments received a very musicianly rendering from the hands of Mr. Burnham Horner. As to the lecture itself, it was a combination of sound critical observation, sympathetic discernment, and genial appreciation of both the man and his music, such as would be expected of so natural, graceful, and accomplished a lecturer as Mr. W. A. Barrett is everywhere known to be. Mr. C. E. Stephens occupied the chair and delivered some interesting observations. Hearty votes of thanks were accorded to the lecturer and to the artists so ably illustrating the admirable paper read. Dr. F. E. Gladstone neatly proposed a vote of thanks to the chairman, which was seconded by Mr. G. A. Osborne, Balfe's fellow countryman and life-long friend, in a speech of much interest and character, in which he paid tribute to Mr. Barrett for his efforts in connection with the Balfe memorial tablet in Westminster Abbey. At the close of the lecture Mr. Barrett kindly displayed a collection of Balfe's scores and musical notes. It was announced that Mr. H. J. Stark will lecture on "Counterpoint" on May 1st.

Passing Events.

Dr. Horton Allison played his new "Lord Wolseley's March" at the banquet recently given in Manchester, in honour of the successful general.

Readers will rejoice to know that Mr. C. Warwick Jordan has returned from America much improved in health.

Señor Sarasate announces an interesting concert on Monday, April 9th, at St. James's Hall, with orchestra, when amongst other solos he is to play Beethoven's Concerto for violin.

Miss Agnes Miller, mentioned in Birmingham letter, p. 194, as resident in that town, has been for some time located in London, though visiting the capital of the Midlands (professionally) one day a week.

Mr. G. A. Osborne charmed the members of the Musical Association on April 2nd by reading a paper in which he narrated many of his personal recollections of some of the great musicians of the last fifty years.

The ninth annual concert by the violin classes in connection with the Birkbeck Literary and Scientific Institution, and under the direction of Mr. W. Fitzhenry, was given on March 31st. The following artists took prominent parts :—Miss Mary Beare, Miss Marian McKenzie, Mr. Edwin Bryant, and Mr. E. Passett, vocalists. Solo violin, Mr. T. E. Gatehouse ; violoncello, Messrs. Kendall and Parker ; pianoforte, Miss Gatehouse and Mr. H. S. Webster. The programme included pieces in which the strings and pianoforte took part.

With much regret it is said that Sir Michael Costa although progressing favourably, is not gaining ground as rapidly as his more sanguine friends desire. It is a great pity that the question of conducting the Handel Festival is not settled negatively. It is sheer madness to expect Sir M. Costa to be prepared to face the serious labours of such an undertaking, and his best meaning friends are anxious that he may be induced to give up all idea of attempting such a task. It is time he had complete rest now.

Captain Evatt Acklom, who is a vigorous, eloquent, and picturesque reader, gave a recital and concert at the Eyre Arms Assembly Rooms, on April 5th. The programme included selections from our best poets, novelists and some music of a popular character. Two songs, "The Kiss," and "We'll never be parted again" (MS.), by Mrs. Henry Scobell were sung, the last having a harp obbligato part. The musical performers were :—Mrs. Shipway, Miss Norah Hayes, Mdme. Inez Bell, Miss Adele Myers, Signor Ria, vocalists. Solo pianoforte, Miss Constance Erica ; solo harp, Herr Carl Oberthur ; conductor and accompanist, Mr. Giuseppe Dinelli.

The London Sunday School Choir (President, Sir Andrew Lusk, Bart., M.P.), gave a concert in aid of the funds of the Royal College of Music, on April 4th, at the Royal Albert Hall. The choir consisted of 1,600 selected voices. The programme included selections from the works of well-known masters, Gounod's "Ave Maria," with organ, pianoforte, and violin obbligati, and also the "Manificat," composed for this choir by Mr. David Davies, to be accompanied by the composer. The artists were :—Señorita Lucia Carreras ; the family quartet ; violin, Miss Maria Schumann, of the Guildhall School of Music. Conductor, Mr. Luther Hinton ; organist, Mr. W. G. Horncastle.

The following is the list of professors at the Royal College of Music :—Violin, Mr. Henry Holmes, Herr Gompertz ; viola, Mr. Gibson, violoncello, Mr. Edward Howell ; double bass, Mr. A. L. White ; pianoforte, Mdme. Arabella Goddard, Herr Pauer, Mr. Franklin Taylor, Mr. John F. Barnett ; organ, Mr. Walter Parratt, Mr. G. C. Martin ; singing, Frau Lind-Goldschmidt, Mr. Albert Visetti, Mr. H. C. Deacon, Miss Mazzucato ; declamation, Mrs. Kendal ; composition and orchestral practice, Mr. C. Villiers Stanford ; counterpoint and organ, Dr. J. F. Bridge ; choral practice and piano, Mr. Eaton Faning ; musical history and composition, Dr. C. Hubert H. Parry ; oboe, Mr. George Horton ; clarinet, Mr. H. Lazarus ; horn, Mr. T. E. Mann ; bassoon, Mr. W. B. Wotton ; Italian language, Signor G. A. Mazzucato.

Service Lists.

SECOND SUNDAY AFTER EASTER.
APRIL 8th.

London.

ST. PAUL'S CATHEDRAL.—Morn.: Service, Te Deum and Benedictus, Stainer in E flat ; Introit, Jesu lives (Hymn 140) ; Communion Service, Martin in C. Even.: Service, Magnificat and Nunc Dimittis, Martin in C ; Anthem, Blessed be the God and Father (Wesley).

WESTMINSTER ABBEY.—Morn.: Service, Calkin in B flat (throughout). Aft.: Service, Garrett in F ; Anthem, O sing unto the Lord (Purcell).

TEMPLE CHURCH.—Morn.: Service, Te Deum and Jubilate, Smart in F ; Apostles' Creed, Harmonised Monotone ; Anthem, Sing, O heavens (Sullivan). Even.: Service, Magnificat and Nunc Dimittis, Smart in F ; Apostles' Creed, Harmonised Monotone ; Anthem, O Lord, Thou hast searched me out (Croft).

LINCOLN'S INN CHAPEL.—Morn.: Service, Steggall in F ; Kyrie, Steggall ; Anthem, I have surely built thee an house (Boyce). Even.: Service, Steggall in F ; Anthem, Thy word is a lantern (Purcell).

ALL SAINTS, MARGARET STREET.—Morn.: Service, Te Deum, Smart ; Benedictus, Simcox ; Communion Service, Hummel in B flat ; Offertory Anthem, But Thou didst not leave (Handel). Even.: Service, Garrett in F ; Anthem, I will mention (Sullivan).

ST. AUGUSTINE AND ST. FAITH, WATLING STREET.—Morn.: Service, Te Deum, Hopkins in C ; Benedictus, Garrett in D ; Communion Service, Hoyte in D ; Offertory, Why seek ye the living (Hopkins). Even.: Service, Garrett in D ; Anthem, Blessed be the God and Father (Wesley).

ST. BARNABAS, MARYLEBONE.—Morn.: Service, Te Deum and Benedictus, Turle in D ; Anthem, Awake, awake (Stainer) ; Kyrie and Nicene Creed, Cooke in G. Even.: Service, Magnificat and Nunc Dimittis, Turle in D ; Anthem, O that I knew (Sterndale Bennett).

CHILDREN'S HOME CHAPEL, BONNER ROAD, E.—Morn.: Service, Anthem, Enter not into judgment (Attwood), and, What are these (Stainer). Aft.: Service, Anthem, Incline thine ear (Himmel), and, Sweet is thy mercy (Barnby).

CHRIST CHURCH, CLAPHAM.—Morn.: Service, Te Deum, Plain-song ; Kyrie and Credo, Weber in E flat ; Offertory Anthem, The Lord is my strength (Monk) ; Sanctus, Benedictus, Agnus Dei, and Gloria in excelsis, Weber. Even.: Service, Magnificat and Nunc Dimittis, Hoyte in B flat ; Anthem, Blessed be the God and Father (Wesley).

FOUNDLING CHAPEL.—Morn.: Service, Garrett in D ; Anthem, Stand up and bless (Goss). Aft.: Service, Garrett in D ; Anthem, But as for His people ("Israel in Egypt," Handel).

HOLY TRINITY, TULSE HILL.—Morn.: Chant Service. Even.: Service, Gadsby in C ; Anthem, O come let us worship (Mendelssohn).

ST. JAMES'S PRIVATE EPISCOPAL CHAPEL, SOUTHWARK.—Morn.: Service, Introit, The strife is o'er (Hymn 127) ; Communion Service, Cherubini in C (No. 2). Even.: Service, Hopkins in F ; Anthem, Strike your timbrels (Schubert).

ST. MAGNUS, LONDON BRIDGE.—Morn.: Service, Opening Anthem, If we say (Reynolds) ; Te Deum and Jubilate, Nares in F ; Kyrie, Boyce. Even.: Service, Cantate and Deus Miseratur, Hayes in E flat ; Anthem, Lift thine eyes, and, He watching over Israel (Mendelssohn).

ST. MARGARET PATTENS, ROOD LANE, FENCHURCH STREET.—Morn.: Service, Te Deum, Smart in F ; Benedictus, Stainer ; Communion Service, Schubert in B flat ; Offertory Anthem, He shall feed His flock (Handel). Even.: Service, Magnificat and Nunc Dimittis, Tuckerman in F ; Anthem, Christ being raised (Elvey).

ST. MARY ABCHURCH, E.C.—Morn.: Service, Chipp in D ; Communion Service, Nares in F. Even.: Service, Magnificat and Nunc Dimittis, Garrett in D.

ST. MARY BOLTONS, WEST BROMPTON, S.W.—Morn.: Service, Te Deum, Armes in G ; Benedictus, Chant ; Communion Service, Kyrie, Credo, Offertory, Sanctus, and Gloria in excelsis, Stainer in E flat ; Benedictus and Agnus Dei, Going in F. Even.: Service, Magnificat and Nunc Dimittis, Stainer in B flat ; Anthem, They have taken away my Lord (Stainer).

ST. PAUL'S, BOW COMMON, E.—Morn.: Service, Te Deum and Benedictus, Stainer in B flat. Even.: Service, Magnificat and Nunc Dimittis, Stainer in E flat ; Anthem, Strike your timbrels (Schubert).

ST. PETER'S (EATON SQUARE).—Morn.: Service, Te Deum, Dykes in F. Even.: Service, Hopkins in F; Anthem, Hear my prayer (Mendelssohn).

ST. PETER'S, LEIGHAM COURT ROAD, STREATHAM, S.W. —Morn.: Service, Mass, Agutter in B flat; Introit, When I wake up (Sutton); Alleluia, Chantwise. Even.: Service, Magnificat, H. J. Stark in D; Anthem, If ye then be risen (Naylor).

Country.

ARDINGLY COLLEGE, SUSSEX.—Morn.: Communion Service, Nares in F. Even.: Service, Arnold in A; Anthem, Worthy is the Lamb (Handel).

ST. ASAPH CATHEDRAL.—Morn.: Service, Tours in F; Anthem, O give thanks (Goss). Even.: Service, Tours in F; Anthem, The Lord is my strength (Smart).

ASHBURNE CHURCH, DERBYSHIRE. — Morn.: Service, Stanford in B flat. Even.: Service, Anthem, Selection from Daughter of Jairus (Stainer).

BEDDINGTON CHURCH, SURREY.—Morn.: Service, Dykes in F; Introit, Alleluia! Hearts to heaven and voices raise (Hymn 137); Communion Service, Dykes in F. Even.: Service, Stainer; Anthem, Whoso dwelleth under the defence of the most high (Maxim).

BIRMINGHAM (ST. CYPRIAN'S, HAY MILLS).—Morn.: Service, Stainer in A and D; Anthems, Why do the heathen, and, Let us break their bonds (Handel). Even.: Service, Smith in B flat; Anthem, This is the day (Elvey).

BIRMINGHAM (S. PHILIP'S CHURCH). — Morn.: Service, Barnby in E; Anthem, I will arise (Creighton). Even.: Service, Barnby in E; Anthem, They have taken away my Lord (Stainer).

CANTERBURY CATHEDRAL.—Morn.: Service, Richardson in F; Introit, Thou wilt keep him in perfect peace (Jarrett); Communion Service, Richardson in F. Even.: Service, Richardson in F; Anthem, He shall feed His flock, and, His yoke is easy (Handel).

CARLISLE CATHEDRAL.—Morn.: Service, Calkin in B flat; Introit, Behold, God is my helper (Stainer); Kyrie, Sir J. Rogers in F; Nicene Creed, Goss in D. Even.: Service, Calkin in B flat; Anthem, This is the day (Turle).

DURHAM CATHEDRAL.—Morn.: Service, Hopkins in B flat; Anthem, If we believe (Goss); Introit, O Lord, we trust (Handel); Communion Service, Armes in B flat. Even.: Service, Hopkins in B flat (Cantate); Anthem, I was in the spirit (Armes).

ELY CATHEDRAL.—Morn.: Service, Te Deum, Walmisley in F; Benedictus, Plain-song.; Kyrie and Credo, Walmisley in F; Gloria, Jackson in E flat; Anthem, From all that dwell (Walmisley). Even.: Service, Attwood in F; Anthem, I have set God (Blake).

EXETER CATHEDRAL.—Morn.: Service, Ouseley in B flat; Communion Service, Ouseley in F. Even.: Service, Ouseley in E flat; Anthem, Praise His awful name (Spohr).

LLANDAFF CATHEDRAL.—Morn.: Service, Dykes in F; Introit, See what love (Mendelssohn); Communion Service, Rogers in D. Even.: Service, The Litany; Anthem, Awake, awake (Stainer).

LEEDS PARISH CHURCH.—Morn.: Service, Attwood in A; Anthem, And the elders (Spohr); Kyrie and Creed, Turle in D. Even.: Service, Hopkins in A; Anthem, The Lord shall reign (Handel).

LICHFIELD CATHEDRAL. — Morn.: Service, Stainer in E flat; Anthem, What are these (Stainer). Aft.: Service, Stainer in E flat; Anthem, God is our hope and strength (Greene).

LIVERPOOL CATHEDRAL.—Aft.: Service, Barnby in E; Anthem, Behold the Lamb that was slain (Spohr).

MANCHESTER CATHEDRAL.—Morn.: Service, Boyce in C; Anthem, Lord for Thy tender mercies (Farrant); Communion Service, Pargy in D. Aft.: Service, Cooke in G; Anthem, Why rage the heathen (Mendelssohn).

MANCHESTER (ST. BENEDICT'S).—Morn.: Service, Kyrie, Credo, Sanctus, Benedictus, Agnus Dei, and Gloria in excelsis, Monk in C. Even.: Service, Magnificat and Nunc Dimittis, Wesley in F.

MANCHESTER (ST. JOHN BAPTIST, HULME).—Morn.: Service, Kyrie, Credo, Sanctus, Benedictus, and Gloria in excelsis, Sutton in F; Agnus Dei, Agutter in B flat. Even.: Service, Magnificat and Nunc Dimittis, Wesley in F.

MUSSELBURGH (LORETTO SCHOOL).—Morn.: Introit, Give peace in our time (Callcott); Service, Stainer in E flat; Anthem, The heavens are telling ("Creation," Haydn). Even.: Service, Anthems, The Hallelujah and Amen Choruses ("Messiah," Handel).

RIPON CATHEDRAL.—Morn.: Service, Chants; Anthem, O Lord, Thou hast searched, and, God is a spirit (Bennett); Kyrie and Credo, Merbecke. Even.: Service, Bridge in E; Anthem, Hear my prayer (Mendelssohn).

ROCHESTER CATHEDRAL. — Morn.: Service, Mendelssohn in A; Jubilate, Chant; Anthems, On Thee each living soul, and, Achieved is the glorious (Haydn). Even.: Service, Smart in F; Anthem, But thou didst not leave, and, Hallelujah (Handel).

SHEFFIELD PARISH CHURCH. — Morn.: Service, Kyrie, Sullivan in D. Even.: Service, Cantate and Deus Misereatur, Chants; Anthem, Blessed be the God and Father (Wesley).

SHERBORNE ABBEY.—Morn.: Service, Te Deum, Herbert in D. Even.: Service, Anthem, Now is Christ risen (Allen).

SOUTHAMPTON (ST. MARY'S CHURCH).—Morn.: Service, Te Deum and Benedictus, Custard in F; Communion Service, Introit, If we believe (Macfarren); Service, Custard in E flat; Offertory; He that soweth (Barnby); Paternoster, Hoyte. Even.: Service, Magnificat and Nunc Dimittis, Stewart in G; Apostles' Creed, Harmonized Monotone; Hopkins.

WELLS CATHEDRAL. — Morn.: Service, Ouseley in G (throughout). Even.: Service, Ouseley in G (throughout); Anthem, Praise the Lord (Croft).

WORCESTER CATHEDRAL.—Morn.: Service, Smart in F; Anthem, Why seek ye (Hopkins). Even.: Service, Smart in F; Anthem, O give thanks (Goss).

[The attention of the several Organists is called to the favour they confer upon their brother musicians by forwarding their notices regularly: this column of the paper is much valued as an index to what is going on in the choice of cathedral music, so much so that intermissions constantly give rise to remonstrance. Lists should be sent in a week in advance if possible.—ED. Mus. Stand.]

*** Post-cards must be sent to the Editor, 6, Argyle Square, W.C., by Wednesday. Lists are frequently omitted in consequence of not being received in time.

NOTICES TO CORRESPONDENTS.

NEWSPAPERS sent should have distinct marks opposite to the matter to which attention is required.

NOTICE.—All communications intended for the Editor are to be sent to his private address. Business communications to be addressed to 185, Fleet Street, E.C.

APPOINTMENTS.

MR. ALFRED B. STUTFIELD to St. Paul's, Addlestone, Surrey.

MR. J. S. LIDDLE, formerly of Basingstoke Parish Church, to be Organist of Halifax Parish Church.

DEATH.

CLARKE.—The death is announced of Mr. Frederic W. Clarke, Mus. Bac., Oxon., of Anerley, a young musician whose career has been watched with great interest by all who knew him.

ERRATUM.—The name of a promising and artistic singer given incorrectly on page 201, col. 2, line 7, should have been Miss Marni, R.A.M.

Printed for the Proprietor by BOWDEN, HUDSON & Co., at 23, Red Lion Street, Holborn, London, W.C.; and Published by WILLIAM REEVES, at
the Office, 185, Fleet Street, E.C. West End Agents:—WEEKES & CO., 14, Hanover Street, Regent Street, W. Subscriptions and Advertisements are
received either by the Publisher or West End Agents.—Communications for the EDITOR are to be forwarded to his private address, 6, Argyle Square, W.C.
SATURDAY, APRIL 7, 1883.—Entered at the General Post Office as a Newspaper.

THE MUSICAL STANDARD

A NEWSPAPER FOR MUSICIANS PROFESSIONAL AND AMATEUR

No. 976. Vol. XXIV. FOURTH SERIES.   SATURDAY, APRIL 14, 1883.   WEEKLY: PRICE 3D.

THE MUSICAL STANDARD· is published every Saturday, price 3d., by post, 3½d.; and may be had of any bookseller or newsagent by ordering its regular supply.

SUBSCRIPTION.—*The Musical Standard* is posted to subscribers at 15s. a year; half a year, 7s. 6d., payable in advance.

The rate is the same to France, Belgium, Germany, Italy, United States, and Canada.

Post Office Orders to be made payable to the Publisher, William Reeves, 185, Fleet Street, London, or to the West-end Agents, Messrs. Weekes & Co., 14, Hanover Street, Regent Street, W.

ADVERTISEMENTS.—The charge for ordinary advertisements in *The Musical Standard* is 2s. 6d. for three lines or less; and 6d. for each line (10 words) in addition. "Organist wanted," 3s. 6d. for 3 lines or less. A reduction is made for a series.

FRONT PAGE.—Concert and auction advertisements, &c., are inserted in the front page of *The Musical Standard*, and charged one-third in addition to the ordinary rates. Other advertisements will be inserted on the front page, or in the leader page, if desired, at the same terms.

Musical Intelligence.

CRYSTAL PALACE CONCERTS.

PROGRAMME.

Overture, "Le Nozze di Figaro"	Mozart.
Symphony in G (composed for the Birmingham Festival of 1882)	C. H. H. Parry.
(First time at the Crystal Palace).	
Aria, "Non mi mir" ("Don Giovanni ")	Mozart.
Miss Annie Marriott.	
Concerto for pianoforte and orchestra, No. 2, in F minor	Chopin.
Mr. Richard Rickard.	
(His first appearance at these concerts).	
Largo in F sharp, for strings................	Haydn.
"Ave Maria"	Gounod.
Miss Annie Marriott.	
Violin obbligato, Mr. Jung; harp, Mr. Lockwood; organ, Mr. Alfred Eyre.	
Selection from the Ballet Airs from "Le Tribut de Zamora"	Gounod.
Danse Espagnole—Danse des Pointes—Danse Italienne.	
Conductor - - - AUGUST MANNS.	

Many years ago I read somewhere the fable of the Nightingale, the Cuckoo, and the Donkey. As far as I can remember it was as follows :—Once upon a time a conceited cuckoo challenged a nightingale to sing, but as it happened late in the evening and far from any frequented path, the only chance person or thing that passed that way was an old donkey, and he was called upon to decide between these songsters of the grove. As soon as the cuckoo had finished his unvaried ditty, the donkey thus commended his performance :—"I admire your efforts greatly, and I like the composition. The form is perfectly simple, and the intervals are natural and very charming." It was now the nightingale's turn to begin, and when the song was ended the donkey said, "I have listened to you, I must confess, with much impatience, for you transgress every kind of rule by your extraordinary modulations and outrageous progressions ; so much so indeed, that I defy any one to follow you, or to comprehend any part of your song. Let the cuckoo come and receive the prize." This fable is by no means flattering to those who, with their so-called "orthodox" views, condemn everything but what is in accordance with certain old rules and regulations, many of which are sometimes "more honoured in the breach than in the observance." On the other hand, the men of the so-called "new school" are so absorbed in the contemplation of their own attainments, and of the present deplorable state of music, that their special mission in this world appears to be that of putting everyone right who ventures to differ from them. Of these two extreme parties—so far as one may judge from his symphony— Mr. Parry evidently steers quite clear. Wagner's style, in a modified form, is at times apparent, it is true ; but the wild uproar, which is supposed by some men of his school or party to make up for lack of ideas, is nowhere to be found in Mr. Parry's music. His phrasing, however, is often designedly interwoven and complex, and this, for the time, prevents the ear from resting upon any individual theme ; but there is no lack of melody, as some may suppose, for the respective parts flow into each other with much freedom, grace, and ingenuity. His over-elaboration is sometimes apparent, and although a fault, it is one into which the best writers occasionally fall—Brahms, to wit. Upon the whole, the work appears to be a happy blending of modern style with the spirit of his great predecessors. The symphony was well played and cordially received, and Mr. Parry showed himself at the end gallery in reply to many calls.

Chopin's concerto was beautifully played by Mr. Richard Rickard, who made his first appearance at these concerts. To a bright and clear tone he adds feeling and high intelligence.

Miss Annie Marriott was not so successful as she often is. Her voice is finer than ever, but the simplicity of style and manner, which until very lately characterized her, are now unfortunately exchanged for a more showy and meretricious manner.   R. S.

Another contributor writes :—

I did not hear Mr. Hubert Parry's Symphony at Birmingham last Autumn, and I cannot, at present, refer to a file of the *Musical Standard*, in order to ascertain what opinion was expressed by your learned correspondent at the time. My own opinion is unbiassed, and I give it—*valeat quantum!* Let me candidly avow a sad disappointment. The symphony struck me as far

too long, generally uninteresting, and often tedious. The gush of genuine inspiration seems to be always wanting ; the scoring, no doubt, scholastic and effective. The first allegro (the "fire" whereof I looked for in vain), is too protracted ; and the *coda* common-place. The andante, mild and Mozartean at the outset, is spoiled by the vague and unmeaning theme of *bruyant* character, which intrudes itself like an unwelcome Paul Pry. The scherzo sounds fresh, yet it is still a steeple-chase after ideas ; the trio is too long. The finale, spirited and well worked out, I esteem the best movement. The annotator "G," himself rather a diffuse writer, has to say, at least twice, that the theme (in question) is "treated at *some* length." Oh, for what grammar books call the "concise" style of writing ! Let Brahms and his imitators read, and get by heart a few chapters of Tacitus. *Breviores esse laborent !*

Mr. Rickard's touch, style, and execution are just adapted for the execution of Chopin's music. The ballet airs of Gounod, especially the Tarantella in A minor (called an "Italian" dance), are very pretty.   A. M.

Enthusiasm plays a still more useful part in criticism than does cynicism, even though praise, like blame, must be guardedly given. A highly esteemed contributor thus writes, anent Mr. Hubert Parry's new work :—It is scarcely in good taste, nor is it complimentary to a true artist for his fellow-countrymen to congratulate themselves on his nationality ; but if some of us may be tempted to rejoice that Mr. Hubert Parry is an Englishman, his works cannot fail to remind us that he claims a higher position than we are giving him, and that he already belongs—not to any particular nation, but to the grand Universal School of Art. Who is conscious that Berlioz was a Frenchman when listening to his "Harold" Symphony ? (to be given at to-day's concert). Who can trace the nationality of Goetz in his one glorious creation in symphonic form ? The whole artistic world, and not in any special degree his native land, claims the artist as its own ; for one touch of genius, like "one touch of nature, makes the whole world kin." That Mr. Parry has this touch of genius that breaks through the barrier of nationality, will hardly be questioned by those who carefully listened to his first symphony last week. I say "carefully," advisedly ; for the work is one of earnest thought and deep feeling—perhaps at times the thought rather overpowers the feeling—and it might not impress a superficial listener. Moreover, like most real thinkers, Mr. Parry has a decidedly original manner, though he is strictly orthodox in his modes of expressing and arranging his thoughts. The melodies are of a broad and noble cast, growing out of each other in the most natural and interesting manner. The parts move with the greatest freedom, and are interestingly woven ; there is no striving after effect, yet the work is truly effective ; it is full of enthusiasm, yet well digested—as far removed from eccentricity as from pretentiousness or triviality ; there is not one unworthy or flippant thought, nor one ineffective phrase from beginning to end.   B. F. WYATT-SMITH.

There can be no better way of closing these different estimations of the new work than by giving the following words of a calm, just, and experienced writer :—

Dr. C. H. H. Parry's Symphony in G is one of the most important works that has proceeded from an English pen. It was, as may be remembered, praised to the echo on its production at last year's Birmingham Festival ; but provincial verdicts in such art matters are lightly esteemed in London, and until the metropolis has placed its *cachet* of approval on a work, its success elsewhere is only a *succes d'estime.* Now, however, that the symphony in question has met with the marked approbation of the critical Crystal Palace Saturday Concerts audience of musicians and amateurs, it will enjoy a renown that Birmingham cannot confer. The work is undoubtedly that of a thoughtful musician, well acquainted with the resources of his art, and possessing considerable experience as to how they can be effectively used. In the general laying out and form of the symphony, there is no breaking away from old bounds, or indulging in the license degenerating into uncouth vagaries, which is so dear to the hearts of certain composers striving hard after an originality. At the same time, Mr. Parry's work has a freshness of thought, a decision of purpose, and an amount of scholarly treatment amply sufficient to please the ear of a general audience, and to satisfy the intelligence of musicians. In saying this, it is not necessarily implied that the work makes a new departure, or is of marked originality. Rather must the critic commend the author in that he has worked mostly in the old form; a shape that some German pseudo-critics have proclaimed exhausted, cramped, and inefficient for complete musical expression. In this abused (though eternally true) form Mr. Parry has written a thoroughly satisfactory work. When we hear these denunciations about worked out and stilted forms, we can but recall to mind with delight the beautiful music that the dead great masters of our art have written on these now despised lines; and further, remember a severe personal proverb anent, "bad workmen finding fault with their tools." Mr. Parry's themes are mostly well-chosen and contrasted; they attack the ear with just that amount of individuality that *leit-motiven* should possess, and are far more grateful than are many of the hideous little phrases which are honoured with that fine sounding appellation. It should, however, be said, that his chief themes are not so concise as they might be, and it may be also remarked that this quality of over-lengthening is to be found throughout the work. The first movement is over developed, and contains too much *remplissage;* but there are many charming thoughts to be found in it, and the coda with the climax growing out of it is masterful. There is a weird uncertainty about the key tonality of the Andante, but this is produced mainly through the free use of suspensions and anticipations; its second subject, in B minor, with its uncommon orchestration, is just one of those rugged pieces of power that might have sprung from the brain of Beethoven. The Scherzo and two Trios are the most striking portions of the Symphony; here the composer's genius is distinctly apparent, and the originality he exhibits is fraught with fair hopes for his future efforts. Purists may object that portions of the movement seem too heavy and coarse for a Scherzo; but it should be pointed out that there is a certain amount of novelty in the form of the movement, as well as in the materials employed; in any case a distinct success is achieved. In the last movement we miss inspiration, and though the score is replete with ingenious scholarship, there is considerable labour exercised over it. The orchestration, moreover, is thick in places, and seems to lack the spontaneity met with elsewhere. The Finale, however, is ambitious and brilliant; it contains clear references to the principal subjects of the earlier movements, and brings the work to a satisfactory ending. In conclusion, it may be added that the symphony gives one to some extent the impression that it has been composed piecemeal, rather than that it has been an unified and rapidly thought out work. Portions of it certainly differ as to the value, but it contains plenty of bright ideas and happy effects; these the composer has caught and fixed on his tone-canvas with so much skill and success, that the musical world will look forward with no small interest to the next symphonic work from his pen.

T. L. SOUTHGATE.

MR. E. AGUILAR'S PIANOFORTE RECITALS.

Mr. Aguilar began his short course of Easter recitals at his own house in Gloucester Crescent, Hyde Park, on Monday afternoon. As usual, he displayed his versatility and catholicity of taste by playing a long list of pieces by "various masters." The list included the ninth number of Sir W. Sterndale Bennett's "Suite de Pièces," in B major; Beethoven's Sonata in A, Op. 101; Liszt's fifth "Rhapsodie Hongroise," in E minor and major; and several of Mr. Aguilar's own works, to wit, the MS. sonata of three movements in A minor; "Arethuse" (a melody) in A major; a Romanza in B flat; the "Day-dream," in E flat; the fantasia on "Lucia di Lammermoor"; the "Pensée Fugitive," in B flat, and the spirited "Carnival Dance" in C major. One of Mr. Aguilar's pupils, Miss A. Gold, was entrusted with Chopin's Polonaise in A flat, Op. 53, and a pretty valse of Janotha in E major. The sonata of Mr. Aguilar in A minor is a very fine work, full of effective contrasts. A bold and impetuous allegro is followed by a flowing cantabile sostenuto in the tonic major, with elegant variations and tenderest modulations. The finale is notable for its nice accentuation, bold left-hand work, and bursts of Beethovian fury. The agreeable recital lasted almost an hour-and-a-half. The second is fixed for Monday, when Schubert's noble Sonata in B major—by some styled the "military" one—is down on the list.

THE CARL ROSA OPERA COMPANY AT DRURY LANE.

The late Vincent Wallace's opera "Maritana" was first produced at Drury Lane Theatre in 1846, and at once gained the success that it deserved, but which, according to Cato, poor mortals do not invariably command. Mr. Carl Rosa revived "Maritana" last Saturday night, for the *début* of Miss Amy Sherwin in the title part. This young lady, evidently a novice, is of pleasing presence and has a light but very sweet soprano of extensive range; the *mezzo voce* is true and clear, and the upper notes of excellent quality. The stage action, as may be supposed, was wanting in colour, but always graceful and unaffected. The most successful points were scored in the two numbers known as "The Harp in the air," and "Scenes that are bright." Miss Sherwin is said to be a native of the United States, but educated—very *well* educated—in the Old World, as the Eastern hemisphere is still honourably called. In a word, although Miss Sherwin excited no actual *furore,* she made, nevertheless, a very favourable impression upon her audience. The other parts of the opera were sustained by Mr. J. W. Turner (Don Cæsar), Mr. H. Pope (Charles II.), Mr. L. Crotty (Don José), and Miss Josephine Yorke (Lazarillo). The recalls cannot be computed; enthusiastic encores were won for Lazarillo's song "Alas, those chimes," the fine trio "Turn on, old Time," "Yes, let me like a soldier fall," and "There is a flower that bloometh." The last *bis,* however, was declined, and very kindly, for these encores are a nuisance to the "wise and prudent."

From another pen are these words:—The production of "Colomba" is another success for all concerned and for English opera. The story of the libretto by Mr. Hueffer, so well-known as a musical editor and prominent critic, is outlined upon the late M. Prosper Merimée's romance, but the librettist has made some considerable alterations in the story and provided an effective opera book. The narrative in its new forms may be briefly stated thus:—The Count de Nevers arrives at Ajaccio as Governor of Corsica, accompanied by his daughter Lydia, and Orso della Rebbia, a Corsican, who has saved the Count's life at Waterloo. Orso is enamoured of Lydia, the Count's daughter, but there is the Corsican custom of the *Vendetta,* of which Orso is reminded on meeting his sister Colomba. Their father has, they believe, been slain by the Barracini, a feud having long existed between the two families. Orso is embarrassed by the urging of his sister on the one hand, and the dissuasion of his betrothed on the other. The Count induces Orso to accept the avowal by Giuseppe Barracini of his innocence. Colomba indignantly asserts his guilt, and appeals to the Savelli, who was near when the murderous shot was fired and found the dying Della Rebbia, who had just time to trace on a page of his pocket-book the letters "Giuseppe Barra." The renewed exhortations of Colomba determine Orso, who threatens the suspected murderer with vengeance, in the shape of a duel, disdaining the office of secret assassin. A meeting and an altercation between Orso and Giuseppe are cut short by a shot fired at the former from behind a wall by the latter's brother Antonio. Orso's left arm is wounded, but with his other arm he shoots Giuseppe, and, on the appearance of Antonio above the wall, fires again with effect. Chilina and her father, the brigand Savelli, are on the spot, and they hasten to the assistance of Orso, who has fainted. They support the wounded man to their retreat. The Count, Colombo, and villagers find the corpse of Giuseppe, with Colomba rejoicing in the accomplishment of the *Vendetta.* She and Lydia seek Orso in his concealment among the brigands, the lovers being left alone. Lydia's horror at Orso's supposed crime and her consequent rejection of him are overcome by his narration of the facts; renewed pledges of troth following. Colomba urges them to flight, soldiers being in pursuit. The two lovers determine to remain, Colomba, Chilina, and Savelli going forth in order to divert the attention of the approaching soldiers. The Count enters and undertakes the establishment of Orso's innocence; the lovers' happiness being clouded by the appearance of Colomba, borne in mortally wounded by a bullet from the soldiers. Colomba's dying expression of contentment at the accomplishment of the *Vendetta,* and the mourning sympathy of the lookers-on, form the final catastrophe of the opera as altered from that of the original narrative. It is to be first noticed with regard to the music, that "Colomba" has no overture, a fashionable omission much to be deprecated as a rule. The Prelude contains some excellent instrumentation, including the *Vendetta leit-motiv* and a general tendency of the composer to adhere very much to the doctrines of the advanced school. This movement, greatly applauded, was, in obedience to the will of the audience, repeated. The first scene, the Market Place of Ajaccio with an effective distant view of the sea, and much colour and animation, has some clever and brilliant dramatic music, with a solo for the brigand's daughter adorned with some charming instrumental effects. An orchestral incidental piece gives us a taste of what is called "martial music." A love scene, with a charming duet, effective declamatory sentences, and striking instrumentation, are present in this act. The second Act takes place on a village green. It opens with a short prelude of a serious tone, and a scena for Colomba with an effective Allegro, some spirited ballet music with a Saltarello, a Rustic March with ingenious and suggestive orchestration, and some good choral music, are to be found in the setting of this scene. The third Act opens with a road scene, and musically, with a brief prelude. Orso has a scena and a somewhat striking love song is included. Chilina is singing behind the scenes a quaint, old-fashioned ballad. The vigorous dramatic music, the attack upon Orso by the two Barracini and their destruction by Orso, the consternation of the country people, and the impressive sounds of a chanted "Requiem," make up this act. The fourth Act opens with another prelude, and has some pleasing duo movements, with effective if not very original sentences, and affording good opportunities for the excellent dramatic and vocal performance they received. The scene is in a valley. Colomba implores the lovers to escape from the soldiers; she is brought back mortally wounded and the work closes with impulsive and well contrasted musical illustrations. Notwithstanding some good dramatic situations, the gloom of the story and the repulsive notion of a systematically pursued vengeance abhorrent to the ideas of cultured English people, make Mr. Mackenzie's task no light one. His music shows good dramatic instincts and much earnestness, which promise well. He is too apt to be restless in his rhythm and to lack clearness of purpose constructively, faults some people are weak enough to regard as virtues. The orchestration is everywhere artistic and masterly. The composer conducted the performance, and was with the poet, manager, and chief singer called for by the audience to be congratulated upon the success of the work. The parts were well sustained by Mdme. Valleria, Mdlle. Baldi, Miss C. Perry, and Mr. B. M'Guckin, Mr. Ludwig, Mr. F. Navora, Mr. H. Pope, Miss E. Collins, Mr. B. Davies, and Mr. W. Esmond.

Another contributor says :—

On Monday night the second great event of the short season came off. Mr. A. C. Mackenzie, a British composer, produced and conducted his new opera "Colomba," entitled a "Lyrical Drama" (in four acts), founded on Prosper Merimée's tale (a twin sister of "Carmen"), and ably adapted for the stage, in English metrical stanzas, by Dr. Francis Hueffer. The story itself is repulsive enough, and so intricate that it may be well to quote the official "argument" at full length.

Orso Della Rebbia, a young Corsican captain, returns to his native country in the company of the Governor, Count Nevers, and his daughter Lydia, with whom Orso is in love. He is met at Ajaccio by his sister Colomba, who speedily indicates to him the sole object of her thoughts, viz., that he shall at once execute vengeance on the supposed murderers of their father—the brothers Barracini. But Orso is not disposed to undertake the task without proof, and is further dissuaded from it by Lydia. All save the latter proceed to the village of Pietranera, home of the Della Rebbia and Barracini families, whom in the second act the Count endeavours to reconcile. The heads of the houses are about to shake hands, when Colomba steps in, and openly accuses Giuseppe Barracini of killing her father, bringing forward as a witness one Savelli, a brigand, who is able to produce proof of the murder. This satisfies Orso, and he challenges his enemies to meet him in open fight, although he still refuses to seek revenge in cold blood; but in the next act, whilst waiting on the road to meet Lydia, he is accosted by Giuseppe Barracini, and suddenly, at a signal from the latter, Orso is fired at. The shot hits him in the left arm; with the right, he lifts his gun and shoots down Barracini, whose brother, next instant raising his head above the neighbouring

fence, receives the contents of Orso's second barrel. Each shot having proved fatal, Orso escapes with the brigand and his daughter into the "macchia," or bush. Hither, in the last act, come Colomba and Lydia, and, after a scene of recrimination and reconciliation between the lovers, the soldiers come to arrest Orso. The Count, however, arrives in time to direct his release, and promises to establish his innocence. Thus Orso and Lydia are made happy, but Colomba has been mortally wounded amid the skirmish with the soldiers, and dies as the curtain falls.

The author of the libretto, in a preface, avows his set "purpose" to discard the existing "Della Cruscan mannerisms of diction in the lyrical drama, as reflected in such "poets" as Bunn and Fitzball, and to write words in accordance with common sense and sound literary taste. Dr. Hueffer has freely introduced lyrical verse forms, with occasional double and triple rhymes, and treated the blank verse "with considerable and intentional liberty." The doctor has also modified the original tale; he kills Colomba in the sequel to meet the requirements of lyrical tragedy, and, in fact, has retained little more than the outline of the story.

The opera is thus cast : Colomba, Mdme. Valleria, Orso, Mr. Barton McGuckin ; De Nevers, Mr. W. H. Pope ; Savelli, Mr. F. Navara ; Chilina (daughter of Savelli), Miss C. Perry ; the brothers Barracini, Messrs. Ludwig and W. Esmond ; and Lydia, Mdme. Baldi.

I now come to the music. Mr. Mackenzie evidently, if not avowedly, adopts the Wagnerian plan of opera, that is to say, a continuity of subject, as contradistinguished from the old stiff and formal "set-piece" system. "Leit-motifs," too, are aptly used. Reserving a full opinion until after a second hearing, it is only just to the composer to acknowledge a fine, and, in some respects, a powerful work, well conceived, consistently carried out, and consummately "finished." The uninteresting, not to say repulsive plot, makes the opera a heavy affair, and the fourth act may be unhesitatingly denounced as a mistake. When the curtain finally dropped on Monday at ten minutes before midnight, the audience were quite exhausted. The opera might easily be made to end with the *vendetta*, the sole end and aim of its heroine, the homicidal Colomba.

A short introduction in F minor and major was unwearyingly encored. It is, nevertheless, pretty *lively* music, with clever modulations, and capitally scored. The chorus of fisherwomen and sailors in G opens the first act, *con spirito*; an obstinate suspension of the third on the dominant chord (G against A), reminds one of a similar device in the laughing chorus of "Der Freischütz" (same key). The succeeding deliverance of Savelli, the brigand, is a good specimen of richly accompanied recitative, and the key (G minor) invests it with a duly sombre colouring. The pretty "Vocero" of Chilina in E flat, "Gentle dove," with harp obbligato, is noticeable for a transition to C flat at the latter end. The *scena* between the lovers, Lydia and Orso, which begins in D and changes to F major (with episode in D flat) is a spontaneous, if not eloquent, dialogue in the accepted Wagnerian style of elaborately accompanied recitative; and at "the sweet words, I love you," the couple sing in unison for some bars. At last Colomba enters on a mule, to the tune of F sharp minor, and a graphic general *scena* ensues, full of dramatic vigour and stir. Colomba now sings a duet with her brother in D minor, a model of fine orchestral writing—(hautboy particularly expressive)—and without any "pull-up." Colomba afterwards sings the end of the "Vocero" (a "leit-motif") in E flat, ascending to G and B flat; and the chorus join in the cry of "Vendetta." A grand quintet and chorus in F, beautifully scored and well worked out, ends the first act.

The other acts are rather shorter. Act II. opens with a dolorous *largo* for Colomba, "What is my home to me," in E minor and major; the rhythm changes as well as the mode, and high B natural is written as "optional," G has also to be held, and a skip of the diminished seventh in descent occurs, from D natural to E sharp, on the word "swallow." No sensation was here excited. The ballet music in B flat and G sounds rather commonplace ; and the hymn in G, "Salve, Regina del Maggio," has (it is presumed intentionally) the same progression of melody, only in different time, as "Alla Trinità Beata" in the "Laudi Spirituali." After a rustic march in E flat comes a quartet in A flat, sung by the Count, Orso, and the brothers Barracini, a smooth suave subject, interrupted by an intrusion of Colomba, whereupon a powerful finale ends the act in E minor. Savelli denounces the two assassins, and Orso resolves to avenge his father. Here may be noted much poetical writing for the strings, and an effective figure drawn.

In Act III., opened by a pretty prelude in G, Orso sings a Corsican love song in G, "Will she come from the hill?" ascending to high G and A. Chilina has a far more beautiful ballad in F sharp minor, "So he thought of his love," certainly *one* gem of the opera. The scene between Orso and his enemy Giuseppe contains some rather coarse writing, relieved by many passages of elegance. The assassin, threatening Orso with death, sings a scale passage (bass clef) from low F sharp to high C natural, at which note the first shot is fired. The harmony changes hereabouts from four sharps to five flats, and the transitions of tonality are incessant. The "Requiem" hymn of the monks, in G minor (written for tenors and basses in thirds), sounds weak; and Colomba's triumphant shout of "Vendetta" on high B natural, blending with the "Requiem" chorus, hardly compensates for the weakness of the (musical) situation.

Act IV., as before hinted, is tedious and redundant. The duet between Colomba and Lydia, in D minor and major, sung on a dark stormy night, evidently wearied the public, and was hardly redeemed by the splendid vocalisation of Mdme. Valeria. The duet between the lovers, long and laboured, arrests the business vexatiously, although it rises to passionate fervour at the latter end. The key changes from G to E flat minor, E major, and E flat major. The scena ends in E flat minor. The lovers are reconciled, and although arrested for murder by the *sbirri*, Orso's two shots are held to be fully justified. Colomba, wounded to death, says that "she dies contented," joins the lover's hands, and expires with the (middle) B flat on her lips, and the word "Remember," the sun rising upon the scene; and a short final chorus, terminates the opera in the key of E flat.

"Colomba" was to be repeated on Thursday. A neat pianoforte score is published by Messrs. Novello, Ewer & Co. Of Mdme. Marie Roze's successful reappearance in "Faust," on Tuesday night, a few words next week—the last of the season.

SENOR SARASATE'S EVENING CONCERT.

The large and extremely enthusiastic audience assembled to do honour to the great Spanish violinist at St. James's Hall, on April 9th, gave distinct evidence of the high appreciation in which the very distinguished *virtuoso* is held here. The programme opened with Schubert's delicious "Unfinished Symphony in B minor," well played by what was practically the Philharmonic Society's orchestra, under the bâton of Mr. W. G. Cusins. The hero of the concert then gave Beethoven's violin concerto with such poetical fire, persuasive eloquence, and perfect technicalities of execution as enraptured his listeners. In a fantasia on themes from "Carmen," written by himself, Señor Sarasate gave a display of the various models of phrasing, bowing, double-stopping, and "harmonics," which was truly remarkable; the perfect tune, pure tone, and accuracy in attack of bow and fingers could not be excelled as an exhibition of virtuosity. The nocturne and scherzo from Mendelssohn's "Midsummer Night's Dream" came next, and, as ever, claimed the admiration which genius and perfect art demand. As exquisite tone pictures, the most hardened and obstinate admirers of the advanced school must surely confess to the power of their witchery. The popular arrangement of Chopin's "Nocturne" and "Spanish Dances," by Señor Sarasate himself, formed the last group of solos. The wonderful playing skill and fascinating power of the artist again aroused the enthusiasm of a discriminating audience; and, after being recalled at the close of every performance, the listeners now succeeded in getting an extra taste of his splendid control over the "king of the orchestra." Weber's "Euryanthe" Overture, spiritedly played, closed the concert. Señor Sarasate has, by general desire, arranged to give a second evening concert on Thursday, April 19th, with the assistance of the same band and conductor, when the programme will include Mendelssohn's "Violin Concerto" and Beethoven's C minor Symphony.

H.R.H. the Prince of Wales has duly applied for, and obtained from the Queen, a charter for the Royal College of Music.

FINSBURY CHORAL ASSOCIATION.

The Finsbury Choral Association gave a performance of the "Elijah" on the 5th inst., at the Holloway Hall. The principal vocalists were Miss Jessie Royd, Madame Florence Winn, Mr. Alfred Kenningham, and Mr. Vaughan Edwardes. The remarkable precision and finish with which the choruses were rendered throughout educed well merited applause. Miss Jessie Royd, though possessed of a fairly good voice, was evidently overtaxed in the air "Hear ye Israel," and her general "get up" and operatic style were certainly out of character with the occasion. Madame Florence Winn was particularly successful in the several contralto solos. Her facile and excellent delivery elicited much applause, and a peremptory recall. She has a rich pleasing voice, and sings like a true artist. The singing of Mr. Alfred Kenningham was much appreciated, notwithstanding an apparent attack of hoarseness. Mr. Vaughan Edwardes was scarcely physically or artistically equal to the arduous task of the Prophet, but nevertheless displayed qualities of promise. The accompaniments were exceedingly well played by Mr. Harding on the pianoforte, and Mr. Marchment on the harmonium, and the conductor, Mr. C. J. Dale officiated with his customary ability. The "Creation" is announced for May 17th.

BEDFORD.

The grand concert held at the Assembly Rooms of this town on the evening of April 5th deserves ample notice. It was patronised by the Hon. W. Lowther, M.P., General Mills, and other local "notables." Mr. Polonaski and Mr. Bond Andrews began with a capital rendering of Beethoven's favourite sonata for piano and violin in F major, whereof the scherzo is alway a *crux* to ordinary performers. Mr. Polonaski afterwards played two violin solos with great taste and finish, to wit, Bach's adagio in C, on the "G" string, and his own "Pensée Fugitive" in E minor, a very poetical effusion. A third piece was the late Henri Wieniawski's "Légende et Mazurka" in G, rather too long for the theme. Mr. Bond Andrews played his own "Grotesque Oriental," No. 2, the "Anglaise," No. 1, "The Return," from the "Maypole," and the "Spinning Song," all characteristic compositions, well conceived and scholastically worked out. Messrs. Polonaski and Bond Andrews finished the concert at half-past ten with Gregoire Leonard's duet on "Tannhäuser," an effective arrangement of the March in B major for piano and violin. Mdme. Aviglioni sang "Batti, batti," and Mr. Charles De Wolfe the serenade of his friend Mr. Bond Andrews, "My lady sleeps."

HIGH WYCOMBE.

On the evening of the 2nd inst. the Choral Association gave their last concert of the season in the Town Hall, before a large audience. The following was the programme:—

"The May Queen"....................	S. Bennett.
Part-song. "Blanche ".	Kucken.
Air, "Love sounds the alarm" ("Acis and	
Galatea ")	Handel.
Pianoforte duet, Slavonic Dances	Dvorak.
Aria, "Non mi dir"	Mozart.
Canon, "Hark to the rolling drum"	Bishop.
Pianoforte Solos—	
"Lieder ohne Wôrte"......................	Mendelssohn.
"Gavotte"............................	Janotha.
Chorus, "Now tramp"	Bishop.

Bennett's charming pastoral is so well known to the readers of the *Musical Standard* that I need not dwell on its many beauties. The performance was a great treat, the choral portion of the cantata being splendidly sung; nor were the artists less successful, Miss Fenna as the May Queen doing full justice to a most charming part, while Miss Webb as the Queen, Mr. Hodgson as the Lover, and Mr. C. Rose as Robin Hood were equally effective. Miss Fenna gave a splendid rendering of Mozart's exacting air, and in response to an enthusiastic encore delighted everyone with Sullivan's "Let me dream again." Mr. J. G. Wrigley, Mus.Bac., Oxon., besides conducting, played three of Mendelssohn's Lieder, Nos. 1, 27, and 30, and a charming gavotte by Jules Janotha, which ought to become popular, and with his brother, Mr. W. A. Wrigley, two of Dvorak's Slavonic Dances, which were much enjoyed. The ladies of the chorus won a well deserved encore for Bishop's canon, and a magnificent performance of "Now tramp" brought a most enjoyable concert to a close.

MUSIC IN READING.

(From our Own Correspondent.)

An important movement in Church music here has recently been successfully inaugurated at St. Mary's Church, where Gounod's "Redemption" has been impressively rendered at two special week-day services.

Part 1 was given on the Tuesday in Holy Week, and Parts 2 and 3 on the Thursday in Easter Week. Large congregations attended the services, and the effect of the music was evidently received as a solemn act of worship. The assistance of members of the Philharmonic Society (by whom the same music was so successfully performed last December), was obtained to form a large special choir, and Mr. Strickland, the organist of the Church, played the accompaniments with a wonderfully good imitation of the orchestral effects, upon the fine four manual organ, by Henry Willis, which the Church fortunately possesses.

I would express the hope that these services may be the first of a series of similar ones, that in Reading, as in other towns of similar resources, the oratorio may be restored to its original purpose.

On Wednesday, 28th ult., Mr. F. J. Read, gave an organ recital at Christ Church, when he played a selection of interesting organ music by Bach, Mendelssohn, Guilmant, &c., artistically and well.

On Wednesday, April 4th, the second subscription concert of the Philharmonic Society was given in the Town Hall, Mendelssohn's "Elijah" being performed with a full orchestra and chorus. The soloists engaged were Mrs. Oswald (substitute for Mrs. F. King), Miss Amy Aylward, Miss Hilda Wilson, and Mr. Henry Guy; and Mr. Burnett (leader); Mr. J. C. B. Tirbutt (organist); and Mr. W. H. Strickland (conductor) occupied their usual posts. The performance was a good one, although one or two choruses went rather unsteadily in some places, and the band occasionally overpowered the soloists; but on the other hand some of the choral numbers were given with a vigorous attack and decided power, and others with appropriate feeling and expression.

Mr. Oswald replaced Mr. King (whose hoarseness necessitated the services of a substitute being engaged the same morning) with considerable success, and I venture to predict that he may become one of the leading exponents of the princicpal parts in "Elijah." Miss Hilda Wilson also made a most favourable impression, and sang the alto music with great effect. Miss Aylward and Mr. Guy both did their work artistically, and upon the whole, I can fairly call the performance one of the best efforts of the Philharmonic Society.

The Duchess of Wellington and many influential people from the town and neighbourhood were present, but the reserved balconies were not so well filled as they should have been.

LIVERPOOL.

(From our Own Correspondent.)

An earnest, practical and sympathetic assemblage of hardworking musicians met in this city on Saturday afternoon last, the occasion being the regular monthly meeting of the Society of Professional Musicians, and the topic for discussion "Local Musical Examinations," propounded by Dr. Henry Fisher, of Blackpool, in a very able speech. There was a lively interest shown in the subject, and a natural curiosity to know to what it would tend. There is not the slightest doubt that the issue will surprise most people and in some quarters perhaps cause consternation; and on the other hand again there are those no doubt who will laugh the scheme to scorn and ridicule the idea, but it cannot be denied that the society is about to take a very important step and one which it is quite competent to carry to a successful issue. Mr. J. Marsden, of Manchester, was voted to the chair, and he in very happy language introduced Dr. Fisher to the meeting.

The following gentlemen, among others, were present: Drs. G. Marsden (treasurer), H. Hiles, Messrs. H. Stevens, C. B. Grundy, J. Thorley, W. J. Young, W. J. Wrigley, and E. Hilton (Manchester); Dr. H. Fisher (Blackpool), A. Alexander, James Dawber (honorary secretary), J. Gaskell and C. D. Mortimer (Wigan); F. Dean (Lancaster), H. Grimshaw, W. D. Hall, F. Haworth, J. J. Monk, and M. Schneider (Liverpool); J. M. Field (Bowdon), R. B. Woodward (St. Helens), T. S. Hill, and

W. H. Hunt (Birkenhead). The Council met before the general meeting and elected Messrs. A. Hague and G. F. Grundy of Manchester, members of the Society. Before the chief business of the evening began, Mr. W. D. Hall (Liverpool), was elected by a large majority, a member of the Council, in the room of the late Mr. J. L. Goodwin (Manchester). Dr. Fisher is a fluent speaker and requires very few notes; he hardly ever pauses to think, but having mastered his subject, he seems to have no difficulty in putting into intelligible language what he wishes to impress upon his audience. It was amusing to see the different phases of expression upon each countenance as startling ideas were thrown out one after the other. Astonishment and surprise were written clearly upon every face, in some cases not unmingled with dismay. As each pet scheme, which some one or other was interested in, was knocked over without ceremony by the speaker, nods, winks, and audible expressions of approval or otherwise were flying about with an alacrity quite out of keeping with the seriousness of the subject. The speaker's high estimation of the system pursued by the late Mr. Curwen was very forcible, but too strong and of too much prominence. His illustration of the parents or the maiden aunt being, in the past, the real local examiners, was very good, and his amusing account of the immense amount of time that used to be spent upon the "Battle of Prague" and the fondness of parents for the piece with its effect of big cannons and rattle of artillery was a very good point, well led up to, culminating in the fact that after all, the Pater and Mater were the real local examiners, even in the present day of official local examiners. Dr. Fisher did not spare the local examiners or local secretaries, and explained that he himself was one, so that what he said equally applied to himself as well as to others holding the same capacity. He gave some very hard knocks on this matter, but no doubt they were well deserved. Of one thing there could be no doubt, and that was that the speaker was thoroughly in earnest, but he spoke so quickly and seemed to hurl one thing after another with such precipitation that the listeners were taken quite aback, and in fact it might be said that Dr. Fisher took the wind completely out of the sails of any objector who intended, or was inclined to develop in that direction. One representative of the R.A.M. got up in wrath, anent the rather hard remarks somewhat reflecting upon the local examiners, but this episode was soon forgotten. Some members objected to the speed with which schemes were promulgated by the society, and also as to the youthfulness of the society and its supposed consequent non-standing, but the Secretary explained the society numbered about eighty members, representing a large area, who were all men of some standing, and that the numbers were being added to day by day; it was only by enrolling and carrying out such schemes that the society could expect any locus standi, and the esteem and support of the entire musical profession. That the board of examiners to be constituted will contain men on whom the public can rely, is admissible, and that the examination will command respect, is I think, conclusive. There was a great feeling that what Dr. Fisher said about "why do we require an examiner to be sent down from London?" was very forcible, true, and conclusive. Dr. Hiles' question as to what was the raison-d'être of the society, if it was not to advance the interest of the musician, and how this was to be done if not by practicable work, was very telling, and make an impression, and was a complete answer to the protests of one or two that the society was travelling at too fast a pace. The fact is, as I hinted a fortnight ago, that no one was prepared for the issue following Dr. Fisher's able speech, but his arguments and resolutions swept away all objections there might have been. The chairman, also very quick to resent any trifling with the subject, kept the members strictly to the matter under discussion, and his admirable firmness saved a deal of valuable time.

The Council are to have a special meeting on the 29th inst., to discuss the whole scheme, including the book of questions to be used for the theoretical examination. The developed scheme will then be laid before the members of the society at the regular meeting in May.   J. J. M.

It may be of interest to state, that a larger sum of money was received for admission to the last Philharmonic concert than has been taken for any previous concert given by the society since its foundation in 1813.

MR. WALTER BACHE'S RECITALS.

Mr. Walter Bache held a second pianoforte recital at St. James's Hall on Monday afternoon. His first (on November 6th, 1882), was duly noticed at the time. On this occasion Mr. Bache temporarily abandoned his master the Abbé Liszt, and took up texts of Beethoven. He chose the two sonatas known as Op. 31, No. 2, in D minor, and Op. 106, in B flat, a tremendous work for brain and fingers. Mr. Bache played magnificently. An enthusiastic University Wrangler, who was present, said that his alternations of mood and variations of style, according to the requirements of the text, might be likened to a rivulet, a storm in the mountains, and—at last—the sweet voice of a woman. Other pieces were the Rondo à Capriccio in G, " Rage over the last penny," and 32 variations in C minor. Mr. Bache was vehemently applauded. Mr. W. Shakespeare sang excerpts from the well-known " Liederkreis " very charmingly.

THE BROUSIL MATINÉES.

At the third " Musical Afternoon " of the family Brousil, on April 5th, Mdme. Wurm and Miss Bertha Brousil began with Beethoven's third sonata for pianoforte and violin in E flat, which was admirably interpreted by both artists. The same master's beautiful pianoforte trio in C Minor, Op. 1, No. 3, which " Papa " Haydn so unsuccessfully advised the composer *not* to publish, concluded the concert at half-past five o'clock. Mdlle. Wurm, the gifted pupil of Mdme. Schumann, and a *protégé* of Dr. George Grove, greatly distinguished herself at this *matinée* as a pianist and a composer. After a very effective execution of Mendelssohn's " Variations Serieuses " in D minor (played out of book), Mdlle. Wurm introduced her own (MS.) sonata for pianoforte and violoncello in G, dedicated to Mdme. Schumann. This fine, and for so young a writer highly creditable work, consists of four movements, viz., an allegro in G, dignified and elaborate, yet never tedious ; a quaint and piquant scherzo in C minor, a (too) short andante in E flat, a cantabile as regards form ; a sort of chorale or canto fermo for the keyed instrument accompanied by the violoncello in triplets ; and a finale in G, a spirited rondo, of which the pretty theme is charmingly varied. The work must be heard again and again ; it only occupies in performance the brief interval of twenty minutes. Mdlle. Wurm plays with power and *aplomb*, and in soft passages displays much of the *finesse* and elegant humoursome style of her mistress. She has an elastic and delicate touch, yet all the sforzandos are effectively and emphatically enunciated. Full chords and rapid scales are executed with equal force and finish. Mdlle. Wurm's sonata evoked much applause. Mr. J. A. Brousil played the violoncello part in first-rate style.

NEWCASTLE-ON-TYNE.

(From our Own Correspondent.)

Our musical season is drawing rapidly to a close, and with the exception of Mr. Ainsworth's Violin Recital on April the 13th, and the Vocal Societies' Invitation Concerts in May, is now almost over as far as concerns any concert of consequence.

Dr. Creser's new work " Eudora," which was performed for the first time in Leeds, on November 28th, last year, will be heard in our Town Hall, on May 1st, when Mr. Albion Alderson's Vocal Amateur Society will give their second invitation concert of the season. Dr. Creser is expected to conduct his own work for the occasion.

Mr. E. Prout's cantata " Alfred," and a selection from Haydn's " Seasons," will be sung at the Newcastle Amateur Vocal Society's second invitation concert, on May 9th, in the Town Hall.

One of the most enjoyable ballad concerts of the season took place in the Town Hall, on March 16th. The vocalists, Miss Anna Williams, Miss Mackenzie, Mr. H. Piercy, and Mr. Maybrick were in their best form, and scored many hearty encores for their excellent singing. Signor Bisaccia, as solo pianist and accompanist, left nothing to be desired. Perhaps the most interesting feature of the evening, was the first appearance of the youthful lady violinist, Miss Maria Schumann, who performed the Andante and Finale from Mendelssohn's Violin Concerto, and a Fantasia on English airs by Weist Hill, (her excellent violin master) in a manner

deserving every praise. Miss Schumann's playing is conspicuous for a rare purity of tone, and true musical feeling. The lady violinist was enthusiastically encored after both pieces.

Notwithstanding the fine weather and many counter attractions, Sullivan's æsthetic opera, performed by D'Oyly Carte's Opera Company, drew a crowded house to the Tyne Theatre, on Monday, April 8th. Miss Ethel McAlpine is a charming Patience, and sings her part admirably. The choruses went well and the orchestra played with spirit and great precision throughout, under the able conductorship of Mr. P. W. Hatton. Sullivan's opera is preceded by a musical farce entitled " Matrimony," composed by Mr. P. W. Hatton. Notwithstanding the music is not free from many reminiscences, it is always pleasing and in accordance with the libretto.

H. W.

WORTHING.—The second concert of the Musical Association was held at the Montague Hall, on Wednesday evening, April 4th. The first part was Mendelssohn's " Athalie," and the second part miscellaneous. The principal vocalists were Mrs. Colin Kerr, Mdme. Clara West, and Miss Lottie West ; organist, Mr. F. J. Sawyer, Mus. Bac. ; pianist, Mr. W. H. Price ; reader, Mr. W. F. Fuller, Esq. ; conductor, Mr. F. D. Carnell, Mus. Bac. The audience was numerous and the concert altogether a success.

GRESHAM HALL BRIXTON, S.W.—At the fortnightly " Musical Evening " of the Surrey County School of Music, held on April 11th, under the direction of Mr. Humphrey J. Stark, Mus. Bac., Oxon., the following artists assisted :—Miss Alma Sanders, Miss Nellie Chaplin, Miss Kate Chaplin (violin), Mr. Asperne Deane (violin), Mr. Joseph Hayes (flute). Vocalists : Miss Evelyn Willoughby, and Mr. Henry Yates. At the pianoforte, Mr. W. E. Stark. The pianofortes were kindly lent by Messrs. Pleyel, Wolff and Co.

SHERBORNE ABBEY.—A concert was given in the Assembly Rooms of the Digby Hotel, on Tuesday evening, in aid of the Abbey Choir Boys' Endowment Fund. The first part consisted of Mozart's 12th Mass (omitting Nos. 5 and 6), with English words, the accompaniments being fairly rendered by an orchestra, which, with the exception of Mr. Ramsay, the leader, was composed entirely of amateurs. The principal vocal parts were taken by Miss May Bell, R.A.M., Mrs. Lyon, Mr. R. W. Mill, and Mr. Witherington. In the second part of the concert (miscellaneous), Miss Bell charmed the audience with her expressive singing, Mr. Mills also gained great applause. The orchestra and chorus numbered nearly 100. The conductor was Mr. G. E. Lyle, organist of the Abbey Church, &c.

SHEFFIELD.—In the presence of a large audience, " Victorian,' a new opera founded on Longfellow's " Spanish Student," was produced last week at the Sheffield Theatre by the Royal English Opera Company. The libretto, which in incident keeps somewhat closely to the poem, is by Mr. J. F. R. Anderson, the composer of the opera being Mr. J. Edwards, who is the conductor of the band, and met with a very cordial reception on entering the orchestra. The overture is tuneful, and there are some skilful choruses and pleasing airs in the opera. As the heroine Miss Lucy Franklein's vocalisation was marked by care and precision, and Mr. Redfern Hollins sang well in the title rôle. The opera, says one writer, in spite of some faults, will probably rank amongst standard English Works.

OLDHAM.—The Vocal Society's concert, the second of the season, was given recently at the Town Hall. As is usual, the members of the society, with their friends, entirely filled the hall, many finding a difficulty in securing seats. The cantata " Psyche " (Gade) is one requiring a fineness of execution which any but a first-rate choir would find it difficult to produce. The solos were well given throughout, all the parts being amply maintained. The second part of the programme, consisting of glees and songs of a miscellaneous character, was given in the very able manner of which the society is capable. The songs deserving special mention are so numerous that we refrain from particularising, while among the part-songs " The Merry March Breeze," and " Winter Days " met with deserved applause. The solos were sung by members of the society, and the conductor was Mr. Joseph Clafton.

HORNS, KENNINGTON.—The Victoria Glee Club of male voices, under the Presidency and Vice-presidency of Drs. J. F. Bridge, and F. E. Gladstone, gave an admirable smoking concert in the above hall on the evening of the 10th inst. The club is making rapid strides in a right direction, singing with much precision and expression. Bishop's name figured conspicuously in the programme, and such names as Pearsall and Beale were not omitted, but the finest performance of the evening was the admirable rendering of Cooke's sterling old glee " Strike the lyre." Great praise is certainly due to the conductor, Mr. W. Sexton. Several songs were contributed. Mr. Bell (of Westminster Abbey), sang in his own artistic style, though his voice on this occasion was not quite under his control. The other soloists were Messrs. Heney, White, Sanderson, and Kersel, all contributing songs which were more or less appreciated, the last named gentleman possessing a splendid tenor voice, but his singing shows a want of voice cultivation and musical declamation. The accompanists were Mr. James Hallé and Mr. Geo. F. Grover.

THE ATHENÆUM, SHEPHERD'S BUSH.—The St. Andrew's Choral Society gave its closing concert of the season, on the 4th inst., and the largeness of the audience allows the thought that the society is flourishing. The conductor, Mr. Kilbey, must have worked hard to get the forces at his disposal to act so well together. A part of Haydn's "Seasons" and a new humorous cantata, by that excellent young musician, Mr. Edmund Rogers, entitled "Beauty and the Beast," constituted the fare provided for the friends and supporters of the society, and to judge from the applause it may be asserted that satisfaction was given. It hardly concerns me to say a word excepting to speak with respect to the cantata. The musicianly skill displayed in a similar cantata, "Blue Beard," to which reference was made last year, predisposed a favourable opinion as to this new work, and the success this new work achieved quite realized our anticipations. Several numbers had to be repeated, including a chorus, a soprano solo, and a recitative for the bass, who of course represented the "Beast." An aria buffa for the bass was also redemanded, but the request was not responded to. With one exception, a notable one, those who took the soli were unknown to me. The chorus and orchestra alike contributed to make the presentation worthy of the work, which I should like to hear a second time in town, before deciding whether it will be likely to be as popular as the composer's "Blue Beard." That the work of a good musician is apparent throughout, may go without question.

ST. LEONARD'S-ON-SEA.—On Tuesday last a most enjoyable morning concert was given in the Royal Concert Hall, in which the following artists took part :—Violoncello, Mons. J. Hollman ; soprano, Miss Beata Francis ; contralto, Miss Annie Layton ; Messrs. Earnest Cecil and Cecil Traherne ; solo pianoforte, Mdme. Mina Gould. Owing to indisposition, the last-named artist was unable to play her solo, but ably assisted in accompanying some of the vocal music. Mr. Arthur L'Estrange kindly consented, at a moment's notice, to play in her stead, and performed with great brilliancy and taste a composition of his own ("Chant des Matelots.") Mons. J. Hollman played in magnificent style a Nocturne of Chopin and a Mazurka by Popper; and in the second an Andante and Finale in A minor (Goltermann). Miss Annie Layton sang with much expression Barnby's pretty song, "When the tide comes in," and also "The three singers," by Berthold Tours. A melodie religeuse "Ave Maria" (Gounod), Bach, sung by Miss Beata Francis, with charming 'cello obbligato by Mons. J. Hollman, was excellently rendered. The other vocalists, Mr. Ernest Cecil and Mr. Cecil Traherne, were both very well received. Special mention may be made of Mdme. Mina Gould's new duet for equal voices, "Eyes," which was sung with much taste by these gentlemen, and also of the pretty song entitled "Stay," by the same composer, in which Mr. Ernest Cecil's fine voice was heard to great effect. It is much to be regretted that such an exhibition of talent was so poorly patronised, and the thinness of the audience seems to speak badly for the appreciation of really good music in such a large place as St. Leonard's. It is, indeed, surprising that such a distinguished artist as Mons. J. Hollman should have to appear before an audience of about only fifty persons, when there should have been hundreds, but those who were fortunate enough to be present last Tuesday afternoon will not soon forget his superb playing, and it is to be hoped that when he next visits St. Leonard's the Royal Concert Hall may be crowded in every part.

The Leeds Orchestral Society gave a performance of Sterndale Bennett's "May Queen," at the Church Institute, on Monday evening. The principal vocalists were Miss Hoyle, Miss Lupton, Mr. G. Wadsworth, and Mr. J. Atha. Mr. W. H. Hanson conducted. The second part of the programme was miscellaneous, and included the March from "Tannhäuser."

It is stated that Sir Michael Costa has sent to the Naples Conservatorium, in which institution he completed his musical education, an autograph copy of his opera "Malek-Adel," accompanied by the following letter :—"This opera of 'Malek-Adel,' composed and copied by me, was represented for the first time in the Italian Opera at Paris, in the Salle Favart, in 1837. After the fire that destroyed that theatre my score was almost miraculously found under the smoking ruins, partly consumed by fire. Having been asked to make a gift of another manuscript to the Royal College of Music in Naples I have re-written that score, and offer it with pleasure to the celebrated archives of the college.— London, 20th March, 1883.—M. COSTA."

SATURDAY POPULAR ORGAN RECITALS, BOW, E.—TO-NIGHT, Mr. W. S. HOYTE. Vocalists, Miss Annie Williams and Mr. W. H. Brereton.

FACTS about FIDDLES.—Violins Old and New, by JOHN BROADHOUSE. Price 6d. ; by post, 6½d. W. REEVES, Fleet Street, London.

FOR SALE.—Organ Music, Violin, and other String Music, Operas, Oratorios, Full Scores, Treatises, Histories, Biographies, and English and Foreign Works in various Branches of Literature.—On Sale by W. REEVES, 185, Fleet-street, London.

PRINCIPAL CONTENTS OF THIS NUMBER.

LONDON: SATURDAY, APRIL 14, 1883.

ORCHESTRAL EFFECTS AND KEYBOARD MANNERISMS.

VI.

IN the transference of orchestral music to either the pianoforte or the organ keyboard, there is nothing deserving of more consideration than the careful comparison of the different mannerisms of tone production. It is quite certain that very little of the tone-colour powers of the orchestra can find any representation on the pianoforte, and in truth the tone-colour of the band is but feebly reflected on the organ; still the key-board performers may with more success imitate the orchestral methods of tone pronunciation, and thereby convey through the power of imaginative association, something of the enunciation and phrasing of the orchestral masses. Yet it must be confessed that too little attention has been turned in the direction of a studied comparison of orchestral versus key-board mannerisms of tone-speech or pronunciation. It may be broadly said that the imperfectly trained performer on any instrument merely produces or plays the notes, but the artistic executant fulfils three conditions in connection with every produced sound : he takes care to effect a true, sharp point of attack ; he firmly maintains the sound during its exact time value, and he takes pains to secure a well defined termination or point of departure to the given sound. Now, the study of the comparative modes of enunciation to be observed in the pronunciation of orchestral and in the tone production of key-board instruments, may be based upon these three essential tone conditions, attack, duration, and termination. Though the tone-producing methods of the orchestra are broadly distinguished by the methods of setting strings and tubes in the act of tone formation, there are numerous modes by which the sound producing conditions are fulfilled. It may be observed here, that much of the life of an orchestral instrument depends upon its self-justification in the three-fold direction of attack, duration, and termination. All instruments fulfil the first-named condition of attack more or less satisfactorily, but some fail in the second and third, as do the harp and pianoforte, in having limited or weak powers of tone duration, and a consequent feeble or uncontrollable method of terminating their sounds. It is the failure of the harp as regards the want of a full power of tone duration, and the subsequent faculty of a sharply defined termination of its sounds, which limits its usefulness and keeps it in the orchestral background, so to speak. The pianoforte gains on the harp, not only through its exquisitely sensitive touch, but by its fuller powers of tone duration. To the organ, with its artificial wind supply and fixed wind pressures, must be assigned the credit of best fulfilling the second of the three conditions of sound production, the power of an even tone sustentation; hence its calm dignity. The bowed instruments have splendid faculties of attack and termination, and only a little less satisfactory power of tone duration. The orchestral wind instruments have well defined powers of attack, excellent powers of tone duration, and perhaps a somewhat less satisfactory command of the terminating points of the notes produced. The history of the orchestra is, quite apart from questions as to the value of given tone qualities, indeed the oft-told story of the "survival of the fittest." In the string family we see the old fashioned six-stringed members of the family, with their want of a strong, nervous power of attack, dismissed at quite an early period in the history of what may be called the modern orchestra. Similarly certain members of the flute and other wind families, producing their tones in such compasses as least suited their peculiar *embouchure* powers of attack, passed away from the roll-call of the orchestra. And the orchestra of our day is simply a collection of the best tone-producing members of the several instrumental types. Only those instruments in fact which are prepared to do earnest, nervous, expressive work have been able to hold their own; and their test of prolonged life has been technically their well developed faculties for the fulfilment of the three-fold tone producing conditions spoken of as the several functions of attack, duration, and note termination.

E. H. TURPIN.

THE LOGIC OF COUNTERPOINT.

THIRD SERIES.

VI.

" IT is permitted," says CHERUBINI, still dealing with four-part counterpoint of the first species, " to pass to " a perfect concord by direct movement between any " two of the three lower or the three upper parts, " this permission not being extended to the relation-

" ship between the two extreme parts, unless such " progressions are absolutely unavoidable." In truth it is no longer possible to avoid passing perfect concords when the vocal score has attained to the number of four or more parts; and it may be remarked that in a fuller harmony, the ear is neither able to trace out passed perfect concords very definitely or consequently any longer conscious of disagreeable effects arising from their presence. It is however still advisable to treat the external parts strictly in this respect, for they outline the moving mass of harmony. With regard to the passing of perfect concords between the two outside parts, it may be noticed that as the bad effect of such progressions is sensibly minimised by the presence of the internal and sympathetic harmony, it is not so large a fault to pass perfect concords in the movements of external parts as it is to permit the presence of such faulty progressions in thin, clear, and palpably transparent two-part counterpoint. Sometimes, too, it happens that the compass of either the soprano or bass part (especially the range of the lower voice) will make it necessary in some positions of the chords to allow passed fifths or octaves between external parts in order to avoid sending the upper part too high or the lower part too low, in endeavouring to escape from covered consecution. The theorist next points out that "the complete common chord " should occupy the first bar, but if this arrangement " will prevent a subsequent and desired flow of the " various contrapuntal melodies in action, then it " would not be wrong to lead off with an incomplete " chord." CHERUBINI even thinks that license in this direction may be carried to the length of allowing all the parts to start from one note sounded in two or three octaves. However, such a liberty could be rarely called for. The observations just made have a direct application to the last bar. It is not without interest to again note, especially with regard to the last bar, that the old masters frequently terminated a piece even in four parts (and apart from any harmonic reason in connection with chords having minor thirds), with a chord lacking its third, while modern composers partly impelled by the cadence form involving the double progression of the leading-note and dominant minor seventh to the key-note and its third, very frequently elect to terminate a movement with a chord having no fifth in it. It seems, the ancients preferred the solid strong effect of the fifth to the sacrifice of the third, while moderns on the other hand choose by preference the sweet sensitive sound of the third to the sacrifice of the firm, strength-giving fifth. This matter might be enlarged upon, as illustrative of the two musical types in which truthful severity and luxurious sweetness have their distinct reigns in the philosophy of the art.

E. H. TURPIN.

The first festival of the Bloomsbury Church Choir Union will take place at St. Giles-in-the-Fields Church, in Broad Street, at the Oxford Street end of Tottenham Court Road, on Thursday, April 19th, at 8. The music will include Smart's Service in F, one of Haydn's motets, and the " Hallelujah " chorus from the "Messiah". The clergy, organists, and choristers of the important district represented, have taken an active interest in the new and useful association, and the Bloomsbury Church Union should have the sympathy of all interested in Church music.

Foreign Musical Intelligence.

"Robin Hood," Herr Dietrich's new opera, has been produced at Cassel.

Eugene d'Albert has given four piano recitals in Dresden with great success.

The new theatre at Prague will open on May 1st with Massenet's "Hérodiade."

A new Mass by Signor Montanelli was recently heard with critical commendation at Pisa.

Le Guide Musical contains a short biographical sketch of Marcella Sembrich, the well-known cantatrice.

Herr R. Franz is suffering from deafness and paralysis of both hands. All will sympathise with the eminent song writer.

Ponchielli's "Miserere," and a "Salve Regina," by Carlotta Ferrari, are among the tokens of a revived interest in church music in Italy.

Fraülein Marianne Brandt, the celebrated German singer, has received gold medals from the Grand Duke of Weimar and the Duke of Sachsen-Altenburgh.

Verdi says "Iago" or "Othello" is not yet written down, though it is asserted that the representative Italian composer has spent much thought upon the proposed work.

Signor T. Mabellini has been nominated Commander of the Order of the Crown of Italy; Signori Gialdino Gialdini, Giovanni Quirici, and Francesco Paoli Tosti have been honoured by similar nominations to different Orders.

It is stated that the principal works at the National Festival at Ghent this year will be Beethoven's Ninth Symphony, Gevaert's "Super Flumina Babylonis," a new composition by Samuel, and Waelput's "Cantate de la Pacification."

It is said that an English lady—Mrs. Florence Steward —is the composer of "La Regina di Scozia," an opera lately produced with success. The lady was the composer of "Suocera," an attractive operetta produced a few years ago at Naples.

"Mademoiselle Dynamite" is the title of a new comic opera awaiting production, words and music by M. Paul Courtois. Notwithstanding the painfully suggestive title, the action does not take place in our day, but is dated for the year 1803, at Bethencourt-sur-Mer.

At Berlin, according to annual custom on Good Friday, the members of the Singakademie, assisted by the Philharmonic Band, gave a performance of Graun's oratorio, "Der Tod Jesu." The large audience showed that the work is still as attractive as ever, though first produced as far back as the 26th March, 1755, in the Berlin Cathedral.

A wish has often been expressed, in our own columns and elsewhere, that the musical authorities at the Universities would arrange to give practical instruction to undergraduates intending to take Holy Orders, and we have therefore great pleasure in announcing that a scheme of this sort is being put forward with the sanction of the Board of Musical Studies at Cambridge. The lectures are to be given by Dr. Garrett, who as a composer, teacher, and organist, is well known beyond the limits of the University city, and the object of the course is stated to be "to convey such musical information as shall enable clergymen to exercise intelligently the large influence on the cultivation of music in the parish schools and its employment in the services of the church which usually attaches to their position.' No previous technical knowledge will be assumed. The following subjects will be treated in the course :—Construction of the scale, grammar, and notation of music, methods of elementary musical instruction for the primary school, choir training, speaking and singing, intoning, chanting, Anglican and Gregorian chants, hymnology, service music, anthems, accompaniment. Gentlemen who desire to attend are requested to leave their names, as soon as possible, with Messrs. Deighton, Bell, and Co., Trinity Street, who will also receive the fee (one guinea and a half) for the course. The musical resources of the University will thus be brought to bear upon a really practical object, and it is to be hoped that the effort will meet with the success which it deserves.—*Church Bells.*

Organ News.

LIVERPOOL.

Mr. W. T. Best gave two organ recitals in St. George's Hall, on Saturday, April 7th :—

AFTERNOON PROGRAMME.

Fantasia in G major	Bach.
Andante (Trio in C minor)	Mendelssohn.
Introduction and Fugue in E minor	Raff.
Barcarolle, "Accours dans ma nacelle"	Rossini.
Andante in A major	Smart.
Finale (Fourth Symphony)	Widor.

EVENING PROGRAMME.

Overture ("Fe Fiddle Burger")	Adam.
Air, "Angls ever bright and fair"	Handel.
Pastorale Russe, "An Village"	Tschaikowsky.
Air with variations in A flat major	Heus.
Prelude and Fugue in D major	Mendelssohn.
Fanfare Militaire	Ascher.

CRYSTAL PALACE.

Mr. A. J. Eyre's programmes on Saturday last were as follows :—

Allegro moderato and Adagio (Sonata No. 1)	Mendelssohn.
Prière et Mélodie	Guilmant.
Bourrée	Saunders.
Serenade from a Quartet	Haydn.
Romanza, "Sie Vendicta " ("Dinorah ")	Meyerbeer.
Selection ("Redemption")	Gounod.
Offertoire	Kühmstedt.
Airs ("Elijah ")	Mendelssohn.
Grand Chœur	Guilmant.
Berceuse	Raber.
Song, "The Lost Chord"	Sullivan.
Andante quasi Allegretto	Stephens.
Operatic selection ("Le Huguenots ")	Meyerbeer.

PRESTON.

The following is the programme of an organ recital given by Mr. James Tomlinson, in the new Public Hall, on Thursday, April 5th :—

Overture in F	Thorne.
Andante (Symphony in D)	Haydn.
Gavotte in B minor	Bach.
Andante (Op. 1)	Mailly.
Overture ("Le Lac des Fêtes")	Auber.
Entr'acte ("La Colombe "), Marche Militaire	Gounod.

And on Saturday, April 7th :—

Overture ("Saul ")	Handel.
Minuet	Mendelssohn.
Triumphal March ("Alfred ")	Prout.
Airs ("Nino ")	Verdi.
Air and chorus ("Placido e il Mar ")	Mozart.
Overture ("L'Etoile du Nord ")	Meyerbeer.

NORWICH.

Annexed is the programme of an organ recital given in St. Andrew's Hall, by Dr. Bunnett, F.C.O., on Thursday, April 5th :—

Overture ("Figaro ")	Mozart.
Russian air in G, with variations.	
Introduction and petit grogre	Banfield.
Andante and Allegro, from a Sonata	Handel.
Offertoire in D	Batiste.
Selection ("Faust ")	Berlioz.
Larghetto in F	Beethoven.
Allegro ("Jupiter " Symphony)	Mozart.
Cradle Song	Lange.
Bourrée in E	Bach.
War March	Mendelssohn.

And on Saturday, April 7th :—

Introduction ("Song of Praise ")	Mendelssohn.
"Come, gentle Spring" ("Seasons ")	Haydn.
Allegro ("Water Music ")	Handel.
Chaconne	Durand.
Larghetto in A (Symphony in D)	Beethoven.
Entr'acte (Gavotte de "Mignon ")	Thomas.
Concerto No. 4, in F	Handel.
Air, "My heart ever faithful"	Bach.
Courante (Suite de Pieces)	Handel.
"Schiller " March	Meyerbeer.

EDINBURGH.

On April 3rd Sir H. Oakeley's recital programme ran thus :—

Chorale, "Christus ist erstanden" (A.D. 1512).	
Chorus, "Worthy is the Lamb " ("Messiah ")	Handel.
Largo (Symphony in D, No. 7)	Haydn.
Adagio and Finale (Sonata No. 1)	Mendelssohn.
Adagio, con sordini (String Quintet, No. 3), and Minuetto e Trio (Symphony in E flat)	Mozart.
Motivo, Op. 17	Guilmant.
Huntsman's Chorus ("Der Freischütz ")	Weber.
Easter March, No. 4, Op. 145	Merkel.

MANCHESTER.

Mr. J. Kendrick Pyne gave an organ recital in the Town Hall, on Saturday, April 7th. Subjoined is the programme :—

Movement, from a Concerto	Handel.
Rhapsodie (" Cantiques Breton," No. 2)	Saint-Saëns.
Sonata in D minor	De Lange.
Humorous Meditation	Ochs.
Passacaille (with couplets)	Couperin.
Concert Piece	Freyer.

BOLTON.

An organ recital was given in the Albert Hall, by Mr. Wm. Mullineux, F.C.O., on Saturday, April 7th. The following was the programme :—

Concerto in D minor (No. 2, 2nd Set)	Handel.
Andante with variations	Lemmens.
March, with Hymn of Priests	Chauvet.
Ancient Dance (" Saltarello ")	Beaumont.
Concert Fugue in G major	Krebs.
Pastorale in A	Guilmant.
Marche Solennelle	Ketterer.

BRISTOL.

Annexed is the programme of the organ recital given by Mr. George Riseley in the Colston Hall on Saturday, March 31st :—

Offertoire in G major	Wely.
Romanza in F major	Beethoven.
Prelude and Fugue in A minor	Bach.
Cantilène Pastorale	Guilmant.
Overture (" Midsummer Night's Dream ")	Mendelssohn.
" Funeral March of a Marionette "	Gounod.
Gavotte, 1774	
Overture (" Zanetta ")	Auber.

And on Saturday last :—

Grand March in D	Schubert.
Largo (Second Sonata)	Beethoven.
Sonata No. 3, in A major	Mendelssohn.
Adagio in D major	Smart.
Fantasia in E	Freyer.
Sonata No. 9 in A	Corelli.
Overture (" Zampa ")	Hérold.

HINDLEY, NEAR WIGAN.

Subjoined is the programme of an organ recital given in St. Peter's Church, by Mr. Chas. D. Mortimer, on Sunday, April 1st :—

Fugue in D major	Bach.
" O Sanctissima "	Lux.
" Hymn of Nuns "	Wely.
Fantasia in E minor (" The Storm,") and Fanfare of Trumpets	Lemmens.

WATERLOO ROAD.

Subjoined is the programme of an organ recital given on Tuesday, April 3rd, at the church of St. John the Evangelist, by Mr. Albert E. Bishop :—

Allegretto in D major	Bach.
Musette in G major	E. H. Turpin.
Sonata in A minor	Rheinberger.
Allegretto in G major	Salomé.
Chorale with variations in E flat major	Smart.
Prayer in F major	Guilmant.
Easter March in F major	Merkel.
" Ave Maria " (adapted by Liszt)	Arcadelt.
Introduction and Fugue in E minor	Raff.
Easter Offertoire in A minor	Batiste.

LEEDS.

A recital was given on the grand organ in the Town Hall (No. 4 of the series), by Dr. Spark, on Tuesday, April 10th, when the programme consisted of works by Haydn, and comprised :—Overture (" Die Zauberflöte ") ; " Un poco Adagio," Symphony in F major ; Motet, " Splendente te Deus" ; Larghetto in D (Clarionet Quintet) ; Chimes for a clock ; Aria, " Agnus Dei " (First Mass ; Quartet, " Benedictus " (Requiem) ; Selection (" Don Giovanni.")

BOW AND BROMLEY INSTITUTE.

Mr. W. G. Wood was the solo organist on April 7th. His first piece was Merkel's Sonata in G minor, a fine organ work, well handled by the player. Wely's Fantasia Pastorale enabled Mr. Wood to display his great skill in producing effective combinations. The organist's three Canons (andante, allegretto, and allegro), proved to be very effective, especially the last of the set, and they were well received. The skill, contrapuntal talent, and courage of the composer in presenting his thoughts in so difficult a form as that of the canon deserves special recognition. A selection from " Faust " as an offering to popular taste, produced much effect, and was excellently played ; further, it must be conceded that there are many sentences in " Faust" which lend themselves advantageously to organic treatment. Bach's Toccata and Fugue in C was omitted for want of time. Weber's overture to " Oberon " was capitally played and received with much applause. Mr. Chaplin Henry sang " Speed on," H. Leslie Elliott's " To the clouds," " The song of Hybrias " and " The Vicar of Bray." Mr. Woodhouse played as his violoncello solos " Souvenir de Spa " (Servias), admirably executed, and " Tarantella " (Popper). The pianist was Mr. C. S. Macpherson. Mr. W. S. Hoyle plays to-night. His programme is an interesting one, including a Sonata for organ by the talented young composer, Mr. C. T. Speer, and his own musicianly minuet and trio. On the 23rd, Haydn's " Creation " is to be performed under the direction of Mr. W. McNaught, with orchestra. It is extremely gratifying to note the efforts made by the committee of the Institute in thus presenting choral works with orchestra, in addition to their other efforts in fostering a love of good music. One is inclined to regret that so earnest and energetic a body of managers cannot be invited to manage some of our other concert-giving institutions for us, as well as control the performances given in the famous East-end concert-room, the fortunes of which they guide so well and to such good artistic results.

PLYMOUTH.

The first of a series of bi-weekly recitals on the grand organ in the Guildhall was given recently by Mr. John Hele, the borough organist. The recital was announced for half-past three, and precisely at that hour the Mayor (Mr. Shelly) ascended the orchestra accompanied by a number of gentlemen of local influence. The audience was a very numerous one. The Mayor remarked that he had been asked to explain before the recital commenced what the arrangements were which had been made by the Corporation in order that the people of Plymouth might, as far as possible, enjoy the music of the organ which, as they all knew, had been presented to the town. Mr. Hele had recently been appointed to that position, and the Corporation believed they had in that gentleman a most capable musician, and one who would give great pleasure and satisfaction to the town by his performances. It had been arranged that on Thursday afternoons at half-past three there should be an organ recital, and in order that everyone might have an opportunity of hearing the music the arcades would be free to the public on those afternoons, while a charge of twopence and threepence would be made for admission to the body of the hall and balcony respectively. On Saturday evenings it was intended that there should be popular recitals, with vocal and organ and other instrumental music. It was hoped that really good, interesting, and valuable music would be made increasingly popular, and that a new and lasting source of enjoyment and, he might add, of instruction, might be opened up to the people of Plymouth. It was the earnest desire of the Corporation that in this way the organ should be made as useful as possible; and it was, at the same time, their hope that the people of Plymouth would more and more appreciate the musical enjoyment and instruction which would thus be provided for them. Mr. Hele then proceeded with the organ recital, and performed several selections with much taste, opening with Mendelssohn's " Midsummer Night's Dream " and concluding with " A March," by Best. The programme was not a " popular " one in the ordinary sense of the term, but the selections were from works of the best known composers, and Mr. Hele did every justice to the occasion, the abilities of the organist and the great merits of the organ being both displayed to the fullest extent.

The *Theatre* for April has excellent photographs of Mrs. Kendal and Mr. W. S. Bennett, so long associated with Mr. A. S. Sullivan. The musical news, contributed by Mr. W. Beatty-Kingston, contain interesting paragraphs about Wagner and the late esteemed pianist Leopold de Meyer. The general contents are of the usual excellence and value.

THE POSITION OF THE CHOIR AND ORGANS IN CHURCHES.

(*Continued from page* 212.)

The choir of Ratisbon Cathedral, which is justly celebrated all over Europe for its efficiency, consists of two separate bodies of voices, one composed of clergy, theological students, etc., who are placed in the stalls in front of the altar, and sing the plain chant ; and the other of professional singers, who sing the harmonised music, and are stationed in the apse, behind the high altar. The organ is immediately behind the reredos : it is a small but singularly good instrument, so far as it goes. Above the stalls, on either side of the choir, are stone galleries bracketed out, which are reserved for the use of the clergy of distinction who are unconnected with the cathedral ; this seems to me to be a very excellent idea,—one which might well be adopted in other places,—because it obviates a difficulty. Strangers ought never to be admitted into the stalls of a cathedral under any condition whatever ; yet it is desirable to have some place for foreign ecclesiastics visiting the church. While I was at Ratisbon I noticed that one of these galleries was occupied by an Armenian bishop and his attendants. I must here call attention to a somewhat remarkable but very successful experiment which was made at this cathedral some years back. The plan of the cathedral is remarkably symmetrical, and when it was restored, numerous positions for the professional choir and the organ were suggested. Both were removed from place to place to discover where they would be most effective. The organ, which is, as I have said, a small instrument, was found to be totally insufficient everywhere, except when placed in the apse, where, owing to some extraordinary acoustic properties of the building, it has the effect of a large and powerful instrument. It was also discovered that the same effect was produced by the choir, so that a body of some twenty voices was found to produce the effect of a very large choir ; it was, however, found necessary to play and sing the music very much slower than it would be ordinarily taken ; a false note or a breakdown would, of course, be multiplied fourfold, and what would be the result of a cypher on the organ I tremble to think. Such things, however, do not happen with the Ratisbon choir, and I do not think that anything could surpass the superb unaccompanied music of Palestrina as rendered by this choir and in this cathedral ; it seems to wind round and about the lofty columns and in and out of the stately arches in a way that baffles all description. I went to the church over and over again before I could discover where these grand waves of harmony proceeded from. This is the only case I known of in which the choir and organ have been placed and arranged with a view exclusively to the acoustic properties of the building, and yet one would naturally have expected to find such a proceeding rather the rule than the exception. The arrangement of organ and choir behind the high altar is not uncommon in France, and wherever I have heard it, the musical effect is remarkably good.

In cruciform churches one of the transepts is an admirable position for the organ. A very fine and effective instrument has been erected in the south transept of Worcester Cathedral.

The aisles of a church are not a good situation for organs without they are like those in the German churches—remarkably lofty. Ancient organs in this position are to be found at St. Afra, Augsburg ; at St. Stephen's, Vienna ; at Norlingen, in Suabia ; at Ingolstadt, in Bavaria ; and at the Cathedral of Erfurth. The organ-lofts in each of these cases are very charmingly designed ; all these churches, however, possess an organ at the West end in addition to that situated in the aisles. There is a gallery at the west end of the north aisle of Winchester Cathedral which was probably formerly an organ-loft, though we know that the principal organ of that church stood on the rood-loft. Another very favourable ancient position for the organ was in a gallery bracketed out from the triforium of the nave. The ancient organs at Chartres, Freiburg, and Strasburg are in this position, and in all probability the so-called minstrels' gallery at Exeter was nothing more than an organ loft. We know also that, in addition to four organs in different parts of the church, Durham Cathedral had an organ corbelled out from the triforium of the nave. Although it is a fairly-good position for a moderate-sized organ, yet it has several drawbacks ; the organ is generally too high up to be quite satisfactory, either for accompaniment or as a solo instrument. Undoubtedly an organ sounds better when raised above the level of the heads of the congregation, but some of its tones must be lost when it is raised some 50 ft. or 60 ft. above the pavement.

Old organs were very frequently placed over the choir-stalls. That of the old Cathedral of St. Paul was in this situation, and the Cathedral of Milan and many Spanish and Italian churches are examples in point. Unless, however, the choir projects west of the transepts, so that the organ can stand under one of the arches of the crossing, there is scarcely sufficient space for a modern organ of large dimensions, and it has led to the very objectionable practice of cutting the organ in half, and placing one half on one side of the choir and the other half on the opposite side, the two being connected by trackers underneath the floor. It is useful, however, sometimes, to have a small organ

over the stalls when there is a large organ in another part of the church. This is the case at Worcester Cathedral.

We sometimes, though very rarely, find old organs placed on the ground to the east of the stalls, and it is to be remarked that the only pre-Reformation organ-case existing in England, that of New Radnor Church, is in this position. Occasionally the organ is placed on a gallery at the back of the altar. Handel's organ at Whitechurch is in this situation ; both organ-case and choir-gallery were designed by Wren. In some of the Lutheran churches in Germany the organ is over the altar. It is so at St. Anne's, Augsburg, but there the altar is the intruder, as the fine old organ holds its original position at the west end of the church, and a modern altar is placed under it. I think it was at Ludwigsburg I saw a singular three-decker arrangement,—one pulpit, reading-desk, and clerk's desk, as one sometimes sees in England,—but an altar below, a pulpit immediately above the altar, and an organ above the pulpit.

It is now customary to place the organ in a chamber at the side of the chancel. I find that this arrangement is almost universally condemned by musicians, and especially by organists. A correspondence upon the subject has recently taken place in the *Musical Standard*, and the veto was strongly against these structures. A very eminent organist lately told me that it was about as bad a position as could possibly be found for an organ, and for his part he would as soon see the organ placed out on the opposite side of the street. I will here relate the objections to organ-chambers which I have heard advanced. (I am not now giving you my own opinions, but that of those who are far more able to judge of the matter). It is advanced that an organ, like all other musical instruments, requires to be placed in an open and isolated position, and that it should never be inclosed or surrounded, except by its own case. We know that when a good pianist wants his instrument to sound well, he draws it away from the wall, and opens the top, so that there shall be nothing to intervene between the instrument and his audience. And it is even more important that an organ should be unencumbered by surrounding objects than a piano, because the organ consists of at least two parts or subdivisions, the most important of which is called "the great organ," and the less important "the swell organ." Now the characteristics of "the great organ" should be power, grandeur, and distinctness of tone, and the "swell" should be more subdued, sweet, and gentle, with a contrivance for producing variety as to *piano* and *forte*. The contrast between the various portions of an organ form one of its greatest merits as an instrument, and these contrasts are affected by certain mechanical means. The "great organ," for instance, demands a clear space to give forth its majestic tones, the "swell" requires to be inclosed, but to be able, when wanted, to break away from this inclosure and give forth a fine *crescendo*. This is effected by a contrivance somewhat resembling Venetian blinds. If there is a choir-organ it should be clear, delicate, and very sweet in tone. Now, when the whole thing is shut up in a box,—and an organ-chamber is really little else,—much of this wonderful contrast is gone, because the very conditions demanded by the instrument are unfulfilled. But some people may say, "Oh, I like the subdued tone of the organ, and cannot bear to hear it when it is loud." An unfortunate organist wrote to the *Musical Standard* a few days back that he was absolutely forbidden by the clergyman to play any but soft voluntaries on the instrument, and was ordered not to play Bach's fugues because the same clerical authority considered them "undevotional" ! Now to such people as this what I should say is, "Why on earth go to the expense of a powerful organ, when, for 8*l*., you can get a harmonium which will be better suited to your taste, or want of taste?" It is surely folly to pay for grandeur of tone and power, and then shut them up in a box where they cannot be heard. Yet this is very frequently done. I have often heard really good organs crammed into organ-chambers, which have, from their unfortunate position, had little more effect than a harmonium. Sometimes, to make matters worse, the organ-chamber will be enclosed by low arches and screens of wood or stone,—all forming a carefully-constructed sound-trap or gag. The fact is, that when the organ is placed in an organ-chamber, the "great organ" is reduced to becoming a "swell organ," without the power of producing *diminuendo*, or *crescendo*. As a rule, also, organ-chambers are far too small to hold an efficient instrument, and the various parts have to be crowded together, and this is always bad. Mr. E. Turpin, writing in the *Musical Standard*, gives 20 ft. by 20 ft. by 20 ft. as the smallest sounding-space for a church organ ; yet how few organ-chambers are of these dimensions. Another defect in organ-chambers is the fact that they are nearly always damp. Now, damp is sure to ruin an organ. Then, also, an organ is difficult to get at when blocked up in a chamber. It is most important that every part of an organ should be easy of access, otherwise it may be absolutely necessary to take down nearly the whole of an organ to remedy some trivial defect which an organist himself could easily rectify if he could obtain access to that part of the instrument where the defect lies. The great organ at the Bois-le-Duc is admirably arranged in this respect, being furnished with a staircase and galleries inside.

From an artistic point of view much has been lost by the organ chamber, which is nearly always an ugly adjunct to a church. Directly organs are relegated to the chamber they no longer come under the attention of the architect, and that singularly-beautiful article of church furniture, the organ-case, is abandoned. But as long as the organ occupies an important position in the building, the case must be carefully designed; and when one sees how magnificently the Mediæval and Renaissance men treated that architectural feature, one cannot help wondering why it so rarely receives any attention at the present time. There are, I am glad to say, some few exceptions, and fine cases have been erected at Worcester, Hoare Cross, and Manchester, and have been designed for St. Margaret's, Westminster, and St. Martin's, Brighton. It is, however, very strange that, as a rule, the only portion of an organ which it is attempted to decorate is the pipes. This is certainly a work of superogation, because the pipes of an organ are sufficiently handsome in their natural condition; whereas the deal-posts and matchboarding, which generally do duty for a case, would certainly be none the worse for what our Yankee cousins call "a lick of paint." If people are very rich and anxious to spend money upon an organ, they should have the pipes embossed. One paints iron to prevent rust, but it seems repugnant to one's feeling to paint tin. I do not, however, propose to detain you by remarks upon the artistic treatment of organ-cases, because this subject is dealt with in a very complete manner by Mr. A. G. Hill, who, in his work upon the organ,—about to be published,—has illustrated and described all the most important examples at present existing in Germany, Holland, Belgium, France, England, and some few even in Italy and Spain. Most of these are reproduced from Mr. Hill's own sketches. By rare good luck Mr. Hill has also become possessed of many curious engravings of old organ-cases now destroyed. To the artistic value of the work he has been able to add much practical information gathered from personal experience as a partner in the well-known firm of Hill & Sons,—which is, I believe, the oldest firm of organ-builders in England.

I now come to the question, "What is the best position for an organ in a church?" And in consulting several eminent organists, I have nearly always received the following reply to the question :—"Either some central position as much isolated as possible, or a western gallery." Now, the objection to a western gallery is, that although it is admirable for sound, people, and especially the Anglican clergy, are opposed to having the choir so far removed from the altar. But I venture to think that the central position might be managed. It certainly suggests a choir-screen of some kind or other; and why should not the choir-screen be constructed in the form of a solid arch or bridge crossing the eastern bay of the nave. This need not occupy any space upon the ground-floor of the church, because the nave benches might be continued under it to its eastern extremity, or the choir might be carried on to its western extremity. If the first plan were adopted the organist would sit in the gallery above the arch; but if the latter were carried out he would play from the west end of the choir-stalls, under the arch. I have ventured to show how this arrangement might be carried out. It may be objected that this scheme gives very great prominence to the organ. But I would ask, why should not an organ occupy a very prominent position in a church? It generally costs more than all the rest of the church furniture put together. It is, as I have shewn, becoming every day a more and more important adjunct to divine worship. It is capable of the highest artistic treatment and architectural development. Why, then, should it not be brought boldly forward and placed in a situation worthy of the king of instruments? In the Middle Ages the organ was regarded with the most extraordinary reverence, and we find St. Peter Damian, in his exquisite hymn "De Gloria Paradisi," enumerates the tones of the organ among the joys of heaven. Now, it so thoroughly describes what an earthly choir ought to be that I venture to quote it :—

> "Novas semper harmonias,
> Vox meloda concrepat;
> Et in jubilum prolata
> Mulcent aures organa."

("Lovely voices make a concert,
Ever new and ever clear;
And in never-ending fœtal
Organs soothe the ravish'd ear.")

CARDIFF.

A concert was recently given at St. John's Schoolroom, Crockherbtown, under the Presidency of the Rev. C. J. Thompson, vicar of St. John's, the financial object being to aid the fund for the enlargement of the parochial schools. There was a large audience, and it was evident that the announcement that Mr. Brinley Richards had kindly consented to take part in the proceedings had had due effect. After several pieces had been given, the Chairman called upon Mr. Brinley Richards to address them. The distinguished musician at once came forward, and was heartily applauded on proceeding to speak from the platform. He expressed the pleasure which he felt in responding to the invitation to attend. He said :—

This being my third, and probably my last, visit to Cardiff,

as the official representative of the Royal Academy of Music, I wish to make some remarks concerning the Local Examinations. I may at once state that the results justify me in making a favourable report of the progress of musical education of Cardiff. I congratulate myself in having had the valuable assistance of Mr. Frederick Atkins, for whom I entertain the respect due to an earnest and intellectual musician. I may describe Mr. Atkins as a jewel in a very unpretentious setting, and if he has a fault, it is that he is too apt to efface himself, and so far does himself an injustice. But I beg to assure him that the hours I have passed with him during the examinations will always be to me a very pleasant memory. To the candidates who are present this evening I would speak as a fellow-student, for though my life has been devoted to music, I still consider myself a student. If we are willing to learn there is no time of life that we may not do so. The best and wisest of us can never live to be more than students, for there is no art, no science, that has yet been perfected. And so with the Divine art of music, with which you of late have been exercising yourselves. The great giants of the art—whose works are left to us as legacies of inestimable value—would tell you, were they here to-night, how far they were from accomplishing perfection. Believe me, this great perfection of all things is reserved for our eternal future, and not to be achieved in this world; and, therefore, our minds are naturally directed to that glorious Heaven to which we all hope, when this student's career of ours is finished, to attain. And now, my young friends—especially those of you whose fingers and brains have been exercised of late in getting up the test pieces which have been so carefully set forth by the Royal Academy for this year's study—I doubt not that most, if not all of you, have studied the whole of the works, and not merely the two which you have had the option of selecting for yourselves. You who have studied the whole will have observed how judicious that selection has been—how every example of technique in the art has been illustrated so far as it was practicable. In fact, the Royal Academy has set before you examples of every style except that which is vulgar—examples which, if you study thoughtfully and diligently, must eventually train your mind to thoroughly enjoy and appreciate all that is beautiful in the art. Believe me that it is of the highest importance what should, or should not, be placed before you for your study and practice—your tastes as well as your fingers have to be educated. Now, had I looked into the music folios a little while ago I doubt not but that I should have found much there that would not have commended itself to the thoughtful and educated musician, and so far you will agree with me, that the Academy has done much for you if it has only set you on the right course of study to become truly educated musicians. And this question, "What is study?" is of immense importance. You may eke out your hour at the piano and accomplish nothing, just as it is possible to wade through volumes of books without acquiring one crumb of solid information. Printers and publishers are responsible as much for the trashy music in circulation as the heaps of trashy books that waste and squander away the youthful hours. Nay, more than waste, they corrupt. Now, there is some difference between amusement and study, although both may be combined. But your practice at the piano, if it has not helped you over some difficult passage or passages, has done little or nothing for you as a student pushing onwards, and I think the Royal Academy has helped both you and your teachers, if they be teachers worthy of the name! and as it is the natural tendency in youth to read light books because they require no effort of the mind, so young pianoforte students, too, catch at the light and frivolous in music for the same reason, as it requires scarcely any care to watch the stuff which many still play, and still less study. Now, these examinations have done all this; they have backed up your teachers against the natural inclination to idle stuff, and they have defined in what they have set before you as proper models for study and practice, and as your ear becomes trained (and it is an organ that can be tutored as well as any other) the more will be your enjoyment of the beauties of such great masters as Beethoven, Mendelssohn, and others, and it will be your duty, as far as you can, to educate others in the same way, not by stooping or pandering to their taste, which has probably not been trained, but to endeavour to raise them to your standard, inasmuch as you have been taught. It is gratifying to see so many ladies going in this year for paper work, and it is moreover somewhat encouraging to the principal and committee of management, who have your interests at heart, for without attention to this department pianoforte playing is reduced to a mechanical operation. The committee have undertaken these examinations purely for the advancement of the art in every part of the kingdom, and the results have been most gratifying. It is the only way open that could possibly reach the masses, and ultimately raise popular taste, and although this is only the third year for these examinations the effect produced has been manifest in every town where the Academy has been operating. The concert was then proceeded with.

The *Leeds Express* treats upon the life and labours of Dr. W. Spark at considerable length in an article, No. 7 of "Local Celebrities," in issue of April 7th.

Correspondence.

THE ORGAN FOR BEVERLEY MINSTER.

TO THE EDITOR OF THE "MUSICAL STANDARD."

SIR,—As a native of Beverley, I wish to endorse the opinion of "One of the Old School" as to the necessity of retaining Snetzler's old work—all that is left of it, if still good and suitable—in the proposed new organ for the Cathedral of that hopelessly dull old town. The wise resolve to replace the organ on the screen, will not, it may be hoped, be abandoned at the last moment; for what other position can compare with it for a Cathedral organ; A handsome case it ought to have, and I am surprised to hear that His Grace of York, who is, I believe, a good musician, should have recommended only "a bare array of pipes." In his own Cathedral of York, the finest in England, the magnificent organ built (on the screen) by Messrs. Hill & Son, would surely demonstrate to His Grace, the advantage and beauty of having even in a smaller Cathedral a large but compact organ, enshrined in a rich case and placed in the position of all positions.

I am, Sir, yours faithfully,

OLD SCHOOL.

Passing Events.

A new opera by Mr. Silas G. Pratt entitled "Zenobia," was produced at McVicker's Theatre, Chicago, U.S., during the past month.

Mr. W. M. Hutchison is announced as engaged in the composition of a humorous cantata having the title of "H.R.H." The words were written by Mr. Edward Oxenford.

A series of highly interesting articles on the treatment of the word "Amen," from the pen of that learned musical critic, Mr. W. A. Barrett, may be read in the pages of the *Musical Review*.

Those who wish to do an obliging and useful man a good turn, and to listen to a pleasant miscellaneous concert at the same time should attend the benefit concert of Mr. Frank Norman, Hall Manager at the Neumeyer Hall, Hart Street, Bloomsbury, on Wednesday next, the 18th inst. The artists include the Misses Ellis Walton, M. Gwatkin, A. Sanders, Mdme. E. Roberts, Messrs. John Cross, H. Carter, H. E. Cooke, and F. Sewell Southgate.

An excellent and useful musical institution, the Clapham Amateur Orchestral Society, gave an excellent concert, on April 11th, at the Kensington Town Hall, in aid of the British Home for Incurables, Clapham Road. The vocalists were Miss Thudicum, Miss Orridge, and Mr. A. Oswald; the conductor was Mr. Ammon Winterbottom. The programme included Schubert's "Unfinished Symphony in B minor," and the overtures "Die Felsenmühle," (Reissiger), and "Merry Wives of Windsor" (Nicolai).

Lincoln's Inn Chapel was reopened on Sunday last, after being closed since August 1881 for enlargement and restoration. The musical part of the service was suitable to the occasion, the anthem sung being that of Boyce, "I have surely built Thee an house." The acoustical properties of the building have been decidedly improved by the enlargement of the chapel. To those who delight in an artistically and devotionally rendered choral service, Lincoln's Inn Chapel, with its excellent and select choir, its classical and accomplished organist, Dr. C. Steggall, presents much that will attract the earnest listener. The services are at 11 and 3 on Sundays.

An important sale is announced. The lease of the business premises, No. 60, Paternoster Row, the goodwill (including the book debts) of the music publishing and general music trade attaching to the well-known business as carried on during the last fifty years, under the style and title of B. Williams, the office and shop furniture and fittings, the extensive and valuable general trade stock, and the extensive and valuable stock of copyright and non-copyright plates, and the music appertaining thereto, etc., will be sold by auction by Mr. William Simpson (of the firm of Puttick and Simpson), with the consent and approbation of Mr. Justice Fry, the judge to whom this action is attached, pursuant to the judgment therein dated the 9th day of January, 1883, at the Gallery, 47, Leicester Square, on the 16th of April, 1883, and the seven following days, at twelve for one o'clock precisely on each day.

The Querist.

QUERY.

BACH AND HANDEL.—Is it correct to say that Handel's setting of the words "HE trusted in GOD" is as good a fugue as any written by Sebastian Bach?—"OLD SCHOOL."

Service Lists.

THIRD SUNDAY AFTER EASTER,

APRIL 15th.

London.

ST. PAUL'S CATHEDRAL.—Morn.: Service, Te Deum and Benedictus, Garrett in F; Introit, Alleluia, Alleluia (Hymn 137); Communion Service, Garrett in F. Even.: Service, Magnificat and Nunc Dimittis, Eaton Faning in C; Anthem, Rejoice, O my spirit, and, The Lamb that was slain (Bach).

WESTMINSTER ABBEY.—Morn.: Service, Garrett in D; Continuation, Bridge in G. Aft.: Service, Attwood in D; Anthem, I was glad (Attwood).

TEMPLE CHURCH.—Morn.: Service, Te Deum and Jubilate, Nares in F; Apostles' Creed, Harmonized Monotone; Anthem, Praise His awful name (Spohr); Kyrie Eleison, Nares in F. Even.: Service, Magnificat and Nunc Dimittis, Stainer in A; Apostles' Creed, Harmonized Monotone; Anthem, Praise the Lord, O my Soul (Purcell).

LINCOLN'S INN CHAPEL.—Morn.: Service, Boyce in A; Kyrie, Clarke Whitfield; Anthem, I was glad when they said unto me (Purcell). Even.: Service, Arnold in A; Anthem, The wilderness (Goss).

ALL SAINTS, MARGARET STREET. — Morn.: Service, Te Deum, Tours in F; Benedictus, Stainer; Communion Service, Silas in C; Offertory Anthem, This is the day (Alewyn). Even.: Service, Martin in C; Anthem, Blessed be the God and Father (Wesley).

ST. AUGUSTINE AND ST. FAITH, WATLING STREET.—Morn.: Service, Stainer in A; Offertory, Since by man came death (Handel). Even.: Service, Garrett in E flat; Anthem, Behold the Lamb (Spohr).

ST. BARNABAS, MARYLEBONE.—Morn.: Service, Te Deum and Jubilate, Aldrich in G; Anthem, How dear are Thy counsels (Crotch); Kyrie and Nicene Creed, Aldrich in G. Even.: Service, Magnificat and Nunc Dimittis, Aldrich in G; Anthem, Rejoice in the Lord (Purcell).

CHILDREN'S HOME CHAPEL, BONNER ROAD, E.—Morn.: Service, Anthems, Grant, O Lord (Mozart), and, Arise, shine (Elvey). Aft.: Service, Anthems, My God, look upon me (Reynolds), and, The Lord is my strength (Monk).

CHRIST CHURCH, CLAPHAM.—Morn.: Service, Te Deum, Plain-song; Kyrie and Credo, Mozart in B flat; Offertory Anthem, Like as the hart (In manus Tuas), Novello; Sanctus, Benedictus, Agnus Dei, and Gloria in excelsis, Mozart. Even.: Service, Magnificat and Nunc Dimittis, Martin in A; Anthem, I will mention the loving kindness (Sullivan).

FOUNDLING CHAPEL. — Morn.: Service, Tours in F; Anthem, O come let us worship (Mendelssohn). Aft.: Service, Cooke in G; Anthem, Worthy is the Lamb, and, Amen (Handel).

HOLY TRINITY, TULSE HILL.—Morn.: Chant Service. Even.: Service, Stainer in A; Anthems, Come, ye children, and, Thou, O Lord, art our Father (Sullivan).

ST. JAMES'S PRIVATE EPISCOPAL CHAPEL, SOUTHWARK.—Morn.: Service, Introit (Hymn 127); Communion Service, Schubert in A flat. Even.: Service, Martin in B flat; Anthem, Saviour of men; The Lord, He is risen; and, From Thy love (Gounod).

ST. MAGNUS, LONDON BRIDGE.—Morn.: Service, Opening Anthem, O Lord, correct me (Coward); Te Deum and Jubilate, Attwood in F; Kyrie, Boyce. Even.: Service, Magnificat and Nunc Dimittis, Attwood in F; Anthem, I will magnify Thee (Goss).

ST. MARGARET PATTENS, ROOD LANE, FENCHURCH STREET.—Morn.: Service, Te Deum and Benedictus, Tuckerman in F; Communion Service, Offertory Anthem, To Thee, Great Lord (Rossini); Kyrie, Credo, Sanctus, Benedictus, Agnus Dei, and Gloria in excelsis, Hummel in B flat. Even.: Service, Magnificat and Nunc Dimittis, Gadsby in C; Anthem, I waited for the Lord (Mendelssohn).

ST. MARY ABCHURCH, E.C. — Morn.: Service, Garrett in D; Communion Service, Armes in A. Even.: Service, Chants.

ST. MARY BOLTONS, WEST BROMPTON, S.W.—Morn.: Service, Te Deum, Armes in G; Benedictus, Chant; Communion Service, Kyrie, Credo, Offertory, Sanctus, and Gloria in excelsis, Stainer in E flat; Benedictus and Agnus Dei, Going in F. Even.: Service, Magnificat and Nunc Dimittis, Stainer in B flat; Anthem, Praise the Lord, O my soul (Goss).

ST. PAUL'S, AVENUE ROAD, SOUTH HAMPSTEAD.—Morn.: Service, Te Deum, Hopkins in G; Benedictus, Barnby; Kyrie, Tours in F; Offertory, Barnby; Credo, Sanctus, and Gloria in excelsis, Tours in F. Even.: Service, Magnificat and Nunc Dimittis, Bridge in C; Anthem, They that go down (Attwood).

ST. PAUL'S, BOW COMMON, E.—Morn.: Service, Te Deum and Benedictus, Chants; Communion Service, Kyrie, Credo, Sanctus, Offertory, and Gloria in excelsis, Stainer in E flat; Benedictus and Agnus Dei, Calkin in B flat. Even.: Service, Magnificat and Nunc Dimittis, Tours in D; Anthem, Glory, honour, praise and power (3rd motet, Mozart).

ST. PETER'S (EATON SQUARE).—Morn.: Service, Te Deum, Sergison in A. Even.: Service, Stainer in A; Anthem, Love divine! all love excelling (Stainer).

ST. PETER'S, LEIGHAM COURT ROAD, STREATHAM, S.W. —Morn.: Service, Mass, Tours in F; Introit, When I wake up (Sutton); Alleluia, Chantwise; Offertory, Charge them (Barnby). Even.: Service, Magnificat, Gadsby in C; Anthem, Then shall be brought to pass (Handel).

Country.

ASHBURNE CHURCH, DERBYSHIRE. — Morn.: Service, Field in D; Kyrie, Credo, and, Gloria, Garrett in D. Even.: Service, Field in D; Anthem, Christ being raised.

ST. ASAPH CATHEDRAL.—Morn.: Service, Gilholy in B flat; Anthem, My soul truly waiteth (Rea). Even.: Service, The Litany; Anthem, O give thanks (Greene).

BEDDINGTON CHURCH, SURREY.—Morn.: Service, Tours in F; Introit, From highest heaven the Eternal Son (Hymn 171); Communion Service, Garrett in F. Even.: Service, Garrett in F; Anthem, I know that my Redeemer liveth (Handel).

BIRMINGHAM (ST. CYPRIAN'S, HAY MILLS).—Morn.: Service, Stainer in A and D; Anthem, Thou wilt keep Him in perfect peace (Jekyll). Even.: Service, Smith in B flat; Anthem, Sing we merrily (Crotch).

BIRMINGHAM (S. PHILIP'S CHURCH). — Morn.: Service, Chipp in D; Communion Service, Woodward in E flat. Even. Service, Barnby in E; Anthem, O rest in the Lord (Mendelssohn).

BRISTOL CATHEDRAL.—Morn.: Service, Wesley in E. Aft.: Service, Wesley in E; Anthem, Hallelujah (Beethoven).

CANTERBURY CATHEDRAL.—Morn.: Service, Te Deum, Barnby in B flat; Jubilate, Hopkins in B flat; Introit, Sleepers wake, a voice is calling (Mendelssohn); Communion Service, Maxted in E flat. Even.: Service, Roberts in G; Anthem, Wherewithal shall a young man (Elvey).

CARLISLE CATHEDRAL. — Morn.: Service, Selby in A; Introit, The Lord hath been mindful (Macfarren); Kyrie, Selby in A; Nicene Creed, Harmonized Monotone. Even.: Service, Selby in A; Anthem, Praise His awful name (Spohr).

CHESTER (ST. MARY'S CHURCH).—Morn.: Service, Goss in in A; Communion Service, Lee in G. Even.: Service, Tearne in A; Anthem, Christ being raised from the dead (Elvey).

DONCASTER (PARISH CHURCH).—Morn.: Service, Wesley in F. Even.: Service, Stainer in B flat; Anthem, Judge me, O God (Mendelssohn).

DUBLIN, ST. PATRICK'S (NATIONAL) CATHEDRAL.—Morn.: Service, Te Deum and Jubilate, Oulton in D; Anthem, God, Thou art great (Part I., Spohr). Even.: Service, Magnificat and Nunc Dimittis, Culwick in A; Anthems, If ye love me (Stewart), and, God, Thou art great (Part II., Spohr).

ELY CATHEDRAL.—Morn.: Service, Te Deum, Plain-song; Kyrie, Stainer in E flat; Credo, Stainer in G; Gloria, Chipp in A flat; Anthem, Jesus said, I am the Bread (Stainer). Even.: Service, Stainer in E flat; Anthem, Awake, awake, put on (Stainer).

LLANDAFF CATHEDRAL. — Morn.: Service, Goss in A; The Litany. Even.: Service, Ebdon in C; Anthems, Then shall be brought to pass, O death, where is thy sting, and, But thanks be to God (Handel).

LEEDS PARISH CHURCH.—Morn.: Service, Gounod in D; Anthem, Rejoice in the Lord (Purcell); Kyrie and Creed, King in C. Even.: Service, Cooke in G; Anthem, Glory, honour (Mozart).

LIVERPOOL CATHEDRAL.—Aft.: Service, Chipp in A; Anthem, Send out thy light (Gounod).

MANCHESTER CATHEDRAL. — Morn.: Service, Te Deum, Jubilate, Kyrie, Creed, Sanctus, and Gloria, Harris in A; Anthem, In Christ dwelleth (Goss). Aft.: Service, Harris in A; Anthem, Send out thy light (Gounod).

MANCHESTER (ST. BENEDICT'S).—Morn.: Service, Kyrie, Elvey; Credo, Sanctus, Benedictus, Agnus Dei, and Gloria in excelsis, Haydn in C (No. 2). Even.: Service, Magnificat and Nunc Dimittis, Bunnett in F.

MANCHESTER (ST. JOHN BAPTIST, HULME).—Morn.: Service, Kyrie, Credo, Sanctus, Benedictus, Agnus Dei, and Gloria in excelsis, Osborne in E flat. Even.: Service, Magnificat and Nunc Dimittis, Willing.

RIPON CATHEDRAL. — Morn.: Service, Chants; Anthem, Rejoice ye with Jerusalem (Stainer); Kyrie and Credo, Merbeck. Aft.: Service, The Litany; Anthem, The sorrows of death (Mendelssohn).

ROCHESTER CATHEDRAL.—Morn.: Service, Attwood in C; Jubilate, Chant; Anthems, This is the day (Croft). Even.: Service, Attwood in C; Anthem, O where shall wisdom (Boyce).

SHEFFIELD PARISH CHURCH. — Morn.: Service, Kyrie, Mozart. Even.: Service, Stainer in D; Anthem, The Lord is my strength (Smart).

SHERBORNE ABBEY.—Morn.: Service, Kyrie, Mendelssohn in E flat; Offertories, Barnby. Even.: Service, Anthem, In Jewry is God known (C. Whitfield).

SOUTHAMPTON (ST. MARY'S CHURCH).—Morn.: Service, Te Deum, Calkin in B flat; Benedictus, Chant; Introit, If we believe (Macfarren); Communion Service, Agutter in B flat; Offertory, While we have time, and, Godliness is great riches (Barnby); Paternoster, Hoyte. Even.: Service, Magnificat and Nunc Dimittis, Smith in B flat; Apostles' Creed, Harmonized Monotone.

WELLS CATHEDRAL.—Morn.: Service, Pyne in C; Introit, Blessed is the man (Stainer); Kyrie, Russian, in D. Even.: Service, Russell in A; Anthem, God is our hope and strength (Greene).

WORCESTER CATHEDRAL.—Morn.: Service, Hopkins in A; Anthem, O taste and see (Sullivan). Even.: Service, Smart in G; Anthem, O come, let us worship (Mendelssohn).

[The attention of the several Organists is called to the favour they confer upon their brother musicians by forwarding their notices regularly: this column of the paper is much valued as an index to what is going on in the choice of cathedral music, so much so that intermissions constantly give rise to remonstrance. Lists should be sent in a week in advance if possible.—ED. Mus. Stand.]

⁎ Post-cards must be sent to the Editor, 6, Argyle Square, W.C., by Wednesday. Lists are frequently omitted in consequence of not being received in time.

NOTICES TO CORRESPONDENTS.

NEWSPAPERS sent should have distinct marks opposite to the matter to which attention is required.

NOTICE.—All communications intended for the Editor are to be sent to his private address. Business communications to be addressed to 185, Fleet Street, E.C.

APPOINTMENTS.

MR. W. H. HOPKINSON, late Organist of St. Peter's, Norbury, Wakefield, has been appointed Organist and Choirmaster for Morningside Parish Church, Edinburgh.

MR. JOHN DING has been appointed Organist of St. Mary's Abbey, Nuneaton.

Printed for the Proprietor by BOWDEN, HUDSON & Co., at 23, Red Lion Street, Holborn, London, W.C.; and Published by WILLIAM REEVES, at
the Office, 185, Fleet Street, E.C. West End Agents :—WEEKES & CO., 14, Hanover Street, Regent Street, W. Subscriptions and Advertisements are
received either by the Publisher or West End Agents.—Communications for the EDITOR are to be forwarded to his private address, 6, Argyle Square, W.C.
SATURDAY, APRIL 14, 1883.—Entered at the General Post Office as a Newspaper.

THE MUSICAL STANDARD

A NEWSPAPER FOR MUSICIANS PROFESSIONAL AND AMATEUR

No. 977. Vol. XXIV. FOURTH SERIES.   SATURDAY, APRIL 21, 1883.   WEEKLY: PRICE 3D.

Musical Intelligence.

CRYSTAL PALACE CONCERTS.

PROGRAMME.

Overture, " Euryanthe " .... Weber.
Selection from the Works of Handel—
    Bourrée from "The Water Music," 1716.
    Overture, " Esther." 1720.
    Aria, " As when the Dove " (Acis and Galatea ").
         Miss Mary Davies.
Symphony, " Harold in Italy " .... Berlioz.
   1. Harold in the Mountains ; Scenes of Melancholy, Happiness,
      and Joy—Adagio, Allegro.
   2. March and Evening Prayer of Pilgrims—Allegretto.
   3. Serenade—the Mountaineer of the Abruzzi to his Beloved—
      Allegro assai, Allegretto.
   4. Orgie of Brigands ; Reminiscences of the preceding Scenes—
      Allegro frenetico.
Songs from "The Maid of the Mill"............. Schubert.
   " Der Neugierige" (The Question).
   " Wohin" (Whither).
         Miss Mary Davies.
Adagio from the String Quintet in G minor........ Mozart.
Slavonian Dances (First Set)...................... Dvorák.

    Conductor - - - AUGUST MANNS.

The old proverb, "A prophet hath no honour in his own country," was, in the case of Berlioz, literally and painfully exemplified. While he lived—though he yearned for their sympathy—the French people treated him with utter contempt, and wounded his spirit with their bitter sarcasms. Berlioz went to his rest in 1869, and no sooner was the Franco-German war concluded in 1871, than they began to perceive that, as Germany could boast of a great and new musical genius in the person of Wagner, France could in Hector Berlioz pride herself on "the chief pillar of modern development." From that time to the present his music has been received in his native country with the greatest enthusiasm, and a monument is now about to be raised there to his memory. In his autobiography he writes, in strange contrast, alas ! to the honours lavished upon him too late, " Behold me, if not at the close of my career, at least on the slope that more and more rapidly leads down to it ; worn out ; consumed, yet always consuming ; and full of an energy that sometimes awakes with a violence that frightens myself. I begin to know French, to write passably a page of score, a page of verse or of prose ; I can direct and animate an orchestra ; I adore and respect art in all its forms. But I belong to a nation which, to-day, concerns not itself at all with noble manifestations of intelligence—a country having the Calf of Gold as its only god."

Having written on "Harold in Italy" for the *Musical Standard* some time ago, I need only now say that the performance was highly satisfactory, although the number of strings was not equal to that required by Berlioz.

Dvorák has now become a well-known name in our programmes, and his music is nowhere more enjoyed than are the Crystal Palace concerts. The selections from Handel and Mozart supplied the wants of those who are fond of variety, and to those who affect the more modern school they could not fail to be welcome. They were not unlike a few exquisite pieces of ancient statuary, placed in a newly furnished drawing-room.

Miss Mary Davies was charming in her three songs, and was twice recalled after Schubert's "Wohin."

           R. S.

MISS SASSE'S MATINEE.

Miss H. Sasse held a matinée on Wednesday, April 11th, at No. 30, Thistle Grove, South Kensington. She played with her sister Miss Grace Sasse, the Variations of M. Saint-Saëns for two pianofortes, on a theme of Beethoven's (trio of scherzo from the Sonata in E flat, Op. 31), a piece by Chopin, Raff, and Mendelssohn. Miss Sasse is rather ambitious in her choice of texts, but she generally plays them with much taste, and if she perseveres in hard study, will no doubt make a name. Miss A. Roselli sang Gounod's "Noël," which effectively displays the dramatic quality of her voice, and Miss Eugenie Kemble's agreeable mezzo-soprano came out well in a song of Behrend. Mr. Poznanski rendered, with customary skill and *savoir faire*, his Romanza and Tarentelle, and joined Miss Sasse in Rubenstein's Sonata for piano and violin, Op. 13. Mr. W. Carter conducted.

THE CARL ROSA OPERA COMPANY AT DRURY LANE.

A second hearing of Mr. Mackenzie's "Colomba," this week, tends to confirm the previous impression of your second contributor in the last issue, and suggests a few additional remarks. As regards the libretto, I agree with the critic of the *Daily Telegraph* that it is absurd to set commonplace dialogue to fine musical phrases; one is reminded of the awkward collision, at a certain Yorkshire Festival, of the *coda* in a crashing Handelian chorus, with the words, uttered simultaneously by two agriculturalists who were talking over a recent dinner—"and apple pie." The line, "It is a lie, you know it is (a) lie," hardly sounds like classical blank verse, and many of the rhymes call for criticism ; such as "stranger and anger," "luggage and baggage," and such like.

To refer to Mr. Mackenzie's music. Nothing can be more graphic and picturesque than the opening chorus of market women. The "Vocero" is very pretty and well scored. The first duet of the lovers (Act I.) makes quite a point of the opera ; and when Colomba joins, the situation rises to a dramatic and musical climax. The finale of this Act is capitally "put up," but rather too protracted, and to leave Orso alone on the stage seems a mistake. In Act II., the opening *scena* of "Colomba," admirably rendered (on Monday) by Mdme. Valleria, claims attention ; the Tarantella is the only part of the ballet music that has struck me on either occasion, the rest sounds commonplace stuff and not new. The quartet of men's voices in A flat is very excellent part writing, preceded by some fine florid scoring of the band, which, in the quartet, subdues its sounds with good effect. Towards the end of Act II. some capital writing is thrown away upon a sort of penny-a-line report of the murder that has provoked Colomba's vengeful wrath ; and the end struck me again as weak, notwithstanding many elegant features of orchestral score.

The Prelude to Act III. is really beautiful, but the "British public," as a rule, vulgarly ignore instrumental music in the opera house, and only hush their silly talk when the *artists* lift up their voices ! I was obliged to change my seat on Monday in order to avoid two prattlers behind, one with a pianoforte score in hand! The orchestral accompaniments of Orso's opening scene should be noticed. His love song in G, and Chilina's ballad in F sharp minor, are recognized as pearls of price, and its publishers already advertise them for separate sale. In the latter will be missed, so far as the *salon* is concerned, the weird undercurrent of the wood wind instruments, so deftly seconded by the strings, with drum *obbligato*. Why does Orso swoon after shooting the two assassins? I continue to think the "Requiem" chant feeble and ineffective ; but Colomba sings with great effect, and here, at the cry of "Vendetta," on the accomplishment of the heroine's object, the opera ought to end.

The duet of Colomba and Chilina in Act IV. has a few passages slightly suggestive of Mozart's "Batti, batti" ; here the clarinet is aptly and charmingly used. The action in the dark; throughout this last act, increases the tedium of the situation. The final duet of the lovers improves on acquaintance, but nothing can remove the impression of *de trop*; one feels impatient for light and the fall of the curtain.

To sum up, "Colomba," as noted by my friend of the *Daily Telegraph*, will not attain the age of an old oak, but the acorns are genuine, and will probably produce good fruit in other forms. Genius is manifest, and the principle on which the composer works a sound one—in my opinion at least. Mdme. Valleria will be indispensable at future representations. An apology was offered for Mr. H. Pope (the Count and Governor) on Monday night. The *Times*, noticing the second performance of Mr. Mackenzie's "Colomba," eulogizes Mdme. Valleria's "creation" of the part as the most artistical of the modern lyrical stage. Mr. McGuckin's Orso, it is said (but herein the writer must differ in opinion), promises to be as perfect, from a histrionic point of view, as it was from the beginning, with regard to the *vocal* part of his task. Judicious excisions, notably of the *ensemble* at the end of Act II., have reduced the time of performance to about three hours ; but it must be stated that, on Monday, the writer could not leave the theatre, without loss of material, before half-past eleven.

The remarks of the *Times* on the *music* of the *opera*

quite coincide with the opinion here, and heretofore, expressed by the writer. "Music of this kind" (says the *Times*) appeals alike to the artist and the intelligent listener . . . We may, however, refer more especially to the *excellency of the instrumentation*—a feature in which, perhaps, more than in any other, Mr. Mackenzie has profited by the study of Wagner's music." (The preludes to Acts I. and III. are specially commended.) All through the work, moreover, the orchestra plays an important part. By its means the *continuity of the musical design is frequently effected*, although, on the other hand, vocal melody was by no means discarded. The voices and the instruments form one harmonious design, and it would be difficult to say which of the two is the more important component."

Mdme. Marie Roze's success in Gounod's "Faust," last week, was brilliant. She again appeared in "Fidelio" on Wednesday. Mr. Goring Thomas's "Esmeralda" was repeated on Tuesday, when Mdlle. Baldi sustained the title part, *vice* Mdme. Georgina Burns. She suffered from nervousness in the first Act, and this affected both her elocution and intonation. In Act II. Mdlle. Baldi recovered herself, and achieved a decisive success later on. A bouquet was presented after Act III., and another at the end of the opera. Mr. Barton McGuckin, in splendid voice, excelled in the air, "And she is true." Mr. Ludwig again made his mark as Claude Frollo.

"Esmeralda" is a pretty and a very clever opera, but might be curtailed. Two young "exquisites," on Monday, were overheard in the lobby to express a preference of this work to "Colomba"! As wisely might one compare a full-blown rose with a tiger-lily! Both operas move on the modern Wagnerian lines with continuity and design, but the styles are essentially different, and "Colomba" is the greater production of the two. A. M.

THE MUSICAL ARTISTS' SOCIETY.

The trial of Saturday last, April 14th, was most satisfactory. Mr. A. Gilbert's Pianoforte Trio in A minor is an unpretentious and very agreeable work, conducted by the composer, with Mr. Ellis Roberts as violinist, and Mr. W. C. Hann, a young player of great promise, as bass string. Mr. W. C. Macfarren's Sonata for pianoforte and 'cello in E minor is a very good specimen of this able professor.

"More suo" is not a new work, but has been published some time. Miss Foskett and Mr. W. C. Hann were its interpreters. Mr. Tobias A. Matthay's "17 Variations for pianoforte, on an original theme" in C, betokens much cleverness, with a decided leaning to modern "notions." Dr. Gustave Wolff's "3 Novelletten" for piano and violin, played by Messrs. E. H. Thorne and Ellis Roberts, is like every other work which I have had the good fortune to hear from the pen of this clever musician, and display a musicianship of a high order, with originality. A theme in No. 3 of the Novelletten recalls an episode in E minor of Schumann's "Arabesque"; but such reminiscences are quite exceptional in the case of Dr. Wolff. Mr. G. Gear's vocal pieces, "A tiny floweret" and "The old journal," deserve notice: they were nicely rendered by Miss Norah Hayes. Mr. Emanuel Aguilar's "Duo Concertante" in C, for two pianofortes, played by the composer and Mr. C. E. Stephens, is a fine and praiseworthy piece of sterling music. The duo begins with a slow movement, with some most captivating melody, and, well contrasted in effects, is followed by an allegro moderato, full of grace and brightness. The work was most cordially received. On a recall to the platform, Mr. Stephens modestly left the composer to respond alone, but he, Mr. Aguilar, on finding himself "unaccompanied," pulled up his worthy coadjutor to share the honours, thus "equally divided," as regards the execution; for both pianists are *du premier rang*. Let me add that I had the opportunity to hear M. Aguilar's duo again (after his own Recital) on Monday afternoon, [and liked it better than before. A. M.

Mr. Geaussent's choir performed Gounod's oratorio "The Redemption" at a recent concert. Opinions differ as to the merits of the performance, but not as to the earnestness of those engaged therein. It was thought that the orchestral and choral forces were not quite strong enough for the work to be done in some departments.

MR. BONAWITZ'S CHAMBER CONCERTS.

At the second concert, on Wednesday, April 11, Mr. Bonawitz played, with immense power and all requisite impetuosity, the "Sonata Appassionata," also Schubert's Impromptu in B flat, Schumann's "Novellette," No. 8; Mendelssohn's "Scherzo a Capriccio" in F sharp minor, and his own effective arrangement of Luther's Hymn. Another acceptable composition of Mr. Bonawitz was the Valse in E flat from his opera "Osnolenka," arranged as a pianoforte duet, and played by himself with Miss Cecilie Brousil. Miss C. Brousil chose two violin solos of Mr. Bonawitz, a Nocturne and a Valse Caprice, and joined him in a fine rendering of Beethoven's duet Sonata in G (No. 3 of the "Emperor Alexander"). A very admirable contralto vocalist, Miss Lena Law, made a deep impression upon a select audience in an air from the "Nitocri" of Mercadante, and "Chi vive amante" from Handel's "Poro." Mr. Bonawitz, on request, transposed Handel's song a semitone, from F to E major.

Mr. Bonawitz's annual *soirée* will be held at the Bluthner Rooms, in Kensington Gardens Square, on May 9.

THE LONDON ACADEMY OF MUSIC.

At a recent concert of the professional students of this Academy, so ably directed by Dr. Wylde, the following pupils distinguished themselves by proficiency as pianists, viz.:—Misses Ida and Ethel Fraser, Miss M. Osborne, Miss R. Griffiths, Miss Ruf, Miss E. Evans, Miss A. Stevens, Miss Hyman, and Miss Titmas. A daily contemporary particularly praises Miss Griffith for her brilliancy and firm execution. She played the first movement of Beethoven's Fifth Concerto—no easy task. Other pianoforte texts chosen by the pupils, were Mendelssohn's "Rondo Brillant" in E flat; his Serenade in B minor, the first movement of Mozart's Concerto in E flat, for two pianofortes and band; Chopin's Valse in A flat; part of a concerto by Dr. J. Hiller, and the adagio and finale of Weber's Concerto in E flat. As violinists, who appeared, with honour, Miss K. Chaplin, Mr. Skuse, and Miss A. Dinelli, and Mr. G. Newman, Miss Dinelli, and Miss Chaplin, deserve special mention. The vocalists were Mr. Reakes, Mr. Ellison, Miss L. Lether Garrod, Miss R. Moss, Mr. O. Noyes Miss L. Carreras, Miss F. Smith, and Miss A. J. Smith, and Miss A. J. Martin, Miss Moss sang, "Va dit elle," from "Robert le Diable." The Academy appears to be flourishing, and the professors to be doing good work. Most of the violins in the band were held by young ladies.

MAIDENHEAD.

The Philharmonic Society brought their season to a close on Tuesday, the 3rd inst., with a concert in the Town Hall. The following formed the programme:—

Allegro Vivace, Sinfonie in C	Mozart.
"Song of Victory"	Hiller.
Overture, "Oberon"	Weber.
Song, "L'Oiseau"	David.
Concerto in C major, for pianoforte and orchestra ..	Mozart.
Part-song, "Drops of Rain"	Lemmens.
Entr'acte in B flat ("Rosamunde")	Schubert.
Chorus, "Forth to the meadows"	Schubert.

A glance at the above will be quite sufficient to show that an interesting selection had been made. Hiller's cantata of course attracted the most attention; it is undoubtedly a fine work, and improves very much on acquaintance. It is rather remarkable that it should have been so very little performed until quite recently, but the last season seems to have brought with it a sudden popularity. The work makes considerable demands on the chorus, the writing being in many cases both brilliant and very effective. "The heathen are fallen" is undoubtedly the finest number, though the final chorus contains some fine passages. The solo parts are not very important. The execution on the whole was very good; both soloist (Miss Jessie Royd) and chorus evidently found it very trying. The second part of the concert was chiefly remarkable for the excellent playing by the orchestra of the "Oberon" overture, and the charming "Entr'acte" from "Rosamunde," which is always enjoyable. Mr. J. G. Wrigley, Mus.Bac., Oxon., was warmly applauded at the close of the piano concerto, and an encore was accorded to Lemmens' part-song, which was exceedingly well sung. The orchestra was led by Mr. J. S. Liddle, and Mr. J. G. Wrigley conducted.

MR. AGUILAR'S RECITALS.

At Mr. Aguilar's second recital, on Monday afternoon, he gave an admirable reading of Schubert's Sonata in B major, of four movements, by some styled the "Military" Sonata, on account of certain passages suggestive of drums and other martial instruments. These occur at the outset, also in the andante (E major), where the auditor is reminded of the cognate movement (same key), in Beethoven's Third Pianoforte Concerto. In the second theme of the first allegro occurs a charming phrase that suggests one in the finale of Beethoven's Sonata in G, Op. 31, No. 1. The scherzo in G is quaint, the rondo very graceful and fluent music. Mr. Aguilar afterwards played Beethoven's Sonata in E flat, Op. 81 ("L'Absence," &c.), with much taste and appreciation of the spirit of the text. His own compositions, on Monday, included the Nocturne in F sharp (major), "Rêve," and "Avere"; a Prelude and Fugue in E minor; the Transcription of "Weber's Last Valse" (*not* by Weber); the "Dream Dance" in A, and the Bolero in D minor. Liszt's Fifth Hungarian Rhapsody, in B flat minor and major, completed the list. Two pupils of Mr. Aguilar acquitted themselves much to the satisfaction of the audience. A very little girl, Miss Mary Troughton, played Sir W. Sterndale Bennett's "Allegro Grazioso" in A, with remarkable correctness and tact; another, Miss Marion Crockenden, chose Chopin's Valse in A flat, and a Nocturne in G, both well executed.

BIRMINGHAM.

(From our Own Correspondent.)

In my last letter I made brief mention of a new "Passion-music," by Mr. Gaul, the organist of St. Augustine's. The following are a few notes made on the occasion of its first production at the Church on Good Friday; but as the composer intends revising and orchestrating the score (the voice-parts on Good Friday having simply the organ accompaniment) criticism can only touch, at present, upon the general construction of the work. The text of the composition, varied and elaborate in its structure, is the compilation of the Rev. J. C. Blissard, who is author also of the original lyrical portions of the work. The course of sacred events connected with the Passion is laid out by the writer so as to form a series of six distinct "scenes." The subjects of these divisions, each occupied with a particular stage of the Mystery, are respectively:—"The Traitor at the Table," "The Denial," "The Condemnation before Pilate," "The Mockery on Calvary," "The Shadow of Death," and "The Holy Sepulchre." Each comprises a prophetic portion preceded by a short chorale, which is retained unaltered throughout the work; a narrative portion dealing with the especial event; and what may be termed the lyrical epode, a hymn embodying the subjective reflection on the preceding passages, in which the whole congregation is supposed to unite. As regards the composer's share in the work it must be noted that, whilst endeavouring to illustrate in the best manner possible the outward course of the events, the dramatic element, properly so called, has been carefully kept out of the work. Individual characterisation has been avoided by allotting the different solo musical passages without regard to any representative character. This arrangement has no doubt been prompted by judicious reasons, and there is much to be urged in its favour. Nevertheless, it may be feared that the distribution of the solo passages among several voices may tend to impair the unity of effect. Mr. Gaul has adopted the *arioso* style of musical setting for the solo portions of his work. In certain parts, as in the melodious solo, "Blessed are the departed," the writing approaches the ordinary *aria* form, but in general the more declamatory style is preserved. In those sections, notably that of the "Unjust Condemnation," where the realistic element is predominant, the composer has manifested his ability to write with dramatic force and intensity as well as with lyric charm. In this respect the choral writing distinguishes itself in comparison with that in the "Holy City" and other of the composer's works. Among the items which impressed me most favourably was the chorus, "The fining-pot is for silver," the beautiful choral passage "Watch and pray," the whole of the choral passages of the condemnation scene; the contralto air, " Oh, hear ye this, all ye people"; the fine chorus, "Consider this," the culminating point of the scene on Calvary; the trio for soprano, tenor, and

bass, "Thou hidest thy face, O Lord"; the quartet, "Hat God forgotten to be gracious"; the strikingly effective chorus, "God is not a man that he should lie"; the solo before mentioned, "Blessed are the departed," with a choral appendage (soli quartet); and last, but not least in merit, the refined setting of Adelaide Proctor's lines "Why shouldst thou fear the beautiful angel Death?" Mr. Gaul has not written new hymn tunes for Mr. Blissard lyrics; the tunes selected for this occasion were from among those in ordinary congregational use. Altogether considered, Mr. Gaul's new work will undoubtedly greatly enhance his already high reputation in the lines of sacred composition. The choir of St. Augustine's (augmented on this occasion) acquitted itself excellently under the direction of Mr. Richard Payne. The principal soloists were Misses Surgey and Wheeler, and Messrs. Breen, Horrex, and Campion. An overflowing congregation testified to the great interest taken in the service. On Saturday evening the work was repeated, the attendance being almost equally large with that of the previous evening.

Miss Miller gave a very interesting concert in the new lecture theatre of the Midland Institute on the 29th ult. The violinist was Miss Skinner (a pupil of Joachim); the vocalist, Miss Edith Santley; and the 'cello, Mr. W. E. Roden. Miss Miller is a representative of the pure, classic order of "pianism." The characteristic beauty of Miss Miller's style resides essentially in her almost ideal precision, in the phrasing and in the *technique* generally. The solo pieces were such not calling for much marked individuality of the performer. Weber's sonata hardly admits of much variation in "reading"; and the lines of the three Schumann items are well worn enough by this time. Altogether considered, conception as well as exposition, I think Miss Miller was faultless. Miss Skinner is a highly-skilled executant, and her performance was a perfectly good one. For the commendable taste shown by Miss Santley in the selection of her songs, and the artistic manner in which they were delivered, too much praise cannot be given. Mr. Roden played with much neatness his little pieces. Schubert's Trio (for piano, violin, and 'cello), a fine specimen of his most mature style, received a perfectly worthy rendition.

An instrumental concert was given on the 12th inst., at the Masonic Hall, by Miss Emily Walker, supported by Miss Lucy Riley, violinist, and Mr. Rowland Winn. The programme was unexceptionable in respect to the artistic worth of the selections made. The pianoforte pieces were sufficiently contrasted to display fully the most varied qualities of the performer, ranging, as they did, from the classic extremes of Bach and Schumann to the *virtuoso* melody embroideries of Thalberg. The pianoforte works of Schumann mainly rely for their full comprehension upon a pre-understanding of the composer's poetical motive; but I can hardly account the pianist to have completely exhibited the full genius of the pieces, though her playing was, in all strictly musicianly respects, perfect and masterly. As regards Miss Walker's interpretation of Beethoven, much the same is to be said as I have just noted with respect to her rendition of Schumann's pieces. Her execution is polished, flawless, and her "reading" of the master thoroughly sound and classic; if any shortcoming there is, it lies in the want of a little more tenderness of treatment, especially in the more lyrical passages. In the second part of the concert Miss Walker's display of *technique* was quite irreproachable. In addition to pieces of Bach, Taubert, and Thalberg, an *étude* of Chopin was also given. The two songs from the collection of Mendelssohn's favourites were those in A flat and A minor (Nos. 19 and 21), well contrasted and well delivered. Of Miss Walker's lady-coadjutor, I am pleased to be enabled to speak in the best terms of encomium. She combines technical qualities of a superior order with earnestness, refinement, and warmth of expression. The charming well-known trifles of the partner-composers, Heller and Ernst (played by Miss Walker and Miss Riley), agreeably concluded the concert. It only remains to say of Mr. Winn that he performed his part with his customary delicacy and taste. The room, though not filled, showed a very good attendance.

Br.

The new Royalty Theatre, now under the management of Miss Kate Santley, has a new comic opera by Mr. G. R. Sims and Mr. Frederick Clay, to be called "The Merry Duchess." Mr. Clay has already written successfully for the stage.

ROYAL VICTORIA COFFEE HALL, S.E.—It is pleasing to note that the Ballad Concerts at the above Hall still attract numerous audiences. That of Thursday was most successful, both s regards selection of music and performers. Miss Hepwell may be congratulated on having provided an entertainment much to the enjoyment of the visitors, and on having been most satisfactorily helped by Mesdames Lynn, Edith Phillips, Alice Cruttenden, Helen Warde, Messrs. Herwen Jones, and Quarternayne, while Messrs. Dinelli and Lindo presided effectively at the piano. It is to be hoped that these concerts which are given on Thursdays will become a regular institution in South London. On Friday April 20th, a number of distinguished members of the legal profession held a grand temperance demonstration.

EALING.—The first concert of the Orchestral Society was given on Tuesday at the Lyric Hall, when an excellent programme was gone through in very creditable style. The orchestra numbered about 24, and amongst the pieces played were the overture to "Prometheus" (Beethoven), and "Esmeralda" (Hermann). A Symphony in E flat by Romberg, and two or three gavottes. Mendelssohn's G minor pianoforte concerto was also played, the solo being admirably rendered by Miss Lottie Harrison, a promising young member of the society. In the vocal music Miss Fuselle sang in a very able manner, an air by Rode's and "The Worker" (Gounod.) Miss Alice Davies was encored for "Fanchiulle il coro," and the Rev. F. G. Elstob sang Bennett's "May Dew," and "Sweet Flower." Mr. Harold E. Stidolph, for whose benefit the concert was announced, conducted carefully and efficiently.

SOUTHEND, ESSEX.—Mr. W. F. Bradshaw's grand Spring concert was held in the Public Hall of this marine resort on April 12. Mdlle. Ida Audain distinguished herself in harp solos, notably Thomas's arrangement of the "Harlech" march, and Oberthür's "La Cascade," which was rapturously encored. Mr. E. Grime, a promising bass vocalist, made his mark in the old air "Down among the dead men," and won a bis for W. H. Jude's song "Deep in the mine." Mr. W. Townsend, Miss Bulloch, Miss H. Hardy, Mdme. Inez Maleska, and Miss L. Robins sang in turn. A selection from "Iolanthe" was given. Miss Audain also played harp solos last week at the Highbury Athenæum, and Mr. E. Grime, whose profound voice reminds one of Signor Foli, sang the song of Polyphemus in G minor, "O, ruddier than the cherry" with éclat. Miss Ida Audain was twice encored at Highbury in her harp solos.

BANBURY.—The Banbury new Philharmonic Society gave their last concert for the season on Tuesday evening, April 10th, in the Exchange Hall. The first part consisted of Stainer's sacred cantata "The Daughter of Jairus" and a miscellaneous selection completed the programme. Miss Ferrari (soprano), Mr. A. S. Fryer (tenor), and Mr. Grice (basso), had been engaged as soloists. Miss Ferrari is of local extraction, a fact that may in some measure account for her very cordial reception. She has a clear and powerful voice of good compass. Mr. Fryer was fairly successful, although his voice appeared to lack strength, while Mr. Grice, a great favourite here, was applauded to the echo for his songs in part 2. It is a pity that a full orchestral accompaniment was not secured for the cantata, the piano and organ (well played by Miss Lewis and Mr. Clough) being barely sufficient. The rendering of the choruses reflects great credit upon Mr. M. J. Monk, Mus.B., the society's excellent conductor.

ACTON.—An excellent concert was given on Wednesday in the Central Hall of the new Board Schools at Acton, a really fine room capable of seating 700 people, which was used for the first time. The first part of the programme was devoted to Stainer's "Daughter of Jairus," sung by a chorus of about 50 voices, the solos being taken by Master Townsend, Mr. Williams, and the Rev. C. M. Harvey. The accompaniments were rendered by Miss Slade on the pianoforte, and Mr. Harold E. Stidolph on the harmonium. The performance of the cantata was eminently satisfactory, and reflected credit on the conductor, Mr. E. H. Sugg. In the second part Miss Annie Lanatt was loudly encored for the rendering of "She wandered down the mountain side" and "Forget and forgive," a similar compliment being paid to Mr. Felix Sumner for his violin solo, and Master Townsend for his singing of "The Liquid Gem." Some part-songs and pieces by local amateurs made up a very agreeable programme, which was thoroughly enjoyed by a large audience.

BRIXTON CHORAL AND ORCHESTRAL SOCIETY.—On April 9th, this Society gave a performance of Mr. Prout's new cantata "Alfred," a work which was criticised in this journal at the time of its production, under the composer's own direction at the Crystal Palace concerts some weeks ago. The present performance appeared to give considerable satisfaction to the large audience which filled the Gresham Hall, the choral numbers and the "Triumphal march" in particular, calling forth loud demonstrations of approval. Mr. Lemare may be congratulated on the decided improvement in his band, which has evidently had some of its weaker constituents weeded out greatly to the general good: indeed were it not for that tendency towards incorrect intonation, that is, alas, so common amongst amateur orchestras, there would be but little fault to find. The chorus

was not altogether satisfactory, appearing to be lacking in finish in piano passages, and showing hesitancy now and then in taking up leads. The chorus "Lift the Raven Standard" was, however, given with commendable crispness and vigour. The soloists, Miss Hilda Coward, Mr. Kenningham, and Mr. Bridson, sang their music in excellent style throughout, although Mr. Kenningham, in the trying music of the part of "Alfred," was obviously struggling against a severe cold. Miss Coward's clear fresh voice told well, and gives promise of a successful career for this young lady in the future. In the second part of the programme Gade's pleasing "Spring's Message" and Handel's organ concerto, No. 5, were performed, the solo instrument in the latter work being efficiently taken by Mr. W. E. Stark. Mr. W. Lemare conducted throughout the evening.

FAVERSHAM.—Mr. C. D. Hobday's third annual classical concert, which took place on April 11th, was highly successful from a musical point of view. The programme was rendered with befitting care and taste from beginning to end, and the lovers of piano, violin, and violoncello had the gratification of hearing those instruments to advantage in the solos of Miss Glyde, Mr. C. M. Gann, and Mr. J. Norman; while the first movements of Hummel's trio in E flat, and the allegro, Andante, and Minuet from Mozart's Quartet No. 14, in the same key (in the latter of which Master Hobday took the second violin and Mr E. B. Norman the viola), afforded instances for the combination of strings. Miss Ambler and Mr. Thompson pleased the listeners by their expressive singing. The audience was highly appreciative, though not large—a fact to be regretted when it is considered how valuable a good exposition of chamber singing is, if only from an educational standpoint.

CORK.—A recital by the pupils of the Cork School of Music was held in the Assembly Rooms on the 10th inst. The programme was miscellaneous.—It is intended by the musical committee of the forthcoming exhibition to hold two concerts on the opening day, with Mr. J. Robinson of Dublin, as conductor; the chorus and orchestra to number 250 performers. Mr. T. J. Sullivan of this city has been appointed choirmaster, the committee have commissioned Mr. Magahy to build an organ for them.—A very fair amateur performance of Messrs. Gilbert and Sullivan's "Sorcerer," and "Trial by Jury," was given on the 16th inst. by Mr. Robert Howard's operatic corps at the theatre. There will be three other performances. This is their third appearance in public, having on two former occasions given Sullivan's "Pinafore" and Reid's "For lack of gold" (MS.). The only fault was the imperfect intonation of the ladies' choruses. Mr. Howard conducted with his usual ability.

BRADFORD.—The Manningham Vocal Union gave a concert in the Bradford Church Institute on April 10th, when there was a very large attendance. Mr. James H. Rooks, the present conductor of the society, has proved no less zealous and enterprising than his predecessor, Mr. F. C. Atkinson; and the concert of Tuesday night will stand forth as perhaps the most important that the society has hitherto given. No effort seems to have been spared to make the concert a success, for not only was a new work of much significance—Hofman's "Cinderella "—selected for performance on this occasion, but valuable outside aid, in the shape of soloists and instrumentalists, had been secured. A small orchestra of two to a part for the strings, with the addition of four wind instruments, harmonium and pianoforte were engaged; and the services of Miss Emilie Norton, Madame Armitage, and Mr. Thornton Wood were secured as solo vocalists. A miscellaneous selection made up the second part of the performance.

STRATFORD.—The Stratford musical competitions were brought to a close on April 14th, when the town-hall was densely crowded, to hear the competition between choral societies for the chief prize. The judges were Mr. Ridley Prentice, Mr. J. F. H. Read, J.P., and Mr. W. G. McNaught. They awarded the prize to the Upton Choral Society (conductor Mr. Proudman). Choirs from Leyton and Plaistow received second and third prizes. On the previous day and on Saturday afternoon the competitions in junior and senior pianoforte performance and sight-playing, in solo singing for all voices, in sight-singing, in quartet singing, and in composition, had been proceeding under the same judges. There were altogether 150 entries, which comprised 350 candidates, all of them resident in the district. The preparation for this event has stimulated the musical talent of the district during the past winter. In giving their awards the judges bore testimony to the high level of attainment reached by the candidates. The originator and director of the competitions is Mr. J. S. Curwen, who describes them as an adaptation of the Welsh Eistedfodd. The proceedings ended amid great enthusiasm with the distribution of prizes.

HULL.—Miss Eva Farbstein gave a grand evening concert on April 13th, at the Jarratt Street Rooms, before a fashionable and highly appreciative audience. The talented concert-giver, who possesses a beautiful and well trained soprano voice, was first heard in Gilbert Byass's new song "For thee"; afterwards in grand scena "Ernani involami" (Verdi), and "Robin Adair," all of them splendidly sung and enthusiastically encored. The refined rendering of the Scotch ballad created quite a furore, and after being recalled, Miss Farbstein gave as a response, "Home sweet home." The other vocalists were : Madame Evans-Warwick, who sang charmingly "Only a child" (Muscat), and "The Ferry of Galloway" (Luard). Mr. Bernhard Lane's artistic singing of Blumenthal's "May Queen" elicited a well deserved encore. Mr. W. Thomas, of Bristol, sang his songs well, by Mattei and Molloy. Among the vocal items were the quartets "God is a Spirit" (Sterndale Bennett) and "Good night, beloved" (Pinsuti). Miss Hildegard Werner's performance of "The moonlight sonata" (Beethoven) and "Polka de concert" (Wallace), was highly appreciated by the evidently much pleased audience. Miss Rose Farbstein efficiently acted as accompanist. The concert concluded with a musical sketch "The Harvest Home," cleverly performed by Mr. M. B. Spurr.

"HORNS," KENNINGTON. — The Kennington Orchestral Club gave their second annual concert at the above rooms on the 17th inst. The programme was an excellent one, and it would be satisfactory if I could speak conscientiously in such eulogistic terms of the performance, when a purely amateur Orchestral Society chooses such works as the overture to "Nabucodonosor Verdi," Mozart's No. 9 Symphony in D, and that lovely Romanze (No. 2), for violin and orchestra. It certainly should be somewhat above the ordinary run of such societies. The Kennington Club is ambitious ; there are many easier and more effective pieces written which Mr. Orbel-Hinchcliff, the conductor, might with advantage put in rehearsal. In Mozart's Symphony the wind instruments were seriously out of tune at times. In Beethoven's Romanze (No. 2), the violin solo was taken by Herr Schöwheyde, who also acted as leader. In his solo he exhibited a large amount of *technique*, but too little "feeling." The vocalists were Miss Edith Luke, Miss Levina Ferrari, and Mr. Alfred Kenningham, the last-named gentleman worthily taking the honours of the evening. The arrangements were most satisfactorily carried out by Mr. Howard Davis, the Secretary, and Mr. Buxton, the worthy proprietor.

GREAT YARMOUTH.—The Great Yarmouth Musical Society are to be congratulated on the result of the concert they gave on April 12th in the Assembly Room of the Town Hall. The oratorio chosen was Handel's "Judas Maccabæus," a composition that they had on two previous occasions performed, and with which they were pretty familiar. The principal vocalists were Miss A. Parry, Miss H. D'Alton, Mr. Dalzell, and Mr. Hilton. Mr. Stonex, the respected and able teacher of the class, conducted. Mr. Lane presided with much ability at the harmonium, and Mr. Cooke was, as usual, leader of the band, which was composed of local musicians—several from Norwich and London. Miss Parry did her best in the difficult music she had to sing. The air "O Liberty!" with the violoncello accompaniment, was one of the principal features of the part ; as were also the airs "So shall the lute and harp awake," "From mighty kings," and "Wise men flattering." Mr. Dalzell took pains to render his part as effective as possible, and his execution of the air "Sound an alarm" was praiseworthy. Miss D'Alton and Mr. Hilton sang in a faultless style. There is very little for the contralto to do in "Judas Maccabæus," but what little Miss D'Alton had to do she did well. Mr. Hilton was in splendid voice on Thursday night. An enthusiastic encore followed his singing of "The Lord worketh wonders," his rendering "Arm, arm, ye brave" and "Rejoice, O Judah," equally effective. Mr. Stonex conducted with care and skill, and the choruses were wel rendered.

GUILDFORD.—The performances held in the Western Hall on April 11 and 12, under the auspices of the Guildford Choral Society, were, in a musical sense, as successful as any that have ever taken place in Guildford. Mr. Prout's fine cantata, "Alfred," which was produced with a power and finish both in its solo, choral, and orchestral portions that would have done credit to the metropolis itself. The cantata will take high rank as a leading English musical composition, and does the highest credit to Mr. Prout's originality and ability. The solo parts were splendidly taken by Miss Annie Marriott, Mr. Alfred Kenningham (tenor), and Mr. H. H. Brereton (bass). The sentinel's part was well sung by Mr. Edwin (Guildford Choral Society). The interest was retained from beginning to end, and the composer and conductor, Mr. Prout, in response to the plaudits, had to bow his acknowledgments. Mendelssohn's beautiful "Hymn of Praise" was first performed, and this, thanks to the efforts of the conductor, Mr. Tiltman, is not new to the Guildford public, but it certainly was never produced in Guildford before with such a thorough completeness and effect as on Wednesday. From first to last, in all its parts, it was thoroughly successful, and the playing of the symphony was marked with precision and care. The difficult chorus "The night is departing" was rendered in such a manner by the choir as to meet with hearty expressions of approval. It is needless to say other than that the tenor singing of Mr. Alfred Kenningham was excellent, whilst in the duet singing Miss Annie Marriott and Miss Sophie Smith gave effect to the chorus, "I waited for the Lord." During the interval on April 11th, Mr. Prout attended in one of the rooms, and, addressing the members of the choir and band, said he wished to offer them his warmest thanks for the way in which they were kind enough to sing his music that afternoon.

He was very pleased with it, and would not have thought could have been done so well in the provinces. He had also thank his friend, Mr. Tiltman, for getting together such an excellent band, as it was a credit to him, and he thanked the gentlemen who composed the orchestra for the way they performed their share of the work. On the evening of April 12th the soloists included Mrs. Jeffries, Miss Sophie Smith, Miss A. Kenningham, and Mr. Brereton. Without going into detail we may mention that the encores included Miss Sophie Smith "Es blinkt der Thau" and "Absent yet present," Mr. Brereton's "To Anthea," and Mr. Kenningham's "Salve dimora" ("Faust"), which were all rendered with great effect. Mrs. Jeffries, who is deservedly popular as an amateur lady vocalist Guildford, sang Diehl's "Going to market," with skill. The overtures to parts 1 and 2 "Masaniello" and "L'Italiana showed the evidences of careful study by Mr. Woods' instrumental class, and were deservedly appreciated.

DUBLIN UNIVERSITY CHORAL SOCIETY.—There is really very little to be said by the press-man, whose business it is to take the rôle of critic on the provincial press. Most, indeed I may say all, musical and dramatic works of any importance are produced in London, or at some of the great English musical festivals, before being presented to the inhabitants of the minor and less favoured portions of the United Kingdom. As the reviews and verdicts pronounced in the leading papers are almost invariably read and digested by musical amateurs in every corner of the Kingdom, these latter are, as a rule, in the awkward position of one who has heard the plot before he read the novel ; saw the drama, or what is worse, knows the melodies before he becomes sufficiently well acquainted with the libretto. The lengthy explanation may be taken as indicating certain disadvantages under which the large audience heard Niels Gade's " Psyche " performed on Saturday last by the Dublin University Choral Society. Sir Robert Stewart, however, spared no effort to reproduce the work, performed at the recent Birmingham festival, in an efficient manner, and with as much completeness as his more or less limited resources could admit. The band was composed of the best instrumentalists that could be procured in the city, but there must always be a disadvantage in listening to any orchestral performance where there is not that complete loss or suppression of individuality that springs from constant discipline and intimate knowledge of leaders and conductors. This defect was noticeable at intervals during the performance on Saturday last. The choir, on the other hand, sang remarkably well, with decision as well as precision. Whilst it was very evident that the members were thoroughly acquainted with their work, I should not like to speak decidedly as to the opinions held by the audience regarding the work itself. But the work did not at any period awaken anything like enthusiasm, and the general effect appeared to be rather disappointing than otherwise. Certainly Gade's cantata will scarcely become as popular here as his chamber music. The vocalists were fairly successful, and Sir Robert Stewart deserves the highest praise for his never-wearying efforts in keeping Irishmen well informed on the musical doings of the European Continent.

Foreign Musical Intelligence.

Liszt has returned to Weimar in excellent health.

Rubinstein's " Dämon " was performed for the first time in Leipzig on the 13th inst.

Mozart's operas are being given in Vienna in chronological order.

A new symphony by Louis Siebert was lately played in Wiesbaden with a fair amount of success.

A new comic opera by Ignaz Brüll, called "Königin Mariette," is to be produced in Munchen early in June.

Peter Benoit's oratorio "Lucifer" will be heard in Paris on May 7th.

Berlioz's "Requiem" was performed at the fourth concert of the Gessellschaft der Musikfreunde in Vienna. The work found more admirers than upon previous occasions of its performance.

The annual gathering of German musicians will this year take place at Leipzig early in May. According to custom, the musical festival will last four days, and an oratorio by Bach will be given in the Church of St. Thomas.

The death is announced at Paris of M. Henri Ketten in his thirty-fifth year. M. Ketten, who will be remembered as a clever pianist and composer, received his training at the Paris Conservatoire, and gained some renown by his playing in London, New York, St. Petersburg, Melbourne, Vienna, and other large cities.

Organ News.

PRESTON.

The following is the programme of an organ recital given by Mr. James Tomlinson, in the new Public Hall, on Thursday, April 12th :—

Second Concerto	Handel.
Andante (Sixth Quartet)	Mozart.
Air with variations (Notturno for Wind Instruments)	Spohr.
Overture ("The Wood Nymphs")	Bennett.
Pastorale	Wely.
Overture ("La Fille du Regiment")	Donizetti.

And on Saturday, April 14th :—

Premiere Meditation	Guilmant.
Overture ("Athalie")	Mendelssohn.
Andante (Symphony in E flat)	Haydn.
Overture ("Merry Wives of Windsor ")	Nicolai.
Allegretto (Chipp)	Chipp.
Fantasia on English airs (MS.).	

NORWICH.

Annexed is the programme of an organ recital given in St. Andrew's Hall, by Dr. Bunnett, F.C.O., on Saturday, April 14th :—

Concertstück	Spark.
"Carillons de Dunkerque"	E. H. Turpin.
Rhapsodie	Saint-Saëns.
Prelude and Fugue	Ouseley.
Romance sans Paroles	Gounod.
"Air du Dauphin"	Roeckel.
Marche Funèbre et Chant Séraphique	Guilmant.
Andante Grazioso in G	Smart.
"Song of Hope"	Batiste.
Allegretto Tranquillamente	Jordan.
Marche Triomphale	Lemmens.

PENDLETON.

An organ recital was given by Mr. S. W. Pilling in the Charlestown Congregational Chapel, Broughton Road, on Saturday, April 7th, with the annexed programme :—

Introduction and Offertoire	Hewlett.
Larghetto	Batiste.
March (with Hymn of Priests)	Chauvet.
Allegro moderato	Deane.
Sonatina	Van den Bogaert.
Andante	Herman.
Petite Fugue in D major	Handel.
"Adeste Fideles"	Adams.
Overture	Suppé.

ESSEX.

Subjoined is the programme of an organ recital given in Holy Trinity Church, Halstead, on Sunday, April 8th, by Mr. G. Leake, A.C.O. :—

Sonata No. 3	Mendelssohn.
Adagia in B flat	Spohr.
Fugue, "St. Ann's"	Bach.
"The Lost Chord"	Sullivan.
March Solennelle	Gounod.
"In native worth," and "The heavens are telling"	Haydn.

The following is the programme of a recital given by Mr. G. Leake, A.C.O., on the fine organ built by Mr. Alfred Kirkland, and erected in the New Congregational Church, Braintree, on Thursday, April 12th :—

Offertoire in G	Wely.
Sonata No. 3	Mendelssohn.
Vesper Hymn	Turpin.
Funeral March and Chorus of Seraphs	Guilmant.
Festal March	Smart.
Coronation Anthem	Handel.
Barcarolle (Concerto for Piano, No. 4)	Bennett.
Fugue in G minor	Bach.
Andante in G	Batiste.
March ("Athalie")	Mendelssohn.

LOUGHBOROUGH.

On Sunday last special choral services were held in Holy Trinity Church for the purpose of reducing the debt on the organ, which was erected about a year ago by Messrs. Porritt & Son. At the conclusion of the evening service a recital was given by Mr. C. H. Briggs, Mus.Bac., Cantab., when the following programme was very skilfully performed :—

Coronation Anthem	Handel.
Adagio	Rinck.
Prelude and Fugue in G	Bach.
Adagio	Beethoven.
First Sonata	Mendelssohn.
Slow Movement Concertante (Quartet in G)	Spohr.
Offertoire No. 4	Wely.
March	Briggs.

MANCHESTER.

Mr. J. Kendrick Pyne gave an organ recital in the Town Hall, on Saturday, April 14th. Subjoined is the programme :—

Marche Religieuse	Salomé.
Nocturne, "La repos de la Sainte famille" ("L'Enfance du Christ ")	Berlioz.
Toccata and Fugue in F major, with Pedal solos ..	Bach.
Concerto in D minor, No. 6	Handel.
Serenata	Braga.
March and chorus (" Ruins of Athens")	Beethoven.

BLACKBURN.

An organ recital was given by Mr. T. S. Hayward in St. John's Church, on Monday, April 9th, and the following selection of music was played upon the occasion :—

Toccata and Fugue in C major	Bach.
"Holsworthy Church Bells"	Wesley.
Sonata in B flat, No. 4	Mendelssohn.
Andante con variazioni	Beethoven.
Fantasia, "O Sanctissima "	Lux.
Gavotte	Thomas.
Grand Chœur in D major	Guilmant.

SUFFOLK.

Mr. Hemstock gave an afternoon and evening recital in the Corn Hall, Diss, on the occasion of a bazaar held on Tuesday, April 10th :—

AFTERNOON RECITAL.

Overture ("Occasional ")	Handel.
Andante in A flat	Sangster.
Fugato	Tietz.
Pastorale	Merkel.
March ("Scipio ")	Handel.
Allegretto and Allegro	Merkel.
"Jerusalem the Go'den "	Spark.
Fantasia	Tours.

EVENING RECITAL.

Concerto in F	Handel.
Andante Grazioso	Smart.
Andante, with variations and Fugue	Rinck.
Allegretto Grazioso	Tours.
March in B flat	Silas.
Concertstück	Spark.
Sonata No 5	Mendelssohn.
National Anthem (arranged by Hesse).	

TRENT COLLEGE.

An organ recital in aid of the Long Eaton Parochial Mission Churches Fund was given in the Trent College Chapel, on Easter Tuesday evening, by Dr. J. H. Gower. The chapel was crowded in all parts, many being unable to obtain admittance. The following programme was admirably performed :—

Sonata No. 1	Mendelssohn.
Concerto	Handel.
Andante ("Evening Prayer ")	Smart.
Anthem, "Thou didst not leave" (" Messiah ")	Handel.
Toccata in F (pedal solo)	Bach.
Air with variations	Best.
Fantasia, the "Storm "	Lemmens.
Offertoire	Batiste.
Anthem, "Abide with me."	
Fantasia	Saint-Saëns.
Adagio (Second Symphony)	Beethoven.
March	Gower.

BURTON-ON-TRENT.

Mr. A. B. Plant, Mus.Bac., Oxon., F.C.O., gave a recital in St. Paul's Institute, on Wednesday, Thursday, and Friday, April 4th, 5th, and 6th. The programmes included :—

Overture (" Caliph of Bagdad ")	Boïeldieu.
Andante	Batiste.
Barcarolle	Bennett.
Gavotte	Thomas.
Gavotte	Martini.
First Movement (" Jupiter" symphony)	Mozart.
Bourrée	Bach.
March of Priests	Mendelssohn.
Overture (" Stradella ")	Flotow.
Andante	Silas.
Gavotte Moderne	Tours.
Marche Religioso	Perelli.
"Military" symphony	Haydn.
Pastorale	Corelli.
Grand Chœur	Salomé.
Overture (" Martha ")	Flotow.
Allegretto in B minor	Guilmant.
First Movement (Concerto in F)	Handel.
Gavotte	Lee.
Sonata in C	Mendelssohn.
Adagio	Beethoven.
Overture in D	Méhul.

BOLTON.

An organ recital was given in the Albert Hall, by Mr. Wm. Mullineux, F.C.O., on Saturday, April 14th. The following was the programme :—

Sonata in B flat, No. 4	Mendelssohn.
Largo (Pianoforte Sonata in A major, Op. 2)	Beethoven.
Canzonet, "My mother bids me bind my hair"	Haydn.
Allegretto vivace ("Jupiter" sinfonia)	Mozart.
Selection ("Maritana")	Wallace.
Dedication March	Bentley.

LEEDS.

Dr. Spark gave a recital on the grand organ in the Town Hall (No. 5 of the series) on Saturday, April 14th, when the programme consisted of works by Beethoven, and comprised :—Overture ("Fidelio"); Romance in F major, Op. 50; Air and variations (Septuor); Marche Funèbre (composed on the death of a hero); Andante in F (Symphony in C); Largo Appassionata in D (Pianoforte Sonata in A); Chorus, "Hallelujáh to the Father."

DORSET.

Appended is a description of the organ designed and built by Messrs. Maley, Young & Oldknow, for St. Mary's parish church, Wareham :—

GREAT ORGAN. CC TO G.

1. Double Open Diap.	16 ft.	6. Harmonic Flute	4 ft.
2. Open Diapason	8 „	7. Fifteenth	2 „
3. Violin Diapason	8 „	8. Mixture (4 ranks)	
4. Clarabella	8 „	9. Posaune	8 „
5. Principal	4 „		

SWELL ORGAN. CC TO G.

10. Contra Gamba	16 ft.	16. Wald Flute	4 ft.
11. Open Diapason	8 „	17. Flageolet	2 „
12. Stopped Diapason	8 „	18. Mixture (3 ranks)	
13. Salcionelle	8 „	19. Cornopean	8 „
14. Voix Celestes	8 „	20. Oboe	8 „
15. Principal	4 „	21. Vox Humana	8 „

CHOIR ORGAN. CC TO G.

22. Open Diapason	8 ft.	27. Gemshorn	4 ft.
23. Dulciana	8 „	28. Harmonic Piccolo	2 „
24. Bell Gamba	8 „	29. Contra Fagotto	16 „
25. Lieblich Gedact	8 „	30. Clarionet	8 „
26. Suabe Flute	4 „		

PEDAL ORGAN. CCC TO F.

31. Open Diapason	16 ft.	33. Violoncello	8 ft.
32. Bourdon	16 „	34. Trombone	8 „

ACCESSORY MOVEMENTS.

35. Swell to Great.	38. Great to Pedals.
36. Swell to Choir.	39. Swell to Pedals.
37. Choir to Great.	40. Choir to Pedals

Four Combination pedals to Great and Pedal organs.
Three   „   „   to Swell organ.

Hore-shoe pedal to Great to Pedals.
Tremulant to Swell organ.

Wind supplied from one large bellows in chamber away from organ, and two reservoirs at different pressures inside organ. Oak case, decorated pipes in front and end.

SALE OF MR. B. WILLIAMS' MUSIC BUSINESS.

With a considerable amount of pluck, Mrs. Mullen (daughter of the late Mr. Benjamin Williams), bid for and became the purchaser at the sum of £5,800, of the good-will of the above old established business, together with the general trade stock. She has also become the purchaser of many of the popular things from the Publishing Catalogue, notably Pinsuti's song "The Bugler" for £215, and Smallwood's "Sea Shells" polka for £336. The sale, which is still proceeding at Messrs. Puttick and Simpson's, will conclude on Tuesday next,

PRINCIPAL CONTENTS OF THIS NUMBER.

LONDON : SATURDAY, APRIL 21, 1883.

THE PRESENT POSITION OF THE COMPOSER.

V.

PERHAPS no difficulty faces the upward progress of the productive artist, whatever may be the medium of his thought presentation, as the public want of faith in new work. "He asked for bread and "they gave him a stone," are words expressing in a single epigrammatic sentence the history of most men of genius ; and the exceptions to the sad rule are for the most part merely the cases of men born to exceptional social advantages, whose friendly aids to fame have enabled them to scale the heights of reputation more quickly by favourably prompting public faith and judgment in their behalf. This want of faith is displayed in all directions. Even a simple witticism palpable enough to all minds, gains zest if attributed to DEAN SWIFT or to SYDNEY SMITH ; a fact probably accounting for many an erroneously assigned *bon mot*. So in music the simplest and most natural 8 or 16 measure melody gives much more enjoyment when the name of some classical or popular composer is placed at the right hand side of its title. This preparedness of the public mind to delight only in what has been already admired, and its accompanying tendency to take no pains to discover what should be admired, is at once the great stumbling-block of the untried composer and the stronghold of the established tone-producer. But further however gifted composers have been and are being ruined as artists, by premature public acceptation brought about usually through the influence and industry of enthusiastic and interested friends in the position to bring social power to the composer's aid. For such premature publicity, as inclining the art-producer to relax his powers of self-examination and self-culture from the knowledge that whatever he may offer to the public, praise and a meed of popularity must follow, is a danger to the artist only second to the more trying peril of a too prolonged neglect; nay as regards the future, prolonged neglect is better far than premature popularity. Not the least treacherous feature of the last-named danger, is its tendency to induce the composer too anxious to get on in the world, to persist in the composition of too many works of the same kind and built upon the same and perhaps for the time being only, popularly accepted model, which may not be an enduring form capable of large art development. Such an error of judgment in the end dwarfs the composer's mental powers and inclination for real art-work, just as the female victim of some perverse and injurious fashionable article of attire is physically punished for the foolish pains she takes in order to be admired. Further, the public mind grows more critical and less grateful with the repeated presentments of a given type of work, in which novelty was likely enough one of the original sources of charm, just in proportion as the composer grows more easily satisfied with his readily repeated labours, and self-deceived, is falling unwarily into the "bed of roses" which will prove, unless he extricates himself in time, an artistic stagnation and perhaps his future downfall. The great composer is, indeed, not only a great artist, but essentially a great man, superior alike to the dangers of adversity and prosperity.

E. H. Turpin.

FORM IN VOCAL MUSIC.

II.

THERE is no doubt that vocal music was in the earlier stages of its development simply a musical expression of the operations of speech. It has been my task more than once to show the affinity. between the melodic formations of music gravitating on scale centres, and the inflections of the speaker's voice, rising above or falling below the ordinary level of his speaking voice. The early musical employments of the voice as still to be noted in the plain song intonations with their medium and grave inflections, were little more than the musical embodiment of the punctuation and expressive inflections of speech. There is a beautiful instance of this dual speech-melody in an ancient monastic form of repeating the confession in which the intonations are at once appropriate and touching. The commas were marked by the fall of a minor third, whilst an expressive turn and a deeper fall to the final note distinguished the more emphatic closes of the complete sentences at each full stop. I give one sentence in illustration of the simplicity and expressive beauty of this early vocal form in which verbal and musical expression and punctuation move together with such truthfulness and eloquence, select-

ing a favourable sentence for the purpose from the middle of the confession.

Mea culpa, mea culpa, mea maxima culpa.

Sung in unison by a body of earnest voices amidst the solemn surroundings of a great church, nothing can exceed the simple eloquence of such early vocal forms. One can only wonder that the fine expressive figures of this speech-melody and others of the same build are not employed in these days of the revival of church art. The earlier chant forms which are still represented by the so-called Gregorian chants to the Psalms, are musically an advance upon the still more primitive half spoken tune figures, which first built up song out of speech, as a higher eloquence built upon eloquence itself.   E. H. Turpin.

M. GOUNOD ON "CRITICISM."

THE distinguished French composer's words on this topic are forcible, but not without a one-sided ring in them. With regard to himself it must be remembered that no composer has been better helped to a high position in his own life-time by the discerning critics. We in England, for instance, know full well that M. Gounod's reputation here was largely contributed to by the persistent and discriminating utterances of the late Henry Chorley in his favour in the columns of the *Athenæum* and elsewhere; not to mention the names of other large-sighted writers who at once recognised M. Gounod's merits. The truth is M. Gounod has been simply declaiming against bad criticism, and unconsciously proclaiming the value of patient, thoughtful, and carefully pronounced judgments. The inconsistency of M. Gounod's position in this matter is aggravated by a presumed desire on his part for literary fame which he would doubtless have purchased to some extent by writing on musical topics, and by the fact that he has himself within the last few weeks undertaken the delicate duties of a musical critic. However, everyone is glad to hear the opinions of such a large-minded and sympathetic artist as M. Gounod is everywhere acknowledged to be. With regard to the cases of Beethoven and Wagner, it may surely be allowed that the geniuses must lead the critics before the critics can lead the public. It is clear that the stumbling-block to the critical mind has ever been either the neglect of, the departure from, or the enlargement of, the ethics of the art; and the attitude of cautious acceptation is on the whole, as M. Gounod himself practically confesses, a desirable position for the critic to assume. However, it is to the enlightened critics the world is chiefly indebted for the after all comparatively prompt recognition of some of the world's most original minds. To turn back to the cases of Beethoven and Wagner, who in the first instance save the critics besought people to listen to their works and who guided the public mind to a larger acceptation of their methods of thought and taught us in the end to admire their most remarkable efforts? There is, nevertheless, a moral in M. Gounod's words; it seems to be this, trust not too much to any impressions built upon critical examination, for no intermediary mind can entirely assess the value to the listener of thoughts intended by the composer to appeal directly to the hearer himself. All the same, the critical function is one of undoubted utility, as leading the public mind by means of experienced, watchful, systematised judgment, to a quicker estimation of art-work than would be attained to without guidance, and as helping to erect art-principles and standards, and so re-acting with advantage to the progress of art upon the minds, habits of thought, and methods of cultivation of the art-producers themselves. Critics, in short, rank among those useful types of the machinery of life which exist to the reduction of labour either mental or physical. The theologian may not be indispensable to those gifted with the spirit of religious faith, but he assists in the enlargement of religious sympathies and knowledge. The critic is to art what the theologian is to religion. Again, as it is deemed necessary to have doctors and lawyers to consult with, so it is well to have critics to guide us in matters which call for the exercise of the understanding at the same time as they appeal to the feelings. Of course there is much bad, interested and ignorant criticism, just as there is much good, disinterested and learned art-examination in our midst. To say this, is merely to advance the self-evident proposition that critics, like composers, are but weak, mortal men, despite their gifts and acquirements. There is a tendency on the part of art-producers now and then to peevishly and impatiently attack the critics, in whom they are wrongly apt to see impediments to popularity; in such cases the artists are forgetting that to critical labour they are indebted for much of the publicity they already enjoy. The power of the critics in the work of enlarging public faith (always timid through prevailing ignorance) in art matters, is alone benefit enough to the world to justify their presence and to claim for them the respect of thinking artists and thoughtful listeners.   E. H. TURPIN.

_____

M. Gounod's words are here quoted:—

Montesquieu said : " The more wise men there are together the less wisdom there is." This means the more particular, exclusive, personal points of view on any question, the more chances there are for discussion, and disturbance of that unity which is Truth. Suppose, for a moment, one critic were called upon to select the paintings for a museum. How many original works would he not reject? The collections that we call museums are nothing else but monuments of that universal judgment which protects master-pieces against personal antipathy, and preserves them for the veneration and instruction of mankind. One advantage painting has over music is that it can express itself by works which appeal directly to the public without those intermediaries which music requires. This is one of the considerations which teaches how delicate a task is that of criticism, and how much the interpretation may mislead us as to the value of a work. While a picture is a permanent work, before which the spectator can pause at leisure, and which presents itself at one stroke in its entirety, the musical work is fugitive and only reveals itself to the intelligence and sensibility of the auditor in a succession of effects which robs most of the details of the value given them by the whole. If one thinks of the part played by memory in the success of a musical work, one must allow that it is very difficult to pronounce on the first hearing of a work in which so many different elements call for attention. How is musical criticism, usually, managed? Who of us who know what it costs to learn, and how much more it costs to conceal the little we know? Who of us, on the morrow of some great work, demanding study of all kinds, of a work where its author has spent perhaps years of his heart and brain—years, not merely of days, but of days and nights—who of us, I ask, would assume the responsibility of an immediate judgment of a work of such compass?

But the critic takes his seat in the stalls, and next morning declares to the readers of his journal that this opera, of which he does not know a note, and which he has heard the evening before for the first time in his life, is a masterpiece or a blunder. What does he know of it? I ask. We men in the business, who wish to understand and who know how to listen, would not express an opinion, much less a judgment, on a work of which we have received only a rapid, fugitive impression. For my part, if fortune had placed me in the delicate situation of having to criticise a dramatic work, I would say to the editor : " Sir, you impose on me a great task. To be honest, I must neither be flippant nor hasty. I must have some days of reflection after the tumult of first impressions, which are necessarily vague. I must have time to disentangle this multitude of airs, duos, choruses and finales. I must put some order into this chaos of situations, characters, and instrumental colours. I do not want to have anything to withdraw or retract. My review must not appear till I can honestly say what I know.

Is criticism useful? I was going to say, Is it good for anything? I doubt it. Criticism is a profession : is it a mission? As for me, I see in it little more than amusement—so much talk. When a man has combatted Eugene Delacroix in the name of Ingres, or Ingres in the name of Delacroix, what will he have proved or produced? Nothing but what is perfectly useless. It might be useful to bring out the qualities of a man or a work. The progress—the movement that produces great men—this growth which creates giants—does not consist in acquiring the gifts which nature has not bestowed on us, but in developing the germs she has given us, and which are the form of our personality.

The artist is nothing but a given manner of thinking, clothed in a certain manner of expressing. Genius is the expression of a certain proportion between two elements ; the element ideal, impersonal which assigns to works their level and their duration; and the real element which is relative and personal and the reason of their novelty. In other terms, genius is " a new manner of saying things that are not new." *Nove non nova.* Do you fancy one can become anything else than what one is? How could the? Progress implies identity. Place on a table a box, on the box a book, on the book a hat, and so on ; you have not a growth, but a heap. Some minds are heaps ; throw what you like into them, nothing germinaets, nothing consequently grows. There is not in all nature, in any forest, on any tree, on any branch two leaves alike ; and you would place the whole human race in uniform and pass it in review! Art is feeling become science ; it is the confused spontaneous element rendering itself precise by intelligence. It is necessary, then, to know much in order to judge, for it is necessary to be able to make the abstraction of one's personal sentiment, which is a prejudice; and it is necessary, at the same time, to be capable of measuring the amount of knowledge contained in a book. If you confine yourself to saying that such or such a thing pleases or displeases you, you teach me nothing ; you express not a judgment, but a sensation, and do not prove that yours is better than mine.

On the other hand, it is useless to pile up argument on argument ; invoke your grammarians to prove to me the merits of a work from which life is absent, or to establish that it does not conform to any of the known and recognised rules. I can reply, in the first place, these rules are not all the rules ; for the present sentiment of higher laws devised by the intuition of genius does not imply the violation of the other law which you invoke. When the great works of Beethoven made their first appearance in France, critics and musicians declared he was a barbarian who did not know how to write, and it required all the tenacity of Habeneck to collect and keep around that barbarian, who was soon to be a standard, the musicians which became the cradle of the famous society of concerts at the Conservatory Girard. The conscientious and intelligent *chef d'orchestre*, who was the successor of Habeneck, told me that after the first trials of the symphonies of Beethoven by the orchestra of the Odeon, the musicians flung from their desks the scores of the Pastoral Symphony, and cried that it was not music. Thanks to the perseverance of Habeneck, the education of musicians, of the public, of the critics, gradually was developed, and the eight first symphonies were recognised as masterpieces. But the ninth ! A celebrated musician said to me : " It is the work of a delirious brain." Then some merit was allowed to the three first movements ; but the last one, it was impossible, ridiculous, cacophonous. Some years later it was the turn of the last quatuors. They were madness—where was melody? No melody—that was the word, no melody. Well, tell me what melody is ! You do not know, nor I, nor anybody, you will reply. It can not be explained ; it can only be felt. It seems to me that it is no more felt than explained for men denied melody to Beethoven yesterday, and grant it to him to-day. Men have denied melody to Rossini's " Barber," after that of Paesiello. After that, one can expect anything.

_____

Mr. Charlton T. Speer announces a pianoforte recital at the Royal Academy of Music Concert Rooms, on May 2nd, with an interesting programme. including a Sonata for pianoforte and flute, by Professor G. A. Macfarren, and a Toccata by Mr. W. Macfarren,

"COLOMBA."
(THE LIBRETTO).

The production last week at Drury Lane of Mr. A. C. Mackenzie's opera "Colomba," has created a veritable stir, and the precise value of this lyrical drama—as its adapter terms it—is a question eagerly discussed in English musical circles. Now that the work has been heard a second and a third time, and its score and words have become more clearly understood, we stand in a better position to assess the merit of the opera, than was the case immediately after its first performance.

This duty of critical examination is indeed thrown upon us by the invitation which Herr F. Hüffer, the writer of the words, practically gives in the preface at the commencement of the book. In order that the value of his share in the work should be properly appreciated, a month ago, the words of the opera were printed, and issued to those persons to whom the task of public criticism is usually committed. Whether this unusual course was inspired by a consideration for the digestive faculties of the critics, or on more purely personal grounds, is of little concern to the general public. Neither is it necessary to notice in detail the controversy (which has now found its way into the columns of the *Illustrated Sporting and Dramatic News*), as to whether it is right for Herr Hüffer to write a work of this character; the ground taken being, that as musical critic of the *Times*, he must either judge his own production, or else vacate the critical chair in favour of a friend for the occasion : and further, that when a professed critic associates himself with a composer in the joint production of an opera, it would be wellnigh impossible for him on a future occasion, in which he was not associated with this particular composer, to criticise adversely his works, if justice necessitated such a course. It may, however, be observed *en passant*, that though the contention has a certain force, if it were to prevail, a critic, whatever ability he might possess, would be prevented from being a producer. The sarcastic doctrine, that critics are those who themselves have failed, is as untrue in music as it is in other arts. To mention one name only, Schumann has shown that the two offices are compatible and may be concurrent, and the biography of prominent members of all the recognised arts show us that they have frequently exercised their critical faculty for the public benefit. There is yet one more matter to which attention may be drawn. In the last issue of Messrs. Novello's new venture, *The Musical Review*, of which it is understood that Herr Hüffer is editor, appears an amateurish article pitched in a shrieking key, abusing those who have unfavourably criticised the libretto of "Colomba." The charge of envy he has brought against some of them is sublime in its absurdity. Criticism has no doubt been severe all round the newspapers; some of the writers have pierced the librettist with a keen rapier, and more than one has knocked him down with a heavy cudgel. It need only be remarked that these gentlemen are perfectly able to take care of themselves. The public will rather form its own judgment over the matter, in preference to merely endorsing the opinion found in an interested journal. Conclusions will also be drawn from the fact that the reprints of the press notices about the work in *The Musical Review*, are extensively garbled, and much important matter is eliminated. However, this aspect of the question may be speedily dismissed. Recrimination settles nothing; it is fairest to Dr. Hüffer to judge his work on its merits, and personalities should be avoided as much as possible.

The Preface to "Colomba" runs as follows :—

In presenting the "lyrical drama" "Colomba," apart from its musical accompaniment, to the general reader of poetry, the author pleads guilty to "a purpose." What that "purpose" is this brief prefatory note is intended to explain. In a literature more developed and more varied than that of any other nation, the art of writing words for music has been strangely neglected. In the age of Tennyson, Browning, and Rossetti, the lyrical drama retains the Della Cruscan mannerism of diction of the "wits" of Pope's time, as reflected in the lofty minds of "the poet" Bunn, and the late Mr. Fitzball. So absolutely identified is that diction with the parlance of the typical librettist, that at last the public itself must have come to the conclusion of its necessity for the purposes of music. To dispel such an idea, prejudicial alike to both arts, the present libretto has been written. It is here attempted to show that the language fitted to musical purposes is not essentially different from that of general common sense and literary taste, that in a libretto it is not necessary for a person or number of persons to ejaculate, "Now good red wine we will be drinking," where every rational being in verse or prose

would sing or say, "Now let me have some good red wine." That turn of phraseology is generally supposed to be necessitated by the scarcity in our language of the feminine or double rhymes and verse-endings so desirable for the rounding off of a musical sentence. That this is a mere prejudice it would be easy to show from the works of our great poets, beginning with Shakespeare. It may suffice, by way of a modest but obvious example, to refer the reader to the Corsican love-song at page 22, and the duet at page 30 of the present work, both of which consist for the greater part of double and even triple rhymes without a single instance of the objectionable present participle.

After some remarks admitting that poetry for music requires a greater freedom and variety than the spoken drama, he continues :—

My intention was to emphasize a difference of system, not to claim exceptional excellence for my individual effort, and with the same intention this little work is submitted to the judgment of the benevolent reader.

It may be mentioned that Herr Hüffer's kind interest in our insular deficiencies is not confined to the improvement of English libretto writing. He has also posed as a reformer of our song music. A set of "Seven Songs, set to music by Franz Hüffer" (Stanley Lucas, Weber, and Co.), reveals him in this benevolent rôle. Our author evidently has a *penchant* for preface writing; for prefixed to this singular collection is a Preface, in which, after severely condemning "the Metropolitan Market muse," he laments, that, "the treasures of English lyrical poetry have scarcely ever found congenial interpreters in the sphere of music, for which they seem so eminently adapted." He then offers his "poetical," "sentimental," "emotional," and "sweet quaint" compositions (as he indirectly designates them), as affording fitting examples of what such music should be. However, these songs are not now under review; but if the readers of the *Musical Standard* want some amusement, let them procure the set. It will be seen that Herr Hüffer did wise to disclaim any "reverential awe for the sacredness of form," the songs presenting an arrangement of notes fearful to contemplate, distressing to hear, and displaying some of the loftiest disregards of grammar trammels to be found in the whole range of printed music.

In the introduction to "Colomba," Herr Hüffer has supplied us with materials for much reflection. His Preface takes very distinct ground, and his remarks naturally fall into three divisions. First, he contemptuously derides our native librettists; secondly, he dogmatically lays down the canons which he assumes ought to govern this species of literary work; and thirdly, with that innate modesty which is regarded as a national characteristic of Teutons of a certain stamp, he calls attention to the naturalness and admirability of his own musico-dramatic treatment. Now let us briefly examine these various pretensions.

In the first place, it will be only just to Dr. Hüffer to remind the readers of the *Musical Standard* that he is a foreigner not long settled amongst us, and that therefore he cannot be expected to have a complete command over our modes of thinking, or of our English diction. Nor would it be fair to suppose that he has an intimate acquaintance with our rich poetical and dramatic literature. Were it otherwise, no comments would be too strong to make on his sweeping condemnation of our librettos, and his statement that the lyrical drama of the day retains the speech and imagery of Bunn and Fitzball. He has evidently erred through ignorance, and not prejudice, for he would not have classed the works of these writers with the librettos of Cumming's "Fairy Ring," Smart's "Bride of Dunkerron," Randegger's "Fridolin," Dr. Bridge's "Boadicea," Cowen's "St. Ursula," Sir Julius Benedict's "Graziella," or the masterly nervous English productions of Prout's "Alfred," and Mackenzie's "Jason" both from the pen of Mr. Grist. However, respecting some of these matters touched on in Herr Hüffer's preface, and his own superior specimen verses, more anon.

We have first to consider the construction of the opera of "Colomba" from a dramatic point of view. As the Argument has already been given in the issue of last week, and is now pretty well known, it is unnecessary to go over the ground again. Prosper Mérimée's novel, from which the idea of the drama is taken, is a truly charming conception. It is as picturesque, as is the same author's popular "Carmen"; the various characters are drawn with the hand of a master, and present carefully finished pictures of Corsican life. But Herr Hüffer has well nigh destroyed the edifice of romance which the brilliant French author has so skilfully built up. He has so mutilated and altered the characters, that, with the sole exception of Colomba, the spectator can feel but a languid interest in any of their doings, as compared with the fascination experienced on reading the novel itself. Moreover, Mérimée is a keen psychologist, and that quality is entirely wanting in Herr Hüffer. The French writer, with delicate skill and truth, depicts the heroine as an ordinary maiden, graced with feminine attributes, of a practical turn of mind, and vengeful towards the murderers of her father simply on account of the traditional *vendetta* of her country. This painful duty satisfied, she returns to the usual avocations of life, and settles down into average respectability. Not so the German adapter's treatment of the subject. He has displayed but one side of Colomba's nature. Omitting entirely her pleasant qualities, and failing to appreciate the valuable touches of contrast that the original author has artistically furnished, he has supplied the girl with a rôle than which surely nothing more repulsive has been seen on the stage! To the exclusion of every other sentiment, she is possessed with an *idée fixe*, viz., fiendish craving for blood. It is impossible to feel any sympathy with a heroine of this offensive type, and perhaps Herr Hüffer was wise to adopt the stock device of weak authors, and cause her to be cleared out of the way by a chance shot. The stage is thus rid of so objectionable a young lady, and the *Deus ex machina* involved in the poetic justice meted out, would have delighted our transpontine theatre-goers, despite the sacrifice of dramatic fidelity over the transaction.

Another mistake of the adapter is seen in the weakness of the love feature. He has entirely altered the character of Lydia, the high-minded daughter of the English Colonel, turning her into a feeble conventional figure of a mild schoolgirl type. An opera ought certainly to contain some important love business, and the more impassioned it is the better; but in the case under examination, one can feel but little interest over the love affairs of Orso and Lydia. Indeed, the lady does not appear at all in the 2nd and 3rd Acts, and we almost forget her existence until she nervously ventures into the Robbers' Camp, and, like another Moses's daughter—as has been wittily said—discovers her lover lying hidden in the bulrushes. The whole matter is managed much more delicately in the novel, Lydia being deceived by Colomba, and brought unknowingly to meet Orso. Again, the evidence on which the Barracini are condemned is too flimsy to satisfy the scant exigences of even a drum-head court martial; while the acknowledgment made by one of the brothers of the supposed crime, is an avowal wholly gratuitous, dictated neither by necessity nor advanced proof. The finishing off of the Barracini betrays a want of stage experience; indeed it almost provokes laughter by its clumsiness, and the modern Irish landlord shooting mode in which the matter is managed, one brother after another dropping to Orso's gun. Corsicans who take pot-shots at their adversaries behind stone walls, and then occasionally pop up, like a Jack-in-the-box, to see how the victim is getting on, might take a valuable lesson in prudence and immediate flight from some of the patriotic brethren of our sister isle. The way in which the stage, representing a road some distance from the village, suddenly becomes filled with the various characters of the play, together with peripatetic monks conveniently provided with biers for the dead bodies, is slightly incongruous with the supposed loneliness of the spot, and affords a startling instance of the rapid spread of bad news. The opera might have ended here, or at any rate, the next Act need have only lasted long enough to get Orso pardoned, and the lovers properly united, according to the design of the original author. But this arrangement did not meet with the approval of the adapter; so in his desire to get rid of the bloodthirsty heroine, he causes her to be shot by accident, gloating in dying over the revenge achieved, and usurping priestly functions so far, as solemnly to join the hands of the lovers. The red glow which blazes up from the foot-lights at the moment, is certainly characteristic of the dying girl's passionate desire for revenge, and her constant whining over "our blood-stained honour"; while the concluding sentiment uttered by the Count "A great and noble heart has passed away," is thoroughly false, hollow, and sophistical.

At the beginning of this act the great mistake is made of repeating, *coram populo*, that which the audience already know respecting the shooting of the Barracini. This long-winded account of an event belonging to ancient history is altogether unnecessary; it not only produces *ennui* and weariness, but exemplifies a serious want of art-construction on the part of the librettist. It was a novel sight on the stage, and indeed touching, to see the wounded tenor condemned to go through his concluding part with an arm in a sling. One could not but feel sympathy with him, and further, regret that he was arranged to sing in an atmosphere of gunpowder smoke.

The stilted and unnatural style of Bunn and Fitzball is not to be commended; but they wrote many admirable lyrics, and their dramatic instinct guarded them against falling into mistakes similar to those which the author of "Colomba" has committed in his libretto.

The diction of "Colomba" next claims our examination. In terming his opera a "lyrical drama," Herr Hüffer evidently imagines that he has created something novel in design. But this is a mistake; his work is not original as to form. Long before he set foot on these shores, we possessed what are more correctly termed "Grand Romantic Operas," by Barnett, Balfe, Wallace, Benedict, and others; their construction was precisely similar to that of "Colomba," viz., a mixture of prose, blank verse, and lyrics. In the remarkable Preface to the work, reprinted above, we read that, "the author pleads guilty to 'a purpose.'" This singular guiltiness takes the form of asserting that in England the art of writing words for music has been strangely neglected; that the lyrical drama has the Della Cruscan mannerism of diction; that the language of a libretto should be the language of general common-sense and literary taste, and that irrational phraseology is supposed to be necessitated by the scarcity in our language of the feminine or double rhymes; finally, that the use of the present participle is objectionable. This serious indictment against our writers, and our defective language having been formulated, Dr. Hüffer goes on to state that, his libretto represents the emphasization of a difference of system, and he points with becoming modesty to his Corsican Love Song, as a satisfactory specimen of art workmanship. Space will not admit of a minute examination of these various charges, so they must perforce be noticed with brevity. As a tree is judged by its fruits, so must the Doctor's libretto be judged by the canons he has laid down, combined with common-sense, and good taste.

A perusal of the Book of Words conveys to one's mind the idea that it has been translated from the German, rather than adapted direct from the French. This impression is further strengthened by the construction of some of the sentences, by the many un-English expressions used, by the odd condemnation "of the objectionable present participle," and further, by the remembrance of the nationality of our author. A few words on the participle question. Dr. Hüffer is evidently unaware that the English present participle is far more elastic than the German. In the latter language it is very rarely used, except adjectively adverbially, or the infinitive of the verb takes its place; in addition to these common variants, other modifications of the sentence are made where we should employ the participle. For instance; the Germans cannot literally translate so simple a phrase as, "Hearing him cry, I ran to him"; they must change it into, "I heard him to cry and ran to him" (*Ich hörte ihn schrein und lief zu ihm*). "Reading good books," must run, "The to read of good books"; "The art of writing," is strictly, "The art to write." Such sentences as "The art of living," and "Up and be doing," samples of strong and good uses of our participle, find no German equivalent. From these examples one can understand how difficult it is for Germans who have not attained a mastery of our language to know when and how to employ our present participle. Herr Hüffer in his wisdom thinks that this is the fault of the unfortunate participle, but others better informed will maintain that this is the fault of the imperfectly educated man. There is no need to refute his supposition that we are poor as to "words for music." When he has time to search, a rapid glance from Shakespeare down to to-day will probably cause him to alter his opinion. While agreeing with him that the language of a libretto should be the language of common sense, it should be pointed out that all opera is conventional, more or less. Though we should laugh over the talking dragons, magic swords, love potions, and thaumaturgical birds, with which certain German operas are adorned, preferring rather dramas of purely human interest, yet in opera we require a certain amount of romance, and with it, flexibility and a greater freedom of language than is current in matter-of-fact life. Herr Hüffer laments the rare employment of so-called feminine rhymes in English, but little real loss is sustained over their restricted use. He condemns mannerisms of diction; and rightly so. Mannerism shows poverty of ideas. On page 12 of his libretto, within the space of a few lines, we find the term "murderous brood" used four times, "murderous hand" twice, and "murderous plot" once, while the word "blood" is employed no fewer than eight times. Such mannerisms are decidedly bad, and betray a singular lack of invention. A few specimens of his lines are given below :—

"Say whose is all this lovely luggage?
Hands off, if you please, you ancient baggage!"

"Until her father's purple stream."

"While I attend to the affairs of state,
And vainly try, with diplomatic ability,
To win the king some hearts, I grieve that your ability
Of public speech has left me to my fate."

"The air of this unhappy island
Is loud as with ill-omened raven's voices."

"Tell him no longer he must tarry
Nor let the shame on our foreheads burn;
Like the royal eagle, he must return
And scare the vultures from their nest;
And with beak and talons that none can parry,
Tear open the hearts of the murderous brood,
Taking life for life, and blood for blood;
That our father's spirit may be at rest,
And the voice of our sorrow drowned in the cries
Of the widowed wives of our enemies!"

"One terrible night
Has blighted all the blossoms of my youth,
And what remains is void of scent and sweetness,
Even as these withered flowers of yester-year,
But what boots it to think!"

"The time is near
When the harvest of murderous seed will appear."

"Father, be with me in this hour of need;
Restrain my hand from soiling our fair fame
With an assassin's venomous blood."

"But this one is safe, he will never rise;
See the bullet-hole right between his eyes;
His villanous tongue will not wag again.
Hallo! here is another one slain,
As dead as a nail. This indeed is sport
A lying lawyer to each barrel.
I call this an excellent retort."

"Say of Love shall he change or alter,
Shall he decay or shall he diminish?
Doomed from his birth to stagger and falter,
Doomed in the end to fail and to finish."

Here is the condemned Della Cruscanism with a vengeance! Space cannot be spared for more extracts. Enough are given to show the extraordinary character of our suggested reformation style. Some lines contain too many, some too few feet; they will rarely scan, and the supposed rhymes are indeed fearful and wonderful. The ludicrous ideas conjured up, and the grotesque language employed are even more absurd than the rubbish to be found in the translations of Italian opera formerly made for the delectation of unlinguistic English people, who desired to know what was taking place on the stage. Herr Hüffer sneers at Bunn and Fitzball, signalling out for special ridicule, "Now good red wine we will be drinking." However, at page 11 of his libretto we find the following line :—

"Rejoice with me, friends, for my brother at last has come;
To unravel the truth he has come,"

again :—

"Like the royal eagle he will return."

and :

"When her friends round the body were assembling."

It will be here seen that the disdainful critic uses precisely the same form of construction (German) as that of the old despised librettists. How their shades must chuckle over this sublime inconsistency! Space will not permit to call attention to the peculiarities of Herr Hüffer's grammar. He has doubtless struggled manfully with the difficulties of English prosody, especially the prepositions and pronouns, but the latter mentioned parts of speech have occasionally been too much for him. There are antecedents lost to view amidst a mass of secondaries, and relatives of so obscure and bigamous a disposition, that they are quite ready to agree with any person or thing preceding them. Such are :—

"The song which on the burial-day
The Signora Colomba did sing and say
When her friends round the body were assembling,
And *which* no Barracini hears without trembling."

"No joy of song is left me,
For the vulture has bereft me
Of the mate I cherished aye,
Piercing his heart, *mine* he cleft me."

As for the double and triple rhymes he claims credit for in the Corsican Love Song, there are no triple rhymes to be found, for "say to her" and "nay to her," is certainly not a true specimen, and of the ordinary rhymes, it must be pointed out that "vendetta" and "faldetta" are foreign words which we term identities, and not true rhymes. The same observation will apply to "dignity" and "malignity," "ability" and "affability," "frightened" and "enlightened," "consolation" and "notion," "intended" and "offended," "assembling" and "trembling," amongst other examples. Attention should also be called to the very large number of foreign words usually employed. Why is "*pomi d'oro*" written instead of "tomatos," "*faldetta*" for "mantle" and "*macchia*" for "the bush"?; and further, why do the chorus (who elsewhere sing in English) suddenly branch into Italian for five lines, lauding their elected Queen of the May in words which are a blasphemous travesty of a Roman Catholic antiphon? The Latin chant of the monks is of course admissible.

From what has already been written, the "benevolent" reader will perceive, that despite the arrogant self-assertion of Herr Hüffer's preface, he has not proved his ability to write good English, or flowing verses adapted for music; nor are his lines free from the reproaches he has thrown on those of other writers. Of course he knows us too well to write the ridiculous stuff that one Hans Von Wolzogen put forth last year as a translation of "The Nibelungen Ring" for the performance of Wagner's operas. Fortunately, the words of an opera are of far less importance than is the music associated with them; this is a thesis that may be safely maintained in spite of the new "unity" theory. But having said this much, let us be just and grant a measure of credit to the *Times* critic for his work. He has failed to reproduce the delicate *nuances* of Mérimée's tale, but the task of putting such a work into a narrative form is a very difficult one. Dr. Hüffer possesses little true poetic feeling, and seems to be entirely ignorant of the lyrical value of alliteration. There is some tedious padding in the work, but his framework is mostly good, and the dramatic character of the opera furnishes the musical composer with just those valuable situations which Mr. Mackenzie has promptly seized, and illustrated with such signal success.

The detailed notice of the music must be deferred until the next issue.   T. L. SOUTHGATE.

Mr. John Stedman's large circle of friends will heartily rejoice in learning, that after a serious illness, which has kept him away from the personal performance of his duties, he will return to town and resume his many responsible engagements next week. Mr. Stedman's restoration to health will be a matter of general congratulation in the musical world; for he has not only won the confidence of the many connected with him as a skilled and experienced concert agent and artist, but he has secured on all sides an enviable reputation as an excellent and very estimable man.

Passing Events.

Amateur Work for April gives the plan and outlines of the violin upon the Stradivarius model.

Mr. George H. L. Edwards announces his Twelfth Evening Concert, to be given at the Town Hall, Poplar, on Monday next, 23rd inst.

A "Musical Evening" was given by the students of the Surrey County School of Music (Principal : Mr. W. Lemare), on April 18th.

At the Annual Conversazione of the Church Guilds Union, at the Holborn Town Hall, April 11th, some good music was given, including organ solos by Mr. Victor Gollmick, part-songs, etc.

The last recital at the Bow and Bromley Institute is to be given on April 28th, by Dr. A. L. Peace of Glasgow. Vocalist Miss Clara Dowle, and violin Miss Marie Schumann, both of the Guildhall School of Music.

Messrs. Willis and Co. have erected a fine and very effective organ in the large new church at the Dominican Priory, Maitland Park, Haverstock Hill. This notably fine church will be shortly opened, and church music of a high order will it is expected be heard there.

At the Stratford Musical Festival held last Friday and Saturday, Miss Adela Duckham, aged 8½ years (who recently was awarded a Corporation Exhibition at the Guildhall School of Music), competed in two classes, and in one for pianoforte solo playing (34 competitors) won a first prize, and in the other for pianoforte sight playing (8 competitors) gained a first-class certificate (second prize).

The Richter Concerts at St. James's Hall will take place on the following Mondays : May 7, 14, 21, 28, June 4, 11, 18, 25, and July 2. The programmes include an "In Memoriam" Wagner selection on the first night, and a choice selection of instrumental and vocal works by Bach, Beethoven, Mozart, Schubert, Mendelssohn, Spohr, Schumann, Berlioz, Cherubini, Raff, and sundry living writers.

At the Boston Symphony Concerts, under the direction of Herr Henschel, a Wagner "memorial concert" was given on the 17th ult. The programme included the Prelude to "Tristan und Isolde," Lohengrin's Legend and Farewell, the "Siegfried Idyll," the air "Dich, theure Halle," from "Tannhäuser," two movements from "Die Meistersinger," the Prelude to "Parsifal," and the Funeral March from "Gotterdämmerung."

The work already accomplished, and now being accomplished by the College of Organists, London, has been and is of a highly valuable character. The number of its members is steadily on the increase, and embraces organists in all countries. The aim has always been to keep up the profession of music in one of its most important branches, and this has been attained by the strict examination those desiring to add the initials F. C. O. after their names, have had to submit to. Such favoured persons must not only play the organ in a capable manner, but must know something about orchestration, counterpoint and fugue, musical history and acoustics. It must be conceded that such musicians scattered everywhere, and labouring in the cause of high art, cannot help but exert a great influence for good upon all with whom they come in contact.—*New York Courier.*

Mr. Henry Leslie's Choir, under Signor Randegger's direction, gave a concert on April 14th, at St. James' Hall. The programme included that famous stock piece of the choir, Mendelssohn's "Judge me, O God," a work which is ever welcome. A new part song by Mr. Caldicott was given with great and deserved success. It is entitled "Winter Days," and has been selected for the competition of choirs at the approaching Eisteddfod at Cardiff. Another pleasing novelty was Mr. J. C. Ward's vocal trio "Hope," which was sung by the Misses Robertson and Mr. J. Robertson, with obbligato concertina accompaniments by the composer and Messrs. Chidley. A third novelty was a graceful and melodious part song, entitled "My Lady Comes," composed by Signor Pinsuti expressly for the choir. The solo vocalists already named contributed other performances, and the vocal music was relieved by Senor Sarasate's admirable violin playing, and pianoforte pieces brilliantly executed by M. Pachmann.

The Querist.

QUERIES.

WALTZES.—There are three well-known waltzes, "Schusuchts, Schmerzens, and Hoffnungs," published by various firms, and ascribed to Beethoven. I seem to have read somewhere that the waltzes are more probably by Schubert, and shall be glad to know if they appear in any authentic list of the former composer's works. Can any correspondent refer me to a printed copy of the old waltz, of which I give the initial figure :—

J. B. S.

PRODUCTION OF THE VOICE.—I should be glad if I could ascertain, through the medium of the *Musical Standard*, what book there is to explain the *production* of the voice, and where published ?—E. A. T.

OBOE.—I should be glad to have the names of one or two of the best oboe tutors (for self-instruction), with the publishers, and prices (moderate ?—A. REED.

Service Lists.

FOURTH SUNDAY AFTER EASTER,
APRIL 22nd.

London.

ST. PAUL'S CATHEDRAL.—Morn.: Service, Te Deum and Benedictus, Barnby in E ; Introit, Alleluia, Alleluia (Hymn 135) ; Communion Service, Barnby in E. Even.: Service, Magnificat and Nunc Dimittis, Barnby in E ; Anthem, Hallelujah to the Father (Beethoven).

WESTMINSTER ABBEY.—Morn.: Service, Mendelssohn in A ; Jubilatte, Boyce ; Continuation, Arnold. Aft.: Service, Oakeley in E flat ; Anthem, The Lord is my strength (Goss).

TEMPLE CHURCH.—Morn.: Service, Te Deum and Jubilate, Attwood in A ; Apostles' Creed, Harmonized Monotone ; Anthem, O come, let us sing (Handel). Even.: Service, Magnificat and Nunc Dimittis, Attwood in A ; Apostles' Creed, Harmonized Monotone ; Anthem, The Lord is my light (Boyce).

LINCOLN'S INN CHAPEL.— Morn.: Service, Distin in C ; Kyrie, Distin ; Anthem, Awake, awake, put on thy strength, O Zion (Wise). Even.: Service, Distin in C ; Anthem, Come unto me (Elvey).

ALL SAINTS, MARGARET STREET. — Morn.: Service, Te Deum, Tours and Benedictus, Stainer ; Communion Service, Schubert in B flat ; Offertory Anthem, Worthy is the Lamb (Handel). Even.: Service, Parry in D ; Anthem, God hath appointed a day (Tours).

ST. AUGUSTINE AND ST. FAITH, WATLING STREET.—Morn.: Service, Garrett in D ; Offertory, But thanks be to God (Handel). Even.: Service, Attwood in F ; Anthem, The trumpet shall sound (Handel).

ST. BARNABAS, MARYLEBONE.—Morn.: Service, Te Deum and Benedictus, Stainer in E flat ; Anthem, See what love (Mendelssohn) ; Kyrie and Nicene Creed, Smart in F. Even.: Service, Magnificat and Nunc Dimittis, Smart in F ; Anthem, Stand up and bless (Goss).

CHILDREN'S HOME CHAPEL, BONNER ROAD, E.—Morn.: Service, Anthems, There is a river (Novello), and, Make a joyful noise (Whitfeld). Aft.: Service, Anthems, Hear my prayer (Kent), and, Through sorrow's path (Sullivan).

CHRIST CHURCH, CLAPHAM.—Morn.: Service, Te Deum, Plain-song ; Kyrie and Credo, Schubert in C ; Offertory Anthem, Christ being raised from the dead (Elvey) ; Sanctus, Benedictus, Agnus Dei, and Gloria in excelsis, Schubert. Even.: Service, Magnificat and Nunc Dimittis, Tours in F ; Anthem, The wilderness (Goss).

FOUNDLING CHAPEL.—Morn.: Service, Te Deum, Barnby in E ; Jubilate, Attwood in B flat ; Anthem, The wilderness (Goss). Aft.: Service, Cooke in G ; Anthems, Hallelujah (Engedi, Beethoven).

HOLY TRINITY, TULSE HILL.— Morn.: Chant Service. Even.: Service, Tours in F ; Anthem, I will give thanks (Hopkins).

ST. JAMES'S PRIVATE EPISCOPAL CHAPEL, SOUTHWARK.—Morn.: Service, Introit Christ is risen (Elvey) ; Communion Service, Beethoven in C. Even.: Service, Barnby in E ; Anthem, The Lord is a man of war (Handel).

ST. MAGNUS, LONDON BRIDGE.—Morn.: Service, Opening Anthem, O Lord, correct me (Coward); Te Deum and Jubilate, Attwood in F; Kyrie, Arnold. Even.: Service, Magnificat and Nunc Dimittis, Attwood in F; Anthem, O that I knew (Bennett).

ST. MARGARET PATTENS, ROOD LANE, FENCHURCH STREET.—Morn.: Service, Te Deum and Benedictus, Tuckerman in F; Offertory Anthem, He shall feed His flock (Handel); Communion Service, Kyrie, Credo, Sanctus, Benedictus, Agnus Dei, and Gloria in excelsis, Mozart in B flat (No. 7). Even.: Service, Magnificat and Nunc Dimittis, Garrett in F; Anthem, Blessed be the God and Father (Wesley).

ST. MARY ABCHURCH, E.C.—Morn.: Service, Nares in F; Communion Service, Merbecke. Even.: Service, Stainer in B flat.

ST. MARY BOLTONS, WEST BROMPTON, S.W.—Morn.: Service, Te Deum, Hopkins in G; Benedictus, Chant; Communion Service, Kyrie, Credo, Sanctus, Benedictus, Agnus Dei, and Gloria in excelsis, Eyre in E flat; Offertory, Stainer. Even.: Service, Magnificat and Nunc Dimittis, Stainer in B flat; Anthem, Praise the Lord, ye servants (Crament).

ST. MICHAEL'S, CORNHILL. — Morn.: Service, Te Deum and Jubilate, Stainer in E flat; Anthem, Fear God, and keep His commandments (Gower); Kyrie and Creed, Thorne in G. Even.: Service, Magnificat and Nunc Dimittis, Hopkins in F; Anthem, Teach me, O Lord (Attwood).

ST. PAUL'S, BOW COMMON, E.—Morn.: Service, Te Deum and Benedictus, Garrett in E. Even.: Service, Magnificat and Nunc Dimittis, Stainer in B flat; Anthem, Children pray this love to cherish, and, God, Thou art great (Spohr).

ST. PETER'S (EATON SQUARE).—Morn.: Service, Te Deum, Goss in A. Even.: Service, Smart in B flat; Anthem, Blessing, glory, and wisdom (Bach).

ST. PETER'S, LEIGHAM COURT ROAD, STREATHAM, S.W. —Morn.: Service, Mass, G. A. Osborne in E flat; Introit, When I wake up (Sutton); Alleluia, Chantwise; Offertory, If we have sown (G. A. Osborne); Communion, Ave verum corpus (Fagan). Even.: Service, Magnificat, Smart in F; Anthem, O give thanks (Goss).

Country.

ARDINGLY COLLEGE, SUSSEX.—Morn.: Communion Service, Hatton in E. Even.: Service, Cooke in G; Anthem, Blessed be the God and Father (Wesley).

ST. ASAPH CATHEDRAL.—Morn.: Service, Clark in G; Anthem, Not unto us (Barnby). Even.: Service, Cooke in G; Anthem, I will sing of Thy power (Sullivan).

ASHBURNE CHURCH, DERBYSHIRE. — Morn.: Service, Hopkins in C. Even.: Service, Gadsby in C; Anthem, The Lord is exalted (West).

BEDDINGTON CHURCH, SURREY. — Morn.: Service, Te Deum, Boyce in A; Benedictus, Burry in F; Introit, Praise my soul the King of Heaven (Hymn 298); Communion Service, Smart in F. Even.: Service, Calkin in D; Anthem, Jesu, Saviour, Thou art mine (Bach).

BIRMINGHAM (ST. CYPRIAN'S, HAY MILLS).—Morn.: Service, Stainer in A and D; Anthem, O give thanks (Greene). Even.: Service, Smith in B flat; Anthem, Blessed be the God and Father (Wesley).

BIRMINGHAM (S. PHILIP'S CHURCH). — Morn.: Service, Chipp in A; Anthem, O be joyful (Palestrina). Even.: Service, Chipp in A; Anthem, Stand up and bless (Goss).

CANTERBURY CATHEDRAL.—Morn.: Service, Smart in F; Introit, O God who hast prepared (Oakeley); Communion Service, Smart in F. Even.: Service, Smart in in F; Anthem, I was in the spirit (Blow).

CARLISLE CATHEDRAL.—Morn.: Service, Smart in G; Introit, Remember me, O Lord (Macfarren); Kyrie and Nicene Creed, Smart in G. Even.: Service, Smart in G; Anthem, As the hart pants (Mendelssohn).

DONCASTER (PARISH CHURCH).—Morn.: Service, Boyce in A. Even.: Service, Hopkins in F; Anthem, The Lord gave the word, How beautiful, and, Their sound is gone out (Handel).

DUBLIN, ST. PATRICK'S (NATIONAL) CATHEDRAL.—Morn.: Service, Te Deum and Jubilate, Gadsby in C; Anthem, The heavens declare (Boyce). Even.: Service, Magnificat and Nunc Dimittis, Smart in B flat; Anthem, As pants the hart (Spohr), and, Blessing, glory, wisdom (Bach).

ELY CATHEDRAL.—Morn.: Service, Te Deum, Garrett in F; Benedictus, Plain-song; Kyrie, Credo, and Gloria, Richardson in F; Anthem, He that shall endure (Mendelssohn). Even.: Service, Garrett in F; Anthem, Glory be to God on high (Haydn).

EXETER CATHEDRAL. — Morn.: Service, Smart in F. Even.: Service, Smart in F; Anthem, Give sentence (Mendelssohn).

HIGH WYCOMBE PARISH CHURCH. — Even.: Service, Chants; Anthem, Blessed be the God and Father (Wesley).

LLANDAFF CATHEDRAL.—Morn.: Service, Smart in F; Introit, How goodly (Ouseley); Kyrie and Credo, Smart in G; Offertory Sentences, Barnby. Even.: Service, The Litany; Anthem, As pants the hart (Spohr).

LEEDS PARISH CHURCH.—Morn.: Service, Hopkins in F; Anthem, Praise His awful name (Spohr); Kyrie and Creed, Garrett in D. Even.: Service, Hopkins in F; Anthem, He sent a thick darkness (Handel).

LICHFIELD CATHEDRAL. — Morn.: Service, King in C; Anthem, Stand up and bless the Lord (Goss). Aft.: Service, Cooke in C; Anthem, Whosoever drinketh, and, Therefore with joy ("Woman of Samaria," Bennett).

LIVERPOOL CATHEDRAL. — Aft.: Service, Fitzgerald in B flat; Anthem, Save me, O God (Balfe).

MANCHESTER CATHEDRAL.—Morn.: Service, Ouseley in G; Anthem, O come, ye servants (Tye); Communion Service, Parry in D. Aft.: Service, Ouseley in G; Anthem, O give thanks (Elvey).

MANCHESTER (ST. BENEDICT'S). — Morn.: Service, Te Deum, Sullivan in D; Kyrie, Credo, and Gloria in excelsis, Seeggall in G; Sanctus, Benedictus, and Agnus Dei, Weber in G. Even.: Service, Magnificat and Nunc Dimittis, Stainer.

MANCHESTER (ST. JOHN BAPTIST, HULME).—Morn.: Service, Kyrie, Credo, Sanctus, Benedictus, Agnus Dei, and Gloria in excelsis, Monk in C. Even.: Service, Magnificat and Nunc Dimittis, Redhead.

ROCHESTER CATHEDRAL.—Morn.: Service, Barnby in E; Anthem, Since by man (Handel). Even.: Service, Barnby in E; Anthem, Be not afraid (Mendelssohn).

SHEFFIELD PARISH CHURCH. — Morn.: Service, Kyrie, Hiles in G. Even.: Service, Magnificat and Nunc Dimittis, Trimnell in F; Anthem, The wilderness (Goss).

SHERBORNE ABBEY. — Morn.: Service, Lyle in E flat. Even.: Service, Anthem, The Lord preserveth the souls of his saints (Hatton).

SOUTHAMPTON (ST. MARY'S CHURCH).—Morn.: Service, Te Deum and Benedictus, Tours in F; Introit, If we believe (Macfarren); Communion Service, Tours in F; Offertory, Charge them (Barnby); Paternoster, Hoyte. Even.: Service, Magnificat and Nunc Dimittis, Tours in F; Apostles' Creed, Harmonized Monotone; Anthem, The radiant morn (Woodward).

SOUTHWELL COLLEGIATE CHURCH, NOTTS.—Morn.: Service, Smart in F; Anthem, Far from my heav'nly home (Pege); Kyrie, Calkin; Creed, Marriott. Even.: Service, Smart in F; Anthem, It is a good thing (Bridge).

WELLS CATHEDRAL.—Morn.: Service, Clarke in F; Introit, The Lord is my light (Macfarren); Kyrie, Rogers in D. Even.: Service, Arnold in A; Anthem, O be joyful (Elvey).

WORCESTER CATHEDRAL.—Morn.: Service, Hopkins in F; Creed, Wesley in E; Anthem, The Lord is in His holy temple. Even.: Service, Hopkins in F; Anthem, Plead Thou my cause (Mozart).

NOTICES TO CORRESPONDENTS.

NEWSPAPERS sent should have *distinct marks* opposite to the matter to which attention is required.

NOTICE.—*All communications intended for the Editor are to be sent to his private address. Business communications to be addressed to* 185, *Fleet Street, E.C.*

APPOINTMENT.

MR. WALTER E. STARK, Organist of the Brixton Choral Society and Assistant Organist of S. Peter's, Streatham, S.W., has been appointed Organist of S. Margaret Pattens, Rood Lane, E.C.

Printed for the Proprietor by BOWDEN, HUDSON & Co. at 22, Red Lion Street, Holborn, London, W.C.; and Published by WILLIAM REEVES, at the Office, 185, Fleet Street, E.C. West End Agents:—WEEKES & CO., 14, Hanover Street, Regent Street, W. Subscriptions and Advertisements are received either by the Publisher or West End Agents.—*Communications for the Editor are to be forwarded to his private address, 6, Argyle Square, W.C*
SATURDAY, APRIL 21, 1883.—*Entered at the General Post Office as a Newspaper.*

A NEWSPAPER FOR MUSICIANS PROFESSIONAL AND AMATEUR

No. 978. Vol. XXIV. FOURTH SERIES. SATURDAY, APRIL 28, 1883. WEEKLY: PRICE 3D.

THE MUSICAL STANDARD is published every Saturday, price 3d., by post, 3½d. ; and may be had of any bookseller or newsagent by ordering its regular supply.

SUBSCRIPTION.—*The Musical Standard* is posted to subscribers at 15s. a year ; half a year, 7s. 6d., payable in advance.

The rate is the same to France, Belgium, Germany, Italy, United States, and Canada.

Post Office Orders to be made payable to the Publisher, William Reeves, 185, Fleet Street, London, or to the West-end Agents, Messrs. Weekes & Co., 14, Hanover Street, Regent Street, W.

ADVERTISEMENTS.—The charge for ordinary advertisements in *The Musical Standard* is 2s. 6d. for three lines or less ; and 6d. for each line (10 words) in addition. "Organist wanted," 3s. 6d. for 3 lines or less. A reduction is made for a series.

FRONT PAGE.—Concert and auction advertisements, &c., are inserted in the front page of *The Musical Standard*, and charged one-third in addition to the ordinary rates. Other advertisements will be inserted on the front page, or in the leader page, if desired, at the same terms.

Musical Intelligence.

CRYSTAL PALACE CONCERTS.

PROGRAMME.

Overture, "Egmont"		Beethoven.
Scena, "From my soul's depths" (" Paradise Lost ")		Rubinstein.
	Mr. Egbert Roberts.	
(His first appearance at these concerts.)		
Concerto for Violin and Orchestra, No. 1, in G		Max Bruch.
	Senor Sarasate.	
Symphony No. 2, in D (Op. 73)		Brahms.
Song, "Bright star of night"		Spohr.
	Mr. Egbert Roberts.	
Solos for Violin		Sarasate.
	Romanza and Habanera.	
	Senor Sarasate.	
Scotch Rhapsody, No. 1		Mackenzie.

Conductor - - - AUGUST MANNS.

The above programme is by no means unattractive, and with Sarasate as solo violinist, a larger audience might reasonably have been expected. We are now, however, approaching a time of year when the counter attractions of the beautiful Crystal Palace gardens, together with the want of ventilation in the concert-room, are sufficient to account for the gradual falling off in the attendance at these concerts. At all times the atmosphere of the concert-room is more or less trying, but on a bright sunny day one feels half suffocated, patiently remaining in a semi-comatose state to the end of the programme, rather than miss the symphony, which is not unfrequently at the very end.

Some six years ago Sarasate performed Max Bruch's concerto No. 1 at the Crystal Palace, and the favourable impression it made at that time was greatly increased on Saturday last. The first movement is imposing, and contains many beautiful and effective points, and the hand of the accomplished musician is shown in its masterly development. The adagio—when played as it was by Sarasate—seems like the embodiment of a prayer. It is full of feeling, and the violins, 'celli, oboi, and corni, in their turn sing in perfect sympathy with the solo instrument, and anon respond to it in a very charming manner. The last movement is brilliant and fantastic, and the thematic treatment is bold and masterly. The performance both of orchestra and soloist was so perfect, that only an extra bilious critic could complain of anything. Sarasate was at the end twice recalled. Later on he played his own Romanza and Habañera, and met with the usual double round of applause, in response to which he gave one of his celebrated gipsy effusions. Under the like circumstances his accomplished contemporary, Dr. Joachim, might have given us one of Sebastian Bach's inspirations by way of contrast. An occasional gipsy piece is all very well, but Senor Sarasate unfortunately gives us so many of that description, that we at times long for something more substantial.

Brahms's splendid Symphony, No. 2 in D, is admired by even those adverse critics who look upon his compositions as "too learned and overwrought." It may not occur to them that learning and inspiration are by no means incompatible, and that Beethoven himself was, amongst other things, accused of over-elaboration in his grand Choral Symphony.

Mr. Mackenzie's Scotch Rhapsody, No. 1, is not in so "advanced" a style as his No. 2, and in consequence met with much greater success.

Mr. Egbert Roberts, who on this occasion made his first appearance at these concerts, exhibited a fine voice, but he has evidently much to learn before he can use it to advantage. R. S.

THE BROUSIL CONCERTS.

At the 4th "musical afternoon," held by Miss Bertha and Mr. A. J. Brousil, on April 19th, were performed Rheinberger's Pianoforte Quartet in E flat, and Mendels-Pianoforte Trio in C minor. Mdlle. Wurm conducted both these works with consummate ability; the strings were held by Messrs. Collins, Channel, and Brousil. Mdlle. Wurm selected for her pianoforte solo Beethoven's sonata in C sharp minor, Op. 27, No. 2; and Mr. J. A. Brousil a violoncello piece of Servais, a fantasia entitled "Le Désir." The Brousils will hold a grand matinée at St. James' Hall on Thursday, May 10th.

THE WESTERN COUNTIES' MUSICAL ASSOCIATION.

The above association held its sixth annual festival at Exeter, on Thursday, April 19th. In the afternoon Haydn's "Creation" was performed at the Victoria Hall. Never before had the oratorio been produced on such a scale in Exeter. Professionals of high rank were engaged for the solos; the chorus parts were sustained by a choir of 360 voices, and the orchestral accompaniments were rendered by a band of nearly 60 performers (including 25 professionals). It is needless to say that with such an array of professional and amateur talent under his control, Mr. D. J. Wood, Mus.Bac., succeeded in securing for the patrons of the festival a gratifying performance.

The soloists engaged in the oratorio were Mdme. E. Wynne, Mr. H. Guy, Mr. Bridson, and Mr. Santley. The composition of the chorus was 140 trebles, 90 alti, 60 tenors, and 70 basses. These had practised at the following branch centres :—Bampton, Budleigh Salterton, Exeter, Exmouth, Honiton, Newton, North Devon, Silverton, Taunton, Teignmouth, Tiverton, Torquay, and Wellington. Mr. Vinnicombe presided at the organ. The sixty instrumentalists forming the band included 11 first violins, 11 second violins, 7 violas, violoncellos, 5 contra bassi, 2 flutes, 2 oboes, 2 clarinets, 2 bassoons, 3 horns, 3 trombones, 2 trumpets, 1 timpani.

The performance as a whole was a very satisfactory one. The band did its work throughout in almost unexceptionable style. Mr. Vinnicombe deserves mention for his skilful playing of the organ accompaniment; the support of the recitatives was in some instances left entirely to him, and in these cases his good taste and judgment were well displayed. The choruses went magnificently; only in a very few places was any symptom of unsteadiness noticed; and when anything of the kind occurred—as in the opening of "The Heavens are telling," and in starting the allegro movement in the final number, "Sing the Lord, ye Voices all "—Mr. Wood quickly succeeded in rectifying the error. The soloists were not heard at their best. Mdme. Edith Wynne was evidently suffering from a bad cold; however, she struggled bravely against the disadvantage under which she was labouring, and was frequently rewarded with warm applause. Mr. Guy was in fairly good voice, and sang well. Mr. Santley, like the soprano, seemed to be suffering from a cold. Mr. Bridson did well in the duets in the third part. Reverting to the work of the chorus, it may be observed that while some disappointment was expressed at the failure of the soloists to come up to the standard expected of them, not a word was heard in disparagement of the chorus. Mr. Wood, of course, deserves much credit for the effective control which he wielded over such a large number of vocalists whom he rarely meets in a body; but praise must also be given to the branch choirmasters, to whose careful training is obviously due much of the success which attended the performances of the choruses in the afternoon. Mr. G. M. Rice led the orchestra with his accustomed skill; and the excellent work done by the leading 'cello and oboe deserves acknowledgment.

Barnett's music to Coleridge's "Ancient Mariner" made up the first, and a miscellaneous selection the second part of the evening programme. The principals were Mdme. Wynne, Miss Marian Mackenzie, Mr. Guy, and Mr. Bridson. These artists brought their best powers to bear on the theme; the band, on the whole, was satisfactory, and the chorus highly efficient. Far more hearty enthusiasm was aroused by this performance than by its predecessor in the afternoon. Mr. Guy delivered the recitatives and airs allotted to him with much taste. "The fair breeze blew," and the last solo, "The seraph band," earned for Mdme. Wynne sterling marks of approval. Miss Mackenzie sang the sweet contralto air, "O sleep, it is a gentle thing," with the genuine sympathetic expression for which she is remarkable. The bass music was given with masterly effect by Mr. Bridson. The duet, "Two voices in," by Mdme. Wynne and Miss Mackenzie, was one of the most charming things of the evening, while the quartets gave unequivocal satisfaction, the final, "Sweeter than the marriage feast," and the concluding chorus being sung in a style worthy alike of the performers and the music. To Mr. D. J. Wood's conductorship too much praise cannot be accorded, nor should it be forgotten that the success of the festival was enhanced by the judicious organ accompaniments of Mr.

E. M. Vinnicombe. The second part of the evening's programme introduced Mendelssohn's Violin Concerto, by Mr. M. G. Rice and the orchestra. Mr. Rice had twice to rise in deference to the rounds of hearty plaudits with which the performance was greeted. Mr. Santley sang Gounod's "Medjé" and M. V. White's "Devout Lover" with the warmth and expression of an artist of the first grade. Applause was enthusiastic and unanimous after each song, and encores were being demanded until Mr. Wood, in a brief appeal to the audience, pointed out that to comply with their wishes would upset the train arrangements of many persons in the orchestra, as well as in the body of the hall. Schumann's "Gipsy Life," with full chorus and band, produced with commendable precision and effect, terminated the concert, during the latter portion of which Miss Lizzie Hicks played the pianoforte accompaniments in a praiseworthy and musician-like manner.

It speaks well for the musical resources of the West, that of the large and efficient orchestra only two members came from London, the first flute and first horn.

MR. AGUILAR'S RECITALS.

At his third and last recital on Monday afternoon, the Egyptian darkness caused by a passing storm of sleet, almost prevented the reading of notes where music-books were required. Mr. Aguilar played (mostly out of book) for about an hour and a half. The scheme included Mendelssohn's Prelude and Fugue in B flat; Chopin's Nocturne in B major (Op. 62, No. 1); Sir Sterndale Bennett's "Three musical sketches" in E major, E minor, and B major (inscribed to Mr. J. W. Davidson), and the Abbé Liszt's "Rhapsodie Hongroise" No. 12, in C sharp minor and D flat major, whereof the peculiar vagueness and uncouth style is partly but barely redeemed by a pretty and plausible Hungarian tune. Musicians who read may have noticed, and some did notice, in this strange rhapsody, truly and etymologically so-called, a remarkable reminiscence of Donizetti's motif in "Lucia di Lammermoor," the dying speech of poor sentimental Edgardo, "fra poco a mi." Equally odd, a far greater man in every respect, Schubert, who died (A.D. 1828) before Donizetti was "born" or at least much thought of, had anticipated the same idea in that pretty symphonic prelude of four bars to the "Morgengrüss" (Morning greeting) of Schubert in C major, transcribed for the pianoforte by Stephen Heller. Mr. Aguilar's own compositions included his fine and masterly Sonata in C major, of four movements, eulogized on previous occasions for its breadth of proportions, great variety of style, and able construction; "Last Look," and "Away"; "Evening" in A flat, the "Valse Brillante" in A major, of which one is never tired, and an etude in A minor. Another of Mr. Aguilar's accomplished young lady pupils, Miss Helen Matthey, had the honour to be entrusted with Schumann's "Faschingsschwank aus Wien" in B flat, a piece of great difficulty, because complex, full of tonal changes, and varieties of rhythm. Miss Matthey is thought, by connoisseurs, to have acquitted herself, as a girl in her teens, very creditably, and with considerable savoir faire, thanks to her "master of arts," or the "art,"—one quite sufficient! An eminent musician and professor (whose esteemed name may not be mentioned) expresses his opinion as follows :—"Miss Helen Matthey, a pupil of Mr. Aguilar, made a most successful first appearance en amateur, performing Schumann's difficult piece (already entitled) with remarkable self-possession, for one so young, and earning great credit, both for herself and her excellent instructor. We look forward with pleasure to hearing this young lady again." The "Faschingsschwank," a fanciful piece of festive character, for it literally means "Carnival Pranks," is an early work, and remarkable, like Schumann's "Kreisleriana," "Carnival" proper, "Humoreske," and "Wald Scenen," for strict adherence to flat keys, chiefly B flat, A flat, F major, D minor, and G minor. A lady complained to the writer, this very week, of a gavotte (by a foreign composer) written in C flat major and A flat minor—seven flats at the signature; but most English writers for the pianoforte are prone to use keys with at least five flats at the signature; the French, on the other hand, seem to prefer the sharp keys, certainly for their chamber songs.

Mr. Aguilar will not resume his excellent recitals before next Christmas, and nobody just now looks forward to another December without shivering and shaking, like 'the man that could never get warm."   A. M.

SENOR SARASATE'S CONCERTS.

Senor Sarasate's second concert, on April 19, was not so fully attended as the first, but it passed off triumphantly. Senor Sarasate's reading of Mendelssohn's concerto in E minor had already been appreciated, as he has played it this season both at the Philharmonic Concerts and at the Crystal Palace. This reading is thought by connoisseurs to be far more satisfactory than the interpretation of the Beethoven Concerto in D, where, as musical opinions go, the brilliant violinist merged the text too much in what Kant and Fichte call the ego, or the "subjective." The cadenza, moreover, struck everyone as poor, trivial, and no recapitulation whatever of the movement in question.

Senor Sarasate's solos, at the second concert, were his own Fantasia on "Faust," and his "Bohemian Airs." I concur with a caustic (daily) contemporary in denouncing the "Faust" piece as utter and unmitigated trash, unworthy alike of the text and the player. The satirical writer says that the applause would have been far louder if Senor Sarasate, after the "Salvation Army" fashion, had played the piece standing on his head ! The "Gipsy" airs were encored, and a Spanish Dance substituted. Nothing can be finer than Senor Sarasate's style; or more brilliant than his executancy; or more ear-piercing than his delicate tone. The piano passages are so subdued, that the proverbial pin might fairly be heard to fall on the floor! But the Senor is a "virtuoso" par excellence, and people find fault with him for playing too much out of the same "book." A third concert, in the afternoon, is already announced. Dr. Sloman will speak of M. Sarasate's doings at Sydenham on Saturday.

It is only due to Mr. W. G. Cusins to notice a capital performance, by his Philharmonic band, of Beethoven's 5th Symphony and the overture to "Oberon." Two pretty ballet airs from Rubinstein's opera "Le Démon," the fiasco of the Royal Italian-Opera season in 1881, were also played in the second part.   A. M.

MISS ZIMMERMANN'S CHAMBER CONCERTS.

Miss Agnes Zimmermann, although of German origin, was educated at our own Royal Academy of Music, of which she is an honourable, as well as an honorary member. Her status as a pianist is established by the fact that Miss Zimmermann is always engaged to play several times in the course of every season at the Monday and Saturday Popular Concerts, both as soloist and as conductor of pianoforte trios, quartets, and quintets. The writer remembers to have heard her, some years ago, at Mr. Ella's "Musical Union," a sort of "Epsom Race" ground, so to speak, where blue ribbons were to be worn, and where merely to appear with fair success was a gold medal of merit.

Miss Zimmermann held the first of three serial chamber concerts at the Tenterden Street Rooms on the evening of April 19th, when she conducted Mr. C. Villiers Stanford's Sonata in D, Op. 11, for pianoforte and violin (Herr Straus), and Rubinstein's Quintet in G minor, Op. 99, of which the string parts were played by MM. Straus, Ries, Zerbini, and Pezze. Miss Zimmermann's solo was Schumann's well-known "Fantasia," in C, Op. 17, marked by a motto of Frederick Schlegel to the effect that through all sounds, in a variegated earth-dream, penetrates a "still small voice" (ein leiser Ton), for which the ear of one in retirement or seclusion listens intently.

Mr. Villiers Stanford's sonata, the only novelty of the concert, has a bright and unaffected character. The first movement in D, 3-4 time, has been quite built on the orthodox plan; the second is a charming, simple melody in G, common time, with two variations and a long episode in the tonic minor, ending with a sort of minuet movement of the original theme. The finale, an allegretto in D, 2-4 time, is also of a gay style, and introduces excerpts from the slow movement, both the major and minor themes happily combined.

The Rubinstein quintet, a fine work, would be improved by curtailment; I esteem the best movements to be the inner ones, a moderato in C minor and major, and an andante variazioni in E flat. These variations, of very charming character, lose effect from their prolixity. Mdme. Sophie Lowe sang six lieder of Schubert and Schumann with the usual taste. The second concert is fixed for May 8th.   A. M.

CHURCH MUSIC AT KENSINGTON.

At St. Matthias, South Kensington, the services are very "musical," and after a laudably short "matins," of about one hour (sermon inclusive), a choral communion is celebrated. The texts of the great masters, and Schubert especially, are freely drawn upon. On Sunday last, the organist, Mr. Mallit Jones, produced a new "Communion Service" in D major, composed by Mr. Frank L. Moir. This comprehends all the movements of the regular "Mass," set to English words. The work is much admired, and a formal review of the score (published by Novello, Ewer, and Co.) will appear in due course. Mr. Mallit Jones conducted the service with consummate ability.

GRAND FESTIVAL CONCERT AT ALBERT HALL.

On Saturday afternoon, April 21 (not the regular "St. George's Day"), Mr. Carter gave a grand English concert at Albert Hall. His own choir and the band of the Scots Guards sang and played several times. English songs, good and indifferent, were rendered by Mdme. Patey, Mdme. Lemmens-Sherrington, Mr. V. Rigby, Signor Foli, Mr. E. Lloyd, Mr. Redfern Hollins, Miss Patti Winter, and Miss Hilda Wilson (a *protégée* of Mrs. Ellicott and a charming contralto). Mr. Poznanski played, as violin solos, his own "Fantaisie Pathétique," with great success, and M. Jacobs, of Brussels, a fine violoncellist, made a *début* of the most satisfactory kind in Schubert's Valse, as arranged by Servais.

MR. NICHOLAS MORI'S OPERA COMIQUE,

"PATTY, OR THE SHIPWRIGHT'S LOVE."

At a miscellaneous concert given at 12, Chepstow Place, Bayswater, on Thursday, April 19th, by the kind permission of J. P. Larkins, Esq., the principal feature was the production of a new opéra comique, the music composed by Mr. Mori, and performed by some of the admirably trained pupils of that gentleman. From so experienced an artist one expected a well-written musicianly work, but was hardly prepared for so many sparkling and charming melodies, which, supported by a background of able scholastic writing, constituted a pleasing, graceful work. Now that Mr. Carl Rosa has so enthusiastically and successfully taken up the cause of English opera, let us hope that other managers may be led to do the same, and they will find that there are many works by English composers that claim a hearing. The singing of Madame Reeves and of other artists was indeed admirable.

FALMOUTH.

The Falmouth Choral Society gave its first concert in the Polytechnic Hall, on Tuesday, April 17th, in aid of the "Cornwall Home for Destitute Girls." The Hall was crammed, the whole of the body having been occupied by reserved seats. The first part consisted of "The May Queen" (Sir Sterndale Bennett). Second part, miscellaneous :—

Mrs. Trelease, R.A.M.	May Queen.
Mr. W. Hearder (Plymouth)	The Lover.
Lieut.-Col. Carlyon	Robin Hood.
Miss H. K. Broad	The Queen.
Mr. W. G. Bishop	Pianoforte.
Mr. J. Pardew (Plymouth)	Harmonium.
Hon. Conductor	Mr. C. W. Robinson.

The concert was a great success, all the performers rendering their respective parts in a manner which evidently gratified the large audience. The "May Queen" choruses, as also the unaccompanied part-songs in the second part, were sung with excellent precision, and with a due regard to light and shade by the class. Mr. J. Parsons's violin solo cavatina (F. N. Lohr), accompanied by Mr. Robinson, was redemanded, as was also the trio for violoncello, pianoforte and harmonium "Meditation," Bach and Gounod, by Messrs. H. and A. Mulder, and Mr. Robinson, Mrs. Trelease also won an encore for "Bid me discourse," and Signor Bechonini for "Infelice." Twenty pounds will be handed over to the charitable institution for which the concert was given. At the last practice the class presented Mr. C. W. Robinson with an ivory *bâton*, gold mounted, and inscribed.

THE ROYAL ITALIAN OPERA.

Mr. E. Gye begins his season on Tuesday next, May 1, with a very strong company, which includes Mdme. Adelina Patti, Mdme. Albani, Signor Nicolini, and most of the old "principals." Mdme. Christine Nilsson's engagement is only, at present, a possibility. The director promises, as a positive novelty, the opera of Ponchielli, "Gioconda," which, brought out at La Scala, Milan, in 1876 (rather a long time ago), has been popular ever since. But what is popular with the Italians may not succeed so well in England, where Wagnerian principles are now rather in the ascendant. Signor Ponchielli, however, although he moves with the Italian groove, is said to have Wagnerian "tendencies."

Mr. Gye also promises Rossini's "La Gazza Ladra" and "Il Comte Ory," with "Le Domino Noir" of Auber. The season will only last twelve weeks.

THE CARL ROSA OPERA COMPANY.

The short season came to an end last Saturday night, when Mr. Carl Rosa, the director, took his place in the conductor's seat, and of course was cordially hailed.

The opera, "Mignon," is well known, both in its English and Italian dress. Madame Marie Roze has invested the title part with a charming significance; first, at Her Majesty's Theatre, in 1879, and since, at the "Opera in English," of Mr. Carl Rosa. On Saturday, Mdme. Roze finished the season with *éclat*. A *débutante*, Miss Leighton, achieved a promising success as Filina ; she has a light flexible soprano voice, and prepossessing presence. The other parts were filled by Mr. L. Crotty, Mr. J. W. Turner, and Miss Josephine Yorke. The short season of four weeks has been one almost exclusively, not only of "opera in English," but English opera *itself, per et absolu*. Poor Wagner has not had a chance this time ; more the pity ! Mr. Carl Rosa, however, deserves praise for the production of two such English operas as "Colomba" and "Esmeralda," sufficiently discussed in these columns.

LEEDS.

Messrs. Gilbert and Sullivan's opera "Iolanthe" was performed at the Grand Theatre, on Monday and during the week. The company engaged by Mr. D'Oyly Carte for taking this opera round the provinces is a first-class one, and principals and chorus are thoroughly efficient. It is rather late in the day to discuss the merits of "Iolanthe," but the general opinion seems to be that in a musical point of view this opera is not equal either to the "Pinafore" or "Patience." At the same time it must be admitted that many of the numbers are melodious and beautiful, and there is no reason why "Iolanthe" should not keep the stage till the new opera promised by the same composers is brought out in London and the provinces. Miss Laura Clement makes a charming Phillis, and sings and acts with grace and refinement. Her song "For riches and rank I do not long," was well received, and she scored a success in her duet with Strephon (Mr. Federici), "None shall part us from each other." Miss Fanny Harrison, as the Fairy Queen, gave an excellent rendering of the pretty song "Oh, foolish fairy." Miss Beatrice Young was pleasing as Iolanthe, and sang with much expression her tuneful ballad "He loves I if the bygone years." Mr. Frank Thornton puts plenty of humour into the part of the Lord Chancellor, and Mr. Geo. Marler, as Private Willis was loudly applauded for his fine rendering of the song at the beginning of Act 2, "When all night long," &c. The pretty chorus of fairies in Act 1, as well as the effective quartet in Act 2, were all given in capital style, and the scenery, costumes, &c., left nothing to be desired.

On Saturday evening last the borough organist gave the sixth of his "Hours with the great Composers," the master with whom the large audience spent a delightful evening being Mendelssohn. The programme was good and interesting, and embraced the military band overture in C, "The Lover's Duet," from the "Songs without Words," the organ Sonata in C minor, a selection from the two-part songs, "The Pilgrim's March" from the Italian Symphony, the "Andante from the violin concerto, which was played with much taste and effect, and finally the "Wedding March" from "A Midsummer Night's Dream."

THE BLOOMSBURY CHURCH CHOIR UNION.

The first festival of this new choral combination was held at the church of St. Giles-in-the-Fields, on April 19th. In the prospectus of the association the following words occur, which describe the position and proposals of the new choral corporation.

The scheme of each year's work includes meetings at each of the Churches represented by the several Choirs, and an Annual Festival taking place between Easter and Whitsuntide.

The immediate government of the Association is vested in the hands of a Committee, formed of the different Church Organists, together with a representative from each Choir of the Union.

The Committee and Association are earnestly engaged in endeavouring to secure the most perfect possible performance of the service Music chosen, and the most devotional rendering of the more general features of a properly-conducted Choral Service.

The success of the first festival showed clearly enough the earnestness of all engaged. During the past few months, meetings for drill in the music chosen for the year, have been held in the churches of St. Giles, St. George, Bloomsbury, St. George the Martyr, and Christ Church, Woburn Square, the choirs of which belong to the B.C.C.U. The selection of music for the festival deserves special notice, as displaying sound judgment and a wide recognition of the multiform types of Church music finding acceptation in the Anglican Church. Of course, the so-called "Tallis Festal" responses were used; the Psalm chants included good specimens by Crotch and Goss; Henry Smart's fine Service in F was sung; Haydn's Motet, now in use with the English words, "Distracted with care," &c., and Handel's "Hallelujah" Chorus, were the anthems given, the latter being sung at the end of the service. The hymns selected were typical specimens of their kind, both verbally and musically. The first was "Praise, my soul, the King of Heaven," to the dignified tune by Goss in the S.P.C.K. collection; the next was "Jesu, my Lord, my God, my all," to Barnby's expressive setting; and during the offertory "O Worship the King, all glorious above" was sung to the strongly built, good old tune, "Hanover." Before and after the service some very admirably rendered organ-music, including Mendelssohn's first sonata, was played by Mr. Constantine and Mr. W. G. Wood, of St. George the Martyr and Christ Church, Bloomsbury. The service was accompanied by Mr. H. Walmsley Little, Mus. Bac., organist of St. Giles-in-the-Fields, with masterly tact, judgment, and skill, and with such courage and care as minimised to an almost imperceptible degree the difficulties arising from the serious distance between the choir and organ. The choristers numbered between 90 and 100. The parts were fairly balanced, save that, perhaps, the alto might have gained from the presence of a few more voices, as is too often the case at Church choral festivals; although the part was, upon this occasion, by no means ineffective, and at times told well. No marked flaw of any kind disturbed the excellent, careful rendering and even flow of the service music, and the singing reflected the highest credit upon the choristers. The responses gained much by the exercise of that desire to secure a devotional enunciation of the whole of the music in an earnest as well as in an artistic manner. If the B.C.C.U. will only firmly keep to the front the admirable proposal to study Church music, with an anxious wish to combine devotional earnestness with artistic excellence, the association will, indeed, not only claim, but will have, the support of all right-minded Churchmen and lovers of ecclesiastical music. Throughout the performance of the Service on the 19th the intonation was good, and only in very rare instances was there any tendency to get out of tune; and this was observable only once or twice even in the boys' part. The general precision was extremely satisfactory. It would be impossible, one thought, on hearing upon this occasion the nervous, dignified sentences, and strong, compact harmonies of Smart in F, heartily and well sung, to name any more characteristic and solid English Church music than this notable work affords. The sympathy of the clergy, churchwardens, and leading inhabitants was shown by their presence; and the kind forethought of the churchwardens and officials of St. Giles, &c., in making efficient arrangements for the reception of the choristers and for the conduct of the service calls for special recognition. The prayers were intoned by the Rev. F. Buller, M.A., and the lessons read by the Rev. N. Bromley and the Rev. J. J. Glendinning Nash, M.A. The sermon was preached by the Rev. Canon Nisbet, rector of St. Giles; and it was an excellent specimen of well-considered pulpit oratory, well adapted for the occasion, its materials being well condensed and not weakened or dispersed by over-much argumentation; and the good points being earnestly, tersely, eloquently, and briefly placed before the hearers.

Canon Nisbet preached from the text II. Chronicles xxix., 30; Colossians iv., 16. He said:—

It is needless that I should dilate to you upon the importance of music as an appropriate accessory of public worship, for your presence here this evening admits it.

It is needless that I should speak of the cultivation of music as a sacred art, for it is an accomplished fact which you yourselves have proved.

"I think," says Luther, "that if David rose from the dead, he would wonder much to find how far we had advanced in music." If this were true in the 16th century, how much more so now? For the time has happily gone by of tame, frigid, drawling, tuneless, tasteless psalmody, for you have resolved to replace it by something which devout hearts may find a support and not a hindrance. It may, however, be well to remind you of some of the dangers to which you are specially liable, and some of the safeguards, by which you may ward off the evils which expose "this noble thing to vile using."

Respecting the dangers to which those are exposed who "invent to themselves instruments of music like unto David." There is the danger-lest the attention should be too exclusively fixed on what I may term the mechanical execution of the art; if, for example, during the celebration of divine service, your thoughts are diverted from its main purpose (which is the worship of God) either excessively to admire the excellence with which it is rendered or possibly, to complain of the faults which accidentally mar it. So also there is a danger lest being sensibly moved by what is purely emotional, you mistake natural feeling for religious feeling. The natural emotions have doubtless a place in our constitution, and it would be an exaggeration to say that they were not to be rightly excited, but it is quite possible for them to be excited, and nothing more. You may rise above mere earthly things without reaching to heavenly; whereas, the tuneless song of the heart may mount to God's throne, while the pealing anthem rises no higher than the vaulted arches of the material building. Then there is another danger, which, as it still exists, must not be unmentioned; and unhappily, I could tell you of cases where I myself have known its pernicious effects. I refer to that vanity which is so easily engendered by proficiency in any art. The preacher may easily become vain of eloquence, real or supposed: the singer may also be elated and puffed up by the admiration which he receives. It is very hard indeed, to try and do your very best and excel in that which you attempt, sometimes without thinking of yourself and how well you do it.

I do not know how I should exactly draw the line between that legitimate pleasure which is allowable from doing anything well and that excessive self-elation which soon becomes the sin of vanity. But being forewarned of the danger, your conscience will generally tell you when you think more of the means than of the end, and consider your own glory rather than the honour of God.

There is one more danger (perhaps I ought to have placed it first, instead of last) for it often begins when the chorister is very young, and that is careless familiarity with things sacred, repeating the holiest words without thinking of their meaning. If the youngest often do this, the oldest of us would admit that we frequently do the same.

It is easy for the voice to say or to sing "My soul doth magnify the Lord." It is not easy thing for the soul itself to rise to such raptures.

I have reminded you of dangers common to all who take part in the services of the Sanctuary: perfunctory exactness, mere emotion, vanity and familiarity.

That these faults may not be found in us, let me say a few words of our safeguards.

Ever cultivate, i.e., studiously discipline your mind to a reverent and awful sense of the great God whom you attempt to worship. "He cannot worthily be praised." The very angels, sinless though they are, veil their faces in His presence. Realise, as far as you can, that presence, His greatness, His Power, His wisdom, His love. Let all these be thought of and adored. Stir up your minds by way of remembrance, and then, and then only, will you be moved to say "What shall I render to my God for all His benefits to me." "Reverence is the angel of the world," so said the renowned Shakespeare. "The least irreverence is the greatest unreason," so lately did I hear from the lips of a young and accomplished prince.

Next cultivate lowly humility. As reverence arises from the contemplation of God, so does humility spring from the consideration of ourselves. Let us ever bow ourselves before the Most High, not only as creatures, but as "miserable sinners" unworthy of the least of His gifts, deserving His displeasure but accepted by His forgiveness, redeemed by His Son, brought near to Him by His Spirit, reinstated into His favour, grafted into His Church, the vessels which he has formed for the reception of His highest attribute of *mercy*, and thus "fulfilled with His grace and heavenly benediction."

Lastly, let us seek from His spirit that *fire of heartfelt fervour* which shall kindle every gift we present. However beautiful the altar, there must be fire to give virtue to the sacrifice. Whatever our prayers may be, however feeble, faltering, imperfect, often lisped by stammering tongues, let them at any rate be heart-prayers, for good is the saying of Bishop Wilson: "They whose hearts desire nothing, pray for nothing." And whatever our praises (whether accompanied by mechanical exactness or not, whether embellished by artistic taste, or devoid of any such accessory), let these also be heart-praises, for good is the saying of John Bunyan: "Let thy heart be without words rather than thy words without heart."

These, then, being your dangers and your safeguards, we bid you God speed in this your good work. Though on your guard concerning it, be not afraid of it. Rejoice in it, take pleasure in it, go on in it, improve in it, reverently, humbly fervently. And, oh! may it be so from the youngest child in his linen ephod to the oldest among you, that you learn in your inmost hearts the old songs of Zion now, and prepare for "the new song of Moses and the Lamb" in the heavenly temple, where "you shall no more go out."

FARNHAM.—Handel's "Messiah" was effectively given, with orchestral accompaniments, before a crowded audience on April 10th. The chief singers were Mrs. Barrington Gore Browne, Miss Aylwin, Mr. Edward Dalzell, and Rev. Clement Powell; organist, Mr. H. Piggott, L.Mus.T.C.L.; leader of the band, Mr. James Brown; conductor, Mr. J· Conway Brown, L.Mus.T.C.L.

SOUTHGATE.—The ninth annual dedication festival was celebrated at St. Michael's, Bowes Park, on Sunday last, the 22nd inst. The services throughout the day were fully choral, and the music included, morning Service, Garrett in D; evening, Stainer in F; anthem, "I will mention the loving kindness of the Lord," the tenor solo being sung with much taste by Mr. Chas. J. Murton. Mr. H. J· Baker presided, as usual, at the organ.

DOUGLAS, ISLE OF MAN.—Miss Wood's fifth popular musical entertainment of the season was given on April 19th. Solos were sung by local singers, and the artistic pianoforte playing of Mrs. Valentine added to the pleasure of the listeners. Miss Wood's classes took part in the performance of part-songs, &c. To the lady just named, much credit is due for her admirably directed and earnest labours in the cause of the art.

ERITH CHORAL SOCIETY.—A highly successful performance of the "Creation" was given at the Erith Public Hall on Friday, the 13th inst., under the direction of Mr. Rich. Lemaire. The soloists were Madam Worrell, Mr. Abercrombie, and Mr. Pyatt. A stringed orchestral accompaniment added much to the success of the performance. The choruses were given with much precision and effect. Mr. Sidney Naylor presided at the pianoforte.

KIDDERMINSTER.—A highly successful concert was given at the Town Hall by the members of the Kidderminster Amateur Instrumental Society, assisted by a picked chorus of about forty voices, on the 5th inst., the programme, which included Haydn's Symphony in D (No. 2 Salomon set), selections from Mendelssohn's "Loreley," part-songs, overtures, &c., gave great satisfaction to a large and appreciative audience. Mr. C. Hayward led the band, and Mr. W. E. Wadely, F.C.O., conducted; after paying expenses, a balance of £15 will be handed over to the Parish Church Tower and Bells Fund.

MR. WILLING'S CHOIR.—The final subscription concert of the season will take place at St. James's Hall on Tuesday, May 1st, when, in addition to a repetition performance of Gade's "Psyche," the programme will contain selections from Sterndale Bennett's "May Queen," Meyerbeer's "Les Huguenots" (including the Rataplan chorus), Gounod's "Reine de Saba," and conclude with Schumann's "Gipsy Life." Mdme. Isabel Howitz will sustain the part of "Psyche," the other principal vocalists being Mesdames Giulia Warwick, A. Ehrenberg, and Ambler, Messrs. Edward Lloyd, Arthur Thompson, and Frederick King. The orchestra will consist of nearly 300 performers, and be conducted by Mr. Willing.

MANCHESTER.—On April 16th the Athenæum Musical Society concluded its sixteenth season with an admirably selected miscellaneous programme. Especially were Smart's "The Shepherd's Lament," Mendelssohn's "The Nightingale," and the chaste and subdued interpretation of "The Wanderer's Night Song," excellent performances. The concert concluded with the fragments of Mendelssohn's unfinished opera. "Loreley," which were sung with all the fire and vigour characteristic of the society. In the "Finale," and throughout the evening, the solo singing was as refined, musicianlike, and in-

telligent as is usual at the Athenæum concerts. Between the parts the ladies of the choir presented Dr. Hiles with a beautiful silver epergue as a mark of "their appreciation of his unremitting kindness and patience."

BURTON-ON-TRENT.—The first concert of the St. Paul's Institute Choral Society took place recently. The programme comprised Handel's "Ode to S. Cecilia's day," Mendelssohn's motet "Hear my Prayer," and a miscellaneous selection, including two movements from Beethoven's Symphony in C. The chorus numbered about eighty voices and the soloists were Miss Eleanor Farnol, Mr. G. H. Welch. The band was an excellent one, and was led by Mr. F. Ward. Mr. George A. Burns officiated as organist, and Mr. A. B. Plant, Mus.Bac., Oxon F.C.O., proved himself to be a painstaking and good conductor. The choruses throughout were well rendered, with an accuracy that bespoke careful and intelligent training. There is clearly a hopeful future before the young society.

MADAME SAINTON-DOLBY'S VOCAL ACADEMY.—The first of three concerts took place at the Steinway Hall on April 19th when a goodly number of Mdme. Sainton's pupils gave abundant evidence of their excellent training. The programme included the following choruses for ladies' voices: "Glorious stand the mountains;" Reinthaler's "Jephtha;" "Ave Maria" (Marchetti). 'Song of the sunbeam," composed expressly for the class by Mr. W. Macfarren; "Our happy home" (first time of performance), Mdme. Sainton-Dolby; "Spinning Chorus," by desire, from Wagner's "Flying Dutchman"; and "Spring's the land" (Raff). Mr. Leipold was the accompanist, and M. Sainton the conductor. The remaining concerts are fixed for April 25th and December 3rd.

LUDLOW.—The Amateur Choral and Orchestral Society (president, the Rev. F. A. Gore Ouseley, Bart., Mus.Doc.) gave its second concert of the season on Tuesday evening, April 17th when Hutchinson's new cantata, "Elaine," and a miscellaneous selection were performed. The soloists were Mdme. Clara West and Miss Lottie West, of London, Mr. H. Byolin, of Shrewsbury, and one or two local amateurs; leader of the band, Mr. T. Watkis; conductor, Mr. R. Bartholomew. Miss Lottie West greatly pleased the audience, being encored in two songs, "The Children's Home" and "Westbury Fair." Mr. H. Byolin met with a similar compliment in "Saved from the Storm," and Mdme. West was greatly applauded in all her efforts. Musically, if not financially, the concert was a great success.

OSWESTRY.—On April 21st the third annual festival of village choirs, held under the auspices of the Oswestry School of Music, took place at Oswestry. Under the presidency of Mr. Henry Leslie the Oswestry School of Music, founded in 1880 has had a prosperous career, and its festivals· attract audiences from far and wide. Amongst those who took part is the festival were Lady Harlech, Mr. Alfred Scott Gatty and Mrs. Gatty, the Hon. G. Spencer Lyttelton, Mr. T. Ratliff, Mr. Lionel S. Benson, Mr. J· Spooner Hardy, and Mr. W. H. Leslie. The competition of village choirs under Government inspection for a prize of £4 resulted in the prize going to the Bronygarth choir. The first part of the programme terminated with the distribution of the prizes and certificates awarded for theoretical knowledge and sight-singing, the recipients receiving their prizes at the hands of the Marchioness of Londonderry. The competition of town choirs for the town banner, which was one of the principal attractions, brought out only one competitor —the Oswestry Philharmonic Society—which was adjudged worthy of the prize. The competition for town choirs under fifteen years' standing resulted in the prize being divided between Oswestry and Llanfyllin choirs, while the prize offered in the competition of town schools under Government inspection was divided between Oswestry National Schools. The chief event of the day was the competition of village choirs for "the Banner of Honour," a second prize, "The Ladies' Banner," also being offered. The prize was won by the Lodge and Brmygarth representatives; the second honours being taken by the Trefonan choir.

EALING CHORAL ASSOCIATION.—On Thursday last the Ealing Choral Association gave their last concert of the season at the Lyric Hall, which was well filled by an appreciative audience. This choral society has now become firmly established; it executes in a thoroughly artistic manner music of interest, and under its present conductor, Mr. Ernest Pease, enables its subscribers to become acquainted with not only the works of the great masters, but also, as was the case this evening, those of composers who are now making history. The cantata "Narcissus," by Massenet, was one of these; the antique idyll commences with a Hymn to Apollo, in which the clear fresh voices of the sopranos and contraltos seemed to revel. Miss Thudichum sang the part of Narcissus, and in the address to the "fountain," as well as where "he" is listening to the chanting of the water nymphs beneath the river, created an enthusiasm. In addition to this charming work, the Association distinguished themselves in one of Mendelssohn's cantatas, "Come, let us sing unto the Lord." Later in the evening they sang a remarkably dramatic chorus, "Liberty," by Eaton Faning, as well as that composer's popular "Song of the Vikings." Mr. Walter Clifford sang the "Valley," by Gounod, and gained an encore for "I fear no foe," by Pinsuti. Mr. George Cox, as well as singing the solo in Mendelssohn's cantata, sang Ernest Ford's song "Dawn," much improved on its original form by the violoncello accompaniment, played by Mr. Whitehouse. Mr. Cox's voice is improving, and he should be more often heard, as he sings with refinement and taste. The choir can be congratulated in having secured the services of Mr. Ernest Ford as conductor, whose Trio for pianoforte, violin, and violoncello, and a chorus for female voices, "Springtime" (also encored), were included in the programme. The interest of the concert would have been enhanced had a book of words been sold, as, however distinct the choir might sing, it was difficult to follow the story of Narcissus or the subject of "Liberty."

PLYMOUTH.—The committee under whose auspices the concert was given on April 18th, at the Plymouth Guildhall must indeed be sanguine men if the realisation did not exceed their highest expectations. Rarely has any concert in the Guildhall secured so well filled a house; the dress seats extended far down the room and were all filled by a highly respectable audience, while the balcony and area were thoroughly crowded. Mr. S. Weekes has secured, as he has assuredly deserved, many triumphs, and this concert was one of them. He conducted with quiet skill and command, the result being a performance of the greatest efficiency and attractiveness. The choral music was rendered with a steadiness and cultivated taste which was almost, except in two or three instances, absolutely perfect. The band was admirable; the organ, played by the Borough organist, Mr. J. Hele, Mus.Bac., greatly enhanced the effect of the choruses, and Mr. Pardew and Mr. Rice were admirably efficient as principal violinists. The choir were in great strength and admirable form. Only once or twice was the least wavering perceptible. In the unaccompanied part-songs—the purity of tone, the perfect steadiness and precision, and intelligent expression once more evidenced that this society is unexcelled in this musical specialty. The solos were taken by professional artists. Mr. Santley was one, and although in his rendering of the airs "The seasons" he seemed at first suffering from slight huskiness, he rose to the full height of his reputation in singing in Gounod's "Nazareth," which was rendered as a solo and chorus. Closely following it in attractiveness was Mendelssohn's cantata, "The Thirteenth Psalm." Miss Mackenzie's vocalisation was tenderly and devoutly impressive, and the choral accompanying music was charming. Miss Mackenzie also won high honours in the second part, her songs being warmly applauded. Mr. Henry Guy was in particularly good voice, and pleased the audience. His scena, " Oh, 'tis a glorious sight " (Weber), was an especially fine performance. Mdme. Edith Wynne was most effective in her dramatic air, " Far greater in his lowly state " which was sung with fervour, and well illustrated her special power.

MR. GEORGE GEAR'S CONCERT.—Mr. George Gear held his annual concert at St. George's Hall, on Tuesday evening, when he achieved a success quite worthy to be so called. This accomplished son of a veteran professor of the vocal art well known as Mr. Handel Gear, proved his proficiency as a composer for, and player on, his own instrument, by a naturally "sympathetic" interpretation of the Sonata of three movements in G, a product of Mr. George Gear's own pen, and a most genial, spontaneous effusion of a really inspired mind. The sonata contains many fine passages, with some effective contrasts. The sequences of the first allegro and certain episodes, would always attract the attention of musicians. The andante cantabile in E flat, dulcet and tuneful, is varied by an agitato in the minor mode; the final rondo, playful, sparkling, and florid, suggests the style of Weber in a well-known scherzo (key of E flat). Mr. George Gear's "fugitive" pieces were Ignace Gibsone's " Saxon Song," Op. 88, and Nicholas Rubinstein's Tarantelle in G minor, Op. 14. Mr. George Gear, apart from his pianoforte, is a pleasing writer of vocal music. Miss Damian, on Tuesday, sang a late effusion "The Old Journal," and Miss Santley gave a very suggestive reading of a positively new song "The Winds," in E flat, with episodes in G major and B flat, the fair vocalist declined to insist, so to speak, on the high (optional) B flat at the end, and was content to make her own pause (without shake) on D, the leading note of the scale. Lady pupils of Mr. Handel Gear sang in the course of this agreeable soirée. Miss Clara Latham afforded much pleasure to the audience in Behrend's " Auntie "; Miss Edith Ruthven made her mark in Mr. W. Coenen's " Lovely Spring," and scored still greater honours in the scena from " Der Freischutz" in E major, where the high B natural was taken without slightest flinching from the "attack." Mr. H. Guy sang Mr. George Gear's air " The White Rose," avoiding the high A natural, and cautiously ending, like a good general, on G (the tonic). In obedience to an encore of Mr. F. H. Cowen's " Last Dream," Miss Damian sang Mr. G. Gear's " Sweet Visions," in E flat, of which Miss Clara Latham is also a capital exponent. Mr. G. Gear's "Hunting Song" (quartet) in B flat, was honoured with an encore d'estime, and might have been repeated.

Foreign Musical Intelligence.

Wilhelmj intends founding a violin school at his villa in Biberich on the Rhine.

Verdi's " Forza del Destino " has been represented at Antwerp, in French, with much success.

Presently a new scheme will be started in Berlin—the performance of classical music at popular prices, under the direction of Herr Carl Blindworth.

The twenty-sixth number of Viotta's " Lexicon der Toonkunst," extending the work to the consideration of the Trumpet-Marine, was lately issued in Amsterdam.

"Le Révérend " is the title of a one-act opera by M. Tandon, recently at Perignan. Bottesini is in Milan superintending the production of his opera " Ero e Leandro."

Wagner's " Götterdämmerung " was lately given in Hamburg for the benefit of Capellmeister Sucher. Frau Rosa Sucher was very successful as Brunnhilde, which part she played for the first time.

It is stated that an adaptation by Mr. H. S. Leigh of Strauss's opera " Prinz Mathusalem," originally produced at Vienna in 1877, will be the piece performed at the reopening of the Folies Dramatiques Theatre, on May 5th.

Wagner's " Nibelungen Ring " has just been given in Bologna and in Venice. The Italians seem generally to find a want of continuous melody in the music, a fault not easily pardoned in the south; and, notwithstanding the enthusiasm of the more pronounced Wagnerites, it is clear that the public remain cold and generally dissatisfied, to quote a leading Italian journal.

The Société des Beaux Arts of Caën offers to French competitors a gold medal (value 300 francs) for a serenade for violin, violoncello, flute, and pianoforte or harmonium. Professor Haftzer's design for the Spohr monument at Cassel consists of a life-size statue of the master in bronze, on a granite pedestal. The composer is standing at a music desk, holding his violin under his arm. A monument is to be erected shortly to Konradin Kreutzer at his native place, Messkirch in Baden. Some of this composer's music suffers from undeserved neglect just now.

M. Delibes' " Lakmé " was produced in Paris on April 14th. The scene is in India. The work, upon which an enormous sum has been spent during the process of production, met with distinct success. Several of the marches and dances are charming, and in the composer's best manner. The action of this opera passes in Hindostan. A Brahmin lives with his daughter, Lakmé, in an Indian cottage near a great town. They possess a lovely garden which has a sacred character. One day in his absence this consecrated spot is invaded by an English officer, his son, two daughters, and their governess. Lakmé flutters about among the flowers. Gerald, the young Englishman, sees her, and falls in love with her. The Indian maid reciprocates his passion. As she avows it in a sentimental ditty the Brahmin returns. He finds the garland of his sacred grove broken down, but as the invaders have flown, he swears vengeance, and resolves to go in search of Gerald. In Act 2, disguised as a beggar, we find him at the fête of Dourga in the neighbouring town. Lakmé is with him as a ballad-singer. Her songs attract the young Englishman. When he sees her he rushes towards her, and is stabbed by the irate father. However, his wound is not fatal. Lakmé stays to nurse him. When she can remove him she leads him into a forest to devote herself to him for life. But a Sepoy revolt obliges him to think of quitting his sylvan paradise. The young girl, noting his painful perplexity, smells a poisonous flower, bids him in song a supreme adieu, and gently expires in his arms. The story is not altogether satisfactory, but the charm of the music will secure a good run for the work.

Figaro has it that at a recent meeting of the creditors of Mr. Franke, Herr Pollini, of Hamburg, made an offer to pay £550 in lieu of all liability as to last season's German opera at Drury Lane. The offer was accepted by the creditors present, but, unless all the creditors agree, the proceeding must fall through. It is stated that if the creditors agree they will (owing to the liberality of Mr. Wedgwood, Mr. Franke's father-in-law, who is willing to forego his own heavy debt, and the salaries of the orchestra, which he has purchased, and to pay £1,000 cash) receive a dividend of about ten shillings in the pound,

BOW AND BROMLEY INSTITUTE.

Mr. W. S. Hoyte was the organist on April 14th. His opening piece was a sonata for organ by the gifted young composer, Mr. Charlton Speer, which was originally published in the *Organist's Quarterly Journal.* Mr. Hoyte well describes the work in his programme notes, thus :—" The 1st Allegro Maestoso in D flat major is full of vigour. The Adagio in C minor is in happy contrast to the breadth and brilliancy of the 1st movement; an introduction of 16 bars (at the conclusion of the slow movement) leads up to a return of the original key (D flat) for the last movement, which is in the orthodox form. A highly effective treatment of the 2nd subject will be observed towards the end, where the melody is accompanied by arpeggioed harmonies."

This excellent and promising work was very warmly received by an appreciative audience. A serenata by Braga, expressively and artistically played and re-demanded and Wagner's "Pilgrims'" chorus from Tannhäuser, were the next organ solo. Silas' clever Fantasia and Fugue in E minor proved to be excellent, and received loud applause. Mr. Hoyte's musicianly minuet and trio was played. The allegretto from Mendelssohn's "Reformation" Symphony and Handel's "Largo," gave great satisfaction. O. Barris's popular March "The Old Brigade" and the march in Berlioz's "Faust," completed the organ pieces. Miss Annie Williams sang two songs nicely. Mr. Brereton sang "O ruddier than the cherry" and Mattei's "Oh, hear the wild wind" excellently, being encored both times, giving in the last case "The Village Blacksmith." Smart's duet "When the wind" was down for the two singers. Mr. W. G. Wood was the able accompanist.

Mr. Founteen Meen, who is not only esteemed as an accomplished organ player, but generally as a painstaking and conscientious musician, whose abilities as an accompanist are also well known, gave the organ recital on April 21st; his selections were much appreciated, especially Hatton's Toccata in F minor. The programme included pianoforte solos by Mdme. Lucie Palicot (a pupil of Mons. Guilmant), introducing the use of the pedalier. The young lady played Bach's Toccata in F, and Grand Prelude and Fugue in A minor, also a Melodie Hongroise of Liszt, in brilliant style, and won an undeniable encore; after several ineffectual bows she played another solo, to the evident gratification of the audience. The pedalier is really a pedal-piano placed under the other piano, and is introduced by Messrs. Pleyel, Wolff, and Co., the player's seat being placed on the pedalier. This arrangement is no doubt very useful, and in the end may advantageously affect some future school of pianoforte music. Miss Florence Norman, a student of the Royal Academy of Music, was the vocalist, and won a *bis* in Handel's air "From Mighty Kings," and was recalled after "In questo semplice." Next Saturday the last recital of the present season will be given by Dr. A. L. Peace, the well-known Glasgow organist, whose sterling playing should command the attendance of students and all interested in good organ music.

On the 23rd Haydn's "Creation" was given with orchestra by the choir of the Institute, under the *baton* of Mr. McNaught. The principal vocalists were Miss Thudichum, Mr. Sidney Tower, and Mr. Robert Hilton. Mr. Alfred Carder was the organist. The orchestra contained some "good and true men," and taken all together the performance was an excellent one, doing much credit to the conductor, band, choir, and managers.

THE PHILHARMONIC SOCIETY'S PRIZE OVERTURE.

An official announcement has been made to the effect that the umpires of the Philharmonic Society, Sir Julius Benedict and Mr. Otto Goldschmidt (the latter kindly acting in the place of Sir Michael Costa), have awarded the prize, offered by the Society for the best overture, to Mr. Oliver A. King, who is now in Canada, and holds the office of pianist to H.R.H. the Marchioness of Lorne, [better known as the Princess Louise ; the overture was played at the concert of Thursday last. Some published works of Mr. King (seen at Novello and Co.'s) show considerable ability ; the earliest of them somewhat crude and strained, but truly promising.   A. M.

PRINCIPAL CONTENTS OF THIS NUMBER.

LONDON : SATURDAY, APRIL 28, 1883.

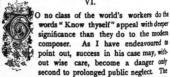

THE PRESENT POSITION OF THE COMPOSER.

VI.

NO no class of the world's workers do the words "Know thyself" appeal with deeper significance than they do to the modern composer. As I have endeavoured to point out, success in his case may, without wise care, become a danger only second to prolonged public neglect. The true composer must stand perforce as much by his moral power over himself and manly conscientious judgment of his own work as by his artistic mastery over the multiform difficulties of his profession. I have already dealt with some of the dangers to the artistic character of a composer which arise from a premature success ; now it seems needful to remark upon the misapprehensions which are co-existent with a present success which may not be afterwards endorsed by public judgment. The young composer is naturally anxious to leap into fame if possible, and believes that the opportunity for the production of a large work should not only be seized, whatever state of preparedness his mind may be in for the present responsibility of such a composition, but should have all possible friendly extraneous aids in order to compass a success. It would seem, indeed, that the composer must regard friendly help, notwithstanding its value in some directions and the pleasure of its possession, with unflinching wariness, as involving peril as regards the attainment of that just assessment of his work which is indispensable to his ultimate success. In no direction is this danger more pronounced than in the case of the production of a new opera. The young compóser must, indeed, possess no small social advantages to succeed in getting his work thought of, and in the end presented. Then it is heard amidst the glamour and excitement attending a stage performance, with all the brilliant, not to say misleading accessories of the arts of the poet, stage-singer, actor, scene-painter, and costumier, before an audience of very decided pleasure-seekers and pre-disposed to be interested, astonished, and delighted. So it is that almost every contribution to the lyric stage, whatever its merits or demerits may be, has a meed of present success, and the composer his sec-tion of determined admirers. But how very few operas live even for twenty years! Time, though the most uncompromising of critics in the end, has the power of alone giving a just and merciful, because true, judgment. To go to a still higher class of music, the oratorio, the composer has again in his favour the presence of friendly enthusiasm. But there are fewer extraneous aids to success in the surroundings of an oratorio performance, and the listeners are necessarily in a more reflective and dis-passionate mood than they would be in the feverish atmosphere of the opera house. So the successful rendering of a new oratorio more surely represents the unbiassed judgment of the future than will even a considerable number of enthusiastic, rather than calmly critical, receptions of a new opera. The suc-cessful production of a new symphony, as demanding a purely musical judgment and some technical know-ledge on the part of the listeners, apart from the ex-citement, sympathies, and associations accompanying the presentation of vocal works, whether sacred or secular, is perhaps the composer's best testing triumph as an artist; for in this case he appeals more entirely upon the strength of his own imagination, intellect, knowledge and skill than he does in any of the other great types of musical expression and constructive power.   E. H. TURPIN.

ENGLISH SUCCESSES.

IT must be a source of no little gratification to the numerous friends of the Royal Academy, whether pupils or appreciative on-lookers, to reflect that both Mr. A. C. MACKENZIE, the composer of "Colomba," and Mr. A. GORING THOMAS, the writer of "Esme-"ralda," were mainly educated within its walls. Their works, which have just been given with such distinct success mark an epoch in our national operatic history; they may prove the beginning of a new, and more independent type than any English operas that have preceded them. Mr. MACKENZIE studied har-mony and composition under that able teacher the late Mr. C. LUCAS; while to Mr. E. PROUT, Mr. THOMAS is mainly indebted for much valuable train-ing. Both these young composers have probably enlarged their powers by a study and observation of the musical types to be found abroad. But this in no way detracts from the value of their English acade-mical training.

Despite the systematic way in which our valuable institution has been traduced, one cannot but be pleased to see its pupils always to the front, whether as players, singers, or composers. During the life of

the last two generations, the Royal Academy has been steadily educating its students in the right and com-plete way. There is not a town in the land, or, indeed, hardly in the colonies, that is not supplied with one of her alumni, thoroughly competent to instruct the youth, and to guide correctly the taste of the neigh-bourhood. To the English musical world this is no news; but it is to be lamented that many of the general public, who are ignorant of these facts, are set against the Academy by the voluble talk of those who, knowing well what the institution has done for the art of music in this country, yet for patent purposes deliberately attempt to convey to provincial audiences a totally different impression. At a money collecting meeting held at Chester a couple of months ago, amongst other statements, the Duke of WEST-MINSTER was pleased to say, that "The Royal "Academy of Music had failed to be a national "institution in the highest sense of the word." His GRACE is not generally recognised as an authority on subjects connected with the art, and so he does not come under the type indicated above; though such reckless statements may also do mischief. If he would supplement his dictum with some arguments advanced in support of his assertions, his confident utterances might possibly be received with more respect than they are at present entitled to. A healthy competition between art training institutions cannot but be beneficial. But to endeavour to foist a new venture into superior notice, by systematic misstatements respecting the results achieved by a rival school, savours rather of—what our transatlantic cousins term—" spread-eagleism," than of that judicial impartiality which ought to characterize an hereditary legislator.   T. L. S.

THE LOGIC OF COUNTERPOINT.

THIRD SERIES.

VII.

ALTHOUGH CHERUBINI does not think it necessary to give new precepts as regards the composition of four-part counterpoint with one voice taking contrapuntal action of either the second or third species, I will venture to offer a few observations upon the employ-ment in a four-part score of the two kinds of counter-point just named. The student should first practise with the voice, taking either the second or third species counterpoint as either the upper or lower part. This is not only a good way of conquering the difficulties of such contrapuntal action by degrees, by placing the moving parts externally where they are best traced out and most manageable, but it is the practice of such action in the parts most likely to be thus employed in actual composition. Having acquired facility in the external use of counterpoint of either second or third species, it is then desirable to gain experience in the use of such counterpoints placed by turns in both of the middle parts. It is not well to relax the important rules necessary for the government of discordant sounds, but it may be observed that as a dissonance is more completely balanced by three other parts in concordant agreement than it could have been in three parts with two parts only in consonant combi-nation, and further, as discords are, generally speaking, less palpable in their effects in the fuller score of four-parts, the writer may be a little less solicitous about the presence of discordant sounds, either as passing between concordant chord elements or attacked occasionally with the other parts at the beginning of a measure. It is of course important in counterpoint, as it is in harmony, to avoid using with any discord the second below such dissonance. Thus counting from the bass or lower part, the second should not be heard with the first, the fourth with the third, the sixth with the fifth as a rule, or the ninth with the octave. The avoidance of such ill-judged combinations will largely help in giving to the harmony freedom from anticipated resolutions, and a general purity and clearness of tone. In points of difficulty a thinning of the harmony secured by the absorption of one part by placing two voices on the same sound, will often be found to be not only a convenient but a satisfactory way of escape. It is perhaps needless to repeat that dissonances are more objectionable, by reason of the greater length of the notes, in counterpoint of the second than in that of the third species. It may also be said, that the crossing of the parts by the more active counterpoint of the second or third kind is not to be so much protested against as would be part-crossing in four-part counterpoint of the first species, for in the case of the more actively moving part the outline of the contrapuntal melody is clearly traceable. The counterpoints of the second and third kinds should as a rule begin with the customary rest in each case ; and should, as being prominent by reason of their distinct activity, take the proper cadence figure if possible, which is peculiar to the species in use at the time.   E. H. TURPIN.

"COLOMBA."

(II. THE MUSIC.)

It has already been shown how faulty is the plot, and absurd the versification of the libretto Dr. F. Hüffer has supplied Mr. Mackenzie with for musical treatment. Remembering what the ancient writer says as to the difficulty of building satisfactorily on a weak foundation, one would suppose that the music of this "lyric drama" could hardly be successful. Happily the reverse is the case ; a work of such very decided merit has been the case, that it may be said without much hesitation, the young Scotch composer has given us the most dramatic, musicianly, and original conception that the English opera stage as yet can boast of. Whether Mr. Mackenzie found much inspiration in the *pabulum* supplied by Herr Hüffer, or whether the success achieved is to be ascribed to his innate genius, is a point not very difficult to settle. As has been pointed out, the work of the German adaptor is not without certain merits ; it is easy to see that the composer has instinctively appreciated the value of the situations the librettist has created, and has done justice, full justice, to the main episodes of the story laid out for illustration. At the same time, there are parts of the opera where his music seems weak, and does not rise up to the very distinct power to be found elsewhere. If the score be examined carefully by the side of the word-book, it will there be seen that these portions are so poor in ideas and clumsy in diction, that it was perhaps impossible for them to convey a spark of inspiration. A hasty generalization, therefore, might assume that the value of the libretto and music was concurrent, but a more careful examination will show that such a supposition is incorrect. There are parts of the libretto wearisome, stilted, and very commonplace ; yet here one occasionally finds admirable music, fresh in tone, full of feeling, and bearing in its phrases the unerring stamp of genius. So that if the scales of judgment be held fairly, one must incline to the impression that it is to the freedom of thought and inborn

strength of the composer's imagination that we owe the excellences of "Colomba" rather than to the suggestiveness of the libretto furnished. What have been the inter-relations between the author and composer I know not, but if a guess may be hazarded from the score, there has been a considerable amount of alteration and revision. Such a course is always a blemish so far as the unity of a work is concerned. In the old Italian operas where music, and music alone, was the attraction, the way in which the various numbers were pieced together was a matter of little moment so that the required contrast of voices and styles was obtained. But the days in which such operas found a ready acceptance are over. The majority of the *habitués* of the modern Italian opera—at least in London—merely go to be amused, and provided they can hear their "stars" they are satisfied. But not so with the outer musical public ; taught by trained thinking critics, the knowledge such opera-goers display is frequently based on the firm ground of naturalness. They are not slow to balance probabilities, perceive incongruities, detect absurdities, and to require an amount of consistence in plot in order to maintain that human interest in a work, without which its days on the stage are numbered. Experience has unerringly taught us that a badly constructed libretto will banish an opera from the stage—Weber's beautiful "Euryanthe" for example. As we turn over the pages of "Colomba" it will be seen that there are sins both of commission and omission ; these together with the repulsiveness of its plot, and the impossibility of feeling any sympathy with the revengeful heroine, may militate sorely against its permanent hold on the affections of the public. In any case, blame cannot be laid on the shoulders of Mr. Mackenzie ; he has done all that a musician could do, but he has clearly been hampered in his task.

Even in the case of a composer displaying marked originality in all he does, it is not easy to describe in words his style, as we use the term in music. Style consists of so many peculiarities, and is built up of materials so intangible and difficult to grasp, that the task of depicting it is well nigh impossible. Without analysing too minutely Mr. Mackenzie's music, and saying what parts resemble and remind one of the styles of the past great masters, it may be said, that though we find reminiscences of Weber, Schubert, Mendelssohn, Gounod, Schumann, Verdi, and Wagner, yet the composer of "Colomba" possesses a distinct type of his own, displaying over and over again the precious gift of originality. If a disciple of Wagner should point out that Mr. Mackenzie's form is that of the so-called infinite *melos* theory of the great Bayreuth master, yet it may be retorted that his *melos* varies considerably from that of Wagner, which, by the way, is frequently so downright ugly, as not to be fairly entitled to the epithet of *melos*, *i.e.*, according to the old Greek meaning "sweetness," at all. It is true that Mr. Mackenzie uses his orchestra in much the same way as Wagner has used it, viz., in telling a continuous tale, recalling past occurrences, and suggesting motives, as well as in the more purely formal duties assigned to it of accompanying the voices, and heightening by its *timbre* the characteristic colour of the situations. All this our young composer has done, but he differs from Wagner mainly in the fact that the partnership between the voices and orchestra is but a limited one, and that strings and wind are rarely allowed to have the best of the co-operation. And further, that though he employs the leitmotive device, he uses it but sparingly, and does not thrust it into prominent notice every few bars, to the dismal discomfiture of the wearied ear, and serious interruption of continuity. It would be folly to assert that Mr. Mackenzie possesses either the marvellous power, or the daring originality in orchestral tone building that all must admit marks Wagner, whatever opinion we may entertain as to the value of his results. But we may maintain that Mr. Mackenzie's method commands respect, and probably conveys more pleasure to the unpledged and unprejudiced mind than the continuous *aria parlante* style of the German composer, with its cynic indifference to the vital importance of the vocal utterances. Thank Heaven ! Mr. Mackenzie has not arrived at the conclusion that infinite *melos* is quite enough for the various phases of musical illustration. He fully recognises the value of recitative and declamation, as exponents of what happens in daily emotional expression. But better than these mechanical forms, he has the rarer poetical gift of melody, and has turned it to good account in the charming solos, the passionate duets, the bright choruses, the piquant dances, and other detachable pieces to be found in his work. So though, perhaps, Wagner is the master chiefly followed, yet it can be truly said that he has likewise afforded an instance of what to avoid, as well as what to adopt. It will thus be seen that Mr. Mackenzie is no slavish copyist. He has adopted the best suggestions of the great masters of the art, blending some of their ideas, together with his own feelings, into an homogeneous mass, distinctly flavoured with his own originality. One of his features, which perhaps strikes one most, is a mastery over dramaticism, combined with a passionate intensity, which reminds one more of the attributes of warm Southern composers, than of the common characteristics of our colder Northern writers. His conception throughout is on a lofty and extensive scale, and in the part-writing, whether of voices or instruments, we perceive that classical turn of mind that bespeaks long training in counterpoint and sentence construction. The orchestral details are masterly worked out, and if the illustrations he supplies of colouring are nowhere startling, they are at least never harsh, thick, or unpleasantly obtrusive. His scoring, indeed, is beautiful throughout; we can listen to it with pleasure, can admire the many original and ingenious figures with which it is studded, can mark its ebullitions of significant sentiment, without losing interest or grasp over the voice parts.

Such is the general impression that Mr. Mackenzie's music conveys to the mind. The opera has already been so carefully noticed in detail in these pages, that it will suffice if attention is now confined to some of its salient members. It seems a pity that the composer has not written a formal overture to his work; surely after the splendid examples we possess of both old and modern overtures, it cannot be said that this free and elastic form is worked out! He has rather preferred to introduce his opera with a brief prelude written in the alternate times of 9-8 and 3.4. It is a well laid out introduction, containing motives connected with the Barracini, the vocero, the love theme, and the concluding prayer on Colomba's death. In the frequent reiteration of some of these leading themes on the brass, and the obstinacy of the orchestral figures employed, we see Wagner's influence strongly reflected. The opening chorus, "Buy, Signori, buy," is a bright, vivid piece of writing, with a singularly dainty accompaniment, just full of that life and vigour natural to the restless throbbing tide of an Italian market-place. Though Herr Hüffer seems to have mistaken the real nature and office of the Corsican "Vocero"—a song improvised at the grave—and has written some absurd lines in the lyric, yet this is one of Mr. Mackenzie's most striking inspirations, alternately so tender and wild is it. The passionate accents of Colombo, as she tells of her anxious watching and waiting for her brother to return home, and her agitated delivery of the final verse of the Vocero, constitute an episode of intense interest; this and the shout of "vendetta," on the high B, with which the number concludes, is indeed a magnificent example of how, by the subtle power of the musician's art, emotions can be heightened, until one thrills with excitement over the scene acted before us. The following quintet with chorus, "There is death in her words," in which the author occasionally writes in ten real parts (independent of the accompaniments) is a piece of remarkably clever construction, and comes out most effectively. The wild bursts of inflamed passion, and the revengeful feeling which it breathes becoming more intensified in every bar till its close. Here, as elsewhere, it may be remarked, that in the sympathetic music which Mr. Mackenzie has assigned to Colombo, he has not sacrificed grace and coherence, to the storm and fury of dramaturgy. It appears a little odd that there is no special theme or leit-motive connected with the heroine herself. The ballet music is elegant, animated, and somewhat fresh as to rhythm; the Saltarello with which it closes seems to have been suggested by Raff's popular Tarantella. However, this form of music is so circumscribed as to its general character, that but little scope is offered for novelty of treatment, so the resemblance here remarked on may have little significance.

Dr. Hüffer's curious whim in making his English-speaking chorus suddenly burst into Italian has already been noticed. It may now be mentioned, that the music to which Mr. Mackenzie has set the rustic chorus, "Salve Regina del Maggio" is an ancient church melody to be found in the *Laudi Spirituali*, and is known under the title "Alla Trinita Beata." Its origin might have been indicated in the composer's score. The florid counterpoint in the orchestra which accompanies the massive harmonies of the old tune is an admirable specimen of Mr. Mackenzie's musicianship, and the same remark applies to the fine male voice quartet, in which the Barracini join Orso and the Count in a hollow ode to peace. The way in which the six-part chorus subsequently join in echoing the phrases of the soloists, occasionally doubling their parts in octaves, is really grand. Such a splendid piece of writing could have come from no pen but that of an Englishman, well acquainted with a school of which we have good reason to be proud. The scene which follows this, where Savelli graphically relates the account of the murder of Orso's father by the deceitful Barracini, is throughout a fine example of vigorous workmanship: the librettist has unduly protracted this business, and in the hands of one not gifted as is Mr. Mackenzie, this scene would probably have wearied the audience; but the rough, and yet pathetic manner in which he has let the brigand chief tell the sad tale, the striking changes in tone, where the Barracini deny their guilt, and the revengeful comments of Colomba, unite in presenting the most powerful and dramatic scene yet witnessed on our native stage. Attention may here be called to the singular breadth and sonority of Mr. Mackenzie's finales: a wonderful massive body of tone comes out from his combination of voices and orchestra, so different to the thin noise that is the characteristic of some well-known Italian stage works, in similar *tuttis*. Musicians will know how to appreciate this valuable feature, and to estimate the hopeful promise it gives of further successes from his pen.

The Corsican love-song in the third act is a rare and beautiful production, possessing some uncommon phrases of melody, and richly decked harmony. But perhaps the gem of the piece is the delicious ballad sung by Chilina, "So he thought of his love." The tender sad flavour that this song possesses, is considerably enhanced by the quaintness of its orchestral support; it is sure to become popular, for its music satisfies the cultured musician, and goes straight to the heart of every hearer. Points to note in this piece are, the happy employment of the augmented second, the breaks in the continuity of the rhythmic metre, the startling effect of the rise from the lower key note (F sharp) to the upper tonic at the close, and the weird warning that lingers on one's ear with the concluding note of the refrain, the voice dying away on the dominant, C sharp.

The ridiculous shooting scene, though it contains some cleverly contrasted music, has not inspired Mr. Mackenzie, but in the finale where the monks conveniently appear, he again shows his power. The Requiem chant of these personages, assisted by the villagers—who are likewise conveniently at the fatal spot—is in thirds and octaves, the orchestra playing an agitated chromatic figure. The scene might well have been more extensively developed, but the advent of that stormy petrel Colomba, now exulting over her satiated revenge, prevents this course; however, her shriek of "vendetta," on the upper B natural, brings the scene to a stirring conclusion. The fourth act is, on the whole, the weakest of the series. Here the inartistic awkwardness of the libretto is apparent. Still, there are two features of special musical interest; the first is the refined and suggestive under-current of music that flows through the orchestra as the two girls, Lydia and Colomba, grope their way amidst the darkness and storm to the robbers' camp. The second point, though we have far too long to wait for it, is a magnificent duet between the lovers "Say of Love, shall he change," a piece full of the warmth and fervour of Italian passion. The music during the flight of the brigands and soldiers is good and stirring, but the conclusion of the opera is too oratorio-like.

If it be stated that Mr. Mackenzie has occasionally written without inspiration, it may in reply be said that in these parts he has had nothing supplied to call up the divine fire; and so one refrains from pointing out in detail certain weaknesses in this opera. But, taken as a whole, his work is the outcome of a masterful, reflective, and original mind; it will command respect from foreign, as it has from critics of his own land. It is evident that in the opinion of the English musical public, "Colomba" can challenge comparison with the contemporary works of any country.

It is not the intention here to describe the performance of the opera at Drury Lane; but it may be said that, thanks to the painstaking care and experience of Mr. Carl Rosa, these were of exceptional excellence. Madame Valleria, by her impassioned singing and powerful acting, has created a Colomba that will not soon be forgotten. She seemed at times to labour under some little difficulty as to the enunciation of the uncouth sentences with which Herr Hüffer had provided her; the rather mixed line :—

"For the *coming of thee* whom to me of all is dearest,"

presenting a crux. One could not but feel amused when watching this most truculent full-aged heroine, to remember that the librettist had playfully termed her "a reckless *child*." Mr. Barton Guckin has risen still higher in public estimation. His fine voice and effective acting contributed in no small degree to the success of the work. But the fool's-cap head-dress with which the librettist had endowed him, made him look like the prize dunce at a school, instead of the hero of a terrible tragedy. The unfortunate Count also commanded sympathy; he was condemned to sing much doggerel, with a huge ornament closely resembling a gorgonzola cheese suspended from his neck. Mr. Novara impersonated the brigand Savelli with signal success. He uses his fine voice with intelligence, and the bluster of his action was capital. The minor parts of Chilina, Lydia, and Guiseppe Barracini, were well sustained; while commendation is justly due to the chorus for their clear spirited singing, and also to the orchestra collectively for the care and delicacy with which Mr. Mackenzie's romantic and elaborate accompaniments were rendered.

T. L. SOUTHGATE.

Organ News.

CRYSTAL PALACE.

Mr. A. J. Eyre's programmes on Saturday last were as follows :—

Elegy in C minor	Stephens.
(In Memoriam, G. W. Reay Mackey, obit 15th April, 1883.)	
Fantasia in F minor	Hesse.
Adagio from Nonetto	Spohr.
Minuet	Bennett.
Occasional Overture	Handel.
Selection, "Carmen"	Bizet.
Graceful Dance (Henry VIII.)	Sullivan.
Larghetto	Rea.
Barcarole	Bennett.
Minuet	Boccherini.
Serenade	Schubert.
Dance Moresque	Killner.

NORWICH.

An organ recital was given at St. Andrew's Hall, Norwich, by Dr. Bunnett, F.C.O. (organist to the Corporation), on Saturday, 21st April. The following was the programme :—

Overture in D	Haydn.
Allegretto Vivace	Morandi.
Quis est homo ("Stabat Mater")	Rossini.
Air, "And God shall wipe away"	Sullivan.
(From "The Light of the World.")	
A Concert on a Lake interrupted by a Thunderstorm	
—A Grand Dramatic Fantasia	Nenkomm.
Larghetto in D (from Clarinet Quintet)	Mozart.
Meditation sur le 1st Prelude, par Gounod	Bach.
Largo in G	Handel.
Gavotte Moderne	Tours.
March (from Cantata, "Lora")	Bunnett.

The recital on Thursday evening, May 3rd, will include several well-known works, and will be of a popular character.

PRESTON.

The following is the programme of an organ recital given by Mr. James Tomlinson (organist to the Corporation), at the New Public Hall, Preston, on Saturday evening, 21st April:—

Overture to "Athalia"	Handel.
(The third of Handel's oratorios.)	
Adagio	Merkel.
Bourrees (Second Violin Sonata)	Bach.
Overture to "Les Huguenots"	Meyerbeer.
Pastorale	Best.
Wedding March	Mendelssohn.

PLYMOUTH.

The Corporation organ recitals, promoted by the Rt. Worshipful the Mayor (J. Shelly, Esq.), Aldermen and Town Council, were resumed on Thursday, April 19th, at the Guildhall, by Mr. John Hele, Mus.Bac., borough organist. Subjoined is the programme :—

Triumphal March ("Alfred")	Prout.
"Angels ever bright and fair"	Handel.
"Gloria in Excelsis"	Weber.
Andante in A	Smart.
Ballad, "Iolanthe"	Sullivan.
Romanza, "Faust"	Gounod.
Offertoire in E major	Batiste.

CASTLE HOWARD.

An organ recital was given in the private chapel at Castle Howard, by Mr. J. R. Brooke, on Sunday, 22nd of April, when he performed the following programme :—

Overture, "Ode on St. Cecilia's Day"	Handel.
Solo and Chorus	Flora.
Stabat Mater	Devorak.
Andante in E minor	Batiste.
Prelude and Fugue in D minor	Bach.
Air and Final Chorus, "Acis and Galatea"	Handel.
Allegretto	Weber.
War March of Priests "Athalie"	Mendelssohn.

CLAUGHTON.

Subjoined is the programme of an organ recital given by E. Townshend Driffield, selected from the works of Handel, on Saturday, 28th April :—

Overture—Andante pomposo—Allegro—Minuetto (Samson).	
Bourree in D minor (Pastor Fido).	
Air in F (Water Music).	
Chaconne in G (Harpsichord Lessons).	
Air, "Lascia ch'io pianga" (Rinaldo).	
Allegro Moderato—Andante maestoso...	} (Fourth Organ Concerto)
Adagio—Allegro	

COLLECTION.

Air, "He shall feed His flock"	} (Messiah).
Chorus, "Hallelujah!"	

The organ has been recently cleaned and repaired, by Messrs. W. and F. Hall, organ builders, Birkenhead.

ALFORD.

The second of the series of musical services in the Parish Church, Alford, was held on Thursday evening, April 19th, at which were sung selections from Haydn's "Creation." The organist on this occasion was Mr. William Wakelin, of Horncastle Parish Church. The organ solos were :—

Larghetto and Allegro (from First Concerto)	Handel.
Larghetto	Merkel.
Fugue in G minor	Bach.
Sonata	Rheinberger.
Pastorale—Andante—Fugue.	
Andante con variazioni	Beethoven.
Offertoire in D	Batiste.

CAMBRIDGE.

The second popular organ recital, by the borough organist, Mr. F. Dewberry, L.R.A.M., took place on Saturday, April 21st, at the Guildhall. The programme included :—

PART I.

Overture, "Occasional Oratorio"	Handel.
Larghetto, in E flat	Rea.
Fugue in G minor	Bach.
Elevation, in A flat	Guilmant.
Allegro Vivace, in A minor	Morandi.

PART II.

Romanza, from Symphony in B flat	Haydn.
Offertoire in G, Op. 35	Wely.
Minuet in A, from Quintet	Boccherini.
March from oratorio, "Abraham"	Molique.

BRISTOL.

Annexed is the programme of the organ recital given by Mr. George Riseley in the Colston Hall on Saturday, April 21st :—

Offertoire in D major	Batiste.
Adagio Sostenuto	Prout.
Fantasia in A	Droning.
Allegro—Andante—Allegro.	
Adagio in B	Spohr.
Air and Fugue, "My heart ever faithful," on St.	
Ann's Tune	Bach.
Air, with Variations	Rode.
Ave Maria	Arcadelt.
Overture, "Le Brasseur de Preston"	Adam.

NOTTINGHAM.

The following is the specification of a chamber organ built by Messrs. Brindley & Foster, of Sheffield, for W. Wright, Esq., Normanton Lodge, The Park, Nottingham. The instrument is blown by Ramsbottom's triple ram hydraulic engine, which is placed with feeders, &c., in a cellar below :—

GREAT ORGAN. CC TO C.

1. Open Diapason	8 ft.	3. Flauto Traverso	...	4 ft.
2. Vox Angelica	8 ,,			

SWELL ORGAN. CC TO C.

4. Lieblich Gedact	... 8 ft.	6. Oboe	...	8 ft.
5. Gamba	8 ,,			

Nos. 2 to 6 enclosed in a swell box.

PEDAL ORGAN. CCC TO F.

7. Lieblich Bourdon	...	...	16 ft.

COUPLERS.

8. Swell to Great.	11. Great Sub-octave.
9. Swell to Pedal.	12. Swell Sub-octave.
10. Great to Pedals.	13. Tremulant.

CHISLEHURST.

On Saturday Evening, April 14th, a recital was given by Fourteen Meen, Esq., on the new organ built by Messrs. Foster and Andrews, of Hull, in the Wesleyan Chapel.

Sonata (" Pontificale ")	Lemmens.
Andante (from Violin Concerto)	Mendelssohn.
Larghetto (from Symphony in D)	Beethoven.
Toccata in F sharp minor	J. L. Hatton.
Canzone in A minor	Guilmant.
Choral Song and Fugue	S. S. Wesley.
Andante with Variations	W. Rea.
Grand Solemn March	H. Smart.

GREAT ORGAN.

1. Large Open Diapn.	8 ft.	5. Harmonic Flute	...	4 ft.
2. Small Open Diapn.	8 ,,	6. Principal		4 ,,
3. Hohl Flöte	8 ,,	7. Twelfth		2⅔,,
4. Gamba	8 ,,	8. Fifteenth		2 ,,

SWELL ORGAN.

9. Lieblich Bourdon	... 16 ft.	15. Stopped Flute	...	4 ft.
10. Open Diapason	8 ,,	16. Piccolo		2 ,,
11. Stopt Diapason	8 ,,	17. Mixture (3 ranks).	various	
12. Salicional	8 ,,	18. Cornopean		8 ft.
13. Vox Celestes	... 8 ,,	19. Oboe		8 ,,
14. Principal	4 ,,			

CHOIR ORGAN.

20. Dulciana	8 ft.	23. Flauto Traverso	...	4 ft.
21. Gedact	8 ,,	24. Flautina		2 ,,
22. Violin	8 ,,	25. Clarionet		8 ,,

PEDAL ORGAN.

26. Open Diapason	... 16 ft.	28. Violoncello	...	8 ft.
27. Bourdon	16 ,,			

COUPLERS.

29. Swell to Great.	32. Choir to Pedals.
30. Swell to Pedals.	33. Swell to Choir.
31. Great to Pedals.	34. Swell Octave.

SUMMARY.

4 Composition Pedals to Great. 3. Composition Pedals to Swell. Great, 8 Stops, 448 Pipes. Swell, 11 Stops, 716 Pipes. Choir 6 Stops, 312 Pipes, enclosed in a Swell Box. Pedal, 3 Stops, 90 Pipes. Couplers, 6.

Total, 34 Stops, 1566 Pipes.

WATERLOO ROAD.

Subjoined is the programme of an organ recital given on Thursday evening, April 19th, at the church of St. John the Evangelist, by Mr. A. Wilkinson Jones, F.C.O.:—

Sonata, No. 2	Mendelssohn.
Christmas Pastorale	Merkel.
Fugue in G minor	Bach.
Andante in A	Smart.
Postlude in E flat	Wely.

NEWINGTON.

The following selections were played at St. Mary's Parish Church on Sunday evenings during March, by Mr. W. Rayment Kirby, F.C.O.:—

Grand Solemn March	Smart.
Andante in F	Merkel.
Aria (from a Sonata)	Paradies.
Andante in E flat	Batiste.
Prelude and Fugue in B flat	Bach.
Air, varied, " Holsworthy Church Bells "	Wesley.
Andante	Dussek.
Andante Pomposo and Allegretto (" Samson ")	Handel.
Selection from the " Messiah "	Handel.

Passing Events.

It is now said that Verdi denies the report, that he is writing a new opera on the story of " Othello."

The organ playing of Mr. E. M. Bowman, A.C.O., in different American cities is highly spoken of.

Messrs. Collard and Co., the pianoforte makers, intend to open their West-end saloons for concert purposes.

The name of Her Majesty the Queen will head the list of patrons of the coming Welsh National Eisteddfod to be held in Cardiff early in August.

The re-opening of the Alhambra is announced to take place in October next. A new spectacular fairy opera by Mr. G. R. Sims and Mr. Frederic Clay will be the first novelty at the new house.

Miss Julia Muschamp's " Soirée Musicale," on April 17th, at Fitzroy House, Primrose Hill, presented a good programme. The lady herself played several pianoforte pieces with much skill and consequent success.

Mr. Mackenzie's new opera " Colomba," which has been so successfully produced at Drury Lane Theatre, is to be the first novelty given by Herr Pollini during his coming autumn season at the Stadttheater, Hamburg.

It seems that at the last Royal Society of Musicians' performance of the " Messiah," a loss of £80 was incurred. This affords further evidence that it is high time to examine into our present costly system of concert-giving.

The Bach Choir, under the baton of Herr O. Goldschmidt, go to Windsor on June 23rd. The Queen has specially requested that Mendelssohn's " Walpurgis Night," shall be included in the programme to be performed before Her Majesty.

The Premier addressed, it is said, a cordial letter to Madame Marie Rose, regretting that the pressure of his work would not permit him to hear her sing in " Fidelio," the other evening, and cordially inviting the lady and her husband to breakfast with Mrs. Gladstone and himself.

Mr. A. Sullivan in the course of his speech at the dinner of the Royal Society of Musicians, noted that in 1707 the opera then had an orchestra of 28 players ; 12 violins, 2 tenors, 5 basses (which I presume, included a violoncello), 4 hautbois, 4 bassoons, and 1 trumpet, with of course the harpsichord in addition.

There were 46 competitors for the Philharmonic Overture Prize. The proposal was praiseworthy on the part of the society, though only a feeble effort after all. However, competitions notoriously fail in art matters, and the right course for the Philharmonic directors to pursue is to offer commissions to English composers.

The musical world has, by the sudden death of Mr. Reay-Mackay, of the Crystal Palace, sustained the loss of a useful supporter. Mr. Reay-Mackay was only 35. He strongly supported the performance of high-class music at the Palace, and was thinking out a scheme for high-class operatic performances to be given there.

The proposal of Dr. George Grove to hold a bicentenary Handel Festival next year, is leading thoughtful musicians to the idea of a really historic festival free from the prevailing abuses of the master's scores and text. It would be very interesting to hear Handel's music thus rendered as in his own day, with largely doubled oboe and bassoon parts, &c.

The prospectus of the eighth Handel Festival at the Crystal Palace has been issued. The festival will be under the sole management of the Crystal Palace company, on Monday, Wednesday, and Friday, June 18th, 20th, and 22nd, 1883, a grand full rehearsal taking place as usual on the Friday previous (June 15th). The solo vocalists engaged are Madame Albani and Madame Valleria, Miss Anna Williams, Madame Clara Suter, and Miss Annie Marriott ; Madame Patey and Madame Trebelli ; Mr. Edward Lloyd and Mr. Joseph Maas ; Mr. Santley, Mr. F. King, Mr. Bridson, and Signor Foli. The chorus and orchestral band will be maintained at the fullest dimensions of previous festivals, numbering about 4,000 performers ; and the whole force will, it is earnestly hoped, be under the direction of Sir Michael Costa. The arrangements for both performers and listeners are ample, and carefully considered, so there is every prospect of a successful meeting.

Beethoven's Choral Symphony has been given in Moscow, under Rubinstein's direction.

Madame Hélène Crosmond will arrive in London from Milan for the season early in May.

A festival of the London Gregorian Choral Association at St. Paul's Cathedral is fixed for May 10th.

Dr. Creser lectured to the members of the Leeds Philosophical Society on "The Life and Works of Henry Purcell," with illustrations.

. Signor Mazzoni is giving musical re-unions at his residence, 15 Charlotte Street, Bloomsbury. A new "Mass" from his pen was lately given by his pupils and friends, and is reported to be a work of musical value.

Some valuable old and new instruments, and a good collection of sterling music, will be offered for sale at Messrs. Puttick and Simpson's, Leicester Square, on Monday next.

It is not often that a musician succeeds in making a fortune out of his profession. Such cases, however, do occur. The will of the late Mr. J. Brockley, well known as a painstaking teacher and writer of some popular songs, has been sworn under £30,000.

Among other new models by the same firm, Messrs. Chappell & Co., have, it is stated, just completed a new oblique grand pianoforte, with dampers in bass. The tone is as powerful as a small grand, and thereby giving greater facility to the player in rendering each note clear and distinct one from the other, and in the execution of *staccato*, or *sostenuto* passages.

By permission of Major-Gen. Smyth, commanding the district, the officers at the garrison at Woolwich are to give, on April 27th, at the theatre in that town, a performance of the drama entitled "Time Tries All." This is to be followed on the same evening by the production of a new operetta written by Mr. T. M. Watson, with music by the Cavaliere Zavertal, bandmaster of the Royal Artillery.

In the number of *Punch* for this week will be found an amusing description of the libretto of "Colomba," together with some clever little woodcuts, illustrative of its queer characters. The German writer is terribly chaffed over his extraordinary production by our witty contemporary, and it is stated that the much criticised *Times* critic, "Humorous Hueffer," has been already engaged to write the next Gaiety burlesque.

The fourth annual report on the music of the past year at St. Paul's Cathedral has been issued by the esteemed succentor, the Rev. Dr. Sparrow Simpson. During the year 129 different services were sung, and it should be added that more than 495 anthems have been given in two years time. T his remarkable record of good work reflects high credit upon the succentor and upon the distinguished organist of St. Paul's, Dr. J. Stainer.

Of the students who went up for examination to the Royal College of Music with the intention of making the violin their principal study, five only succeeded in satisfying the examiners. Among the names of those elected is found that of Master Percy Victor Sharman, of Gipsy Hill, a pupil of Mr. E. Eberwein. About two years ago, the remarkably clever playing of this lad at a concert was noticed in this journal, and a bright future predicted for him.

Mr. C. Vincent, Mus.Bac., for many years the efficient organist of Tavistock parish church, has obtained an appointment at Hampstead, and having been equally fortunate in securing the good opinion of the people of Tavistock, of whom he is now taking his leave, he has recently been the recipient at their hands of a gratifying testimonial. For five years Mr. Vincent has acted as the conductor of the Tavistock Musical Society, the members of which initiated and promoted the movement which resulted in the presentation. The fund was so liberally subscribed to that its promoters were able to purchase a handsome silver-mounted ivory *baton*, and a silver teapot. The teapot bore the inscription, "Presented, with a *baton*, to Charles Vincent, Esq., Mus.Bac., Oxon., by the members of the Tavistock Musical Society, of which he was for five years the conductor, Easter, 1883," and the presentation was made by Mr. M. T. Leamon, late president of the Society, accompanied by the heartiest wishes for Mr. Vincent's future success.

The Querist.

REPLIES.

"PRODUCTION OF THE VOICE." E. A. T. will find Behnke's "Mechanism of the Voice," 3rd edition (Curwen and Sons), the most philosophical, lucid, and practical of any work on the subject.—E. ROBINSON—E. S. writes to the same effect: "The Mechanism of the Human Voice," by Emil Behnke, 3s. (Curwen and Sons, 8, Warwick Lane, E.C.); but a new work by the same author is in hand, which I believe will contain photographs of the interior of the larynx, while in the act of singing.

OBOE.—"A Complete Method," by Barret, 16s. (Lafleur and Son, Green Street, Leicester Square). There is also a small one, a number of the "Bandsman," published by Rudall and Co., but Barrett's book is the thing, if "A. Reed" means serious study.—E. S.

Service Lists.

FIFTH SUNDAY AFTER EASTER,

APRIL 29nd.

London.

ST. PAUL'S CATHEDRAL.—Morn.: Service, Te Deum and Benedictus, Prout in F; Introit, Christ the Lord is risen to-day (Hymn 131); Communion Service, Prout in F. Even.: Service, Magnificat and Nunc Dimittis, Steggall in C; Anthem, When Israel out of Egypt came (Mendelssohn).

WESTMINSTER ABBEY.—Morn.: Service, Turle in D. Offertory, Collard in D. Aft.: Service, Turle in D; Anthem. Hear my prayer (Mendelssohn).

TEMPLE CHURCH.—Morn.: Service, Te Deum Laudamus, Garrett in E; Apostles' Creed, Harmonized Monotone; Anthem, Hear my prayer (Mendelssohn). Even.: Service, Garrett in E flat; Apostles' Creed, Harmonized Monotone; Anthem, I will love Thee, O Lord (Clarke).

LINCOLN'S INN CHAPEL. — Morn.: Service, Aldrich in G: Kyrie, Aldrich in G; Anthem, O how sweet are Thy words (Steggall). Even.: Service, Aldrich in G; Anthem, Call to remembrance, O Lord (Battishill).

ALL SAINTS, MARGARET STREET. — Morn.: Service, Te Deum, Gauntlett in F; Benedictus, Monk in F; Communion Service, Weber in G; Offertory Anthem, This is the day (Alwyn). Even.: Service, Gounod in D; Anthem, In the beginning, and The heavens declare (Haydn).

ST. AUGUSTINE AND ST. FAITH, WATLING STREET.— Morn.: Service, Stainer in E flat; Offertory, Let your light (Stainer). Even.: Service, Gadsby in C; Anthem, My hope is in the everlasting (Stainer).

ST. BARNABAS, MARYLEBONE.—Morn.: Service, Te Deum and Benedictus, Hopkins in F; Anthem, Turn thy face (Attwood); Kyrie and Nicene Creed, Harvey Löhr in A minor. Even.: Service, Magnificat and Nunc Dimittis, Hopkins in F; Anthem, The wilderness (Goss).

ST. BOTOLPH, ALDGATE.—Morn.: Service, Te Deum, Dykes in G; Anthems, Now we are ambassadors, and How lovely are the messengers (Mendelssohn); Kyrie, Hoyte. Even.: Service, Magnificat and Nunc Dimittis, Stainer in A; Anthem, The wilderness (Goss).

CHILDREN'S HOME CHAPEL, BONNER ROAD, E.—Morn.: Service, Anthems, Holy is the Lord (Vogler), and, All ye nations praise the Lord (Müller). Aft.: Service, Anthems, Lo! my Shepherd's hand (Haydn); O praise the Lord (Mifils).

CHRIST CHURCH, CLAPHAM.—Morn.: Service, Te Deum, Plain-song; Kyrie and Credo, Weber in E flat; Offertory An, them, I know that my Redeemer liveth (Handel); Sanctus, Benedictus, Agnus Dei, and Gloria in excelsis, Weber. Even.: Service, Magnificat and Nunc Dimittis, Stainer in A; Anthem, Great and marvellous are Thy works (Boyce).

FOUNDLING CHAPEL.—Morn.: Service, Te Deum, Goss in F; Benedictus, Smart in F; Anthem, Blessed be the God and Father (Wesley). Aft.: Service, Cooke in G; Anthem, Sing praises (Gounod).

HOLY TRINITY, TULSE HILL. — Morn.: Chant Service. Even.: Service, Stainer in E flat; Anthem, Praise the Lord, O my soul (Stark).

ST. JAMES'S PRIVATE EPISCOPAL CHAPEL, SOUTHWARK. —Morn.: Service, Introit, Saviour of men (Gounod); Communion Service, Weber in G. Even.: Service, Gadsby in C; Anthem, Rejoice, O my spirit, and The lamb that was slain (Bach).

ST. MAGNUS, LONDON BRIDGE.—Morn.: Service, Opening Anthem, O Lord, correct me (Coward) ; Te Deum and Jubilate, Attwood in F ; Kyrie, Arnold. Even.: Service, Magnificat and Nunc Dimittis, Attwood in F ; Anthem, Blessed be the God (Wesley).

ST. MARGARET PATTENS, ROOD LANE, FENCHURCH STREET.—Morn.: Service, Te Deum, Sullivan in D ; Benedictus, Dykes in F ; Communion Service, Offertory Anthem, Incline thine ear (Himmel) ; Kyrie, Credo, Sanctus, Benedictus, Agnus Dei, and Gloria in excelsis, Schubert in B flat. Even.: Service, Magnificat and Nunc Dimittis, Oakeley in E flat ; Anthem, Hear my prayer (Mendelssohn).

ST. MARY BOLTONS, WEST BROMPTON, S.W.—Morn.: Service, Te Deum, Hopkins in G ; Benedictus, Goss in C ; Communion Service, Kyrie, Credo, Sanctus, Benedictus, Agnus Dei, and Gloria in excelsis, Eyre in E flat ; Offertory, Stainer. Even.: Service, Magnificat and Nunc Dimittis, Gounod in D ; Anthem, Fear not, O land (Goss).

ST. MICHAEL'S, CORNHILL. — Morn.: Service, Benedicite, Best ; Jubilate, Boyce in A ; Anthem, All Thy works ; Praise thee, O Lord (Thorne) ; Kyrie and Creed, Marbecke. Even.: Service, Magnificat and Nunc Dimittis, Hoyte in B flat ; Anthem, Thou, O God, art praised in Zion (Greene).

ST. PAUL'S, BOW COMMON, E.—Morn.: Service, Te Deum and Benedictus, Chants ; Communion Service, Kyrie, Credo, Sanctus, and Gloria in excelsis, Garrett in E flat ; Benedictus and Agnus Dei, Verulam in F ; Offertory, Calkin. Even.: Service, Magnificat and Nunc Dimittis, Tours in F ; Anthem, On thee each soul awaits, and Achieved is the glorious work (Haydn).

ST. PETER'S (EATON SQUARE).—Morn.: Service, Te Deum, Garrett in F. Even.: Service, Tours in F ; Anthem, The wilderness (Wesley).

ST. PETER'S, LEIGHAM COURT ROAD, STREATHAM, S.W. —Morn.: Service, Kyrie, Credo, Sanctus, and Gloria in excelsis, Dykes in F ; Benedictus and Agnus Dei, Sutton in F ; Alleluia, Chantwise ; Offertory, Christ being raised (Elvey) ; Post Communion, The eyes of all (Redhead). Even.: Service, Magnificat, Gladstone in F ; Anthem, Blessed be the God and Father (Wesley).

ST. PETER'S, VERE STREET, W.—Even.: Service, Magnificat and Nunc Dimittis, Tours in F ; Anthem, If ye love me (Monk).

ST. PAUL'S, AVENUE ROAD, SOUTH HAMPSTEAD.—Morn.: Service, Te Deum, Calkin in B flat ; Jubilate, Boyce in A. Even.: Service, Magnificat and Nunc Dimittis, Gounod in D ; Anthem, The Lord is loving unto every man (Garrett).

Country.

ARDINGLY COLLEGE, SUSSEX.—Morn.: Communion Service, Calkin in G. Even.: Service, Walmisley in D minor ; Anthem, Fear not O land (Goss).

ST. ASAPH CATHEDRAL. — Morn.: Service, Whitfeld in E ; Anthem, Awake up My glory (Wise). Even.: Service, The Litany ; Anthem, O give thanks (Sydenham).

ASHBURNE CHURCH, DERBYSHIRE. — Morn.: Service, Garrett in F (throughout). Even.: Service, Garrett in F ; Anthem, selections from Last Judgment (Spohr).

BEDDINGTON CHURCH, SURREY. — Morn.: Service, Te Deum, King in F ; Benedictus, Tuckerman in F ; Introit, Lord in Thy name (Hymn 143) ; Communion Service, Garrett in F. Even.: Service, King in F ; Anthem, I will give thanks (Barnby).

BRISTOL CATHEDRAL.—Morn.: Service, Attwood in F. Aft.: Service, Attwood in F ; Anthem, Praise the Lord (Mozart).

BIRMINGHAM (ST. CYPRIAN'S, HAY MILLS).—Morn.: Service, Stainer in A and D ; Anthem, Why do the Heathen and Let us break their bonds (Handel). Even.: Service, Smith in B flat ; Anthem, O clap your hands (Stainer).

CANTERBURY CATHEDRAL.—Morn.: Service, Hopkins in G ; Te Deum, Hake in G ; Jubilate, Behold, now praise (Oakeley) ; Sanctus and Communion, Rogers in D. Even.: Service, Goss in A ; Anthem, O where shall wisdom be found (Boyce).

CARLISLE CATHEDRAL.—Morn.: Service, Barnby in E ; Introit, We wait for (Armes) ; Kyrie, Barnby in E ; Nicene Creed, Harmonised Monotone. Even.: Service, Barnby in E ; Anthem, The wilderness (Goss).

CHESTER (ST. MARY'S CHURCH).—Morn.: Service, Tearne in C ; Communion Service, Tearne in A. Even.: Service, Barnby in E ; Anthem, O taste and see, and How gracious the Lord is (Goss).

DONCASTER (PARISH CHURCH).—Morn.: Service, Boyce in F. Even.: Service, Hopkins in F ; Anthem, They that go down (Attwood).

DUBLIN, ST. PATRICK'S (NATIONAL) CATHEDRAL.—Morn.: Service, Te Deum and Jubilate, Mendelssohn in A ; Anthem, The wilderness (Wesley). Even.: Service, Cantate Deus Miseratur, Hayes in E flat ; Anthem, Grant, we beseech Thee (Mendelssohn) ; I behold, and lo (Blow).

EXETER CATHEDRAL. — Morn.: Service, Gilbert in E. Even.: Service, Gilbert in E ; Anthem, Come hither (Crotch).

ELY CATHEDRAL.—Morn.: Service, Roberts in D ; Kyrie and Credo, Roberts in D ; Gloria (Ely) ; Anthem, O Lord, how manifold (Barnby). Even.: Service, Roberts in D ; Anthem, O clap your hands (Stainer).

HIGHFIELD, SHEFFIELD (ST. BARNABAS' CHURCH).—Morn.: Service, Introductory Voluntary, Hopkins ; Responses, Tallis ; Te Deum, Jackson ; Jubilate, Woodward ; Anthem, The glory of the Lord (Goss) ; Kyrie and Gloria Tibi, Tallis. Even.: Service, Introductory Voluntary, Merkel ; Responses, Tallis ; Deus Miseratur, Pring ; Anthem, The Grace of God that bringeth Salvation (Barnby).

LEEDS PARISH CHURCH.—Morn.: Service, Mendelssohn in D ; Anthem, O come, let us (Mendelssohn) ; Kyrie and Creed, Turle in D. Even.: Service, Walmisley in D minor ; Anthem, In the beginning (Haydn).

LICHFIELD CATHEDRAL.—Morn.: Service, Smart in F Anthem, O Lord, have mercy (Pergolesi). Even.: Service, Cantate and Deus Miseratur, Hayes in E flat ; Anthem, Distracted with care and anguish (Haydn).

LIVERPOOL CATHEDRAL. — Aft.: Service, Magnificat and Nunc Dimittis, Stainer in E flat ; Anthem, Thou, O God, art praised in Zion (Burstall).

LLANDAFF CATHEDRAL.—Morn.: Service, Goss in A ; The Litany. Even.: Service, Hopkins in F ; Anthem, Then shall the righteous, and He that shall endure (Mendelssohn)

MANCHESTER CATHEDRAL. — Morn.: Service, Wesley in F ; Anthem, O Lord how manifold (Barnby). Aft.: Service, Wesley in F ; Anthem, Hear my Prayer (Stroud).

MANCHESTER (ST. BENEDICT'S). — Morn.: Service, Te Deum, Sullivan in D ; Kyrie, Credo, and Gloria in excelsis, Steggall in G ; Sanctus, Benedictus, and Agnus Dei, Weber in G. Even.: Service, Magnificat and Nunc Dimittis, Stainer.

MANCHESTER (ST. JOHN BAPTIST, HULME).—Morn.: Service, Kyrie, Credo, Sanctus, Benedictus, Agnus Dei, and Gloria in excelsis, Tours in F. Even.: Service, Magnificat and Nunc Dimittis, Bunnett in F.

SHEFFIELD PARISH CHURCH. — Morn.: Service, Kyrie, Tours in F. Even.: Service, Cantate Domine and Deus miserreatur, Chants ; Anthem, Plead thou my cause (Mozart).

SHERBORNE ABBEY. — Morn.: Service, Kyrie, Lee in D ; Offertories, Barnby. Even.: Service, Anthem, I will lift up mine eyes (Whitfeld).

SOUTHAMPTON (ST. MARY'S CHURCH).—Morn.: Service, Te Deum and Benedictus, Stainer in E flat ; Introit, Jesus said (Stainer) ; Communion Service, Stainer in E flat ; Offertory, Let your light (Stainer) ; Paternoster, Hoyte. Even.: Service, Magnificat and Nunc Dimittis, Stainer in E flat ; Apostles' Creed, Harmonised Monotone ; Benedictus and Agnus Dei, Agutter in B flat ; Anthem, O taste and see (Goss).

WELLS CATHEDRAL.—Morn.: Service, Bennett in E ; Introit, Blessed are the pure in heart (Macfarren) ; Kyrie, Clarke in E. Even.: Service, Elvey in A ; Anthem, Lift up thine eyes (Goss).

WORCESTER CATHEDRAL. — Morn.: Service, Smart in F ; Anthem, From the rising of the sun (Ouseley). Even.: Service, Smart in F ; Anthem, Hear my prayer (Mendelssohn).

APPOINTMENT.

Mr. JOHN SYMONS has been appointed Organist and Choirmaster of St. Katherine Cree Church, London.

Particulars of Charter of the Royal College, and several important articles are held over.

ERRATUM.—An awkward error in the notice of last week may have puzzled many readers. Mr. Walter C. Macfarren's sonata in C minor, for piano and 'cello, should have been said to have been written *more suo*, or, in his own individual style ; but " more suo " was given as the title of the sonata.

Musical Standard

A NEWSPAPER FOR MUSICIANS PROFESSIONAL AND AMATEUR

No. 979. Vol. XXIV. FOURTH SERIES.   SATURDAY, MAY 5, 1883.   WEEKLY: PRICE 3D.

THE MUSICAL STANDARD is published every Saturday, price 3d., by post, 3½d.; and may be had of any bookseller or newsagent by ordering its regular supply.

SUBSCRIPTION.—*The Musical Standard* is posted to subscribers at 15s. a year; half a year, 7s. 6d., payable in advance.

The rate is the same to France, Belgium, Germany, Italy, United States, and Canada.

Post Office Orders to be made payable to the Publisher, William Reeves, 185, Fleet Street, London, or to the West-end Agents, Messrs. Weekes & Co., 14, Hanover Street, Regent Street, W.

ADVERTISEMENTS.—The charge for ordinary advertisements in *The Musical Standard* is 2s. 6d. for three lines or less; and 6d. for each line (10 words) in addition. "Organist wanted," 3s. 6d. for 3 lines or less. A reduction is made for a series.

FRONT PAGE.—Concert and auction advertisements, &c., are inserted in the front page of *The Musical Standard*, and charged one-third in addition to the ordinary rates. Other advertisements will be inserted on the front page, or in the leader page, if desired, at the same terms.

CRYSTAL PALACE,—SATURDAY CONCERT, MAY 5th, at 3.10.—The programme will include Overture, "Les Deux Journées" (Cherubini); Ballade and Polonaise for Violin and Orchestra (Vieuxtemps); MS. Symphony in R, No. 1 (Schubert), completed by J. F. Barnett (first time of performance); Solo for Violin, "Airs Russes" (Wieniawski). Vocalist, Miss Thudichum (her first appearance at these Concerts); Solo Violin, Mdlle. Teresa Tua (her first appearance in England). Conductor, Mr. August Manns. Seats, 2s. 6d., 2s., and 6d.

PHILHARMONIC SOCIETY.—Patroness, Her most Gracious Majesty THE QUEEN.—Conductor, Mr. W. G. CUSINS. FIFTH CONCERT, ST. JAMES'S HALL, WEDNESDAY NEXT, May 9th.—Pastoral Symphony (Beethoven); Motett (Cherubini); Violin Concerto, No. 1 (Max Bruch); Pianoforte Concerto in F minor (Chopin); Marche Hongroise (Berlioz); and Symphonic Ballad, written expressly for the Society by A. C. Mackenzie (first performance). Signor Merzwinsky, Mr. Vernon Rigby, M. De Pachmann, and Signorina Teresina Tua (her first appearance in London).—Tickets, 2s. 6d. to 15s., of the usual agents. Admission, 1s.

By order, HENRY HERSEE, Hon. Sec.

In the High Court of Justice, Chancery Division: Blockley v. Blockley.—Stock of Copyright and non-Copyright Music Plates, Lease, Goodwill, &c.

MR. WILLIAM SIMPSON (of the firm of Puttick and Simpson), the person appointed by the Judge in the above action, will SELL by AUCTION, at the Gallery, 47, Leicester Square, London, W.C., on Monday, June 11th, 1883, and following days, at 10 minutes past 1 o'clock precisely each day, the LEASE of the PREMISES situate and being No. 3, Argyll Street, Regent Street, W., together with the trade furniture and fittings, goodwill, and book debts of the music publishing business, so successfully carried on by the late Mr. John Blockley. Also (in lots) the important stock of copyright and non-copyright music plates, and the printed stock attaching thereto.—Catalogues will shortly be ready, and may be had on receipt of six stamps, of Messrs. Pritchard, Englefield, & Co., Solicitors, Painter's Hall, Little Trinity Lane, E.C.; or of the Auctioneer as above.

COLLEGE OF ORGANISTS.

TUESDAY, June 5th, "Some Musical Ethics and Analogies." H. C. BANISTER, Esq.—TUESDAY, July 3rd, a Paper will be read by F. J. SAWYER, Esq. Mus.Bac.
N.B.—These Meetings will take place at the NEUMEYER HALL, Hart-street, Bloomsbury, W.C., commencing at 8.
The Midsummer Examination will be held on July 10th and 11th for Associateship, and on July 12th, for Fellowship.

E. H. TURPIN, Hon. Secretary.

95, Great Russell-street, Bloomsbury, W.C.

KING'S COLLEGE, CAMBRIDGE.—A CHORAL SCHOLARSHIP (for a tenor voice), value £90 a year for three years, will be offered for competition on July 11, 1883, among candidates under twenty-five years of age. Besides proficiency in music, a knowledge of elementary classics and mathematics will be required. Further information will be given by the SENIOR DEAN, King's College, Cambridge, to whom testimonials as to character and musical ability should be sent not later than June 12.

SOCIETY OF ARTS' PRACTICAL EXAMINATIONS in VOCAL and INSTRUMENTAL MUSIC.—The Examination for the London Centre will this year commence on Monday the 11th June. Full particulars on application to the Secretary.
H. TRUEMAN WOOD, Secretary.
Society's House, Adelphi, London, W.C.

VIOLIN.—HERR POLONASKI (Violinist), open to ENGAGEMENTS for Concerts, Musical At Homes, and Violin or Accompaniment Lessons.—For Terms, please Address, HERR POLONASKI, 16, Wharfdale-street, South Kensington, S.W.

A FREE EDUCATION is offered to BOYS WITH GOOD VOICES in the Choir of S. Luke's, Kentish Town.—Apply to CARLTON C. MICHELL, 31, Oseney Crescent, Camden Road, N.W.

WANTED immediately, TWO LEADING BOYS for the Choir of S. Luke's, Kentish Town; £10 a year and education free.—Apply to CARLTON C. MICHELL, 31, Oseney Crescent, Camden Road, N.W.

ORGANIST, who will also act as CHOIRMASTER, WANTED in July, for the Baptist Chapel, West Street, Rochdale. Instrument new, three manuals, thirty-nine stops.—Applications, with testimonials and stating salary required, to be sent not later than May 15th, to Mr. RICHARD WATSON, Thrum Hall, Rochdale.

B. WILLIAMS, PATERNOSTER ROW.—Having purchased the lease and goodwill of the above old-established business, together with the very extensive trade stock, I beg to announce that, with the old staff of assistants which I have specially retained, I shall endeavour to carry on the concern with as much satisfaction as heretofore. The publishing department (of which I have had the sole management since the death of Mr. B. Williams) will receive every attention.
LUCY J. MULLEN, (Daughter of the late Mr. B. Williams).

ALL WHO POSSESS A PIANOFORTE and canot play it, may now play at once, without any previous knowledge of Music, by ROYLANCE'S NUMERICAL SYSTEM, which contains a FIGURED DIAGRAM to fit on the Keyboard of any Pianoforte or Harmonium, and a choice selection of forty SACRED and SECULAR MELODIES, composed for the use of those who have no time to study Music. Thousands are now able to play who did not believe such a thing possible. The diagram alone will be found most useful to Professors for teaching purposes. 6d. nett.—Price 2s. 6d. nett; post free 33 stamps.
C. ROYLANCE, 184, Tottenham Court-road; and all Music Sellers.

Musical Intelligence.

CRYSTAL PALACE CONCERTS.

PROGRAMME.

Overture, "Walpurgis Nacht" .... Mendelssohn.
Recit. and Air, "Lascia ch'io pianga" Handel.
         Miss Mary Lemmens.
   (Her first appearance at the Crystal Palace.)
Concerto for pianoforte and, or-
   chestra, in D minor.......... Mozart.
Solo Piano .... M. Vladimir de Pachmann.
    (His first appearance at the Crystal Palace.)
Symphony No. 4, in D major...... Thomas Wingham.
     (First time of performance.)
Ballade de la Mandragore, "Jean
   de Nivelle" .... Leo Delibes.
        Miss Mary Lemmens.
Solos for Pianoforte .... Chopin.
     Nocturne in F minor.
     Etude, Op. 10, No. 12.
     Etude, Op. 25, No. 9.
     Tarantella, Op. 42.
     M. Vladimir de Pachmann.
Hungarian Rhapsody, "Teleki" .. Liszt.

Conductor   -   -   -   AUGUST MANNS.

The idea of foreign musicians being preferred by the British public to their own countrymen, is now, happily, an exploded one. Years ago, doubtless, there were many silly people who thought it fine to praise them at the expense of talented Englishmen. This kind of prejudice, was, on the other hand, also frequently manifested against foreigners ; even accomplished organists, as well as their bellows-blowers, have been known to treat them with some degree of contempt. Take the following as an example :—Mendelssohn was once playing upon one of our church organs, and after giving out the subject of the Hundredth Psalm, proceeded to extemporize upon it, but in the middle of his grand performance came suddenly to a stop for lack of wind in the bellows. The blower could by no means be induced to resume his exertions, but coolly sitting down protested that he could not be dictated to by any foreigner "whatsomever," and that having been blower there for thirty years, he ought to know how many strokes it took to do the Old Hundredth. Having already given the proper number and two over, no more was on any consideration to be got out of him. Happily we have lived to see Englishmen and foreigners treated pretty much alike. Certainly it is so at the Crystal Palace, both as regards composers and professors generally. During the last few months many works by English composers, including three symphonies, have been produced here, so that no complaint can be made of the compositions of our own countrymen being set on one side.

Of Mr. Wingham's symphony I cannot unfortunately say much at this time, for although through the courtesy of Mr. Manns I can attend the private rehearsals, I was on this occasion unable to do so. I have therefore only heard it once, and without the aid of a score. I am, however, convinced that it is the work of a highly accomplished and very able orchestral composer. In the first movement—which contains many beautiful and spontaneous passages—the influence of Mozart is distinctly felt, and the development of the two principal themes seems almost worthy of that great master. In the adagio the light and graceful manner of Bizet may be traced, but in the finale a more ambitious and less successful attempt is made in the way of effect. I must not forget to mention the scherzo and trio as being perfect models of Mr. Wingham's own happy manner of writing. The performance of the work was very successful, and Mr. Wingham, who was present, was cordially cheered by the audience.

M. De Pachmann was no less appreciated here for his charming performances on the piano than he has lately been at St. James's Hall ; and Miss Mary Lemmens, though at first suffering from slight nervousness, was very successful in her well chosen songs.   R. S.

Respecting the symphony, Mr. T. L. Southgate writes :—
In Mr. Wingham's new symphony another English success has been scored. In this work the composer has revealed the possession of yet higher powers than he has hitherto been credited with. The favourite pupil of Sterndale Bennett, in the pieces that he has as yet produced, one sees a reflection of the grace and refinement of feeling that is characteristic of our lamented English composer's music. But in this, No. 4 Symphony, Mr.

Wingham has apparently taken up new ground, and shown an amount of originality, vigour, and heroic strength, that he has not before exhibited. The main themes employed are, in almost every instance, remarkable for their striking freshness and novelty of form. They are subjects that a widely read and trained musician on hearing would at once exclaim, "Here indeed is something new." But more than mere leading themes, however good they may be, are required to make a satisfactory symphony. There is the treatment and elaboration of the themes, the episodial work, and the orchestration ; and, independently of these requisites, a composer must have the gift of flowing thought, and power to knit his materials into a continuous texture, or his work will be but fragmentary, and lack unity in design. Mr. Wingham's symphony certainly possesses these qualifications, besides other features of considerable importance. Noteworthy is the vigour and fire of his episodes, especially those in the first movement, their remarkable treatment setting off to advantage the clear-cut main themes. Both the first and last movements contain an astonishing amount of energy and vigour, the violin parts being brilliantly written, particularly in the upper part of the register. The principal subject of the slow movement is a theme of much intensity and passion, while its second subject (allotted to the 'celli), is a placid, refined thought, in marked contrast with its predecessor. The whole of the andante is delicately conceived and coloured, being more expressive of sweet pastoral grace, than of any special striving after depth of feeling. The minuet is singularly quaint ; noteworthy in the trio is the wild rush of the fiddles, as against the quiet passages written for the other instruments. The march-like subject of the finale with its strong diatonic harmonies appears a little heavy for the last movement of a symphony, but the second subject presents a grateful contrast, and the spirited coda brings the work to a brilliant ending. Mr. Wingham's symphony may perhaps sound too bright to ears accustomed to much of the plodding dulness founded on modern German models, but the ingenious construction and ripe scholarship it exhibits, together with its spontaneity, combine to place it in the very front rank of English symphonic works. It is to be hoped that Mr. Manns will soon accord it another hearing. . . . .

THE PHILHARMONIC SOCIETY.

The programme of the fourth concert given at St. James's Hall, April 25th, was as follows :—

PART I.

Overture ("Hermann und Dorothea")............ Schumann.
Concerto, Pianoforte, in E flat .... Beethoven.
       Madame Sophie Menter.
Vocal Scena (MS.) ("Mary Stuart's Farewell ") .. Benedict.
      (First time.)
       Madame Patey.
The Prize Overture .... Oliver A. King.

PART II.

Symphony in A (No. 7)......................... Beethoven.
Canzonet ("She never told her love ")......... Haydn.
       Madame Patey.
Prelude in A .... Bach.
Barcarole .... Schubert.
Solo, Pianoforte ("Wedding March").......... Mendelssohn.
       Madame Sophie Menter.
Rhapsodie Hongroise (No. 4) .... Liszt.

Schumann's overture, with which the concert opened, is but a dry production, and is certainly not written in his best manner. It was intended as the introduction to an operetta founded on Goethe's poem, the commencement of which represents the departure of the French troops for the war. This accounts for the employment of the Republican hymn, the Marseillaise, fragments of which are interwoven with the music of the overture. Schumann was apparently fond of the theme, for it may be remembered he uses it with admirable effect in his fine song of "The two Grenadiers." The treatment of it in the overture is singularly mild for so warlike a subject ; it is almost always given *piano*. Although the overture contains some ingenious polyphonic writing, the work seems to have been done without much inspiration, and lacks the brightness and warmth of the life scenes it is intended to illustrate. Beethoven's grand Concerto in E flat, the last of the noble five that the master wrote for the piano, and worthily termed the "Emperor," demands for its due rendering an "Empress" of the instrument. And just such an artiste is Madame Sophie Menter. She is confessedly at the head of the fair sex players, and it would be difficult to name a piece better suited for the display of her exceptionally gifted powers. The grandeur of the first movement, the serene tenderness of the second, and the energetic gladness of the rondo found alike a satisfactory exposition in her playing. Her delivery of the opening of the allegro may have seemed a little hard, and she certainly took some liberties with the *tempo*, so far as the precise time of the respective note-divisions was concerned; but looking to the powerful majestic nature of the opening—as soon as the grand arpeggios are over—it will be seen that firmness and dynamic power are demanded of the player, rather than mere formalness. Sympathetic appreciation was shown to perfection in the noble hymn-like adagio, while the rhythmical phrasing of the brilliant finale afforded an exhibition of rare union of technical skill combined with the perfection of taste. Of the lady's subsequent solos, she gave an excellent rendering of Bach's fine Prelude in A, and of Schubert's delicate little barcarolle; but the choice she made of Liszt's florid fantasia on Mendelssohn's "Wedding March" is to be condemned. It is nothing better than an act of offensive charlatanry to treat this gorgeously coloured orchestral piece from the wondrous "Midsummer Night's Dream" music as a vehicle for pianism. No doubt the fearful difficulties that Abbé Liszt has introduced into his arrangement are calculated to excite astonishment among the Philistines, but the hisses which greeted Madame Menter at the close of the display were significant of the opinion formed by a Philharmonic audience over the achievement. Surely, this great artiste must know that there are hundreds of real pianoforte pieces far more worthy of her powers than was the acrobatic travesty she had selected to play on this occasion.

The symphony chosen for the concert, the No. 7 of Beethoven, is ever welcome and popular, chiefly perhaps on account of the singular contrast that its movements present to one another. The solemn tone of its lovely slow movement, with its heavenly melody in the major, breaking on the ear with singular charm after the close, rich harmony of its mysterious opening, is indeed a revelation of highest genius. The feelings that the last movement induces, with its bright gaiety and powerful rhythmic accents, are of a very different type to those the allegretto calls forth. To the contemplative hearer, the latter may suggest the subject of a placid lake embosomed amidst lofty many hued mountains; the tints of its calm surface changing ever and anon with each passing cloud. But when, through a rift, the glorious sun lights up the scene, a marvellous change takes place. The clear bright colours of the major mode have supplanted sombreness, and the warmth of glowing life has taken the place of cold, though majestic contemplation. The *brio* of the concluding allegro calls to mind the incessant movement and unrestrained gaiety of some country fair, with its picturesque assembly bent on through enjoyment. Notable in this movement to the musician, is the remarkable descent of the five chromatic intervals of the melody at the end of the second section of the main theme; this passage going down chromatically from F sharp to D natural, instead of conveying (as do most chromatic indulgences) a sense of weakness and effeminacy, really give a feeling of strength and determination, marvellous in its power.

The two novelties the programme contained attracted a considerable amount of attention. The chief was the performance of the overture which gained the prize offered by the Philharmonic Society. The author of the work, selected from among the forty-six sent in for competition by Sir Jules Benedict and Mr. Otto Goldschmidt, was Mr. Oliver King. This gentleman was formerly a choir-boy of St. Andrew's Church, Wells Street. He was afterwards a pupil of Mr. J. Barnby, and subsequently studied at the Leipsic Conservatoire; he is now residing at Ottawa, Canada. If truth be meted out with justice, it is impossible to report favourably of Mr. King's essay. The form of his overture is orthodox, the coda however being but indistinctly marked; the themes are trivial, while their treatment and working out is poor, and exhibits neither freshness nor profound scholarship. There is much repetition in the overture; the work is of course correctly written, but its general tone is so monotonous and wanting in contrasts, that its performance excited but little interest. It must be allowed that Mr. King writes with clearness, and his treatment is never harsh or unpleasant; but these qualities, it may be pointed out, do not compensate for a lack of inspiration, and that prime requisite has been denied to him, so far as this new overture is concerned.

The second novelty was a new vocal MS. *scena* illustrating the monologue delivered by Mary Stuart, translated from Schiller's famous tragedy of that name. The piece is written in a lengthened and ambitious form. It commences with a recitative, occasionally interrupted with brief orchestral sentences; to this succeeds a more formal melody, and this is followed by a short intermezzo leading to a finale. The words roam over so wide a field and are so very varied in sentiment, that the excerpt from the play seems hardly fitted for close musical treatment. This comment, however, applies only to the concert-room; on the stage, the Wagnerian theory might be employed with better chance of success. Sir Jules Benedict's setting is marked by that elegant grace, smoothness, and thorough musicianship that characterizes all he writes; but viewed as a whole, it can hardly be accepted as a faithful reflection of Schiller's singularly touching words. The declamatory phrases are not intense enough, and there was too much of cold uniformity to illustrate the alternate tenderness and passion of the scene. Madame Patey's fine voice was heard to advantage in the piece, the composer conducting it himself; the orchestral accompaniments were very raggedly played. In Haydn's favourite canzonet, the lady had the advantage of Mr. C. E. Stephens's refined accompaniment on the pianoforte. Liszt's remarkable and original Hungarian rhapsody (No. 4), through its performances at the Crystal Palace concerts, has now become pretty well known to Londoners. The band, under their able chief, Mr. Cusins, gave a spirited rendering of the piece, but the tempo at the close was hardly accelerated enough. The wild fury with which the Hungarians themselves play such music electrifies their audience, but this sort of fervid rendering cannot be reproduced by foreigners to the Maygar land. Cherubini's MS. motet is promised for the next concert.
T. L. SOUTHGATE.

MUSIC IN READING.

(From our Own Correspondent.)

A morning concert, of more than ordinary importance, was given here, in the New Town Hall, on Thursday, April 26th, in aid of the fund for founding a Berkshire Scholarship at the Royal College of Music.

The Berkshire Musical Association, including the Windsor and Eton Amateur Madrigal Society, the Berkshire Amateur Musical Society, and the Wallingford Philharmonic Society, together with amateur members of the Oxford and other musical societies, formed the chorus; and a complete band of forty instruments, principally selected from the Crystal Palace orchestra, and led by Herr Rosenthal, occupied the orchestra. With Mr. Arthur Sullivan, Mr. John Francis Barnett, and Mr. Walter Parratt, as conductors, the material gave promise of a musical performance of unusual interest and effect; and the result was a concert of a kind seldom heard in provincial towns, except at the great festivals.

"The Martyr of Antioch," conducted by Mr. Sullivan, was the principal attraction of the programme, and there is no need to refer in detail to that well-known work, one of the few great examples of English composition. With the advantage of the composer's direction, the many striking points of the instrumentation were well brought out, and the singing of the chorus was most praiseworthy. In the more difficult parts of the great "Chorus of Sun-worshippers," an occasional want of decision and unsteadiness were noticeable with the tenors and basses, who were the weaker part of the chorus; but the sopranos and contraltos sang with remarkable brightness and a careful observance of all marks of expression.

The unaccompanied "Funeral Anthem" was the triumph of the choral singing, and much care had evidently been given to its preparation. In the "Chorus of Heathen Maidens and Christians," the voices were drowned by the orchestra, but this would be rather the fault of the chorus being disproportionately small. The solo vocalists were Miss Annie Marriott, Miss Josephine Cravino, Mr. Harper Kearton, and Mr. Barrington Foote. Miss Marriott earned every acknowledgment of her earnest and successful efforts with the difficult and dramatic music of the soprano, and Mr. Harper Kearton sang the tenor music with a purity and refinement which was especially applauded. Miss Cravino also made a good impression, but the voice and style of Mr. Barrington Foote seemed scarcely in sympathy with the bass solo music. Upon the whole the performance was an excellent one, the dramatic force of the music appealing irresistibly to a "morning" audience, fashionable, and therefore inclined to be somewhat cold. But the genius of the composer was recognized by a most hearty recall at the conclusion of the work.

The second part opened with Mr. J. F. Barnett's "Symphonic Poem" for orchestra, with organ and chorus, "The Harvest Festival," also conducted by the composer. Produced at the Norwich Festival in 1881, this cannot yet be called a familiar work, but, notwithstanding the lengthy idyllic poem by Mary Mark Lemon, of which it is a musical illustration, Mr. Barnett has written a charming set of four movements, which would appeal favourably to any audience by their simplicity and melodious gracefulness. The "Dance of Reapers and Gleaners" is quite "dainty" in its melodies and instrumentation. The chorus is only utilized to sing a "Hymn of Thanksgiving" in plain harmonies above the orchestral figure of the concluding movement.

After what had gone before, it seemed hardly fair to produce the "Invocation to Harmony" (by desire, and for the first time in public), composed by H.R.H. the late Prince Consort. Beginning with a chorus, allegro maestoso, in C major, common time, which consists of thirty-one bars of simple chords, an allegretto in three-four time follows, which is really the theme of the work. But it is no more than a simple melody, most simply harmonized, and not remarkable for any originality ; the orchestra playing *con voci* throughout. As this is repeated, allegro and piu allegro, over and over again, it becomes certainly too familiar, especially as the short solos for soprano, tenor, and bass, which are inserted between the choral movements, afford very little relief either in key, melody, or rhythm. Such a work might be very useful to small choral societies of most limited resources, but as everyone knew that H.R.H. the late Prince Consort was an educated musician, one cannot see the use of producing a simple work which does not show any unusual skill or ability, at an important concert such as the one under notice. Mr. Walter Parratt, the organist of St. George's, Windsor, was the conductor of this part of the performance, and I should not omit to mention that he presided at the organ in the preceding items of the programme.

A good rendering of Mendelssohn's "Ruy Blas" overture by the band, under Mr. J. F. Barnett, concluded the concert. It seemed improbable, with the heavy expenses incurred, that the local Scholarship Fund for the Royal College of Music would derive any advantage from the concert, as the reserved balconies showed many vacant seats, but I believe this the first concert of the Berkshire Musical Association is intended to be, if possible, a sign of the revival of the triennial festivals which were held in Reading with great success thirty or forty years ago. Whether such an enterprise can be supported in these days, with so many altered circumstances, remains to be proved ; but the experiment is in the best hands with the new Musical Association ; and in wishing it all success, I can only say that the more of such performances we can have here, or in any other provincial towns, the better for musical art and education in every way.

SOUTH LONDON CHORAL ASSOCIATION.

By the earnestness of the members and the painstaking skill of Mr. L. C. Venables, this choir has been raised to a foremost place in the list of London choral bodies. The fifth annual concert of the institution was given on April 26th at St. James's Hall. The programme opened with J. Stafford Smith's noble and too much neglected glee, "Blest pair of Sirens." The programme included such specimens of vocal harmony as H. Smart's "The water nymphs," S. Webbe's "The mighty conqueror," Pearsal's "Light of my soul," Pinsuti's "In April time," Archer's "Kate Dalrymple," Mr. Venable's "Song of the trees," etc. The performance of Eaton Faning's dramatic chorus, "Liberty," was chorally the weakest performance of the evening. Generally the intonation of the choir was excellent, the quality of the voices bright and fresh, and the careful observance of light and shade, together with excellent precision in attack, were alike commendable. The soloists were Miss Clara Samuel, Miss Josephine Cravino, Mr. Harper Kearton, and Mr. Barrington Foote. Mr. W. H. Harper was at the pianoforte. Mr. Venables ably conducted. Handel's "Your voices tune," closed an enjoyable performance.

WOLVERHAMPTON CHORAL SOCIETY.

On Monday evening, April 23rd, this society brought a most successful season to a close by a performance of Macfarren's "St. John the Baptist," and Haydn's "Imperial" Mass. The principals on the occasion were Miss Anna Williams, Miss Helen Dalton, Mr. Vernon Rigby, and Mr. Frederic King, with the band and chorus of 300 performers. Dr. Swinnerton Heap conducted, as usual. The artists were all in excellent voice, and did full justice to the music set down for them. Special mention should be made of Miss Williams's performance of Macfarren's air, "I rejoice in my youth," which was most brilliantly rendered, and fairly brought down the house, in spite of the edict against applause issued by the committee. Mr. Vernon Rigby has never been heard here to better advantage than on this occasion. The choruses were not quite up to their usual standard of excellence, but they made ample atonement for their slight defects by their fine renderings of several items, conspicuous amongst these being the chorus, "Lo, the daughter of Herod cometh in." Dr. Heap, to whom much of the success of the past season is due, conducted with the taste and judgment which always characterize him. There was a very large audience on the occasion.

The triennial festival in connection with this society takes place in the coming autumn on an enlarged scale, and promises to be a highly successful one.

SACRED HARMONIC SOCIETY.

The music chosen for the concert of the 27th of April at St. James's Hall gave at once works of distinct interest and pleasant familiarity in Schubert's Mass in E flat and Mendelssohn's ever fresh "Hymn of Praise." Schubert's noble Mass is one of his most characteristic and beautiful sacred works. It abundantly displays his perfect gift of tune, his earnestness and dramatic feeling, as it also shows his tendency to diffuseness, even to weakness, and want of systematic contrapuntal training. All the same, it is a glorious piece of Church music. The lovely and tender "Et incarnatus est" and the vocal "Benedictus" are after the composer's best manner. The fine "Kyrie eleison," the broad solemn "Agnus Dei," and the beautiful "Dona nobis pacem" are all notable movements of their kind. The instrumentation of the work, again, is of a most interesting character. Not only does it present many delicate and charming effects, but it displays many points in the use of the trombones, &c., which at the time of its composition (1828) were enlargements of treatment although not newly invented effects. The work, on the whole, was admirably presented ; although with regard to the band, the strings were somewhat too weak and the brass at times too ostentatious. The many charming effects for the wood, wind, and combined instruments were well pronounced, and showed care. The soloists of the evening were Miss Annie Marriott, Mrs. Suter, Miss Hancock, Mr. H. Kearton, and Mr. R. Hilton. Mr. Charles Hallé conducted. The symphony of the "Hymn of Praise" received, on the whole, a good and careful rendering, though the brass department was again too assertive. To the chorus this work was clearly a familiar and welcome friend, and the choral movements were excellently taken. The "Messiah" will be given on May 11th.

THE BACH CHOIR.

At the third and last concert of the season, given on the afternoon of April 28th at St. James's Hall, Bach's great Mass in B minor, was performed. This gigantic work was written by the great cantor of Leipzig when he had reached the ripest and most prosperous part of his career, after accepting office as chapel-master to the court at Dresden in 1736. The present performance was only the seventh in London. Though admiring the spirit and judgment of the Bach Choir in presenting this noble work from time to time, one must regret that it is deemed necessary to curtail portions of two or three of the solo movements. It is quite true that modern taste demands a more dramatic, terse type of solo, duo, etc. ; all the same, the performances of the Bach Choir are of the dignity of being historical performances, and as such demand the utmost completeness and the strictest integrity with regard to the composer's text. The opening chorus was well rendered, and the beautiful fugal chorus, "Kyrie eleison," was given with an evident feeling for the expressive . contrapuntal idioms of the movement. The whole of the "Gloria," with its varied and complex movements, was finely rendered. The *obbligato* passages for flute, oboe, and horn (this last most trying from the extended compass and technically difficult figures employed), were most artistically rendered by Mr. Radcliffe, M. Lebon, and Mr. Mann. Equally excellent was the general rendering of the colossal setting of the "Credo," the solos of which were sung by the ladies previously mentioned and by Mr. Brereton. The effect of the closing chorus was indeed superb. The Sanctus was admirably given. The presence of two such experienced artists as Mr. W. H. Cummings and Mr. Carrodus, as singer and violinist in the graceful setting of the "Benedictus," secured a rendering of much eloquence, tempered with sound judgment. The "Agnus Dei," contralto solo, and "Dona nobis pacem," final chorus, were both well performed. The B minor Mass reveals to the listener a mine of pure melody and contrapuntal power. It was the first of the great modern settings of the office; in grandeur of design it is alone equalled by Beethoven's Mass in D. As regards length (which alone would make its use as Service music impossible), it is one of the longest settings of the Mass in existence, the longest being probably Bach's Mass in B minor, Beethoven's in D, Schubert's in E flat, Mozart's so-called No. 12, and Cherubini's Mass in D minor. It is, in the interest of the art, to be hoped that the Bach Choir will from time to time present this great Mass, which is one of the highest exemplifications of the genius of Bach; who, Catholic-minded in the largest sense of the word, as men of genius usually are, notwithstanding the cramping effects of local surroundings, wrote for the Roman and Lutheran branches of the universal Church with equal earnestness and power. The organ on the 28th was in the capable hands of Mr. T. Pettit, and Herr Otto Goldschmidt occupied his usual place as conductor. That the Bach Choir will again come forward with their useful and artistic efforts next season with undiminished earnestness will be the hope of all lovers of the art.

MR. WILLING'S CHOIR.—On May 1st Gade's "Psyche," a portion of Bennett's "May Queen," and Rossini's "William Tell" Overture, etc., formed the attractive programme of a concert given in St. James's Hall. The music for the most part received a careful and artistic rendition. The Princess of Wales honoured the performance by her presence.

SOUTH NORWOOD.—A sacred concert was given in the Wesleyan Church, 26th of April. The singers were, Miss Evelyn Bawtree, Mdme. Jennie Bawtree, Mr. E. Putman, and Mr. A. W. Owen. Mr. H. T. Pringuer played the following organ solos :—Overture in C (Mendelssohn); Andante in A flat (W. S. Hoyte); Fugue in G (Krebs); Barcarolle (W. S. Bennett), and Organ Concerto, No. 2 in B flat (Handel).

ROYAL ITALIAN OPERA.—The short season at Covent Garden of the now limited liability company commenced on May Day. The theatre has been provided with numerous doors in order to facilitate a more comfortable ingress and a quicker egress. Precautions of an elaborate kind have also been made again st dangers from fire. The opening opera was Verdi's "Aïda." Mdme. Fursch-Madi and Mdlle. Stahl, with Signori Cotogni and Sochara, efficiently undertook the leading parts. Signor Bevignani conducted the large and excellent orchestra. The other operas of the week were "M arta "and " L'Africaine."

SCHUBERT SOCIETY.—The second concert of the 17th season was given at St. James's Hall, on April 19th. Schumann's Pianoforte Quartet, Op. 47, a just now neglected composition, by the way, opened the concert, being well rendered by Messrs. Carl Hasse, Henkel, Witt, and Schuberth. Mdme. Zimeri contributed several songs, singing with much artistic power. Miss Eva Thompson played Schumann's "Ambesque" and Handel's Fugue in E minor. Several young artists made their first appearance upon this occasion; but they were too nervous to do themselves justice. Herren Henkel and Schuberth played in good style solos for violin and violoncello.

CLAPHAM POPULAR CONCERTS.—A most successful series of entertainments, which have been given weekly for the last five months, was brought to a conclusion on Saturday. The directors (Mdme. Louisa Vernon and Mr. Douglas Vernon) were on this occasion assisted by Miss Edith Luke, Miss Laura Clare, Mr. George Batchelor, Mr. Charles Weller, Mr. Henry Canter, Miss Alice Bertram (piano), and the Semper Paratus Quartet (mixed voices). All acquitted themselves in a very excellent manner. The services rendered by those engaged throughout the series were acknowledged by the clergy of Holy Trinity, and the treasurer to the fund; and Mr. Vernon, in reply, expressed the great pleasure it had been to provide from week to week for the enjoyment of an audience so appreciative.

DOUGLAS, ISLE OF MAN.—Mr. Walter Lucas, organist of St. Thomas's Church, gave an excellent concert on April 17th. His pianoforte solos were a selection of four of Mendelssohn's " Songs without Words" (Nos 1, 23, 18, and 34), and Beethoven's "Sonata Pathétique." Mr. Lucas proved himself to be a performer of power and judgment. His execution and touch were indeed admirable; and the audience greeted him with much applause. The vocalists were Miss Fanny Bristowe, Miss Howard Dutton, Mr. Seymour Jackson, and Mr. John Barrow. The vocal music was a miscellaneous assortment of good and popular pieces, mostly English.

RICHMOND.—The Kew Road Musical Society gave an excellent performance of Haydn's " Creation" on Thursday evening, April 26th. The soloists were Madame Clara West, Mr. J. Williams, and Mr. W. Forrington; organist, Mr. J. F. Goodban, R.A.M.; conductor, Mr. F. A. Crew. For her rendering of the airs " With verdure clad " and ' On mighty pens," Madame West received an outburst of applause; a scarcely less marked compliment being paid to the other soloists for some of their numbers. The choruses were nearly all admirably rendered under the able conductorship of Mr. Crew, and Mr. Goodban accompanied with taste and judgment.

PRINCES' HALL.—The new art galleries, which include the handsome concert-room to be known by the title given above, were opened on April 27th, in the presence of the Prince and Princess of Wales, the Duke of Edinburgh and other members of the Royal Family. The acoustical properties of the concert-room are admirable, and are as satisfactory as are the elegant decorations of this luxurious abode of the arts. A vocal and instrumental concert commenced with a verse of the National Anthem and a glee was given by the Vocal Union Choir, under the direction of Mr. Fred. Walker. Miss Santley, Signor Piatti, Mdme. Patey, M. V. de Pachmann, and Signor Foli also assisted during the evening; Mr. Fred. Cowen presiding at the pianoforte, during the proceedings. The royal party was conducted through the three galleries, and displayed much interest in the 900 pictures exhibited. The new room is another fact contributing to the growing evidence of the co-operation and mutual assistance characterising the advancement and relationship of the sister arts in these days of earnest artistic progress.

ROYAL VICTORIA COFFEE HALL.—The ballad concert given on Thursday, April 26th, at the above Hall, was one of the most successful of the season. M. Sainton conducted with great vigour and affability, and the choir of ladies (pupils of M. Sainton), sang with remarkable artistic power and precision. The ballad concerts for May at the above Hall will be under the direction of Madame Osborne Williams, Mr. Clement Hoey, Signor D'Havet Zeccara, and Mr. J. Greenhill. This gentleman is arranging a concert to illustrate the vocal music of Shakespeare, arranged in chronological order, with biographical sketches and anecdotes of the various composers. On 22nd Mr. W. Carter's choir of 300 voices will give a performance of "Placida," under Royal and distinguished patronage. In consequence of the large audiences that have attended on the Wednesday and Friday Penny Nights' Entertainments, Tuesday will be added to the third night in the week, and from the 12th inst. the prices on Saturday, Monday, and Thursday nights are to be lowered for the summer season.

GLASGOW.—A performance of Handel's "Messiah" was given on April 25th, by the South-side Choral Society. The soloists were all local, and among them were two members of the Glasgow Select Choir. Mrs. Smith, Miss Fyfe, Mr. Howell, and Mr. James Fleming, were the principals, and Mr. James McKean the conductor. Mr. W. Davidson was the organist, and the orchestra was made up of resident performers. The performance was in many respects highly creditable, and much praise is due to the chorus for the firm and vigorous style in which many of the numbers were rendered. An occasional roughness and tardiness in the attack were the only noticeable drawbacks. The principals were all successful; but Miss Fyfe showed to much less advantage than was to be expected from the beautiful quality of her voice. Her inexperience of oratorio music in a measure qualifies her shortcomings. The orchestra played remarkably well, and the organist was equally good. The Glasgow Select Choir has been invited to repeat the Hymn Music programme, previously noticed, at several of the larger Scottish towns, and will no doubt aid in effecting the much needed reformation in Scottish psalmody. Professor Bruce is delivering lectures with the same laudable object in view. There is a scheme afloat here to establish a branch college in connection with the London Tonic Sol-fa body, and a meeting in furtherance of the same has already been held.

ECCLES, NEAR MANCHESTER.—On Tuesday evening the members of the Eccles District Vocal Union had their first open meeting at the Eccles Town Hall. The first part of the programme consisted of Gaul's cantata, " The Holy City," which was rendered with great precision and effect. The choruses, "They that sow in tears," and "Great and marvellous," were much appreciated. The solos were taken by the following members of the union : Miss A. Rawson, of the Royal Academy of Music, Miss Hibbert (pupil of the musical director, Mr. R. F. Coules, F.C.O.), Mr. G. S. Ball, Mr. T. Hibbert (pupil of Mr.

Coules), and Rev. C. Heath, M.A. Miss Rawson sang "Eye hath not seen" with admirable taste, as did also Mr. Hibbert the solo "Thus saith the Lord of hosts," the chorus singing the Sanctus *pianissimo*. The cantata was evidently much enjoyed by the audience, as was shown by the hearty applause at the conclusion of the work. The second part of the programme opened with a part-song, "Wake, to the hunting," by Smart, and "The lullaby of life" (Leslie), followed by a pianoforté solo by Mr. R. F. Coules : (*a*) March Funebre from Sonata in B flat minor, Chopin (*b*) "Jagdlied" (Schumann), both of which were well received. Miss A. Rawson sang "Orpheus with his lute" (Sullivan), and Mr. T. Hibbert sang "The roll call" (Pinsuti), for which he was recalled, and sang "The warrior bold." The Rev. C. Heath, Mr. G. S. Ball, and Mr. Watson contributed songs in a praiseworthy manner. The concert concluded with the exquisite glee "When wearied wretches" (Bishop). The hall was filled. The Rev. F. Coules, F.C.O., conducted the choruses, accompanied the songs, and played the above pianoforte solos.

TOTTENHAM.—On Tuesday evening, April 24th, the Tottenham Wesleyan Musical Society gave a most successful concert to a crowded audience. The first part was of a miscellaneous character, consisting chiefly of sacred songs and choruses from well-known oratorios. Mr. James Budd rendered Handel's two fine solos, "Arm, arm, ye brave" and "Honour and arms," in his usual artistic manner, while Miss Coyte Turner sang with great taste the lovely air from Costa's "Naaman," "I dreamt I was in heaven." Mr. Edward Dalzell sang "In native worth," but his lack of expression must have been keenly felt by all those who were able to appreciate the beauty in good old father Haydn's music. Certainly the most unsatisfactory thing in the first part was the attempt on the part of Mr. Kessell to sing "If with all your hearts"; there are certain mistakes which very often summon up a smile from the most stern musician, but anything short of contempt could not have existed in the hearts of those who boasted of the largest amount of charitableness. We must not forget to mention with great commendation the admirable violin playing of Mr. Arthur Payne, a young man in possession of indubitable talent. The second part of the concert opened with Suppé's overture to the "Poet and the Peasant," well rendered by the band ; but the prominent feature was Macfarren's "May Day." Without any undue praise, we may say that a finer rendering of this work has never been achieved by an amateur choir, though do not let it be imagined from the prefix that it should take a secondary position in the *rôle* of choirs. Too much praise cannot be accorded to Mr. R. J. Pitt for the great attention he has given to the choir during the past season, and the high state of proficiency his musical talents has been able to bring it to. Miss Rissel took the part of the May Queen ; Mr. Jefferys was organist, and Mr. Geo. F. Grover presided at the piano.

Foreign Musical Intelligence.

(*From our Own Correspondent.*)

PARIS, May 1st, 1883.

It is always a good thing to allow one's self a little time for reflection before expressing a decided opinion about so important an effort as a new opera. First night audiences and their impressions are often critical, but, as a general rule, they are not trustworthy. We know from repeated experience that a second and third nights public often reverses the verdict of the critics and "society," and the time has gone by, at least in Paris, in which it was possible to force people, by ingenious puffery or depreciation, into swallowing the ready-made views of the small body which is supposed to set the fashion in music, and which too frequently records its views, favourable or unfavourable, under the influence of prejudices, tastes, personal likings, dislikings, or hatreds, unshared by the greater, vulgarer public which comes after, and comes to the new thing set before it with an honest determination to enjoy it if that be possible, and if that be impossible, to make the fact as clear as silence, or sibillation, can.

Having relieved myself of these generalities, perhaps I may be permitted to say a few words about the new Anglo-Indian opera of M. Léo Delibes, "Lakmé," although you have already devoted some of your space to its discussion last week. "Lakmé" is, musically speaking, in many respects a disappointing work, and has certainly been overpraised by the critics. The two first acts, though pleasing enough, I admit, are dreadfully wanting in depth and originality ; while the third, charming as it is, undoubtedly, would certainly be far less interesting were it not for the charming poetry of the libretto which has inspired it, and with which it shares the applause. I, for

one, ungrudgingly gave, and am ready again to give u, when I hear it. Briefly : "Lakmé" without this third act would be a decided failure. The success of the third act is due in a great measure to Messrs. Gille, Gordinet, and Mortier, the librettists. Wherever M. Léo Delibes has succeeded, it is because he has managed to thoroughly identify himself with the touching and tender scenes imagined of this triumvirate of librettists. Wherever he has failed, or seems weak, he may ascribe the fact to his having ceased to be in harmony with his subject. The libretto, in fact (you were rather disdainful in speaking of it last week, I noticed) is the making of this opera, and the best thing in it. As to the music—if you press me for an opinion, I will confess it is poetic and pretty. But if you press me just a little more, I will have to own that it is no less shallow. The orchestration, from beginning to end, is ingenious and agreeable. The melody is facile too, save here and there, where the composer has been carried away by his orientalism and dreamy sentiment. But there are shocking faults of taste and judgment in several of the *morceaux*, especially in the second Act which contains a "Legende" (written "expressly to suit the gifted little Lakmé, Mdlle. Marie Vanzandt), so thoroughly out of keeping with all that goes before and comes after it, that it is impossible to avoid getting rather angry and disgusted with M. Léo Delibes. He might be doing better than humoring the caprice and peculiarities of even so delightful a little tyrant as Mdlle. Marie Vanzandt. And talking of this, I should very much like to know why Lakmé deliberately departs from the dramatic proprieties at this particular point, to sing *at* the audience instead of *to* the mottley group of Hindoos and English who have assembled on the stage to listen to her trashy "Legende."

Despite these criticisms, and despite, or perhaps in consequence of my being more correct in saying because, of its very facility and lightness, "Lakmé," seems to be a remarkable success. It is studded with musical pearls which will certainly be most popular in all drawing-rooms, and is one of the most pleasing works that any lazy amateur of the divine art could wish to hear. Now most opera-goers in all countries—Italy, perhaps, excepted—are lazy.

It will be interesting in the extreme to compare "Lakmé" with Felicien David's "Perle du Brésil," which is really to be revived this week for the *début* of Miss Emma Nevada (*née* Wixom) of Nevada city, the *prima donna* who is to succeed Marie Vanzandt at the Opera Comique. Most good judges of Felicien David set far greater store on this opera than on "Lalla Rookh," by which he is better known to the present generation. Nous verrons.

M. Pasdeloup deserves great credit for having at last bravely broken free from routine, and determined to give us a chance of hearing good orchestral concert music in May, as well as April, March, or February. He has arranged for a series of afternoon concerts this month at the Eden Theatre, and as there is not one music-lover less in Paris than there was a month ago, while the number of entertainments for the aforesaid music-lovers has been very largely reduced, there appears to be no reason whatever for his not drawing crowded houses and doing well. *Apropos* of all this, the subscription for the shares of the Concert Populaire Company makes headway but slowly, a matter which on every account is to be regretted.

M. Guilmant has given the first of his interesting organ recitals at the Trocadéro, with the assistance of M. Colonne's orchestra and several distinguished artists. The concert was well attended.   C. H. MELTZER.

Reviews.

Messrs. Duncan Davison, of Regent Street, publish three compositions by Mr. Georg Asch. *Hide and Seek* is the title of a song in F, with limited compass, which the public have heard through the medium of such interpreters as Mdlle. José Sherrington and others. Miss Meysell sang it at her late concert. Two easy pianoforte pieces from the pen of Asch are the *Danse des Sauvards*, a sort of polka movement, in F, and *Feuilles Mortes*, a reverie in B flat, of very simple style, but smooth and flowing. He also gives to the public, through Messrs. Willey & Co., two new Gavottes, both pretty and suited to amateur players. They are entitled *Vive is Reine*, in F, and *Sonata Sophia*, of oriental colour, in B flat.

A Lullaby. By W. W. Hedgcock. (Augener & Co.)—A melodious setting of Barry Cornwall's well-known lines. The song presents variety as to its mode of treatment, and the accompaniment is well laid out, displaying in places freshness and originality.

The Lord is with thee, Anthem. By G. A. Osborne. (Novello & Co.)—This is a thoughtfully written anthem, in which flowing melody plays an important part. Far too many of our modern pieces of this form depend for their effect chiefly on highly coloured and elaborate organ parts. While fully recognising the use and importance of the accompanimental settings, the mission of which is but to enshrine and assist in displaying the vocal parts, Mr. Osborne has also been mindful to give us good pure melody and smooth part-writing. The full choral portions of the work are well contrasted and relieved by solos for tenor, bass, and soprano. The anthem is decidedly effective, and seems likely to become a favourite.

Chant du Pêcher, Pour Piano per Francesco. Berger. (Lamborn Cock.)—A well constructed and melodious song without words, in which the interest is equally divided between both hands.

Minuet and Trio, for the pianoforte. By C.'H, Couldery. —*Vittoria,* air. By Carissimi. Arranged for the pianoforte. (Lamborn Cock.)—The first-named piece revives an old form which has furnished many clever and pleasing specimens of the art. The above can, however, hardly be classed under either one or the other of these heads. The air of Carissimi does not lend itself readily to the modern pianoforte treatment, and is not improved by its new dressing.

Sonata (in G), for the pianoforte. By Domenico Scarlatti. Marked and fingered by Florence May. (Lamborn Cock.)—This is a specimen of the sonata form in its earliest days, and, after the manner of D. Scarlatti, consists of but a single movement. The treatment of the subject is in the simplest style of imitation in two parts, and will be found an excellent study for the young student. The editing is judiciously carried out.

Gavotte and Courante. By J. S. Bach. (The Fan Series.) (Lamborn Cock.)—Under the fanciful title of the "Fan Series" a good selection of ancient and modern authors is in preparation—Handel, Rubinstein, Dussek and the above two movements from the French suite in G being already published. This last appears to be carefully fingered and is particularly clear as to print.

Transactions of the National Association for the Promotion of Social Science, 1882. (Longmans & Co.)—A valuable volume, containing full reports of the proceedings last year in Nottingham. The papers and discussions on art matters include Mr. C. H. Lloyd's Lecture "On the Royal College of Music," given at length in these columns. The matter bearing upon Education, Art, and various subjects of social and artistic importance, contained in this volume, forms indeed a mine of thought well deserving the attention of intelligent readers.

Higher Examination of Papers of Trinity College, London, 1874-82. (W. Reeves, Fleet Street; and A. Hammond & Co., Vigo Street.)—To musical students, this collection of examination papers, as set by some twenty-nine of the leading men of our day, will be most acceptable, as containing a very mine of musical thoughts and technical suggestions. To the musical world generally, the book offers undeniable evidence of the general excellence, earnestness, and thoroughness of the examination work undertaken by the spirited institution in Mandeville Place.

Agnes of the Sea. By Louis Liebe. (Stanley, Lucas, Weber & Co.)—This cantata presents a peculiarity which, under certain conditions, will be readily appreciated. Its characters are two, viz., soprano and contralto, while the chorus is written in two parts only, instead of three, as is customary in works of this character. Short cantatas for ladies' voices are now much affected at the breaking-up concerts (as they are termed) of schools. Those who have conducted such works can bear testimony to the considerable difficulty experienced in getting a satisfactory representation of the third voice part. Two parts pretty well exhaust the voices at disposal, and the school, or vocal class, is a large one, and the contralto element strong. For this reason, Mr. Liebe's cantata will be welcome. The story is founded on a Norsk legend of a maiden lured by the songs of the sirens to dwell in the depths of the sea. But the fickle fair one hears the church bells of her native village, and quitting the mermaids, returns to her home again. Miss Johnstone has told the poetical story in good English, and it may in some quarters be deemed an advantage that the usual love element is absent from the tale. Mr. Liebe's music is satisfactory, though it presents no features of striking novelty. A ballad, "A maiden sat by the shining strand," is good; and towards the end of the work happy use is made of the melody of "Home, sweet home." Most of the choruses and airs are simply constructed, the only ambitious piece in the work being a somewhat independently written duet, "Farewell." The composer is a little fond of enharmonic changes, and a considerable amount of the cantata is written in 6.8 time; but this conventional barcarole form seems to be inseparable from sea music. The accompaniment is for the piano alone. Would it not be well for the writers of pieces of this kind to employ an harmonium in conjunction with the eternal pianoforte? By this means an agreeable colour of tone can be got, which would certainly heighten the effect of the music written. The value afforded by the contrast and mixture of these two household instruments may be commended to the notice of writers of works of this character.

True Love to Win. By G. Benson, Mus.Bac., Cantab. (Lamborn Cock.)—We have here a smoothly written glee for four male voices. Mr. Benson's work shows that though this form of composition seems, from various causes, to be dying out among us, we still possess composers who can write melodious, richly harmonized music in this peculiarly English form.

The Mermaids' Invitation. By Ridley Prentice. (Lamborn Cock.)—An admirable trio for ladies' voices. There is so much excellent musicianly work in this, that if nicely sung it is bound to satisfy hearers of every type

Elementary Exercises on the Rudiments of Music. By E. Ellice Jewell. (Lamborn Cock.)—"The Catechism on the Rudiments of Music," of which these exercises now form a continuing portion, has already been noticed with approval in this journal. The exercises are well designed for impressing on pupils the cardinal features of the art they are studying. The quicker these essentials are appreciated and fixed on the memory, the more rapid will the progress of the student become. The book consists mainly of ruled music staves for the pupil to write the various exercises directed to be worked out. The plan is a good one; the directions printed before each exercise are so lucid, and the work so cheap, that Miss Jewell's exercise-book ought to be gone through by every pupil who is studying intelligently.

Epitaph on a Robin. By C. A. Ranken. (Lamborn Cock.)—A simple little song, aptly illustrating Samuel Roger's pathetic words. To those who can command an obbligato violin accompaniment, the ballad will prove welcome.

The Hidden Land. By Livesey Carrott. (Lamborn Cock.)—A song, the words of which are of the semi-mysterious type much in vogue at the present day. However, the idea conveyed is poetical, and Mr. Carrott's music has a healthy freshness about it that ought to render the song popular.

Harmony. By Carl Mangold. (W. Morley & Co.)—The composer of this little work is professor at the Guildhall School of Music, and is favourably known as an able, conscientious teacher, long settled in this country. The treatise, though small, is singularly complete, and appears to be the outcome of a life's study of the best writers on harmony and counterpoint, educed by a lengthened experience of tuition. The explanations given on the various branches of the science are so clear and distinct, though brief, that nothing a student ought to know is omitted. The illustrations printed, are admirably chosen to fix the rules touched on firmly in the mind. An appendix gives a mass of valuable information in question and answer form. The treatise, lucid and complete in itself, may be recommended as a useful introduction to the more elaborate works on the subject by Fux, Albrechtsberger, Cherubini, and G. Weber.

Mr. Sims Reeves gave a concert on May 1st, at St. James's Hall. He had the assistance of some of our leading singers and the "Anemoic Union."

A COMPLAINT ANENT INCOMPETENT CONDUCTORS.

Only those who are habitually playing on orchestras, operatic or otherwise, can have the least idea of the amazing difference there is in that art called "Conducting"; and though old stagers like the writer are perfectly well aware that a great conductor "is born, not made," yet, strange to say, the greater the number of great qualities required to make a great conductor, the more numerous are the aspirants who pant and yearn to wield the *bâton*. Almost every organist or musician of a leading social position, whatever may be his powers or experience, assumes that he can conduct the "Messiah" or "Elijah," or some such work. Every aspiring non-professional, especially of the vocal order, seizes the earliest opportunity of conducting part-songs, small cantatas, etc. Only those who have played under really competent conductors can perhaps see and feel acutely the shortcomings of vain, inefficient leaders. Conductors of the last-named type, as a rule, know little or nothing about the band parts and the complex effects of high-class orchestration; two out of three sing, while conducting, the chorus part of their own particular vocal compass, and, as a rule, are serenely unconscious of the shortcomings or reliability of the strings, wood, or brass, I could unfold some stories of incompetent conductors had space permitted such narrations. Surely it is high time musicians studied the art of conducting systematically, especially now the growth of orchestral music is so rapidly advancing from day to day.

J. R.

COLLEGE OF ORGANISTS.

On Tuesday last, Mr. H. J. Stark, Mus.Bac, &c., delivered a very useful and excellent lecture on the subject of "Counterpoint" at the Neumeyer Hall. The living interest taken in this great subject was evidenced by the large assembly of members and friends present. The course adopted by the lecturer was to plead for a moderate reformation of the contrapuntal laws in certain directions. This position he strengthened not only by presenting examples (lithographed copies of which were liberally supplied to the audience), but by a thoughtful and clever exposure of the discrepancies and evasions so constantly to be noticed in the too free examples all the contrapuntal theorists illustrate their rules with, to the dire confusion of thoughtful students, who not unnaturally expect men to practise what they preach. This is perhaps not the place to point out, that though great value must be attached to the fact that gifted, shrewd men like Mr. Stark are disposed to lead the way towards the imparting of what may be taken as broader, freer principles in counterpoint, the contrapuntal art, as Dr. F. E. Gladstone, the learned and able chairman, pointed out with much force and perspicuity, must largely be regarded as a means to an end, that end being composition. Further, there is a danger in telling students of the supposed advantages of contrapuntal freedom, which is parallel with the policy of letting boys advance to manhood free from the restraints absolutely necessary to form upright men and to prepare them for the enjoyment of a righteous freedom. Grammatical strength is essential in all art, and so felt some of the eminent musicians present, although they cordially hailed Mr. Stark's courageous and masterly advocacy of an enlarged contrapuntal policy with much satisfaction. The speakers, during the very useful discussion following the lecture, were Dr. Gladstone, Mr. Higgs, Mus.Bac., Mr. G. A. Osborne, Mr. A. C. Cooper, Mr. Bradbury Turner, Mus.Bac., Mr. James Turpin, Mus.Bac., and Mr. F. Davison (Messrs. Gray and Davison). Summed up and fairly balanced, the opinions of the lecturer and various speakers really accorded in the desire for a thoughtful, careful, widely based, and generous study of the great art, which in the main, to quote the thoughtful opinion of Mr. James Higgs, elsewhere expressed, is the department of the art most beyond the reach of change and fashion. The lectures remaining are "Some Musical Ethics and Analogues," Mr. H. C. Banister, on June 5th; and "The Organ Writers of the Nineteenth Century," Mr. F. J. Sawyer, Mus.Bac., July 3rd. The very interesting meeting terminated with the usual and well-deserved vote of thanks.

LONDON: SATURDAY, MAY 5, 1883.

PROFESSIONALS AND NON-PROFESSIONALS.

GAIN the vexed question of the distinction between the "Regulars" and "Volunteers" of the art intrudes itself; this time the matter is urged to the front by the letter of an esteemed correspondent and occasional contributor, which will be found elsewhere. Until the points in dispute are fully and amicably settled, it may be presumed that the delicate questions involved will arise from time to time. It is less my present purpose to endeavour to frame a reply to "H. E. S.," than it is to try to show how difficult any settlement of the questions at issue must be, and how tenderly and courteously such questions must be considered, as concerning the relationship between two indispensable and mutually essential bodies of the artistic world. To begin, there is a danger of setting up some needless irritation in the Quixotic idea that a strongly marked line of demarcation between our professionals and amateurs is essential to the well-being of the art and necessary for the due recognition of the interests of its followers. The truth is, the setting forth of a distinct line of demarcation between the two great artistic divisions is an impossibility; and the two bodies are, through the growth of a general culture, chiefly advanced by our excellent professional teachers themselves becoming more and more intimately connected and interlaced from day to day. The history of all the arts will show the same processes of artistic life. First, in its rudimentary forms a given art is practised without systems and without full appreciation and consequent rewards,; then an acknowledged profession of its principles and practice does not practically exist. In process of time the development of such art is sufficiently advanced to require the ministrations of artists pledged to a life-time of earnest and highly skilled service, whose rewards grow with the advancing appreciation of their labours. As appreciation gains ground, the professors of the art are inevitably called upon to teach its mysteries they best understand to those most willing to appreciate; and thus the army of non-professional artists, consisting of those who being most anxious to appreciate are also desirous to be doing active service, is definitely raised. When the given art has reached a ripened period of its existence, the tide of general culture sweeps away many artificial distinctions, and in the end all participate more or less in the exercise of the artist's gifts and in the enjoyment of an art grown to be universal in its influence. There was a time when only clerks and scholars could read and write, now their once special avocations are exercised by all. Likely enough the professors of reading and writing at one period of the history of the growth of literature jealously cried out for the impossible line of demarcation; but what would be now thought of a protected interest in, for instance, that humble branch of the literary avocation, letter writing ! "Wherever there is power, there will "be activity," is an axiom true in every form of natural, social, and artistic life. The musical art has reached that full-grown epoch of its existence, when the warmth and light of its sun-like rays of life-giving beauty are disseminated far and wide, to the vivifying of all who have ears to hear and minds to cultivate. The weeds of the artistic garden are neither to be described as professional or amateur, but are recognised as those who impede the growth of art, or choke the virgin soil by doing false, misleading, and purely self-interested art work; and the flowers and fruit are those, be they professionals or amateurs, who, largely forgetting self-interest, exist primarily for the benefit of the art and its followers. If we look around, the presumably protected professions offer corresponding evidence of the natural effects of growth. The clergy are not able to do the work of evangelizing the world without extraneous aid ; so on all sides we find earnest laymen, exhorting, lecturing, and teaching. The medical men are likewise being largely aided by a generally increased knowledge of the laws of sanitation, by the labourers in the cause of temperance, by scientific lecturers and by writers on medical topics. In short, the law of development, by which knowledge becomes power, and power necessitates activity, affects all professions alike, and I venture to assert is beneficially affecting music in our midst. The arguments anent the difficulties of the professional concert-room performers with regard to so-called amateur pretensions, are more specious than accurate. One natural result of a rapid musical growth in this country has been the creation of a perhaps unduly large class of artists whose eagerness of fame has outstripped artistic prudence. Much of the music performed at concerts, again, is of an inferior type, and not equal to the requirements of the present time. Indeed, it would not be difficult to show that good artists and good music find a just, not to say generous, appreciation, and consequently the building up of substantial art claims upon solid merit will leave the complaints alluded to but little force. At the same time, the whole question of concert-giving demands, I know, serious consideration. However, in this, as in every department of the art; ability and earnestness will ever secure a fair success, at least for the good artist, even though there are some abuses and misunderstandings to be cleared away. As regards the broad aspect of the question, skilled work such as calls for a life-time's experience, will always be wanted, and the friendly aid and art-devotion of the non-professional artist will also not cease to be essential requirements of a truly healthy national art-life. It is our business to reconcile the several duties of the two classes of art workers and to effectually dove-tail their mutual interests. Such a course will alone bring real strength to all, and the various members of the same artistic body must learn to be mutually useful, and to accept in its widest and best possible meaning the motto, *Dum vivimus vivamus.*   E. H. TURPIN.

INTONING.

THE satisfaction and glory of crowning the edifice of clerical ignorance in musical matters and congregational bigotry, would seem to have been reserved for the chief minister and the more narrow-minded section of a certain congregation attending an important church in one of the leading sea-ports of the south of England. This triumph of needless, bigoted selfishness and blindness to the requirements of the age we live in, is narrated in the letter signed "A Country Organist" which appears in the correspondence section of this week's issue. The eager bigotry of the document now bequeathed to the history of our boasted progress in church music, over-reaches even the narrow-minded intentions of its compiler or compilers. Not contented to ask the choristers to read, rather than intone (to use the verb which is presumed to best express the process of *reading* on one given sound for the sake of decency and order in the conduct of public worship), this unfortunate notice insists that the reading is to be as *unmusical* as possible. What, now, is the full meaning of this expression? and what must be the spirit of the writer or compilers ? The choristers are not only to be effectually snubbed in the proper discharge of their duties as leaders of the voices of the people, but are called upon to obstreperously and ostentatiously proclaim the temporary strength of the more heedless as the more short-sighted section of the worshippers. Instead of the seemly, orderly self-abnegation implied in the symbolic unity of all voices centred upon a given sound, as expressing the many hearts centred in one sacred act, the choristers are to encourage the congregation to self-actuated, self-inflected, unseemly and disorderly utterances of the most solemn public acknowledgments of human helplessness and divine power. The confession of sins innumerable, demanding a complete self-abnegation, without which the confession is in truth not made at all, and the call for grace which without charity has no practical manifestation, are alike —according to these in all likelihood sincere, but certainly misguided and injudicious, declaimers against "decency and order,"—to be made with an ostentation of self-will, with an expression of the determination of a faction, which must be dangerously irritating in one direction, and dangerously destructive of such real humility as may be possessed by the advocates of "Indecency and disorder" in the conduct of public worship themselves. Truly, there can be no greater misfortune to a church than that it should be allowed, from the want of a strong, sensible guiding mind, to become an arena for the evil disposed and uncharitable actions of the victims of that hateful spiritual or rather mental disease, the *Odium theologicum.* Then, without daring to judge, one pauses with dread to think of the possible thoughts of recrimination and resistful intolerance, such directions and their determined carrying out may give rise to, at the very moment when all should kneel before the Most High in single-hearted abasement and self-sacrificing humility, and with "one voice" to seek for mercy. It is high time that moderate men stepped forward to check the fanaticism of both "high" and "low," and to enforce, wherever possible, such practices as are sensible and seemly, apart from all thoughts of "Ritualism or Puritanism." It is high time, too, to insist upon the general musical education of our clergy, who without such training are not duly prepared for the complete discharge of their high duties and sacred calling. Not less is it the time to teach the people that the uplifting of their voices on regulated musical tones, is the true technical distinction between the functions of united public worship and individual private prayer, and that such musical reading was not only practised in the early Christian Church, but was in prevailing use in the pre-Puritanical days of the Anglican Church. The spirit of the directions to read as *unmusically* as possible is of the cold, bad, selfish, intermediary period of Church history, when the "quality" slept comfortably in big, square, high-backed pews and the poor sat shivering in "free and (very) "open seats." Perhaps the author or authors of the sage document now being considered meant to direct the unhappy choristers merely to read naturally and in the ordinary speaking voice; but the tone of the directions appears distinctly to betray a wish that the *sensational* qualification is to be unmistakeably evident, and consequently to some offensively prominent. However, we are advancing in happier days when the fever of faction fanaticism will, it is to be hoped, be reduced to a bare existence, if not entirely destroyed, and when service uses will be based alone upon sound and charitable judgment. There are signs of more light, warmth, earnestness, and common-sense in the consideration of matters of church discipline arising from day to day; and soon it will be impossible to address to choristers so stupid, foolish, and weak a manifesto as one requesting them to read as *unmusically* as possible.   E. H. TURPIN.

FORM IN VOCAL MUSIC.
III.

THE study of antique melodic idioms is one of much profit and interest, and goes far to show how universal and how very old many of the still and ever-to-be useful tune germs are. SHAKESPEARE tells us of the folly of paying undue respect to antiquity for its own sake :—

> "What custom wills in all things should we do it,
> The dust on antique time would be unswept,
> And mountainous error be too highly heaped
> For truth to over-peer."

All the same "truth" may often be hidden under the dust of antiquity; and in the study of art, history has the two-fold function of showing us what our fore-fathers did, and teaching us something of the power of art-forms and thought expressions, by showing how long such forms have successfully influenced the human mind. In our pride at the possession of express trains and mighty steam-ships, we are too apt, perhaps, to forget that wood and iron, hammers, screws and wheels played an important part in the early history of the world, and by their presence in all ages have greatly helped forward—and have ever been and are still absolutely essential—to the growth of mechanical power. So it is in art : certain primary sources of power and action are all-pervading in the development of all types of art ; and in none more so than in music, which, although often spoken of as the most modern of the arts, is in its fundamental and primary powers nearly as ancient as speech from whence it sprang. Although the works of the great masters of modern times may truly be said to embody all that is good and powerful in music, the study of ancient musical figures and forms is necessary, in order that the student may be duly impressed with the unalterable value of many of the melodic impulses and constantly applied effects in both tune and harmony; which by reason of their universality are neither to be overlooked or rejected, but which if rightly and duly valued are a precious heritage to the composer, and in his hands, as in the hands of his predecessors, are an invaluable source of eloquence and power.
    E. H. TURPIN.

MRS. LAMBORN COOK'S CONCERT.

Mrs. Lamborn Cock's orchestral concert on Monday evening was fully attended. A band, selected from the Philharmonic corps, and conducted by Mr. G. W. Cusins, played the overture to "Egmont" and the March of "Athalie." Mr. Cusins played Sir Sterndale Bennett's lovely Pianoforte Concerto in F minor, No. 4, in scholarly style ; he might have produced his own in A minor without offence. The eminent Spaniard, Senor Sarasate, introduced a Suite of Raff, for violin and band, including a prelude, a minuet, and a moto perpetuo. The suite, which will be liked and fully appreciated on further acquaintance, was announced as a "first time performance." The Senor, who played some of his Spanish dances, of course electrified his audience. Miss Hilda Wilson's sweet, rich voice was heard to advantage in the air from Mr. Cusins' "Gideon," "The eyes of the Lord are over the righteous" (Psalm xxxiv.). Mr. E. Lloyd sang Wagner's air from "Die Meistersinger," "Morning was gleaming," and Mr. Santley an air from Gounod's "Mireille"; Miss Santley also appeared and sang the air from "Joshua," "Oh, had I Jubal's lyre." Mr. John Thomas played the harp solos.

Mdme. Dukas gave at the Steinway Hall, on April 26th, a miscellaneous concert, the third of a series, primarily intended to afford her pupils opportunities for public appearances. Of the vocalists the Misses Esther Joseph, Emmie Lane, Amy Hussey, and Mdlle. Angèle Prudhomme gave many signs of proficiency and promise. A juvenile pianist, Miss Ada Fraser, played a polonaise by Chopin in good style.

Organ News.

NORWICH.

An organ recital was given at St. Andrew's Hall, Norwich, by Dr. Bunnett, F.C.O. (organist to the Corporation), on Saturday, 28th April. The following was the programme:—

Overture in F	Vincent.
Cantabile Pastorale	Guilmant.
Minuet in C	Boccherini.
Cujus Animam ("Stabat Mater")	Rossini.
Ave Maria	Bunnett.
O Isis und Osiris ("Die Zauberflöte")	Mozart.
Selections from "Le Prophète"	Meyerbeer.
(Including "Coronation March.")	
Andante Cantabile	Mendelssohn.
Air from "Dinorah" (Shadow Song)	Meyerbeer.
Overture, "Oberon"	Weber.

BRISTOL.

At the organ recital on Saturday, April 28th, at the Colston Hall, Mr. George Riseley performed the following programme:—

Coronation Anthem, "God save the King"	Handel.
Andante in D major	Silas.
Grand Fantasia in F minor	Mozart.
Allegro—Andante—Allegro.	
Momens Musicaux { u Andantino } { v Allegretto }	Schubert.
Overture, "William Tell"	Rossini.
Magnus Dominus	Carmusci.
The Storm (by desire)	Lemmens.

NOTTINGHAM.

Mr. G. H. Porter (organist of the Louth Parish Church), gave two organ recitals in the Car Colston Church, from the works of Handel, Beethoven, Mendelssohn, Merkel, Smart, Page, Gower, Rea, Archer, Calkin, Barnby, Raff, Haydn, &c., in aid of the Organ Restoration Fund, on April 26th and 27th.

TUNBRIDGE WELLS.

A new organ in the Vale Royal Wesleyan Chapel was opened by Mr. W. T. Best, organist of St. George's Hall, Liverpool, on the 3rd May. Mr. Sweetland, of Bath, has supplied the organ. The following is the specification:—

GREAT ORGAN, CC TO G.

1.	Open Diapason	8 ft.		5.	Viol de Gamba	8 ft.
2.	Dulciana	8 „		6.	Principal	4 „
3.	Clarabel Flute (treble)	8 „		7.	Harmonic Flute	4 „
				8.	Fifteenth	2 „
4.	StoptDiapason(bass)	8 „		9.	Clarionet	8 „

SWELL ORGAN, CC TO G.

10.	Bourdon	16 ft.		16.	Harmonic Piccolo	2 ft.
11.	Open Diapason	8 „		17.	Mixture (3 ranks)	
12.	Keraulophon	8 „		18.	Oboe	8 „
13.	StoptDiapason(bass)	8 „		19.	Cornopean	8 „
14.	Lieblich (treble)	8 „		20.	Vox humana	8 „
15.	Principal or gemshorn	4 „		21.	Tremulant to swell.	

PEDAL ORGAN.

22.	Open Diapason	...	...	...	16 ft.

Total 1083 pipes.

The couplers are: Swell to great, swell to pedals, and great to pedals. There are two composition pedals to great and two to swell organ. The lowest octaves (CC to G) of viol de gamba, harmonic flute, clarionette, keraulophon, and oboe, are prepared for and will be added as the funds permit. The vox humana stop is Mr. Sweetland's patented invention; it is enclosed in a separate swell box. The organ has a double swell box, with Mr. Sweetland's patented swell front. It is built upon the College of Organists' regulations. The following programme was performed by Mr. W. T. Best:—

Organ Sonata (No. 2 B flat major)	Mendelssohn.
Andante Cantabile (A flat major)	Guiraud.
Prelude and Fugue (F minor)	Bach.
Siciliana	Weber.
Tema con Variazioni	Weber.
Toccata (A flat major)	Hesse.
Andante Cantabile (G major)	S. S. Wesley.
Introduction and Fugue on a Trumpet	W. T. Best.
Fanfare	W. T. Best.
Marche Religieuse	A. Chauvet.
Finale—Allegro Assai (C major)	H. Smart.

Mr. Best's masterly and finished execution, as an organist, would doubtless elicit unqualified admiration.

LEEDS.

Dr. Spark gave a recital on the grand organ in the Town Hall (No. 7 of the series) on Saturday, April 28th, when the programme consisted of works by Spohr and Weber, and comprised:—Overture to the opera "Jessonda"; Adagio in A flat, from the "Notturno," for wind instruments, Op. 34; cradle song, "Andantino," from the symphony "The power of sound"; song, "Rose softly blooming" ("Azor and Zemira"); polacca, from the opera "Faust."—Part Second: overture to the opera "Der Freischütz"; cavatina; reminiscences of the opera "Oberon."

BOW AND BROMLEY INSTITUTE.

The organ recitals were brought to a worthy conclusion last Saturday by Dr. Peace, the well-known Glasgow organist, who received a hearty welcome from a crowded house, every seat being occupied. During the present successful series the engagements have included several of the leading organists of the day, and, in addition, some rising players have been opportunely presented to the public. The opening solo played by Dr. Peace was Handel's "Cuckoo and Nightingale" Concerto, most admirably rendered. Merkel's "Pastorale" in G, Op. 103, and "March for Eastertide" came next. A "Berceuse," by M. Alex. Guilmant, proved to very attractive. An Offertoire, by G. Morandi, in E flat, and Haslinger's "Jubilee" Overture on the Austrian hymn, completed the organ solos, all of which were finely played, and at the close the audience, filling every seat in the hall, warmly acknowledged the performer's great skill by what may be described as quite an ovation. Miss Clara Dowle was the vocalist. She sang Weber's "Softly sighs," showing much promise, but apparently suffering from nervousness. The young lady sang Handel's "Angels ever bright and fair," with organ accompaniment. In this there was a want of understanding between singer and organist, who anxiously rendered such obvious though doubtless well meant assistance, to the vocalist as was clearly as perplexing in its way as a due want of support would have been. "Within a mile of Edinbro'" was another song given. Miss Maria Schuman played her violin solos "Andante Rigoletto" (Alard), and "Bird in the tree" (Hauser), with such pure tone, grace, and finish as secured for the talented violinist a very full meed of approval from the audience. So closed the performances of another season. The committee, artists who have appeared, and the thousands of listeners, are to be earnestly congratulated upon the highly satisfactory results gained through such spirited and excellent management. To the Bow and Bromley Institute not only belongs the credit of the establishment of the most varied, successful, and valuable organ recitals to be heard in the whole world, but praise for the erection of an admirable scheme for the propagation of a love of high-class music judiciously dashed with the enjoyment of an admixture of the popular element, which has already done an enormous amount of good. Organ students, lovers of organ music, and the general public, owe to the committee of the institute and their indefatigable, courteous, and far-sighted hon. secretary, Mr. W. Foster, grateful thanks for a series of performances which are unequalled as displaying the largest amount of organ-playing skill ever yet heard in one room, and which have conferred an immense amount of instruction and pleasure upon all classes of society. It is a pity the committee of this notable institution—now famous as a musical nursery wherever art newspapers are read in the English language and Anglo-Saxon lovers of music are to be found—cannot be asked to do for the world and the West End what they have accomplished in the East, by being asked to manage the Albert Hall and its great organ. However, may every success any way attend their valuable labours at the Bow and Bromley Institute, will be the earnest wish of every one interested in the progress of the art and in the advancement of popular taste.

The Redhill Harmonic Society performed Gounod's oratorio "The Redemption," on April 24th. The principal vocalists were: Miss Adela Vernon, Miss Emily Dones, Mr. Harper Kearton, Mr. J. Bridson. The orchestra contained some leading players, and the conductor was Mr. Henry T. Pringeur, Bac.Mus. (Oxon), F.C.O.

THE ROYAL COLLEGE OF MUSIC.

The following are the leading points of the Royal charter granted upon the petition of H.R.H. the Prince of Wales :—

The purpose for which the Corporation is founded are, first, the advancement of the art of music, by means of a central teaching and examining body charged with the duty of providing musical instruction of the highest class, and of rewarding with academical degrees and certificates of proficiency and otherwise persons, whether educated or not at the College, who on examination may prove themselves worthy of such distinctions and evidences of attainment ; and, secondly, the promotion and supervision of such musical instruction in school and elsewhere as may be thought most conducive to the cultivation and dissemination of the art of music in the United Kingdom ; and, lastly, generally the encouragement and promotion of the cultivation of music as an art throughout Our dominions.

The first President shall be His Royal Highness the Prince of Wales.

The Vice-Presidents shall be appointed by the President, and their number after the first appointments shall not exceed 15.

Any vacancy in the office of Vice-President may be filled up by the President for the time being, but it shall not be incumbent on the President to fill up any such vacancy so long as the number of Vice-Presidents holding office is not less than four.

The Council shall consist of two ex-officio members and of 24 ordinary members.

The ex-officio members shall be the President for the time being and the Lord Mayor of London for the time being.

The first ordinary members of the Council shall be the persons in that behalf named in the first part of the schedule hereto, and such four other persons as may be appointed members of the Council by the President.

At the first general meeting held after the expiration of the fifth year from the date of Our Charter, and at the first general meeting held after the expiration of every succeeding third year, one-third of the ordinary members of the Council shall retire from office, but any member so retiring shall be eligible for re-election.

The offices of retiring members of the Council shall be filled up by the members of the Corporation in general meeting assembled by the election of such persons, whether members of the Corporation or not, as the members of the Corporation may think expedient. The ordinary members of the Council to retire at the two first elections of members in general meeting under this Our Charter shall, unless they agree among themselves, be determined by ballot. At every subsequent election of members in general meeting the one-third who have been longest in office shall retire. A member of the Council elected at a general meeting of the Corporation to fill the place of a retiring member shall hold his office for nine years.

The first Director shall be George Grove, of Sydenham, in the county of Surrey, D.C.L. Subsequent Directors shall be named by the President out of a list of five names to be submitted to the President by the Council. The Director shall hold his office during the pleasure of the Council.

The Board of Professors shall consist of such number of teachers, to be styled Professors, as may from time to time be determined by the Council. The Professors shall hold their offices during the pleasure of the Council. The Professors constituting the first Board shall be named by the President on the recommendation of the Director. Subsequent Professors shall be chosen by the Executive Committee of the Council hereinafter mentioned on the recommendation of the Director, a list of not less than three persons being submitted to such Committee by the Director on the occasion of each vacancy in the office of Professor.

The pupils shall consist of scholars, exhibitioners, and students. The scholars and exhibitioners shall be pupils who have obtained scholarships and exhibitions entitling them wholly or partially to the privileges of gratuitous education and maintenance, or one of such privileges, or to some description of aid in their education. The students shall be pupils who have obtained neither scholarships nor exhibitions.

A person becoming entitled to a scholarship or exhibition who declines to accept the emoluments thereof by reason of his being able to pay for his education or maintenance, may bear the title of honorary scholar or honorary exhibitioner, or such other title as may be determined by the Council.

The Council may cause medals, prizes, or other like rewards to be conferred on deserving pupils.

The Council shall have power to cause examinations to be held of pupils of the College and of other persons who may present themselves for examination, and after examination to confer, in such conditions as they may from time to time determine, all or any of the degrees of Bachelor in Music, Master in Music, and Doctor in Music.

At the conclusion of every examination of the candidates the examiners shall declare the name of every candidate whom they deem to be qualified to receive any of the said degrees, together with such particulars as the Council may from time to time direct, and every such candidate shall receive a certificate under the seal of the Corporation, and signed by the President or by one of the Vice-Presidents, in which the degree conferred by the Council shall be stated, together with such particulars (if any) as the Council may determine.

The Council may confer the honorary degrees of Bachelor, Master, or Doctor in Music on such persons distinguished in music, and whether educated or not at the College, as the Council may, with the sanction of the President, determine.

The Council shall have power to cause examinations to be held of pupils of the College and of other persons who may present themselves for examination, and after examination to grant, in such mode and on compliance by the candidate with such conditions as they may from time to time determine, certificates of proficiency in such branches of music as the Council may from time to time determine.

At the conclusion of every examination of the candidates, the examiners shall declare the name of every candidate whom they deem to be qualified to receive any such certificate, together with any such particulars as the Council may from time to time direct, and every such candidate shall receive a certificate under the seal of the Corporation, signed by the President or by one of the Vice-Presidents, in which the branch of music in respect of which such candidate has been granted a certificate of proficiency shall be stated, together with such particulars (if any) as the Council may determine.

The Council may authorise the holders of certificates of proficiency to call themselves Associates of the College, or such other title as the Council may think fit to confer.

Contributions for Fellowships to be acquired by competition and to be held by graduates of the College who have distinguished themselves in music, may be received by the Council and applied by them in such manner as may be determined by the Council, or agreed upon between them and the contributors.

Annual subscribers to the funds of the College of £100 or upwards during the period of their subscriptions, and contributors at one time of £50 or upwards, or its equivalent, shall be deemed to be donors within the meaning of this Our Charter.

The instruction of the pupils shall be conducted under the direction and superintendence of the Director and Board of Professors, with the assistance of such teachers, to be styled Assistant Professors, Assistant Masters, Assistant Teachers, or of any of such names, as may be required, subject to the regulations made by and to the control of the Council. Any difference which may arise between the Director and the Board of Professors in respect of the instruction of the pupils shall be decided by the Council.

The Council may negotiate with any musical bodies as to the conditions on which they will be willing to join with, or be amalgamated wholly or partially with, the Corporation.

The Council may establish Scholarships, Exhibitions, and Fellowships. They may make terms with any donors as to the appropriation of their donations for a building fund, or the endowment of Fellowships, Scholarships, or Exhibitions, or otherwise as they may think expedient. The Council may affiliate any musical schools or societies with the Corporation.

The Council may enter into any arrangements with the Government respecting musical instruction in elementary or other Government schools, including the inspection of schools, the conduct of examinations, the providing wholly or partially for the supply or education of musical teachers, the appropriation of Scholarships or otherwise to persons educated in such schools, and any other matter in relation to the promotion of music in connection with Government aid which may be thought expedient.

The Council may from time to time agree with any Department of the Government to secure to such Department such official representatives on the Council as may be thought expedient.

The following persons shall be members of the Corporation, that is to say—(1) the President for the time being ; (2) the Vice-Presidents for the time being ; (3) the members of the Council for the time being ; (4) the Director and members of the Board of Professors for the time being ; (5) the graduates ; (6) the donors.

A general meeting of the Corporation shall be held once a least in every year at such time as they may be fixed by the Council. Special general meetings shall be held whenever summoned by the President or the Council.

The Council shall meet for the despatch of business, and shall from time to time make such regulations with respect to the summoning, notice, place, management, and adjournment of such meetings, and generally with respect to the transaction and management of business.

The Corporation shall provide for the instruction of their pupils, whether scholars, exhibitioners, or students.

"The Corporation " means the Royal College of Music, established by this our Charter.

"Graduates" means persons who have attained the degree (whether honorary or not) of Bachelor, Master, and Doctor in Music, or any of those degrees.

Words in the masculine gender include the feminine, it being intended that women should be admitted to membership, scholarships, exhibitions, fellowships, professorships, degrees certificates of proficiency, and all other privileges under this our Charter in the same manner as men.

First Ordinary Members of the Council named in Charter.— The Duke of Edinburgh, K.G., Prince Christian, K.G., the Archbishop of Canterbury, the Archbishop of York, the Duke of Westminster, K.G., Earl Cadogan, Lord Charles Brudenell-Bruce, M.P., the Right Hon. Lyon Playfair, M.P., Sir Thomas Gladstone, Bart., Sir Richard Wallace, Bart., K.C.B., M.P., Sir John Rose, Bart., G.C.M.G., Sir Thomas Brassey, K.C.B. M.P., Sir Julius Benedict, Thomas P. Chappell, Esq., Otto Goldschmidt, Esq., Charles Hall, Esq., Q.C., Attorney-General to His Royal Highness the Prince of Wales, E. W. Hamilton, Esq., Charles Morley, Esq., Kellow Pye, Esq., Dr. Stainer.

Members named in Charter of the First Executive Committee of the Council.—Prince Christian, K.G., the Archbishop of York, Lord Charles Brudenell-Bruce, M.P., Thomas P. Chappell, Esq., E. W. Hamilton, Esq., Charles Morley, Esq., Dr. Stainer.

Members named in Charter of the First Finance Committee of the Council.—The Duke of Edinburgh, K.G., the Duke of Westminster, K.G., Lord Charles Brudenell-Bruce, M.P., the Right Hon. Lyon Playfair, C.B., M.P., Sir Richard Wallace, Bart., C.C.B., M.P., Sir John Rose, Bart., G.C.M.G.

The total original number of applications for scholarships was 1,588. These were reduced by the preliminary local examinations to 480, divided as follows: Pianoforte—Females, 185; males, 49; total, 234. Singing—Females, 124; males, 13—137. Violin—Females, 16; males 35—51. Composition—Females, 8; males, 22—30. Organ—Female, 1; males, 20—21. Violoncello —Males, 3. Clarinet—Male, 1. Oboe—Male, 1. Flute—Male, 1. Harp—Female, 1.

These 480 selected candidates have been recently under examination by the professors of the College in the various branches, at the College and in the Albert Hall; they were reduced to seventy-six, and out of these, the professor selected the final number of fifty. The professors present were Madame Lind-Goldschmidt, Madame Arabella Goddard, Mr. Paner, Mr. Deacon, Mr. Holmes, Mr. Walter Parratt, Mr. Martin, Mr. Stanford, Mr. Hubert Parry, Dr. Bridge, Mr. Franklin Taylor, Mr. John F. Barnett, Mr. Eaton Faning, Mr. Visetti, Mr. Gompertz, Mr. John Thomas, Mr. Lazarus, and Mr. Barrett.

The following are the names of the successful candidates and of the proxime accesserunt :

Pianoforte Scholarship—Ellen E. Asbin, aged 15, Jersey; Marmaduke M. Barton, 17, Leeds; William W. Cook, 15, Halifax; Lily A. Crabtree, 18, Manchester; Sarah T. F. Crowdy, 13, Weybridge; Emily E. Daywood, 16, Reading; Emily C. Few, 16, Leytonstone; Annie C. Fry, 18, London; Annie M. Grim son, 13, London; Beatrice E. Halbert, 14, Norwood; Frances M. E. Hime, 14, Londonderry; Chas. H. Holden-White, 14, London; Louisa F. Kellett, 17, Dublin; Mary C. Macd-onald, 17, Chester; Edith E. Manning, 16, Bexley Heath; Edith Oldham, 17, Dublin; Marian P. Osborn, 14, Shorncliffe. Proxi me accesserunt—Eugenie E. L. Benard, 18, London; Wm. J. Chrisman, 10, London; Emily L. Gilloch, 18, London; Ada H. Green, 16, New Barnet; Atalanta K. Heap, 17, Walmer; Clara Howard-y-Gomez, 16, London; Lucy Kaye, 18, Leicester; Mabel R. Lyons, 13, London; Hannah A. Parry, 12, London; Mary B. Sanderson, 17, London; Catherine Smith, 14, Leeds; Olive B. St. Clair, 17, London; Simeon Vantyn, 14, London; Henrietta Van- Velthusen, 13, Newton Abbott; Thomas J. Woolall, 16, West Bromwich.

Singing Scholarships.—Julie Albu, 19, London; Amanda C. E. Aldridge, 17, London; Annie Belcher, 19, Brighton; Sarah Berry, 18, Heywood; Thomas C. Frost, 22, London; Annie H. Harding, 20, Reading; Thos. W. Page, 19, Dartford; Dan Price, 20, Dowlais; John A. Ridding, 20, Birmingham; Bertha Risch, 19, Charlton; Edith F. Robilolio, 18, London; Anna M. Russell, 20, Limerick; Emily L. Stewart, 19, Birkenhead. Proxime accesserunt—Sarah A. Armitage, 17, Newcastle; Florence C. Boxell, 18, London; Kate E. Burrage, 21, London; Ellen M. Conway, 21, London; Ada Elkington, 17, London; Keturah Evans, 18, Dowlais; Dora M. Mawhinney, 21, London; Kate Y. McKrill, 19, London; Francis H. M. Summers, 20, Cottenham.

Composition Scholarships.—Francis J. Barat, 20, London; William Duncan, 16, Sale; James McCunn, 14, Greenock; Arthur W. Smith, 20, Windsor; Sidney P. Waddington, 13, Leicester; Charles Wood, 16, Armagh.

Organ Scholarship.—Alfred H. Brewer, 17, Oxford.

Clarinet Scholarship.—Francis D. Balkley, 16, Dublin.

Flute Scholarship.—Hubert J. Lambach, 13, Edinburgh.

Harp Scholarship.—Allen M. Smith, 15, Taunton.

Violin Scholarships.—Arthur C. Bent, 16, London; Winifred R. Holliday, 17, London; Henry H. Inwards, 17, Luton; Emil Kreuz, 15, London; Arthur C. Rush, 14, London; Percy V. Sharman, 13, London; Wm. M. Stephenson, 9, Bingley; Jasper Sutcliffe, 14, Oldham. Proxime accesserunt—Jessie C. Hudson, 17, Twickenham; Annie E. E. Norledge, 13, London.

Violoncello Scholarships.—Joseph F. Field, 16, London; Wm. Henry Squire, 11, Exeter.

Correspondence.

Correspondence.

PROFESSIONAL AND AMATEUR ARTISTS.

TO THE EDITOR OF THE "MUSICAL STANDARD."

SIR,—I have no doubt many of your readers have seen the remarks that Mr. H. Irving made recently at the dinner given at the Freemasons' Tavern upon the subject of amateurs. His remarks were naturally intended for amateurs in his own profession, but I think they may very well be applied also to the musical profession, and even with greater force. If it be true that the extraordinary large number of amateurs coming upon the stage seems to threaten to sweep away professional actors altogether, how much more truly it may be said that the large number of amateurs and solo instrumentalists who appear in our concert-rooms threaten to ruin the professional artists who find the bread taken out of their mouths? Is it not a fact that many an artist is often induced to sing for very low terms, or even for mere expenses—or for nothing—in order that he or she may keep their name before the public, because they know that if they do not sing or play their part will be taken by some aspiring amateur? I cannot help thinking that the so-called popular entertainments, which have been so plentiful all over the country during the past winter or two, have had much to do in depreciating artistic talent in our concert-rooms. Wherever they have been established, hosts of amateurs, some good, some indifferent, and the majority bad, have come forward, the consequence being that when a concert has been given at which only professional artists have appeared, the attendance has been of the scantiest, and loss has resulted to the concert-giver. That this is attributable to the reason that people prefer to pay their sixpence or shilling at one of these popular entertainments, where they can hear and criticise their own friends, and perhaps enjoy some really good music from two or three professionals, I, for one, have not the least doubt. The remedy Mr. Irving proposed in the case of actors is also applicable to musicians. If professional artists of whatever standard would resolutely refuse to sing or play at a public concert without a fee, I believe the incompetence and self-assurance, which are the chief characteristics equally of amateur actors and musicians, would soon be recognised by the public, and they would tire of attending performances at which only these miserable travesties of the musical art were the only inducements to attend. I am speaking now from experience. During the past winter I have conducted a series of these popular entertainments, for which, I may add, I have received a fee. I had nothing whatever to do in getting up the weekly programme, but whenever artists were announced whose capabilities were known and appreciated there was invariably a much larger attendance than on other occasions. The amount of incompetence on the part of many of the performers whom I have been called upon to accompany or to listen to is simply appalling. On one occasion I got into hot water with the committee for firmly declining to play a comic song, but I maintained my position, and the consequence was that for the rest of the season no comic song of the same type appeared in the programmes. It seems to me that if artists would be true to themselves, to their confrères, and to their art, they would strengthen their position, and by refusing to appear without their usual fee side by side with miserably incompetent amateurs, they would give a death blow to the system by which now-a-days a professional musician is expected to give his services upon every occasion upon which he may be asked.

I am, sir, yours truly,

April 19th. H. E. S.

INTONING versus READING.

TO THE EDITOR OF THE "MUSICAL STANDARD."

SIR,—I think the accompanying "notice" will be interesting to some of your readers, and worthy of being placed on record. It was issued to the members of a choir in a large town in the south of England, with a request, "Please let everyone see this," the words in italics being carefully underlined :—

"NOTICE.—As the Rector and many of the congregation strongly dislike intoning, or anything approaching thereto, and as the present musical way of reading has been mistaken by the congregation for intoning, I must request all members of the choir for the future to read their part in a loud voice, not on one note, but to vary the pitch continually and read as unmusically as possible."

I make no comment, but subscribe myself,

April 30th, 1883. A COUNTRY ORGANIST.

At the dedication festival of St. Mary, Newington, on Tuesday, May 8th, Dr. Bridge's oratorio "Mount Moriah," will be sung, under the direction of Mr. W. Rayment Kirby, F.C.O. Mr. E. H. Turpin, will preside at the organ, and Mr. E. Deane will play the harp.

Passing Events.

Gounod's "Redemption" is to be performed by the Oxford Choral Society on May 17th.

Mr. W. de Manby Sergison announces his first evening concert, at St. James's Hall, on May 29th.

Herr Wilhelmj intends, it is said, to turn his villa at Biebrich into a conservatoire for violin students.

To-day the ninth annual students' concert of the Academy for the Higher Development of Pianoforte Playing takes place at the Marlborough Rooms, at 3.

The death is announced of M. Octave Foncqué, a highly distinguished Parisian composer and musical critic.

Mr. Jerome Hopkins has produced a child's opera in New York called "Taffy and Munch," as a feature of his eighteenth season there.

Mr. Silas G. Pratt's "Zenobia" was produced lately at Chicago. The composer is known already as the author of several works of merit.

A "Sir Julius Benedict Pianoforte Exhibition," and a "Sims Reeves Vocal Exhibition" have just been added to the prizes previously established in connexion with Trinity College, London.

Mr. George H. L. Edwards gave his twelfth evening concert, on April 23rd, at the Town Hall, Poplar, with an admirable classical and miscellaneous selection, and an excellent list of performers.

Jean Jaques Rosseau's "Devin du Village" is to be given at the Châtelet, Paris, presently, in aid of the fund for the erection of a statue to celebrate the memory of the composer and philosopher.

The music for the Sons of the Clergy Festival on Wednesday next, at St. Paul's, includes Sullivan's "In Memoriam" Overture, an effective Service in A by Mr. Myles Birket Foster, and Hiller's "Song of Victory."

The London Literary and Artistic Society held, on April 25th, an interesting monthly conversazione at St. James's Hall. The music was under the direction of Herr Immanuel Liebich.

The Brixton Choral Society give "St. Paul," on Monday next, at the Gresham Hall, under the *baton* of Mr. W. Lemare, who has done much for the art in the South of London, and deserves the earnest support of the concert-going public.

At the Church of St. Mary Abchurch with St. Laurence Pountney, a special service was held on the evening of Ascension Day. The music included Magnificat, Nunc Dimittis, Stainer in B flat, and a selection from the "Messiah."

At a concert given at the Holborn Town Hall, under the direction of Mr. Farquharson Walen, a trio written by that gentleman (the organist at St. Alban's, Holborn), for violin, violoncello, and pianoforte, was a feature of the programme. The work, composed during Mr. Walen's student days, has three movements, and is both shapely and interesting, giving promise of future efforts of still greater excellence.

A concert was given on May 1st, at the Holborn Town Hall, in aid of the Fox Court Ragged Schools. The artists were : Miss Fanny Perfitt, Miss Mary Warner, Mrs. Thomas Bound, Miss Ada Robertson, Miss Jessie Dixon, Mr. W. G. King, Mr. C. J. Clarke ; pianoforte, Miss Mary L. Harris, R.A.M., and Miss Marian Robbins ; cornet, Mr. E. C. F. Hare ; organ, Mr. W. C. Harris ; conductor, Mr. Thomas Bound.

Sir Michael Costa continues, all will regret to learn, to advance but slowly towards convalescence. He has set his heart upon conducting the Handel Festival if possible, and will, it is said, have the assistance of Mr. Willing at the rehearsals. It is a thousand pities, the best friends of the conductor agree, that he has not given up all thought of undertaking a responsibility now far beyond his age and powers. It is much to be lamented, that the ill-advised and inartistic parade happens just now, and it seems to be a heedless and cruel proposal to call upon the invalid musician to undertake a duty far too onerous for a man who should now be enjoying a complete and well-earned rest.

The Querist.

REPLY.

J. G. W.—A good average height for an organ stool is 2 inches and ¼ -ths, or from 25 to 26 inches. Care should be taken by the player to avoid sitting too high. A position should be chosen which keeps the hands well at the natural level of the middle row of keys, and enables the player to place his feet closely upon the pedals, so as to secure a smooth action of the feet from the ankle joints.—ED. *Mus. Stand.*

Service Lists.

FIRST SUNDAY AFTER ASCENSION.

MAY 6th.

London.

ST. PAUL'S CATHEDRAL.—Morn.: Service, Te Deum and Benedictus, Calkin in B flat ; Introit, See the conqueror mounts in triumph ; Holy Communion, Mozart in B flat. Even Service, Magnificat and Nunc Dimittis, Smart in B flat ; Anthem, He in tears that soweth, Mighty is our God (Hiller).

WESTMINSTER ABBEY. — Morn.: Service, Garrett in F Continuation, Jekyll. Aft.: Service, Tours in F ; Anthem The wilderness (Wesley).

LINCOLN'S INN CHAPEL.—Morn.: Service, Steggall in F Kyrie, Steggall ; Anthem, Sing to the Lord a new made song (Mendelssohn). Even: Service, Steggall in F ; Anthem, God is gone up (Croft).

TEMPLE CHURCH.—Morn.: Te Deum Landum Mendelssohn in A ; Apostles' Creed, Harmonized Monotone Anthem, He was cut off (Handel). Even.: Service, Magnificat and Nunc Dimittis, Mendelssohn in A ; Apostles' Creed, Harmonized Monotone ; Anthem, Let God arise (Dr. Greene).

ALL SAINTS, MARGARET STREET. — Morn.: Service, Te Deum, Mendelssohn in A ; Benedictus, Garrett in D ; Holy Communion, Haydn's Imperial Mass ; Offertory Anthem, Unto ye Portals, from "Redemption" (Gounod). Even.: Service, in flat (Barnby) ; Anthem, King all glorious (Barnby).

CHRIST CHURCH, CLAPHAM.—Morn.: Service, Te Deum, Plain-song ; Kyrie and Credo, Schubert in B flat ; Offertory Anthem, O risen Lord (Barnby) ; Sanctus, Benedictus, Agnus Dei, and Gloria in Excelsis (Schubert). Even.: Service, Magnificat and Nunc Dimittis, Smart in B flat ; Anthem, God Thou art Great (Spohr) ; during Offertory, Hallelujah Chorus (Messiah).

FOUNDLING CHAPEL.—Morn.: Service, Te Deum, Dykes in F ; Jubilate, Attwood in F ; Kyrie, (H.R.H. Princess Beatrice Anthems, If with all your hearts, and Cast thy burden (Mendelssohn) ; Aft.: Service, Garrett in D ; Anthem, Then round about the starry throne (Handel).

HOLY TRINITY, TULSE HILL.—Morn.: Chant Service Even.: Service, Gadsby in C. ; Anthem, Thou art gone up on high, and Lift up your heads (Handel).

ST. JAMES'S PRIVATE EPISCOPAL CHAPEL, SOUTHWARK.—Morn.: Service, Introit, (processional) Hail the day ; Communion Service, Cherubini's Coronation Mass ; Even.: Service, Thorne in D ; Anthem The Apostles, &c., Unfold ye portals everlasting, "Redemption." (Gounod).

ST. MAGNUS, LONDON BRIDGE.—Morn.: Service, Opening Anthem, If we say (Coward) ; Te Deum and Jubilate, Attwood in F ; Kyrie, Arnold. Even.: Service, Magnificat and Nunc Dimittis, Attwood in F ; Anthem, God is gone up (Croft).

ST. MICHAEL'S, CORNHILL.—Morn.: Service, Te Deum, Jubilate, Wesley in F ; Anthem, God is gone up (Croft) ; Kyrie, Evison ; Creed, Stainer. Even.: Cantate Domino, and Deus Miseratur, Goss in C ; Anthem, O sing unto God (Blow).

ST. MARY ABCHURCH, E.C.—Morn.: Service, Boyce in C ; Communion Service, Garrett in E flat. Even.: Service, Tours in D.

ST. MARY BOLTONS, WEST BROMPTON, S.W.—Morn.: Service, Te Deum, Smart in F ; Benedictus, Goss in C ; Holy Communion Service, Kyrie, Credo, Sanctus, and Gloria in excelsis, Smart in F ; Offertory, Barnby, Benedictus, and Agnus Dei. Even.: Service, Magnificat and Nunc Dimittis, Smart in F ; Anthem, God is gone up (Croft).

ST. PAUL'S, BOW COMMON, E.—Morn.: Service, Te Deum and Benedictus, Chants ; Communion Service, Kyrie, Credo, Sanctus, and Gloria in excelsis, Stainer in A ; Offertory, Stainer in A ; Benedictus and Agnus Dei, Eyre in E flat. Even.: Service, Magnificat and Nunc Dimittis, Hopkins in F ; Anthem, King all glorious (Barnby).

ST. PETER'S, VERE STREET, W.—Even.: Service, Magnificat and Nunc Dimittis, Parry in D; Anthem, If ye love me (Monk).

ST. MARGARET PATTENS, ROOD LANE, FENCHURCH STREET.—Morn.: Service, Te Deum, Smart in F; Benedictus, Dykes in F; Communion Service, Offertory Anthem, Lift thine eyes (Mendelssohn); Kyrie, Credo, Sanctus, Benedictus, Dei, and Gloria, Weber in E flat. Even.: Services, Magnificat, and Nunc Dimittis, Gadsby in C; Anthem, King all glorious (Barnby).

ST. PAUL'S, AVENUE ROAD, SOUTH HAMPSTEAD.—Morn.: Service, Te Deum, Smart in F; Benedictus, Goss; Kyrie, Mendelssohn in G. Even.: Service, Magnificat and Nunc Dimittis, Smart in F; Anthem, Lift up your heads, "Messiah" (Handel).

ST. BARNABAS, MARYLEBONE.—Morn.: Service, Te Deum and Jubilitate, Boyce in A; Anthem, God is gone up (Croft); Kyrie and Nicene Creed, Harvey Löhr, in A minor. Even.: Service, Magnificat and Nunc Dimittis, Arnold in A; Anthem, But Thou didst not leave, and Lift up your heads (Handel).

ST. PETER'S, LEIGHAM COURT ROAD, STREATHAM, S.W.—Morn.: Holy Eucharist, I saw water (Novello); Introit, Hearken unto my voice (Sutton); Mass, Hoyte in D; Hallelujah (Sutton); Communion, Hail, Thou living Bread (Corke). Even.: Magnifcat, Martin in A; Anthems, God is gone up (Croft); Lift up your heads (Handel).

ST. AUGUSTINE AND ST. FAITH, WATLING STREET.—Morn.: Service, Tours in F; Offertory, O risen Lord (Barnby); Even.: Service, Martin in A; Anthem, Thou art gone up on high, Lift up your heads (Handel).

Country.

ARDINGLY COLLEGE, SUSSEX.—Morn.: Communion Service, Hatton in E; Gloria, Wesley in C. Even.: Service, Stainer in E flat; Anthems, King all glorious (Barnby); Lift up your heads (Handel).

ST. ASAPH CATHEDRAL.— Morn.: Service, Lewis in C; Anthem, The Lord is exalted (West). Even.: Service, The Litany; Anthem, King all glorious (Barnby).

ASHBURNE CHURCH, DERBYSHIRE. — Morn.: Service, Smart in F; Kyrie, Credo, and Gloria, Garrett in E flat. Even.: Service, Garrett in E flat; Anthem, Leave us not (Stainer).

BEDDINGTON CHURCH, SURREY. — Morn.: Service, Dykes in F; Communion Service, Dykes in F. Even.: Service, Stain er in F; Anthems, But Thou didst not leave, and Lift up your heads (Handel).

BRISTOL CATHEDRAL.—Morn.: Service, Attwood in D. Aft.: Servi ce, Attwood in D; Anthem, The earth is the Lord's (Spohr).

BIRMINGHAM (ST. CYPRIAN'S, HAY MILLS).—Morn.: Service, Field in D; Anthem, O God the King of glory (Smart). Even.: Service, Clarke-Whitfeld in E; Anthem, Thou art gone up on high (Croft).

BIRMINGHAM (S. PHILIP'S CHURCH). — Morn.: Service, Chipp in A; Holy Communion, Woodward in E flat. Even.: Service, Chipp in A; Anthem, O risen Lord (Barnby).

CARLISLE CATHEDRAL.—Morn.: Service, Best in D; Introit, Why stand ye gazing (Macfarren); Kyrie, Best in D; Nicene Creed, Harmonized Monotone. Even.: Service, Macfarren in E flat; Anthems, He was cut off, and Lift up your heads (Handel).

DONCASTER (PARISH CHURCH).—Morn.: Service, Wesley in F; Anthem, God is gone up (Croft). Even.: Service, Calkin in B flat; Anthem, Blow ye the trumpet (Taylor).

DUBLIN, ST. PATRICK'S (NATIONAL) CATHEDRAL.—Morn.: Service, Te Deum and Jubilate, Mendlessohn in A; Anthem, Behold the Lamb that was slain (Spohr); Kyrie, Creed, and Sanctus, Smith in C; Gloria, Stewart in G. Even.: Service, Magnificat and Nunc Dimittis, Smart in G; Anthems, Happy and blest are they (Mendelssohn); Unto which of the angels; Let all the angels; and Lift up your heads (Handel).

EXETER CATHEDRAL. — Morn.: Service, Hopkins in C; Communion, Aldrich in G; Anthem, O Lord we trust (Handel). Even.: Service, Goss in E; Anthem, God is gone up (Croft).

ELY CATHEDRAL.—Morn.: Service, Walmisley in D; Kyrie and Credo, Walmisley in D; Gloria, Chipp in D; Anthem, If ye love me (Monk). Even.: Service, Walmisley in D; Anthem, Thou art gone up, and Hallelujah (Handel).

HIGH WYCOMBE PARISH CHURCH. — Morn.: Service, Kyrie, Faning in C; Offertory, Attwood in E flat. Even.: Service, Anthems, From Thy love as a Father; Unfold ye, portals everlasting, "The Redemption" (Gounod).

LEEDS PARISH CHURCH.—Morn.: Service, Smart in F; Anthem, 148; Communion, Dykes. Even.: Service, Wesley in E; Anthem, He was cut off (Handel).

LICHFIELD CATHEDRAL.—Morn.: Service, Turle in D; Communion Service, Turle in D; Anthem, Lift thine eyes, and He watching over Israel (Mendelssohn). Even.: Service, Turle in D; Anthem, King all glorious (Barnby).

LIVERPOOL CATHEDRAL. — Aft.: Service, Magnificat and Nunc Dimittis, Smart in G; Anthem, King all glorious (Barnby).

MANCHESTER CATHEDRAL. — Morn.: Service, Goss in D (throughout); Anthem, O God the King of glory (Smart). Aft.: Service, Goss in E; Anthem, Thou art gone up on high (Handel).

MANCHESTER (ST. BENEDICT'S). — Morn.: Service, Kyrie, Credo, Sanctus, and Gloria in excelsis, Stainer in A; Benedictus Agnus Dei, Woodward in E flat. Even.: Service, Magnificat and Nunc Dimittis, Bunnett in F.

MANCHESTER (ST. JOHN BAPTIST, HULME).—Morn.: Service, Te Deum and Benedictus, Stainer; Kyrie, Credo, Sanctus, Benedictus, Agnus Dei, and Gloria in excelsis, De la Hache in B flat; Post Communion, I am the living bread (Hoyte. Even.: Service, Magnificat and Nunc Dimittis, Bunnett in F; Anthem, Incline thine ear (Himmel).

ROCHESTER CATHEDRAL.—Morn.: Service, Hopkins in D; Anthem, God is gone up (Gibbons); Communion Service, Hopkins in D Even.: Service, Attwood in D; Anthem, Lift up your heads (Handel).

SHEFFIELD PARISH CHURCH. — Morn.: Service, Kyrie, Hiles in G. Even.: Service, Magnificat and Nunc Dimittis, Hopkins in F; Anthem, King all glorious (Barnby).

SHERBORNE ABBEY. — Morn.: Service, Kyrie, Lee in D; Offertories, Barnby. Even.: Service, Anthem, Thou art gone up on high (Herbert).

SOUTHAMPTON (ST. MARY'S CHURCH).—Morn.: Service, Te Deum and Benedictus, Woodward in E flat; Introit, The Lord reigneth (Macfarren); Communion Service, Woodward in E flat; Offertory, Whoso, Blessed is the man (Barnby); Paternoster (Hoyte). Even.: Service, Magnificat and Nunc Dimittis, Woodward in E flat; Apostle's Creed, Harmonized Monotone.

WELLS CATHEDRAL.—Morn.: Service, Rogers in F; Introit, Remember me, O Lord (Macfarren). Even.: Service, Rogers in F; Anthems, He was cut off; But Thou didst not leave; and Lift up your heads.

[The attention of the several Organists is called to the favour they confer upon their brother musicians by forwarding their notices regularly: this column of the paper is much valued as an index to what is going on in the choice of cathedral music, so much so that intermissions constantly give rise to remonstrance. Lists should be sent in a week in advance if possible.—ED. *Mus. Stand.*]

* *Post-cards must be sent to the Editor, 6, Argyle Square, W.C., by Wednesday. Lists are frequently omitted in consequence of not being received in time.*

NOTICES TO CORRESPONDENTS.

Next week's issue will contain an article of exceptional interest on "Mozart's Organ Works," by Mr. F. J. Sawyer.

CITY ORGANIST.—The gentleman in question insists that he has a Doctor's degree, but does not say what science or art the diploma refers to. Your letter is too personal as it stands, though your ideas are just. I will keep the matter in view.—ED. *M.S.*

NEWSPAPERS sent should have *distinct marks* opposite to the matter to which attention is required.

NOTICE.—*All communications intended for the Editor are to be sent to his private address. Business communications to be addressed to* 185, *Fleet Street, E.C.*

Printed for the Proprietor by BOWDEN, HUDSON & Co., at 23, Red Lion Street, Holborn, London, W.C.; and Published by WILLIAM REEVES at the Office, 185, Fleet Street, E.C. West End Agents:—WEEKES & CO., 14, Hanover Street, Regent Street, W. Subscriptions and Advertisements are received either by the Publisher or West End Agents.—*Communications for the EDITOR are to be forwarded to his private address, 6, Argyle Square, W.C.*
SATURDAY, MAY 5, 1883.—*Entered at the General Post Office as a Newspaper.*

The MUSICAL STANDARD

A NEWSPAPER FOR MUSICIANS PROFESSIONAL AND AMATEUR

NO. 980. VOL. XXIV. FOURTH SERIES.   SATURDAY, MAY 12, 1883   WEEKLY: PRICE 3D.

Musical Intelligence.

CRYSTAL PALACE CONCERTS.

PROGRAMME.

Overture, "Les deux Journées"	Cherubini.
Recit. and Air, "Infelice"	Mendelssohn.
Miss Thudichum.	
(Her first appearance at the Crystal Palace.)	
Ballade and Polonaise, for violin and orchestra..	Vieuxtemps.
Signorina Teresina Tua.	
(Her first appearance in England.)	
Manuscript Symphony in E, No. 7	Schubert.
(First time of performance.)	
Song, "Knowest thou the land" ("Mignon") ..	Ambroise Thomas.
Miss Thudichum.	
Solo for Violin, "Airs Russes"	Wieniawski.
Signorina Teresina Tua.	
L'Invitation à la Valse........................	Weber.

Conductor - - - AUGUST MANNS.

Only a few men have been really successful in writing a grand symphony. Many have tried and failed. Even Weber, with all his dramatic power and perfect knowledge of the orchestra, was unsuccessful. If, then, it be the lot of the few only to succeed in this, which is universally acknowledged to be the highest branch of modern musical art, who can ensure success in such a work as has been undertaken by Mr. J. F. Barnett? Mendelssohn once contemplated finishing Schubert's Symphony, No. 7, and Mr. Sullivan was, I am informed, asked to do so; but bearing the Italian proverb in mind, *A cader va, chi troppo alto sale*, he declined the task, for much remained to be done. Very little, indeed, even of the first movement is really complete, and in the andante the bare subject is merely given for violins, and repeated for flutes, whilst in the scherzo a few leading passages only are written for violins and clarinets. The finale is still more difficult to deal with, as it contains only the barest fragments to work upon. Some pages of the score are, with the exception of a solitary horn or violin passage, absolutely bare. It will be thus seen how extremely difficult and hazardous Mr. Barnett's undertaking really was. Of the chain of thought which possessed Schubert, when the scraps which have been mentioned were hurriedly jotted down, it is, of course, utterly impossible to conceive. We often hear of sketches and skeleton copies of compositions, but in this case even the outline is unfinished, leaving each to imagine for himself the idea intended to be conveyed by the finished picture. The words, therefore, which naturally occur to one on contemplating so arduous a task are, Who is sufficient for these things? In Mr. Barnett we have, no doubt, a clever and skilful man, hard-working and ambitious, and he has brought to bear on his impossible task a vast amount of thoughtful and affectionate labour. But even this must tell against him; for there is a readiness of invention and spontaneity of manner in Schubert's works which distinguish them from those of a more laboured character. In Mr. Barnett's work there are, of course, some indications here and there of Schubert's style, amongst which the andante, with occasional passages for clarinets and horns, is a good specimen; but, on the whole, the absence of Schubert's manner and inventive genius is but too evident. The symphony was fairly well played, and not unfavourably received.

Signorina Teresina Tua was most successful in her first appearance, and one may hope ere long to hear her again, and in at least one piece of music of a more severe and sterling character than those chosen on this occasion.

Miss Thudichum, who is a pupil of the Royal Academy, and who also made her first appearance at the Crystal Palace, acquitted herself with marked success.

R. S.

Of Schubert's Symphony, Mr. T. L. Southgate writes:—

The manuscript Symphony in E, which Dr. Grove designates No. 7, instrumented and completed from the composer's outline by Mr. J. F. Barnett, adds but little to its author's fame. It was sketched out before Schubert had emancipated himself from the influence of the great masters who had preceded him. The Handelian opening, the Haydn-like themes, the Mozartean treatment—so far as the sketchy working can be traced, all betray that Schubert had not yet learnt to think and rely on himself alone. The slow movement is in its way a gem, and though it contains no deep feeling or shows power, its dreamy pastoral tone is very pleasing. The scherzo and trio are the most original portions of the symphony, and in their individuality recall to mind his subsequent workmanship. The finale, is, exceedingly weak; there is no inspiration in this movement, and it altogether lacks the bright, ringing spontaneous tone that we find in the onward fiery march of his C Symphony, for instance. The movement is ill constructed, becoming towards the end very vague in its general plan. The brilliancy of the coda must be ascribed entirely to Mr. Barnett's cleverness. There are occasionally true Schubert touches in the skeleton, and one can see his customary fondness of repetition and diffuseness, but there is little of special fresh interest to chronicle. Dr. Grove's enthusiasm for all that Schubert has written is too well known to need comment; whether wisdom has been shown in finishing and giving to the world a work the composer himself practically declined so to do, is open to question. But there can be no doubt as to the very great ability and loyal skill with which Mr. Barnett has performed the task set him. On hearing what he has done, it is difficult to believe that we are listening to a joint production. Only a long, faithful study of the master's works could have led to so homogeneous a result. All the Schubert charms are there. The only difference is, that Mr. Barnett is a contrapuntist, and Schubert was rather a melodist and fanciful colourist; so in this symphony, while the old maestro is never obscured with over learning, we see the pen of a practised scholar, filling in and adorning with science the fragmentary work left us. It was significant that the performance excited no enthusiasm.

THE PIANOFORTE PLAYING ACADEMY.

At a *matinée* of the "Academy for the Development of Pianoforte Playing," in Hinde Street, Manchester Square, held last Saturday in the Marlborough Rooms, Regent Street, the following pupils displayed more or less proficiency, viz., Misses M. Mackeson, Moore, H. M. Wilkinson, Perman, Farrer, Hartog, Hayter, Youle, A. Stewart, McMahon, Hickson, Warren, Rosselli, and Rottenberry. The pieces were chosen from texts of Scarlatti, Mozart, Weber (the Sonata in C, Op. 24), Chopin, Henselt, Schumann, Liszt, and Mendelssohn (first movement of first concerto). Miss Youle particularly excelled in "The Concert Studies" of Liszt; Mr Clinton played the pianoforte concerto. The performance gave proof of steady work and good teaching under the direction of those excellent professors, Messrs. Franklin Taylor and Oscar Beringer.

MONS. VLADIMIR DE PACHMANN'S RECITAL AT ST. JAMES'S HALL.

PROGRAMME.

Sonata in B minor (Op. 58).....	Chopin.
Allegro maestoso—Scherzo—Largo—Finale, presto non tanto.	
Nocturne in F (Op. 15, No. 1)	Chopin.
Fantaisie in F minor (Op. 49)................	
Mazurka in C sharp minor (Op. 41, No. 1)	
Scherzo in C sharp minor (Op. 39)	
Ballade in G minor (Op. 23) ...	
Bolero in C (Op. 19)	
Prelude in E flat (Op. 28, No. 19)	
Etude in E flat (Op. 10, No. 11)	
Valse in A flat (Op. 42)	
Polonaise in A flat (Op. 53)	

There was a time when the fact of a man being able to play, like this gifted Russian, 250 pieces by heart, would have seemed sorcery (Bülow, by the way, boasts of 570 pieces, which he has by heart), but, astonishing as the fact is in itself, it falls into complete insignificance when we consider the exquisite manner in which Pachmann interprets every work. The poetry of his conceptions is as ideal as his execution is marvellous. His shading is unique, there never was such a *pianissimo*. His touch is of the most refined. Gifted with much physical strength, he remains always well within the capabilities of the instrument. As a Chopin interpreter he is perhaps unrivalled, and to hear him play Henselt, for whom also he has a great reverence, is a treat of the rarest. The encores, of which there were three, and the enthusiasm of the audience, amongst which we counted most of the prominent pianists of London, testified to the high rank that he, comparatively a new comer, has by extraordinary pianistic genius attained. FERDINAND PRAEGER.

RICHTER CONCERTS.

The presence of Herr Hans Richter among us tends to enliven, in a very marked degree, a musical season which would otherwise (as regards orchestral performances at least) be a remarkably dull one. The programme of the first concert, given last Monday, was in memory of the master with whose latter years the name of Richter has been so closely associated; whom Richter, undoubtedly, beyond any other, has taught us to understand and appreciate; and by whose lifeless body (the grand heart and soul work finished) Richter has stood with sorrowful reverence since we last gave him our hearty welcome.

The programme opened with a "Faust" Overture; which is, formally, one of Wagner's most orthodox productions; though the spirit of it is restless, striving, desponding to an almost painful degree. It is rightly called, as "C. A. B.," the thoughtful annotator of the Richter programmes, points out, "A 'Faust' Overture," for it depicts the typical Faust—the Faust-like character, not the individual Faust of Goethe, or of any other writer. It might have been added that Wagner invariably deals with something vaster than individual lives; for, like Nature herself, he ever appears only:—

Careful of the type,
Careless of the single life.

Next in order came the prelude to "Parsifal," which again impressed me with its religious solemnity. But it was in the following number, the Prelude and Isolde's "Liebestod," that Herr Richter showed his full power of appreciating Wagner, and revealing him as he is but rarely revealed to us. We have all heard this Prelude and "Liebestod" under several conductors, including Herr Richter himself, but the perfection of this performance has surely been very rarely attained.

The vigorous outpouring of melody, which we have gradually learned to understand and follow, "each moment growing more and more intensely emotional" (I quote from the programme), leads to a climax which the programme calls a "phrenzy." But it was the very absence of "phrenzy" or anything approaching passion in tatters that rendered this performance a memorable one. The reins were firmly held even in the most intensely emotional passages, and the effect of this self-restraint in conductor and performers was to enhance the power, the impressions, and the purity of the music in a scarcely credible degree. The Funeral March from the "Götterdämmerung" brought the Wagner portion of the programme to a close. "C. A. B." has indicated the leading themes of which this most solemn Death Scene is composed; but such an index can at best be but unsatisfactory. It is, for example, scarcely correct to call the first subject given "Siegfried's death-blow"—that was given before the so-called Funeral March begins; for Siegfried survived after receiving it long enough to live over again in thought the happiest moment of his life—the awakening of Brünnhilde. The real death-blow, when heard in the concert-room, is perhaps equal led for thrilling effect only by the "Barabbas" in Bach's "Passion" (St. Matthew); yet when heard in connection with the action, it appears so natural and perfectly in its place as to be scarcely noticed. The subject alluded to might with greater propriety be called the "presence of death," rather than the "death-blow"; for it pervades the scene, like a dire spirit, crushing out the life of even the fresh, youthful Siegfried subject, rising from a low dirge to a fierce agony of struggle with that motive which "C. A. B." calls "Siegfried, the Warrior"; but which is in reality a wonderful amplification of the motive Siegfried plays on his horn. "C. A. B." does not call attention to that touching return of this "horn" motive, brokenly in the minor, near the close of the scene, preceded by the motives of the "Curse" and the "Ring," showing whence death had come to that vigorous, beautiful young spirit; nor does he notice the allusions to the restless questioning of human nature, so well known by Wagner, "Wiss't ihr wie das ward?" to be answered later by Brünnhilde. But who could tell the whole of this wonderful story, so full of detail, when it is never heard without some new point coming to light in each individual listener? The second part of the programme was devoted to Beethoven's C minor Symphony; which, like the earlier numbers, served to reveal the full strength of the well-balanced orchestra, as well as to show in the most favourable light the powers of the conductor.

F. B. WYATT-SMITH.

MDLLE. IDA HENRY'S CONCERT.

The concert of this clever pianist, given at the Prince's Hall, Piccadilly, on the 8th of May, was the second that has taken place in this new building. Spacious and in every respect well appointed, it will no doubt prove a great acquisition to concert-givers. The audience cannot fail to be delighted with the luxurious seats provided for them, and when the glaring white of the walls is softened by ornamental devices, which we understand is the proprietor's intention, it certainly will be the best concert-room in the metropolis.

Mdlle. Ida Hénry is evidently quite at home in chamber music, as her performance of Beethoven's Trio, Op. 11, a sadly antiquated one, by the way, and Schumann's beautiful Quartet, fully proved, and she also fully deserved the applause of her audience for the solo performances, which required the technique of a first-rate pianist.

Miss Thekla Friedländer's excellent rendering of German songs is well known, and was duly appreciated, albeit the choice of Rubinstein's songs was not a happy one. This prolific composer has written some pretty songs, but a great number of them seem to have been suggested by pianoforte passages which often are wire-drawn, and to which he has provided a more or less common and as often unvocal melody.

Mdlle. Henry was assisted by Messrs. Ludwig, Hollman, and Zerbini, the latter of whom also accompanied the songs in his able manner. The solos for violin and violoncello proved most effective, as could not be expected otherwise from two such first-rate artists. If I object already to transcriptions of Chopin's Pianoforte Nocturne for stringed instruments, I must positively avow a contemptuous dislike to Popper's soul-less concoctions, even when so skilfully rendered. Herr Ludwig's violin playing is of the most refined, his tone noble, his intonation faultless, and his bowing so exceptionally perfect that it might serve as a model to many other violinists of repute. The Caprice by M. Saëns, bristling with difficulties, was masterly executed, but no part of the praise due to the performer can be awarded to so dry a composition. How voluminous and superior the catalogue of pianoforte music is to that of the stringed instruments shows itself at once by comparing the solos, all of artistic merit, which were so ably rendered by Mdlle. Ida Henry—pieces by Mendelssohn, Chopin, Liszt; how different, and yet how interesting every one of them!

FERDINAND PRAEGER.

MUSIC IN CORK.

A series of four Italian concerts, commencing on April 30th, have been given at the Opera House, under the direction of Signor A. de Gabriele. The programme each night was different, agreeing only in the plan, viz.: First part: miscellaneous; second part: an act from some well-known opera in costume, with chorus, scenery, etc. The following artists appeared during the week: Mdme. Vogri, Mdlles. de Laporte, Manes, and Revelli; Signors A. Byron, A. Salvini, Bolli, V. Bellati, Benghardi, and Breunelli. On Friday night the entire programme consisted of Verdi's "La Traviata" (played in four acts), for the benefit of the conductor, Signor de Gabriele. The three principal parts were cast as under: Alfredo, Sig. A. Salvini; Germont, Sig. Bellati; and Violetta, Mdlle. de Laporte. Mdlle. de Laporte has one of the most beautiful voices that I have had the good fortune to hear from time to time. Thoroughly cultivated, it is perfectly under her control, and one does not require to be much of a prophet to foretell a brilliant career for the talented lady. Several times during the progress of the opera she reached a D flat with greater ease than most average sopranos would sing B flat. Her acting, though good throughout, was not equal however to her singing, although in several parts of the opera she showed a high appreciation of the scenes she was engaged in. Signors Salvini and Bellati also acquitted themselves very well, the latter obtaining a well merited encore for his singing of "De Provenza il mar." The chorus was very faulty, and a piano which the conductor used in the orchestra instead of the usual harmonium had a most ridiculous effect. Before the curtain rose Signor Enrico Bernini (of Cork), played a fantasia for clarinet and orchestra, founded on airs from Bellini's "La Sonnambula." The house was very well attended. The Carl Rosa Opera Company are expected here on the 21st inst.

F. ST. JOHN LACY.

M. EUGÈNE WAGNER'S RECITAL.

M. Eugène Wagner, a native of Alsace, held a recital on Thursday afternoon, May 3rd, at the rooms of Messrs. Collard and Co., in Grosvenor Street. M. Wagner is a pianist of considerable ability, and plays very excellent music, his own inclusive. Great power is combined with a fine touch, and nice observance of *nuances*. The scheme included Schumann's "Arabesque" and Nachtstück Liboff's "Spinnlied," a nocturne of Chopin, a study of Raff, and A. Henselt's "Poeme d'Amour." M. Wagner's own pieces (all played without a book) were a barcarolle in D flat, "Sur le Lac Léman," a soft melody, with an imitative "current" of semiquavers; a "Menuet Bijou"; a ballade, "Souvenir de la Baie des Anges"; and the "Valse Royale," in D flat, a very pretty *pièce de circonstance*. Miss Carlotta Peretti, an agreeable mezzo-soprano, sang a *lied* of Spohr, Gounod's "Au Rossignol," and Mignon's air "Connais tu le pays." Signor Ria made his mark in Tosti's "Good bye," and a romance of Campana. The grand Collard used on the occasion is a fine specimen of the firm's excellent manufacture.

LIVERPOOL.

(*From our Own Correspondent.*)

Another comic opera by a local musician saw the light last Wednesday, at the Prince of Wales's Theatre. "Foxglove, or the Quaker's Will," is styled an opera in three acts, but it is hardly of sufficient importance, either musically or literally. The dialogue is of a very ordinary character, and the music throughout is of rather too fragmentary a character, notwithstanding the fact that it bears the stamp of a musician, though the flavour of the music is somewhat ancient. Dr. Rohner's best efforts are perhaps in the choral numbers, although some of the solos should not be passed over without a favourable remark; for instance, "The sweet birds are warbling" is a sweet sentimental song, though rather old fashioned, and "Oh dear, if you only but knew," and "'Tis surprising, tantalising," are thoroughly catching in character, and liven up the work considerably. The effect of the first part of Mendelssohn's "Wedding March," sung in four vocal parts in the third act, was not effective. Surely Dr. Rhoner is capable of writing a village wedding march? Mr. Chas. Dyall has been more successful in his lyrics than his dialogue. The work was very well represented by a body of amateurs, if we except the representative of Gerald, who might appropriately be styled a tenor in miniature, or a pocket tenor; the character is an important one, and ought to have been in more capable hands. The choruses were well sung by a body of fresh voices, evidently well trained. The composer conducted the two performances (Wednesday and Thursday), and both he and the author were warmly applauded at the first representation. Dr. Rohner is a professor well known and highly respected in this city, and produced some time back an oratorio, "Moses," and a "Stabat Mater." It would rather appear that Dr. Rohner's greater success was in the more solid works. The melodious comic operas by Mr. W. H. Jude and Mr. Frost, produced some little time ago, were, it must be admitted, more successful in catching the public taste than this last effort of a more learned musician, though, no doubt, if it were given with a good professional staff of actors who could also sing, it would be a greater success.

The following is the programme of an interesting concert given by the pupils of the School for the Blind this (Tuesday) afternoon, under the direction of Mr. W. D. Hall:—

Anthem, "I was glad"	Elvey.
Anthem, "Why seek ye the living?"	Hopkins.
Recit., "For behold darkness"	
Air, "The people that walked"	} Handel.
Chorus, "For unto us"	
Organ Solo, cantata, "May Day"	Macfarren.

Mr. Martin Schneider, of this city, an organist of great skill and tasteful accomplishments, has been appointed to the organistship of Mossley Hill Church. There is a fine organ, by Willis, and the church, architecturally, is one of the finest about Liverpool, and has a large and fashionable congregation. The appointment is a valuable one.

T. F. M.

BRIXTON CHORAL & ORCHESTRAL SOCIETY.

At the concert at Gresham Hall, on the 7th inst., Mendelssohn's "St. Paul" was given in its entirety, with Mesdames Worrell and Raymond, and Messrs. Henry Yates and Lewis Thomas as principal vocalists, Mr. W. Lemare occupying his usual post of conductor. The improvement in the playing of the orchestra (leader, Mr. Decker) noticeable at the last concert, was fully maintained; on the present occasion, and considerable care had evidently been taken with the work as a whole. The two grand choruses "Rise up, arise," and "Oh, great is the depth" especially, were given with commendable force and precision, whilst the more placid attributes of "How lovely" and "See what love" produced the impression which such truly beautiful music always has done and always will. Weak spots in the execution were not wanting, however, notably in the duet "We verily" which was attempted—it cannot be said to have been performed —by two members of the chorus, whose names were mercifully omitted from the programme, in a truly deplorable manner. Mr. Lemare ought to have more care for his reputation than to have permitted such an exhibition of incompetence. The beautiful choral "Sleepers, awake" too, was shorn of much of its effect by being accompanied throughout, whereby much of the charm of contrast was lost. In the solos, Madame Worrell gave general satisfaction, her rendering of "Jerusalem" being most admirable; Madam Raymond displayed a powerful voice of the genuine contralto *timbre*; and Mr. Lewis Thomas was, of course, thoroughly at home in all his work. Of the tenor, Mr. Yates, all that can be said is that he tried to do his best, but that he was evidently over-weighted with his part. His voice is too light for such work, and his style is quite unformed at present. The hall, which has recently been undergoing structural improvements, was crowded by an appreciative audience.

THE ROYAL ITALIAN OPERA.

Flotow's "Marta," on Thursday, May 3rd, introduced Mdme. Repetto in the title part. She has a light flexible soprano voice, and warbles like a bird. On Monday this lady undertook the part of the Queen in "Les Huguenots, when Mdme. Furschmedi, the Austrian *prima donna* sang splendidly as Valentine, and quite electrified the house. Her voice has great power, and also sweetness of quality. M. Gresse was the Marcel on Monday, and Signor De Reszke the Comte di San Brio. Signor Mierzwinski (Raoul) rather forced his voice, but otherwise did well. Signor Bevignani conducted.

On Saturday, Meyerbeer's heavy opera, "L'Africaine," a posthumous work that had better, perhaps, have been left on the shelf, served for the *rentrée* of that admirable artist, Mdme. Pauline Lucca, in the title part of Selika, an uncommonly silly one if the libretto alone be looked to. The Slumber Song in Act 2 and the grand dying *scena* were both magnificent displays of vocal brilliancy and histrionic genius, for Mdme. Lucca is a thoroughly dramatic artist. M. Devoyod, a new baritone, who enacted Nelusko, has a fine voice, but spoils the effect by his French *tremolo*; he sang well, however, in the prison scene. Signor Mierzwinski, as Vasco di Gama, executed his notes unevenly, and forced his high notes *di petto* most distressingly; his Italian orthoepy, too, is open to improvement.

Mdme. Repetto filled the small part of Inez. Signor Bevignani took the time of the famous passage for strings in unison decidedly too fast.

The new tenor, Signor Marconi, achieved a fair success last week as Lionel in "Marta." He has an imposing presence, because tall and of dignified deportment. He dragged the time of the hackneyed air in F, "M'appari tutt' amor," and the action at times betrayed lack of stage experience. Mdme. Tremelli was a smart and pert Nancy. Signor Cotogni won the only encore of the evening for the "Beer Song" of Plunkett.

On Tuesday, "I Puritani" was reproduced, with Signor Marconi as Arturo, and Mdme. Sembrich, another splendid singer, as Elvira.

The production of Bellini's last and best work, "I Puritani," on May 8th, furnished Mdme. Sembrich with an excellent opportunity for vocal display. Her pure, fresh voice, graceful, brilliant singing, and finished phrasing, proved irresistible. Signor Battistini, an excellent baritone, made a good first appearance. "Faust" and "L'Etoile du Nord" were down for performance on the 10th and 12th.

MUSIC IN · DUBLIN.

A more enjoyable concert than that given by Miss Adelaide Mullen, on the 1st inst, at the "Antients," it has seldom been my good fortune to listen to. With most becoming modesty, Miss Mullen allowed the remainder of her profession to take their annual concert before she ventured to seek support for her "first," and from the large attendance and well deserved encouragement she received, I am convinced it will not be difficult to induce her to make the event an annual one also. The talented young artist was supported by the highest members of her profession here, and contributed very largely herself to the rendering of a very select programme. Her selections were "Genevieve," by Sullivan ; " Bright days," by Berthold Tours, to which Dr. Smyly played a violin obbligato ; "The birds were telling one another," by Smart; she also took part in Sir R. Stewart's exquisite quintet, "The Bells of St. Michael's Tower." Miss Mullen's rendering of the above was in her usual cultured style, and deserving of naught but the highest praise. Mr. Bapty, of whose sweet tenor voice one never wearies, was heard to good effect in C. Villiers Stanford's trying song, "A valentine," and also took part in some concerted music. Mrs. Scott Fennell's singing of "Aprendimi qual," by Rossi, and "Always together," by Molloy, was a faultless piece of vocalism. "The two chords" (Hutchinson), was given by Mr. Grattan Kelly. Two piano solos, by Miss Newcombe would have been most enjoyable, but the effect was entirely marred by the piano being out of tune. A word of praise is certainly due to Mr. Arthur Patton, for the admirable manner in which he conducted the concert, as also to Mr. Williams for his assistance in the concerted music.

The St. Patrick's Oratorio Society are busily engaged in the rehearsal of "St. Paul," which they intend producing at the Cathedral, on 11th inst.

The Carl Rosa English Opera Company are fulfilling a three weeks' engagement here, at the "Gaiety," and, though last not least, the Dublin Orchestral Union again appear before the public, on the 15th inst., with a strong programme.   T. J. B.

SWANSEA.—The Glee and Madrigal Society held its second concert on the 4th, in the Albert Minor Hall, under the conductorship of Mr. J. Matthews. The various pieces were well rendered, before an appreciative audience, by the members of the society. The programme included madrigals, glees, etc., by Walmisley, Callcott, Hatton, Leslie, and a part-song, "The Well of St. Keyne," by Mr. J. Matthews.

BUXTON.—The second popular concert of the season was given at the Buxton gardens, on Saturday evening, May 5th, under the direction of Mr. Karl Meyder. The band played very effectively the overtures to "Marítana " and " William Tell," the March from "Athalie," etc. The vocalist was Miss Clara Wollaston, whose charming rendering of the popular ditties, Molloy's "Punchinello," Hutchinson's "Side by side to the better land," and Watson's "Wayside Posy," gained for her the most enthusiastic applause.

BETHNAL GREEN CHORAL SOCIETY.—A concert, consisting of Mendelssohn's " Hear my prayer," Macfarren's "May Day," etc., etc., was given May 1st, the soloists being Madame Clara West, whose artistic rendering of the soprano solos greatly pleased the audience ; Miss Annie Smith, in place of Miss Lottie West, who was unavoidably absent ; Mr. C. J. Murton, and Mr. Bernard Fountain ; conductor Mr. R. A. Slater ; pianoforte, Mr. W. West ; harmonium, Mr. E. T. Temple. The concert was very successful, especially from a musical point of view.

ST. MARY'S, NEWINGTON.—The annual festival in connection with the dedication service of the first week in May, was held in this church on May 8th. The feature of the service was Dr. J. F. Bridge's oratorio "Mount Moriah." This was sung by the large and efficient choir of the church, the various solos and choruses being carefully rendered. Mr. W. Rayment Kirby, F.C.O., conducted. Mr. E. Deane played the harp obbligato parts, and Mr. E. H. Turpin accompanied upon Lewis's fine toned organ.

HALSTEAD.—An evening concert, announced by Mr. George Leake, A.C.O., organist of Holy Trinity and conductor of the Halstead Musical Society, was held on April 26th. The audience were highly gratified, the concert proving to be the best of the season ; the efforts of Miss Agnes Lidel, and Miss Ada Earée, both of the Guildhall School of Music, especially contributing to the success of the evening. The programme, a miscellaneous one, included Haydn's Symphony, No. 4, as a quintet, Guonod's Berceuse, and Chopin's Fantasia Impromptu, admirably played by Mr. Leake. The concert was an enjoyable one.

HULL.—On the evening of April 19th, at the Baker Street Hall, was produced for the first time in Hull, Dr. Stainer's sacred cantata, "The Daughter of Jairus." The soloists were Miss Cheape (soprano), Mr. Russell (tenor), and Mr. Ditchbourn (bass). The chorus numbered fifty voices. Mrs. Scott presided at the piano, and Mr. Hoskins at the harmonium. Mr. Porter, F.C.O, (organist of St. Mary's, Hull) conducted, and the performance was a success. The cantata was succeeded by a miscellaneous selection.

SONS OF CLERGY FESTIVAL.—The annual gathering was held at the Metropolitan Cathedral on May 9th. Sullivan's "In Memoriam" overture, in which the majestic and expressive blending of orchestra and organ produces an effect which makes the work a happy prelude to any cathedral festival, was the first piece. The Service was a setting in A by Mr. Miles Birkett Foster. This is a most attractive work, tuneful, picturesque, expressive by turns, and its composition reflects much credit upon the composer—the organist of the Foundling Chapel. Hiller's " Song of Victory" was the anthem, and Handel's " Hallelujah " Chorus was, as usual, a feature of the service. The fine choir and excellent orchestra were under Dr. J. Stainer's charge, Mr. G. C. Martin being the organist.

STRATFORD, E.—A concert was given at the Stratford Town Hall, on Thursday, the 3rd last., under the conductorship of Mr. Sidney Vernon. The vocalists were Miss Clara Dowle, soprano ; Mi-s Minnie Hyem, contralto; Misses James, Foot, and Bloom, and Messrs. Westlake and Waters. Miss Marie Schumann, violin ; Miss Emily Fehr and Miss Adela Duckham, pianoforte. Miss Doyle sang, "Softly Sighs" (Weber) and It was a dream" (Cowen) and greatly pleased the audience. Miss Hyem's contributions were " Heaven and Earth " (Pinsuti) and .'' Two's company" (Roeckel). The violin solos of Miss Marie Schumann were well rendered. Miss Adela Duckham, a child of eight years old, who lately obtained an exhibition at the Guildhall School of Music and afterwards the first prize for piano playing, at the Stratford Musical Festival, performed a solo in a remarkable manner, and Miss Fehr's piano solo, in "Midsummer night's dream" (Mendelssohn) was splendidly given.

THE UPTON CHORAL SOCIETY.—The second concert of this very flourishing society was given on May 1st, at the Stratford Town Hall, to a crowded audience, and like its predecessor was characterised by marked success throughout. Under the very excellent direction of Mr. Joseph Proudman, the choir recently gained the first prize at the late musical festival held at Stratford, and the society is certainly to be much congratulated for having so rapidly attained such distinction. The programme was composed of Mendelssohn's " Hear my prayer," Macfarren's "May Day," part-songs and, songs. The soloists were, Miss Mary Davies, Miss F. Jones, and Mr. Alfred Kenningham, each of whom sustained the well-merited reputation they have all achieved ; the recitatives, sung by Miss M. Davies, being rendered with much feeling and good taste. Mr. A. Kenningham sang in admirable style. The choir, among other part-songs, gave that for which they recently received the first prize, 'viz, "Now the grass with dew is wet," and were much praised. A duet, "Marche solennelle," was played by Mr. T. C. Kitson (pianoforte), who accompanied during the evening, and Mr. G. B. Gilbert (harmonium) ; this was effective and much appreciated. Mr. J. Proudman accompanied.

ISLE OF MAN.—The Popular Entertainment Choir and the Douglas Singing Class, conducted by Miss Wood, gave a concert in Ramsey, on Tuesday week last, the Hall being crowded to its utmost capacity. The choir comprised about seventy voices, and the programme included a series of popular pieces, which were fairly well rendered. Mr. G. B. Cowen's song, with choral accompaniment, "Alone at midnight," was well received, as was likewise Mrs. Stanley Nelson's piece, "The Children of the City." Mrs. Valentine charmed her audience with two pianoforte solos, which were brilliantly rendered, and Miss Wood's song, "Going to market," was one of the most successful in the evening's entertainment. "Kate Dalrymple," was sung by the ' Popular Entertainment Choir in good style. "Punchinello," a solo, by Miss Marion Smith, was sung with charming sweetness, and was rapturously applauded. Mr. J. E. Bowman's piece, " For ever and for ever," was followed by an amusing glee, " Old Daddy Long-legs," the rendering being very spirited. A duet, "My boat is waiting here for thee," was charmingly given by Miss Idaline Gilder and Miss Marion Smith. Miss Wood is to be warmly congratulated on the great success of her teaching, and also for resolutely declining encores.

MR. CHARLTON T. SPEER'S CONCERT.—Mr. Charlton T. Speer gave an interesting pianoforte recital at the Academy Rooms, on May 2nd. A varied and well-selected programme of works by Bach, Beethoven, Chopin, Liszt, and other representative composers gave the young artist ample display for his facile execution, power and delicacy of touch, truthful expression, and well prepared technicalities. In G. A. Macfarren's scholarly Sonata, in B flat, for flute and piano, Mr. Oluf Svendsen proved an able *collaborateur*, both parts being rendered with artistic taste and skill. Mr. Charlton T. Speer's cleverly written impromptu, romance, and polonaise, exhibiting talent of a high order, and of a somewhat advanced type. His effective song "Oh, songs of the olden time," was admirably rendered by Mr. W. H. Brereton, whose other solo, "O ruddier than the cherry," also deserves praise. Mr. Charlton T. Speer is in many ways an accomplished artist, and has, for so young a man, secured a high place in the estimation of a large number of those interested in the progress of English art and artists. His annual recital is a courageous presentation, amply justified by his marked and varied powers, and is an annual exposition of English skill and earnestness which calls for a cordial public recognition.

COVENTRY.—The programme provided by the Coventry Musical Society, on April 30th, attracted a large attendance at the Corn Exchange. The concert commenced with Parts I. and II. of the "Creation," Haydn's first oratorio, and for generations the only rival to the "Messiah" in the favour of the English public. The artists announced were Miss Agnes Larkcom, soprano ; Mr. Harper Kearton, tenor ; and Mr. Henry Cook, basso ; but the latter gentleman was too unwell to appear, and his place was taken by Mr. W. H. Ward, a member of the society. The band was above the average. The chorus sang in good tune and fairly good time, the most noticeable effort being "Achieved is the glorious work." Miss Agnes Larkcom fairly delighted the audience—notwithstanding a cold, which necessitated some apologies on her behalf by the president. After a short interval, Mendelssohn's "Lobgesang" ("Hymn of Praise") was performed. The band performed the symphony in a masterly style throughout. The chorus music was also firmly sustained, the choir showing more "attack" and life than in the first part of the programme ; the chorale, "Let all men praise the Lord" (the first part unaccompanied), was especially worthy of note, as also the final chorus, " Ye nations, offer to the Lord." Miss Larkcom's efforts were well appreciated, and the duet, "I waited for the Lord," by this lady and Miss F. E. Hill, was loudly applauded. Of Mr. Arthur Trickett's conducting, little need be said. His patient work was evident in the chorus, and in the *verve* with which the whole performance was given, abundantly proving that as a conductor he is in his right sphere.

Foreign Musical Intelligence.

Signor Ciro Pinsuti has been named a Commander of the Order of the Crown of Italy.

Verdi has, according to *Le Ménestrel*, declined to write a work for the next Birmingham Festival.

Mr. Mackenzie's "Colomba" will be heard in Hamburg next autumn.

Weber's "Oberon" was lately given in Cologne for the first time, with recitatives by Franz Wüllner, the "Hofkapellmeister" of Dresden.

"The Poor Student" is the title of an opera by Herr Milloecker, of Vienna, which has already been represented more than fifty times in Berlin.

An imposing monument is to be erected in Vienna to the memory of Mozart, who, living there in poverty to receive at the end an unknown grave, is, after the manner of the world, to be now duly honoured, having previously built an imperishable monument to himself in his works.

Le Guide Musical criticizes at some length Gounod's "Redemption," which was performed in Brussels the other week under the composer's direction, and remarks that the solitary specimen of fugue at the end of the work must have been written as a concession to the taste of the English public, who have a particular adoration for Handel, the great master of oratorio and choral polyphonic writing.

The following is a list of the posthumous works of Flotow :—1. "Sacountala," five-act opera, completed ; 2. "The Musicians," comic opera on an incident in the life of Mozart ; 3. "The Vengeance of the Flowers" and "The Deserter," melodramas ; 4. Two concertos for the piano ; 5. A Mass ; 6. Sixteen songs, and also a bolero for soprano, believed to have been his last composition. A comic opera in two acts is also known to have been completed by Flotow some years previous to his death.

A new humorous cantata, "Miss Kilmansegg," the work of Miss Holland, was performed by that lady's choir at a concert given for a charitable purpose, on May 4th. Miss Holland's setting of Tom Hood's well-known poem is tuneful and appropriate to the spirit of the words. The cantata, published by Messrs. Weekes and Co., will be useful to small choral societies.

Organ News.

CRYSTAL PALACE.

Mr. Eyre's organ recitals on Saturday week included the following :—

Overture, "Prometheus"	Beethoven.
Andante, "Evening Prayer"	Spohr.
Air, "Love in her eyes sits playing " ("Acis ")	Handel.
Chorus, "Let their celestial concerts" ("Samson")	
Grand Prelude in E flat	Bach.
Allegretto from Symphony No. 4 ("Lobgesang")	Mendelssohn.
Bourrée in D	Saunders.
March from "Abraham"	Molique.
Grand Chorus	Guilmant.
Serenade from a Quartet	Haydn.
Variations on a Theme by Hesse	Freyer.
Turkish Patrol	Michaelis.
Procession March	Batiste.

And on Saturday last :—

Overture, "Henry VIII."	Hatton.
Grand Prelude in D minor	Mendelssohn.
Larghetto from Symphony in D	Beethoven.
Fugue on "St. Ann's" Tune	Bach.
La Berceuse	Gounod.
Gradino in B flat, and Moto Continuo in G	Hopkins.
Procession March, "Meistersinger "	Wagner.
Introduction and Pastorale	Bennett.
Overture, "Poet and Peasant"	Suppé.
Coronation March	Meyerbeer.
Funeral March of a Marionette	Gounod.
Festival March	Wischeate.

NORWICH.

An organ recital was given in St. Andrew's Hall, Norwich, by Dr. Bunnett, F.C.O., on Thursday evening the 3rd May. The following was the programme :—

Overture, "Maritana "	Wallace.
Danse des Gavots	Löhr.
Selections from "Martha "	Flotow.
Andante, "Romanunde "	Schubert.
"Harmonious Blacksmith" (arranged by Chipp)	
Silver Trumpets	Viviani.
Overture, "Huguenots "	Meyerbeer.
Rousseau's "Dream," with variations	
Gavotte, "Mignon "	Thomas.
English Airs (varied)	
Shadow Song, "Dinorah "	Meyerbeer.
Cornelius March	Mendelssohn.

PRESTON.

On Thursday evening, May 3rd, an organ recital was given by Mr. James Tomlinson. The following is the programme :—

Overture in D	Spohr.
Romanm in G	Beethoven.
(Violin and orchestra.)	
March from "Alfred "	Prout.
Overture to "Othello "	Rossini.
Berceuse	Guilmant.
Festival March	Carter.

And on Saturday evening, May 5th :—

Grand Fantaisie	Calkern.
Adagio for violin and organ	Merkel.
Fugue in E flat	Bach.
Airs from "Euryanthe"	Weber.
Chœur des Anges	Clark.
Military March	Pauer.

SOUTHAMPTON.

An organ recital was given in St. Mary's Church on May 3rd, by Mr. R. Sharpe. Annexed is the programme :—

Allegro Pomposo	Smart.
"Quis est Homo "	Rossini.
Larghetto from Symphony in D	Beethoven.
Poco Adagio from Quartet	Haydn.
Toccata e Fuga in D minor	Bach.
Andante in F	Batiste.
March, "Polycarp"	Ouseley.

BRISTOL.

At the organ recital on Saturday, May 5th, at the Colston Hall, Mr. George Riseley performed the following programme :—

March, "Eli"	Costa.
Adagio, "Maid of Orleans "	Bennett.
Organ Sonata, No. 2, in C minor	Mendelssohn.
Grave—Adagio—Allegro—Fugue.	
Largo, "O ruddier than the cherry "	Handel.
Motet, "Hear my prayer "	Mendelssohn.
Postlude, in E flat	Wely.
Agnus Dei	Mozart.
Overture, "Sophonisbe "	Paer.

BOLTON.

Mr. William Mullineux, F.C.O., gave an organ recital in the Albert Hall, on Saturday, April 28th, when the following programme was performed:—

Organ Concerto in A major (No. 2—and set)...... Large—Allegro—Minuetto—Fugue.	Handel.
Communion for the organ in F major	Grison.
Gospel Prelude and Fugue in B minor	Bach.
Air with Variations from the Symphony in D	Haydn.
Barcarolle	Gounod.
Military March in D major	Beethoven.

And on Saturday, May 5th :—

Grand Organ Sonata in D major	Mendelssohn.
Echo in B minor	Bach.
Serenade, "Wake in all thy beauty"	Cowen.
Overture in D major (Op. 13)	Spohr.
Gavotte and Musette in A	Smith.
Air, "But thou didst not leave" } Chorus, "Lift up your heads" }	Handel.

HIGH WYCOMBE.

On Monday evening, the 7th inst., a recital was given on the organ in the Parish Church, by Mr. J. G. Wrigley, F.C.O., Mus.Bac., Oxon. The following formed the programme:—

Marche Triomphale	Lemmens.
Andantino in B flat	Schubert.
Toccata et Fuga in D minor	Bach.
Offertorium sur des Noëls	Guilmant.
Andante espressivo	Salomé.
Gavotte	Raisch.
March, "Athalie"	Mendelssohn.

LEEDS.

Dr. W. Spark closed his season of recitals on the Town Hall organ on May 5th, playing a selection of Hebrew tunes and music by the Jewish composers, Meyerbeer, Costa, and Benedict. One feature of the performance was the presentation of an illuminated address to Dr. Spark from some of the members of the Great Synagogue, Leeds, in recognition of his services on the occasion of Hospital Sunday. Mr. Edward Butler (chairman of the Leeds School Board), who presided, said he was exceedingly glad that there was so large an audience to testify their gratitude to the borough organist for the recitals. The Rev. J. Groves endorsed Mr. Butler's remarks. The Leeds Corporation have decided upon spending £750 in repairing and cleaning the organ.

AYLESBURY.

Mr. August Gern, of Boundary Road, Notting Hill, has completed an excellent example of a chamber organ, for Charles Threlfall, Esq., of Aylesbury. Although not so large as that built by the same maker for Thomas Threlfall, Esq., of Holland Park, and of which a description was given in a former number; in quality of tone and general effect it is by no means inferior, while the case, which is of walnut, with burnished tin pipes, is one of the handsomest the writer, in the course of a long experience, has ever seen. This instrument, like that above referred to, has been built under the direction of Dr. Steggall, who has expressed his entire approval of the work, both in respect of the mechanism and of the general tone-quality. The builder's improved tubular pneumatic action is applied to the Pedal Organ and also to the front speaking pipes, by means of which the use of long conveyances is obviated. The following is a list of the stops :—

GREAT ORGAN. CC TO A.

1. Bourdon	16 ft.	5. Principal	4 ft.
2. Open Diapason	8 „	6. Flûte Harmonic	4 „
3. Clarabella	8 „	7. Fifteenth	2 „
4. Dulciana	8 „	8. Cremona	8 „

SWELL ORGAN. CC TO A.

9. Open Diapason	8 ft.	13. Full Mixture (3 ranks)
10. Stopped „	8 „	14. Horn .... 8 „
11. Gamba	8 „	15. Oboe .... 8 „
12. Gemshorn	4 „	

PEDAL ORGAN. CCC TO F.

16. Bourdon	16 ft.	17. Bass Flute	8 ft.

COUPLERS.

18. Swell to Great (sub-octave)	20. Great to Pedals.
19. Swell to Great.	21. Swell to Pedals.
	22. Tremulant.

SUMMARY.

4 Composition Pedals to Great. 3 Composition Pedals to Swell.

Both Swell and Great are in swell boxes.

RICHMOND, YORKSHIRE.

On Easter Tuesday, a new organ, built by Abbott, of Leeds, for the Parish Church of the above-named place, was formally opened by the organist, Mr. James Callow, with the immortal "Hallelujah" Chorus. The Service used on the occasion was Woodward in D. Henry Smart's charming "Quasi Allegretto" in G was played during the offertory. The Archbishop of York, who preached, ably sustained the position of music as an important element in Divine worship. The glorious "St. Anne" fugue closed the Service. In spite of a certain roughness (probably inseparable from a new organ), the inhabitants of the ancient borough may be congratulated on possessing an instrument worthy of their fine parish church. The one which it replaced was by G. P. England, and the more valuable portions of his work have been retained. The specifications are as follows :—

GREAT ORGAN.

1. Double Open Disp.	16 ft.	7. Harmonic Flute ...	4 ft.
2. Large Open Diap..	8 „	8. Twelfth	2½ „
3. Small Open Diap..	8 „	9. Fifteenth	2 „
4. Salicional	8 „	10. Mixture (4 ranks)	
5. Hohl Flöte	8 „	11. Posaune	8 „
6. Octave	4 „	12. Clarion	4 „

SWELL ORGAN.

13. Bourdon	16 ft.	20. Harmonic Piccolo...	2 ft.
14. Geigen Principal ..	8 „	21. Fifteenth	2 „
15. Stopped Diapason..	8 „	22. Mixture (3 ranks)	
16. Dulciana	8 „	23. Contra Fagotto......	16 „
17. Voix Celeste	8 „	24. Horn	8 „
18. Octave	4 „	25. Oboe	8 „
19. Wald Flute	4 „	26. Clarion	4 „

CHOIR ORGAN.

27. Gedact	16 ft.	31. Lieblich Gedact ...	8 ft.
28. Pierced Gamba....	8 „	32. Gedact Flute.......	4 „
29. Dolce	8 „	33. Gemshorn	4 „
30. Flauto Traverso ..	8 „	34. Clarionet	8 „

PEDAL ORGAN.

35. Sub Bass	32 ft.	39. Flute Bass........	8 „
36. Open Bass........	16 „	40. Violoncello	8 „
37. Violone	16 „	41. Trombone	16 „
38. Bourdon..........	16 „		

COUPLERS.

42. Swell to Great.	45. Great to Pedals.
43. Swell to Choir.	46. Swell to Pedals.
44. Choir to Great.	47. Choir to Pedals.

COMPOSITION PEDALS.

4 Acting on Great and Pedal Organs.
3   „   „   Swell Organ.

A Double-action Foot Pedal is applied to the Great to Pedal Coupler, also one to Swell to Great Coupler.

SUMMARY.

Great Organ...	12 stops.	Choir Organ..... 8 stops.
Pedal Organ...	7 „	Sounding Stops.. 42 „
Swell Organ...	14 „	Couplers ...... 6 „
Compass of each Manual................		CC to A.
Compass of Pedals		CCC to F.

The cost of the organ was £1,100. In the afternoon a recital was given by Mr. Best, which was numerously attended.

BECKENHAM, KENT.

The following is the specification of an excellent new organ, built for H. R. Mark, Esq., of Cheriton House, Albermarle Road, Beckenham, by Mr. R. O. Welsman, 47, Mansfield Road, N., and of Poppleton, near York:—

GREAT ORGAN. CC TO G.

1. Open Diapason......	8 ft.	5. Principal	4 ft.
2. Stopped Diapason ..	8 „	6. Fifteenth	2 „
3. Dulciana	8 „	7. Mixture (3 ranks).	
4. Clarabella	8 „	8. Trumpet	8 „

SWELL ORGAN. CC TO G.

9.*Open Diapason......	8 ft.	12.*Oboe	8 ft.
10.*Stopped Diapason..	8 „	13.*Vox Humana.......	2 „
11.*Hohl Flöte...........	4 „	14. Tremulant on Swell.	
	* Enclosed in an inner Swell box, 2 inches thick.		

PEDAL ORGAN. CCC TO F.

15. Bourdon...................		30 pipes.

COUPLERS.

16. Great Organ to Pedals.	18. Swell to Great.
17. Swell to Pedals.	

There are 3 composition pedals on Great, 2 pedals on Swell, and 2 crescendo pedals. The organ is blown by a gas engine, and fitted with two reservoirs, and two pressures of wind. The whole organ is enclosed in an elaborate burnished tin front, with oak case.

MUSIC AT ST. PAUL'S CATHEDRAL.

The Succentor of St. Paul's Cathedral, the Rev. Dr. W. Sparrow Simpson, has recently printed and issued his fourth biennial Report to the Dean and Chapter; and, since he has intimated that a copy will be sent to any clergyman, precentor, or organist who may apply for one before the stock is exhausted, it will not perhaps be a breach of courtesy to offer a few remarks in these columns on the contents of the Report, intended, as it no doubt is, for external perusal, although at first sight of a semi-private nature.

The first page of the Report contains a warm advocacy of the claims of octavo scores over single voice parts, and here all that I can imagine can be urged in favour of the former over the latter is eloquently put forward by the Succentor. Undoubtedly, "to read the score of a great work is part of a musical education," and, under the system of voice parts, "when a singer's thoughts should be raised to the heavenly ideas presented by the words and by the music, they are reduced to the low level of counting *one, two, three, four*"; yet, as church music is at present published, nearly all the works of Boyce, Croft, Greene, Gibbons, Hayes, and Purcell, not to mention any of the lesser lights of long ago, must be shelved if the octavo score is to reign paramount; and on referring to the appendices to the Report I see, unfortunately, a pretty clear indication of this fact as the result of the principles advocated on the first page. I do not for a moment profess a veneration for the names mentioned merely because they happened to flourish when the nineteenth century was not; on the contrary, I believe that nothing is more common than to overrate very grossly the "old school" of English church music: still, it appears that the modern school may be fostered, "part of a musical education" afforded to vocalists, and even very young composers encouraged at too dear a price, if that price be the almost entire exclusion from such a service as that of St. Paul's of the works of the fathers of Anglican Church music.

Some excellent remarks will be found on the second page of the Report, *apropos* of the purchase of music, which I cordially recommend some of our cathedral chapters and their supporters to read, mark, and inwardly digest:—" Nor ought there to be in the case of any cathedral any serious difficulty" as to funds "in this matter of the provision of an adequate library. If the true position of the cathedral as the mother church of the diocese were realised there could be no difficulty; the loyal laity of the diocese would resolve that in each department the cathedral should realise the ideal of divine worship; her services should be the grandest, her music the noblest, as the material shrine is the most magnificent in the district of which she is the centre." Would that they did!

Next follows, of more than local interest, a record of the musical services in St. Paul's during the past two years, and then an interesting page, on which is tabulated the various works given at the Sons of the Clergy Festival since 1860, which will doubtless be useful for reference. The appendices contain a scheme of services for sixteen weeks, which is scarcely as commendable as might be wished; and, with other lists of minor importance, a complete table of the anthems sung in the cathedral during the past year. It would materially add, I venture to suggest, to the interest of the Report another year if the *number* of times each anthem, and, more particularly, each service has been sung, were also given.

Let me not be misunderstood in any remarks I have now made, or as to any apparent blemishes I have endeavoured, in no spirit of ill-feeling, to point out. That St. Paul's Cathedral has done, and is doing, noble service in the cause of English Church music is beyond question, and most gladly and emphatically do I echo the closing words of the Succentor, "May God bless 'the grand Cathedral of St. Paul and all who minister within its walls!"

MRS. GENIUS.

(Song of a Sorrowful Hero-Worshipper.)

AIR—"Mrs. Johnson."

Great Mr. Genius takes a bride,
Through life to struggle at his side,
By law, and her own heart-strings tied
  To mighty Mr. Genius.
Her task to feed his spirit's flame,
To mend his breeks, and mark his fame,
To meet all bother, bear all blame,
  Oh, happy Mrs Genius!

He to his desk devotes the day;
Shall he be plagued with bills to pay,
Costers or cats to scare away?
  Leave that to Mrs. Genius!
His duty is big books to write,
Which give Society delight;
To tend the house from morn till night
  Is task for Mrs. Genius.

To halls of light he may repair,
His name is famous everywhere;
She stays at home and suffers there,
  Poor jealous Mrs. Genius!

Shall he stint ease or pleasure? No!
She cannot soar, then let her sew,
And sup on porridge; 'twill keep low
  The pulse of Mrs. Genius?

He's of an atrabilious mood,
At bearing pain he is not good,
But given to grumble and to brood
  And worry Mrs. Genius.
He growls much like a bee-stung bear,
Denouncing all to earth and air,
She loves—and listens; that's the share
  Of lucky Mrs. Genius.

Among earth's stars he'll sidle to roam,
Sirens his shaggy locks will comb.
Dames pet him. She can patch at home
  The dressing-gown of Genius.
Of letting her make friends he's shy,
No, let her feeble fingers try
To wring wet sheets (with wetter eye)
  Poor, lonesome Mrs. Genius!

    —Punch.

PRINCIPAL CONTENTS OF THIS NUMBER.

LONDON: SATURDAY, MAY 12, 1883.

OPENING OF THE ROYAL COLLEGE OF MUSIC.

THE Charter granted by her Majesty to the Royal College of Music was formally issued last week, and on Monday his Royal Highness the Prince of Wales inaugurated the new institution with a speech singularly graceful and redolent of English common sense. The lofty mission of our art was thoroughly recognised by his Royal Highness; in pointing out in eloquent terms the elevating effect upon the best feelings of the human heart that the cultivation of music produces, he displayed a breadth of view, which distinguishes the true thinker, from the conventional talker. The readers of this journal do not require to have again detailed the various steps of the movement which has culminated in the ceremony of Monday last. The course of the scheme has from time to time been brought under notice, and subjected to criticism in these pages. Now that the institution is a *fait accompli*, we must first thank the Prince for the persistent energy he has shown in striving for the accomplishment of the scheme unfolded at St. James's Palace; and further congratulate him on the success achieved in the raising of so large a sum as £110,000, and the opening of the school within so short a period as that of fourteen months. The hearty response that the country has accorded to his appeal shows, that at the time of the now historic meeting he had correctly gauged both the wants of the people, and also their ready appreciation of the plan there enunciated. In the second place, now that the machinery has been completed, and the school has commenced its active duties, it behoves all to whom music is dear, in the words of Sir Frederick Leighton at the banquet of the Royal Academy of Arts the other evening, to wish God-speed and every prosperity to the infant just launched on the world. There are many among us who feel that the Royal Academy of Music has not been fairly treated. It has been maintained that if this old institution, which, by its art-fruits, has established an enduring claim on the country, had received an adequate measure of support, allowing it to offer free scholarships to meritorious but poor pupils, all (and even more than) the advantages claimed for the new school would have been completely achieved. But a different course has been taken. The time has not yet come to make public the negotiations between the supporters of the two schemes. While simply remarking that union has failed, it will suffice to observe that the rivalry between the schools need not necessarily be of an unfriendly character. The lines they respectively run on are parallel rather than divergent, and so the goal reached in both cases is much the same. It is therefore of no use bewailing the fact that the Royal Academy has not been selected to carry out the task his Royal Highness has mapped out. A new departure has been made, and it becomes those who have not looked with favour on the novel scheme, but who still have the true welfare of music at heart, to assume at least an attitude of benevolence towards the school just opened. If a cordial support cannot as yet be universally accorded to it, let those who have—not without many good reasons, doubtless—felt constrained to oppose it, remember that we English pride ourselves on a fair hearing ; the authorities of the Royal College of Music are at least entitled to expect this from all. They will have plenty of thorny questions to trouble them in the future, both internal and external ; wherever therefore it is possible, let a generous support be given by musicians to their endeavours so long as an earnest striving for the best interests of the art is apparent.

The establishment of the College undoubtedly marks an epoch in the history of English music ; whether under its fostering care a truly national school of music, national in all the branches of the art, will be created, is doubtful. But this may be pointed out: the native element is strong, very strong, both on the council and teaching staff; its director, though not a practical musician, is an Englishman of undoubted talent. It is an open secret that we have been saved from the ignominy of having some third-rate German foisted on us by the practical sense and strong national instinct of the Prince of Wales.

. In the various phases and details connected with all the arts opinions will vary, and conflicting ideas always exist ; such a condition indeed is of vital necessity if we are to enjoy healthy progress, instead of somnolent satisfaction. There is plenty of room for discussion as to the best modes of tuition, and the right course of study. Such discussions can do no harm, and will rather aid in helping to produce the concrete results of experience and wide culture. It is but natural that the governing body of the College

should have faith in themselves; that quality is the prime factor in ultimate success. But they must also beware of the dangers of optimism, and should welcome, rather than repel, criticism on their doings. Faddism is becoming one of the unpleasant features of the age ; it must certainly not be allowed to obtain at the Royal College of Music. However clever a teacher may be, he must subordinate his purely private opinions to the methods generally accepted by a united staff. If one teaches harmony according to a system which another professor sturdily combats, the house will be divided, to a certain extent, against itself, and we have good authority for predicting what the result will be. In the precise value to be attached to the works of the masters of various countries, in the selection of suitable pieces, in the way in which musical history is read, in pointing out to the student and impressing on him the true principles which underlie and should ever govern true progress in all branches of the art, in the determination of the right length of lessons, as well as on many other points, conflicting opinions will probably prevail. It will be the duty—not an easy one—of the council and director to discriminate on such matters, and institute a judicious uniformity in system that should be observed by all the staff. This plan of a set method obtains at the Paris Conservatoire, and its advantages are too obvious to need comment. Thoughtful musicians know well of what vital importance it is that the course of study should be rigorously systematic, and not desultory, just at the whim of either master or pupil. There should be a prescribed period for the study of the works of each prominent builder up of the edifice of music. 'Every step in the onward march of the art should be appreciated, and mastered before proceeding to the next standpoint. This straightforward course the "fad" professor objects to. If his clever pupil can get through a Liszt concerto, he deems it waste of time to detain him over the earlier works of such pioneers as Mozart and Hummel. Another master will concentrate all his energy in teaching his pupil well-known excerpts from popular operas, ignoring with disdain the great teaching value of the pure works by the Italian masters of a generation ago. Yet another, will encourage a student to essay orchestral crudities, who has not yet mastered the art of writing simple vocal flowing sentences. These few instances show the necessity of an early regulation of the course of study to be followed, and an insistence of the abnegation of crotchets, from those who suffer from this common form of conceit. All the details of the teaching will soon become known to the outer world, and with that knowledge will inevitably come criticism. But this is not to be deplored; it ought to do good all round, it should spur on sluggish pupils, revivify tired teachers, and animate the staff to fresh striving after healthful progress.

The criticisms that from time to time have appeared on the scheme generally have been of decided utility, various modifications that have thus been suggested having been adopted. And here one may remark that efforts should be made to disabuse the minds of many of the public of the crass idea, that the institution will supply us with shoals of Beethovens, or

"Max Bruchs," as one speaker, with delicate irony, put it. The primary object of the Royal College is to discover and train latent talent. When its old pupils are scattered over the country, they can then diffuse a true appreciation and correct knowledge of the art around their several centres. Geniuses are the works of Providence, and not the productions of schools. It is remarkable that no great musician has ever come out of a musical conservatoire; our own R.A.M., with Macfarren, Sterndale Bennett, Sullivan, Mackenzie, and some others, probably scoring the best. Fancy fifty Beethovens turned out per annum! What would they do? And if each one made as wide a departure from previous types as the greatest of tone-poets did, what a fearful condition poor Music would get into! Happily, such a plethora seems a physical impossibility; during the last four hundred years, the united civilized world has not produced a dozen men of this exalted type. Such tall talk as has been indulged in on this head, should be discouraged. It savours too much of trade advertising.

There are several points in the Charter that offer suggestions for comment, but space does not permit to notice them in detail. Conspicuous, however, is the clause directing that the Board of Professors is to be subject to the Council. Those who are acquainted with the history of the Royal Academy will remember that when it seemed the end had come, it was found that the amateur Directors were responsible for the condition of things, and not the Professors. Contrary to general opinion, the amateurs proved themselves to be worse men of business than the teachers; their ornamental dis-ability nearly wrecked the institution. Professional men are rightly jealous of amateur interference. When it is remarked, that out of the twenty names that constitute the members of the Council, only three can claim to be professed musicians, it will be observed that here is an element of weakness, if not of absolute danger. The degrees which the institution is empowered to confer are wisely not to be limited to the students educated within its walls. All in the country worthy of the honour are eligible, and one is glad to see that the legitimate claims of women have been recognized. As independent examiners are to take part in the distribution of these distinctions, it practically places the Royal College in the position of an University, in connection with all the schools, and so its degrees and certificates will be valued and recognized throughout the land. Nothing is said in the Charter as to for whom the benefits of the institution are to be reserved for. His Royal Highness intimated in his speech that it was intended to be Imperial, and that all who owned the sway of her Majesty were eligible. It would be well to set this matter clearly forth, for complaints are already rife that some of its students are foreigners; if this is so, it will certainly stop the further flow of English subscriptions. In another column will be found a letter as to the fees charged for paying pupils. This matter requires careful consideration. The terms fixed are higher than those charged at the R.A.M., where more is given for the money, without taking into account other advantages it offers to students. Moreover, the charge is much higher than that which obtains at the foreign conservatoires, and we were told, among other things, that this new school would prevent English students from going abroad for musical instruction. No mention is made in the scheme for provision of studies in opera. A national school where the national drama in conjunction with music can find a home, will eventually have to form a necessary addendum.

The conclusion of the Prince of Wales' speech, which he stated that Her Majesty graciously intend to signalise the event of the day by conferring honour of knighthood on Dr. G. A. Macfarren, A. Sullivan, and Dr. G. Grove, will strike a sympathetic chord wherever the English language is spoken In the case of the doyen of our realm of music, honour is not only a tribute of admiration for genius, but in decorating the worthy head of the Royal Academy and Cambridge Professor, it is shown that while honouring the new school, the old one is not been slighted, and the graceful distinction conferred is a formal mark of the value in which the so popular art of our country is held. In Dr. Arthur Sullivan we possess a genius in the prime of life whose facile pen has ranged over the whole field of the art, giving us in the "In Memoriam" overture and "The Light of the World," true music ranking far above the trifles of comic opera. The untiring energy and enthusiasm which Dr. Grove has long exhibited in the cause of music, independently of his brilliant literary qualities, mark him out for distinction. To his perseverance and great devotion, must be attributed in no small degree the firm and speedy establishment of the new school of music.

'. T. L. SOUTHGATE.

OPENING OF THE ROYAL COLLEGE OF MUSIC

The College, situated close to the Royal Albert Hall was opened on May 7th, at noon, by the Prince of Wales (the President), who was accompanied by the Princess of Wales, the Duke and Duchess of Edinburgh, and the Princess Christian. Among those present were, Mr. Gladstone and Miss Gladstone, the Archbishop of Canterbury, Lady Folkestone, Baron Ferdinand de Rothschild, Sir C. J. Freake and Lady Freake, Mr. Courtenay, the Lord Mayor, Alderman Sir Whittaker Ellis, Sir H. Thring, Sir Richard Wallace, M.P., Sir John Rose, Mr. Charles Morley (Hon. Secretary), and Mr. H. Morley, Dr. George Grove (Director of the College), Sir Cunliffe Owen, Mr. Arthur Sullivan, Dr. Bridge, Mr. Joseph Barnby, Sir Julius Benedict, Mr. Otto Goldschmidt and Mdme. Goldschmidt the late Randall Davidson, Mr. T. P. Chappell, Mr. E. W. Hamilton, Mr. Henry Leslie, Dr. Stainer, Mr. Charles Hallé, Sir George Elvey, Mr. Charles Godfrey, and Mr. Albert Lowe. The Royal Highnesses were received by the trustees, the director, and the honorary secretary, by whom they were conducted to seats in the corridor on the second floor, where suitable preparations had been made for the inaugural ceremony. The pupils of both classes—students holding scholarships and paying students—were all assembled in rooms at the side of the corridor, and they witnessed the proceedings of the day. The ceremony commenced with the offering by the Primate of the following special prayer for the opening of the College :—

O God, who art the only Author of order and beauty, bless, we beseech Thee, this College to the perfecting of science and skill in Thy honour of music; and grant that the good intent of its founders may be answered in the diligence and virtue of its students that both the restful delight of music and the glory of the Divine worship may be enhanced ever more and more, through Jesus Christ, our Lord. Amen.

This was followed by the Collect, "Prevent us, O Lord," and the Lord's Prayer.

Dr. Grove (the Director of the College) read an address. He commenced by alluding to the meeting held at St. James's Palace on the 28th of February, 1882, at which the scheme of founding the College was launched, and to the numerous meetings held subsequently in London and many provincial towns in support of the object. By these meetings, continued Dr. Grove, and by the personal exertions of your Royal Highness and your illustrious brothers, a sum of money, amounting to over 110,000*l.*, has been raised, of which nearly £6,000 was due to the gracious action of Her Royal Highness the Princess of Wales. Included in this are four private scholarships, founded by the generosity of private individuals, viz. :— The Courtenay Scholarship, founded by Miss Courtenay in memory of her brother, Frank Courtenay, Esq.; the Wilson Scholarship, founded by Sir Erasmus Wilson, F.R.S., F.R.C.S.; the Morley Scholarship, founded by Samuel Morley, Esq., M.P., and two sons, Howard and Charles; the Elizabeth Pringle Memorial Scholarship, founded by her daughter, Lady Harvey, of Langley Park, Slough; and two others have even been founded in Australia, one by Sir W. J. Clarke for the southern colony of Victoria, and one by Sir Thomas Elder for that of South Australia. The scholar for the former of these was elected on the 1st of February, and is now on her way from Melbourne to the College. These funds, though not half what are necessary for the complete realisation of your Royal Highness's plan, have enabled you to take possession of this building erected by Sir Charles Freake, and munificently presented by him to your Royal Highness. They have also enabled you to begin the College with a considerable instalment of the entire plan by founding 50 scholarships for tuition, 15 of which include maintenance. The professors selected are such as to give confidence as to the high character of the instruction. The piano is in the hands of Mr. Pauer, Mdlle. Arabella Goddard, Mr. Franklin Taylor, and Mr. John Francis Barnett. To forward our interests, Mdme. Lind-Goldschmidt has emerged from her retirement, and singing will be taught by her, Mr. Deacon, and Signor Visetti. The violin is in the charge of Mr. Henry Holmes and Mr. Gompertz, the organ of Walter Parratt. Counterpoint and composition are taught by Dr. Bridge, Mr. Villiers Stanford, and Dr. Hubert Parry; while among the professors of other instruments are the honoured names of Harper, Lazarus, Thomas, and other ornaments of the English school. Declamation will be specially cared for, and for this the names of Mrs. Kendal and Mrs. Arthur Stirling are sufficient guarantee. The competition which has taken place throughout the country for the 50 scholarships is in itself ample proof, if proof were needed, of the justness of your Royal Highness's idea. Following the method adopted in launching the institution, your Royal Highness appealed to the mayors, corporations, and local boards throughout the country, and in the metropolitan districts to the vestries, to make known the fact of the competition, and to organize the preliminary examinations, selecting the examiners from the most eminent local musicians. The result was as successful as might have been anticipated. The Municipal Buildings were put at the disposal of the College, and the best musicians were prompt to give their services as honorary local examiners to a task which in many cases involved great labour and severe sacrifice. Dr. Grove gave an account of the recent examination. He continued :—Time will not allow me more than an allusion to various acts of private generosity by which the College has benefited. Prominent among them is the gift of the library of the late Sacred Harmonic Society through Sir Philip Cunliffe Owen, and various other gifts of pianos, furniture, etc., by Sir Charles Freake, Messrs. Broadwood, Messrs. Erard, Messrs. Chappell, Messrs. Holland, Feltham, and others. The professors, scholars, and students are awaiting your Royal Highness's notice at the close of these proceedings, and I trust your Royal Highness will believe that we are all alike animated by a sincere and enthusiastic desire to carry out to the full those wise and gracious designs which have brought us to this first step in our career. That your Royal Highness may long live to preside over us and guide us in the right path, is our humble and earnest hope and prayer.

The PRINCE OF WALES said :—I have heard your address with pleasure, and I feel great gratification in opening to-day the Royal College of Music, in the promotion of which I have taken so deep an interest. I avail myself of this the first public opportunity that has offered itself of expressing the deep personal gratification I feel at the manner in which the country has replied to my appeal for aid in establishing the College. There is no class of her Majesty's subjects capable of affording assistance to which I have addressed myself in vain. The Corporation of London and the London Companies have led the way in giving pecuniary assistance; and I owe a debt of gratitude to the mayors throughout the kingdom for the valuable aid they have afforded by granting facilities for holding local examinations essential to the proper selection of scholars. I thank these great bodies for their services, and I trust that I may yet expect from them further help in completing the task so auspiciously begun; I thank the donors of scholarships for their liberality; I thank the general public for the sums they have subscribed at a time when agriculture has been depressed and the prospects of trade have not been encouraging; and, above all, I thank the many kind friends who have responded so cordially and liberally to my appeal for assistance. I have noticed also with the greatest pleasure the contributions for Colonial scholarships that have

been given by two eminent colonists, the one on behalf of the colony of Victoria, and the other on behalf of the colony of South Australia. The object I have in view is essentially Imperial as well as National, and I trust that ere long there will be no colony of any importance which is not represented by a scholar at the Royal College. Much indeed, has been done, but I am aware that much remains to be done. I am conscious that I may be thought to have taken a bold step in beginning so great an enterprise with only the resources at present at my command. But I am unwilling that any delay should take place in giving effect to the generous intentions of those who have already contributed so liberally. I am sanguine enough to think that the example set during the last year by corporate bodies, representatives of the colonies, private donors, and the general public will be followed in ensuing years. Ours is an institution which admits of almost indefinite extension, for wherever a scholarship is founded, we know now that we shall find a deserving candidate to hold it. Let me now pass to an account of what has been actually accomplished. Fifty scholarships have been established, of which 35 confer a free education in music, and 15 provide not only a free education, but also a maintenance for the scholars. Of these scholarships half are held by boys and half by girls. I observe with pleasure that the various districts from which the scholars are drawn indicate the widespread distribution of a taste for music throughout the United Kingdom. London with its vast population, sends only 12 out of the 50. The remaining 38 come as follows:—Twenty-eight from 14 different counties in England, two from Scotland, six from Ireland, one from Wales, and one from Jersey. The occupations of the scholars are as various as the places from which they come. I find that a mill-girl, the daughter of a bricklayer, and the son of a blacksmith, take high places in singing, and the son of a farm-labourer in violin playing. The capacities of these candidates has been tested by an examination of unusual severity. Each of these scholars who returns to his native place furnished with the highest instruction in music will form a centre from which good musical education will spread around; while those who obtain musical engagements elsewhere will stimulate and encourage by their success the cultivation of music in the places whence they have come. Surely, then, it is not too much to expect that many years will not pass away before our College has so popularized music as to place England on a par with those countries on the Continent which have acquired the distinction of being called musical peoples. I feel, then, that one great object of a College of Music has been secured—namely, the discovery of latent musical ability, and the extension to those who, with great natural gifts, have been blessed with little of this world's goods, the opportunity of obtaining instruction in music, to say the least, not inferior to any which this kingdom can afford. That these words are not the language of exaggeration will be apparent to those who read the names of the eminent staff who have placed their services at the disposal of the College. Side by side with these scholars will be educated a group of paying pupils, who think that music is an art which, if worth studying at all, is worth studying well. They are then prepared to enter upon a systematic course of instruction, of less severity and continuance than that of the scholars, but still far removed from the musical dilettanteism of those who, induced by fashion, not by taste, to study music, make progress enough to torment themselves and distract their friends. (Laughter.) I lay great store by the meeting of the various classes of society in pursuit of a common yet elevating study. Such a union softens asperities, inspires kindly feeling between various classes, and proves that all mankind are akin when engaged in an art which gives the highest expression to some of the best and purest feelings of the human heart. The observations I have hitherto made relate only to the Royal College of Music as a teaching body. It is not proposed, however, that the functions of the College should be restricted to teaching. The charter under which we are incorporated provides that the Council are to cause examinations to be held of pupils of the College, and of other persons who may present themselves for examination, and after examination to confer on those who deserve such distinctions the degrees of Bachelor of Music, Master of Music, and Doctor of Music, certificates of proficiency, and other rewards. I propose that this power should be exercised by an independent board of examiners chosen by the Royal College in conjunction with the universities, and after consultation with the great musical authorities in the United Kingdom. I trust thus to secure an examining body whose impartiality will be above suspicion and capacity above all question. I hope thus, through the instrumentality of the Royal College, to raise the standard of music throughout the United Kingdom, and to create a central influence which may be beneficially exercised over all music-teaching bodies who recognise the advantage of a common system of examination. Beyond and above all this, I trust, as I stated on a previous occasion, that the College will become the recognised centre and head of the musical world in this country. It has been a reproach to England that with her vast resources, her large benevolence, her eagerness to instruct all classes of society in other branches of knowledge, one thing has hitherto been wanting—a national institution for music. Yet music is in the best sense the most

popular of all arts. If that government be the best which provides for the happiness of the greatest number, that art must be
the best which at the least expense pleases the greatest number.
I trust that to-day we have removed the reproach. England, by
a national subscription, has acquired an institution worthy to be
called national, and with the establishment of such an institution
we may look forward with confidence to the creation of a
National School of Music. England has the composers already;
all she wants is a general centre, such as the Royal College of
Music, to which they may resort for mutual aid and common
inspiration. (Cheers.) Such are the aims, not mean nor ignoble
aims, proposed for the College which we open to-day. It remains
for you, gentlemen of the council, to be careful that these aims
are fully realised. A young institution requires fostering care
and constant supervision. You must not relax your efforts. No
pains must be spared to gain fresh support, and obtain the
establishment of new scholarships. We want much—we are, I
trust, entitled to ask for much—of the public. In addition to
scholarships we want more extended premises, a music hall,
lodgings for our scholars, houses for masters, and all the appurtenances of a great college. I am sure I may trust to the
generosity of the public to supply these wants ; but you, gentlemen, must by your careful supervision make our institution
worthy of support, and no efforts of mine shall be wanting to
secure the objects we have in view. (Cheers.) I will say only
one word in conclusion. The establishment of an institution
such as I open to-day is not the mere creation of a musical
society. The time has come when class can no longer stand
aloof from class, and that man does his duty best who works
most earnestly in bridging over the gulf between different classes
which it is the tendency of increased wealth and increased civilization to widen. I claim for music the merit that it has a voice
which speaks in different tones, perhaps, but with equal force,
to the cultivated and the ignorant, to the peer and the peasant.
I claim for music a variety of expressions which belong to no
other art, and therefore adapts it more than any other art to
produce that union of feeling which I much desire to promote.
Lastly, I claim for music the distinction which is awarded to it
by Addison—that it is the only sensual pleasure in which excess
cannot be injurious. What more, gentlemen, can I say on behalf
of the art for the promotion of which we are to-day opening this
institution—an institution which I trust will give to music a new
impulse, a glorious future, and a national life? Before I quit this
room, a further duty devolves on me—a most gratifying one, I
admit. I am called upon to announce a most gracious act by
which the Queen has been pleased to mark her interest in the
opening of the Royal College. Her Majesty authorises me to
say that she proposes to confer the honour of knighthood on
Professor Macfarren and Dr. Sullivan. (Cheers.) If anything
could add to my satisfaction in making this statement, it is this,
that these honours are bestowed by the advice of the Prime
Minister, who has taken so kind an interest in the promotion of
the Royal College, and who could have devised no better mode
of celebrating its opening than by recommending that honour
should be done on this occasion to music by conferring knighthood on men so celebrated in their art as Professor Macfarren
and Dr. Sullivan, and that honour should be done to our College
by awarding a like distinction to its director, Dr. Grove
(renewed cheering)—who, eminent in general literature, has
specially devoted himself to the preparation and publication of
a Dictionary of Music, and has earned our gratitude by the skill
and success with which he has worked in the difficult task of
organizing the Royal College. I have only to add that the
Prime Minister by his presence to-day proves that neither the
cares of State nor the overwhelming press of business by which
he is surrounded, prevent him from giving personal countenance
to a national undertaking which, if I am right in what I have
said, is calculated to advance the happiness and elevate the
character of the English people. (Cheers.)

At the close of his Royal Highness's reply the professors proceeded with their pupils to the various class-rooms, which were
afterwards visited by the Prince and Princess of Wales and the
other Royal visitors. Their Royal Highnesses spent altogether
about an hour in the building ; and before leaving signed their
names in the visitors' book.

The work of the College starts with the fair number of 92
students, including 42 paying scholars. Most of course are
devoted either to pianoforte or singing. The result of the labours
of the professors and the future of the institution will be looked
forward to with no small amount of public interest.

On May 8th, H.R.H. the Prince of Wales gave what may
be almost called a Royal College of Music dinner party, the
guests including the following musical men : Prof. G. A. Macfarren, Sir J. Benedict, Dr. J. Stainer, Dr. Sullivan, Mr. J.
Barnby, Herr Otto Goldschmidt, Mr. George Mount, Mr. W. G.
Cusins, Mr. Mackenzie, Mr. T. Chappell, Dr. George Grove,
Mr. C. Morley, and Mr. Kellow Pye.

Madame Nilsson made her first appearance since her
recent return to England, at the Albert Hall on May 9th,
at a concert given by Messrs. Austin and Watts.

THE NEW MUSICAL KNIGHTS.

The bestowal of the honour of knighthood upon Prof.
G. A. Macfarren, Dr. A. S. Sullivan, and Dr. G. Grove, is
a gratifying incident of the time chosen for the opening
of the Royal College of Music. In the case of Prof. Macfarren, knighthood is honoured ; the cause of honest
artistic labour, and England as an artistic nation too, are
alike honoured by the bestowal of a title upon Prof.
Macfarren, as a man of genius, unswerving earnestness
and faithfulness to the best interests of an art which is
one of the mightiest engines of the world's civilisation.
To Dr. Sullivan the honour is a recognition of well cul-
vated gifts. As a popular English composer, Dr. Sullivan indeed stands in a position which can only be
described as unique. It is true he has enjoyed unparalleled opportunities and advantages, but it is equally
true that he has never failed to make good use of them ;
and it has been his task to successfully prove how wide
popular the name of an English composer can be made.
The claims of Dr. G. Grove are intimately connected
with the progress of music in English during the last
twenty years, as in his labours in connection with the
popularization of high-class orchestral music at the
Crystal Palace ; in the bringing forward of much English
and German music, and notable in his share of the work
of unearthing Schubert's great works, in the compilation
of his valuable "Dictionary of Music," and as regards
his acceptance of the high position of Director of the
Royal College of Music. Viewed broadly, the bestowal
of these honours will aid in the social and artistic advancement of English music and musicians ; and not
only are the recipients to be congratulated upon the
occasion, but the entire profession, as upon the receipt of
what is at once a new token of the advancing status of
the musician here, and an acknowledgment of the daily
increasing popularity of music in our midst.

Below is added a brief biographical account of the
three gentlemen.   E. H. T.

Mr. George Alexander Macfarren was born in London in
1812; he was educated at the Royal Academy of Music, and he
produced several operas, oratorios, and a large number of musical compositions of all descriptions. Fifty years ago, when he
a student, he composed his "Chevy Chase" overture, and it
was performed under Mendelssohn's conducting at the concerts
of the Gewandhaus, Leipzig. Under the direction of Dr.
Macfarren, Mendelssohn's "Antigone" music was first performed in London. Forty-two years ago he composed a
cantata in honour of her Majesty's marriage ; and since that
he has written a large number of works in one style and
another. To speak of his operas alone, he brought out in the
"Don Quixote," at Drury Lane ; in 1849 " King Charles II."
at the Princess's ; in 1860 "Robin Hood," at Her Majesty's;
and in 1864 "Helvellyn," at Covent Garden. Among his great
works are two admirable oratorios, "John the Baptist" and
"Joseph," and of his cantatas, "May Day" holds the chief
place. Dr. Macfarren has also wielded the critical pen, and the
poetical analyses of musical works that he has done for the
Philharmonic Society's programmes are singularly valuable. The
works he has written on the science of Harmony, chiefly
on the Day theory, constitute a most important English contribution to the scientific aspect of the art. Dr. Macfarren is well
known as a powerful and successful lecturer on music. In 1834
he was appointed a member of the board of professors at the
Royal Academy of Music, and in 1875, on the death of Sir Sterm-
dale Bennett, he was elected to the Professorship of Music at
Cambridge University, and was created Doctor of Music the same
month. Although Professor Macfarren labours under the
severe affliction of blindness, as a teacher, he has been very
successful. His thorough grasp over all that comes before him,
and his marvellous memory excite the astonishment of those who
are brought into relation with him.

Mr. Arthur Sullivan was the son of the Principal of the Knel-
Hall establishment. He was born in 1844, and entered the
Chapel Royal, St. James's, as a choir-boy. On leaving there,
he became a pupil of the late Sir John Goss, and in his early
compositions has caught no small reflection of that master's
lofty and beautiful church style. He afterwards briefly studied
music, in Germany, and entering our Royal Academy gained the
Mendelssohn Scholarship. He soon became famous for his
compositions. "The Tempest music," the "In Memoriam
overture," and his first symphony showed his striking ability.
Since the production of these earlier works, his genius has ranged
over a wide extent of subjects. His contributions to comic opera,
"The Contrabandista," "H.M.S. Pinafore," "Trial by Jury,"
"Patience," and "Iolanthe," have obtained for him a wide celebrity on both sides of the Atlantic, and no small amount of
wealth, it may be added. But in his "Festival Te Deum," "The
Prodigal Son," "The Light of the World," and "The Martyr of
Antioch," as well as in his numerous Anthems, he has displayed

till higher qualities. He was the director of the National Training School for Music, the embryo of the New Royal College ; the hon. degree of Doctor in Music was conferred on him by the University of Cambridge in 1876.

Mr. George Grove, D.C.L., was born at Clapham, in 1820. He was educated for a civil engineer, and was employed on the staff of Mr. Robert Stephenson, in the construction of the Chester and Holyhead Railway, and the Britannia Bridge. In 1850 he was appointed secretary to the Society of Arts, and shortly after, became secretary to the Crystal Palace Company, an office he held for many years, and with no little advantage to the cause of good music. On leaving Sydenham, he joined the firm of Messrs. Macmillan, of whose eclectic Magazine he is editor. He is also the compiler of the valuable "Dictionary of Music and Musicians," still unfinished, and he took an active part in the ormation and management of the Society for the Exploration of Palestine. In 1875 the University of Dublin conferred on him he honorary degree of D.C.L.

HENRY PURCELL

In the course of his lecture upon the "Life and Dramatic Compositions of the English Mozart," recently delivered at Leeds, Dr. W. Creser said:—

A consideration of the life and dramatic works of one who had long been regarded as the representative or type of English composers would probably be interesting. Unfortunately for dramatic musical art in England, Purcell died at the early age of 37, and before he had fully established his style. This misfortune, and the prevailing fashion for Italian and French music, completely overwhelmed the English school. Nevertheless one other composer of sterling merit did follow Purcell, namely, the gifted Arne, the composer of "Rule Britannia." He might have placed the English school on a firm basis, but failed to do so, owing to a too great adherence to the musical idioms of the rival schools of France and Italy. At the present time there was a great hope of a resuscitation of the true English school. He used the term resuscitation advisedly, for it was certain that during the reigns of King Henry VIII. and Queen Elizabeth the English school was equal in point of genius and national character to that of any other nation, and he took it that that character should be a blending of deep musical thought with much tenderness and grace. Purcell's genius was indeed altogether in advance of his time. Its character was such as to show that a composer had arisen possessing the necessary genius to build up, or at least to lay the foundation of, English opera. In 1681, at the age of 23, he ventured upon his first publication—a set of sonatas. In 1690, in addition to much laborious work in connection with his appointment as organist, he appeared to have worked assiduously for the theatres, and it was at this period he produced the "Tempest," from which specimens were given by the choir. Another great work next dwelt upon was "The Prophetess, or the history of Diocletian," from which illustrations were given, and also that of "King Arthur, or the British Worthy," which was first performed in 1691. It was to be regretted that a part only of the latter opera survived. That was but an instance of his usual custom, for Purcell published almost nothing compared with what he wrote. He neglected the most ordinary precautions for the preservation of his works, as well as those which would ensure him personal emoluments by their publication. It would seem as if the view Purcell had obtained of the power and resources of his art, and his conviction of what it might hereafter accomplish, led him to regard all that he produced as but the efforts of a learner capable of giving but a brief and transient impulse to its advancement ; and having accomplished this, fit only to be forgotten. After 80 years of neglect, however, that opera was revived, a fact without a parallel in the history of dramatic music.

The members of the St. George's Glee Union held their usual monthly concert at the Pimlico Rooms on the 4th inst. The programme was miscellaneous, and gave great satisfaction. The artists were Miss E. Phillips, Miss J. Rosse, Mr. Arthur Thompson, Master Frank Charlton, and Mr. Chaplin Henry. In the second part of the programme the chief item was the cantata "May Day" (Macfarren), the soprano solos being well rendered by Miss Phillips. The part-singing by the choir, throughout the evening, was well up to the society's standard, and included "Now is the month of Maying" (Morley), "The Nightingale" (Mendelssohn), "Now Tramp" (Bishop), and "The Song of the Vikings" (Eaton Faning), the latter receiving an encore. The accompaniments were played by Miss Edith Mahon and Mr. F. R. Kinkee, and Mr. Joseph Monday conducted.

Correspondence.

THE ROYAL COLLEGE OF MUSIC.

TO THE EDITOR OF THE "MUSICAL STANDARD."

SIR,—The publication of the Royal Charter granted to the Royal College of Music induces me to make the following remarks, in the hope that you will give them publicity in the interests of the unsuccessful candidates for scholarships. One of my sons passed the preliminary examination, and went up for the final, as appointed, but was not successful in obtaining a scholarship. The intimation of non-success was accompanied by a suggestion from the director that "it might be worth the candidate's while to enter the College as a paying student." That, Sir, my son would be glad to do, but, unfortunately, the high fee charged and the conditions of payment render that impossible. The fee for paying students is fixed at £40 per annum, and the whole amount to be paid in advance.

Now, Sir, the latter is a prohibitory condition to most of the unsuccessful candidates. From the number of my son's receipt, I estimate that 500 candidates went up to compete for 50 scholarships, consequently there are 450 disappointed, and among that number there is probably not more than one-fifth that can afford to comply with the suggestion of the director. If the Royal College of Music is really intended to foster a love for the art among the struggling classes it must open its portals a little wider than its present prospectus indicates, and if it sincerely wishes to help the young musicians of this country to obtain a thorough training under its roof it must both reduce the fees and modify the mode of payment.

The fees as fixed at present are higher than the highest in the country, and nearly treble those of any conservatoire abroad, so that the unsuccessful candidates for scholarships are driven from the doors of the Royal College of Music, which is said to be national, to seek admission to cheaper establishments at home or in a foreign land.

The Royal College of Music might easily establish its national character, fulfil its necessary functions, and receive nearly all the unsuccessful candidates by reducing its charges, and making them payable on easier terms. Indeed there is nothing to prevent, if the governing body have the will, reducing the fees to half the fixed amount to the unsuccessful candidates, so as to keep them in good practice and training until other scholarships are open for competition, and that would be a concession that would secure the training of the most promising musical talent in the country, and make the Royal College of Music worthy of the national character it assumes.

I am, Sir, yours, &c.,

PATER.

Passing Events.

"David, the son of Jesse," is the title of a Scriptural operetta produced in New York on April 16th.

Miss Agnes Larkcom and Miss Clara Myers (a rising young singer) announce a morning concert on May 23rd, at 19, Harley Street, with a strong list of good artists.

The Metropolitan Opera House in New York, one of the largest theatres in the world, is rapidly approaching completion. A roomy seating is a welcome feature of the new house.

The authorities of the Tonic Sol-fa College have invited the Cologne Choir to a breakfast at Exeter Hall during their forthcoming visit. The kindly thought of the invitation has been accepted.

Messrs. Wadsworth, Brothers, of Manchester, have just built an effective organ at Brighouse, Leeds. It was opened by Dr. W. Creser, Mr. S. E. Woxton playing on the following Sunday.

Dr. Creser's cantata "Eudora" was performed at Newcastle last week, the composer himself conducting. The local press speaks most highly of the work itself as well as of the performance.

The Guildhall School of Music gave on the 5th an excellently rendered concert at the Mansion House under the experienced direction of the principal, Mr. H. Weist Hill.

Mr. Goring Thomas's opera "Esmeralda," is to be given at the Stadt Theatre, Cologne, in the autumn. English music is now finding acceptance on the continent pretty freely.

Herr Max Bruch has recently conducted some of his own music in New York with success. Balfe's "Satanella" was to be revived in New York on May 7th.

An excellent institution in its way, the "Academy for the Higher Development of Pianoforte Playing," held its ninth annual students' concert at the Marlborough Rooms on the 5th inst. President, Mr. Franklin Taylor; Director, Mr. Oscar Beringer.

The Kyrle Society gave an efficient rendering of Mendelssohn's "Elijah" at Christ Church, Poplar, on the 2nd; Mr. Probert and Mr. A. G. Herbert artistically took the tenor and bass parts. Mr. M. L. Lawson conducted, and Mr. E. H. Turpin was the organist.

The Ecclesiastical Commissioners propose a codification and issue of fresh regulations for the governance of the St. Paul's Cathedral staff. In the event of this scheme being adopted, the Corporation of the Vicars Choral will be dissolved.

The large and fine new organ built by Messrs. Brindley and Foster in the stately old parish church of Bakewell, Derbyshire, was opened on the 10th. A choral service was celebrated in the morning. In the afternoon Mr. E. H. Turpin gave a recital. In the evening another choral service was held at which Mr. T. B. Mellor, the organist of the church, was the player.

Music appears to be a prominent plank in the eccentric platform of the Salvation Army people. "General" Booth has stated that the army had 45 paid bandmasters, and 250 bands. As within the last nine months £9,000 has been spent in the purchase of instruments, it is evident that the movement has been of considerable value to the manufacturers of musical instruments.

At the last concert of the Brousil family, on May 3rd, Miss Wurm repeated her fine Sonata in G for pianoforte and violoncello (Mr. J. A. Brousil). The work, already discussed, improves on acquaintance and is in every respect creditable to Mdme. Schumann's accomplished pupil. Miss B. Brousil, her brother, and Miss Wurms gave a capital reading of Beethoven's Pianoforte Trio in B flat. Op. 97.

An excellent concert was given on the 7th in aid of the Choir Fund of St. Jude's Church, Grays Inn Road. Miss Thudichum and Miss Ida Igguiden of the R.A.M. assisted as principal singers. The concert was under the direction of Mr. Ford, the able and much esteemed organist of St. Jude's, who has done much to advance the interests of the choir and to improve the musical services of the Church. Mr. Ernest Ford played the accompaniments very artistically. The choir sang several part-songs, and the listeners were much gratified.

At the 7th concert of the West London College of Music, at No. 31, Colville Gardens, on the evening of May 3rd, Miss Lynn distinguished herself both as pianist and singer, choosing the "Sonata Pathétique," and the air, "O mio Fernando." Miss Josephine Agabeg played most artistically Chopin's Polonaise in A flat and a Rhapsody of Liszt. Miss E. Dashwood, has a clear soprano, and tastefully sang "Couvien partir" from "La Figlio del Reggimento," also a lied of Jaubert. Mr. Warre, a fine baritone, sang Mr. Hall's "Vanity," and Mrs. Shipway won a bis for "Tit for Tat." Mr. Beresford, a professor of the violin at the College, gave a fine rendering of Ernst's "Carnaval de Venise." Some fine part-singing relieved the solos.

Mr. Charles Mackeson's valuable "Guide to the London Churches" is now out. Year by year this useful compilation is full of renewed interest. The Guide contains particulars of some 928 churches. For statistical purposes of comparison, the number is corrected to 920. As regards music the following calculations are highly interesting. In 379 churches, more than two-fifths, the service is fully choral, and in 316, more than one-third, it is partly choral; so that in 695 churches, or three-fourths, there is a musical service more or less elaborate. The Gregorian tones are used for chanting in 133, one-seventh; the choir is paid in 254, more than one-fourth, and voluntary in 477, more than half, the choir in the remaining one-fourth being partly paid or partly voluntary, or consisting of school children. In 502 churches, considerably more than half, the choir is surpliced. A new feature of the book is an index to the work done by the organ builders in the London churches.

Service Lists.

WHIT SUNDAY.
MAY 13th.

London.

ST. PAUL'S CATHEDRAL.—Morn.: Service, Te Deum and Benedictus, Best; Introit, Come, Holy Ghost (Attwood); Holy Communion, Weber in E flat. Even.: Service, Magnificat and Nunc Dimittis, Stainer in B flat; Anthem, The wilderness (Wesley).

WESTMINSTER ABBEY. — Morn.: Service, Smart in F (throughout). Aft.: Service, Garrett in F; Anthem, I was in the Spirit (Blow).

LINCOLN'S INN CHAPEL.—Morn.: Service, Rogers in D; Kyrie, Rogers; Anthem, O Lord, Thou hast searched me out and God is a Spirit (Bennett). Even: Service, Rogers in D; Anthem, I was in the Spirit (Blow).

TEMPLE CHURCH.—Morn.: Service, Te Deum Laudamus, Turle in D; Athanasian Creed, Tallis; Anthem, Come, Holy Ghost (Attwood). Even.: Service, Magnificat and Nunc Dimittis, Turle in D; Apostles' Creed, Harmonized Monotone Anthem, God is a Spirit (Bennett).

ALL SAINTS, MARGARET STREET. — Morn.: Service, Te Deum and Benedictus, Stanford in B flat; Holy Communion, Guilmant in E flat; Offertory Anthem, Lovely appear, from "Redemption" (Gounod); Communion, Ave Verum (Mozart). Even.: Service, Smart in F; Anthem, selection from "The Pentecost," Part III. of "Redemption" (Gounod).

CHILDREN'S HOME CHAPEL, BONNER ROAD, E.—Morn.: Service, Anthem, Pray for the peace (Novello); Come, Holy Ghost (Attwood). Aft.: Service, Anthems, Sweet is Thy mercy (Barnby); What are these (Stainer).

CHRIST CHURCH, CLAPHAM.—Morn.: Service, Te Deum, Plain-song; Kyrie and Credo, Schubert in B flat; Offertory Anthem, Come, Holy Ghost (Attwood); Sanctus, Benedictus, Agnus Dei, and Gloria in excelsis (Schubert). Even.: Service, Magnificat and Nunc Dimittis, Smart in F; Anthem, God is a Spirit (Bennett); The Lord descended from above (Hayes) during Offertory, Sing to the Lord with joy and gladness (Haydn).

FOUNDLING CHAPEL.—Morn.: Service, Te Deum, Smart in F; Anthem, I was in the Spirit (Blow). Aft.: Service, Foster in A; Anthem, As the hart pants (Mendelssohn).

HOLY TRINITY, TULSE HILL.—Morn.: Chant Service. Even.: Service, Cantate and Deus Misereatur, Attwood in D; Anthem, His salvation is nigh them, and God is a Spirit (Bennett).

ST. GEORGE THE MARTYR, QUEEN SQUARE.—Morn.: Service, Te Deum and Benedictus, Tours in F; Kyrie, Schubert. Even.: Service, Magnificat and Nunc Dimittis, Smart in F; Anthem, I waited for the Lord.

ST. JAMES'S PRIVATE EPISCOPAL CHAPEL, SOUTHWARK.—Morn.: Service, Introit, Come Holy Ghost; Communion Service, Schubert in E flat; Even.: Service, Field in D; Anthem, The Pentecost, "Redemption" (Gounod).

ST. MAGNUS, LONDON BRIDGE.—Morn.: Service, Opening Anthem, If we say (Coward); Te Deum and Jubilate, Attwood in F; Kyrie, Arnold. Even.: Service, Magnificat and Nunc Dimittis, Attwood in F; Anthem, God is gone up (Croft).

ST. MICHAEL'S, CORNHILL. — Morn.: Service, Te Deum and Jubilate, Sullivan in D; Anthem, Come, Holy Ghost (Attwood); Kyrie and Creed, Thorne in E flat. Even.: Service, Cantate Domino, and Deus Misereatur, Attwood in D; Anthem, The wilderness (Wesley).

ST. MARY ABCHURCH, E.C.—Morn.: Service, Wesley in F; Communion Service, Garrett in D. Even.: Service, Chants.

ST. MARY BOLTONS, WEST BROMPTON, S.W.—Morn.: Service, Te Deum, Smart in F; Benedictus, Chants; Anthem, Come, Holy Ghost (Attwood); Holy Communion, Kyrie, Credo, Sanctus, and Gloria in excelsis, Smart in F; Offertory, Stainer; Benedictus and Agnus Dei, Eyre in E flat. Even.: Service, Magnificat and Nunc Dimittis, Tours in D; Anthem, The heavens are telling (Haydn).

ST. PAUL'S, BOW COMMON, E.—Morn.: Service, Te Deum, Smart in F; Benedictus, Chants; Holy Communion, Kyrie, Credo, Sanctus, Benedictus, Agnus Dei, and Gloria in excelsis, Eyre in E flat; Offertory, Stainer in A; Paternoster, Stainer. Even.: Service, Magnificat and Nunc Dimittis, Tours in D; Anthem, God is a Spirit; And blessed be the Lord God of Israel (Bennett).

ST. MARGARET PATTENS, ROOD LANE, FENCHURCH STREET.—Morn.: Service, Te Deum, Sullivan in D; Benedictus, Dykes in F; Communion Service, Offertory Anthem, Come, Holy Ghost (Attwood); Kyrie, Credo, Sanctus, Benedictus, Agnus Dei, and Gloria, Hummel in B flat. Even.: Service, Magnificat and Nunc Dimittis, Tuckerman in F; Anthem, God is a Spirit (Bennett).

ST. PETER'S, VERE STREET, W.—Even.: Service, Magnificat and Nunc Dimittis, Parry in D ; Anthem, Come, Holy Ghost (Attwood).

ST. PAUL'S, AVENUE ROAD, SOUTH HAMPSTEAD.—Morn.: Service, Te Deum, Hopkins in G ; Benedictus, Stainer in E flat ; Anthem, God is a Spirit (Bennett) ; Kyrie, Tours in F ; Offertory, Barnby ; Credo, Sanctus, and Gloria in excelsis, Tours in F. Even.: Service, Magnificat and Nunc Dimittis, Gounod in D ; Anthem, God came from Teman (Steggall).

ST. BARNABAS, MARYLEBONE.—Morn.: Service, Te Deum and Jubilate, Wesley in E ; Anthem, Come Holy Ghost (Attwood) ; Kyrie and Nicene Creed, Wesley in F. Even.: Service, Magnificat and Nunc Dimittis, Wesley in F ; Anthem, Be thou faithful, and See, what love (Mendelssohn).

ST. PETER'S, LEIGHAM COURT ROAD, STREATHAM, S.W.—Morn.: Holy Eucharist, I saw water (Novello) ; Introit, The Spirit (Anon) ; Mass, Mozart in C (first Mass) ; Hallelujah ; Sutton ; Sequence, Veni, Sancte Spiritus. Even.: Magnificat, Stark in D ; Anthems, Veni Creator (Attwood) ; Hallelujah Chorus, "Messiah" (Handel).

ST. AUGUSTINE AND ST. FAITH, WATLING STREET.—Morn.: Service, Te Deum and Benedictus, Garrett in F ; Communion Service, Schubert in G ; Offertory, If ye love me, Monk.. Even.: Service, Attwood in C ; Anthem, The wilderness (Wesley).

S. MILDRED'S, LEE, S.E.—Morn.: Service, Te Deum Barnby in B flat ; Benedictus, Goss in E ; Introit, Above the starry ; Communion Service, Calkin in D. Even.: Service, Magnificat and Nunc Dimittis, Bunnett in F ; Anthem, God is a Spirit, from the "Woman of Samaria" (Bennett).

Country.

ARDINGLY COLLEGE, SUSSEX.—Morn.: Communion Service, Hayne in G. Even.: Service, Martin in B flat ; Anthems, God came from Teman (Steggall) ; How lovely are the messengers (Mendelssohn).

ST. ASAPH CATHEDRAL.—Morn.: Service, Garrett in D ; Anthem, God is a Spirit (Bennett). Even.: Service, The Litany : Anthem, I was in the Spirit (Blow).

ASHBURNE CHURCH, DERBYSHIRE.—Morn.: Service, Tours in F ; Sanctus and Gloria in excelsis, Marbecke. Even.: Service, Tours in F ; Anthem, God came from Teman (Steggall).

BABBACOMBE (ALL SAINTS).—Morn.: Service, Matins, Plain Song ; Communion Service ; Kyrie, Credo, Sanctus, Benedictus, Agnus Dei, Gloria in excelsis, Mozart in C ; Post Communion, Soul of Jesus (Fowles) Even.: Service, Magnificat and Nunc Dimittis, Faux Bourdons, on V. Tone and VII. Tone.

BEDDINGTON CHURCH, SURREY. — Morn.: Service, Dykes in F ; Communion Service, Dykes in F. Even.: Service, Stainer in F ; Anthems, But Thou didst not leave, and Lift up your heads (Handel).

BRISTOL CATHEDRAL.—Morn.: Service, Smart in F. Even.: Service, Smart in F ; Anthem, The wilderness (Wesley).

BIRMINGHAM (ST. CYPRIAN'S, HAY MILLS).—Morn.: Service, Field in D ; Anthem, Send out Thy light (Gounod). Even.: Service, Clarke-Whitfeld in E ; Anthem, I was in the Spirit (Blow).

BIRMINGHAM (S. PHILIP'S CHURCH). — Morn.: Service, Best, Chant Service ; Holy Communion, Barnby in E. Even.: Service, Chipp in A ; Anthem, God came from Teman (Steggall).

CANTERBURY CATHEDRAL.—Morn.: Service, Calkin in B flat ; Anthem, O Lord, give Thy Holy Spirit (Buck) ; Communion, Calkin in B flat. Even.: Service, Calkin in B flat ; Anthem, The Lord gave the word ; How beautiful (Handel).

CARLISLE CATHEDRAL.—Morn.: Service, Stanford in B flat ; Kyrie and Nicene Creed, Calkin in B flat. Even.: Service, Stanford in B flat ; Anthem, God is a Spirit, and Blessed be the Lord God (Bennett).

CHESTER (ST. MARY'S CHURCH).—Morn.: Service, Wesley in F ; Communion Service, Lee in G and Stuart in G. Even.: Service, Wesley in F ; Anthem, Come, Holy Ghost (Attwood).

DONCASTER (PARISH CHURCH).—Morn.: Service, Wesley in F ; Anthem, God is gone up (Croft). Even.: Service, Calkin in B flat ; Anthem, Blow ye the trumpet (Taylor).

DUBLIN, ST. PATRICK'S (NATIONAL) CATHEDRAL.—Morn.: Service, Te Deum and Jubilate, Garrett in D ; Anthem, Night falleth round me, and Behold, God the Lord passed by (Mendelssohn) ; Kyrie, Creed, and Sanctus, Garrett in D. Even.: Service, Cantate, Deus Misereatur, Stewart in E flat ; Anthems, God is a Spirit (Bennett) ; Let God arise (Greene).

EXETER CATHEDRAL. — Morn.: Service, Roberts in D ; Communion, Rogers in D ; Introit, Ward ; Anthem, If ye love me. Even.: Service, Walmisley in D minor ; Anthem, The Lord gave the word (Handel).

ELY CATHEDRAL.—Morn.: Service, Steggall in G ; Kyrie, Credo, and Gloria, Steggall in G ; Anthem, God is a Spirit (Bennett). Even.: Service, Steggall in G ; Anthem, God came from Teman (Steggall).

GLOUCESTER CATHEDRAL.—Morn.: Service, Smart in B flat ; Anthem, God is a Spirit (Bennett). Aft.: Service, Smart in B flat ; Anthem, God came from Teman (Steggall). Even.: Service, Goss in E ; Anthem, From Thy love ; Unfold ye portals (Gounod).

HIGH WYCOMBE PARISH CHURCH. — Morn.: Service, Smart in F ; Communion, Kyrie, and Offertory, Stainer in E flat. Even.: Service, Stainer in A ; Anthem, God came from Teman (Steggall).

LLANDAFF CATHEDRAL.—Morn.: Service, Smart in F ; Introit, Hymn 156 ; Kyrie, Arnold in B flat ; Creed, Harmonized Monotone ; Offertory Sentences, Barnby. Even.: Service, Goss in E ; Anthem, Come, Holy Ghost (Attwood).

LEEDS PARISH CHURCH.—Morn.: Service, Stanford in B flat ; Anthem, How lovely (Mendelssohn) ; Kyrie and Creed, Wesley. Even.: Service, Attwood in A ; Anthem, O where shall wisdom (Boyce).

LICHFIELD CATHEDRAL.—Morn.: Service, Hopkins in F ; Anthem, God is a Spirit (Bennett). Even.: Service, Hopkins in F ; Anthem, The wilderness (Wesley).

LIVERPOOL CATHEDRAL.—Aft.: Service, Oakeley in E flat ; Anthem, Come, Holy Ghost (Hatton).

MANCHESTER CATHEDRAL.—Morn.: Service, Kempton in B flat ; Full Communion, Hoyte in B flat ; Anthem, God is a Spirit (Bennett). Aft.: Service, The Litany ; Anthem, Blessed be the God and Father (Wesley).

MANCHESTER (ST. BENEDICT'S). — Morn.: Service, Kyrie, Credo, Sanctus, and Gloria in excelsis, Stainer in A ; Benedictus and Agnus Dei, Woodward in E flat. Even.: Service, Magnificat and Nunc Dimittis, Bunnett in F.

MANCHESTER (ST. JOHN BAPTIST, HULME).—Morn.: Service, Te Deum and Benedictus, Stainer ; Kyrie, Credo, Sanctus, Benedictus, Agnus Dei, and Gloria in excelsis, Agutter in B flat. Even.: Service, Magnificat and Nunc Dimittis, Bunnett in F ; Anthem, And when the day of Pentecost (Simper).

NORTH BERWICK, N.B. (S. BALDRED'S).—Morn.: Service, Te Deum, Tours in F ; Anthem, O Holy Ghost (Macfarren) ; Introit, When God of old (Hymn 154) ; Kyrie, Nares in F. Even.: Service, Garrett in F ; Anthem, If ye love me (Monk).

PETERBOROUGH CATHEDRAL.—Morn.: Service, Boyce in A ; Anthem, As pants the hart (Spohr) ; Communion Service, Smart in F. Even.: Service, Tours in F ; Anthem, In the beginning (Haydn).

ROCHESTER CATHEDRAL.—Morn.: Service, Goss in A ; Chants, Jubilate ; Anthem, God is a Spirit (Bennett) ; Communion Service, Armes in A. Even.: Service, Stainer in A ; Anthem, And the Spirit of God, and The heavens are telling.

SHEFFIELD PARISH CHURCH.—Morn.: Service, Sullivan in D (throughout). Even.: Service, Trimnell in D ; Anthems, Holy, Holy (Handel) ; What are these (Stainer).

SHERBORNE ABBEY. — Morn.: Service, Kyrie, Lee in D ; Offertories, Barnby. Even.: Service, Anthem ; Thou art gone up on high (Herbert).

SOUTHAMPTON (ST. MARY'S CHURCH).—Morn.: Service, Te Deum and Benedictus, Dykes in F ; Athanasian Creed, Helmore ; Introit, The Spirit of the Lord (Macfarren) ; Communion Service, Monk in C ; Offertory, Lay not up (Barnby) ; Paternoster, Hoyte. Even.: Service, Magnificat and Nunc Dimittis, Stewart in G ; Apostles' Creed ; Harmonized Monotone, Hopkins ; Anthem, If ye love me (Monk).

ST. LEONARDS-ON-SEA (ST. MARY MAGDALENE).—Morn.: Versicles, Tallis' Festival ; Te Deum, Tozer in C ; Benedictus, Garrett ; Anthem, Grieve not the Holy Spirit of God (Stainer) ; Kyrie, Mendelssohn in A flat ; Credo, Monotone ; Offertory Sentences, Martin. Even.: Service, Versicles, Tallis ; Magnificat and Nunc Dimittis, Tozer in C ; Anthem, God is a Spirit (Bennett).

TAUNTON (ST. MARY MAGDALENE).—Morn.: Service, Communion, Hayne in G ; Te Deum, Steggall in G. Even.: Service, Bridge in D ; Anthem, Come, Holy Ghost (Attwood).

WOLVERHAMPTON (ST. PETER'S COLLEGIATE CHURCH).—Morn.: Service, Te Deum, Steggall in G ; Benedictus, Gauntlett ; Anthem, O Holy Ghost (Macfarren) ; Communion Service, Dykes in F. Even.: Service, Magnificat and Nunc Dimittis, Stainer in A ; Anthem, God came from Teman (Steggall).

WELLS CATHEDRAL.—Morn.: Service, Travers in F (throughout) ; Introit, The Lord hath been mindful (Macfarren). Even.: Service, Travers in F ; Anthem, I was in the Spirit (Blow).

WORCESTER CATHEDRAL.—Morn.: Service, Garrett in E ; Creed, Lloyd in E flat ; Anthem, Come, Holy Ghost (Attwood). Even.: Service, The Litany (Tallis) ; Anthem, The wilderness (Goss).

APPOINTMENT.

Mr. H. C. TONKING, R.A.M. (pupil of Dr. Chas. Steggall), has been appointed Organist and Choirmaster of Westminster Chapel, London.

Printed for the Proprietor by BOWDEN, HUDSON & Co., at 93, Red Lion Street, Holborn, London, W.C.; and Published by WILLIAM REEVES, at the Office, 185, Fleet Street, E.C. West End Agents :—WEEKES & CO., 14, Hanover Street, Regent Street, W. Subscriptions and Advertisements are received either by the Publisher or West End Agents.—*Communications for the EDITOR are to be forwarded to his private address, 6, Argyle Square, W.C.*
SATURDAY, MAY 12, 1883.—*Entered at the General Post Office as a Newspaper.*

The MUSICAL STANDARD

A NEWSPAPER FOR MUSICIANS PROFESSIONAL AND AMATEUR

No. 981. Vol. XXIV. FOURTH SERIES.   SATURDAY, MAY 19, 1883.   WEEKLY: PRICE 3D.

THE MUSICAL STANDARD is published every Saturday, price 3d., by post, 3½d. ; and may be had of any bookseller or newsagent by ordering its regular supply.

SUBSCRIPTION.—*The Musical Standard* is posted to subscribers at 15s. a year ; half a year, 7s. 6d., payable in advance.

The rate is the same to France, Belgium, Germany, Italy, United States, and Canada.

Post Office Orders to be made payable to the Publisher, William Reeves, 185, Fleet Street, London, or to the West-end Agents, Messrs. Weekes & Co., 14, Hanover Street, Regent Street, W.

ADVERTISEMENTS.—The charge for ordinary advertisements in *The Musical Standard* is 2s. 6d. for three lines or less ; and 6d. for each line (10 words) in addition. "Organist wanted," 3s. 6d. for 3 lines or less. A reduction is made for a series.

FRONT PAGE.—Concert and auction advertisements, &c., are inserted in the front page of *The Musical Standard*, and charged one-third in addition to the ordinary rates. Other advertisements will be inserted on the front page, or in the leader page, if desired, at the same terms.

CHOPIN IN SOCIETY.

[Translated from the *Deutsche Musiker Zeitung*, by Miss Edith E. Southgate].

The Marquis de Custine, of Prague, celebrated for his many literary works, the best known of which is that on Russia, possessed a large fortune, an aristocratic name, and inhabited a splendid mansion in Paris. At the brilliant soirées he gave, one met the greatest artists and foremost men of science in the French capital. I cannot quite remember, relates Friedrich von Flotow in his "Recollections," how I, at that time unknown as I was, received an invitation to that circle of renowned and eclectic people. I only knew the Marquis by name, and was quite a stranger to him. The well-known French fashion of a servant announcing the name of each guest upon his entrance into the drawing-room would, I knew, help me to a certain extent to learn the names of the distinguished persons who were to appear. In order that I should succeed in this, I determined to be one of the first to enter the Hotel de Custine. I was the first, and was so early, indeed, that there was not even a servant present in the anteroom, and I walked into the drawing-room without being announced. I told my name to the friendly Marquis, who advanced towards me, and introduced myself as a German. He perceived my embarrassment, and came at once to my help, praising the punctuality of my countrymen in general, and above all that of the German artists. They certainly never seek to produce a sensation in a drawing-room, through an affected late appearance.

After a short time the arrivals commenced, and I heard the name of Horace Vernet, the celebrated battlefield painter; he looked like a Bedouin sheik, so dark was the colour of his face. Then came Baron Marochetti, the sculptor, a young but already famed artist; Graaf von Nieuwerkerke, his colleague; the sea painter, Gudin; Tissot, professor and member of the Institut de France; Balzac the author; Appert, who, through his active exertions to better the French prisons, received the name of "*Bienfaiteur des prisonniers*"; Artôt the violin player, and Franchomme the violoncellist.

At last I heard the name of Chopin announced, and my entire interest became centred in him. He appeared to me suffering and nervously excited; in stature he was large, but at the same time painfully thin. He quickly approached the Marquis, and I heard him ask quietly, "Is she coming?" "I hope so," was the answer. I asked of a gentleman standing near me who this referred to. "Do you not know," was the reply, "that the Baroness Dudevant is expected?" Finding that I was utterly ignorant as to the significance of this name, he added, "The Baroness Dudevant is the most celebrated authoress, and signs her works with the name of George Sand." This *nom de plume* was certainly well known to me, I had read and admired most of her works. In the course of conversation with my friendly neighbour, I discovered that George Sand had taken up the literary career in the later years of her life, and that she was separated from her husband. The well-known man of letters, Sandeau, first discovered her great talent, called her attention to it, and directed her steps up to the first stage of fame. Out of gratitude to him, she adopted the first half of his name, and signed her works with "Sand." Just at this time, I was told, she was at variance with her friend and admirer, and this was perhaps the cause of his absence at the soirée in the Hotel Custine. Whether this statement was true or not, I cannot say, but I heard later from others the same tale with little variation. Informed by the servant of fresh arrivals, the Marquis de Custine hurried away, and immediately appeared again, having a lady on his arm, the servant following behind, and with a stentorian voice announcing, "Madame George Sand." All hurried to meet her. Each wished to be the first to greet, or see, the honoured one. Here she accorded a little laugh, there friendly words, and to the special favourites she offered her hand. To the last-named category belonged Chopin. After the first excitement was over, I succeeded in obtaining a favourable place from which I could watch the distinguished authoress. She was not beautiful, and not young, I could perceive nothing out of the ordinary in her outward appearance.

The concert then began; after a few pieces had been given, Chopin was called upon to play. He seated himself at the pianoforte and performed one of his much-admired mazurkas. His friends declared that upon the evening there was a greater depth of feeling in his music than usual. I had never before heard him, so could offer no opinion; but I was enraptured with his playing. After Chopin had finished, there was a pause and then something happened which at that period was, indeed most peculiar and extraordinary. George Sand demanded a cigar! Not a lady's paper cigarette, with perfumed contents; no! a real, full-sized man's cigar. Those who had lived thirty years in Paris can well understand what an impression such a demand (and especially from a lady) must have made at that time on the assembled guests of the Marquis de Custine. We young people, when we approached a lady carefully avoided carrying with us even the smell of cigars. We did not even smoke in the morning, when we intended going into society the same evening. Since that period it is indeed, otherwise in Paris.

The cigar which George Sand had desired was brought; the door which led to the garden of the mansion was opened, and the "performance" began. Furnished with hat and cloak (for it was cool outside), the celebrated lady, without anyone to attend her, walked up and down puffing mighty clouds of smoke in the air. Unconcerned she stood the glance of hundreds of eyes, which were directed on her through the windows. The young lads found it original, the elders unfitting; the young men were enchanted, the married men were uneasy, chiefly on account of the bad example. Everything in the world comes to an end, and so did the cigar of Madame Sand. She threw the fragment left on one side, and returned to the company.

Chopin was now called upon to play something; at first he declined, but afterwards he declared himself ready to improvise; an universal bravo rewarded him in advance. He was about to begin, when he suddenly got up, and whispered to the Marquis that his inspiration could only be created by the eyes of the celebrated authoress; she was to be asked to sit opposite him. George Sand granted his request, and took a seat at the end of the piano; she gave a long look at the music improvisator, which the latter answered, and began. The remaining mortals, or immortals, stood or sat in a circle around. Expectations were raised to the highest. Since that evening forty years have fled, nevertheless I remember Chopin's improvisation as if I had only heard it yesterday. He began with the lowest bass notes of the pianoforte, and by judicious employment of the pedals worked up a stormy roll, leading into a tender melody in the minor; the whole concluded with a very brilliant and triumphant coda. The long continued applause of his audience, and a warm shake of the hand from George Sand (who felt herself very flattered at the distinction which Chopin had thus accorded her) was the reward of the great virtuoso. He left the piano exhausted and languid. The guests departed, and I took leave, delighted to have found in the Marquis de Custine an accomplished gentleman, to have heard the celebrated Chopin, and to have seen the most famous authoress of France smoke a cigar.

THE ROYAL COLLEGE OF MUSIC.—The new musical college—musical university it may almost be called, since it has the power of conferring degrees—will, for so long as it comes to be identified with the name of its founder and patron, the Prince of Wales. Indeed, he is more than its patron and founder—he has displayed in its cause a persevering energy, and power of organizing that ought to assure to any institution a successful start. But, without prejudice to Dr. Grove, the director, or to Dr. Sullivan, as representing the training school now merged in the new college, the most graceful act of the occasion was the statement, that one of the three new knights is to be Dr. Macfarren. Unquestionably, if the Royal Academy of Music, which he represents, had received some fragments of the money and influence which has been showered upon the new institution, the Royal College of Music would have been little needed, had it been needed at all. People often talk as if England had been till now without the machinery for producing good musicians. In truth, she has long possessed an admirable machine—it is the money and the influence that alone have been wanting. The pittance of a very few hundreds a year, which has been grudgingly given to the Royal Academy, has been earned a thousand-fold; and it is well, therefore, that the original school of nearly all the English musicians of distinction whom we have had for some 60 years should not, on the occasion of yesterday, have been wholly forgotten. If the Royal Academy has done so much without aid, there is no limit to what the Royal College ought to do.—*Globe.*

Musical Intelligence.

CRYSTAL PALACE CONCERTS.

PROGRAMME.

Concert-Overture, "Mein Heim" .... Dvorak.
　　First time in England.
Air, "Love in her eyes" ("Acis and Galatea ").... Handel.
　　Mr. Harper Kearton.
Concerto for Violin, No. 7 .... C. De Beriot.
　　Signora Teresina Tua.
Duet, "In Questo Suolo " ("La Favorita ") .... Donizetti.
　　Miss Orridge and Mr. F. King.
Aria, "Deh ! vieni, non tardar," ("La Nozze de
　Figaro") .... Mozart.
　　Miss Annie Marriott.
Solo for Violin, "Airs Hongroises" .... Ernst.
　　Signorina Teresina Tua.
The Choral Symphony .... Beethoven.
　Miss Annie Marriott, Miss Orridge, Mr. Harper Kearton,
　　Mr. F. King, and the Crystal Palace Choir.

Conductor ... ... AUGUST MANNS.

To the London Philharmonic we owe a deep debt of
gratitude, for the first performance in this country of the
"Choral Symphony." In March, 1823, this fine old society
gave Beethoven fifty pounds for the use of the manuscript for a limited time, and it was performed by them
in London in 1825. The Viennese public however, much
to the disappointment of our Philharmonic, had first the
honour of hearing it in 1824, at the Kärnthnerthor
Theatre. In speaking of the progress of orchestral music
in this country during the past fifty years, Professor
Macfarren stated last year, on the interesting occasion of
the presentation of Mr. Manns' testimonial, at the Crystal
Palace, that although this great symphony had in years
past been creditably performed in London on several
occasions, it remained for Mr. Manns and the Crystal
Palace orchestra to make it better understood, and more
thoroughly appreciated than it had been. We owe to
them therefore an equal debt of gratitude with the Philharmonic, for most of us remember when even the
majority of musicians looked upon it as a strange and
unintelligible thing, a kind of poem recondite and
æsthetic problem.

The performance, on Saturday last was very satisfactory as far as the orchestra was concerned, but
the vocal parts left much to be desired. The quartet
voices were individually good, but many of the most
beautiful passages were marred from want of consen-
taneousness ; and in the chorus parts a few additional
high and fresh treble voices would have been acceptable.

Dvorak's Concert-Overture was another beautiful specimen of this gifted man. It is full of brightness and
enthusiasm, and made a most favourable impression.

I have again to record a decided success by the very
young and talented violinist, Signorina Teresina Tua.
The grace and freedom of her bearing, her marvellous
execution, and her tender expression, produced a very
marked effect upon her audience.

It may be well to state that the next Saturday concert
will not take place until the 26th of May, when Berlioz's
"Grand Messe des Marts," will be performed for the
first time in England. One may hope that on this
occasion the directors may think fit to make use of the
great Handel orchestra, not only for the comfort of the
audience, but to prevent the overcrowding of performers
in the concert-room orchestra, as a much greater number
of instruments must be employed, and probably a much
larger choir.　　　　　　　　　　　　　R. S.

Another contributor writes :—

Mr. Manns may be congratulated on a capital performance of the "Choral Symphony" last Saturday. It was
well, however, as Spohr opined, if the long work terminated
with the three masterly orchestral movements. The
choral part, generally rendered in a style the reverse of
satisfactory, is quite an anti-climax, and Mr. John Oxenford's unhappy version of Schiller's "Ode to Joy," still
does duty at Sydenham, if not elsewhere. "Here's a kiss
for everyone," sounds rather school-girlish ; and to rhyme
"millions" with "pavilion," reminds one of a certain
libretto recently put before the public.

Signorina Tua played with taste and mastery of mé-
canique De Beriot's violin concerto. Ernst's Hungarian
airs, in nowise remarkable, were also executed with clearness and taste. Considering the limited repertoire of
violin (solo) music, De Beriot, Kreutzer, and Meyseder
might be more frequently heard. The inevitable "Spanish
-dance" was played by Mdlle. Tua on a bis.　　A. M.

THE PHILHARMONIC SOCIETY.

The programme of the fifth concert, given on the
evening of the 9th inst., was open to objection on account
of its length. It is true the directors had provided
a banquet of dainties. But Solomon declares that dainties
are oft "deceitful meats," and the surfeits that are likely to
ensue from over-indulgence of them, so far as a long
course of concert listening is concerned, renders probable
the literal fulfilment of Shakespeare's dictum :—

"Surfeited grooms
Do mock their charge with snores."

The scheme was as under :—

Symphony, No. 6, in F, "Pastoral" .... Beethoven.
Motet for tenor, solo, and chorus .... Cherubini.
　Mr. Vernon Rigby, and the Philharmonic Choir.
Concerto, Violin, No. 1 .... Max Bruch.
　　Signorina Teresina Tua.
Romanza, "O mio, all !" "Guillaume Tell" .... Rossini.
　　Signor Mierzwinsky.
Ballad for Orchestra, "La belle dame sans merci".. Mackenzie.
Concerto Pianoforte in F minor .... Chopin.
　　M. Vladimir de Pachmann.
Aria, "Fra poco a me" ("Lucia"). .... Donizetti.
　　Signor Mierzwinsky.
Violin Solos, { (a) "Cavatina" .... Raff.
　　　　　　{ (b) Spanish dance," "Zapateado" .. Sarasate.
Marche Hongroise, "La damnation de Faust " .... Berlioz.

Beethoven's ever fresh and delightful Pastoral gives
one new pleasure, and fresh interest in its manifold beauties, each time that the masterpiece is heard. It presents
indeed a perfect exemplification of the maxim, Ars celare
artem. So simple does the score for the most part appear,
that a hasty perusal, or a listless hearing, might lead one
to imagine that the production was little more than a
slight piece of agreeable music. But when the thoughtful student looks below the pleasing surface of this
"expression of feeling, rather than a painting," as its
author expressly terms it, he will find hidden the most
consummate art. The genius of the great tone-poet
carries us away with him into the country, and as we
drink in the fresh air we listen to the sweet songs of the
birds, observe the simple gaiety of the country-folk, perceive with awe and wonder the terrible storm, and join
with the herdsmen in their thankful feelings after the
tempest is over. Despite Beethoven's appropriations of
woodland minstrelsy in the express reproductions of the
songs of the yellow-hammer, nightingale, quail and cuckoo,
there is no realism in the whole work. He has but taken
these fragments as themes for treatment ; so intertwined
are they with the logical sequence of the movement, that
they form an integral part of it, variegating it with beautiful and vivid colouring. None but a true genius artist could
have so successfully blended such unrhythmical elements,
with the strict texture of scientific music. The culminating
point of the storm, coincident with the grand introduction of the trombones, just after the steady chromatic descent of the bass, is perhaps the most sublime thing the master has written. And then after the depth of the gloom, how
singularly bright and hopeful is the broad theme of the
oboes and flute, giving the first ray of sunshine and glad
thankfulness ! There are other symphonies of Beethoven
more ambitious than the "Pastoral," but none that show
more skill, or deeper human sympathy than this vivid picture
of country-life exhibits. The symphony is one requiring
great care in its performance. Its delicate points and
varieties of sentiments were satisfactorily brought out by
the band under Mr. Cusins' careful direction.

Cherubini's Motet in F, which was performed for the
first time in England, was written in 1818 for the French
Chapel Royal. The original score was acquired by the
late Prince Consort, and it was graciously lent by the
Queen from the Buckingham Palace library for performance. The work is written for tenor solo, four-part
chorus, and full orchestra. It reflects throughout the
religious and elevated spirit of the great Florentine's
sacred music. The opening solo, "Adjutor in oppor-
tunitatibus," a smooth piece of writing, leads into two
choruses ; in the second of these, to the words, "De
profundis clamavi," the choir sing (in F minor) some
short detached chords, remarkable for the tone of heartfelt sorrow they express. The final chorus, "Quia apud
te propitiatis," forms a skilfully written and florid conclusion to the motet. The orchestration of the motet is
deliciously coloured, and exhibits that fertility of resource
and refined skill so characteristic of Cherubini's scoring.
Max Bruch's Violin Concerto, No. 1, in G minor, is a

work of a different nature to that of the ridiculous Scotch fantasia, which recently set the Philharmonic audience laughing. It cannot, however, take rank as a fine composition; but considering the somewhat limited repertoire of concertos for the violin, it will find acceptance as worthy to be occasionally heard. Its themes are for the most part heavy and uninspired, and there is a great sameness about the tone of its orchestral setting. What little impetuosity it possesses, seems rather to be manufactured, than to grow spontaneously out of the texture itself. Still, there is musicianly work in it, but scholarship does not make up for want of inspiration. The concerto served to introduce to a London audience Signorina Teresina Tua, a young lady of some seventeen summers, who comes to us with a great, and, apparently, well-deserved reputation from the continent. Her playing of this (and the subsequent solo, Raff's beautiful "Cavatina") was an exact reflection of the mode of singing current among the best artists of her native land. It was marked by the same passion, excessive refinement, and sympathy that is to be found there. Young as she is, she has already studied to such good purpose, that she has apparently mastered all technical difficulties, and acquired a pure, silvery, if not large, volume of tone. Her bowing is free, and her stopping singularly accurate. Although she plays with great brilliancy, and dash enough almost to startle one, yet she exhibits those little touches of delicate fancy, *rubato*, and exquisite expression that mark the intelligent sympathetic artist. Her dynamic power is as yet naturally limited, but from that shown in the double stops, it promises to be as satisfactory as are her other qualities. Until one has heard Signorina Tua play Mendelssohn's violin concerto, or in a Beethoven quartet, it is not easy to fix the precise place she is entitled to in violin hierarchy, but it promises to be a high one. She must have worked up Sarasate's "Spanish Dance" since she came over here; her rendering of it was a clever imitation of the style of its author, and it was played with just that gest and *abandon* which he exhibits.

Mr. Mackenzie's orchestral piece, "La belle dame sans merci," is inspired by Keats's beautiful words. The piece has but just been written for the Philharmonic Society. Why the author should term it a "ballad for orchestra," is difficult to discover. Editors of musical dictionaries will henceforth have to add a new meaning to the old appellation. Herr Hüffer (the writer of the Society's programme books) says, but few remarks should be expected from "a discreet analyst," so that the audience is left in doubt as to the particular portions of the tale sought to be illustrated. From a certain point of view, however, this is as well; the listeners then have the advantage of exercising their imaginations, and it takes the piece out of the comparative low category of "programme" music. Mr. Mackenzie's work belongs rather to the class of illustrative tone-pictures, of which Mendelssohn's "Calm sea and prosperous voyage," Wagner's "Siegfried's death march," and our own countryman, Sterndale Bennett's ethereal "Paradise and the Peri" overture belong. Mr. Mackenzie's deep and expressive music requires more than a single hearing in order to appreciate it, but apparently it is an advance on anything that the gifted author of "Columba" has yet written. From its impressive opening phrase for the 'cello, to the closing clever and picturesque working out of a remarkable agitated theme first enunciated on the oboe, the ballad is full of the highest and unflagging interest. The poetry of this music, the breadth of its melodic phrases, as well as the technical skill shown over its workmanship, will become more and better appreciated on a second hearing. Mr. Cusins gracefully resigned the *bâton* to the composer, under whose direction the work was carefully given.

One of the few of Chopin's friends left, himself a distinguished musician, declared that to hear M. Vladimir de Pachmann play, was to listen to the wonderful Pole himself. And we of this generation who have not heard Chopin, but have listened to many of his interpreters, can quite believe that this is true. M. Pachmann is evidently one of the very few who possess the gift of entire sympathy with the ideas and feelings of his renowned countryman. His playing has been already so carefully analysed and described, that it is needless to dwell upon its features. Chopin's F minor concerto, in which are to be found some of his happiest thoughts, most exquisite embroidery, surprising modulations, and untrammelled passion, found indeed a sympathetic player in M. de

Pachmann. Specially commendable in his playing is the fact—unhappily rare to chronicle in these days—that he never thumps the keys. All grades of tone and necessary power are obtained without descending to this blacksmith-like resort.

Signor Mierzwinsky's method of singing is more peculiar than pleasant. He exaggerates expression, uses his head voice unskilfully, and indeed often unnecessarily, and his tone frequently degenerates into coarse shouting. Berlioz's forcible Hungarian march from the "Faust" music came from tired players upon a tired audience, and wanted *verve*.

The concert of May 30th, at which Madame Menter and Signorina Tua are again to play, will be the last of the season.   T. L. SOUTHGATE.

CONCERT AT DUDLEY HOUSE.

On Saturday afternoon, May 5th, a concert was given in aid of the General Lying-in Hospital, York Road, Lambeth. This ancient Hospital, established in 1765, is fortunate in having upon its staff Dr. F. H. Champneys, who is not only Doctor of Medicine, but also learned in music, and has under his command an excellent amateur choir of ladies and gentlemen. The concert opened well with a psalm (127th), for quartet and chorus, "Nisi dominus ædificaverit domum." It was sustained by Miss Hardy, Miss Annie Williams, Mr. H. E. Wooldridge and the Hon. Spencer G. Littleton. The performance was at times somewhat unsteady, but the choir soon settled down to their work, and entirely redeemed their character in the next item, an unpublished motet, "Tu es Petrus" composed by Leonardo Leo, which was sung in a manner which reflected great credit upon them and their able conductor, Dr. Champneys. Astorga's "Stabat Mater" followed; this was composed for chorus, solo-voices, and orchestra, but accompanied on this occasion by the piano-forte. The solo music in this work was sung by Miss Robertson, Miss A. Williams, Mr. H. E. Wooldridge, and the Hon. Spencer G. Lyttleton. The tenor music had been allotted to Mr. Lionel Benson, but he was disabled by a severe cold, and his part was kindly taken by Mr. Wooldridge, although it was evident that the inclement weather had been only too successful in its attacks upon *his* voice. Miss Robertson's voice was in excellent condition, and was heard to great advantage in the soprano solo, "Sancta Mater."

The second part of the programme consisted of an interesting collection of secular music, commencing with the well-known, but ever fresh madrigal by John Wilbye, "Flora gave me fairest flowers," with which was coupled an excellent choral composition from the pen of Dr. Champneys, called "Lalage," which may be most aptly described as a madrigalian part-song; the words are the well-known lines by S. T. Coleridge: "I asked my fair, one happy day, what I should call her in my lay," &c. and have been very happily treated throughout. Besides the above, Wilbye's madrigal "Sweet Honey-sucking Bees," and Bennet's "Thyrsis, sleepest thou," as also Danby's glee "Awake, Æolian lyre," interspersed with various solos rendered by Mrs. Lymedoch Moncrieff (who contributed a composition of her own); Miss Robertson, Miss Colthurst, Miss Annie Williams, Mr. Wilfred Ward, Mr. Walter Marnock, and Signor Pacisotti; while Handel's Violin Sonata in A was played by Herr Rowe. The pianoforte accompaniments were played by Signor Romili.

The attendance was so numerous as to warrant the hope that the funds of the hospital have materially benefited by the concert.

MISS ZIMMERMANN'S CHAMBER CONCERTS.

At Miss Agnes Zimmerman's second concert, on the very wet evening of May 8th, she played, with Miss J. Skinner, Mozart's Sonata in E flat, Op. 2, No. 6, for pianoforte and violin; Schubert's Fantaisie in C, Op. 15, for the same instruments (with Herr Straus); and Joachim's "Theme and variations" in E, Op. 10, for pianoforte and viola (Herr Straus). The "recalls" need not be counted. Miss Zimmerman's solos were Brahms' Rhapsodie in G minor, Op. 79, No. 2; his Intermezzo in A flat, Op. 76, No. 3; and the Hungarian Dance in D flat, No. 6. On a rapturous encore, Miss Zimmerman played another "dance" from the same set. The *soirée* was altogether a delightful one.

RICHTER CONCERTS.

The second of these concerts, which took place on Thursday in last week, introduced nothing absolutely new, but much that was interesting. The programme was as follows:—

Overture, "Coriolan"	Beethoven.
Concerto, for Violin and Orchestra	Brahms.
Gospodin Adolph Brodsky.	
Overture and "Venusberg" (Bacchanale) Music	
("Tannhäuser")	Wagner.
Recit. and Air, "Che faro senza Euridice" ("Orfeo")	Gluck.
Miss Orridge.	
Symphony, "Im Walde" (In the Forest)	Raff.

The two first numbers formed a striking contrast in every way, but the whole may be summed up in this:—Beethoven has said much in few words in his overture; Brahms has said little in many words in his concerto. Altogether this concerto is a painful subject, because there are passages in the first movement that make the hearer wish it were possible to care for the work as a whole; but they are only the faintest gleams of sunshine through a murky sky; and the general impression is of a wearying, depressing monotony, to which even a sharp pain would be preferable. The days for writing purely bravura passages, no matter how clever, how difficult, or how novel they may be, have passed away; but in this, if in nothing else, Brahms is sadly behind the age. The slow movement is even more heavy and uninteresting than the first, the subjects being of the mildest kind. The finale opens promisingly, for there is a Hungarian boldness in the leading melody, and in his imitations of national airs Brahms is always bearable. But before long he again becomes entangled in passages which have literally no vitality and no beauty; merely scales and exercises that should have no place outside an instruction book; for we do not conjugate our verbs and repeat declensions when we are conversing with our friends in any language — still less when we are attempting to instruct and elevate mankind. Herr Joachim introduced this concerto at a Crystal Palace concert when it was in MS., and unfortunately it does not improve on further acquaintance. M. Brodsky is so thorough, and so manly a performer, so entirely free from trickery, that his selection is the more to be regretted.

The new "Venusberg" music reveals to those who are thoroughly acquainted with the scene as it was first written Wagner's wonderful advance in those sixteen years of his life after its completion and before its revision; it is thus full of instruction to the student. The new themes introduced are of the breadth and fervency of the "Nibelungenring" and "Meistersinger" music, to which an occasional resemblance may be traced; the orchestration is almost fearful in its power of depicting licentiousness, for it is Wagner's great mission to show us the horrors of vice as clearly as the beauties of virtue, in which particular he stands almost alone among our great teachers.

Raff's "Im Walde" Symphony was splendidly rendered; and how glorious an inspiration it is from beginning to end! The orchestration alone is a study and a poem. Surely none but Schubert can be compared to Raff for apparently instinctive and spontaneous orchestral effects! and even in Schubert there is not always the same unity of design (if the expression will be understood) that we meet with in Raff. But the orchestration is not Raff's only beauty. Transcribed for the piano, this symphony would be of exceptional interest: the melodies are so broad, so earnest, and so striking, that in no form could it be robbed of all its beauty. The slow movement bears the stamp of Raff's peculiar genius in a remarkable degree: it is one of his many subjects that cannot be compared to the melodies of any other musician, and that would make the loss of Raff's name among the list of tone-poets a wholly irreparable one.

Miss Orridge was artistic, if somewhat cold and formal, in her rendering of Gluck's touching song. The splendid band was most strikingly successful in the "Tannhäuser" music, the Pilgrims' Hymn being entirely free from that dragging effect that often makes the intelligent listener question what the highly original violin accompaniment can mean. It is certainly calculated to puzzle the hearer when it is made too prominent; but many things that are bad as masters are useful as servants; and the effect produced on this occasion was undoubtedly just what the author conceived when he gave his broad grand chant to the brass, never intending it to struggle against, but to reign over, the counterpoint that he entrusted to the violins.

B. F. WYATT-SMITH.

SIGNOR TITO MATTEI'S CONCERT.

Signor Tito Mattei, a general favourite in the musical world, held a grand *soirée* at St. James's Hall last Saturday evening. He played his own pieces, all very pretty and effective, to wit: "L'Elégante," a saltarello, a valse-galop, and his grand fantasia on a subject hardly worthy of the composer's notice, namely, the hackneyed and now colourless opera of Bellini, "I Puritani." A song of Signor Mattei, "Death or glory," written expressly for M. Foli, was sung by that *basso profondo* and encored. A capital septet, "I am shocked," from a MSS. opera comique, written by Messrs. Farnie and Murray, and composed by the Signor, was sung by Mdlle. Marimon, Miss Santley, Mdlle. Trebelli, Mr. Lloyd, Mr. Santley, Signor Zoboli, and Signor Foli. The success was signal. Madame Tito Mattei was recalled for a fine version of Rossini's Romance in A flat, "Selva opaca." Mdlle. Marimon, in excellent voice, was encored in Mozart's florid air, "Non paventar," and sang a valse instead. Mdme. Trebelli won a *bis* for Rossini's "Pensa alla patria," and substituted the Habañera from "Carmen." Mr. E. Lloyd had two "calls" in favour of Signor Mattei's new song (for him composed), "Whither, who can tell?" Mr. Santley sang "The devout lover"; and Signor Guido Papini, the eminent violinist, played his own "Pensée Fugitive" and "Garty. Owen." Signors Li Calsi and Tito Mattei wound up a splendid concert with the March from "Marie di Gand," arranged for two pianofortes.

THE ROYAL ITALIAN OPERA.

"L'Etoile du Nord" was unavoidably postponed on Saturday, by reason of Signor Frapelli's indisposition, and in place of Meyerbeer's opera the directors mounted "Lucia di Lammermoor," with Mdme. Sembrich in the title-part. The music of this part, as in the case of "Il Puritani," is admirably adapted to Mdme. Sembrich's peculiar, light and brilliant soprano voice, and her appearance in "L'Etoile du Nord" is anxiously expected. The part of Edgardo, on Saturday, was well sustained by a tenor whom Mr. Mapleson first introduced to the public at the theatre in the Haymarket, Signor Rovelli; and Signor Cotagni was the Enrico.

On Thursday, May 10th, Mdme. Pauline Lucca appeared in Gounod's "Faust," to realise Goethe's interesting "creation" of feminine gentleness and frailty with the consummate skill and intuitive discernment of a genuine histrionic artist. The passionate outbursts in the cathedral-scene stood in bold relief against the tenderness of love passages in the garden-scene, the coquettish by-play on the first encounter with Dr. Faustus, and the unaffected gush of girlish joy when the jewels are discovered. The "Jewel Song" and the "King of Thule" ballad (which Gounod writes in A minor, and Berlioz in F major), were salient points of a capital "all round" performance. The new tenor, Signor Marconi, sang "Salve dimora" with taste. M. Gailhard made an excellent Mephistopheles, and M. Devoyod, the French baritone, resumed what it is the fashion to term his "original" part of Valentine, Marguerite's brother.

"Il Trovatore" was down for Tuesday, with Mdme. Lucca as Leonora, and Mdme. Albani will make her first appearance to-night (Saturday), in Verdi's "Rigoletto."

ST. AUGUSTINE AND ST. FAITH, WATLING STREET.—On Friday next, May 25th, being the eve of St. Augustine, there will be a special full choral service in the above church, at 7.30 p.m. The Magnificat and Nunc Dimittis will be Stainer in B flat, and the anthem "How lovely are the messengers" from Mendelssohn's oratorio "St. Paul." At the conclusion of the service Hiller's sacred cantata "A song of victory" will be sung, and the ordinary choir will be augmented by several members of that of St. Paul's Cathedral.

WIMBLEDON MUSICAL SOCIETY.—On Wednesday, 9th inst., this society completed its third season by a good performance of "Elijah." Miss Alice Parry, Miss Emily Dones, Mr. Harper Kearton, and Mr. Frédéric King, being the principals, it is needless to say that the solos were all well rendered, especially so, "Woe unto them," and "O rest in the Lord" by Miss Emily Dones; "Is not His word like a fire" and "It is enough," by Mr. King; and "Then shall the righteous," by Mr. Kearton. The double quartet, "For He shall give His angels," was sung by members of the choir, and was one of the gems of the performance. Miss Whitehead sang the part of the "youth" correctly and well. One of the special features of the society's performances is the excellence of its chorus-singing; on this occasion it was even better than usual ; he choruses " Baal, we cry to thee," " Blessed are the men," " Thanks be to God," " He, watching over Israel," " Behold, God the Lord passed by," and " Then did Elijah the Prophet break forth like a fire," showing to perfection the versatile powers of this well-drilled choir. The orchestra played exceedingly well, rendering the accompaniments to the solos with much care and attention to expressional effects, the brass being most judicious in this respect, never overpowering the solo voices, but never lacking power when volume was required, Mr. Sumner conducted. The hall was full. At the last rehearsal on the Saturday preceding the performance, an interesting presentation, at the hands of James Ranken, Esq., took place, of an ivory silver mounted *bâton* and a gold keyless watch by Benson, bearing the following inscription :—" Presented by the members of the Wimbledon Musical Society to their conductor, William Sumner, Esq., May 5th, 1883." Next season the society proposes giving " Jephthah," " Messiah," and " St. Paul," in addition to one or two orchestral works.

Reviews.

History of the Boehm Flute ; with illustrations exemplifying its origin by progressive stages, and an appendix containing the attack originally made on Boehm, and other papers relating to the Boehm-Gordon controversy. By CHRISTOPHER WELCH, M.A. (Rudall Carte, and Co.—1883).

This title sufficiently indicates the object and scope of the treatise. The writer is a distinguished amateur performer on the flute. His views and opinions may therefore be fairly accepted as being free from professional bias, or influenced by the pecuniary interests of a manufacturer in conducting his examination of the documents relating to the Boehm-Gordon controversy. Opinions are, even at the present time, divided as to whom is to be awarded the merit of the production of the comparatively perfect instrument which we now possess.

No musical instrument has undergone so many progressive changes as the flute, embracing, as they do, the material, the tube and bore, the position of the holes, and the mechanism of the keys. For material we have now metal and india-rubber (vulcanite) as well as wood. Tubes are now made cylindrical, as well as conical, with the head-joint of a parabolic form. The holes are now pierced as nearly as possible in their true nodular position, corresponding to successive organ pipes, irrespective of the natural capabilities of the fingers of the performer ; while the keys are suited, by ingenious mechanism, to the fingers. Unlike the old eight-keyed flute, all the notes are open, which, it is asserted, imparts a freer tone. With these advantages, we have now an almost perfect instrument.

The merit of the first suggestion of these improvements lies between Captain Gordon and Mr. Boehm. Since their first production various additions have been suggested, more or less successful, such as by Card, Siccama, Clinton, Carte, Radcliff, and lately by Collard, who has adopted the Carte 1867 pattern and added duplicate holes to the lower C, D, and E. Again, professors, and amateurs, have devised additional keys to carry out some real or imaginary improvements of their own. Mr. Welch informs us that he has himself devised various additional keys which gave additional facilities. The result is that every flute-player must now take about with him his own instrument, since he never can be certain of meeting with one suited to his previous practice.

All these innovations are based on Boehm's fundamental principles, hence the great controversy to whom the credit is due for the original suggestions on which all our present flutes are based—to Gordon or to Boehm ? With strict impartiality Mr. Welch lays before his readers all the evidence he has been enabled to collect on the subject. The weight of evidence seems to be in favour of Boehm. Be this as it may, few persons now living have probably seen a Gordon flute, while the Boehm flute is in extensive use, more particularly on the continent. Not only flute players, but every lover of music, will derive pleasure and instruction in the perusal of Mr. Welch's book.

Beyond the immediate examination of the question of the merit of the invention generally, the relative merits of the cylindrical and conical bore are considered. But perhaps Mr. Welch has gone a little too far in stating that our great artist Mr. Radcliff gave a decided pre-

ference to the cylinder. For a long time he adopted the conical bore ; but if I mistake not Mr. Radcliff now more frequently performs in public on the cylinder flute. All our old masters played with surprising effect on the cone flute. In the hands of a professor in constant practice, though it may require more management, I think a decided preference is to be given to the cone Boehm introduced the open G sharp key. Mr. Radcliff has gone back to the shut G sharp key. Here, again, a controversy might arise as to the relative merits of the two systems. Mr. Welch considers the "return to the closed G sharp key" to be "a great relief to the little finger" ; that may be true with respect to the pure Boehm in the flat keys, but great facilities are imparted in the sharp keys, and the inconvenience suggested has been fully superseded by Carte in his 1867 pattern, and with this improvement on the Boehm flute we have a decided advantage in retaining the open G sharp key.

One other subject I must note, referred to by Mr. Welch, and which naturally suggests itself to every flute player, namely, to account for the fact that the Boehm principles of improvements are not generally adopted by players on the clarionet, oboe, and bassoon. Mr. Welch informs us that Messrs. Rudall, Carte and Co. have made a clarionet successfully on the Boehm principle, and that he has seen a bassoon on the same principle, and that the great performer on the oboe, Lavigne, had adopted it on his instrument with marked success. Clarionets on the Boehm system, modified by Klosé, are used in military bands in France ; and I believe Mr. Clinton now plays on such an instrument.

The refusal generally to adopt these improvements is thus accounted for by Mr. Welch :—" The explanation usually given is, that it is impossible to improve these instruments ; that with them improvement would be destruction, *as their essential character lies in their imperfections*. Perhaps, however, the cause of this absence of reform may rather be traced to the want of a sufficiently large number of amateurs to break down, by their influence, the conservatism of professional players, and to overcome their disinclination to change. A musician who has spent his youth *in learning to conceal the defects of an instrument*, has but little inclination to give up the vantage he has gained, nor has he time, amidst the engagements of his professional career, to learn a new system of fingering. Still less can he be expected to place in the hands of a young player (soon perhaps to become a rival) an instrument which may be the means of enabling him to come to the front in the race for artistic distinction."

Not only is this work tastefully got up, but the portraits and diagrams give it an additional value and interest.

The Communion Service (Kyrie, Credo, Sanctus, Benedictus, Agnus Dei, and Gloria), set to music in the key of D. By Frank L. Moir. (Novello, Ewer & Co. 1883).—The successful production of this Service (or Mass) at St. Matthias' Church, South Kensington, was noticed last week. The work is characterised by an unaffected simplicity of style, without the slightest descent from the dignity of the great "argument." The subdued passages of the Service are smooth, melodious, and vocal; the climaxes bold, yet never extravagant ; the modulations effective ; and withal, *pace* modern composers of the feverish or restless school, the tonality homogeneous. The key of D, with one exception, is consistently maintained, so that the signature really denotes a definite tonality, without being contradicted, as by Wagner, Liszt, and others, in the very first bar. It must be remembered on the other hand, that old friend Beethoven, choosing the "natural" key of C for his overture to "Prometheus," begins with a hanging chord of the 6-4-2 on B flat, and is fond, in his concertos, of enharmonic changes. The "Kyrie eleison," of necessity, is here used for the responses after the Ten Commandments. It is melodious, but not striking. The "Credo" opens with "full" choir in 3-4 time ; at the phrase "God of God" (the "of" here is emphatic and equivalent to the Latin *de*), the four voices sing A (the dominant) in unison, and interrupt it on a (minim) B flat, whilst the organ plays (after A in unison) the full chord of G minor, followed, in contrary motion, by the harmony of D minor. At the passage "Very God," &c., the D minor chord is succeeded by the 6-4 on E, with a view to a change to the dominant key. A tenor and bass solo intervene, and at the resumption of the "full," an effective pause (with swell reeds and pedal) is made on Mr. Moir's evidently favourite harmony of F sharp major. This naturally introduces the "Crucifixion" episode in the relative (B) minor, and at the words "was buried," the four voices drop simultaneously from F sharp to low B. The key of D major recurs at the "Resurrection," with a modulation to the subdominant (G). A fine burst of full harmony at the end of the "Credo" forms a grand climax. On a pedal E are here piled the chord of E minor; and the same harmony with the superadded discords of D natural and B flat; the voices taking B flat in unison and revolving on A, the cadence is plagal.

The "Sanctus," in D, 6-4 time, a movement of breadth and solemnity, is remarkable for its "Amen," first harmonized with the chords of G minor and D major, and lastly on a tonic pedal, with flowing inner parts. The "Benedictus" is varied with short solos. The "Hosanna" will be thought remarkably fine. Towards the close the organ, with "swell to great full" and pedal, gives out high A on a chord of the 6-4-2 with C natural as bass; and the C is revolved on two other inversions of diminished and dominant sevenths, whereof the basses; B natural and B flat, at last find a pled d'terre on A, with the 6-4 harmony of the cadence in D, again interrupted by G minor.

The "Agnus Dei," (which follows the Collect, "We do not presume," &c.), is a duleet strain in D minor allotted to the tenor and bass solo in succession. This adagio is followed by an andante tranquillo for soprano solo in the tonic major; the chorus come in at the end with long holding notes, on dominant and tonic pedals; the cadence is here "authentic"; but the final clause, "dona nobis pacem," is repeated on a tonic pedal of six bars, the sopranos ending on the mediant note (low F sharp).

The (according to the English Service) final "Gloria in Excelsis," begins with arpeggios on the organ (soft swell), which cannot but suggest the opening of Handel's anthem, "Zadok the Priest." The voices enter with long holding notes, and a pause occurs at "on earth, peace," with the chord of F sharp major. The time-mode then changes from triple to common, and some effective tonal changes startle the ear. Thus, B major is followed by the second inversion of E flat, in which key a cadence is made at the passage, "For Thy great glory, O God," &c. The bass now sings a short solo as an episode, mezzo forte, in B flat minor, and the full choir modulate into F. The flat keys are persisted in, with an excursion so far as G flat, of which, at a point, the organ "augments" the fifth (from D flat to D natural). The key of D major is not resumed until the final clause, after a pause (of the organ) on a diminished seventh (G sharp in the bass, with F natural above). The cadence is again plagal, the sopranos ascending from B to D, and the basses falling from G to D.

That Professor Macfarren should have lived to his present age untitled even by the modest prefix which is given on the slightest provocation to successful tradesmen in the metropolis and the suburbs, while foreign professors have been freely dubbed knight, has excited considerable surprise, and it is only an act of grace that he should be included in the new trio. Sir Arthur Sullivan has so long been connected with princely music-making, that the title will well harmonise with his character as a court musician, although his best friends will still regret that the commercial success of his comic operas, and the attractive pursuit of writing royalty-ballads for the music shops, should have led him away from the higher paths of the art on which in earlier days he seemed to have set out. To Mr. George Grove the honour comes at a suitable moment, on his assumption of the duties of Director of the Royal College, while, as a reward for much earnest devotion to music, everyone will admit that he has earned all he receives. On general grounds it is satisfactory to see that music is being gradually raised to her rightful place by the side of the sister arts of painting and sculpture; and although the Royal College has yet to make good its claim to confidence by real work, and by sending forth not merely a few brilliant executants, but a body of well-trained musicians, the prestige of royal favour will give it a welcome stimulus. That such encouragement has practically been withheld from the Royal Academy of Music cannot unfortunately be forgotten, nor are the professors or students of the old school likely to look at first with any great favour upon the new institution.—*Church Bells*.

ASMODEUS IN THE MUSICAL WORLD.

CHAP. III.

"Nay, Don Cleofas," said Asmodeus, "the fable thou hast so pleasantly narrated is inapplicable, for these foreign gentry often add ingratitude to assumption. The sturdy and truly gifted man, now comfortably dining with the quiet fellow of perfectly good breeding in the corner of the most imposing room in this well-known hostelry, which is one of the chief places of entertainment in Madrid, is roundly abusing the whole body of your native musicians. At this same time he is anxiously grasping the leadership of every Spanish musical institution he can put his hands on. And he would have the public believe he had forsooth cordially accepted the nationality even of the country he is so much indebted to, but which he affects artistically to despise." "From whence, friendly demon," cried Don Zambullo, "are we to expect gratitude, if it may not be found in the breast of the alien, who has received from the land of his adoption a cordial and generous support?" Asmodeus smiled quietly as the young student grew more vehement in his denunciation of one of the most common sins, ingratitude. "Truly," said that wily personage, "no class suffers so much from foreign invasion as do the musicians. The priest, the doctor, and the notary practise in such well-guarded preserves as offer an almost inviolable security from foreign domination. Even the poet and the painter are for the most part free from the foreign competitor, be he Jew or Gentile. But the musician, following a profession easily entered and generally overcrowded, must, forsooth, have to endure the competition of a never-ending influx of alien composers, singers, and players, who are, to aggravate the sharpness of the struggle for success, much patronised, to the detriment of native talent, by a court with not unnatural foreign sympathies, and by an aristocracy deeply smitten with a fondness for the alien professor. One of the strangest features of foreign musical dictation in this happy city of Madrid," continued Asmodeus, "is the fact that the leading journal employs a foreigner to administer its musical opinions, who, though doing his best with a considerable mastery over a strange language, cannot be said either to understand or to sympathise very earnestly with Spanish art." [The intelligent reader, including, of course, all who take the trouble to read, will either be surprised at the opinions just enunciated, or be led to suspect that this narrative is the work of a satirist, who, as is often the case with such writers, has in pursuit of his object overstrained the boundary line of the probable. It is well known that the Spanish people are not, and never were, anxious to encourage in their midst the presence of foreigners. The Spanish aristocracy, with much pride and exclusiveness, have been less inclined to form alien connections and to encourage the influx of strangers, than have the society leaders of other lands. So the disclosures of the M.S. are remarkable, and the commentator takes this opportunity of assuring the reader that the printers have played no tricks with the statements of the author, and that the original is here given in all its integrity. The mention of a "leading journal" seems also to call for some comment. Everybody knows the date of Le Sage's famous book, and no one will be misled into the notion that so obvious an imitation of that remarkable work, as the present narrative undoubtedly is, could have been written prior to the production of that meritorious romance. Without following these speculations further, for the reader must be naturally impatient at what he may be pleased to consider the impertinent interpolations of a wordy commentator only too anxious to air his own opinions, it may be remarked that it would be strange indeed if, generations back, Madrid actually possessed a "leading journal" (an expression now common enough in London), with sufficient enterprise to search the world through for a truly universal genius to write its musical criticisms, and a journal far-sighted enough to secure a writer for this purpose with such marvellous powers of comprehension as would enable him to fully appreciate his own merits and partially to understand the misty merits of the advanced musical thinkers of his own native land. The sneering tone of Asmodeus will not affect the English reader, for here we are sufficiently enlightened at any rate to know that, in art matters, we ought to despise everything produced by our own countrymen, and to welcome with open arms everything and everybody coming from abroad; and we know, further, that we should accept in all humility the performances of foreign artists, who graciously offer their sublime efforts to us for such paltry returns as fame, fortune, and a never-changing, blindly generous reception]. "So it comes to pass," said Asmodeus, "that, under such influence, the good people of Madrid not only accept with the utmost cordiality the performances of all the artistic locusts from abroad (this expression seems needlessly harsh, but is certainly in the original MS.], but, as has been before noticed, they eagerly. A place, their souls and daughters under the tuition and guidance of these foreign professors, without waiting to ask whether their antecedents and characters are good, bad, or indifferent, or whether they be Jews or Gentiles; taking care, however, in the most inconsistent manner conceivable, to employ their native musicians reluctantly, and after careful enquiries into their private characters and artistic qualifications." [The narrow-minded doctrine that a nation ought to employ and duly encourage its native artists with at least as much consideration as would be shown to invading adventurers and settlers with or without merit, is too obviously implied in the foregoing words of Asmodeus to require comment.] "Here," said Asmodeus, "lives a foreign artist of high distinction, of Jewish extraction, and gifted with a sharp eye for business, and who has practised in Madrid for a long space of time. This gentleman teaches the favourite domestic instrument, the guitar, upon the principles and according to the mannerisms employed a generation ago in the manipulation of this enchanting musical medium. This ancient artist is hard at work teaching a good many hours daily for the not incontemptible sum of 100 reals per lesson." [If the author does not here purposely conceal the period of his production, the comfortable sum named as the reward for the skilled guidance and patient listening of an artist for the space of an hour, as being expressed in Spanish money not in use, would denote the date of the work now being printed as of a period dating from before our own times. The reader will not fail to form his own conclusions upon this and other statements made in the course of this delectable narrative.] "This distinguished professor, a type of a class of successful artists and teachers, is naturally solicitous of being identified with every prominent scheme of the artistic republic, and rightly judges that men do well to keep their names perpetually before the eyes of the world." "Who is that elderly man to whom so many musical people are now offering a double tribute of appreciative applause, and a substantial testimonial in gold?" "Ah, truly!" rejoined Asmodeus; "he is a noteworthy man and an artist of undoubtedly high distinction. You are witnessing, in a well-known musical academy, the acknowledgment by an assembly consisting of most of the eminent musicians of the day, of the unselfish, earnest, unflagging labours of a truly great artist and learned man. He has been surprised, in the midst of his faithful work, by this admiring, loving crowd of artistic disciples and fellow musicians, who desire to testify to him their appreciation of a really noble life. This great artist is a native of Madrid, who, in spite of every prejudice and difficulty, and without one motive false to the art he serves so well, has not only largely contributed in every way to the advancement of national art at home, but has done much to make that art respected all over the world." "This, indeed," cried Don Zambullo, "is a spectacle to reconcile one to many apparent inconsistencies to be seen in the midst of much noble suffering and manly strife in a pure and good cause." "Say, Asmodeus," presently said the young student, "who is that distinguished looking man now crossing the street? Is he not the famous singer Senor Xacarero?" "Thou hast guessed aright, Don Cleofas," returned Asmodeus; "it is that popular songster, whose career forms a notable illustration of the fact that much may be made out of little, seeing that the gentleman in question has made a handsome fortune, for the most part by the constant repetition of some half-dozen songs, which not only he but his imitators have been performing ad nauseam for the last fifteen or twenty years."

It is satisfactory to learn that Mr. Goring Thomas's opera "Esmeralda," produced by Mr. Carl Rosa at Drury Lane last month, has been accepted by Herr Julius Hofmann for the Stadt-Theater, Cologne, where it will be given some time next autumn.

LONDON: SATURDAY, MAY 19, 1883.

MOZART'S ORGAN WORKS.

NOT inaptly one might term the present period of "musical resurrection." During the last few years the creative activity which spread abroad such a lustre on the art-life of the early part of this century seems to have lulled for a time, and thus the musical gaze from an ever-intent prospect of the future, or, even of the present, has become reflective, and returns to take a more thorough inspection of its already created treasures. This it is, doubtless, that accounts for the resuscitation of works and facts which forms one of the most promising features of the musical life of the last two decades. From Carissimi's "Jonah," and Bach's Mass in B Minor to Berlioz's "Faust," a long chronological list might be made of the many great and good works which, thanks to this retrospective tendency, have once more obtained a hearing. Yet, perhaps, while this "resurrection," if I may be allowed the term, has taken place in the other branches of music, organ writings have been, unfortunately, sadly neglected. Except the works of Bach and those of Mendelssohn—a pair whom we may rightly call the Elijah and Elisha of the organ art,—no pains seem to have been taken to obtain for the present generation of organists anything like a correct or even moderately full edition of the writings for the "king of instruments" of our great classic writers. Even our boasted love of Handel has not saved for us his collection of twelve original voluntaries. Of Mozart the organ world knows less, imagining that he wrote nothing for the instrument. With what surprise therefore will the announcement be greeted that Mozart wrote *seventeen sonatas for the organ,* or, as their nature will explain, perhaps more correctly termed *short concertos for organ and orchestra?* Yet the industry of Herr Köchel in the compilation of his thematic catalogue of Mozart's works brings this before us. While awaiting their publication by Messrs. Breitkopf and Härtel (for they are all still in manuscript), we have much interesting information respecting them. They were written to fill up the gap at high mass between the Gloria and Credo, and were, thus intended to form part of the Church Service. They consist of one movement only, the form being that of the ordinary sonata. The first three of these seem to have been written in the year 1769, when Mozart, aged thirteen, returning from Vienna, received from the Archbishop of Salzburg the post of concertmeister. The first of these is in E flat (andante), the second in B flat (allegro), and the third in D (allegro), all being for organ, two violins, and bass. We then find nothing composed for the organ until in 1775, four more appear to have been written in that period of great activity, which lasted till 1777, and which during two and a half years saw the production in all of no less than ten sonatas. No. 4 (allegro, D major) and No. 5 (allegro, F major) open with genuine Mozart unison phrases. No. 6, composed in July, 1775, at Salzburg, is in B flat major. Nos. 7 and 8 are respectively in F and A, the opening of the latter being particularly bold. The following year, 1776, produced No. 9 in G major, No. 10 in F, No. 11 in D, and No. 12 in C major. The last of these proves the most interesting, since the accompaniment is increased by the addition of two trumpets. During the first nine months of 1777, until he started on his travels with his mother in September, two more appear to have been written, the first in G major, the second in C, while the accompaniment of the latter is still farther increased to two violins, 'cello, bass, two oboes, two trumpets, and drums. Then followed the journey of Mozart to Munich, Mannheim, and finally Paris, where his mother died. June, 1779, saw him once more in Salzburg, and appointed successor to Adlgasser, organist at the court and cathedral, with a salary of £40. Then were written the last three organ sonatas, the first being in C major, opening with a final staccato passage for the strings. The second, also in C major, has accompaniment of two violins, bass, two oboes, two horns, violoncello, trumpets, and drums. To this Köchel appends a note: "The longest and most developed"; while to the last and seventeenth sonata (C major), composed in March, 1780, at Salzburg, the note is made: "In this the organ is treated as chief instrument and obbligato throughout." With Mozart's final departure from Salzburg his organ compositions come to an end. It is difficult at first to see how they have all remained so long in manuscript. It is not improbable that the displeasure of Archbishop Colloredo, who objected to all instrumental music in the Church, and commanded the disuse of these sonatas, may have had something to do with this. It was the same prelate who ordered Michael Haydn to compose choral pieces to Church text in place of them. Of the

sonatas, Otto Jahn "finds in them nothing that reminds him of the church," while the instrument is "never treated with virtuosity." Yet, notwithstanding this, the publication of Mozart's seventeen organ sonatas will be awaited by the host of organists with more than usual curiosity and interest.

FRANK J. SAWYER.

"PALMAM QUI MERUIT FERAT."

ALTHOUGH everyone would respect the exercise of Professor G. A. MACFARREN's private judgment in not at first wishing to accept the honour of knighthood, there is a general feeling of satisfaction in the fact that he has given up his original personal reluctance to accept a new dignity, and has, in what may be fairly termed the general interest of the art and to the gain perhaps of the institutions he is intimately connected with, decided to accept a graciously thought of and well meant honour. The world has long since decided very properly upon placing such a high value upon the noble artistic labours of the great English composer, theorist, writer, musical chief, and large-minded teacher, that no external honours or title could add force to the esteem in which Sir GEORGE MACFARREN is held. But it is a good thing for the art and for artists, that so true and good a man should be thus honoured, and by his good name lending honour to honour itself. Not only is the example of such a well-bestowed title an encouragement and new strength to the brother artists of the previously highly distinguished musician, but the judicious bestowal of the title exercises real power in the social uplifting of the followers of the art. Sir ARTHUR SULLIVAN and Sir GEORGE GROVE are to be congratulated upon similar grounds, and as bearing company with the great English artist, whose name calls up thoughts of an earnest, laborious, patient life, adorned by high gifts and great virtues, a life which every lover of English music must contemplate with national pride and affectionate admiration.

That Sir GEORGE ALEXANDER MACFARREN may live long to benefit English art by his earnest and distinguished labours, will be the earnest hope of all who love the art and can appreciate the good done by gifted, earnest, noble-hearted, and self-sacrificing artists.   E. H. TURPIN.

THE LOGIC OF COUNTERPOINT.

THIRD SERIES.

VIII.

WITH regard to the intermingling of the first three different species of counterpoint in four parts, a matter Cherubini deems it unnecessary to discuss, it is well to remind the student that the intermixture should be practised with every possible interchange of position in the score. The following table, in which the *canto fermo* is expressed by the line, will suggest a fairly complete and sufficiently exhaustive interchange of species (1st, 2nd and 3rd) between the various voices of a four part score :—

1	2	3	3	1	2	1	1	3	3	3	1	3
2	1	2	1	3	1	3	2	1	2	1	—	—
3	3	1	2	2	—	—	—	—	—	—	2	2
—,	—,	—,	—,	3,	2,	3,	2,	1,	2	3,	1,

```
 2  3  —  —  —  —  —  —
 —  —  1  2  3  3  1  2
 3  1  2  3  2  1  3  1
 1, 2, 3, 1, 1, 2, 2, 3
```

Although these and other scoring plans may be adopted for practice, it should be remarked that the least effective intermixtures and, perhaps, the most difficult combinations to manipulate, are those in which the *canto fermo* and first species counterpoint occupy the next nearest parts, whether in the upper or lower portions of the score. There is the least objection to such proximity between the two middle parts. It will, of course, be apparent that the best arrangements will be those in which the contrapuntal layers are relieved and contrasted by placing alternately active and inactive parts, thus—

```
2
1
3
```

I would venture to suggest that the student will gain some useful practice, by writing examples in which two of the parts move at the same time with the same degree of activity, in contrast with two conjointly moving parts in long notes, thus—

```
—  1  2  3  2  3
1  —  2  3  1  —
2  3  1  —  —  1
2, 3, —, 1, 2, 3.
```

The student will also gain by working these different combinations in triple measure, and so increasing the number of notes of the second and third species by one-half. As the power of moving with grace and ease in the time quantities of threes and sixes is nearly or quite as essential to the composer as is the faculty of proceeding in twos and fours, contrapuntal practice in triple time should be regarded as being nearly, if not quite, as necessary as is the practice of moving with the different types of active counterpoints in duple measures. E. H. TURPIN.

Organ News.

BRADFORD.

The opening of the new organ in St. Andrew's Church, Lister Hills, by Mr. A. Marchbank (organist and choir-master of the above church), took place on Sunday, May 6th. Organ recitals were given on May 8th by Mr. W. T. Best (organist of St. George's Hall, Liverpool) ; on May 9th the organist was Mr. A. Marchbank ; on May 10th the organist was Mr. Jeremiah Rhodes, Bradford. Mr. Best played the following programme :—

AFTERNOON RECITAL.

Overture, "Die Lustige Dinge"	Sporv.
Andante in B flat major	Widor.
Toccata and Fugue in C major	Bach.
Andante Cantabile in G major	Wesley.
Scherzo for the Organ in A minor	Best.
Siciliana, and Tema con Variazioni	Weber.
Festive March	Smart.

EVENING RECITAL.

Fantasia in F minor	Mozart.
Adagio in E major	Merkel.
Chorale with Variations, and Fugue in C minor	Bach.
Andante in A major	Smart.
Toccata in A flat major	Hesse.
Andante in D flat major	Chauvet.
Introduction and Fugue on a Trumpet Fanfare	Best.
Fantaisie in E flat major	Saint-Saëns.

WREXHAM.

An organ recital was given in St. Mary's Church, Bersham, by Mr. Edwin Harriss, on Thursday last, the following being the programme :—

Occasional Overture	Handel.
Marche Funèbre de Chant Séraphique	Guilmant.
Organ Sonata, in B flat	Mendelssohn.
Siciliana	Hopkins.
Marche for Eastertide	Merkel.
Cujus Animam	Rossini.
"O rest in the Lord"	Mendelssohn.
Fanfare	Lemmens.
Fugue in G minor	Bach.

NORWICH.

Dr. Bunnett gave an organ recital at the St. Andrew's Hall, on May 12th, the following was the programme :—

Overture, "Poet and Peasant"	Suppe.
Canzone	Guilmant.
Prelude and Fugue	Bach.
Romanza in F	Beethoven.
"Cuckoo and Nightingale" Concerto	Handel.
"The Lost Chord"	Sullivan.
Lieder, "The Duetto"	Mendelssohn.
"The Chapel by the Sea"	Barnett.
Andante con Moto	Smart.
Allegro Marziale	Dense.

HAVERSTOCK HILL.

An organ recital was given by Dr. A. L. Peace, in the Priory Church, Haverstock Hill, on Tuesday, May 8th. The vocalists were Master Hannagan, Mr. Charles Lyall and Mr. De Vere. The programme included :—

Organ Concerto, F major	Handel.
Organ Solo, { (a) Pastoral in G, Op. 105	} Merkel.
{ (b) March for Eastertide	}
Organ Solo, "Prelude and Fugue" ("St. Ann's")	Bach.
Organ Solo, "Bercuese"	Guilmant.
Organ Solo, "Offertorio," E flat major	Morandi.
"Jubilee Overture," E major	Haslinger.

PRESTON.

On Thursday evening, May 10th, an organ recital was given by Mr. James Tomlinson, in the new Public Hall. The following is the programme :—

Concertante	Handel.
Allegro—Largo—Allegretto—Fugue.	
Adagio, "Fourth Symphony"	Haydn.
Grand Choeur et Cantilène	Salomé.
Airs from "Ballo in Maschera"	Verdi.
Marche Cortège from "Irene"	Gounod.

And on May 12th the programme included :—

Overture to the Oratorio, "The Fall of Babylon"	Spohr.
Andante con variazioni	Beethoven.
Marche Religieuse	Adam.
Fantasia Pastorale	Wely.
Musette from the Sixth Concerto for Strings	Handel.
Overture to "Nachtlager in Granada"	Kreutzer.

ALFORD.

The third and last of the series of musical services and organ recitals took place in the Parish Church, on May 10th. A selection from the "Messiah" was sung. The organist was Mr. G. H. Gregory, Mus. Bac., Oxon, of Boston Parish Church. The organ solos were :—

Sonata (No. 1) in F minor	Mendelssohn.
Emperor's Hymn (varied from a quartet)	Haydn.
Prelude and Fugue in D	Bach.
Allegro Moderato in B flat	Chauvet.
"Pastorale," from a sonata	Guilmant.
Andante in F	Smart.
Concerto in A	Handel.

MAXWELL.

An organ recital of sacred music was given in the Parish Church on Friday evening, May 4th, by Mr. Jas. Pattinson, Mus. Bac., Cantab. (organist of the church) assisted by the augmented choir. The following was the programme :—

Organ Solo, Sonata No. 1 in F	Mendelssohn.
Allegro Moderato—Adagio—Andante—Allegro.	
Anthem, "Blessed be the God and Father"	Wesley.
Organ Solos—	
Prayer in E flat	Pattison.
Marche Funèbre et Chant Séraphique	Guilmant.
Recit. and Air, "I feel the Deity within," and	
"Arm, arm, ye brave" ("Judas Maccabæus")	Handel.
Anthem, "As pants the hart"	Spohr.
Organ Solos—	
Gavotte de "Mignon"	Thomas.
Allegretto Villereccio	Funapft.
Song, "The Golden Ladder"	Cowen.
Chorus, "Judge me, O God"	Mendelssohn.
Organ Solos—	
Cantabile (Sonate "O Fili")	Lemmens.
March	Smart.
```
```

NEW YORK.

Messrs. Hook and Hastings' fine new organ for St. Francis Xavier's Church (R.C.), was opened on Jan. 23rd by admirable performances by Messrs. John White and F. E. Whiting. The generally excellent specification is somewhat wanting in 32ft. pedal power. Now the manuals are provided with 16ft. tone, the presence on the Pedal organ of sufficiently counterbalancing 32ft. stops has become a necessary feature of a completely built up harmonic system. In a few years time all large organs must indeed have such harmonic provision.

GREAT ORGAN.

Open Diapason	16 ft.	11. Gambette	4 ft.
Quintation	16 „	12. Octave	4 „
Open Diapason	8 „	13. Twelve	$2\frac{2}{3}$ „
Viola da Gamba	8 „	14. Fifteenth	2 „
Doppel Flote	8 „	15. Mixture (5 ranks)	
Gemshorn	8 „	16. Acuta (5 ranks)	
Claribella	8 „	17. Bombard	16 „
Viol d'Amour	8 „	18. Trumpet	8 „
Quint	$5\frac{1}{3}$ „	19. Clarion	8 „
Flute Harmonique	4 „		

SWELL ORGAN.

0. Bourdon	16 ft.	30. Nazard	$2\frac{2}{3}$ ft.
1. Open Diapason	8 „	31. Flautina	2 „
2. Violoncello	8 „	32. Mixture (4 ranks)	
3. Salicional	8 „	33. Dolce Cornet (5 ranks)	
4. Æoline	8 „	34. Contra Fagotto	16 „
5. Stopped Diapason	8 „	35. Cornopean	8 „
6. Quintadena	8 „	36. Oboe (with Bassoon)	8 „
7. Flauto Traverso	4 „	37. Vox Humana	8 „
8. Violina	4 „	38. Clarion	4 „
9. Octave	4 „		

CHOIR ORGAN.

9. Lieblich Gedacht	16 ft.	45. Fugara	4 ft.
0. Geigen Principal	8 „	46. Flute d'Amour	4 „
1. Open Diapason	8 „	47. Hohlpfeiffe	4 „
2. Melodia	8 „	48. Piccolo	2 „
3. Rohr Flute	8 „	49. Clarinet	8 „
4. Dulciana	8 „		

SOLO ORGAN.

0. Stentorphon	8 ft.	53. Flauto Traverso	8 ft.
1. Viola	8 „	54. Octave Viola	4 „
2. Philomela	8 „	55. Tuba Mirabilis	8 „

PEDALE.

6. Bourdon	32 ft.	62. Violoncello	8 ft.
7. Open Diapason	16 „	63. Super Octave	4 „
8. Violone	16 „	64. Trombone	16 „
9. Bourdon	16 „	65. Posaune	8 „
0. Quint	$10\frac{2}{3}$ „	66. Fagotto	8 „
1. Octave	8 „	—	

MECHANICAL REGISTERS.

67. Gt. Organ Separation.	73. Swell to Choir Coupler.
68. Swell to Grt. Coupler.	74. Great to Solo Coupler.
69. Choir to Grt. Coupler.	75. Great to Pedale Coupler.
70. Solo to Great Coupler.	76. Swell to Pedale Coupler.
71. Chr. to Gt. Sub-Octve.	77. Choir to Pedale Coupler.
72. Octave Coupler Great on itself.	78. Solo to Pedale Coupler.

(These Couplers are operated by pneumatic power and controlled by thumb-knobs, placed over the Great Organ keyboard).

79. Tremolo.	81. Pedal Combination Separation.
80. Bellows Signal.	

(Detaching the Pedale registers from the Pedal movement at will, controlled by a thumb-knob over the Swell Manual).

PEDAL MOVEMENTS.

1. Fortissimo Pedal, drawing all registers and couplers at once.
2. Crescendo Pedal, drawing all registers from softest to loudest at will.
3. De Crescendo Pedal, reverse of No. 2,
4.*Forte Great, giving full Great organ.
5.*Mezzo Great, giving all 8 and 4 foot registers.
6.*Piano Great, giving a soft combination.
7.*Forte Swell, giving all swell registers.
8.*Mezzo swell, giving all 8 and 4 foot registers.
9.*Piano swell giving a soft combination.
10.*Forte Choir, giving all choir registers.
11.*Piano Choir, giving a soft combination.
12. Reversible Pedale to operate No. 75.
13. Adjustable Swell Pedal.

* Nos. 4 to 11 also give an appropriate pedale.

Pneumatic motors are applied to the Great organ and all its couplings, the Pedale organ, the Swell, and to the register action. The action is extended and reversed. The motive power for blowing the organ is the Boston Hydraulic Motor, which is supplied with water from a tank placed in the attic above the organ.

RECAPITULATION.

Great Organ	19 stops	1,566 pipes.
Swell „	19 „	1,508 „
Choir „	11 „	638 „
Solo „	6 „	348 „
Pedale	11 „	330 „
Mechanicals	14 „	......
Totals	80 stops	4,390 pipes.

13 pedal movements.

EXPERIENCES OF AN ORGANIST.

VI.

Having now plenty of available material, and being assisted by the prejudices before alluded to in favour of new brooms, I got together a large choral class, or rather psalmody class (some of our Presbyterian friends had conscientious objections to our calling it by any other name), and we practised with assiduity and enthusiasm, devoting part of our time to works of the great masters, and part to the music which was used at the Sunday services. This latter, when I first came to the church, was of the old-fashioned kind. Tunes now, almost, if not quite, obsolete, such as Cranbrook, and Devizes, and Cambridge New, were in use. But the congregation had evidently begun to grow sick of this vulgar stuff, and soon after my arrival, to my great relief, a new tune-book was introduced. Even this improvement was not made without some opposition on the part of one or two conservative members, who objected to all improvements on principle; and there was one obstinate old gentleman who, for many weeks after the change was made, refused to stand during the singing, but stuck rigidly to his seat as a mark of his disapproval. After this everything went on smoothly for a considerable period. There was a critical lady in one of the side pews who occasionally complained that I played too slowly, but as she was counterbalanced by another critical lady sitting exactly opposite to her, who complained that I played too fast, I concluded that I was giving satisfaction, and congratulated myself accordingly. My position was, indeed, a very comfortable one. Not only did the congregation generally seem satisfied, but, by using the organ cautiously, selecting my voluntaries carefully, and not playing too loudly, I even succeeded in winning the approbation of those who had at first been most strongly opposed to the introduction of the instrument. They began to modify their views, and I was told by one of them that I played very judiciously, and that he found the organ much less objectionable than he had anticipated.

Two years passed away, and there was no quarrelling or bickering among my Presbyterian brethren. All was calm and peaceful, and I began to think it must be true, as I had been informed, that in Presbyterian churches the form of church government was so superior to that of Congregational chapels that the dissensions which were liable to arise in the latter were entirely unknown in the former. But I was mistaken. Presbyterianism is not without its imperfections, which, when a favourable opportunity presents itself, can sometimes be seen easily with the naked eye. In our church the opportunity would appear to have been lacking for some time, but it came at last. Among the various religious societies which flourished in our midst was one calling itself the Christian Young Men's Early-rising Presbyterian Sabbath Morning Fellowship Association. I am not quite sure that I have accurately recollected the title. I fancy I am wrong about the words "Early-rising," but in other respects I believe I have put it down correctly. This body had got it into its head that our parson was growing too old for his work, and that he needed a coadjutor. Most persons, it may be supposed, would feel a delicacy in telling any one for whom they professed to have any regard that he was growing old, and would hesitate a long while before doing it. Not so the young men of the Sabbath Morning Fellowship Association. They loved their pastor dearly. Nobody could be more devoted to him than they were. But they had weighed him in the balances, like Belshazzar, and had found him wanting. His health and strength, they were sure, were failing, and his spiritual power was almost gone. He was over sixty years of age, and it was evident to them that he was rapidly "breaking up," and for the sake of the church, whose interests they had so much at heart, they thought they had better tell him so without delay. So they called together the elders of the church and laid the matter before them for their prayerful consideration. Perhaps it may be as well to explain, for the benefit of the unenlightened, that in Presbyterian churches the office of elder is equivalent to that of deacon. Our Scotch friends seem to think that deacons are unscriptural, and no doubt they very often are. I am afraid, however, that elders too are sometimes open to the same charge. Our elders were particularly favourable specimens of their kind, and yet I think that even they were not always either quite as wise as serpents or quite as harmless as doves. But be that as it may, having heard all that their young friends had to tell them, and the conclusions to which they had come, and being themselves of the same mind, they decided that a deputation, consisting partly of elders and partly of members of the Sabbath Morning Fellowship Association, should wait upon their dear minister, gently remind him of his advancing years and decreasing strength, and propose that he should be assisted in his ministerial work (and relieved of a portion of his salary) by a co-pastor. Accordingly they repaired at once to the house of the reverend gentleman, and proceeded to make known the purpose of their visit. Their beloved pastor being a strong and active old gentleman, was, as may be supposed, greatly surprised and not a little mortified on being told that his health was failing and his powers declining. At first he stoutly denied the impeachment, and declared that he was fully capable of continuing his work without assistance. Ultimately, however, he was induced to consent, though with great reluctance, that the matter should be referred to the congregation, and that a meeting for this purpose should be convened at an early date.

It is not necessary that I should give an account of this meeting, or endeavour to picture the scenes to which it gave rise, especially as I have already portrayed similar scenes in a former chapter. Suffice it to say that there was much disputation and not a little recrimination, for Presbyterians when once they let their angry passions rise, are little or no better than other and more benighted communities. The elders made long speeches, in which they proved very clearly that their much esteemed minister was too old for his work, and their much esteemed minister made a long speech in which he proved with equal clearness that he was not. Then the congregation took sides, one part supporting the minister and the other part supporting the elders. The result of the fight was that the elders, although their party was in the majority, failed to carry their point. Some of the discontented ones, however, including an elder or two and a goodly portion of the Christian Young Men's Sabbath Morning Fellowship Association, severed their connection with the church, and betook themselves to a hall in the neighbourhood, where they preached to one another, and had "a little heaven below" all to themselves.

The church, which up to this period, was in a flourishing condition, was much weakened by this rupture. The congregation grew thinner, and many empty pews were to be seen. Now congregations are necessarily very much like the individuals of which they are composed, and when they begin to fall into bad health, they are apt to become querulous and captious. It was so with us. Everybody began to find fault with everybody else, and as a matter of course, the organist did not altogether escape censure. For instance, he was told that he was not sufficiently circumspect in the selection of his voluntaries, some of which, it was asserted, were of a light and frivolous character and only fit for dancing purposes. Haydn's air "In native worth" was put down as one of this class. He was also accused of introducing ritualistic practices into the church because, on one special occasion, the choir sang an anthem at the conclusion of the service. Such a thing had never been heard of before in a Presbyterian sanctuary. True, it was admitted in palliation of the offence, that the performance had taken place after and not during divine service, but nevertheless as was sharply remarked by a sour little Scotchwoman with a narrow mind and a broad accent, it was "bordering on ritualism" and "wouldna do." Other equally serious accusations were brought against him. Still it must be acknowledged that the complaints in

this direction were never either very loud or very frequent. Whether they would have become more so after a while I cannot say, for about this time I received the offer of an appointment as professor of harmony at a school of music in Ireland together with that of organist and choir-master of a church in the same region, and fearing that in consequence of the unsatisfactory condition into which our church had fallen, my position there was not quite so stable as it had formerly appeared to be, I resolved, after much consideration, to leave it and to try my fortune in the amiable sister isle.

A HOME FOR ENGLISH OPERA.

Are we never to have a theatre especially devoted to English opera? Is it possible to collect money from every other description of entertainment, and to find men willing to contribute large sums in support of schools of instruction; and yet refuse their sympathy to that which alone can afford opportunities for young aspirants to exhibit their abilities? Until we have a home especially devoted to musical works in our own language we cannot expect to have either singers or composers devoting their lives to an art which has been, and continues to be, barbarously neglected in this country. Instrumental music receives its fair share of patronage; and we have, during the past ten years, a remarkable exhibition of progress in English instrumental writers and players, and we can also say they have received a satisfactory amount of patronage; but the poor vocalist has had to devote himself for the most part to singing concert-ballads and occasionally taking part in a cantata, or to be content with foreign music wedded to foreign words. At one time the cry was—You have no English composers; but this was never true, for, as early as the 17th century a school of English music existed, and we can point to particular forms of composition that healthily supported the theatre as the year 1600. It is folly to talk of compositions or composers when you are without an audience to listen to them. As readily might you expect the flower to grow, or a tree to thrive, when planted in an uncongenial soil. We have had plenty of good trees, but we have been without sunshine; and even when the plant has been watered, and has only been done by fits and starts, and the flowers that were forced into bloom have died as soon as created for want of sympathetic culture and care. The 19th century has given us plenty of opera writers': Bishop, with his wealth of melody; Rooke, with his charms of construction; Balfe, with his light but ever tuneful phrases. The names crowd upon us, and we have the music of Wallace, Loder, Macfarren, Barnett, and many others vibrating still in our ears at the present moment. To say nothing of the well known works of Balfe and Wallace, can we forget "The Mountain Sylph"? are we never again to hear the "Charles the Second," "Robin Hood," and, above all, the "Don Quixote" of George Macfarren? I cannot trust myself to talk of these works; but England would be much richer and a much happier nation if we heard them at the present day. I am not forgetting Arthur Sullivan, for he has made comic operetta respected in this country. He has written music that is refined, although it makes us laugh, and he has written carefully, taking the greatest pains with his score. And now we have Mr. Villiers Stanford, and Mr. F. H. Cowen ready to show us that the lyric drama is not dead in England, if it only had a theatre suitable for its performance. We look to Mr. Carl Rosa, whose short season at Drury Lane is sure to interest us, and we ask ourselves again and again, Are operas in English never to have a permanent home amongst us?

The second cry that has been raised is, that we are without dramatic vocalists. I think that any reasonable musician, who watches the horizon and knows anything about the human voice, can prove to the world that we have plenty of vocal ability; the astonishment is that we possess so many singers, when we consider the small encouragement given to them. Only let the want be exhibited, and I guarantee we shall find the supply. We may not have very many large voices at present occupying themselves with public singing, but if you hear as much as I do of the amateur, you will acknowledge that we are not without them in private.

Another remark we hear made on every possible occasion is, that English operas have never been made to pay in this country. In a former communication I have tried to disprove this assertion, and I think that I am prepared to demonstrate to any reasonable enquirer that, when worthy of patronage, operas in English do not spell "loss." Mr. Bunn was not a perfect manager, and yet a great deal of money was taken at Drury Lane when he was there. Mr. Bunn was too egotistical to be a liberal manager, and unless his own words were included in the libretto he took but little interest in the production. The history of Macfarren's "Don Quixote" has yet to be written to clearly prove how good English works are sometimes treated by the management. Mr. Maddox, the first lessee of the Princess's Theatre, told me himself that, after paying all expenses and painting new scenery, he cleared £5,000 in his first season. Jullien's tenure of Drury Lane was cut short by his extravagance and the losses resulting from other speculations. Every one connected with music knows that Mr. Harrison was ruined at Covent Garden, but the fact is hardly so well understood that Mr. Harrison plotted in himself what he never would have allowed any one else. Had he been manager only and not a singer, we have every reason to believe that his efforts to revive English opera would have been successful. As to the Opera Company, Limited, although they are to be thanked for the manner in which Macfarren's "Helvellyn" was produced, their expenses in salaries alone swallowed up all the receipts. If Mr. Carl Rosa can be successful in the provinces, he should be successful in London. It must all depend on good management. We have plenty of theatres of moderate size where music could be better enjoyed, better heard, and better put on the stage than in opera houses like Covent Garden, with its gigantic stage, its numerous band, chorus, and ballet. It has been over and over again demonstrated that small houses can be made to pay where large ones perish. A good orchestra is needed, it is true, but can't it be constructed on a less extensive scale? A moderate chorus frequently gives more satisfaction than a large one; while the principal singers that can work in the provinces, with all the worry of change of place and extra rehearsal, should be sufficient for London. Better, that we should commence on a more moderate scale and continue all the season, than open in a larger house with extra singers that in salaries alone drain the treasury, however liberally the public may support the undertaking. With all the experience of past years, and with the appreciation of music at the present day, with the number of patrons that surround us and profess to be animated by an ardent desire to advance the arts that civilize,—with institutions springing up to teach the higher forms of poetic expression,—are we never to have a home where the works of our own land can be cherished and matured? or are we ever to be saying, "A prophet is not without honour, save in his own country and in his own house,"? I am thoroughly convinced that the day will come when we shall regard with astonishment our own paqueness, and when our encouragement of everything that is foreign will no longer be the fashion or the profitable weakness that it now appears to be regarded by most of our countrymen.—"PHOSPHOR," Brighton Guardian.

It is stated that H.R.H. the Prince of Wales has joined the committee of the Park Band Society, and has sent a contribution to its funds. The band of the Middlesex Yeomanry Cavalry (bandmaster, Mr. W. T. Graves, late of Life Guards) has been engaged by the society to play in Victoria Park, E., from 4 p.m. to 7 p.m. every Sunday, commencing on the 13th instant, until Sunday, September 6th. Arrangements have also been made with the 1st Essex Volunteer Artillery for the band of this corps to play in West Ham Park every Thursday from 6.45 till dusk, commencing on the 17th instant, and finishing in September. In Regent's Park the society's own band will play (under the conductorship of Mr. Hiram Henton, the bandmaster of the London Rifle Brigade), after the 13th instant, as last year, on Tuesday and Thursday afternoons, between 4 p.m. and 7 p.m., till further notice. In Hyde Park, where the society's band has already been playing every Sunday since April 1st with marked financial success, the band will begin on next Saturday its daily performances, and will play, as last year, on Sundays, Tuesdays, Wednesdays, Fridays, and Saturdays, between 3 p.m. and 7 p.m. till further notice. All communications, subscriptions, and donations should be forwarded to the secretary, Park Band Society, 51, Strand, W.C. The Sunday Band question is a delicate one to discuss. However, it is time that our military bands were employed in the performance of week-day concerts.

Correspondence.

INTONING.

TO THE EDITOR OF THE "MUSICAL STANDARD."

SIR,—You will doubtless be interested in hearing that your well-deserved castigation of an ill-advised rector in "one of the leading sea-ports in the south of England" got copied into at least one of the local papers, which identified the performance with a church not a hundred miles from the heart of the aforesaid ancient town. The meeting of the choir of that church following the exposure was, a little bird informs me, anything but harmonious—the grievance apparently being that these gross offenders against common sense had been "found out" and exposed to the contempt of the educated. Oddly enough, the said rector, attending his first meeting of the kind—I should say in my five-and-twenty years' experience here—at a neighbouring church, where an effort was made to clear off the debt on a new organ, seemed to take it as a virtue that he was as fond of good organs as anyone, and he believed he was the first to bring a real (sic) good one to our town. I don't read in the report of the meeting that the rev. gentleman went on to say how he used the "real good one." Possibly his modesty restrained him; but if I may testify from personal experience, I should say a barrel pricked with half-a-dozen tunes and chants would abundantly suit all the demands made for years past upon the "real good" instrument by the alleged introducer of it into the town. So much for self-glorification from a place where awkward questions cannot be asked. If the "unmusical" method of following the prayers was not a thing to be ashamed of, where was the need of making any mistake about it?　　OBSERVER.

Passing Events.

Mr. F. H. Pocock gives an organ recital on the 21st., at the Lancaster Hall, Notting Hill.

The Rev. Sir F. A. Gore Ouseley has recently delivered an interesting lecture on motets at Oxford.

Mr. F. Clay is announced as musical director of the Alhambra Theatre, now in course of re-erection.

At Paris, on the 5th inst., died in his 83rd year, Monsieur Louis Viardot, husband of Mdme. Viardot Garcia.

A good concert was given on May 16th at the Birkbeck Institution under the direction of Mr. J. Stedman.

The degree of LL.D. has been conferred upon the Rev. Sir F. A. Gore Ouseley, Bart., by the Cambridge University.

A tolerably complete series of performances of Wagner's operas will be given during the next few weeks in Hamburg.

An opera, "Fenice," by the late gifted English composer, Henry Hugh Pierson, has been produced at Dessau, it is reported, successfully.

Signor Spinelli's comic opera, "Il Carnavale di Piripicchio," has been heard with approval in Rome. The composer has only just attained the age of 18.

Ponchielli's "Gioconda" is in active preparation at Covent Garden, and will, it is expected, be produced on the 24th or 26th of this month.

An eminent living composer was much amused the other day by hearing a request in a well-known music shop in Regent Street for Wagner's "Nibelungen Ring" arranged for two flutes!

The prize for the best ballet offered by the Monnie, Brussels, has been awarded to M. Paul Bertier for his "Bulbul, ou le Poeté et l'Etoile." The number of competitors was eleven.

The aggregate receipts of the three concerts given by Sarasate amounted to little short of £1,000. Since the visit of Paganini to this country, no violinist has ever attracted such remunerative audiences as Sarasate.

It is stated that, owing to a variety of untoward circumstances, not the least being the illness of Mr. G. Wills the librettist, Mr. Frederick Clay has felt himself obliged to abandon his new secular cantata, "Sardanapalus," which he was writing for the Leeds Musical Festival. Mr. Clay has offered to take a subject and begin another cantata de novo, but the Festival Committee do not feel justified in running the risk which this would involve.

Mr. J. L. Hughes, a well-known Liverpool tenor, and highly successful choir-trainer, has just been appointed choirmaster of the principal Episcopal church in Chicago (U. S.), at a salary of 1,000 dollars (£200) per annum.

Mortier de Fontaine, whose death in London was announced last week at the age of 71, was a pianist of some renown in Vienna some forty years ago, and made his *début* at the Musical Union in 1849, and afterwards visited America.

The Taunton Philharmonic Society gave Haydn's "Creation" on May 10th, under the able conductorship of Mr. T. J. Dudeney. The orchestra was complete and well balanced, and the chorus singing is reported as being most excellent. The society is doing really good work in the cause of art.

At St. Stephen's Church, South Kensington, on Whit-Sunday afternoon, the second part of Gounod's "Redemption" was rendered with orchestral accompaniment under the direction of Mr. Stedman, to a large congregation. This service will be repeated on Sunday next, with the addition of the third part of the oratorio.

Although the organ is daily gaining friends in the north, it appears that the names of 50,000 members and adherents of the Free Church of Scotland have been placed upon a petition asking the General Assembly of that Church to withhold all sanction to the introduction of instrumental music into the services. However, this does not mean much; every question is a battle-field in these days.

The closing concert of the season of the Borough of Hackney Choral Association, on May 7th, under the thoughtful and excellent direction of Mr. E. Prout, was a representation of modern English music, including works by Sir A. Sullivan, Mr. A. C. Mackenzie, Mr. Prout, Mr. C. V. Stanford, Mr. Goring Thomas, Mr. Cowen, and Dr. C. Swinnerton Heap.

Dr. Arnold's choir gave a concert at the Guildhall, Winchester, on May 10th. The admirable finish, refinement, light and shade of the choir singing abundantly testified to the thoughtful and valuable training of the conductor, Dr. Arnold. The programme included several fine old madrigals, and was made up of an excellent selection of sacred and secular works. The choir forms, indeed, a noteworthy and very useful musical institution in Winchester.

The Wolverhampton Triennial Musical Festival will be held on the 13th and 14th September, and the works to be performed are: Mendelssohn's "Elijah," Beethoven's "Mount of Olives," Gounod's "Messe solennelle," Hummel's "Alma Virgo," Macfarren's "Lady of the lake," and Mackenzie's "Jason." Soloists: Mesdames Anna Williams, Mary Davies, Patey; Messrs. Lloyd, Maas, King, and Foli. Leader, Mr. Carrodus. Conductor, Dr. Swinnerton Heap.

Mr. George Gear, whose pianoforte works and execution thereof, at his own concert, were recently noticed in eulogistic terms, came out as a vocalist at the Vestry Hall, Turnham Green, on May 10th. He sang "Les Rameaux," of Faure, and Hatton's "Simon the Cellarer," with great success, and was re-called. Mr. G. Gear also played, with *éclat*, his fantasia on "Faust"; and his song, "The rose is dead," well rendered by Miss Edith Ruthven, was honoured with a *bis*.

Mdme. Florence Winn held her annual evening concert at the Athenæum, Camden Road, on the 5th inst. The hall was crowded with a most appreciative audience, which is scarcely to be wondered at when her list of artists included the names of Miss Mary Davies, Miss Damian, Mr. Alfred Kenningham, Mr. Sidney Tower, and Signor Foli. The concert throughout was such a complete success that it is almost impossible to particularise. Mdme. Winn delighted her audience with her artistic rendering of "The Storm" (Hullah), which she gave with true dramatic fervour. Miss Mary Davies and Signor Foli were never heard to greater advantage. Particular mention should be made of Miss Ethel Headley, a young artist of great promise, whose rendering of Bishop's "Tell me, my heart" could hardly be surpassed. Mr. Turle Lee and Mr. Bending conducted with their accustomed ability. We are pleased to think that this concert—one of the best ever given in the North of London—has been as satisfactory to Mdme. Florence Winn as it was gratifying to her numerous audience.

At the Richter Concerts now in course, will shortly be heard a new pianist of great pretension, Mdme. Vera Stepanoff, a young Bessarabian lady, and pupil of Professor Dachs at Vienna. Mdme. Stepanoff enjoys highest reputation on the continent, and has played with brilliant success in all the large cities and musical centres such as Vienna, Berlin, Leipsic, Dresden, Salzburg, Austria, Bremen, and Cassel. The *Signale* (music journal), of Vienna, praises Mdme. Stepanoff's performances in glowing terms.

At the *matinée* of Mdlle. and M. Brousil, held at James's Hall on May 10th, a quartet for violin, viola, violoncello, and contra-basso, by J. I. F. Dotzauer, produced, Mdlle. Bertha Brousil leading the strings. It is a work of sterling material, and stands steadily on "ancient ways." Miss Maria Wurm, who held not enticed a bouquet, but a regular flower-basket, played her own mazurka, a nocturne of Chopin in D flat, and (with J. Adolphe Brousil) her duet sonata in G, already spoken of as admirable music. The sonata was heartily applauded by veteran *connoisseurs*. A string quartet of Julius Benedict, Op. 87, concluded the *séance*.

Mdme. Jenny Viard-Louis held her (public) concert on May 10th, at St. James's Hall. She gave her well-known grand reading of Beethoven's Sonata in D minor, Op. and afterwards played fugitive pieces by E. Grieg and Liszt. Mdme. Viard-Louis introduced and conducted a peculiar but very interesting work, by Niels W. Gade (another Scandinavian composer), called "Novelletten," a sort of "suite" in several movements, running one into the other, and very well worked out. Mdlle. Isidore Levallois was recalled for a capital execution of H. Wieniawski's Polonaise for the violin, and Miss Victoria Brinsen won rapturous applause for the favourite concert-song from "Dinorah," and some of her charming Swedish songs. Mr. Wm. Carter conducted the concert.

Mr. J. B. Bonawitz held his final concert on the evening of May 9th, at the Blüthner Rooms, Kensington Gardens Square. The scheme comprised his own Piano-Quintet in G minor, already noticed as a splendid composition, three pieces of Chopin, the "Festspiel" of "Brantlied," from "Lohingren," as arranged by Liszt, and Mr. Bonawitz's Duet for the Pianoforte, Op. 10, played by him and Mdlle. Cecilia Brousil. Mdlle. C. Brousil led the strings in the quintet, and played, as a solo, Bonawitz's clever "Concert Dramatique." The other "strings" were, Messrs. D'Egville, Alois Brousil, etc. Mr. J. F. Rudersdorff. Miss E. Selim, a fine contralto, sang with taste and feeling Mr. Bonawitz's song "The Orphan," and two other pieces by A. E. Tozer and Gregh. The concert unfortunately fell on a "Philharmonic" night.

The Querist.

QUERY.

THE RESONATOR.—Can anyone give me any information concerning an instrument invented by Signor Albert Bach, called the Resonator, for magnifying the sound of the voice? If there is such an instrument, I should like to know where to obtain one, and what is about the cost.—A. P.

Service Lists.

TRINITY SUNDAY.
MAY 20th.

London.

WESTMINSTER ABBEY.— Morn.: Service, Calkin in B flat; Continuation, Garrett in E flat; Aft.: Service, Walmisley in ...; Anthem, " The Lord is very great " (Beckwith).

LINCOLN'S INN CHAPEL.—Morn.: Service, Gibbons in F; Kyrie, Gibbons; Anthem, Blessed be the God and Father (Wesley). Even: Service, Gibbons in F; Anthem, Praise the Lord, O my soul (Croft).

TEMPLE CHURCH.—Morn.: Service, Te Deum Laudamus, Hopkins in C; Athanasian Creed, Harmonised Monotone; Anthem, Behold the Lamb that was slain (Spohr). Even: Service, Cantate Domino, and Deus Misereatur, Kent in C; Apostles' Creed, Harmonized Monotone; Anthem, I have surely built Thee an house (Boyce).

CHRIST CHURCH, CLAPHAM.—Morn.: Service, Te Deum, Plain-song; Kyrie and Credo, (Gounod) Messe Solennelle; Offertory Anthem, Sing to the Lord with joy and gladness, (Haydn); Sanctus, Benedictus, Agnus Dei, and Gloria in excelsis (Gounod). Even.: Service, Magnificat and Nunc Dimittis, Smart in B flat; Anthem, The heavens are telling (Haydn).

FOUNDLING CHAPEL. — Morn.: Service, Garrett in D; Anthem, God is our hope and strength (Greene). Aft.: Service, Garrett in D; Anthem, Let all men praise the Lord (Mendelssohn).

ST. GEORGE THE MARTYR, QUEEN SQUARE.—Morn.: Service, Te Deum, Tours in F; Kyrie, Tours. Even.: Service, Magnificat and Nunc Dimittis, Foster in A.

ST. JAMES'S PRIVATE EPISCOPAL CHAPEL, SOUTHWARK. —Morn.: Service, Introit Athanasian Creed (Tallis); Communion Service, Hummel in E flat. Even.: Service, Barnby in E flat; Anthem, Holy, holy, and Hallelujah (Handel).

ST. MAGNUS, LONDON BRIDGE.—Morn.: Service, Opening Anthem, To the Lord our God (Ouseley); Te Deum and Jubilate, King in F; Kyrie, Ebdon. Even.: Service, Magnificat and Nunc Dimittis, King in F; Anthem, I was in the Spirit (Blow).

ST. MICHAEL'S, CORNHILL.—Morn.: Service, Te Deum and Jubilate, Smart in F; Anthem, Whatsoever is born of God (Oakeley); Kyrie and Creed, Wesley in E. Even.: Service, Magnificat and Nunc Dimittis, Naylor in C; Anthem, I saw the Lord (Stainer).

ST. MARY BOLTONS, WEST BROMPTON, S.W.—Morn.: Service, Te Deum, Smart in F; Benedictus, Chant; Holy Communion, Kyrie, Credo, Sanctus, Benedictus, Angus Dei, and Gloria in excelsis, Eyre in E flat; Offertory, Stainer; Paternoster, Stainer. Even.: Service, in B flat; Anthem, To Thee Cherubim and Seraphim (Handel).

ST. PAUL'S, BOW COMMON, E.—Morn.: Service, Te Deum, Benedictus, Chants; Holy Communion, Kyrie, Credo, Sanctus, Benedictus, Agnus Dei, and Gloria in excelsis, Mozart in B flat; Offertory, Garrett; Paternoster, Stainer. Even.: Service, Magnificat and Nunc Dimittis, Hopkins in F; Anthem, I saw the Lord (Stainer).

ST. MARGARET PATTENS, ROOD LANE, FENCHURCH STREET.—Morn.: Service, Te Deum, Sullivan in D; Benedictus, Dykes in F; Kyrie, Credo, Sanctus, Agnus Dei, Benedictus, and Gloria in excelsis, Mozart; Offertory Anthem, God is a Spirit (Bennett). Even.: Service, Magnificat and Nunc Dimittis, Garrett in F; Anthem, The word is flesh become Redemption" (Gounod).

ST. PETER'S, VERE STREET, W.—Even.: Service, Magnificat and Nunc Dimittis, Wood in G; Anthem, Come, up hither "Last Judgment" (Spohr).

ST. PAUL'S, AVENUE ROAD, SOUTH HAMPSTEAD.—Morn.: Service, Te Deum, and Benedictus, Calkin in B flat; Kyrie, Tours in F; Offertory, Barnby; Credo, Sanctus, and Gloria in excelsis, Tours in F. Even.: Service, Magnificat and Nunc Dimittis, Bridge in C; I am Alpha and Omega (Stainer).

ST. BARNABAS, MARYLEBONE.—Morn.: Service, Te Deum and Jubilate, King in F; Anthem, From all that dwell (Walmisley); Kyrie and Nicene Creed, Merbecke. Even.: Service, Magnificat and Nunc Dimittis, King in F; Anthem, Awake, awake (Stainer).

ST. PETER'S, LEIGHAM COURT ROAD, STREATHAM, S.W. —Morn.: Holy Eucharist, Purge me with hyssop (Novello); Introit, Blessed be the Holy Trinity (Aguiter); Mass, Tours in F, gradual; Blessed art thou, O Lord (Sutton). Even.: Magnificat, Smart in F; Anthem, in humble faith (Garrett).

ST. AUGUSTINE AND ST. FAITH, WATLING STREET.— Morn.: Service, Smart in F (throughout); Offertory, Blessing and glory (Boyce). Even.: Service, Smart in F; Anthem, Praise his awful name (Spohr).

ST. SAVIOUR'S HOXTON.—Morn.: Service, Te Deum, Smart in F; Athanasian Creed, Best; Holy Communion, Kyrie, Credo, Sanctus, Gloria in excelsis, Smart in F. Even.: Service, Magnificat and Nunc Dimittis, Dykes in F; Anthem, With Angels and Archangels (Hopkins).

Country.

ARDINGLY COLLEGE, SUSSEX.—Morn.: Communion Service, Tours in F. Even.: Service, Tours in F; Anthem, I saw the Lord (Stainer).

ST. ASAPH CATHEDRAL.—Morn.: Service, Nares in D; Anthem, I am Alpha and Omega (Stainer). Even.: Service, The Litany; Anthem; I beheld, and lo! (Blow.)

ASHBURNE CHURCH, DERBYSHIRE. — Morn.: Service, Dykes in F; Kyrie, Credo, and Gloria, Woodward in E flat. Even.: Service, Lloyd in E flat; Anthem, selections from Last Judgment (Spohr).

BEDDINGTON CHURCH, SURREY. — Morn.: Service, Smart in F; Introit, Holy, holy, and blessing and glory (Spohr); Communion Service, Smart in F. Even.: Service, Smart in B flat; Anthems, Let the bright Seraphim, and Let their celestial concerts (Handel).

BIRMINGHAM (ST. CYPRIAN'S, HAY MILLS).—Morn.: Service, Field in D; Anthem, I saw the Lord (Stainer). Even.: Service, Clarke-Whitfeld in E. Anthem, I beheld, and lo, a great multitude (Blow).

BRISTOL CATHEDRAL.—Morn.: Service, Walmisley in B flat. Even.: Service, Walmisley in D minor; Anthem, I saw the Lord (Stainer).

CANTERBURY CATHEDRAL.—Morn.: Service, Goss in F; Te Deum, Oakeley in F; Jubilate; Anthem, Whatsoever is born of God (Oakeley); Communion Service, Elvey in E flat. Even.: Service, Elvey in F. Anthem, I saw the Lord (Stainer).

CARLISLE CATHEDRAL.—Morn.: Service, Hopkins in C; Te Deum and Nicene Creed, Best in G. Even.: Service, Attwood in C. Anthem, Come, said a voice, and Behold the Lamb that was sacrificed (Spohr).

DUBLIN, ST. PATRICK'S (NATIONAL) CATHEDRAL.—Morn.: Service, Te Deum and Jubilate, Smart in F; Holy Communion, Kyrie, Creed, and Sanctus, Smart in F; Anthem, and God saw everything (Haydn). Even.: Service, Magnificat and Nunc Dimittis, Ebdon in C. Anthems, Above Him stood the Seraphim (Mendelssohn); and In the beginning (Haydn and Stevenson).

EXETER CATHEDRAL. — Morn.: Service, Roberts in D; Communion, Rogers in D; Introit, Ward; Anthem, If ye love me. Even.: Service, Walmisley in D minor; Anthem, The Lord gave the word (Handel).

ELY CATHEDRAL.—Morn.: Service, Plain Song; Kyrie and Credo, Stainer in B flat; Anthem, Holy, Holy, Holy (Stainer in B flat). Even.: Service, Stainer in E flat; V. Crea. and Gloria, Jackman in D; Anthem, To Thee all Angels, To Thee Cherubim (Handel).

LLANDAFF CATHEDRAL.—Morn.: Service, Stewart in G; Introit, Hymn 161; Communion Service, Parry in D. Even.: Service, the Litany (Tallis); Anthem, In humble Faith (Garrett).

LICHFIELD CATHEDRAL.—Morn.: Communion "Service, Barnby in E; Veni Creator, Palestrina; Anthem, Let all men Praise the Lord (Mendelssohn). Aft.: Service, Stainer in A; Anthem, Hallelujah to the Father (Beethoven).

LIVERPOOL CATHEDRAL.—Aft.: Service, Magnificat and Nunc Dimittis, Collingwood Banks in E flat; Anthem, I am Alpha and Omega (Stainer).

MANCHESTER CATHEDRAL.—Morn.: Service, Barnby in E; Holy Communion, Pyne in A flat; Anthem, Come, Holy Ghost (Attwood). Even.: Service, Barnby in E; Anthem, How lovely are the Messengers (Mendelssohn).

MANCHESTER (ST. BENEDICT'S). — Morn.: Service, Kyrie, Credo, Sanctus, Benedictus, Agnus Dei, and Gloria in excelsis, Monk in C. Even.: Service, Magnificat and Nunc Dimittis, Bunnett in F.

MANCHESTER (ST. JOHN BAPTIST, HULME).—Morn.: Service, Kyrie, Credo, Sanctus, and Gloria in excelsis, Williams in D; Benedictus, and Agnus Dei, Eyre in E flat; Offertory, Holy, Holy, (Handel). Even.: Service, Magnificat and Nunc Dimittis, Stainer; Anthem, In Jewry is God known (Clarke-Whitfield).

MUSSELBURGH (LORETTO SCHOOL).—Morn.: Introit, God is a Spirit, Woman of Samaria (Bennett); Service, Stainer in E flat; Anthems, Holy, holy, holy (Handel), and Hallelujah ("Mount of Olives," Beethoven). Even.: Service, Anthem, There is none like unto the God of Jeshurun (Goss and Sullivan).

ROCHESTER CATHEDRAL.—Morn.: Service, Barnby in D; Anthem, Above Him stood (Mendelssohn). Even.: Service, Hatton in E; Anthem, To Thee all Angels, and To Thee Cherubim (Handel).

SHEFFIELD PARISH CHURCH.— Morn.: Service, Kyrie, Elvey in A. Even.: Service, Cantate Domine and Deus Miseratur Chants; Anthem, I am Alpha and Omega (Stainer).

SHERBORNE ABBEY. — Morn.: Service, Te Deum, Lyle in E flat; Athanasian Creed, Lyle in G; Anthem, Holy, Holy (Spohr); Kyrie, Mendelssohn in E flat; Offertories, Barnby. Even.: Service, Anthem, Holy, Holy (Mozart).

WELLS CATHEDRAL.—Morn.: Service, Boyce and Arnold in A; Anthem, O, how amiable (Richardson); Veni Creator Spiritus (Attwood). Even.: Service, Cooke in G; Anthem, I saw the Lord (Stainer).

WORCESTER CATHEDRAL.—Morn.: Service, Skelton in D; Anthem, And lo! a throne (Spohr). Even.: Service, The Litany (Tallis); Anthem, I saw the Lord (Stainer).

APPOINTMENT.

Mr. G. COOPER has been appointed Organist and Choirmaster of St. Anne and St. Agnes, Gresham Street, E.C.

NOTICES TO CORRESPONDENTS.

ORGANO's request has been attended to.

A CORRESPONDENT desires to know where, and at what cost, Handel's "Water Music" can be obtained?

Printed for the Proprietor by BOWDEN, HUDSON & Co., at 23, Red Lion Street, Holborn, London, W.C. ; and Published by WILLIAM REEVES at the Office, 185, Fleet Street, E.C. West End Agents :—WEEKES & CO., 14, Hanover Street, Regent Street, W. Subscriptions and Advertisements received either by the Publisher or West End Agents.—*Communications for the EDITOR are to be forwarded to his private address, 6, Argyle Square, W.C.*

SATURDAY, MAY 19, 1883.—*Entered at the General Post Office as a Newspaper.*

THE MUSICAL STANDARD

A NEWSPAPER FOR MUSICIANS PROFESSIONAL AND AMATEUR

No. 982. Vol. XXIV. FOURTH SERIES.   SATURDAY, MAY 26, 1883.   WEEKLY: PRICE 3D.

ULRICH'S "FLORA MACDONALD."

Just now when the setting of one of the most glorious of earth's musical stars has cast over the world a pall of gloom and sadness, it may not be inopportune to turn our glance from the desolation wrought by death's cruel grip to the hope that lives in the future of the rising generation of composers who have already begun to make their mark in the musical centres of Germany and Italy. Amongst these I would single out a young composer of the German school whose name is not quite unknown to the English public, some of his earlier compositions having been already performed in London.

John Ulrich, born in 1850, of German parents in an English island of the West Indies, who studied music first at the Stuttgardt Conservatorium, and later in Paris under Damcke, Rubinstein's professor, has this last winter achieved a brilliant success in Bologna in the production of his first grand opera which had to undergo the trying ordeal of being played after two masterpieces, Gouhod's "Faust" and Wagner's "Tannhäuser," and yet came off with flying colours.

Some details of this new musical production which has for its subject a page of English history, and bears the title of "Flora Macdonald," can hardly fail to interest the readers of our English musical papers.

I quote from the *Arpa* "Giornale litterario, artistico, teatrale uffiziale, per la publicazione degli atti della Reale Academia filarmonico di Bologna."

The public settled down with the gravest attention to listen to the short overture, which met with general appreciation; then an attentive silence was maintained until the love duet between Signorina Bulichioff and the tenor Novelli, which was applauded at several parts, the union of the two voices occasioning the most vociferous applause, and calling the composer to the Proscenium. Previous to that duet however the intelligent public had greatly admired several very fine choruses, also a Scotch song, sung by the tenor Novelli, which has all the character, all the special melancholy type, of the music of those Northern regions.

The martial air which Novelli sings as he grasps the national standard is remarkably fine, and a word of praise is also due to Macdonald's Grandiose Hymn. At the end of the first act the applause was renewed, and the young author was again obliged to present himself to the public.

The 2nd act contains a beautiful patrol, played first behind the scenes, and a terzetto between Signora Leavington, Novelli, and Wilmant, a delicious melody which is entrusted to the violins. The Reveillé, which is sung first by the baritone, and repeated in an harmonious theme by the trombones with harp accompaniment, is most striking, fresh, and pleasing. The enthusiastic reception that it met with left no doubt of the opinion of the audience, forced at last to throw away its last vestige of coldness and reserve, and call again vociferously for the Maestro.

Wilmant was encored, the trombones also, then followed a *crescendo ensemble* of the whole orchestra, with an elaborated instrumentation of marvellous sonorous effect.

This Reveillé is original in its conception, original in its form, and is really what may be called a musical gem. After its encore the young composer was again obliged to appear.

The rest of the act passed in silence, till towards the end, but the grandiose finale was well received, and the curtain fell in the midst of universal applause, the composer being again called for. I noticed besides this a fine march, but was specially struck with the masterful style of the finale.

Almost all the 3rd act was listened to in silence, but the various dance intermezzi are delicate, elegant, and original. There are some, specially the 3rd, which somewhat recalls the style of Mozart. These beautiful pages of dance music will certainly live in the future.

The 4th act proceeds in silence until the prayer of Novelli, which again arouses the audience by the beauty of the music, and its exquisitely artistic execution. The celebrated tenor is immensely applauded—the composer is again enthusiastically called for.

This act finishes with a symphony descriptive of a battle, the chief part of which is executed with the curtain down; when it is raised the battle-field covered with the dead and wounded carries the spectator far on in the story of the piece.

This symphonic work is one of the most happily elaborated passages of the whole opera, and is a creation that would do honour to the most distinguished composer. The descriptive character is a complete success. The cry of the Macdonald rushing to the rescue of the King, breaking in upon the confused noise of battle, and the groaning of the dying, carries its passionate thrilling effect through the house, so that the act closes in the midst of tumultuous rapture, the young Maestro being again called vigorously.

The 5th act, with Flora's exquisitely harmonised air, the effective terzetto which the soprano, tenor, and bass gave with wonderful power, and the finale, which they also sang together, and which was grand and imposing, brought the opera to a close, which was the signal for continued and rapturous applause.

This real success was a triumph (wrested not from the indulgence of the audience, which at Bologna always shows itself very difficult to be pleased, but due entirely to the real merit of the work), to the masterly power possessed by Herr Ulrich to produce grand musical harmonies. When Gounod, truly one of the most competent judges we have, asserted that Herr Ulrich was destined to a great future, I think he was certainly not mistaken, for the opera of "Flora Macdonald" shows in making of a real artist—of a composer that is on the right road to fame.

The opera has too many prayers in it—though then possess a special local character— a young composer's first grand work is generally an assemblage of different disconnected passages, but "Flora Macdonald" is quite of another build: it is a complete work, through which a dominant idea is running, developing itself gradually to the end. The instrumentation is worked out with infinite skill and great effect; one sees that Herr Ulrich has studied his classic authors well, and follows carefully the rules of modern melodramatic composition. In the whole opera there is nothing common-place—all is delicate, refined, fresh, and further performances will undoubtedly bring into relief many beauties which necessarily escape the audience at a first performance.

The critic must be allowed however to remark upon the lengthiness of the recitatives; the march in the 2nd act is also too spun out, creating some sense of weariness; also I consider that in some parts a more synthetic system of composition would better bring together in one frame the beauties of the music. But this is Herr Ulrich's first grand opera—and if as in all things perfection is the result of experience, in art above all things experience is the most certain and effectual master.

The *Arpa* continues to describe the artists and their specialties, but I have quoted enough to prove that a serious work of real merit has seen the light at Bologna, and has been accorded a most appreciative reception, and if the verdict of the music-loving Bolognese may be accepted, I hope that the music of the future may yet find many gifted exponents though the Mausoleum at Bayreuth has closed over the mortal remains of Germany's favourite composer.

The programme of the Gloucester Festival, fixed for September 4th, 5th, 6th, and 7th, has now been definitely settled, and will include the Mass in C (Beethoven), "The Redemption" (Gounod), "Sennacherib" (Arnold), "Elijah," "Messiah," "St. Mary Magdalen" (Stainer), "Lobgesang" (Mendelssohn), "Psyche" (Gade), and "Acis and Galatea." The principal singers will be Miss Anna Williams, Miss Mary Davies, Madame Patey, Miss Hilda Wilson, Mr. Lloyd, Mr. King, Mr. Brereton, and Mr. Santley. Mr. Carrodus will be the leader of the orchestra, and Mr. C. L. Williams, the organist of the cathedral, will conduct the Festival for the first time. Mr. Williams has already displayed his abilities as a conductor to advantage.

Musical Intelligence.

MR. CHARLES HALLE'S CHAMBER MUSIC CONCERTS.

As last year, Mr. Charles Hallé holds his chamber concerts on the evenings of Friday, at the Grosvenor Gallery in New Bond Street. Eight concerts are announced, and the first, on May 18th, was honoured by the Princess of Wales. Mr. Hallé's "good work" ought by this time to be as well known as "Oliver Blake's," recorded by Mr. J. Cordy Jeaffreson. The scheme included Schubert's String Quintet in C, Op. 163; Schumann's "Three Fantaisie Stücke," Op. 73, in A minor and major, for pianoforte and violin; and Gade's Pianoforte Trio in F, Op. 42. Mr. Hallé, as before, was assisted by Mdme. Norman-Néruda and Herr F. Néruda. MM. Ries, Straus, and Robert Mendelssohn played the inner parts of the quintet. It will be noticed that Mr. Hallé has here made an exception from his rigid rule that all the concerted works at his chamber concerts shall include the *keyed* instrument (a grand iron concert Broadwood). Vocal pieces are still very properly banned. Mr. Hallé chose for his solo the charming "Sonata Caracteristique" of Beethoven in E flat, and could hardly have done better. The concerts will be continued every successive Friday until July 6 (inclusive).

THE ROYAL ITALIAN OPERA.

Mdme. Albani had her *rentrée*, after a successful campaign in America, last Saturday evening, in "Rigoletto," of course in the part of Gilda, the jester's daughter. In excellent voice, and a most interesting impersonator of the poor betrayed damsel, Mdme. Albani's reception, in the second scene, was so cordial, that the business of the stage had to be suspended for a short interval. The air in E, "Caro nome," evoked loudest applause, and, in short, the evening, was a series of triumphs for the fair Canadian. A good "all-round" performance of the opera may be recorded. The title-part found a good, if not a perfect, representative in the French baritone, M. Devoyod, and Signor Ravelli was the libertine Duke, an Italian Don Giovanni of the vilest type. His "original," Francis I. of France, has been grossly libelled in this respect by Victor Hugo, for according to all accounts Francis, if a gay man, fond of nocturnal adventures like the Caliph Haroun Alraschid, was not a deliberate and systematic seducer of innocence or a thorough scoundrel, like the utterer of the monstrous sentiments in "Quest, o quella," and "La donna è mobile"! Mdlle. Tremelli made a smart Maddalena.

"La Favorita," Donizetti's heaviest opera, was performed on Monday with Mdlle. Tremelli as Leonora, Signor Marconi as Fernando, and Signor Battistini as the King of Spain.

On Whit-Monday, "La Favorita" was suspended (for reasons), and "Marta" substituted, with Mdme. Stahl, *née* Mdlle. Tremelli, as Nancy.

Mdme. Pauline Lucca, on Tuesday, repeated her peculiarly analytical representation of "Carmen," and scored several "honours," especially in the coquettish scene with that silly soldier, Don José, at once a sentimentalist and a suicide, in that he ruins himself, soul and body, for a "gipsy's lust," to quote the memorable phrase of Shakespeare from "Antony and Cleopatra." The climax of the evening, perhaps, was attained by Mdme. Lucca in the card-playing scene, where Carmen, in spite of her assumed nonchalance and *insouciant* "don't care for anything," evidently foresees the scissors of Atropos, and probably (a little beyond that) the terrible scourge of the Eumenides, goddesses only to be propitiated, even when Orestes committed his justifiable matricide, by the intervention and coaxing of Pallas Athene. Signor Del Puerte, the *only* "Toréador," appeared at the Royal Italian Opera for the first time, and his famous song with chorus) the poorest, because so sensational a number of the opera, secured the usual encore.

Boïto's "Mefistofele" was down for Thursday night, with Mdme. Albani, Mdlle. Tremelli, Signor Marconi, and M. Gailbard as "principals in front." Mdme. Semyrich is announced to appear on Monday in "L'Etoile du Nord."

RICHTER CONCERTS.

There was a very decided weakness about the first part of last Monday's programme, which caused the noblest of Beethoven's purely instrument symphonies to stand out more prominently than ever in its unapproachable grandeur.

PART I.		
Overture, "Anacreon"	....	Cherubini.
Scotch Rhapsody, "Burns," No. 2, in B flat, Op. 24	....	A. C. Mackenzie.
"Schicksalslied" ("Song of fate"), Op. 54. for Orchestra and Chorus	....	Brahms.
PART II.		
Symphony, No. 7, in A	....	Beethoven.

Beethoven entertained the highest admiration for Cherubini, and, as is well known, wrote in a letter to him, "You are, among all my contemporaries, the man that I most esteem." But it must have been the very opposite character of his talent which created that esteem; for there is none of the romanticism and freedom from conventionality to be found in Cherubini which alone could have won the heart of Beethoven, as distinct from his admiration. No better criticism of the "Anacreon" Overture could be given, than that provided in the programme:—"The excitement throughout is due to the masterly contrapuntal and polyphonic treatment of the themes, rather than to the themes themselves, which, it must be confessed, are somewhat trite in character."

I regret to say that Mr. Mackenzie's second Scotch Rhapsody does not impress me favourably. The materials are not crushed into atoms and then reforged into something absolutely new, as is the case with Liszt's Hungarian Rhapsodies; but three Scotch tunes are treated in turn ("Scots! wha hae wi' Wallace bled," "She's fair and fause that causes my smart," and "I coft a stane o' haslock woo'") in three distinct movements, which follow each other without pause. The programme says: "Mr. Mackenzie seems to have aimed at furnishing a musical portrayal of three leading phases of Scottish national character, viz., the martial, the pathetic, and the jovial. This he has effected by successively bringing before us a war-song, a love-song, and a humorous song"; but, beyond the tunes themselves, I fail to find anything national, or in any way characteristic about this Rhapsody; moreover, it is not rhapsodical enough to deserve its name, nor, perhaps, formal enough to claim any other. And having said that it has no local habitation, though it is called "Scotch," and no name, though it is called a "Rhapsody," I have said all. Mr. Mackenzie, who was complimented after the performance, bowed from below the conductor's desk.

How few there are who can succeed in being calm without being insipid! The dreariness of the first part of Brahms's "Schicksalslied," which represents "the blissful repose of the Olympian deities," causes one to welcome with something like a sigh of relief the turmoil, the uncertainty, the passion, and the poetry of human life which follows; thus the effect produced is in exact opposition to what the composer intended. But it is rare indeed to find *rest* effectively conveyed in any art! We know so little of the feeling; for, in our present state of being, our ideas of repose and ease are too closely associated with indolence and selfish apathy; and as our own art, more than any other, has a tendency to reflect the unpleasing phase of ease, it requires a stronger man than Brahms to give us a notion of the ethereal peace of another state of existence. This composition served to bring the Richter Choir to the front for the first time this season. Unfortunately, they cannot be complimented on their performance. The parts are not well balanced; there is no light and shade; the words are most indistinctly pronounced, and the rendering generally was unfinished. Alas! for the promised 9th Symphony, if rapid progress is not made!

I have listened to a finer performance under Herr Richter of the A major Symphony than that of this week. The strings were not particularly steady in their semiquaver figure in the introduction, and again in the working out of the first movement a slight unsteadiness was apparent. On the other hand, a magnificent *pianissimo* was obtained in the slow movement—one of those distinct whispers that we rarely hear from a soloist, still less from an orchestra. The scherzo left nothing to be desired, and the impassioned delivery of the finale made one gladly forget the undeniable flatness that had hung over the first part of the concert, and that seemed to cling even to the first movement of the Symphony.

B. F. WYATT-SMITH.

MADAME MENTER'S RECITALS.

Mdme. Sophie Menter held a first recital last Saturday afternoon. Her wonderful powers of executancy excited the admiration, even the marvel, of *connoisseurs* last season, and the sensation was renewed on May 19th. Dr. Johnson, on hearing a "fire-eating" pianist of the period play a tremedously difficult piece, uttered a wish that it were impossible! A veteran critic, last Saturday, lifted up his eyes, at a certain crisis, with the ejaculation, "How can it be done?" Sundry detractors who have libellously insinuated that Mdme. Menter, although possessed of immense force, lacks feeling and sensibility, would do well, in future, to be reticent, for they have "all England" and half the continent of Europe against them. A respected weekly contemporary noticing this recital, remarks that Mdme. Menter is not so fine an artist as Herr De Pachmann; but that she is equal to Rubinstein as an executant, and superior to him in respect of exactness and *aplomb*, never alighting on wrong notes, by "mistake," in the excitement of the minute. The beautiful and expressive emphasis of Mdme. Menter's *cantabile*, the tender deliverance of the softer subjects, and the versatility of treatment, sufficiently show that her *forte* is not exclusively the energetic style. Mdme. Menter might adopt the two Latin mottoes of Virgil and Ovid: *Vires acquirit eundo*, and *Gutta cavat lapidem, non vi, sed sæpa cadendo.*

The scheme of Saturday may be printed *seriatim* for the information of absentees. It was as follows: Sonata Quasi una Fantasia, Op. 27, No. 2 (Beethoven); Gavotte in D minor (Bach); Variations in E (Handel); Sonata in C, Allegro Vivacissimo (Scarlatti); Moment Musical, Op. 94, No. 6; Impromptu, Op. 90, No. 4 (Schubert); "Ave Maria," "Ich Hörte ein Bächlein Rauschen" (Schubert-Liszt); Military March (Schubert-Tausig); "Lied ohne Worte" in A, No. 30, Op. 62; "Lied ohne Worte" in E, No. 36, Op. 67 (Mendelssohn); Novelette in E, Schumann; Etude in C, Op. 10, No. 7; Etude in C minor, Op. 25, No. 12; Etude in F, Op. 10, No. 8; Mazurka in C sharp minor, Op. 41, No. 1, Mazurka in B minor, Op. 33, No. 4, Scherzo in C sharp minor, Op. 39 (Chopin); Etude in D flat, Rhapsodies (Liszt); and lastly, Wedding March ("Midsummer Night's Dream") (Mendelssohn-Liszt).

The sonata of Beethoven probably gave less satisfaction than the other pieces, except in the second (scherzo) movement, which was played with exquisite gracefulness. The "attack" of the two crashing dominant chords which occur in the finale, at the end of the opening bars, sounded rather as if the first quaver were a dotted one; and the effect, therefore, lacked crispness. The "Blacksmith" piece of Handel was quite a treat, notwithstanding painful recollections of the impostor Powell at mendacious Edgware. The left-hand work in Liszt's two transcriptions of Schubert had absolute organ power, whilst the *cantabile* of Mendelssohn's "Spring" Lied in A major so moved the audience that a recall (one of many) ensued. Chopin's Scherzo in C sharp minor was a climax of very fine interpretations. Liszt's Study would have been preferred to his Rhapsodies; the transcription of the "Wedding March," as at the Philharmonic concert, not only "made the judicious grieve," but has again provoked severe comments from strictly classical contemporaries. The Abbé, indeed, has here made quite a *travesty* of Mendelssohn's beautiful subject, but the executancy of any pianist who is able to surmount the difficulties, does not the less call for acknowledgment. Mdme. Menter literally astonished the public. At her second recital, on June 2nd, Mdme. Menter will play a far better arrangement of Liszt, to wit, the marvellous Transcription, with all its unutterable effects, of the overture to "Tannhäuser."　　　　A. M.

LEEDS.

The Headingley Choral Society lately gave a concert in the Leeds Church Institute. The programme included Mendelssohn's "Athalie," and a miscellaneous selection. It is a pity that such a splendid work as "Athalie" should have been put down as the last item of a rather long programme; the performance, however, was, on the whole, a creditable one, the solos being taken by Miss G. Dixon, Miss Gisburne, Mrs. T. Appleyard, and Miss Cheveley. In the miscellaneous part the principal vocalists were Miss G. Dixon, Miss Gisburne, Mr. Holmes, and Mr. Fred. Walker, all of whom acquitted themselves

to the satisfaction of the audience. Miss G. Dixon sang with great taste Cowen's song, "It was a dream," and Miss Gisburne was loudly applauded for her excellent rendering of Weber's charming song "Softly sighs" from "Der Freischütz." Messrs. Holmes and Fred. Walker were successful in the music allotted to them, the latter especially distinguishing himself in the song "The Desert," by Louis Emanuel. These two gentlemen also sang the duet "Love and War" (Cooke) in a highly creditable manner. Special mention must be made of the trio "The Three Dreams," by G. A. Macfarren, sung with excellent effect by Miss Gisburne, Mr. Dixon, and Mr. Wood Higgins. The members of the chorus, numbering upwards of fifty, did their share of the work in a manner that reflects the highest credit upon their conductor, Mr. James Broughton. Their rendering of the part-songs, "Lovely night" (Chawtal) and "Parting" (F. Otto), left nothing to be desired, while in Schumann's "Gipsy Life" they were heard to great advantage. The instrumental music included a pianoforte duo (Schubert) played by Messrs. J. and A. Broughton, and two pieces for piano and violin, played by Messrs. Sutcliff and Gaitcliff; Schubert's Sonata, No. 3, Op. 137, and Raff's "Marcia," all given with great taste and skill. I must not omit to mention the duet, "Maying" (Alice May Smith), sung by the Misses Dixon in charming style, Mr. James Broughton conducted in a thoroughly efficient manner, and the concert was a decided success.

ALEXANDER KUMMER.

This excellent violinist gave his annual concert, at the Rooms of the Royal Academy, on Tuesday evening last. The performance began with Beethoven's Sonata in C for piano and violin, which certainly might be mistaken for one of Gyrowet or Pleyel. Neither in invention nor logical development does it contain a tithe of the great Beethoven. The solo pieces for Herr Kummer were arrangements of the Prize Song from "Die Meistersiger," and the Spinning Song from the "Flying Dutchman," which were given with that breadth of expression and refinement of bowing and intonation which we are accustomed to look for from this artist. His playing, too, of that very difficult new set of Hungarian Dances by Brahms and Joachim was perfect. One would certainly think it would have been advisable if Messrs. Brahms and Joachim had stopped after their first successful collaboration of Hungarian dance forms instead of giving us diluted imitations. Another of the solo violin pieces was a Romance by E. Shute, which deserves the fullest praise. It is full of pure feeling, musicianly work, and altogether a gem of its kind.

The pianist was Mdme. Haas, who, determined not to be behind others of her sex, did her utmost to rival the stronger sex by an extreme effort of physical power. What they gain in this direction they lose in expression, certainly the all-important consideration. The vocalist, Miss Mackenzie, has a splendid contralto voice, but she must endeavour to overcome the conventional coldness from which she seems to suffer. M. Albert's two solos deserve special mention.　　FERDINAND PRAEGER.

THE PACHMANN PIANOFORTE RECITAL.

A most varied programme, which was performed at St. James's Hall last Tuesday, afforded the pianist an opportunity of advantageously displaying his high artistic gifts and executive skill. Of the pianist's interpretation of the "Fantaisie Chromatique," as edited by Bülow, I have to accord the satisfaction of the entire audience. The performance was a strikingly grand one, and well deserved the applause it elicited. The same serious earnestness which characterised the interpretation of this monumental work of the old Protestant master was evident in the performer's reading of the whole of the pieces set down, but I must take exception to the *prestissimo tempo* in which the Chopin Impromptu and Valse were taken. The Valse was encored, and again it was played with the same excessive speed. The performance of the Sonata brought out the weak side of its creator. It is beyond question that in the severer forms of art, *e.g.*, the concerto and sonata, Chopin was not so great as in works of smaller dimension of the impromptu and valse kinds. There was developed in the master's sensitiveness akin to the emotional in woman, which was not counterbalanced by the powerful logic of man. Of this onesidedness, perfect as it is, we have several examples in the sister art. Alfred de Musset, with all his genius in light pieces, could never have written a Hugo drama ; nor Meissonnier delineate with any power a stirring historical scene ; nor Heinrich Heine, the most perfect master of lyrics, indite an epic. And yet how truly great are all these masters in their sphere ; and thus it was with Chopin.

Nothing could more fully illustrate the powerful individuality of the pianist than his characteristic rendering of Mendelssohn's Rondo, which, worn threadbare by the everyday performance of myriads of schoolgirls, was galvanised into new life. Mons. Pachmann, is, indeed, a great artist.   FERDINAND PRAEGER.

MUSIC IN DUBLIN.

It is most encouraging to notice the success which has attended the St. Patrick's Oratorio Society in their efforts to attain for classical music that recognition and popularity which has so long been denied it. Not that I would wish to convey from this observation that the taste of the people was unfavourable to its production, but rather that sufficient opportunity had not been afforded them in the past of familiarising themselves with the works of the master hands. True, the Dublin Musical Society have been working faithfully in this direction for some years, but it must be borne in mind that the subscription to their concerts is such as to preclude a very large section of the community from enjoying the performances. I am sure it would have delighted the heart of Mendelssohn himself to witness the vast and eager crowd assembled in St. Patrick's Cathedral on the 11th inst. to listen to the production of " St. Paul," and methinks he would have been equally pleased at the very creditable rendering of his work by a society of such infant growth as St. Patrick's. Started but three years ago, it has achieved a measure of success quite beyond my most sanguine expectation, and here I would accord a word of praise, nay, more, if space permitted, to its talented conductor, Mr. C. Marchant, for the energy, zeal, and musician-like qualities he has displayed in his guidance of the society. The performance of " St. Paul" was, with scarce an exception, an unqualified success. The soloists were Miss Russell, soprano ; Mr. Bapty, tenor ; and Mr. T. Marchant, basso. Miss Russell rendered her music in a most finished and artistic manner, and Mr. Bapty, whose voice is admirably adapted to sacred music, was heard to beautiful effect. Mr. Marchant, who is coming well to the front as a basso, gave his music with a precision and faithfulness highly commendable. The choruses were admirably rendered, tunefully, in good time, and, what is most essential, the voices were fairly balanced. Especially fine was the singing of the chorus, " Stone him to death," and " Oh, great is the depth." The conductor presided at the organ with marked ability.

I have also to chronicle the performance of another youthful society, this being but its fourth season. I allude to the Dublin Amateur Orchestral Union, whose concert took place on the 15th inst., at the Antient Concert Rooms. The formation of this society has supplied a want long felt in Dublin, and I sincerely hope now that it is in good working order it will not be allowed to lapse into obscurity for want of permanent support. The programme was as follows :—

Overture, " Mireille "	Gounod.
Song, " Golden Love "	Wellings.
Minuet (for strings)	Boccherini.
Song, " My heart is like a singing bird "	Mrs. Moncrieff.
Entr'acte, " Don Cæsar "	Massenet.
Song, " Never again "	F. Cowen.
Concerto, D minor	Mendelssohn.

Pianoforte and orchestra.

Symphony, No. 6	Mozart.
Song, " Forget, forgive "	Wellings.
Suite de Ballet, " Language of flowers "	F. Cowen.
Solo Piano, " Rhapsodie Hongroise "	Liszt.

The execution of the above by the Amateur Orchestral Union was in every way a highly successful performance, and would have done credit to a society of far more mature years. It was not, as could hardly be expected, entirely faultless, but the defects noticeable were slight, and remediable, and have not, I am sure, escaped the quick ear of the respected conductor. I could not if I would be captious with this society. It has fought its way through great difficulties and discouragements, the principal one, alas, being want of support, and on this score I have to own to a sense of tenderness for it.

For their latest performance I have to heartily congratulate them ; items 7, 8, and 10 were delightful pieces of orchestration, nor should I omit to mention the valuable assistance rendered by Miss Ella Rosenthal at the piano. To the conductor, Mr. Telford, the lovers of orchestral music must ever feel grateful for his untiring exertions in promoting the success of the society.   F. J. B.

EAST DULWICH.—The St. John's Choral Society gave the final concert of their sixth season, at the Parochial Schools, East Dulwich, on Thursday the 17th inst., the works performed being Rossini's " Stabat Mater " and Sterndale Bennett's " May Queen." The rendering of the first work was particularly good throughout, and the choruses of the " May Queen " were sung with great precision. Miss Emily Gillock presided at the piano, and Mr. Charles Hancock, Mus.Bac., Oxon, of Leicester, at the harmonium, while Mr. Charles Lawrence, Mus.Bac., Oxon, conducted. At the conclusion of the concert Mr. Lawrence, who has been organist and choirmaster at St. John's Church for upwards of nine years, was, on his retirement, presented by the vicar, the Rev. Dr. Warburton, on behalf of the congregation, with a valuable gold watch and chain and an illuminated address on vellum, in token of their esteem.

CHRIST CHURCH, FOLKESTONE.—An organ recital was given at this church on Tuesday evening, 22nd inst., by Miss Theresa Beney, A.C.O., lately appointed organist. There was a large and appreciative audience. The programme was a well selected and varied one, and in the execution of the several items Miss Beney showed a thorough command of the instrument in all its parts. The manipulation of the more delicate portions of the selection was especially noticeable, at the same time that there was no lack of ability to bring out the larger and grander features of the various works. Connoisseurs would have noticed especially the power Miss Beney displayed in the pedalling of the Toccata in F by Bach, while an andante by Batiste, and a minuet and trio by Sterndale Bennet, made perhaps the most impression on the general audience. The recital was relieved by the introduction of one or two anthems, which were satisfactorily rendered by the choir of Christ Church, the solo in Spohr's " As pants the hart " being expressively and well sustained.

HOLBORN TOWN HALL.—On Tuesday evening, May 22nd, the annual concert in aid of the funds for the Butcher's Charitable Institution was given to a crowded, though not an enthusiastic audience. Mr. R. J. Pitt, under whom was the direction of the concert, managed to gather a large body of well trained vocalists and instrumentalists for the carrying out of his programme. Among the instrumental music we must mention the admirable violin playing of Mr. Arthur Payne in Mendelssohn's well-known Andante and allegro (violin concerto), Glinka's " Pas de Patineurs," a Russian dance for orchestra with piccolo obbligato, carefully played by Mr. H. W. Hollis ; and it is with pleasure we have to notice the playing of Mr. John Jeffreys in Mendelssohn's Capriccio in B minor for piano and orchestra ; this gentleman is well known as a careful accompanist, but his talents for this particular kind of performance, are as yet not quite so universal, though he has a very large field to work, yet the workmen are numerous, and indeed many proficient ; knowing this, Mr. Jeffreys will doubtless take it as an incentive—his technical power was complete but yet there was somewhat a lack of finality and rest, which only experience in this style will produce. Among the most successful vocalists were Mrs. Merton Clark, Miss Thelenberg, and Mr. A. Reynolds. The concert concluded with a splendid rendering of Macfarren's " May Day," Miss R. Kinel sustaining the part of the queen with great force. The accompanist was Mr. Geo. F. Grover.

ST LEONARD'S-ON-SEA.—The third of the special services held from time to time in St. Mary Magdalen's Church, took place on Thursday evening last, the 17th inst. Evensong was sung at 8 o'clock, and the Service included a setting of the Magnificat and Nunc Dimittis in D, by G. C. Martin. The anthem was the greater part of Gaul's " Holy City," and the numbers selected were those comprised in Part I, and the bass solo with choral sanctus and the chorus " Great and marvellous are Thy works," from Part II. The tenor solo, " My soul is athirst for God," was sung with much expression by Mr. Alfred Kenningham, of St. Paul's Cathedral, who also sang (by kind permission of the composer), " Eye hath not seen," transposed into the key of C major. The long and important bass solo was well rendered by Mr. Geo. Hawkins, a member of the choir, and the unaccompanied trio " At Eventide " was sung by some of the boys with much taste and feeling. The choruses were all rendered with the requisite light and shade, a special feature being a most artistic interpretation of the unaccompanied " For God so loved the world." The introduction to the first and second parts were played by Mr. A. E. Tozer, who accompanied the whole service as well. The S. Mary Magdalene choir have, during the last eighteen months, sung on various occasions the greater part of Mendelssohn's " St. Paul," the whole of the " Lauda Sion," Stainer's " Daughter of Jairus," and Spohr's " God, Thou art great " ; and with the exception of Mr. Kenningham, who at three of these special services has taken the tenor solos, the different numbers have been sung entirely without extraneous help.

Organ News.

NOTTING HILL.

The programme of the organ recital at the Lancaster Hall, given on Monday, May 21st, by Mr. Francis H. Pocock, who is a promising pupil of Mr. Russell Lochner, was also adorned by the artistic efforts of Herr Wiener, Miss Frances Hipwell, and Mr. Russell Lochner. The organ solos were :—

Toccata in F	Bach.
Trio	Smart.
Sonata, No. 3	Mendelssohn.
Minuet in C	Guilmant.
Andante in E minor	Batiste.
Fugue in G minor	Bach.
Andante Cantabile	Ren.
Jubilant March	Stainer.

BRISTOL.

The following is the programme of the organ recital, given on Saturday, May 19th, by Mr. George Riseley, at the Colston Hall.

Organ Concerto in B flat	Handel
Allegro—Larghetto—Allegro.	
Adagio, Third Symphony	Mendelssohn.
Prelude and Fugue in A minor	Bach.
Largo and Chorus, "Wretched lovers"	Handel.
Entr'acte and Ballet music "Rosamunde"	Schubert.
Air, with variations	Haydn.
Overture, "Masaniello"	Auber.

CRYSTAL PALACE.

Mr. Eyre's programme, on Saturday last, included the following :—

Procession March	Sullivan.
Chorale	Haydn.
Concerto Fugue in G	Krebs.
Intermezzo	Macbeth.
Andante Cantabile	Smart.
Air, "Sound an alarm"	Handel.
Chorus, "See the conquering hero"	
Selection, "Faust" (Judas)	Gounod.
Gavotte, "Heimliche Liebe"	Resch.
Song, "The Lost Chord"	Sullivan.

WATERLOO ROAD.

An organ recital was given on Thursday, May 17th, at the Church of S. John the Evangelist, by Mr. A. A. Yeatman. The following was the programme :—

Organ Concerto, No. 2	Handel.
Allegro—Andante—Adagio-Allegro.	
Adagio (from a quartet)	Spohr.
Song, "The peccato"	Rossini.
Prelude and Fugue in C major	Krebs.
Sonata in G minor	Fink.
Song, "Maestro"	Gounod.
Larghetto (from a quintet)	Mozart.
Fantasia, with Chorale	Smart.

LLANELLY.

An organ recital was given in the Hall Street Wesleyan Chapel, by Mr. J. Matthews, on Friday, May 18th. The following was the programme :—

Toccata and Fugue in D minor	Bach.
Song, "O rest in the Lord"	Mendelssohn.
Pastorale	Guilmant.
Song, "O thou that tellest"	Handel.
Song, "Angels ever bright and fair"	Handel.
Festive March	Smart.
Song, "The Lost Chord"	Sullivan.
Recitand	Fennick.
Duet, "O lovely peace"	Handel.
Miss Williams, and Miss Davies.	
Song, "Let the bright Seraphim"	Handel.
Allegro, "Cuckoo and Nightingale Concerto"	Handel.

NORWICH.

An organ recital was given by Dr. Bunnett, F.C.O., at St. Andrew's Hall, on Saturday, May 19th. The following was the programme :—

Overture in F	Welz.
Pastorale, Prelude	Gordigiani.
Allegretto in G	Frost.
Pastorale in F	Welz.
Organ Concerto in C	Bach.
Adagio, "Moonlight Sonata"	Beethoven.
Canzonetta del Salvator Rosa	Liszt.
Sylvana, Menuet d'amour	Lee.
Andantino	Chauvet.
Fanfare	Lemmens.
Overture, "Guglielmo Tell"	Rossini.

WESTMINSTER ABBEY ORGAN.

Messrs. W. Hill & Son are now engaged upon the reconstruction of the above instrument, in order to make it thoroughly suited to modern requirements, and to the demands made by a cathedral service. For some years the necessary rebuilding has been contemplated, and the work is now being finally carried out. Originally built by Schreider about the year 1730, it remained unaltered till 1790, when Avery added a set of pedal pipes to CC. In about 1828 Elliott added new bellows and a trumpet stop. In 1830, Elliott and Hill built a new Swell with an octave of large Pedal pipes to GGG, 20 feet. In 1848 the organ was moved from the centre of the screen and placed at the two extremities, N. and S.; the compass of the Great organ extended to CCC, that of the pedal from tenor C to CC, and that of the Pedal double diapason to CCCC, 32 feet. With the exception of the subsequent addition by Hill of a Solo manual, the organ remained until now as it was after the alterations in 1848. The inconvenience of the CCC manuals, and the want of a separate pedal organ, together with the natural decay through age of various portions of the action, have necessitated a thorough rebuilding of the instrument, such as is now being carried out. The organ will be re-erected in its old position at the N. and S. extremities of the screen, but will be very considerably increased in height, though not in depth, the narrowness of the church forbidding any extra projection, for appearance sake, though the great height will be a vast architectural improvement, more particularly because Mr. J. L. Pearson, R.A., the architect, has designed two fine cases to enclose the two divisions of the organ. These are somewhat after the model of the old Gothic buffet in the Cathedral of Chartres. Almost entirely new action of all kinds is being provided, of the most approved modern description, pneumatic apparatus being largely used. It is proposed to supply blowing power by means of a gas-engine. Those pipes that are in good condition will be used again, while old new ones will be supplied, both as additions and as substitutions for damaged ones. Many of the new reed stops will be on a heavy pressure of wind. The organ, when rebuilt, will, it is hoped, be a representative cathedral instrument of the best type.

The following is the new scheme of stops :—

GREAT ORGAN, CC TO A.

1. Double Open Diap.	16 ft.		8. Twelfth		
2. Open Diap., No. 1.	8 „		9. Fifteenth		
3. Open Diap., No. 2.	8 „		10. Mixture (4 ranks)		
4. Open Diap., No. 3.	8 „		11. Double Trumpet		
5. Stopped Diapason	8 „		12. Posaune		
6. Principal	4 „		13. Clarion		
7. Harmonic Flute	4 „				

CHOIR ORGAN, CC TO A.

14. Gedact	16 ft.		20. Nason Flute		
15. Open Diapason	8 „		21. Flautina		
16. Dulciana	8 „		22. Dolcan		
17. Keraulophon	8 „		23. Bassoon		
18. Stopped Diapason	8 „		24. Cor Anglais		
19. Principal	4 „				

SWELL ORGAN, CC TO A.

25. Double Diapason	16 ft.		32. Principal		
26. Open Diapason	8 „		33. Fifteenth		
27. Dulciana	8 „		34. Mixture (3 ranks)		
28. Salicional	8 „		35. Double Trumpet		
29. Vox Angelica	8 „		36. Cornopean		
30. Höhl Flute	8 „		37. Oboe		
31. Dulcet	4 „		38. Clarion		

SOLO ORGAN, CC TO A.

39. Gamba	8 ft.		42. Clarionet		
40. Harmonic Flute	4 „		43. Vox Humana		
41. Orchestral Oboe	8 „		44. Tuba Mirabilis		

PEDAL ORGAN, CCCC TO F.

45. Double Open Diap.	32 ft.		50. Violoncello		
46. Open Diapason	16 „		51. Viola		
47. Open Diapason	16 „		52. Ophicleide		
48. Bourdon	16 „		53. Clarion		
49. Principal	8 „				

Wind of various pressures.

COUPLERS.

54. Great to Pedals.	59. Swell to Great.
55. Swell to Pedals.	60. Swell to Choir.
56. Choir to Great.	61. Solo to Great.
57. Solo to Pedals.	62. Swell Octave.
58. Solo to Pedals, 8ve.	

Various combination arrangements.

It is hoped the work will be completed during the autumn.

FRODSHAM, CHESHIRE.

The new organ, built by Mr. J. J. Binns, of Bramley, near Leeds, was formally opened on the 18th inst. by F. W. Hird, Esq., of Leeds. The Rev. Canon Gore, Vicar of Bowdon, preached in the afternoon, and the Rev. H. B. Blogg, Vicar of Frodsham, in the evening. An organ recital was given at the close of each service by Mr. Hird. The organ has been erected at a cost of about £800, the front being in plain oak, slightly carved, with plain spotted metal pipes; altogether the whole forms a marked feature in the church. The tone of the organ was greatly admired by a large congregation, among whom were several organ builders. A striking characteristic of the organ is the full and ringing tone of the diapasons, resembling in this particular (as well as in the clearly defined individuality of the flue work generally), the tone produced by the late eminent organ builder, Edmund Schulze. The reeds also are excellent, the oboe being specially charming, and the pedal stops are quite on a par with the rest of the work. The preacher in the evening paid a high tribute to the untiring energy and ability of Mr. Binns. The organ is placed in the Helsly Chapel of the recently restored edifice, which is now one of the finest churches in the county. The following is a specification of the organ :—

Compass of each Manual, CC to G. in alt., 56 Notes.

GREAT ORGAN.

1.	Bourdon	16 ft.	6.	Octave	4 ft.
2.	Large Open Diapn.	8 „	7.	Twelfth	2⅔„
3.	Small Open Diapn.	8 „	8.	Fifteenth	2 „
4.	Stop D'apason	8 „	9.	Mixture, 3 ranks	
5.	Harmonic Flute	4 „	10.	Trumpet	8 „

SWELL ORGAN.

11.	Bourdon	16 ft.	16.	Octave	4 ft.
12.	Open	8 „	17.	Harmonic Piccolo	2 „
13.	Dulciana	8 „	18.	Mixture, 3 ranks	
14.	Voix Celestes	8 „	19.	Horn	8 „
15.	Hohl Flöte	8 „	20.	Oboe	8 „

CHOIR ORGAN.

21.	Lieblich Bourdon	16 ft.	25.	Lieblich Flöte	4 ft.
22.	Violin Diapason	8 „	26.	Flautino Dolce	2 „
23.	Dolce	8 „	27.	Clarionette	8 „
24.	Lieblich Gedact	8 „			

PEDAL ORGAN.

28.	Open Diapason	16 ft.	30.	Flute Bass	8 ft.
29.	Bourdon	16 „			

COUPLERS.

31. Swell to Great.	34. Great to Pedals.
32. Swell to Choir.	35. Swell to Pedals.
33. Choir to Great.	36. Choir to Pedals.

4 Composition Pedals to Great Organ.
3 Composition Pedals to Swell Organ.

SUMMARY.

Great Organ	10 Stops	672	Pipes
Swell Organ	10 „	662	„
Choir Organ	7 „	382	„
Pedal Organ	3 „	90	„
Couplers	6 „	...	„
Total	36 Stops	1806	Pipes.

FISHERIES EXHIBITION.

Mr. Frank Bradley gave the following organ recitals, on Monday and Wednesday, at the above Exhibition, on Messrs. Lewis's and Henry Jones's organs.

MONDAY.

Gigue in D major	Bach.
Fugue in D major	Archer.
Gavotte	Thomas.
Air and variations	Chipp.
Gavotte and Musette	Raff.
Fugue	Bach.
Extempore	} Bradley.
Gavotte and Musette	
Fusiliers	Lemmens.

WEDNESDAY.

Concerto	Handel.
Dances	Dvorak.
Gavotte in D and A	{ Bach.
	Gluck.
Polish Dances	Scharwenka.
Air and Variations	Lux.
Fugue in G minor	Bach.
Overture, "Merry Wives"	Nicolai.
Pastorale and Canon	Salomé
Chorus, in D major	Guilmant.

Academical Intelligence.

SOCIETY OF ARTS.

The next Practical Examination in Vocal or Instrumental Music in London will be held at the House of the Society of Arts, 18, John-street, Adelphi, W.C., during the week commencing on the 11th June, 1883.

HONOURS.

The Examination in Honours will consist of three sections, viz., a paper to be worked, an examination similar in form to the practical examination for a First and Second Class, and a *viva-voce* examination.

FIRST AND SECOND-CLASS.

Vocal.

Candidates for a First or Second Class Certificate in Vocal Music will be required—
1. To sing a solo, or to take part with another candidate in a duet, already studied.
2. A key-note being sounded and named by the Examiner, the candidate to name sounds or intervals, or successions of sounds or intervals, played or sung by the Examiner.
3. To sing or sol-fa at sight passages selected generally from classical music.

Instrumental.

Candidates for a First or Second Class Certificate in Instrumental Music will be required—
1. To play a short piece, or a portion of a larger work, already studied.
2. A key-note being sounded and named by the Examiner, the candidate to name sounds or intervals, played by the Examiner.
3. To play a piece or portion of a piece at sight.
Full particulars can be obtained on application to the Secretary.

THE TONIC SOL-FA COLLEGE.

The annual meeting was held at Exeter Hall on Tuesday evening, May 22nd, the chair being taken by Mr. Henry Leslie. A very enthusiastic, crowded audience testified to the hearty character of the meeting. Mr. R. Griffiths read the highly satisfactory report of the year. Addresses were delivered by the chairman, Mr. J. Spencer Curwen, the Rev. Professor Davis, and the Rev. R. C. Billing. The sight-singing test was an anthem, "Arise, shine," by W. Meston. This was cleverly gone through. Proceedings were opened by an organ recital, Miss Mary Harris and Mr. W. C. Harris : "Cornelius" March (Mendelssohn) ; Andante in G, Batiste ; Allegro and Fuga from No. 2 of Organ Sonatas (Mendelssohn) ; Gavotte Moderne in *Ut* (Berthold Tours). The United choirs (conductor, Mr. J. Proudman ; organ, Mr. J. Thomson) sang chorus, "The many rend the skies" (Handel). Mr. McNaught's choir (conductor, Mr. W. G. McNaught) gave part-song, "A rose of the garden" (Henry Leslie). The South London Choral Association (conductor, Mr. L. C. Venables) sang part-song, "Zephyr, taking thy repose" (G. A. Macfarren). The Tonic Sol-fa Choral Association (conductor, Mr. J. Proudman) gave part-song, "The lullaby of life (Henry Leslie). Mr. McNaught's choir sang part-song, "The silent Land" (Alfred R. Gaul). The Tonic Sol-fa Choral Association, part-song, "In vain you tell" (J. L. Hatton). The South London Choral Association sang the clever humorous part-song, "Kate Dalrymple" (Frederick Archer).—The Sight Test. The United Choirs (conductor, Mr. W. G. McNaught) performed part-song, "The Pilgrims" (Henry Leslie). The Tonic Sol-fa Choral Association, part-song, "Take thy banner" (James Coward). Mr. McNaught's choir, Madrigal (8 parts), "Lay a garland" (R. L. de Pearsall). The South London Choral Association, chorus, "The halt of the caravan" (Sir H. R. Bishop). The United Choirs (conductor, Mr. L. C. Venables), chorus, "We never will bow down" (Handel).
It would be impossible to do justice to the united, earnest enthusiasm of the audience. Clearly tonic sol-fa interests are in good hands, and the future of the cause as a powerful educational influence is fully assured.

Reviews.

The Eleventh Annual Festival Service Book of the London Gregorian Choir Association for the current year, is perhaps musically the most satisfactory issue of the kind yet offered to the members. The book has designedly an Eucharistic character. The preface gives brief and sensible directions anent the performance of plain-song, which display real knowledge and sound judgment, as do the rules to sing ascending passages with increased force to climax points, and descending sentences towards repose points with decreased intensity; and to sing to closing *Pneumas* with lightness and delicacy. The Eucharistic tone of the contents of this Service Book tends to show that the Gregorian movement in the Anglican Church is too much in the hands of one section of the Church; or perhaps High Churchmen join and influence the movement largely as one of mediæval picturesqueness, and so impart to what should be a broadly Catholic movement the elements and tendencies of a religious faction. It would be difficult otherwise to account for the presence of the prose for Corpus Christi Day "Laudi Sion salvatorem," and the side-notes: "The words in *italics* are sung only on the festival of Corpus Christi." Now is that great Roman festival of the earlier part of Trinitytide ever celebrated in the Anglican Church? Or is the doctrine of transubstantiation, which it practically celebrates, accepted fully in the English Protestant section of the one body, which, as regards its broader principles, exists "throughout all the world?" Surely there can but be a negative reply to both these questions, and such a negation with equal certainty shows a want of judgment, or the presence of a prejudicial leaning in a given direction on the part of the Committee of the L.G.C.A. The music of the Church, the common heritage of all, should be nurtured upon broader principles than these, and the sooner the Committee of the L.G.C.A. change their tactics, the better for the cause they so earnestly advocate; unless, indeed, they are determined to promulgate given doctrines as part and parcel of the mediæval arts of the Church, in which case the public will doubtless decide how to view the claims of those who thus ostensibly seek to forward a revival of the Church's musical heritage—plain-song. Another complaint may here be registered against the stiff and often inelegant translations of some of the finest of the ancient metrical hymns; some of them are unhappy enough to have been the work of the author of the libretto of a recently produced English opera. One innovation of ritual is the introduction of antiphons before the psalms and canticles after the manner of the Roman Church, a matter involving no doctrinal consideration, but showing an anxious desire to revive or transplant ancient formularies. As regards the music, there is little but praise. The plain-song (which is, however, not very pure) of the responses has been judiciously placed in the upper part, where it is much more available for congregational purposes than when sung in the tenor part. The harmonies, although they might have been still more set upon the old modes than they are with advantage, are laudably diatonic in character, and show a desire to permit the grand old and never-fading melodic idioms to find their way to the human heart as they should, as unadorned and as naturally as possible. The book contains such gems as the hymn, "Pange lingua," the old notes to the "Preface" and "Lord's Prayer," destined to last, as long as the Church remains on this earth, the tune of "Laus devote mente," and other priceless treasures of ancient song. The modern anthem given was Dr. Gauntlett's dignified setting of the words, "I will go unto the altar of God." It may be added that the L.G.C.A. have issued adaptations to the Communion office of two plain-chant "Masses," Nos. 1 and 2 of "Series of Plain-Song Masses." The first is a beautiful specimen of French ornate plain-song, the second is the well-known "Missa de Angelis," which furnishes in the initial themes of its "Gloria and Credo" the priest's intonations so universally used in the Roman Church. The accompanying harmonies are good.

Mendelssohn's "Elijah" was well given by the Kyrle Society at St. Barnabas, King's Square, on May 26th, under the direction of Mr. M. L. Lawson. Mr. E. H. Turpin was the organist.

PRINCIPAL CONTENTS OF THIS NUMBER.

ULRICH'S "FLORA MACDONALD."
MUSICAL INTELLIGENCE:—Mr. Charles Hallé's Chamber Music Concerts—The Royal Italian Opera—Richter Concerts—Madame Mera—Recitals—Leeds—Alexander Kummer—The Pachmann Pianoforte Recital—Music in Dublin.
ORGAN NEWS :—Notting Hill—Bristol—Crystal Palace—Waterloo Road—Llanelly—Norwich—Westminster Abbey Organ—Frodsham, Chester—Fisheries Exhibition.
ACADEMICAL INTELLIGENCE :—Society of Arts—The Tonic Sol-fa College.
REVIEWS OF BOOKS AND MUSIC.
EDITORIAL :—Berlioz.
BERLIOZ'S " REQUIEM " MASS.
THE LATE M. MORTIER DE FONTAINE.
CERTAIN OBSERVATIONS CONCERNING HYMN-TUNES. By "Old School."
ROYAL ACADEMY OF MUSIC.
PASSING EVENTS. Service Lists, &c.

LONDON : SATURDAY, MAY 26, 1885.

BERLIOZ.

DISTINGUISHED writer holds that "without BERLIOZ there would have been "no Wagner." This observation, when limited to the matter of orchestration, is not without force. Undoubtedly the great French composer contributed enormously to the modern supremacy of instrumentation as an essential art in the history of the music of the present era. So the performance of his "Requiem" Mass at the Crystal Palace to-day is a matter of special interest. It may be that the effect of the work will not altogether answer the expectations of the many enthusiastic and expectant listeners. In two directions such a disappointment is possible. In the first place, the human mind is apt through the deceptive powers of the imagination to overleap its own faculties of comprehension. A man might propose to himself to see such a vast area of landscape as would necessitate his being carried up a great height in order that his sight may compass so large an expanse. As his power of vision will not permit the definite inspection of a too extended area, he would inevitably lose much of many beauties spread before him. So it is in art, and a too extensive and overloaded score is often a practical failure. The conception of the mind surpasses its own power for the receptivity of details; and it is the artist's real business to attain to great thoughts through limited means, rather than to hope to secure commensurate results through means too extensive for the grip of the but limited powers of hearing and seeing. Again, BERLIOZ was the exponent of a department of the art rather than a complete master of the entire art; and notwithstanding his undoubted genius, he was afflicted with that

> Vaulting ambition which overleaps itself.

In his impetuous tone-colour power he often sought to over-dress ideas which only could be properly attained with the simplest tone-colour raiments; he would gild the very nails and screws of his musical structure. This tendency to overdress his ideas did indeed lead to the larger development of orchestral power; but it is a question whether music has gained as much from his labours as would have been secured by a more complete all-round attention to the duties of the composer's workmanship. By the splendour of his over-drawn pictures he certainly showed to the world the possible importance of a department of the art. Perhaps he also furnished the musical student with a warning not to bestow too much power in any one given direction, or to rely too much upon effects which may not always have beneath their glittering surface real, solid, and shapely thoughts.

Critically it must be allowed that some of BERLIOZ's effects display a want of acoustical knowledge; as his employment of drums in chords, for the indefinite nature of the sounds produced by those instruments and their harmonic peculiarities somewhat unfit them for such use. Again, some of his effects are extensions of other men's ideas rather than inventions of his own; as the use of the trombone foundation tones (which he calls pedal notes) with high chords for flutes to prompt the formation of harmonic suggestions, a device not very modern and beautifully illustrated in Mendelssohn's "Andante" of the "Italian" Symphony.

Fair justice demands, indeed, that BERLIOZ should be acknowledged as a man of real power and inventive strength in his way. His orchestral combinations and inventions have indeed uplifted instrumentation to a science in itself almost. The graphic and interesting account of the great artist's composition and preparation of the "Requiem"—the score of which, like the score of some other works of his, will continue to be regarded by musicians as affording valuable examples for thought and study—as expressly translated for this paper by Mr. SOUTHGATE, will be found to reveal much, both of the artist and of the man.

E. H. TURPIN.

BERLIOZ'S "REQUIEM" MASS.

(Translated from "Mémoires de Hector Berlioz," cap. 46.)

By T. L. SOUTHGATE.

In 1836 M. de Gasparin was Minister of the Interior. He belonged not only to the small number of our statesmen who felt interest in music, but also to the number still smaller who had a real love for the art. Religious music had for a long time past ceased to occupy an honourable position in France. M. de Gasparin, being desirous of reinstating it, determined that from the funds at the disposal of the Department of the Fine Arts, a sum of 3,000 francs should be allocated every year to a French composer, designated by the minister, to write either a mass or a grand oratorio. According to the scheme of M. de Gasparin, the department was, moreover, to be answerable for the performance of the new work, which was to be given at the cost of the government. "I am going to commence with Berlioz," said he; "he must write a

requiem mass, I am sure that he will succeed." These particulars were given me by a friend of M. de Gasparin that I knew. My surprise was as great as my joy. In order to be quite certain as to the truth, I solicited an audience of the minister. On seeing him, he confirmed the correctness of the details I have given above. "I am about to quit the ministry," he added, "this will be my musical testament. You have received the formal order concerning the Requiem?" "No, monsieur! and it is only chance that has permitted me to know your kind intentions towards me. Indeed! How can this be? a week ago I gave directions that you should be sent for. The delay must have been caused by the carelessness of my officials. I will see to this."

Nevertheless, several days passed, and no order arrived. Full of uneasiness, I addressed myself to M. de Gasparin's son, who informed me of an intrigue of which I had not the slightest suspicion. M. XX . . .,* the Director of the Fine Arts, did not approve of the minister's project relative to religious music; still less the choice he had made that I should lead the way among our composers, and inaugurate the scheme. He knew, besides, that in a few days M. de Gasparin would be no longer in office. Now in delaying until after the minister's departure the issuing of the decree which founded the project and invited me to compose the music, it was easy to secure the failure of the scheme, and dissuade the new minister from attempting to realize it. This is what monsieur the director had in his head. But M. de Gasparin would not permit anyone to play with him. On learning from his son that no steps had as yet been taken, the day before he left the ministry he sent at the last moment to M. XX . . . a command very severely expressed, to issue the decree instantly, and to send it to me; so this was done.

This first check to M. XX . . . could not but increase his bad feelings towards me; indeed, it eventually had such a result.

This arbiter of art and the fate of artists vouchsafed to recognise true value in music in Rossini alone. One day after having expressed before me in a lengthy disdainful way an appraisement of all the ancient and modern masters of Europe, with the exception of Beethoven, whom he had *forgotten*, he suddenly changed his tone, saying :—"However, it appears to me there is still another one . . . it is . . . . there . . . ., what is he called? A German whose symphonies are played at the Conservatoire, . . . You ought to know *that* M. Berlioz . . . Beethoven? Yes, Beethoven. Ah, well! that person is not without some talent."—I actually myself heard a Director of the Fine Arts thus express himself. He graciously admitted that Beethoven *was not without talent!*

And in this, M. XX . . . was only the representative of the musical opinions of all the French bureaucracy of the period. Hundreds of amateurs of this type occupied all the avenues through which artists had to pass, and set in motion the wheels of the government machine by which proper support ought to be accorded to our national institutions.—To-day . . . .

As soon as I was furnished with the decree, I commenced to work. I regarded the text of the "Requiem" as a prey long coveted, which was delivered to me at last, and on which I threw myself with a sort of fury. My head seemed ready to burst through the effects of seething over thoughts. The plan of one piece was no sooner sketched, than that of another presented itself. Owing to the impossibility of writing quickly enough, I adopted short-hand signs, which (especially for the "Lacrymosa") proved to be of great assistance. Composers know the torment and despair caused at the remembrance of the loss of certain ideas, which one has not had time to write down, and which escape one for ever. I have consequently written this work with great rapidity; I may add, that I made but few modifications afterwards. These are to be found in the second edition of the score published by Messrs. Ricordi of Milan.

[NOTE.—Is it not strange that at that period, when I was writing this grand work and was married to Miss Smithson, twice I had the same dream? I was in the little garden of Madame Gautier at Meylan, sitting beneath a charming drooping acacia alone, Mdlle. Estelle not being there, and I said, "Where is she? Where is she?" Who can explain that? Sailors perhaps,

* There seems to have been no reason why Berlioz should have affected any mystery over the name of the Director of the Department of the Fine Arts. He had been dead a dozen years when the "Memoires" were written, and the date given, 1836, is sufficient to indicate to the curious the identity of the *bête noir.*—T. L. S.

or scientific men, who have studied the movements of the magnetic needle, and who know that the heart of certain men resemble it. . . .]'

The ministerial order directed that my "Requiem" should be performed at the cost of the Government on the day of the funeral service celebrated every year for the victims of the revolution of 1830.

When the month of July, the period of that ceremony, approached, I had copies of the chorus and orchestral parts of my work made, and by the advice of the director of the Fine Arts, commenced the rehearsals. But almost immediately came a letter from the office of the minister, informing me that the funeral ceremony for the July victims would be held without music, and ordering me to suspend all my preparations. The new minister of the interior was, however, by that time responsible for a considerable sum due to the copyists, and to the two hundred choristers who, on the faith of the decree, had given up their time to my rehearsals. For five months I begged without effect for the payment of these expenses incurred. As to that which was owing to me, I did not venture to mention it; they seemed not even to dream of it. I was beginning to lose patience, when one day, as I was going out of the cabinet of M. XX . . . , after a lively discussion I had had with him on the subject, the canon of the Invalides announced the capture of Constantine. Two hours after, I was asked in great haste to return to the minister. M. XX . . . had found the means to get rid of me. General Damrémont having fallen under the walls of Constantine, a solemn service for him and the French soldiers who had died during the siege was to be held in the Church of the Invalides. This ceremony concerned the Minister of War, and Gen. Bernard, who then occupied that post, consented to have my "Requiem" performed. This was the unhoped for news which I learnt on arriving at M. XX . . .'s.

But here the drama became complicated, and incidents of the most serious kind succeeded one another. I recommended the poor artists who worked with me to profit a little by my experience, and to meditate upon that which had already happened. I advise those who read this to acquire the sad advantage of mistrusting all and everything, when they find themselves in an analogous position; to regard written orders with no more faith than mere words, and to entertain as much caution against heaven as against hell.

Hardly had the news of the approaching performance of my "Requiem" as a part of the grand and official ceremony which was to take place, been told to Cherubini,* than it threw him into a perfect fever. It had already long been the custom that in like cases one of his two funeral masses should be executed. Such a decision irritated him profoundly. He considered it as a blow struck at that which he regarded as his rights, his dignity, his just celebrity, his incontestable value, in favour of a young man hardly yet at the beginning of his career, and one, moreover, who was credited with having introduced heresy into the school. All his friends and pupils, Halévy at the head, partook of his vexation; they endeavoured to raise a storm and direct it on me, seeking everywhere for aid to depose the young man for the old one's profit. One evening I was at the office of the *Journal des Débats,* to the staff of which I was already attached (M. Bertin, the director, regarding me with the most active benevolence), when Halévy presented himself. I divined at a glance the object of his visit. He came to have recourse to the powerful influence of M. Bertin to aid in the realization of Cherubini's projects. A little disconcerted, however, to find me there, and still more at the air of coldness with which M. Bertin and his son Armand received him, he instantly changed the direction of his batteries.

Halévy having followed M. Bertin, senior, into the next room, the door of which was open, I heard him say, "that Cherubini was so extraordinarily affected over the matter, that it was feared he would be confined to bed through illness. He (Halévy) had consequently come to beg M. Bertin to use his influence and endeavour to obtain, as a consolation, the commander's cross of the Legion of Honour for the illustrious master." The stern voice of M. Bertin then broke in these words:—"Yes, my dear Halévy, we will do what you wish in order to obtain a distinction that Cherubini well merits. But if

* The published "Memorials of Cherubini," who at that period was head of the Paris Conservatoire, show that the relations between the two composers were very strained.—T. L. S.

there is any question about the 'Requiem,' and propositions are to be made to Berlioz respecting his work, and he had the weakness to yield a hair, *I would never speak to him again in my life.*"—Halévy retired a little more than confused at this response.

So the good Cherubini, who had already wished to make me swallow, as it were, ever so many little adders, was himself compelled to receive from my hand a huge boa constrictor, which he never digested.

Now for another intrigue, more cleverly plotted, the deep wickedness of which I hardly dare to fathom. I incriminate nobody, merely recounting roughly the facts, but with the most scrupulous exactitude, without making the least commentary.

General Bernard having announced personally to me that my "Requiem" would be executed on the conditions already related, I was about to commence the rehearsals when M. XX . . . sent for me.—"You know," said he, "that Habeneck * has been charged to direct the music of the grand official fêtes?" (Good gracious, I thought, another blow has fallen on my head!) "Certainly, you are at present in the habit of conducting the performance of your own works, but Habeneck is an old gentleman" (another stroke), "and I know that he will experience considerable pain if he does not preside at the conductor's desk for your 'Requiem.' On what terms are you with him?" On what terms? We had quarrelled, I don't know why; during the last three years he had ceased to speak to me; I altogether ignore his motives, and, to tell the truth, have not deigned to inform myself of them. He commenced by brusquely refusing to direct one of my concerts. His conduct towards me is as inexplicable as uncivil. However, as I plainly see that on this occasion he desires to figure at the ceremony connected with Maréchal Damrémont, and that this appears to be equally agreeable to you, I consent to yield the bâton to him, reserving to myself at all times the direction of the rehearsals. "That, of course, belongs to you," answered M. XX . . ., "I will give him notice."—The divisional and general rehearsals were held with much care. Habeneck spoke to me, as if our relations had never been interrupted, and it appeared that the work ought to proceed well.

On the day of the performance, in the Church of the Invalides, before the princes, ministers, peers, deputies, all the French press, the correspondents of foreign journals and an immense crowd, it was imperative that I should have a great success; a mediocre effect would be fatal, and for a still stronger reason, a bad effect would be annihilation to me.

But now listen to this :—

My performers were divided into several groups, placed at a distance from one another; and it was necessary also that the four orchestras of brass instruments, which I had employed in the *Tuba mirum,* should each occupy corners at the angles of the grand mass of vocal and instrumental performers. At the point of their entry, the commencement of the *Tuba mirum,* which is connected with the *Dies iræ* without break, the movement becomes enlarged; all the brass instruments first bursting forth at the same time. Afterwards they challenge and answer one another in the distance, their successive entries on the major third, thus gradually building up the scaffold of vivid tone, and so intensifying the effect.† It is, therefore, of the highest importance clearly to indicate the four beats of the new movement, and give the cue to the respective orchestras at the moment when they should come in. Were this neglected, this terrible musical cataclysm, where means quite exceptionable and formidable in their proportions, and combinations that have never before been tried, would produce only an immense and frightful cacophony. I trust that this musical picture of the last judgment will always remain as an example of the greatness of our art.

* Habeneck, though of German parentage, was born in France. He was a fair musician, and enjoyed the reputation of being an unprejudiced man. It was through him that Beethoven's symphonies were introduced to the Parisians.—T. L. S.

† It may be mentioned that the "Tuba Mirum," the most extraordinary number of this original work, is an Andante Maestoso in E flat, led up by a sudden chromatic rush up of the strings. The score directs that on the entry of the new movement shall be regarded as equivalent to two of the preceding one. The introduction is entirely allotted to the four separate orchestras of brass. The eight sets of kettledrums, from which velvety chords are called *pianissimo* by drumsticks with sponge ends, enter later on with the chorus, wood-wind, strings, and other instruments of percussion. The whole conception requires great care and skill to direct successfully; one can only appreciate the agony Berlioz experienced when he saw Habeneck's nonchalance at the critical moment.—T. L. S.

On account of my habitual mistrust, I was standing behind Habeneck, turning my back on him. I surveyed the group of kettle-drummers, which he could not see, the time approaching when they have to take part in the general conflict.

There are perhaps a thousand bars in my "Requiem." Precisely on that of which I have above spoken, where the time becomes doubled, and where the brass instruments launch out with their thrilling tones, on that special bar, where the action of the conductor is absolutely necessary, Habeneck *dropped his bâton, calmly drew out his snuff-box, and took a pinch of snuff.* I had kept an eye on him; instantly I turned rapidly on my heel, and dashed in front; I stretched out my arms and marked the four leading beats of the new movement. The orchestra followed me, each part entering in order; I conducted the piece until the end, and the effect that I had long dreamt of was produced. When Habeneck saw that the *Tuba mirum* was saved, he said to me,—"What a cold perspiration I had, without you, we should have been lost!" "Yes, I understand that well," replied I, fixing my eyes steadily on him." I did not add a word.—Could he have really done it? Was it possible that this man, in accord with M. XX..., who detested me, together with the other friends of Cherubini, had dared to plan, and attempted to carry out this base wickedness? I do not wish to think it, but I have little doubt. May God pardon me if I do him any injury!

The success of the "Requiem" was complete, in spite of all the conspiracies, cowardly or atrocious, officious and official, which had opposed the production of the work.

I will now speak as to the terms the minister of war had agreed to respecting the performance. Here they are:—"I will give," said the honourable General Bernard to me, "10,000 francs for the execution of your work; but this sum will only be delivered to you on the presentation of a letter from my colleague the minister of the interior, by which he will engage to pay you, first that which is due for the composition of the "Requiem," according to the decree of M. de Gasparin, and afterwards that which is due to the choristers for the rehearsals they attended in July last, and likewise to the copyists."

The minister of the interior had verbally engaged to General Bernard to discharge this triple debt. His letter was already issued, it only wanted his signature. To obtain it, I waited in his antechamber with one of his secretaries armed with the letter and furnished with a pen, from ten o'clock in the morning until four in the afternoon. At that time the minister came out, and the secretary, detaining him, got him to attach to the letter his very precious signature. Without losing a minute, I ran to General Bernard, who, after having read with attention the order of his colleague, delivered to me 10,000 francs.

I expended this sum entirely in paying my executants; I gave 300 francs to Duprey, who had sung the solo of the "Sanctus," and 300 francs to Habeneck, the incomparable snuff-taker, who had used so appropriately his box. There remained for *me* absolutely nothing. I supposed that I should eventually be paid by the minister of the interior, who was doubly obliged to take to this debt, first by the decree of his predecessor, and secondly by the engagement that he had personally contracted with the minister of war. "Holy simplicity!" as says Mephistopheles. One month, two, three, four, eight months passed, without me being able to obtain a sou. Through supplications, recommendations of various friends of the minister, and a course of complaints written and verbal, at last the rehearsals of the choristers, and the costs of the copies, were paid. I was thus freed from the intolerable persecution which I had already so long been compelled to undergo, from many people wearied of waiting for their due, and perhaps prejudiced against me by suspicions, the very idea of which still brings up the blush of indignation.

I, the author of the "Requiem," to suppose that I attached any value to vile gold! For shame! This was indeed a calumny. Consequently, people were very careful as to paying me. I now, however, take the opportunity of recounting at full length as to the accomplishment of the ministerial promises. I had an imperial want of gold. So again I was compelled to resign myself to laying siege to the cabinet of the director of the Fine Arts. Many weeks passed in fruitless solicitations. My anger grew, I became thin, I was unable to sleep. At last, I arrived one day at the ministry, blue, pale with fury, resolved to make a disturbance, determined for anything. On entering, to M. XX.... I said,—"Ah, now it decidedly appears that they *will* not pay me!"—"My dear Berlioz," replied the director, "you know it is not my fault. I have taken much trouble, I have made the most searching investigation. The funds which were destined for you have vanished, they have had another destination. I do not know in what office this has been done. Oh! if such things were to happen in mine!..." —"Indeed, how is this! Funds destined for the Fine Arts can then be employed outside your department without you knowing it?... Your budget is then at the disposition of the first comer?... But that is of little importance to me! I never intend to trouble myself over such questions. A 'Requiem' has been commissioned of me by the minister of the interior at an agreed price of 3,000 francs; I want my 3,000 francs."—"Good heavens, have a little more patience! One must consider. It is already a question elsewhere as to you receiving the Cross.... To the d—— with the cross."... "Give me my money."— "But.."—"There is no *but*," cried I, in knocking over a chair, "I will give you till midday to-morrow; and if at midday precisely I have not received the sum, I will create for you and the ministry such a scandal as has never yet been seen! And you know well that I possess the means to carry this out."

M. XX... agitated, forgetting his hat, rushed to the staircase which led to the minister, and I pursued him, crying,—"Tell him plainly that I should be ashamed to treat my bootmaker as he treats me, and that his conduct will soon acquire wide notoriety."

[NOTY.—And yet he was an excellent man, full of good intentions.]

This time I had discovered the weakness in the armour of the minister M. XX.... Ten minutes afterwards he returned with a bill for 3,000 francs on the treasury of the Fine Arts. Some one had found the gold.... See what artists sometimes have to do to get justice rendered to them in Paris! There are yet other means more violent which I can, if necessary, show you not to neglect.

Later on, when the excellent M. de Gasparin had resumed the portfolio of the interior, he appeared desirous of making amends to me for the abominable denial of justice which I had suffered over the "Requiem," by causing the famous cross of the Legion of Honour to be given to me. At one time this would have represented a value of 3,000 francs to me, and when it was thus offered I would not have given 30 sous for it. This vulgar distinction was accorded to me at the same time as to Dupouchel, then director of the opera, and to Bordogni, the best singing-master of all the teachers of the period. As soon as the "Requiem" was engraved I naturally dedicated it to M. de Gasparin, though he was no longer in power.

That which renders piquant in a high degree the conduct of the minister of the interior towards me in this affair, was, that after the execution of the "Requiem," when the musicians, the choristers, the carpenters who had constructed the temporary orchestra, Habeneck, Duprey, and all the rest were paid, I had still to try and and obtain for myself the 3,000 francs. Certain spiteful opposition journals took advantage of this to stigmatize me as one of the favourites of the authorities, comparing me to a silkworm living on the leaves of the budget, and it was seriously stated that I had received for the "Requiem" 30,000 francs.

They had only added a nought to the sum that I had not received! It is in this way that history is written.

THE LATE M. MORTIER DE FONTAINE.

M. Mortier de Fontaine died at the age of 67. He was a native of Warsaw, and so highly esteemed by Fétis as to be classed superior to Liszt and Thalberg. A fine and conscientious interpreter of Beethoven's music, M. de Fontaine was the first to play (in Germany) the tremendous Sonata in B flat, Op. 106. He also proved himself a capital "reader" of Bach and Chopin. Some one, possibly Fétis, has styled him "the best pupil of the great Sebastian." Renowned as a pianist, M. Mortier de Fontaine also excelled as a composer; a grand orchestral work, called "The Arab Ride," may be cited as a specimen of his genius.

CERTAIN OBSERVATIONS CONCERNING HYMN-TUNES.

By "OLD SCHOOL."

A rumour, not contradicted, was current a short time ago, to the effect that the collection of sacred music and words, known as "Hymns Ancient and Modern," will be followed at no distant date by another work of a similar kind. Such an announcement may be of little interest to those whose longings for a perfect Hymnal are already satisfied; and it is almost certain that attempts on the part of an individual to depopularise such an established favourite would occupy a foremost place among futile undertakings.

It will be conceded, however, by many, that the Hymnal under consideration is scarcely perfect; that, while there is very much good matter in it, there is also a considerable quantity of "padding," and not a little poor music. Such faults as these in a work whose meridian of popularity has been reached, would naturally incite novelty-mongers, or revivalists, or improvers, to publish a rival collection of Hymns with music destined possibly to supplant the cherished favourite.

Pending the result of any such contemplated scheme, and doubting, as we may, whether it is not too soon to start it, I propose to consider briefly whether our Hymnal, of which the scope is sufficiently comprehensive to please differing tastes, is put to such varied use as might help to prolong its popularity (assuming that to be threatened); whether certain tunes in the book have not been too much favoured, to the exclusion of others equally valuable, and in many cases more so; whether, in short, the good resources of the work are fairly and fully developed?

It can scarcely be doubted that, as regards its use in a great many churches, the very title of the book is a misnomer: "Hymns Modern (and Ancient)" would be a far more appropriate name to give it. For, how seldom it is that such excellent tunes as Tallis' Ordinal, Crasselius, London New, Vienna, and Tallis' Canon are permitted to enhance the beauty of a Church service! Further, why should we be compelled to go through the six weeks of Lent, year after year, without the companionship of St. Mary's or Windsor? and where shall we go for better Lenten music—where indeed? There is also in "Hymns Ancient and Modern," a remarkably fine tune called Breslau, and another called Lubeck: in how many churches in England are we ever allowed to sing either? This last complaint might be answered by the assertion that such tunes, belonging, as they do, to the bone-and-muscle *genus* in church music, are not in accordance with modern thought. Indeed, most churchmen are too prone now-a-days to think of the Saviour as he was in His humiliation —as agonized in the garden, as hanging on the Cross. But what if one prefers to think sometimes of the Saviour as "Great David's Greater Son,"—as the Lion of the Tribe of Judah—as greater than the Samson of the Tribe of Judges, who slew more at His death than He did during His life? What then? To worship and extol Him as such, one must needs have recourse to music of something like appropriate grandeur. Nor can it be said with any truth that admiration for grand hymn-tunes is at all inconsistent with decency, or even with reverence, in praise.

Again, the variety of opinion as to the beauty and value of the several tunes in a collection is remarkable, and illustrations of it are seldom wanting. For instance, I know a clergyman whose *beau-ideal* of a good hymn-tune would seem to be the music to "O happy band of pilgrims" (No. 224): he will put it into the programme two or three days in succession—and what he sees to admire in it, I, for one, cannot: the ugly little sequence in the third clause, and the impertinent note (in the treble) at the end of it, are quite enough to condemn the whole thing, not to mention the naughtiness of the second clause. And yet, good taste the rev. gentleman must have, for one of his favourites is Narenza—right good music, quite the St. Ann's of the short metres. But, as with individuals, so with congregations. To go back a few years: most of us can remember the time when people affected to love the music to "Sun of my soul," and no organist or choirmaster was supposed to have done his duty unless he had imported it into the service-list at least once a fortnight. Congregations were charmed with it, or fancied they were, which was much the same thing. At length, fashion chose to relinquish

the wretched drawl: it then got from bad to worse, and now few people, if any, care to resuscitate it. Later, popular fancy was exercised with the music to "Hark, hark my soul" (No. 223)—surely one of the weakest things the great Henry Smart ever did in his life: the setting of the words "Angels of Jesus, Angels of Light" is good, but for the rest, which is the greater twaddle—the words or the music? It is what I call school-girl music—the kind of music that a fashionable young lady of 16 or 17, just about to leave school at St. Leonards or Richmond, would pretend to admire immensely, knowing perfectly well, if her musical education has been worth a sixpence, that Ely, St. James's, or Vienna is each worth a dozen of it.

Quite recently, however, popular taste would appear to have undergone improvement. It has made a friend of Dr. Irons' taking music to Hymn No. 20, "At Even"— which is now frequently to be heard in provincial churches on Sunday evenings. More than once have I found it very soothing to the patience after too long a sermon. The music is devotional and pleasing, and, though not a model tune, it is one of considerable value:—but is it not rather too soon to change the key (even if the change be only to the dominant) before the composer has reached the end of the 1st clause? Some favour continues to be shown to Mr. H. Lahee's music to "Come, let us join"; this again is not a model tune, but there is a good deal of music in it. Improvement in the popular taste should go on, and then, one result, among others, would be the more frequent hearing of such music as Dundee, Crüger, St. Magnus, Bedford, Hanover, York, St. Hulbert, and Westminster (by Turle). For until more favour is shown to such tunes as these, it cannot be said that "Hymns Ancient and Modern" is made a proper use of, or a *fair* use of.

With regard to the time in which hymn-tunes should be sung, I would refer to certain letters of Mr. R. J. Hopper, who was, I believe, sometime organist of St. Matthias', Richmond. This gentleman, writing to the *Musical Standard* some months ago, advocated earnestly the cause of *slower* time. To his opinion I give my support, such as it is—with the reservation that due respect must be paid to the intentions of composers, and to the spirit of the words. Not all hymn-tunes can be taken slow. But Mr. Hopper has doubtless done good work in pointing out the mischievous tendency to hurry, which is still unchecked in many churches.

Before the singing has time to begin, however, I would say a word concerning the organist's duty in giving out the hymn-tune. What is this unamiable custom which is so prevalent—the custom of previously playing over the tune too hurriedly on the soft stops of the swell closed? True, it *may* suffice to remind the choir, sitting near the organ, what they have been practising during the week— but there are some of the congregation at the far end of the church, and they must be told what they have to sing. Let the tune then be given out deliberately on a solo stop, if the melody is of the right character, which need not be *too* loud, with a subdued accompaniment and 16-ft. bass, or else play it over on the diapasons of the great organ alone in four part harmony: this done, the remote congregation, instead of having to catch up the choir as best they can, will be prepared to join in immediately. I protest altogether against hymn-tunes being given out in a confidential whisper between the organist and the blower. The *allegro* and *piano* enunciation of chant and hymn-tune is one of those amenities of new school lore which is supposed to command unqualified respect and approval. Art may have a "commercial basis," but it has also a common-sense one: and singers among the congregation must know what the tune is to be before they can sing it.

Concerning variedness of accompaniment, this may safely be left to the accomplished organist, who, untrammelled by fashion, can treat the words, interpret the music, and apply the resources of the organ with proper discernment and skill. The recommendation of some authorities that one or more verses be sung in unison, with varied harmonies, is entitled to respect: but certainly a more decided relief from monotonousness can be secured by the choir *alone* taking some one verse (say the last but one) in harmony, *without accompaniment*.

Keep the congregation quiet, if you can: and then let the four principals of the choir sing *alone*. Some tunes are shown off to the greatest advantage by such means— Ely, for example. The time being very *moderato*, and the voices good, a beautiful effect is gained by slightly dwelling on the harmony of the 3rd clause. Or let the whole choir sing together the unaccompanied verse, due regard being had to balance, as well as to light and shade. In a large church or cathedral this would be the better plan in any case.

As against unison singing, I would recommend all the verses to be sung in harmony, such gradations and varieties of organ-tone being added as may be most agreeable to the subject. For, of unison or octave singing there is more than enough among the congregation, without the choir leading in octaves. At Christ Church, Reading, we have an organ wretchedly placed, but it is presided at with much taste and ability by Mr. F. T. Reade, Mus. Bac. Oxon., a young man who is certainly an admirable church-musician, while his choir is second to none in the town. Entering this church, as it were accidentally, about a year ago, just in time for St. Magnus, I found that Mr. Reade was not too fashionable to choose such good old music, nor too conceited to take pains with it when chosen ;—I have, therefore, attended his church ever since.

But, to resume very briefly : Can we sufficiently deplore the inconsistency and, I may say, the stupidity, of an English congregation in the matter of singing ? They will take great interest in the church choir, and will in some cases contribute handsomely towards their services : what next ? the male parishioners then go regularly to church and do all they can to neutralize every effect of harmony by 300 men out of 400 all singing the soprano : and they would do just the same, if every member of the choir were a professional singer in the first rank : as if a church, nearly half full of women, whose treble voices are led by the 20 trained sopranos of the choir, were not of themselves more than enough to destroy all balance ! Such is the hopelessness of getting people to understand that if they wish to join in the music of the sanctuary there is such a thing as singing *in the heart*, until such time as they have sufficiently cultivated their knowledge of music and their voices, wherewith they may supplement, not overwhelm, the harmonies of the choir.

In conclusion, I return for a moment to the principal topic of this paper, and once again plead earnestly for the more frequent use of "ancient" tunes.

With those who, like myself, prefer St. James's at Westminster Abbey, to Sullivan's " Onward, Christian Soldiers " at St. Paul's—who, with me lament that the modern composer could not do in 1880 as well as Raphael Courtville did in 1680—the foregoing observations may have some little weight. They are mainly intended to show how much the service of the Church suffers by neglect of music which, having stood the test of time, is still as fresh and as appropriate as when it was first made known one, two, and even three hundred years ago.

If any readers of my little essay should be disposed to lay aside " Hymns Ancient and Modern," I would advise them to re-open the excellent book of hymn-tunes compiled some 25 years ago by Mr. T. L. Forbes. This publication, which is one of sterling merit, and got up in a very attractive form, was, I believe, frowned upon by that thing you call fashion, an influence which to this day is the author of more mischief than enough in the Church musical world. How else could Mr. Forbes's work have fallen into disuse?

But what more can I say against that baneful influence ! I desire to hear much oftener than I do such music as Nuremza, London New, The Old Hundredth, St. James's, and Windsor—and I am told that I cannot see that the world of music is " progressing." Is not this enough to make one wish that the world of music was in some respects " progressing " backwards ?

ROYAL ACADEMY OF MUSIC.

The following is the report of the Committee of Management to the Directors of the Royal Academy of Music, for the year, 1883.

Your committee are happy to report the continued fiscal and technical prosperity of the Royal and National Institution you commit to their management.

The financial welfare of the Academy is evinced in the fact that there is a surplus over the expenses of the year 1882, which is recorded in the balance sheet. This is largely consequent on the increased number of students, which at the close of July last was greater than at any other period. Some of the then pupils have since left the Academy, but have been to a great extent re-

placed by the entrance of seventy-three strangers in the Michaelmas Term, besides the new comers of the present term, who are not yet counted. Some profits accrued from the local examinations of musical students, throughout the country, in the spring of 1882, which was entered by 1,245 candidates, of whom 143 obtained honours, and 698 passed in various branches of music. The Metropolitan Examination of Artists and Teachers, held in January, 1882, yielded also a small amount to the Academy funds. Of the sixty-eight candidates who submitted to this ordeal, fourteen were approved by the examiners, and were consequently created licenciates of the Royal Academy of Music.

The tokens of the musical success of the institution are :—

The public reception of young artists who have recently completed their training here ; the welcome to several singers, instrumentalists, and even composers, at important performances, who are still pursuing their studies ; more than one application from establishments in good esteem for the services of the Operatic Class ; the warm encouragement experienced by the solo performers, the band and the chorus, at the Academy concerts, in St. James's Hall, and in the Academy room ; and the conscientious opinion of the professors and friends of music, who witnessed the talent displayed at the fortnightly meetings which are held throughout the year.

Your committee are happy to record the munificence of Lady Goldsmid, who has again presented a Free Scholarship, to be competed for in April, by female pianists who have been studying for two years in the Academy, this being designed to facilitate to the most deserving the continued pursuit of excellence.

Prizes of ten guineas each were given last year, and are promised for this, by Dr. Lewellyn Thomas to a female student for declamatory English singing ; by Mr. Henry Evill to a male student for the same ; by Mr. Heathcote Long, to a male student for pianoforte playing ; by Mr. Chas. Santley, to students of either sex for accompaniment ; and by Mr. Bonamy Dobree, to a student for violoncello playing. There are several individuals who pay the entire fees of one or more students, but withhold their names from public announcement. The Potter Exhibition, which is the oldest endowment at present on the books, the Westmorland, the Sterndale Bennett, the Parepa-Rosa, the Sir John Goss, the Balfe, and the Thalberg Scholarships, are permanently secured. It is to be regretted that no additions have been made to the reserve fund for reducing the fees of deserving and necessitous students, and the amount as yet collected is insufficient for investment.

It has been found desirable to appoint a finance committee, to have special charge of the monetary arrangements, and Messrs. J. Lamborn Cock, J. F. H. Read, and Chas. E. Sparrow have been kind enough to accept the onerous and troublesome duties of this office. The examinations for the Memorial Prizes have been conducted by musicians *not* teaching in the Academy, and those gentlemen have always given their gratuitous services.

It will be necessary, during the summer vacation, to enter upon heavy expenditure for the re-decoration of the concert-room, which will seriously intrench on the funds at the disposal of your committee.

An application was made, in the autumn, to Sir Henry Ponsonby, asking whether her Majesty might probably accept a request, were it preferred by the body of directors, to allow a concert to be performed by Academy pupils in the presence of the Queen. Such a boon was granted by George IV., who received the pupils in Carlton Palace ; such, again, was granted by William IV., and Queen Adelaide, who visited the King's Theatre, to witness the pupils' performance ; it was therefore supposed a hope might not be groundless that a like grace might be accorded by the present Sovereign. The reply of Sir Henry was however to the effect that her Majesty was too much engaged to entertain the proposal, were it to be officially made.

Your committee regret the letter, which will be read to you, from Mr. George Wood, resigning his two-fold office of director, and member of the committee, and which will, according to the charter, necessitate his ceasing to act as auditor. This resignation, on your acceptance, will cause a vacancy in each of the positions held by Mr. Wood, and the committee beg to nominate the present director, Mr. J. F. H. Read, for the places in the committee and the auditorship, and Mr. P. Stainton, for the place on the direction—who have both stated their willingness to serve if you appoint them.

Your committee have to state that the communication to H.R.H. the Prince of Wales, embodying the resolution passed at your adjourned meeting on March 25th, 1882, has been acknowledged by the secretary of his Royal Highness, without comment. This communication included a transcript of your reply to the invitation of the Lords of the Privy Council, your remarks on the petition of his Royal Highness for a charter for a Royal College of Music, in June, 1880, stating the elasticity of the charter of this institution, and offering to modify the working of the Academy in any way, according to this charter, that might meet the views of the Prince of Wales.

In conclusion, your committee wish openly and strenuously to declare that this Academy, honoured as it is by the patronage of the entire Royal Family, and strengthened by the confidence of the musical profession and the British public, is capable of everything that is desirable for the furtherance of its grand National and educational object so far as its pecuniary means extend.

Passing Events.

"Zenobia," the American opera by a native composer, Mr. Pratt, has suffered reverses from various causes, but its author announces that he intends to continue the presentation of the work.

The *Court News*, of May 22nd, reports that Mr. G. A. Macfarren, Mus.Doc., Mr. G. Grove, D.C.L., and Mr. Arthur Sullivan, Mus.Doc., received from Her Majesty the Queen the honour of knighthood.

In consequence of the recent successful performances of "Ajax" at Cambridge, the "Birds of Aristophanes" will be produced next October term. The music to the play will be written by Dr. Hubert Parry.

On Trinity Sunday, Mendelssohn's "Hymn of Praise," including the whole of the symphony, was given after the evening service at St. Luke's, Chelsea. The band, numbering about forty performers, was complete, both in wind and strings.

The sale at Messrs. Puttick and Simpson's, on Tuesday next, of the library of the late Mr. John Brockley, is one of special interest. The effects include several series of MS. lectures by Dr. Crotch, Sir H. Bishop, and Henry Phillips.

The attention of those interested in music may be directed to the Pitt-Rivers ethnological collection now being exhibited at the South Kensington Museum. There will be found here some cases of musical instruments from various parts of the world, showing the gradual development of instruments of various types from the rudest beginnings up to the period of comparative civilization.

Lady Goldsmid has made another generous contribution to the Royal Academy of Music, a gift to be applied to scholarships for female pianists to be contended for in 1884 and 1885. The last-named is the tenth year of bounty from the same source, besides the scholarship of the late Sir Francis Goldsmid and certain generous assistance given by Lady Goldsmid to meritorious students, not publicly announced.

Among deaths recently chronicled is that of Signor G. Marras, at Nice, aged 73; his "Apresmidis" obtained much favour in London a few years ago; and that of Sir Thomas Barnard, who passed away at a very advanced age. The deceased gentleman was for many years a director of the Royal Academy of Music, and gave hearty support to the art; he represented Aylesbury in Parliament for a considerable period.

Under the title of "The Tale of Troy," an attractive dramatic entertainment will be given on May 29th and 30th, at Cromwell House, South Kensington, by the kind permission of Sir Charles Freake, Bart., for the benefit of the Building Fund now being raised for "The Ladies' Department of King's College." The performances will be organised under the superintendence of Prof. C. T. Newton, C.B., and Prof. George C. Warr, M.A., of King's College. The representation will consist of tableaux and scenes from the "Iliad" and "Odyssey" of Homer, to be acted by ladies and gentlemen. The first performance will be given in English, the second in Greek. The English performance will take place on the afternoon of Tuesday, May 29th, at three o'clock. The Greek performance will take place on the evening of Wednesday, May 30th, at half-past eight. The scenic effects and tableaux will be designed with the assistance of Sir Frederick Leighton, P.R.A., Prof. E. J. Poynter, R.A., Messrs. Edwin Long, R.A., G. F. Watts, R.A., George Simonds, and Prof. P. H. Delamotte, F.S.A., of King's College. The scenery will be painted by Mr. J. O'Connor. The descriptive and vocal music will be specially composed by Messrs. Otto Goldschmidt, Malcolm Lawson, Theo. Marzials, Walter Parratt, and Prof. W. H. Monk, Mus.D., of King's College. The dramatic arrangements will be superintended by Mr. Hermann Vezin, and by Messrs. C. P. Colnaghi and J. M. Thomson (stage managers). The music of the first part "The Iliad" has been written by Herr Otto Goldschmidt and Mr. W. Parratt, Dr. W. H. Monk has composed the "Spinning" Song for "Penelope's Maidens," and Mr. M. L. Lawson (who is acting as general musical director) is responsible for the music of the second part, "The Odyssey."

The Querist.

QUERY.

AMERICAN ORGAN.—Would some fellow-reader kindly tell me a little about the history of the American Organ. Who was the first maker, etc.?—ORGANO.

REPLY.

HANDEL'S "WATER MUSIC."—In answer to a correspondent, seeking information on the subject of Handel's "Water Music," I beg to state that a very capital little selection therefrom appeared in the *Musical Library*, published in 1845, and consisted of the following movements:—Maestos, Andante Quasi Allegretto, Aria, and Vivace. All of these are as Handelian as they possibly can be. The *Musical Library* is still in print, and can be had of Messrs. Augener, of Newgate Street, in two vols., price 7s. 6d. each. They comprise selections from the works of the great composers, arranged for piano, &c. I am not aware, at the present moment of writing, of the existence of a complete modern edition of the "Water Music." In addition to the movements mentioned in the *Musical Library*, I have also, in an old M.S. music book, a Largo, and a March.—J. S. BUMPUS.

Service Lists.

FIRST SUNDAY AFTER TRINITY.

MAY 27th.

London.

ST. PAUL'S CATHEDRAL.—Morn.: Service, Te Deum and Benedictus, Calkin in B flat: Introit, Blessed is he who cometh (Gounod); Holy Communion, Schubert in C. Even.: Service, Magnificat and Nunc Dimittis, Foster in A; Anthem, Sing to the Lord a new made song (Mendelssohn).

WESTMINSTER ABBEY.— Morn.: Service, Turle in D, (throughout). Even.: Service, Walmisley in D minor; Anthem, O God, when Thou appearest (Mozart).

FOUNDLING CHAPEL.—Morn.: Service, Te Deum, Sullivan in D, and Jubilate, Smith in B flat; Anthem, As pants the hart (Spohr). Aft.: Service, Magnificat and Nunc Dimittis, Smith in B flat; Anthem, I will exalt Thee (Hummel).

TEMPLE CHURCH.—Morn.: Service, Te Deum Laudamus, Goss in D; Apostles' Creed, Harmonised Monotone; Anthem, I was in the Spirit (Blow). Even.: Service, Magnificat and Nunc Dimittis, Cooke in C; Apostles' Creed, Harmonised Monotone; Anthem, Heaven and earth display (Mendelssohn).

LINCOLN'S INN CHAPEL.—Morn.: Service, Boyce in A; Kyrie, Steggall; Anthem, In that day (Elvey). Even: Service, Boyce in A; Anthem, Wherewithal shall a young man (Boyce).

ALL SAINTS, MARGARET STREET.— Morn.: Service, Te Deum, Smart in F, Benedictus, Simcox; Holy Communion, Hoyte in D; Offertory Anthem, As the hart pants (Mendelssohn). Even.: Service, Hoyte in B flat; Anthem, Rejoice in the Lord (Martin).

CHRIST CHURCH, CLAPHAM.—Morn.: Service, Te Deum, Plain-song; Kyrie and Credo, Mozart in B flat; Offertory Anthem, Blest are the departed (Spohr); Sanctus, Benedictus, Agnus Dei, and Gloria in excelsis (Mozart). Even.: Service, Magnificat and Nunc Dimittis, Tuckerman in F; Anthem, As pants the hart (Spohr).

ST AUGUSTINE AND ST. FAITH, WATLING STREET.— Morn.: Service, Calkin in B flat; Offertory, O taste and see (Goss). Even.: Service, Calkin in B flat; Anthem, Now we are ambassadors (Mendelssohn).

ST. BARNABAS, MARYLEBONE.—Morn.: Service, Te Deum and Jubilate, Rogers in D; Anthem, Incline thine ear (Himmel); Kyrie and Nicene Creed, Rogers in D. Even.: Service, Magnificat and Nunc Dimittis, Rogers in D; Anthem, from the rising of the sun (Ouseley).

ST. GEORGE THE MARTYR, QUEEN SQUARE.—Morn.: Service, Te Deum, Smart in F; Kyrie, Gounod. Even.: Service, Magnificat and Nunc Dimittis.

ST. JAMES'S PRIVATE EPISCOPAL CHAPEL, SOUTHWARK. —Morn.: Service, Introit, Hymn; Communion Service, Marbecke. Even.: Service, Porter in D; Anthem, If thou shalt confess (Palestrina).

ST. PETER'S, VERE STREET, W.—Even.: Service, Magnificat and Nunc Dimittis, Garrett in D; Anthem, Rejoice in the Lord alway (Purcell).

ST. MICHAEL'S, CORNHILL.— Morn.: Service, Te Deum and Jubilate, Dykes in F; Anthem, The heavens declare (Boyce); Kyrie, Creed, Stainer in E flat. Even.: Service, Magnificat and Nunc Dimittis, Ouseley in B flat; Anthem, I was in the Spirit (Blow).

ST. MARGARET PATTENS, ROOD LANE, FENCHURCH STREET.—Morn.: Service, Te Deum, Sullivan in D; Benedictus, Dykes in F; Offertory Anthem, Lord at all times (Mendelssohn); Kyrie, Credo, Sanctus, Benedictus, Agnus Dei and Gloria, Schubert in B flat. Even.: Service, Magnificat and Nunc Dimittis, Tuckerman in F; Anthem, I will mention (Sullivan).

ST. MARY ABCHURCH, E.C.—Morn.: Service, Garrett in D; Communion Service, Armes in A. Even.: Service, Chants.

ST. MARY BOLTONS, WEST BROMPTON, S.W.—Morn.: Service, Te Deum and Benedictus, Goss in C; Holy Communion, Kyrie, Credo, Sanctus, Benedictus, Angus Dei, and and Gloria in excelsis, Eyre in E flat; Offertory, Barnby; Evensong, Mag., and Nunc Dimittis, Parisian Tones, Stainer; Anthem, O clasp your hands (Stainer).

ST. MAGNUS, LONDON BRIDGE.—Morn.: Service, Opening Anthem, To the Lord our God (Ouseley); Te Deum and Jubilate, King in F; Kyrie, Ebdon. Even.: Service, Magnificat and Nunc Dimittis, King in F; Anthem, I waited for the Lord (Mendelssohn).

ST. PAUL'S, AVENUE ROAD, SOUTH HAMPSTEAD.—Morn.: Service, Te Deum, Dykes in F, Benedictus, Barnby; Kyrie, Nares in F. Even.: Service, Magnificat and Nunc Dimittis, Stainer in A; Anthem, The wilderness (Goss).

ST. PAUL'S, BOW COMMON, E.—Morn.: Service, Te Deum, and Benedictus, Smart in F. Even.: Service, Magnificat and Nunc Dimittis, Tours in F; Anthem, the Lord is a man of war, and Thy right hand O Lord "Israel in Egypt" (Handel).

ST. PETER'S, LEIGHAM COURT ROAD, STREATHAM, S.W.—Morn.: Holy Eucharist, Purge me with hyssop (Novello); Introit, O Lord my trust (Chantwise); Mass, Osborne in E flat; Gradual, I said, Lord (Chantwise); Communion, Ave Verum Corpus (Fagan). Even.: Magnificat, Stainer in A; Anthem, Praise the Lord, O my soul (Stark).

ST. SAVIOUR'S, HOXTON.—Morn.: Service, Te Deum, Smart in F; Holy Communion; Kyrie, Credo, Sanctus, Gloria in excelsis, Smart in F. Even.: Service, Magnificat and Nunc Dimittis, Dykes in F; Anthem, Thine O Lord (Kent).

Country.

ST. ASAPH CATHEDRAL.—Morn.: Service, Calkin in B flat; Anthem, Blessed is the people (Claxton). Even.: Service, Calkin in B flat; Anthem, Send out Thy light (Gounod).

ARDINGLY COLLEGE, SUSSEX.—Morn.: Communion Service, Calkin in G. Even.: Service, Wood in F; Anthem, Bring unto the Lord (Gladstone).

ASHBURNE CHURCH, DERBYSHIRE. — Morn.: Service, Garrett in D (throughout). Even.: Service, Turle in D; Anthem, Whatsoever is born of God (Oakeley).

BEDDINGTON CHURCH, SURREY.—Morn.: Service, Te Deum, Garret in D, Benedictus, Barry in F; Introit, Sing praise to God; Communion Service, Calkin in D. Even.: Service, Calkin in D; Anthems, God is a Spirit, and Who is the image (Bennett).

BIRMINGHAM (ST. CYPRIAN'S, HAY MILLS).—Morn.: Service, Field in D; Anthem, O praise God in His holiness (Clarke-Whitfeld). Even.: Service, Clarke-Whitfeld in E; Anthem, Praise the Lord (Garrett).

BIRMINGHAM (S. PHILIP'S CHURCH). — Morn.: Service, Best, Chant Service; Anthem, Come up hither; Holy, Holy, Holy (Spohr). Even.: Service, Barnby in E; Anthem, O Lord, Thou hast searched me out, God is a Spirit (Bennett).

BRISTOL CATHEDRAL—Morn.: Service, Croft in A; Even.: Service, Elvey in A; Anthem, Blessing and glory (Bach).

CANTERBURY CATHEDRAL.—Morn.: Service, Smart in F; Anthem, in my Father's home (Calcott); Communion Service, Smart in F. Even.: Service, Smart in F; Anthem, Holy, Holy, Holy, and Lord our Creator, "Elijah" (Mendelssohn).

CARLISLE CATHEDRAL.—Morn.: Service, Dykes in F; Introit, God is my helper (Stainer); Kyrie and Nicene Creed, Dykes in F. Even.: Service, Gadsby in C; Anthem, Glory to God (Haydn).

DUBLIN, ST. PATRICK'S (NATIONAL) CATHEDRAL.—Morn.: Service, Te Deum and Jubilate, Stainer in E flat; Holy Communion, Kyrie, Creed, and Sanctus, Stainer in E flat; Anthems, O Lord, Thou hast overthrown, and thanks be to God (Mendelssohn). Even.: Service, Magnificat and Nunc Dimittis, Smart in G; Anthems, Not unto us O Lord (Robinson), and The Wilderness (Wesley).

DONCASTER (PARISH CHURCH).—Morn.: Service, Tours in F; Anthem, O Lord, Thou hast searched (Bennett). Even.: Service, Tours in F; Anthem, God is a Spirit (Bennett).

DURHAM CATHEDRAL.—Morn.: Service, Wesley in F; Anthem, He watching over Israel (Mendelssohn); Introit, Blessed is the man (Wesley); Communion Service, Nares in F. Even.: Service, Wesley in F; Anthem, In humble faith (Garrett).

EXETER CATHEDRAL. — Morn.: Service, Boyce in A; Communion, Wesley and Travers in F. Even.: Service, Elvey in A; Anthem, O Lord Thou hast searched (Croft).

ELY CATHEDRAL.—Morn.: Service, Garrett in E; Anthem, In humble faith (Garrett). Even.: Service, Garrett in D; Kyrie and Credo, Garrett in]D; Gloria, Richardson; Anthem, I will give thanks (Barnby).

GLOUCESTER CATHEDRAL.—Morn.: Service, Selby in A; Communion service, Wesley in E; Anthem, Turn Thee again (Attwood). Aft.: Service, Selby in A; Anthem, The Wilderness (Wesley).

LLANDAFF CATHEDRAL.—Morn.: Service, Garrett in D. Even.: Service, Garrett in D; Anthem, Blessed be the God and Father (Wesley).

LIVERPOOL CATHEDRAL.—Aft.: Service, Magnificat and Nunc Dimittis, Hatton in E flat; Anthem, God is our hope and strength (Greene).

LEEDS PARISH CHURCH.—Morn.: Service, Boyce in A; Anthem, The Souls of Righteous (Nares); Kyrie and Creed, Dykes in F. Even.: Service, Calkin in B flat; Anthem, Wherewithal.

MANCHESTER CATHEDRAL.—Morn.: Service, Gounod in C; Holy Communion, Masse Solomnelle (Gounod); Anthem, Praise His awful name (Spohr). Aft.: Service, Gounod in C; Anthem, In the beginning (Haydn).

MANCHESTER (ST. BENEDICT'S). — Morn.: Service, Credo, and Gloria in excelsis, Williams in D; Kyrie, Sanctus, Benedictus, and Agnus Dei, Mozart in B flat. Even.: Service, Magnificat and Nunc Dimittis (Willing).

MANCHESTER (ST. JOHN BAPTIST, HULME).—Morn.: Service, Kyrie, Credo, Sanctus, and Gloria in excelsis, Steggall in G; Benedictus, Thorne; Angus Dei, Miné. Even.: Service, Magnificat and Nunc Dimittis (Jordan).

ROCHESTER CATHEDRAL.—Morn.: Service, Barnby in E; Anthem, He watching over Israel (Mendelssohn). Even.: Service, Barnby in E; Anthem, I was in the Spirit (Blow).

SHEFFIELD PARISH CHURCH. — Morn.: Service, Kyrie Trimmell in F. Even.: Service, Magnificat and Nunc Dimittis; Anthem, I have surely built Thee an house (Trimmell).

SOUTHAMPTON (ST. MARY'S CHURCH).—Morn.: Service, Te Deum and Benedictus, Woodward in D; Introit, They that put their trust (Macfarren); Communion Service, Woodward in A; Offertory, Not every one (Barnby); Paternoster, Field. Even.: Service, Magnificat and Nunc Dimittis, Smith in B flat; Apostles' Creed, Harmonised Monotone.

SHERBORNE ABBEY.—Morn.: Service, Tozer in F. Even.: Service, Anthem, If ye love me (Monk).

WELLS CATHEDRAL.—Morn.: Service, Arnold in D; Introit, Drop down, ye heavens (Macfarren); Kyrie, Mendelssohn in G. Even.: Service, Arnold in D; Anthem, Thy word is a lantern (Purcell).

WORCESTER CATHEDRAL.—Morn.: Service, Stainer in E flat; Anthem, The Lord is in His holy temple (Thorne). Even.: Service, Stainer in E flat; Anthem, Blessed be the God and Father (Wesley).

APPOINTMENTS.

Mr. ALEX. G. HAYS (pupil of James Stimpson, Esq.), has been appointed Organist and Choirmaster of the Parish Church, Hay.

Mr. FREDERICK A. JEWSON has been elected by the Trustees Organist and Director of the Music to the Wesleyan Chapel, Great Queen Street.

Mr. JOHN DENHAM has been appointed Organist and Choirdirector of St. Osburg's Church, Coventry.

NOTICES TO CORRESPONDENTS.

"Form in Vocal Music" and other articles are this week crowded out.

Printed for the Proprietor by BOWDEN, HUDSON & Co., at 23, Red Lion Street, Holborn, London, W.C. ; and Published by WILLIAM REEVES, at the Office, 185, Fleet Street, E.C. West End Agents :—WEEKES & CO., 14, Hanover Street, Regent Street. Subscriptions and Advertisements are received either by the Publisher or West End Agents.—*Communications for the EDITOR are to be forwarded to his private address, 6, Argyle Road, W.*
SATURDAY, JUNE 2, 1883.—*Entered at the General Post Office as a Newspaper.*

The Musical Standard

A NEWSPAPER for MUSICIANS PROFESSIONAL AND AMATEUR

No. 985. Vol. XXIV. FOURTH SERIES   SATURDAY, JUNE 16, 1883.   WEEKLY: PRICE 3D.

THE VOICE

MUSICALLY AND MEDICALLY CONSIDERED.

BY

ARMAND SEMPLE, B.A., M.B., Cantab., M.R.C.P., Lond.,
Physician to the Royal Society of Musicians.

(*Continued from page 351.*)

The full extent of male voices is shown in the following
table :—

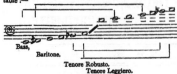

Bass,

Baritone.

Tenore Robusto.
Tenore Leggiero.

FEMALE VOICES.

THE CONTRALTO VOICE.

Quality.—This voice is powerful, and not very flexible ;
and its musical construction being strong, the acute sounds
are usually harsh, or weak, and deficient in flexibility. It
is exceedingly difficult to render it full and of equal power
throughout the whole of its compass.

Its quality varies in strength and extent according to
the construction of the organ. It is usually strong from
Sol (G) to Sol (G)

occasionally full from Sol (G) to Re (D)

but frequently weak on Mi (E), and Fa (F)

It is very uncommon to meet with a contralto voice
which is not shrill, harsh, or indistinct, from Re (D) to
Sol (G)

It sometimes happens that it is weak even from Sol (G)
to Sol (G)

Extent.—This is very great when the voice has been
judiciously trained, since the compass may then reach
from Mi (E) to Si flat (B♭)

Cultivation. — Very great care is required in developing the contralto voice, since by nature it is not
endowed with much flexibility, and if the extremes be at
all forced, the quality rapidly degenerates, the muscles
becoming weak, and the power of vibration is destroyed.

At first this voice should be limited from Sol (G) to
Mi (E)

It is a matter of extreme difficulty to render the contralto voice smooth and equal, since its quality is indistinct, hard, or hollow ; when, however, the power of
modulation within the above limits has been acquired, it
may be extended gradually to its high and low extremes.

The following table shows the compass of the Contralto
voice :—

Low Extreme. Limits in Cultivation. High Extreme.
Do (C)

or

(*To be continued.*)

PRESENTATION TO MR. W. R. ATKINS.

A meeting of the Cork Orchestral Union was held on
June 7th, at the Mayor's Office, for the purpose of
presenting a diploma, conferred by the Academy of the
Royal Institute of Music in Florence on Mr. William
Ringrose Atkins, conductor of the Cork Orchestral Union.
The Mayor presided.

The Mayor said that he received a letter from the
Marquis of Torrigiani, dated the 22nd of May, which was
formally acknowledged by him. Mr. Atkins happened
to be in London when he received that letter, and so he
was unable to present the diploma which he had received
from the Academy of the Royal Institute of Music in
Florence. He communicated with Mr. Atkins, and from
documents he had received from the Marquis, and papers
that had come to his hand, he thought the occasion was
one that demanded of anyone in his position a formal and
a public presentation to Mr. Atkins. The documents
which he would read would prove that this was merit of
very high distinction, and had been conferred on some of
the most distinguished men in Germany and Italy. He
then read the following communication :—

" From the Marquis of Torrigiani, President of the Academy
of the Royal Institute of Music, Florence, to the Right Worshipful the Mayor of Cork.

" Florence, 22nd May, 1883.

" I beg, illustrious Sir, that you be kind enough to remit the
enclosed letter, with a diploma and a pamphlet that will reach
you with the same, to Mr. Wm. Ringrose Atkins, Director of
the Orchestral Society of Cork, with the distinguished consideration. I am, etc.

" TORRIGIANI, Marquis, President."

" Letter from the Marquis Torrigiani, to Mr. Wm. Ringrose
Atkins :—

" Florence, May 22nd, '83.

" At the meeting of the Musical Academy of this Institute,
held on the 6th inst., you, Sir, were elected Honorary Acade-
mician. In sending the accompanying diploma, it gives me
great pleasure to congratulate you on this work of esteem
deservedly offered to you by our Academy, while I must congratulate the Academy as well on the acquisition it has gained
in having admitted you amongst its members. I am, etc.,

" TORRIGIANI, Marquis, President."

He (the Mayor) was sure they all joined in the Marquis's congratulations to Mr. Atkins on this distinguished
compliment which had been paid to him. It was not
only that they congratulated him personally, but also
with his connection with the musical people of Cork, and
they congratulated him that the City of Cork through one
of her sons had been complimented in this manner. He
was sure all his friends in Cork—and they were all
interested more or less in the advancement of music—
felt proud in seeing Mr. Atkins' name connected with
that distinguished Institute. The Mayor then handed
the diploma to Mr. Atkins.

Mr. Atkins said he felt very much obliged to the Mayor
for having summoned that meeting, and for the kind
manner in which he had spoken about him.

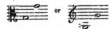

Musical Intelligence.

CRYSTAL PALACE CONCERTS.

PROGRAMME.

Symphony No. 8, in B minor (Unfinished)....	Schubert.
Allegro moderato—Andante con moto.	
Recit. and Aria, "Leise, Leise" ("Der Freischütz ")	Weber.
Madame Leideritz.	
Romance, "When the Orb of Day" ("Euryanthe ")	Weber.
Mr. Edward Lloyd.	
Selection from "Colomba"	A. C. Mackenzie.
Prelude to the First Act.—Andante moderato e grave.	
Vocero, "Gentle dove, thy voice is sad."	
Madame Valleria.	
Ballet Airs and Rustic March	
Allegretto grazioso in B flat, Saltarello in G minor.	
Andantino in G major, Rustic March in E flat.	
Old Corsican Ballad, "So he thought of his love."	
Miss Annie Marriott.	
Duet, "Oh, Orso, see me here."	
Madame Valleria and Mr. Barton McGuckin.	
Capriccio Brilliant for Pianoforte and Orchestra (Op. 22.)	Mendelssohn.
Mdlle. Clotilde Kleeberg.	
Recit. and Air, "O Vision entrancing" ("Esmeralda")	A. Goring Thomas.
Mr. Barton McGuckin.	
Prelude to "Parsifal"	Wagner.
Solos for Pianoforte—	
Nocturne in E flat	Field.
Valse in A flat	Chopin.
Mdlle. Clotilde Kleeberg.	
Overture, "Tannhäuser"	Wagner.
Conductor	AUGUST MANNS.

The above attractive programme was, without exception, most successfully performed, and gave unfeigned pleasure to those who assembled on the occasion of Mr. Manns's annual benefit. Of Schubert's Unfinished B minor Symphony, it is scarcely needful to say anything, as it is so often performed and so well known ; but of the composer himself much might still be written in admiration of his unbounded love for his profession, as shown by his incessant labour, in spite of many difficulties and disappointments. The following beautiful quotation from the preface to Coleridge's poems strikes me as being peculiarly applicable to Schubert, and indeed with perfect truth might have formed the preface to his musical works : "I expect neither profit nor fame from my writings, and I consider myself as having been amply repaid without either. My work has been to me its own exceeding great reward ; it has soothed my afflictions ; it has multiplied and refined my enjoyments ; it has endeared solitude ; and it has given me the habit of wishing to discover the good and the beautiful in all that meets and surrounds me."

Notwithstanding the disadvantage of performing extracts from an opera, the selections from Mr. Mackenzie's "Colomba" were listened to with admiration, and produced a most favourable impression. Mdme. Valleria's singing of the Vocero, "Gentle dove," was extremely charming, and her fine voice was again heard to advantage with Mr. McGuckin in the duet "Oh, Orso." Both the prelude to the first act and the ballet music were superbly played.

Mendelssohn's Capriccio in B seldom finds a better interpreter than Mdlle. Clotilde Kleeberg, who appeared here for the first time. Although young in years, she has an intelligent appreciation of the requirements of the respective composers whose music she so judiciously selected for her *début*, and this, combined with a most perfect *technique*, insured for her an undoubted success.

I must not forget to mention that Mdme. Leideritz and Mr. E. Lloyd appeared, in addition to the vocalists already mentioned. Of the latter, who is an old friend here, one need only say that he was in fine voice, and never sang better ; and of the lady, who is new to us, it is my pleasing duty to say, that although at first suffering slightly from nervousness, she made a very favourable impression.

The Saturday concerts will be resumed in October.

R. S.

Miss Alma Sanders recently gave a concert of excellent quality at 26, Harcourt Terrace, Redcliffe Square. The programme included two movements from a musicianly pianoforte of her own composition.

RICHTER CONCERTS.

PROGRAMME.

Overture, "Die Tragische"	Brahms.
"Siegfried Idyll"	Wagner.
Concerto, No. 2, in G minor, for Pianoforte and Orchestra	Saint-Saëns.
Pianoforte, Madame Stepanoff.	
Introduction to Act III. of "Die Meistersinger."	Wagner.
Slavonic Rhapsody, No. 2.	Dvorak.
(First performance in England.)	
Symphony, No. 4, in B flat	Beethoven.

The "Tragic" overture was rather apathetically received. The subjects themselves awaken no interest ; and their treatment, though elaborate, is tedious ; for few of us are philanthropic enough to care about the doings and the fate of those who fail to appeal in some degree to our sympathies. Brahms would have a better chance of satisfying others if he were not so pre-eminently satisfied with himself. He seems to have completely lost out of his nature the desire to please—a desire that is born in every true artist, and that dies only with his death.

M. Saint-Saëns's Concerto is not of a character to bring out the higher qualities of a pianist ; it is, therefore, impossible to say more at present about Mdme. Stepanoff's playing than that she has a remarkably firm, brilliant, clear touch, and that her execution is faultless. The work is splendidly written for the solo instrument, and the orchestration shows an abundance of tact, *savoir faire*, and a certain amount of thought. But beyond this, Charity herself could find nothing to praise. The analysis given (from a new Philharmonic programme and signed "H. W.") spends much time in endeavouring to manufacture an excuse for M. Saint-Saëns, because he has made his middle movement a scherzo, instead of the usual adagio. The excuses offered may be satisfactory ; but an unanswerable one might have been added— M. Saint-Saëns could not write a slow movement such as we have been taught to look for in a concerto if he tried. The musician who could perform a Beethoven Sonata with a lack of appreciation that would not have been creditable to a school-girl of ordinary intelligence (and in such a manner I have heard him play the "Waldstein"), is scarcely the man to whom we should look for the slow movement to succeed those contained in the concertos of the classical masters. One is at least satisfied to accept a scherzo in place of the attempt, especially as the scherzo is the most agreeable movement of the three. The first does not seem to aim at anything, and certainly does not attain it ; while in the finale there is more noise than effect, and more effect than cause. It is to be regretted that so flimsy an affair should have introduced us to a pianist whose fame preceded her.

"C. A. B." provides a careful analysis of Dvorak's Rhapsody. He begins by telling us what a "Rhapsody," as applied to music, is :—"The word, which is strictly classical in its derivation, signifies the stringing together of verses or tunes. A work of this kind, which may be defined as an emanation from the variation form, may be briefly described as consisting of a series of movements, or rather changes of tempo, fused into one single and continuous movement, the leading subjects of one or the other of which, by a process of metamorphosis or thematic development, are made to serve as primary or secondary subjects in the others, in company with more or less matter of an incidental and independent character introduced transitionally."

I quote the passage at length because it would be impossible to explain better in so few words what a "Rhapsody" is. Its present perfected form (though, like all that is beautiful, it has been of gradual growth), we owe to Liszt.

Naturally, a "Slavonic" Rhapsody cannot carry away the hearer in the same way as a "Hungarian" Rhapsody does ; because it does not deal with the music of a people, full of poetry, unbound by the laws of civilization. But this rhapsody left the impression on me of being too studied—not sufficiently extravagant. The melodies used are not of a striking or a particularly pleasing character ; and the treatment, though clever and in its dissecting tendency—*i.e.*, the tendency to make entire phrases and new themes out of two or three notes of the principal melodies—highly suggestive of Liszt, yet seemed to lack that inspiration and spontaneousness which alone can give life to such a work. A second hearing might, however, remove this impression : for Dvorak is so eminently agreeable a writer, and there is so much that is pleasant in this rhapsody, that any disparaging remarks, however well considered, seem to savour of ingratitude.

The two Wagner numbers and the Symphony met with the usual reception the works of Wagner and Beethoven enjoy at these concerts : they were applauded with an enthusiasm and persistency which in the case of the "Meistersinger" Prelude amounted to a demand for a repetition. Nothing could exceed the calm, contemplative peace of the "Siegfried Idyll," so perfectly reproduced in every beautiful detail. This, the most lyric of Wagner's writings, is the strongest proof he has left us that he could, when he chose, write without the fire of dramatic action to inspire him.

B. F. WYATT-SMITH.

M. VLADIMIR DE PACHMANN'S THIRD RECITAL.

M. de Pachmann is the crowning success of the season, and the undoubted favourite, among many favoured ones, of musical London. He is thoroughly worthy of the distinction ; for the most lavish praises of him that we constantly hear are but poor and cold reflections of the admiration that he awakens. Two of the chief causes of his popularity are, however, not usually pointed out ; these are, his excessive and unaffected modesty, and his child-like enjoyment of the passing moment, without apparently a thought or care, beyond the endeavour to give, not so much a perfect, as an enjoyable rendering of the work in hand. This simple wish, to be pleased and give pleasure, has, in the rare cases when it outlives childhood, a fascination peculiarly its own. In M. De Pachmann, it distinguishes him from Von Bülow, whose manner offended some of the critics, because he seemed to say, "Listen to the beauties that I will reveal to you in this work " ; it distinguishes him in a more marked degree from Rubinstein, who, with his followers, seems to imagine that his extraordinary power creates rather than reveals the hidden poetry ; for M. de Pachmann seems to say, "This is beautiful ; let us hear it and enjoy it together ! " His manner thus tends to establish an altogether unusual sympathy between himself and his audience, a sympathy that deepens into admiration with closer acquaintance.

His programme, last Saturday, was of varied interest.

Toccata and Fugue	Bach—Tausig.
Sonata (Op. 101)	Beethoven.
Novelette, (No. 4)	Schumann.
Variations, (Op. 104, No. 2)	Rubinstein.
(First time in England.)	
"Danklied nach Stürm "	Henselt.
Etude en forme de Valse	Saint-Saëns.
Nocturne, (Op. 27)	Chopin.
Mazurka, (Op. 33, No. 1)	"
Valse, (Op. 64, No. 1)	"
5 Etudes	"
Op. 10, Nos. 3 and 4, Op. 25, Nos. 2, 6, and 8.	
Polonaise, No. 8	"

The Chopin numbers, as usual, called forth the loudest expressions of approval ; and the valse was repeated, as well as two of the most fatiguing études.

Rubinstein's Variations are founded on a sufficiently pleasing melody ; but as its attraction lies in agreeable though rather cloying harmonies, and these harmonies are repeated in most of the variations, the interest rather diminishes than increases as the work proceeds.

Schumann's Novelette, No. 4, was included by M. de Pachmann in the programme of his first recital here, last year. It is indeed charming in his hands, though it would be difficult for a less gifted performer not to reveal some of its simple melodic beauty.

Henselt is, as M. de Pachmann reveals him, almost as individual and poetic as Chopin himself, though, of course, moving in a smaller circle.

M. de Pachmann's innate modesty prevented him from accepting the uproarious applause that greeted him when he had reached the end of his programme, as a natural tribute to his genius—a well earned ovation—but he considered it simply a request for more ; so, with the good nature that those who know him say is characteristic of him, he re-seated himself at the piano, and played one more piece to an audience who were preparing to leave, but who gladly, one and all, stayed a few minutes more to hear the last notes from the pianist whom, a musician remarked, he " could listen to for ever ! "

B. F. WYATT-SMITH.

The blind pupils of the Royal Normal College, the institution so admirably directed by Dr. E. J. Campbell, gave a morning concert at Grosvenor House on June 9th.

ROYAL ITALIAN OPERA.

" La Gioconda " was repeated on Saturday and Tuesday. Madame Durand firmly maintains her position. This opera of Signor Ponchielli will certainly constitute a regular number of the *repertoire.*

"L'Etoile du Nord " at last was produced on Monday night, with Madame Sembrich as Caterina ; the Hungarian *prima donna* seemed to be very nervous, but she warmed up to the business of the scene in the Camp, and in the "mad " business of the last Act, already painfully overdone in "Lucia di Lammermoor" and other operas, a fair climax was attained. A *débutante*, Mdlle. Gini, who represented Prascovia, can hardly be reported as the *conquérante* of operatic spoils. M. Gailhard represented the part of Peter the "Great" (anything but " great") with dignity.

The Directors announce an extra performance of " Carmen " to-day at 2 o'clock, with Madame Pauline Lucca as the Gipsy. " Lohengrin " was done last week, with Mr. Maas in the title part ; he was a success. Mdme. Albani is thought to have been too demonstrative as Elsa.

A. M.

MR. BONAWITZ'S CONCERTS.

Mr. J. B. Bonawitz held a sort of historical pianoforte recital at the Bluthner Rooms, Kensington Gardens Square, on Tuesday evening, when he played for two hours a long and interesting list of pieces with wonted energy and remarkable skill in respect of difficult executancy. The selections included many notable works of what Mr. A. G. Chappell calls " various masters."

Full and free drafts were made upon texts of Frohberger, Muffat, Couperin, Rameau, Scarlatti, Bach, Handel, Mozart, Haydn, Mendelssohn, Beethoven, Schubert, Schumann, and Chopin. The list is worthy of record.

Andante and Canon	Frohberger.
Gigue	Muffat.
Re Reveil—Matin	Couperin.
Le Tambourin	Rameau.
Allegro in G minor	Scarlatti.
Fuga in D major	Bach.
Suite in G minor	Handel.
Fantasia in D minor	Mozart.
Sonata, Op. 27, (No. 2)	Beethoven.
Impromptu in B flat major	Schubert.
Scherzo a Capriccio	Mendelssohn.
Novellette (No. 8)	Schumann.
Nocturne in D flat major }	
Mazurka in F minor }	Chopin.
Scherzo in B flat	
Wedding March, from Mendelssohn's " Midsummer Night's Dream "	Liszt.

Miss Helen Akroyd sang some solos.

THE COLOGNE CHOIR OF MEN'S VOICES.

The Cologne Choir, known (*Germanicè*) as the Kölner-*Männer*-Gesang-Verein," is again in our midst, and held the first of eight serial concerts last Monday afternoon, at St. James's Hall. The ninety-two members of the choir are all amateurs, and their laudable purpose is the erection and establishment of an "Anglican Church " in their great cathedral city. The society was formed in 1842 by a number of musical enthusiasts in Cologne, anxious not only to promote the interests of high art, but to aid charitable institutions—it is to be hoped only such as are really worthy of support, for the abuses of benevolent contributions in England are known to be enormous and abominable.

The Choir, on Monday and Tuesday, sang with excellent effect and *ensemble.* The scheme of Monday included Kreutzer's " Sabbath Song " (erroneously so entitled, seeing that the " Sabbath " to Christians is a *dies non*, or common-place " Saturday "); Mendelssohn's " Wasserfahrt "; Max Bruch's " Vom Rhein "; Schubert's " Gondolier ;" the old Dutch song, founded on a Rembrandt etching, " Homm, O Homm, holdes Kindahen"; and " Corinthian Courtship," whereof the very "low" or *patois* German has been rendered into equally poor " Lowland Scotch " by F. Corder. Violin solos by M. Olive Musin, accompanied on the pianoforte by Mr. W. Ganz, agreeably relieved the choruses. M. Musin introduced a Romance in G, by M. De Lange (first time in England).

These Cologne choralists command the notice of the British public. They ought to be heard, by " practitioners " especially, at this time, when the Handel Festival at the Crystal Palace is about to challenge the criticism of the wide, wide world.

A. M.

READING ORPHEUS SOCIETY.

The first open meeting of the Reading Orpheus Society was held, by invitation, in the New Town Hall, on Monday evening, and was attended by a large and fashionable company, including many of the clergy and principal inhabitants of the town. The society, which includes about thirty-five adult members, was established last autumn for the purpose of practising glees, part-songs, and choruses for male voices only, the members mostly belonging to Church choirs in the town. Mr. F. J. Read, Mus.Bac., organist of Christ Church, is the director. On this occasion a small band, led by Mr. Rippon, took part, and played an overture and symphony, besides accompanying the last chorus. Mr. Read was conductor, and Mr. C. H. H. Sippel (organist of St. Lawrence's), accompanied the songs. The programme included :—

Overture, "Italians in Algieri"	Rossini.
Part-song. "Summer Eve"	Hatton.
Glee, " Queen of the Valley "	Callcott.
Pianoforte solo, " Invitation pour la Valse "	Weber.
Part-song, "Tar's Song"	Hatton.
Introduction and Allegro " Symphony in D "	Haydn.
Part-song, "The Lifeboat "	Hatton.
Glee, " Peace " (a fable)	Bridge.
Quartet, " By Celia's Arbour "	Horsley.
Solo and chorus, " My task is ended "	Balfe.

Miss Margaret Hoare is an accomplished vocalist, and made a very pleasing impression upon her audience, eliciting hearty applause by her excellent rendering of the two songs, the last being re-demanded. Miss Stokes sang very nicely, and was enthusiastically applauded—Milton Welling's song, " Tell me again," being encored. Of the part-singing of the Orpheus Society, one can scarcely speak too highly. The several numbers were given with excellent precision, well in tune, and with a remarkable degree of expression, and effect of light and shade. At the close of the programme Dr. Wells explained the objects of the society, and said they hoped next season to give two or three subscription concerts.

VARIOUS CONCERTS.

Signor Ria held a *matinée* on June 7th at the Marlborough Rooms. He sang Campana's Romance, " Mi credena in Paradiso " (by desire); also Castaldon's " Musica Proibita "; and a duet of Donizetti with Signor Susini. A cordial reception greeted this favourite tenor vocalist. Miss José Sherrington, Mdme. Rose Hersee, and other artists appeared; Mdme. Hersee chose the " Dove " song from "Colomba," and illustrated it. Signor Tito Mattei evoked much applause for his grand Fantasia on " I Puritani," and his new " Saltarello." Herr Oberthür's harp solo on " Marta " was another good hit.

Mrs. Edmund A. Netherclift held a concert on the afternoon of May 31st at Willis's Rooms. This lady sang, with taste and feeling, Vaccaj's air, " Ah, se tu dormi," and was much applauded. A ladies' chorus sang Romer's " Golden Summer," and Professor G. H. Macfarren's " Mermaid." Miss Santley, Miss Wakefield, and Mr. L. Thomas sang choice pieces, and Miss Madalena Cronin, whose successful concert was noticed a fortnight ago, played, in her always admirable style, Chopin's " Andante Spinato and Polonaise," Op. 22, and Rubinstein's Valse, " Le Bal." Mr. R. Blagrove favoured the audience with a solo on the concertina (Regondi's " La Sonnambula "), but the instrument itself is simply an infliction to " ears polite."

Mdlle. Clotilde Kleeberg held a pianoforte recital at the Marlborough Rooms, Regent Street, on the afternoon of June 4th, and will hold a second on Thursday, June 21st. Mdlle. Kleeberg is an excellent artist, of strictly classical style, and a refined as well as an emphatic executant. The scheme comprised Beethoven's Sonata in C sharp minor; five pieces of Chopin (inclusive of the " Study " in G flat), a Fugue of J. S. Bach, and several fugitive pieces by " Russian " Field (the Nocturne in E flat), Schubert, S. Heller, Mendelssohn, Schumann, Henselt, Hiller, and T. Dubois.

Miss Josephine Agabeg held her annual concert at St. George's Hall on Thursday evening, June 7th Miss Agabeg played Beethoven's Sonata in A flat, Op. 26 ; Chopin's Nocturne in C minor ; and Schumann's " Études Symphoniques," in C sharp minor, for which she was much applauded, and received a bouquet. Miss Agabeg is recognized as a pianist of no small pretensions. Miss Mackenzie won a *bis* for Mr. W. Ganz's song " Forget me not." Mr. O. Musin played violin solos, and assisted

Miss Agabeg and M. Gustave Libotton in an able interpretation of Schubert's Pianoforte Trio in E flat. Mr. Ganz conducted the concert, and played, with Miss Agabeg, Mendelssohn's " Allegro Brillante " in A, for two pianofortes.

At Mr. F. Von Zastrow's "drawing-room concert" on June 8th, Miss Mabel Bourne played Chopin's Scherzo in B minor, and Weber's Polonaise in E with *éclat*. Herr Polonaski entertained a select audience with violin solos by Schumann and Brahms, modestly introducing his own " Chanson du Nord," which ought to be in the publisher's hands if still in MS. Miss Bourne and Herr Polonaski played together a well-known Sonata of Handel in A major.

MUSIC IN DUBLIN.

The pupils' annual concert in connection with the Royal Irish Academy of Music was held on the 8th inst., in the large concert hall of the Royal University Buildings. If any evidence were wanted of the interest taken by the public in this institution, certainly the attendance at this concert would have been evidence abundant, not a vacant seat being visible in the building. The orchestra was remarkably well furnished ; and viewed from the centre of the hall, produced a very elegant effect —the ladies appearing all in uniform costume (white dress and green sash). The programme opened with a Largo, by Handel for violins, organ, and piano, which was very creditably performed ; and a Romanza from " L'Ombra," by Flotow, received a very good interpretation at the hands of Mrs. MacMullen. A special interest is always felt in the piano pupils, for it stands unsurpassed as a school of pianoforte playing. The performance of the pieces on this season's programme will, I am sure, tend to increase its high repute. The items were as follows :—" La Campanella " (Taubert), Miss Stirling ; Scherzo in B flat minor (Chopin), Miss Krügger ; " D'Après la Tarentelle " (Liszt), Miss Douglas ; and Etude, in F sharp (Sgambato), Miss Walker. Miss Krügger's performance displayed all the qualifications of an excellent pianist, and the careful and beautifully finished manner in which she rendered her selection elicited very hearty applause. The other ladies were equally successful in their performances, and must have quite pleased the estimable professors of the Academy to whom this branch of their musical training is entrusted. I should not forget to mention that Miss Douglas, in addition, played an organ Prelude and Fugue by Hesse, and acquitted herself with great credit. Mr. Cox, who, by the way, possesses a nice baritone voice, which showed every sign of careful training, rendered " Awake, thou golden blush of morn," by Cushman, in a very superior style ; Mr. Webb sang the aria, " No more sorrow languish," by Handel, but did not come up to my expectation. He has, nevertheless, a sweet tenor voice, though by no means promoted, and I doubt not that, with careful study, and a more judicious selection of a song, I shall have the pleasure of noticing him more favourably at the next Academy concert. " Thou fair and happy boy " (Hiller), was tunefully rendered by Miss Harris ; and the recit. and aria, " Non paventar ah ! infelice," from Mozart's " Flauto Magico," was undertaken by Miss Egerton. Truly it recalled the days of Italian opera, at the Old Royal, now a mass of ruins, and by a strange coincidence it was Miss Egerton's father, then stage manager, who perished in the flames in his endeavours to stay the action of the fire. To return to Miss Egerton, her voice is one of great flexibility ; and her thoroughly artistic rendering of the above called forth an encore, which could not be denied. A pretty duet by Schumann, " La Villanelle," was done full justice to by Miss Goulding, and Miss Lynch ; and a quartet by Wallace, " Though the world," was an equally meritorious production ; the soprano part was sustained by Miss Kearne, with her usual ability. Miss O'Hart, who possesses a sweet contralto, nicely cultivated, rendered her part with a grace and judgment that makes one regret her name did not appear on the programme for a solo. Messrs. Marks and O'Farrel contributed their parts in good style. A violin solo, " Fantaisie," by Leonard, was capitally played by Mr. Richardson, and very warmly applauded ; and a ladies' violin class gave a very successful rendering of a composition for strings by Steibelt, " Pezzo D'Assieme." " Benedizione dei Pugnali " (Meyerbeer), was well rendered by Messrs. Marks, O'Farrel, Whelan, and Foy, with chorus and orchestra ;

chorus and air, " Deh placatevi con me," by Glück, was
very artistically got through by Miss Windsor, who was
well supported by the chorus. The piece of the evening
however, was the motet, " Gallia," by Gounod, which was
composed for the opening of the International Exhibition,
London, 1871 ; but this is the first time it has been performed in Dublin. The Dublin musical public are
therefore highly grateful to the Academy for bringing
forward what to the major portion was entirely new. It
is written for soprano solo, chorus and orchestra, and, it
must be said, received an excellent rendering upon this
occasion. Miss Keane gave her music in a most artistic
manner, and shewed what a careful study she had made
of her part. The chorus performed its work in excellent
style, and shewed a thorough knowledge and appreciation of the beautiful work. The orchestra was quite up
to the requirements of the composition, and acquitted
itself in a praiseworthy manner. The conductor, Signor
Bozelli, is to be congratulated on the general success of
the concert, a success he has been labouring so assiduously
to bring about.   T. J. B.

OXFORD.—The entertainments belonging to commemoration
time are always more or less musical. A concert was given at
Jesus College on June 6th. The Pembroke Musical Society
gave a concert on June 7th in their Hall. Haydn's " Seasons "
formed the programme of the Philharmonic Society's concert in
the Sheldonian Theatre, on June 11th. Magdalen College gave
a concert on June 13th. All these performances have displayed
much artistic excellence.

EDINBURGH.—Prejudice dies hard. The instrumental music
question, supposed to have been settled at the Assembly of the
Free Church, is to be immediately revived. At a meeting of the
minority opposed to the organ in church, it was resolved to form a
Purity of Worship Defence Association, with branches throughout the country, and to adopt measures with a view to secure the
reversal of what is described as the unsound decision of the
General Assembly. That the cause of music will ultimately
triumph, no sensible person will question, with all respect to
worn out yet no doubt honest prejudices.

ST. MARY'S NEWINGTON CHORAL SOCIETY.—On Tuesday
evening, June 12th, the above society gave its second concert in
the parochial room adjoining the Church. Though it is of a very
recent growth, it shows signs of much improvement. The
members should feel gratified in having for their conductor Mr.
W. Rayment Kirby, F.C.O., and knowing that under his careful
guidance this class will grow, and in time perform music in a
style worthy of the Church with which they are connected. The
principal work was Bennett's " May Queen," the chorus, though
rather weak, sang with a certain amount of precision, and a conscientious knowledge of the work, which, by the way, reflects no
small amount of credit on the conductor. The soloists were
Madame Worrell, who, as the May Queen, sang in her usual
artistic style, while the remaining soloists, Miss Gatland, Mr.
J. R. Jekyll, and Mr. H. Wilson, call for no special mention.
The second part of the programme was of a miscellaneous
character.

WORCESTER.—Nearly 1,800 members of Church choirs attached
to the Worcester Archidiaconal Church Choral Association held
their fourth triennial festival in the cathedral at Worcester
recently, and notwithstanding a rainy morning, the cathedral
doors were besieged early, and there was a complete rush to
obtain seats, the portion of the cathedral not occupied by the
choirs being quickly filled. The number of Church choirs joining
in the festival was 63, and the total number of choristers more
than 1,700, of which number a thousand were surpliced, one
choir wearing blue cossacks under their surplices and birettas.
The procession of choirs and clergy into and out of the church
was the spectacle of the day for the congregation. Anthems by
Walmisley and Barnby were given, the latter at the morning and
the former at the afternoon Service. The general secretary to
the association, Rev. H. H. Woodward, Mus.Bac., and minor
canon of the cathedral, wrote a special Te Deum and Benedictus
for the festival, and Mr. Lloyd, Mus.Bac., and organist of Oxford
Cathedral, contributed a Magnificat and Nunc Dimittis. The
whole went off well, although only one rehearsal of the united
choirs had been possible.

A statue of Auber has been placed in the Theatre of
Caen. The official inauguration on the 10th was attended
by several notable French musicians. The music performed included a violin concerto by the author of " Mas-
saniello."

A festival will be held at Ghent on the 1st and 2nd of
July. The first day will be devoted to Belgian composers.
The performers number 500. The new works to be per-
formed include "La Pacification de Gand" cantata by
M. Walput, and "Amor lex æterna," a lyrical cycle in
six episodes, composed by M. Adolphe Samuel.

Organ News.

LIVERPOOL.

Mr. W. T. Best gave an organ recital in the St.
George's Hall, on Thursday June 7th. The following
is the programme :—

Overture, "Athalie"	Mendelssohn.
Romanza, "The Fishermaiden"	Meyerbeer.
Passacaglia (Variations and Fugue on a Pedal-Bass)	Bach.
Pastorale	Moriconi.
Military March, "La Garde passe"	W. T. Best.
Scherzo-Symphonique	Alex. Guilmant.

On Saturday afternoon, June 9th :—

Overture, "I Lituani"	Ponchielli.
Andante in G major	H. Smart.
Fantasia in the Style of Bach in F minor	Mozart.
Chaconne with Variations in G major	Handel.
Romanesca (Italian Dance of the Sixteenth Century. Anciently accompanied by Singing)	
Toccata for the Organ in B minor	Boëly.

CRYSTAL PALACE.

Mr. Eyre's recent Saturday programmes have included
the following pieces :—

Concert Fugue in G	Krebs.
Andante Cantabile	Smart.
Fantasia in C minor	Hesse.
Adagio in E flat	Hopkins.
Fantasia	Lemmens.
Wedding March	Gounod.
Theme and Variations	Hesse.
Grand Prelude and Fugue in D	A. W. Bach.
Danse Ancienne	Sanders.
Allegretto in A	Henselt.
Pastorale	Guilmant.
Hero's March (Op. 92)	Mendelssohn.
Andante in G and Soprano Melody	Smart.
Barcarolle	Spohr.
Pastorale Sonata (1st movement)	Rheinberger.
Fantasia with Choral	Smart.

FISHERIES EXHIBITION.

An organ recital was given on Thursday, June 7th, by
Mr. James Loaring. The following was the programme :—

Overture ("Masaniello")	Auber.
Adagio from Symphony	Haydn.
Organ Concerto (No. 2)	Handel.
Gavottes { 4 in B	Gluck.
{ 3 in F	Martini.
Selection from "Madame Favart"	Offenbach.
Fugue	Bach.
Festive March in D	Smart.

The organ recital on Friday June 8th, was given by
Mr. James Loaring. The following was the programme :—

Overture, "L'Italiana"	Rossini.
Marche Heroique	Schubert.
Fugue in E flat	Bach.
Chorus, "Zadok the Priest"	Handel.
Andante and Allegro	F. E. Bache.
Selection from "La Perichole"	Offenbach.
March of the Crusaders	Churchill Sibley.

The recital on Tuesday, June 12th, was by Mr. T.
Pettit. The following was the programme :—

March in D major	Smart.
Nocturne	Mendelssohn.
Gavotte in D	Bach.
Andante in G	Batiste.
Postlude	Wely.
Overture, "Le Cheval de Bronze"	Auber.
Pastorale	Handel.
March, "Tannhäuser"	Wagner.

PRESTON.

The following is the programme of the organ recital
given by Mr. James Tomlinson, in the new Public Hall,
on Thursday evening, June 7th.

Marche Religeuse	Chauvet.
Scherzo	Guilmant.
Adagio and Finale, from the Quartet in C	Spohr.
Overture to "Rosamunde"	Schubert.
Chaconne	Durand.
Cornelius March	Mendelssohn.

On Saturday evening, June 9th :—

Overture to the Oratorio "The Last Judgment"	Spohr.
Larghetto (Clarionet Quintet))	Mozart.
Selection from the "Water Music"	Handel.
Maestoso—Air—Minuetto—Allegro—Finale.	
Fantasia on the "Vesper Hymn"	E. H. Turpin.
Ballet Music from "Sylvia"	Delibes.
Overture in F minor	Morandi.

NORWICH.

Dr. Bunnett gave an organ recital at the St. Andrew's Hall, on June 9th, the following was the programme :—

Overture, " Don Pasquale "	Donizetti.
War March	Lichtenstein.
Adagio and Finale (from Quartet)	Spohr.
Air, Favori de Marie Antoinette	
Gavotte in D	Bach.
Organ Concerto	Crotch.
Musette, Andante, and March	Handel.
Adagio Religioso (Hymn of Praise)	Mendelssohn.
Air in A (with variations)	Haydn.
Overture, " Egmont "	Beethoven.

BRISTOL.

Mr. George Risely gave an organ recital at the Colston Hall, on June 9th. The following was the programme :—

Festival March	Mendelssohn.
Momens Musicaux .. { a Andantino / b Allegretto }	Schubert.
Sonata, No. 4, in B flat	Mendelssohn.
Allegro—Andante Religioso—Allegretto—Allegro	
Barcarolle	Sir S. Bennett.
Overture, " Midsummer Night's Dream "	Mendelssohn.
Andante in G major	Batiste.
Grand March, " Schiller "	Meyerbeer.

BOLTON.

An organ recital was given in the the Albert Hall, by Mr. William F. Mullineux, on June 9th. The following was the programme :—

Organ Concerto in G minor, (No. 4, and set)	Handel.
Allegro—Variations on a Ground-Bass Fuga.	
Minuetto Romantique	Smith.
Fantasia on English Airs—	
"Old King Cole."	
"Home, Sweet Home."	
"Rule Britannia."	
Overture, " Le pré aux clercs "	Hérold.
Air, "O ruddier than the Cherry" (pedal solo)	Handel.
Romanza, " Rose softly blooming "	Spohr.
Fanfare Militaire	Ascher.

RAMSEY.

Miss Wood gave a recital on the new organ built by Messrs. Forster and Andrews, of Hull, in the St. Paul's Church, on Thursday, June 7th. The following was the programme :—

Four Preludial Pieces	E. J. Hopkins.
Adagio—Grazioso—Siciliano—Moto Continuo.	
"Placido e il Mar," Mozart	Arr. by Hopkins.
Andante con Moto	Guilmant.
Priere	Lemmens.
Pastorale	Zipoll.
Toccata and Fugue in D minor	Bach.
Andante in A major	Smart.
Carillons de Dunkerque	E. H. Turpin.
Fanfare	Lemmens.
Andante in F major	Merkel.
Organ Sonata { Grave, Adagio, Allegro Maestoso } No. 2. { e Vivace, Fuga	Mendelssohn.

ROCHDALE.

The opening of the new organ in the Presbyterian Church (built by Alex. Young and Sons, of Manchester), took place on May 6th. The following is a synopsis of the organ :—

GREAT ORGAN.   CC TO G, 68 NOTES.

1. Open Diapason.. ..	8 ft.	3. Wald Flöte	4 ft.
2. Dulciana	8 „		

SWELL ORGAN.   CC TO G, 68 NOTES.

4. Gamba	8 ft.	6. Hautboy	8 ft.
5. Lieblich Gedact	8 „		

PEDAL ORGAN.   CCC TO F.

7. Bourdon	16 ft.

COUPLERS.

8. Great Octave on itself.	11. Swell to Pedals.
9. Swell to Great.	12. Great to Pedals.
10. Swell Octave on itself.	

A recital on the new and effective organ, lately erected by Mr. Alfred Kirkland, of Wakefield, was given by Mr. E. H. Turpin, on June 12th, at the Wesleyan Church, Holly Park, Crouch Hill, N. Some excellent vocal music was added to the programme.

CANTERBURY.

The effort which Dr. Longhurst is making to obtain for Canterbury Cathedral an organ adequate for the performance of the highest class of sacred music, is being warmly supported. The total amount required to provide an organ cased in accordance with the designs of the late Sir Gilbert Scott, is about £3,500. Of this sum over £1,000 has been promised. Dr. Longhurst and the Rev. W. D. Wardell are secretaries to the committee, and will gladly receive subscriptions. The present instrument is supposed to have been built in 1661, and rebuilt in 1753, and 1784. Seven pedal pipes were added by James Longhurst, in 1825 ; and the organ was finally rebuilt, and a few additions made, by W. Hill, in 1841. It is wholly unfit for the performance of much of the music which the improved Services of the Cathedral require. It is inferior to the organs of most of the English Cathedrals. The following lists of organs and stops will show how far Canterbury is behind other cathedrals in this respect :— Canterbury, 34 ; Lincoln, 38 ; Gloucester, 40 ; Oxford, 40 ; Bagnor, 45 ; Westminster Abbey, 47 ; Llandaff, 48 ; Exeter, 48 ; Ely, 50 ; Rochester, 51 ; Carlisle, 52 ; Peterborough, 54, Wells, 54 ; Ripon, 56 ; Hereford, 65 ; Lichfield, 68 ; Winchester, 71 ; Worcester, 71 ; Durham, 76 ; Chester, 81 ; St. Paul's, 82 ; Salisbury, 86 ; and York, 87. Canterbury is the only one of these places with an organ built earlier than 1847. The following is the scheme proposed :—It is intended that all the stops should go through, and to consist of four complete manuals, from C C to A, 58 notes and two-and-a-half octaves of pedals, C C C to F 30 notes.

GREAT ORGAN.

1. Double Open Diap.	16 ft.	9. Twelfth	3 ft.
2. Open Diapason	8 „	10. Fifteenth	2 „
3. Open Diapason	8 „	11. Piccolo	2 „
4. Gamba	8 „	12. Mixture (4 ranks)	
5. Stopped Diapason	8 „	13. Double Trumpet	16 „
6. Claribel Flute	8 „	14. Cornopean	8 „
7. Principal	8 „	15. Clarion	4 „
8. Flûte Harmonic	4 „		

SWELL ORGAN.

16. Double Open Diap.	16 ft.	23. Mixture (3 ranks)	ft.
17. Open Diapason	8 „	24. Contra Fagotto	16 „
18. Lieblich Gedact	8 „	25. Trumpet	8 „
19. Salicional	8 „	26. Hautboy	8 „
20. Vox Angelica	8 „	27. Vox Humana	8 „
21. Octave	4 „	28. Clarion	4 „
22. Flageolet	2 „		

SOLO ORGAN.

29. Flûte Harmonic	8 ft.	32. Corno-de-Bassetto...	8 ft.
30. Concert Flute	4 „	33. Tuba	8 „
31. Orchestral Oboe	8 „	34. Clarion	4 „

CHOIR ORGAN.

35. Lieblich Gedact	16 ft.	40. Flûte Harmonique..	4 ft.
36. Lieblich Gedact	8 „	41. Gemshorn	4 „
37. Open Diapason	16 „	42. Corno-de-Bassetto ..	8 „
38. Salicional	8 „	Clarinet or Cremona	
39. Flauto Traverso	8 „		

PEDAL ORGAN.

43. Double Open Diap.	32 ft.	48. Octave	8 ft.
44. Open Diapason	16 „	49. Flute	8 „
45. Open Diapason	16 „	50. Mixture (4 ranks) ...	
46. Violono	16 „	51. Posaune	16 „
47. Bourdon	16 „	52. Clarion	8 „

COUPLERS.

53. Swell to Great.	58. Swell to Pedals.
54. Swell to Great.	59. Great to Pedals.
55. Swell to Great.	60. Choir to Pedals.
56. Choir to Great.	61. Solo to Great.
57. Solo to Pedals.	62. Swell to Choir.

Tremulant to Swell Vox Humana.

4 Pneumatic Combination Pistons to each Clavier, and 4 Combination Pedals to Pedal Organ. A double-acting Pedal to Great to Pedal Couplers.

That the Metropolitan Cathedral shall indeed have a worthy organ, is a matter calling for speedy fulfilment, and the proposal deserves earnest support.

In Memoriam.—On the 7th inst. Charles Luders died. A native of Germany, he resided for many years in this metropolis. He was a musician of rare skill, and as honest a soul as ever trod this earth. He needs no monument to extol his many noble virtues, for his memory will ever live in the hearts of all who knew him.—FERDINAND PRAEGER.

PRINCIPAL CONTENTS OF THIS NUMBER.

LONDON: SATURDAY, JUNE 16, 1883.

THE POSITION OF THE CATHEDRAL ORGANIST.

THAT complaints should have to be made anent the treatment and position of those important servants of the Church and nation, our cathedral organists, is indeed a scandal, even though it is true that exceptional cases show that surrounding circumstances have much to do with the difficulties the occupants of too many cathedral organ seats are called upon to face. In the very selection in early and unsettled times of quiet nooks, away from the turbulent tides of commercial life for the most part, the foundations of some of the disadvantages attending the life of the Church artist were laid; and the tide of modern busy life following generally the ancient streams, has rather drifted further from than more nearly approached many of our old cathedral cities. With the exception of such great centres as London, Manchester, Bristol, etc., the distinguished and often highly cultured musicians who consent, often to their own professional and artistic loss, to become our cathedral organists, have no proper opportunities for the full exercise, and for securing consequent due reward, of their self-denying artistic labour. The word "consent" was used advisedly, for the artist of distinction has hardly any chance of a due appreciation in a sleepy cathedral city, while, on the other hand, the cathedral atmosphere is by no means detrimental to the due advancement of its clerical staff. For the average pay of an express engine-driver, and in some cases for less remuneration still, an educated gentleman, and highly cultured artist, is called upon to undertake never-ending and such very responsible duties as uplift him into a national rather than a purely local position. In the midst of all his daily and anxious work, usually involving such ungrateful labour as everyday choir-boys' drill, the cathedral organist is generally denied the sympathy, and largely shut out from the proud, exclusive society, of his fellow and clerical cathedral officials, who are apt to forget the words, "All of you " be subject one to another," and who are called upon to teach that " he that humbleth himself shall be " exalted," and to proclaim and practise the virtues of brotherly love, hospitality, charity in thought, word, and deed, and humility in all things. Truly, we have much cause to be grateful to our cathedral organists for their patient, resigned self-abnegation and admirable devotion to their high and too little appreciated labours. Now and then it is hardly possible to avoid a feeling of indignation when some revelation or other comes into daylight in connection with our leading ecclesiastical musicians. In a recent instance the conditions of the acceptance of office by an incoming cathedral organist were degrading in their nature. The organist, to begin with, is practically to be shut out from the just advantages of a cathedral office as a life elected officer, and is to be liable to be discharged at three months' notice. The Dean and Chapter again impose the condition, that the organist shall not be absent without their consent, and only then by providing a deputy having their approval. Thus they take the power of refusing to allow their organist to be absent from, say, a week-day service, and may enforce their tyrannical, and if they choose impossible, condition by declining to permit anyone else, save, say Mr. BEST for the sake of the argument, to release their hard-worked organ player even for a single day. Had these well meaning but ill-advised ecclesiastics advertised for a groom, or gardener, their anxiety to secure a due sense of the best possible candidates for the organist's post. Perhaps the Dean and Chapter of the cathedral in question do not know of the existence of the detective clock, as used in our large prisons, by which the warders hourly register their presence and attention to duty. Had they possessed this knowledge, possibly such a mechanical register would have been adopted, whereby their to be pitied new organist might have been called upon daily to notify his presence at the organ key-board. This same severely conscientious Dean and Chapter are, however, possibly not unaware of the existence of a much easier form of cathedral officialism, and, it may be, have heard of clerical pluralists, and canons in occasional residence, to whom, in some instances, the environs of

the clubs about Pall Mall are as familiar as the not too much frequented precincts of their several cathedrals. It is not my present purpose to probe further into a matter which can only be written about with much pain and dissatisfaction. It might, however, be told, how all the accumulations of Church property and changes in money value had been from age to age carefully assessed and balanced in favour of the leading clerical members of our cathedral staffs, and just as carefully discounted and re-adjusted to the loss and disadvantage of the organist and choristers. Such statements might be startlingly illustrated were I to place before my readers a comparison of the salaries paid to the deans and canons before the middle of the 16th century in several of our chief cathedrals and the salaries of the organ-playing priests of the same pre-Reformation period, with the like stipends paid to the clerical dignitaries and organists of the same cathedrals now. The subject should claim the attention of our legislative authorities. There is much to be done, indeed, before the "chief musicians" of our cathedrals are duly esteemed, honoured, and rewarded for their self-denying noble discharge of their trying and never-ending duties, and before cathedral worship stands forth in all its true beauty and grandeur.

E. H. TURPIN.

THE LOGIC OF COUNTERPOINT.

THIRD SERIES.

IX.

THE conduct of the fourth order in four parts necessarily calls for special observations, seeing that the additional or fourth part when employed in connection with the use of syncopations affecting triads must naturally add to the complication of the part movements. Expressed briefly, one of the four parts is apt to be in the way sometimes, in dealing with suspended harmonies. CHERUBINI's first rule anent the conduct of fourth species counterpoint in four parts runs thus : " The chord should always be com- " plete in a bar whether the syncopated part forms a " discord or a concord ; in the latter case, if the chord " be not complete on the accented part of the measure, " it must necessarily be so at the unaccented portion." Read between the lines, this merely means, there is no excuse for incomplete harmony in a four-part score. The theorist continues to explain, that the chords are not complete at the occurrence of the discords, because the discords are simply the suspensions of concords ; so if the discord in each instance is omitted and the resolution substituted for it, the particular complete chord will appear at once, having only been held in abeyance by the discord as it were. The idea of this kind of held-back harmony may be conveyed in the following repeated trite and simple words. The four parts represent four friends walking abreast. A prepared discord is one of the friends lagging behind the other three friends pausing in their progress until their lagging companion is again level with them. CHERUBINI goes on to say (doubtless bearing in mind that one of the four parts may be in the way so to speak, or may be utilised in adding fulness and completeness to the harmony formed), "The resolution of a discord may even be altered by exceptionally allowing the use of minims in one or more of the parts not engaged in the formation of syncopations. The following scheme in letters is an illustration :—

```
      — C       C    B
        G       F
        E       A    D
        C       D
```

The theorist gives examples of such licenses applied to the discords of the fourth, seventh, and ninth. It is needless to add that the licenses so employed of extra minims may in this way lead to an unexpected change of root at the point of a resolution. Such an introduction of original minims in the parts usually taking one note only in each bar would seem to be of only rare use, as disturbing the accustomed flow of the several parts, and, what is of more consequence, accelerating the even procession of chord roots bar by bar. Further, such part actions belong naturally to the intermixture in four parts of second and four species counterpoint. There is a certain gain in the presence of a fourth part in the way of forming short pedal passages, as the fairly complete harmony may be successfully carried forward by three parts during a brief sentence in which a fourth part is stationary. One of the best means of escape from complications in four parts is by the process of absorption—that is, by a temporary reduction of the score, or a putting away of one part for an instant, by assigning two parts for the moment to one sound, thus—

```
      A B       B A
      F         E
      D         E
      D         C
```

E. H. Turpin.

EXPERIENCES OF AN ORGANIST.

VIII.

When I had been a few months in my new position, our leading soprano, the lady about whose musical talents I had heard so much, and who, as I have already said, was absent from home when I first came to the church, returned to town, and was much chagrined on learning that the duties of choirmaster, which she had hitherto undertaken of her own accord, as a free-will offering, and which she had always fulfilled to her own perfect satisfaction, were now entrusted to the organist, who, presumptuously preferring to take upon himself the responsibilities of accompanist and conductor combined, had had the temerity to stipulate for and assume the control of both offices. She complained to the select vestry, as our board of directors was called, and informed the head of that rather weak-minded body that she entirely disapproved of their proceedings, not so much because they had superseded her as choirmistress (that, in her humble opinion, was quite a minor consideration), but rather because, in bringing over an Englishman to play the organ, they were taking the bread out of an Irishman's mouth (she said bread, but of course she meant potatoes) and pursuing what she felt bound to stigmatize in the very strongest parliamentary language as a most unpatriotic course. But it was too late for her complaints to be of any avail. The vestry had committed itself. The Saxon intruder was encamped upon the soil, or, to be more precise without being much less figurative, enthroned upon the organ-stool, and could not be immediately got rid of. To dislodge him from his position must be a work of time. Meanwhile, however, it was easy to harass the enemy, and that was what this feminine patriot, this Irish Joan of Arc, determined to do. When

the happy thought occurred to her she regained her equanimity, and attended the choir-practices with a light heart and a smiling face.

The lady's antipathy to me was so marked, and she took so little pains to conceal it, that it was impossible not to perceive it at once. At the same time, as I was not conscious of having done anything to incur her displeasure, I could not understand it, for I would not at first allow myself to believe that my nationality was likely to create any prejudice against me in Irish minds. This patriotic prejudice, however, as I afterwards found, was not the only cause of her hatred of me. There was a disappointed candidate in the background, and she, in sporting phraseology, was his heaviest backer. In other words, among those who had made application for the post which I occupied, there had been one whom she had done the vestry the honour to recommend to them, and she had taken it as a matter of course that the appointment would have been made in his favour. Her candidate was a youth with whose father, an organist in the neighbourhood, she had been on intimate terms for what may be considered in her case as a long period, viz., several months. They had arranged the whole matter between them. The son was to have the organ ; she was to continue to direct the choir, and the father was to give his assistance on festival-days and other special occasions. That they had the true welfare of the church at heart there can be no doubt, and it certainly was provoking to find their good intentions frustrated. But such is the ingratitude of human nature generally, and especially of vestries and churchwardens ! I do not blame her for being angry with it or with them, but I do think it was a little unreasonable of her to be so inimical to me, whether from pique or patriotism, or both. It was not my fault that I was born in London. That was owing to circumstances over which (for obvious reasons) I had no control. Neither was it my fault (though, perhaps, it may be considered my misfortune) that I was elected organist of the church which she was good enough to patronize. I heard of the vacancy, and fondly imagining myself competent to fill it, and being, moreover, instigated by one or two Irish friends, who must, I suppose, have been entirely wanting in that lofty patriotism for which the Green Isle is so famous, I ventured to offer my services. " The very head and front of my offending had this extent, no more." Hence I cannot see why this musical matron should have been so determined to treat me as her mortal antagonist. Since, however, she was resolved to do so, it only remained for me to accept the inevitable as calmly as I could.

The principal sin which she laid to my charge was that of playing too slowly, and as she was considered by the congregation to be a great musical authority, and was looked up to, in fact, as the musical oracle of our little temple, it soon became a generally accepted fact that I did play too slowly. It seems somewhat strange that I, who had formerly been found fault with for playing much too fast, should now be accused of playing too slowly. But tempora mutantur, as (if I remember rightly) Valpy's Latin Delectus tells us. The times are changed, and it may be that I have not changed with them, as according to that delectable authority, that ancient proverbial philosopher, we are all expected to do. This is a fast age ; an age of steam and electricity. Lightning-speed is what the world is striving after, and the Church, in this respect, is not behind the world. She is no longer content to "sit and sing herself away to everlasting bliss" at the same slow pace as she was accustomed to fifty years ago. Then she went to one extreme, and sang her "cheerful songs" like funeral dirges. Now she goes to the other extreme, reads her "title clear" with marvellous rapidity, and wipes her "weeping eyes" with an alacrity verging on indecency, taking all her "griefs and fears," and "rattling them off to a popular tune," like the "heavy dragoon" in the comic opera.

My protests against this irreverent style of singing, and my attempts to check it, were quite sufficient, even if there had been nothing else, to bring me at once into collision with our late choirmistress, seeing that her views on the subject were diametrically opposed to mine. Sometimes she positively refused to sing a note because I ventured to act upon my own judgment in preference to hers. At other times she would sing in advance of the organ, and try to get neighbouring members of the choir to do the same. Of course I could not tolerate this, and I had therefore to request her more than once not to sing so fast, but to endeavour to keep with the organ, which request I was generally careful to put as politely as possible. I must admit, however, that on one such occasion, when she declared, as she had so often done before, but this time with more asperity than usual, that she would rather not sing at all than sing so slowly (the hymn being a particularly solemn one), my natural politeness momentarily forsook me, and I replied that in that case I would prefer her silence to her assistance. I did not lose my temper : perhaps it would have been better if I had ; for my calm and Christian bearing, combined with the epigrammatic way in which I expressed myself, was, I am afraid, not calculated to make us better friends. In fact, as time wore on, her enmity towards me increased, and she sought to undermine my influence in every possible way. She got up a concert in the neighbourhood of the church, and having arranged that the choir should sing some concerted music, she invited the organist of an adjacent church to act as conductor. Handbills were distributed, and placards posted up, announcing that on a certain date a concert would be given in a certain hall for the benefit of our organ-fund, and that the choir of our church, "and other distinguished amateurs," would perform certain pieces, conducted by a certain gentleman, who was no other than the father of the disappointed candidate before mentioned. I must confess that I was considerably annoyed, as well as somewhat astonished, on seeing these public announcements, and on finding that all the arrangements had been made without consulting me. It was also a matter of regret to me that any members of my choir could be found to support an undertaking which, as they must have been aware, was got up in a spirit of insubordination and opposition to their recognized leader. It is true that I was, almost at the last moment, though before the bills were printed (or, at least, before they were out), asked to conduct ; but after I had undertaken to do it, at great inconvenience, since I had to alter and re-arrange, on this account, my classes at the college at which I was engaged, the night was suddenly and unaccountably changed, so that it was impossible for me to be present. The promoters of the concert then refused to again alter the night to suit me, and immediately made arrangements, as though in accordance with some preconcerted plan, to secure the services of the gentleman above alluded to.

I now began distinctly to perceive what I had surmised long before, that between a section of the choir and myself there existed no sympathy whatever, and, on reflection, I concluded that, as time went on, we were likely to become more and more estranged. I therefore resolved that I would sever my connection with the church before there was any serious disagreement between us. I was particularly anxious not to have it reported, as it had been in the case of each of my predecessors, that there had been any quarrelling, and I thought that the best, if not the only way to avoid such a report, would be to leave as soon as possible. Accordingly I sent in my resignation, giving, as my reason, that which was but one of several, and not the most important, viz., that I was residing at a considerable distance from the church, and that I would like to get a position nearer my house, as the time occupied in travelling to and from the church was more than I could conveniently spare. When I had done this I felt somewhat easier in my mind, and indulged in some self-congratulations, as I thought that, while former religious had every one of them quitted this scene of their labours only after much strife, I, in my superior wisdom, had been enabled to foresee the coming storm, like the prophet Elijah, while the cloud was "no bigger than a man's hand"; and that without being obliged to gird up my loins and take my departure at the same rate of speed as that ancient seer had found necessary, I should yet contrive to escape before the rains descended and the floods came ; in other words, before I got into hot water. But my self-congratulations were premature. The "stars in their courses" fought against me as they did against Sisera, and my hopes of being able to depart in peace were not realized.

And this brings me to the last and worst of my experiences—an experience of a particularly unpleasant kind, the relation of which, while it will afford some relief to my ruffled spirit, may also prove not uninstructive to the incipient musician who reads these pages, as it will show him, more clearly perhaps than anything which has yet been revealed, that there is a kind of discord sometimes to be met with by organists, which,

although it is much more easily explained than many of those which are to be found in scientific treatises on the art, is nevertheless much more difficult to resolve. We had been for some months practising and preparing for the harvest festival service which was shortly to be held, and on the Saturday night of the week preceding that in which the special service referred to was to take place we had a full rehearsal. In the course of this rehearsal I had occasion to correct the choir concerning the chanting, and to make some remark as to how a certain passage should be "pointed." Our disaffected soprano leader objected to what I had said, and expressed her opinion that the choir were right and I was wrong. At first I took no notice of her observation, and merely continued my instructions as to the singing of the passage, but when she repeated it, I answered somewhat curtly, having by this time lost a good deal of that amiability which I formerly possessed, that I thought I knew my business, and that, if I did not, I was sure she was not competent to teach me. Now as this lady considered herself quite competent to undertake *anybody's* musical education, and as her friends had for many years encouraged her in her humble opinion, she was, I suppose, mortally offended. She said nothing, but forgetting, in her indignation, that she was a woman and not a war-horse, snorted defiantly and pranced out of the church, with her bosom-friend the near-sighted contralto at her heels. On the Sunday following we had two more practices, one in the morning and one in the afternoon, both of which passed off without further disagreement between me and the fair matron whom I had so grievously offended on the previous evening, although, in consequence of what had occurred, the relations between us were, to speak in political phraseology, considerably strained. At the conclusion of the last practice, however, the bosom friend, prompted by her lady superior, asked me when they could have another practice. I said that I did not think that another practice was necessary ; but they both declared that it was, and that they could not sing at the service without it, and demanded that we should have it either on Tuesday or on Wednesday, the service being fixed for Thursday. I replied that I could not conveniently come on either of those days, as it would interfere with my other engagements, and would occupy more of my time than I could spare. Nothing more was said then, but in the course of the evening I received a visit from the clergyman's wife. I am going into this matter somewhat minutely because, although it may seem unimportant, if not trivial, it led to serious results. The reverend lady (not to speak disrespectfully) brought me a note from her husband, in which he expressed a hope that I would give the choir another practice, rather than that there should be any unpleasantness. His wife, too, said she thought that as on the whole we had got on pretty amicably together up to the present, and as I was about to leave shortly, it was a pity that there should be any quarrelling at the last moment. I said I thought so too, and that was one reason why I was desirous of having no more practices than necessary. This was a sarcastic allusion to the Saturday evening duel between our leading songstress and myself. Ultimately, however, to satisfy my visitor, who was a very affable and lady-like woman, I agreed to give the choir another practice, on Thursday, an hour before the festival service commenced. As I heard nothing further about the matter on Monday, I took it for granted that it was settled, but on Tuesday morning, much to my surprise, I received a letter from the clergyman, informing me that "the choir" (by which I suppose he meant the rebel lady-leader and her hench-woman above-mentioned) had refused to practise on Thursday morning, on the ground that if they practised then they would afterwards be too tired to sing at the Service ; that they, the choir, said they must have another practice ; that he had, therefore, arranged with another gentleman to give them a rehearsal on Wednesday, and to conduct the music on Thursday, and that consequently my services would be dispensed with on the latter day. The gentleman whom he had thus engaged was, as I suspected, and as I afterwards learned, the same gentleman who had conducted the concert, and who was considered, and, I am sorry to say, seemed to consider himself, my rival. It was of course quite out of the question that I could willingly accept this arrangement, and indeed it was hardly to be expected that I should care to allow anyone to officiate in my place on an occasion of so much importance to our small, but genteel community, as the harvest festival Service. Moreover, it was easy to guess at whose suggestion the arrangement had been made, and to perceive that it was simply one more attempt, coming from the same rebellious quarter, to oust me from my position, and supersede me in my work. I therefore wrote, not without some indignation, that I certainly could not consent to any gentleman's taking my place at the organ on the occasion referred to, and that, if this were done in spite of my protest, I must decline to play any more in the church from that date ; should consider myself summarily dismissed, and should claim, besides the salary then due, a further three months' salary in lieu of notice. In reply, I received a letter from the clergyman, in which he expressed regret that I should feel annoyed by the arrangements made, but, at the same time, defended the course he had taken and refused to alter it.

Immediately after the festival Service had taken place, I wrote to the select vestry, calling their attention to what had transpired, and informing them of my determination not to play again at the church. As it had previously been arranged, with my consent, that a candidate for the appointment was to play on the following Sunday, my refusal to officiate further as organist did not put the vestry in any difficulty as regards the obtaining of an immediate substitute, and therefore, considering the treatment I had received, I do not see that they could have had any reason to think that I had acted unjustifiably. I told them that, on its being found that I was unable to give the choir another rehearsal except on Thursday morning (no further practice whatever being in my opinion necessary), it had been decided, without my consent and in spite of my protest, to invite another gentleman to take my place at the organ on Thursday afternoon, and that I considered this tantamount to a summary dismissal, as it was not to be expected that I could resume my duties after such an insult. I concluded by saying that I trusted that they would feel, as I did, that I had taken the only dignified course. The vestry, however, did not adopt this view of the case. Perhaps, looking at the matter in its financial aspect (for they were business men), they considered it wiser not to admit that I had any ground of complaint. Be that as it may, they simply sent a cheque for the amount due, and took no further notice of either me or my grievance. A great deal has been said by philosophers in praise of silence, and undoubtedly it is a very good thing sometimes (especially among musical people), but it is often exceedingly provoking. In this case it was not at all calculated to tranquilize my feelings or allay my irritation. Had they acknowledged that I had been badly treated and expressed any regret, I should have probably let the matter drop. As it was, knowing as I did that former organists had been subjected to similar ill-usage, I thought it only right that such treatment, even though it might remain unpunished, should not be allowed to pass unexposed. I therefore put the matter into the hands of a solicitor, through whom I requested payment of an additional quarter's salary, in lieu of notice, and whom I instructed to take proceedings in a court of law, if necessary. In spite of his letter, which they probably regarded as an idle threat, the vestry still refused to entertain my claim, or even to acknowledge the reasonableness of my complaint, and so I brought my action.

The case was tried at the county court, in due course. My solicitor, being a musical man, was well able to understand and appreciate the circumstances in which I had been placed, and knew how to put my case in the most favourable light. His opening statement was all that the most fastidious client could have desired. The opposing solicitor, on the other hand, did not appear to me to make even so plausible a defence as he might have done, for although his clients were, as I believe, morally in the wrong, it was quite possible, so I am given to understand, for a painstaking and conscientious lawyer to prove that they were legally in the right. I was therefore agreeably surprised at the weakness of his defence. But when the Recorder began to deliver his judgment, I was still more agreeably surprised, as I had been told over and over again by all my counsellors, legal and otherwise, that my hope of success was a forlorn one. He said he was perfectly satisfied of my being fully qualified for the position which I held, and he considered that, as choirmaster, I was the proper person to decide how many practices were requisite for the occasion referred to, and when they should be held. It seemed to him that a choir was something like a regiment of soldiers, in which implicit obedience to the commanding officer was absolutely necessary to ensure success. In the case before him,

however, instead of the choirmaster controlling the choir, the choir appeared to think it their duty to control the choirmaster. Well, the select vestry chose to approve of that sort of thing, and his worship thought that the organist was justified in the letters he wrote. He then proceeded to comment on the letters, remarking that it was evident to him, on reading them, that the organist's position had been rendered intolerable by some of the choir. Ultimately, after referring to the passage in which I stated that I thought the course which had been taken by the clergyman was tantamount to a summary dismissal, he said, "And I think so, too." He then announced that he should give a decree in my favour for the full amount claimed, viz., £15, with costs.

In spite of its triumphant issue, this last experience of mine is by no means a satisfactory one, and I look back upon it with regret. But it is possible that, among those who read these pages, there may be some who either are, or have been, placed in circumstances similar to mine, and it will assuredly be to their advantage that they should know what are the rights as well as the wrongs of organists. For this reason I have felt justified in making revelations which, on account of their extremely disagreeable nature, it might otherwise have been desirable to suppress. I hope, however, that I have not wearied my readers by entering too much into detail, for I should be sorry if that which has been a trial to me should also prove a trial to them.

Not many months after the occurrence just related I left Ireland and returned to my native land. I had private reasons for doing so, but as I have already made a confidant of the reader as regards other private matters, I will not leave him (or her) entirely in the dark concerning this one. The fact is, I had news of a certain young lady, with whom it will be remembered I used to play pianoforte duets in years gone by. Her venerable progenitor, the oracular and dogmatic old gentleman whom I had found, or who (as some prejudiced people think), had found me so intractable, was dead, and thinking that I might be able to offer her some consolation in her bereavement, I proceeded with all speed to London. I found her in a somewhat low state of health, but am happy to say that she is now considerably better.

I have not yet obtained another organ appointment, and my experiences as an organist are therefore at an end for the present. I think, however, that what I have written is sufficient to prove the truth of my opening statement, that the organist is not without his full share of " the cares of this world." Whether it is any satisfaction to him to know that, in his case, those cares are not likely to be associated with " the deceitfulness of riches " is a question which I am not called upon to answer. Of one thing I am certain, namely, that while from a pecuniary point of view his position is rarely all that it should be, in other respects it is often all that it should not be. This being so, it is scarcely to be wondered at if he should sometimes have been found to have "left undone those things which he ought to have done," and to have " done those things which he ought not to have done " (like an orthodox Churchman) ; for even organists, though an exemplary body, are not absolutely impeccable, and it must not be expected that they should all of them act with that circumspection which, as will doubtless readily be admitted, has distinguished the present writer throughout his chequered career. In conclusion, however, let me venture to hope that every organist who reads these pages will in future always display similar circumspection, and that it may lead to less unfortunate results.

Sir Michael Costa's "Eli" is to be given at the St. James's Hall on Saturday morning the 16th inst., at 3 o'clock by Mr. Willing's Choir. Coming, as it will, the day after the full rehearsal of the Handel Festival, of which it is not necessary to remind readers, Sir Michael Costa has been the conductor since the initial performance in 1857. It is a happy thought of Mr. Willing thus to do honour to the composer-conductor by giving a performance of the work at such a time, and doubtless many of the chorus, as well as the general public who will be in London for the purpose of attending the Festival, will avail themselves of the opportunity to be present and to join in the demonstration of regard and esteem towards the renowned musician which the occasion will so opportunely permit.

Correspondence.

THE HENRY SMART MEMORIAL FUND.

TO THE EDITOR OF THE "MUSICAL STANDARD."

SIR,—Without doubt, many of your readers would feel astonished, if not humiliated, when reading the announcement you made in your issue of June 2nd, relative to the sum that has been collected towards the Henry Smart Fund. How is it that such apathy has been shown to the memory of so great a man? The influence of his high-toned manly writing is not lost, but remains with us. Musicians have just cause to be proud, yet grateful, for what he has accomplished. It is, however, painful and humiliating to reflect, that the efforts of this truly great man were neither appreciated nor remunerated as they ought to have been during his life. It is well known that those who aspire to write sacred music must devote their lives to studying the highest and most difficult branches of the science before they feel themselves competent to write worthily for the Church. Our Church authorities ought to feel grateful to Henry Smart for what he contributed to their Services, he rendered to the Church, or in contributing to the Memorial Fund? Nothing!! They were, however, most energetic a few years ago, which shows what they can accomplish in soliciting subscriptions, preaching sermons and having collections in their churches, to form an annuity in, aid of the wife and family of one of their brethren (the Rev. Dr. Dykes, of Durham). The result of their combined efforts was most gratifying—the sum of "ten thousand pounds" being subscribed. What have the music publishers done to perpetuate the memory of Smart? They have been vying with each other recently with their "hundreds" and their "thousands," in response to the invitation from the Prince of Wales, in founding a new College of Music. Their generosity has been heralded far and wide. The advocacy of the "Sailor" Prince (who is one of the Henry Smart Committee), does not appear to have attracted any attention. The "Sailor" Prince, unfortunately for the fund, went on a cruise, and the memorial fund, I fancy, followed his example; that is why we have heard so little respecting it of late.

It appears only the other day since a Mr. Moleneux, of Manchester, presented (shall I call it the "princely" sum of) 1,000 guineas towards a London Benevolent Musical Institution. Yet the combined efforts of Henry Smart's admirers, including our English publishers and English professors, can only manage to subscribe one-half that sum.

Oh, that there were other generous patrons of the Moleneux type to aid in an effort in perpetuating the names of those who have, and who may yet earn, our gratitude and esteem, by rendering true and noble service to the Art we follow.

As I before stated (see Dr. Spark's "Life of Henry Smart," page 350), "The influence of his high-toned, manly writing is not lost, but remains with us as a pattern for imitation, emulation, and perhaps development; and proves beyond doubt to the world that we in England have just cause to be proud, yet grateful, in possessing our own distinctive and characteristic school of music." We know quite well that our "men of mark," be they poets, musicians, or painters, have each their own peculiar individuality, their own distinctive style, or mode of thought and feeling. Therein lies the value of their productions. This power—or shall we call it originality?—cannot be transmitted or taught; it dies with its possessor. The outer world appear to forget this fact, and cannot be made to understand why a man of genius like Henry Smart, having such great ability for composition, should have persistently devoted himself to composing for the Church, writing organ voluntaries, and other high-class music, for which there would undoubtedly be appreciation, but very little remuneration.

Pardon me for my digression in introducing the name of a composer of a very different calibre to Henry Smart. M. Offenbach was considered (in a monetary sense) the most successful composer the world ever produced. The *Musical Standard* told us in November, 1874, "Opera-bouffe would appear to be a very lucrative property. . . . Within 1873, according to the *Belgian Times*, M. Offenbach received £80,000 for the author's rights of only three of his pieces!" In contrast to this statement, I would ask what kind of remuneration is there awaiting sober-minded Englishmen who strive to elevate their art? All the musical efforts of M. Offenbach during his life never approached the calm dignity, the chaste beauty, and the learning of our English master, who, had he descended to the "frivolous," could, without doubt, have written reams of tuneful wriggle, good enough, if not too good, for the easily-pleased audiences who generally assemble to see the showy girls who are engaged to sing and dance (it does not matter which) to the "high sentiment" (?) usually embodied in the librettos of so-called opera bouffe. The Divine Art is used for strange purposes in these enlightened days. We are told that music has the power of intensifying language; granted, but if the words are inane, what then? Music can have no meaning, but it is degraded and out of place by the association. Many examples might be quoted where other successful authors besides M. Offenbach have enriched themselves (but not

their art) by adapting light, "pretty wriggle," called music, to the veriest nonsensical rubbish, which is nothing more than an insult to common sense. Yet it is received nightly with loud acclamations. I am afraid there is much truth in Thomas Carlyle's estimate of the inhabitants of this island. Surely the self abnegation, as shown by Henry Smart's unselfish life and the high tone of his writing, deserves something more than the barren laurels of journalistic commendation! I would respectfully suggest to the Committee of the Henry Smart Memorial Fund, that they delay disbursing the small sum they have in hand. Efforts should be made to add to the fund, and make it a more worthy offering to the memory and the honour of England's greatest musicians.

The proceeds of our musical festivals could not be more worthily bestowed than in aiding the formation of a "Henry Smart Benevolent Fund," for the use and encouragement of those who have, and who may yet distinguish themselves as composers of high-class music.

A re-issue in cheap pamphlet form of the letters that were addressed to the *Musical Standard* on the above subject, would prove of interest to many, who might be induced to add to the fund.

I am, yours truly,
THOS. HOPKINSON.

4, Pryme Street, Hull,
June 11th, 1883.

"THE GREGORIAN ASSOCIATION FESTIVAL BOOK."

TO THE EDITOR OF THE "MUSICAL STANDARD."

SIR,—"Mus. Bac. Oxon." is right in saying that religious controversy is out of place in the columns of the *Musical Standard*, but your reviewer did not enter into any controversy; he merely and rightly stated that the celebration of the Festival of Corpus Christi is not sanctioned by the Church of England as established by law. "Mus. Bac." has no argument with regard to dedication and harvest festivals, for these do not involve the surreptitious introduction of doctrine or practice not in harmony with the Protestant position of the Anglican Church, as does the celebration of the Corpus Christi Festival, of the Roman branch of the Christian community. The Corpus Christi Festival was unknown in the earlier and purer ages of the Church, and only established as late as 1264 (some authorities with less evidence say 1249), and the festival was rejected by the reformers of the 16th century. If, as "Mus. Bac." asserts, the festival is now largely honoured in the Anglican Church, two propositions are set forth, viz., that law is powerless to direct the changing opinions of the religious world, and that the Anglican Church shelters within her fold many persons who have little sympathy with her tenets as legally established, and doubtless from earnest conviction are determined to make her conform more and more to the practices of the Roman Church. Like your reviewer, I offer no opinion and decline to enter into any controversy, merely contenting myself with the assertion that the Committee of the Gregorian Association can find no legal sanction for the recognition of the festival in question in the Protestant Anglican Church; while dedication, harvest, and musical festivals, as involving no outside doctrine, may be celebrated, and illustrate that freedom of action, peculiar to the Anglican Church, the elasticity of which the Gregorian Association seems inclined to overstrain. I do not venture to say what is right, or what is wrong spiritually or morally; I only refer to the question of legality. It would be a matter of interest to know why the Gregorian Association Festival at St. Paul's was, to use a polite expression, "unavoidably postponed"; and whether or not there is any truth in the idea that the Service Book involved too great a doctrinal flavour to justify the consent of the Cathedral authorities, usually so cordially given, and under the expectation of a possible disturbance to so cause the Association to retreat to St. Alban's, Holborn. Musically, I can but wish that every success will attend the labours of the Gregorian Association, and trust that every branch of the One Catholic Church will be taught to make a discreet and earnest use of the grand old ecclesiastical melodies.

Yours, etc.,
AN ORGANIST.

SUNDAY SCHOOL FESTIVAL.

TO THE EDITOR OF THE "MUSICAL STANDARD."

SIR,—Kindly permit me, through your columns, to invite the aid of tenors and basses of Church choirs for the annual Festival of the Church of England Sunday School Choirs, to take place at the Crystal Palace, on the afternoon, of Saturday, July 21st. A rehearsal will take place, at Albion Hall, London Wall, E.C., on the 9th of July, at 7.30 p.m., a ticket for which I will gladly forward to any gentleman who will forward me his name and address. The music consists of anthems, hymns, glees and part-songs, and will be issued to those taking part in the festival at a small charge.

Yours, &c.,
T. EARLE.

Passing Events.

Mozart's "Idomeneo," after a neglect of more than 20 years, has been revived at Munich.

There is a sense of relief in the practical retirement of Sir M. Costa from the conductorship of the Handel Festival.

The retirement of Mr. Cusins, a step to be regretted just now, puts another anxious burden upon the Philharmonic directors in the appointment of a successor.

A selection from Mendelssohn's "Hymn of Praise" will be sung at Christ Church, Clapham, on Sunday evening, the 24th inst., St. John the Baptist's Day, under the direction of Mr. William·Sewell.

Mr. Thomas and Dr. Damrosch, with their respective orchestras, have been, and are still, touring through America, giving admirable concerts, and playing a good deal of high-class music.

Mr. W. S. Hoyte, one of the few artists who make both organ and pianoforte their special study with marked success, announces an attractive recital, at which he will perform Bennett's "Maid of Orleans" sonata.

Mr. Henry Bird, at once an accomplished pianist and organist, gave his fifth annual concert at Collard's Rooms, on June 14th. The programme had, as two interesting features, a pianoforte Quartet in A minor by F. Kiel, and a similar work in E flat by Rheinberger.

The Dean and Chapter of York have announced their intention of advertising for candidates for the vacant organistship in their cathedral—a not very wise or necessary proceeding, because the question should surely be reduced to the examination of the names of a few men of repute who may choose to consider the appointment desirable.

The performance of the "Imperial" or "Nelson" Mass at a recent Richter concert was by no means a satisfactory undertaking, although the choir fairly claim praise for their department. The fantastic *tempi* the conductor chose to adopt was often utterly destructive to the character of the music, and the unfortunate departures from the composer's clear design in the use of the organ many critics cannot altogether overlook.

At Madame Antoinette Stirling's recent morning concert at St. James's Hall, a formidable array of singing stars appeared. The lady herself sang charmingly, though perhaps succeeding best in English music. Mr. Sims Reeves was in good voice. Mr. Santley also sang. The "Family Quartet" (the Coward family), gave much pleasure by their artistic performances. An interesting feature to musicians was the performance of Schumann's "Dichter-liebe" (1840), a cyclus of songs and a work of much character and beauty.

Selections from Mendelssohn's "Elijah" were given at St. John's Cathedral, Denver, Colorado, U. S., on May 25th. The Dean delivered a short synopsis of the intention of the oratorio, pointing out the salient features of the parts to be rendered. The soloists were Miss Callie Brinker, Miss Etta Butler, Mr. W. C. Nevin, Mr. Benj. Ives. Mr. Walter E. Hall was the organist, and Mr. Frank Damrosch, the son of Dr. Damrosch, acted as conductor. The chorus consisted of the Damrosch choral society and members of the cathedral choir. The skill of the organist and the many artistic features of the performance gave much pleasure.

The Querist.

QUERY.

ORCHESTRA v. PIANOFORTE.—Is it *necessary, advisable,* or *correct* to use a piano in a string band numbering twenty-two performers, unless the piano has a special and solo part?—W. T. J.

REPLY.

W. T. J.—The pianoforte should not be used save when a properly written part has been assigned to it by the composer. The instrument has but little sympathy with the orchestral functions, and is absolutely injurious to the development of a young orchestra, save when used with rare discretion.—EDITOR.

Service Lists.

FOURTH SUNDAY AFTER TRINITY.
JUNE 17th.

London.

ST. PAUL'S CATHEDRAL.—Morn.: Service, Te Deum and Benedictus, Garret in F; Introit, Lead us, Heavenly Father; Holy Communion, Weber in E flat. Even.: Service, Magnificat and Nunc Dimittis, Gadsby in C; Anthem, Whoso dwelleth under the defence (Martin).

WESTMINSTER ABBEY.—Morn.: Service, Turle in D; Continuation, Bridge in G. Even.: Service, Attwood in A; Anthem, Praise the Lord, O my soul (Mozart).

TEMPLE CHURCH.—Morn.: Service, Te Deum Laudamus, Cooke in G; Apostles' Creed, Harmonised Monotone; Anthem, Glory, honour, praise and power (Mozart). Even.: Service, Magnificat and Nunc Dimittis, Cooke in G; Apostles' Creed, Harmonized Monotone; Anthem, Ascribe unto the Lord (Travers).

LINCOLN'S INN CHAPEL.—Morn.: Service, Hatton in E; Kyrie, Steggall; Anthem, I beheld, and lo, a great multitude (Blow). Even: Service, Goss in A; Anthem, God came from Teman (Steggall).

CHRIST CHURCH, CLAPHAM.—Morn.: Service, Te Deum, Plain-song; Kyrie and Credo, Weber in E flat; Offertory Anthem, In the sight of the unwise (Ouseley); Sanctus, Benedictus, Agnus Dei, and Gloria in excelsis, Weber. Even.: Service, Magnificat and Nunc Dimittis, Smart in F; Anthem, What are these that are arrayed (Stainer).

FOUNDLING CHAPEL.—Morn.: Service, Barnby in E; Te Deum and Jubilate, Sullivan in D; Anthem, I was glad (Attwood). Aft.: Service, Dykes in F; Anthem, Blessed be Thou (Kent).

HOLY TRINITY, TULSE HILL.—Morn.: Chant Service. Even.: Service, Magnificat and Nunc Dimittis, Garrett in D; Anthem, Remember now my Creator (Steggall).

ST. MICHAEL'S, CORNHILL.—Morn.: Service, Te Deum and Jubilate, Thorne in C; Anthem, I have set God (Goldwin); Kyrie, Sullivan; Creed, Stainer in G. Even.: Service, Magnificat and Nunc Dimittis, Garrett in F; Anthem, Praise the Lord (Croft).

ST AUGUSTINE AND ST. FAITH, WATLING STREET.—Morn.: Service, Te Deum, Walmisley in F; Benedictus, Hopkins in F; Communion Service, Eyre in E flat; Offertory, Blessed are they (Tours). Even.: Service, Attwood in F; Anthem, How lovely are Thy dwellings (Spohr).

ST. PETER'S (EATON SQUARE).—Morn.: Service, Te Deum, Sergison in A. Evensong: Service, Eaton Faning in C; Anthem, O where shall wisdom (Boyce).

ST. MAGNUS, LONDON BRIDGE.—Morn.: Service, Opening Anthem, I will arise (Cecil); Te Deum and Jubilate, Travers in F; Kyrie, Mendelssohn. Even.: Service, Magnificat and Nunc Dimittis, Travers in F; Anthem, I was glad (Horsley).

ST. JAMES'S PRIVATE EPISCOPAL CHAPEL, SOUTHWARK.—Morn.: Service, Introit, O Lamb of God (Mozart); Communion Service, Garrett in F. Even.: Service, Garrett in F; Anthem, Rejoice in the Lord (Purcell).

ST. SAVIOUR'S, HOXTON.—Morn.: Service, Te Deum, Goss in F; Holy Communion; Kyrie, Credo, Sursum Corda, Sanctus, and Gloria in excelsis, Dykes in F. Even.: Service, Magnificat and Nunc Dimittis, Parry in D; Anthem, O taste and see (Goss).

ST. PAUL'S, AVENUE ROAD, SOUTH HAMPSTEAD.—Morn.: Service, Te Deum, Hopkins in G; Benedictus, Barnby; Kyrie, Merbecke; Offertory, Barnby; Credo, Sanctus, and Gloria in excelsis, Merbecke. Even.: Service, Magnificat and Nunc Dimittis, Smart in F; Anthem, He watching over Israel, from "Elijah" (Mendelssohn).

ST. SEPULCHRE'S, HOLBORN.—Morn: Service, Nares in F; Anthem, O taste and see (Goss). Even.: Service, Cooke in G; Anthem, Blessed be the God and Father (Wesley).

ST. PETER'S, LEIGHAM COURT ROAD, STREATHAM, S.W. —Morn.: Holy Eucharist, Purge me with hyssop (Chantwise); Introit, The Lord is my light (Chantwise); Mass, Osborne in E flat; Gradual, Be merciful (Chantwise); Offertory, If we have sown (Osborne). Even.: Service, Magnificat, Gadsby in C; Anthem, As pants the hart (Spohr).

ST. PAUL'S, BOW COMMON, E.—Morn.: Service, Te Deum and Benedictus, Chants; Holy Communion; Kyrie, Credo, Sanctus, Benedictus, and Gloria in excelsis, Garrett in D; Agnus Dei, Monk in C; Offertory, Calkin. Even.: Service, Magnificat and Nunc Dimittis, Parry in D; Anthem, What are these (Stainer).

ST. MARY BOLTONS, WEST BROMPTON, S.W.—Morn.: Service, Te Deum and Benedictus, Dykes in F; Holy Communion, Kyrie, Credo, Sanctus, Benedictus, Agnus Dei, and Gloria in excelsis, Monk in C; Offertory, Barnby. Even.: Service, Magnificat and Nunc Dimittis, Parry in D; Anthem, What are these (Stainer).

ST. MARGARET PATTENS, ROOD LANE, FENCHURCH STREET.—Morn.: Service, Te Deum and Benedictus, Tuckerman in F; Communion Service: Offertory Anthem, On Thee each living soul (Haydn); Kyrie, Credo, Sanctus, Benedictus, Agnus Dei and Gloria, Hummel in B flat. Even.: Service, Magnificat and Nunc Dimittis, Garrett in F; Anthem, I will mention (Sullivan).

ST. BARNABAS, MARYLEBONE.—Morn.: Service, Te Deum and Jubilate, Travers in F; Anthem, Turn thy face (Attwood); Kyrie and Nicene Creed, Travers in F. Even.: Service, Magnificat and Nunc Dimittis, Travers in F; Anthem, Be thou faithful; and See what love (Mendelssohn).

ST. PETER'S, VERE STREET, W.—Even.: Service, Magnificat and Nunc Dimittis, Gadsby in C; Anthem, Rejoice in the Lord alway (Purcell).

ALL SAINTS, MARGARET STREET.—Morn.: Service, Te Deum and Benedictus, Stainer; Holy Communion, Weber in G'; Offertory Anthem, From Thy love as a Father, from "Redemption" (Gounod). Even.: Service, Garrett in F; Anthem, Hear my prayer (Mendelssohn).

Country.

ST. ASAPH CATHEDRAL.—Morn.: Service, King in C; Anthem, Sweet is Thy mercy (Barnby). Even.: Service, The Litany; Anthem, The Lord is my light (Hiles).

ASHBURNE CHURCH, DERBYSHIRE — Morn.: Service, Steggall in G; Kyrie, Credo, and Gloria, Eyre in E flat. Even.: Service, Thackwray in C; Anthem, Blessed be the God and Father (Wesley).

BEDDINGTON CHURCH, SURREY.—Morn.: Service, Garrett in F; Introit, O what the joy and the glory; Communion Service, Garrett in F. Even.: Service, Garrett in F; Anthem, I will alway give thanks (Whitfeld).

BIRMINGHAM (ST. CYPRIAN'S, HAY MILLS).—Morn.: Service, Field in D; Anth. m. I waited for the Lord (Mendelssohn). Even.: Service, Clarke-Whitfeld in E; Anthem, Unto Thee have I cried (Elvey).

BIRMINGHAM (S. ALBAN THE MARTYR).—Morn.: Service, Holy Communion: Introit, Kyrie, Credo, Offertory, Sursum Corda, and Sanctus, Smart in F; Benedictus and Agnus Dei, Redman in F; Paternoster and Gloria, Smart in F. Evensong: Magnificat and Nunc Dimittis, Barnby in E.

BIRMINGHAM (S. PHILIP'S CHURCH). — Morn.: Service, Best, Chant Service; Holy Communion, Woodward in E flat. Evensong: Service, Hopkins in F; Anthem, O come, let us worship (Mendelssohn).

BRISTOL CATHEDRAL.—Morn.: Service, Garrett in D. Even.: Service, Garrett in D; Anthem, Hear my prayer (Kent).

CANTERBURY CATHEDRAL.—Morn.: Service, Barnby in B flat; Te Deum, Hopkins in B flat; Jubilate, Praise the Lord (Scott); Communion. Even.: Service, Roberts in G; Anthem, Ponder my words (Corfe).

CARLISLE CATHEDRAL.—Morn.: Service, Mendelssohn in A; Introit, Blessed is the man (Stainer); Kyrie, Mendelssohn; Nicene Creed, Harmonized Monotone. Even.: Service, Cooke in C; Anthem, Come, said a voice, and Behold the Lamb that has sacrificed (Spohr).

DONCASTER (PARISH CHURCH).—Morn.: Service, Boyce in C. Even.: Service, Ebdon in C; Anthem, O taste and see (Goss).

DUBLIN, ST. PATRICK'S (NATIONAL) CATHEDRAL.—Morn.: Service, Te Deum and Jubilate, Stanford in B flat; Communion, Kyrie, Creed, and Sanctus, Stanford in B flat ;.Anthem, Blessing, glory, wisdom (Bach). Even.: Service, Magnificat and Nunc Dimittis, Stanford in B flat; Anthems, O Lord, my God, hear Thou (Stewart); The Lord is a man of war (Handel).

EXETER CATHEDRAL.—Morn.: Service, King in C; Communion, Gilbert in E. Even.: Service, Hopkins in F; Anthem, O come hither (Crotch).

ELY CATHEDRAL.—Morn.: Service, Ouseley in C; Kyrie and Credo, Ouseley in G; Gloria, "Ely"; Anthem, I know that the Lord (Ouseley). Even.: Service, Ouseley in G; Anthem, As pants the hart (Spohr).

GLOUCESTER CATHEDRAL. — Morn.: Service, Te Deum and Jubilate, Mendelssohn in A; Kyrie and Creed, Turle in D; Anthem, In Thy sight (Ouseley). Aft.: Service, Walmisley in D; Anthem, Let us lift up (Wesley).

LLANDAFF CATHEDRAL.—Morn.: Service, Te Deum and Jubilate, Smart in F; Introit, I am the bread of life (Stainer); Holy Communion, Smart in F. Even.: Service, Anthem, Wherewithal shall a young man (Elvey).

LIVERPOOL CATHEDRAL.—Aft.: Service, Magnificat and Nunc Dimittis, Calkin in B flat; Anthem, Plead Thou my cause (Mozart).

LEEDS PARISH CHURCH.—Morn.: Service, Chants, 100, 101, 155; Anthem, O rest in the Lord (Mendelssohn); Kyrie and Creed, King in C. Even.: Service, Cooke in G; Anthem, The souls of the righteous (Nares).

LICHFIELD CATHEDRAL.—Morn.: Service, Calkin in B flat; Anthem, He that shall endure (Mendelssohn). Even: Service, Calkin in B flat; Anthem, What are these? (Stainer).

MANCHESTER CATHEDRAL.—Morn.: Service, Tours in F; Holy Communion, Tours in F; Anthem, As pants the hart (Spohr). Aft.: Service, Tours in F; Anthem, Remember now (Steggall).

MANCHESTER (ST. BENEDICT'S). — Morn.: Service, Kyrie, Credo, Sanctus, Benedictus, Agnus Dei, and Gloria in excelsis, Monk in C. Even.: Service, Magnificat and Nunc Dimittis, Wesley in F.

MANCHESTER (ST. JOHN BAPTIST, HULME).—Morn.: Service, Kyrie, Credo, Sanctus, and Gloria in excelsis, Dyke in F; Benedictus and Agnus Dei, Calkin in B flat. Even.: Service, Magnificat and Nunc Dimittis, Redhead.

PETERBOROUGH CATHEDRAL.—Morn.: Service, Goss in A; Anthem, As pants the hart (Spohr); Communion Service, Tours in F. Even.: Service, Fitzgerald in B flat; Anthem, Praise the Lord (Mozart).

SHEFFIELD PARISH CHURCH. — Morn.: Service, Kyrie, Sullivan in D. Even.: Service, Trimnell in D; Anthem, O rest in the Lord (Mendelssohn).

SHERBORNE ABBEY.—Morn.: Service, Te Deum, Chants; Kyrie, Howells; Offertories, Barnby. Even.: Service, Anthem, O Lord the protector (Corfe).

SOUTHAMPTON (ST. MARY'S CHURCH).—Morn.: Service, Te Deum and Benedictus, Woodward in E flat; Communion Service: Introit, They that put their trust (Macfarren); Service, Woodward in E flat; Offertory, Barnby; Paternoster, Field. Even.: Service, Magnificat and Nunc Dimittis, Woodward in E flat; Apostles' Creed, Harmonized Monotone; Anthem, Blessed be the God (Wesley).

WELLS CATHEDRAL.—Morn.: Service, Rogers in G; Introit, Behold, to obey (Macfarren); Kyrie, Browne in G. Even.: Service, King in A; Anthem, O Lord my God (Nares).

. Post-cards must be sent to the Editor, 6, Argyle Square, W.C., by Wednesday. Lists are frequently omitted in consequence of not being received in time.

NEWSPAPERS sent should have distinct marks opposite to the matter to which attention is required.

NOTICE.—All communications intended for the Editor are to be sent to his private address. Business communications to be addressed to 185, Fleet Street, E.C.

[The attention of the several Organists is called to the favour they confer upon their brother musicians by forwarding their notices regularly: this column of the paper is much valued as an index to what is going on in the choice of cathedral music, so much so that intermissions constantly give rise to remonstrance. Lists should be sent in a week in advance if possible.—ED. Mus. Stand.]

Printed for the Proprietor by BOWDEN, HUDSON & Co., at 21, Red Lion Street, Holborn, London, W.C.; and Published by WILLIAM REEVES, at the Office, 185, Fleet Street, E.C. West End Agents:—WEEKES & CO., 14, Hanover Street, Regent Street, W. Subscriptions and Advertisements received either by the Publisher or West End Agents.—*Communications for the EDITOR are to be forwarded to his private address, 6, Argyle Square, W.C.*
SATURDAY, JUNE 16, 1883.—*Entered at the General Post Office as a Newspaper.*

The MUSICAL STANDARD

A NEWSPAPER FOR MUSICIANS PROFESSIONAL AND AMATEUR

No. 986. Vol. XXIV. FOURTH SERIES.   SATURDAY, JUNE 23, 1883.   WEEKLY: PRICE 3D.

Musical Intelligence.

THE HANDEL FESTIVAL AT THE CRYSTAL PALACE.

Beautiful and unique as the Crystal Palace is, with all its lovely surroundings; with its countless attractions within the building; with its large and efficient staff of professors and teachers in arts and science, and with its powerful influence, exerted on behalf of the best possible music; the bare fact of its being able only to keep its head just above water, financially, is not an agreeable one to digest, and reflects not a little on our refined and æsthetic age. The shareholders of the Crystal Palace may, however, have this consolation, that the work carried on there is bearing fruit, the result of which will have a most refining influence on their children and others. With regard to music, it has for nearly a generation been associated with our greatest composers, several of whom have found an English home there, and nowhere in the world has Handel's music been given with such magnificence and grandeur. Such performances as those given at the Handel festival are impressive in the highest sense, and notwithstanding the much talked of "new departure" from antiquated paths, we become more than ever devoted to the grand old master, whose works were often feebly and inadequately interpreted in the days of our youth. But on the other hand it is to be regretted that this very perfection makes us less tolerant of more humble attempts in Handel's music, and the introduction of noisy brass bands in our villages, with harmoniums in our village churches superseding the old-fashioned strings and reeds, has, alas! caused Handel's music to become quite a thing of the past in many places where he was once thoroughly enjoyed. Formerly the greatest achievement of a country choir was to be able to prepare a few of Handel's songs and choruses, for what was called the "charity sermon," and Handel himself must have heard and encouraged humble efforts of this kind, as the following true anecdote will show :—Going along a country road one evening, he overtook an aged rustic, with a 'cello under his arm, and asked him where he was going with his instrument. "I'm going, sir to practise Mr. Handel's music, for next charity sermon." Handel : "Don't you find his music rather tough, especially when you get much among the sharps and flats ?" Rustic : "Well, sir, some on it is tough enough ; but we generally stick to his easy pieces, and when we get to an out-of-the-way thing, with a many sharps or flats, we follow Jack the blacksmith's rule." Handel : "Ah, and what's that ?" Rustic, emphatically : "Why, sir, *he leaves 'em all out, and so do we.*" Handel laughed heartily, but warmly urged the old man for the future to steer clear of hard keys and frequent accidentals.

The history of Handel's compositions is well known to all musicians, but his fine example as a man can never be sufficiently estimated. Tortured by his frequent failures, by bitter persecution and bodily anguish, he suddenly became inspired with a noble desire to devote himself entirely to the production of grander works than his former ones, thereby soothing his afflictions, and procuring fame to a greater extent than he could ever have anticipated. But fame was the result of his magnificent labours, not the object of them. His desire, as he himself tells us, was to compose music, "not merely for the entertainment of his hearers, but to make them better." How grand and touching, therefore, to see this honest, truth-telling, God-fearing man, in the midst of adversity, nobly struggling at first to obtain a hearing for those grand conceptions which were destined to become as immortal as the works of Homer or Shakespeare. "It is always interesting," writes Mr. Besant, in one of his new works, "to read in the biographies of writers, great or small, how at the outset the candidate for glory is invariably received with a most prodigious quantity of cuffs, *coups de pied,* thwacks, black eyes, snubs, disgraces, disappointments, down knockings, out kickings, rebuffs, rudenesses, broken promises, prejudices, cheats, robberies, rejections, woundings of vanity, pullings down of pride, dampings of ambition, and so forth. The most curious thing is that all these kicks seem in the long run to be good for a man. They teach him, I believe, to feel for other people, and so help him to get a hold of them. And presently his wounds heal up, and you would never think, to see him, now so

magnificent and triumphant, that he was once a mere down-trodden, squirming worm. Behold him ! He leadeth the people by the ear, just as in old days they used to lead their captives by a hook in the nose, or as all-conquering Venus still drags her prisoners by a single hair."

One of the great features of Handel's oratorios, as differing from other sacred music of those days, was their preponderance in the way of choruses ; he also greatly augmented the instrumentation, and it is amusing to find that he is often accused of excess and violence in his powerful choral combinations, and reproached with having exaggerated the orchestra ; but no one ever dreamt of his impoverishing the vocal parts for the mere sake of orchestral effects, as some of our recent composers are doing. This is very much like making the instruments represent the statue, and the voices the pedestal ; but as this question would occupy too much space if properly dealt with, I hasten to speak of

THE GRAND REHEARSAL.

The glowing sky with which we had become so familiar of late did not greet the visitors who, on the morning of the rehearsal, poured into the Crystal Palace, and the graceful summer costumes of the ladies consequently did not appear to so great advantage, especially when in a short time the rain came pouring down and so cooled the air, that on leaving the Palace those wise persons who had brought warm wraps were only too glad to make use of them. Some 6,000 persons more were present than on the corresponding day in 1880, and the scene, as witnessed from the galleries, was a very impressive one. The thousands of human beings in the orchestra, all more or less skilled musicians ; the still larger number assembled in the nave, were all gathered together for one purpose, and that to honour the memory and to listen to the works of a man who died more than a century ago, and who, until past the middle age of life, was comparatively little appreciated by his contemporaries. The large audience was anxiously waiting to give Sir Michael Costa a hearty greeting, when it became generally known that he was too ill to undertake the weighty responsibility of the festival ; but as the services of Mr. Manns, the able conductor of the Crystal Palace concerts, were available, no misgivings were felt as to the success of the undertaking. Doubtless the choir and orchestra who have so long enjoyed the advantage of Sir Michael's steady hand and unfailing tact, felt a slight pang of regret, but that was soon dispelled by their successful achievements in what may be called the test choruses ; indeed, one of the most complicated, "Wretched lovers," was never better sung or more thoroughly enjoyed. The solos were entrusted to Mdme. Valleria, Mdme. Trebelli, Mdme. Patey, Mr. E. Lloyd, Mr. Maas, Mr. Barton McGuckin, and Mr. Santley,—Mdme. Albani, the prima donna, reserving herself for the "Messiah." Of course at a rehearsal criticism would be in bad taste, but the above names are a guarantee that the solo singing was quite worthy of the occasion.

One of the ladies was just a little disappointing in her rendering of one of the songs which Mdme. Adelina Patti sings so exquisitely, and comparisons, though forbidden, were very naturally made ; but the voice, as we know, is a most delicate organ, and is not always equal to the demands made upon it.

THE "MESSIAH."

Perhaps in some respects the "Messiah" is the most impressive performance of the whole festival, inasmuch as the subject of it transcends all others, and in these days, when infidelity is but too common, it is a sight one may well be thankful for, to behold thousands of persons listening with rapt attention to a work whose subject is the sum and substance of the Christian religion.

Seldom have the beautiful gardens of the Crystal Palace appeared more lovely than on Monday last—the shrubs and flowers, all refreshed by the rain of last week, so welcome after the long drought that in this neighbourhood preceded it. The sun for the most part shone brightly, and the occasional clouds tempered the heat that might otherwise have been too great. Most delightful was it during the interval, to enjoy the air and the extensive view from the balcony, to those especially who, coming from the crowded cities of our busy nation, seldom have time or opportunity to enjoy a view such as this. Within the Palace everything appeared admirably arranged, and, assisted by the courteous officials, both audience and performers, in spite of the crowd, made their way to their seats with but little difficulty. The enthusiasm with which the National Anthem was received must have been gratifying to those members of the royal family who honoured the performance by their presence. Immediately at its close, Mdme. Trebelli, Mr. Maas, and Signor Foli entered, and the overture began.

The "Messiah," which was at first rejected in London, April 12th, 1741, and afterwards was received at Dublin, and became the corner-stone of Handel's fame, was on no occasion in the history of the Handel festival more grandly performed than on Monday last. To speak of the different numbers in detail, both solos and choruses, with a string of adjectives, would occupy too much space, and perhaps savour too much of the penny local paper; I will, therefore, content myself by saying that the effect produced by the choir in the jubilant choruses: "For unto us," "Lift up your heads," the "Hallelujah," and "Worthy is the Lamb," with its "Amen," was grand and overwhelming; that in contrast, the pathetic choruses, "Behold the Lamb of God," and "Surely he hath borne our griefs," produced an impression of a more deep and solemn character; and that in none of the other choruses was there a single hitch to call for remark.

The efforts of the eminent soloists were also crowned with success, and it was interesting to notice the sympathy shown by each division of the choir to the vocalist whose compass of voice was similar to their own, Mdme. Trebelli and Mdme. Patey being the favourites of the altos, whilst Signor Foli and Mr. Santley were much applauded by the basses, and so on throughout. The greatest impression of all was made by Mdme. Albani's chaste and fervent interpretation of "I know that my Redeemer liveth," the effect being deeply and unanimously felt by the entire choir and audience.

The *tempo* of Mr. Manns was, taken as a whole, in strict accordance with Handelian traditions; two exceptions, however, were noticeable. The chorus, "And with His stripes"—one that cannot be hurried with impunity —was taken faster than usual; and the tenor solo, "But Thou didst not leave," suffered from the same cause, but in this case the alteration may possibly have been suggested by Mr. Maas, who sang the tenor part throughout, as Mdme. Albani did the soprano. Mdme. Trebelli and Signor Foli were succeeded in the second part by Mdme. Patey and Mr. Santley.

The organ, at which Mr. Willing ably presided, was heard to great advantage, having been entirely reconstructed and improved since the last festival. Of the admirable performance of the orchestra it is needless to speak, and my last words must be of congratulation to Mr. Manns, who conducted with such readiness and efficiency, that, though the absence of Sir Michael Costa was regretted, his presence could have added nothing to the perfection of this grand performance.　　R. S.

P.S.—The Selection day was a great success, but details cannot be given until next week.

RICHTER CONCERTS.

Last Monday, Herr Richter and his magnificent orchestra fairly surpassed even their own high standard of excellence; consequently expressions of approval, more fervent and prolonged than those which usually reward their ever-warmly appreciated efforts, proceeded from their highly critical audience. The overture to Tannhauser, as originally written, and as it must ever remain for concert-room purposes, headed the programme, and called forth an enthusiasm which was little short of an ovation; an enthusiasm which, once aroused, scarcely grew less throughout the evening. With this overture, perhaps the best known of Wagner's writings, the performers are, of course, thoroughly at home, and at one with their conductor; but even taking these facts into consideration, there remains something so unusually excellent in the performance, as to render it a memorable one. The return of the Pilgrim's Chant, above all, was given in a manner that Wagner himself must have pronounced perfect, and that vividly brought before the mind's eye his own picture of the scene :—"Day at length begins to dawn, and the song of the returning pilgrims is heard in the distance. As their song draws nearer, and day succeeds to night, that whirring and murmuring in the air, which but just now sounded to us like the horrible wail of the damned, gives way to more joyful strains, till

at last, when the sun has risen in all its splendour, and the pilgrims' song with mighty inspiration proclaims to the world and to all that is and lives, salvation won, its surging sound swells into a rapturous torrent of sublime ecstasy."

"Perfection," however, is but a relative term, or one might be tempted to say of such a performance as this, "we can no further go." But all true artists have an unattainable goal, be they creators or interpreters. Like Mazeppa and his steed :—

> "Dans le désert immense,
> Dans l'horizon sans fin qui toujours recommence,
> Ils se plongent."

PROGRAMME.

Overture, "Tannhaeuser"......................	Wagner.
Concerto in A minor, Op. 129, for Violoncello and Orchestra.............................	Schumann.
Violoncello, Herr Hausmann.	
Preislied, "Die Meistersinger"................	Wagner.
Mr. Edward Lloyd.	
Symphonic Poem, "Mazeppa"...................	Liszt.
Symphony, No. 2, in D	Brahms.

Schumann's concerto is more in the style of his beautiful sonatas for violin and piano, than of his symphonies, or his pianoforte works. The three movements of which it consists, follow each other without pause, and abound in expressions characteristic of their author; though, judged as a whole, the concerto cannot be said to rank among Schumann's most genial productions. Herr Hausmann has already established his position as an artist of the first rank. He was twice recalled at the conclusion of his difficult and grateful (though not so considered by Sir G. Grove), task. A similar compliment awaited Mr. Edward Lloyd for his rendering (in English !) of Walther's Prieslied. Mr. Corder had a hopeless task in hand when he undertook to re-produce this wild effusion in matter-of-fact English. There is something irresistibly ludicrous about the lines :—

> "By rugged way
> My feet did stray
> Towards a mountain,
> Where a fountain
> Enslaved me with its sound."

and

> "She stood beside me,
> Who shall my bride be ?" &c.

It is doubtful whether Walther would have obtained the prize if, like Mr. Lloyd, he had delivered his address in English.

Thanks to Mr. Bache, and Mr. Manns, Liszt's "Mazeppa" is not altogether unknown to us. Like Schumann's concerto, which preceded it, it consists of three movements; the first and last in quick time, and the second slow; but in the case of Liszt the movements are more closely linked, and each is more absolutely and indivisibly a part of the other. One may hope that it is not necessary now to defend "music with a poetic basis," or to renew the contest of some years ago, for or against so called "pure music;" but "C. A. B." says a few words on the subject, wisely and well, in his analysis of "Mazeppa."

The term, "Symphonic Poem," it will be remembered, is of Liszt's creation; and, like his other invention, the Rhapsody, it has been found so happy, that composers in abundance have adopted it as applicable to their own writings.

Wagner, in his warm-hearted criticism of these "Symphonic Poems," insists on their most powerful characteristic; which is, their extreme melodiousness. This characteristic, he says, cannot fail to secure for them a speedy popularity with the great mass of musicians. Wagner may, or may not, be right in his conclusion (though Liszt has to fight every inch of ground with the *critics*); but he is certainly right in his main fact. Liszt's melodies are of the most downright, straightforward, description : melodies which, whatever we may think of them, are living realities, that take their allotted place fearlessly, and with unadorned simplicity.

An amusing misprint crept into the earlier advertisements of this concert, and remained unaltered throughout in the announcements posted at St. James's Hall. Instead of Brahms's second symphony, the printer promised us "Beethoven's symphony, No. 2, in D." As Beethoven's second symphony, like Brahms's, happens to be in D, and as the opus number was not given, the announcement passed unchallenged; though some of us probably wondered that Herr Richter chose to give unpromised works, when so many promises for the season remained unfulfilled.

Especial care had evidently been bestowed on this symphony, and "Mazeppa" in rehearsing, and the result was all that the most exacting could desire. It is necessary again to raise a protest against Sir G. Grove's misleading remarks (reprinted from a Crystal Palace programme), that preface his analysis of this symphony. Once more then, be it said, that Schumann did not seriously "fear that the name of symphony" would in the future belong only to history at the very moment when he was reviewing a new symphony with enthusiastic admiration ; and that we have to thank a publisher (not an uncommon occurrence) for the title, " Concert sans orchestra" applied to Schumann's Op. 14, and not the wish even, far less a settled theory, of the author.

B. F. WYATT-SMITH.

THE HANDEL SOCIETY.

This society was established last year by Mrs. Ellicott, wife of the Bishop of Gloucester and Bristol ; she is a highly accomplished musician, and boasts of a daughter who composes very clever and agreeable songs for the chamber. A first concert was held by the society on June 14th, when the director, Mr. Docker, performed a selection from "Belshazzar"; a selection from the "Water Music"; Gluck's overture to "Iphigenia in Aulis," and (unaccompanied) part-songs of Brahms. "Belshazzar" bears the date of A.D. 1745, four years after "The Messiah" (1741), and one before "Judas Maccabeus" (1746). In "Belshazzar" Miss Ellicott sustained the part of Nitocris, alternately with Miss May Moon ; Miss Wakefield enacted Cyrus ; Mr. Harper Kearton, Belshazzar ; and the Hon. Spencer G. Lyttleton, Daniel. Miss Ellicott proved her proficiency as a vocalist, and was much applauded. Miss May suffered from a cold. Miss Wakefield excelled, and Mr. Kearton is known as a professional, therefore bound so to do. The choruses were finely sung, but how long the programme ! The oratorio did not come to an end until nearly eleven o'clock. The most impressive choruses were "Recall, O King, thy rash command" (sung by the Jews), and "By slow degrees the wrath of God." Miss Wakefield's best achievement was in the air "O God of truth," and Mr. Lyttleton scored a point in the "interpretation" recitative of Daniel the Seer. The German lieder were delicately rendered. The lateness of the hour prevented many of the audience from waiting to hear the beautiful "Water Music." Why will the projectors of concerts thus " spoil sport " ? People will not sit up half the night even for Handel ! Most concerts are too long by a third at least.

THE COLOGNE CHOIR.

The Cologne Choir should be heard by all admirers of genuine vocal music. Six concerts have already taken place. The ensemble and balance of tone are perfect. The tenors have been complained of as unduly prominent, but they are only too powerful in the episodial quartets, not in the choruses ; the tenor voices are pure, fresh, and penetrating ; the basses deep and sonorous. A baritone soloist came out well in "D'Hamkehr." Three pieces were encored on June 15th, viz., Schubert's "Der Entfernten," and Veit's "Schön-Rohtraut." Some delicious effects of piano were heard in the "Old Dutch Song" of Kremser (also encored). Herr W. Hoss played violin solos of Bruch and Brahms-Joachim ; and with Fräulein Johanna Hesse, two movements from a sonata of Gade in D minor.

On Saturday evening M. de Lange, the able conductor of the choir, played a Toccata of Bach for the organ in splendid style, and on Monday Mdlle. Heimlicher introduced some pianoforte pieces on a very stiff "Steinway," whereby the Polonaise which follows Chopin's "Andante Spianato" suffered loss. An air of Pergolesi and Rubinstein's "Valse Caprice" were also played by this lady.

MR. CHARLES HALLE'S CHAMBER CONCERTS.

These go on swimmingly. At the soirée of June 15th, Spohr's string quartet in E minor was performed, and Fibich's pianoforte quartet in the same key repeated by desire. The pianoforte solos were Beethoven's "Rondo à Capriccio" in G, Op. 129, and the Fantasia, Op. 77. Last (Friday) evening Schumann's "Humoreske" in B flat was set down for Mr. Hallé as solo ; the concerted works were Dvorak's string quartet in E flat, Op, 71, and Haydn's pianoforte trio in E flat, Op, 12.

ROYAL ITALIAN OPERA.

A morning performance of "Carmen" took place on Saturday, June 16th, and in the evening Mdme. Adelina Patti made her rentrée for the season, with splendid success, in our old friend "Il Barbiere di Siviglia." The voice is in fine condition, and the execution, as ever, unrivalled. The "Lesson Scene" of Act 2, the grande situation of the opera, was made a medium for the introduction of the florid air from "Ernani," "Ernani involami," one of Titiens' triumphant achievements, and the very poor English ditty, "Home, sweet home," quite out of place at the Italian Opera, and, weighed on its own abstract merits, worthless, because intrinsically vapid, common-place, and indeed almost vulgar. The sentiment, "There's no place like home" (not always true by the way), of course appeals to the soft brains and flabby hearts of ordinary humanity. Signor Nicolini is not thought to have made a very brilliant Almaviva on this occasion. Signor Cotogni and Signor De Reszke completed the caste as Figaro and Bartholo. The Prince and Princess of Wales were present. Mdme. Patti appeared on Tuesday in Verdi's naughty opera "La Traviata." A. M.

MR. CHARLES GARDNER'S MATINEE.

Mr. Charles Gardner gave a matinée at the Prince's Hall, on Monday last. The vocalists were Miss Mary Davies, Mdlle. Etty, Miss Marian McKenzie, Mr. Arthur Thompson, and Mr. W. H. Cummings. M. Albert contributed a violoncello solo, and joined Mr. Gardner and Mr. Egerton in Beethoven's Trio, Op. 11, for piano, clarionet, and violoncello. Mr. Gardner played several solos with finish, and was ably assisted by Miss Florence May in duets for two pianofortes. A noteworthy feature of the concert was the production for the first time in England, of Mendelssohn's second Duet, Op. 114, for clarinet and corno di bassetto. Mr. Egerton and Mr. Maycock gained well earned applause for their artistic rendering of this, a work of singular interest, originally written for two celebrated performers on these two of Mozart's favourite instruments. Mr. C. E. Stephens, Mr. H. Deacon, and Signor Randegger assisted with the accompaniments in their usual efficient manner.—F. E. T.

MISS AGNES BARTLETT'S RECITAL.

This was given on June 15th at the Alexandra Hall, Blackheath. The young lady hails from the Dresden Conservatorium. She possesses an excellent technique, and a charming touch. Her first piece was Beethoven's Sonata in C sharp minor, Op. 27. The melancholy of the adagio, the grace of the scherzo and the fire of the finale were admirably expressed by Miss Bartlett. Mendelssohn's fine Prelude and Fugue in E minor was rendered with much breadth and power. Three of Chopin's Etudes, and several other works of his, including the Preludes in C and G, displayed Miss Bartlett's poetical feeling to advantage, and the Ballade in A flat was given with admirable finish, light, and shade. A Polonaise by Liszt was played with much brilliancy and fire, and Miss Bartlett claims, for her excellent and varied performances, a high place in the list of our more promising pianists. Miss Carlotta Elliott, though suffering from a cold, sang several songs in an artistic manner.

MR. AND MRS. GEORGE HENSCHEL'S VOCAL RECITAL.

Mr. and Mrs. George Henschel's vocal recital at St. James's Hall on Saturday, 16th inst., was a really musical treat ; indeed, it was quite a bonne-bouche for the connoisseur. The rendering of the programme was as felicitous as it was rare. Mr. Henschel's versatility is surprising ; he is a composer, conductor, singer, and last, but not least, a pianist. Indeed, in the first and last of these qualities, he will appear at the Richter concert on Monday night next, where he will perform a pianoforte concerto of his own composition. Mrs. Henschel has undoubtedly made great progress since her last début in the metropolis.

I cannot help thinking that a repetition of such a charming concert would meet with general approbation.

FERDINAND PRAEGER.

ST. CECILIA SOCIETY.

The fourth concert was given on June 14th at St. James's Hall. It would be difficult to name a better programme of the kind. Marcello's Psalm "Jehovah's Power," came first with organ accompaniment, and served to display a good body of pure, fresh, well trained female voices. The most important feature of the scheme was Pergolesi's "Stabat Mater." This work had been re-scored by Mr. Lawson for strings (in which he followed pretty closely the composer's own parts), and organ (which was treated freely, and not from the figured bass so much as the means of supplying a certain amount of wind tone-colour). The lovely melodies, quaint grace, and inexhaustible power of the composer in the invention of detail even with but limited executive means, were felt and enjoyed. The performance reflected high credit upon Mr. M. L. Lawson the able conductor and his highly intelligent executants. It did, indeed, seem strange, to see and hear the ladies' orchestra, playing with remarkable skill, generally good intonation and reliable firmness. The solos were expressively and artistically rendered by Miss Edith Phillips (a rising soprano of excellent gifts), Miss Emily Lawson, Miss Howell (a young lady with an excellent contralto voice), etc. The chorus singing was throughout of an admirable character ; and the fine old poetical work proved most attractive, and thanks are due to the society for its presentation. The second part opened with Bach's F minor Concerto for pianoforte and strings. The solo part was neatly executed and artistically expressed by Miss Mary Carmichael. Another feature of special interest was a solo and chorus from C. V. Stanford's "Veiled Prophet," a movement of much variety, well-sustained interest, and musicianly workmanship. The solo part was gracefully sung by Miss Everett Green, to whom the society is much indebted for a great deal of earnest, well directed labour as Hon. Secretary. This performance did not fail to create a desire for a hearing of the complete opera. Wuërst's "Russian Suite" for violin, solo, and strings, was, on the whole, piquantly and prettily played. Miss Amy Hickling sustained the solo violin part, with a pure tone and graceful style. Some short excerpts from Mr. Lawson's music to "The Tale of Troy" for soli voices and chorus, were very tuneful, graceful, and expressive. Several songs, well sung by Mr. Probert, varied the programme, which closed with two of Lachner's part-songs. Miss Mary Carmichael was the painstaking pianoforte accompanist, Mr. E. H. Turpin was the organist and Mr. Lawson occupied his usual post as conductor. A large, and evidently much pleased audience attended the performance.

NEWCASTLE-ON-TYNE.

A Dramatic and Choral Amateur Festival in aid of the Newcastle fund of the Royal College of Music has been recently held at the Tyne Theatre. On Wednesday and Thursday nights Sophocles' "Antigone," with Mendelssohn's music, was given ; on Friday night dramatic recitals by Mrs. Scott-Siddons, with music by a choir, and on Saturday night, June 16th Sullivan's operetta "Cox and Box," and Byron's comedy "Old Soldiers," were performed by members of the Northumberland Amateur Dramatic Club.

The performance of Sophocles' "Antigone" with Mendelssohn's music may be considered as generally satisfactory. The chorus, of upwards of sixty performers, was led by Mr. James Dick, and the orchestra, consisting mostly of professional players from Manchester, Newcastle, and the district, was under the painstaking conductorship of Mr. W. Rea. The fine singing of the choir, was, perhaps, the principal feature of the performances, and on Thursday night the singers received well-merited encores for "O Eros" and "Hymn to Bacchus," which were sung with fine effect. The playing of the orchestra was on the whole very satisfactory, but occasionally too loud in the accompaniments, and in some of the piano passages in the overtures, and the first two movements from the Italian Symphony, by Mendelssohn, performed before and between the parts of the tragedy.

The part of Antigone was taken by Mrs. Scott-Siddons, and that of Creon by Mr. R. W. Younge, the energetic manager of the Tyne Theatre. The other parts of the tragedy were rendered by amateur performers. The

houses have not been so well filled as they ought to have been, considering the efficient way in which the drama was put before the public ; but, somehow, every scheme of furthering the fund in aid of the Royal College of Music has only received an inadequate support here. The lack of interest evinced in the matter by the public may possibly arise from h .ving not a single representative from Newcastle, nor even the whole of Northumberland and Durham, among the successful candidates who gained scholarships of the Royal College of Music.

Messrs. Howard and Wyndham are the new managers of the Theatre Royal, and Mr. W. H. Bachelor, a musician of ability, the new musical director of the establishment. A few weeks ago Miss Lila Clay, the clever lady conductor, and her company of ladies performed with great success the musical oddity, "An Adamless Eden."

Last week "H.M.S Pinafore," the most popular work by Messrs. Gilbert and Sullivan, proved to be as attractive as ever, for it drew good houses, notwithstanding Sophocles' "Antigone" was performed at the Tyne Theatre. The principal characters by Miss Rivers (Josephine), Miss M. Stavart (Buttercup), and Henry Walsham (Rackstraw), were well rendered, and the singing of the choruses excellent. The cast altogether was exceptionally strong.　　　　　　　　　　　　H. W.

The *Newcastle Daily Journal* says : "Antigone" was first heard in this country on Thursday, January 2nd, 1845, at the "Old" Covent Garden Theatre, under the direction of Sir (then Mr.) George A. Macfarren. On this occasion, it is said, Mendelssohn wrote a highly complimentary letter to Mr. Macfarren acknowledging and thanking him for his services. The work has been but rarely heard in this country since the occasion of which we have been speaking, the most notable performances, probably, being those which took place at the Crystal Palace on December 14th, 1875, and at the Theatre Royal, Newcastle-on-Tyne, in 1876.

The same journal, speaking of the second performance, observes : Excellent as was the performance of "Antigone" at the Tyne Theatre, that of last night may be said to have surpassed it. The artists—professional and amateur—engaged in the performance appeared one and all to exert themselves to their utmost to make the representation as perfect as possible, the result being that none but a pessimist could, with any degree of fairness, discover a fault worth mentioning. The choruses were rendered in a manner even more effective than upon the previous occasion of their performance. "O Eros" and the "Invocation to Bacchus" were so finely sung that they were re-demanded in a most unmistakable manner, and had to be repeated. It would be a great pity to allow so fine a choir of male voices to quietly disperse, now that the "Antigone" performances are over.

The orchestra, led by Mr. J. H. Beers, gave a splendid performance of Mendelssohn's fine orchestration. In addition to the music of "Antigone," the band also played with excellent effect the march from Gounod's "La Reine de Saba," the overture to Mozart's "Die Zauberflote," and Mendelssohn's overture to "Athalie." Mr. James Dick, as leader of the chorus, sang exceedingly well ; and Messrs. Idle and Lohmeyer sang their parts with capital effect. To Mr. Dick a large share of the success of the festival is due ; for he has laboured incessantly in its cause. Mr. Rea, who conducted the performance, performed his arduous duties as perhaps few could have done. It may be said that the whole of the success of the actual performance depended upon him ; but he has proved himself in the past, and it is to be hoped will yet again and again prove himself, capable of guiding to a successful issue many a great undertaking.

VARIOUS CONCERTS.

Herr S. Lehmeyer held his annual concert on June 12th, when he played Chopin's Ballade, Op. 47, a Fugue of Bach, and Handel's Variations in E major, falsely ascribed to a mythical "blacksmith," who did *not* live at Edgware, although the impudent impostor's tombstone, in Whitchurch Yard, still asserts the falsehood. Some of Herr Lehmeyer's pupils played with proficiency, to wit : Miss E. D'Egville, Miss Furness, Mr. G. Sumpter, and Miss Elcock. The last-named lady joined Herr Lehmeyer in Erkel's "Grande Marthe Hongroise."

Mr. W. G. Cusins, whose retirement from the Philharmonic Society as conductor is felt to be a great loss, held a *matinée* on June 8th at St. James's Hall. Hummel's superb Septet in D minor, for pianoforte, wood-wind, and strings, headed the scheme, and was very welcome, as the work could never, or only very seldom be heard, except at the "Grande Matinée" of Mr. Ella's "Musical Union," which has unfortunately ceased to exist. Mr. Cusins executed the pianoforte part of the Septet with great efficiency; he afterwards played J. S. Bach's grand Fantasia and Fugue in G minor (arranged by Liszt), and Chopin's "Andante Spianato and Polonaise," also Thalberg's Fantasia on "Mosé." Part of the "Kreutzer" sonata was played by Mr. Cusins, with Mdlle. Levallois as violinist. Mdme. Marie Roze sang deliciously Gluck's "Divinités du Styx," and with Mdme. Trebelli, the pretty duet from "Mefistofeles," "Canta, o Sirena." Mdme. Trebelli chose for solo an air of Bizet's, and Mdme. Sembrich Délibes' "Air de la Clochette" (first time in England). Mdlle. Levallois, whose *avenir* (as foreseen by Mdme. Viard-Louis) is ensured, played a violin piece of Von Wieniawski with *éclat*. The assistant artists in Hummel's Septet were Messrs. Svendsen, Lebon, Paersch, Blagrove, Heygesi, and Progratzky.

At a quiet "reception," held by the Rev. Alfonso and Mrs. Matthey on the afternoon of June 13th, in Warwick Gardens, Kensington, several pianists of note were present, viz., Mr. Eugène Wagner, Mdme. Viard Louis, Miss M. Cronin, Mr. J. B. Bonawitz, &c. M. Wagner played some of his own pleasing compositions, and Miss Cronin delighted the assembly so much with her readings of Chopin (the "Andante Spianato" especially), that she was detained, perforce, at the pianoforte, a "fine grand iron drawing-room" of Messrs. Collard and Collard. Miss Helen Matthey repeated her careful and correct version of Schumann's "Faschingsschwank aus Wien," so much admired by professors and "lay people" at Mr. Aguilar's recital on April 23rd. The three Misses Matthey sang together some very pretty German and French part-songs. Mr. W. G. Cusins was unable to be present from the pressure of "Palace" and other engagements. Mrs. Meadows-White, the composer of "The Ode to the Passions," was one of the guests, with her husband, Mr. Meadows-White, Q.C.

Mr. Harvey Löhr held his annual *soirée* on June 13th. He conducted with ability Götz's pianoforte trio in G minor, Op. 1, and played Schumann's "Faschingsschwank" in B flat with Herr A. Hummer. M. Lohr played Beethoven's sonata in F, Op. 24. M. Hummer won a *bis* for a Gavotte of Franz Ries in G, and Mr. W. E. Whitehouse played M. Lohr's Ballade for violoncello, "Liebes-Geständniss."

Mdlle. Victoria Bunsen gave a grand "Scandinavian" concert on Tuesday afternoon at Portman House, Portman Square, W., which, although a palatial mansion, the writer was only able to find after fifty inquiries, for even the flunkeys of houses in the square did not know the house by name, nor the carriage-drivers either. Gross ignorance of topography marks the English, alike in town and country! Miss De Bunsen sang most splendidly, and *con amore*, as a fair Swede should do, several Scandinavian airs, notably, "The ocean's lovely maiden," a Swedish "Dancing Song," and "Little Ole," whereof (*pace* Herr Andersen), the words are supremely silly. Miss De Bunsen's rich lower notes came out well. Miss Felicia De Bunsen accompanied her sister on a grand Broadwood, on which Mr. W. G. Cusins afterwards played a Notturne of Chopin and his own Valse in F flat with good effect. Many more national ditties were sung by other artists. Mdme. Marie Roze, radiant and lovely, sang with *éclat* a grand air from Poniatowski's *Pierre de Medicis*, "Doux rêve de ma vie" in E flat and D flat, with a range from low D to B flat in alt. The *cadenza* was a splendid display of vocalisation, and a recall ensued. Part of Niel Gade's pianoforte trio in F, Op. 42, was performed by Miss Felicia De Bunsen, Herr W. Hess, and Herr Hollman. Herr Hess and his sister, Mdlle. Johanna Hess (who has recently appeared at the Cologne Choirs concerts with *éclat*), played together two movements in F. The concert went off well.

A concert in aid of a hospital (S. Raphael's, Torquay), was held at Prince's Hall, on Thursday, June 14th. The vocalists included Mdme. Antoinette Sterling, Miss Santley, Miss Wakefield, Mr. Edward Lloyd, Mr. J.

Robertson, and Mr. Santley. Mr. Santley was much applauded on his two solos, especially in "The Devout Lover" (M. V. White), accompanied by the composer; the song won a *bis*. Mdme. Antoinette Sterling evoked comparatively little applause, although she sang beautifully. Miss Santley was encored and sung a second song. Mr. E. Lloyd sang "I will come," by Mr. Cowen, also a trio with Mr. and Miss Santley. Miss M. V. White played a solo on the piano, and was well received. Mr. Sutton played a violin solo.

CORK.—In consequence of the continued severe illness of Mr. T. J. Sullivan, the Musical Committee of the Exhibition sometime ago asked Herr Swertz to take his place as choirmaster, to which he consented. How happy they have been in their choice was shown by the fact that when last down, Mr. Robinson complimented Herr Swertz on the admirable manner in which he had trained the voices under his care. Mr. Sullivan is rapidly recovering from the severe attack of fever with which he was struck down.

CAMELFORD.—The annual festival of the Trigg Minor Church Choir Union was held on Wednesday, when the following parishes were represented :—St. Breward, Forrabury and Minster, St. Juliot, Lanteglos and Advent, Lesnewth, Michaelstow, St. Teath, Tintagel, and Trevalga. The service, which was very attractive, was held in the parish church of Lanteglos, in the evening. The first lesson was read by the Rev. E. Townend, Lesnewth, and the second by the Rev. E. A. Hammick, Forrabury and Minster. The anthem, "Hear the voice and prayer," by J. L. Hopkins, was well rendered. The sermon was preached by the Rev. V. H. Aldham, M.A., rector of Boconnoc, who took for his text 2nd Chronicles, xxix. chapter, and part of the 27th and 28th verses. The singing of the choirs was excellent throughout. Mr. C. Bate led on the harmonium, accompanied by the following brass instruments—Cornets by Messrs. H. Bray and A. Cann, tenor baritone by Messrs. W. Langdon and J. Bate, and euphonium by Mr. A. Langdon.

WEYBRIDGE.—The first concert of the Weybridge Amateur Musical Society took place on Tuesday evening 12th inst. The first part of the programme consisted of an excellent performance of Dr. Stainer's cantata "The Daughter of Jairus," the solo parts being undertaken by Madame Talbot Cherer, Mr. Alfred Kenningham, and Mr. Adam Longmore. The orchestral accompaniments were played by a small but effective string band under the leadership of Herr Silberberg, the lack of wind instruments being supplied by Mr. W. T. Russell on the American organ, Mr. Burnell (pupil of Mr. G. E. Lake) ably presiding at the pianoforte. The whole performance reflects great credit on the conductor Mr. G. E. Lake, the choruses especially being admirably rendered, and shewing evidence of a very careful and judicious training. The second part of the programme consisted of a miscellaneous selection, in which Miss More deserves great credit for her admirable rendering of Cowen's beautiful song "Light and Darkness." Mr. Longmore, a gentleman well known among musical circles in Edinburgh, and possessed of a very fine bass voice, is much to be commended for the way in which he sang "Rocked in the Cradle of the Deep," and Mozart's "Qui sdegno." Mr. G. E. Lake gave an artistic rendering of Beethoven's pianoforte sonata Op. 90 No. 1, besides accompanying the songs with great taste. The choir also contributed two part-songs, which were noticeable for the excellent way in which they were phrased, the pianos and fortes being most judiciously attended to.

STEINWAY's Astoria factories contain eight steam boilers of the aggregate power of 500 horses, by which the necessary amount of steam is generated for the 60,000 feet of pipe used in heating the drying-rooms and workshops, and driving four steam-engines aggregating 300 horse power, which in turn put in motion the various labour-saving machines. In the extensive lumber-yards, located between the dock, basin, and these factories are constantly stacked upward of 5,000,000 square feet of the choicest kind of lumber in the open air for seasoning purposes, each separate piece of which is exposed to all the atmospheric changes for two years, and then kept in the steam-drying kilns for three months prior to being used in the factory.—*Art Journal*.

READING Henry Vizetelly's "Berlin Under the New Empire" the other day we were struck with his description of one of the Conservatories at Berlin as described to the writer by a young Englishman, who had enrolled his name as a pupil, and who states that he was admitted without any preliminary examination, except the merely farcical one of being asked to play any tune he liked on the piano, upon doing which he was told that at the end of two years he would be a first-class musician. Whilst the pupils play, the master sits in a chair beside them—asleep! In fact, soporous professors are the rule; for a gentleman, who is one of the lights of Stern's Conservatorium, and indeed of the musical world of the Prussian capital, slept regularly throughout the lessons during the time the writer attended the institute—a period of six months. Certainly the learned professor must have considered his "bread and water sure."—*Musical Opinion*.

Foreign Musical Intelligence.

"King Lear" is the subject of a new opera by Signor Cagnoni.

The composer, Vincenzo De Meglio, died recently at Naples, aged 50.

A new opera by Suppé will probably be presented in Vienna in September.

Wagner's son, Siegfried, was confirmed on June 20th at the Protestant Church, Bayreuth.

A statue of Auber was recently unveiled at Caen, his birthplace, amid great festivities.

A new opera, "Eugéne Onegrin," by Ischarkowski, has been well received in St. Petersburg.

The performances of Wagner's "Nibelungen Ring" in Italy have not been financially successful.

"The Queen of Scotland" is the title of a new opera for Turin, by a lady composer, Signora F. M. Stresa.

Mr. S. P. Warren, a prominent New York organist, is giving just now an interesting series of organ recitals in his church there.

A new symphonic poem called "Tamara," by a Russian composer, M. Balakireff, has been received with considerable favour in St. Petersburg.

Three madrigals, by John Dowland, John Wilbye and Thomas Morley, were sung at a recent concert of the Leipsic Bach Society.

The well-known composer Merkel, who is court organist at Dresden, has been decorated by the King of Saxony with the Albrecht order.

The death is announced at Trieste, of Madame Hedwig Reicher-Kindermann, the talented prima donna of Wagnerian opera, at the early age of thirty.

A Mozart Festival will be held in Vienna in the autumn. Artists of all nationalities have been invited to assist, and Rubinstein has promised his co-operation.

After an interval of twenty years, Mozart's "Idomeneo," has been heard in Munich, for which city it was originally written. The leading parts were taken by Herr and Madame Vogl.

The Belgian Musical Festival will take place on July 1st and 2nd in Ghent, under the direction of M. Waelput. The first day is to be devoted to modern Belgian music, the second to classical works.

M. Gounod has been engaged to write a new work for the next Birmingham festival. Report says that it will be a sequel to the "Redemption." Mr. Villiers Stanford has also been asked to write a choral work for the same occasion.

Gounod's oratorio of "The Redemption" was given for the first time at San Francisco on the 8th of May, in the First Congregational Church, by the Choral Society of the said church under the direction of the pastor, Rev. Chas. Dana Barrows. It is to be repeated next fall.

The Orchestral Union of San Francisco lately gave the third and last concert of the fourth series. These amateur musicians are doing excellent work. They number about forty-five active members. Prof. Wm. Toepke, their leader, leaves for Europe in June, for further study. Herr Fredick Zech, Jr. (pianist and composer), will be their musical director next season. It is mainly supported by associate or subscribing members.

Says the New York *Courier:* The nomenclature of organ stops and their arrangements is a matter of much importance. It is, however, like most things relating to the instrument, in an unsettled condition. In many organs the printed label on the stop-handle does not correctly indicate its character. With regard to the arrangement of registers, much might be, as much has already been, written, but organ-builders do not appear to care to adopt some general plan (with only little variation), and thus things remain for ever *in statu quo.*

The Kyrle Society gave "Samon" at St. John the Evangelist's, Grove Street, Commercial Road, on June 20th. Mr. M. L. Lawson conducted, and Mr. E. H. Turpin was the organ player.

NOTES OF THE CUCKOO.

Gilbert White, of Selborne, affirms that the cuckoo in his time, was heard to sing at various intervals, from a major second to a perfect fifth—a margin of five semitones. Beethoven in the "Pastoral" adopts the *major third* (D natural to B flat) in his second movement. The writer, with an experience of some sixty "summers," (such as "summers" are in England), can state that the general (or average) interval *is* this major third. He has never, so far as memory will serve, heard the *perfect fourth* more than twice or three times, and only on damp gloomy days, a compromise between the major and *minor* third, for the lesser interval was never quite exact or decisive according to "commas."

Another question is about the *key.* The writer has almost always fixed the tonality of the cuckoo's third in D major, (F sharp to D) *never in C,* which he thinks is the key noticed by Gilbert White. An interesting variation, however, may be noticed. Last Saturday, in a remote village in south Essex, near the sea, the cuckoo was heard at 7 o'clock P.M., to sing in D *major,* the next day (Sunday, June 17th) at about 2.15 P.M., with the sun brightly shining, and a change of wind from cold N.W. to balmy W.S.W., the cuckoo (suspected to be the same), sang in D *flat,* and again on Monday morning. The high pitch is referred to, but not the operatic.   A. M.

EXTRAORDINARY DISPUTE IN A CHURCH.

An extraordinary dispute has arisen in connection with the parish church of St. James, Taunton. Desirous of making some alteration in the nature of the musical services, the churchwardens of St. James's served a notice to leave on the organist (Mrs. Chapman), who, bye-the-by, is the wife of the sexton, bellringer, vestry clerk, and assistant overseer of the parish, practically giving her three months' notice. This seems to have met with the disapproval of the parishioners, and a crowded vestry meeting called by the overseers was held, at which it was unanimously resolved that the appointment of the organist should be confirmed. On the same day as the meeting was held, the organist received a demand from the vicar and the church-wardens, who did not attend the meeting, to deliver up the keys of the organ. This she refused to do, acting under legal advice. On Wednesday evening, last week, at the usual weekly service, the organist was in her place at half-past six o'clock, and a large congregation had assembled in anticipation of a scene. The vicar accompanied by the new organist who had been appointed, walked up to the organ and asked the lady to resign her seat. This she firmly refused to do, and the vicar then retired with the newly-appointed organist to the vestry. He next demanded that the sexton, the lady's husband, should order her off her seat, but he declined to do so, stating that he had nothing to do with the office of organist. The vicar then sent for the organ blower, and ordered him not to supply any wind for the instrument. Matters remained in this position for some time, the people anxiously waiting until the service should commence. Ultimately the vicar and the new organist walked off, and no service was held. The congregation dispersed, and the sexton and organist were left in possession of the building. The sexton locked the doors of the church and went home. Sunday morning there was a crowded congregation in anticipation of a repetition of the scene. The church doors were opened at ten o'clock, and the vicar, the churchwardens, and the newly-appointed organist proceeded to the organ, when to their astonishment they found Mrs. Chapman already there. She refused to give way, and the organ having been locked by the churchwardens, the service was held without music. Not a single chant was sung, and the hymns went by default. The new organist during the service remained in the vestry of the church. A strange incident in connection with the affair is that the new organist, who has been organist to the Temple Wesleyan church, seems to have given no notice of his intention to absent himself from that place of worship on Sunday morning, and the consequence was that there also the service proceeded without the instrumental music. The congregation were, however, not to be done out of their singing, and they rendered their psalms and hymns under the direction of a voluntary precentor, and without the organ. John Mattock Chapman, the sexton, was charged on Wednesday, with riotous, indecent, and insolent conduct in the church, but the magistrates dismissed the case.

LONDON: SATURDAY, JUNE 23, 1883.

THE HANDEL FESTIVAL.

THIS event, now fully established as one of the recurrent incidents of the cycle of English musical life, has taken place with no diminution of *éclat* and enthusiasm. Even though HANDEL's position in the world of art has suffered some modification of late years, and it is now conceded that he did not alone possess the secrets of grandeur and contrapuntal power, it remains undeniably true that he had, perhaps, pre-eminently, the faculty of reaching the largest proportion of musical minds by the creation of colossal effects through the well applied agency of clear decisive harmonies and of those musical powers, as rhythm and strong accentuation, which are not in themselves the highest and most abstract powers of the divine art. HANDEL in his nervous sentences relies much upon the "long "pull, strong pull, and a pull all together" type of writing. Herein lies much of the source of his popularity, for his sledge-hammer power of striking out effects sublime in their way, does and will ever continue to, appeal to the majority of minds who would fain rise into heights of musical eloquence upon the wings of physical health and strength. So the great, sturdy Saxon will naturally command more admirers for his trenchant thoughts, the highest expression of the age of carved fat-faced Cherubim and bag-wig mannerisms, while the most abstract sublimities in which high spiritual thought is present with a comparative absence of the more physical sources of musical power, such as may be found in the works of HANDEL's kindred geniuses PALESTRINA and BACH, will only command the appreciation of the comparatively few cultured and thoughtful intellects.   To enter upon the questions here indicated would be to advance into a dissertation concerning the connection between body and soul, and their mutual sources of re-action and influence, and their mutual relationship in art through the intervening power of the mind, a matter in which, as my readers well know, I should at once be out of my depth.   Briefly, HANDEL has, with a strong hand and a REMBRANDT-like vividness amounting at times almost to a coarseness of manner, grandly struck out such half-physical and half-spiritual musical truths, as have with more or less success called for such a mighty exposition of material musical force, as no other composer has hitherto claimed.   This is not the time either to discuss another of our complex mental phenomena, the fact that results in art are by no means governed by the measure of means employed, as our conception of what is sublime greatly surpasses our but limited powers of seeing, hearing, and realising, and mighty thoughts are beyond the application of any accumulated forms of practical expression.   Still, though the cathedral choir may at times uplift us with heaven-bound aspirations when the great army on the HANDEL Festival Orchestra might fail to do more than astonish us with a weight of tone probably without a parallel in the history of musical festivals, the HANDEL celebration presents effects calling for the attention of both artist and layman.   What has been noted before has been noted again.   Certain great orchestral effects, for the strings as the violin figures, and the moving basses in certain of the splendid chain of descriptive choruses in "Israel in Egypt," have never produced anything but comparatively small effect. It may be somewhat unfair criticism to point out, that such failures are easily to be explained when it is borne in mind that the effects have been sought for from the wind or rather military band point of sight; that the orchestra contained flutes, piccolos, and drums enough to make up a drum and fife band for a regiment of the Foot Guards, granting certain differences in pitch, and that there were brass instruments in a sufficient abundance to make brass bands for two cavalry regiments.   Naturally, development in such directions demoralizes the sense of hearing, and no effect is sufficiently spiced without the keen pointing of the wind instruments notwithstanding the presence of a large array of strings, which however included many players of feeble grip and indifferent bow discipline.   On the other hand some of the more purely choral effects were truly imposing.   The ungracious and possibly affected surprise expressed by some critics who have been accustomed to belaud unduly the eminent conductor, Sir MICHAEL COSTA, that the Festival could be carried forward successfully even in the lamented absence of the veteran *chef-d'orchestre*, only serves to show up an unfortunate tendency to judge by precedents rather than by reason. And it is to be hoped that the present occasion will administer a severe blow to the absurd spirit of conductor worship, even while furnishing an opportunity for the congratulation of Mr. A. MANNS upon his vigorous and courageous assumption of a trying position.   Sensible people know that in the matter of conducting, as in every other walk of life, there is an abundance of the necessary ability, though there are but few opportunities for its exercise.   It is to be hoped that the proposal to celebrate HANDEL after his own manner by a Festival, with an orchestra built up as he knew and expected it to be built up, will indeed, be arranged for in the course of the next two years.   Such an event would be a matter of special interest to the musician.

E. H. TURPIN.

___

HENRY SMART.

THE long-continued Henry Smart Memorial Fund movement has been successfully brought to an issue by the few earnest friends who were determined to perpetuate the appreciation in which the distinguished English composer and organ-player was held in during his own time.   Now his memory will be celebrated in two of our musical institutions, the authorities of Trinity College having, with commendable spirit and liberal forethought, already erected a Henry Smart Scholarship, and now, by the decision of the meeting held in Trinity College on the 19th, a scholarship will commemorate the manly artist and noteworthy composer within the walls of the Royal Academy of Music.   There is no present opportunity to dilate upon the genius, mental power, and remarkable acquirements of Henry Smart.   He is, as a composer, one of the men to whom time must be gracious, for he sought not to discount public favour in advance by friendly influences.   Henry Smart's music has never been performed, it may be fairly said, save upon the strength of its own merits, and a future is assured to it such as may not await the works of men who in their personal careers seem to the casual observer to have been more fortunate than was the composer of "Jacob" and "The Bride of Dunkerron."   The life of Henry Smart is not without lessons for the student.   His artistic conscientiousness and earnest perseverance, despite many difficulties, will not be forgotten.   Again, his manly independence by which, together with his splendid abilities, he contrived to build up a great name without the external influences of the world's favour peculiar to our immediate times, in the shape of a specially conspicuous official position, University popularity, patronage in high places, and "troops of busy friends," should indeed encourage the English musical student who will elect to stand chiefly upon his own merits.   Such an example in these days, when happily art is in fashion and carefully nurtured by colleges and musical corporations, is not without power and significance, and teaches us that however valuable the extraneous and rightly sought-for advantages modern appreciation of art has secured for the artist may be, the real foundation of the good artist will still in any case be built upon the rock-like strength of an independent, manly love of art for its own sake. So the works and example furnished by the labours of Henry Smart are to be ranked among the honourable records of English art; and it is gratifying and satisfactory to know that loving admirers have succeeded in perpetuating his memory in so honourable a manner.

E. H. Turpin.

FORM IN VOCAL MUSIC.

IV.

That the development of form in vocal music should have proceeded not only through the simple process of reiteration or re-presentation of the early song plans, but also should have grown through the complex counterpoint of the church is a matter of much interest, and the task of tracing such growth would be doubtless an undertaking of much instruction. Without dipping too deeply into this profoundly interesting matter, it is well to notice that in proportion to growth of contrapuntal power the advance of the constructive or architectural faculty in music was a slow process, while in modern times, as the contrapuntal genius grow more neglected, the growth of form advanced with seemingly accelerated rapidity. But in the transition period, towards the close of the seventeenth and at the beginning of the eighteenth century, it is of moment to note that counterpoint, in its highest demonstration the fugue, had arrived at the three general principles of form, presentation, development, and recapitulation. Thus the fugal exposition corresponds with the primary presentation of the leading theme or themes; the episodes in effect answer to the employment of developed and episodical thoughts as propounded in the modern musical constructions; the processes applied to the fugue subject, as augmentation, diminution, the formation of new counter subjects, etc., take the place of the function of development, or the "Free Fantasia" as some authorities call the specially set aside section for development and modulation; the counter exposition and fugal stretto are the contrapuntal equivalents for the recapitulation of the various architectural schemes; and the listener to the fugue is brought finally home by such devices as the pedal point, just as the coda of the different constructive forms furnishes the listener with a satisfactory and final assertion of tonic harmonies.

E. H. Turpin.

Reviews.

The Technics of Violin Playing. By Karl Courvoisier, translated by H. E. Krehbiel. (W. Reeves.)—One of those somewhat rare, but useful books, which give us valuable but well condensed information. The chapters on intonation, and the various departments of the art of bowing, are very valuable.

The Child's Pianoforte Book. By H. Keatley Moore, B.A. (W. Swan Sonnenschein & Co.)—A really charming book for small children, with nice little tunes, pretty little pictures, and clearly written little lessons, something after the Kindergarten method. To the musical mother, anxious to teach her own children, and to elementary teachers, this handsome, instructive, and entertaining book ought to be a treasure.

Organ News.

NORWICH.

Dr. Bunnett gave an organ recital at the St. Andrew's Hall, on June 16th; the following was the programme:—

Offertoire in F	Wely.
Pastorale in G	Merkel.
March (from "Tannhäuser")	Wagner.
Organ Concerto in D	Handel.
Allegro—Andante con Moto, and Fuga.	
Andante in C (from a Concerto)	Mendelssohn
Postlude in D	Smart.
Studio per Flauto	Fumagalli.
Grand Chœur in D	Lemmens.
Gavotte, from the opera "Ortone," Siciliana and }	Handel.
Allegro from the "Fire Music" }	
Hallelujah Chorus, "Messiah"	Handel.

PRESTON.

The following is the programme of the organ recital given by Mr. James Tomlinson, in the new Public Hall, on Saturday evening, June 16th.

Concerto in C minor	Handel.
Maestoso—Allegro—Minuetto—Allegro	
Andante con Moto	Beethoven.
(Symphony in C minor.)	
Fugue in D	Bach.
Grand Fantasia, "The Storm"	Lemmens.
Rigaudon	Silas.
Overture to "L'Etoile du Nord"	Meyerbeer.

LIVERPOOL.

Mr. W. T. Best gave an organ recital in the St. George's Hall, on Thursday evening, June 14th. The following is the programme:—

Overture, "Maria di Rohan"	Donizetti.
Prelude, (D flat major, Op. 28)	Chopin.
Organ Sonata, (No. 1, F minor)	Mendelssohn.
Mazurka, (G minor, Op. 21)	Saint-Saëns.
Andante (Six Concert Pieces, No. 3)	W. T. Best.
Toccata (A flat major)	Adolph Hesse.

On Saturday afternooon, June 16th :—

Ouverture Solennelle	Flotow.
Gavotte (E major), and Fugue (A minor)	Bach.
Offertorio, (E flat major)	Morandi.
Allegro Scherzoso, (F minor)	Schubert.
Andante Cantabile, (E major)	C. V. Alkan.
Hungarian March, ("Rakoczy")	Liszt.

HIGH WYCOMBE.

On Monday evening June the 4th, a recital was given on the organ in the Parish Church, by Mr. J. G. Wrigley, Mus.Bac., Oxon., F.C.O. The following was the programme :—

Choral Song and Fugue	S. S. Wesley.
Allegretto Cantabile	Lemmens.
Tema con Variazioni (from the Sinfonie in D)	Haydn.
Marche Funebra et Chant Seraphique	Guilmant.
"Ave Maria d'Arcadelt" (16th Century)	Liszt.
Heroic March in D	Schubert.

CHRIST CHURCH, NEWGATE STREET.

An organ recital will be given by Dr. Charles Joseph Frost, at Christ Church, on Monday evening, June 25th, to commence at 7.30 p.m. The following was the programme :—

Organ Solos, Toccata and Double Fugue	Eberlin.
Fantasia (on the Choral "St. Mary")	Stephens.
Marche Religieuse	Baptiste Calkin.
Organ Solos, Sonata	Westbrook.
Allegro—Moderato—Adagio—Menuetto—Finale	
Marche Funebre	Gigout.
Organ Solos { a Andante in G }	Frost.
{ b Allegretto in F }	
Marcia di processione	Morandi.

BOLTON.

An organ recital was given in the Albert Hall, by Mr. Wm. Mullineux, F.C.O., on June 16th. The following was the programme :—

Chorus, "See ! the proud Chief advances now"	
("Deborah")	Handel.
Adagio for the Organ (D major)	Morandi.
Grand Organ Sonata in D minor (No. 6.)	Mendelssohn.
Chorale with Variations and Fugue—Andante.	
Serenade " L'Enfance du Christ "	Berlioz.
Serenade " Good night ! Good night I beloved "	Balfe.
Postlude in D	Smart.

OXFORD.

No one who cares for the organ in its modern form could willingly omit from his programme of commemoration proceedings the organ recital given by Mr. Dodds, Mus.Bac., the College organist, in Queen's chapel. The instrument is by far the largest in Oxford, containing four rows of keys, over sixty actual stops (besides couplers, etc., etc.), all of which run throughout the entire compass of the instrument, and possessing, moreover, one of the most splendid swell organs in England. The programme, which, in at least two pieces, was identical with that performed in the Sheldonian on Wednesday, was as felicitously chosen as it was ably performed, and adapted to show off to the utmost the unusual capacity of the enormous instrument. The following is the programme :—

Concerto (No. 2.)	Handel.
Air with Variations	Wely.
Overture (Occasional)	Handel.
Fugue in E flat	Bach.
Fantasia Pastorale	Wely.
March, from Molique's Oratorio "Abraham" arranged by Best.	

FISHERIES EXHIBITION.

The recital on Wednesday, June 13th, was by Mr. Wm. H. Stocks. The following was the programme :—

Motet ("Deus Tibi")	Mozart.
Placidamente in A, and Grazioso in B flat	E. J. Hopkins.
Fugue in D minor	Bach.
Quasi Pastorale in G	H. Smart.
Chorus, "And the Glory" ("Messiah")	Handel.
Prelude and Fugue in G	Mendelssohn.
Prelude in C minor, (Op. 28, No. 20.)	Chopin.
(Arranged for the Organ by W. H. Stocks.)	
Quoniam ("Second Mass")	Haydn.

An organ recital was given on Thursday, June 14th, by Mr. James Loaring. The following was the programme :—

Overture "Guy Mannering"	Bishop.
Organ Concerto (No. 1.)	Handel.
Gavotte in G minor	Bach.
Prelude and Fugue	Loaring.

The organ recital on Friday June 15th, was given by Mr. James Loaring. The following was the programme :—

Prelude and Fugue	Bach.
Offertoire in F	Clark.
Andante Grazioso	Smart.

On Monday June 18th, an organ recital was given by Mr. Frank Bradley. The following was the programme:—

Overture ("Semele")	Handel.
Marcia Eroica and Finale	Best.
Prelude and Fugue in G major (1st Book)	Bach.
Harmonious Blacksmith, (with variations) !	Chipp.
Intermezzo in E major—Scherzo in A minor, and Passacaglia in E minor (from 7th Sonata for Organ)	Rheinberger.

And on Tuesday Mr. Bradley gave the following :—

Overture ("Amadige")	Handel.
Choral Study, eleven Variations	Merkel.
Trio in C minor, Adagio and Allegro	Bach.
Fugue in G major (from the 9th Volume.)	
Marche de Procession and Grand Chorus in F	Guilmant.
Concert Variations on an Original Theme	Archer.

HALSTEAD, ESSEX.

The following is the programme of an organ recital given by Mr. G. Leake, A.C.O., at Holy Trinity Church, after the evening service on Sunday, June 17th :—

March, "St. Polycarp"	Ouseley.
Sonata, No. 4	Mendelssohn.
The Lost Chord	Sullivan.
Funeral March and Chorus of Seraphs	Guilmant.
Concerto, No. 2	Handel.
"If with all your hearts" ("Elijah")	Mendelssohn.
Grand Offertoire in D	Batiste.

CRYSTAL PALACE.

Mr. Eyre's programme on Saturday last was as follows :—

Concerto Fantasia in C minor	Hesse.
"My heart ever faithful"	Bach.
Overture, "Henry VIII."	Hatton.
Finale and Fugue on the 8th Tone	Rheinberger.
Bourrée in D	A. Sanders.
Adagio in E flat	Hopkins.
Intermezzo	A. Macbeth.
March from a Capriccio	Mendelssohn.

PADFIELD, NEAR HADFIELD.

The opening of the new organ for the Wesleyan Chapel (built by Alex. Young and Sons, of Manchester), took place on March 23rd. The following is the specification of the organ :—

GREAT ORGAN.   CC TO G, 56 NOTES.

1. Open Diapason	8 ft.	5. Principal	4 ft.
2. Stopped Diapason	8 „	6. Harmonic Flute	4 „
3. Clarabella	8 „	7. Fifteenth	2 „
4. Dulciana	8 „		

SWELL ORGAN.   CC TO G, 56 NOTES.

8. Spitz Flöte	8 ft.	11. Gemshorn	4 ft.
9. Salcional	8 „	12. Hautboy	8 „
10. Voix Celestes	8 „		

PEDAL ORGAN.   CCC TO F, 30 NOTES.

13. Bourdon	16 ft.

COUPLERS.

14. Swell to Great (unison).	16. Swell to Pedals.
15. Swell to Great (super-octave).	17. Great to Pedals.

Two Composition Pedals to Great Organ.

NETHERWARDEN.

The new organ (built by Alex. Young and Sons, of Manchester) for Netherwarden Church, near Hexham, was opened on April 21st. Mr. William Metcalfe, of Carlisle, presided at the organ. The following is a specification of the instrument :—

GREAT ORGAN.   CC TO G, 56 NOTES.

1. Open Diapason	8 ft.	3. Dulciana	8 ft.
2. Clarabella	8 „	4. Principal	4 „

SWELL ORGAN.   CC TO G, 56 NOTES.

5. Gamba	8 ft.	7. Flute	4 ft.
6. Lieblich Gedact	8 „	8. Hautboy	8 „

PEDAL ORGAN.   CCC TO F, 30 NOTES.

9. Bourdon	16 ft.

COUPLERS.

10. Swell to Great.	13. Great to Pedals.
11. Swell to Great Octave.	14. Swell to Pedals.
12. Great Octave.	

Two Composition Pedals to Great Organ.

STUDY.

As a rule the casual observer of art is not satisfied with its productions, and for this reason, that a man, unless he be an artist, or rather theoretically understands an art, is never gratified with a work of artistic merit; it is something beyond him; something he cannot grasp; he beholds the work with astonishment at first, and probably becomes infatuated with its beauties, but this infatuation, like all spontaneous delight, withers and departs in as short a space of time as it took to take possession of him. An observer of this kind looks upon art in the same way as the fox looked upon the grapes, and, on finding they were out of its reach, walked away, endeavouring to convince itself they were sour. And the man, in turning his back upon a work of art which he cannot appreciate, will look upon it as something ridiculous, whereas if he examined himself carefully, he would most probably discover that it was his own stupidity, and lack of knowledge and study, which is the stumbling block to his appreciating that which is artistic. It is through our imagination, if refined, that we are enabled mentally to behold things that are beautiful, things that are heavenly; but we must have something to feed and guide it, as humanity is naturally prone to evil, there is something required to direct our footsteps into a right channel, and this I hold is the indirect cause of crime that exists in our midst. If an imagination be left to itself, it of course inclines to that which is human, and that is sin, "humanum est errare." It is the training that an infant mind will receive which will find for it either a good or bad path through the world, and thereby decide its future lot. There are two things which a child first feels, pleasure and pain. It has its passions and its pains, and when excited vent is given unto them. The things of the world crowd so suddenly upon the little brain, that reflection is out of the question.

As time goes on fear takes possession of the child, and teaches it to modify its feelings. It is chastised when it attempts to return displeasure, and through harshness a child will become deceitful, from the fact that when a thing is promised, and the promise is not kept; when a child is threatened and the threat is not carried out, the timidity becomes cruelly and falsely excited, and the childish wish, built upon the highest pinnacle of hope, is wilfully broken down, so the child, being terribly satiated with disappointment and delusion, its young mind cannot fail to become deceitful.

Reid, on the human mind, aptly remarks: "From being forced into concealing the thoughts which we conceive, we begin to affect those which we do not. So early do we learn the two main tasks of life, to suppress and to feign, that our memory will not carry us back beyond that period of artifice to a natural state when the twin principles of veracity and belief were so strong as to lead philosophers of a modern school into the error of terming them innate."

The basest of criminals possess an imaginative power, as we do ourselves; but it is the terribly wrong groove into which their imagination has been allowed to move, that has led them to crime of the worst description. What is crime but indiscretion and lack of knowledge? It is proved without doubt daily. Criminals and indiscreet persons are their own dupes in the long run. It has truly been said that man is his own sharper and bubble, and the sharpest of men in course of time outwit themselves; they become so entangled in their own vice, that as time goes on they are quite powerless to free themselves from the maze of sin and wrong in which they are held. In his own peculiar way the criminal is a philosopher; he invents laws, ways, and means by which he can find an excuse for crime, and gets so thoroughly permeated with his own special code of order, and having become so used to cheat others, he invariably, and I think quite naturally, cheats himself.

Bad emanates from idleness and lack of study, neglect which, in progress of time, will ruin our mind, and thereby stop our right imaginative power; for the brain is a machine which requires to be carefully and regularly fed to begin with, but when it is thoroughly in working it will go, and nothing will stop it; but if neglected nothing will make it go, the machinery will become rusted and clogged up.

Now this brain motive power is *study*. A studious life need not necessarily be a secluded one, although learning and knowledge of all description is best grasped in solitude; but am I right in speaking of solitude in connection with study? There is nothing like learning to drive away loneliness, for in the depth of knowledge and science the student is in the realm of happiness, and where true happiness exists, there can be no solitude.

There are students of thought and students of imagination, and in both instances, before they are able to reach anything that is at all reasonable, they must dive deep into the stream of metaphysical investigation, so as to find the origin of intellect, and if we do this we shall find that our studies will greatly strengthen our principles and establish whatever good may exist within us. It is by study of the arts, music, painting, poetry, sculpture, &c., that we learn to look upon virtues in their true light. The virtues in uneducated people arise from emotion, but in the learned from principle. It may be remarked that, apart from the origin of the virtues in learned and unlearned, the effect is the same in each; not so, principle is to be relied, emotion is not. Those who have not studied are very apt to draw false conclusions from nature, which conclusion study can prove to be untrue. There can be no education in which the lessons of the world do not take a part, for it is by study that we become acquainted with the world, and learning in whatever sphere of life we may be placed should bring content.

"Of all that belongs to us the least valuable parts can alone fall under the will of others; *whatever is best is safest*, lies out of the reach of human power, can neither be given nor taken away. Such is this beautiful work of nature, the world. Such is the mind of man which contemplates and admires the world, whereof it makes the noblest part. These are inseparably ours, and as long as we remain in one, we shall enjoy the other."

Has not the student moments of secret and overflowing delight; the glory of gratified research; lightnings of pleasure, which fully repay the loneliness of thought, "and light up his solitude as a revel"?

Lord Lytton observes, "If the certainty of future fame bore Milton rejoicing through his blindness, or cheered Galileo in his dungeon, what stronger and holier support shall not be given to him who has loved mankind as his brother and devoted his labours to their cause? Who has not sought but relinquished his own renown? Who has braved the present censures of men for their future benefit, and trampled upon glory in the energy of benevolence? Will there not be for him something more powerful than fame to comfort his sufferings and to sustain his hopes?"

Virtue has been compared to the precious odours as being most fragrant when crushed, for prosperity does so well discover vice; but adversity does best discover virtue, and it is in possession of certain expedients which lie buried deep within itself waiting until the time may come when they shall be summoned from their hiding places.

In my opinion it is the good that exists in the world working out in its pure and holy path, not only among the cultured, but the most uncivilised. Have you not, reader, ever observed with a certain amount of awe and wonder when gazing upwards, during a severe storm, the blackness that pervades the firmament on all sides; the utter and hopeless solitude that exists around, and suddenly from out the midst of the murky darkness, and when you are beginning to feel that the sky has been shut off from the gaze for ever and ever, there appears a flash of lightning, illuminating the whole heavens, and for the moment the black darkness (which an instant before seemed impenetrable) is forgotten on beholding this sudden dart of fire. And indeed can we not observe the working of the Seraph Virtue, in this way among the most degraded, and where we should least expect to find it? Virtue has truly been called the realm of God; it is the guardian angel of civilisation, the ruling power of knowledge. Verily there is virtue in wisdom; and can we not observe in a benevolent and studious genius the self-sacrificing nature, the high and lofty virtue? A man of this description will (unlike an untutored genius) give up his time to sound reading and reason rather than to fiction and fancy; principle will overrule his inclination, and his love for others will predominate over that of himself. These men, rare though they are, make human misery the object of their search, and the happiness of humanity their sole desire—who, "by a zeal and labour that brings to habit and inclination a thousand martyrdoms, makes their lives a very hour-glass in which each sand is a good deed of a virtuous design." Study and research into wisdom, however shallow, can never be undeserving of attention. Though at first the road of study is hard and laborious to travel, we may depend upon it that sooner or later we shall meet with a sign-post to direct us into the paths of wisdom and into the avenue of learning; we are sure by careful study to find the Garuda stone of knowledge which will act as a future talisman against unhappiness and sin. However great a genius a man may be, unless he possesses application and is fond of study, his talents must become misguided, for genius is little else than "natural inclination," and this, if not properly guided, will most assuredly fail. But in our studious genius we have our natural knowledge converted into natural wisdom, and such characters may be said to make life beautiful; when we behold the utter ignorance that exists, these men indeed act as a consolation, for however black the darkness we still feel the effects of the light. Such men are called proud by the world, but men of genius open to their own interest a world in themselves, and so become consoled for the ill-feeling in the world without; they teach us to love the vanities of earth for their graces and not for their utility. The loves of the world, coarse and low, feed their rank fires from an unmingled and gross depravity; but these men show us the serpent's teeth in such errors and point out the sublime extreme. Though wisdom and genius be scattered by the wind, still the seeds are dispersed by unselfish hands to hearts which would willingly forego the whole harvest of their labours upon those who know not the good intent of the workmen. As I have before observed, genius must be nurtured and guided by study before it can hope to succeed, and then its progress will be limited unless modesty be associated with it, for a vain man can never hope to reach a successful standard of excellence, from the fact that he will never listen to the advice of others; he never knows peace of mind because he is sure to find someone who will excel him in something. Vanity is a growing and insatiable disease, for what it prizes to day to-morrow it will reject as useless. Yet there are vain men who are not blind to the glories of Virtue, but not until they become matured in years and see the follies of vanity, do they avail themselves of their perceptions.   But let us not mistake a vain for an ambitious man ; the difference is this, a man whose failing is vanity requires an immediate reward for labour done, he cannot wait, and that which he attempts he must at once seize ; nor are his cravings easily satisfied, unless they procure all, and so his whole time is taken up, and wasted away by stretching out for that which is hopelessly beyond the power of his reach. It has been remarked that there are certain characters which in the world are evil, and in seclusion are good. These persons are of such a morbid sensitiveness that they are perpetually galled by the collision of others. Such men are under the dominion of vanity ; and that vanity, never at rest in the many competitions of society, produces nothing but hatred. But often in solitude the good dispositions, with which our vanity or self love no longer interferes, have room to expand and ripen without being cramped by opposing interests ; yet with all this a ruling passion in a man will never part from him, he may modify it, but rid himself—never ! A vain man is detestable to society, for vanity often brings with it that most despicable of weaknesses " Jealousy."   Yet how often it exists in men of talent, and it must show itself.   But vanity and jealousy I care not how deftly they may be practised, must in the end bring discontent with the things of life.   Jealousy and vanity can only exist in selfish people, but I hold that studious men of genius are not in possession of these petty trifles ; we may be certain that a man so vain of his work lacks knowledge, and in whatever sphere of art he may move in or whatever talents he may be in possession of, he must study to become proficient.   How often do we not see in painters and musicians lives wasted for the want of knowledge to direct the talent, and these are the men whose very life desire is fame ; it is the one hope always present, yet never realized ; it is present in the dreams, it darkens the thoughts, shuts out entirely the energies and enjoyments of life.   Such characters as these do not possess that vanity and jealousy of which I have spoken, but the greater weakness, *contempt;* they look upon humanity as beneath themselves yet they forget that they themselves make up a portion of the one sordid mass which they are so willing to condemn. The thirst for fame in an untutored genius is a deadly plant, which grows up to the exclusion of all else, but in a studious genius it shelters rather than withers the virtues by which it is encompassed, and is a means of binding such an one by charity closer to mankind ; in the former it produces a disgust to his species, but in the latter a love, with the one, power has " the badge of distinction, with the other the means to bless."

Fame is a passion which should not be suppressed but directed, and to clothe oneself with hope and humility is the surest way of winning it.   Then may we look for a brilliant future, which, though it *may* place us a step above our fellow-men, will bring charity and not pride with our success.   G. J. GROVER.

HENRY SMART MEMORIAL FUND.

At a meeting of the subscribers to the "Henry Smart Memorial Fund" (the Rev. Canon Duckworth, D.D., in the chair), held on the 19th inst. at Trinity College, Mandeville Place, W., it was resolved that the amount available after expenses, about £500, should be devoted to the establishment of a perpetual exhibition at the Royal Academy of Music bearing the name of Henry Smart.   It had been found impracticable to carry out the original idea of establishing a Musical Scholarship at Oxford or Cambridge.   The committee having expressed their great disappointment at the smallness of the sum contributed, it was resolved by the meeting that the trustees, in whose names the capital sum will be invested, be empowered to receive and add thereto any additional contributions which may be offered them.   The musical public which has so largely profited by the genius of Henry Smart will thus still have an opportunity of doing honour to the memory of one of the most gifted English composers. Contributions may still be paid to the "Henry Smart Memorial Fund" at Messrs. Coutts's, 59, Strand, W.C.

Academical Intelligence.

CAMBRIDGE UNIVERSITY.

The following result of the preliminary examination for the Degree of Mus.Bac. and special examination for the ordinary B.A. degree has been issued :—

Class 1 (in order of merit) : James ; Karn ; Pluine, Corpus ; Frye ; Ewer, Trinity ; Skynner ; Sykes. *Class* 2 (in alphabetical order) : Bullock, Trinity ; Capel-Cure, King's ; Hulburt, Corpus ; Merrick, Trinity ; Reichardt, Corpus ; Vasper ; Walters, Emmanuel. *Examiners :* Sir G. A. Macfarren, F. E. Gladstone, Mus.Doc., R. Pendlebury, M.A.

Correspondence.

NATIONAL COLLEGE OF MUSIC.

TO THE EDITOR OF THE "MUSICAL STANDARD."

SIR,—The establishment of a National College of Music, so universally responded to, induces me to ask " what will ultimately be the fate of its scholars ? "   The College will be the means of, firstly—educating, and secondly—throwing upon the musical world, a vast number of instrumentalists.   The fact appears to be ignored that there is already in London alone a considerable number of talented English players who cannot obtain a living, owing to the distinguished patronage lavished on foreign artists.   British musicians naturally look forward to the London season for their harvest, but as regularly as the season approaches we find two Hungarian bands located here, advertising themselves "*under the immediate patronage of His Royal Highness the Prince of Wales, and the nobility,*" engaged day and night at various garden parties, dinners, balls, &c., to the exclusion of the English musician. There is also another band here from Vienna, whose arrival has thrown an entire orchestra out of employment, as they first play at a theatre, and afterwards at an aristocratic club, recently formed.

The manifest injustice to English artists must be apparent, and I feel sure the facts need only to be brought under the notice of those who have the power of bestowing their patronage on native talent to remedy the evil.

By kindly inserting these few remarks in your influential paper, you will greatly oblige a large section of the musical profession.

I am, sir, yours obediently,
AN ENGLISH MUSICIAN.

Passing Events.

The Tonic Sol-fa College gave an enjoyable breakfast to the Cologne choir at Exeter Hall, Strand, on June 15th, 1883.

Sunday concerts are being given at New Brighton, Liverpool. Last Sunday the programme included the vocal portion of Mendelssohn's " Hymn of Praise."

A new Mass by Signor Mazzoni, for male voices, orchestra, and organ, will be used for the first time at the Italian Church, Hatton Garden, on Sunday, July 1st.

The number of MSS. sent in for the Cardiff Eisteddfod in August is no less than 317, including 17 cantatas. The gathering will, it is believed, be one of much importance.

Mr. Gabriel Thorp gave an evening concert on June 12th at the Steinway Hall. A good miscellaneous programme was well gone through, Mr. Gabriel Thorp himself sang several songs, French, Italian, and English, and proved himself to be a useful and promising vocalist.

The *Scarborough Daily Post* speaks highly of the abilities of Miss Gertrude Jackson, a young artist and daughter of a local professor, who has attained distinction at the recent R. A. M. Examination in Harmony and Pianoforte Playing.

The days of the Leeds Triennial Musical Festival are October 10th, 11th, 12th, and 13th. The programme includes Mendelssohn's " Elijah " and " Lobgesang," Raff's symphony oratorio, " The End of the World," which will then be performed for the first time in England ; Niels Gade's secular cantata, " The Crusaders," Sir G. A. Macfarren's oratorio " King David," and Rossini's " Stabat Mater." Sir A. Sullivan will conduct,

Mr. Russell Lochner and Herr Alto Booth give violin and organ recitals at the Lancaster Hall on June 30th, July 7th, and 14th. The first performance was given on June 16th.

The London Music Publishing and General Agency Company propose to meet two important requirements now pressing upon the musical world. The publication of meritorious compositions, by young composers, is a matter sure to command public sympathy. The systematic construction of good and cheap pianofortes may also be productive of good. It may be that company's scheme will call for further consideration at an early opportunity.

Mr. C. F. South, the esteemed organist of St. Augustine and St. Faith's, City, has been appointed organist of Salisbury Cathedral. Mr. South, hitherto an amateur organist, will henceforth take rank, it may be presumed, as a professional artist. He has done much good work in his London appointment during the past thirteen years. He is an excellent organ player, and an earnest and accomplished church musician.

The College of Organists meeting on July 3rd at the Neumeyer Hall will be one of special musical interest. Mr. F. J. Sawyer will speak about Mozart's "Organ Concertos" and selections from those hitherto overlooked works will be given by the lecturer, upon a small organ built by Mr. A. Kirkland, of Wakefield, and supplied through Messrs. Weekes and Co. expressly for this occasion, and by several stringed instrumentalists.

Oxford has wrested from Cambridge the honour of first properly recognising a distinguished and highly esteemed musician. In a Congregation held on June 14th, the honorary degree of Doctor of Music was conferred upon Charles Villiers Stanford, M.A., organist of Trinity College, Cambridge. He was presented for the degree by Mr. C. H. Lloyd, organist of Christ Church, in the absence of the professor of music. Mr. Lloyd, in a short Latin speech, alluded to the reputation Mr. Stanford's compositions had obtained, especially in Germany, and to the lustre he had already shed on the English musical name, expressing the wish that an opportunity could have been given those present of hearing some of his compositions performed.

Miss Eva Lynn gave her first matinee musicale on June 20th, at 26, Cambridge Square, Hyde Park, W. The artists included Mdme. Liebhart, Miss Edith Phillips, Miss Adèle Myers, Miss Eva Lynn, Mdme. Olga de Morini, Signor Ria, Mr. Levetus, Mr. Hirwen Jones, and Mr. Arthur Oswald. The instrumentalists were : solo pianoforte, Signor Tito Mattei ; harp, Mr. F. Chatterton ; violin, Mr. Bernhard Carrodus. Miss Eva Lynn sang several songs effectively, including Mozart's "Addio" and Mr. Salaman's "Hebrew Love Song." Miss Edith Phillips gave an artistic rendering of Buoncini's "Per la gloria." An instrumental feature of interest was the excellent violin playing of Mr. Bernard Carrodus, a son of the eminent English violinist. The duet, "Una Notte a Venezia," was excellently sung by Miss A. Myers and Mr. Levetus. A good miscellaneous programme was well gone through.

On June 15th a number of ladies waited on Mr. Monk at the Philharmonic Hall, Liverpool, where the examinations in connection with Trinity College, London, have been carried on during the week, for the purpose of presenting him with a testimonial of their esteem. The subscribers, about forty in number, past and present pupils of Mr. Monk, who has occupied the position of honorary local secretary to the college for several years. The testimonial took the form of an illuminated address, the work of Mr. Thomas Eyres, Church Street, and was a most artistic work of art. The address conveyed the subscribers' appreciation of Mr. Monk's earnest and untiring efforts towards the improvement of musical art in this city, expressing a hope that he might be long spared to labour as successfully as he had done in the past. Major R. E. Stewart occupied the chair, and the presentation was made, on behalf of the subscribers, by Humphrey J. Stark, Mus.Bac. Oxon., who spoke of Mr. Monk's musical ability, adding that his exertions as honorary local secretary had made Liverpool the most important centre of Trinity College in the whole country. The presentation was acknowledged in feeling terms.

The Querist.

REPLY.

E.B.—"ALLEGRO VIVACISSIMO," Scarlatti, played by Madame Menter, at her pianoforte recital, on May 19th, is only published in the original edition. Madame Menter played her own arrangement, and this is not published.—WILLIAM H. STOCKL.

Service Lists.

FIFTTH SUNDAY AFTER TRINITY.
JUNE 24th.
London.

ST. PAUL'S CATHEDRAL.—Morn.: Service, Te Deum and Jubilate, Oakeley in E flat ; Introit, Lo, from the desert homes ; Holy Communion, Oakeley in E flat. Even.: Service, Magnificat and Nunc Dimittis, Barnby in E flat ; Anthem, Behold, God hath sent Elijah (Mendelssohn).

WESTMINSTER ABBEY.—Morn.: Service, Mendelssohn in A; Continuation, Garrett in D. Even.: Service, Cooke in C; Anthems, O Praise the Lord of heaven (Goss), and I waited for the Lord (Mendelssohn).

TEMPLE CHURCH.—Morn.: Service, Te Deum Laudamus, Attwood in A ; Apostles' Creed, Harmonised Monotone; Anthem, The wilderness (Wesley). Even.: Service, Cantate Domino and Deus Misereatur, Attwood in D ; Apostles' Creed, Harmonized Monotone ; Anthem, Sing, O heavens (Sullivan).

LINCOLN'S INN CHAPEL.—Morn.: Service, Steggall in D; Kyrie, Steggall; Anthem, O praise the Lord of heaven (Goss). Even: Service, Turle in D ; Anthem, I will sing of Thy power (Greene).

CHRIST CHURCH, CLAPHAM.—Morn.: Service, Te Deum, Plain-song; Kyrie and Credo, Schubert in B flat ; Offertory Anthem, In the sight of the unwise (Ouseley) ; Sanctus, Benedictus, Agnus Dei, and Gloria in excelsis, Schubert. Even.: Service, Magnificat and Nunc Dimittis, Bunnett in F ; Anthem, A selection from Mendelssohn's "Hymn of Praise."

FOUNDLING CHAPEL.—Morn.: Service, Nares in F ; Anthem, How beautiful are the feet (Handel). Aft.: Service, Foster in A ; Anthem, Hallelujah (Handel).

HOLY TRINITY, TULSE HILL. — Morn.: Chant Service. Even.: Service, Magnificat and Nunc Dimittis, Gregory in E flat; Anthems, Comfort ye, and, And the glory of the Lord (Handel).

HIGH WYCOMBE PARISH CHURCH. — Even : Service, Anthems, From Thy love as a Father, and, Unfold ye portals everlasting, "The Redemption" (Gounod).

ST. MICHAEL'S, CORNHILL. — Morn.: Service, Te Deum and Jubilate, Wesley in F ; Anthem, Awake, awake (Wise); Kyrie, and Creed, Thorne in G. Even.: Service, Magnificat and Nunc Dimittis, Attwood in C; Anthem, Prepare ye the way (Wise).

ST. PETER'S (EATON SQUARE).—Morn.: Service, Te Deum, Garrett in F. Evensong: Service, Smart in B flat ; Anthem, Blessed be the God and Father (Wesley).

ST. MAGNUS, LONDON BRIDGE.—Morn.: Service, Opening Anthem, I will arise (Cecil) ; Te Deum and Jubilate, Travers in F; Kyrie, Mendelssohn. Even.: Service, Magnificat and Nunc Dimittis, Travers in F ; Anthem, Thou wilt keep him (Wesley).

ST. JAMES'S PRIVATE EPISCOPAL CHAPEL, SOUTHWARK. —Morn.: Service, Introit, Blessed is he that cometh (Mozart); Communion Service, Mozart. Even.: Service, Calkin in B flat ; Anthem, Jerusalem, happy and blest (Mendelssohn).

ST. SAVIOUR'S, HOXTON.—Morn.: Service, Te Deum, Goss in F; Holy Communion ; Kyrie, Credo, Sursum Corda, Sanctus, and Gloria in excelsis, Dykes in F. Even.: Service, Magnificat and Nunc Dimittis, Parry in D ; Anthem, And the Glory (Handel).

ST. PAUL'S, AVENUE ROAD, SOUTH HAMPSTEAD.—Morn.: Service, Te Deum, Sullivan in D ; Jubilate, Helmore ; Kyrie, Nares in F. Even.: Service, Magnificat and Nunc Dimittis, Walmisley in D minor ; Anthem, What are these, that are arrayed (Stainer).

ST. SEPULCHRE'S, HOLBORN.—Morn : Service, Barrow in F; Anthem, Incline thine ear (Himmel). Even.: Service, Nares in F ; Anthem, How lovely (Mendelssohn).

ST. PETER'S, LEIGHAM COURT ROAD, STREATHAM, S.W. —Morn.: Holy Eucharist, Purge me with hyssop (Novello) ; wise) ; Introit, The Lord hath called me (Chantwise); Mass, Hoyte in D ; Gradual, Before I formed thee (Chantwise) ; Even.: Service, Magnificat, Stainer in A; Anthem, Comfort ye (Handel).

ST. PAUL'S, BOW COMMON, E.—Morn.: Service, Te Deum and Benedictus, Chants; Holy Communion; Kyrie, Credo, Sanctus, Benedictus, Agnus Dei; Offertory, and Gloria in excelsis, Calkin in B flat. Even.: Service, Magnificat and Nunc Dimittis, Tours in D; Anthems, Blessed are they, Among those that are born, and There is not a greater prophet, from "St. John the Baptist (Macfarren).

ST. MARY BOLTONS, WEST BROMPTON, S.W.—Morn.: Service, Te Deum and Benedictus, Dykes in F; Holy Communion, Kyrie, Credo; Offertory, Sanctus, and Gloria in excelsis, Stainer in E flat; Benedictus, and Agnus Dei, Goring in F. Even.: Service, Magnificat and Nunc Dimittis, Gounod in D; Anthem, Prepare ye the way of the Lord (Crament).

ST. MARGARET PATTENS, ROOD LANE, FENCHURCH STREET.—Morn.: Service, Te Deum and Jubilate, Sullivan in D; Communion Service: Offertory Anthem, Comfort ye (Handel); Kyrie, Credo, Sanctus, Benedictus, Agnus Dei and Gloria, Schubert in B flat. Even.: Service, Magnificat and Nunc Dimittis, Hopkins in F; Anthem, as pants the hart (Spohr).

ST. PETER'S, VERE STREET, W.—Even.: Service, Magnificat and Nunc Dimittis, Hopkins in F; Anthem, The Lord is my shepherd (Macfarren).

ST. MARY ABCHURCH, E.C.—Morn.: Service, Wesley in F; Communion, Garrett in D. Even.: Service, Stainer in A.

Country.

ST. ASAPH CATHEDRAL.—Morn.: Service, Boyce in C; Anthem, Listen, O Isles (Allen). Even.: Service, Roberts in F; Anthem, Prepare ye the way (Garrett).

ASHBURNE CHURCH, DERBYSHIRE. — Morn.: Service, (throughout), Garrett in F. Even.: Service, Garrett in F; Anthem, The voice of one crying (Garrett).

BEDDINGTON CHURCH, SURREY.—Morn.: Service, Smart in F; Introit, Lo, from the desert homes; Communion Service, Calkin. Even.: Service, Stainer; Anthems, Comfort ye, every valley, and The Glory of the Lord (Handel).

BIRMINGHAM (ST. CYPRIAN'S, HAY MILLS).—Morn.: Service, Field in D; Anthem, O be joyful (Hayes). Even.: Service, Clarke-Whitfeld in E; Anthem, The Heavens declare (Boyce).

BIRMINGHAM (S. PHILIP'S CHURCH). — Morn.: Service, Chipp in A; Anthem, O be joyful (Palestrina). Even.: Service, Hopkins in F; Anthem, O that I knew where I might find Him (Sterndale Bennett).

BRISTOL CATHEDRAL.—Morn.: Service, Garrett in F. Even.: Service, Garrett in F; Anthem, And to a mighty host (Spohr).

CANTERBURY CATHEDRAL.—Morn.: Service, Smart in G; Anthem, Blow ye the trumpet (Leslie); Communion, Smart in G. Even.: Service, Smart in G; Anthem, Comfort ye my people, And the glory (Handel).

CARLISLE CATHEDRAL.—Morn.: Service, Smart in F; Introit, The Lord is in His Holy Temple (Thorne); Kyrie, and Nicene Creed, Dykes in F. Even.: Service, Hopkins in F; Anthem, The voice of one crying (Garrett).

CHESTER (ST. MARY'S CHURCH).—Morn.: Service, Boyce in C; Communion Service, Lee in G. Even.: Service, Barby in E; Anthems, Comfort ye, Every valley, And the glory of the Lord ("Messiah," Handel).

DONCASTER (PARISH CHURCH).—Morn.: Service, Boyce in C. Even.: Service, Ebdon in C; Anthem, What are these? (Stainer).

DUBLIN, ST. PATRICK'S (NATIONAL) CATHEDRAL.—Morn.: Service, Te Deum and Jubilate, King in D; Communion, Kyrie, Creed, and Sanctus, King in C; Anthem, What went ye out into the wilderness to see (Macfarren). Even.: Service, Magnificat and Nunc Dimittis, Stainer in A; Anthems, And sorrow and sighing (Wesley), Be thou faithful unto death (Mendelssohn).

EXETER CATHEDRAL.—Morn.: Service, Travers in F; Communion, Wesley in F. Even.: Service, Travers in F; Anthem, Comfort ye my people (Handel).

ELY CATHEDRAL.—Morn.: Service, Te Deum, Barnby in E; Benedictus, Plain-song; Kyrie and Credo, Thorne in E flat; Gloria, Chipp in A flat; Anthem, It is high time (Barnby). Even.: Service, Barnby in E; Anthem, Jerusalem I thou that killest, Happy and Blest (Mendelssohn).

LLANDAFF CATHEDRAL.—Morn.: Service, Te Deum and Benedictus, Stainer in E flat. Even.: Service, Magnificat and Nunc Dimittis, Stainer in E flat; Anthem, Prepare ye the way (Wise).

LIVERPOOL CATHEDRAL.—Aft.: Service, Magnificat and Nunc Dimittis, Farebrother in B flat; Anthem, Prepare ye the way of the Lord (Wise).

MANCHESTER CATHEDRAL.—Morn.: Service, Stainer in A; Holy Communion, Stanford in B flat; Anthem, Listen O Isles (Allen). Aft.: Service, Stainer in A; Anthem, This is the record of John (Gibbons).

MANCHESTER (ST. BENEDICT'S), — Morn.: Service, Kyrie, Credo, Sanctus, Benedictus, Agnus Dei, and Gloria in excelsis, Monk in C. Even.: Service, Magnificat and Nunc Dimittis, Wesley in F.

MANCHESTER (ST. JOHN BAPTIST, HULME).—Morn.: Service, Kyrie, Credo, Sanctus, Benedictus and Agnus Dei, Tours in F. Even.: Service, Magnificat and Nunc Dimittis, Bunnett in F; Anthem, Praise the Lord (Scott).

NORTH BERWICK, N.B. (S. BALDRED'S).—Morn.: Service, Te Deum, Steggall in G; Kyrie, Mendelssohn. Even.: Service, Chants; Anthem, What are these? (Stainer).

PETERBOROUGH CATHEDRAL.—Morn.: Service, Stainer in E flat; Anthem, Listen, O Isles (Allen); Communion Service, Thorne in E flat. Even.: Service, Stainer in E flat; Anthem, Comfort ye (Handel).

SHEFFIELD PARISH CHURCH. — Morn.: Service, Kyrie, Sullivan in D. Even.: Service, Chants; Anthem, O Lord our governor (Marcello).

SHERBORNE ABBEY.—Morn.: Service, Te Deum, Lyle in D. Even.: Service, Anthem, Come, mighty Father (Handel).

RIPON CATHEDRAL.—Morn.: Service, Boyce in C; Anthem, Be thou faithful (Mendelssohn); Kyrie and Credo, Garrett in F. Aft.: Service, Stainer in E; Anthem, What are these? (Stainer).

ROCHESTER CATHEDRAL.—Morn.: Service, Dean in A; Anthem, From the rising of the sun (Ouseley). Even.: Service, E. J. Hopkins in B flat (cantata); Anthem, Stand up and bless (Goss).

WELLS CATHEDRAL.—Morn.: Service, Bryan in G; Introit, Let us not be weary (Macfarren). Even.: Service, Stacy in A; Anthem, I was glad (Purcell).

*** *Post-cards must be sent to the Editor, 6, Argyle Square, W.C., by Wednesday. Lists are frequently omitted in consequence of not being received in time.*

NEWSPAPERS sent should have *distinct marks* opposite to the matter to which attention is required.

NOTICE.—*All communications intended for the Editor are to be sent to his private address. Business communications to be addressed to* 185, *Fleet Street, E.C.*

[The attention of the several Organists is called to the favour they confer upon their brother musicians by forwarding their notices regularly: this column of the paper is much valued as an index to what is going on in the choice of cathedral music, so much so that intermissions constantly give rise to remonstrance. Lists should be sent in a week in advance if possible.—ED. *Mus. Stand.*]

	NETT. s. d.
73. Haydn's Fantasia in C	4 0
74. Chopin's Polonaise in A. Op. 40	3 0
75. Scarlatti's Sonata in A. No. 31	3 0
76. Hummel's Rondeau villageoise. Op. 122	4 0
77. Mendelssohn's Andante in E minor. Op. 7, No. 1	3 0
78. Bach's Prelude in B flat. 1st Partita	2 0
79. Dussek's Adagio from "L'Invocation." Op. 77	3 0
80. Chopin's Berceuse. Op. 57	3 0
81. Weber's Adagiofrom Sonata. Op. 24	3 0
82. Hummel's La bella capricciosa. Op. 55	6 0
83. Bach's Allemande in B flat. 1st Partita	3 0
84. Mendelssohn's Andante and Rondo capriccioso. Op. 14	4 0

Printed for the Proprietor by BOWDEN, HUDSON & Co., at 23, Red Lion Street, Holborn, London, W.C.; and Published by WILLIAM REEVES, at the Office, 185, Fleet Street, E.C. West End Agents:—WEEKES & CO., 14, Hanover Street, Regent Street, W. Subscriptions and Advertisements are received either by the Publisher or West End Agents.—*Communications for the EDITOR are to be forwarded to his private address, 6, Argyle Square, W.C.*
SATURDAY, JUNE 23, 1883.—*Entered at the General Post Office as a Newspaper.*

THE MUSICAL STANDARD

A NEWSPAPER FOR MUSICIANS PROFESSIONAL AND AMATEUR

No. 987. VOL. XXIV. FOURTH SERIES.   SATURDAY, JUNE 30, 1883.   WEEKLY: PRICE 3D.

THE MUSICAL STANDARD is published every Saturday, price 3d., by post, 3½d. ; and may be had of any bookseller or newsagent by ordering its regular supply.

SUBSCRIPTION.—*The Musical Standard* is posted to subscribers at 15s. a year ; half a year, 7s. 6d., payable in advance.

The rate is the same to France, Belgium, Germany, Italy, United States, and Canada.

Post Office Orders to be made payable to the Publisher, William Reeves, 185, Fleet Street, London, or to the West-end Agents, Messrs. Weekes & Co., 14, Hanover Street, Regent Street, W.

ADVERTISEMENTS.—The charge for ordinary advertisements in *The Musical Standard* is 2s. 6d. for three lines or less ; and 6d. for each line (10 words) in addition. "Organist wanted," 3s. 6d. for 3 lines or less. A reduction is made for a series.

FRONT PAGE.—Concert and auction advertisements, &c., are inserted in the front page of *The Musical Standard*, and charged one-third in addition to the ordinary rates. Other advertisements will be inserted on the front page, or in the leader page, if desired, at the same terms.

YORK ORGAN FACTORY,

BLENHEIM PLACE, MONKGATE.

SPECIFICATION of NEW ORGAN, built by the late ROBT. POSTILL, in Pitch Pine Case, Stained and Varnished, with Spotted Metal Speaking Pipes in Front.

GREAT ORGAN.

Open Diapason	8 feet.	56 Notes.	
Salcional	8 „	44 „	
Stop Diapason	8 „	56 „	
Principal	4 „	56 „	
Flute Harmonic	4 „	56 „	
Fifteenth	2 „	56 „	
Sesquialtra	—	112 „	
Pasoune..	8 „	56 „	

SWELL ORGAN.

Double Diapason	16 feet.	44 Notes.	
Open Diapason	8 „	44 „	
Stop Diapason	8 „	12 „	
Clarabella	8 „	44 „	
Gemshorne	4 „	56 „	
Viol de Gamba	8 „	44 „	
Echo Dulcet	8 „	44 „	
Hautboy	8 „	56 „	

PEDAL ORGAN.

Bourdon (large scale)	16 feet.	30 Notes.	

COUPLERS.

Swell to Great.   Swell to Pedals.
          Great to Pedals.

Three Composition Pedals for Changing the Stops.
Two Octaves and a third of German Pedals for the Feet.

Front of Organ	10 feet 3 inches.	
Front to Back	9 „ 6 „	
Height	16 „ 6 „	

The above Instrument is for SALE, and may be seen and heard by applying at the Works, or Mrs. J. POSTILL'S, 25, Monkgate.

MR. HUMPHREY J. STARK begs to announce his REMOVAL to 12, Norwood Road, Herne Hill, S.E.

WANTED a CHAMBER ORGAN. Must be by a good maker and in good condition.—Address, Mrs. SIMONDS, Fishtoft, Boston.

WANTED, by the Advertiser, PRACTICE on an ORGAN, three manuals, near Cannon Street or Charing Cross Stations.—Address, "F. D.," care of Davies & Co., Finch Lane, Cornhill.

GENTLEMAN (well recommended), with thorough knowledge of music, DESIRES SITUATION in a London house (publishing department preferred).—Address E. G., care of Mr. REEVES, 185, Fleet Street, E.C.

AN ORGANIST will shortly be open to RE-ENGAGEMENT, in or near London preferred. 1st Class Certificate from Society of Arts ; good testimonials and references.—Address, F. J. PARKER, 20, Sangora Road, New Wandsworth, S.W.

A CLERGYMAN wishes to recommend an EX-PUPIL TEACHER as CLERK or ASSISTANT in a Firm where he could obtain employment and also further instruction in music.—Address Rev. E. HARMAN, Pickwell Rectory, Oakham

---

TO SOLO BOYS.—A Professional Organist wishes to meet with a BOY having GOOD SOPRANO VOICE for Church Choir. In return first class tuition on organ, piano, and singing is offered, with expenses. — "ORGANIST," Beaconsfield House, Iverson Road, Kilburn, N.W.

Post 8vo., boards, 2s. 6d., post free.

TECHNICS OF VIOLIN PLAYING, by KARL COURVOISIER. Edited and translated by H. E. Krehbiel. Numerous illustrations.

Joachim says : "It is my opinion that this book will offer material aid to all violin players.

W. REEVES, 185, Fleet Street, London, E.C.

THE ORGANIST and CHOIRMASTER of Cirencester Abbey desires RE-ENGAGEMENT. 14 years' Cathedral experience.—Address as above.

JUST PUBLISHED, "MORNING and EVENING SERVICE," set to music for the especial use of Parish Choirs, by FREDK. HUNNIBELL, F.C.O. Price, 1s. ; or separately, 8d. and 6d.
London : NOVELLO, EWER & CO.

FIRST AND SECOND GRADES JUST PUBLISHED.

PRICE TWO SHILLINGS EACH.

Under the Sanction and Approval of the Rev. Sir FREDERICK A. GORE OUSELEY, Bart., M.A., Mus.Doc. Oxford, and of Sir G. A. MACFARREN, Mus.Doc., Cambridge.

THE MUSICIAN.

A GUIDE FOR PIANOFORTE STUDENTS.

Helps towards the Better Understanding and Enjoyment of Beautiful Music.

BY RIDLEY PRENTICE.

"We are far from suggesting that there is any royal road for acquiring technical knowledge, but we are quite certain that Mr. Ridley Prentice's road is in every way the pleasantest that has yet been laid before any piano-forte student. If anyone will work through this first grade conscientiously, by the time he has reached the end of it he will have mastered many difficulties in harmony and musical form which he might have hitherto thought were almost insurmountable. The work supplies a deficiency in musical literature which has long been felt ; and we earnestly recommend the study of it to all those who wish to become intelligent pianoforte players."—*Saturday Review.*

"A knowledge of form is imparted in simple and pleasant language. This is the right sort of instruction book, for it teaches people to think and study for themselves. We heartily commend it to all who desire to understand, satisfactorily interpret, and enjoy beautiful music."—*Academy.*

SECOND EDITION READY.

THE CHILD'S PIANOFORTE BOOK; a First Year's Course of the Piano, by H. K. MOORE, Mus.B., B.A., Illustrated, 4to, 3s. 6d.

W. SWAN SONNENSCHEIN & CO., Paternoster Row
And all Book and Music Sellers.

Musical Intelligence.

THE HANDEL FESTIVAL AT THE CRYSTAL PALACE.

THE SELECTION DAY AND "ISRAEL IN EGYPT."

The grand success of the eighth triennial Handel Festival is now more than a thrice told tale, and it would be both stale and unprofitable to write more than a few words on the subject.

The selection was, as usual, made up from opera, cantata, and oratorio, with the G minor concerto for the organ. The advantage which Handel gained in an artistic point of view, from writing no less than thirty-nine operas, is not to be lightly esteemed. Some writers have drawn a striking parallel between the operas of Handel and the comedies of Shakespeare, and think that the early schooling both had in these forms of art, was the very means by which they gained so complete a mastery of them, as to enable them hereafter to free themselves from their constraining influence. This they would never have effected in so remarkable a degree, if they had from the first devoted themselves to the highest form of their respective arts, but as in Shakespeare comedy preceded tragedy, so with Handel did oratorio succeed to opera, and I cannot but think that in both instances the lighter style was the foundation of nobler and grander productions. On the part of Handel the advantage was even greater, for in many of his oratorios we find whole songs of a suitable character transferred from his secular works and adapted to sacred words, and many of his instrumental pieces, as is well known, were changed into choruses; indeed much honest labour that at one time seemed destined to be forgotten, was utilized for a nobler purpose. Thus it is with all honest and conscientious work. Sooner or later the time will come when the labourer shall meet with his reward.

In the selection both the sacred and secular parts were sung with wonderful precision. Only in one—"Oh the pleasure of the plains"—did Mr. Manns feel it necessary to beat his book, and in that but for a few bars. With regard to the numerous solos, Mdme. Valleria was heard, if not to perfection, certainly to much greater advantage, in the song "From mighty kings" than on the rehearsal day. Mdme. Albani was charming in "Let the bright seraphim" as well as in "Angels ever bright and fair," transposed by the orchestra into six sharps. Mdme. Trebelli and Mdme. Patey were no less successful in their respective songs, and Mr. E. Lloyd, Mr. Barton McGuckin, and Mr. Santley did not fail to do justice to some of the finest and most exacting of Handel's songs. One of the most beautiful features of the programme was the organ concerto No. 1, and of Mr. Best's admirable performance of it, it would be impossible to speak too highly.

"ISRAEL IN EGYPT."

The broad grand choruses which occupy the chief part of this mighty work, with their varied and skilful treatment, make it especially interesting to musicians, and the fact that on this day there was a larger attendance at the Crystal Palace than on any other of the Festival, is not to be passed over, for it is a sure sign that we are not yet indifferent to the effects produced by combined human voices, effects often more grandly impressive than those of any orchestra.

Of the performance, a word or two will suffice. Absolute perfection was scarcely to be expected, but it was little short of this. I have attended four of these festivals, and on no occasion has the choir reached so high a standard of perfection. This remark is not only applicable to "Israel in Egypt," but to the other performances. A friend of mine has taken the trouble to count over the names in the choir list, in order to ascertain the proportion the contingent from the provinces bears to that of London, and I am told that including the names of men from nearly all our cathedrals, only about one-sixth of the whole are from the country. London may, therefore, be justly proud of what she has achieved, and it would, I think, be quite practicable to have in each of the two

years succeeding the Handel Festival, a musical festival at Sydenham, at which both symphonies and the choral works of our greatest composers might be performed. London, with its wonderful resources, its unbounded wealth, and its growing musical taste, is more than able to effect this desirable object, especially with a conductor who has proved himself so skilful and efficient as Mr. Manns has done, in conducting not only a large orchestra, but also in the less familiar task of commanding so large a body of voices as that gathered together at the Handel Festival.　　　　　R. S.

M. SAINTON'S FAREWELL CONCERT.

ALBERT HALL, JUNE 25TH.

PROGRAMME.

PART I.

Overture, "Zampa"	Hérold.
Part Song, "Fair and Young"	J. Coward.
The Coward Family Quartet.	
Aria, "Caro mio ben"	Giordani.
Miss Annie Lord.	
{ a. Serenade, "Through the night"	Schubert.
{ b. Song, "Devotion"	Schumann.
Mr. Vernon Rigby.	
Air, "Creation's Hymn"	Beethoven.
Miss Damian.	
Concerto (Andante and Finale)	Mendelssohn.
Mons. Sainton.	
Song, "I will come"	Cowen.
Mr. Edward Lloyd.	
Aria, "Ah, quel giorno" ("Semiramide")	Rossini.
Madame Trebelli.	
Romanza, "Salve dimora" ("Faust")	Gounod.
Signor Scovello.	
Couplets, "Aux bruits des lourds Marteaux"	
("Philémon et Baucis")	Gounod.
Mr. Santley.	
Song, "The Days that are no more"	Blumenthal.
Madame Sainton-Dolby.	
Air, "Sweet Saint" ("St. Dorothea")	Mme. Sainton-Dolby
Mr. Edward Lloyd.	
Violoncello obbligato, Mons. Lasserre.	
(Accompanied by the Composer.)	
Suite de Pièces "Language of Flowers"	F. H. Cowen.
No. 2. Lilac (First emotion of love).	
No. 3. Yellow Jasmine (Elegance and grace).	
No. 5. Lily of the Valley (Return of happiness).	

PART II.

Overture, "William Tell"	Rossini.
Aria, "La bella mea"	Schira.
Madame Trebelli.	
"Ave Maria," on a Prelude by	Bach.
(arranged by Gounod for voice, violin, piano-	
forte, and harmonium.)	
Mdme. Adelina Patti, Mons. Sainton, Mr. Leipold,	
and Mr. Louis Engel.	
Duo Concertante, for two Pianofortes.	
Variations in B flat	Schumann.
Miss Margaret Gyde and Miss Cantelo.	
Song, "Save me, O God"	Randegger.
Miss Mary Davies.	
Nocturne, Violoncello	Chopin.
Mons. Lasserre.	
Song, "Here's a health unto his Majesty"	Old English.
Mr. Santley.	
Ballad, "Strangers yet"	Claribel.
Madame Sainton-Dolby.	
Solos, Violin { a. "Un rien"	Sainton.
{ b. "Valse"	
Mons. Sainton.	
Song, "The Nightingale's Trill"	Gana.
Miss Hilda Coward.	
March from "Le Prophète"	Meyerbeer.
Conductors :—Sir Julius Benedict, Mr. Frederick Cowen, Mr. Leipold,	
Mr. Willing, Mr. Sidney Naylor, and Mr. Randegger.	

As might have been expected, the leave-taking from the public of so popular an artist as M. Sainton has ever been from the beginning of his career in the metropolis, was of more than usual interest. Admired as a *virtuoso*, respected and beloved as a man, and united to a lady who, as a vocalist, held for many years the first rank—and by her noble qualities endeared herself to all who had the good fortune of knowing her—the worthy pair not only enchanted their audiences but created a school by transmitting their excellent methods to a large number of pupils.

The great popularity of these distinguished artists could not have been better proved than by the fact, that when M. Sainton came forward as an apologist for Mdme. Adelina Patti and Mr. Sims Reeves, both artists, who, amongst the many "ills that flesh is heir to," had been visited—Mdme. Patti by "un enroument," whilst Mr. Sims Reeves had been assailed with "hay fever"—the announcement, excepting a general titter when the great English tenor's name was mentioned, caused no visible sign of disappointment.

M. Sainton's vigour, brilliant execution, and sympathetic tone, found full scope in Mendelssohn's Concerto and two of his own graceful compositions. His pupils of the Royal Academy, represented by Mdlle. Vaillant, presented him a wreath of golden laurel leaves amid the enthusiastic and overwhelming applause of the whole audience, who rose *en masse*.

Nothing could better show the excellence of Mdme. Sainton-Dolby's method than her rendering of the two popular songs, which she accompanied herself in an admirable manner. Her full clear notes and her remarkably distinct enunciation and impressive declamation might well serve as a valuable lesson to many vocalists of the present day. The floral gifts, in the form of magnificent bouquets, were as plentiful as the ovations were enthusiastic.

Cela va sans dire, that all the artists, who assisted, did so *con amore*, and were at their best.

FERDINAND PRAEGER.

Another contributor says:—

The writer has known and borne willing testimony to the merits of this eminent violinist for the last twenty-five or thirty years, and remembers him in his heyday of summer. M. Sainton, a Frenchman by birth, has long been a leading man amongst us, and for some years acted as *chef-d'orchestre* at Her Majesty's "Opera" (formerly yclept Her Majesty's *Theatre* and the *King's* Theatre), under Sir Michael Costa. As a soloist, M. Sainton always commanded splendid successes, notably in classical music, and the severe "quartet" department of art. The veteran, who married a favourite and super-excellent contralto, well-known as Miss Dolby, took his farewell of an admiring public last Monday afternoon at the Albert Hall, and was favoured not only with a large audience, but a cordial and enthusiastic greeting. How M. Sainton played his own part at this farewell concert, it boots not to say. *Ca va sans dire /* He chose the andante and finale from Mendelssohn's (one) violin concerto in E minor, and two solos from his own pen, "Un rien" and a Valse. Part of the finale, in the concerto, was repeated by express "desire." Madame Sainton-Dolby, reappearing for this great success only, condescended to sing, and in finest style, Blumenthal's air "The days that are no more," and Claribel's "Strangers yet." How melancholy to think that we must, henceforth, submit to miss two so great artists, vocal and instrumental !

Mdme. Trebelli volunteered "Ah quel giorno" (Rossini), and Schira's "La bella mia." Mr. Sims Reeves could not appear as announced. Mr. Edward Lloyd sang Mdme. Dolby's "Sweet saint," and Mr. Santley Gounod's "Hammer song." A band of 100 performers was engaged. The conductors of the concert were Sir Julius Benedict, Mr. F. Cowen, Mr. Leipold, Mr. Willing, Mr. Sidney Naylor, and Mr. Randegger. M. Sainton retires full of years and honours.   A. M.

The Times thus notices the antecedents of M. Sainton, and the facts are sufficiently interesting :—

"It was in 1844 that M. Sainton, at that time a young and promising artist of continental repute, made his first appearance in London at a Philharmonic concert, and the reception he met with led to his return in the next season, and finally, to his permanent settlement amongst us. M. Sainton appeared before the public in various capacities, and was successful in each of them. His *technique*, acquired under Habeneck at the Paris Conservatoire, and his highly cultivated taste, enabled him to interpret the great classical masters, and he was one of the original members of the Beethoven Quartet Society, in which he acted as 'first violin.' The same important post he occupied frequently at the late 'Musical Union,' founded by Mr. Ella, the 'Monday Popular,' and other high class concerts, besides continuing his activity as a solo player. But perhaps the most signal and permanent services to the cause of music M. Sainton has rendered are as first violinist,' or as it is technically called the 'leader' of orchestras. In that capacity his name will always be connected with that of his famous chief, Sir Michael Costa, under whom he worked with unwearying zeal at the Italian operas of Covent Garden and her Majesty's, the Sacred Harmonic Society, and the great provincial festivals, and whom he now follows into well-merited *otium cum dignitate*. At Monday's concert a large and distinguished audience had assembled to do honour to a 'good and faithful servant.'"

The Continental and American sea-side and pleasure places of resort announces their summer musical arrangements. We may well ask here, is anything being done to make the bands at certain of our waterside places more complete, better balanced, and more generally effective? and further, are steps being taken to secure the performance of higher class music than one generally hears at our sea-side pleasure places?

BRIGHTON.

The newly formed Musical Society gave their first concert recently at the Hove Town Hall, under the able direction of Mr. F. J. Sawyer, Mus.Bac. The programme included Attwood's "Coronation Anthem," the overture to Spohr's "Last Judgment," the 1st movement from Mozart's G minor Symphony, Romberg's "The Transient and the Eternal," and several vocal pieces, including two old madrigals. This interesting programme was admirably performed, the chorus singing being exceptionally good ; and the enthusiastic recall of Mr. Sawyer at the end of the concert showed how well the audience appreciated the performances under his *bâton*. Madame Rose Kœnig played Mendelssohn's G minor pianoforte concerto in good style and the band accompaniments were very satisfactorily rendered.

MR. W. CARTER'S CHOIR.

Mr. William Carter held another grand concert at the Albert Hall on June 16th, when his choir sang Auber's chorus in E flat, known as the "Prayer," from "Masaniello," otherwise "La Muette de Portici," a gem of that beautiful opera ; also Mendelssohn's "Farewell to the forest," "Rule Britannia," and E. Bending's grand "Patriotic March." The united bands of the three regiments of foot-guards played pieces at proper intervals. Miss Ellicott, daughter of the Bishop of Gloucester, gave a very intellectual and effective reading of Handel's air in A, "From mighty kings." Mdme. Trebelli, Mr. Foli, Mr. Maybrick, Mr. Barrington Foote, and Miss A. Larkcom, sang in turn. Haydn's "Toy" symphony had the honour to be performed by Sir Julius Benedict, Mr. W. Ganz, Signor Tito Mattei, M. Poznanski, M. Jacob (of Brussels), Mr. Lindsay Sloper, Mr. E. Bending, Mr. W. Carter, and Mr. C. Oberthür ; the vocalists were Mr. Foli, Mr. Barrington Foote, and Mr. Maybrick. Mr. Oberthür and Mr. Poznanski played solos on harp and violin with their customary success. The recitations, always *de trop*, do not, happily, lie within my province. At private parties they are simply inflictions, "cruelty to animals" of the higher order !

ROYAL ITALIAN OPERA.

Nothing particularly new this week. "La Gioconda" (repeated on Monday), continues to draw the public, and no wonder. Last week the directors revised Mozart's genuine Italian opera, "Le Nozze di Figaro," with Mdme. Albani as the Countess Almaviva, Mdme. Repetto as Susanna, Signor Cotogni as Figaro, Signor De Reszke as the Count, and last, not least, Mdme. Pauline Lucca as the love-sick page Cherubino, whose "Voi che sapete," with its delicious change of tonality (on the same vocal note), from C minor to A flat major, made a deep impression from the finished phrasing and expressive delivery of the text. Mdme. Albani sang her music with consummate skill. Signor De Reszke makes the Count rather too stiff and statuesque for the character. Almaviva, after all, is something of a libertine, and libertines, if jealous of wives, seldom rise to the dignified grandeur of the "injured husband." How rotten the morality of an age when such "fine gentlemen" as Don Juan, Almaviva, and the like, were not only tolerated, but popular ! A French revolution of morals, no less than politics, are certainly called for ; and Beaumarchais gave the movement a hard shove !

Mdme. Patti on Friday, June 22nd, appeared in the title part of "Semiramide," the dismal and dreary tragic opera of Rossini, which it is impossible to sit out without yawning. A dull repulsive plot is not redeemed by florid vocalisation on texts whereof the style now sounds vapid, effete, and utterly out of date. "Bel raggio," of course, excited applause, and the duet "Giorno d'orrore" (with Mdme. Scalchi as Second) went well as usual. M. Gailhard was the Assur.   A. M.

MOZART'S definition of *prima vista* reading is one which musicians in general, and young students in particular, should commit to memory. It is this:—To play the piece in the time in which it ought to be played, and to express all the notes and appoggiaturas, etc., with proper taste and feeling, as written, so that it should give the impression of being composed by the person who plays it. This is an art in itself, and can only be acquired by faithful, persistent study.—*Church's Musical Visitor*.

MUSICAL ARTISTS' SOCIETY.

The twenty-ninth performance of new compositions took place at the Royal Academy of Music, Saturday evening, June 23rd. Three very charming English dances, for pianoforte duet (Algernon Ashton), were played by the composer, and Mr. E. H. Thorne, the second one narrowly escaping a *bis*. A pianoforte trio in E flat (Dr. Jacob Bradford), was played by Miss Emily Lawrence, Mons. Victor Buziau, and Mr. Edmund Woolhouse. Mr. H. C. Banister presented his own Romance and Tarantella, No. 2 ; and four melodious and poetical characteristic pieces (E. H. Thorne), were sympathetically performed by Miss Edith Goldsboro. Songs by Oliveria Prescott, and C. J. Read, were sung by Mr. Arthur Jarratt, and Miss Von Hennig. " The Safeguard," a sea song (Duncan Hume), sung by Mr. W. J. Fletcher, was redemanded and repeated. Through some misunderstanding the string quartet, by F. Adler, was not played.

CAMBRIDGE UNIVERSITY MUSICAL SOCIETY.

Mr. Hubert Parry's " Second Symphony in F," was given with very encouraging success at a recent concert. The first movement is tuneful and charming, though here and there a little overwrought perhaps. The Scherzo in D minor and major is piquantly instrumented. The Larghetto in B flat is a charming and characteristic movement. The finale is an interesting movement, though perhaps less spontaneous in its themes than are the preceding pieces. The whole work is one of remarkable musicianship, with not too much obscured form outlines. The composer was enthusiastically received. Other items of the concert were Schumann's highly characteristic " Pilgrimage of the Rose," and Brahms's " Schicksalslied." The chief vocalists were Miss Amy. Aylward, Miss Helen Arnim, Mr. Walter Ford of King's College, and Mr. Herbert Thorndike. Both band and chorus, under the very excellent beat of Mr. C. V. Stanford, did their parts very satisfactorily. The' Society deserves much praise for consistent efforts in the production of new and little used musical works.

THE COLOGNE CHOIR.

Recent concerts have fully maintained the reputation of this famous choral society. The members had the honour of a " command " to sing before the Prince of Wales and the Royal Family at Marlborough House last Saturday afternoon. On June 21st, when the writer was present for the last time, the Choir sang pieces by Kreutzer, Mendelssohn ("Wasserfahrt" and "Wanderlied "), Schubert, Rietz, Herbeck, Koschat, &c. The fine tone, the *nuances*, and the *crescendo* of the Choir, were particularly noticeable in Mendelssohn's part-song " Der Frohe Wandersmann." Signor Eugenio Pirani and Mr. W. Ganz played an effective pianoforte duet, a Polonaise and Valse composed by the first-named gentleman, who had previously introduced his own "Fantasia," Op. 16, also a Prelude and a Study of Chopin. Concerts were held on Friday afternoon and Saturday evening, when this interesting series was to terminate. It is suspected, however, that extra concerts will be asked for by the public. Herr De Lange deserves the highest praise for his able direction.

Another contributor says :—
The Cologne Choir's visit has been one of the most important events of the season. It has shown us the perfection to which part singing by a large body of men can be brought, when each individual that makes up the whole is an enthusiast and a musician. How thoroughly they were appreciated was proved by the fact that at the last concert there was a strong tendency to encore each number on the programme. The very way the whole Choir rise as one man at the instant the conductor gives the signal, the attention with which they watch his movements till the moment to begin arrives, shows how, one and all, they are heart and soul in their work. Their influence has been good, for it has given us a higher ideal of part-singing ; and they may reckon on a hearty welcome when they shall again visit our metropolis.

B. F. WYATT-SMITH.

The next students' invitation orchestral concert at Trinity College will take place on July 3rd, at eight o'clock.

MDLLE. KLEEBERG'S RECITALS.

Mdlle. Clotilde Kleeberg, although her patronymic is obviously Teutonic, happens to be a Parisian by nationality, and a pupil of M. Massart. Her second pianoforte recital, held at the Prince's Hall, Piccadilly, on the afternoon of Thursday, June 21st (the longest day, alas !), passed off with the greatest *éclat*. Mdlle. Kleeberg, it may be repeated, is an artist of the first rank, and seems to have a special aptitude for the exposition of modern pianoforte literature, especially the works of Schumann and Chopin. The scheme included Beethoven's Sonata in E flat, Op. 31, No. 3, which the writer had the misfortune to miss (" such a busy life "), Fugues of J. S. Bach in F sharp and B flat, an Impromptu of Schubert in E flat, Wehle's " Berceuse," a Romance by Mendelssohn in A minor, Rubinstein's Barcarolle in G minor, " La Fille des Aulnes " by G. Pfeiffer, and four pieces of Chopin, viz.—two Preludes in A flat and B flat minor, two Mazurkas in B minor and A flat, an Etude in C minor, and Ballade in G minor. Schumann's " Carnival " supplied, about half way, the *pièce de résistance*, and excellent, in every sense, was the interpretation by this accomplished and exceedingly modest young French lady. Brilliant execution and *aplomb;* force, defined purpose, and decision ; flexibility, versatility of style, and delicate colouring, may be noted as essential qualities—not to deal in vague generalities, or to be content with eulogy which, if not analytical, conveys no compliment to the performer. The " Carnaval " piece requires as many different "humours " as the spangles of friend "Arlequin's" particoloured suit of tights. The recital only lasted an hour and a half, and the public were delighted. Mdlle. Kleeberg played upon an iron-grand Erard. A. M.

RICHTER CONCERTS.

A notice was given with the programmes last Monday to the effect that, " owing to unforeseen circumstances, Herr Henschel's concerto, Herr Richter regretted to say, could not be included in the programme ; the 'Vorspiel und Isolde's Liebestod ' would therefore be substituted.' The "unforeseen circumstances' are much to be deplored ; for so unusual an event as the appearance of a successful singer in the character of instrumentalist was looked forward to with great interest ; the more so as those who had the privilege of being present at Herr and Mdme. Henschel's Vocal Recitals were struck with the distinguished vocalist's power—not only as an excellent accompanist, for that was known before ; but— as a pianist with no inconsiderable amount of executive ability.

The programme was given in the following order :—

Symphony, No. 6, in C ("Lins")	Mozart.
Walther's Probelieder (Trial Songs,) from " Die Meistersinger "	Wagner.
a. " Am stillen Herd " (" By silent hearth in winter-tide ")	
b. " Fanget an ! " (" Now begin ! ")	
Mr. Edward Lloyd.	
Vorspiel und Isolde's " Liebestod " from " Tristan und Isolde"	Wagner.
Symphony, " Harold en Italie," Op. 16.	Berlioz.
Viola, Herr B. Hollander.	

Mozart's Symphony cannot be said to rank among the noblest of his works ; it was, however, admirably performed and much applauded. Mr. Lloyd's rendering of Walther's songs was earnest and appreciative, well meriting the double seal that testified to his success. The introduction and closing scene of "Tristan und Isolde " was again, as at the first concert of the season when it was given, the most impressively perfect performance of the evening. The Harold Symphony has been heard to as great advantage in England on previous occasions. Possibly insufficient time was given to rehearsing ; for the more than average excellence that Herr Richter accustoms us to expect was not attained. Those who have heard the work under Mr. Manns would not only fail to find anything particularly striking in the performance of last Monday, but might not improbably, be disposed to give the preference to the interpretation presented at the Crystal Palace. There appeared to be a lack of that repose which is born of perfect trust and confidence between conductor and performers ; consequently, the delicate attention to detail, into which Herr Richter throws his whole soul when he has nothing else to think of, was to a great extent absent. Herr Holländer's part was, however, in every respect, all that could be desired : he is an artist of the first rank.

Probably most of us can say now, with Schumann :—"Berlioz is as clear to me as the blue sky above me." But it is only within the last few years that he has been allowed to make headway among us ; and—"Honour to whom honour is due"—it was the Wagner Society that kept the name of Berlioz before the musicians of London by including his works in their programmes more often than those of any master but Beethoven and Wagner, at a time when his compositions were not to be heard here by any other means.

It is to be regretted that our leading musicians should as "C. A. B." has done in our programmes, take up Dr. Hiller's unworthy and ignoble version of the well-known story relating to Paganini's gift of 20,000 francs to Berlioz. We have been taught to believe—what indeed it was perfectly natural for anyone possessed of a spark of generosity to believe—that Paganini, in an overflow of enthusiastic admiration for the master whom he considered was the worthy successor of Beethoven, proved his admiration in the substantial way that was most acceptable to the struggling artist. Not so ! We learn in these wise latter days that the "gift was by no means a voluntary one, but was extorted from him by Jules Janin, the editor of the *Journal des Débats*, then the source of all artistic fame in Paris. Paganini, fearful of losing his prestige with the public if the *Débats* should turn against him, yielded to Janin's persuasions, and sent the sum named to Berlioz." This is one version of an old and honourable story. Dr. Hiller says it was Armand Bertin, the proprietor of the paper, who obliged Paganini to send the money. But neither version agrees very well with Paganini's own remarks :—"It is the profoundest satisfaction I ever felt in my life," and "Now all those who are in league against you will dare to say nothing more ; for they know I am not *easy*." (Fr. *aisé* ; probably meaning here "easily parted from my money.")

We know that Berlioz's gratitude to Paganini never grew less ; that he had no greater wish than to prove himself worthy of his benefactor's generosity by some musical offering noble enough to be dedicated to him : we know further that the "Romeo and Juliet" symphony was inspired by this high-souled artistic gratitude : and shall we say now that Berlioz was only the dupe of a kindly-meant, but none the less vile plot ; that Paganini was no more capable of artistic enthusiasm and self-forgetfulness than we are of appreciating such feelings ; that all the "calumnious insinuations" against him referred to by Berlioz as having arisen at the time, are solid truths ; and that it is a duty we owe our fellow-creatures to discover a base, despicable motive for everybody's actions, there being nothing pure, unselfish or honourable under the sun ? Each one of us must decide in this matter as his own heart directs him.

B. F. WYATT-SMITH.

MUSIC IN DUBLIN.

The University Choral Society concluded the present season on 22nd instant with an evening concert in the Dining Hall of Trinity College. By comparison with what the Society has previously produced, it must be confessed, that the programme on this occasion was of a somewhat modest character. At their first concert for this season they produced "Acis and Galatea" (Handel), and the oratorio "Jonah," by Carissimi, and their second performance was Gade's "Pysche." The concert under notice consisted principally of solos, part songs, and glees, with a departure which I am delighted to chronicle, viz., the introduction of orchestral music. The concert opened with Haydn's No. 12 Symphony in B flat. The venture was indeed a bold one, as the orchestra was composed chiefly of amateur talent ; all the more credit is therefore due for the admirable manner in which the symphony was performed. The composition is brimful of melody and delicate orchestration, and was rendered with excellent effect, and listened to with very marked attention. The ballet from Schubert's "Rosamunde" was also very tunefully rendered by the orchestra. For the production of some of the vocal music the society procured the services of Mrs. Scott Fennel and Miss Keane, both professionals. Mrs. Scott Fennel sang "How Like a Flower" (Schumann), "A Dream on the Waters" (Schubert), "When the Tide comes in " (Barnby), and "Fond and Firm " (E. H. Seymour), and were one

and all rendered by her with that grace and finish which characterises the true artist. A special interest attaches itself to the last song, " Fond and Firm," the composer being a member of the University Choral Society Committee, and for which song he obtained the first Balfe Memorial Prize. Miss Keane rendered "Thou Fair and Happy Boy," from Hiller's "Lurline," and " For Pity's sake " (Adams), in a very agreeable manner, and was warmly applauded. A gentleman amateur possessed of a nice quality tenor voice, sang with great expression " Sweet Morn of May " (Sir Robert Stewart), also " The Paradise in Herrenalf," by Mr. Arthur Patton ; the composer in each case playing the accompaniment. A member of the Society rendered " Droop not, Young Lover " (Handel), in commendable manner, but it was quite apparent that the bass music of Handel is not suited to his voice. Another member of the Society sang an Aria by Handel in a very good style. Two part-songs "The Hawthorn Tree" and " The Hawthorn in Berry," both by Sir R. Stewart, were given in excellent style by the chorus, as was also "The Song of the Vikings," by Eaton Faning. I should not forget to mention a violoncello solo, " The Last Rose of Summer," and a " Gavotte," from Carolan's Concerto, which was exquisitely played by an amateur. The foregoing comprised the principal items of the programme. It is to be hoped the Society will continue to introduce into its programme the production of classic orchestral music, which I am sure would be very successful under the able guidance of its esteemed conductor, Sir R. Stewart.

T. J. B.

LIVERPOOL.

(From our Own Correspondent.)

June 26.

The Liverpool Philharmonic Society has undergone several changes lately. The proprietors held meetings and denounced the doings of the committee, and ousted several of them, when the election of members to serve on the committee occurred ; the other members resigned, and so there is now an entirely new committee elected by the enraged proprietors. The cry was, that there was too much of the foreign element in the concerts, and that an English conductor ought to be engaged ; and yet the very first thing that this new committee does is to elect Mr. Hallé as the new conductor, thereby lowering the Liverpool society to that of second fiddle to Manchester ! Mr. Hallé's terms are that he continues his own concerts as before, and introduces some drastic change into the chorus. Why this worship of Hallé? Is there no Englishman equal to conducting the musical affairs of the Liverpool Harmonic Society? The re-election of the committee is to be ratified by the proprietors to-morrow (Wednesday) if they agree to their insane arrangement ; if the proprietors do confirm the committee's nomination, it will be an evil day for the Liverpool Harmonic Society.

I cannot do better than give a few quotations from a letter which appears in the *Liverpool Daily Post* of to-day :

" The new committee of the Philharmonic Society have issued a circular calling an extraordinary general meeting for Wednesday next, the 27th inst., at which meeting they will submit for the consideration and approval of the proprietors an appointment of a conductor.

" No name is mentioned in this circular; but it is an open secret by this time that the committee will propose on Wednesday to offer the post to Mr. Charles Hallé, of Manchester, and to omit from his contract the principal clause imposed an all former conductors—viz., that the conductor shall not arrange to give, or conduct, any orchestral or other concerts in Liverpool or the immediate neighbourhood, excepting those of this society or in connection with it.

" As to Mr. Hallé's' pre-eminence as a conductor there can scarcely be two opinions. But, notwithstanding our unbounded respect for Mr. Hallé, there exists an opinion that his appointment to the conductorship of the Philharmonic Society will prove an irretrievable mistake.

" There are many persons who share in the opinion that the Liverpool Philharmonic Society is something more than a concert-giving society—that, as the leading musical society, it exerts a fatherly protectorate over musical matters in this city ; that it is the recognised home of local musicians ; and that it is and should remain essentially a Liverpool institution. Such it has been for over forty years, and now it is proposed to merge the individuality of our musical life into that of Manchester,

"One might understand this eagerness to secure the services of Mr. Hallé if we had not already the opportunity to enjoy his concerts in our own hall : but the policy of handing over unconditionally the management of our society to a gentleman, however eminent he may be, who represents Manchester if he represents anything, and who will continue to give a series of concerts in our own hall for his own benefit, is to many most unintelligible. What would the shareholders of the National Steamship Company say if it were proposed that Mr. Guion should manage their company for a small salary, and at the same time be allowed to continue his business in their office? By men of business that would be called a suicidal policy. I see no difference between that and what is proposed by the new committee of the Philharmonic Society.

"That the fullest control should be given to the conductor over all the musical arrangements of our society—in fact, that his authority should be commensurate to his responsibilities—is a policy generally acknowledged to be essential ; but no man can serve two masters equally well, and our conductor, if invested with the unlimited powers that are his due, should be ours only. There should be no possibility of any suspicion that such a thing as a rival interest could ever stand between him and our society.

"Let the best man be chosen that can be found, or let us be as patriotic as we like in our choice; but above all let us remain loyal to our society and to our city, and do not let us sell our birthright for a mess of pottage."

Mr. Martin Schneider gave an organ recital upon the organ in Mossley Hill Church (to the organistship of which he has just been appointed) on Saturday afternoon, which was very successful in every way. Mr. Schneider's playing is always of a refined and artistic character. The programme of the recital will be found in the proper column. J. J. M.

Mr. Willing's Choir.—By a graceful thought, Sir M. Costa's "Eli" was given on June 16th, at St. James's Hall. Miss Robertson announced to take the soprano part did not appear, but Miss Griffin took her place. The soloists were Mdme. Patey, Mr. Vernon Rigby, Mr. Ludwig, and Mr. Lewis Thomas. The oratorio, on the whole, was well rendered.

Norwood.—The St. Luke's summer concert was given at the Institute, Lower Norwood, on Monday evening, June 25th, under the able direction of Mr. R. Sloman, Mus. Doc., Oxon, the principal vocalists being Mdme. Clara West, Miss Lottie West, Miss A. Percival, Mr. F. J. Smith, Mr. C. G. Goodall, and Mr. H. Hancock ; flautist, Mr. H. Pope ; pianists, Miss Plowright and Dr. Sloman. Everything passed off admirably and there was a good attendance.

Guildhall School of Music.—A Students' concert was given at the City of London School, on Wednesday evening the 20th inst. Mr. Weist Hill conducted and Mr. J. Henry Leipold was the accompanist. A large number of students took part, and their efforts were much appreciated by a crowded audience. After two songs—those of Miss Clara Dowle and Mr. Sydney Beckley—demands for encores had to be submitted to. Mr. Beckley gave "The Bedouin's Love Song" (Pinsuti), in very good style, and displayed the quality of his fine baritone voice; Miss Clara Dowles' "Softly Sighs" (Weber) was given in an excellent manner, her voice being heard to much advantage. This was her first appearance at a Students' concert, and she was warmly congratulated on her successful debût.

St. Mary, Hornsey Rise.—This church was formally reopened for divine service on Wednesday morning, June 20th, the anniversary of the Queen's accession, and the 22nd of the consecration of the church. It has been enlarged, cleaned, and has undergone considerable structural alterations. The organ, a two-manual instrument, which was greatly in need of repair, has at the same time been thoroughly overhauled and cleaned by Mr. Henry Willis, the original builder, under the direction of Mr. Thos. H. Bunbury, the organist and a special committee. The organ chamber has been entirely re-built and enlarged, the pedal organ re-modelled, and its tracker work dispensed with by Mr. Willis's admirable pneumatic apparatus. A violoncello stop has been added to the pedal organ and a new set of Bourdon pipes substituted for the old ones. The new case of pitch pine, designed by the architect, with its beautifully surmounted pipes of spotted metal, forms an elegant feature in the north transept. The tone quality of the instrument is vastly improved, and its power considerably augmented. Mr. C. W. Pearce, Mus. Bac., Cantab., F.C.O., presided at the organ and played a selection of music after the service. The Sermon was preached by the Bishop of Bedford.

Exeter.—An organ recital was given on the 23rd at the Victoria Hall, by Mr. Harold Ryder. The organist made a very favourable impression, and he was warmly applauded at the close of each piece ; two or three times, in fact, the audience wished to have the piece repeated, but Mr. Ryder wisely refrained from yielding to the wish, and thereby unduly prolonging the performance. His programme opened with an Allegretto in E flat, by Wely,

played in a style which showed that the organist was master of his subject, and which promised a careful and intelligent rendering of the other selections. No. 2 was Beethoven's beautiful Andante con Variazione in G. This Mr. Ryder performed with great skill, and the piece was long and loudly applauded. C. J. Frost's March in B flat was well rendered, the rhythm being excellently marked. In Pleyel's Variations on the German Hymn the pedal part in the last variations was finely done. Guilmant's Caprice in B flat, with its taking echo effects, proved a delightful morceau. Here again the performer might have interpreted the sustained applause of his audience as an encore, but after a brief interval he passed on to the extract from Handel's Concerto in G minor—allegro, adagio, and andante—which was given with admirable manipulation. E. H. Turpin's fantasia on a Theme by Weber was effectively treated. The performance concluded with a fine rendering of Bach's Toccata and Fugue in D minor.

Glasgow.—By the death of Mr. Thos. Logan Stillie on June 6th, Glasgow has lost sight of its best known musical worthy. He was for a considerable time musical critic of the Glasgow Herald, in which capacity he gained the esteem of many of the famous artists who visited Glasgow, and did much to make known what is good and classical in music by his admirable writings. His valuable library of musical works is bequeathed to the Glasgow University, a fact which is not altogether satisfactory in itself, inasmuch as the bequest will be practically inaccessible to musical students. This places Glasgow in the peculiar position of having the most extensive musical libraries, both of which are carefully packed from the public reach. We understand that the Ewing library in Anderson's University is still unarranged, though it was bequeathed and catalogued many years ago. There is nothing stirring in the music section of Glasgow at present, nor is there much likelihood of anything occurring till after the holidays. J. B.

Notts Church Choral Union.—The twenty-sixth annual festival of the choirs comprising the Notts Church Choral Union was held in the Collegiate Church of St. Mary's, Southwell, better known as the Minster. The musical portion of the morning service was admirably rendered. Mr. A. Marriott presided at the organ, and the Rev. W. G. Croft, of Edwalton, Nottingham, conducted. The service was intoned by the Rev. R. F. Smith, minor canon of Southwell Minster. The afternoon service had evidently more attractions for the general public than the morning, for long before the hour fixed for service the Minster was crowded. At half-past three there was not standing room to be obtained, and probably such an immense concourse of people has never been seen at the festival before. The musical portion of the programme was again well rendered, even better than in the morning. The anthem, "The God of Jeshurun," was admirably sung, the quartet deserving special mention. The whole of the services were most successful. A large number of the clergy from the neighbourhood were present, and with but few exceptions all the clergy came with their various choirs. The organ was played throughout by Mr. A. Marriott, of the Minster. The choirs present (including that of Southwell Minster), numbered 30, and consisted of some 685. As usual the alto part was too weak in numbers for the securing of a just tone balance, and the trebles in the same way just as much too strong in proportion. All things considered the music was effective.

Foreign Musical Intelligence.

"Königin Mariette," a comic opera by Ignaz Brull, has been successfully played in Munchen.

A large new organ, built by the firm of Merklin, for Rouen Cathedral was opened by M. Guilmant the other week.

It is announced that Madame Augusta Holmes has finished an opera, "La Montagne Noire," of which according to custom she has written both words and music.

The Concordia Society of Prague offered a prize for the best essay on the music of Richard Wagner and its national character. Ten manuscripts were sent in, and the prize was awarded to M. Louis Nohl, who is already favourably known by his works on Beethoven and Mozart.

The three-act opera "Sappho" of Charles Gounod, which was almost forgotten after its production in Paris in 1851, will, in the ensuing winter, be again given at the Grand Opera House at Paris. Emile Augier (the author of the words) and Gounod, have through an entire alteration and the addition of a fourth act, given a new form and interest to the work.

In the well-known instrument manufactory of Biese, in Berlin, there has been lately two pianos completed, which are, in their way, the only types existing. Their oak cases, as the inscription on them states, are cut from parts of the wooden Rhine bridge which Claudius Nero Drasus built between Mainy and Castel in the last century before the birth of Christ, fragments of which were discovered in 1880. The wood is of a dark and in some places, black colour, and is exceedingly hard. This peculiar condition intensifies the tone of the instruments, which are to be exhibited in the Nüremberg Exhibition for a short time. The inscription runs : "Once on the bottom of the Rhine I served the Roman war god, now in this new form I am content to assist in the battle of music."

A highly interesting autograph is in the possession of Herr Carl Kindworth, namely a copy of Beethoven's "Meeresstille and Glückliche Fahrt" ("Calm Sea and Prosperous Voyage" cantata), corrected by his own hand. The copy, in oblong quarto, belonged formerly to Richard Wagner, who seems to have considered it of little value in comparison to the original score of his "Reingold." Wagner has written on the title-page, with reference to exchanging Beethoven's MS. for his own score, which Klindworth had obtained : "Willst du für 'Wagner' der was Koofen, gewinnst du sicher mit Beethoven. Auf Wiederschen."—R. W. (By disposing of Wagner thou wilt surely gain Beethoven. To meeting again.—R. W.) Upon the lower margin of the first page of the manuscript Beethoven had written in red ink : "N.B.—There are again 150 florins already sunk on me up to the present date, *mea culpa, mea maxima culpa.* Upon the remembrance of this the old mountain again poured out fire and flames.—Junna, 19th Dec. 1822." From the 28th to the 30th bars the copyist had written the second chord of D major in demi-semiquavers, *tremolo.* Beethoven has crossed out this, and instead of it put long holding notes, tying the chords for three bars together. As a marginal note appears the following words : "N.B.—It sounds too powerful; how could it be said directly afterwards 'locked in slumber is each wave'?" The repetition of this part occuring again in the bars from 36 to 38 is crossed through and marked : "Exactly as before." In the second part the corrections are more numerous. In the bars 82 to 85, where the copyist had written chords for the upper part, is remarked : "The wind whistles are an octave too low." Beethoven put them an octave higher, and wrote underneath, "Oh you stupid." In the bars 108 to 111, the bass part to the passage "The billows divide" was written an octave too high. Beethoven made his corrections, and remarked in a marginal gloss, "Oh! you merry rabble." Wagner had the volume bound in red morocco leather, and labelled in large gold letters, "Autograph of Beethoven."

COMPETITION FOR DESIGNS IN ARTISTIC PIANOFORTE CASES.

The jury appointed to decide the competitive merits of the designs sent in for an artistic cottage pianoforte case for the firm of Rud. Ibach Sohn of Barmen, report thus :—

The number of the competitive designs amounted to 133. In accordance with the main conditions laid down, the designs were to be sketched according to a given measurement, provision being made for sufficient space, as specified, for the admittance of the instrument. And further, the several kinds of wood proposed were to be specified, or indicated in the drawing. These conditions have been observed by all the competitors, with a few trifling deviations. The conditions were :—(1) Artistic beauty, (2) originality in conception, and (3) the case not to exceed the sum of £12. 10s in value.

After careful inspection, the jury were unanimously of opinion that not one of the designs met all the conditions required, and they felt sorry that those who entered the lists as competitors, paid no attention to the manufacture of the cases, and that they have thus neutralised the object in view. The jury were compelled to decline adjudicating the prize. But in order some way to utilize the labour bestowed on these designs, they have induced Mr. Ibach to buy up eleven of the designs by distributing among the competitors the sum total originally intended for the successful competition. It is of course evident that the purchase of these designs depend upon the consent of the respective competitors, and as the jury declined to open the letters corresponding to the mottoes, Mr. Ibach desires to know the names of the respective parties by publication of these particulars, with a view to obtaining their consent.

THE DANGER OF LOCAL REPORTS.

All who love the art of music for the sake of itself, and therefore have its general welfare in their innermost hearts, must admit that its age of conventionalism is now fast drawing to a close, and that quite a new era is awaiting us, though it will not necessarily be a Wagnerian epoch in the annals of music (which to a certain extent would mean a tendency for violating and setting aside many accepted rules based upon sound principles), but rather a time when all true musicians, professional and amateur, shall be of one mind as to music's future career, and in this revolution the Press should not occupy an inferior position. It is admitted by many true artists that the greatest lessons they have learned, and the most valuable hints given, have been brought home and pointed out to them by true criticism. Let the student study as hard as he may, and as long as he pleases, he will look forward with anxious hope to what the papers have to say of his first performance, and if he be a sensible man he will at once see that an unbiassed rebuke in a paper of good reputation is not an act of unkindness, but one of true charity—yet at the same time I would warn those who set a value on criticism not to shut their eyes to the fact that biassed praise is just as uncharitable and insulting as prejudicial condemnation, that is such praise as most local reports contain.

Then, again, inferior critics, owing to their ignorance, are often deterred from venturing on a fair criticism for fear of opening up a controversy on a subject quite unknown to themselves.

Let us consider the word "criticism," and we shall find that its accepted meaning is "judgment." Now, it is plainly an absurdity to attempt to judge and form an artistic opinion upon that of which we are quite ignorant. George Macdonald remarks, "Unless a man be a musician, he cannot criticise music ; he can simply say whether he likes it or not." Now local musical reporters, of course, thoroughly ignore this axiom ; hence, art is maltreated and writers devoid of trained judgment are dangerous, and I contend that their ridiculous flattery is often detrimental to the real progress of many young artists who form the class which suffers most from false notices. Professional people of good standing are quite independent of inferior criticism, and should accept as a great compliment the absence of their names from reports written by biassed or ignorant critics ; it would take a thousand stupid notices to destroy a Sims Reeves, but one paper might contain sufficient to seriously injure the future prospects of a hundred young artists. Or, again, such reporters cannot harm an established artist, neither could a whole regiment of prejudiced reporters establish a single performer. Flattery and encouragement are as different as dark from light, for when we flatter we may, perchance, insult ; but when we encourage we truly acknowledge that ability exists. With flattery the majority of these local notices are crowded, but of encouragement but little is seen. We should with a firm hand endeavour to stop the mischievous habit of writing fulsome notices, for we cannot be blind to the fact that the harm they do to young beginners is a matter for grave consideration. I will give an example : A young lady leaves school, having at her fingers' ends a few valses, etc., and who, by the advice of her friends, determines to try a public performance. What is the result? her playing, which only approaches mediocrity, and is void of all feeling and expression, is applauded by the local press as a grand performance, and by upholding the girl as a musical prodigy. So, fondly imagining all this to be true, she forthwith turns her attention to music "as a profession," refuses every advice, until she finds that she is not so successful as she anticipated ; and when she appears in the big world of music, she learns how utterly helpless she is, and looks back with regret to find that the valuable time she has wasted in one profession cannot be made up by another. I have seen such palpable untruths in local reports that I endeavour to impress upon my pupils and all whom I may know who are "fighting for fame," not to heed such notices as criticisms, but to reject them as insults. Want of sense of duty is at the bottom of much defective criticism. Byron, smarting under bad criticism, said—

A man must serve his time to ev'ry trade,
Save censure ; critics all are ready made.
Take hackneyed jokes from Miller, got by rote,
With just enough of learning to misquote.
Care not for feeling, pass your project jest,
And stand a critic, hated yet caress'd.

GEO. F. GROVER.

LONDON: SATURDAY, JUNE 30, 1883.

THE CARDIFF EISTEDDFOD.

AN Eisteddfod is no new event. For generations the music loving Welsh people have maintained with unabated enthusiasm their great music and literary competitions. And such meetings have undoubtedly done much to preserve and foster the musical and artistic instincts of the inhabitants of the Principality. But the National Eisteddfod to be held during the first week of next August promises to be a meeting of exceptional interest and one likely to leave a permanent mark for good upon the history of art in Wales. Nations and cities, like men, have their duties, responsibilities, and opportunities. This year the task of holding with due dignity and liberality the great Welsh meeting has fallen to the lot of rich, prosperous, energetic, hospitable, and art-loving Cardiff; and the men of that ancient and now powerful port—where commercial prosperity advances "by "leaps and bounds"—know full well how to do their duty, and how to carry forward to a successful issue every cause they take in hand. The fame of Cardiff, and the high reputation of its inhabitants for spirited, energetic and judicious activity in matters of education and art, have invoked expectations and called forth indeed responsibilities which will neither be neglected or unfulfilled, as those who are acquainted with the ancient town know just as well as they know the sun will continue so long as the world lasts to rise and set. The arrangements made justify large expectations, and promise a truly memorable Eisteddfod. Not only are the usual features of such a gathering amply provided for, as may be seen by a glance through the long list of prizes and by the numerous entries of choirs, and competitors of all types, but there are special features which it cannot but be assumed will make the meeting one of special artistic value and interest. In the first place, the Committee have determined upon giving a series of orchestral performances during the week by a select, complete, and well-balanced orchestra of distinguished London players. At these concerts, Symphonies by BEETHOVEN, SCHUBERT, MENDELSSOHN, SPOHR, and STERNDALE BENNETT will be given. Concertos for organ, pianoforte and violin by HANDEL, MENDELSSOHN, etc., may also be included in the scheme. The best typical overtures by MOZART, MENDELSSOHN, SPOHR, WEBER, ROSSINI, WAGNER, STERNDALE BENNETT and Sir G. A. MACFARREN are likewise included in the scheme. The introduction of high class orchestral music for the first time in an Eisteddfod scheme is a matter of high import as regards the future of art in Wales. It is a step in strict keeping with the liberal traditions of these great meetings, at which both vocal and instrumental music stand side by side in the annals of the arena of Welsh art. Further, it is an advance which must bear much good fruit as calculated to disseminate throughout the Principality a love of the art in some of its highest, purest, and grandest forms. The significance of the introduction of good, classical orchestral music in competent hands at the forthcoming Festival is already felt by the shrewd, art-loving people of Wales; and it is no mere figure of speech to say that the eyes of all the many thousands of singers, players, and listeners in our sister land are fixed upon this notable feature of the Cardiff scheme. Another gain upon this occasion will be the presence of a large concert organ temporarily secured from Messrs. BRINDLEY and FOSTER with an ample specification, including a large pedal organ, as will make the organ recitals and performances to be given highly satisfactory illustrations of the noble music written by BACH, MENDELSSOHN, etc. for the "King of instruments." A leading musical authority of North Wales has testified to the writer of these words as to the real interest felt by some of the influential Welsh music lovers in the liberal scheme of the Cardiff committee, especially in the addition of orchestral performances. The lead thus taken by the great commercial centre of South Wales will surely bear good fruit, and is nothing short of a national service in the cause of the art. The umpires chosen by the Cardiff committee include such men as Sir G. A. MACFARREN, Mr. J. BARNBY, Mr. J. BENNETT, and Mr. JOHN THOMAS ; so the decisions arrived at will be awaited with confidence. From every point of sight, therefore, the Cardiff National Eisteddfod promises to be a specially satisfactory and notable meeting. The old town too, comprising Llandaff within its rapidly extending area, has rare attractions, both architectural and artistic. The lovely surrounding country, and the excellent railway facilities are such as should tempt many visitors. Those who go will not fail to see and hear much which will be gratifying to the admirers of scenery, antiquities, and artistic and commercial progress. And visitors may rest assured that the good accounts so often given of the hospitality and earnest love of art of the now University town of Cardiff, will be duly justified by any amount of personal experience. That success may attend the artistic efforts of the Cardiff Eisteddfod will surely be the wish of all anxious for the progress of music in our midst.

E. H. TURPIN.

ARTISTIC CONSCIENTIOUSNESS.

No charge is to be preferred against any individual or against any collective body of artists in these words. But as we are all of one common weak nature composed of many delicately balanced characteristics of good and evil, it is well to contemplate even the possibilities of our inherent tendencies to err. There can be no grander tribute to the greatness of art than the acknowledgment of the fact, that its successful pursuit can only be hoped for on the part of the artist by his complete self-abnegation and by the exercise of the noblest of our moral qualities. However advantageous selfish considerations may seem at the moment, they are in the long run destructive to the high, pure motives of the true artist and inimical to real lasting success. The composer who descends to a low type of popular taste in his writings, the organist who does not take the trouble to always play with the same determined accuracy because he does not know that any of his listeners are critical, the singer who thinks the stale song and the royalty ballad form the best means of success and the orchestral performer who thinks because he plays on an instrument of soft tone qualities that he may unobserved spare his efforts and even not play at all in some of the forte passages, all furnish familiar types of the unconscientious artist, who, reaping the just punishment of their neglect, wonder how it is they are less fortunate than their neighbours. Shortsightedness ever accompanies selfishness. So the composer madly hunting for popularity fails to see that the only safe course for the productive artist is to write for the future and according to the highest standards of the art, the indifferent organist discovers too late, that people have "ears to hear" with, the silly singer who seeks for a butterfly popularity finds that the fame of a great executive artist can only be built up by the performance of great music, and the negligent orchestral player discovers that conductors will in the end only pin their faith upon men who do not spare their fingers or breath. The true artist is in the highest sense of the term a good soldier who spares not himself for the cause he follows, and gives his first thought and strength to his duty and concerns himself least of all about his pay. Some one says " mankind is divided "into two classes, those who will and those who will "not advance." This saying may be well applied to the artist's career ; for without wishing to discourage the exercise of worldly prudence, a necessity and a virtue when governed under high motives, there is no lasting fame or success obtainable, save by the power of noble, self-sacrificing motives ; and it is of the highest importance that young artists should be taught the splendid morality of art while they are studying the technicalities of its power, for in art moral worth and artistic beauty are inseparable companions.   E. H. TURPIN.

Organ News.

NORWICH.

Dr. Bunnett gave an organ recital at the St. Andrew's Hall, on June 23rd; the following was the programme :—

Overture, "Stradella"	Flotow
Reverie Cantabile	Jordan.
Introduction and Fugue in F (by request)	F. R. Greenwood.
Andante con Moto	Bodly.
"May no Rash Intruder" ("Solomon")	Handel.
Offertoire in F	Batiste.
Ave Maria	Bunnett.
Finale to Organ Concerto	Handel.
"O Rest in the Lord"	Mendelssohn.
Marche Religieuse de "Lohengrin"	Wagner.
Overture, "Fidelio"	Beethoven.

PRESTON.

The following is the programme of the organ recital given by Mr. James Tomlinson, in the new Public Hall, on Saturday evening, June 23rd.

Overture to the Oratorio "St. Paul"	Mendelssohn.
Air with Variations (Notturno)	Spohr.
Allegro Maestoso (from the Serenade for Wind Instruments)	Mozart.
Overture to "Preciosa"	Weber.
Air from the Opera "Serse" (Largo)	Handel.
Military March (Posthumous Work)	Beethoven.

FISHERIES EXHIBITION.

Mr. James Loaring, F.C.O., gave organ recitals last week. The following amongst other pieces were included in the programmes :—

Organ Concertos (Nos. 3 and 4)	Handel.
Air with Variations from Overture in D	Haydn.
Flute Concerto	Rink.
March Heroique in C	Schubert.
Festive March in B flat	Loaring.

An organ recital was given on Thursday, June 21st, by Mr. James H. Rooks. The following was the programme :—

Overture, "Zanetta"	Auber.
Andante and Allegro	Bache.
Allegro Cantabile (from 5th Symphony)	Widor.
Gavotte	Benedict.
No. 5 of "Original Compositions"	Batiste.
March from "Herne the Hunter"	W. Meyer Lutz.

On Monday June 25th, two organ recitals were given by Mr. Frank Bradley. The following were the programmes :—

Overture, "Die Zauberflöte" (arranged by Best)	Mozart.
Schiller March	Meyerbeer.
Adagio from Symphony in C (arranged by Dr. Stainer)	Schumann.
Rhapsodie No 1.	Saint-Saëns.
Prelude and Fugue in C minor, (No. 6)	Bach.
Postlude in E flat, Andante and Allegro	Smart.
Double Fugue in B minor	Kühmahdt.
Sonata in D minor (3 movements)	A. Mailly.
Allegro Maestoso—Andante—Allegro con Brio.	
Andante in A minor	Merkel.
Toccata and Fuga in F	Bach.
Rhapsodie No 2.	Saint-Saëns.
Chaconne in A major	Handel.
Fantasia in A flat	Guiraud.
Grand Chorus in E flat	Guilmant.

SHERBORNE.

The following is the programme of an organ recital given in the Abbey Church on Thursday, June 21st, by Mr. C. E. Lyle.

Overture to "Athaliah"	Handel.
"Chœur des Anges"	Scotson Clark.
Offertoire in C minor	Batiste.
Andante	Haydn.
Fanfare	Lemmens.
Air, "Thou shalt bring them in" } ("Israel in Egypt")	Handel
Double Chorus, "Sing ye to the Lord" }	
"La Carita"	Rossini.
"Ave Maria"	Schubert.
A Concert on a Lake interrupted by a Thunderstorm	Neukomm.
"God Save the Queen," varied by G. E. Lyle.	

CRYSTAL PALACE.

Mr. Eyre's programme on Saturday last included the following :—

Motet, "Deus tibi"	Mozart.
Aria from a Sonata	Paradies.
Offertoire in C	Wely.
Serenata	Kullak.
Introduction and Fugue, alla Marcia	Tiley.
The Turkish Patrol	Michaelis.
Spring Song	Hensaelt.
Hungarian March ("Faust")	Berlioz-Liszt.

BOSCOMBE.

An organ recital was given in the Church of St. George's-in-the-Wood, on the new organ, on Thursday, June 7th, by Mr. T. A. Aldridge. The following is the programme :—

PART I.

Præludium in G major }	Bach.
Fugue in G minor }	
Andante in A	Smart.
Barcarole (from 4th Concerto)	S. Bennett.
Air, "O Rest in the Lord"	Mendelssohn.
March in D	Smart.

PART II.

Air, "But the Lord is Mindful"	Mendelssohn.
Cantilene Pastorale	Guilmant.
Grand Chœur in D }	
Air, "I Dreamt I was in Heaven"	Costa.
Marcia Religiosa	Meyerbeer.

LICHFIELD.

Messrs. Hill and Son have received instructions to rebuild and enlarge the organ at Lichfield Cathedral. Subjoined is the specification.

GREAT ORGAN. CC TO A.

1. Double Diapason	16 ft.	9. Harmonic Flute	4 „
2. Large Open Diapn.	8 „	10. Twelfth	2⅔ „
3. Small Open Diapn.	8 „	11. Fifteenth	2 „
4. Clarabella	8 „	12. Grave Mixture (4 ranks).	
5. Bell Gamba	8 „	13. Mixture (3 ranks).	
6. Stopt Diapason	8 „	14. Grand Posaune	8 „
7. Octave	4 „	15. Clarion	4 „
8. Octave Gamba	4 „		

SWELL ORGAN. CC TO A.

17. Double Diapason	16 ft.	25. Mixture (3 ranks)	ft.
18. Open Diapason	8 „	26. Mixture (2 ranks)	
19. Pierced Gamba	8 „	27. Contra Fagotto	16 „
20. Voix Celestes	8 „	28. Trumpet	8 „
21. Stopped Diapason	8 „	29. Oboe	8 „
22. Principal	4 „	30. Cornopean	8 „
23. Celestina Flute	4 „	31. Clarion	4 „
24. Fifteenth	2 „		

CHOIR ORGAN. CC TO A.

32. Lieblich Bourdon	16 ft.	37. Principal	4 ft.
33. Open Diapason	8 „	38. Wald Flöte	4 „
34. Dulciana	8 „	39. Piccolo	2 „
35. Stopped Diapason	8 „	40. Clarionet	8 „
36. Keraulophon	8 „		

SOLO ORGAN. CC TO A.

42. Harmonic Flute	8 ft.	45. Corno-de-Bassetto	8 ft.
43. Concert Flute	4 „	46. Grand Tuba	8 „
44. Orchestral Oboe	8 „		

PEDAL ORGAN. CCC TO F.

48. Double Open Diap.	32 ft.	53. Bass Flute	8 ft.
49. Open Diapason	16 „	54. Fifteenth	4 „
50. Open Diapason	16 „	55. Mixture (4 ranks)	
51. Bourdon	16 „	56. Trombone	16 „
52. Principal	8 „	57. Trumpet	8 „

COUPLERS.

58. Great to Pedal.	65. Swell to Great (Sub octave).
59. Great to Pedal.	
60. Choir to Pedal.	66. Swell to Choir.
61. Solo to Pedal.	67. Choir to Great.
62. Swell to Great.	68. Solo to Great.
63. Swell to Great.	69. Swell to Pedal.
64. Swell to Super-octave.	70. Pedal Ventil.

TEN PNEUMATIC COMBINATION PEDALS.

4 to Great and Pedal Organs combined.
4 to Swell Organ.
1 to Choir Organ.
1 to reduce Pedal Organ to soft 16 ft.
Double acting pedal for "Great to Pedal."

To be blown by gas engine. Solo organ to be placed in separate swell box, with separate crescendo pedal ; stops to be placed at an angle of 45°.

Pneumatic action to great, swell, and pedal organs. The whole of the action throughout the organ to be new, and the instrument to be built on the plans adopted by the College of Organists.

His Grace the Archbishop of Canterbury has accepted the office of President of the College of Organists, a position held by his predecessors in the Primacy since the foundation of the College.

LIVERPOOL.

Mr. W. T. Best gave an organ recital in the St. George's Hall, on Thursday evening, June 21st. The following is the programme :—

Fantasia and Fugue (E minor).....................	Best.
Canzonetta, "In distant lands I rove"............	Taubert.
Marche et Cortège de Bacchus ("Sylvia").........	Delibes.
Prelude and Fugue (D major)	Mendelssohn.
Andantino. (1. Cradle Song. 2. The Dance. 3. Serenade.)	} Spohr.
From the Symphony "The Power of Sound"	}
Finale :—Allegro Vivace (A minor)................	Morandi.

On Saturday afternoon, June 23rd :—

Fantasia with Chorale (G major)..................	Smart.
Scherzo from the Music to "A Midsummer Night's Dream "	} Mendelssohn.
Adagio and Fugue (C minor)......................	Mozart.
Romanza, "Arpa gentil ".........................	Rossini.
Andante from an Organ Sonata....................	H. Mailly.
March from the Third Organ Symphony	Widor.

WARE PARISH CHURCH.

An organ recital was given in this church on Tuesday, June 26th, by Mr. James L. Gregory, A.C.O. The following was the programme :—

Minuet from Overture to "Joseph"	
Fuga (No. 4 of Six "Petites Fugues" for the Harpsichord.)	} Handel.
Adagio in E (Op. 35)	Merkel.
Prelude and Fugue in G..........................	Mendelssohn.
Adagio from Sonata in G minor for Violin and Piano	Bach.
Grand Chœur in D	Guilmant.
Andante from Quartet in D minor	Mozart.
Fantasia on "Vesper Hymn"	Turpin.

WEYBRIDGE.

The following is the specification of the new organ erected by Messrs. Brindley and Foster in the church of St. Michael and All Angels, from designs by Mr. G. E. Lake, organist of the parish church.

GREAT ORGAN. CC TO G, 3.

1. Open Diapason......	8 ft.	5. Principal	4 ft.
2. Hohl Flöte	8 „	6. Piccolo	2 „
3. Dulciana	8 „	7. Clarionet	8 „
4. Wald Flöte	4 „		

SWELL ORGAN. CC TO G, 3.

8. Lieblich Bourdon ...	16 ft.	12. Flauto Traverso ...	4 ft.
9. Violin Diapason ...	8 „	13. Mixture (3 ranks)	
10. Lieblich Gedact · ...	8 „	14. Oboe	8 „
11. Voix Celestes.	8 „	15. Horn	8 „

PEDAL ORGAN. CCC TO F.

16. Contra Bass	16 ft.	18. Flute Bass	8 ft'
17. Sub Bass	16 „		

COUPLERS.

19. Swell to Great.		22. Great to Pedals.
20. Swell to Super Octave		23. Tremulant to Swell.
21. Swell to Pedals.		

Self balancing swell pedal, pedal board concave, "College of Organist's measurement." The tone of the instrument is pronounced to be very pure and round.

In his new book "From Ponkapog (a little New England village) to Pesth," Mr. T. B. Aldrich, an accomplished American author, thus speaks of Arab music :—" Looking at it carelessly, it struck me that Moorish enjoyment was composed of very simple ingredients ; but, looking closer, I suspected there were depths and qualities in this profound and nearly austere repose, in this smouldering passion, with its capricious fiery gleams, which I had not penetrated. Perhaps it was the drug in the tobacco, or perhaps it was the pungent property in the coffee, that sharpened my sense ; but, presently, I began to detect in the music, which had rather irritated me at first, an undercurrent of meaning, vague and perplexing. The slow dragging andante and the sudden wailing falsetto seemed half to assist and half to baffle some inarticulate spirit that strove to distil its secret into the ear. Something that was not the music itself was struggling to find expression through it,—the pride, the rage, the inertia, the unutterable despair of an ancient and once mighty people passing away."

Reviews.

X. Y. Z. Railway Guide.—Musicians do not employ the final letters of the alphabet in their art, but they travel extensively, and will be glad to know that X. Y. Z. is a conveniently arranged time table for the railways radiating out of London, at the remarkably small cost of one penny.

Elementary History of Music. By N. D. Anvers, edited by Owen J. Dulled. (Sampson Low, Marston, Searle & Rivington).—A useful and well got up little book, giving its information in a clear, concise manner. The book is adorned by some well selected, and well engraved illustrations. Though its pages only number about 100, the work is so well planned and condensed that it contains a really large amount of information.

The Pianoforte Teacher's Guide. By L. Plaidy, translated by Fanny Raymond Ritter. (W. Reeves).—A sign of the increased interest in art is the studied advance in the appliances for learning and teaching. This valuable work deals concisely and happily with the technicalities and mannerisms of the leading household musical instruments. The work should be in the hands of all who play, or hope to be able to play, or who wish to teach with every advantage and knowledge.

The Girl's Own Annual.—(56, Paternoster Row, E.C.) —It would be impossible to over-estimate the value and usefulness of this admirably got up and artistically illustrated annual. The variety of the information given, the sensible guidance afforded throughout its pages in the formation of female character upon a good, sound basis, and the endless entertainment and artistic delight the volume provides for our girls, make the book a veritable home treasure. The list of writers includes many of eminence in their several ways. The illustrations, including a dozen handsome coloured and toned paper plates, are excellent and abundant. Interspersed through the book are admirable articles on the performance of given schools of music, and anent different instruments and musical topics ; in addition to this valuable instruction, there are charming songs from the pens of well known and esteemed composers. Every girl should, in short, possess "The Girl's Own Annual."

SIR WALTER SCOTT'S PIANO.

At a marriage which took place in Edinburgh a short time ago, the presents received by the bride embraced an old piano, prized as having been a gift to her mother's family, so far back as the year 1817, from Sir Walter Scott. It was understood to have been the instrument on which Sir Walter's daughters, Anne and Sophia, had received their first instruction in music ; but having only thirty-six notes, it had been replaced by a more modern piano suitable to their advancement. It is of the spinet form, and looked, at the date referred to, as if it had belonged to the middle of the last century, the name it bore being "John & Hugh Watson, Edinburgh, makers, from London." For twelve years the piano again did service in the school-room, but was again deposed to meet the requirements of advanced pupils. Yet it retained an honoured place in the heart, especially of one who had enjoyed the friendship and confidence of Scott before he was recognized as the author of "Waverley." It was always spoken of as "Old Sir Walter," and accompanied its owners in many changes long after it had ceased to "discourse sweet music ;" though, sooth to say, for many years it occupied the place of a lobby table. In 1854 the instrument descended to the second generation, which necessitated a long and weary journey. Age had brought infirmities and very shaky legs, but no better refuge was forthcoming than the corner of a bath-room. Here it remained undisturbed until 1872, when another change brought it back to Edinburgh, when, alas ! the new owner could not afford even standing-room. An asylum was sought in the relict-room of the Scott monument, but the piano was deemed too large for admission. Only one alternative remained—that of amputation. The legs were taken off, and for nine years dangled from the roof of a butler's pantry, while the honoured trunk was deposited under a bed. Now the instrument, as a heirloom, descends to the third generation, and brighter days are apparently in store for it.—The Musical Visitor.

THE EFFECT OF OHORUS SINGING UPON THE VOICE.

Anent Mr. Deaken's articles on singing in Grove's Dictionary, the *Tonic Sol-fa Reporter* says :—

It would be hiding the truth not to point out to the writer of the article that his views had been anticipated by Mr. Curwen by nearly forty years ; and that his remedy has been applied for that period by an army of several thousand teachers. On every side of them have existed "Choral Societies," whose members have been accepted on their own opinions of their abilities, without test of question of any kind. In such societies many promising voices have been ruined by the absence of the restraining effect of a course of elementary lessons. It is a common thing for those having a taste for singing and some amount of voice, to be *snapped up* by the local society, thrust into the middle of an oratorio or cantata, and expected to read their notes and control their voices by *intuition*, supplemented by large doses of instrumental aid. When there is no individual certainty of the sounds to be produced notes will be "taken by hook or by crook and voice production forgotten." The conductor must then concentrate all his attention upon cramming the music into their heads, and forcing it out of their throats. He will fly for aid to the most powerful instrument he can command, a three-manual organ for preference. What consideration have the pipes of an organ for the delicately-constructed human larynx ? "The sopranos are wrong," shouts the conductor, " put on the full organ, Mr. Diapason." "The tenors are all at sea—add the trumpet." Fierce wages the conflict ; fragile throats and weak lungs *versus* huge metal pipes and hydraulic blown bellows. A good knowledge of notation (singing from notes) must precede a proper delivery of the voice when the music is difficult either in interval or pitch. If an instrument is played with the singers, to lead them, it must be with much greater force than they are using or it would not be heard by them. In proportion to the strength of the accompaniment (?) will be utterances of the choir. The conductor then gets "the maximum of effect out of his little army of singers." Away they go, basses roaring, tenors shouting, altos bleating, and sopranos shrieking.

"Much overdrawn," some may say. Perhaps so. But can it be denied that the modern rage for the "Dramatic" in music—works with difficult music, huge bands, violent contrasts—leads to high pressure both at rehearsals and concerts. Excited by the orchestral din singers exert themselves to the utmost, perpetrating sounds which, if heard without the instruments, they would be quite ashamed of.

The decrease of all unaccompanied part-singing is to be deplored, for the reason (amongst many others) that those forms of choral music *compel* the conductor to care for "individual voices." There, one strained chest A¹ by a tenor in the midst of the pure, natural "thin " register of his companions will stand out as distinctly as a black cloud against a blue sky. Not less distinctly can the heavy forced G's be heard of a contralto voice, the possessor of which is either desirous of coming out as a prima donna, or is too indolent to master her proper (albeit much more difficult) part. Soft singing abounds in unaccompanied choral music. There is an indefinable charm about the pianissimos of a number of voices, of which composers of all periods and styles have largely availed themselves. Rarely is the sign *ff* to be found in a motet or madrigal. Singers of this class of music instinctively listen to the effects they are creating. The parts follow each other in melodious strains delightful to the ear as a stream winding through a fertile valley is to the eye. Listening to the general effect leads them to give attention to their own voices. Then badly-formed tones are corrected, and "forced" voices almost impossible. Compare motet, madrigal, glee and part-song with the awkward, instrumental-like parts of the declamatory chorus or the "*fff* tuttis " of the "dramatic cantata." Gone is the sweetness of tone and the delicate feeling induced by the pastoral character of the music ; in place of it there is noisy, strained singing and evident physical exertion which, without heavy accompaniments would be simply unbearable.

Much harm may be done to young and untrained voices by joining choral societies which may be engaged upon heavy works, and that all singers should be educated up to the standard required for the complete mastery of the music they may be called upon to perform. On the other hand there can be no harm in allowing a number of young and immature voices to sing choral music, if the latter be within their ascertained means, and be guided by a conductor who knows the danger of misusing a voice—who recognizes the fatigue induced by long continued vocal exercises, and has the tact to give his choir sufficient variety in their work and rest between their pieces—who is in fact a singer, feels as a singer, and acts as a singer.

The Church of England Temperance Chronicle for June 23rd has a portrait of Mr. W. H. Jude, the Liverpool organist, with a biographical notice and a spirited part-song from his pen.

THE RESTFULNESS OF MUSIC.

By Paul Pastnor, in *The Musical Visitor.*

Rest is a process, not a product. It restores to body and mind expended energy, but itself is not this energy,—only the means of obtaining it. We ought not, in strictness to say that we are *rested*, but renovated, rather. Our natural forces recover their tone and vigour through a period of quiet, but no vital force is added to them by rest. Indeed, it is questionable whether rest, so called, has any objective reality at all, and is not altogether a state, and a variable state at that.

Music as a means of restoring expended vigour of mind and body—music at rest—has long been acknowledged to be one of the most natural and available methods. Its qualities are such as to induce the pleasurable quiet and soothing repose which are necessary for mental and physical recuperation. How naturally music aids itself to sleep. The first melody that floats in consciousness, and will always remain there, as one of the sweetest reminiscences of life, is the lullaby crooned by the mother over the cradle of her babe. We are all familiar with the fairy tales and the romances, where the queens and the princes, and the maidens are wooed to sleep in fragrant bowers, by soft, sweet strains from hidden players. All romance is idealized common life, and so it is here. The hidden players and the fragrant bowers are all that give the tale its glamour. Music soothes the weary and the care burdened to sleep, as truly as it does the beautiful people in the stories. The strain must be soft and slow and of no great range. Let it be monotonous, the more so the better—a singing and a re-singing of a plaintive gentle theme. Such music, run in the thoughts, will put one, however restless, speedily to sleep. Some birds, I have heard, sing themselves to sleep—why should not we ?

But music is useful otherwise than a composer to sleep. In this manner it is chiefly a physical rest ; but in another manner it is more restful to the mind.

I think that very few who have a natural taste and love for music, and yet neglect it, for very weariness sake, realize that it is more useful than absolute quietness itself. There are hundreds and thousands of brain-weary and heart-weary men and women, who will doze and wake by the fireside all the evening and go to bed more weary than at first, who might be rested and refreshed and prepared for sweeter slumber by their latent or forgotten love of music. If there be any employment in our homes during the evening, it is apt to be reading ; and people think that reading rests, because it requires no movement of the body. The fact is that reading is tiresome, compared with music. Not that I would cry down reading, but I say it should have the best hours of the day, when the mind is fresh, for it is an appropriative act, and requires energy. Almost anybody will gape over a book that is really worth reading, after nine o'clock in the evening. The attempt to incorporate another's thoughts exhausts the already weary mind, and, almost before the reader knows, the sense has run away and is lost.

But it is otherwise with music. Music rests the mind. It does not require a mental process to appropriate it. The heart-mind—the spirit—apprehends music, and it does it intuitively, without the use of the reasoning power. Do you ask why it rests us more than absolute quietness does? I answer, because as we have seen, rest is a process, not a product ; we must make use of some *means* to reinvigorate our powers. What we may call "absolute quietness" does not exist—only relative quietness ; and while the mind and body are relatively quiet, they are only preying upon themselves by a sort of ceaseless subjective activity. What is needed is not complete relaxation of nerve and muscle, but something to tone these up and restore wasted energy.

The conductors of the Philharmonic concerts next season are to be, it is said, Sir A. Sullivan, Dr. Stainer, Messrs. Mount, Cowen, Barnett, and C. V. Stanford.

It seems that Mr. Willing was engaged at the Handel Society in association with Sir M. Costa and retained his engagement naturally, although his chief and friend was unfortunately prevented from attending in consequence of ill health. Otherwise no doubt Mr. A. Eyre, the admirable and gifted organist of the Crystal Palace, would have been invited to take some part in the Festival.

THE EXTRAORDINARY DISPUTE ABOUT AN ORGANIST.

The service of St. James's, Taunton, have been again conducted without either organ or accompaniment. The psalms were not chanted, nor were any hymns sung. Mrs. Chapman, the late organist, was at 'her seat at the organ 20 minutes before 11 o'clock, but the instrument was still locked, and the key in possession of the churchwardens. Mr. Dudeney, the new organist was not present. Mr. Dudeney has published a letter, in which he states that he made no application for the appointment, which was voluntarily conferred upon him. He understood that deafness was the cause of Mrs. Chapman leaving, and was not aware that there would be any unpleasantness. Indeed, he had offered to give £5 5s. towards a testimonial to her, and a concert in aid of the same object. Mr. Hitchcock, one of the churchwardens, writes to say—"It is true that Mrs. Chapman has held the position of organist for more than 20 years, but it is equally true that she suffers from deafness, according to her own admission to myself, and such an infirmity must necessarily interfere with a person who would have the training and management of a large choir."—A vestry meeting of the parishioners was held on Monday under the presidency of Councillor George Webber, for the purpose of considering the conduct of the vicar and churchwardens towards the parishioners, and of considering various questions and business matters relating to the parish. There was a good attendance, but the proceedings were not so lively as on some former occasions. It was resolved, "That this vestry views with commiseration and alarm the destitute and hopeless condition of the service and attendance at St. James's Church, in this large and increasing parish, and desires to express its regret that the vicar and newly-appointed churchwardens should continue to ignore the unanimous voice and decision of the parish, in vestry assembled, by creating. a scandal and attempting during the hours of Divine service to deprive the congregation of the organist of their selection—one who has at all times given the greatest satisfaction—and also by attempting to force upon the congregation another organist ; and that to prevent further scandal, this vestry is of opinion that the time has arrived when an inquiry should be instituted by the bishop, and the cause of the wholesale digressions from the church of a number of ratepayers, and also as to the legality of the appointment of Mr. S. Farrant as churchwarden." A deputation was appointed to visit Wells and lay the whole of the facts before the bishop.

Says a musical contemporary—When John Jacob Astor went to America he took with him six flutes, which his brother in London had made. He started his modest little business in furs with the proceeds of the sale of these instruments. A hundred years ago the box-wood flute with six keys was considered a great improvement on anything of the kind then made, four keys, in addition to the ten holes, being the highest number then in use, and each of Mr. Astor's flutes was priced at seventy-five dollars. Of the six original flutes with which Mr. Astor began his career in New York, one, bearing the mark of the maker, "Astor, No. 6, W. Y. C. R. Street, London," fell into the hands of a gentleman of Hoboken, and by him was sent to a flute maker for repairs. Time had cracked the old flute, and the keys were bent and worn. It has been made whole again and restored to its pristine vigour, though its value lies in its associations rather than in its musical qualities.

The growth of large musical festivals in this country is an encouraging sign. Although many faults are to be discerned in their management, together with some crudeness in the musical performances thereof, these festivals indicate the extent to which musical taste is developed, and the sterling worth of the material taking part in them. That they have even been as financially successful as they have proves the deep and keen interest taken by a large mass of the American public in performances given on a grand scale. If we are not, as yet, a nation of music producers, we can claim to be a nation of good music listeners, and from these must future creators evolve. The future of this country, with regard to music and musicians, is indeed bright for those who will come after us, and although people do not generally care to work for posterity's sake without present reward, it is as well for all earnest musicians to remember that what they can do to help the good work along, without undue sacrifice, will redound to the credit of their native or adopted country.—*New York Courier.*

SUGGESTIONS TO SINGERS.

Never breathe through your mouth in walking, especially at night, or on coming out into the open air after singing. Keep the lips closed, and inhale the air through the nostrils. This is easily acquired, and to be able to do this will be found of great service in taking breath for singing ; but, out of doors, it is most important, for the immediate rush of cold or damp air to the delicate organs of the throat, especially when the latter have been excited by the exertion of singing, is dangerous.

It is a good plan, and a profitable use of the time, to practise breathing while walking, by filling the lungs and utilising each inspiration for as long a distance as possible. Nothing can be said in favour of our climate for singing. With proper precaution, however, a great deal of trouble arising from this cause may be averted.—In summer as well as in winter, the writer would strongly urge the wearing of moderately thick-soled boots or shoes. Then, again, the neck and chest should never be exposed alike to a June sun and a December frost, but instead, it should be moderately and reasonably covered.

Great care should be taken never to get wet, especially wet, or damp feet.

In going out of a hot room into the open air, much pains should be exercised to keep the throat and chest covered up with an overcoat or cloak, however warm the weather may be.

In *very severe* winter weather, the singer will derive much comfort by wearing a flannel chest-protector.

Sitting about in gardens and on lawns in the evenings, on even the warmest days, is not a safe indulgence for the student who is in earnest in the pursuit of his art. One caution is necessary as to "wrapping up," however. Do not overdo it. The constant use of a "comforter" renders the throat delicate and susceptible. All you have to fear is *damp*, not cold, in the atmosphere. A comforter closely wound around the throat promotes perspiration, and the risk of chill in removing it is greater than in not wearing it at all. Common sense must guide every one. It is impossible to make a rule for all.

Never practise or sing upon an empty stomach or soon after a meal. Either of these habits will unfairly tax your digestive organs, and in so doing damage your voice. After a meal, all the energy of the body is required for the stomach. In a healthy person, the extremities will generally be cold after a full meal ; and the reason is that the digestive organs are using all the blood that the body can give for their special work. Nature thus points to a rest of every other organ at that time, and you must not fight against nature by attempting any such severe physical strain as the practice of the voice demands.

Avoid late hours. You require not only a certain amount of sleep, but to take that sleep before the body and mind are at all overtasked.

From many causes, it is well known, the human frame is always at its lowest from about 2 A.M. till 5 A.M.; and the nearer you approach those hours in going to bed, the less able are you to derive all the benefit you require from sleep.—*Musical Herald, U.S.*

OCEAN VOICES.

(For Music.)
[Copyright.]

Like a stately monarch resting,
   Lay the ship awaiting him,
And anon it lifted anchor
   While my straining eyes grew dim ;
Slowly fading from my vision
   Sailed the goodly barque away,
As I stood in yearning fancy
   Watching from the silent bay.
      Suddenly I heard a whisper,—
      'Twas a promise breathed to me
      In the cadences of twilight
      Coming from the placid sea!

Roll ye billows, swell beneath me !
   Once soft ripples made me glad ;
Now I love the waking storm-blast,
   Softer music makes me sad ;
There's deceit in your fond wooing
   Like the summer skies of youth ;
But when tempest fights with tempest
   There's a voice that speaks the truth !

Yes ! I know that thou wilt never
   Come across the deep to me,
But when raging winds are blowing
   Then I seem more near to thee ;
So whene'er I sail the ocean
   Swell ye billows as I go,
For I hear another whisper
   Coming from the depths below :
      Some day I shall reach my haven,
      After one fierce storm is past ;
      I shall hear a dear voice calling,
      And shall find my love at last !
                              Edward Foskett.

Passing Events.

The Richter concerts have this year resulted in a financial loss.

"L'Orfèvre du Roi" is the title of the Marquis d'Ivry's new opera. The story is built upon Balzac's "Désespérance d'Amour."

The death of Mr. Matthew Arbuckle, a well known American bandmaster and cornet soloist, is announced, says the *New York Tribune.*

The Society of Arts have awarded their silver medal to Mr. A. J. Hipkins for his interesting lecture on the history of the pianoforte, which he read before the Society on March 7th.

Mr. Sims Reeves recently played Tom Tug in "The Waterman" at Mr. Toole's Theatre, and the pretty old-fashioned musical burletta seems not to lose its charm and freshness.

At Mr. F. Von Zashow's drawing-room concert on Tuesday last, a fashionable audience were regaled with several pieces by standard composers. Miss Mabel Bourne and Herr Polonaski played artistically.

A gratifying proof of successful training of the talented students of the Royal Normal College for the Blind is testified to in the invitation from Herr Richter to a gifted young pianoforte pupil to play a concerto at one of the eminent German conductor's concerts.

Miss Ellaby's fifth annual pupils' concert at Bath on the 27th of June consisted of a miscellaneous programme of well selected pianoforte works and songs. The young ladies acquitted themselves very satisfactorily, and did credit to their able and industrious instructress.

It is stated that a sacred song, composed by King Alfonso the Wise of Castile (thirteenth century), and modernized by Hilarion Eslava, together with a "Stabat Mater" by the latter, was recently performed, under the direction of the Chevalier van Elewyck, at St. Peter's, Louvain.

The second annual entertainment of the Browning Society was to take place at University College last night. The programme consists of songs from Mr. Browning's works, and readings and recitations. Mr. Malcolm Lawson was to direct the musical part. Mr. Gabriel Thorpe sing the solos in Mr. Stanford's cavalier songs which were given last year.

The desirability of introducing a compact theoretical and practical examination, the College of Organists offers the particular model to be discussed, into the various professional departments in America is to be considered at the forthcoming meeting of the Teachers' Association there, and the proposal is a sign of the musical earnestness of our relations across the Atlantic.

Mr. A. Manns' courageous and successful conductorship of the Handel Festival was not unaccompanied by much plotting and antagonism, when only help and support should have been given. However, it is satisfactory to know that Mr. Manns did his work just as well as ever the same work was done by Sir M. Costa, and so administered a severe practical rebuke to the foolish conductor worshippers.

A despatch from Boston conveys the intelligence that a bill in equity has been filed, praying for an injunction to restrain the Music Hall Corporation from removing the big organ from the hall. The big organ belongs to Boston, and Boston to the big organ. Mankind can no more think of Boston without the big organ than they can think of Hero without Leander, or of Paul without Virginia, or of Mason without Dixon, or of Chang without Eng.

The other week the lady orchestra of the St. Cecilia Society attracted attention. Now Viscountess Folkestone gives concerts with a lady orchestra of some 47 strings, very fairly balanced, one taking place on June 29th, in aid of the funds of the St. Andrew's Convalescent Home, Folkestone, and the People's Entertainment Society. Such efforts call for cordial encouragement, and our aristocracy, both ladies and gentlemen, are doing well in making such good use of their talents and acquirements.

The Querist.

QUERY.

VOLUNTARIES.—Would any of the musical readers of the *Standard* kindly favour me with the names and publishers of some pretty, effective, and pleasing Voluntaries, either in volume or in sheets ?—VERITAS.

Service Lists.

SIXTH SUNDAY AFTER TRINITY.
JULY 1st.
London.

ST. PAUL'S CATHEDRAL.—Morn.: Service, Te Deum and Benedictus, Prout in F ; Introit, Blessed is he who cometh (Gounod) ; Holy Communion, Schubert in G. Even.: Service, Magnificat and Nunc Dimittis, Thorne in D ; Anthem, God is a Spirit, and, Blessed be the Lord God (Bennett).

TEMPLE CHURCH.—Morn.: Service, Te Deum Laudamus, Smart in F ; Apostles' Creed, Harmonised Monotone ; Anthem, I was glad (Purcell). Even.: Service. Magnificat and Nunc Dimittis, Smart in F; Apostles' Creed, Harmonized Monotone ; Anthem, God is our hope (Greene).

LINCOLN'S INN CHAPEL.—Morn.: Service, Aldrich in G; Kyrie, Aldrich ; Anthem, Sing to the Lord a new made song (Mendelssohn); Even.: Service, Aldrich in G ; Anthem, Unto Thee will I cry (Calkin).

FOUNDLING CHAPEL. — Morn.: Service, Garrett in D; Anthem, The wilderness (Goss). Aft.: Service, Children's Service, Chants and Hymns.

CHRIST CHURCH, CLAPHAM.—Morn.: Service, Te Deum, Plain-song; Kyrie and Credo, "Messe Solennelle" (Gounod); Offertory Anthem, Blessed be the Lord God (Nares); Sanctus, Benedictus, Agnus Dei, and Gloria in excelsis, Gounod. Even.: Service, Magnificat and Nunc Dimittis, Hoyte in B flat ; Anthem, O taste and see (Goss).

HOLY TRINITY, TULSE HILL.— Morn.: Chant Service. Even.: Service, Magnificat and Nunc Dimittis, Gadsby in C; Anthem, Sing praises unto the Lord (Gounod).

ST. AUGUSTINE AND ST. FAITH, WATLING STREET.—Morn.: Service, Stainer in E flat, Offertory, O love the Lord (Sullivan). Even.: Service, Smart in B flat; Anthem, Whoso dwelleth (Martin).

ST. PETER'S, LEIGHAM COURT ROAD, STREATHAM, S.W. —Morn.: Holy Eucharist, Purge me with hyssop (Chantwise); Introit, How dreadful is this place (Agutter); Mass, Schubert in G ; Gradual, This place was made by God (Sutton); Communion, "Ave verum corpus" (Fagan). Even.: Service, Magnificat, Stark in D; Anthem, The Lord is with thee (Osborne) ; Solemn Te Deum, Hopkins in G.

ST. PETER'S, VERE STREET, W.—Even.: Service, Magnificat and Nunc Dimittis, Hopkins in F ; Anthem, Staud up and bless the Lord (Goss).

ST. PAUL'S, AVENUE ROAD, SOUTH HAMPSTEAD.—Morn.: Service, Te Deum, Dykes in F ; Benedictus, Lawes ; Kyrie, Stainer in E flat. Even.; Service, Magnificat and Nunc Dimittis, Gounod in D ; Anthem, God came from Teman (Steggall).

ST. PAUL'S, BOW COMMON, E.—Morn.: Service, Te Deum and Benedictus, Chants ; Holy Communion ; Kyrie, Credo, Sanctus, Benedictus, Agnus Dei and Gloria in excelsis, Verenham in F ; Offertory, Calkin. Even.: Service, Magnificat and Nunc Dimittis, Tours in F ; Anthem, Here by Babylon's wave (Gounod).

ST. JAMES'S PRIVATE EPISCOPAL CHAPEL, SOUTHWARK. —Morn.: Service, Introit, O Lamb of God (Gounod) ; Communion Service, Messe de Orphéonistes (Gounod). Even.: Service, Stanford in B flat ; Anthem, O rest in the Lord (Mendelssohn).

ST. MARY BOLTONS, WEST BROMPTON, S.W.—Morn.: Service, Te Deum and Benedictus, Smart in F; Even.: Service, Magnificat and Nunc Dimittis, Smart in F ; Anthem, I was glad (Elvey).

ST. MARY ABCHURCH, E.C.—Morn.: Service, Boyce in C and Stainer in A; Holy Communion, Smart in F. Even.: Service, Garret in D.

ST. MARGARET PATTENS, ROOD LANE, FENCHURCH STREET.—Morn.: Service, Te Deum, Smart in F ; Benedictus, Dykes in F ; Communion Service : Offertory Anthem, For the mountains shall depart (Mendelssohn) ; Kyrie, Credo, Sanctus, Benedictus, Agnus Dei and Gloria (Mozart). Even.: Service, Magnificat and Nunc Dimittis, Hopkins in F ; Anthem, His salvation, and, God is a Spirit (Bennett).

ST. MICHAEL'S, CORNHILL. — Morn.: Service, Te Deum and Jubilate, Dykes in F; Anthem, In Christ dwelleth (Goss); Kyrie, and Creed, Marbecke. Even.: Service, Magnificat and and Nunc Dimittis, Nares in F; Anthem, O Lord; give ear (Greene).

ST. MAGNUS, LONDON BRIDGE.—Morn.: Service, Opening Anthem, I will arise (Cecil); Te Deum and Jubilate, Travers in F; Kyrie, Mendelssohn. Even.: Service, Magnificat and Nunc Dimittis, Travers in F; Anthem, God is gone up (Greene).

ST. SAVIOUR'S, HOXTON.—Morn.: Service, Te Deum, Hopkins in G; Holy Communion; Kyrie, Credo, Sanctus, and Gloria in excelsis, Smart in G. Even.: Service, Magnificat and Nunc Dimittis, (Best); Anthem, Holy, holy (Spohr).

ST. SEPULCHRE'S, HOLBORN.—Morn.: Service, Sullivan in D; Anthem, I know that the Lord (Ouseley) Even.: Service, Cooke in G; Anthem, We will rejoice (Croft).

Country.

ST. ASAPH CATHEDRAL.—Morn.: Service, Ordination Service, " Veni Creator" (Palestrina). Even.: Service, The Litany; Anthem, Now we are ambassadors (Mendelssohn).

ASHBURNE CHURCH, DERBYSHIRE. — Morn.: Service, Dykes in F; Holy Communion, Lloyd in E flat. Even.: Service, Lloyd in E flat; Anthem, Sing a song of praise (Stainer).

BIRMINGHAM (S. ALBAN THE MARTYR).—Morn.: Service, Plain-song; Holy Communion; Kyrie, Credo, Sanctus, Gloria, Garrett in D; Benedictus and Agnus Dei, Redman in D. Evensong: Magnificat and Nunc Dimittis, Tours in F.

BIRMINGHAM (ST. CYPRIAN'S, HAY MILLS).—Morn.: Service, Field in D; Anthem, Praise the Lord, O my soul (Mozart). Even.: Service, Clarke-Whitfeld in E; Anthem, Be Thou my 'udge (Corfe).

BIRMINGHAM (S. PHILIP'S CHURCH). -- Morn.: Service, Chant Service (Best); Holy Communion, Best in G. Evensong Service, Chipp in A; Anthem, Blessed are they (Tours).

CANTERBURY CATHEDRAL.—Morn.: Service, Te Deum, Hopkins in G; Jubilate, Hake in G; Anthem, O Lord we trust (Handel); Communion, Garrett in D. Even.: Service, Goss in A; Anthem, The glory of the Lord (Goss).

DUBLIN, ST. PATRICK'S (NATIONAL) CATHEDRAL.—Morn.: Service, Te Deum and Jubilate, Smart in F; Communion, Kyrie, Creed, and Sanctus, Smart in F; Anthem, Grant us Thy peace (Mendelssohn). Even.: Service, Magnificat and Nunc Dimittis, Smart in F; Anthems, Distracted with care (Haydn), and, I looked, and lo, a Lamb (Stevenson).

DURHAM CATHEDRAL. — Morn.: Service, Calkin in D (throughout); Anthem, for this mortal must put on immortality (Wesley); Introit, O taste and see (Rogers). Even.: Service, Anthem, On Thee each living soul (Haydn).

ELY CATHEDRAL.—Morn.: Service, Te Deum, Hopkins in E flat; Benedictus, Plain-song; Kyrie and Credo, Arnold in B minor; Gloria, Jackman in E flat; Anthem, Thou visitest the earth (Greene). Even.: Service, Arnold in F; Anthem, I will sing of thy power (Greene).

GLOUCESTER CATHEDRAL — Morn.: Service, Te Deum and Jubilate, Stanford in B flat; Kyrie and Creed, Stanford in B flat; Anthem, O Lord, my God (Wesley). Aft.: Service, Stanford in B flat; Anthem, Hear my prayer (Mendelssohn).

LEEDS, ST. MARTIN'S CHURCH (POTTERNEWTON). — Te Deum and Benedictus, Chants; Introit, I will wash my hands in innocency (Wesley); Kyrie, Torrance in D; Nicene Creed, (Marbeck); Offertory Sentences (Farebrother). Even.: Service, Magnificat and Nunc Dimittis, Chants; He in tears that soweth (Hiller).

LICHFIELD CATHEDRAL—Morn.: Service, Tuckermann in E flat; Communion Service, Tuckermann in E flat; Anthem, Praise the Lord (Hayes). Even.: Service, Turle in D; Anthems, Whosoever drinketh, and, Therefore with joy "Woman of Samaria " (Bennett).

LLANDAFF CATHEDRAL.—Morn.: Service, Te Deum and Jubilate Garrett in D; Introit, O Saviour of the world (Goss); Holy Communion, Garrett in D. Even.: Service, The Litany; Anthems, Now we are ambassadors, and, How lovely (Mendelssohn).

LIVERPOOL CATHEDRAL.—Aft.: Service, Magnificat and Nunc Dimittis, Smart in E flat; Anthem, I was glad when they said unto me (Horsley).

MANCHESTER CATHEDRAL.—Morn.: Service, Attwood in F; Anthem, There is Joy (Sullivan); Holy Communion, Parry in D. Aft.: Service, Attwood in F; Anthem, Glory be to God (Haydn).

MANCHESTER (ST. BENEDICT'S). - Morn.: Service, Kyrie, Credo, Sanctus, Benedictus, Agnus Dei, and Gloria in excelsis, Thorne in G. Even.: Service, Magnificat and Nunc Dimittis, Bunnett in F.

MANCHESTER (ST. JOHN BAPTIST, HULME).—Morn.: Service, Kyrie, Credo, and Gloria in excelsis, Stainer in A; Sanctus, Benedictus and Agnus Dei, Gounod. Even.: Service, Magnificat and Nunc Dimittis, Bunnett in F; Anthem, I will lift up mine eyes (Clarke-Whitfield).

RIPON CATHEDRAL.—Morn.: Service, Chants; Kyrie and Credo, Armes in B flat; Anthem, O Saviour of the World (Goss). Aft.: Service, Haynes in E; Anthem, The wilderness (Wesley).

ROCHESTER CATHEDRAL.—Morn.: Service, Goss in A; Anthem, O Father, blest (Baum); Holy Communion, Hopkins in G. Even.: Service, Hopkins in A; Anthem, Blessed be the God (Wesley).

SHEFFIELD PARISH CHURCH. — Morn.: Service, Kyrie, Tours in F; Even.: Service, Magnificat and Nunc Dimittis, Barnby in C; Anthems, Then shall the righteous, and, He that shall endure (Mendelssohn).

SHERBORNE ABBEY.—Morn.: Service, Te Deum, Chants, Kyrie, Goss in G; Offertories, (Barnby). Even.: Service, Anthem, O God who hast prepared (Corfe).

SOUTHWELL COLLEGIATE CHURCH, NOTTS.—Morn.: Service, King in C; Kyrie, Calkin in B flat; Creed, Marriott in F. Even.: Service, Walmisley in D minor; Anthem, Ascribe unto the Lord (Wesley).

SOUTHAMPTON (ST. MARY'S CHURCH).—Morn.: Service, Te Deum Calkin in B flat; Benedictus, Aldrich; Holy Communion; Introit, O how amiable (Macfarren); Service, Monk in C; Offertory, "Charge them " (Barnby); Paternoster, Field. Even.: Service, Magnificat and Nunc Dimittis, Steward in G; Apostles' Creed, Harmonized Monotone.

WELLS CATHEDRAL.—Morn.: Service, Banks in G (throughout). Even.: Service, Aldrich in A; Anthem, Praise the Lord (Mozart).

WORCESTER CATHEDRAL.—Morn.: Service, Garrett in F; Anthem, Holy, holy (Crotch). Even.: Service, Garrett in F; Anthem, Send out Thy light (Gounod).

APPOINTMENTS.

Mr. RICHARD LEMAIRE has been appointed Choirmaster at the Royal Military Chapel (the Guards' Church), St. James's Park. Mr. Lemaire will continue to hold his present appointment at St. John's, Horsleydown, S.E.

Mr. C. A. HODGKINSON has been appointed Organist and Choirmaster of Christ Church (Parish Church), Bexley Heath.

Mr. ALFRED A. PHYSICK has resigned the organistship of the Church of the Ascension, Lavender Hill; and has been appointed Organist and Director of the Choir, to Holy Trinity Church, Upper Tooting. Mr. Hand, late Organist of S. Chad's, Haggerton, succeeds Mr. Physick at Lavender Hill, upon his leaving there during the next month.

. *Post-cards must be sent to the Editor, 6, Argyle Square, W.C., by Wednesday. Lists are frequently omitted in consequence of not being received in time.*

NEWSPAPERS sent should have *distinct marks* opposite to the matter to which attention is required.

NOTICE.—*All communications intended for the Editor are to be sent to his private address. Business communications to be addressed to* 185, *Fleet Street, E.C.*

[The attention of the several Organists is called to the favour they confer upon their brother musicians by forwarding their notices regularly: this column of the paper is much valued as an index to what is going on in the choice of cathedral music, so much so that intermissions constantly give rise to remonstrance. Lists should be sent in a week in advance if possible.—ED. *Mus. Stand.*]

The

Musical Standard,

A NEWSPAPER FOR MUSICIANS,

PROFESSIONAL AND AMATEUR.

VOL. XXV. NEW SERIES.

JULY TO DECEMBER, 1883.

"The powers of music are felt or known by all men."—SIR W. TEMPLE.

LONDON:

WILLIAM REEVES: "MUSICAL STANDARD" OFFICE, 185, FLEET STREET.

Price Nine Shillings, bound in cloth.

INDEX TO VOL. XXV. NEW SERIES.

The Musical Standard

A NEWSPAPER FOR MUSICIANS PROFESSIONAL AND AMATEUR

No. 988. VOL. XXV. FOURTH SERIES.   SATURDAY, JULY 7, 1883.   WEEKLY: PRICE 3D.

THE MUSICAL STANDARD is published every Saturday, price 3d., by post, 3½d.; and may be had of any bookseller or newsagent by ordering its regular supply.

SUBSCRIPTION.—*The Musical Standard* is posted to subscribers at 15s. a year; half a year, 7s. 6d., payable in advance.

The rate is the same to France, Belgium, Germany, Italy, United States, and Canada.

Post Office Orders to be made payable to the Publisher, William Reeves, 185, Fleet Street, London, or to the West-end Agents, Messrs. Weekes & Co., 14, Hanover Street, Regent Street, W.

ADVERTISEMENTS.—The charge for ordinary advertisements in *The Musical Standard* is 2s. 6d. for three lines or less; and 6d. for each line (10 words) in addition. " Organist wanted," 3s. 6d. for 3 lines or less. A reduction is made for a series.

FRONT PAGE.—Concert and auction advertisements, &c., are inserted in the front page of *The Musical Standard*, and charged one-third in addition to the ordinary rates. Other advertisements will be inserted on the front page, or in the leader page, if desired, at the same terms.

YORK ORGAN FACTORY,

BLENHEIM PLACE, MONKGATE.

SPECIFICATION of NEW ORGAN, built by the late ROBT. POSTILL, in Pitch Pine Case, Stained and Varnished, with Spotted Metal Speaking Pipes in Front.

GREAT ORGAN, EIGHT STOPS.   SWELL ORGAN, EIGHT STOPS.

PEDAL ORGAN.

Bourdon (large scale).... 16 feet .... 30 Notes.

COUPLERS.

Swell to Great.   Swell to Pedals.
Great to Pedals.

Three Composition Pedals for Changing the Stops.
Two Octaves and a third of German Pedals for the Feet.

Front of Organ.................. 10 feet 3 inches.
Front to Back .... 9 ,, 9 ,,
Height .... 16 ,, 6 ,,

The above Instrument is for SALE, and may be seen and heard by applying at the Works, or Mrs. J. POSTILL'S, 25, Monkgate.

COLLEGE OF ORGANISTS.

TUESDAY and WEDNESDAY, July 10th and 11th, Examination for Associateship.—THURSDAY, July 12th, Examination for Fellowship.—TUESDAY, July 17th, at 8, Annual General Meeting.

The above Meetings will be held at the NEUMEYER HALL, Hart Street, Bloomsbury.

E. H. TURPIN,
Hon. Secretary.

95, Great Russell Street, Bloomsbury, W.C.

THE ORGANIST of the PARISH CHURCH, TIVERTON, DEVON, offers his HOUSE to anyone who would take his duties during the month of August; or would exchange with organist at seaside, or deputise.—Address, T. RUSSE, Tiverton, Devon.

WANTED, a VIOLIN ASSISTANT, who must be a really good performer. Salary about £120 a year, which might largely be increased.—Apply, T. RUSSE, Tiverton, Devon.

TO CONNOISSEURS.—A splendid CHAMBER ORGAN, built recently by one of the first London firms. Contains TWENTY STOPS (including two on the pedal organ) and TWO COMPLETE MANUALS. Pedal board radiating and concave according to the revised scale (Coll. Organists). The METAL throughout is of the very best quality. Blown by one of Duncan's patent hydraulic engines. This instrument, having been specially designed regardless of expense, is, for completeness of workmanship and quality of tone, one very seldom to be met with, and commends itself to the notice of those who may desire to possess a really fine and complete instrument.—Address for full particulars, price, &c., 73, Park Road South, Birkenhead.

MR. HUMPHREY J. STARK begs to announce his REMOVAL to 12, Norwood Road, Herne Hill, S.E.

MAKERS AND REPAIRERS.

GEORGE WITHERS & CO.

(Late of Coventry Street),

WHOLESALE IMPORTERS OF

MUSICAL STRINGS,

From Rome, Padua, and Naples.

A FINE COLLECTION OF ITALIAN INSTRUMENTS.

Bows, Cases, Music Stands, &c. See Price Lists.

51, ST. MARTIN'S LANE, LONDON.

LEEDS TRIENNIAL MUSICAL FESTIVAL, October 10th, 11th, 12th, and 13th, 1883.

Conductor—SIR ARTHUR SULLIVAN.

OUTLINE PROGRAMMES may now be had on application, All communications to be addressed "FRED. R. SPARK, Esq., Hon. Sec. Musical Festival, Leeds."

MISS NORAH HAYES, CONTRALTO VOCALIST of the Albert Hall and St. James's Hall Concerts, is open to engagements for Concerts, Soirées, and At Homes. Good Press opinions. Services given free for Charities.—Address, 95, Edgware Road.

VIOLIN.—HERR POLONASKI (Violinist), open to ENGAGEMENTS for Concerts, Musical At Homes, and Violin or Accompaniment Lessons.—For Terms, please Address, HERR POLONASKI, 16, Wharfdale-street, South Kensington, S.W.

FISHERIES EXHIBITON, SOUTH KENSINGTON.—Mr. FRANK BRADLEY, Professor of the Organ, Trinity College, London, &c. (concert organist), will give RECITALS on MONDAYS and WEDNESDAYS, on the Organs of Messrs. Lewin, and Henry Jones & Sons, during the Exhibition.—Programmes gratuitously given in the Building.

For Concerts and Recitals, address Beaconsfield, Gunnersbury, W.

INTERNATIONAL FISHERIES EXHIBITION.—ORGAN RECITALS daily, upon the fine-toned Organ, in West Gallery. Supplied to the Executive Committee by HENRY JONES & SONS, 136, Fulham Road, South Kensington.

MR. E. DAVIDSON PALMER, Mus.Bac., Oxon., author of " What is Falsetto ?" " Pronunciation in Singing," etc., gives LESSONS in VOICE TRAINING and SOLO SINGING, at his residence, 10, Gladesmore-road, Stamford Hill, N.

THE ORGANIST and CHOIRMASTER of Cirencester Abbey desires RE-ENGAGEMENT. 14 years' Cathedral experience.—Address as above.

ORGANIST and CHOIRMASTER. — Newington United Presbyterian Church, Edinburgh. Salary, £70 per annum.—Applications, with testimonials, to be lodged, on or before the 1st August next, with JAMES PATERSON, 16, Dick Place, Edinburgh, from whom copies of the conditions of engagement may be obtained.

JUST PUBLISHED, "MORNING and EVENING SERVICE," set to music for the especial use of Parish Choirs, by FREDK. HUNNIBELL, F.C.O. Price, 1s.; or separately, 8d. and 6d.
London : NOVELLO, EWER & CO.

Post 8vo., boards, 2s. 6d., post free.

TECHNICS OF VIOLIN PLAYING, by KARL COURVOISIER. Edited and translated by H. E. Krehbiel. Numerous illustrations.
Joachim says : " It is my opinion that this book will offer material aid to all violin players.
W. REEVES, 185, Fleet Street, London, E.C.

Second Edition, Revised and Enlarged, cloth, 3s. 6d.

BEETHOVEN'S PIANOFORTE SONATAS, explained by ERNST von ELTERLEIN, translated by E. Hill. Preface by E. Pauer.
W. REEVES, 185, FLEET STREET, LONDON.

Foreign Musical Intelligence.

Massenet's new opera is to be given in Paris next winter.

M. Louis Deffès is the new director of the Conservatoire in Toulouse.

Signori Ferrari and Faccio are appointed respectively manager and conductor of La Scala, Milan.

Herr Paulli, the "kapellmeister" of Copenhagen, has lately retired, after a service of over fifty years, at the Royal Theatre.

The municipal council of Paris have contributed the sum of 200 francs to the fund for erecting a memorial to Hector Berlioz.

M. Félix Clement has lately brought out the second edition of his valuable work of reference the "Dictionnaire des Opéras."

"Isona di Provenza" is the title of a new opera by Signor Mancinelli, composed as a commission from the well-known house of Ricordi.

A Dresden manufacturer has invented an instrument of the harmonium species, to which he has given the singular name of "Cantus transcendentalis."

Amongst Raff's papers were found two operas, "Benedetto Marcello," and a comic opera, "Die Eifersuchtigen," of which last he had himself written the libretto.

Wilhem Krüger died at Stuttgart on June 20th. The funeral was one of an imposing character, and the departed composer and pianist was held in high esteem in Germany.

An English composition was given at a recent state concert, Mr. M'Guckin and Mdme. Valleria singing the love-duet from the fourth act of Mr. Mackenzie's "Colomba."

It is announced that at two concerts recently given by Rubenstein at St. Petersburg, 16,207 roubles were realised, 5,000 of which he has devoted to a fund for the erection of a monument to Michael Glinka, the father of Russian opera.

From Brussels comes the story of the discovery of an autograph MS. concerto by Mozart for pianoforte and violin with orchestra. The work is dated 1778, is said to have been composed at Mannheim, and the MS. occupies some fifteen pages only.

Before the close of the season two new works were produced at the Paris Opéra Comique. "Matthias Corvin," a comic opera in one act, the music by M. de Bertha, is described as the writing of a promising composer. The other novelty, a two act comic opera called "Le Portrait," is the work of M. de Lajarte, whose music is light and pleasing.

The French papers give the following list of the chief provincial Conservatoires of France, with the dates of foundation attached:—Aix, 1850; Angers, 1857; Besançon, 1861; Bordeaux, 1852; Boulogne, 1829; Caen, 1835; Cambrai, 1821; Douai, 1799; Dunkirk, 1863; Lille, 1801; Marseilles, 1820; Nantes, 1844; Nimes, 1864; Toulon, 1866; Toulouse, 1830; Valenciennes, 1836.

The Festival of the Girls' Friendly Society was held in St. Paul's Cathedral on Thursday the 14th inst., in the presence of a large congregation. The service opened with the singing of the Te Deum (Smart in F). The celebration of the Holy Communion was then proceeded with, the music selected being Stainer's fine service in A. The anthem, "Blessed be the God and Father" (Wesley) was sung during the offertory, and the "Veni Creator" was also given. The choir was composed of the boys of St. Peter's Church, Eaton Square, and gentlemen from St. Paul's, Westminster Abbey, the Chapel Royal, St. Peter's, Eaton Square, &c., and the service was rendered in a most satisfactory manner. Mr. W. de M. Sergison, of St. Peter's, Eaton Square, presided at the organ, as he has done at these Festivals on previous occasions.

Organ News.

LIVERPOOL.

Mr. W. T. Best gave an organ recital in the St. George's Hall, on Thursday evening, June 28th. The following is the programme :—

Toccata for the Organ (F sharp minor)	Hatton.
Romance in G major (Violin and Orchestra, Op. 40.)	Beethoven.
Fantasia in the Style of Handel (F minor)	Mozart.
Prelude and Fugue (B flat major)	Bach.
Duet, "Quis est homo" (" Stabat Mater ")	Rossini.
Festal March	Best.

On Saturday afternoon, June 30th :—

Overture "Le Médecin Malgré Lui"	Gounod.
Adagio from the Third Symphony	Mendelssohn.
Sicilienne and Fugue (G minor)	Bach.
Trio, "Sott' altro ciel" (" Guglielmo Tell "	Rossini.
March (A minor. Theme in the Pedal-Bass)	W. T. Best.

NORWICH.

The last of the afternoon organ recitals of the season was given by Dr. Bunnett, on Saturday afternoon, 30th of June, at the St. Andrew's Hall. The following was the programme :—

Overture, " Samson "	Handel.
Marche Religieuse	Chauvet.
An der Wiege (Cradle Song)	Lange.
Barcarole (from Fourth Concerto)	Bennett.
Aria, " Verdi Prati "	Handel.
March to Calvary, " Redemption "	Gounod.
Andante and Allegretto	Bunnett.
Air, " My heart ever faithful " and }	
The Giant Fugue }	Bach.
Andante in B flat	Mozart.
Andante and Allegretto	Mendelssohn.
From Organ Sonata.	
Jubilee Overture	Weber.

This recital made the thirty-second since November last. Nearly 300 pieces have been performed, which have been selected from 100 composers, representing 39 English, 25 German, 24 French, and 13 Italian, many pieces being quite new, while many of a standard classical character have not been forgotten. The organ works of Bach, Handel, and Mendelsohn have been well represented.

PRESTON.

The following is the programme of the organ recital given by Mr. James Tomlinson, in the new Public Hall, on Saturday evening, June 30th.

Concerto in F major	Handel.
Adagio—Allegro—(Cuckoo and Nightingale movement)—Allegretto—Fuga.	
Romance (Violin and Orchestra)	Beethoven.
Andante (Symphony in E flat)	Romberg.
Airs from " Faust "	Gounod.
Sketch in D	Chipp.
Marche Celebre	Lachner.

BRISTOL.

Mr. George Risely gave an organ recital at the Colston Hall, on June 23rd. The following was the programme :—

Marche Heroique	Schubert.
Andante from the First Symphony	Mozart.
Grand Sonata, No. 1.	Mendelssohn.
Allegro—Adagio—Andante—Allegro	
Andante in F sharp minor	S. S. Wesley.
Postlude in E flat	Wély.
Sarabande et Gavotte, "Oliva"	Roeckel.
Overture "Don Pasquale "	Donizetti.

BOLTON.

An organ recital was given in the Albert Hall, by Mr. Wm. Mullineux, F.C.O., on June 23rd. The following was the programme :—

Wedding March	Best.
Operatic Selection "Ernani "	Verdi.
Mélodie in A flat	Guilmant.
Organ Concerto " The Nightingale and Cuckoo "	Handel.
Gavotte in G	Smith.
Song, " Eve's Lamentation "	King.
Chorus, "Zadok the Priest " (Coronation Anthem).	Handel.

HINDLEY, WIGAN.

The following is the programme of the tenth monthly organ recital given by Mr. Chas. D. Mortimer, in St. Peter's Church, on Sunday, July 1st.

" Funeral March " and "Hymn of Seraphs "	Guilmant.
Fantasia on a Theme by Weber	E. H. Turpin.
" Pilgrim's Song of Hope "	Batiste.
Andante in E minor and major	Batiste.
Festive March in D	H. Smart.
Preludium in G	J. S. Bach.

FISHERIES EXHIBITION.

Mr. James Loaring, F.C.O., gave two organ recitals on Thursday, June 28th. The following pieces were included in the programmes :—

Overture, " Fra Diavolo "	Auber.
March from the " Ruins of Athens "	Beethoven.
Organ Concerto (No. 5)	Handel.
Andante from " Surprise Symphony "	Haydn.
Festive March in B flat	Loaring.
Overture " Semiramide "	Rossini.
Adagio from 7th Symphony	Haydn.
Rigaudon from " Ariodante "	Handel.
Coronation March	Meyerbeer.
Tema for the Organ in G	Loaring.
Chorus, " We never will bow down "	Handel.
Festive March in D	Smart.
March from the " Ruins of Athens "	Beethoven.
Organ Concerto (No. 5)	Handel.
Prelude and Fugue	Loaring.
Andante from " Surprise Symphony "	Haydn.
Festive March in B flat	Loaring.

And on Friday June 29th, Mr. James Loaring gave the following programme :—

Overture (" Semiramide ")	Rossini.
Adagio from 7th Symphony	Haydn.
Rigaudon	Handel.
Tema for the Organ in G	Loaring.
Festive March in D	Smart.

The following is the programme of a recital given on Friday afternoon, June 29th, by Mr. Wm. Sewell, A.R.A.M., organist of Christ Church, Clapham :—

Fugue in D minor	Bach.
March in G	Smart.
Adagio	Mozart.
Fanfare	Lemmens.
Marche Militaire	Gounod.
Andante in G	Smart.
Postlude in E flat	Batiste.

Mr. Frank Bradley gave an organ recital on Saturday June 30th. The programme consisted of the following selections from Handel, arranged by Mr. W. T. Best :—

Concerto in F, for Strings, etc., Largo—Siciliana—Fuga.	
Andante in F, from Oboe Concerto	
Tambourine, " Alcina " in G	
Minuet, from Grand Concerto in D major	
Fuga in B flat, from snd Oboe Concerto	
Allegro from " Water Music " in F	
Gavotte from " Lotario," in D	
Passacaille in G minor, from 7th Suite for Harpsichord	
Fantasia in C major, for Harpsichord.	
Sonata in D, " Il Trionfo-del-Tempo."	

Recitals were also given in the course of the day by Mr. Roger Askham. The following is the programme :—

Pastorale-Sonata (Op. 88)	Rheinberger.
Pastorale—Intermezzo—Fugue.	
Andante Piacevole	E. J. Hopkins.
Funeral March from Sonata (Op. 35)	Chopin.
March in C	R. Askham.
Andante in G	Smart.
Fugue in G minor	Bach.
Allegretto in B minor (Op. 19)	Guilmant.
Grand Chorus (Op. 18)	Guilmant.
Gavotte in A	Hollins.
Coronation Anthem, " Zadok the Priest "	Handel.
(Arranged by Dr. E. J. Hopkins).	

And Mr. Edward J. K. Toms also gave a recital. The following was the programme :—

March in D	Smart.
Andante Pastorale	G. E. Stephens.
Bourrée	Handel.
Barcarolle	S. Bennett.
Chilian National Hymn	F. Beyer.
Prelude and Fugue	Bach.
Gavotte	Tours.
Danse	S. Smith.
March (" Eli ")	Costa.

Mr. Frank Bradley gave organ recitals on each day of the past week. Want of space prevents the insertion of the programmes, which were of the usual interesting character.

TUNBRIDGE WELLS.

The fine organ at Trinity Church built by Messrs. J. W. Walker and Sons, and the gift of a munificent donor, was opened on June 27th. In the afternoon Mr. E. H. Turpin gave a recital before a very large number of listeners. In the evening an impressive service was held. The music included Tours' Service in F, an Anthem by Goss, and Handel's " Hallelujah Chorus." These were admirably rendered by a choir of 70 or 80 voices (ladies and gentlemen). The music was conducted by Mr. N. Elvey Irons, the much esteemed organist of the church, with so much quiet firmness, tact, and success, as clearly showed the presence of a very capable musical chief. A very large congregation listened to this really impressive service, which was pointed and garnished by a thoughtful sermon on church music by the greatly valued vicar, the Rev. Canon Hoare. Several Voluntaries were played during and after the service by Mr. E. H. Turpin, which served to display the various beauties of the singularly fine instrument ; such an organ indeed as was to be expected from the hands of so distinguished and painstaking a firm as that of Messrs. J. W. Walker and Sons. The diapason work proved to be deliciously full, round and smooth. The characteristic solo stops were found to be delicate and effective in tone. In general tone-balance and as regards the presence of some fine reeds, the organ is also a most satisfactory instrument, while very high finish characterises the mechanical movements. The Great organ has 11 stops, the Swell 12, the choir 6, the pedal 4, and there are 5 couplers, 6 composition pedals, Tremulant to Swell, pneumatic lever to Great organ and couplers. The stops number 38 and the pipes 1956. The people of Tunbridge Wells are to be congratulated upon the possession of another ecclesiastical and musical advantage in their town.

NEW KENT ROAD, S.E.

Dr. G. C. Martin gave an organ recital at St. Andrew's Church, on Wednesday evening, July 4th, on the occasion of the opening of the new organ. The following is the programme :—

Overture, " Athaliah "	Handel.
Andante from " Septuor "	Beethoven.
Introduction to " Passion "	Haydn.
Romanza in E flat	Haydn.
Minuet in B flat	Handel.
Fantasia and Fugue in D minor	Bach.

MORNINGSIDE, EDINBURGH.

An organ recital was given in the United Presbyterian Church, on Saturday afternoon, June 30th, by Mr. Wm. Blakeley. The following was the programme :—

Organ Concerto in F major (No. 5)	Handel.
Larghetto, Allegro, Alla Siciliana, Presto.	
Andante Cantabile (from Trio No. 13)	Haydn.
Concert Fugue in G major	Krebs.
Fantasia, " Vesper Hymn "	E. H. Turpin.
Andante, " First Symphony "	Beethoven.
" Ave Maria "	Cherubini.
Fantasia upon Two English Melodies	Guilmant.

BRADFORD.

Specification of three-manual pedal reed organ, built for C. H. Barker, Esq., organist, by E. W. Snell, of Camden Town :—

GREAT ORGAN. CC TO C. 61 NOTES.

1. Diapason	8 ft.	4. Flute	4 ft.
2. Principal	4 „	5. Vox Humana (mechanical)	
3. Oboe	8 „		

SWELL ORGAN. CC TO C. 61 NOTES.

6. Gemshorn	8 ft.	8. Euphone	8 ft.
7. Lieblich Bourdon	16 „		

CHOIR ORGAN. CC TO C. 61 NOTES.

9. Dulciana	8 ft.	11. Tremulant	
10. Voix Celestes	8 „		

PEDAL ORGAN. CCC TO F. 30 NOTES.

12. Bourdon	16 ft.	13. Violoncello	8 ft.

COUPLERS.

14. Swell to Great.	15. Great to Pedal.

ACCESSORY PEDALS.

Full organ, crescendo (Venetian swell), front and side blowers, beat keys, overhanging fronts, ivory draw-knobs, placed right and left of player, straight pedals, radiated sharps.

All scales, positions, and measures, strictly in accordance with the resolutions of the council of the College of Organists.

The numerous readers and contributors to *Notes and Queries* and many musical friends will regret to learn the very sudden death of the editor of the journal just named, Mr. Henry Frederic Turle, on Thursday last, of heart disease. A son of the well-known musical composer, the late organist of Westminster Abbey, Henry Turle was himself an " old Westminster," and ever retained the warmest affection for his former home. His devotion to the work which he had carried on since Dr. Doran's death will be patent to all who are familiar with *Notes and Queries*.

THE TONIC SOL-FA MOVEMENT.

In the course of his advocacy of the Tonic Sol-Fa movement, Mr. Sedley said in a lecture, given in Manchester, and now printed in pamphlet form :—

" No one travelling by railway at night can have failed to notice how the nearer and remoter lights visible from the line seem to be thrown into independent motion of their own, and to be executing about each other some complicated and bewildering kind of dance. A very simple real movement executed uniformly in a straight line by a spectator is thus shown to be capable of producing a complex-looking, unreal, but nevertheless seeming or *apparent* set of movements on the part of the objects at which he looks. If our traveller were not aware that his train was in motion, he would confidently assert on the direct evidence of his own senses that the objects which he observed really moved in the manner in which they appeared to move. Let us next replace this simple case by one somewhat more complex. Suppose that an observer is stationed at night on the deck of a steamer traversing a crowded waterway, and that he watches the lights of other vessels within sight. The observed motions of these objects will clearly be made up of two different elements, the real movements actually executed by the other ships, and the apparent movements which they seem to execute in consequence of the observer's station being itself in motion. The observer, if he is not aware of his own state of motion, will necessarily take the composite apparent movements thus produced for the real movements of the vessels in his field of view.

In these obvious considerations lies the reason why the proper motion of the planets formed an insoluble problem from the dawn of Astronomical Science down to the middle of the sixteenth century. During all this period the problem was studied on the assumption, which then appeared self-evident, that the earth was immovably fixed. The old observers were, therefore, exactly in the position of our supposed unconsciously moving steam-boat passenger.

At last came the great step which created modern Astronomy. Copernicus, who was a canon of a cathedral, in an outlying corner of what is now called North-Eastern Prussia, originated, or as he modestly preferred to put it, derived from a vague hint in some ancient writer, the idea that the earth was not fixed, but in motion, and that the apparent movements of the planets were essentially affected by that fact. By a simple application of geometrical principles to the problem before him Copernicus deduced from the apparent motions of the planets what must be their real motions on the assumption that the earth described a circle about the centre.

It was thus by substituting the conception of a movable for that of a fixed earth that planetary Astronomy was brought out of confusion and obscurity into order and light. A change no less salutary is wrought on vocal music when the conception of " movable doh " displaces that of " fixed doh."

Now what is the principle which lies at the root of the distinction embodied in these technical terms ? Take the simplest form of a melody, such as the notes of our National Anthem. When we hear them we at once recognise the tune, whether it be sung in the shrill notes of a child's voice, or in the deep tones of a manly bass. In short, the tune remains the same on whatever part of the scale we "pitch " it, *i.e.*, on whatever note we lead it off. Whether that note be in itself shrill or grave no more affects the tune than the scale on which a portrait is painted or drawn affects its likeness to the person whom it represents. Thus, in order that a melody may remain unchanged, fixed relations of pitch must connect the sounds of which it is made up, but the whereabouts of these sounds in the general scale—their absolute pitch as it is called—may be altered without altering the identity of the melody heard.

Let us see to what a tangle of difficulty and confusion the adoption of the opposite, or "fixed doh " system, as embodied in the ordinary staff notation, necessarily leads.

That notation begins by singling out a sound of assigned pitch and arbitrarily erecting the group of which that sound is the tonic into the " standard " key of C. All other keys, although inherently no whit less well entitled than it to an independent existence, are henceforth to be represented as merely altered forms of that one privileged key, the variations on its notes being indicated by a smaller or larger group of sharps or flats, forming what is technically called the "signature" of the altered key. How immediately this perverse arrangement acts, to the singer's detriment, may be seen by a moment's consideration. Suppose that a simple air, comprising the seven notes of the gamut has been written down in the key of C, and that the vocalist wishes to pitch the air half a note higher—nothing less than an array of seven sharps, or five flats, will suffice to direct such performance. If the pitch is to be lowered by half a note, the services of five sharps must in a like manner be called in. Thus, what to ninety-nine trained ears out of a hundred would be recognised as practically one and the same tune, is to be indicated on paper in three or four totally distinct ways, all but one of them involving very considerable complexity.

When a modulation affects a key already garnished with several accidentals, it is often necessary to neutralize these by the action of sharps, called a " natural," the remarkable feature about which is that it may indicate either a rise or a fall of the semitone, and that you can only ascertain by reference to the key-signature, or it may be to preceding notes, which of these two diametrically opposite processes is intended. It will be readily understood that these arbitrary and most un-scientific devices may, and often do, pile up such a heap of gratuitous complication, that a reader of the staff has no small difficulty in making out what note it is that he is directed to sing. When this obstacle is surmounted an even more serious one presents itself. The established notation, while communicating much irrelevant information as to the relation borne by the constituent sounds of a melody to one fixed and probably quite insignificant note (C), vouchsafes no direct information as to the relation in which those sounds stand to their own tonic for the time being. It is, however, only by knowing or feeling beforehand precisely what this relation is to be, that accurate sight-singing is possible. Accordingly a notation, for vocal purposes, must be pronounced bad on the face of it if it fails to indicate tonic relationship in a direct and rapidly recognisable fashion. The ordinary staff is at once condemned on an appeal to this principle. Its tonic character is exceedingly inferential, and can be but precariously made out from a single voice-part, even by a singer who is helped by a knowledge of harmony. Its notation indicates directly only absolute pitch. Inasmuch, however, as the great bulk of musically endowed persons do not possess the faculty of reproducing absolute pitch, a notation which indicates nothing but absolute pitch leaves the vocalist without instruction how to hit the note which he is directed to sing. Such instruction can only be efficiently supplied by a system of notation which enables the performer to recognise by simple inspection the relative pitch of the sounds he is to produce, *i.e.*, their respective positions in the group of notes constituting the key in which the passage to be executed is for the moment moving.

As regards a time-notation, Tonic Sol-fa appealing directly to the eye, and getting rid at one stroke of " semibreves," " minims," " crotchets," " quavers," and so forth, the corresponding array of "rests " which appear on the staff, are rendered needless by the very simple expedient of instructing the performer to hold his tongue wherever nothing is set down for him to sing. But, though the simplification thus effected is of the utmost importance to the beginner, it appears to me an open question whether, when applied to rhythms of great complexity, this " graphic " time notation is or is not an improvement on that in ordinary use. But in its notation for pitch, the Tonic Sol-fa system, by practically embodying and keeping constantly in view the identity of every key in the gamut, as to internal constitution, necessarily possesses for the singer an overwhelming superiority over the established notation."

The Brisbane Courier tells of a pleasant and informal meeting on May 14th, at the office of Mr. W. H. Wilson, the object of which was to welcome Mr. Walter G. Wilmore back again and to present to him a handsome diamond ring and an address of cordial welcome after his visit to England. Mr. Wilmore (who belongs to the College of Organists) has many admiring and appreciative friends in England, and Mr. Wilson is also known here as an earnest lover and cultivator of good music.

GOUNOD'S "REDEMPTION."

BY AN ENGLISH MUSICIAN.

SUFFICIENT time has now elapsed to enable the musical world to assess the merits of Gounod's chief essay, 'The Redemption,' which, it may be at once said, is a stagey imitation of Bach's sublime *Passions Musik* from a Roman Catholic point of view. The composer himself disarms us by saying that we are not to glance at it from an old-fashioned oratorio standard. He describes it as a 'Trilogy.' It is even more than a triangular arrangement, having a Prologue, and starts with that misty foundation of matter, 'Chaos,' which is tortuously begotten of ascending and descending chromatic gamuts played together, making us all regret the archaic picture at the commencement of the 'Creation' by that departed master, Haydn. Gounod is his own Laureate, and tells us he wrote the words when lodged in Rome at the Academy of France, situate on that favourite promenade of the modern Romans, the Pincian Hill.

What the text may be like in the original, cannot be hazarded, —what it is through the medium of an uncouth and unmusical translation we certainly do know; such doggerel has rarely met the eye in works of a sacred character. The entire concoction bears remarkable likeness to the Biblical "dramas," in which the younger members of our Sunday Schools take a demure delight. With a proviso. Well known hymns of the Latin Church are cunningly interlarded and sung to the dreary strains of the Roman Plain-Chant, as the "Vexilla Regis" and "Stabat Mater," the latter, with a noteworthy reading, which may be commended to Anglican clergymen who contemplate improving their congregations by a performance of the work. Gounod's attempts at choral writing are of the most humble description, resembling brief "part songs" and without the slightest address in the march of the inner parts. Out of a series of more than twenty short choruses, almost all are in simple counterpoint, note against note, syllable to syllable, as in operatic music; and on such ignoble *pabulum* as this, our trained bodies of singers are invited to exist! Are then the wonderful pages of Bach's *Passions Musik*, as well as the choral splendours in the oratorios of Handel and Mendelssohn mere sound and fury, signifying nothing? It may be that the composer devoutly wishes to contribute in winning this country back to the "Roman Obedience" by his pious hymns, sung to a nursing organ accompaniment. They have not, it is true, the cloying fervour of the Hymn tunes by Dykes among our native harpers, but it is doubtful whether M. Gounod will bring many lambs into the Roman fold from the ranks of our choristers, who insist on being well cared for when making up their minds for a scientific shout in any large sacred work, and are hardly to be appeased by copious doses of ordinary psalmody.

It would be unfair to dismiss the clerical translator without a sample of his wares; the Disciples here reply to the holy women—

> "Though we fain would have believed you,
> Some form surely has deceived you,
> Some phantom seen in the night.
> From trusting what you have told us
> Lack of witness must withhold us :
> We rely on hearing and sight."

It can hardly be said that these words fall grandly on the ear, and they are average specimens of the prevailing bathos. Another quotation has a strong favour of H.M.S. Pinafore—the allusion is to our common progenitor, the primeval Adam—

> "And he, placed in a land of abundance and beauty,
> Lived a pure happy life, under guidance of duty."

Surely such a subject demands grave and noble diction. In the art of marrying words to music, a new revelation is made as to the word "possession," usually accented on the second syllable; but in the first short chorus the translator regales himself by placing the accent, with hideous musical effect, on the *last*, and that to a note on the strongest musical accent known, viz., the first note in any time-bar. This offence against the quantities is carefully repeated a little further on; subsequently, the same word is set as we always hope to find it; therefore both ways cannot be correct even from a "precenting" point of view. To return to the music.

The impression, after listening to Gounod's *ouvrage de ma vie*, must be faithfully chronicled—it is one of dull monotony, nor does a second hearing dispel the uncomfortable feeling; the air-form of composition has almost been tabooed, while extreme and irritating weariness is caused by the endless sing-song of those bores, the narrators, who cling with dreadful pertinacity to the two or three notes doled out to them by the composer, who frequently surrounds their utterances with humorous figures on accompanying violins, when not busy with his sour and diminished discords. It was to be expected that such an expert in the art of instrumentation as Gounod would leave a powerful impress upon the orchestral details of his score; and this is undoubtedly the case; in fact it may be predicted that a performance of the "Redemption," without a fully equipped band, is out of the question, and would hardly be undertaken or tolerated anywhere. From this cause, and the fragmentary character of the choral music, it cannot obtain vogue at those numerous singing-meetings where social groups of either sex, duly fortified with friendly but chest-contracting "octavos," stand to their work round a well-thumped piano, and make night hideous in neighbouring areas. The influence of Wagner in Gounod's work is paramount, so we are all prepared for that baleful and pantomimic nostrum, a *leit-motif*, which accompanies all allusions to the Saviour, and here consists of a passage for the orchestra repeated *rosalia* fashion, *i.e.*, a note higher each time, with a final cadence. The device of repeating short phrases in this manner is an infallible sign of creative decay, and is profusely employed ; many chromatic orchestra passages with ugly diminished harmonies, rise upon the ear "high and ever higher," but exactly the reverse as to the artistic value of the procedure, which has long ago been condemned by the school-men. The orchestral figure before alluded to—a dominant point of a few bars—has since been diverted from its purpose to do publishers duty as a song ! the translator supplying words under the rather absurd title of "Power and Love ;" more recently a well-known singer attempts to accommodate this *leit-motif* to devout Latin words. It is much to be regretted, that at the very outset the Saviour is introduced as one of the *dramatis personæ*, having many solo entrances assigned throughout. As a matter of notoriety, Beethoven's "Mount of Olives," and Spohr's "Calvary" were remodelled in this respect before a performance in England was permitted, and it is a curious aspect of the times to find responsible Anglican clergymen sanctioning a performance of the "Redemption" in well-known edifices without having this unseemly feature eliminated, not to mention others which plainly stamp the work as being more suitable to congregations who frankly own the Roman obedience. Owing to the undue prominence given to the orchestra by M. Gounod, a want of elevation of style is generally apparent ; for instance, the passage given to the mocking Jewish priests, " Can he not save himself," is dangerously similar to the profane *Habanera* in "Carmen." Again, the composer can hardly expect us to accept the theatrical and tawdry strains of his march to Calvary as "typical" of the dead march of the ancient Romans. The portentous darkness during the Crucifixion affords excuse for a very sinuous orchestral movement, described by the analytical commentator as a "study in dissonances," and must have cost the composer a deal of midnight oil ; in comparison with this "study," contrast the sublime effect of a few master-strokes in "He sent a thick darkness," from Handel's "Israel in Egypt ! ' The separation of groups of trumpet players at opposite wings of the orchestra, first practised by Berlios and continued by Verdi with splendid effect in his "Requiem," has been followed by Gounod in the chorus, "Saviour of men," where the only two notes played easily lend themselves to changing harmonies. The opening passages of this movement for the horns are very suggestive of Weber's overture to "Der Freyschütz," where the cadences for the instruments are much alike. In the symphony to the solo with chorus, "Ye mountains, ye perpetual hills," in E major, Gounod takes without compunction Mendelssohn's melodious theme from "St. Paul," "Be thou faithful unto death," for tenor, with violoncello *obbligato*, but hesitates to give the audacious crib to the singer ; so it is relegated to the violins before the vocal entry.

It will be seen from this notice that a high place is not accorded to Gounod's sacred work. The composer, it is unquestionable, has done conspicuous service to musical art in its operatic and secular branches, but in essaying the highest form has not been successful. In conclusion it may be said that although the "Redemption" will keep a place during a special season in certain quarters, it is destined to fall into the *désuetude* which so rapidly overtook the composer's unfortunate Wedding Marches, produced to royal order ; and the grounds for this estimate may thus be summarised:—(1) Absence of sustained melodic'interest ; (2) Insignificant and trivial character of the choral music ; (3) Negation of the air or song-form, superseded by tedious singsong in a declamatory style, and destitute of melodious grace ; (4) Undue prominence given to the orchestra throughout, surely contributing to a want of elevation in the music. It remains to be seen whether the work will be accepted and utilised by the Roman Catholic Church abroad, a matter very problematical, as it is known that "orchestras" in sacred buildings are out of favour and generally discouraged in the chief cities of the continent—a remarkable sign of the times.—*St. Cecilia's Magazine.*

Mr. and Mrs. F. Sewell Southgate gave an interesting concert of a miscellaneous kind at the Cavendish Rooms on the evening of June 20th. Moscheles' duet for two pianos, "Hommage à Handel," was brilliantly played by Mr. and Mrs. Sewell Southgate, and the former contributed a solo, Chopin's "Ballade" in A. Miss Kate Chaplin's violin solos were also a welcome addition. Some excellent singing of ballads, duets, and quartets was given by the Misses Ellis Walton, Eleanor Faulkner, Fusselle, Marian McKenzie, Jeanie Rosse, and Henden Warde, Mr. John Probert, Mr. Kirwen Jones, Mr. Franklin Clive, Mr. Quatremayne, and Messrs. Cecil and Ernest Traherne. Mr. E. Morton, Mr. Walenn, and Miss Nellie Chaplin assisted as accompanists.

WOMEN AS PIANO-TUNERS.

Every piano has one inherent weakness, which has to be repaired once or twice every year. Under the stress of time, use, and the weather, it loses tone. To restore the instrument to its proper condition is the art of the tuner. In the smaller cities and in the country, it often happens that the tuner is also obliged to be a repairer of the action of pianos.

The business of piano-tuning is another of the employments to which women are beginning to aspire. There is in Boston a school where, for some time, tuning has been regularly taught to both men and women. The objection that women have not the requisite fineness of ear is met by the fact that of the applicants for admission to this school only a small proportion fail to enter by reason of any aural defect. The sense of tune or harmony appears to exist in greater or less degree in the majority of civilized people, and, if there is but a germ, it can be educated into something practically useful, be the pupil man or woman. The objection that women have not the strength required in the art is nonsense, for, with the proper tools, a child can break a piano-string with ease. The time required by a young woman to perfect herself in the art of tuning the piano, the pipe or reed organ, is about one year. The course of study begins with a systematic training of the ear in pure unison. For this purpose the pupil is provided with a piano from which the action has been removed. The three strings for each note are plucked with the fingers, and alternately tightened or loosened with the proper lever or key, till the pupil's ear clearly apprehends the difference between unison and discord. No attention is paid to pitch, as the sole aim is to train the ear to a true unison of tones. If the pupil fails in this stage of the work, it is hopeless to go on. She is simply "harmony-blind," precisely as one may be colour-blind.

The next step is the training of the ear in pure harmony. For this work a piano is used having a worm and gear in place of the usual friction-pin for tightening the strings, so that the work of tuning is very light, the slightest movement of the hand controlling the instrument perfectly. The pupil now learns the relations of tones in a true major third. Then thirds are added together till the (tempered) octave is reached. Here the pupil discovers that the pure harmony does not bring the unison she had expected (from her previous studies) in the octave. In this manner the pupil discovers for herself the science of temperament. She soon hears the growl of the "wolf," and learns to catch the wailing "beats" of the interfering sounds. Then the science of tuning must be explained, and this leads to the study of acoustics in their relation to keyed instruments. Lectures and demonstrations in harmony and music are a part of the course. Having made some progress in tuning pianos, the pupil then takes up the tuning of the reed and pipe organ, with daily practice upon both instruments. During the entire course there is also drill in the gymnasium, with proper appliances for strengthening the hands and wrists. A good tuner also should know how to repair a piano. To equip the young woman for this work, there is regular practice upon models of all kinds of piano and organ actions. These are taken to pieces and put together with the usual tools till the mechanism is clearly understood. The action of a piano is easily taken out for repairs, and, as all the parts are interchangeable (for the same style and manufacture), it is not difficult to purchase the various parts and put them in their place when necessary. It is true the action is heavy, but there is always some one near who will lend a hand in lifting it out of the instrument. Piano-tuning is both a healthful and a profitable occupation, and a study of tuning trains the ear to good music.

At a soirée musicale at Mr. Klein's, Belsize Park, on Tuesday, Mr. Aptommas gave two solo performances on the harp. Alvard's fantasie on themes from "I Montechi e Capuletti" and his own Welsh melodies, and in conjunction with Mr. Harold E. Stidolph played two duets for piano and harp, "O dolce concento" (Henz), and "Tarentella" (Aptommas). Miss Mary Davies sang "Thou'rt like unto a flower" (Rubinstein), "Dedication" by Franz, and other songs, and M. Stidolph played Raff's "Rigandon." Mr. Corney Grain also gave two or three of his amusing and clever sketches.

LONDON : SATURDAY, JULY 7, 1883.

WHAT WILL THEY DO WITH IT?

HEN it was publicly announced that the "Sacred Harmonic Society" had determined on committing suicide, the question as to what was to become of their valuable Library excited much interest in the musical world. A comprehensive view, and examination of all the circumstances in connection with the dissolution of the Society has yet to be made. There is no intention to enter on the task here; but it may be pointed out, that the plea put forth to the effect that it had completely accomplished the work for which it was founded, its mission thus coming to a natural end, probably deceived no one. Briefly admitting that the institution during its fifty years' life has undoubtedly helped to advance the music-art in this country, it must yet be remembered that art is progressive, and that it is always presenting new worlds to conquer. The repertoire of the defunct Society was but a limited one. The authorities relied chiefly on the ordinary stock works, varied occasionally by an experiment from the pen of their own conductor; they touched but the fringe of the vast field of sacred music. The moribund condition into which the Society fell, was but the natural sequence of biological laws, and the "happy despatch" with which it terminated its existence, a weak act significant of the effeteness of mind that usually characterizes suicide.

All are pretty well agreed that the Sacred Harmonic Society has benefitted music generally, aided charity, assisted in raising a higher standard of taste in our land, and had a useful educating influence. On the question, as to why was it dissolved? there is not a consensus of opinion. The response to this question is probably tinctured by the particular bias of each one who answers it. But among the replies that have been given, a strange one found occasional utterance, viz., that the Society was broken up, so that its members might realize for their individual benefit the value of the property that from time to time had been accumulated. There must of course be a motive in every human action; though one may smile at the flimsy pretext, officially put forth, of "mission accomplished"; yet we cannot accept as a solution so mean and greedy a motive as this particular one would seem to imply, despite the fact that avarice not infrequently comes with old age, and is a weed that will grow in a barren-soil. In this case, such a selfish reason is certainly not correct in the aggregate, however true the implication may be in some individual cases. An old writer says:—"Avarice is one of the "most stupid and senseless passions, and the surest "symptom of a sordid and sickly mind."—Surely such a spirit as this could not obtain among the members of so respected a body as the old Sacred Harmonic Society! One of its early rules runs thus:— "No persons to be permitted to join the Society but "such as are strictly moral characters."—What was the precise standard of the morality necessary to acquire membership is an unrevealed mystery, and little concerns the public. It is sufficient to note that the Society made a certain parade of its goodness. To suggest then, that (like many of the mushroom Companies of the day) professional wreckers were to be found on its list, is really to charge the Society with being rotten to its foundation, and corrupt to the core. Such selfishness as this could hardly exist in a Society that carried its morality so far as to carefully eschew the term "Mass," adopting in its place the Protestant title of a "Service;" and further, to sternly prohibit applause at its concerts. The Society can fairly claim to be judged by its works, just as a tree is by its fruit. It will not be unfair then to apply this test, and see what has happened over the disposal of its noble Library.

The history of this unique collection is pretty widely known, so that it is only necessary for our purpose here briefly to mention a few particulars culled from the Catalogue, prepared by the librarian, Mr. W. H. Husk. In felicitous language he describes some of its treasures, showing that proud appreciation of them characteristic of an enthusiastic custodian and cultured man of letters. The catalogue is a portly volume of four hundred pages, and gives an account of upwards of four thousand works. These are classified under the heads of Printed Music, MSS., and Musical Literature, the divisions being further subdivided for convenience into thirty-one sections. The wealth of these is indeed great. The madrigal and glee collection is a perfect one. Here are to be found all the productions of the golden age of our own great madrigal writers, as well as a large number of works of this type from the pens of the distinguished Flemish and Italian composers of the sixteenth and seventeenth centuries. Ecclesiastical music is well represented; there are here early editions of Palestrina's Motets, Willaert's Psalms, published at Venice in 1565; early English Masses; and eight volumes of that scarce work, Rev. John Barnard's selection of "Church Musick," printed in 1641. Probably every oratorio that has been written is on the shelves. Of English Operas there are as many as four hundred catalogued, besides a multitude of pieces of all kinds by our native composers. When a complete history of the English school of music comes to be written, this invaluable collection of national music will be the mine of stored up materials that will be chiefly worked. Among other interesting MSS. there are some Missals, the score of Haydn's unheard opera "Armida," the copy of "Elijah" that Mendelssohn made for its first performance at Birmingham in 1846, besides many compositions and autograph letters of the great composers from an early period down to modern times. Perhaps, however, it is in the division entitled "Musical Literature," that the library is the richest. Nearly every work that has been issued on the History, Theory, and Practice, Biographies of its Professors, as well as on the drama, and other miscellaneous works treating on the art and science of music, are to be found in this superb collection. Space does not permit to name a tithe of these treasures, but the comprehensive nature of the gathering may be imagined by the statement that, from the very rare work of Gaforius, published at Naples in 1480, Holborne's "Cittarn Schoole," 1597, and an early "Modulorum Hortus," down to works issued from the presses of to-day, hardly any *lacuna* exist. In the department of pure music, there is a goodly number of orchestral scores; and the sections containing poetry, word-books, and miscellaneous pamphlets, are large and most useful for historical purposes.

One can now form a rough idea of the great value of this fine library to the musical world; a few words will not be out of place as to the way in which it has been gathered together. The commencement was a modest purchase of fifty standard works out of the profits of the season of 1836, the year the youthful Society boldly ventured on giving concerts in the large room at Exeter Hall. It must be noted that the library has grown up, and been formed from three distinct sources of supply : 1st. The general funds of the association; 2nd. The gifts of individual members; 3rd. Donations from outside musicians and the general public. In the examination of this question, it is of some importance to ascertain from which of the three sources the major part of the works has come. Taking the Catalogue as a guide, it would seem that the library has been chiefly enriched from the 3rd source, viz., that of benevolent friends. In any case it may be safely assumed, that the various donors gave to an institution which appeared to be a permanent one, and that the books were given for the use of all members, whether present or to come. The committee took a liberal view of their trust duties, and frequently conceded the privilege of research and reading to students, who were not members of the association. A consideration of these circumstances can but lead one to see that the collection partook of the nature of a common library, rather than as belonging to a few privileged individuals. Though these persons were undoubtedly its legal owners, they were owners chiefly in the sense of trustees, not in that of sole *bénéficiaires*.

When it was decided that the Society was to be dissolved, the question as to the disposal of its accumulated property came to the front. According to the rules, the existing members were entitled to participate in certain proportions in any division of the property; and in taking the steps they eventually did, it may be admitted that they were within their legal rights. But the question has a moral, as well as a legal bearing. This aspect of the case seems to have been overlooked, and thus the action of the members is calculated to cause a serious scandal in connection with the art they profess to love and serve. It is a common thing for private persons to bequeath their libraries to public institutions, and there are not wanting precedents as to the disposal of public music libraries. On the dissolution of the Bach Society, founded by Sir Sterndale Bennett, its library was presented to the Royal Academy of Music; that of the defunct Musical Union was given by Mr. J. Ella, its founder, to the authorities at South Kensington. It is said that at one period the Sacred Harmonic Committee offered their collection free to the Corporation of London for the Guildhall Library, but for some inscrutable reason it was declined. The president, committee, and officials of the Society are credited with having all along taken the view that the library should be handed over to some analogous institution, instead of adopting the mercenary plan of selling it and dividing the proceeds. But good intentions alone are not sufficient: some of the members objected to this arrangement; they cared more for their pockets than for the good of music. As the Scotch proverb runs :—" It is hard for a greedy eye to hae' a leal heart." Besides, the question became complicated by deaths, and the duties of executors, so a purchaser was sought for. The British Museum declined to treat; the Royal Academy had no funds to spare; Trinity College made no sign, and the Universities slumbered. On an appeal being made in the newspapers to the authorities of the Royal College of Music to purchase the library in its entirety, and not allow it to be dispersed by auction, or go abroad, Sir George (then Mr.) Grove formally stated that the new school "had no funds available to such a "purpose." How such an accomplished *litterateur*, and one who knows full well the desirability of pupils becoming acquainted with the history and progress of the art, and the necessity of studying the works of the great masters, can have put forth such a statement astonishes one! As well might he have declared that no portion of the hundred thousand pounds subscribed to the institution was to be devoted to the purchase of musical instruments, lesson and exercise books, or school furniture. (It may just be mentioned that the library of the Paris Conservatoire de Musique contains 15,000 volumes.) Besides technical skill, Sir George thoroughly appreciates the advantage of wide culture: it seems therefore likely that his statement was ingeniously designed to attain the very object in view, viz., the acquisition of the coveted library by the Royal College—only, at the expense of friends of the institution, instead of out of its own funds. A certain amount of mystery has been maintained as to where the money came from for the purchase. Dr. J. Stainer and Mr. W. H. Cummings were commissioned to examine and value the library on behalf of the Royal College, and the matter was negotiated through Sir Philip Cunliffe Owen, who is generally looked upon as a prominent representative of the new College. However, the purchase was completed, the books removed to Kensington Gore, and an agreed sum of upwards of £3,000 paid into the treasury of the Sacred Harmonic Society. This amount (together with the proceeds of other realized property) has just been distributed to the members.

Now comes the question, set out at the head of this article—"What will they do with it?" There can be very little difficulty in deciding what they ought *not* to do with it, viz., to retain it in their own pockets. According to "Cherubino" in the *Figaro*, some old members have received as much as £200, the junior ones proportionately less; he goes on to say that, such an appropriation of funds is an artistic scandal. And such it undoubtedly would be, were they to persist in such a disingenuous proceeding. It is impossible to believe that a body of educated English people can reap, and deliberately retain for their own benefit, the proceeds of a harvest they have not sown. If so, they will earn the contempt bestowed on Trustees who realize property formally committed to them for their enjoyment and care, but likewise, unquestionably intended to be for the benefit of all in perpetuity. In whatever light the matter is looked at, it is certain that the donors to the library of a Society, established for art purposes only, never intended that those who chanced to be members at a particular period, should obtain a pecuniary advantage through their gifts. That there is right feeling among some of the members, is evidenced by the fact, that a few cheques have been sent to the Royal Society of Musicians, and to the new Sacred Harmonic Society. But the great bulk of the members have as yet given no signs that they understand the responsibility cast upon them to give up what seems almost public money that they happen to have received privately. Surely, it is the duty of the officials of the old Society at once to call a meeting of the members at which schemes for founding scholarships, or giving handsome donations to some of our established musical institutions can be discussed and settled. Before the cry of shame is further raised, time must be given for reflection, and the members be recommended to do privately, but unitedly, that which they were legally unable to do in their corporate capacity. Until such an opportunity has been afforded them, it is better to refrain from further comments.

The President of the Association in his brochure on the history of the Society, gracefully speaks of "the power of music to raise and refine the moral "tone." Let us wait and see, what is the outcome of its practical effect on the members of his Society, who have so long been under the sway of this valuable power. What will they do with the money which accident has brought to them?   T. L. SOUTHGATE.

THE PRESENT SEASON.

UNDER the surface of the artistic and fashionable turmoil we speak of as the "London Season," there are doubtless many lessons to be learnt. The musician, although he can attach no importance to much that is proceeding during the brief annual metropolitan fever, finds nevertheless some yearly indications regarding the progress or decadence of different departments of his art, which are not to be disregarded. The present season has shown the growth of what may be called free trade in concert giving, and the corresponding decadence of the long continued protectionist policy, by which only a few reputations were possible and by which a few interested agents, concert givers, and business men contrived very largely to govern the concert-room platform. Still the prospect, though improved and improving, is not without its anxieties. Every year multiplies the long lists of vocal and instrumental executants; and it must be feared that we are in danger of having more artists than we can properly support. This seems especially to be the case as regards singers and pianists; the latter class of performers having largely increased lately and the old pianoforte playing monopolies being nearly at an end. One lesson to be gathered from the present state of affairs seems to be that of warning anxious young people of talent not to enter rashly or hurriedly a profession daily becoming more and more overcrowded. A truly gratifying feature of the season's work has been the clear indication that in spite of much competition and feverish experiments intended to establish alien conductors during the past few years, the sound love of orchestral music is steadily gaining ground. That once absolutely essential feature of the London season, Italian Opera, has been again a not unimportant characteristic of the season; though its glory, in spite of the presence of a fair number of stars, is evidently much diminished, if not on the wane. The Handel Festival has been naturally a prominent event of the season, even remembering that performances on so gigantic a scale and under such conditions are to be looked upon rather as musical sensations than as artistic expositions. On the whole, while the past season has produced little to chronicle, it has satisfactorily shown that music is growing steadily in many directions which denote a gratifying and healthy advance in public taste. E. H. TURPIN.

The London Literary and Artistic Society, which "provides a centre where men of letters and of science, also artists and others not engaged in these professions, but having literary, scientific, musical, and artistic tastes, meet for social intercourse," held a conversazione recently at the studios of the Mediæval and Industrial Art Society, New Bond Street. In the course of about three hours the studios, which were decorated with beautiful specimens of "painted tapestry"—*tentures artistiques*—were visited by five or six hundred ladies and gentlemen. A programme of music was well rendered, Herr Immanuel Liebich eliciting much admiration, while Signor di Giambattista, a celebrated pianist from the Neapolitan Academy, created astonishment by his left-hand performance on the piano. It is proposed that the premises in which the conversazione was held should be secured as the permanent home of the society, for new premises have become necessary owing to the large increase in the number of the members.

Reviews.

The Musician; a Guide for Pianoforte Students.—By Ridley Prentice. Grades I and II. (W. Swan, Sonnenschein & Co.)—This work is comprised in six grades. Its design, as stated in the preface, is to "help pianoforte students to become musicians, by acquiring, through careful study and analysis of well known pianoforte works, some insight into musical forms." By a simple, but unique system, the author contrives to present, in a pleasing manner, information regarding harmony and form. Brief biographical notes, entertaining anecdotes of famous musicians, and interesting, if somewhat fanciful interpretations of some of the pieces will doubtless serve to fix the students' attention. It may be questioned whether Mr. Prentice, in his zeal to make the public intelligent, has not crowded too much into his two grades. Be that as it may, if the success of the work is equal to its merits, its success will be great.

The Mechanism of the Human Voice. Second edition. By Emil Behnke. (J. Curwen & Sons, Plaistow, E.)—Herr Behnke has, with others, succeeded in revolutionising the art of teaching singing in our midst. His popular work now being noticed has but one weak point, a tendency to treat upon other people's methods by way of defending his own, when indeed his own book requires no defence at all. Herr Behnke's observations upon breathing, and upon the different registers are deeply interesting, and very conclusive. The earnestness and clearness of his style, and the evidently remarkable pains he has taken with a truly difficult subject, are everywhere manifest. All interested in that important subject, the voice, should read this book, which in its second edition, has been enlarged and improved upon. Its subject matter has an important bearing upon the art, and the spread of knowledge, as to the construction and treatment of the vocal instrument, will bear good fruit in many ways.

Academical Intelligence.

TRINITY COLLEGE, LONDON.

The following new Regulation for the Local Examination in Instrumental and Vocal Music has just been issued, and will come into operation after the long vacation :—

A satisfactory performance of the selected solo—vocal or instrumental, is *absolutely essential*. Candidates must therefore obtain 50 per cent. of the maximum marks in this section (performance of selected solo) in order to qualify for a pass certificate, or 75 per cent. for a certificate of honour. The *gross total* of marks (i.e. upon the whole examination) required to gain a pass certificate, is 50 per cent., and for a certificate of honour 75 per cent.; but a high per centage of marks in other sections will not be allowed to compensate for failure in the performance of the selected solo. No candidate above the age of 16 is eligible for a certificate of honour in any Junior Division, with the exception of singing, the limit of age in this instance being 18 years.

COLLEGE OF ORGANISTS.

The lecture of July 3rd was indeed one of rare interest. Mr. H. J. Sawyer, who has already contributed so much to our knowledge of organ music and organ players, found in "Mozart's organ works" a congenial subject, and he was in his happiest mood. His excellent discriminating and deeply interesting lecture was listened to with marked pleasure. The specimens performed were No. 9, in F (most probably not heard since it was played by its great composer, in Salzburg Cathedral in 1780); No. 10 in D, 13 in C, 14 and 15. All these were capitally played by Mr. Sawyer himself (on a small chamber organ of excellent tone, by Mr. A. Kirkland of Wakefield, and lent through Mr. Kirkland's London agents, Messrs. Weekes and Co.); Mr. J. M. Gray, first violin; Mr. Parkes, second violin; and Mr. Crapps, F.C.O., violoncello. Though secular and lively in character, these works are thoroughly Mozartian and contain beautiful ideas, and points of masterly workmanship. Mr. C. E. Stephens occupied the chair with his accustomed tact and ability; and with Messrs. Crapps, Stokoe, C. W. Pearce, and E. H. Turpin, addressed the attentive and enthusiastic listeners. This meeting was announced as the last of the session, the College Examinations taking place on July 10th, 11th, and 12th, and the Annual General Meeting on July 17th, closing the season. And during no year of the college's existence, has a more brilliant and valuable series of lectures been brought before the members and their friends. Mr. Sawyer's lecture will appear in our columns at a future date.

ORCHESTRAL CONDUCTING.

A correspondent has sent the following extract translated from a pamphlet by Wagner :—

"Robert Schumann once complained to me in Dresden, that at the Leipzig concerts Mendelssohn had deprived him of all enjoyment in the ninth symphony, by taking the first movement at a too hasty tempo. I myself was once present in Berlin at a rehearsal of Beethoven's eighth symphony (F major) under Mendelssohn's direction. I observed that he, as if according to humour, here and there seized upon a detail and laboured with a certain amount of obstinacy to obtain a clearness of execution, and that this detail was then so excellently rendered, that I did not quite understand why the same amount of attention was not granted to other portions. Altogether, this incomparably bright symphony was performed in an uncommonly smooth and entertaining manner. He on several occasions gave me to understand, with respect to direction, that a too slow tempo was the most detrimental, and that he himself would rather recommend a too hasty performance. Mendelssohn's scholars must have heard him make further and more precise remarks upon the subject, for this could not have been a casual view, imparted to me alone, for I had further opportunities of learning the results and lastly the grounds of that maxim.

I observed a striking exemplification of the former in the performance of the orchestra of the London Philharmonic Society. Mendelssohn had directed it for some considerable time, and it appeared that the tradition of Mendelssohn's style of performance had been firmly adhered to, this, on the other hand, had so accommodated itself to the usages and peculiarities of the concerts of this society, that the conjecture that Mendelssohn's manner of directing may have been suggested to him through this means, is not without a certain amount of probability. As in these concerts an unusual quantity of instrumental music is performed and only one rehearsal bestowed upon it, I myself was often obliged to allow the orchestra to follow its traditions, and by that means I became acquainted with a style of performance which much reminded me of the remarks which I had heard from Mendelssohn. It flowed like water from a town pump, an attempt to check it was not even to be thought of, and every allegro concluded as an undeniable presto. The trouble of struggling against this was painful enough, for it was really when a correct and modified tempo was secured that the further faults in the execution, hidden until then, beneath the general waterfall, discovered themselves. The orchestra never played otherwise than 'mezzoforte,' it neither attained to a real forte nor to a real piano. So far as it was practicable, I took care in the important cases to adhere to that manner of execution which seemed to me to be correct, and at the same time to be the suitable tempo. The able musicians had no objection, in fact were sincerely pleased at it ; the public also appeared to be perfectly satisfied. The critics alone became furious over it, and intimidated the directors of the society to that extent, that I on one occasion was really requested by them to allow the second movement of the E flat symphony of Mozart to be played again in that hasty manner in which they were accustomed to hear it, and as indeed Mendelssohn himself had allowed it to be played.

But at last the fatal maxim presented itself quite literally in a request made to me by a very friendly disposed old contrapuntist, Mr. Potter (if I mistake not), whose symphony I had to direct, and who heartily entreated me to take the andante at a good speed, as he was greatly afraid that it might otherwise become tedious. I demonstrated to him that his andante, however short a time it might last could not be otherwise than tedious if it were played without expression and insipidly, whereas, on the other hand, it might be attractive if the pretty naive themes were performed by the orchestra, for instance alter this manner, as I then sang to him, for he doubtless had meant it so. Mr. Potter was evidently moved, owned that I was right and excused himself with the remark that he was no longer accustomed to take into consideration this style of orchestral performance. In the evening, immediately after this andante, he joyfully squeezed my hand."

Mr. H. Weston Eve, M.A., Head Master of University College School, has been appointed Dean of the College of Preceptors, in place of Mr. A. K. Isbister, deceased.

Correspondence.

SUGGESTIONS TO SINGERS.

TO THE EDITOR OF THE "MUSICAL STANDARD."

SIR,—I take the liberty of pointing out to you that the extract from the *Musical Herald*, U.S., in last Saturday's *Musical Standard* entitled "*Suggestions* to Singers," is simply copied from "*Advice* to Singers" by a singer, published by Messrs. Warne & Co. (pages 16—18).

    I am Sir,
        Your obedient servant,
            MAURICE PUCKLE.

[Though sorry that the too common habit of printing extracts without an acknowledgment led me to unconsciously quote from an English work without proper recognition, I am glad to be able to point out that, judging from the extract given in this paper, "Advice to Singers" must be a useful work.—ED, *Musical Standard*.]

AMERICA AND THE COPYRIGHT LAW.

TO THE EDITOR OF THE "MUSICAL STANDARD."

SIR,—You quote the *Musical Herald*, U.S., in your last issue, and from such quotation I learn that that excellent periodical has been doing me the very empty honour of appropriating my little work "Advice to Singers," the first edition of which was published by Mr. Reeves, the enlarged and extended book being now one of Warne's series of "Useful Handbooks." To musical houses, publishing firms, writers, and others here, who wish to appropriate my writings, I say do so to your heart's content ; but as regards America a larger question is involved. For years past there has been an endeavour on this side, and to some extent on *that* side, to bring about a copyright law, which, however, still is not. I am one of those who think that the American nation is specially interested in frustrating the progress of such a law—for the reason that my friends on that side can buy the latest book or piece of music issued here and reprinted there, at a much lesser rate than I can obtain it here, with all the advantages of "25 off," and other facilities open to me. Three of my larger musical books have been published in serial form, and subsequently in volume shape by separate American publishers, and for these I have received no, or very scanty, acknowledgment. Nor can I, under the existing fitness of things, demand anything, not even a copy of such pirated editions. So, then, you may imagine that when I read in your journal certain extracts from my book, while you, with just zeal, credit the *Musical Herald*, U.S., with the same, I am not particularly overjoyed. On the contrary, I feel that America is sufficiently indebted to me in having appropriated my volumes without a standard journal on this side going out of its way to credit my shrewd cousins with ideas which originally emanated from this side, and which belong none the less to me because they happen to be issued under an anonymous, or perhaps no title. Such a slip needs, I feel, correction. I only trouble you with this to show how very important a subject this "Copyright" question between England and America really is, and how important it is that we on this side should stir ourselves and do something that will bring about some protection to authors and musicians from the gross injustice which we are suffering at the hands of the American book and newspaper publishers.

    I am Sir,
        Your obedient servant,
            FREDERICK T. CROWEST.

Among the foreign visitors to London this season are three violoncellists of repute, viz.— Hollmann, from Holland ; Fischer, from Paris ; and De Munck, from Brussels, the latter with his wife, Carlotta Patti, sister of Adelina, *prima donna* of the Italian Opera.

Among the latest arrivals of artists of distinction and renown from the Continent is M. Blumer, a pianist favourably noticed during the past musical season in Paris, where he is already re-engaged to appear at the concerts of Cologne. M. Bulmer, a native of Zurich, after completing his education at Leipsig, visited Rome, and enjoyed the friendship of Liszt, and useful instruction from the illustrious master. Since his arrival in London, he has had the honour of playing before Royalty and at private parties of the musical aristocracy. He is a thorough artist of sensibility and intelligence, and of his executive powers *nulli secundum*. It is to be regretted that such an exceptional pianist arrived too late to be heard at the orchestral concerts of the present London season.

Passing Events.

Dr. John Hullah is spending a few months at Nice.

Signorina Luisa Cognetti recently gave a pianoforte recital at the Prince's Hall, with a programme of interest.

It is gratifying to know that the Philharmonic Society has this season a balance on the right side.

The death of Mr. S. N. Barber of Denmark Hill, removes an earnest lover of organs and organ music and an esteemed friend of many artists.

Mr. Barnby's new Service and Dr. Stainer's " Daughter of Jairus " were to be sung at St. Peter's, Eaton Square, yesterday, at the evening Service.

It is announced that a new opera by Herr Ignaz Brüll, " Königin Mariette," was lately produced with success at Munich.

At the last concert of the season given by Mr. Henry Leslie's choir, a manuscript motet for two choirs by M. Gounod (written in 1851) was sung. The choir propose next season to sing Spohr's neglected " Vocal Mass."

Mdlle. Clotilde Kleeberg recently gave a second pianoforte recital at the Prince's Hall. She played a number of pieces with much grace and finish, but was judged to be least successful in Beethoven's Sonata in E flat, Op. 31, and Schumann's " Carnaval."

Carl G. P. Grädener, who was a composer and theorist of solid reputation, died at Hamburg on June 10th, at the age of seventy-one. He will be succeeded as professor in the Conservatorium of that city by Dr. Hugo Riemann.

On June 11th, St. Barnabas' day, at St. Barnabas' Church, Bell Street, Marylebone, Mendelssohn's " Hymn of Praise " was sung by the choir of the church, assisted by that of All Saints', Margaret Street, under the direction of Mr. W. S. Hoyte. Mr. Hoyte presided at the organ, and Dr. J. F. Bridge conducted.

Readers will receive with much regret the news that Mr. W. Lemare of Brixton is suffering from an " overstrained nervous condition," and after twenty-five years of hard and useful professional work, will most probably have to go away into the country and sever his connection with South London.

Mr. W. S. Hoyte gave an afternoon pianoforte recital at Collard's rooms on June 27th, and was assisted by Mr. Charlton Speer, Mr. J. Marsh, and Miss Kate Bompas as pianists, and the following vocalists : Madame Edith Wynne, Miss Clara Samuell, and Mr. Harper Kearton. Mr. Hoyte played admirably a number of solos, as also a sonata by Rubinstein for piano and violin, Op. 13, in conjunction with M. Victor Buziau.

Says Figaro : Mr. A. C. Mackenzie is in a fortunate, and in one sense in an enviable, position. The musical critics of both the Times and the Daily Telegraph are, I hear, writing librettos for him. The Times libretto will be an opera for the Carl Rosa company. The Daily Telegraph libretto will be an oratorio for next year's Norwich Festival. The subject of each work is at present a secret.

It is definitely settled that Paris is to have an Italian opera-house. A new theatre will be built for this purpose, and in the mean time the Théâtre des Nations is to be engaged for the company. It is stated that Signor Faccio will be the conductor. The names of Mesdames de Reszké, Corelli, and Donadio, and of Signori Gayarré Stagno and Maurel are mentioned as likely to be connected with the new enterprise.

Says the Musical Times : The fine organ in Salisbury Cathedral has at last received what it has long needed— namely, a case. This work has just been effected, at a cost of nearly £1,000, from designs prepared by the late Mr. G. E. Street, R.A. To those who sympathise with such a laudable expenditure of money we venture, unasked, to commend an exactly similar want which at present exists in the neighbouring Cathedral of Chichester. The case of the present organ, which only needs a small outlay to make it a very fine instrument, was destroyed by the collapse of the spire twenty years ago, and has never since, owing to lack of diocesan funds, been replaced.

The Derby Choral Union propose to perform Gounod's " The Redemption " next season.

The Tonic Sol-fa Reporter for July, contains a useful article on " Harmonium Playing," by Mr. Reah, junr.

The Irish Presbyterian Church, following the Scotch example, concede the introduction of organs to the judgment of the different congregations.

The late William Spottiswoode, was, as is wellknown, a learned supporter of the art of music, especially from the more scientific aspect. His death is, therefore, a distinct loss to the musical world.

Mr. C. E. Miller will compose the service for the festival of the London Church Choir Association, for which occasion Dr. Stainer has also promised to write an anthem.

The service at Westminster Abbey will be sung on Wednesday afternoons in future by men's voices only, in order to give the boys a holiday, a practice which has prevailed on one week day at St. Paul's for a considerable time now.

The organ at Christ Church, Burton-on-Trent, has been entirely rebuilt and enlarged by Mr. A. Kirkland of Wakefield, and was opened last Sunday, July 1st, by Mr. Graham, the organist of the church. The organ has two manuals and pedals, with 17 sounding stops, 3 couplers, and 3 composition pedals.

Rignold's panorama of the Arctic regions will be exhibited at the Royal Victoria Hall during July. This panorama was painted by the late Clarkson Stanfield, R.A., and has the reputation of being the finest marine painting extant.

Princess Christian of Schleswig-Holstein assisted on June 30th at two grand concerts given in aid of the Royal College of Music at the Albert Institute, Windsor, the hall of which was tastefully decorated for the occasion with bunting, evergreens, and flowers.

It is satisfactory to note the general belief in the critical world that, in the event of another Handel Festival, some of the ill-judged additions and alterations made to the scores by Sir M. Costa will be either modified or swept away by Mr. Manns, in accordance with his reputation as a conductor duly respecting scores and historical traditions.

On Sunday week Mr. Dudeney, the newly appointed organist at St. James's, Taunton, conducted the musical portion of the service. Mrs. Chapman presented herself, but was told that her services were not required. The Bishop and the Archdeacon have been appealed to, and it is likely that an investigation into the whole circumstances of the case will be made.

A military musical fête was given in the grounds of the Royal Hospital, Chelsea, on June 29th. The combined bands of the foot-guards played, under the direction of the bandmasters, Messrs. D. Godfrey, C. Thomas, and J. P. Clarke. The object of the fête was that of aiding the funds of the Royal Army Coffee Tavern Association. The music given was for the most part of a popular type.

Miss Adelaide Thomas gave her second recital on Saturday last at the Marlborough Rooms. This lady does great credit to her instructor, Herr Pauer, and plays the works of the great masters with rare intelligence, and promises to rank among the best female pianists of this country. If not misinformed the writer understands that Miss A. Thomas obtained a scholarship, and completed her education at the late Training Schoo for Music at Kensington.

At the Students' (Orchestral) Concert, held on Tuesday, July 3rd, the following formed the programme :—Symphony in B minor, unfinished (Schubert) ; song, " My beloved spake," Miss Maud Vernon (Gounod) ; violoncello obbligato, Mr. J. H. Callcott ; movements from Concerto in D for, pianoforte and orchestra (Mendelssohn)— pianoforte, Miss Bessie Walker ; movements from " The Lay of the Last Minstrel " (J. F. Barnett) ; song, " O Fatima," from " Der Freischutz," Miss Grosvenor Gooch (Weber) ; concertstück for pianoforte and orchestra (Weber)—pianoforte, Mr. Arthur L'Estrange ; overture, " Rosamunde " (Schubert). The pianoforte accompaniments to the songs were played by Mr. R. Frederick Tyler, A.Mus., T.C.L, and the whole was under the direction of the conductor, Mr. George Mount, who is to be congratulated on the growing efficiency of the students' orchestra under his most efficient training.

The Tonic Sol-fa breakfast to the Cologne Choir gave the utmost satisfaction and pleasure to the guests. Excellent speeches in German were given by Mr. J. Curwen, Mr. A. Ellis, and Herr Behnke ; and equally effective speeches in English were delivered by Dr. Max Pensqueens, Herr Putz, and Herr Heimann. Such friendly meetings, in the interest of pure, cosmopolitan art, do an immense amount of good.

The "Annuaire Général de la Musique de France," for 1883, is a large 8vo volume, of nearly 600 pages, filled with an immense amount of information relating to music and musicians in France, including a list of all the Choral Societies of the land, with extracts from competent judgments on their singing at public competitions. There are also lists of the music trade and profession, of new music, &c. The editor of this useful compilation is H. A. Symon.

An afternoon concert was given by Mr. John Thomas at St. James's Hall on June 23rd. A band of harps, chiefly lady performers, played several arrangements in good style ; and Mr. John Thomas gave several harp solos of his own composition which were much appreciated, and also two duets in conjunction with Signor Lebano and Mr. T. H. Wright. Mr. Santley was at his best in Gounod's "Maid of Athens," with the harp accompaniment of Mr. John Thomas. The other vocalists were Mesdames Edith Wynne, Enriquez, Rose Hersee, and Hope Glenn ; and Mr. W. H. Cummings.

It is told that the proceeds of the Nilsson Concert, given by Messrs. Austin & Watts at the Albert Hall came to 1500. The expenses were £800, and the concert givers cleared £700.' A comparison between this performance, musical and commercial, and the work being done by our leading societies and the poor results obtained, would be instructive. In connection with this star concert, it is said that Mdme. Nilsson received 200 guineas, Mr. Sims Reeves 100 guineas, our most favoured baritone 50 guineas, our most popular contralto 25 guineas, and our most favoured tenor after Mr. Reeves has been mentioned 25 guineas.

The balance sheet of Trinity College, as audited by A. E. Drinkwater, Esq., and Messrs. Ward and Wilding (public accountants) is a very satisfactory document, showing as it does the steady growth of the institution and its consequent advance financially to a position of assured strength and usefulness. It is most gratifying to see our public institutions devoted to musical education, standing so well as do the Royal Academy of Music, the College of Organists, Trinity College, and the Guildhall School of Music. Presently, it may be hoped, the first report of the Royal College will also swell the list of successful institutions.

A large educational tourist party of Americans, above one hundred in number, organized by Dr. Eben Tourjee, of the Conservatory of Music in Boston, and travelling under the arrangements of Messrs. Caygill and Co., arrived at the Midland Grand Hotel on June 30th, and on Sunday morning, under the conductorship of Mr. John Ripley, who has accompanied them from America, they went to the Metropolitan Tabernacle to hear Mr. C. H. Spurgeon. On Monday the party visited the exhibition of pictures at the Albert Hall, and they were photographed in a group on the steps of the Albert Memorial. On Tuesday evening two sections of them started for the Continent—one via Paris and the other via Belgium and the Rhine, to be followed by the remainder in a few days, visiting Rome, Naples, Venice, Vienna, Amsterdam, &c., after which they return in September to America.

ORPHAN SCHOOL FOR DAUGHTERS OF MUSICIANS.—Miss Helen Kenway has taken a house in London, and hopes to open her orphan school in September. There are five orphans to be provided for, but boarders and day-pupils will also be received, to whom a good general education, with special opportunities for the study of music, are offered on moderate terms. All fees to be used for the benefit of the Charity. Subscriptions and applications must still be addressed to Miss Helen Kenway, South Hill House, Bath, until Aug. 11th, after which date the address will be, 8, Lupton St., Kentish Town, N.W. Two definite promises of money, and several small presents, such as a tea service, a bedstead, two teapots, two quilts, and a blanket have been received, and kind volunteers are making the linen. Further gifts of furniture, standard books, and music, will be gratefully received.

The Querist.

QUERY.

INFORMATION WANTED.—Publishers, sizes, and prices of the following pictures on musical subjects :—Thos. Webster's "Village Orchestra and Choir" (Oleograph) ; Frank Dicksee's "Harmony" (Etching and Photograph) ; Quartet of Amateurs (Litho).—J. MATTHEWS, 35, Henrietta Street, Swansea.

Service Lists.

SEVENTH SUNDAY AFTER TRINITY.
JULY 8th.

London.

ST. PAUL'S CATHEDRAL.—Morn.: Service, Te Deum and Benedictus, Selby in B flat ; Introit, Holy, holy, holy ; Holy Communion, Calkin in B flat. Even.: Service, Magnificat and Nunc Dimittis, Calkin in B flat ; Anthems, How great, O Lord, is Thy goodness, and, The Lord be a lamp (Bennett).

WESTMINSTER ABBEY. — Morn.: Service, Tours in F (throughout) ; Cooke in G ; Anthems, Happy is the man (Bridge), and Blest are the departed (Spohr). Even.: Service, Walmisley in D minor ; Anthem, O how amiable (Wesley).

TEMPLE CHURCH.—Morn.: Service, Te Deum Laudamus, and Jubilate Deo, Boyce in C ; Apostles' Creed, Harmonised Monotone ; Anthem, Teach me, O Lord (Boyce). Even.: Service, Magnificat and Nunc Dimittis, Goss in E ; Apostles' Creed, Harmonized Monotone ; Anthem, O where shall wisdom be found (Boyce).

LINCOLN'S INN CHAPEL.—Morn.: Service, Steggall in A ; Kyrie, Clarke-Whitfield ; Anthem, Sing unto God, O ye kingdoms (Croft). Even: Service, Goss in A ; Anthem, Blessed is the man (Goss).

ALL SAINTS, MARGARET STREET.—Morn.: Service, Te Deum (Smith) ; Benedictus, Cobb in G ; Holy Communion, Schubert in B flat ; Offertory Anthem, God is a Spirit (Bennett). Even.: Service, King in D ; Anthems, All ye that cried, and, I waited on the Lord (Mendelssohn).

FOUNDLING CHAPEL. — Morn.: Service, Dykes in F ; Jubilate, Attwood in F ; Anthem, O come, let us worship (Mendelssohn). Aft.: Service, Chants and Hymns.

CHRIST CHURCH, CLAPHAM.—Morn.: Service, Te Deum, Plain-song ; Kyrie and Credo, Smart in F ; Offertory Anthem, Not unto us, O Lord (Walmisley) ; Sanctus (Smart) ; Benedictus, and Agnus Dei, Eyre in A flat ; Communion, Hail, Thou living bread (Foster) ; Gloria in excelsis, (Smart). Even.: Service, Magnificat and Nunc Dimittis, Martin in A ; Anthem, O clap your hands (Stainer).

HOLY TRINITY, TULSE HILL. — Morn.: Chant Service. Even.: Service, Magnificat and Nunc Dimittis, Agutter in D ; Anthem, Hear my prayer (Mendelssohn).

ST AUGUSTINE AND ST. FAITH, WATLING STREET.— Morn.: Service, Tours in F ; Offertory, Barnby. Even.: Service, Garrett in F ; Anthem, I will mention (Sullivan).

ST. BARNABAS MARYLEBONE.—Morn.: Service, Te Deum and Jubilate, Aldrich in G ; Anthem, Lord, who shall dwell (Rogers) ; Kyrie and Creed, Aldrich. Even.: Service, Magnificat and Nunc Dimittis (Aldrich) ; Anthem, If with all your heart, Cast thy burden (Mendelssohn).

ST. PAUL'S, AVENUE ROAD, SOUTH HAMPSTEAD.—Morn.: Service, Te Deum, Calkin in B flat ; Benedictus, Garrett ; Kyrie, Nares in F. Even.: Service, Magnificat and Nunc Dimittis, Calkin in B flat ; Anthem, He watching over Israel "Elijah" (Mendelssohn).

ST. PAUL'S, BOW COMMON, E.—Morn.: Service, Te Deum and Benedictus, Hopkins in F. Even.: Service, Magnificat and Nunc Dimittis, Hopkins in F ; Anthem, Hear my prayer (Mendelssohn).

ST. PETER'S (EATON SQUARE).—Morn.: Service, Te Deum, Dykes in F ; Holy Communion, Stainer in A. Even.: Service, Stainer in A ; Anthem (Stainer).

ST. JAMES'S PRIVATE EPISCOPAL CHAPEL, SOUTHWARK. —Morn.: Service, Introit, Lord have mercy (Gounod) ; Communion Service, "Missa Iste Confessor" (Palestrina). Even.: Service, Arnold in A ; Anthem, In exitu Israel (Wesley).

ST. MARY ARCHURCH, E.C.—Morn.: Service, Garrett in D ; Communion, Armes in A.

St. Mary Boltons, West Brompton, S.W.—Morn.: Service, Te Deum, Smart in F; Benedictus, Chants; Holy Communion, Kyrie, Credo, Sanctus; Offertory and Gloria in excelsis, Stainer in E flat; Benedictus and Agnus Dei, Going in F. Even.: Service, Magnificat and Nunc Dimittis, Smart in F; Anthem, Great is the Lord (Hayes).

St. Michael's, Cornhill. — Morn.: Service, Te Deum and Jubilate, Sullivan in D; Anthem, O God, Thou art my God (Purcell); Kyrie, and Creed, Stainer in E flat. Even.: Service, Magnificat and Nunc Dimittis, Hoyte in B flat; Anthem, Rejoice in the Lord (Purcell).

St. Magnus, London Bridge.—Morn.: Service, Opening Anthem, to the Lord our God (Calkin); Te Deum and Jubilate, (Whitfield) Kyrie, (Armes). Even.: Service, Magnificat and Nunc Dimittis, (Whitfield); Anthem, How dear are Thy counsels (Crotch).

St. Saviour's, Hoxton.—Morn.: Service, Te Deum, Hopkins in G; Holy Communion; Kyrie, Credo, Sursum Corda, Sanctus, and Gloria in excelsis, Smart in G. Even.: Service, Magnificat and Nunc Dimittis (Best); Anthem, Lord of all power (Mason).

St. Sepulchre's, Holborn.—Morn.: Service, Nares in F; Anthem, Lord of all power (Mason). Even.: Service, Nares in F; Anthem, Thy word is a lantern (Purcell).

Country.

St. Asaph Cathedral.—Morn.: Service, Roberts in D; Anthem, The Lord is great in Zion (Best). Even.: Service, Roberts in D; Anthem, The Glory of the Lord (Goss).

Ashburne Church, Derbyshire. — Morn.: Service, Smart in F (throughout); Even.: Service, Hopkins in F; Anthem, Withdraw not Thou Thy mercy (Attwood).

Beddington Church, Surrey.—Morn.: Service, Tours in F; Introit, O what the glory; Communion Service, Tours in F. Even.: Service, Bunnett in F; Anthem, O taste and see (Goss).

Birmingham (S. Alban the Martyr).—Morn.: Service, Plain-song; Holy Communion; Kyrie, Credo, Sanctus, Gloria, Garrett in D; Benedictus and Agnus Dei, Redman in D. Evensong: Magnificat and Nunc Dimittis, Tours in F.

Birmingham (St. Cyprian's, Hay Mills).—Morn.: Service, Field in D; Anthem, In that day (Elvey). Even.: Service, Clarke-Whitfield in E; Anthem, God is our hope and strength (Greene).

Birmingham (S. Philip's Church). — Morn.: Service, Barnby in E; Anthem, I will arise (Creighton). Evensong Service, Barnby in E; Anthem, Stand up and bless (Goss).

Canterbury Cathedral.—Morn.: Service, Te Deum, and Jubilate, Dykes in F; Anthem, God so loved the world (Tuckerman); Communion, Dykes in F. Even.: Service, Dykes in F; Anthem, I praise Thee, O God (Mendelssohn).

Carlisle Cathedral.—Morn.: Service, Sullivan in D; Introit, We wait for (Armes); Kyrie, and Nicene Creed, Best in G. Even.: Service, Attwood in F; Anthem, Praise the Lord (Goss).

Chester (St. Mary's Church)—Morn.: Service, Cooke in G; Communion Service, Tearne in G. Even.: Service, Turle in D; Anthem, Lift up your head (Hopkins).

Doncaster (Parish Church).—Morn.: Service, Calkin in B flat. Even.: Service, Stainer in E flat; Anthem, Blow ye the trumpet (Taylor).

Exeter Cathedral.—Morn.: Service, Rogers in F; Communion, Best in B flat. Even.: Service, Gilbert in E; Anthem, I will love Thee (Clarke).

Gloucester Cathedral.—Morn.: Service, Te Deum and Jubilate, Turle in D; Kyrie and Creed, Turle in D; Anthem, Blest are they (Spohr). Aft.: Service, Magnificat and Nunc Dimittis, Turle in D; Blessed be the God (Wesley).

Harrogate (St. Peter's Church). — Morn.: Service, Te Deum and Benedictus, Chants; Anthem, Teach me, O Lord (Attwood). Even.: Service, Magnificat and Nunc Dimittis, Ebdon in C; Anthem, Abide with me (Bennett).

Leeds Parish Church.—Morn.: Service, Garrett in F; Anthem, O give thanks (Elvey) Kyrie and Creed, Walmsley in F. Even.: Service, Garrett in F; Anthem, The Lord is righteous (Handel).

Leeds, St. Martin's Church (Potternewton). — Te Deum, Wesley in F; Benedictus, Chant; Anthem, Holy, holy, holy (Spohr). Even.: Service, Magnificat and Nunc Dimittis, Garrett in F; Anthem, Lead me, Lord, in Thy righteousness (Wesley).

Llandaff Cathedral.—Morn.: Service, Te Deum and Benedictus, Hopkins in F. Even.: Service, Magnificat and Nunc Dimittis Hopkins in F; Anthem, awake, awake, put on thy strength, O Zion (Stainer).

Liverpool Cathedral.—Aft.: Service, Magnificat and Nunc Dimittis, Garrett in D; Anthem, Wherewithal shall a young man (Elvey).

Manchester Cathedral. —Morn.: Service, Te Deum, Jubilate, Kyrie, Creed, Sanctus and Gloria, Garrett in D; Anthem, For He shall give His angels (Mendelssohn). Aft.: Service, Garrett in D; Anthem, I beheld, and lo ! (Blow).

Musselburgh (Loretto School).—Morn.: Service, Introit, O praise God in his holiness (Weldon); Communion Service, Garrett in F; Anthem, Blessed be the God and Father (Wesley). Even.: Service, Anthem, hear my prayer (Sinead).

Rochester Cathedral.—Morn.: Service, Nares in F; Anthem, O most merciful (Hullah). Even.: Service, Heathcote in B flat; Anthem, O where shall wisdom (Boyce).

Sheffield Parish Church. — Morn.: Service, Kyrie, Sullivan in D; Even.: Service, Bunnett in F; Anthem, the glory of the Lord (Goss).

Southampton (St. Mary's Church).—Morn.: Service, Te Deum and Benedictus, Custard in F; Holy Communion; Introit, O how amiable (Macfarren); Service, Custard in E flat; Offertory, "Whatsoever" (Barnby); Paternoster, (Hoyte). Even.: Service, Magnificat and Nunc Dimittis, King in F; Apostles' Creed, Harmonised Monotone (Hopkins).

Southwell Minster, Notts.—Morn.: Service, Attwood in F; Kyrie, Mendelssohn in G; Creed, Calkin in B flat. Even.: Service, Attwood in F; Anthem, Blessing, glory (Bach).

Wells Cathedral.—Morn.: Service, Hudson in E flat; Introit, Remember me (Macfarren); Kyrie, Weber in E flat. Even.: Service, Turle in D;. Anthem, The heavens declare (Boyce).

Worcester Cathedral.—Morn.: Service, Smart in F; Anthem, Let all men praise (Mendelssohn). Even.: Service, Mann in E; Anthem, Lead kindly light (Stainer).

NOTICES TO CORRESPONDENTS.

W. S.—The next Examination for Associateship at the College of Organists, takes place on Tuesday and Wednesday next; see advertisement.

The "Logic of Counterpoint," and other articles, etc., are crowded out this week.

⁎ Post-cards must be sent to the Editor, 6, Argyle Square, W.C., by Wednesday. Lists are frequently omitted in consequence of not being received in time.

Newspapers sent should have distinct marks opposite to the matter to which attention is required.

Notice.—All communications intended for the Editor are to be sent to his private address. Business communications to be addressed to 185, Fleet Street, E.C.

A NEWSPAPER FOR MUSICIANS PROFESSIONAL AND AMATEUR

No. 989. VOL. XXV. FOURTH SERIES. SATURDAY, JULY 14, 1883. WEEKLY: PRICE 3D.

THE MUSICAL STANDARD is published every Saturday, price 3*d.*, by post, 3½*d.* ; and may be had of any bookseller or newsagent by ordering its regular supply.

SUBSCRIPTION.—*The Musical Standard* is posted to subscribers at 15*s.* a year ; half a year, 7*s.* 6*d.*, payable in advance.

The rate is the same to France, Belgium, Germany, Italy, United States, and Canada.

Post Office Orders to be made payable to the Publisher, William Reeves, 185, Fleet Street, London, or to the West-end Agents, Messrs. Weekes & Co., 14, Hanover Street, Regent Street, W.

ADVERTISEMENTS.—The charge for ordinary advertisements in *The Musical Standard* is 2*s.* 6*d.* for three lines or less ; and 6*d.* for each line (10 words) in addition. " Organist wanted," 3*s.* 6*d.* for 3 lines or less. A reduction is made for a series.

FRONT PAGE.—Concert and auction advertisements, &c., are inserted in the front page of *The Musical Standard*, and charged one-third in addition to the ordinary rates. Other advertisements will be inserted on the front page, or in the leader page, if desired, at the same terms.

YORK ORGAN FACTORY,
BLENHEIM PLACE, MONKGATE.

SPECIFICATION of NEW ORGAN, built by the late ROBT. POSTILL, in Pitch Pine Case, Stained and Varnished, with Spotted Metal Speaking Pipes in Front.

GREAT ORGAN, EIGHT STOPS. SWELL ORGAN, EIGHT STOPS.
PEDAL ORGAN.
Bourdon (large scale).... 16 feet. .... 30 Notes.
COUPLERS.
Swell to Great. Swell to Pedals.
Great to Pedals.
Three Composition Pedals for Changing the Stops.
Two Octaves and a third of German Pedals for the Feet.
Front of Organ .... 10 feet 3 inches.
Front to Back .... 9 ,, 6 ,,
Height .... 19 ,, 6 ,,

The above Instrument is for SALE, and may be seen and heard by applying at the Works, or Mrs. J. POSTILL'S, 25, Monkgate.

COLLEGE OF ORGANISTS.

TUESDAY, July 17th, at 8, Annual General Meeting.
The above Meeting will be held at the NEUMEYER HALL, Hart Street, Bloomsbury.
E. H. TURPIN,
Hon. Secretary.
95, Great Russell Street, Bloomsbury, W.C.

MR. HUMPHREY J. STARK begs to announce his REMOVAL to 12, Norwood Road, Herne Hill, S.E.

NEW ORGAN PIECE, by M. GUILMANT.—SPOHR'S 24th PSALM (English words), 9d. and 2s. Ditto arranged for Organ Solo by M. GUILMANT, 1s. 6d.
London : NOVELLO, EWER & CO.

HANDEL'S FIRST ORGAN CONCERTO, with Orchestral Accompaniment, as performed at the Handel Festival, Crystal Palace, edited, arranged, and supplemented with a Cadenza by W. T. BEST. Organ Score, 1s. 6d. ; Orchestra Parts, 2s. ; complete, 2s. 6d. nett.—AUGENER & CO., 86, Newgate Street, Foubert's Place, and 81, Regent Street, London.

MISS NORAH HAYES, CONTRALTO VOCALIST of the Albert Hall and St. James's Hall Concerts, is open to engagements for Concerts, Soirées, and At Homes. Good Press opinions. Services given free for Charities.—Address, 95, Edgware Road.

VIOLIN.—HERR POLONASKI (Violinist), open to ENGAGEMENTS for Concerts, Musical At Homes, and Violin or Accompaniment Lessons.—For Terms, please Address, HERR POLONASKI, 16, Wharfdale-street, South Kensington, S.W.

PRIZE TUNES and CHANTS.—THREE PRIZES for the BEST TUNES in the order of merit. See the " ORCHESTRA, CHOIR, AND MUSICAL EDUCATION," for April, May, June, and July, price 3d.
W. REEVES, 185, Fleet Street, London, E.C.

TO MUSIC PUBLISHERS and OTHERS.— A GENTLEMAN, a Mus.Doc. (Oxon.) of some years' standing, and holding an appointment as Organist and Choirmaster at an important church in the country, being desirous of moving to the neighbourhood of London, would be glad to enter into NEGOTIATIONS with a well-established MUSIC PUBLISHING FIRM, or to act as GENERAL MANAGER or SECRETARY to a MUSICAL ASSOCIATION, at a fixed salary. A few hundred pounds could be invested in a safe concern.—Apply, in the first instance (by letter), to A. B., 8, Averne Road, Grantham.

INTERNATIONAL FISHERIES EXHIBITION.—ORGAN RECITALS daily, upon the fine-toned Organ, in West Gallery. Supplied to the Executive Committee by HENRY JONES & SONS, 136, Fulham Road, South Kensington.

THE ORGANIST and CHOIRMASTER of Cirencester Abbey desires RE-ENGAGEMENT. 14 years' Cathedral experience.—Address as above.

JUST PUBLISHED, "MORNING and EVENING SERVICE," set to music for the especial use of Parish Choirs, by FREDK. HUNNIBELL, F.C.O. Price, 1s. ; or separately, 8d. and 6d.
London : NOVELLO, EWER & CO.

Post 8vo., boards, 2s. 6d., post free.
TECHNICS OF VIOLIN PLAYING, by KARL COURVOISIER. Edited and translated by H. E. Krehbiel. Numerous illustrations.
Joachim says : " It is my opinion that this book will offer material aid to all violin players.
W. REEVES, 185, Fleet Street, London, E.C.

THE VOICE

MUSICALLY AND MEDICALLY CONSIDERED.

BY

ARMAND SEMPLE, B.A., M.B., Cantab., M.R.C.P., Lond.,
Physician to the Royal Society of Musicians.

(*Continued from page 366.*)

THE MEZZO-SOPRANO VOICE.

Quality.—This voice is usually of a full and round quality, and is capable of being rendered very flexible.

It may sometimes be mistaken for a soprano on account of the ease with which it can take the upper notes ; but, since its muscular construction is strong, if at first it is exercised too much upon the upper notes, true intonation, and the power of expansion in the middle part of the voice, will be destroyed.

This voice is of stronger and clearer quality than any other from Do (C) to Sol (G)

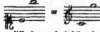

It is, however, difficult to make it full and equal.

Extent.—This is generally from Si flat (B♭) to Si flat (B♭).

The acute sounds, nevertheless, in some Mezzi-Soprani appear natural to a much greater extent.

In the lower sounds this voice may even sometimes produce the Sol (G)

Cultivation.—The Mezzo-Soprano voice should at first be limited from Do (C) to Sol (G)

When it has acquired sufficient firmness, flexibility, and vibratory power within this compass, it may be extended with a fair amount of ease to the extreme sounds.

The following table shows the compass of the Mezzo-Soprano voice :—

Do (C)   Low Extreme.   Limits in Cultivation.   High Extreme.

OR

THE SOPRANO VOICE.

Quality.—The voice of the soprano is thin and light throughout, and in its lower part limited. It is not possessed of muscular strength, and consequently not capable of sustaining sounds with effect, or giving much declamatory power, but when carefully developed it is exceedingly brilliant. Its organisation is very delicate. The vocal organ is situated high in the throat, and therefore is incapable of vibration in the lower sounds. It can scarcely produce a distinct sound on Do (C), Re (D), Mi (E), and Fa (F).

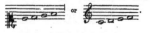

It is weak even from Sol (G) to Si (B),

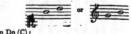

from Do (C) ;

and as far as it can be extended its tone is firm, clear, and silvery.

Extent.—In some cases the compass is limited from Do (C) to Do (C).

In others, however, it may be extended from Do (C) to Mi (E).

Cultivation.—The soprano at first should be exercised only from Do (C) to Sol (G).

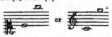

The extension must be made very gradually and carefully, for otherwise the voice will become shrill, weak, and tremulous instead of acquiring power.

The following tables show the compass of the soprano voice :—

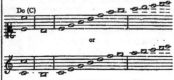

Do (C)

or

The following table shows the full extent of the female voices :—

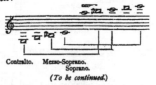

Contralto.   Mezzo-Soprano.   Soprano.

(*To be continued.*)

An exceedingly good concert was given at the Walworth Lecture Hall on Monday, July 2nd, under the direction of Mrs. Yell, for the benefit of the St. Paul's Girls' Friendly Society, when the following distinguished amateurs gave their services :—Lord Brabazon, Princess Ghika, Lady Colin Campbell, assisted by Mesdames Gwynne, Green, Wheelwright, and Messrs. Barrington, Foote, Thomas, Smith, and Owen. Mr. Smith accompanied.

A morning concert was given at the Steinway Hall by the pupils, past and present, of Madame Sainton Dolby's Vocal Academy on July 5th. Reinecke's new cantata for female voices, "The Enchanted Swans," was excellently given under the bâton of M. Sainton. This was announced as the first time of performance in England. The soli parts were well sung by Misses Hilda Coward, Mary Willis, Amy Carter, and Madame Henrietta Whyte. Mr. Leipold was, as before, the able accompanist.

THE LATE REV. SCOTSON CLARKE.

The lamented and rather sudden death on July 5th of the Rev. Scotson Clarke at a comparatively early age, has removed a somewhat prominent figure from the musical world. The Rev. Scotson Clarke was a man of varied talents and attainments without being, perhaps, a musician of great profundity. As a composer, he belonged to the school who ever do injustice to their own gifts by writing down to the level of popular requirements. He wrote facile, tuneful music, which bore its impressions on the surface. He was a performer of much skill and possessed to a considerable extent the power of playing pleasant and ready extemporaneous organ pieces. He took much interest in the proceedings of the recent Organ Conference and offered as one of the invited attendants at the meetings, a goodly number of suggestions which showed earnest thought upon the questions at issue. The Rev. Scotson Clarke founded a school for the study of the organ in London. His death will be regretted by a pretty wide circle of friends and pupils, who duly recognised his exceptional gifts and acquirements.

Musical Intelligence.

ROYAL ITALIAN OPERA.

It is supposed that Mdme. Adelina Patti induced the directors to revive Rossini's very old opera "La Gazza Ladra," for the display of herself. At all events, the public were pleased to patronize the performance on July 5th, for the theatre was full, and the audience unusually inclined to exact *encores*. The overture, full of sparkling melody, and in spite of many faults an effective if sensational piece of orchestral writing, was repeated ; also the *caballetta* of "Di piacer," and the duet "Ebben la tua memoria," sung by Mdme. Patti and Mdme. Skalchi (as Povero Pippo). Mdme. Patti greatly excelled both as a vocalist and actress in the trial scene, and the "Prayer" ejaculated in prison. The famous trio, a "canon on the octave," "O nume benefico," made less impression than other numbers of the opera ; the theme is in nowise striking, but the piece has generally caught the popular ear. How inferior, in every respect, to that other canon (a quartet) in Beethoven's "Fidelio," which now hardly raises a hand in money-grubbing London. The cast of the opera was completed by M. Gailhard, who made a passable Podesta, Signor Frapolli, and Signor Cotogni. M. Bevignani conducted. "Aïda" was played for the last time on Friday (July 6th), and "La Gioconda" repeated for the penultimate time on Monday. On Tuesday the directors chose to revive Wagner's most interesting opera, the "Flying Dutchman," with Mdme. Albani as Senta, but such a work naturally finds more congenial interpreters among the Germans. Mr. Carl Rosa with an English company and Mdme. Valleria as Senta has made the opera a thing of note at Her Majesty's Opera, and elsewhere. "Il Vascello Fantasma"—to adopt the Italian title—was first heard in England at Drury Lane Theatre, under Mr. G. Wood's management in 1870, with Mr. Santley in the title part, and Mdme. Ilma di Murska as Senta. Mr. Carl Rosa afterwards mounted the opera, and splendidly, at the Lyceum, and at the large theatre in the Haymarket. He was also able to "ring the changes" upon it in 1880 and 1881. Last spring, at Drury Lane Theatre, German opera was suspended in favour of old and new works by English composers. The "Flying Dutchman" was mounted at the Royal Italian Opera some six or seven years ago, and then withdrawn. The season will soon be over. A. M.

THE SOUTH KENSINGTON SCHOOL OF MUSIC.

After a very long interval, Mr. Richard Dressel held his 17th recital at the "school" in Thistle Grove, Kensington, on July 5th. Several of the pupils were allowed to display their progress in the art, and played pieces which no doubt delighted their friends, and did not fail to interest lovers of the art. A certain limit, however, should be imposed on the performance of young persons, here and elsewhere, for the public at large complain, and their complaints must be listened to, if not echoed by the press. Mr. Dressel played in excellent style, and most

unobtrusively, solos by Heller, Le Couppey, H. Scholtz, Jensen, and Chopin (the Valse in E minor). An original composition, "Rocked by the waves," has been published by Stanley, Lucas, Weber, & Co., and is well worth its "exchange value" in money. Mrs. Dressel sang "lieder" of Schubert and Taubert with taste and expression. Herr Bonawitz, a "lion" of the day, took his audience by storm in three pieces of Chopin and Beethoven's Sonata in E, Op. 90. Mdlle. C. Brousil played two violin solos (one a valse of Herr Bonawitz), and took part with her friend in a sonata of Beethoven.

MR. CHARLES HALLE'S CHAMBER CONCERTS.

These excellent and instructive concerts came to an end on Friday July 6th, when the scheme included "Papa" Haydn's string quartet in E flat, Op. 71, and Brahms's pianoforte quartet in A, Op. 26. Mr. Charles Hallé's solo was Beethoven's sonata in E major, Op. 109 (the "air with variations.") Mdme. Norman-Néruda played two violin pieces of Spohr.

M. HOLLMAN'S ANNUAL MORNING CONCERT.

M. Hollman's annual morning concert, which took place, by the kind permission of the Earl and Countess of Denbigh, at 2, Cromwell Houses, South Kensington, on Thursday, the 5th inst., gave this celebrated violoncellist ample opportunity of exhibiting his remarkable execution, and what is worth infinitely more than that, his artistic expression. M. Hollman performed a varied programme of J. Sebastian Bach, Moscheles, Schubert, Rubinstein, Saint-Saëns, and the seemingly unavoidable Popper. Is it that the public are to be judged by their liking of such *Fanfaronade?* There must be a great dearth of 'cello music, as most of the performers on that instrument have recourse to arrangement of pianoforte works to which certainly objection may be taken. There is, however, no denying that Schubert's "Serenade," as performed by M. Hollman and Signor Lebano, was as striking as it was charming. In Signor Lebano one welcomes one of the best harpists I have heard for a long time. Mdlle. Scharwenka was the vocalist, and Herr Blumer was the pianist.

FERDINAND PRAEGER.

Mdlle. Jeanne Douste, a juvenile pupil of Mdlle. Gayrard-Pacini, aged only 14, was introduced by her accomplished mistress on July 4th at Mrs. Reuben Sasson's, No. 1, Belgrave Square. Mdlle. Douste played Bach's "Italian" Concerto, pieces of Handel, Mendelssohn (the "Spinnlied" in C), and the last movement of Weber's Sonata in C major. Her poetry of style and exquisite sensibility were greatly extolled in the artists' room by competent judges. Mdlle. Douste and Mdlle. Gayrard-Pacini played together an "Impromptu," arranged for two pianofortes, on a theme from Schumann's "Manfred," and a duet (for one pianoforte) entitled "Reveil des Oiseaux" by a composer named Tresvaux de la Roselaye. Mdme. Rose Hersee was one of the successful vocalists. She chose Gounod's Barcarolle, "Ou voulez vous aller," to which the gallant response might naturally have been, "Avec toi" ; also "La Mandolinata," which the reporter cannot accept even as ordinary "concert" music. Mdlle. Gayrard-Pacini gracefully withdrew her own name from the programme-head in favour of her pupil, Mdlle. Douste, but she will suffer no loss from this worthy sacrifice of self.

Mdlle. Avigliana's *matinée* on July 2nd was a success. She sang the air "From mighty kings," and Sullivan's song, "My dearest heart," by request ; also Bach's air, "My heart ever faithful," and "Comin' thro' the rye." Signor Tito Mattei played pianoforte solos. Rossini's trumpery trio, "Pappataci" was one of the most loudly applauded numbers !

LIVERPOOL.

(*From our own Correspondent.*)

JULY 11TH.

Mr. Hallé's appointment as conductor to the Liverpool Philharmonic Society was confirmed at the last meeting of the proprietors. This being the case, the Liverpool Philharmonic Society, as a separate and Liverpool Musical Society, *is dead ;* it will for the future be simply a *branch* of Mr. Charles Hallé's Manchester concerts. Mr. Hallé is to receive double the salary paid to Sir Julius Benedict when he was the conductor, or double the income for which Mr. Randegger or Mr. Cowen would have accepted the position. *On dit*, that all the Liverpool contingent of the late Philharmonic orchestra have received notice of dismissal, and their places are to be supplied by Mr. Charles Hallé's Manchester band, which said performers are to appear every other week as rivals to themselves ! In other words, Mr. Hallé has stipulated that he continue his own concerts, given alternately with the Liverpool Philharmonic Society's concerts ! One Tuesday evening Mr. Hallé will appear as the conductor of the Liverpool Philharmonic Society, and the same night week as a rival to the same !

More than rumour says that the local chorus is to be replaced by Mr. Hallé's choir, and, in fact, a meeting of the male members of the local chorus was held last night at which the members agreed to resign in a body, owing to the fact that the several advantages which have been granted to them since the foundation of the Liverpool Philharmonic Society are under the new management to be abolished.

It is a lamentable affair altogether, and Liverpool musicians may now bow their heads with shame and sorrow. I believe that the committee also treated with Mr. Hecht, and wished to engage him as the chorus-master, but this has fallen through, and the only local man engaged by the wise (?) directorate is Mr. Brans-combe as chorus-master, who, it is stated, has had no previous knowledge of chorus training.

Altogether the whole affair is a great muddle, and another blow at English musical art and English musicians.

It is whispered that Mr. Best may resign the organist-ship of the Society ; but this waits confirmation.

In my last letter, by a printer's error, Liverpool *Harmonic* Society appeared instead of Liverpool *Philharmonic* Society.   J. J. M.

MUSIC IN CORK.
(*From our Own Correspondent.*)

It is a long time since such a display, musical and otherwise, has been witnessed by the people of this city as was presented to them on Tuesday (July 4th), the opening day of the Cork Industrial Exhibition. Previous to describing the purely musical portion of the festival, a few words as to the opening itself may not be out of place. At a quarter before one o'clock, a procession was formed, consisting of the members of the Executive and Ladies' Committees, the two Hon. Secretaries, the Architect and the Builder, the Mayor, and the Earl of Bandon (president of the Exhibition). On the entrance of the procession into the main hall it was greeted by a fanfare from the orchestra, which continued until all the members of it (the procession) had taken their places.

Part I. consisted of selections from "The Hymn of Praise" (Mendelssohn), and from Haydn's "Creation"; and Part II. of a miscellaneous selection, including "The March of the Priests" ("Athalie") (Mendelssohn).

The entire strength of the orchestra was as follows : principals 6, soprani 86, contralti 53, tenori 46, bassi 58, and band 52, making the respectable total of 301 persons engaged in the musical portion of the opening.

Too much praise can not be given to the chorus for the manner of their singing throughout, but in particular I must mention the rendering of the opening chorus from the "Lobgesang" "All men, all things," which was simply perfect. Though the tenori were a trifle weak, and the soprani a little too strong in point of numbers, yet they seemed to be thoroughly aware of their shortcomings in that respect and managed so that it was hardly noticeable. I am sorry I can not speak so highly of some of the principals. Miss Annie Williams was all that could be desired, and her part was a very hard one, having to appear in eight of the principal items, but she sang very well and judging from the way in which she was received, the audience was of the same opinion. Miss Helen D'Alton was also very successful in the two items she was down for, and narrowly escaped an encore for her singing of "The Lost Chord" with organ obbligato by Herr Swertz. Mrs. Langfield, an amateur, sang her part of the duet for two sopranos very well, her voice, though not very powerful, being of a sweet quality and in perfect tune ; she appeared to be a little nervous in the morning, but in the evening she sustained her part right well. Mr. Bernard Lane had either a cold, or had not recovered from the

fatigue of travelling, for he was very husky all through, and Mr. Griffin sang several times out of tune ; with the exception of his singing of one piece, which was really very good, and Mr. Lane's singing of "In splendour bright," which was also very fair, I cannot conscientiously praise either of them. What I have said above with regard to the singing of the chorus applies equally well to the playing of the band, which was excellent. The overture to "William Tell," went admirably, as did also the march from "Athalie." The same programme was repeated at the evening concert, which I think was a great mistake, as it had the effect of keeping away a great many of those who were present in the morning. The only difference was that the encores were many, and were nearly all responded to, and that Miss Helen D'Alton sang in addition "Creation's Hymn" by Beethoven.

To sum up. Cork has reason to be proud of being able to bring together such a body of musical amateurs as sang and played on that day, for nearly two-thirds of the performers were localists. Herr Swertz is to be congratu-lated on the success of his labours in bringing the mass of voices under such perfect control ; and Mr. Robinson is to be congratulated for the admirable manner in which he conducted the whole performance, to the chagrin, no doubt, of many who were opposed in the first instance to his being brought down. Herr Swertz presided at the organ during the morning and evening concerts.

"H.M.S. Pinafore" is at the theatre, but on Tuesday, on account of the instrumentalists being required at the Ex-hibition, they were obliged to perform with only the aid of a piano. They have a very good caste.

The excellent organ, built by Mr. Magahy, of Cork, has 3 manuals and pedals, 34 stops, with the usual pro-portion of couplers and composition movements.
            F. S. JOHN LACY.

EASTBOURNE.—The musical season under the direction of the popular conductor and pianist, Mr. Julian Adams, commenced with a capital concert, at which the orchestral features were the overtures "Ruy Blas" and "Tännhauser" and Schubert's Sym-phony in C. A concert has been given in aid of the Royal College of Music. The orchestra is again in excellent form, and one can but wish that every pleasure resort possessed the still rare musical advantages enjoyed by Eastbourne.

THE MUSIC TEACHERS' NATIONAL ASSOCIATION, U.S.—The seventh annual session of the organization was held at Providence, R. I., July 4th, 5th, and 6th. The programme con-sisted of essays, discussions, vocal and instrumental concerts, &c. Distinguished musicians from all parts of the country were present and took part in the exercises. The call was issued and signed by the President, E. M. Bowman, of St. Louis ; W. F. Neath, Secretary, Ft. Wayne, Ind. ; and the Exe-cutive Committee, Robert Bomner, Providence, R. I. ; H. E. Holt, Lexington, Mass. ; Albert A. Stanley, · Provi-dence, R. I.

ROYAL ACADEMY OF MUSIC LOCAL EXAMINATIONS, MANCHESTER CENTRE.—The annual distribution of certificates to successful candidates at the Local Examinations held during the year, in connection with the Royal Academy of Music, was made on July 5th, in the large rooms of the Town Hall, Man-chester. Alderman Bunnett was in the chair. A selection of classical music, performed by some of the candidates, gave great satisfaction to a large audience. Miss E. H. M. Hochstetter (one of the junior candidates), a rising young pianist, played Weber's Polonaise, Op. 72, with so much brilliancy as to secure an *encore*, and in response played Handel's Fantasia in C. Miss Biddolph, one of the senior Honours candidates, also received a well-merited *encore* for her artistic performance of Chopin's Nocturne, Op. 27, No. 2.

GWENNAP, CORNWALL.—A new organ was opened last week at Gwennap Church, by Mr. J. Hele, junr., organist of St. Peter's, Plymouth. It consists of Great organ with open diap-son, gamba, dulciana, fluto traverso, principal harmonic, piccolo; swell organ, with open diapason, salicional, gedact, gemshorn, and oboe ; pedal, bourdon 30 notes, couplers, swell to great, swell to pedals, great to pedals. The organ has spotted metal front pipes, and all stops are through. Mr. Hele played with his usual excellence. Following is the programme :—Sonata No. 1— Allegro con Brio, Andante religioso, Allegretto, Allegro Maes-toso (Mendelssohn) ; Pastorale in G (Merkel) ; Solo, No 9 (Corelli) ; Occasional overture (Handel) ; "Qui est homo" ("Stabat Mater"), (Rossini) ; Grand Chœur (Guilmant) ; Ro-manza in G (Beethoven) ; Offertoire in D (Batiste) ; March in E flat (Wely).

CITY OF LONDON COLLEGE.—On the occasion of the inauguration of the City of London College, last Saturday, by the Prince of Wales, some of the students from the Guild-hall School of Music rendered a selection of· vocal music.

The artists were Miss Clara Dowle, Miss Newman, Miss Armstrong, Miss Umpleby, Misses Nellie and Annie Sheldon; and Messrs. Boulcott-Newth, Sackville Evans, and Caston. Miss Clara Dowle's rendering of "Softly Sighs" (Weber), was much admired, and she was loudly applauded. Miss Helen Armstrong sang "The last dream" (Cowen); Miss Newman "Since then" (Roeckel); Misses Sheldon Pinsuti's duet, "Cantiam l'Amore," and Messrs. Boulcott-Newth and Evans the duet "Love and war" (Cooke). Mr. J. H. Leipold accompanied.

SOUTHEND.—Madame Maleska's matinée musicale took place at her residence, on July 7th. Madame Morini, though announced, was absent; but in her place Miss Howard sang a couple of songs with great expression, though showing a want of vocal strength. Miss Bath played and accompanied, but her touch was heavy, and somewhat wanting in variety. Miss Maria Schumann's violin solos gave golden hope of the future, and those that heard her on this occasion must wish to hear her again. Messrs. Lewis and Dunn sang with ability, but Mr. Russell sang "Honour and Arms," rather stiffly; however, in his second solo he quite redeemed himself, and shewed dramatic qualities of no mean order, linked to a voice that is pleasing and strong. Madame Maleska and Mdlle. Spontini sang with taste and were well received. The performance concluded with the famous quartet from "Rigoletto," which certainly would have gone better had some rehearsal taken place.

NOTTINGHAM.—A recital of chamber music was given on Tuesday evening, in the Albert Hall, by Mr. John Farmer and others, to a numerous audience, at which the following programme was performed:—Quartet in E flat, Op. 47, for violin, tenor, violoncello and pianoforte (Schuman), Miss M. Farmer, MM. Gibson, Cave, and Albert; Rondo in B minor, for violin and pianoforte, Miss Bateman and Mr. Gibsone; Quartet in G minor, Op. 25, for pianoforte, violin, tenor and violoncello, Miss M. Farmer, M.M. Gibson, Cave, and Albert; Etude in C minor (Chopin); "Abends" (Schumann), and Etude in G flat (Chopin), Miss M. Farmer; Etude in F major (Henselt), selections from Schumann's "Carnival," &c., Miss Bateman; and Septet, No. 2, for two violins, tenor, violoncello, double-bass and flute (John Farmer), Mr. John Farmer and the instrumentalists already named. The performance gave perfect satisfaction, especially Mr. John Farmer's "Septet," which was well received; but not more favourably, says *The Nottingham Guardian*, than its merits demanded.

KENDAL.—The Church of St. George has been restored. Foremost among the many eminently satisfactory features in the alterations is the substitution of a new organ for the old instrument, which in its day had done good service, but which can no longer be retained in its accustomed site to mar the full effect of the greatly improved appearance of the interior of the church. For some time past it has been known that the concealment of many blemishes and shortcomings in the part it sustained in the services was entirely due to the judicious handling of Mr. Smallwood. Messrs. Wilkinson and Son, of this town, who have now a wide reputation for exceptional excellence in this branch, undertook to supply the want, and they have succeeded in doing so in a manner which has brought the new instrument forward as a real acquisition to the town. In external appearance the work is altogether of a sumptuous character, no pains having been spared to make it artistically complete, and certainly nothing could be added that would in any way enhance the beauty of its design, while it is needless to say that nothing has been gained in point of show at the expense of the more important internal properties. In the latter respect nothing is wanting. As the reader will remember, a conference upon organ building was held under the auspices of the College of Organists, at which resolutions and recommendations were adopted, and these have been studiously observed in the matter of the relative positions of the manuals, pedals, composition pedals, &c., the organ in every detail giving ample evidence that the aim of the builders has been to ensure as high a degree of perfection as is possible. While Messrs. Wilkinson are to be congratulated upon their work, they may also be congratulated that it is in the hands of a gentleman who will not allow any of its beauties to go undemonstrated. The organ is admirably balanced and contains many excellent effects. It has 3 manuals, and pedal organ, 37 stops, and 2026 pipes. The church was re-opened by an impressive thanksgiving service on July 5th.

Says the *Daily News*: In conversation with a French correspondent M. Gounod stated that the works upon which he is busily engaged for the Birmingham Festival of 1885 will be entitled "Death and Life," and will be in two parts. The first part, "Death," will be a species of Requiem. The second, "Life," will be a description of the New Jerusalem, taken from the Revelations, and in it the *motifs* used in the first section will be repeated, but developed "in such a way as to express the joy of the souls of the saved in the heavenly Jerusalem of Saints." M. Gounod added that he intended to write no more for the operatic stage.

foreign Musical Intelligence.

The health of Hans von Bülow has greatly improved. He is now staying in Switzerland.

An international musical competition will be held at Amsterdam early next September.

The death is announced of Wilhelm Krüger, court pianist, of Stuttgart.

M. Gregoir, of Brussels, has published a biography of the composer Grétry.

Pauline Lucca has gone to Ischl for the benefit of her little daughter's health.

Spohr's "Jessonda" is to be revived on the re-opening of the Dresden Theatre.

Max Zenger's oratorio, "Kain," was given last month at Innspruck.

M. Gounod is re-arranging "Sapho" for the Paris Opera.

"Venetianische Nächte," the new buffo-opera, by Johann Strauss, will be produced first at Hamburgh.

At the Brussels Monnaie Theatre, Litolf's opera, "Die Templer," will shortly be produced, to be followed later by Reyer's "Sigurd."

Rubinstein's "Verlorenes Paradies" will be heard next winter in Berlin, under the direction of Herr Alexis Holländer.

An opera, by Hector Berlioz, "Benvenuto Cellini," is to be produced at the Leipsic Theatre at the end of this month for the first time.

The orchestra of the Wagner Theatre has been disbanded after giving several concerts, under the direction of Herr Anton Seide, the pecuniary result of which was far from satisfactory.

Having returned from America, Max Bruch has attended the Coblentz Musical Festival, and thence proceeds to Breslau, where he has been chosen to succeed Bernhard Scholz.

The Italian opera company at St. Petersburgh will begin their performances on October 1st, with a one act opera, by Salvayre, called "Richard III." and Rubinstein's "Demon."

A FURTHER DEVELOPMENT OF PROGRAMME MUSIC.—A Missouri composer has written a symphony entitled "The Mule." It is an admirable piece of descriptive music. It opens with an easy, moderate movement, intended to represent the animal jogging contentedly along the road. A few grace notes indicate his reaching to one side to nab a thistle as he passes. The road grows harder, and the movement slower. Then the driver encourages the mule. The cluck and the crack of the whip is heard. But the movement doesn't increase in rapidity. It stops short; and then, the middle brasses take up one note and hold it through the rest of the symphony, to indicate that the mule has balked and won't move. Meanwhile, the strings give expression to the efforts of the driver to beat the obstinacy out of the beast with the whip, a few sharp taps of the bones soon coming in to indicate the breaking of the whipstock. Dull blows upon the kettle drum tell that the driver has taken up the cushion of the waggon-seat, and is whacking the mule round the tail with it. However, the mule remains firm; and the cushion is thrown aside, and the driver goes to a fence to get a board. The tearing of his clothes in the wayside bushes and his ripping the board from the fence are clearly defined by the trombones and lower strings. He returns and belabours the mule with the board ; and this is one of the most lively and pleasing movements of the work, and is continued until the mule begins to kick. Then, the melody becomes somewhat obscured, but the force and speed of the movement are greatly accelerated. The waggon begins to break. First, the dash-board goes, then the seat, then the wiffletree,—a sharp clang of the triangle denoting the breaking of the ironwork. So it goes, till the mule has freed itself from the waggon. Then, it kicks the man over the fence ; and he falls in a hog-wallow. Then comes the finale—the triumphant bray of the mule. This is a wondrous bit of composition, so natural and true to life that a listener with his eyes closed would think himself in close proximity to the living animal. The roar is something tremendous, and can only be produced by an orchestra of ninety-two pieces ; while the conductor has to be strapped down to obviate his throwing himself off his feet.—*Boston Post*.

Organ News.

BOLTON.

An organ recital was given in the Albert Hall, by Mr. Wm. Mullineux, F.C.O., on July 7th. The following was the programme :—

Dead March ("Saul")	Handel.
Introduction (Extempore)	} Bach.
Fugue in E Flat (St. Ann's)	
Motet, "O Salutaris Hostia"	Gounod.
Overture, "Die Zauberflöte"	Mozart.
Air, "If with all your hearts"	Mendelssohn.
Chorus, "Blest be the man" (Joseph)	Handel.
Marche Funèbre et Chant Séraphique (by desire)	Guilmant.
Festival March	Dunster.

BRISTOL.

Mr. George Riseley gave the last organ recital for the season at the Colston Hall, on Saturday, June 30th. The following was the programme :—

Air, varied, "Partant pour la Syrie"	Haynes.
Andante, (Symphony No. 4)	Mendelssohn.
Fantasia, et Fuga in G minor	J. S. Bach.
Pastorale	Wely.
Sonata, No. 9, in A	Corelli.
Romance	Hime.
Overture, "Les Huguenots"	Meyerbeer.

COVENTRY.

The new organ erected by Porritt, of Leicester, in the Church of All Saints, Coventry, was opened by Dr. Charles Joseph Frost, on Wednesday evening, July 4th. The following was the programme :—

Toccata in A flat	Hesse.
Introduction and Fugue	Raff.
Marche Religieuse	Chauvet.
Fantasia Sonata in A flat	Rheinberger.
(Grave—Allegro—Adagio expressivo—Fuga).	
Grand Marche	Merkel.
Allegretto Villareccio	Fumagalli.
Maestoso in C, and Allegretto in D	Frost.
Marcia Religiosa	Perelli.
Allegretto Vivace in A minor	Morandi.

CRYSTAL PALACE.

Mr. A. J. Eyre's programme on Saturday, July 7th, included the following :—

Overture, "Henry VIII."	Hatton.
Adagio from a Symphony	Haydn.
Air, "My heart ever faithful"	Bach.
Grand Prelude in D minor	Mendelssohn.
Fugue in D major	Bach.
Romance, "Rose, softly blooming"	Spohr.
Postlude in C	Bartley.
Finale from an Orchestral Suite	Schumann.

EXETER.

Mr. Claude R. Fowles gave an organ recital at the Victoria Hall, on Saturday evening, June 30th. The following was the programme :—

Introduction and Allegro in D	F. E. Bache.
Romance for Violin, Op. 40	Beethoven.
Fugue in D minor	J. S. Bach.
Andante Tranquillamente	Hy. Smart.
Siciliana	E. J. Hopkins.
Chorus, "The Heavens are telling"	Haydn.
Meditation (on 1st Prelude, J. S. Bach)	Gounod.
March, "Cornelius"	Mendelssohn.
Cantilene Pastorale	A. Guilmant.
Impromptu	
Overture, "Peter Schmoll"	Weber.

FISHERIES EXHIBITION.

The following is the programme of a recital given on Tuesday, July 3rd, by Mr. James Halle, on Henry Jones and Sons' organ.

Marche, "Cornelius"	Mendelssohn.
Overture, "Tancredi"	Rossini.
Offertoire in G	Batiste.
Organ Concerto, No. 4	Handel.
Pilgrim's Song	Batiste.
Airs Impromptu	
Marche from "Le Prophète"	Meyerbeer.

Mr. James Loaring, F.C.O., gave his twelfth organ recital on Thursday, July 5th. The programme included:—

Overture, "Artaxerxes"	Dr. Arne.
Organ Concerto, No. 2	
Overture, "Les deux Avengles"	Méhul.
Prelude and Fugue in D minor	Bach.
The Bride's March	Loaring.

EALING.

An organ recital was given on Monday, the 9th inst., at Christ Church, by Mr. Harold E. Stidolph, and was largely attended. The programme was as follows :—

March from Joshua	} Handel.
March from "Ode to St. Cecilia"	
Romanzo Affettuoso	Cramer.
Concerto (No. 5)	Handel.
"I waited for the Lord" ("Lobgesang")	Mendelssohn.
Storm Fantasia	Lemmens.
Andantino, from Quartet	Pleyel.
Wedding March	Mendelssohn.

HIGH WYCOMBE.

On Monday evening the 2nd inst., a recital was given on the organ in the Parish Church, by Mr. J. G. Wrigley, F.C.O., Mus.Bac., Oxon. The following formed the programme :—

Sonata (No. 2) Op. 65	Mendelssohn.
(Grave—Adagio—Allegro maestoso e vivace—Fuga).	
"Carillons de Dunkerque"	Carter.
"Air du Dauphin"	Roeckel.
Overture	Flotow.
Grand Fantasia, "The Storm," in E minor	Lemmens.

PRESTON.

The following is the programme of the organ recital given by Mr. James Tomlinson, in the new Public Hall on Saturday evening, July 7th.

Sixth Symphony	Haydn.
(Adagio—Allegro—Andante—Minuetto—Vivace).	
Adagio (Quartet in E flat)	Mendelssohn.
Overture to "The Crown Diamonds"	Auber.
Chorus and Air, "Idomeneo"	Mozart.
Military Overture	Mendelssohn.

CHILDREN'S VOICES.

The *Century Magazine* has a paper dealing with the question of training children's voices from the pen of Mr. William L. Tomlins, a well-known worker in the cause in America, and preceded by a few observations from Mr. Theodore Thomas.

Mr. Tomlins debates the question whether in truth the method commonly adopted in these seminaries is not harmful to the voice and destructive to artistic singing in the future. " Briefly mentioned," he says, "The faults of current instruction are these : Everything is sacrificed to a knowledge of musical notation. The voice is developed only in respect to power, and this, unfortunately, in a way which must be entirely undone whenever the study of artistic singing is begun. Instead of soft, pleasant, expressive voices, one hears in school almost universally a hard, shouty tone, unsympathetic and inexpressive. " All of these shortcomings," he tells us, " finally reduce themselves to two—namely, ignorance of, or indifference to, the physiological relation between singing and the vocal organs; and, second, apathy with regard to all kinds of musical relations beyond the simplest and most obvious. This state of things, which prevails for the most part throughout the country, is to be accounted for, or at least has been influenced by, two or three circumstances. The music-teachers are chosen mainly for their knowledge of notation and the sight-reading of music. They are generally earnest, practical teachers, with perhaps a turn for music, but with no systematised training in the physiology of the vocal organs, and without practical acquaintance with the technic of vocal culture." He mentions the Sunday school singing-books and the Moody and Sankey hymns as being written down for the class-singing market; but works of this kind are perhaps more supplied to school children in America than in England. Some good observations are made, too, upon the habit of coupling physical exertion with singing; and the author very truly says "The panting of the breath directs the blood to the throat and lungs, and involves an action of the extrinsic muscles of the throat which directly antagonises the proper act of singing." Mr. Tomlins observes that the only way of altering the received method of teaching children singing at large schools is by the dissemination of proper knowledge of vocal culture amongst the teachers themselves; for if the attention of young people is solely directed to notation and sight-singing, he who can shout the correct interval the loudest is certain to be considered the best singer. Mr. Theodore Thomas was present during an exhibition of some 200 or 300 children singing at Chicago. "The singing of the children," he says, "as I heard it on that occasion, demonstrated the soundness of Mr. Tomlins's theories and his rare abilities as a teacher. They showed ease, spontaneity, warmth, expression, accuracy of pitch, precision—in fact, came so near to perfection that I assured them I had never before heard such beautiful singing."

THE HARP.

The following extracts are from an article by a "Foreign Professor" in *St. Cecilia Magazine.*

Some imagine that the harp had its origin in the bow of an antediluvian Nimrod, who, finding the string emitted a note, added others. The new instrument thus formed must have pleased "the giants in those days" of dim and dawning history, for by degrees the frame was broadened and hollowed out (sometimes above, sometimes below) to give the infant harp a deeper, stronger resonance. The learned and enterprising Scotch traveller, Bruce, found at Thebes, among the sculptured records of that splendid Egyptian civilisation, which was the cradle of the Hebrew and Greek, paintings apparently as old as the 13th century before the Christian era, in which harps of surprising size and beauty figure among the favorite instruments used by the Imperial Egyptian. The harp of the mystic Chaldean, though it had the sound-board or resonance-box above instead of below, resembled the Egyptian harp in the absence of the pole or pillar, which in the Gothic harp forms the third arm of the triangle. By this important addition to the frame of the harp, the Goths, and other Scythic emigrants from Asia,—whose incursions into Western and Northern Europe carried the harp even as far as "Caledonia, stern and wild,"—not only completed the beauty and symmetry of its outward form, but gave the frame of the instrument sufficient strength to bear the tension of those thicker, longer, more tightly drawn strings, whether of sinew or metal, from which the harp derived a power of tone suited to the wild vigorous genius of its new masters, the Goth, Teuton, Celt, and Saxon. As the traveller who crosses a broad stream at twilight, steps from one fragment of rock to another, so here and there a vague allusion, a scanty hint, a rude monument, aids us in tracing the uncertain path of the harp's progress over the dim mediæval period of history. High and clear, at a very early stage of this dark road, rises the majestic figure of the Celtic Druid of Britain, and his disciple the Druid of Gaul. The brief hierarchy of these gifted men—divines, philosophers, judges, physicians, poets, seers, and harpists,—seems not to have extended to Caledonia, where their hardly less versatile successors, the Bards, were represented by Merlin and others. About this period we find the Irish Bard rising into such eminence that Galileo, the astronomer's father, and Dante, acknowledged them as the instructors of tuneful Italy itself on the harp, and speak in high terms of the size and beauty of that instrument, which even now is the national emblem of the country where the mediæval harp rose to its summit of beauty and power in the "Regina Cithararum,"—the "Galway" harp of 1621. Nor must I pass over in silence the gifted bard of the rich-voiced *telyn* or Welsh harp.

The harpist's art, that once formed so picturesque a feature in the story of Royal Saxon Alfred, was again cultivated by a Royal student, James I. of Scotland, and it appears to have even enjoyed high favour both in the Highlands and Lowlands of Scotland until the French cornemuse (bagpipe) players in the train of Mary Queen of Scots succeeded in introducing into this country the latter instrument. No wonder, that having received this impetus, the shrill and warlike bagpipe should speedily have gained favour with the savage chieftains, who, then and long after, formed the nobility of Scotland. But in our milder age, when war is regarded rather as an evil than as a favourite pastime, we might hope to hear again much oftener the gentle voice of the harp. And if the French brought in the semi-barbaric bagpipes, to them also we owe the latest and most perfect form of the harp. The mediæval harp, whose simple diatonic scale was unfit for modern instrumental music, was first improved by an ingenious Tyrolese, who inserted little crooks into the neck, so as to shorten the strings and add other semitones to the scale. Hochbrucker in 1720, gave the harp the power of modulation by connecting these crooks with pedals, thus leaving the hands free. Then the Frenchman Cousineau contrived to produce semitones without the jarring, inconvenient crooks (which pulled the string out of its level) and by adding another row of pedals, constructed, in the year 1782, the first double-action harp. A few years afterwards, the great Sebastian Erard invented that beautiful contrivance, the fork mechanism, which has raised the harp to its present state of perfection, and superseded all the cumbrous and jarring machinery of which the harpists of his day had so long complained. Since Erard invented the double-action harp, (1810), a *new world* has been opened up to the harpist. The instantaneous and perfect production of all the chromatic semitones places within the performer's reach those beautiful enharmonic effects, the "synonyms," obtained by throwing the whole scale into one chord, which the hand of the performer sweeps, now loudly, now softly, as the sigh of the Æolian harp. These and other peculiar effects, such as the bell-like harmonics, the "etouffées," drum-notes, the distant rumble of the skilfully swept bass notes (imitating the "thunder stop" of the organ, the bray of trumpet-like "mordente" produced *presso la tavola*), all these, and many more, are enhanced in brilliancy and facility by the exquisitely perfect construction of the sound-board and other adjuncts equally due to the inventive genius of the great Alsatian. The manufacture of harp-strings, now much improved, has removed another obstacle to the general adoption of the harp for solo performances and concert and chamber music. A few chords, a simple melody, played in that style which Italy teaches to instrumentalists as well as vocalists, is immediately felt by all to be something—*non so che*—quite unique in its charm. The harp has been found a beautiful adjunct to Church music on the continent of Europe, and lately on that of America, where, as in southern Europe, the feelings of religious devotion seek a more varied, picturesque expression than would please those men would condemn us to a psalmody graphically described by Sir Jasper Cranbourne, in "Peveril of the Peak." Meyerbeer, has employed the harp in his orchestral effects with an art which consoles the harpist for the uncouth orchestral tricks of Berlioz and Wagner.

POPULAR SONGS.

(Extracted from an American Paper.)

"Auld Lang Syne" is popularly supposed to be the composition of Burns, but, in fact, he wrote only the second and third verses of the ballad as commonly sung, retouching the others from an older and less familiar song. "The Old Oaken Bucket" was written by Woodworth in New York City during the hot summer of 1817. He came into the house and drank a glass of water, and then said: "How much more refreshing it would be to take a good long drink from the old oaken bucket that used to hang in my father's well." His wife suggested that it was a happy thought for a poem. He sat down and wrote the song as we have it. "Woodman, spare that tree," was the result of an incident that happened to George P. Morris. A friend's mother had owned a little place in the country which she was obliged, from poverty, to sell. On the property grew a large oak which had been planted by his grandfather. The purchaser of the house and land proposed to cut down the tree, and Morris's friend paid him ten dollars for a bond that the oak should be spared. Morris heard the story, saw the tree, and wrote the song. "The Light of Other Days" was written to be introduced into Balfe's opera, "The Maid of Artois."

Payne wrote "Home, Sweet Home" to help to fill up an opera he was preparing, and at first it had four stanzas. The author never received anything for it, but though the opera was a failure when played in the Covent Garden Theatre the song took, and over one hundred thousand copies were sold the first year. In two years the publishers cleared over two thousand pounds by the publication. Payne was afterwards appointed American consul in Tunis, where he died, and whence his remains the other day were sent to America. Some of his miseries may be guessed from his own words: "How often have I been in the heart of Paris, Berlin, London, or some other city, and have heard persons singing or hand-organs playing 'Home, sweet home,' without having a shilling to buy myself the next meal, or a place to lay my head." "Rock me to sleep," was written by Mrs. Allen, of Maine. She was paid five dollars for it, and Russell and Co., of Boston, who had in three years gained four thousand dollars by its sale, offered her five dollars apiece for any songs she might write. Some years after, and when a poor widow and in need of money, she sent them a song, which was promptly rejected. "A Life on the ocean wave," by Epes Sargent, was pronounced a failure by his friends. The copyright of the song became very valuable, though Sargent never got anything from it himself. "What are the wild waves saying?" was suggested to Dr. Carpenter by a scene from Dickens's novel, "Dombey and Son," and the music was by Charles Glover. "Poor Jack," was from the pen of Charles Dibdin, the author of "The Lamplighter." "Poor Jack" netted £5,000 for its publishers and almost nothing for the author. "Love's young dream" was one of Moore's best, but the tune to which it is commonly sung is from an Irish ballad called "The Old Woman." Moore sang his own songs so well that both the auditors and himself were often moved to tears. "Kathleen Mavourneen" was sold by Crouch, the author, for £5, and brought the publishers as many thousands. Crouch was hopelessly improvident, and now in his latter days is in poverty. When Madame Tietjens was in America a few years ago she sang "Kathleen Mavourneen" in New York, when a wretched-looking individual introduced himself as Crouch, was recognized, and thanked her for singing the song so well.

There is a story afloat that when Lord Wolseley visited Dublin lately, it was thought he would go to hear Service at St. Patrick's Cathedral. As a delicate compliment to the successful general and his colleagues, the anthem (so runs the story) was chosen from Handel's "Israel in Egypt," the words being "Egypt was glad when they departed."

Mr. Musgrove Tufnail, a pupil of Mr. Frederick Walker, has succeeded in winning the Parepa-Rosa gold medal at the Royal Academy of Music. The judges were Mr. R. Hilton, and Signori Arditi and Bevignani. Mr. Tufnail has also won the Evill prize at the same institution, and was the prize winner for baritone singers at the Carmarthen Eisteddfod.

PUBLIC SINGING.

The following words are taken from an article by Madame Nilsson, in the *North American Review*:—

To the public singer, more perhaps than to any other artist, sympathetic appreciation quickly and naturally manifested by the audience is everything. The painter and the poet, if they have the courage that comes from a complete consciousness of their peculiar gifts, may work on in the solitude of their studies, confident that what one generation refuses to consider another may give a rightful place among the immortal achievements of human genius and skill.

The composer may be misunderstood, misinterpreted, neglected; but his score survives him, and may yet be rendered to an admiring world by some musician who had not begun the first music of the cradle when its author became silent in the grave. Even the actor, though his success depends largely upon sympathy in his audience, is not under so great obligations to it as the singer, by as much as the dramatist and the scene-painter play a more important and observable part than the composer.

Words may express an idea, however clumsily or coldly spoken; but the expression of the more delicate and fleeting emotions and suggestions of songs must be created almost entirely by the singer, who is all the while conscious that unless they fall upon sensitive and sympathetic ears, they pass for ever out of existence with their own brief echoes. The audience that exhibits the most sympathetic appreciation gets the best music. There is no power in mechanical singing, and the hearers will always feel its lifelessness, whether they understand its cause or not. Singing may be said to find its level. It cannot stir the nature of the hearer to any deeper depth, or exalt his enthusiasm to any higher height, than the depth and height of the singer's own heart and soul.

From the nature of the case, there must be a certain amount of tediousness or weariness in singing the same piece many times over. Yet a song which gives fitting expression to any genuine emotion of the human heart, which in any way arrives at that touch of nature that makes the whole world akin, is one of the most durable of all things in art or literature. And it must be remembered that each public rendering is an experience more or less peculiar to itself.

INTERNATIONAL COPYRIGHT.— The following, from the American point of view, is of interest. "It is a well-known fact among those interested in this subject—and one that we have taken pains to substantiate while contemplating the publication of this article—that our leading book-publishers and authors are strongly in favour of the passage of an international copyright law. There is no doubt that the music-publishers and composers are also anxious to secure such an obvious protection for their publications. It is understood that the opposition to the passage of an international copyright law comes from England, and for this reason : English publishers insist upon retaining the publication at home, thus securing to their own printers, binders, paper-makers, etc., the manufacture, to the great injury of American industries. In this lies the true cause of the delay. English authors and composers are very prolific in brain-work, and it seems strange that they should not unite to protect their interests in this country, and secure additional income from their works. In conversation with a Boston manager who has within a few days returned from London, he said : " I heard several new operas which I very much wished to bring out in Boston, but knowing that there is no international copyright law to protect me, I declined to purchase them. Any unprincipled manager could have them 'memorized,' and produce them here in advance of my authorized presentation of them. This, of course, keeps a good many dollars out of the pockets of English writers, and deprives our public of the pleasure of hearing the new English operas presented as they should be. This opinion is corroborated by the various other responsible managers, who would all be glad to assist in the bringing about of a law that shall protect them in their ventures, and shall give the public the benefit of throughly first-class representations. It is to be hoped that the authors, composers, and publishers will make a renewed and combined effort to secure the making of the law. It is difficult to imagine a reason why English authors and composers do not memorialize Parliament to pass an international copyright law. So obvious a benefit to all, would, it is believed, have but to be presented in its proper shape, in order to secure their prompt and emphatic approval. The present agitation must, it seems to us, result in the framing of a new law, that shall, by just provisions, guarantee the brain-workers of either country a reward for their labour."—*Musical Record.*

Miss Alice Sydney Burvett (the Australian pianist) will give a concert at the Princes' Hall, Piccadilly, on July 18th. The vocalists, from Paris, are Madame Georges Clément and Monsieur Georges Clément; violin, Mr. Carrodus.

PRINCIPAL CONTENTS OF THIS NUMBER.

LONDON : SATURDAY, JULY 14, 1883.

ORCHESTRAL EFFECTS AND KEYBOARD MANNERISMS.

VIII.

THE direct, or more or less direct, to speak more accurately, orchestral representations of the tone colour of the organ have, as has been shown, considerable sympathy with sundry orchestral functions. And without detracting in any way from the self-possessed grandeur and calmness of the organ, such varied tone-colour representations are of high value in the list of the organist's ample resources. Such effects are not to be found on the key-board of the pianoforte, but in orchestral representation the last-named instrument becomes, by reason of its wonderfully susceptible touch and extraordinary powers of executive facility, no mean reproducer of orchestral idioms. Now, in the absence of direct tone-colour faculties, the pianoforte touch is exalted into a rare and precious gift. If the pianoforte lacks the power of giving the more positive tone qualities, it certainly possesses to a larger extent than the organ the faculty of readily producing varied light and shade, such as are constantly present in the phrasing of the orchestral masses. The reader need not here be reminded of the comparison that the orchestra produces a picture and the pianoforte an engraving, but the comparison may be emphasized by adding that though the engraving reproduces no colour it may be made by the skilful engraver to represent nearly all the lights and shades of the original picture. This is exactly the position of the pianoforte as a reproducer of orchestral effects ; for though it is incapable of suggesting any of the decided tone colours of the orchestra, its delicate and ready sense of touch enables the skilful pianist to typify many of the expressive phrasings of the orchestra. The one art most required in such work is the faculty of "singing" or tone sustaining. Those who knew MENDELSSOHN have remarked upon his extraordinary power of "singing" on the pianoforte key-board, whereby he succeeded in suggesting some of the effects produced by the sustained soft notes of the orchestral wind instruments as well as the *legato* bowing of the strings. This artistic power over the fading tones of the pianoforte must be sought for with care and taste. Its production may be generally indicated by telling the student to attack the keys softly, but to press them with extreme firmness. The attack should be made in piano sentences from the soft part of the fingers, a mode of attack best secured by stretching the fingers slightly forward, and by lowering the wrist. The three methods of approaching the pianoforte keys should be carefully studied not only by the performer anxious to typify orchestral effects, but by the soloist pure and simple, for the best pianoforte music, as BEETHOVEN's Sonatas, are full of the purest orchestral idioms. The methods alluded to are these, the *legato* and "singing" style, expressed by firm, soft pressure from the slightly extended fingers with the wrist held down so as not to interfere in any way with the free subtle movement of the fingers. The *staccato* or semi-staccato, produced by the decided yet free employment of the wrist, with the hand slightly raised, so as to enable the wrist to lift the fingers lightly and promptly from the keys. Then at times, in heavy chords, *sforzando* figures and broad massive effects, some strength may be borrowed from the front part of the arm just beyond the wrist. The wrist, too, it should be remembered plays a delicate but important function in the art of phrasing. A more enlightened view of the relationship of "Orchestral Effects and "Key-board Mannerisms" has of late, shown the wisdom of key-board performers bestowing some attention upon both the typical instruments with keys. Thus the study of the organ has been found to lend to the pianist considerable power in the attainment of a perfect *legato* touch ; and on the other hand, the practice of the pianoforte assists the organist in obtaining a prompt, clean, bright action of the fingers. The large intermixture in modern music of orchestral idioms in the literature of both organ and pianoforte certainly claims from the key-board performer of either kind a careful study of the varied methods of expression and phrasing which are chiefly the heritage of the orchestra, duly remembering that this is to be done without in any way sacrificing the special characteristics and individualities of the distinct keyboard instruments.   E. H. TURPIN.

Madame Antoinette Sterling, Messrs. Sims Reeves and Santley, sang at the public dinner given in honour of Mr. Henry Irving on July 4th.

Mr. J. Stedman, the much esteemed concert agent, is conducting the business arrangements in connection with the orchestral concerts to be given at the forthcoming Cardiff Eisteddfod.

THE LOGIC OF COUNTERPOINT.

THIRD SERIES.

X.

THE fourth species in four parts seems specially to favour the employment of brief pedal passages, by reason of the natural grace secured by a chain of suspended harmonies being dropped step by step, over a stationary sound. CHERUBINI reminds the student of the rule which he first applies to three part counterpoint of the fourth species and which formulates the principle, that a succession of discords and concords with discords sometimes prepared and followed by other discords, when forming links of the same conjunct descending chains of suspensions and their resolutions, may be placed over or under a sustained pedal note, providing the first discord be prepared by a concord and the last discord be resolved by a concord, that is, that the external points of the chain be consonant harmonies. He continues, similar harmonic formations may be produced in four part counterpoint of the species under consideration. The theorist quotes examples from PALESTRINA, in which the discord of the fourth is boldly taken without preparation in order that it may become as it were its own preparation, thus :—

$$
\begin{array}{c|c|c}
\begin{array}{l} B\ C \\ G \\ D\ C \\ G \end{array} &
\begin{array}{l} C\ B \\ G \\ D \\ G \end{array} &
\begin{array}{l} C \\ G \\ E \\ C \end{array}
\end{array}
$$

the unprepared fourth being shown in the second beat of the first measure. This progression was indeed in the sixteenth century an established cadence formation ; and most probably the progression was already a trite one in PALESTRINA's day, having been in use some years before his time it may be fairly assumed. Similarly the tritone was, at a little later period than the just quoted progression, allowed to appear in conjunct movement thus :—

$$
\begin{array}{c|c}
\begin{array}{l} C \\ E\ F \\ A \\ A \end{array} &
\begin{array}{l} D\ C \\ F\ C \\ G \\ B\ C \end{array}
\end{array}
$$

The theorist proceeds to show that the conduct of the fourth species counterpoint in four parts may be characterised by much greater freedom than would be the formation of the same contrapuntal genus in three parts, as in two and three parts minims could not be employed save in the part carrying the syncopations. "This practice may be employed" continues our author, "for dissonant as "well as for consonant syncopations ; therefore, by "the help of such permissible devices, it is possible "to introduce discords whenever they may occur with "difficulty and easily secure the means of escape from "embarrassing passages." The judiciously added words are not to be unheeded, "These means should "however be employed with reserve and without "abuse of the permission." For it is clear that a too abundant use of such exceptionally allowed figures would tend to detract from the clear design and outline of the counterpoint, and to impart harmonic complexities and sometimes laboured progressions to the stream of even contrapuntal action. [E. H. TURPIN.

THE PRESENT POSITION OF THE COMPOSER.

VI.

It is sometimes questioned whether the present age is or is not one of great productive power in art. Certainly these high-pressure days present many difficulties in the career of the productive artist, who requires time for thought, and to whom the irritating turmoil and trying, monotonous routine of modern life are by no means conducive to health and mental freshness. If the great masters of the past could be called upon to lead the feverish, overstrained lives which seem now to be the inevitable lot of our London and Parisian artists of reputation, it may almost be questioned whether they would have succeeded in pouring forth masterpiece after masterpiece. Again, it may be that in the balance of the seemingly conflicting and varied events and developments which make up the life of this world, one age is called upon to produce, and another to employ and use what has already been produced. It seems any way to be true that the various arts have their cycles, and it is possible that music has attained its highest productive power. However, it is not for the artist "having put his hand to the plough" to stop in his course to enquire as to the nature of the age in which he lives, but it is his task to work on hopefully, and to remember that there is always room for good, honestly done work. It seems, indeed, not out of place to point out the importance to the composer of carefully steadying and guiding his mind through all the multiform causes of irritation and prostrating pressure which the actively engaged artist must encounter. The temperament of the composer's mind should be one of a great abiding calmness; heshould learn so to fight the battle of life that he can step aside out of the conflict at almost any time, with an unimpaired serenity and with a sweetened patience. One of the chief difficulties in his way, is the large call teaching makes upon his time and mind. Most musicians must teach, undoubtedly, though it is greatly to be deplored that our composers are so little encouraged for the most part, as to be unable to rest from labours so exacting as are those of the teacher of music. One remedy is the persistent determination never to teach a note of badly-written music; a resolution happily more possible in these days of advanced education than it was some years ago. Such a determination saves the musician from much that is trying to his mind and temper. A kindred good resolution is that of determinedly declining to teach unsympathetic and incapable pupils. It is possible by a thoughtful and well-planned method of employing the mental faculties in teaching, to preserve them, nay, possibly to develope and strengthen them. Perhaps the subject will call for more thought and consideration presently.   E. H. Turpin.

Mr. Bright, M.P., has consented to deliver the annual address and present the prizes at the annual prize festival of the Royal Normal College and Academy of Music for the Blind, on July 18th. The chair will be taken by the Duke of Westminster.

"COUNTERPOINT."

By H. J. Stark, Mus.Bac.

A Paper read before the College of Organists, on May 1st, 1883.

The progress of the art of music in this country during the past fifteen or twenty years has been marked by many features of interest, but amongst these it is hardly possible to select for consideration a more gratifying circumstance than the increased attention which has been given to the *theory*, as distinguished from the *practice*, of the art. The fact that students now feel it incumbent upon them to undergo a proper training, not only in the elementary principles of music, but also in its higher and more abstruse theories, may be accepted as a sure proof that the present revival of music in England has taken firm root; indeed, it may be said that already we are beginning to reap the fruit of so much earnest and devoted study.

The theoretical training of the English musician may be generally described under the following heads :—(i.) Harmony, (ii.) Counterpoint, (iii.) Form, (iv.) Instrumentation. These subjects are usually studied in the order just given, although not unfrequently Harmony and Counterpoint are taught simultaneously, a plan which I venture to think preferable to any other. A little consideration will show that, with respect to Harmony, very much has been done by means of improved text-books to bring theory as far as possible on a level with the requirements of modern practice. It is even possible that in this respect theorists have to some extent overshot the mark, especially by attaching undue importance to arguments based upon mathematical ratios, which can have little or no bearing on our existing scale system; so that, like the dog in the fable, we may run the risk of losing the substance whilst grasping at the shadow. If any danger of this kind really exists, we may safely trust to the stern logic of time and facts to correct such irregularities, and our feelings of gratitude need be in no way lessened towards those who have striven to throw the light of truth upon the dark and obscure corners of our art.

Whilst, however, the study of Harmony has developed to an extent which could hardly have been predicted a quarter of a century ago, we find that Counterpoint, the sister branch of study, remains very much where it was. There is, it is true, an intense desire on the part of students to thoroughly master the subject, and a very large amount of valuable time is expended upon it; but the result achieved is, I venture to think, altogether out of proportion to the attention which it receives.

The truth is that, whilst all other branches of study have progressed side by side with the art itself, Counterpoint alone has been allowed to lag behind.

The old restrictions, many of them unnecessary or inapplicable to modern tonality, are still in full force; and students seem doomed to an endless repetition of vain and unprofitable exercises, invariably based upon themes of inconceivable dulness, and having little or no pretension to melodic form. In the hope of directing attention to the shortcomings of the existing method, and thereby preparing the way for such changes and modifications as will enable the student to obtain real and lasting benefit from a course of Contrapuntal study, I have selected this subject as the theme of my paper this evening. Let me ask you to bear in mind that it is a matter which peculiarly concerns us as organists and Church musicians, since the music to which our attention is so frequently directed is mainly contrapuntal in its construction. I do not mean that the rules of Counterpoint are to any great extent observed in the actual composition of organ or Church music, for this indeed would be impossible. Still, what may be called the *spirit* of Counterpoint appears to pervade all well-written works of this class, and my object is to call attention to the discrepancies which are admitted to exist between Contrapuntal theory and practice, so that, as far as possible, the path of the student may be cleared of all unnecessary complications. Some of my conclusions may appear, at first sight, strange, and even revolutionary in their character, but I would bespeak for them a calm and impartial consideration, believing that in the end they will not be found so remote from the truth as might at first sight appear.

As I am addressing an audience composed for the most part of professional musicians, it will be unnecessary to say much concerning the early history of Counterpoint. I may, however, remind you that it is generally assumed to have taken its rise from the ancient Diaphony, or Descant, which consisted of fifths and octaves added to the plain-song melodies of the Church. Diaphony was thus a first rude attempt at harmony, and previous to its invention we have no certain trace of anything but unison singing. A distinction is drawn by some writers between Diaphony and Descant, the latter being considered as a later development of the art, if such it can be called. There can be little doubt, however, that the principle of adding fifths and octaves to a given theme was common to both methods, and they appear to have existed without much modification to about the end of the twelfth century. A curious use of this ancient system in our own day will be found in the final "Celestial Chorus" of Gounod's "Faust," but in this case the chords are made complete by the addition of the third.

The history of the gradual growth and development of harmonized music from the ancient Descant will be familiar to most of my hearers, and I shall therefore at once proceed to a consideration of the present contrapuntal system.

In the first place, it will be instructive to examine the usual definitions of the term Counterpoint.

Originally derived from the Latin, *punctum, contra-punctum*—point against point, or, in modern parlance, note against note—it is now generally considered as implying the combination of melodies in two or more parts. Exception has, however, been taken to this view by at least one writer, in terms which I venture to quote. "The common definition of Counterpoint as the 'art of combining melodies' is not strictly logical, unless the word 'melody' has a definition not generally accepted; because distinct melodies are never given to the student to combine unless they have been previously proved capable of combination; and if a composer should attempt to combine two distinct melodies in accordance with the laws of strict Counterpoint he will probably find it necessary to eliminate so much of one or both of his subjects that little real musical melody is left. The contrapuntist's notion of a melody is—a succession of sounds which does not infringe certain theoretical laws." This is, I conceive, a strictly logical view of the case, and appears to demand more attention than it has hitherto received.

Counterpoint exercises are usually constructed upon the following plan :—A certain theme or subject, generally called the *canto fermo*, is given to the student, who composes upon it an additional melody or melodies, according to the number of parts required. Until quite recently, two-part Counterpart may be said to have been written with little or no regard for the harmonic combinations which must inevitably be suggested by the simultaneous sounding of any two notes. A Counterpoint exercise written on this system can

never be more than a dry combination of intervals, and it is probable that the majority of students are in the habit of constructing two-part Counterpoint without the least thought of any higher artistic purpose. If this is the case, and I appeal for confirmation to experience of every teacher and student, it may be easily perceived that such a course of study is in the highest degree damaging, since, by ignoring every natural aspiration far harmonic completeness, it tends to blunt and deaden the very feeling which it should be the aim of all sound teaching to encourage and develope.

In dealing with Counterpoint in more than two parts, the law-givers have been compelled to recognise the fact that musical sounds cannot be combined without having regard to the chords which are, either actually or by implication, conveyed to the [mind of the auditor. It is characteristic of the system, however, that from first to last we are strictly limited to *one chord*, the triad ; and even this combination is only permitted in *two* of its *three* available positions.* I am quite prepared to admit that in early exercises some restriction of this kind is highly desirable, but it is only reasonable to expect that when the student is able to deal satisfactorily with the simplest combinations, he should be gradually instructed in the application of contrapuntal principles to all chords in general use. With the triad, however, the system begins and ends, so that one who has practised the art for years, and has acquired a full knowledge of its details, is allowed no more freedom than the student of a few weeks' standing.

Let me not be understood as throwing contempt upon the use of simple chord formations. The triad is, and must ever remain, the best and most satisfactory harmonic combination. It is not only perfect in itself, but it is also the essential, firm, and solid basis of every existing fundamental chord. Its treatment should be the subject of special study, particularly at the outset of a student's career. Let us give it all the respect and attention which it deserves, but at the same time remember that a complete and satisfactory theory must deal with *all* the materials at command, and not merely with *one* combination, however important it may be.

The usual plan of writing Counterpoint in five distinct "orders" or "species" has much to recommend it. These orders, as I may remind you, are as follows :—(i.) Note against note, (ii.) Two notes to one, (iii.) Four notes to one, (iv.) Syncopation, (v.) Florid counterpoint. The amalgamation of the second and fourth "orders" has been strongly advocated, but this, in my opinion, can only be ventured upon with advantage after both have been practised independently.

Good examples of the first, third, and fifth "orders" of Counterpoint will be found in Mendelssohn's sixth organ sonata ; there is a fine specimen of the second order in Bach's "Passion" (St. John), at the chorale "O Mighty King." I have been unable to find an instance of Counterpoint in the fourth order, except when used by amalgamation with others, and this seems to confirm the argument that it really has no separate existence. A very near approach to the continuous use of the fourth "order" will be found in the middle movement of Beethoven's Pianoforte Sonata in G, Op. 14, No. 2. 'It is to be regretted that so little attention is given to Counterpoint in triple time—three notes to one—since this form is undoubtedly one of great strength.

Familiar examples may be found in Mendelssohn's chorus, "But our God abideth in Heaven," from "St.

* The term "position" is not here used as implying the various methods of arranging the *upper* notes of a chord ; it refers to the three harmonic positions of the triad $\frac{8}{5}$, $\frac{5}{3}$, $\frac{8}{3}$

Paul," and in the same composer's chorus " Dogma datus Christianis," from the Church cantata, " Lauda Sion."

Reference has already been made to the dry and uninteresting character of the so-called " melodies " which are furnished to the student as the basis of his exercises. This peculiarity may be traced to three distinct causes :—(i.) the invariable use of notes of uniform length, (ii.) the neglect of all recognised principles of melodic form, (iii.) the fact that many of the ancient themes are constructed on scales which have long since been discarded. The student on being informed that all Counterpoint must be regarded from a melodic rather than from a harmonic stand-point, naturally turns to the themes supplied to him, expecting to find fulfilled in them all the conditions of a good and satisfactory melody. Am I overstating the case by asserting that in no single instance is this expectation realized ? If any doubt exists on this point let reference be made to any Counterpoint text-book, and a slight study of the Canti Fermi thereon given, will probably convince the most sceptical. No wonder, indeed, that Counterpoint is voted " dull," and that little or no life can be infused into the dry bones of an art which, if judged by text-book theories, must be pronounced as extinct as the dodo !

I have refrained from noticing in detail the usual text-books on the subject of Counterpoint, because they will be found, on examination, to be merely re-productions of the well-known work of Cherubini. There is one exception, however, which is worthy of more than passing notice—I refer to Professor Mac-farren's treatise, published in 1879. This work is generally supposed to represent a very decided advance upon the school of Cherubini, and it has been adopted as a teaching work by very many pro-fessors. A careful perusal will show, however, that the author had no intention of extending the study of Counterpoint beyond the limits previously assigned to it ; indeed, at the outset he expresses a hope that the work may be found to contain " nothing new in fact."

On two points, however, we may notice a distinct advance. First as regards the rule for figuring two-part Counterpoint with the object of indicating the complete harmony ; and, secondly, by providing rules for the proper treatment of the minor key. With these exceptions the work is a disappointing re-enactment of the old restrictions, and, like all previous text-books, fails to carry the student beyond the mere mechanical combination of intervals.

▶ The matter contained in Chapter 17 (Counterpoint in the modern free style) is by far the most important part of the work, but even here we find many pedantic and wholly unnecessary restrictions. Further reference will presently be made to this work.

(To be continued).

At the annual general meeting of the Philharmonic Society held at Trinity College on Saturday, June 16th ult., the following gentlemen were elected honorary directors for the ensuing season :—Sir Julius Benedict, Mr. Francesco Berger, Mr. W. H. Cummings, Mr. Charles Gardner, Mr. George Mount, Mr. Charles E. Stephens and Mr. John Thomas. Honorary membership was bestowed upon Madame Sophie Menter and Senor Sarasate.

The love of rare fiddles seems not to languish. At the sale of violins of the late Joseph S. Hulse by Messrs. Puttick and Simpson on Monday week, the following lots realized high prices :—Lot 5, a violin by Joseph Guarnerius, 1738, £290 ; lot 7, a violin by Antonius Stradiuarius, 1687, known as the " Spanish Stradiuarius," £500 ; lot 13, a violin by Carlo Bergonzi, £90 ; lot 41, a violin by Joseph Guarnerius, 1739, £245 ; lot 104, a violin by Francesco Rugerius, stated to have been for-merly the property of George IV., £330.

THE ÆSTHETIC EFFECT OF ALTERED KEY.

Some time ago I wrote with reference to the key of A minor as being curiously vigorous and brilliant, a favourite key ; but here we have the great and fresh keys of E and A major coming in as auxiliaries. D minor I should describe rather as pathetic ; with the power that belongs to simple pathos.[*]

With regard to B flat, which has E flat and F for auxiliaries, the casting vote is on my side. (Some time ago your Crystal Palace critic described Beethoven's B flat Symphony as perhaps the most Spring-like of all music :—*toto coelo* our votes would be together also as regards A minor. Another writer also considers B flat as " mellow and brilliant " (meaning, of course, in com-parison with C, whatever the pitch of C may be.) With regard to Beethoven's colossal " Waldstein " (the first movement—*that* is Beethoven ; and the too-brief Inter-mezzo) 'tis true it starts in the key of C—but how long does it keep in it ? how soon does it not dash (or thunder) off into D minor, C minor, and other keys, some remote, *ad lib. !* The phrase " in the key," as applied to a move-ment, is often a slovenly conventionality—a great piece is in many keys—like some equatorial Alp shoring up and " bearing all the zones on its flanks." *Au reste*, I think we all agree rather than differ. Practically, pitch is key : *va sans dire* that so long as the pitch fluctuates there can be no fixing the absolute character of key. To quote from the same article (*Mangi muss Gewisse Dinge wieder holen*, says Goethe) " of course the effect is relative, and more apparent by comparison." Again : " On the other hand, on Beethoven's piano the key of D corresponded perhaps to that of our C ; this proves that the effect is not absolute, nevertheless " (and here is the point) " it remained D to him as to us, perchance produced the same relative impression ; his key of C being bald to him as it is to us, and D flat noble," &c. If our C were raised to C sharp, nevertheless the C sharp to that C, and the the keys of E and A, &c., would be relatively more bril-liant, as now, on account of the pitch. Yes ; but it may still be doubted whether the idea that there is something idiosyncratic in key itself is not rather a scientific (and therefore poetic) suspicion (*Ahnung*) than mere musician's fancy. A Helmholz alone can answer whether the *timbre* or idiomorphism (*form* of the air-wave) of each key differs as well as the pitch. Again, such a fact as this may " give us pause." The chord of C sounded in the key of G is nothing like so noble as in the key of A flat. Again, the so-termed " equal temperament " is (repre-sentatively) a compromise. It is not equal. A recent correspondent pointed out that the (slight) difference in the vibrating ratios would account for the difference in key-character.

One writer surely goes too far when he says the emotional effects (key affects our mood) are " not in any way caused by the key used as the medium." Let us take a test. If a bright and vigorous thought (I almost want a new word to express what a musical idea is—it is thought and feeling—and often picture—in one) " came into his head," as the little ones say, would the same writer employ natural selection in his key, or not ? Would he write it in C minor, or C or D ? Would he not write it in E or A, for example. Why did Ernst choose C minor for his feeling " Elégie " ? Is the unapproachable " Dead March " in " Saul " grander in D or C ?—in which key I *have* seen it sold. Mendelssohn's " Wedding March " actually begins (that the trumpet notes) not in C, but with that grand crash in B. Nevertheless, once more we agree rather than differ, " The time being the same, a noble or pathetic melody will remain so in whatever key, almost in whatever octave. The music is, of course, infinitely more important than the key," (as it is than the fiddlesticks) " difference in key is not of vital, but æsthetic importance." It may be compared, perhaps, like Rhyme, to style and manners ; it is something like what Style is to Thought (the *suaviter in modo fortiter in re*) Manners to Character.

[*] It would, however, be easy enough to write vigorous music in D minor. Scarlatti's Fugue in D minor is an instance that the musical world will not willingly let die. Beethoven's first movement in his " Tempest " Sonata Op. 31 is an essence of pathetic power.

It must be reflected, that when a key is termed brilliant, vigorous, expressive, &c., it is meant *by comparison*, especially with C ; not "in itself," for "the great globe itself" is but an island, the home of a family, and in it all beings and things are related. Nothing is, in, or by itself ; nothing would have meaning so, for the same reason—that of infinite consanguinity—the intentions and phrases of poetic perception which apprehends allusion and seizes relation in all things, not least in colour, fragrance, and tone, are not lightly to be nicknamed "fudge" (by the Philistine it might be related—it is a hazardous thing to call names). It is certain that many would likewise select their key according to their music ; though, undoubtedly, nobody ever dreamt of the contrary ; the brilliance, pathos, power, beauty, &c., belong infinitely more to the music than to the key. The key only enhances, delicately contributes—powerfully contributes, if we are to call the minor mode the minor key. The Coryphæus of modern orchestration gives an elaborate list of the keys according to their character. Alloyed as Berlioz's inspiration was by insanity, he was nevertheless a judge on this point. But half the positions are already conceded, by the opponents of the chromatic or picturesque terminology. They grant that "in the orchestra" one thinks of *Hamlet* with Hamlet left out ; keys are bright and vigorous according to the open strings (they might add, and the favourite keys of the wind and wood-wind) ; and they allow that the practical tuning of the household orchestra, the pianoforte, occasions slight (quite enough) difference in key character. They also grant that pitch affects character—*Ecco !* This is all that is demanded ; and Mendelssohn will eternally be allowed to have shown an exquisite instinct in having selected the key of E for his "Midsummer Night's Dream" Overture ; Beethoven an inspired one in selecting C minor for his Fifth and A for his Seventh Symphonies—those colossal revelations of the soul and heart of man.

Correspondence.

THE SACRED HARMONIC SOCIETY AND THE LIBRARY MONEY.

TO THE EDITOR OF THE "MUSICAL STANDARD."

SIR,—One is glad to see that the question as to the disposal of the money the members of the Sacred Harmonic Society have received for the sale of their splendid library, has now been formally brought before the public. It is indeed no private affair, but one of general interest, the donors of the books having practically given them for the use of all musical students, and not for an exclusive few to turn into money and retain for their own benefit. The writer of your article on the subject last week comments severely on the questionable morality of the proceeding, and asks the pertinent question, as to what is proposed to be done with the money so received. It should be known that this matter has already been considerably discussed among the members themselves, and it is believed that few of them wish to retain the money which has thus accidentally come into their possession. On the contrary, it is generally felt that it should be devoted to some scheme that will benefit the art, and aid in the cause of spreading a love of good music among the people. Hitherto, such talk has been desultory and purposeless, chiefly for the reason that no recognised leader has placed himself at the head of the movement to formulate a definite scheme, and also because the members have not been formally called together to consider the matter. Give them time and opportunity, and the public will find that they are not all greedy of gain and selfish. They are quite ready to recognise the responsibility that has been cast upon them, and doubtless will do their duty in accordance with the fair fame and healthy traditions of the old society. It has been suggested that a thousand pounds should be given to the new Royal College of Music, and a similar sum to the Royal Academy ; at both these institutions scholarships could thus be founded in remembrance of the Sacred Harmonic Society. If sufficient funds were returned, the claims of the Royal Society of Musicians, the College of Organists, and sundry other kindred associations would not be overlooked. Mr. D. Hill, the President of the Society, should lose no time in calling his members together, and I have little doubt but that a hearty response would be given to any scheme that a committee, appointed by the members, would put forth. The public should know that at the dissolution, there were certain liabilities that had to be provided for. As to the dissatisfaction which

was rife in some quarters respecting the large amount of £500 voted to one officer, the thing has been done, and it is useless to comment further on it. And the same may be said as to the threat of an application for a *mandamus* by some old members who had left the society before the division took place. They contend, perhaps with some justice, that as some of the books were purchased out of the profits of concerts at which they formerly sung, that therefore they should share in the division. Legally the rules are against them, but no doubt they have a sort of moral claim. The question as to what is to be done with the Benevolent Fund, amounting to upwards of £4,000, and who are going to take this, will probably prove a troublesome one to settle satisfactorily.

Yours truly,
S. M. EAGLETON.

Passing Events.

Herr Hans Richter has left London for Vienna.

The Musical Examinations in connection with the College of Preceptors were this Midsummer conducted as before by Dr. Westbrook and Mr. E. H. Turpin.

Students' concerts of an interesting character were on the list of Royal Academy of Music engagements, and the prize distribution takes place on July 28th.

"Silver Rock," a musical comedy, written by Sam. V. Steele, of Chicago, Ill., for Miss St. Quinten, was produced for the first time on any stage at the Pickwick Garden, St. Louis, U.S.A., June 11.

The College of Organists' examination took place on July 10, 11 and 12. A large number of candidates presented themselves. A list of passed candidates will be given next week.

The examinations at Trinity College have been numerously attended, and have occupied several days during the past week. A list of successful candidates will be duly presented to our readers.

The Prince of Wales caused to be conveyed to Mr. Julian Adams's his appreciation of the music provided by Mr. Adams' orchestra on the occasion of the recent Royal visit to Eastbourne.

The number of competitors entered for the National Eisteddfod at Cardiff number no less than 3,000 for musical prizes, &c., and some 500 for the literature and art prizes.

The new Westminster Town Hall will be opened on the 19th by the Duke of Buccleuch, K.G. The room will doubtless be of great use for musical purposes. London is greatly in need of convenient and sufficiently spacious concert-rooms.

A window to the memory of the late Mr. James Turle has just been placed in the musicians' corner, close to the grave of Croft, at Westminster Abbey. It is by Clayton and Bell, and is the gift of the late organist's son, Mr. J. R. Turle. A portrait of Mr. Turle is inserted.

Herr Schalkenbach is now giving the visitors to the Crystal Palace an opportunity of seeing to what a variety of purposes electricity may be applied. The agent he employs—his own invention—is designated' "The Orchestre Militaire, or Electro-Moteur," and by means of it almost all the most modern developments of electricity are applied to musical science and to much less euphonious uses. The invention, which about twenty years ago was shown in its original crude form to the Emperor Louis Napoleon, and appears to have been receiving improvements ever since, is a combination of the organ, the harmonium, and the piano, and various percussion instruments employed to produce military and other effects are so placed under the hands of the performer that he can easily use them without any interruption to his playing. Thus at intervals round the front of the theatre gallery different kinds of apparatus produced under the influence of keys or pedals the playing of musical bells, the blowing of a row of trumpets, the grating sound of a mitrailleuse in battle, the firing of pistols and guns, the rotation of an electric railway, the lunar lighting up of clouds, and other phenomena. It would be difficult to decide whether the military or the orchestral effects are most surprising.

Mason and Hamlin have sent Liszt a cabinet organ for the use of the music school at Weimar.

The Council of the Scottish Musical Society have postponed the opening of the new Academy of Music till next year. A sum of about £4,000 will be required to meet the liabilities of the first four years, and nearly two-thirds of this has been already subscribed.

Dr. Walmisley, M.A., of Cambridge, it is said upon the best authority, possessed an autograph MS. copy of Mendelssohn's three Preludes and Fugues. It so happened that the great composer of "Elijah" lost his own copy and re-wrote the whole work from memory. Wonderful to tell, the new copy corresponded almost note for note with the original as possessed by Dr. Walmisley, save that in the C minor Fugue the new copy had a bar less towards the end than had the first version.

The Tonic Sol-fa Reporter says that it has been decided to repeat the Stratford Musical Festival next spring. No details are fixed, but the advisability has been discussed of adding to the scheme prizes for choirs from elementary schools, and for adult elementary singing classes, the award in these classes to depend equally upon sight-singing and upon good performance. A special pianoforte class for married ladies has been proposed, as it is considered that they are handicapped in the race with girls whose whole time is devoted to study.

Miss Mabel Bourne's *matinée musicale* took place on Tuesday, 10th July, at the Glendover Mansions, South Kensington, before a crowded and fashionable audience. The well arranged programme was carried out to the letter. The clever young pianist played Bach's Prelude and Fugue à la Tarantelle in A minor, Chopin's Valse in F, Nocturne in E flat and Etude in C sharp minor, and from her own pen "Three Sketches" previously already favourably noticed. She was assisted in Rubinstein's Trio in B flat, Op. 52 for piano, violin and violoncello by Messrs. Polonaski and Whitehouse, the latter two artists playing each a solo by Vieuxtemps and Popper respectively. The trio, a very intricate composition, was a masterpiece of *ensemble* playing and secured the greatest attention and general applause. The vocalists were Miss Agnese Thorndike, Mdme. Polonaski, and Mr. Jos. Tapley, whose artistic merits are already well known. Miss Thorndike had a special success in a new song, "Springtide," by Mdme. Polonaski, a very poetical and well written composition, and Mr. Tapley sang with great effect Miss Mabel Bourne's previously well criticised song " My Lady Queen."

The thousandth anniversary of the foundation of the Parish Church at Chester-le-Street, near Durham, will be commemorated by a series of festival services on Wednesday, July 18th, and four following days. The anthems, to be performed by a choir of about fifty voices, will be Sir F. Ouseley's " It came even to pass," Dr. Boyce's "I have surely built thee an house," Mendelssohn's 95th Psalm, "Come, let us sing," and a new anthem, "O God, thou hast cast us out," which has been composed for the occasion by Mr. Arthur Prendergast (whose Te Deum obtained last year the prize offered by the London Church Choir Association), and will be sung on the first and fourth days of the Festival ; the words having been chosen by the Rector, the Rev. W. O. Blunt, Honorary Canon of Durham, with special reference to the history of this Church, which was founded A.D. 883, by the Monks of Lindisfarne, who, cast out of their establishment by the Danes, wandered about for some years and eventually re-settled themselves at Chester-le-Street, whither they brought the body of S. Cuthbert, and where the Cathedral of the North was established for 113 years. Another feature of the festival will be an organ recital, to be given by Dr. Armes, of Durham, at the service of Friday evening, the 21st inst.

The Querist.

QUERY.

ANALYSIS.—Is there any work specially dealing with analysis ? I want one to help trace the chords and progressions of classical works, as well as their form.—SLOW AND SURE.

Service Lists.

EIGHTH SUNDAY AFTER TRINITY.
JULY 15th.

London.

ST. PAUL'S CATHEDRAL.—Morn.: Service, Te Deum and Benedictus, Selby in A; Introit, Three in One, and One in Three; Holy Communion, Alwyn in C. Even.: Service, Magnificat and Nunc Dimittis, Selby in A; Anthems, Remember Lord, and, Lord before Thy footstool bending (Spohr).

WESTMINSTER ABBEY. — Morn.: Service, Smart in F; Even.: Service, Smart in F; Anthem, The wilderness (Wesley).

FOUNDLING CHAPEL. — Morn.: Service, Te Deum and Jubilate, Smart in F; Anthem, Hear my crying (Hummel). Aft.: Service, Chants and Hymns.

TEMPLE CHURCH.—Morn.: Service, Te Deum Laudamus, and Benedictus, Hopkins in F ; Apostles' Creed, Harmonised Monotone ; Anthem, Hear my prayer (Mendelssohn). Even.: Service, Magnificat and Nunc Dimittis, Stainer in A ; Apostles' Creed, Harmonised Monotone ; Anthem, Blessed be the God and Father (Wesley).

LINCOLN'S INN CHAPEL.—Morn.: Service, Boyce in A; Kyrie, Distin; Anthem, O give thanks unto the Lord (Greene). Even: Service, Arnold in A ; Anthem, His salvation is nigh them that fear Him (Bennett).

CHRIST CHURCH, CLAPHAM.—Morn.: Service, Te Deum, Plain-song ; Kyrie and Credo, Mozart in B flat ; Offertory Anthem, I will magnify Thee, O God (Goss); Sanctus, Benedictus, Agnus Dei, and Gloria in excelsis (Mozart). Even.: Service, Magnificat and Nunc Dimittis, Tours in F; Anthem, Lead kindly light (Stainer).

HOLY TRINITY, TULSE HILL. — Morn.: Service, Chant Service. Even.: Service, Magnificat and Nunc Dimittis, Stainer in A ; Anthem, The heavens declare (Boyce).

ST. BARNABAS, MARYLEBONE.—Morn.: Service, Te Deum and Benedictus, Hopkins in F ; Anthem, If we believe that Jesus died (Goss) ; Kyrie and Creed (Merbecke). Even. : Service, Magnificat and Nunc Dimittis, Hopkins in F; Anthem, Rejoice in the Lord (Purcell).

ST. MAGNUS, LONDON BRIDGE.—Morn.: Service, Opening Anthem, to the Lord our God (Calkin); Te Deum and Jubilate, Whitefield in F ; Kyrie, (Armes). Even.: Service, Magnificat and Nunc Dimittis, Whitfield in F ; Anthem, O taste and see (Goss).

ST. MARGARET PATTENS, ROOD LANE, FENCHURCH STREET.—Morn.: Service, Te Deum, Smart in F ; Benedictus, Dykes in F ; Communion Service : Offertory Anthem, Cast thy Burden (Mendelssohn) ; Kyrie, Credo, Sanctus, and Agnus Dei Mozart in B flat ; Gloria, Schubert in F. Even.: Service, Magnificat and Nunc Dimittis, Tuckermann in F ; Anthem, Praise the Lord, O my soul (Goss).

ST. MARY BOLTONS, WEST BROMPTON, S.W.—Morn.: Service, Hopkins in G ; Holy Communion, Kyrie, Credo, Offertory, Sanctus, and Gloria in excelsis, Stainer in E flat ; Benedictus and Agnus Dei, Going in F. Even.: Service, Magnificat and Nunc Dimittis, Hopkins in F; Anthem, Stand up and bless the Lord (Goss).

ST. PAUL'S, AVENUE ROAD, SOUTH HAMPSTEAD.—Morn.: Service, Te Deum, Sullivan in D ; Benedictus, Goss ; Kyrie, Tours in F ; Offertory, Barnby ; Credo, Sanctus, and Gloria in excelsis, Tours in F. Even.: Service, Magnificat and Nunc Dimittis, Arnold in A ; Anthem, God is a Spirit, " Woman of Samaria " (Bennett).

ST. PAUL'S, BOW COMMON, E.—Morn.: Service, Te Deum and Benedictus, Chants ; Holy Communion, Kyrie, Credo, Sanctus, and Gloria in excelsis, Smart in F ; Benedictus and Agnus Dei, Veulham in F ; Offertory (Calkin). Even.: Service, Magnificat and Nunc Dimittis, Parry in D ; Anthem, O where shall wisdom be found (Boyce).

ST. PETER'S (EATON SQUARE).—Morn.: Service, Te Deum, Sergison in A. Even.: Service, Tours in F ; Anthem, As pants the hart (Spohr).

ST. PETER'S, LEIGHAM COURT ROAD, STREATHAM, S.W.—Morn.: Service, Holy Eucharist, Purge me with hyssop (Chantwise) ; Introit, We wait (Chantwise) ; Mass, E. A. Sutton in F ; Gradual, Be Thou (Chantwise) ; Offertory, Charge them (Barnby) ; Communion and Post Communion. Even.: Service, Magnificat, Agutter in D ; Anthem, Lead, kindly light (Stainer).

ST. PETER'S, VERE STREET, W.—Even.: Service, Magnificat and Nunc Dimittis, Wood in F ; Anthem, The Lord is with thee (Osborne)

ST. JAMES'S PRIVATE EPISCOPAL CHAPEL, SOUTHWARK. —Morn.: Service, Introit, God my King (Bach); Communion Service, Nares and Garrett in F. Even.: Service, Stanford in B flat; Anthem, O Lamb of God (Mozart).

ST. MICHAEL'S, CORNHILL. — Morn.: Service, Te Deum and Jubilate, Boyce in A; Anthem, I will wash my hands in innocency (Hopkins); Kyrie, and Creed, Thorne in E flat. Even. Service, Magnificat and Nunc Dimittis, Thorne in E flat; Anthems, Thou wilt keep him in perfect peace (Wesley).

ST. SEPULCHRE'S, HOLBORN.—Morn: Service, Sullivan in D; Credo, Lott in F; Anthem, I will sing (Greene). Even.: Service, Gibbons in F; Anthem, Then shall the righteous (Mendelssohn).

Country.

ST. ASAPH CATHEDRAL.—Morn.: Service, Colbrne in C; Anthem, Thou wilt keep him (Calkin). Even.: Service, The Litany; Anthem, O come let us worship (Mendelssohn).

ASHBURNE CHURCH, DERBYSHIRE. — Morn.: Service, Field in D; Kyrie, Credo and Gloria, Garrett in D. Even.: Service, Field in D; Anthem, The Lord is exalted (West).

BEDDINGTON CHURCH, SURREY. — Morn.: Service, Te Deum, Boyce in A; Benedictus, Tuckermann in F; Communion Service, Smee in E. Even.: Service, Ebdon in C; Anthem, Praise the Lord, O my soul (Buny).

BIRMINGHAM (S. ALBAN THE MARTYR).—Morn.: Service, Te Deum and Benedictus, Dykes in F; Holy Communion; Kyrie, Credo, Sanctus, Gloria, Garrett in D; Benedictus and Agnus Dei, Redman in D. Evensong: Magnificat and Nunc Dimittis, Tours in F.

BIRMINGHAM (ST. CYPRIAN'S, HAY MILLS).—Morn.: Service, Field in D; Anthem, Sing, O heavens (Kent). Even.: Service, Cobb in D; Anthem, Plead Thou my cause (Mozart).

BIRMINGHAM (S. PHILIP'S CHURCH). — Morn.: Service, (Best); Chant Service; Holy Communion, Barnby in F; Evensong Service (Best); Chant Service; Anthem, O give thanks (Rea).

BRISTOL CATHEDRAL.—Morn.: Service, Attwood in D; Even.: Service, Attwood in D; Anthem, O God, when Thou appearest (Mozart).

CANTERBURY CATHEDRAL.—Morn.: Service, Calkin in B flat; Anthem, Behold now praise the Lord (Rogers); Communion, Calkin in B flat. Even.: Service, Calkin in B flat; Anthem, Behold the Lamb of God (Handel).

CARLISLE CATHEDRAL. — Morn.: Service, Selby in A; Introit, Blessed is the man (Stainer); Kyrie, Selby in A; Nicene Creed, Harmonised Monotone. Even.: Service, Selby in A; Anthem, O give thanks (Purcell).

DUBLIN, ST. PATRICK'S (NATIONAL) CATHEDRAL.—Morn.: Service, Te Deum and Jubilate, Stanford in B flat; Holy Communion, Kyrie, Creed, and Sanctus, Stanford in B flat; Anthem, Hear my prayer (Mendelssohn). Even.: Service, Magnificat and Nunc Dimittis, Stanford in B flat; Anthems, Above him stood the Seraphim (Mendelssohn), and, I have surely built Thee an house (Boyce).

ELY CATHEDRAL. — Morn.: Service, Walmisley in F; Kyrie and Credo, Walmisley in F; Gloria, Cambridge in C; Anthem, Teach me, O Lord (Atwood). Even.: Service, Attwood in F; Anthem, Wherewithal (Elvey).

HARROGATE (ST. PETER'S CHURCH). — Morn.: Service, Te Deum, (Helmore); Benedictus, Chants; Anthem, The Lord is my strength (Monk); Kyrie and Credo, Tours in F. Even.: Service, Magnificat and Nunc Dimittis, Turle in D; Anthem, The Lord shall preserve, and, Blessed is the man "Mount Moriah" (Bridge).

LICHFIELD CATHEDRAL. — Morn.: Service, Boyce in C; Anthem, Rejoice in the Lord (Purcell). Even.: Service, Walmisley in D minor; Anthem, O Where shall wisdom (Boyce).

LLANDAFF CATHEDRAL.—Morn.: Service, Te Deum and Benedictus, Prout in F; Introit, Ponder my words (Gadsby); Holy Communion, Prout in F. Even.: Service, The Litany; Anthem, Blessed is the man (Goss).

LIVERPOOL CATHEDRAL.—Aft.: Service, Magnificat and Nunc Dimittis, Burstall in D; Anthem, Ascribe unto the Lord (Travers).

MANCHESTER CATHEDRAL. — Morn.: Service, King in F; Kyrie, Creed, Sanctus and Gloria, Ross in G; Anthem, Come unto me (Smith). Aft.: Service, King in F; Anthem, Send out Thy light (Gounod).

MANCHESTER (ST. BENEDICT'S). — Morn.: Service, Kyrie; Credo, and Gloria in excelsis, Stainer in A; Sanctus, Benedictus, and Agnus Dei, Guilmant in E flat. Even.: Service, Magnificat and Nunc Dimittis, Bunnett in F.

MANCHESTER (ST. JOHN BAPTIST, HULME).—Morn.: Service, Kyrie, Credo, Sanctus and Gloria in excelsis, Steggall in G; Benedictus and Agnus Dei, Eyre in E flat. Even.: Service, Magnificat and Nunc Dimittis, (Gregorian).

MUSSELBURGH (LORETTO SCHOOL).—Morn.: Service, Introit, Incline Thine ear (Himmell); Communion Service, Stainer in E flat; Anthem, Plead Thou my cause (Mozart). Even.: Service, Anthem, The Heavens are telling "Creation" (Haydn).

ROCHESTER CATHEDRAL.—Morn.: Service, Cooke in G; Chant and Jubilate in C; Anthem, O Lord, my God. Even.: Service, Cooke in G; Anthem, Praise the Lord (Hayes).

SHEFFIELD PARISH CHURCH. — Morn.: Service, Kyrie, Trimnell in F; Even.: Service, Magnificat and Nunc Dimittis, Chants; Anthem, They that go down to the Sea (Attwood).

SHERBORNE ABBEY.—Morn.: Service, Te Deum, Chants; Kyrie, Mendelssohn in E flat; Offertories (Barnby). Even.: Service, Anthem, Blessed be Thou (Kent).

SOUTHAMPTON (ST. MARY'S CHURCH).—Morn.: Services Te Deum and Benedictus, Woodward in D; Holy Communion; Introit, Jesus said (Stainer); Service, Stainer in E flat; Offertory, Not every one, and, While we have time (Stainer); Benedictus and Agnus Dei, Agutter in B flat; Paternoster, (Hoyte). Even.: Service, Magnificat and Nunc Dimittis, Spark in D; Apostles' Creed, Harmonized Monotone; Anthem, The radiant morn hath passed away (Woodward).

SOUTHWELL MINSTER, NOTTS.—Morn.: Service, Gates in F; Kyrie, Mendelssohn in D; Creed, Goss in D; Sanctus and Gloria, Elvey in F. Even.: Service, Arnold in F; Anthem, Let the righteous be glad (Arnold).

WELLS CATHEDRAL. — Morn.: Service, Garrett in D; Introit, Blessed is the man (Stainer). Even.: Service, Garrett in D; Anthem, Praise the Lord (Croft).

WORCESTER CATHEDRAL.—Morn.: Service, Hatton in E; Kyrie, Creed and Sanctus, Wesley in E; Anthem, All glory to the Lamb (Spohr). Even.: Service, Hatton in E; Anthem, Why rage fiercely the heathen (Mendelssohn).

APPOINTMENT.

Mr. GEORGE FLETCHER (pupil of Mr. Arthur Marriott, Organist of Southwell Minster), has been appointed Organist of All Saints Church, Stamford.

ERRATUM.—Line two, page six, read Mr. Sedley Taylor.

*** *Post-cards must be sent to the Editor,* 6, *Argyle Square, W.C., by Wednesday. Lists are frequently omitted in consequence of not being received in time.*

NEWSPAPERS sent should have *distinct marks* opposite to the matter to which attention is required.

NOTICE.—*All communications intended for the Editor are to be sent to his private address. Business communications to be addressed to* 185, *Fleet Street, E.C.*

THE MUSICAL STANDARD

A NEWSPAPER FOR MUSICIANS PROFESSIONAL AND AMATEUR

No. 991. VOL. XXV. FOURTH SERIES.   SATURDAY, JULY 28, 1883.   WEEKLY: PRICE 3D.

"COUNTERPOINT."

By H. J. STARK, MUS.BAC.

A Paper read before the College of Organists, on May 1st, 1883.

(Continued from page 28.)

Having ventured to challenge the expediency of many contrapuntal rules, I must expect to be called upon for some tangible proof of their inaccuracy. This can be easily supplied, but in order to make my position perfectly clear I must ask your indulgence whilst I set before you a few necessarily dry, but I hope not uninteresting, technical details.

Cherubini's rules for the construction of Counterpoint in two parts may here be examined with advantage.

Rule I. provides that the commencement and close must be in perfect concord. Whilst admitting the more satisfactory effect of a termination upon the tonic, there is absolutely no justification for disallowing a commencement upon the *third* of the key-note chord. Instances of good and satisfactory melodies beginning in this way are so common that it is unnecessary to quote an illustration.

Rule II. :—" The parts should progress always by concords." Now, bearing in mind that in Counterpoint the term " concord " merely includes the thirds and sixths—major and minor—together with the octave and perfect fifth, we are reduced by this rule to the wearisome reiteration of *four* intervals, the whole of the remainder being put aside as useless ! This rule strikes at the root of all that is good and effective in two-part writing, and it is a simple fact that the great composers, from Bach downwards, have systematically disregarded it.

Rule III., which admits the occasional crossing of the parts, is, of course, unobjectionable.

Rule IV. states the well-known prohibition against consecutive fifths and octaves. There can be little doubt that octaves should be disallowed on the ground of weakness of effect, the interval being, as Cherubini says, " well nigh void of harmony."

In moving Counterpoint, however, it will be found that they can be avoided by the use of an intermediate note.

The consecutives between the alto and bass of the example, I here quote from Bach, would be condemned by every text-book, but probably I shall not stand altogether alone in preferring the authority of Bach to all others. It may be urged that the quotation is in four parts, whilst the rule refers only to two-part writing, but the rules of four-part Counterpoint most clearly ! prohibit progressions of octaves with only one intervening note, so that the force of the illustration is in no way lessened.

Consecutive fifths require more attention. That they are frequently used with good effect is an undeniable fact, so that their absolute prohibition cannot reasonably be maintained. Theoretical writers have apparently failed to discriminate between good and bad fifths, and have taken refuge in a rule entirely forbidding their employment. In spite of all that has been written on the subject, no perfectly satisfactory explanation of the harsh effect of bad consecutive fifths has yet been given. Cherubini argues that fifths are bad " because the upper part progresses in one key at the same time that the lower part progresses in another. For example, if in the key of C an upper part be added, which gives a perfect fifth in each bar, it follows that one part would be in C while the other would be in G. It is from this concurrence of two keys that the discordance arises."

This explanation cannot be accepted as satisfactory,

for the rule forbids the employment of *any two* successive fifths, and not merely that of scale passages in fifths. It is only when we arrive at the penultimate bar of Cherubini's example that we have an indication of the scale of G, all the other notes belonging strictly to the scale of C.

For further information we must consult the works of classical composers.

The above examples, I have shown to you, may be held to prove that consecutive fifths may be used (i.) for the purpose of satisfactorily resolving a discord (ii.) when one of the notes employed is a " passing" note. One Example is particularly interesting, as it shows the direct resolution of the so-called " German sixth " to the dominant chord, a progression which must inevitably result in consecutive fifths. Progressions of fifths are invariably bad between chords having little or no harmonic relationship to each other, and this would seem to indicate that it is not after all the mere *interval* which is in fault, but rather that the harsh effect is due to the absence of any proper or agreeable connection between the *chords* employed. In any case we shall act wisely by refraining from an indiscriminate condemnation of progressions involving consecutives merely because a rule exists which forbids them. I conclude this portion of my paper by referring you to an example of four-part florid Counterpoint, by Sir John Goss, which appears on page 67 of Dr. Bridge's treatise on Counterpoint. In almost every part we find violations of the rule forbidding consecutives, yet it is good Counterpoint, and will probably outlive the law which it transgresses.

Cherubini's fifth rule forbids the employment of " hidden " fifths and octaves. This rule is so persistently disregarded in actual composition that I refrain from giving examples—the student will find ample illustration of its uselessness (as it now exists) without further assistance.

Rule VI. forbids the employment of any intervals of melody except the following :—Major and minor 2nds and 3rds, perfect 4ths, 5ths, and 8ths, and minor 6ths. In more recent works we find the major 6th and imperfect 5th are also allowed, but even with these the list of available intervals of melody is very inadequate. The characteristic intervals of the minor key, the augmented 2nd and its inversion, the diminished 7th, are entirely overlooked, with the result that exercises ostensibly in the minor key are in reality in the so-called " relative " major, except at the commencement and conclusion. The proper treatment of the minor key is fully dealt with in Professor Macfarren's work, but for an illustration of allowable intervals of melody I refer you again to Example 2.

This sixth rule also forbids the employment of more than three 3rds or 6ths (harmonically) in succession. Professor Macfarren (sec. 80) adopts this view, but in the very first example which he gives we find this progression :—

Rule VII. deals with the false relation of the octave, and also that of the tritone. With regard to the former, so many exceptions must be allowed that anything like a strict observance of the rule seems well-nigh impossible. An instance of the use of this false relation as an interval of melody will be found in Example 2, but similar passages exist in abundance in nearly all classical compositions. The false relation of the tritone, and its treatment, has ever been a source of trouble to the student of Counterpoint. It is unquestionably bad under certain conditions :—

Other tritones, usually condemned as bad, will be found perfectly harmless :—

At *a* and *b* the bad effect entirely disappears when the harmony is completed as follows :—

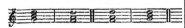

Whilst that at *c* is good even in two parts if treated as follows :—

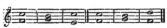

Cherubini's assertion, that "all successions of chords of which one contains an F and the other a B, and *vice versa*, indisputably bring about the false relation of the tritone," is, of course, literally accurate, but to condemn all such progressions as bad is far too sweeping. In the very first example of Cherubini, which he expressly tells us is "in conformity with the rules of strict Counterpoint," we find the following :—

Instances of the *melodic* use of the tritone are so abundant that it is unnecessary to quote them.

(*To be continued.*)

PIANOS AND NOVELS.—Says an American paper : The modern novel, particularly the "novel of society," is full of piano playing. No parlour is complete without the piano, and it assists materially in love-making scenes. A travesty of one of Disraeli's novels, "Coningsby," burlesques the gorgeousness with which Beaconsfield fits up all his interiors by making a young lady play to her lover on a piano cased in ivory, with mother-of-pearl keys and pedals of pure gold. And all the surroundings are similarly sumptuous, and so, of course, the youth declares his intentions at once. Columns might be filled with excerpts from popular novels to show how largely the piano is made a factor in bringing about the right understanding between young couples. But this only shows that it is so in the actual life which the stories attempt to pourtray. But while the piano has been the means of drawing many a young man into a declaration, the elder Weller conceived that it might be the instrument of getting old Pickwick out of the difficulties resulting from the breach of promise suit of Mrs. Bardell. The immediate difficulty to be got out of was the Fleet Prison, which could be done, as Mr. Weller conceived, if Mr. Pickwick was willing, by a "plany-forty as von't play, and vith no vorks in it ; but as vill hold him easy, vith his hat and shoes on, and breathe through the legs, vich is holler." Thus did Mr. Weller "dewise" with a cabinet-maker. It was Mehamet who believed that piano playing might be taught by proxy, but when the late Felicien David was in Cairo, and was engaged by his highness to give music lessons to the ladies of the harem, he found five fat negro eunuchs, the chief of whom told him to begin his lessons at once to them, and they in turn would teach them to the ladies. We need no more than note the important part which the piano now literally plays on the stage. The modern melodramas and the best comedies are much assisted by this instrument. The piano is nowhere so truly pathetic as it is in the last scene where consumptive Camille sits down to it for the last time ; it is very effective in "Ours," just before the to-be heroes go to the Crimea. Between these two extremes, through the long list of the plays of our day, the piano is as common as it is in what Thalberg calls "the cultivated classes of society."

ROYAL ITALIAN OPERA.

The short season of 1883 ended last Saturday night (July 21st.), with "Il Barbiere di Siviglia," and Mdme. Patti as the Rosina. The only novelty this year has been "La Gioconda" of Signor Ponchielli, repeated several times with uniform success. The work has already been fully discussed in these columns, and no more remains to be said. Auber's charming opera "Le Domino Noir" had been promised, but was not produced. Why Mozart's early and very pretty opera "Il Seraglio" (revived in 1882) has not been repeated this season, deponent cannot say, but "more's the pity." A tribute has been paid to Wagner by the revival—for one night only—of "The Flying Dutchman." "Italicè," "Il Voscello Fantasma," and "Lohengrin" were performed twice or three times. The Italian company, however, are not "at home" with Richard Wagner's texts and never will be. Rossini's opera "La Gazza Ladra," full of sparkling tunes that are now utterly worn out and used up, was twice performed for the pleasure of Mdme. Patti. Böito's "Mefistofele" and Bizet's "Carmen" were notable operas, and worthily represent what is called the "modern element." The mainstays of the Royal Italian Opera have been Mdme. Patti, Mdme. Albani, and M. Gailhard. Mdme. Durand in "La Gioconda" excelled, notwithstanding an over-worn voice. The new tenor, Signor Marconi, cannot be reckoned a great gain to the establishment. The chorus, as a rule, have sung much more precisely this season, except in the German operas. It is evident that the old "star" system of the Italian Opera is at last to collapse, and the present artificial monopoly cannot be thought conducive to the interests of high art. The following caustic remarks of the acute and discerning critic who writes for the *Times*, an orthodox disciple of Wagner, but yet of cosmopolitan taste, deserves to be read with attention. Says *The Times* of Monday :—

"To tell the truth, the system to which the original rise and subsequent decline of this theatre (the Royal Italian Opera) have been due has not in any perceptible degree been modified. *Stars* continue to be the main centres of attraction. They monopolise the attention of the public, and to their share a vast proportion of the available resources must, of necessity, be allotted. Knowing that they are indispensable, they make their terms accordingly, and those terms have, in the course of time, grown to be exorbitant, and promise to be still more ruinous since the competition of the American market has begun to assume gigantic proportions. It does not require the gift of prophecy to predict that such a system cannot last much longer ;* that, indeed it will collapse on the day when Mdme Patti retires from the stage or loses her voice—*for the latter does not necessarily imply the former.* That famous *prima donna* has for years been the mainstay of an establishment which without her could scarcely be imagined. Even if an equally great vocalist and much greater actress were to arise, it may be well doubted whether she would rouse and retain public favour to a similar degree and for a similar period. The absolute reign of the *singer* on the operatic stage is a thing of the past, as far at least as the *intelligent* portion of the musical public is concerned. We shall still require great artists, much *greater and more universally gifted* artists, indeed, than in times gone by, but they will no longer be allowed to make *individual display* their sole aim and purpose. The *works* to be interpreted will, in fine, be regarded at least as much as the *interpreters.* With this fact plainly discernible to those who can read the signs of the times, even the managers of the Royal Italian Opera *in England* will have to reckon. Fortunately, there is reason to hope that Italian art will not fail to supply the stage with operas well worthy of the most careful study that can be bestowed upon them. Italy can boast in Signor Böito of one of the most interesting composers of modern times, and in Signor Faccio of a conductor second to Herr Richter alone. Perhaps at some future time. the 'land of song' will once again produce singers worthy of the traditions of Farinelli and Grisi, and of Mario."

The italics are marked by the writer.   A. M.

---

* The committee of the forthcoming Leeds Festival, it is known, have declined the services of Mdme. Albani on account of the extravagant sum demanded.—ED., *M.S.*

MR. MORI'S NEW OPERETTA.

Mr. N. Mori's operetta, "The Shipwright's Love," was repeated at his residence on the 18th inst., and confirms my previous opinion of its merits. It is full of melodies, which would not fail to become popular. Mr. Henry Quirke, who read the dialogue, also recited Longfellow's "King Robert of Sicily," in a most impressive and admirable manner, and cannot fail to make his mark. . . . . FERDINAND PRAEGER.

MR. VON ZASTROW'S DRAWING ROOM RECITAL.

At the concert held at the Glendower Mansions, South Kensington, on Thursday, July 19th, Miss Mabel Bonne played "Le Carnaval" of Schumann and several pieces by Chopin and J. F. Barnett. On a previous occasion Miss Ellen Norton, a Gold Medallist of the London Academy of Music, played some classical texts, inclusive of Chopin, with great taste. Mr. De Wolfe, often referred to in eulogistic terms, sang a new song of Mr. Cowen, and Fesca's "Spring Song." Miss Lucy Francis, a youthful authoress of classical proclivities, recited Tennyson's "Revenge" and the trial scene from Shakespeare's "Henry VIII." This recital was thought to be so excellent a performance that it is exceptionally reported in these columns. Mdme. Polonaski sang several German and English songs with her usual taste and finish.

VARIOUS CONCERTS.

Mrs. Fairfax Ball, the eminent professor of elocution, held a reception at her house in Holland Road, Kensington, on Friday evening, July 20th. Mr. Carl Hause and Mdlle. Gayrard-Pacini played pieces on the pianoforte—below concert-pitch, by the way—with great brilliancy. Mr. J. A. Browell executed two violoncello solos with his wonted ability. Miss Zimeri and M. F. Quatremayne sang several times in admirable style. The trio was protracted to a late hour. The fair hostess gave two splendid recitations—one of these turned upon the false worship of earthly kings, the second was a notable extract from Thackeray's "Vanity Fair."

Signor Villa held a matinée at the Collard Rooms, Grosvenor Street, on July 18th, in conjunction with Mr. Churchill Sibley. He sang Gounod's Canzone in E, "Flo masso nuove corde," "The Bells of St. Paul's," and Salamen's Arab song "Zahra" which was accompanied by the composer and encored by acclamation. Mdme. Rosell excelled in Mr. C. Sibley's ballad "With thee," Miss Helen Meikson, in spite of a cold, sang Mr. W. Carter's air "Loved for ever," with great taste. Miss L. Rivers and Miss Berta Francis also appeared with honour. Signor Tito Mattei played two pieces from his own pen, and M. Poznianski a Fantasia of Vieuxtemps on "Il Lombardi" of Verdi. The concert proved a complete success.

A grand concert was held on Saturday afternoon, July 21st, at the Prince's Hall, in aid of the sufferers from the late "Dreadful disasters at Sunderland and on the river Clyde. The projector, Mrs. Florence Graet, an amateur of great taste and a generous patroness of art and artists, sang Robandi's air "Alla stella confidente" in exquisite style; she also sustained the second parts of Mozart's duet "Sull' aria" (with Miss Samuell), and the duet from "Mefistofele" "La luna immobile." Lady Colin Campbell was unable to sing as announced. Mr. Bernand Lane and Mr. J. Robertson won much applause for their songs. Miss Clara Samuell sang Rossini's "Non più mesta" (from "La Cenerentola") in the key of E flat instead of E major—the range is from low G to high B, and Alloni, years ago, made a great effect by dropping a double octave. Signor Monari Rocca won a bis for a rollicking French song of Herr Schubert, and Mdlle. G. Ameris sang the "Santo Spirito" of Marius. Herr Schuberth played part of Goltermann's second concerto for violoncello, and the Earl of Mar an "Elegy" for violin by Del Nero. Mr. Kuhe played two pieces, his own "Etude du Concert" and a Notturne of Chopin. Mrs. Florence Grant allowed the children of the St. Marylebone Charity Schools to attend the concert, and provided a basketful of buns for their refreshment.

"The Three Beggars" is the title of a new comic opera by V. Dunn and E. Belleville, to be given as a "costume piece" at the Royal Academy of Music to-night.

BERMONDSEY.

On Monday evening, the 23rd inst., the Bermondsey branch of the "People's Entertainment Society," Metropolitan Choral Union, gave its first soirée in St. Mary Magdalene Schools. Mr. W. H. Leslie is the enterprising conductor of this scheme, and he deserves great congratulation in bringing a body of singers together in such a neighbourhood to perform part-singing so very satisfactorily. Mr. Leslie during the evening contributed two violin solos, which were warmly received, as they well deserved to be. Mr. John Jefferys gave two pianoforte solos, which were equally welcomed; but the great attraction was the artistic and sympathetic singing of Viscountess Folkestone. She received quite an ovation, everyone being equally delighted with her simple yet careful rendering of the four songs she so kindly gave. Lady Folkestone also took part in Leslie's popular trio, "Memory," with Messrs. Geo. F. Grover and R. J. Pitt. The audience were most enthusiastic, and a recall was speedily demanded and given. Mr. Arthur Reynolds, the well-known baritone, sang two songs in his usual artistic style, while Miss Rosa Kissel's singing was very much appreciated. Messrs. J. Jefferys, Geo. F. Grover, and R. J. Pitt acted as accompanists.

LEEDS MUSICAL FESTIVAL.

On Friday and Saturday of the last week, Sir Arthur Sullivan, who has been appointed conductor of the above festival, visited Leeds, and attended two full chorus rehearsals. There were 395 members of the chorus present, out of a total of 314. Sir Arthur was received with prolonged applause, the whole chorus rising and cheering for some time. He was accompanied by the Mayor (Councillor Woodhouse), Mr. Thomas Marshall (chairman of the Executive), and Mr. Fred. R. Spark (hon. sec.). The Mayor having introduced the conductor to the chorus, Sir Arthur Sullivan spoke a few words. He remarked that the echoes of the last festival seemed scarcely to have died away, when they were called upon once more to make preparations for the next. Those echoes were still ringing in his ears, bearing with them memories of the happiest associations of his life. He was reminded that there were displayed on that occasion work, discipline, enthusiasm, and—he could hardly call it talent, he could only call it with reference to the choral singing genius, which marked one of the proudest times of his musical history. This was scarcely the time for speechmaking, but he could not begin his work without thanking them sincerely and heartily for the extraordinarily kind way in which they had received him. He still bore in mind their kindness on the last occasion, and he could not help thinking this new example of it was not only personal to him, but an expression of confidence that he would do his best to lead them to victory. To say that no efforts would be wanting on his part was unnecessary, because any one placed in that proud position must, of course, do his best. He only hoped to find the same attention, discipline, and extraordinary power and brilliance of work, coupled with the same remarkable results, if not greater, than were seen at the last festival. He congratulated them on again having the powerful and experienced aid of Mr. James Broughton, their chorusmaster. There was a good deal of work in the world for which those who did it did not always get the just kind glory and reputation. They who were working within knew exactly the worth of Mr. Broughton's work, and that without his patient care and very great intelligence it would be impossible, even with that splendid material in the way of chorus, to obtain the results they did. These remarks were frequently cheered. The rehearsal was then proceeded with. The choruses in Joachim Raff's oratorio, "The World's End; Judgment; and the New World," were taken, under the direction of Mr. Broughton; and afterwards, with Sir Arthur conducting, the important chorus with which Bach's cantata, "Thou Guide of Israel," commences, and the lovely chorale with which it concludes, were gone through. Beethoven's Grand Mass in D was taken on Saturday afternoon, the enormous difficulties of which seemed to be well overcome by the Yorkshire choralists.

Covent Garden Theatre is again given over to the carpenters, Mr. A. Gwyllim Crowe having determined to give a promenade concert season there, commencing early next month.

LIVERPOOL.

(From our own Correspondent.)

JULY 24th.

The position of the Liverpool Philharmonic Society (now so miscalled) is in the same chaotic state as described in the two last numbers of the *Musical Standard*. The only difference, if any, is that the estrangement between the "amateur members of the orchestra" and the newly elected committee, is complete. It appears from a long letter which has been addressed to the local press, by the "Hon. Secretary, Philharmonic Chorus," that the chorus were in existence as the Philharmonic Society before the Philharmonic Hall was built, and before any arrangement was entered into with them by the proprietors.

The letter goes on to state that :—"This is clearly evidenced by the following extracts from the rules governing the 'amateur members of the orchestra.'" The preamble reads as follows :—

"The following rules for the regulation of the amateur members of the orchestra have been adopted by the committee, to take effect from the 26th of May, 1856, and all the gentlemen who are now members of the orchestra, or who may hereafter join, will be furnished with a copy hereof :—

RULE I.

" * * * Subscribing members shall pay to the funds of the general society an entrance fee of 10s. 6d., and two-fifths of the subscription paid by proprietors and annual subscribers to the extent of a double subscription; a corresponding deduction to be made in the price of tickets for all extra concerts to be given by the society.

RULE XX.

"The general committee shall have power, either to frame new laws or alter any of those existing. But previous notice of any proposed alteration or addition shall be posted on the notice board on two consecutive rehearsal nights, and the next succeeding rehearsal night the practical members may hold a meeting and determine by vote whether any suggestions or objections respecting them shall be made on their part to the general committee. Any proposed alteration or addition which is objected to by a majority of the practical members shall be withdrawn.

"It is therefore clear that, whatever the legal rights of the question may be, the intention of the arrangement at the time that the same was entered into with the members of the Philharmonic Society was that they should exist as the chorus of the Society under the rules which were then adopted, and that these rules should not be abolished or amended without the mutual consent of the parties affected thereby.

"Notwithstanding this, however, the general committee have decided to do away with these rules in order that they may establish the society on entirely new lines and principles.

"Matters having reached this stage, the representatives of the chorus on the general committee took the first opportunity of pointing out the difficulty which existed in the way of any amendment or abolition of the rules upon which the society has been established, in view of the stipulation in Rule XX. above quoted; that this cannot be done without the assent of a majority of the practical members; and the committee, in order to get over this difficulty, accordingly passed the following resolution :—'That any arrangement which may have been entered into between the Liverpool Philharmonic Society and the vocal members of the orchestra be rescinded.' The representatives of the chorus, on the general committee, appreciating the position of affairs in consequence of the passing of the above resolution, and in view of the fact that the general committee had themselves declined to convene a meeting of the chorus, then decided that the general body of the practical members should be acquainted with the facts, and accordingly summoned a meeting to consider what action should be taken."

The result of the meeting here referred to I have already given in a former letter.

A local contemporary, in a leading article upon the affair, sums up as follows :—

"Supposing, however, the action of the committee to be good, the society is at this moment in the happy position of a body of proprietors of a concert-room. Having neither band nor chorus, they have no longer any pretensions to the standing of the leading musical society in Liverpool. They ought, therefore, to abdicate the high-sounding title they have hitherto held, and to adopt the more modest designation of the Hope Street Music Hall Company (Limited). One hoped for a decided improvement upon the unsatisfactory state of things that existed prior to the recent alterations in the *personnel* of the committee, and the only explanation to account for the conduct of the new committee, is that their success in ousting their predecessors has had the effect of slightly turning their heads. If so, their case is but another illustration of the old proverb, *Quem deus vult perdere, prius dementat.*"

It is rumoured that the chorus intend starting a fresh society under the title of the present society, which they claim to be theirs.

This would be hazardous, but plucky certainly; and it is questionable whether it would pay its way, but still there are plenty of people who just now would, assuredly support warmly such a scheme. On the other hand, if the funds were forthcoming for the establishment of a new society, where would the concerts be given? There is no other concert hall suitable for the carrying out the intended programme, except the Philharmonic itself.

It is an extraordinary affair altogether, and a disgrace to the city of Liverpool.

Mr. Hallé's salary as conductor to the new *régime* is £600! Sir Julius Benedict got £300. It is expected to make the difference up by the doing away with the privileges hitherto accorded to the late chorus. J. J. M.

SOUTH NORWOOD.

The study of music in ladies' colleges has ceased to be of the old routine character, when mere "piece-work" was the rule of the master, taught by rote. Mr. Robert Beringer, brother of Mr. Oscar Beringer, whose annual classical pianoforte recitals in London are renowned, has rendered good service as a professor at South Norwood, where on Tuesday evening, in the South Norwood Hall, he held a concert, mainly supported, as regards the performance, by the young lady pupils of the Chagford College in that suburb, directed by the Misses Green. Mr. R. Beringer himself conducted the overture to "Der Freischütz," arranged as a quartet for two pianofortes, and he also played with Miss Mabel Green, Lindberg's duet in "Don Juan." Weber's overture was most effectively rendered by Misses Stotter, Ross, and Coles, their master keeping them well "up to time" and effectively emphasising the text. Miss Mabel Green excelled in Chopin's Berceuse, Op. 57, and Miss Bastard, a very young lady, achieved a fair success in Mr. Alfred Cellier's "Danse Pompeuse." Misses M. and A. Asta played some of Brahms's "Hungarian Dances" with great spirit and aplomb. A pianoforte trio (a march of Goblaerts) found apt exponents in Misses Letts, E., Ross and G. Stainer, and M. Bartholomew's piano sextet, "Les Six Amies" was executed in dashing style by Misses Parsons, Foster, Hatcher, Kershaw, M. Ross, and L. Woodhead; Mdlle. Clauda Nicolle and Miss Williams sang airs of Gounod and Goglielmo. Miss Westacott, to be commended for her reading of Schumann's lied "Ein Traum," should be advised to avoid the illegitimate practice—not even allowable as a musical licence—of pronouncing "ich" as if it were spelt "isch"—a too common fault. Mr. W. P. Mills, an amateur, from London, sang a tenor song, "O maiden mine," which was encored, and played a flute solo of Reichert with fine taste. A recitation of S. H. Cowan's "Becalmed," was *de trop*, and the reporter avoided it. In Part II., Franz Abt's pretty cantata for ladies' voices "Rübezahl," Op. 593, was performed, the English words are from the pen of Mr. W. Grist of the Crystal Palace. Miss Aste sustained the soprano solos; the other vocalists were Misses Williams, Nicolle, and Howarth. Miss Howarth was reader (of the explanatory text), and Mrs. Worthington, a highly accomplished amateur pianist, accompanied the voices. Mr. R. Beringer conducted the cantata. It includes eight numbers, solos and choruses in C minor and major, A, D minor, G and E major. The concert lasted over two hours. Mr. Beringer may well be proud of his pupils.

A new *opéra bouffe*, "Virginia and Paul," by Messrs. Stephens and Solomon was brought out at the Gaiety Theatre on Monday week, not altogether successfully. The libretto is a satire on one of the follies of the day, and to this Mr. Solomon has written music which if not original is in parts decidedly pretty. Although the adverse verdict of the audience was not wholly undeserved, many much worse pieces have been more favourably received.

Foreign Musical Intelligence.

A Philharmonic Society has been formed in Seville.

Sarasate has been named honorary professor of the National Music School, Madrid.

Boïto's "Mefistofele" is to be given at the Teatro Colon, Buenos Ayres.

Yet another biography of Franz Liszt is being written, this time by Augusto Trinchieri.

Donizetti's "Linda di Chamounix" was found attractive lately at the Teatro del Principe Alfonso, Madrid.

Sarasate, the eminent Spanish violinist, has returned to Pampeluna. A large crowd welcomed him at the railway station, and he was afterwards serenaded.

The Réunion Chorale of Schaarbeck carried off the first prize at the recent Orpheonic competition held at Amsterdam.

M. Kowalski has written a new opera, "Vercingétorix," which the authorities at the Château d'Eau Theatre, Paris, have accepted.

At Meszkirch, a monument has been erected to the memory of Konradin Kreutzer. Like Rembrandt, he was the son of a miller, and was born in his father's mill near Meszkirch in 1780.

At Würzburg, a committee has been formed to raise funds throughout Germany to defray the expenses of a monument which is to be erected to the Minnesinger Walther von der Vogelweide.

The editor of *Die Neue Zeitschrift für Musik*, Professor Dr. Hermann Zopff, died at Glogau at the age of fifty-seven. He was an excellent musician, and a most conscientious critic.

M. Peter Benoit's "Lucifer" is to be produced at La Scala, Milan, in October next. A committee has been formed with a view to presenting the Duke of Campo Felice with the composer's bust in bronze as a mark of gratitude for the interest he has always taken in all Belgian artists, and in Benoit particularly.

An interesting little work by Signor Pasolini Zanelli, called "G. Sarti, musicista del secolo XVIII," has just been published. Sarti was one of the most remarkable dramatic composers of the eighteenth century, and to his personal renown added that of being the master of Cherubini, who was warmly attached to him.

It is stated that the first of this year's performances of Wagner's last work, "Parsifal," which took place at Bayreuth, created comparatively small interest, about 900 persons only attending. Many foreign dilettanti were present, as were press representatives from most of the European cities. The audience, which included Siegfried Wagner, made little demonstration, and, indeed, the atmosphere of the theatre could not have been more sombre had "Parsifal" been "In Memoriam." Many visitors made a pilgrimage to Wagner's grave after hearing his work.

CHURCH SUNDAY-SCHOOLS' CHOIR.—The fifth annual festival of this choir was held at the Crystal Palace on July 21st. About 100 schools within the metropolitan area belong to the organization, which is connected with the Church of England Sunday-School Institute. Its chief object is to spread a knowledge of vocal music—especially sacred music; but its secondary object is to promote unity and good-feeling among Sunday-School workers by means of innocent and wholesome recreation. Nearly 20,000 persons were present at the festival. The chief event of the day was a concert by 5,000 children, who quite filled the Handel orchestra, and presented an attractive and almost impressive spectacle. With Mr. W. Stokoe as conductor, and Mr. R. Stokoe, as organist, the concert was a success; the children sang well together, showing an improvement upon their performance at some previous festivals. The sopranos, it is true, rather overpowered the other voices, but that was inevitable. Besides the attractions provided by the Palace Company themselves, there were athletic sports (with 250 entries and 30 prizes), and music by the bands of St. Phillip's, Kensington, and St. Dunstan's, Stepney. In the evening a meeting was held in the Concert Theatre, where the prizes were distributed to the winners in the athletic sports, and a picked choir of adults gave a selection of music.

Reviews.

How to Learn the Pianoforte. By Emanuel Aguilar. (Groombridge & Sons, 1883.)—A new edition of this excellent little manual has been called for. Its utility is recognized by a host of our contemporaries in London and the provinces, and their favourable opinion can be endorsed without scruple. The author speaks direct to the point, and expresses his views with great lucidity. The book comprises five chapters, with daily exercises and manual illustrations. The illustrations are both "mechanical" and "mental." M. Aguilar is a very original writer, but he modestly quotes rules and remarks from the works of Bach, Mozart, Clementi, Cramer, and other great authorities.

Researches into the Early History of the Violin Family. By Carl Engel. (Novello, Ewer & Co., Berners Street.) —This valuable and able work has a melancholy interest, as appearing much in the light of a posthumous work, as the author, to quote Mr. Hipkins's preface, "has gone to his rest before the last revision of it." The same friendly pen calls "attention especially to the interesting chain of reasoning which derives the Mediæval Rotte from the old Greek Lyre." The book, as Mr. Hipkins adds, contains other features of discerning and judicious investigation. The author leads the way and strikes the key-note of his arguments by first dealing with the story of that true distinctive feature of the violin *genus*, "The Fiddle-Bow." In this chapter he very clearly traces the development, from the plectrum to the bow of that little but powerful engine of musical emotion. Next the Crwth is dealt with in a very interesting chapter. Step by step, through the crowd, the rotte, the rebec, etc., to the viol, the author advances to his final chapter, a clever "Retrospect," in which he briefly states the main features of the development of the true "king of instruments" to its present perfection of simplicity and expressive power. Mr. Gladstone has told us that as much thought has been bestowed upon the perfecting of the violin as has been devoted to the development of the locomotive engine. This remark embodies a profound truism. Some one has shown that a musical instrument is perfected truly as it advances towards a condition of absolute simplicity. The machine which regularly performs the business and obeys the will of man is widely distinguished from the instrument which is called upon to express his very thoughts and emotions. Thus, the violin has passed through its varied career to arrive at the simplest instrumental form we know of; but a form which, by reason of its very simplicity, is the one which comes most nearly to the man's own heart-strings. The Italians say that the violin has a soul; anyway, it furnishes the readiest exposition yet found for the soul of the instrumental performer. Hence the value of the lamented Carl Engel's "Violin Family" cannot well be overrated as a concise, clear, thoughtful, logical guide to one of the most remarkable and noteworthy developments the art has known. The book, it is needless to add, is admirably printed and got up, and it is adorned by sundry curious and instructive illustrations.

Life of Handel. By W. Rockstro. (Macmillan & Co.) —Though it may be said that when a man sits down to write a biography, he is already in love with his subject, or he would not elect to undertake it, it is only fair to recognize the fact, that without pre-existent enthusiasm an author would find it very difficult to arouse and sustain the reader's interest in his work. Now, Mr. Rockstro has this necessary enthusiasm, but it is tempered by much sound judgment. One can hardly pay him a higher compliment than by saying that he accompanies his Saxon hero in his daily life with something of the affectionate observation of a Boswell, whilst he examines his artistic work with much of the critical discrimination of a Macaulay. The book opens with a graceful and appreciative notice from the pen of no less an authority than Sir George Grove. Then the author, after a brief preface, plunges into his subject with so much skill that the reader almost seems to live in the musical world of the dawn and first half of the eighteenth century. In matters of doubt and controversy, Mr. Rockstro at times almost disappoints one in not pronouncing a decided opinion, when he might fairly claim to do so, but this feeling passes away when it is discovered how carefully he balances the evidence, and how modestly he declines to assume the position of a judge whenever the sifted evidence is too nearly balanced to permit of a dictatorial opinion being given, at least by a discreet writer. It is in this spirit that Mr. Rockstro deals with the famous Harmonious Blacksmith legend. At other times Mr. Rockstro gives us details which are not to be considered perhaps as established truths, because he honestly desires to present every side of the composer's character and career before us. In the artistic analysis of the master's works, Mr. Rockstro, displays a rare and practised power of inspection, and his criticisms have a charm and clearness quite refreshing. In dealing with the comparative merits of Bach and Handel, Mr. Rockstro, perhaps, leans too much towards the latter. The questions involved in such a discussion extend beyond the artistic attainments of the two giants, and involve a full consideration of their respective characters. From such a point of sight Bach shines more brightly than Handel, for the latter composer obviously intended to push his way in the world and to bend his splendid talents to the practical purpose of getting a quick return for his labours ; hence he studied to write for the masses with forcible, strong, clear idioms, whilst his great compeer quietly pursued his nobler artistic career with little or no thought of fame or gain. With all deference and respect for the genius of both men, it is impossible not to see the influence of personal character in their different methods of workmanship. People do not suppose that " H.M.S. Pinafore " is written from the same point of sight as Gounod's " Faust ;" and we know, too, that Handel meant to get on, and to make money, and this is said with all respect for his gifts, and that Bach was comparatively indifferent to the possession of this world's good things. Mr. Rockstro's comparative definition of the two men's contrapuntal methods is thoughtful. The following sentences embody the gist of his opinion, which, however, deserves to be read very carefully at full length. He says :—" Bach's fugal subjects are remarkable for their ductility. They go where he will make them to go. Handel's subjects are different. Though their subjection to the recognised laws of art is so great, that they avoid many collisions which Bach treated as lawful, and therefore, by his authority made lawful, the last thing one thinks about is their artistic perfection. They savour, not of the studio, but of nature." Of course the advocate of Bach could triumphantly point to instances of his fugal work which are not to be excelled in naturalness, even if equalled. Mr. Rockstro's work contains an immense amount of information, table of compositions, with dates, etc., etc ; and its details have been clearly collected with a surprising amount of painstaking care. The volume is one, in truth, of real value, and admirably sustained interest ; and as such, will, it may be fairly expected, meet with an appreciative reception from the public, both musical and general.

THE SACRED HARMONIC SOCIETY.

The musical critic of the *Figaro*, writes :—
The discussion as to the division of the funds of the defunct Sacred Harmonic Society has been taken up by the musical papers. The members have, it seems, pocketed the money, and, although a majority are willing to devote the whole sum to some art purpose, the minority appear to consider that charity beginneth at home. Still, there is no doubt the whole transaction savours of lawful dishonesty. The library was largely contributed by friends of art, who assuredly had no idea that at a certain period the members would sell it for what it would fetch, and appropriate the cash. £500 has, it is understood, been voted to one officer of the society, and the public would be glad to learn what is to be done for the subordinate officers who have served the society so faithfully and for so many years. Surely the members do not intend to pocket the " swag," and turn their old officers out into the street.

That the dissolution of the old Sacred Harmonic Society was brought about owing to inactivity and mismanagement after Bowley's death, has often been stated and as often denied. For many years before the dissolution the season was an annual loss. In Bowley's time it was different. I have before me the balance sheet for 1859. The total receipts were £10,000 odd, and out of the profits the society invested £3,000 in Consols, £1,000 in New Three Per Cents., and carried forward a cash balance of £1,534 which with the estimated value of library, etc., £3,500, and other things, gave the society in 1859 a total property of about £8,500. Bowley's successors lost a good deal of these savings, and the present generation of members have pocketed the balance.

WAGNER'S " PARSIFAL."

Says the *Daily News : * The report that it is intended to perform Wagner's last opera " Parsifal " as a sacred cantata at the Royal Albert Hall next winter, is received in Berlin with absolute incredulity. Although the intention may exist in London, it is considered altogether unlikely that the late composer's representatives will accord their permission for a performance so entirely opposed to Wagner's intentions and theories. The possibility of performing the work will depend on their permission, , even in the absence of legal protection in England, for the reason that the Mayence publishers of the " music-drama " are not allowed to sell the score—the orchestral and solo parts—without the consent of Wagner's heirs. It is therefore pretty certain that Englishmen who may desire to hear and see " Parsifal " will still have to make the pilgrimage to Bayreuth.

SIR GEORGE GROVE, says, "I like the look of it."
Send one to MACFARREN.

SIR GEORGE MACFARREN writes, "The Handel
is quite a Creation. Send one to GROVE."

SIR ARTHUR SULLIVAN has already received
several anonymously in registered envelopes.

THE ORPHEUS' HAIR-BRUSH.—Keep ordering
of your Musical Publisher until you get it.

WASHING WANTED.—A Graduate who has taken
high honours in Harmony at the Royal College of Music, having,
owing to the unexpected return of his Oratorio, several suspended chords in
his back-garden for which he has no further use, will be happy to make
arrangements with families for taking in their washing.—Address, B. Piver,
Mus. Doc. Nightingale, Lane.

TO THE INFIRM AND AGED.—A powerful and
accomplished kettle-drum player (Savage-Club Student, Chinese-
Gong Medallist, First-class Prizeman in Strepitous Poluosmorivos,
Mus. B. and S. of Oxford and Cambridge) is desirous of meeting with
an aged couple a little hard of hearing, to whose declining years his constant performance on two full-sized Bavarian kettle-drums might prove an
agreeable and stimulating solace. Can do Thunder-salvos, double-side
tattoo, the Storm a surprise, dog-beating, and give a capital imitation of the
Storming of Rangoon. Open to any offer. Would not object to taking
terms with a Regent on a Channel steamer.—By letter, X., Post Office,
Dagenham.

ZOOLOGICAL AND URGENT.—An Indian Rajah,
anxious, in response to the appeal of a distinguished personage, to
assist the Royal College of Music, has, through a mistaken translation of the
list of wind instruments, presented it with a large consignment of full-grown
Cobras. As the Secretary is greatly hampered by the presence of these fine
but deadly creatures, who are now loose in the dormitory, and greatly excited
by the practice of the Violoncello Class, he will be happy to part with them
on easy terms for the purpose of founding a Scholarship on the proceeds.

MUSICAL PITCH.—A large Surplus Stock of this
useful commodity now on hand, and to be disposed of at less than
cost-price. As the pitch is in very fine condition, Amateur Yachtsmen who
have been hitherto unable to go to °C comfortably, should order without
delay. Apply, enclosing remittance, to the Secretary, as above.

THE ROYAL COLLEGE OF MUSIC ALE.

THE ROYAL COLLEGE OF MUSIC ALE is a
fine classic beverage.

THE ROYAL COLLEGE OF MUSIC ALE is much
stronger than Treble X.

THE ROYAL COLLEGE OF MUSIC ALE is far
superior to Double Bass.

THE ROYAL COLLEGE OF MUSIC ALE is more
sparkling than Monday Pop.

THE ROYAL COLLEGE OF MUSIC ALE can be
had in barrel organs.

THE ROYAL COLLEGE OF MUSIC ALE may be
ordered in octaves.

THE ROYAL COLLEGE OF MUSIC ALE is supplied in reputed counterpints.

THE LANCET says, "We have tested the Royal
College of Music Ale, and, for dancing purposes, consider it equal to
Hop Bitters."

SIR JULIUS BENEDICT writes, "I prefer it to
Meyer-beer."

THE ROYAL COLLEGE OF MUSIC.

GRADUATES IN DIFFICULTIES from having
been unable to dispose of their own musical compositions, can by
applying to Mr. F. Sharp, be assisted in effecting one on easy and harmonious terms with their creditors, as above.—Ledger Line Row, E.C.

WHY NOT HAVE A MUSICAL FUNERAL?
Anyone sending three postage stamps to "Maestoso, care of the
Secretary, &c., &c., College," will receive by actual return of pamphlet
satisfactorily answering this trite and cheerful little question.

CAUTION TO TRAVELLING FELLOWS. The
Peninsular and Oriental, Orient, White Star, and National Ocean
Steamer Companies, give notice that on and after the first of next month
they decline to carry in any part of their vessels, under any pretence whatever, holders of Travelling Fellowships of the Royal College of Music
without receiving a written undertaking that they bring with them no
ophicleide, bassoon, double bass, piccolo, triangle, cymbals, side-drum,
trombone, or other dangerous instrument, and are willing, if desirous of
practising their scales at sea, to be let down into the hold, with sealed
hatchways.

A RURAL DEAN in a large and populous neighbour-
hood, to whom it has been intimated that an exalted Royal personage
would be gratified by his making some special effort to raise funds for the
Royal College of Music, will, on the termination of the Evening Service on
Wednesday next, endeavour to stand on his head in his own pulpit. As it is
his first essay at any feat of the kind, it is confidently hoped that the attendance will be proportionately large, and that his parishioners will contribute
to the Offertory on the occasion, which will be devoted solely to the establishment of a Triangle Scholarship, tenable for life. Further particulars
will be announced shortly.

A BROKEN-DOWN QUEEN'S COUNSEL, re-
quiring immediately a few Bars' rest, will be glad to hear from the
Secretary, 94A, Lower Serjeants' Inn.   PUNCH.

PRINCIPAL CONTENTS OF THIS NUMBER.

LONDON: SATURDAY, JULY 28, 1888.

FOREIGN MUSICAL PRODUCE.

A MEMBER of Parliament, dating from the
House of Commons, puts forth the following plea for British musicians:—

"Many persons interested in the progress and
"development of native musical talent have viewed
"with dissatisfaction and apprehension, the exten-
"sive and exclusive patronage which so-called
"'London Society' has given to foreign musicians during
"the current season, and for my own part I must express my
"surprise that the chief promoters of the Royal College of Music
"should have failed to practise the doctrines which they have
"so loudly preached, and have gone to sleep while the bread was
"being taken out of the mouths of their own countrymen by the
"strong force of Hungarian and other foreign competition. A
"case in point occurred on Wednesday night, at the entertain-
"ment given at the Fisheries Exhibition. Two foreign bands
"and two English bands were engaged for the occasion. Fair-
"play would have given to each band an equal chance; but, as a
"matter of fact, while the 'post of honour' in the conservatory
"and main building were respectively assigned to the foreigners,
"the English were relegated to obscure positions in the garden
"grounds, where their presence was not realized until late in
"the evening. Comparisons, no doubt, are odious; but no
"impartial musical expert would venture to attribute inferiority
"to English bands, and unless the managers of the entertainment
"can urge extenuating circumstances, they must stand convicted
"of having acted with manifest injustice towards a deserving
"class of artists whose interests it was their special duty to
"protect."

The neglect with which our native musicians are
frequently treated has often been commented upon in
these columns. But little further need be said over
the patent case to which an M.P. has drawn attention.

It represents but one of the many injustices that the
partial patronage of "fashion" exercises on music in
England. While it may be admitted that a good
Hungarian band can naturally play Hungarian music
—but a mere provincialism in art—better than performers of any other nationality, it can yet be fearlessly and truthfully maintained, that our English
regimental bands are altogether better than those of
foreign countries. Their rich *ensemble* and artistic
finish affords a marked contrast to the slovenly out-
of-tune tone of the German *Kapellen*, the brassy
thinness of the French, the weak volume of the
Austrian, and the rough *brilliant* quality of the Belgian
military bands. Unfortunately, but few of the units
which go to make up "London Society" are capable
judges in this matter. Their whirl of, more or less
inane, amusements leaves them little time to study
what is eclectic in art. With most of them, the term
"music", is too frequently synonymous with weak
opera tunes, and the *fioriture* of some petted prima
donna. Such people as these are mainly responsible for
the indifference and negligence with which much good
English music is treated. The ignorance they exhibit
of what their country has done, and, day by day, can
still better accomplish in music, is somewhat amusing
to cultured people. But one of its constants is, to
discourage preludes chiefly the pretentious, and sometimes the incompetent section, to presume on pampered
mediocrity, and to foist themselves, their
productions, into a position over
here, to which their precise merits by no means entitle
them. It is for the delectation of listeners of this class
that the programmes of our State Concerts,—programmes that are the ridicule of the musical world
—are chiefly drawn up. Happily, there is some
hope of general improvement looming in the
future. The long continued teachings of Professor Hullah have leavened the mass. The
study, slight though it be, of music in all our normal
schools, and especially the serious attention now
devoted to it at Eton, Harrow, Marlborough and
other great public schools of the country, must eventually work a great change in public taste. Then,
perhaps, English music and English musicians will
have fair play. More than this we should not desire,
for no one country has ever had the exclusive monopoly of art; genius, whether in its creative or executive phases, will ever compel appreciation and
command support. Those who possess such qualities
may be sure of always finding a welcome on these
shores, be their nationality what it may.

It was mainly on account of the absurd depreciation
of the Royal Academy, its staff, and its system, and
the extravagant laudation of foreign institutions, that
the new Royal College of Music has been regarded
among thinking people with coldness, and hardly concealed jealousy. The ridiculous fables as to the condition of English musical matters, with which gaping
provincial audiences have been sedulously fed, may
have been successful from a pecuniary point of view,
but the self-depreciation indulged in showed much
ignorance, co-mingled with motives palpably interested.

In connection with "London Society" patronage
of music, attention may be called to the concert
recently given at the Guildhall in aid of the funds for
the new College. The programme was little above
that of the "penny-reading" type, the artists were
chiefly Italian soloists, and so thoroughly did our
foreign residents consider, that the whole of the arrangements ought to be undertaken by them, that one,
HERR LOUIS ENGEL, the critic of the *World*, has
printed a lengthy invective against the PRINCE OF
WALES, and others, because, he states, His Royal
Highness sent his secretary to desire PATTI to sing
some insignificant song, in place of a royalty ballad,
(originally put down) from the pen of the modest
HERR ENGEL himself. On glancing over the programme of this concert, the thought crosses one's
mind as to whether our merchant princes have ever
heard of, or know, the value of the orchestral symphonies of the great masters. Probably not, or else they
lack the power to appreciate them. It was hardly so
in former times. Their forefathers imported from the
Italian republics and the Low Countries madrigals
and instrumental *ricercari*, as well as other produce
from abroad :—by the way, sending in exchange the
remarkable Fancies and sonatas of our own prolific
JOHN JENKINS, who seems to have supplied the best
part of the civilized world of that day with music for
viols and other stringed instruments. That works of
this character, whether brought from abroad, or
written at home by the composers of our own Third
Period, were performed and enjoyed by our London
merchants, is clear from the Diary of gossiping old
PEPYS. And even fifty years ago, there were excellent
concerts given in the City under the patronage of
the Duke of Sussex and the city magnates ; at these,
good music all round was given, instead of Italian
hackneyed, and shop royalty ditties.

It probably never occurred to the mind of the civic
authorities that in MR. WEIST HILL, the principal
of their Guildhall Music School, they possessed a
thoroughly able conductor, or they would hardly have
engaged two Italian conductors for the very difficult
duties of this remarkable official concert. However, we
read that "a large assembly of fashionable people"
came to meet the Royalties assembled, and, as a thousand pounds were netted for the scheme, the promoters,
performers, and audience, were probably, delighted
with the result. But the question has yet to be
answered, as to how much art in this country has
been advanced by such an exhibition.

T. L. SOUTHGATE.

THE LOGIC OF COUNTERPOINT.

CHERUBINI quotes from the much quoted FUCHS
some examples of the employment of fourth species
counterpoint in four parts, observing that "two
"minims are rarely substituted for a semibreve" in
any of the parts not engaged in enunciating the
syncopated counterpoint, "and this reserve in the
"use of such license must be observed," continues
the theorist, "in order to become accustomed to the
"control of the difficulties to be encountered in
"having semibreves only in the parts not occupied in
"conducting the syncopation." Next, CHERUBINI
remarks, that "these examples present some unisons

" upon the unaccented beat of the bar in the synco-
" pated, and between the two middle parts"; adding,
" these unisons are, in some sort of way, tolerated in
" this order, owing to the restraint which arises from
" the obligation to have all the syncopations in the
" same part. At the same time I would advise the
" exercise of much discretion in the use of such
" unisons, which should only be introduced when all
" means of avoiding them have been fruitlessly tried."
It is true that such coincident unisons should be
sparsely employed. Still, the theorist would seem to
display an excessive anxiety in this matter. For,
though there are just objections against the disappearance for the moment of a given part, especially when
that particular voice is carrying an important and characteristic counterpoint, it is reasonable to allow that
an occasional thinning of the harmony is rather a
gain than a loss in actual effect. Again, four-part
harmony is sufficiently solid to fairly tax most listeners'
attention when set contrapuntally, consequently an
occasional reduction for a moment of so solid and
contrapuntal a structure as a wall of four-part counterpoint presents, may be not only a convenient *lapsus*,
but a welcome and well-advised rest for the ear. All
the same, be it remembered, the theorist is right in
restricting such practice to that of an exceptional use,
but he seems hardly logical in displaying too much
anxiety as regards the employment of a license which
may now and then not only release the writer's hands,
but also furnish the listener with a pleasant sense of
relief from the weight of a harmony which may
possibly be too fully sustained.   E. H. TURPIN.

WHERE THE OLD PIANOS GO!

HAVING been applied to for a number of second-hand
pianos for school-practice, I went to a large firm and
inspected their second-hand stock, sent a descriptive
list of their quality and price to the applicants—it was
a pure work of charity, or else I would have refused
the mission—and waited for their decision. The
answer was long in coming, and begged of me to close
the bargain. But imagine my surprise when I found
that all the pianos had been sold to one buyer. To
save me time and trouble, the firm advised me to offer
the buyer of these pianos an inducement to part with
them. Thither I went and found at least one answer
to the heading of these lines. The pianos in question
were to have new life infused into them by means of
new barrels. The purchaser of them was an Italian,—
evidently well-to-do,—who was a lively, chatty little
man, and glibly entered into a dissertation on music,
of which art he called himself a professor. " I am
" going to have a grand piano arranged for myself,
" and intend to give concerts." Till then he had not
given me an opportunity to edge in a word, nor had I
any wish to enter into so unpalatable a subject as
that of concerts must ever be to a critic. But when
from sheer politeness I offered some remarks, I discovered that my *pseudo*-professor of the piano based
his professorship on his skill in turning the handle of
the intended automaton grand piano. My face must
have expressed what I refrained from saying, for the
son of the sunny South archly remarked, " I have
" been to many concerts and heard many pianists,

" and whilst some of them are considerably less
" correct in execution than my automatons, they are
" not a whit above them in expression, and so I am
" going to have BEETHOVEN'S Op. 106, and *tutti*
" *quanti* barrels prepared for a concert tour." Up to
the present moment, I do not know whether the
Signor was serious or joking, but the frightful
prospect of such an addition to our concerts caused
me to make a hasty retreat without even attempting
to complete the purpose of my visit.
. . . . .   FERDINAND PRAEGER.

Organ News.

LIVERPOOL.

An organ recital was given on Saturday afternoon, July
21st, at St. George's Hall, by Mr. W. T. Best. The
following was the programme :—

March from the Symphony, "The Power of Sound"	Spohr.
Andante (No. 2, A major)	Smart.
Prelude and Fugue (A minor)	Bach.
Overture, "A Midsummer Night's Dream"	Mendelssohn.
Selection from the "Water Music"	Handel.

And on Thursday evening, July 26th :—

Toccata con Fuga (D minor)	Bach.
Romanza, "Lonely though I wander"	Weber.
Overture, "Marco-Spada"	Auber.
Prelude and Fugue (G major)	Wesley.
Rondo dei Campanelli	Morandi.
Fantasia (No. 1)	Best.

FISHERIES EXHIBITION.

Mr. James Loaring's programmes, on the 16th and
19th inst., included the following :—

Overture, "Il Barbiere"	Rossini.
Introduction and Fugue in E flat	Albrechtsberger.
Chorus, "How excellent" ("Saul")	Handel.
"With Verdure Clad" ("Creation")	Haydn.
March, "Cornelius"	Mendelssohn.

Overture, "Crown Diamonds"	Auber.
Organ Concerto (No. 5)	Handel.
Andante from "1st Symphony"	Beethoven.
Selection from "Le Prophète"	Meyerbeer.
Grand March in C	Loaring.

And on Tuesday, July 17th, by Mr. C. E. Miller :—

Occasional Overture	Handel.
Introduction—Allegro—Adagio—March.	
Slow Movement, from Symphony No. 7	Haydn.
Gavotte in D major	Bach.
Ballet Music, from "Rosamunde"	Schubert.
Allegretto from Four Sketches for a Pedal Piano }	
Adantino, "Chansons Orientale" }	Schumann.
Prelude and Fugue in D minor	Bach.
Fanfare, Cantabile, and March Triomphale	Lemmens.

And on Friday, July 20th, by Mr. Percy H. Fell :—

Postlude (in the form of a March)	Battley.
Andante	Mendelssohn.
Gavotte	Zimmermann.
"Air du Dauphin"	Roeckel.
"Fix'd in his Everlasting Seat"	Handel.
Offertoire	Hewlett.
Gavotte, "Mignon"	Thomas.
Fantasia, "Alla Marcia"	Wesley.

And on Monday, July 23rd, by Mr. C. E. Miller :—

Overture, "Samson"	Handel.
Romanza, from Symphony, "La Reine de France"	Haydn.
Short Prelude and Fugue in B flat	Bach.
Cantilene	Guilmant.
Gavotte, in D (No. 2)	Bach.
Pastorale (No. 7)	Kullak.
Triumphal March	Calkin.

CRYSTAL PALACE.

Mr. Eyre's programmes on Saturday last included
the following :—

March Religieuse	Guilmant.
Allegretto, "Lobgesang"	Mendelssohn.
"Swell the full chorus"	Handel.
Intermezzo	Macbeth.
Fugue on "Wir glauben all' au einen Gott"	Bach.
Gavotte, Moderne	Tours.
Spring Song	Henselt.
Finale from an Orchestral Suite	Schumann.
Andante in D	Smart.
Overture, "Henry VIII."	Hatton.
Grand Chorus	Guilmant.
Selection, "Messiah"	Handel.
Trumpet March	Jude.

CHATTERIS, CAMBRIDGESHIRE.

The following is the programme of an organ recital given in the Parish Church, by Mr. John Thomas, on Friday, July 13th :—

Processional March	Clark.
Largo	Handel.
Prelude in G	Mendelssohn.
March "Rothaine"	Gounod.
Andante in G	Wareing.
"March of Flambeaux"	Clark.
Grand Chorus in D	Guilmant.

PRESTON.

The following is the programme of an organ recital given by Mr. James Tomlinson, in the New Public Hall, on Saturday evening, July 21st :—

Sixth Sonata	Mendelssohn.
Choral with Variations—Fuga—Andante.	
Fantasia, on the Prayer from "Freischütz"	Lux.
Andante Cantabile (Symphony)	Mozart.
Overture to "La Dame Blanche"	Boieldieu.
Pastorale	Best.
Grand Solemn March	Smart.

WARE.

An organ recital was given on Thursday, July 26th, at the Parish Church, by Mr. Malcolm Heywood, A.R.A.M. The following was the programme :—

Sonata in C minor	Mendelssohn.
Grave—Adagio—Allegro maestoso e vivace—Fuga.	
Andante con variazioni	Beethoven.
Andante	Guilmant.
Prelude and Fugue	Krebs.
Barcarolle from 4th Concerto	Bennett.
Marche Religieuse	Guilmant.

And on the same occasion by Mr. J. L. Gregory :—

Andante in F	Waly.
Fugue in E	Bach.
Andante, from the 5th Quintet	Mozart.
March, " Leonidas "	Trembath.

WICK.

An organ recital was given at the Parish Church, on Friday evening, July 13th, by Mr. Arthur H. Collier, Mus.Bac. The following was the programme :—

Sonata (No. 6)	Mendelssohn.
Adagio, "Sonata Pathétique"	Beethoven.
March of Israelites ("Eli")	Costa.
Concerto in B flat	Handel.
Theme with variations, "Septuor"	Beethoven.
Lord God of Abraham, "Elijah"	Mendelssohn.
" Let the Bright Seraphim"	Handel.
"Hallelujah Chorus	"

CORK.

Programme of recitals given by Mr. T. J. Sullivan, on the organ of the Exhibition, on Monday, 16th inst. :—

Overture, " Cenerentola "	Rossini.
Romanza in G (violin and orchestra)	Beethoven.
March	Spohr.
Allegretto, " Hymn of Praise "	Mendelssohn.
Prelude and Fugue, G major	Bach.
Irish Melodies	
Air, with variations	Hesse.
Cavatina	Raff.
Coronation March	Meyerbeer.

And on Tuesday, 17th inst. :—

Overture, "Figaro "	Mozart.
Concertante	Handel.
Fugue, D major	Bach.
Irish Airs	
March	Spohr.
Andante (3rd Symphony)	Haydn.
" Ah ! che la morte "	Verdi.
Schiller March	Meyerbeer.

The new Westminster Town Hall was opened on the 19th inst. by the Duke of Buccleuch (High Steward of Westminster). An anthem; " Behold, how good and joyful a thing," was sung, prayer was offered by Archdeacon Farrar, and various addresses were made. The building has cost about £30,000. It contains a large room and a good sized board-room, and the structure will doubtless be of great service for musical and artistic purposes as well as for general use. The movement which is supplying London with local town halls may be one of enormous service to the art as furnishing good sized, but not too large, concert-rooms. Architects and committees should be duly impressed with the importance of providing properly arranged orchestral space in view of the musical employment of these useful structures.

THE VOICE

MUSICALLY AND MEDICALLY CONSIDERED.

BY

ARMAND SEMPLE, B.A., M.B., Cantab., M.R.C.P., Lond.,

Physician to the Royal Society of Musicians.

(*Continued from page 18*).

Extent of Voices.

It must be borne in mind that, no matter what the extent, the absolute and real power of expression resides in the middle quality of every voice; force will not render this middle quality full and round, but the ease and steadiness by which the sounds are produced and sustained will give simultaneously capability of expansion and power of vibration. As soon as the middle quality has become full and firm, the muscles will have gained so great a degree of flexibility that the extreme sounds, both high and low, may be acquired with a fair amount of ease. Nevertheless, the extreme sounds of any voice, even when gained, should be carefully nursed, and employed chiefly for ornament and brilliant effect.

Styles of Music.

The adoption of the style of music best adapted for any individual voice demands the exercise of common sense and experience. The voice should be cultivated for that particular style for which nature formed it. No full or strong voice can give much effect to pieces requiring difficult execution, and on the other hand no thin or light voice can be so effective in the sostenuto style as in more brilliant music.

Again, the selection of songs is a matter of importance. Male singers commit an egregious error in singing songs especially written for females, and the latter a similar mistake in singing those written for males. How ridiculous it is to hear a gentleman singing "I'm a merry, merry Zingara," or "I dreamt that I dwelt in marble halls"; or a lady contributing " My pretty Jane," or "Come into the garden, Maud,". Again, how ludicrous is the effect of a ponderous bass singing, " Ever of thee I'm fondly dreaming," like a war song, and a languid dandy with the lightest of tenor voices simpering, " Yes ! Let me like a soldier fall."

To attempt the cultivation of a voice for any particular style, either English, Italian, or German, is an absurdity. The language of music is always the same, no matter in what language the words are. The voice is only able to sing to the utmost advantage in the style for which its organisation is suitable, whether for execution, brilliancy, or sostenuto. The music of every nation will resolve itself into one of these styles.

Management of the Breath.

Few singers acquire the easy management of the breath, and thus many vocalists, in their endeavours to express themselves with effect, give utterance to sounds harsh to the ear, and produce contortions unsightly to the eye. Many singers think that a long breath should be taken before commencing a passage of sustained sound or of rapid divisions, thus losing sight of the fact that by such a proceeding they of necessity lose the very power they are in the hope of gaining, for by distending the lungs to such an extent, these organs become oppressed by too great a volume of air, and the natural tendency is to throw out the breath with rapidity and force ; thus the singer is unable to guide his voice with ease, but is compelled either to inspire at once with an effort, or by restraining the air on the lungs violently to contort the mouth and stretch the neck, by which actions distinct vibration and equal quality are destroyed, and articulation impeded, and in extreme instances the violence of the effort may even lead to bursting of the smaller veins of the head, throat, or breast.

The breath should invariably be taken without the slightest visible effort. In the pronunciation of the open Italian A (*Anglicè, Ah*), the mouth by nature assumes a smiling or easy appearance, neither too much closed nor too open, and by this means the lips are prevented from projecting, or from extending too far in a lateral direction, the former action rendering the sound throaty or guttural, the latter giving it a thin character. The tongue lies flat and free in the mouth, touching gently the lower front teeth.

Every sound at first should be produced lightly, expanded gradually to its full power, and then diminished gradually.

Two figures are employed to indicate the crescendo and diminuendo, viz.

Piano. Crescendo. Forte Diminuendo. Piano.

the latter, resembling the form of the eye, appears best to illustrate the action.

The length of time of respiration varies in different individuals, according to the power possessed by the lungs, and according to the period over which the amount of practice has extended. The lungs acquire strength by practice. It is highly important that the breath should never be taken in the middle of a word, and as in reading prose or poetry the various stops indicate the temporary degree of suspension, so in reading music the unaccented parts point out the point of suspension, and in these the breath may be taken with propriety. The reading of musical phrases, however, depends much upon the intelligence and taste of the singer.

(*To be continued.*)

A REMINISCENCE OF HEINE.

BY FREDRICH KÜCKEN.

The following was given in the New York Courier.

After I had become comfortably settled in Paris, my first duty was to call on Meyerbeer. I counted upon a hearty welcome, for when I made his acquaintance in Berlin, at the house of his mother, he had treated me with great kindness and consideration. To my regret, I found him occupied—rehearsing with some fair vocalist—but he begged me to repeat my visit in the evening at seven o'clock. As a matter of course, I came promptly at the appointed time.

Clouds of thick smoke poured out of the fireplace as I entered the parlour, during stormy weather a common occurrence in Paris, and I found myself very much annoyed by the smoke, in the presence of eight or ten gentlemen, who had evidently dined with Meyerbeer. He introduced me by his most charming manner as a young song-writer, who had already achieved great popularity in Germany. I then heard him pronounce the names: Scribe, Jules Janin, Alexander Dumas, Berlioz, Pixis and others, which I cannot recall. I knew but one of the gentlemen, Pixis, whose acquaintance I had made in Baden the previous summer. He approached me, and in order to avoid a general conversation in French, which, owing to a superficial knowledge of the language at that time, would have been very embarrassing, I purposely prolonged our *tête-à-tête*.

In the meantime I hardly noticed how a not particularly striking personage turned towards us, remained standing at a distance of a few feet, and then abruptly turned upon his heel. In departing, Meyerbeer invited me to listen to a few acts of the "Huguenotten" from his private box at the opera-house, the same evening. We came in time to witness a complete butchery of the second finale. Grieved and frightened that this unfortunate event should have happened in the presence of the master, I glanced toward Meyerbeer, who, however, did not seem to be concerned in the least. He turned around and said, "Do not give yourself any uneasiness. These accidents are liable to happen occasionally when the same opera is repeated so many times. The public does not mind it, however, for it knows that the next performance will run smoothly; after the thorough overhauling it will have received in the meantime." Thus I spent my first evening in society, and at the opera.

Next, it was the desire of my heart to make the acquaintance of Heinrich Heine. His residence happened to be near mine, and the very next morning I knocked at his door at the usual hour for receiving callers. A servant appeared. I gave my name and begged to be announced. To my regret, she returned with the message, "Herr Heine is not at home." The following day I called again; again I was dismissed with "Herr Heine is not at home," and this repeated itself at least a dozen times.

I now allowed several weeks to pass, hoping that chance would throw him into my way before long. Vain hope!

Once more I began making my periodical visits to Heine's door. One day a man answered my wrappings in place of the maid-servant, and just as I was on the point of rapturously greeting him as Heine, he cried out indignantly, "Herr Heine is not at home!" No doubt remained but that Heine himself had slammed the door in my face. Six months passed, when an accident brought us together at last. The well-known—at that time given—celebrated music publisher, Moritz Schlesinger had arranged to publish a French translation of several of my most popular songs. In order that we might talk over the matter at our leisure, he invited me to breakfast one morning. A gentleman appeared, unannounced, whom Schlesinger received with the words, "Good for you, my dear Heine? I am glad you happen in just at this time, for Kücken here is the most unhappy mortal alive—simply because he has not made the acquaintance of his favourite poet." Heine, though he saw how delighted I was, said, stiffly, "We know each other already, my dear Kücken" —my surprise was great—" have you forgotten the evening with Meyerbeer, when he introduced you, and then called out the names of all present? Old Pixis captured you at once, but I thought to myself, Go, greet the countryman by all means. I went to you, and although I listened to the *tête-à-tête* of the *débutante's* father for some time, you did not think it worth while to notice me. Of course, I turned my back upon you and returned to my Frenchmen. Alexander Dumas did not allow this to escape him, and I want you to understand, Alexander Dumas is a brazen-tongued scoundrel! He said, 'My dear Heine, your popularity in Germany cannot amount to much, for this fellow does not even know you!' You see, my dear Kücken, in Paris we do not submit to these things!" Here, then, was the explanation of the everlasting "Herr Heine is not at home," as well as of the personal slamming to of the door.

I resided in Paris for several years, and after this meeting a relation of true friendship sprang up between us. I might relate many interesting anecdotes of him, but for this time I will close by adding the following little letter which once accompanied a parcel of new poems :

"Dear Kücken—Here are a few eggs for you to hatch. Do not cackle over them too long, and let me hear from you soon.

"Ever your   "H. HEINE."

MUSIC IN LADIES' SCHOOLS.

There are doubtless seminaries in which the arts are taught as such, while in others they occupy rather an unfavourable position for their development. A great deal of musical instruction is imparted year after year in these schools and it is desirable that it should be made as perfect and efficient as possible. It is surprising to find among those who preside over educational institutions men and women who have no correct appreciation of the nature and influence of art culture. Some regard music merely as an accomplishment designed to entertain and to enable young ladies to appear with credit to themselves in society. In how many schools of this sort is music placed on a level with other studies? It generally passes under the name of an "extra," and as an "extra" it has not the same rights which other branches of learning have. It is, perhaps, unreasonable to expect that ladies' seminaries, which are, as a rule, but poorly endowed, should make music a study free for all, just as Latin or mathematics is free to every student that enters the school; but it is not unreasonable to ask that music should be regarded as a regular study. The art furnishes a good revenue to many schools, and even when viewing the question from this standpoint, one would suppose that it would be placed on a level with all other branches of curriculum.

A teacher of music in a ladies' seminary finds himself at times in an embarrassing position. Indeed, outsiders can not fully appreciate what it means to teach music in such institutions. The department must be made self-supporting and that teacher who is unable to raise it to that position is not the man of reason that is wanted. Teachers in the regular or collegiate department, as a rule, are more independent. They have better control over pupils for the simple reason that the branches which they teach are not "extras." Young misses may or may not study music. They fully understand, that studying music adds so much "extra" revenue to the income of the school. If a music teacher resorts to discipline, or pursues a course of instruction that is in a measure distasteful to pupils, he is straightway threatened with the prospect of their stopping their lesson. This places the teacher in an embarrassing position. Complaints are made against him to president, parents, and teachers, and these complaints are generally of such a nature that the true facts can scarcely come to light. Would that parents could see their own interests better, and sustain faithful teachers; at any rate, that they would thoroughly investigate the complaints offered by their daughters before they arrive at a decision. If teachers could be assured of the support of parents, if they could follow out, without danger of complaints, that course which is best for pupils, much better work would be done in a number of schools of this kind.

Another impediment to the advancement of genuine art education is the fact that in some seminaries students are so overcrowded with work that very little time or energy can be devoted to the study of music. Students rush through a course as rapidly as possible, and in order to please them and to keep them in the school, their wishes in this particular are often indulged. What can be expected of musical students that are overworked with other studies, that hurry, so to speak, through their education? The study of music requires leisure as well as application. Many of those attending such schools would do better to let music alone, for their money and time is not unfrequently wasted. Unless music can be accorded as much time as other studies, not much good can come out of it. If any study must be neglected it is almost sure to be the study of music. Many pupils take up music as a sort of a side issue, or because it is fashionable, and the position accorded to the art among other studies is calculated to encourage them to do so.

Despite these difficulties, much is expected of teachers of music. When a young miss comes home from the boarding-school fond parents do not examine into her knowledge of Latin or mathematics, but they are quick to invite her to the piano where she is expected to give evidence of her musical progress. At parties, her friends expect great results from her educational advantages abroad, and at the earliest opportunity she is asked to step to the instrument to astonish the cousins and the aunts. Observing teachers are aware of this fact, and "prudently" provide for such occasions. Thus many ladies are allowed to spend their time on pieces which they ought to devote to the playing of exercises. Parents are often unreasonable in their expectations of one year's musical instruction, especially when it has to be imparted under such disadvantageous circumstances. No matter how little talent Miss Julia may have, she is expected to come home an accomplished artist ; no matter how little she knows when going to boarding-school, she is expected to know all when she comes back.

Music is called an "extra," and is not accorded that position among the regular studies which it deserves, for all it is diligently used as a means to advertise the school, and to bring it before the public.

School libraries are not supplied with musical books, nor are musical journals to be found in the reading-rooms of scarcely any of these institutions. Other points might be mentioned, as for instance the use of inferior instruments for practice and the employment of deficient teachers for beginners, etc. Enough has been said to show that music in ladies' boarding-schools is not in all respects what it ought to be. Nothing is further from the purpose of these words than a fault-finding spirit or a disposition to belittle the noble work many such institutions are doing. The editor of a musical journal, has a right to inquire into the welfare of music, no matter where it is taught or by whom.—*Brainard's Musical World.*

Correspondence.

THE INTERNATIONAL COLLEGE OF MUSIC.

TO THE EDITOR OF THE "MUSICAL STANDARD."

SIR,—In your last number I read a paragraph from "J.J.M." of Liverpool, which would lead the public to infer that the International College of Music had received payment of fees for a Practical Examination, without such examination having taken place. Now, if "J.J.M.," who lives in Liverpool, had seen all his local newspapers, he would have seen that the examination, postponed more than a month ago through the action of our late local secretary, is to be held on September 5th and following days.

In addition, I must state, in justice to myself, that not one of the fees said to be missing has ever reached the College, and I had actually left my house *en route* for Liverpool, when a messenger overtook me, with a telegram from our late secretary, requesting me not to leave London that night, the examination being put off, which will account for my non-appearance on the scene.

Of course, no college can be answerable for the actions of its local representatives ; all that we can do in this case is as far as possible to atone for the disappointment of the numerous candidates by giving them their examination as if the College had received their fees. My personal loss will naturally be a heavy one, but as I, like fair play myself, I always endeavour to give it to others.

Mr. W. Henry Dreaper, of Bold Street, Liverpool, the present admirable local secretary for the Musical International College, will, I am sure, be happy to give "J.J.M." or anyone else any further information.

Yours truly,
EDWIN M. LOTT,
Examiner.

279, Cornwall Road, Notting Hill,
July 23rd, 1883.

ORPHAN SCHOOL FOR DAUGHTERS OF MUSICIANS.

TO THE EDITOR OF THE "MUSICAL STANDARD."

SIR,—In the notice which appeared in the *Musical Standard* of July 7th, the address of the Orphan School was given as 8, Lupton Street, Kentish Town, but it was found that that house could not be used for a school.

I have, however, secured another, which I hope will answer the purpose ; and after August 15th my address will be 10, Daraley Road, Royal Crescent, Notting Hill, W.

I am, Sir, yours truly,
HELEN KENWAY.

South Hill House, Bath, July 24th.

THE SACRED HARMONIC LIBRARY QUESTION.

TO THE EDITOR OF THE "MUSICAL STANDARD."

SIR,—As a former member of the Sacred Harmonic Society, I have read with much pain and some shame of the division among the existing members of the money received from the sale of their fine library. The article commenting on the greed and impropriety of this step that has appeared in your journal, and the various comments on the job in that of other musical papers, are too just to be resented. The matter, unfortunately, is not a private affair, to be smoothed over, hole and corner fashion, but it is practically a violation of a public trust, that one could never have thought the members of the old Sacred Harmonic Society would have been guilty of. At the same time, it should be known that it was by no means the generally-expressed wish that the library should be sold and the money divided, but is no secret that there were not half-a-dozen members who reminded this if pressed of firstly according to the bond. The great bulk of them, and notably the executive officers, were opposed to this mean proceeding. Here are the names of the committee from our last published list, and if those of your readers who may happen to know any of those gentlemen will personally urge them to take immediate action in the matter, the reproach brought against us may yet be wiped away. T. Hill, president ; Messrs. J. Carmichael, G. Dennison, H. Durlacher, S. Foster, J. Frye, M. Hanhart, N. Hanhart, W. H. Harrison, J. Kitcat, G. T. Maddox, W. Pattinson, T. Sherard, G. M. Smith, F. W. Wilcocks, T. Williamson, W. H. Withall, committee ; W. H. Husk, hon. librarian, and E. H. Mannering, secretary. If only some one with authority will take the matter up, and consult the old members, it will doubtless be found that there is no desire to retain money they have never earned, and the Royal College of Music, the Royal Academy, and other established musical institutions, will receive a handsome portion of the funds now gone wrong.

To shew that there was far from unanimity over what was done, it may be mentioned that Sir Michael Costa removed his books and arrangements from the Society, and would not allow them to be sold. It may also be said, that the old officers of the Society have been provided for, and not ignored, as the musical critic of *Figaro* infers ; and further, that his particulars of former profits made is over-estimated. Still, his statement, that the dissolving members are putting into their private pockets the value of the books bought out of ancient profits made from the public by old members long since retired, correctly represents what has actually taken place. It is not pleasant to anticipate what the foreign art-world will say of this ugly musical scandal.

Yours, etc.,
AN OLD MEMBER, S. H. S.

Academical Intelligence.

TRINITY COLLEGE, LONDON.

The following is a list of the successful candidates at the Midsummer examinations held by Trinity College for diplomas and other higher musical certificates ; the names being placed in order of merit :—

LICENTIATES IN MUSIC.

Richard Frederic Tyler, Trinity College, London ; Henry Edgar Hyatt, Trinity College, London ; Lucy Elinor Hatchett Jackson, Oxford.

ASSOCIATES IN MUSIC.

Lewis E. Lewis, Meopham Vicarage, Gravesend ; Jane T. Bird, Berwick-on-Tweed ; Herbert Robb, Trinity College, London ; John Freeman Downton, London ; Henry Pickford (B.A. Cambridge), Trinity College, London ; Francis Wilmot, Heslington, York ; John Matthew Ennis, University of London ; Emily Asquith, Barnsley ; Robert Reith, South Shields ; Joseph Walsh, Trinity College, London ; Alfred Frederick Tindall, London ; Henry Glasspoole, London ; Emily Champion, Trinity College, London ; Philip Sharpe, Bishop Stortford.

PRELIMINARY EXAMINATIONS FOR ASSOCIATESHIP.

James Stewart Henderson, London ; Henry Palmer, Kettering ; E. Augusta Walker, Birmingham ; Eva Tindall, Barrow-in-Furness.

On behalf of Academical Board,
H. G. BONAVIA HUNT,
Warden.

The solo singers at the Cardiff Eisteddfod concerts of the first week in August include Mdme. Edith Wynne, Miss Anne Marriott, Miss Anna Williams, Miss Spencer Jones, Mr. Barton McGuckin, Signor Foli, Mr. Lucas Williams, Mr. ApHerbert, etc. The conductor will be Mr. E. H. Turpin.

Passing Events.

Mr. C. Mackenzie has declined to write for the Birmingham Festival, being already too much occupied.

A pianoforte recital was given by Herr S. Lehmeyer, at 62, Harley Street last week.

Messrs. Brainard, of New York, offer 200 dollars for the best five anthems for a prize anthem book to be published next year.

The new Metropolitan Opera House in New York is to be opened on October 22nd with "Faust." The house seats an audience of 3,200.

"Le Diable à Quatre" is the title of MM. Najac, Toché, and Jonas's new comic opera which is to be produced on the re-opening of the Nouveautés in Paris this autumn.

"The British Patrol," a descriptive allegro, by Mr. George Asch, and a sequel to the popular "Turkish Patrol," has been recently performed at the Crystal Palace and the Fisheries Exhibition with great success. It is understood that at least 4,000 copies of the composition have been already sold.

Miss A. S. Burvett, a talented and skilled pianist from Australia, gave a very successful recital at Prince's Hall the other evening. Her rendering of the "Kreutzer" Sonata, Gottschalk's "Dernier Amours," and a caprice by Raff showed her powers to the best advantage. Miss Burvett has already made for herself a position claiming respect in Belgium and elsewhere.

It is unnecessary to criticise an Italian opera called "La Regina di Scozia," which was produced at the Folies Dramatiques Theatre the other week. The words and music are both by Mrs. M. F. Stuart Stresa, the subject, of course, being Mary Queen of Scots. The work is amateurish in character, and the statement that it was well received at Turin and Milan excites some surprise. A very efficient company interpreted the opera, and the conductor, Signor Furlotti, is evidently a man of talent.

The proceeds of the entertainment given by the Savage Club at the Albert Hall on the 11th inst. did not amount to sufficient for the purpose intended, i.e., the founding of a scholarship in the Royal College of Music, with a preference for sons and daughters of club members. It has been proposed that the deficiency shall be covered by taking a "show" through the larger provincial towns, on the model of that which collected over two thousand pounds for the Cotton Famine Fund some twenty years ago.

The balance sheet of the annual Pilots' Concert, held in Hengler's Circus, in connection with the Liverpool Seamen's Orphanage, on Easter Monday, has been published, from which it appears that after paying expenses, the sum of £358 18s. 11d. has been handed over to the treasurer. When it is added that over £200 was turned away from the doors, some idea may be entertained of the popularity of the institution. Mr. S. Claude Ridley, the well known organist of the institution, was the director of the entertainment.

One of the oldest violins in the United States is in the possession of Mr. W. Y. Macpherson, of Owensboro'. It is known to have been in his family over 100 years. The violin is 266 years old, having been made by Nicolaus Amati, of Cremona, Italy, one of the most celebrated violin makers in the world. He was born in 1587, and was thirty years old when the violin was made, just in his prime. One characteristic of his make was in the varnish used, the art of making it having died with him. It consists in the beautiful shading, which in this particular violin could not be surpassed, and it no doubt is one of his best.

The rector and churchwardens of St. George's, Hanover Square, have recently set a good example, and acknowledged the ability of their organist, Mr. W. Pinney, Mus.B., Oxon., in a complimentary manner. A few Sundays since the Rev. E. Capel Cure, prefaced his sermon by saying that "the offertory in the morning would be for the purpose of supplementing the organist's stipend, in recognition of his great and valued services." The offertory amounted to about £40. For two or three years past this plan has been adopted, following the usual Easter-day offertory for the assistant curate, and it is a plan which deserves general adoption.

The Querist.

REPLY.

M. K.—Gounod's "March Cortège," from "Irene," is published by Augener, of Newgate Street, and arranged by Naumann.—J. S. B.

Service Lists.

TENTH SUNDAY AFTER TRINITY.

JULY 29th.

London.

ST. PAUL'S CATHEDRAL.—Morn.: Service, Te Deum and Benedictus, Stainer in E flat; Introit, To the name of our salvation; Holy Communion, Stainer in E flat. Even.: Service, Magnificat and Nunc Dimittis, Stainer in E flat; Anthem, The wilderness (Goss).

TEMPLE CHURCH.—Morn.: Service, Te Deum Laudamus, and Jubilate Deo, Nares in F; Apostles' Creed, Harmonised Monotone; Anthem, Praise the Lord (Goss). Even.: Service, Magnificat and Nunc Dimittis, Arnold in A; Apostles' Creed, Harmonized Monotone; Anthem, The King shall rejoice (Handel).

LINCOLN'S INN CHAPEL.—Morn.: Service, Steggall in G; Kyrie (Steggall); Anthem, Whosoever drinketh of this water (Bennett). Even.: Service, Tuste in D; Anthem, Wherewithal shall a young man (Elvey).

CHRIST CHURCH, CLAPHAM.—Morn.: Service, Te Deum, Plain-song. Kyrie and Credo, Schubert in B flat; Offertory Anthem, How goodly are thy tents (Ouseley); Sanctus, Benedictus, Agnus Dei, and Gloria in excelsis (Schubert). Even.: Service, Magnificat and Nunc Dimittis, Smart in F; Anthems, Come unto Him, and, With Cherubim and Seraphim (Handel).

FOUNDLING CHAPEL.—Morn.: Service, Goss in F; Benedictus, Smart in F; Anthem, Hear my prayer (Mendelssohn). Aft.: Children's Service.

HOLY TRINITY, TULSE HILL.—Morn.: Chant Service. Even.: Service, Magnificat and Nunc Dimittis, Hopkins in F; Anthem, I will extol Thee, and Hosanna (Costa).

ST AUGUSTINE AND ST. FAITH, WATLING STREET.—Morn.: Service, Smart in F; Introit, Behold, O God, our defender; Communion Service, Smart in F; Agnus Dei, Monk in C. Even.: Service, Martin in A; Anthem, O clap your hands (Stainer).

ST. BARNABAS, MARYLEBONE.—Morn.: Service, Te Deum and Jubilate, Clarke-Whitfield in E; Anthem, Woe unto them, and, He that shall endure; Litany. Even.: Service, Magnificat and Nunc Dimittis, Hoyte in B flat; Anthem, Stand up and bless (Goss).

ST. JAMES'S PRIVATE EPISCOPAL CHAPEL, SOUTHWARK.—Morn.: Service, Introit, Author of life divine; Communion Service, Mozart's Twelfth Mass. Even.: Service, Stainer in E flat; Anthem, How lovely (Spohr).

ST. MAGNUS, LONDON BRIDGE.—Morn.: Service, Opening Anthem, to the Lord our God (Calkin); Te Deum and Jubilate, Boyce in A; Kyrie, (Armes). Even.: Service, Magnificat and Nunc Dimittis, Arnold in A; Anthem, Lord, how are they increased (Kent).

ST. MARGARET PATTENS, ROOD LANE, FENCHURCH STREET.—Morn.: Service, Te Deum, Sullivan in D; Benedictus, Stainer; Communion Service: Offertory Anthem, How beautiful are the feet (Handel); Kyrie, Credo, Sanctus, Benedictus, Agnus Dei, and Gloria, Mozart in B flat. Even.: Service, Magnificat and Nunc Dimittis, Garrett in F; Anthem, To Thee, great Lord (Rossini).

ST. MARY BOLTONS, WEST BROMPTON, S.W.—Morn.: Service, Te Deum, Armes in G; Benedictus, Chant; Holy Communion, Kyrie, Credo, Sanctus, and Gloria in excelsis, Smart in F; Offertory (Barnby); Benedictus and Agnus Dei (Redhead). Even.: Service, Magnificat and Nunc Dimittis, Arnold in A. Anthem, I will give thanks (Hopkins).

ST. MICHAEL'S, CORNHILL. — Morn.: Service, Te Deum and Jubilate, Dykes in F; Anthem, Now we are ambassadors (Mendelssohn); Kyrie, and Creed, Thorne in G; Offertory Sentences (Barnby). Even. Service, Magnificat and Nunc Dimittis, Naylor in C; Anthem, Ascribe unto the Lord (Travers).

ST. PAUL'S, AVENUE ROAD, SOUTH HAMPSTEAD.—Morn.: Service, Te Deum, Thomd in F; Benedictus, Garrett; Kyrie, Mendelssohn in G. Even.: Service, Magnificat and Nunc Dimittis, Bridge in C; Anthem, The Wilderness (Goss).

ST. PAUL'S, BOW COMMON, E.—Morn.: Service, Te Deum and Benedictus, Chants; Holy Communion; Kyrie, Credo, Offertory, Sanctus and Gloria in excelsis, Stainer in A; Benedictus, Agnus Dei, Eyre in E flat. Even.: Service, Magnificat and Nunc Dimittis, King in D; Anthem, In Thee, O Lord (Weldon).

ST. PETER'S (EATON SQUARE).—Morn.: Service, Te Deum, Tours in F. Even.: Service, Smart in F; Anthem, Art Thou weary (Lloyd).

ST. PETER'S, LEIGHAM COURT ROAD, STREATHAM, S.W.—Morn.: Service, Holy Eucharist, Purge me with hyssop (Novello); Introit, When I called (Chantwise); Mass, Kyrie Credo, Sanctus and Gloria, Dykes in F; Benedictus and Agnus, Dei, Sutton in F; Gradual, Keep me (Chantwise); Offertory; Communion and Post Communion. Even.: Service, Magnificat, Gadsby in C; Anthem, As pants the hart (Spohr).

ST. PETER'S, VERE STREET, W.—Even.: Service, Magnificat and Nunc Dimittis, Tuckermann in F; Anthem, O taste and see (Goss).

ST. SAVIOUR'S, HOXTON.—Morn.: Service, Te Deum, Hopkins in G; Holy Communion; Kyrie, Crédo, Sursum Corda, Sanctus, and Gloria in excelsis, Smart in G. Even.: Service, Magnificat and Nunc Dimittis (Best); Anthem, O praise the Lord (Wilton).

ST. SEPULCHRE'S, HOLBORN.—Morn.: Service, Sullivan in D; Anthem, Rejoice greatly (Handel); Credo, Lott in F; Offertory Anthem, Let your light (Haydn). Even.: Service, Arnold in A; Anthem, Blessed be Thou (Kent).

Country.

ST. ASAPH CATHEDRAL.—Morn.: Service, Calkin in B flat; Anthem, O send out Thy light (Calkin). Even.: Service, The Litany; Anthem, God be merciful (Lloyd).

ASHBURNE CHURCH, DERBYSHIRE. — Morn.: Service, Throughout, Hopkins in C. Even.: Service, Walmisley in D; Anthem, O that men would praise the Lord (Bartholomew).

BEDDINGTON CHURCH, SURREY.—Morn.: Service, Garrett in D; Communion Service, Calkin in D. Even.: Service, Calkin in D; Anthem, O clap your hands together all ye people (Stainer).

BIRMINGHAM (S. ALBAN THE MARTYR).—Morn.: Service, Te Deum and Benedictus, Dykes in F; Holy Communion; Kyrie, Credo, Sanctus, Gloria, Garrett in D; Benedictus and Agnus Dei, Redman in D. Evensong: Magnificat and Nunc Dimittis, Tours in F.

BIRMINGHAM (ST. CYPRIAN'S, HAY MILLS).—Morn.: Service, Field in D; Anthem, Give the King Thy judgments (Boyce). Even.: Service, Cobb in G; Anthem, O Lord, Thou hast searched me out, and God is a Spirit).

BIRMINGHAM (S. PHILIP'S CHURCH). — Morn.: Service, Barnby in E; Anthem, I will give thanks (Palestrina). Evensong Service, Chipp in A; Anthem, O be joyful (Smart).

CANTERBURY CATHEDRAL.—Morn.: Service, Smart in F; Communion, Smart in F; Anthem, Thou will keep him in perfect peace (Jarrett). Even.: Service, Smart in F; Anthem, This is the day (Oakley).

CARLISLE CATHEDRAL.—Morn.: Service, Hopkins in C; Introit, I will love Thee (Macfarren); Kyrie, Hopkins in C; Nicene Creed, Harmonized Monotone. Even.: Service, Macfarren in E flat; Anthem, Lead kindly light (Stainer).

CIRENCESTER (HOLY TRINITY).—Morn.: Service, Smart in F; Even.: Service, King in F; Anthem, How lovely are Thy dwellings (Spohr).

DONCASTER (PARISH CHURCH).—Morn.: Service, Tours in F. Even.: Service, Tours in F; Anthem, Wherewithal (Elvey).

DUBLIN, ST. PATRICK'S (NATIONAL) CATHEDRAL.—Morn.: Service, Te Deum and Jubilate, Mendelssohn in A; Holy Communion, Kyrie, Creed, Sanctus, Rogers in D; Anthem, Judge me, O God (Mendelssohn). Even.: Service, Magnificat and Nunc Dimittis, Smith in B flat; Anthems, Father, Son and Spirit guide (Dicinkson), and, Blessing, glory, wisdom (Bach).

ELY CATHEDRAL.—Morn.: Service, Te Deum Smart in F; Benedictus, Plain Song, Kyrie and Credo, Smart in F; Gloria, (Richardson); Anthem, How lovely (Salaman). Even.: Service, Anthem, Praise the Lord (Mozart).

EXETER CATHEDRAL.—Morn.: Service, Boyce in C; Communion, Smart in F. Even.: Service, Cooke in G; Anthem, God is my hope (Greene).

FOLKESTONE (ST MICHAELS).—Morn.: Service, Te Deum and Benedictus, Tours in F; Anthem, These are They (Dykes). Even.: Service, Magnificat and Nunc Dimittis, Stainer in B flat; Anthem, He that sitteth on the throne (Dykes).

HARROGATE (ST. PETER'S CHURCH). — Morn.: Service, Kyrie (Mendelssohn); Credo (Goss); Anthem, O how amiable (Richardson). Even.: Service, Magnificat, and Nunc Dimittis, Best in E; Anthem, The Lord is great in Zion (Best).

LEEDS PARISH CHURCH. — Morn.: Service, Boyce in A; Anthem, Lift Thine eyes (Mendelssohn); Kyrie and Creed, Walmisley in F. Even.: Service, Calkin in B flat; Anthem, O where shall wisdom (Boyce).

LICHFIELD CATHEDRAL. — Morn.: Service, Hopkins in C; Anthem, But the Lord is mindful, and See what love (Mendelssohn). Even. Service, Cantate and Deus Misereatur, Haynes in E flat; Anthem, The wilderness (Goss).

LIVERPOOL CATHEDRAL.—Aft.: Service, Magnificat and Nunc Dimittis, Calkin in B flat; Anthem, Praise the Lord (Elvey).

LIVERPOOL (ST. CUTHBERT'S, EVERTON).—Morn.: Service, Stanford in B flat. Even.: Service, Cantate and Deus, Attwood in D; Anthem, Blessed be the God and Father (Wesley).

LLANDAFF CATHEDRAL.—Morn.: Service, Te Deum and Jubilate, Lloyd in E flat: Introit, One thing have I desired (Macfarren); Holy Communion, Stainer in E flat. Even.: Service, The Litany; Anthem, Lead, kindly light (Stainer).

MANCHESTER CATHEDRAL. — Morn.: Service, and Full Communion, Tours in F; Anthem, Incline Thine ear (Himmel). Aft.: Service, Tours in F; Anthem, Draw near, ye people (Mendelssohn).

MANCHESTER (ST. BENEDICT'S). — Morn.: Service, Kyrie; Credo, Sanctus, Benedictus, and Gloria in excelsis, Thorne in G; Agnus Dei, Miné in F. Even.: Service, Magnificat and Nunc Dimittis (Stainer).

MANCHESTER (ST. JOHN BAPTIST, HULME).—Morn.: Service, Kyrie, Credo, Sanctus, Benedictus, Agnus and Gloria in excelsis, Monk in C; Even.: Service, Magnificat and Nunc Dimittis (Jordan).

PETERBOROUGH CATHEDRAL.—Morn.: Service, Boyce in C; Introit, I am the bread of life (Stainer); Communion Service, Stainer in A. Even.: Service, Stainer in E flat; Anthem, Hear my prayer (Mendelssohn).

SALISBURY CATHEDRAL. Morn.: Service, Te Deum and Jubilate, Cooke in G; Kyrie and Credo, Dykes in F; Offertory, (Redhead). Aft. Service, Cooke in G; Anthem, Hear my prayer (Mendelssohn).

SHEFFIELD PARISH CHURCH. — Morn.: Service, Kyrie, (Redhead). Even.: Service, Cantate Domine and Deus Misereatur, Chants; Anthems, Holy, holy! (Handel), and, What are these (Stainer).

SHERBORNE ABBEY. — Morn.: Service, Te Deum, Lyle in D. Even.: Service, Anthem, Sing a song of praise (Stainer).

SOUTHAMPTON (ST. MARY'S CHURCH).—Morn.: Service, Te Deum and Benedictus, Tours in F; Holy Communion; Introit, Jesus said (Stainer); Service, Tours in F; Offertory, God is not unrighteous, and, To do good (Barnby); Paternoster (Field). Even.: Service, Magnificat and Nunc Dimittis, Tours in F; Apostles' Creed, Harmonized Monotone.

WELLS CATHEDRAL. — Morn.: Service, Clarke in E; Introit, O magnify the Lord (Macfarren). Even.: Service, Clarke in E; Anthem, O worship the Lord (Hayes).

WORCESTER CATHEDRAL.—Morn.: Service, Hopkins in F; Anthem, Thou visitest the earth (Greene). Even. Service, Hopkins in F; Anthem, They that go down to the sea (Attwood).

APPOINTMENT.

Mr. C. E. MILLER has been appointed Organist to St. Augustine and St. Faith, Watling Street, E.C.

ERRATUM.—In report of College of Organists' examination last week, one name should be that of C. H. H. Sipple, and not C. H. Hayler Tipple as reported.

THE MUSICAL STANDARD

A NEWSPAPER FOR MUSICIANS PROFESSIONAL AND AMATEUR

No. 992. VOL. XXV. FOURTH SERIES. SATURDAY, AUGUST 4, 1883. WEEKLY: PRICE 3D.

"COUNTERPOINT."

BY H. J. STARK, MUS.BAC.

A Paper read before the College of Organists, on May 1st, 1883.

(Continued from page 47.)

One great feature of the Macfarren system of Counterpoint, the figuring of incomplete chords for the purpose of showing the full harmony, deserves careful attention. If this idea were thoroughly and consistently carried out its value would be self-evident, but, unfortunately, this is not the case. The object sought to be gained is, as Professor Macfarren remarks, "to secure the student's constant sense of the entire harmony, which will often be incompletely represented, and to direct necessary attention to the radical succession of chords." The working out of this idea presents some curious inconsistencies, especially as regards the second inversions of triads, and the second inversions of dominant sevenths, both of which are unquestionably used in the examples, although forbidden in the text. On page 27, for instance, we meet with the following :—

In all fairness, I would ask, how can the fourth chord be considered in any other light than as the second inversion of the tonic triad? To figure it $\frac{8}{4}$ is a simple begging of the whole question, and if the figuring is "to secure the student's constant sense of the entire harmony," the ordinary figuring of a second inversion should be adopted. To first condemn a chord, and afterwards write it in a mutilated form, with a misleading figuring, is in the highest degree illogical and inconsistent.

Again, in Counterpoint of the second order, we find the following :—

These progressions are given as allowable instances of the use of two chords in the same bar, the first interval being considered as representing a chord of the 6th, and the second a triad. In the first two cases the root of the whole bar is unquestionably F, and I am inclined to think that most people would give B flat as the root of the others. Professor Macfarren says :—"Fanciful disputants assume that the second inversion of a concord is implied on the first note of each of these instances, but such fancy outruns reason."

A little further on we find the following examples of cadence :—

On this Professor Macfarren remarks as follows :—"Although at A the leading note precede not the key-note immediately, its effect rests on the memory, and at B the fundamental character of the dominant is equally remembered, and so the single melody gives much of the effect in both instances of the fuller har-

mony, with both the root and the 3rd in the chord." Now, if the effect of the first minim "rests on the memory" in one instance, why not in the other? In which case the "fanciful disputants" would be right in assuming that the $\frac{6}{4}$ chord is distinctly implied in Example 21. Here is another example, from page 33 of the same work :—

If the third bar does not contain the second inversion of the key-note triad, I confess I am at a loss to account for it in any other manner. In the same way the following—

contains in the third bar either the second inversion of the key-note triad, or a chord of the dominant 13th. If the object of the chord-figuring is "to secure the student's constant sense of the entire harmony," it must be admitted that in all these cases it obviously fails in its purpose. Another absurdity is the treatment, in Counterpoint, of the incomplete $\frac{6}{4}$ on the supertonic as the *first inversion of a triad*. Without doubt, the dominant is the root, for the leading note can bear no harmony of its own ; yet, because the interval of a fourth is said to be forbidden in Counterpoint, we find this chord shorn of one of its intervals, and presented in an altogether erroneous light. I am fully aware that this chord is generally used in an incomplete form by Handel and his contemporaries, but in modern times a better knowledge of chords and their roots has led to the employment of this harmony in its complete and more satisfactory aspect. This feeling against second inversions finds no place outside text-books.

Having thus very briefly pointed out a few of the inconsistencies of text-book Counterpoint, I venture to suggest the following modifications as being likely to lead to better results than could be obtained by the existing method. First, let the themes supplied to students be real living melodies, constructed according to the principles of melodic form, and with due regard to the scale-system now in use. Secondly, let nothing be written without full knowledge on the part of the student of the harmonic combinations resulting from the incomplete chords used in 2 and 3 part Counterpoint, so that the chord-figuring becomes a reality instead of a misleading sham. Thirdly, the contrapuntal system should deal satisfactorily with all recognised chord-formations, so that students may become gradually familiar with the application of Counterpoint to all the resources of modern harmony. These suggestions appear to comprise all that is necessary for lifting Counterpoint out of the rut into which it has fallen.

I had originally intended to add to this paper a few examples of Counterpoint constructed according to what I believe to be the true principles of the art. Such examples, however, belong more properly to a treatise on the subject than to a paper, which from its necessarily limited space can touch little beyond the mere outline of the question. The great point to be insisted upon is that the works of classical composers, and especially those of the great John Sebastian Bach, must form the basis of any satisfactory system of

Counterpoint. If I have ventured to call the existing rules into question, it is because I find them to be constantly at variance with all that we are taught to accept as good and beautiful in music, and in no single instance have I omitted to quote the highest possible authority for my statements. These illustrations are not to be put aside as exceptional cases, that in no way affect the soundness of the rules which they violate; on the contrary, such infractions of rule form part of the every-day literature of the art. If it is still contended that the text-books are right, we must conclude that Bach and his later followers have written exceedingly bad Counterpoint; if, on the other hand, we prefer to take our stand upon those imperishable treasures which have descended to us as models of contrapuntal excellence, we must perforce abandon a system of teaching with which they are in conflict. From this position we cannot logically and consistently escape.

It has been asserted that the rules of strict Counterpoint are not intended to apply to actual composition, but are merely useful as a mental exercise. If this be so, one is tempted to ask, *Cui bono?* Surely the object of all teaching should be to impart *useful*, as distinguished from *useless*, knowledge, and this is especially true when dealing with the highly technical matters involved in the training of a musician. If the rules are not intended to be observed, they certainly ought not to be taught, and the attempt to train composers upon the existing laws of Counterpoint may be likened to teaching the use of the modern rifle by a course of instruction in the handling of the antiquated cross-bow.

There is an art of Counterpoint, which all must study to attain excellence, but that art is not to be found in the text-books. It exists in the undying creations of the great masters, whose teaching and practice we may with advantage strive to imitate, even though we can never hope to rival the results which their genius has enabled them to achieve.

DISTRIBUTION OF PRIZES AT THE ROYAL ACADEMY OF MUSIC.

On the afternoon of July 28th, a large assemblage of the pupils of this institution and their friends attended in the hall of the Academy to receive the prizes gained by the successful pupils during the year. The Principal, Sir G. A. Macfarren, presided, Mrs. Ellicott, the wife of the Bishop of Gloucester and Bristol, distributing the prizes. After a selection of vocal music had been rendered by the pupils, the Principal opened the proceedings with a brief address to the Professors and the many other musical celebrities present. The standard by which the pupils were judged had been raised year by year, and, according to the report of the examining board, a higher average than ever had been reached this year. The prizes were then distributed. Amongst those who most highly distinguished themselves was Mr. G. J. Bennett, who, after taking every honour that could be awarded, received from the examiners a certificate that he continued to progress in knowledge of harmony, counterpoint, and composition. Among the lady prize-winners was Miss Frances Smith, who gained the Sterndale-Bennett prize of ten guineas for the pianoforte, and a certificate of merit, the highest possible award. A cordial vote of thanks was given to Mrs. Ellicott. Bishop Ellicott, in returning thanks for Mrs. Ellicott, said he "must congratulate all present on the great advance music had made in the last twenty years; and he could not but attribute that great progress to the steady, persistent, work of a central institution like the Academy. He was glad also to observe some very cheering signs that music was making a definite progress nationally. Our Royal family were giving earnest help in this direction, and he was proud to have a connection with a society—the English Ballad Society—which had discovered that in what were called by some people the lower classes there was a growing taste for music of the very highest order."

Musical Intelligence.

LANCASTER HALL.

Recently a successful concert was given by the pupils of Mr. Russell Lochner, who has done so much to elevate musical taste in the neighbourhood, at the above hall, before a full and appreciative audience. The programme opened with Schubert's "Marche Heroïque," a duet for pianoforte and organ, which was played by Miss Arliss and Mr. Sirkett, the latter of whom afterwards gave two organ solos, an Andante in E of Batiste, and a Postlude in C by Smart, of which the former was very well executed. After a tasteful performance of a Pastorale of Smart's, by Master Rideout, on the organ, a march of Hofman's was played as a pianoforte duet by Miss Mabel Tibbs and Miss Laura Vernon with much spirit. This was followed by the "Children's Queen," sung by Mr. Biss, who was succeeded by Miss J. Gill, who gave a very fair rendering of the andante and variations withthe "Marche Funèbre" from Beethoven's Twelfth Sonata. Of the other pianoforte pieces, the most noticeable were a Nocturne by Le Gran, very well played by Miss M. Hunnard; "Speranza" (Jules Cohen), by Master Rideout; and Chopin's Valse in C sharp minor, given with excellent effect, despite extreme nervousness, by Miss Rose. The most popular *morceau* in the programme was a violin solo—"Fantaisie" by Dancla—played by Master Felix Lochner, a pupil of Mr. R. W. Buttery, which received very great applause. Miss Robinson contributed Wély's "Offertoire in A," which, being charmingly played, met with general approval. The programme concluded with the overture to "Euryanthe" (Weber) for eight hands on two pianos, very accurately rendered by the Misses Pratt, Hunnard, Banke, and Peache. On the whole, Mr. Lochner may be again congratulated on the creditable manner in which his pupils showed the progress made in their musical studies under his careful tuition.   L. S. D.

THE WEST LONDON COLLEGE OF MUSIC.

Signor E. P. Casano and Captain Evatt Acklom held a joint benefit concert last Monday night, at the College, Colville Gardens, Bayswater. A large audience, with several pertinacious talkers of the "mash" or "masher" species in the lobby, assembled on the occasion. The director, Signor Casano, sang his own melody "Un Voce" accompanied by himself, and made a deep impression by his sonorous voice, expressive style, and emphatic delivery. Mdme. Liebhardt sang three times with *éclat*, choosing Lotti's "Pur dicesti," G. B. Allen's "In silence and in tears," and a trifle called "No, sir." The fascinating Miss Gertrude de Lille, whose face may be said to be "her fortune" as well as her voice, sang two airs of Mr. F. Cowen, "If love were what the rose is," and "Better far" in B major, also Tosti's "Aprile," a rather trivial effusion, but not the less applauded by the unreflecting; the *music* alone of course is here referred to, for Miss de Lille's rendering could not fairly be criticized. Mdlle. Blanche Navarre chose "Oh! had I Jubal's lyre," but thought proper to change her second piece, a license always resented, and very properly, by audience, who insist on hearing what is set down in the scheme, and in regular rotation. The title of the second song is purposely suppressed *in terrorem* against future offenders. Miss Helen Meason scored a point in Mr. Wm. Carter's song "Loved for ever." Signor Ria excited a *furore* in "Mi credeva in Paradiso," a sentiment doubtless shared by all the young ladies of the assembly. Signor C. Ducci, Mr. A. Brousil, Herr Oberthür, and Mr. Beresford, played solos on their own instruments, the pianoforte, the violoncello, the harp, and the violin. At the fag end of a very long *soirée*, Misses Gertrude de Lille and H. Meason sang the favourite duet from "Mefistofele," and Signor Casano, a musical veteran, no more fatigued than the Duke of Wellington after the campaign of six years in the Peninsula, sang "Alla Stella confidente," with violoncello accompaniment by Mr. A. Brousil. Captain Acklom gave a recitation but this happily lieth not within the "province" of the musical reporter. The writer left the artists still hard at work, so late as eleven o'clock, with many others of the company, naturally anxious to catch last and if possible *fast* trains.

LIVERPOOL.

(From our own Correspondent.)

JULY 31st.

Mr. E. M. Lott's letter in last week's issue of the *Musical Standard*, does not in the least do away with the truth of my remarks anent the International College of Music and the announced local examination. It is absurd for any person to argue that "no college can be answerable for the actions of its local representatives." It is bad law, as well as being against common-sense and honesty.

I notice that the title of this institution is changed to "Musical International College." I have no wish to cross swords with Mr. Lott, but I cannot allow him to impugn my veracity, or to gloss over a glaring fact by asserting his own law, which would not hold water. If the people like to patronise a series of examinations having no legal status, and the Principal of which says he cannot be answerable for the action of local representatives, well and good.

There is nothing fresh respecting the Liverpool Philharmonic Society. The correspondence on the question of the chorus goes on in the local papers, day by day, but nothing seems to come of it. A great many people call the action of the chorus Quixotic, and I think, not without reason.   J. Ji M.

MR. VON ZASTROW'S DRAWING-ROOM CONCERTS.

Mr. F. Von Zastrow held his benefit concert on Friday July 27th, at the Glendower Mansions, South Kensington. Miss Mabel Bourne and M. Hann began with Mendelssohn's Romance in D for violoncello, which was substituted for a piece of Chopin, announced in the scheme. The burden of the afternoon rested on Miss Mabel Bourne and Mr. Hann. Miss Bourne played for solos her own "Three Sketches," and Chopin's Ballade in G minor. M. Hann, on the violoncello, played a Berceuse and a Tarantelle of Dunkler, and Herr Polonaski Bach's Adagio on the fourth (violin) string, in a masterly style, and a Legende of Wieniwaski, with his own pieces—a "Pensive Fugitive," and the "Chanson du Nord." Mrs. Florence Grant sang "Alta Stella confidente" and "Home, sweet home." Mdme. Polonaski chose her own Reverie "Spring Tide," and Braga's Serenata in G. A good *pièce de résistance* was Rubinstein's beautiful Pianoforte Trio in B flat, with Miss Bourne, Herr Polonaski, and M. Hann as interpreters. This work had been done before at the Glendower Mansions. If the reading was imperfect, partly no doubt, from want of sufficient rehearsals, the audience nevertheless, might fairly appreciate the work. But to those who have heard Rubinstein play the pianoforte part at the Musical Union, comparisons could not fail to be suggested. The audience at this concert was numerous and brilliant.

VARIOUS CONCERTS.

Mr. D'Arcy Ferris held his annual concert in the afternoon of July 36th, at Lord and Lady Spencer Churchill's house in Manchester Square. Mr. D'Arcy Ferris sang with taste R. B. Addison's "Serenade" in D, and Blumenthal's "Across the far blue hills." He also produced and sang the tenor part of a new trio composed by himself "In memoriam," to the memory of the late Duke of Marlborough. More might be said for the music (in A minor and major) than for the stanzas, which are but sorry specimens of versification. Mr. D'Arcy Ferris was aided by Miss Helen Arnim, Miss B. Navarre, Signor Ria, Miss Beata Francis, Mdme. Osborne Williams, and Mdlle. De Vaney, who, with Mr. D'Arcy-Ferris, sang the "Garden Scene" from "Faust." Mr. W. Ganz, Signor Samuelli, Mr. Lindo, and Sir Julius Benedict were the conductors.

The Misses Poole held a final reception (for the season) on Monday, at their residence in St. Paul's Road, Camden Road. Miss Mina Poole sang a pretty Serenade in D flat of Mr. Otto Booth, the violinist, with violin obbligato (played by the composer). The Rev. Mr. Taylor, the Chaplain of Gray's Inn, and a very clever amateur vocalist, greatly amused the company with a setting of a song of Spanish colour and French words. Mdme.

Viard-Louis played. Litolff's pianoforte piece "La Petite Fileuse" and might have been asked to resume her seat, but some tiresome and most unwelcome "recitations" were held to be more acceptable—a great mistake. The intelligent public, it may be repeated, dislike these recitations exceedingly, unless, indeed, they are delivered by superior elocutionists, such as Mrs. Fairfax Bell. True, that this was only a private reception."

GLOUCESTER MUSICAL FESTIVAL.

The principal artists engaged for the Gloucester festival are Miss Anna Williams, Mdlle. Avigliana, and Miss Mary Davies, Mdme. Patey and Miss Hilda Wilson, Mr. Edward Lloyd and Mr. Boulcott Newth, Mr. Frederick King, Mr. W. H. Brereton, and Mr. Santley; organist, Mr. Langdon Colborne, Mus. Bac.; pianoforte (and organ, Wednesday evening), Mr. W. Done; leader and solo violinist, Mr. Carrodus; conductor, Mr. Charles L. Williams, Mus. Bac. Many of our most eminent instrumentalists will appear in the band; the organ will be specially erected by Messrs. Willis, of London.

The following is a list of the works to be performed: on Tuesday morning, Sept. 4th, "Elijah" (Mendelssohn). Wednesday morning, Sept. 5th, "St. Mary Magdalene" (Stainer), composed for this festival, and conducted by the composer; "Bow thine ear" (Bird, 1560), unaccompanied; "Hosanna, to the Son of David" (Gibbons, 1604) unaccompanied; "Mass in C" (Beethoven). Wednesday evening, Sept. 5th, "Sennacherib," (Arnold), composed for this festival, conducted by the composer; "Hymn of Praise" (Mendelssohn). Thursday morning, Sept. 6th, "Elegiac Symphony" (C. V. Stanford)—allegro appassionata, lento expressivo, scherzo, adagio, allegro—conducted by the composer; and "Redemption" (Gounod). Friday morning, Sept. 7th, "Messiah" (Handel).

The programme on Tuesday evening includes Symphony in G minor (Mozart) and overture, "Anacreon" (Cherubini). On Thursday evening, overture, "Jessonda" (Spohr), and "The First Walpurgis-Night," or, "The Eve of the First of May" (Mendelssohn). On Friday evening there will be a grand nave service, to include organ voluntary; prelude, "Last Judgment" (Spohr); Magnificat; Nunc Dimittis; anthem, "Blessed is the man that considereth the poor and needy" (C. H. Lloyd), and "Hallelujah" (Beethoven).

Convenient railway arrangements have been made for the four days, and every action taken to secure a successful meeting and to obtain due comfort for visitors.

NEWCASTLE-ON-TYNE.

The great interest taken in the choral festival in connection with Newcastle Cathedral was remarkably displayed on Thursday, July 26th, when the first festival was held in the Cathedral Church of St. Nicholas. Before the hour announced for the commencement of the service, all the available space was fully occupied, and the scene was one of impressive solemnity as the long line of surpliced choristers wound their way through the crowded audience to their appointed places, to the voluntary played by the cathedral organist, Mr. M. W. J. Ions. Five cathedral choirs were present—Newcastle, Durham, York, Ripon, and Carlisle—and they were assisted by several local choirs in the district, and also by some female choristers and lady amateur singers. Among the clergy present were the Bishop of Newcastle, the Dean of York, Archdeacon Hamilton, and the Vicar of Newcastle (Canon Lloyd). The service consisted of evening prayer, Tallis's Preces being used throughout. Between the lessons the Magnificat and Nunc Dimittis were sung to the music in G, specially composed for the occasion by Mr. Ions. The service contains many beautiful and effective passages, and Mr. Ions has certainly proved his fitness for the office he occupies by this admirable contribution to Church music, and to the beautiful Service of the Church of England.

In the place of an anthem, Dr. Gladstone's new Church oratorio, "Philippi," was sung, the words selected from the Scriptures by the Rev. J. Powell Metcalf, M.A. It opens with a prologue, in which the choirs unaccompanied sing the two well-known verses from Isaiah, "How beautiful upon the mountains." This chorus is an excellent example of four-part writing, full of harmony and sweetness, and was sung by the choirs—as were, in fact, all the choruses—with a power and precision which left nothing to be desired.

The cantata is divided into seven parts :—I. The Call to Macedonia ; II. The Conversion of Lydia ; III. Casting out the Spirit of Divination ; IV. The Fury of the People ; V. In the Prison ; VI. The Keeper of the Prison ; VII. Sweet Counsel with the Brethren. These divisions describe the chief incidents in the narrative ; and to four of the cathedral choirs were allotted the solo pieces—the Newcastle choir, with Mr. F. Mace, 1st tenor ; Mr. T. Thompson, 2nd tenor ; Master J. Dewar, soprano, and Mr. E. Perry, bass, had the first and fifth divisions. York, with Mr. MacDonald, tenor ; Master Sheffield, soprano ; and Mrs McCall, bass, had the second and sixth. Durham, with Mr. Whitehead, tenor ; Master J. Walker, contralto ; and Mr. Nutton, bass, the third and fourth division, and Ripon the seventh division. The solo members of the Ripon choir deserve great praise for the refined way in which they sang the beautiful quintet (unaccompanied), "Rejoice in the Lord." In fact, both soloists and choristers rendered the music of Dr. Gladstone's new oratorio in a way that evoked the greatest praise from its composer, who conducted his own work. Mr. Ions presided at the organ, and played with great taste and precision the accompaniments.

"Philippi," is an admirable work which will compare favourably with many of similar character which have preceded it. The style is a purely religious one, and notwithstanding some of the recitatives and solos are very finely written ; the choruses are decidedly the most interesting and dramatic numbers in the work. Special mention must be made of "Praise the Lord, O my soul," "For of Him and through Him," and perhaps the grandest of them all, "Why do the heathen rage?" preceded by a contralto recitation "And the multitude rose up," which was admirably rendered by Master J. Walker. The chorus was splendidly sung. The festival concluded by the singing of the festival hymn," "Hail, festal day ! for ever sanctified," music by Dr. Armes, of Durham.

The success which attended this festival has been so great, that it is to be hoped it will be an annual event—more so considering the beneficial effect it will have upon the manner in which the musical portions of Services are rendered in the various Churches in the district.

Dr. Gladstone has in a letter to our esteemed cathedral organist, Mr. Ions, expressed his delight in seeing the "evident enthusiasm which was thrown into the work by everyone, both in the choruses and in the solos," and Dr. Gladstone further adds :—" I feel deeply grateful to all who so kindly assisted in the first performance of 'Philippi.' My letter would, however, be incomplete if I failed to offer to you personally my warm thanks, not only for the pains which you must have taken in organising the festival, but also for your much valued aid at the organ."

Mr. T. Albion Alderton's amateur choir will perform during the season, 1883—84, the following works, all by English composers :—"The Sun Worshippers," by Goring Thomas ; "The Rose Maiden," by Cowen ; "The Fairy Ring," by Cummings, and "Jason," by Mackenzie.

The Tyne Theatre will open the season with Messrs. Gilbert and Sullivan's fairy opera, "Iolanthe" ; and the Theatre Royal, with "Rob Roy." During the vacation, both the theatres have undergone complete renovation, and, many alterations have also been made for the comfort and safety of the audience.

The deepest sensation was created amongst all sections of the temperance party of Newcastle and the religious bodies in the town at the news that Mr. Rowland Lambert had expired suddenly at his residence, Villa de St. George, on July 30th. He was the energetic originator and sole manager of the so-called Blue-Ribbon Concerts, which have been held here every Saturday night, at the Central Hall, during several years, and with the greatest success—the place being invariably crowded to the door by a delighted audience, consisting mainly of working men and their families. In Mr. R. Lambert's death the cause of temperance has sustained a loss that appears irreparable, and the poor a friend whose sympathy and help were always available in their distress.

H. W.

Madame Lind Goldschmidt (Jenny Lind) was one of the artists who gave their services at the grand concert at the Royal Spa Hall, Malvern, for the benefit of the Widows and Orphans of the Great Western Railway Servants on July 23rd. Her fresh and vigorous singing in Mendelssohn's trio "Lift thine eyes," and Rubinstein's "Song of the Birds," completely astonished the audience.

Foreign Musical Intelligence.

Samuel David's opera "Bianca Capello" will be given in Paris next winter.

The "Societa Musicala" of Rome recently performed Schumann's "Paradise and the Peri" very successfully.

The Vienna Court Opera re-opened on the 16th ult. with Meyerbeer's "Huguenots."

Milan is having a summer operatic season, Donizetti's "La Fille du Regiment" being one attraction.

The "Parsifal" performances at Bayreuth appear to be financially a failure. However, the King of Bavaria has undertaken to pay the deficit.

Verdi's "Don Carlos" will be heard next season at La Scala, Milan. The composer hopes by that time to have completed his new opera, "Othello."

It is announced that Dr. Hermann Zopff, well known as a musical critic in Leipzig, died on the 12th of July at the age of fifty-seven.

Dr. Hans von Bülow, who is at present staying at the Lake of Geneva, has, it is said, so far recovered his health that he hopes to be able in the autumn to resume his duties at Meiningen.

The German rights in "The Nibelungs Ring" have been sold by Herr Neumann, to the Prussian Intendant-General for £1,000. However Wagner's family intend to dispute the transfer in a court of law.

Here is a promising bit of news for the lovers of Italian opera. Signor Cagnoni, whose opera "Don Bucefalo," it is stated, has been very successful in Italy, has written an opera on the subject of "King Lear," which will be produced at the opening of the new theatre at Novara.

A recent number of the Muskalisches Wochenblatt contains a report from the pen of Herr Richard Pohl of the present performances of "Parsifal" in Bayreuth. The writer pronounces them even more nearly perfect than those which were given last year.

An Italian journal gives the following account of a musical invention by a priest named Bartolomeo Grassi-Landi. It concerns a reform in the present manner of writing music, the invention itself being a chromatic keyboard which may be applied to organs, pianos, and harmoniums. The octave is divided into twelve sounds, and with the present system we have seven names, ut, re, mi, fa, sol, la, si, which represent the natural scale. These notes may be raised by the sharp and double sharp, or lowered by the flat and double flat. This makes thirty-five names, which in reality only represent twelve sounds. M. Grassi-Landi abolishes sharps, flats, and naturals, giving to the twelve sounds the following names, Ba, Be, Bi, Bo, Da, De, Di, Do, La, Le, Li, Lo. Each name represents a sound which never varies. In writing M. Grassi-Landi retains the old system, with the modification that the value of the notes is exclusively shown by quavers and semi-quavers, the heads being either white or black, indicating the sound. All the white ones, on, or between the lines represent the white keys, the black ones the black keys.

TRINITY COLLEGE, LONDON.—At the recent examinations for Musical Diplomas at Trinity College, London, the following gentlemen acted as examiners :—Sir Julius Benedict (Musical Form and Orchestration), R. W. Crowe, Mus. D., Cantab. (Harmony), A. H. Mann, Mus. D., organist of King's College, Cambridge (Choir Training, &c.), E. H. Turpin (Counterpoint and Fugue), James Keene, F.R.C.S. Eng. (Vocal and Aural Physiology), and W. H. Walshe (Musical Acoustics).

ROYAL COLLEGE OF MUSIC.—The Prince of Wales presided at a meeting of the Council, held at Marlborough House on Monday, July 30th. There were present : Prince Christian, the Earl Cadogan, Lord Charles Bruce, M.P., Baron Ferdinand Rothschild, Sir John Rose, Sir Henry Thring, Sir Julius Benedict, Sir Arthur Sullivan, Mr. Cusins, Mr. Thomas Chappell, Mr. Otto Goldschmidt, Mr. E. W. Hamilton, C.B., Mr. Charles Morley, Mr. Kellow Pye, and Dr. Stainer. The director, Sir George Grove, was in attendance. The following were unavoidably absent : The Duke of Edinburgh, the Archbishop of Canterbury, the Archbishop of York, the Duke of Westminster, Sir Lyon Playfair, M.P., Sir Thos. Gladstone, Sir Richard Wallace, Sir Thomas Brassey, M.P., and Mr. Charles Hall.

Organ News.

PRESTON.

The following is the programme of an organ recital given by Mr. James Tomlinson, in the New Public Hall, on Saturday evening, July 28th :—

Grand Concerto in G minor	Handel.
(Larghetto—Allegro, introducing the Cadenza written by Mr. Best for the recent Handel Festival.—Adagio—Andante.)	
Pilgrim's March (Fourth Symphony)	Mendelssohn.
Andante (Quartet in C)	Mozart.
Turkish March from the "Ruins of Athens"	Beethoven.
Liebesfrühling	Unger.
Overture to "Cenerentola"	Rossini.

MANCHESTER.

On Sunday evening, the 29th inst., at the Holy Innocents' Church, Fallowfield, Mr. W. A. Wrigley gave an organ recital after evening service. The programme included :—

Minuet ("Samson")	Handel.
Bénédiction Nuptiale	Saint-Saëns.
Cantilène Pastorale	Guilmant.
Grand Chœur in D	,,

HALSTEAD, ESSEX.

The following is the programme of an organ recital given after the service on Sunday evening, July 29th, by Mr. G. Leake, A.C.O.

The Prophet's March	Meyerbeer.
Adagio from C minor Symphony	Beethoven.
"My hope is in the Everlasting" ("Daughter of Jairus")	Stainer.
Gloria, 12th Mass	Mozart.
Song, "The Better Land"	Cowen.
The Vesper Hymn	Turpin.

FISHERIES EXHIBITION.

Mr. Loaring's programmes, on the 23rd and 26th inst., included the following :—

Overture, "Zampa"	Hérold.
Organ Concerto (No. 6)	Handel.
Offertoire in B flat	Collin.
Concert Fantasia in C minor	Reese.
March Héroïque in D	Schubert.

Overture, "Le Cheval de Bronze"	Auber.
March Funèbre	Chopin.
Offertoire in F	S. Clark.
"Hallelujah Chorus"	Handel.
March "Tannhäuser"	Wagner.

CORK.

Programme of recitals given by Herr H. C. Swertz, on the organ of the Exhibition, on Saturday, 21st inst :—

*March	Swertz.
Sonata, No. 1	Mendelssohn.
Adagio from Op. 65	Rheinberger.
*Valse	Swertz.
Overture, "William Tell"	Rossini.
*Fantasia	Swertz.
* These were Improvisations.	

And on Tuesday, 24th inst. :—

Prelude in E minor	Mendelssohn.
Overture, "William Tell"	Rossini.
Valses, No. and 3, Op. 34	Chopin.
"Hymn to the Night"	Swertz.
(For soprano solo, chorus, and orchestra).	
Sonata, No. 1, Op. 8	Beethoven.
Finale (Improvisation)	Swertz.

BRADFORD.

An organ which has been erected in the Leeds Road Baptist Chapel was formally opened on July 26th. The instrument, which was built by Gray, of London, and afterwards enlarged by Hill and Sons, occupied the Trinity Church, Halifax, for some years. It has two Manuals and Pedal organ, with some 24 stops, including couplers. The Pedal organ, the Swell organ, and three of the soft stops were put in by Messrs. Hill, and two composition pedals for the Swell and three for the Great organ have yet to be added by Mr. F. W. Nicholson, who has re-erected the instrument. The opening recital was given by Mr. J. H. Rooks, who brought out with excellent judgment and taste every available portion of the instrument. Mr. Rooks' masterly rendering of "The Giant" was exceedingly enjoyable. He also gave a fine performance of the fantasie "O Sanctissima" (F. Lux), some parts of which are difficult, and in this and the "La Clemenza" overture (Mozart) he thoroughly displayed the resources of the instrument, bringing out well the good tone of some of the soft stops which were put in by Messrs. Hill. In addition to the organ recital there were vocal selections from Sir M. Costa's "Naaman."

A MUSIC LECTURE OF THE OLDEN TIMES.

In the course of an interesting article under the above title in the *Musical Review*, Mr. W. Barclay Squire says :—The establishment of the music lecture at Oxford by Dr. Heather, in 1626, is almost the only fact that is known of the routine of university instruction in music, though the position which the art held in the Trivium and Quadrivium—which in those days formed the basis of the whole curriculum of a liberal education—render it tolerably certain that, in Oxford at least, there must have been some regular system of musical education authorised by the university. Dr. Heather's foundation came at almost the close of the period of musical activity which produced the greater musicians who are the chief glory of the English school; nor does the roll of professors who occupied the musical chair at Oxford during the seventeenth century comprise any very distinguished names, and therefore any glimpse, however faint and indefinite, of an earlier state of things, cannot fail to possess a certain amount of interest. Such a passing glimpse is afforded by a letter from that admirable correspondent, Sir Dudley Carleton, to his friend Mr. John Chamberlain, which is preserved in the still almost unexplored mine of historical treasures, the State Papers in the Record Office. The letter, the original of which will be found in the Domestic State Papers, James I., volume xxxv., runs as follows :

Sir,—Though I am presented by Mr. Gent who hath sent you the Act questions and Oxford newes, yet I can not forbeare my relation likewise, because you may be the better-informed of our Universitie proceedings, wch were cheefly memorable at this time for a deluge of Doctors ; there being 22 of all professions, but none almost of note or apparence. I had the goode fortune to meete with Sr John Bennet with whom I spent the small time I was there, wch was monday and tuesday. Sr Will Paddie was no small grace to the towne, who made a solemne entrie in a coach with fower white mares and six men in liuerie, well mounted. The Saturday exercise was not much spoken of, only the musike lecture wch was read in the morning by one Sheapheard sownded long after, who tooke vppon him a Cambridge quarrel, first remembering a ballet that was made there in disgrace of the king's entertainment at Oxford, and then answering one Cecill the Proctor of Cambridge who in their last commencement inuayed against a booke sett out by the Orator of Oxford touching the exercise that was there performed before the king. And for the first part he sayde it was nether cantus, nor cantio, cantibula, nor cantilena, nor anything in Latin but Anglicè—a Ballet, and those that made it might properly be called Balatrones. The ditie he turned into Latin :—

Istibani oppidani
Qui dicuntur Aldermani, &c., &c.

the tune he putt to it was 'To the Parlament the Q(ueen) is gone,' and because being in a narrow pue he sayde it was not '*locus ad agenda amplissimus*,' he came out into the schoole and there playde it upon a viol. 'But' (sayde he) 'since now *Sicelide musae doc paulo maiora canere*,' he would deale with Cecill, and reciting all the inuectiues made by Tullie in his oration against Cecilius he sayde they were prophesies of this man, and went on with more than an howers speach all in this mad merrie tune, and had great audience as well of Cambrige men as others. In the monday exercise there were likewise many inuectiues, as the Philosophers in the question '*An terra sit naturae magnetica*,' against D : Gilbert and all his sectaries wch they call Gilbertinos, wherein *il y va de vostre* interest, the Phisitians against the Ciuilians, and the Ciuilians against poore woemen. The diuines descanted one uppon an other, as D : Thornton had his name diuided into *Spina* and *dolii*, and it was made a wonder why he should hold that we could not *perfectè implere legè* when *dolii* might be so easely both fild and emptied, and many such yong conceits not so well befitting theyr grauities and professions. At supper in Christchurch it was my hap to lite in a mess with D : White, D : Perin, and Sr Ed : Ratliff, whose wittes and fooleries did so well encounter that I made goode amends for our long sitting up wch was fully past midnight before we rose frō the table.

"I am now here againe at goode leisure as by my scribling unto you you may well coniecture, and purpose to spend a month yf not more betwixt this place, the Grange, and Ascott. Sr Michell and my Lady goe on Saturday next to Hampton poyle and I differre my going to them till theyr returne frō thence because I would not so soone part frō thē. Sr Hn : Saville and my La : come about a fortnight hence to Oxford there to stay for a month. My Ld : Norreys was gone to the Bath before I came into this cuntrie and doth there purpose to stay as yet fiue weekes. Sr Michell Dormer doth threaten a Jornie to go see him and I haue halfe past a promise to accompanie him, wch I shall the better performe with my wifes leaue if you come into the cuntrie in good time, that you may moderat matters betweene such disputants as 'I doubt' the woemen will proue at Ascott about theyr little faiths. We perswade our selfs you will hasten yr cuming for our sakes ; as I assure you it is for yours that we doe the more linger, in hope to see you before we return and thus wth all kind remembrances to yrself and the two goode societies of Knebworth and Ware parke I comitt you to Gods protection.

"frõ Huntercomb,
"this 14th day of July 1608
"Yrs most assuredly
"DUDLEY CARLETON.
" To my very louing frend
Mr. John Chamberlain at Wingfield
house on St Peters hill give these,
London."

Enclosed in the above letter are some Latin verses in Sir Dudley Carleton's handwriting, headed "Licet marito uxorem verberare," the humour of which is of a description more relished in those days than it would be in our own time.

To the student of the history of English music, the chief interest in the above letter lies in the individuality of "one Sheapheard," as to whom there is some little difficulty in identification. Sir Dudley Carleton was a distinguished diplomatist of the seventeenth century. He was born in 1573, educated at Westminster and Christchurch, where he took his B.A. degree in 1595 and his M.A. in 1600. He was successively secretary to the Embassy to France, to Henry Earl of Northumberland, and sat for St. Mawes in the first Parliament of James I. In 1605 he went to Spain with Lord Norris. He was imprisoned on suspicion of being concerned in the Gunpowder Plot, but was soon afterwards released. He married a niece of Sir Maurice Carey in 1607, and the remainder of his life was principally spent as Ambassador in Holland, from which country his letters to England— which have been edited and published—are a valuable contribution to the history of the period. He was created Viscount Dorchester by Charles I. He died February 15, 1631-2, and is buried in Westminster Abbey. There is a large collection of Carleton's letters preserved in the State Papers, many of which are addressed (like the one we have already given) to his friend John Chamberlain. This John Chamberlain was born in 1552, and educated at Cambridge. He possessed a considerable private fortune, and spent most of his life at his country residence, from which he kept up a constant correspondence with Carleton, Sir Henry Saville, and many other distinguished persons. He died between 1626 and 1631. Sir John Bennet was the grandfather of the Earl of Arlington. He was the second son of Sir Richard Bennet, was educated at Oxford, where he filled the office of Proctor for some time, and received the degree of Doctor of Laws in 1589. He was knighted at the coronation of James I., and was distinguished as a judge, though, like his contemporary Bacon, he fell into the habit of taking bribes, for which he was fined the enormous sum of £20,000. He died in 1627. William Gilbert was born at Colchester in 1540, and educated at Cambridge. He was admitted a Fellow of the College of Physicians in 1573, and achieved considerable scientific reputation from his discoveries with regard to the magnet. He died November 30th, 1603. Sir William Paddie was a celebrated doctor of the day, physician to the King, and President of the College of Physicians. He bequeathed his valuable library to St. John's College, where he also left funds to endow an organist and provide for the performance of choral service. He died in 1634, and is buried in the College Chapel. His portrait may still be seen at St. John's. The "D: White," of Sir Dudley Carleton was probably Dr. Thomas White, a Canon of Christchurch at the beginning of the seventeenth century. "D: Perin" was Dr. John Perin, who was sometime Fellow of St. John's, Regius Professor of Greek in 1597, and installed a Canon of Christchurch in 1604. He died in 1615, and is buried in the Cathedral. "Lord Norreys or Norris," was, as we have seen, an old friend of Carleton's ; Sir Michael Dormer came of a city family, and Sir Henry Saville (1549-1621) was Warden of Merton and Provost of Eton. As to the Cambridge Proctor, "One Cecill," he was possibly Thomas Cecill, a Fellow of St. John's, but the Cambridge records of this time are unfortunately not so numerous and accessible as those of the sister university. "The booke sett out by the orator of Oxford" can be identified with tolerable certainty as a quarto volume which appeared in 1607, and ran through some six editions. It is an account of the celebrated visit of James I. and his court to Oxford in 1605, by Isaac Wake of Merton, and is entitled "Rex Platonicus : sive de Potentissimi Principis Jacobi Britanniarum Regis, Ad Illustrissimam Academiam Oxoniensem, Adventu, Aug. 27, Anno MDCV. Narratio ab Isaaco Wake," etc., etc.

With regard to Shepherd, there was an eminent composer of this name living at Oxford about fifty years earlier than the date of Sir Dudley Carleton's letter, and many of his works are preserved in the Music School and Christchurch collections, as well as in the British Museum and other libraries. This John Shepherd—or Sheppard, as it is often spelt—was a Fellow of Magdalen, where he was appointed Instructor of the choristers in 1542. In the following year his place was taken by one Preston, but Shepherd was reinstated in 1545 and held the office until 1547. He was also organist of the College Chapel, which post he seems to have occupied until 1595, when Richard Nicholson was appointed. On April 21, 1554, Shepherd, according to Anthony à Wood's "Fasti Oxonienses," presented a petition that he might be admitted to the degree of Mus. Doc., stating that he had been a student in music for twenty years, but there is no record that his prayer was granted. On the 2nd June, 1555, it is recorded in the Magdalen registers that Master Shepherd was fined for having kept an unfortunate chorister in chains, "et eundem contra formam statuti ad pernoctandum admiserit," a fact which throws some light upon the manner in which choristers were punished in those days. On the 15th of the same month, Master Shepherd was again accused "quod puerum quendam pauperem vinctum miserè traheret a Maumsberge Oxoniam usque "—a method of obtaining recruits for the choir which was too scandalous even for those days.

At a first glance, the singular behaviour of this Shepherd would seem to tally with the description given of the "one Sheapheard" of Carleton, but (if the facts given by Wood are correct) it is hardly possible that they can be the same person. But there is some evidence that about this time there lived another John Shepherd, who was also a musician, for in the Cheque Book of the Chapel Royal a person of this name was sworn as a "Gentleman Extraordinary" on December 1, 1606, "who, at the takinge of his othe, did voluntarilie binde himselfe thereby not to sue by any meanes direct or indirect, as by friendes or otherwise, to be admitted into an ordinarie place of paye in his Highnes sayd Chappell, untill he shalbe called and approved fitt for the same by the Deane, the Sub-Deane, and the major part of the Gentlemen then beynge." As his name does not occur again in the Cheque Book, it is not improbable that this Shepherd never became an ordinary member of the Chapel, and that it is he whose jests Carleton chronicled for the benefit of his friend. It would be interesting to examine the extant compositions which bear the name of Shepherd, to see whether it may not be possible that some of the compositions of the later musician of that name (none of which are recorded to exist) have not been included in the works of the Magdalen organist mentioned by Wood.

TONIO SOL-FA COLLEGE.

On July 7th the Council of the Tonic Sol-fa College held its half yearly meeting at 186, Aldersgate-street. After some preliminary business the consideration of the proposed staff notation certificates was resumed, the discussion ending in its rejection by a considerable majority. It was then resolved that the possession of the elementary certificate be a preliminary to the staff notation certificates, which the executive were requested to draw up for the consideration of the Council. A motion by Mr. Hardcastle (Liverpool), requiring the examination for the elementary and intermediate certificate to be completed always at one sitting was discussed, and by leave withdrawn. A motion by Mr. Bonner, for holding a choral competition in London in June, 1884, was lost. The Report to be presented to the shareholders was approved, and the Council adjourned.

The annual meeting of shareholders was held in the same building in the evening, when there was a good attendance. After the appointment of scrutineers, Mr. R. Griffiths, secretary, read the annual report and financial statement. The report mentioned the chief events of the year. The new shares issued were 189, to 164 persons, making a total of £2,576 shares issued to more than 1,000 shareholders. The certificates issued were 16,047 against 11,881 last year, an increase of 4,166. The income from examinations was within a few pounds of covering the necessary expenditure, but left no margin for new schemes. Mr. D. S. Allan (Glasgow), moved the adoption of the report and financial statement which had been read. He remarked on the increase in certificates, and said that it was in the power of teachers still further to promote their use. Mr. Adamson (Dundee), in seconding this, bore out what Mr. Allan had said. He believed that the 6d. tax had greatly raised the value of the certificates in Scotland. The resolution was unanimously carried. The election of Mr. Henry Leslie as an honorary member was moved by Mr. A. J. Ellis, F.R.S., who spoke of Mr. Leslie's weight in the musical world, and of the importance of his adhesion to our movement. Mr. Thomas (Manchester) in seconding, recalled the time when it required a sacrifice to be a Solfaist ; things were changed now. Before the resolution was put, Mr. McNaught mentioned a phrase in Mr. Leslie's Exeter Hall speech which was likely to be misunderstood. Mr. Leslie had spoken of a Sol-faist having to unlearn the Tonic Sol-fa in order to proceed to the staff. Mr. Leslie had explained to him that all he meant was that a Sol-faist in this position had to set to work to become accustomed to new signs and nomenclature. The resolution was carried amid cheers. The election of Mr. Sedley Taylor of Cambridge, was moved by Mr. Ashcroft, who said he had that week been reading Mr. Taylor's pamphlet, and felt that the College would strengthen itself by closer association with such an authority in scientific circles. Mr. John Bell (Glasgow) seconded, and the resolution was unanimously passed. Thanks to the auditors were moved by Mr. Coventry (Manchester), seconded by Mr. T. Austin (Bedford) and carried. Mr. Venables spoke of the work of his Association. Mr. McNaught addressed the meeting at some length, on the condition of music in schools and Training Colleges. Mr. Ashcroft urged the issue of a circular to Training Colleges which had not adopted Tonic Sol-fa, and moved a resolution to that effect. Mr. J. A. Birch (Chapel Royal) seconded, describing the admirable sight-singing of the children in the London Board Schools. Mr. W. Bond thought it a pity that so few pupil-teachers took the music paper. Some inspectors discouraged it. As to the Training College course, he had come across many teachers who had passed through College and had yet no idea of the practical teaching of singing. After a few words from Mr. Ellis, Mr. Curwen said he doubted the wisdom of addressing the Colleges, as he thought they would very soon spontaneously adopt the Tonic Solfa system. The resolution was then modified, asking the executive to consider the advisability of issuing a circular, and unanimously passed. Mr. A. J. Wilson moved, and Rev. C. Livermore, vicar of Norley, seconded, the appointment of Mr. Warner as shareholders' auditor for the year. Thanks to the scrutineers were moved by Mr. G. Merritt, and seconded by Mr. W. D. Oliver (Newcastle). Mr. Proudman moved, and Mr. A. J. Ellis seconded, thanks to the officers, to which Mr. Curwen and Mr. Griffiths briefly responded, and the meeting ended.

At a meeting of the Council on the 21st July, the president and treasurers were re-elected, and the following members of Council were chosen by ballot :—Messrs. Bonner, W. C. Harris, Coward (Sheffield), Jenkins (Aberystwyth), Adamson (Dundee), Cowley (Dublin).

Mr. Curwen reported that the summer term had commenced most auspiciously. The students were more numerous than they had been for several years, 33 having entered already. They were, moreover, of high average ability, and of much earnestness.

The following letter from Mr. Henry Leslie was read—

Bryn Tanat, July 20th.

Dear Sir,—I am much flattered and gratified at the honour conferred upon me by being elected an honorary member of your College, and gratefully accept the position. I doubt not I shall have in the future to speak frequently on the happy results of your system, for a movement which has done so much good in the diffusion of elementary choral singing in the past is not in the least likely to retire into the background, but will continue in the front rank of workers, carrying good results wherever it is used. I shall be much obliged if you will convey my best thanks to your Council at the earliest opportunity. I am, Dear Sir, faithfully yours,

Robert Griffiths, Esq. HENRY LESLIE.

—Tonic Sol-Fa Reporter.

PRINCIPAL CONTENTS OF THIS NUMBER.

LONDON : SATURDAY, AUGUST 4, 1883.

THE PRESENT POSITION OF THE COMPOSER.

VI.

CERTAIN recent incidents have called my attention more forcibly to the want of knowledge of the world and its ways displayed by many of our young composers. Many prevalent disappointments and disasters await the young artist through that *ignis fatuus* of the art world—the belief that unaided merit will in the end be sure to claim a due public recognition. How many weary years are wasted even by good and sensible artists, in vain efforts to clutch at seemingly hopeful opportunities ! How many friendless young composers dream of the possible chances of a commission to write an opera, or the chances of getting the oratorios performed which are to place their happy authors at once on the pinnacle of fame ! It may be well that hopes do thus buoy up human hearts and so lead to untold efforts of perseverance and patience. Still, it would surely be better if it were more generally understood that, as a rule, there is no pathway to reputation save that which is hedged in by favourable surrounding circumstances and smoothed by friendly hands. Genius and talent, and the still rarer virtues of patience and clear sighted resolution, are after all common enough, and the "mute inglorious MILTONS" exist in myriads; but the presence of genius in exactly the right mind, and its possession by the person so placed socially as to command the first population on the stream of public favour, presents a picture of comparative rarity. It is ordained that millions of the choicest flowers shall grow year by year, bloom and pass away, never seen by mortal eye. Similarly there are millions of highly artistic minds which never come within the range of cultivation and opportunity. Then, again, alas! there are thousands who persist for years in mistaking the glow of enthusiasm for the rapture of genius, and only find out too late, after perhaps a wasted life-time and through painful disappointments, that the "fond imagination" of hopeful natures and the kindly folly of surrounding friends, are responsible for many a wrecked career to be seen on the shore which separates time from eternity. It is a moot question, indeed, whether even in aristocratic England, where native talent is much too little appreciated, it is not much easier to win a peerage, starting from the clerk's stool of a country lawyer's office, than it is, without the requisite social advantages, to secure a recognised position as a composer whose works will be performed and listened to. At the present time, with an increased encouragement, the annals of the art can show no single instance of a composer of estimation in public opinion who has not had such advantages either in the good station of his parents, or by the timely encouragement of influential friends, or through the fostering shelter of the cathedral or public institution. So the man why is fully conscious of the possession of sound ability and yet lacks such advantages, should take care to advance step by step from small to great things and above all to assiduously make friends, for without them in modern society no talents or gifts, however great, have any value, inasmuch as they can have no friendly recognition. One prevalent idea now is the notion that the competitive opportunities presented from time to time are calculated to benefit both the art and composers. It is quite true that they do a certain amount of good in the way of encouraging young writers to make definite efforts, but as a general principle these competitions lead to but little result. If it happens that a prize is gained by a well known writer (be it observed, however, that well-known musicians are generally much too busy to enter into competitions), then the usual result of having gained public favour follows the publication of such a work, and a success is a natural result. If, however, the prize has been honourably gained by an unknown hand, then the writer's labour is soon to be lost, and the object of the well-disposed donors is defeated, for the reason that the writer lacking the very "breath of life" to the artist—a secured friendly recognition, his work excites no stimulated public curiosity and interest, and even if performed or published, or both, and in spite of very remarkable merits, is speedily forgotten. It seems, and it is a trite truism to say, that no short road to success can be devised, and the wise artist plods along, not caring to turn aside to pluck the flowers which are within his grasp, but which will fade within an hour. So success or want of success in the competitive schemes of the day should not give the art producer one moment's solicitude in his onward march to the summit of Mount Parnassus.

E. H. TURPIN.

A GOOD EXAMPLE.

THE MUSICAL STANDARD has never yet hesitated to give publicity to any scheme obviously framed for the good of the art and of artists; and no plans for the advancement of the art have a better claim to such publicity than proposals for the popularization of good orchestral music. The orchestra has been not inaptly spoken of as the sun of music, for it is not only the sole source of tone-colour power, but in phrasing, in expression, and supremely as the grandest manifestation of life and combined mental power in music, it is indeed and ever must be the greatest engine of modern art. Therefore, it may be fairly questioned whether any work done for the advancement of the art can exceed in value and importance the development in our midst of sound orchestral music.

So true to the best interests of the art are orchestral manifestations, that it may be safely conceded that there can be no solid progress without their presence. Indeed, our national and musical authorities should regard the encouragement of competent orchestral performances as being quite as essential as is the development of general musical education to the artistic well-being of the nation. Great strides have been lately taken in London for the advancement of this class of music—where skilled performers have been counted by tens, they are now to be found in twenties. And increased travelling facilities have made the large number of our distinguished orchestral artists here, a very useful nucleus for the orchestral permeation of our national musical body. Our great provincial commercial centres are rapidly gaining orchestral power, and have probably also doubled their instrumental resources in the past twenty years. Our University centres, too, are well to the front, as the admirable orchestral concerts of Oxford and Cambridge plainly demonstrate. Now, the people of Wales are advancing on the same pathway by a very decided movement, after long years of patient and intelligent cultivation of the art in both its vocal and instrumental departments. The vigorous town of Cardiff, now the great outlet for the vast mineral wealth of the Principality and the youngest of our University centres, has, as already told, decided upon setting a good example by introducing at the National Eisteddfod of next week a series of orchestral performances of high-class and standard works, by a well-balanced and fully competent body of leading London performers. The beneficent and liberal action of the committee in this matter deserves very high praise, and the introduction of orchestral music upon so efficient a basis is an educational advance of distinct importance, especially remembering the large number of listeners concerned who come from all directions and may be said to represent the whole of Wales. To attempt to point out, again, the features of the eloquent and intellectual power of the best instrumental music, would be an act of supererogation here. Still, one or two brief thoughts are not perhaps out of place. Quite apart from the power and charm of tone-colour, orchestral music has the function of displaying such a concentrated vitality as may alone demonstrate the full force of great musical thoughts. This vitality is intensified by the fact that its expression is conveyed through so many combined mediums. Thus the glories of the composer's art are perhaps only fully realized by the orchestra, seeing that concentration, variety, phrasing power and individual expression, here find their most complete assertion and most effective setting forth by combination and contrast. The duty of encouraging orchestral growth is indeed a paramount obligation which falls upon all interested in the real progress of the art. E. H. TURPIN.

THE SOCIETY OF ARTS.

The Society of Arts' Conversazione was held at the International Fisheries Exhibition, South Kensington, by permission of the Executive Committee, on Wednesday evening, the 25th July. The reception was held near the entrance, by Sir William Siemens, the Chairman of the Council, assisted by the following Vice-Presidents and members of the Council :—Lord Alfred S. Churchill, Lord Sudely, Sir Philip Cunliffe-Owen, Sir Frederick Abel, Sir Edward Inglefield, Captain Douglas Galton, Sir John Hawkshaw, Sir Frederick Leighton, Sir John Lubbock, Sir Richard Temple, Mr. B. F. Cobb, Mr. W. H. Perkin, Mr. R. Rawlinson, Dr. Richardson, Mr. Carpmael, Mr. H. Doulton, Mr. T. V. Lister, Mr. J. M. Maclean, Mr. Matthey, Mr. Loftus Perkins, Mr. W. H. Preece, and Mr. Owen Roberts.

Their Royal Highnesses the Prince of Wales, President of the Society, and the Princess of Wales, accompanied by H.R.H. Prince Christian, and the Hereditary Princess of Saxe-Meiningen, and attended by Colonel Arthur Ellis, the Hon. Mrs. A. Hardinge, and Fraülein von Cohausen, arrived at half-past ten, and were escorted through the building by Sir William and Lady Siemens, Sir Philip Cunliffe-Owen, and the members of the Council, after which their Royal Highnesses proceeded to the Royal Pavilion.

The Exhibition Buildings, the Conservatory of the Royal Horticultural Society, &c., were lighted up by the electric light, and the gardens were illuminated throughout with coloured lamps, as well as four large Siemens electric lights, put up for the occasion.

The band of the Grenadier Guards, conducted by Mr. Dan Godfrey, performed in the gardens. The band of the Royal Artillery, conducted by Cav. L. Zavertal, the band of the 6th (Thuringian) Regiment of German Infantry (by kind permission of His Imperial Majesty, the Emperor of Germany), and the Hungarian band, performed within the buildings.

A vocal and instrumental concert, consisting of glees, &c., was given by the Royal Criterion Handbell Ringers, under the direction of Mr. Harry Tipper, in the Conservatory, from 9 to 11 p.m.

Refreshments were supplied at buffets arranged at various parts of the building. The number of visitors attending the Conversazione was about 6,500. A large number of scientific, literary, and artistic celebrities were present.

After the Conversazione, Sir William and Lady Siemens entertained the members of the Council and a company of friends at supper.

The novel concert arranged by the Saltaire Park Band Committee, Bradford, for the evening of July 26th, was a decided success. There was a large attendance in the park while the Saltaire band played through their portion of the programme, and when the combined glee unions from Bradford and Shipley afterwards took seats on board the river steamer the river banks were lined with spectators who were sufficiently interested to keep their places until the close of the concert. While the boat steamed up the river the band performed additional selections, the singers giving their glees as she drifted slowly down again. The sound of the voices on the water was very pleasing, and the vocalists were rewarded with hearty applause for their rendering of " Comrades in Arms," and " Wanton Gales." The steamer was decorated with Chinese lanterns. The success of this experiment will, it is hoped, induce the committee to give another similar concert.

THE MUSIC OF THOUGHT.

The Universe may be described as precipitated thought—incarnate, transubstantiated thought, and the history of humanity, of progress, has been the history of thought, of reason—alas, also, and of insanity (it is spoken in all seriousness, with too profound conviction)—if reason far from fully developed, and therefore as much misused, and abused, as used. Man, in short, has done what a brute would do if he could. Hence his cannibalism and fetishism, with all their hideous and miserable manifestations. The history of religion may be described as the history of man's progress towards God, a higher conception of God, and consciousness of himself. His art, above all, his music, goes *pari passu*, with this. At a time, then, when the Book itself has just been revised (by no means inspiredly), and when the Liturgy is on the imminent brink of revision, of re-formation, it savours of suspicion that the order of the day is urged—" Church music in the style of the middle ages !" But we can no more go back to another in art than in geology, than the chalk period can go back to the carboniferous. Essentially, we can no more alter ourselves to their music than we can step into their shoes, or put on their doublets. Why? *Because we do not think like them*, and, therefore, do not feel like them (and *vice versâ*). Let any man read the " Storia d'Italia," for instance, Guicciardini's (an ancestor I presume, of Beethoven's Countess Giulia), in the 15th and 16th centuries, and then see if he can write music, express himself in art like the men of that period—bigotted, bloody, and rotten. Italy possessed its Savonarola, but no Luther, and hung and burnt that poor imitation, that degenerate specimen. Why should we be urged to go back to the art of Savonarola (or his *alter ego*) and not utter ourselves in the art of Luther, develop'd? For Luther set a glacier going (or stood on the head of one going) which he could by no means stop. Professor Tyndall planted his stakes in the glacier at Chamounix, but he was far too wise to imagine they would stop there; on the contrary, he expected (and proved) they would be carried forward by the icy irresistible current.

Palestrina and his compeers might set the Gospel genealogies to "sublime music," but it was, after all, a foolish proceeding. What would a Beethoven think if you were to demand of him to set the Te Deum, *e.g.* in that archaic style ! For style is thought, as the pious and celebrated Spanish writer says, citing Balzac :—

" El estilo nacu de las ideas y non de las palabras.
Le style vient des idées et non des mots."

But further, and more pertinently for us, what would a Beethoven think if you were to demand of him to set, *e.g.*, the Athanasian Creed ? The fiery energy of French genius incontinently boils forth in a damnation of Faust, but its revolting sensationalism is only too typical of the period. Real religion would shudder at reproducing it. Our watchwords are—Poor Humanity and Progress; hence above all in music, our pathos and triumph, these the fountains of our great deep ! The consequence of compelling Church music to be written in the style of exploded thought would simply be to shock and disgust the best musical minds from writing it at all. The common chords and counterpoint, grand as they may be, of that period, are not essentially—in a scientific or pyschologic *all-umfassened* sense—style. Style is belief. Neither art nor the man would be benefited, expressed so. Why should the living tone-poet be prohibited from his idiom, or rather language ? Why should he not write rather in the style of the " Missa Solennis " and Schumann's " Pater Profundus " (the religious music of the future according to Brendel) than of Lassus and Hasler ? The pure thinker will write pure music, equally as good in its way as Palestrina's, and better in so far as it is more appropriate, the *alter ego* of truth. Wisdom is better than knowledge, but without knowledge wisdom also is impossible. This is the gist of knowledge, and its art as much as its religion must flow from that. The Church is the last place where freedom (clear, is, truth) should be prohibited. Music—above all, religious music—is philosophic feeling; if it is really to progress it must do so by being this more and more. In the Church or out of the Church, it will strive, above all, to be sincere, and will repose as on a Rock of Ages, in " measureless content " ; in this,

" Work well done exempts itself from fear."

JOHN FIELD AND HIS HABITS.

The celebrated pianist, John Field, was a man that the public talked much about while he lived, and even after his death. The anecdotes that are attributed to him are very numerous, and a volume could be formed of those that are said to be genuine. As to the others, every journal has invented them to amuse its readers, and thus the number published cannot be counted.

John Field was one of the best pianists and brightest men of his day, as all confessed who knew him. What is not so widely and generally known is that he was also one of the greatest drinkers of champagne in Russia, where he had established himself, and where a greater quantity of champagne is drunk than in all the other European countries put together.

He became intoxicated quite easily with an inferior bottle of this sparkling wine, yet after dinner Field was rather in a state of merriment than drunkenness—at least, in the majority of instances. Every day he indulged his appetite for exhilarating drink, especially, so it seemed, when he had to appear in public the same night. The story goes, that when he had the honour to play at a Paris Conservatory concert, on which occasion he obtained a great success, Liszt and Chopin were forced to take him by the arms after his performance, in order to safely lead him to his hotel. Another time, at a minor German court, he became so thoroughly confused in the middle of a "Concerto" of his own composition that he made a sign for the orchestra to stop, put out the lights that were burning on the piano, and wrought up the public to a pitch of enthusiasm by a remarkable improvization, which, in any other condition, would hardly have been possible. His best work was the result of a partial dulling of the senses.

Field made a good deal of money. He went from house to house giving lessons, followed by two enormous English bull-dogs, which he liked very much. He received twenty-five rubles (or fifteen francs) every lesson. When he returned to his residence in the evening, he threw his receipts into a corner of his room. The pile of francs did not increase, however, for when he died he did not leave a cent.

In spite of his drinking and disorderly habits, John Field worked with an enthusiasm that was never abated. No pianist ever practised on his chosen instrument with so tenacious a per-severance. When he was studying a new piece, he had near him upon a little table at his left hand two hundred counters. Every time he recommenced a passage he took one of the counters and placed it upon another small table at his right hand, until all the counters had been conveyed from the left to the right table. It often happened, when the passage was difficult, that he transferred the counters from one table to the other eight or ten times.

Yet, John Field was an unrivalled pianist among the great pianists that form that remarkable galaxy of performers in which shone with such lustre Thalberg, Liszt, Chopin, Hers, and Prudent.—*New York Courier.*

Says an American journal :—"The first organ ever brought to this country is still in constant use in St. John's Chapel, Portsmouth, N. H. The Hon. Henry K. Oliver, of Salem, Mass., thus gives its history :—' It is sometimes known as the Brattle organ, having been the property of the Hon. Thomas Brattle, who was born in Boston in 1658, and was treasurer of Harvard College (where he graduated in 1676, one of a class of only three members) from 1693 till 1713, the year of his death (unmarried), in Boston. Brattle Square and Brattle Street, and the now extinct Brattle Street Church, Boston, of which he was the leading founder, giving the land on which it was built, take name from him. The organ (not large) referred to was of English make and imported. Mr. Brattle, in his will, says : " I give, dedicate and devote my organ to the praise and glory of God in the said church [Brattle Street], if they shall accept thereof, and within a year after my decease procure a sober person that can play skilfully thereon with a loud noise; otherwise to the Church of England [King's Chapel] in this town, on the same terms and conditions, and on their non-acceptance or discon-tinuance to use it as above, unto the college, and on their non-acceptance, to my nephew William Brattle." Brattle Street Church refused the gift, the opposition to organs in dissenting churches being then as it is now in churches in Scotland. But the parish of King's Chapel (Stone Chapel) accepted the gift, complying with the terms and procuring a "sober person," Mr. Edward Enstone, from England, on a salary of £30 per annum. Here it was used till 1756, when it was replaced by a new and larger one from Eng-land. It was then sold to St. John's Church, in Ports-mouth, though rumour has it that it was for a while in a church in Newburyport. It is now at least 175 years old, and yet in good order. Why, on "its discontinuance," it did not go to Harvard College, according to the terms of the will, is not known.' "

THE HISTORY OF THE PIANOFORTE.

By A. J. HIPKINS.

[*A Paper read before the Society of Arts, March 7th,* 1883].

As this paper is composed from a technical point of view, some elucidation of facts, forming the basis of it, is desirable before we proceed to the chronological statement of the subject. These facts are the strings, and their strain or tension ; the sound-board, which is the resonance factor ; and the bridge, connecting it with the strings. The strings, soundboard, and bridge are indispensable, and common to all stringed instruments. The special fact appertaining to keyboard instruments is the me-chanical action interposed between the player and the instrument itself. The strings, owing to the slender surface they present to the air, are, however powerfully excited, scarcely audible. To make them sufficiently audible, their pulsations have to be communicated to a wider elastic surface, the soundboard, which, by accumulated energy and broader contact with the air, rein-forces the strings' feeble sound. The properties of a string set in periodic vibration are the best known of the phenomena appertaining to acoustics. The molecules composing the string are disturbed in the string's vibrating length by the means used to excite the sound, and run off into sections, the comparative length and number of which depend partly upon the place in the string the excitement starts from ; partly upon the force and the form of force that is employed ; and partly upon the length, thickness, weight, strain, and elasticity of the string, with some small allowance for gravitation. The vibrating sections are of wavelike contour ; the nodes or points of apparent rest being really knots of the greatest pressure from crossing streams of molecules. Where the pressure slackens, the sections rise into loops, the curves of which show the points of least pressure. Now, if the string be struck upon a loop, less energy is communicated to the string, and the carrying power of the sound proportionately fails. If the string be struck upon a node, greater energy ensues, and the carrying power proportionately gains. By this we recognise the importance of the place of contact, or striking-place of the hammer against the string ; and the necessity, in order to obtain good fundamental tone, which shall carry, of the note being started from a node.

If the hammer is hard, and impelled with force, the string breaks into shorter sections, and the discordant upper partials of the string, thus brought into prominence, make the tone harsh. If the hammer is soft, and the force employed is moderated, the harmonious partials of the longer sections strike the ear, and the tone is full and round. By the frequency of vibration, that is to say, the number of times a string runs through its complete changes one way and the other, say, for measurement, in a second of time, we determine the pitch, or relative acuteness of the tone as distinguished by the ear.

We know, with less exactness, that the sound-board follows similar laws. The formation of nodes is helped by the barring of the sound-board, a ribbing crosswise to the grain of the wood, which promotes the elasticity, and has been called the "soul" of stringed musical instruments. The sound-board itself is made of most carefully chosen pine in Europe of the *Abies excelsa*, the spruce fir, which, when well grown, and of light, even grain, is the best of all woods for resonance. The pulsations of the strings are communicated to the sound-board by the bridge, a thick rail of close-grained beech, curved so as to determine their vibrating lengths, and attached to the sound-board by dowels. The bridge is doubly pinned, so as to cut off the vibration at the edge of the bearing the strings exert upon the bridge. The shock of each separate pulsation, in its complex form, is received by the bridge, and communicated to such undamped strings as may, by their lengths, be sensitive to them ; thus producing the Æolian tone commonly known as sympathetic, an eminently attractive charm in the tone of a pianoforte.

We have here strings, bridge, and sound-board, or belly, as it is technically called, indispensable for the production of the tone, and indivisible in the general effect. The proportionate weight of stringing has to be met by a proportionate thickness and barring of the sound-board, and a proportionate thickness and elevation of the bridge.

The tension of the strings is met by a framing, which has be-come more rigid as the drawing-power of the strings has been gradually increased. In the present concert grands of Messrs. Broadwood, that drawing-power may be stated as starting from 150 lb. from each single string in the treble, and gradually in-creasing to about 300 lb. for each of the single strings in the bass. I will reserve for the historical description of my subject some notice of the different kinds of framing that have been introduced. It will suffice, at this stage, to say that it was at first of wood, and became, by degrees of wood and iron ; in the present day the iron very much preponderating. It will be at once evident that the object of the framing is to keep the ends of the strings apart. The near ends are wound round the wrest-pins, which are inserted in the wooden bed, called the wrest-plank, the strength and efficiency of which are most important for the tone and durability of the instrument. It is composed of layers of wainscot oak and beech, the direction of the grain being alter-nately longitudinal and lateral. Some makers cover the wrest-plank with a plate of brass ; in Broadwood's grands, it is a plate of iron, into which, as well as the wood, the wrest-pins are screwed. The tuner's business is to regulate the tension, by turning the wrest-pins, in which he is chiefly guided by the beats which become audible from differing numbers of vibrations. The wrest-plank is bridged, and has its bearing like the sound-board; but the wrest-plank has no vibrations to transfer, and should, as far as possible, offer perfect insensibility to them.

I will close this introductory explanation with two remarks, made by the distinguished musician, mechanician, and inventor, Theobald Boehm, of Munich, whose inventions were not limited to the flute which bears his name, but include the initiation of as important change in the modern pianoforte, as made in America and Germany. Of priority of invention, he says, in a letter to an English friend, "If it were desirable to analyse all the inventions which have been brought forward, we should find that in scarcely any instance were they the offspring of the brain of a single individual, but that all progress is gradual only; each worker follows in the track of his predecessor, and eventually, perhaps, advances a step beyond him." And concerning the relative value of inventions in musical instruments, it appears from an essay of his, which has been recently published, that he considers improvement in acoustical proportions the chief foundation of the higher or lower degree of perfection in all instruments, their mechanism being but of secondary value.

(To be continued.)

The pleasure of hearing Madame Marie Roze in "Carmen" (says a contemporary), is to be afforded the British public, Mr. Carl Rosa having acquired the sole right of representing the opera in English, and almost as a matter of course entered into an engagement with the celebrated prima donna to play the title-rôle. Bizet composed "Carmen" specially for Madame Marie Roze. He had a thorough knowledge of her capabilities and a great admiration for her artistic power, which resulted in the creation of a character moulded on his daily—almost hourly—observation of the development of her powers. In her studies she was constantly assisted by the composer, who in this way obtained a perfect realisation of his intentions, and the success which Marie Roze afterwards achieved in her representation of the heroine was amongst the greatest of her triumphs. Bizet showed his regard for his pupil and friend by preparing a MSS. of the opera carefully and copiously annotated and margined with stage directions and hints to keep his instructions fresh in the memory of the debutanté. This interesting mémento is now, no doubt, in the possession of Colonel Mapleson, Mdme. Roze's husband. The libretto of the opera for Mr. Rosa has been written by Mr. H. Hersee and the first representation will take place on Aug. 20th.

The great organ will go, but not out of Boston. An agreement has been concluded between the Music Hall Association and the persons who had applied for an injunction to restrain the association from making any disposition of the instrument, one of the terms of that agreement being the withdrawal of the suit. As has already been announced, the organ will be set up in the new hall at the South End to be built by the New England Conservatory of Music. The work of removal must begin on May 15 of next year, and the organ and all its appurtenances must be out of the hall on or before July 1 succeeding. The Music Hall Association will, however, if it shall be found necessary, provide storage room for portions of the instrument during the summer months. When ready for use in its new home, the organ will have many important and greatly needed additions in the way of registers, especially of the sort known as mixtures, which will probably be furnished by the builders of the organ, Walcker & Co., of Ludwigsburg, Germany. The expression of a hope that no feeling of jealousy, growing out of national pride, will prevent the use of the best system of action known in France is in order, as well as of one that the architecture of the new hall will be more in harmony with the design of the "organ-house," as the Germans call it, than is that of its present abiding place. Mr. William O. Grover is the purchaser of the organ, and the responsible party in the matter of removal. His connection with the matter is purely to save the great organ in the public interest, and those who deplored the threatened loss of the famous instrument from Boston have him to thank for its preservation here as one of our boasts as a musical centre. Mr. Grover is not only an amateur of music, but serves its cause practically as a trustee of the New England Conservatory of Music, which he hopes to see take its place in the highest class of such institutions, and as a director of the Philharmonic Society. —*Boston Transcript (U.S.)*

Passing Events.

Dr. Hullah is now residing at Nice.

There are more than nine thousand brass bands in the United States.

Mdlle. Marie Litta, the operatic singer, died lately in New York. Her death was attributed to over-work.

The *World* says that not a note of Sir A. S. Sullivan's new opera has yet been written.

The Duchess of Beaufort has given a new organ to the parish church at Baddington on the ducal estate.

The opera, "Rip van Winkle" has been given more than 250 times at the Comedy Theatre.

The (reduced) orchestra have been re-engaged for the Royal Italian Opera season of 1884.

A comic opera, "The Three Beggars," by Messrs. Sinclair, Dunn, and Belville, was produced at the Royal Academy of Music on July 28th.

Theodore Thomas, with his orchestra, opened the third annual season of summer nights' concerts at the Exposition Building, Chicago, recently.

The Charles Lucas Medal was awarded at the Royal Academy of Music on July 21st to Frederick Hilvington Hattersley.

Mdme. Trebelli sails for New York October 2nd, and Mdme. Valleria October 13th, both to join Mr. Abbey's troupe.

Mr. Theodore Thomas has been giving successful orchestral concerts lately at Chicago, U.S., these forming part of his scheme of a provincial tour.

In 1885 will occur the bicentenary of the births of both Handel and Bach. Surely neither giant will be forthcoming!

Sir R. Stewart has awarded the prize offered by the Hibernian Band of Hope Union for a temperance song to Mr. T. Simpson, of Burnley.

Signor Arditi is now looking out for new artists on the continent, and Lieutenant-Colonel J. H. Mapleson will start on a similar hunting tour in a fortnight.

Herr Franke proposes to give a season of German opera next year in London with the Pollini troupe under Herr Reichter. With this view he is now in Germany making arrangements.

It is said Sir Michael Costa is letting his house in Eccleston Square and proposes to reside at Brighton for three years. He is in excellent general health, though still suffering from paralysis of the tongue.

Félicien David's symphonic ode "Le Désert," first performed at (the old) Her Majesty's in 1845, may probably be revived in the course of the season at the Crystal Palace under Mr. Manns.

Only twenty operas have been given at Covent Garden this season. Four years ago, when Mr. Mapleson competed with Mr. Gye, thirty operas were given during the season at the Royal Italian Opera.

An American writer advises singers to practise breathing while walking, by filling the lungs, and using each inspiration for as long a distance as possible. This will inevitably strengthen the lungs.

Mdme. Patti is to sail for New York to join Mr. Mapleson's company on October 22. Mesdames Gerster, Pappenheim, and Signor Bertini, a clever Viennese tenor, are also engaged in the same company.

ST. PETER'S COLLEGIATE CHURCH, WOLVERHAMPTON.— On Wednesday, 25th July, there was a special full choral Evening Service in the above church, in aid of the additional Curates' Aid Society, in which the choirs of St. John's, All Saint's, and Penn Churches joined, there was a crowded congregation. The choirs, under Mr. J. Roper's, F.C.O. (organist of St. Peter's) careful training, were fully up to the occasion. The service taken was Stainer in A, and the anthem "Send out Thy light" (Gounod). In all that they did the choirs showed the effects of the excellent training they had received. Mr. Roper, who conducted, must be congratulated on the success of the festival. Mr. Halford, F.C.O., organist of St. John's, Wolverhampton, ably presided at the organ.

Hand and Heart for August has an account of Mr. James A. Birch with a portrait. Mr. Birch is editor of the *Standard Book of Song,* and has rendered valuable aid to the cause of temperance as a composer, conductor, and teacher.

The choral works to be done at the Glasgow Orchestral concerts include Berlioz's " Messe de Morts," Félicien David's " Le Désert," Gounod's " Redemption," Mendelssohn's " Walpurgis Night," and Handel's " Acis and Galatea " and " Messiah."

An Italian opera season will be given in Berlin from Sept. 16th to Oct. 16th, with Signor Bimboni as conductor. The repertoire is to include Verdi's operas, " Hamlet " by Thomas, and Rossini's " Othello " and " Semiramide."

The Union of Church Choirs in New York has grown in three years to a membership of more than four thousand. At the recent annual concert 3,400 singers took part. The work of the union is certainly doing much to improve congregational singing.

The large American organ, built by Messrs. Estey and Co. for the Festival at Bayreuth has been purchased by Messrs. Haynes & Co., musical instrument merchants, of Cecilia Hall, Malvern, for the Rev. E. Ford's new private chapel at his College, Hillside, West Malvern.

The following advertisement in the *Church Times* of July 20th deserves to be recorded :—

" A YOUNG MAN, aged 30, who understands waiting at table, &c., is anxious to obtain a situation in a clergyman's family in a country parish. He is competent to instruct a choir, and take the organ, &c."

The Council of the Scottish Musical Society met at Edinburgh and decided to postpone the starting of a musical academy for Scotland, and to cancel and abandon their arrangement with Mr. F. H. Cowen as principal. But arrangements are now in progress to start an academy for Glasgow under the auspices of the Choral Union.

The Covent Garden Promenade Concerts begin to-night under the direction of Mr. Freeman Thomas, Mr. Gwyllym Crowe as before conducting the splendid orchestra. The band will be almost identically the same as that of last year, with Mr. Carrodus for leader. A new Bow Street entrance to the Floral Hall has been made, and the building is lit by fifty arc and a hundred incandescent Jablochkoff lights. The stage is decorated like a Chinese pavilion. The issue of guinea season tickets is another special feature.

A Parochial Choir Festival was held at Chester Cathedral on July 18th. The organist arranged the processional hymns for the local Militia bands, big drum and all. This is taking the wind out of the sails of the " Salvation Army " with a vengeance. Will General Booth meet his defeat with a counterfeit movement and try to start a cathedral choir ? Clearly the Church means to leave no advantages to outsiders. The general's bandmaster is thought to be scoring for the next turn-out of the army, " Salvation ! Oh, the joyful sound."

The *Athenæum* says, that Verdi has remodelled his " Don Carlos," which is, to be given next season at the Théâtre Italien, Paris. He has suppressed the whole of the first act, excepting the romance for the tenor, which has been transferred to the second act. A new introduction has been written for the former third act, which is now the second, and the whole of the dance music in this act has been cut out. The *finale* of the last act has been re-written and much shortened ; and besides several other modifications of more or less importance, the composer has in many places changed the orchestration.

The chief works to be performed at the Leeds Musical Festival are as follows :—Wednesday morning, October 10th, Mendelssohn's " Elijah " ; evening cantata, " Gray's Elegy ". (A. Cellier ; written for this festival), and Beethoven's Symphony in D (No. 2). Thursday morning, October 11th, Rah's Symphony-oratorio, " The End of the World " (first time of performance in England). Thursday evening, 97th Psalm (Barnby) ; third motet (Mozart) ; Bach's cantata, " O Shepherd of Israel," and Rossini's " Stabat Mater." Friday morning, Macfarren's new oratorio, " King David " ; evening, Gade's cantata, " The Crusaders," and a miscellaneous selection. Saturday morning, Beethoven's " Grand Mass in D," and Mendelssohn's " Hymn of Praise " (" Lobgesang ").

The *Times,* says that Mr. William Gilstrap, of Fornham Hall, Bury St. Edmunds, Suffolk, and Newark-on-Trent, Notts, who last year gave £1,000 to the funds of the Royal College of Music, has now added £2,000 to that sum, with the view of founding a scholarship in the College, in his own name, to be awarded (1) to natives of Suffolk, or failing them (2) to natives of Nottinghamshire, or failing them (3) to the country at large. The Prince of Wales has accepted this munificent offer, and it is to be hoped that so excellent an example of public spirit may be followed in other counties.

The Choral Festival of the Aldershot, Farnham, Farnborough, and Crookham Church Choir Association was held in All Saints' Military Church recently. The performers numbered 150, including the string bands of the 1st Scottish Rifles and the 2nd York and Lancaster Regiment. Band-Sergeant Bampton played the organ, Mr. J. Conway Brown, L.Mus., T.C.L, conducted. Sir R. Stewart's Service in G was sung, and the anthem was " The watching over Israel," from " Elijah." The Service was opened by the adagio from Haydn's 7th Symphony, and closed by the march in " Athalie."

The first of the autumn concerts proper will be the Crystal Palace Saturday concerts under Mr. Manns, probably beginning on October 6. Richter's three autumn concerts will take place October 29, November 3 and 10. Herr Joachim will probably again appear before Christmas, and it is anticipated that, in the course of the season, Madame Essipoff and other favourites will be heard. The Albert Hall concerts, November 7 to April 11, have already been announced. The Sacred Harmonic Society will start their next season under Mr. Charles Hallé on November 16, " Messiah " being performed December 19, followed by other concerts.

The funeral of the late Mr. Joseph Williams, the well known and long established music publisher, of Berners Street and Cheapside, took place on Tuesday last, at Marylebone Cemetery, Finchley. The deceased occupied a high position in the esteem of those with whom his extensive business and artistic relations brought him in contact, and the respect which was entertained for him as a man was shown in the large and influential attendance at the mournful ceremony. Many well known professional men and a very general representative of the music trade assembled to pay their last respects to his memory.

The *Era* says that the National Opera House on the Thames Embankment, after standing idle for so long a period, will be soon put to practical use. It is expected that it will be completed in time for next season, and it is intended to have a three months' season of Italian Opera, three months' German Opera, three months' French Opera, and two months' English, the other month being devoted to promenade concerts. Should Mr. Carl Ross' take part in the scheme, it is anticipated that a longer time will be devoted to English Opera and less to French ; but, whatever arrangements may ultimately be made, the theatre will be kept open throughout the year.

The death of Mr. Samuel Pearsall, the senior Vicar Choral of Lichfield Cathedral, is announced with regret. The deceased gentleman, who was advanced in years, was generally well known as an accomplished, though florid, tenor singer. In early life he had the advantage of tuition, and certainly during the days of Mr. Pearsall and Mr. Machin, Lichfield Cathedral boasted of a tenor and bass of very rare excellence. Prior to the rise of Mr. Sims Reeves, Mr. Pearsall was esteemed as a leading tenor of the day ; a reference to programmes of the principal London and provincial concerts and festivals will demonstrate the position he then held in the world of song. A not-to-be-forgotten association was his well known musical lecture, in which he was assisted, season after season, by the various members of the Cathedral Choir.

A grand Mass and Benediction were held at the Roman Catholic Church at Sclerder, Cornwall, on Sunday, the 15th inst., the occasion being the Bishop of Plymouth's visit for the purpose of holding a confirmation. The church, which is dedicated to " Our Lady of Light," is one of the most ancient shrines in England, and people formerly resorted there to seek restoration from blindness. Bordese's fine Mass was splendidly sung. The leading vocalist was Mdlle. Alice Roselli, whose dramatic and artistic singing was well displayed in the solos. The offertory, "Veni, Spiritus Sancte" (Rossi), employed the great compass of her fine voice to advantage. At the Benediction, Mdlle. Roselli again sang admirably in Bordèse's lovely "O Salutaris," and Neukomm's "Tantum Ergo," which she rendered magnificently.

Sir Herbert Oakeley writes thus of the Handel Festival :—" It is refreshing to be reminded, at least once in three years, of the supremacy of Handel as a choral writer, and it is good 'to inhale his bracing mountain air. His music beats with the strong pulse of a wholesome humanitarian, universal feeling. No theme too great for him ; he moves at home among miracles ; he has music fit for Sinai and the passage of the Red Sea ! His is music to make us grow strong as we sit and listen.' And in these latter days, during prevalence of some music without form and void, like to—

' Rich windows that exclude the light,
And passages which lead to nothing,'

the grand and broad Handelian strains and his superb counterpoint, now a neglected art, his marvellous power of word-painting, and of producing the greatest effects with the simplest means—in such times as these of ' Musikalische Krankheit' the grand old master's nobility of style and elevation of thought seem to give listeners special and renewed edification."

On July 24th Miss Laura Willock gave a soirée at her own residence, 2, Anson-road, N. The young lady has lately returned, handsomely certificated, from the Leipzig Conservatoire. The pianoforte solos played by Miss Willock evinced not only much talent and care, but very conscientious cultivation and excellent power of expression and phrasing. Her critical friends present displayed their satisfaction and pleasure, called forth by her artistic performances. The programme included :—Song, recit. and aria from "Galatea" (Handel), Miss Johnstone ; song, "To Anthea" (Hatton), excellently sung by J· Henry ; pianoforte solo, Ballade in A flat (Reinecke), played by Miss Willock with much finish, breadth, excellent tone and touch ; song, "At thy casement waiting," sung by Mr. Knight, who has a good tenor voice ; vocal duet, "In the dusk of the Twilight" (Offenbach), Miss Carr Shaw and Miss Brown ; song, "Sunshine and Rain " (Blumenthal), Mrs. Carr Shaw ; pianoforte solo, Etude (F. Walenn), admirably rendered by Mr. F. Walenn ; song, "None shall part us " (" Iolanthe") (A. Sullivan), Miss Carr Shaw ; pianoforte solo, Ballade in A flat (Chopin), played by Miss Agnes Bartlett with fine delicacy, expressive phrasing, and genuine power ; song, " Pur dicesti " (Lotti), admirably sung by Mrs. Carr Shaw ; pianoforte solo, "Warum" (Schumann), artistically rendered by Miss Willock ; and pianoforte solo, Norwegian Dance (Grieg), played by Mr. F. Walenn.

Correspondence.

THE MAJORITY OF THE " MUSICAL STANDARD."

TO THE EDITOR.

SIR,—As a "Reader from the first," permit me to offer my congratulations on the occasion of the *Musical Standard* attaining its majority. The first number, August 2nd, 1862, is now before me, and it would be interesting briefly to survey its progress since. One remark only can I now make. Owing in some measure to the exertions of the *Musical Standard*, the College 'of Organists came into existence in 1863 ; afterwards the tone of the paper altered, and exhibited the greatest hostility to the young institution ; now poetical justice has been wrought, and the Hon. Sec. to the College of Organists is Editor of the *Musical Standard !* With every good wish for its future prosperity,
I am, Sir, yours faithfully,
STEPHEN S. STRATTON.
Birmingham, Aug. 2nd, 1883.

[The kindly words of Mr. Stephen S. Stratton, a much esteemed contributor from time to time, demand my grateful and heartfelt acknowledgment. Such words not only touch all connected with the paper, but serve to supply those engaged upon it with new strength.—ED.]

The Querist.

QUERY.

ORGANO would be glad to hear what is the best edition of J. S. Bach's works for the organ. He wants to purchase them bound neatly in one volume, as complete as possible. Please say name of publisher, and price.

[Peters's edition is perhaps the best complete available copy. Messrs. Bridge and J· Higgs are producing a new English edition, published by Novello & Co.]—ED.

Service Lists.

ELEVENTH SUNDAY AFTER TRINITY.

AUGUST 5th.

London.

ST. PAUL'S CATHEDRAL.—Morn.: Service, Te Deum and Benedictus, Hopkins in F ; Introit, We pray Thee, Heavenly Father ; Holy Communion, Barnby in E. Even.: Service, Magnificat and Nunc Dimittis, Hopkins in F ; Anthem, Walk ye on in love and truth, and, God Thou art great (Spohr).

TEMPLE CHURCH.—Morn.: Service, Te Deum Laudamus, and Jubilate Deo, Barrow in F ; Apostles' Creed, Harmonised Monotone ; Anthem, O, how amiable (Greene). Even.: Service, Magnificat and Nunc Dimittis, Barrow in F ; Apostles' Creed, Harmonized Monotone ; Anthem, O give thanks (Boyce).

LINCOLN'S INN CHAPEL.—Morn.: Service, Barrow in F ; Kyrie (Nares) ; Anthem, O clap your hands (Greene). Even.: Service, Barrow in F ; Anthem, Remember now thy creator (Steggall).

ALL SAINTS, MARGARET STREET.—Morn.: Service, Te Deum and Benedictus (Stainer) ; Holy Communion Service in D (Hoyte) ; Offertory Anthem, Praise the Lord (Mendelssohn). Even.: Service, King in D ; Anthem, Lift thine eyes, and He, watching over Israel (Mendelssohn).

CHRIST CHURCH, CLAPHAM.—Morn.: Service, Te Deum, Plain-song ; Kyrie and Credo, Schubert in F ; Offertory, Anthem, Enter not into judgment (Attwood) ; Sanctus, Benedictus, Agnus Dei, and Gloria in excelsis (Schubert). Even.: Service, Magnificat and Nunc Dimittis, Goss in A ; Anthem, Behold, how good and joyful (Clarke-Whitfield).

FOUNDLING CHAPEL.—Morn.: Service, Te Deum and Jubilate, Nares in F ; Anthem, The heavens are telling (Haydn). Aft. : Children's Service.

HOLY TRINITY, GRAY'S INN ROAD.—Morn.: Service, Te Deum, Hopkins in G ; Jubilate, Chant. Even. : Service, Magnificat, Bunnett in F ; Nunc Dimittis, Chant ; Anthem, The Lord is loving unto every man (Garrett).

HOLY TRINITY, TULSE HILL.—Morn.: Chant Service. Even.: Service, Magnificat and Nunc Dimittis, Parry in D ; Anthem, Plead Thou my cause (Mozart).

ST AUGUSTINE AND ST. FAITH, WATLING STREET.—Morn.: Service, Hopkins in F ; Introit, Be merciful unto me (South) ; Communion Service, Eyre in E flat (throughout). Even.: Service, Smart in F ; Anthem, O come, let us worship (Mendelssohn).

ST. BARNABAS, MARYLEBONE.—Morn.: Service, Te Deum and Benedictus, Dykes in F ; Anthem, Thou wilt keep him in perfect peace (Wesley) ; Kyrie and Nicene Creed, Dykes in F. Even. : Service, Magnificat and Nunc Dimittis, Hoyte in B flat ; Anthem, Stand up and bless (Goss).

ST. JAMES'S PRIVATE EPISCOPAL CHAPEL, SOUTHWARK. —Morn.: Service, Introit, I am not worthy, Holy Lord ; Communion Service, Stainer in A. Even.: Service, (Mendelssohn) ; Anthem, Come unto Him (Gounod).

ST. MAGNUS, LONDON BRIDGE.—Morn.: Service, Opening Anthem, If we say (Calkin) ; Te Deum and Jubilate, Nares in F ; Kyrie (Nares). Even.: Service, Magnificat and Nunc Dimittis, Nares in F ; Anthem, Incline Thine ear (Himmel).

ST. MARGARET PATTENS, ROOD LANE, FENCHURCH STREET.—Morn.: Service, Te Deum, Sullivan in D ; Benedictus, Stainer in A ; Communion Service : Offertory Anthem, Os Thee each living soul (Hoyte) ; Kyrie, Credo, Sanctus, Benedictus, Agnus Dei, and Gloria, Hummel in B flat. Even.: Service, Magnificat and Nunc Dimittis, Garrett in F ; Anthem, I waited for the Lord (Mendelssohn).

ST. MARY BOLTONS, WEST BROMPTON, S.W.—Morn.: Service, Te Deum, Armes in G ; Benedictus, Dykes in F ; Even.: Service, Magnificat and Nunc Dimittis, Arnold in A ; Anthem, Give peace in our time (Callcott).

ST. MICHAEL'S, CORNHILL. — Morn.: Service, Te Deum and Jubilate, Smart in F; Anthem, How dear are Thy counsels (Crotch); Kyrie, and Creed, (Marbecke). Even. Service, Magnificat and Nunc Dimittis, Ouseley in B flat; Anthem, Thou, O God (Greene).

ST. PAUL'S, AVENUE ROAD, SOUTH HAMPSTEAD.—Morn.: Service, Te Deum, Dykes in F; Benedictus, Barnby; Kyrie, Arnold in A; Offertory (Barnby). Even.: Service, Magnificat and Nunc Dimittis, Stainer in A; Anthem, O taste and see (Goss).

ST. PAUL'S, BOW COMMON, E.—Morn.: Service, Te Deum and Benedictus, Chants: Holy Communion; Kyrie, Credo, Offertory, Sanctus, Benedictus, Agnus Dei, and Gloria in excelsis, Calkin in B flat. Even.: Service, Magnificat and Nunc Dimittis, Dykes in F; Anthem, Lift Thine eyes, and He, watching over Israel (Mendelssohn).

ST. PETER'S, VERE STREET, W.—Even.: Service, Magnificat and Nunc Dimittis, Tuckermann in F; Anthem, I waited for the Lord (Mendelssohn).

ST. SAVIOUR'S, HOXTON. — Morn.: Service, Te Deum, Smart in F; Holy Communion; Kyrie, Credo, Sursum Corda, Sanctus, and Gloria in excelsis, Tours in F. Even.: Service, Magnificat and Nunc Dimittis, Stainer in F; Anthem, O give thanks (Tucker).

ST. SEPULCHRE'S, HOLBORN. — Morn.: Service, Dykes in F; Anthem, Praise the Lord (Wilton). Even.: Service, Porter in D; Anthem, O taste and see (Goss).

Country.

ST. ASAPH CATHEDRAL.—Morn.: Service, Goss in F; Anthem, O Lord my God (Wesley). Even.: Service, The Litany; Anthem, O Lord, Thou art my God (Lloyd).

ASHBURNE CHURCH, DERBYSHIRE. — Morn.: Service, Stanford in B flat; Kyrie and Credo, Wesley in E. Even.: Service, Stanford in B flat; Anthem, Selection from "Elijah" (Mendelssohn).

BEDDINGTON CHURCH, SURREY.—Morn.: Service, Garrett in D; Communion Service, Calkin in D. Even.: Service, Ebdon in C; Anthems, God is a Spirit, and Who is the image of the invisible God (Bennett).

BIRMINGHAM (S. ALBAN THE MARTYR).—Morn: Service, Te Deum and Benedictus, Dykes in F; Holy Communion; Kyrie, Credo, Sanctus, Gloria, Dykes in F; Benedictus and Agnus Dei, Redman in D. Evensong: Magnificat and Nunc Dimittis, Parry in D,

BIRMINGHAM (ST. CYPRIAN'S, HAY MILLS).—Service, Cobbe in G (throughout); Anthem, I was glad (Elvey). Even.: Service, Cobb in G; Anthem, My song shall be of mercy (Kent).

CANTERBURY CATHEDRAL.—Morn.: Service, Richardson in F; Anthem, He is risen (Gadsby); Communion, Richardson in F. Even.: Service, Richardson in F; Anthem, This is the day (Oakley).

CARLISLE CATHEDRAL. — Morn.: Service, Dykes in F; Introit, Remember, O Lord (Macfarren); Kyrie, Dykes in F; Nicene Creed, Harmonized Monotone. Even.: Service, Hopkins in E flat; Anthem, Hear, O Thou Shepherd (Walmisley)

DONCASTER (PARISH CHURCH).—Morn.: Service, Whitfield in E. Even.: Service, Cantate and Deus Misereatur, Hopkins in B flat; Anthem, I am Alpha and Omega (Stainer).

DUBLIN, ST. PATRICK'S (NATIONAL) CATHEDRAL.—Morn.: Service, Te Deum and Jubilate, Smart in F; Holy Communion, Kyrie, Creed, Sanctus, and Gloria, Smart in F; Anthem, Why rage fiercely the heathen (Mendelssohn). Even.: Service, Magnificat and Nunc Dimittis, Smart in F; Anthems, Sleepers wake (Mendelssohn), and I beheld, and lo (Blow).

ELY CATHEDRAL.—Morn.: Service, Te Deum, Ross in G; Benedictus, Plain Song, Kyrie and Credo, Ross in G; Gloria, Jackman in D; Anthem, I will magnify (Goss). Even.: Service, Anthem, Blessed be Thou (Kent).

EXETER CATHEDRAL.—Morn.: Service, Smart in F; Communion, Wesley in F; Introit, O Lord, we trust (Handel). Even.: Service, Smart in F; Anthem, Wherewithal (Elvey).

HARROGATE (ST. PETER'S CHURCH). — Morn.: Service, Harvey in G; Benedictus, Chant; Anthem, The Lord is my Shepherd (Macfarren); Kyrie and Credo, Tours in F; Sursum Corda, Sanctus, and Gloria in excelsis, Woodward in E flat. Even.: Service, Magnificat, and Nunc Dimittis, Russell in A; Anthem, Blessed be the God and Father (Wesley).

LEEDS PARISH CHURCH.—Morn.: Service, Prince Consort in A; Anthem, O Lord, how manifold (Handel); Communion Turle in D. Even.: Service, Russell in A; Anthem, Come unto him (Gounod),

LEEDS, ST. MARTIN'S CHURCH (POTTERNEWTON). — Te Deum and Benedictus, Chants; Kyrie (Garrett); Credo (Marbeck); Offertory Sentences (Farebrother). Even.: Service, Magnificat and Nunc Dimittis, Chants; Anthem, O rest in the Lord, and Cast thy burden (Mendelssohn).

LICHFIELD CATHEDRAL. — Morn.: Service, Garrett in D; Communion Service, Garrett in D; Anthem, Blest are the departed (Spohr); Garrett in D; Anthem, I know that my Redeemer (Handel).

LIVERPOOL CATHEDRAL.—Aft.: Service, Magnificat and Nunc Dimittis, Turle in D; Anthem (unaccompanied) God is a Spirit (Bennett).

LIVERPOOL (ST. CUTHBERT'S, EVERTON).—Morn.: Service, and Holy Communion, Calkin in B flat. Even.: Service, Ebdon in C; Anthem, I was glad (Elvey).

LLANDAFF CATHEDRAL.—Morn.: Service, Te Deum and Benedictus, Dykes in F; The Litany. Even.: Service, Magnificat and Nunc Dimittis, Garrett in F; Anthem, Praise the Lord (Goss).

MANCHESTER CATHEDRAL. — Morn.: Service, and Full Communion, Garrett in D; Anthem, Jesu, word of God (Husband). Aft.: Service, Garrett in D; Anthem, The wilderness (Wesley).

MANCHESTER (ST. BENEDICT'S).—Morn.: Service, Te Deum, Sullivan in D; Kyrie Credo, Sanctus, Benedictus, and Gloria in excelsis, "Messe des Orphéonites" (Gounod). Even.: Service, Magnificat and Nunc Dimittis (Stainer).

MANCHESTER (ST. JOHN BAPTIST, HULME).—Morn.: Service, Kyrie, Credo, Sanctus, and Gloria in excelsis, Dykes in F; Benedictus, and Agnus Dei, Calkin in B flat. Even.: Service, Magnificat and Nunc Dimittis (Willing).

PETERBOROUGH CATHEDRAL.—Morn.: Service, Barnby in E; Introit, To Father, Son, and Holy Ghost (Bach); Communion Service, Elvey in A, and Goss in D. Even.: Service, Barnby in E; Anthem, Ascribe (Travers).

ROCHESTER CATHEDRAL.—Morn.: Service, Smart in G; Anthem, O living Saviour (Gounod); Holy Communion, Smart in G. Even.: Service, Smart in G; Anthem, Stand up and bless (Goss).

SALISBURY CATHEDRAL. Morn.: Service, Te Deum and Jubilate, Hopkins in A; Kyrie and Credo, Walmisley in D; Offertory (Barnby). Even.: Service, Smart in B flat; Anthem, Praise His awful name (Spohr).

SHERBORNE ABBEY. — Morn.: Service, Te Deum, Chants; Kyrie (Howells); Offertories (Barnby). Even.: Service, Magnificat and Nunc Dimittis, Hopkins in B flat; Anthem, Sing unto God (Lyle).

SOUTHAMPTON (ST. MARY'S CHURCH).—Morn.: Service Te Deum and Benedictus, Woodward in E flat; Holy Communion, Introit, O how amiable (Macfarren) Service, Woodward in E flat; Offertory (Barnby); Paternoster (Field). Even.: Service, Magnificat and Nunc Dimittis, Woodward in E flat; Apostles' Creed, Harmonized Monotone.

WELLS CATHEDRAL.—Morn.: Service, Roberts in D. Even.: Service, Goss in E; Anthem, O give thanks (Purcell).

WORCESTER CATHEDRAL.—Morn.: Service, Garrett in E; Communion Service, Tours in F; Anthem, Incline thine ear (Himmel). Even. Service, Tours in F; Anthem, In that day (Elvey).

THE MUSICAL STANDARD

A NEWSPAPER FOR MUSICIANS PROFESSIONAL AND AMATEUR

No. 993. VOL. XXV. FOURTH SERIES. SATURDAY, AUGUST 11, 1883. WEEKLY: PRICE 3D.

THE VOICE
MUSICALLY AND MEDICALLY CONSIDERED.
BY

ARMAND SEMPLE, B.A., M.B., Cantab., M.R.C.P., Lond.,
Physician to the Royal Society of Musicians.

(*Continued from page 56*).

Ear and Tune.

A good voice is, of course, the first requisite for a vocalist, but next in importance, if not quite equal in importance, is the possession of an accurate ear for tune.

A singer endowed by nature with the most beautiful voice must fail to produce a pleasing effect if there is the slightest fault in his or her intonation ; and the individual on whom natural gifts have been far less liberally bestowed may, nevertheless, always ensure considerable success by perfect intonation, *i.e.*, by singing absolutely in tune.

No doubt many persons by nature possess a keen ear for tune ; but, I believe, in many cases this faculty is acquired.

It is possible that the child of non-musical parents, or one who is not thrown in the way of hearing musical strains, who never hears its nurse sing, may show the possession of a good ear for music when later in life the opportunity of hearing music is obtained ; but I am strongly of opinion that such a case is extremely rare. I believe that an ear for music is acquired in early life, I may say, in infancy, the mother or nurse of the child being always in the habit of lulling it to sleep with some popular refrain. I have heard a child of under two years of age give utterance to such tunes, as "Oh, my little darling," and "Over the garden wall,"—melodies at one time to be heard on every street organ—with perfect intonation, these being tunes which, no doubt, this child had been sung to sleep by, night after night, and day after day.

There can be no doubt that the auditory-nerve fibres in infants and young children are acutely sensitive to impressions, and that they become readily attuned to sweet sounds, and cannot do otherwise than keenly appreciate any deviation from a correct interval.

I have seen instances, over and over again, in different families, of the keen perception of tune and the reverse.

In one family, the father and mother being both fond of music, there were several children, every one of whom could hum a tune perfectly. In another, both parents being unmusical, not one of the children had the slightest idea of tune, and in fact their efforts were positively unpleasant to a musical ear ; and in another, where the children had been played to and sung to by both parents from the time they were born, every individual member picked up a tune with remarkable facility. I have also known instances where individuals have positively been unable to recognise the difference between the melodies, "God save the Queen" and "Rule Britannia," and one gentleman, of very brilliant attainments, was so disagreeably affected by music in any shape or form, that he told me he was obliged to leave the room when any was about to be performed. I am perfectly certain that the above-mentioned cases were those of non-acquirement, and had these persons as children, been brought up in an atmosphere of music, they would, in all probability, have had quite as much appreciation of the beautiful art as others placed under more favourable circumstances.

Change of Voice, or Transition Period.

In the Female the voice undergoes no marked change at any time, with the exception that it loses the acute sounds possessed by many in very early youth ; the quality, however, remains the same, and as the vocal organ becomes firmer and stronger, so proportionally do the sounds increase in fulness and power.

In the Male, on the contrary, the vocal organ is subject to very remarkable alterations during its passage from boyhood to manhood. This change usually takes place at some period between thirteen and fifteen years of age. It is, however, in some cases, considerably protracted. The acute, or high sound of the voice, at first becomes weak, since the muscles are relaxed ; and a certain amount of hoarseness is observed, which somewhat resembles an ordinary cold, the sound frequently going off with a kind of squeak at the end of a sentence. During this period of change, the entire vocal organ by degrees becoming enlarged and descending in the throat, there is a complete inability of fixing the voice, even during the act of speaking.

When the vocal organ is thus relaxed, it should never be *much* exercised, for, although it is true that, in some instances, in consequence of the strength of the muscles, it is tolerably evident what quality the voice will ultimately assume, still it is usually a matter of difficulty to determine its character until it has finally settled. Whatever may be the quality of the voice, in the majority of cases it becomes firm at first in the lower sounds. In the Tenore Leggiero the organ descends but little in the throat, and as its muscular construction is slight, it is possible to recognise its character during the period of change, which is rarely very marked.

During this transition period, it is advisable, if the voice is exercised at all, to treat it with the utmost care, and sedulously avoid the use of the extreme sounds, especially the high ones, for any straining at this time may occasion mischief which is irretrievable. It is judicious to turn the attention more to an acquirement of the theoretical principles of the art than to abuse a highly precarious gift by premature exhibition.

Many teachers are opposed to the voice being used at all during the transition period, and will not even allow young girls to sing, as they consider this proceeding is calculated to spoil the voice in after years ; but so long as the voice is carefully guarded against any strain, and the *middle portion* is almost exclusively used, every piece of music being transposed so that the highest note shall be easily within the compass of the individual, it is fair to anticipate that the muscles will acquire power and the voice firmness. No reasonable person would oppose a child running about, or taking a fair amount of exercise, for by so doing the muscles occupied in locomotion are improved in firmness and strength, and may not the same argument apply to the muscles of the throat and the larynx.

(*To be continued*).

PROMISING PRIZE PUPILS OF THE ROYAL ACADEMY OF MUSIC.

The report of the interesting ceremony last week may be fitly supplemented by a cursory notice of some of the promising pupils in the Royal Academy of Music. Miss Thudicum is already known as a singer on the concert platform ; she has a fine soprano voice, but appears to be too self-conscious, or as the Germans would say, subjective, a fault to be rectified. Miss M. Burton, who received a bronze medal for singing, has an organ of much power and sweetness, with distinct articulation. Miss Alexandra Ehrenberg distinguished herself for declamatory English vocalization, and received the "Llewelyn Thomas" gold medal accordingly. Miss Frances Powell stands in the first division of "commenced" singers ; she has a splendid soprano voice, of extensive compass, and is likely to succeed in her own chosen department of the art, to wit, operatic concerts and oratorios. Miss Powell is much esteemed by the Principal of the Academy, and by her own particular professor. Miss Eleanor Rees, silver medallist, has a rich sympathetic contralto.

As regards pianists, Miss Dora Bright, a silver medalist, is a fine executant, and plays with confidence. At the June concert she was entrusted with the andante and the rondo vivace of Chopin's Concerto in E minor, Op. 11.

Amongst the gentlemen pupils may be named Mr. Musgrave Tufnail, who won the "Carl Rosa" gold medal for the singing of selected pieces ; he also carried off the Evill Prize, a purse of ten guineas for good declamatory English singing. Mr. Tufnail sang Mozart's fine air from "Figaro," "Vedro', mentr' io sospiro," at the June concert. Mr. William Lucas won a silver medal for singing. The "Heathcote Long" prize, a purse of ten guineas, for selected pianoforte pieces, was worthily won by Mr. C. W. P. Crowther, who has great sensibility. Alexander Christian and Jesse W. Buckland also deserve honourable mention. *Vix tenent lacrymas, quia nil lacrymabile cernunt.*

Musical Intelligence.

THE WELSH NATIONAL EISTEDDFOD.

(From the "Daily Telegraph.")

CARDIFF, Monday.

The energetic and flourishing town in which I write has put on its bravest apparel to honour the National Eisteddfod of Wales. Even the most benighted dweller in Saxon Britain must know that while every year many places in the principality get up Eisteddfods on their own account, one is chosen for the national celebration, the rule being to favour the north and south alternately. It has now come to the turn of the south, and of Cardiff, which shows, I am bound to say, a very thorough appreciation of its good fortune. At the present moment it seems bent upon suggesting to thoughtful minds the question whether the National Eisteddfod, when visiting the south, could find such a welcome and such good quarters anywhere else. The local Eisteddfod committee, as worthily representing a wealthy town, has devoted an unusually large amount to the encouragement of excellence in various branches of literature, science, and art. Some of the prizes are valuable enough to bring the best talent into the lists : thus, £100 is offered for the best essay on the history of Welsh literature during a certain period ; a like sum for the best choral singing ; £50 for the best musical setting of a dramatic poem, and so on. As for the subjects in which competition is stimulated by smaller though still desirable amounts, their name is legion. They do not, however, comprise the homely and common-place themes that on former occasions have excited sarcasm. It has been too much the fashion at Eisteddfod meetings to judge according to conditions dictated rather by regard for the competitors than for absolute merit. Hence a contentment of mediocrity with itself, and an absence of striving after a superior condition, the existence and necessity of which are kept out of evidence. The Cardiff committee have taken pains to avoid this mistake. Not only do observers find the character of the competitions raised, but they note the engagement of adjudicators who are not likely to forget, in consideration for the candidates, what is due to the literature, science and art they represent. In respect of music, always prominent at an Eisteddfod, even more has been done by the engagement of a first-class London orchestra, nearly sixty strong, and the making of programmes that are most instructive. An orchestra of some kind is no novelty on occasions like the present, but I believe that such a body of instrumentalists as that brought down here is without precedent in Eisteddfod history. Unique also will be the performance during the week of works like Spohr's "Power of Sound," Schubert's symphony in B minor, Mendelssohn's concerto in G minor, the overtures to "Leonora," "Der Freyschütz," "Die Zauberflöte," and other compositions of a similar class. It is by thus setting before a local public the highest examples of universal art that the existence of shortcomings is demonstrated, and wholesome dissatisfaction with actual attainments encouraged. On the whole the Cardiff Eisteddfod bids fair to prove most valuable as a stimulus to Welsh culture. Its general tendency is less national, and therefore less narrow, than of many gatherings in the past. The Eisteddfod opened this morning with the ceremonies that never vary and have often been described. The Marquis of Bute, president of the day, was escorted from the Castle to the "Pavilion," a huge engine shed not yet occupied by the railway company, the Mayor and Corporation in full municipal state taking part in the pageant. An immense crowd watched this public display, to which all the resources of the town contributed, including even the Fire Brigade. The ancient and significant ceremonies of the gorsedd followed, presided over by the venerable chief bard, Clwydfardd, whose fourscore years and four sit lightly upon him ; and then an adjournment to the pavilion was made, for the purpose of carrying out the programme of competitions and adjudications. Lord Bute's reception by an audience numbering some 5000 or 6000 persons was enthusiastic. Hearty, likewise, was the greeting bestowed upon Lady Bute by the Mayor of Cardiff, the venerable Archdeacon of Llandaff, and the many Welsh notables who presently filled the platform. The National Anthem having been played by Mr. E. H. Turpin upon the organ specially erected by Messrs. Brindley and Foster, Lord Bute delivered an address which showed very considerable and painstaking research into the past of the Welsh nation. His speech would perhaps have better suited the Cymmrodorion Society now in session here, but it was heard with laudable attention by the noble president's very miscellaneous audience, and obtained, as it deserved, frequent applause. The judications then proceeded, those in literature, science, painting, &c., having been, of course, determined beforehand ; but the musical competitions, as far as they entailed performance, went on then and there, some in separate rooms, others on the great platform, the judges being Sir G. A. Macfarren, Messrs. Barnby, Bennett, Evans, Jenkins, Brinley Richards, Turpin, and John Thomas. They comprised an orchestral performance of the overture to "Masaniello," for which bands entered from Cardiff, Merthyr, and Treherbert. This was most interesting, as demonstrative of the attention paid to instrumental music in its highest and most complicated form. It was also gratifying as proving that attention to be neither slight or fruitless. The Cardiff string band, to which Sir G. A. Macfarren awarded the first prize, played really well, while much credit, in addition to the second prize, was earned by the amateurs from Merthyr. In other competitions, in the singing of "Quando Corpus," in playing pianoforte solos, which brought to the front a clever Newport lad, named Try, and in the singing of an anthem by church or chapel choirs, the result was not quite satisfactory. Prizes for sight-singing, offered by Mr. S. Aitken, chairman of the Musical Committee, were not contested, the choirs entered failing to make an appearance, much to general disappointment. Altogether the music of the morning sitting was not remarkable. Apart from the playing of the two prize bands it lacked the superior merit which confers distinction by marking its purposes out from the common run.

The evening sitting was presided over by Sir E. J. Reed, M.P. for Cardiff, and had music for its chief attraction, there being competitions for brass bands, solo violinists, organists, pianists, harmonium players, string quartets, &c., in addition to which performances were given by Signor Foli, Mr. Brinley Richards, Mr. John Thomas, Mr. Turpin, Mr. Ap Herbert, and the local Blue Ribbon choir, whose ladies wore Welsh costume.

CARDIFF, Tuesday.

In my letter of yesterday I said that the musical adjudicators engaged here were not men likely to be influenced by mere sentiment in coming to conclusions. Their decisions have again and again proved that I was right. Some prizes have been withheld altogether, others have been reduced in value, while in certain cases the second prize has become the first, and the advertised first has disappeared. Possibly one result is soreness of spirit here and there, but I feel sure that public common sense approves a course which, if in itself disagreeable, tends to bear good fruit by and by. Let it be declared again, as a fact beyond dispute, the lenient judgment in past times is answerable for much mischief. Unfriendly critics of the Eisteddfod sometimes assert that the institution has really done very little of a noticeable character. I should answer that often the best work is not noticeable, but the fact remains, and a habit of praising everything and everybody has tended to restrain the spirit of progress by inspiring content with present achievement. The Eisteddfod now in session may be said to mark a new departure ; its discipline many will find to be not joyous but grievous ; but all this is worth undergoing for the sake of the conviction that there is not only a higher good unattained but that the good in question is demanded by the standard applicable to Eisteddfod exercises.

To-day's weather was much more favourable than that of yesterday. Nevertheless, the attendance at the morning session, which was mainly devoted to adjudications and competitions, fell short of the expected number. This, however, is not unusual at Eisteddfodau on the second day. The public reserve themselves for the session whereat the winner of the choir prize is inducted into his distinguished place with the ancient form and ceremony. In the present case they held back also for the admirable concert of this evening, which promised a first-class London orchestra, and such excellent vocalists as Miss Annie Marriott, Mr. Barton McGuckin, and Signor Foli. But if the immense engine shed, capable of receiving 20,000 people, was not crowded, a large and greatly distinguished audience assembled, watching the proceedings hour after hour with unflagging patience. The chairman of the day, Lord Aberdare, having been duly installed, and his address delivered, business went rapidly and smoothly on. The literary adjudications were many, and their subjects various, ranging from the libretto of a pantomime up to the condition and prospects of King Cole. The interest of the morning sitting chiefly gathered, as usual, round the musical competitions, some of which were necessarily conducted in private, only the results being made known and the winners heard in public. Some very satisfactory work was done. For example, an instrumental solo competition, choice of instrument open, showed a good average of merit, the first prize being taken by a clever Swansea boy named Griffiths (flute), and the second by an excellent, though self-taught trombonist (Mr. Foxwell), of Newport. A madrigal and part-song competition also showed valuable results, as did in special measure a competition amongst male voice choirs. The winners of the first prize in the last-named case were a party of sixteen colliers from Rhondda Valley. Anything more admirable than the singing of these underground workers I do not expect to hear in London. Power and delivery, precision and artistic freedom were conspicuous to a degree which filled strangers with amazement. That the decision of the judges in favour of the Rhondda men was endorsed by a delighted audience goes without saying—let the so-called musical countries show anything better among their miners and I will admit their supremacy without further cavil. Time and space fail me to tell of other excellent work such as was done in vocal duet competitions, in a choral competition which brought bodies of singers, all working men and women, from Abergavenny, Dowlais, Merthyr, Neath, and Tregedar. Merit varied, of course, but was never entirely absent, and ever deserved the praise due to a good attained in despite of untoward circumstances. All things considered, it created astonishment and a profound belief that a country able to show such results in the "green tree" of actual conditions will take a brilliant place in the good time coming.

This evening was devoted to an orchestral concert, in which a band of sixty London players made a first appearance here, conducted—and well conducted, too—by Mr. E. H. Turpin. The connection of such an orchestra with the Eisteddfod is an event calling for hearty congratulation, and reflects the utmost credit upon the Cardiff committee, who are showing themselves worthy to represent a university town. These eminent London performers—among whom are Messrs. Pollitzer, Lazarus, Barret, Reynolds, and many others equally well known—come down not only to delight unaccustomed ears, but to show what excellence is, and thus to stimulate effort by setting up a more exalted standard. Their playing this evening was a grand lesson, worth all the sacrifice entailed. It opened the eyes of many to see that which theretofore had been unimagined, and made a distinct step towards the highest good. The works performed included Beethoven's C minor Symphony and "Leonora" overture; Handel's first organ concerto, solo by Mr. Scott, a local professor of high attainment both in an executive and artistic sense; the overtures to "Der Freyschütz" and "Semiramide;" Mendelssohn's scena, "Infelice," sung most admirably by Miss Annie Marriott; a harp solo by Mr. John Thomas, who again demonstrated his dexterous skill; and songs in which Mr. Barton McGuckin and Signor Foli brought down the house. Altogether the first classical concert was a brilliant success, auguring well for those to follow.

BISHOP'S STORTFORD.

The annual festival usually held at the end of the Midsummer term of the High School took place on Tuesday, the 31st ultimo. At 2.30 p.m. a full choral and orchestral service was held in the fine old parish church, when the combined choirs of the church and the school were reinforced with members of St. Paul's Cathedral, the Temple, and St. James's Chapel Royal, London, and of St. George's Chapel Royal, Windsor. The principal musical items were Dr. Stainer's Service in B flat, Mendelssohn's 115th Psalm, "Non Nobis Domine" as the anthem, and Handel's "Hallelujah Chorus." The solo portions of the works were taken by two of the Temple choristers, and by Messrs. Kenningham and Kempton,

of St. Paul's Cathedral. A select orchestra accompanied, which included the well known names of Val. Nicholson, Doyle, Ould, Woolhouse, Harper, Lazarus, Barrett, Horton, Hutchings, Anderson, Matt, and many others with Mr. Warwick Jordan at the organ. In the evening a concert was given in the Gospel Hall, at which the same artists, both vocal and instrumental, performed, with Mrs. Scales, Miss Baldock, and Mr. Frost as additional solo vocalists. A highly interesting and well diversified programme was thoroughly well rendered, including notably amongst the orchestral numbers, Schubert's unfinished symphony in B minor, and amongst the vocal solos "From mighty Kings," "Deeper and deeper still," and "Waft her, angels." Beethoven's "Hallelujah Chorus," which concluded the first part, and Faning's "The Vikings" at the end of the second part, deserve also especial notice. Mr. Lewis Marcus, the organist of the parish church, conducted both the service and the concert, and he is to be congratulated on the fact that the performances which he had been at the pains of producing are rarely excelled in any provincial town.

CORK.

(*From our own Correspondent.*)

On the 26th ult., the members of the Cork Orchestral Union gave a grand concert in the great hall of the Exhibition, when they performed the following programme :—

Overture, " Le Puito d'amour "	Balfe.
Ballet Music, " La Reine de Saba "	Gounod.
Allegro Moderato, Concerto in E minor	} Prout.
Andante for organ and orchestra	}
Marche, " Firenze "	Atkins.
Concert Overture, " Queen Marie Stuart's hunt "	Zoeller
Fantasia de Concert, " Souvenir d' Irlande "	Bonicoll.
Tonbild, " Die Turkish Scharwache "	Michaelis.
Overture, " La Gazza Ladra "	Rossini.

The programme was lengthened by songs of Sir R. P. Stewart, C. Dick, B. Tours, etc., sung by Mr. W. Ellis, Miss Colthurst, and Mr. Longfield.

Herr Swertz presided at the organ, and played the concerto remarkably well, and Mr. Ringrose Atkins conducted as usual. The only fault to be found was that the andante of Prout's concerto was taken much too slow.

On Friday evening the 27th ult., Mr. G. F. Moran gave a piano recital in the Exhibition hall. The programme, which is too long for entire quotation, was very well received, Mr. Moran showing great power as a pianist. The following were the principal items played by him.

" Ruy Blas," Overture	Mendelssohn.
Allemagne, Valse	Rubinstein.
Valse, Op. 34. No. 1	Chopin.
La Bella Capricciosa	Hummel.
Andante from Sonata, Op. 110	Beethoven.
"Tannhauser," March	Wagner-Liszt.

He also gave an organ recital on the 28th ult., showing as an organist even to greater advantage than as a pianist.

Rigoletto (*Verdi*) was produced on the 30th ult., at the Opera House, in Italian. The principal characters were well sustained by Mdlle. de Laporte, Mdlle. Mosinas, Signor Bellatti, and Signor Arturo Salvini.

Verdi's "Trovatore," (Tuesday), and Bellini's "Sonnambula" (Wednesday), have been also produced by this company.

F. ST. JOHN LACY.

LEEDS ORGAN SCHOOL AND ACADEMY OF MUSIC.

The half-yearly students' concert and award of certificates of honour took place on Saturday afternoon at the Institution in Great George Street, in the presence of numerous friends. The programme was an unusually good and interesting one. Most of the pieces embraced in it were difficult works by the great masters, and their performance might not have been satisfactorily accomplished by the students ; but it must be allowed that they were one and all given in a creditable manner, and with appropriate taste and expression. Special mention may be made of Miss Greenwood's organ playing, Mr. Arthur Elvey's performance of Bach's great organ Fugue in G minor and Weber's fine "Concert-Stuck" for the pianoforte. Towards the end of the programme the Rev. J. Bewley, M.A., of St. Martin's Church (chairman), proceeded to distribute the awards.—*Yorkshire Post.*

PROMENADE CONCERTS, COVENT GARDEN.

A season of Promenade Concerts, under the direction of Mr. A. G. Crowe, appears to be an established annual institution—proving the successful manner of conducting former series, and inspiring confidence in the management of the one which commenced on Saturday evening last. The orchestra comprises most of the eminent performers who have been marshalled under Mr. Crowe's *baton* before, with Mr. J· T. Carrodus at the head of the strings. On Wednesday evening there was a crowded house, attracted by the first classical programme of the season. The orchestral numbers of the first part were : Overture, " Der Freischütz" (Weber) ; Ballet music, " Faust " (Gounod) ; Danse des Sylphes, " Faust " (Berlioz) ; and "The Italian Symphony " (Mendelssohn). Mr. J· T. Carrodus gave an excellent performance of Mendelssohn's Violin Concerto, which met with warm appreciation. The interest which the audience manifested in the performance of these works was evidence of the development of a wide appreciation of the higher class of musical art, and which, it is to be hoped, will tend to an increase of the classical element in the programmes of the Promenade Concerts. The vocal numbers in this part of the programme were Beethoven's " Creation's Hymn," well sung by Madame Fassett ; a scena from Gounod's " La Reine de Saba," for which Mr. Joseph Maas received a determined *encore*, which, however, he wisely and firmly declined ; and Handel's charming *aria*, " Lascia ch'io pianga," from " Rinaldo," contributed by Miss Mary Lemmens. The second part comprised, Overture, " Maritana " (Wallace) ; new Waltz, by A. G. Crowe ; Polka, " Grelots' (Villac) ; Operatic Selections, " L'Italiana in Algieri," and " Lucia di Lammermoor," and Berlioz's " Hungarian March." Madame Fassett sang " Jock o' Hazeldean" ; Mr. Maas gave Balfe's " Come into the garden " ; and Miss Lemmens, " Away to the mountain's brow," by Lee.

Foreign Musical Intelligence.

The death of Dimitri Glinka, brother of the Russian composer, is announced from Lisbon.

An international meeting of bands and choirs will be held in Amsterdam next month.

Cagnoni, the composer of " Don Bucefalo," is writing an opera on the story of " King Lear."

Le Ménéstrel has an appreciative article on " Parsifal," from the pen of Victor Wilder.

The distribution of prizes at the Paris Conservatoire took place on August 4th.

It is stated that several architects have gone to Bayreuth to ascertain if it be possible to transport to Monaco the theatre constructed by Wagner for himself.

The *Gazetta Musicale di Milano* says that not Berlin, but Vienna, will have the first representation of the new operetta of G. Strauss, " Le Notti Veneziani."

Formerly the direction of the Court Theatre in Sweden was the exclusive right of the Swedish nobility. Breaking through tradition, King Oscar has this year entrusted the management to Anders Willman, an esteemed artist of the opera at Stockholm.

All the French newspapers, in noticing the memorial stone in honour of Rameau in the church of St. Eustache, Paris, have suggested that Rameau was organist there. This is incorrect ; Rameau was only buried in the Church of St. Eustache, Sept. 13th, 1764.

The subscriptions opened in France for a monument to Berlioz have already reached a large sum, sufficient to ensure the completion of the work. So much cannot be said of the monument to Félicien David, which remains incomplete for want of funds.

Petrella's " Ione " has been revived, after the lapse of several years, at the Teatro del Principe Alfonso, Madrid. This opera, a great favourite in Italy, was produced in Madrid in 1863. It became the rage and was performed over fifty times.

It is announced that Franz Liszt has been presented by Messrs. Mason and Hamlin, of Boston, U.S., with a fine chamber organ, which is said to be worth 6,000 dollars. Liszt has transferred the present, according to his usual practice, to the music-school at Weimar.

Professor Dr. Hermann Zopff, a composer of talent, and for some time editor of a leading German musical journal, and one of the most eminent musical theorists in Germany, died at Leipzig on the 12th ult. Besides numerous instrumental and vocal works, he composed several operas.

The following is a list of the chief provincial Conservatoires of France, with the dates of foundation attached : Aix, 1850 ; Angers, 1857 ; Besançon, 1861 ; Bordeaux, 1852 ; Boulogne, 1829 ; Caen, 1835 ; Cambrai, 1821 ; Douai, 1799 ; Dunkirk, 1863 ; Lille, 1801 ; Marseilles, 1820 ; Nantes, 1844 ; Nimes, 1864 ; Toulon, 1866 ; Toulouse, 1830 ; Valenciennes, 1836.

Massenet's new opera, " Manon Lescaut," it is reported, is to be put into rehearsal at the Opéra Comique, Paris, next October, and it is hoped that it will be produced about the end of the year. The principal part is to be " created " by Mdme. Heilbronn. It will not be overlooked that Auber has written an opera on the same subject to a libretto by Scribe.

In the course of the season just ended at the Royal Opera House of Vienna, 303 performances took place, comprising a *répertoire* of 78 different works. Of these 42 evenings were devoted to Meyerbeer, 41 to Wagner, 31 to Verdi, 23 to Mozart, 21 to Gounod, 16 to Donizetti, 15 to Adam, 14 to Boïto, 10 to Gluck, and 9 only to Weber. Beethoven, with " Fidelio," 2.

The Italian season in St. Petersburg commences on the 1st of October, and terminates on the 2nd of March, 1884. The band will number ninety performers ; the chorus, ninety voices. The ballet-master is M. Petipa ; the conductors, Bevignani and R. Driga. The novelties will include Anton Rubinstein's " Nerone " (first time in Italian) ; " Richard III.," grand opera in four acts, book by M. E. Blavet, music by G. Salvayre (first performance) ; " I Lituani," four-act opera by Ponchielli ; " Philémon et Baucis," three-act opera by Gounod (first time in Italian) ; and " La Moglie Rapita," three-act buffo opera by R. Drigo (first performance). The general repertory includes : " Mefistofele," " Carmen," " La Gioconda," " Lohengrin," " Les Huguenots," " Robert le Diable," " L'Africaine," " L'Etoile du Nord," " Guillaume Tell," " La Muette de Portici," " Faust," " Mignon," " Zampa," " Fra Diavolo," " Aïda," " Rigoletto," " La Traviata," " Don Giovanni," " La Favorita," " Norma," " La Juive."

ORPHAN SCHOOL FOR DAUGHTERS OF MUSICIANS.

Miss Helen Kenway, who with the assistance of friends has during the last five years educated a few fatherless girls in Bath, is now making arrangements to take a house in London, and hopes to open the Orphan School in September. The school is intended to provide—1. Free board and education for *orphan* and indigent daughters of musicians. 2. Board and education at a moderate cost for daughters of musicians, or girls with musical abilities whose means are limited.

The pupils will receive a good general education, with special opportunities for the study of music in preparation for the Royal Academy or Royal College, together with some training and practice in the art of teaching. Orphans without musical ability will be trained for some other profession or business. All fees payable in advance, and to be devoted to the benefit of the charity. Accounts subjected to a public auditor, and the school examined annually. Some subscriptions to meet the increased expenses of furnishing, etc., have been received, also several small gifts of furniture, but further donations of money, furniture, standard books, or music, are earnestly solicited. Five orphans are waiting for admission, and three others have been under Miss Kenway's care in Bath.

Until Aug. 15th, the address will still be—Miss Helen Kenway, South Hill House, Bath. After Aug. 15th, the address will be 10, Darnley Road, Royal Crescent, Notting Hill, W.

Organ News.

HALSTEAD, ESSEX.

An organ recital was given at the Parish Church on Thursday, August 2nd, by Mr. Thomas Adams, A.C.O., the organist of the Church. The following was the programme :—

Prelude and Fugue in B min r	Bach.
Andante in D 8	Robinson.
Hokeworthy Church Bells	Wesley.
Prelude and Fugue in G	Mendelssohn.
March Romaine	Gounod.
Organ Sonata, No. 9	Mendelssohn.
Festival March	Pinsey.

FISHERIES EXHIBITION.

Mr. James Loaring, F.C.O., gave recitals every day last week on Messrs. Henry Jones and Son's organ, the programmes being selected each day respectively from the works of Handel, Haydn, Mozart, Beethoven, Mendelssohn and Bach.

Mr. Loaring's programme, on the 30th ult., included :—

Overture, "La Clemenza di Tito"	Mozart.
Lieder ohne Worte { (a) The first Violet..... } { (b) The Garland ...... }	Mendelssohn.
Chorus, "Immortal Lord" (" Deborah ")	Handel.
Prelude and Fugue in D minor	Bæh.
The " Midnight March "	Williams.

STOKE DAMEREL.

An organ recital was given by Mr. John Hele, Mus.Bac., in the Parish Church, on Friday, July 27th. The following was the programme :—

Overture, " Occasional "	Handel.
Air	Lachner.
Installation Ode	Bennett.
Air, " With verdure clad "	Haydn.
Duet, " Quis est homo "	Rossini.
Finale from 3rd Symphony	Mendelssohn.

And on Friday, August 3rd :—

Marche Religieuse	Gounod.
Movement from an "Ode"	Bennett.
Air, " There is a green hill "	Gounod.
Benediction Nuptiale	Saint Saëns.
Chorus, "Disdainful of danger " (" Judas Maccabeus ")	Handel.
Air, " But the Lord is mindful " (" St. Paul ")	Mendelssohn.
"Silver Trumpets"	Viviani.

LEEDS.

An organ recital was given on Wednesday, August 1st, by Alfred Benton, Esq., on the new organ in St. Martin's Church. The following was the programme :—

4th Concerto (major)	Handel.
(Allegro Moderato—Andante—Adagio—Allegro—Fuga).	
Allegretto and Grand Chœur	Salome
Andante from the 5th Quintet	Mozart.
Fugue in G Major	Krebs.
"Marche Funèbre et Chant Séraphique"	Guilmant.
March in E flat major	"

CORK INDUSTRIAL EXHIBITION.

The following are the programmes of the organ recitals given in the main hall of the Exhibition on July 28th, by Mr. G. F. Moran :—

Prelude and Fugue in E	Bach.
" See the proud chief (" Deborah ")	Handel.
Two Andantes { No. 1 in G ...... } { No. 2 in E minor }	Batiste.
Sonata in B flat	Mendelssohn.
" Pater in manus Tuas " (last seven words)	Haydn.
Grand Offertoire in G	Wely.
Andante (Quartet in F)	Haydn.
" Hallelujah." Chorus (" Messiah ")	Handel.
War March of the Priests (" Athalie ")	Mendelssohn.

And on July 30th by Signor Cellini :—

Grand March in D	Cellini.
Overture " Nabuco "	Verdi.
" La Passione "	Coop.
Selection, " Alda "	Verdi.
Melodie in C minor	Croiser.
Potpourri, " Sapho "	Paccini.
Fugato e Finale	Cellini.

And on July 31st, by Mr. H. Daly :—

Marche Romaine	Gounod.
Grand Offertoire in G	Wely.
Adagio, Op. 47	Spohr.
Gloria, 12th Mass	Mozart.
Fantasia, Op. 40	Tutz.
Offertoire in C minor	Batiste.
Festival March	Best.
" Hallelujah " Chorus (" Messiah ")	Handel.

NORTH BERWICK.

An organ recital was given on Monday July 30th, at St. Baldred's Church, by Mr. T. S. Guyer. The following was the programme :—

Overture, " Messiah "	Handel.
Larghetto, and Symphony	Beethoven.
Sonata, No. 1	Mendelssohn.
(Allegro—Adagio—Andante—Allegro).	
Air, " Holy, Holy "	Handel.
Andante con moto	Haydn.
Fugue in G minor	Bach.
Andante in G	Smart.
Chorus, "from the Censer" (" Solomon ")	Handel.

YARMOUTH.

An organ recital was given at the Parish Church, on Tuesday evening, by Mr. H. Stonex. The following was the programme :—

Andante in A (Posthumous work, No. 1)	Smart.
Offertoire in A flat	Batiste.
Ave Maria in F (" 16th Century ")	Arcadelt.
Offertory in F, No. 2	Wely.
Barcarolle in F, 4th Concerto	Bennett.
Cantilene Pastorale in B minor	Guilmant.
Meditations in B flat	Clark.
Concertstück for the organ	Spark.

BAMBURGH.

The organ in the fine old Church of St. Ardan, Bamburgh, Northumberland, has recently been moved from the west end to the Chancel. Special services in connection with the re-opening of the instrument took place on the 24th, Mr. J. Collinson, Mus.Bac., organist of St. Mary's Cathedral, Edinburgh, presiding at the key-board. The services, which were of the usual festal nature, included the anthem, "O how amiable" (Richardson), and Dean Alford's fine processional hymn, "' Forward ' be our watchword," with its stirring tune by H. Gadsby. Mr. Collinson gave two organ recitals, the playing of this gentleman giving the greatest pleasure to the crowded congregation and fully sustaining the reputation he has earned during the time he has officiated as organist of St. Mary's Cathedral, Edinburgh, where, as perhaps some of our readers are aware, Mr. Collinson presides at a very fine four-manual organ by Henry Willis.

The work of removing the organ was entrusted to Messrs. Harrison, of Durham, who have re-constructed and re-modelled the instrument, which consists of 2 manuals with pedal organ, about 15 sounding stops, with the usual couplers, composition pedals, &c.

AN ORGAN PERFORMANCE ON BANK HOLIDAY.

On Monday, the Bank Holiday, Mr. Edwin Bending held two recitals on the great organ of the Royal Albert Hall, at noon, and again at four o'clock. The British public, alas! attended in very weak force, numerically speaking, for only the arena or floor of the hall was occupied ; the reporter, who sat in the amphitheatre, was quite alone in his glory. Mr. Bending had been engaged to play pieces suited to the popular taste. He chose Guilmant's " Marche Funèbre et Chant Séraphique," a dance air by Czibolka, a " Fantasia Pastorale " of Wély, the overture to " Semiramide," and an (extempore) " Marche Militaire." In a set of ingenious pot-pourri, Mr. Bending introduced a snatch of " Rule Britannia," " Auld Robin Gray," and " God bless the Prince of Wales," with imitations of Church bells in octaves, and the note of the cuckoo (a major third). A selection from Mendelssohn's works was omitted, but the beautiful minuet from Sir W. Sterndale Bennett's Symphony in G minor (first heard as a separate piece at the Cambridge Institution in 1862) must have charmed every sensitive auditor. Mr. Bending made good use of his soft stops, but the solo organ utterly failed to produce the proper effect in Rossini's grand overture. A professor once spoke of the organ as all " soot and snow," in this case it is all daub and smear; the rapid scale passages for the violins were quite lost, and the upward rush of the octave passage at the coda sounded like a " caution." Mr. Bending ascribes the failure, mainly if not entirely, to the acoustical faults of the Albert Hall, and of course no one would blame this esteemed organist. It may be suspected, however, that even modern " solo " organs are inadequate to the due expression of delicate orchestral passages. The organ is fitted to sustain sound, not to execute runs with nice accentation and point. The recital lasted only an hour, yet the " British public " held a " processional march " in and out of the arena nearly the whole time.

WINDSOR CASTLE.

The following is the specification of the organ just completed by Messrs. Gray and Davison in St. George's Chapel. The cases and most of the pipes of the old organ, which were mostly Gray and Davison's make, are incorporated in this instrument.

GREAT ORGAN.

1. Double Open Diap.. 16 ft.	8. Twelfth .... 2⅔ft.
2. Large Open Diap. 8 „	9. Fifteenth .... 2 „
3. Open Diapason ...... 8 „	10. Sesquialtera (3 ranks)
4. Stopped Diapason... 8 „	11. Mixture (2 ranks)
5. Clarabella .... 8 „	12. Posaune .... 8 „
6. Principal .... 4 „	13. Clarion .... 4 „
7. Harmonic Flute ... 4 „	

SWELL ORGAN.

15. Leiblich Bourdon .. 16 ft.	23. Mixture (3 ranks)
16. Open Diapason...... 8 „	24. Contra Fagotto ...... 16 ft.
17. Stopped Diapason... 8 „	25. Cornopean .... 8 „
18. Dulciana .... 8 „	26. Oboe .. .. 8 „
19. Voix Celestes......... 8 „	27. Vox Humana....... 8 „
20. Principal .... 4 „	28. Clarion .... 4 „
21. Octave Dulciana ... 4 „	29. Tremulant
22. Fifteenth................ 2 „	

CROFT ORGAN.

31. Dulciana............... 8 ft.	35. Flute .... 4 ft.
32. Keraulophon ...... 8 „	36. Piccolo .... 2 „
33. Stopped Diapason.. 8 „	37. Corno di Bassetto ... 8 „
34. Principal .. .. 4 „	

SOLO ORGAN.

39. Harmonic Flute ... 8 ft.	41. Tromba .... 8 ft
40. Orchestral Oboe ... 8 „	

PEDAL ORGAN.

43. Open Diapason ... 16 ft.	46. Violoncello......... 8 ft.
44. Violone .. .. 16 „	47. Trombone .... 16 „
45. Bourdon .... 16 „	

COUPLERS.

49. Solo to Great.	52. Swell to Pedal.
50. Swell to Great.	53. Great to Pedal.
51. Solo to Pedal.	54. Choir to Pedal.

Four Manuals CC to A, 58 Notes.
Pedals CCC to F, 30 Notes.
Four Composition Pedals, to Great and Pedal.

Three	„	„	to Swell.
One	„	„	to Great to Pedal.
One '	„	„	to Pedal Organ.

Pneumatic action to great organ and its couplers, stops draw-ing at an angle, keys overhanging and near each other, pedals concave, not radiating ; keys, &c., at south end, enabling organist to see toward either choir or nave ; wind reservoirs near the sound boards, swell pedal on new system, so as to remain wherever left by the organist's foot ; draw stop knobs of solid ivory, stool made so that the seat may be raised or lowered, swell shutters facing both south and west.

[A somewhat serious and obvious defect in this otherwise excellent scheme is the want of 32-feet pipes in the Pedal organ, such tone being necessary in all important instruments having 16. feet stops on the manuals.—ED. M.S.]

BEAUTY IN MUSIC.

Writing upon the philosophy of music a "Scottish Graduate" says in the *St. Cecilia Magazine* :—

Some philosophers have accounted for art by declaring that the nature of beauty is simply the beauty of nature ; for this is tantamount to saying that art only imitates nature. This was Aristotle's doctrine. He says (Phys. II. 8):—"Art is wholly concerned with supplementing nature when it is found wanting, and with imitating it." By the art which is supplementary of nature's deficiency, he understands industrial art. Fine art, according to him, is imitative. Now, painting may imitate the varied hues of nature in colour, sculpture may imitate the pose and gesture of nature in effigy ; but can it be said that music imitates the sounds of nature or the harmonies of nature, further than for those adventitious effects which have been already considered ? It is only by a metaphor that the breeze is said to be musical, the running brook melodious, the plash of breaking waves rhythmical. Goethe's saying, that beauty is a manifestation of hidden laws of nature, which, but for this phenomenon, would have been for ever hidden from us, is an excellent observation as regards natural beauty ; but, if applied to art, all it can mean is

that æsthetic beauty cannot be explained by any reference to the .laws of nature. There is nothing like a tune in nature ; it has no harmonies. Whatever the other arts may be, music at least, is not imitative of nature, but creative of beauty, not,—if the reader will pardon the pedantry of a neologism—physicomimetic, but callopoetic. Aristotle, indeed, when face to face with what under a solely imita-tive theory is a paradox, i.e., that the work of art may be beautiful, although the object imitated be of the most ordinary sort, modifies his doctrine so that not so much the particular, as the essential, of the special object is to be imitated by the artist. This is much nearer the truth, and in this sense we might say that music imitates in objective sound subjective feeling ; but even in this account no notice is taken of the artistic regulation of the emotions to be imitated, and the subjective feeling can-not be spoken of as part of any other nature than human nature. Music is therefore not imitative of nature, but seeks a higher beauty. The beauty of art is for human beings a light of something higher than the beauty of nature. In nature we are never fully assured, as in art, that the beauty is the creation of mind in thorough sym-pathy with our own, seeing with the same eyes, feeling with the same heart as we do. Art is beautiful because of the palpable presence in it of an informing human mind, with all its aspirations and failings, all its vast possibilities and littleness of realization. Nature has none of this : it is perfect, passionless. "Nature," says Novalis, "is an Æolian harp, whose tones again are keys to higher strings in us."

In music, beauty is form. No musical sound or note has in itself what we call artistic beauty. This, as regards the particular notes, and in most instances as regards phrases and movements, is a quality relative to the po-sition occupied by the note, phrase, or movement, as com-pared with other notes, phrases, and movements, and with the whole work. The number of single notes which are recognised as musical is extremely limited as compared with the number of musical compositions ; but the modes of arrangement and rearrangement, the forms of music, are inexhaustible. But this is crude theorizing. If we recall the logical distinction between matter and form, our enquiry will be more philosophical, for this distinction is as clearly established for the imagination as for the reasoning powers. The matter is what of the product is given *to* the thinking or imagining faculty ; as in a pro-position, the subject ; in a representation of the imagina-tion, the original representation in sense-perception. The form is what is given *by* the thinking or imagining faculty ; as, in a proposition, the quantity or quality predicated of the subject ; in a representation, the mode and variety in the selection by which the sense-presentations are revived. Thus, in music, nature supplies the necessary, permanent, material factor, sound. But in addition to this original matter, there is a derivative matter supplied to the artist. This derivative matter has in the development of our art, been added to the primary *Stoff* by the action of formative processes working upon it. To the original sounds of nature the form of notes has been given, these again have been fashioned into scales, moulded into modes, rough cast and chiselled into all the *technique* of the art. The theory of music, the mechanism of thoroughbass and counterpoint, have been developed by what we may call æsthetic selection. Æsthetic selection is a good enough name for the process ; genius is the name given to those in whom the process works unconsciously. Kant defines genius as that talent or endowment of nature which gives rules to art. All this theory, then, is so much matter given to the composer, and has not in itself what is most essential to musical beauty ; for one can write with the strictest attention to all the rules and maxims of theoretical music without inspiring his hearers with that impression of grace or power which the lightest lyric of a musical genius awakens. All this matter, therefore, has to pass through the creative mind of the artist. It is fictile and receives the impression of all his inner life, all his fulness of knowledge and deftness of practical skill. The artist's mind is plasmic, and superinduces on the material object the subjective quality of artistic form or beauty—the total effect in which the *rudis indigestaque moles* is reduced to the unity of musical charm.

Artistic beauty, then, is not something having an objec-tive existence in the beautiful thing, but a subjective quality, form, superinduced on the matter by the artist's mind. This inversion, though it can hardly be called Copernican, as being neither original nor revolutionary, may yet explain some problems which in the other view are paradoxical, and is moreover in harmony with the teaching of some great philosophers. As an instance of a paradoxical problem solved, take the difference in musical tastes which resolves itself into the radical and derived differences between different individuals, inasmuch as the subjective quality, the effect of the whole mind of the artist on his work, will at once appeal to those mentally constituted similar to the artist himself and to one another. Plato and Kant may be instanced as maintaining the subjective nature of beauty. For Plato, the beautiful is that idea which imparts to its sensible copies the highest brilliancy, since it, most of all ideas, shines through its copies. For Kant, the beautiful is that which through the harmony of its form with the human faculty of knowledge awakens a disinterested, universal, and necessary satisfaction.

So much for the nature of beauty. We now pass to the last question which shall be raised here : What is the function of music as an art? Here we must revert to that essay of Mr. Herbert Spencer's which we quoted in our first part. While disagreeing with him as to the origin of music, we cannot but admire his account of its function. Using the word cadence as comprehending all modifications of voice, he says :—" Cadence is the commentary of the emotions upon the propositions of the intellect. Beyond the direct pleasure which it gives, music has the indirect effect of developing the language of the emotions. Modifications of voice are the chief media of sympathy, and the tendency of civilization is more and more to repress the antagonistic elements of our nature and to develope the social ones." He concludes his essay in terms highly laudatory of the art, thus :—" In its bearings on human happiness, we believe that this emotional language which musical culture develops and refines, is only second in importance to the language of the intellect, perhaps not even to it."

The doctrine of emotional education as the function of music may be compared with Aristotle's κάθαρσις τῶν παθημάτων, which he holds to be the function of tragic poetry. The expression has puzzled the commentators. It means purification of the emotions. κάθαρσις means a purifying or purging, and has been imported into our language in the nomenclature of pharmacy. But although many medical properties have been ascribed to music by learned doctors, although music has been prescribed for sciatica, viper-bites, gout, and insanity—as to which, see the paper, " Medical Music," in Disraeli's " Curiosities of Literature" —yet Aristotle's κάθαρσις is moral, not physical. It has been variously interpreted as bringing the emotions to their ethical mean, the elimination of all painful ingredients in the emotions, and the provisional satisfaction of a regularly recurring emotional instinct. All these functions music may be said to fulfil, but this is not what the composer has in view when he sets to work. For him, the end of art is beauty as a product and pleasure in the beautiful, implying judgment, as an effect.

This thing of beauty, art's product, is no mere flash of pretty fancy, nor does it come at once into the world. It was Minerva who sprang all armed from the head of Jove. Apollo had a longer and more laborious birth. By patience and long musing the artist knows or feels those of our fleeting emotions which are at one with the ideal, that beacon of the onward progress of humanity. He knows—

" Such harmony is in immortal souls,
But, while this muddy vesture of decay
Doth grossly close it in, we cannot hear it."

He feels the great love which reconciles aspiration and realization, and, music and love being type and ante-type, translates his inner feeling into the one language which is universally intelligible. But his translation, being man's work only, is imperfect. Yet he will try again. So the artist works towards an ideal. The ideal, the god-like beautiful in its singleness of form, strikes upon him as on a harp, and he recognises a concord from the symphony of the universe. He gives his life to reconstruct the symphony ; and, after his life his work, stays, like the fabled tomb of Memnon, to give forth sweet harmony when the sun has risen upon another day.

With regret the lamented death of Mr. Joseph Wallis, the well known musical instrument manufacturer and importer, is announced as having occurred at Ryde on July 31st.

PRINCIPAL CONTENTS OF THIS NUMBER.

LONDON : SATURDAY, AUGUST 11, 1883.

ON MUSICAL THINKING.

IS it possible to turn to practical and profitable account the processes of tone-thought? All are familiar enough with the phenomenon of thinking verbally in silent words, and all recognize the undoubted utility of such a mental operation.

Surely, then, the mind stocked with musical idioms, and ever alive to musical impulses, may be encouraged to the systematic direction and assortment of the toneless tones of musical thought. As a matter of fact, no form of thinking produces more haunting, fascinating impressions than does the exercise of imaginative thought in unheard musical sentences. It is unnecessary to assert that all mental achievements must originate in that great human motive power, thought. Musical people will also duly remember the saying attributed to SCHUMANN, that it was comparatively easy to think extemporaneously, but the real mental difficulty was that of successfully consigning ideas to paper. Still, it may be urged, that systematic musical thinking is not as much practised as it might be with advantage, seeing that it must inevitably lead to the development and strengthening of those qualities which are essential to the composer, whose task it is to conduct musical thoughts into shapely forms by means of a strong mental grip upon his own imagination and to fix them upon his listeners' minds through the formation of a memory in part created and chiefly sustained by the operation of such forces, as evolution, development, proportion, and recapitulation. There is abundant evidence to show that many of the great masters did assiduously cultivate the art of musical thinking; we can all call to mind the shaping of a goodly number of masterpieces by the force of systematised thinking. However, the object of my present words is less that of advising prolonged meditation before composition on paper, than it is to suggest the systematic utilization of musical thinking at such times as when composition may not be conveniently pursued. To this end it is suggested that the precipitation of musical ideas upon the mind should neither be neglected or resisted. The recipient should endeavour to form them into definite rhythmical periods; should especially seek to define the sources of such impulses; try to clothe them with suitable if imaginary harmony, and endeavour before dismissing them to find subjects of a companionable type, just as it is the business of the composer to place in conjunction themes on paper which may serve to secure that necessary contrast which is ever essential to the maintenance of the listener's interest and to the due refreshment of his mind. There may be times when such exercise as this can be conducted to special advantage, when it is even well for the thinker to be at rest and away from the actual machinery of composition. Thus, in the enjoyment of the beauties of Nature, the musician may draw extemporaneous music which will strengthen his powers of perception; enrich the storehouse of his mind and enable him to realise more and more the universality of his art, and teach him much valuable self-knowledge as to his own powers of mind and memory.

Surely Beethoven, Mendelssohn, and many others must have practised such an art of thought-cultivation as this; and as the painter loves to seek Nature, so the composer should also study her powers and moods and learn to apply his knowledge, through the process of musical thinking, to the production of music strong and pure.

E. H. TURPIN.

FORM IN VOCAL MUSIC.

VI.

THAT the principles of Form—as musicians understand the word in its large, architectural sense—should have been of slower growth, save in the contrapuntal department, in vocal than in instrumental music, is a matter easily to be realised. In vocal music the expression of verbal thoughts would naturally overrule and supersede the exigencies of musical shapeliness for ages, and it was chiefly through the advances made in the instrumental forms that the application of the processes of musical architecture gradually made themselves felt as—to a large extent—essential features in the logical conduct of the vocal branch of the art. But ultimately we arrive late in the eighteenth century at the anomalous position of the subjugation of the verbal text, even when it consisted of sacred words of the most solemn import, to the musically effective plans now fully adopted from the instrumental structures. Such an obvious abuse of the reverent and common-sense treatment of words

will often be observable in the Masses and other Church works of the Viennese school of the period just spoken of. The modern English school of Church music has in the directions of a dignified treatment of the verbal text, and a subjective as well as objective use of form in vocal music, exercised a real and beneficial influence in the art of our own times, an influence which has carried weight further away from home than many of us are apt to think likely or possible. It is of importance, however, to remember, that the principles of form not only show themselves at an early period of the history of vocal music, but have had no insignificant influence through vocal moulds in the domain of instrumental art, as in the formation of *cantabile* subjects often assigned to instruments, and as in the meditative instrumental sentences of the unaccompanied or accompanied monologue and recitative types of musical thought.

E. H. TURPIN.

THE MAJORITY OF THE "MUSICAL STANDARD."

THE reference made to the twenty-one years' existence of the MUSICAL STANDARD in last week's issue by Mr. STEPHEN S. STRATTON, to whom the readers of this paper are indebted for valuable contributions and information from time to time, claims a word or two. It must, in justice to my predecessors and colleagues, be asserted that the vitality of the paper has been owing to their ability, skill, and watchfulness, and to the fact that they have ever striven to keep the paper apart from unworthy selfish interests, and honestly endeavoured to advance true art. All connected, too, with the MUSICAL STANDARD desire to join me in gratefully recording our lasting indebtedness to our many occasional contributors, correspondents, supporters, and last but not least, to our faithful subscribers; to whom, indeed, much of the power of carrying forward our good work is owing. Readers may feel assured that the efforts made in past times to make the MUSICAL STANDARD useful to both Art and Artists will be earnestly continued. The staff will not only be diligent in endeavouring to increase the general utility of the paper, but will strive to make it more and more of practical value to the musician, in the hope that the MUSICAL STANDARD will advance with no diminution of energy, but with increased vitality, as having increased usefulness, along the course of time, again and again to be congratulated by its constant and faithful readers upon the attainment of such further epochs and landmarks as time may apportion to us mortals whose business here is to think and to work.

E. H. TURPIN.

A description of the superb home of Gounod, in Paris, suggests the individual character which the master likes to give to his surroundings. The exterior has the severely solemn aspect of a monastery. One enters through grim iron gratings, fastened with stern-looking locks, and comes through gloomy passages to a huge, mysterious staircase. But here comes in the spirit of the composer —locks and gratings are adorned with graceful female heads, the passages are ornamented with beautiful pictures and statuary, and the stairs, richly carpeted, lead up to the great, light, airy apartment, handsomely furnished, where Gounod sits at his desk-piano, and, as he composes music, writes it down.

Academical Intelligence.

OXFORD UNIVERSITY.

EXAMINATIONS FOR DEGREES IN MUSIC.

The second examination for the degree of Bachelor in Music will commence on Tuesday, October 9th. In addition to the usual subjects, there will be required a critical knowledge of the full scores of Beethoven's symphony, No. 6 (Pastorale), and Mozart's Motet "Misericordias Domini." The examination for the degree of Doctor in Music will commence at the same time. Candidates are required to give in their names to the clerk of the Schools on or before October 1st.

TRINITY COLLEGE, LONDON.

The following address has been issued to the Honorary Officers and Council of Trinity College, London :—

MY LORDS AND GENTLEMEN,

At the close of another academical year, a brief retrospect of the work of this College during the past twelve months is due to those who have taken an active part in that work ; and may also be interesting to many others outside the governing body who have most kindly concerned themselves in the welfare of the institution.

It is with deep thankfulness that I place upon record the fact that the past year has been one of solid growth and prosperity. It is a matter of sincere gratification to us all to learn that the balance-sheet just issued by the auditors is of a highly satisfactory character, and leads us to hope that in the course of a very few years there will be a sufficient surplus to allow of some further additions being made to the Scholarships tenable at the College.

The Session which has just closed has been marked by the establishment of three such Scholarships :—1st. The Henry Smart Scholarship, founded in 1882 in memory of the great musician of that name, who was connected with the College as a member of this Council, and also as an Examiner for our diplomas. It will be felt by all that it is most fitting so good and staunch a friend to the College, whose official connection with the institution was terminated only by death, should be thus remembered by his grateful colleagues. It is to be hoped that this Scholarship will be the means of helping forward many a promising young student in the future, and so prove to be no unworthy perpetuation of the memory of Henry Smart.

During the present year, two free Exhibitions have been constituted, one for Pianoforte Students, the other for Vocalists ; and these have been associated (by kind permission in each case) with the names of two eminent members of the Council, Sir Julius Benedict and Mr. Sims Reeves. There is good reason to believe that a large number of candidates will compete in September next for the honour of holding either the Sir Julius Benedict or the Sims Reeves Exhibition. I should add that these Exhibitions, as well as the Henry Smart Scholarship, are by no means restricted to the present students of the College, but are open to all British subjects, under certain necessary conditions named in the published regulations.

In the course of the Session great improvements have been made in the organization of the teaching department. Very much is due to Mr. Bradbury Turner, Mus.B., who, as Director of the Musical Studies, is not only zealous in the interests of the institution, but is most popular with the students. The curriculum has been carefully systematized, and brought into closer harmony with the requirements of the public examinations ; and while the number of the students has been well maintained, the tone and status of the students themselves as a class show a marked improvement of late years, doubtless owing in a great measure to the distinctive lines on which our work is conducted—namely, the promotion of musical education on a basis of general culture. Before leaving this branch of my subject, I must not omit to state that the reputation of Trinity College as a Musical School has now spread, not only through the United Kingdom, but abroad to other countries, and that amongst the more recent *alumni* are students from the Continent, from India, and from Australia.

A brief reference should here be made to the goodly accession of subscribing members. The number on the books reaches the very respectable total of six hundred and fifteen members. These were formerly designated "Honorary Members" but lately the Academical Board obtained the necessary authority to discontinue the term "Honorary," as liable in some cases to be misunderstood. Members by the revised regulations are eligible for election on presenting certificates (easily procurable by any really suitable candidate) of educational and moral fitness. Although about forty Board meetings have been held during the year, only two meetings have passed without election of new members. I may also state that 430 Local Institutions, Schools, and Societies are now enrolled in union with the College, thus representing a very large and widespread constituency.

Not less encouraging have been the results of our efforts in the department of Examinations during the Academical year now ended. Upwards of one hundred and seventy candidates have entered at the Higher Examinations of the College, and of these a fair proportion have passed with distinction. It is extremely satisfactory to note that the matriculation or entrance examination in arts, which, following the enlightened lead of Sir Robert Stewart at Dublin, this institution initiated in our own division of the United Kingdom 'as the necessary complement of a professional qualification for musicians, has proved no bar whatever to real musical merit, and that the number of candidates for matriculation is steadily on the increase. There can be no doubt that this effort to place the holders of our professional diplomas on an educational footing with those of the sister professions has added greatly to the value of our higher examinations. At the same time their technical efficiency has been thoroughly guaranteed by means of friendly co-operation, as Examiners, of some of our most eminent musicians, including Sir Julius Benedict, Sir George Elvey, Dr. Hopkins, of the Temple Church, Dr. Mann, of Cambridge, Dr. Hubert Parry, Mr. F. H. Cowen, Mr. E. H. Turpin, Mr. James Higgs, Mr. Walter Parratt, and many other distinguished men, to whom our warmest acknowledgments are due for their able assistance during the past year.

But it is in the field of Local Examinations that our most signal successes have been achieved. No less than 3,900 candidates have entered at the examinations in Elementary Musical Knowledge, while 1,640 have been examined in Instrumental and Vocal Music, making a grand total for the year of 5,540 local candidates, as against 5,275 last year. This, as has been demonstrated on a previous occasion, places the College far ahead of all other examining bodies engaged in the same branch of musical work—a well-known institution standing second with about one-fifth of the number. It must be borne in mind, however, that Trinity College was the first by several years to hold these examinations on a considerable scale, and that this lengthened experience has enabled the Academical Board, with the most valuable help of the Registrar, Mr. Humphrey Stark, Mus.B., to bring every detail of the work to a high degree of perfection. Our grateful acknowledgments are also due to the Local Secretaries of the 250 Local Centres of the College for the zeal and ability with which they have aided us in our operations, and to the influential Local Committees, who have assisted in maintaining the public character of the examinations.

It will thus be seen that the prestige of the Trinity College Certificate has in no way been affected by the flattering imitation of certain older musical bodies. On the contrary, though our standard is as high—to say the least—as that of any similar system, the number of candidates has continued to increase year by year. This fact must prove one of two things—either that the competition (if in no invidious sense I may so term it) has been commenced too late, or that the field is amply wide enough for more than one examining body. For myself, I am fully convinced that the latter is the true state of the case. The oft-repeated question, "Why multiply institutions?" is on the face of it a very sagacious one, but it has lost much of its force by being too frequently asked by those who desire nothing less than a monopoly of the field for some one institution. On the other hand, there are those who believe Oxford to be the better for the friendly rivalry of Cambridge, and both these the better for the enterprise of the younger Universities. It is no secret that Trinity College has aroused certain other organizations from the comparative stagnation into which they had lapsed ; and even from this point of view our College may be considered to have done good service to the public. Since the foundation of our Society new musical institutions have been established—notably the Royal College of Music—and we can only rejoice that in the ever widening arc of musical enterprise other zealous and distinguished workers have been found willing to share our labours. Recent events, in addition to previous experience, have confirmed us in the belief that there is abundant scope for every existing institution, and that persistent emulation conduces to the public benefit, so long as a narrow-minded and short-sighted hostility is not imported into such operations. The community as a whole is quick to appreciate the efforts of those who honestly endeavour to meet a public want—and has little concern—and less sympathy—with the position of isolation favoured by a few over-zealous partisans; and I am enabled to assert, from no small acquaintance with what I may term the musical laity, that our own College owes very much of the popularity it has obtained throughout the country to the readiness of the governing body to co-operate in a thoroughly friendly spirit with its accredited fellow-workers in the common cause.

Our obituary record for the year is happily but small in point of numbers. Yet ours is a heavy loss, since it includes one which is deeply mourned by greater societies and worthier men, and our regrets for ourselves are augmented by those which we must needs feel in respectful sympathy with others. William Spottiswoode, P.R.S., who, as an honorary Fellow of this College, signalized his connection with the institution by many acts of kindness, which (like the late Sir John Goss and Henry Smart, and like others whom I see around me) he took care to show chiefly at a time when we stood most in need of sympathy and support, has left us a memory which we shall ever gratefully treasure and an example which the best of us may well aspire to follow. Our roll of Honorary Fellows is thus bereaved of an illustrious name, which the Council will find it difficult to replace. Before I leave this sad page of our annual register, regretful allusion must be made to the loss which the Council has sustained in the lamented death of George Critchett, F.R.C.S., and to the late John Owen, of Chester, one of the most highly esteemed of our local representatives.

To return, in conclusion, to a brighter key, our Council has lately been reinforced by several members, with whose valuable aid in the various departments of our work the College will surely continue to extend its usefulness and add to its achievements; profiting in the course of the second decade on which it has now fairly entered, by the experience it has gained during the past eleven years. I have the honour to be,

My Lords and Gentlemen,
Your most obedient servant,
H. G. BONAVIA HUNT,
(Chairman of the Council.)

July 14, 1883.

THE HISTORY OF THE PIANOFORTE.

By A. J. HIPKINS.

(Continued from page 72.)

I will now proceed to recount briefly the history of the pianoforte from the earliest mention of that name, continuing it to our contemporary instruments, as far as they can be said to have entered into the historical domain. It has been my privilege to assist in proving that Bartolommeo Cristofori was, in the first years of the 18th century, the real inventor of the pianoforte, but with a wide knowledge and experience of how long it has taken to make any invention in keyed instruments practicable and successful. I cannot believe that Cristofori was the first to attempt to contrive one. I should rather accept his good and complete instrument as the sum of his own lifelong studies and experiments added to those of generations before him which have left no record for us as yet discovered. The earliest mention of the name pianoforte (piano e forte), applied to a musical instrument, has been recently discovered by Count Valdrighi in documents preserved in the Estense Library, at Modena. It is dated A.D. 1598, and the reference is evidently to an instrument of the spinet or cembalo kind; but how the tone was produced there is no statement, no word to base an inference upon. The name has not been met with again between the Estense document and Scipione Maffei's well-known description written in 1711, of Cristofori's "gravecembalo col piano e forte." My view of Cristofori's invention allows me to think that the Estense "piano e forte" may have been a hammer cembalo, a very imperfect one, of course. But I admit that the opposite view of forte and piano, contrived by registers of spinet-jacks, is equally tenable.

Bartolommeo Cristofori was a Paduan harpsichord maker, who was invited by Prince Ferdinand de Medici to Florence, to take charge of the large collection of musical instruments the Prince possessed. At Florence he produced the invention of the pianoforte, in which he was assisted and encouraged by this high-minded, richly cultivated, and very musical Prince. Scipione Maffei tells us that in 1709, Cristofori had completed four of the new instruments, three of them being of the usual harpsichord form, and one of another form, which he leaves undescribed. It is interesting to suppose that Handel may have tried one or more of these four instruments during the stay he made at Florence in 1708. But it is not likely that he was at all impressed with the potentialities of the invention any more than John Sebastian Bach was in after years, when he tried the pianofortes of Silbermann. The sketch of Cristofori's action in [Maffei's essay, from which I have had a working model accurately made, shows that in the first instrument the action was not complete, and it may not have been perfected when Prince Ferdinand died in 1713. But there are Cristofori grand pianos preserved at Florence, dated respectively 1720 and 1726, in which an improved construction of action is found, and of this I also exhibit a model. There is much difference between the two. In the second, Cristofori had obtained his escapement with an undivided key, reconciling his depth of touch, or keyfall, with that of the contemporary harpsichord, by driving the escapement lever through the key. He had contrived means for regulating the escapement distance, and had also invented the last essential of a good pianoforte action, the check. I will explain what is meant by escapement and check. When, by a key being put down, the hammer is impelled towards the strings, it is necessary for their sustained vibration that, after impact, the hammer should rebound or escape; or it would, as pianoforte-makers say, "block," damping the strings at the moment they should sound. A dulcimer player gains his elastic blow by the free movement of the wrist. To gain a similarly elastic blow mechanically, in his first action, Cristofori cut a notch in the butt of his hammer, from which the escapement lever, "linguetta mobile," as he called it—" hopper," as we call it—being centred at the base, moved forward when the key was put down to the extent of its radius, and after the delivery of the blow returned to its resting-place by the pressure of a spring. The first action gave the blow with more direct force than the second, which had the notch upon what is called the underhammer, but was defective in the absence of any means to regulate the distance of the "go-off," or "escapement" from the string. In the second action, a small check before the hopper is intended to regulate it, but does so imperfectly. The pianoforte had to wait for 50 years for satisfactory regulation of the escapement.

In the first action, the hammer rests in a silken fork, dropping the whole distance of the rise of every blow. The check in the second action, the "paramartello," is next in importance to the escapement. It catches the back part of the hammer at different points of the radius, responding to the amount of force the player has used upon the key. So that, in repeated blows, the rise of the hammer is modified, and the notch is nearer to the returning hopper in proportionate degree.

I have given the first place in description to Cristofori's actions, instead of to the "cembalo" or instrument, to which they were applied, because piano and forte, from touch, became possible through them, and what else was accomplished by Cristofori was due, primarily, to the dynamic idea. He strengthened his harpsichord sound-board against a thicker stringing, renouncing the cherished sound-holes. Yet the sound-box notion clung to him, for he made openings in his sound-board rail for air to escape. He ran a string-block round the case, entirely independent of the sound-board, and his wrest-plank, which also became a separate structure, removed from the sound-board by the gap for the hammers, was now a stout oaken plank, which, to gain an upward bearing for the strings, he inverted, driving his wrest-pins through in the manner of a harp, and tuning them in like fashion to the harp. He had two strings to a note, but it did not occur to him to space them into pairs of unisons. He retained the equidistant harpsichord scale, and had, at first, under-dampers, later, over-dampers, which fell between the unisons thus equally separated. Cristofori died in 1731. He had pupils, one of whom made, in 1730, the "Raffael d'Urbino," the favourite instrument of the great singer Farinelli. The story of inventive Italian pianoforte making ends thus early, but to Italy the invention indisputably belongs.

The first to make pianofortes in Germany was the famous Freiberg organ builder and clavichord maker, Gottfried Silbermann. He submitted two pianofortes to the judgment of John Sebastian Bach in 1726, which judgment was, however, unfavourable; the trebles being found too weak, and the touch too heavy. Silbermann, according to the account of Bach's pupil, Agricola, being much mortified, put them aside, resolving not to show them again unless he could improve them. We do not know what these instruments were, but it may be inferred that they were copies of Cristofori, or were made after the description of his invention, by Maffei, which had already been translated from Italian into German, by König, the court poet at Dresden, who was a personal friend of Silbermann. With the next anecdote, which narrates the purchase of all the pianofortes Silbermann had made by Frederick the Great, we are upon surer ground. This well accredited occurrence took place in 1746. In the following year occurred Bach's celebrated visit to Potsdam, when he played upon one or more of these instruments. Burney saw and described one in 1772. I had this one, which was known to have remained in the new palace at Potsdam until the present time unaltered, examined, and, by a drawing of the action, found it was identical with Cristofori's. Not, however, being satisfied with one example, I resolved to go myself to Potsdam, and being furnished with permission from H.R.H. the Crown Princess of Prussia, I was enabled in September, 1881, to set the question at rest of how many grand pianofortes by Gottfried Silbermann there were still in existence at Potsdam, and what they were like. At Berlin there are none, but at Potsdam, in the music-rooms of Frederick the Great, which are in the town palace, the new palace, and Sans Souci—left, it is understood, from the time of Frederick's death undisturbed—there are three of these Silbermann pianofortes. All three are, with unimportant differences having nothing to do with structure, Cristofori instruments, wrest-plank, sound-board, string-block, and action, the harpsichord scale of stringing being still retained. The work in them is undoubtedly good ; the sound-boards have given in the trebles, as is usual with old instruments, from the strain : but I should say all three might be satisfactorily restored. Some other pianofortes seem to have been made in North Germany about this time, 'as our own poet Gray bought one in Hamburg in 1755, in the description of which we notice the desire to combine a hammer action with the harpsichord, which so long exercised men's minds.

(To be continued.)

PROFESSIONALS AND AMATEURS.

In the course of an article contributed to the *Musical Times*, Dr. W. Pole, himself a distinguished amateur, writes thus :—

Let us endeavour to distinguish clearly between the different classes of people who have to do with music. In the first place, there is a very large and meritorious body of persons, deserving of all respect, who make their livelihood solely by occupation in some branch of music, chiefly by teaching or public performance. These are properly distinguished as "professional" people ; though their assumption of the title " Professor " is unfortunate ; it has no precedent in other professions ; it clashes with the legitimate use of the term, and it has given rise to some ridiculous parodies, such as "Professors" of gymnastics, hair-dressing, or conjuring. "Professional Musician," "Teacher of Music," are honourable and intelligible terms. "Professor of Music" has either a false meaning or none at all.

Then, secondly, there is the great class of the music-loving public, who take interest in the art but do not make any use of it for the purpose of money-making. These are the true "Amateurs."

So far all is simple, but such is the complex nature of our social system that in this, as in all other attempts at statistical classification, we soon come upon anomalous relations which destroy the sharpness of any line of demarcation it is attempted to draw.

Music offers great attractions to minds sensitive to it, and if it happens that persons so constituted are intelligent and persevering, they may, without any intention of making a living by the profession, carry their study and practice so far as to obtain a knowledge and proficiency fully equal to that of many professional men. Now, undoubtedly, such persons are not "professional musicians" in the sense that they depend on music for their subsistence ; but are they to be thereby debarred from exercising their musical abilities, or from reaping any profit that is obtainable therefrom ? The class of persons in question becomes more numerous in lower ranks. A young man, for example, who is a poorly paid office clerk, may by-dint of hard practice have become a clever organ-player : is he to be forbidden to take a paid office at a church if he can play well enough to obtain one? Or a man engaged in a shop all the day may have acquired considerable proficiency on the violin : may he not be allowed to take a place in a paid orchestra in the evening ? Or a young girl in a Magazin des Modes has learnt how to manage well a naturally fine voice : is it a social crime for her to form the first soprano of a paid choir? It may have been distasteful to English professional composers that a young German amateur should have been given a large sum for composing "Elijah" for the Birmingham Festival, but if the Birmingham people have been satisfied, one can hardly see in either case an

infraction of any rule of justice or propriety. The same thing occurs continually in analogous cases. It is difficult to draw a parallel with the clerical, legal, or medical professions, as the practising of these is necessarily hemmed in by special restrictions ; but in literature and art the parallel exists abundantly. Could we deny the right of anybody to publish a profitable book or a paid magazine article, if he did not depend entirely on literature for his living ? or to sell a picture or a bust, if he were not strictly a professional artist ? or to take an engagement as an actor, if he had any other means of support ?

The regulating check must obviously be the competence of the person for the duty he undertakes to do. The semi-professional must recollect that if he enters into competition with *bona fide* professional men on their own ground, he must expect no favour—on the contrary, he fairly provokes hostile criticism ; and if the Liverpool musicians have good reason to complain of the undue encouragement of incompetence in their semi-professional rivals, no one can object to their using strong language, or to their taking any means to expose the injustice. And, again, the semi-professionals should bear in mind that in entering the field against professional musicians they ought to compete with them on equal terms, and not (if I may be pardoned the expression) to *undersell* them. It is hardly fair for an amateur who is able to do profitable musical work to do it for less remuneration than would be reasonably paid to the professional man whom he supersedes, so taking advantage, to the prejudice of the latter, of his less need of the pay. It is probable that this condition has not always been borne in mind, particularly by amateur organists, who, I fear, are often tempted to undertake duties for remuneration often below what ought fairly to be paid. No doubt cases arise where, from scarcity of funds, offers of this kind are encouraged ; but the wisdom of the policy is doubtful, and church authorities would do well to recollect that the labourer is worthy of his hire, and that work underpaid is seldom heartily done. I should say that the professional musicians may reasonably demand this ·recognition of their position, and would be justified in publishing and holding up to reprobation any clearly proved cases, not only of incompetence for musical duties undertaken, but of their being done for obviously inadequate pay.

If these conditions are carried out, it is difficult to believe that professional men have much to fear from their semi-professional rivals. The cases of real competence are rare, and these must be almost entirely confined to *performance*. One cannot think that *teaching* can be carried on to any extent by such persons, who would have neither time nor inclination for it, and we know that teaching is the main source of income to professional men.

The often mooted idea of forming a strictly professional body, with the view of excluding all others from undertaking profitable musical work, is a delusion ; no such thing would be practicable. It is quite practicable and expedient to promote the issue of certificates of competence, from properly constituted authorities, and to encourage the public to rely on them, or to demand them, before entrusting important work to unknown hands ; but it is obvious that this system would in no wise exclude really competent semi-professional men, but would rather improve their position, for no respectable examining body could refuse them certificates for any special branch of music in which they were properly qualified.

A word or two may perhaps be added as to the general relations between professional men and amateurs, properly so called. It would be salutary for the latter class to bear in mind that in the matter of *performance*, they must of necessity be much behind professional men. Speaking generally, I am afraid the standard of amateur musical performance, is in this country, deplorably low. This cannot be due to want of the necessary mental qualification : it must arise either from bad teaching or from ignorance, bad management, bad taste, or bad judgment on the part of the learners or their friends—probably more or less from all combined. However, the question of general improvement is far too large to enter upon here. I would refer more to the rarer cases of fairly good performance which an educated musician can listen to with interest or pleasure. The more such cases can be encouraged and multiplied the better for the cause of music in society. But there is always a tendency for the performers to presume too much on their own merits ; they should recollect that, notwithstanding all their talent and industry, it is scarcely possible for them to approach the standard of the professional performer, whose life has been devoted to the cultivation, in the most favourable manner, of his technical skill. For this reason amateur performance ought generally to be confined to private society ; it would seem to be a mistake to thrust it into public positions, which must provoke invidious comparisons with the members of the profession. Public solo concerts by amateurs are usually got up more for the gratification of the performers than the hearers, and I should say the fewer of them there are the better.

There are, however, many right-thinking people who will cordially echo the wish expressed by a writer in this magazine, that the tone of the musical profession could be raised by the introduction into it of persons of higher culture, of superior social standing, and of broader and more enlightened views. The new Royal College might do much towards this ; but, alas ! they seem to think the low social origin of their scholars a subject for congratulation, and there is, at present at least, no evidence of an intention to adopt a higher education than mere technical training.

ASMODEUS IN THE MUSICAL WORLD.

IV.

" Truly," said the wily Asmodeus, " thou art innocent, indeed, friend Zambullo, not to know that no musical institution, like any other human organization, can be other than imperfect, both as regards motives and designs. The society of the Musical Brotherhood in Madrid is no exception to the rule ; though it is but fair, thou descendant of a much more astute ancestor, to say that from the first day of the existence of this society it has ever been well served by good and true men." " But," quoth the descendant of Don Cleofas Leandro Perez Zambullo, " the worthies who now guide the destinies of the Brotherhood are not only doing good service to the art, but are working for no self gain." " Far be it from your impish friend," cried Asmodeus, " to gainsay your, in the main, true and well meant words. Let us however take a flight through mid-air, and alight at the college where music holds its sway, and where the learned directors of the Brotherhood are wont to meet." Zambullo, as he has been often known to do before in the annals of this diverting history, resigned himself to the supernatural agency of the very reliable demon of friendly impulses, and presently the worthy pair were listening, unseen, to the disputations of the excellent chiefs of the Brotherhood of Harmony. It concerneth not the reader to disclose all that was said upon this occasion, especially as, like most human discussions, there was much said that Time will, through the want of human foresight, unsay at no very remote date. Suffice it to assert that the chief object of the meeting was the settlement of the claims of sundry well known professors of the art to the musical leadership of the company, a matter made necessary by the somewhat paradoxical and striking discovery that the eminent artist who had for many years led the Musical Brotherhood was neither too old or too little appreciated, but was reluctant for some reason or other to again allow himself to be nominated for one of the greatest positions of the kind in Europe. The end of this discussion was the decision to invite some half-dozen much esteemed musicians to act by turns as musical leaders of the famous Madrid Brotherhood of Harmony. (The commentator ventures to ask the reader to pause in his perusal of this delectable narrative, in order to contemplate another proof of the remarkable way in which history persists in repeating herself in the resemblance between the details just given and certain recent proceedings of our own much valued Philharmonic Society. The resemblance is striking enough to induce the wary to suppose that this passage is probably an interpolation by some unscrupulous modern hand, and is intended to reflect satirically upon the doings of an existing body of professional gentlemen. The commentator, however, desires to assure the reader that there are no signs of any such tampering with the MS., and as he has been previously prompted to add, the reader must draw his own conclusions upon this matter.) " Truly," cried Asmodeus, " though it is only fair criticism to question the wisdom of the proposal to invite six musical generals to alter, or it may be, to undo each other's. work, and possibly to introduce an element of weakness and confusion in the ranks of those to be subjected to the inconveniences of a mixed and complicated leadership. These directing worthies have many interests of level power to balance, and probably only such a course as that proposed could save the Brotherhood from falling into the hands of an alien leader, a contingency which would now be deplorable, seeing that Spain is once more learning to be true to her own children of song. Anyway, Don Zambullo, these same directors have gracefully contrived to bell one cat likely, before, to give the Brotherhood no little trouble. They have, with a liberality not often exercised in such a direction, secured the valuable literary services of the musical dictator of the 'leading journal' of Madrid, who, once devoted to alien interests, is now engaged upon the pleasant and profitable task of writing gossiping accounts of the music to be rendered by the instrumental servants of the Brotherhood, and thus doing a judicious stroke of policy fairly identified with the objects of the harmonious society."

Correspondence.

"COUNTERPOINT."

TO THE EDITOR OF THE "MUSICAL STANDARD."

Sir,—I have, with much pleasure, read Mr. Stark's paper on "Counterpoint" (as given in your columns) and I am thankful for having his able help in the crusade against antiquated dogmas which, for some thirty years, I have been waging. In the *Musical Record*, in *The Choir*, in my " Grammar of Music," and in many other ways, I have striven to show the absurdity of endeavouring to perpetuate a bondage which neither we nor our fathers have been able to bear. It is truly wonderful how, without the addition of a single new idea, people multiply modern editions of those dry-as-dust old rules that were long ago thrust aside by all practical musicians For nothing is clearer, or more indisputable, than that the rules still given in the text-books of so-called "counterpoint" were not submitted to even by the men to whose modes of writing they are supposed to afford a clue.

What an amount of nonsense has been written about second inversions ! Yet how absolutely clear it is that, in itself, the second inversion of a consonant triad is more satisfactory than the first, and more nearly resembles the natural form of the chord.

And what a subject of ridicule a University examination becomes when Beethoven's Ninth Symphony is scrutinized to detect its author's varied modes of treating second inversions, all of "which are generously ' passed ' as satisfactory, although ' exceptional.'"

Or how can a student respect a system (!) which, only at the end of his training, confesses that his surmises have been right all along, and that that puzzling "first inversion" of a chord that may not be used in any other shape is really the second inversion of the familiar dominant seventh chord, with the root omitted ; and that the dissonant sound thus smuggled in (because the queerly sensitive ears of the ancients could not tolerate a consonant fourth) may actually be doubled, contrary to all his modern harmony notions of well-balanced chords.

And with what delight a sharp pupil points to the delightfully excruciating "false relation" quoted by Mr. Stark from page 27 of Macfarren's "Counterpoint," and to many other instances, of broken rules found in that work.

I heartily wish Mr. Stark " God speed ! " And, if he will refer to the " Grammar " already alluded to, he will, I think, find some further ground for, and help in, fighting against 'the groundless and ridiculous theories about consecutions, &c., still prevalent.

Yours truly,

HENRY HILES.

Osborne House, Penmaenmawr,
August 6th.

It will be remembered that at Bayreuth considerable trouble was occasioned by the difficulty of securing an instrument to execute the four notes of the bell-motive in the finales of the first and third acts. Actual bells, besides being too expensive, were not available, on account of the harsh, dissonant overtones which always accompany their proper tone. Hans Richter's " bell-piano," which contained four thick strings consisting each of several ordinary strings twisted into one, did not prove a success, and the tamtams substituted for them did not indicate the pitch with sufficient distinctness. In place of these Mr. Thomas, the eminent New York conductor, conceived the happy idea of getting four steel bars of different thicknesses, which are carefully tuned, and, on being struck with a wooden hammer, give forth a silvery sound as free from overtones at a distance as tuning forks, and strikingly suggestive in their sound of actual cathedral chimes.

Passing Events.

The Buffalo (U. S.) Sangerfest was held on July 16th, 17th, and 18th.

The New York Musical Critic has just entered upon the fifth year of its existence.

A new comic opera by an American composer, Mr. Robert Stoepel, "All about a Bonnet," will be shortly produced.

At the Welsh National Eisteddfod, at Cardiff, it was announced that funds had been collected to found a scholarship for Welsh boys and girls at the Royal Academy of Music.

The "Sterndale" School of Music, Wallington, under the direction of Mr. Herbert Green, had a pupils' matinée on July 28th. The programme included some excellent classical pianoforte music.

The service at Gloucester Cathedral on Wednesday afternoon will in future be sung by the lay vicars only, thus allowing the choir boys a weekly half-holiday. This change has been adopted on the recommendation of Mr. C. L. Williams, the organist.

English opera is very popular in America, as indeed it has become in England. Mr. James C. Duff is organising an English opera company for next season. This will add yet another company to the already considerable number before the American audiences.

Messrs. James Nisbet & Co. have recently published the Bible Psalter, being the authorized version of the Psalms, pointed for chanting, and with chants adapted thereto, or specially composed for this work by Sir Herbert Oakeley, Mus.Doc., etc. The pointing of the "Anglican" Psalter, or Prayer Book version, is in contemplation, with the same selection of chants and under the same editorship.

The proprietors of the *Orchestra, Choir and Musical Education*, have determined to offer prizes for all kinds of musical composition. For the best setting of songs (words given) for a single voice with pianoforte accompaniment, a prize of £3 3s. and 100 printed copies of the song (words and music) will be accorded, subject to the following conditions:—1. The melody must not exceed one octave and three notes in compass. 2. The accompaniment must not present any technical difficulties.

It is stated that the directors of the Crystal Palace have arranged with Mr. Faulkner Leigh to give a second series of twelve grand operas, commencing the 21st inst. The following artists are already engaged:—Mdme. Rose Hersee, Miss Emily Parkinson, Mdme. Cave-Ashton, Miss Josephine Yorke, Miss Helen Armstrong, and Miss Palmer; Messrs. J. W. Turner, Walter Bolton, Lansmere, Aynsley Cook, and Faulkner Leigh. The following operas are to be performed:—"Maritana," "Faust," "Lurline," "Rose of Castille," and "Favorita" (first time at the Palace). Sterndale Bennett's "May Queen" and Benedict's "Graziella" are to be placed on the stage for the first time in England. The chorus has been engaged from the Royal Italian Opera, Covent Garden, and the band will consist of the Crystal Palace Orchestra; the series will be conducted by Mr. August Manns.

A fine carillon of twenty-five bells is now on its way to Philadelphia to be placed in Holy Trinity Church. The bells were cast by Severin van Aerschodt, the celebrated founder, of Louvain. Before leaving the foundry they were examined by Dr. Stainer on behalf of the Philadelphia committee, and he expressed a very high opinion of their merit, both as to workmanship and beauty of tone. The carillon is a gift to the church by Mr. Joseph E. Temple, in memory of his late wife. Each bell is ornamented with a medallion portrait of both Mr. and Mrs. Temple in bas-relief. There will be a keyboard acting upon the bells, constructed on the Belgian principle. The weight of the largest bell is rather more than one ton and a quarter, its diameter is four feet four inches, and it gives the note F of the old organ pitch, nearly E flat concert pitch. The smallest bell weighs half a hundredweight. The whole of the bells are designed with great taste, and, according to the custom of the country, have been carefully polished.—*Musical Times.*

Mr. H. C. Tonking, R.A.M. (pupil of Dr. Charles Steggall) will give an Organ Recital at the Fisheries Exhibition on Monday, 13th.

Wagner never enjoyed jokes against himself. Alexander Dumas, calling upon him, made some good-humoured remarks about his own ignorance of music, which he had once defined as "the most expensive of noises," but his pleasantries were listened to with such a smileless stolidity that he went home in a huff, and wrote his contemptuous protest against "Wagnerian din—inspired by the riot of cats scampering in the dark about an ironmonger's shop." On the day before this was printed in *l'Opinion Nationale*, Wagner returned Dumas's visit, and was kept waiting for half an hour in an ante-room. Then the author of "Les Trois Mousquetaires" marched in, attired in a plumed helmet, a cork life-belt, and a flowing dressing-gown. "Excuse me for appearing in my working dress," he said, majestically. "Half my ideas are lodged in this helmet, and the other half in a pair of jack boots, which I put on to compose love scenes." Snubs of this sort, of which Wagner encountered many, rankled deep in his mind and made him say that the French were vandals.—*Boston Transcript.*

Service Lists.

TWELFTH SUNDAY AFTER TRINITY.

AUGUST 12th.

London.

St. Paul's Cathedral.—Morn.: Service, Te Deum and Benedictus, Stainer in E flat; Introit, Jesu, gentlest Saviour; Holy Communion, Stainer in E flat. Even.: Service, Magnificat and Nunc Dimittis, Stainer in E flat; Anthem, God is our hope and strength (Greene).

Holy Trinity, Gray's Inn Road.'— Morn.: Service, Te Deum, Jackson in F; Jubilate, Chanted. Even.: Service, Magnificat, Chanted; Nunc Dimittis, Bunnett in F; Anthem, The Lord is my strength (Lowe).

Holy Trinity, Tulse Hill.—Morn.: Chant Service. Even.: Service, Magnificat and Nunc Dimittis, Gregory in E flat; Anthem, The wilderness (Goss).

St. James's Private Episcopal Chapel, Southwark. —Morn.: Service, Introit, O food that weary pilgrims love; Communion Service, Schubert in C. Even.: Service, Calkin in G; O Lord, the maker ("King Henry VIII.")

St. Magnus, London Bridge.—Morn.: Service, Opening Anthem, If we say (Calkin); Te Deum and Jubilate, Nares in F; Kyrie (Nares). Even.: Service, Cantate and Deus Miseratur, Goss in C; Anthem, Thou visitest the earth (Greene).

St. Margaret Pattens, Rood Lane, Fenchurch Street.—Morn.: Service, Te. Deum, and Benedictus, Tuckerman in F; Communion Service : Offertory Anthem, Lovely appear (Gounod); Kyrie, Credo, Sanctus, Benedictus, Agnus Dei, and Gloria, Schubert in B flat. Even.: Service, Magnificat and Nunc Dimittis, Steggall in C; Anthem, O Lord, have mercy (Pergolesi).

St. Paul's, Avenue Road, South Hampstead.—Morn.: Service, Te Deum, Smart in F; Benedictus, Lawes; Kyrie, Stainer in E flat. Even.: Service, Magnificat and Nunc Dimittis, Gounod in D; Anthem, O send out thy light (Gounod).

St. Paul's, Bow Common, E.—Morn.: Service, Te Deum, Nares in F; Benedictus, Dykes in F. Even.: Service, Magnificat and Nunc Dimittis, Stainer in A; Anthem, As pants the hart (Spohr).

St. Sepulchre's, Holborn. — Morn: Service, Dykes in F; Anthem, Lord, for Thy tender (Farrant). Even.: Service, Cooke in C; Anthem, "In Jewry" (Clarke-Whitfeld).

St Augustine and St. Faith, Watling Street.— Morn.: Service, Stainer in E flat; Introit, The Lord is my light (South); Communion Service, Stainer in E flat. Even.: Service, Garrett in E flat; Anthems, How lovely are Thy dwellings fair; and Happy who in Thy house reside (Spohr).

St. Saviour's, Hoxton. — Morn.: Service, Te Deum, Smart in F; Holy Communion; Kyrie, Credo, Sursum Corda, Sanctus, and Gloria in excelsis, Tours in F. Even.: Service, Magnificat and Nunc Dimittis, Stainer; Anthem, They that wait upon the Lord (Stainer).

ST. MARY BOLTONS, WEST BROMPTON, S.W.—Morn.: Service, Te Deum. Armes in G; Benedictus, Dykes in F; Holy Communion, Kyrie, Credo, Sanctus, and Gloria in excelsis, Thorne in G; Benedictus and Agnus Dei, Monk in C; Offertory (Barnby). Even.: Service, Magnificat and Nunc Dimittis, Arnold in A; Anthem, O taste and see (Goss).

Country.

ST. ASAPH CATHEDRAL.—Morn.: Service, Atkins in C; Anthem, Sing ye praises (Mendelssohn). Even.: Service, Bridge in C; Anthem, Thou wilt keep him (Gauntlett).

ASHBURNE CHURCH, DERBYSHIRE. — Morn.: Service, Garrett in E; Continuation Lloyd in E flat. Even.: Service, Lloyd in E flat; Anthem, I will mention (Sullivan).

BIRMINGHAM (S. ALBAN THE MARTYR).—Morn.: Service, Te Deum and Benedictus, Dykes in F; Holy Communion; Kyrie, Credo, Sanctus, Gloria, Dykes in F; Benedictus and Agnus Dei, Redman in D. Evensong: Magnificat and Nunc Dimittis, Parry in D.

BIRMINGHAM (ST. CYPRIAN'S, HAY MILLS).—Morn.: Service, Cobb in G (throughout); Anthem, Thy word is a lantern (Purcell). Even.: Service, Cobb in G; Anthem, Ascribe unto the Lord (Travers).

BIRMINGHAM (S. PHILIP'S CHURCH). — Morn.: Service, Stainer in A; Anthem, Blessed are they (Tours). Evensong Service, Hopkins in F; Anthem, The wilderness (Goss).

CANTERBURY CATHEDRAL. — Morn.: Service, Porter in D; Anthem, Thou wilt keep him (Jarrett); Communion, Porter in D. Even.: Service, Porter in D; Anthem, Wherewithal shall a young man (Elvey).

CARLISLE CATHEDRAL. — Morn.: Service, Ouseley in G; Introit, Behold, God (Stainer); Kyrie, Ouseley in G; Nicene Creed (Goss). Even.: Service, Chipp in A; Anthem, The Lord is loving (Garrett).

CHESTER (ST. MARY'S CHURCH).—Morn.: Service, Hopkins in F; Communion Service, Tearne in G. Even.: Service, Goss in E; Anthem, O how amiable are Thy dwellings (Barnby).

DUBLIN, ST. PATRICK'S (NATIONAL) CATHEDRAL.—Morn.: Service, Te Deum and Jubilate, Stainer in E flat; Holy Communion, Kyrie, Creed, Sanctus, Stainer in E flat; Anthem, We have heard with our ears (Sullivan). Even.: Service, Magnificat and Nunc Dimittis, Smart in B flat; Anthems, Happy and blest are they (Mendelssohn), and The heavens declare (Boyce).

ELY CATHEDRAL.—Morn.: Service, Te Deum, Boyce in C; Kyrie and Credo, Arnold in B minor; Gloria, Monk in A; Anthem, O how amiable (Barnby). Even.: Service, Goss in E; Anthem, The glory of the Lord (Goss).

FOLKESTONE (ST. MICHAELS).—Morn.: Service, Te Deum and Benedictus, Smart in F; Anthem, Lead, kindly light (Stainer). Even.: Service, Magnificat and Nunc Dimittis, Smart in F; Anthem, The Lord is my Shepherd (Gaul).

LEEDS, ST. MARTIN'S CHURCH (POTTERNEWTON). — Te Deum and Benedictus, Chants; Anthem, Lift thine eyes (Mendelssohn). Even.: Service, Magnificat and Nunc Dimittis, Chants; Anthem, Blessed be the God and Father (Wesley).

LIVERPOOL CATHEDRAL.—Aft.: Service, Magnificat and Nunc Dimittis, Stewart in G; Anthem, I have surely built Thee an house (Boyce).

LIVERPOOL (ST. CUTHBERT'S, EVERTON).—Morn.: Service, Turle in D. Even.: Service, Turle in D; Anthem, The Lord will comfort Zion (Hiles).

MANCHESTER CATHEDRAL. — Morn.: Service, Boyce in A; Full Communion Service, Cobb in G; Anthem, Save me, O God (Boyce). Aft.: Service, Arnold in A; Anthem, Sing praises unto the Lord (Gounod).

MANCHESTER (ST. BENEDICT'S).— Morn.: Service, Kyrie, Credo, Sanctus, Agnus Dei, and Gloria in excelsis, second "Messe des Orphéonistes" (Gounod). Even.: Service, Magnificat and Nunc Dimittis (Stainer).

MANCHESTER (ST. JOHN BAPTIST, HULME).—Morn.: Service, Kyrie, Credo, Sanctus, and Gloria in excelsis, Dykes in F; Benedictus, and Agnus Dei, Calkin in B flat. Even.: Service, Magnificat and Nunc Dimittis (Willing).

ROCHESTER CATHEDRAL.—Morn.: Service, Travers in F; Anthem, Lord, for Thy tender mercies (Farrant). Even.: Service, Travers in F; Anthem, They that go down (Attwood).

SALISBURY CATHEDRAL. Morn.: Service, Te Deum and Jubilate, Attwood in C; Kyrie and Credo, Gadsby in C; Offertory (Barnby). Even.: Service, Magnificat and Nunc Dimittis, Attwood in C; Anthem, I will mention (Sullivan).

SHERBORNE ABBEY. — Morn.: Service, Te Deum, Tozer in F. Even.: Service, Anthem, Trust in the Lord (Lyle).

SOUTHAMPTON (ST. MARY'S CHURCH).—Morn.: Service, Te Deum and Benedictus, Custard in F; Holy Communion, Introit, O how amiable (Macfarren); Service, Custard in E flat; Offertory, Be merciful; and Bleased is he (Barnby); Paternoster, Field. Even.: Service, Magnificat and Nunc Dimittis, Russell in A; Apostles' Creed, Harmonized Monotone.

WELLS CATHEDRAL.—Morn.: Service, Bennett in E; Introit, Blessed are the pure in heart (Macfarren); Kyrie, Mendelssohn in G. Even.: Service, Elvey in A; Anthem, O be joyful (Boyce).

WORCESTER CATHEDRAL.—Morn.: Service, Lloyd in E flat; Anthem, O taste and see (Sullivan). Even. Service, Lloyd in E flat; Anthem, God is our hope (Greene).

** Post-cards must be sent to the Editor, 6, Argyle Square, W.C., by Wednesday. Lists are frequently omitted in consequence of not being received in time.

NEWSPAPERS sent should have distinct marks opposite to the matter to which attention is required.

NOTICE.—All communications intended for the Editor are to be sent to his private address. Business communications to be addressed to 185, Fleet Street, E.C.

MUSICAL STANDARD

A NEWSPAPER FOR MUSICIANS PROFESSIONAL AND AMATEUR

No. 994. VOL. XXV. FOURTH SERIES. SATURDAY, AUGUST 18, 1883. WEEKLY: PRICE 3D.

GASPARO SPONTINI, AND HECTOR BERLIOZ.

(Translated from the *Deutsche Musiker Zeitung*.)

BY MISS EDITH E. SOUTHGATE.

The cómpositions of Spontini and Berlioz were, during their life time, the subject of constant notice, either of praise or censure. The value of their various works was often discussed, and the novelty of the forms in which they were cast afforded a theme for much critical disputing. Spontini, who had won a place of honour among his contemporaries by his operas, " La Vestale," and " Ferdinand Cortez," and had achieved triumphs of all kinds, was at last himself compelled to acknowledge that everything on this earth is transient. He had to admit that even the fame of a composer, won after much labour, energy, and many trying conflicts, rarely endures for long. The stirring and rapidly changing period during which he lived was a remarkable one : it affected him to a considerable extent, and its prominent features are to be seen reflected in his music. His fame rose rapidly, and, in consonance with the transientness of the time, as rapidly fell. A brief consideration of the current circumstances will assist us in forming a correct estimate of his art works, and assessing their real value.

Spontini was born at Jesi, in the Italian Papal States, in 1778. He went to Paris at the time when France was preparing herself for the last great scene with which the drama of the French Revolution ended, namely, the crowning of Napoleon, which took place on 2nd December, 1804. The splendour which attended the creation of the realm, the effulgence which surrounded the new chief officer of the young state, and the recollection of the glorious achievements of the various wars, radiated far and wide through this brilliant time, and had a marked effect on Spontini. The glamour of the Empire fascinated a character so ambitious and thirsting for glory as was his : thus, it is easy to understand that this important epoch had a great influence on the ardent spirit of the young Italian, and distinctly affected the peculiar path of his genius. Public attention was first directed to his ability by the appearance of his successful opera, " Iphigenie in Aulis," which was frequently given at the Grand Opéra. In 1807, appeared that remarkable fruit of his inspiration, the opera, " La Vestale," causing a great sensation. The national feelings of the French, which had been called forth by the victories of Napoleon and the glory of the period, found utterance in the opera, " Ferdinand Cortez," which followed the " Vestal," in 1808, and with this Spontini had reached the highest point of his fame. Those that he brought out afterwards, the opera, " Olympia," which appeared at the time of the Restoration ; and again later oh, in 1822, " Lalla Rookh," produced at Berlin ; " Nurmahal," given in 1825, and others, possessed but little imagination or constructive ability ; and were but a re-echo of his former greatness. The power he had once possessed disappeared more and more, for these latter works were produced at the time when Napoleon's glory began to decline, and gradually lose its former splendour. In sympathy with this altered condition of public affairs, the incentive that Spontini once had to compose existed no longer ; thus, his genius faded with the setting of the Napoleonic star.

With Berlioz it was altogether different. Spontini, during his youth, enjoyed the tuition of such celebrated masters as Padre Martini, Sala, Traëtta, and Cimarosa, and even before he went to Paris was celebrated for his works, written for the Italian stage. Berlioz, who was born in 1803, at a French village, in the Dauphine La Côte Saint André, received his first musical instruction from his father, who was a physician. He learnt to play the flute, and afterwards took lessons on the guitar, from a musician of Lyons, who had settled himself in the village, by the persuasion of Berlioz's father. It is difficult to decide how much of the real art of music the youth obtained from the knowledge of this instrument. As a boy he occupied himself with small compositions for home use. But as his father became aware of the boy's passionate inclination for music, he set him to anatomical studies, hoping to turn him from his love for art, and induce him to follow the profession of a physician. In 1822, he sent him to Paris, to study medicine, but music attracted young Berlioz so strongly, that he left everything else, and, against the will of his parents, gave himself up entirely to the study of the art. His masters at the Conservatoire were Lesueur and Reicha. He especially applied himself

to the study of Gluck's works, a design he carried on with great and continuous industry. He also studied the symphonies of Beethoven, the works of Spontini, and Weber, and in fact everything that seemed 'to indicate a new departure in the art. His restless and eccentric ideas found an approximate image in the exclamation of Chateaubriand's Réné, " Un instinct secret me tourmente." A mysterious feeling seems indeed to have troubled him, and examples of its cryptic voice may be found in nearly all his works. When he, for the third time, hoped to obtain the chief composition prize at the Conservatoire, many of his works had already attracted notice, and in consequence of this it was hinted to him from different quarters that he would be sure to receive the prize this time. This expectation excited him to the composition of the cantata on the history of Cleopatra—who kills herself by means of a poisonous adder—and he essayed to illustrate the theme in music, according to what he thought displayed a Shakesperian imagination and influence. He loftily ignored any consideration or concession to the ruling tastes and musical forms of the day. But the work made such a bad impression, that the prize judges determined to award no prize on this occasion. Boieldieu, the well-known opera composer, one of the judges, had the following conversation with Berlioz the next day.—" Mon Dieu ! what have you done ? You had the prize within your grasp, and have thrown it away." " Yet I can assure you that I have done my best." " It is just that with which we have to reproach you. You should not have done your best, because your best is the enemy of good order. How could I call anything like that good? I love above all music which moves me, and excites me agreeably." " Well, but it is difficult to compose music, to lull one pleasantly, when the Queen of Egypt, frightened by her guilty conscience, and poisoned from the bite of a venomous snake, is sinking in the moral and physical agony of death." " You always know how to defend yourself, but that does not prove anything ; one cannot be calm and graceful in all situations." " Yes, the gladiators of old knew how to die with grace, but Cleopatra was not so trained, because it was not her office. She did not die either, as they did before an audience." " You exaggerate, we do not ask that you should set the scene in dance rhythm. On the other hand, what possessed you to put such out-of-the-way, perfectly incomprehensible harmony ? And then this peculiar rhythm in the accompaniment, which one has never heard of !."—" I don't see why one should eschew new forms in composition, where one is happy enough to hit upon such, and bring them in in the right places."—" My young friend, Madame Dobadie, who sang your cantata, is a capital musician, but one could see that she had to use great effort and attention to keep herself correct."—" Upon my honour, I did not know that music is intended to be performed without taste or attention."—(*Memoires de Hector Berlioz*, I. 142.) Boieldieu drew the conversation to a close with the significant remark, that Spontini might make good use of these observations in writing for the prize of next year. This he appears to have done, for after having tried for it four times, the coveted distinction was presented to him in 1830. It is worth noting, and seems indeed remarkable, that Berlioz should have shown such a strong original tendency, surrounded as he was by a musical atmosphere of quite a different character.

Symphony concerts were not given in Paris until the year 1848. The Parisians only heard music in their theatres and ball-rooms ; they took interest chiefly in the music of the Opéra Comique, and afterwards favoured the dance music of the composer Musard. The various pieces given at the virtuoso concerts, which took place at this time, were mainly selected from one or other of these types. In consequence of this, the public were not music enough to hear with interest and properly appreciate, foreign, or peculiar original music. How this condition was felt here and there, may be illustrated by the following account of what happened at the theatre in the Palais Royal. During the scene in a play represented, some journeymen were seen at their work. One of them sings a song ; after he has finished, a companion wishes to know by whom this song is, and receives as a reply, " De Mosard." " You are mistaken," the other replies—who was most likely an Alsatian, for he gave the right sound to the German z—" we French say Musard, but the Germans say Mozart."

It was acknowledged on all sides that Berlioz was a

talented author. His witticisms were treasured and feared; but, as a composer, he never secured a marked success with his countrymen. Unhappily, it is too often the case that celebrated men are really honoured only after their death. Public appreciation, which would have been sunlight to them during their creative period, is frequently denied them. It is hardly possible to believe the many disappointments this man had to contend against when he wished to bring out one of his works. The collecting of so great an orchestra, choir, and soloists as was necessary for the performance of his pieces, caused a great many difficulties. The mass of performers could only be obtained from different theatres, and this necessitated a perfect understanding with the directors of the theatres. Nor was the difficulty over when the period of rehearsal arrived. The aversion to his music was not confined only to its practising : the performers also had to suffer, for the aversion to it was shared by the audience, most of the listeners only coming out of curiosity in the hope of hearing all sorts of curious effects, which one could joke about afterwards. Neither the artistic nor material results rewarded the trouble which such a performance entailed. The energy and activity which, in spite of this, Berlioz exhibited, is really to be admired. He accepted most of the barren results with calmness ; but at the same time he watched his enemies with a sharp eye, and at times found the opportunity of revenging himself with his pen. His concerts in Germany at once met with approbation, and this induced him to continue his concert tour. The art-loving public of Austria, Hungary, Russia, and England, willingly took him up, and he found everywhere that which had been denied to him in Paris, viz., appreciative notice, general acknowledgment of his merits, and pecuniary gains. Encouraged by these unexpected results, he again appeared at Paris as a concert-giver. Soon after the revolution of 1848, it so happened that Berlioz arranged a concert the programme of which included the first scene of the second act from Spontini's opera, "Ferdinand Cortez." Berlioz, who had a great admiration for Spontini's genius, invited him to its rehearsal, and Spontini, who felt the negligence of the administration of the theatre keenly, was very willing to accept such an invitation. When the rehearsal was about to begin, Spontini asked for the music, feeling himself once again in the exercise of his beloved art. Various copies of his score were placed before him, but all to no avail ; his eyes were dim with age, rendering the reading of the notes impossible. Full of sadness, he rubbed his eyes and polished his glasses, but all to no purpose. Like a brave champion who, having the goal of victory before him, never thinks of the loss of the battle, but keeps his place firm, so Spontini pushed the score from him and took his place in front of the orchestra.

The rehearsal began; it was touching to notice how the enthusiasm of the old man was roused, and at the same time, the physical strength to direct was denied to him. He lifted his trembling hands in the air as if he implored the aid of the Muses ; then he rubbed convulsively his face and forehead, and fell back almost fainting in a chair which his companion had pushed towards him. The martial introduction of the scene had, during this painful proceeding, arrived at the part in which the Spanish officer exclaims " Dans un piège fatal ! " This awakened the fiery old man from his lethargy, and, greatly excited, he listened as well as his strength allowed him. But when the chorus answers the soldiers so decidedly, " Quittons ces bords," he could not contain himself any longer ; springing up, with an effort he walked towards the singers, and with an angry " Halt ! " accompanied by movements of his arm, indicated to them that their rendering was too tame, and that they as mutineers ought to sing more peremptorily and to speak their words firmer and with more spirit. He went on to say, " Have you already forgotten the recent barricades ? " Here there was a pause as if he felt that he had, in his eagerness, gone too far with his searching question ; he then tried to sing their parts to them, but his voice failed him. The aged composer quickly tore the cravat from his throat, as if it had affected his voice, and when he could no longer sing, he seemed to be in doubt as to what to do. Berlioz and Spontini's companion tried to quiet him, but the great exertion had undergone had completely unstrung him, and left him powerless. After resting a few minutes, he was led from the room, and lifted into his carriage.

Spontini, who had begun by a brilliant career in Paris, and later on spent many years in active service at Berlin, where he attained to the post of General Music Director, lived eventually at Paris, quite retired from the excitement of the day. The same jubilations with which Spontini had been honoured, now fell to the lot of his countryman, Rossini, as Berlioz stated in the *Figaro*. But this supremacy was soon disputed, for Meyerbeer obtained the first position at the chief place, viz., the Grand Opéra. Rossini wrote only one opera for this institution, that was "Wilhelm Tell," in 1829. Meyerbeer, who with his first opera, "Robert the Devil," gained almost undisputed pre-eminence, published in 1836 "The Huguenots," a work which surpassed the former. His creative power was exerted to the greatest extent, and he brought before the never tired Parisians, "The Prophet," 1849, "The Star of the North," 1854, and others, mainly preserving through the various compositions the old order of things.

The French composers, who, according to the wish of Boieldieu (with the sole exception of Berlioz), only composed music *qui berce*, were, through the influence of Meyerbeer, roused from their musical slumber, somewhat confused. They found that the old-fashioned form in which they had been working was now effete, and their goal being no longer recognized, their aims became obliterated. It was not until after the appearance of Gounod's "Faust," in 1859, at the Théâtre Lyrique, that the charm which Meyerbeer had exercised seemed to fade. The power which he displayed had caused the French composers to almost disappear from the stage for a short time. Under such circumstances it is not to be wondered at that Spontini, who had never won a genuine triumph with his works, was somewhat forgotten. It also appears quite natural, that Berlioz could not succeed in attracting general notice during this period, for he was not only in continual opposition to the art tendency of his countrymen, but also in collision with the concert arrangements of the Paris musical world. Had he directed his aims to the composing of opera music, and worked at this branch with the same perseverance that he displayed in the construction of symphonies (which at this day occupy a peculiar place in art), he would, perhaps, during his lifetime have obtained an honourable position in the general musical life of Paris. But although those remarkable and highly characteristic works, which he wrote for his concert rooms, and which he called, symphonies, are in their way grand and show much imagination and intellectual power, they are too deep for the every-day musical understanding of the Parisian public. When his opera, "Benvenuto Cellini" (1836), was given at the Grand Opéra, the set opinions of the French were too deeply rooted to appreciate its value. The work was a complete failure. Hereupon followed—in 1841-2—the exciting journeys. The triumphs which he achieved at this time won for him the respect of his countrymen, and when his second opera, "Les Troyens à Carthage" (1863), was given at the Théâtre Lyrique, instead of the Grand Opéra, he was in a measure made happy, for it was performed twenty times, and brought him in a good sum. He, being the author both of the words and music, received all the fees. Before this (1862), one of his comic operas, "Béatrice et Bénédict," had been given in Baden, then at Weimar, and met with approval.

Berlioz seemed to the Parisians like two separate persons, who, continually finding fault with one another, do not appear at their best, despite the fact that they acknowledge one another's good qualities on either side. And after death there was also a great difference between Berlioz and Spontini. The Parisians can now hardly hear enough of their gifted countryman's symphonic music. In honouring him with enthusiasm as a composer, we must take it that there exists yet another reason, viz., that they at last acknowledged the true art and greatness of this man. Just as the French call the violinist Gaviniés their Tartini, and celebrate Méhul as their Mozart, so they have eventually discovered in Berlioz their Wagner.

———

The splendid enthusiasm of the Welsh people continued to burn brightly to the very end of the Eisteddfod proceedings. Several of the successful candidates, as the young harpist hailing from Caerphilly, were received with every manifestation of delight upon returning home. On the return, on August 10th, of the North Wales choir gaining the £100 prize, and the gold medal, the members were received by admiring thousands, with the attending demonstrations of bands, triumphal arch, etc., and at night bonfires lit up the surrounding mountains.

Musical Intelligence.

CARDIFF.

Concerts were given on Saturday the 11th and Monday the 13th, by the Blue Ribbon Choir, ably conducted by Mr. Jacob Davis, and the band of the Black Watch, 2nd Battalion Royal Highlanders, conducted by Mr. Walter G. Buck, the bandmaster. The choir distinguished itself by singing, with excellent effect, several choruses, part-songs, &c., and the band played a number of overtures and selections, greatly pleasing the audiences by their performances. The programmes included vocal solos, and organ solos were given by Mr. E. H. Turpin. The concerts, which were for the benefit of the local Infirmary, were largely attended, taking place in the immense Eisteddfod building, the large and fine organ built by Messrs. Brindley and Foster for the recent festival being used upon these occasions.

PROMENADE CONCERTS, COVENT GARDEN.

The programme on Wednesday was comprehensive, both vocally and instrumentally, the vocalists being Miss Mary Lemmens, Mdme. Enriquez, and Signor Foli ; and the chief solo instrumentalists, Mr. J. T. Carrodus (violin), Mdme. Frickenhaus (pianoforte), and Mr. Howard Reynolds (cornet) ; Mr. J. M. Carrodus leading the orchestra of 100 performers, the band of the Coldstream Guards playing under the direction of Mr. C. Thomas, Mr. F. Clyffe being the pianoforte concert accompanist, and Mr. John Cheshire playing the harp. Mr. A. Gwyllym Crowe was the conductor of the concert. The first, or "classical" part included the overture to "Anacreon" (Cherubini), and the succeeding pieces included some ballet music from "Rosamunde" (Schubert) ; Concerto in A minor (Schumann), in which Mdme. Frickenhaus admirably illustrated her well-known powers on the pianoforte ; Allegro from violin concerto (Beethoven), the soloist being Mr. J. T. Carrodus, who was rapturously applauded ; and the unfinished symphony in B minor (Schubert) ; the conclusion of the first part being the overture to "Rosamunde." The "miscellaneous" programme constituting the second division of the concert, included a selection, "L'Italiana in Algieri" (Rossini), in which the orchestral and Coldstream bands united. This was succeeded by a tarantella from "Venezia e Napoli" (Liszt), in which Mdme. Frickenhaus again appeared as pianoforte soloist ; and after, an entr'acte from "Lohengrin," the orchestral and military bands again joining. The remaining pieces embraced a new waltz "In the Moonlight" (A. G. Crowe), the quick march, "Habt Acht," or "Attention" (Gung'l), forming with the combined strains of the bands a pleasant finale to a concert, the interest of which never flagged for a moment.

BEVERLEY.—Dr. Spark gave an organ performance recently in St. Mary's Church. The profits of the performance were given in support of an educational institution. Dr. Spark's treatment of the classical programme was highly appreciated by the large and studious audience.

CARNARVON.—The North Wales Musical Eisteddfod opened at Carnarvon on August 6th, under the presidency of Mr. Rathbone, M.P. The Festiniog choir won the fifty guinea prize in choral competitions, the Llanberis band winning twenty guineas in brass band competitions. Mr. Henry Leslie and Dr. F. G. Rogers, organist of Bangor Cathedral, were chief adjudicators. Sir Llewellyn Turner presided at the evening concert.

MELBOURNE.—The last of the Kennedy concerts, which was given in the Town Hall on June 9th, attracted the largest audience yet assembled to enjoy these popular entertainments. The pieces in the programme, which had been selected by the audience, included some of the most popular songs given by the Kennedy family, and were received with enthusiastic applause. Mr. Kennedy at the conclusion of the entertainment, after thanking the public for their patronage, made the pleasing announcement that he would return in twelve months' time, and bid a final farewell to Melbourne. Mr. R. Kennedy, who during the week had become a Benedict, had an old shoe with a bouquet attached thrown at him in accordance with the time-honoured custom, which regards such a missile as a token of good fortune. Mr. and Mrs. R. Kennedy intend to take a tour round the world, which will occupy about five years. This is a proper kind of honeymoon, is it not ?—*Melbourne Herald*, June 11th, 1883.

LONG EATON.—A new organ, built by Messrs. Brindley & Foster, of Sheffield, for Zion Chapel, Long Eaton, was opened on July 29. The chapel was also re-opened after having been closed for repairs and cleaning, etc. Sermons were preached by the Rev. T. Rushworth. Mr. S. W. Pilling, of Bolton, presided at the organ in the morning and afternoon, and Mr. W. Gad-by, of Ilkeston, in the evening.—An organ recital was given on August 4th by Mr. Pilling. The following is the specification of the instrument : Great organ CC to C, 61 notes, 6 stops : Swell organ, CC to C, 61 notes, 6 stops ; pedal organ, CCC to F.—*Nottingham Guardian*.

CARMARTHEN.—A musical matinée was given on August 1st at the Assembly Rooms, by Mrs. Prince, principal of the High School in this town. The programme was gone through by the pupils in a manner reflecting credit both on themselves and their teachers. Without being invidious, we feel compelled to mention Miss F. Steele's artistic performance of Beethoven's Sonata in A flat (Op. 26) ; and the singing of Mendelssohn's duet, "I would that my love," by Misses E. Tudor Thomas and Ch. Williams. The concert concluded with "God save the Queen," after which the Vicar proposed a vote of thanks to Mrs. Prince, the pupils, and teachers, and to Mr. Cooke, the zealous conductor.—A concert was given at the Assembly Rooms on the evening of August 2nd by Miss Ellis, R.A.M. She was assisted by a number of competent artists, and patronised by the nobility and gentry of this and the neighbouring counties.—The Eisteddfod, held in a spacious marquee at New Quay, on July 31st, proved a great success. There was a large attendance.—*Carmarthen Journal*.

Foreign Musical Intelligence.

An International Music Meeting has recently been held at Bayonne, under the presidency of M. Gounod.

A musical institute has been founded at Cordova. The Governor of the Province has contributed to the cost 30,000 francs.

An opera, entitled "L'Alcade de Zalaméa," book by Détroyat and Silvestre, music by Benjamin Godard, will be produced during the coming winter in Antwerp.

It is reported that Spondrini, architect of the Teatro Costanzan, Rome, will be entrusted with the task of building the new Italian Opera-house, Paris.

A memorial is to be erected to C. M. von Weber in his native town, Eutin, and will be unveiled on the 18th December, 1886, the 100th anniversary of his birth.

Wagner's "Ring des Nibelungen" and "Tristan und Isolde" will probably be heard, it is stated, ere long at the Theatre Royal, Dresden.

Berlioz's "Benvenuto Cellini" is attracting attention just now in Germany. Flotow's posthumous opera, "The Count of San Megrin," is to be given presently in Cologne.

At the seventh Silesian Musical Festival, to be held, it is said, next Whitsuntide, at Breslau, Blumner's oratorio, "Der Fall Jerusalems," will be performed on the first day under the direction of its composer.

It is extraordinary how wide the artist will open his mouth when America is mentioned. Signor Fancelli, who is, perhaps, the most sweet-voiced tenor of the present day, being approached, replied that he understood Signor Campanini was to get half a million of francs (£20,000), and, therefore, he would want three quarters of a million (£30,000) for the season. The story goes that a stipulation was likewise made that the tenor should not be obliged to attend rehearsals, nor to learn new parts, and that scented soap and cigars were to be provided gratuitously. He expressed an opinion that his voice would suffice to divide America in twain, and render all current talk about the Panama Canal superfluous. Another great tenor has asked the more moderate price of £275 per night, and he will probably be accepted.—*Figaro*.

Among the solo performances of the recent Cardiff concerts are noticed the splendid artistic playing of Herr Pollitzer (violin), Mr. Lazurus (clarionet), in concertos by Mendelssohn and Weber and Mr. W. Morrow, as trumpet obbligato in "Let the bright Seraphim."

Organ News.

FISHERIES EXHIBITION.

Mr. James Loaring, F.C.O., gave his 40th recital last week. The programmes included :—

Overture, "Crown Diamonds"	Auber.
Toccata and Fugue in D minor	Bach.
Organ Concerto, No. 1	Handel.
Andante, from Quintet in C minor	Mozart.
"Sound an alarm"	Handel
Festive March in D	Smart.

Overture, "Occasional"	Handel.
Allegro Vivace, from "Jupiter" Symphony	Mozart.
Andante in G	Batiste.
"Hailstone" Chorus	Handel.
"With verdure clad"	Haydn.
March from "Fidelio"	Beethoven.

Mr. S. Claude Ridley gave organ recitals on Thursday and Friday, August 9th and 10th. The following are the programmes :—

Triumphal March and Ballet Music	Verdi.
Romance "Feuille de Rose"	Voss.
Concert Fugue in G	Krebs.
Gavotte, "Mignon"	Thomas.
Fantasia, "The Storm"	Lemmens.
"Air du Dauphin"	Roeckel.
Overture to "Zampa"	Hérold.

Processional March in E flat	Wely.
Andante, with variations in A	Haydn.
Selections from the "Pirates of Penzance"	Sullivan.
Prelude and Fugue in B flat	Bach.
Offertoire in D, No. 5	Batiste.
Gavotte, "Louis XV."	Lee.
Overture to "Masaniello"	Auber.

Hymne, Marche Triomphale	Verdi.
Andante with variations	Haydn.
Prelude and Fugue in B flat	Bach.
Gavotte, "Louis XV."	Lee.
Overture to "Masaniello"	Auber.
Romance in A flat	Voss.
Offertoire in D	Batiste.
Chorus, "Lift up your heads" ("Messiah")	Handel

And on Monday, August 13th, by Mr. W. H. Hedgecock:—

"Occasional" Overture	Handel.
"Evening Prayer"	Smart.
March, "Naaman"	Costa.
Ballet Air, "Rosamunde"	Schubert.
Allegro in D	Tours.
Melody in C	Silas.
Gavotte in G	Handel.
Selection, "Carmen"	Bizet.

And on Monday, August 13th, by Mr. H. C. Tonking, R.A.M.:—

Concerto for Organ, No. 2	Handel.
Postlude in C minor	Steggall.
Gavotte in F	Martini.
Gavotte, "Mignon"	Thomas.
Postlude in D	Smart.
Toccata and Fugue in D minor	Bach.
March from "Ode to St Cecilia"	Handel.
March from "Occasional Oratorio"	Handel.
Grand Chorus	Guilmant.

GODALMING.

A short organ recital was given by Humphrey J. Stark, Esq., Mus.Bac., Oxon., in the Parish Church, on Sunday, August 12th. The following was the programme :—

Andante with variations	Beethoven.
Fugue in G minor	Bach.
Offertoire in D major	Batiste.

WISBECH.

Mr. Jude has been lately visiting Wisbech, which is his native town, and the opportunity was taken by Mr. Chas. King, the organist of the Parish Church, to obtain his consent to the giving of a recital. A very large number of people assembled in the church, and Mr. Jude delighted his audience with his talented performances. The recital lasted rather more than an hour, but the interest was fully sustained by the variety of the compositions, which were from the works of such distinguished composers as Handel, Mendelssohn, Sterndale Bennett, Guilmant, Wesley, and one piece, a Trumpet March, of Mr. Jude's own composition. The following was the programme :—

Chorus, "When His loud voice"	Handel.
Barcarolle, from the 4th Concerto	Bennett.
Chorale, with variations, in D minor	Mendelssohn.
Trumpet March, "La Garde Passe"	Jude.
"Holdsworthy Church Bells"	Wesley.
Grand Sonata for the Organ	Guilmant.

CARDIFF.

The following is the specification of the organ supplied for the Eisteddfod (Cardiff, 1883), by Brindley and Foster of Sheffield :—

GREAT ORGAN. CC TO C.

1. Double Stopt Diap..	16 ft.	6. Harmonic Flute ...	4 ft.
2. Open Diapason	8 „	7. Grave Mixture (2 ranks)	
3. Viola	8 „	8. Full Mixture (3 ranks)	
4. Hohl Flöte	8 „	9. Double Trumpet ...	16 „
5. Principal	4 „	10. Trumpet	8 „

SWELL ORGAN. CC TO C.

11. Bourdon	16 ft.	17. Fifteenth	2 ft.
12. Open Diapason	8 „	18. Mixture (4 ranks)	
13. Gamba	8 „	19. Cornopean	8 „
14. Voix Celestes	8 „	20. Oboe	8 „
15. Gedact	8 „	21. Space Slide	
16. Principal	4 „		

CHOIR ORGAN. CC TO C.

22. Salicional	8 ft.	25. Lieblich Flute	4 ft.
23. Lieblich Gedact	8 „	26. Piccolo	2 „
24. Dulciana	8 „	27. Clarionet	8 „

PEDAL ORGAN. CCC TO F.

28. Sub Bourdon	32 ft.	30. Sub Bass	16 ft.
29. Open Diapason	16 „	31. Trombone	16 „

COUPLERS.

32. Swell to Great.	37. Swell Super.
33. Swell to Choir.	38. Great Super.
34. Swell to Pedal.	39. Pedal Super
35. Great to Pedal.	40. Tremulant.
36. Choir to Pedal.	

Three Composition Pedals, to Great and Pedal.
Three   „   „   to Swell.

Drawstop action diagonal ; pedal board, concave ; "College of Organists'" resolution ; case and decorated front pipes to design sent.

LIMERICK.

The following is the synopsis of the new organ just erected in the new Parish Church (R.C.) of S. Michael, by Messrs. Telford and Telford, of Dublin :—

GREAT ORGAN. (CC TO G IN ALT).

1. Open Diap. (No. 1)	8 ft.	6. Octave	4 ft.
2. „ (No. 2)	8 „	7. Fifteenth	2 „
3. Bourdon	16 „	8. Mixture (4 ranks).	
4. Gamba	8 „	9. Trumpet	8 „
5. Stopped Diapason..	8 „		

SWELL ORGAN. (CC TO G IN ALT).

10. Open Diapason	8 ft.	15. Octave	4 ft.
11. Dulciana	8 „	16. Fifteenth	2 „
12. Voix Celeste	8 „	17. Mixture (3 ranks).	
13. Bourdon	16 „	18. Oboe	8 „
14. Double Gedact	16 „	19. Cornopean	8 „

CHOIR ORGAN. (CC TO G IN ALT).

20. Stopped Diapason...	8 ft.	23. Dulciana	8 ft.
21. Flute Harmonic	4 „	24. Clarinet	8 „
22. Piccolo Harmonic...	2 „		

PEDAL ORGAN. (CCC TO F).

25. Bourdon	16 ft.	27. Double Open	16 ft.
26. Open Diapason	8 „		

COUPLERS.

28. Swell to Choir.	30. Swell to Great.
29. Swell to Pedal.	31. Great to Pedal.

Accessory Stop, Blower.

Great	648	Pipes.
Swell	592	„
Choir	256	„
Pedal	90	„
Total	1,586.	

No. of Stops 32

The Swell-box has *vertical*, instead of *horizontal*, shutters. The organ is an excellent instrument, the Pedal organ being very fine, and the whole of the reeds good and well voiced. The case is of stained pine, with diapered open diapason pipes in front. The instrument stands in the choir gallery, over the South transept. The church has just been erected at a cost of about £14,000, and is considered to be one of the finest in the South of Ireland.

BAKEWELL.

An organ recital was given in All Saint's Church, on Wednesday, August 1st, by S. W. Pilling, Esq. The following was the programme :—

Organ Sonata (No. 2 in C minor) .... (Grave—Adagio—Allegro—Maestoso—Fuga).	Mendelssohn.
Pastorale .... Caprice in B flat .... }	Guilmant.
Allegro Pomposo	Smart.
Air, "O God have mercy" ("St. Paul")	Mendelssohn.
Fantasia	Guiraud.
Prelude and Fugue in G minor	Bach.
March, with "Hymn of Priests"	Chauvet.
Cavatina	Raff.
Andante con moto	Boely.
Elevation and Finale..............................	Saint-Saëns.

And on Wednesday, Aug. 8th, by Mr. J. F. Dovaston :—

Introduction and Allegro..........................	Wood.
Andante con moto	Smart.
Andante quasi Adagio	Calkin.
Recit. and Air (Vocal) "O come hither"	Elvey.
Air (Vocal) "Gracious is the Lord"	Harris.
Allegro Pomposo	Smart.
Prelude and Fugue	Mendelssohn.
Barcarole	Bennett.
Moderato Maestoso	Hoyte.
Air (Vocal) "Lord, what is man?"	Handel.
Solo (Vocal) "Be Thou faithful"	Mendelssohn.
Triumphal March	Lemmens.

THE HISTORY OF THE PIANOFORTE.

By A. J. HIPKINS.

(Continued from page 88.)

The Seven Years' War put an end to pianoforte-making on the lines Silbermann had adopted in Saxony. A fresh start had to be made a few years later, and it took place contemporaneously in South Germany and England. The results have been so important that the grand pianofortes of the Augsburg Stein, and the London Backers, may be regarded, practically, as re-inventions of the instrument. The decade 1770-80 marks the emancipation of the pianoforte from the harpsichord, of which before it had only been deemed a variety. Compositions appear written expressly for it, and a man of genius, Muzio Clementi, who subsequently became the head of the pianoforte business now conducted by Messrs. Collard, came forward to indicate the special character of the instrument, and found an independent technique for it.

A few years before, the familiar domestic square piano had been invented. I do not think clavichords could have been altered to square pianos, as they were wanting in sufficient depth of case, but that the suggestion was from the clavichord is certain, the same kind of case and key-board being used. German authorities attribute the invention to an organ builder, Friederici of Gera, and give the date about 1758 or 1760. I have advertised in public papers, and have had personal inquiry made for one of Friederici's "Fort Bien," as he is said to have called his instrument. I have only succeeded in learning this much, that Friederici is considered to have been of later date than has been asserted in the text-books. Until more conclusive information can be obtained, I must be permitted to regard a London maker, but a German by birth, Johannes Zumpe, as the inventor of the instrument. It is certain that he introduced that model of square piano which speedily became the fashion, and was chosen for general adoption everywhere. Zumbe began to make his instruments about 1765. His little square, at first of nearly five octaves, with the "old man's head" to raise the hammer, and "mopstick" damper, was in great vogue, with but little alteration, for forty years, and that in spite of the manifest improvements of John Broadwood's wrest-plank, and John Geib's "grasshopper." After the beginning of this century, the square became much enlarged and improved by Collard and Broadwood, in London, and by Petsold, in Paris. It was overdone in the attempt to gain undue power for it, and, about twenty years ago, sank in the competition with the latter cottage pianoforte which was always being improved.

To return to the grand pianoforte. The origin of the Viennese grand is rightly accredited to Stein, the organ builder, of Augsburg. I will call it the German grand, for I find it was as early made in Berlin as Vienna. According to Mozart's correspondence, Stein had made some grand pianos in 1777, with a special escapement, which did not "block" like the pianos he had played upon before. When I wrote the article "Pianoforte" in Dr. Grove's "Dictionary" no Stein instrument was forthcoming, but the result of the inquiries I had instituted at that time ultimately brought one forward, which has been secured by the curator of the Brussels Museum, M. Victor Mahillon. This instrument, with Stein's action and two unison scale, is dated 1780. Mozart's grand piano, preserved at Salzburg, made by Walther, is a nearly contemporary copy of Stein, and so also are the grands by Huhn of Berlin, which I took notes of at Berlin and Potsdam; the latest of these is dated 1790. An advance, shown by these instruments of Stein and Stein's followers, is in the spacing of the unisons, the Huhn grands having two strings to a note in the lower part of the scale, and three in the upper. The Cristoforio-Silbermann inverted wrest-plank has reverted to the usual form ; the tuning pins and downward bearing being the same as in the harpsichord. There are no steel arches as yet between the wrest-plank and the belly-rail in these German instruments. As to Stein's escapement, his hopper was fixed behind the key ; the axis of the hammer rising on a principle which I think is older than Stein, but have not been able to trace to its source, and the position of his hammer is reserved. Stein's light and facile movement with shallow key-fall, resembling Cristofori's in bearing little weight, was gratefully accepted by the German clavichord players, and, re-acting, became one of the determining agents of the piano music and style of playing of the Vienna school. Thus arose a fluent execution of a rich figuration and brilliant passage playing, with but little inclination to sonorousness of effect, lasting from the time of Mozart's immediate followers to that of Henri Herz, a period of half a century. Knee-pedals, as we translate "génouillères," were probably in vogue before Stein, and were levers pressed with the knees, to raise the dampers, and leave the pianoforte undamped, a register approved of by Carl Philip Emmanuel Bach, who regarded the undamped pianoforte as the more agreeable for improvising. He appears, however, to have known but little of the capabilities of the instrument, which seemed to him coarse and inexpressive beside his favourite clavichord. Stein appears to have made use of the "una corda" shift. Probably by knee-pedals, subsequently by foot-pedals, the following effects were added to the Stein pianos. The harpsichord "harp"-stop, which muted one string of each note by a piece of leather, became by the interposition of a piece of cloth between the hammer and the strings, the piano, harp, or celeste. The more complete sourdine, which muted all the strings by contact of a long strip of leather, acted as the staccato, pizzicato, or pianissimo. The Germans further displayed that ingenuity in fancy stops Mersenne had attributed to them in harpsichords more than a hundred and fifty years before, by a bassoon pedal, a card which, by a rotatory half-cylinder just impinging upon the strings, produced a reedy twang; also by pedals for triangle, cymbals, bells and tambourine, the last drumming on the sound-board itself. Several of these contrivances may be seen in a six-pedal grand pianoforte belonging to the Queen, at Windsor Castle, bearing the name as maker of Stein's daughter, Nannette, who was a friend of Beethoven.

We gather from Burney's 'contributions to "Rees's Cyclopædia," that after the arrival of John Christian Bach in London, A.D. 1759, a few grand pianofortes were attempted by the second rate harpsichord makers, but with no particular success. If the workshop tradition can be relied upon that several of Silbermann's workmen had come to London about that time, the so-called "twelve apostles," more than likely owing to the Seven Years' War, we should have here men acquainted with the Cristofori model, which Silbermann had taken up, and the early grand pianos referred to by Burney would be on that model. I should say the "new instrument" of Messrs. Broadwood's play-bill of 1767 was such a grand piano ; but there is small chance of ever finding one now, and if an instrument were found it would hardly retain the original action, as Messrs. Broadwood's books of the last century show the practice of refinishing instruments which had been made with the "old movement." Burney distinguishes Americus Backers by special mention. He is said to have been a [Dutchman. Between 1772 and 1776, Backers produced the well-known English action, which has remained the most durable, and one of the best up to the present day. It refers in direct leverage to Cristofori's first action. It is opposite to Stein's contemporary invention, which has the hopper fixed. In the English action, as in the Florentine, the hopper rises with the key. To the direct leverage of Cristofori's first action, Backers combined the check of the second, and then added an important invention of his own, a regulating screw and button for the escapement. Backers died in 1776. It is unfortunate that we can refer to no pianoforte made by him. I should regard it as treasure trove if one were forthcoming in the same way that brought to light the authentic one of Stein's. As, however, Backers' intimate friends, and his assistants in carrying out the invention, were John Broadwood and Robert Stodart, we have, in their early instruments, the principle and all the leading features of the Backers grand. The increased weight of stringing was met by steel arches placed at intervals between the wrest-plank and the belly-rail, but the belly-rail was still free from the thrust of the wooden bracing, the direction of which was confined to the sides of the case, as it had been in the harpsichord. Stodart appears to have preceded Broadwood in taking up the manufacture of the grand piano by four or five years. In 1777, he patented an alternate pianoforte and harpsichord, the drawing of which patent shows the Backers action. The pedals he employed were to shift the harpsichord register, and to bring on the octave stop. The present pedals were introduced in English, and grand pianos by 1785, and are attributed to John Broadwood, who appears to have given his attention at once to the improvement of Backer's instrument. Hitherto the grand piano had been made with an undivided belly-bridge, the same as the harpsichord had been ; the bass strings, in three unisons, to the lowest note, being of brass. Theory would require that the notes of different octaves should be multiples of each ,other, and that the tension should be the same for each string. The lowest bass strings, which at that time were the note F, would thus require a vibrating length of about twelve feet. As only half this length could be afforded, the difference had to be made up in the weight of the strings and their tension, which led, in these early grands, to many inequalities. The three octaves towards the treble could, with care, be adjusted, the lengths being practically the ideal lengths. It was in the bass octaves (pianos were then of five octaves) the inequalities were more conspicuous. To make a more perfect scale, and equalise the tension, was the merit and achievement of John Broadwood, who joined to his own practical knowledge and sound intuitions the aid of professed men of science. The result was, the divided bridge, the bass strings being carried over the shorter division, and the most beautiful grand pianoforte in its lines and curves that has ever been made was then manufactured. In 1791, he carried his scale up to C, five and a half octaves; in 1794, down to C, six octaves, always with care for the artistic form. The pedals were attached to the front legs of the stand, on which the instrument rested. The right foot pedal acted first as the *piano* register, shifting the impact of each hammer to two unisons instead of three; a wooden stop in the right hand key-block permitted the action to be shifted yet further to the right, and reducing the blow to one string only, produced the *pianissimo* register, or *una corda*, of indescribable attractiveness of sound. The cause of this was in the reflected vibration through the bridge to the untouched strings. The present school of pianoforte playing rejects this effect altogether, but Beethoven valued it, and indicated its use in some of his great works. Steibert called the *una corda* the *celeste*, which is more appropriate to it than Adam's application of this name to the harp-stop, by which the latter has gone ever since.

(To be continued).

MODESTY IN CONNECTION WITH MUSIC AND ITS SISTER ARTS.

PAPER II.

It is generally accepted by all who labour mentally or bodily, that there is a certain amount of self-assurance necessary if we wish to make headway in our respective avocations. Yet at the same time we must be very discreet in saying such a thing, for fear it should be misunderstood; for this self-assurance if misapplied is the seed of vanity. It is observable from the highest to the lowest: we see it playing about the work of the common labourer, on the canvas of the successful artist, in the lives and works of musicians of accepted fame, in the mendicant whose canvas is the London flagstones, endeavouring to convince the public of the artistic merit that exists in his work by writing the words "I am an artist." I was rather amused a few weeks back, by observing the conceit of an itinerant street singer. He was a man, I should say, who had seen "brighter days," but whose present degraded position was due to a "common weakness;" after going through some hackneyed ballad, he solicited alms of those who were standing round, evidently thinking he had well earned the right of asking. And judging from his exertions, he had; but the crowd was not appreciative—the people seemed reticent to encourage his "talent." So after returning his almost penniless hat to its accepted place of location, he remarked (with an air of injured talent, as he turned on his heels once more) "and this is artistic England!" I felt greatly inclined to remark, "It is," but such men as this we pity, and as they can hardly be said to enter the pale of art, we must dismiss them from our subject; but we are inclined to look upon conceited and egotistical art workers with great contempt. It is quite necessary for an artist to feel his ability and to feel a natural degree of pride from the fact of his being in possession of talent; but the gift is not his own—he is simply the instrument through which it has pleased the "Giver" that art should flow.

If we take a glass of pure water, and mix it with a dirty substance, it at once becomes impure, but the impurity is in the dirty substance, not in the water; it is so with music, which in itself is so pure, but if it mingles with impurities it becomes unclean. Pride is this impurity, which is the great opposite to music and crushes with relentless hatred its loving influence. How many clever men we see utterly ruined, how many lives wasted, by this greatest of humanity's failings! This pride in some men will very often get to such a pitch that they will in course of time begin to look upon art as something which in their "exalted positions" they deign to patronise. We cannot indeed be too careful when we praise people—even encouragement may be too lavishly bestowed; let us leave the young artist alone, let him work on in the realms of "art" undisturbed. Let him, I say, work on for the love of that which he follows, instil into him that he is but a poor journeyman in "His" workshop. Tell him not that the pinnacle of fame is easy to reach, but rather impress upon his youthful imagination that it is a road which is hard and stony at first to travel, but as he gets on he will find that it becomes easier and smoother to traverse. Conscientious *art workers* need neither praise or encouragement from human lips. Art will whisper words of consolation which will urge on energy, and as time goes on, he will find a world of such resplendent beauty open to him such as he has never seen before. It will be always present with him; it will enable him to appreciate that which before he was unable to. Charity will be his *watchword*, and art his *companion*. The ore of humanity (instead of being crusted over with the rust of conceit) will shine out with dazzling brightness; he will feel that emotion, half rapturous, half sad, that can fill one's soul when listening to some great masterpiece—it may be of music, poetry, or perchance a splendid outburst of eloquence, and he may have this same feeling come over him at the sight of a marvellous picture. With what rapture does he listen devoutly to the lofty strains of that massive master Beethoven, to the tender soul-stirring music of Mendelssohn!—the rapture of gratitude to Him for sending such great spirits whose ears have heard such inscrutable things, which *they* can but translate into sound for us! What beautiful things Beethoven must have heard if his music is but an echo of his thoughts! Yet, nevertheless, we feel a little sad, for one cannot help feeling such a feebleness of stature—there is the thought, subdued, perhaps half latent, yet none the less real—and why does this feeling come over us? it is because we are but children grouping in semi-darkness—using what? the prattling language of children. Yet we have been in the presence of "men heroes" whose eyes are opened to see that which is nearly obscure to us. We have heard with bated breath their bold strong utterances. What *shall* we do? What *can* we do? What is left for us to do? Why, to strive with unflinching ardour, to follow in their wake. Who can tell but that some day we may find this great era of recognised childhood, the precursor, or as our Teuton friends would say, the apprenticeship, of full manhood. Even in this life, modest art-workers will tell us that through art we may have glimpses short but clear of the higher realities, *and as we see*, so we interpret to others by means of art. I say, even *here* we may have partial sight, and catch a reflection from that "*glory*" that will make us truer, nobler, and more courageous. From the angels who see this glory is evoked the angels' song; from us who see so dimly, is evoked what?

Do not such thoughts as these make us abhor conceited people? Do not they make us feel, that to touch them, we shall become contaminated? All these thoughts, however small they make us feel, yet in our littleness tell us we may be real; they should also bring comfort, for we must remember "No man has a right to underrate *honest* work, whether his own or another man's." When Shakespeare remarked "that to be honest is to be one man picked out of ten thousand," he was not more harsh than true. The paucity of such men make them so precious; if we could pick up diamonds as easily as we do the particles of sand on the sea-shore, they would at once lose their value. This seems strange to us, but it has always struck me as being a dispensation of Providence that His faithful servants should stand out, with exceptional prominence. With all art there should be a feeling of rest, of consolation, and of peace, in which nothing becomes a man so much as modesty and humility. Let us strain our ears to catch the song of love, which is sung continually by the angels; let us try with a common brotherhood, those of us who are here below, to encourage this modest love; let us join hands and hearts in sending up *our* portion, that with one grand and exultant pean of joy we may mingle our hearts' song with those above, that *the* one anthem of devotion may echo through the arches of heaven with a resonance transcending the power of human words to describe, that our one great "mission" may resound o'er the Paradise hills with such grandeur that as it ascends onwards and upwards to the Eternal Throne we may trace a smile of recognition and delight on the countenance of Him who has bestowed on us such power of praise. Who is it that would dare to be vain that can appreciate such thoughts as these, for it is only by looking at such a virtue as "modesty" from the highest stand-point that we are enabled to find something which is detrimental to the progress of its opposing vice.   GEO. F. GROVER.

A PROPOSED WELSH MUSICAL FESTIVAL.

Mr Brinley Richards's suggestion that Cardiff should, like several English towns, get up a musical festival, is well worthy of consideration. There are several reasons why the effort should be made, and there are also substantial reasons for expecting such an effort to prove successful. We mention Cardiff rather than any other town in Wales simply because Mr. Richards named it, but any considerable town might take the hint and try the experiment. Of material there is no lack. If such an institution as an Annual or Triennial Musical Festival can find the necessary material anywhere, it ought to find it with greater facility in this part of the country than anywhere else. Wales abounds in large and well-trained choirs. Every town, every village, almost every place of worship, has its choir. All that is needed is co-operation under one conductor. But here we come face to face with an obstacle, which. we fear, no ordinary effort will push out of the way. Mr. Brinley Richards has suggested the institution, and we have every reason to believe that, coming from him, the suggestion will be received throughout the Principality with great respect. But he would need go a step further. He would, in our opinion, require to show the advantages which music-loving Wales would gain from such an institution, and further how the object would most likely be made successful. At present the choirs in different localities are trained by their leaders quite independently of one another. Each choir makes its selection of musical compositions, and gets them up. Very frequently they have entered the lists as competitors at some local eisteddfod and of course, they practise separately, and with a view to win a prize. The difficulty of amalgamation under such circumstances must be obvious. Local eisteddfodau and consolidation or amalgamation of choirs are, we fear, hostile to each other. That very competition that acts as a stimulus to the several choirs acts also as a hindrance to their amalgamation. In England it can hardly be said that such an obstacle exists, so that large choirs are possible there. At the same time the advantages of the institution which Mr. Richards so strongly recommends are such as to make it desirable that the genuine lovers of music in Wales should set themselves to see if nothing whatever can be done. We believe that Wales suffers from its neglect of great musical compositions. That is to say, the time and labour of the choirs are spent upon detached choruses and similar compositions, to the neglect of the works from which the composition has been taken. We do not say this is a fault everywhere. At Swansea several works have been got up from beginning to end by a choral society which practises in that town. But there is no denying the assertion that the usual custom is to learn extracts. A chorus is selected from the " Messiah " or from " Acis and Galatea," or other work, and much time is devoted to it. But how can a detached chorus be fully appreciated? It occurs only as a part of a whole, as a portion of a complete edifice. To understand it, to know precisely what it means, and consequently to know how it should be sung, it should be studied in its place. The composer inserted it in his work to fit a certain place. It is built, so to speak, on what preceded it, and is made to correspond with its surroundings. In order, then, to give it the force intended by the composer, it should be studied in, and not out of, its own place. How can one give due effect to such pieces unless he knows what effect was intended, and how can he discover the intention without studying the work as a whole? In delivering their verdict on the singing of the choirs, the adjudicators laid stress upon the fact that the intention of the composer was evidently misunderstood in some of the passages. But how can this mistake be avoided? Of course, it may, to a large extent, be avoided, if the conductor, having thoroughly studied the composition himself, takes good care to impart his ideas to his choir. But we are firmly persuaded that our great composers will never have ample justice done to them until the rendering of their chief productions in their entirety becomes more common. We hope, therefore, that Mr. Brinley Richards, having thrown out a happy suggestion, will endeavour, for the sake of the musical reputation of his own country, to strive to realise it.—*South Wales Daily News.*

Dr. J. Stainer's new work for the Gloucester Festival is reported to be a composition of much interest and effect.

PRINCIPAL CONTENTS OF THIS NUMBER.

LONDON : SATURDAY, AUGUST 18, 1883.

A MUSICAL EXPERIENCE IN WALES.

ANNUALLY much is written and said about the recurring ancient Eisteddfod. The importance of the meeting of the present year has perhaps caused more than usual to be both written and said about it. To some extent, the special character and importance of the Eisteddfod just concluded are to be ascribed to the fact that the meeting took place at Cardiff. The Festival, like that ancient and now chief town of south Wales, had some contrasts to present and much of encouragement to show. Just as at one side of Cardiff stands the quiet, stately old castle, emblem of the still life of a once existing picturesque, but now impossible, feudalism, and on the other side of the town is found the busy life of a huge commerce, congested and partly strangled for want of space—so the Eisteddfod as an institution shows in one direction a weak craving after art forms which are primitive, and of the past, whilst in the other direction there is the presence of a real, living, healthy enthusiasm, and a downright, honest, earnest desire to cultivate the divine art upon a wide and sensible basis. Those who have read the admirable comments of the shrewd special correspondent of the *Daily Telegraph* will at once realise the situation. The Welsh Eisteddfodau are indeed institutions requiring the full light of day, and the nourishment of vigorous modern thought, in order that they may not only continue to exist; but grow into a timely and beneficent gain, not only to the inhabitants of the Principality, but to the whole world of art. It is, of course, not unnatural that many will still persist in ascribing to the Eisteddfod an archaic character. To carry this doctrine too far, as many well-meaning supporters of the Eisteddfodau still do, is to take a position as absurd in its way as would be a proposal to return to any of the other typical forms of mediæval life. The Welsh Eisteddfodau would indeed cease, save that a more generous policy has prevailed to a considerable extent, and been the means of more or less adapting such meetings to the exigencies of modern artistic life. One has nothing to urge against the picturesque retention of old features and the performance of traditional Welsh melodies; but it is important that so valuable an institution as the Eisteddfod may be made, should not be lost in that exclusive and hopeless clinging to effete and worn-out forms and customs which in the end would, unless modified by a recognition of present art requirements, destroy the very institutions it was intended to preserve. The bringing of the Eisteddfodau to towns having such a wholesome admixture of modern artistic impulses and earnest belief in the progress of institutions intended to benefit the human race as are possessed by Cardiff and Liverpool, has practically brought to an issue the questions, Is the Eisteddfod to droop away in the Welsh mountains and be lost in the mists of that mistaken antiquity-loving spirit which embraces rather unconsciously to destroy than to preserve? or, Is it to be supported with a combined spirit of reverence for its age and long continued national service, and to be strengthened by judicious and earnestly applied modern thought into a powerful engine for the artistic development of one of the most musically gifted races to be found on the face of the earth? Despite certain shortcomings ever attending the control of large meetings, Cardiff has displayed that public spirit which may always be confidently expected of one of the grandest centres of healthy, vigorous, commercial life to be found in the United Kingdom. An enormous building, with a fine large concert organ by BRINDLEY and FOSTER, an ample staff of English and Welsh musical and literary adjudicators, and a series of high-class concerts, were awaiting the beseiging army of competitors and listeners. A London orchestra formed a notable feature of the exhaustive scheme. Under the management of the able concert agent, Mr. J. STEDMAN, this department was as perfect as it could well be, and included such leading players as Herr POLLITZER, Messrs. WATSON, Herr BERNHARDT, Messrs. WOOLHOUSE, REYNOLDS, BARRY, G. HORTON, H. LAZARUS, WOOTTON, WENDLAND, W. MORROW, CHATTAWAY, SMITH, &c. The welcome innovation of such an array of instrumental skill in the exemplification of the orchestral masterpieces of MOZART, BEETHOVEN, SCHUBERT, MENDELSSOHN, WEBER, &c., was an effort indeed worthy of art-

loving Cardiff, and for this the town and visitors were chiefly indebted to Mr. S. AITKEN, the esteemed and able Chairman of the Music Committee, whose earnestness, large-sightedness and musical experience were simply invaluable. This gentleman is not only an enthusiastic caterer for the public but an accomplished and talented musician, playing the organ part in SULLIVAN's "In Memoriam" overture at one of the recent Cardiff concerts with admirable judgment, and giving other practical proofs during the Eisteddfod of his artistic taste and musical skill. Nor must the artistic support of such men as Mr. BROOKSBANK, Mus. Bac. (organist of Llandaff Cathedral) and Mr. W. SCOTT (whose admirable performance of HANDEL's 2nd Organ Concerto was a principal feature of one of the concerts) be overlooked. Mr. S. AITKEN's forethought in the provision of such illustrations of the great composers' choicest works presented in their entirety, furnished a memorable precedent at perhaps the most memorable Eisteddfod yet held; and greatly helped to weld the ancient institution to the exigencies of the art of our own times; and by this happy adaptation of the purposes of the venerable Welsh nursery of vocal and instrumental music to the present requirements of living Welshmen, such worthy to be recorded judgment and energy has, whatever the heedless lovers of antiquity for its own sake may assert, helped not a little to satisfactorily solve the question of the future hopeful existence of the Eisteddfodau. The admirable precision, excellent discipline and earnestness of some of the competing choirs again showed the real life of Welsh musical instincts. To see an audience of many thousands patiently seated through a long and severely contested trial of vocal skill was truly an invigorating spectacle. The leading merits of the different choirs were displayed in the directions of certainty of attack and a watchful unity of purpose. Their defects were a proneness to sing out of tune usually on the sharp side through the application of a too abundant energy and the in itself excellent habit of sharply defining the pronunciation of the consonants, and the occasional want of a well sustained *piano*. The singing of a choir of male voices; the in every way admirable performance of the successful Penrhyn Choir (under the leadership of Dr. ROLAND ROGERS, of Bangor, who conducted with rare tact and judgment); and the singing of the Llanelly Choir (taking the second prize at the great choral competition) were efforts to be duly remembered. The successful performances of the Cardiff string quartet party and of the Cardiff Orchestral Society were characterized by much power and promise. The wisdom of the introduction of good orchestral concerts found an indirect though emphatic justification in the competitions upon various instruments; these revealing, among other tokens of progress, excellent performers on the piccolo, flute, trombone, &c., and illustrating the preparedness of the Welsh people for the development of instrumental music. The solo vocal trials brought to the front some good singers, one, Miss IDA BROWN, attracting much attention by her capital contralto singing. The quartet singing again brought forward some talented displays of the vocal art. The solo performances on the organ, pianoforte, and harmonium also showed much skill. The prizes for the cantata, anthem and duet for pianoforte and harmonium were withheld ; and the chief bardic prize being also withheld, the Eisteddfod lost in consequence the picturesque old custom of chairing the bard. The Marquis of BUTE presided upon several occasions and took a large interest in the proceedings, attending almost every meeting in a most praiseworthy manner. This was as it should be, for upon this esteemed nobleman, the "King of South Wales," has fallen a commercial and artistic responsibility almost unique. The eyes of the world indeed look to him not only to aid by large personal sacrifices in freeing great commercial interests from the thraldom of territorial restrictive interests, but to assist in the due development of Welsh art of all kinds by the exercise of an intelligent patronage and encouragement. There are hopeful signs that the Marquis of BUTE will, indeed, do his best to foster the commerce and art of the Principality. The other presidents included Dean VAUGHAN, Archdeacon GRIFFITHS, Sir E. REED, &c.

Among the Welsh musicians present were Mr. BRINLEY RICHARDS, who urged upon one occasion the institution in rich Cardiff of a musical festival, Mr. JOHN THOMAS, who has succeeded in raising a scholarship for Wales at the Royal Academy of Music, to be held alternately by vocal and instrumental students, Mr. JENKINS, Mr. E. EVANS, &c. The English musicians assisting included Sir G. A. MACFARREN, Mr. J. BARNBY, Mr. JOSEPH BENNETT, &c. The disappointments of the Festival were centred in the proceedings of the last day, when the vast surging audience of some 20,000 took possession of the entire building, including the orchestra, so that the leading features of the final scheme of a concert of combined choirs had to be abandoned, an unfortunate termination which was chiefly brought about by allowing, from the first day onwards, the occupiers of the shilling places to clamber over the barriers to the higher priced seats, an irregularity which naturally led to a kind of demoralization, though it must be noted that the public behaved with much more patience and forbearance than might have been expected under their disappointment ; and in certain of the fruitless competitions in which the prizes remained unawarded from the lack of works of sufficient merit to justify the favourable judgment of the adjudicators. However, the national Eisteddfod of 1883 was a grand and striking event, proving abundantly the presence in the sister country of remarkable musical gifts, extenive cultivation, and unmistakable earnestness. That the artistic power of the Principality will be discreetly fostered, that the ancient Eisteddfodau will continue under wise guidance to promote the development of Welsh talent, and that these interesting and important meetings will still fulfil their original purposes upon a sufficiently enlarged and enlightened basis to expand their objects in accordance and in just proportion with the exigencies of our rapidly advancing artistic life, must indeed be the earnest wishes of all anxious for the highest attainable growth and welfare of the talented people of Wales, and of those near neighbours whose interest is ever onwards, bound up in the doings of the gifted, hospitable, kindhearted inhabitants of the Cambrian plains and mountains.

E. H. TURPIN.

AN OBSERVATION ANENT MILITARY BANDS.

THE growth of brass instruments played with valves has assumed something of the form of an abuse, as having invaded in many military and brass bands the entire brass family. Some recent experience induces me to urge upon military authorities the importance of retaining the older members of the brass genus, as the French horn, trumpet, and trombone, with slides; not only as regards the superiority of their tone-qualities, but as the means of imparting a better and more elastic temperament, so to speak, to the military orchestra. I fully concede the necessary employment of brass instruments of such executive facilities and manipulative conveniences as are obviously possessed by those playing chiefly in the second and third octaves of their respective harmonics, and having a complete and handy chromatic compass by means of valves ; but on the other hand, the exclusive use of valve brass instruments tends to a lack of pure and varied tone, to a loss, in consequence, of some power, and to the presence of a defective temperament, inasmuch as the valve instruments, even in the hands of experienced players, are rarely, if ever, in perfect tune with each other in the mass. The employment of valve trombones in a complete military band of much excellence especially called my attention to this matter, and convinced me that in this department alone it was a mistake to sacrifice a group of instruments possessing a pure, free tone, and by the simple medium of the slide having the power of infusing into the general mass of sound strong triads in perfect tune. The observation must also be extended to the group of French horns, and even to the re-introduction of the old slide trumpets, for which parts could easily be added to the usual score. The use of these instruments with a large number of open sounds presents a distinct gain, for the wood instruments with keys are also somewhat wanting in elasticity of temperament, and the powerful and to be made perfectly in tune chords of the trumpets, horns, and especially trombones with slides, will be found to permeate and draw together the whole of the mass of military instruments into one perfectly harmonious, ringing sound ; a function performed by these same instruments in the stringed, or what Mr. H. CHORLEY sometimes called the "civil orchestra." It is needless to point out that the power of the military band is obviously increased in this way, not only by the direct presence of true tune, but by the increased confidence gained by performers, sensitive as to tonality, feeling the wholesome presence of a massive body of naturally well-tuned sound. In the brass band pure and simple the retention of the slide trombones at least lends purity and brightness to the general level monotony of a body of valve brass instruments. I duly recognise the difficulties of lipping to be encountered on horseback or on the march by performers playing for the most part in the upper octaves of the harmonic range under conditions of movement involving lip disturbance. Still, it must surely be worthy of the attention of military musical authorities to duly consider the importance of retaining the presence of instruments boasting the advantage of such perfect and simple mechanisms. E. H. T.

THE OPERA: PAST, PRESENT, AND FUTURE.

" RUMOUR, full of tongues," may lie through the throat as in SHAKESPEARE'S time, but one thing seems to be certain : the monopoly of "Italian " Opera" can no longer be maintained. The air, of late, has been pregnant with warnings, and signs of the times. The *Times* (quoted in these columns) had a significant "last notice" of the theatre in Covent Garden a few weeks ago, and we hear, now, that the immense building on the Thames Embankment is to be completed in time for the season of 1884, with a view to the performances of *European* opera, French, German, Italian, and it may be hoped, English. Every accommodation will be provided for the public, and it is said—almost too good to be true—that the extravagant prices of admission (to the *stalls* for instance), will be reduced 50 per cent.

Good news, this, for the long suffering and severely fleeced inhabitants of West London. The "stars," great and little, must hide their diminished rays ; vocalists may no longer rely on the trickery of roulades and *fioriture ;* the barrel-organ tunes of BELLINI, MERCADANTE, and other degenerate descendants of the old Italian school, will give place to the "leit-" "motifs " of WAGNER, and it may be Mr. A. C. MAC-KENZIE ! The sunny land of ague, malaria, earth-quakes, and chronic mendicancy already sees the hand-writing on the walls, not in Hebrew characters to be deciphered by a second DANIEL, but in letters to be "read" by those that "run." The reign of humbug and imposture draws towards its ignominious end. A brighter day is about to dawn. It may be remembered that the "King's Theatre" in the Hay-market had a monopoly of Italian opera for a long period. Fashion supported the establishment far more than music. The five gentlemen stood up and displayed their frilled shirts and diamond studs in "fops' alley ;" and the ladies glittered with diamonds in the boxes on the evening of a "Drawing Room" day. "Full dress" was so rigorously enforced that on one occasion, in 1817, five gentlemen were turned back from the *gallery* because they wore coloured neck-ties ; and a seat in the gallery then cost five shillings ! The pit, however, occupied half the floor of the auditorium, and admission to that part of the house might be secured, through the medium of a music-seller, for about eight shillings, the "regulation" price being ten.

The writer remembers to have seen his father's opera hat, a fashionable head-gear at the beginning of the century, in the form of the military "cocked" covering for the head. SPAGNOLETTI then acted both as conductor and "leader," altenately waving his fiddle-stick and playing on the violin. At Boulogne-sur-Mer, in 1838, the same phenomenon was seen by the writer. No regular conductor was to be found anywhere ; but Mr. COSTA, who took the "chair" at the King's Theatre between 1820 and 1830, "changed all that," as SGANARELLE says in " Le Médécin malgre lui." A Frenchman named LAPORTE directed the King's Theatre up to the year 1841. He was always in difficulties, and the artists were obliged to dun

him for their salaries. Mr. LUMLEY, LAPORTE'S lawyer, took the theatre in 1842, and went on swim-mingly until 1846, when he quarrelled with his con-ductor, Mr. COSTA, and a secession took place. COSTA retired in triumph, carrying with him GRISI, PERSIANI, TAMBURINI, MARIO—in fact, all the "stars" except old LABLACHE.

The "Royal Italian Opera" was established by the seceders in 1847, and still exists under the GYE dynasty. Mr. LUMLEY still held on at the old house in the Haymarket, called, after the accession of QUEEN VICTORIA in 1837, "Her Majesty's Theatre ;" and introduced the famous JENNY LIND in 1847 ; but in spite of her success, as a "star," fortune frowned upon the old Opera, and poor LUMLEY failed. The theatre was closed for a time and then re-opened, with Signor ARDITI as conductor. It was burnt down in December, 1867.—Mr. MAPLESON has come con-spicuously to the front, and after a brief coalition with Mr. GYE, at Covent Garden, engaged "old " Drury," and held annual seasons of opera (on the retirement of Mr. WOOD), from 1871 up to 1877, when he returned to the rebuilt theatre in the Haymarket. Mdme. CHRISTINE NILSSON was always a staunch supporter and pillar of this institution. After several successful summer and winter seasons, Mr. MAPLESON retired at the end of 1881, and it is understood that he made some arrangement with the GYE's to the effect that no *opera* of any kind or nationality should be performed at Her Majesty's for the time being. Mr. GYE, accordingly, has enjoyed a monopoly for the last two years, 1872 and 1873.

The new theatre on the embankment, it is supposed, will be under the direction of Mr. MAPLESON, but this matters little so long as the public are properly treated, and the "star" system is put down. Mr. CARL ROSA has still golden opportunites before him at Drury Lane Theatre, but his seasons are too short. Herr FRANKE, too, promises to come forward again next Spring at the same house, and with WAGNER's texts "interpreted" by a man like Herr RICHTER. Let all hope that he may find ample compensation for the (*pecuniary*) non-success of his spirited enterprise in 1882.

Gross personalities disfigured the crisis in 1847, when LUMLEY was left in the cold. The late Mr. GRUNEISEN, then critic of the defunct *Morning Chronicle*, took up the cudgels for Mr. COSTA (now Sir MICHAEL), and attacked LUMLEY's management with some acerbity. Even JENNY LIND was found fault with, and at length Mr. LUMLEY withdrew the daily advertisement. Of course at the "Royal " Italian" all was gold that glittered, in our friend GRUNEISEN's eyes ; and it ought to be stated in his favour, that he introduced the famous contralto, Mdlle. ALBONI, as he afterwards brought over to England Dr. HANS VON BULOW, the pianist. GRU-NEISEN was ever at war with the GYES, and paid for his admission to their theatre. The *Morning Chronicle*, moreover, during a short interregnum of sacerdotal or "ritual" churchianity, sternly refused to accept any honorary admissions for their musical reporter. Many years ago, some one suggested an omnibus box for the use of all the critics, but the objection that some of them would play the "bear and lion," as in Dr. Watts's nursery line, was held to be fatal. One critic had personally abused another in print ; the assailed one retorted by ridiculing his adversary's articles, in which, sad to relate, appeared such solecisms as the key of A *sharp*, and E *sharp*, (for A and E *major*).   A. M.

THE VOICE

MUSICALLY AND MEDICALLY CONSIDERED.

BY

ARMAND SEMPLE, B.A., M.B., Cantab., M.R.C.P., Lond.,

Physician to the Royal Society of Musicians.

(*Continued from page* 78).

The accompanying plate shows the parts of the throat and mouth which are brought into action during the development of the voice.

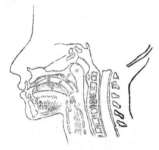

While the mouth remains shut, the tongue takes the form A, B, C. At E is seen the Uvula, a small appendage attached to the Soft Palate F, and which may be seen at the back of the throat.

The passage behind the uvula and communicating with the nose is shown at G.

The Larynx, or Vocal Organ, is represented at H. I is the Epiglottis. K is the Trachea (Windpipe). L is the Rima Glottidis (chink of the glottis), the inlet of the larynx, through which vocal sounds are produced by the air ascending from the lungs. The letters M, M, M, indicate the spinal vertebræ. N is the expansion of the throat ; and O, O, O, the cavity of the mouth.

The trachea (windpipe) is capable by nature of rising and falling, and this action conveys to the larynx (vocal organ) a motion, either upwards towards the cavity of the mouth (O) or downwards towards the expansion of the throat (N). In the production of the grave sounds the windpipe (K) descends, and the inclination of the larynx (H) is towards the expansion of the throat (N). In the passage from the grave to the acute sounds, the windpipe (K) rises gradually, and the larynx (H) ascends, inclining towards the cavity of the mouth (O), thus causing the so-called head-vibration. During this action, the internal muscles of the larynx (K) either contract or dilate, gradually contracting for the acute sounds and dilating for the grave.

This elastic property of the muscles endows the rima glottidis (entrance of the glottis) with the power of forming itself into various spaces. Now every sound is generated in a space, and from these various spaces the different sounds of the voice take their origin, the *quality* of each individual voice being declared by the natural position of the organ in the throat.

The Different Positions of the Mouth, and the Effects Resulting from each Position.

When pronouncing the opening sound of the Italian A (*Anglice Ah*), the tongue lies nearly flat in the mouth, as represented at A, D, C. The uvula (E) and the soft palate (F) recede towards (G), the passage which communicates with the nose, thus causing a space of sufficient calibre to allow the sound to pass with perfect freedom, and with capability of vibration. At the commencement of the cultivation of a voice, this is perhaps the best position for practice, but the continuous habit of practising upon this position exclusively, is in my opinion injudicious if not positively injurious, especially in the production of the higher notes, as it throws the voice too far back in the throat and renders its quality too open. This subject will, however, be treated more fully hereafter.

The results which are obtained by singing in other positions are given below :—

1. The pronunciation of the sound O. Here the lips project. The muscles of the throat are compressed, and thus a free expansion of the sound is prevented. The sound is thick in quality, and is not capable of any vibratory power.

2. When the lips are extended too far laterally, a thin quality of sound is produced, since in this case the muscles of the throat and mouth are rendered stiff, and thus the sound possesses no capability of expansion and very little power of vibration.

If the teeth are too much closed, nearly the same effect is produced as when the mouth is shut, for the whole space is then compressed. The tongue curves in the direction A, B, C, and the soft palate (F) and the uvula (E) descend. The sound is thus prevented from issuing freely, and makes its way through the passage (G) which communicates with the nose. The sound thus becomes of a nasal quality.

If the construction of the vocal organ is not understood, and the voice is not formed on correct principles, the organ always remains in an imperfect condition, and this leads to incorrect intonation. The slightest effort or compression either disturbs or obstructs natural action ; at first the effect is not felt, but very soon the muscles become relaxed, and their flexible powers are lost. The voice becomes harsh, and the sounds are more and more imperfect, until the loss of correct intonation is attributed to want of ear in the singer, whereas the fault really consists in improper development of the organ, by which all sounds can be made only with effort.

In all uncultivated voices defects exist, and these defects are the same in all the different qualities of voice in the organs both of the female and of the male ; the same method of cultivation consequently must be employed in each, the only difference being that the male organisation is more rigid than that of the female, and therefore male voices cannot so easily be rendered flexible and extensive.

From what has been stated in earlier pages, it will be seen that the different voices may be classified as follows :—

1. Bass, Baritone, and Contralto.
2. Tenore Robusto and Mezzo-Soprano.
3. Tenore Leggiero and Soprano.

The organ of the Bass, Baritone, and Contralto being of strong muscular construction and difficult to render flexible, produces the most effect in sustained singing —*canto di portamento*. The Baritone is, however, softer and more flexible than the bass, and is therefore more adapted for dramatic effects and is of greater brilliancy.

The Tenore Robusto and Mezzo-Soprano are of full quality and capable of considerable flexibility. They are the most suited for the expression of the stronger as well as the more delicate sentiments and passions, especially in the recitative, which calls for energy and declamatory power. These voices are therefore cultivated for sacred music and grand opera (*opera seria*).

The Tenore Leggiero and Soprano, from their delicate muscular construction, are thin and light in quality, and usually weak or indistinct in the lower notes, since the vocal organ is situated high in the throat. They are not effective in the *canto di portamento*, and seldom even in drama. From their brilliancy of execution and clearness, they are chiefly cultivated for light opera and *opera bouffa*.

As a memento of his visit to Windsor Castle, the Queen has presented Mr. Baillie Hamilton with her portrait and autograph set in rich velvet and encased in a frame of silver filigree work, as a souvenir of his performance before Her Majesty on the vocalion at Windsor.—*Musical World.*

Correspondence.

"COUNTERPOINT."

TO THE EDITOR OF THE "MUSICAL STANDARD."

SIR,—I take an early opportunity of thanking Dr. Hiles for his manly and outspoken letter in your last issue It is only by means of very plain speaking that we can hope to make an impression on teachers who have for years been travelling along the old paths; but I believe that, in the end, the true principles of art will prove triumphant, and our present counterpoint text-books will be consigned to a well-deserved oblivion. Unfortunately for my argument, considerations of space appear to have forbidden the insertion in the *Musical Standard* of most of the examples with which I have illustrated the text of my lecture. My object was to prove the falsity of most contrapuntal rules by an appeal to the works of the great masters; and at the College of Organists I had lithographed copies of these extracts from classical authorities freely circulated amongst the audience. Owing to the omission of these illustrations, readers of my paper in the *Musical Standard* can hardly form a fair idea of the real strength of the position which I have felt bound to take up; but in order that the matter may be properly placed before the musical world, I am now making arrangements for the production of my paper in pamphlet form, with all the musical examples properly set out.

It certainly appears strange that musicians still continue to use books which not only abound with glaring contradictions and inconsistencies, but are also known to be founded on principles directly opposed to the works of the great composers. How can we profess to admire a symphony of Beethoven, and at the same time uphold a system of study which is in conflict with every page of the score? Yet musicians of good repute are doing this every day, and appear to think that the obsolete rules of bygone ages must remain in force for all time. The present system of examinations for degrees in music has much to answer for in this respect, and although I have been a consistent advocate of the examination system, I am bound to say that it is at present working badly for the cause of musical progress. The fault is not in the system itself, but in the misuse of it on the part of the powers that be, and to this result the plan of selecting text-books has largely contributed. Candidates should be judged by their *works* rather than by their *faith*, yet the text-book system offers a direct encouragement to the "crammers," who lose sight of the artistic aspect of music in a vain and unprofitable adherence to the shibboleths of the examination room. Those who plead for some reasonable revision of the contrapuntal system are gravely informed that counterpoint is a "means to an end," and that, although the rules may be opposed to truth, yet a course of study under their guidance is likely, in some mysterious way, to benefit the student. It is possible that those who do not care to look beneath the surface may be content with such an explanation, but the "means to an end" argument is in reality the strongest condemnation of the existing system. We may fairly ask, What is the "end" sought to be achieved? and we shall of course be told that the object of all musical theory is to place the learner in a position to compose music if he has the genius requisite for the task, or at least to understand and appreciate the works of the great masters. Here, then, is the *reductio ad absurdum* of the argument. A student is trained to compose music by a system of restrictive rules, yet it is admitted that he can only produce satisfactory and original work by a consistent violation of the dogmas which he has been taught. One might as reasonably expect a child to walk after having his legs tied together, or a grown man to acquire the art of swimming with the assistance (?) of a millstone around his neck. To put the case in another way, would any sane person attempt to teach astronomy, geography, or indeed any subject of general education, by means of text-books dated two centuries back? This is, however, the present condition of the art of counterpoint, and so it will remain unless a determined effort is made to shake off the obsolete fetters of a bygone age.

The fatal influence of the text-book system is directly responsible for the perpetuation of these errors, since students are compelled to work according to the ideas of the University Professors for the time being, and frequently to confess an adherence to views which are known to be erroneous. Sir George Macfarren's work was selected for criticism solely because it might be taken to represent the latest ideas of the most recently appointed University Professor; but I venture to say that if any other Cambridge text-book were found to contain a tithe of the errors and contradictions to be found in this work, it would be very quickly suppressed by the authorities.

I am aware that the enunciation of views such as these may place one, for a time, in a somewhat unenviable position, but that is a very small matter as compared with the interests of truth. Let it be remembered that the reform for which I am contending is no new thing. It dates from the writings of John Sebastian Bach, and our justification is to be found in every page of his incomparable Counterpoint."

As Dr. Hiles refer me to his own book on counterpoint, I may say that 'it was shewn to me a few weeks ago by a professional friend, and since then I have made a careful study of it. I earnestly advise every musician to do the same, and I believe most persons will rise from its perusal with a conviction of the truth of Dr. Hiles' theories, and a strong inclination to make a bonfire of any other counterpoint text-books which may happen to be in their possession.

I am Sir, yours faithfully,
HUMPHREY J. STARK.

Passing Events.

Sir G. A. Macfarren's oratorio, "David," written for the Leeds Festival, is in print, and is a work of a very high character.

The band of the Grenadier Guards, under the direction of Mr. D. Godfrey, gave a concert in Cardiff on August 15th.

Mr. J. Barnby's new psalm, written for the Leeds Festival, is said to be a work of much excellence, and to contain some effective choral writing.

The new oratorio, by Dr. G. B. Arnold, for Gloucester Festival, is being looked forward to as a work of much character and excellence.

The music trade season seems about to set in with considerable activity, and a large crop of new works, some of much importance, will be issued presently.

The new organ, built by Messrs. Brindley and Foster (consisting of 3 Manuals and Pedal organ, with some 40 stops), for the Albert Hall, Nottingham, will, it is said, be heard there for the first time next month.

It is said that the masterly pen of Mr. Joseph Bennett is secured for the analysis of the new and leading works to be performed at the approaching Leeds Festival; the works thus to be written about are Sir G. A. Macfarren's "David," Mr. Barnby's new "Psalm," etc.

The orchestra engaged for the Gloucester Festival includes many of our leading performers, and will doubtless prove an effective body of instrumentalists. Mr. C. L. Williams, the cathedral organist, has already proved himself to be an able conductor, and a notable Festival may be confidently expected.

Lord Garmoyle, the eldest son of Earl Cairns, is announced as about to be married to Miss Fortescue, a beautiful and clever actress at the Savoy Theatre. The lady, whose real name is Finney, and who is the daughter of the head of a large coal firm (Finney, Seal, & Co.), has, in the short time she has been upon the stage, won the respect and esteem of all who know her.—*Musical World*.

Speaking at the recent Eisteddfod, at Cardiff, Sir G. A. Macfarren strongly defended the claims of the old stave notation to general use, as most fully representing to the eye the multiform effects of sound, and as including many ingenious inventions. Upon the same occasion the Professor deprecated the habit, which prevails extensively in Wales, of singing too much from memory, and laid much stress upon the importance of constant practice in sight-seeing.

Despite the busy lives led by our leading musicians, and the still too largely prevailing neglect of our native composers, it is probable that no other country can, at the present time, show such a display of composing activity as is now being exhibited in England, and which will with due encouragement be enormously increased in the immediate future. Undoubtedly England is gradually taking up a leading position as a musical country, both from the productive and executive points of sight.

During the now fast departing summer season an unusually large number of American organists and musical people have visited England and the European continent, partly from motives of observation, and partly for pleasure. This aptitude for travelling on the part of our cousins, will undoubtedly be attended by the gain of enlarged views and a usefully extended experience; and to some extent will tend to rectify the prevailing leaning towards modern German art and art theories, which is now noticeable in the musical doings of the United States.

The Temple Church is now closed for the long vacation. The services will be resumed on October 7th.

The projected tour of Mr. Sims Reeves, which was to begin this week, will extend to the middle of October.

The programme of the Society of Arts Examinations for 1884 is now ready. Copies can be obtained gratis on application to the secretary.

A Musical Lectureship is part of the academical scheme of the new University College of South Wales and Monmouthshire. The College opens in Cardiff with the next term.

English opera is to be produced in New York next fall by Messrs. Brooks and Dickson at the Standard Theatre. Max Maretzek will be conductor, and a number of prominent artists will be members of the company. Two or three of Balfe's operas will be produced.

It is stated that Mr. F. H. Cowen is about to undertake a professional tour in the United States, on the invitation of Dr. Damrosch and Mr. George Henschel. He will conduct his cantata "St. Ursula," the "Scandinavian" Symphony, and other works.

The library of music of the late William Laidlaw, Esq. (of Liverpool), comprising full and vocal scores of operas, oratorios, and other works, publications of various musical societies, Handel's works by Arnold, orchestral parts of a large selection of compositions, theoretical treatises, etc., was to be sold by auction by Messrs. Puttick and Simpson on August 17th.

The *Athenæum* has it that the various Wagner societies in Germany have sent delegates to the number of 180 to Bayreuth to discuss the important question as to the future of the theatre in that town. It is said that the representations for next year are already assured, thanks to the disinterestedness of the artists, who will be content with a simple indemnity against loss in return for their services.

The Sacred Harmonic Society's offices have been removed to 12, John Street, Adelphi. The prospectus for the ensuing season will be ready early in September next, and will, it is thought, be found to contain works of such interest to the subscribers and friends of the society, and to the musical public and profession generally, as will command their hearty co-operation and support; and the council look forward with confidence to a success attending next season's concerts even greater than that attained by the last. It is announced that Mr. Charles Hallé will act as conductor, and Mr. W. H. Cummings as assistant conductor.

Not long ago, at a wedding in a village church, an amateur organist, in honour of the occasion, agreed to herald the entry of the bride into church and her exit therefrom by appropriate selections. The bride and bridegroom, and, indeed, all the persons immediately concerned, were what is known in society as "good" people, and there was a large assemblage of friends. The organist was equal—more than equal—to the occasion. As the bride, followed by her bridesmaids, entered the church, he crashed out the familiar strains, "See, the conquering hero comes." Perhaps it was a delicate attention on the part of the player with a view of inspiring courage into the bridegroom's heart.

In addition to being a thorough musician, Mdme. Rudersdorff was a most entertaining woman. The stories of her life are full of interest. She was a great favourite with the Princess Royal of England, who is now the Crown Princess of Prussia. Shortly after the marriage of the Princess, Madame Rudersdorff sang at a Court concert at Berlin, and was invited by the Crown Princess to breakfast with her. They breakfasted together informally, and afterwards madame sang several songs of Handel, the Princess's favourite composer, her royal hostess playing her accompaniments. After a while, the Princess proposed a visit to the nursery. As madame was sitting on the floor, with one child playing with the charms on her watch-chain, another hanging over her shoulder, and the baby in her arms, the door opened, and the Crown Prince walked in. The Princess arose and introduced her visitor. Madame looked up, and, with her ready tact and wit said, "Your Royal Highness, I must either disregard Court etiquette or drop the baby." The Prince bowed courteously, and said, with a smile, "Do what you like with etiquette, but regard the baby."

Dr. Spark, of the Leeds Town Hall, is giving a series of organ recitals in North Yorkshire, including Saltburn, Whitby, Market Weighton, Driffield, Beverley, Hull, etc. The first recital took place in the Parish Church, Saltburn, the programme including a concerto by Handel, a fugue by J. S. Bach, and other important and interesting works by Mendelssohn, Beethoven, Guilemont, Rossini, Batiste, and the performer himself, was highly appreciated by the audience. In the evening Dr. Spark presided at the organ at a festival of choirs, consisting of about 200 voices, and amongst the pieces sung with great effect was the new festival anthem, entitled, "And now, Israel, what doth the Lord thy God require of thee?" This piece, which formed quite the feature of the evening concert, is melodious and effective, and will be found useful for choirs. During the evening Dr. Spark performed several voluntaries of a character well suited to display the excellent organ built by Messrs. Foster and Andrews, Hull.

Surely the *claque* might be dispensed with at the opera! The *claquers* do their duty vigorously, but they check genuine applause, and this must, I should fancy, be of very much more value to singers than the applause they buy—for I take the individual singer, or her friends, to be responsible for the business. It is done in France, of course, and I gather from a recent event that it is now the habit in Italy. I judge so, because of what took place on the first night of a composition called "La Regina di Scozia" at the Folies Dramatiques. A lady dressed in black was seated in a stage-box. She had a large fan. When she opened the fan and used it, applause came from a section of the gallery in accordance with the vigour with which the fan was waved. When the instrument was 'elosed the applause ceased. All this was so neatly done that it must have been practised, and, as the company came from Italy, I assume that it was practised there.—*Illustrated Sporting and Dramatic News.*

Service Lists.

THIRTEENTH SUNDAY AFTER TRINITY.

AUGUST 19th.

London.

St. Paul's Cathedral.—Morn.: Service, Te Deum and Benedictus, Smart in F; Introit, Now my tongue, the mystery telling; Holy Communion, Smart in F. Even.: Service, Magnificat and Nunc Dimittis, Smart in F; Anthem, How beautiful are the feet, and Break forth into joy (Handel).

Foundling Chapel.—Morn.: Service, Tours in F; Anthem, God is our hope and strength (Greene). Aft.: Children's Service.

Holy Trinity, Gray's Inn Road.— Morn.: Service, Te Deum, Dykes in F; Jubilate, Chanted; Nicene Creed (Merbecke); Offertory Sentences (Grainger). Even.: Service, Magnificat, Parry in D; Nunc Dimittis, Chanted; Anthem, Solo and Chorus, Sing ye then, Let all men praise the Lord (Mendelssohn).

Holy Trinity, Tulse Hill.— Morn.: Chant Service. Even.: Service, Magnificat and Nunc Dimittis, Agutter in D; Anthem, How lovely are Thy dwellings (Spohr).

St. James's Private Episcopal Chapel, Southwark. —Morn.: Service, Introit, He is blessed that cometh (Mozart); Communion Service, Mozart in C, No. 1. Even.: Service, Stainer in E flat; Anthem, Hallelujah (Beethoven).

St. Magnus, London Bridge.—Morn.: Service, Opening Anthem, If we say (Calkin); Te Deum and Jubilate, Goss in A; Kyrie (Nares). Even.: Service, Cantate and Deus Misereatur, Goss in C; Anthem, To the Lord God (Goss).

St. Michael's, Cornhill. — Morn.: Service, Te Deum and Jubilate, Thorne in C; Anthem, Awake up my glory (Wise); Kyrie, Arnold in A; Creed, Stainer in G. Even.: Service, Magnificat and Nunc Dimittis, Thorne in E flat; Anthem, Thou, O God, art praised in Zion (Greene).

St. Margaret Pattens, Rood Lane, Fenchurch Street.—Morn.: Service, Te Deum, Smart in F; Benedictus, Dykes in F; Communion Service: Offertory Anthem, Lift thine eyes (Mendelssohn); Kyrie, Credo, Sanctus, Benedictus, Agnus Dei, and Gloria, Schubert in B flat. Even.: Service, Magnificat and Nunc Dimittis, Steggall in C; Anthem, From Thy love as a Father, "Redemption" (Gounod).

ST. PAUL'S, AVENUE ROAD, SOUTH HAMPSTEAD.—Morn.: Service, Te Deum, Tilleard in F; Benedictus, Turle; Kyrie, Tours in F; Offertory (Barnby); Credo, Sanctus and Gloria in excelsis, Tours in F. Even.: Service, Magnificat and Nunc Dimittis, Arnold in A; Anthem, Blessed are they (Tours).

ST. PAUL'S, BOW COMMON, E.—Morn.: Service, Te Deum and Benedictus, Chants; Holy Communion, Kyrie, Credo, Sanctus, and Gloria in excelsis, Dykes in F; Benedictus and Agnus Die, Redhead in F; Offertory (Stainer). Even.: Service, Magnificat and Nunc Dimittis, Tours in F; Anthem, O rest in thd Lord, and He that shall endure to the end (Mendelssohn).

ST AUGUSTINE AND ST. FAITH, WATLING STREET.—Morn.: Service, Garrett in E; Introit, The Lord is the strength (South); Communion Service, Smart in F (throughout). Even.: Service, Gadsby in C; Anthem, Praise His awful name (Spohr).

ST. SAVIOUR'S, HOXTON. — Morn.: Service, Te Deum, Smart in F; Holy Communion; Kyrie, Credo, Sursum Corda, Sanctus, and Gloria in excelsis, Tours in F. Even.: Service, Magnificat and Nunc Dimittis, Stainer in F; Anthem, Lord how long (Mendelssohn).

ST. MARY BOLTONS, WEST BROMPTON, S.W.—Morn.: Service, Te Deum, Benedictus, Goss in C; Holy Communion, Kyrie, Credo, Sanctus, and Agnus Dei and Gloria in excelsis, Monk in C; Offertory (Barnby). Even.: Service, Magnificat and Nunc Dimittis, Arnold in A; Anthem, He that shall endure to the end (Mendelssohn).

ST. SEPULCHRE'S, HOLBORN. — Morn: Service, Dykes in F; Anthem, Call to remembrance (Farrant). Even.: Service, Porter in D; Anthem, O taste and see (Goss).

Country.

ST. ASAPH CATHEDRAL.— Morn.: Service, Tours in F; Anthem, The Lord is my Shepherd (Macfarren). Even.: Service, The Litany; Anthem, Praise the Lord (Elvey).

ASHBURNE CHURCH, DERBYSHIRE. — Morn.: Service: Garrett in F; Kyrie, Credo and Gloria, Garrett in B flat. Even.: Service, Musgrave in F; Anthem, O come, let us worship (Mendelssohn).

BABBACOMBE (ALL SAINTS).—Morn: Service, Plain Song; Communion Service; Kyrie, Credo, Sanctus, Benedictus, Agnus Dei, Gloria in excelsis, Mozart's 1st Mass in C. Even.: Service, Magnificat and Nunc Dimittis, Faux Bourdons; Anthem, Hear my prayer (Mendelssohn).

BIRMINGHAM (S. ALBAN THE MARTYR.—Morn.: Service, Te Deum and Benedictus, Dykes in F; Holy Communion; Kyrie, Credo, Sanctus, Gloria, Dykes in F; Benedictus and Agnus Dei, Redman in D. Evensong: Magnificat and Nunc Dimittis, Parry in D.

BIRMINGHAM (ST. CYPRIAN'S, HAY MILLS).—Morn.: Service, Cobb in G; Anthem, O clap your hands (Stainer). Even.: Service, Cobb in G; Anthem, This is the day (Elvey).

DONCASTER (PARISH. CHURCH).—Morn.: Service, Calkin in B flat. Even.: Service, Calkin in B flat; Anthem, The Lord is King (Trimnell).

DUBLIN, ST. PATRICK'S (NATIONAL) CATHEDRAL.—Morn.: Service, Te Deum and Jubilate, Aldrich in G; Holy Communion, Kyrie, Creed, Sanctus, Aldrich in G; Anthem, Rejoice in the Lord (Purcell). Even.: Service, Magnificat and Nunc Dimittis, Wheeler in C; Anthems, Distracted with care (Haydn) and O Lord Thou art my God (Haydn and Gaudry).

ELY CATHEDRAL.—Morn.: Service, Te Deum, Leslie in D; Benedictus, Plain Song; Kyrie, Credo, and Gloria, Richardson in F; Anthem, O that I knew (Bennett). Even.: Service, Anthem, The Lord hath done great things (Smart).

FOLKESTONE (ST. MICHAELS).—Morn.: Service, Communion Service, Mozart in C. Even.: Service, Magnificat and Nunc Dimittis, Garrett in F; Anthem, Come unto me (Husband).

HARROGATE (ST. PETER'S CHURCH). — Morn.: Service, Te Deum (Helmore); Benedictus, Chant; Anthem, Out of the Deep (Mozart); Kyrie (M. S.); Credo (Goss). Even.: Service, Magnificat and Nunc Dimittis, Tours in F; Anthem, As pants the hart (Spohr).

LLANDAFF CATHEDRAL.—Morn.: Service, Te Deum and Jubilate, Smart in G; The Litany. Even.: Service, Magnificat and Nunc Dimittis, Ebdon in C; Anthem, O Lord, how manifold (Barnby).

LICHFIELD CATHEDRAL. — Morn.: Service, Barnby in E; Communion Service, Barnby in E; Anthem, My song shall be of mercy (Kent). Even.: Service, Barnby in E; Anthem, O, God, when Thou appearest, "Splendente Te Deus" (Mozart).

LEEDS (ST. LAURENCE CHURCH, PUDSEY). — Morn.: Service, Te Deum and Jubilate, Chants; Kyrie and Credo, Best in F; Sanctus, Gibbons in C; Offertory Sentences, Strickland in D. Even. Service, Magnificat and Nunc Dimittis, Chants; Anthem, Lord God of Heaven (Spohr).

LIVERPOOL CATHEDRAL.—Aft.: Service, Magnificat and Nunc Dimittis, Banks in E flat; Anthem, The healing of blind Bartimaeus (Burstall).

LIVERPOOL (ST. CUTHBERT'S, EVERTON).—Morn.: Service, Holy Communion, Smart in F. Even.: Service, Smart in F; Anthem, O where shall wisdom (Boyce).

MANCHESTER CATHEDRAL.—Morn.: Service, Full Communion Service, Stainer in E flat; Anthem, O taste and see (Goss). Aft.: Service, Stainer in E flat; Anthem, How lovely are Thy dwellings fair (Spohr).

MANCHESTER (ST. BENEDICT'S).—Morn.: Service, Te Deum, Sullivan in D; Kyrie and Credo, (Mercadante); Sanctus, Benedictus, and Agnus Dei, "Messe Solennelle" (Rossini). Even.: Service, Magnificat and Nunc Dimittis, Tours in F.

MANCHESTER (ST. JOHN BAPTIST, HULME).—Morn.: Service, Kyrie, Credo, Sanctus, Benedictus, Agnus Dei, and Gloria in excelsis, Agutter in B flat. Even.: Service, Magnificat and Nunc Dimittis, Bunnett in F.

PETERBOROUGH CATHEDRAL.—Morn.: Service, Ross in G; Introit, Send out Thy light; Communion Service, Smart in F. Even.: Service, King in C; Anthem, Wherewithal (Elvey).

ROCHESTER CATHEDRAL. — Morn.: Service, Smart in F; Anthem, O come every one (Mendelssohn). Even.: Service, Smart in F; Anthem, The Lord is very great (Beckwith).

SALISBURY CATHEDRAL. Morn.: Service, Te Deum, Benedictus, Kyrie and Credo, Parry in D; Offertory (Stainer). Aft.: Service, Magnificat and Nunc Dimittis, Parry in D; Anthem, Come let us sing (Mendelssohn).

SHERBORNE ABBEY. — Morn.: Service, Te Deum, Chants; Kyrie, Smart in G; Offertories (Barnby). Even.: Service, Anthem, O sing unto the Lord (Lyle).

WELLS CATHEDRAL. — Morn.: Service, Mendelssohn in A; Introit, Drop down ye Heavens (Macfarren); Kyrie, Cooke in G. Even.: Service, Smart in F; Anthem, I was in the Spirit (Blow).

WORCESTER CATHEDRAL.—Morn.: Service, Smart in F; Anthem, Cast thy burden (Mendelssohn). Even. Service, Smart in F; Anthem, Praise His awful name (Spohr).

APPOINTMENT·

Mr. ERNEST SLATER, R.A.M., A.C.O. (late Assistant Organist of Exeter Cathedral), has been appointed Organist and Choir Master of Lambeth Palace Church.

Printed for the Proprietor by BOWDEN, HUDSON & Co., at 23, Red Lion Street, Holborn, London, W.C. ; and Published by WILLIAM REEVES, at
the Office, 185, Fleet Street, E.C. West End Agents :—WEEKES & CO., 14, Hanover Street, Regent Street, W. Subscriptions and Advertisements are
received either by the Publisher or West End Agents.—*Communications for the EDITOR are to be forwarded to his private address, 6, Argyle Square, W.C.*
SATURDAY, AUGUST 18, 1883.—*Entered at the General Post Office as a Newspaper.*

The MUSICAL STANDARD

A NEWSPAPER FOR MUSICIANS PROFESSIONAL AND AMATEUR

No. 995. Vol. XXV. FOURTH SERIES. SATURDAY, AUGUST 25, 1883. WEEKLY: PRICE 3D.

MOZART'S ORGAN WORKS.

By FRANK J. SAWYER, B.Mus. Oxon., F.C.O.

[A Lecture delivered at the College of Organists.]

LADIES AND GENTLEMEN,—In coming before you to-night, I feel that my first duty is to make some sort of explanation of the sudden change that has come over the subject of my lecture from that first announced—"The Organ Writers of the Nineteenth Century"—to that with which I hope to interest you, viz., "Mozart's Writings for the Organ."

It is not saying, I feel sure, too much, if I assert, that a few months ago, out of every hundred organists, barely one, if indeed *one*, had the slightest idea that Mozart had, with the exception of a work for the "king of instruments." To such ignorance I must myself plead guilty. Imagine, then, my surprise, when, on searching "Köchel's Thematic Catalogue of Mozart's Works," I accidentally found allusion made to 15 organ sonatas ; all, however, with the note "unpublished."

A preliminary notice of the scope of these compositions appeared, by kindness of the editor, in the columns of the *Musical Standard*, while an enquiry at the firm of Messrs. Breitkopf & Härtel, of Leipzig, elicited a reply and copy of these sonatas, recently printed in the complete edition of all Mozart's works now being prepared by that firm. Still further allusion was made to them in a paper read before the Musical Association by Mr. Prout, and entitled "The Use of the Organ with the Orchestra," an article subsequently reprinted in the pages of the *Musical Record.*

So far the subject had advanced when I suggested to the Council of the College of Organists that I might be allowed to take it up in lieu of that already announced; a suggestion which, I need not say, was accepted.

I propose first of all to see the state of organ music when these 15 organ sonatas, which form the special topic of this evening's lecture, were written. Mozart, born Jan. 27, 1756, must at a very tender age have begun his studies on the organ, since we find that when only seven years old he performed in the chief churches of the towns through which, in his early travels, he passed. The first question naturally is: From what had he studied? Bach had been dead then about 12 years; and there would, perhaps, be little possibility, in those days of heavy locomotion, of the great Leipzig cantor's works being widely dispersed, especially as, perhaps then as now, they were "too good for the money." Froberger and Frescobaldi would doubtless in his studies have represented the early school, together, perhaps, with pieces by Pachelbel and Kerl; still, these could scarcely represent the entire scope of his studies for the organ, and one must therefore suppose that other works were then to hand of which we at present know nothing. Organ music occupies, undoubtedly, an anomalous position among the various branches of the art. While the early writers for the voice, the piano or harpsichord, the violin, the opera, and the oratorio, have received attention—first at the hands of the archæologist, and lastly at the hands of the more general public—the past of organ music has remained almost a blank. It is not, perhaps, difficult to trace the reason of this. An organist's performances are almost entirely in Church, and at a time when little particular attention is paid and no enthusiasm evinced. In fact, as some clergy would put it, the organist's performance is merely a noise to cover the tread of the approaching or departing congregation.

Again: there was always up to the beginning of this century, with the exception of the Handel school, a seriousness and earnestness in organ music that would not arouse public interest. Hence we of to-day are left to solace ourselves with merely the name and none of the works of many a great composer. Let us hope, however, that as the position of the organist is gradually bettering itself, so the scope of organ music will extend, reaching not only forward to the moderns but backwards to the ancients.

That the music Mozart studied made, comparatively speaking, no influence on his organ compositions, those performed to-night will testify, for in them we find no traces of any one, save "Mozart himself" pure and simple.

Whatever works may have formed the infant prodigy's organ practice, the fact remains that at the early age of five years he must have devoted himself to the instrument. His father, Leopold Mozart, is known to us only as a violinist, yet he, too, was, according to Otto Jahn, an "excellent organist," and thus doubly well fitted to fill the post he so self-sacrificingly occupied of tutor to his marvellous little son. And so readily had the son profited that, when at the age of seven, he set out on his first travels, we read, "At the monastery of Ips, while their travelling companions, three monks, were saying mass, Wolfgang mounted to the organ loft, and played so admirably that the Franciscan friars, and the guests they were entertaining, rose from table and came open-mouthed with astonishment to listen to him."

The next interesting point in Mozart's organ life we find in a letter of his father. On their second journey from Salzburg in 1763, the carriage broke down at Wasserbrunn, thus delaying them. "The last new thing is," writes the father, "that in order to pass the time, we went to look at the organ, and I explained the pedals to Wolferl. He set to work on the spot; pushed the stool away, and preluded, always standing, using the pedal as if he had practised it for months. We were all lost in astonishment. What has caused others months of practice, comes to him as a gift of God." Another hidden point of interest lies in this narrative: had the organs previously used possessed pedals, the inquiring mind of Mozart would never have left them even so long unused, but even if unable from his youthful stature to reach them, would have *understood* their use. Hence we may perhaps surmise that in 1750 pedals were *not* universal to organs.

During this journey, "Wolfgang performed on the organ constantly, and was even more admired as an organist than as a clavier player"; for instance, "Making an excursion to Heidelberg, Wolfgang played the organ at the Church of the Holy Spirit, and so astonished his audience that the Dean ordered his name to be inscribed as a memorial on the organ." The announcement of his last Frankfort concert, as "the boy who is not yet seven summers,—he will finally, both on the harpsichord and the organ, improvise as long as may be desired, and in any key; thus proving that he is as thoroughly acquainted with the one instrument as with the other, great as is the difference between them."

Again, when, after the Paris visit, he arrived in London, and was received in such a friendly manner by George III. and Queen Charlotte, we find when summoned to the court he played various pieces by Bach, Abel, and Handel, at sight, at his Majesty's request, and then "surpassed his clavier playing when he sat down to the King's organ."

On his return through Holland, we find him playing on the organ at the Church of S. Bernhard, and at Haarlem.

During the period of quiet study in Salzburg we find nothing of special note to us to-night, nor during the production of his earliest operas in Vienna.

In December, 1769, we find him starting for Italy with his father. His reception was marvellous. At Roveredo, "when he wanted to play the organ at the principal church, the report of it spread through the town, and the church was so full that it took two strong men to clear the way to the choir, and then it was a quarter of an hour before they could get to the organ, they were so besieged by the audience." When he played at the church of St. Thomas, at Verona, the scene was repeated. "The press was so great that they were obliged to get into the church through the monastery, and even then they could hardly have reached the organ had not the monks formed a ring round them, and so made a way through the crowd." "When it was over the noise was still greater, for every one wanted to see the little organist."

But we have not time to-night to watch the youthful Mozart through all his organ triumphs. In 1775 we find the first definite trace of a composition for the instrument that had been the means of bringing him so many laurels.

In July of that year the first dated sonata appears, and here it becomes necessary to explain the nature and scope of these works, which cannot be better done than by quoting the passage *in extenso* from Jahn:—" At Salzburg, as Mozart told Padre Martini, a sonata was introduced between the Epistle and the Gospel, until Archbishop Hieronymus (or Colloredo) replaced it by a gradual in 1783."

Kochel, in his great thematic catalogue of Mozart's works, says:—"The organ sonatas were introduced at High Mass between the Gloria and the Credo."

To continue from Jahn:—"They are all inscribed as sonatas, and all consist of a lively movement of moderate length in two parts, and in regulation sonata form. The Church sonatas (*sonati di chiesa*) differ, indeed, from the chamber sonatas (*sonata di camera*) in being serious, dignified, often fugued and in counterpoint, but the style has nothing that suggests a sacred performance. The tone is neither solemn nor devotional, nor the style severe. The tone and treatment of the commencement remind us of the first movements of the smaller sonatas and quartets; the subjects are, sometimes, very pretty; the treatment is free and skilful, and in the later pieces not without touches of Mozart's originality. They are usually written for two violins and violoncello, to which the organ part was always added, but never obbligato (?), nor with any regard to executive display; it has often only its customary office of accompaniment to the 'cello, in which case a figured bass part is written. Even when the organ part is independent, it is for the most part limited to what the skilful organist can make out of the *continuo;* its independence is very modest, and it never aspires to a solo or any passages."

So Jahn says, but I think you will shortly agree with me, that these strictures are not merited.

(To be continued.)

It seems that the projected Italian season at Paris is to consist of from twenty to twenty-five performances, which are to be held at the Théâtre des Nations. The direction is in the hands of MM. Corti. Their artistic representative is the excellent baritone M. Maurel; Signor Faccio has been secured as musical conductor; and among the singers already engaged or likely to be engaged are Mesdames Devriès, Tremelli, Reske, and C. de Vère, and MM. Gayarré and Reske. Wagner's "Lohengrin" will be one of the attractions. The prices are fixed as follows : Avant-scène, 35 francs; Loges de face, 30 francs; Loges de côté, 25 francs; Loges de 1re galerie, 20 francs; Loges de 2de galerie, 15 francs. The price of the fauteuils has not yet been fixed, but will probably be 20 francs.

Musical Intelligence.

LEEDS MUSICAL FESTIVAL.

The first great musical festival in Leeds was held as part of the inaugural ceremony, when the Town Hall was opened by the Queen, on September 7th, 1858. The four days following were devoted to the festival, Professor W. Sterndale Bennett being the conductor. The works produced on that occasion included "Elijah," the "Messiah," "Israel in Egypt," "Mount of Olives," "Stabat Mater," Haydn's "Seasons" (Spring and Summer), Bach's "Passions Music" (St. Matthew), and Bennett's "May Queen," then produced for the first time. In September, 1860, a public meeting, convened by the mayor, also resolved to continue the festivals. A committee was formed, and Dr. Bennett was again invited to become the conductor. Many of the works were selected, and preliminary arrangements were entered into with the principal singers. Unforeseen difficulties, however, arose, which were of so serious a nature that in May, 1861, the committee passed the following resolution :—" That considering all the circumstances and difficulties attending the organization of the arrangements of the musical festival, and the doubts entertained of its success, it is desirable that no festival be held this year." From that period no attempt was made to revive festivals in Leeds till 1874, when the then mayor (Ald. Marsden), convened a meeting of the principal inhabitants, and again it was determined to establish, if possible, Leeds Triennial Musical Festivals. Under the conductorship of Sir Michael Costa, a festival was held. The chief works produced were "St. Paul," the "Messiah," part of "Israel in Egypt," Mendelssohn's "Lobgesang," Henry Smart's "Bride of Dunkerron," Macfarren's oratorio "St. John the Baptist," "Stabat Mater," and Schumann's "Paradise and the Peri." Three years afterwards (1877), the committee felt justified in giving a commission to Professor Macfarren to write a new work. On that occasion the oratorio of "Joseph" was written, and was for the first time produced. The other works included "Elijah," "Solomon," Mozart's "Requiem," Beethoven's "Mount of Olives," Mendelssohn's "Walpurgis Night," and Bach's Magnificat in D. Sir Michael Costa was the conductor. In 1880 the festival was in every way a great success. Mr. (now Sir Arthur) Sullivan accepted the important position of conductor. The band and chorus were enlarged to 420 performers. Mr. Jas. Broughton being the chorus-master, and Mr. J. T. Carrodus the principal of the violinists. The chief works were—the "Elijah," Handel's "Samson," Beethoven's Mass in C, Haydn's "Creation" (Parts 1 and 2), Spohr's "Last Judgment," Sullivan's "Martyr of Antioch" (written for the festival), Bennett's "May Queen," Beethoven's Choral Symphony, and a new cantata by J. F. Barnett, "The Building of the Ship." For the festival arranged to be held this year, three new works have been composed. These are—"King David," an oratorio by Sir George Macfarren; "Gray's "Elegy," a cantata, by Alfred Cellier; and the 97th Psalm, by Joseph Barnby. The composition by the late Joachim Raff, which may properly be termed a symphony-oratorio, was the last great work of that prolific German musician. When the committee in the early part of last year decided to perform the oratorio at the next festival, they invited the composer to conduct his own work. Shortly afterwards, the death of Herr Raff ensued; but the following extract from a letter shows that it was his intention to comply with the committee's request :—Mdme. Raff wrote on July 24th, 1882, as follows :—" It was one of his last occupations to enter the excellently translated words of his oratorio 'Weltende,' into the manuscript, in order to get the work ready for the Leeds Musical Festival. He had quite made up his mind to attend the performance at Leeds personally, and this occasion would have been his first visit to England. But, alas ! it was not to be so." The band will comprise the best London instrumentalists, and a few local players. It will be seen that the chorus has been selected from Leeds and various towns in the West Riding. There were 700 applicants in response to an advertisement ; and every one of these was tested individually and alone, both for voice and reading ability. Of these, the best 320 were engaged. Already, up to the issue of this programme, 29 full rehearsals have been held, members of the chorus being brought by railway from parts of the Riding outside Leeds. Before the festival takes place, about 44 full chorus rehearsals will have been held, besides several sectional rehearsals. The programme is here outlined:—Wednesday morning, October 10th, Oratorio, "Elijah" (Mendelssohn); organist, Dr. Spark. Wednesday evening, Cantata (written for this festival), "Gray's Elegy" (Alfred Cellier), conducted by the composer, and a miscellaneous selection; organist, Mr. Walter Parratt. Thursday morning, Symphony-oratorio, "The World's end, the Judgment, the New World" (Joachim Raff) (first time in England); organist, Mr. Walter Parratt. selection from the works of Handel, organist, Dr. Spark. Thursday evening, 97th Psalm, "The Lord is King" (Joseph Barnby), conducted by the composer (written for this festival), organist, Dr. Spark; Motet No. 3 "Glory, Praise, and Honour" (Mozart); Sacred cantata, "Thou Guide of Israel" (Bach) (first performance in this country); Oratorio, "Stabat Mater" (Rossini), organist, Dr. Spark. Friday morning, Oratorio "King David" (Sir George Macfarren), (written for this festival), organist Mr. Walter Parratt. Friday evening, secular Cantata "The Crusaders" (Niels Gade), and a selection. Saturday morning, Grand Mass in D (Beethoven); Symphony cantata "Hymn of Praise" ("Lobgesang"), (Mendelssohn). Saturday evening, extra miscellaneous concert, consisting of selections from the Festival works. Band, chorus, and principals.

CORK.

(From our own Correspondent.)

On Sunday, the 12th inst., the Exhibition buildings were thrown open to the public, notwithstanding a determined opposition on the part of some of the exhibitors. The sequel proved the committee to have been right, as an immense crowd paid for admittance on that day. At 3 p.m. Herr H. C. Swertz gave an organ recital of a sacred character, of which the following were the principal pieces played. Overture, "Last Judgment" (Spohr); air, "I waited for the Lord" (Mendelssohn); "March to Calvary" ("Redemption") (Gounod); "Cum Sancto Spiriti" (3rd Mass) (Cherubini). On Monday evening following, he gave another recital, of a mixed character, consisting of pieces by Hérold, Chopin, Weber, Mendelssohn, etc., and was much applauded, one of the items being encored.—The students of the Cork School of Music, under the conductorship of Mr. T. J. Sullivan, gave a concert on Tuesday evening, consisting of Spohr's "Last Judgment," and a second part, miscellaneous. They were not, however, as successful as one could wish, the number of voices employed failing to fill the hall, besides being very unevenly balanced. The orchestra was also too large in parts, quite drowning the voices. The second part was much better, and as deserving of special praise I must mention the following: Miss O'Connell and Mr. FitzGibbon for their singing of the duet from Spohr's oratorio, "Forsake me not;" and Miss Bayly, Miss O'Keefe, and Miss Weekes for their piano playing. Miss O'Hanlon was also very successful in Bishop's song, "Tell me, my heart"; her voice, though not very powerful, being exceedingly well cultivated. Mr. FitzGibbon also sang "Salve Dimora" from Gounod's "Faust," with violin obbligato by Capt. Haynes.

F. ST. JOHN LACY.

The recent performances of "Parsifal" at Bayreuth appears to have given much artistic satisfaction to the disciples of the departed master. The principal parts were this year distributed as follows:—Parsifal, Herren Winkelmann, of Vienna, and Gudehus, of Dresden. Kundry, Mmes. Materna, of Vienna, and Malten, of Dresden. Gurnemanz, Herren Scaria, of Vienna, and Siehr, of Munich. Amfortas, Herr Reichermann, of Vienna. Klingsor, Herren Fuchs of Munich, and Degele of Dresden. Titurel, Herr Fuchs of Munich. The orchestra consisted of thirty-six violins, twelve violas, twelve violoncellos, eight double basses, four flutes, four oboes, one alto oboe, four clarinets, one bass clarinet, four bassoons, one double bassoon, six horns, three trumpets, four trombones, one bass tuba, two drummers (kettle-drums), and four harps. Herren H. Lewi and Franz Fischer, of Munich, were the conductors.

Foreign Musical Intelligence.

MUSIC IN PARIS.

(From our Own Correspondent.)

PARIS, August 21st, 1883.

It may seem rather early to speak of the novelties, or quasi-novelties, with which we are to be entertained in Paris during the approaching season: but so dull, flat, and uneventful has this Summer been here, so devoid of the faintest musical interest; so drearily, drowsily, and dismally unmusical, indeed, that there is nothing else worth writing to you about at present. With a free and easy disregard of its duty which we have for years past somehow tolerated and grown resigned to, the management of the Opéra Comique has closed the doors of that theatre for a couple of months, and will not re-open them for another ten days or so. The Opéra has been open three times weekly, as usual at this season; but, ever since the June sun drove Parisians to the sea-side, M. Vancorbeil has offered us wretched casts and the stalest of *repertoires*. Of concerts (unless those at the Jardin d'Acclimation and the parks be accepted) we have had none—none at least worthy the name; for really one cannot apply the word to the sinister rubbish played and sung in the Champs Elysées of nights; and even at the Trocadéro, where we *do* occasionally hear an organ recital in August, nothing has been done this year. A stupid tradition still prevents. *impresarii* from venturing on the experiment of Summer classical concerts. The Paris Biergarten is, and bids fair long to be, a dream of the future. For "the quarter of an hour" we are all supposed to have forgotten Beethoven, and to have developed a taste for the prurient balderdash now dignified by the name of *chansonettes*, and until September comes, bringing back the scattered Parisians to their beloved asphalte, we shall have to "possess our souls in patience."

Early in September, however, the Opéra Comique will give us a revival of Félicien David's "Perle du Brésil," for the *rentrée* of Miss Emma Nevada (who, by-the-by, has been winning golden opinions lately at Aix-les-Bains.) This may be followed by the production of a new opera, by M. Poise, the composer of so many charming and delicate trifles, and by the revival (not a very much needed one) of M. Joncières' "Dimitre." But the event of the season at the Opéra Comique will doubtless be the first performance of a new 3-act opera by M. Massenet, founded on the fascinating story of Manon Lescaut, and entitled "Manon." In deference to the nice morals of the age, the librettists of "Manon" have altered the characters of the Abbé Prévost's hero and heroine considerably. We are to be shown a revised, reformed, and respectable Chevalier des Grieux, at all events, and his light-o'-love will be made as decorous as may be humanly possible. M. Massenet has been working at the opera in the sunny South for some time past, but is expected back in Paris within the fortnight.

At the Opéra, with all respect to M. Dubois and his ballet "La Farandole," the most interesting feature by far of the season will probably be the long hoped for revival of Gounod's "Sapho." Not that I anticipate it will prove a success, however carefully or splendidly it may be put upon the stage. There is a monotony about its beauty—a weariness of nobleness, if I may use the expression—which will, I fear, always prevent its being "popular." Still, judging from the fragments we have heard on several occasions lately at the Conservatoire, to all true lovers of music, to all artists and people of delicate culture, the reappearance of "Sapho" on the stage, after all these years of oblivion, will be looked forward to with delighted curiosity, and overshadow all other events at the Opéra—even the possible production of M. Salvayre's "Richard III.," of which there has been some talk again.

The Théâtre Italica—as the Théâtre de Nations (the ex-Lyrique) will shortly be rechristened—is likely to open with the revised versions of "Simon Boccanegra" and "Don Carlos." These may be followed by the "Herodiade" of M. Massenet, and, it is hoped, by the production (at last!) of M. Boito's "Mefistofele."

A fourth opera-house, doomed only too certainly to speedy failure, is to be given us at the Chateau d'Eau, where we are promised a revival of Mermet's "Roland à

Roncevaux"—which, I fear, will seem rather antiquated to the ears of this generation. The Chateau d'Eau management, mindful of the passing triumph scored by the fortunate impresario who introduced Paris to M. Prevost some years ago, will trust for its chances of success more to a marvellous new tenor, named Rouvière, who is to be the "star" of its company.

I need scarcely trouble you with very particular details of the opéra bouffes which are to be given us next season. Amongst them is a new work by M. Hervé, entitled "Vertigo," and one by M. Sellenick, the well-known bandmaster, to be called "Le fou Chopine."

M. Ambroise Thomas has been seriously ill for weeks past ; but I am glad to say he is now better.

C. HARRY MELTZER.

Selections from Berlioz's works have been given lately at the concerts in Brussels.

The *Courier de la Meuse* speaks highly of the quartet performances of MM. Wolf, E. Ludwig, Ender, and Jules Thys at Maestricht, in Holland, at a concert recently given there.

The concerts of the sea-side season at the Casino, Ostend, are said to be excellent. The singing of M. and Mdme. Padilla Artôt there is reported as being artistic and successful.

The death of Antony Mocker took place in Paris on July 26th. He was born at Marseille in 1795, and was an esteemed pianist, composer for the pianoforte, and professor at the Conservatoire, Paris.

The Opéra Comique, Paris, will be re-opened in the beginning of September. The rehearsals of "Joli Gilles," by MM. Monselet and Poise, will presently be resumed, so as to be ready for performance in September.

It is reported that besides Reyer's "Sigurd," the Théâtre de la Monnaie (Brussels) will probably next winter bring to a hearing a grand opera by Henri Litolf, entitled "Les Templiers."

Among the victims of the terrible catastrophe at Casamicciola were Giovanni de Monte, violoncellist, L. Gravina, announced in the Italian papers as an English composer and pianist, and several well-known nonprofessional performers of talent.

Upon the façade of 202, Rue Saint Honoré, Paris, an inscription has been placed, stating that the old theatre once standing there was occupied by Molière's company in 1641 and by the Royal Academy of Music (or opera) from 1673 to 1781.

François A. d'Albert Doppler died at Baben near Vienna, on July 28th. He was born in 1821, and was a composer of ability, a good flute player, chef d'orchestre at the Court Theatre, and a professor at the Conservatoire, Vienna.

It is stated that Gounod has for the summer months taken up his abode at Nieuport. On a former occasion he finished there his opera "Zamora" ; this time he will be busy with the alteration of "Sapho," and no doubt with his new oratorio for the next Birmingham Festival.

M. Mathis Lussy, one of the contributors to *Le Ménestrel*, is writing on "Musical Rhythm." He rightly attaches high importance to the full consideration of this subject, which, notwithstanding its necessary presence in all music, is much neglected as a systematic study.

La Tribune de Genève tells that the Lutheran Church of that town is preparing to celebrate the 400th anniversary of the Reformer by the performance of a kind of oratorio entitled "Luther at Worms." This work, by Meinardus, has been written some years, and will be executed, it is reported, in a large number of towns.

The question of continuing the Bayreuth Theatre performances has been seriously discussed by the various Wagner Societies, and, as the artists have agreed to perform with salaries for the next year, it is hoped that afterwards an arrangement will be made so that the theatre may become a permanent institution.

Suppé has completed some time ago his operetta "The Blue Rose," and it will be given in Vienna. The scene is laid in Russia, and a love episode between the Empress Katherine and the Potemkin furnishes the plot. Suppé is now engaged, it is stated, on a serious work for the Vienna Grand Opera, "The Vendetta." The plot is laid in Corsica, the home of Napoleon I.

The *Grand Prix* of the Conservatoire, Paris, has been won by M. Vidal, a pupil of Massenet ; the *Premier Second Grand Prix* by M. Dubussy, a pupil of Guiraud ; and the *Deuxieme Second Grand Prix* by M. René, a pupil of Léo-Delibes. Their task consisted in the setting to music the lyric scene "Le Gladiateur," by M. E. Moreau.

A new Wagner society, it is announced, has been founded. Its object is the continuation of Bayreuth dramatic festival performances. The rules, which were put into circulation some weeks ago, comprise 24 paragraphs. The contribution of members is four shillings per annum, and the *Bayreuther Blätter*, the organ of the society, will be supplied to them at the reduced price of six shillings.

The German theatres announce operatic performances of interest. At Berlin Lortzing's "Ondine," and possibly Delibes's "Lakmé" ; at Cologne, A. G. Thomas's "Esmeralda" and Delibes's "Lakmé"; at Hamburg, Rubinstein's "Sulamite" and Mackenzie's "Colomba"; at Frankfort, Dresden, Munich, Leipzic and Prague, "Lakmé" will be given ; at Bremen, F. Thomas's "Mignon" ; at Vienna, Wagner's "Tristan" and most likely "Lakmé," etc. Of all recent works, "Lakmé" appears to have attained the largest popularity in Germany.

A BIRTHDAY LETTER.

In a recent issue of the *Deutsche Rundschau* was published a letter, written by Richard Wagner to his mother upon her birthday. Herewith is appended a literal translation, from an American musical contemporary :—

My DEAR MOTHER :—It is so long since I have offered you my congratulations on your birthday, that I am really glad for this once to avail myself of the right day—which the pressure of business has so often in former years caused me to overlook—and to tell you how rejoiced I am that you are still spared to us—that I can still look forward to sitting with your hand in mine, recalling the days when my youth was nourished and fostered by your tender care. Nothing but the consciousness of your presence among us would suffice to unite your children into a family ; we, driven hither and thither by the winds of life, ever forming new ties, new interests, find our bond of union in the thought of the dear old mother who has never had a tie but that which bound her to her children. God grant that this happiness may be ours for many years to come, and may He long preserve in you so clear a mind that the only earthly joy which remains for you—the joy and sympathy in the well-being of your children—may be yours to the very end ! Perplexed, as I often am, by the riddle of life, now urged forward, now held back, always striving after perfection, seldom attaining the success I long for, wearied and disgusted by contact with the outer world, and by the contradiction of my dearest hopes, the only pleasure that never fails me is in the enjoyment of nature. When I fling myself with bitter tears and lamentations into her arms, she consoles and strengthens me by showing me what fancied sorrows they are that oppress mankind. We lose ourselves in striving after an impossible ideal ; then Nature calls us gently back, and would fain convince us that we are her children as surely as the trees and plants which spring from seed and shoot upwards, warmed by the sun and strengthened by the fresh air, to live on until they have scattered the seed which is to renew the eternal youth of all created. If I can once grasp the idea that I, too, belong to this bountiful Nature, my thoughts are no longer centered on self ; I am conscious of my fellowship with all that is good in mankind. And how can this feeling exist without bringing with it a yearning love for the mother who bore me, and who withers while I bloom ? We, dear mother, can afford to smile at the wayward mistakes and follies of human society, tormenting itself to invent new theories of life, which tend only to confuse, destroy, or sever the loving ties of Nature ! How surely are all the trifling differences that have come between you and me dissipated by these thoughts. Turning my back upon the turmoil of the city, I wander into a lovely wooded valley, stretch myself upon the mossy turf, admire the freshness of the foliage, and listen to some sweet wood-bird's song, till tears, but not of sorrow, start unbidden to my eyes. Just so, I feel when through the mass of wayward folly which clings to me, I stretch my hand to lay hold upon yours, and cry, "May God preserve my dear old mother, and when it pleases Him to take her from me may it be gently, and without pain." We need not speak of *death*, for do you not live on in your children a richer, fuller life than yours ever could be ? Thank God, that he has blessed thee in thy children ! Farewell my dearest mother.

Your son, RICHARD.

Dresden, September 19th, 1846.

Organ News.

LIVERPOOL.

An organ recital was given in St. George's Hall, by Mr. W. T. Best, on Thursday, August 16th. The following was the programme :—

Fantasia Cromatica in A minor	Thiele.
Serenade, "Through the night"	Schubert.
Pastorale (Cor Anglais and Flute) }	Gambini.
Military March in G major	}
Toccata and Fugue in C major	Bach.
Musette, from the 6th Concerto	Handel.
Cornelius March	Mendelssohn.

And on Saturday afternoon, August 18th :—

Organ Sonata (No. 2 in C minor)	Mendelssohn.
Pastorale and Ronde Militaire, "Jean d'Arc"	Gounod.
Fantasia in F minor	Mozart.
Andante from the 4th Symphony	Haydn.
Overture for the Organ, C major, Op. 106	Gambini.

FISHERIES EXHIBITION.

The following organ recitals have been given during the last week.

Mr. Loaring's programmes included the following :—

Overture, "Le Nozze di Figaro"	Mozart.
Chorus, "The King shall rejoice" ("Dettingen Anthem ")	Handel.
"La Carita"	Rossini.
Chorus, "Happy Pair" ("Alexander's Feast ")	Handel.
Adagio from "Sestet," Op. 81	Beethoven.
Double Fugue, "Baumgarten"	
Overture, "Il Turco in Italia"	Rossini.

Overture, "Zauberflöte"	Mozart.
Prelude and Fugue in D minor	Bach.
Chorus "From the Censer" ("Solomon ")	Handel.
"Cujus Animam"	Rossini.
Chorus, "The King shall rejoice" ("Coronation Anthem ")	Handel.
Melody from a Motet, "Jepthe"	Paer.
Overture, "Pré aux Clercs"	Hérold.

The programmes of the recitals by Mr. H. C. Tonking, R.A.M., on Wednesday, August 15th, were :—

March in B flat	Silas.
Postlude in C minor, (introducing "Jerusalem on High ")	Steggall.
Gavotte, "Mignon"	Thomas.
Finale from 1st Sonata	Mendelssohn.
Barcarolle, from the 1st Concerto	Bennett.
March from "St. Cecilia"	Handel.
Andante in F	Wely.
Fugue in E major	Best.
Gavotte in F	Martini.
Grand Chorus	Guilmant.

On Saturday, August 18th :—

Allegro from Sonata in D	Mozart.
"Air du Dauphin"	Roeckel.
"Hercules" March	Trembath.
Air, "Che faro"	Gluck.
"War March of the Priests"	Mendelssohn.
Gavotte, "Mignon"	Thomas.
"Scotch Airs"	
Festal March in D	Smart.

On Monday, August 20th :—

Allegro from Sonata in D	Mozart.
"Air du Dauphin"	Roeckel.
Fugue in G minor	Bach.
Aria, "Che faro," from "Orfeo "	Gluck.
"War March of the Priests"	Mendelssohn.
Pastorale, Op. 57	Kullak.
Grand Sonata in A	Mendelssohn.
Postlude in D	Smart.
"Lascia ch'io pianga," from "Rinaldo"	Handel.
Festal March in D	Smart.

The programme of the recital by Mr. Harry Dancey, F.C.O., on Monday, August 20th, was :—

Allegro, from Concerto in G minor	Handel.
Pastorale	Kullak.
Allegro Vivace	Moranill.
Allegretto in C major	Gade.
Andante in G	Batiste.
Gavotte in G major	Dancey.
Vesper Hymn, with variations	Turpin.
Triumphal March, from "Alfred"	Prout.

On Monday, Aug. 20th, by Mr. W. W. Hedgecock :—

March in D	Best.
Entr'acte, "Rosamunde," (No. 2)	Schubert.
Allegro in E flat	Batiste.
Minuet	Schubert.
Granovo in F	Smart.
Gavotte in C minor	Saint-Saens.
March, from "The Camp of Silesia"	Meyerbeer.

ACCRINGTON.

On Wednesday evening, August 1st, Mr. Tattersall, the organist at the Parish Church, gave an organ recital and performed the following pieces :—6th Sonata (Mendelssohn) ; Air, with variations ; Pleyel's hymn-tune ; Organ Concerto in D (Handel) ; and Fantasia Pastorale (Lefébure-Wely). There was a large attendance.

ST. LEONARD'S-ON-SEA.

An organ recital was given on Tuesday evening, by H. C. Nixon, Esq., in St. Paul's Church. The following was the programme :—

Overture, "Athalie"	Mendelssohn.
Chorus, "Give unto the Lord ("The Widow of Nain ")	Abram.
Andante in D major, ("Pianoforte Quintet ")	Nixon.
Air, with variations, in F major, from the "Nonette "	Spohr.
Prelude and Fugue in C minor	Bach.
Andante in F major, from the 4th Symphony	Mozart.
Funeral March and Scherzo, ("Pianoforte Quintet ")	Schumann.
Notturno in E major	Mendelssohn.
"Coronation March"	Meyerbeer.

MAIDSTONE.

Mr. W. de M. Sergison, of St. Peter's, Eaton Square, gave an organ recital upon the fine instrument by Lewis, on the 15th ult., at the Parish Church, which was attended by over 1,000 persons, and £18 was collected towards establishing a surpliced choir, the formation of which will be entrusted to Mr. Sergison. The following was the programme :—

Concerto in D minor	Bach.
Introduction—Fugue—Largo—Finale.	
Sonata	Mendelssohn.
Chorale and Variations—Fugue—Andante.	
Concerto in B flat	Handel.
Andante—Maestoso—Allegro—Largo Allegro.	
Andante	Wesley.
"March "Nuptiale"	} Guilmant.
Pastorale and Finale from 1st Organ Sonata	

BRIGHOUSE.

An organ recital was given on Tuesday evening last August 21st, in St. James's Church, by C. W. Pearce, Esq., Mus.Bac. Cantab. The following was the programme :—

Overture, "Samson"	Handel.
Romanza, "La Reine de France "	Haydn.
"Spring Song"	Pearce.
Air, "Angels ever bright and fair "	Handel.
Concert Fantasia	Stewart.
Andante from Organ Sonata	Macfarren.
Postlude in C	Smart.
Anthem, "Blessed be the God"	Wesley.
Grand March	Silas.

ROYAL ALBERT HALL.

Two organ recitals were given by Mr. S. Claude Ridley, on Thursday, August 23rd, in the above Hall. The following were the programmes :—

Overture to "Zampa "	Hérold.
Air, "My heart ever faithful "	Bach.
Fanfare of Trumpets	Lemmens.
Prelude and Fugue in E minor	Bach.
Andante from 5th Symphony	Haydn.
Chorus, "See the Conquering Hero"	Handel.
Sonata in C (No. 2)	Mendelssohn.
Gavotte in A	Gluck.
Grand Pageant March	Gounod.

Festival March	Smart.
"Love Song	Henselt.
Prelude and Fugue in D	Bach.
Gavotte, "Mignon"	Thomas.
Chorus, "Fixed in His everlasting seat "	Handel.
Nocturne in G minor	Chopin.
Military March	Schubert.
Andante in F sharp minor	Wesley.
Overture to "Guillaume Tell "	Rossini.

CHELMSFORD.

Special interest was attached to the services at the Unitarian Chapel, Legg Street, New Street, on Sunday, when a new reed organ, by Messrs. E. and W. Snell, of London, was used for the first time. The organ, which is of great sweetness and purity in tone, contains five sets of reeds, with ten stops and knee action, and is enclosed in a handsome Gothic case. Mr. E. Snell, of London, presided at the morning and evening Service, giving at the close of each an organ recital, which embraced the following selections :—Choral Fugue (Mozart) ; Prelude by Chopin ; March from "Athalie" (Mendelssohn) ; Adagio (Guilmant) ; Morçeau" Fugue (Matthias van den Gheyn) ; Lento in E flat (Scotson Clark) ; Procession March (Scotson Clark). Miss E. Maddocks presided in the afternoon. Each service was well attended ; and the cost of the new instrument, with the exception of a small sum, has been defrayed by subscriptions and the collections on Sunday.

SANDRINGHAM.

An organ recital was given in Sandringham Church on Wednesday, August 8th, by Mr. Arthur H. Crosse. The following was the programme :—

Grand Sonata in A	Mendelssohn.
Andante in D ... Con moto maestoso—Andante tranquillo.	Gladstone.
Aria, "My heart ever faithful" }	Bach.
Fugue in G minor ... }	
Andante con moto in A	Smart.
Grand Offertoire in G	Wely.
Organ Sketch in G minor	Chipp.
Offertoire in A flat	Batiste.
"Gloria in Excelsis" ("Mass in G")	Weber.

WEST NEWTON.

An organ recital was given in the West Newton Church, on Wednesday, August 15th, by Mr. Arthur H. Crosse. The following was the programme :—

Grand Sonata in C minor	Mendelssohn.
Pastorale in F	Merkel.
"La Carita"	Rossini.
Fugue in D	Bach.
Melody for the Organ	Westbrook.
Grand Offertoire in A	Batiste.
Allegretto Cantabile in D	Hopkins.
Aria in F	Gluck.
March, "Albert Edward"	Elvey.
"Vivat Regina"	

ASTBURY CHURCH.

The following is the specification of the new organ, now being built by Mr. Stringer, of Hanley :—

GREAT ORGAN. CC TO G.

1. Open Diapason	8 ft.	6. Wald Flute	4 ft.
2. Stopped Diapason	8 „	7. Fifteenth	2 „
3. Clarabella	8 „	8. Mixture (2 ranks).	
4. Keraulophon	8 „	9. Trumpet	8 „
5. Principal	4 „		

CHOIR ORGAN.

10. Dulciana	8 ft.	13. Harmonic Flute	4 ft.
11. Gamba	8 „	14. Clarinet	8 „
12. Stopped Diapason	8 „		

SWELL ORGAN. CC TO G.

15. Bourdon	16 ft.	20. Gemshorn	4 ft.
16. Open Diapason	8 „	21. Harmonic Piccolo	2 „
17. Lieblich Gedact	8 „	22. Mixture (2 ranks).	
18. Salcional	8 „	23. Hautboy	8 „
19. Vox Angelica	8 „	24. Cornopean	8 „

PEDAL ORGAN. CCC TO F.

25. Grand Open Diap.	16 ft.	27. Bass Flute	8 ft.
26. Grand Bourdon	16 „		

Three Composition Pedals, to Great Organ.
Three   „   „   to Swell.
And Five Couplers.

The Great, Choir, and Pedal Organs will be placed on the north side of the chancel, supported on two pillars, about twelve feet from the floor, and rising up to the clerestory. The Swell will open from the north aisle to the chancel arch.

The annual Welsh musical festival of North Wales choirs, numbering six hundred voices, was held within the ancient walls of Harlech Castle. The weather was delightfully fine, and special trains being run from the watering places, the old castle was crowded with a vast audience. At the morning and afternoon performances, English, Irish, and Welsh airs, together with anthems from the great masters, were rendered by seven choirs. The principal vocalists were—Miss Annie Marriott, Mr. Byfed Lewis, and Mr. Lucas Williams. Sir Richard Wyatt presided. Mr. Samuel Holland, M.P., said, "Now that musical colleges were being established, we should doubtless become a thoroughly musical community." In the evening Handel's oratorio "Judas Maccabœus" was performed by the united choirs, led by Eos Morlais. Mr. Samuel Pope, Q.C., presided, and said no one felt more interested in the promotion and cultivation of music than himself. Excepting the people of Lancashire—his native county—he knew no people who possessed more of the whole heart and soul of music than Welshmen. He hoped when the colleges for higher education in the Principality were erected, students of music would not be forgotten-

THE LATE SCOTSON CLARK.

The *Musical Record* has the following particulars of the late popular composer and organ player :—

He was born on the 16th of November, 1840, and received his earliest musical instruction from his mother, the daughter of Richard Cusack Kearney, an Irish landed proprietor ; she had studied with Mrs. Anderson, and had, it is said, also received lessons from Chopin. At the age of ten Master Clark played the violin ; at the age of twelve he took the service at the parish church of Ewell, whither he had been sent to school ; at the age of fourteen he was appointed organist at Regent Square church ; and at the age of eighteen he became a teacher in the Royal Academy, where he had studied under the late Sterndale Bennett, the late Sir John Goss, Engel, Pinsuti, and Pettitt.

Before he was twenty years old he had to undergo an operation for cataract ; through the skill of Mr. W. Bowman, his sight improved, although he was always afterwards obliged to wear powerful glasses.

In the year 1865 he founded a College of Music, a special feature of which was the advantage offered to students of the organ and of church music. He was for some time organist of Exeter College, Oxford ; and in 1867 he took the degree of Mus.Bac. In the same year he was appointed Head Master of St. Michael's Grammar School, Brighton. About this time Mr. Scotson Clarke took holy orders, after which he went to Leipzig, where, besides doing duty at the English Church, he devoted himself with fresh energy to the study of music, and for two seasons had the advantage of being under Richter, Reinecke, and other eminent professors. From Leipzig he went to Stuttgart, and continued his studies with Lebert, Kruger, &c. In 1873 he returned to London, and for two years he occupied himself almost exclusively with composition. In 1875 he resumed his connection with the London Organ School. In 1878 he was one of the organists at the Paris Exhibition ; he gave an organ performance at the Trocadéro, and received a gold medal. With regard to memory he was exceptionally gifted. He could play Bach's fugues by heart, and could learn any new piece in an incredibly short time. A distinguished organist and composer once wrote a successful and difficult organ piece, which he refused to publish, wishing to keep it specially for his own use at concerts. Mr. Scotson Clarke went to hear him perform it ; and so, it is said, immediately afterwards played it from memory.

REMINISCENCES OF AN OLD REPORTER.

I first went to a theatre, even old Covent Garden, on Friday, January 18th, 1828, when the "play" was Mozart's opera "Il Seraglio," with an altered plot, and the pantomime "Harlequin and Number Nip of the Giant Mountain." Head over (*years*) in love with a little fairy of 10 or 11 summers, and uncomfortable for 48 hours : *anno statis*, nine. In this pantomime occurred performances on the slack and the tight rope ; the slack rope man played the "Copenhagen" valse on a horn whilst suspended, like St. Peter, with his head downwards ! The pantomimists then changed their costumes for the harlequinade on the stage ; brand-new "personages" now lazily slipped on from the sides. The music of "Il Seraglio" seemed to be fairly appreciated by the "pittites," amongst whom I sat. The Processional Chorus in C, "Singt dem grossen Basha lieder," took my fancy as a boy, for my father, a "whole-hog" Mozartean, had taught me the tune at home. The opera was capitally performed by a German company at old Drury in 1854 ; it was done at the Royal Italian a year ago. The libretto, like "Die Zauberflöte," was originally German, the title of the work "Die Entführung aus dem Serail" (The abduction from the Seraglio). Osmia's song in D "O wie will ich triumphiren," is strangely neglected by concert singers. Staudigl, and afterwards Formes, made a great hit with this piece 40 years ago. I shall never forget the "run" of Auber's opera "Gustavus III." in the winter of 1833-34. It went on from the middle of December until the next May, at Covent Garden, and afterwards at Drury Lane, for Mr. Bunn held a lease of both houses. The masquerade scene was a marvel of scenic effect. Henry Phillips, Mr. Templeton, Miss Inveraritz, and Mr. Warde were the "principals," and a Miss Shirrett, Oscar the page. Tom Cooke, the conductor, had the *brass* to manufacture a song for Phillips from the first few bars of the overture in E flat, where Auber effectively uses augmented fifths. The title of this piece was "When time hath bereft thee of charms now divine," and every amateur baritone bought it for domestic use. Phillips was fortunate with his operatic airs. John Barnett gave him the fine song of Hela in the "The Mountain Sylph," "Farewell to the Mountain" (A.D. 1834), and Balfe, in 1836, wrote for him "The light of other days is faded," in "The Maid of Artois ;" the air was twice or thrice encored nearly every night, and the other principals were savagely jealous—*genus irritabile vatum!* Phillips also scored a point in "The Siege of Rochelle" (A.D. 1835), where he sang a piece, "When I beheld the anchor weighed." His sudden production of two pistols from his boots, on a threat of assassination with a dagger by the villain of the opera (Mr. Giulilei), created a tremendous sensation. I was melted to tears on hearing Phillips's exquisite reading of John Barnett's air in A major from his opera "Fair Rosamond" (A.D. 1837), "Sweet Rose of the World," and used to sing it at home—how weakly in comparison, alas!

At old Drury in 1835, Mr. Bunn produced "La Juive" of Halévy, as a grand *spectacle* and *without the music!* This was no loss, for Halévy had little melody in his soul; the opera is dulness itself, and the bass air, too often sung by Mr. Foli at concerts, an infliction. Halévy's Shakesperian opera "The Tempest," produced at Her Majesty's Theatre in 1850, with old Lablache as Caliban, fell to the ground still-born—a *dead* failure. Hector Berlioz and other French critics came over from Paris to witness the performance, and to write *feuilletons* for their own papers. Berlioz greatly pitied the reporters of the London daily papers, then compelled to write a column or two about a new opera the very same night, and within the interval of an hour and a half to two hours. Poor old Hogarth of the *Morning Chronicle* and the *Daily News,* left the Italian Opera on the first night of the season in 1842, at one o'clock, to write his notice, and the morning papers then went to press at about two at the latest. Hector Berlioz and the foreign critics produced their *feuilletons* at present, once a week, in the form of a general "musical review," or *omnium gatherum.* So now in London, a first performance is dismissed with half-a-dozen lines, and the details are given a few days afterwards. Mr. James Davison, of the *Times,* knocked off one night nearly two columns of an excellent notice on Spohr's "Faust;" the newspaper was exhibited some years afterwards at the Kensington Museum amongst other "curiosities." I myself have sat up until half-past one or two after attending an opera or a grand concert, and written a long notice, either at the newspaper office or at some coffee-house hard by, sipping green tea at intervals, and I had to walk or cab it to Hackney afterwards. "Think of that, Master Brook!" Mr. Tyas, as the head of the parliamentary staff of reporters on the *Times,* one night fell asleep in a cab, engaged to drive him from the Palace at Westminster to Printing House Square, and was woke up in the Mile End Road, some three miles off, his copy yet unwritten! At musical festivals in the country, reporters for the London papers often write the notice on their hats during the morning performances in the cathedral or town hall, so as to be "up to the collar." At the Worcester Festival of 1845, I was scribbling my notice every day from about one o'clock until five in the afternoon, so as to catch the train which left at the latter hour; then a hasty dinner, and a rush to the evening concert at eight. Observe that I had to "lamp in" the concert notice of the *preceding* night with the *critique* on the next day's morning performance in the cathedral! Newspaper reporters must not feel drowsy, and there is no time to take snuff, however much they may be "*up* to it."

A long and formal notice of an opera announced, but *suspended on the actual night,* appeared in the *Morning Herald* (A.D. 1856). The reporter had been left in the lurch; he was at once dismissed, but subsequently re-appointed. Many reports of concerts have been written on speculation. Mr. Oxenford of the *Times* used to say, "go to the concert-hall for a few minutes, if only to see that the house is not burnt down !"

I saw Mendelssohn at Exeter Hall during his visit to England in 1842, also at the Philharmonic concert of June 13th, when he conducted his Symphony in A minor. At Exeter Hall I scrutinized him closely, within a few feet of distance, in the artists' row, where he conversed affably with Muller the organist, Mr. Henry Phillips, and other musicians. Mendelssohn looked pale, and his handsome features struck me as of a rather feminine type. He played variations of *his own* on "The Harmonious Blacksmith," and made the large organ "speak" that evening. Other organ recitals in the City churches made a great noise at the time, and were eulogised by Mr. H. F. Chorley.

Auber used to praise the Stilton *cheese* as the "perfect cadence" of our English dinners. Mine is only a half cadence, or *suspension* of the final tonic chord.   A. M.

PRINCIPAL CONTENTS OF THIS NUMBER.

LONDON : SATURDAY, AUGUST 25, 1883.

SOME ACCOUNT OF AN ANCIENT INSTITUTION.

THE season of the Welsh Eisteddfodau affords a timely opportunity to say something concerning one of the most ancient series of musical gatherings the world can point to. The word is Eisteddfod, derived from eistedd "to sit," denoting a session of bards. The word bard is of uncertain etymology. LUCAN (Liber 1) writing about A.D. 60 has a passage in which the word occurring in the Latin plural, and in one the common of ancient bardic functions is pourtrayed

"Vos quoque, qui fortes animas, belloque peremptas
Laudibus in longum vates dimittitis ævum
Plurima securi fudistis carmina Bardi."

In these prosaic but far more sensible days, poets and musicians have other tasks than that of celebrating the "patriot souls in battle slain," and in pompous stately periods glorying in various deeds. According to TACITUS, the ancient Germans had warlike songs, called "barditus" by the Latin author. Bards were intimately associated with the daily lives and early art aspirations of the different Celtic tribes. Originally spread over a great part of Western Europe, the bardic race found a last retreat in Wales and Ireland, and now from the ashes of the past, or rather in the glimmering of an unbroken poetical chain of meetings and traditions, the literature, music, and art of the imaginative Welsh people are being fostered in the more than ever popular Eisteddfodau. According to WHARTON, and there is much shrewdness in his conclusion, the bards were in the first instance a "constitutional appendage of the Druidical hierarchy." The ruins of an archdruid's house the "Trer Drew" existed in, and probably may still be seen in, the parish of Llanidau in the Isle of Anglesey. Near this spot is the "Hamlet of Bards," or "Trer Beird." So strong was the Welch love of poetry and song, that all the changes of ages, the acceptation of the Christian religion, and new political conditions failed to shake, though they modified, the national position of the bards. It may be that the artistic life of a nation is indeed indestructive and plastic, surviving alike decay and change and endowed with a never-ending youthfulness. The domination of the Romans in Britain did, indeed, as far as we know, crush out the primitive songs and art-life and all but destroy the very language of the ancient Britons; but no such results occurred in Wales, where the people, jealous of the encroachments of aliens, whether Romans or Saxons, remained faithfully attached to their songs and Celtic habits. The laws of HOEL DHA, promulgated about the year 940, or 950, recognise the courtbard or "Bardd Teulu." As an officer of an important position in the household, he enjoyed very special court privileges and ranked as worthy of the eighth place in the court of the prince. When the three great feasts of Christmas, Easter, and Whitsuntide came round, he sat next to the prefect of the palace, who delivered the harp to the bard. The bard who gained the chief badge in a musical contest, or Eisteddfod, was supposed to be prepared to sing a hymn to the glory of God, a song in honour of the prince, and the bard of the hall (TEULUWR) sang a song upon a chosen topic. The person and property of the bard were sternly and anxiously protected, rigorous laws being enacted to this end. One of the higher and most privileged of the domestic bards was the PENCERADD GWLAD, though he was not a regularly appointed member of the household. The bards were anciently supposed to be endowed with a sort of a prophetic inspiration. Doubtless they were expert flatterers, as they made a special study of genealogy, a craze characteristic of other than ancient days, and affording, even in modern times a ready access to the pride of birth. They were diligent students of their specially famed predecessors, MYRDDVN AP MORFRYN, MYRDDYN EMRYS, and TALIESIN BEN BEIRDD. About 1080, or as some say in the year 1078, GRYFFTH AP CONAN, KING or Prince of WALES, re-constituted and reformed the bardic hierarchy. In the early history of the Eisteddfodau, the judges were appointed by commission from the princes. One of the last occasions upon which such a commission was granted or deemed necessary, occurred sometime in 1568. It would not interest the reader to go further into this matter. It may however be noted that players on the harp were held to be supreme as instrumentalists, and that performers upon the crwths (or ancient violins with three or more strings), tabor, or pipe were held to be artists of an inferior grade. Four degrees were allowed in

the poetical and five in the musical faculty. PENNANT has much to tell upon these matters. A word or two on the Welsh harp may not be out of place, especially as the instrument seems now to be a thing of the past. Though the Welsh, like the Irish, had some form of harp at a very early period, the Welsh triple-stringed harp is not after all a very ancient instrument. Its compass ranged recently from G G to about G in altissimo on the right hand side, and from gamut G to a similar height on the left hand side. The outside strings proceeded in unison, diatonically, and the semitones (moving a semitone higher than the adjacent notes in each case) were placed upon the middle row of strings; thus in modulating from C to G, the F sharp was found upon the middle string level with the two outside strings sounding F natural. The instrument attained some importance by being written for by HANDEL. However, it was an inconvenient, though ingenious instrument in some respects. The infinite superiority of the modern double-action harp as heard under the fingers of so artistic and accomplished a performer as Mr. JOHN THOMAS (himself a Welshman), has convinced all but the most wrong-headed lovers of antiquity, that it is absolutely necessary now, even in Wales, to adopt the modern and improved instrument. The above particulars suggest one thought beyond the interesting testimony they offer as to the early and universally prevailing power of the divine art. This is the question, Have not our musicians in modern days rather lost than gained ground socially speaking? It may be that our princes and nobles seek other pleasures than the pure delights of music; still, all the same, it seems clear that the musician has even now some ground to recover, and the listening patron has yet some lesson to learn, before the old reverence of the art and its professors is fully re-established. On the other hand, it must be allowed that the artist is no longer under the obligation of seeking help and shelter under the patronising wing of the prince or noble; he may now best appeal to the public at large for appreciation and support. All honour is however due to men of olden time who so earnestly supported music and song; and similar honour is also due to the men who still in Wales carry forward the same good work by annually holding the valuable and interesting meeting still dignified by the ancient title of the Eisteddfodau. It is, in conclusion only to be hoped that they will be faithfully continued in the full daylight of modern artthought.   . E. H. TURPIN.

A FEW WORDS OF REGISTRING ON THE ORGAN.

OWING to such changes in the construction of the modern organ as increased wind pressure, the importation and invention of novel stops, and the large extension of orchestration of late years, the art of applying tone-colour to organ music has undergone some decided changes during the past half-century. Mr. JAS. HIGGS has already alluded to this matter in a highly interesting paper on "Organ Arrangements." It is certain that the old directions, such as a preceding generation were familiar with in such works as NOVELLO's Select Organ Pieces, are things of the past. It is also true, that there is a feeling against the too slavish use of the stereotyped composition pedal combinations. Providing this new feeling for nice tone gradations and frequent modifications of the tone qualities of the organ is not carried to a feverish point, it is an undoubtedly artistic advance. One would jealously watch a movement which would induce our organ players to sacrifice anything of that spirit of calmness which arises from the occasionally prolonged use of registers of the diapason genus. Still, it is clear that our organs are in future to contain a larger admixture of 8-feet and soft 4-feet stops, and that the art of organ playing will involve a more and more skilled employment of soft mixed tone qualities of these types, and a decreasing tendency to handle the organ as an instrument of fixed combinations and effects. The combinations up to principal or to principal and fifteenth, have become of less frequent use for instance, partly from the introduction of stops of the harmonic flute type, which are so useful in the performance of contrapuntal music, as throwing forward without too much sharpness the outlines of the moving parts. The presence of more soft reeds again, and the introduction of the stringed-toned family of stops, have in different directions tended to create new effects in the art of registring, and the presence of soft doubles of 16-feet pitch has also resulted in adding richness to certain organic effects. It may be that increased wind pressures have had much to do with a changed taste in stop manipulation, but it is also evident that the future of skilled organ playing will require the careful cultivation of the art of judiciously mixing the softer tone-qualities. This subject may receive further attention presently.

E. H. TURPIN.

THE CONCERT SEASON OF 1883–84.

THE "recess," in respect of musical business, is not quite so long as the parliamentary one. Even now, activity prevails at the Crystal Palace, where Mr. A. MANNS, untiring, and unfatigued by the exhausting labours of the last ten months, is holding weekly concerts on Saturday evenings, and performing standard operas every afternoon, beginning with WALLACE'S "Maritana" last Tuesday, and promising AUBER'S "Fra Diavolo," Sir JULIUS BENEDICT'S "Graziella," and Sir W. STERNDALE BENNETT'S "May Queen," which may be mounted for the stage. The autumnal season of Saturday afternoon concerts will begin at the end of the first week in October.

With November, not always so "dark and dreary" as the song suggests, will come forward Herr RICHTER and Mr. ARTHUR CHAPPELL. Herr RICHTER, in addition to his nine Spring concerts, now gives three "extras" in the Autumn, and might, probably, increase the number, without pecuniary loss. The three concerts of this "fall" are fixed for October 29, and November 3 and 10. The materials are sure to be of stirling value. The "Popular" Concerts, no longer "Monday Popular," for one is held every Saturday afternoon, have taken deep root in the ground, and fully deserve the patronage which the public, not always disposed to support classical enterprises, so liberally bestows. It might be, and has

been, hinted to the worthy Director of the "Popular" Concerts that the repertoire would be improved by an extension, to include more new compositions of acknowledged merit on the Continent. Mr. CHARLES HALLE has set a good example in this respect at his own annual Recitals, now held in the Grosvenor Gallery. Mr. ARTHUR CHAPPELL, moreover, might provide a greater variety of pianists and solo players.

Mdlle. JANOTHA, Miss ZIMMERMANN, and Miss KREBS are admirable exponents of classical texts; the first is now famous. Mr. CHARLES HALLE, of course, may rest content with his laurels. Nevertheless, several eminent European pianists remain to be heard; the engagement of Herr VLADIMIR DE PACHMANN, last winter, was a good move in the right direction, and holds out a fair prospect for future seasons. It would be invidious to name individual artists, not hitherto engaged at the "Popular," but their names are familiar in the wide, wide (musical) world.

Everyone is glad to be informed that the old Philharmonic Society, the friend and in one sense the foster-mother of BEETHOVEN, has done well this year in the financial department. The energetic Treasurer, Mr. CHARLES E. STEPHENS (ably seconded by the Honorary Secretary, Mr. HENRY HERSEE), has restored the fortunes of the Philharmonic; so, in 1842, Sir ROBERT PEEL by his Budget—(no thanks for the permanent Income Tax)—converted the annual deficits of the ministry of the day into a respectable surplus. The Philharmonic Directors had prudently widened their boundaries, so as to comprehend more modern works, many of them quite new to the English public. It is to be regretted, on the other hand, that so much money is squandered for the engagement of "star" vocalists, however eminent. The motive of the directors is, no doubt to draw audiences, but if fine symphonies and cantatas do not suffice to fill St. James's Hall, it is to be feared that the "occupation" of the Society is "gone," like OTHELLO'S.

Mr. WILHELM GANZ of the "Orchestral," once the "New Philharmonic," concerts, has abandoned his enterprise after some years of valiant campaigning. The public thus lose the opportunity of hearing fine compositions splendidly performed, with a leader like Mr. POLITZER, on Saturday afternoon, and by daylight. But Mr. GANZ cannot be expected to pay the piper at the expense of a certain deficit. He is entitled to many thanks for the production of HECTOR BERLIOZ'S "Symphonie Fantastique" with the two big bells, and the engagement of fine pianists, such as Mdme. MENTER, Herr DE PACHMANN and Herr LOEWENBERG.

Very early in the Spring of 1884—leap year, by the way—the Philharmonic concerts will be resumed, and Herr RICHTER is to follow suit in May. The "Monday Pops" will go on from the end of October until the Monday in Passion, or as the Ritualists term it, "Holy" Week, which, next year, is on April 7th, as Easter Day falls on April 15th, or three weeks later than in 1883. The "Ballad" concerts are good of their kind, and splendid pianists, such as Mdme. MENTER, have been engaged of late years.

The Royal Albert Hall must not be forgotten. Mr. BARNBY will, as before, hold an oratorio concert once a month, beginning in November. It is hoped and expected by the sanguine, that he will perform "La "Messa des Morts" of HECTOR BERLIOZ, the general execution of which colossal work last Spring at Sydenham failed to satisfy *connoisseurs*, notwithstanding the laudable efforts and clever conducting of friend MANNS. Fortune does not always favour the bold ; for a good general must be backed by a serviceable and efficient army !

The autumn season of this year will comprise two "provincial" festivals at Gloucester and Leeds, to take place respectively in September and October. The old festival of the "Three Choirs" rather lives on a respectable reputation than on present prowess, but the managers certainly endeavour to maintain vitality by the infusion of fresh blood, not always of the purest or *bluest !* Formidable, indeed, to musical reporters, for the list of important novelties at this forthcoming festival, is truly terrific in the eyes of unfortunate · men who will be obliged to scribble off slips of "copy" by the hundred, for transmission to London by express, and to dash off telegrams, for the composition of which in elegant terms, time always fails.   A. M.

THE VOICE
MUSICALLY AND MEDICALLY CONSIDERED.
BY
ARMAND SEMPLE, B.A., M.B., Cantab., M.R.C.P., Lond.,
Physician to the Royal Society of Musicians.

(*Continued from page* 104).

The Various Organs concerned in Vocalisation.

Hitherto in speaking of the voice, the larynx has been almost exclusively discussed, but it must be mentioned that various other organs are concerned in vocalisation, viz. :—

1. The Lungs, or Bellows, or Organs of Air-Supply.
2. The Larynx, or Organ of Vibration.
3. The Pharynx, or Organ of Reflection.
4. The Mouth providing the organ of articulation, viz., the Lips, Tongue, Palate, and Teeth.

The Lungs, the Air-Supplying Organs.

These organs are two in number, one on each side of the chest ; they are the essential organs of respiration, are situated underneath the vocal organ, and perform an office exactly analogous to that of the bellows of an harmonium or church organ supplying the air or wind requisite to throw the vocal cords into vibration. From the lungs the air passes through a number of small tubes, termed the ramifications of the bronchi (bronchial tubes), which converge into one bronchus or bronchial tube on each side, the two bronchi at last meeting to form an extremely elastic tube, termed the trachea or windpipe, which ascending the anterior surface of the neck in a vertical direction terminates in the larynx.

The lungs are frequently but very erroneously imagined to give rise to the sounds commonly known as *Chest Notes.* This fallacy originates in the fact that men, certainly not women, perceive in the act of speaking or singing, in the lower tones, a powerful feeling in the chest and back; but the chest has no power to create these sounds, the vibrations of which are simply transmitted, and in reality the chest under these circumstances may be compared to the harmonic or sounding-board of a violin or piano.

The lungs simply act as receptacles for the accumulated air ; they are enclosed by the ribs and lie upon the diaphragm, by which structure they are separated from the abdomen. The lungs are developed during the act of inspiration simultaneously and conjointly from above downwards through the contraction of the diaphragm, and laterally by the ribs becoming distended. It is uncertain whether these two acts could take place independently of one another, but it is exceedingly probable that upon their conjoint action depends perfect inspiration. The inspiratory act in the female subject is more frequently effected by the elevation of the chest or thorax, hence their breathing is known as thoracic.

The Larynx.—The Vibrating Organ.

This organ is the generator of the voice, and forms in the male the protuberance in the front of the throat, to which the name of Pomum Adami or Adam's apple has been given. In the centre of the larynx is a narrow passage formed by two membranes spread horizontally across it, having a common attachment at the pomum and passing backwards one on each side. These are the vocal ligaments or true cordæ vocales (vocal cords). The aperture between these ligaments is called the glottis or rima glottidis (chink of the glottis), and these cords are therefore frequently called the lips of the glottis. To these lips or ligaments the vibrations of the voice are solely due. During inhalation the shape of the glottis is nearly triangular, but in the act of phonation (speaking or singing) it assumes a linear form, the ligaments being closely drawn together. The vocal cords are not similar in structure throughout their entire length, the anterior three-fifths being composed of ligament, and their posterior two-fifths of cartilage. Situated above the vocal ligaments are two oblong cavities termed the ventricula laryngis, or ventricles of the larynx, one on each side, each being surmounted by a fold or band, the position of which is parallel to the vocal cord. The space between the folds is termed the superior upper or false glottis. This orifice is far wider than the inferior true or real glottis, and it never closes. The office performed by the upper glottis is to circumscribe an elliptical space immediately above the lower lips, enlarging and contracting this space, so that when desired the quality and volume of the voice may be capable of modification. During the emission of vocal sounds the superior opening of the larynx is free, but during deglutition it is completely closed by the epiglottis, a kind of small heart-shaped lid, which is situated behind the tongue. The registers, the brightness or dulness of sounds, and their volume and intensity are entirely formed by the larynx.

The Pharynx.—The Reflecting Organ.

This is an elastic cavity situated at the back of the mouth, between the tongue and the arch by which the circumference of the palate is formed. The voice on its issue from the glottis is echoed and reflected by this cavity, and since the pharynx can assume numerous forms it communicates a distinctive character to the sounds generated by the larynx.

The Mouth.—The Articulating Organ.

This is composed of divers movable parts, viz., the tongue, jaw, palate, and lips, the special function of which is to render the vowels precise, and to make the process of articulation perfect by the addition of the consonants.

Register. Timbre. Intensity.

Every sound is possessed of these three attributes. The Registers are 3 in number, viz. :—
1. The Chest Voice or Voce Di Petto.
2. The Falsetto Voice or Voce Di Fasetto.
3. The Head Voice or Voce Di Testa.

Timbre or Quality.

The leading qualities are 2 in number.
1. The Open or Clear.
2. The Closed or Muffled.

(*To be continued*).

A medal has been awarded to the celebrated export pianos manufactured by Weidenslaufer, Berlin, by the international jury of the Colonial Exhibition in Amsterdam.

At the recent temperance fête held at the Crystal Palace, and at which fifteen bands competed, Messrs. Besson and Co. not only presented a large proportion of the instruments which were contested for, but exhibited near the centre transept a case containing their latest productions in brass and wood instruments, and distributed circulars to all the musicians, inviting them to. inspect their factory and show-rooms.

Reviews.

Vive La Reine. Gavotte for Pianoforte. By George Asch. (Willey & Co., 1883.)—An effective specimen of the *genre* in the key of F, with very pretty "motives."

The British Patrol. By George Asch. (Riviere and Hawkes).—This "Descriptive Allegro" is a sequel to the popular *Turkish Patrol.* It is performed every week at the Fisheries Exhibition and at the Crystal Palace, by a military band, and invariably envokes enthusiastic applause. The key is F.

Geh' Perlen Suchen; Der Tochter Klage. German Songs. Composed by Richard Dressel. (Stanley, Lucas and Co., 1883).—The first of these *lieder*, "Seek pearls upon the barren strand," is a pretty, sentimental effusion in E flat, but the signature is almost immediately contradicted by a C flat; as at the outset of Schumann's pianoforte quintet, and a touch of change to B flat minor. The range is from E natural to G natural above the lines. The second song, "Motherless," is short and pathetic; the key D minor; the range from C to F natural. The composer, as in the first song, shows a predilection for skips of the *minor* sixth; here, from G natural to E flat. Mr. Dressel's other German *lieder*, sung at his last concert, were reviewed about a fortnight ago.

Organ Cases and Organs of the Middle Ages, etc. By Arthur Hill, B.A., F.S.A. (David Bogue, 3, St. Martin's Place, Trafalgar Square).—An imposing volume, large folio size, and a handsome drawing-room or library book. The author well prepared for his task by earnest, antiquarian and technical study, opens with a chapter "On the Destruction of Ancient Organs"; which, although interesting, betrays the common error of describing all kinds of artistic neglect and wilful destruction to the period of the Commonwealth, an error it is now time to shake off. Mr. Hill has, however, much to say of organs which were not destroyed, and does not confine himself to the usual course of quoting prejudiced and not unnaturally spiteful Royalist accounts of certain ill-advised fanaticisms of the Commonwealth period. Indeed, he has something to say against vandalism of more modern times. The chapters on "Remarkable Organs of early and late times," "English Organs of the Middle Ages," "The Organ Case," etc., are admirably written, and very interesting. With regard to the more technical chapters, the name of the author is a sufficient guarantee for their accuracy and utility. In dealing with "The Position of the Organ in our Churches," Mr. Hill gives some sensible suggestions without confining himself to an advocacy of any fixed position for all large churches alike. The question is one of much importance; and it is not a little curious that the natural greed for large, open spaces in our great churches, makes it as difficult to properly place an organ in a cathedral as in a village church. A large portion of the volume is occupied by plates of the more famous organs and organ cases in England, Germany, France, Italy, etc., together with descriptions of and remarks upon their constructional peculiarities and contents. One reflection arises from a perusal of details : surprise at the skill, artistic power, and liberality of the people of former days ; and the counter reflection also arises, that in these boastful times we are apt to be over fussy and to cackle exceedingly when we chance to build an organ of anything more than respectable dimensions. The thanks of the musical and architectural worlds are due to Mr. Arthur Hill for his painstaking labour, enterprise, and excellently written chapters of this notable work. The handsome volume previously issued by Mr. John Norbury, perhaps, to some extent, anticipated Mr. A. Hill's work ; but Mr. Hill's valuable addition to the literature of the "King of Instruments" is exceedingly welcome, and, it is to be hoped, will receive a due public appreciation.

Franz Liszt, Artist and Man. By L. Ramann, translated from the German by Miss Cowdery. (W. H. Allen and Co., 13, Waterloo Place).—It is not often that the influence of the artist is great enough, or his life long enough, to justify so complete, so frank, and so thoroughly personal a narrative as is to be found in the well got up and interesting volumes now under notice. That there

are errors of detail and misprints, that the work is one of considerable partisanship, are matters which go without saying. On the other hand, there is every sign, on the part of both author and translator, of painstaking enthusiasm, careful investigation, and appreciative thought. It is, indeed, a rare thing to find a book, entering as this does, most fully into an examination of the works, life, nay, very thoughts of the genius to be pourtrayed. What will be Liszt's ultimate position in the world of art, is a question often thought of, doubtless. His talents are of a most exceptional type truly, and as an executant he occupies a standing place all but unique. As a composer, and this is probably the department in which he wishes himself to claim the widest recognition, his long life and splendid reputation, have not even now secured for him a very exalted position. It cannot be denied that he possesses abundantly the faculty of being picturesque, and at times even poetical ; but his want of constructive power, the art of saying only the right thing at the right time, and a consequent diffusive vagueness of manner, it must be allowed, have tended to deny to him the power and popularity his otherwise exceptional gifts and eloquence might have secured. Our author begins with Liszt from his birth, tracing very fully the development of his talents ; his growth as an executant ; his advance as a composer ; his concert tours ; his Parisian experience ; his religious, political, and social thoughts and actions, and his loves and friendships. All these are gone into with a frankness and clearness at times damaging, and at times engaging. The artist and the man are indeed very minutely examined and pictured. To the student about to enter the world, to the artist already in the world, to the musician desirous of reading about the opinions and doings of the past great artistic generation, these volumes will be very welcome and of distinct use. Despite an occasional proneness to a rather excessive affectionate sentimentality not unnatural in a sincere admirer of a truly gifted man, the author writes with clearness and purpose ; and the work fascinates the reader in its well sustained general and artistic interest.

CREMONAS.

The Rev. H. Haweis recently contributed an article to the *Gentlemen's Magazine* upon this topic, from which the following passages are extracted :—

At the beginning of this century, hidden away in old Italian convents and wayside inns, lay the masterpieces of the Amati, Stradivarius, Guarnerius, and Bergonzi. But Tarisio's eye was getting cultivated. He was learning to know a fiddle when he saw it. "Your violinio, Signor, requires mending?" says the itinerant pedlar, as he salutes some monk known to be connected with the sacristy or choir of Pisa, Florence, Milan. "I can mend it." Out comes the Stradivarius, with a loose bar or split rib, and sounding abominably. "Dio mio !" says Tarisio, but your violino is in a bad way. My respected father is prayed to try one that I have, in perfect and beautiful accord and repair, and permit me to mend this worn-out machine. And Tarisio, whipping a shining clean instrument out of his bag, hands it to the monk, who eyes it and is for trying it. He tries it ; it goes soft and sweet, though not loud and wheezing, like the battered old Stradi. Tarisio clutches his treasure. The next day back comes the pedlar to the cloister, is shown up to the padre. "But" he exclaims, "you have lent me a beautiful violino and in perfect order." "Ah! if the father would accept from me a small favour," says the cunning Tarisio. "And what is that?" "To keep the violinio that suits him so well, and I will take in exchange the old machine which is worn out, but with my skill I shall still make something of it !" A glass of good wine or a lemonade or black coffee clinches the bargain. Off goes Tarisio, having parted with a characterless German fiddle—sweet and easy going and "looking nice," and worth now about £5—in perfect order, no doubt—and having secured one of those gems of Cremona which now run into the £200. Violin collecting became the passion of Tarisio's life. The story has been told by Mr. Charles Reade, and all the fiddle world knows how Tarisio came to Paris with a batch of old instruments, and was taken up by Chanot and Villaume, through whose hands passed nearly every one of those *chefs-d'œuvre* recovered by Tarisio.

Mr. Theodore Thomas has received a copy of the new symphonic poem by Franz Liszt, entitled "From the Cradle to the Grave," which his orchestra will bring out in Chicago.

THE MUSIC OF A HUNDRED YEARS AGO.

The following extracts are quoted from the *Nineteenth Century* :—

Music is a better test of the moral culture of an art age than its painting or its sculpture, or even its architecture. Music, by its nature, is ubiquitous, as much almost as poetry itself, and in one sense more so, for its vernacular tongue is common to mankind. Music in its nature is social, it can enter every home, it is not the privilege of the rich ; and thus it belongs to the social and domestic life of a people, as painting and sculpture—the arts of the few —never have done or can do. It touches the heart and the character as the arts of form have never sought to do, at least in the modern world. When we test the civilization of an age by its art we should look to its music next to its poetry, and sometimes even more than to its poetry. One wearies of hearing how grand and precious a time is ours, now that we can draw a corn-flower right. Music is the art of the eighteenth century, the art wherein it stands supreme in the ages—perfect, complete, and self-created. If one thinks of the pathos of those great songs, of the majesty of those full choirs, of the inexhaustible melody of their operas and all that Bach, Handel, Haydn, Mozart, Gluck, and the early years of Beethoven gave us, it is strange to hear that that age was dead to art. Neither the age which gave us Rheims and Westminster Abbey, nor even the age which gave us the Parthenon, did more for humanity than the age to which we owe the oratorios and the operas, the sonatas, symphonies, and masses of the great age of music. Not merely was music of the highest order produced, not merely did that age create almost all the great orders of music, but the generation gave itself to music with a passion such as marked all ages wherein art reaches its zenith. When Handel and Buononcini, Gluck and Piccini, divided the town, it was not with the languid partisanship which amuses our leisure, but with the passions of the red and green factions in the circus of Byzantium. England, it is true, had few musicians of its own, but Handel is for practical purposes an English musician, and the great Italian singers and the great German masters were never more truly at home than when surrounded by English admirers. Our people bore their fair share in this new birth of art, especially if our national anthem was really the product of this age. And not our people only, but the men of culture, of rank, of power, and the Court itself. And the story that the King caused the whole house to rise when the "Hallelujiah Chorus" was heard is a happy symbol of the enthusiasm of the time.

THE APPROACHING CHURCH CONGRESS.

Earnest people who are accustomed by long experience to disappointments regarding the conduct of the Church, and the intense difficulty to be encountered in making our clergy alive to the wants of our times, have special cause for disappointment in the stale, poverty-stricken scheme of the Church Congress at Reading from October 2nd to 5th. Of course there will be the usual overplus of clerical talk, and the chatter of those who think they are able to talk upon every subject it is possible for man to talk about. But, alas ! there is hardly a sign of any sensible and gainful discussion as to the necessary steps whereby to increase the national affection for the Church, to intensify, and where necessary (especially as regards the prevailing plethora of talk upon every possible subject in the pulpit during divine worship) to abbreviate and improve her Services, and to purify and enlarge the scope of sacred art. More love, more earnestness, more beauty in that precious heritage of the Christian religion ; music : less talk, less wrangling, less of clerical professional interests, these are the imperative calls now being made ; yet year after year passes by, and little or nothing is done. The only hopeful sign of the approaching meeting in which, as usual, clerical obtuseness and the clerical tendency to talk, rather than to listen now and then and to learn something of the people's religious wants, form the "dead flies in the ointment," is the consideration for two hours and a half only of the vital question, "the Services of the Church and their adaptation to modern needs."

Mr. Theodore Blockley, music publisher, has removed his stock to his new premises at 72, Berners Street, W.

Mr. James J. Monk presided at the organ at St. Peter's, Church Street, Liverpool, last Sunday morning and evening. Advantage was taken of the occasion to do Travers' rarely-sung anthem, "Ascribe unto the Lord" and Hatton's fine E flat Service. The Service altogether went well, and was an enjoyable change from the usual humdrum style of the parish services.—*The Liverpool Musical and Dramatic World.*

Passing Events.

An American musical paper asks, Was Rubinstein's opera "The Demon" composed as an "imp"-romptu?

The band and chorus at the Leeds Festival consist conjointly of 425 performers, of which the orchestra will number 112 players.

An American journal says, an operetta has been composed with the title of "In a Dilemma." Of course, the orchestral score will include two horns.

Messrs. Neumeyer and Co. are again to the front, this time having a show of their pianofortes and Bell organs at the Building Exhibition, which opened at Manchester recently, and is to continue for six weeks.

Five of the "Gala Cars" of the Rock Island, Chicago, and Pacific Railway Company, are named respectively after Adelina Patti, Clara Louise Kellogg, Anna Louise Cary, Emma Abbott, and Christine Nilsson.

The Archbishop of Canterbury and the Bishops of London, St. Albans, and Rochester, have become patrons of the London Church Choir Association. The annual festival takes place at St. Paul's Cathedral on November 8th.

The Americans are adopting the titles "Mus. Doc." and "Mus. Bac." At the recent commencement of Racine College the degree of Doctor of Music was conferred upon George W. Warren, organist of St. Thomas's Church, New York.

The West End (London) Welsh Eisteddfod is to be held at the Vestry Hall, Kings Road, Chelsea, on Dec. 4th, the prize compositions being sent in by Nov. 12th. Particulars may be obtained of Mr. W. M. Jones, 197a, Buckingham Palace Road, S.W.

Readers will regret to learn that it is understood that Sir Michael Costa has been unfortunate in some important investments. The testimonial to the esteemed *chef d'orchestre* is likely presently to take a practical form. Sir Michael Costa, one is grieved to add, is still suffering from paralysis of the organs of speech.

In spite of the local competition of the Prince's Hall, and the multiplication of concert-rooms, the shares of St. James's Hall paid 8 per cent this year. It is true they produced 10 per cent two years ago, but on the other hand there has been a large outlay upon the hall during that period.

On Tuesday evening next, at St. John's, Waterloo Road, Mr. Samuel Millar, professor of the trombone at the Royal College of Music, will join Mr. H. J. B. Dart, in giving an organ recital, including a grand Fantasia and Chorale, "Ein feste burg" (Braüer) ; "Marche Funebre," from Concerto (David) ; and Prayer (Michael), for trombone and organ.

The *Trovatore* makes out the following thirty-five composers as having written operas on the subject of "Semiramide" : Andrea Ziani (1671), Strungk (1684), Aldovrandini (1701), Pollaroli (1714), Destouches (1718), Vinci (1723), Caldara (1725), Porpora (1729), Vivaldi (1732), Aroja (1738), Aliprandi (1740), Hasse (1747), Gluck (1748), Delle Dame (1750), Jomelli (1752), Cocchi (1753), Graun (1754), Sacchini (1762), Guglielmi and Traetta (1765), Sarti (1765), Paisiello (1773), Salieri (1774), Prati and Martellari (1785), Gyrowetz (1790), Nasolini (1792), Himmel (1795), Bianchi (1798), Cimarosa (1799), Portogallo and Catel (1802), Meyerbeer (:819), Rossini (1823), Garcia (1828).

Thomas Hamilton Murray, writing, for the *Home Journal* of the private libraries of Boston, U.S., says :— Dr. Eben Tourjée, of the New England Conservatory of Music, has a splendid collection of several thousand volumes, which comprises the finest music library in the United States. It includes, among other features, the extremely valuable collection of the late Dr. Tuckerman, and contains the complete scores of many of the great masters. There is also in the library a vast amount of interesting rarities, both in the line of music literature and in that of a general nature. In addition to the collection of works on music, there is also a fine library of historical and philosophical works, belles lettres, and books of reference.

Correspondence.

ORGAN RECITALS AT KENSINGTON.

TO THE EDITOR OF THE "MUSICAL STANDARD."

SIR,—For the national credit and out of respect for some gentlemen of acknowledged ability whose names are on the list of performers, cannot some supervision be exercised in the selection of those who are permitted to give organ recitals at the International Fisheries Exhibition ?

It was my misfortune to pass both the organs the other day, between six and seven o'clock. Recitals were in progress. In both instances the element of correct time was conspicuously wanting, and one was being concluded by a rendering of the "Wedding March" which baffles description. "Finis coronat opus." (There was no indication that it was intended by the performer as a comic reading of the work).

Yours, etc.,
AN ORGAN STUDENT.

London, August 20th.

ROYAL ACADEMY PUPILS.

TO THE EDITOR OF THE "MUSICAL STANDARD."

SIR,—You kindly mention my name as classed in a first division of commenced singers at the Royal Academy of Music. The printer should have printed it commended singers, a slight difference, as I am not a mere novice or freshwoman, but a pupil of two years' standing. Please correct this error, as it spoils the effect of your valuable notice.

Yours truly,
FRANCES POWELL.

5, Gledhow Terrace, South Kensington.
August 16th.

ON THE TEACHING OF COUNTERPOINT.

TO THE EDITOR OF THE "MUSICAL STANDARD."

SIR,—A few words from me upon this subject, recently discussed in your columns, may not be inappropriate.

The discussion seems to resolve itself into two questions : firstly, the desirableness, for students, of a course of strict (as distinguished from free) Counterpoint, using those terms in their precise, technical sense ; secondly, the validity, goodness or badness, of the various notes given by writers of books on Counterpoint.

Eleven years ago, I wrote : "The study and practice of strict Counterpoint is adapted to cultivate a pure and solid manner of writing. Free Counterpoint is soon learned after the student has subjected himself to the discipline of a course of strict Counterpoint ; from the restrictions of which he will then easily emancipate himself, with greatly increased power, from having worked under them ; albeit that they may have seemed to him somewhat arbitrary and irksome."—("Text book of Music," p. 119). From that main position I see no reason to recede, after some thirty-three years of professional experience.

Moreover, I think there is a pretty general consent among musicians to the conjoint study of Harmony—(chords, and their treatment)—and Counterpoint (see p. 41 of "Text book.")

Now, seeing that in studying Harmony the learner will in all probability be kept for some time at triads and their inversions, and that, in strict Counterpoint, triads and their first inversion are the only chords usually authorized, it will follow that the student's early contrapuntal work will be of the nature of strict Counterpoint, and, in the preface to my "Text book," (p. vii.), I endeavoured to sketch a plan for the side-by-side study of Counterpoint and harmony, as the student advanced with the latter. Undoubtedly, if the study of Counterpoint is not commenced until the learner has made considerable advance with harmony—mastering not only all the chords and their treatment, but also suspensions, passing-notes, etc., it will seem to him a most depressing repression to be held in with the bit and bridle of strict Counterpoint ; and that, moreover, in two parts. The harness will chafe.

But, five years ago, I wrote,—(I must be forgiven for quoting myself)—"There is nothing revolutionary in suggesting the enlargement of the basis of contrapuntal study, in conformity with the wider range of harmonies now recognized. There is really no justification for the perpetual and rigid exclusion, all through the student's contrapuntal course, of the chord of the 7th and its inversions. Or, to put the matter in another way : if, ... the study of Harmony .... be pursued in conjunction with that of Counterpoint, there is no valid reason why the rules should not be so far elasticized as to be progressively adapted to the further insight of the student into the various essential chords ..... The subsequent application of the rules respecting passing-notes, suspensions, etc., need be of no practical difficulty under a judicious teacher. .... If all this is done, with a wise, progressive conservatism, there will be no real provocation of the frequent complaints of students against the stringent exclusion of dissonant harmonies from their early exercises."—(Preface to seventh edition, pp. xiii.-xiv.)

I venture to submit, Mr. Editor, that these suggestions, thrown out years since, anticipated somewhat the matters that have been lately under discussion, and pretty well cover the ground. If any teachers, now-a-days, insist upon the study of strict Counterpoint exclusively, without extending their pupils' horizon beyond those narrow limits, or illustrating the application of the principles (not the rules, especially the prohibitory rules)—to modern, free writing, such musical Tories fail in their duty to those entrusted to them, through failure to apprehend, with their own minds, the philosophy of Counterpoint. But, though I am aware of the influence of certain examinations in perpetuating a somewhat antique rigidity, I believe that intelligent teachers are, now-a-days, more ready to proceed with what I have called a "progressive conservatism."

I may add that it is the "go-a-head" tendencies of the present day which have imbued students with a certain unsubmissive erraticism, necessitating more restrictiveness on the part of watchful teachers than might otherwise have been requisite.

I remain, dear Sir,
Yours faithfully,
HENRY CHAS. BANISTER.

August 21st, 1883.

Service Lists.

FOURTEENTH SUNDAY AFTER TRINITY.

AUGUST 26th.

London.

ST. PAUL'S CATHEDRAL.—Morn.: Service, Te Deum and Benedictus, Selby in A ; Introit, O God unseen, but ever near ; Holy Communion, Alwyn in C. Even.: Service, Magnificat and Nunc Dimittis, Selby in A ; Anthem, Whosoever drinketh of this water, and Therefore with joy (Bennett).

FOUNDLING CHAPEL.—Morn.: Service, Te Deum, Goss in F ; Jubilate, Sullivan in D ; Anthem, The Wilderness (Goss). Aft.: Children's Service.

CHRIST CHURCH, CLAPHAM.—Morn.: Service, Te Deum, Plain-song ; Kyrie, Credo, Sanctus, Benedictus, Agnus Dei, and Gloria in excelsis, Tours in F, and Eyre in A flat. Even.: Service, Magnificat and Nunc Dimittis, Tours in F ; Anthem, Great and marvellous (Boyce).

HOLY TRINITY, GRAY'S INN ROAD.—Morn.: Service, Te Deum, Dykes in F ; Jubilate, Chanted. Even. : Service, Magnificat, Chanted ; Nunc Dimittis, Parry in D ; Anthem, In the beginning was the word (Allen).

HOLY TRINITY, TULSE HILL.—Morn.: Chant Service. Even.: Service, Magnificat and Nunc Dimittis, Garrett in D ; Anthem, O that Thou hadst hearkened, and There is joy in the presence (Sullivan).

ST. JAMES'S PRIVATE EPISCOPAL CHAPEL, SOUTHWARK.—Morn.: Service, Introit, Blessed is he that cometh (Gounod) ; Communion Service, Haydn in B flat, No. 1. Even.: Service, Aldrich in G ; Anthem, Plead Thou my cause (Handel).

ST. MAGNUS, LONDON BRIDGE.—Morn.: Service, Opening Anthem, If we say (Calkin) ; Te Deum and Jubilate, Goss in A ; Kyrie (Goss). Even.: Service, Cantate and Deus Misereatur, Goss in C ; Anthem, O praise the Lord (Goss).

ST. MARGARET PATTENS, ROOD LANE, FENCHURCH STREET.—Morn.: Service, Te Deum, Sullivan in D ; Benedictus, Dykes in F ; Communion Service ; Offertory Anthem, To Thee, great Lord (Rossini) ; Kyrie, Credo, Sanctus, Benedictus, Agnus Dei, and Gloria, Hummel in B flat. Even.: Service, Magnificat and Nunc Dimittis, Steggall in C ; Anthem, O love the Lord (Sullivan).

ST. PAUL'S, AVENUE ROAD, SOUTH HAMPSTEAD.—Morn.: Service, Te Deum, Hopkins in G ; Benedictus, Goss ; Kyrie, Nares in F. Even.: Service, Magnificat and Nunc Dimittis, Bunnett in F ; Anthem, Incline Thine ear (Himmel).

ST. AUGUSTINE AND ST. FAITH, WATLING STREET.—Morn.: Service, Te Deum, Tours in F ; Benedictus (Gounod) ; Introit, Behold, O God (South) ; Communion Service, Tours in F. Even.: Service (Gounod) ; Anthem, I will mention (Sullivan).

ST. SAVIOUR'S, HOXTON. — Morn.: Service, Te Deum, Smart in F ; Holy Communion ; Kyrie, Credo, Sursum Corda, Sanctus, and Gloria in excelsis, Tours in F. Even.: Service, Magnificat and Nunc Dimittis, Stainer in F ; Anthem, The Lord is exalted (West).

ST. SEPULCHRE'S, HOLBORN. — Morn: Service, Boyce in A ; Anthem, From the rising (Ouseley). Even. : Service, Porter in D ; Anthem, Thy word is a lantern (Purcell).

Country.

ST. ASAPH CATHEDRAL. — Morn.: Service, Whitfeld in F; Anthem, Grant us Thy peace (Mendelssohn). Even.: Service, Whitfeld in F; Anthem, I will wash my hands (Hopkins).

ASHBURNE CHURCH, DERBYSHIRE. — Morn.: Service, Kempton in B flat, without accompaniement. Even.: Service, Arnold in B flat; Anthem, O taste and see (Goss); without accompaniment.

BIRMINGHAM (S. ALBAN THE MARTYR).—Morn.: Service, Te Deum and Benedictus, Dykes in F; Holy Communion; Kyrie, Credo, Sanctus, Gloria, Dykes in F; Benedictus and Agnus Dei, Redman in D. Evensong: Magnificat and Nunc Dimittis, Parry in D.

BIRMINGHAM (ST. CYPRIAN'S, HAY MILLS).—Morn.: Service, Cobb in G; Anthem, Wherewithal shall a young man (Elvey). Even.: Service, Cobb in G; Anthem, The Lord is my Shepherd (Kent).

CHESTER (ST. MARY'S CHURCH).—Morn.: Service, Boyce in C; Introit, O food that weary pilgrims love; Communion Service, Tuckermann in F. Even.: Service, Turle in D; Anthem, O rest in the Lord, and He that shall endure unto the end "Elijah" (Mendelssohn).

DONCASTER (PARISH CHURCH).—Morn.: Service, Calkin in B flat. Even.: Service, Stainer in E flat; Anthem, In humble faith (Garrett).

DUBLIN, ST. PATRICK'S (NATIONAL) CATHEDRAL.—Morn.: Service, Te Deum and Jubilate, Wesley in F; Holy Communion, Kyrie, Creed, Sanctus, Wesley in F. Even.: Service, Magnificat and Nunc Dimittis, Ebdon in C; Anthems, As pants the hart (Spohr), and Lord how they are increased (Stevenson).

ELY CATHEDRAL.—Morn.: Service, Walmisley in D; Kyrie and Credo, Walmisley in D; Gloria, Monk in A; Anthem, From all that dwell (Walmisley). Even.: Service, Walmisley in D; Anthem, Ye shall dwell in the land (Stainer).

HARROGATE (ST. PETER'S CHURCH). — Morn.: Service, Te Deum and Benedictus, Chants; Anthem, Come unto me (Smith); Kyrie and Credo, Wesley in E. Even.: Service, Magnificat and Nunc Dimittis, Turle in D; Anthem, O taste and see (Goss); Sullivan's arrangement of St. Ann's tune before Sermon.

LICHFIELD CATHEDRAL. — Morn.: Service, Calkin in B flat; Anthem, Rejoice ye "The morning stars" (Stainer). Even.: Service, Calkin in B flat; Anthem, Ascribe unto the Lord (Travers).

LEEDS PARISH CHURCH.—Morn.: Service, Garrett in F; Anthem, Lo, star led chiefs (Crotch); Introit, Blessed are they (Wesley), Kyrie and Creed, Dykes in F. Even.: Service, Garrett in F; Anthem, Blessed be the God (Wesley).

LEEDS (ST. LAURENCE CHURCH, PUDSEY). — Morn.: Service, Te Deum and Jubilate, Chants; Kyrie (Mendelssohn); Credo, Best in F; Sanctus, Marbeck in C; Offertory Sentences, Strickland in D. Even. Service, Magnificat and Nunc Dimittis, Chants; Anthem, Praise His awful name (Spohr).

LEED's (ST. MARTIN's, POTTERNEWTON).—Morning Service, Te Deum (Merbecke); Benedictus (Crouch); Anthem, The Lord is great (Best). Even.: Service, Magnificat and Nunc Dimittis, Tours in F; Anthem, Wherewithal shall a young man (Elvey).

LIVERPOOL CATHEDRAL.—Aft.: Service, Magnificat and Nunc Dimittis, Fitzgerald in B flat; Anthem, O sing unto the Lord (Purcell).

LIVERPOOL (ST. CUTHBERT'S, EVERTON).—Morn.: Service, Barnby in E. Even.: Service, Barnby in E; Anthem, O where shall wisdom (Boyce).

MANCHESTER CATHEDRAL.—Morn.: Service, Ouseley in G; Full Communion Service, Jeykll in C; Anthem, As for me (Wesley). Aft.: Service, Ouseley in G; Anthem, Proclaim ye this (Pyne).

MANCHESTER (ST. BENEDICT'S).—Morn.: Service, Credo and Gloria in excelsis, Williams in D; Kyrie, Sanctus, Benedictus, and Agnus Dei, Mozart in B flat, No. 7. Even.: Service, Magnificat and Nunc Dimittis, Tours in F.

MANCHESTER (ST. JOHN BAPTIST, HULME).—Morn.: Service, Kyrie, Credo, Sanctus, Benedictus, and Agnus Dei (Gounod); Gloria in excelsis, Tours in F. Even.: Service, Magnificat and Nunc Dimittis, Tours in F.

PETERBOROUGH CATHEDRAL.—Morn.: Service, Boyce in A; Introit, Give ear; Communion Service, Tours in F. Even.: Service, Hopkins in F; Anthem, The wilderness (Goss).

SALISBURY CATHEDRAL.—Morn.: Service, Te Deum, Jubilate, Kyrie and Credo, Wesley in F; Offertory (Stainer). Aft.: Service, Wesley in F; Anthem, How lovely are Thy dwellings (Spohr).

SHERBORNE ABBEY. — Morn.: Service, Te Deum, Clarke-Whitfield in E. Even.: Service, Magnificat and Nunc Dimittis, Chants; Anthem, Bring unto the Lord, O ye mighty (Limpus).

SOUTHAMPTON (ST. MARY'S CHURCH).—Morn.: Service, Te Deum and Benedictus, Garrett in D; Holy Communion, Introit, They that put their trust (Macfarren); Service, Monk in C; Offertory, Lay not up (Barnby); Paternoster (Field). Even.: Service, Magnificat and Nunc Dimittis, Garrett in D; Apostles' Creed, Harmonized Monotone. Anthem, In Jewry (Whitfeld).

WELLS CATHEDRAL.—Morn.: Service, Croft in A; Introit, Blessed are they (Macfarren). Even.: Service, Attwood in D; Anthem, Hear, O Thou Shepherd (Walmisley).

WORCESTER CATHEDRAL.—Morn.: Service, Stewart in G; Anthem, See what love (Mendelssohn). Even. Service, Stewart in G; Anthem, We will rejoice (Croft).

ERRATUM.—In paragraph number 10 of Passing Events, in last issue, page 105, for sight-seeing read sight-singing.

. Post-cards must be sent to the Editor, 6, Argyle Square, W.C., by Wednesday. Lists are frequently omitted in consequence of not being received in time.

The MUSICAL STANDARD

A NEWSPAPER FOR MUSICIANS PROFESSIONAL AND AMATEUR

No. 996. Vol. XXV. FOURTH SERIES. SATURDAY, SEPTEMBER 1, 1883. WEEKLY: PRICE 3D.

MOZART'S ORGAN WORKS.

BY FRANK J. SAWYER, B.Mus. Oxon., F.C.O.

[*A Lecture delivered at the College of Organists.*]

(*Continued from page* 111).

Although Sonata No. 6 is the first bearing a distinct date, July, 1775, yet Röchel arranges five others before this in point of age. Of these, No. 1 in E flat is the only one in a slow *tempo* andante, the organ part expressed solely by the words—*Bassi ed Organo*—to the bass line.

No. 2 in B flat (allegro) is more florid, but similarly marked as regards organ, as, indeed, is No. 3 in D. No. 4, likewise in D, opens with a vigorous staccato passage, and contains the addition of a figured bass to the organ part.

. No. 5 in F has no *tempo* mark, but is undoubtedly allegro moderato. Here we first meet with the word *tasto solo*, as well as the figured bass, yet strangely the re-entry of the 'cello is not marked.

No. 6 in B flat (allegro) marks again a progress in the greater freedom and scope left for the organ in the accompanying passages to the violins.

To the same date, 1775, belong No. 7 in F, and 8 in A. The period of 1775 and '76 and '77, as far as September, spent at Salzburg, mark perhaps the only period of quiet in the life of Mozart. Then he would, from his father's duties, be brought frequently to the Cathedral. Hence we find the organ used during 1775 not only for the three sonatas, but also in a Mass in C, a Kyrie with organ accompaniment, an Offertorium and an "Osanna."

The first sonata in the following year, 1776, is not .ncluded in the Breitkopt and Hartel Edition; it was in E major allegro.

In March we find Mozart again at the organ, using it in the accompaniment to a Litania de Venerabili, and in April writing Sonatas 9 and 10, which shall furnish our first practical examples of his works.

That they may be the better understood I will first lay before you a short analysis of each.

No. 9 in F major, ¾-time allegro, opens with a pleasing theme announced by the first violin, the second violin playing a broken accompaniment, the 'cello reiterating the bass notes, and the organ—marked "copula alone," being an 8-foot flute stop—filling up much in the way that the wood wind in an orchestra would support the strings. At the eighth bar the theme is repeated, overture fashion, but this time it is given to the organ, the violins, and 'cello, merely accompanying until six bars later Mozart's usual progression to the dominant C takes place. Then the second theme starts with three staccato notes for the first violin, the use of the organ again being simple but excellent. The second phrase of the theme repeated, and six bars coda lead us to the double bar with its repeat.

The development in the second section is of much interest. The opening skip of the octave in the first theme forms the first material, and is at the fifth bar treated in canon at the fourth below between the first and second violins; then the second bar of the second theme and the second phrase before mentioned come in for treatment, and with a passage of descending chords of the sixth the return of the first subject comes. This section is in the usual style of this period, the repetition down to the close in C before the entry of the second theme being an exact copy, and from there to the end merely a transposition into the key of F.

I will now ask you to listen to the sonata.

[*Sonata No.* 9.]

It is with perhaps pardonable pride that I take the liberty of supposing that this performance of it, with which you have so approved, is probably the first time the sonata has been heard in public, since in about 1780 it was placed amongst the lumber of Salzburg Cathedral, by the order of Archbishop Colloredo.

No. 10 in D forms in many respects a contrast to its predecessor. Opening with a bold unison phrase on the tonic chord, the theme proper seems to start at the third bar, where the organ, in imitation of the wood wind, doubles the violins in the octave. A bold passage for all the instruments, forte, with the introduction of the second theme, with one of the most charming effects to be found in the sonatas. The organ, like a horn, holds on the dominant E, the violin's staccato giving out the elegant little second subject with its strange accented note in the second beat of the second bar, the whole passage being repeated. Then follows a forte phrase, and with a unison passage taken from the episode following the first subject, we reach the double bar. The development, starting in the key of A minor, is chiefly formed on this same phrase, treated in imitation between the first violin and 'cello. Then we reach the first pedal note, or rather note for the pedals, which we have yet met with, the dominant A, and which serves, after a curious use of the organ, to accompany the strings, to reintroduce the first theme; the repetition takes place exactly in the usual way, the only special point being the addition of a lower third octave to the sustained A of the organ during the entry of the second subject, an early use of the inverted pedal, to the beauty of which I have already drawn attention.

[*Sonata No.* 10.]

One more sonata (in C major, common time, allegro) was composed during this period, but is for some reason not contained in the Breitkopf and Härtel Edition. This is to be regretted, as in it we find the addition of two trumpets to our previous instruments.

Mozart, in his letter to Padre Martini, September 4, 1776, writes:—

" I live in a place where music prospers but little, although we have some good musicians, and some especially good composers of thorough knowledge and taste. The theatre suffers from want of singers; we have few male sopranos, and are not likely to have more, for they require high pay, and over liberality is not our weak point. I busy myself with writing Church and chamber music, and we have two capital contrapuntists, Haydn and Adlgarrer. My father is Capellmeister at the Cathedral, which gives me the opportunity of writing as much as I like for the Church. But as my father has been thirty-six years in the service of the Court, and knows that the Archbishop does not care to have people of an advanced age about him, he takes things quietly, and devotes himself chiefly to literature, which has always been his favourite study. Our Church music differs widely and increasingly from that of Italy. A Mass with Kyrie, Gloria, Credo, the Sonata at the Epistle, the Offertorium or Motet, Sanctus and Agnus Dei, must not last longer than three-quarters of an hour, even in festivals, when the Archbishop himself officiates. This kind of composition requires special study."

Hence we again find from Mozart's own pen that these sonatas formed part of the service itself. One other point I would wish to mention. I remember to have read on several occasions that *concertos* were not performed in church; this is erroneous, as Burney even mentions them, while Jahn (vol. 1, page 286), says:—" Distinguished instrumental performers also were allowed to add their share to the attractions of Divine worship. Instrumental concertos were played at the conclusion of the Service, without any regard to an ecclesiastical character." This, therefore, would settle the point.

The following Sonata, No. 11 in the Breitkopf Edition, has only a figured bass line, though the figuring is copious. It is in G major, and opens with a unison theme. This was composed in 1777, together with No. 12 in major. Here again the organ part is restricted to a figured bass line, but the sonata becomes, by the addition to the score of two oboes, two trumpets and drums, virtually a small concerto. It contains so many points of interest, that I greatly regret that adequate means are not possible to-night for a complete rendition. The opening theme is bold and healthy in vigour. From the fulness of the figured bass line, it is evident that the organ part when performed was far more full than the scanty organ parts of Sonatas 9 and 10 would lead one to suppose. Hence I felt justified in filling up the bareness occasionally met with.

The following year, 1777, saw Mozart's meeting with the first of those unpleasantnesses that seem so to have embittered his life. To quote from Herr Pohl :—"All that teaching could do for him had been done in Salzburg ; the time had now come for him to go out into the world and let the discipline of life complete the work. His existence at Salzburg had long become intolerable to him ; beyond a few intimate friends, he had no society ; he was disgusted at the want of appreciation for art, and his position with regard to the Archbishop Hieronymus became daily more critical." The father asked for leave to accompany his son on a professional tour. The Archbishop refused, saying that "he could not bear to see people going about begging in that fashion." Mozart applied for his discharge, and on September 23, 1777, set out with his mother—first to Munich, then to Augsburg.

In the latter place he made the acquaintance of Stein, the instrument maker. One scene of their meeting Mozart shall narrate in his own words :—"When I told Herr Stein that I should like to play upon his organ (in the Barfüserkirche), for that I had a passion for the organ, he was greatly astonished, and said : ' What ! a man like you, a clavier player, willing to play on an instrument with no douceur, no expression ; which allows of neither *piano* nor *forte*, but goes on always the same !' ' All that has nothing to do with it. To my mind, the organ is the king of all instruments.' ' Well, do as you like.' So we went together. I could guess from his way of talking that he did not expect me to do his organ much credit ; he thought I should play clavier-fashion. He told me how he had taken Choberl to the organ, according to his request. ' And I was sorry,' said he, ' for Choberl had told everybody, and the church was full. I had imagined the fellow would be full of spirit, fire, and rapidity, and that would tell on the organ ; but as soon as he began I changed my opinion.' I only said, ' What do you think, Herr Stein ? are you afraid that I shall come to grief on the organ ?' ' Ah, you ! that is quite different.' We went into the choir ; I began to prelude, at which he laughed with delight ; then followed a fugue. ' I can well believe,' said he, ' that you enjoy playing the organ, when you play like that.' At first I did not quite understand the pedal, because it was not divided. It began C, then D E in a row. With us D and E are above where E flat and F sharp are here. But I soon got accustomed to it."

The latter remarks evidently refer to a short octave pedal board. Again, he took the monks of St. Ulrich and of the Monastery of the Holy Cross by storm. The Dean, who, he says, is "a jolly good fellow," was quite beside himself.

It is stated that Franz Liszt is at present in Weimar, where he is hard at work upon the composition of a new oratorio, " St. Stanislas."

Musical Intelligence.

OPERA AT THE CRYSTAL PALACE.

Mr. Manns is carrying on an active campaign at Sydenham in the general operatic line of action. He began on Tuesday afternoon, August 21, with Wallace's "Maritana," first heard at Drury Lane theatre in 1846, and ever since a "trump card" for theatrical managers. The performance was a very successful one, chiefly on account of Mr. J. W. Turner's rendering of the part of Don Cæsar. Mr. Turner sang in splendid voice, and was honoured with encores of most of the popular tenor airs.

On Saturday (August 25), " Il Barbiere di Siviglia " was performed, when Mr. W. Bolton appeared to great advantage as Figaro, both in a musical and a dramatic sense ; and Mr. Griffin, a *basso profundo*, made a successful *début* in the part of Don Basilio, singing the famous air "La Calunnia" with great effect. Mr. Griffin has a voice of great power and compass ; his concert was recently noticed in these columns. Signor Zoboli did well as old Bartolo. Mr. Faulkner Leigh cannot be complimented for his impersonation of the Count Almaviva, in the (rather disgusting) drunken scene ; his odd attitudes provoked the mirth of some experienced operagoers, who sat near the reporter. The Helots of Sparta could hardly have done more to make folks laugh. Madame Rose Hersee carried off the honours of the day. Her charmingly sweet and flexible voice was displayed to perfection in Rode's air, but Mdme. Hersee might have chosen a better and less hackneyed piece.

On Thursday (August 23) appeared a truly fascinating Margherita in Gounod's " Faust." Madame Marian Hood *looks* the interesting girl, so exquisitely pourtrayed by Goethe, to the very life, and as "to the manner born ;" Mdme. Christine Nilsson alone stands on a loftier level. Mdme. Hood has a beautiful, delicately feminine physiognomy, and a most winning manner. Every heart must have been moved by her pathos and passion. The voice is a pure, liquid, silvery, and "sympathetic" soprano, super-excellent in the higher register, and very even throughout ; the execution facile, unconstrained, and exact : the production admirable. Mdme. Hood made a great point in the "Jewel song" and the "King of Thule" ballad, which Hector Berlioz, unlike Gounod, writes in the major (F) mode. The action in the Cathedral scene was a severe test of histrionic talents—denoted close study and intuitive conception ; but the Prayer-book was made rather too much of. The dying scene constituted a fine climax to a magnificent performance. Faust might have thought of Phœbus Apollo, in pursuit of Daphne, as he regarded Margaret's flowing hair and other charms.

" Spectat *inornatos* collo pendere capillos,
　Et, Quid ? Si *comantur*, ait. Videt igne micantes,
　Sidenbus similes oculos ; videt oscula . . . . .
　　　　　　　. . . . Laudat digitosque, manusque,
　Brachiaque . . . ."

Of the other artists, only Mr. W. Bolton, the Valentine of the opera, can be commended. Mr. Faulkner Leigh's Faust is ineffective, and his *physique* fails to realize the mouldy old philosopher in his state of magical rejuvenescence. One pitied Gretchen at having to be wooed by such a lover. Mr. Lansmere, as the fiend Mephistopheles, left out a portion of his music in a certain scene, and sang, in the Cathedral situation, behind a wall instead of in view of the audience ! "Don Giovanni" and "Figaro" were down for the week ; and Auber's "Fra Diavolo" should not be deferred.

The Saturday evening concerts are going on prosperously, and deserve public patronage if only for the excellence of the programmes.

On Thursday, Friday, and Saturday, August 23rd, 24th, and 25th, a Swiss Bazaar was held in the Town Hall, Folkestone, in aid of the funds for the completion of St. Michael's Church, the Incumbent of which, the Rev. E. Husband, is a well-known musical man, the Services at whose church are much admired. During the bazaar, Viscountess Folkestone gave a series of concerts to crowded audiences, and her Ladyship (whose singing was loudly applauded) was assisted by the Hon. Wilma Pleydell Bouverie, the Hon. Jacob Pleydell Bouverie, Mr. Robert J. Pitt, and the Rev. E. Husband. The amount realized was about £250, and much of this gratifying result was due to the great kindness of Lady Folkestone and her friends.

AVENUE THEATRE.

On August 25th, a farcical extravaganza, called "A Bunch of Keys," was here presented as a "musical comedy," by the Anglo-American company now in possession of this theatre. Neither the words, by Mr. C. Hoyt, or the music, by Mr. G. L. Gordon, pretend to any exaltation. The main object of the piece, as regards the literary department, is to make people laugh; musically, the presence of catching tunes and pretty dance measures, with occasional effective touches of orchestration, are the paramount features of the work, which only pretends to be a "musical comedy." A number of eccentric people, including a good stage lawyer, at cross purposes, and now and then disguised, with an admirably constructed bar scene in an American hotel, form the ingredients of the dramatic action. The leading parts were admirably played by Mr. Willie Edouin (who sustained the lawyer's part with capital spirit), Mr. J. S. Powers (an actor possessing an abundant sense of broad humour), Miss Alice Atherton (who sings and dances with much piquancy and grace). The other clever performers included Mr. F. Desmond, Mr. C. B. Stevens, Mr. A. Sims, Miss J. Verona, Miss H. Chapman, and Miss V. Reynolds. "A Bunch of Keys" wants a little weeding with regard to certain passages not in perfect taste. The piece, however, will be found one of real laughter-provoking power, with some pleasant, tuneful music, and it will most likely hit the public taste.

THE GLOUCESTER FESTIVAL.

The full rehearsals for this the 160th meeting of the three choirs will begin in earnest on Monday next. The scheme of the Festival is one of remarkable interest, both as regards the number of novelties to be given, and the wide historical basis of the programme, including standard works of all schools of the past 300 years, from Bird and Orlando Gibbons to our own day. Such a selection reflects the highest credit upon the authorities concerned; and with the proved skill of an excellent conductor, Mr. C. L. Williams, and a capital staff of skilled executants, including some 65 instrumentalists, a very successful meeting seems to be a foregone conclusion. Cathedral Services : Choral Service each morning in the Cathedral, by the three choirs; Tuesday morning at ten o'clock, the other three mornings at eight o'clock. Usual choral services on Tuesday, Wednesday, and Thursday evenings at 5 o'clock. Special nave service on Friday evening, at 6.30, with full band and chorus. On Tuesday morning, a sermon will be preached by the Very Rev. C. J. Vaughan, D.D., the Dean of Llandaff, in aid of the widows and orphans of the poorer Clergy within the Diocese of Gloucester, Worcester, and Hereford. All the Services, except that of Friday evening, will be held in the choir. Service music : Tuesday morning, Service, Smart in F; Anthem, "This is the day" (Oakeley). Wednesday morning, Service, Walmisley in D; Anthem, "Thou Judge of quick and dead" (Wesley). Thursday morning, Service, Garrett in E; Anthem, "Blessed be the God" (Wesley). Friday morning, Service, Travers in F; Anthem, "O Saviour of the world" (Goss). Organ, Mr. W. Done. Tuesday morning, September 4th, "Elijah" (Mendelssohn). The programme on Tuesday evening, September 4th, includes "Symphony in G minor" (Mozart); violin solo, "Concerto in D," 1st movement (Beethoven), Mr. Carrodus; new choral work, "The glories of our blood and state" (Parry), composed for this concert; overture, "Anacreon" (Cherubini); chorus, "I wish to tune my quivering lyre" (Dyer); pianoforte solo, "Ballade in G minor," Op. 23, No. 1 (Chopin), Miss Amy Hare, and "Allan a Dale" (Lloyd). Wednesday morning, September 5th, "St. Mary Magdalen" (Stainer), composed for this Festival, conducted by the composer; part 2, "Bow thine ear" (Bird, 1560); "Hosanna to the son of David (Gibbons, 1604); and, "Mass in C" (Beethoven). Wednesday evening, September 5th, part 1, "Sennacherib" (Arnold); composed for this Festival, conducted by the composer; part 2, "Hymn of Praise" (Mendelssohn). Thursday morning, September 6th, "Elegiac Symphony" (Stanford), conducted by the composer; "Redemption" (Gounod). The programme, on Thursday evening includes : overture, "Jessonda" (Spohr); "Song of the heart" (Tennant), Miss Hilda Wilson; "The First Walpurgis night" (Mendelssohn); overture, "Prometheus" (Beethoven); madrigal, "Why weeps, alas! my lady love?" (Pearsall); and march, "Tannhäuser" (Wagner). Friday morning, September 7th, "The Messiah" (Handel). Friday evening, special nave Service, organ voluntary; overture, "Last Judgment" (Spohr); Magnificat, Walmisley in D minor; Nunc Dimittis, Walmisley in D minor; Anthem, "Blessed is the man that considereth the poor and needy" (Lloyd), and, "Hallelujah" Beethoven). Doubtless such a scheme will be duly appreciated.

THE CHURCH CONGRESS.

The brief article of last week's issue, calling attention to the poverty (from the musical point of view) of the scheme for the Reading meeting, has given rise to further accusations of neglect, and to some explanations. It appears that the want of a thorough, painstaking consideration of the position of music in the Church has not only been felt, but urged, and the blame of the neglect would seem to lie at the door of the Subject Committee. It is thought by some that the members of that committee are either anxious to promote the consideration of questions of more burning and personal interest to the clergy, or desirous of securing topics upon which they can best talk about themselves. Thinking people agree that the studied neglect of musical questions at these meetings is a blind, wilful, and foolish policy it is high time now to reverse.

SWANSEA MUSICAL EISTEDDFOD.

On the 21st of August, an interesting Musical Eisteddfod was held in the grounds of Oystermouth Castle : there were about 7,000 visitors. Mr. Charles Gold presided, and the adjudications were given by Eos Morlais and Mr. W. T. Samuels; the Rev. E. Edwards was the conductor. The chief competitions and results were as follows :—£10 to a choir of not less than 60 voices, for the best rendering of "I was tossed by the winds." Five competed, and the successful choir was declared to be the California (Clydach). To the choir of not less than 30 voices for the best rendering of "Jerusalem, my glorious home," Cwmbwrla was successful. Duet, "Maying," Mr. J. Edwards and Miss Mary Charles. Tenor solo, "If with all your hearts" (Elijah). G. T. Davies, Morriston. Bass solo, "Honour and Arms" (Samson), Hy. Rees, London. Prize for sight-singing divided between W. Thomas, Cwmbwrla, and D. Lloyd, Crossland. There was a successful concert in the evening.

FESTIVAL OF ASSOCIATED CHOIRS AT WHITBY.

For some time past there has been evinced in more than one quarter of the Whitby Rural Deanery, over which the Rector of Whitby presides, a desire to bring together at one grand service all, or at any rate a large proportion, of the choirs connected with the churches within the limits of the Deanery. The idea has been brought about, and the success which attended the festival given in St. Michael's Church augurs well for the construction of a most useful association on a wide and firm basis, whose annual festival may be looked forward to with positive pleasure. The festival was held on August 21st., and St. Michael's was crowded in every part, the large congregation including many of the visitors now sojourning at this charming resort. The choirs which took part in the service were :—Grosmont, 26; Lythe, 24; Fylingdales, 20; St. Michaels, 25; St. Ninian's, 16; Iron Church, 20; Parish Church and St. John's, 8; Ruswarp, 14; total, 133. These were under the direction of Mr. Henry Hallgate, the conductor, to whom praise is justly due for the very indefatigable manner in which he performed the arduous task of training the scattered choirs for this service. A word of praise is also due to Mr. Carr, choirmaster. The organ accompaniment was rendered in the most efficient manner possible by Mr. H. R. Bird, organist of the Parish Church, Kensington. The prayers were intoned by the Rev. S. Flood Jones, precentor of Westminster Abbey, who shewed a laudable desire to render valuable help in preparing for the service. Special psalms were sung to chants by Elvey and Jones, and the Magnificat and Nunc Dimittis were Lloyd's. The anthem was "From all that dwell below the skies," by Dr. Walmisley. Hymns were also sung before the sermon, and while the offertory was being taken. The musical portion of the service was rendered with much taste and judgment throughout, and reflected the greatest possible credit upon all who took an active part in it; and this remark applies with all the more force, when it is considered that there were necessarily many drawbacks to encounter in connection with this, the first festival given by these associated choirs.

GLASGOW.

The musical season is once more at hand, and evidences are not wanting to show that a considerable amount of stir and activity already exists. The Choral Union will perform, among other works, Mendelssohn's "Walpurgis Night," Gounod's "Redemption," Berlioz's "Messe des Morts," Felicien David's "The Desert," and Handel's "Messiah" and "Acis and Galatea." Mr. Manns will again act as conductor, and M. Victor Buziau as leader. The orchestral works and leading performers will be announced in due course. The City Hall concerts in connection with the Abstainers' Union will commence on September 15th. The Musical Union, under the new conductor, Mr. William Moodie, is going to study three Handelian works, the "Messiah," "Acis and Galatea," and the "Dettingen Te Deum." The Glasgow and South-Western Railway Musical Association will study Van Bree's "St. Cecilia's Day," and other works. Dr. A. L. Peace is giving organ recitals in the Cathedral; and Mr. John Fulcher, a well-known Glasgow professor of music, has announced concerts in the City Hall. The Royal Italian Opera company is coming to the Royalty theatre on September 10th.

WHITBY.—On Sunday August 12th, at St. Michael's Church the Services were of a remarkably bright and hearty character. They were fully choral, and were rendered in the most effective manner. Mr. Bird, the organist of the parish church, Kensington, presided at the organ in the absence of Mr. Clark. At the evening Service the prayers were intoned by the Rev. S. Flood Jones, precentor of Westminster Abbey, and the Rev. A. G. Austen; the anthem was "O how amiable," by Mr. John Storer, Mus.Bac., a former organist of the church, and now organist of the Parish Church, Scarborough.

OLDHAM.—At the Exhibition now being held here the organ recitals recently given have been very successful, larger audiences attending every day. Upon one occasion Mr. C. Bloomfield Bumstead performed Weber's overture, "Preciosa;" Mendelssohn's "Sonata No. 2;" etc. Mr. Bumstead is a very highly-finished player and reflects credit on the eminent masters under whom he has studied. Mr. Joseph Clafton, who gave an organ recital upon another occasion and in the evening of the same day a concert assisted by his son, Mr. William Clafton, on the violin, and Miss Johnson and Mr. R. L. Whittaker as vocalists, needed no introduction to an Oldham audience. Mr. William Clafton's mastery of the violin in the difficult solos he rendered was pleasurably evident to all; and the singing of Miss Johnson, and Mr. R. L. Whittaker was all that could be desired. Mr. Clafton has also conducted a grand concert given by the members of the Oldham Vocal Society. —On August 22nd, at the Exhibition, a short organ recital was given by Mr. Herbert Chadwick, who displayed considerable taste and skill in his performance.—A concert was given by the Vocal Society recently to a large and appreciative audience. The most striking feature of the concert was undoubtedly the excellent part-singing of the choir. In consequence of the absence of a number of members, the effect at times was not quite satisfactory, this being noticeable more especially in the last movement of Hill's "Hushed in Death"; but in the passages requiring soft, delicate, and expressive singing the effect was admirable in every way. The selection of the choral pieces was admirable, containing pieces by Macfarren, Hatton, Stewart, &c. The programme contained Cowen's "Unfinished song." This is a charming song, and was sung by one of the contraltos with great taste and expression. Mr. Clafton conducted and accompanied with much skill and judgment.

F. Townsend Southwick, organist of the Congregational Church, Oswego, N.Y., recently gave three organ recitals in that church. His programmes were very interesting, and according to all accounts, well rendered. Some of the pieces played were Rheinberger's "Pastoral Sonata," Bach's Fugue in C minor and Dorian Toccata, Eugene Thayer's variations on "Pleyel's Hymn" and "Ave Maria"; Gustav Merkel's three grand Choral Preludes; Handel's Concerto in F, Mendelssohn's Organ Sonata in C minor, No. 2; Thiele's "Chromatic Fantasie," and Hesse's Fantasie for two performers, in D minor. In the interpretation of the latter work, Mr. Southwick had the assistance of Prof. H. B. Huerter, organist of St. Mary's Church. These recitals have interested the public, have had their influence for good, and have furnished evidence of the advance of organ playing in America, where indeed many excellent organists are to be found.

Foreign Musical Intelligence.

Lortzing's "Ordine" is to inaugurate the season at Berlin.

Berlioz's "Benvenuto Cellini" has been successful in Leipzig.

"Mazeppa," Tschaïkowsky's new opera will be shortly performed in St. Petersburg.

Herr A. Thierfelder's new opera, "Der Trentdjäger," has been given in Brandenburg.

Dr. Hugo Riemann, of Hamburg, announces a supplement to his "Musik-Lexicon."

M. Lavastre, the decorator of the Paris Opera House, died recently at the age of 56.

Giuseppe Del-Maino, a distinguished professor of the violin and viola, died on August 14, at Parma.

That Rubinstein's "Sulamite" will be given at Hamburgh in the autumn, seems to be accepted as a certainty.

A concert is to be given at Aix-les-Bains for the benefit of the sufferers by the catastrophe at Casamicciola.

Popular concerts are being successfully given in Marseilles after the manner of our promenade concerts.

Mr. F. Besson has obtained a diploma of honour for the construction of brass instruments at the Exhibition at Amsterdam.

The Choral Society of Dijon, together with the local Musical Union, announced a concert in the wood of the park there, the other day.

Flotow, it is said, besides the opera "Count of San Megrin," has also left a comic opera in three acts, called "The Miller of Meunier."

O Mundo Artistico is the title of a new journal published in Lisbon and dedicated to art matters. The paper is excellently got up, with admirably lithographed front page.

Ferdinand Hiller has requested the editor of Le Ménestrel to deny the report of his retirement from the direction of the Conservatoire at Cologne and the Gürzenich concerts given in the same city.

At Sondershausen lately a concert was given under Herr Schröder, at which Tschaïkowsky's overture to "Romeo and Juliet" was performed.

An out-door concert upon a large scale was given in Venice on the 15th of August, in aid of the sufferers at Ischia. Some 300 performers assisted.

M. Benjamin Godard is reported to be engaged upon the composition of an opera, "Don Pedro de Zalamea," which will be first produced at Antwerp. The libretto is by Messrs. Sylvestre and Detroyat.

A new Mass in F, by Mdlle. Angelina Henn, was given at Bonne-Nouvelle on August 15. The "Kyrie," "Benedictus," and "Agnus Dei" are specially commended, though the whole work is much praised.

The new Conservatoire opened only last April in Sondershausen, under the direction of Herr Carl Schröder, has, it is said, made a very successful commencement, eighty-five pupils having already entered it.

An excellent new organ has been built by the Brothers Lingiardi, of Pavia, for the parish church of Saint Eulalia, Cagliari. The tone of each department is spoken of by the Italian local press as very admirable.

M. Jules Blüthner, of Leipzig, has obtained a diploma of honour for his pianofortes at the Amsterdam Exhibition; and a gold medal has been awarded at the same place to MM. Th. Mann and Co., of Bielfefeld for their iron pianofortes.

On August 24th a concert was to be given in Milan in aid of sufferers at Ischia. The chorus of 350 voices was under the direction of Signor Cairati, the orchestra consisted of 100 performers, and the conductor was Signor Raffaele Kuon.

It is authoritively stated that Herr Angelo Neumann has undertaken the direction of the Bremen Opera, and will during the coming season produce there, in addition to the standard classical works of the répertoire, the "Rheingold," "Walküre," and "Tristan und Isolde." Herr Anton Seidl is engaged to conduct Wagner's works.

Organ News.

LIVERPOOL.

An organ recital was given in St. George's Hall, by Mr. W. T. Best, on Thursday, August 23rd. The following was the programme :—

Overture, "Regenella"	Braga.
Adagio from the Sestet for Horns and Stringed Instruments	Beethoven.
Introduction and Fugue in G major	Best.
Allegretto and Adagio Religioso, from the Symphony to the "Lobgesang"	Mendelssohn.
March for the Organ in E flat major	Salomé.

And on Saturday, August 25th :—

Organ Sonata, No. 2 in A minor	Capocci.
Andante Cantabile in G major	Wesley.
Selection from the music to "A Midsummer's Night's Dream "	Mendelssohn.
Prelude and Fugue in C major	Bach.
Overture, "L'Ombra"	Flotow.

FISHERIES EXHIBITION.

The following organ recitals have been given during the last week.

Mr. Loaring's programmes included the following :—

Overture, "La Gazza Ladra"	Rossini.
Gavotte	Bach.
Prelude and Fugue	Baumgarten.
Selection from "Le Prophète"	Meyerbeer.
"Let the bright Seraphim," and "Let their celestial concerts"	Handel.
Grand March, "La Festa"	Westbrook.
Overture, "The Poet and the Peasant"	Suppé.

Overture, "Sophonisbe "	Paer.
Gavotte in D	Loaring.
Fugue in E flat	Bach.
Selection from "H.M.S. Pinafore "	Sullivan.
Organ Concerto, No. 6	Handel.
March "Placida"	Carter.
Overture, "Il Tancredi"	Rossini.

The programme of the recitals by Mr. H. C. Tonking, on Wednesday, August 22nd, were :—

Overture, "Occasional Oratorio"	Handel.
Offertoire in G	Batiste.
Fugue in E major	Bert.
Festal March in F	Smart.
"Hercules" March	Trembath.

On Friday, August 24th :—

Andante in F, No. 2	Smart.
Concert Fugue in G	Krebs.
Postlude in D	Smart.
Canon in A	Salomé.
Fantasia on a Welsh March	Best.

On Saturday, August 25th :—

March in B flat	Silas.
Fanfare	Lemmens.
Andante in F	Wely.

The programme of the recital by Mr. Clough, on Thursday, August 23rd, included :—

Offertoire in F major	Wely.
Toccata in D minor, and Fugue in B flat major	Bach.
"March Triomphale"	Clough.
Andant't, with variations	Batiste.
Fanfare and Final	Lemmens.

And by Mr. J. Loaring :—

Overture, "Il Tancredi"	Rossini.
Organ Concerto, No 2	Handel.
Andante from 1st Symphony	Haydn.
Offertoire in F	Clarke.
Grand March, "La Festa"	Westbrook.

And by Mr. Theo. Ward :—

Grand March	Clarke.
Prelude and Fugue	Bach.
"Improvisation "	

And by Mr. E. H. Sügg :—

Grand Chorus	Guilmant.
Andante, with variations	Haydn.
Grand March	Sögg.
Prelude and Fugue, No. 2	Mendelssohn.
Offertoire in A	Clarke.
Gavotte	Sögg.
Offertoire in E major	Batiste.

WARE.

An organ recital was given at the Parish Church on Thursday, August 23rd, by Mr. Geo. Herbert Gregory, Mus. Bac., F.C.O., Mr. James L. Gregory, F.C.O., and Mr. Alfred E. Gregory, A.Mus. T.C.L. The programme included :—

Concerto in A	Handel.
Grave—Allegro—Minuet e Trio—Fuga.	
Andante in A (Posthumous)	Smart.
Larghetto from the 2nd Symphony	Beethoven.
Romanza from Symphony in E flat	Haydn.
Two Nocturnes in E flat and F minor	Chopin.
Minuet and Trio	Çalkin.

DEVONPORT.

An organ recital was given in the Albert Road Chapel, Morice Town, on the new organ, erected by Messrs. Hele and Co., Plymouth, by Mr. John Pardew, on Friday, August 24th. The following was the programme :—

Offertoire	Wely.
Andante	Guilmant.
Chorus, "Sing unto God"	Handel.
Cavatina	Raff.
Allegro	Lemmens.
Gavotte	Ghys.
"Waft her, Angels"	Handel.
March	Mendelssohn.

BERKELEY SQUARE.

The following pieces were played by Mr. P. de Surpis, the hon. organist of St. Mary's, after service on Sunday evening, the 5th inst., on the occasion of the completion of the organ, by Bryceson Brothers :—

March, "Abraham "	Molique.
Offertoire, in D minor	Batiste.
Andante in A	Smart.
March, "Cornelius "	Mendelssohn.

GLASGOW.

An organ recital was given on Monday, August 6th, in the Cathedral, by Dr. A. L. Peace. The following was the programme :—

Organ Concerto, "Cuckoo and Nightingale "	Handel.
Meditation in F sharp minor	
Cantilène Pastorale, op. ...	Guilmant.
Grand Chœur in D major	
Grand Prelude and Fugue in D major	Bach.
Cantique Religieuse, "Notre Dame des Petits Enfants "	Gounod.
Rondo, "Con L'Imitazione de Campanelli "	Morandi.
March, "King David"	Harley.

And on Monday, Aug. 20th :—

Organ Sonata, No. 2	Chauvet.
Allegro—Andante con espressione—Sonata	
Adagio (Quartet in B flat, No. 3)	Mozart.
Prelude and Fugue in D major	Mendelssohn.
Song, "Ave Maria"	Schubert.
"Post Communion," per Organo	Morandi.
Marche Héroïque	Saint-Saens.

FRIERN BARNET.

A fine organ of 3 manuals and pedal, with 29 sounding stops, and the usual number of couplers and accessory movements, has just been erected at All Saints' Church, by Messrs. Bryceson, Bros. It was opened with a special service and recital, on Thursday evening, August 23rd, Mr. J. C. B. Tirbutt, organist of All Saints', Reading, being the organist. The following was the programme :—

Introduction and Air, varied	Hesse.
Two Andantes	Batiste.
Fugue in E flat, "St. Ann"	Bach.
Fantasia, "O Sanctissima "	Lux.
Air, "Let the Bright Seraphim "	Handel.
Andante Cantabile, from 4th Concerto	Bennett.
"Romance sans Paroles"	Guilmant.
Festival March in D	Smart.
Hallelujah Chorus ("Messiah")	Handel.

HARWICH, ESSEX.

On Wednesday, August 22nd, Mr. Joseph White, of Teignmouth, gave an organ recital, at the Wesleyan Church here, before a large and appreciative audience, who listened throughout with the greatest attention. The organ has two manuals and pedals, and was built by Mr. George Tucker, of Plymouth. The following was the programme :—

March Militaire	Gounod.
Allegretto Villeroccio	Franggili.
Fugue in G major	Bach.
Air, with variations	Carter.
Offertoire in C minor	Batiste.
Air, with variations	Haydn.
Cantilène	Salomé.
Overture in E	Morandi.

HOLLOWAY.

On Sunday, August 12th, special services were held in the united Methodist Free Church, for the purpose of opening a new organ, which has been given to the church by Mr. R. Wildgoose. Mr. F. G. Painter, of London, presided at the organ, and played several pieces, bringing out the good points of the instrument with success. For the anthems, the choir selected two pieces from Mozart's 12th mass, that in the morning being "Gloria in Excelsis," and in the evening, "I will call upon the Lord." Messrs. C. Lloyd & Co., of Nottingham, are the builders of the organ. On the following Monday evening, in the same place, a musical festival was given, when selections of music were rendered by the choir, interspersed with organ solos by Mr. F. G. Painter.—*Nottingham Guardian.*

PELYNT, CORNWALL.

On August 8th, the new organ was opened. The instrument has been built by Mr. George Tucker, of the Octagon Organ Works, Plymouth, and there was a general expression of opinion on the part of those present that the vicar and committee were to be congratulated on securing such an excellent instrument. It has two manuals, the Swell and the Great, each consisting of 56 notes, CC to G, and pedals. The general tone of the instrument is very full and sweet, the Clarabella stop being especially good. After a brief dedicatory service, Mrs. R. H. Carter, of Kenwyn, who had kindly consented to act as organist for the day, opened the recital with Mendelssohn's march "Cornelius," in which she was accompanied by the string band of the Royal Marines. This was followed by an organ solo, the Adagio from Beethoven's 6th quartet, Op. 18 ; the Allegretto and Adagio, from Sinfonia of "Lobesang," given by the organ and band. The march from Schiller, "Meyerbeer," was the next item, and this was followed by Sullivan's "Lost chord," arranged for organ and band, and in which Mr. Elford's cornet part was most effective. The recital closed with the hymn "Hark ! hark ! the organ loudly peals." There was full evening Service at 7.30, when the church was crowded by an attentive congregation. In every respect save the weather the day's proceedings were a success.

HELENSBURGH.

The new and artistically constructed organ for the Episcopal Church, built by Mr. August Gern, was opened on the 18th and 19th inst., by Dr. W. Spark. The recital of the 18th had a capital programme carefully executed. The organ has two manals and pedals, with 28 stops. It is constructed upon the tubular system, and the workmanship reflects high credit upon the builder, who is a truly artistic and painstaking maker of organs.

REMINISCENCES OF AN OLD REPORTER.

As continuity is one law of music (not always observed, by the way), let me proceed to speak of Miss Shirreff. After making a great hit as Oscar the page, in "Gustavus III." (A.D. 1833—34), she assumed the higher position of prima donna at Covent Garden Theatre, four years afterwards (A.D. 1838½) in an opera called "Amilie, or the Love Test," composed by one M. W. Rooke, of the Royal Academy, and the instructor of William Harrison, the tenor singer. The music of "Amilie" was very pretty, and the opera well mounted, but its term of life did not endure beyond the season. I heard the work on Friday, April 20th, 1838 ; the name of the tenor vocalist, a young soldier who tests the love of Amilie in disguise—no "new thing," I unfortunately forget ; and indeed, only remember one sparkling soprano song, "To the Vine Feast," allotted to a "second lady." It appears that Rooke was much surprised at his success ; he wrote very slowly, and took a long time to bring forth his ideas, like the old parliamentary speaker who "conceived" three times, to produce—nothing !

Henry Westrop, for many years "second fiddle'' at the opera and the Philharmonic concerts, had a very good MS. opera on the stocks for some years, but although the "Harrison and Pyne" company looked at the score with favour in 1861, the work was never produced—a great pity. One heard "elegant extracts" in the salon : and Westrop composed admirable music for the Chamber.

English opera, however, has not always been kept out in the cold. John Barnett scored a splendid success with "The Mountain Sylph" in 1834 ; and in 1837, another triumphal entry took place at old Drury on the shoulders of his "Fair Rosamond."

Edward Loder, junior, opened the new Lyceum Theatre in July, 1834 (under Arnold's management), with "Nourjahad," an oriental tale ; Miss Romer, Henry Phillips, and a Miss Fanny Healey were principals. Henry Phillips, always fortunate, took the town with a song, "There's a light in her laughing eye," but "Nourjahad's" life could not, as it is in the story, be prolonged. Mr. Loder did better, in 1846, at the Princess's Theatre with the "Night Dancers," an opera highly extolled by the critics of the daily press, particularly Mr. Jas. Davison and Mr. Grüneisen. In this opera, poor Leffler, the bass singer, was engaged to take the part of a foolish and

besotted beadle. At the end of the last act, somebody on the stage expressed a fear (according to "copy") that he had been drowned ! "Then it must have been in gin, brandy, or whiskey" (retorted a saucy girl), "for he never allows any water to come near him." The audience broke out into roars of laughter, and poor Leffler—(I witnessed the scene on October 24th, 1846)—looked uncommonly sheepish. It was too bad ; but Leffler had become notorious as a lover of strong waters. One night, he wrote a short note to the (then) manager of the Lyceum, enriched with expletives, (usually printed with hyphens), to the effect that he had drunk so much claret that he could not possibly sing. The letter was read aloud to the audience, who sympathized with the manager, but hissed poor Leffler to the ceiling. Talking of expletives, I have always longed to hug the inimitable humourist who, when in Holland, carefully dated his epistles to friends in England from " Rottend——— !" Pious, reverent, prudent soul, with a nice appreciation of the proprieties !

Leffler had a pretty daughter who sang at concerts for a short time, attired in deep mourning, about the year 1846—7.

I heard the once great Grisi sing a ballad in the course of a concert held by Mdme. Rudersdorff at St. James's Hall in May, 1865. The poor prima donna looked ghastly pale and could not sing even the simple English music in perfect tune. Alas ! Mrs. Alfred Shaw, who, at Covent Garden in 1841 achieved a triumphant success as Azsace in "Semiramide," was another melancholy instance of rapid decline, after a most successful début, and one or two brilliant seasons. When Grisi lost her temper, the opera had to be changed : was present at a morning performance of the Royal Italian in 1849, when, to the horror and indignation of classical people who had come from the suburbs expressly to hear "Don Giovanni," Rossini's "La Cenerentola" was substituted, at a "short notice." Alboni, however, must have compensated the disappointed ones in a degree : she sang splendidly, and in "Non più mesta," dropped a double octave—no easy feat !

On Easter Tuesday, April 10th, 1849, a "row" occurred at the Royal Italian Opera. Mr. Delafield had allowed a number of professional persons, critics, and others, to gain access to the stalls, (then all, or mostly, unreserved), through the saloon, so as to anticipate ordinary outsiders. The suspension of this privilege provoked a noise ; one pertinacious gentleman had his coat torn to pieces in the struggle, and made a speech to "Messrs. Delafield and Webster" from the upper boxes : he was mollified, or at least removed, before the opera began, and Mr. Delafield, wisely withdrew the ill-advised suspension. The opera that night was "Linda di Chamouni," and served to introduce Miss Catherine Hayes in the title-part.

"La Donna del Lago" was a successful revival in 1849 ; the mise en scene magnificent. "La Muette di Portici," or "Masaniello," made the fortune of the theatre the same year. In "Lucrezia Borgia," Alboni, when she sang the famous "Brindisi" in C, shook on the high G, at the end, and of course raised loud cries of brava ! An old aunt used to say that she must be careful to know what word to use at the opera, whether bravo, brava, or bravi ! It is certainly an adjective, and must therefore be declined.

When Jenny Lind made her début at Her Majesty's Theatre, in May, 1847, the House of Lords actually adjourned at an earlier hour, in order to hear her. The Lords never, as a rule, sit very late. Lind chose "Robert le Diable," as her opera d'intrata, taking the part of Alice. A weak Bishop of Norwich, one Dr. Hinds, afterwards made her go into another line, and she appeared in "Die Zauberflöte" with concert costume ; the opera was mounted on the stage as a Cantata ! A dead failure soon stopped this nonsense. The Jenny Lind mania ruined Lumley in the sequel. The public were so eager for "new things" and terrestial "stars," that they cried, like the horse-leech, "give, give," and Lumley could give no more. In June, 1850, he introduced a lady of colour, who played trumpery tunes on a guitar between the acts, but the exhibition proved a woful failure ; the audience only laughed. "Florinda," Thalberg's opera, produced in 1851, fell flatly. The managers, in that (the Exhibition) year thought to make fortunes—but no ; the vast crowd that flocked to Hyde Park in the day-time were too tired to do more, at six o'clock, than go home to supper and bed !

A. M.

Academical Intelligence.

COLLEGE OF ORGANISTS.

Examination for Associateship, July 10, 1883.

PAPER WORK AT ORGAN.

The candidates commence at the organ by the performance of an organ piece, or a selection of not more than two movements from a composition written for the instrument, with a pedal obbligato part. The organ works of Bach and Mendelssohn afford the best examples for the candidates' selection. The examiners reserve to themselves the power to stop any candidate as soon as their judgment is formed.

The first six verses of the "Venite" were to be accompanied to the music of a given chant.

A hymn-tune was to be given out, and one verse accompanied.

A given passage was to be transposed at sight, the new keys being named by the examiners :—

An example of vocal score-reading was to be played at sight on the two diapasons of the Great organ only, and without the use of the pedals.

And a figured bass to be filled up at sight in four parts.

M.M. ♩=69.

$\begin{smallmatrix} 5 & 6 & 5 \\ 3 & 4 & 3 \end{smallmatrix}$ $\begin{smallmatrix} 6 & 5 \\ 4 & 3 \end{smallmatrix}$ — $\begin{smallmatrix} 6 & 9 & 6 \\ 4 & 3 & 4 \end{smallmatrix}$ $\begin{smallmatrix} 6 & 7 & 9 & 8 \\ 5 & 7 & \end{smallmatrix}$

PAPER WORK AWAY FROM ORGAN.

A melody was to be harmonisd in four parts in vocal score, with proper clefs.

A bass to be harmonised in four parts in vocal score, from the figures, with proper clefs.

The candidates was to write out the bass of a given passage, figure it according to the harmonies given, and name the root notes of the different chords employed.

To add two simultaneous counterpoints of first species, and above and one below, to a given *canto fermo*.

To add three simultaneous counterpoints of any species, two above and one below, to another *canto fermo*.

To give answers to two fugue subjects.

And to answer as many of the succeeding questions as possible.

1. What are combinational or resultant tones ?

2. How is the pressure of organ wind estimated? and what does the expression three inches of wind mean ?

3. About what date did the orthodox compass or organ manuals and pedals begin to prevail in England ?

4. Describe the chord known as the Neapolitan sixth, and say on which degree of the scale it is commonly used.

5. Say which individual species of counterpoint most frequently supplies the beginning and ending of examples of florid counterpoint.

6. Show the structure of a double chant, giving the bar divisions and indicating the position of the several reciting notes.

7. Name the pitch of the open strings of the violin, viola, and violoncello.

8. Give the name of the first Italian opera composed by Handel in England, and the date of its composition.

9. Give a list of Mendelssohn's chief sacred choral works, with dates of composition.

(To be continued).

Messrs. Wilkinson and Sons, of Kendal, re-opened two of their organs, after enlargement, on Sunday, August 26th. One at Cautley Church, Yorkshire, containing one manual, with general swell ; and the other at Skelsmergh Church, Westmoreland, with great and swell, 14 stops.

Messrs. G. R. Sims and F. Clay's new opera "The White Queen," forms the opening piece at the re-built Alhambra on October 22nd.

PRINCIPAL CONTENTS OF THIS NUMBER.

LONDON : SATURDAY, SEPTEMBER 1, 1883.

PURPOSE IN THE COMPOSITION OF MUSIC.

I.

THAT " purpose in art may supersede techni- "cal law," would seem to be an undisputed axiom ; and this is but allowing that the object to be attained must be superior to the means employed. The courageous opening up of the questions concerning the contrapuntal laws by Mr. H. J. Stark in his paper recently read before the College of Organists, and the consequent valuable letters from Dr. H. Hiles, Mr. H. C. Banister, and Mr. C. E. Stephens, will, it is hoped, lead to a further timely discussion upon a subject of much importance with respect to the future best interests of the art. Such a discussion could be widened out with advantage into the consideration of the broad question, " Can " purpose in art justifiably supersede technical law ? " A modern poet makes one of his characters say philosophy is an enemy of the State, weakening faith and converting the people into a nation of talkers. Now, without wasting space in these columns by diving into polemics, it may be safely asserted that in music we do want philosophy rather than theories; and prolonged discussions on matters in which the due expression of thought is to be considered as against the strict observance of the technicalities of the art, cannot fail to be beneficial to the future of music. As in literature and in all the arts, so in music, there are undoubtedly times when the strong tide of thought will bear down the barriers which are none the less of general utility in the shaping, assertion, expression, and even restraining of exuberant ideality. The whole question of law *versus* license seems to include the following subdivisions. Under what circumstances may rules be temporarily disregarded? What class of art-producers may be considered to be entitled to so disregard technical laws? and what is the position of the student with regard to such liberty of action? It would seem, indeed, that the whole question hinges upon the word "purpose." I propose to offer a typical passage as an illustration, which involves in the natural form of its enunciation a repeated violence of the rule musicians most universally elect to abide by the law which directs the avoidance of consecutive perfect concords in part-writing.

In the version A the eye of the musician will at once detect decided purposes, such as are often found in the compositions of men of high genius, writing skill and decided thoughts. The scale sentences in the lower parts are harmless when taken apart from the shake figure of the upper tone *stratum*; it is the persistent purpose of this upper part which introduces the illegal element; and such results from the use of the common ornament, the shake, are frequent enough, though but little noticed, as they usually do not actually appear on paper. Now, the question arises. Which of the three *strata*—all having decided "purpose" in their lines—is to give way in order to secure the customary respect for a truly essential law? or, on the other hand, are the outlines so truly decisive in their naturalness as to justify the repeated breach of an obviously good rule? or, again, is it, or is it not, a wise policy on the part of the writer to here permit such a patent disregard of a strong law, lest by shrinking from the sternly natural character of the combined tone actions, he will not only hopelessly weaken the general idea of the sentence (which is as nothing without "purpose"), but will also show up by such studied avoidance of a plain course the very stumbling blocks he does not desire the listener to observe? The straightforwardness of the first version of the passage carries honest, decided "purpose" in its courageous, unbroken lines with such a decided *strength* of will as seems to make the undoubted *weakness* of certain points of the sentence all but

logically imperceptible. To put the matter in other words, the irregularities of the road have not stood in the way of the strong-built vehicle passing over it.

Now, in version B, the material, without being actually altered, has lost much by the dodging delays and—what may be dignified as tact, but hardly spoken of as "purpose"—an obvious cringing from decision of outline in order to secure the respectability which is presumed to arise to the gain of the law-abiding writer. On the other side, arguments could be presented to show that version B, to the educated ear, presents an unbroken, harmonious continuity which cannot be claimed for version A, and this very harmonic integrity is after all a strength of its kind of a very high character. The arrival at any decision in the contemplation of such a passage must, to some extent, depend upon the temperament, will, or sensitiveness of the writer. I venture to think the student may ponder over this and similar sentences to be found in the more freely written works of the great masters of the art with some advantage as regards the building-up of his own musical mind and will.

E. H. TURPIN.

MUSIC NOT AN AMUSEMENT.

INDULGENT readers will not pass over the "Reminiscences of an Old Reporter," printed in this and the last edition of the *Musical Standard*, and to be continued, as some people would say, if the *fates* will. The facts recorded by the writer have suggested the title of this article and the few remarks that follow. Ignorant and superficial people with minds—if they have minds—incapable of reflection, indulge in a notion that music is merely a pastime, and that musical reporters have rather a gala time of it. Idiotic simplicity! Beautified innocence of green-sick girlhood! The "Old Reporter" tells a very different tale, and his colleagues on the press would be ready, if asked, to corroborate his evidence.

That learned etymologist the (Protestant) Archbishop of Dublin, Dr. TRENCH, has shewn that to call anyone of the fine arts an "*a*-musement" is a stupid contradiction in terms. *Ex vi termini,* "*a*-musement signifies to be away, or absent from the MUSES, who preside individually over particular departments of Art and Science. It follows, therefore, that if music be an *amusement*, the devotee to the pursuit must run away from and dispense with the aid of EUTERPE and POLYHYMNIA. The ancients knew better. Life with them, as with us, was short, but art was long. They laboured like slaves at the arts, and *amusement* was the unbending of that bow which PHŒBUS himself cannot venture to keep in rigid tension at all times. SOCRATES gave his lectures, and then *amused* himself with a game at marbles!

The professor, of course, is too well aware that music, like painting and sculpture, is a tremendous toil, and exacts the assiduous devotion of an anchorite. Slip-slop boarding- school and "bread-and-butter" girls hammer at a few flimsy tunes to please papa and mamma or may be a *côterie* of flirting "mashers," but the regular student must practise his instrument seven or eight hours a day; study the theory of the art, know all the mysteries of harmony and counterpoint; and if he be worth his salt, be ready to extemporise on a figured bass at a moment's notice. The greatest geniuses are not exempt from this toil and trouble. Their ideas are inspired, but the development and "working out" of those ideas is a climbing of the steepest Parnassus. MOZART shortened his life by the severity of his studies, and BEETHOVEN would note pages of music before he adopted the precise form of thought.

Then with respect to the musical reporter. He must not only be well versed in the theory of the art, have some knowledge of all the *technique*, and be deeply read in classical texts, but also work hard outside in the public service. LORD LYNDHURST, at a dinner of the Newspaper Press Association in 1839, gave a faithful representation of the Parliamentary reporter, who, apparently at his ease in the gallery of the House, was "obliged to sit for hours afterwards "in a close office, lighted with gas, writing out his "hieroglyphics for the printer." So the musical critic, as our "Old Reporter" testifies, was compelled, not so many years ago, to write a column or two of minion type after midnight, in order that the public might have on their breakfast tables, at nine the next morning, a full account of some new opera or oratorio, with careful criticism and minute analysis of details. *Punch*, in 1850, had a skit on some city clerk, envious of a friend who often went to the opera as a reporter for the press, and found the task anything but an *amusement*. It is fair to say that a man must and does *like* the duty, and of course enjoys great pleasure, of the highest kind, on hearing fine compositions, but then the alloy! The ordinary auditor listens, applauds, goes home to supper humming the haunting airs of the new work, and there an end. The reporter, on the contrary, takes copious notes, like a judge on the bench, and if not obliged to pen his lengthy notice the same night, must keep his memory green, and not lose the impressions made upon the ear, and through the ear upon the mind. ALBERT SMITH used to say that the pleasure of seeing a pantomime was spoiled by his foreknowledge of the "notice" to be written thereafter for the press; and what is a Christmas pantomime in comparison with a grand opera like "Lohengrin," or an oratorio such as "Elijah"?

The mention of oratorio reminds one that at the provincial festivals, reporters must needs scribble their column of notice off-hand, and send the copy up to London by an afternoon train. No time to be lost; even on a hasty plate of soup! It is news of the day and hour. In London, as already stated, a brief summary usually suffices on the actual night; in fact, a long notice, if written at once, runs a great risk, especially during the session, of being "crowded out." This occurred many years ago, in the *Times* office, when the editor gave the substance of a long notice by Mr. J. W. DAVISON in a few lines, apologizing for the necessity—want of space. The full notice appeared next day. Some editors used to be very exacting, and the complaints of "old re-"porters" on the daily press have been deep, if not so loud as the roar of Niagara. Music, then, the reader may now admit, is certainly not an amusement, but a very serious business to all who are *earnestly* concerned.   A. M.

THE LOGIC OF COUNTERPOINT.

THIRD SERIES.

XII.

THE combination of second, third, and fourth species counterpoint in a four-part score affords the student one of the best possible forms of exercise, not only as regards the practical mastery of the art from the scholastic point of sight, but as a valuable means of enlarging the mental resources of the future composer, called upon to be prepared to face part-complications and knotty fugal points. This contrapuntal drill should of course be practised with every possible variety of position; but the best models of distribution are those in which the contrapuntal activity is most equally spread throughout the score. The following scheme of arrangements will be found to embrace all the necessary scoring plans. The *canto fermo* is distinguished, as before, by the short horizontal line, and the figures denote the several species by their cardinal numerals.

$$
\begin{array}{cccccc}
2 & 3 & 4 & - & 4 & 2 \\
3 & 2 & - & 2 & 3 & 4 \\
4 & - & 3 & 3 & 2 & - \\
- & 4, & 2, & 4, & - & 3, \\
\\
3 & - & 4 & 2 & 3 & - \\
- & 4 & 2 & 3 & - & 2 \\
4 & 3 & 3 & - & 4 & 4 \\
2, & 2, & - & 4, & 2 & 3 \\
\\
3 & - \\
4, & 3 \\
2 & 2 \\
- & 4 \\
\end{array}
$$

In practising the different scoring schemes the student will, as in similar previous drill with mixed counterpoints, speedily find a special aptitude for given arrangements. The plans placing the third and fourth species in the inner parts will most likely give the student the most trouble, from the cramped melodic action of the middle parts and because both active movement and suspended action are perhaps more liable to disturb the chord progressions when employed internally than when used externally. There seems to be no objection in the writing of mixed counterpoints to the introduction of rests, but these should not exceed a bar and a-half, or two bars in a given part at a time.

CHERUBINI suggests that in beginning the third species we may commence with a crotchet rest, and the start of the second species counterpoint be delayed until the end of the second bar. There could be no logical objection to the commencement of the fourth species counterpoint in the second instead of in the first measure. Still, as the activity of the third species and the piquancy of the fourth species lend so much character, not to say vitality, to a group of mixed counterpoints, it does seem reasonable to regard the second species counterpoint as the one least to be missed from the general movement, and therefore, the part to which rests may be best assigned without damage to the general interest of the structure. Such considerations as these must depend, however, upon the comparative brevity or length of the examples being worked out. With regard to the cadence point, the fourth species would naturally seem to be the one kind claiming the retention of its accustomed cadence figure in either of the suspensions seven-six or two-three according to the position of part carrying this type of counterpoint. When the fourth species counterpoint is in the lowest part this practice may be perhaps best departed from; and it may be a convenient device in the case of such a departure, to temporarily convert the second species which is being conducted in one of the three upper parts, into a bearer of the fourth species cadence, by the introduction of a suspended note into the second contrapuntal order in the last bar but one. The point of this suggestion lies in the fact that suspended harmony has a special value at a cadence point, and should be retained at such a point, even if it is found convenient—in order to secure more solid dominant harmony by giving the root to the lowest tone stratum—to transfer the suspension for the moment from the fourth species line to the part carrying the second contrapuntal order.

E. H. TURPIN.

THE VOICE
MUSICALLY AND MEDICALLY CONSIDERED

BY

ARMAND SEMPLE, B.A., M.B., Cantab., M.R.C.P., Lond.,
Physician to the Royal Society of Musicians.

(Continued from page 119.)

Intensity or Volume.

The voice exhibits different characters, such as dulness or brightness, and also different degrees of intensity or volume.

Timbre or Quality.

The sound is modified by the pharynx or reflecting organ, and by it are produced the various qualities of the voice. The term Timbre implies the peculiar and variable quality which each register can assume, even the forming of the different vowels.

Difference of timbre is caused by the various methods of vibration of which the larynx is capable, and by the modifications produced upon the issuing sounds through the reflecting capacity of the pharynx.

Timbres are due to two Conditions.

1st. Those of which the nature is fixed, and which characterise every individual voice, viz.: form, volume, capacity, firmness, and the healthy or unhealthy condition of the organ.

2ndly. Variable conditions, viz.: The direction taken by the sounds during their emission, whether through the mouth or nose; the capacity or shape of the vocal organ; the tension of the sides; the width between the lower and upper jaws; the action of the soft palate; the position of the lips; and the extent to which they can be opened, and finally the depression or elevation of the tongue.

Timbres may be divided into two leading Classes.

1. The Open, Clear, or Bright Timbre.
2. The Closed, Muffled, or Sombre Timbre.

Every sound emitted must belong to one of these classes, the whole compass of the voice being impressed with its character.

Much brilliancy is given to the voice by the open timbre, but if exaggerated it renders the voice shrill and shrieky; roundness and breadth are imparted by the closed timbre; by which alone can the voice attain rich quality. If the closed timbre is exaggerated, the sounds become muffled, dull, and hoarse, an effect more observable in the high than in the low part of the register. In the falsetto the close timbre is well defined, although not so strikingly as in the chest voice. In the head voice it occasionally produces a very remarkable effect, imparting a pure and limpid character to this register, resembling the tones of the harmonica.

The Formation of Sounds.

The mechanical actions by which "voice" is solely formed are by periodical compressions and expansions of air during its passage from the glottis. The two lips (vocal cords) in the interior of the larynx, which constitute the glottis or breath-passage close one upon the other, creating beneath them an accumulation of air, and this, in consequence of the pressure which it undergoes in that situation, becoming elastic, and by the sudden expansion of the glottis, escapes through the lips. By the alternate dilatations and contraction, which produce regular and successive expansions of air, the voice originates. The height or lowness of a sound is dependent upon the rapidity with which the glottis opens and closes. It must also be noticed, that the rapidity of the alternations increases in the inverse ratio to the length of the vibratory aperture.

The Do; (C$_1$) requires per second 132 vibrations.

Do, (C$_2$)	"	"	264
Do, (C$_3$)	"	"	528
Do, (C$_4$)	"	"	1056
Do, (C$_5$)	"	"	2112

It will thus be seen that each octave takes double the number of vibrations to that immediately below it.

The dimensions of the glottis are shortened by the following process:—

During tranquil breathing the shape of the glottis is triangular, but the moment that sound is emitted it changes its shape for a linear form which is assumed during phonation; its sides being fixed, and the vocal cords meeting at both their extremes, a space is left at the centre only for air to escape when required. The anterior extremities are always fixed, the posterior, the substance of which is cartilaginous, alone are capable of motion, the glottis being opened by their separation, and closed by their collapsing.

During the production of the deepest note of the voice the vocal cords are in action throughout their entire length; both the ligamentous and cartilaginous parts are set in motion. As the voice commences its ascent in the scale the cartilaginous parts progressively come into contact from behind forwards until they approximate throughout their whole length. By this movement the length of the glottis is, of course, gradually diminished, and it is reduced to the dimensions which can be afforded by the ligamentous parts only. By these latter parts being acted upon from behind, the length of the vibratory aperture is still further diminished.

THE TESTIMONIAL TO SIR MICHAEL COSTA.

The form which the testimonial in contemplation is to assume, says the *Musical World*, has not yet been decided on; but at a second meeting opinions may coincide, and unanimous consent be awarded to one or other scheme proposed. Meanwhile the names of those who have taken upon themselves the responsibilities involved will suffice to show that the work in hand will earnestly and intelligently carried out.

Julius Benedict, Joseph Bennett, Francesco Berger, Hums Burnley, E. Chappell, W. G. Cusins, J. W. Davison, J. W. Dow, A. Durlacher, John Ella, L. Engel, George Grove, M. Hanhart, H. B. Heath, Rev. Thomas Helmore, D. Hill, H. W. Hill, W. H. Husk, H. Lazarus, Henry Leslie, J. M. Levy, Henry Littleton, Stanley Lucas, G. A. Macfarren, E. H. Mannering, A. Manns, W. Mitchell, J. M. P. Montague, Costantino Perugini, Captain Philips, A. Randegger, P. Sainton, C. Santley, F. Schira, T. Sherrard, G. M. Smith, John Stainer, Arthur Sullivan, F. W. Willocks, and C. E. Willing ("with power to add to their number").

In the course of the official statement prefixed to the foregoing, the following words occur:—"Sir Michael Costa came to England in 1829, and made his first appearance in this country at the Birmingham Musical Festival of that year. By a curious coincidence his last appearance in public was as conductor of the Birmingham Musical Festival of 1882. He therefore continuously pursued his profession in England for the long period of fifty-three years. The committee solicit subscriptions from Sir Michael Costa's friends and admirers for carrying it into effect. The desire of the committee is to procure the contributions of as large a number of persons as possible, in order to testify to the wide esteem in which Sir Michael Costa's services are held."

SIR G. A. MACFARREN ON THE CARDIFF EISTEDDFOD.

Professor Macfarren has addressed a letter to the *Western Mail*, which appeared on the 18th inst. with an explanation from the editor, in which occur the following words :—" It will be remembered that full adjudication was delivered on the great Choral Competition at the National Eisteddfod of Wales, which was held in Cardiff during last week. The excitement and noise which followed the announcement of the names of the successful choirs was so great that Sir George Macfarren could not make himself heard, and was, therefore, compelled to withhold the remarks which was his intention to make. This was much regretted by everyone who had an interest in music in Wales, inasmuch as it was felt that a criticism upon Welsh choral singing would have been of immense value." In answer to a request for his opinion Sir G. A. Macfarren replied in a letter in which are to be found the following important and valuable sentences :—

" SIR,—In compliance with your request, I will state, more or less, what I might have said had it been possible to speak through the tumult of the enthusiastic audience when I announced the adjudication on the choral contest at the Cardiff Eisteddfod last Thursday. The grounds whereon the unanimous verdict of the seven judges was founded, and which, in their estimation, raised the Penrhyn Choir far above all its competitors, were purity of tone, correctness of time, precision in the taking up of points, musicianliness of phrasing, and just variety of power. The Llanelly United Choir, though remote in merit from that which honourably won the first prize, was, in the particulars that have been named, deemed superior to the others. The tendency, whether resulting from excessive ardour or from whatever cause, to force the voice, induced always harshness of quality, and often falseness of intonation—the last sometimes to such an extent as to change the key that should prevail—and this tendency was manifest occasionally to an extent that disabled the instrumental accompanist from continuance, and that was painful to the hearers. Too much praise cannot be awarded to those conductors of choirs who, without special musical education, had educed from their singers good points which must not be ignored even in the least meritorious of the six performances. An obvious conclusion from the morning's experience is, however, that a trained musician is in all likelihood the ablest teacher of music, and that the excellence of a performance is in most instances commensurate with the technical skill of its director.

" It will not be irrelevant to remark generally on the musical proceedings of the very important and highly-interesting meeting at which it has been my happy privilege to be present. First, then, let it be said in the face of the whole world that the allegation is totally false which denies the musical capacity as a possession of the natives of this island. The long roll of names of singers of the present generation who have come from Wales, and who command the admiration of the whole country, gives living proof that the vocal faculty is strong in the ancient British race—the faculty that comprises sweetness of the voice, distinctness of enunciation, intelligence of declamation, and, above all, the power of sympathy which magnetises the hearers and holds their attention enchained to the executant and to the music he animates. Lovers of art must rejoice in the valuable sign of progress evinced in the exhibition of instrumental skill that has of late been witnessed. It is not to speak of individual merit, examples of which may be found here, or there, or everywhere, when nature has been generous and study assiduous ; but of the highly-important advance displayed in the performance of orchestral music in which many a talent is united to produce one effect. Science reveals not a sublimer or more wonderful phenomenon than the rhythmical unity of multitudinous performers who join in time and in tune with such accurate exactness as proves the dominion of a single all-pervading will. The marvel is the greater when the diverse qualities of tone that characterise the several instruments which constitute a complete band are combined, and musical executancy reaches its highest perfection in this combination. In declaring the award for orchestral performance mention was made of the historical order of instrumental development—a conception, nay more, a discovery that is due to Mr. J. F. Rowbotham, a writer now engaged on a new history of music—this is, that instruments are struck, such as drums and cymbals, which mark measure but not pitch, are the earliest inventions of barbarous nations ; that instruments which are blown, such as pipes with or without reeds, next follow ; and that instruments which are bowed, such as the whole of the viol series, are the latest fruit of musical civilization. All these classes are combined in the modern orchestra. The composer who can employ them consentaneously must have large knowledge and keen sight, and the band comprising them that can play unanimously presents in itself an epitomized chronology of instrumental art. Applause is due, then, to the bands that competed, much for what was accomplished, and very far more for what is promised by the fact of the competition, since this fact points

more directly to musical proficiency in Wales than does any other incident of the Eisteddfod. Bearing on this point is the acceptance by the unaccustomed audiences who were present of the classical works that were rendered in full completeness by an adequate number of the best masters of their respective instruments ; this acceptance proved interest in the performance such as is apt for cultivation and probable of yielding richest fruit. In the department of composition, Welshmen generally have not taken such high ground as in executancy, but there are two who have taken university degrees, and two who have attained to widest popularity, and the deserved success of these proves that the land has ore ready for refining.

" The absence of competitors for a sight-singing prize is the least favourable sign in the whole course of the proceedings. In all the choral competitions many of the singers were without copies, and many looked not at those they held. This implies memory, but memory is not musicianship. It is a ludicrous mistake in many of our elementary schools for a teacher to play a part in a musical composition again and again till the pupils know it by ear, and can sing it by heart, or—as Cobbett derides the last [term—' by hear it.' Thus bullfinches are taught, and thus parrots learn to shriek fragments of melody. As sensible would it be to pretend to teach children to read by frequently reciting to them a sentence until they could repeat it by memory ; but they would be ignorant of the look of the letters or the principles of joining them into words. Oh ! Welshwomen and Welshmen, you of the beautiful voices and the strong musical instinct, believe that if there be truth this is one of the truest, namely, that to be able to read music as easily as words will largely augment your power of pleasing others, of joining in harmony with one another, and of deriving delight to yourselves through the mind's ear from the written characters which are the types of unuttered sounds. The master will render you more real service who will teach you to read one phrase from the musical staff, the staff which was in use in England before ever it was known in Italy, than he who parrots you into singing a whole oratorio by rote.

" The thoughtful must deprecate a wish, strongly expressed by one or two persons, that the obsolete Welsh harp may be perpetuated, not for its musicality, but for its nationality. As reasonably might be desired the restoration of the crwth which has been supplanted by the violin. In like manner the pedal harp has superseded the triple-string harp of Wales, as this did the harp without the fore-pillar of primitive Ireland, which was in its day a modernization of the Hebrew harp, and so on in backward line with the harps of Egypt and Assyria. Jealousy of other branches of our united nation, and the desire to keep Welsh honours for the Welsh, and Wales itself exclusively for Welshmen, betoken a spirit adverse to progress, and uncongenial to that which, on the other side of the mountains, is what will be the better for us all if we regard each other as brethren of one nation, and if we feel and act with a patriotism common to us all. Truly, the Cymric race ruled here prior to the Saxon, but the Finnish is shown to have preceded the Cymric. Antecedent history, which is written by the glacier on the living mountains, proves that time was when earlier races than humanity itself solely populated the island. It could scarcely be contemplated on archæological grounds to re establish the sway of the ichthyosaurus and plesiosaurus over the contemporary subordinate population of Britain. Let the Welsh preserve their leek, which renews itself from spring to spring, and, fresh as the glistening sunbeam, will twine with the rose and the thistle to form a single emblem of an undivided people.

" Some persons say—and they say much other than their prayers—that musical culture is in a bad state in this country. The fallacy of the saying is proved by the musical advances in our public schools, by the musical advances in our private families, and—most remarkable of all—by the musical advances in the mining and quarrying districts that have sent their toilers to the recent competitions. The circumstance which alone may seem to render this denial equivocal is the preference often shown for foreigners to our land, as composers, singers, and players, over musicians of our own breeding ; and the persons who say what has been cited of our musical culture are they who do the most to promote this preference. The same persons say that hundreds of Englishmen go yearly to Leipsic for musical education because none is to be obtained here ; but statistics disprove this by showing that the number of English musical students in foreign countries may be counted by tens or units, instead of by hundreds, and evidence could be adduced of other reasons for their self-exile than the want of educational means at home. The same persons say that England owns no school wherein music can be taught ; but the advantages adduced above date from the institution of the Royal Academy of Music sixty-one years since, which has trained the best talent of all England, including those distinguished musicians of Welsh birth or parentage whose praises are familiar on every lip, and whose presence as performers, and still more as adjudicators, has been the brightest ornament of the Cardiff Eisteddfod.—I am, &c.,

" August, 16th. G. A. MACFARREN."

The *Western Mail* sensibly calls attention to the chief points of Sir G. A. Macfarren's letter in a leader containing the following words :—"Unquestionably the most important part of the whole letter is that wherein the writer touches upon the sore point of Welsh jealousy and exclusiveness. Art *must* be first in the affections of her devotees, let who or what will be second. And Art has a right to her place, for Art, being Truth, is Divine. Love of country even must not be allowed to stand between her worshippers and her glorious self, and this, we take it, is the occult meaning of the President of the Royal Academy herein. Lord Bute had before this told the Welsh nation that its individuality need not stand between it and excellence ; Sir George Macfarren now says *it must not.*"

The *Musical World* adds the comment now given :—"Thus it may be seen how Welshmen can receive admonishment and advice with the same cordiality as that with which they welcome praise, when addressed to them by competent authority and clothed in sympathetic language. This event alone would suffice to perpetuate the remembrance of the Cardiff Eisteddfod of 1883. Every one of the appointed judges gave his opinion impartially, heedless of what might or not be said ; and the judgment of the combined tribunal was respected and acclaimed. *Sic itur ad astra.*"

TRADE PROSPECTS IN AMERICA.

I contend that the piano and organ trade is in its infancy ; that more musical instruments will be manufactured in this country during the next five years than have been manufactured during the last ten. At the Music Teachers' National Convention, held a few weeks ago, several of the teachers were telling me their estimates of the number of persons engaged directly in the profession. "There are more than 100,000 music teachers in this country," said a Western teacher, and he was correct. I take it that there are at least 150,000, and their number is rapidly increasing. This is only one basis for a calculation of the number of persons engaged in giving piano, organ, and singing lessons. We can easily understand that there must be many pupils, and these pupils all use instruments to play upon. But I have something more definite to prove that the business is prospectively much greater than it has been in the past. According to an estimate made after a searching examination, there are not 1,000,000 pianos in this country ; there are only about 800,000 pianos in use. Many of these were imported forty to eighty years ago, before any number of pianos were made here. From 1840 to 1860 the industry began to assume large dimensions ; but the bulk of American pianos were made since 1855—say during the past thirty years. The production last year was greater than for the preceding year ; in fact, more than twelve times as many pianos were made than in any one year thirty or so years ago. Now let us see. Many of the 800,000 pianos in use now are very old, and are being replaced constantly by new ones. The exchange of old for new pianos is a daily occurrence with large houses all over the country, and makes a large item. But the chief business is done in sales to families who are about to have children taught, or pianos sold to young people just married, or going to housekeeping. There are about 52,000,000 people in this country. It is difficult to get at the number of families ; but say, there are only 2,500,000 that are or will be able to buy pianos, including amongst these 2,500,000 also the many single men and women who will purchase pianos. A part of this number is only supplied new. That is enough to keep business booming. It will keep the manufacturer busy to supply the annual number of purchasers who are comprised in this class, not taking into consideration the rapid increase of the population, which alone creates a large part of the piano purchasers every year. I have not said a word about the export of pianos, but this branch of the business has been gradually increasing, and many instruments made here are annually exported, and this export will continue to expand. From all this we can gather, as I said before, that the pianoforte business is in its infancy. The younger members of the trade will come into handsome business properties, and if they manage with discretion their future is assured.—*Musical Courier.*

A sister of Offenbach, now Mrs. Maas, has lived, says an American journal, in Galveston, Texas, for many years.

Correspondence.

THE SECOND INVERSION OF THE DOMINANT SEVENTH.

TO THE EDITOR OF THE "MUSICAL STANDARD."

SIR,—I quite agree with Mr. Stark and Mr. Hiles about the fingering and treatment of the second inversion of the dominant seventh, commonly called the chord of the 6.4.3. The fourth or *root* of the chord, ought *not*, I contend, to be omitted ; the only reason for the required omission appears to be an old prejudice on the part of pig-tail "contrapuntists" against the use of the 4th, which is treated by them as a *discord.*

When, 40 years ago, I first studied harmony or "thoroughbass," the "Thorough Bass Primer" of the late Mr. J. T. Burrowes was put into my hands as a text book, and an excellent manual it is. But poor old Burrowes, alas ! supports the old notion of the pig-tailed and *pig-headed*, that in the discord of the 6.4.3 "the octave of the root should be omitted," *ex gra.:—*

(Key of C major.)

Omitting the root-note (G), he is obliged to make the discord (F) *ascend*, relying on the license of resolving it on the E (or mediant) in the bass.

My first master, Mr. Stenson Major, never insisted on this absurd restriction. Many years afterwards, when helping a full-grown sister in her "through-class" exercises, I came across the old "Burrowes," and recorded (August, 1861), the following remark on the page of the book itself :—" *This I deny ; the root IS generally doubled.*" A few minutes afterwards I casually took up a score of Mendelssohn—no authority, of course—and found a full chord of the 6.4.3, (D, F, G, and B, *in the key of C*) at the very outset. But such instances of doubling the root might be multiplied a hundredfold. If the fourth is to be omitted, why figure the chord 6.4.3 ? The contrapuntists find a hole of escape in the way so justly derided by Mr. Stark ; they figure the chord a 6.3 ! Where is the *root* ? G, of course, as B natural, bears an imperfect fifth, and cannot, therefore, be a "radical " or bass of B minor. Mr. J. A. Hamilton, in his "Catechism of Harmony," allows the full chord of a 6 = 4 = 3, and offers no objection to the doubling of the root. A *reductio ad absurdum* has been made by doubling the fifth for bass, which is monotonous, or even the *discord* (F) which is monstrous.

I can never forget the "frivolous and vexatious " rules of counterpoint, with its tiresome "species " in several parts. Take up any ordinary duet and what do you find ? "Two-part writing " in thirds and sixths, the thirds and sixths being often consecutive five or six times, *not* according to rule ! Rossini's duet in E "Quis est homo," is a case in point, and George Hogarth of the *Morning Chronicle* and the *Daily News*, once pointed out that the composer had blown the trumpet so loudly (and *literally*) in order "to conceal the poverty of his counterpoint." Mr. Hastings of the *Morning Herald*, criticising the defunct opera of Verdi "I Masnadieri" (the Robbers), in 1850, caustically reported that in the duets there were "plenty of thirds and sixths." It is high time to knock off the fetters of this false "counterpoint," as all masters of the art *do* and have done for ages past.

It occurs to me, on glancing over "Hamilton's Catechism " and other manuals, that some of our musical terminology is grossly absurd. For instance, why call an augmented interval a *superfluous* sixth ? If "superfluous," it ought surely to be struck out of the staff. Then the pupil is puzzled by "minor and major semitones," elsewhere called "chromatic and diatonic " ! The *fifths* are regular puzzle-monkeys, that beat the araucarias by "chalks." "Perfect, imperfect, minor, major, augmented, and diminished "—who is to decide? Only the practical "fifth-catchers," I trow ! My own plan would be to classify the fifth thus :—

(Key of C major.)

Perfect. Imperfect. Diminished. Augmented.

(Rationale) No. 2 is *naturally* imperfect *from the scale*, but in No. 3 the interval is reduced by a *sharp*, and from *below*. No. 4, Mendelssohn's "Pet " speaks for itself. I hardly know whether to call the F *flat*, which so deliciously colours the melody at the outset of Rossini's air in A flat, "Sombre forêt " ("Guillaume Tell "), a *minor* or a *diminished* fifth ; it *is* diminished, but not like the other fifth of my example (No. 3) *from below*, or after the cognate example of the diminished *seventh*, where (key of A minor) the lower note is G *sharp* and the upper one F *natural*.

Your obedient Servant,
ALFONSO MATTHEY,
Foggy Lane, Far West, Aug. 15th.

Passing Events.

Mr. Eugene d'Albert is to compose, or is now writing, a new symphony for the Festival at Birmingham in 1885.

It is said Mr. Joseph Bennett spoke at the recent festival at Harlech. His remarks, which would undoubtedly be valuable, have not come to hand.

The late Dean Boyd, of Exeter, amongst other benevolent bequests, left £5,000 towards a fund for apprenticing the cathedral chorister boys and boys of the cathedral school.

Readers will regret to hear of the death of Mayer Randegger, elder brother of the well-known composer and conductor, Alberto Randegger, for so many years a resident of this country.

Upon the occasion of the visit of the Duke and Duchess of Connaught to Norwich Cathedral on the 22nd inst., Bennett's "God is a Spirit" was sung by the choir, though it was not Service time.

The reconstruction of Verdi's "Don Carlos" by the composer includes its condensation from 5 to 4 acts, the omission of the interpolated ballet, and an extensive alteration of some of the movements.

It is stated that the Archbishop of Canterbury, the Bishops of London, St. Albans, and Rochester have become patrons of the London Church Choir Association: The annual Festival in St. Paul's Cathedral is announced for November 8.

From Lincoln comes the intelligence of the death of Edwin Aspa, the composer of "Endymion," "The Gipsies," and other works. He died on the 17th inst., at the early age of 47, and his loss will be regretted by a wide circle of friends in the Midland Counties.

An American contemporary tells the world that there are 9,000 bands in the United States. Perhaps the number given includes military bands, etc. The test question is, in any country, how many properly balanced and complete orchestral bands are there to be found?

Says the *Athenæum*: The performances of "Parsifal" announced for next year at Bayreuth are to be given in August, instead of in July as this year. It is stated that King Ludwig of Bavaria intends to have a private performance of the work at Munich in the course of next May.

The lamented death of Mr. J. Wallis, of 135, Euston Road, has made no difference in the arrangements and conduct of the well-known musical instrument business carried on at the above address under the title of J. Wallis and Son. The members of the family of the late Mr. Wallis have received much wide spread sympathy in their recent loss.

H. Clarence Eddy and Frederick Grant Gleason's "Church and Concert Organist," published by Ed. Schuberth and Co., of New York, has reached its second edition. These well known and able musicians are now compiling a second volume, which is to appear about Christmas. They both bring experience to their work, and the two volumes should become as valuable as they are interesting.

The *Weekly Dispatch* seems to be sceptical about the new Italian Opera house on the Thames Embankment, but Mr. Mapleson is not a man to disappoint the public. The doubt is suggested by the existence of a (supposed) agreement between Mr. Mapleson and Mr. Gye, which would, greatly to the public detriment, ensure a continued monopoly of the Italian opera : impossible, after all, with Mr. Carl Rosa and Drury Lane theatre as *derniers ressorts*. The *Weekly Dispatch* is not alone however in its exception with regard to this scheme.

At the dedication of a new stained-glass window lately at Beetham, Milnthorpe, an excellent and carefully rendered choral service was held. On a following day an organ recital was given, in which the "Andante" from Mendelssohn's violin concerto, "Meditation of Bach's First Prelude" by Gounod, and "Cavatina" (Raff), were admirably played on the organ and violin by Mr. Randolph Hall, formerly deputy organist, Ely Cathedral, and Mr. G. Robinson the organist of the Church.

Ambroise Thomas has been indisposed, but recent accounts, it is said, represent him as now convalescent.

A reception was held last Saturday afternoon at the residence of Mrs. Stretton, Edwardes Squire, Kensington, when Mrs. Hitchcock and Miss Constance Hitchcock played a tarantelle of Raff's in splendid style, also other pianoforte pieces. Mrs. Stretton sang one or two English songs with great sweetness and expression, and Miss Annie Baldwin gave an excellent "reading" from the text of Shakespeare. Some of the Kensington clergy were present.

An important sale of musical property, including pianofortes by Broadwood, Collard, Erard, Hermann, and others, harmoniums, harps, Italian and other violins, violas, violoncellos and double basses, the remainder of the library of music of the late William Laidlaw, Esq., of Liverpool, chiefly comprising manuscript scores and parts (many being original and bearing autographs), also the excellent library of Wm. Lemare, Esq., of Brixton, were to be sold by auction, by Messrs. Puttick and Simpson, on August 22nd.

Max Strakosch has been making extensive preparations at the Twenty-third Street Theatre, New York, for the production of S. G. Pratt's opera "Zenobia," which took place on August 20th. The opera was rehearsed under the direction of Signor de Novellis. The chorus numbered some sixty voices. The soloists were Miss Henninges, Miss Rosalba Beecher, Miss Bertha Ricci, Signor Montegriffo, Brignoli, Mr. Stoddard, John Gilbert and Mr. Bordemann. After "Zenobia" the "Bohemian Girl" was produced, then "Martha" in English. Signor Operti's new opera, "A Merry Prince," will probably be represented at this theatre some time next season.

The Querist.

QUERY.

CIPHERING.—We—myself and some professional friends—appeal to you to settle a much disputed question, viz :—"What is the correct way of spelling the word Ciphering, known to all having much to do with cheap organs? What's its origin? Does it come from Siphon ?"—AN OLD SUBSCRIBER.

To an "OLD SUBSCRIBER": I regret that I cannot offer any decisive information. The word sipho, or siphon, from the Greek, and incorporated into the Latin language, was one of quite universal use, and frequent application anciently in connection with tubes, etc. And as the organ grew up in the church where the Latin language prevailed, the idea of "An Old Subscriber" is one of much shrewdness. Perhaps some one learned in organ-building matters will kindly come forward and throw some definite light upon a subject of some interest. ED.—*Mus. Stan.*

Service Lists.

FIFTEENTH SUNDAY AFTER TRINITY.

SEPTEMBER 2nd.

London.

ST. PAUL'S CATHEDRAL.—Morn.: Service, Te Deum and Benedictus, Tours in F ; Introit, Then we adore; Holy Communion, Tours in F. Even.: Service, Magnificat and Nunc Dimittis, Garrett in D ; Anthem, Ye people, If with all your hearts, Cast thy burden on the Lord (Mendelssohn).

FOUNDLING CHAPEL.—Morn.: Service, Sullivan in D; Anthem, Send out Thy light (Gounod). Aft.: Children's Service.

ST. JAMES'S PRIVATE EPISCOPAL CHAPEL, SOUTHWARK. —Morn.: Service, Introit, I am not worthy, holy Lord; Communion Service, Hummel in B flat. Even.: Service, Proul in F ; Anthem, Save me, O God (Balfe).

ST. MAGNUS, LONDON BRIDGE.—Morn.: Service, Opening Anthem, I will arise (Creyton); Te Deum and Jubilate, Goss in A ; Kyrie (Nares). Even.: Service, Cantate and Deus Misereatur, Goss in C; Anthem, Awake, awake (Wise).

ST. MARGARET PATTENS, ROOD LANE, FENCHURCH STREET.—Morn.: Service, Te Deum, Sullivan in D; Benedictus, Dykes in F; Communion Service ; Offertory Anthem, Whosoever drinketh (Bennett); Kyrie, Credo, Sanctus,

Benedictus, Agnus Dei, and Gloria, Schubert in F. Even.: Service, Magnificat and Nunc Dimittis, Stark in D; Anthem, Praise the Lord, O my soul (Goss).

ST. PAUL'S, AVENUE ROAD, SOUTH HAMPSTEAD.—Morn.: Service, Te Deum, Dykes in F; Benedictus (Garrett); Kyrie, Mendelssohn in G; Offertory Sentences (Barnby). Even.: Service, Magnificat and Nunc Dimittis, Arnold in A; Anthem, Behold now praise (Calkin).

ST. PETER'S, VERE STREET, W.—Even.: Service, Magnificat and Nunc Dimittis, Tuckermann in F; Anthem, O come, let us worship (Mendelssohn).

ST. AGNES, KENNINGTON PARK, S.E.—Morn.: Service, Holy Communion, Kyrie, Credo, Sanctus, Gloria in excelsis, Distin in C; Benedictus and Agnus Dei, Eyre in E. flat.

ST AUGUSTINE AND ST. FAITH, WATLING STREET.—Morn.: Service, Calkin in B flat; Introit, Be merciful (South); Communion Service, Calkin in B flat. Even.: Service, Calkin in B flat; Anthem, Blessing, glory, honour, power (Spohr).

ST. SEPULCHRE'S, HOLBORN. — Morn: Service, Nares in F; Anthem, In Thee (Weldon). Even.: Service, Cooke in G; Anthem, If with all your hearts (Mendelssohn).

Country.

ST. ASAPH CATHEDRAL.—Morn.: Service, Garrett in D; Anthem, O give thanks (Sydenham). Even.: Service, The Litany; Anthem, Blessed is the man (Goss).

ASHBURNE CHURCH, DERBYSHIRE. — Morn.: Service, Kempton in B flat; Kyrie, Credo, Gloria, Woodward in E flat. Even.: Service, Arnold in B flat; Anthem, Turn thee again (Attwood).

BIRMINGHAM (S. ALBAN THE MARTYR).—Morn.: Service, Te Deum and Benedictus, Dykes in F; Holy Communion; Woodward in E flat. Evensong: Magnificat and Nunc Dimittis, Tours in F.

BIRMINGHAM (ST. CYPRIAN'S, HAY MILLS).—Morn.: Service, Cobb in G; Anthem, Praise the Lord (Elvey). Even.: Even.: Service, Clarke-Whitfield in E; Anthem, O come, let us worship (Mendelssohn).

CANTERBURY CATHEDRAL. — Morn.: Service, Dykes in F; Anthem, Above all praise (Mendelssohn); Communion, Dykes in F. Even.: Service, Dykes in F; Anthem, He shall feed his flock, and His yoke is easy (Handel).

CARLISLE CATHEDRAL.—Morn.: Service, Walmisley in F Introit, God is my helper (Stainer); Kyrie, Walmisley in F; Nicene Creed, Harmonised Monotone. Even.: Service, Garrett in E flat; Anthem, Plead Thou my cause (Mozart).

DUBLIN, ST. PATRICK'S (NATIONAL) CATHEDRAL.—Morn.: Service, Te Deum and Jubilate, Stainer in E flat; Holy Communion, Kyrie, Creed, Sanctus, Gloria. Stewart in G; Anthem, Grant us Thy peace (Mendelssohn). Even.: Service, Magnificat and Nunc Dimittis, Stainer in E flat; Anthems, Holy, holy, holy (Mendelssohn), and O Lord our Governor (Stevenson).

ELY CATHEDRAL.—Morn.: Service, Te Deum, Chipp in E; Benedictus, Plain Song; Kyrie and Credo, Roes in G; Gloria, Ouseley in E flat; Anthem, Pray for the peace (Novello). Even.: Service, O sing unto the Lord, No. 15 (Greene).

HARROGATE (ST. PETER'S CHURCH). — Morn.: Service, Te Deum and Benedictus, Dykes in F; Anthem, Turn Thy face (Attwood); Kyrie Credo, Sursum Corda, Gloria in excelsis, Woodward in E flat. Even.: Service, Magnificat and Nunc Dimittis, Ebdon in C; Anthem, They have taken away my Lord (Stainer).

LICHFIELD CATHEDRAL. — Morn.: Service, Hopkins in F; Communion Service, Dykes in F; Anthem, O, come let us worship (Mendelssohn). Even.: Service, Elvey in A; Anthem, O clap your hands (Stainer).

LIVERPOOL CATHEDRAL.—Aft.: Service, Magnificat and Nunc Dimittis, Burstall in C; Anthem, I will extol Thee (Hatton).

LIVERPOOL (ST. CUTHBERT'S, EVERTON).—Morn.: Service, and Communion, Tours in F. Even.: Service, Tours in F; Anthem, The wilderness (Wesley).

MANCHESTER CATHEDRAL.—Morn.: Service, Hopkins in F; Holy Communion Service, Cobb in G; Anthem, Then round about the starry throne (Handel). Aft.: Service, Hopkins in F; Anthem, O hadst thou hearkened (Sullivan).

MANCHESTER (ST. BENEDICT'S).—Morn.: Service, Credo and Gloria in excelsis, Williams in D; Kyrie, Sanctus, Benedictus, and Agnus Dei, Mozart in B flat, No. 7. Even.: Service, Magnificat and Nunc Dimittis, Tours in F.

MANCHESTER (ST. JOHN BAPTIST, HULME).—Morn.: Service, Kyrie, Credo, Sanctus, Benedictus, Agnus Dei and Gloria Gloria in excelsis, Sutton in F. Even.: Service, Magnificat and Nunc Dimittis, Wesley in F.

SALISBURY CATHEDRAL.—Morn.: Service, Lloyd in E flat; Offertory (Lloyd). Aft.: Service, Lloyd in.E flat; Anthem, In that day (Elvey).

SHERBORNE ABBEY.— Morn.: Service, Te Deum, Chants; Kyrie, Smallwood in F; Offertory (Barnby). Even.: Service, Anthem, Sing unto God (Lyle).

SHEFFIELD PARISH CHURCH. — Morn.: Service, Kyrie, Weber in E. Even.: Service, Magnificat and Nunc Dimittis, Barnby in C; Anthem, The glory of the Lord (Goss).

WELLS CATHEDRAL. — Morn.: Service, Boyce and Hayes in G; Continuation, Travers in F. Even.: Service, Hayes in E flat; Anthem, Awake, awake put on thy strength (Wise).

WORCESTER CATHEDRAL. — Morn.: Service, Dykes in F; Anthem, The Lord is in His holy temple (Thorne). Even. Service, Dykes in F. In that day (Oakeley).

₊ *Post-cards must be sent to the Editor,* 6, *Argyle Square, W.C., by Wednesday. Lists are frequently omitted in consequence of not being received in time.*

NOTICE.—*All communications intended for the Editor are to be sent to his private address. Business communications to be addressed to* 185, *Fleet Street, E.C.*

NEWSPAPERS sent should have *distinct marks* opposite to the matter to which attention is required.

ERRATA.

"A few words on Registering on the Organ" should have been the title of the first leaderette in last week's issue on page 117.

Read lines 9, 10, and 11 of leader, "Some account of an Ancient Institution" (page 116), as follows :—"has a passage in which the word occurs in the Latin plural, and in which one of the most common of bardic functions is portrayed."

In line 7 of Mr. H. C. Banister's letter in *Musical Standard* of last week, for "notes" read "rules."

APPOINTMENT.

Mr. J. J. LISHMAN, has been appointed organist and choirmaster to Christ Church, Bermondsey.

Printed for the Proprietor by BOWDEN, HUDSON & Co., at 23, Red Lion Street, Holborn, London, W.C.; and Published by WILLIAM REEVES, at the Office, 185, Fleet Street, E.C. West End Agents:—WEEKES & CO., 14, Hanover Street, Regent Street, W. Subscriptions and Advertisements are received either by the Publisher or West End Agents.—*Communications for the* EDITOR *are to be forwarded to his private address*, 6, Argyll Square, W.C.
SATURDAY, SEPTEMBER 1, 1883.—*Entered at the General Post Office as a Newspaper.*

The Musical Standard

A NEWSPAPER FOR MUSICIANS PROFESSIONAL AND AMATEUR

No. 997. Vol. XXV. FOURTH SERIES. SATURDAY, SEPTEMBER 8, 1883. WEEKLY: PRICE 3D.

MOZART'S ORGAN WORKS.

BY FRANK J. SAWYER, B.MUS. OXON., F.C.O.

[A Lecture delivered at the College of Organists.]

(*Concluded from page 127*).

From Augsburg, Mozart's journey led him to Mannheim ; here, while content with the secular music, the Church music seems to have disgusted him. Of the choir he writes :—

"Six soprani, six alti, six tenore, six bassi to twenty violins, and twelve basses, stand just in the proportion of 0 to 11" .Of the organists : "They have two organists here, for whose sake alone it would be worth taking the journey to Mannheim. I had a good opportunity of hearing them, for it is the custom here to omit the Benedictus, and for the organist to go on playing instead. The first time I heard the second organist, and the next time the first; but I have a better opinion of the second than of the first. When I heard him I asked, 'Who is at the organ?' 'Our second organist.' 'He plays wretchedly.' When I heard the other I asked, 'Who is that?' 'Our first organist.' 'He plays more wretchedly still.' I suppose if they were shaken up together the result would be something still worse. It makes one die of laughter to see them. The second goes to the organ like a child to the mud; he shows his trade in his face. The first wears spectacles. I stood at the organ and watched him for the sake of instruction."

Again he gives a humorous account in a letter to his father of the effect of his organ playing, soon after his arrival (Nov. 13, 1777):—

"Last Sunday I played the organ in the chapel for a joke. I came in during the Kyrie, played the end of it, and, after the priest had given out the Gloria, I made a cadenza. Nothing like it had ever been heard here before, so that everybody looked round, especially Holzbauer. . . . The people were inclined to laugh, because every now and then, when I wanted a pizzicato effect, I gave little bangs to the notes. I was in my best humour. A voluntary is always played here instead of the Benedictus; I took the idea from the Sanctus, and carried it out as a fugue. There they all stood and made faces."

On the opening of a new organ, Dec. 18th, at the Lutheran Church, he again played, but greatly disliked the Abbé Vogler, who performed also on it.

From Mannheim, after falling in love with Aloysia Weber, he journeyed to Paris, where his poor mother breathed her last. In the French capital we find no organ playing, but at length, by his father's careful management, Wolfgang is appointed Organist and Deputy Capellmeister at Salzburg Cathedral, by the Archbishop, at a salary of 500 florins. Thither he therefore returned, though with a strong dislike to the town, its authorities, and its inhabitants. To quote again from Jahn (vol. ii., 92) :—

"As organist, Mozart was, under the necessity of playing the organ at festivals, but as a rule only for accompaniments and for interludes at set-places, which gave him opportunity for improvising—his special delight. We have some organ sonatas with orchestral accompaniments belonging to this time (Nos. 13, 14, and 15), quite in the style of those already noticed; compositions after the fashion of, the first movement of a sonata, without a trace of ecclesiastical severity either in the technical construction, which is very light, or in the style, which is brilliant and cheerful. The organ occurs as an obbligato instrument only in one of these sonatas (the last, No. 15), which is the most elaborated, but still very moderate in style, and without any florid passages."

It will be my next pleasant duty, having now traced Mozart from the last period, to place before you, with the help of my friends, these three concluding sonatas of the series.

No. 13 opens (in C major allegro) with a quaint theme alternately staccato and legato. The form is perhaps least clear in this of all that have come before us tonight. Immediately after the fourth bar a *forte* passage of four bars' length enters, which gives way to a third phrase of a soft, melodious character, forming thus three separate sections to the first theme. This latter phrase then appears at once in E major on the 'cello, ultimately leading by a passage derived from a part of the second phrase to a pedal on the super-tonic C of the key, thus reintroducing E major with the second theme, *forte* ; but after eight bars still another pretty little passage occurs in the same key. A pedal phrase on E leads to the cadence and double bar. From this it will be seen that the form is not so distinct in this movement.

After the double bar comes the most interesting section. The development opening boldly leads to a strain where the sustained organ part, blending with the short light phrases of the strings, forms an exquisite piece of tone colour. The third section contains the usual repetitions of the first.

[*Sonata No.* 13.]

As we have thus traced Mozart to his appointment as organist of Salzburg Cathedral, it may not be uninteresting to us to see what sort of instrument he had to play on. Marpurg describes it thus:—"The cathedral contains a large organ at the back of the entrance, four side organs in front of the choir, and a little choir organ below the choir, where the choristers sit. The large organ is only used on grand occasions, and for preludes ; during the performance one of the four side organs is played, generally that next to the altar on the right side, where the solo singers and basses are. Opposite, by the left side of the organ, are the violinists, &c., and on the other two sides are two choruses of trumpets and drums. The lower choir organ and double bass join in when required." Mattheson gives a similar description.

Sonata No. 14, to which we now turn our attention, was composed soon after his return from Paris and introduces us for the first and only time to a somewhat full orchestral accompaniment. It is scored for 2 oboes, 2 horns in C, 2 trumpets in C, 1st and 2nd violin, organ, 'cello and bass. Röchel remarks, that this is longest and most developed of all the organ movements, but without any special thematic development.

We cannot have the means to-night of representing this sonata as intended, but as the horn and trumpet parts are all contained in the organ part, if you will permit me to weave in the oboe parts into my own, while our two violinists and 'cellist give the string parts, your fertile imaginations can picture the drums, and thus a mutilated, but nevertheless slight idea, can be given you of Sonata 14.

The opening theme is one of those bold yet simple strains that Mozart so often made out of the tonic triad.

The second theme, reached after some development of the first by the 'cello, is given out by first violin, replied to by the oboes ; the organ joins in in imitation of the strings; and there succeeds to a bold passage, *forte* in E major, an exquisite phrase for the reeds and violins, still in the key of the second subject, the organ pedals strengthening the bass. Six bars' modulation reintroduces the first theme, repeated as usual with the second theme and episode in its transposed key. The effect as written with brass, reeds, drums, strings, and organ, must be undoubtedly grand.

[*Sonata No.* 14.]

Before playing to you the last example that we have to bring before you to-night, two other interesting little stories of Mozart as an organist should be related.

In 1789 he made his sixth professional tour, visiting Berlin, Dresden, and Leipzig. At the latter place, to give an eye-witness's account, "On April 22, he played the organ in the Thomas Kirche, without previous notice, and gratuitously. He played finely for an hour to a large audience. The then organist, Görner, and the cantor, Doles, sat near him and pulled out the stops. I saw him well; a young, well-dressed man of middle height. Doles was quite delighted with the performance, and declared that his old master, Sebastian Bach, had risen again. Mozart brought to bear all the arts of harmony with the greatest ease and discrimination, and improvised magnificently on every theme given—among others on the chorale, "Jesu, meine Zuversicht."

Lastly, Hesse became acquainted in Frankfort, as he tells us, with an old superannuated organist of the Katharinenkirche, who in 1790 had been the pupil of his predecessor; the old man said :—"On Sunday, after service, Mozart came into the choir of S. Catharine's, and begged the old organist to allow him to play something. He seated himself on the stool and gave the reins to his fancy, when the organist suddenly pushed him off the stool in the rudest manner, and said to his pupil standing by : 'Mark that last modulation which Herr Mozart made; how can he profess to be a musician and commit such grave offences against correct composition?' The pupil did mark the modulation, and Hesse thought it a fine one, and by no means unusual."

Turning now to the last sonata, we find, undoubtedly from the organ point of view, the most interesting of the whole series. The accompaniment is once more for two violins and bassi, but the organ part is written out in full, and is here and there only a solo instrument, with accessories. Kochel notes :—"Probably Mozart wrote this sonata for himself, it being composed during the time of his Court organistship at Salzburg."

That the organ part bears a strong resemblance to to Mozart's piano style, becomes evident at once.

To describe the form. The first ten bars given to the strings announce the theme *piano*—an elegant and smoothly written cantabile. At the eleventh bar the organ enters and takes it up, the other instruments simply following in accompanying passages of the pure concerto style. The second subject is given out by the upper notes of the organ, the first and second violins playing to it in thirds below. The section in the dominant is of long duration, and introduces beside the theme two other delightful phrases—one before, one after a *tutti*. The latter, thirds on the organ with detached string chords and long sustained notes alternating between organ and violins, leads to the resumption of the first subject, and consequent repetition of the first part, the organ passages being made slightly more florid.

[*No.* 15.]

And now, in making a *resumé* of what has been before us to-night, we find, firstly, that Mozart was as great an organist as pianist. He was so great an extemporaneous performer on the organ that Doles said his old master, Bach, had risen again.

It is then plainly evident that his own playing must have been widely different from the organ parts of the sonatas which have been before us to-night. To extemporise fugues on any subject given him, seems to have been but child's play, while his performances of chorales in Lutheran Leipzig resembled those of Bach himself. In Mozart the learned and the passionate

meet ; what grandeur must there then have been in his unfettered phantasy on the king of instruments. Yet, strange to say, the latter part of his life he seems entirely to have neglected the organ ; for in his Vienna life we find no allusion to it.

Finally, the question will naturally be asked, how have these excellent organ sonatas or miniature concertos remained in oblivion so long? After Mozart had left Salzburg, Archbishop Colloredo or Heirony-mus—the same who had been such a thorn in the side of the composer during his residence in the town, took a dislike to all pure orchestral music in the Church, and consequently ordered the discontinuance of the organ sonatas, ordering Michael Hadyn to compose choral movements to ecclesiastical text to be used in their stead. Hence arose, says Köchel, the many graduales of that composer.

Though they have rested now in oblivion for nearly a century, I feel that their resurrection to-night may bring a fresh period of life to them, of which your applause has shown them worthy.

The score is not expensive—only 4s. 6d.—and to all those—and there are many who for a relief against the pure organ music, and glad for variety to combine other instruments with it—I heartily commend these sonatas as a source of much pleasure to all concerned.

Finally, in thanking you for the patient hearing you have accorded me, I would ask you to accord with me your warmest thanks to Mr. Crapps, F.C.O., Mr. Gray, and Mr. Parks, for so kindly giving up so much time and labour to the rehearsals and performance of the sonatas, which have proved the relieving, if not indeed the redeeming feature, of what would otherwise have been, I fear, a dry discourse.

ANOTHER CRITICISM BY SIR GEO. MACFARREN.

It will be recollected that some considerable local disappointment was occasioned at the Cardiff Eisteddfod several weeks since, by the brevity with which Sir George Macfarren expressed the verdict of the adjudicators in the great choral competition. Sir George has now offered a supplementary statement in response to the conductor of one of the choirs, and speaking for himself only, he says, under date of August 23 :—"The point most to blame in some of the performances was a tendency to force the voices, especially among the boy singers. That boys may sing with beautiful effect, is proved daily in our cathedral Services ; but this effect is produced by an easy emission of tone, without tightening of the throat and with natural effortless management of the breath, which should be impelled from the diaphragm, and never influenced by the rising of the shoulders. Disregard of these principles by female and male adults, as much as by boys, induces hardness of tone to the extent of harshness, and causes the rising of the pitch, which in some instances at Cardiff proceeded into strange keys, and rendered the singing impossible of instrumental accompaniment. Noise is not power, and the best quality attained is with the least physical exertion. The fault I have named, and certainly not an incorrect knowledge of the music, was the cause of the singing being out of tune on the occasion. By musically phrasing, I mean the taking of breath at the natural reading places in the musical sentences—analogous to observing the punctuation of words—the giving more or less emphasis to words according to their significance in the musical sense. By just variety of power, I mean regard to the directions for loudness and softness, and the gradations between the extremes, avoiding to sink in pitch with the diminution of tone, and beginning every phrase with distinct firmness, whether it be soft or loud." The writer concludes with a testimony to the musical aptitude of the Welsh.

Musical Intelligence.

GLOUCESTER MUSICAL FESTIVAL.

The one hundred and sixtieth meeting of the rotatory festivals of the three choirs of Gloucester, Worcester, and Hereford, is by this time an accomplished fact. Originating in meetings of the three cathedral choirs only, these festivals, as our readers well know, have arisen to a large artistic importance, with a benevolent purpose, an orchestra and solo singers being engaged, the performances of sacred music being given in the Cathedral, and miscellaneous concerts of secular music in the Town Halls—collections being made after the Cathedral services and the oratorios, the proceeds of which are applied in aid of the widows and orphans of the poorer clergy of the three dioceses. These purposes have been largely served by the three-choir festivals.

The list of stewards for this year's festival gives the names of upwards of 200 gentlemen so acting, headed by that of the Earl of Ducie, the Lord-Lieutenant of the county, and including those of many of the neighbouring gentry.

The band upon the present occasion consisted of some 65 players and comprised many of the most eminent members of the best London orchestras, led by Mr. Carrodus. The nucleus of the chorus was formed by the associated Cathedral choirs of the three cities, these singers being reinforced by choristers from various other quarters. The solo singers engaged were Misses A. Williams and M. Davies, Mdlle. Avigliana, Mdme. Patey, Miss H. Wilson, Mr. E. Lloyd, Mr. B. Newth, Mr. F. King, Mr. Brereton, and Mr. Santley.

Monday was devoted to the serious hard work of rehearsing in the Cathedral and Shire Hall. The proceedings, as far as the public were concerned, commenced on Tuesday morning with the Service which was held in the choir of the Cathedral, at 10 o'clock, the members of the three choirs joining in the choral portions. The Service was intoned by the Revs. B. K. Foster (Precentor), and J. P. Bowen. The anthem was Oakeley's "This is the day," and after the sermon and during the offertory a new setting of the hymn, "Crown him with many crowns," by Mr. Williams, the able organist of Gloucester Cathedral, was sung. The Deputy Mayor and Corporation attended in state. The sermon was preached by the Rev. Dr. Vaughan, Dean of Landaff, who took for his text, Psalm lxxxvii. 7, "As well the singers as the players on instruments shall be there ; all my springs are in Thee."

Next followed a luncheon, given by the Mayor of Gloucester. At half-past one on Tuesday Mendelssohn's "Elijah," was admirably performed, and those who now heard an oratorio in a Cathedral for the first time experienced a sensation never to be forgotten, and realised that noblest triumph of art, "a musical sermon."

The music of the Prophet was sung by Mr. Santley, its finest living exponent ; the tenor solos by Mr. E. Lloyd ; the soprano music was divided between Miss M. Davies and Miss A. Williams, as was that for contralto between Miss H. Wilson and Madame Patey. Noteworthy *solo* and *soli* pieces were the duet, "Zion spreadeth her Hands"—Misses M. Davies and H. Wilson ; the air, "If with all your Hearts"—Mr. E. Lloyd ; the declamatory bass solo, "Is not His Word like a Fire "—Mr. Santley ; the soprano air, "Hear ye, Israel "—Miss A. Williams ; "O Rest in the Lord "—Madame Patey ; and the trio, "Lift thine Eyes "—Misses A. Williams and H. Wilson, and Madame Patey. Some of the concerted pieces claimed the help of Mdlle. Avigliana, Mrs. Whitaker, Mr. B. Newth, Mr. F. King, and Mr. Brereton. "Thanks be to God," the chorus "Be not afraid," "And then shall your light," and other choral passages were finely sung. Mr. C. L. Williams was the conductor ; leading with remarkable forethought and skill, though at times choosing somewhat feverish *tempi* considering the acoustic properties of a building with an aptitude for the preservation, or rather prolongation, of sound. Mr. Williams has already proved himself to be an excellent and trustworthy conductor, and Gloucester must be congratulated upon the presence of so gifted, complete, and useful an artist. The orchestral detail and the contrapuntal overture, a masterpiece of its kind, were admirably produced. The evening concert in the Shire Hall contained one novelty of interest, Dr. C. Hubert Parry's setting for chorus and orchestra of James Shirley's poem, "Death's Final Conquest," a fine, thoughtful poem, admired even by that worthless monarch, Charles II. The music by Dr. Hubert Parry is large in its thoughtfulness, gloomy in its general complexion, but orchestrated with a rare mastery. One passage is of great beauty and grace—this is the setting of the oft-quoted words, "Only the actions of the just smell sweet and blossom in the dust." The piece was conducted by the composer, and was received, it need not be said, with applause. Further particulars must be reserved for next week.

EASTBOURNE.—The cause of the overwhelming success attending the Devonshire Park concerts is not far to seek. It does not consist in the simple gratification of a desire among visitors to assemble where others in the same social grade are wont to meet together, nor can it be said to have its origin in the circumstance that other and counter attractions are wanting ; it may be safely concluded that the pre-eminent reason of such highly satisfactory results as are placed on record in our columns week after week—and this, be it remembered, in the height of summer —is the really superior character of the entertainment provided. While the daily performances of Mr. Adams's orchestra are listened to with exceeding pleasure by admiring and critical assemblies, the Saturday evening special vocal and instrumental concerts have up to the present not unnaturally enlisted the highest degree of public patronage. It is now no uncommon thing to find the Floral Hall crowded to its fullest capacity on the occasion of these weekly concerts. The other Saturday, so great was the crush that many had to content themselves with standing-room, while not a few were unable to gain admission at all. The principal orchestral number was Mozart's Symphony, No. 3 in E flat, which closed the first part of a very excellent programme. This was the first occasion of the production of this classical work in Eastbourne. A prominent feature in the programme was the performance of two numbers from F. H. Cowen's "Language of Flowers," which was received with manifest tokens of appreciation, and among the other orchestral numbers to which Julien Adams's band did full justice, were the march, "Tannhäuser" (Wagner), Rossini's overture, "Semiramide," and the overture by Weber, "Oberon." Each of these was played with that *verve* and precision characteristic of this orchestra under its able conductor, who directed the entire programme from memory.—*Eastbourne Chronicle.*

A NEW AMERICAN MUSICAL PITCH.

It has long been known that the present pitch in America is too high, and affects particularly European singers ; we, therefore, quote with pleasure the following as a movement in the right direction :—

Some time ago several members of the musical profession held a meeting in Boston, to consider the subject of the present high and constantly rising pitch. In proof of the need of some immediate effort being made to adopt a standard pitch or fundamental keynote, it was stated that the celebrated Music Hall orchestra in that city, under the leadership of Carl Zerrahn, in the last year had risen a quarter of a tone above the already high pitch of the Great organ. Accordingly, a committee of seven of the best known musicians was appointed to arrange for another and more public public gathering of the Profession and the manufacturers of musical instruments, to agree upon a common standard. The first two members of this important committee were Carl Zerrahn and Lyman W. Wheeler, both of whom are well known in Detroit. In the circular which was issued by the committee, the following interesting figures were given, showing the present variations in pitch, or keynote—the number of vibrations per second for middle C.

Boston Great organ	...	...	...	271·2
Chickering pianos	...	...	...	273·9
Hook and Hastings' organs	...	...	270
New York highest	...	...	...	273·9
Steinway pianos	...	...	...	273·2

At the final meeting of all persons interested, held at the New England Conservatory of Music, a resolution was adopted to lower the pitch and to make 262 vibrations a second the standard for middle C. This is not so low as the standard in many parts of Europe. The Konig pitch is but 256·1. This is a movement, therefore, in the right direction, and if this standard becomes general in the United States, it will be of very great value and convenience to American vocalists.—*Music and Drama* (New York).

Lecocq's newest work, "Le Grain de Sable," will, it is stated, be first produced at the Theatre des Galeries Saint-Hubert, Brussels.

Foreign Musical Intelligence.

Peter Benoit's "Lucifer" is to be brought out at La Scala, Milan, next month.

In Luttich, died recently, aged 84, Victor Massart, a highly-esteemed teacher of the double bass and a pupil of Cherubini.

A monument to the memory of Theodore Kullah, erected by his friends and pupils, is to be unveiled in Berlin on September 12th.

New Italian operas are "King Lear," by Cagnoni; "Edmea," by Giuseppe Anteri; "Salambo," by Nicolo Massa; "Baldassare," by Villate.

Hans von Bülow has returned to Meiningen in excellent health, and is expected to resume his artistic activity as a pianist and conductor next winter.

The King of Saxony has conferred upon Herr Capell-meister Carl Reinecke, of Leipzig, the order of _Ritter-kreuz erster Classe des Albrechtsordens._

Victor Nessler, composer of the "Rattenfanger des Hameln," is now engaged on a new opera to be produced at the Leipsic Town Theatre in November.

New German operas are "Der Trompeter von Sack-ingen," by Victor Nessler, and "Eine Nacht in Venedig," by Johann Strauss to be first produced at the Friedrich-Wilhelmstadtischen Theater, Berlin.

The _Eastern Express_ of August 7th announces that M. Adolphe Terschak, the Hungarian flautist, lately played before his Majesty the Sultan; the latter was so pleased with the performance that he conferred upon M. Terschak the order of the third class of the Médjidié.

Berlin is to have a month of Italian opera, from 16th September to 16th October. Bimboni will be the con-ductor. The _répertoire_ includes Rossini's "Semiramide" and "Othello," Ambroise Thomas's "Hamlet," Halévy's "La Juive," and several of Verdi's operas.

Neue Zeitschrift für Musik tells that the new Concert Hall at Leipzig is advancing towards completion. Statues of Mozart and Beethoven are to adorn the front, statues of Bach, Handel, Haydn, and Schubert the sides, and probably statues of Mendelssohn and Schumann the foyer.

The Musical Institute of Florence offers prizes for Church music, for a setting of the Antiphon "Hosanna! Filio David" in five parts, the last sentence, "Hosanna in excelsis," to be set as a Fugue for five voices. The competition is to be open until the end of next June. The first prize is 200 lire.

Among the unpublished works of the late Joachim Raff are said to be four operas; two of these are "Die Eifer-süchtigen," a comic opera in four acts, and "Benedetto Marcello," a lyric opera. An orchestral work, an Italian Suite, entitled "Im Süden" (In the South), which consists of a Barcarolle, Policinella, Notturno, and Tarantella, will be performed, it is said, at Professor Wüllner's concerts in Berlin.

It is announced that the Bach Choir will give two concerts next season, on March 19 and May 14. Pales-trina's Mass, "Assumpta est Maria," for six voices; S. Wesley's motet, "Exultate Deo;" a hymn, "Awake, my heart," for bass solo, chorus, and organ, by Mr. C. V. Stanford; and works by Bach, Mozart, and Schumann, are to be given. Mr. Otto Goldschmidt will be musical director, as usual.

At Belzig, a small town in the Wittenberg district, a memorial tablet was lately placed on the house in which the composer Reissiger was born. The following words are inscribed on it with golden letters: "_Hoffcapellmeister C. G. Reissiger, geb. den 31 Juli, 1798, gest den 7 Nov., 1859._" Vocal performances, in which 300 singers took part, a banquet, and a festive procession, celebrated the memory of the estimable musician.

The Royal Orchestra of Kalakawa, King of the Sand-wich Islands, is at present giving concerts at San Fran-cisco. It is said that the orchestra, numbering about forty performers, proposes to visit Europe. The musicians are natives, but their conductor, Heinrich Berger, is a German, who was formerly an oboist in a regiment of the Prussian Guard, but who has devoted some years now to the cultivation of music and the formation of bands in the Sandwich Islands.

Two distinguished flute players and composers for that instrument have been lost to the world lately. Joseph Fahrback died on the 7th of June, aged seventy-nine; Franz Doppler on the 27th of July, aged sixty-one. The latter made himself a name as a composer of several popular operas and ballets. His most successful works of this description are the operas "Ilka" and "Wanda," and his ballets, "In Versailles" and "Melusine."

Between August 23, 1882, and June 13, 1883, 237 per-formances of operas have been given at the Berlin Court Opera House. The works performed numbered 56, and were by 29 composers. 32 evenings were devoted to Wagner, who was represented by 6 works. Next came Mozart, with 21 performances and 5 works; after him Meyerbeer, with 18 and 5; Lortzing, with 18 and 2; Bizet, with 18 and 1; Weber, with 16 and 3; Gluck, with 11 and 4; Auber, with 11 and 4; Verdi, with 9 and 3; Nicolai, with 7 and 1; Beethoven, with 6 and 1; Perfall, with 6 and 1; Nessler, with 6 and 1; Rossini, with 6 and 1; Donizetti, with 6 and 2; Klughardt, with 5 and 1; Brüll, with 5 and 1; Ambroise Thomas, with 5 and 2; Goldmark, with 4 and 1; Flotow, with 4 and 2; Conradin Kreutzer, with 3 and 1; Halévy, with 3 and 1; Spontini, with 2 and 1; Boieldieu, with 2 and 1; and Spohr, Marschner, and Cherubini each represented by one work.

THE ANNUAL MUSICAL FESTIVAL OF THE NORTH AMERICAN SÆNGERBUND.

The twenty-third Sängerfest of the North American Sænger-bund, took place in the city of Buffalo, N.Y., from Monday, July 16th, to Wednesday 18th. It excited unusual interest, and called forth great enthusiasm. There were no great novelties given among the musical compositions, nor great or prominent works executed, but the festive tone given to the meeting, the good general musical choice, the large choruses, and Dr. Damrosch's orchestra, gave the whole "Fest" a character of unity, which will do much to still increase a desire for musical improvement.

Buffalo, with its decorations, its triumphal arches, its flags and banners, looked like a German city; and its festive appear-ance was enhanced by the presence of a host of visitors, estimated at from 50,000 to 75,000, most of whom were Germans. The new hall accommodates in its main room about 5,000 people, and the spacious corridors easily contain 3,000 more. The stage accommodates 2,000 singers and an orchestra of 100 instruments. The building is in the French renaissance style of architecture, and is at present gay with all sorts of flags and mottoes. The legend that appears on all sides is "Wilkommen Sænger."

The association have reason to feel proud of this festival, and what they have attained since their organization. The first "Sängerfest" known in America was held in Cincinnati in June, 1849. At that time there were five singing societies, with 118 singers, representing the cities of Cincinnati, Louisville, and Madison, Ind. On June 2nd of that festival, the association was formally organized. From 1849 to 1860 a festival was held each year. The festival of 1860 was held at Buffalo, and was both artistically and popularly one of the greatest festivals of the association.

The continuity of these festivals was broken by our civil war, and five years elapsed before the next festival, which was held at Louisville, Ky. From this time the association became national both in its scope and its representation. In Chicago, in 1869, fifty-eight societies were represented, with 1,200 singers. In Cincinnati, the following year, 1,800 singers, representing sixty-one societies, were present. For a few years after this, owing principally to the sudden popularity of the May festival, interest in the "Sängerbund" declined.

The artistic merits of the association have, however, greatly advanced of late years, owing to a rule adopted in '75, excluding from the "Bund" societies of less than twelve voices, and admitting none whose musical fitness was not certified by the festival director. The festivals have been again growing in popularity for the last few years, and the last one held in Chicago two years ago was remarkable for its artistic success. Nothing had been left undone to make the festival a great suc-cess and a memorable meeting of the "Saengers," or "Singers." The soloists engaged for the festival were Mme. Gabriella Boema, Mdme. Marie Schell-Graham, Mrs. Wells B. Tanner, Joseph Benedict, Christian Fritsch and Max Heinrich.

The directors of the various special concerts were Carl Adam, (Monday evening) Joseph Mischka (Tuesday afternoon and Wednesday evening), Frederick Federlein, (Tuesday evening and Wednesday afternoon.)

The societies present were from Cincinnati, Cleveland, Columbus, Dayton and Tiffin, O.; New York, Dunkirk, Rochester, Elmira, of this State; Allegheny, Erie and Phila-delphia, Penn.; Chicago, Ill., Indianapolis, Ind.; Louisville, Ky.; Detroit, Mich.; St. Louis, Mo.; Milwaukee, Wis.; Wheeling, W. Va.; Newark, N.J.; Hamilton and Waterloo, Ontario.—_Music and Drama_ (New York).

Organ News.

FISHERIES EXHIBITION.

The following organ recitals have been given during the last week.

Organ recitals were given by Mr. J. Loaring, F.C.O., on August 27th, 29th, and September 1st. The following were the programmes :—

Overture, "L' Italiana "	Rossini.
Adagio, from "Sonata Pathétique "	Beethoven.
"So shall the lute," and "Sing unto God "	Handel.
Selection from 1st Rondo	Mendelssohn.
March, " Heroïque " in D	Schubert.

Overture, "Masaniello "	Auber.
Andante from Quartet in D minor	Mozart.
"Gipsy" Rondo	Haydn.
Selection from the opera, "Cymbia "	Pascal.
"The Bride's March "	Loaring.

Overture, "Zampa "	Hérold.
Gavotte	Corelli.
Organ Concerto, No. 3	Handel.
"Gloria in excelsis " (" 12th Mass ")	Mozart.
March, " Heroïque " in C	Schubert.

The programme of the recital by Mr. Hedgecock, on Tuesday, August 28th, was :—

March of the Crusaders	Liszt.
Slow Movement, from a Trio	Hummel.
Postlude in D	Smart.
Pastorale	Kullak.
Chorus, "Fixed in His everlasting seat " (" Sampson ")	Handel.
Fantasia in F	Best.
Theme in A	Hird.
March in B flat	Silas.

The programme of the recital by Mr. H. C. Tonking, R.A.M., on Wednesday, August 29th, was :—

Organ Concerto, No. 2	Handel.
Offertoire in G	Batiste.
Fanfare in D	Lemmens.
Andante in F	Smart.
Fantasia on a Welsh March	Best.
"Hercules " March	Trembath.
Grand Chorus in D	Guilmant.

And on Thursday, August 30th :—

Fugue in D	Bach.
Andante in F	Wely.
Offertoire in G	
Postlude in C minor, introducing " Jerusalem on High "	Spragall.
Fantasia on a Welsh March	Best.

Grand Chorus	Guilmant.
Offertoire in G	Wely.
En Forme d'Ouverture in D minor	Smart.
Postlude in D	Smart.

And on Friday, August 24th, by Master Henry J. Wood, whose programme included :—

Offertoire in B minor	Lott.
Trio, Moderato, Theme var., No. 4	Beethoven.
Movement from a Sonata	Beethoven.
Chorus from " Harvest Cantata "	Weber.

An organ recital was given on September 4th, by Mr. E. Taunton. The programme included :—

War March, " Athalie "	Mendelssohn.
Andante (P. F. Sonata)	Mozart.

And by Mr. H. E. Warner :—

Offertoire in F	Batiste.
Chorus, " Worthy is the Lamb "	Handel.
Gavotte in G	Warner.

And by Mr. Percy H. Fell :—

Andante in F minor	Batiste.
Largo	Handel.
Gavotte in F	Fell.
Prelude and Fugue, No. 6	Bach.

NORTH BERWICK.

An organ recital was given in St. Baldred's Church, by Mr. T. S. Guyer, on Wednesday, August 22nd. The programme included :—

Overture, " Samson "	Handel.
Largo in C	Handel.
Toccata and Fugue in D minor	Bach.
Largo in D	Haydn.
March in G	Smart.

GLASGOW.

An organ recital was given on Saturday, September 1st, in the Cathedral, by Dr. A. L. Peace. The following was the programme :—

Overture, "The Last Judgment"—Andante—Grave—Allegro.	Spohr.
Adagio from the Septet	Beethoven.
"Faith, Hope, and Charity"—three sacred choruses..	Rossini.
"Allegretto Villereccio "	Fumagalli.
"March to Calvary" ("Redemption ")	Gounod.

CRYSTAL PALACE.

Mr. Cedric Bucknall, Mus.Bac., played the following programme on Saturday week :—

March Cortège, "Irene"	Gounod.
Andante from 10th Trio	Reissiger.
Sonata, No. 3, in A	Mendelssohn.
Con moto maestoso—Andante tranquillo.	
Prelude and Fugue in E minor	Bach.
"Impromptu "	
Offertoire in F	Batiste.
"Invocation "	Guilmant.
Choruses, " He spake the word," and "But the waters "	Handel.

WATERLOO ROAD, S.E.

An organ and trombone recital was given in the Church of St. John the Evangelist, by Messrs Henry J. B. Dart, and Samuel Millar, on Tuesday, August 18th. The following was the programme :—

*Fantasia in C minor	Behrens.
Marche Funebre, from Concerto	David.
*Romanza	Beethoven.
Grand Fantasia on Chorale, " Ein feste bürg "	Brafler.
*Air and variations in A	Hesse.
Prayer	Michael.
*Sonata, No. 6	Mendelssohn.
Chorale and variations—Fuga—Andante.	
Polonaise in A	Chopin.
Pieces marked with an asterisk for organ solo.	

MALVERN.

An organ recital was given at the Priory Church, by W. H. Speer, Esq., on Wednesday, August 29th. The following was the programme :—

Toccata and Fugue in D minor	Bach.
Minuet and Trio (Symphony in G minor)	Bennett.
" My heart, ever faithful "	Bach.
Sonata in D	Guilmant.
Andante in A flat	Hoyte.
Andante in F, Op. 35	Beethoven.
" Let their celestial concerts "	Handel.

OLDHAM.

On the 1st inst., an organ recital was given by Mr. W. A. Wrigley (organist of Holy Innocents', Fallowfield, Manchester) in the concert room attached to the Fine Art Exhibition. The room was crowded in every part. The programme included :—

March and Chorus, " Ruins of Athens "	Beethoven.
Prelude and Fugue in B flat	Bach.
Andante Cantabile in E flat	Weber.
Grand Chœur in D	Guilmant.
Allegretto in B minor	
"Heroic " March in D, No. 3	Schubert.

LEEDS.

The organ of St. George's Church, after being silent for nearly two months, undergoing extensive repairs, was re-opened by Dr. Spark, the organist, the other Sunday, when special music was performed. The organ was built by Holt Brothers, in 1850, and was opened by Dr. Samuel Sebastian Wesley. A few years afterwards, at the suggestion of the present organist, the instrument was entirely rebuilt, and several new and beautiful stops were added by Messrs. Gray and Davison, the builders of the Town Hall organ. The new work, including nearly all new action, three new sets of ivory keys, thorough cleaning, and general repairs, has been executed by Messrs. Wordsworth and Maskell, Leeds, and so far as can be ascertained from a couple of days' experience and trial, with much credit to them, and with satisfaction to Dr. Spark. In the morning the Te Deum was Smart in F, and Kyrie and Credo (Wesley). The voluntaries were by Silas, Smart, and Dr. Spark. In the evening there were Wesley's Service in F, and Goss's anthem, "Praise the Lord." The voluntaries were, andante, sonata (Bach), the organist; and for the collection, Handel's Coronation Anthem, "Zadok the Priest." The organ opening proper was followed with a recital of "organ music," by Mr. Walter Parratt, Mus.Bac., organist of St. George's Chapel Royal, Windsor. The following was the programme :—

Organ Concerto in A major	Handel.
Fantasia in E flat	Saint-Saëns.
Overture in C major	Adams.
Canon in B minor	Schubert.
Fugue in D major	Mozart.
Passacaglia	Bach.
Pastorale in G major	Widor.

In all the pieces Mr. Parratt showed himself an able and accurate exponent of the works of others. The finest specimen of Mr. Parratt's playing was in the last piece, the sublime " Passacaglia," by Bach.

SCHOLES.

The new organ, in the Church of SS. Philip and James, was opened on August 24th, by Dr. Creser (Leeds Parish Church), who performed the following selection :—

Musette	Turpin.
Barcarolle	Bennett.
Variations on a Theme by Handel	Creser.
Grand Chorus	Guilmant.
Andante	Archer.
" War March of the Priests " (" Athalie ")	Mendelssohn.

The organ, built by Messrs. Booth and Hepworth, has two manuals and pedals.

ROTHERHAM.

An organ recital was given by Mr. S. W. Pilling, of Bolton, in the Congregational Church, on Wednesday, August 21st. The following was the programme :—

Prelude	Hird.
Sonatine	Bogaert.
Pastorale	Wely.
Offertoire in C major	Haydn.
Air, with variations	
Andante from Violin Concerto	Mendelssohn.
Allegro maestoso...Fuga.	
Introduction and Offertoire	Hewlett.
Andante Grazioso }	Smart.
March in D major }	

The above church, after having been closed for eleven weeks, for repairs, and for the enlargement and completion of the organ, was re-opened for divine worship August 29th. The interior arrangements of the organ have been altered, and the mechanism improved, besides some important additions. The work has been very satisfactorily carried out by the makers, Messrs. Brindley and Foster, of Sheffield. The specification is as follows, the asterisks indicating the additional parts :—

GREAT ORGAN. CC TO G3.

1.*Double Diapason	16 ft.	6.*	{ Twelfth	3 ft.
2. Open Diapason	8 „		{ Fifteenth	2 „
3. Rohr Gedact	8 „	7.*Mixture (4 ranks)	
4. Viola di Gamba	8 „	8.* Trumpet	8 „
5. Principal	4 „			

SWELL ORGAN. CC TO G3.

9. Bourdon	16 ft.	13.*Mixture (3 ranks)	
10. Gemshorn	8 „	14. Oboe	8 ft.
11.*Vox Angelica	8 „	15.*Trumpet	8 „
12. Principal	4 „		

CHOIR ORGAN. CC TO G3.

16. Lieblich Gedact	8 ft.	19. Lieblich Flöte	4 ft.
17.*Dulciana	8 „	20.*Clarionet	8 „
18. Gemshorn	4 „		

PEDAL ORGAN. CCC TO E.

21.*Open Diapason	16 ft.	22. Bourdon	16 ft.

COUPLERS.

23. Swell to Great.	25. Swell to Pedal.
24. Swell to Choir.	26. Great to Pedal.

Three composition Pedals to Great Organ.

The re-opening services commenced yesterday afternoon, when an organ recital was given by Mr. S. W. Pilling, an eminent organist, of Bolton. An admirable plan for bringing out the different qualities of the organ had been prepared, and was gone through with exquisite taste. Mr. Pilling rendered the various works selected with great effect. In the evening divine service was held in the church, when Mr. C. H. Perrott presided at the organ.

Nearly a quarter of a century ago, says a recent number of the Halifax *Mail*, Canada, at the urgent request of the clergymen and a number of leading citizens of Halifax, Gen. Sir Hastings Doyle, then in command of the garrison at that city, made an order by which the military bands were relieved of the duty of entertaining the crowds while marching to the garrison on Sundays. On a certain Sunday, Gen. Russell, now in command, who always worships at the bishop's chapel, attended the garrison church for a change, and he was shocked at the small attendance of officers and men, and the want of discipline exhibited. What was still worse, the garrison chaplain, Rev. Mr. Townsend, was absent without leave, having gone fishing on that day. The general has now made an order, revoking that of Doyle issued so long ago, and in future all troops not absolutely employed must attend Church. Guards will not be mounted until 2.30 p.m., and two bands will play on the way to and from service. The new order has taken the garrison by surprise, and is the principal subject of gossip about the city and in the barracks.

COLLEGE OF ORGANISTS.

(*Continued from page 132.*)

EXAMINATION FOR ASSOCIATESHIP, JULY 11, 1883.

PAPER WORK AT ORGAN.

The first six verses of the " Venite " were to be accompanied to the music of a given chant.

A hymn-tune to be given out, and one verse accompanied.

A given passage to be transposed at sight, the new keys being named by the examiners.

A given example of vocal score-reading was to be played at sight on the two diapasons of the Great organ only, and without the use of the pedals.

A figured bass was to be filled up at sight in four parts.

PAPER WORK AWAY FROM ORGAN.

A melody was to be harmonised in four parts in vocal score, with proper clefs.

A bass to be harmonised in four parts in vocal score, from the figures, with proper clefs.

The bass of the following passage to be figured according to the harmonies given, and name the root notes of the different chords employed.

The candidates were to add two simultaneous counterpoints of first species, one above and one below, to a given *canto fermo*.

To add three simultaneous counterpoints of any species, two above and one below, to a given *canto fermo*.

To give answers to two fugue subjects.

AND TO ANSWER AS MANY OF THE SUCCEEDING QUESTIONS AS POSSIBLE.

1. Describe the tones said to have been discovered by Sorge and made generally known by Tartini.

2. Describe the pneumatic action ; give the name of the inventor, and date of invention.

3. Distinguish between the nature and use of ventils and sound-board pallets.

4. What is a ground bass? Name any example.

5. On which degree of the scale is the chord of the augmented sixth most frequently placed ? and under what circumstance is the degree on which it is so placed chromatically altered?

6. Say which of the first four species of counterpoint may be said to be chiefly used in forming the figures of florid counterpoint.

7. Explain the following metres, L.M., S.M., C.M. ; say, are they iambic or trochaic in their several methods of accentuation?

8. Say how the strings of the double bass are tuned in England, Germany, Italy, and France, and which string is sometimes lowered in pitch in England.

9. Give the name of Handel's last oratorio, and the date of its composition.

EXAMINATION FOR FELLOWSHIP, JULY 13, 1883.

PAPER WORK AT ORGAN.

The first six verses of the "Venite" were to be accompanied to the music of one of two given chants.

A choral was to be given out, and one verse accompanied.

A given passage was to be transposed at sight, the new keys being named by the Examiners.

An example of vocal score-reading was to be played at sight on the two diapasons of the Great organ only, and without the use of the pedals.

Candidates were desired to extemporise upon a given phrase for about sixteen bars.

The candidates were to harmonise a given melody.

A figured bass was to be filled up at sight in four parts.

PAPER WORK AWAY FROM ORGAN.

A melody was to be harmonised in four parts in vocal score, with proper clefs.

A bass to be harmonised in four parts in vocal score, with proper clefs.

1. The candidates were to add two simultaneous counterpoints to a given Canto Fermo, in F, in the second and fourth species respectively.

2. Transpose the Canto Fermo into C, place it in the bass, and add three upper parts in florid counterpoint.

Counterpoint of various kinds and in any number of parts were to be added to a given canto.

The candidates were asked to write a fugal exposition on a given subject in four vocal parts, with proper clefs.

The candidates were asked to score a passage, from an Andante by S. S. Wesley in G, for 2 flutes, 2 oboes, 2 clarionets, 2 bassoons, 4 horns, 2 trumpets, 3 trombones, drums, and the usual stringed instruments.

AND TO ANSWER AS MANY OF THE SUCCEEDING QUESTIONS AS POSSIBLE.

1. What is the difference between a major and a minor tone called? Show relative value by figures.

2. What is the difference between a diatonic and a chromatic semitone called? Show relative value by figures.

3. What practical difference would it make in organ pipes and orchestral instruments (other conditions remaining as at present) if the velocity of sound in air were three times as rapid as it is?

4. Say upon what principle the organ stops tuned above the unison registers are employed.

5. Describe the several kinds of discords, and the general methods adopted in their treatment.

6. Name some particular use for the chords $\frac{6}{4}$ and $\frac{4}{2}$.

7. Say what harmonic successions are to be avoided in double counterpoint of the tenth.

8. Say how triple and quadruple counterpoints are formed.

9. Explain the differences between the oboe and corno di bassetto, and between the clarionet and cor Anglais.

10. State what symphony the trombones were first used in; and say what composer sometimes used two instead of three of those instruments.

11. Give the names of composers of following oratorios, and approximate date of their composition; "Samson," "Mount of Olives," and "Last Judgment."

12. Give the names of composers and approximate dates of composition of following operas: "Die Zauberflöte," "Der Freischütz," "Jessonda," and "Guillaume Tell."

Edgar S. Kelley is an American composer of some promise, according to reports. Thomas was to have played an overture of his, "Macbeth," at his series of concerts in Chicago. Mr. Kelley had a string quartet performed in Stuttgart, which was much praised. He is a native of Wisconsin, and was formerly a pupil of H. Clarence Eddy, and afterwards of Seifriz, Rheinberger, and other German musicians.

LONDON: SATURDAY, SEPTEMBER 8, 1883.

FORM IN VOCAL MUSIC.

VII.

AS before observed, the examination of the mutual action between instrumental architectural development and the application of form to vocal music affords a deeply interesting study. Historically, it is a matter of astonishment to note how very soon "form," as we understand the word, begins to appear in the sacred department of the art, even though its growth was a matter extending over so long a period. The student will, perhaps, find the greatest profit from a consideration of the development of "form," in the sacred music—to take only one large department; of the art—of the great transition period beginning with the Italian Church writers of the end of the seventeenth century; then advancing onwards through the great choral works of BACH and HANDEL, on to our own day. Through this long growth, there has been a marked gravitation to the episodical outline as being generally more plastic and convenient, in its application to vocal music than any other type of structural method. Thus, we find in the sacred choral works of MEN-

DELSSOHN, SPOHR, and still more recent writers, a large proportion of choruses written according to this pattern. In the setting of sacred words, the composer is undoubtedly pledged by a due sense of earnestness and propriety to primarily regard the meaning and expression of the words. This is a matter of the highest importance, and the student must not allow himself to be misled by the fascinating laxity to be observed in the Church music of the Viennese school, extending from HAYDN and MOZART to the "Masses" and Motets of HUMMEL and others of less note. It may be, that the splendid development of the same school and period in instrumental music furnished the temptation to apply in too wholesale a fashion the general principles of "form" to the requirements of sacred vocal music; and most probably the habit of employing given patterns happened to be so strong, and was found so convenient as saving much thought in the use of the ready-to-hand "forms" even to the skilled composer, that the abuse of "form" in the Church music of the time was a natural outcome of its almost slavish adoption by both writers and listeners. It may be safely asserted that we are now actuated in these matters by better taste, and a modified judgment. In all save the fugal forms—which, as I have shown, are also expressive in their way of the general principles of musical architecture—the composer is called upon to carefully examine the doctrinal and expressive outlines of the words forming the sacred text to be set. To do this thoughtfully is not so easy a task as it might appear to be at the first sight. Take one case in point, the setting of the "Nicene Creed." The just expression of the passage referring to the Incarnation of our Lord, breaks up the doctrinal division thereof, though it actually in practice assists in deepening the theological statement. This instance alone seems to show that in dealing with sacred text an earnest desire to express the words must take precedence over any proposal to consult too exclusively either doctrinal divisions or musical form outlines. Still, this theory of a careful verbal expression seems liable to a kind of abuse. Take the constant habit of the "Mass" composers of the Viennese school and, it must be added, their predecessors and followers who, treating the "Gloria in excelsis Deo" episodically, persist in dividing the words most illogically in the middle of a doctrinal sentence, by commencing the episode—generally a slow movement of distinct style and tempo—with the words, "Qui tollis peccata mundi"; and, often aggravating this violation of good sense and judgment by the intersection of a symphony between the two musical divisions. The proper management of the words in this case would be—and one rejoices to add this is the method adopted by M. GOUNOD and often by our common sense English composers—that of commencing the episode at the words "Domine Fili unigenite." By this means the essential doctrinal divisions will be alone duly regarded. This remark I have applied to the Latin of the "Mass"; of course, it has the same application in the case of the treatment of the same words in English in our Anglican Communion Service.

E. H. TURPIN.

THE TRIPLE-STRINGED HARP.

TRULY, those who either desire to stand still or to look back in matters artistic or mechanical, have no solid ground for the soles of their feet to rest upon. Just now there is, on the part of a few devoted lovers of Welsh archæology, an evident hope that the so-called national or triple-stringed harp of the Principality may be saved from the wreckage of time, and, to this end an attempt is being made to revive the all but departed interest in this instrument. Now, those who read the history of music aright, are well aware, as thinking people are concerning all other things of this changeable world, that no musical instrument can exist without such development as will secure its permanent usefulness in a rapidly advancing art. The "survival of the fittest", is an essential law, in the story of instrumental music, those instruments alone remain which by their powers of expression and convenience of manipulation may duly enunciate the musical idioms of the time; and as judiciously pointed out in a Welsh paper lately, one may as well hope to revive the spinet and harpsichord, as to preserve the Welsh harp. So it came to pass that at the recent Cardiff Eisteddfodd, candidates for performance on that now bygone instrument were not forthcoming. Earnest patriotic zeal, even when misguided by reason of its very devotion to a given cause, commands respect; still, it is a positive duty to point out that this very zeal may, by being judiciously and thoughtfully corrected to the requirements of the age we live in, become a real, living, and precious faculty. These remarks are called for by the following advertisement extracted from the *Cambrian* and forwarded by a distinguished artist and esteemed correspondent:—

"WELSH HARP COMPETITION.—Prizes to the "amount of £40 will be given by the Most Noble "Marquis of BUTE and the Right Hon. Lady LLAN-"OVER, for competition, on the triple-stringed harp, "the national instrument of Wales, at the Musical "College of Wales, Swansea, on October 25th, under "the presidency of Sir HUSSEY VIVIAN, Bart., M.P. "No one will be qualified to compete who has been a "player on the pedal harp, the object of these prizes "being to restore to its proper position the National "(Portable) Instrument of the Principality, and to "encourage the cultivation of the pure and simple "style in which ancient Welsh music ought to be "played. All Welsh harpers intending to compete "will be required to send in their names and ad-"dresses to the Right Hon. Lady LLANOVER, Llan-"over, Abergavenny, South Wales, on or before the "25th September, 1883, from whom correct copies of "the Welsh airs may be obtained, gratis, on applica-"tion by post.—Adjudicator: Dr. Joseph Parry, "Principal of the Musical College of Wales, Swansea."

The sentence restricting the competitors to those who have not played the pedal harp, was surely not sufficiently thought over. It could not be the design of so amiable and worthy a lover of her country as Lady LLANOVER is, or the wish of such an enlightened nobleman as the Marquis of BUTE, to so cramp the harp playing talents of the Welsh by confinement to an all but obsolete instrument, that they would be reduced to living upon stray halfpence gained by performances in the streets or public-houses! With the eminent example of Mr. JOHN THOMAS before them, who by his artistic skill on the now only possible harp has not only gained for himself a high position in the world of art, but founded a useful Welsh scholarship at the R.A.M., with other instances of the development of the national talent to high positions and fame, as in the case of Mr. BRINLEY RICHARDS, it cannot be seriously intended to discourage the direction of Welsh instrumental ability to any channel, save one from which the tide of artistic life has ebbed away never more to flow into. That HANDEL once wrote for POWELL, a Welsh harpist, says nothing, for the pedal harp, to begin with, was not known in his day; and, again, the most sanguine of patriots would never dream now of the possible adoption of the Welsh harp in London, and the composer of to-day expects his harp music to be played as it is played by Mr. JOHN THOMAS, a Welsh artist, on the pedal harp. There is no question about the antiquity of the harp as a Welsh national instrument. JONES'S "Relics of the Welsh Bards," the "Leges "Wallicæ," and PENNANT alike offer testimony to the effect, that the instrument is not only ancient, but has probably borne its present outward form for a thousand or even fifteen hundred years. At the same time, be it remembered, the triple-stringed harp now fast passing away is after all not a very ancient instrument; so that to push this archaic idea to its reasonable limits, the advertisers of the approaching competition should insist upon a restoration of a still more ancient form of the instrument; for to accept one development in the triple-stringed harp is logically to justify the adoption of a further development, the invention of the pedal harp. When the enthusiastic devotees of the Welsh harp are prepared to return to the most ancient form of the instrument, with, as an authority asserts, probably only nine strings, then alone will reason be fairly displayed in this matter from their point of sight. Of course, there can be but one consistent method of giving encouragement to the undoubtedly gifted Welsh musicians: they must be placed in the ranks of the artistic army, armed to do their work with the most improved and fully developed instruments of their several kinds.

E. H. TURPIN.

MUSICAL FESTIVALS AND THEIR FRUITS.

THIS year the public are invited to two Musical Festivals, at Gloucester and Leeds. The meeting in the Cathedral city will be at an end by the time that these remarks attract the reader's eye; the more important reunion in the smoky town where "sharp blades" have ceased to be manufactured, as the writer knows to his cost, is fixed for next month.

Musical Festivals in the so-called "provinces" have been materially modified, like most other sublunary institutions, by the "chances and changes of this mortal life."

Half a century ago, at Birmingham, the triennial "meeting" held for the benefit of the General Hospital, was an event of great æsthetical importance; not so much on account of the actual performances,

then held (the sacred portion at least) in the parish church of St. Philip, but because London had lagged behind, and possessed no regular societies, as now, for the production and execution of oratorios, always the great feature of the country "Festivals." Birmingham, moreover, has always been a musical focus, and of late years the absolutely first performance of "Elijah," under MENDELSSOHN'S own direction (A.D. 1846) has naturally made the manufacturing town especially famous. Leeds and Bradford have since entered the lists; the discontinuance of the excellent festival at the latter town is merely owing to its contiguity to Leeds. Dr. SPARK, in the large west Yorkshire emporium, renders the same service to the art, by his talents and indefatigable labours in the cause, as old JOSEPH MOORE, the master of the ceremonies at Birmingham did some sixty years ago.

The Festivals of the Three Choirs, as before said, drag on a dwindling existence, and do little for music in the highest sense. They hardly pay their way, although last year at Hereford it is understood that the treasurer had rather less reason to complain, but it must be remembered that a "guarantee fund" exists at the expense of persons rich enough or foolish enough to lend their names. The "widows and "orphans" dependent on the Three Choirs have very little to be thankful for. The Worcester Festival was suspended in 1875, by the bigotry of the Dean and some of the local clergy; its revival in 1878 and 1881 was rather in an ecclesiastical or "Church Service" direction. Norwich appeared to be doomed as a musical institution in 1875, when the petty "Jacks-in-office" disgusted the gentlemen of the London press by their stupid arrogance and gross incivility; but two years ago a revival was reported—whether by natural causes or by some sort of artificial galvanic action, such as makes a dead frog jump about as before, the writer avows that he is ignorant.

And now for the *fruits* of these festivals, not from a banker's point of view but with respect to art. The great standard works continue to be performed; the "Messiah" and "Elijah" are stereotyped on the schemes, and a clever writer in the *Daily Telegraph* offered strong objections to this incessant repetition of familiar oratorios, to the exclusion of other not necessarily *new* works, when reporting the two festivals of 1872. People can now hear the standard oratorios in St. James's and the Albert Halls, whilst country folks come to London so often and remain there so long, that to perform the "Messiah" or the "Creation" in the rural districts seems like "taking coals "to Newcastle" or "oysters to Whitstable." It may be replied that HANDEL, HAYDN, and MENDELSSOHN pay, and thus the "main chance" is not missed. On the other hand, the truth must be told, that most of the new works, even compositions on a large scale such as oratorios and cantatas, either fall still-born to the earth or die a natural death within the twelvemonth. "Elijah" and Professor G. A. MACFARREN'S "St. John the Baptist," produced at the first Bristol Meeting in 1873, are two grand and noble exceptions. Yet the world has not since heard too much of the Professor's second oratorio, "Joseph," which the writer rejoiced to report well of at the Leeds Festival of 1877. A third essay in oratorio is about to be made by the Professor at Leeds, and the result is anxiously awaited. Dr. STAINER's fate is already decided at Gloucester this week. Sir ARTHUR SULLIVAN's oratorios, "The Light of the World" and "The Resurrection," owe their occasional repetition, it is suspected, to the "flukes" of fashion and a popular name. Sir JULIUS BENEDICT, does not find any eager demand for his "St. Peter," produced at Norwich some eleven years ago, and heard *once* by the writer the same autumn at St. James's Hall. The "Redemption" of GOUNOD has been severely criticised by learned musicians who do not admire or even understand its eccentricities, but GOUNOD has a great name and his oratorio is sure to be on the "stock" list for half a generation at least. Then, alas! for the, cantatas—"our cantatas, where are they?" In MILTON's "Paradise of Fools" or in the waste-paper cupboard? Some of these cantatas are really clever compositions, notably the recent works (all written for festivals) of M. RANDEGGER, Signor SCHIRA, Mr. J. F. BARNETT, not to omit Mrs. MEADOWS-WHITE, so successful at Hereford last year. The "May Queen" of Sir STERNDALE BEN-NETT, and Professor MACFARREN's "May Day," are exceptionally excellent, *hors de la ligne*, as the French say, and therefore likely to be permanent. The cantata, all the same, is an anomalous affair in point of form, neither dramatic nor concert music "pure and " simple." The cantatas are usually very long, and the subjects uninteresting. They come before the public at the festivals, obtain a *succès d'estime*, and are forgotten! Such will no doubt be the case this year, at Gloucester and Leeds.

To sum up: the provincial meetings in the cathedral cities exist on sufferance and live from hand to mouth. They have had their day and are effete. Birmingham and Leeds do well, for two reasons: they secure composers, as a rule, of the first order; they provide great variety, and, above all, they can rely on a larger popular inrush of paying visitors. May they go on and prosper!   A. M.

Mdme. Minnie Hauck received an official request from the committee of the great Aix-la-Chapelle competitions, asking her to act as one of the musical judges. Mdme. Hauck declining, sent a large medal of Handel surrounded by a laurel wreath of gold as a prize for the best singing of Handelian choruses. She was invited by the burgo-master to be the honorary guest of the city during the festival. It is said that upwards of forty choirs, comprising about 7,000 choristers, make up the strong list of competitors.

The *Evening Standard* says:—"A praiseworthily emphatic announcement has been made by the Manager of Drury Lane Theatre, to the effect that the sale of pro-grammes is in future prohibited in his establishment. Hitherto notices to the effect that "No Fees" are to be inflicted upon visitors to many of the London Theatres have been issued; but, in defiance of this loosely-worded edict, black mail has been generally levied by the atten-dants who show the audience to their seats and attend them in the cloak-rooms. Mr. Harris has, however, given strict orders that the attendants in the front of his house are to receive no donations; and if the *habitués* of Drury Lane only second the manager's efforts, the system, which is not only unfair, but irritating as well, will speedily come to an end. Other managers, it is to be hoped, will follow Mr. Harris's energetic example." It is to be hoped too, that Mr. Harris's forethought for the interests of the public will produce good fruit in the concert-room as well as in the theatre.

THE VOICE

MUSICALLY AND MEDICALLY CONSIDERED.

BY
ARMAND SEMPLE, B.A., M.B., Cantab., M.R.C.P., Lond.,
Physician to the Royal Society of Musicians.

(*Continued from page* 135.)

Registers.

The term Register implies a series of homogeneous and consecutive sounds which take their origin from the same mechanical means, but which essentially differ from other sounds produced by mechanical agencies of a different nature; hence, all sounds of the same register are similar in their nature and quality, no matter what modifications of power or quality they may undergo.

The Chest Voice (Voce di Petto) Register.

In the Male Voice, this is the principal Register and is of the following extent, viz.: from Re flat, (D flat,), Re$_1$ (D$_1$), or Mi flat$_2$ (E flat$_2$), to Si$_2$ (B$_2$), Do$_4$ (C$_4$), or D sharp$_1$ (C sharp$_4$)

Within this gamut of 3 octaves the compass of every individual voice may be found; this is generally from a twelfth to two octaves.

In the Female Voice the chest register commences according to the character of the organ, with one of the sounds between Mi$_2$ (E$_2$) and La$_2$ (A$_2$)

Extending to Si$_3$ (B$_3$) Do$_4$ (C$_4$) Do sharp$_4$ (C sharp$_4$) or Re$_4$ (D$_4$)

Every octave in Acoustics is designated by a number; to the octave from Do (C) to Si (B)

the number 1 is applied, thus Do$_1$ Si$_1$; to the octave above

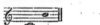

the number 2 is given thus, Do$_2$, Si$_2$ the octave above this 3, Do$_3$, Si$_3$, as below, and so on.

The Falsetto (Voce di Falsetto) Register.

This register commences in both sexes at about Sol$_2$ (G$_2$)

Ascending to Do sharp$_4$ (C sharp$_4$), or Re$_4$ (D$_4$)

and extending to a twelfth on the same notes as in the chest register. This latter register alone is able to descend below Sol$_2$ (G$_2$).

The Head Voice (Voce di Testa) Register.

The sounds of the head voice are the next to the fal-setto, and range from Re$_4$ (D$_4$), to Do$_5$ (C$_5$), Do sharp$_5$ (C sharp$_5$), Re$_5$ (D$_5$), Re sharp$_5$ (D sharp$_5$), Mi$_5$ (E$_5$), Fa$_5$ (F$_5$)

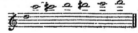

In the Male, these sounds are but the remains of the boys' voice; they can only be used by very high tenors, and then very exceptionally, or by the so-called *Buffi Caricati* singers.

It may be observed that the chest register descends lower in the male than in the female, that the falsetto is common to both voices, and that in the female the extent of the head voice is greater than in the male.

These points may be shown diagrammatically thus:—

FEMALE VOICE: Chest Voice.

          | | Head Voice.

       Falsetto Voice.

MALE VOICE: | | Head Voice.

    Chest Voice.   Falsetto Voice.

The following is the general scale of the 3 registers:—

Two or three notes are here given as the possible limits in each register, since, on account of the elasticity of the organ, it is by nature subject to fluctuation.

The illustrations above given are of course merely intended to indicate the possible degree to which human voices may be extended, but in the cultivation of any individual singing voice it is never of that compass in practice, since all voices do not use all the registers indiscriminately, and to employ the extremes of each register is always fatiguing to a singer.

Correspondence.

"COUNTERPOINT."

TO THE EDITOR OF THE "MUSICAL STANDARD."

SIR,—Absence from home has prevented me from replying to Mr. H. C. Banister's letter in your issue of the 25th ult. Whilst fully admitting that the quotations which Mr. Banister gives from his own work are on some points considerably in advance of the laws of Fux and Cherubini, I fail to see that they fairly "cover the ground of discussion." Mr. Banister's contrapuntal *rules* are in the main those of Cherubini—although some useful and sensible modifications are introduced; so that, if the laws of Cherubini are shown to be defective or erroneous, it stands to reason that a modern reproduction must share the same condemnation. The chief defects of the Cherubini school are (i) unnecessary restrictions as to chords; (ii) absence of any proper recognition of implied harmony in two-part exercises; (iii) construction of exercises upon *canti fermi*, which are "melodies" in name only, and upon which no student can be expected to write satisfactory studies. It will be seen that Mr. Banister's quotations touch only on the *first* of these matters, and I have searched his book in vain for any indications of advance as regards the second and third points, without which a "wider range of harmonies" would be of no practical use to the student. It is true, on page xiv (preface to the 7th edition), we find the following:—" In connection with this branch of study, I may give it as a strong recommendation that students should *figure* the lowest part of their counterpoint exercises: especially those in only two parts, where the harmony is less clearly or completely defined." This, however, is clearly an afterthought; for the rules given in the body of the work contain no reference to the subject of contrapuntal chord figuring, nor do we find that the more advanced views embodied in the preface are turned to any practical account. The "unsubmissive erraticism" of which Mr. Banister complains, might be reasonably condemned if the laws to which submission is invited were founded on principles of artistic truth; but the errors and contradictions of the lawgivers are so self-evident that no person of ordinary intelligence can be expected to accept without question the theories which are so complacently enunciated. Mr. Banister's remedy appears to be "more restrictiveness on the part of watchful teachers." This reminds one of the Israelites, who justly complained to Pharaoh of the hardness of their tasks, and were immediately commanded to produce the same work under conditions of increased hardship and difficulty. "Progressive conservatism" is highly desirable, provided there is anything really worth conserving; but text-book Counterpoint presents very little that will stand the test of careful enquiry and research.

Mr. Banister agrees with me in condemning the examination system as applied to Counterpoint, but he refers only to "certain" examinations, as though there are some systems wherein the subject *is* treated satisfactorily. May I ask where these examinations are to be found? I make a point of studying the papers issued from time to time by the Universities, and other institutions, and I confess I have never been able to discover a trace of even the "progressive conservatism" advocated by Mr. Banister. If an intelligent and reasonable system of contrapuntal examination really exists, Mr. Banister will confer a favour on musicians by making the fact more generally known.

Under the present system of text-books, progress of any kind is impossible, as I endeavoured to show in my remarks upon the work issued by the Cambridge professor; for the system fetters the examiner equally with the student. An examiner setting a paper is bound, in fairness to the candidates, to restrict his questions to the matter contained in the books authorized for study; and to judge of the work submitted by the rules therein laid down. Thus it comes to pass that exercises containing progressions of inconceivable barbarity—such as may be found in the books—are accepted and passed as "good Counterpoint"; whilst passages which might be fully justified by the writings of the great masters would be unhesitatingly condemned.

Every teacher knows the importance of instructing a pupil in the proper use of the various chord formations, commencing of course with the simplest combinations, and gradually introducing those demanding greater care and experience for their proper and effective employment. There is, however, no reason why the principles inculcated in a final lesson should be inconsistent with those taught at the commencement of a course of study; and it is because I find this unnecessary and objectionable feature in the more generally recognized Counterpoint text-books, that I have been compelled to condemn the whole system as illogical and absurd.

It would be a great pity if the interest which has been excited on this important subject were allowed to die out without the attainment of some practical result. I therefore venture to suggest that the Council of the College of Organists should take steps to organize a series of meetings—on the plan of those held in connection with the Organ Conference—with the object of formulating some really sound rules for contrapuntal study. I feel sure our leading musicians would gladly aid in such an undertaking, and the result of their deliberations would probably be accepted as a satisfactory settlement of the question, even by those who shrink from committing themselves to theories opposed to the established text-books. I need scarcely say that I shall be glad to aid in the work, and to promote its success by every means in my power. I take this opportunity of expressing my gratification at the discussion which has been provoked by the publication of my paper in your columns. So far, professional opinion appears unanimously in favour of reform; for no one has ventured to defend the existing contrapuntal system. There is, therefore, every encouragement to press forward; and although it may take some time to overcome the prejudice of centuries, yet in the end success is certain. *Magna est veritas, et prævalebit.*

I am, Sir, yours faithfully,

HUMPHREY J. STARK.

TO THE EDITOR OF THE "MUSICAL STANDARD."

SIR,—I note with satisfaction that you have opened your columns to correspondence on the subject of Mr. Stark's paper on Counterpoint, read at the College of Organists in May last, when I regretted my inability to attend. I learnt that in the discussion which ensued there was considerable diversity of opinion. Had I been present, I should most certainly have ranged myself on the side of the lecturer. It seems to me a grievous error to teach counterpoint solely in view of bygone periods of musical art, and to pertinaciously adhere to the exclusion of certain things now, solely because they were excluded in those bygone periods. Mr. Stark has ably exposed this as it applies to "second inversions." In University or College examinations in Music, any candidate who would presume to write as follows would probably fare ill at the hands of most examiners:—

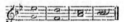

It would doubtless be said, firstly, that in the second bar above there is an implied $\frac{6}{4}$, which is "forbidden"; and, secondly, that even if this chord could be tolerated in Counterpoint, as its fourth should descend to A, the F must not proceed to that note, as this would be an implied doubling of the leading note. To this I would reply, firstly, that I consider the implied $\frac{6}{4}$ wholly unobjectionable; and, secondly, that as the A is *not doubled* (and no amount of argument can show that it *is*), there is no error whatever.

Mr. Stark's animadversions on the figuring, $\frac{6}{4}$, in certain examples which he quotes, are all to the purpose. This figuring *is transparently disingenuous* in those examples—it does not there fulfil its profession of setting forth the chords of which the actual notes employed form only a part ; and, taking advantage of general usage to omit the figure 3 in denoting chords of ⁴⁄₂ it slyly evades the real point at issue. I also agree with Mr. Stark that the following are not necessarily instances of two chords in a bar (though, if they were so, I certainly should not object on that account) :—

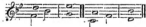

and not only that it is *not* " fanciful " to assume that the second inversion of a chord is implied on the first note of each of these examples, but, again, that such second inversion, whether implied or actual, is quite unobjectionable, if introduced in a proper manner. We must, of course, guard against a similar scanning throughout, in such an example as the following :—

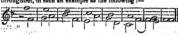

Scholastic discipline is one thing, but the prohibition of what is perfectly good is another, and may involve the serious evil of inculcating narrow and prejudiced views of art. I therefore think that much praise is due to Mr. Stark and Dr. Hiles for their bold attack on a system which has so long " held its own," in defiance of rational progress, and it is eminently satisfactory to find a sympathizer in so excellent an authority as Mr. Banister.

I am, Sir, faithfully yours.
CHARLES E. STEPHENS.

37, Howley Place, Maida Hill, W.
August 25th, 1883.

DR. TUCKERMAN.

TO THE EDITOR OF THE " MUSICAL STANDARD."

SIR,—In your issue for August 25th, under the heading of " Passing Events," is a misstatement regarding myself, which, for the present moment, at least, calls for the most unqualified denial. The article in question, speaking of the private musical libraries of Boston, U.S., refers to my own collection of full scores and other valuable works connected with the art, as being now in the possession of Dr. Eben Tourjée, principal of " The New England Conservatory of Music." This fact is beyond all question ; but the writer of the article in the " Home Journal " is mistaken in speaking of me as " the *late* Dr. Tuckerman ; " therefore, in my anxiety to avoid causing unnecessary alarm to relatives and friends by a premature announcement of my decease, I desire to contradict this report under my own signature. It may be remembered that Byron's definition of fame was to be killed in battle, and have one's name misspelt in the newspapers, but my case is far more serious, inasmuch as I have been killed before my decease, though I feel grateful to the slayer, for at least spelling my name correctly in the article under notice.

Yours faithfully,
S. PARKMAN TUCKERMAN.

[Dr. Tuckerman's correction is inserted with very great pleasure and every apology.—ED. *Mus. Stand.*]

"CYPHERING."

TO THE EDITOR OF THE " MUSICAL STANDARD."

SIR,—In reference to notes sticking in organs, to which the term " cyphering," or " ciphering " is generally applied, I shall be glad to know how this expression came in use. The suggestion of the word put forth by your correspondent last week, I think is most likely, but how it is in anyway applicable to denote stickings I cannot make out. As to the mode of spelling " cyphering ", in the organ trade, it is generally spelt as just given. Hoping to see this question determined in your valuable paper (as I think it is a matter that should be settled),

I remain, Sir, yours faithfully,
A. C. A.
Sept. 3rd, 1883.

THE WINDSOR ORGAN.

TO THE EDITOR OF THE " MUSICAL STANDARD."

SIR,—I fully endorse your note (in issue of Aug. 11th) respecting the absence of a 32-ft. in the organ at St. George's, Windsor, recently re-constructed. Having been acquainted with the organ for some years, I was greatly astonished at the removal of the large pedal pipes, which went down to FFFF. I can only assume that want of funds is the cause, and that when an opportunity occurs it is the intention of the authorities to insert a complete set of 32-ft. pipes in this noble instrument.

I am, Sir, yours faithfully,
A. A.

Aug. 30th, 1883.

Passing Events.

The " Reminiscences of an Old Reporter," will be continued next week, and from time to time.

Figaro has an appreciative account of Mr. A. C. Mackenzie as one of the " coming men."

Mr. E. Aguilar will probably resume his pianoforte recitals at Christmas. He remains in London.

It is said that Mr. Carrodus has recently bought the Stradivarius violin once owned by Paganini at a cost of £680.

Suppé's new opera, " Africa-Reise," has been well received, it is said, at the Stadttheater, Baden, near Vienna.

Signor Casano intends to open a branch of the " West London College of Music " at Ealing, and possibly in other suburbs of London.

Mr. Viard-Louis proposes to hold public lectures on pianoforte music, with illustrations on the instrument, in the ensuing month of November.

One of the American Conservatoires has followed the example of Trinity College, London, by the formation of a class for the study of the conductor's art.

Another token of the healthy growth of orchestral music is the scheme for four concerts at Birmingham arranged for by Messrs. Harrison and Harrison, which includes Mr. C. Hallé's orchestra.

Miss Florence St. John, Miss C. Merivale, M. Marius, and the members of the Avenue Theatre Company, have appeared with success at the Grand Theatre, Leeds, in " Madame Favart " and " Lurette."

Mr. H. Lazarus, since his professional visit to Cardiff, has been visiting at Castle Cary (Torquay), and at Rhyl (North Wales). During the Gloucester Festival Mr. Lazarus has been the guest of the Bishop and Mrs. Ellicott.

Lord and Lady Clarence Paget, both accomplished amateurs, have been entertaining guests on board their steam-yacht the " Miranda " at Ryde, Isle of Wight. Among the party last week were Prince Edward of Saxe-Weimar, Prince William of Hesse, Maria, Marchioness of Aylesbury, Mr. Kemp, and Mr. Brinley Richards.

People's Concerts are given at the Victoria Hall, Exeter, on Saturday evenings. The first of the series took place on Sept. 1st. The vocal artists were Miss Marian McKenzie, Miss Ambler, Mr. Harper Kearton, Mr. W. H. Brereton. Instrumental artists : Miss Annie Williams, Miss Marie Schumann, violin ; Dr. Hillier, clarionet ; and Mr. Harold Ryder, pianoforte.

Herr J. B. Bonawitz intends to give a series of four " Historical Pianoforte Recitals," at the Blüthner Rooms, Kensington Gardens Square, on Oct. 17, Nov. 7 and 21, and Dec. 5. Herr Bonawitz will review deceased, as well as living, composers at every recital. He begins a long list with Frescobaldi (1591—1654), and concludes with Brahms, F. Hiller, Zopff, Sgambati, and the Abbé Liszt.

At the recent Carnarvon Eisteddfod, Mr. Henry Leslie, in delivering his adjudication on the rendering of " 'Twas then, ye Sons of God," from the cantata " David and Saul," by Mr. D. Jenkins, Mus. Bac., of Aberystwith, said, he was bound to pay great tribute to the Principality for the learned and classical composition that had been rendered by the choirs. He had been greatly pleased by it, and it was a credit to the country that it possessed such an excellent composer.

Sir Michael Costa has presented to the Naples Royal College of Music the manuscript score of four operas and four ballets. The operas are " L'Imagine," " Il Sospetio Funesto," " Il Delitto Punito," and " Don Carlos," of which the first was performed for the first time in 1825 and the second in 1826 by the pupils of the College of St. Sebastian. The ballets are " Il Castello di Kenilworth," " Un'ora a Napola," " Sir Huon," and " Alma." On the first page of each score Sir Michael has written : " To the famous archives of the Naples Royal College of Music. In memory of M. Costa. London, August 15, 1883." At the same time the illustrious director presented the *bâton* used by him for ten years. It is of ebony, with a coral pommel, and at the tip has an effigy of Garibaldi, also in coral.

A musical contemporary of authority has it that the result of the twelve performances of Wagner's " Parsifal," at Bayreuth, seems to have been financially as well as artistically satisfactory. At any rate, the reopening of the theatre next summer has been decided upon. The artists, who have formed a society under the presidency of Liszt, will give their services, as heretofore, most disinterestedly.

The new comic opera which Mr. Desmond L. Ryan has written, and Signor Schira has set to music, has been in hand for some months. It is entitled "The Isle of Beauty," and it includes a good deal of the humorous and the serious elements. These two gentlemen have already collaborated for an important musical work the clever cantata " The Lord of Burleigh," produced some years ago at a Birmingham Festival.

The Times, as duly expected by musical men, has a characteristic, not to say vicious, notice of the new works produced at Gloucester, on Wednesday. The writer is good enough to use the expression, " organists' music," as a happy medium for politely stigmatising music as at once ambitious, pedantic, and valueless. Possibly he forgets that Gibbons, Purcell, Bach, Handel, Mozart, Mendelssohn, and in our own day, Smart, Saint-Saëns, Guilmant, Hopkins, Best, Stainer, Ouseley, Sullivan, Stanford, etc., were—and are—organ players and, wrote, and one is glad to add, some are still writing, " organists' music."

A rumour has been extensively circulated to the effect that Mr. Horatio Chipp is about to retire from his profession. There is no truth in the report, which Mr. Chipp asks us to deny. The following is a copy of a letter bearing on the subject which he has received from Sir Arthur Sullivan :—" Mr. Spark, of Leeds, has forwarded me a note from you which I read with surprise and regret. It is my fault that you were not offered an engagement at the forthcoming Leeds Festival, as I was told that you had retired from the active pursuit of your profession. It is too late now, I fear, to remedy the matter, but I write you these few lines to show you my great regret that I shall not have the pleasure of seeing you at Leeds, and so explain to you why your name was omitted."

The United States Music Teachers' National Association will hold its eighth annual session in Boston next year, the recent convention at Providence having so decided. Another important result of the recent meeting was the appointment of a committee of five persons as follows :—E. W. Bowman, of St. Louis, N. Coe Stewart, of Cleveland, Wm. H. Sherwood, Carlysle Petersilea, and S. B. Whitney, of Boston, to consult with other eminent musicians of the country at large as to the advisability of establishing a College of Musicians much upon the plan of the English College of Organists ; to be incorporated and impowered to examine candidates for the position of teachers of theory, voice, piano and organ, enabling the public to know that any person holding a certificate from the college is qualified and entitled to confidence. An additional duty of this committee is to formulate a plan for the establishment of State and district boards of examiners, that all sections and all branches of the music profession may be reached.

The Querist.

QUERY.

THE HALT OF THE CARAVAN.—Can any of your readers inform me whether Sir H. R. Bishop's glee, "The Halt of the Caravan," appeared in either of his operas, or merely as a separate piece.—C. T. JOHNSON.

REPLY TO G. L.

DUTIES OF A CHOIRMASTER.—I am unaware of the existence of any work dealing with the duties of a Choirmaster, and his relations with the other officials. When the organist is choirmaster, then the choirmaster should undoubtedly have full control over the choir, but under other circumstances, choirmastership must be based upon considerations of an exceptional character. The dual arrangement rarely works well, for unlike the conductor of an orchestra dealing with fixed orchestration, the choirmaster has no power over the accompaniments. A full consideration of this subject would be a real gain to the profession.—ED. *Mus. Stand.*

Service Lists.

SIXTEENTH SUNDAY AFTER TRINITY.

SEPTEMBER 9th.

London.

ST. PAUL'S CATHEDRAL.—Morn.: Service, Te Deum and Benedictus, Stainer in E flat ; Introit, O saving victim ; Holy Communion, Stainer in E flat. Even.: Service, Magnificat and Nunc Dimittis, Stainer in E flat ; Anthem, Ascribe unto the Lord (Wesley).

FOUNDLING CHAPEL. — Morn.: Service, Smart in F ; Anthem, Remember, O Lord (Hummel). Aft.: Children's Service.

HOLY TRINITY, GRAY'S INN ROAD.—Morn.: Service, Te Deum, Chanted. ; Jubilate, Best in A. Even. : Service, Magnificat, Chanted ; Nunc Dimittis, Tours in F ; Anthem, Incline Thine ear (Himmel).

HOLY TRINITY, TULSE HILL.—Morn.: Chant Service. Even.: Service, Magnificat and Nunc Dimittis, Gadsby in C ; Anthem, Consider the lilies, and Doth not wisdom cry (Haking).

ST. JAMES'S PRIVATE EPISCOPAL CHAPEL, SOUTHWARK. —Morn.: Service, Introit, He is blessed that cometh " Requiem " (Mozart) ; Communion Service, Schubert in B flat. Even.: Service, Tours in B flat ; Anthem, The earth is the Lord's (Spohr).

ST. MAGNUS, LONDON BRIDGE.—Morn.: Service, Opening Anthem, I will arise (Creyton) ; Te Deum and Jubilate, Goss in A ; Kyrie (Goss). Even.: Service, Magnificat and Nunc Dimittis, Ebdon in C ; Anthem, Out of the deep (Mozart).

ST. MARGARET PATTENS, ROOD LANE, FENCHURCH STREET.—Morn.: Service, Te Deum, Smart in F ; Benedictus (Stainer) ; Kyrie, Credo, Sanctus, Benedictus, Agnus Dei, and Gloria, Schubert in C ; Offertory Anthem, O rest in the Lord (Mendelssohn). Even.: Service, Magnificat and Nunc Dimittis, Stark in A ; Anthem, Blessed be the God and Father (Wesley).

ST. PAUL'S, AVENUE ROAD, SOUTH HAMPSTEAD.—Morn.: Service, Te Deum, Tilleard in F ; Benedictus (Goss) ; Kyrie, Nares in F. Even. : Service, Magnificat and Nunc Dimittis, Bunnett in F ; Anthem, I am Alpha and Omega (Stainer).

ST. PETER'S (EATON SQUARE).—Morn.: Service, Te Deum, Garrett in F ; Jubilate, Calkin in B flat ; Anthem, Comfort ye, my people (Handel).

ST. PETER'S, VERE STREET, W.—Even.: Service, Magnificat and Nunc Dimittis, Wood in F ; Anthem, O come let us worship (Mendelssohn).

ST. AGNES, KENNINGTON PARK, S.E.—Morn.: Service, Holy Communion, Kyrie, Credo, Sanctus, Gloria, Armes in A ; Benedictus and Agnus Dei, Monk in C.

ST AUGUSTINE AND ST. FAITH, WATLING STREET.— Morn.: Service, Barnby in E ; Introit, The Lord is my light (South) ; Communion Service, Garrett in E flat. Even.: Service, Barnby in E ; Anthem, Praise the Lord (Goss).

ST. SAVIOUR'S, HOXTON. — Morn.: Service, Te Deum, Goss in F ; Holy Communion ; Kyrie, Credo, Sanctus, and Gloria in excelsis, Ouseley in C. Even.: Service, Magnificat and Nunc Dimittis, Bunnett in F ; Anthem, O love the Lord (Sullivan).

ST. SEPULCHRE'S, HOLBORN.—Morn : Service, Rogers in D. Even. : Service, Arnold in A ; Anthem, We will rejoice (Croft).

Country.

ST. ASAPH CATHEDRAL.—Morn.: Service, Walmisley in F ; Anthem, O rest in the Lord (Mendelssohn). Even.: Service, Hall in C ; Anthem, Hearken unto my voice (Sydenham).

ASHBURNE CHURCH, DERBYSHIRE. — Morn. : Service, throughout (Dykes in F). Even.: Service, Musgrave in F ; Anthem, Give peace, O Lord (Calcott).

BELFAST (ST. GEORGE'S).—Morn.: Service, Te Deum, Chipp in D, No. 80 ; Jubilate, Stewart in G ; Apostles' Creed, Harmonised Monotone ; Full Communion Service, " Celebration Choral," Tours in F ; Offertory, Let your Light (Monk). Even.: Service, Magnificat and Nunc Dimittis, Stanford in B flat ; Apostles' Creed, Harmonized Monotone, Anthem, O give thanks (Elvey).

BIRMINGHAM (S. ALBAN THE MARTYR).—Morn.: Service Te Deum and Benedictus, Dykes in F ; Holy Communion ; Woodward in E flat. Evensong : Magnificat and Nunc Dimittis, Barnby in E.

BIRMINGHAM (ST. CYPRIAN'S, HAY MILLS).—Morn.: Service, Cobb in G ; Anthem, Daughters of Jerusalem, and Yea, though I walk (Sullivan). Even.: Service, Cobb in G ; Anthem, Hear my prayer (Mendelssohn).

CANTERBURY CATHEDRAL. — Morn.: Service, Goss in F ; Te Deum, Oakeley in F ; Anthem, O Lord, pour out Thy Holy Spirit (Buck) ; Communion, Whyley in D. Even.: Service, Longhurst in E ; Anthem, The Lord is my Light (Boyce).

CARLISLE CATHEDRAL.—Morn.: Service, Lloyd in E flat; Introit, We wait for (Armes); Kyrie and Creed, Lloyd in E flat. Even.: Service, Stainer in E flat; Anthem, Praise His awful name (Spohr).

DONCASTER (PARISH CHURCH).—Morn.: Service, Calkin in B flat; Kyrie and Creed (Hopkins); Introit, O Lord, my God (Wesley). Even.: Service, Magnificat and Nunc Dimittis, Hopkins in F; Anthem, The wilderness (Goss).

DUBLIN, ST. PATRICK'S (NATIONAL) CATHEDRAL.—Morn.: Service, Te Deum and Jubilate, King in C; Holy Communion, Kyrie, Creed, Sanctus, King in C; Anthem, O God, Lord God (Mozart). Even.: Service, Magnificat and Nunc Dimittis, Stainer in B flat; Anthem, Cast thy burden (Mendelssohn), and I will love Thee (Clarke).

ELY CATHEDRAL.—Morn.: Service, Roberts in D; Kyrie and Credo, Roberts in D; Gloria, Monk in A; Harvest Thanksgiving, Special Sermon, Hymn, Benedicite; Anthem, Give unto the Lord (Bridge). Even.: Service, Songs of gladness, &c., from "Naomi" (Chipp).

HARROGATE (ST. PETER'S CHURCH). — Morn.: Service, Te Deum Harvey in G; Benedictus, Chant; Anthem, Arise, Shine (Elvey); Kyrie and Credo, Wesley in E. Even.: Service, Magnificat, Peregrine Tone, Harmony by Bach; Nunc Dimittis, Haynes in G; Anthem, Comfort ye (Handel).

LEEDS PARISH CHURCH.—Morn.: Service, Hatton in E; Anthem, Send out Thy light (Gounod); Introit, Blessed is He (Gounod); Kyrie and Creed, Walmisley in F. Even.: Service, Gounod in D; Anthem, The Lord is righteous (Handel).

LICHFIELD CATHEDRAL. — Morn.: Service, Cooke in G; Anthem, As pants the hart (Spohr). Even.: Service, Cooke in G; Anthem, Stand up and bless (Goss).

LIVERPOOL CATHEDRAL.—Aft.: Service, Magnificat and Nunc Dimittis, Stainer in E flat; Anthem, Hear my prayer (Mendelssohn).

LIVERPOOL (ST. CUTHBERT'S, EVERTON).—Morn.: Service, Turle in D (unaccompanied). Even.: Service Bridge in C (Festal Service) Anthem, In that day (Elvey).

MANCHESTER CATHEDRAL.—Morn.: Service, Te Deum, Benedictus, Kyrie and Creed, Goss in D; Gloria, Hopkins in D; Anthem, Like as a father (Hatton). Aft.: Service, Goss in E; Anthem, Lift Thine eyes (Mendelssohn).

MANCHESTER (ST. BENEDICT'S).—Morn.: Service, Kyrie (Elvey); Credo, Sanctus, Benedictus, Agnus Dei, and Gloria in excelsis, Farmer in B. flat. Even.: Service, Magnificat and Nunc Dimittis, Tours in F.

MANCHESTER (ST. JOHN BAPTIST, HULME).—Morn.: Service, Kyrie, Credo, Sanctus, and Gloria in excelsis, Williams in D; Benedictus and Agnus Dei, Anguter in B flat. Even.: Service, Magnificat and Nunc Dimittis, (Willing).

NORTH BERWICK, N.B. (S. BALDRED'S).—Morn.: Service, Te Deum, Garrett in F; Anthem, If ye love me (Mark); Kyrie (Stainer). Even.: Service, Chants; Anthem, Thou that killest, and To Thee, O Lord "St. Paul" (Mendelssohn).

ROCHESTER CATHEDRAL. — Morn.: Service, Dean in A; Anthem, Come unto me (Smith). Even.: Service, Ebdon in C; Anthem, Be not afraid (Mendelssohn).

SHERBORNE ABBEY. — Morn.: Service, Te Deum, Jackson in F. Even.: Service, Chants; Anthem, God is gone up (Croft).

SOUTHAMPTON (ST. MARY'S CHURCH).—Morn.: Service, Te Deum and Benedictus, Woodward in D; Holy Communion, Introit, Like as the hart (Hoyte); Service, Woodward in A; Offertory, Not every one (Barnby); Paternoster (Hoyte). Even.: Service, Magnificat and Nunc Dimittis, Walmisley in D minor; Apostles' Creed, Harmonized Monotone.

WELLS CATHEDRAL.—Morn.: Service, Wesley in F; Introit, Behold to obey (Macfarren). Even.: Service, Arnold in D; Anthem) I will love Thee (Clarke).

WOLVERHAMPTON (ST. PETER'S COLLEGIATE CHURCH).— Morn.: Service, Te Deum, Stainer in E flat; Benedictus, Gauntlett in E; Anthem, Send out Thy Light (Gounod). Even.: Service, Responses, Tallis; Magnificat, Hopkins in G; Nunc Dimittis, Barnby in E; Anthem, Blessed be the God and Father (Wesley).

WORCESTER CATHEDRAL.—Morn.: Service, Smart in G; Anthem, O worship the Lord (Thorne). Even. Service, Smart in G; Anthem, Sing ye praise (Mendelssohn).

*** Post-cards must be sent to the Editor, 6, Argyle Square, W.C., by Wednesday. Lists are frequently omitted in consequence of not being received in time.

NEWSPAPERS sent should have distinct marks opposite to the matter to which attention is required.

APPOINTMENT.

Mr. A. S. ROUND, A.C.O., has been appointed Organist of the Parish Church, Wick.

THE YOUNG ARTIST.
A selection of Classical Works for the
PIANOFORTE.

1. SONATA in C, Op. 20, No. 2 ...	... L. Kozeluch	4
2. SONATA in G, Op. 4. No. 1 ...	... G. F. Pinto	4
3. SONATA in G, Op. 23, No. 3 ...	... J. B. Cramer	4
4. SONATA in C, Op. 8, No. 1 ...	... L. Kozeluch	4
5. SONATA in B flat, Op. 60 ...	... J. Woelfl	4
6. SONATA in C flat, Op. 37. No. 3 ...	... D. Steibelt	4
7. SONATA in E flat, Op. unknown ...	... L. Kozeluch	4
8. SONATA in C, Op. 37. No. 1 ...	... D. Steibelt	4
9. SONATA in C, Op. 9. No. 2 ...	... J. B. Cramer	4
10. SONATA in G, Op. 8, No. 2 ...	... L. Kozeluch	4
11. SONATA in C, Op. 4. No. 3 ...	... G. F. Pinto	4
12. SONATA in G, Op. unknown ...	... J. B. Cramer	4

EDITED AND FINGERED BY
W. J. WESTBROOK, Mus. Doc., Cantab.
London: EDWIN ASHDOWN, Hanover Square, W.

Printed for the Proprietor by BOWDEN, HUDSON & Co., at 23, Red Lion Street, Holborn, London, W.C.; and Published by WILLIAM REEVES, at the Office, 185, Fleet Street, E.C. West End Agents:—WEEKES & CO., 14, Hanover Street, Regent Street, W. Subscriptions and Advertisements received either by the Publisher or West End Agents.—Communications for the Editor are to be forwarded to his private address, 6, Argyle Square, W.C.
SATURDAY, SEPTEMBER 8, 1883.—Entered at the General Post Office as a Newspaper.

THE MUSICAL STANDARD

A NEWSPAPER FOR MUSICIANS PROFESSIONAL AND AMATEUR

No. 998. VOL. XXV., FOURTH SERIES. SATURDAY, SEPTEMBER 15, 1883. WEEKLY: PRICE 5d.

THE MUSICAL STANDARD is published every Saturday, price 3d., by post, 3½d.; and may be had of any bookseller or newsagent by ordering its regular supply.

SUBSCRIPTION.—The Musical Standard is posted to subscribers at 15s. a year; half a year, 7s. 6d., payable in advance.

The rate is the same to France, Belgium, Germany, Italy, United States, and Canada.

Post Office Orders to be made payable to the Publisher, William Reeves, 185, Fleet Street, London, or to the West-end Agents, Messrs. Weekes & Co., 14, Hanover Street, Regent Street, W.

ADVERTISEMENTS.—The charge for ordinary advertisements in The Musical Standard is 2s. 6d. for three lines or less; and 6d. for each line (10 words) in addition. ("Organist wanted," 3s. 6d. for 3 lines or less. A reduction is made for a series.

FRONT PAGE.—Concert and auction advertisements, &c., are inserted in the front page of The Musical Standard, and charged one-third in addition to the ordinary rates. Other advertisements will be inserted on the front page, or in the leader page, if desired, at the same terms.

SOME MUSICAL ETHICS AND ANALOGIES.

[*A Paper read before the College of Organists, June 5th, 1883.*]

BY HENRY C. BANISTER.

IN announcing, as the subject of my Paper, "Some Musical Ethics and Analogies," I have proposed to myself some treatment of our beautiful art other than technical : some considerations concerning it which shall be a relief from that theoretical method of speaking about it to which our professional habits render us so liable ; and, moreover, some way of looking at and treatment of it which shall not lead us into the region of pure æsthetics—whatever that may be—any more than into the technical region, which we know only too well. I have thought that the terms *Ethics* and *Analogies* may be sufficiently elastic to include such informal and untechnical considerations as those which I propose submitting to you.

By *Ethics*, we understand, speaking generally, *moral laws* : by the Ethics of any subject, the moral laws affecting, or exemplified by that subject. By *Analogy*, we understand the *resemblances* between any two matters, or rather, between their *relationships*, bearings, influences, and the like.* By *Musical Ethics and Analogies*, or, better still, the *Ethics and Analogies of Music*, then, it is implied that, in certain important senses, Music does not stand alone, isolated, independent : *moral considerations* affect it, as they do other matters ; and that, on the other hand, although it is in some respects *unique*, it has counterparts and analogies which may serve to illustrate it, clear our perceptions about it, and increase our interest in it. For I have always found that my acquaintance with Musical Art has enhanced my enjoyment of all else that is imaginative, ideal, and artistically structural. And there may be a *vice versâ* : a reflex process.

All of you musicians are familiar enough with, and know what I mean when I talk of the *German* 6th, the *French* 6th, the *Italian* 6th, the *Neapolitan* 6th, the *Major* and *Minor* Triads, the *Diminished Triad*, the *Augmented ·Triad*. I doubt, however, whether you will feel quite so much at home if I venture to refer to the *Welsh Triads*. Pardon me if I do you injustice : but of course you do not all come from the Principality, nor have you all been to an *Eisteddfod*. These *Welsh Triads* are, I understand, a collection of poetical histories, mythologies, ethical and legal maxims, &c., tersely expressed, and all in groups of three : hence their name. Now one of these *Triads* enunciates "*the three excellencies of Poetry : simplicity of language, simplicity of subject, and simplicity of invention*." And it strikes me that musicians should be the last to decline to accept, in the form of a *Triad*, and appropriate to their own Art, the terse enunciation of one of the first foundation principles of all true Art. Simplicity in character and life all right-minded men approve : simplicity of purpose, manner, and speech : whether as opposed to obscurity, mystery, or to duplicity : not at all to *profundity*. For the man of true simplicity, in character and life, has principles so profound, so deep down, that the waves of fashion, and the gusts of passion, do not disturb the consistent stedfastness of his career. It is a mistake, and an offence against the morality of words, to speak of a certain sort of bad man as *deep*, and *cunning*. The man of *ken*, the *knowing* man, in the right sense of the word, is really deep and profound. And yet the man with deep knowledge, and profound principles and character, is, in the truest sense, superficial : that is, there is nothing that need be buried and concealed :

* "Analogy does not mean the similarity of two *things*, but the similarity, or sameness of two *relations*. There must be more than two *things* to give rise to two relations : there must be at least three ; and in most cases there are four." (Copleston's *Four Discourses* : note to Disc. iii.)

therefore it *comes to the surface* : you see, by and on the surface, what there is deep down. For when we characterise a life as marked by "*simplicity and godly sincerity*," we use two words which mean, respectively, *without fold*, and *without wax*. Duplicity, doublefoldedness, which we all abhor—in others, at least—stands opposed to *.simplicity* : and *sincerity* just expresses what the finest honey is : no residuum of wax : all sweet and pure.

And this simplicity is a *moral* quality : therefore it finds its place in this treatment of *ethics*. For if there is to be simplicity of language, subject, invention, there is to be, of course, definiteness of aim : and this must be, clearly to express a pure idea. *A pure idea :* no attempt to invest the impure with interest. "To be for ever true is the Science of Poetry."* Mendelssohn detested the having to write an overture to that which he designated the "*odious play*" of "Ruy Blas." And yet, quite recently, in an able journal, distinguished for its high tone, it has been declared that "music is neither good nor bad, any more than poetry or eloquence, but is a method of expression which to many organisations is capable of conveying higher, more delicate, and, above all, more exact meanings than any other. But it can convey any meaning, and does very often convey a sensual one."† That it should have been possible to write this, may well be laid to the charge of certain composers who have debased the art by vile associations. But it has yet to be proved, I venture to submit, that music can, with definiteness or otherwise, "convey a sensual meaning." More of this, anon.

But, "*simplicity of invention*": does it exist in music ? Yes. Bach could, with the honesty and conscience which characterised the *simple-minded* man, call his two-part, and three-part movements for the clavichord, INVENTIONS. Not *Transcriptions* : oh! no. Not "*Pensées fugitives*": no! These pieces were not mere transient, unworked, unthought effervescences, or off-shoots : they were *inventions*. He *came upon* these pieces :—*discovered* them, in the *inventory* of his marvellous mind. They were his own. And there was "*simplicity of subject*" : merely a few notes,—perhaps a section of the scale. And, further, "*simplicity of Language.*" Not, indeed, without *folds* : these two part, three-part, double-contrapuntal *Inventions*. But it was the *many-sidedness*, not the evasiveness of thought : *manifold* beauty : beauties to be unfolded.

For this simplicity, it is not paradoxical to assert, by no means excludes the *complex*, or *complicated*. The very mention of Bach brings the two elements to one's mind : he being such an exemplification of the union of true, honest simplicity with the utmost, profoundest complicatedness. It has been well said, "True simplicity does not consist in what is trite, bald, or commonplace. So far as regards the thought, it means, not what is already obvious to everybody, but what, though not obvious, is immediately recognised, as soon as propounded, to be true and striking. As regards the expression, it means, that thoughts worth hearing are expressed in language that every one can understand. In the first point of view, it is opposed to what is abstruse ; in the second, to what is obscure. It *is* not what some men take it to mean, threadbare commonplace, expressed in insipid language. . . . True simplicity is the last and most excellent grace which can belong to a speaker, and is certainly not to be attained without much effort."‡ And for "speaker," here, one may substitute "musician," or any other productive artist. And all this agrees with the *Welsh Triad* : "simplicity of language, subject, invention."

* Hunt's *Poetry of Science*. Introd. p. xi.
† *Spectator*, May 12th, 1883, p. 606.
‡ *Edinburgh Review*, Oct. 1840, pp. 94-98.

Of course, then, no one supposes that objection is here raised to that complexity which may be inevitably associated with elaboration. It goes without saying that in a *Fugue*, or other developed contrapuntal work, there will be the involvements proper to such work. But, amidst all these, that which is pleaded for is simplicity in the subject : definiteness : and, above all, non-ambiguity, non-evasiveness : non-requirement of justificatory explanation. This is a matter which, I am persuaded, from constant experience, needs impressing upon musical students, and young composers, just now. Students seem to be liable to two extremes of danger : that of thinking that knowledge alone will stand them instead of genius : and that of thinking that imagination must not be curbed by pedantic rules. Some come to us to be taught, with the charmingly naïve ingenuousness so quaintly expressed by the old poet—

"O! my dear master, cannot you" (quoth I)
"Make me a poet? do it if you can,
"And you shall see I'll quickly be a man."*

This really is hardly an exaggeration of the sanguineness of some who come expecting that, though unable to put two chords together, a few months' easy study are to thoroughly equip them for their Bachelor's degree. On the other hand, some are so impatient of restraint, or so marvellously well-read in all the exceptions to rules, and in all just possible, though rare, progressions, that every bar exemplifies a rarity or a license : and, moreover, brings into play all the student's capacity for exceptional justification, often by equivocation : theoretical equivocation. All springs from the lack of simplicity : simplicity of thought, plan, purpose, design, language or mode of expression : the poverty or ambiguity of the thought being disguised by eccentric, unsimple presentation,—so often the refuge of poor, or confused, or shallow thinkers, in literature, and in music.

What do we mean by *Classical*, as applied to music? With what does it stand in contrast? In scholarly pursuits, of course, the term has defined application to certain languages and productions, which are in a *class* by themselves, needing no other specification. But, in modern use of the term, is not the contrast between two manners or styles of writing, the *Classical* and the *Romantic*? Speaking of the difference, with regard to literature, and with the view to enunciate that it need not be merely an essential characterisation of the Classical and Romanesque *languages* and *ages*, respectively, one well endowed with the faculty to pronounce, says—

"The classical, like the heroic age,
"Is past ; but poetry may re-assume
"That glorious name with Tartar and with Turk,
"With Goth or Arab, Sheik or Paladin,
"And not with Roman or with Greek alone.
"The name is graven on the workmanship."†

On which, an eminent critic remarks - "To define for our present purpose the difference between the classical and the romantic modes of workmanship : in classical writing every idea is called up to the mind as nakedly as possible, and at the same time as distinctly : it is exhibited in white light, and left to produce its effect by its own unaided power. In romantic writing, on the other hand, all objects are exhibited as it were through a coloured and iridescent atmosphere. Round about every central idea the romantic writer summons up a cloud of accessory and subordinate ideas for the sake of enhancing its effect, if at the risk of confusing its outlines. The temper, again, of the romantic writer is one of excitement, while the temper of the classical writer is one of self-possession. No matter what the power of his subject, the classical writer does not fail to assert his mastery over it and over himself, while the romantic writer seems as though his subject were ever on the point of dazzling and carrying him away. On the one hand, there is calm, on the other hand enthusiasm : the virtues of the one style are strength of grasp, with clearness and justice of presentment : the virtues of the other style are glow of spirit, with magic and richness of suggestion."*

(*To be continued*).

Musical Intelligence.

GLOUCESTER MUSICAL FESTIVAL.

Before proceeding from the notice of last week, one must praise a natural and effective chorus by Dr. A. E. Dyer, "I wish to tune my quivering lyre." Miss A. Hare's rendering of Chopin's "Ballade" for pianoforte was an admirable piece of tasteful and artistic playing. Mr. Carrodus gave an exceptionally good reading of the first movement of Beethoven's "violin concerto," with Molique's cadenza, rendered with perfect skill and fine tone. Mozart's G minor Symphony, played with the composer's additional clarionet parts, and Cherubini's "Anacreon" overture, were well played, with perhaps a little more enthusiasm than with due regard for light and shade. Dr. J. Stainer's cantata, "St. Mary Magdalen," was produced on Wednesday morning. The words were compiled by the Rev. J. Sparrow Simpson, who tells us in a prefatory note that "it would be out of place in a work of this character to discuss the identity of the woman who anointed the feet of Christ in the house of the Pharisee with St. Mary Magdalen. The ancient opinion of the Church was that they were one and the same, and this opinion has been followed in the present work. It is an opinion not only the most ancient, but also dear to the Church, and consecrated by the belief of many teachers, including St. Ambrose, St. Jerome, St. Augustine, St. Gregory Magnus, St. Bonaventura, and the great body of the Fathers and saintly writers down to the sixteenth century. It has "impressed itself upon the very language " of the Church, and has further been advocated by the writers of the Acta Sanctorum," &c. Opportunity will doubtless come in which to review the work fully. It is satisfactory to note that the cantata is thoughtful and scholarly without being dry, and effective. As in the case of many other modern works, there is a manifest desire to strike the listener by little innovations and dramatic surprises, although these are, as might be expected, in the work of so well trained and thoughtful a writer as Dr. Stainer, managed with extreme care and good taste. Nevertheless, in " St. Mary Magdalen " there are points when these efforts in search of effect somewhat interfere with the musical continuity. The interspersed recitative passages of the overture are cases in point. One can understand the prologue before the overture to " Elijah " as a preparation by announcement, but it is not so easy to endorse the insertion in a piece of one form of ideas of another type. One may speak at the wrong time, and "there is a time and place " for everything ; or to run some distance for a metaphor, "there is no use for a locomotive engine on the deck of a steamship." This spirit of innovation and departure from accepted types, although evidently controlled by the strong hand of a clever composer, mars much of Dr. Stainer's good work. The overture is, however, admirable in its general musicianship and judicious orchestration. The solo for Mary Magdalen, " Ah ! woe is me," is touching. The choruses, " This man if he were a prophet," and " Let Christ the King," are instances of a want of more continuous treatment, and the tendency shown here and there to sacrifice art to the exigencies of dramatic realism. An excellent and better sustained chorus, on the other hand, is " For none of us liveth to himself." In the second part there are some charming and natural movements, as "O Jesu Lord, Jesu behold me," as the tenor solo " O thou that weepest." The chorus of combined effects sung by Roman soldiers and christians (female voices) is clever, but disappointing in general effect. A feature of much beauty is the solo, " They have taken away," which is full of natural,

---

* Michael Drayton. *Epistle to Henry Reynolds.*
† W. S. Landor. *Epistle to Author of " Festus."*

* Prof. Sidney Colvin. Preface to "*Selections from Landor.*"

pathetic expression, heightened by a truly charming accompaniment. The work concludes with some fine choral writing and effective vocal points. Dr. Stainer has in this cantata distinctly added to his position as a composer, and given a valuable work to our limited stores of the kind, even though it is not perhaps a landmark in the annals of the art. On the whole, the work is a distinct advance upon any preceding composition by Dr. Stainer; it has signs of increased earnestness, decision of purpose, and increased writing experience; so it is a welcome addition to the stores of sacred music already accumulated.

Another new work was Dr. G. B. Arnold's "Sennacherib." Without proposing to notice this at length here, it is necessary to convey some impressions of the work upon its production. The contemplation of this new oratorio calls for a few words as to the attitude of the composer of the day. It is quite natural that a commission to write a large choral work for a Festival will stimulate the composer to special exertions. Unfortunately, however, this very anxiety to make the most of an opportunity is very apt to induce an overwhelming ambition to produce as many striking effects as possible. Now, the result of composing under the pressure of putting one's best leg foremost, especially when one is not engaged in daily composition, is the loss of a certain naturalness, without which music has no real value. Rossini was wise when he stated that his success was rather owing to his determination to be *natural* than from any desire to be *original*. The wish to attain originality rather than write naturally is the *ignis fatuus* of every producing artist not possessing the strong, balanced mind, which comes of special and daily devotion to a given task. There are but few specially written Festival works to which these words do not apply with more or less force. With the application of this thought, it seems comparatively easy to understand why an accomplished musician, and, certainly experienced writer, like Dr. Arnold, should overreach himself in his very earnestness to do his best. People in art do not, beyond a slight impetus arising from healthy excitement, rise to any special occasion; the artistic growth is ever a slow and gradual advance. "Sennacherib" opens with a slow introduction, with the programme title of "The besieged city." Herein Dr. Arnold has displayed at once the keynote of what disappoints one in "Sennacherib." The thoughts are in themselves nervous and excellent, but they are overstrained and made uncomfortable by needless and unnatural modulations and harmonic surprises. The "March of the Assyrians," which follows, is in some respects one of the best movements of the work, and one which may attain to some popularity; though it is over-orchestrated. A chorus, "Behold the Assyrians," has purpose in it, and some dramatic power. The succeeding solos, with good points, are somewhat ungainly from the vocal point of sight. The duet, "O House of Jacob," has tuneful figures. "O Lord, Thou art great," is an effective chorus on the whole. There is a vigorous though somewhat overwritten bass solo; then the introductory symphony is in part resumed. The trio, "O Lord God of Hosts," has a choral sentences interspersed. The chorus, "The proud are robbed," opens with a needless and melo-dramatic symphony, which much weakens the piece as a whole. The final chorus has a fugal movement of interest, and contains some clear contrapuntal writing. Dr. Arnold has undoubted power as a writer, and the present work has specimens of natural writing and some well laid out contrapuntal work, which justifies a hope that he will give to the world still more attractive works than the one under notice. The new works were, considering all things, well rendered, the composers conducting. Beethoven's Mass in C was, on the whole, excellently given. Byrd's Anthem, "Bow thine ear," and Orlando Gibbon's magnificent "Hosanna," were admirably sung, as they should be, without accompaniment, and finely testified to the real life of the early English Church school. It should be noted that Mendelssohn's "Hymn of Praise" stood out gloriously as "A thing of beauty and a joy for ever." Dr. C. V. Stanford's "Elegiac Symphony," a work of four divisions, is an admirable production. There is undeniable earnestness and beauty in the "Lento," and some passionate sentences in the opening "Allegro," though the work has an evident tendency to display too much effort and a restlessness at times from the use of broken rhythm here and there. The work is artistically scored, and it was conducted, in the absence of the com-

poser, by Mr. C. H. Lloyd. M. Gounod's "Redemption" proved the greatest attraction of the Festival; and the music gained upon one with singular force. The excellent performance of this work was ably and carefully conducted by Mr. C. L. Williams. Mendelssohn's "Walpurgis Night" was excellently rendered, the fine overture being in every way admirably played. The selection of songs for the miscellaneous concerts was, on the whole, an unworthy one. However, a few classical vocal pieces were included in the list. On Friday morning the "Messiah" was given. In the evening at the Special Service, with orchestra and chorus, a new Anthem, "Blessed is he that considereth the poor," by Mr. C. H. Lloyd was given. The first movement is of well-sustained interest, and the final chorus, with fugal termination, has many evidences of strong contrapuntal thought and sound musicianship. T. A. Walmisley's Evening Service, the overture to Spohr's "Last Judgment," and Beethoven's "Hallelujah Chorus," were features of this grand service, wherein a noble use of a great cathedral was fully illustrated. Mr. L. Colborne, Mr. Done, and Mr. Lloyd rendered valuable aid at the organ and pianoforte during the Festival, and Mr. C. L. Williams proved himself to be an admirable musical director. Mr. Gardom, the Hon. Sec., deserves much praise for his administrative care and labours.

A meeting of the stewards of the late Gloucester Festival was held at Gloucester on Sept. 8th, at which a rough debtor and creditor account was laid before them by the secretary. The total amount received for the charity was only £490 against £600 at the previous festival in 1880. At the 1880 gathering, however, the stewards each contributed £5; which with subsequent receipts from other sources made a total of £1,656. If, as is anticipated, the present stewards follow the example of their predecessors it will add £1,000 to the amount already secured; and as a few sums always drop in after the close of the festival it may be expected that the total amount realised for the Clergymen's Widow and Orphan Charity will fall little short of that of 1880. The amount collected at the closing special church service at the Cathedral on Friday night was £53 15s. 8d., which exceeded the amount collected after Wednesday morning's oratorio. The amounts received for the clergy charity in the last six years have been—At Worcester in 1878, £1,504 10s.; at Hereford in 1879, £971 6s. 1d.; at Gloucester in 1880, £1,656 9s. 10d.; at Worcester in 1881, £1,116 7s. 5d.; at Hereford in 1882, £867 5s. 2d.; and at Gloucester last week up to the close of the festival, £490 12s. 7d. The largest amount ever derived from any of these meetings was at Gloucester in 1877, when £1,885 10s. was received.

THE CRYSTAL PALACE
SATURDAY EVENING CONCERTS.

The concerts on Saturday evening continue their course successfully. Last Saturday Mr. Manns provided a programme of capital quality. He performed the overture to "Der Freischütz"; the introduction to Act III. of "Lohengrin;" "Dreams, a Study to Tristan and Isolde;" the gavotte, "Yellow Jasmine," from Mr. F. H. Cowen's "Language of the Flowers;" the march movement from Raff's "Lenora;" and the ballet, "Spring," from Verdi's "I Vespri Siciliani." Mdme. Marian Hood, recently so successful at the Crystal Palace opera, in "Faust," was one of the vocalists on Saturday, and sang splendidly—a more flattering reception could not have been recorded. Mdme. Marian Hood was in fine voice; Mr. J. W. Turner sang his pieces well; Miss Mary M'Clean has a fine complete voice, of much power and volume, but the quality rather coarse.

Mr. Manns may be congratulated on his autumnal career; the winter season, alas! is not afar off. Sydenham has no outside attractions in October and November, and the train service being so inefficient entails a sad loss of time.

Mrs. Marion Hood had a good choice of *material*. She sang Dr. Arne's popular air, "The Soldier tired of War's Alarms" and Pinsuti's "Heaven and Earth." Miss McClean sang Gluck's "Che faro' senza Euridice," and Mr. J. W. Turner, "Lend me your aid" from Gounod's "Irene." The scheme, comprising sixteen numbers, was rather too long.   A. M.

Offenbach's "La Vie" is to be produced next month at the Avenue Theatre, with a splendid mounting, it is said.

BIRMINGHAM.

(From our own Correspondent.)

Once more the concert-managers in Birmingham plan their campaign of the coming season. Though we have no such splendid feast spread for us as we had last year—no "opus vitæ meæ" to adjudicate upon, among other things—yet as the following outline of the different schemes will perhaps sufficiently show, in musical as well as in general doings, we are still going 'forward" in obedience to the municipal motto.

The Festival Choral Society will give again four concerts this season. Mendelssohn's "St. Paul" is a welcome announcement for the first performance, to take place Oct. 4th. At the next concert, in November, Mr. Cowen's cantata, "St. Ursula," will be performed for the first time in Birmingham; and a selection —"Spring and Summer"—from Haydn's "Seasons." In accordance with a general desire, Gounod's "Redemption" will be again repeated this season. The greatest novelty on the list is Dvorak's "Stabat Mater;" this, together with Schubert's "Song of Miriam" (another pleasing selection), and Mendelssohn's "As the Hart pants," will be given at the final concert of the series, March, 1884. As heretofore, the conductor will be Mr. Stockley. To give a list of the principal vocalists would be simply to print the names of pretty well all the leading singers of the day.

The Philharmonic Union will enter into close rivalry this time with the elder society, as both "St. Paul" and the "Redemption" are also to be performed under Dr. Swinnerton Heap's conductorship. They have the start in this, however, of the Festival Choral Society, the "St. Paul" performance being announced for the 27th of this month, and that of Gounod's oratorio for the 27th of December. Schumann's "Paradise and the Peri" (which has not been heard here for some years) will, along with an extract from Max Bruch's "Odysseus"—the banquet scene—be presented at the concert of the series in April next, on which occasion Ferdinand Hiller's Concerto in F sharp minor will be performed, with Mr. G. Halford as pianist. At a miscellaneous concert, to be given in the month of February, a very notable novelty will be introduced—Spohr's "Nonette"—a work only rarely heard, indeed, in this country; and for this performance the services of some of the leading instrumentalists of the day have been enlisted. On this occasion the programme will also include Leslie's "Resurgam," Wesley's "In exitu Israel," a pianoforte solo by Dr. Heap, and various part-songs, glees, instrumental selections, &c.

Mr. Stockley's Orches'ral Concerts, which have become, by this time, well established in the favour of the public, will be continued on the same plan as hitherto. Instrumental works will form the chief items of the programme of each concert, these, however, being agreeably varied by vocal solos. Two eminent vocalists are, as before, engaged for each concert. The instrumental selections already announced are as follow: Beethoven's "Eroica" Symphony (to be viewed quite as a musical "revival," in Birmingham); Schumann's B flat symphony; Mendelssohn's "Scotch" Symphony; Dr. Stanford's "Serenade;" Mackenzie's Scotch Rhapsody; and Svendsen's Norwegian Rhapsody; Sullivan's "Tempest" Music; a new overture by Mr. Herbert Wareing, Two Sketches by Mr. Anderton, and an Intermezzo by Edward Elgar. The instrumental soloists engaged are Miss Agnes Miller (piano), Mr. Carrodus (violin), and Mr. Reynolds (contrabasso). Undoubtedly the director is justified in his remark that "he may now fairly consider that the reproach to the town—of not having an efficient orchestra—has been removed."

Messrs. Harrison's programme as usual offers great attraction. In the lengthy list of artistes d'élite appears again the name of Mdme. Adelini Patti, who will be the bright particular star at the opening concert, Oct. 2nd. Mdme. Albani appears at the next performance of the series. To Messrs. Harrison we shall be indebted for the pleasure of hearing M. Pachmann (who has not yet been heard in Birmingham). Mr. Charles Hallé and his orchestra, as customary, will make the grand feature of one out of the four concerts of this series.

Mr. Stratton has issued the prospectus for the fifth season of his popular Chamber Concerts. Six concerts are announced to take place, the subscription for the series being almost too-absurdly low—ten shillings and five shillings, namely, seats being numbered and reserved throughout. As well known, one great feature of these concerts is the introduction on each occasion of a work by some British composer. The selections made this time for this department will be most interesting. The MS. composition by the Birmingham composer, F. E. Bache (which was postponed from last season), will be performed; a Pianoforte Trio by Cowen; a Sonata for piano and 'cello, by Mr. Edward Sharp (who will take part in the performance); a Sonata f-r piano and violin, by Dr. Heap; Mackenzie's pianoforte Quartet in B flat; and a new string Quartet by Mr. Thomas Anderton. Among the classic works to be produced are Haydn's Quartet in D (Op. 64, No. 5); Beethoven's Quartet in C (Op. 59, No. 3); Schubert's Quartet in A minor (Op. 29); Mozart's quintet in G minor, and Mendelssohn's Quintet in B flat; Schumann's Quintet in E flat (Op. 44); and Schubert's Octet (the repetition of this by general desire); while some novelties will be introduced, including a sonata for piano and 'cello, by Mr. F, Praeger,

the piano trio, by Fanny Hensel (Mendelssohn's sister), and Raff's Octet for string instruments.

The first concert of the series takes place on Tuesday, Oct. 16th, with Mr. Rowland Winn for pianist. Mr. Winn will be followed by Dr. Heap, Miss Constance Bache (who will perform in the piece of her late brother's), Miss Agnes Miller, Mr. Sharp, and Mr. Stratton. In the other instrumental departments the artistic personnel will remain unchanged, Messrs. Ward and Abbott, as before, alternating as leaders.

The directors of the Musical Section of the Midland Institute offer a most interesting scheme for the coming season. Great stress is laid by the directors upon the educational importance of the programme. To aim at teaching, as well as "amusing," the musical listener is, of course, only in conformity with the character of the institution in connection with which these most enjoyable concerts are given. A madrigal society has lately been formed (under the conductorship of Mr. Stockley), whose performances will add novel interest to these entertainments.

May I just append a little note in reference to the article in the MUSICAL STANDARD of last week, by A.M.? The oratorio "The Resurrection" is by Professor Macfarren, not by Sullivan; and Sir Julius Benedict's "St. Peter" was first heard in Birmingham, not at Norwich. Both being Birmingham Festival works, I am, perhaps, in place in making this correction of my confrère's error. B. T.

LIVERPOOL.

(From our own Correspondent).

SEPT. 12.

The Carl Rosa Opera Company opened at the Alexandra Theatre here on Monday week. The performances have been eminently successful in every way.

Thomas's "Esmeralda" has been an unqualified success, and has taken the public fancy in a marked manner. "Columba" was produced on Monday evening, but it did not meet with the same enthusiastic reception accorded to "Esmeralda." The other operas given were "Mignon," "Faust" (with Madame Roze as Marguerite), and the inevitable "Bohemian Girl." Mr. Goossens has conducted all through.

A new comic opera by Mr. Fred. Solomon, brother to the composer of "Billee Taylor," was produced for the first time on any stage on Monday evening, at the Prince of Wales Theatre. It is entitled "Captain Kidd, or the Bold Buccaneer," but I am afraid it will not have any success, as it is anything but entertaining, musically or otherwise.

The fifteenth annual children's Festival of Sacred Song was held last evening in St. George's Hall before an audience which entirely filled the large building. The performance was a great success. Mr. J. B. Clarke conducted, and Mr. W. T. Best presided at the organ.

J. J. M.

FOLKESTONE.—A concert was given in the Town Hall on August 30th, by Miss Theresa Beney, A.C.O., organist of Christ Church. Miss Beney was assisted by Miss Clara Ross (soprano), Miss Clara Myers (contralto), Signor Palmieri (tenor), Mr. Bicknell Young (baritone), Mr. Ernest Crooke (violin), and the well known, able accompanist, Mr. Chas. Marshall. Among the more successful items of a most interesting programme was the beautiful Trio "Il desiderio" (Gordigiani), sung by Miss Ross, Messrs. Palmieri and Young—a new song, "The Mower and the Lass" (Milton Wellings), sung for the first time and with great taste by Miss Clara Myers—Signor Palmieri's excellent rendering of "Questà Quella" (Verdi)— "The Harbour lights" (Pinsuti), splendidly sung by Mr. Young —and a new song by Theresa Beney (words by Kinloch Cooke), entitled "Farewell, for ever," well sung by Miss Clara Ross— all of which were re-demanded. The excellent violin playing of Mr. Ernest Crooke was deservedly appreciated, his solos being "Zigeunerweisen" (Sarasate), and Léonard's "Souvenir de Haydn." As an encore he played Gounod's charming little lullaby, "Peacefully slumbering." Miss Theresa Beney's pianoforte solos "Ballade in A flat" (Chopin), "Novelette in E" (Schumann), and the "Norwegian Bridal March" (Grieg), were well received, the pianiste being twice recalled. Gounod's "Ave Maria" and "La Colombe," for violin, pianoforte, and harmonium, formed a pleasing contrast, and the quartet from "Rigoletto," "Un di si ben" (Verdi), sung with great effect by Misses Ross and Myers, Messrs. Palmieri and Young, brought to conclusion a most successful concert.

Mr. Alex. Henderson has entered into an arrangement to bring out, at the Avenue Theatre, on or about the 1st October, "La Vie," a comic opera in three acts, written by Mr. H. B. Farnie, the music composed by Offenbach. The opera will be previously played at Brighton on the 17th inst. Report says the costumes are to exceed in taste and costliness anything hitherto seen on the London stage.

Foreign Musical Intelligence.

MILAN.

An English musician writing from Italy, thus gossips about music in Milan :—Musical doings here are at a standstill just now. The theatres are closed : the Dal Verme opens on the 8th, whilst the Scala is closed until December. Last Friday week, we had a grand concert at La Scala for the Ischia benefit. It was a good performance for a scratch team. The artists all, of course, gave their services ; the band was very rough and over-weighted the voices. Many good artists sang in the chorus, in pieces from various operas : "Inflammatus" from "Stabat Mater," Rossini, "Chorus of Conspirators" from "Huguenots," etc. The Milanese want "Gioconda" produced. It has been done a good deal in Italy, I think, but I fancy never here. I do not consider musical art in Italy is at a very high standard.

The organ playing in the churches here is poor, and the singing worse. They give some very good little instrumental concerts in the Cafés here ; the two principal are the Biffi and the Cova, also Gnocchi ; there are small orchestras at each, and the style of music is good and well selected. Perhaps it is hardly fair to criticise a place out of its season.

The operatic artists are here in force, looking for engagements. The Dal Verme opens with "I Promessi Sposi," by Petrella. The musical world here is over-stocked as at home. Everything is opera.

The novelty next season at the Teatro Real, Madrid, will very likely be Ponchielli's "Gioconda."

Saint-Saëns has returned to France, having recovered from his recent illness.

"Mazeppa," a new opera by Tschaikowsky so called, will be heard in St. Petersburg before long.

The Quartet Society of Milan have given a prize for a pianoforte Trio to Signor E. F. da Crema.

Signor Benacchia's opera "Ectore Fieramosca," was favourably noticed on its recent production in Padua.

A Conservatorium has been founded in Cordova under the direction of a violinist named Van Mark, a pupil of De Beriot and Léonard.

One of the new operatic successes is Gabais' new opera, "Gilda di Guascogna," which has been well received at the Politeama, Placenza.

The academical course of the Rossini Conservatoire at Pesaro is announced. It includes all branches of solo singing, composition, organ playing, and the study of orchestral instruments.

The well-known English baritone, Mr. Frank Quatremayne, has been for some time in Milan, studying opera with Sangiovanni. Mr. Quatremayne returns to London for an engagement on the 24th.

Anton Rubinstein is expected in Germany by the end of this month. His opera "Die Maccabaer" will be given at Frankfort on October 28th, and the "Sulamite" in Hamburg on November 8th.

These novelties are promised for the forthcoming opera season at Cologne : Goring Thomas's "Esmeralda," Flötow's "Der Graf von St. Megrin" and Delibes' "Lakmé." Schumann's "Genoveva" is also to be revived.

It is said that the right of performing Wagner's "Nibelungen Tetralogy" has been acquired for the Prussian Theatres Royal in Berlin, Hanover, Cassel, and Wiesbaden.

It is announced that Millöcker's "Bettelstudent" is as successful in Hamburgh as elsewhere, having already run upwards of a hundred nights at the Carl Schultze-Theatre.

M. Halévy, a well-known writer of dramatic and other works, has died at St. Germain-en-Laye. He was the brother of the composer of the same name, and father of the scarcely less famous M. Ludovic Halévy, who, chiefly in collaboration with M. Henri Meilhac, has written some of the most successful pieces of modern time. M. Léon Halévy wrote several plays, which were played with success at the leading Paris theatres.

A FEW REMARKS ON DR. STAINER'S CANTATA, "ST. MARY MAGDALENE."

The work of an artist may be said to be but a reproduction of himself, however dexterously he may try to disguise it ; a little careful study into the works of a man and the man will show a very striking resemblance : they are sure to bear a tint of the composer's innate character, and there it will remain, irrepressible, never dormant ; we examine the work, we behold the man ; we love the work, we reverence the artist ; our sympathies are with the composition, we feel with the writer ; the defects of the work are but symbols of the artist's weakness, while the good qualities are but a portrait of his talent and skill. With the "Messiah," with Handel ; and all who have read about the lives of Mendelssohn, Beethoven, and Mozart, must feel that their works are but echoes of the lives of the men themselves. In this cantata, then, Dr. Stainer has written himself, which fact speaks everything in favour of the composition under notice.

It is not my intention to critically expatiate on every number contained therein, but to take a general view without unnecessary signalising. The story of St. Mary Magdalen is so well known as not to need recapitulation here ; suffice it to say, that in the hands of the Precentor of St. Paul's Cathedral the libretto is everything that can be desired. The cantata is divided into three scenes, "Magdalen in the house of Simon," "By the Cross," and "At the Tomb." The work opens with an overture, which (although it is broken here and there by the introduction of a recitative for the purpose of explanation) enables us fully to realise the scene : in this it can be at once seen that Dr. Stainer has commenced as he means to go on—viz., whenever he hits upon a theme which treats of a subjective portion of one narrative he still keeps his mind's eye firmly fixed on the objective. In the solos of the Magdalen (soprano), "Ah ! woe is me," this is again depicted at the words, "Yet, O Thou Saint." Another beautiful air in the first scene is given to "an angel" (contralto), "Happy art thou." Our Lord's words throughout are entrusted to a tenor, while the narrative and other portions are left in the hands of a bass voice. This scene is dismissed with a really most effective chorus, "For none of us liveth to himself," the change of subject at the words, "And that the Spirit," stands out with due prominence from the bold theme preceding it. Again the first subject returns, and is artistically worked out to a final exultant climax. The second scene, "The Magdalen by the Cross," contains numbers replete with points of musicianly skill and artistic interest. The solo, "O Thou that weepest," doubtless will be hailed with delight by aspiring tenors, though I must remind them of that ambition which is proverbial for o'erleaping itself before they attempt it. This scene closes with a carefully written chorus, "Rest in peace," full of modesty, beauty and tenderness. In the opening chorus, "Awake, awake," of the third scene, we at once recognise Dr. Stainer. This is the commencement of the end—the one object in the cantata—and not until we come to the words of Mary, "I will rise now and go about the city," are we able fully to realise the love which she had for her Divine Saviour ; but the only regret which is to be felt is that Dr. Stainer did not deem it necessary to make this passage longer. Shortly after follows a chorus by a choir of angels, with contralto solo. An artistic end is here gained, in spite of the difficulty which must necessarily exist in writing so-called celestial music. It is so essentially conjectural, and at the same time fertile a laoj, that every new workman has a perfect right to enter its domains. After our Lord has been recognised by the Magdalen, comes the final chorus, splendidly worked out, and which affords ample means both for the chorus and orchestra for displaying their respective powers. The cantata is brought to an original climax by a recitative and closing "Amen."

Although Dr. Stainer has not altogether adhered to the strict and conventional school of Church music, with which he has been so much associated, his departure in this instance at once stamps him as being in possession of a creative musical power of a high order. This departure may at first sight appear to the eyes of my more musically conservative contemporaries as a violation of the artistic principles of his school, yet, at the same time, they must admit that successful departure in any form is an artistic gain we should do well to prize. In this cantata the composer excels without being pretentious, and by steadily and modestly aiming at the *highest* motive he becomes successful in every way, and when I remark that Dr. Stainer has brought this cantata to a successful issue I am only saying that which he has, as an experienced English musician, faithfully earned, and he eminently deserves a full recognition as a genuine composer and artist.

GEO. F. GROVER.

Organ News.

FISHERIES EXHIBITION.

The following organ recitals have been given during the last week.

Organ recitals were given by Mr. J. Loaring, F.C.O., last week. The programmes included :—

Overture, "Preciosa"	Weber.
Offertoire in D minor	Batiste.
Andante from the Grand Symphony, No. 1	Haydn.
March Cortege from "Irene"	Gounod.
Overture, "Masaniello"	Auber.
Overture, "Iphigenie en Tauride"	Gluck.
Gavotte Moderne in Ut	Tours.
Overture, "Le Cheval de Bronze"	Auber.

On September 7th, the programme by Mr. Ernest Taunton, included :—

"War March of the Priests" ("Athalie")	Mendelssohn.
Andante	Mozart.

And by Mr. Churchill Sibley :—

"Improvisation"	
Offertoire	Batiste.
Cathedral March	Sibley.

And by Master Henry J. Wood :—

March, "Lebanon"	Smallwood.
"Wedding March" ("Midsummer Night's Dream")	Mendelssohn.
Sinfonia, from Opera of "Almira"	Handel.

And on Saturday and Wednesday, September 8th, and 12th, by Mr. Freeman Dovaston, A.C.O. :—

March in B minor	Schubert.
Introduction and Allegro	Wood.
Andante Sostenuto	Batiste.
Danse Gracieuse	Wellings.
Triumphal March	Sainton-Dolby.
Allegro Moderato	Mendelssohn.
Andante in C	Smart.
Postlude in D	Greenish.
Overture, "Saul"	Handel.
Tocata and Fugue in C	Bach.
Sonata in C minor	Mendelssohn.
Andante in C	Smart.
"March Militaire"	Schubert.
Canzohe	Guilmant.

LIVERPOOL.

An organ recital was given in St. George's Hall, by Mr. W. T. Best, on Thursday, September 6th. The following was the programme :—

Organ Concerto in D minor	Handel.
Andante—Aria—Fuga.	
Meditation on Bach's 1st Prelude	Gounod.
Sarabande ("Euryanthe")	Weber.
Fugue in A minor (Con moto continuo)	Bach.
Andante con Variazioni, from the "Notturno"	Spohr.
Finale, "Allegro Marziale" in D major	Best.

And on Saturday, September 8th :—

Overture, "I Lituani"	Ponchielli.
Siciliana, and Tema con Variazione, Op. 60	Weber.
Prelude and Fugue in G major	Wesley.
Romanza, "The wished for land is near"	Curschmann.
Tocata in A flat major	Hesse.
Pastorale (Cor Anglais and Flute) } Military March in G major }	Gambini.

CRYSTAL PALACE.

Mr. Eyre's organ recital, on Saturday last, included the following :—

Sixth Organ Sonata (Chorale and variations)	Mendelssohn.
Andante from a Quartet	Rossini.
Canzona in D minor	Bach.
Solo and Chorus, "La Carita"	Rossini.
Offertorium in B flat	Stark.
Selection, "Don Giovanni"	Mozart.

MARGATE.

An organ recital was given at St. Paul's, Cliftonville, by Mr. John C. Ward, on September 10th. The programme included a selection from Handel's works, and a miscellaneous selection, embracing :—

Sonata No. 1	Mendelssohn.
Pastorale in G	Hopkins.
"Homage à Haydn"	Calkin.
March from "Abraham"	Molique.

WELFORD.

A recital of sacred music was given in the Parish Church on September 6th, by Mr. Geo. Herbert Gregory, Mus.B., F.C.O, Mr. Jas. L. Gregory, F.C.O., A.Mus., T.C.L., and Mr. John B. Roberts. The following pieces were included in the programme :—

Postlude	Kettle.
Concerto in A	Handel.
Largo—Allegro—Minuetto e Trio—Fuga.	
Andante from quartet in D minor	Mozart.
"Marche Religieuse"	Guilmant.
Adagio in E	Merkel.
"Harvest Thanksgiving" March	Calkin.
Larghetto from 2nd symphony	Beethoven.
"War March of the Priests"	Mendelssohn.

A NOVEL ORGAN SCHEME.

It may interest readers to examine the specification of the first organ to be built upon the system of Mr. Thomas Casson, of Denbigh. It has been commenced, and will be ready for exhibition within twelve months. It will be divided and separated from the Console, the Great and Choir with their Pedal organs being grouped separately from the Swell with its Pedal organ. The Great and Choir have only one manual ; it is not pretended that this is superior to two, but the object is to show how several manual organs, say six, or eight, with their respective Pedal organs and couplers, may all be perfectly controlled from two or three manual claviers, and one pedal clavier.

GREAT ORGAN.

1. Bourdon	16 ft.	4. Principal .... 4 ft.
2. Open Diapason ...	8 „	5. Mixture (3 ranks)
3. Flute Harmonique..	8 „	6. Trumpet .... 8 „

GREAT PEDALIER.

7. Open Diapason	16 ft.	9. Trombone .... 16 ft.
8. Quint	10⅔„	

Great pedalier coupler, Great to Great pedalier.

ACCESSORIES.

Two combination pedals, giving nine combinations for Great organ, Great pedalier and manual and pedal couplers, one retaining pedal, one attaching and detaching piston.

CHOIR ORGAN.

10. Dulciana	8 ft.	12. Flute Douce .... 4 ft.
11. Stopt Diapason.....	8 „	

CHOIR PEDALIER.

13. Bourdon	16 ft.	14. Clarion .... 4 ft.

Choir pedalier coupler, Choir to Choir pedalier.

ACCESSORY.

One attaching and detaching piston.

SWELL ORGAN.

15. Bourdon	16 ft.	19. Gemshorn .... 4 ft.
16. Viol di Gamba ...	8 „	20. Mixture (2 ranks)
17. Voix Celestes	8 „	21. Cornopean............ 8 „
18. Hohl Flöte	8 „	22. Vox Humana ....., 8 „

SWELL PEDALIER.

23. Sub-Bass	16 ft.	24. Euphonium .... 16 ft.
In swell box.		

Swell pedalier coupler, Swell to Swell pedalier.

ACCESSORIES.

Two combination Pedals to Swell, Swell pedalier and coupler, giving six combinations, one retaining pedal, one attaching and detaching piston, tremulant to 22.

MANUAL COUPLERS.

25. Swell to Great.	27. Swell to Choir.
26. Choir to Great.	

Manuals, CC to G, 56 notes.
Pedals, CCC to A, 34 „

This is merely an illustrative organ, and it contains only one pedal stop "for melodic use."

LEEDS.

The Town Hall organ has been re-opened by Dr. Spark, after partial re-construction and thorough renovation by the builders. The estimated cost of the improvements contemplated in the original contract between the Corporate Property Committee and the builders was £700. The concert took place on Monday last, and the admission was free. The enormous audience evinced perfect satisfaction with the improved quality of the instrument. The programme afforded ample scope for displaying its completeness and power. Dr. Spark gave three organ solos. The first of these, Handel's concerto in G minor. On this occasion the organist added a cadenza, in which the subjects of the concerto were skilfully introduced. A feature of the concert was the second of the organist's contributions, an andante in A flat, and an allegro in F major, from a fantasia in F major, " composed for this occasion by Dr. Spark." The full composition comprises three movements, but the final section was not given on account of its length. The composition, very creditably represents Dr. Spark's fanciful treatment of organ pieces, and the effect which it produced on the audience ought to have gratified him both as a composer and performer. The third of the organ solos was of the French school—Batiste's "Angelic Voices," two andantes in E flat and A flat. It may be added that the concert was attended by the Mayor, the Town Clerk, and other representatives of the Corporation.

BOW AND BROMLEY INSTITUTE.

The invaluable work done in the past by the excellent management of this admirable and truly popular institution inclines the public mind to regard with every confidence and satisfaction the proposals for the season now about to commence. The renowned organ recitals, which have long been maintained as the most varied and remarkable performances of the kind in existence, will recommence on Sept. 22nd, and the committee are negotiating with some of our most eminent organists for their appearance during the season. Of special musical arrangements the following may be stated :—On Monday, Sept. 24th, the opening concert will be given. Vocalists : Miss Anna Williams, Miss Grace Damian, Mr. Redfern Hollins, Mr. Chaplin Henry. Solo violin, Signor Erba ; conductor, Mr. Fountain Meen.—The Institute Choir and Music Classes are under the direction of Mr. W. G. McNanght, and contribute important services. The pianist will be Mrs. W. G. McNaught, and the organist Mr. Alfred Carder. Dr. Stainer's new oratorio, "St. Mary Magdalen," is in rehearsal, with a view to performance with full orchestra on (probably) Tuesday, October 30th. On October 22nd the Operatic Class of the Royal Academy of Music will perform a selection of standard operas. On Nov. 12 the Royal Albert Hall Amateur Orchestral Society, under the presidency of H.R.H. the Duke of Edinburgh, will give an Orchestral Concert, under the conductorship of Mr. George Mount ; and on December 10th the Concluding Concert, will be given by the choir of the Institute, with Mendelssohn's "Hymn of Praise," and Haydn's "Spring ;" conductor, Mr. W. G. McNaught. The educational and class arrangements embrace every science and art, are under competent guidance, and would not disgrace one of our universities. Music is judiciously and fairly represented in the scheme. One feature is the tuition by Mr. Alfred Carder, of pianoforte playing and solo singing. Mr. W. Foster, the energetic hon. secretary, is again at his post, and a strong working committee are engaged in the management, so the hopes of a good and useful season rest upon an experienced controlling power, tried judgment, recognised energy and tact, and upon an established reputation which trained audiences and a well-served public know how to gratefully support.

A Musical Festival is to take place in Quebec on the 3rd and 4th of next month.

The *Musical Record*, Boston, U.S., has a paragraph showing the extension of the movement for a return to the ecclesiastical style of the sixteenth century :—The American St. Cecilian Society was to hold a convention at Cleveland, Aug. 21st, 22nd, and 23rd, when works of Palestrina, Antonio Lotti, De Witt were to be performed. Professor Singenburger, who was created Knight of St. Gregory by Pope Pius IX., is president of the society and directs the choral work at the Convention. The St. Cecilian Society is labouring earnestly to banish from the services of the Catholic church all popular and unworthy music, and to reinstate the old school compositions of a more devout character, or new music conceived in a similar vein. The movement, though originally a German one, has been joined in by the English speaking churches ; it is endorsed by the Pope and has the patronage of all the bishops ; and what is equally, or more, important, it has the support of some eminent and influential musicians.

PRINCIPAL CONTENTS OF THIS NUMBER.

LONDON : SATURDAY, SEPTEMBER 15, 1883.

PURPOSE IN THE COMPOSITION OF MUSIC.

II.

ALTHOUGH people have little difficulty in deciding the question, "What class of art-"producers may be entitled to disregard "technical laws?" as regards its application to literature, there is a strange general misconception as to the permissible freedom in this respect of the painter, musician, or architect. This arises, no doubt, from the possession on the one hand of a standard of popular judgment attained through the daily and personal use of the verbal language, and on the other side from a general want of knowledge as to the technical requirements of the musician, painter, and architect. Hence it comes about that people sensible enough not to commit themselves to paper from the literary point of sight without some acquaintance with the necessary grammatical rules and practices governing the verbal language, are nevertheless weak enough to suppose they can express their musical thoughts with but little or no technical knowledge. Unfortunately these irreconcilable notions prevail beyond the ranks of the musically ignorant being in part fostered by the deeply engrained vanity which, common to all weak mortals, prompts us to suppose that our inborn, shapeless thoughts, which we nurse with so much self-complacency, may be received as tokens of genius. The vanity of being thought rich in mental gifts is akin to the more vulgar vanity of being esteemed as of good society and well-to-do in the world. So it comes to pass that the most precious lesson the art-producer has to learn is that of gaining the virtue of humility, without which, indeed, the artist has no self-knowledge, no power of selection and rejection as regards the use of his own mental materials, and little faculty for that artistic sympathy with the rest of mankind without which the artist misses the principal function of his career. It was the possession of this very artistic humility which prompted BACH to walk miles to hear the best organ players of his time, to listen with interest to the instrumental compositions of VIVALDI, and to study with intense care and application. This same spirit prompted HANDEL to learn much from the works of CARISSIMI and PURCELL, and made MOZART, BEETHOVEN, and MENDELSSOHN not only diligently examine the works of their predecessors, but studiously drill themselves in the use of the machinery of the art. Such men, it is unnecessary to point out, were certainly entitled to disregard upon occasion the technicalities of their craft; for they knew well how to balance loss and gain, and could discern the difference between a vapoury, deluding fancy, and a real, strong purpose. No master has probably exercised the minds of pedants than has the JOHN SEBASTIAN BACH; and those who have from time to time desired the advance of artistic freedom have turned for justification to the grand Cantor who, writing some hundred and fifty years ago, still stands out as a gigantic figure beckoning us forward. This great man in short presents the most prominent instance of the possession of a splendidly trained and powerful mind, thoroughly in earnest; and fully understanding what is the real position of purpose in the composition of music. A distinguished living authority—adapting in part a saying originally directed to JOSQUIN DES PRES, has told us that "Whilst counterpoint conquers most men, BACH "conquers counterpoint." These words point to the fact, that having become a master of his craft, BACH wrote not without definite purposes and definite thoughts; so his counterpoint is at once objective and subjective. His purpose is ever so decided that he will drive what he duly recognises as a worthy musical thought through every obstacle, and count disonances most men writing long after his time would shrink from using of as little account as the soldier on the march will heed the stinging nettles which may lie in his pathway. But let us before passing on see how this great and determined contrapuntal thinker practically regarded the more essential rules of the art. With all his courage and decision of purpose, how rarely he admits a brace of consecutive fifths or octaves into the tissue of his musical lace work; and how rarely he permits the presence of a discord he does not either resolve, or use in the act of passing through as it were, or allow merely because he elects not to break up a thought or disarrange a sequence! When therefore the student has attained such a mastery as BACH secured before beginning the great writing tasks of his life, surely he may then claim to be entitled to disregard in the same judicious spirit

technical laws when occasion for increased freedom may arise. In other words, when the student can write scores of complicated pages without a single case of ill advised or accidental consecution escaping his eye and full control, when he can lay out a network of parts of cable-like strength and perfect independence, and when he can plan a fugue with all the ramifications of exposition, counter-exposition, stretto and other more minor fugal devices, without finding his hands entangled by any intrusive, obstinate discords, then he is certainly strong enough to deserve as much freedom as the carrying forward of strong purposes may call for; and he is also surely entitled to disregard all those technical laws which only exist for the true artist as the means by which strength and clearness may be created to help in the building up of definite objects. E. H. TURPIN.

The institution the great master was certainly
artistic, and the art of instruction of the

TIN-KETTLE PIANOFORTES

A CORRESPONDENT hailing from a rural rectory complains bitterly that two "cottage" pianofortes, loudly puffed by the owner, are both so out of tune that the proverbial cow, even with its nine lives of a cat, would be killed without the butcher's assistance. Nor is this an uncommon case in the country. The English laity are not sensitively musical; they are either too ignorant, or too stingy to hire a tuner from the nearest town, and the poor pianoforte consequently degenerates into an acetous quality of tone. JEAN JACQUES ROUSSEAU, in his "Emile" (a work on Education), places his hero in a remote villa, where a pianoforte is found, considerably the worse for wear, and a worthy companion of the tin-kettle in the kitchen. But "Emile" is an adept, able to put his hand to anything; he tunes the instrument, and forthwith sings serenades to his Sophie, or mayhap accompanies her sweet songs with all the sympathy of an adoring lover. Poor BEETHOVEN, in the last year of his life, resided in a village near Vienna. A friend, visiting the great man one wet day, was grieved to hear that his only pianoforte could no longer emit dulcet sounds, but made the strangest mixture of sharps and flats. BEETHOVEN, however, suffered from deafness.

Even in London, fashionable folks neglect their pianofortes, and often expose their ignorance or want of acute ear by asking for official information about the state of the grand ERARD or the iron drawing-room COLLARD.

Some have the effrontery to invite their friends to an afternoon tea-fight, or a soirée, to hear a little "music," and when the guests are assembled, coolly announce, with or without apology, that the pianoforte is rather out of tune! Happily, half the company, or may be more, could not for their lives sake detect the faulty intonation.

How strange it seems that the best tuners do their work empirically, without, as a rule, any knowledge of music itself. Old THOMAS HAYDON, the professor, once asked his tuner, a clever fellow enough, to express an opinion on some new composition; the tuner excused himself on this very ground—that he knew nothing of the art itself. The question of "temperament" has been recently discussed, and much remains to be said; but this is not to the present question. Reserving the theory of keys, and their supposed *qualities*, the compromise, so much ridiculed by the acoustical doctors, is confessedly indispensable : the pianist, therefore, contents himself with maintaining the accepted and allowable inconsistencies of temperament (erroneous only in a *scientific* sense), by means of the screw and the fork. The rules for preserving a pianoforte, so far as possible, from the influences of damp, cold draughts, and other atmospheric annoyances, are old as the hills. I would advise that all pianofortes be tuned up to the high "Philharmonic" pitch.

One of the tin-kettle pianofortes complained of by my unfortunate friend in the country is a *rara avis*, one of the old fashioned "six octaves," from F to F; the form is semi-grand, but these six-octave instruments are usually square. We had a cabinet "Rolfe" pianoforte, at home, some forty or fifty years ago, of five five-eighth octaves, to wit, from F to C; it would now, of course, be utterly useless for modern pianoforte music. You rarely find now-a-days the six six-eighth octave pianofortes, from C to A; even the cottage instruments have, usually, the full extension of seven octaves, from A to A; but this extension hardly answers, unless the action be very fine, and the tuner in frequent attendance. The very high notes sound like wood, and merely produce a *thud*, whilst the deep bass notes are almost invariably out of tune.

The old "square" pianoforte had one advantage over the "cabinet," you could see and *sing* across it without the obstruction and acoustical absorption of the "upright." I remember how convenient these "squares" proved to be at dances, so far back, alas ! as the Christmas of 1826-27. The gentleman quadrille-player, plentifully supplied with hot water, sugar, and brown brandy, sat in a corner, whence he could see the movements. This was very necessary, as the "figures" of the quadrille, then quite new, were not generally known to the dancers. Fancy a man calling out, at intervals, and in a stentorian voice of command : "lady advance"; "gentlemen to the right," "pous-sette"; "chassez-croisez," and so on ! Stately minuets and country dances were still the vogue up to the year 1820, or thereabouts. I am shocked, speaking of quadrilles, to remember (in 1825-26) a "first set" on themes from "Der Frei-schütz," including the famous *motif* of the *scena* (for Agnes) in E major (orchestrally enunciated *à l'ouverture*, in E *flat*), and the rollicking song of Caspar in B minor (Act I).

A. M.

A SINGULAR CAREER.

The *Daily Telegraph* has a picturesque leader on the career of the composer of "Kathleen Mavoureen." It may be questioned whether the successful author of only one or two melodious songs can fairly claim much attention from the musical world on the ground of his achieved work. Further, and the present writer speaks alas ! from an extensive knowledge of many cases, the life failure of an artist with gifts small or great, almost invariably arises from his own uncorrected faults of temperament or character, and through his indolence, pride, or neglect of work and artistic opportunities. However, the story so neatly told by the *Daily Telegraph* is interesting and perhaps instructive. Says that journal in the course of the article in question :—

"Mr. F. Nicholls Crouch is seventy-five years of age. " He has been the contemporary of Braham and Cramer, " of Mori and Dragonetti. He may have known " Storace and Catalani, Sapio and Incledon. When " he first became noted as a composer, our favourite " English female vocalists were Miss Paton and Miss " Maria Tree, Madame Vestris, and Mrs. Waylett. " He had reached the maturity of his powers before Miss " Bruce and Miss Birch, Miss Dolby and Miss Louisa " Pyne were known in London concert-rooms. And now " this old-world musician starts up, to the general sur- " prise, from the 'tenebræ' of years, and the individuality " of the writer of 'Kathleen Mavourneen,' which was " growing as dim as that of the composer of " Through " 'the wood' and 'I'd be a butterfly,' is revealed very " sharply and picturesquely indeed in the broad light of " the American press.

" The lives of authors and painters, it is commonly said, " are most graphically written in the books which they " have composed, or in the pictures which they have " painted ; but the story of the life of the author of " 'Kathleen Mavourneen,' must be sought for far beyond " the range of his songs. A highly eventful and deeply " troubled life-journey it would seem to have been. Born " in 1808, and a musician almost from his infancy, it is " said that at the age of nine he was playing the bass in " the orchestra of the Royal Coburg Theatre, afterwards " the Victoria. Then, while still a mere child, he was " attached to the King's Theatre, now Her Majesty's, and " had the honour of playing a solo on the violin in the " presence of Rossini. The conductor of the orchestra, " Bochsa, a well-known harpist, who married one of the " sisters of the notorious Harriette Wilson, recognising " the talent of young Crouch, gave him lessons, and pro- " cured his admission to the choir of Westminster Abbey. " When the Royal Academy of Music was founded by " George IV., Crouch, then a boy of fourteen, qualified " himself by the hardest of hard work for a Royal " studentship, and after the death of the king, the young " Academy student attended professionally the corona- " tion of William IV. and Queen Adelaide, and was sub- " sequently appointed a member of the Queen's private " band. He had already become a composer, and had " written his first ballad, 'Zephyrs of Love' for Miss " Tree, and a 'Swiss Song' for Madame Malibran. All " at once Mr. Crouch deserted his art for the most prosaic " of metallic industries, and, in conjunction with other " speculators, set up some large rolling mills for zinc in " the county of Kent. The concern collapsed, and Mr. " Crouch found himself ruined. He returned to London " and to the pursuit of his profession, and, to some very " pretty words sent to him by Mrs. Crawford, he set the " delightful melody of 'Kathleen Mavourneen.' The " success of this song woke the dormant fires within him, " and in rapid succession he produced many more ballads, " the most popular of which was 'Would I were with " 'thee,' written to words by Caroline Norton. Then he " accepted a seven years' engagement, at an annual " salary, with a firm of music publishers, Dalmaine & Co., " in Soho Square, who, in consideration of the stipend " which they paid him, were to have the benefit of all " the compositions which he produced. He continued to " write not for seven but for nine years, and, in addi- " tion to twelve 'volumes' of songs, composed two " operas, 'Sir Roger 'de Coverley' and 'The Fifth of " November.' In 1849 it occurred to Mr. Crouch to visit " the United States, the well-known 'impresario,' Max

"Maretzek, having offered him the post of conductor of 'the orchestra at the New York Opera House.

"The venture proved a failure, and Max Maretzek's "troupe was scattered to the winds. The next appear- "ance of Mr. Crouch was as a lecturer on music at Port- "land, in the State of Maine. Subsequently he became "conductor to the concerts of the Portland Sacred Har- "monic Society; produced for the first time in the Eastern "State the 'Stabat Mater' of Rossini; composed glees "and madrigals;' sang in a church choir on Sundays; "and gave music lessons during the week. He made "some money in Portland; but, when the gold mines "of California were discovered, imprudently realized all "he had amassed by the toilsome practice of his pro- "fession, and set sail for the land of El Dorado. He "failed to obtain any nuggets on the Pacific slope, and "was fain to retrace his steps, first to Washington, "where he was master of the choir of a Roman Catholic "church, and next to Richmond, in Virginia. On the "breaking out of the Civil War, the composer, although "long past the age of military service, volunteered in "the ranks of the Southern army, giving up, it is "said, an income of four thousand dollars a year for "the promise of twelve dollars a month as a private "'Grayback.' He carried a musket from the beginning "of the war till the battle of Appomattox, and then, hav- "ing apparently got into very low water, he took service "with a Mr. Perkins as 'a gardener and farm hand' at "Buckingham Court House. Thence, broken in health "and pocket, he found his way back to Richmond, and "afterwards to Baltimore, in Maryland, in which last- "named city for nearly twenty years he struggled pain- "fully to obtain a livelihood for himself, his wife, and five "children. No later than the 7th of June last came a "remarkable epilogue to the poor worn-out composer's "weary life-drama. On the date mentioned a petition "was filed in the Circuit Court of Baltimore by an indi- "vidual styling himself James Marion Roche Crouch. "The petitioner prayed that his change of surname from "Marion to Crouch might be sanctioned on the ground "that he had become attached to the composer of 'Kath- "leen Mavourneen' and his family in their adversity, and "that he felt 'that by adopting the name of Crouch he "could the better look after and care for his adopted "father in his declining years, and after he was gone his "children could have a brother to look up to, and call "upon for aid and protection.' The gentleman who, with "exceptionally sympathetic munificence, has thus en- "larged on that principle of adoption so curiously and so "beautifully interwoven with the manners of the Ameri- "can people is, it is stated, an officer in the United States "Navy Yard. So there is an end to the indigence of Mr. "Frederick Nicholls Crouch; and the veteran composer, "naturally exhilarated by the prospect of better fortune, "is about to make a tour through the Sothern States, and "to publish his biography."

"The sorrows of popular song writers have come to be as "familiar in our mouths as household words. Sometimes "it is the poet and sometimes the musician whom the world "unconsciously elects shall starve; sometimes the writers "both of the words and of the melody who come to grief; "occasionally it is the poet who gets the oyster-shell, and "the composer the oyster. The 'poet' Bunn did not do so "very badly by his 'libretti.' They were laughed at, but "they sold wonderfully well, whereas the great composers "of the 'Bohemian Girl' and 'Maritana' were remunerated "at a rate which, in these days, would be thought simply "wretched. Vincent Wallace died weighed down by the "icy hand of poverty; and the competence which shed "sunshine over the closing years of the life of Michael "William Balfe was certainly not the result of his profes- "sional earnings. George Linley, the author and composer "of 'Constance' and the 'Spirit of Love,' was glad to get "twenty pounds for a ballad, words and music to boot; "the author of 'Home, Sweet Home,' John Howard Payne, "led a struggling and precarious life until, in his old age, "the Government of the United States made him a consul "in North Africa; while the writer of the music of the "sweet, natural, and pathetic ditty in question, Henry R. "Bishop, was 'stock' composer to a London theatre; "and when in his declining years he received the honour "of knighthood might almost have said 'ditto' to Oliver "Goldsmith à propos of giving ruffles to a man who had "no shirt. In the case of the fascinating English opera "of 'The Night Dancers,' the poet and the musician "were both equally and desperately impecunious. The "latter, Edward Loder, was almost as shabbily treated "by his contemporaries as Wallace had been; while the "author of the libretto, Mr. George Soane, a scholar of "high attainments, had been literally 'cut off with a shil- "ling' by his father, the celebrated architect Sir John "Soane, and condemned to the life-long misery of a lite- "rary hack for the dire offence of having written disparag- "ing criticisms of his sire's architectural performances. "Not much more fortunate was the career of a song writer "whose lays had brought thousands upon thousands of re- "cruits to the British Navy, and whose patriotic verse stirred "the whole heart of the country when our very national "existence was threatened. When Charles Dibdin could "be no longer of service to the Government, the meagre "pension of two hundred pounds per annum, which he "had enjoyed for a few years, was ungraciously with- "drawn, and he was left to struggle with poverty and to "die in mean lodgings in Camden Town in the year of "Waterloo, 1815. The lives of English composers in "times past—never, it is to be hoped, to return—form, it "must be admitted, a long and mournful chronicle of "neglected genius and unrewarded merit; yet the gloomy "calendar may be marked with at least one white stone, "when we find an enthusiastic young American claiming "the composer of 'Kathleen Mavourneen' as his adopted "father, assuming his name, and undertaking to provide "not only for his declining years but for the loved ones "whom he may leave behind him."

It is only just to the world to add the comments of an esteemed and reliable veteran artist upon the subject matter of the above notice. "My early recol- "lection of him (CROUCH)" says this gentleman in a letter, "is that he was an indifferent musician and a "very ordinary violoncello player. He allowed such "grammatical errors as the presence of objectionable "consecutive fifths to remain without correction in the "many editions of his celebrated song 'Kathleen "'Mavourneen' for many years. He disappeared "from this country, and it is even believed allowed "himself to be announced in the obituary notices of "the newspapers soon afterwards as a dead man. "No one ever heard of him for a long time, until the "singing of his chief song by TITIENS some years ago "at Boston, U.S., once more brought him forward as "in the act of thanking the singer personally."

The story should be a warning to young composers who may dream of that delusive hope, making a hit and may be a fortune, by a song which will take but little thought and trouble to write. No one could be so unkind as to wish to upbraid the composer of "Kathleen Mavourneen" for not being able to secure the professional success his talents are presumed to have deserved. Still, he himself would doubtless be one of the first to desire to warn students against hoping to build up reputations upon adventitous suc- cesses, and to earnestly urge the persistent persevering cultivation of art from the highest point of sight. "Excelsior" should ever be the artist's only watchword. Further, it is important to bear in mind that small efforts, even if crowned with such hardly to be explained success as has attended certain modern songs, cannot lead in themselves to any really great and lasting artistic positions. Such a success may indeed equally with a complete absence of reward, delude and ruin the producing artist; who must be something of a pioneer, or he is not a true artist; and who must exercise a far-sighted wisdom, self-knowledge, and self-respect, which will stand out in due proportion with his genius, talent, and artistic skill.

E. H. TURPIN.

Reviews.

King David. By G. A. Macfarren. (Stanley, Lucas, Weber & Co.).—Surely no finer example of earnest, thoughtful, dutiful, artistic labour can be presented for the student's contemplation, than that of Prof. Sir G. A. Macfarren, who, burdened with large responsibilities, and all but overwhelmed by routine labours, contrives to think out and to produce important contributions of various kinds to the literature of the art he has magnificently served so long. To his oratorios (to speak of only one type of work), "St. John the Baptist," "The Resurrection," and "Joseph," he has now added "King David," composed for the approaching Leeds Festival. The title chosen, "King David," is a fitting one, for we have placed before us the great man, the chosen king from the beginning of his kingly career. Samuel once pointed out to the people the consequences of having an earthly king of tyrannical greed, who would take their sons and rob them of their hard-earned wealth; still, they would have a king. Saul, the son of "a mighty man of power," an aristocrat and "a choice young man and a goodly" reigned disastrously over them. Then God chose for Israel a king after His own heart, selecting the man of humble origin and position, the simple shepherd, but withal the man of real governing power, the man of genius, mental strength and eloquence, born to rule by force of heavenly gifts, and not the mere apex of existing society and the royal puppet of circumstances. Such is the grand figure of Prof. Macfarren's new work, and the composer has felt the dignity of his task in pourtraying such a stately character. The composer starts his subject after the death of Saul, and continues the work rather as a series of detached scenes, than as the unrefined action of one and the same recital. The first scene opens with the acclamations of the people, after which the ceremony is performed of bringing in the ark. Then follows the prophecy of Nathan. The choruses are much used in a declamatory sense. A large part of the first section of the work recounts the story of David's sin with the wife of Uriah, the Hittite, as it is told by the narrator, while the chorus sings, "Remember not, Lord, our offences," from the Litany. Then Nathan recounts the parable of the one ewe lamb, and in a duet the parable is applied to David, who is sorrowing for his sin. A contralto solo, "What is a man profited?" and a chorus, which declares the vengeance of God upon sinners, close the first part. The second part is taken up with the story of the rebellion of Absalom, the son of David. This comprises a scene between the widow Tekoah and David; a solo voice and chorus describe the forces of Absalom, and after a contralto song, the retreat of David's army across the Jordan is narrated. The defeat of Absalom is told by dialogue, and the oratorio ends with a pathetic lamentation of David, his prayer for mercy, and the doxology.

One notes with thankfulness that Prof. Macfarren adds in the prelude to "King David" another fully planned overture to the limited list of sacred compositions of that type. This is built upon well-defined subjects and according to the orthodox lines, and it contains some musicianly development. The overture in its chief subjects and development expresses forcibly a musical description of David's shepherd life, the summons to battle, David playing before Saul, the King's envy and his death,

a musical process introducing the listener to the immediate period of the action of the oratorio. The first chorus opens with Mozartean dignity and has a pastoral movement with an effective accompaniment. In the succeeding recitative, David appears as a bass or baritone rather. The song "I will not suffer mine eyelids" has a broad and vigorous melody. The following chorus, a "Psalm at the bringing in of the Ark," opens dramatically with trumpet phrases, and is characterised by much grandeur of a healthy diatonic character. Taking the keynote of this chorus C, as the mediant of A flat, we are led straight into the succeeding graceful soprano song, "The path of the just." "The Prophecy" with recitative for Nathan (tenor) and chorus is finely conceived, striking in effect, and contains fragments of previously heard thoughts. The next chorus, "The seed of David is great," has some dignified sentences and a clearly written fugal movement. In the succeeding "Narration" begins the story of Uriah's wife. In the treatment of narrative passages of this type, the composer shows much aptitude for a refined dramatic power, great powers of expression, and a large skill in intermingling sentences of great variety in style. "Remember not, Lord, our offences," the next movement, is an unaccompanied chorus of the smooth vocal type of Bennett's "God is a Spirit." The borrowing of the words from the Anglican Litany most likely suggested the adoption of one of the musical responses as a subordinate subject to the words "Spare us, good Lord." Now comes Nathan's parable, a duet for David and Nathan, and a contralto solo, "What is a man profited?" all characteristic pieces; "Vengeance belongeth to the Lord," a fine dramatic and vigorous chorus terminates the first part. The second part opens with a narration beginning the story of Absalom; then comes a long dramatic duet between David and the widow of Tekoah. "Absalom prepareth" is the next piece, a fine chorus written in a clearly outlined form with two episodes. A recitative and song for Absalom, and a new but not dissimilar choral treatment of the words "Absalom prepareth," bring us to the highly picturesque chorus, "Give ear, all ye tribes." An important and characteristic solo, "Woe unto them that call evil good," offers an unusually dramatic employment of the contralto voice. There is much life and activity in the succeeding chorus, "Arise, and let us flee." The following brief narration has, as is usually the case in this work, some effective instrumental passages. The chorus, "Thou, a king, shall not go forth into battle," is expressive and tuneful. "What seemeth you best, I will do," are the opening words of the next recitative and song for David, containing a strong individuality and dramatic element. A pleasing duet for female voices, "Like as a father," succeeds this scene. The next dialogue for David and the chorus of female voices is admirably thought out, and its closing sentences for male chorus announcing that the battle is won but Absalom is lost, are strikingly earnest. "O Absalom, my son," is David's following pathetic lamentation; this is continued in the chorus (with solo) "Behold, he weepeth," which has some charmingly expressive harmonies. "Despise not thou the chastening of the Lord" is a gracefully accompanied and effective soprano solo in two movements with a brief return to the first idea by way of coda. The chorus, "Arise, come forth," opens like the first chorus. David's highly expressive prayer, "Have mercy upon me," follows this, ending with a ray of strong hope in the fine setting of the words, "And my tongue shall sing." A graceful chorus and quartet, "Joy is in Heaven," now follows. The doxology which closes the oratorio opens fugally. As the movement proceeds, many passages of great power and dignity are disclosed, and the final coda is formed of pure church-like harmonies, which most effectively terminate the work. Though it is perhaps proper to await the verdict of the first public performance in Leeds of "King David," it is the duty of the reviewer to announce the fact that Professor Macfarren has indeed produced a really fine, ripe, and scholarly work in this oratorio. There are abundant signs of rare naturalness in its figures, which show how much the composer has learnt after a long experience to trust—as all true composers must learn to trust—in the simplest resources for the production of the greatest effects. The details are everywhere of a remarkable and thoughtfully sustained interest, without being too laboured in manner. The work will add much to the well earned renown of the veteran and nobly in earnest composer, theorist, writer, and affectionately regarded teacher and artist.

Correspondence.

ON THE TEACHING OF COUNTERPOINT.

TO THE EDITOR OF THE "MUSICAL STANDARD."

DEAR SIR.—It was not my intention to trouble you with any further remarks upon this subject ; but some observations in Mr. Stark's letter in your last issue seem to invite some reply, and I am unwilling to ignore that invitation. No less unwilling, however, am I to prolong any discussion on any such matter, in connection with any personal references to myself or my book. I will only say, firstly, that in my preliminary chapter (*xxxvii.*) on Counterpoint, I expressly say—" It is considered advisable, as a mental discipline, for a musical student to pursue, in the first instance, a course of SIMPLE or PLAIN COUNTERPOINT, in the STRICT STYLE " (p. 118). My object was not to inaugurate a revolution, but to summarise and elucidate the generally accepted views. Therefore the three chapters that follow treat of *strict Counterpoint* : the advantages of the study of which, as "adapted to cultivate a pure and solid manner of writing," I remark on (p. 119). But even in that introductory chapter I briefly expound *Free* Counterpoint, as including "Chromatic progressions and combinations, as well as Essential Discords ;" and, at page 149, I again refer to that style, advise the student to exercise himself therein, " subject to *principles*," previously laid down : not re-iterating *rules*, such as that essential discords should be resolved, &c. And I also add : " he [the student] may write Counterpoint, not only, as hitherto, to a *Canto Fermo*, but, likewise, to subjects consisting of notes of unequal length :" a point referred to by Mr. Stark, if I rightly understand his remarks upon *Canti Fermi.*

Moreover, though Mr. Stark says that he has "searched [my] book in vain for any indication of advance as regards the second and third points," mentioned by him,—the second point being the "defect of the Cherubini school" in the "absence of any proper recognition of implied harmony in two-part exercises,"—yet, at p. 120, occurs the following paragraph : " In all two-part writing, the *two* notes in combination must be considered as representing, in incomplete form, a complete and defined harmony. And the harmonies so represented must succeed one another according to the various principles which have been explained in connection with the different chords. There should be no ambiguity as to the harmony intended ; but it should be understood how it should be filled up, were the complementary parts added. And there should be no *False Relation* between successive combinations."

Rest assured, Mr. Editor, that I make these references and quotations solely in order to show that the "sympathy" with "rational progress," which Mr. Stephens justly credits me with, has been felt for many years ; and, I may add, has been acted upon in professional work. My object is addressing you at all has not been *controversial* : rather *suggestive* as to the *line of reform*, which line should be parallel with that of *Chord* and *Harmony* study. I regret the implied distinction : *Harmony* and *Counterpoint* are two phases of *Music.*

I observe that all references, now-a-days, are to *Cherubini.* I believe that it is pretty certain that Cherubini himself did not write the book which bears his name ; but let that pass. Cipriani Potter told me that, in the early days of the Royal Academy of Music, a conference of the Professors was held, at which, after examination, it was declared that *Albrechtsberger's* book should be the authorised manual for the students in that institution, Cherubini's being considered a less safe or orthodox guide. And yet the present Oxford Professor's book is, avowedly, " on the basis of Cherubini." How is this? The two books already mentioned were, I suppose, "on the basis of Fuchs," and so on, backwards. The fact appears to be that, gradually, the need of enlargement, to meet growing perceptions of the art, has been felt ; and so fresh books have been written, advancing *a little*, somewhat timidly, perhaps. I think that the *feeling* and the *practice* of musicians has been increasingly progressive of late years ; but this progressive instinct has hardly found much expression or exposition in the text-books. Indeed, the most recent book on Counterpoint, to which much reference has been made in this discussion, is rather *retrogressive* so far as *rules* and *restrictions* are concerned ; though marked by much power, as need hardly be said.

After all, the matter is one of *teaching policy* ; and I reiterate that I think competent teachers will enlarge their basis of instruction, and adapt their counsels to their pupils' requirements, undeterred by any books, and, most assuredly, uninfluenced by any "Conference." If preparing a candidate for an examination, of course regard must be had to the known proclivities of the Examiner. Will any Conference undertake to *reform the Examiners ?*

Many other points might be touched upon, did time and space permit.

Yours faithfully,
HENRY CHAS. BANISTER.

Sept. 10th, 1883.

DR. ARNOLD'S NEW SACRED CANTATA "SENNACHERIB."

TO THE EDITOR OF THE "MUSICAL STANDARD."

SIR,—Referring to the very severe criticism of the London press on Dr. G. B. Arnold's Cantata, " Sennacherib," permit me, as a casual observer at the recent Gloucester Festival, to say that I dissent from the view taken by the London critics. There were two distinct opinions expressed in Gloucester at the time, eminent professors of music (whose names I can give) declaring that the work was not only original, but that in point of merit it was above the average. None of the critics have analyzed the music. The work will, I think, compare favourably with most productions of the same class and length that have appeared of late years. I may specify three "numbers"—"The soul in anguish" (worthy almost of Spohr), " O House of Jacob," and "God breaketh the battles." Dr. Arnold conducted his work, it struck me, with exceptionable ability. The organist of Winchester Cathedral has proved that he is capable of undertaking one of the most difficult forms of composition. See his eight-part fugue, which closes his oratorio of " Ahab."

I am, Sir, your obedient servant,
CHARLES T. GRINFIELD, R.A.M.

Weston-super-Mare, Sept. 11, 1883.

Passing Events.

Herr Engel is daily expected in town from Vienna.

Dr. John Hullah has returned to London, one is glad to add, in better health ; though he is still something of an invalid and requiring rest.

Messrs. Hueffer and Mackenzie's " Colomba " has been successfully produced in Liverpool by the Carl Rosa Opera Company.

Saturday Evening Concerts at the Glasgow City and St. Andrew's Halls commence to-night. These are admirably managed by the local caterers. Popular Saturday concerts are spreading everywhere apparently.

The Committee of the Glasgow Choral Union have been actively engaged in negotiations, with vocal and instrumental artists for the forthcoming season.

Music and charity ever go hand in hand. Numerous concerts have been given in Glasgow in aid of the Daphne disaster fund, and with marked pecuniary success.

Mr. Edward J. Spark announces his Subscription Concerts at Worcester, on Oct. 30th, Nov. 27th, and Feb. 4th, with a list of eminent artists which promises well for the success of his scheme.

Messrs. Boosey and Co., writes to the *Musical World* to say that Balfe's " Come into the Garden, Maud " was first printed on the royalty system, and the royalty, was afterwards sold to them for £100.

Messrs. Cassell and Co's long list of new and forthcoming books includes among other works of interest, Dr. J. S. Bristowe, F.R.S., " On the Throat and Voice," as part of the " Book of Health."

Mr. Carrodus proposes to conduct a string quartet party during the winter season through the provinces ; accepting engagements for chamber, drawing-room, miscellaneous concerts, and oratorio performances.

The sale of tickets for the Leeds Festival has been unprecedentedly large. Sir Arthur Sullivan has conducted another choral rehearsal, and Mr. J. Barnby conducted a practice of his 27th Psalm on Tuesday last.

The Princess Mary Adelaide, Duchess of Teck, has transmitted to the honorary secretary of the Kew Church Enlargement Fund the sum of £1,062, being the net proceeds of the concert organized a few months ago by her.

The performances of " Rip Van Winkle " at the Comedy Theatre have been suspended during the past week, during which the theatre was closed for redecoration. The company will return on the 17th, and in the meantime they have been giving performances of Mr. Planquette's popular opera at Brighton.

Sir M. Costa is understood to have sustained the money losses before alluded to through unfortunate investments in Spanish and Egyptian affairs. Sir M. Costa is now living at the Hove end of Brighton, where it is hoped he will find benefit from the rest gained. He has furnished a villa taken on lease, for a permanent abode.

Mr. Edwin M. Lott held examinations in Liverpool in behalf of the International College of Music on Sept. 5th and 6th. The pass list gives a goodly array of successful candidates, some having specially distinguished themselves. Dec. 6th and Feb. 13th are, according to the *Liverpool Mercury*, fixed for forthcoming examination days.

Mr. Stephen S. Stratton has issued the prospectus of his admirable Birmingham Chamber Concerts. The scheme refers to one of the most important and art serving institutions of its kind in the kingdom. Mr. Stratton has rendered invaluable services too, locally, by making known standard and new works, and by bringing forward local artists of merit.

On Sunday, August 26th, Mr. Henry Farmer's Mass in B flat was given with orchestra at St. Barnabas (Roman Catholic Cathedral) Nottingham, with admirable effect, upon the occasion of the Anniversary Festival of the church. The composer himself conducted. The church, a large and stately building, has a fine organ, and orchestral use prevails there at the great Festival Services.

The Musical Lectureship of the New South Wales and Monmouthshire University at Cardiff has been assigned to Mr. Clement Templeton, M.A., Secretary of the Harrow Music School. There were 11 candidates. Mr. Templeton has a rare field in musical Wales for the exercise of his talents and learning; that he may have a full meed of success will be the wish of all lovers of the art. Mr. Clement Templeton, M.A., who is a gentleman of large culture and experience, gained honours at Cambridge and the Leipzig Conservatoire, and has been engaged for some time with Mr. John Farmer in the musical department of the Harrow school.

The 176th monthly concert of the St. George's Glee Union was held at the Pimlico Rooms on the 7th inst. The soloists were Miss Annie Matthews, Miss Nellie Watts, Miss Jeanie Rosse, Mr. Reginald Groome, and Mr. Theodore Distin. The part-singing by the choir, included—"O my love's like a red red rose" (Garrett), "When the sun sinks to rest" (Bridge), "All among the barley" (Stirling), "The sea hath its pearls" (Pinsuti), "Love you for beauty" (Clarke), and "The shepherd's lament" (Smart). The pianoforte accompaniments were played by Miss C. Ogilvie, Miss Louisa Distin, and Mr. F. R. Kinkee. Mr. Joseph Monday conducted.

The prospectus of the thirteenth season of the Albert Hall Choral Society, which will shortly be issued, contains a feature of more than common interest. Mr. Barnby, the energetic and skilful conductor of the society, intends to produce as an oratorio Wagner's "Parsifal," which has never been heard out of Bayreuth. The experiment is a bold one, and will, no doubt, attract all the more attention, as there is at present little chance of Wagner's sacred drama being seen on the London stage. Beethoven's great mass in D will also be included in the scheme. From the appearance of this statement, it may be concluded that legal and local difficulties with regard to the English performance have been removed.—*Times.*

Prof. John Ella is remaining in town. He bears his years gallantly, entertaining his friends from time to time. It is gratifying to add that Prof. Ella is in the enjoyment of excellent health, and continues to relate with extraordinary vigour and clearness the varied details of his exceptionally large artistic experience. A man who has taken an active part in the advancement of art in England, who has with keen powers of observation carefully watched the unexampled growth of music during the past 60 years, and has personally known every great musician from the time of Rossini and Weber, to our own days, has something to say, and Prof. Ella does say that something to those who enjoy his friendship, with shrewdness and effect.

The Wolverhampton Musical Festival took place during the past week. There were four performances—Thursday and Friday, morning and evening, the works chosen being Mendelssohn's "Elijah," Gounod's "Messe Solennelle," Beethoven's "Mount of Olives," and an offertorium by Hummel, "Alma Virgo." The chief secular pieces were Mackenzie's cantata "Jason," and Macfarren's "Lady of the Lake." The leading vocalists were Miss Anna Williams, Miss Mary Davies, Madame Patey; Mr. E. Lloyd, Mr. Maas, and Signor Foli. Dr. Swinnerton Heap was conductor. The band was under the leadership of Mr. Carrodus, and the chorus numbered about 250 voices. Earl Dartmouth was the President. An account of the Festival will be duly presented.

The Querist.

QUERY.

CANTATAS.—Can any of your readers give me the titles of any cantatas within the compass of an ordinary Parish Church Choir? We have already sung Stainer's "Daughter of Jairus," Spohr's "God, Thou art great," the greater part of Gaul's "Holy City," and Mendelssohn's, "Lauda Sion." I have looked through other works, but they either make too great a demand upon the soloists (especially the boys, who of course, sing the soprano solos), or else the choir is sub-divided so much for double choruses, or quartets and chorus, that all good effect is lost, as the total number of singers is not more than about thirty. Stainer's "Daughter of Jairus," was exactly the style of thing for us, and my desire is to find something equally "taking," and at the same time equally good music. For any suggestions I shall be very grateful.—F.C.O.

REPLIES.

H. E. S.—The outside cover of your communication came to hand by post without the contents.

The *Orchestra, Choir, and Musical Education* has a capital translation by Mr. Whittingham, of Fétis's "Treatise on Accompaniment from Score," and other valuable articles.—ED. *Mus. Stand.*

C. T. JOHNSON.—The following, from Professor Macfarren's papers and Bishop's "Glees," *Musical Times*, (1864-5) may be of service to your correspondent, Mr. C. T. Johnson. It is all the information I am able to give on the subject :—" The half of the Caravan,' a chorus for two female and three male voices, interspersed with solos with accompaniments, is from some dramatic work, of which I cannot ascertain the name. It is gay and not without melodic prettiness, but it can have little or no effect away from the stage."—S. S. S.

Service Lists.

SEVENTEENTH SUNDAY AFTER TRINITY.
SEPTEMBER 16th.
London.

FOUNDLING CHAPEL. — Morn.: Service, Garrett in D; Anthem, O come, let us worship (Mendelssohn). Aft.: Children's Service.

CHRIST CHURCH, CLAPHAM.—Morn.: Service, Te Deum, Plain-song; Kyrie, and Credo, Schubert in B flat; Offertory, Anthem, Grant, O Lord, we beseech Thee (Mozart); Sanctus, Benedictus, Agnus Dei and Gloria in excelsis (Schubert). Even.: Service, Magnificat and Nunc Dimittis, Hoyte in B flat; Anthem, Praise the Lord, O Jerusalem (Hayes).

HOLY TRINITY, TULSE HILL.— Morn.: Chant Service. Even.: Service, Cantate Domino, and Deus Misereatur, Attwood in D; Anthem, Blessed be the God and Father (Wesley).

ST. JAMES'S PRIVATE EPISCOPAL CHAPEL, SOUTHWARK.—Morn.: Service, Introit, Blessed is he that cometh (Hummel); Communion Service, Weber in G. Even.: Service, Hopkins in F; Anthem, Sanctus, sanctus, Osanna in excelsis (Bach).

ST. MAGNUS, LONDON BRIDGE.—Morn.: Service, Opening Anthem, I will arise (Creyton); Te Deum and Jubilate, Goss in A; Kyrie (Goss). Even.: Service, Magnificat and Nunc Dimittis, Ebdon in C; Anthem, I will lift up mine eyes (Clarke).

ST. MARGARET PATTENS, ROOD LANE, FENCHURCH STREET.—Morn.: Service, Te Deum and Benedictus, Tuckermann in F; Communion Service, Offertory Anthem, He in tears (Hiller); Kyrie, Credo, Sanctus, Benedictus, Agnus Dei, and Gloria, Schubert in C. Even.: Service, Magnificat and Nunc Dimittis, Hopkins in F; Anthem, O give thanks (Elvey).

ST. PAUL'S, AVENUE ROAD, SOUTH HAMPSTEAD.—Morn.: Service, Te Deum, Calkin in B flat; Benedictus (Havergal); Kyrie, Tours in F; Offertory (Barnby) ; Credo, Sanctus, and Gloria in excelsis, Tours in F. Even.: Service, Magnificat and Nunc Dimittis, Gounod in D; Anthem, Ascribe unto the Lord (Wesley).

ST. PETER's (EATON SQUARE).—Morn.: Service, Te Deum, Garrett in F. Even.: Service, Dykes in F; Anthem, Awake, awake (Stainer).

ST. PETER's, VERE STREET, W.—Even.: Service, Magnificat and Nunc Dimittis, Wood in F; Anthem, Ye shall dwell in the land (Stainer).

ST. AGNES, KENNINGTON PARK, S.E.—Morn.: Service, Holy Communion, Kyrie, Credo, Sanctus, and Gloria, in excelsis, Distin in C; Benedictus and Agnus Dei, Eyre in E flat.

ST. AUGUSTINE AND ST. FAITH, WATLING STREET.—Morn.: Service, Stainer in A; Introit, The Lord is the strength (South); Communion Service, Stainer in A. Even.: Service, Walmisley in D major; Anthem, Lead kindly light (Stainer).

ST. SEPULCHRE'S, HOLBORN.—Morn: Service, Te Deum and Jubilate, Nares in F ; Credo, Agutter in B flat. Even. : Service, Nares in F ; Anthem, Lord, we pray Thee (Haydn).

Country.

ST. ASAPH CATHEDRAL.—Morn. : Service, King in C ; Anthem, Be merciful unto me (Sydenham). Even.: Service, The Litany ; Judge me, O God (Mendelssohn).

ASHBURNE CHURCH, DERBYSHIRE. — Morn. : Service, Laurence in D ; Kyrie, Credo, and Gloria, Wesley in E. Even.: Service, Garrett in E flat (Cantate) ; Anthem, Blessing, honour, glory (Spohr).

BELFAST (ST. GEORGE'S).—Morn. : Service, Te Deum, and Benedictus, Woodward in E flat ; Apostles' Creed, Harmonized Monotone : Litany (Helmore) ; Offertory (Barnby). Even. Service, Magnificat and Nunc Dimittis, Chipp in A ; Apostles' Creed, Harmonized Monotone, Anthem, I will always give thanks (Calkin).

BIRMINGHAM (S. ALBAN THE MARTYR).—Morn.: Service, Te Deum, Boyce in C ; Benedictus, Steggall in G ; Holy Communion, Kyrie, Credo, Sursum Corda, Sanctus, Benedictus, Agnus Dei and Gloria, Redman in F throughout. Evensong.: Magnificat and Nunc Dimittis, Redman in F.

BIRMINGHAM (ST. CYPRIAN'S, HAY MILLS).—Morn.: Service, Cobb in G ; Anthem, All ye that cried, and I waited for the Lord (Mendelssohn). Even.: Service, Smart in F ; Anthem, I know that my Redeemer liveth, and Since by man (Handel).

BRISTOL CATHEDRAL.—Morn.: Service, Mendelssohn in A ; Even.: Service, Goss in E ; Anthem, O Thou Shepherd (Walmisley).

CARLISLE CATHEDRAL.—Morn.: Service, Chipp in A; Introit, Blessed is the man (Stainer) ; Kyrie, Chipp in A ; Nicene Creed, Harmonized Monotone. Even.: Service, Stainer in A ; Anthem, The wilderness (Goss).

DONCASTER (PARISH CHURCH).—Morn.: Service, Wesley in F. Even.: Service, Hopkins in F ; Anthem, I will mention (Sullivan).

DUBLIN, ST. PATRICK'S (NATIONAL) CATHEDRAL.—Morn.: Service, Te Deum and Jubilate, Dykes in F ; Holy Communion, Kyrie, Creed, Sanctus, Dykes in F ; Anthem, Judge me, O God (Mendelssohn). Even.: Service, Magnificat and Nunc Dimittis, Dykes in F ; Anthem, O come everyone (Mendelssohn), and O where shall wisdom (Boyce).

EDINBURGH (ST. JOHN'S).—Morn.: Service, Anthem, By the waters of Babylon (Boyce). Even. : Service, Rejoice in the Lord (Purcell).

ELY CATHEDRAL.—Morn.: Service, Te Deum, Hopkins in E flat ; Benedictus, Plain-song ; Kyrie, Credo, and Gloria, Jackman in E flat ; Anthem, from the rising of the sun (Ouseley). Even.: Service, Jackman in E flat ; Anthem, The righteous shall flourish (Calkin).

FOLKESTONE (ST. MICHAEL'S).—Morn.: Service, Holy Communion, Introit, Bread of Heaven ; Kyrie, Credo, Sanctus, Gloria, &c. (Mozart). Even.: Service, Magnificat and Nunc Dimittis, Garrett in F ; Anthem, But as for His people (Handel).

LICHFIELD CATHEDRAL.—Morn.: Service, Stainer in E flat ; Communion Service, Stainer in E flat ; Anthem, Come unto Him (Gounod). Even. : Service, Stainer in E flat ; Anthem, These are they (Dykes).

LIVERPOOL CATHEDRAL.—Aft.: Service, Magnificat and Nunc Dimittis, Gadsby in C ; Anthem, The Lord will comfort Zion (Hiles).

LIVERPOOL (ST. CUTHBERT'S, EVERTON).—Morn.: Service, Holy Communion, Calkin in B flat. Even.: Service, Stanford in B flat ; Anthem, as pants the hart (Spohr).

MANCHESTER CATHEDRAL.—Morn.: Service, Te Deum, Jubilate and Full Communion, Barnby in E ; Anthem, The Lord is my Shepherd (Macfarren). Aft.: Service, Barnby in E ; Anthem, Praise the Lord, O my soul (Goss).

MANCHESTER (ST. BENEDICT'S).—Morn.: Service, Kyrie (Elvey) ; Credo, Sanctus, Benedictus, Agnus Dei, and Gloria in excelsis, Farmer in B flat. Even.: Service, Magnificat and Nunc Dimittis, Bunnett in F.

MANCHESTER (ST. JOHN BAPTIST, HULME).—Morn.: Service, Kyrie, Credo, Sanctus, and Gloria in excelsis, Williams in D ; Benedictus and Agnus Dei, Agutter in B flat. Even.: Service, Magnificat (Bradford) ; Nunc Dimittis (Monk).

PETERBOROUGH CATHEDRAL.—Morn.: Service, Mendelssohn in A ; Anthem, Come unto him (Gounod) ; Communion Service, Thorne in E flat. Even.: Service, Stainer in E flat ; Anthem, This is the day (Elvey).

ROCHESTER CATHEDRAL.—Morn.: Service, Walmisley in C ; Anthem, The earth is the Lord's (Hopkins). Even. : Service, Walmisley in C ; Anthem, O Lord, how manifold (Handel).

SHEFFIELD PARISH CHURCH. — Morn.: Service, Kyrie, Hayne in G. Even.: Service, Trimnell in D ; Anthem, O Lord, our Governor (Marcello).

SHERBORNE ABBEY. — Morn.: Service, Kyrie, Roe in E flat ; Offertories (Barnby). Even.: Service, Chants ; Anthem, reat is the Lord (Lyle).

SALISBURY CATHEDRAL.—Morn.: Service, Barnby in E ; Offertory (Barnby). Alt.: Service, Barnby in E ; Anthem, The Lord hath done great things (Smart).

SOUTHAMPTON (ST. MARY'S CHURCH).—Morn.: Service, Te Deum and Benedictus, Tours in F ; Holy Communion, Introit, Like as the hart (Hoyte) ; Service, Tours in F ; Offertory, Zacheus stood forth (Barnby) ; Paternoster (Hoyte). Even.: Service, Magnificat and Nunc Dimittis, Tours in F ; Apostles' Creed, Harmonized Monotone ; Anthem, O Lord how manifold (Macfarren).

WELLS CATHEDRAL.—Morn.: Service, Hall and Hine in E flat ; Introit, Let us not be weary (Macfarren) ; Kyrie, Aldrich in G. Even.: Service, Ebdon in C ; Anthem, Behold how good (Battishill).

WOLVERHAMPTON (ST. PETER'S COLLEGIATE CHURCH).—Morn.: Service, Te Deum, Smart in F ; Benedictus, Matthews in E ; Communion Service, Stainer in E flat. Even.: Service, Responses, Tallis ; Magnificat, Camidge in E flat ; Nunc Dimittis, Wickes in G ; Anthem, Lord of all power (Mason).

WORCESTER CATHEDRAL. — Morn.: Service, Stainer in E flat ; Anthem, O that I knew (Bennett). Even. Service, Stainer in E flat ; Anthem, Hear, O Thou Shepherd of Israel (Walmisley).

* * Post-cards must be sent to the Editor, 6, Argyle Square, W.C., by Wednesday. Lists are frequently omitted in consequence of not being received in time.

NEWSPAPERS sent should have distinct marks opposite to the matter to which attention is required.

APPOINTMENT.

Mr. C. E. MELVILLE, of Leeds, Associate of the College of Organists, has been appointed Organist and Choirmaster to St. Mary's Church, Harrogate.

Printed for the Proprietor by BOWDEN, HUDSON & Co., at 23, Red Lion Street, Holborn, London, W.C.; and Published by WILLIAM REEVES, at the Office, 185, Fleet Street, E.C. West End Agents—WEEKES & CO., 14, Hanover Street, Regent Street, W. Subscriptions and Advertisements are received either by the Publisher or West End Agents.—*Communications for the EDITOR are to be forwarded to his private address, 6, Argyle Square, W.C.*

SATURDAY, SEPTEMBER 15, 1883.—*Entered at the General Post Office as a Newspaper.*

The MUSICAL STANDARD

A NEWSPAPER FOR MUSICIANS PROFESSIONAL AND AMATEUR

No. 999. VOL. XXV. FOURTH SERIES. SATURDAY, SEPTEMBER 22, 1883. WEEKLY: PRICE 3D.

THE MUSICAL STANDARD is published every Saturday, price 3d., by post, 3½d.; and may be had of any bookseller or newsagent by ordering its regular supply.

SUBSCRIPTION.—*The Musical Standard* is posted to subscribers at 15s. a year; half a year, 7s. 6d., payable in advance.

The rate is the same to France, Belgium, Germany, Italy, United States, and Canada.

Post Office Orders to be made payable to the Publisher, William Reeves, 185, Fleet Street, London, or to the West-end Agents, Messrs. Weekes & Co., 14, Hanover Street, Regent Street, W.

ADVERTISEMENTS.—The charge for ordinary advertisements in *The Musical Standard* is 2s. 6d. for three lines or less; and 6d. for each line (10 words) in addition. "Organist wanted," 3s. 6d. for 3 lines or less. A reduction is made for a series.

FRONT PAGE.—Concert and auction advertisements, &c., are inserted in the front page of *The Musical Standard*, and charged one-third in addition to the ordinary rates. Other advertisements will be inserted on the front page, or in the leader page, if desired, at the same terms.

LEEDS MUSICAL FESTIVAL, 1883.
October 10th, 11th, 12th, and 13th.

Conductor—SIR ARTHUR SULLIVAN.
BAND AND CHORUS OF 425 PERFORMERS.
Detailed Programmes may be had on application to
FRED. R. SPARK, Hon. Sec.
Festival Office, Leeds.

BOROUGH OF HACKNEY CHORAL ASSOCIATION.—Season 1883-4.
Conductor—Mr. EBENEZER PROUT, B.A.

FOUR CONCERTS will be given in the SHOREDITCH TOWN HALL, with Full Band and Chorus, as follows:—

Monday, Oct. 29th, "Hereward" .. .. .. E. Prout.
,, Dec. 10th, "Stabat Mater" .. .. Rossini.
,, ,, ,, Symphony in D .. .. Mozart.
,, ,, ,, Selection, "Oberon" .. .. Weber.
,, Feb. 25th, "Jason" .. .. .. A. C. Mackenzie.
,, ,, ,, Selection, "Rosamunde" .. Schubert.
,, April 28th, "St. Paul" .. .. .. Mendelssohn.

Subscription, £1 1s., giving Two Numbered Seats for each concert.

For full copy of Prospectus, and further particulars, apply to the Hon. Secretary, 31, Fountayne Road, Stoke Newington.

SOUTH LONDON CHORAL ASSOCIATION and INSTITUTE OF MUSIC, Camberwell New Road, S.E.

Principal—Mr. LEONARD C. VENABLES.

The Sixteenth Season will be inaugurated on TUESDAY, October 2nd, 1883, with a Lecture by Emil Behnke, Esq., on "SCIENCE and SINGING," illustrated by Photographs of the Throat in the act of singing, thrown upon the Screen by means of the Oxy-Hydrogen Light.

Dr. JOHN STAINER, M.A., H.M. Inspector of Music, will take the chair at eight o'clock.

Classes are held, and Private Tuition given, in all branches of Musical Education, under competent Professors, for particulars of which see Prospectus, post free on application.

ORCHESTRAL BAND (Conductor, Mr. Leonard C. Venables; Leader, Mr. T. E. Gatehouse). There are vacancies for Clarionets, Bassoons, Horns, and Euphonium.—Apply to Edward Simpson, Hon. Sec.

MUSICAL INTERNATIONAL COLLEGE, LONDON.

Founded for Examining purposes only.
Principal—EDWIN M. LOTT.

PRACTICAL EXAMINATIONS in INSTRUMENTAL and VOCAL MUSIC throughout the kingdom, conducted personally by the Principal. Next LOCAL THEORETICAL EXAMINATION, DECEMBER 6, 1883.

For particulars, address SECRETARY, Musical International College, 270, Cornwall Road, Notting Hill, W.

MAKERS AND REPAIRERS.

GEORGE WITHERS & CO.
(Late of Coventry Street),
WHOLESALE IMPORTERS OF

MUSICAL STRINGS,
From Rome, Padua, and Naples.
A FINE COLLECTION OF ITALIAN INSTRUMENTS.
Bows, Cases, Music Stands, &c. See Price Lists.

51, ST. MARTIN'S LANE, LONDON.

THE ORPHAN SCHOOL FOR DAUGHTERS OF MUSICIANS will be opened SEPTEMBER 17TH. Boarders and Day Pupils also received on moderate terms. Special musical advantages.—Address, Miss Helen Kenway, 10, Darnley Road, Notting Hill, W.

ORGANIST WANTED AT ONCE. Good Church-man. Gregorians used.—Apply and send references to the Vicar, St. Bartholomew's, Dover.

WANTED MUS.BAC. to CORRECT EXERCISES IN COUNTERPOINT, by applicant intending to work hard for a Degree.—Apply to Omega, at the Office of *Musical Standard*.

ORGAN FOR SALE, suitable for Church, Chapel, or large Chamber, by Hill & Son. In handsome mahogany case, with gilt pipes, 3 Manuals, 11 Stops in Swell, 11 in Great Organ, and 8 in Choir, 4 Stops on the Pedals, 4 Couplers, and 6 Composition Pedals, all modern improvements. Blown by Gas Apparatus, or in the ordinary way, the property of the late S. N Barber, Esq. May be seen at 174, Denmark Hill, on Tuesdays and Fridays, before one o'clock, or by special appointment, during the months of September and October.

ORGAN FOR SALE (New), Two Manuals, Twenty Stops, suitable for Church or Chapel. Must be Sold.—Ginns Brothers, Organ Builders, Briscoe Road, Merton, London, S.W. Nearest Station, Tooting Junction.

JUST PUBLISHED. NEW HARVEST ANTHEM.

" THOU VISITEST THE EARTH," composed by by E. H. Turpin. Price 6d.

WEEKES & CO.: 14, Hanover Street.

Second Thousand.

W JOHNSON'S HARVEST ANTHEM, "I WILL MAGNIFY." Easy and effective. Price 3d.

London: NOVELLO, EWER & CO., 1, Berners Street, W.

JUST PUBLISHED.—Full Anthem, "BE NOT DRUNK WITH WINE, WHEREIN IS EXCESS." For Temperance Services, etc., by E. H. TURPIN. Price 4d. net.—Messrs. WEEKES & CO., 14, Hanover-street W

NEW ORGAN PIECE, by M. GUILMANT.— SPOHR'S 24th PSALM (English words), 9d. and 2s. Ditto arranged for Organ Solo by M. GUILMANT, 1s. 6d.

London: NOVELLO, EWER & CO.

THEORY OF MUSIC, BOOKS I., II., III., by LOUISA GIBSON. "FIRST BOOK" Revised (not Catechetical). Popular Edition, 1s.; A. B. C, 6d.; "Musical Examiner" shortly.

London: WEEKES & CO.; NOVELLO & CO.

For Sale.

COSTA'S "ELI": an ORATORIO, FULL SCORE, folio, Beautiful Copy, in olive morocco, gilt edges, for £1 12s. (pub. £3 3s. unbound, the binding worth about £1 18s.), £1 12s.—W. Reeves, 185, Fleet Street, London, E.C.

TE DEUM LAUDAMUS in A, for Congregational Use, by W. de M. SERGISON.

London: NOVELLO, EWER & CO.

THE VOICE

MUSICALLY AND MEDICALLY CONSIDERED.

BY

ARMAND SEMPLE, B.A., M.B., Cantab., M.R.C.P., Lond.,

Physician to the Royal Society of Musicians.

(*Concluded from page 152.*)

The Formation of Registers.

The Chest Voice (*Voce Di Petto*), possessing far greater vibratory power than the Falsetto, (*Voce di Fasetto*) requires far firmer contraction or "*pinching*" of the glottis. This "pinching" is more easily brought about by the use or enunciation of the Italian I (*Anglice* E).

The Falsetto Voice is usually more veiled than the Head Voice (*Voce di Testa*), and a greater expenditure of air is required in its production.

These last two registers are frequently confounded together; the term falsetto is commonly misapplied. In male singers it is the head voice, to which in them there are many objections, which is usually misnamed the falsetto. In reality the greatest beauty of voice, especially in Tenor Voices, is the union or wedding of the chest and falsetto registers, and by this perfect union some of the greatest operatic singers (notably Rubini and Mario) established a world-wide reputation.

The Chest and Falsetto registers in the emission of their lower notes throw into vibration the whole length of the vocal cords; in gradually ascending the vocal scale, the cartilages are brought more and more into approximation until at last vibration is produced by the ligaments only. By the ligaments, in Tenor Voices, the glottis forms, between Mi₃ (E₃) and Do₄ (C₄).

The notes which have been termed Mixed Voice or Mezzo-Petto; and in Female Voices between Mi₄ (E₄) Do₅ (C₅), an octave higher, those termed the Head Register

When the ligamentous portions only of the vocal cords are occupied in circumscribing the glottis (the summits of the cartilages still vibrating), these portions do not always compress one another with sufficient firmness for the requirements of the beats; as a result, the notes of the Male Voice, between Si₂ (B₂) and Re sharp₃ (D sharp₃)

and in the Female, between Si₃ (B₃) and Re sharp₄ (D sharp₄)

in some cases exhibit tremulousness and weakness on account of the organ being unsteady. Directly the vibrations ceased to be affected by the cartilages—and this event takes place in the voice of the male on reaching Mi₃ (E₃) and that of the female, Mi₄ (E₄)—the sounds usually become pure and quite steady.

To correct this weakness the best method is to contract or "*pinch*" the glottis firmly.

Occasionally when the Soprano voice attempts the sounds Si₄ (B₄) and Do₅ (C₅)

It rises unintentionally to Re₅ (D₅) and Mi₅ (E₅)

in a pure thin tone, and with less effort than would be required in taking the notes below. The mechanism of

such sounds has been explained as follows:—The lips of the glottis are stretched, and perfectly, though gently, touch one another while the space between the vocal cords is considerably lessened. In this condition the organ the least pressure of air will cause it to rush through a minute aperture of the glottis which, however narrow, serves to produce the most rapid beats with extreme facility. The pressure of the air, however, should be very slight when the aperture of the glottis is to be minute. The above process is also capable of application by the male voice. It will communicate clearness to the high notes of the bass, and enable tenors to extend the compass of the chest register, and sing the high notes in Mezzo-Voce. It is not necessary that perfect closure of the glottis should take place after each partial opening; it is only requisite that an opening shall exist of sufficient smallness to develop the elasticity of the air which is opposed to it. Any rush of air escaping through the half-opened orifice will be very perceptible, and communicate to the sound a veiled or muffled and sometimes exceedingly dull character. This result often happens with the falsetto. Hence it follows that brilliancy of voice depends upon the entire closure of the glottis after each beat, and by this perfect closure the breath is also economised.

Volume and Intensity of Voice.

The intensity of a sound is dependent upon the quantity of breath which is employed to produce a pure vibration—after each vibration the glottis should close perfectly, for if it were continually open, the notes emitted undoubtedly would be weak instead of strong in consequence of the waste of breath. In proportion, therefore, to the pressure upon the breath, must the glottis be contracted or "*pinched*."

Formation and Characters of Timbres.

The Timbres of the voice may be modified by many different causes.

1. According as the *glottis* is half-opened or closed, the notes will be either bright or dull.

2. The folds or upper tendons by which the glottis is surrounded may, either by closing, yield a stifled tone, or by retiring, give volume to the sounds.

3. Varied qualities of timbres may be rendered by the *pharynx* to the sounds during their passage through this situation; the varieties of timbres correspond to the multifold mechanical changes of which this vocal tube is susceptible.

The Pharynx may be regarded as a deep and extremely elastic tube, commencing inferiorly at the larynx, forming a curve at the arch of the palate, and terminating superiorly at the mouth. The Pharynx at its shortest dimension forms only a slight curve, but at its longest dimension almost a right angle; in the former case the larynx rising towards the soft palate which drops to meet it; in the latter case, the larynx dropping and the soft palate rising.

The *bright* timbre is produced by the short and gently curved condition of the pharynx. The *sombre* timbre by its elongated, and strongly curved state. The various vowel-sounds and the various forms which the pharynx may assume are closely related.

Every alteration in the method of producing vibration may occasion a difference in timbre, and every modification undergone by a sound whilst passing through the vocal tube changes its quality and character.

A New York paper recently had the following:—"The morning *stars* sang together," exclaimed a preacher with great emphasis, "And there didn't three or four giggling *stars* stick themselves up before all the rest and monopolize the music and worship of Heaven! Our next hymn will be 'Coronation'; let everybody sing." By all means let everybody sing when everybody has been taught how to sing. The most prominent, self-seeking, jealous, for the time un-christian as forgetful of decent forethought for his neighbour and probably unconsciously worldly-minded *star* of the story, was most likely the would-be-witty-at-the-wrong-time preacher himself; who possibly monopolised in his sermon upon the same occasion much more of the time for worship than was assigned to the divinely appointed exposition of praise—music, or was desirable from any point of sight whatever.

MUSICAL FESTIVALS.

The remarks on "Musical Festivals and their Fruits" by that worthy contributor, "A. M.," are so *pessimist* in spirit that one might infer that they were the result of an attack of indigestion. I feel strongly inclined to "break a lance," but have not time to enter at length into details. Let me, however, say that so far as I know provincial matters musical, we need neither the pity nor greatly mind the "lash" of "A. M."

That institutions come into being, flourish, and die, is a truism unnecessary to enlarge upon; that all our provincial music meetings (Birmingham and Leeds excepted) have reached the last stage, is so far from being the case that last week witnessed a remarkable display of vitality at Wolverhampton. A few notes may possibly supplement the report you may present. The Festival was established in 1868, when a performance of the "Messiah" was given in aid of the Wolverhampton and South Staffordshire Hospital, conducted by Signor Randegger, and including Mr. Sims Reeves among the vocal principals, with leading London players in the band. From that time it has been held triennially with gradually augmented artistic resources. A local Festival Choral Society has been created, consisting in a great measure of people of education and cultured feeling, and their singing, for refinement and delicacy, is something not easy to surpass, while they only want numbers to equal the tone and weight of our Birmingham Chorus. To Mr. W. C. Stockley, of Birmingham, belongs the credit of forming and training this admirable body of singers, and much of the success of preceding Festivals. Dr. Heap, who succeeded him as conductor a year ago, has not only maintained the reputation of the Society, but increased it. Last week the number taking part in the Festival was about 250, and the band was nearly 60 strong, made up principally of local performers, led by Mr. Carrodus, with Mr. Hann, viola; Messrs. M. Vieuxtemps, violoncello; Neuwirth, double-bass; Dubrucq, oboe; Trout, bassoon; and Mrs. Priscilla Frost, harp, as the only other "outside" assistants. Sir George Macfarren, who was present at the rehearsal as well as the first day's performances, congratulated his London friends upon being in such excellent company, and called the performers "a magnificent orchestra," besides paying a high compliment to Dr. Heap as a musician and conductor. Well, the committee, without great preliminary fuss, this year ventured upon a two days' Festival with the programme inserted last week. The large Agricultural Hall was well filled at every performance—twice, indeed, being crowded. While everything was well done, the cantata "The Lady of the Lake" received the best treatment it has yet met with—so said its experienced composer. The rendering of "Jason" completely retrieved the Bristol disaster of last year, and enabled us at last to hear a work that will assuredly escape the fate "A. M." seems to predict for all cantatas. Now here is a great artistic triumph achieved with very little aid from the metropolis. The vocal principals London cannot claim as her own. London, in fact, acts as a great magnet, but its productive powers do not equal those of its *attraction*. The London press gave no attention to this Festival beforehand, but the able critic of the *Daily Telegraph* enters upon the subject of centralisation and its attendant evils, with both justice and generosity. Again, the London press need not flatter itself that without its approval all things provincial must wither and die. While no words are too strong to express indignation at the blundering and stupidity in the arrangements at times for the accommodation of gentlemen invited to witness and record the provincial celebrations, on the other hand we need not hang our heads in despair because we are told by some of them that many of our institutions are effete, or exist on sufferance. As to the novelties produced, and their fate, I will leave that for another occasion; I hope my present words may provoke a little discussion, for the matter may profitably be considered from both metropolitan and provincial points of view.

STEPHEN S. STRATTON.

Messrs. Henderson and Farnie's version of Offenbach's opera "La Vie," produced at Brighton on the 17th, and subsequently brought out at the Avenue Theatre, has undergone some alterations, including the changing the locality to England, and the representing of one of the principal scenes as taking place at Charing Cross.

A NEW OPERA SCHEME.

Many doubt the realisation of the scheme for the completion of the proposed Opera House on the Thames Embankment, but another proposal is even said to be on the *tapis;* this one to be under the management of a lady who has some influence in the musical world it is claimed, and who is to be backed and supported by a rich and sanguine man. This new idea proposes the formation of an operatic "School of Music," the training of an exceptionally efficient chorus of 120 selected voices, the formation of an orchestra of 105 players, and the performance annually of Italian opera for four months, and English opera for a like period. The propounders of this new scheme are so much in earnest as to be bent, it is said, upon the engagement of some large existing theatre (the Opera House in the Haymarket has even been named) so that the work may not be delayed by having to wait for a suitable home and training place. The staff of the Opera Conservatoire is, according to rumour, to consist of twenty competent teachers of voice production, singing in Italian and English, acting, etc. It is only necessary to add that a scheme which would employ a capital of some £500,000, involve an expenditure of about £130,000 annually, and counts upon a return in the end, of course of something in excess of that sum annually, must be regarded by those who know anything of operatic and theatrical matters to be chimerical in the extreme. History has scores of schemes to record of this dreamlike character which have come to nothing as naturally as rain descends. Seriously, opera, like every other commodity to be created and paid for, does not live satisfactorily upon the exotic basis. Even the operatic establishments in part supported upon State subventions, are by no means at all times healthy institutions; as being in the anomalous position of not always duly considering critical and public tastes, and being, further, now and again too independent of public support, to efficiently provide for changing and exacting tastes. The rich Quixotic gardener, who, as the fable runs, determined upon supplying people solely with his own favourite vegetable, learnt too late that the public appetite must be taken into account, and that the laws of demand and supply must be kept in harmony for success to be attainable. There is no desire here to "throw cold water" upon any reasonable proposal for the advancement of the art in any direction; but hobbies are not to be accepted as schemes fairly claiming support, neither will money unaided by sound judgment and timely action furnish a lasting motive power.

Says the *Daily News* :—Mr. Gilbert's and Sir Arthur Sullivan's new comic opera in preparation at the Savoy Theatre will probably take the place of "Iolanthe" early in November. It is founded, we understand, like a former piece from the same pen, upon Mr. Tennyson's poem of "The Princess." The earlier work, brought out at the Olympic Theatre in January, 1870, has been described by the author as a "respectful perversion of Mr. Tennyson's poem"; but in the play-bill of the time attention was claimed for it as "an attempt to reform a much-abused branch of dramatic entertainment, not only by the selection of a high-class work for its subject, but by treating it with refinement and elegance." Nor was this claim without substantial foundation. When the history of dramatic fashions in recent times comes to be written Mr. Gilbert's "Princess" will claim a place not only by reason of its intrinsic merits, but also because it marked a very noteworthy departure from the senseless pattern of the burlesques then in full favour with the public. It followed pretty closely the Poet Laureate's story, though it did not employ Mr. Tennyson's lines, nor did it profane or vulgarise the fanciful legend of the college of learned ladies, unless the substitution of a clownish porter for the college portress who in the poem admits Cyril and Florian into the sacred precincts, is open in any degree to that objection. The merriment was, as a rule, derived from heightening the poet's picture of the "sweet girl graduates," their contempt for men, their pedantry, and ignorance of the world, and contrasting these with a stronger dash of the alleged weakness and vanities of the sex. It may perhaps be assumed that the new comic opera will treat the story somewhat in the same vein.

Musical Intelligence.

WOLVERHAMPTON.

This last developed festival was held last week under conditions of a most encouraging nature. The excellent orchestra and the capital chorus were under the artistic foresight and musicianly grip of Dr. Swinnerton Heap. At the Thursday night's performance Sir G. A. Macfarren's "Lady of the Lake" was excellently given. This is in every way one of its veteran composer's most picturesque and effective works, and it is gaining that public favour it deserves. At the performance of the work, the author was called for from the orchestral ranks as well as by the audience, and acknowledged the applause by bowing his thanks. On Friday, the morning performance consisted of the following interesting selections, Beethoven's "Mount of Olives," in which Miss Anna Williams and Messrs. Maas and Foli were the chief singers; Hummel's "Alma Virgo" the solo part by Miss Mary Davies, and Gounod's "Messe Solennelle," Miss Mary Davies, Mr. Maas, and Mr. F. King sustaining the beautiful solo sentences. Much has been written with regard to the appropriateness of the chosen text and its setting in Beethoven's "Mount of Olives," but there can be no question as to the rare beauty and even impressiveness of much of the music contained therein. Hummel's motet, an effective piece of showy Church music, which shows the hand of the practised writer, deserves to be heard to advantage from time to time, as it was heard on this occasion. Gounod's "Mass," putting aside certain inventions of questionable taste, always attracts, as it did upon the occasion of its first hearing in England, at a private performance given under the direction of Dr. Hullah, in St. Martin's Hall, some five-and-twenty years ago. The chief feature of the evening performance was Mr. Mackenzie's "Jason," a work of exceptional power and interest. The solo parts were admirably sustained by Miss Davies, Mr. E. Lloyd, and Mr. F. King. The band and chorus did their work for the most part very efficiently, and the work was received with much satisfaction by a greatly interested audience. That the Wolverhampton Festival is now to be regarded as an established and permanent institution, is indeed a matter of much artistic importance, and one upon which the congratulations of the artistic world must be offered to the spirited, hard-working, and musically appreciative town.

LEEDS GRAND THEATRE.

The comic opera "The Merry Duchess" has been performed here during the week, with great success. The libretto is by Mr. G. R. Sims, and as the piece appeals to the English love of horse-racing, and the words are wedded to pretty, tuneful music, it is just the sort of thing to take with the public. "The Merry Duchess" is set to music by Mr. Frederic Clay, who is already known as the composer of "Princess Toto," "Lalla Rookh," and other works. The music altogether is of a decidedly pleasing character, several of the numbers being above the usual average of comic opera. Miss Kate Santley's part of Rowena was taken by Miss Ruby Stuart, who sang and acted in charming style. Her opening song, "A Maiden is like the Bird that's free," was given in a manner that at once made her a favourite with the audience, and this lady deserves praise for her share in the duet with Brabazon, "Love's Memories," which was encored, also for her exquisite rendering of the pretty Spanish love-song, "I'm the gay Chatelaine." Miss Haidee Crofton played the Duchess of Epsom Downs in a bright and intelligent manner, and sang with excellent effect, "A Duchess, I've an easy task," and was heard to advantage in the sestet and chorus "Oh, cruel day!" Mr. Joseph Pierpont as Captain Walker, was encored for his song "Take me a Message, oh, Bird of the Sky!" Mr. Sidney Harcourt was sufficiently amusing as Brabazon, and was very successful in the vocal portions that fell to his share. The choruses and concerted pieces were all rendered in capital style, notably "The Tigers' Chorus," "Love's Memories," the chorus of jockeys and girls, the pretty vocal waltz "Love is a fairy," and others. Altogether, "The Merry Duchess," both as regards words and music, is just the style to suit the public taste, and there is no reason why this opera should not become as popular in the provinces as it has been in London.

BOW AND BROMLEY INSTITUTE.

On Monday, September 17th, a good concert was given in the above Institute, the vocalists being Madame Clara West, Miss Lottie West, Mr. Bevan Jones (in place of Mr. Fredericks), Mr. Frederick Bevan, and the St. Paul's Glee Union; solo pianist, Miss Ettie Wieland; accompanist, Mr. Arthur Dorey. Encores were deservedly scored by Madame and Miss West, Mr. Bevan and Miss Wieland, and the concert was altogether a musical success, although the attendance was not quite so large as could have been desired.

LIVERPOOL.

(From our own Correspondent).

SEPT. 18.

The Carl Rosa English Opera season came to an end on Saturday evening last with a scratch performance of "Mignon" in place of the announced "Maritana," several of the artists being indisposed. Madame Roze scored another triumph in the assumption of Colomba during the engagement. It is a character well suited to her and gives scope for her artistic acting; she also gained golden opinions for her fine conception of Marguerite in Gounod's "Faust." Madame Burns as Esmeralda has also a part in every way fitted to her, and she has also the proud position of being able to count another success among the many already won. Mr. Ben Davies is making rapid progress in his profession; his voice is gaining strength and his acting more finish.

The remaining old members of the troupe still retain all their many excellences. Mr. Goosens is sole conductor now, and thoroughly up to his work. Every opera has been thoroughly well staged, and the season of a fortnight has been a great success in every way. The Company return to Liverpool at Christmas for a six weeks season at the Court Theatre.

The new Philharmonic Choral Society (the old chorus of the Liverpool Philharmonic Society) have secured Mr. A. Randegger for conductor. It is said that the guarantee fund is very large and that the Society has met with much sympathy and support.

J. J. M.

ELY CATHEDRAL.—The mother church of the diocese has set the example of again commemorating the annual in-gathering of the harvest, by special thanksgiving services. A special and appropriate Service was given. The anthem was a selection from Dr. Chipp's oratorio, "Naomi," being three choruses, "Songs of gladness," etc., "To the Lord of the Harvest," etc., and "Blessed be the name," etc. It was very effectively rendered and strongly impressive by its individuality both of conception and treatment. Generally the style is distinctly Mendelssohnian. During the offertory, hymn No. 365, Ancient and Modern, was sung, then followed the benediction, by the Very Rev the Dean. The recessional hymn was No. 386, Ancient and Modern.

BRAY, DUBLIN.—A very pleasant and excellent concert was given in the New Town Hall, Bray, on September 5th. The tasteful and careful performance of the various pieces gave much satisfaction to the audience. The programme included: chorus, "All people that on earth do dwell" (Tallis); solo, recit. "Alas! I find," and aria "If guiltless blood" (Handel), Miss Adelaide Mullen; chorus, "Morning Prayer" (Mendelssohn); solo, "Bussiled" (Beethoven), Mr. Walter Bapty; solo, "O trusting heart" (Bach), Mrs. J. Bewley; duet, "Children, pray this love to cherish" (Spohr), Miss Adelaide Mullen, and Mr. Walter Bapty; quartet, "Vintage Song" (Mendelssohn); solo, "Oh! who can guess my emotion" (Mendelssohn), Mrs. J. C. Manley; duet, "When the wind bloweth in from the sea" (Smart), Mrs. J. Bewley, and Mr. R. Blair White; chorus, "Come, Dorothy, come" Swabian volkslied. Miss Ffennell and Miss Barrington were the pianists.

In the *Voyage of the Wanderer*, a new and interesting book of travels by C. and T. Lambert, a performance on the nose flute, an instrument to be found in the Islands of the Eastern seas, is thus described: "Now we hear a deep whistling sound, varying up and down only two or three notes, and find a lot of natives playing on nose flutes made of bamboo. To perform on these you block up one nostril with your thumb, while the fingers belonging to the same hand extend along the instrument, and with the other nostril you play your tune—if you know how! The effect produced is very like that of the sign of contempt called by boys 'taking a sight.'"

Foreign Musical Intelligence.

"PHOSPHOR'S" ACCOUNT OF MUSIC ABROAD.

I have written so many articles about music in the metropolis, that I think I may be allowed now in the off-season to describe familiarly an *al fresco* concert abroad. In these pages have appeared some remarks on the condition of musical taste in Holland. Let us now turn to Germany, the land of highly classical performances, and see what they give their admirers on warm summer evenings to satisfy their harmonious longings.

The ecstasy of some people when they speak of *al fresco* entertainments generally, and open-air concerts abroad in particular, is, to say the least of it, embarrassing. Take that well-known pleasure town, Baden-Baden, and let us see what entertainment is afforded, particularly to the tourist who visits there. We recal Campbell's well-known line :—"'Tis distance lends enchantment to the view," and we feel inclined to say that perhaps Baden-Baden round the corner might meet with a more qualified approval.

I had so frequently heard of the charms of these meetings in the open air, not only from those who had visited the place, but from glowing newspaper paragraphs, that the words "enchanting," "fairy-like," somehow came to be associated in my mind with these assemblies. I had heard that the music played in the Kiosk was perfection, the promenade delightful, and the whole thing a scene of intoxicating revelry.

When Baden-Baden was a very haughty place, and visited by very haughty people, we had plenty of evidence to prove that it had its peculiar attractions ; but all these have been so eloquently described that I don't think any one would thank me if I tried to repaint an old picture. I want more particularly to speak of Baden-Baden, the sedate, the demure—in a word, the Baden-Baden of the present day, and especially to note its musical attractions.

He must indeed be a barbarian who cannot enjoy its lovely walks, its salubrious atmosphere, and its hundred healthy substantial charms. All this I allow, but these are its daylight amusements, and I would speak of its evening attractions, its *al fresco* concerts, its lamp-lit promenades, and its lovers' seats. I would write of its thousands of cane-bottom chairs, its hundreds of street lamps, and its interminable winding walks, laid out with tables like an extended tea garden. I would visit its restaurant, drink of its questionable coffee, smoke its bad cigars, and occasionally indulge in its raw ham sandwiches. Baden-Baden is indeed now demure ; she is more, she is shy. Walk through the splendid rooms of the "Conversation House," you will hear nothing but the sound of your own footfall. Try to conjure up the perturbed ghosts that perhaps look down upon the scene of their destruction ; the gambling tables are empty, the very air of the rooms has a vault-like odour about it, and you half expect to see a mildew gathering on the neglected walls.

But something still remains for those who do not care about perpetually walking, like Vathek, through these halls of Eblis. It has its celebrated orchestra, and we have come expecting to hear a grand concert. Our landlord of the Victoria has prepared us for a treat ; besides, the "Badeblatt" has a startling announcement in large type, "Grosses Solisten—concert des Stadtischen Orchesters," under the direction of Kapellmeister Kœnnemann, and Herr Kœnnemann had written a grand symphony (so it was named to me). Great interest was exhibited by the inhabitants of the place and the visitors, and even the members of the orchestra regarded it as a work of some pretensions.

Let me try and describe this novelty. It was divided into four parts, the first, opening with a chorus of huntsmen, a long way off, who, not contented with remaining at a distance, soon made themselves thoroughly heard, and vigorously engaged the attention of every member of the orchestra. This, after a good many modulations, lapsed into a kind of Tyrolese waltz, and so brought the first part to an end. The second seemed to resemble a shepherd's festival, and the oboe had a long solo, then came a chorus with a good many born passages in it. It was called in the programme *Landliche scene*, but it can hardly be said to have come to a conclusion peaceably, and I at once felt convinced that a storm was brewing, which proved to be correct, for no sooner had the third part commenced with the waltz-like movement of the first part than it was interrupted by a burst of the most startling character. I have heard a good many storms illustrated by music, but they have been mere tea-cup convulsions when compared with this commotion. Not only did the conductor keep his instrumentalists hard at work, but he introduced a lively accompaniment of theatrical wind and pea-pattering rain. The lightning was rather vague, but the thunder made up for it, and seemed to shake the very kiosk. I was only delighted when it was somewhat abated, and a full peal of church bells chimed out their thankfulness, which was evidently shared by some of the audience. But the storm was not fully vanquished until the fourth part commenced, without a pause, and human voices, in conjunction with the orchestra, burst into a grand "Te Deum."

So came to conclusion a work that had not only exhausted the members of the orchestra, but the patience of some of the audience also, many of whom, remembering a celebrated "Pastoral," could not help asking themselves whether the present work was intended as a burlesque. A great deal that would have delighted the Wagnerites was decidedly in it, and much that emulated the genius of Liszt with a strong dash of Jullien's method was there ; but, shade of Beethoven ! is this the serious music of the great German school? Herr Kœnnemann might repeat the words of an obscure symphony writer, who after waiting ten years, got one of his works produced, and exclaimed joyfully, at the conclusion, "When it was finished the audience said they were delighted."

The maestro Ponchielli has written a new opera with the title "Marion Delorme."

Planquette's "Cloches de Corneville" has been played 900 times at the Folies Dramatiques, Paris.

Méhul's semi-sacred opera "Joseph" has been given lately in Berlin with success, Herr Schott taking part in the performances.

Benjamin Godard is at work on a new opera called "Pedro de Zalamea," which is to be produced in Antwerp in January, 1884.

The late examination of pupils at the Conservatoire in Paris gives promise of vocalists of both sexes likely to prove a valuable acquisition to the lyrical theatres.

The Cologne Town Theatre began a course of opera on August 31st with Meyerbeer's "Huguenots." During the winter Liszt's "St. Elizabeth" will be given.

The Bremen Town Theatre opened its first season this month with a good performance of "Demetrius," directed by Angelo Neumann. The next opera given was Gluck's "Armida."

A new musical and theatrical paper, entitled *Frou-Frou*, has been started at Buenos-Ayres. It is printed in no less than four languages : English, French, Italian, and Spanish.

Teresina Tua, the violinist, will give two concerts in Leipsic next month in conjunction with the pianist Robert Tischof. The two artists have already accepted eighty-three engagements.

The Hamburg Town Theatre began its tenth season on Sept. 1st, under the direction of Herr Pollini. The subscriptions reached the sum of half-a-million marks. Next month a new opera, "Schloss de l'Orme," by Herr Kleinmichel will be produced.

During the past week, "Lohengrin," "Oberon," and "The Flying Dutchman," have been admirably performed at Frankfurt, attracting many visitors from Homburg, among the latter, Mr. and Mrs. Arthur Coleridge and their accomplished daughters.

An obliging friend sends programmes of music performed recently by small orchestras in two of the chief Cafés in Milan. These include overtures "Otello" (Rossini), "La Figlia del Raggimento" (Donizetti) ; "Polinto," by the same composer "Euryanthe" (Weber) ; and "Giralda" (Cagnoni) ; "Dance of Sylphes" (Berlioz) ; with Marches, etc., from the works of Meyerbeer, Verdi, etc., together with operatic selections and good specimens of the Austrian school of dance music, by Strauss and others.

The life of Tourguénief, the recently departed great Russian novelist, contains one passage which reveals much of the cause of the success of that painstaking *littérateur ;* he was in the habit of writing out his works at great length, then he "boiled them down" by careful weeding and reduction into short stories. Would that our composers might be induced to bestow the same care over their works. Cipriani Potter is said to have been told by Beethoven that he wrote out his Second Symphony six times over before he was satisfied with it. Such examples ought to be of guidance and encouragement to the producing artist.

An American writer says : "In the history of great campaigns we often read of the useless destruction of fine art works, through the mistaken zeal of soldiers. They mean to do their duty and aim to serve their country well, yet who can excuse such vandalism ? So critics often injure artists and art-works, meaning, no doubt, well, and desiring to advance the interests of the art they love. Still, theirs is vandalism, only in a different direction." Was this thought evolved after reading the *Times ?*

Organ News.

LIVERPOOL.

An organ recital was given in St. George's Hall, by Mr. W. T. Best, on Thursday, September 13th. The following was the programme :—

Military March (Posthumous Work)	Beethoven.
Adagio (F sharp major) }	W. T. Best.
Allegro Maestoso (C minor) }	
Bourrée (B minor) and Organ Fugue (G major)	Bach.
Romanza—" Spirto Gentil"	Donizetti.
Marche Funèbre (B flat minor)	EugèneGigout.
Overture, " Zanetta "	Auber.

And on Saturday, September 15th :—

Overture, " Idomeneo "	Mozart.
Pastorale (E major)	C. Franck.
Prelude and Fugue (A minor)	Bach.
March—" La Garde passe "	W. T. Best.
Adagio Solenne (D flat major)	Dussek.
Rondo de' Campanelli	Morandi.

CRYSTAL PALACE.

Mr. Eyre's programme, on Saturday last, included the following :—

Fantasia and variations	Freyer.
Barcarolle, " Ou voulez vous aller "	Gounod.
Overture, " Egmont "	Beethoven.
Fugue in D minor	Bach.
Air, " Nazareth "	Gounod.
Andante from D minor (Concerto)	Moranz.
" Schlummerlied "	Schumann.
Elevation (Romanza and Choral)	Stark.
Gavotte, " Mignon "	Thomas.
Grand Chœur	Salomé.

OLDHAM.

Recent recitals upon the organ built by Conacher and Co., at the Fine Art Exhibition have included :—

By Mr. W. Standsfield :—

Introduction and Double Fugue	Merkel.
" March Triomphale "	Lemmens.

By Mr. Wm. Mullineux, F.C.O. :—

Fantasia de Concert sur " O Sanctissima ! "	Lux.
Grand March Triomphale in A flat	Mullineux.
" Improvisation "	
Organ Sonata in F minor	Mendelssohn.
Toccata and Fugue in D minor	Bach.
Canzone in A minor	Guilmant.
Grand Fantasia in E minor (representing a storm)	Lemmens.
Overture, " Jubilee "	Weber.

By Mr. Herbert Chadwick :—

Adagio	Best.
Larghetto	Richardson.
March, upon a Theme of Handel	Guilmant.

By Mr. W. A. Wrigley :—

Largo and Allegro (Concerto in D)	Handel.
Allegro in B minor	Guilmant.
Gavotte in C	Tours.
Slow Movement (Symphony in D)	Beethoven.
Air, " In native worth "	Haydn.
Impromptu in G	Hiles.
Air with variations	Lemmens.
Selection, " Pinafore "	Sullivan.

CORNWALL.

The re-opening of the organ and the in-gathering of the harvest were celebrated yesterday in Morval Church. There has been an organ in this church for many years, but some five months ago it was found necessary to entirely reconstruct it. The work was entrusted to Messrs. Hele and Company, of Plymouth, and with most satisfactory results. The old organ has really been absorbed in a new and larger one. The organ is built in a handsome and costly oak case, chastely carved. It is a complete instrument, with two Manuals, the front pipes being of spotted metal.

ABERDARE.

Mr. Alfred Monk, of London, has just built and erected the new organ in Aberaman Church. The organ has two Manuals and Pedals, with some twenty-six stops and six composition pedals. Case of pitch pine, front pipes decorated in gold and colours. The organ is blown by hydraulic engine.

LEEDS.

An organ recital was given in the Town Hall, on Sept. 15th, by Dr. Spark. The programme ran thus :—

Fantasia with a Chorale in G major	Smart.
Andante in C major	Mendelssohn.
Funeral March in B flat minor	Chopin.
Andante, " The hymn of Nuns "	Wely.
New Concert-satz for the organ	Dienel.
" Reminiscences of the Opera " (" Don Giovanni ")	Mozart.

FISHERIES EXHIBITION.

The following organ recitals have been given during the last week by Mr. J. Loaring, F.C.O. The programmes included :—

Overture, " Crown Diamonds "	Auber.
Gavotte, " Daphne "	Sturges.
Fugue in G minor	Bach.
" La Caritá "	Rossini.
Offertoire in B flat	Collet.
Grand March from " Carmen "	Bizet.

Overture, " Semiramide "	Rossini.
Gavotte, " La Fontaine "	Arnaud.
Fugue in D minor	Bach.
Adagio from 6th quartet	Beethoven.
Minuet	Kontski.
March, " Aux Armes "	Farráis.

Overture, " Sophonisbe "	Paer.
Danse Antique	Greebe.
Fugue in E	Bach.
Andante in G	Batiste.
Allegro con brio	H. H. Turpin.
March Past	Laimothe.

And on Friday, September 14th, by Mr. Harry Witmer.—

Grand Offertoire	Batiste.
Andante in G	"

And by Master Henry J. Wood :—

" Marche des Jacobins "	Scotson-Clark.
Offertoire in G	Lott.
Andante	Beethoven.
March, " Lebanon "	Smallwood.
" March aux Flambeaux "	Scotson-Clark.

And by Mr. Ernest Taunton :—

" The Bride's March "	Loaring.
" March of the Crusaders "	Sibley.

And by Mr. Churchill Sibley :—

Cathedral Melody, " The Reaper "	Meir.
" March of the Crusaders "	Sibley.
" Improvisation "	
Cathedral March	Sibley.

And on Saturday, and Tuesday, September 15th and 18th, by Mr. Freeman Dovaston, A.C.O. :—

Festal March	Hivey.
Andante in E minor	Batiste.
Postlude in E flat	Wely.
Organ Voluntary	Heron.
March in C	Grunnes.
Allegro Pomposo	Smart.
Triumphal March	Doll.

Allegro from " P. F. Sonata "	Mozart.
Introduction, air and variations	Chrahne.
Adagio	Beethoven.
March from " Elf "	Costa.
Offertoire in F	Batiste.
Postlude in E flat	Wely.

The programme of the recital by Mr. Edward J. K. Toms, R.A.M., on Wednesday, September 19th, was :—

March in F	Wallis.
Allegro Moderato, in A	Smart.
Air à la Bourrée	Handel.
March," Eroica,"	Hime.
Andante Cantibile, from 4th Concerto	Bennett.
Allegro con Spirito	Gladstone.
March (Festive)	Elvey.

And by Mr. Edwin Barnes :—

Organ Sonata	Mendelssohn.
Adagio in F minor	C. E. Stephens.
Fugue, " St. Ann's "	Bach.
Allegretto, from " Lobgesang "	Mendelssohn.
March, " Undine "	Bénedict.
Andante, from Symphony	Haydn.
Overture, in E minor	Morandi.

And by Mr. Harold Stidolph :—

Offertoire in F	Batiste.
Finale to 3rd Symphony	Mendelssohn.
Andante	Wely.
Adagio from Quartet in E flat	Schubert.
Offertoire in E	Batiste.
Andante from 3rd Symphony	Haydn.

And by Mr. Churchill Sibley :—

Cathedral March	Sibley.
March of the Crusaders	Sibley.

COPPERHOUSE.

An organ recital was given in the Wesleyan Chapel on September 14th, by Mr. H. C. Tonking, R.A.M. The programme included :—

Overture, " Occasional Oratorio "	Handel.
Postlude in D	Smart.
Andante in F	Wely.
Postlude in C minor	Smart.
Fantasia on a Theme by Weber	E. H. Turpin.
Grand Chorus	Guilmant.
" Hallelujah Chorus "	Handel.

BECKENHAM, KENT.

Mr. Eustace Ingram has just completed an effective organ for the New Baptist Chapel. The instrument has two manuals and pedals, 22 stops, and five composition pedals.

GLASGOW.

An organ recital was given in the Cathedral, on Sept. 15th, by Dr. A. L. Peace. The following was the programme:

Offertoire in D—minor and major	Wely.
Pastorale and Scherzo (organ symphonies)	Widor.
Aria, " Pietà Signore" ("San Giovanni Batista ")	Stradella.
Toccata and Fugue in F major	Bach.
Song without words	Mendelssohn.
March of the Crusaders ("St. Elizabeth ")	Liszt.

TOWCESTER.

On Thursday, Sept. 13th, the renovation of the fine old Church was fitly completed by re-opening Services, and an organ recital was given in the afternoon by Mr. E. H. Turpin, with another short recital after the Evening Service. The church-goers of Towcester are numerous and in earnest, making good use of their beautiful, ancient church, which is at last again to be seen to advantage with its fine nave and stately proportions, its old monuments and choice carved wood-work. The choir is under the careful training of the painstaking organist, Mr. Edwin Hunt, who ably presided at the organ during the Services upon this occasion. The organ, which is a truly musical one, with some fine toned and carefully voiced stops, has been rebuilt, and this work has been admirably executed by Mr. W. J. Richardson, of Camberwell Road. The instrument has now 3 Manuals and Pedal organ, with some 37 stops, and the usual array of composition pedals. The exquisitely carved old case has not been thrown aside but utilized to advantage. The instrument now stands on the north side of the chancel, close to the choir seats. The opening Services were continued on Sunday last.

BIRMINGHAM.

Recently a special musical service was held in St. Martin's Church, Bull Ring, in connection with the re-opening of the organ, which has recently been renovated and enlarged, and by the introduction of many modern improvements made a more complete instrument than it formerly was. The attractive nature of the Service, coupled with the announcement that the sermon would be preached by the Very Rev. the Dean of Lichfield, induced the attendance of a crowded congregation. The opening portion of the ordinary form of evening prayer was used, stopping at the third collect, and in place of the anthem, there was substituted Mendelssohn's "Lauda Sion" (Praise Jehovah). This beautiful composition was admirably rendered throughout by the choir. Immediately after the "Lauda Sion," followed the sermon, which was preached, according to announcement, by the Very Rev. the Dean of Lichfield. Many of the congregation remained to hear the organ recital by Mr. W. Brookes, R.A.M., who rendered, among other selections, Macfarren's Religious March, andante con moto (Guilmant) and a piece by Merkel was admirdbly renoered. These compositions were well calculated to test the enhanced capabilities of the organ, and it was admitted to have been made into a really fine instrument. It is a great pity that upon these occasions better arrangements are not made, whereby the people may hear their organists fully employ the resources of the instrument. A long sermon, in a close, hot church, and the wrong-headed closing of the Service, when the clergyman has had his say, disorganizes the congregation, and the music which they came to listen to as part of the Service is not fairly treated.

Organ builders and Church authorities, etc., should read Mr. George H. Birch's interesting Cantor lecture on the "Decorative Treatment of Metal in Architecture," now printed in the *Journal of the Society of Arts*.

At the Bow and Bromley Institute, to-night, the first organ recital of the season will be given by that accomplished player, Mr. Walter Parratt, with an admirable, classical programme, the correct key will be found. On Monday next, the opening concert will take place. Vocalists :—Miss Anna Williams, Miss Damain, Mr. Redfern Hollins, and Mr. Chaplin Henry. Solo violin, Signor Erba; piano and organ, Mr. F. Meen,

POINTS IN PIANOFORTE TEACHING.

By HENRY G. HANCHETT.

It can scarcely be maintained that the teaching of musical theory is properly to be expected of those who engage to give piano lessons. Musical theory is a subject by itself, and should be taken up as a separate branch by those who expect to become musicians. Still, there are certain matters of theory that it is necessary for any person to know in order that he should be able to study piano compositions intelligently, and fully comprehend criticisms and the remarks of a good teacher, and the object of the present article is to call attention to some of these points that are too often neglected.

The theoretical distinctions in melodic notes are rarely explained to pupils, but they ought to understand which notes are harmonic, which passing notes, and which appoggiaturas at least, especially as these can be easily defined and easily remembered. An harmonic note is accented and harmonized, a passing note is neither accented nor harmonized, and an appoggiatura is accented but not harmonized. A pupil who can distinguish these notes by their definitions can tell, in studying a composer who wrote in the last century, whether any small notes that may be found are to be regarded as appoggiaturas or grace notes, that is, whether such small notes are to have half the time of the following notes, or to be merely hurried over as embellishments.

Again, this knowledge helps when small notes are written, and it becomes a question whether they are to be played in advance of the whole chord in large notes, or only in advance of one note of that chord, and *with* all the remaining notes. Scales, too, especially the minor scales, are very poorly understood by the ordinary piano pupil. Why are there three minor scales? Why do they borrow their signatures instead of having one of their own? And why does the same scale consist of two sets of notes, according to some instructors, which are different according as the scale goes up or down?—an arrangement that is in my opinion all nonsense. These questions, perhaps, never occur to the pupil, but they should be suggested and answered by the teacher.

Then in connection with the scales comes the question of embellishments that are founded on a part of the scale, like the turn and trill. Most pupils are guided entirely by their ears in forming these graces, not knowing that they must be formed from the notes of the scale, unless accidentals occur in connection with the signs, indicating that an alteration is desired.

Even the key of some more elaborate compositions is not readily decided by pupils for lack of systematic instruction as to how it is determined. Where there is but one key used in a composition it is an easy matter to decide what it is ; but some pieces are in minor and end with a major concord, others begin in one and end in another key, and still others never seem decided. In all such cases it is the last tonic in connection with the signature that must decide the matter. Thus a Bach fugue in minor ending in a major chord always has the tonic and not the relative major concord. This was because the theorists of Bach's time held that the minor chord was imperfect, and not to be used in a final cadence. This use of a single major chord, however, does not make the key of the piece major, but taking the tonic in connection with the signature, the correct key will be found. In pieces like Chopin's Scherzo, Op. 31, which is in different keys, the last key must always govern in giving a name to the piece. This is often called the Scherzo in B flat minor, but it is the Scherzo in D flat major, and I do not know of a single musical authority that does not so make the rule. Some say that the key of a piece is that in which it both begins and ends, but *all* say that it is that in which it ends. There are a few pieces like Schumann's "Child falling asleep" in the "Kinderscenen," that never end, but simply stop. In such cases the ear must decide the key, which it is not often difficult to do.

Different forms and styles of compositions should be explained as they are met in practice, and in this connection some idea of a composer's nationality and period should be given, and his preference in composition. Moreover, every pupil should know the difference between a concord and discord, at least ought to recognize that the one may be, and the other can never be, a satisfactory concluding chord. The distinction between a resolution and a modulation, and the difference between different kinds of chords would not carry the teacher too far into musical theory, and would be of great service to the pupil.—*American Art Journal.*

NEW ENGLAND CONSERVATORY OF MUSIC.

BOSTON, UNITED STATES.

The handsomely got up prospectus says that " The Conservatory System of musical instruction was first introduced by the Director into America in 1853. The Musical Institute in which this advance was made, chartered by the Statein 1859, soon developed into the Providence Conservatory of Music, at Providence, R.I. To secure advantages nowhere to be found outside of the largest cities, the institution was, in February, 1867, removed to Boston, where commodious quarters were secured in the famous Music Hall ; and in 1870, by a special act of the legislature of Massachusetts, incorporated under the name of the New England Conservatory of Music. Here its growth was such that it soon became the largest music school in the world. In the brief history of the school more than 30,000 have enjoyed its advantages, and gone forth to exert their influence for good, in the refinement of public taste and in the elevation of society. Of its graduates, many are filling responsible and lucrative positions as teachers, organists, etc., while others, as solo artists and professors, have attained a most honorable distinction at home and in foreign countries. So high is the esteem in which the training is held, that even the large numbers graduated from year to year do not suffice to supply the public demand for teachers who have enjoyed it. This growth and the needs and possibilities of the Conservatory System and of the combination of musical with general culture, led to the purchase of its new estate on Franklin Square, forming the New England Conservatory.

" The new building is on Newton and James Streets, fronting on Franklin Square,—a beautiful park adorned with fountains, flowers, trees, etc. The building has seven stories and a dome, is 185 feet on Newton Street and 210 feet on James Street, and has rooms for 550 lady students. The new concert-hall will have a large organ, stage, etc., and seats for 2,500. Besides library, reading-room, parlours, offices, etc., there are steam laundries, bath-rooms, hot and cold water, steam heat, gas, and two elevators, and three broad, easy flights of stairs running from basement to attic. Telephone office is in the building.

" The branches of instruction embrace fifteen separate schools in all ; viz :—

" A school for the piano.
" A school for the organ.
" A school for singing, formation and cultivation of the voice, lyric art and opera.
" A school for the violin, orchestra, quartet, and *ensemble* playing.
" A school for all orchestral and band instruments, and art of conducting.
" A school for harmony, composition, theory, and orchestration.
" A school for church music, oratorio and chorus practice.
" A school for training music teachers for public schools, etc.
" A school for tuning pianos and organs.
" A school for physical culture.
" A college of music.
" A school for common and higher English branches, and, for those who are fitted for it, a college course in connection with the college of liberal arts of Boston University.
" A school of languages, especially Italian, German, and French.
" A school of elocution and dramatic action—the largest of its kind in America.
" A school of fine arts."

The admirable and educational Orchestral Concerts, 1883-4, given in the Town Hall, Birmingham, under the very able direction of Mr. Stockley, are to be continued this season in a series of four concerts, to take place on Nov. 8th, Dec. 13th, Feb. 7th, and April 24th. The vocalists will be Mdme. Lemmens-Sherrington, Miss Anna Williams, Miss Clara Samuell, Mdme. Patey, Mr. Edward Lloyd, Mr. Maas, Mr. Franklin Clive, and Signor Foli. Solo pianoforte, Miss Agnes Miller ; solo violin, Mr. Carrodus ; solo contrabasso, Mr. Reynolds ; solo organ, Mr. Stimpson ; duet violin, Messrs. Abbott and Ward. The selections for the season are to include the " Eroica " Symphony (Beethoven) ; B flat Symphony (Schumann) ; the " Scotch " Symphony (Mendelssohn) ; Serenade (Stanford) ; Scotch Rhapsody (Mackenzie) ; Rhapsody Norwegienne (Svendsen) ; "Tempest " Music (Sullivan) ; New Overture (Herbert Wareing) ; Two Sketches (Anderton) ; Intermezzo (Edward Elgar) ; etc.

PRINCIPAL CONTENTS OF THIS NUMBER.

LONDON : SATURDAY, SEPTEMBER 22, 1883.

FORM IN VOCAL MUSIC.

VIII.

THE musical setting of the Canticles is comparatively rarely done in the Roman Church, in the Liturgy of which the Canticles occupy a less prominent position than elsewhere ; but this is a constant musical necessity in the Anglican Church ; and is a matter calling for much constructive thought and skill.

No greater difficulty in the architectural laying out of Church music can indeed be named probably than the one to be encountered in the construction of the " Te Deum." This fine Canticle, so full of glorious praise and prayerful fervour, has a want of coherent continuity in its construction ; and terminating as it does with a prayerful attitude without recovering the glow of thankful praise with which it opens, it presents, to the composer a juxtaposition of verbal sentiments which in their proper treatment disarranges the usual musical principles of the presentation, development, and recapitulation of ideas. It has been my privilege to know something of a learned, thoughtful, and masterly analysis of the "Te Deum laudamus" by Mr. H. S. HUME. The author in this essay explains with much clearness the historical development and doctrinal growth of this venerable and precious heritage of the Church. Though commonly ascribed to the time of ST. AMBROSE, its origin must be dated from a much earlier period, when the Christians made their belief in the divinity of their great Master the watchword of their lives, and when the full doctrinal position of the Church was, though acknowledged, not formulated as in after ages. The original fragments of the great hymn of the Church militant forming a post-communion hymn addressed with gladdened hearts to CHRIST, and triumphantly declaring that, "we praise Thee, O GOD, " we acknowledge *Thee* to be the LORD," were incorporated into the complete doctrinal exposition as now in daily use in Church. This growth of the hymn, by the involution of a wide doctrinal scope, and the consequent changed nature of what was in the first instance a fervid, adoring personal address, has undoubtedly complicated the composer's task of treating the words with judgment and effect. It would repay the thoughtful composer, indeed, if he were closely to examine the structure of the hymn as it now stands, and compare it with its more primitive outlines. As now read, the "Te Deum laudamus" has several distinct outbursts of praise combined with, the doctrinal recognition of the three-fold Unity of the Blessed Trinity. Thus, we have the opening sentences, next the "Ter Sanctus," then the separate acknowledgment of the three persons of the Trinity in Unity; and, lastly, the outburst, "Day by day " we magnify Thee." Here, then, are several distinct and emphatic utterances calling for dignified, grand and praiseful musical periods, and these passages form the bright lights so to speak of the hymn. Then, it is the composer's task to distinguish solemnly the central doctrine of the Incarnation and the prayerful address to the Incarnate One, during the rendering of which in ancient times and still in the Roman Church, the people kneel in solemn meditation. Then there are to be severally treated the general and personal sentiments of prayer which bring the hymn to a close. The simplest and perhaps most obvious method of musically treating the "Te Deum laudamus" is by the adoption of either a modified binary or episodical form. Thus the primary subject of praise may be brought round again at the words "Day by day"; the "Ter Sanctus" naturally receives a distinct treatment, and the setting of prayerful sentences following the declaration of the Incarnation, may with judicious modification be resumed, in manner if not in actual detail, at the pronunciation of the closing sentences. The setting of this great Canticle, the "Te Deum laudamus," may call for some further consideration presently.

E. H. TURPIN.

THE LOGIC OF COUNTERPOINT.

THIRD SERIES.

XIII.

NATURALLY CHERUBINI does not find it necessary to give further rules for the conduct of florid or fifth species counterpoint in four parts. His directions for the practice of writing florid counterpoint, however, are judicious, and deserve notice. He proposes that the student shall first write such a counterpoint in one part, then in two parts, and lastly in three parts, occupying, of course, all the voices save the one sustaining the *canto fermo.* Thus the student is led on to the composition of the only contrapuntal combination of general utility. It may, perhaps, be asked, Why is it necessary to spend so much preliminary thought and labour on the practice of the different species preceding the fifth, when the last-named species is the only one in constant use, and when the other kinds are only exceptionally employed at any sustained length?. It would be impossible to answer so wide a question to the satisfaction of all, for no two minds can be measured together as regards their aptitude for unaided production, clear-sightedness, or sense of reliance upon rules or advice. However, the importance of practising the composition of the different contrapuntal species in any number of parts, may surely be realised by the usually stated theoretical truism that florid counterpoint is made up of a mixture of the foregoing species garnished with a modicum of quavers. So that the power acquired by sustained effort and practice in the treatment of notes of any distinct kind or value must be useful and requisite mentally, just as the executant physically requires to have a greater command over the mechanisms of a given musical instrument than may be absolutely called for, to all appearance, in the texture of the music to be performed. Again, the practice of writing the different contrapuntal species exercises an influence over the writer's mind in the production and development of a readiness and alertness of thought which is invaluable to the composer. A well drilled contrapuntal mind—this is said, be it observed, without implying pedantic training—is not only strong in the sense of being able to control with definiteness of purpose and clearness of outline the parts forming the melodic *strata* of a score, but it is stored with a faculty and aptitude for the utilization of particles of musical ideality which is indeed one of the most necessary functions of the useful composer. The mind of the productive artist has been compared, as regards its fructifying powers and cultivation, to land. It is true that natural power produces trees, herbs, and grass, but the successful growth of corn and fruit, more especially necessary as food for mankind, can only come of a painstaking cultivation under which lies the Divine ordinance, not to say consecration, "labour." The land must be ploughed, and the seed sown before there can be any hope of a harvest. So the composer must cast his ideas into the well prepared and receptive ground of a trained musical mind. The would-be inspired — without effort—genius, may, after a struggle ten times more trying than such an effort would be to a musical and mental athlete, knock together an indifferent royalty song; which, from the hand of an untrained writer, must have its construction revised and its accompanying harmonies made ship-shape by the publisher's musical "reader"; but such a self-satisfied composer is helpless when he thinks of approaching the vocal or orchestral score. Action and re-action are usually close upon each other's heels; so now we have the advance of art by earnestly developed technical training met by the Bohemian spirit of artistic license. The contrapuntist must not be misled into such lifelong errors as mistaking training for slavery, license for freedom. So it is well to practise diligently the conduct of the different species *ab uno disce omnes*, first separately, then mixed together, before working at florid counterpoint in four parts, which forms for the most part the staple commodity of the contrapuntal writer; seeing that its successful handling calls for the strong, ready use of all the species, and that quick apprehension and habitual contrapuntal thought which prompts the appropriate application of the types best suited to express or adorn the thought to be enunciated at the time.　　　E. H. TURPIN.

REMINISCENCES OF AN OLD REPORTER.
THE PHILHARMONIC SOCIETY.

The letter of Mr. Charles E. Stephens in your issue for Sept. 8th, reminds me of the "Old Philharmonic" Society, of which this gentleman is now the active and efficient treasurer. My father was a subscriber to the Society for many years, and remembered the meetings in the Argyll Rooms, Regent Street. At that time (1820-40), the subscription for "outsiders" was four guineas for eight concerts, which usually began in March and ended in June. My father was present at a concert when "the finest gentleman in Europe," then Prince Regent, honoured the Society with his presence; one of his black silk stockings, for His Royal Highness appeared in full court dress, had a long "ladder" at the back, but as my father said, "what mattered the unravelled silk with such legs to display!" It is well known that George IV. liked music and was an adept at the violoncello.

The Old Philharmonic went on prosperously, with various conductors, until 1845, when sundry critics of the press made a "dead-set" against the alternate holders of the ivory *baton*, especially poor Sir Henry Bishop, whose taking of the time was always either too slow or too fast! The directors seem to have been intimidated by the "thunder" of the (no longer *leading*) "Jupiter," and they appointed Sir Michael Costa as sole conductor in 1846. Even Sir Michael was assailed with fiery bolts and the "rows" were incessant. Sir Michael, however, weathered the storm, and at last retired spontaneously at the end of a long and honourable reign. He became musical director of the new "Royal Italian Opera" in 1847, and had plenty of work on his hands. Sir Michael signalised his first year at the Philharmonic by producing all the nine Symphonies of Beethoven in rotation; a "sensation" was naturally created in the musical world.

I witnessed the *début* of Vieuxtemps at the Philharmonic concert on Monday, April 19th, 1841, and sat near Mr. Thos. Alsager, then the musical reporter of *The Times*: he wrote nearly a column of complimentary criticism in favour of the famous Belgian, which appeared on the Tuesday; reporters at that time could not put off their notices. Vieuxtemps, in the ensuing month of June, appeared in the course of a *matinée* at Her Majesty's Theatre, which then had a regular concert-room with tiers of boxes. In the course of his solo Vieuxtemps broke a string and retired. A vocalist stood forth like "Moses in the gap," and Vieuxtemps afterwards came on again to conclude his piece. He was a fine fiddler, but a dreadfully dry composer.

It was my good fortune, on June 13th, 1842, to see Mendelssohn conduct his Symphony in A minor, yclept the "Scotch"; his organ performances that year have already been referred to. In the spring of 1847, the year of his untimely death, I heard the great master play Beethoven's Fourth Concerto in G; he had composed about half-a-dozen cadenzas at rehearsal, but at the very last

moment improvised a new one, and kept Sir Michael Costa waiting, at the end of the first movement, for a space, benignantly smiling at the necessarily passive conductor and his trial of patience.

The Society left the Hanover Square Rooms for St. James's Hall about the year 1859 or 1860, but I was then an absentee. After Sir M. Costa's resignation, Wagner and Sir Sterndale Bennett wielded the stick; Wagner only one season, when he encountered a storm of hostile, and I fear spiteful, criticism.

Thirty or forty years ago, the programme always included *two* symphonies, two overtures, and *two* concertos, for violin or pianoforte. The concert was too long, yet it never lasted more than three hours, and was over at about eleven o'clock. Even now, I can never get out of St. James's Hall before that hour, unless I choose to miss some last notable number, a most objectionable proceeding.

Mr. Anderson, the *then* treasurer, was a very agreeable man, and a fundamental believer in the Old Philharmonic. He had very hard work as conductor of the Queen's private band, and like Mahomet's coffin, fluctuated between Windsor and London. Mrs. Anderson will long be remembered as a favourite pianist. She had the honour of giving lessons to the Queen.

I should have said, when speaking of *Mäestro* Mendelssohn, that on one occasion—(I was not present and forget the date)—he ran up the steps of the orchestra, in the Hanover Square Rooms, to reprove one of the players after the performance of his overture, probably the "Isles of Fingal," but no matter. Every artist trembled and turned pale, until the sovereign conductor accosted poor Chipp, of the double drums, who blushed like a peony in buxom May. Chipp had failed to produce one of Mendelssohn's peculiar effects; the master briefly explained his wishes, ran back, smiled at Chipp as much as to say "do you twig?" and repeated the overture, which the audience had encored. The late Dr. Doran, rather prone to "additions and embellishments," told me that Mendelssohn stopped the band in full career when Chipp made this trifling mistake, but the fact is denied, and I reject it accordingly. Mendelssohn once came rather late to a rehearsal, and one of the artists, a wealthy and consequential man, exclaimed: "Mr. Mendelssohn, you have kept the band waiting." Henry Westrop, then a "second fiddle," related the circumstance to me. He added that Mendelssohn urged the directors to dismiss the offending artist, but they declined to do so as he was not only rich but a very valuable servant. Poor Grattan Cooke, the hautboy player, was not so fortunate. The directors got rid of him in 1850, and Cooke wrote a protest, which he sent round to the papers, my own amongst the number. I then wrote for the *Era*. Grattan Cooke used to "play the fool exceedingly" in the orchestra, and neglected his business. Mendelssohn once told him "to go home and practise." The directors made the excuse that Cooke had accepted the leadership of the 2nd Life Guards Band, and could not, therefore, properly fulfil his duties at the Philharmonic. At the Norwich Festival of 1845 Grattan Cooke came forward as a tenor *singer* between the two *bassi* Staudigl and Machin, but the experiment was a failure.

George Hogarth was Secretary of the Society in 1854, or about that time. He wrote the musical notices for the *Morning Chronicle* up to 1846, when he joined the *Daily News*, and Mr. C. L. Grüneisen succeeded him on the *Chronicle*. I sat by Hogarth at one of Mr. Henry Leslie's concerts in 1855, when he was much annoyed at an alteration made in the text of Burns's "Tam O'Shanter," set to music by Howard Glover, the then critic of the *Morning Post*, and a thorough "Jenkins" in style: he used such words as "riant" for smiling—*par example!* Howard Glover was cashiered in 1866, and died almost a pauper, in America. The cause of his dismissal is well known to the initiated; he was a self-conceited, superficial, fellow. Mr. Ella once excluded him from the "Musical Union," whereat poor Howard Glover was dreadfully irate, and wrote a venomous article in his paper. Mr. Stanley Lucas succeeded Mr. Hogarth as Secretary, and Mr. Henry Hersee now fills the post to the satisfaction of every one concerned.

The annotated programmes of the Philharmonic concerts used to be written, at great length, and very ably, by Professor G. A. Macfarren. Dr. Hueffer is now responsible for the editorship; and to him the words of Horatius Flaccus, "brevis esse laboro" are not inapplicable. Long analyses, however, are a mistake, unless the book be supplied to subscribers *before the concert*, so that they may make themselves *au fait* at home. On the same principle, I dislike to see people poring over scores, and pretending to follow the performance. The task must distract the attention and naturally mar the enjoyment. I believe that a great authority, Mr. James Davison, holds the same opinion; Sir George Grove is on "the other side," but the doctor's *dictum*, often laid down in Crystal Palace programmes, has not yet convinced me. Former directors of the Philharmonic, highly respected as musicians, were Mr. McMurdie, Mr. Anderson (already spoken of) and Mr. Williams, the clarinet player.

Spohr played a violin concerto at the Philharmonic some thirty-five years ago, and I heard Moscheles play a pianoforte concerto in the summer of 1861, his last appearance in London.

One fine night, in June, 1842, Sigismond Thalberg was actually hissed, for insulting the classical Philharmonic Society with some sorry *virtuoso* stuff. The Sibilants I happen to know; and one of them still glories in the avowal of the deed.

I heard Thalberg again, in June, 1850, when he was *not* hissed, although he chose so trivial a theme for his variations as the song of Dulcamara the quack-doctor, "Io son ricco," so well rendered by Ronconi at the Royal Italian Opera. I never could bear the *compositions* of Thalberg; his execution is another matter.

A scene occurred at the Philharmonic in 1848 or 1849. Sir Sterndale Bennett's overture, "Parisina," was on the cards, but the composer either found fault with Sir Michael Costa's *tempo*, or sent some curt verbal message to the conductor, expressive of his wishes. Sir Michael took offence, and when the overture came on, walked away, down the stairs that lead to the artists'-room. Mr. Lucas then stepped forward and assumed the *bâton* for the occasion. I was and am still ashamed of the unseemly affair, highly discreditable to *some*-body.

The Philharmonic is prospering under present management. May the Society continue its career, with three cheers for Messrs. C. E. Stephens and Hersee! A. M.

AN EXPERIENCE IN PIANOFORTE PLAYING IN NEW ORLEANS.

"I was loafing around the streets last night," said Jem Nelson, one of the oldest locomotive engineers running into New Orleans, "and as I had nothing to do, I dropped into a concert and heard a slick-looking Frenchman play a piano in a way that made me feel all over in spots. As soon as he sat down on the stool I knew by the way he handled himself that he understood the machine he was running. He tapped the keys way up one end, just as if they were gauges and he wanted to see if he had water enough. Then he looked up, as if he wanted to know how much steam he was carrying, and the next moment he pulled open the throttle and sailed out on the main line as if he was half an hour late.

"You could hear her thunder over culverts and bridges, and getting faster and faster, until the fellow rocked about in his seat like a cradle. Somehow I thought it was old '36' pulling a passenger train, and getting out of the way of a 'special.' The fellow worked the keys on the middle division like lightning, and then he flew along the north end of the line until the drivers went around like a buzz-saw, and I got excited. About the time I was trying to tell him to cut her off a little, he kicked the damper under the machine wide open, pulled the throttle valve way back in the tender, and—Jerusalem—how he did run! I couldn't stand it any longer, and yelled to him that he was pounding on the left side, and if he wasn't careful he'd drop his ash pan.

"But he did not hear. No one heard me. Everything was flying and whizzing. Telegraph poles on the side of the track looked like cornstalks, the trees appeared to be a mud bank, and all the time the exhaust of the old machine sounded like the hum of a bumble bee. I tried to yell out, but my tongue would not move. He went around curves like a bullet, slipped an eccentric, blew out his soft plug, went down grades fifty feet to the mile, and not a confounded brake set. She went by the meeting point at a mile and a half a minute, and calling for more steam. My hair stood up like a cat's tail, because I knew the game was up.

"Sure enough, dead ahead of us was the tail-light of the 'special.' In a daze I heard the crash as they struck, and I saw cars shivered into atoms, people mashed and mangled and bleeding, and gasping for water. I heard another crash as the French professor struck the deep keys away down on the lower end of the southern division, and then I came to my senses. There he was at a dead standstill, with the door of the fire-box of the machine open, wiping the perspiration off his face, and bowing at the people before him. If I live to be a thousand years old, I'll never forget the ride that Frenchman gave me on the piano."—*American Journal.*

TRINITY COLLEGE, LONDON.

The Examiners acting for the Academical Board unanimously decided that no candidate examined displayed such conspicuous merits as to justify the award of the Henry Smart Scholarship, tenable for three years. The Sims Reeves Exhibition, tenable for one year, was awarded to Miss Maud Lee, with high commendation to Miss Eugenie A. Faull. The Sir Julius Benedict Pianoforte Exhibition, tenable for one year, was also awarded to Miss Olive B. St. Clair. In connection with this competition, Miss Maud E. Quick was highly commended, and commendation was bestowed upon Miss Snudden. The members of the Academical Board present were, Messrs. H. J. Stark, Mus.B., Chairman, Gordon Saunders, Mus.D., Bradbury Turner, Mus.B., J. Stedman, and E. H. Turpin, with Mr. Shelley Fisher, the College Secretary.

TWO LETTERS WRITTEN BY WAGNER.

The *Musical Record* gives a translation of two letters. The first letter is addressed to Herr Schelper, the well-known baritone singer:—

Most worthy Herr Schelper,—I hope you will not be in any doubt as to the interest which I take in you. Even if the names of your associates in the performance of the "Ring des Nibelungen" at the Leipzig Theatre were unknown to me, the name alone of the distinguished artist whom I so joyfully greeted a few years ago as Hans Sachs in Bremen, would suffice to assure me of a successful interpretation of the most difficult part of my work. I knew that I was not deceiving myself: everything unanimously confirms my favourable presupposition. I heartily welcome you once more !

I frankly confess to you that the bold line of conduct pursued by your manager causes me great joy. As the matter thus interests me, I would venture to express the wish that there might be a clearer agreement between the scenic action and the orchestra. I am speaking of matters which were only learnt and attended to at the rehearsals which I myself conducted. Try and get your manager (specially for the proposed Berlin performances) to summon to Leipzig the ballet-master, Herr Fricke, from Dessau, and the music-director, Seidel (here), both of whom are intimately acquainted with my wishes; and to give, under their direction, some extra rehearsals, so as to remove imperfection.

With the best good wishes, I remain, yours very truly,
RICHARD WAGNER.
Bayreuth, May 14th, 1878.

The second letter is addressed to Director Franz Jauner, in Vienna, in answer to one written to Wagner giving an enthusiastic account of the success of "Siegfried" in Vienna (November, 1878).

But, dearest friend, how can you be in doubt as to my feelings? Most wonderfully am I affected by performances such as yours in Vienna. Do you think I am blind to the meaning of this success, and to the extraordinary good will which caused it? Formerly, when I published the poem of this work, no one believed in the possibility of its production; this I remember, but still more so the fact that I myself could not dare to hope to be able to give to the public of our theatres the various portions of the work as opera performances. Such a complete and satisfactory performance as that of "Siegfried" to the opera-going public of Vienna was considered ten years ago—yea, think of that!—an almost incredible event, and I am now of the same opinion. I can only say that I am lost in amazement; and how can I be otherwise than thankful !

However, I also know that I could only get the work performed to perfection with the extraordinary contrivances which I have provided for it in Bayreuth. Should I or my successors one day have the opportunity of repeating these stage festival plays, it must then be remembered that some means will have to be employed to replace that which is quite impossible for performances in provincial theatres. Therefore, guided by common sense in the matter, I was the first to propose 'cuts' for ordinary theatre performances, as lately for the "Gotterdämmerung." Siedel, and I think also Richter, know them. That I am forced to regard this as necessary, is indeed the reason why I do not attend these performances, and why I am most unwilling to hear details respecting these changes. This weakness must be forgiven me. A young enthusiast, quite unconnected with the stage described to me the painful impression which the changes in the great concluding scene of "Siegfried" had made on him. It was unpleasant for me to hear of it. Then came to my remembrance my faithful and clever Materna, who from her heart has learnt of me more than any other; I felt persuaded that it must grieve her to sacrifice all the tender transitions

(Uebergänge), which she performed with so much willingness, to a rough pell-mell (Durcheinander); and expressed to her my real regret for what had to be done. Well, that's all!

Oh, L: quite understand that the Viennese, especially those who frequent the pit, want something good to eat and drink about eleven o'clock. I know that perfectly well, and we confess to ourselves that it is unreasonable to demand efforts even for its own enjoyment from a town theatre (evening) public; to meet this difficulty, I especially established my Bayreuth stage festival performances.

I have told you this, dear friend, on the last Vienna evening before the whole public, that only you could have persuaded me to assist an opera theatre in the ennobling of its efforts. I assure you that since then you were not and are not the cause of my refusing to co-operate. Our first attempts and their wonderful success at once convinced me that the state of our modern theatres; and the publicity influencing them on all sides, would render a lasting sympathy on my side impossible. Therefore, all the better if you at least do not lose courage; and if from these wonderful circumstances you gain from time to time something like these "Siegfried" performances, I congratulate you from the bottom of my heart.

I have to beg of you, for the intended representation of the whole work, to give very careful extra study to the "Rheingold"; and, as would seem necessary, in every particular. The fault of giving this prelude between the first and second principal piece is one which you most probably have discovered yourself, and would have remedied even without a suggestion without me.

So good luck to you! You have accomplished much: do still more. From his heart greets you, your devoted

RICHARD WAGNER.

Bayreuth, November 18th, 1878.

Correspondence.

"COUNTERPOINT."

TO THE EDITOR OF THE "MUSICAL STANDARD."

SIR,—I have been away from home, taking a rest from my usual work, or I should have written earlier on the above question. I am very glad, indeed, that you have opened your columns for discussion, and I trust some good may be done by it. I have read all the letters that have appeared, and it would seem, that there is a desire on the part of your correspondents to advocate a system of Free Counterpoint only, based, of course, on Harmony. This is what all musicians desire in the end, and it is generally believed that the study of Strict Counterpoint is the very best means to bring about this freedom in writing. It must be remembered, however, that freedom without power, or force, will be weak and uninteresting. I must also say, that all our greatest composers, Wagner also,—the freest of all,—have been great contrapuntists, and I believe, for one, that the study of Strict Counterpoint cannot be dispensed with.

It is all very well for men who have been training themselves for years to cry out for freedom now; but ask any young gifted composer to write good Free Counterpoint, before he has written a note of Strict, and bad work may with certainty, be predicted. Is it possible for a raw, or average recruit, to fight as well on the battle-field, as a well-trained soldier? Consult any general.

But, supposing we turn again to music, and in doing so we put aside, for a moment, Fugues, etc., and give our attention to that part of a Sonata which is sometimes called the "free fantasia" or the "development portion." I will go a little further, and imagine two musicians, of equal natural ability, engaged in developing and elaborating the two foregoing subjects. If one of these men were a good Contrapuntist, and the other only a good Harmonist, it would soon be found which could produce the best development. There can be no question but that the work of the former would possess more backbone and sinew than that of the latter. It would be seen at once that he (the former), would handle and stick to his themes like a good debater, that he would most likely present one as a bass to the other (if such a combination were possible), and he would do many other things which fancy dictates, because his musical strength would enable him; and this strength would be the natural result of the constant habit of writing one melody against another in Strict Counterpoint. It is, no doubt, very high sounding, to hear Mr. Stark recommend living melodies as canti fermi, but upon a moment's consideration, it will be admitted that this would be more difficult for a beginner than the present system.

It would be nearly equivalent to what is known as writing the 5th Species in several parts. I wish Mr. Stark had practised his system upon some of his pupils before he read his paper, as it would have been exceedingly interesting to have learned the result of his labour.

Apologising for the length of this letter,

I remain, Sir, your humble servant,

X. Y. Z.

"SENNACHERIB."

TO THE EDITOR OF THE "MUSICAL STANDARD."

SIR,—Since the production of the sacred cantata "Sennacherib" by Dr. Arnold at the Gloucester Musical Festival, on the evening of the 5th Sept. last, I have observed the varied and adverse opinions upon the new work, some of which I feel assured were written not with a spirit of premeditated harshness, but in haste and a want of a better acquaintance with the score, and Dr. Arnold's style in former compositions. For some years I have known his "Ahab," and his 23rd Psalm, the latter work being the superior composition (although brief). I have now also before me "Sennacherib," in the performance of which I aided at its production, and my opinion of the work was confirmed by many of my orchestral colleagues, that its merits would be much more fully appreciated upon a second hearing.—Hundreds rejected the works of Spohr and Wagner upon a first hearing, who since have become their most ardent admirers. That the Biblical story of "Sennacherib" was an unfortunate choice for a libretto, is undeniable; therefore admitting that, I think Dr. Arnold has shown considerable skill in its treatment, more especially in the fugal and contrapuntal portions, nor is it deficient in melodic power, as instanced in the Soprano and Tenor Duet.

I am glad to find that the Musical Standard has approached the work in a fair and impartial spirit. Time alone will prove the artistic value of the work.

Yours faithfully,

CARITA.

Sept. 17th, 1883.

Passing Events.

There is reason to doubt the reports of capital being subscribed for the immediate completion of the great opera house on the Thames Embankment.

It would be most desirable to secure a theatre of moderate dimensions for a permanent series of operas in English, at reasonable prices of admission. In London we are already surfeited with musical burlesques of the Offenbach school.

The Social Science Congress is to be held at Huddersfield, from Oct. 3rd to 10th. Art and musical matters are not overlooked by this important and useful body. The President this year is Sir R. Temple, and the President of the Art section will be Sir Rupert A. Kettle.

Mdme. Fraziska Ellmenreich, an eminent German actress, of whose talent report speaks in the highest terms, will make her début on the English stage at the Gaiety Theatre, at a special matinée, on Wednesday, the 26th inst. Mdme. Ellmenreich is said to have a wonderful command of the English tongue.

Mr. Abbey's operatic troupe at the New Metropolitan Theatre, New York, will include the following, Mdmes. Nilsson, Sembrich, Fursch-Madi, Valleria, Scalchi, Tremelli, and Lablache; MM. Stagno, Capoul, Campanini, Kaschmann, Del Puente, Guadagnini, Maini, Novara, and Mirabella. Signor Vianesi will be the conductor.

"Falka," now in rehearsal for the Comedy Theatre, is an adaptation of "Le Droit d'Alnesse," by MM. Leterrier and Vanloo, and music by M. Chassaigne, a Belgian composer. It was produced at the Paris Nouveautes last January. Falka is a young Magyar girl, who by adopting male attire contrives to personate her cowardly brother and take his inheritance, while her lover, who has a beardless face, is sent back to the convent school in mistake for her. The part of the heroine, taken in Paris by Mdlle. Marguerite Ugalde, will be played at the Comedy by Miss Violet Cameron.

The annual festival of Diocesan Church Choirs was held in the Cathedral, Cork, on the 23rd ult., at 3 p.m. A procession was formed in the Cathedral yard of the Bishop, clergy, and one hundred singing men and boys, all surpliced. Evening prayers were then said, and Hymns 41, 356, 448, and 36, of the Irish Church Hymnal, were sung at different parts of the Service. The anthem was Dr. Boyce's "I have surely built," and "Hallelujah to the Father," from Beethoven's "Mount of Olives." The Canticles were sung to Martin's Service in A, and before the Benediction Handel's "Hallelujah Chorus" was sung with grand effect. Mr. J. C. Marks, Mus.Bac. Oxon., presided at the organ with his usual ability. The sermon was preached by the Bishop from the words, "Sing ye praises with understanding" (Psalm xlvii. 7).—Church Bells.

By the advice of his physicians, Sir Michael Costa has resolved to leave Brighton, and to spend the winter in his native Italy.

There seems to be some hope that Sir A. Sullivan's long promised grand opera may now be completed, possibly in time for the next season at the Royal Italian Opera. The work is understood to be "Mary Stuart," which was projected many years ago, and the English libretto of which was sketched by the late Mr. H. F. Chorley, who was one of Sir A. Sullivan's most ardent admirers, and who during the early part of the composer's career and largely advanced his reputation in the columns of the *Athenæum* and elsewhere.

An American musical journal sensibly objects to too much high-flown nonsense being directed against the existence of dance music, and quotes Mozart's saying that "no one can be a good composer who cannot write a good tune." The dance was indeed the progenitor of instrumental music. Mendelssohn delighted in occasional refreshment in the way of a dance with a good tune ; and students of composition may learn much about the management of rhythm, etc., from the dance music of Strauss, Labitzky, Gungl, and Lanner.

At the second concert of the late Gloucester Festival (on Sept. 8th), a striking feature was the production of a new song composed by Miss Rosalind Ellicott, daughter of the Bishop of Gloucester and Bristol. The song, carefully scored for the full band, was rendered with great *verve* and expression by Miss Hilda Wilson, the principal contralto vocalist at the Festival. The first few lines of the song are chiefly accompanied by the bassoon, the reeds, and violoncello, and when the subject changes, there is a pizzicato accompaniment of the strings, with an effective passage for the horns. The second verse is in a more lively measure, and the climax bold and effective.

With much and sincere regret the death of the young and popular contralto, Miss Orridge, is announced. Towards the middle of August Miss Orridge joined her family at Guernsey for a short holiday, but two days afterwards she was seized with an illness which terminated fatally last Sunday, Sept. 16th. Miss Orridge was born in London, in 1856, and was a pupil of Senor Manuel Garcia, at the Royal Academy of Music, carrying off the bronze medal in 1876, the silver medal and Llewellyn Thomas gold medal for declamatory singing in 1877, and the certificate of merit, the Parepa Rosa gold medal, and the Christine Nilsson prize in 1878. She has since then enjoyed a high position as an oratorio and concert singer, which her rich voice, charming and individual manner, and artistic accomplishments fully justified. She will be long missed by our concert-room audiences, and by her numerous friends, both in public and in private life. Miss Orridge was only 27.

Madame Lemmens Sherrington's farewell appearance in Birmingham is announced, and it is understood as a preliminary step towards the artist's retirement from public life. Madame Lemmens Sherrington was born at Preston in 1834, and after studying at Brussels she made her *début* here in 1856. She married the late M. Lemmens in 1857, and since then she has been a favourite soprano, not only at festivals and at concerts, but also in English and Italian Opera. Two of her daughters, the Misses Mary and Ella Lemmens, have already appeared in London concert-rooms.

This year the lectures founded by Sir Thomas Gresham will be read to the public on the following days, in the months of October and November, 1883, in English, at six o'clock p.m., in the theatre of Gresham College, Basinghall Street, in the following order:— Physic—Dr. Symms Thompson, Oct. 2 ; Wednesday, 3rd ; Thursdays, 4th ; Friday, 5th. Rhetoric—Mr. J. E. Nixon, M.A., Tuesday, Oct. 9 ; Wednesday, 10th ; Thursday, 11th ; Friday, 12th, Astronomy—The Rev. E. Ledger, M.A., F.R.A.S., Tuesday, Oct. 16th ; Wednesday, 17th ; Thursday, 18th ; Friday, 19th. Geometry —The Very Rev. B. M. Cowie, D.D., Dean of Manchester, Tuesday, Oct. 23rd ; Wednesday, 24th ; Thursday, 25th ; Friday, 26th. Law—Dr. J. T. Abdy, LL.D., Tuesday, Oct. 30th ; Wednesday, 31st ; Thursday, Nov. 1st ; Friday, 2nd. Divinity—The Very Rev. J. W. Burgon, B.D., Dean of Chichester, Monday, Nov. 5th ; Tuesday, 6th ; Wednesday, 7th ; Thursday, 8th. *Music —Mr. Henry Wylde, Mus.D., Tuesday, Nov. 13th ; Wednesday, 14th ; Thursday, 15th ; Friday, 16th.*

The Querist.

Replies.

F.C.O. is desirous of finding a Cantata within the compass of a Parish Church Choir, and which is to be "taking" and at the same time good music. I beg to suggest that he could not do better that try the sacred cantata, "God is love," by the late Mrs. Robinson, wife of Joseph Robinson, Vicar Choral of St. Patrick's Cathedral, Dublin. The words are selected from the sacred poets, Keble, Monsell, Bonar, and others. Throughout the music is bright, tuneful and effective, and no very great difficulties are anywhere presented ; it would be the very thing for a Parish Choir. It is published by Chappell and Co., in folio size, price 10s. 6d., but some of the movements may, I believe, be had separately. I also venture to recommend for similar use, "The Vision of St. John Divine," by Dr. Iliffe, formerly organist of St. Barnabas Church, but now of S. John's Coll., Oxford ; likewise "Nichodemus and Phillip," by Dr. Gladstone, and "S. John the Evangelist," by Dr. Armes, of Durham. All these contain much excellent writing. Some of our grand church anthems are quite little cantatas in themselves, such as : "Lord, Thou hast been our refuge," "Blessed is he that considereth," by Boyce ; "I was glad," by Attwood ; "Behold, now praise the Lord," by Sir F. Ouseley," and "The Lord will comfort Zion," and "If the Lord Himself," both by Thomas Atwood Walmisley. These last two are especially grand. It is a matter for much regret that some of our fine old English anthems are not more drawn upon than they appear to be in our Cathedrals and Churches. Excerpts from the oratorios of Handel, Haydn, Mendelssohn, Spohr, and others are far too prevalent. This should not be, while we have such an inexhaustible mine of wealth in the composers for our Anglican Church. We can point with just pride to such names as Tallis, Gibbons, Childe, Rogers, Purcell, Blow, Croft, Greene, King, Boyce, Hayes, Battishill, Attwood, Crotch, Goss, the Wesleys, the Elveys, Hopkins, Monk, Barnby, Garrett, Steiner, and a host of other, ancient and modern, too numerous to mention. Well may English Churchmen take courage and say that the school of composers for the Service of their Church has the merit of having outlived all other schools which have been founded, have had their day, and have decayed.—J. S. Bumpus.

Cantatas.—Your correspondent, F. C. O., might find among the following something sufficiently effective and not too difficult: Spohr's "Christian's Prayer," Farmer's, "Christ and His soldiers," some of Mendelssohn's psalms, Bennett's, "Woman of Samaria," Gounod's "Redemption " (for three separate occasions).—J.T.A.

M. M. W.—I regret I am unable to give particulars of the proposed Teachers' Registration Bill, or to say, at present, what qualifications will be required of the recognised teacher of music. Doubtless, however a musical degree or diploma from one of the Universities ; the Royal Academy of Music, the College of Preceptors, the College of Organists; Trinity College, London, or the Royal College of Music, will furnish the required *status*. In accordance with the spirit of our legislation it cannot be supposed that the proposed Act will interfere with teachers, holding or not holding diplomas, who are already established and previously in practice for some such given period as a year.—[Ed, *Mus. Stand.*]

Service Lists.

EIGHTEENTH SUNDAY AFTER TRINITY.
SEPTEMBER 23rd.

London.

St. Paul's Cathedral.—Morn.: Service, Te Deum and Benedictus, Stainer in B flat ; Introit, Blessed is He who cometh (Gounod) ; Holy Communion, Stainer in A. Even.: Service, Magnificat and Nunc Dimittis, Stainer in B flat ; Anthem, Lord, at all times I will bless Thee ; By His care are we protected, Praise Jehovah, bow before him "Lauda Sion." (Mendelssohn).

Christ Church, Clapham.—Morn.: Service, Te Deum, Plain-song ; Kyrie, and Credo, "Messe Solonnelle " (Gounod) ; Offertory Anthem, Thine, O Lord, is the greatness (Kent) ; Sanctus, Benedictus, Agnus Dei, and Gloria in excelsis (Gounod). Even.: Service, Magnificat and Nunc Dimittis, Martin in A ; Anthem, God came from Teman (Steggall).

Holy Trinity, Gray's Inn Road,— Morn.: Service, Te Deum, Jackson in F; Jubilate, Chanted. Even. : Service, Magnificat, Purry in D ; Nunc Dimittis, Chanted ; Anthem, If with all your hearts (Mendelssohn), and Teach me, O Lord.

Holy Trinity, Tulse Hill.—Morn.: Chant Service. Even.: Service, Magnificat and Nunc Dimittis, Hopkins in F ; Anthems, In His hands, and For His is the sea (Mendelssohn).

St. James's Private Episcopal Chapel, Southwark. —Morn.: Service, Introit, From Thy love as a Father (Gounod); Communion Service, Haydn's Imperial Mass ; Even.: Service, Tours in F ; Anthem, The Lord great wonders (Hiller).

St. Magnus, London Bridge.—Morn.: Service, Opening Anthem, I will arise (Creyton); Te Deum and Jubilate, Goss in A; Kyrie (Goss). Even.: Service, Magnificat and Nunc Dimittis, Ebdon in C; Anthem, The Lord descended (Hayes).

St. Margaret Pattens, Rood Lane, Fenchurch Street.—Morn.: Service, Te Deum, Sullivan in D; Benedictus, (Stainer); Communion Service, Offertory Anthem, Cast thy burden (Mendelssohn); Kyrie, Credo, Sanctus, Benedictus, Agnus Dei, and Gloria, Schubert in F. Even. Service, Magnificat and Nunc Dimittis, Garrett in F; Anthem, The marvellous worth (Haydn).

St. Michael's, Cornhill. — Morn.: Service, Te Deum and Jubilate, Stainer in E flat; Anthem, In Thee, O Lord (Weldon); Kyrie, and Creed, Thorne in G. Even.: Service, Magnificat and Nunc Dimittis, Hopkins in F; Anthem, I will love Thee, O Lord (Clarke).

St. Paul's, Avenue Road, South Hampstead.—Morn.: Service, Te Deum, Smart in F; Benedictus (Barnby); Kyrie, Stainer in E flat, No. 2. Even. : Service, Magnificat and Nunc Dimittis, Bridge in C; Anthem, Remember now thy Creator (Steggall).

St. Peter's (Eaton Square).—Morn.: Service, Te Deum, and Jubilate, Goss in A. Even.: Service, Garrett in D; Anthem, I will wash my hands (Hopkins)

St. Peter's, Vere Street, W.—Even.: Service, Magnificat and Nunc Dimittis, Parry in C; Anthem, To Thee, great Lord (Rossini).

St. Agnes, Kennington Park, S.E.—Morn.: Service, Holy Communion, Kyrie, Creed, Sanctus, and Gloria, Garrett in D; Benedictus and Agnus Dei, Redhead in F.

St. Augustine and St. Faith, Watling Street.—Morn.: Service, Garrett in E; Introit, Behold, O God (South); Communion Service, Garrett in E flat. Even.: Service, Stainer in A; Anthem, Lord, before Thy footstool bending (Spohr).

St. Saviour's, Hoxton. — Morn.: Service, Te Deum, Goss in F; Holy Communion; Kyrie, Credo, Sanctus, and Gloria in excelsis, Ouseley in C. Even.: Service, Magnificat and Nunc Dimittis, Bunnett in F; Anthem, O Saviour of the world (Goss).

St. Sepulchre's, Holborn.—Morn.: Service, Nares in F; Credo, Agutter in B flat. Even.: Service, Nares in F; Anthem, How lovely (Mendelssohn).

Country.

St. Asaph Cathedral.—Morn.: Service, Ordination Service. Even.: Service, The Litany; Anthem, Awake, awake, put on thy strength (Wise).

St. Leonard's-on-Sea (St. Mary Magdalene).—Morn.: Service, Tallis'; Harvest Festival; Benedicite, Best in C; Benedictus, (Baumer); Anthem, O taste and see (Sullivan); Kyrie, Mendelssohn in A flat; Offertory Sentences, Calkin and Redhead; Even.: Service (Tallis); Magnificat and Nunc Dimittis, Martin in D; Anthem, Ye shall dwell in the land (Stainer); Te Deum, Dykes in F.

Ashbourne Church, Derbyshire. — Morn.: Service, Smart in F, throughout. Even.: Service, Gadsby in C; Anthem, Doth not wisdom cry (Haking).

Belfast (St. George's).—Morn.: Service, Te Deum, and Jubilate, Garrett in F; Apostles' Creed, Harmonized Monotone; Kyrie, Spohr in E flat; Gloria, Gratias and Creed, Dykes in F; Offertory (Barnby). Even. Service, Magnificat and Nunc Dimittis, Goss in A; Apostles' Creed, Harmonised, Monotone, Anthem, The strain upraise (Sullivan).

Birmingham (S. Alban the Martyr).—Morn.: Service, Te Deum, Boyce in C; Benedictus, Steggall in G; Holy Communion, Kyrie, Credo, Sursum Corda, Sanctus, Benedictus, Agnus Dei and Gloria, Redman in F throughout. Evensong. Magnificat and Nunc Dimittis, Redman in F.

Birmingham (St. Cyprian's, Hay Mills).—Morn.: Service, Cobb in G; Anthem, Thou wilt keep him in perfect peace (Tekyll). Even.: Service, Smart in F; Anthem, O praise God in His holiness (Clarke-Whitfield).

Canterbury Cathedral. — Morn.: Service, Smart in F; Anthem, In my Father's house (Callcott); Communion, Smart in F. Even.: Service, Hayes in E flat; Anthem, I saw the Lord (Stainer).

Carlisle Cathedral.—Morn.: Service, Garrett in E; Introit, Blessed is the Lord God (Ouseley); Kyrie, Cooke in G; Nicene Creed, Stainer in G. Even.: Service, Garrett in F; Anthem, O where shall wisdom (Boyce).

Doncaster (Parish Church).—Morn.: Service, Wesley in F; St. Ann's Hymn Tune, with Sullivan's accompaniments; Even.: Service, Tours in F; Anthem, Judge me, O God (Mendelssohn).

Dublin, St. Patrick's (National) Cathedral.—Morn.: Service, Te Deum and Mendelssohn in A; Holy Communion, Kyrie, Creed, Sanctus, Garrett in D; Anthem, Not unto us (Robinson) Even.: Service, Magnificat and Nunc Dimittis, Garrett in D; Anthem, As pants the hart (Spohr), and By the waters of Babylon (Stevenson).

Edinburgh (St. John's).—Morn.: Service, Anthem, O where shall wisdom be found (Boyce), and O come, let us worship (Mendelssohn).

Ely Cathedral.—Morn.: Service, Plain Song; Introit, Hymn, 297; Kyrie, and Credo, Stainer in E flat; Gloria, Chipp in A flat; Anthem, O come ye servants (Tye). Even.: Service, Stainer in E flat; Anthem, The Wilderness (Goss).

Leeds Parish Church — Morn.: Service, Garrett in F; Introit, Come, Holy Ghost (Attwood); Kyrie and Credo, Tours in F. Even.: Service, Garrett in F; Anthem, The souls of the righteous (Nares).

Lichfield Cathedral. — Morn.: Service, Goss in C; Anthem, Remember, O Lord (Himmell); Ordination (Attwood). Even. : Service, Hayes in E flat; Cantate and Deus Misereatur; Anthem, Blessing, glory, wisdom and thanks (Bach).

Linlithgow Abbey.—Morn.: Service, Anthem, O Lord how manifold (Barnby). Even. : Service, Anthem, In Jewry is God known (Clarke-Whitfield).

Liverpool Cathedral.—Aft.: Service, Magnificat and Nunc Dimittis, Stewart in G; Anthem, Fear not, O Land (Goss).

Liverpool (St. Cuthbert's, Everton).—Morn.: Service, Dykes in F. Even.: Service, Ebdon in C; Anthem, Motet, Hear my prayer (Mendelssohn).

Manchester Cathedral.—Morn.: Service, Te Deum, Jubilate, Pyne in D; Kyrie, Creed, Sanctus and Gloria, Pyne in A flat; Anthem, Now we are Ambassadors (Mendelssohn). Aft.: Service, Pyne in F; Anthem, The Lord is my Shepherd (Macfarren).

Manchester (St. Benedict's).—Morn.: Service, Kyrie (Elvey); Credo, Sanctus, Benedictus, Agnus Dei, and Gloria in excelsis, Haydn in C, No. 2. Even. : Service, Magnificat and Nunc Dimittis, Bunnett in F.

Manchester (St. John Baptist, Hulme).—Morn.: Service, Kyrie, Credo, Sanctus, and Gloria in excelsis, Steggall in G; Benedictus and Agnus Dei, Eyre in E flat. Even.: Service, Magnificat and Nunc Dimittis, Bunnett in F.

North Berwick, N.B. (S. Baldred's).—Morn.: Service, Champneys, Stainer, etc.; Anthem, The Lord is loving (Garrett). Even.: Service, Garrett in F; Anthem, Blessed be the name (Gadsby).

Rochester Cathedral.—Morn.: Service, Walmisley in E; Anthem, Lord, for Thy tender (Farrant). Even.: Service, Hatton in E; Anthem, Rejoice in the Lord (Purcell).

Sheffield Parish Church. — Morn.: Service, Kyrie, Schubert in F. Even.: Service, Magnificat and Nunc Dimittis, Chants; Anthem, The Lord is King (Trimnell).

Sherborne Abbey. — Morn.: Service, Te Deum, Nares in F; Even.: Service, Chants; Anthem, O Lord, my God (Malan).

Salisbury Cathedral.—Morn.: Service, Te Deum and Jubilate, Walmisley in B flat; Kyrie and Credo, Stanford in B flat; Offertory (Barnby). Aft.: Service, Walmisley in B flat; Anthem, Whoso dwelleth (Martin).

Southampton (St. Mary's Church).—Morn.: Service, Te Deum and Benedictus, Dykes in F; Holy Communion, Introit, Like as the hart (Hoyte); Service, Dykes in F; Benedictus and Agnus Dei, Gray in F; Offertory, O God, and If we have sown (Barnby); Paternoster (Hoyte). Even.: Service, Magnificat and Nunc Dimittis, Dykes in F; Apostles' Creed, Harmonized Monotone.

Wells Cathedral.—Morn.: Service, Nares in F, throughout; Introit, Blessed are the pure (Matfarren). Even.: Service, Arnold in A; Anthem, The wilderness (Wesley).

Wolverhampton (St. Peter's Collegiate Church).—Morn.: Service, Te Deum, Goss in C; Benedictus, Goss in C; Even.: Service, Tallis's Responses; Magnificat, Camidge in E; Dimittis, Wickes in G; Anthem, O Lord, how manifold (Barnby).

Worcester Cathedral. — Morn.: Service, Hopkins in A; Anthem, Sleepers wake (Mendelssohn). Even. Service, Stewart in G; Anthem, Plead Thou my cause (Mozart).

*** *Post-cards must be sent to the Editor, 6, Argyle Square, W.C., by Wednesday. Lists are frequently omitted in consequence of not being received in time.*

Newspapers sent should have *distinct marks* opposite to the matter to which attention is required.

APPOINTMENTS.

Mr. Wm. Lee Jones, Assistant Organist and Choir Trainer for Dr. Monk, at King's College, London, and St. Matthias, Stoke Newington, N., is appointed Organist to the Church of S. Mary Magdalene, Enfield Chase, London.

Mr. A. Fowles has been appointed Solo Bass and Choirmaster, to Wimborne Minster.

Mr. C. H. Kempling, R.A.M. late of St. Mary's, Balham, has been appointed organist to St. John's the Divine, Kennington.

Printed for the Proprietor by BOWDEN, HUDSON & Co., at 23, Red Lion Street, Holborn, London, W.C.; and Published by WILLIAM REEVES, at the Office, 185, Fleet Street, E.C. West End Agents:—WEEKES & CO., 14, Hanover Street, Regent Street, W. Subscriptions and Advertisements are received either by the Publisher or West End Agents.—Communications for the EDITOR are to be forwarded to his private address, 6, Argyle Square, W.C. SATURDAY, SEPTEMBER 22, 1883.—Entered at the General Post Office as a Newspaper.

THE MUSICAL STANDARD

A NEWSPAPER FOR MUSICIANS PROFESSIONAL AND AMATEUR

No. 1,000. Vol. XXV. FOURTH SERIES. SATURDAY, SEPTEMBER 29, 1883. WEEKLY: PRICE 3D.

THE MUSICAL STANDARD is published every Saturday, price 3d., by post, 3½d.; and may be had of any bookseller or newsagent by ordering its regular supply.

SUBSCRIPTION.— *The Musical Standard* is posted to subscribers at 15s. a year; half a year, 7s. 6d., payable in advance.

The rate is the same to France, Belgium, Germany, Italy, United States, and Canada.

Post Office Orders to be made payable to the Publisher, William Reeves, 185, Fleet Street, London, or to the West-end Agents, Messrs. Weekes & Co., 14, Hanover Street, Regent Street, W.

ADVERTISEMENTS.—The charge for ordinary advertisements in *The Musical Standard* is 2s. 6d. for three lines or less; and 6d. for each line (10 words) in addition. "Organist wanted," 3s. 6d. for 3 lines or less. A reduction is made for a series.

FRONT PAGE.—Concert and auction advertisements, &c., are inserted in the front page of *The Musical Standard*, and charged one-third in addition to the ordinary rates. Other advertisements will be inserted on the front page, or in the leader page, if desired, at the same terms.

THE WELSH MUSICAL CONTROVERSY.

There are idiosyncrasies of men, and there are idiosyncrasies of race. In neither case must one offer criticism unkindly, as while we know that we are peculiarly fallible ourselves, we must also recollect that unkindness can never effect a satisfactory reform in others. Dictation is not acceptable even to those who may become convinced of the unsuitability of their purposes, and sneering criticism is apt to produce nothing better than resentment. When, therefore, we hear of what appears to us to be retrograde tendencies, let us consider that all history teaches us that backward movements are repeated from time to time, if only that a more conspicuous march forward shall afterwards take place ; and that if we would say anything in the way of criticism or remonstrance, we have no need to be harsh, and that we gain nothing if we fail to be considerate towards those with whom we, peradventure, may not agree. With these few remarks I will take leave to refer to the position of Wales in regard to matters musical. Although reputedly a land where the love of poetry and music is predominant, Wales is, just now, giving the musical world some little trouble and fear ; and the outbreak on the part of those who claim to be the leaders of Welsh thought cannot be lightly overlooked, while, however, it ought not to be treated in an arbitrary manner. We must not seek to suppress, so much as to convince, a proud little nationality like this of what we may believe to be its errors. When we hear of an inclination being manifested on the part of Welshmen to reject ennobling orchestral music on the ground that the ancient Welsh harp ought to be more prominently before the public as a representative instrument, let us bear in mind for one moment that the old traditions of independence and minstrelsy have a strong influence in Wales, even at the present time. This harp is to many the relic of a bygone day, which Welshmen love to look back upon as glorious. The national instinct is yet strong, and the old harp is a revered symbol, around which there clings many a hallowed poetical fancy, which is cherished from age to age, and takes the mind back into the memorable circumstances of the distant past. As late as the 14th century, there lived the " greatest of the Welsh lyrists "—the famous Dafydd ab Gwillim, and he was a noteworthy resident in the county where the last National Eisteddfod was held. Ab Gwilim had enrolled himself in the order of minstrels, who made each year, like the Provençal troubadours, a circuit of their patrons. Not only in Glamorganshire, where he was recognized as laureate of the shire, but in all South Wales, and especially at Llewellyn's house at Emlyn, the minstrels (with their trichord harps), found a warm welcome. Listen to the poet's fervent sentiments towards his favourite county, and consider how great a hold he—a typical poet—must have obtained upon the affections of his countrymen :—

Hear me, Summer, thou shalt be
Bounteous messenger for me.
Fly to Essyllt : hasten forth ;
From the rude land of the North ;
Go, until thou reach the sea,
And the land beloved of me ;
Take my greeting, kindly told,
To Glamorgan twenty-fold ;
Twice a hundred blessings bear
To Glamorgan true as fair.
From the mountain to the strand,
Pass and compass all the land.
Let her grasses stay thy feet,
Bless her fields of corn and wheat,
Fruitful lakes and fertile dells,
Marble halls where kindness dwells.
There her lords for poets' meed,
Pour the wine and pour the mead ;
There in bright continuous hand
Orchards stretch across the land ;
Birds that sing from tree to tree,
Fill the air with love and glee ;
Tangled branches cluster o'er
Leafy wall and flower'd floor ;
There the fields as tribute pay
Eight kinds of corn and three of hay—
Fields that stretch from hill to sea,
A cloth of trefoil tapestry.
There the Lord does not withhold
From his poet mead and gold ;
Through the palace ever rings
Music of the voice and strings ;
Day by day from out the toil
Spring the crops to guerdon toil—
Wheat beneath the labourers' hands,
Wheat to spare for other lands.
Dear Glamorgan by the sea,
Other lands rejoice for thee.

The lays of other days, with their accompaniments, no doubt still ring in the ears of the imaginative Welshman, and he suddenly wakes up to the fact that his beloved harp has been superseded. Then he who, be it observed,

in this 19th century, does not forget to stoutly assert his right to claim Monmouth as one of the counties of his native land, reproachfully considers that he has been forgetful of his old traditions. The harp must be replaced, and national institutions must not be Anglicised. Well, in answer to all this, I respectfully submit that the union of England and Wales was accomplished long since, and that, generally speaking, England herself is not more loyal to the British Constitution than Wales. Wales herself has progressed with England in many things ; Wales has, to a large extent, adopted the English language, and many of the great Welsh mining districts and ports have been developed by men from other parts of the country. In Wales, as in England, the day of troubadours has gone out of fashion, and the desire for patronage is not now prominent. Neither am I aware that for the sake of " national " sentiment, old tapestries and sculptural remains are searched by modern nations for the correct form of a national instrument. And as to patronage—an idea which, it must be confessed, is associated with the old Welsh harp—are not the colliers about to establish for themselves labour scholarships at the new University College of South Wales ? Welshmen do not necessarily lose their nationality by speaking English. Will they lose it by accepting a new meaning in the old dictum recognised by all civilised countries that art belongs to no age ? It is almost idle to fondle the antiquated belongings of the past. Let us respect the music of an earlier day, and let us not be ashamed to recognise the progressive efforts of our ancestors, but do not let us deceive ourselves with false sentiment. The retention of old customs is not an abstract good. Great revolutions are constantly being wrought in society, and all nations undergo changes. Comparing the Welsh nation with what it was several centuries since, the contrast is indeed remarkable. Wales has grown and developed new customs and conditions. Welsh and English are being assimilated, and although certain marks of nationality still remain, the chief distinctions are surely wearing out, and in time the whole of this island will be the abode of English-speaking people. The increased facilities of locomotion lead to this. To put forward, therefore, old theories and symbols is scarcely worthy of the people recently born in Wales. They must recognise the importance and the teaching of the times, and, while tenderly regarding their past history and achievements, they must be up and doing, and ready to show the world that they are not narrow conservatives in art matters ; but that, as Welshmen, they are able to hold their own in all respects against all comers. They must not encourage a tendency to rest satisfied with what history says their forefathers accomplished. No one can afford to live in the past. We have improved on the works of others, and we desire that the work of progression will be continued. If conclusion —a National Eisteddfod cannot be creditable unless it is conducted in a broad and liberal spirit. The good that men do lives after them, but to insist not be cribb'd, cabin'd and confin'd," for reposeful admiration—I should rather be recognised as a strong incentive to further deeds of good. The Welsh language, although said to have been spoken in Paradise, is not the universal tongue. Welshmen themselves speak English more and more. In this manner the greatest social barrier is being voluntarily overcome. And the old Welsh harp, no doubt an advance at a remote period, on previous productions, cannot seriously be put forward by an intelligent nation as an instrument for " all eternal time."

JOHN G. E. ASTLE.

The musical services at St. Catharine's, Liverpool, will after to-morrow become a thing of the past, Mr. Banner, the liberal art amateur, who for so long has borne the whole expense of the choir which bears his name, and whose object, and that of his lieutenant, Mr. S. Cooke Ridley, has been to render the best ecclesiastical Service and Anthems, having been informed that he must either make the Service so low that any singing at all would be an absurdity, or—go. There is scarcely another town in the kingdom where a gentleman would be found willing to spend hundreds of pounds on such a laudable object as providing the best music for Church-goers, and it is to be hoped that this powerful combination will not be lost to Liverpool, but that another Church may be found where Mr. Banner's devotion to Church music may be better appreciated.

REMINISCENCES OF AN OLD REPORTER.

THE NEW PHILHARMONIC SOCIETY.

The "*New* Philharmonic" Society was started by Dr. Wylde, and the concerts, at first, were held in Exeter Hall, now not only the occasional, but the exclusive *locale* of the pious folks that attend the "May" and other "religious" meetings in the Strand. Dr. Wylde, to be esteemed by me as a musician of genius and an old *confrere* of the *Corps de Critiques*, conducted the "New Philharmonic" concerts, and brought out in 1854 a masterly version of Milton's "Paradise Lost."

After several seasons the Doctor coalesced with M. Wilhelm Ganz, and held a series of "Orchestral" concerts in St. James's Hall. Some differences unhappily arose after a time, and M. Ganz was "left alone in his glory." I much regret the discontinuance of the "Orchestral Concerts" held on the Saturday afternoon, but, as before hinted, M. Ganz could not be expected to entertain the British public at his own and at a very heavy expense. For his "leader," M. Pollitzer, I entertain the highest respect.

Old enough is this poor and nearly superannuated "Reporter" to remember M. Ganz's worthy father as conductor of the German Opera at old Covent Garden Theatre in 1841 and 1842. He was an able *chef*, and I shall not forget his performance of "Die Zauberflöte," on Saturday, May 21, 1842. Madame Stoeckel Heinefetter, and Herr Staudigl undertook the leading parts of these German operas as soprano and bass; the tenors I forget, except one, Tichatschek, spoken of by the reporters as "the German tenor with the unpronounceable name." Staudigl afterwards appeared at Drury Lane. I met him at the Worcester Festival of 1845, where the good-humoured man declined to sing an "extra," at one of the evening concerts, even to oblige the ladies. They had asked for "Der Wanderer" of Schubert. Staudigl lost his hat at one of the "receptions" in the College Hall, held after the evening concerts. His successor, Formes, had a stentorian voice, and looked Caspar (in "Der Freischütz"), to the life. A very bad Caspar spoiled Weber's opera at Covent Garden in 1842; but I forget his name. Staudigl could sing down to low D, and always did so at a certain recitative in "The Creation," which ends with a line about the "sinuous" course of the worm! Poor Staudigl, in the sequel, lost his reason, and was confined in a *Maison de Santé* at Vienna, where he still sang his songs on occasion. His brain had softened.

An Amateur Orchestral Society, conducted by Mr. Alfred Mellon, came to grief for want of support. I remember to have heard at one of the last concerts, in November, 1865, Mrs. Meadows-White's pretty overture to "Lalla Rookh," very cordially received. Mr. Henry Leslie conducted another Amateur Orchestral Society for a few seasons about the years 1853-56, but this too proved a failure. It was a rule that either the composer of each number must be an amateur, or, if not, the artist (singer or player). A musical Jew, Mr. Simon Waley, often played concertos on the pianoforte; one wet night, in Dec., 1856, I heard him execute, with M. Sainton, Beethoven's beautiful Sonata for pianoforte and violin in F. An amateur player on the hautboy, Mr. Alfred Pollock, occasionally, played a piece of Handel; with whom, as well known, it was a favourite instrument. This Pollock's version of "Swallow, swallow flying south," is now quite superseded by the very superior setting of Signor Piatti. One night, in the year 1860, at a private party, Alfred Pollock met with a dire mishap. A careless lady sat down upon his hautboy, a valuable French one, and broke it. A provoking incident, but Pollock boasted that "he bore it like an angel."

The "Concerts of Ancient Music" were famous for many years, and they ought never to have been allowed to drop. The title of this Society sufficiently explains the purpose of its institution. I was present at one concert during the very last season, A.D. 1846, held at the Hanover Square Rooms. A number of "notables," including the (then) Speaker of the House of Commons (afterwards Lord Eversley) were present. George Hogarth was chaffed by Mr. Gruneisen when Avison's trumpery piece, "Sound the loud timbrel," came on, for Hogarth hated it, and took good care next day to "pitch into" the work; he had just joined the *Daily News* (started in 1846). Mr. Parry, father of John Parry, of comic song celebrity, acted as cicerone to the press at this concert, gave them a list of the visitors, and otherwise made himself useful.

Tea and coffee were provided between the parts, at the Society's expense. Poor *John* Parry I first heard at the Hanover Rooms in 1840; he was often engaged at benefit concerts, and too often the proprietor of the concert impudently put down his name when he was not to appear at all. His favourite songs were, "Wanted, a Governess," "Mamma is so very particular," "Berlin Wool," and others that I cannot remember. Albert Smith wrote the words, "John Parry was a superior musician; to hear him only touch the pianoforte was worth half a guinea." He suffered much from nervousness, and at one of his own "benefit" concerts in 1843 or 1844, I heard that he burst into tears, and was quite unstrung, in the artists' room, merely from "stage fright." How extraordinary this, for Parry enjoyed an unbounded popularity, and carried all the "public" away with him. Parry afterwards gave elaborate "Entertainments" *à la* Matthews, with imitations and feats of mimicry. I heard him at the old Assembly Rooms, Hackney, in January, 1851. Having invited him to sing at a private party at Hackney about this time (of course "on terms"), Parry most politely replied that he had given up such engagements, and therefore could not oblige me.

On that same night I engaged for the delectation of my friends, Henry Westrop and George Genge, the tenor vocalist. They sang, with my sister, Barnett's Trio in G, "This magic wove scarf," and Genge kindly introduced a song of my own composition, "The Warrior's Serenade," accompanied by Westrop. I had taken the trouble at Genge's request to transpose the (published) song from A major to C (one-third higher). Genge gave a capital reading, but told me that he should have preferred even a higher key.

Speaking of John Parry and his popularity, it may be remembered that the bulky Lablache, at the Italian Opera, frequently indulged in what are called *lazzi*, but I never heard one of these. that was not very "poor wit," such as calling out "Good night," (*Anglice*) in the Serenade scene of "Don Giovanni." The silly British public laughed loudly, nevertheless. Lablache, one night (after dinner), sang for a street "ballad" squeaker, and handed him a hatful of silver, bestowed by the delighted audience.

I have yet to speak of more modern Institutions, such as the "Musical Union," and the "Monday Popular" Concerts. *Jam satis.* A. M.

Church Bells says:—"Some indignation has been expressed, and not altogether without reason, at the omission of the Sunday evening services at Westminster Abbey during this season of the year." The same paper further complains that another "serious grievance is the non-performance by the Canons of the preaching duty, which forms almost the only return they give for their handsome stipends. At the best of times the Canons of Westminster compare far from favourably in this respect with the dignitaries of other foundations, but when Society is out of town they are more than ever conspicuous by their absence." Truly an establishment with the ample income of some £30,000 a year, ought to do much more for the cause of religion and for the benefit of the nation than is done at Westminster Abbey. For years past, another serious charge has been made against the Abbey authorities, this has been the neglect of the week-day choral Services during the holiday season; a time, indeed, when thousands of visitors from all parts throng the great city of the world, who, in many cases are only able at that season and on week-days to attend the Services held in our great churches.

Cassell's Saturday Journal, a new serial starting next month, appears to be designed on something like parallel lines to those on which the *Family Paper* was founded, making due allowance for the enormous development in popular taste which has been effected during the last twenty-five years. There will be an abundance of fiction and amusement in its pages, as well as entertainment of more substantial kind; and as it will not be illustrated, all the available space will be filled to the advantage of its readers. Doubtless the enterprising publishers will duly remember the claims of Music in some way or other in their new venture.

The Church of St. Agnes and St. Anne, Gresham St. City, is now re-opened, the organ having been repaired and improved, and the piper re-voiced by Messrs. Lewis and Co.

Musical Intelligence.

MANCHESTER.

Mr. Carl Rosa's opera troupe are here for a fortnight. The repertory comprises, "Mignon," "Esmeralda," "Faust," "The Bohemian Girl," and "Carmen." Place for "Columba" could not be found. "Esmeralda" scored a great success, though Madame Burns (Mrs. Crotty), who played the title part, did not appear in it to so great advantage as she does in such artificial parts as Filina. Miss Annie Albu made her first appearance as Marguerite, and was distinctly successful. This is much to say when one remembers all the great artists who have appeared as the heroine of Goethe's legend. In Mr. Leumane, Mr. Rosa seems to have gained an important acquisition to the vocal strength of his company.

On Friday, the 21st, a most interesting experiment was made by a scientific gentleman interested in local telephony. By means of telephones placed on the stage of the theatre and the usual conducting wires he conveyed the opera to his residence some two miles distant, and not only the music, but the dialogue as well as the applause of the audience could be perfectly heard. The only difficulty was with the orchestral bass, which could not be easily distinguished. Does the telephone reduce the limits of audibility in the human ear? Mr. Rosa was present, and able to criticise his artists easily, thus upsetting the time-honoured saw about the absence of the cat.   C. J. H.

THE IMPERIAL THEATRE.

Mr. J. W. Currans, acting manager at this theatre, took his benefit last Saturday, when special attractions were announced in the shape of three new pieces, the authors having consented to appear in their respective plays. The farce, "Blonde and Brunette," by Mr. John Augustus O'Shea, was, however, withdrawn, and it is almost a subject of regret that the same policy was not pursued with the remaining pieces. "Auld Robin Gray," a one-act drama, adapted by Mr. George Roy from Jean Marie, proved dull and uninteresting, nor was it redeemed by some very indifferent acting; while Mr. H. P. Grattan's three-act comedy, "Ye Legende: or, The Four Phantoms," chiefly caused amusement by the absurdity of its construction, and the many slips and unintentional comicalities by which it was accompanied. A poorer performance has seldom been in London, though it must be admitted that the comedy had not a fair hearing owing to its unfinished mode of presentation, the actors generally being defective in their parts, and the prompter's services in constant requisition. Mr. John Hudspeth formed a bright exception to the general mediocrity, his really excellent and humorous acting of John Thomas, the butler, gaining almost the only genuine applause of the evening. The theatre was so scantily attended that it is to be feared Mr. Currans would not realise much from his benefit. On another occasion of the kind he would do well to provide some more solid attraction.

F. E. T.

Mr. Willing's Choir will be well to the front during the coming season. The concert scheme includes, Sir George Macfarren's oratorio "King David," for the first time in London, on Dec. 11th, Mendelssohn's "Walpurgis Night," and a miscellaneous selection on Jan. 15th, Mendelssohn's "Elijah" on March 25th, and a new cantata, "Perizabeh," by Mr. Wilfred Bendall, on April 22nd.

In the course of the New York *Tribune's* criticism of Mr. S. G. Pratt's opera of "Zenobia" the writer observes "As for the invention, his score contains several numbers which the most captious critic must admire—the opening chorus of priests, and the contrast of the padres' chorus following; Zenobia's air at the beginning of the second act, and the exquisite slumber-song which precedes it; the finale of that act; the quartet of the third act; Zenobia's song in the fourth act, with the pathetic return of the slumber-song as accompaniment; the fine 'Ode to Immortality,' and its treatment; and the finale of the opera, all require sincere commendation." Perhaps Mr. Carl Rosa has already thought of this work; if not, his attention, or the like forethought of some other English opera manager, would be at once a courageous recognition of merit and a graceful compliment to our cousins across the Atlantic.

BOSTON, LINCOLNSHIRE.

Elsewhere appears the specification of a new organ recently erected at the Boston Chapel of Ease, one of the ugliest specimens of "little Bethel" architecture that could be imagined by any architect in a fit of dyspepsia. The organist, Mr. T. H. Scott, last week, displayed the qualities of this instrument, the manufacture of Mr. T. H. Nicholson, in presence of the writer. Mr. Scott played the Offertorium of Lefébure-Wély in G, and another of Edward Batiste in D, besides other pieces of minor pretension, with all the skill and *technique* of an experienced musician. The effect of the "mixtures" was exquisite. The "Röhr Flote" and the "Flute" are deliciously smooth and dulcet; the "Oboe" (Swell organ) struck the writer as slightly nasal in tone, but the "orchestral Oboe" has put this old stop quite out of joint. Mr. Nicholson is to be complimented on his production.

Mr. Scott also favoured the writer with a "discourse" on one of the harmoniums, to be viewed at the handsome rooms of Messrs. Hildred Brothers, Market Place, Boston. Here, indeed, is a harmonium worthy to redeem the ordinary "cheap-Jacks" of country Churches, condemned last week. The instrument is greatly superior to the so-called American and other "organs" that are really of the same species, and not organs at all. There are twenty stops, and two manuals. Mr. Scott afterwards played in the same rooms, on a octave "upright iron-overwrought pianoforte" (manufactured in Germany), which sufficiently exemplified the competency of the craft to produce the finest "action." Mr. Scott, in a *Lied ohne Worte* of Mendelssohn (the one in A major from Book V) gave practical proof of the touch and tone. Mr. Scott's own German grand "iron-overstrung horizontal" pianoforte is a powerful "concert-orchestral" instrument, worthy so to be called, at the same time that the soul of expression may be evolved by velvety hands and judicious pedalling.   A. M.

CORK.

An interesting feature of the musical portion of the Cork Industrial Exhibition was a band contest held on the 21st and 22nd inst. in the great hall.

On the first day, which was set apart for the military, seven bands entered for the contest. Each band was required to perform the overture to "Oberon," and, in addition, a piece of their own selection, the prizes being £20, £10, and £5 respectively for the first, second, and third best bands. Messrs. J. Smith, Mus. Doc. T.C.D.; J. P. Smith, bandmaster Scots Guards; J. C. Van Maanen, bandmaster Royal Irish Constabulary, acted as judges. Having ballotted for places, the playing commenced at one o'clock and continued until six. On the conclusion of the contest, Mr. J. P. Clarke delivered judgment as follows:—"Ladies and Gentlemen,—The judges are unanimous in awarding the first prize to the third band in the order in which they played, namely, the 2nd Batt. Oxfordshire Light Infantry. The second prize we are equally unanimous in adjudging to the band which played fifth in order, and that we find to be the band of the 20th Hussars. We also desire specially to commend the band which played fourth in order, the 1st Batt. Lincolnshire Regiment, and, on our representation, the Exhibition Committee have consented to give them the third prize. We desire to compliment all the bandmasters on their various performances." Besides the money prizes mentioned above, each of the successful bandmasters was presented with a medal.

On the second day, for Civilian Reed Bands, there were only four entries, two local and two from Dublin. The first prize was awarded to the Barrack Street Band, the same band which was victorious at the Dublin Exhibition band contest; the second was divided between the two Dublin bands. These bands were required to play a selection from Rossini's "Mosè in Egitto," and a piece of their own choice.   F. St. John Lacy.

The excellent performance recently at the Promenade Concerts of Mendelssohn's "Midsummer Night's Dream" music, recalls to old concert-goers the admirable rendering of this delicious music at the Covent Garden Concerts under Alfred Mellon, some 15 years ago, with a band containing such artists as Pratten, Barrett, Nicholson, Lazarus, Winterbottom, and the Harpers.

Mr. Villiers Stanford will, it is understood, compose a Cantata for the next Festival at Birmingham.

LIVERPOOL

(From our own Correspondent).

Sept. 26th.

The Liverpool Philharmonic Society begin the 1883-4 season on Tuesday, October 9th, when Mr. Charles Hallé will make his first appearance in the capacity of conductor to the society. During the first half of the season, the sixth concert taking place on the 18th December, the following symphonies are to be performed :—Mozart's No. 6, in C major ; Haydn's "Oxford" in G ; Mendelssohn's "Scotch," and Goldmark's "Rustic Wedding ;" while among the overtures announced are Beethoven's "Leonora" No. 3 ; Mendelssohn's "Hebrides," Auber's "Zanetta," Spohr's "Jessonda," Schubert's "Italian," Rade's "Hamlet," Cherubini's "Lodoiska," Gounod's "Mirella," and Sterndale Bennett's "Naiades." An orchestral and choral selection from Beethoven's "Ruins of Athens" also figures in the scheme, and other composers mentioned as contributing to the programme are Gluck, Wagner, Ernst, Wieniawski, Hummel, Molique, Svendsen, Eliasz, Hiller, and Saint-Saëns—names which suggest varying degrees of merit. Mr. Hallé will be prominent in the pianoforte music of the season, and Madame Norman-Néruda and Mr. L. Straus not less conspicuous—the one in Spohr's Ninth (D minor), and the other in Molique's Fifth Violin Concerto (A minor). The "Messiah" is to be performed on December 18th, when the newly-formed chorus of the society will appear for the first time.

It will be to news to the readers of the Musical Standard to inform them that English music is notoriously absent in the above scheme, if they have watched the scheme of the Manchester concerts under the direction of the same conductor. It is an admitted fact amongst Manchester musicians, that whatever Mr. Hallé has done for musical art in general, he has never given a helping hand to the musical works of Englishmen. At Mr. Hallé's own orchestral concerts, which alternate with the Philharmonic Concerts, Beethoven's nine symphonies are to be played in chronological order, and form a strong contrast to the meagre scheme of symphonies set down for performance at the Liverpool Philharmonic Society's concerts.

Mr. Joseph Maas sang at a concert given in the Philharmonic Hall, on Saturday evening last, and created a furore, being recalled four times.   J. J. M.

GLASGOW

The Glasgow Select Choir give a concert on Sept. 22nd, under the auspices of the Abstainers' Union, in St. Andrew's Hall, which forms the first of a series organised by that body to take place on Saturdays. The programme consisted of part-songs, glees and solos, by Cowen, Smart, Weber, Bishop, Blumenthal, Fasing, Booth, Behrend, Callcott, Hume, Mendelssohn and Spofforth. Dr. Peace contributed several pieces on the organ, in his usual faultless manner, and Mr. W. D. Swan acted as accompanist. There is a marked improvement in this latter gentleman's style of performance, and study will soon place him in the foremost rank of West of Scotland pianists. The solos were all of a most satisfactory character, the contralto being especially happy. Mr. James Allan, as usual, conducted.

Mr. David Baptie, of this city, has published with Messrs. W. Morley & Co., of London, a "Handbook of Musical Biography," in which will be found a large amount of useful information in a condensed and easily accessible form. Few names of importance are wanting ; and though no pretence is made of giving a full account of each musician noticed, the book will serve as a very handy manual, as, which the chronology is sufficiently accurate for all ordinary purposes. The work can be recommended for the eclectic spirit which it shows, and for the notice bestowed on contemporary musicians.   J. B.

CHICAGO

The average attendance at Theodore Thomas's Orchestral Concerts at Chicago recently has been from 3000 to 5000. Among the works, all of which were admirably rendered, were the following symphonies : the Sixth and Seventh of Beethoven, the No. 3 in C major, of Schumann ; the "Leonore" of Raff ; the "Unfinished" and the great Symphony in C ("Jupiter") of Mozart ; and the following, which were heard for the first time in Chicago : Symphony in F, No. 9, by Goetz ; Symphony in D minor, No. 1, by Volkmann, and Symphony in D, by Dvorák, the Slavic composer. Overture, "Mein Heim," by Dvorák ; the "Manfred" music, by Schumann ; the "Intermezzo Scherzando," by Reinhold ; "Scenes Alsaciennes," by Massenet ; the "Good Friday's Spell," from Wagner's "Parsifal" ; "Bal Costume," a most charming masquerade of material dances, by Rubinstein, originally written as a four-hand piece for piano ; a gavotte, by Saambehl ; a setting by Mr. Thomas for full string quartet, No. 9, in G ; Liszt's brilliant Tarantelle, adapted for orchestra by Berghaus Muller, who also adapted the Second Rhapsody ; a concert overture, "The Princess," by Mr. Whiting, the organist ; overture to "Macbeth," by Kelley, a young musician in San Francisco ; who recently studied music

with Mr. Eddy, in this city, an "Alla Mazurka," by Gernsheim ; a prelude from the manuscript opera of "Montezuma," by Mr. Frederic Grant Gleason, "Em Marchen," a violin obbligato by Templeton Strong, and a serenade by Robert Fuchs.

TAUNTON.—The annual harvest thanksgiving services in connection with St. James's Church, Taunton, were held on Sunday last. The services throughout the day were full choral, and were sustained by a strong choir, Mr. T. J. Dudeney presiding at the organ. The following was the order of musical services :—Morning : Anthem, "O Lord, how manifold," J. Barnby ; Kyrie, T. J. Dudeney ; Credo, J. Merbecke. Evening : Anthem, "We give Thee thanks," G. A. Macfarren. The organist, Mr. Dudeney, selected voluntaries of a festive character for the day. In the morning he played in fine style, as an opening voluntary, the chorus, "Lift up your heads," from the "Messiah" ; and as a concluding voluntary the "Hallelujah Chorus," from Beethoven's "Mount of Olives," otherwise known as "Engedi." At the evening service he opened with the chorus, "Thanks be to God," from Mendelssohn's "Elijah," and concluded with Handel's "Hallelujah Chorus." During the subsequent recital he played his Andante con Variazioni e Fuga, a composition which has won the highest encomiums from some of the first musicians of the day. The church in the evening was crowded to such an extent that forms had to be placed in the aisles, and many persons were content to stand up during the whole of the service. The singing, which has vastly improved in this parish recently, was of an exceptionally high order.

Reviews.

Compendium of Thorough Bass and Patent Chord Denoter. By F. W. von Kornatzki. (Weekes & Co., Hanover Street).—Anything more ingenious in the way of practically teaching harmony has never yet been invented. The Compendium and Chord Denoter is not a book. Outwardly it is a case in book form. The contents consist of a guide connecting the principles of harmony with the author's scheme, and the mechanism planned for its expression. A framework with the two musical staves painted on glass and arranged so as to admit the insertion of the cards underneath forms a leading feature of the invention. The printed cards are covered by details connected with scale formations, chords, sequences, &c., all duly classified and arranged with astonishing skill and forethought so as to present—when placed under the glass and moved from note to note as may be desired—all the possible positions and ramifications connected with the scale or chord to be illustrated. To young students the "Chord Denoter" will be found to be simply invaluable, especially as conveying to the inexperienced mind such logically arranged information as awakens and strengthens the student's faculties and creates such an insight into the wondrous subtle beauty of the harmonic system and its heaven-born proportions, as cannot fail to enlarge the mind and impress the imagination. All teachers should forthwith make the acquaintance of this thoughtful and valuable invention.

To the Immortals. Song. Words by D. F. Blomfield, Music by R. F. Ellicott. (Enoch & Sons, Holles Street, 1883.)—This is a pianoforte edition of a song produced at the late Gloucester Festival, with full orchestral accompaniment (noticed under the head of "Passing Events" in last week's issue). The stanzas are supposed to be the prayer of a lover to "the gods" to the effect, that when his fair one "wakes from dreams in the silent night, she may think awhile on him," and that when the deities are pleased to remove the lady, "from this dull earth into their land of mirth," they will take him as well ! The first part of Miss Ellicott's composition is in the quiet sostenuto preghiera style ; but at the invocation of the Gods, the tone becomes more passionate, and some effective modulations colour the text. Thus, at the words, "Grant, O ye Gods," a pause on the chord of C major (the dominant of the dominant), leads to a passage in F minor and A flat. The "working up" displays much skill and savoir faire, but Miss Ellicott is known to be an accomplished musician and elegant song-writer. Key B flat, range from low C to E flat or F (Optional). Miss Ellicott uses the chord of the 6—4—3, so strongly objected to by pig-tail contrapuntists, with a suspension of the root in the treble clef.

Organ News.

NOTTINGHAM.

The Albert Hall was crowded on September 24th by a delighted audience, and it is questionable whether during the concert season of 1883—84 a couple of hours will be spent more pleasantly by lovers of music than the time was passed by those who were fortunate enough to secure seats on this occasion. The new organ could hardly have been opened under more favourable circumstances. The reputation of Mr. W. T. Best as a brilliant and accomplished organist is so well known that it is needless almost to speak in his praise. It goes without saying that he showed to perfection the power and charming tunefulness of the new organ, and that no one could have been chosen more fitted to perform the task. The greatest skill, experience, and ability have been exercised in the construction of the new organ, and the result is an instrument which is perfect. It is built by Messrs. Brindley and Foster, of Sheffield.

The programme of the music given by Mr. Best was as follows :—

Organ Sonata, No. 2, in C minor	Mendelssohn.
Andante in A major	Smart.
Turkish March, "Ruins of Athens"	Beethoven.
Siciliana and Fugue in G minor	Bach.
Andante, with variations and finale	Best.
Fugue in G major	Wesley.
Bell Rondo	Morandi.
Overture (founded on the "Austrian Hymn")	Haslinger.

The "Turkish March" enraptured the audience. It permits a gradual increase of the organ tone to be made from the opening *pianissimo*, leading by degrees to the full power of the instrument, after which the tone is gradually diminished to the end of the more. The brilliant style in which Mr. Best played this famous march was a treat to listen to ; the audience showed their appreciation of his performance by loud and continued applause, signifying that they wished to hear it again, and Mr. Best kindly acceded to their wishes. His wonderfully clever rendering of the "Bell Rondo" showed again to great advantage the powers of the organ, and he was loudly applauded. These two selections afforded the greatest pleasure to the audience, but the whole programme was listened to with feelings which high-class music alone can excite, and, on the whole, a more admirable entertainment of the kind could hardly be expected. During an interval in the performance it was announced that another eminent organist will shortly preside at the organ, and when the time, which will be duly advertised, arrives, we have no doubt that the Albert Hall will be again filled by a similarly appreciative audience to that which so heartily welcomed Mr. W. T. Best.

The *Nottingham Daily Express*, from which the above account is extracted, also gives a complete scheme of the fine organ the town now boasts the possession of, and which has already appeared in these columns. The presence of such an instrument in a fine room will doubtless tend to increase the local love of organ music.

LIVERPOOL.

An organ recital was given in St. George's Hall, by Mr. W. T. Best, on Thursday, September 10th. The following was the programme :—

Organ Concerto in G major	Handel.
Largo—Ciaconna—Andante—Fuga.	
Andante in A major	Smart.
Prelude and Fugue in C minor, No. 6	Bach.
Legende :—"La Prédication aux Oiseaux" ("St. Francis of Assisi preaches to the birds ")	Liszt.
Overture, "La part du Diable "	Auber.

And on Saturday, September 22nd :—

Organ Sonata, No. 3, in A major	Mendelssohn.
Con moto maestoso—Andante tranquillo.	
Introduction and Pastoral Chorus, "Le Prophète"	Meyerbeer.
Hymn sung in the Cathedral	
Air, Variations, and Finale Fugato	Smart.
Adagio in E major	Merkel.
Introduction and Allegro Marziale	Bache.

The new organ at St. Martin's Church, Birmingham, has been rebuilt by Mr. J. C. Banfield with admirable skill and judgment. The instrument has now three Manuals and Pedal organ, and some 40 stops.

FISHERIES EXHIBITION.

The following organ recitals have been given during the week by Mr. J. Loaring, F.C.O. The programmes included :—

Overture, "Griselda "	Paer.
Organ Concerto, No. 7	Handel.
Gipsy Rondo	Haydn.
Offertoire in G	Wely.

Organ Concerto, No. 1	Handel.
Rondo con Imitazione da Campanelli	Morandi.
Chorus and Fuga, from Grand Mass in D	Righini.
" Bridal March"	Edwards.

Organ Concerto, No. 2	Handel.
" Cujus Animam "	Rossini.

An organ recital was given on Friday, September 21st by Mr. Freeman Dovaston, A.C.O. The programme comprised :—

Marche d'Eglise	Saville.
Organ Voluntary	Havco.
Offertoire in A	Batiste.
Allegro, from F.F. duet	Mozart.
Introduction and Allegro	Wood.
Postlude in C	Batiste.

Also by Master Henry J. Wood :—

"The Old Abbey March "	Wagner.
Cathedral Melody	Mozart.
Offertoire in O	Lott.
Andante, No. 2	Batiste.
March of the Crusaders	Sibley.

And by Mr. Churchill Sibley :—

" Cathedral March	Sibley.
Trumpet March	Jude.
Cathedral March	Sibley.

And by Mr. H. C. Tonking, R.A.M. :—

Overture, " Occasional Oratorio "	Handel.
Offertoire in G	Wely.
Postlude in D	Smart.
Postlude in C minor	Steggall.
Fantasia on a Welsh March	Best.

Organ recitals were given on Tuesday, September 25th, by Mr F. Dovaston, A.C.O. The programmes included :—

March in B flat	Silas.
Offertoire in F	Wely.
Organ Voluntary	Burrowes.
Allegretto	Gladstone.
Festive March	Smart.
Allegro vivace	Mozart.
Posthude in E flat	Wely.

Andante and Allegro	Bache.
March in C	Grunnen.
" Danse Royal "	Watson.
Offertoire in C	Wely.
Andante con moto	Smart.
Chorus, " Put the waters " (" Moses and the children ")	Handel.
Minuet and Trio	Hoyte.
" Austria," with variations	Haydn.
" Song of Peace "	Roeckel.
" March of the old Brigade "	Barri.

And on Wednesday, September 26th :—

Allegro Pomposo	Smart.
Minuet and Trio	Hoyte.
Andante in D	Silas.
Prelude and Fugue in C	Bach.
Allegro Moderato, from 1st Sonata	Mendelssohn.
Song for Tenor	Smart.
Introduction and Allegro	Wood.

BERKELEY SQUARE, W.

The new organ, built by Bryceson Bros., for St. Mary's Church, has two pitch-pine cases, each 22ft. high, 7ft. 6in. wide, 9 ft. deep, and 9ft. apart, to show west window. The Manuals, Great organ, Pedal open, and 'cello are on north side ; Swell organ, sub-bass, and bass flute on south side of gallery. The swell organ, CC to G, has eight stops ; the great organ has also eight stops ; the pedal organ, CCC to F, has four stops, and there are four couplers, &c.:—Swell to great, swell to pedals, great to pedals, bellows signal.

PRESTON.

Mr. James Tomlinson (organist to the Corporation), resumed his Saturday evening recitals, in the New Public Hall, on Saturday, September 22nd. The following was the programme :—

Marche Religieuse	Adam.
Andante (Violin Concerto)	Mendelssohn.
Toccata and Fugue in D minor	Bach.
Overture to " Mirella "	Gounod.
Communion	Orison.
Hungarian March	Berlioz.

The tasteful manner in which Mr. Tomlinson rendered " Communion " (Grison), elicited a well-deserved *encore*. There were a very large number of persons present.

BOW AND BROMLEY INSTITUTE.

Thanks to the spirited and enlightened action of the Committee of the Institute, the first organ recital given here after the holidays has come to be regarded as a sort of opening day of the musical season, as affording the earliest sign of earnest, active, musical life. On Saturday last, Mr. Walter Parratt, of Windsor, a most finished performer and an accomplished musician, gave the recital. His programme was worthy of his artistic reputation. It opened with Mozart's Introduction and Fugue in D, originally written for orchestra. Next was a movement by Lemmens. The great feature of the recital, however, was a fine performance of a new organ Sonata in E minor by Rheinberger, a work of high purpose and skilful writing. Mr. Parratt says of it in his notes : "It is in four numbers—1. A solemn Adagio with Fugue, which is three times interrupted by a second theme not treated fugally ; 2. A graceful Intermezzo ; 3. A Scherzo entirely devoted to the development of one theme, and leading to 4, a Passacaglia, a series of clever variations upon a ground bass, the Sonata being rounded off by a repetition with slight variations of the Introduction." Other organ solos were "Grand Chœur Dialogue" by Eugène Gigout, a good specimen of the French school, and Bach's wonderfully wrought out "Toccata and Fugue in C major." All these works received ample justice from the head and hands of the organist, whose playing gave very great pleasure to his audience. Miss Florence Norman sang nicely and was once recalled. Mr. Fountain Meen was the excellent accompanist. To-night Mr. W. S. Hoyte will play. On Monday, Mr. R. Ganthony gives a reading and musical entertainment.

TEWKESBURY.

In connection with the Commemoration Services celebrating the anniversary of the re-opening of the Abbey Church, a grand Festival of Parochial Choirs was held on Tuesday, September 25th. Above 400 choristers assembled, and testified to the judicious care with which they had been prepared by their choirmaster, Mr. Hemingway, F.C.O., who conducted the festival, with the exception of the Magnificat and Nunc Dimittis, which, being written for the occasion, was conducted by the composer, Dr. C. J. Frost. This, a work containing effective yet not difficult work for the voices, and an independent organ accompaniment, together with parts for cornets, horns, trombones, bass and drums, produced an admirable effect, and is unquestionably a welcome addition to the small list of practicable easy Services. In the evening an organ recital was given by Dr. Frost, who played in admirable style the following pieces :—

March in D	Best.
Fantasia in F	Volckmar.
Sonata in C	
Introduction—Allegro—Andante—Finale.	
Andante in G, and Larghetto in F	Frost.
Hommage à Handel	Moschales.
Cantata, "God, Thou art great"	Spohr.
Allegro vivace ("Reformation Symphony")	Mendelssohn.
Andante Grazioso in E, and Moderato con moto in A minor	Smart.
Allegro vivace in A minor	Morandi.
Chorus, "Hallelujah" ("Messiah")	Handel.

On Thursday, September 27th, a harvest thanksgiving service was held at 7.30 p.m. ; and on Sunday, September 30th, at 6.30, Evensong, the Festival Service will be repeated, with band and organ. Anthem, "The Wilderness" (Wesley).

OLDHAM.

An organ recital was given by Mr. Wm. Mullineux, F.C.O., on Friday, September 21st, at the Industrial Exhibition. The programme included :—

March for the organ in D major	Best.
Prelude and Fugue in D major	Bach.
Chorus, Symphonie au Concertato	Lemmens.
Organ Sonata in B flat, No. 4	Mendelssohn.
Introduction, Variations and Fuga on the Hymn-tune "Jerusalem the golden"	Dearnsley.
"Adoremus," Melodie Religieuse	Ravina.
"Improvisation"	
Grand Fantasia and Fugue in G minor	Bach.
Grand Chœur in D	Guilmant.

And by Mr. Fred Turner :—

Sonata No. 4, in B flat	Mendelssohn.
Barcarolle from a Concerto	Bennett.
Andante in G	Smart.
Toccata and Fugue in C major	Bach.
Andante in A	Hopkins.
Fanfare in D major	Lemmens.
Grand Chœur in D major	Guilmant.

BRADFORD.

An organ recital was given on the rich new organ at St. Mary's Church, by Mr. James H. Rooks, of St. Paul's, Manningham, Bradford, in the presence of a large and fashionable audience. The programme had evidently been chosen with great care and taste, for it was of such a kind as enabled the organist to bring out the full, rich, and varied tones of the fine instrument to perfection. Sir R. Stewart's "Pastorale," Mozart's overture, C major, Smart's "Fantasia," with chorale, and the "Storm Fantasia," were all performed with remarkable brilliancy. The programme finished with Handel's "Hallelujah."

The annual choir services at St. Thomas's Church, were celebrated on Sunday in the presence of large congregations. In the evening, when the sacred edifice was crowded from end to end, the choir was strengthened by about fifty members of the Bradford Festival Choral Society, and Mendelssohn's "Hymn of Praise" was sung after the sermon. A temporary platform had been erected in the chancel for the accommodation of the singers. The soloists were Miss Clara Marshall, soprano ; Mrs. Clarke, contralto ; and Mr. Wm. Coates, tenor. Mr. J. H. Rooks presided at the organ, and Mr. W. H. Emsley, choirmaster of St. Thomas's, conducted. At the morning service, which was also fully choral, Goss's anthem, "The Wilderness," was given by the church choir.

HIGHER BLACKLEY.

An organ recital was recently given by Mr. W. Mullineux, F.C.O., in the Methodist New Connection, Zion Chapel. The programme included :—

Organ Sonata, in F minor	Mendelssohn.
Pastorale in A major	Guilmant.
Canzone in A minor	
Fantasia and Fugue in G minor	Bach.
Grand Fantasia in E minor	Lemmens.
March for the organ, in D major	Best.

ABERFELDY.

The following is the programme of an organ recital given by Mr. Jesse Timson, in the Episcopal Church, of St. David's, Weem, on the 21st ult. :—

Organ Concerto in B flat, No. 6	Handel.
Allegro—Larghetto—Allegro Moderato.	
Roco Adagio	Smart.
Triumphal March from "Naaman"	Costa.
Andante in F	Gritton.
Fugue in D minor	Bach.
Postlude in C	Smart.
Andante, from 11th Symphony	Mozart.
Festal March	Calkin.

PERTH.

On Saturday, September 15th, Mr. Woodthorpe Browne resumed the series of monthly organ recitals, in the Parish Church, Kinnoull. The programme included the following :—

Overture in E minor	Morandi.
Air in E flat	Mozart.
Adagio Cantabile	Haydn.
Organ Sonata	Mendelssohn.
Andante in A minor and major, and in B flat	Batiste.
Grand Schiller March	Meyerbeer.

ECCLESHALL.

The organ of Eccleshall Church, after being silent for nearly two months, undergoing thorough reparation and improvement, was re-opened recently by Mr. J. E. Jefferies, organist of St. Matthew's Parish Church, Walsall, who gave two recitals to large congregations. The programmes included :—Afternoon : Overture to "Samson" (Handel) ; Sonata in C minor, No. 2 (Mendelssohn); Toccata et Fugue in D minor (Bach) ; Andante from Sonata in E minor Op. 70 (Weber). Evening : Overture to the " Occasional Oratorio " (Handel) ; Prelude and Fugue in D (Bach) ; Larghetto from Symphony in D (Beethoven) ; Offertoire in D (Batiste) ; "Schiller March" (Meyerbeer). In all the pieces Mr. Jefferies proved himself to be a thorough executant, receiving afterwards hearty congratulations for his masterly performance. W. Addenbrooke, Esq., sang the solos with great taste and finish, adding much to the pleasure of the recitals.

The death of Mr. C. S. Packer, for many years organist of St. Mary's, Reading, is announced with regret.

The new organ for the Royal Naval Hospital Chapel at Plymouth is being built by Messrs. Hele and Co., to whom the order was given by the Admiralty authorities.

Foreign Musical Intelligence.

M. Guilmant has been playing recently at the Trocadéro, Paris.

A new opera "Tommaso il Gobbo," by Signor Luigi Tem is announced.

Concerts have been given at Amsterdam by the Bilse Orchestra from Berlin.

Brahms has left Vienna, where he resided many years, and settled at Wiesbaden.

Felix Weingartner has completed the words and music of a new opera, "Sakuntála."

M. Adolphe Samuel, director of the Ghent Conservatoire, is writing a new opera.

Miss Grieswold, the American cantatrice, recently made a successful début in Brussels as "Mireille."

The friends and pupils of Theodore Kullak have erected a monument over his grave in the Berlin cemetery.

Ponchielli has finished his "Marion Delorme," and is about to compose another opera to be called "Janko."

A very successful performance of the opera of "Benvenuto Cellini" by Berlioz, was given recently at Leipsic.

Herr Carl Kuntze, very well known as a conductor and organist, in Berlin, died on Sept. 7th. He was born in 1817.

In November, Nessler's new opera, "Jung Werner, der Trompeter von Säkkingen," will be given at the Leipsic Town Theatre.

M. Salvayre's "Richard III." will, it is said, be included in the repertory of the coming season at the Italian opera, St. Petersburgh.

At Madrid a new musical drama has been produced, entitled "Un Lio en el Ropero"; the music has been composed by Reig.

The Théâtre de la Renaissance of Brussels, will have several novelties this season, chiefly comic operas by Belgian composers.

The "violin fairy," Teresina Tua, has sustained an irreparable loss in the death of her mother, to whom she was fondly attached.

It is proposed to celebrate the two hundredth anniversary of Handel's birth next year, by a grand musical festival in Hamburg.

A committee has been formed in Eutin with the view of erecting a memorial to Weber on the centenary of his birth, December 18th, 1886.

"Jery and Bätely," one-act opera, with libretto founded on Goethe's text, and music by Mdme. Ingeborg von Bronsart, will, it is stated, shortly be produced in Leipsic.

At the recent Ghent Festival, given under the direction of M. Waelput, interesting music by Gevaert, Benoit, and a new cantata by M. Samuel, received an excellent rendering.

Herr Angelo Neumann has, says the *Athenæum*, commenced his management of the Opera at Bremen by a performance of Gluck's "Armida," in which the title part was sustained by Frau Antonie Schreiber.

The Società de Quator, of Milan, has awarded the first prize for the best trio in four movements for piano, violin, and violoncello, to Signor Martucci, of Naples. Forty-four manuscripts were sent in competition.

The tenth and last volume of Wagner's "Gesammelten Schriften" will be published by E. W. Fritzsch, of Leipsic, next month. This will include the master's contributions to the Bayreuth papers written in the last year of his life.

De Fossez, the French opera impresario, is in New Orleans preparing for his coming season of opera. The répertoire will include "Le Roi de Lahore," "Le Prophète," "L'Etoile du Nord," "Le Cheval de Bronze," and "L'Héro_diade."

A Wagner Society has been formed in Amsterdam for the purpose of giving dramatic performances of Wagnerian opera in the concert hall with orchestra, to the end of diffusing an increased knowledge and a better understanding of his works.

PRINCIPAL CONTENTS OF THIS NUMBER.

LONDON: SATURDAY, SEPTEMBER 29, 1883.

PIANOFORTE PEDALS.

MR. JOSEPH HATTON described Miss Tippets in his little society story, "Kites and Pigeons" as seated at the pianoforte, "with her foot on the soft "pedal playing a new set of waltzes "*pianissimo*, that no one may be disturbed by the music, and also that "her mistakes may be less noticeable;" they "would be under the influence of the *soft* pedal." But musicians well know that the abuse of the so-called *forte* pedal commonly arises from an instinctive feeling on the part of badly trained pianists that the damper pedal affords the readiest means of sheltering all sorts of defects of playing technicalities; although the popular novelist is right so far as he pictures the would-be fashionable young lady as putting down the soft pedal when she desires to feel her way with dreamy, cat-like softness of touch through a new piece ; the abuse of one of the pianoforte pedals is, indeed, not unusual, and it is here shrewdly hit off. The use of and abuse of the pianoforte pedals would indeed furnish food for an essay on the helplessness and perversity of the human mind under the influence of badly formed habits, or the half-unconscious consciousness of the advisability of employing any means we may have within reach, whereby we may nervously shelter ourselves from the unpleasant risk of bringing down public judgment upon our own defective talents, or acquirements. The pedals of the pianoforte—beyond of course an allowed conscientious desire to employ them effectively—are to the inefficient or imperfectly trained pianist just what the walking-stick and umbrella are to nervous awkward people who do not know what to do with their hands when walking out. And the comparison may be pushed further; for in both cases the existing awkwardness is not really hidden from observant listeners or spectators, by either the uncalled for employment of the damper pedal, or the awkward handling of walking-stick or umbrella. Seriously, the modern abuse of the pianoforte pedals is a matter calling for the earnest attention of both teachers and pupils, and this same abuse is so prevalent that only our most accomplished players can be said to use the damper pedal judiciously. And this judicious employment of the pedal being almost impossible of attainment without the previous formation of a perfect finger mechanism, the pianoforte teacher's duty is either to watch most carefully the formation of the habit of properly using the pedals, or to forbid their employment entirely until the student is prepared by a mastery of the finger mechanisms to be better able to bestow the necessary attention upon the artistic use of the pedals and is fully able to control the desire to put down the damper pedal as a ready means of producing stronger tones and sheltering imperfect fingering. The best way, as everybody agrees, to combat an evil is to first discover its origin. In the present matter, want of command over nerves and mechanisms is the root of the evil. The consequent defects are involved in the too hurried formation of the player's style, in the general eagerness for results, which pervades the artistic just as it does the commercial world. Instead of striving to attain a perfectly true, strong action of the fingers, we are too anxious to cultivate music which displays a more cheaply bought power, springing from the already strong wrists and arms ; a misled taste modern writers pander to, as saleable new music usually means that which produces an apparent maximum of result from a minimum of labour. The fingers indeed should be trained to express every possible light and shade, from *fortissimo* to *pianissimo*, as a matter all important to the earnest executant. Beethoven and other classical composers for key-board instruments ask in their works for this necessary power, which is a much higher qualification than the deceptive power we meet with in the banging of big heavy chords from the wrist and arm. Composers naturally borrow orchestral, as the highest of instrumental idioms in writing for the pianoforte. Now, a rapid passage in single notes assigned to a mass of violins looks to be a slender matter on paper, but when springing from a number of equally handled

bows, whether the notes are taken delicately or forcibly, such a sentence presents a striking effect to listen to. So the fingers of the pianist should be strong and true enough to bring forward such passages relying solely upon finger power, as may be found, to give only one instance, in the first movement of BEETHOVEN's Sonata in G, Op. 49, No. 2. The thoroughly trained artist is never unwilling to play such music, but the sham cheap-jack performer would shrink from such a piece and would select something of the prevailing written-to-show-off-without-much-preparation school of music. Then one cause of the abuse of the damper pedal arises from the natural feeling for rhythmical distribution being generally more developed than is the judgment and knowledge of the progress of chord roots and the division of their several harmonic *strata.* How to effectually conquer habits so strong as to frequently defy the utmost determination and defeat the greatest care of their unfortunate student victim, is a matter which must often seriously engage the attention of the conscientious teacher. Without going into details, I will venture upon a few suggestions with regard to the conquering of the acquired habit of misusing the pianoforte pedals. At first the teacher or the earnest student anxious to correct himself, should entirely forbid or forego the use of either pedal, by having both taken off the pianoforte. Then a course of thorough finger training should be inaugurated, which to be complete should include the study of the organ or harmonium, in order to secure a perfect nervous, strong, legato touch. Next, the practice of BACH's "Preludes and Fugues," and even vocal fugues with a careful sustenation of the parts, should be undertaken. Then HAYDN and MOZART's Sonatas, and other music thinly laid out for pure finger work, should be practised without the pedals. So much for the task of eradicating a bad habit ; now for the building up of a good one in connection with the use of the pedals of the pianoforte. A few exercises should be compiled with marks for the damper pedal to be put down to chords on accented, then on uncented beats, to be alternated with exercises for the same pedal to be put down during rests between chords. Next, a few passages with the occasional employment of the pedals should be rehearsed ; and, lastly, sentences from CHOPIN, LISZT, and other modern composers should be given for study, involving the dexterous and frequent use of the damper pedal and the occasional employment of the soft pedal in *con sordini* passages. Even after much painstaking drill, great care will have to be exercised, lest a relapse into old and not easily conquered habits sets in. The difficulty chiefly concerns the use of the damper pedal, but the student should be trained to use both pedals at exactly the right times, and their employment should be absolutely confined to the passages which are specially marked for their use. The questions connected with the mental and mechanical operations of the instrumental performer are many, and are important in their bearing upon the artist's success as well as interesting in their consideration. I hope presently to venture to offer further thoughts in this direction.

E. H. TURPIN.

"NOSE" MUSIC IN CHURCH.

THE musical world is indebted to MR. T. L. SOUTH-GATE, an able and learned contributor to this journal, for the term "nose" music, derisively applied to a certain absurd fashion imposed upon vocalists by M. GOUNOD. Apart from the practice of singing, or trying to sing, with closed lips, we all know what is meant by "singing through the nose". For the present, I propose to speak solely of "nose" music in the *instrumental* sense.

Last week, a few remarks were made respecting "tin-kettle pianofortes" in the country, also pianofortes out of condition, that is to say, out of tune, *hic et ubique*. But worse remains behind. At home, in the rural rectory, or the dull country house, "a little music," of nights, may, if officiously proposed, be sternly interdicted by Paterfamilias as a bore. On the first day of the week, however, ignorantly miscalled, by Judaizing Christians, the "Sabbath," Papa is impotent, and his "interdict" as invalid as the POPE'S in Protestant and enlightened lands. The Church bells begin to chime for morning service, and gloomy thoughts, of a sceptical kind, at once intrude themselves upon the mind as it reflects on its "possibilities," or impossibilities, of the musical portion of Divine Service, at the sanctuary in SLOSHY-CUM-STARVATION, or WILDERNESS-ON-THE-WOLDS.

The Ritualists and other Reformers of the *Services* (I speak of forms, not doctrines)—have put a stop to many anomalies, such as *reading* of the Psalms and Canticles, the duet between the literate clergyman with his accurate pronunciation and the ignorant clerk with his hopeless provincialisms. The school children are generally drilled at a choir's practice on the Friday, and there *may* be a tolerable player on the organ, in the person of the schoolmaster or the clergyman's wife. But then the instrument itself! What of *that*?

Heaven save us from the ordinary harmonium! No musical ear could even be taught to tolerate the nasal tone of this most offensive wind instrument. True, that fine harmoniums, of sonorous quality, enriched with numerous and effective stops, may be purchased in Paris for fifty guineas and upwards, and I heard a very fine one at Boston (of foreign manufacture) ten days ago. I now refer to the "cheap "Jacks" which the indigence, or niggardly spirit, of rural parishes, provides for Church worship. Better to have voices unaccompanied than these pseudo-*sirens*. The harmonium is only one of a very disagreeable family. I may be wrong, but all these peculiar wind instruments, where the sound is derived from the action of the wind upon metallic tongues or plates, made me feel like MOZART, at the sound of the trumpet, when blown a few commas on the "wrong side of the post." In the words of my friend Mr. SOUTHGATE, the harmonium is *nose* music; the effect intensely disagreeable, and provocative of irritable temper rather than fervent devotion. Hector BER-LIOZ, in his valuable book on the orchestra, speaks of other obnoxious instruments of the "species"; I include within my own ban, the seraphine, the apollonicon, the concertina—in fact all machines where the sound is produced in the manner specified.

Suppose that an *organ* is found in the village Church. Well, or ill: there are organs and organs, good, bad, and indifferent. At present, I am doomed to hear a small organ, of fairly suave and agreeable tone, but with only one manual, and four stops! This, too, in a comparatively large Church. The choir of school children, supported by this limited accompaniment, chant the Canticles and Psalms, and intone the Responses. In other places, I have heard horrible organs, not only weak, but out of tune, and in the last grumpy stage of decay! The execution of the player too, often aggravates the nuisance. The parsons' wives and squires' ladies may, or may not, know something about "music." When they don't, heaven help you; when they do, "a little knowledge" leadeth to presumption and bad practice. I remember a shallow-pated self-conceited lady of the manor, in the wilds of Northamptonshire, who used to write "*chaunt*" for "chant," and at the end of the final, or playing "out" "Voluntary, on the Sunday," lifted her hands suddenly from the keys as soon as she saw the "last" silly sheep "out" at the door! The effect of this *staccato*, on the organ, may be imagined. Speaking of grammatical, in addition to musical, ignorance, I may mention that one clergyman's wife, in Bucks, used to "hand" out the list of hymns, on the Sunday, with such solecisms as "the FOUR FIRST verses of Hymn, No. LVI.," &c.! Dean ALFORD boldly defended this monstrous contradiction in terms, but in MR. MOON, who wrote a book called "The Dean's English," the unfortunate master of Canterbury Cathedral caught a veritable Tartar! There cannot be four *first*, or even fifty *first* verses! Or is it—to answer fools according to their folly—a case of *primus inter pares*?

By the way of a solatium, I am going to hear MR. SCOTT, one of the organists at Boston, who will kindly show off his instrument, and play select pieces (at my request); by LEREBURE-WELY (the Offertorium in C major) and BATISTE'S Offertorium, No. 3. The organ in the immense mother church of Boston, quite a cathedral, will be duly discussed; Mr. SCOTT'S own organ is a new one, erected in the Chapel of Ease. Mr. SCOTT also proposes to play on his new German "iron-overstrung" grand pianoforte, so that I may expect a treat.

A "specification" of Mr. SCOTT'S organ and some account of his performances at Boston, appear this week in another column of the *Musical Standard*.

J. H.

NOISE *versus* MUSIC.

MODERATION in music, as in everything else, would seem to be the golden rule. On the one hand, it is important to avoid the sickly sentimentality which prompts feeble folk to a preference for very soft, sweet, slow music, and on the other side, it is equally necessary to steer clear of that boisterous love of powerful tones which especially characterizes vigorous and youthful artists, and which is so apt to cross the border line separating music from noise. Power loses something of its force unless it is conserved and reserved for use at the right moments. This lesson is more easily learnt in the practical affairs of daily life than it is in the less trodden pathways of art. The man who over-drives his horses, the engineer who wastes his steam, and the gaby who spends his money recklessly, are all objects of instantaneous and sharpest criticism; but the ignorance and stupidity of the composer who habitually employs an excess of instrumental power, and of the organist who is incessantly employing the full organ, are less amenable to public judgment, although hardly less objectionable to public taste. In the case of the composer suffering from an exuberant love of noise, society may readily protect itself by, not taking the trouble to listen to his music; but in the case of the youthful organist who thinks he can best scale the heights of public estimation by firing off his artillery all at once, people have not the same chance of escaping from his organic broadsides. Lest I should be deemed impertinent for any observations I may make upon the performances of my brother organists, I must here protest that my present words are written at the prompting of a clerical friend, whose forethought, kindly interest in the organist's profession, and good taste are undeniable. And further, as I fear much unkind secret criticism in this direction is offered to the professional detriment of the criticised, I venture to think a little openly expressed advice will be readily forgiven, if not accepted. If it well to add, that the criticisms anent this matter, refer chiefly to, the art of accompanying. The philanthropic costermonger, who, according to schoolboy traditions says—

"If I'd a donkey which would'nt go,
Would I thrash him, no, no, no."

is a gentleman claiming general estimation. Similarly the organist who is thoroughly experienced in the art of accompanying, and rarely puts his foot upon the composition pedal which throws out all the stops, is much more likely to be esteemed as an artist, than is the organ player who musically "thrashes" and "kicks" both choir and congregation, as they travel along, or it may be, limp through their chants, hymns, and anthems. The organist is ever something higher than the mere executant. He is either the composer's best friend and "aide-de-camp," or his worst enemy, for he practically decides the qualities and amount of the tone-colour to be employed in illustrating the composer's ideas. More than this, the organist in church is a musical general, disposing of his forces as he will, throwing one line forward, strengthening another, and ever anxiously holding together his vocal army with such tact and prudence as will secure the most efficient, orderly and precise movements "en masse." The true economy of such a position is that of learning how to boldly use that which is obviously wanted; and at all times inclining to the sparing and reserving of that which can be safely dispensed with. The prudent organist will build up a system of careful observation; he will learn how to pick up his fast singing choristers by the use of clear rather than powerful sounding stops, especially using for this purpose the softer stops of 4-feet pitch; he will be equally expert in knowing how to calm down excited sharp singing by lessening the power employed. He will also be reserved in the employment of either strong reeds or

screaming mutation stops, and will discover that judicious variety affords the best possible power. The question as regards the organist has a bearing upon the organ also. The skilful, prudent player is the only fit person to be entrusted with a large and powerful instrument; and the people who can thoroughly rely upon the judgment of such an artist, will, as far as means go, be always willing to provide an instrument worthy of such a player. All organs ought to be ample enough to flood the buildings in which they are placed with majestic tones, and to have variety enough to produce every shade of sound down almost to a distant echo. Organists ought, especially as regards the delicate art of accompanying, to learn how to completely control and judiciously utilise all the varied powers of such an instrumental giant; and this matter of use and control deserves more serious study than is generally accorded to it. One thing seems absolutely necessary, this is the careful study of the instrumental accompaniments to be found in the scores of the greatest masters.

T. H. TURPIN.

MUSIC.

The influences of music, although its language is more vague and subtle in its expression, are in some sort analogous to those of literature. It feeds the imagination, and awakens and gives play to slumbering thoughts. It stirs the finer emotions of the soul, and kindles the inspiration which belongs to poetry. Creating a sympathy with the beautiful and sublime in nature, it sharpens the sensibilities and stimulates the fancy, until it blooms into the imagery of forms of material, intellectual, and moral beauty. Like literature, music gives renewed life and vigour to daily existence, and strengthens the hopes and aspirations of humanity. Dispelling the gloom which occasionally shrouds the mind, it carries the soul gently from extreme depression to supreme content. How many congenial images of beauty it suggests to the mind! And upon how many nations does its plastic power leave the impress of its refining touch? Whatever the effect of music, whether it be of a sensuous, emotional, or intellectual character, its subjective influences are unmistakable, transporting us at times into a mighty realm of dreams, and tingeing with the deepest hues the primary elements of our nature, the sympathies and emotions of the heart, the imagination, the passions of the soul, and the manifestations of the religious sentiment. The influences of music are felt around the firesides of the poor as well of those of the rich; and the young, flushed with the spirit of youth, and the old, even if hardened by experience, yield alike to its mystic charms. It is curious to reflect upon the variety of thoughts and the varied emotions which find their source in music. In vain have writers sought to discover the secret of its power, and to define with anything like precision its subtle effects upon the heart and mind. The radical difficulty which at first presents itself in any attempt to solve this problem is that the effect and influence of music depend upon the temperament and the physical, mental, and moral condition of the individual. To a certain extent, the same may be said in respect to some forms of poetry, and prose. But an effort to analyze the meaning of the most imaginative and mystical passages in literature would meet with a success far beyond what has yet been achieved by those who have essayed to interpret the language of the art divine. While descriptive music has undoubtedly many admirers, and has a prominent place in the works of the great masters, it has always seemed to us that the mind and feelings become fettered by being chained to the ideas of the composer. Who can listen to a fine opera without at times confessing it to be a privilege to be ignorant of the libretto? And who can listen to the music of a great master set to the words of a sickly sentimentalist without being conscious that disturbing influences are at work on both mind and body? — *Providence Evening Bulletin* (U.S.).

Passing Events.

Madame Nillson is now on her way to America.

Ch. Lecocq's opera, " Le Cœur et la Main," has been recently successfully produced at Daly's Theatre, New York.

It seems, unfortunately, that the Three Choirs Festival at Gloucester has left a deficiency of £515 to be met by the stewards.

The September number of *Brainard's Musical World*, U.S., gives a short biographical notice, with portrait, of Sir Arthur Sullivan.

The Guide to the Church Congress at Reading has been again prepared by that able *littérateur* and editor Mr. Charles Mackeson.

Mr. Ebenezer Prout is said to be writing an orchestral work for the Birmingham Festival of 1885. This is good news, as a musical contemporary observes.

It is stated as probable that the first performance in London of Raff's " World's End," to be produced at the Leeds Festival, will be at the Crystal Palace.

It is announced that the Birmingham Festival Committee have decided on asking Dvorák to write a work for the Festival to be held in that town in 1885.

At St. James's Hall Mr. Chas. Du Val is giving nightly at present an entertaining and spirited " Monologue of Music, Mimicry, and Character Delineation."

The Duke and Duchess of Connaught were present at a concert at Norwich lately. They congratulated Dr. Bunnett, from whom, some years ago, the Duke took lessons.

Englacher's opera, " The Prince Consort," has been translated into English, and will, it is announced, be produced this season by the Wilbur Opera Company in America.

The New York papers say, there was recently placed in the office of the County Clerk the certificate of incorporation of the Grand Conservatory of Music of the city of New York.

Mr. J. Conway Brown proposes to publish by subscription, his Sonata for pianoforte and violin which gained the prize of 10 guineas and the gold medal recently at Trinity College, London.

A young lady pianist, Miss Neally Stevens of Chicago, is returning home from Europe with the most flattering testimonials and encouragement from some of the most eminent German composers and *virtuosi*.

Our greater music schools are again getting into working trim, and the well-sustained influx of students at the various institutions, prove that there is no diminution in our natural love of the art.

The Ballad Concert Committee propose to extend their concert scheme this year by the performance of the " May Queen" and by the introduction of classical nights, under the direction of Mr. W. H. Thomas.

The ever hard at work Sir G. A. Macfarren has written a part-song to the words of Burns' poem, " To Mary in Heaven," for the Glasgow Select Choir, who will sing it at Mr. Austin's St. Andrew's Festival at St. James's Hall, Nov. 30th.

Mr. Mapleson has, it is said, obtained the requisite capital to enable him to finish building the new opera house on the Thames Embankment, which he proposes to open in June, 1884. This statement is, however, doubted by some.

A prospectus has been issued announcing that the Liverpool Philharmonic Concerts are to take place under Mr. Charles Hallé, on Oct. 9th, 23rd; Nov. 6th, 20th; Dec. 4th, 18th; Jan. 8th; 22nd; Feb. 5th, 19th, March 11th, and April 1st.

The Brisbane *Daily Observer* tells of a local meeting held under the chairmanship of Mr. W. H. Wilson, a much esteemed supporter of the art, at which it was decided to raise a fund with the object of placing a gifted young artist, Miss Fanny Atkinson, in the Royal College of Music as a New Zealand representative. The scheme has been warmly taken up.

Messrs. Alderson and Brentnall, of Newcastle-on-Tyne, announce three Subscription Concerts at the Town Hall, with Mr. Chas. Hallé's excellent band, on Nov. 13th, Jan. 14th, and Feb. 25th. The same firm also give a special Chamber Concert Dec. 7th, the artists being, Mr. Chas. Hallé, Mdme. Norman-Neruda, and Miss Santley.

The proceedings of the Musical Association are in print under the care and the admirable conduct of the hon. sec., Mr. James Higgs. Papers are included by Messrs. F. Praeger, G. N. Carpari, E. J. Breakspeare, J. Turpin, G. A. Osborne, S. S. Stratton, and D. J. Blaikley. Stanley Lucas & Co. are the publishers.

Another new instrument is announced in the advertisement that " Herr Karl Hahn is playing at Crystal Palace this day, on his new instrument, the Cantus Transcendentalis, Ancient Melodies, Chinese, Hindustani, Hebrew, and Arabian, and Modern Melodies, Hungarian, Russian, and Gipsy songs from the " Tatra."

The Parish Church, Leeds, after being closed for some weeks, was re-opened on Wednesday, and a special series of services were arranged for the occasion. On the first day, Gounod in D and Barnby in E flat were sung. Anthems by Wesley, Stainer, etc., have been given during the week. During the recess the fine organ has been greatly improved.

A veteran correspondent remembers the father of Crouch (the composer of " Kathleen Mavourneen ") as a violoncellist at the Ancient Concerts. In the days of the Ancient Concerts, about 1821, the violoncellists were the two Lindleys (father and son), Crouch, Ely, and Brooks. Thanks to progress and to Costa, our strings are much stronger and better balanced now.

The funeral of Miss Ellen Dividge, the lamented, much esteemed, and greatly gifted young contralto singer, took place on the 21st, at Kensal Green, in the presence of a large number of professional and private friends. Among others present were Mr. Santley, Signor Foli, Mr. Maybrick, Rev. Edward White, Mrs. Mudie-Bolingbroke, Mr. Stanley Lucas, Mr. Vert, and Mr. Barnard.

Pitman's *Musical Monthly* has appeared for Oct. It is edited by Mr. T. Crampton, and issued at 7d., with some 8 pages of music in both notations, a pages of well assorted literary matter, and an admirable portrait of Madame Georgina Burns, not to add a goodly number of business announcements; the paper is good and remarkably cheap. Such a spirited start deserves well of the public, and fairly claims, a future of usefulness and success.

Says Cherubino in *Figaro*.—Contrary to report, I believe Mr. A. C. Mackenzie has not yet begun the new opera for the Carl Rosa Company. Mr. Hueffer has, however, finished the libretto, and the composer will have to set to work at once to deliver the work in the course of the present year. Mr. Mackenzie's Norwich cantata, the libretto of which is from the pen of Mr. Joseph Bennett, is more forward, and the first part is, it is understood, already completed.

Mr. Walter Macfarren has been paying a series of visits in Yorkshire, Flintshire, Somersetshire, and Cornwall. On Sept. 20th, he gave a pianoforte recital at Falmouth, for the benefit of the Cornwall Home for Destitute Little Girls, and his appeal was liberally responded to by a delighted audience, who warmly appreciated the rich musical treat provided for them. The programme comprised pieces from the works of Haydn, Beethoven, Chopin, Mendelssohn, Schumann, Sterndale Bennett, and Walter Macfarren himself.

The *Banner* has the following " case which is suggestive to persons about to marry, and to all who are meditating the purchase of a new pianoforte, came before the court at the Old Bailey recently, when William Rutley, printer, and Telemachus Collard, carpenter, were indicted for forging and counterfeiting the trade mark of Messrs. Collard and Collard, pianoforte makers, in Cheapside. The prisoners were ultimately discharged, after giving a positive undertaking that in the future this system of imitating the trade-marks of the prosecutors should be stopped, and Collard also consented to give up the labels still in his possession, by removing them from all the pianos upon which they had been placed under his control. Although the defendants were thus acquitted, the fact remains that the system of imitating trade-marks is adopted more widely than is generally supposed.

On Sept. 6th, the organ of St. Leonard's Church, Newark, which has undergone extensive alterations, was re-opened, and a special service was held. There was a crowded congregation. In addition to the organ the band of the Yeomanry Cavalry, under the direction of the Bandmaster, Mr. Lilley, played selections of sacred music. The work of re-building was entrusted to Messrs. Hasston and Sons, of Newark. They have added a swell organ with nine stops, with three additional couplers.

After passing through the fire of a natural reaction,—after undergoing the abuse of the long-haired advanced school, who apparently hate the notion of a gentleman and a man of large general culture proving himself to be a tone-poet of a high order,—Mendelssohn's best music is still holding its own, and, further, it is noticed that his best works are being actually more and more performed, and are finding an undeniable general acceptance from day to day. This is the case, too, with the greatest works of Mozart.

The prospectus of the Sacred Harmonic Society has been issued for the season. Mr. C. Hallé is again conductor, and Mr. W. H. Cummings, assistant conductor. On Nov. 16th, Macfarren's "King David," will be given under Sir A. Sullivan's direction, as he is preparing its production in Leeds. Other features of the season will be Bach's "Christmas Oratorio," Mendelssohn's "Walpurgis Night," and Gounod's "Redemption." The concerts will be given at St. James's Hall, and the conversazione at Prince's Hall, Piccadilly.

A choral festival will be held at the Church of SS. Augustine and Faith, Watling Street, E.C., on Friday evening next, the 5th October (being the eve of St. Faith's day), commencing at half-past seven. The music will consist of Villiers-Stanford's Evening Service in A, Schubert's Psalm "The Lord is my Shepherd," a short selection from the oratorio's of "St. Paul," and the whole of Dr. Stainer's cantata "The Daughter of Jairus"; the choir of the church being slightly augmented for the occasion, and Mr. C. E. Miller, the organist, presiding at the organ. This little church, hestling under, and almost hidden by, the neighbouring cathedral of St. Paul, was twenty years ago a pioneer of choral services in London, and is now justly noted both for its high-class and well-rendered music.

Says the Banner :—A considerable measure of success attended the second annual open-air concert at Wakefield, held on Sunday, Sept. 9th, in aid of the funds of the Clayton Hospital in that town. The weather was most favourable, and upwards of 25,000 persons attended the performance, in which between five and six hundred vocalists and instrumentalists took part. The programme included several choruses from Handel's "Messiah" and "Judas Maccabæus" and three well-known hymns. The conduct of those present was all that could be desired, and a large sum was realised for the benefit of the hospital, the offering being received in boxes and sheets. The proceedings were opened by prayer by the Rev. A. Chalmers, Unitarian minister, and closed in a similar manner by the Rev. A. T. Curtis, vicar of St. Michael's Church. This example will very likely be followed in other towns, next season it may be fairly assumed.

With regret is announced the death of Mr. George Forbes, who, for forty-five years, was organist at St. Mary's Church, Bryanston Square. The deceased gentleman was in his seventy-first year, and for some time previous to his death had been suffering from a complication of internal complaints. It was not, however, until lately that his illness caused any anxiety to his friends, as he seemed as strong and hearty as ever. On Sunday, August 5th, the induction day of the new Rector, the Rev. the Hon. Canon Leigh—after presiding at the organ, Mr. Forbes complained of feeling very ill, and, at his request, two of his friends connected with the church saw him safely to his residence. After a rest of some days, Mr. Forbes resumed his duties as organist, but on Sunday, the 26th ult., he had a relapse, and never again left his bed. The loss sustained by St. Mary's will be very deeply felt, as both in and out the church deceased's genial nature and kindliness of heart were well known and appreciated by a large circle of friends. Mr. Forbes was a talented and industrious musician, composing, arranging, playing, and teaching with such marked ability, as to have secured the estimation of a large musical connection.

It is announced that Herr Pollini, the director of the Hamburg Theatre, has been fortunate enough to discover a new tenor of the first rank, Herr Gustav Memmler, who has just made a brilliant *début* in the very trying part of Tristan.

The evenings following the days of military display in the neighbourhood of Homburg have been devoted to plays and operas performed before the imperial and royal visitors. On the 22nd was given a gala performance of "Carmen," with Mdme. Trebelli in the title part, at the Kurhaus Theatre.

La Gazetta Musicale of Milan, in reviewing Sir A. Sullivan's "Martyr of Antioch," says "The appearance of a new work from one of the most illustrious of English composers is to be regarded as an event of great importance;" says further "The work is most beautiful, the style elevated and good in character;" and concludes "we offer hearty congratulations to Sir A. Sullivan."

The statement that the Vatican archives will shortly be opened to the public, and that the only thing necessary to gain admission will be sending a note to the librarian stating the kind of study about to be undertaken, are matters of exceptional interest to the students of all branches of science, literature, and art. It is indeed a matter of congratulation that His Holiness, the Pope, has thus departed from the old restrictive and protective policy, and, decided upon allowing the world to know something of the unequalled treasures of the Vatican. Musicians will anxiously look forward to some information to be gained from the visits of experts regarding the musical works, and books yielding information concerning the art to be found in the Vatican.

One characteristic feature of the recent German military manœuvres was the performance, on the evening of the 20th, by way of welcome to the German Emperor, of the great tattoo by the combined bands of the Army Corps, massed as one band, and numbering no less than 1,012 bandsmen, fifers, and drummers. The programme includes—March, "Queen of Saba," by Gounod; Festival-Overture, by Fisher; Finale of 3rd act of "Rienzi," by Wagner; Fanfare militaire, by Asher; and the great tattoo. It is strange that a similar combination of military bands is not attempted elsewhere, though in England it is to be feared unexpected difficulties would arise in the way of ill-advised selections of instruments, and want of agreement as regards pitch.

M. Louis Besson of the Paris *Evénement*, tells the following pleasant little story :—"The other day a poor woman was endeavouring to earn a little money by singing in the Rue de Sentier. She was enfeebled with cold and hunger, and her voice was hoarse with the effects of a sore throat. Suddenly her strength failed and she sank on the pavement. At this moment a young pupil at the Conservatoire, Mdlle. Anna Drousart—why not tell her name?—came out of the opposite house and perceived the unfortunate singer. She tended her with every possible care and gave her money. But, not being very rich herself, she conceived the idea of putting herself in the woman's place. So the inhabitants of the street were surprised to hear all at once a fresh and lovely soprano voice singing without accompaniment Gounod's "Ave Maria" and the "Berceuse" from "L'Africaine." All the windows were thrown open, as may be imagined, and contributions poured in so liberally, that the poor woman returned home with the sum of eighty-five francs, which Mdlle. Drousart had thus cheerfully earned for her."

The London Music Company, having commenced operations at 54, Great Marlborough-street, have issued a wonderfully cheap list of useful pianofortes. But as regards the advancement of the art, their proposals attend the publishing of new music, are perhaps the most important. They announce that a jury of three musicians will examine works offered for publication, the decision of these gentlemen being accepted by the company, who are already prepared to receive MSS. This scheme is one likely under good management to exercise an important influence for the good of the art, and the proposal claims public attention and support.

APPOINTMENT.

Mr. J. Flavell, pupil of Hugh Brooksbank, Esq., Mus. Bac., of Llandaff Cathedral, has been appointed Organist and Choirmaster of Worksop Abbey.

The Querier.

QUERY.

BOOK FOR LEARNING MUSIC.—Would some one be kind enough to inform a reader of the best book for learning music; also, where it is to be obtained, and the price.—A LOVER OF MUSIC.

[No more suitable work could be found than Mr. H.'C. Banister's "Music," advertised in another portion of this paper.—ED. *Mus. Stand.*]

Service Lists.

NINETEENTH SUNDAY AFTER TRINITY. SEPTEMBER 30th.

London.

ST. PAUL'S CATHEDRAL.—Morn.: Service, Te Deum and Benedictus, Lloyd in E flat; Introit, O saving victim (Gounod); Holy Communion, Schubert in B flat. Even.: Service, Magnificat and Nunc Dimittis, Barnby in E flat; Anthem, O come before His presence with singing (Martin).

FOUNDLING CHAPEL.—Morn.: Service, Dykes in F; Benedictus, Smart in F; Anthem, God is our hope and strength (Greene).—Aft.: Children's Service.

ALL SAINTS, MARGARET STREET.—Morn.: Service, Te Deum Tours in F; Benedictus (Stainer); Holy Communion, Weber in G; Offertory Anthem, O pray for the peace (Thorne). Even.: Service, Garrett in F; Anthem, Hear my prayer (Mendelssohn).

CHRIST CHURCH, CLAPHAM.—Morn.: Service, Te Deum, Plain-song; Kyrie, and Credo, Mozart in B flat; Offertory Anthem, For He shall give His angels "Elijah" (Mendelssohn); Sanctus Benedictus Agnus Dei, and Gloria in Excelsis (Mozart). Even.: Service, Magnificat and Nunc Dimittis, Stainer in A; Anthem, O praise the Lord, all ye His angels (Barnby).

HOLY TRINITY, GRAY'S INN ROAD.— Morn.: Service, Te Deum, Boyce in A; Jubilate, Chanted; Nicene Creed, Stainer in A. Even.: Service, Magnificat, Tours in F; Nunc Dimittis, Chanted; Anthem, The wilderness (Goss).

HOLY TRINITY, TULSE HILL.—Morn.: Chant Service. Even.: Service, Magnificat and Nunc Dimittis, Stainer in A; Anthem, Praise the Lord, O my soul (Goss).

ST. JAMES'S PRIVATE EPISCOPAL CHAPEL, SOUTHWARK. —Morn.: Service, Introit, O Lamb of God (Hummel); Communion Service, Stainer in A. Even.: Service, Barnby in E flat; Anthem, Lord vouchsafe ("Cujus Animam") (Rossini).

ST. MARGARET PATTENS, ROOD LANE, FENCHURCH STREET.—Morn.: Service, Te Deum, Wesley in E; Benedictus, Dykes in F; Communion Service, Offertory Anthem, Jesu, Lord of Life (Nauman); Kyrie, Credo, Sanctus, Benedictus, Agnus Dei, and Gloria, Mozart in B flat. Even.: Service, Magnificat and Nunc Dimittis (Tuckermann); Anthem, Whosoever drinketh, and God is a Spirit (Bennett).

ST. MARY BOLTONS, WEST BROMPTON, S.W.—Morn.: Service, Te Deum, Hopkins in E; Benedictus, Chant; Holy Communion, throughout, Redhead in F; Offertory (Barnby). Even.: Service, Magnificat and Nunc Dimittis, Gounod in D; Anthem, To Thee Cherubim (Handel).

ST. MAGNUS, LONDON BRIDGE.—Morn.: Service, Opening Anthem, I will arise (Creyton); Te Deum and Jubilate, Goss in A; Kyrie (Goss). Even.: Service, Magnificat and Nunc Dimittis, Eldon, in C; Anthem, Come holy Spirit (Hatton).

ST. MICHAEL'S, CORNHILL.—Morn.: Service, Te Deum and Jubilate, Sullivan in D; Anthem, I have surely built Thee a house (Boyce); Kyrie and Creed, Thorne in E flat. Even.: Service, Magnificat and Nunc Dimittis, Hopkins in F; Anthem, O, praise the Lord (Handel).

ST. PAUL'S, AVENUE ROAD, SOUTH HAMPSTEAD.—Morn.: Service, Te Deum, Tours in F; Benedictus (Barnby); Kyrie, Boyce in A. Even.: Service, Magnificat and Nunc Dimittis, Smart in F; Anthem, Lead kindly light (Stainer).

ST. PAUL'S, BOW COMMON, E.—Morn.: Service, Te Deum and Benedictus, Chants; Holy Communion, Kyrie, Credo, Sanctus, Benedictus and Gloria in excelsis, Eyre in E flat; Offertory (Garrett). Even.: Service, Magnificat and Nunc Dimittis, Stainer in E flat; Anthem, O clap your hands (Stainer).

ST. PETER'S (EATON SQUARE).—Morn.: Service, Te Deum, Dykes in F. Even.: Service, Hopkins in F; Anthem, Blessed be the God and Father (Wesley).

ST. PETER'S, VERE STREET, W.—Even.: Service, Magnificat and Nunc Dimittis, Parry in D; Anthem, I will magnify Thee (Goss).

ST. AUGUSTINE AND ST. FAITH, WATLING STREET.— Morn.: Service, Smart in F; Introit, O praise the Lord (South); Communion Service, Smart in F. Even.: Service, Stuart in B flat; Anthem, O praise the Lord, all ye His angels (Barnby).

ST. SAVIOUR'S, HOXTON. — Morn.: Service, Te Deum, Goss in F; Holy Communion; Kyrie, Credo, Sanctus, and Gloria in excelsis, Ouseley in C. Even.: Service, Magnificat and Nunc Dimittis, Bunnett in F; Anthem, With angels and arch-angels (Hopkins).

ST. SEPULCHRE'S, HOLBORN.—Morn.: Service, Smart in F; Even.: Service, Cooke in G; Anthem, and the glory (Handel).

Country.

ST. ASAPH CATHEDRAL.—Morn.: Service, Whitfeld in E; Anthem, This is the day (Gaul). Even.: Service, The Litany; Anthem, Not unto us (Barnby).

ASHBURNE CHURCH, DERBYSHIRE. — Morn.: Service, Hopkins in C. Even.: Service, Hopkins in F; Anthem, God Thou art great (Spohr).

BIRMINGHAM (S. ALBAN THE MARTYR).—Morn.: Service, Te Deum, Boyce in G; Benedictus, Steggall in G; Holy Communion, Kyrie, Credo, Sursum Corda, Sanctus, Benedictus, Agnus Dei and Gloria, Redman in F throughout. Evensong. Magnificat and Nunc Dimittis, Redman in F.

BIRMINGHAM (St. CYPRIAN'S, HAY MILLS).—Morn.: Service, Cobb in G; Anthem, O come let us worship (Mendelssohn). Even.: Service, Smart in F; Anthem, The heavens declare (Barnby).

BELFAST (ST. GEORGE'S).—Morn.: Service, Te Deum and Jubilate, Garrett in F; Apostles' Creed, Harmonized Monotone; Litany (Helmore); Kyrie (Spohr); Gloria, Gratias and Creed, Dykes in F; Offertory (Stainer). Even.: Service, Magnificat and Nunc Dimittis, Goss in A; Apostles' Creed, Harmonized Monotone; Anthem, Lord, for Thy tender mercies' sake (Farrant).

CANTERBURY CATHEDRAL.—Morn.: Service, Richardson in F; Anthem, O praise the Lord (Oakeley); Communion, Richardson in F. Even.: Service, Richardson in F; Anthem, Holy, holy, holy, Lord our Creator (Mendelssohn).

CARLISLE CATHEDRAL.—Morn.: Service, Tours in F; Introit, I will love Thee (Macfarren); Kyrie and Nicene Creed, Tours in F. Even.: Service, Tours in F; Anthem, God is a Spirit, and Blessed be the Lord God (Bennett).

CHESTER (ST. MARY'S CHURCH).—Morn.: Service, Garrett in F; Communion Service, Tearne in G. Even.: Service, Barnby in F; O taste and see how gracious the Lord is (Goss).

DONCASTER (PARISH CHURCH).—Morn.: Service, Tours in F; Even.: Service, Calkin in B flat; Anthem, Blow ye the trumpet (Taylor).

EDINBURGH (ST. JOHN'S).—Aft.: Service, Anthem, Sing praises to the Lord (Croft). Even.: Service, Anthem, The Lord is my Shepherd (Macfarren).

ELY CATHEDRAL.—Morn.: Service, Clarke in E; Kyrie and Credo, Clarke in E; Gloria, "Ely"; Anthem, Unto which of the angels (Handel). Even.: Service, Anthem, To Thee all angels (To Thee, cherubim (Handel).

FOLKESTONE (ST. MICHAEL'S).—Morn.: Service (Gounod); Anthem, And God made the Firmament, and The Marvellous Works (Haydn's "Creation"). Even.: Service, Magnificat and Nunc Dimittis, Sceberras in F; Anthem, Rejoice, O Judah, and Hallelujah, Amen (Handel's "Judas Maccabæus"). After the sermon, Rejoice greatly (Handel's "Messiah").

HARROGATE (ST. PETER'S CHURCH). — Morn.: Service, Te Deum Helmore, No. 1; Anthem, Enter not into judgment (Attwood); Kyrie, Davy in F; Credo (Goss). Even.: Service, Magnificat, and Nunc Dimittis, Garrett in F (Edison); Anthem, I will sing of Thy great mercies (Mendelssohn).

LLANDAFF CATHEDRAL.—Morn.: Service, Te Deum and Jubilate, Stanford in B flat. Even.: Service, Magnificat and Nunc Dimittis, Stanford in B flat; Anthem, Fear not, O Land (Goss).

LEEDS PARISH CHURCH. — Morn.: Service, Mendelssohn in A; Anthem, If with all (Mendelssohn); Communion, Wesley in E. Even.: Service, Barnby in E flat; Anthem, Awake, awake (Stainer).

LINLITHGOW ABBEY, W.B.—Morn.: Service, Anthem, Behold God (Stainer). Even.: Service, Anthem, How lovely are Thy dwellings (Spohr).

LIVERPOOL CATHEDRAL.—Aft.: Service, Magnificat and Nunc Dimittis, Hatton in E flat; Anthem, O praise the Lord of heaven (Elvey).

LIVERPOOL (ST. CUTHBERT'S, EVERTON).—Morn.: Service, Te Deum and Jubilate, Barnby in E; Kyrie and Credo, Smart in F; Anthem God is a Spirit, unaccompanied (Bennett). Even.: Service, Cantate e Deus, Attwood in D; Anthem, How lovely I Happy who in Thy house; Lord God of hosts, hear thou my prayer; and Lord God of hosts; that reigneth on high (Spohr); Concluding Anthem, Hallelujah, "Mount of Olives" (Beethoven).

MANCHESTER CATHEDRAL.—Morn.: Service, Te Deum, Jubilate, Kyrie, Creed, Sanctus and Gloria, Chippy in A; Anthem, But He shall give His angels (Mendelssohn), Aft.: Service, Chipp in A; Anthem, And there was war in heaven (Allon).

MANCHESTER (ST. BENEDICT'S).—Morn.: Service, Kyrie (Elvey); Credo, Sanctus, Benedictus, Agnus Dei, and Gloria in excelsis, Haydn in C, No. 2. Even.: Service, Magnificat and Nunc Dimittis, Bennett in F.

MANCHESTER (ST. JOHN BAPTIST, HULME).—Morn.: Service, Te Deum and Benedictus (Gregorian); Kyrie (Meyerbeer); Credo, Sanctus and Gloria in excelsis, Garrett in D; Benedictus, Thorne in B flat; Agnus Dei, Mind in A flat; Paternoster, Hoyte in G. Even.: Service, Magnificat and Nunc Dimittis, Tours in F.

MITCHAM PARISH CHURCH.—Morn.: Service, Te Deum, Dykes in F; Anthem, Fear not, O land, be glad and rejoice (Garrett). Kyrie, Thorough B flat; Creed (Goss). Even.: Service, Magnificat and Nunc Dimittis, Garrett in F; Anthem, Thou visitest the earth (Greene).

PETERBOROUGH CATHEDRAL.—Morn.: Service, Keeton in B flat; Anthem, Teach me, O Lord (Attwood); Communion Service, King in C. Even.: Service, Keeton in B flat; Anthem, God is our hope (Greene).

ROCHESTER CATHEDRAL.—Morn.: Service, Cooke in G; Anthem, Above Him stood, holy holy (Mendelssohn). Even.: Service, Cooke in G; Anthem, I was in the Spirit (Blow).

SHEFFIELD PARISH CHURCH.—Morn.: Service, Kyrie, Tours in F. Even.: Service, Trimnell in F; Anthem, How lovely are Thy dwellings (Spohr).

SHERBORNE ABBEY.—Morn.: Service, Te Deum, Lyle in D; Anthem, Thou, O God, art praised in Zion (Coste). Even.: Service, Chants; Anthem, This is the day (Elvey).

SALISBURY CATHEDRAL.—Morn.: Service, Selby in A; Offertory, Selby in A; Service, Selby in A; Anthem, O praise the Lord of Heaven (Goss).

SOUTHAMPTON (ST. MARY'S CHURCH).—Morn.: Service, Te Deum and Benedictus, Custard in F; Holy Communion, Introit; Therefore with angels (Novello); Service, Custard in E flat; Offertory, He that soweth (Barnby); Paternoster (Hoyte). Even.: Service, Magnificat and Nunc Dimittis, Walmisley in D minor; Apostles' Creed, Harmonised Monotone; Anthem, Ye shall dwell in the land (Starnes).

WELLS CATHEDRAL.—Morn.: Service, Barnby in E; Introit; The Lord has been mindful (Macfarren), Even.: Service, Goss in D; Anthem, I beheld, and lo (Blow).

WORCESTER CATHEDRAL.—Morn.: Service, Garrett in D; Anthem, See what love (Mendelssohn). Even.: Service, Garrett in D; Anthem, Praise the Lord (Hayes).

*** Post-cards must be sent to the Editor, 6, Argyll Square, W.C., by Wednesday. Lists are frequently omitted in consequence of not being received in time.

NEWSPAPERS sent should have distinct marks opposite to the matter to which attention is required.

NOTICE TO CORRESPONDENTS—Letters on Counterpoint (from Dr. Hiles, Mr. H. J. Stark, and X. Y. Z.), with other matter, are held over till next week.

Printed for the Proprietor by BOWDEN, HUDSON & CO., at 23, Red Lion Street, Holborn, London, W.C. ; and Published by WILLIAM REEVES, at the Office, 185, Fleet Street, E.C. West End Agents:—WEEKES & CO., 14, Hanover Street, Regent Street, W. Subscriptions and Advertisements are received either by the Publisher or West End Agents.—Communications for the EDITOR are to be forwarded to his private address, 6, Argyle Square, W.C.
SATURDAY, SEPTEMBER 29, 1883.—Entered at the General Post Office as a Newspaper.

The MUSICAL STANDARD

A NEWSPAPER FOR MUSICIANS PROFESSIONAL AND AMATEUR

No. 1,001. Vol. XXV. FOURTH SERIES.　　SATURDAY, OCTOBER 6, 1883.　　WEEKLY: PRICE 3D.

A DREAM.

I amuse myself sometimes in the sleepless hours of night, when the simpler devices of counting a flock of sheep leaping over a style, or saying the alphabet backwards, fail to bring the sweet god of forgetfulness, by picturing to myself what I would do if I had a great fortune ; till presently I fall into a kind of waking dream which usually takes something like the following shape :—

I have been left a comfortable competency of a million a year safely resulting from a respectable investment in Government three-per-cents. I very naturally ask myself what I can do with the money so as to secure the greatest enjoyment for myself coupled with a certain amount of good to my fellow men. As I am a musician, it equally naturally follows that I determine to endow a musical institution, and as I am a Wagnerian *pur sang*, the form that institution takes is a theatre on strict Wagnerian principles, where, however, not only the master's works, but really great operas of all other schools shall be performed, totally regardless of expense, in strict and reverend accord with the intentions of their creators. To this end the first object is the building. This is to be erected on a gentle eminence which rears its modest head close to Sherborne, for Sherborne presents many advantages which even Bayreuth cannot boast of. It lies but three hours from London ; it lies on the main line of the South-Western Railway, so that all who care to come to my performances can get here easily ; the hotel accommodation is good ; but of that I cannot speak more particularly lest I be accused of insinuating a cheap advertisement into these widely-read columns. But the main thing in its favour is, that the inhabitants of this town—as indeed all West-country folk—are passionately fond of music and are also very proud of all their town institutions ; witness the noble abbey, the town-hall, and the Digby Memorial-hall, which latter has not been built yet, but is vastly talked about. Here, then, on this pleasing eminence, I will erect a noble theatre that shall in all its essentials conform strictly to the Bayreuth original, while in its details, and especially in the materials of which it is built, it will far transcend its prototype. Everything about it is to be massive and rich, but nothing gaudy or luxurious ; indeed, the ornamental accessories shall be confined mainly to the exterior, which cannot be too handsome. The auditorium, on the other hand, is to be left as plain as possible, having regard to the strict requirements of good taste only. Nothing meretricious, nothing that shall for a moment attract the eye from the stage, shall find any tolerance. The stage, indeed, is to be the main object of the whole building, and on it all that modern engineering skill, all that modern art and science are capable of, shall be freely lavished. The mechanical arrangements are to be as nearly perfect as anything human can be, and I rely upon electricity not only for illumination but for many other aids undreamt of even by Wagner. The scenery is to be entirely under the control of the prompter, so that the most elaborate sets can be removed and others equally elaborate put in their place merely by touching a knob,—and all instantaneously and noiselessly. Such a thing as a carpenter's scene will be quite unknown ; on the other hand, by calling in the assistance of the very greatest artists only, I hope to produce pictures in "Parsifal" and the "Nibelungen" such as the wildest idealism must be content with. I calculate that for about £250,000 I ought to get the kind of building I want, but of course I am prepared to go to any further sum that may be needed. Grouped round my theatre there will be a small city of tasteful detached houses, in which all my artists will live, each receiving a house and garden suited to his wants rent free. And this brings me to the most elaborate and costly part of my scheme —though money is really no object whatever—the constitution and maintenance of my *personnel*. My orchestra, (the most important part of any operatic establishment, though it has not hitherto been recognised as such) will consist of about 25 first and 25 second violins, 20 violas, 20 'cellos and 25 basses, of which 12 will use the 4-stringed instruments. There will also be two 'contra double basses of 32-feet tone, 6 flutes, 4 oboes, 4 clarinets, 2 bass clarinets, 2 corno inglese, 4 bassoons, 2 contra bassoons, 6 harps, 8 horns, 6 trumpets, 8 trombones, 2 serpents, 2 tubas, 2 sets of kettle-drums (3 in each set), big drum and cymbals, triangle, tam-tam, etc., making with extras a respectable total, of say, 180 performers for

the orchestra before the stage. But, of course, I shall have a splendid organ on the stage and a complete military band, so that the total may reasonably be placed at 240 members. These will receive a liberal salary, graduated upon the importance of their various instruments and also upon their own individual merits, but no member of my orchestra shall receive less than £500 a year, which, with a house, rent free, coal and gas and perquisites (including tax, being paid by me), ought to enable him to live like a gentleman. Indeed, very important qualifications for membership in my orchestra will be—gentlemanliness of behaviour, a generous instinct for art, and the loftiest moral tone. On the stage, the establishment will consist of 50 picked artists of the highest calibre, not including, however, stars of such prodigious vocal powers as to absorb an unfair amount of attention, and a carefully chosen chorus of 150 voices. These shall also receive salaries beginning at £500, with the same privileges in the way of house-rent, etc. as the orchestra. I shall altogether expect to have a pleasant little salary list of about £500,000 or £600,000 a year ; but in return for that, I shall have gathered together such a body of artists as will be quite unmatched. While the theatre, and the city are being built, this great phalanx will be set to work studying some of the first works of our future *répertoire*, and getting acquainted with each other. When the theatre is ready, what a festival we shall have at the opening ! Imagine the sight ! There on the pleasing hill will tower the lofty edifice, standing alone on a fair lawn set about with flowers and fountains and approached by gently sloping carriage-drives. Round it, in a semicircle, cluster the pretty villas of the artists. There will be no Churches, because the various places of worship in Sherborne will amply suffice for all our needs, but there will be a special school in which every form of useful knowledge will be taught, including music, both theoretical and practical. Imagine the beautiful town, in which architecture shall be encouraged to display its fairest forms, even on the humblest building, so that it shall be a model for all the world; swarming with bright-faced artists; safe from all anxiety (I need not say that anyone found worthy to join the Sherborne Theatre will never be dismissed), and mingling freely with the guests who have come from all the ends of the world to assist at our opening performance of "Parsifal."

As rest is as needful to the body and mind as air, there will only be three operatic performances a week in the theatre, the intervals being dedicated to enjoyment or to needful rehearsals. No work will be presented before it has been rehearsed, with full accessories, at least twelve times, but of course nothing will be produced till there is absolutely no flaw whatever in the performance. And what a *répertoire* we shall have ! The operas of Gluck, Mozart, Beethoven, one or two of Meyerbeer's, one or two of Verdi's, one or two of Gounod's, and, of course, all Wagner's, will form the foundation ; but I shall rely upon a great school of dramatic composition, springing up almost immediately in England ; for every work sent in will be carefully and fairly examined, and if found answering the first requirements, will be as carefully rehearsed, as if for a long run, and will then be produced *in the presence of the composer only*. And if he likes it, it will find a place in the general *répertoire*.

I have not quite settled yet on what system the public is to be admitted to my theatre. There is a doubt in my mind whether I will admit them at all in a general sense. Of course, all admission will be free, if there is any, and students from distant countries will indeed receive subsidies to enable them to assist at our performances. But one class, the critics, will be required to pay, and pay rather heavily, for their places ; in the first place, because, as I shall only employ the greatest performers, and produce the greatest masterpieces, critics will be quite unnecessary ; and in the second because this is the only safe means of ensuring a perfectly unbiassed report.

My brain is in a whirl when I think of the blessings my theatre will bring upon England. She will spring at once into the foremost place among musical nations : composers, dramatic singers, orchestral players, will occupy a new position, and an era will dawn for my beloved art such as it has never yet passed through.

Have I forgotten anything ? Oh yes, the conductor ! At this point, I grieve to say, my waking dream gradually slips into a waking nightmare, and I finish by picturing MYSELF conducting this vast and glorious combination ; and daring the performance of one of my own operas,—I fall gently asleep. LOUIS N. PARKER.

THE CANTUS TRANCENDENTALIS.

The *Orchestra* thus describes a new instrument : The Cantus Transcendentalis, an invention of Mr. Karl Hahn from Blasenwetz near Dresden, has attracted considerable attention in the musical circles of Germany. The highest testimonials and approbations have been granted to Mr. Hahn by Professor J. Joachim, Professor von Helmholtz, H.M. the King of Saxony, and the press. The Cantus contains five octaves of keys, from F to F, and resembles in shape a small table standing on two legs. The principal novelties and improvements are :—1. A singular tone, very noble, impressive, and with a great variety of expression. 2. An apparatus to vibrate slowly or quickly like a human voice, and to regulate the vibration according to the required expression or to cause the vibration to cease. 3. A sounding-board, directing the full sound towards the hearer, and avoiding any loss of tone. 4. A prolongation, which enables the player to keep as many tones as he likes sounding and increasing to any length, without resting the fingers on the keys. This contrivance replaces the pedal effect in many cases and allows the player to produce chords five octaves in compass. Mr. Hahn produced this instrument for the first time at the Crystal Palace, where it was highly appreciated by the audience. It is said that Mr. Hahn will reside for a short time in London, 36, Oxford Terrace, W., where the new instrument may be seen and further particulars obtained. The price, it is understood, will be about fifteen guineas.

NOTES ABOUT PAGANINI.

The succeeding extracts are reprinted from *Musical Opinion* :—

The singular personality of Paganini displayed itself in his private, no less than in his artistic life ; and a few out of the many anecdotes told of him will be of interest, as throwing fresh light on the man. Paganini was accused of being selfish and miserly, of caring little even for his art, except as a means of accumulating money. While there is much in his life to justify such an indictment, it is no less true that he on many occasions displayed great generosity. He was always willing to give concerts for the benefit of his fellow artists, and for other charitable purposes, and on more than one occasion bestowed large sums of money for the relief of distress. We may assume that he was niggardly by habit and generous by impulse. Utterly ignorant of everything except the art of music, bred under the most unfortunate and demoralising conditions, the fact that his character was on the whole so *naïve* and upright speaks eloquently for the native qualities of his disposition. His eccentricities, perhaps, justified the unreasoning vulgar in believing that he was slightly crazed. His appearance and manner on the platform were fantastic in the extreme, and rarely failed to provoke ridicule, till his magic turned all other emotions into one of breathless admiration. He talked to himself continually when alone, a habit which was partly responsible for the belief that he was always attended by a familiar demon. When a stranger was introduced to him, his corpse-like face became galvanized into a ghastly smile, which produced a singular impression, half fascinating, half repulsive. He was taciturn in society, except among his intimates, when his buoyant spirits bubbled out in a polyglot tongue, for he never knew any language well except his own. Naturally irritable, his quick temper was inflamed by intestinal disease, which racked him with a suffering that was aggravated by a nostrum, in the use of which he indulged freely. Indeed, it was said by his friends, that his death was accelerated by his devotion to medical quackery, from a belief in which no arguments could wean him.

To his fellow artists he was always polite and attentive, though they annoyed him by their persistent curiosity as to the means by which he produced his unrivalled effects—effects which the established technique of violin-playing could not explain. An Englishman, named George Harris, who was an attaché of the Hanoverian Court, attended Paganini for a year as his private secretary, and he asserts that Paganini was never seen to practise a single note of music in private. His astonishing dexterity was kept up to its pitch by the numerous concerts which he gave, and by his exquisitely delicate organization. He was accustomed to say that his whole early life had been one of prodigious and continual study, and that he could afford to repose in after years. Paganini's knowledge of music was profound and exact, and the most difficult music was mere child's play to him. Pasini, a well-known painter, living at Parma, did not believe the stories told of Paganini's ability to play the most difficult music at sight. Being the possessor of a valuable Stradiuarius violin, he challenged our artist to play, at first hand, a manuscript concerto which he placed before him. "This instrument shall be yours," he said, "if you can play in a masterly manner that concerto at first sight." The Genoese took the violin in his hand, saying :

"In that case, my friend, you may bid adieu to it at once," and he immediately threw Pasini into ecstatic admiration by his performance of the piece. There is little doubt that this is the Stradiuarius instrument left by Paganini to his son, and valued at about £6000.

He was very fond of his little son Achille. A French gentleman tells us that he called once to take Paganini to dine with him. He found the artist's room in great disorder. A violin on the table with manuscript music, another upon a chair, a snuff-box on the bed along with his child's toys, music, money, letters, articles of dress—all pell-mell ; nor were the tables and chairs in their proper places. Everything was in the most conspicuous confusion. The child was out of temper ; something had vexed him ; he had been told to wash his hands ; and, while the little one gave vent to the most violent bursts of temper, the father stood as calm and quiet as the most accomplished of nurses. He merely turned quietly to his visitor, and said, in melancholy accents : "The poor child is cross ; I do not know what to do to amuse him ; I have played with him since morning, and I cannot stand it any longer."

In the early part of the present century the facilities for travel were far less convenient than at the present time, and it was always an arduous undertaking to one in Paganini's frail condition of health. He was, however, generally cheerful while jolting along in the post-chaise, and chattered incessantly as long as his voice held out. Harris tells us that the artist was in the habit of getting out when the horses were changed, to stretch his long limbs after the confinement of the carriage. Often he extended his promenades, when he became interested in the town through which he was passing, and would not return till long after the fresh horses had been harnessed, thereby causing much annoyance to the driver. On one occasion Jehu swore if it occurred again he would drive on and leave his passenger behind to get along as best he could. The secretary, Harris, was enjoying a nap, and the driver was true to his resolution at the next stopping place, leaving Paganini behind. This made much trouble, and a special coach had to be sent for the enraged artist, who was found sputtering oaths in half a dozen different languages. Paganini refused to pay for the carriage, and it was only by force of law that he reluctantly settled the bill.

His baggage was always of the plainest description ; in fact, ludicrously simple. A shabby box contained his precious Guarnerius fiddle, and served also as a portmanteau wherein to pack his jewellery, his linen, and sundry trifles. In addition to this he carried a small travelling bag and a hat-box. Mr. Harris tells us that Paganini was in eating and drinking exceedingly frugal. Table indulgence was forbidden him by the condition of his health, as any deviation from the strictest diet resulted in great suffering. He was a thorough Italian in all his habits and ideas. Among other traits was a great disdain for the lower classes, though he was by no means subservient to the people of rank and wealth. It was his habit, when an inferior addressed him, to enquire of his companion, "What does this animal want with me ?" If he was pleased with his coachman, he would say, "That animal drives well." This seemed not so much the vulgar arrogance of a small nature, elevated above the class in life from which it sprang, as that pride of great gifts, which made the freemasonry of genius the measure by which he judged all others, noble and simple. Like all men of highly nervous constitution, he was keenly susceptible to both enjoyment and suffering. He was so sensitive to atmospheric changes that his irritability was excessive during a thunderstorm. He would then remain silent for hours together, while his eyes rolled and his limbs twitched convulsively. Such fragile, nervous, highly sensitive organizations are not unfrequently characteristic of men of great genius, and in the Italian violinist it was developed in an abnormal degree.

The circumstances accompanying the last scenes of Paganini's life are very interesting. He had been intimate with most of the great people of Europe, among them, Lord Byron, Sir Clifford Constable, Lord Holland, Rossini, Ugo Foscolo, Monti, Prince Jerome, the Princess Eliza, and most of the great painters, poets, and musicians of his age. For Lord Byron he had a most ardent and exaggerated admiration. Paganini had stopped at Nice on his way from Paris, detained by extreme debility, for his last hours were drawing near. Under the blue sky and balmy air of this Mediterranean paradise the great musician somewhat recovered his strength at first. One night he sat by his bedroom window, surrounded by a circle of intimate friends, watching the glories of the Italian sunset that emblazoned earth, air, and sky, with the richest dyes of nature's pallet. A soft breeze swept into the room, heavy with the perfumes of flowers, and the twittering of the birds in the green foliage, mingled with the hum of talk from the throngs of gay promenaders sauntering on the beech. For a while Paganini sat silently absorbed in watching the joyous scene, when suddenly his eyes turned on a picture of Lord Byron that hung on the wall. A flash of enthusiasm lightened his face, as if a great thought were struggling to the surface, and he seized his violin to improvize. The listeners declared that this "swan song" was the most remarkable production of his life. He illustrated the stormy and romantic career of the English poet in music. The accents of doubt, irony, and despair, mingled with the cry of liberty, and the tumult of triumph.

Musical Intelligence.

NEWCASTLE-ON-TYNE.

Our coming musical season promises to be one of great interest and activity. The second series of Mr. Charles Hallé's Grand Orchestral Concerts, promoted by Messrs. Alderson and Brentall, will take place in the Town Hall, on November 12th, 1883, January 14th, and February 25th, 1884. Among the items on the programme, for the first concert, are:—Beethoven's "Pastoral" Symphony, one of Svendsen's "Rhapsodies Norvegiennes," and Mendelssohn's "Serenade and Allegro Giojoso," with orchestral accompaniment. Mr. Hallé will be the solo pianist, and Mr. Straus the leader of the orchestra. The vocalist engaged for the first concert is Mr. Santley.

Another great feature during the coming season will be the Special Chamber Concert, promoted by Messrs. Alderson and Brentnall, which will be held in the Town Hall, on December 7th. The artists engaged are :— Mdme. Norman-Néruda (violin), Mr. Charles Hallé (pianoforte), and Miss Santley (vocalist). As the pieces are truly popular, and the artists of first rank, the Town Hall is likely to be crowded to the doors.

The prospectus of Mr. W. Rea's three Subscription Concerts has been issued; but the dates have not yet been fixed for them. No doubt the concerts will be worthy of the reputation of their able and experienced conductor.

The first of the Chamber Music Society's concerts will take place on November 19th. Among the artists engaged are :—Herr Joachim, Mr. Henry Holmes, Signor Piatti, etc. Mr. Henry Holmes will lead the violin quartet which perform at the first concert.

The Annual General Meeting of the Newcastle Amateur Choral Society was held on September 27th, in the Church of England Institute. The works for this season are:—Van Bree's Dramatic Cantata "St. Cecilia's Day," Lock's "Macbeth," and a special arrangement of the choruses from Rossini's opera "La Donna del Lago." Notwithstanding this society has laboured under many disadvantages, it has wonderfully improved under the bâton of its talented conductor, Mr. J. McCallum.

"The Liebe-Heimlicher Trio," Mdme. Terese Liebe (violinist), Mdme. Heimlicher (pianist), and Mr. Liebe (violoncellist), have been performing last week, before crowded and delighted audiences, at the Promenade Concerts, given at the Central Exchange Art Gallery. Mdme. Terese Liebe is a great favourite here, where her talent as violinist is much admired.

After being completely renovated during the vacation, the Theatre Royal, with its chastely decorated interior, and many beauties, is a perfect little gem of its kind; and Messrs. Howard and Wyndham may be heartily congratulated on the success of their venture.

Lately Miss Florence St. John and her Comic Opera Company (under the management of M. Marius), have played with the greatest success, at the Theatre Royal, two of Jenback's operas, "Lurette" and "Madame Favart." And during this week Miss Kate Santley's Opera Company has been performing the clever production of Messrs. Fred. Clay and George R. Sims, entitled "The Merry Duchess," before delighted and crowded houses. The pleasing music, well rendered by a good company, combined with the witty libretto, and fine mounting of the whole, is likely to make this opera as popular in the provinces as it has been in London.

H. W.

The complaints as to the continued absence of any consideration of the vital subject of Church Music at the Church Congress are heard on every side. The special correspondent of a contemporary writing from Reading says :—To the regret of very many, for some years now, a charming item has been cut out of the scheme—namely, the evening devoted to church music, with illustrations by such choirs as were available. The practice was begun at Manchester just twenty years ago, and the Rev. Sir F. A. G. Ouseley, Dr. E. G. Monk, and Mr. W. H. Monk read the papers. Dr. Dykes was the lecturer at Norwich, and the following year the present Lord Chancellor, then Sir Roundell Palmer, read a most interesting paper on Hymnology. Next year, Ouseley and Helmore were the chief speakers. At subsequent congresses Dr. Gauntlett, E. H. Bickersteth, Drs. Stainer, Spark, Hullah, and Mr. Barnby spoke upon the art in which they were masters. Since Swansea no special place has been given to church music in the Congress programme.

CORK INDUSTRIAL EXHIBITION.

On Tuesday evening, the 25th inst., the greatest musical event of the Exhibition, viz., the performance of Mendelssohn's "Elijah," came off in the large hall of the building before an audience numbering several thousand persons. The oratorio, with the exception of two slight cuts of part of each of the choruses "Woe to him" and "But the Lord," was performed entire by the members of the "Cork Musical Society," under the bâton of Mr. J. C. Marks, Mus. Doc., Oxon. The following vocalists were engaged as principals :—soprani, Misses Marian Fenni and Lucy Ashton Hackett ; contralto, Miss Helen d'Alton ; Mr. Walter Bapty, bass, Mr. J. Sullivan, the minor parts being taken by Miss F. C. Marks and Messrs. R. M. Keatinge, D. F. Shea, and E. Hackett. The chorus consisted of 294 voices divided, as follows: Soprani, 104 ; contralti, 59 ; tenor, 53 ; bassi, 80 ; which together with the orchestra, numbering 52 members, made the very respectable ensemble of 346, exclusive of principals.

The faults to be found with the performance itself were, I am happy to say, but few and far between. The contralti were decidedly weak, as were also the tenori, though not so noticeably as the former, their apparent knowledge of it themselves unfortunately, however, provoking a tendency to force the tone at times.

The orchestra, owing probably to the number of extra hands got for the occasion, was not altogether as perfect as could be wished. This was plainest to be seen in the recitative "Now Cherith's Brook," and the aria, "Lord God of Abraham," the instruments not playing well together. Here, also, in the accompaniments of some of the recitatives, one of the principal defects in the organ showed up in its not speaking quick enough in answer to the pressure of the keys, causing a short series of syncopations never dreamt of by the composer. Neither was the band powerful enough for such a mass of voices. For instance : the ornate accompaniment to the chorus "Baal! hear and answer," and the beautiful figure for the strings in the chorus; "Behold, God the Lord" (Novello's ed., p. 160, bar 13 to end of movement) being, except to those seated quite close to the orchestra, undistinguishable amid the mass of voices and instruments. This, however, is partly due to the acoustical properties of the hall not being very good. The choruses were rendered throughout with an excellence and precision that speaks well for the care taken with the rehearsals by the conductor.

Of Miss Helen D'Alton's singing of her part it is almost unnecessary to speak, but it would be unfair not to refer to her excellent rendering of "Woe unto them" and "O, rest in the Lord," to the former of which, if there was any choice, I should most unhesitatingly give the palm. Miss Fenna throughout sustained her part as first soprano very well, "Hear ye Israel" being deserving of praise. Miss Hackett, though not having a heavy part did what she had to do with a conscientious regard for the intentions of the composer. Of Mr. Sullivan, as Elijah, the hardest work naturally fell, and right well he acquitted himself. In the aria, "Is not his word like a fire?" he was not so successful, his voice not being flexible enough to give the running passages with the necessary vigour, and they were somewhat slurred over in consequence, but, in "Lord God of Abraham," and "It is enough," his really magnificent voice showed to great advantage. Mr. Bapty was also very successful in his singing, particularly in "With all your hearts," gaining over the audience thus early in the evening. Mr. J. Osborne Marks, Mus. Doc., T.C.D. presided at the organ.

It is a great pleasure to think that such a number of amateurs can, in a provincial city like Cork, be got to work together so earnestly in the production of a work like the "Elijah," and with such excellent results. It only proves what the writer has held forth all along : that the stuff is there and all that is wanting is the raison d'être for putting forth their strength. It is only natural that when the singers see the conductor going through the rehearsal in a slovenly manner that they should also fall into a slovenly way of following him ; but, so also, as in the present instance, when they see their conductor going energetically to work, they begin to take an interest in what they are doing with the result of a good performance.

Unfortunately, too, the generality of the local press do nothing but praise both bad and good, with, it is needless to say, the result of making the performers quite careless.

F. St. John Lacy.

ST. JOHN'S, ANGELL TOWN.—The Harvest Festival commenced on St. Michael's day, September 29th. The music included Stainer's Service in A ; Anthems, "Glorious is Thy Name" (Mozart), and "O Lord, how manifold " (Barnby). Mr. W. J. Winbolt conducted with care and skill. Mr. E. H. Turpin was the organist. The Rev. Dr. Sparrow Simpson intoned the prayers, and the Rev. R. B. Dowling was the preacher.

TAUNTON.—A concert was given on September 27th, in aid of the funds of the Philharmonic Association, by a number of ladies and gentlemen, under the conductorship of Mr. T. P. Dudeney. Two chief items of the programme were G. A. Macfarren's Trio in A, for violin, violoncello and pianoforte, and Mendelssohn's Duet Sonata in B flat, for violoncello and pianoforte. Many of the pieces were well rendered to the pleasure of the audience, which it is to be regretted was not a larger one.

BURTON-ON-TRENT.—The annual thanksgiving services for the in-gathering of the harvest, were held in St. Paul's Church, last Sunday. The order of service for the evening was as follows :—"Magnificat and Nunc Dimittis," Tuckermann in E flat; Anthem, "O how amiable," "Out Thee each living soul awaits," and chorus, " The heavens are telling," (Haydn), Bach's "Toccata and Fuga in D minor," was played as a concluding voluntary by the organist, Mr. A. B. Plant, Mus.Bac, Oxon., F.C.O.

DECLINE OF CONGREGATIONAL SINGING.

A discussion, it is announced, on the decline of congregational singing took place at the recent meeting of the South-Eastern Clerical and Lay Church Alliance, held at Canterbury. The Rev. J. B. Whiting, vicar of St. Luke's, Ramsgate, said that in the last twenty years he had visited 600 parishes, and his experience was that choral singing was increasing, and congregational singing was very much diminishing. A spirited discussion followed, which, however, turned upon small points of ritual, and consequently bore little or no fruit. That congregations sing less need not be taken as a sign of decadence in any direction. It may indeed be a hopeful proof of increased intelligence in listening, combined with a lively desire to fulfil the Apostolic injunction to sing with the " understanding," as well as with the heart. Although the people have a right to join in singing certain things, they have no more just right to monopolise the ministry of singing than they have that of preaching. It has been observed that the more people know of music, the less inclined are they to rashly intrude their unprepared efforts in that ill-regulated institution, congregational singing ; again, it is said, " musicians rarely sing in Church, they know how to behave." So it may be hoped that indirectly the recent discussion will lead to some good. And much good would, be realised if the whole question could be judiciously approached, apart from all prejudices and habits, both doctrinal and musical.

THE HISTORY OF THE PIANOFORTE.

The following words are extracted from an appendix to Mr. A. J. Hipkins's paper, with corrections, from the *Journal of the Society of Arts :—*

The analysis of my paper, by Mr. Victor Mahillon, while occupied with the French translation of it, has shown the necessity of further revision than was possible at the time of publication. The most important correction is this—" Now if the string be struck upon a loop." The statement thus introduced must be brought into agreement with Thomas Young's law which I had, for the moment, overlooked. According to this law, a stretched string set in vibration by percussion, or otherwise, loses, if the disturbance takes place upon a nodal division, not only the harmonic proper to that node, but all the harmonics which have a node corresponding to the same point. The usual striking place in a piano being on or near one of the most important nodal divisions, either the eighth or the ninth, it results that augmentation of intensity may be attributed to the greater amplitude and vibrating energy of the larger segment of the string produced by the suppression of the harmonic proper to the node. As to the relative value of the different harmonic divisions arising from the varying position of the point of disturbance, the first division, that of the octave, which takes place at the half of the string, and completely annuls the even series of harmonics, engenders a *timbre*, or sound quality, resembling that of the clarinet, fuller and richer than any other to be obtained from the instrument. The next best measurements, tried dulcimer fashion with a suitable hammer, are those which correspond to the third, fourth, sixth, and eighth of the string. Of all these, the last division only, from obvious reasons of construction, is possible in a pianoforte. The fifth and seventh are less favour-

able than the third or fourth. At the ninth the quality of tone becomes harder, as the tone regulator well knows. This tendency increases in proportion with the diminution of the division for the striking place, until the oboe quality is attained, due to the favouring of the very high harmonics at the expense of the deeper. The " lute " stop of a harpsichord with the quill plectrum acting close to the bridge might be appropriately called the " oboe " stop from this peculiar nasal quality.

While harpsichords and spinets had their strings agitated mechanically, at distances varying between a fourth and a seventh, I have not myself met with an example of a grand pianoforte struck so low down even as the seventh. In Broadwood's grand pianos, now struck exactly at the eighth, the seventh and ninth harmonics are distinctly audible, while the eighth is obliterated ; the forte of the blow at the eighth division does not therefore annul the neighbouring harmonics—that is to say, the seventh and the ninth. In old spinets and harpsichords no attention was paid to the point of disturbance, although we find the younger Hans Ruckers obtaining a modification in quality by using two registers of crowquill *plectra* on one string. His nephew, Jan Couchet, went further with this idea of varying lengths of string and striking place, an idea which Huygens fostered (" Jongbloet " and Land's Collection of Huygens' Musical Correspondence.") In the grand pianoforte, John Broadwood's division of the sound-board bridge rendered a more favourable striking-place for the bass strings possible. I believe John Broadwood was the first to carry out, in grand and square pianos, the idea of a rational striking distance. A few years later (A.D. 1800), Young formulated his law, already referred to. Kützing (" Das Wissenschaftliche der Fortepiano Baukunst.") Berne, 1844, was subsequently empirically enabled to assert that the best quality was obtained in a pianoforte at the eighth of the string, without having recourse to a softening of the hammer covering—indispensable when the blow was directed to the ninth. From what precedes, it may be asserted that there is no foundation whatever for the current notion, which Helmholtz has reproduced, that pianoforte makers have sought the seventh or ninth of the string, in order to banish one of those comparatively dissonant harmonics, and leave the concordant eighth to form part of the harmonic sheaf combined in the note. Where they have used the ninth, and even shorter divisions—as has been customary in the trebles—it has been done, without theory, to gain a more brilliant effect.

The sentence, " has been called the soul," should be, " may be called the nervous system." I have made inquiry about the wood used in America for pianoforte sound-boards, and learn from Mr. Dolge, who is a practical authority, that it is the *Abies alba*, a wood of rather softer texture than the European *Abies excelsa*, the spruce, which includes the *Haselfichte* of the Bavarian highlands, used in the best fiddle making.

The acquisition, since my paper was read, by Mr. Victor Mahillon of an upright grand piano by Friederici, of Gera, dated 1745, corrects my information as to date ; moreover, on this instrument he inscribed his name, Friederici. The mechanism of this upright grand piano is very simple, the hammer action resembling that German clock-bell action which Mr. Mahillon, having seen another example at Nuremberg, suggests may have been transferred to the piano ; of course independent of Cristofori's invention, to which it would be mechanically inferior.

Nannette Stein's six pedals are thus arranged, beginning from the left foot :—1, shift pedal ; 2, bassoon ; 3, damper ; 4, half-celesta ; 5, full celeste ; 6, drum, Steibelt, " Methode de Piano." Paris, 1805, describes the first four pedals only, and gives signs for their employment.

The treble dampers were first omitted in grand pianos about 1809. In the original square pianos of Zumpe, the dampers were used throughout. In John Broadwood's square piano of 1780 one note is left undamped, the highest. In 1792 he had the eight highest notes undamped in a similar instrument, evidently to gain "ring," as with his brass damper it was not a question of convenience.

The Lyre pedal was introduced in its first form in 1809-10.

The promised production of the late Sir Sterndale Bennett's cantata " The May Queen," for the first time on the stage, is postponed to October 16th.

The Saturday afternoon concerts at the Crystal Palace will enter on their twenty-eighth season on October 13th—nine more performances taking place before Christmas, the remaining ten concerts beginning on February 16th and ending on April 19th ; the usual supplemental performance for the benefit of Mr. Manns, the conductor, being announced for April 26th. Among the specialties are the orchestral symphony, " Zur Herbstzeit " (Autumn), and an Italian suite by the late Joachim Raff, a pianoforte concerto by Anton Dvorak, Sir Arthur Sullivan's incidental music to the " Merry Wives of Windsor," and a repetition of Berlioz's " Messe des Morts." Accepted classical works will not be overlooked in the scheme of these famous performances.

Organ News.

COLLEGE OF ORGANISTS.

The arrangements for the season run thus :—Examination for Associateship, January 8th, 9th, and July 8th, and 9th. Examination for Fellowship, January 10th and July 20th. The lectures, and members' meetings, are on Tuesdays, November 6th, December 4th, February 5th, March 4th, April 1st, May 6th, June 3rd, July 1st ; and the Annual General Meeting, for business purposes of the College, takes place on July 29th.

LIVERPOOL.

An organ recital was given in St. George's Hall, by Mr. W. T. Best, on Thursday, September 27th. The following was the programme :—

Overture, " Ruy Blas "	Mendelssohn.
Benediction Nuptiale (for the Organ)	Saint-Saens.
Double Fugue in F minor	Krebs.
Romanza, " Deserto in terra "	Donizetti.
Finale, Allegro con brio in E major	Best.

And on Saturday, September 29th :—

Overture, " Le Serment "	Auber.
Andante in E flat, No. 5	Best.
Toccata and Fugue in C minor	Bach.
Andantino in D flat major	Chauvet.
Marche Religieuse in A major }	
Allegro Maestoso, with Trumpets and Horns, from the " Water Music "	Handel.

WALMERSLEY.

An organ recital was given in Christ Church, on Tuesday, September 25th, by Mr. W. T. Best, on the new organ (which has two manuals and Pedal), built by W. Hill and Son, London, and presented to this Church by James Jardine, Esq., of Alderley Edge, Manchester. The following was the programme :—

Organ Sonata, No. 5, in D major	Mendelssohn.
Andante in A major	Smart.
Bell-Rondo (" Rondo de Campanelli ")	Morandi.
Fugue in G major	Wesley.
Adagio Solenne	Dussek.
Prelude and Fugue in C minor	Bach.
Festal March	Best.

BOW AND BROMLEY INSTITUTE.

On September 29th, Mr. W. S. Hoyte was the organist. A very large and enthusiastic audience attended. Miss Helen D'Alton was the vocalist, singing the evergreen " Lost Chord " with much effect, and, of course, with the inevitable and enthusiastic *encore*. Mr. Hoyte's first piece, a " Grand Fantasie de Concert," by M. Callaerts, the organist of Antwerp Cathedral, was admirably performed, and loudly applauded. The next solo, a Polonaise, by Rubinstein, was so effectively rendered as to secure an *encore*. Guilmant's " Canzone " and Best's masterly " Scherzo " were capitally received. A fine performance of Krebs' Prelude and Fugue in C minor, was also well received. Guilmant's " Grand March Triomphale " closed a very effective series of organ pieces, well calculated to display Mr. Hoyte's broad, vigorous style, and excellent execution. The arrangements for the future interlude, Mr. W. S. Best, on October 20th, and Dr. Peace, on the 27th. The organist, this evening, will be Mr. Walter Wesche, who makes his first appearance upon this occasion.

CRYSTAL PALACE.

Mr. Eyre's programme, on Saturday last included the following :—

Grand Offertoire in F	Wely.
Minuet and Trio, from G minor Symphony	Bennett.
Aria, " Che faro Senza Eu'ydice " (" Orpheus ")	Gluck.
Grand Prelude in E flat	Martini.
" The Lost Chord "	Sullivan.
Intermezzo	Macbeth.
Larghetto, from a Trio	Mozart.
Allegretto, " Aurelois "	Richards.
Polonaise in C	Rubenstien.

And on Saturday, the 22nd ult. :—

" Cornelius " March	Mendelssohn.
Adagio from a quartet	Onslow.
Elegy in C minor	Stephens.
(In memoriam, Ellen A. Orridge, died 16th September, 1883.)	
Offertoire in G	Kuhmstedt.
Cradle Song	Lange.
March from Suite No. 2	Lachner.
Organ Concerto No. 2, in B flat	Handel.
Selection of Airs, " Faust "	Gounod.
Chorus, " Welcome mighty king " (" Solomon ")	Handel.

FISHERIES EXHIBITION.

The following organ recitals have been given during the week by Mr. J. Loaring, F.C.O. The programmes included :—

Overture, " Semiramide "	Rossini.
Gavotte in D	Loaring.
Organ Concerto, No. 1	Handel.
Triumphal March, " Alfred "	Prout.

Overture, " Men of Prometheus "	Beethoven.
Prelude and Fugue in E	Bach.
Organ Concerto, No. 2	Handel.
Marche Romaine	Gounod.

Toccata et Fuga in A minor	Bach.
Organ Concerto, No. 1	Handel.
The " Bride's March "	Loaring.

An organ recital was given on Saturday, September 27th, by Mr. Walter Clough. The programme included :—

Grand Chorus in D major	Guilmant.
Gavotte (Pastorale)	Muscat.
March Triomphale	Clough.
Prelude in B flat major, and Fugue in G minor	Bach.
" The Language of Flowers " (" The Lilac ")	Cowen.
March and Chorus, " Tannhäuser "	Wagner.

BOLTON.

An organ recital was given in the Albert Hall, by Mr. W. Mullineux, F.C.O., on Saturday, September 29th. The following was the programme :—

Organ Concerto in D major	Handel.
Allegro—Andante—Fuga.	
Gavotte, " Heimliche Liebe "	Resch.
Variations on the Hymn, " O Sanctissima " (" Sicilian Mariner's Tune ")	Lux.
Double Chorus, " The Horse and his Rider "	Handel.
Grand March Triomphale	Mullineux.

OLDHAM.

On Friday, September 28th, organ recitals were given in the Industrial Exhibition by Mr. Alfred Smith. The programmes included :—

Festival March	Dunster.
Melody in A flat	Guilmant.
Chorus, " Fixed in His everlasting seat "	Handel.

Grand Organ Sonata, No. 1	Mendelssohn.
Allegro—Adagio—Andante—Allegro assai vivace.	
Andantino	Schubert.
Marche Funèbre et Chant Séraphique	Guilmant.

And by Mr. James Lowe, on the same day :—

Grand Solemn March in E flat	Smart.
Andante in D	Archer.
Cantilène Pastorale	Guilmant.
Grand Sonata in E flat	Bach.
Andante con moto in A	Smart.
Caprice in B flat	Guilmant.
" La Prière "	Thayer.
Brilliant March in B flat	Wely.

WARE.

An organ recital was given on Tuesday, September 25th, by Mr. James L. Gregory, F.C.O., assisted by Mr. Trelawny Cobham. The following was the programme :—

Concertante in C major (1st movement)	Handel.
Recit., " Ye people, rend your hearts "	
Air, " If with all your hearts " } (" Elijah ")	Mendelssohn.
Andante con moto in E	Guilmant.
Harvest Thanksgiving March	Calkin.
Meditation on Bach's 1st Prelude	Gounod.
Andante con moto in A	Smart.
Romanza in G, Op. 40	Beethoven.
Grand Offertoire in D	Batiste.

BURTON-ON-TRENT.

An organ recital was given on Saturday, September 29th, by Mr. A. B. Plant, Mus.Bac., Oxon., F.C.O., in St. Paul's Institute. The following was the programme :—

Overture, " La Clemenza di Tito "	Mozart.
Offertoire upon two Christmas Themes	Guilmant.
Sonata in C minor	Mendelssohn.
March, with " Hymn of priests "	Chauvet.
Gavotte	Bach.
Fuga in C	Buxtehude.
Adagio	Beethoven.
March to Calvary	Gounod.

POOL.

An organ recital was recently given on the new organ at Pool Church, by Mr. John Hele, junr., with the following as the programme :—

Overture to " Otho "	Handel.
" Berceuse "	Guilmant.
Andante in D	Silas.
Minuet and Trio	Bennett.
Grazioso	Smart.
Offertoire, No. 5	Wely.
Gavotte	Thomas.
" March Triomphale "	Lemmens.

REIGATE.

An organ recital was given by Mr. J. W. Gritton, F.C.O., at St. Mark's Church, on the occasion of the re-opening of the organ, after enlargement, alterations, and additions by Mr. A. Kirkland, Wakefield. The following was the programme which was admirably executed :—

Andante in A flat	Hoyte.
Andante and Allegro	Sachs.
"As pants the hart"	Spohr.
Harvest Thanksgiving March	Calkin.
" Slumber Song	Gounod.
Allegro in D	Tours.
Sonata, No. 1	Mendelssohn.
Larghetto from Trio in B flat	Mozart.
Marche Religieuse	Guilmant.
Andante from 10th Trio	Rheinger.
Toccata and Fugue in D minor	Bach.

BIRKENHEAD.

A new organ is now in course of erection at St. Michael's Mission Church, Claughton. The organ is being erected by Messrs. Wm. and Frank Hall, organ builders, Birkenhead, and will be formally opened next week. The manuals extend to upper C, thus making the super octave really useful. The Great organ sound-board comes outside the recess of the organ chambers. The organ has two manuals and Pedal. There are 2 Couplers and the same number of composition pedals, balance Swell, perpendicular shutters, upper keyboard projecting, couplers over Swell keyboard.

PRESTON.

On Saturday evening, Sept. 29th, Mr. Tomlinson, organist of the Corporation, gave his usual weekly recital in the New Public Hall, on the grand organ. The programme was as follows :—

Cantilene in D minor	Salomé
Fantasia on a Theme of Weber	E. H. Turpin.
Barcarolle	Spohr.
Overture to "La Sirene"	Auber.
Pastorale Symphony, from the "Light of the World"	Sullivan.
Grand March, from "La Reine de Saba"	Gounod.

Mr. Tomlinson rendered the "Fantasia" in a most pleasing manner. The compositions of the composer of this piece are always well received at these recitals. The "Barcarolle" was given in equally good style, and the organist received a well-merited encore, to which he responded. The recital concluded with the Grand March from "La Reine de Saba," played in a very spirited manner. On Thursday, Sept. 27th, at a meeting of the Town Council, Mr. James Tomlinson was re-appointed organist to the Corporation.

BLUNDELLSAND.

Annexed is the programme of an organ recital given at St. Nicholas' Church, on September 26th, by Mr. Fred. H. Burstall, Mus.

Overture for the Organ	Morandi
Air with variations in A major	Haydn.
Grand Fugue in G major	Krebs.
Romance sans Paroles	Gounod.
Festive March in D	Smart.

GALASHIELS.

An organ recital was given by Mr. John W. Oxley, L.Mus., T.C.L., on Wednesday, September 26th, in St. Paul's Church. The programme included :—

Organ Concerto in F	Handel.
Solo " Angelic Voice"	Batiste.
Offertoire in A major	Wely.
Solo, "Nuptial March"	Guilmant.

BOSTON.

The following specification of the new organ for the Chapel of Ease is supplied by the organist, Mr. Scott :—

SWELL ORGAN.

1. Bourdon	56 pipes.
2. Open Diapason	56 „
3. Lieblich Gedact	56 „
4. Principal	56 „
5. Mixture	168 pipes
6. Oboe	56 „
7. Cornopean	56 „

GREAT ORGAN.

8. Open Diapason	56 pipes.
9. Rohr Flöte	56 „
10. Dulciana	56 „
11. Principal	56 pipes.
12. Fifteenth	56 „
13. Flute	56 „

PEDAL ORGAN.

14. Open Diapason	16 ft.

COUPLERS.

15. Swell to Great.	17. Swell to Pedals.
16. Great to Pedals.	

GLASGOW.

An organ recital was given on Saturday, September 29th, by Dr. A. L. Peace, in the Cathedral. The following was the programme :—

Overture and March, "Hercules"	Handel.
Andante (Symphony in D)	Haydn.
Prelude and Fugue in E minor	Mendelssohn.
March and Chorus, Duet, and Prayer, ("Moses in Egypt")	Rossini.
Study No. 9 and Canzo Popolare	Schumann.
Triumphal March ("Naaman")	Costa.

BELFAST.

An organ recital was given on Tuesday evening, the 18th inst., by Master Alfred Hollins, of the Royal Normal College for the Blind, Upper Norwood, a pupil of Dr. E. J. Hopkins, on the fine organ built by Peter Conacher & Co., Huddersfield, in the Carlisle Memorial Methodist Church. His programme included :—

PART I.

Motet, "Deus Tibi"	Mozart.
Funeral March	Chopin.
Allegretto in B minor	Guilmant.
Grand Chœur in D	
Two short pieces in A and D	Hopkins.
Pastorale Sonata, Op. 88	Rheinberger.

PART II.

Gavotte, "M. Antoinette"	
Gavotte, "Air du Dauphin"	Roeckel.
Gavotte in A	Hollins.
Grand Fugue	Bach.
Cantabile and Fanfare	Lemmens.
Prelude, No. 10	Chopin.
"Wedding March"	Mendelssohn.

It will be seen from the above, that great variety was presented. Left alone as he was, and comparatively new to the instrument, loss of sight did not seem to interfere with Master Hollings and his many beautiful combinations and at all times "clean" playing, showed rare talent. His rendering of Lemmens' lovely cantabile, Guilmant's well-known allegretto and "Grand Chœur" (splendidly played), the last movement of Rheinberger's sonata, and the G minor fugue, are worthy of particular mention. A gavotte of his own composition was also an attractive item. His talented master's graceful pieces in A and D were beautifully played. Altogether the recital was a rare treat, and the youth is to be heartily commended on his really good performance. Several private recitals given here on different instruments have shown more evidence of his skill both as an organist and pianist. The organ is an effective instrument of two manuals and Pedal organ with some 37 stops.

Mr. A. C. Mackenzie's orchestral ballad "La Belle Dame sans Merci," which was so successfully performed by the Philharmonic Society last season, will, it is understood, be included in the first concert of Mr. Theodore Thomas's orchestra in the coming season in New York.

Says the Musical Times :—The details of Mr. Mackenzie's new oratorio (to be produced at the Norwich Festival next year) being now settled, and the work considerably advanced, amateurs may feel interested to know some particulars connected therewith. It is called "The Rose of Sharon," and presents in a dramatic form the argument of the Song of Solomon. The compiler of the book, Mr. Joseph Bennett, has adopted Ewald's reading of the Hebrew poem—a reading with which Renan substantially agrees—but has permitted himself to take certain liberties with the arrangement of the scenes, showing in action, for example, events that the original simply describes. Mr. Bennett's book is in four parts, respectively entitled "Separation," "Temptation," "Victory," "Reunion," and there are four principal characters—the Sulammite (soprano), a First Attendant (contralto), the Beloved (tenor), and Solomon (bass). The action opens in Lebanon, is then transferred to Jerusalem, and finally returns to the vineyards and cedar groves where it began. Throughout each scene the simple object is to illustrate the moral of the Song of Songs—"Love is strong as death and unconquerable as the grave." The Sulammite is taken by Solomon from her native mountains to Jerusalem, and sees the King "in all his glory." But she remains faithful, her one answer being, "My beloved is mine, and I am his." Strong in this strength she resists, and is at last permitted to return to her village and her vineyard, to be united to him whom her soul loveth. We believe that Mr. Mackenzie finds all his sympathies aroused by the beautiful story, and the no less beautiful Scriptural text.

Foreign Musical Intelligence.

The original manuscript of Spohr's "Faust" has been presented to the library of the Paris Conservatoire.

Johannes Brahms intends conducting the performance of his new Symphony to be given at a forthcoming concert in Berlin.

Anton Rubinstein has recently been made by the Emperor of Russia a Knight of the Wladimir Order, Class III.

It is stated that Peter Benoit's "Lucifer" will be performed in the course of October at Milan under Faccio's direction.

The composer Herr Xavier Scharwenka and Emile Sauret project a concert tour in Switzerland, presently.

News from Paris announces the death of Charles Thomas, a brother of Ambroise Thomas.

At the Théâtre des Galeries St. Hubert, Brussels, Lecocq's new opera, "Le Grain de Sable," is being rehearsed.

August Pott, formerly the Grand-Ducal Court Capell-meister at Oldenburg, died at Graz on the 27th of August. He was an esteemed pupil of Spohr and an admirable violinist.

At Liège recently died Victor Massart, honorary professor of the Conservatoire of that town, a brother of the still better known Jean Lambert Massart, professor of the Paris Conservatoire.

The *Melomane*, a well conducted Parisian journal recently started, has for its chief concerts well assorted music. It says in its weekly budget of news, that a great novelty is a new opera, "Egmont," by M. Gaston Salvayre.

Another book having Wagner for its subject is printed in Dutch, and written by G. Viotta. "R. Wagner: Zijn leven en zijne werken geschetst," that is, "R. Wagner: A criticism of his life and works" (Amsterdam: Van Dauben in Smock).

Since the 31st of August, Meyerbeer's "Robert le Diable" has, it is stated, been performed at Vienna 403 times; so it is clear that the advanced operatic school has so far been unable to shake the popularity of old favourites.

The four hundredth anniversary of Luther's birth is to be celebrated at Geneva by a musical festival. An important feature in the proceedings will be the performance of an oratorio, "Luther at Worms," by Meinardus. This work, written fourteen years ago, has hitherto only existed with the original German words, which have now been ably translated into French by M. A. Köckert, for use at the approaching festival.

Rubinstein has been visiting in Konigsburg at the house of Herr Ernest Wicherts, who supplied the composer with the libretto of his latest work, a comic opera. According to the German papers the opera treats of an exciting episode of Spanish robber life, and Rubinstein has set this to music with appropriate local colouring. The work will probably be produced at the Hamburg Town Theatre for the first time on November 8th, together with the same composer's "Sulamith."

At the Italian Opera, Paris, the conductors will be M. Franco Faccio, MM. Cisalino Cialdini and Luigi Corti. The ballet will consist of twenty-four *danseuses* chosen from the pupils of the Milan School. The chorus will number seventy-five, and the orchestra will consist of seventy performers. Of works new to Paris are promised: "Simon Boccanegra," by Verdi; "Erodiade," by Massenet; and "Gioconda," by Ponchielli. Among the well-known works of the *répertoire* are mentioned: "Rigoletto," "Ballo in Maschera," "Ernani," "Puritani," "Martha," "Barbiere," "Nabucco," "Don Juan," "Luisa Miller," "Linda di Chamounix," "Saffo," "Lucrezia Borgia," "Semiramis," "Poliuto," "Maria di Rohan," "Lucia," "Anna Bolena," "Ceperentola," etc.

An experienced married lady has observed that the way to manage a husband is to "feed him and flatter him." This saying has been successfully paraphrased by one who has had experience in the concert-giving world, who says the way to manage an artist is to "fee him and flatter him."

PRINCIPAL CONTENTS OF THIS NUMBER.

LONDON: SATURDAY, OCTOBER 6, 1883.

THE CHURCH CONGRESS AND CHURCH MUSIC.

THE annual meeting of clergymen at Reading, this week, is not likely to do much good either theologically or æsthetically. The public press have already pointed out the poverty of the "subjects" on hand, and their inutility to serve any practical purpose. The president will pour forth the usual platitudes of conventional pulpit oratory. Small men will air their crotchets, and be obliged to keep in *time*. Self-conceited and consequential laymen, may lecture the community at large without convincing a single soul. The readers of this journal are more concerned to inquire what the Congress will do for the improvement of the *Church Service*, especially the musical part, now so essential. The answer, it is to be feared, must be, nothing.

The subject of Church music does not appear to be down on the list of papers. How is this? *Tempora mutantur*, within the last thirty years, and many of the clergy are now not only fair musicians, but clever composers of ecclesiastical works. I remember the

time when, as a rule, the ablest preachers, the most
learned divines, took no interest in Church music at
all. Most of them confessed that they had no ear,
that they could not "turn a tune." The late Mr.
HARNESS, a schoolfellow of Lord BYRON, at Harrow,
and an editor of SHAKESPEARE, was minister of St.
Peter's, Regent Square, in 1835, and thereafter. My
father, a member of the congregation, often complained of the organist, a poor player, wise in his own
conceit; but HARNESS avowed his own incompetence
"to interfere about objects of musical ignorance,
and asked my father to act as his deputy." Such interference, on the part of a private, however, would
have been a breach of etiquette, and nothing was
done. Other respectable and erudite ministers rowed
in the same boat as poor HARNESS; they knew not
one note from another. The services were shorn of
all music except the Psalms of DAVID—the abominably bad "Old and New Versions," of STERNHOLD
and HOPKINS, TATE and BRADY, sung to tunes good,
bad, and indifferent. The prose Psalms of the Prayer
Book were read by parson and clerk, in a dreary duet
—fideles tacebant! The Canticles and Versicles underwent the same treatment.

At St. Peter's, Regent Square (A.D. 1835-37), the
"Kyrie Eleison," after the Ten Commandments in
the Communion Service, was spoken by the charity
children in the gallery; but after the tenth, the
organist broke out with a peculiar response, which
occurred an unmeaning burst at the passage "in our
hearts," followed by an equally unmeaning "break"
before the words, "we beseech Thee."—The "old
Advent" Hymn "Lo! He comes," horrified all
musical ears at the beginning of December, TERRY,
the able organist of Hackney Church, positively
refused to play it, at the request of the (then) rector,
one GOODCHILD, who, by the way, served Mr. HAR-
NESS at Regent Square Church, as curate, and
resigned because (he said), he was tired of playing
second fiddle! Then, as now, poor curates were
only allowed to preach to servant-maids and common
people, as the affluent and fashionable absented
themselves. Even TERRY, although he wrote several
capital Canticles for his Church, could or would do
no better on such Festivals as Christmas and Easter,
than play, for the climax, before the sermon, Psalm
xcvii. with a "got up," Hallelujah for the charity
children at the close! In country Churches, a small
band of clarinet, violoncello, and bassoon, accompanied the choir of charity girls and boys.

Nous avons changé tout cela; but musical reformers
know nothing of finality: they decline, like Earl
RUSSELL, to "rest and be thankful." The Church
Congress might have discussed several important
questions within the province of ecclesiastical music.
The merits, or demerits, of the so-called "Gregorian"
System, for example, would have supplied a bonne
bouche, or rather a hard nut to crack. The prevalent
ignorance on the subject, even amongst professionals,
can hardly be thought creditable. The misnomer has
been sufficiently exposed; and S. GREGORY dragged
down from his eminence. The almost rabid enthusiasm of ultra-Ritualists for the ancient "Modes"
strikes moderate men as supremely ridiculous. Without absolutely condemning them, I incline to the

opinion of learned professors (if such term might
be named) that the Greek "Modes" are really relics
of barbarism; in a sense aesthetical, quite out of keeping with the present generally adopted scale, and often
positively ugly. The "augmented Fourth and the flat
seventh of the two "Lydians" are not agreeable to
ears refined. CHARLES CHILD SPENCER, of Hackney,
who wrote an able pamphlet on the "Modes," cried
them up to the sky; but SPENCER boasted that he had
found a key to the peculiar harmonies required for the
accompaniment of ancient scales, and he certainly, in
my hearing, produced some good effects on the organ.
The "Gregorians," I hold, should be very sparingly
used, if tolerated at all. The notion that any
sacred or celestial character is attributable to these
strains is a matter about which opinions differ.

Other points besides the question of the "Modes"
may occur to your readers. The Canticles too often
are made mediums to show off the composer; they
are then styled "Services"—Services in which few of
the people can take part, and therefore unsuitable to
ordinary Common Prayer. The "Chant" form
ought to be used in Parish Churches. The Psalm-
singing varies, after the fashion of the abolished
uses. The Rev. Sir F. GORE OUSELEY, I think, laid
down the rules (in a Lecture), that the words going to
the "Recitation" note of the Chant ought not to be
hurried over, but sung slowly, whereas the following
scale passages in minims should be accelerated. The
hurrying over referred to sounds irreverent. The same
gentleman, or some other eminent authority, has also
declared against double chants: they ought always to
be single. The Responses after the Commandments
sometimes savour of sugar-candy secularity; the Hymns
still now so. I object to most of the current Hymn-
ologies, both words and music. The Hymns
Ancient and Modern hover on the confines of
heterodox doctrines, whilst the "Evangelical"
manuals such as KEMBLE's for instance, are tainted
with the unctuous gushing style which unfits them
for men and women. Then too many verses are sung,
and the congregation kept standing too long in consequence. I have often cut out a few verses from
these lengthy Hymns for the benefit of the poor
tired sheep. The formula of the clerk, "Let us sing
to the praise and glory of God" has been happily
abolished, and the clergyman always gives the notice.
As regards organ Voluntaries, I am in favour of a
short one at the beginning, and a long, elaborate one
at the end of the Service. Many of the congregations
may be seen sitting in their pews, Sunday after
Sunday, until the sweet end of the final Voluntary,
when played, on a fine organ, by one of the many
excellent musicians that now abound in London and
also in the larger provincial towns. Some narrow-
minded clergymen dislike th' "entrance" Voluntary.
I remember that at Regent Square Church, St. Pancras,
forty years ago, the organist was allowed a margin
for instrumental play of some eight to ten minutes
between Psalms and the first Lesson, so that the overtasked officiating minister, obliged to read the Psalms,
might take breath, or perchance retire to his vestry
for the refreshment of a glass of water. The Ritualist
priest would be aghast at such a licence!

A. M.

A GROUNDLESS ALARM.

THE assertion is not unfrequently made that the melodic devices to be formed on the diatonic scale are pretty well nigh exhausted. The young composer may well ask, Is this true? and if true, what are the future resources of the composer seeking to be original? To grant the truth of the assertion is just as damaging to the statement as would be arguments of denial proving the endless expansion of the powers of tune. For if it is asserted that tune is exhausted by reason of the limited powers of the available scale materials it is only logical to concede that this exhaustion must have occurred at a very early date in the history of the art, and indeed would naturally come about in primitive days long antecedent to the days of Plain-song, if not even before the days of JUBAL or when the Lydian shepherds piped their flocks together. Indeed, it would seem that this alarming exhaustion of tune, in view of the apparently slender materials tune is made of, must be dated before music, as we know it, came into existence. Well, if this is so, the composer may calm his fears and learn to be indifferent to the from time to time reiterated cry, Tune is exhausted! The truth is this probably, thought is interminable and illimitable, and the means ordained for the expression of thought are as wonderful in their economical adaptability as they are marvellous in their endless powers of thought-suggestiveness and definition of ideality. The subject approaches the mysteries which surround the wondrous scheme of life in production and reproduction. One may examine the question from another point of sight. The cry has not yet been raised which would inform the world that orchestral effects and combinations are exhausted; on the contrary, we are taught to regard instrumentation as a new-born science destined to throw a flood of light upon the other resources of the art. Now, the primary divisions of the orchestral powers are even less in number than are notes of the diatonic scale. Yet orchestral effects are now regarded as exhaustless, just as they were deemed to be before BEETHOVEN wrote; and WAGNER, the latest exponent of the myriad functions of the orchestra, is even now accepted as the founder of a new school and not believed to be the last workman in an exhausted mine. The alarmist cry has not yet been raised in this direction, but it would be quite as reasonable to say that the resources of instrumentation are already worked out as it is to assert that Melody is exhausted. The reputed words of BEETHOVEN, himself a most painstaking employer of means, that it was the thoughts lying under the notes and not notes themselves he wanted, point to the direction in which the student may find a solution of this question ; for so long as he has thought to express, he will surely find the means for its enunciation more than sufficient. The CREATOR Himself in limiting the most beautiful of all musical instruments—the human voice—to an average range of some twenty notes, and by ordaining that the principles of tone gravitation shall still more limit all true melodic inspirations, has indeed for once and for all time put an end to the mistrustful doctrine of exhaustion ; and the earnest student will find out, as BEETHOVEN said

he had found out, that all the great effects in music were—and one may safely add ever will be—clustered together in that marvel of tone eloquence, the diatonic scale. So the composer need not fear to ever have to cry out as regards the sources of melody, *ipsi iam fontes sitiunt*, for the unseen springs of tune are of everlasting fertility, beauty, and strength.

E. H. TURPIN.

THE LOGIC OF COUNTERPOINT.

THIRD SERIES.

XIV.

BEFORE proceeding to the consideration of the conduct of Counterpoint in more than four parts, which will bring my work to a close, I venture to offer a few more thoughts on counterpoint in four parts, the most useful and consequently the most important of all contrapuntal score arrangements.

It seems reasonable to object to the fourth in the preliminary course of two-part counterpoint of the first species, unless in rare instances it may be either taken in passing as a discord—though the assumed length of the notes in most species points against such a proceeding—or else resolved in the usual way. When, however, the fourth appears in three-part counterpoint, modified by the addition of the sixth, it does not seem unreasonable to raise objections against its occasional appearance. The fourth may well appear indeed in such a figure as in the second chord of this passage, with the two upper parts ascending and the lower voice is descending :—

B	C	D	E
G	A	B	C
G	E	D	C

and there are other ways of using the chord six-four, even in three parts. But in a score of four parts there are still more favourable opportunities for the occasional appearance of the second inversion of the common chord without regarding it as an objectionable interloper. An enlargement of the passage just sketched, with the chord twice introduced, will illustrate such a possibility :—

B	C	D	E
G	A	B	C
D	E	G	G
G	E	D	C

And it will be noticed on trial that the six-four chords in this passage are still less objectionable if a few more five-three and six-three chords follow on. It must be conceded that the fourth to the lower part presents a combination requiring management and discretionary power. Certain it is, moreover, that there has been in all the contrapuntal ages, a not altogether unreasonable objection to the use of the six-four chord, and it seems now the time to duly consider and modify the objection. MERSENNE, writing two hundred and sixty years ago, has, in his "Harmonie "Universelle," many arguments to prove that the fifth is sweeter than the fourth, and takes pains to show why the fourth is not so good against the bass as the fifth. Then, again, he enters at length in the discussion of the proposition that "the fourth is sterile, that "it engenders nothing good by its multiplication, nor

" by its division." It is of course unnecessary to recapitulate the stated rules concerning this combination as given by more recent theorists. The student must neither hastily reject such lines of reasoning, or confine himself too rigidly to rules which exceed in prohibitive force their logical power and explanatory clearness. Perhaps a still more important matter to be considered, and one which modern theorists are still better agreed upon, is the question of the use of the minor mode from the modern point of sight, which calls for a modification of the old contrapuntal assimilation of that scale form to the—from the harmony point of sight—indefinite method of an ancient mode. One way of marking the satisfactory treatment of the modern minor diatonic scale, is the determination to incline at suitable cadence points and other progression to the due recognition of dominant harmonies involving the presence of their major thirds as affording the truest approach to the chord of the tonic. The spirit of sober quaintness which prompts the composer in writing church music and in other contrapuntal uses, to assume an old world, venerable tone-flavour is perhaps to be respected ; and this tendency is secured most readily by allowing one's thoughts—especially when employing the minor scale —to drift in the idioms more or less peculiar to the ancient modes. Such a method of thought naturally leads to the, at least partial, exclusion of bran new harmonies and progressions more securely based upon the increased modern knowledge of true harmonic relationship. Such an assumption of old idioms and mannerisms may be based upon a natural inclination to look back through the past ages as well as look forward with hope in all art expressions of religious emotions and religious faith. And as we do not chide our church architects for gathering inspiration from our solemn old cathedrals and churches, we are not at liberty to find fault with our ecclesiastical composers for their parallel tendencies to assume musical mannerisms cast in the mould of grave and antique thought. Such considerations will naturally affect the true use of the minor mode as now generally accepted. Still the student is called upon to learn the truth about the materials he uses, and further to know why he makes use of given forms and mannerisms. Without the imposition of too many restrictions, he should study the different methods of treating passages in the minor mode, whether their inclination be ancient or modern. One useful form of exercise might be that of taking *canti fermi* in major keys and changing them into minor themes. Such practice would help to clearly show the complete and responsible relationship between the harmonies of the two pillars of both major and minor scales, the chords of the tonic and dominant.   E. H. TURPIN.

Among other places at which Gounod's sacred trilogy, "The Redemption," will be performed, during the ensuing season, may be mentioned : Paris, (two performances), Vienna, London (two performances), Birmingham (two performances), Bristol, Burton-on-Trent, Cardiff, Cheltenham, Cork, Derby, Glasgow, Gravesend, Ipswich, Manchester, Middlesbro', Newcastle, Northampton, Nottingham, Plymouth, Stockport, Swansea, Wolverhampton, Trinidad, Melbourne, and Sydney, and many cities in the United States of America.

Correspondence.

"COUNTERPOINT."

TO THE EDITOR OF THE "MUSICAL STANDARD."

SIR,—I fear that by writing to congratulate Mr. Stark upon his paper on the teaching of so-called counterpoint, I have involved him in an unwelcome controversy. But it is abundantly evident that Mr. Stark can argue his case ably, and I hope he will not grudge the time.

It was scarcely fair for the writer of the letter in to-day's *Musical Standard*—especially when writing anonymously—to insinuate that Mr. Stark has been unfolding an untried theory. I have tried all methods of teaching part-writing—or "Counterpoint," if you choose so to call it—and I declare, unhesitatingly, that any successful explanation of its true principles must be based upon modern harmony. It is of the utmost importance that the teacher should show what combinations are suitable for each pattern of writing, and may be sufficiently delineated by the number of parts engaged. No part-writing worth a button could be managed without a full knowledge of dissonance.

I deny that "it is generally believed that the study of *strict* Counterpoint [than which nothing could be less strict] is the best means to bring out freedom in writing." It would be difficult to find any accomplished musician who would own to such a belief. This controversy has not, so far, disclosed the name of such a man.

The fact is that, although during the last quarter of a century there has been a wonderful increase of power and perspicuity in the teaching of almost every other branch of knowledge, our rules for part-writing are still of the feeblest and most childish description. They do not represent the actual knowledge of any age, however remote and dark ; for it does not appear that they ever were obeyed by any musician of higher standing than that astounding genius JOHAN JOSEPH FUX, their renowned sponsor.

We are told that a soldier should be well trained. Certainly ! But how ? If he is to wield a sword, ought he to be exercised in handling a broom ? Just such an absurdity is advocated in schooling our young musicians. They are to be prohibited from using the most effective and puzzling chords during their tutelage, in order that they may effectively and confidently employ them when deprived of all guidance. In order to fit them for the responsibilities of adult life, we are enjoined to seclude them in the nursery, and feed them upon spoon meat. In the worship of the august FUX, they are to be absorbed, till suddenly they emerge as the teachers and guides of an age full of life, and vigour, and animation. To-day they are to see nothing but beauty and grace in Albrechtsberger and Cherubini ; to-morrow they will be expected to explain Schumann, to be wrapped up in Brahms, and to adore Wagner.

Mr. Banister sarcastically asked—Whether we expect to "reform the examiners ?" Certainly ! that is just what we do expect, and intend to do. With a flood of ridicule we will wash away their nonsense. We are tired of the " progressive conservatism" that is ever conserving, and never progressing.

What a keen and graphic exposition of the absurdity of the position Mr. Banister unconsciously and innocently gave, when he wrote that, "gradually, the feeling and practice of *musicians* has been increasingly progressive ; but the most recent book on Counterpoint is retrogressive so far as rules and restrictions are concerned."

Yours truly,
HENRY HILES.

Manchester, Sept. 22nd, 1883.

TO THE EDITOR OF THE "MUSICAL STANDARD."

SIR,—Your correspondent, "X.Y. Z " appears to have taken a somewhat peculiar view of my remarks upon the present contrapuntal system, and, as I should be sorry to allow an erroneous impression to exist upon any point raised in the recent discussions, I must ask leave to again trespass on your space. Let me assure "X. Y. Z." that nothing has been farther from my intention than to advocate the abolition of a strict style of Counterpoint for those who are commencing their studies. If your Correspondent will kindly refer to my paper, and to my subsequent letters in your columns, he will find many passages completely exonerating me from such a charge. The art of counterpoint must indeed be taught by first instructing the student in the use of the simplest materials at command, and until he can deal satisfactorily with these elementary combinations, it would be highly injudicious to allow the introduction of anything of a more complicated nature.

My charge against the contrapuntal system is not that it begins by teaching elementary principles—for every well considered system of study must proceed in this manner—but rather that the principles taught are erroneous, and stand self-condemned by the manifest errors and contradictions of the textbooks. "X. Y. Z." appears to uphold the present system, but has he the courage to defend its shortcomings ? Will he enter upon a defence of the peculiarities noticed in my paper, and afterwards so ably dealt with by Dr. Hiles and Mr. C. E. Stephens? Let him refer again to the letters of those gentlemen who have devoted such an amount of time and attention to the subject as to cause my own small effort to sink into insignificance, and ask himself whether a system founded on such a complication of absurdities is really worth preserving. Let us have strictness by all means, but let us at the same time stipulate for truth. There can be no possible good, but rather absolute harm, in teaching that which is known to be false. As the case stands, I contend that any person entering the lists in opposition to reform is bound, in the first instance, to disprove the charges brought against the accuracy of text-book Counterpoint. If this can be done, well and good, but the fact remains that no ardent devotee of Cherubini or Macfarren has yet attempted the task. I claim, in fact, to have proved my case; indeed, up to the present time there has, been nothing said in defence of the existing system.

Let me say, once and for all, that I believe—with your correspondent "X. Y. Z."—that the study of strict Counterpoint "cannot be dispensed with," and further, that I have never advocated its abolition. I do not, however, accept the Counterpoint of text-books or examinations as in any sense an equivalent for the thorough artistic training which every musician must undergo. It is not even satisfactory if considered as an introduction to a higher course of study, seeing that it is in direct conflict with much that a student subsequently learns.

One word as to the adoption of "living melodies" in place of the soulless successions of sounds now generally used. "X. Y. Z." asserts that a "living melody" would be "more difficult for a beginner than the present system." This I entirely deny. Certainly, the mechanical operator, who constructs his exercises after the manner of a sum in simple addition, would be unable to write satisfactory Counterpoint on a genuine melody, either at the beginning or end of his training. He cannot, of course, bring into play a feeling for artistic form, seeing that he does not possess the power of appreciating those beautiful combinations which we know under the term of "melodies." But the true art-worker would find his faculties quickened and developed by a course of contrapuntal study on "living melodies," instead of being dragged down—as he is at present—to the level of the mechanical manufacturer of Counterpoint. "X. Y. Z." doe not, however, appear to claim for text-book Counterpoint that it possesses any "artistic merit" of its own; but only that it may be useful as a "mental training." Accepting this ground of argument, the question then arises: "Is the present system the best mental training that can be provided?" I unhesitatingly affirm that it is not, and I have endeavoured to justify this assertion by the arguments used in my paper, and in the course of this correspondence. To assert that text-book rules—as they now exist—are necessary as a preliminary "mental training," is equivalent to saying that the juvenile game of "noughts and crosses" is an indispensable prelude to the study of arithmetic! "X. Y. Z." speaks of the "constant habit of writing one melody against another in Strict Counterpoint," ; but the student never arrives at such a thing as melody in a text-book. Will your correspondent kindly quote eight, or even four bars, of good rhythmical melody from any text-book in existence? It is impossible to do so; unless, indeed the term "melody" is held to bear a totally different meaning from that usually assigned to it. "X. Y. Z." remarks that all our greatest composers have been "great contrapuntists," and such is indeed the case. We can only arrive at a knowledge of the principles on which the great composers have worked by a careful study of the results of their labours. If these principles, when ascertained, are found to be in conflict with the recognised systems of study, so much the worse for the text-book manufacturers.

Your correspondent suggests that I should practise my system on my own pupils, with the object, I presume, of ascertaining whether the result would show an advantage over the ordinary method. Let me point out that work produced by the aid of common-sense rules would be unhesitatingly condemned by the "tie-wig" school, whatever might be its merit from an artistic point of view. In addition to this, the majority of pupils will be found to have some examination in view; and they not unnaturally regard any tuition outside the lines of their text-books as beside the purpose. It is the hardship of the present examination system that no discretion of any kind is allowed to teachers. They are condemned to impart that which they know to be false, and they thus become the unwilling slaves of an absolute despotism.

I am, Sir, yours obediently,

HUMPHREY J. STARK.

TO THE EDITOR OF THE "MUSICAL STANDARD."

Sir,—Following up the discussion which has appeared in your paper, on the teaching of Counterpoint, I think it rather a pity that the conversation which took place at the College of Organists, after the reading of Mr. Stark's paper, has not been published. I, for one, feel very sorry that such a paper was ever penned, and I really regret that it was ever inserted in the *Musical Standard.* I know, for a fact, that this periodical is

widely read by young musicians, by men who have lately been under examination, and by others who are about to be.

It is then highly important that nothing should appear (whether written by Mr. Stark or any one else), which is likely to injure our rising generation.

I cannot reply to *all* that Mr. Stark's paper contains, in one letter, but I will write to-day upon *one* of the things which has troubled him very much, viz., the chord of eight-six, which is sometimes found on the dominant of the minor key. In speaking of the minor key, we must remember, at the outset, that the Art and Science of music contain many things which have not yet been explained. Indeed, the very existence of the minor key has not yet been satisfactorily accounted for. It is not to be wondered at, then, if we in our research should come across some anomalies. Some years ago, I went through a long course of contrapuntal study. However, after reading lately Professor Macfarren's book on Counterpoint, it seems to me now very strange that Cherubini, Albrechtsberger, and Fuchs should never have pointed out any of the difficulties which the minor key presents. These theorists, and others too, were constantly in the habit of avoiding them. I do not mean by this, that there is no good whatever to be found in their works,—far from that; but, by turning to Albrechtsberger's book (Novello's edit.), and examining Ex. 719, which is professedly in the key of E minor, we find that in a piece of music of fifteen bars, only three of them are in the key of E minor. The same thing may be said of the next example (720), and of a great many others. Surely it was not necessary nor desirable, in so short a piece of music, to modulate at all. Modulation, like all the other good things in this world, should be used, but not abused. It is, in these examples, a sign of weakness, and it is clear that a change of key has been made to avoid the trouble of keeping in the original key. Moreover, it is extremely doubtful if any hearer could fully realise the sense of the key of E minor if the above short pieces were performed. Cherubini does something similar to Albrechtsberger every time he writes a Counterpoint to a minor canto. Mr. G. C. Banister has really produced, in some respects, an admirable Text-book on "Music," and yet he has not given a single example of Counterpoint in a minor key. Sir Frederick Ouseley, in his book, inserts examples from Fuchs in the Dorian mode, which are practically useless to students, now that the old church modes are obsolete. It has always been a wonder to me why these examples should have been given at all. It must be quite evident that there is nothing to be learnt about the minor key from them. Where, then, can I turn to get any instruction in writing Counterpoint to a minor canto? If any one will show me, I shall feel extremely obliged. At the present time I know of no book but the one lately issued by the worthy Professor of Music in the University of Cambridge. He, like the late Alfred Day, seems to me to have probed to the uttermost everything in connection with Harmony and Counterpoint. In consequence of this, the difficulties of the minor key have been manfully met, and a complete list of all the attendant harmonies has been made out.

By going into the matter rather closely, we can soon discover, immensely to the gain of the student, what harmonies every note of the minor scale will bear, and it is very curious that the dominant should give us some trouble. This note gives its own harmony, a major triad, most satisfactorily; but, at the same time, it would appear that it resented any other complete concordant harmony. If we try to write a chord of the 6th, we have a major 3rd and a minor 6th to the bass, and these together are so very discordant, that the combination is not available in strict Counterpoint. Still there is no reason why these same notes may not be used together in Free Counterpoint as Bach has done. In the 10th bar of the Great G minor Fugue, there is the following notable instance:—

The Counterpoint is here in three parts, and at the X there is a chord of the 6th on the dominant.* At this part of the subject, the key of G minor prevails, and this is the way that Bach keeps within his key without using a second inversion. Again, in the 15th bar, 4th beat, there is another similar combination of notes. The key is changed to D minor, and the number of parts increased to four. It is very remarkable that Bach should have made such a persistent use of this chord, but it proves that he knew, in this, as in everything else, what he was doing; and it is quite certain that he preferred this discord to a second inversion.

But I must return to strict Counterpoint, and in our desire to discover new concords for this purpose without changing the

* I wonder how many organ students have stopped at this place to consider what this chord is.

key, we find that, besides the true dominant harmony, there is nothing left in the shape of a concord on the dominant, except an isolated 6th. This 6th, with the 8th above it, is the chord which figured eight-six, and although it sounds rather thin, yet it is eminently smooth and pleasant in its effect.

This is the chord which Mr. Stark chooses to laugh at, but he takes good care not to throw any additional light upon this, or any other chord. It is unfortunate that we cannot ask Bach anything; it is also very much to be lamented that he has left us no treatise; but we can, however, appeal again to his imperishable works. I quite agree with Mr. Stark that the works of Bach should form the basis of any satisfactory system of Counterpoint, and I believe that if Bach were asked a question about the above chord, eight-six, he would sanction its use; for I have found it in his works over and over again. By referring again to the G minor Fugue bar, 30, we find the following :—

At the third quarter of this example, marked with a X, here is the identical chord of eight-six, which proves beyond a doubt that Bach preferred the chord in this form to a second inversion. Later on, in this Fugue, there are other instances of the same thing. Had Bach chosen to insert a fourth, it would have been quite easy for him to have done so, *but he did not do so*, and I fancy it would be AT THE PERIL of any organist to play such a note. As actions speak louder than words, Bach shows that this chord of eight-six had its place in Counterpoint, and that its effect justifies its use.

The example from the 30th bar, as well as the one from the 10th bar, proves that Mr. Stark is in error when he says that this feeling against second inversions finds no place outside text-books.

He is also very severe, and blames Professor Macfarren for mutilating the chord which is figured eight-six; but why does not Mr. Stark blame Bach for doing precisely the same thing? I have thus been led on to write somewhat at length about this chord, and I trust I have been successful in showing that there is no other concordant combination on the dominant of the minor key available for strict Counterpoint, save the true dominant triad before mentioned. I think it manifestly unjust to blame any man for mutilating or robbing this chord; for if only two different concords can be found on the dominant of a minor key, is that anybody's fault? A natural philosopher cannot create anything; he can only treat of such things as he finds in nature. But some people may say, "Why not use a chord of six-four on the dominant?" Why?

I have referred you to one of Bach's grandest compositions, one which is played more now than ever it was since it was composed, and there is not a single second inversion in it. In fact, at the very end (in the last chord but two), where we would most naturally expect a cadential six-four, the fourth from the bass is studiously and most carefully kept out of the chord. It is veritably another eight-six. The reason for this, it seems to me, is that the chord of six-four produces a light, trivial effect, and seriously disturbs the dignity and majesty of good Counterpoint. The old masters felt the same, and thus they considered the fourth from the base a discord, and required it to be prepared; Bach and Handel, and scores of others, were of the same opinion, as their works incontestably prove. If Mr. Stark had only made a Code of Rules from analysing Bach's works, there would not be such great differences between his (Mr. Stark's) views and those of Professor Macfarren. I do not mean to say that everything found in Bach could be embodied in a book of rules, but those peculiar chords on the dominant given above are to be found in many other of Bach's works, so that it is not a mere whim or caprice on the part of this composer, but a matter of musical faith. Trusting you will pardon the length of this letter, and hoping you will sympathise with me, in my not being able to make it shorter.

I remain, Sir, your humble servant,
X. Y. Z.

The *Musical Times* is glad to find that Mr. A. C. Mackenzie's cantata "Jason" is steadily making its way among Choral Societies. Its success at the recent Wolverhampton Festival has been recorded, and during the forthcoming season London amateurs will have an opportunity of making the acquaintance of the work, performances being promised by the London Musical Society and the Borough of Hackney Choral Society. Besides these, it will be heard during the winter at Edinburgh, Blackburn, Bishop Auckland, and Bradford.

Passing Events.

"The Reminiscences of an Old Reporter" will be resumed next week; and from time to time.

The Sherborne Abbey Choir, strengthened for the occasion to about 80 voices, and aided by an amateur orchestra, will shortly produce at a concert in aid of the Choir Boys' Endowment Fund, a new cantata, "Nina," composed by the organist of the Abbey, Mr. G. E. Lyle.

A contemporary has it that Mr. James Mitchell, of Coatbridge, near Glasgow, has invented a metronome which, by means of faint and strong ticks, distinguishes pulses from measures. He calls it a "Time Meter," and proposes to bring it out as soon as he has enough subscribers.

A clever and effective operetta, "The Maid of Arcadie," by Mr. C. J. B. Meacham, Mus.Bac., has been given with much success at the St. Alban's Bazaar, Curzon Hall, Birmingham. This striking little musical drama was composed for the occasion.

A really healthy sign of musical enterprise in Bristol is the establishment of Saturday evening concerts, at which oratorios are performed with an orchestra, in Colston Hall, Bristol. No less than two thousand seats are available at threepence each, and the reserved seats are only one shilling.

American papers announce that the Boston Symphony Orchestra will enter on its third season this autumn and winter and will be directed as heretofore by Mr. George Henschel. Mr. Henry L. Higginson, the founder and patron of the enterprise, has decided to sell the tickets by auction, rather than in the usual way.

It is stated that the chorus choir of the Church of the Immaculate Conception, Boston, U.S., under the direction of Signor Leandro Campanari, is to be increased to eighty voices, and many works of note will be sung during the coming months, Schubert's mass in E flat having been selected for the Christmas Service.

Sir Julius Benedict's "Graziella" has been put on the stage at the Crystal Palace, the composer conducting the first performance on Saturday last. The effect of the music was not on the whole enhanced by the transference of the work to its new *locale*.

Mr. G. H. Gregory, of the Parish Church at Boston, gave a recital on his fine organ on Wednesday, which will be duly noticed in the *Musical Standard* presently. The specification of Mr. Scott's smaller organ at the Chapel of Ease, was crowded out on Sept. 29th; it appears to-day under "Organ News."

During last month yellow fever has been causing fearful ravages at Guaymas, in Mexico, and had up to Sept. 17th included in its victims twelve of the members of an opera company. The inhabitants were fleeing from the country. The opera troupe whose ranks were so greatly thinned by the disease only arrived a day or two before the virulent epidemic broke out.

The President of Queen's College, Galway, in his recent annual report, says :—" I am strongly of opinion that the efficiency of our examination would be much increased by considerably enlarging the *viva voce* part in certain departments, and assigning it a higher value in the aggregate of marks." Dr. Moffett adds, " I am also inclined to think that too much advantage is occasionally given to quickness of writing and readiness in producing knowledge by the number of questions proposed to be answered in a given time. Examination tests memory and power of book-work, as well as rapidity of penmanship, all of which are more or less estimable faculties, but may be possessed in a high degree by persons of very moderate capacity, while they may be far less conspicuous in real workers and thinkers. An examination should not be turned into 'A Great Writing Race,' as Professor De Morgan used to style the examinations at Cambridge." These words deserve the attention of all concerned in musical examinations. To encourage genuine intelligence rather than special cram, and to discover what a candidate does know, rather than to trouble about what he does *not* know, should be the characteristic method of every examination. It may be questioned, however, whether in art the *viva voce* system is of the same value as in other departments of knowledge.

One of the curiosities of the Amsterdam Exhibition is an instrument made of 25 large flints, suspended from two parallel rods, and struck by two smaller flints by way of hammers. M. Baudre the inventor, of St. Florent, has spent 30 years in perfecting the instrument, which presents some curious acoustical and tone-producing results.

The Archbishop of Canterbury has been preaching earnestly against the selfish, snobbish "dangerous class barriers" now existing. The encouragement of music, the formation of choral societies, and the employment of all talents, especially in the Services of the Church, are to be ranked among the means for drawing the different classes together.

It is stated that there were 195 candidates at the recent music examination of the Society of Arts. Of these all but 13 obtained certificates, 45 being first class, 92 second, and 45 third. Many sol-faists are among the successful candidates. No prizes were given. So large a number of candidates shows the continued determination of our musical people to abide by the reigning inclination towards the examination system.

On Saturday Oct. 13th, the 1st and 2nd parts of Haydn's "Creation" will be performed, under the direction of Mr. Humphrey J· Stark, Mus.Bac., at Holy Trinity, Tulse Hill, on the occasion of the annual Harvest Festival. A complete orchestra of about 30 instrumentalists will assist; and the choir will number about 70 voices, including some of Mr. J· Stedman's choir boys. The solos will be undertaken by Mr. J· Stedman, Mr. Robert Poole, and Masters Townsend, Hull, and Wallum. Messrs. W. E. Stark and E. J· Quance will preside at the organ. Mr. Stark's orchestral setting of the Magnificat will be used on this occasion. The Service commences at 7.30 p.m.

The candidates for the position of organist of York Minster, vacant by the resignation of Dr. Monk, are more than 50, of whom several are at present organists of cathedrals or of parochial choirs of much repute. The Dean and Chapter of York have appointed a small committee from their body to examine and report on the testimonials of the several candidates, after which probably about half-a-dozen of the most eligible will be invited to present themselves for individual competition, both as instrumental performers and trainers of choirs, on separate days. The election will take place on the 17th October.

Useful work is being done by the Popular Ballad Concert Committee, who have commenced their new season of work for providing a cheap musical entertainment for the people, and at the same time organising centres of instruction in vocal and instrumental music, and the formation of choral and orchestral classes. Lady Colin Campbell, Miss Ambler, Miss Edith Phillips, Mdme. Frances, Mr. Bartrum, Mr. Prenton, Mdlle. Brousil, and Mr. Aylmer took part in the first concert of the Third Winter Series, which was given at the Foresters' Hall, Clerkenwell, on Monday last. Two new centres have been organised at Shoreditch and Bermondsey, and musical entertainments will be given throughout the season at these respective town halls. Choral classes will be trained at Clerkenwell, Bermondsey, and St. Giles's. Orchestral classes are likewise being formed at Clerkenwell and Bermondsey. The hon. secretary of the committee is Mrs. Ernest Hart, 38, Wimpole-street; and the hon. musical directors are Mr. Clement Hoey, Mr. Armine Bevan, Mrs. Mallett, and Mrs. Ernest Hart.

The *Tewkesbury Register*, speaking of the recent Choral Festival at the Abbey there, observes :—One of the most interesting features in this year's Choral Festival is the fine setting of the Canticles, "Magnificat," and "Nunc Dimittis," undertaken very kindly by Dr. Chas. Joseph Frost, at the request of the precentor and the organist. The writer is well-known as an organist of the first rank and a skilful composer of church music, several anthems among other works bearing his name. The "Magnificat" is scored for brass instruments, organ, and drums. There is some most effective unison writing throughout, diversified by verses in harmony, with a theme recurring now and again beautifully marked out. The "Nunc Dimittis" is smooth and melodious in its treatment, while the "Gloria" is similar to that written for the "Magnificat." We heartily thank Dr. Frost for his compositions, and we only wish that they may frequently be heard elsewhere. The pieces were conducted by himself.

"La Vie," altered from Offenbach's opera of 1866, was heard for the first time in London on Oct. 3rd, under the direction of M. Jacobi, at the Avenue Theatre.

The Hackney Choral Society announce a spirited scheme for the season, starting with Mr. E. Prout's "Hereward." That gentleman, as heretofore, will conduct the performances.

Bord's pianos have been awarded the gold medal at the Amsterdam Exhibibition and the great merit of the maker, has received deserved recognition at the hands of the President of the French Republic, who, at the recommendation of the Minister of Commerce, has conferred on Mr. Bord the title of Chevalier of the Legion of Honour.

The Highbury Philharmonic Society have issued their prospectus for the sixth season. The conductor as before will be J· Frederic Bridge, Mus.Doc. Sub-conductor, David Beardwell; honorary accompanist, Mrs. C. J· Birch. The energetic and enthusiastic society has already selected for the ensuing season, Mendelssohn's "Athalie," Schumann's "Pilgrimage of the Rose," and selections from Weber's "Euryanthe," and Beethoven's "Fidelio."

The London rehearsals for the Leeds Festivals of next week were held during the past week, at St. James's Hall, and fully demonstrated the fine properties and excellent balance of the orchestral forces. Sir Arthur Sullivan conducted the practice of Sir G. A. Macfarren's "King David," the composer being present; Raff's oratorio, "The World End," etc. Mr. Cellier directed the rehearsal of his "Gray's Elegy," and Mr. Barnby led the practice of his 97th Psalm. The rehearsals gave promise of a real musical success.

The Royal Albert Hall Choral Society (conducted by Mr. Barnby) opens its thirteenth season on November 7th with a repetition of Berlioz's "Faust" music, the dates of the other nine concerts being November 28th, December 12th, January 1st and 16th, February 7th and 27th, March 13th, April 2nd and 11th. M. Gounod's oratorio "The Redemption" will be given, in addition to several standard works by classical composers of the past, including Beethoven's "Missa Solennis" in D. A special feature in the prospectus is the promised production of the late Richard Wagner's closing "opera drama" "Parsifal," which will be performed without stage accessories.

The Querist.

QUERY.

MUS.BAC. DEGREE.—Will some kind reader inform me whence I may obtain a list of the requirements for Mus.B. Degree, and also state the names of the text-books necessary for a good study of the subjects for examination ?—G. W.

REPLY TO E. R.

"Gallia" is the ancient name of France. The motet gracefully and sadly points to France, as modern Gaul. The composer writing just after the Franco-German war, mourned in this cantata the sorrows of his beloved country.—ED. Mus. Stand.

Service Lists.

TWENTIETH SUNDAY AFTER TRINITY.

OCTOBER 7th.

London.

TEMPLE CHURCH.—Morn.: Service, Te Deum Laudamus, and Jubilate Deo, Boyce in A ; Apostles' Creed, Harmonised Monotone ; Anthem, Thou visitest the earth (Greene). Even.: Service, Magnificat and Nunc Dimittis, Arnold in A ; Apostles' Creed, Harmonized Monotone; Anthem, Praise the Lord, O Jerusalem (Hayes).

FOUNDLING CHAPEL.—Morn.: Service, Tours in F ; Anthem, Hear me when I call (Hummel). Aft.: Children's Service.

ALL SAINTS, MARGARET STREET.—Morn.: Service, Te Deum and Benedictus, Stanford in B flat ; Holy Communion, Hummel in B flat ; Anthem, I waited for the Lord (Mendelssohn. Even.: Service, King in D ; Anthem, Quod in orbe (Hummel).

CHRIST CHURCH, CLAPHAM.—Morn.: Service, Te Deum, Plain-song; Kyrie, and Credo, Schubert in B flat; Offertory Anthem, O Lord, how manifold (Barnby); Benedictus, Agnus Dei, and Gloria in excelsis (Schubert). Even.: Service, Magnificat and Nunc Dimittis, Smart in F; Anthem, O be joyful in G (Smart).

HOLY TRINITY, GRAY'S INN ROAD. — Morn.: Service, Te Deum, Chanted; Jubilate (Best); Nicene Creed (Merbecke). Even.: Service, Magnificat, Bunnett in F; Nunc Dimittis, Chanted; Anthem, In Jewry is God known (Clarke).

HOLY TRINITY, TULSE HILL. — Morn.: Chant Service. Even.: Service, Magnificat and Nunc Dimittis, Tours in F; Anthem, The heavens declare (Boyce).

ST. BARNABAS, MARYLEBONE.—Morn.: Service, Te Deum and Benedictus, Turle in D; Anthem, Rejoice in the Lord alway (Purcell). Even.: Service, Magnificat and Nunc Dimittis, Turle in D.

ST. JAMES'S PRIVATE EPISCOPAL CHAPEL, SOUTHWARK, —Morn.: Service, Introit, Offertory and Communion Service, Silas in C. Even.: Service, Gadsby in C; Anthem, Gloria in excelsis (Gounod).

ST. MARGARET PATTENS, ROOD LANE, FENCHURCH STREET.—Morn.: Service, Te Deum, Wesley in F; Benedictus, Stainer; Communion Service, Offertory Anthem, To Thee great Lord (Rossini); Kyrie, Credo, Sanctus, Benedictus, Agnus Dei, and Gloria, Mozart in B flat. Even. Service, Magnificat and Nunc Dimittis, Gadsby in C; Anthem, O give thanks (Elvey).

ST. MARY BOLTONS, WEST BROMPTON, S.W.—Morn.: Service, Te Deum and Benedictus, Chants. Even.: Service, Magnificat and Nunc Dimittis, Dykes in F; Anthem, It shall come upon you in the last days (Garrett).

ST. MAGNUS, LONDON BRIDGE.—Morn.: Service, Opening Anthem, I acknowledge (Calkin); Te Deum and Jubilate, Turle in D; Kyrie (Turle). Even.: Service, Magnificat and Nunc Dimittis, Turle in D; Anthem, Sing, O heavens (Kent).

ST. MICHAEL'S, CORNHILL. — Morn.: Service, Te Deum and Jubilate, Dykes in F; Anthem, I will wash my hands in innocency (Hopkins); Kyrie and Creed (Marbecke). Even.: Service, Magnificat and Nunc Dimittis, Garrett in F; Anthem, Thy word is a lantern (Purcell).

ST. PAUL'S, AVENUE ROAD, SOUTH HAMPSTEAD.—Morn.: Service, Te Deum, Smart in F; Benedictus (Goss); Kyrie, Arpold in A. Even.: Service, Magnificat and Nunc Dimittis, Stewart in G; Anthem, God came from Teman (Steggall).

ST. PAUL'S, BOW COMMON, E.—Morn.: Service, Te Deum, Smart in F; Benedictus, Dykes in F; Holy Communion Kyrie, Credo, Sanctus, Benedictus and Gloria in excelsis, Mozart in B flat, No. 7; Offertory (Garrett). Even.: Service, Magnificat and Nunc Dimittis, Tours in D; Anthem, God said behold I have given you every herb (Macfarren). After Service, Solemn Te Deum.

ST. PETER'S (EATON SQUARE).—Morn.: Service, Te Deum, Sergison in A. Even.: Service, Turle in D; Anthem, as pants the hart (Mendelssohn).

ST. PETER'S, VERE STREET, W.—Even.: Service, Magnificat and Nunc Dimittis, Garrett in F; Anthem, Thy word is a lantern (Purcell).

ST. AUGUSTINE AND ST. FAITH, WATLING STREET.— Morn.: Service, Barnby in E; Introit, He fed them (South); Communion Service, Eyre in E flat, throughout. Even.: Service, Stanford in A; Anthem, Be thou faithful, See what love, happy and blest (Mendelssohn).

ST. SAVIOUR'S, HOXTON. — Morn.: Service, Te Deum, Gadsby in E flat; Holy Communion; Kyrie, Credo, Sursum Corda, Sanctus, and Gloria in excelsis, Smart in F. Even.: Service, Anthem, Fear not, O land (Goss).

ST. SEPULCHRE'S, HOLBORN.—Morn: Service, Dykes in F. Even.: Service, Cooke in G; Anthem, From the rising (Ouseley).

Country.

ST. ASAPH CATHEDRAL.—Morn.: Service, Tours in F; Anthem, Incline thine ear (Himmel). Even.: Service, ; The Litany; Anthem, Seek ye the Lord (Roberts).

ASHBURNE CHURCH, DERBYSHIRE. — Morn.: Service, Laurence in G; Kyrie, Credo and Gloria, Wesley in E. Even.: Service, Thackwray in C; Anthem, I will mention (Sullivan).

BEDDINGTON CHURCH, SURREY.—Morn.: Service, Garrett in D, throughout. Even.: Service, Garrett in F; Anthem, Praise the Lord (Hayes).

BIRMINGHAM (S. ALBAN THE MARTYR).—Morn.: Service, Te Deum, Boyce in C; Benedictus, Steggall in G; Holy Communion, Kyrie, Credo, Sursum Corda, Sanctus, Benedictus, Agnus Dei and Gloria, Redman in F throughout. Evensong.: Magnificat and Nunc Dimittis, Redman in F.

BIRMINGHAM (ST. CYPRIAN'S, HAY MILLS).—Morn.: Service, Cobb in G; Anthem, Thou visitest the earth (Simms). Even.: Service, Smart in F; Anthem, This is the day (Elvey).

CANTERBURY CATHEDRAL. — Morn.: Service, Porter in D; Anthem, O praise the Lord (Goss); Communion, Porter in D; Anthem, Thou, O God, art praised in Zion (Greene). Even.: Service, Smart in G; Anthem, Try me, O God (Hake); Communion, Smart in G; Anthem, Ascribe unto the Lord (Travers).

CARLISLE CATHEDRAL. — Morn.: Service, Selby in A; Introit, Remember me, O Lord (Macfarren); Kyrie, Selby in A; Nicene Creed, Harmonized Monotone. Even.: Service, Selby in A; Anthem, I praise Thee, O Lord (Mendelssohn).

DUBLIN, ST. PATRICK'S (NATIONAL) CATHEDRAL.—Morn.: Service, Te Deum and Jubilate, Stainer in A; Holy Communion, Kyrie and Creed, Stainer in A; Sanctus and Gloria, Stewart in G; Anthem, Be thou faithful unto death (Mendelssohn. Even.: Service, Magnificat and Nunc Dimittis, Stainer in A; Anthem, Distracted with care (Haydn); and God is our hope and strength (Greene).

DONCASTER (PARISH CHURCH).—Morn.: Service, Tours in F; Even.: Service, Tours in F; Anthem, They that go down (Attwood).

EDINBURGH (ST. JOHN'S). — Aft.: Service, Anthem, I beheld and lo (Blow); Even.: Service, Anthem, O how amiable (Barnby).

ELY CATHEDRAL.—Morn.: Service, Stainer in A; Kyrie, Credo and Gloria, Cambridge in C; Anthem, The Lord is loving (Garrett). Even.: Service, Stainer in A; Anthem, Praise the Lord (Garrett).

HARROGATE (ST. PETER'S CHURCH). — Morn.: Service, Te Deum and Benedictus, Dykes in F; Anthem, Come unto Him, Kyrie, Credo, Sursum Cords, and Gloria in Excelsis, Woodward in E flat. Even.: Service, Magnificat, and Nunc Dimittis, Hopkins in B flat; Anthem, Blessed be the God and Father (Wesley).

LEEDS PARISH CHURCH — Morn.: Service, Smart in F; Anthem, If with all your hearts (Mendelssohn); Communion, Smart in F. Even.: Service, Garrett in F; Anthem, Lord God of heaven (Spohr).

LIVERPOOL CATHEDRAL.—Aft.: Service, Magnificat and Nunc Dimittis, Whitfeld in F; Anthem, They that go down to the Sea (Attwood).

MANCHESTER CATHEDRAL.—Morn.: Service, Te Deum, Benedictus, Kyrie, Creed, Sanctus and Gloria, Stainer in E flat; Anthem, O Lord, how manifold (Barnby). Aft.: Service, Stainer in E flat; Anthem, Fear not, O land (Goss).

MANCHESTER (ST. BENEDICT'S).—Morn.: Service, Kyrie (Elvey); Credo, Sanctus, Benedictus, Agnus Dei, and Gloria in excelsis, Haydn in C, No. 2. Even.: Service, Magnificat and Nunc Dimittis, Bunnett in F.

MANCHESTER (ST. JOHN BAPTIST, HULME).—Morn.: Service, Te Deum and Benedictus (Gregorian); Kyrie (Meyerbeer); Credo, Sanctus, and Gloria in excelsis, Garrett in D; Benedictus, Thorne in B flat; Agnus Dei, Miné in F Even.: Service, Magnificat and Nunc Dimittis (Jordan).

ROCHESTER CATHEDRAL.—Morn.: Service, Hopkins in D; Anthem, O, most merciful (Huliah); Communion Service, Hopkins in D; Anthem, Here by Babylon's wave (Gounod).

SHEFFIELD PARISH CHURCH. — Morn.: Service, Kyrie, Gounod in G. Even.: Service, Cantate Domine and Deus Misereatur, Chants; Anthem, O Lord, how manifold (Barnby).

SHERBORNE ABBEY. — Morn.: Service, Chants; Kyrie, Lee in D; Offertories (Barnby). Even.: Service, Magnificat and Nunc Dimittis, Lyle in D; Anthem, God came from Teman (Steggall).

SALISBURY CATHEDRAL.—Morn.: Service, Garrett in E, and E flat; Offertory, Garrett. Aft.: Service, Garrett in E flat; Anthem, O be joyful (Elvey).

SOUTHAMPTON (ST. MARY'S CHURCH).—Morn.: Service, Te Deum and Benedictus, Woodward in E flat; Holy Communion, Introit, Holy, holy, holy; Service, Woodward in E flat; Offertory, Let him that is taught (Barnby); Paternoster (Field). Even.: Service, Magnificat and Nunc Dimittis, Woodward in E flat; Litany, Tallis' "Ferial."

WELLS CATHEDRAL.—Morn.: Service, Travers in F, throughout. Even.: Service, Aldrich in A; Anthem, God is our hope and strength (Nares).

WOLVERHAMPTON (ST. PETER'S COLLEGIATE CHURCH).— Morn.: Service, Te Deum, Stainer in F; Benedictus, Chant, Gauntlett in E; Communion Service, Stainer in E flat. Even.: Service, Responses (Tallis's); Magnificat, Chant, Goss in E; Nunc Dimittis, Barnby in D; Anthem, The Lord is my Shepherd (Macfarren).

WORCESTER CATHEDRAL. — Morn.: Service, Croft in A; Anthem, Blessed are they (Wesley). Even.: Service, Elvey in A; Anthem, How lovely are thy habitations (Salaman).

. Post-cards must be sent to the Editor, 6, Argyle Square, W.C., by Wednesday. Lists are frequently omitted in consequence of not being received in time.

NEWSPAPERS sent should have distinct marks opposite to the matter to which attention is required.

Printed for the Proprietor by BOWDEN, HUDSON & Co., at 23, Red Lion Street, Holborn, London, W.C., and Published by WILLIAM REEVES, at the Office, 185, Fleet Street, E.C. West End Agents—WEEKES & CO., 14, Hanover Street, Regent Street, W. Subscriptions and Advertisements are received either by the Publisher or West End Agents—Communications for the EDITOR are to be forwarded to his private address, 6, Argyle Square, W.C.
SATURDAY, OCTOBER 6, 1883.—Entered at the General Post Office as a Newspaper.

The MUSICAL STANDARD

A NEWSPAPER FOR MUSICIANS PROFESSIONAL AND AMATEUR

No. 1,002. VOL. XXV. FOURTH SERIES. SATURDAY, OCTOBER 13, 1883. WEEKLY: PRICE 3D.

Musical Intelligence.

"NOTES" OF THE CHURCH CONGRESS AT READING.

(From our own Correspondent).

From a musical point of view there has been far too little of general interest to report in connection with the proceedings of the Church Congress, and, so far as any practical effect upon church music is to be considered, I am afraid the future will unfortunately be quite barren of results from the Reading meeting. If I may be allowed to record my notes of the week it will be seen how meagre has been the musical fare.

To begin at the beginning of Congress week. On Sunday, Sept. 30th, special Choral Services were held in most of the churches, at which the Annual Harvest Festivals were combined with special preachers to mark the opening of the Congress Services, which were continued in the same churches on the Monday evening. On Tuesday morning the opening Services were confined to the three old parish churches in the town—those dedicated respectively to St. Mary the Virgin, St. Giles, and St. Laurence. As the Archbishop of Canterbury was to preach at St. Mary's, that became the most attractive church, and it was filled to overflowing by members of Congress only a very few minutes after the doors were opened. It is a fine old church, with a large four-manual organ by Willis (at which Mr. W. H. Strickland has long ably presided), and this Service seemed to obtain appropriate dignity by the presence of the Mayor and Corporation in state, as well as many of the greater dignitaries of the Church.

Sometime before eleven o'clock Mr. Strickland played some soft voluntaries, commencing with Schubert's Andantino in A flat, No. 2 of "Momens Musicals." As the Mayor and Corporation entered the church the "Old Hundredth" was given out, and by the time the choir and clergy were visible at the west entrance, a fine volume of tone arose from "all the people." Tallis's Festal Responses were used, preceded by the Ely harmonized confession—a modern innovation which, I regret to say, is a sort of Diocesan use in Oxford and Reading. The Psalms and Canticles were chanted to single chants by Jones, Turle, Hayes, etc., and being taken very rapidly by the choir, it was soon apparent that the large congregation meant to have its full share of the singing at its own time, and the consequence was that the choir and organ were usually taking one part of the chant, while the "congregational singing" followed one or two notes after. This was an unfortunate blemish upon the whole service, which might have been avoided by the organist and choir "humouring" the important congregation a little more.

Our critical friend, "Old School," was standing a few paces from my seat, and it was sad to see the wrathful glances which he frequently directed both upon the choir and organist, and upon the more vigorous of the worshippers around him. I should not be surprised if another periodical complaint should be already forwarded by him to the Musical Standard.

The anthem was Clarke Whitfeld's "Behold how good and joyful," and it was very well rendered by the voluntary choir, but it did sound rather old-fashioned for the occasion. I could not help mentally contrasting this service with one which I heard in the same church on the previous Friday evening, when, at the Harvest Festival, the choirs of St. Mary, All Saints, and St. Saviour's, were combined with grand effect, and the rendering by the large body of voices of Tours' "Praise God in his Holiness," was strikingly effective. But the admirable sermon of the Archbishop compensated one entirely for any defects in the preceding Service, and the organist "played us out" with a good performance of Beethoven's "Hallelujah," in which the power and resources of Willis's fine organ were fully displayed.

For the Congress meetings a large wooden hall was erected to seat an audience of 3000, while the Town Hall, close at hand, was utilized for the Sectional meetings. As each meeting has been opened and closed by a hymn, the organ of the Town Hall has been regularly used, but in the large Congress Hall only an Estey organ was available, as the Committee declined to reserve sufficient space for an organ to be specially erected. The leading organists of the town—Messrs. Davis, Read, Strickland, and Tirbutt—have alternately given their services at the two

halls, but short organ recitals were, of course, only possible at the Town Hall.

I believe it is customary to commence the Congress Meeting with the Apostles' Creed, as well as prayers and hymns, and on Tuesday the recital of the Creed in the Congress Hall, by a crowded gathering of at least 3,000 people, was very impressive. To me it seemed the most convincing argument for congregations saying their responses in *monotone* rather than *speaking* them, independently of all time and rhythm. What a "hubbub" would have resulted from such "speaking" in this instance, while the "monotoning" produced a most impressive effect.

I must also mention the wonderfully grand "congregational singing," which I heard at the meeting on Wednesday evening, when the Hall was packed with over 3,000 working men for their especial meeting. The hymns "All people" (Old Hundredth), "O God our help" (St. Ann), and "Glory to Thee" (Tallis's Canon), were sung, as it had not been my lot to hear them before, the sound rolling out in a slow, broad, and dignified unison, which is only possible with sound, majestic tunes, sung by an immense body of men's voices. At such a time one forgot all about sentimental refinement, strict time, and startling contrasts, and only joined with heart and voice in swelling out God's praise in all possible grandeur.

At the meeting in the Town Hall on Thursday evening, the subject of discussion was "The Services of the Church, and their Adaptation to Modern Needs," introduced by papers from the Bishop of Bedford, Canon Medd, Rev. Berdmore Compton, and Mr. Sydney Gedge. Upon this meeting my hopes were centred for something interesting to us church musicians, but, alas ! I was disappointed, for only the smallest reference was made to what might have been the most important part of the subject. It seems to me, that the clergy do not realize the influence which music has, or should have, in their church Services, however much they are alive to the importance of the prayers and sermons.

In the course of his paper the Bishop of Bedford truly remarked upon the necessary differences to be observed in services at Mayfair and Bethnal Green respectively, and rightly protested against the continual elaboration of the musical part of the Services, so that they went beyond the understanding of the congregations, and the Rev. Berdmore Compton agreed with him in fearing that the musical services at present were becoming too elaborate. But Mr. Sydney Gedge, who appears to be a very "protestant" layman, simply objected to anything but the most simple musical service, holding up intoning and monotoning by choir and clergy to the very easy ridicule of senseless jokes. Supposing, said Mr. Gedge, that we had an earnest request to make of the prime minister, should we make it more earnest or effective by intoning it? And this idea (very old, by the way) was received with great laughter and applause. But is not such a comparison of our forms of prayer and praise somewhat irreverent, and is it possible to argue effectively against such bigoted intolerance of decent forms as is evinced by such church people as Mr. Gedge and his sympathisers? At any rate no real notice was taken of these remarks in the discussion which followed them, and only Canon George Venables ventured to remark that the Psalms were written for singing, and could not be properly expressed by reading.

The clergy who joined in this discussion devoted all their time to pleading for greater freedom in using and adapting the prayer-book, and in increasing the number of Services ; but not a suggestion was made as to the power of music in adapting the Services to modern needs; not a voice was raised to advocate the performance of oratorios in churches as a most attractive act of worship; not an attempt was made to explain the meaning and intention of the more elaborate musical Services, which are surely not everywhere inappropriate to modern needs ; and, in fact, it was evident that not one of the speakers considered the Service music as at all important in connection with the subject.

Mr. Beresford Hope mentioned (although he did not suppose it had really anything to do with the subject), that the introductory sentences might be set to music, and sung as anthems, and so used to commence the Service instead of the processional hymn to which some objected ; and another speaker, a clergyman, thought that there should be no loud organ playing whatever after the Services, but that soft music should be played, while the clergy could go and quietly converse with those who had been affected and brought to repentance by the soul-stirring praying and preaching just concluded! Indeed, the great idea seemed only to make the evening Services mission Services for the poor, and to make as prominent as possible the sad and awful side of religious thought and feeling.

But where were all our musical clergy and our prominent church musicians? How I longed to hear the well-known name announced of someone with a position sufficient to assert his right to be heard in behalf of the *musical* Services of the church, and *their* adaptation to modern needs. The hall was full, crowded in fact, with an assemblage of church-goers anxious to hear of something practical, and there was a splendid opportunity for a church musician, either clerical or lay, to explain and plead for the musical service. As it was the idea of "Congregational singing" was narrowed down to the simplest chanting and hymn singing, and a fine opportunity for suggesting some advancing movement was lost. And now we can but hope for something better—far better—from the Congress meeting of Carlisle a year hence!

THE LEEDS FESTIVAL.

The preparatory rehearsals were duly, and on the whole, very satisfactorily accomplished. On Wednesday, Oct. 10th, the real work of performance commenced, and the remarkably fine mass of skilled instrumentalists and good, healthy, well-trained Yorkshire voices, very soon demonstrated their strong points and good qualities. London can neither claim a monopoly of good music or the possession of a vested right in dense fogs. The arrival in Leeds on Wednesday morning of the Duke and Duchess of Albany; and their official reception by the corporation, practically opened the festival; but unfortunately the royal couple entered Leeds in a fog fairly to be called dense, and in an atmosphere made all the more miserable by drizzling rain. However, the fine Town Hall, lit up by electricity (which, however, like the elements outside, was not altogether propitious to the interests of the meeting, for the lights at one time approached a failure), presented a nobly animated scene. An audience packed to the very doors, showed the unfailing popularity of Mendelssohn's "Elijah"—that finest work, in which voices are used vocally and the best resources of the art are legitimately employed, of the present century,—and a notable performance gave proof that the popularity of "Elijah" is well founded. Costa's dressing of the National Anthem opened the festival, but before proceeding the warm-hearted reception of the chief actors of the week's musical drama, including an enthusiastic greeting for Sir Arthur Sullivan, must be recorded. The fine tone of the band, the equally fine and well-balanced chorus instantly made their mark. The chorus, indeed, more than equalled the high expectations of those who attended the last Leeds Festival, and was, in short, finer than ever. The singing of Madame Valleria proved that the meeting could get on very well, indeed without Madame Albani. Madame Patey sang admirably as she always does; Mr. Maas was most efficient, and Mr. Santley warmed up to one of the finest readings of the prophet yet heard. The choruses were sung with an attack, with a richness of tone, and a living enthusiasm well worth a long journey to hear. The very small number of signs of hesitation or of error, were too trifling to call for a word, only congratulations are to be offered for a superbly fine choral performance. Dr. Spark was the organist, taking the monster organ with a familiar hand. Sir A. Sullivan conducted with complete success. At the evening concert Mr. Cellier's setting of "Gray's Elegy" was produced, this work taking the place of Mr. F. Clay's originally proposed "Sardanapalus." The new work was necessarily written to time, so perhaps is not to be criticised too sharply. It may be questioned whether the selection of the words was one suited to the clever composer's talents. The "Elegy" is one of those efforts of genius which like "Hamlet" in a larger way, has its strength in its appeal to the innate reflective powers of the reader or listener. The soul of the poet is in communion with that of the reader, and the display of imagination and descriptive power is external and only secondary to the greater depths of philosophical, passive thought. It is a question whether such a poem can ever be satisfac-

torily set — certainly not by the composer, who with facile tune and technical skill approaches his task by wading in a sort of up to the knees prettiness, and has not had either time or perhaps inclination to swim out breast high into the strong tide of deep musical emotions. Mr. Cellier's attempts to regain strength by the use of small imitative realisms, by pretty orchestral devices, is at once directly contrary, if not impertinent to the really deeply contemplative character of the poem. The realisation of the natural and local sounds should rather have been avoided, and the composer practically fell into a trap of his own making. His workmanship is undeniably good, and he has the gift of pleasant, fluent melody ; his harmonies are good and well chosen, and his orchestration shows everywhere an experienced hand. The superficial beauties and good qualities of Mr. Cellier's music won for him a sincere congratulation from an audience well disposed to accept and be pleased. The vigorous and well marked chorus, "Let not ambition," proved to be one of the most effective numbers of the work. The solo and chorus, "Full many a gem," and the tenor solo, "Some village Hampden," were among the pieces making a good impression. The soloists were Miss A. Williams, Miss H. Wilson, Messrs. Lloyd and King ; these artists sang earnestly and well. The chorus singing was here and there fine, but the display in this department was not equal to the work of the morning concert ; neither was the band so much on fire as in the rendering of "Elijah." Mr. Cellier conducted, with excellent skill, and was much applauded. The second part of the concert included a good performance of Beethoven's second symphony, the effects of which here and there are, however, better suited to a smaller orchestra. We are indeed in some danger, with our exceptionally large modern orchestras, of doing violence to the more delicate effects of scores originally intended for an orchestra not exceeding sixty players, with all departments properly proportioned. The soloists were Madame Valleria, and Mr. Lloyd. Choral and instrumental pieces were alike well rendered.

NEWCASTLE-ON-TYNE.

One of the great features of our musical season, will be Mr. W. Rea's Subscription Concerts. At the first of these —on Nov. 21st,—will be given Mendelssohn's oratorio, "St. Paul," not heard here for some time. The artists engaged for "St. Paul" are Miss Marriott, Miss Palmer, Mr. Joseph Maas, and Mr. Brereton. The second concert, on February 11th, 1884, will be a miscellaneous one, and at the third concert, which will take place about the third week of March, 1888, Mr. Rea intends to give Gounod's oratorio, "The Redemption." As this will be the first performance of "The Redemption" in our city, it will doubtless prove to be to music lovers in this district the most interesting concert of the series.

Mr. Rea also intends to give "The Messiah" on December 26th, and "Israel in Egypt" on April 14th, 1884. In all these concerts Mr. Rea's excellent and well-trained choir will assist.

A grand popular concert is announced to take place in the Town Hall on October 19th, in aid of the Organ Fund of St. Dominic Church. Miss Helen D'Alton, Miss Powell (violin), and Madame Gould (pianoforte) are among the artists engaged.

Harvest festivals have been the order of the day during the last weeks, and these thanksgiving Services are still performed in our churches, both in Newcastle and its neighbourhood. Beside the special musical Services, the churches have also been tastefully decorated with fruits, flowers, &c.

During next month the Carl Rosa Opera Company will appear here during one week, at the Tyne Theatre (a theatre especially well adapted for large operas—on account of its excellent stage, &c.), when we are promised "Esmeralda," and "Colomba," with Madame Marie Roze as the heroine, in the latter opera. This is indeed good news to lovers of English operatic music, and a welcome change in the usual repertoire of "Maritana," the "Bohemian Girl," etc.

In the musical intelligence from Newcastle, which appeared last Saturday, in the *Musical Standard*, by misprint, I was made to say—concerning the special chamber music, promoted by Messrs. Alderson and Brentnall—that "the *pieces* are truly popular," should have been, the *prices* are truly popular. The programme of this concert has not yet been issued.   H. W.

BELFAST CHORAL ASSOCIATION.

On Sept. 6th the annual conversazione in connection with this association was held in the Assembly Hall, May Street. There was a large attendance. After tea the chair was taken by Mr. Thomas H. Browne, T. C., who expressed the pleasure it gave him to see such a large gathering. It was with great pleasure he learned of the additions which had lately been made to the membership of the society. He hoped it would continue to prosper. After referring in eulogistic terms to the conductor of the association, Mr. W. J. Kempton, to whom he said the success of the organization was largely due, he called upon Mr. George H. Scrivenor to read an address to Mr. Kempton from the members.

Mr. Scrivenor then read the following address:—

"Dear Sir,—At the opening of another season we take the opportunity of congratulating you on the success which has hitherto attended your labours in connection with our association, and tendering to you our best thanks for the uniform courtesy, unremitting care, and unfailing kindness we have experienced at your hands. We wish also to express our appreciation of your great musical talent, your unstinted use of which has so much conduced to the better knowledge and cultivation of high-class music; and we bear our testimony to the consummate tact and ability you have invariably exercised in the discharge of your onerous duties as conductor, the exercise of which has led you to be regarded with feelings both of esteem and admiration. We bear in mind the many sacrifices you have made to serve us, and to advance the knowledge and practice of music. We quite recognise how impossible it would be to adequately thank you for all you have done, but we beg you will accept from us the expression of our deep indebtedness, and of the high regard in which we hold you, and, as a souvenir of bygone happy days and pleasing associations, the accompanying baton. We trust you may long be spared to wield it among us, and that our intercourse together may continue of the same agreeable nature which has up to the present characterised it.—On behalf of the association, we beg to subscribe ourselves, yours, under deep obligation, A. E. Cheyne, hon. secretary; & W. Mathews, hon. treasurer."

Mr. Kempton made a suitable reply.

A select programme of music was afterwards rendered. At the request of the chairman, the choir sang "Auld Lang Syne," and the proceedings concluded with "God save the Queen."—*The Northern Whig.*

EXETER.

Exeter churchgoers were treated to a musical novelty on Sept. 29th, on the occasion of the Dedication Festival at the Church of St. Michael and All Angels, built by the late Mr. Gibbs, of Tyntesfield, as a chapel-of-ease for the parish of St. David's. There has been a change of organists during the past 12 months, and the new organist, Mr. W. H. Richmond (late of Dundee Cathedral), resolved to make this year's Dedication Festival unusually bright and attractive, and conceived the idea of engaging a military orchestral band for the evening Service. The idea was adopted, and the result was a crowded church and a highly gratified congregation. A new processional hymn, by Mr. Tuttel, to music written by Dr. Hopkins, especially for this Festival, was used both morning and evening; and among other original music used for the first time were a "Te Deum" and "Jubilate" by Mr. W. H. Richmond, both of which were well sung by the little choir. Mr. Richmond presided at the organ at the morning service, playing with much taste.

In the evening 15 members of the Royal Marine Band, in uniform, were placed in the chancel. They comprised two first violins, two seconds, one viola, two violoncellos, one double bass, two cornets, two horns, two trombones, one euphonium, and two kettledrums the organ being relied upon to supply the wood and reed elements. The combination proved to be very effective, the only fault being that the brass was too weighty. The service was opened with a cleverly-written prelude for orchestra and organ, in which the composer (Dr. Harding) conducted, and Mr. Richmond played the organ part. The piece was excellently rendered. As in the morning, the processional hymn used was Tuttel's "We march with glad devotion," Dr. Hopkins's inspiriting phrases being enriched by the tasteful accompaniments written for orchestra and organ by Mr. Richmond, who, it may be mentioned here, arranged the whole of the instrumental music with the exception of the prelude and concluding marches. Two of the three proper Psalms were sung to Battishill's Chant, the band joining in the glorias, which were sung in unison against an elaborate instrumental part. In the third Psalm (150th), sung to the Grand Chant, the orchestra was employed, the various instruments being introduced at places where they seemed to be called for by the words. While the 4th and 5th verses (beginning "Praise Him in the cymbals and dances") were being sung, the first violins played an old Hebrew air said to be used at feasts of the Armenian Jews.

The Cantate and Deus Misereatur were by Dr. Hopkins. Here Mr. Richmond's ability in instrumentation was well displayed, and again in Mr. T. Tallis Trimnell's anthem, "I have surely built Thee an House," where, indeed, the orchestral part seemed to be richer and better balanced than in the previous items of the Service. Much praise is due to Mr. Richmond for his successful training of the choir, which, with but little extraneous help, performed its part with precision and taste, observing well the various gradations of tone. The tenor solo in the anthem was well sung by Mr. Truscott. There remain to be noticed the hymns sung before and after the sermon. They were three, viz., "We plough the Fields and scatter," "All People that on Earth do dwell," and "Stars of the Morning." The well-known tunes were taken up by the large congregation with really grand and impressive effect. After the sermon Mr. Richmond's "Te Deum" was repeated with organ and band accompaniment. It is an excellent work. While elaborate, joyous, and richly harmonised, it never loses the dignity and devotional feeling which should mark every setting of the grand hymn; and it was heard with evident pleasure. The Triumphal March in "Naaman," and Mendelssohn's "Cornelius" March, were played after the Service. Mr. Richmond conducted throughout after the prelude, his seat at the organ being occupied by Mr. Craddock, Mus. B., of Torquay, who played in masterly style.

HORNS ASSEMBLY ROOMS.—The first of a series of six Smoking Concerts took place on Thursday, the 4th inst., at the above Hall, under the direction of Mr. George F. Grover. Though there was not a very large audience present, the concert nevertheless was very much appreciated. A new vocalist at this hall, Mr. H. Setton, sang two songs in admirable style; he possesses a bass voice of splendid quality. Mr. Arthur Reynolds sang with his proverbial "go," which is so much enjoyed at concerts of this description. Mr. Charles Bradberry contributed two violin solos with success, and a solo by Mr. Wilkins's cornet-à-pistons was greatly applauded. Two American organ solos were given by Mr. George F. Grover—the remaining vocalists, Messrs. Bowden, Thornton, and Kersel were fairly successful. Mr. George F. Grover was accompanist throughout the evening. If the remaining five which are to be given, prove equally successful from a musical point of view, those who are partial to this class of music may with safety become subscribers.

NANTWICH.—In connection with the Harvest Thanksgiving Services in the Parish Church of Nantwich, on Thursday, the 27th ult. Weber's "Jubilee Cantata" was given as the anthem, with organ and orchestral accompaniments, by the Church Choir, assisted by several ladies and gentlemen of the town and neighbourhood. The work, which is a difficult one, was exceedingly well rendered; the solo parts being sustained in good style by Master Rory Waleen (from Mr. Stedman's choir) of London (treble); Mr. Hitchcock, of Crewe (tenor); and Mr. J. Dunning, of Nantwich Choir (bass). The effective way in which the choruses were sung reflected great credit on the organist of the church, Mr. G. D. Harris, who conducted the performance, and on whom has devolved the training of the choir. The Rev. Hylton Stewart, Precentor of Chester Cathedral, ably presided at the organ.

LEEDS PARISH CHURCH.—This church was reopened on Wednesday morning, Sept. 26th, after being closed for some months for repairs and alterations. The opening Service consisted of a Service of Blessing, which was conducted by the Bishop of Bedford, who was accompanied by the vicar and curates of the Parish Church. Several of the local clergy were also present in surplices. The "Te Deum" was sung to Gounod in D, and the music to the Holy Communion was Wesley's fine service in F. In the evening the Bishop of Bedford preached to a large congregation, and the anthem was "Awake, Awake" (Stainer). The organ, which has been improved at an expense of £1,600, is now one of the finest church organs in the kingdom. The instrument has some 75 stops and 4,164 pipes.

BELFAST.—The conductor and members of the Choral Association may be congratulated on the success of the first popular concert of the season recently given in the Ulster Hall. The building was well filled in every part, and the applause evoked at intervals indicated that the efforts of Mr. Kempton and the committee were fully appreciated. The occasion was the first appearance in the hall of the band of the Inniskilling Fusiliers, under Mr. M'Laren. The manner in which the various selections and accompaniments were played was skilful and judicious. The tendency to loudness, so frequently noticeable where a band comprising the heavier brass instruments is employed indoors, was carefully guarded against. The part songs and glees rendered by the chorus, were well chosen, and served excellently to display the culture of the singers, who promise this winter to sustain their old reputation for refinement and precision. One of the most successful items was "Three Doughtie Men," the chorus's part song composed for the association by Mr. W. W. Pearson. The concert, which was under the patronage of Colonel Stokes and officers of the Royal Inniskilling Fusiliers, was an auspicious opening for the season of a society of recognised musical standing.

Academical Intelligence.

ROYAL ACADEMY OF MUSIC.

Sir G. A. Macfarren's address is always looked forward to with interest, and the one delivered on Sept. 29th, as an exposition of the Professor's views on a burning question, will be thought over with marked attention. The following extract will fully display the speaker's ideas anent the question of "the music of the future":—

"Orchestration one might describe as the chemistry of sound —the learning how to balance different qualities of tone so as to produce new effects of sound from their combination. The greatest art of the orchestral writer was to produce such a variety of tone, yet to make for ever the distinctness of its several parts apparent to the hearer. Such they found to be the case in the orchestration of Mozart, who was—and must, he thought, remain—the greatest model for them all. No one had produced more beautiful effects of musical combination than Mozart; but there was never an occasion when one could not distinctly trace by the ear, in performance, the distinct walk in every part of the score, as one could trace it by the eye if one examined the musical construction on paper. In the composer whose name he had mentioned—Wagner—there was not a variety of sound. The same quality of tone prevailed throughout an opera of four hours' length. One had but the variety which was made by striking more forcibly or less forcibly on the pianoforte—of loud and less loud—but the constancy of the same tone of brass and reed instruments prevailed from beginning to end, and with such indistinctness of part writing that when the music had been committed to memory by a listener he could not, in many instances, trace the elements of the score. On that ground he feared that this writer had exercised a bad influence to the musical history of the present, though he would have had no influence but for the genius he had manifested, which he (the speaker) most distinctly wished to acknowledge. The beautiful passages which appeared in the course of his works dazzled them and benumbed the sense for the moment to those large portions which were unequal to them. It was particularly to be desired that they should watch his moments of beauty with circumspection, and in comparison with the writings of other men. Another element of this author's writing was his discarding the principles of musical construction, grounding his practice upon the idea that music was but a portion of the work presented to the public, that it was dependent on the words, that it was dependent on the dramatic action, that it must work together with these to complete the composition presented, and that the trammels, as they were called, of art-forms were fetters to genius, and hindrances to the just development of the musical idea. A work of art without plan, design, or form could not exist. A work of nature presented to us most distinct evidences of plan, design, and form; and art could only emulate nature when it went on principle and when it constructed its productions with this ideal of principle at its very root. Musical design should be built upon the exigencies of the situation that had to be illustrated, but that situation was at the heart of the musical plan, and musical plan might be thoroughly designed, thoroughly fulfilled, if the peculiarities of the text (if it referred but to words), if the dramatic action (if extended over single sentences) were made the groundwork of musical plan.

TRINITY COLLEGE, LONDON.

The inaugural address of the session of Trinity College, London, was delivered on Tuesday, Oct. 2nd, by the Rev. H. G. Bonavia Hunt, Mus.B.Oxon. (warden of the College), after the diplomas, certificates, medals, etc., had been distributed to the candidates.

SOCIAL SCIENCE CONGRESS.

At the Social Science Congress at Huddersfield, the Warden of Trinity College, London (Rev. H. G. Bonavia Hunt) contributed, by request, a paper on the special question, "What constitutes a School of Music; and how far can the formation of an English School be encouraged?" Such a paper from one who has thought much about and done admirable work for musical education, would naturally prove an essay of value and interest, and it will presently be laid before the reader.

Signor Bimboni has gone to Bucharest, there to direct the orchestra of the Theatre Royal. During his stay in the Roumanian capital he will mount an opera of his own, "l'Aiddúck," which is written on a national subject. The season at Bucharest will last till the middle of February, and on March 15th an Italian opera season will open at the Vienna Imperial Opera under the musical direction of Signor Bimboni.

Foreign Musical Intelligence.

M. Brunel, of Paris, has written an operetta called "Alter Ego."

The people of Berlin propose to erect a monument to Beethoven.

Rendano, the pianist, commences a tour through Italy in November.

Filippo Romagnoli has been nominated a cavalier of the order of the crown of Italy.

Brahms has finished his Third Symphony, which will presently be performed in Berlin.

The death is announced of Carl Kuntze, composer and organist, at the age of sixty-six.

The death of the organist, Signor Cesare Carini, at the age of fifty-seven, is announced from Milan.

A new Spanish opera, "San Francisco de Sena," by Senor Arrietta, has been composed for Madrid.

Signor Meucci has composed a new opera entitled "Annalena," which is to be produced during the present month.

Jules de Swert has finished a four act opera, "Graf Hammerstein," which will probably be given this season in Weimar.

Enrico Piatti, the brother of the distinguished violoncellist, Alfred Piatti, and himself a violoncello player, died recently at Brescia.

The "Walhalla," a new theatre devoted to operetta in Berlin, has mounted a novelty called "Nanon," words and music by Richard Genée.

A new work called "Helianthe," words and music by Adalbert von Goldschmidt, is announced for performance at the Vienna Court Opera during the season.

The monument to be erected to the memory of Weber in his native town, Eutin, will, it is hoped, be inaugurated on December 18th, 1889, the centenary of the composer's birth.

At the funeral of Tourgenieff at St. Petersburg on Oct. 9th, Russian musical societies joined the other artistic, literary and scientific bodies, in paying tribute to the memory of the great novelist.

Signor Alberto Mollini has written an opera, in four acts, "Bocca degli Abbati," the action being of the date of the thirteenth century. Signor Mollini is both a librettist and a composer.

Rubinstein's opera, "Der Haufmann Kalaschnikow," which was for some years interdicted in Russia on political grounds, is now to be heard in Moscow and St. Petersburg. The Russian Emperor personally gave the composer this permission.

Liszt's birthday, October 22nd, will be celebrated in Weimar by a performance of his oratorio, "St. Elizabeth," the composer assisting on the occasion. This summer Liszt has written several pieces, and has twice a week instructed a large number of pupils, about thirty-two.

It is announced that the tenth Middle Rhenish festival is to be held next July at Mayence. Among the chief works given will be the "Triumphlied" of Brahms, one of Schumann's symphonies, the "Faust" overture of Wagner, and Handel's "Messiah." Herr Friedrich Lux will be the conductor.

Forty-four pianoforte trios were sent in to compete for the prizes offered by the Quartet Society of Milan. The work composed by Signor Martucci, of Naples, received the first prize. The second prize was not awarded, as the next work in merit proved to be by a German, and the competition was confined to Italians.

Says the *Athenæum* :—"A new theatre, the Deutsche Theater, has just been opened in Berlin, at which a plan has been adopted worthy of general imitation. All the performers have resolved that they will not allow any recalls, except on benefit nights, and on the first production of new works. We fear that the recall and encore nuisance has taken too firm a hold of our English public to offer much hope that the excellent example of the Berlin artists will be followed here."

Organ News.

LIVERPOOL.

An organ recital was given on Thursday, October 4th, in St. George's Hall, by Mr. W. T. Best. The following was the programme :—

Organ Sonata, No. 3, in A minor	Eyken.
Andante in F major, from the 4th Symphony	Mozart.
Scherzo-Symphonique	Lemmens.
Pastorale, "Villanella"	Fumagalli.
Overture, "Lurline"	Wallace.

And on Saturday October 6th :—

Allegro Moderato in A major	Smart.
Air and Chorus of Priests, "O Isis and Osiris"	Mozart.
Organ Concerto in D major	Handel.
Andante for the organ, in B flat major	Dubois.
Fugue in G major, Vol. 9, No. 4	Bach.
Overture, "Luisa Miller"	Verdi.

BOLTON.

An organ recital was given in the Albert Hall, by Mr. W. Mullineux, F.C.O., on Saturday, October 6th. The following was the programme :—

Processional March	Eyken.
Andante from the Pianoforte Sonata in C	Beethoven.
Pastorale in A major	Guilmant.
Toccata in F major (with Pedal solos)	Bach.
Improvisation on "The Last Rose of Summer"	
Overture, "Le Pré aux Clercs"	Hérold.

CHARLTON.

An organ recital was given on Saturday, October 6th, by Dr. Charles Joseph Frost, Cantab., in St. Paul's Church, together with sacred musical selections. The programme included the following :—

Toccata and Fugue in C major	Bach.
Moderato in A, and Alla Marcia in F	Frost.
March, "Funebre"	Gigout.
Fantaisie	Guiraud.
Communion	Grison.
Grand Offertoire in G	Wely.

ILKESTON.

A new and effective organ, with two manuals and Pedals, was opened here on Monday, September 24th, at the Wesleyan Methodist Chapel, Bath Street. There was a special Service in the afternoon, and in the evening a recital was given by Mr. E. H. Turpin. Upon both occasions the attendance was large. The instrument was built by Messrs. Forster and Andrews, of Hull. The preacher at the afternoon Service was Dr. Melson, of Birmingham, who with Mr. Smith, of Langley Mill, addressed the congregation during the evening recital.

OLDHAM.

On Saturday, the 6th inst., Mr. W. A. Wrigley, organist of Holy Innocents, Fallowfield, Manchester, gave two recitals on the organ in the Fine Art Exhibition. The programmes included :—

March in F	Wallis.
Cavatina	Raff.
Minuet	Boccherini.
Prelude and Fugue in G minor	Bach.
Allegretto in E	Schubert.
"Wedding March"	Mendelssohn.
Andante in G	Batiste.
"Cujus Animam"	Rossini.
Overture "Calif of Bagdad"	Boildeau.
March in D	Smart.

HIGH WYCOMBE.

On Monday evening the 24th ult., a recital was given on the organ, in the Parish Church, by Mr. J. G. Wrigley, F.C.O., Mus.Bac., Oxon. The programme included :—

March Religiosa	Parelli.
Andante quasi Larghetto	Ouseley.
Teman con Variazione	Beethoven.
Prelude and Fugue in B flat	Bach.
"Wedding March"	Mendelssohn.

HINKLEY.

An organ recital was given in the Parish Church, on Sunday evening, October 7th, by Mr. Chas. J. King. The following was the programme :—

Sketch "Ave Maria"	Chipp.
Concert Fantasia in D	Stewart.
Andante con variazioni in A	Rea.
"The Harmonious Blacksmith"	Chipp.
Allegro in A minor	Gade.

BOW AND BROMLEY INSTITUTE.

On Saturday last Mr. Walter Weschd made a good first appearance as solo organist, handling the instrument with much skill and considerable taste, though showing perhaps a little want of a full and perfect control of the louder passages, possibly in consequence of a slight nervousness. The first solo was an overture in C minor by Himmel, which makes an effective organ piece. Next came Bach's Fugue in D major. Then "Variations Moderne" of the player's own, consisting of seventeen changes upon an original theme. This is a clever and promising work, was well handled by the player, and was duly appreciated by a critical audience. The other organ solos were the andante from Haydn's "Surprise Symphony" of Gavotte, by M. Lee, and Flotow's favourite overture to "Stradella." The accomplished violoncellist, Mr. E. Woolhouse, played most artistically Servais's "Concerto Militaire," for which he was recalled, and "Chanson a boire" (Dunckler), which was encored. Mr. George Cox has a good tenor voice of excellent quality, and sang carefully and well. His first song was "Deeper and deeper still." The next was Sullivan's "A maiden sat at her door," which was encored, and then Allen's "Maid of Athens." Mr. Wood was the painstaking accompanist. Mr. W. T. Best is to play next Saturday, and Dr. A. L. Peace will be the soloist on Oct. 27th. Both announcements will give pleasure to the organ world. To-night Mr. Albert E. Bishop will be the organist.

FISHERIES EXHIBITION.

The following organ recitals have been given during the week by Mr. J. Loaring, F.C.O. The programmes included :—

Organ Concerto, No. 3	Handel.
Bell-Rondo	Morandi.
Prelude and Fugue	Bach.
March Cortège from "Irene"	Gounod.

Overture, "Il Turco in Italia"	Rossini.
Organ Concerto, No. 4	Handel.
Prelude and Fugue	Bach.
"Marcia de Processione"	Morandi.

BRISTOL.

An organ recital was given in the Colston Hall on Saturday, October 6th, by Mr. George Riseley. The following was the programme :—

Offertoire, No. 4, in G minor	Batiste.
Allegro—Andante—Allegro.	
Adagio, 3rd Symphony	Mendelssohn.
Organ Concerto, No. 4, in F	Handel.
Allegro—Andante maestoso—Adagio—Allegro.	
Adagio	Beethoven.
Overture, "Midsummer Night's Dream"	Mendelssohn.
Marche Religieuse	Chauvet.
March, "Tanahauser"	Wagner.

EXETER.

An organ recital was given on Wednesday, September 19th, in the Queen Street United Methodist Free Church, by Mr. Harold Ryder, organist of Southernhay Congregational Church. The following was the programme :—

Overture to "Athalie"	Handel.
Allegro—Grave—Allegro—Adagio.	
"Hymn of the Nuns," with variations	Wely.
Larghetto from the Symphony in D	Beethoven.
Concert-stuck	Spark.
Fantasia on the "Vesper Hymn"	E. H. Turpin.
Flute Concerto	Rink.
Preludium et Fuga ("pro organo pleno")	Bach.
Air, with variations, and Finale Fugato	Smart.
Offertoire in E flat major	Batiste.
Sonata, No. 1, in A minor	Mendelssohn.

The organist is reported as playing admirably.

PRESTON.

On Saturday evening, October 6th, Mr. J. Tomlinson, organist of the Corporation, gave his usual weekly recital in the New Public Hall. The programme was as follows :—

Concerto in D minor	Handel.
Larghetto from the 2nd Symphony	Beethoven.
Scherzo	Best.
Airs from the opera, "Stradella"	Flotow.
Serenata	Braga.
"Fanfare Militaire"	Archer.

The andante movement in the concerto in D minor was rendered in a very pleasing manner. "Serenata" (Braga), was, however, the piece of the evening, for the audience received it with loud applause, and were not satisfied until Mr. Tomlinson repeated the whole of it. The airs from "Stradella," and "Fanfare Militaire" were also well received. The attendance was good.

WORMLEY, HERTS.

An organ recital was given at St. Laurence, on October 9th. Mr. Swift, the organist of the church, presided at the morning and evening services. The programme included :—

Toccata and Fugue in D minor	Bach.
"Austrian Hymn," with variations	Haydn.
Barcarolle	Spohr.
Fugue in E	Bach.
Grand Chœur in D	Guilmant.
Grand Offertoire in D	Batiste.

The organ has two manuals, and Pedal organ, with three couplers, and two composition pedals. The builder is Mr. Speechly, of Camden Town, London.

DUNDEE.

Mr. Horton resumed the series of organ recitals in St. Mark's Church, on Wednesday, Sept. 26th. The vocalists were Miss Winton, and Mr. James Stephen. The programme included :—

"Meditation in a Cathedral"	Silas.
Minuet and Trio	Bennett.
Overture for Organ in E minor	Morandi.
Adagio in B flat	Spohr.
Military March	Beethoven.

MORNINGSIDE, EDINBURGH.

An organ recital was given in the United Presbyterian Church, on Monday, October 8th, by Mr. William Blakeley. The following was the programme :—

Organ Concerto, No. 4	Handel.
Adagio in D major	Mozart.
Prelude and Fugue in G minor	Bach.
Aria, "How beautiful are the feet"	Handel.
Pastorale, from the 8th Concerto	Corelli.
Introduction and Fugue in C minor	Gaebler.
Allegretto in G major	Blakeley.
Entr'acte	Gounod.
Overture in F minor	Morandi.

BOSTON.

Mr. G. H. Gregory (the organist) gave a performance at the great church of Boston on October 3rd, when he played, in masterly style, Handel's concerto in A, of four movements ; Sir Michael Costa's "March of Israelites" from "Eli," Batiste's Offertoire in D, Smart's "Song for Tenor," and the final chorus in C, from "The Mount of Olives." This fine organ, which stands in a low gallery over the north transept (approached by a very awkward staircase) was originally built in 1717 by Christian Schmidt (or Smith), nephew of the famous "Father Smith." Its great glory consists of its magnificent diapasons, which, aided by the excellent acoustical properties of the church, produce an effect rarely to be equalled. The organ has been restored and enlarged from time to time ; the last occasion was in 1871, when it was completely re-constructed by Messrs. Brindley and Foster of Sheffield. It now contains forty-one sounding stops, viz. : thirteen on the Great Organ, thirteen on the Swell, eight on the Choir, and seven on the Pedal, besides the usual couplers. Perhaps the most justly admired stops (after the diapasons before mentioned) are the German Flute (by Bishop), the clarinet and bassoon, and the oboe on the Swell organ. One of Smith's original (four feet) stops remains ; it is labelled " Flute-i-Bec," but has nothing very special in its tone, and merely supplies the place of a second Principal on the Great Organ. The Pedal organ is very bold and massive, but suffers from the confined space in which it is placed. The organ, according to Mr. Gregory, is heard to the best advantage about half-way down the lengthy nave.

A small curiosity in Boston Church may be passed over by visitors. This is a monumental tablet at the west-end of the building, to the memory of some unknown individual, with an inscription of the melody of Balfe's song, "Then you'll remember me," from "The Bohemian Girl." The carver, however, like some modern "arrangers" has taken the liberty to change the key D flat to D major.

The project for building a new organ for Canterbury Cathedral hangs fire. Only about £1,200 out of the required £3,500 have been raised. Possibly people are reluctant to give because they believe the revenues of the cathedral are large enough to cover any cost in connection therewith.

BRISBANE.

The first organ recital given in this enterprising centre of a distant colony, took place on July 31st, at the Presbyterian Church. The executants were Madame Mallalieu, (reported to be an admirable pianist as well as an accomplished organ player), Mr. Walter Willmore (an organist well known in London and a member of College of Organists); Mr. Atkinson, and Mr. Scott. One feature of the programme was Merkel's "Duo Sonata," excellently played by Madame Mallalieu and Mr. Willmore. Compositions by Smart, Freyer, Guilmant, and Hiles were also given.

HOPE, DERBYSHIRE.

The Parish Church of Hope has just been enriched by the erection of an excellent organ, by Messrs. Brindley and Foster, of Sheffield, of which the following is the Specification :—

GREAT ORGAN. CC TO G.

1. Open Diapason	16 ft.		4. Principal	4 ft.
2. Stopped Diapason	8 „		5. Harmonic Flute	4 „
3. Dulciana	8 „		6. Harmonic Piccolo	2 „

SWELL ORGAN. CC TO G.

7. Violin Diapason	8 ft.		11. Twelfth	3 ft.
8. Lieblich Gedact	8 „		12. Fifteenth	2 „
9. Vox Angelica	8 „		13. Trumpet	8 „
10. Principal	4 „			

PEDAL ORGAN. CCC TO F.

14. Sub-Bass	16 ft.

COUPLERS.

15. Swell to Great.	17. Great to Pedal.
16. Swell to Pedal.	18. Great Sub-Octave.

Two composition pedals.

The pedals are straight and concave, the Swell shutters vertical, and the Great to Pedal coupler has a draw knob on either side of the Manuals.

The instrument, which is the gift of W. J. Marrow Esq., of Liverpool, is most effective, the soft stops being particularly well and delicately voiced.

At the request of the vicar, the Rev. H. Buckston, Mr. W. H. Tutt, Mus.Bac., Cantab., L.R.A.M., gave, on the 18th inst., a recital, of which the following is the programme :—

Andante and Allegro	Bach.
Larghetto from clarinet quintet, Op. 108	Mozart.
Fugue in E minor	Bach.
Largo from string quartet	Haydn.
Offertoire in G minor	Wely.
Two slow movements, from violin duets	Spohr.
March	Rowber.
Andante	Wely.
"Hallelujah" ("Messiah")	Handel.

BEVERLEY MINSTER ORGAN.

The fine old instrument in Beverley Minster, built originally by Shetzler, is now being re-constructed and enlarged by Messrs. W. Hill and Son. The old pipes will be carefully preserved, intact, and used again, but entirely new action of all kinds, on the most scientific principles, will be provided, and the organ will be blown by hydraulic power. The present instrument stands in the nave, but the newly constructed one will be arranged partly on the choir screen, and partly at the southern extremity of the same, in the choir aisle, where will be placed the 32 ft. Pedal and organ pipes. Tubular pneumatic apparatus will be used for much of both the key and drawstop action. The following is the scheme, as being carried out :—

GREAT ORGAN. CC TO A.

1. Bourdon	16 ft.		8. Wald Flute	4 ft.
2. Open Diapason	8 „		9. Twelfth	3 „
3. Open Diapason	8 „		10. Fifteenth	2 „
4. Open Diapason	8 „		11. Sesquialtera (3 ranks)	
5. Gamba	8 „		12. Mixture (4 ranks)	
6. Stopped Diapason	8 „		13. Posaune	8 „
7. Principal	4 „		14. Clarion	4 „

CHOIR ORGAN. CC TO A.

15. Open Diapason	8 ft.		20. Flute	4 ft.
16. Dulciana	8 „		21. Fifteenth	2 „
17. Stopped Diapason	8 „		22. Sesquialtera (3 ranks)	
18. Clarabella	8 „		23. Cremona	8 „
19. Principal	4 „			

SWELL ORGAN. CC TO A.

24. Bourdon .... 16 ft.	31. Oboe .... 8 „
25. Open Diapason ...... 8 „	32. Trumpet .... 8 „
26. Stopped Diapason... 8 „	33. Vox Humana......... 8 „
27. Principal .... 4 „	34. Clarion .... 4 „
28. Fifteenth .... 2 „	35. Tuba Mirabilis ...... 16 „
29. Sesquialtera (4 ranks)	36. Tuba Mirabilis ...... 8 „
30. Horn .... 8 „	

PEDAL ORGAN. CCCC TO F.

37. Double Open Diap. 32 ft.	40. Violoncello .... 8 ft.
38. Open Diapason ... 16 „	41. Trombone .... 16 „
39. Violone .... 16 „	

COUPLERS.

42. Swell to Great.	46. Great to Pedal.
43. Swell to Choir.	47. Choir to Pedal.
44. Swell to Pedal.	48. Choir to Great.
45. Swell Octave.	49. Tremulant.

The two Tuba stops are novelties, and are taken from those made many years ago for York Minster, by Messrs. Hill, the original inventors of the heavy pressure reed, the first ever made being still in the large instrument in the Town Hall, at Birmingham. The present Swell by Snetzler goes only to tenor C.

CHURCH MUSIC AND CONGREGATIONAL SINGING.

It is well that we should distinctly recognize the difference between secular music and that which is specially intended for the service of God.

"The intent of singing is by a musical pronunciation of affecting truth, to render it still more affecting." To accomplish this end the music ought, at all events, to be adapted to the sentiments. As in speaking, the sound or modulation of the voice conveys to us the sentiment the speaker wishes; so, to a great extent in singing, there are certain tones which are naturally expressive of joy, sorrow, indignation, &c., and the grand art of psalmody consists in applying these to the sentiments of the various hymns. Ordinary music provides only a high intellectual enjoyment, whilst church music is an offering dictated to God, and as such must be redolent of the incense of worship and adoration.

It has sometimes been argued, that, because a congregation sings a certain tune with evident enjoyment, the tune must be good. Such an argument would hold good if personal enjoyment were the end and aim of church music. But it entirely falls to the ground if we proceed on the principle that the singing of every hymn is an act of worship. Our method as a rule is not good. It frequently happens that someone who has a taste for music composes a tune, a mere tune, without any sentiments to be expressed. The poet then, instead of going before the musician, comes after him; and a hymn is conformed to the tune, instead of a tune to the hymn. The tune being composed to four, six, or eight lines, is applied to any hymn that is written in these respective measures, and repeated over, without any regard to the meaning, as many times as there stanzas to be sung.

There is no need to object to the division of music into parts or breaks, so as to make proper places for pausing; but this division ought not to be uniform, but governed to some extent by the matter to be sung. There ought to be no pauses in music, any more than in speaking, save at the conclusion of a sentence, or of some lesser break in the division of it; and the length of the pause ought to be governed by the meaning, in some proportion as it is in reading. Nothing can be more unnatural than for a congregation to dwell in a long swelling sound upon such words as in, and, from, &c., while they skip over words expressive of the very burden of the hymn, as if they were of no account; yet this will frequently be the case, if we make hymns to tunes instead of tunes to hymns. It would be difficult to find a better definition of a good hymn tune than Mr. Barnby's, and I make no apology for quoting it in full. "The true test of a hymn tune is that it shall equally satisfy the worshipper, a better musician or amateur. It should be capable of embodying the purest thoughts and noblest aspirations of both religion and art. But if, after a fair trial, it fails, through its too great severity, to stimulate the best f elings of the amateur, or if it offend the susceptibilities of the musician, by an excess of laxity, it is surely unfit for its high purpose."   ERNEST BIRCH.

PRINCIPAL CONTENTS OF THIS NUMBER.

LONDON: SATURDAY, OCTOBER 13, 1883.

SIGNS OF MISTAKEN CLANSHIP.

A YOUNG GENTLEMAN has gained a musical degree. Very great credit is due to this young gentleman, therefore; but the circumstance is not so remarkable in these days as to call for special notice. However, this really talented and musically well-informed artist has thought fit to make an observation, which seems to call for some comments. He has attributed the criticisms of the London press regarding certain recently-heard new music, the composition of a distinguished musical graduate, to what he is pleased to consider the persistent prejudices against and consequently vindictive onslaughts upon those martyrs of culture, the gentlemen holding degrees, by the wild Indians of the press in that wicked, presumptuous, ostentatious, and stony-hearted place, London, who practise predatory warfare with that dreadful weapon, the pen. Those who know the world of science, literature, and art, know well enough that there is no truth whatever in the allegation of the young musical graduate. However, the young gentleman holds to his own opinion; it is useless there fore to bring forward any testimony to the contrary, and one is inclined to quote the caustic words, *Plus negabit unus in centum horæ, quam probaverint in centum annis.* Now, no import ance whatever is to be attached to this matter in itself; still it is an incident which shows the want in a certain direction of a little breezy common sense; just as does the absurd story of a musical doctor who was so impressed with the dignity of his position as a holder of the awe-striking diploma, that he was constrained to decline to be introduced to those benighted musicians of this happy land who have neglected to become musical graduates, and very likely he would add also, to those artists who like M. GOUNOD, M. AMBROISE THOMAS, and Signor VERDI &c., have had the misfortune to be born in lands where the effulgence of the glory of musical graduateship is unknown. This story should not be told without the witty comment of a celebrated musi cian, who observed "The doctor evidently wants to reduce all of us to one level." But it is not fair to cite such palpable cases of weakness; for the many distin guished artists and estimable men who hold University diplomas would themselves be the first to condemn this new form of British snobbishness. Personally I feel pained to be constrained to write about this matter, and only a sense of duty compels me to notice the subject. It is important to point out the necessity there is for doing all possible honour to those who have earnestly and ... achieved the distinction of ... ... honourable degrees. And to urge all young ... entering the profession that it has indeed ... absolutely necessary for their future ... recognition and welfare, that they prepare themselves ... duly to pass the Examinations held at our Universi ties and at such incorporated or chartered institutions as the Royal Academy of Music, the College of Organists, Trinity College London, and the Royal College of Music in ... ... seniority. All the same, it should be borne in mind that this is a transition age, and that it will be time enough for the next generation to talk about the necessary universality of musical graduateship, and to devise special titles of honour to take the place of the titles which are very properly becoming merely the means of duly registering with attainable high credit the names of their holders as qualified members of the musical profession. And it must be remembered that the highest of these diplomas have been given *honoris causâ* to most of our eminent musicians—hold ing them, as in the cases of STERNDALE BENNETT, G. A. MACFARREN, E. J. HOPKINS, ARTHUR SULLIVAN, VILLIERS STANFORD, OAKELEY, G. C. MARTIN, &c. Further, no man in his senses could sup pose it to be necessary for their distinguished

musicians not holding such high diplomas to begin life again by throwing themselves into the crowd of young aspirants, who are now with true sense of self-respect and with a high sense of the dignity of their art, preparing to take their degrees and diplomas by examination. Further, in the name of common sense, where are the tribunals before which such gifted, influential and highly cultured men as, in the field of composition HENRY SMART, J. HATTON, G. A. OSBORNE, C. E. STEPHENS, EBENEZER PROUT, W. MACFARREN, JOSEPH BARNBY, HENRY GADSBY, COWEN, MACKENZIE, T. WINGHAM, and A. GORING THOMAS,—such poetical, powerful, and critical writers and teachers, as JOSEPH BENNETT, J. DAVISON, HENRY C. BANISTER, H. J. LINCOLN, C. A. BARRY, W. H. CUMMINGS, and H. F. FROST,—such a stan dard organ player and composer for the instru ment as W. T. BEST, and such a typical per former as J. CARRODUS, can be called upon to display their art? ... ... These, indeed, have been leaders in the van of the musical army which has been more uplifted musical England, and raised the position of the musical graduate into one of universal respect and substantial dignity. These men, forming an unequalled phalanx of English musical strength, are working side by side with such distinguished musical graduates, as those previously named, and as F. A. GORE OUSELEY, R. STEWART, J. STAINER, JAS. HIGGS, W. A. BARRETT, G. M. GARRETT, ... BRIDGE, C. STEGGALL, F. E. GLADSTONE, H. HILES, W. PARRATT, and others who have well earned academical honours, for the advancement of the art and for the welfare of its professors. For the benefit of the young musical graduate, now taken to task and as a protest against any injurious, uncalled for, and mis taken snobbery, it may be well to repeat what has been pointed out by abler writers than myself, that granting the dignity and power of Oxford and Cambridge, and duly recognising the important functions our grand and noble universities exercise in the academical preparation of the athletes of the intellectual and artistic world, London must, from its pre-eminent position as a scientific, intellectual, political, and artistic centre, remain the arbiter of British merit and skill. It is the place for men of tried and proved strength; and its vastness has reflected a vagueness of mind, a capacity for true and generous criticism, and a sense of responsibility upon most of the men who have risen to do work for the world, far above the petty schoolboy notions which prompt such non sense as the weak dictum of one who supposes that musical graduates well able to hold their own high positions, were being sat upon by the London press, because forsooth they are honourable scholars. There always will be doctors and doctors, men and men; but let those earnestly interested in the advance of the art, learn to see clearly, despite the clouds of ignorance and prejudice; and learn too that those soldiers of the artistic army who have in their long experience acquired the power of distinguishing good work from bad, are ever the first to rejoice in new found treasures from whatever mine they may be brought to light.   H. TURPIN.

PURPOSE IN THE COMPOSITION OF MUSIC.

III.

WITHOUT any rhetorical exaggeration, it may be asserted that the presence of purpose as well as character in their music has been the chief source of the individual reputations of the great masters. The determined definiteness of the yearnings for dramatic effects, which characterised the labours of MONTEVERDE, LULLI and HENRY PURCELL, furnished the seeds from which sprang modern opera—purpose, as is usually the case, making history. The different idiosyncrasies of BACH and HANDEL will ever live in their distinct methods and ideas of purpose in music; and the comparison of their labours or achieved purposes have frequently furnished the writer on music with abundant subject matter for consideration. Even the distinct types of the men's lives told upon their work. Thus, we find in BACH the retired, conscientious artist, who could exercise an infinite amount of painstaking without any desire for immediate recognition or reward. On the other hand, note the resolute struggles and restless determination of HANDEL to succeed from the worldly point of sight. So the one composer gives to the world thoughts overwhelmingly rich in contrapuntal power and only to be fully accepted after generations of art progress; whilst the other turns counterpoint to a more immediately practical result, combining it with such clear rhythmical outlines and striking, nervous harmony, as at once to secure popular respect, recognition, and due reward. To examine the various methods of the great masters would perhaps be a needless task, though I will venture to remind the student of the impression of HAYDN's clear-sighted orderly mind, and the consequent gain to the departments of proportion in form and appriateness in orchestration arising from his exercise of purpose in music. Similarly one could point to the delicate, sensitive thought evolutions and exquisite finish which MOZART impressed upon all his work; making it the most perfect study in the way of placing the right idea in the right place, and in the direction of perfectly proportioned construction; here, again, is the exaltation of purpose in music. Then, again, no composer ever stamped the genius of purpose more definitely upon his work than did BEETHOVEN. This power enabled him to create atmosphere in music, as in the persistent figures of the Pastoral Symphony, in which by gentle monotony and by harmonies deeply and strongly laid out upon Nature's own purest harmonics, he wafts the tired brain into thoughts of the silence which is refreshment itself because it is never silent, into dreams of sunny green meadows, waving corn, clear skies accompanied by the delicious humming of birds and insects. Again, see the master with another purpose, worked out with a giant's will. Listen to that tone manifestation of magnificent self-will the Fifth Symphony. Hear the stern, strong accents of the first movement with the rugged unisons, and the unflinching clashing in seconds and fourths of the brass and drums against the stalwart unison of the other orchestral masses, chords which no other man hardly ever dared to use without preparation and resolution. Note the exultant determination of the horns and trumpets in the slow movement. Observe the varied, yet determined accents of the Scherzo and the almost appalling energy and almost savage yet well controlled self-will of the Finale! Here we have a truly magnificent exemplification of purpose in music. Here we find purpose exalted into a distinct principle which pervades, I had nearly said overrides, the music itself.

E. H. TURPIN.

TONE versus COLOUR.

THE subject of identity of effect between sound and colour has again cropped up, in the *Standard* this time. The now ancient story of the blind man comparing the sound of the trumpet to scarlet, has been brought forward, and a corresponding incident, that of a deaf girl making a similar comparison, has also appeared. These comparisons point to the real source of similarity. For as pointed out elsewhere in these columns, in a review of Mr. F. HUGHES's new work on the subject, colour on a picture is neither form or design, but an accompanying quality by which form and design are made apparent. So in music, colour refers to the quality of the tones engaged in the act of enunciating melodic and harmonic figures and designs. However, the desire to compare scale and chord structures with colour effects prevails with an earnestness of purpose which will either lead to the establishment of some fixed principles of comparison, or will demonstrate the fixed and ingenious obstinacy of a certain class of speculative theorists. The Rev. A. P. BETHELL, a Priest of the Roman Catholic Church, has a long letter in the issue of the paper previously named, of Saturday last, in which are the following passages :—

"It is now more than sixteen years since I invented "for my own use a system of Scale-colour, or, as I prefer "to call it, Colour Music, so perhaps a few words from "me may prove of interest to some of your corre- "spondents.

"I doubt very much whether the science of optics can "as yet assist us much in establishing an exact correla- "tion between the notes of music and the hues of colour, "and therefore I have not approached the subject from "the scientific side. The view with which I started was "more psychological. I asked myself the question why "are musical sounds capable of suggesting to the mind "ideas of a much higher order, or, in other words, how "is it that they speak a language in which they merely "act the part of signs, like the letters I am writing on "this paper? The only answer I could find to this "question came in the shape of a conviction that the "mind attaches a transcendental value to its comparison "of the intervals between musical notes, dependent "partly on their relative magnitudes, and partly also on "the agreeable physical effects produced on the ear by "concords.

"In 1879 I happened to find a musical passage in "Macfarren's 'Lectures on Harmony' (page 14), taken "from Beethoven's quartet in A minor, which is given as "a specimen of the ancient Lydian mode, and is un- "doubtedly to be considered, as Dryden has it—

'Softly sweet in Lydian measure.'

"I therefore translated the passage into colour, according "to the dictates of my diagram, and was surprised to find "the result, in the opinion of everyone who has seen it, "undeniably 'soft and sweet.' I hope soon to publish in "some magazine such a sketch of my system as will enable artists to form some opinion upon it.

"I am little concerned with absolute pitch, and there- "fore not disposed to enter into a controversy with Mr. "Foxell as to the correctness of my correlative in colour "for the note G flat. Of course it must vary with the "pitch of the standard A, and also with the key in "which it is taken. But if, as I assume, Schönfield's "'Rosa Krapp' may be taken as the proper representa- "tive of Mozart's A, then, reckoning downwards by fifths "to G flat as the tonic of its key, 'Chalons Brown' is the "colour which I should propose as the equivalent of "Mozart's tonic G flat.

"The chief advantage to be derived by artists from a "system of colour-music depends, however, in my "opinion, upon their recognising the truth that the "value of any colour in a picture is determined by its "surroundings, and I think it will be found that the "musical system is the only one which will give any "trustworthy guide to the results which may be expected "from different combinations. To take a simple illus- "tration—if yellow be used as the third of a major "chord (i.e., in my system, with azure as its root, and "scarlet as the fifth), it will bear out brilliantly and "forcibly, but if taken as the third of a minor chord "(with blue as its root and red as the fifth) it must "needs be somewhat sad and subdued. I am quite "ready to let any artist paint up a scarlet coat to the "extreme of brilliancy, and then undertake to subdue it "simply by painting on other portions of the figure the "colours necessary to make it count as the third of a "minor chord, or by reckoning it as a fifth of a major "chord, and adding to it the root and the third. For "the accent is always attracted by the third, whether "for joy or for sadness, and the fifth is nothing but a "make-weight, which can never be accented by any bril- "liancy of the pigment used for it. I am making experi- "ments at present to determine the corresponding values "of colours when used as sevenths and ninths; and as I "am never satisfied till I have gone all round the circle, "taking at least twelve colours, and finding the same "result with each, it is obvious that I must have some "reason to remember the saying, 'Ars longa, vita brevis.' "Perhaps it may be as well to give roughly my equiva- "lent for musical notes, which run thus: Red, A; "Crimson, B flat; Purple, B; Mauve, C; Azure, C sharp; "Blue, D; Deep Green, E flat; Green, E; Yellow, F; "Buff, F sharp; Orange, G; and Scarlet, A flat. The "seven naturals are what are usually called the seven "colours of the spectrum, viz.: Red, Purple, Mauve (or "Indigo), Blue, Green, Yellow, and Orange. There is a "difference of tone between my Mauve and the Indigo "of the spectrum, but I think experience justifies me in "making it. Violet Carmine may be taken as the repre- "sentative of Mauve, although the aniline colour is often "required in painting costumes, &c. The others may "be taken roughly thus: Red, Rosa Krapp; Crimson, "Magenta; Purple, Dahlia Carmine; Azure, New Blue, "Blue, Ceruleum; Deep Green, Viridian; Green, Schön- "field's 'Hill-grün Zinnöber; Yellow, Italian Pink; "Buff, Chalons Brown; Orange, Reeve's Pure Orange; "Scarlet, Orange Scarlet Madder. In each case I only "indicate the hues, which may be darkened or lightened "as required, but are subject to alteration in different "keys."

These definitions differ entirely from those given by Mr. F. Hughes. Certain of the statements herein made, such as the writer's estimate of the position of the fifth in the chord, show to the musician that these speculations are, at least, open to question. Every intelligent mind inherits that glow of delight which attends the intimation or actual discovery of some one or more of the wonderful affinities of the universe, a glow of feeling which is in its recognition of the sys- tematic power shown in the CREATOR's works, a truly religious impulse as well as a glimpse of that power of apprehension which uplifts man into the regions of infinite life. So the eagerness with which such specu- lative knowledge is pursued, does not always corres- pond with the real amount of light the investigator is able to throw upon his subject. Still the present discussion is one of interest. And it has at least as evidence of the importance of its nature, such facts as the inherent tendency of music to shape itself into fixed scales, to select modes presumably appropriate to the expression of given ideas by temperament, or pitch, or both, and above all the clustering together of closely related harmonic strata in all intelligible and accepted tone progressions.

E. H. TURPIN.

HYMNOLOGY.

Mr. Gladstone has lately translated in the Nineteenth Century, Cowper's Hymn, "Hark! My soul, it is the Lord" into Italian. The Daily Telegraph improves upon the incident, and in an article of interest observes:—

"The power of the hymn was recognized by so celebrated a divine as St. Augustine, who said :—'One feels that song softens the heart, and makes pious emotions rise in it. Words when sung, speech when kindled by music, lay hold of the mind more powerfully than oratory; and therefore it was that the ancient Eastern custom to sing hymns and anthems in churches in order to tune the hearts to devotion had been introduced into the Western Church also at the time of Ambrose.' From that day to this the hymn revival has been steadily progressing. No Catholic service in Germany is complete without its hymn in the vernacular; and in English Catholic churches, throughout the land, translations of the best-known Latin hymns, as well as the modern religious poetry of singers like Faber and others, occupy their appointed place in the ordinary services of the Sunday and week-day. Indeed, the most popular of all Roman Catholic services in this country are those which adopt the German cus- tom of singing hymns in all but the most solemn and silent por- tions of the mass. In a paper read before the Social Science Congress of 1881 at Dublin, Sir Robert Stewart made pointed allusion to this revival. 'Among the Catholics,' he said "the effort to purify and improve the music of the sanctuary made within the short space of 15 years is more remarkable than any. By one bold move of a musical priest, the Rev. Franz Witt, of Lower Bavaria—a move fortified by the sanction of the highest ecclesiastical authorities—they have established Cecilian So- cieties, similar to those founded in the year 1868 on the continent and in the United States of America, whose object it is to remove from their services the florid church music known and practised from the eighteenth century down to quite a recent period, and to replace these scarcely veiled opera strains which once deformed their worship by the purest forms of Gregorian or music of a similar type, which, even if polyphonic, shall be of the highest class of its school, and must be marked by sobriety as well as by grandeur.'

"It is not in Anglican or Evangelican services alone that we find the power and purpose of the hymn revival. We may step into a High church and find the congregation uplifting their hearts and voices to the stirring strains of 'Jerusalem the Golden,' or "Abide with Me, fast falls the Eventide,' or 'Sun of my Soul, Thou Saviour dear.' We may repair to a Low church and discover just as much energy and emotion bestowed on the 'Old Hundredth' or the good old 'Evening Hymn,' or even the unmetrical strains of Tate and Brady; but it is rather to the unorthodox churches that we must look to find the power of the hymn and the excitement of unison singing as an incentive to popular religion.

"The mere fact of singing collectively exerts a great power of attraction over persons of all kinds who have tunable voices and are susceptible of the graver emotions. Their human needs should be satisfied in the best and simplest way."

Says the Lute: Italian opera may be going down in England, but it seems to be going up elsewhere. As our readers know, a house will soon be ready for it in Paris, and we learn that Signor Bimbino was to open a month's campaign in Berlin during September. It will be curious to note now "Semiramide" and "Othello" are received in the German capital at this time of day.

Reviews.

Harmonies of Tones and Colours developed by Evolution. F. J. Hughes. (Marcus Ward & Co., Chandos Street.)—This large and handsomely got up book deals with a subject science can hardly be said, as yet, to have fairly examined. Under the warmth of his delight in the discovery of—or rather under the impression of sundry suggested—analogies, the author writes with a glow of enthusiasm which is catching. And throughout the work there is an edifying belief in the Creator's unity of purpose in the government of all things by laws which are universal, and a keen pleasure in the contemplation of natural and artistic wonders, which make the book pleasant reading. But the work is, for the most part, too purely of a speculative type, though the author has evidently read pretty extensively a goodly number of metaphysical and scientific works in the course of some fifty years' experience. The style of his writing may be seen by a few quotations. In his introduction he observes—

The following scheme endeavours to show that the development of the musical gamut and the colours of the rainbow are regulated by the same laws. I wish it to be clearly understood that I have gained the evolutions from the mysterious type of Life—a golden thread running throughout the Scriptures.

Again he observes—

It is my firm belief that if a powerful intellect takes up the radical idea contained in the following pages it will be found to be the directing force or general key-note which will gradually disentangle intricacies in all the natural sciences, and link, by the same mode of physical evolution, the past, the present, and the future.

Such writing lacks logical clearness. Then, again, the following words have in them a flavour of musical empiricism, or, at any rate, a groping about things commonly understood in connection with musical theory. Says Mr. Hughes—

I wrote down the development of the seven major keys of the white notes in keyed instruments. I was perplexed by the movement as of "to and fro," but the development of numbers explained this point, and I found that the method of development in colours, tones, and numbers agreed. I remembered the keys with sharps, but had forgotten that B flat belonged to the key of F, and here I thought that the laws failed. But I found, by reference, that all were correct, the eighth being the first of a higher series, the laws having enabled me to distinguish between sharps and flats, whether veering round or advancing and retreating in musical clef.

And—

I had forgotten all the minor keys, except that A is the relative minor of C major; but although I had only faint hopes of success, I determined to try, and I gained the twelve keys correctly, with the thirteenth octave. I found also that E flat was usually printed as a minor key-note, Nature's laws having shown that it must be D sharp.

These are words of a more definite import—

As knowledge increases, may not the beginning of every physical science be traced first as a trinity, springing from a trinity in unity, followed by a second, partaking of the nature of the first, so as to unite with it in complementary pairs, as here described, in tones and colours, trinity in unity being the germ of never-ending developments?

Also the following—

The inequality of the equinoctial points is a well-known fact. It will be seen how apparent this is in the development of harmonies. From the moment that trinities depart from unity the balance is unequal, and the repeated endeavours after closer union cause a perpetual restlessness.

This is a sample of the author's speculative manner of dealing with the theory of musical scale system and its adjacent harmonies—

On a keyed instrument only twelve are major key-notes, but as the double tones C sharp-D flat and F sharp-G flat are roots, there are fourteen different chords. As an example of the major chords in the different keys, we may examine those in the key of C. A major fifth includes five out of the seven of its key; with the third or central note it is the threefold chord, or fourfold when the octave note is added. Including the silent key-notes, a threefold chord embraces eight, or, counting the double tones, not including E sharp, eleven. The first and second chords of the seven of the harmony are perfect major chords in the key of C; the central note of the third chord, being C sharp-D flat, is a discord. The first pair of fifths in the scale, with its central note, is a chord of the key; if we include the octave, the last pair of fifths, with its central note, is the same chord an octave higher than the lowest chord of the seven.

The application of the author's theory of colour in harmony with tone, as regards the scale formation, illustrates at once the difficulties of his position. He employs the three primary colours with their secondary developments. Twice three can only make six; consequently an extra tint must be brought into the scheme to yield seven parallelisms of colour and tone. The following extract from a given diagram will explain itself:—

Red.	Orange.	Yellow.	Green.
C,	D,	E,	F,
Blue.	Violet.	Ultra-Violet.	
G,	A,	B.	

Now, these primary colours here fall prettily enough to the notes of the common chord. But as the distances between C and E and E and G represent different types of imperfect concords, the colour system given is not in harmony with the divisions of the notation; and, as a result, while two tints of two of the primary colours (red and yellow) are given, three tints of the other primary colour (blue) are employed. A really just division would place the primary colours a major third apart, thus—

Red.	Yellow.	Blue.
C,	E,	G sharp,

with the intermediate sounds represented by the secondary and tertiary shades of the primary colours. The entire scheme, chromatically given, would therefore run thus :—

Red.	Deep-orange.	Orange.	Light-orange.	Yellow.
C,	C sharp,	D,	D sharp,	E,
Light-green.	Green.	Dark-green.	Blue.	
F,	F sharp,	G,	G sharp,	
Purple.	Violet.	Crimson.		
F,	A sharp,	B,		

By this arrangement the primaries fall at equal distances of major thirds apart to C, E, G sharp, and the secondary colours also lie at the same distances apart on D, F sharp, and A sharp. This scheme, though, represents no affinity between colour and harmony. Then, again, can it be maintained that the different tone intensities of the different octaves are to have no corresponding changes of colour intensities in any complete system of analogy? To proceed, all Mr. Hughes' circular diagrams furnishing his analogies are based upon this unevenly-balanced system of employing red and yellow with their secondaries, and blue with both secondary and tertiary developments. Ingenious in elucidation and beautiful in thought as such proposals of colour and tone often are, no satisfactory conclusions have, apparently, yet been drawn therefrom. Perhaps the base of such logic is at fault ; for colour is not form, nor is melodic design tone-quality. If we compare like with like, as in putting colour side by side with tone-quality and pictorial design side by side with musical design, the genius of comparison does indeed find much scope for instructive and interesting analogies. Mr. Hughes enjoyed the (at least corresponding) friendship of Dr. Gauntlett, and quotes copiously from his letters. The Doctor is interested, if not a little fascinated, by Mr. Hughes' doctrines. In one letter Dr. Gauntlett says : "Why you should be able to explain the much-quarrelled-over connections (between tones and harmonies) is beyond my comprehension, and if I could discover the key, the result would be most important for the well-being of music. With this view, your system always interests me. I suspect it lies in that wonderful adaptability of the *order* of numbers." Putting aside a flavour of self-complacency in Dr. Gauntlett's words, or, it may be, a self-consciousness of ability to do great things with new tools, it does seem clear that Mr. Hughes' system had not produced upon the mind of his friend very definite results. No one can condemn Mr. Hughes' earnest, thoughtful speculations; especially as they are indeed earnest enough to incline the student to take a deeper interest in the mysteries of the art. Some of the diagrams want more fully entered-upon explanations ; others express but little of practical value. They all show much thought and not a little ingenuity. Mr. Hughes says (quoting Dr. C. W. Siemens): "In the great workshop of Nature there are no lines of demarcation between the most exalted speculation and common-place practice, and that knowledge must lead up to one great result—that of an intelligent recognition of the Creator through His works." Still it is important that speculation shall be subjected to scientific proof, and common-place practices also be deduced from fixed principles, in order that really gainful knowledge may be secured. It cannot be said that Mr. Hughes' work realizes either positions. He has done good work, at least, in making some such advance upon his subject as may lead to further investigations. The work is richly and very handsomely got up, and in every way a credit to its publishers.

The Church Congress Hand-Book. By C. Mackeson. (Parker and Co.)—This useful and admirably conducted annual, which faithfully and carefully accompanies the migrations of the great ecclesiastical court of church opinion from year to year, gives a guide to the recent congress, an interesting description of the churches, etc., of Reading, biographical sketches of readers and speakers, together with valuable information of the past congress doings. In process of time these ably conducted records will, from their intelligent faithfulness and unbiassed clearness, become matters of great value, and readers should collect them from time to time. The type, portraits, and views are all excellent in their way.

An Ecclesiastical History of Reading. Edited by the Rev. P. H. Ditchfield, M.A. (E. J. and F. Blackwell, Market Place, Reading).—A well got up and interesting hand-book, including accounts of local churches, etc., mostly by clerical writers. From this work readers will learn, as they would from Mackeson's "Church Congress Guide," what a large amount of history the old town has been the scene of, and what a noble structure the Abbey was once upon a time. To musicians the most interesting chapter of the book, perhaps, is a well written account of local "Church Music," from the pen of Mr. F. J. Read, F.C.O., Mus.Bac. This shows that the good cause is flourishing fairly well in Reading, and that the town has some excellent organs. Mr. Read reminds us that a monk of Reading composed the earliest of known canons, "Sumer is icumen in." Some of the entries of the old churches are curious, as "1505.—Payed to the clerk for syngyng of the Passion on Palm Sunday, in all id." 1541.—Payd for a quart of malmesey for the clerk on Palm Sonday, iiijd." Intoning during the season of fasting was evidently regarded as laborious and exhausting work. Then in 1549, when the English liturgy comes into use, are the following:—"Paid Sir Will'm for c'tayne songs that he bought for the church, viz." "Paid to Sir Richard a Deane, for ridyng to Windesor for the s'vice in Englishe, iiijs."; and "Paid for paper and inke for pricking the songs in Englishe, viijd." These items show how early in the reformed church music took an honoured place. There are items concerning the purchase of pairs of organs, and for "playing upon the orgayns," and for "syngyng in the quere," which points also to the cultivation and preservation of church music at that period.

The Maidenhead Philharmonic Society announce their first concert for Nov. 25th. The programme will include a selection from Sir Arthur Sullivan's oratorio, "The Light of the World." Mr. J. G. Wrigley, Mus.Bac.Oxon., will conduct, and Miss Fenna, Miss Eliza Thomas, Mr. Alfred Kenningham, and Mr. Musgrove Tufnail, will be the principal soloists.

The committee of the Annual Festival of the Worcester County Musical Association, U.S., has made strenuous efforts to make its festival in 1883 a notable occasion, not only for the eminent artists engaged, but also for the excellent choice of works to be performed. It is scarcely possible to praise these efforts too highly. The festival was held in the afternoons and evenings at the Mechanic's Hall, Worcester, Mass., from Monday, Sept. 24th, to Friday, Sept. 28th. The works performed comprised the following numbers : Sept. 25th—Gounod's "St. Cecilia Mass" and miscellaneous selection. Selection from Handel's "L'Allegro et Il Penseroso," and miscellaneous selection; Wednesday—Schubert's Symphony in B minor and selection. Berlioz's "La Damnation de Faust." Thursday—Bruch's "Fair Ellen," and selection. Selections from Wagner's "Lohengrin," and miscellaneous. Friday—Beethoven's Ninth (Choral) Symphony and selections. Saturday—Handel's oratorio, "Samson." The chorus comprised five hundred selected voices. Mr. Frederic Archer presided at the organ. Mr Carl Zerrahn conducted.

M. Vladimir de Pachmann will presently pay a professional visit to this country.

Miss Alice Aloof gives the first of three concerts at the Brixton Hall on Oct. 16th.

Dr. Horace Hill, of Norwich, is about to publish an oratorio, "Nehemiah."

The Temple Church and the St. James's Chapel Royal resumed their choral services on Sunday last.

F. Lux has written a comic opera in two acts, "Die Fürsten von Athen."

Mr. Villiers Stanford will compose a cantata for next Birmingham Festival.

The Skinners' Company contribute £500 to the Royal College of Music in five annual instalments.

A new pianist, Miss Josephine Lawrence, has played at the Covent Garden Concerts with a good measure of success.

The *Yorkshire Post* has an excellent and lengthy analysis of Macfarren's "King David," from the pen of Mr. T. J. Dudeney.

Weber's "Jubilee Cantata" was sung with augmented choir at the Harvest Festival, St. Mark's, Myddleton-square, on Oct. 11th.

Mdme. Ellen Hopekirk will play at the Crystal Palace and in several provincial towns, before her visit to America next month.

The jurors of the Cork Exhibition have awarded a medal for a violin made by Mr. Walter H. Mayson, stating that this is the highest they have given.

The report is that the recent Eisteddfod meeting in Cardiff, notwithstanding the enormous outlay and expenses, resulted in a clear profit of some £550.

People's Concerts of excellent character are being given in Exeter. Mr. D. J. Wood, Mus.Bac., Mr. Harold Ryder, and other local professors, take part in these performances, as well as artists from London and elsewhere.

Mr. Walter Bache, Liszt's chief supporter here, gives his annual Pianoforte Recital on the birthday of his musical idol, Oct. 22nd, when Liszt enters upon his 73rd year. Mr. Bache confines his programme to the works of his favourite master.

It is understood that Mrs. Dutton Cook, the widow of the late Mr. Dutton Cook, the eminent dramatic critic, contemplates re-entering the profession. Before her marriage, as Miss Linda Scates, this lady was heard at the Philharmonic, Crystal Palace, Saturday, and other concerts, and was recognized as a pianist of very exceptional ability.

On Wednesday evening, Oct. 3rd, the first of a series of high-class "Entertainments for the People," was given at the Bethnal Green-road Congregational Church, Hackney. This was a grand ballad concert, the vocalists being Mdme. Clara West, Miss C. Wollaston, Miss Lottie West, Mr. W. Doble, and Mr. A. Tucker; pianist, Mr. W. West; organist, Mr. John E. West, A.C.O. There was a numerous and appreciative audience.

Mr William Lemare announces that, being ordered by his physician to take absolute rest, it is with feelings of regret that he finds it necessary to sever his connection of many years' standing in Brixton, and seek retirement in the country. Mr. Humphrey Stark, Mus.Bac.Oxon., will, for the present, represent Mr. Lemare as Principal of the Surrey County School of Music. Readers will be glad to know that Mr. Lemare's health is improving.

The case of Mr. Edward Solomon was brought before the Court of Bankruptcy, on Oct. 5th. The debtor was described as a musical composer, of Oxford-mansions and Bloomsbury-place, also of 272, Strand, and of Warwick-street, Pimlico. The liabilities were returned at £1,406, and assets £75, and resolutions were passed for the liquidation of the estate by arrangement, with Mr. James Waddell as trustee. Mr. James Davis explained that Mr. Waddell had not accepted the office. His Honour ordered a new first meeting to be held.

Mr. C. L. Williams, the esteemed organist of Gloucester Cathedral, has made a valuable and thoughtful suggestion to the effect that symphonies and instrumental works be written suitable for Service and Church Festival use. A modern form of the "Sonata di Chiesa," would indeed, be welcome, and would open up to the composer a field for the employment of his talents.

On September 23rd forty-eight years had elapsed since the death of Bellini. The anniversary was celebrated in Naples by a concert and other performances of his music, the occasion being made one of some little additional interest by an Elegy, composed by Florimo, a skilful transcription of one of Bellini's melodies, for violoncello solo, and by excellent solo singing, and a fine rendering of the beautiful quartet in "Il Puritani."

On St. Luke's Day, Thursday next, the 18th inst., the Harvest Festival will be celebrated at St. Margaret Pattens Church, Rood Lane, Fenchurch-street. Weber's Mass in E flat will be sung at 12 noon. After the Evensong at 7.30, Mendelssohn's "Hymn of Praise" will be given. Mr. Alfred Kenningham will sing the tenor solos, and Mr. Walter E. Stark will preside at the organ. The arrangements, as usual, will be under the direction of Mr. Stedman.

The annual thanksgiving for the ingathering of the harvest was held in the Wimborne Minster on Sunday last. The order of service was as follows :—Morning, Boyce in C; anthem, "O Lord, how manifold," by Barnby. Evening service, Arnold in A; anthem, "Ascribe unto the Lord," by Travers. After evening service Mr. Smith, the organist, played Rossini's "Cujus animam" with much effect.

The Royal Victoria Coffee Hall re-opens for the winter season in October with a most attractive programme. On Thursday evenings, for a few weeks, a musical entertainment entitled the "Rose Queen" will be given. It includes soloists, choruses and ballets, and represents the old English customs of dancing round a maypole, crowning a village maiden, and Morris dances. On Tuesday evenings, through the kindness of the Trustees of the Gilchrist Fund, the Committee of the Hall have been able to arrange for the delivery of Penny Science Lectures by eminent lecturers. The Park Band Society will give a performance before and after each lecture.

The Harvest Festival at St. Michael's, Bowes Park, Southgate, was held on the 3rd inst, the services including a full choral Evensong at 7.30 p.m. The music sung at the latter service included Magnificat and Nunc Dimittis, by W. G. Wood in F; Anthem, "I will give thanks," (Barnby); and Te Deum, Smart in F, the choir numbering as usual on these occasions, over forty voices. Mr. Henry J. Baker presided at the organ. It may be mentioned as an interesting fact worthy of notice, that St. Michael's is now, one of the *few* churches in the northern suburbs at which there is a choral celebration every Sunday at mid-day.

Service Lists.

TWENTY-FIRST SUNDAY AFTER TRINITY.

OCTOBER 14th.

London.

St. Paul's Cathedral.—Morn.: Service, Te Deum and Benedictus, Stainer in B flat; Introit, O Lamb of God (Schubert); Holy Communion, Schubert in G Even.: Service, Magnificat and Nunc Dimittis, Faning in C; Anthem, Awake, awake put on thy strength (Stainer).

Temple Church.—Morn.: Service, Te Deum Laudamus, and Jubilate Deo, Turle in D; Apostles' Creed, Harmonised Monotone; Anthem, Thy word is a lantern (Purcell). Even.: Service, Magnificat and Nunc Dimittis, Turle in D; Apostles' Creed, Harmonized Monotone; Anthem, O where shall wisdom (Boyce).

All Saints, Margaret Street.—Morn.: Service, Te Deum, Gauntlett in F; Benedictus, Monk in F; Holy Communion, Hoyte in D; Offertory Anthem, Quod in orbe (Hummel). Even.: Service, Tours in F: Anthem, Rejoice in the Lord (Martin).

All Souls, London Road, South Hampstead, N.W.—Morn.: Service, Te Deum, Tours in F; Benedictus, Chant; Anthem, I will magnify (Goss); Kyrie, Thorne in E flat; Creed (Marbecke). Even.: Service, Magnificat and Nunc Dimittis, Tours in F; O Lord, how manifold (Barnby).

Christ Church, Clapham.—Morn.: Service, Te Deum, Plain-song; Kyrie, and Credo, Weber in E flat; Offertory Anthem, Achieved is the glorious work (Haydn); Sanctus, Benedictus, Agnus Dei, and Gloria in excelsis (Weber). Even.: Service, Magnificat and Nunc Dimittis, Barnby in E flat; Anthem, a selection from the "Creation"; during the Offertory, Fear not, O land (Goss).

Holy Trinity, Gray's Inn Road.— Morn.: Service, Te Deum, Dykes in F; Jubilate Chanted. Even.: Service, Magnificat, Chanted; Nunc Dimittis, Tours in F; Anthem, Behold, how good and joyful (Whitfeld).

Holy Trinity, Tulse Hill.— Morn.: Service, Harvest Festival. Special Even.: Service, with full orchestral accompaniment; Magnificat Stark in D ;. Anthem, The 1st and 2nd part of Haydn's "Creation."

St. Barnabas, Marylebone.—Morn.: Service, Te Deum and Benedictus, Dykes in F; Anthem, With verdure clad (Haydn), O Lord, how manifold (Barnby); Kyrie and Nicene Creed, Dykes in F. Even.: Service, Magnificat and Nunc Dimittis, Hoyte in B flat; Anthem, Thou visitest the earth (Greene); Te Deum, Smart in F.

St. Botolph, Aldgate.—Morn.: Service, Te Deum, 'Smart in F; Anthem, Fear not, O land (Goss). Even.: Service, Magnificat and Nunc Dimittis, Bridge in C; Anthem, O Lord, how manifold (Barnby), and God Thou art great (Spohr).

St. James's Private Episcopal Chapel, Southwark, —Morn.: Service, Introit, The sower went forth sowing; Communion Service, Cherubini in C, No. 4. Even.: Service, Prout in F; Anthem, All men, all things (Mendelssohn).

St. Margaret Pattens, Rood Lane, Fenchurch Street.—Morn.: Service, Te Deum, Sullivan in D; Jubilate, Sullivan in D; Communion Service, Offertory Anthem, Jesu, Lord of life (Naumann); Kyrie, Credo, Sanctus, Benedictus, Agnus Dei, and Gloria, Hummel in B flat. Even. Service, Magnificat and Nunc Dimittis, Hopkins in F; Anthem, O love the Lord (Sullivan).

St. Mary Boltons, West Brompton, S.W.—Morn.: Service, Te Deum and Benedictus, Stainer's 4th series of Tones; Holy Communion, Kyrie, Credo, Sanctus, Benedictus, Agnus Dei, and Gloria in excelsis, Eyre in E flat; Offertory (Stainer). Even.: Service, Magnificat and Nunc Dimittis, Stainer's 4th series of Tones; Anthem, Glorious is Thy name (Mozart).

St. Magnus, London Bridge.—Morn.: Service, Opening Anthem, The sacrifices of God (Calkin); Te Deum and Jubilate, Turle in D; Kyrie (Walmsley). Even.: Service, Magnificat and Nunc Dimittis, Turle in D; Anthem, As pants the hart (Spohr).

St. Michael's, Cornhill. — Morn.: Service, Te Deum and Jubilate, Smart in F; Anthem, O Lord, my God (Wesley). Kyrie and Creed, Thorne in E flat. Even.: Service, Magnificat and Nunc Dimittis, Ouseley in B flat; Anthem, Praise the Lord (Croft).

St. Paul's, Avenue Road, South Hampstead.—Morn.: Service, Te Deum, Sullivan in D; Benedictus, Bennett in A; Kyrie, Nares in F. Even.: Service, Magnificat and Nunc Dimittis, Stainer in A; Anthem, He is watching over Israel "Elijah" (Mendelssohn).

St. Paul's, Bow Common, E.—Morn.: Service, Te Deum and Benedictus, Stainer in B flat. Even.: Service, Magnificat and Nunc Dimittis, Stainer in B flat; Anthem, Whosoever drinketh, and Therefore with joy shall ye draw water (Bennett).

St. Peter's (Eaton Square).—Morn.: Service, Harvest Thanksgiving; Holy Communion Tours in F; Te Deum, Boyce in A; Anthem, O Lord, how manifold (Barnby). Even.: Service, Lloyd in F; Anthem, Fear not, O land (Goss).

St. Peter's, Vere Street, W.—Even.: Service, Magnificat and Nunc Dimittis, Garrett in F; Anthem, . I will give thanks unto thee (Goss).

St. Augustine and St. Faith, Watling Street.— Morn.: Service, Garrett in F; Introit, The Lord is my light (South); Communion Service, Garrett in F. Even.: Service, Hopkins in F; Anthem, Rejoice in the Lord (Martin).

St. Saviour's, Hoxton. — Morn.: Service, Te Deum, Gadsby in E flat; Holy Communion; Kyrie, Credo, Sursum Corda, Sanctus, and Gloria in excelsis, Armes in A. Even.: Service, Magnificat and Nunc Dimittis, Smart in G; Anthem, The Lord is exalted (West).

St. Sepulchre's, Holborn.—Morn.: Service, Dykes in F. Even.: Service, Porter in G; Anthem, O praise the Lord (Wilton).

Country.

St. Asaph Cathedral. — Morn.: Service, Benedicte, Chant; Anthem, Thou wilt keep him (Calkin). Even.: Service, Whitfeld in E; Anthem, I am Alpha and Omega (Stainer).

Ashburne Church, Derbyshire. — Morn.: Service, Garrett in D throughout. .Even.: Service, Jackson in G; Anthem, Blessed be the God and Father (Wesley).

BEDDINGTON CHURCH, SURREY. — Morn.: Service, Te Deum and Benedictus; Garrett in D; Introit, Bread of heaven; Communion Service. Calkin in D. Even.: Service, Garrett in D; Anthem, God, Thou art great (Spohr); After Sermon, O lovely peace, Rejoice O Lord, and Hallelujah, Amen, "Judas Maccabaeus" (Handel); Te Deum.

BIRMINGHAM (S. ALBAN THE MARTYR).—Morn.: Service, Te Deum, Boyce in C; Benedictus, Steggall in D; Holy Communion, Dykes in F. Evensong.: Magnificat and Nunc Dimittis, Barnby in E.

BIRMINGHAM (ST. CYPRIAN'S, HAY MILLS).—Morn.: Service, Cobb in G; Anthem, The Wilderness (Goss). Even.: Service, Smart in F; Anthem, O give thanks (Greene).

BRISTOL CATHEDRAL.—Morn.: Service, Garrett in D; Anthem, The King shall rejoice (Handel) Aft.: Service, Garrett in D; Anthem, O God, when Thou appearest (Mozart).

CANTERBURY CATHEDRAL. —Morn.: Service, Smart in G; Anthem, Try me, O God (Hake); Communion, Smart in G; Even.: Service, Smart in G; Anthem, Ascribe unto the Lord (Travers).

CARLISLE CATHEDRAL.—Morn.: Service, Best in D; Introit, Remember Lord (Verrinder); Kyrie, and Nicene Creed, Turle in D. Even.: Service, Macfarren in E flat; Anthem, Hear my crying (Hummel).

CHESTER (ST. MARY'S CHURCH).—Morn.: Service, Tearne in A; Anthem, Thou visitest the earth (Greene); Communion Service, Tearne in A. Even.: Service, Goss in A; Anthem, O lovely peace (Handel), and Fear not, O land (Goss).

DUBLIN, ST. PATRICK'S (NATIONAL) CATHEDRAL.—Morn.: Service, Te Deum and Jubilate, Stewart in E flat; Holy Communion, Kyrie and Creed, and Sanctus, Cambridge in C; Anthem, Hallelujah (Beethoven). Even.: Service, Cantate and Deus Miserateur, Stewart in E flat; Anthem, Grant us Thy peace (Mendelssohn), and O God of my righteousness (Greene).

DONCASTER (PARISH CHURCH).—Morn.: Service, Te Deum and Jubilate, Calkin in B flat; Introit, O Lord, my God (Malan); Kyrie and Creed (Hopkins); Anthem, I was glad (Purcell). Even.: Service, Magnificat and Nunc Dimittis, Calkin in B flat; Anthem, I have surely built Thee an house (Boyce), and Hallelujah (Handel).

EDINBURGH (ST. JOHN'S).—Aft.: Service, Anthem, Ascribe unto the Lord (Wesley). Even.: Service, Anthem, Thine O Lord is the greatness (Kent).

ELY CATHEDRAL.—Morn.: Service, Benedictus, Plain-song; Jubilate, Clarke-Whitfeld in E flat; Kyrie and Credo, Clarke-Whitfeld in E flat; Gloria, Ouseley in C; Anthem, In Thee O Lord (Tours). Even.: Service, Clarke Whitfeld in E flat; Anthem, I waited for the Lord (Mendelssohn).

GLOUCESTER CATHEDRAL. — Morn.: Service. Te Deum, Lloyd in E flat; Benedictus, Lloyd in E flat; Introit, He that shall endure (Mendelssohn); Communion Service, Wesley in E. Aft.: Service, Magnificat and Nunc Dimittis, Lloyd in E flat; Anthem, The Wilderness (Wesley).

HARROGATE (ST. PETER'S CHURCH). — Morn.: Service, Te Deum and Benedictus, Chants; Anthem, O Holy Ghost (Macfarren). Even.: Service, Magnificat, and Nunc Dimittis, Tours in F; Anthem, God is gone up (Croft).

LEEDS PARISH CHURCH.—Morn.: Service, Stanford in B flat; Anthem, Saviour of sinners (Mendelssohn); Kyrie and Creed, Turle in D. Even.: Service, Barnby in E flat; Anthem, The wilderness (Wesley).

LICHFIELD CATHEDRAL. — Morn.: Service, Hopkins in C; Anthem, The Lord be a lamp (Benedict). Even.: Service, Oakeley in E flat; Anthem, Lead kindly light (Stainer).

LIVERPOOL CATHEDRAL.—Aft.: Service, Magnificat and Nunc Dimittis, Calkin in B flat; Anthem, The Lord is very great and terrible (Beckwith).

MANCHESTER CATHEDRAL.—Morn.: Service, Te Deum, Jubilate, Kyrie, Creed, Sanctus and Gloria, Ouseley in G and D; Anthem, How goodly are thy tents (Ouseley). Aft.: Service, Ouseley in G; Anthem, Out of the deep (Hatton).

MANCHESTER (ST. BENEDICT'S).—Morn.: Service, Te Deum, Sullivan in D; Kyrie, Credo, Sanctus, Benedictus, and Gloria in excelsis, Thorne in G; Agnus, Dei, Miné in F. Even.: Service, Magnificat and Nunc Dimittis, Tours in F.

MANCHESTER (ST. JOHN BAPTIST, HULME).—Morn.: Service, Te Deum and Benedictus (Gregorian); Kyrie, Credo, Sanctus, Benedictus and Agnus Dei (Gounod); Gloria in excelsis, Tours in F. Even.: Service, Magnificat and Nunc Dimittis (Redhead).

PETERBOROUGH CATHEDRAL. — Morn.: Service, Ross in G; Anthem, If ye love me (Monk); Communion Service, Armes in A. Even.: Service, Parry in D; Anthem, Send out Thy light (Gounod).

ROCHESTER CATHEDRAL.—Morn.: Service, Garrett in D; Anthem, Remember, O Lord (Himmell). Even.: Service, Garrett in D; Anthem, In the beginning, And the Spirit of God, The heavens are telling (Haydn).

SALISBURY CATHEDRAL.—Morn.: Service, Te Deum and Benedictus, Hopkins in F.; Kyrie and Creed, Oakeley in E flat; Offertory (Barnby). Aft.: Service, Hopkins in F; Anthem, Praise the Lord (Goss).

SHERBORNE ABBEY. — Morn.: Service, Te Deum, Boyce in C. Even.: Service, Chants; Anthem, O Saviour of the world (Goss).

SOUTHAMPTON (ST. MARY'S CHURCH).—Morn.: Service, Te Deum and Benedictus, Garrett in E; Holy Communion, Introit, O how amiable (Macfarren); Service, Agutter in B flat; Offertory While we, and Godliness is great riches (Barnby); Paternoster (Field). Even.: Service, Magnificat and Nunc Dimittis Garrett in D; Apostle's Creed, Harmonized Monotone (Cooper); Anthem, Wherewithal shall a young man (Elvey).

WINCHESTER CATHEDRAL.—Morn.: Service, Skelton in D; Creed, Oakeley in E flat. Even.: Service, Russell in A; Anthem, Glory, honour (Mozart).

WELLS CATHEDRAL.—Morn.: Service, Kent in D; Introit, Remember me, O Lord (Macfarren); Kyrie, Pilbrow in B flat; Even.: Service, Kent in D; Anthem, Blessing, glory (Bach).

WOLVERHAMPTON (ST. PETER'S COLLEGIATE CHURCH).—Morn.: Service, Te Deum. Smart in F; Benedictus, Barnby in D (Chant); Anthem, I have set God always before me (Goldwin); Litany, Barnby in A. Even.: Service, Responses (Tallis's); Magnificat, Smart in G (Chant); Nunc Dimittis, Stevens in A flat; Anthem, Now we are ambassadors, and How lovely are the messengers (Mendelssohn).

* * *Post-cards must be sent to the Editor, 6, Argyle Square, W.C., by Wednesday. Lists are frequently omitted in consequence of not being received in time.*

NEWSPAPERS sent should have *distinct marks* opposite to the matter to which attention is required.

NOTICE TO CORRESPONDENTS.—Proceedings of meeting of Society of Professional Musicians, and other important matter, crowded out until next week.

APPOINTMENTS.

Mr. S. BATH, late of St. Saviour's, Denmark Park, has been appointed Organist of Maidstone Parish Church.

Mr. ROBERT J. PITT, Assistant Conductor of the Metropolitan Choral Union, has been appointed Director of the Choir of St. Giles', Cripplegate, E.C.

Printed for the Proprietor by BOWDEN, HUDSON & Co., 2127, Red Lion Street, Holborn, London, W.C.; and Published by WILLIAM REEVES at the Office, 185, Fleet Street, E.C. West End Agents:—WEEKES & CO., 14, Hanover Street, Regent Street, W. Subscriptions and Advertisements are received either by the Publisher or West End Agents.—Communications for the EDITOR are to be forwarded to his private address, 6, Argyle Square, W.C.
SATURDAY, OCTOBER 13, 1883.—Entered at the General Post Office as a Newspaper.

The MUSICAL STANDARD

A NEWSPAPER FOR MUSICIANS PROFESSIONAL AND AMATEUR

No. 1,003. Vol. XXV. FOURTH SERIES.   SATURDAY, OCTOBER 20, 1883.   WEEKLY: PRICE 3D.

SOME MUSICAL ETHICS AND ANALOGIES.

[*A Paper read before the College of Organists, June 5th, 1883.*]

BY HENRY C. BANISTER.

(*Continued from page 159.*)

Now, if this is in the main true, and applicable, with some technical deviations, to Musical Art, it will not be difficult—nay, I fancy it will be almost inevitable —at once to associate certain modern names with the Romantic, the iridescent, school : the school of excitement, dazzle, enthusiasm, glow : in all of which there may be, let us remember, life : reactionary life : reaction against pedantry, stiffness, formalism, conventionalism, stagnation, and artificialism ; even as was the case with the rise of the modern Romantic School of Poetry ; and so far, so good. But it is of the Classical that I am speaking, specially : and about this, let it be repeated,—

"The name is graven on the workmanship."

But then that workmanship is not the idiom or manner of an age, a country : but is the outcome of genius, and of truth and beauty, which are of and for all time.

Bach, in the case supposed, does present the idea in its unadorned purity, strength, suggestiveness. It need not shrink thus to stand : it is true : suggestive and susceptible of true harmonies. It needs no iridescence : only white light. But then follows,—not clothing to cover it, not apology to excuse it : but trial to prove it : as though it were the stern goodness of a righteous man. And, like that, it comes forth as gold, " purified seven times" : tested by *counterpoint*, by *tonal alteration* or modification, by *inverse movement*, by *augmentation*, by *diminution*, by *modulation*, by *stretti*. Those are seven ways : but, after all, seven is the perfect number ; and the test is perfect.

Is there not some analogy to all this, for instance, in the longest poem by Mr. Browning? Firstly, he arrests you, accosts you with—

> " Do you see this Ring?
> 'Tis Rome-work, made to match
> (By Castellani's imitative craft)
> Etrurian circlets found, some happy morn,
> After a dropping April ; found alive
> Spark-like 'mid unearthed slope-side fig-tree roots
> That roof old tombs at Chiusi : soft, you see,
> Yet crisp as jewel-cutting. There's one trick,
> (Craftsmen instruct me) one approved device
> And but one, fits such slivers of pure gold
> As this was,—such mere oozings from the mine,
> Virgin as oval tawny pendent tear
> At beehive-edge when ripened combs o'erflow—
> To bear the file's tooth and the hammer's tap :
> Since hammer needs must widen out the round,
> And file emboss it fine with lily-flowers,
> Ere the stuff grow a ring-thing right to wear." *

And then he describes what that "trick" is : and in this, the analogy fails, by the way, for the trick is to " melt up wax with honey, so to speak " :—to " mingle gold with gold's alloy." But then, the ring presented, he goes on—" What of it ? "

Yes : just what the shallow, without intuitive perception, say of an unadorned, plain musical subject:—

> " What of it ?
> 'Tis a figure, a symbol, say ;
> A thing's sign : now for the thing signified."

> "Do you see this square old yellow book, I toss
> I' the air, and catch again, and twirl about
> By the vellum covers,—pure crude fact
> Secreted from man's life when hearts beat hard,
> And brains, high-blooded, ticked two centuries since?"

Then he proceeds to give the narration of the history, the germ of all : but still "crude fact." He has given the subject : the answer : the countersub-

---

* *The Ring and the Book.*

ject : philosophizes about, hints at, suggests the possibilities, the potentialities enclosed in that history, —even as the *Exposition* of a Fugue does with what the uninitiated, the unsusceptible, regard as like " pure crude fact." But, then, after the speculations of " *Half-Rome*" and " *The other Half-Rome*,"—just the *Episode* that succeeds the *Exposition*—he proceeds to give the relation of that same history, in various ways, by the various characters, with various prominences, and, perhaps, various suppressions, even distortions : but the same history, the same subject, in various lights : only,—mark you !—with a *bias*, in every case. Now, on the other hand, when the honest musician presents an idea, a musical thought to you, —he says, as it were,—" Do you see this Ring ?—this Book ? Do you hear this subject ? "

" What of it ?" say you. " Well, I will shew you what of it." And then he proceeds to shew you its richness and many sidedness : not to leave you in bewilderment : not to suppress the weak points, exaggerate the strong, distort the doubtful,—but to shew you strength and truth, all round and all through.

I do not know whether this seems to you a fancifully-wrought analogy : a mere *conceit*, in the old sense of that term. But, I confess, again, that it is because I have learned something, practically, theoretically, and by observation, of the mode of presenting, carrying out, and developing a germ-thought, in music, that I can, with the enhanced pleasure that I have referred to, follow a train of thought, and to some extent enter into and apprehend an artistic production, in verse, in prose, in any art in which continuous thought, and varied, many-sided presentation, may find its expression. It makes me feel in sympathetic brotherhood with all true human intellects.

And this varied presentation is Classical : not ornamental. It is not polish : not external chasing, however elegant, on a surface. It is not sensuous : iridescent. It is hardly rhetorical : it is logical : it is a development of innate truth. It is presentation in *white light*, according to the previously cited definition.

But be it observed, " the re-assumption of the glorious name " of Classical is of little avail unless there be the animating spirit and power. Heroic verse presupposes, necessitates, heroes and heroic deeds ; or it becomes mere bombast, or schoolboy-exercise. And this reassumption, moreover, is a different thing from, and is not to be attained by, the donning of the antique garb : by prattling in bygone speech and idiom. Fascinating indeed is it, to any of us who have any measure of the historical imagination, to transport ourselves into old times, old scenes, old manners, old modes of thought and of expression. This is one reason why we experience such peculiar pleasure in visiting ruined abbeys, castles, and the like :—our historical imagination seems to be thereby kindled and helped. It is in proportion to the extent of this element,—is it not ?—that we have the sense of the *picturesque* in a scene. It is this element in our minds, in a more or less exaggerated or distorted form, that has given rise, I suppose, to the—shall I say ?—*fads* or *crazes* for blue china, or for so-called æsthetic furniture or dress. And is there not, in our art, something of an analogous kind, in the *anachronism*, artistically speaking, of writing, now-a-days, pieces of music in the obsolete *dance-measures ?* We may build Queen Anne houses : but then we can inhabit them. But why write *Gavottes*, *Bourrées*, and the like, when they are not danced, now ? No dance-motion such as the old writers witnessed, and were at least *prompted* if not *inspired* by, now impels our writers. Manufactured picturesqueness is surely a strange fad. I know a house, by the side of a London Canal, where there is a manufactured ruin, of an abbey, I believe made of virgin cork, with vacant window frames, and so on, on a slope down to the water's edge. I am not impressed by it, neither am I carried back to old times by a modern Gavotte. Does any one say Oh! I like the quaintness of it? Ah! listen to what an authority on philology says about that word quaint—

"Its primary meaning is artificially [not artistically] elegant, or ingenious, then affectedly artificial, and finally, odd, antique, yet retaining always an element of the pleasing. The idea of quaintness belongs at present most commonly to style of thought and verbal expression in which appears a combination of fancy, originality, delicacy, and force, yet a disharmony with present modes. Quaint architecture, for instance, is in detail antiquated and curious, showing an obsolete beauty and an unfashionable ingenuity."

Now, rest assured, I make no personal allusions, and have not any personal references in my mind. I freely acknowledge the charm of some modern movements of this class that I have heard: and I know what a pleasurable pastime it is, in one's lighter moments, to exercise one's fancy and ingenuity in writing such pieces. I only would, with all kindness, caution young writers against throwing dust into their own eyes, by disguising, perhaps, very ordinary thoughts in this quaint garb. "Quaint," and, as Sterndale Bennett used to say to me, "characteristic," are rather dangerous words.

These attempts to reproduce old manners are not often successful. Even so great a man as Spohr, in his Historical Symphony, is generally considered not to have reproduced anything, from Handel to Auber, but to have re-illustrated his own versatility in conjunction with his mannerism: the movements, after all, only represent Spohr in different suits of clothes. Those of us who remember the man, know very well that Mozart's clothes would have been a misfit: and so with Mozart's style: that would not fit the musician, Spohr.

There are many other analogies and ethics to which I might draw your attention; but time warns me that I must hardly even venture upon the summing-up of what I have, as it may seem to you, somewhat discursively, advanced.

What is idealising? Is it not the elimination from the object presented of all that is unbeautiful, unattractive, seizing hold of and presenting all in it that is admirable, and, moreover, the discernment and making evident of all the potentialities of good, the latent beauty, pruned of that which is accidental and of the nature of excrescence: and so presenting not a false, not a distorted, not an exaggerated, not even a one-sided view: but the view of the rich possibilities, rather than the actual; because the blemishes in the actual are from outside: the beautiful, the good, is from within? Is not this what we mean by an idealised portrait? Is it not the kind of portrait that we should like our friends to take of us, of our characters; and which it would be better for our charity to take of our friends?

Now music is not an idealising art: it is itself, not a selective, nor an eliminatory art: it is itself in its essence, ideal. It is a yearning art: actually expressive of the sensual, it cannot be. Music is a sentient art: it appeals to us through one of our senses: but sensual it is not. It may be that certain composers have presented it in highly-wrought sensuous fashion: and we are sentient beings. It may be that, as I said before, some have associated music with sensual surroundings. But are we to say, with the writer that I referred to, that "Music is neither good nor bad?" Because "out of the same mouth proceedeth blessing and cursing," is Language the less a Divine gift: a good, therefore?

Archdeacon J. Smith, Synonyms Discriminated.

And so, music is good,—a Divine gift and endowment.* That patriarch who to so many of you is only a name, but to those of us who knew him a name always pronounced with reverence—Cipriani Potter—used to say to me—"All good music is melancholy." I fancy that what he really meant was that it is ideal. And inasmuch as the ideal is not realised: is not the actual, the real,—but the ideal still,—there will be associated with it that kind of undefined melancholy, that sense of something that might have been but is not, that wistfulness which the Laureate expresses in asking

> "Who can tell
> Why to smell
> The violet
> Recalls the dewy prime
> Of youth and buried time?"

Yes: and anything which does this,—engenders at once the dissatisfaction and the yearning, in this grovelling, sensuous, nay, sensual world,—is so far purifying. Only it is Music, true Music that must do this. After that, if we have ears to hear, do we not feel that which another poet has expressed, only with mythological phraseology (we can substitute Beethoven or Handel for Apollo)—

> "Oh! ecstasy,
> Oh! happiness of him who once has heard
> Apollo singing! For his ears the sound
> Of grosser music dies, and all the earth
> Is full of subtle undertones, which change
> The listener and transform him. As he sang—
> Of what I know not, but the music touched
> Each chord of being—I felt my secret life
> Stand open to it, as the parched earth yawns
> To drink the Summer rain; and at the call
> Of those refreshing waters, all my thought
> Stir from its dark and secret depths, and burst
> Into sweet odorous flowers, and from their wells
> Deep call to deep, and all the mystery
> Of all that is, laid open." †

And again, the same poet, of the vocation of poet, artist, or musician:—

> "To be fulfilled with Godhead as a cup
> Filled with a precious essence, till the hand,
> On marble or on canvas falling, leaves
> Celestial traces, or from reed or string
> Draws out faint echoes of the voice Divine
> That bring God nearer to a faithless world.
>
> Or, higher still and fairer and more blest,
> To be His seer, His prophet; to be the voice
> Of the Ineffable Word; to be the glass
> Of the Ineffable Light, and bring them down
> To bless the earth, set in a Shrine of Song." ‡

Mr. Thomas, bandmaster of the Coldstream Guards, has been presented by the Duchess of Cambridge with a splendid pearl and diamond scarf pin, and the band-sergeant with a handsome pin set with diamonds and lapis lazuli. Her Royal Highness has also made a substantial donation to the widows and orphans funds of the Nulli Secundus (Coldstream Guards) Band Club.

A correspondent says with regard to Mr. Banner's Liverpool Choir, that it has been decided since leaving St. Cuthbert's not to offer the services of this able choir to any other church, at all events for the present; but, under the direction of Mr. Claude S. Ridley, they will proceed to rehearse Spohr's "Last Judgment," which will probably be rendered with orchestral accompaniments at a future date.

---

* "There is this peculiar advantage about melody, that per se, it is absolutely pure and remote from trivial ideas. The song and the dance may have their associations, good or evil; but the pure melody in itself is pure indeed: it is gay, or pathetic, or stately or sublime, but in any case there is something in the thrill of a choice chord, and the progression of a perfect melody, which seems to raise the hearer above the trifling affairs of life. At times it 'brings all Heaven before our eyes.' . . . Music is naturally more pure and removed from the concrete and sensuous ideas of ordinary life than a drama can usually be."—Prof. W. Stanley Jevons's "Methods of Social Reform," pp. 9, 11.
† Epic of Hades, p. 90.
‡ Epic of Hades.

Musical Intelligence.

THE LEEDS FESTIVAL.

The constitution of the Leeds orchestra for large choral works has proved as before to be a satisfactory one; and generally it is that adopted at Birmingham, with the wood wind doubled. Sir M. Costa's first experiment included the doubling of the brass as well, but experience proved this to be unnecessary, so the brass remains the same as usual, save that two trumpets and two cornets are secured to form the upper group. Sir Arthur Sullivan deserves to be complimented upon his efforts to secure the proper trio of alto, tenor, and bass trombones. The French custom of using three in B flat, and the usual plan in England of employing two tenors and one bass, are not altogether satisfactory. The bass trombone in G is necessary to do justice to the lower notes below F, and the alto is equally necessary for the proper sustentation of the upper part, for the tenor cannot produce with effect the high B natural, C, etc., which appear in the scores of the great masters, as in "Elijah." The doubled wood wind is a gain perhaps in the choral and fugal movements as giving additional, without intrusive, strength; the flutes and oboes in contrapuntal work generally doubling the soprano, the clarionets taking the alto, and the bassoons dividing the tenor and bass. *En passant*, unfortunately, the wood wind players not regarding their instruments as so essential as they really are in *forte* passages, at times neglect their responsibilities by taking rests not in the score; such occasional negligence always causes a sensible deterioration in the orchestral tone. When all is said and done, it is true that no orchestra is so expressive, elastic in action, passionate withal, and so pure in tone as one not much exceeding 60 players, and without doubled wind in any department. All the same, the combined effect of the Leeds orchestra and chorus was for the most part excellent. Thursday's morning concert brought to light Raff's "Weltende, gericht, Neue Welt." There is no question about the high claims made and earned by Raff in this noble piece of tone-thought. Whether the experiment of an orchestral supremacy in oratorio will be followed is not a matter for present discussion. Suffice it to say that the grandeur of the newly heard oratorio; the complete contempt of the composer in his tone-painting for the opinion of worldlings yearning only for pretty music; the elevation and combination of fine counterpoint with lofty picturesque thought; and the magnificent orchestral effects, will make Raff's last not only his greatest work, but an epoch in modern art forms. The composer has in plan enlarged upon Beethoven's Choral Symphony, and Mendelssohn's Symphony-Cantata, "The Hymn of Praise," and now the latest sign of the modern supremacy of orchestral function is the setting up of the Symphony-Oratorio. That Raff entered deliberately into such a scheme must be accepted as true, for he well knew how to write for voices, and was one of the most accomplished, if not quite the most skilled, of modern composers since Mendelssohn's time in the handling of practical, living counterpoint. His power over the orchestra, too, was truly remarkable; so he was fairly equipped for the composition of oratorio upon the lines left by the great composer of "St. Paul" and "Elijah," had he chosen to follow the usual oratorio plan. In the "World's End," there is practically only one character, that of St. John, to whom is assigned two solos, and the recitation of his vision of the last days. Three other airs are given to the contralto as "A Voice" occupying a sort of reflective position. Neither soprano nor tenor solos appear in the score. Throughout the work the orchestra is indeed the supreme musical medium. The section of the work actually treating of the end of the world is subdivided into four. In the second of these are four orchestral intermezzi describing the horsemen of the Apocalypse; thus pestilence, war, famine, death and hell are depicted with a strong hand, recalling the pictorial power of the painter Martin. Wonderful passages for the violins whirl the listener's spirit into the realms of imagination, and the varied powers of the orchestra are handled with striking boldness. Choruses of Martyrs, a petition for judgment, and a thanksgiving for the granting of the petition, are exceedingly impressive in parts. The despair of mankind and the last throes of nature are pourtrayed; then comes an expressive intermezzo, and a chorus of despair representing the people calling upon the rocks to fall upon

them and to hide them. There is much power and some strongly-built contrapuntal work here. The second section is "The Judgment." An intermezzo describes the Resurrection with dexterous skill, cries of despair and celestial strains are heard, intermingled. A double chorus is introduced of the Righteous and the Wicked, with strains of joy and cries for mercy. This section terminates with a chorus of praise. The third section contains three choral numbers, two of joy and one of a prayerful type built upon the sentence, "The grace of our Lord be with us all, Amen." Some fine contrapuntal writing and an impressive coda close the work. The band was admirable throughout this trying music, and no small thanks are here due to Sir A. Sullivan's care and firmness. The chorus, though evidently well prepared for their work, were not always happy in the most trying sentences, and at times sang out of tune. Miss Damian and Mr. Santley executed the soli parts admirably. The second half of this concert was devoted to, Handel, in a selection from his works. On the whole the committee do well to avoid giving that master's well-known works in full; people want upon these occasions to move somewhat out of the beaten track, and to advance their knowledge of the riches of the musical world. The soloists in the selection were Miss A. Marriott, Miss H. Wilson, Messrs. Mass and Blower. At the evening concert, Mr. Barnby's Ninety-seventh Psalm was produced and distinctly added to his reputation as a composer. The movements are instrumental Prelude, chorus, soli work for baritone, soprano with chorus (a movement of melodious power and likely to become very popular) and contralto. An orchestral interlude, some graceful writing but nothing of particular interest is introduced. There is an admirably written double quartet, a March and chorus setting of the "Gloria Patri," this being worked up with much power and skill. The composition is one doing much credit to the English school; and it displays a character and dignity the composer has hardly before attained to. The adaptation of one of the choruses from Mozart's "King Thamos," as the so-called "Third Motett," was capitally rendered, though adaptations should be eschewed at great festivals. Bach's cantata, "Thou Guide of Israel," and Rossini's "Stabat Mater," compositions of a widely different character, were finely performed. The famous chorus exceeded themselves at this concert. The organists, Dr. W. Spark and Mr. Walter Parrott, have shared the playing duties in connection with the instrument they are such well-known professors of. Each of the days' performances showed unabated sign of the enthusiasm of a large assembly of listeners.

The proceedings of Thursday were pleasantly diversified by the Mayor's luncheon, at which not only many distinguished visitors were invited, but very properly the guest list included the chief artists engaged at the Festival. Friday morning was a decided improvement in the weather. The Duke of Albany attended the first part of the performance of Macfarren's "King David." The Duchess being absent through indisposition. The performance was quite a memorable one for English art. For consistent treatment, with applied science, and thorough musicianship, "King David" takes rank as one of the most satisfactory oratorios the world has welcomed for many years. "David" has already been noticed in these columns, and will soon be heard in London, so it is not necessary here to enter largely into the performance of Friday week, though it is important to say that the impressions of the performance even exceeded those arising from a previous book inspection of the work. Prof. Macfarren's well chosen plot bearing upon the story of the King's sin and repentance is already familiar to all. From cover to cover the score of the oratorio displays the composer at his very best. Fine, vigorous choral writing; clever, healthy, frankly conducted forms; real dramatic power when required; and thoroughly masterly instrumentation make up a work which must not only gratify but astonish all who remember the composer's age, affliction of blindness, and laborious life. Principals, band and chorus, did their utmost to secure this first performance, which reflected much credit upon the firm, intelligent, painstaking direction of the conductor, Sir A. Sullivan. At the close of the work, ending with a magnificent doxology, the composer received such an ovation as falls to few artists. The performers and audience out-vied each other in their enthusiastic and admiring applause. So terminated a truly notable occasion as regards English art." Gade's "Crusaders" was the chief feature of the evening concert, this being performed because its author had not been able to undertake a new composition for the Festival. Miss Annie Marriott, Messrs. Lloyd and King sustained the chief parts most artistically. The delicate and finished instrumentation was delightfully rendered, and the chorus excellent. Beethoven's Mass in D; and Mendelssohn's "Hymn of Praise" formed the programme of Saturday morning. Certainly the performance of the great "Mass" was one of the best yet given; there were however a few inaccuracies in the band parts. The chorus, notwithstanding an occasional unsteadiness in this and in the still more familiar "Hymn of Praise," did wonders. The perfection of their intonation, their attention to light and shade, their splendid attack and superb quality of tone, call for the warmest congratulations and praise. The concert was closed with the National Anthem, and Sir A. Sullivan and Mr. Broughton, the able chorus master, received fitting ovations for their successful labour.

"With regard to the last popular concert of the Festival, the local correspondent of the *Musical Standard* writes :— Saturday night's concert was very well attended, and the programme consisted mainly of excerpts from the more important works of the Festival. The chorus sang selections from Macfarren's "King David," Raff's "End of the World," Barnby's Ninety-seventh Psalm (conducted by the composer), Cellier's "Gray's Elegy" (also conducted by the composer); and other works. Solos were sung by Miss Anna Williams, Miss A. Marriott, Miss Hilda Wilson, and Miss Damian. Mr. Maas sang with much sweetness and expression "Cujus Animam" from the "Stabat Mater," and "Lend me your aid" (Gounod). Mr. King was loudly applauded for his fine rendering of Sullivan's "Henry the Eighth's Song." The band and chorus all did their work in splendid style. The concert was brought to a close by the singing of the National Anthem, conducted by Sir Arthur Sullivan, the audience all standing; and few who were present will forget the scene of excitement that ensued as the last strains of the chorus died away. The Festival has been the most successful ever held in Leeds, and it is expected that more than £2000 will be handed over to the charities of the town; after paying expenses.

As regards Madme. Valleria, the committee evidently made a wise choice in selecting her as *prima donna* for the Festival. In the "Elijah" on the opening day she produced a most favourable impression, and in the later concerts, as she became accustomed to the size of the hall, and thus gained confidence, she more than justified the highest anticipations. I have no hesitation in saying that this accomplished vocalist is destined to make her mark in oratorio music, as she has already done on the operatic stage.

The world knows, well the extremes which characterise mankind; as the man who can only enjoy accepted types and the goahead, to whom pure thought is nothing apart from progress, and progress present is as nothing as compared with some advance or other to come. Shakespeare has been often improved for such restless spirits, and Wagner has in the interests of such people improved the scores of Gluck and Beethoven. The conceit of being wise beyond one's generation adds always to the strength of the so-called advanced school. Progress, by all means, but let us not mistake eccentricity for genius or novelty for originality. A writer in a Leeds daily paper has nothing encouraging to say with regard to the English works produced at the recent festival; his great spirit disdains the beautiful and yearns for the vast. Raff's experimental exaltation of the orchestra in the domain of oratorio, however, appeals to his mind; apparently he hardly knows why, for he says the composer "has found in discords his richest resources." We shall next hear of the man of business who prefers copper to gold and silver to bank notes. It suffices for this writer that the music in question is implied; progress, merely because it proved to be experimental. However, the writer's words may be given.

"Raff has found in discords his richest resources and most "effective materials. His work has been a rod too hard for the "musical critics to crack. Last week the newspapers teemed "with the cant of criticism. Criticisms were written in the usual "style and were quite as long as ordinary compositions "were dealt with. But Raff was a complete puzzle to the

"*Telegraph,* (the *Times* (what will Herr Hueffer say to this?), "the *Standard, &c.* Because his methods clashed with their "preconceived ideas, and with the musical laws they had "been for years laying down to admiring readers, they "made the terrible mistake of trying to extinguish him by "ridicule, and by continuous asseveration that his aims were "beyond the province of music. Further reflection has probably changed their views, and they would give much to "recall their utterances of Thursday, Oct. 11. But it would "never do for the great London critics, who fancy they lead "England by the nose in musical matters, to cry *peccavimus*. "That Raff's work will influence composition in England is "perhaps too much to expect, for we have no English composer "fit to wear his mantle. The next performance of the 'World's "End' in England will be an event to note; and we predict "that before that occurs, the great London critics will have "wholly changed their tune."

The truth is, no one has sought to disparage Raff's work, which contains some noble music as everybody allows and—possibly this information will be unpalatable in some quarters—some superb contrapuntal writing upon the purest classical lines. The great critics the learned writer in Leeds speaks so glibly about, and thinks so little of, will be among the first to welcome Raff's great work in London or elsewhere undoubtedly, and will in due time enlarge more upon its contents. They could hardly be expected to write more fully than they did under the pressure of a busy week, writing at midnight and under the necessity of transmitting their opinions as briefly as possible by the telegraph wires.

CRYSTAL PALACE CONCERTS.

PROGRAMME.

Festival Overture, "Jubilee"		Weber.
Concerto for Pianoforte and orchestra in G minor, Op. 33		Dvorak.
(First time in England).		
Pianoforte—Mr. Oscar Beringer.		
Recit. and Cavatina, "Hide me from day's garish eye" ("Il Penseroso")		Handel.
Mrs. Hutchinson.		
Symphony, No. 4, in B flat, Op. 60		Beethoven.
Bolero, "Zaïde"		Berlioz.
(First time).		
Mrs. Hutchinson.		
Overture, "King Lear"		Berlioz.
(First performance at the Saturday Concerts).		
Conductor — AUGUST MANNS.		

An assemblage, not very numerous, welcomed with satisfaction the commencement of the twenty-eighth series of Saturday concerts at the Crystal Palace. For the first time in England, Dvorak's concerto in G minor was performed. This composition is one of his early ones—Op. 33—and was written long before he became known to Brahms, who was the first to recognise his great talents and obtain for him the desire of all young composers, a generous and appreciative publisher. This is another instance of a timely intervention by which failure in the life of a genius has been prevented. The early history of Dvorak brings the following quotation from Mr. Irving Montague to mind : "That there is a Divinity which shapes our ends, rough hew them as we may, is never more clearly demonstrated than when in the shifting scenes of an eventful life one finds circumstances, as welcome as they are unexpected, crop up at that particular moment when the intervention of nothing else could have prevented a failure. Many such instances must take place with the most prosaic, but with those to whom fortune has been fickle, those who buffeted about from pillar to post, at home and abroad, have had to fight tooth and nail from their youth up, it must be strangely manifest."

The honour of having been the first to introduce Dvorak's works in England belongs to Mr. Manns, who in 1879 introduced his first set of Slavonic Rhapsodies at the Crystal Palace. A symphony and an overture and other shorter pieces have since that time been performed here. Dvorak is at present an organist and teacher at Prague. It is well to make this known, as it has very recently been said by one of our leading critics, that an organist can hardly be expected to write anything worth hearing, especially in the way of orchestration.

The concerto in G minor is, as I have already said, one of Dvorak's early works. There is a freshness and charm about it, but at the time of writing it, he had yet—like other young artists—to see his touch gain firmness, the grasp of his art stronger, and his powers more developed. It contains nothing of the old forms with the exception of the introduction, and as is the case with most concertos of the new school, the pianoforte is subordinate to the orchestra. The first movement is long and tedious, the andante is rather more interesting, with some Schubert-like combination for reeds and horns, but in the *finale* the young composer shows much ingenuity and individuality, and the Bohemian gipsy element which abounds in some of his later works is here charmingly manifested. The work upon the whole was fairly well received, but failed to make a deep impression. Mr. Beringer was deservedly recalled after his masterly performance of it.

The other numbers in the programme call for no special remark, but at least a word of praise must be given to Mrs. Hutchinson for her artistic singing of Handel's and Berlioz's songs.   R. S.

Another contributor writes :—

The new pianoforte concerto of Dvorak, the Bohemian composer, pleased me, in common with other *connoisseurs*. It is bright, melodious, and finely scored for the band, *if* a little rhapsodical in parts. The andante in D major, opened by the horn, is thought to be the best of the three movements, all of which, by the way, are in common time. Mr. Oscar Beringer, as usual, played admirably, and with laudable self-control. The execution of the No. 4 symphony was so exquisite as to evoke an extra demonstration of approval. I have rarely, if ever, heard finer violin playing than in the *finale* at the episodes. The overture of Berlioz, performed by Mr. Dannreuther at a "Wagner Society" concert in November, 1873, struck me as dramatic, but dull and laboured. The subject certainly does not inspire cheerful ideas. The introductory movement is too protracted; the composer has here made good use of the hautboy. The late Raff's "Autumn" symphony No. 10 in F minor, will be in good keeping with the sere and falling leaves this (Saturday) afternoon, and Wagner comes to the front.   A. M.

BRIGHTON.

The Autumn festival in connection with the Brighton, Hove, and Preston Church Choir Association was held on Oct. 11th, in St. Martin's Church, Lewes Road. The Association was formed last year to endeavour to raise the standard of Church music in the town by periodical festivals in the larger churches. The first was held at St. Peter's in the autumn of last year, and the second in the spring of the present at St. Mary's. The number of choirs affiliated has steadily increased, but are not so large as might be wished, considering the comprehensive basis of the Association. Since the last festival some alterations in the rules have been made, calculated to bring about the more harmonious working of the body. The post of conductor and choirmaster is now filled by Mr. Alfred King, Mus.Bac., who must be congratulated upon the improved order of service which he has complied. Mr. Charles Bailey, the organist of St. Martin's, was organist of the festival. The number of choristers was 350. The choirs represented were those of Hove Parish Church, St. Andrew's, Hove; St. Peter's, St. Nicolas', Christ Church, Chapel Royal, St. John's, Carlton Hill; St. Mary's, St. Martin's, St. James's, St. Luke's, St. Saviour's, and the Holy Trinity, Ship Street. The choirs of the Church of the Annunciation, All Soul's, and All Saint's would have joined but for unavoidable circumstances. The festival commenced with a celebration of the Holy Communion at eight o'clock in the morning, the remaining Services being two evensongs, one at four, and the other at eight. At the afternoon Service, the organist, Mr. C. Bailey, opened with a voluntary, an Andante by Gladstone, and the choirs then entered singing the hymn "Onward, Christian Soldiers," set to a new tune by Mr. Alfred King, the conductor, thoroughly martial in its character, the harmonies being splendidly arranged, with the introduction of two or three unison bars. The anthem was Barnby's "I will give thanks," the "Magnificat" and "Nunc Dimittis" being sung to H. Smart's Service in G. The strength of the choir at the afternoon Service was not sufficiently represented to give any fair idea of their capabilities, and this seriously interfered with the general success of the service. The "Magnificat," sung to H. Smart's arrangement, was sung most effectively, the unison passages being given with very fair precision. In the "Gloria," however, there was a tendency to drag, but this was quickly set right by Mr. King. The anthem was sung in excellent time, the rich harmonies of the semi-chorus and the chorale being most masterly. The sermon was preached by the Ven. Archdeacon Walker. He selected as his text Psalm cvi. 12 : "Then believed they His words, they sang His praise." At the close of the service, an offertory was taken in aid of the funds of the Association, and the organist played the March from "Scipio" (Handel) as the congregation left the church. In the evening the church was filled in every part. The Band of the 4th Royal (Irish) Dragoon Guards assisted, accompanying the principal pieces. This proved specially effective in the Canticles and Anthem, the large attendance of the members of the choirs also adding to the general effect, which was simply grand. The whole of the band accompaniments were written by Mr. Alfred

King, the conductor. The entire service was characterised by great heartiness. The festival was one of the most successful ever held by the Association, Mr. Alfred King's conductorship greatly aiding this result.

BRIXTON.—Madame Worrell gave her annual concert at the Brixton Hall, on Thursday, 11th inst., which proved very successful. The programme, a somewhat lengthy one, was tolerably free from usual royalty songs; the various items on the whole were judiciously selected. Madame Worrell, who is justly very popular, was received with great fervour by the numerous audience assembled, and encored in each of her songs; Gounod's "O that we two were mapping," creating the most impression. Madame Osborne Williams sang "Fanciulle che il core" ("Dinorah"), with much taste, and joined Madame Worrell in Rossini's "Quis est homo" ("Stabat Mater"). The other vocalists were Miss Matilda Roby, Miss Maud Cameron, Miss Annie Butterworth, Messrs. Henry Guy, F. H. Cozens, Fred'k. Bevan, and J. Budd; all of whom acquitted themselves with much success, especially Miss Maud Cameron in "O Roberto che adoro," and Mr. Henry Guy in "Oh, 'tis a glorious sight" ("Oberon"). Mention should be made of Mr. H. Guy's charming trio "Reflection," which was well rendered by Madame Worrell, Miss Butterworth, and the composer. Mons. Albert contributed with great skill two solos on the violoncello, and Mr. Turle Lee ably conducted.

St. Botolph, Aldgate, E.C.—Harvest Thanksgiving Services were held in this, the parish church, on Sunday last. In the morning the Te Deum was sung to Smart's setting in F, and the anthem was "Fear not, O Land" (Goss). At the evening Service Spohr's cantata "God, Thou art great," was rendered in place of the anthem, by an augmented choir under the direction of Mr. W. T. Goold, organist and choirmaster. The treble solos were sustained with much ability by Master Willie Hollis (of Mr. Stedman's choir), and Mr. C. T. Grimsditch rendered valuable assistance in the duet.

St. Paul's, Avenue Road, N.W.—The Harvest Festival will be held on Sunday next, the 21st inst. The first evensong of the festival will be held at 7.30 p.m. on Saturday, at which service a full band will accompany the choir as well as the organ. Mr. E. M. Lott, F.C.O., will assist Mr. W. H. Carpenter at the organ, and the Rev. J. W. Bennett, M.A., will conduct. The Magnificat and Nunc Dimittis will be Gadsby in C, and Mendelssohn's "Lauda Sion" will be given, at the anthem, Handel's "Hallelujah Chorus" will be sung after the sermon.

Tulse Hill.—It is with feelings of satisfaction that one has to chronicle from time to time individual efforts to restore oratorio to its rightful home, the Church. At the Harvest Festival on Saturday the 13th inst., at Holy Trinity Church, the 1st and 2nd parts of Haydn's "Creation" were performed at the evening Service with full orchestra, under the able direction and chiefly through the energy of the esteemed organist, Mr. Humphrey J. Stark, Mus. Bac. The choir numbered 70 voices, including Mr. Stedman's choir of boys. The Service consisted of the shortened form of Evening Prayer, unlike "Magnificat" was sung to Mr. Stark's skilful and effective service in D, which was originally composed for full orchestra. The oratorio took the place of the sermon, and between the parts a collection was made and hymns sung. The choruses were all admirably rendered, no doubt the sacred character of the building and the devout demeanour of the large congregation greatly enhancing the effect; in fact, the choruses of The Heavens are telling," and "Achieved is the glorious work," were rendered with excellent precision and taste that could vie with many of our best choral societies. The soprano solos were divided between Misses H. Townsend, W. Hall, and R. Weleen, who acquitted themselves with great success. Mr. Stedman sang "In native worth" very artistically, and also the remainder of the tenor music. Mr. Robert Poole likewise well sustained the bass solos. The service commenced and finished with processional hymns, which were the least successful of all that preceded, followed them, the organ, orchestra, and choir occasionally not keeping together. Messrs. W. E. Stark and E. J. Quance presided; at the organ and Mr. Victor Buziau very ably led the orchestra. After the service Mendelssohn's "Cornelius March" was played; the overture to "Athalie" and Romanza in G (Beethoven) was also announced to be performed, but omitted for want of time.

Preston.—On Sunday, October 14th, the annual Harvest Festival was celebrated at Holy Trinity Church. The choir was augmented, and there was also a full band of 30 performers. The morning Service opened with an organ solo, Adagio from violin concerto (Spohr), rendered with great taste by the organist, Mr. W. B. Norwood. The anthem, morning and evening, was "O Lord, how manifold are Thy works" (Sir G. A. Macfarren). The evening Service commenced with a clarionet solo. With verdure clad" (Haydn). At the conclusion of the services the band played in a spirited manner, "Cornelius March" (Mendelssohn), the Mr. L. Norwood wielded the baton. There were very large congregations in both services. Mr. Norwood announces that he will give a grand concert on Monday next, the 22nd inst., in aid of the Preston Infirmary, when "The

British Army Quadrilles" will be rendered for the first time in Preston, with all the original effects. Miss Lillie Snowden, R.A.M., a Preston lady, and Signor Foli, will be the vocalists.

HIGHER BROUGHTON, MANCHESTER.—A Harvest Thanksgiving Service was held on Oct. 12th, in the Church of St. John the Evangelist. The processional hymn was No. 480, the tune being "St. Gertrude" (Sullivan). The chants were Higgin in T, Lawes in C, and Smith in A flat. Weber's harvest cantata, "Jubilee," took the place of the anthem. The music is characteristic throughout, and in many parts is exceedingly striking and impressive. There are recitatives and airs for soprano, tenor, and bass, a duet for soprano, and no fewer than six choruses, and the scoring is occasionally somewhat elaborate, and severely taxes the powers both of the choir and the organist. With a few trifling exceptions the singing was admirable. Mr. W. Mulineux, F.C.O., officiated as organist and director of the choir. The anthem during the offertory was "Unfold, ye portals everlasting," from Gounod's "Redemption."

MOULSHAM.—The annual Harvest Thanksgiving Services were held at Moulsham Church on Sunday last. The church had been tastefully decorated. The service was commenced with the stirring hymn "Come, ye thankful people, come," in which the congregation joined heartily with the choir. The musical portion of the service was ably rendered by the choir. The "Venite" was sung to Jones in C, for the "Te Deum" Dr. F. Iliffe's Service in A was used, and the "Jubilate" was sung to Wesley in F, Joseph Barnby's anthem, "O Lord, how manifold are thy works," was given with excellent effect, the verse parts being taken by Master Alfred Pilgrim, Messrs. G. Hayward, C. W. Barnard, and F. Hayward. An appropriate sermon enforcing the duty of thanksgiving to God was preached by the vicar from the words, "Do all in the name of the Lord Jesus, giving thanks to God and the Father by Him" (Colossians, iii. 17). In the evening, when, despite the inclemency of the weather, the church was crowded, the vicar read the prayers and the Rev. S. W. W. Wilkin and the Rev. J. A. Kershaw, head-master of Chelmsford Grammar School, the lessons. Sir John Goss's anthem, "I will magnify thee, O God, my king," was sung with care and precision. The psalms were sung to Hy. Smart in G and Lemon in G, the "Cantate" to Dr. Stainer's fine double chant in C, composed for Chelmsford Choral Festival in 1882, and the "Deus Misereatur" to a very pleasing double chant in B flat, composed for the occasion by Mr. A. G. Barnard, the organist. At the close of the Service Helmore's "Te Deum" in E flat was sung. Mr. Barnard, the organist, who efficiently accompanied the singing, played the following voluntaries :—Pastorale in G (Henry Smart), march in G (Henry Smart), Andante cantabile (Gustav Hermann); chorus, "Quoniam tu solus" in C from Haydn's 2nd Mass.

WATFORD.—On Friday evening, the 12th inst., the annual Harvest Thanksgiving was held in St. Andrew's Church, and more than usual interest was imparted to the occasion by the opening of the new organ built by Messrs. Brindley and Foster, of Sheffield, in accordance with a specification prepared by Mr. James Turpin, Mus.Bac., the organist at the church. The music in the service comprised Proper Psalms to Chants by Turton, Towle, and Humphreys, an evening service especially composed for the occasion by Mr. James Turpin, and the anthem "Fear not, O land" by Goss. After the service, Mr. James Turpin played a selection of pieces showing the excellent qualities of the organ, to the large congregation which filled the church, and who were evidently interested in the newly acquired instrument, which will be the means of enhancing the services of the church. The rendering of the vocal part of the services by the choir was excellent, showing devotional earnestness and careful attention to the requirements of the music selected, which were of a sufficiently exacting type to thoroughly test the choir. The whole service gave the utmost satisfaction.

BEDDINGTON, SURREY.—The Harvest Thanksgiving Services at the beautiful Parish Church of Carew notoriety (which by the way, is one of the most noted for its highly decorated and unique interior), were held on Sunday, Oct. 14th. As usual at each service, immense congregations assembled. The excellent choir the church possesses was heard at its best, both at the morning and evening services. At the latter, the anthem was Spohr's "God, Thou art great;" and after the sermon Handel's duet "O lovely peace," and "Hallelujah, Amen," from "Judas Maccabeus," was performed. The principal treble at the evening service was Master H. A. Burry, of St. Paul's Cathedral, who is the son of the organist of Beddington... Mr. Burry's services in the post of organist and choirmaster at this church date back some eighteen years, and at that time the musical part of the service was rendered in the most primitive style; the Rev. Canon Bridges, the rector, having during that time, by his munificence, added to everything that is beautiful in the church and its services.

The Owl Club gave their opening concert on Oct. 15th, at the Cannon-street Hotel, thus inaugurating their tenth season.

SOCIAL SCIENCE CONGRESS.

ART DEPARTMENT.

The following abstract version of the paper on "What constitutes a 'School of Music,' and how far can the formation of an English School be encouraged?" By the Rev. H. G. Bonavia Hunt, Mus.Bac., F.R.A.S., Warden of Trinity College, London, will be found interesting :—The author, after referring to the variety of senses in which the term "school" is commonly employed, trusted his hearers would at least agree to define "a school" as the creation of a group of artists whose work possessed in common some distinctive characteristic. This distinctiveness might lie either (1) in the kind of subject chosen, or (2) in the mode of treatment adopted, or again (3) in a subtle aroma pervading all, no matter what the class of subject or the mode of treatment. Any special cult of the first mentioned order would be essentially narrow, because necessarily exclusive. A school of the second description would be less restricted as to subject, but still fettered by forms. But if we apprehend a School of Music as comprising every kind of work, and at the same time possessing the nameless but unmistakable quality imperfectly defined as a "subtle aroma," our art horizon at once expanded on all sides, and we felt it could enclose nothing less than a complete world. In speaking, therefore, of an "English School of Music," we should regard it not as characterised by more or less rigid adherence to some system of treatment, still less to any one branch of composition, but as covering the whole field of art work, and at the same time setting its distinctive mark on everything which its hand had touched, so that all men might say of it "this is English work." In former times nationality was necessarily far more marked than it could be now. The difference between the Dutch School of painters and the Italian was not merely one of method, but of ideal. The former with its fruit and vegetables aimed at literalness; the Italian School had a higher, because a more poetical, ideal, appealing as it did to imagination and emotion. But now-a-days people travelled more, saw and heard more. With wider knowledge the mind expanded, and the greater the intellectual environment the more lofty would be the ideal. The musical student of this and other nations is early familiarised with all the "schools," and his efforts may be moulded in this or that cast according to his predilections. Nevertheless his nationality would assert itself in his works, and his genius, if he possess it, would individualise all he wrote. The conception of a lofty ideal, and the power to reach it by one way or another, could not and should not be the monopoly of any one small section of the human race. If therefore we were led to see that the development of an isolated and exclusive school of music was not only under present conditions impracticable, but also unworthy of the catholicity of all true art, we should rise to a higher view of the subject and ask, how can England best contribute to the future literature of the one common language of mankind? It might serve to clear the ground a little if we summarised our musical past. While rendering all homage to our great musicians, we must admit that there is not one amongst them of whom we can declare that he has given to the world a new revelation. And in making such an admission our national pride need not suffer; we should only look with fuller assurance to the future. Already there were abundant signs that after long years of lethargy, and consequent musical stagnation, new life was beginning to stir in old England. For many years past the Royal Academy of Music had given to the nation a splendid race of teachers. Our cathedrals had not only supplied some of our greatest composers, but had really kept the art of music alive during long periods of utter apathy. Within recent times the work of the older bodies had ripened into the foundation of the College of Organists with its well-devised and carefully executed scheme of examinations; of Trinity College, London, with its teaching staff of some fifty professors, and its higher and local examinations resorted to by over 5,000 candidates annually; of the Guildhall School of Music, which owed its existence to, and was well subsidised by, the Corporation of London; and last, but by no means least, of the Royal College of Music with its numerous free scholarships for the encouragement and support of able and deserving English students. Yet, although this systematic seed sowing was indispensable as a preliminary, far more was needed to develope our

English School of Music. We must give greater opportunities to our young musicians. At present they are compelled to spend their whole time in teaching for a livelihood. The long-established endowments of learning had recently been supplemented by aids to scientific research, in all which it had been recognised that ability must have free play in a certain amount of assured leisure. Some such provision should be made for our composers—a scheme of fellowships, or, perhaps, something more akin to the *Prix de Rome.* Another means of encouragement would undoubtedly be the formation of an Academy of Musicians upon the lines of the Royal Academy of Arts, or the Royal Society of London—a body into which a composer who had "made his mark" could be "co-opted" by his brethren. Lastly, while placing the greatest value on sound scholarship and the study of the classical models of musical structure, let us hesitate to pounce down upon our young composers for any variation from established lines, at least until we have assured ourselves that it is a deterioration, lest we should incur the responsibility of obstructing the progress of the highest art the world can ever know.

MUSIC IN NEW YORK.

A correspondent of the Detroit *Every Saturday,* thus writes of music in New York, and says of that city:—"It has the reputation of sustaining with no unsparing hand whatever is meritorious and ennobling in the divine art. Being the landing-place, so to speak, of the finest European talent and the centre from which ability of the highest order radiates in every direction, the material for perfecting every species of musical organization is complete indeed." That the German element, present as it is in so large a force in New York, is entitled to much of the credit which the city everywhere gets for its music is the deserved acknowledgment of a simple fact. In orchestral and piano playing the Teuton is everything; while the Englishman seems to carry off the palm in all that is meritorious in organ performances. Neither the churches nor the theatres appear at their best just now, but the music I have listened to—at the new R. C. cathedral on Fifth avenue, under Dr. Peche; at Old Trinity, Broadway, under Mr. A. H. Messiter, and at Trinity chapel, Madison Square, (at which church Mr. W. B. Gilbert, Mus. Bac., Oxon, and the compiler of one of the finest hymnals with music ever presented to the Episcopal church in America, is the organist and choirmaster) was very excellent. The services both at Old Trinity and Trinity chapel are so soul-inspiring as to make one feel all the better for attending them. The boy choisters at Trinity are, I am informed, well paid, chorus singers receiving $300, while soloists are paid as much as $500 and $600 a year. Trinity Church Corporation believes the organist as well as the minister to be worthy of his hire, and pays the "man on the bench" almost as many thousands as hundreds of dollars fall to the lot of some "poor hirelings." Outside of Trinity, liberal salaries are paid, in a few instances only, to several organists, but the majority of performers are so poorly paid, and their tenure of office so thoroughly dependent upon the caprices of too many church musical nobodies, that sterling organists and musicians fight shy of church positions altogether. That such a state of things should exist in a community where church millionaires can be counted by the hundreds, and where the parson who "draws" receives salary enough to run a "monetary institution" all by himself, is discouraging, if not reprehensible in the highest degree."

To some extent a similar state of things prevails here. Still it is pleasant to find some good organists in America, commanding salaries averaging from £400 to £700 and £1,000 a year. Though it must be borne in mind that the cost of living is greater in America in some directions than in England,

Messrs. G. Sims and F. Clay are engaged upon another new opera.

On Tuesday, Oct. 16th, there was an important sale of musical instruments, including pianofortes, harmoniums, a 2-manual chamber organ, double-action harps, Italian and other violins, violas, violoncellos, and double basses, wind instruments, etc., etc., and also a small library of music, at Messrs. Puttick and Simpson's establishment.

PRINCIPAL CONTENTS OF THIS NUMBER.

LONDON : SATURDAY, OCTOBER 20, 1883.

ON THE ORIGIN OF A FAMOUS TUNE.

RECENTLY the story of the air so charmingly varied by HANDEL in a suite de pièces and known as the, most probably mythical, "Harmonious Blacksmith" has attracted attention. Without being in the position of being able to add to the stores of evidence already presented, I wish merely to offer what may tend to induce the reader to either accept or decline the hypothesis that HANDEL did adopt—great men do not steal but adopt, says a German writer—the melody forming the theme of the movement in question. To accuse a man of plagiarism merely because he employs accepted and floating musical idioms is obviously unfair ; but when the general outline of a melody is followed, there seems *prima facie* cause to believe that the composer accused of borrowing had seen or heard a musical construction which he consciously or unconsciously repeats. The matter, used similar tricks as those employed by another would not be judged, thereby, but a man who builds his house something after a previously adopted plan may be fairly accused of some kind of pre-knowledge which he has taken advantage of, more or less unfairly perhaps. I have looked through a copy of "Les Pseaumes de David, mis en rime Françoise per CLEMENT MAROT et THEODORE DE BEZE," printed in Paris in 1662, and here give the melody to the 130th Psalm which forms the basis of the statement regarding HANDEL'S adopted melody. This Psalm, there is evidence to show, was put into metre by MAROT in Geneva in 1543, the year before his death and several years before BEZA's visit to the headquarters of Calvinism. How soon after the music was adapted to the words I am unable to show. The tune is as follows:—

This is printed in the diamond shape notes of the period; the dots denote cadence points, and the natural was not in the original, as that sign was not then in general use if invented, but is here introduced, as there is internal evidence in the book to ...

... come to HANDEL in the progress ... metrical version of the Psalms was ... Dutch and German Lutheran Churches ... copy I have, entitled "Psalmen Des Propheten DAVID," rendered from the French version in corresponding Dutch metre by PETRUM DATHENUM, the music edited by a musician, one CORNELIS ... printed at Schiedam in 1686, the above melody is given note for note. Now, it is conceivable that HANDEL might know and even be familiar with this tune, in consequence of its prevailing use in Protestant Germany. He might model it, or build his own version upon a half-forgotten recollection of the church tune he knew in his early days; or it is possible the tune itself had undergone revision and modification before he knew it. In such a way as to bring it nearer his own treatment. The advance of the tune, to a condition of greater rhythmical shapeliness would yield interesting matter for study. The compression and alteration into the dominant cadence of the first part, the repetition and extension of figures, the omission of a note to secure a dominant half cadence, and some slight changes towards the last cadence would be interesting features of such development.

Many of the plain song and other traditional melodies have undergone such transformations; and

such tunes have in process of time lost something of their character by the subtraction of some of their conjunct intervals, peculiar to the plain chant, and earlier contrapuntal ages, and have assumed bolder forms with the presence of more disjunct intervals. Such appears to have been the case with the original outline of the theme of the so-called Harmonious Blacksmith. CLEMENT MAROT'S melody, possibly not the original itself, but an adaptation from plain song, was fairly wedded to his words at an earlier period than the date of the book I copy it from. Mr. W. H. CHAPPELL says, in a letter addressed to Professor J. ELLA, that it was first published in 1565 by BALLARD in a collection of French chansons. It may be that this book was really the metrical Psalms, or that the version named by Mr. W. CHAPPELL was another adaptation of a traditional tune. Prof. ELLA went into the question now being discussed in 1865, printing the version of the French song given first in the Records of the Musical Union in 1862, and again in 1865, from the ...

NEW MUSIC.

... harmonised by WEKERLIN and printed in Paris ... being the leading place, so to speak, of the most Europian talent ... highest order ...

Prof. ELLA, as other writers have done, disposes of the tradition respecting the mythical Blacksmith and gives the story of LUTHER, of BACH, bestowing the popular title containing the tune was written. On ... HANDEL went to Cannons; it was possibly composed some little time before he knew of the existence of the Blacksmith, at whose forge ...

Curiously enough there is a plain song tune still in the same ... which leads us ...

A striking resemblance to the second portion of the theme now in question. But most probably, however, only another proof of the universality of plain particles. Alone nevertheless; an interesting fragment in being French, and as indicating the presence in France of another possible basis of the traditional theme. Several developments of the old Psalm tune first appearing to CLEMENT MAROT'S words could doubtless be traced. I seem to recollect seeing one somewhere, but unfortunately cannot verify my impression. A true Dutch version of the tune was probably used soon after the National Synod in 1578 ...

1619. It may be presumed that the French version with the corresponding notes was known to the Swiss Calvinists and the French Huguenots some time before the close of the sixteenth century. Mr. ROCKSTRO, in his life of HANDEL, prudently declines to pronounce finally in this matter. I venture no more than to point out observations personally made. There might be some interest in an attempt to trace the use of the tune in the German Lutheran Church about the beginning of the eighteenth century; to track down any changes made in the outline of the melody, and to point a decided knowledge of HANDEL'S acquaintance with it in his youth. Then there would indeed be some sort of solid ground for the assertion that the French tune was, as a half remembered association of his younger days or as a distinctly remembered and deliberately improved melody, the real basis of the world famous air, so dexterously set with "doubles" or variations in the first of the two sets of "Suites de Pieces," the two sets being first printed, respectively, in 1720 and in 1733.

E. H. TURPIN.

THE LOGIC OF COUNTERPOINT.

THIRD SERIES.

XV.

THERE is one matter calling for consideration before leaving the ordinary domains of counterpoint, as exemplified in the four-part score; this is the character of the canto fermo. As an institution, this is nearly always set in semibreves or in dotted semibreves when the counterpoint is in triple measure. Again it is usually purely diatonic, and almost invariably—following the ancient method of approaching the final note of a "mode" from the second above—ends by falling from the supertonic to the tonic. Now it is surely time to consider whether it is wise to confine the student to such a restricted, stiffly set form of canto fermo, which, in consequence of its very confined methods of formation, has rarely any tuneful grace and withal can rarely be described as a melody. It is to be feared too, that theorists have got into the way of writing canti fermi very mechanically from the not unnatural idea, that rigidly set out forms are not intended to be spontaneous or tuneful productions. When the student comes to the fugue however, he is expected to compose subjects of a well-marked character, which from their well-distributed figures—in parts formulated upon given well-marked uses of different time values, which at all points arrest the ear of the listener on the qui vive for subject entrances. Now, one cannot but think the confinement of the student through his preliminary contrapuntal training to themes of the orthodox and time-honoured canto fermo type, must not only tend to increase his impatience to escape from the trammels of the stricter forms of contrapuntal drill, but deprive him of the benefit of some experience in the manipulation of repeated melodic figures and variations of the notes forming the theme as regards their time value. It seems to me, therefore, that it would be well to employ throughout the student's contrapuntal course, not only the orthodox type of canti fermi, but also melodies as

themes in which the changes, graces, and variations in the time value of the notes used impart so much character to tune. There would be good practice even in two-part writing in pitting strictly carried out counterpoints of various species against more or less ornate melodies used as canti fermi. Such drill, continued through the various contrapuntal stages in combination with a fair proportion of exercise in treating themes of the old orthodox kind, would not only furnish much useful, not to say graceful, strength in part-writing, but would decidedly supply an excellent preparation for the practice of double counterpoint and fugue. In the real business of composition the strict, uncompromising canto fermo rarely finds a place, but there are distinct and not unfrequent opportunities—as in moving basses for the use of different orders of counterpoint in combination with natural, graceful, and varied melodies and harmonies.

E. H. TURPIN.

THE AUTUMN SEASON.

THE autumnal season of classical concerts may be said to begin with the admirable performances on Sydenham Hill every Saturday afternoon. The first Crystal Palace Concert took place last Saturday, and the second, to-day, will be signalized by the production of Raff's "Anthem" symphony. The scheme for the year 1883-84 has not yet come before me, but the repetition of HECTOR BERLIOZ'S "Messe des Morts" promises to be one, most interesting feature. Mr. MANNS will recognise a room for improvement after the practical failure of last spring. The chorus must be well looked after. The "Old Reporter's" protest against the annoyance inflicted upon attentive auditors at the Crystal Palace by the noisy intrusion of late comers, and the intolerable chattering in the gallery, may be strongly backed up. The directors have issued an "order of the day" for the prevention of the nuisance, but it is not always respected. The concerts will go on until Christmas and then a suspension of some weeks ensue. The omission of all "royalty" vocal numbers would be advisable, and the length of the concert should be limited to about an hour and a half or three quarters.

Mr. ARTHUR CHAPPELL will not be far behind with his Saturday and Monday "Populars;" he began last year before the usual time, to wit, at the end of October, but then Easter fell early. This year, 1883-84, a wider margin is available, for Easter does not fall until April 13th, or three weeks later than in 1883. What novelties may be expected remains to be seen. A more extensive choice of pianists, from the large host available on the continent, has already been suggested. One more point: the connoisseurs would like to hear more sonatas, and fewer of the pieces recently in fashion, however good they may be. SCHUBERT'S sonatas would be "special business" at the Monday Popular, and Mr. HALLE cannot expect to appease the healthy appetite of that composer's numerous admirers with an occasional reading of No. 10 or No. 11. How is it that DUSSEK so seldom comes to the fore? His "Plus Ultra" and "Invocation" sonatas used to be played regularly, but they have been lying on the shelf for too many years.

Mr. BARNBY promises a good season at the Albert Hall, to begin early in November. He has been asked to perform the "Messe des Morts" and must do so. The "Redemption" of Gounod will be repeated as a matter of course. The "Requiem" Masses of MOZART, CHERUBINI, and VERDI, cry loudly for repetition, and some of HANDEL'S more rarely heard oratorios would be the better for an airing. The three RICHTER concerts will come off within a month of this date. May they prove successful in a financial sense. They surely deserve to be.

A. M.

THE LATE SIGNOR SCHIRA.

READERS will be sorry to learn that Signor FRANCESCO SCHIRA died at his London residence on Monday night. He had only recently returned from Milan, where he had completed a new comic opera. Signor SCHIRA was born at Malta in 1815, and was educated at the Milan Conservatorio. In 1842 he came to London, here teaching many artists of eminence. He was successively conductor of the English opera season at the Princess's, under MADDOX, at Drury Lane in 1844, under BUNN, and at Covent Garden. Under his direction many of the operas of BALFE, WALLACE, G. A. MACFARREN, and others were produced. For the Princess's Theatre he wrote "Mina" in 1843, and "Theresa" in 1850, which were performed with Miss LOUISA PYNE in the chief parts. In 1865, his opera "Niccolo di Lapi" was produced at Her Majesty's, with TITIENS and Mdlle. TREBELLI in the leading parts. His cantata, the "Lord of Burleigh," founded on TENNYSON's poem, by MR. DESMOND RYAN, was written for the Birmingham Festival of the year. The lamented composer and teacher was a man of rare musical gifts. His devotion to teaching naturally led to his neglect of composition. This is, alas! a common story to tell of musical men. His rare faculty for impassioned melody, his admirable sense of proportion, yet bold use of form, his intimate acquaintance with the voice, knowledge of the orchestral effects, and generally sound judgment as a writer, would, had he given more time to musical composition, produced results which could only have been anticipated by those who knew his exceptional talents. As a teacher of singing Signor SCHIRA had long held an honoured position in England, and his many pupils and many admiring friends will not forget him now. He lives here only by the memory of his works, and in the tender regard of those who claimed his friendship and recognised his great talents.

H. TURPIN.

Paul VIARDOT has returned to Paris from a successful tour in Germany and Russia.

Messrs. Gilbert and Sullivan's opera, "Iolanthe," is at the Grand Theatre, Leeds, last week on a return visit. The part of Phyllis is now played by Miss Osmond, who acts in a charming and intelligent manner, while vocally she is fully equal to the requirements of the part. Her songs are all well received, and her pretty duet with Strephon, "None shall part us from each other," as one of the gems of the opera. Miss Fanny Harrison as the Queen, and Miss Beatrice Young as Iolanthe, are both thoroughly efficient. The choruses were all given in capital style.

SOCIETY OF PROFESSIONAL MUSICIANS.

The first annual general meeting of this Society was held in the Old Town Hall, Manchester, on a recent Saturday afternoon. There was a large attendance. Mr. Wrigley, M.R.A.M., occupied the chair. The treasurer (Dr. Marsden) read a report, which showed that there was a balance in hand of about £100. The following report was read by the hon. secretary, Mr. J. Dawber, of Wigan, and adopted:—

There is much to be said... Alone, among the arts and sciences, had music been left, without any association regular intercourse, or co-operation of its professors and teachers. To supply this lack, the Society of Professional Musicians has been formed. The aims of the society are—(1) To bring into close contact those who, by the nature and restrictions of their quiet, often solitary, and for that most part solitary work, have few opportunities of joining in friendly discussion and interchange of ideas. (2) To disseminate among those holding chief influence over the spread of musical knowledge the latest and best information. (3) To consider all legislative and other proposals affecting the interests of musicians. (4) To labour earnestly and perseveringly for the full recognition in the highest and widest of the education system of the highest character; and (5) to establish a system of graded examinations which shall (by its obvious fairness, independence, and completeness) command the confidence of students, and the respect and loyal support of all teachers.

The monthly gatherings of the association have been held in various centres of large population, and it is intended as far as the place of meeting as to render them easily accessible to musicians throughout the kingdom. During the very first year of the existence of the society, abundant evidence has been supplied of the keen-felt need of such an association, and of the good that may be done by the united efforts of its members. Busy men—previously labouring isolated and without the aid of the ready sympathy awaiting full knowledge of their views and exertions—have been enabled to work unitedly, more hopefully, and therefore more zealously. Much progress has been made towards ridding the teaching and study of music of those uncertainties which surround the chief... the chief readiness to zeal union, and in cultivating catholicity and greater breadth of purpose. The earnest thought of the members has been directed to inevitable and rapidly advancing changes and to the necessity for a united course of action in view of certain legislative probabilities. Attention has been called to the alteration from their legitimate purpose of endowments intended for the advance of musical knowledge, and efforts have been made to bring about a more systematic and thorough teaching of music in its various education departments. The... registration of teachers has also been considered, and much time has been occupied in preparing a better system. Finally, very considerable and self-denying labour has been bestowed in the elaboration of a scheme for a just examination of students in different localities, in all sections of theoretical and practical musical knowledge. It is proposed, that in the early... probably in June of the next and each succeeding year, in Manchester, Liverpool, and in all places where such help may be desired, examinations should be held of all students of music presenting themselves, and that success should be testified by certificates of various degrees, signed by the head of the society. For the guidance of teachers and candidates the qualifications necessary in competition for the different grades of certificates are laid down as exactly stated as to leave no room for uncertainty as to the conditions, or as to the efficiency and openness of the inspection, which will in each centre be conducted by three selected examiners, striving to do the totality and entirely without interest in the success or failure of the candidates. For the examinations in harmony, etc., a book has been compiled (and is to be drawn up) containing the questions from which (by number) a selection will be made on the very day of each examination. This plan has been adopted (1) in order to put all candidates and tutors upon an equal footing; (2) to relieve the test questions of the whims of particular teachers, or the followers of any particular school of theory; and (3) to avoid the possibility of perplexing students by placing before them (as is too often done) similar questions obscured by their vague and unfamiliar form and phraseology. The questions (from each section of which some two or three will be chosen each year) have been arranged to avoid any attempt, while including all essential points, and are in each chapter so numerous that far less time and trouble would be required in order properly to prepare students by thorough and honest teaching of the whole subject than to accept ill-grounded candidates for probable and deserved failure. It is confidently believed that a society, showing such evidence of unity, forbearance, and mutual goodwill, and displaying the earnest and zealous co-operation of musicians throughout the realm.

The following gentlemen were elected upon the council: Dr. Fisher (Blackpool), Mr. F. Dean (Lancaster), Mr. Marsden (Salford), Mr. J. Charton (Oldham), and Mr. S. Myerscough (Rochdale), Dr. Marsden, and Mr. Dawber.

248

were re-elected treasurer and secretary respectively. A considerable time was then devoted to the consideration of the contents of an "examination book," which is to be published for the society by Messrs. Novello and Co.

Organ News.

HAWORTH CHURCH.

Organ recitals were given in Haworth Church, on Tuesday, October 16th, by Mr. Best, of Liverpool. The programme included :—

Allegretto and Adagio Religioso, from the Symphony to the Lobgesang	Mendelssohn.
Fugue in G major	Wesley.
Adagio Solenne	Dussek.
Vestal March	Best.
Legende, "La Prédication aux Oiseaux"	Liszt.
Overture, founded on the "Austrian Hymn"	Haslinger.

BOW AND BROMLEY INSTITUTE.

Mr. A. E. Bishop was the soloist on Saturday last. He played with much care and taste, though at times perhaps his performance wanted a little more impulse, possibly through nervousness upon a strange organ. His solos were "Offertoire sur des Noels" (Guilmant), "Fantasia and Fugue" (Merkel), an Adagio of his own, a work of much promise, printed in "English Organ Music," a Pastorale by Salomé, a very interesting introduction and Fugue by J. Raff, an "Elevation" by Guilmant, and a March by Wely. These pieces were rendered excellently with admirable care and considerable taste. Miss Ambler sang well, but nervously, her songs winning very solid compliments. Mr. W. H. Brereton sang remarkably well. One of his songs was Mr. C. T. Speer's "Sea King," a new work. Mr. Van Praag was the violinist, his solo, "Fantasia Militaire" by Leonard being admirably played and very warmly received. Mr. W. T. Best will be the organist to-night.

FISHERIES EXHIBITION.

Mr. James Loaring, F.C.O., gave an organ recital on Saturday, October 13th. The following is the programme :—

Overture, "Le Cheval de Bronze"	Auber.
Organ Concerto, No. 2	Handel.
Minuet and Trio from Symphony in E flat	Mozart.
Marcia Villereccia	Fumagalli.
Overture, "Zampa"	Herold.

And on Monday, October 15th, by Mr. James Loaring, F.C.O. :—

Prelude and Fugue in E flat	Oxley.
Fantasia Alla Marcia	Burnell.
Andante con moto and Fuga	Allison.
Minuet and Trio	Hoyte.
Sketch, "The Lake"	Spark.
Postlude in C minor	Steggall.
Andantino Alla Candele	Stephens.
Gavotte Moderne	Peace.
March of King David's Army	Longhurst.

And by Mr. W. A. Roberts :—

"March of the King of Spain"	Vilbac.
Chorus of Shepherds, "Rosamunde"	Schubert.
Marche in G minor	Saint-Saëns.
Graceful Dance	Smart.
Prelude and Fugue in E minor	Bach.
Church Festival March	Best.
Overture, "King Harry Wild"	Hatton.

And by Mr. G. Hedges :—

March, "Midnight"	Williams.
Gavotte, "L'Ecolier"	Tyson.
Overture, "Guillaume Tell"	Rossini.
"Festal March"	Clarke.
Overture, "Die Zauberflöte"	Mozart.
Grand Offertoire in G	Wely.

ASTBURY CHURCH.

An organ recital was given in Astbury Church, by Mr. A. Benton, on Wednesday, October 19th. The following was the programme :—

Organ Concerto in F major	Handel.
Allegretto—Andante—Adagio—Fuga.	
Allegretto in B minor	Guilmant.
Grand Fugue in G minor	Bach.
Romanza in E flat	Haydn.
Austrian Hymn (varied)	Haydn.
Nocturne	Field.
Marche in E flat	Salomé.

The local press speaks well of the instrument and of Mr. Benson's playing.

NOTTINGHAM.

BURTON-ON-TRENT.

The following organ recitals were given in St. Paul's Institute, on Wednesday, Thursday, Friday, and Saturday, October 10th, 11th, 12th, and 13th, by Mr. A. B. Plant, Mus. Bac., Oxon. The programmes included :—

Allegretto in B flat	Lemmens.
Barcarolle	Bennett.
Sonata in C minor	Mendelssohn.
Gavotte (Modern)	Bach.
Adagio Sonata Pathetico	Beethoven.
Marche Funebre et Chant Seraphique	Guilmant.
Jupiter March, from "Sappho"	Gounod.

And on Thursday, October 11th :—

Bell Rondo	Morandi.
Larghetto from Symphony in D	Beethoven.
Gavotte	Bach.
Concerto in F	Handel.
"Carillon de Dunkerque"	Turpin.
Fugue in D minor	Bach.
March, "Naaman"	Costa.
Overture in C	Adam.
Andante from 1st Symphony	Beethoven.
Fugue in A minor	Bach.
March Religieux	Guilmant.
Elevation	Guilmant.

And on Saturday, October 13th :—

Overture, "Martha"	Flotow.
Selection, "Faust"	Gounod.
Cantilene Pastorale	Guilmant.
Concerto, "Cuckoo and Nightingale"	Handel.
Bourrée	Bach.
Improvisation on National Airs	
Overture in E minor	Morandi.

MILLSIDE.

The following is the programme of an organ recital given by Mr. George Leake, A.C.O., in Holy Trinity Church, at the evening Service on Sunday, October 14th :—

Fugue in C major	Bach.
Sonata, No. 6	Mendelssohn.
March, "Scipio"	Handel.
Air with variations, from Symphony in D	Haydn.
Chorus, "The horse and his rider" (Israel in Egypt)	Handel.
Grand Chorus alla Handel	Guilmant.

BOLTON.

An organ recital was given in the Albert Hall, by Mr. W. Mullineux, F.C.O., on Saturday, October 13th. The following was the programme :—

March, composed in honour of the painter Cornelius	Mendelssohn.
Offertoire in A major	Wely.
Air, varied, "Harmonious Church Bells"	
Morceau Capriccio "Redemption"	Gounod.
Air, from "Thy love as a Father"	Gounod.
Chorus, "Unfold ye portals everlasting"	
Adoremus, "Messe solennelle"	Rossini.
Scherzo Symphonique, Concertant	Lefébure-Wély.

BRISTOL.

An organ recital was given in the Colston Hall on Saturday, October 13th, by Mr. George Riseley. The following was the programme :—

Overture, "Semiramide"	Rossini.
Largo in D major, Op. 9	Beethoven.
Fantasia in F minor	Mozart.
Allegro—Andante—Fuga.	
Largo	Handel.
Fantasia et Fuga in G minor	Bach.
Romance	Home.
Grand March, "Alford"	

BIRKENHEAD.

Annexed is the programme of an organ recital given in Christ Church, Claughton, on Saturday, October 13th, by Mr. E. T. Driffield :—

Concert Fantasia	Best.
Melody in D	
Postlude in E flat	Silas.
Slow Movement from Quartet in G minor	Haydn.
Sonata, No. 4	Mendelssohn.
"Pastorale and Variations"—Fugue—Andante.	
Scherzo in A minor	Best.

GLASGOW.

An organ recital was given on Saturday, October 13th, in the Cathedral, by Dr. W. H. Peace. The following was the programme :—

Overture in D major	Spohr.
Andante—Allegro molto.	
Pastorale and Finale, Organ Sonata, No. 4	Mendelssohn.
Toccata and Fugue in D minor	Bach.
Chopin, "Polonaise"	Chopin.
Grand Fantasia, "The Storm"	Lemmens.
Funeral March, "On the death of a hero"	Beethoven.
Grand Chorus, "Hallelujah to the Father"	Beethoven.

NOTTINGHAM.

On October 15th, Mr. C. H. Turpin gave an organ recital upon the fine organ by Messrs. Brindley and Foster, first used at the National Eisteddfod, Cardiff, and now permanently fixed in the Albert Hall, Nottingham, a new and imposing concert-room.

BRIGHTON.

The Corporation organ recitals were given in the Dome, Royal Pavilion, by Mr. King, Mus. Bac., honorary organist, on Saturday, October 13th. The programme included :—

Fantasia in C minor, Op. 40 .... *Thiele.*
    Andante maestoso—Allegretto—Allegro con fuoco.
Toccata in F, No. 2 .... *Bach.*
Barcarolle from the 4th Pianoforte Concerto .... *Bennett.*
Grand Solemn March in E flat .... *Smart.*
Match Funebre et Chant Seraphique (Fantaisie), Op. 17. *Guilmant.*
Overture to " La Clemenza di Tito " .... *Mozart.*

AMSTERDAM.

Mr. E. M. Lott recently gave a recital on Cavaillé-Coll's large organ in the Exposition. The programme was as follows :—

Overture, " Guillaume Tell " .... *Rossini.*
Andante from 5th Symphony .... *Beethoven.*
Fanfare .... *Lott.*
Fugue in G minor .... *Bach.*
Selection, " Carmen " .... *Bizet.*
March, " Schiller " .... *Meyerbeer.*

Academical Intelligence.

UNIVERSITY OF OXFORD.

FACULTY OF MUSIC.

The following have satisfied the examiners :—

FOR THE DEGREE OF BACHELOR IN MUSIC.

F. R. GREENISH, New College, and St. Martin's, Haverfordwest.
W. G. MERRIKIN, New College, and St. Jude's, Hull.
J. H. RIGHTON, New College, and Westward Ho ! N. Devon.
L. J. ROGERS, Scholar of Balliol College.
A. H. STEVENS, B.A., Worcester College and Dovey.
W. A. WRIGLEY, New College, and Greenheys, Manchester.

FOR THE DEGREE OF DOCTOR IN MUSIC.

H. T. PRINGUER, New College, and Stoke Newington, N.
F. J. SAWYER, New College, and Brighton.
E. W. TAYLOR, New College, and Stafford.
R. M. WINN, New College, and Harborne, Birmingham.

Foreign Musical Intelligence.

Suppé's " Juanita " is shortly to be produced in Brussels.

The Symphony Concerts at Angers have recommenced under M. Gustave Lelong.

A new lady singer in Paris, Mdlle. Adler, a very young artist, is attracting attention and preparing for the opera.

M. Vidal's new prize Cantata " Le Gladiateur " has been executed in Paris at the annual public séance of the Institut.

A new edition of M. Lussy's masterly work " Le Rythme Musical " is out. The book will be presently noticed.

M. Pasdeloup's concerts have recommenced. Schumann's Symphony in C is included in Sunday's programme.

The Society of the Friends of Music at Vienna have issued a spirited prospectus. Their concerts are conducted by M. Gericke.

On Sunday, there was to be a grand concert in the Trocadéro. M. Guilmant was the organist. The orchestra was complete, and the choir consisted of 200 voices.

Meyerbeer's " Dinorah " has been recently well played at its first home, the Opéra Comique, Paris, under the original title " Le Pardon de Ploërmel." Six of the principals were educated at the Conservatoire, Paris.

Passing Events.

After Evensong on Sunday next at St. Margaret Pattens, there will be given a selection of sacred music under the direction of Mr. Stedman.

Bizet's " Carmen," with Mdme. Marie Roze and the Carl Rosa Company, has created an enormous success in Bristol. People are nightly turned away from the doors of the theatre.

Dr. Stainer's " St. Mary Magdalen " will be given at the Bow and Bromley Institute, with Mr. W. G. McNaught, the composer, taking the organ, on Oct. 30th. There will be a complete and most efficient orchestra.

The Metropolitan Opera House in New York is to be opened on the 22nd by a performance of " Faust ". The staff of principals is a strong one ; the orchestra will consist of 60 players, and the chorus of 80 singers.

The Manchester Athenæum Society opened their seventeenth season on Oct. 15th, under the very able direction of Dr. H. Hiles. The chief feature of the programme was Gade's cantata " The Erl-King's Maiden."

A lecture entitled " Why learn to Sing ? " by Anthony Roskilly, Esq., has been given in connection with the new singing classes at St. James-the-Less, Victoria Park. A selection of music was performed during the entertainment.

There is a movement, inaugurated by Sir A. Sullivan, to erect in some suitable locality a memorial of some kind to the late Sir John Goss. To this end, a preliminary meeting will be held at the College of Organists on Monday next, at 5.30.

Mr. F. W. Chanot, jun., will publish early this month, his catalogue of new music for the violin. The music plates are each numbered uniformly with the numbers in the catalogue, so that ordering new copies will be a certain and easy process.

The *Leeds Daily News* expresses a regret that no organ solo was included in the scheme of the Festival. Dr. Spark or Mr. W. Parratt, or both gentlemen, might surely have been induced to play some organ work with orchestral accompaniment.

On Wednesday, Oct. 10th, a Grand Evening Concert was given at the Institute, Chelmsford. The artists were, Mdme. Clara West, Mrs. Sydney Barnby, Mr. H. Parkin, Mr. Lovett King, and Mr. H. Preston. The audience was numerous and appreciative.

The advertisement of a soprano French horn with a chromatic compass of 5 octaves is the last exposition of mechanical ingenuity in the invention of musical instruments. Applications concerning this novelty are to be made to E. G. Heidrich, at Breslau, Germany.

At Mr. Stedman's concert, at the Birkbeck Institution on Wednesday next, the programme will be rendered by the following admirable list of artists : Miss Carlotta Elliott, Miss Polak, Miss Ellen Marchant, Mr. Arthur Oswald, M. Victor Buziau, with Mr. Stedman, and his popular choir boys.

No one appeared the other day in support of the application by the Royal Academy of Music for its licence. Several of the magistrates, however, considered that this must be due to some mistake or other. On the motion of Mr. Galsworthy, the standing orders were suspended to meet the case, and the licence was renewed.

A Vocal and Instrumental Concert was given in the Town Hall, Newbury, on Tuesday evening, Oct. 9th, in connexion with the Newbury Literary and Scientific Institution. The vocalists were Mdme. Clara West, Miss C. Wollaston, Mr. H. Parkin, and Mr. H. Prenton. Solo violinist, the Chevalier Niedzielski, leader and conductor, Mr. Lovett King. There was a large and appreciative audience.

On Wednesday, the 17th inst., an Evensong with instrumental accompaniment was held as part of the Harvest Festival at Allhallows Church, Southwark. The anthem was Barnby's " O Lord, how manifold," and the " Te Deum," Dykes in F. The service was well rendered by the choir, conducted by Mr. C. J. Viner, organist of St. John's, Red Lion-square, and the accompanists, soli and voluntaries were admirably played by Mr. F. J. Perry, organist and choir-master of the church.

Mr. James Peck; to whose courtesy those who frequented the old Sacred Harmonic Concerts were for many years indebted, solicits employment as a steward at concerts, or a copyist of music. It seems scandalous that the members of the Society have pocketed money earned by their predecessors, and have turned both the officers out into the world.—*Figaro.*

The prospectus of the Ealing Choral Association has been issued for the coming season, and includes some interesting and unfamiliar works, amongst which may be mentioned the Requiem for "Mignon" of Schumann, the "Schicksalslied" of Brahms, and Raff's "Morning Song." The list of artists includes Miss Thudichum, Mr. Walter Clifford and others, whilst Mr. Ralph leads the band, which with the chorus, numbers about 150. Mr. Ernest Ford, is the able conductor.

The Exposition and Music Hall Building, now erecting in St. Louis, will cover the entire square bounded by Olive, Thirteenth, St. Charles and Fourteenth Streets, heretofore occupied by the Missouri Park. The extreme dimensions will be three hundred and twelve by four hundred and eighty feet. The main front will be on Olive-street, and the great Exposition Hall will run east and west through the middle of the block, from Thirteenth to Fourteenth Streets. The Music Hall will be on the St. Charles-street side, away from noise and disturbances. The floorage of the building is over nine acres, of which over one-half is devoted to Exposition purposes. All of the numerous departments of an Exposition have been carefully looked after, not excepting the Art and Floral Departments. The Music Hall has two grand vestibule approaches. These are wide corridors, and capable of seating four thousand persons, and a stage capable of accommodating one thousand choristers and grand organ.

The Querist.

QUERY.

ANTHEMS.—Can any reader of the *Musical Standard* inform me who publishes the following anthems, and the prices of each: "Thou judge of quick and dead" (Wesley), and "Behold, how good and pleasant" (Smart).—J. I. F.

ANCIENT MARINER.—Would any Musical Society lend, or on very low terms, or sell at a very low price, twenty-five, or even as many as fifty, vocal scores of Barnett's "Ancient Mariner?" Anyone willing to do this will benefit greatly a music loving body of singers, who are, and have been for sometime, debarred from taking the work in hand, owing to the copies being so dear in price.—CONDUCTOR.

ORGAN PLAYING.—What is considered the "broad" style of organ playing? We often read of recital givers displaying a broad, vigorous style. Is it intended to mean a "coarse" and vulgar style, for this is the meaning of the word "broad."—IRISH ORGANIST.

Perhaps the critics, now and then, use the expression without attaching the full dictionary meaning to the words, and at other times employ the phrase as their way of denoting an excess of noise and unmeaning vigour.—ED. *Mus. Stand.*

REPLY.

ADAGIO.—The pronunciation of "Weber" depends according to as *v*, and the first *e* as a broad *a*, with the accent on that syllable, thus: "Vaben." (My idea of the genius of the English language is to assimilate the pronunciation of foreign words to its own methods; still, I venture to think we should retain the original pronunciation as far as possible.—ED. *Mus. Stand.*

Service Lists.

TWENTY-SECOND SUNDAY AFTER TRINITY.
OCTOBER 21st.

London.

ST. PAUL'S CATHEDRAL.—Morn.: Service, Te Deum and Benedictus, Stanford in B flat; Introit, "Word of God incarnate, No. 572 (Gounod); Holy Communion, Jekyll in C. Even.: Service, Magnificat and Nunc Dimittis, Stanford in A; Anthem, O come let us worship, In His hands, For his is the sea (Mendelssohn).

TEMPLE CHURCH.—Morn.: Service, Te Deum Laudamus and Jubilate Deo, Nares in F; Apostles' Creed, Harmonized Monotone; Anthem, I will love Thee (Clarke). Even.: Service, Magnificat and Nunc Dimittis, Nares in F; Apostles' Creed, Harmonized Monotone; Anthem, Ascribe unto the Lord (Travers).

FOUNDLING CHAPEL.—Morn.: Service, Sullivan in D; Anthem, Come unto him (Gounod). Aft.: Children's Service.

ALL SAINTS', MARGARET STREET.—Morn.: Service, Te Deum, Goss in A; Benedictus, Smith in E flat; Holy Communion, Standford in F; Benedictus and Agnus, Niedermeyer; Offertory Anthem, Praise thou the Lord (Mendelssohn). Even.: Service, Smart, in F; Anthem, The wilderness (Wesley).

CHRIST CHURCH, CLAPHAM.—Morn.: Service, Te Deum, Plainsong; Kyrie and Credo, Tours in A; Offertory Anthem, O praise God in His Holiness (Weldon); Sanctus (Tours); Benedictus, and Agnus Dei, Eyre in A flat; Communion, Jesu, Word of God incarnate (Mozart); Gloria in excelsis (Tours). Even.: Service, Magnificat and Nunc Dimittis, Tours in F; Anthem, The Lord is my Shepherd (Macfarren).

HOLY TRINITY, GRAY'S INN ROAD.—Morn.: Service, Te Deum, Chanted; Jubilate (Deil); Nicene Creed, (Percival). Even.: Service, Magnificat, Louis in F; Nunc Dimittis, Chanted; Anthem, I will lift up mine eyes (Walmisley).

HOLY TRINITY, TULSE HILL.—Morn.: Service, Chant. Even.: Service, Magnificat and Nunc Dimittis, Gadsby in C; Anthem, O Thou each living soul, and Achieved in the glorious work (Haydn).

ST. GEORGE'S, HANOVER SQUARE.—Morn.: Service, Stainer in C; Kyrie, Pinney in G; Offertory Sentences (Tours). Even.: Service, Barnett in F; Anthem, O give thanks (Sydenham).

ST. JAMES'S PRIVATE EPISCOPAL CHAPEL, SOUTHWARK.—Morn.: Service, Introit, and magnify (They (Palestrina); Communion Service, Schubert in G. Even.: Service, Attwood in F; Anthem, Agnus Dei (Barthovan).

ST. MARY'S, BERKELEY SQUARE.—Morn.: Service, Steggall in A; Kyrie, Pinney in F; Nunc Dimittis in F; Even.: Service, Wesley in E; Anthem, O Lord, How manifold (Barnby).

ST. MARGARET PATTENS, ROOD LANE, FENCHURCH STREET.—Morn.: Service, Te Deum and Jubilate, Sullivan in D; Communion Service, Offertory, Anthem, O Thou each living soul (Haydn); Kyrie, Credo, Sanctus, Benedictus, Agnus Dei, and Gloria, Weber in E flat. Even.: Service, Magnificat and Nunc Dimittis, Gadsby in C; after the Service, a selection of sacred music.

ST. MARY BOLTONS, WEST BROMPTON, S.W.—Morn.: Service, Te Deum, Smart in F; Benedictus, Chant; Anthem, God said, Behold I have given you every herb (Macfarren); Holy Communion, Kyrie, Credo, Sanctus, Offertory, and Gloria in excelsis, Stainer in E flat; Benedictus and Agnus Dei, Eyre in E flat. Even.: Service, Magnificat and Nunc Dimittis, Gadsby in G; Anthem, Ye shall dwell in the land (Stainer); at conclusion of Service, Solemn Te Deum (Chants).

ST. MAGNUS, LONDON BRIDGE.—Morn.: Service, Opening Anthem, The sacrifices of God (Calkin); Te Deum and Jubilate, Turle in D; Kyrie (Walmisley). Even.: Service, Magnificat and Nunc Dimittis, Turle in D; Anthem, I was glad (Havergal).

ST. PAUL'S, AVENUE ROAD, SOUTH HAMPSTEAD.—Morn.: Service, Te Deum, Calkin in B flat; Benedictus, Calkin in B flat; I will magnify Thee (Goss). To Thee, O Lord, our hearts we raise (Gerrard); Kyrie, Stainer in E flat, No. 2; Offertory, Stainer; Credo, Sanctus, and Gloria in excelsis, Stainer in B flat. Even.: Service, Magnificat and Nunc Dimittis, Gounod in D; Anthem, Ye shall dwell in the land (Stainer); Te Deum, Hopkins in F; Processional, Now thank we all our God (Mendelssohn).

ST. PAUL'S, BOW COMMON, E.—Morn.: Service, Te Deum and Benedictus, Chants; Holy Communion, Kyrie, Credo, Sanctus, Benedictus, Agnus Dei and Gloria in excelsis, Eyre in E flat; Offertory (Stainer). Even.: Service, Magnificat and Nunc Dimittis, Hopkins in F; Anthem (unaccompanied), I wrestle and pray (Bach).

ST. PETER'S, EATON SQUARE.—Morn.: Service, Te Deum, Goss in A. Even.: Service, Garrett in F; Anthem, Hopkins in F; Anthem, I will wash my hands in innocency (Hopkins).

ST. PETER'S, VERE STREET, W.—Even.: Service, Magnificat and Nunc Dimittis, Garrett in F; Anthem, Ye shall dwell in the land (Stainer).

ST. AUGUSTINE AND ST. FAITH, WATLING STREET (South).—Morn.: Service, Selby in A; Introit, Be merciful unto me (South); Communion Service, Martin in C. Even.: Service, Martin in C; Anthem, Ho! every one that thirsteth (Martin).

ST. SAVIOUR'S, HOXTON.—Morn.: Service, Te Deum, Gadsby in E flat; Holy Communion; Kyrie, Credo, Sursum Corda, Sanctus, and Gloria in excelsis, Smart in F. Even.: Service, Magnificat and Nunc Dimittis, Smart in G; Anthem, O praise the Lord (Goss).

ST. SEPULCHRE'S, HOLBORN.—Morn.: Service, Smart in F; Credo, Introit in B flat. Even.: Service, Cooke in G; Anthem, As pants the hart (Spohr).

Country.

ST. ASAPH CATHEDRAL. — Morn.: Service, Atkins in C; Anthem, How lovely are the messengers (Mendelssohn). Even. Service, The Litany; Anthem, Ye shall dwell in the land (Stainer).

ASHBOURNE CHURCH, DERBYSHIRE. — Morn.: Service, Steggall in G; Kyrie, Credo and Gloria, Byrie in E flat. Even. Service, Stainer in A; Anthem, Thou earth, waft sweet incense (Spohr).

BEDDINGTON CHURCH, SURREY.—Morn.: Service, Tours in F; Communion Service, Smee in E. Even.: Service Stainer; Anthem, O clap your hands together all ye people (Stainer).

BELFAST (ST. GEORGE'S). — Morn.: Service, Te Deum Woodward in E flat; Jubilate, Garrett in F; Apostles' Creed, Harmonized Monotone; Anthem, God said, behold I have given you (Macfarren); Offertory, Let your light (Monk). Even. Service, Magnificat and Nunc Dimittis, Arnold in A; Apostles' Creed, Harmonized Monotone; Anthem, I will give thanks (Barnby); Hymn, The strain upraise (Sullivan).

BIRMINGHAM (S. ALBAN THE MARTYR).—Morn.: Service, Te Deum, Boyce in C; Benedictus, Steggall in G; Holy Communion, Dykes in F. Evensong, Magnificat and Nunc Dimittis, Barnby in E.

BIRMINGHAM (ST. CYPRIAN'S, HAY MILLS).—Morn.: Service, Nares in C; Anthem, The Lord is my Shepherd (Kent). Even.: Service, Ebdor in C; Anthem, Plead Thou my cause (Mozart).

BRISTOL CATHEDRAL.— Morn.: Service, Hopkins in F. Even.: Service, Hopkins in F; Anthem, And God said (Haydn).

CARLISLE CATHEDRAL.—Morn.: Service, Stewart in G; Introit, Blessed be the Lord (Ouseley); Kyrie and Creed, Best in G. Even.: Service, Prout in F; Anthem, Teach me, O Lord (Attwood).

CANTERBURY CATHEDRAL.—Morn.: Service, Hopkins in G; Te Deum, Hake in G; Jubilate, Give peace in our time (Callcott); Communion, Elvey in E flat. Even. Service, Stainer in E; Anthem, O rest in the Lord (Mendelssohn).

DONCASTER (PARISH CHURCH).—Morn.: Service, Boyce in A; Introit, rend your heart (Calkin); Kyrie and Creed (Hopkins). Even.: Service, Ebdor in C; Anthem, I was glad (Purcell).

DUBLIN, ST. PATRICK'S (NATIONAL) CATHEDRAL.—Morn.: Service, Te Deum, Haydn in C; Jubilate, Smart in F; Holy Communion, Kyrie, Creed, and Sanctus, Smart in F; Anthem, And God saw everything that He had made (Haydn). Even.: Service, Magnificat and Nunc Dimittis, Stainer in B flat; Anthem, All men, all things (Mendelssohn), and In the beginning (Haydn), and The heavens are telling (Stevenson).

EDINBURGH (ST. JOHN'S).—Aft.: Service, Anthem, Fear not, O land (Goss). Even.: Service, Anthem, The Lord is loving (Garrett).

ELY CATHEDRAL.—Morn.: Service, Leslie in D; Kyrie Credo and Gloria, Richardson in F; Anthem, O give thanks (Rea). Even.: Service, Colborne in D; Anthem, Fear not, O land (Goss).

GLOUCESTER CATHEDRAL.—Morn.: Service, Hopkins in A; Kyrie and Creed, Stainer in A; Anthem, Holy, holy (Spohr). Aft.: Service, Hopkins in A; Anthem, Sing ye praise (Mendelssohn).

HARROGATE (ST. PETER'S CHURCH).—Morn.: Service, Te Deum, Harvey in G; Benedictus, Chant; Anthem, Come unto me (Smith); Kyrie and Credo, Wesley in E. Even.: Service, Magnificat and Nunc Dimittis, Turle in D; Anthem, The Lord is loving (Garrett).

LEEDS PARISH CHURCH.—Morn.: Service, Gounod in D; Anthem, His salvation is nigh (Bennett); Introit, Thou visitest the earth (Greene); Kyrie and Credo, Garrett in D. Even.: Service, Stainer in A; Anthem, Sing, O heavens (Sullivan).

LINLITHGOW ABBEY, W.B.—Morn.: Service, Anthem, Be merciful comfort, O Lord (Crotch). Even.: Service, Anthem, How lovely are Thy dwellings (Spohr).

LIVERPOOL CATHEDRAL.—Aft.: Service, Magnificat and Nunc Dimittis, Smart in G; Anthem, Lead, kindly light (Stainer).

MANCHESTER CATHEDRAL.—Morn.: Service, Full Service, Stanford in B flat; Anthem, My song shall be of mercy (Hiles). Aft.: Service, Stanford in B flat; Anthem, By Babylon's wave (Gounod).

MANCHESTER (ST. BENEDICT'S).—Morn.: Service, Te Deum Dykes in F; Kyrie, Credo, Sanctus, Benedictus and Gloria in excelsis, Thorne in G; Agnus, Dei, Mind in F. Even.: Service, Magnificat and Nunc Dimittis, Tours in F.

MANCHESTER (ST. JOHN BAPTIST, HULME).—Morn.: Service, Te Deum and Benedictus (Gregorian); Kyrie, Credo, Sanctus, Benedictus and Agnus Dei (Gounod); Gloria in excelsis, Tours in F. Even.: Service, Magnificat and Nunc Dimittis, Wesley in F.

NEWINGTON (ST. MATTHEW'S).—Morn.: Service, Anthem, The Lord is loving unto every man (Garrett). Even.: Service Magnificat and Nunc Dimittis, Smart in B flat; Anthem, The Wilderness (Wesley).

ROCHESTER CATHEDRAL. — Morn.: Service, Smart in F; Anthem, O Lord we trust (Handel). Even.: Service, Smart in F; Anthem, They that go down (Attwood).

SALISBURY CATHEDRAL.—Morn.: Service, Wesley in E; Offertory (Redhead). Aft.: Service, Wesley in F.; Anthem, Hear my crying (Hummel).

SHEFFIELD PARISH CHURCH.—Morn.: Service, Kyrie Elvey in A. Even.: Service, Cantate Domino and Deus Misereatur, Trimnell in E flat; Anthem, Blessed are they that dwell in Thy house (Tours).

SHERBORNE ABBEY. — Morn.: Service, Te Deum and Jubilate, Chants; Kyrie, Howells in G; Offertories (Barnby). Even.: Service, Anthem, O Lord, How manifold (Barnby).

SOUTHAMPTON (ST. MARY'S CHURCH).—Morn.: Service, Te Deum and Jubilate, Whitfeld in E; Holy Communion, Introit, With hearts renewed; Service, Monk in C; Offertory, Charge them (Barnby); Paternoster (Field). Even.: Service, Magnificat and Nunc Dimittis, Field in D.

WINCHESTER CATHEDRAL.—Morn.: Service, Goss in A; Creed, Banks in G. Even.: Service, Tours in F; Anthem, The Lord is my Shepherd (Arnold).

WELLS CATHEDRAL.—Morn.: Service, Banks in G (through-out; Introit, O send out Thy light (Macfarren). Even.: Service, Attwood in F; Anthem, Plead Thou my cause (Mozart).

WOLVERHAMPTON (ST. PETER'S COLLEGIATE CHURCH).—Morn.: Service, Venite, Chant, Barnby in E; Te Deum, Stainer in E flat; Benedictus Chant, Garrett in G; Communion Service, Stainer in E flat. Even.: Service, Magnificat Chant, Wesley in G; Nunc Dimittis, Gilbert in G; Anthem Blessed are the men (? Elijah).

WORCESTER CATHEDRAL. — Morn.: Service, Smart in F; Anthem, Cast Thy burden (Mendelssohn). Even.: Service, Smart in F; Anthem, O where shall wisdom (Boyce).

*** Post-cards must be sent to the Editor, 6, Argyle Square, W.C., by Wednesday. Lists are frequently omitted in consequence of not being received in time.

NEWSPAPERS sent should have *distinct marks* opposite to the matter to which attention is required.

Printed for the Proprietor by BOWDEN, HUDSON & CO., at 23, Red Lion Street, Holborn, London, W.C.; and Published by WILLIAM REEVES, at the Office, 185 Fleet Street, E.C. West End Agents:—WEEKES & CO., 14, Hanover Street, Regent Street, W. Subscriptions and Advertisements are received either by the Publisher or West End Agents.—*Communications for the EDITOR are to be forwarded to his Private Address, 6, Argyle Square, W.C.*
SATURDAY, OCTOBER 20, 1883.—*Entered at the General Post Office as a Newspaper.*

The Musical Standard
A Newspaper for Musicians
Professional and Amateur

No. 1004. VOL. XXV. FOURTH SERIES. SATURDAY, OCTOBER 27, 1883. WEEKLY; PRICE 3D.

THE PROPOSED GOSS MEMORIAL.

A very influential meeting in support of the erection of some suitable monument to the memory of Sir John Goss was held at the College of Organists last Monday.

The proceedings opened by the Hon. Secretary of the College suggesting that the only preliminary course before the meeting would seem to be that of inviting the illustrious pupil and friend of the departed musician (Sir Arthur Sullivan) to preside.

This was unanimously agreed to.

Sir ARTHUR SULLIVAN, who was warmly greeted, claimed the indulgence of the meeting, as he was suffering from a throat attack, which made speaking a matter of some difficulty and pain. He pointed out, in well-chosen words, the reputation of the departed great ecclesiastical composer, saying that, like the famous architect of the metropolitan cathedral in which Sir John Goss passed most of his professional life, the musician could claim to have it said of his works, *Si Monumentum quæris, circumspice,* or rather *audi.* Sir Arthur dwelt upon the pure character of Goss's Church music, and said that some permanent memorial was called for whereby to express the esteem and admiration of his contemporaries, pupils, and fellow-workers. He therefore moved—

That, in the opinion of this meeting, it is desirable that the long and beneficial services rendered to music in this country by the late Sir John Goss, the distinguished Church composer, and the high esteem and regard in which he was uniformly held, should be publicly expressed by the erection of some suitable Memorial in St. Paul's Cathedral, where he was organist for a period of 34 years.

And he made the observation that large sums were not wanted ; it was chiefly desirable that the many should be represented by small amounts.

The Chairman's proposal was seconded by Dr. J. F. BRIDGE very heartily.

This resolution was carried unanimously.

Sir G. A. MACFARREN moved.—

That a Committee, consisting of the following gentlemen, with power to add to their number, be forthwith nominated, for the purpose of carrying out this design.

He recalled, in expressive words, his personal connection with Sir John Goss, and felt all would act with loving esteem to forward the proposal to so perpetuate the memory of one whose services to the art, and sweet character, so fully called for due honour. He felt also that it was important that the habitual attendants and strangers visiting St. Paul's should see a memorial to Goss. Sir G. A. Macfarren referred to the presentation of the Cambridge Doctorship to Sir J. Goss and Sir A. Sullivan.

The resolution was seconded by Mr. J. BARNBY, and unanimously carried.

Mr. C. E. STEPHENS moved—

That Subscriptions be invited to defray the cost of the memorial and incidental charges.

This was seconded by Mr. H. LITTLETON (Novello and Co.), and carried.

Mr. E. H. TURPIN proposed—

That Mr. W. H. Cummings be requested to act as hon. treasurer of the fund, and Mr. T. L. Southgate to undertake the duties of hon. secretary connected with the matter.

This proposal was seconded by Dr. E. J. HOPKINS, and carried forthwith unanimously.

The Rev. T. HELMORE, in proposing a vote of thanks to the Council of the College of Organists for the use of the room, &c., dwelt upon the character of Sir John Goss, and laid stress upon his prayerful and earnest attitude as a Church composer.

Mr. W. H. CUMMINGS, in seconding this vote of thanks, also recalled characteristics of the departed composer. In his remarks, he said he thought that a suitable monument in the National Cathedral would be as an example to choir boys, showing them a high standard to aim at.

Dr. J. STAINER proposed a vote of thanks to Sir Arthur Sullivan for occupying the chair. The speaker, in his remarks, dwelt also upon the career of the amiable, good man the meeting was pledged to do honour to. He

recalled his personal knowledge of Sir John Goss from the time he (the speaker) was a chorister of seven years of age. He thought Sir John Goss had hardly a fault, save that he had not enough rough metal in his constitution to fully assert himself in the world. His great tenderness of character the speaker thought to be most attractive and endearing.

Dr. E. J. HOPKINS seconded the vote of thanks to the Chairman.

Sir A. S. SULLIVAN, in replying, said he felt grateful for the kind words uttered. He felt with gratitude that he had a right to call himself Sir John Goss's favourite pupil. So thoughtfully and tenderly did Sir John Goss treat him, that he could recall many lessons being given in the evening, outside the usual routine of student life. Sir A. Sullivan also pointed out that the departed composer and organist was a man of most liberal ideas, possessed of great artistic knowledge, and ahead of most of his compeers in his appreciation of new works. In conclusion, he expressed the great pleasure he had had in presiding over a meeting of so distinguished and representative a character.

The following are the names of the Committee, having power to add to their number:—

Sir Arthur Sullivan.	E. H. Turpin.
Sir George Macfarren.	H. Gadsby.
Sir Robert P. Stewart.	Dr. C. J. Frost.
Sir George T. Elvey.	C. J. Jekyll.
Dr. J. Stainer.	W. A. Barrett.
Dr. J. F. Bridge.	W. C. MacNaught.
Dr. E. J. Hopkins.	J. B. Calkin.
Dr. F. E. Gladstone.	C. H. Lloyd.
Dr. G. G. Verrinder.	H. Littleton.
Dr. W. H. Monk.	Albert Lowe.
J. Barnby.	C. Warwick Jordan.
E. Prout.	Dr. H. T. Pringner.
E. H. Cowen.	A. H. Mann.
G. A. Osborne.	Dr. H. Hiles.
C. E. Stephens.	W. H. Gladstone, M.P.
W. H. Cummings.	M. E. Wesley.
H. C. Banister.	A. Randegger.
Dr. C. Villiers Stanford.	H. Weist Hill.
J. Higgs.	Rev. H. G. Bonavia Hunt.
Dr. C. Steggall.	F. Walker.
C. King Hall.	J. Spencer Curwen.
W. Parratt.	J. F. Barnett.
Dr. J. Bradford.	E. Faning.

A GOSS REMINISCENCE.

At the meeting held at the rooms of the College of Organists on Monday last, to consider the steps to be taken for placing a tablet in St. Paul's Cathedral to the memory of the late esteemed organist and composer Sir John Goss, the chairman, Sir Arthur Sullivan, spoke in glowing but by no means too warm terms of the affectionate regard in which that good man was held equally by his *cotemporaries* and by his *juniors* and pupils.

To know whether this feeling was extended to him throughout life, many would doubtless be interested to learn how he stood in his comparatively early days in the opinion of his *seniors ;* and to the great esteem in which he was universally held, I, as a youthful chorister, was a witness on numerous occasions.

For some years,—in 1830 and for some time before and after that date,—I, as a Chapel Royal boy, attended the meetings of the Noblemen and Gentlemen's Catch Club, the Concentores Society, the Glee Club, the Madrigal Society, &c., for the purpose of singing the treble part of any music that might be " called," having a part for that voice. At these meetings Mr. Goss was a frequent attendant ; and I well remember the cordial manner in which his unobtrusive entry into the room was invariably welcomed by such men as Sir George Smart, Attwood, Bellamy, Linley, Knyvett, Sale, Sir John Rogers, Cartwright, and any other influential musicians, singers, or patrons of the musical art who might be present.

On one of these occasions Mr. Goss's quiet humour nearly brought the performance of a glee to an abrupt termination. A "serious" glee had been "called,"—one of Spofforth's,—the sloping desk supporting the copy had been placed before Mr. Goss who was to sing one of the tenor parts, and the other singers stood around him. When they had sung the music about half way through, a tiny spider let itself down from the ceiling on to the book and commenced performing a series of extraordinary evolutions. Goss following the little creature with his little finger as it run its course up and down the score, disturbed the gravity of his colleagues quite sufficiently. Presently he had a bar's rest, when, instead of observing the customary silence, he said in a voice sufficiently loud to be heard by those immediately around him, " The glee we are singing is a Spofforth, but this spider evidently takes it for *a Webbe*." This was quite too much for his colleagues, who, from that point to the end, sang the " serious " glee with grinning faces and tittering voices.

What followed was equally amusing. The ever sensitive Mr. Goss, finding that his witticism had caused a much greater departure in deportment and manner from that which he thought should occur when singing a serious glee, generously volunteered to apologise to his colleagues all round, which offer of course was received with a shout, and simply led up to further pleasantries.

E. J. HOPKINS.

THE LATE CHARLES S. PACKER.

The *Musical Standard* of September 29th announced, with regret, the death of Mr. C. S. Packer, for many years organist of St. Mary's, Reading. The passing away of one who under happier circumstances would doubtless have done even more for art than he actually accomplished, is worthy of more notice than has been accorded him. In the hope that some friend may give us some particulars of his career (his name appears in none of our Dictionaries, English or Foreign), I send a few extracts from my note books.

" Charles S. Packer was educated at the Royal Academy of Music, and made his mark at a pupil's concert given at the Hanover Square Rooms, December 20th, 1827, when a *Scena* " Basta ! Basta ! " from Metastasio's " Morte d'Abelle " was produced. This was described as full of talent and judgment, the accompaniments of the most masterly kind, and the harmonies, in many instances, absolutely new and highly effective. The *Harmonicon* (July, 1828), concludes a highly eulogistic review with these words : ' Let us indulge a hope that some munificent patron, some musical Mecænas, will take by the hand a youth who holds out the fairest promise of becoming, and that in a short time, an ornament to his art and to his country. Let him be snatched from the impending slavery of teaching—a drudgery which impairs the imaginative faculty, damps that noble ambition which alone leads to excellence, and in most cases finally extinguishes every spark of genius."

Three years later, the same journal, in reviewing another work, *Scena ed tria* " Crudo Ciel," refers to the former notice, and expresses regret that no singer had since brought forward that work, and goes on to remark the general neglect of native genius. I have no further memoranda available, but some one will, I trust, furnish the readers of the *Musical Standard* with some further particulars of an English artist whose name ought not entirely to perish from memory.

STEPHEN S. STRATTON.

SACRED MUSIC IN THE ROMAN CHURCH.

The *Observatore Cattolico* of Milan publishes the following article, which will be found interesting as bearing on the question of Gregorian music and on recent decisions of the Sacred Congregations of Rites concerning the Roman Church.

" To prevent all doubts as to the bearing of the Decree of April 10th, 1883, relating to the authority of the Edition of the Roman Chant, as printed by Pustet of Ratisbon and approved of by the Sacred Congregation of Rites, we think it well to reproduce the following documents,

" The first is an article published in the Review of Liturgical Music, entitled *Musica Sacra*, printed at Milan, as the official organ of the Italian General Association of S. Cecilia. The following is the article :—

" ' We are requested to throw light upon, and to explain some words of the Decree of the Sacred Congregation of Rites.

" ' This is our opinion on the subject.

" ' Firstly, That the disapproval, expressed in the above Decree, is limited to certain of the wishes expressed, and does not apply to all indiscriminately.

" ' Secondly, That the Decree is not unfavourable to the study, past or future, of ancient liturgical music.

" ' Thirdly, That the Decree does not in the least condemn the method of executing Plain Chant according to the method of Guido d'Arezzo.

" ' Fourthly, That the Decree does not forbid the publication, and distribution of new editions, whether already made or to be made in the future, for the purpose of facilitating the historical or archæological study of Plain Chant.

" ' Another very important question which has been submitted to us concerns the practical use which may now be made of the Original Chants of S. Gregory, *i.e.*, whether by the Decree it is intended to forbid it altogether for liturgical purpose, or to allow or tolerate it in the same way as the music of Palestrina ; the use of the organ and of orchestral music by composers not only modern but even unknown, is allowed, even when much longer than the original liturgical music. Certainly the chant need not fear comparison with the above-named music, either for the beauty or fitness of its liturgical melody. We therefore think there is no reason why the Holy See (after having examined and ascertained that it is genuine) should not, if it saw fit under special circumstances, allow the use of this music in the Divine offices, especially as we suppose it would be accompanied by the organ. It seems to us that it would be injurious to the Holy See to imagine that it intended to exclude entirely from Divine worship the more ornate kind of plain chant which was used with so much edification throughout the Church during so many centuries, and from which modern plain chant has come, having been simplified for the sake of convenience.'

" The above article had the approval of the Cardinal Prefect of the Sacred Congregation of Rites, as may be gathered from the following letter :—

" ' I congratulate you on the articles published in the *Bulletin Officiel* for May and June. In this Decree, which you considered it your duty to publish, the Sacred Congregation has entirely confirmed its former views on the subject of plain chant.

" ' Continue confidently the work which you have begun for the reformation of Church music, for it is truly desirable. As I said to you on a former occasion, there are two ways of doing this, viz., the study of Palestrina's music, so eminently ecclesiastical, and of music with an accompaniment for the organ or orchestra, after the manner of the compositions of the great masters of the seventeenth and eighteenth centuries. There are few places where Palestrina's music is properly executed ; and as far as I know, it can best be heard in the Papal Chapel and in Ratisbon Cathedral. The rareness with which it is heard may be attributed to the heavy expenses which its execution entails and the want of the necessary trained voices. To escape this last difficulty it would be advisable to bring up young men carefully, as Palestrina did in his day. We have an example of this in the Gregorian capella *All' Anima*, which you helped to found, and where carefully taught youths execute Palestrina's sublime compositions with great effect.

" ' But the Italian ear, too much accustomed to the sounds of the organ, feels no pleasure in the beautiful harmonies of Palestrina when unaccompanied by instrumental music, whilst to the true lover of music the effect is wonderful. The ordinary run of hearers, unacquainted with the art, think that these beautiful compositions—echoes of the melodies of Paradise—are only a confusion of voices. Hence, if Palestrina's music were much used, there would be a danger that the faithful, generally unable to appreciate what is sublime, would not attend services where music was used which would not be fortunate enough to please them. But when the organ is used, the music is more pleasing as a rule, and becomes almost enchanting when it is accompanied by other instruments. This kind of music was customary among the Jews, as the pages of the Old Testament bear witness ; and the Psalms were sung in the Temple to the accompaniment of instruments.

" ' The compositions of Haydn, and the Masses of Mozart, of Cherubini, and of others, are choice and serious compositions, and are far from being unbecoming to the holiness of the Church.

" ' To avoid contradictions, we ought to abstain from blaming composers, but ought to invite them courteously to imitate the style of the masterpieces we possess. I am convinced that with good management and the periodical publishing of the music of Palestrina with organ accompaniment, the desired reform would gradually take place.

" ' In the above sense, I am ready to give your plans the support you think necessary, &c.

" ' D. CARD. BARTOLINI.

" ' Rome, 15th July, 1883.

" ' To M. le Professeur, Guerrino Amelli,
" ' Vice-Librarian of the Ambrosian Library, Milan.' "

The above liberal letter shows a healthy feeling against the too narrow tendency on all sides to check the progress of ecclesiastical music.

Musical Intelligence.

CRYSTAL PALACE CONCERTS.

PROGRAMME.

Overture, "The Magic Flute" .... Mozart.
Symphony, No. 10, in F minor, Op. 213, "Zur Herbst-
　zeit" (Autumn) .... Raff.
　　Impressions and Feelings—Dance of Phantoms—
　　Elegy—The Hunt. (First time in England).
Recit. and Air, "Lend me your aid" .... Gounod.
　　　Mr. Maas.
Concerto for Pianoforte and Orchestra, No. 5, in E flat　Beethoven.
　　Madame Helen Hopekirk.
　　(Her last appearance before her departure for America).
Walther's prize song, "Die Meistersinger" .... Wagner.
　　　Mr. Maas.
Introduction to the Third Act, Dance of Apprentices,
　　Procession of the Mastersingers ("Die Meister-
　　singer") .... Wagner.
　　　Conductor　-　-　AUGUST MANNS.

On Saturday last the leading feature in the programme was Raff's "Autumn" symphony. As is well known, the ideas of each of the four seasons have been embodied by him in a series of four symphonies, of which the three first are now already known to us, the fourth, "Winter," still remaining to be performed. The "Autumn" symphony, of which we now speak, is divided into four movements, and a heading at the top makes known to us the ideas which it is intended to depict in each of these. An analogy is to be discerned between these ideas and those of the earlier symphonies which would doubtless appear more strongly if we could hear them all performed in close succession, when we should doubtless find that they are intended to constitute an organic whole. The style is a mixture of the "New German School," with the old classical. Although most of Raff's symphonies, including the present one, contain much of what is called "programme music," yet he does not forsake the old traditional lines; in fact, the ancients themselves, with all their glorious laws and contrivances of counterpoint, have perhaps never used them so advantageously as he does.

The "Autumn" symphony was an undoubted success, and was received with unbounded applause, both by the general audience and by the connoisseurs who were present in great force. There are, nevertheless, weak points in it, which ought not to be passed over. The scenes described and depicted sometimes border very closely on the ridiculous. The rattling of dead men's bones by the violins playing col legno—striking with the back of the bow—and the yelping of the hounds by the piercing high notes of the same instrument, cannot but provoke a smile. Our feelings were also appealed to in the first movement by the heading, "feelings and impressions." Now, let us compare this style of writing with the spirit of the greatest master of symphony. In the "Eroica," the C minor, A major, and the Choral, we see a noble character struggling with adversity, surmounting all obstacles and breaking forth from bondage to liberty, out of darkness into light; sometimes through the changing scenes of happiness and sorrow to the sublimest visions of bliss. Surely this was a grander idea to work out than most of those depicted in the modern programme music.

That Raff, like Berlioz, was a perfect master of all the resources of the orchestra, there can be no doubt, and his effects are always telling and often very lovely. Take, for instance, the third movement called the "Elegy," which is full of melody of the most charming kind, given to the most sympathetic instruments—here the combinations for the wood-wind are of the loveliest description. From first to last, the work is indeed most interesting; and often very beautiful, and in every passage we see the hand of a master and a genius.

Beethoven's E flat Concerto was played with commendable success by Mdme. Helen Hopekirk, and was much applauded. Mr. Turner, who sang in the place of Mr. Maas, gave much pleasure in his songs.　　R. S.

Another contributor writes :—

I agree in the main with the critic of the Daily Telegraph respecting Raff's "Autumn" symphony, of which the doctor must give details. It is not a great work, and in nowise suggestive of autumn on the "programme music" theory. Raff, as our contemporary remarks, had evidently fallen into the "sere and yellow leaf" himself, and worked out his mine. After "Leonora" the symphony sounds weak ; but I must admit that it is not uninteresting or untuneful. The "long-drawn out" melody of the first movement, in A flat, for violin and flute, struck me as

very pretty. The "Dance of Phantoms," in A minor, bids fair to take the popular ear; if a trifle tricksy ; the trio for three flutes is a good point, and indicative of the actual meaning of the term "trio" in this department of the art. The "Elegy" in C sharp minor and major, a sort of "song without words," is too long. Raff enunciates the theme equivocally, and suggests E major, until a B sharp in the bass asserts the relative minor ; an enharmonic change occurs in a "complement," from A flat to G sharp; the movement closes in the tonic major. "The Hunt" is commonplace stuff, and not new; the trumpet call at the close is ineffective as a climax. Musicians would notice the non-relation of the keys in the various movements ; the first and the final correspond "relatively," but the composer elsewhere changes from F minor to A minor, and from A minor to C sharp minor. Raff uses the B flat clarinet in the first and last movements, so as to "read" in B flat and G ; in the "Dance of Phantoms" and the "Elegy" the A clarinet comes into play, so as to "read" in C and G.

Mdme. Helen Hopekirk has received, and deservedly, full homage for her reading of Beethoven's 5th Concerto. I am happy to endorse other golden opinions. Sir George Macfarren's Symphony in E minor (first time) will be a bonne bouche for this (Saturday) afternoon. By the way, the overture to "Zauberflöte" was taken at much too great a pace.　　A. M.

MR. WALTER BACHE'S PIANOFORTE RECITAL.

Last Tuesday, in commemoration of Liszt's birthday, a recital of some of his pianoforte compositions was presented by Mr. Bache before a large audience at St. James's Hall. The programme included :—

Sarabande and Chaconne. (From Handel's Singspiel "Almira").
Études de Concert, Nos. 1 and 3. (Dedicated to E. Liszt).
Sonate B minor. (Dedicated to Schumann).
"Bénédiction de Dieu dans la Solitude."
Rhapsodie Hongroise. No. XI.
Ungarischer Sturm Marsch. (Edition of 1876).

Liszt's "Loreley" was sung by Miss Ambler, after the sonatas to Mr. Bache's artistic rendering of the accompaniment. This refined, delicious tone picture (more elegant, to my mind, in its simple pianoforte dress than with orchestral accompaniment), was somewhat beyond the powers, physical and mental, of the lady, who, nevertheless, possesses some attractive, though undeveloped, qualities.

A more varied programme than the above from the works of any one man could by no possibility be arranged, and Mr. Bache had the reward of discretion and good taste by retaining the attention of most of his audience from the first note to the last. The interest naturally centred round the Sonata, but the variety produced by the song and the lighter pieces following prevented one from feeling that the object of the day was over when the Sonata had been heard. The "Bénédiction de Dieu" is a most entrancing flow of melody : rarely has such a long, restful strain touched the heart of a poet !

"D'où me vient, O mon Dieu, cette paix qui m'inonde ?
D'où me vient cette foi dont mon cœur surabonde ?"

These are the lines of Lamartine that the musician has chosen as a motto, and nobly (yet how simply and gracefully !) illustrated.

"C. A. B.'s" able analysis of the Sonata was given with the programmes, as on a former occasion. Mr. Bache is anxious that others, like himself, should understand the musician, as whose prophet in this country he has fully established his claim to be accepted ; he does not wish them either blindly to worship, or ignorantly to condemn. Mr. Bache has, in a remarkable degree, made this noble work his own. One feels as if it were the author himself to whose interpretation one is listening ; so earnestly, so lovingly, and with such firm faith, is every detail set forth. This complete self-identification with the writings of another is a power second in importance only to the highest creative genius. Those who do not appreciate Liszt through Mr. Bache's reading of his works will certainly never learn to appreciate them through any other interpreter ; their only chance will be by a quiet and conscientious study of them at their own piano.

　　　　B. F. WYATT-SMITH.

A new Communion Service by Mr. Warwick Jordan, will be sung at St. Stephen's, Lewisham, at the 11.45 morning Service, on Sunday week, the 4th prox. In addition to the organ accompaniment, special parts are written for trumpet and trombone.

MR. J. B. BONAWITZ'S "HISTORICAL RECITALS."

Mr. J. B. Bonawitz began his four "Historical Recitals of Pianoforte Music" on Wednesday evening, Oct. 17th, at the Blüthner Rooms, Kensington Gardens Square. These recitals should be attended by all who desire to cultivate a fine taste, and to be "well read" in the literature of the pianoforte. Mr. Bonawitz does not utter one word as a regular "lecturer" would, but he so faithfully and so eloquently expounds his elegant extracts as sufficiently to inform those who, having ears, *will* to hear, and what is more, to bear in mind the impressions received. The scheme of this first recital deserves to be specified. The numbers were as follows : Canzona in G minor (Frescobaldi), (1591-1654); Gigue in B flat major (Muffat), (1650-1702); Fugue in D major (Bach), (1685-1750); Suite in G minor (Handel), (1685-1759); Fantasia, in C minor (Mozart), (1756-1791); Sonata, Op. 27, "Moonlight" (Beethoven), (1770-1827); Andantino from the Sonata in A major, No. 10 (Schubert), (1797-1828); Caprice, in E minor (Mendelssohn), (1809-1847); Nachtstuck, in F major (Schumann), (1810-1856); Fughetta in G minor (Schumann), (1810-1856); Nocturne, in F minor (Chopin), (1809-1849); and Scherzo, in B flat minor (Chopin). So much for deceased writers. The works of living composers were : "Preghiera" (Rubinstein); Spring melody (Agnes Zimmermann); "Yellow Jasmine" (from the "Language of Flowers "), (F. H. Cowen); Tarantelle (Immanuel Liebich); Albumblatt (Theodore Kirchner), and the Wedding March from Mendelssohn's "Midsummer Night's Dream" (Liszt). The names of the above composers (two excepted), are familiar to educated persons ; the notice is not written for the non-musical. The gigue of Muffat and Bach's fugue sensibly stirred the audience, and Mozart's Fantasia or "quasi-sonata" excited a *furore*; in Mr. Bonawitz's hands the work fully asserted its power and meaning. The second movement from Schubert's 10th sonata (there is a shorter and slighter one of earlier date in the same key) might have moved a marble Niobe. How remarkable in this piece, as in the fragmentary Symphony No. 8 (B minor), the alternation of melting pathos with fierce and stormy outbursts of impatient rage! Schumann's little "Fughetta" is a gem, too short by half; it ought to have been encored. The living composers were worthily represented. Rubinstein's "Prayer" in B flat has all the devotional fervour of its subject ; Miss Zimmermann's "Melody," in the bright key of D major, made one sigh to think that it was the season of the "sere and yellow leaf." Mr. Cowen's sweet floweret, odoriferous in an analogous sense, diffused its fragrance through the room, and Herr Liebich's spirited Tarantelle in B flat minor, will no doubt, induce some visits of ladies to the well-stored *librairie* of Messrs. Augener & Co. The Abbé Liszt concluded the *soirée* with a crashing climax. Mr. Bonawitz played with intense energy and marvellous versatility, for nearly two hours, and was rewarded with frequent demonstrations of approval and admiration. The next recital is fixed for Nov. 7th.

LEEDS.

A People's Concert was given in the Town Hall, on Saturday evening, before a crowded audience. A special feature of the concert was the exquisite violin playing of Mr. Bernhardt Carrodus (a son of Mr. J. T. Carrodus), who made his first appearance before a Leeds audience. This young gentleman played Vieuxtemp's "Air Varie in D," which being encored, he gave a piece from Gounod ; and in the second part of the programme, De Beriot's "Scene de Ballet," all played with great taste and skill, to the evident delight of the audience. A new song of Dr. Spark's entitled "Life," composed for and dedicated to Madame Valeria, was efficiently sung by Miss Bristow. The song is a composition of great merit and was encored. Another interesting item was the unaccompanied chorus from Macfarren's new oratorio "King David," "Remember not, Lord." This was sung as a quartet by Miss Bristow, and three members of the Leeds Arion Octet, and was given in a most impressive manner. Miss Bristow also sang "Hear ye, Israel" from the "Elijah," and one or two other pieces, all being given in excellent style. The remaining soloists were Messrs. Northrop, Vernon Williams, and D. Billington, and the members of the Leeds Arion Octet sang a couple of glees in a manner that showed very careful training. Mr. J. P. Bowling played the pianoforte accompaniments, and Dr. Spark ably presided at the organ, and played as organ solos selections from "Lohengrin" and the overture to the opera "Martha."

J. D. T.

RECEPTION AT KENSINGTON.

Mrs. Williams and Mdme. De la Baume held a reception last Saturday evening, Oct. 20th, in Lower Phillimore Place, Kensington. A number of professional musicians and a large *corps journalistique* were present. Mdlle. Lebrun, known as a pianist, but at present acting as vocalist, with a fine mezzo-soprano voice, sang with much emphasis and passion Denza's air in D, "Si tu m'aimais," ranging from low C natural to F sharp, also a MS. English song of Carlo Ducci (who conducted), entitled "'Twas not to be "; Mdlle. Lebrun's pronunciation of the (to her) foreign words was remarked with admiration by the audience. Mdlle. Lebrun afterwards sang, with Signor Ria, a favourite tenor *des salons*, the duet in G, from "Il Trovatore," between Manrico and his gipsy mother. Signor Ria, in finest voice, sang for solos "Musica Proibita," taking high G at the end, and Campana's air "Mi credeva in Paradiso." Mr. Quatremayne excited a sensation by his genuine dramatic delivery of Blumenthal's song, "Across the far blue hills, Marie," where the composer, fond of modulation, makes an excursus from G (the original key) to B major. Mr. Quatremayne achieved equal success in another elaborate piece, the title of which was unfortunately not noted at the time, and is consequently forgotten. The sonorous basso, Signor Mcnari-Rocca, almost shook the roof with "Largo al factotum," and the stirring "gallop-along" song "Les Muletiers de Calabre," one of his *specialité*. Miss Davey sang Donizetti's air "E morta " in E minor and major, holding finely the high G and A natural that occur. An amateur young lady, who sang an English ballad out of time, and in the worst style, is only referred to as a caution against the impertinent intrusion of utterly incompetent persons, in the presence of eminent professionals, who can only pity them and pass by. The audience and the reporter were sorely disappointed not to hear the young American soprano, Miss Griswold, disabled by hoarseness. This charming cantatrice is likely, if allowed an opportunity, to achieve great success on the stage of lyrical theatres, and her personal appearance must always command the "sympathy" of a large audience. Signor Carlo Ducci, who conducted the concert, played some pretty solos on the pianoforte, inclusive of a characteristic gipsy air, "Tziganeska," in E minor and common time. This is published. The MS. English song should also be handed to the engraver forthwith.

CHRIST CHURCH, WOBURN SQUARE.

On Oct. 18th the annual festival and harvest thanksgiving service was held. The different local choirs, St. Giles in the Fields, St. George, Bloomsbury, Christ Church, &c., formed a body some seventy strong. The service was W. G. Wood's effective Magnificat and Nunc Dimittis in F. The anthems were E. H. Turpin's "Thou Visitest the Earth" and Handel's "Hallelujah" chorus. The whole of the music was carefully and excellently rendered. Mr. W. G. Wood presided most ably at the organ, and Mr. E. H. Turpin conducted. A large congregation attended the service.

WANDSWORTH.

At the Wandsworth Town Hall on the 18th inst., an evening concert was given, when the following works were performed. Mendelssohn's "Hymn of Praise," commencing with the chorus "All men, all things "; in this and the succeeding one, the choir were in excellent form, and did great credit to their conductor. The soloists were Miss Perfitt, who was deservedly applauded, and Mr. J. Heald, who was also heard to advantage, rendering the tenor solos with great taste. Mrs. Farley, Mrs. O'Donoghue, Messrs. Minot and Furmage, sang the quartet "I waited for the Lord," and Mrs. O'Donoghue and Mr. Garratt the duet "My song shall be always thy Mercy," in a pleasing manner. A sacred cantata "Babylon's Wave," by E. M. Flavell, first time of performance, a work shewing evidence of power, was well received, the soprano solo sung by Miss Perfitt being encored. The second part of the programme consisted of a pianoforte solo, Polonaise in A flat (Chopin), by Miss Rozel Ayots, another cantata by E. M. Flavell (words by F. J. Brebner), "The Fairy King" (soloists, Misses Perfitt, Coyte Turner, Fincham, and Messrs. Garratt and Hodges), and miscellaneous selections.

The stage performance at the Crystal Palace of Sterndale Bennett's beautiful cantata, "The May Queen," proved to be a mistake, as everyone who knew the character of the music might have foretold.

BIRMINGHAM.

The musical season of Birmingham may be said to have opened with the performance of Mendelssohn's "St. Paul," by the Philharmonic Union, on the 27th ult. The chorus, under the conductorship of Dr. Heap, did its part of the work thoroughly well, the rendering of the magnificent choral finale to the first part, "O great is the depth," sufficiently attesting the good "stamina" and training of this now fully-matured musical corps. This is the eighth series of concerts, by the way, which has now been entered upon ; and the perfect efficiency of the chorus reflects the utmost credit upon the worthy conductor, who has held his post from the birth of the institution up to the present time. The soloists on this occasion were Misses Clara Samuell and Dones, and Messrs. Kenningham and Blower. The first-named artist sang her beautiful opening solo, "Jerusalem, thou that killest the prophets," in a manner truly charming, as indeed the whole of her music ; of the other vocalists it need only be said of them that their efforts were satisfactory in their respective departments, though Mr. Blower, by his display of an upper F sharp, without sufficient authority, incurred the displeasure of some. There are some passages, certainly, in which the logical conduct of a melody demands the higher note instead of its octave below, which it seems the composer must have written in order to spare the voice. Where this is obviously the case, no one, I am of opinion, need stickle at a slight change of the kind. It is different where the melody is affected characteristically, to suit the singer and his "top-note." That many evils are likely to creep in if points such as this are left'to the discretion of the vocalist, there can be no doubt ; and as I have no wish to incur a charge of heterodoxy and want of respect for the "classics" simply to shield Mr. Blower, I will leave the point open to general question. The alteration made was in the *aria,* "O God, have mercy ;" the three notes D, F sharp, and E before the first double bar may or may not seem to allow of being sung in the upper octave. The question is not whether such alterations should be deprecated "on principle," but whether it is possible to distinguish such passages where the composer has only been deterred, for practical reasons, from writing a note in the upper range of the voice. If the latter is possible, such alterations would, instead of mutilating the strain, simply restore the original and obvious intention of the composer.

On the same evening (Thursday) of the week following, the Festival Choral Society gave a performance of the same oratorio. Under the conductorship of Mr. Stockley, the work went, of course, admirably. Whatever is undertaken by this Society is done, as a general rule, perfectly. There *was* a little shortcoming last season, but that may have been owing to the strain of the festival performances. It would be unprofitable, apart from the question of bad taste, to institute comparisons between this performance and that of the week previous. It may be said, without offence, however, that the voices in the older society are a little better balanced. In Dr. Heap's choir the alto section seemed, to my thinking, rather weak. The soloists, on this occasion, were certainly *sans reproche*—Mesdames Anna Williams and Enriquez, and Messrs. Edward Lloyd and Ludwig. After such a lapse, two performances of "St. Paul," so very close together, was, perhaps, not an event unacceptable to some. I doubt whether the two societies *intended* this rivalry.

The first concert of the musical section of the Midland Institute took place on the 6th inst. The programme (wholly orchestral) included Bennett's lovely Symphony in G minor. We have had no greater treat for some time than was afforded by the performance of this work. Messrs. Ward and Abbott played Spohr's Duo Concertante for two violins (Op. 88). This is the piece I mentioned some time ago when it was first played by these two clever artists at a concert given by Mr. Stockley. It went excellently well. The Andante (from unfinished Symphony) of Schubert, and the overtures to "Athalie" and "Ruins of Athens," together with the "Turkish March," belonging to Beethoven's work, were the other items of the programme.

Mr. Stratton's first concert of the present series took place on the 16th inst. The principal work performed was the Piano Quintet of Herman Goetz (Op. 16). Though new to the performers as well as the audience, the work altogether received a worthy rendering, and was most appreciatively received. Mr. Cowen's early Trio in C minor, for piano, violin, and 'cello, was welcome as an interesting specimen of the work, though immatured as yet, of this elegant composer, who has not at present forsworn his nationality. Haydn's well-known Quartet (Strong's) in D (Op. 64) was excellently rendered by Mr. Ward and party ; and the artist named took for his solo a *romance,* "L'Adieu," by Mr. Carrodus. Dr. Rowland Winn played an Impromptu Caprice, by Oliver A. King—not a very good selection, if intended to exhibit British art—and a Capriccio in E, by Scarlatti. In both works he did justice to his own reputation as a clever executant, and in the concerted pieces he was, of course, "everything to be wished." BR.

Concerts for young people are being organized in New

LIVERPOOL.
(From our own Correspondent).

Oct. 23rd.

Musical matters are getting brisk in this city. The Philharmonic Society opened its doors for the first season a fortnight ago, when the principal artists were Mr. Charles Hallé and Signor Foli, the whole under the direction of Mr. Charles Hallé the new conductor to the Society. To-night the second concert takes place, the principal artists being Madame Patey and Mr. Ludwig Straus. The concert is to be under the conductorship of Mr. Edward Hecht in consequence of (according to the advertisement) "Mr. Hallé being absent owing to an engagement contracted by him prior to his appointment to the Conductorship of the Society"! I Comment is unnecessary ! In any other business arrangement would such a thing be allowed! I trow not. The Liverpool Philharmonic Choral Society are preparing for their campaign. The first concert is announced for November 3rd and the oratorio of "Elijah" has been selected for the opening night. Mr. Randegger will conduct and Mr. W. T. Best will be at the organ. It is also stated that there will be a full band. The works underlined for future concerts are the Messiah, and "Israel in Egypt."

Mr. Branscombe has been giving organ recitals on the fine organ in St. Margaret's Church, Princes Road.

Mr. Martin Schneider gave a recital on the organ in the Church of St. Matthew and St. James, Mossley Hill, on Saturday last. The programme will appear in the "Organ News" column next week. J.·J. M.

GLASGOW.

Among forthcoming concerts and musical events may be mentioned the following :—A chamber concert, by Mr. Charles Hallé and Madame N. Néruda, on the 19th ; a rendering of the "Creation," by the Tonic Sol-fa Association, with Madame Ilma di Murska, Mr. R. Hilton, &c., on the 25th ; and, on the same day, the Glasgow Select Choir will sing Smart's "Jacob," accompanied by Messrs. Berry and Swan, Mr. Allan, as usual, conducting. Miss Agnes Liddell, of this city, gave a concert on the 16th in the Queen's Rooms, assisted by Miss Ada Earee, Mr. George Perrin, Mr. Bantock Pierpont, Mdlle. H. Lippmann, and Herr A. Gallrein ; Signor Alberto Visetti conducted. Mr. J. T. Carrodus will appear at the St. Andrew's Hall on Saturday the 20th.

The Glasgow Choral Union sang at the ceremony of laying the foundation stone of the New Municipal Buildings on Saturday the 6th ; but, being environed by bands playing, and the distracting sounds attending a congregation of many thousands, the effect was neither sublime nor audible. The programme consisted of a few psalms, the "Hallelujah" chorus, and "Rule Britannia."

An amateur orchestral society has been commenced in the west end, under the conductorship of Mr. W. T. Hoeck ; but it is understood to be a semi-private concern. It is raised from the ruins of a former association, and has already been practising.

DERBY.

A successful amateur concert was given at St. James's Hall on October the 19th, in aid of the restoration of a local church. The performers were, almost exclusively, amateurs. Under the circumstances, severe criticism would be misplaced. The following ladies and gentlemen took part :—Lady Florence Duncombe, Mrs. Milnes, Mrs. Osborne Bateman, Mrs. Curgenven, Rev. T. F. Jones, Mr. Edward M. Wass, Rev. H. M. Willoughby, Mr. J. V. Woodward (violoncello), Rev. S. Bengough (accompanist). The vacancy caused by the absence of Miss Milnes through indisposition was kindly filled up by Mrs. Curgenven, whose rich, mellow voice, and cultured style, was shown to advantage in Gounod's pathetic setting of "Oh ! that we two were maying." Lady Florence Duncombe possesses a voice of good quality, but scarcely powerful enough to tell well in so large a room. It is a matter for regret that her ladyship should not employ her talents upon better material than the two songs she chose on this occasion. Mrs. Bateman is most deservedly a favourite with a Derby audience. Perhaps the most pleasing of her contributions was the song with 'cello obbligato, although Handel's "Lascia ch'io pianza" was carefully well rendered. The gentlemen, one and all, did excellent service. Special mention should perhaps be made of

HEATON.—In connection with the annual harvest festival at St. Barnabas's Church a selection of music from "The Creation" was performed the other Saturday evening in the presence of a large congregation. The principal parts were sustained by the Rev. R. W. Easton, Miss Cockcroft, and Mr. Charlesworth Prince, whilst Mr. James Rooks, of St. Paul's, most efficiently presided at the organ. The choruses were well rendered by the choir, assisted by several members of the Bradford Festival Choral Society, the whole being ably led by Mr. Alfred Padfield, the choirmaster of the church.

PRESTON.—On Saturday evening, Oct. 20th, Mr. James Tomlinson gave his usual weekly organ recital. The programme was as follows : Overture to "Lodoiska" (Cherubini), "Cuckoo and Nightingale" concerto (Handel), Fantasie (Guiraud), Overture "The Naïdes" (Sterndale Bennett), Barcarolle (Spohr), March from the 1st Suite (Lachner). The "Cuckoo and Nightingale" concerto was received with loud applause. The Fantasie was rendered with great feeling, and elicited a well merited encore, to which Mr. Tomlinson responded. The march was rendered in a spirited manner. There was a moderate attendance.—On Monday, Oct. 22nd, Mr. Norwood gave a grand military and orchestral concert in aid of the Infirmary. Signor Foli sang "The Shipwright," "The Vikings." Miss Snowden, R.A.M., a Preston lady, sang very sweetly "Kathleen Mavourneen," "Second thoughts are best," "The Lost Chord." The orchestra, consisting of 40 performers, rendered overture "William Tell," gavotte "Mignon," selections from "Carmen" and "Iolanthe," and "The British Army Quadrilles." The Gordon Highlanders' Pipers and three other military bands took part in the "Quadrilles." The concert was a success, and it is expected that the Infirmary will receive a handsome sum.

BATH.—Mr. Oliver's concert took place at the Assembly Rooms, on Friday evening, Oct. 19th, but without Mr. Sims Reeves, who pleaded illness as the reason of his absence. It was the first time that Miss Ella Lemmens had sung in Bath, and she received a cordial welcome. Her voice is a soprano, flexible, sweet in tone, and well under control. Miss De Fonblanque sang very beautifully. The songs were good, and the duets, Mozart's "Su l'Aria" with Miss Lemmens, and "Crudel Perchè" with Mr. Barrington Foote, were delivered with perfect taste and finish. Mr. Barrington Foote is a great favourite here. He sang an effective composition of Mr. Herbert Reeves, "Highwayman Jack," receiving a unanimous encore. Signor Pinsuti was pianist. He played one of Mendelssohn's "Songs without words," and a brilliant "Saltarello" by Mattei ; also Liszt's "Rhapsodie Hongroise," for which he received an encore. The veteran Nicholson took part in the programme. It was altogether an enjoyable entertainment. This being the first concert of the season, it may be well to mention that the entrances to the rooms, which have always been more or less gloomy, are now brilliantly lighted by three of those splendid lamps which the Council have placed in convenient positions in the city.

Academical Intelligence.

TRINITY COLLEGE, LONDON.
LIVERPOOL CENTRE.

In the small concert room of St. George's Hall, on Saturday afternoon, the prizes and honour certificates gained by the candidates of the Liverpool centre at the examinations in elementary musical knowledge and in instrumental and vocal music, held in connection with Trinity College, London, were distributed by Mrs. Palgrave Simpson. The chair was taken by Mr. Palgrave Simpson, and with him on the platform there were Sir James Picton, Rev. T. Major Lester, Major R. E. Stewart, Dr. Utting, Mr. H. Grimshaw, Rev. S. Armour, Mr. Franklin Haworth, Dr. R. H. D. Johnson, Messrs. W. D. Hall, John Wrigley (Manchester), R. Burgess, A. E. Isaac, Theo. Goebbells, W. H. Maxfield (Altrincham), Higgins, H. E. Rensburg, Malcolm Guthrie, J. Sanders, G. Holden, A. W. Newell (Wigan), J. B. Mackenzie, C. K. Bryan (Southport), G. Miller, H. Kinsey, Holmes, Edwards, J. H. Kelley, H. Thornborough, J. H. W. Biggs, &c.

The local hon. secretary (Mr. J. J. Monk) intimated that letters had been received from Lord Claud Hamilton, M.P., the Rector of Liverpool, Mr. Santley, Mr. E. R. Russell, the Warden and the Registrar of the College, and others, expressing regret at their inability to be present. He afterwards read the report for the year 1882-3, stating that, for the sixth time, the annual report was presented with a favourable result. *During the past year only three gained first senior honours in the United Kingdom, and one of the three is a Liverpool candidate.* Out of ten candidates who gained second senior honours, one also belongs to Liverpool, and of twenty-nine gaining third senior honours, four represent the Liverpool centre. At the June theoretical examinations, the senior honour candidates complained that the paper could not be done in the time allowed (two hours) ; and that the matter will, in the future, not be over-

looked by the examiners who set the papers. The visiting examiner, in the person of Mr. Humphrey J. Stark, remains unchanged ; and, on all sides, it is hoped that that arrangement will be continued in the future. It would be impossible for any visiting examiner to give more satisfaction than Mr. Stark has done, and the encomiums passed upon his method and manner of examining candidates, by both teachers and students, are a very pleasing and well-deserved feature. With regard to the examinations in instrumental and vocal music, two or three notable improvements will be introduced in the coming examinations. Certain privileges have also been accorded to candidates who have passed the senior local examinations with high honours, in entering for the higher examinations held only at the College, in London, every January and July. The best thanks of the committee are due to one of their own body, the Rev. T. Major Lester, for acting as visitor at the two examinations which were held in this room.

The CHAIRMAN, after commenting upon the satisfactory character of the report, said there had of late years been a remarkable extension of musical culture in this country.

A selection of music was next given.

Mrs. PALGRAVE SIMPSON then distributed the prizes.

Foreign Musical Intelligence.

MUSIC IN PARIS.
(From our own Correspondent).

PARIS, OCT. 23rd, 1883.
The concert season opened brilliantly on Sunday, when full houses welcomed back M. Pasdeloup and M. Colonne at the Cirque and Châtelet. The programme at the Cirque was excellent, though the only novelty provided was an Andante Symphonique from the pen of M. Léon Husson, a young and rising composer. It is dramatic in character, and gives promise of better things. The influence of Wagner is evident in M. Husson's somewhat intemperate use of the brass wind instruments. Here and there the work lacks clearness ; but the orchestration is, even when most pretentious, both ingenious and uncommon. I am sorry to say the andante was not received with great enthusiasm.

The *pièce de résistance* was Schumann's ever delightful Symphony in C major, to which succeeded (besides the andante of M. Husson), the Theme and Variations from Beethoven's Serenade for violin, alto, and violoncello, Mozart's B flat pianoforte Concerto (admirably played by M. Theodore Ritter), and Berlioz's overture to "Le Carnaval Romain." The popular *chef d'orchestre* had a most flattering reception.

At the rival Châtelet, M. Colonne led off with one more performance of the "Damnation de Faust," which is all I need say about the concert, except that Berlioz's masterpiece was executed as faultlessly as ever, and that, like M. Pasdeloup, the young conductor who has so often led his followers of the Association Artistique to victory was loudly applauded on stepping forward, bâton in hand, into his old place.

M. Pasdeloup's arrangements for the season promise us an excellent series of concerts. They will hardly be satisfactory, however, to the countless French composers who have works ready for production, as M. Pasdeloup announces that he intends to devote particular attention this year to the Italian and Russian Symphonists, and will, consequently, be compelled to disregard the claims of many native musicians. We are also, as usual, to be afforded opportunities of renewing our acquaintance with many old and forgotten favourites. Gluck, Rameau, and Lulli will all of them be remembered, and several long neglected pianoforte compositions of Mozart will be "revived," and represented to us by that erudite and gifted artist, M. Theodore Ritter.

It is now nearly twenty-three years since M. Pasdeloup founded the Paris Popular Concerts. Although the competition of enterprizing rivals like MM. Colonne and Lamoureux has often threatened his work with disaster, it still lives and flourishes.

After several years' absence, Mdlle. Galli-Marié, one of the most original and delightful artists on the lyric stage, will make her reappearance at the Opéra Comique, in Bizet's "Carmen." I hardly know which will be the more welcome—the work or its interpreter. Mdlle. Galli-Marié, as you are doubtless aware, "created" the part of Carmen when Bizet's opera was first produced in Paris. She has few, if any, equals in one or two rôles. Even Miss Marie Vanzandt is scarcely a more charming "Mignon."

The management of the Theatre Lyrique Populaire (otherwise the Château d'Eau) is making a gallant struggle against fearful obstacles, and doing its best to supply the want of cheap and good performances of opera.

Mermet's "Roland à Roncevaux" has been revived with some success, and we are shortly to have a revival of "Le Brasseur de Preston," which, by-the-bye, most of us could have done very well without.

At the Opéra the preparations for the coming production of

"Sapho" are being hurried forward. Gounod will probably conduct the first performance of the work himself. His views on the subject which divide him from Sir Michael Costa and most other *chefs d'orchestre* do not appear to have altered.

The Hillemacher brothers (both *prix de Rome*, and now studying in the "Eternal City") have, I hear, nearly completed their opera, "Henri III. et sa Cour." The libretto is founded on Alexandre Dumas' drama.   C. HARRY MELTZER.

FOREIGN VIEWS OF THE LEEDS FESTIVAL.

A London correspondent of the *Independance Belge* (the leading journal of Brussels) writes as follows on the late Leeds Festival:—

"The unanimous opinion is that the 'King David' of Sir G. A. Macfarren is the most powerful work hitherto conceived by the composer of 'The Resurrection' and 'St. John the Baptist.' The overture has 'allusions' to the pastoral life of David, and his relations with King Saul. The most remarkable number is the lamentation of David on the death of Absalom, treated with a fine feeling of dramatic effect. This *English* work indemnified and consoled the public for the deception that they had been made to experience by the Cantata of M. Cellier, based on Gray's "Elegy." The financial results of the Festival, moreover, attest the development of the taste for classical music at home."

The writer seems to be unaware that Mr. Cellier is a native of England, if of French extraction. Like other Gallican writers, he also blunders about *dates*. He compares the receipts of the late Leeds Festival, for example, with the tributes rendered *last year* (1882), in 1881, and 1880, whereas the meeting is only a triennial one. The actual dates of the four Festivals hitherto held were 1874, 1877, 1880, and 1883. *L'Indépendance Belge* is worthy of more correct correspondents, and the proprietors will be advised accordingly.

M. Gounod is said to have completed his new oratorio.

Rubinstein's "Demon" has been given in Leipzig, lately.

Gevaert's "Quentin Durward" is to be given shortly at Weimar.

Kleinmichel's opera, "Schloss de l'Orme," has been given in Hamburg.

Lecocq's "Marcotte" has enjoyed, in Barcelona, an extraordinary success.

Herr Martin Röder's oratorio, "Maria Magdalena," will be presently produced in Berlin.

Nesling's "Jung Werner der Trompeter von Säkkingen" will be heard, it is said, in Leipzig, next month.

Rubinstein's opera, "Kalaschinoff the Merchant" is shortly to be given in St. Petersburg and in Moscow.

The Russian Musical Society in St. Petersburg proposes some good symphony concerts during the season.

"Le Serment" is announced abroad as "un petit acte," by a very rich Englishman, John Urich, set to music by an amateur.

Nohl has published his work (a brochure of some 70 pages) on Wagner and his influence upon national German art.

The concerts at Leipzig are now setting in, and the performances in St. Thomas's Church have been recommenced.

The bi-centenary of Bach's birth will be celebrated next year by the erection of a colossal statue at Eisnach, his native town.

Cornelius's "Der Barber von Bagdad," Wagner's "Walkure," and Schumann's "Genoveva," are announced at Karlsruhe.

M. Paul Samuel, a Belgian, has invented an electric "Batteur de mesure," for marking the time for band and chorus in large theatres.

Breitkopf and Härtel, of Leipzig, announce among other recently published works of the composer, Raff's "Weltende, Gericht, Neue Welt."

The introduction of Wagner's music into the programmes of the Brussels Conservatoire, is described as, under M. Gevaert's direction, a veritable revolution.

It is said a mass by that interesting composer, Méhul, may be sung at the St. Cecilia Festival, at St. Eustache, n Paris. The work is dated 1804.

PRINCIPAL CONTENTS OF THIS NUMBER.

LONDON: SATURDAY, OCTOBER 27, 1883.

JOHN GOSS.

MORE striking testimony to the unanimity of the English musicians when called upon to recognise artistic merit and high social character, could hardly be pointed out than was afforded by the representative meeting at the College of Organists on Monday last. To Sir ARTHUR SULLIVAN and to Mr. T. L. SOUTHGATE must be ascribed the honour of leading the way towards an exceptional recognition of one whose talents as an artist, and admirable qualities as a man, were balanced with an evenness rarely to be recorded. JOHN GOSS was born at Fareham in Hants, 27th December, 1800, and he died at Brixton, May 10, 1880. In 1811 he became one of the Children of the Chapel Royal, studying under JOHN STAFFORD SMITH, and afterwards ARTWOOD. In 1824 he was appointed organist of St. Luke's Church, Chelsea, quitting there in 1838 for St. Paul's Cathedral.

He officiated there for thirty-four years, retiring in 1872. He also occupied the post of State composer at the Chapels Royal. His public services therefore extended over a period of sixty-one years. On the occasion of writing the Te Deum, and the Anthem, "The Lord is my strength," for the Thanksgiving Service held for the recovery of the Prince of Wales in 1872, he received the honour of Knighthood.

In a volume of "The Harmonicon," for the year 1827, will be found a Motet from his pen, "Requiem Æternum," composed in memory of the Duke of York. His State services as composer may thus be said to have lasted forty-five years. After his retirement from active work at the cathedral, he enjoyed his well earned leisure for seven years before he died, still, however, teaching until within a short period of his death.

The value of his works must not be measured by a long list of opus numbers, but rather by their intrinsic merit. Of the thirty Anthems, he composed, the best known are "If we believe," "Praise the Lord, O my Soul," "The Wilderness," "The Lord is my strength," "O taste and see," "Almighty and Everlasting God." These are distinguished for their breadth, religious beauty, and simple grandeur. He wrote twelve Services, besides setting separate Canticles. Of his eight Glees, "O thou whose beams," and "There is beauty on the mountain," are exquisite specimens of unaffected grace and glowing melody.

In 1833 he published "An Introduction to Harmony and Thorough Bass," a second edition in 1847, and this widely known and popular work has now reached its 15th edition. In 1841 he edited a collection of "Chants, Ancient and Modern." In 1854, in conjunction with the Rev. W. Mercer, was brought out "The Church Psalter and Hymn Book."

The series of volumes of "The Organist's Companion" led the way to the various collections of *** for the Instrument which have appeared *** that period. Of his secular compositions, The Sergeant's Wife, enjoyed a great *** years ago. An overture in F minor *** at a Philharmonic concert in 1827, and another in E flat was written for performance at one of the "British Concerts" in 1835.

Sir John Goss was for many years a Professor at the R. A. M., a member of various Glee Clubs, and up to the time of his death President of Trinity College, London. At the Cathedral, the Academy, and privately by his compositions and teachings, his influence on English music has been considerable. Forty is hardly a church in the kingdom, where some of his music is not performed weekly. After his retirement from official life, he was entertained at a public banquet at the Albion Tavern, Mr. W. H. Gladstone being the chairman. A public subscription was subsequently opened, for the purpose of endowing an Exhibition at the R. A. M. connected with his name. The personal esteem with which he was regarded, and the admiration felt for his professional talents, found illustration in the considerable sum that was collected to endow the Goss Scholarship at that Institution. This exhibition is suitably administered through the College of Organists, an institution which, like the Royal Academy of Music, the eminent Englishman duly honoured, ***

The general tone of the meeting of Monday last showed in a touching manner how largely the fine music and the no less distinguished amiability of the departed organist of St. Paul's had appealed to the admiration and esteem of his contemporaries and immediate professional successors. Everyone had felt the beauty of his "pure Church music" to quote Sir A. Sullivan's happy expression,—music in which the severer dignity of the older school is happily softened and tempered by the cultivated judgment and tuneful, solemn grace of the learned yet unostentatious composer, and of the high-souled yet lowly-minded man. Many present could offer personal testimony with regard to the tender beauty of the character of the man whom they sought to honour. That there are many organists, choirmen and choristers, who will desire to join in the present opportunity for the permanent honouring of a great and loved name, cannot be doubted, and as Sir G. A. Macfarren, Sir A. Sullivan, and other speakers felt, it will be well to arrange the conduct of the subscription so as not to freeze out by a large moneyed generosity, however commendable, that may be, the companionship of the equally generous and well meant small sums which may be offered from those who appreciate, and in gratitude than they are in this world's good.

The Treasurer of the Fund, Mr. W. H. Cummings (Brackley Villas, Dulwich), or the Secretary, Mr. T. L. Southgate (Epsledale, Jasper Road, Gipsy Hill), will doubtless gladly acknowledge even the smallest sums which may be sent in aid of a notable scheme, whereby the memory of a good and faithful Artist, a true and tender-hearted man, may be placed before the world as a shining example by the grateful recognition of many friends and of a host of admirers.

E. H. Turpin.

"VAIN REPETITIONS."

Idle words, tedious reiterations, and hammerings of malleable material until it is almost attenuated into unsubstantiality, have been condemned by the highest authorities (ancient and modern). How many otherwise fair speeches are spoiled by reversions to previous sentiments! What pious church goer trembles not like St. James' devils that vainly believed when Dryasdust, too idle or too ignorant to compose his sermon, attempts to preach extempore, and, in order to fill up the time, ekes out his thirty-two "sections" with one or two "points more," which—nön remi acu tangit—turn out to be mere repetitions of a very trite old story. Some ordinary (not) "Conversation Kengés" have a trick of saying an emphatic sentence twice: the writer knew a gentleman—a reductio ad absurdum—who invariably, repeated the last word, as, for instance: "Will you have the kindness, Sir, to pass the bottle bottle?"

And now comes forward a formidable champion of Christendom to protest against repetitions in the domain of music. A real dragon—M. Dannreuther's "Nibelungen" monster—inspired with life by some process in la Frankenstein, would shrink into its cavern, and bury its forked tail in the sand, rather than bear the brunt of Mr. Ferdinand Praeger's sharp-pointed spear. Polemics, in such a case, are out of the question. Suffice it to blow the trumpet before him as he triumphantly rides "conquering and "to conquer." Let the poor humble henchman be allowed, at the same time, to whisper, if only as a friendly hint, the warning enjoined by the haughty potentate of ancient Macedon, "*Philippe, hamo es!*"

Mr. PRAEGER'S opinions must always command respectful attention ; he is master of his art, a musician of eminence, and a philosopher by nature. His contributions to this journal may be referred to without reserve, since the accomplished writer always signs his name in full. The question at issue was raised by Mr. PRAEGER during the 9th session of the "Musical "Association," when he read a paper on "the Fallacy "of the repetition of Parts in the classical Form."

Musicians are cognizant of the "form" condemned by Mr. PRAEGER. He holds that the first impression made by a "part" is weakened by its reproduction, and he adduces the analogy of a poet repeating half his poem, a dramatist one whole act, and a novelist one whole chapter. The opening phrase of BEETHOVEN'S Fifth Symphony, "It is Fate knocking at "the door," is cited as a case in point. "The re"appearance of Nemesis reminds one strongly of the "return of BASILIO, with his repeated 'good night,' in 'The Barber of Seville.'" Mr. PRAEGER will not allow the precedents of the great masters, HAYDN, MOZART, and BEETHOVEN, to be made musical law. He would dare to "improve upon" them : "only "make the experiment." To the plea that repetition is required to make the ideas of the composer clearly comprehensible, Mr. PRAEGER replies with this advice : "Let those who cannot understand music "performed in public take the scores home, and "study and practise them *at home*." He knows some of SWINBURNE'S poems that you have to read over a dozen times to see their full beauty ; and SHAKESPEARE, after 300 years, still gives rise to fresh publications every month, especially in Germany. Mr. PRAEGER explains that his contention does not apply to *rhythmical* compositions, such as marches and dances, because in *them* music only holds a *subordinate* position.

In the discussion that ensued, Mr. PROUT (the chairman), Mr. BANISTER, Mr. C. E. STEPHENS, Mr. G. A. OSBORNE, Dr. GLADSTONE, Dr. W. H. MONK, Mr. MOSELEY, and Mr. SHEDLOCK took part. The paper (published by the Association as a pamphlet) deserves an attentive perusal. Mr. PROUT, in an able and argumentative address, apologized for taking up a distinctly hostile line to Mr. PRAEGER ; but other members thought that there was "much to be said "on both sides" ; and that a very strong case had been made out by the author of the paper. Mr. CHARLES STEPHENS thought that in many cases the "repeat" was only a fashion of the day, but urged that in some cases, notably the "Scotch" Symphony, and MOZART'S Pianoforte Quartet in G minor, there were clear indications that the author really intended the parts to be repeated. Mr. PRAEGER, it will be seen, overrules this plea of authority and precedent. Dr. GLADSTONE remarked that in classical overtures there is no specimen of a repeat to be met with, but the Chairman (Mr. PROUT) quoted MENDELSSOHN'S

"Military Overture," Op. 24, as an exception. Mr. PROUT also explained the difference between the overture and the sonata. In the former, with very rare exceptions, the middle portion, or "free fantasia," is either omitted altogether, or cut down to very short limits, as in MOZART'S "Figaro" for example.

It is quite an exceptional thing to have much development ; you get back to the first part almost immediately, with very little development, and this may be a reason why a repetition of the first part is not necessary in an overture as in a sonata. It may be remembered that a new overture, produced at one of the Philharmonic concerts last summer, was found fault with by *connoisseurs* for this very reason, that the first part was formally repeated. Mr. PROUT reminded the meeting that the famous overture to "Die Zauberflöte" has no repeats ; the motive of the *allegro* is gracefully vari ed, with a delicious colouring by use of the minor mode, in the second part.

The writer, with bated breath, and modest as the herald of him against whom DEMOSTHENES launched his glowing periods of Attic Greek, would simply speak as followeth. *Formal* repetitions, especially of plain straightforward subjects, should be avoided, as a rule. In the case of vocal pieces, many of HANDEL'S to wit, they are felt to be positively wearisome and altogether redundant. Much depends on the length of the theme, and, as shown by Mr. PROUT, on the *form* of the composition itself. Reminiscences, of frequent recurrence, seem to be not only allowable, but agreeable to the ear : note, as one instance that occurs *en passant*, the final movement of BEETHOVEN'S Sonata in G, Op. 31, No. 1. This is the "Rondo" form, and between "Rondo" and "Repetition" no comparison is admissible. Any hard and fast rule, after all, would be felt as a tyranny. Taste must ever be the supreme *arbiter elegantiarum.*   A. M.

Herr Rudwick, an organist of Landsberg, has composed a cantata which is well spoken of, with the title of "Armin's Kampfruf."

The post of organist of York Minster has been offered to, and accepted by, Dr. Naylor, of Scarborough, who is already recognised as a valuable Church musician. Every one will wish the doctor success in his new and responsible sphere of labour. The salary at York is at present £300, and may in time be raised to £400 per annum. The appointment was made by the whole body of the Chapter headed by the Dean, Precentor, etc., and it may therefore be presumed was settled by voting. The absurd statement made in the London papers that the salary will ultimately be £700, hardly requires contradiction. The fact is as here stated, the present salary is £300, and may in the end, on the expiration of Dr. Monk's pension, be raised to £400.

On Thursday, Oct. 18th, an organ recital was given at Christ Church, Broad Green, Croydon, by Mr. F. Cambridge, organist of the parish church. The following was the programme :—Overture, "Samson" (Handel); sanctus, "Messe Solennelle" (Gounod) ; fugue, "St.Ann's Tune" (J. S. Bach); andante, "Dramatic Concerto" (Spohr); Triumphal March in D (Moscheles); Selection, "Athalie" (Mendelssohn); Hallelujah, "Mount of Olives" (Beethoven). The harvest festival at this church took place on Friday, Oct. 12th, and was repeated on Sunday. The Service was choral, the choir being slightly augmented, and was very effectively rendered, the solo being sung by Master H. Townsend, of Mr. Stedman's choir, who has a splendid treble voice. Mr. J. H. W. Oclee, one of the most prominent of the local organists, played an effective selection of suitable music.

Organ News.

BOW AND BROMLEY INSTITUTE.

Mr. W. S. Best had, on Saturday last, the deserved compliment of a crowded house, and he was in his best playing form. It is quite unnecessary to offer any observations upon his performance. The opening piece was his own, "Adagio and Finale Allegro con brio," which was loudly applauded. The fine Fugue in G major, by S. Wesley, was much appreciated. Listz's, "La Prédication aux Oiseaux," came next. A "Siciliana and Fugue" in G major in twelve-eight measure of a gigue type, by J. S. Bach, were very finely rendered and encored. Mr. Best then played "The Trumpet Fugue."] Morandi's attractive "Rondo de Campanelli" was the final solo. Miss Carlotta Elliot gave great pleasure by her very artistic singing, and was encored in one song, of which she repeated the last verses. Mr. F. Meen accompanied. To-night Dr. Peace, of Glasgow, will be the soloist.

ST. LEONARD'S-ON-SEA.

Organ recitals were given on Monday, October 22nd, by Mr. W. T. Best, in St. Paul's Church. The following were the programmes :—

AFTERNOON.

Organ Sonata, No. 3, in A major	Mendelssohn.
Con moto Maestoso—Andante Tranquillo.	
Fugue in G major	Wesley.
Bénédiction Nuptiale (" Piece d'Orgue)	Saint-Saëns.
"Festival March"	Best.
Legende, "La Prédication aux Oiseaux"	Liszt.
(St. Francis of Assisi preaches to the birds).	
Andante in G major	Smart.
Scherzo Symphonique	Guilmant.

EVENING.

Organ Concerto in D minor	Handel.
Andante—Aria—Fuga.	
Andante in B flat major	Dubois.
Siciliana and Fugue	Bach.
Andante in E flat major	Best.
"Rondo de' Campanelli (" Bell Rondo")	Morandi.
Offertoire Funèbre	Wely.
Overture, founded on the "Austrian Hymn"	Haslinger.

HAWORTH CHURCH.

Organ recitals were given in Haworth Church, on Tuesday, October 16th, by Mr. Best, of Liverpool. The programmes included :—

AFTERNOON.

Allegretto and Adagio Religioso, from the Symphony to	
"the Lobgesang"	Mendelssohn.
Fugue in G major	Wesley.
Adagio Solenne	Dussek.
Festal March	Best.
Légende, "La Prédication aux Oiseaux"	Liszt.
Overture, founded on the "Austrian Hymn"	Haslinger.

EVENING.

Organ Concerto in D minor	Handel.
Andante—Aria—Fuga.	
Andante (G major)	Smart.
Rondo de Campanelli (" Bell-Rondo ")	Morandi.
Siciliana and Fugue	Bach.
Andante, with variations and Finale	Best.
Organ Sonata, No. 5, in D major	Mendelssohn.
Chorale—Andante—Allegro con brio.	

The organ, built by Mr. J. P. Jepson Binns, of Bramley, near Leeds, has three Manuals and Pedal and forty stops.

FISHERIES EXHIBITION.

Mr. Loaring, F.C.O., gave recitals on Monday, Thursday and Friday, October 15th, 18th and 19th. The following were the programmes :—

Gipsy Rondo	Haydn.
Organ Concerto, No. 1	Handel.
The Bride's March	Loaring.
Grand March in C	"
Gavotte in D	Loaring.
"Marcia di Processione"	Morandi.
Organ Concerto, No. 2	Handel.
Festive March in D	Smart.
Overture, "The Poet and the Peasant"	Suppé.
Gavotte in G	Handel.
Rondo de Campanelli	Morandi.
March, "Militaire"	Gounod.
Andante in G	Batiste.
Allegro con Spirito	Bache.

Organ recitals were given on Monday, October 22nd, by Mr. E. H. Sugg, organist of Parish Church, Acton ; Mr. Gregory, F.C.O., organist of Ware Parish Church ; Mr. J. Loaring, F.C.O., &c. ; Mr. G. Hedges, organist, Wycliffe Con. Ch., Stepney ; and by Mr. E. Willmott Renshaw, organist, St. Luke's, Fulham Road.

CRYSTAL PALACE.

Mr. Eyre's programmme on Saturday, 13th October, included the following :—

"Cum Sancto Spiritu," from 2nd Mass	Cherubini.
Adagio from the Octet	Schubert.
Air, "My heart, ever faithful"	Bach.
Prelude and Fugue in G	Mendelssohn.
Introduction, Church Scene and Finale (" Faust ")	Gounod.
Grand Offertoire in F	Wely.
Chorus, " Sing unto God " (" Judas ")	Handel.
Adagio from a quartet	Spohr.
Concert Fugue in G	Krebs.
Air, "If with all your hearts" (" Elijah")	Mendelssohn.
Military March	Schubert.
Gavotte, "Heimliche Liebe"	Resch.
Procession March	Sullivan.

And on Saturday, October 20th :—

Postlude in D	Smart.
Adagio from a quartet	Spohr.
Fugue in G minor	Bach.
Minuet from G minor Symphony	Bennett.
Serenade	Schubert.
Pastoral from a Sonata	Guilmant.
Selection, "Redemption"	Gounod.
Overture, "Prometheus"	Beethoven.
Andante, "Evening Prayer"	Smart.
Air, "Love in her eyes sits playing (" Acis ")	Handel.
Allegretto, from Symphony No. 1 ("Lobgesang")	Mendelssohn.
Bourrée in D	Saunders.
March from "Abraham"	Molique.

WATERLOO ROAD, S.E.

An organ recital was given on Tuesday evening, October 23rd, in the Church of St. John the Evangelist, by Mr. Humphrey J. Stark, Mus.Bac., Oxon. Miss F. Rivers was the vocalist. The programme included :—

Concert Fantasia	Stewart.
Adagio in C major	Schubert.
Prelude and Fugue in D minor	Hesse.
Adagio, from the quartet in G minor	Spohr.
Communion }	
Minuet and Trio }	Stark.
Bourrée in B minor	Bach.
March of Crusaders	Liszt.

CHESTER.

Two organ recitals were given in St. Mary's Church, on Sunday, the 14th inst., by Mr. H. W. Radford, organist and choirmaster. The programmes included the following :—

AFTERNOON.

"In native worth"	Haydn.
"Austrian Hymn," with variations	Haydn-Chipp.
Festal March in D	Radford.
"The War March of the Priests"	Mendelssohn.

EVENING.

"Festal March"	Elvey.
Festal March in D	Radford.
"With verdure clad"	Haydn.
March in C	Radford.
Andante in G ("Clock Symphony in D," No. 4)	Haydn.
Fugue ("St. Ann's Tune ")	Bach.
Minuet and Trio in B flat	Bennett.
March (" Sennacherib ")	Arnold.
"Hallelujah Chorus"	Handel.

PEEL.

An organ has just been erected in the New Church, Peel, by Messrs. Brindley and Foster, of Sheffield. The following is the specification :—

GREAT ORGAN. CC TO A.

1. Open Diapason	... 8 ft.	5. Harmonic Flute	... 4 ft.
2. Stopt Bass, and Cla-		6. Twelfth	... 3 „
rabella	... 8 „	7. Fifteenth	... 2 „
3. Gamba	... 8 „	8. Mixture (3 ranks)	
4. Principal	... 4 „	9. Trumpet	... 8 „

SWELL ORGAN. CC TO A.

10. Double Diapason ..	16 ft.	15. Gemshorn	... 4 „
11. Open Diapason	... 8 „	16. Piccolo	... 2 „
12. Stopt Diapason	... 8 „	17. Mixture (3 ranks)	
13. Dulciana	... 8 „	18. Cornopean	... 8 „
14. Voix Celestes	... 8 „	19. Oboe	... 8 „

PEDAL ORGAN. CCC TO F.

20. Open Diapason	... 16 ft.	22. Principal	... 8 ft.
21. Bourdon	... 16 „		

CHOIR ORGAN. CC TO A.

23. Leiblich Gedact......	8 ft.	25, 26, 27, and 28, Spare Slides
24. Flauto Traverso ...	4 „		

COUPLERS.

29. Swell to Great.	34. Swell Super-octave
30. Swell to Pedal.	to Great.
31. Swell to Choir.	35. Great to Pedal.
32. Choir to Pedal.	36. Tremulant.
33. Swell Sub-octave.	

Seven composition Pedals.

TAUNTON.

The harvest festival, and the opening of the new organ took place at S. Andrew's, Rowbarton, on Sunday, October 7th. Recitals were given by Mr. W. W. Hedgecock, organist of St. Agnes' Church, Kennington Park, London. The programme included :—

Triumphal March, "Nanman"	Costa.
" Evening Prayer "	Smart.
Allegro in D	Tours.
Air, " O rest in the Lord " ("Elijah ")	Mendelssohn.
" Coronation March "	Meyerbeer.

And on Tuesday afternoon, October 9th :—

" March of the Crusaders "	Liszt.
Grazioso in F	Smart.
Fugue (" St. Ann ")	Bach.
Melody in C	Silas.
Allegro Giojoso	Best.
Theme in A	Hird.
Pastorale	Kullak.
March (for a Church Festival)	Best.

The organ has been built by J. W. Walker and Sons. It has two Manuals and Pedal, with eighteen stops. The instrument is, for its size, very effective.

MANCHESTER.

Two recitals were given on the new organ now building for St. James's Church, Daisy Hill, Westhoughton, at the Central Organ Works, Mulberry Street, Hulme, by the following gentlemen :—Wednesday, October 4th, Mr. J. Kendrick, Manchester Town Hall ; Thursday, October 25th, Mr. Wm. Mullineux, organist, Bolton Town Hall. The instrument was built by Messrs. W. E. Richardson and Sons, London, Manchester, and Preston. The organ has three Manuals and Pedal, and some thirty-four stops.

The organ is constructed on W. Richardson and Sons' principle, having two bellows with regulating valve for regularity of pressure, the action of which works on pivots. The case is of pitch pine, being very choice, with spotted metal front pipes and of a beautiful design. The whole of the action is bushed with cloth, and the squares, backfalls, &c., made of mahogany.

WATFORD.

The following is the specification of the new organ in St. Andrew's Church, built by Messrs. Brindley and Foster, of Sheffield, and opened by Mr. James Turpin, Mus. Bac., Cantab., at the Harvest Thanksgiving on Friday evening, October 12th :—

GREAT ORGAN. CC TO C. 61 NOTES.

1. Bourdon	16 ft.	5. Principal	4 ft.
2. Open Diapason	8 „	6. Twelfth	3 „
3. Hohl Flöte	8 „	7. Fifteenth	2 „
4. Gamba	8 „	8. Trumpet	8 „

SWELL ORGAN. CC TO C.

9. Leiblich Bourdon	16 ft.	14. Mixture (3 ranks)	ft.
10. Violin Diapason	8 „	15. Oboe	8 „
11. Echo Gamba	8 „	16. Cornopean	8 „
12. Voix Celestes	8 „	17. Vox Humana	
13. Salicet	4 „		

CHOIR ORGAN. CC TO C.

18. Lieblich Gedact	8 ft.	21. Piccolo	ft.
19. Dulciana	8 „	22. Clarionet	8 „
20. Harmonic Flute	4 „		

PEDAL ORGAN. CCC TO F.

23. Sub-Bass	32 ft.	26. Principal	8 ft.
24. Open Bass	16 „	27. Flute Bass	8 „
25. Sub-Bass	16 „	28. Trombone	

ACCESSORY MOVEMENTS, ETC.

29. Great to Pedal.	34. Great to Pedal.
30. Swell to Pedal.	35. Swell to Great.
31. Choir to Pedal.	36. Swell to Choir.
32. Pedal Super-octave.	37. Swell Super-octave.
33. Tremulant.	38. Great Super-octave.

Three composition pedals acting on Great and Pedals organs, and three acting on the Swell organ.

The arrangement of Manuals, Pedals, draw-stops, etc., are in accordance with the resolutions of the College of Organists ; and the drawstops are placed at an angle facing the player. A case of elegant design, with spotted metal pipes, encloses the instrument, which slightly projects into the chancel. Special commendation should be accorded to the characteristic and level excellence of the various registers, and the smooth unfailing accuracy of the intricate mechanisms, which have been put to a ...

Correspondence.

SCALE COLOUR.

TO THE EDITOR OF THE "MUSICAL STANDARD."

SIR,—I have only time this week to say that I concur with Dr. W. J. Foxell, of Amersham, with respect to his opinion (expressed in the *Mus. Stand.* of Oct. 3rd), that any representation of the notes in our musical scale by colour is unscientific and absurd. The analogy between colour and pitch may be poetical and pretty, but is it exact ? The " equal temperament " of the scale is still a vexed question, and I wish that Mr. A. Ellis, Dr. Stone, Mr. C. E. Stephens, or Dr. E. Hopkins, or some other learned pundit, would thoroughly sift it. I have always leaned to the opinion that there is no different *character* of keys, that to term D major a "bright," and E flat or D flat a "soft" key, is nonsense. Helmholtz's authority should be sufficient ; but doctors, as ever, disagree. The temperament on the pianoforte and the organ is not exactly " equal," owing to certain compromises, a mystery of the tuning art. And again, I have been informed by players in the orchestra of the opera that a different " colour " or character of key, is produced by using the *open*, or *stopped* strings of the violins and violoncellos. Without "stopped" strings and accommodations of temperament, the difference between D and E flat, or between B major and D flat, would be simply a difference of *pitch*. In a word, the vibrations may be more *rapid*, hence the rising of the pitch ; they may be more *ample*, and hence louder or more sonorous ; and lastly the *mutable form* of the vibrations, or different directions of the sound waves, produces the well known varieties of *tone*, *cæteris paribus*, the pitch and the intervals remaining the same. But I wish rather to inquire than to dogmatise.

Yours faithfully,
ALFONSO MATTHEY.

COLOUR-MUSIC.

TO THE EDITOR OF THE "MUSICAL STANDARD."

SIR,—I cannot expect to be allowed to intrude as far upon your space as to put down even a tithe of the thoughts suggested by your notice of my letter to the *Standard*, and your review of Mr. Hughes' work. But perhaps you will be able to find room for a very few words just to explain my position.

It is my firm conviction, based on experience, that the system of musical intervals may be used with good effect by artists, to secure the harmony of their colours, and having established, provisionally, a basis of correspondence between colours and musical notes. I have long been engaged in testing its truth by actual experiment, that is, by colouring pictures so as to display given chords, and observing, with the help of others, how far they exhibit the same character as their musical counterparts. Whatever doubt may, as yet, be attached to my experiments with such chords as that of the dominant ninth, there can be none as to the correspondence of my colours with musical notes in respect of this quality, as major or minor. It was therefore a disappointment to me to find that Mr. Hughes follows so many previous writers in the error of reckoning the ascending scale *down* the solar spectrum, from red, through orange, to yellow, etc., instead of in the contrary direction, as I do. For the effect of this error is to invert the music, and substitute minor chords for major. Thus he makes red, yellow, and blue a major chord, whereas if he put it on a picture and compared it with blue, buff, and red (my D, F sharp, and A), he would find that it is palpably minor, and corresponds, as I give it, to D F A. His system, if *inverted*, will be almost the same as mine. This error, however, is founded on the notion that we ought to compare the number of undulations for second in light with the vibrations of sound. And in fact, it is not the number of undulations but the length of the waves (which are in inverse ratio to the number of undulations) by which we should reckon, since the longer the wave the greater is the impression which it makes on the retina of the eye, and the "sharper," in musical language, is its effect.

You object, not unnaturally, to my speaking of a common chord as " a mere make-weight." Of course I was not then speaking of musical notes, but of the notes in colour, and I am free to confess that this description is somewhat rough, and requires limitation, for which I had not space at my command. Nevertheless, there is a great difference in this matter between music and colour. In the former you may find four notes to a chord a very bare minimum, whilst in a picture it is sometimes impossible to use more than two with good effect. I say this, not so much from the observation of my own poor attempts at painting, as from the consideration of pictures by great masters, who generally syncopate their chords. I am not so foolish as to suppose that it is possible, by means of any theory, to teach artists a new system of colouring quite unknown to them at present. As music existed long before the rules of harmony were discovered, so it must be with colouring, and any the....

essence of the chord still remains, then you will have little difficulty in finding many of the chords in my system already in constant use by artists. In pictures where the artist limits himself to three colours in one chord, of which an exhibition at the Royal Academy generally supplies a considerable number, you will find the fifth, but in many of the more ambitious flights, such as those of Sir F. Leighton, you will find more than one chord, yet seldom a fifth, as far as I have hitherto observed, with any of them. Perhaps I should have better expressed my meaning by saying that in colour the fifth is always *implied* by the rest and the third ; but as I am afraid I have already trespassed too much on your kind indulgence, I will only add that in some points there must needs be a difference between musical chords and chords of colour, whilst it may be quite possible to show, as I hope to do, when not pressed for elbow-room, that such differences involve no discrepancy of fundamental principles.

I am, Sir, your obedient servant,
A. P. BETHELL.

Genoa-road, Anerley, S.E.
October 15th, 1883.

Passing Events.

Signor Vianesi conducts the new opera in New York.

Herr Franke will again be associated with the management of the Richter concerts.

The Howlers Club gave a smoking concert on Oct. 18th. Mr. W. W. Robinson was the pianist.

Mr. Cowen's "St. Ursula" is to be given by the New York Oratorio Society on Nov. 21st and 22nd.

Le Ménestrel is enthusiastic in its praise of Leeds Festival, both as regards composers and executants.

Mr. Mackenzie is fortunate enough to have Mr. Joseph Bennett as his librettist for his oratorio for Birmingham.

Mr. F. Amor has recovered his health and is again to enter his profession as a violinist. A subscription has been started as an expression of sympathy.

The total number of listeners at the Leeds Festival came to 13,984 for the seven performances. Upon several occasions the audience numbered 2000.

Sir Julius Benedict is said to be composing incidental music for the new poetical drama by Messrs. Wills and Herman, now in preparation at the Princess's Theatre.

The "Birds" of Aristophanes will be represented at Cambridge this term. The performance will take place on the evenings of November 27th, 28th, 29th, and 30th, and on the afternoon of December 1st ; and great care is being taken to secure a thoroughly efficient cast. Mr. Hubert Parry supplies the music.

Mr. and Mrs. German Reed at their entertainment, St. George's Hall, have produced an entirely new musical sketch, by Mr. Corney Grain, entitled "On the Thames ;" and a new after piece, by Mr. Arnold Felix, music by Mr. George Gear, entitled "A Water Cure." The highly successful "Treasure Trove" still retains its place in the programme.

Brainard's Musical World has an interesting account of the various portraits of Beethoven, in the course of which it says :—Only three oil paintings were taken from life. The first of these represents the master when thirty years of age. It is considered an inferior work, and but few engravings have been made from it. The second was executed by Schimon when Beethoven was forty-nine years of age. The third was still later in life and is the work of Stieler, of Munich.

The passion for theatrical realism is naturally bringing its accompanying dangers. A terrible accident is reported to have occurred in the Grand Theatre, Moscow, on the occasion of the last representation of M. Rubinstein's opera of "The Demon." A platform suspended by cords, and supporting seven little girls—pupils of the Dramatic School—figuring as genii, suddenly gave way through the snapping of the cords. The children, who fell from a height of about 17 feet on to the stage, were found to have suffered more or less from concussion of the brain. Two of the victims were also seriously wounded. Surely the authorities ought to be well taken to task for allowing children to be so placed.

Says the *Athenæum*, it is possible that two of the most esteemed of living continental composers will visit London next season, thanks to the initiative of the Philharmonic Society. Eduard Grieg has accepted an invitation to play a new pianoforte concerto, and overtures have also been made to Anton Dvořák to compose and conduct an orchestral work.

The Annual Festival of the Guild of St. Luke, was held at St. Paul's Cathedral, on Thursday evening, the 18th inst. The musical portion of the service was carried out by the London Gregorian Choral Association, with about 150 voices, under the direction of Mr. C. Warwick Jordan, who very ably presided at the organ. The sermon was preached by the Bishop of Bedford.

On Tuesday, October 16th, on the occasion of the fourth annual general meeting of the Ware Musical Society, the members presented their honorary conductor, Mr. James L. Gregory & Co. with a valuable gold watch and chain, as a token of their esteem and appreciation of his musical talent. The works selected for practice and performance by the society during the present season are Gade's "Erl-King's Daughter," Macfarren's "May-day," and Haydn's "Spring."

Mr. Willing's Choir at St. James's Hall, announce a very spirited prospectus. The subscription will comprise a series of four concerts, as follows :—Tuesday, 11th Dec., 1883, Sir George Macfarren's "King David." Tuesday, 15th Jan., 1884, Mendelssohn's "Walpurgis Night," 57th Psalm, by E. H. Thorne, and Selection. Tuesday, 25th March, 1884, Mendelssohn's "Elijah." Tuesday, 22nd April, 1884, Wilfred Bendall's cantata, "Parizadeh," and an operatic selection. The orchestra is of the best possible quality.

Some time ago Mr. N. Holmes, offered to the Dean and Chapter of Canterbury, his grand four-manual organ, which is now in the concert-room at Haverstock Hill. The organ was built at a cost of £8,600, but it has been offered to the Dean and Chapter for a sum considerably less than the original cost. The principal objection the Chapter had to the instrument being placed in the cathedral was that it would mar the architecture of the building, and would obstruct the fine view of the nave which is now obtained from both aisles. This objection Mr. Holmes thinks may be obviated, and a mock representation of the appearance of the organ and the space it would occupy, is now being placed in the cathedral.

Says a contemporary, "Sing a Song of Sixpence" is as old as the sixteenth century. "Three Blind Mice," is found in a music-book dated 1609. "The Frog and the Mouse" in 1580. "Three Children Sliding on the Ice" dates from 1639. "London Bridge is broken down" is of unfathomed antiquity. "Girls and Boys, Come out to Play" is certainly as old as the reign of Charles II., as is also "Lucy Locket lost her Pocket," to the tune of which the American song of "Yankee Doodle" was written. "Pussy Cat, Pussy Cat, Where have you been?" is of the age of Queen Bess. "Little Jack Horner" is older than the Seventeenth Century. "The Old Woman tossed in a Blanket" is of the reign of James II., to which monarch it is supposed to allude.

Says the *Huddersfield Daily Chronicle*, In the list of candidates for the degree of musical doctor who have satisfied the Oxford University examiners, was the name of R. M. Winn, New College, and Harborne, Birmingham. Rowland Mellor Winn is a nephew of our veteran organist, Mr. Richard Mellor, and also a nephew of Mr. William Winn, of Her Majesty's Chapel Royal, St. James's, and St. Paul's Cathedral, London. He obtained the degree of Mus. Bac. at Oxford before he was 20 years of age. He has composed an oratorio, "The Sea of Galilee," for his university test of Doctor of Music, this term. This oratorio, with full orchestral accompaniments, is to be performed at Oxford. Dr. Winn will take his singers and orchestra from Birmingham. The doctor is another proof of what natural talent, coupled with good training, will do. From a child he was taught the piano by his mother—who will be well-known to some of our readers as Miss Mellor—a clever pianoforte player and organist in Huddersfield above 30 years ago. This lady is still in the full possession of all her powers, as was shown by her playing, as duets, with her brother (Mr. Richard Mellor) some of Handel's choruses on the organ at our Exhibition a few weeks ago.

The Querist.

QUERY.

MUSICAL DEGREE.—At what University in Great Britain, or Ireland, can a Musical Degree be taken without passing an Arts Examination, and what are the best books for study for that University?—ORGANIST.

EXPENSE OF INSTRUCTION, ETC. — What would a lady's yearly expense be for a course of instruction and living in London, at the R.A.M., or R.C.M. in piano and organ; or at Berlin, under Kullauk and Lange, amount to?—PROVINCIAL.

REPLY.

J. I. F.—" Thou Judge of quick and dead" forms the concluding movement of S. S. Wesley's eight-part anthem, "Let us lift up our heart," but is not published separately. The complete anthem is to be had of Novello and Co., in folio size, price 4s. As to "Behold, how good and pleasant," I am unable to say whether it is by Henry or Sir George Smart. There is no mention made of it in the life of the former composer by Dr. Spark, neither can I find it in any music catalogue. I should think it was most probably by Sir George Smart, who composed some Cathedral music, and of which I once saw a list, but am unable to recollect whether the anthem in question was in it. Addison and Co., were, I think, the publishers.-J. S. BUMPUS.

CONDUCTOR.—The Leamington Philharmonic Society has set of copies of "The Ancient Mariner," including orchestral Parts. Will "Conductor" communicate with A. E. Gibbs, Hon. Sec., who will make any reasonable arrangement.

Service Lists.

TWENTY-THIRD SUNDAY AFTER TRINITY.
OCTOBER 28th.
London.

ST. PAUL'S CATHEDRAL.—Morn.: Service, Te Deum and Benedictus (Gounod); Introit, Word of God Incarnate, No. 572 (Gounod); Holy Communion, Martin in C. Even.: Service, Magnificat and Nunc Dimittis (Gounod); Anthem, They were lovely and pleasant (Stainer).

TEMPLE CHURCH.—Morn.: Service, Te Deum Laudamus and Jubilate Deo, Barrow in F; Apostles' Creed, Harmonised Monotone; Anthem, The Lord is my light (Boyce). Even.: Service, Magnificat and Nunc Dimittis, Barrow in F; Apostles Creed, Harmonized Monotone; Anthem, I will sing of Thy power (Greene).

FOUNDLING CHAPEL.—Morn.: Service, Te Deum, Calkin in G; Benedictus, Smith in B flat; Anthem, When I call upon Thee "Mass in C" (Beethoven). Aft.: Children's Service.

CHRIST CHURCH, CLAPHAM.—Morn.: Service, Te Deum, Plain-song; Kyrie, and Credo, Schubert in F; Offertory Anthem, In the sight of the unwise (Ouseley); Sanctus, Benedictus, Agnus Dei, and Gloria in excelsis (Schubert). Even.: Service, Magnificat and Nunc Dimittis, Hoyte in B flat; Anthem, Sing a song of praise (Stainer).

HOLY TRINITY, GRAY'S INN ROAD. — Morn.: Service, Te Deum, Boyce in A; Jubilate, Chanted. Even.: Service, Magnificat, Chanted; Nunc Dimittis, Bunnett in F. Anthem, Now we are ambassadors, How lovely are the messengers (Mendelssohn).

HOLY TRINITY, TULSE HILL. — Morn.: Service, Chants. Even.: Service, Magnificat and Nunc Dimittis, Gregory in E flat; Anthem, Now we are ambassadors, and How lovely are the messengers (Mendelssohn).

ST. JAMES'S PRIVATE EPISCOPAL CHAPEL, SOUTHWARK, —Morn.: Service, Introit, What are these (Stainer); Communion Service, Haydn in C, No. 2. Even.: Service, Thorne in D; Anthem, Lovely, appear "Redemption" (Gounod).

ST. MARGARET PATTENS, ROOD LANE, FENCHURCH STREET.—Morn.: Service, Te Deum, Wesley in F; Benedictus, Dykes in F; Communion Service, Offertory Anthem, How beautiful are the feet (Handel); Kyrie, Credo, Sanctus, Benedictus, Agnus Dei, and Gloria, Schubert in B flat. Even.: Service, Magnificat and Nunc Dimittis, Hopkins in F; Anthem, Lovely appear "Redemption" (Gounod).

ST. MARY BOLTONS, WEST BROMPTON, S.W.—Morn.: Service, Te Deum, Smart in F; Benedictus, Chant; Holy Communion, Kyrie, Credo, Offertory, Sanctus, and Gloria in excelsis, Stainer in E flat; Benedictus and Agnus Dei, Eyre in E flat. Even.: Service, Magnificat and Nunc Dimittis, Gadsby in G; Anthem, It came to pass (Ouseley).

ST. MAGNUS, LONDON BRIDGE.—Morn.: Service, Opening Anthem, If we say (Calkin); Te Deum and Jubilate, Turle in D; Kyrie (Walmisley). Even.: Service, Magnificat and Nunc Dimittis, Turle in D; Anthem, Save, Lord, and hear us (Hayes).

ST. MICHAEL'S, CORNHILL. — Morn.: Service, Te Deum and Jubilate, Dykes in F; Anthem, Teach me, O Lord (Attwood); Kyrie and Creed, Thorne in E flat. Even.: Service, Magnificat and Nunc Dimittis, Attwood in C; Anthem, Now we are ambassadors (Mendelssohn).

ST. PAUL'S, AVENUE ROAD, SOUTH HAMPSTEAD.—Morn.: Service, Te Deum, Dykes in F; Benedictus, Stainer in E flat; Kyrie, Tours in F; Credo, Tours in F. Even.: Service, Magnificat and Nunc Dimittis, Walmisley in D minor; Anthem, How lovely are the messengers "St. Paul" (Mendelssohn).

ST. PAUL'S, BOW COMMON, E.—Morn.: Service, Te Deum and Benedictus, Chants; Holy Communion, Kyrie, Credo, Offertory, Sanctus, and Gloria in excelsis, Stainer in A; Benedictus and Agnus Dei, Eyre in E flat. Even.: Service, Magnificat and Nunc Dimittis, Stainer in E flat; Anthem What are these that are arrayed (Stainer).

ST. PETER'S (EATON SQUARE).—Morn.: Service, Holy Communion, Stainer in A; Te Deum, Tours in F. Even.: Service, Stainer in A; Anthem, Hallelujah, power and glory (Beethoven).

ST. PETER'S, VERE STREET, W.—Even.: Service, Magnificat and Nunc Dimittis, Goss in A; Anthem, I waited for the Lord (Mendelssohn).

ST. AUGUSTINE AND ST. FAITH, WATLING STREET.— Morn.: Service, Selby in A; Introit, Thou shalt make them (South); Communion Service, Garrett in E flat. Even.: Service, Selby in A; Anthem, The wilderness (Goss).

ST. SAVIOUR'S, HOXTON. — Morn.: Service, Te Deum, Gadsby in E flat; Holy Communion; Kyrie, Credo, Sursum Corda, Sanctus, and Gloria in excelsis, Smart in F. Even.: Service, Magnificat and Nunc Dimittis, Smart in G; Anthem, The Lord is my Shepherd (Macfarren).

ST. SEPULCHRE'S, HOLBORN.—Morn.: Service, Smart in F; Anthem, Lord for Thy tender (Farrant). Even.: Service, Porter in D; Anthem, Now we are ambassadors, and How lovely (Mendelssohn).

Country.

ST. ASAPH CATHEDRAL. — Morn.: Service, Boyce in A; Anthem, The Lord preserveth (Hatton). Even.: Service, Arnold in A; Anthem, The Lord is the portion (Webbe).

ASHBURNE CHURCH, DERBYSHIRE. — Morn.: Service throughout, Garrett in F. Even.: Service, Garrett in F; Anthem, Hallelujah! What are these (Stainer).

BELFAST (ST. GEORGE'S). — Morn.: Service, Te Deum, and Jubilate, Smart in F; Communion Service, Woodward in E flat; Offertory (Monk). Even.: Service, Magnificat and Nunc Dimittis, Arnold in A; Anthem, Give unto the Lord the glory (Bridge).

BIRMINGHAM (S. ALBAN THE MARTYR).—Morn.: Service, Te Deum, Boyce in C; Benedictus, Steggall in G; Holy Communion, Dykes in F. Evensong: Magnificat and Nunc Dimittis, Barnby in E.

BIRMINGHAM (ST. CYPRIAN'S, HAY MILLS).—Morn.: Service, Nares in C; Anthem, Put me not to rebuke (Greene). Even.: Service, Ebdon in C; Anthem, When the Son of man shall come (Kent).

CARLISLE CATHEDRAL.—Morn.: Service, Hopkins in C; Introit, We wait for (Armes); Kyrie and Nicene Creed, Dykes in F. Even.: Service, Attwood in C; Anthem, Praise the Lord (Wesley).

CANTERBURY CATHEDRAL. —Morn.: Service, Dykes in F; Anthem, Let thy merciful ears (Ashley); Communion, Dykes in F. Even.: Service, Dykes in F; Anthem, The Lord gave the word, How beautiful, &c. (Handel).

CHESTER (ST. MARY'S CHURCH).—Morn': Service, Tearse in C; Introit The Heavenly word proceeding forth; Communion Service, Tuckerman in F. Even.: Service, Turle in D; Anthem, O how amiable are Thy dwellings (Barnby).

DONCASTER (PARISH CHURCH).—Morn.: Service, Whitfeld in E. Even.: Service, Whitfeld in E; Anthem, Now we are ambassadors, and How lovely are the messengers (Mendelssohn).

DUBLIN, ST. PATRICK'S (NATIONAL) CATHEDRAL.—Morn.: Service, Te Deum, and Jubilate, Stanford in B flat; Holy Communion, Kyrie, Creed, and Sanctus, Stanford in B flat; Anthem, The Wilderness (Wesley). Even.: Service, Magnificat and Nunc Dimittis, Stanford in B flat; Anthem, How lovely are the messengers (Mendelssohn), and I beheld, and lo (Blow).

EDINBURGH (ST. JOHN'S).—Aft.: Service, Anthem, Jerusalem thou that killest "St. Paul" (Mendelssohn). Even.: Service, Anthem, How lovely are the messengers, "St. Paul" (Mendelssohn).

ELY CATHEDRAL.—Morn.: Service, Wesley in F; Kyrie and Credo, Wesley in F; Gloria, Tours in F; Anthem, The Lord redeemeth (Wesley). Even.: Service, Wesley in F; Anthem, Blessed be the God and Father (Wesley).

FOLKESTONE (ST. MICHAEL's). — Morn.: Service, Kyrie, Credo, Sanctus and Gloria in excelsis (Gounod); after the Consecration, O saving victim (Gounod); after the Blessing, O Lord, save me (Gounod). Even.: Service, Magnificat and Nunc Dimittis, Gounod in D; Anthem, Send out Thy light (Gounod); Concluding Voluntary, Marche Militaire (Gounod).

HARROGATE (ST. PETER'S CHURCH).—Morn.: Service, Te Deum, and Athanasian Creed, Chants; Anthem, Lead me, O Lord (Attwood). Even.: Service, Magnificat and Nunc Dimittis, Wesley in F; Anthem, The Lord shall preserve, and Blessed is the man (Bridge).

LLANDAFF CATHEDRAL.—Morn.: Service, Te Deum and Benedictus, Stainer in E flat. Even.: Service, Magnificat and Nunc Dimittis, Stainer in E flat; Anthem, What are these (Stainer).

LEEDS PARISH CHURCH—Morn.: Service, Boyce in A; Anthem, The depths have covered (Handel); Kyrie and Creed, Best in E. Even.: Service, Bridge in G; Anthem, In that day (Elvey).

LICHFIELD CATHEDRAL. — Morn.: Service, Sullivan in D; Anthem, O praise the Lord of Heaven (Elvey). Even.: Service, Stainer in B flat; Anthem, By Babylon's wave (Gounod).

LINLITHGOW ABBEY, W.B.—Morn.: Service, Anthem, O Lord, my strength (Auber). Even.: Service, Anthem, Whosoever drinketh of Thy water (Bennett).

LIVERPOOL CATHEDRAL.—Aft.: Service, Magnificat and Nunc Dimittis, Banks in E flat; Anthem, I beheld and lo (Elvey).

MANCHESTER CATHEDRAL. — Morn.: Service, Te Deum Jubilate, Creed, Sanctus, and Gloria, Tours in F; Anthem, Incline thine ear (Himmel). Aft.: Service, Tours in F; Anthem, Remember now thy Creator (Steggall).

MANCHESTER (ST. BENEDICT'S).—Morn.: Service, Te Deum Sullivan in D; Kyrie, Credo, Sanctus, and Gloria in excelsis, Steggall in G; Benedictus, and Agnus Dei, Woodward in E flat. Even.: Service, Magnificat and Nunc Dimittis, Tours in F.

MANCHESTER (ST. JOHN BAPTIST, HULME).—Morn.: Service, Te Deum and Benedictus (Stainer); Procession, "Lauda Sion " (Cobb); Kyrie, Credo, Sanctus, and Gloria in excelsis, Stainer in A; Benedictus and Agnus Dei, Tours in F; Offertory Anthem, Thou visitest the earth (Greene); Paternoster and Post Communion (Hoyte). Even.: Service, Magnificat and Nunc Dimittis, Tours in F; Anthem, Ye shall dwell in the land (Stainer); Te Deum (Stainer).

MUSSELBURGH (LORETTO SCHOOL).—Morn.: Service, Introit, Incline Thine ear (Himmel); Service, Stainer in E flat; Anthem, O clap your hands (Stainer). Even.: Service, Anthem, Sing to the Lord, our King and Maker (Haydn).

ROCHESTER CATHEDRAL. — Morn.: Service, Elvey in A; Anthem, How goodly (Ouseley). Even.: Service, Elvey in A; Anthem, God is a Spirit (Bennett).

SHEFFIELD PARISH CHURCH. — Morn.: Service, Kyrie, Elvey in A. Even.: Service, Magnificat and Nunc Dimittis, Chants; Anthem, Blessed are the merciful (Hiles).

SHERBORNE ABBEY. — Morn.: Service, Te Deum, Lyle in F. Even.: Service, Chants; Anthem, Thou visitest the earth (Greene).

SOUTHAMPTON (ST. MARY'S CHURCH).—Morn.: Service, Te Deum and Benedictus, Stainer in E flat; Holy Communion, Introit, Jesus said (Stainer); Service, Stainer in E flat; Offertory (Stainer); Paternoster (Hoyte). Even.: Service, Magnificat and Nunc Dimittis, Stainer in E flat; Apostle's Creed, Harmonized Monotone; Anthem, Behold, how good and joyful (Whitfeld).

WELLS CATHEDRAL.—Morn.: Service, Ouseley in A; Introit, O magnify the Lord (Macfarren). Even.: Service, Barnby in E; Anthem, Be merciful (Purcell).

WOLVERHAMPTON (ST. PETER'S COLLEGIATE CHURCH).—Morn.: Service, Te Deum, Steggall in G; Benedictus, Goss in C. Even.: Service, Magnificat, Wooward in A; Chant; Nunc Dimittis, Stevens in A flat; Anthem O taste and see (Marn).

WORCESTER CATHEDRAL. — Morn.: Service, Jackman in D; Anthem, Blest are the departed (Spohr). Even.: Service, Jackman in D; Anthem, Then shall the righteous (Mendelssohn).

. Post-cards must be sent to the Editor, 6, Argyle Square, W.C., by Wednesday. Lists are frequently omitted in consequence of not being received in time.

APPOINTMENTS.

Mr. CHAS. J. MARVIN, has been appointed Organist and Choir-master of St. Paul's, Balls-pond.

Mr. ALFRED PAWSEY has been appointed Alto to St. Paul's, Great Portland Street, W.

NOTICE TO CORRESPONDENTS.—"Form in Vocal Music," and several other articles, are this week crowded out.

NEWSPAPERS sent should have distinct marks opposite to the matter to which attention is required.

Printed for the Proprietor by BOWDEN, HUDSON & Co., at 23, Red Lion Street, Holborn, London, W.C.; and Published by WILLIAM REEVES, at the Office, 185, Fleet Street, E.C. West End Agents:—WEEKES & CO., 14, Hanover Street, Regent Street, W. Subscriptions and Advertisements are received either by the Publisher or West End Agents.—*Communications for the Editor are to be forwarded to his private address, 6, Argyle Square, W.C.*
SATURDAY, OCTOBER 27, 1883.—*Entered at the General Post Office as a Newspaper.*

THE MUSICAL STANDARD

A NEWSPAPER FOR MUSICIANS PROFESSIONAL AND AMATEUR

No. 1005. VOL. XXV. FOURTH SERIES. SATURDAY, NOVEMBER 3, 1883. WEEKLY: PRICE 3D.

THE VOICE
MUSICALLY AND MEDICALLY CONSIDERED.
BY
ARMAND SEMPLE, B.A., M.B., Cantab., M.R.C.P., Lond.,
Physician to the Royal Society of Musicians.

(*Continued from page 174.*)

CLASSIFICATION OF CULTIVATED VOICES.

MALE VOICES.

As has been already stated, these voices may be classified as *Bass* (the lowest in the male vocal scale) ; *Baritone* (one-third above the bass) ; *Tenor* (one-third above the baritone) ; *Contraltino* or *Counter-tenor*, one-third above the tenor, and highest in the male vocal scale.

The BASS VOICE should be confined to the Chest register, which may in the most fortunate case be extended from Re flat$_1$ (D flat$_1$) to Mi$_2$ (E$_2$).

It experiences considerable difficulty in reaching the falsetto notes, which extend from Si flat$_2$ (B flat$_2$) to Sol flat$_2$ (G flat$_2$).

The BARITONE VOICE may be extended from Sol$_1$ (G$_1$) to Sol$_2$ (G$_2$) in the chest voice. The Falsetto extends from Si$_2$ (B$_2$) to Si$_3$ (B$_3$) thus

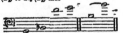

Baritone, Tenor, and Counter-Tenor Voices can produce falsetto notes with almost the same ease as Female Voices.

The TENOR VOICE may extend from Do$_2$ (C$_2$) to La$_3$ (A$_3$) in the chest.

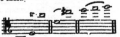

The Falsetto extends from Re$_3$ (D$_3$) to Do sharp$_4$ (C sharp$_4$).
The Head voice extends from Re$_4$ (D$_4$) to Mi$_4$ (E$_4$) and Fa$_4$ (F$_4$).
Tenors can combine the chest and falsetto registers with more ease than Baritones, since the pitch of modern music being too high for Tenor singers, they are compelled to fall back upon the Falsetto ; but the employment of this register ought in every case to depend upon the aptitude of the voice in blending the *timbre* of the chest and the falsetto registers.

The CONTRALTINO or COUNTER TENOR is the highest voice in the male scale. Its quality is light and clear ; the Chest voice may extend from Re$_3$ (D$_3$) to Do$_4$ (C$_4$) ; the Falsetto from Re$_3$ (D$_3$) to Do sharp$_4$ (C sharp$_4$) and the Head from Re$_4$ (D$_4$) to Fa sharp$_4$ (F sharp$_4$) thus

Chest Voice.   Falsetto.   Head Voice.

This voice can combine the chest and falsetto registers with more ease than other male voices. It is the thinnest and most effeminate of the male voices.

FEMALE VOICES.

In women there are four kinds of voices.
The *Contralto*, the lowest in the female vocal scale.
The *Mezzo Soprano*, one-third above the Contralto.
The *Soprano*, one-third above the Mezzo Soprano.
The *Soprano-Sopracuto* (rare) one-third above the soprano and the highest in the female scale.

The Chest (Voce di Petto) Register.

This register more exclusively belongs to the Contralto voice. It is of less importance in the Mezzo-Soprano, and Soprano. It is, however, the basis of the female voice. Including the deepest voice, the compass of this register is from Mi$_2$ (E$_2$) to Re$_4$ (D$_4$).

The highest note of this register should never go beyond Mi$_3$ (E$_3$) or Fa$_3$ (F$_3$)

since any straining above these sounds might entirely destroy the voice.

The Falsetto (Voce di Fasetto) Register.

This is the most remarkable part of the Mezzo-Soprano voice. It descends nearly as low, and ascends quite as high as the chest register. The notes, however, between Sol$_2$ (G$_2$) and Re$_3$ (D$_3$)

are usually weak, and wanting in energy. Although the registers of the chest and falsetto possess the same compass, the character of the former is vigorous, sonorous, and penetrating, whilst, on the contrary, that of the latter is soft and veiled.

The notes from Sol$_3$ (G$_3$) to Re$_4$ (D$_4$).

when produced in the chest register, call for so much effort, that their employment in this manner for a few years might probably destroy the voice permanently. These notes are, however, sung with perfect ease in the falsetto register ; to obviate weakness in the low notes of the scale the compass should be formed by uniting the two registers. The chest being employed from Fa$_2$ (F$_2$) to Fa$_3$ (F$_3$), the Falsetto from Re$_3$ (D$_3$) to Re$_4$ (D$_4$), thus—

Chest.   Falsetto.

four sounds being thus reserved which are common to the two registers. The capability of changing the registers on any of their notes is thus retained.

The Head (Voce di Testa) Register.

The brilliancy of Soprano Voices is chiefly due to the ease with which they can produce the high sounds. These voices in the lower sounds are comparatively weak.

The following tables show the Registers of the Female Voices :—

The Contralto.

Chest.   Falsetto.   Head.

Perilous.

The Mezzo-Soprano.

Chest.   Falsetto.   Head.

The Soprano.

Chest.   Falsetto.   Head.

The Soprano Sopracuto.

Chest.   Falsetto.   Head.

In these tables, in each register three or four notes are allowed as the limit since every individual possesses varying capabilities of extension.

(*To be continued.*)

REMINISCENCES OF AN OLD REPORTER.

I must begin by reverting to the Philharmonic Society, and a certain incident which I assumed to be founded on fact, a few weeks ago. A learned authority, a veritable "book in breeches," as Sydney Smith used to call Babington Macaulay, doubts, if he does not directly deny, that Mendelssohn asked the directors of the Society to dismiss an artist who had presumed to call him to account for "keeping the band waiting" at rehearsal. I can only repeat that Henry Westrop, the "second violin," gave me the information, and Westrop was not a man to circulate idle gossip. Perhaps Mr. Charles E. Stephens, who knows everything about the Philharmonic, may be able to decide this dispute *de facto*.

A highly respectable Society, called the "British Musicians," flourished for awhile about the years 1840—46. The object, as one of the Westrops said, was to give professionals an opportunity of "playing their own things"; and several excellent works for the chamber were produced from time to time. The Society included amongst its principal members G. A. Macfarren, Cipriani Potter, H. Westrop, T. Westrop, James Davison, Lucas, and other notables. I have before spoken of one Alsager, on the staff of the *Times*, as City Correspondent and musical reporter; but he subsequently gave up the latter duty in favour of his nephew, John Oxenford, who knew as much of music (until he took lessons in the theory of the art) as Mr. Snodgrass did of skates ! What induced Alsager to make an attack upon the Society of British Musicians, deponent cannot testify ; but the deed was done. One foggy morning in December, 1844, there appeared, in the *Times*, a column of minion type, "leadlined," in which the leading members of the Society were sharply assailed in turn, especially Lucas and Cipriani Potter. Those of your readers who wish to read this article may go to Peele's Coffee House or the British Museum. I forget the details. The gist of the article was that the composers referred to had done nothing to advance the art, and that the Society itself was practically worthless for that purpose. James Davison and Mr. Macfarren were let off with a bit of cautionary advice to mind their p's and q's. Alsager, although he deceived none of the *initiated* by the crafty device, was so mean as to add a postscript to his article, which informed the public that it had not been written by the regular musical reporter, but by a gentleman of authority, to be relied on as evidence ! Oxenford at this time wrote the *critiques* for the *Times*, doing double duty at the opera and the theatres, both lyrical and dramatic : the *drama* was his *forte*. James Davison succeeded him in 1846, and began his work with a masterly analysis of "Elijah," which appeared in long primer type a week before the performance at Birmingham, also reviewed in detail by Mr. J. Davison. Reverting to the "British Musicians," I heard that Cipriani Potter had offended Alsager by declining, on religious grounds, to play at his Sunday receptions in Queen Square, Bloomsbury. If this be true, the worse for poor Alsager's reputation. I remember Cipriani Potter well ; I had not known him personally up to the year 1868.9, but I then encountered the venerable musician at Mr. Hallé's recitals, and also at the Crystal Palace Concerts. At the Recitals he once kindly lent me his Programme Book (presented to him as a mark of respect by one of Mr. Chappell's *employés*), with the observation that he discerned my deep interest in the performance. I had, as usual, been taking copious notes. Potter told me a personal anecdote. He had received a stall for the Italian Opera, at Drury Lane Theatre, and presented himself, at eight o'clock, without the compulsory "swallow-tail" coat. The officials refused to admit him in his surtout, and Potter retired in discomfiture. But Balm in Gilead ! On reading the large post-bills outside the theatre, Potter saw that the opera of the night was "Rigoletto." This work of

Verdi's did not satisfy the old musician's severe tastes, and he thus rejoiced in the gain of a loss. Potter did not explain to me why he neglected to read the advertisement of the theatre in the morning papers, or why, a veteran "about town," he failed to don the regular evening dress always insisted on at the Opera. *Aliquando Homerus dormitat !* When Cipriani Potter honoured Mr. Hallé with his attendance, that great pianist was running through the eleven sonatas of Schubert in rotation ; he repeated them regularly for a few years, in 1867-69. I wish that he would revert to them once more, for they are rarely to be heard. All have their merits, but commend me to Nos. 10 and 11 in A major, and B flat. Like the little girl's affection for her papa and mamma, "I like *both* best." The "Fantasia Sonata" in G, the three in A minor, and the so-called "Military Sonata" in B major, are also pearls of price. Sir George Grove and Mr. Manns should make some of their pianists play these sonatas at the Crystal Palace on Saturdays, instead of the often hackneyed "fugitive" solos.

Ecce iterum Crispinus ! Alsager once more, for he had much to do with music, and deserves his meed of praise. He founded the "Beethoven Quartet Society," and so paved the way for the proper performance of the five "Posthumous" quartets, now annually reproduced by Mr. Arthur Chappell on a festival Wednesday afternoon in March. These and other classical chamber compositions were rendered at Alsager's house by the finest artists in London. Scipion Rousselot, the violoncellist, dedicated his splendid edition of the "Posthumous" quartets to "his friend Alsager" as a grateful recognition of the good work by him achieved. Alsager played the violoncello fairly well, but said that he could no longer bear to hear *himself*, after Rousselot, Lindley, and other grand artists. Alsager sometimes devoted the Sunday to Mass Services. On one occasion, full forty years ago (or more), Spohr was entertained, in Queen Square, together with a host of musical notables, on a fine Sunday in the height of summer. A grand concert, which lasted some hours, was agreeably relieved with a superb banquet ; both the programme and the *menu* were printed in gold letters. The selection of music I forget, but you may rely on my word that no grinding ballads or "royalty" songs found a place in the scheme ; most of the numbers would, of course, be instrumental and concerted. Alsager, although he cared little for theology or dogma, usually invited a clergyman, his friend, whom he addressed, at table, as "Mr. Chaplain," and asked him to say grace. I met this worthy pastor in 1840 and 1841, at Alsager's house, and believe that he is still alive, as the Rev. Charles Perring, once assistant minister of Regent Square Chapel, St. Pancras, but now "unattached." Spohr, on this golden Sunday, of course received all honour, and his health was drunk in bumpers of champagne *con amore*. After the death of Mrs. Alsager, the widower gave up his receptions, lost his spirits, and finally, as I have before related, destroyed himself, on his dismissal from the post of City Correspondent to the *Times*, in November, 1846. Two years before, when a grand dinner took place at the London Tavern in honour of the *Times* newspaper, whose Paris correspondent had exposed an infamous conspiracy, to the detriment of the mercantile and commercial interests. Alsager, on returning thanks for the toast to himself, boasted that he had written the City Article for twenty-seven years. How slippery are the paths of life ! What dreadful *cadences* in this world, from high estate, that do *not* end in the major mode !

Cipriani Potter's adventure at Drury Lane Theatre reminds me of Auber. That great French composer was one night "kept out in the cold" at the Opéra Comique, not for incorrect costume, but because he had arrived late ; and it was the rule to refuse admission to all tardy ones—most properly—until the particular piece was over. Mr. Walter Bache and Mr. Dannreuther, of the Wagner Society, have followed the good example. The Directors of the Crystal Palace might follow suit. They ought to, and indeed *do*, insist on the exclusion of visitors during the actual performance of a number at the Saturday concerts. The first overture, or symphony, used to be accompanied by an *obbligato* stampede of elephantine tramps, and the incessant talking would irritate even the passive turtle-dove which, naturalists say, will allow its eyes to be plucked out, yet offer no resistance !

I must defer my references to the "Musical Union" until I can have an interview with Professor Ella, now, alas ! afflicted with blindness, but otherwise hale and hearty.   A. M.

Musical Intelligence.

CRYSTAL PALACE CONCERTS.

PROGRAMME.

Festival March. "Edinburgh"	Oakeley.
Fantasia-Overture, "Paradise and the Pen"	Bennett.
Recit., "Confounded be all," and Air, "They shall be turned back" (" Naaman ")	Costa.
(Her first appearance at these Concerts).	
Miss Hilda Coward.	
Symphony in E minor	Macfarren.
(First time at these Concerts).	
Recit. and Evening Prayer (" Eli ")	Costa.
Madame Patey.	
Concerto for Violoncello and Orchestra, No. 3, in B minor......................................	Golterman.
(First time at these Concerts).	
Mr. Edward Howell.	
(His first appearance at the Crystal Palace).	
Song, " Lo ! here the gentle lark "	Bishop.
Miss Hilda Coward.	
Flute obbligato, Mr. Alfred Wells.	
Orchestral Prelude, "The Eve of St. John "	Stewart.
(First time at these Concerts).	
Solo for violoncello, " Andante and Allegro "	Boccherini.
Mr. Edward Howell.	
Song, " By the Sad Sea Waves "	Benedict.
Madame Patey.	
Overture, " Di Ballo "	Sullivan.
Conductor - - AUGUST MANNS.	

Sir George Macfarren's symphony was written for the British Orchestral Society, and produced at their concert on the 26th of March, 1874. Many works are brilliant and clever, but few are really artistic. No one can suppose that Sir G. Macfarren is deficient in this respect. The controversy which still goes on between the old school and the new, and in which Sir G. Macfarren is a leading champion of the former, naturally provokes many of the new lights to criticize in the severest manner every work of his. Too harsh a line is perhaps drawn between these two apparently opposite schools by the accomplished professor. It is maintained by his opponents—and with some show of reason—that rules are liable to continual change, that genius is a certain latitude makes its own rules, and that an instrumental work should not only rest upon a poetic basis, but its form also should be dictated by the nature and order of the poetical material. He who does this is supposed to make a more exalted view of art than one who plays a perpetual sort of game of skill in accordance with certain fixed rules. Last week I spoke of Raff as being a mixture of the two, and had he possessed the genius of Mozart or Beethoven, two contending schools might have been happily blended and so have put an end to the strife. In the symphony above alluded to, we have an example—perhaps not one of the best—of a stern uncompromising adherence to old forms and ancient regulations, the only exception being the substitution of the gavotte for the minuet. It was an appeal to the intellect rather than to the emotions, and the general impression made by it must, I fear, have been disappointing to the talented composer, who was present on the occasion. English musicians were abundantly represented. Amongst other things I must not forget to mention one of ,the most perfect gems, Bennett's overture, " Paradise and the Peri." This alone was worth going to hear. Sir R. Stewart's work was an agreeable surprise. It is bright, brilliant, clever, and artistic. Of Mr. E. Howell's performance on the 'cello, I cannot speak too highly. His success and the appreciation he met with were most emphatic. Miss Hilda Coward is fast coming to the front. Her voice is heard to advantage even in this large concert-room, and her enunciation—a thing too often neglected—is most perfect. Mdme. Patey of course came in for her full share of admiration. R. S.

Another contributor writes :—

I am rather amused at the chaffing of some of your daily contemporaries with respect to the "titular" prefixes of the composers. All of them certainly have handles to their names, although to be called "Sir" can hardly be reckoned an exalted honour, not at least when the word merely signifies a knight bachelor. What's in a name, however, if the music be good? Sir Herbert Oakeley's march in E flat, a mere *piece d occasion*, has a bold, broad, and striking subject, rather alloyed by reiteration ; the passage for flute and hautboy with moving bass *pizzicato*, struck me as excellent. The numbers to which are appended the honoured names of Sterndale Bennett and Arthur Sullivan, have always been heard with admiration. Sir A. P. Stewart's " Orchestral Prelude" in D is not a strong specimen of "programme music," although tune-ful, nicely scored, and marked by striking contrasts. Mr. E. Howell achieved a signal success and to him is due the patient hearing of Goltermann's dreadfully dull concerto, whereof the commonplace finale reminds one of " Draw the swords of Scotland " ! Boccherini proved to be a still greater bore.

Sir G. A. Macfarren listened to his own symphony from the gallery, with the orchestra in full front. I heard the work when first produced at a concert of the British Orchestral Society in March, 1874. The first elaborate allegro stamps the symphony as a *chef-d'œuvre*. The " Serenade," in C, has a reminder, doubtless accidental, of the Count of Luna's air in " Il Trovatore," " Il balen del suo sorriso," the hautboy comes in very prettily in the "Musette" of the 3rd movement, with an effective bassoon part below. The use of bright major keys (E and B) in the finale, tends to relieve the grave, if not sombre, character of the first movement. Miss Hilda Coward has a clear, rather shrill soprano, but must study her shakes, and other details. Mdme. Patey's revival of Sir Jules Benedict's " Sad Sea Waves" song, was most acceptable. " The First Walpurgus Night " is down for this afternoon, and Mr. Carrodus will play a " Fandango" by Molique, I hope something lively, for Molique is usually dry as a stick. A. M.

RICHTER CONCERTS.

The autumn season, of three concerts, began last Monday, with the following programme :—

Huldigungs-Marsch	Wagner.
Overture, "Die Akademische"	Brahms.
Introduction to Act III., " Die Meistersinger"	Wagner.
Der Ritt der Walkuren, " Die Walküre"	,,

Symphony, No. 6, in F (" The Pastoral ") Beethoven. So thoroughly familiar a scheme calls for but little comment, the performance being above criticism. The band was in splendid form, the brass showing to extraordinary advantage in the opening number. Herr Richter was received with the customary enthusiasm : his presence among us is productive of good results, and his audience, well knowing this, does not fail to acknowledge its indebtedness. In spite of the Wagner mania that has occasionally possessed us, in spite of the conscientious efforts of some able musicians in our midst to familiarise us with his music, we should even now know but little of the inexpressible beauty of Wagner's works, heard as music pure and simple, were it not for the periodical visits of Hans Richter. Our English artists are undoubtedly aware of this, or they would not have assembled so numerously to listen with unwavering attention to music that they could probably hum through from beginning to end. There is always something new to be learnt by those who hear aright ; for music is inexhaustible, boundless, divine, as Nature herself. Who can say that he has discovered the last beauty that is revealable in a perfect performance of—for example—the Huldigungs-March ?—not only the finest " occasional piece " that was ever written, but one of the most perfect and attractive specimens of polyphonic composition in existence.

Some critics have thought fit to blame Herr Richter for bringing with him " nothing new " ; others complained a few seasons ago because he came laden with novelties. Fortunately for us Herr Richter follows his own counsel : he tells us of Wagner (and perhaps also of Beethoven) what we do not hear elsewhere. Of "novelties" from Wagner's writings, he could give us only the Cantata of " The Last Supper " (an early work that we scarcely hear), or some numbers from " Parsifal,"—and perhaps —who can prophecy ?—that last unapproached, sacred work had better be left for performance amid the solemnising influences of Bayreuth ! Mr. Barnby will soon give us an opportunity of judging how far we may be capable of supplying for ourselves the want of scenic illusions, how far we can forget what the tyrant, custom, has taught us, and (as Jarno said to Wilhelm Meister) "not cavil at the form "—the rest being left to our "own good sense and feeling"; how far we shall "prepare ourselves by reading and meditation for the great religious drama which we are to witness,"[*] as was the practice of the more serious of the Beyreuth audience. Herr Richter, at all events, arranged a programme which satisfied his audience : for the "Meistersinger" number was redemanded and repeated, while there was an unopposed call

---

[*] Rev. H. R. Haweis at Bayreuth, 1883.

for a repetition of the "Walkürenritt," which was hushed only when Herr Richter had by frequent bows and reappearances testified his unwillingness to go through any more of his numbers a second time.

It is a pity that the doors are not closed during the performance of each piece : the practice not only gives comfort to those who arrive in proper time, but engenders a feeling of reverence for art, respect for artists, and consideration for our fellow-auditors, beneficial to the art-world at large.

A few words on the Pastoral Symphony and "programme" music may be offered for consideration next week.   B. F. WYATT-SMITH.

THE ROYAL ACADEMY OF MUSIC.

The first "Students' Chamber Concert" was held last Friday afternoon (Oct. 26), at St. James's Hall, under the direction of Mr. Wm. Shakespeare. Purcell's Anthem, "O sing unto the Lord a new song," opened the business at half-past two o'clock, and went well. Another sacred number was Brahms's Psalm XIII., "O Lord, how long, &c.," for choir of ladies. Here might be noticed a good balance of tone and effective *crescendos* at the proper place.

Some original compositions of the students were produced. Mr. E. Kiver's tenor song, "If ye love me," denotes good style : smoothness and fluency, but no novelty. Mr. Hulbert Fulkerson was the exponent. Mr. Kilvington Hattersley's setting of Longfellow's Serenade (from "The Spanish Student"), although mild, soft, and pretty, has not sufficient variety for so many stanzas ; this theme, a poor one in itself, has been quite overdone by our song-writers. Mr. G. J· Bennett's first song, "The road to Slumberland," suffers from the very childish words, only fit, indeed, for "babies" on their way to "*Bed*fordshire." The second effusion, "As spirits watch from above," has a certain colouring of the German *lied*, and won an *encore d'estime*, as no actual encores are allowed. These pieces were fairly interpreted by Miss L. Pople and Miss Kate W. Payne.

The pianists played very well. Miss Annie Mukle (Lady Goldsmid scholar), chose Mendelssohn's "Seventeen Variations" in D minor ; she has neat, distinct, enunciation, but is a little too automatic. Miss Alice Dyer read Mendelssohn's Fantasia in F sharp minor, Op. 28, with much delicacy and *finesse*, displaying good technical execution in the florid passages. Mr. C. S. Macpherson played part of Sir G. A. Macfarren's third Sonata in G minor, clever but rather dry, music, with a happy humouring of the text, an incisive touch, and firm grasp of the key-board. Miss Dora Bright's (own) "Two Sketches" in F sharp minor, and A, are elegant little *esquisses* ; a loud and most improper recall failed to induce a reappearance of the young lady. Mr. H. C. Tonking was applauded for his execution of H. Smart's "Con moto moderato" in D minor, and Mr. Richardson, for his performance of two pieces for the violin, composed by Mr. German E. Jones (student). Other numbers, by well-known composers, completed a too long scheme.

ST. PAUL'S, BOW COMMON.

The Dedication Festival of this church took place on Tuesday last, Oct. 30th, the services commencing at the early hour of 7 a.m. with a choral celebration, at which the choir sang for the first time, Mozart's 4th Mass in C, arranged for the English service by Mr. Horace Buttery, organist and choirmaster of the church. At the evening service the choir was augmented to about 140 voices by the aid of the choirs of St. Mary's, Boltons, S.W., St. Peter's, South Kensington, and St. Mary's Haggerston, and others. The Rev. J· B. Powell's Processional "Salve Festa dies," opened the service with fine effect. The canticles were sung to Stainer in B flat, and the anthem was Mendelssohn's noble eight-part Psalm, "Sing to the Lord a new made song," which was sung as written, that is, the first two movements unaccompanied, the organ coming in at the third movement with splendid effect, the large choir not having in the least sunk in pitch ; and the whole service (concluding with Handel's "Hallelujah"), was rendered with the greatest vigour and precision. Mr. Buttery conducted the anthem and accompanied at the organ other parts of the service, being assisted by Mr. Mortimer J. Dudman ; and Mr. Chas. W. Pearce, Mus.Bac., played at the conclusion of the service one of Mendelssohn's organ sonatas and a march by E. Silas. The dedication services were to be continued on Wednesday by a performance by the St. Paul's, Bow Common, choir alone, of Dr. Ferdinand Hiller's "Song of Victory" at 8 p.m., and the list of music for the continuation of the festival on Sunday next will be seen in another column.

On Oct. 22nd, the same combination of choirs as above assisted at the Dedication Festival Evensong at St. Mary's, Boltons, the arrangements of the service and music selected being almost identical, and under the same musical direction, Mr. Buttery being organist and director of the choir at both churches. At St. Mary's, at the conclusion of the service, Mr. J· M. Crament, Mus.Bac., organist of Holy Trinity, Brompton, gave a short recital on Messrs. Hill's new organ.

MUSIC AT ST. GEORGE'S HALL.

Mr. and Mrs. German Reed are themselves good musicians, and at their "Entertainments," always popular and amusing, good care is taken to provide a variety of sweet sounds. At the Hall, in Langham Place, may now be witnessed, twice a day, the "Treasure Trove," written by Mr. A. Law, with music by A. J· Caldicott. Also, a "New Second Part," entitled, "The Water Cure," words by Arnold Felix, and music by Mr. George Gear. The slight plot of this funny piece runs on some absurd mistakes made in a hydropathic establishment. Mr. George Gear, well known as an elegant composer of sonatas for the pianoforte, and many very superior vocal pieces, has written some sprightly music for the little extravaganza. The overture in G, gives good promise ; the duet in D, "Her anger I'll brave," deserves the applause always liberally bestowed ; and the trio in G, "Think what misery and shame," with an episode in the tonic minor, rises to a climax. An *ensemble* in G, and a final laughing quartet, complete the score, except a "Lullaby," which is, for the present, omitted. W. G. Goss accompanies his songs on a grand Erard, with the aid of a harmonium. The characters of "A Water Cure" are sustained by Miss F. Holland, Miss M. Wardroper, Mr. North Hope, and Mr. Alfred Reed. Mr. Corney Grain appears in the "Treasure Trove," which is opened by a pretty instrumental prelude.

VICTORIA COFFEE HALL.

For several months past a movement has been on foot at the above hall, for the purpose of organising a permanent choir, that the frequenters of the "Old Vic." might smoke their pipes, sip their coffee, or partake of a "revolutionary cup of tea" and enjoy good music at the same time. The idea is a commendable one, which deserves encouragement. The conductor of the choir in question is Mr. W. Sexton (lay vicar of Westminster Abbey) who took his Benefit Concert here on Thursday, Oct. 25th ; it was announced as "a grand operatic night," and thus I was induced to pay a visit. The first part of the programme was occupied by a musical piece entitled "The Wreck of the Argosy," but neither the composition, or the performance call for any special notice. The second part was taken up by a grand musical spectacle "The Rose Queen"; this, I think, requires a little comment. The music comprises a mixture of Macfarren's "May Day" and Bennett's "May Queen"; it also contains selections from Bishop, Blumenthal, and Mendelssohn, together with commonplace tunes for skipping-rope, and eccentric dances, and conventional arrangements for a "Corps de Ballet" (8 in number) ; this was to be performed with full stage effect. Before remarking on the performance, I would wish to say a few words to this effect. At one time a lover is serenading his mistress, but has his back turned on her, all through his love refrain. Again, the stage is crowded with choristers, ballet girls, and country clod-poles (a strange combination truly), while the majority of the chorus evidently not accustomed to the stage or stage clothing, stroll about at leisure regardless of anything or anybody, in the midst of which a lady walks on, and without any apparent reason, obliges with a song. It is also somewhat embarrassing to see a priest associating with ballet girls ; it may be all right off the stage, but on the "boards" it does not look well. I must, however, pass on to something more serious than these comparatively petty faults. Can anyone imagine, who has the slightest artistic taste, Mendelssohn's lovely trio, "Lift thine eyes," figuring in the same programme as "A Skipping-rope dance by Little Flo," but thus it was. Again, I *do* maintain that it shows lack of respect, and want of refinement, to have an eccentric dance by three exhilarated villagers follow on immediately after the performance of Bennett's beautiful trio which occurs in his Cantata. Variety, which is proverbially charming, was (to me) most objectionable and irritating. Such things are not consistent with artistic ideas.

With regard to the actual performance—I must commend Mrs. Merton Clark for her very careful and artistic rendering of "Lo ! here the gentle lark." The rendering of "My Queen," by Mr. J· Wenham Walker, the aforenamed impolite wooer, was not altogether satisfactory. Mr. Lansmere sang his music with great care, but I would remind him that the art of acting does not consist of rushing about all over the stage. Miss Annie Daymond "The Rose Queen," sang her music very tastefully. With regard to the ballet (alas !) considering their small number, they went through their usual movements with success. The choir, in one or two instances did their work (musically) admirably. The singing all through seemed to be much appreciated by "Ye Gods." This kind of thing, without such depressing stage effects, is all right, and tends, no doubt, to do a lot of good ; but when lovely music is burlesqued, and lovers turn their backs on those they are supposed to love, when ballet girls not only become the companions of choristers, but hover around and the steps of a sacred edifice—then such performances become detrimental to artistic progress. I should wish to impress upon the management of Thursday week, that with ignorant people, no art suffers from association, like music. Bennett's "May Queen" was performed without orchestral parts. Why was this   GEO. F. GROVER.

WELLINGTON BARRACKS.

A Military Harvest Festival was held last Sunday at the Wellington Barracks. At the evening service the three bands of the Foot Guards, with the choir formed of soldiers, boys and men, took part in the Festival. The effect of the wind instruments as employed at the ordinary services of this chapel is remarkably effective and striking. The harmonies produced are so firm and rich, as to point out that much may be done in Service Music by the judicious employment of wind instruments, especially in conjunction with the organ. It may be well to remind readers that the public are admitted every Sunday to the services at the Wellington Barracks. The morning service is at 10.30, and visitors should be in their places a little before that time.

LEEDS.

(From our own Correspondent).

The Carl Rosa Opera Company were at the Grand Theatre last week, and the production of the new operas, "Esmeralda" and "Colomba" was looked forward to with much interest, every available seat having been booked in advance, while on each night the house was crowded. The cast in "Esmeralda" was the same as when the piece was originally brought out at Drury Lane a few months ago. Madame Georgina Burns delighted every one by her fine acting in the title rôle, while as a vocalist she has few equals on the operatic stage.

In Mr. Mackenzie's "Colomba," the title character was entrusted to Madame Marie Rose, who was in splendid voice, and acted magnificently, and at the close of the long, trying scene in the finale to the third act, she was received with loud applause. Miss Clara Perry, as Chilina, sang the beautiful " vocero " with much expression, and Mr. Barton McGuckin's fine tenor voice was heard to advantage in the music allotted to Orso. Both operas were splendidly mounted. Madame Marie Rose also appeared in "Trovatore" and "Carmen."

Dr. Spark's recital on the Town Hall organ last Saturday evening was devoted to reminiscences of the Musical Festival, and was well attended. The programme included, among other items, selections from the "Elijah," from Barnby's 97th Psalm, and from Raff's oratorio, "The End of the World," and though the latter work is unsuited to the organ, those who were not at the Festival would be able to form some idea of the kind of music that has excited so much interest and controversy. The "War March of Priests" from "Athalie" brought the concert to a close. The same programme was repeated on Tuesday. Prior to the recital, a presentation was made to Dr. Spark as a token of esteem from his past and present pupils, the presentation taking the form of a handsome album, which contained the portraits of several of his numerous pupils. At the presentation there were present the Rev. Canon Bullock, Vicar of Holy Trinity (who presided), and others. The Rev. Chairman, in presenting the birthday token, expressed his great pleasure at having afforded to him an opportunity of publicly expressing his appreciation of the great services rendered to the town by Dr. Spark. He spoke of the fact that Dr. Spark had had the honour of imparting some instruction in oratorio music to the late Mdlle. Titiens. Dr. Spark was not only famous as a teacher and as a musician, but also as a composer. The rev. gentleman presented the album to the Doctor amid much applause. Mr. Oldroyd, an old friend of the Borough Organist, endorsed all the remarks of Canon Bullock, and bore his testimony both to the private worth and public work of Dr. Spark. Dr. Spark, on rising to acknowledge the present, was received with great enthusiasm. In the course of his reply he said it was a pleasant thing to find that, after a career of twenty-five years, containing its usual share of difficulties and misrepresentations, so kind a present should have been made to him by his old and present pupils.

SOUTHAMPTON.

Says a local journal, a large audience assembled in the Hartley Hall on Oct. 25th, to hear Dr. Arnold's "Sennacherib." The different numbers were received with marked discrimination and acceptance, beginning at the picturesque march following the orchestral prelude introducing the work, and culminating in, for a Southampton audience, the rare re-demand of the chorus in about the middle of the cantata, "O Lord Thou art great "—a solid piece of writing, which the chorus of 150 voices brought together from the two towns gave with marked vivacity and power. It was introduced by a charming duet, "O house of Jacob " for soprano and tenor, in which these solo voices were heard to their best ; the band, however, which, composed for the most part of the players at the Gloucester festival, had necessarily been brought together without practice in a body, manifesting considerable unsteadiness and uncertainty in the other chief concerted piece for the soloists, a trio, "O Lord God of Hosts," leading to a smooth piece of four-part harmony for the chorus, "Save us out of his hand." A song of triumph for the soprano, "God breaketh the battles," well written for the display of the voice, and powerfully given by Mdlle. Avigliana, who sang the music at Gloucester, led to the final chorus, containing a fugue, commencing with the words "His name alone is excellent," the work concluding with a sound piece of writing, "The

sword of the enemy "—a form of thanksgiving to the Almighty. The hearty applause which greeted Dr. Arnold, who confia.ced the performance, both at the close, when the chorus markedly supplemented the plaudits of the audience, and following individual numbers of the work, testified the gratification which the cantata gave.

WINCHESTER.

A large audience was present at the Guildhall on Oct. 26th at Dr. Arnold's concert. The principal interest centered in the firs part, which was taken up entirely by "Sennacherib," a sacred cantata from the pen of the conductor, which was first produced at the last Gloucester Festival. The solo parts were taken, as ca the previous evening, at Southampton, by Mdlle. Avigliana and Messrs. H. Kearton and W. H. Brereton. The band, led by Mr. Fletcher, though not complete, was sufficient to indicate many of the beauties of the instrumentation, which is very elaborate throughout. The chorus of 170 voices was much strengthened by a contingent from Southampton. The choruses showed signs of careful rehearsal, and left nothing to be desired in their performance—in fact, a better choral performance has never been heard in Winchester. The hearty reception of Dr. Arnold, and frequent applause, showed that the verdict of the public on this his last work, was a favourable one.

LIVERPOOL.

(From our own Correspondent).

Oct. 31.

The initial of the series of Mr. Charles Hallé's orchestral concerts took place last evening in the Philharmonic Hall. There was a crowded attendance.

The programme was enjoyable, containing as it did Beethoven's first symphony, Mendelssohn's violin concerto, overture to " Oberon," &c.

An interesting work of Dvorak's for the orchestra (Rhapsodie Slave, in G minor, Op. 45, No. 3) was given for the first time. It is characteristic of the composer and a refreshing change from the ordinary colour scoring.

Madame Norman-Néruda was the solo violinist, and in addition to the charming interpretation of Mendelssohn's concerto, essayed a Sonata of Rust's. It is very antiquated, but makes a good violin item, and certainly requires a good player and clever executant. Need I chronicle the reception given to the gifted lady who played this suite (for it is not a sonata) in such a perfect style ? No! enough, that it was played (and it embraces a fugue almost without any accompaniment) by Madame Norman-Néruda. The vocalist was Miss Thudichum who sang with great success Meyerbeer's " Come rapido " ("Il Crociato"), Handel's " Lusinghe piu care," and Spohr's " Rose, softly blooming" (which last, by-the-way, seems to be a favourite with Royal Academy students of the fair sex).

Sir Julius Benedict presided at the Royal Academy of Music's local distribution on the 22nd inst., and made some very pertinent remarks. The following notes upon his speech contain the whole thing in a nutshell :—" How is it that a city of the dimensions and wealth of Liverpool is so lamentably behind in everything connected with the most entrancing of all arts? Are we to suppose that the merchants of Liverpool are less intellectual than the cotton spinners of Manchester or the wool weavers of Leeds. Or to take a nearer parallel, Bristol, with little more than one-third the population, can set on foot a musical festival to which Liverpool can show no rival. Some cause there must be for such a marked inferiority, and it probably lies in a lack of the sympathy and spirit of mutual co-operation, which is necessary to draw into a focus the individual atoms that must exist in so large a community. The result we see in the fact, so feelingly alluded to by Mr. Palgrave Simpson, that Liverpool cannot produce an orchestra of her own, but has to import one from Manchester, and to place the affairs of her principal musical society under the absolute control and direction of a Manchester conductor, without regard to the competent representation of works of the highest order. Of course, if Liverpudlians choose to submit to such a humiliating state of things it does not concern the remainder of the empire in any way: But there are in Liverpool many to whom the making such a confession is a cause of shame and heart-burning. It is for them to combine together to remove such a reproach from their city, and it cannot be but that by strenuous exertion and patient perseverance it could in time be done. The Philharmonic Society has abdicated its position as a distinctly local leader in music. Its old place untenanted. Will none step forth to assume the mantle it has cast away ? "

Messrs. Alfred Burnett and Ridley Prentice announce their intention of giving another series of their excellent chamber concerts at the Alexandra Hall, Blackheath during the coming winter. Four concerts will, it is said, be given, and the programme of each evening is to include one work by an English composer.

GLASGOW.

(From our own Correspondent.)

The programme of Mr. Charles Hallé's concert on Oct. 19th, was as follows :—

Fantaisie Sonata in G, Op. 78	Schubert.
Solo (violin) " Fantaisie caprice "	Vieuxtemps.
Duet (pf. and violin) Andante and Rondo	Mozart.
Sonata in C minor, Op. 30, No. 2	Beethoven.
Berceuse in D flat	Chopin-Gluck.
Larghetto in A	Nardini.
Polonaise in A	Wieniawski.

Mr. Hallé was assisted by Madme. Norman-Néruda, and performed with his usual power to an appreciative audience.

A most satisfactory performance of Haydn's " Creation " was given by the Glasgow Tonic Sol-fa Choral Society, on October 25th, to a crowded audience. The soloists were Mdlle. Ilma de Murska, Mr. Leonard E. Auty, and Mr. Robert Hilton. The orchestra was composed of local performers, under the leadership of Mr. T. Smyth, and the style of the rendition was all that could be desired. Dr. Peace was organist, and Mr. W. M. Miller, as usual, conducted. The chief noticeable defects in the choral portions of the work were an occasional lack of sympathy or unanimity between the various parts, and a decided weakness among the tenors. In other respects, the performance was highly successful, and Mr. Auty secured the inevitable encore for the air " In native worth." Mdlle. de Murska was not so happy in her singing if she had been in the more congenial sphere of opera, and her quality of voice has manifestly deteriorated since she formerly sang in Scotland. The society are rehearsing for production Handel's " Athaliah " and " Messiah."

The Glasgow Select Choir gave a performance of Smart's " Jacob " in the City Hall, and again manifested the power to do justice to choral works of considerable size and difficulty. The present performance was an advance in some slight particulars on the former production of the work, and the choral portions of the work were faultless. The solos were likewise commendably good, and the accompaniments by Messrs. Swan (harmonium), and Berry (piano), were able and judicious. Mr. Allan conducted. The choir is expected to appear twice in London this season, and we believe, thanks to the untiring zeal and energy of the conductor, that an improvement on some of the features of the choral singing will be apparent.

The scheme of the Saturday evening concerts in St. Andrew's Hall, past and to come, includes among other singers and performers, the following : Miss Mary Davies, Miss Carlotta Elliot, Miss K. W. Payne, Miss Clara Samuell, Miss Agnes Larkcom, Madme. Isabel Fassett, Miss M. Mackenzie, Miss Helen D'Alton, Mr. George Perren, Mr. R. Hollins, Mr. H. Guy, Mr. B. Foote, Mr. C. King, Mr. R. Hilton, Mr. T. Beale, Mr. J. T. Carrodus, Miss Marie Schumann, Dr. A. L. Peace and many others.

Madam Helen Hopekirk is announced to give a farewell concert previous to her departure for America. The Council of the Choral Union have republished for circulation among the members an *aid* to the comprehension of Berlioz's " Messe des Morts," in the shape of an article which appeared in the *Saturday Review.*   J. B.

Foreign Musical Intelligence.

Verdi completed his 70th year last month.

Rubinstein's " Tower of Babel " will be given shortly in Dresden.

Gounod's " Redemption " will be performed in Vienna on Nov. 4th.

Rubinstein's " Maccabäer " was given at Frankfort-on-Main, on Oct. 27th.

A monument is being erected to Glinka, the Russian composer, at Smolenski.

Suppé's new three-act opera, " Juanita," is attracting much attention in Brussels.

Under the direction of M. Paul Martin, the popular concerts at Lille are to be as good as they are successful.

Dr. J. Schucht contributes an interesting article on " The Tremolo in Singing " to the " Neue Zeitschrift für Musik."

" Loreley," that favourite German mythical subject, is the title of a new opera by Herr Mohr, which is presently to be produced at Breslau.

MM. Meilhac and Gille are said to be busy adapting into French Mr. Farnie's new comic opera, " Nell Gwynne," the intention being to perform the work simultaneously in Paris and London early next year. M. Planquette will compose the music.

Organ News.

CRYSTAL PALACE.

Mr. Eyre's programmme on Saturday, October 27th included the following :—

Double Chorus, " Fixed in His everlasting seat "	Handel.
Grand Prelude in D minor	Mendelssohn.
Larghetto from Symphony in D	Beethoven.
Short Prelude and Fugue in E minor	Bach.
Serenade	Gounod.
Grazioso in B flat, and Moto Continuo in G	Hopkins.
Procession March, " Die Meistersinger "	Wagner.
Overture, " Egmont "	Beethoven.
Barcarolle in G	Spohr.
Intermezzo, " Forget-me-not "	Macbeth.
Marche de la Caravanne, " Le Désert "	David.
Adagio and Allegro from and Organ Sonata	Mendelssohn.
" Slumber Song "	Schumann.
Fantasia, with Chorale in G	Smart.

STEPNEY.

A fine organ has been erected by Messrs. Peter Conacher and Co., of Huddersfield, in Stepney Meeting House, one of the oldest of the Nonconformist churches in London. The instrument has three manuals and Pedal and some thirty-one mounted stops. The case is of pitch pine, with eighty-five speaking pipes. The whole presents a very handsome appearance, and the tone of the organ is exceptionally good. In accordance with the Puritan traditions of the church, the organ was opened with a somewhat grave service, in which a sermon, by Dr. Allon of Islington, took a prominent part. Mr. Minshall, of the City Temple, presided at the organ.

LAMBETH ROAD.

A notably fine organ, by Messrs. Brindley and Foster, at the Upton Chapel, Lambeth Road, was opened on October 31st. The vocalists were Miss Roby, Miss Williams, Messrs. Cornwall and Chaplin Henry. Mr. E. H. Turpin was the solo organist, and Mr. W. Taylor, of St. Matthew's, New Kent Road, was the accompanist.

BEDFORD.

An organ recital was given at the Wesley Chapel on Tuesday, October 16th, by Mr. A. Margeson, F.C.O. The vocalists were Miss Carter and Mr. Margeson. Movements by Bach, Wesley, Guilmant, Wely, and Lux were played.

BROAD GREEN.

An organ recital was given in Christ Church, by Mr. F. Cambridge, on Thursday, October 18th. The programme was as follows :—

Overture, " Samson "	Handel.
Sanctus, " Messe Solennelle "	Gounod.
Fugue on " St. Ann's Tune "	Bach.
Andante in F (Dramatic Concerto)	Spohr.
Triumphal March in D	Moscheles.
Selection " Athalie "	Mendelssohn.
Hallelujah, " Mount of Olives "	Beethoven.

BRIGHTON.

The Corporation organ recitals were given in the Dome, Royal Pavilion, by Mr. J. Crapps, F.C.O., on Saturday, October 20th. The programme included :—

Sonate Pontificale	Lemmens.
Allegro moderato—Adagio—March Pontificale.	
Grand Fantasia and Fugue in A minor	Bach.
Cantailne Pastorale, Op. 15	Guilmant.
Grand Study, " Hosannah "	Lemmens.
Fantasia for Organ, on Mozart's celebrated duet in " Il Flauto Magico "	Hepworth.
Grand Offertoire in F No. 6	Batiste.
Air varie, Allegretto in B flat	Lissant.
" War March of the Priests " (" Athalie ")	Steggall.

Mr. Crapps's performance is spoken of as in every way admirable.

ALYTH.

An organ recital was given in the Episcopal Church, on Thursday, October 18th, by Mr. C. J. Smith. The programme included :—

Largo in B flat	Smith.
Prelude and Fugue in F	Bach.
" March of the Crusaders "	Sibley.
Overture to " Athalia "	Handel.
Andante in G	Batiste.
" Tuba Mirum " (Requiem)	Mozart.
Andante (1st Concerto)	Mendelssohn.
Largo (Violin and Organ)	Handel.
" Wedding March "	Mendelssohn.

The organ recitals at Holy Trinity Church, Gray's Inn Road, will be recommenced on Sunday next, by Mr. Stretton Swann, and will be continued during the winter season, on the first Sunday in every month, after the evening Service.

BOW AND BROMLEY INSTITUTE.

The soloist on Saturday was Dr. Peace of Glasgow; in whose performance there is nothing to criticise but everything to admire. The calm mastery and high finish of his playing, which so forcibly struck the present writer upon the first appearance here of the eminent organist, were upon the present occasion abundantly displayed. The pieces given were the Rev. Sir F. A. G. Ouseley's fine Sonata No. 2; Rondo in A minor and major, (G. Morandi); Bach's great Toccata and Fugue in F; "Rhapsodie," No. 3, Saint-Saëns; and overture, "The Erl King"(Kuhlau). The vocalist was Miss Emily Jones, who was encored in Hullah's "The Storm"; Mr. Fountain Meen accompanied. To-night a pianoforte recital will be given by Herr Bonawitz, aided by sundry well known string players, with Miss A. South as vocalist. It cannot now be more than recorded that an excellent rendering of Dr. J. Stainer's "St. Mary Magdalene" was given on Tuesday last at the Institute. The performance was given under Mr. W. G. McNaught, by the choir of the Institute, now an admirable and enthusiastic body of singers, doing excellent work from time to time in the cause of the art. The orchestra was a thoroughly representative one, and the entire performance was another good thing scored to the credit of the Institute. The esteemed composer of the new work played the organ part.

FISHERIES EXHIBITION.

Mr. Ernest Slater, R.A.M., A.C.O., organist of Lambeth Parish Church, gave an organ recital on Monday, October 29th. The folllowing is the programme :—

Chorus, "Heaven and earth display"	Mendelssohn.
Andante in F	Batiste.
Fugue in G minor	Bach.
Andante in F sharp minor	Wesley.
"War March of the Priests"	Mendelssohn.
Andante and Fugue	Slater.
Grand Chorus	Guilmant.
Andante in F	Smart.
Chorus, "And the glory of the Lord"	Handel.

BOLTON.

An organ recital was given in the Albert Hall, by Mr. W. Mullineux, F.C.O., on Saturday, October 20th. The following was the programme :—

Prelude and Fugue in C minor	Bach.
Andante from the Symphony in C major	Mozart.
The "Bell Offertoire"	Batiste.
Overture for the organ in F minor	Morandi.
Song, "The Chorister"	Sullivan.
March Posthume	Rossini.

SHEFFIELD.

Mr. James Hallé gave a recital on the grand organ on Saturday, October 20th, at the Albert Hall. The Yorkshire St. Cecilia Quartet, of Leeds, made their first appearance upon this occasion. The programme included :—

Overture, "Semiramide"	Rossini.
Barcarolle in F (4th Piano Concerto)	Bennett.
Grand Fantasia, "The Storm"	Lemmens.
"Improvisations on National Airs"	
Grand Offertoire in C minor	Batiste.
"Tannhäuser" March	Wagner.

OORK INDUSTRIAL EXHIBITION.

On Saturday, the 13th inst., the Exhibition was opened to the public for the last time. There was no closing ceremony, properly speaking, a series of military bands playing throughout the day doing duty for it. The attendance was immense, everybody wishing to have a last look before the place was closed. At three o'clock Mr. T. J. Sullivan performed the following selection on the organ :—

Overture, "Zauberflöte"	Mozart.
Irish Melodies	Moore.
Selection, "Maritana"	Wallace.
Andante con moto, Symphony in C minor	Beethoven.
Allegretto, from "Hymn of Praise"	Mendelssohn.
Hallelujah Chorus, "Messiah"	Handel.

At four o'clock the combined bands of five regiments played—

British Army Quadrilles	Jullien.
Grand March, "Tannhäuser"	Wagner.
Overture, "Fra Diavolo"	Auber.
Fantasia, "Reminiscences of Ireland"	Godfrey.

A somewhat similar programme was performed in the evening, with the exception of the substitution of a selection played by a military band for the organ recital.

Mr. Cowen's visit to America to conduct some of his own works has, it is stated, been postponed.

PRINCIPAL CONTENTS OF THIS NUMBER.

LONDON : SATURDAY, NOVEMBER 3, 1883.

A NOTABLE PROGRAMME.

THE esteemed conductor Mr. A. Manns and the authorities of the Crystal Palace achieved a quiet, but none the less significant triumph on Saturday by the successful performance of a genuine English programme. The leading feature was Sir G. A. Macfarren's Symphony in E minor, written years ago for the then existing British Musical Society. This fine work, with its finely expressed thoughts, its admirably contrasted movements and sound musicianship, astonished not a few present last Saturday who had perhaps overlooked the existence of the work. Sir R. P. Stewart's excellently scored and characteristic Prelude to "The Eve of St. John" proved a most welcome novelty. Sir H. Oakeley's vigorous "Edinburgh" March was also found worthy of a place in the Crystal Palace scheme.

To speak of the brightness, gaiety and freshness of Sir A. SULLIVAN'S overture, "Di Ballo," is now to talk of a fully accepted delight. It is well, perhaps, to say that satisfactory as the entire selection of English music proved to be on the occasion now referred to, the programme also served to show how much good English music is still being neglected, and that the Crystal Palace authorities have yet much to do in the way of making amends for long continued sins of omission. The performance at an early date of one of the late Sir JOHN Goss's much neglected and musicianly orchestral works, is one thing to be looked for. There is nothing boastful in the assertion that at the present time, England can produce music not to be excelled, and in some respects even hardly to be equalled, by the music of any other existing school. The result of last Saturday's selection was a proof of the truth of the assertion. The word school now-a-days, be it remembered, implies little more than the grouping together of a national musical party; for the universal language, music, has naturally, in this period of the quick electric intercourse of thought, led the way in the interchange and mutual adoption of idioms. But, though all modern music seems destined to wear the same universal tokens of thought kinship, the obligation of the distinct cultivation and encouragement of its own national school of music which rests upon each separate nationality is not a whit the less serious. We have long in England welcomed all men of genius and their works; but this feeling has, through divers causes not now to be discussed, been carried to a length which has stultified and degraded our own home art productions. We have laid ourselves open by our want of discernment to an invasion of all kinds of second and third rate composers, conducting adventurers who confidently come to lead our own bands for us with more or less success, and legions of singers and players, who can show no claims which can in any way justify the heedless, cruel, silly neglect of our own native artists. Now, we are happily modifying our policy; not rejecting all that is really good that is brought to us, for England ever has an open, generous hand, but learning to better appreciate and reward our own true artists; who have to accuse us in their noble, patient, striving attitude of bitterly neglecting a precious heritage of goodly gifts and earnest cultivation. It is therefore to be hoped that the example set at the Crystal Palace on Saturday last will be followed far and wide.

E. H. TURPIN.

FORM IN VOCAL MUSIC.

IX.

IN setting the great Church Hymn the "Te Deum laudamus," due regard must of course be maintained as to the character of the Services in which it is to be used. The hymn indeed has quite a distinct use in the Anglican Church from that which prevails in the Roman and some other branches of the Christian Church. Whilst in the English Church the "Te Deum laudamus" forms an abiding feature in the daily form of morning prayer, elsewhere it has a special character and a reserved employment for great occasions and special festivals. So the settings by HAYDN, GRAUN, ROMBERG, and others do not exactly furnish models for the English Church composer, any more indeed than do the almost parallel settings in English by PURCELL, HANDEL, and quite recently by Sir A. SULLIVAN. It may here be observed, however, that no feature of our too long morning Services displays so painfully the weak compression of the musical portion of the office as does the hurried, brief setting generally made to the words of the "Te Deum." The great imagery of its different clauses, its varied attitudes of praise and prayer and points of doctrinal exposition, cannot be justly dealt with in the ordinary brief, compressed musical scamper which forms the "Te Deum" in most of our English Services. Such unworthy treatment of impressive words would be impossible anywhere but in an English Church; alas! that this is so. How to offer suggestions to the student as to the treatment of the glorious hymn to a musical setting which could find no favour, save upon the condition that it is to be written so as to be rattled through in about five minutes, is indeed an anomalous perplexity I have no intention of trying to solve. At the same time it is necessary that any setting intended for ordinary Anglican use shall be fairly in keeping with the surrounding conditions and elements of frequent public worship.

E. H. TURPIN.

THE ITALIAN OPERA IN BOTH WORLDS.

OUR learned contemporary of the *Times* has returned to the charge, and favoured the public with a most interesting article on the future of "Italian Opera in England and America," suggested by the recent opening of the "New Metropolitan Opera House" in New York, said to be one of the largest and most magnificently appointed theatres in the world. Here, on the opening night, Mdme. CHRISTINE NILSSON, who sang in GOUNOD's "Faust," received the present of a real *golden* girdle. On the same night our old friend Colonel J. H. MAPLESON began his season at the "Academy of Music," hitherto the home of Italian opera in New York, with Mdme. GERSTER as his *prima donna*, and a splendid success rewarded the fair Hungarian lady's remarkable vocal achievements. The shrewd writer in the *Times*, on these premisses, proceeds to discuss the question whether the "ingenuous reader"—(as much a *rara avis* as the "intelligent foreigner,")—can discover in these events the beginning of a new era in the history of Italian opera in America; and whether—for this is really a main question—this fashionable Institution will recover in the New World the ground that it has notoriously lost in the Old.

A musical pessimist (continues the writer of the article in the *Times*), well acquainted with the ways and means of modern opera, would probably be the reverse of sanguine. For a very sufficient reason. Under the existing most absurd, even abominable, "Star" system, the expenses of an Opera house are so enormous that an *impresario* must be a veritable *millionaire*, like Mr. VANDERBILT, the presenter of the golden girdle, if he would secure a "public" by engaging eminent *prime donne* at fabulous prices.

To Mdme. ADELINA PATTI it is said that Colonel MAPLESON has made the unprecedented offer of £1,100 a night; and how, it is pertinently asked, could even the most crowded houses under such circumstances pay expenses and yield a profit? The old plan of a "first lady" and four dolls, will no longer answer, for even the *poupées* expect to be well paid; the chorus and band, moreover, must be first-rate, and are not to be had for nothing. It is thought, therefore, that the matter resolves itself into a financial struggle between Col. MAPLESON and Mr. ABBEY, and that the final victory of the Metropolitan Opera house *or* the Academy will depend upon the amount of available "chink."

But this is a side issue: the main point, the future prospects of Italian opera in the abstract, remains for consideration. This main point involves two secondary questions. There is on one hand, an almost ruinous expenditure on "Stars" and manifold modern necessities; on the other, a growing indifference of the public to the old form and style of "Italian" opera pure and simple.

The Times, notwithstanding a tendency to pessimism, opines that the magnitude of the evil as regards expenses will make its speedy removal "a matter of " absolute and immediate necessity." "The *prima* " *donna*, to speak plainly, is no longer worth the " money she asks. The intelligent portion of the " public has at last grown tired of old-fashioned operas " indifferently mounted, for the sake merely of serving " as a foil to the *salti mortali* of accomplished singers." The two or three great vocalists who still draw large audiences by their own unsupported efforts are not likely to have any successors. After quoting the precedent of a male *figurante* in the "Ballet" once *à-la-mode* at the "King's Theatre" in the Haymarket, it is suggested that the modern *prima donna* may, at no distant date, be as unknown as the male dancer. Great singers, of course will be required, engaged, and fairly remunerated, but not according to mere tricks of technical skill, or at the expense of *high works of art*, of which after all, they are only the interpreters.

The writer of the essay in the *Times* has no faith in these grand doings on the other side of the broad Atlantic. He looks nearer home. Mr. Gye, of our own "Royal Italian" Opera, is reminded of certain facts. He has no CRŒSUS like Mr. VANDERBILT at his back, but he is supported by a *clientèle* of "con-" servative subscribers," and he has the field to himself for the present. All that is needed is an intelligent selection of operas, *ancient* and modern, provided with due attention to a perfect *ensemble* of which *individual* great artists shall form important, but not all-engrossing components.

So far the *Times*. Concurring with the writer on the main point, it may be thought that a monopoly is not the most likely stepping-stone to a radical reform of the existing system, whilst the precedents of past seasons hardly inspire very sanguine hopes. Rather let us look to the healthy stimulus of fair competition; to a second or third opera house established on sound cosmopolitan principles; above all to the permanent performances of companies such as Herr FRANKE and Mr. CARL ROSA have already brought before the public; the latter with success so signal, notwith-

standing his English *libretti* and English artists. At all events, the *repertoire* of opera must be enlarged so as to include WAGNER (*properly interpreted*), and all eminent modern composers of the continent, especially the German school. "For each and for all," should be the director's motto. Let all tastes be suited, but as the chorus in the "Agamemnon" of ÆSCHYLUS, repeatedly exclaim, "Let the *good* prevail and con-" quer."　　　　　　　　　　　　　　　　　　A. M.

Reviews.

High Festival Communion Service. By George Carter. (Novello, Ewer, & Co).—Mr. George Carter, a brother of Mr. William Carter, was formerly organist of St. Luke's, Chelsea, and the Cathedral of Montreal in Canada. He is also honourably known as a composer of Cantatas, two whereof, "Evangeline" and a "Sinfonia Cantata" on Psalm CXVI, have already been published. Mr. Carter has "on the anvil" another Cantata suggested by Longfellow's later poem "The Golden Legend."

This Communion Service in E major has been heard at St. Paul's Cathedral and other churches. On Sunday, Oct. 14th, the writer had the pleasure of hearing the Service at St. Matthias, South Kensington, where the organist, Mr. Mallitt Jones, has a capital choir under his control. The Service comprises the "Kyrie Eleison," the "Credo," the "Sanctus," the "Benedictus," the "Agnus Dei," and the final "Gloria in Excelsis." On Sunday, Oct. 14, for reasons, the "Agnus Dei" had to be omitted. Mr. G. Carter has composed a very interesting and excellent work, full of striking contrasts, learned, yet never dry, a clever combination of the old severer style of Anglican Church music with the more florid modern forms of thought brought into fashion by Gounod and the French School. The short "Kyrie" (after the Commandments), has been set in the key of G, and the "Gratia Tibi" (after the Gospel) in B major. The "Credo" in E major, a very fine and bold movement, is remarkable for a correct emphasizing of the passage "God *of* God, Light *of* Light," &c., by means of the unison, and the same device marks the declaration of the Father and the Son's consubstantiality; here the harmony changes to F sharp minor, but reverts at the clause "By Whom all things were made," to E major. The tenor and bass sing (*quasi recitative*) "Who for us men," and the bass (solo), intones the "Incarnatus;" the chorus enter at the clause "And was made man," with a pause on the chord of C sharp *major;* the alto then sings the words "And was crucified." Here occur some striking harmonic progressions and bits of contrapuntal imitation on a discord of the diminished seventh. At the "Resurrection" episode comes a fugue, led off by the sopranos and afterwards produced by the basses in the forms known as "inversion" and "augmentation." A florid accompaniment of quavers, which begins the "Credo," is resumed at the second paragraph of the Creed, "And I believe in the Holy Ghost," and the bass (of organ) moves contrapuntally independent of the voice parts. The concluding passage "And I look," &c, is in the *alla capella* style, with full chords for organ, and the fugue is resumed (*stretto*), at the final clause. A plagal cadence, where the extraneous notes D natural and C natural have been used effectively in the tenor part, brings out the closing chord of E major with happy prominence and emphasis.

The "Sanctus" in A major and 3-4 time, is a smooth and tuneful movement, opened by the tenor solo with a pretty flowing accompaniment (afterwards transferred to the bass). At the "full" occurs a change to G flat *major;* the moving figure of accompaniment was well played by Mr. Mallitt Jones. The voices sing the final "Glory be to Thee, O Lord" in unison, and an ingenious suggestion or suspicion of the key of B flat incidentally colours the text.

The "Benedictus" in C major, is opened by the tenor solo on the lowest pedal bass for the organ; an (orchestral) harp effect is produced by the "harmonic flute" on the great organ. The choir make a grand climax at the end of the second page on the chord of E flat, and at the "Hosanna" comes a short *fugato* accompanied by a florid counterpoint on the pedals, continued by the "trumpet stop," here happily used by the composer. Some horn effects are rendered by the "swell reeds." The sopranos sing the final words "In the highest," to the notes C, the high A, and the high G natural (held as semibreves). The "Agnus Dei" in A, esteemed by the composer the most important part of this particular Service, most felicitously combines the penitential and prayerful with the more tuneful cantabile style; phrases in D and E minor *ex. gra.*, are succeeded by responses in C major, a most graphic representation of the "Peace of God" after the agony of appeal to the Lamb. Frivolity is carefully avoided; the choir end in unison. The "Gloria in Excelsis" in C, opens with a brilliant chromatic phrase of octaves, followed (when the voices enter), with a *forte* of ponderous chords. The *quasi* andante at the words "In earth peace," where the voices are in unison for two bars, has a delicious effect; this unison has been subsequently employed without accompaniment, but the organ takes "revenge" in a brilliant passage for the pedals. The words of the "Gloria" suggest a marked contrast of jubilant tone with prayerful tenderness, and the composer has not been slow to avail himself of this opportunity. At the end of the clause "At the right hand of the Father" the soprani skip from high G to C, and Mr. Carter, like Beethoven, in the concluding chorus of the "Mount of Olives," interrupts the cadence with a chord of the 6-4-2 on B flat which he resolves on the first inversion of F minor, but not finally. The opening theme of the "Gloria" is resumed at the passage "For Thou only," but without the brilliant chromatic passage, which Mr. Carter reserves for the "Amen." The cadence is plagal, but the chord F major is followed by a feint of D minor, and is resolved really as a chord of the 6-4-3, on a tonic pedal (C). Mr. Carter, in his various keys, has always retained the note E natural. The organ stops (some of those referred to), are "analogues" of the orchestral score. Performances in a church may not be criticised, but it is only fair to report favourably of the organist and the choir at St. Matthias. Many difficult passages and some long "skips" are written for the voices, and these were well seized. The tenor soloist, too, deserves commendation for his part of the service.

On Sunday, Oct. 21st, Mr. Mallit Jones performed Schubert's fine Mass in G, and used the one in B flat. On Oct. 28th, the Festival of St. Simon and St. Jude. On Sunday evening Mr. Jones played, as a postludium, Léfébure Wély's splendid Offertorium in G major, and many of the congregation remained to hear this popular piece of organ music.

Academical Intelligence.

UNIVERSITY OF CAMBRIDGE.

The Final Exam. for the degree of Mus. Bac. takes place on Thursday and Friday, Dec. 6th and 7th, 1883. The work for analysis is Mozart's Symphony in C, No. 49 ("Jupiter?") in full score.

UNIVERSITY OF OXFORD.

Degrees in Music.

In a congregation held on Thursday, Oct. 25th, the following were admitted to the degree of

Bachelor in Music:—

FREDERICK R. GREENISH, New College, and Haverfordwest.
WILLIAM G. MERRIKIN, New College, and Hull.
ARTHUR H. STEVENS, B.A., Worcester College, and Dover.

The following is abstracted from the papers set at the recent examinations at Oxford :—

EXAMINATION FOR THE DEGREE OF DOCTOR IN MUSIC, OCTOBER 9, 1883.

HARMONY.

1. Compose a movement of not less than sixteen bars, for six voices, in open score and proper clefs.
2. Harmonise a given theme in the tenor, in G minor, in three different ways, for eight voices, in open score and proper clefs.

3. Write twenty-four bars on a given short ground bass of four bars in six vocal parts, inclusive of the bass, never repeating the same harmonic treatment.
4. Analyse passages from various points of view, which are extracted from the finale of Beethoven's Sonata in B flat, Op. 22, and from Mozart's Quintet in E flat, No. 5.

COUNTERPOINT, &C.

1. Add seven upper parts to a given Canto Fermo in G minor, all strictly in counterpoint of the first species, in open score and in proper clefs.
2. Compose a fugue in D major, in simple triple time, on two original subjects, introducing counterpoints at the octave, tenth, and twelfth, and any other ingenious devices. It must not be less than thirty or more than forty bars in length.
3. Continue and conclude either of two given canons, in sixteen bars.

INSTRUMENTATION AND ACOUSTICS.

1. Give the formula for finding equal temperament.
2. Explain the characteristics of the various systems of unequal temperament (*e. g.* Kirnberger's, Euler's, Herschell's), or the system of absolutely pure intervals.
3. Give the fractions representing the ordinary comma, the Pythagorean comma, and the Enharmonic diesis ; and explain the meaning of those terms.
4. Give a list of the principal overtones (or harmonics) of G, and shew which of these are available in practical harmony.
5. Explain the phenomena of the vibrations of :—i. Stretched strings ; ii. Flue-pipes ; iii. Reed-pipes ; iv. Plates (square or circular) ; v. Stretched membranes.
6. Harmonise a given melody in E minor, for two violins, two violas, violoncello, and double bass, introducing imitations, &c.
7. Score a given sketch in B minor, the melody and a figured bass being set, for full orchestra, introducing imitations, &c.

SECOND EXAMINATION FOR THE DEGREE OF
BACHELOR IN MUSIC.

HARMONY.

1. Add an alto and tenor part in their respective clefs to a given melody in D minor.
2. Add four upper parts in their proper clefs to a given figured bass in E flat, and give roots.
3. Harmonise a given passage for five voices, imitating as nearly as possible the Church style of Palestrina, the treble and bass of fourteen bars from Palestrina's "Dixit Dominus" being set.
4. Add three parts, in short score, to a given figured bass in A flat.
5. Explain certain bars marked in a given passage from Pierson's "Jerusalem," giving roots, &c.

COUNTERPOINT AND FUGUE.

1. Write simultaneous counterpoints of the third and fourth species on a Canto Fermo in F, together making three parts.
2. Add four parts in the first species to the bass Canto Fermo in D.
3. Write a short fugue in four parts on a given subject in F, pronounced by the tenor for the first time, and introduce the subject by inversion.
4. Give tonal answers to four given subjects.

HISTORY, INSTRUMENTAL, &C.

1. Give a list of the principal Madrigalian composers in England during the reigns of Queen Elizabeth and James I.
2. Give the name and date of the work which first introduced the Italian Madrigalian composers to the English public.
3. What was the influence of the Commonwealth upon music, and the progress of the art in England ?
3. What kind of overture did Lully prefix to his operas ? Was his method followed by any great composers in other countries ?
5. What was the "Beggar's Opera"? Who compiled it ? What influence had it on English Art ?
6. What celebrated compositions have been written in upwards of sixteen real vocal parts ?
7. Give examples of the effective employment of the piccolo.

8. In one of his oratorios Handel has written unusually difficult passages for horn and trumpet in the introductory symphony of a chorus. Give the names of both chorus and oratorio.

9. Name any instances in which the usual form of the finale of a symphony has not been adhered to.

10. State the several methods in which the two treble parts, the alto, tenor, and the bass parts of a vocal quintet may be scored for the stringed quartet and the double bass.

11. Describe the leading characteristics of J. S. Bach's organ sonatas, and of Mendelssohn's organ sonatas.

12. Arrange the Old Hundredth Psalm tune as follows :—i. with the melody for a solo stop, accompanied by varied harmonies ; ii. for full organ in simple harmony. Both examples with pedal obbligato.

13. Define rhythm in its fullest meaning as applied to musical composition.

RAPHAEL'S MUSICAL INSTRUMENTS.

In Messrs. J. A. Crowe and G. B. Cavalcaselle's "Raphael : his Life and Works," the account of his sketches for the Assumption or Coronation of the Virgin is as follows :—"One of the boys plays the tambourine. Another pose of the same youth yields an angel playing a pocket-viol. But instead of looking up, as we find him in the Pesth design, he looks down musingly, and the slight interval which parts the two drawings in date of execution indicates the moment when the idea of an 'Assumption' was given up and that of a 'Coronation of the Virgin' was adopted, for in the 'Coronation' the tambourine player bends his face towards the ground, and not towards the sky. Hardly had the original design been put aside when Raphael recomposed the whole of it. He lightly threw on a sheet, now at Lille, two contours of boys, one of whom sits and prays with joined hands, whilst the other likewise sits and holds a crown over his neighbour's head. Hastily drawn with a pen, this sketch scarcely looks so good as Raphael should have made it. Better, yet also from the model, and with very rapid strokes, Raphael outlined a boy touching the strings of a mandoline, which he put aside for one playing a violin, on the skeleton of whose frame the drapery hangs in folds, flapping in the wind. Both sketches on the same paper are exhibited at Lille. Even these efforts did not prove entirely suitable ; the head of the boy had been bent to the left ; a better effect might be got if it were turned to the right. A model now sat, but only for the head and the hand, with the bow. The type of the face, in itself lovely, is realized with marvellous skill, and this perfect and inimitable study adorns the British Museum. To the left of the Virgin and Christ in the 'Coronation,' the studies for the tambourine and viol players at Lille do service, but in this wise, that whereas the latter stands to the left and the former to the right in the design, their position is reversed in the picture—the viol is turned into a harp, and both figures are clothed in ample drapery."

The new work, "Voice, Song, and Speech," by Messrs. Lennox Browne and Emil Behnke, advertised to appear on the 1st of November, will be delayed for a few days in consequence of Messrs. Putnam and Sons of New York, having taken half the first edition on condition that publications in this country be postponed for fourteen days after the date of shipping to America, so that the work may make its appearance simultaneously in both countries.

Says *Church Bells :* "A bright contrast to the obstinacy and parsimony which have prevented the progress of the Free Library movement is, however, furnished at Watford, in Hertfordshire, where a local school of music has been established in accordance with the spirit, if not absolutely within the terms of the letter, of the Act. Some years ago a suggestion was made that each parish might place an organ in its vestry hall, if the consent of the ratepayers could be obtained ; but the *Athenæum*, if we recollect aright, argued that it would scarcely be legal to take such a course. If, however, the inhabitants of a parish or a borough can rate themselves for the establishment of a school of music, there would seem to be no valid reason why they should not resolve to purchase a musical instrument, which would contribute to the public pleasure and improvement."

Correspondence.

JOHN SMITH'S DOCTORATE.

TO THE EDITOR OF THE "MUSICAL STANDARD."

SIR,—In the "Dictionary of Music and Musicians" (Macmillan & Co.) under the heading of SMITH, JOHN, it is stated that "about 1826 he assumed the title of Doctor, but it is doubtful if the degree was ever conferred on him, no record of it existing."

No such record does exist ; but a further search in the minute-books of Trinity College, Dublin, has discovered a resolution of the Board, dated July 7, 1827, *agreeing to give* the degree of Doctor of Music to Mr. Smith. No other entry on the subject can be found ; but as a resolution similar to that referred to appears to have been the usual way of conferring the degree of Mus.Doc. in Dublin at that time, there seems to be no doubt that Mr. Smith was virtually entitled so to style himself.

As Editor of the "Dictionary of Music and Musicians," I regret that any doubt should have been cast on the validity of Mr. Smith's title.　　Yours truly,

GEORGE GROVE.

Lower Sydenham, Oct. 26, 1883.

HARMONIUMS.

TO THE EDITOR OF THE "MUSICAL STANDARD."

SIR,—Not only as an advertiser and reader of your journal, but also as a player and admirer of that somewhat misunderstood, and consequently much maligned instrument, the Harmonium, will you allow me to say that I think the article in the above paper (Sept. 29th), signed "A.M.," on "Nose Music in Church," insulting to English makers ; incorrect—and, to my mind, written in bad taste. The writer refers to "this most offensive wind instrument" with a "nasal tone," and then proceeds to say, "fine harmoniums, of sonorous quality, may be purchased in Paris," etc., etc.

Now, any one understanding the subject is perfectly aware that the French instruments of this class are the most "nasal"-toned of any in the world. He then speaks of "this disagreeable family of pseudo-*sirens*," and says, "all these peculiar wind instruments, including the seraphine" (completely out of date and forgotten), "and the Apollonicon" (which really was a barrel and finger *organ*, containing 1,900 *pipes*, and 45 stops, and was built in 1812), "and, in fact, all machines where the sound is derived from the action of the wind on metallic tongues or plates" (why not have included the American organ ?) "make me feel, like Mozart, at the sound of the trumpet when blown a few commas on 'the wrong side of the post.'"

Of course it is to be regretted that the author of "Nose Music in Church" should be of such exceeding nervous temperament, and suffer from defective memory ; but I would suggest that before he writes concerning free-reed instruments again, he should make inquiry into the facts and relative characteristics of the various "species."　　Yours faithfully,

Hampstead Road.　　E. S.

P.S.—The late Scotson Clark, who *did* know something of harmoniums, says, "No organist should be without one."

[A. M. has a personal objection to the Harmonium. E. S. has a direct interest in its artistic development and popularity. Each writer is fairly entitled to his own opinion. The popularity of so useful an instrument as the Harmonium is not likely to suffer abatement. The various forms of this reed instrument, from the cheapest keyboard type in existence to the superb Mustel organ, the large amount of good tone produced from such a portable instrument, its organ-like power of sustaining sounds, and its admirable effects in good hands, will secure an unshakable position for the Harmonium.—ED. *Mus. Stand.*]

ORCHESTRAL TUNING.

TO THE EDITOR OF THE "MUSICAL STANDARD."

SIR,—May I be allowed, through the medium of your valuable paper, to call the attention of conductors of orchestral concerts to an evil the magnitude of which it is not easy to over-rate. I refer to the practice, very common among members of an orchestra, of tuning their instruments between the numbers of a programme. Recently I heard a fine performance in London of Weber's overture to "Oberon," the effect of which was quite spoiled by a vigorous "tuning " on the part of the whole orchestra, which began immediately after the last chord of the overture. The effect of this would have been ludicrous had it not been very distressing to the hearer. I feel sure it is only necessary to bring this evil before the notice of conductors to ensure an effort on their part to avoid it.

I am, Sir, your obedient servant,

F. C. O.

On Oct. 25th a Welsh harp contest was held at Swansea, Dr. Parry of that town being the adjudicator

"THE COMING OPERA."

Judging from the signs of the times, and the indications of approaching activity of prominent impresarios, the probabilities point strongly toward the rapid growth and expansion of the English as the coming opera, especially with English-speaking people. We think this is as it should be, and is but the natural desire of the people to hear that which they can understand.

There is, of course, always a certain toady element that reaches after and apes the foreign; but the real solid and sensible element are beginning to give more decided tokens of a pronounced desire for that which most readily furthers their understanding and enjoyment of what they hear.

Foreigners are to a fault exacting and uncompromising in their adherence ¦to their mother tongue; and it would be quite as unlikely to expect an Italian to enjoy his music in any other than his beloved language as to expect the Chinese, with their ancient and heathen traditions, to admire and enjoy the music of civilized nations.

There is undeniable evidence of the adaptation of certain languages to musical sounds, and of others as being radically unsusceptible and unfitting to musical expression. These peculiarities are quite palpable even to those of only ordinary observation.

The German is manifestly harsh and guttural, and many beautiful effects of musical expression are well-nigh ruined by this harshness, inseparable from the articulation of the language.

Also, French is totally inadequate as the vehicle of pathetic or sustained expression by reason of its constant use of the anterior organs of speech—the lips and teeth—and as a consequence there is a mincing, crisp, and forceless effect.

The English is considerably better, although partaking of some peculiarities of both, which does not make it the most euphonious language for song. But, on the contrary, all the Latin languages, as the Italian, Spanish, and even the Welsh, strange as the latter may seem, on account of their softness and predominating vowel sounds and terminations, determine such as being the best vehicles of pure musical expression.

I remember, some years since, hearing the Russian male choir on the occasion of their first visit to this country, and was pleasantly surprised to hear softness and smoothness where I had, from an observation of their language, been led to expect harshness.

In no tongue are there more mistaken notions of euphony than in the Welsh, which upon a view of the extraordinary doubling and trebling of vowels and consonants in such words as llyr, ddadblyylad, ynghyd, gymmhuys, ngogoneddu, etc., etc., gives the impression of an impossible articulation ;—and it was with me an abiding impression, until I had more direct opportunities of information and enlightenment, that the attempted articulation of such a language would involve writhings, distortions, tongue-tyings, and throat convulsions appalling to contemplate. But in no idea was I more in error, as the actual effect was soft and euphonious.

It is overwhelmingly apparent that most Asiatic languages are totally unsusceptible of adaptation to music—as, for example, the Chinese and Japanese.

We do not wish our remarks understood as being an arraignment of the English language as unfitting for musical expression, but as not being the best one for such purpose, judging from a purely musical standpoint. It is, however, the one with which we have the most to do, and the one which is bound, in the nature of the case, to supersede and crowd out all others, and consequently be the paramount reason for the growth and ultimate supremacy of the English opera.

The most renowned artists of the world are gradually becoming converted to this view ; and although, while a few of the greatest will scorn the use of any other than the Italian, yet the potent majority are placing themselves in harmonious sympathy to the pronounced demands of the people, and of the best paying policy.

In our own land, Caroline Richings (since deceased), the glorious and lamented Parepa, and, latterly, Emma Abbott, have striven earnestly in the cause of their mother tongue—notably the former, who can be rightfully regarded as the pioneer in this musical path.

It is certain, however, that Mr. Carl Rosa has been, and is, doing the most powerful and educating work in this branch of the art, and is conspicuously prominent among his operatic *confrères* in the encouragement and engagement of English and American talent, and the production of strictly English operas by native composers. Mr. Rosa has but just brought out two new works—" Esmeralda " and " Colomba "—the products of Mr. Goring Thomas and Mr. Mackenzie, in accordance with an engagement so to do by him. Both of these works mark an era in English opera, and are the forerunners of an epoch the like of which has as yet been unrealised, and which bids fair to blossom and expand into splendid fruition.

The action of Mr. Rosa, with its attendant success, has already had its stimulating effect in America, where Mr. Silas G. Pratt, a native of Chicago, has taken the initiative, and imitated the example furnished by the husband of the adored Parepa.

It is conclusively evident to our mind that the time is rapidly approaching when we shall have a distinctive America opera, furnished and equipped by American brains and talent. This is a " consummation devoutly to be wished."—*American Art Journal.*

Passing Events.

Gade's " Psyche " has been performed by the Shrewsbury Harmonic Society.

On Monday last the new opera comique, " Falka," for which Mr. Farnie has written the libretto to Mons. F. Chassigne's music, was produced at the Royal Comedy Theatre.

The Goss Memorial Committee met on Tuesday last at the College of Organists. Sir A. Sullivan occupied the chair, Mr. Cummings taking his place during the closing part of the meeting.

Mr. Charles King gave a miscellaneous concert at Wisbech the other evening. Miss Marianne Fenna, Mr. E. Dunkerton, Miss A. Ward (violin), Mr. King, and Mr. W. H. Jude, were the performers.

The Rev. E. W. Bullinger, D.D., has set to music Mr. Martin F. Tupper's poem on Luther, presumably with a view to use at the forthcoming London recognition of the reformer's 400th birthday anniversary on the 10th.

That excellent society the Borough of Hackney Choral Association, under the direction of Mr. E. Prout, commenced the season on Monday last with a performance of their conductor's cantata " Hereward," at the Shoreditch Town Hall.

The Kyrle Society have recently given Mendelssohn's " St. Paul " at All Saints, Haggerston, and at Christ Church, Watney-street, Commercial-road. Upon both occasions Mr. M. L. Lawson was the conductor, and Mr. E. H. Turpin, the organist.

A contemporary says : A neat little operetta, " The Sergeant's Ruse," cast for four characters, two of each sex, has been written by Mr. Panting for Miss Cameron's operetta company, by whom it found intelligent interpretation at the Surrey Masonic Hall, on Tuesday evening. Miss Horton, who possesses an agreeable contralto voice, is, perhaps, the most meritorious of the quartet. The music, by Mr. T. Merton Clarke, is bright and catching.

On Tuesday evening, Oct. 30th, a concert in aid of the Church Schoolmasters and Schoolmistresses' Benevolent Institution, was given in St. Michael's Hall, Hackney. The vocalists were Mdme. Clara West, Mdme. Christine Wallace, Miss Annie Cole, Mr. Mullerhausen, Mr. Stanley Cockton, Mr. Pegler, and the St. John's College (Battersea) Glee Party. Buffo, Mr. H. P. Matthews ; pianists, Miss Pharoah, and Mr. Sharp ; concertina, Mr. Hobday. There was a very large and appreciative audience.

Mr. J. S. Curwen closed on Saturday last a fortnight's lecturing tour in Durham and Northumberland. Large and successful gatherings were held at Stockton, West Hartlepool, Middlesbrough, Sunderland, Wallsend, Newcastle, North and South Shields, Jarrow, Bishop Auckland, Durham, and Darlington. These meetings took the form of musical demonstrations of the Tonic Sol-fa system by choirs of children specially trained, Mr. Curwen giving the necessary explanations. At Durham Mr. Curwen addressed the students of the University in one of the lecture-rooms.

Under the title of " The Musical Year " a new work is being issued from the pen of Mr. Joseph Bennett, which will contain selections from his criticisms. There can be no doubt about the usefulness of such a book ; for however valuable good criticisms may be in our widely-spread newspapers, they are there read in the midst of a number of varied surroundings and impressions, and there will be distinct gain in having opinions upon important artistic productions and performances placed upon permanent record in book form. It is needless to add, that Mr. Joseph Bennett is known to be a writer of such unimpeachable judgment, critical experience, verbal clearness and shrewd observation, that the work must needs be both instructive and pleasant reading.

It is reported that Franz Liszt is engaged on the composition of a new pianoforte concerto, his third work of this type.

It is stated that Senor Sarasate will go to Russia next month, with the intention of remaining there throughout the winter season. He will probably return to Paris about March, and may be shortly afterwards expected in London.

A correspondent writes of the following services of musical interest, at St. Mary-of-the-Angels, Bayswater. On Saturday the 3rd, the First Vespers of the Feast of St. Charles will be sung at 4.30. p.m. The music will consist of Mozart's setting of the Vesper Psalms in C, with the exception of the "Laudate Pueri," which will be by Capocci, the Maestro di Capella of St. John's Lateran. On Sunday the 4th, the music at the High Mass (11 a.m.), will consist of Haydn's Mass in C (No. 2), with Mozart's Offertorium, "Splendente te Deus." Mozart's Vespers will be sung again in the evening at 7 p.m.

Musicians will be glad to hear that a neat and simple little contrivance for turning over the pages of music has been invented by an Armenian mechanic, named Erghanian, and patented in several European countries. This small apparatus is worked silently by a treadle, and gently picks up the page, which it lays smoothly on the opposite one. It can be applied to any ordinary music stand, and will doubtless be of great use in orchestras, avoiding by its use, the pause and flapping of leaves, when the players have to wait and turn over the pages of their music.—Chambers's Journal.

The great success which has been achieved by the reproduction of Balfe's "Mazeppa" at Margate has awakened the attention of other choral societies to the value and interest of the work, so that there is a prospect of its becoming as popular and as well known as it deserves. It should be stated in connection with the revival that great credit is due to Mr. Frank Bodda for his exertions in the matter. In his desire to bring Balfe's music to the place it should occupy in public estimation, he has shown himself in every way a worthy partner of his talented wife, formerly Miss Louisa Pyne, who, in conjunction with the late Mr. William Harrison, played many of Balfe's operas on the stage at the Lyceum and Covent Garden Theatres.—Morning Post.

The Dean and Chapter of Canterbury have apparently discovered there is some truth in the saying that "The larger the church the less room there is for the organ." A meeting was held on Saturday last for the purpose of coming to a final decision as to the purchase or rejection of the organ offered them by Mr. Holmes. A representation of the organ had been placed on each side of the choir, and also in the north and south transepts. These were so arranged that persons could pass beneath, but they completely obstructed the view from the transepts to the nave, and besides presenting an incongruous appearance, and it was thought greatly marred the architectural beauty of the building. So after a minute inspection and long consideration the Chapter declined the offer.

Mendelssohn's "Lauda Sion" was given with orchestral accompaniments at S. Stephen's, Gloucester Road, South Kensington, on Sunday evening, the occasion being the Harvest Festival. It was also repeated on All Saints' Day. The vocal parts were taken entirely by the members of the choir, under the direction of the newly-appointed organist, Mr. Alfred J. Caldicott, Mus.Bac., Cantab.

The Querist.

QUERY.

BURIAL PLACE OF DR. MAURICE GREENE.—I have never been able to find any record of the burial place of Dr. Maurice Greene. Can any of your readers inform me where he was interred ?—Q. R.

REPLY.

J. L. F.—It is possible that the anthem enquired after by J. L. F., "Behold, how good and pleasant," is the unaccompanied chorus forming No. 19 of Henry Smart's cantata, "Jacob." I have heard it on one occasion in Birmingham employed as an anthem. "Jacob" is published by Cramer and Co., but I do not think this chorus is issued separately.—S. S. S.

Service Lists.

TWENTY-FOURTH SUNDAY AFTER TRINITY.
NOVEMBER 4th.
London.

ST. PAUL'S CATHEDRAL.—Morn.: Service, Te Deum and Benedictus, Prout in F ; Introit, Comfort the soul of thy servant (Crotch) ; Holy Communion, Prout in F. Even.: Service, Magnificat and Nunc Dimittis, Elvey in A ; Anthem, my song shall be alway Thy mercy and Ye nations offer to the Lord (Mendelssohn).

TEMPLE CHURCH.—Morn.: Service, Te Deum Laudamus and Benedictus, Hopkins in C ; Apostles' Creed, Harmonised Monotone ; Anthem, As pants the hart (Spohr). Even.: Service, Magnificat and Nunc Dimittis, Cooke in C ; Apostles' Creed, Harmonized-Monotone ; Anthem, The Heavens declare (Boyce).

FOUNDLING CHAPEL. — Morn.: Service, Te Deum, Nares in F ; Anthem, If with all your hearts, and Cast thy burden " Elijah " (Mendelssohn). Aft.: Children Service.

ALL SAINTS, MARGARET STREET.—Morn.: Service, Te Deum, Gounod in C ; Benedictus, Garrett in D ; Holy Communion, Alwyn in F ; Offertory Anthem, Who are these, like stars appearing (Redhead). Even.: Service, Miller in D ; Anthem, It came even to pass (Ouseley). Te Deum, Gounod in C.

CHRIST CHURCH, CLAPHAM.—Morn.: Service, Te Deum, Plain-song ; Kyrie and Credo, " Messe Solennelle (Gounod). Offertory Anthem, Hallelujah, from the " Messiah " (Handel) ; Sanctus, Benedictus, Agnus Dei, and Gloria in excelsis (Gounod) Even.: Service, Magnificat and Nunc Dimittis, Smart in B flat ; Anthem, On Thee, each living soul, and sing to the Lord (Haydn).

HOLY TRINITY, GRAY'S INN ROAD. — Morn.: Service, Te Deum, Hopkins in G ; Jubilate, Chanted. Even. : Service, Magnificat and Nunc Dimittis, Parry in D ; Anthem, Solo, O Lord Thou hast searched me out (Bennett), and Chorus, Enter not into judgment (Attwood).

HOLY TRINITY, TULSE HILL. — Morn.: Service, Chants. Even.: Service, Magnificat and Nunc Dimittis, Garrett in D ; Anthem, Consider the lilies, and doth not wisdom cry (Haking).

ST. AGNES, KENNINGTON PARK, S.E.—Morn.: Service, Holy Communion, Kyrie, Creed, Sanctus, and Gloria, Gadsby in C ; Benedictus and Agnus Dei, Hedgecock in C.

ST. JAMES'S PRIVATE EPISCOPAL CHAPEL, SOUTHWARK. —Morn.: Service, Introit, Come, ye sin defiled " St. Mary Magdalen " (Stainer) ; Communion Service (MS.) Even.: Service, Tours in B flat ; Anthem, Gloria in excelsis (Bach).

ST. MARGARET PATTENS, ROOD LANE, FENCHURCH STREET.—Morn.: Service, Te Deum, Wesley in F ; Benedictus, Dykes in F ; Communion Service, Offertory Anthem, Blest are the departed (Spohr) ; Kyrie, Credo, Sanctus, Benedictus, Agnus Dei, and Gloria, Schubert in F. Even.: Service, Magnificat and Nunc Dimittis, Stark in D ; Anthem, Holy holy (Mendelssohn).

ST. MARY BOLTONS, WEST BROMPTON, S.W.—Morn.: Service, Te Deum, and Benedictus, Goss in C. Even.: Service, Magnificat and Nunc Dimittis, Hopkins in F ; Anthem, What are these that are arrayed (Stainer).

ST. MAGNUS, LONDON BRIDGE.—Morn.: Service, Opening Anthem, If we say (Calkin) ; Te Deum and Jubilate, Turle in D ; Kyrie (Walmisley). Even.: Service, Magnificat and Nunc Dimittis, Turle in D ; Anthem, Thy word is a lantern (Purcell).

ST. PAUL'S, AVENUE ROAD, SOUTH HAMPSTEAD.—Morn.: Service, Te Deum, Smart in F ; Benedictus (Langdon) ; Kyrie Tours in F. Even. : Service, Magnificat and Nunc Dimittis, Smart in F ; Anthem, What are these (Stainer).

ST. PAUL'S, BOW COMMON, E.—Morn.: Service, Te Deum Smart in F ; Benedictus, Chant ; Holy Communion, Kyrie, Credo, Sanctus Benedictus, Agnus Dei, Gloria in excelsis, Mozart's 4th Mass in C ; Offertory, Stainer. Even. : Service, Magnificat and Nunc Dimittis, Barnby in E flat ; Anthem, I have surely built Thee an house (Boyce).

ST. PETER'S, VERE STREET, W.—Even.: Service, Magnificat and Nunc Dimittis, Goss in A ; Anthem, As pants the hart (Spohr).

ST. AUGUSTINE AND ST. FAITH, WATLING STREET.— Morn.: Service, Stainer in E flat ; Introit, Let us all rejoice (South) ; Communion, Stainer in E flat. Even.: Service, Attwood in C ; Anthem, These are they (Dykes).

ST. SAVIOUR'S, HOXTON. — Morn.: Service, Te Deum, Hopkins in G ; Holy Communion ; Kyrie, Credo, Sursum Corda, Sanctus, and Gloria in excelsis, Armes in A. Even.: Service, Magnificat and Nunc Dimittis (Parry) ; Anthem, What are these (Stainer).

ST. SEPULCHRE'S, HOLBORN. — Morn: Service, Te Deum Jubilate, and Kyrie, Sullivan in D ; Credo, Agutter in B flat ; Anthem, O taste and see (Goss). Even. : Service, Magnificat and Nunc Dimmittis, Arnold in A ; Anthem, In Jewry (Clarke-Whitfeld).

Country.

ST. ASAPH CATHEDRAL. — Morn.: Service, Gilholy in B flat ; Anthem, I will go unto the altar of God (Gauntlett). Even.: Service, The Litany ; Anthem, The Lord is in His holy temple (Saunders).

ASHBURNE CHURCH, DERBYSHIRE. — Morn.: Service, Boyce in C ; Kyrie, Credo and Gloria, Martin in C. Even.: Service, Goss in E ; Anthem, Selection from " Last Judgement " (Spohr).

BABBACOMBE (ALL SAINTS).—Morn : Service, Plain Song ; Communion Service ; Kyrie, Credo, Sanctus, Benedictus, Agnus Dei, and Gloria in excelsis, " Messe Solennelle " (Gounod); Offertorium, Ave Verum, Jesu, Word of God (Gounod). Even.: Service, Magnificat and Nunc Dimittis, Stainer in B flat ; Anthem, What are these that are arrayed in white (Stainer) ; after sermon, Worthy is the Lamb, and Hallelujah, " Messiah " (Handel).

BEDDINGTON CHURCH, SURREY.—Morn.: Service, Tours in F ; Communion Service, Calkin in D. Even.: Service Garrett in D ; Anthem, Whoso dwelleth within the defences of the most high (Martin).

BELFAST (ST. GEORGE'S). — Morn.: Service, Te Deum, and Jubilate, Sullivan in D ; Apostles' Creed, Harmonized Monotone ; Litany (Helmore); Communion Service, Woodward in E flat ; Offertory (Stainer). Even.: Service, Magnificat and Nunc Dimittis, Barnby in D ; Anthem, The Lord is my Shepherd (Macfarren).

BIRMINGHAM (S. ALBAN THE MARTYR).—Morn.: Service, Te Deum, and Benedictus, Dykes, in F ; Holy Communion, Kyrie, Credo, Sanctus and Gloria, Dykes in F ; Agnus Dei and Benedictus (Redman). Evensong.: Magnificat and Nunc Dimittis, Barnby in D.

BIRMINGHAM (ST. CYPRIAN'S, HAY MILLS).—Morn.: Service, Nares in C ; Anthem, Hear my prayer (Kent). Even.: Service, Ebdon in C ; Anthem, My soul truly waiteth (Kent).

BRISTOL CATHEDRAL.— Morn.: Service, Attwood in F ; Even.: Service, Attwood in F ; Anthem, Blessed be the God (Wesley).

CARLISLE CATHEDRAL.—Morn.: Service, Calkin in B flat ; Introit, Come ye blessed (Barnby) ; Kyrie, Calkin in B flat ; Nicene Creed, Harmonized Monotone. Even.: Service, Stainer in B flat ; Anthem, Come, said a voice, and Behold the Lamb that was sacrificed (Spohr).

CHESTER (ST. MARY'S CHURCH).—Morn.: Service, Goss in C ; Communion, Tearne in G. Even.: Service, Garrett in F ; Anthem, Rejoice, O Judah, Unto which of the Angels, and Let all the Angels (Handel).

DONCASTER (PARISH CHURCH).—Morn.: Service, Whitfeld in E ; Introit, God so loved the world (Goss) ; Kyrie and Creed (Hopkins). Even.: Service, Whitfeld in E ; Anthem, The Wilderness (Goss).

DUBLIN, ST. PATRICK'S (NATIONAL) CATHEDRAL.—Morn.: Service, Te Deum, and Jubilate, Mendelssohn in A. Holy Communion, Kyrie, and Creed, Stainer in A ; Sanctus, and Gloria, Stewart in G ; Anthem, Elijah, Get thee hence, For He shall give His angels (Mendelssohn). Even.: Service, Magnificat and Nunc Dimittis, Chants ; Anthem, The Lord is good (Costa), and Come let us worship (Gick).

EDINBURGH (ST. JOHN's).—Aft. : Service, Anthem, O God, Thou art my God (Purcell). Even.: Service, Turn thy face from my sins (Attwood).

EDINBURGH (CHRIST CHURCH, MORNINGSIDE).—Morn. : Service, Te Deum, and Jubilate, Chant. Even. : Service, Whitfeld in E ; Anthem, In Jewry is God known.

ELY CATHEDRAL.—Morn.: Service, Garrett in F ; Kyrie, and Credo, Thorne in E flat ; Gloria, " Ely " ; Anthem, How lovely (Salaman). Even.: Service, Garrett in F ; Anthem, Lead kindly light (Stainer).

HARROGATE (ST. PETER'S CHURCH).—Morn. : Service, Te Deum, and Benedictus, Dykes in F ; Anthem, The Lord is my Shepherd (Macfarren) ; Kyrie, Goss in F ; Credo, Sursum Corda, Sanctus, and Gloria in excelsis, Woodward in E flat Even.: Service, Magnificat, Nunc Dimittis, Ebdon in C ; Anthem, I will give thanks (Barnby).

LLANDAFF CATHEDRAL.—Morn.: Service, Te Deum and Benedictus, Dykes in F ; Introit, O Lord, my God (Wesley) ; Holy Communion, Prout in F ; Offertory Sentenees (Barnby). Even.: Service, Anthem, Praise the Lord (Garrett).

LEEDS PARISH CHURCH.—Morn.: Service, Garrett in F ; Anthem, come, let us worship (Mendelssohn) ; Communion Service (Wesley). Even.: Service, Garrett in F ; Anthem, I that day (Elvey).

LICHFIELD CATHEDRAL. — Morn.: Service, Attwood in F ; Communion Service, Dykes in F ; Anthem, Lo ! my Shepherd is divine (Haydn). Even.: Service, Attwood in F ; Anthem, My God, why, O why, hast Thou forsaken me (Mendelssohn).

LINLITHGOW ABBEY, W.B. — Morn.: Service, Harvest Thanksgiving ; Te Deum, Irons in E ; Anthem, Let us now fear the Lord, No. 62 (Sewell). Even. : Service, Anthem, Ye shal dwell in the land, No. 75 (Stainer).

LIVERPOOL CATHEDRAL.—Aft.: Service, Magnificat and Nunc Dimittis, Turle in D ; Anthem, The souls of the people are in the hand of God (Rea).

MANCHESTER CATHEDRAL. — Morn.: Service, Te Deum, Jubilate, Creed, Sanctus, and Gloria, Garrett in D ; Anthem, Doth not wisdom cry (Haking). Aft.: Service, Garrett in D ; Anthem, Jerusalem (Mendelssohn).

MANCHESTER (ST. BENEDICT'S).—Morn.: Service, Kyrie, Sanctus, Benedictus, and Agnus Dei, Monk in C ; Credo and Gloria in excelsis, Williams in D. Even.: Service, Magnificat and Nunc Dimittis, Wesley in F.

MANCHESTER (ST. JOHN BAPTIST, HULME).—Morn.: Service, Te Deum and Benedictus (Stainer) ; Kyrie, Credo, Sanctus, Benedictus, Agnus Dei and Gloria in excelsis, De la Hache in B flat. Even.: Service, Magnificat and Nunc Dimittis, Simper in F ; Anthem, What are these (Stainer).

ROCHESTER CATHEDRAL. — Morn.: Service, Wesley in F ; Anthem, Blessed are they (Hopkins) ; Holy Communion, Smart in F. Even. : Service, Cooke in C ; Anthem, Give ear, O ye heavens (Armes).

SALISBURY CATHEDRAL.—Morn.: Service, Garrett in F ; Offertory (Garrett). Aft.: Service, Garrett in F ; Anthem, Jehovah, Lord God of hosts (Spohr).

SHEFFIELD PARISH CHURCH. — Morn.: Service, Kyrie, Trimnel in F. Even.: Service, Magnificat and Nunc Dimittis, Trimnell in F ; Anthem, O praise God in His holiness (Trimnell).

SHERBORNE ABBEY.—Morn.: Service, Te Deum, Chants ; Kyrie, Mendelssohn in G ; Offertories (Barnby). Even. : Service, Magnificat and Nunc Dimittis (Arnold) ; Anthem, I was glad (Callicott).

SOUTHAMPTON (ST. MARY'S CHURCH).—Morn.: Service, Te Deum and Benedictus, Dykes in F ; Holy Communion, Introit, The souls of the righteous (Macfarren) ; Service, Dykes in F ; Benedictus and Agnus Dei, Gray in F ; Offertory (Barnby) ; Paternoster (Hoyte). Even.: Service, Magnificat and Nunc Dimittis, Dykes in F Apostle's Creed, Harmonized monized Monotone.

WELLS CATHEDRAL.—Morn: Service, Smart in F, throughout. Even.: Service, Smart in F ; Anthem, O Lord, our governor (Stevenson).

WINCHESTER CATHEDRAL.—Morn.: Service, Tuckermann in F. Even.: Service, Arnold in F ; Anthem, Hear, O Thou Shepherd (Walmsley).

WORCESTER CATHEDRAL. — Morn.: Service, Lloyd in E flat ; Anthem, O worship the Lord (Thorne). Even.: Service, Lloyd in E flat ; Anthem, In that day (Elvey).

APPOINTMENT.

Mr. GEORGE RYLE has been appointed Organist and Choirmaster to Christ Church (Episcopal), Morningside, Edinburgh.

Printed for the Proprietor by BOWDEN, HUDSON & CO., 23, Red Lion Street, Holborn, London, W.C ; and Published by WILLIAM REEVES, at the Office, 185, Fleet Street, E.C. West End Agents :—WEEKES & CO., 14, Hanover Street, Regent Street, W. Subscriptions and Advertisements are received either by the Publisher or West End Agents.—*Communications for the EDITOR are to be forwarded to his private address, 6, Argyll Square, W.C.*
SATURDAY, NOVEMBER 3, 1883.—*Entered at the General Post Office as a Newspaper.*

THE MUSICAL STANDARD

A NEWSPAPER FOR MUSICIANS PROFESSIONAL AND AMATEUR.

No. 1,006. Vol. XXV. FOURTH SERIES. SATURDAY, NOVEMBER 10, 1883. WEEKLY: PRICE 3D.

THE VOICE
MUSICALLY AND MEDICALLY CONSIDERED.
BY
ARMAND SEMPLE, B.A., M.B., Cantab., M.R.C.P., Lond.,
Physician to the Royal Society of Musicians.

(*Continued from page 271.*)

All uncultivated voices invariably present certain marked defects, or are unequally developed in parts. Many are deficient in compass, steadiness, power, mellowness, flexibility, and elasticity, whilst others are tremulous, throaty, nasal, harsh, veiled, or piercing. Many persons, possessed of a good ear and genuine love for music, are deterred from singing because they find that their voices appear harsh and unmusical when attempting certain notes, and, in consequence, they will make no attempt to sing, conscientiously believing that they have no voices at all; but almost every individual possesses a voice suitable for singing, although of course of variable capacity, quality, and beauty, and with care and perseverance, under the watchful eye of an experienced master, the power of producing a pleasing effect in the majority of cases is almost sure of attainment.

The commonest defects, by which the beauty of the voice may be impaired, are the following :—

The *Guttural or Throaty Timbre :* occasioned by the rising or swelling of the tongue at its base, the epiglottis being thus driven back upon the column of ascending air, and causing the voice to be emitted with a choked sound. To correct this fault, the plan sometimes adopted is to practise singing with the handle of an ordinary silver spoon in the mouth, which should press down the base of the tongue.

For the transformation of sounds into vowels the tongue is undoubtedly the great agent, but this change should be effected mainly by the movements of the *edges* of the organ ; its *base* should always remain in repose. In the formation of all vowels the degree of separation of the jaws should be almost uniform for each.

The *Nasal Timbre :* probably caused by too much relaxation of the soft palate, the column of air being either reflected or immediately echoed into the nasal cavities before its exit by the mouth. This fault may be obviated by merely raising the soft palate by a deep inhalation, the mouth being at the same time well opened.

The *Cavernous, Hollow or Veiled Timbre :* may arise from any obstruction to the advance of the sound-waves, such as the rising of the tongue at its apex ; the voice may also be rendered muffled by enlargement of the tonsils—the almond-shaped structures to be seen at the back of the throat, one on each side. This latter condition presents an additional difficulty in the formation of the head voice and the extension of the compass. This veiled character may be corrected by the firm contraction or pinching of the glottis, which is best accomplished by the enunciation of the Italian I (Anglice E).

In the act of singing, the mouth *should not be too open,* since if the jaws are too widely separated, the pharynx becomes tightened, losing its arched or vaulted form, and thus all the vocal vibrations are arrested. If, on the other hand, the teeth are too nearly approximated, a peculiar grating quality is communicated to the voice, which has not inaptly been compared to the sound produced when singing through a comb. If the mouth takes an oval shape, the character of the voice is rendered gloomy and dull, the vowels becoming indistinct, and the expression of the face hard and unpleasing. If the lips are projected so as to form a funnel, the sound of the voice becomes heavy.

In opening the mouth the jaw should fall by its own weight, the corners of the lips slightly receding ; thus the lips are kept pressed lightly against the teeth, and the mouth assumes an agreeable form ; the tongue should be without motion and loose, no effort being made to elevate it, either at its apex or base, and the throat-muscles should be relaxed.

Absolute control over the breath is most essential to singing. The head should be erect, and not thrown back, but in the position it would naturally assume when addressing an individual of the same height as the singer.

The shoulders should be thrown back firmly, but without stiffness, and the chest steadily expanded. The diaphragm—the wide muscle by which the lungs are separated from the abdomen—should be steadily lowered, and the chest slowly and regularly elevated. The air is thus retained without effort ; the passage of air through the glottis should never be accompanied by any noise, since this not only produces a wheezing sound, distressing to the ear, but also renders the throat stiff and dry.

The power and elasticity of the lungs may be greatly increased by submitting them to the following exercises, as recommended by the celebrated Manuel Garcia.

1st. Gently and slowly inhale, for a few seconds, as much air as the chest will contain.

2nd. After taking a deep breath, exhale again very gently and slowly.

3rd. Fill the lungs, and keep them inflated for the longest possible time. And

4th. Exhale completely, and leave the chest empty as long as the physical powers will conveniently allow.

It must, however, be admitted that all these exercises will, at first, be very exhausting, and must be practised separately, with long intervals of rest.

The first two actions, viz. : the gentle inspiration and expiration will be effected equally by nearly closing the mouth, so as to leave only a very slight opening for the passage of air. The pupil will, by these means, acquire steadiness of voice.

The breath influences the method or character of vocal execution ; having the power of rendering it either steady or vacillating, connected or unconnected, feeble or powerful, expressive or expressionless.

(*To be continued.*)

At a meeting of the Liverpool Committee of the Royal College of Music recently, it was announced that the amount necessary to form a Liverpool Scholarship, £3,000, had been subscribed.

Messrs. Novello and Co. have secured Sir M. Costa's version of "God Save the Queen." It is to be regretted that a more satisfactory setting could not be made. The score is of little use with a limited orchestra, and is only complete when used by a very large festival orchestra ; as for instance, not only are trumpets employed, but two cornets are, in addition, absolutely indispensable. With Sir M. Costa's known love of noisy orchestration and really splendid knowledge of instrumentation, it is quite surprising that he did not produce a larger amount of richness and sonority than he has chosen to impart to his version of our National Anthem ; his favourite trombone parts even would be condemned as a very poor specimen of student harmonization, whether judged in connection with the brass mass only or as essential to the complete score. Perhaps the version was written under pressure of time. However, it is well to know that now the version, poor as it is, is available for use, so that some general standard may be hoped for. The distinguished and enlightened publishers would have done better had they commissioned some English composer to have re-scored the piece ; for it will be a poor compliment to English art not to ultimately adopt a version of our glorious National Anthem, which has sprung from an English heart, head, and hand.

The Dean of Wells, Dr. Plumptre, has been giving an interesting lecture in the Chapter House of Gloucester Cathedral on "Cathedral Singers in Times Past and Present ;" in which, after conveying much valuable historical information, he proceeded to make several practical suggestions for the management of the musical staff of our cathedrals. Where there is a Theological College in a Cathedral city, the Dean suggests that some of the students should be drawn in on musical grounds, by what may be termed Choral Exhibitions ; and he believes that, with such a system, the withdrawal of the choir at the celebration of the Holy Communion would no longer be permitted. For the chorister boys, Dr. Plumptre desiderates something more than general education and musical instruction ; he asks that they shall receive adequate pastoral supervision on the part of the Chancellor or Precentor. The Dean has a genuine sympathy with the boys, and it is a welcome evidence of the new life which is welling up in our old cathedrals that one of their chief officers should write and speak in this way.—*Church Bells.*

Musical Intelligence.

CRYSTAL PALACE CONCERTS.

PROGRAMME.

In Memoriam:—Mendelssohn died 4th November, 1847.
Symphony in A, "Italian" .... Mendelssohn.
Air, "O God, have mercy" ("St. Paul") .... "
　　　　Mr. Santley.
Concerto for violin and orchestra .... "
　　　　Mr. Carrodus.
"Creation's Hymn" .... Beethoven.
　　　　Miss Hilda Wilson.
Serenade, "Good Night" .... Balfe.
　　　　Mr. Charles Chilley.
Solo for Violin, "Fandango" .... Molique.
　　　　Mr. Carrodus.
Ballad, "The First Walpurgis Night" .... Mendelssohn.
　　Druid Woman　..　Miss Hilda Wilson.
　　Christian Guard　..　Mr. Charles Chilley.
　　Druid Priest　..　Mr. Charles Santley.
　　Druids and Christians　The Crystal Palace Choir.
　　Conductor　-　-　AUGUST MANNS.

If any of those who are in the habit of depreciating Mendelssohn were present on Saturday last, they must have felt that, so far from his music dying out, or becoming stale and unpopular, it invariably attracts a large audience. But it does more than this, for the more frequently it is heard, the more it seems to excite the musical appetite to fresh enjoyment of its many beauties and glories. The "Italian" symphony was as fresh and lovely as ever, and was played on this occasion as though every man in the orchestra knew it from beginning to end. The concerto for violin was intrusted to Mr. Carrodus. And here it is gratifying to observe that at two consecutive concerts we have had Englishmen as soloists. Mr. Carrodus played his part in a masterly manner and achieved a success; but with due deference to the opinion of some who think the *finale* is generally taken too fast by our great violinists—Sarasate is one who is said to transgress in this respect—I cannot but think that Mr. Carrodus would have done better to have taken it faster. The very character of the movement, with its marked "Allegro molto vivace," seems to demand an impetuosity aptly called "fiery."

As the "First Walpurgis Night" is not so frequently performed as some others of Mendelssohn's works, it may not be amiss to recall the leading subjects of the work. The night between the 30th April and the 1st May is called the "Walpurgis Night," the name being derived from Walpurga or Werburga, sister to Boniface, the great apostle of Germany. On this night popular tradition imagines a kind of witches' carnival to be held on the Harz mountain. Goethe, in his poem, set to music by Mendelssohn, probably wishes to show us how this superstition arose out of the mystic rites secretly celebrated by the Druids on that night. In the instrumental introduction we have the stormy blasts followed by the soft and genial air of spring, and then the Druid priest with his chorus appears on the scene and calls the people to sacrifice and not to fear their Christian foes, who would fain uproot every remnant of the old faith. After some dramatic choruses, the Christian guard appears, but mistaking the dark figures seen only by the lurid light of the sacrificial flame and enveloped in smoke, for demons, they turn and fly, leaving the Druids to finish their rites at their leisure.

The "First Walpurgis Nacht" was first publicly performed in England by the Philharmonic Society on the 8th July, 1844, having been privately performed on the 14th June at the house of Mr. Hullah, in the presence of several distinguished men, most of whom are now, alas! gone over to the great majority.

Careful rehearsals and untiring drilling of the chorus on the part of Mr. Eyre insured for it a commendable freedom from *taches*. The instrumental part was of course everything that could be desired. The solo vocalists, both in this work and in the other selections, were very successful.　　　　　　　　　　　　　　R. S.

Mr. Stephen Stratton (an excellent musician and a contributor to the *Musical Standard*), has it is said, resolved and actually begun to abolish "part repetitions" at his chamber concerts. It seems, says an influential writer, that the time is ripe for the innovation, as it now comes out that for many years musicians (including Sir Sterndale Bennett) have wished for "nothing less than the abolition of all part repetitions," though they had either not the courage or not the opportunity to bring it about.

MONDAY POPULAR CONCERTS.

The first concert of the 26th season was held on Monday evening before a densely packed audience. The following was the programme:—

Part 1.

Quartet in C major, Op. 59, No. 3, for two violins,
　viola and violoncello .... Beethoven.
　Madame Norman-Néruda, MM. L. Ries, Straus, and Piatti.
Songs, "There is dew for the flow'ret," and "Absence" Cowen.
　　　　Miss Santley.
Ballade in G minor, Op. 42, for violin, with pianoforte
　accompaniment .... F. Néruda.
　　　　Madame Norman-Néruda.
Barcarolle in F sharp major...................... Chopin.
Wiegenlied in C flat (for pianoforte alone) .... Henselt.
　　　　M. Vladimir de Pachmann.

Part 2.

Nocturne, for violoncello, with pianoforte accompa-
　niment .... Lachner.
　　　　Signor Piatti.
Song, "Oh! had I Jubal's lyre" ("Joshua") .... Handel.
　　　　Miss Santley.
Quintet in A major, Op. 114, for pianoforte, violin,
　viola, violoncello, and contrabass .... Schubert.
　M. Vladimir de Pachmann, Madame Norman-Néruda, MM. Straus,
　　　　Reynolds, and Piatti.
Accompanist　..　..　..　Signor ROMILI.

Behold in this scheme, a "feast of fat things," a few of which, perhaps, might have been reserved; for the concert lasted longer than usual, and such music as the director so properly provides may not be taken in too large doses. What remains to be said of the actual performance? But little that has not been repeated again and again! The 3rd "Rasoumowsky" quartet, with its beautiful andante in A minor, and dashing fugal finale, just served to remind the world that a colossal genius flourished in Europe during the first quarter of the nineteenth century; also to attest the fact that the artists, all favourites and familiar to their admiring public, had not lost "cunning" in respect of their right (or *left*) hands. Mdme. Norman-Néruda's fine silvery tone might have asserted her presence, had the auditor been blindfold. Her brother's "Ballade," an agreeably wild, weird, and romantic sort of "gipsy" story, composed two years ago, displayed some of the lady's most salient qualities, only to note the exquisite trills, and the delicate *pianissimo* at the close.

Signor Piatti, "Richard himself," obliged the subscribers by introducing Ignaz Lachner's Nocturne in F, a *dolce cantabile* in 2-4 time, with a well-contrasted episode in the relative minor. The violoncello has here a fair range. The adagio is the second of three "Characteristic Pieces," and seems to deserve more favourable notice than it has received elsewhere.

Place for Herr Vladimir de Pachmann, happily engaged by Mr. Arthur Chappell for the very first *soirée*, and for two more (Nov. 10th and 12th). This gifted Russian gentleman has been so frequently and so lavishly eulogized in your columns and elsewhere, that a full endorsement of previously expressed opinions seems to be best becoming. The *connoisseurs*, between the parts, were all extolling the marvellous executancy, soft liquid touch, and delicate gradations of tone. M. de Pachmann chose two consecutive pieces in (practically), the same key, F sharp major and G flat; the effect, it must be admitted, was slightly monotonous. Chopin, by the way, has chosen G flat for a delightful "Etude" No. 5, the *motif* whereof strongly suggests the *vivace* (finale) of Beethoven's Sonatina in G, Op. 79. Henselt's "Cradle Song" reminds the musician of Schumann's "Schlummerlied"; also, as some say, of Chopin's "Berceuse": no matter, for the piece is prettiness itself, and should be heard before bed-time, as a preventive of prevalent insomnia. The melody, in 6-8 time, is formed of holding notes (dotted crotchets), with a peculiar syncopated accompaniment of quavers, on a tonic pedal bass. Henselt, (a Russian), visited England in 1867, but declined to play in public. Of course M. de Pachmann was *bissé*, when he once more sat down to the grand Broadwood and played an "extra," a quick movement in C minor, the authorship whereof was not recognised by any of the pundits, although one a very learned man, was inclined to give the credit to Henselt. M. de Pachmann is to play Schubert's Rondo in A flat, Op. 90 (first time), and Mozart's "Fantasia" in C minor, on Monday next.

Miss Santley was much applauded and recalled. Schubert's pianoforte quintet, first introduced at the "Popular" by MM. Hallé and Joachim, so far back as January 1867, has only been repeated four times (including last Monday). The work bears date A.D. 1819, *anno*.

ætatis 22. The "Trout" theme of the Variations in D stamps the composition. Herr de Pachmann led the quintet with sympathetic grace, expression, and sensibility, and Mr. Reynolds played the double bass effectively. The new conductor, Signor Romili, is likely to satisfy his audiences.

RICHTER CONCERTS.

Programme of the second concert, held Saturday, 3rd inst.:—

Overture, "Tannhäuser"	Wagner.
Introduction and Closing Scene, "Tristan und Isolde"	,,
Preislied, "Die Meistersinger"	,,
Mr. Edward Lloyd.	
Hungarian Rhapsody, No. 2	Liszt.
Symphony, No. 5, in D minor	Beethoven.

There is a most delightful sense of rest in one's enjoyment of these familiar programmes, familiar to the audience through many hearings, and familiar to the orchestra through careful study with a conductor who has mastered the scores, not only in their musical, but also in their poetical aspect. The hearer forgets even the possibility, which usually haunts him, of a blurred impression arising from a particular phrase not coming out with due prominence; of an effect being spoilt through the failure of horns or trumpets; of a want of steadiness troubling his serenity; and ceasing to look for any of these casualties, he abandons himself unreservedly to his delight in the performance. Certainly it is still possible for a string to break at an unlucky moment (proof thereof was given at this concert), but all avoidable imperfections seems to be successfully excluded. To say that a particular part of the programme was given to greater perfection than the rest, can, when all is perfect, simply be to affirm that our individual mind happened to be more in accordance with the spirit of one piece or another at the moment of performance, and therefore was much more alive to its beauties as they are set forth.

A truly representative audience (from Royalty and distinguished artists downward), completely filled the hall, at both first and second concert. The third and last is announced to take place to-night.

Liszt's second Hungarian Rhapsody, given at one of the summer concerts and then criticised, is the only unfamiliar piece presented, and therefore the only one needing comment, for Mr. Lloyd's careful rendering of the "Prize Song" is not unknown among us, nor is it ever unappreciated.

Those who heard the Rhapsody last season could scarcely fail to have been impressed with the vastly more finished and appreciative reading of last Saturday. Whether we do or do not admire the work, we must all feel that everything was done for it that could be done in the performance. And it requires no small amount of tact to play a Liszt rhapsody aright—to give it life, energy, unlimited spontaneousness, and yet to steer clear of any approach to grotesqueness.

Liszt, the inventor of the Rhapsody, remains its only successful author; others have succeeded in what they have called rhapsodies, but which might as well have been called caprices or fantasias. No other writer has caught the improvisation-like character, the quaint entry of subject after subject, the designed failure of ideas when a subject has been as it were, "talked out" among the instruments, till just at the moment when the pause in the conversation is becoming embarrassing, some one hits on a happy idea; others discourse on it till it soon engages the attention of the entire orchestra; other thoughts arise, or perhaps an old idea comes back with a new light on it, there seems to be absolutely no forethought, and yet who can say with how vast an amount of thought this apparent freedom from law and design has been attained? Liszt's Rhapsodies will make many enemies, but they will not fail to find many friends.

B. F. WYATT-SMITH.

Another Reporter writes:—

The second concert on Nov. 3rd surpassed the first, if that be possible. I make it a religious rule never to miss the magnificent overture to "Tannhäuser," a composition at once unique in respect of the music, and a sublime symbol, in celestial tone-poetry, of the still enduring contest between the powers of good and evil, light and darkness. The persistent Chorus of Pilgrims, so pertinaciously self-asserting against the bright, but heathenish and voluptuous "Song" of the as yet unconverted hero, always suggests to my mind the "war in heaven" and the final conquest of the

TRUTH. The performance was perfect, but the enjoyment much alloyed by late comers, who stumbled over your feet, and had the impudence to greet their gossiping friends aloud *en passant!* Why does not Herr Franke bar the doors of the hall for the time being, like M. Dannreuther? The other Wagnerian numbers are both golden specimens. I admire the excerpt from "Tristan und Isolde" again and again; and on this occasion, the rapture of delight was renewed. The "Death Song," however, certainly loses some of its effect off the stage, where the "situation" (*teste* the Drury Lane season of 1882), equals any cognate crisis in the records of the lyrical theatre. What do pundits say to the changes of tonality (in the "Death Song"), from four flats to five sharps, and the harmonic progressions in the 2nd and 4th bars of the "Sehr Massig" (page 49 of Programme Book), where (transient) perfect fifths, in similar motion, occur on the accents of the measure? Beethoven, who "asked after" the prohibitors of these fifths, has not scrupled to use them *twice*, in the slow moment of the Sonata Appassionata, although, theoretically, the first fifth is made a *doubly* "augmented" *fourth* by the B♭ *double* flat in the bass. When Smellfungus sneers at Wagner for lacking vocal melody, let us point to the delicious "Prize Song," in C, from "Die Meistersinger," beautifully rendered by Mr. E. Lloyd. I have already noted the "Prayer" of Elizabeth, and Wolfram's "Abendstern" song in "Tannhäuser," and the "Spinning Chorus" from "Der Fliegende Holländer" as models. Liszt's "Rhapsody" in D delights the ear, *my* ear at least, by repetition: the music is so characteristic and varied. All the same, it must be allowed that this Gipsy stuff—call it "Lassans," "Frischkos"—or what not, is pitched in a very low key. Mr. Oluf Svendsen here played his flute *obbligato* most effectively. Beethoven's 5th Symphony had been heard several times before under Herr Richter's *bâton*. A significant testimony to the great Viennese conductor may be reported. All the *connoisseurs*, and the mass of the audience, remained in the hall to the very last. Such execution, for homogeneity, baffles mere pen-and-ink sketching. Herr Richter and his band were to appear at Manchester on Wednesday night. A. M.

ROYAL ALBERT HALL.

A fine performance of "La Damnation de Faust" took place on Wednesday evening under the direction of Mr. Barnby, conductor of the Royal Albert Hall Choral Society. The Hall was crowded to the doors, and the fine work of Hector Berlioz seemed to be fully appreciated—witness the (customary) *encores* of the March in A; the Sylphs' Dance in D; and the Serenade of Mephistopheles in B major. Mdme. Albani, Mr. E. Lloyd, Mr. Pyatt, and Mr. Santley were the solo "principals." The performance lasted three hours, and many of the audience left long before the end.

BOW AND BROMLEY INSTITUTE.

The entertainment on Saturday last was one of chamber music, and included a Trio by Herr Bonawitz for pianoforte, violin, and violoncello, played by himself, Mdlle. C. Brousil, and Mr. H. Trust; Mozart's Trio in B flat, and the *finale* from one of Haydn's trios, were also included in the programme. Herr Bonawitz played admirably, one of his solos, the Liszt version of Mendelssohn's "Wedding March," and was encored. He also gave other solos by Frohberger, Mendelssohn, and Chopin. Mdlle. Brousil played effective violin solos. Miss Ada South sang nervously, but was encored in one song. To-night Stainer's "Mary Magdalen" will be repeated. Now the institution boasts of a fine choir as well as of the possession of a splendid organ, it might be well worth while to increase the number of choral concerts given under Mr. McNaught's able direction. However, the Committee have proved themselves so able to judiciously foster the artistic growth in their hands, that they may be left safely to do or not to do as they see best.

Sub rosa, it is said that the welcome announcement of the publication of Mr. Joseph Bennett's "The Musical Year," is in a great measure due to the thoughtful suggestion of a distinguished non-professional lover and patron of the art, who has himself done the cause of music good service during the past year.

WESTERN MADRIGAL SOCIETY.

The excellent performances of this society have recommenced under the conductorship of Dr. Bridge, whose knowledge, skill, and tact are everything that could be desired for the due rendering of the choice works given. The programme on October 3rd, ran thus :—

Madrigal,	" Now tune the viol "	Camio.
,,	" Ah, me! where is my true love "	Anerio.
,,	" Lady unkind "	Ferretti.
,,	" Your shining eyes "	Bateson.
Anthem,	" Hear my prayer "	Haydn.
Madrigal,	" Soon the silver moonbeams "	Gastoldi.
,,	" Ah, me! she frowns "	Pilkington.
,,	" Now let us make "	Weelkes.
Motet,	" Jehovah reigns "	Palestrina.
Madrigal,	" Hard by a fountain "	Waelrent.
,,	" Adien, my joy "	Virchi.
,,	" April is in my mistress' face "	Morley.
,,	" Ye pearls of snowy whiteness "	Croce.
,,	" Flora gave me fairest flowers "	Wilby.
,,	" Spring returns "	Marenzio.
Ballet,	" What saith my dainty darling "	Morley.

MANCHESTER.

By the 22nd of October all our musical societies and agencies are in full swing, and the present season forms no exception to the rule.

Glancing at last Saturday's newspapers I find no less than six concerts announced to be given in the space of as many days, and this may be taken as a fair sample of the state of musical activity in Manchester during the winter.

Mr. Hallé has already given two concerts, the " Redemption " (with Miss Mary Davies, Miss Hilda Wilson, Mr. Lloyd, and Mr. Santley as principals), having been performed last Thursday ; and Mr. De Jong a couple. It is to be hoped that Mr. Hallé will not disappoint those of his subscribers who justly expect that this season shall be more fruitful in the production of novelties than the last few years have been. Mackenzie's " Jason " is, I believe, to be given.

The " Royal " English Opera Company have been performing at the Prince's Theatre for the last week. With Mesdames Gaylard, Cole, and Franklein, and Messrs. Packard, Sauvage, and Lyall in the troupe, one looked for good things, but it takes more than a few competent singers to constitute a good opera company. The chorus was not fair to look upon nor to hear, and the band was unsatisfactory, a result partly attributable to the conductor. The repertoire included " Mignon " (in Italian), and the " Piper of Hamelin." Madme. Gaylard was as successful as ever in her charming impersonation of the heroine in Thomas's opera, whilst Mr. Sauvage and Mr. Lyall were both conspicuously excellent in the " Piper."

That ancient institution the " Gentleman's Concerts," which has now been in existence for a century and more, is threatened with extinction. Under the present management the concern has languished for some years past, and the directors now propose to wind it up. Such a result would be a lasting disgrace to Manchester, and a committee of the subscribers are endeavouring to prevent such an undesirable consummation, and give the concerts a new lease of life. I have reason to hope that their efforts will be successful. Under proper management these entertainments occupy a most useful place, but as at present conducted they can only end in failure.

I am glad to hear that M. Guilmant is to pay us a visit next month.

It is not good that the Town Hall organ should be under the exclusive control of one individual, however eminent he may be, and the Corporation may be reminded that it is two years since the keys of their fine instrument were touched by a stranger's hand.

C. J. H.

GLASGOW.

The prospectus of the Choral Union Concerts just issued is of great uniform excellence, both as regards the vocalists and instrumental performers and the works selected. There will be twelve concerts this season, eight being orchestral and four choral. Herr August Manns, of the Crystal Palace, will again conduct, and, with an augmented orchestra should once more give delight to Glasgow music-lovers. The vocalists are as follows : Miss Mary Davies, Mrs. Hutchinson, Mdlle. Warnots, Miss C. Samuell, Miss Robertson, Miss H. Coward, Miss Thudichum, Miss C. Elliot, Miss H. D'Alton, Madame Patey, Miss M. McKenzie, Miss G. Damian ; Messrs. M'Guckin, C. Chilley, E. Lloyd, J- Maas, Santley, Bridson, and King. Solo violinists : Herr H. Heermann and Signor Papini. Solo violoncellist : Signor Piatti. Solo pianists : M. Vladimir de Pachmann, Mdlle. Janotha, Madame Montigny-Rémaury. Organist : Dr. A. L. Peace. Chorus-master : Mr. Allan Macbeth. The choral works are Mendelssohn's " Walpurgis Night," Handel's " Acis and Galatea," Handel's " Messiah," Gounod's " Redemption," Berlioz's " Messe des Morts " ; and on an orchestral night F. David's symphonic ode, " The Desert." The scheme of orchestral works includes symphonies by Beethoven (" Eroica " and " Pas-

toral "), Bennett, Mendelssohn (" Italian "), Mozart (" Jupiter "), Schubert, and Schumann. Concertos by Beethoven, Chopin, Mendelssohn and Piatti. Overtures by Beethoven, Berlioz, Brahms, Cherubini, Macfarren (" King David "), Rossini, Wagner and Weber. Other orchestral works by Cowen, Delibes, Gluck, Haydn, Liszt, Macbeth, Mackenzie, Raff, Stanford, Sullivan and Wagner. There is nothing absolutely new in the scheme, unless so far as Glasgow is concerned, all of the principal works having been produced elsewhere. The first concert takes place on December 4th, and the last February 5th, 1884.

The following Musical Associations, under the conductorship of Mr. W. T. Hoeck, will this season produce the undermentioned works—Pollokshield's Musical Association : Smart's " Bride of Dunkerron." Hillhead Musical Association : Schumann's " Song for the New Year," and Miscellaneous. Bothwell Musical Association ; " The Erl-King's Daughter " (Gade, etc.) Queen's Park U. P. Church Choir : Gade's " Christmas Eve," and Gounod's Third " Messe Solonnelle." The Glasgow Amateur Orchestral Society : Symphony No. 2 in A, (Haydn); and Cherubini's " Lodoiska " and Mendelssohn's " Hebrides " overtures, etc.

Madame Helen Hopskirk gave a farewell concert in St. Andrew's Hall, on November 2, previous to her departure to America. The programme consisted of selections from Mendelssohn, Bach, Brahms, Mozart, Beethoven, Schumann, Gluck, Nicodé, Chopin, Field, and Rubinstein, played from memory.

J. B.

St. George's Glee Union.—The 178th monthly concert of the St. George's Glee Union was held at the Pimlico Rooms on the 2nd inst. The chief feature of the programme was " John Gilpin," a comic cantata by George Fox. The soloists were Miss Kate Hardy, Miss Mary Belval, Mr. Arthur Thomas, and Mr. Theodore Distin. The first part of the programme consisted of a miscellaneous selection, songs being contributed by, the artists before mentioned, and Mr. Hirwen Jones. The part singing was good, and included " Hark ! the lark " (Dr. Cooke), " Damon and Phyllis " (Theodore Distin), and a chorus " The Charge of the Light Brigade " (Hecht). The accompaniments were played by Mr. Kinkee and Mr. F. R. Kinkee, and Mr. Joseph Monday conducted.

Mile End.—On Saturday evening, Nov. 3rd, a performance of Handel's " Messiah," was given in the Great Assembly Hall, Mile End. The principal vocalists were Madme. Clara West, Mrs. Day Winter, Mr. H. D. Field, and Mr. C. T. Marriner, most of whom acquitted themselves admirably, Madme. West especially charming the audience in " Rejoice greatly," and " I know that my Redeemer liveth," and Mr. Marriner in " The trumpet shall sound," which had to be repeated. The band and chorus were fairly good. Conductor, Mr. G. Day Winter ; organist, Mr. Bellman. There was a very large attendance on the occasion.

Claremont Lecture Hall.—A concert, forming the first of a series of winter entertainments, was given in Claremont Lecture Hall, Pentonville Road, on Monday, the 5th inst., at eight o'clock. Solos were ably rendered by Misses Ethel Harwood, George, and Goudge ; Messrs. W. H. Glanvill, W. H. Mason, and Jas. Strugnell. Duets were also given by the Misses Pettit and Latham, and by Miss Harwood and Mr. Mason. Mr. W. L. Frost contributed to the success of the evening by giving a selection of Scotch airs, arranged by himself, on the piano and harmonium, and he and Mr. Percy Collins accompanied throughout. Next entertainment takes place on the 3rd prox., when readings and recitations will be given by Messrs. Fred. W. Broughton and T. Grahame Plumber ; songs by Miss Minnie Gwynne and Mr. Brandon ; and Messrs. W. L. Frost and Percy Collins at the piano and organ.

New Barnet.—A concert was lately given at the Parochial school rooms, New Barnet, in aid of the funds for the Church of England Temperance Society. The credit of this successful concert, for such it was, rests with Mr. W. D. Herbert together with Mr. G. D. Taylor, whose efforts were rewarded by a crowded room and appreciative audience. The performers included Mrs. Langley and Miss Alice Taylor, accompanists ; Madme. Ashton, and Mr. Arthur Thompson, and Mr. Chaplain Henry, whose names alone are sufficient guarantee for the quality of the vocal music. Miss Cartwright, a young amateur of promising talent, also sang. Miss Hilda French, an amateur pianist of much talent, residing at New Barnet, played with success, grand fantasia " La Valse de Faust " (Liszt) and a tarantelle. Mrs. W. D. Herbert being unable to sing through illness, Mr. Henry kindly volunteered " The Old Brigade " in her stead. Some excellent duets and trios, in which Mr. G. D. Taylor joined, contributed to the successful issue of this concert.

St. Mary of the Angels, W.—On Nov. 3rd, Mozart's Vespers in C were sung (probably for the first time in England) at this church, it being the Eve of the Feast of St. Charles. Mozart's ever fresh and beautiful music was capitally rendered by the choir of the church. A word of special mention is due to the exquisite singing of Master Charles Crowther in the various soprano solos throughout the Psalms, notably in the fifth—

"Laudate Dominum," which was beautifully rendered. Mr. John Probert (tenor) sang the melodious, but trying " Laudate pueri " of Capocci (with treble and alto chorus), with great spirit, his beautiful, sympathic voice showing to much advantage. Master C. Burton and Mr. T. Fraser took the incidental alto and bass solos. On Sunday morning Haydn's fine mass in C, No. 2, was splendidly sung ı y the choir, the above-named singer taking the solos. Mr. Fraser rendered the lovely " Qui tollis " one of the finest movements of the mass, in a feeling and artistic manner. Mozart's " Splendente te Deus" was sung at the Offertory. Next Sunday the choir will sing Cherubini's Coronation Mass in A, and a special sermon will be preached in aid of the choir by the Rev. R. B. Sankey, Mus.Bac., Oxon.

Organ News.

LIVERPOOL.

An organ recital was given in St. George's Hall, by Mr. W. T. Best, on Saturday, October 6th. The following was the programme :—

Overture, " Athalie "	Mendelssohn
Romanza, " Deserto in terra"	Donizetti.
Fugue in G major	Wesley.
Légende, " La Prédication aux Oiseaux "	Liszt.
Sarabande, " Dorothea "	Parker.
Military March, " The British Guards "	Pauer.

And on Saturday, November 3rd :—

Overture in D major, Op. 15	Spohr.
Benediction Nuptiale	Saint-Saëns.
Tempo di Ballo, " Brave Fantasia "	Fumagalli.
Trio for Flutes and Harp (" L'Enfance du Christ ")	Berlioz.
Scherzo-Symphonique	Guilmant.
Adagio and Finale	Best.

NORWICH.

An organ recital was given in St. Andrew's Hall on Thursday evening, November 1st, by Dr. Bunnett, F.C.O. The programme included :—

An Air composed for Holsworthy Church Bells, varied for the organ	Wesley.
Canzone	Guilmant.
Grand Offertoire in F	Batiste.
Preludium and Fuga in D minor	Bach.
Offertoire in G	Wely.
English Airs, varied	Bunnett.

And on Saturday afternoon, November 3rd :—

Allegretto Vivace from Jupiter Symphony	Mozart.
Serenata	Braga.
Grand Offertoire in C minor	Batiste.
Organ Concerto in B flat, No. 2	Handel.
Andante Maestoso—Allegro—Adagio and Allegro.	
Andante Cantabile in B flat	Mendelssohn.
Prelude and Fugue in G major	Bach.
Andante and Allegro in A, from Sonata	Handel.
" March of the Israelites " (" Eli")	Costa.

MANCHESTER.

Two recitals were given by Mr. J. Kendrick Pyne, organist, Manchester Town Hall, and Mr. Wm. Mullineux, organist, Bolton, on the 24th and 25th inst., at the Central Organ Works of Messrs. Richardson and Sons, upon the large organ for St. James Church, Westhoughton.

PRESTON.

An organ recital was given on Wednesday evening, October 31st, by Mr. James Tomlinson, organist to the Corporation, on a new organ, at Messrs. Ainscough and Co.'s Organ Works, Derby Street. The organ has two manuals, and is enclosed in a case of elegant design. The instrument is, for its size, very effective.

On Saturday evening, November 3rd, Mr. James Tomlinson, organist to the Corporation, gave his usual weekly recital in the New Public Hall. The programme was as follows :—

Andante	Wesley.
Overture to " Jessonda "	Spohr.
Bell Rondo	Morandi.
Marche Funebre et Chant Seraphique	Guilmant.
" The British Patrol " (Descriptive Allegro)	Asch.
Airs from " Les Hugenots "	Meyerbeer.

The " Marche Funebre " was rendered with great feeling, and was received with loud applause ; as was also the " Bell Rondo." The piece of the evening was, however " The British Patrol," for the spirited rendering of which Mr. Tomlinson secured a well merited *encore*. The recital concluded with some of the most pleasing airs from the popular opera, " Les Hugenots." There was a moderate attendance.

WOOLWICH.

The new organ at St. Andrew's Presbyterian Church was opened by Mr. E. H. Turpin on Nov. 5th. The instrument is very effective and of good tone. The maker is Mr. W. E. Richardson, of Camberwell and Manchester. The organ has two manuals and pedal. During the Recital, the choir sang three movements from Mozart's 12th Mass.

PRESENTATION TO MISS BERTIE STEPHENS

This young and much esteemed artist was the recipient of a truly munificent gift on Saturday, Nov. 3rd, when her friends and pupils presented her with an excellent and highly-finished chamber organ, handsomely decorated in black and gold. The presentation took place at the young lady's residence and organ studio, Downham Road, Islington. The instrument, built by Mr. E. Ingram, and very delicately voiced, has two manuals and pedal. The Rev. J. W. Horne, Vicar of St. James the Apostle, Islington, at which church Miss Stephens is organist, made the presentation, and Mr. E. H. Turpin gave a short Recital to display the powers of the instrument. To Mr. Harry Sullivan the greatest credit is fairly due for having brought this gratifying and well-deserved presentation to so successful an issue. Miss Bertie Stephens will now be able to receive organ pupils with exceptional advantages at her own home.

CRYSTAL PALACE.

Mr. Eyre's programmes, on Saturday, November 3rd, included the following :—

" Hero's March "	Mendelssohn.
Fantasia in C	Tours.
Andante in G	Maclaren.
Fugue in D minor	Bach.
Motet, " Hear my prayer "	Mendelssohn.
Entr'acte in B flat, " Rosamunde "	Schubert.
Grand Offertoire in G	Wely.
Jubilant March	Steiner.
Larghetto from the Clarinet Concerto	Mozart.
Barcarolle, in G	Spohr.
Finale from a Suite for Orchestra	Schumann.

MAIDSTONE.

An organ recital was given at the Parish Church, by the organist, Mr. S. Bath. Subjoined is the programme:—

Toccata in F	Bach.
Barcarolle	Bennett.
Organ Sonata, No. 6	Mendelssohn.
Quasi Pastorale	Smart.
Andante in G	
Offertoire in D	Batiste.

BRISTOL.

An organ recital was given in the Colston Hall, on Saturday, October 27th, by Mr. George Riseley. The following was the programme :—

Offertoire in D major	Batiste.
Romanza	Mozkwen.
Organ Concerto	Handel.
Allegro—Andante maestoso—Adagio—Allegro.	
Barcarolle	Bennett.
Prelude and Fugue in D major	Bach.
" Cradle Song "	Lange.
Overture, " Zanetta "	Auber.

And on, Thursday, November 1st :—

Overture, " Samson "	Handel.
Largo in D major	Beethoven.
Organ Sonatas, Nos. 4 & B flat	Mendelssohn.
Allegro—Andante—Allegretto—Allegro.	
Largo	Handel.
Fantasia et Fuga in G minor	Bach.
Minuet and Trio	Bennett.
Overture, " Midsummer Night's Dream "	Mendelssohn.

And on Saturday, November 3rd :—

March in E flat	Ketterer.
Andantino and Allegretto, " Momens Musicaus "	Schubert.
Prelude and Fugue in A minor	Bach.
" Ave Maria "	Cherubini.
Organ Sonata, No. 5 in D major	Mendelssohn.
Andante—Andante con moto—Allegro.	
" O ruddier than the cherry "	Handel.
" But the waters	
Gavotte, " Mignon "	Thomas.
Overture, " Zampa "	Herold.

OLDHAM.

On Wednesday evening, October 31st, Mr. W. A. Wrigley, organist of Holy Innocents, Fallowfield, Manchester, gave a recital on the organ in the Fine Art Exhibition. The programme included :—

Offertoire in D minor	Batiste.
Air varied, in B flat	Haydn.
" Cornelius " March	Mendelssohn.

BRIGHTON.

The Corporation organ recitals were given in the Dome, Royal Pavilion, by Mr. A. King, Mus.Bac., on Saturday, November 3rd. The programme included :—

Andante in G	Smart.
Fantasa and Fugue in G minor....................	Bach.
Andante in C, from 3rd Symphony	Haydn.
Fantasia in E flat	Saint-Saens.
Con moto—Allegro di molto.	
Overture in F	Morandi.

The new organ in the Chapel Royal, was opened on All Saints' Day, November 1st. Mr. F. Butler, A.C.O. and organist, gave admirably rendered organ recitals. The programmes included :—

Offertoire in C	Wely.
Andante con moto	Calkin.
Toccata and Fugue in D minor....................	Bach.
Cantilene Pastorale	Guilmant.
Andante in F	Smart.
" Festal March "	Calkin.
" Occasional Overture "	Handel.
" Weihnachtspastorale "	Merkel.
" Song without words "	Calkin.
Fugue in G minor	Bach.
Offertoire in G	Batiste.
Offertoire in D minor..............................	
Priere	Hauser.
Minuet and Trio	Bennett.

The organ was built from a specification by Mr. J. Baptiste Calkin, F.C.O., by Messrs. Henry Willis and Son. It consists of three complete manuals, from CC to G, 56 notes ; and two octaves and a half of concave and radiating pedals, from CCC to F, 30 notes, and has some thirty-two stops.

UPTON CHAPEL, LAMBETH.

In connection with the opening of the new organ, which has been erected in this Church by Messrs. Brindley and Foster, of Sheffield, a recital was given on Wednesday, October 31st, by Mr. E. H. Turpin, before an audience which filled the spacious and handsome edifice to overflowing. The programme contained several items of interest, among them being a contribution in MS. from Mr. E. J. Hopkins, " Adagio in D, for organ," which was received with delight, as it deserved to be. The vocalists who assisted were, Miss Annie Williams, Miss Matilda Roby, R.A.M., Mr. Chaplin Henry, and Mr. John Cornwall, the accompanist being Mr. W. Taylor. Mr. Chaplin Henry especially distinguished himself by his splendid rendering of Gounod's " Nazareth." The following was the programme of organ pieces—

Organ Sonata, No. 5	Mendelssohn.
Andante Op. 16	Beethoven.
Fugue in G major	Bach.
Air, with variations	Haydn.
Allegro Vivace	Morandi.
Adagio in D (MS.).................................	Hopkins.
Variations on a Ground Bass (5th Concerto, and Set) ..	Handel.
Andante, Symphony No. 6	Mozart.
Overture, " Harmonie Musik "	Mendelssohn.

The organ is a very effective and fine toned one, with concave pedals, and all the latest improvements ; it is enclosed in a very massive and highly ornamental case, and altogether has a very imposing appearance. The instrument certainly reflects great credit upon the builders, being undoubtedly one of their happiest efforts. The organist, who has just been appointed, is Mr. Henry Ford Benson, of Cambridge University, and late organist of Shoreditch Tabernacle, London. The following is the Specification :—

GREAT ORGAN. CC TO G.

1.	Open Diapason	... 8 ft.	5.	Principal	4 „
2.	Viola	8 „	6.	Flute	4 „
3.	Dulciana.............	8 „	7.	Harmonic Piccolo ...	2 „
4.	Hohl Flöte	8 „	8.	Trumpet	8 „

SWELL ORGAN. CC TO G.

9.	Double Diapason ...	16 ft.	13.	Principal	4 ft.
10.	Violin Diapason ...	8 „	14.	Mixture (3 ranks)	
11.	Vox Angelica	8 „	15.	Cornopean	8 „
12.	Gedact	8 „	16.	Oboe	8 „

PEDAL ORGAN. CCC TO F.

17. Open Diapason ... 16 ft. | 18. Bourdon .... 16 ft.

COUPLERS.

19. Swell to Great.	21. Great to Pedal.
20. Swell to Pedal.	

Three Composition Pedals to Great, and two to Swell.

Dr. W. Spark of Leeds, has been visiting Exeter, playing there at the Victoria Hall, and lecturing with success.

ST. LEONARD'S-ON-SEA.

An organ recital was given in St. Paul's Church, by Mr. A. E. Tozer, on Wednesday, October 31st. The following was the programme :—

Prelude and Fugue in C	Bach.
Pastorale in C	Wely.
Andante in D	Silas.
Cantilène in A minor..............................	Salome.
Marche Funèbre et Chant Séraphique..............	Guilmant.
Offertoire in D	King.
Largo in G	Handel.
Intermezzo, " Adoration "	Gaul.
Fantasia in C minor................................	Tietz.
Andante maestoso—Allegretto—Allegro con fuoco.	

GREENOCK.

A recital was given in Finnart United Presbyterian Church, on Thursday, November 8th, by Dr. A. L. Peace, on the occasion of the inauguration of the new organ. The following was the programme :—

Overture and March, " Hercules "	Handel.
Pastorale in G, Op. 103 }	Merkel.
March for Easter-tide }	Mendelssohn.
Prelude and Fugue in D major	Morandi.
Allegretto Vivace in A minor and major	Guilmant.
Caprice in B flat	Haslinger.
Jubilee Overture	

WARE.

An organ recital was given on Tuesday, October 30th, in the Parish Church, by Mr. H. C. Tonking, and Mr. James L. Gregory, F.C.O. The programme was as follows :—

Sonata in F minor	Mendelssohn.
Soft Movement in F sharp minor	Wesley.
Grand Chœur in D.................................	Guilmant.
Romanza from Symphony in E flat	Haydn.
Gavotte..	Thomas.
Fugue in G	Krebs.
Postlude in D	Smart.

INDIA.

Messrs. P. Conacher and Co., of Huddersfield, have just shipped a fine three-Manual organ, to Madras. It is intended for St. Andrew's Scotch Church in that city, and is a very highly-finished instrument All the pipes are of spotted metal, and the timber has been carefully selected to withstand the severe climate. The instrument has some thirty-two stops with three manuals and Pedal.

PORTSMOUTH.

The first of a series of organ recitals was given in St. Mark's Church, on Thursday, October 11th, by Mr. A. Blissett, before a large congregation. Annexed is the programme :—

Allegretto	Lemmens.
Schiller March	Meyerbeer.
" The Storm "	Lemmens.
Concerto in C	Bach.
" Austrian Hymn "	Chipp.
Offertoire	Wely.

LEEDS.

A recital was given on the grand organ in the Town Hall, by Dr. Spark, organist to the Corporation, on Saturday evening, October 27th. The programme included :—

March and Chorus, " Gloria Patria " (from the Psalm " The Lord is King ")	Barnby.
Allegretto, from " The Hymn of Praise " (" Lobgesang")	Mendelssohn.
Selection from the oratorio, " The End of the World "..	Raff.
Selection from the oratorio, " Elijah "	Mendelssohn.
Air, " What though I trace " (" Solomon ")	Handel
The War March of Priests (" Athaliah ")	Mendelssohn.

CAMBRIDGE.

An organ recital was given in the Guildhall, on Tuesday, October 30th, by Mr. F. Dewberry, L.R.A.M. The following was the programme :—

Triumphal March, " Alfred "	Prout.
Andante Cantabile, from 9th Symphony	Haydn.
Organ Concerto, No. 2, in B flat	Handel.
Andante maestoso—Allegro—Adagio—Allegro.	
Rondo—Gavotta, " Mignon "	Thomas.
Minuette-Grazioso in G............................	Gluck.
" Lied ohne Wörte," Book 3, No. 6	Mendelssohn.
Gavotte e Rondo in E	Bach.
Song, " The Better Land ";	Cowen.
Fantasia, on Theme by Weber	E. H. Turpin.
Overture, " Guglielmo Tell "	Rossini.

There is a growing use of the pianoforte with organ in a goodly number of American churches ; the two instruments being thought of good effect in the presentation of sacred works originally scored for an orchestra.

ST. MARY, BROOKFIELD, HIGHGATE.

The organ commenced at this church by Messrs. Brindley and Foster, of Sheffield, in 1880, has been recently completed and was opened on Thursday, Nov. 1st, and the following Sunday. The music on All Saints' Day was excellently rendered. The organist Mr. G. E. Blunden is evidently not only a skilled player, but a painstaking choirmaster. Smart's Service in B flat and Wesley's anthem, "The Wilderness," were the chief features of the service. Mr. Blundell, whose decided talents and attainments as an organist are already recognised, gave two short recitals upon the two opening days. The first programme included Guilmant's D minor Sonata and Bach's A minor Prelude and Fugue, and the second list contained Mendelssohn's "Ruy Blas" Overture by desire, and pieces by Guilmant and Salomé, etc. The congregation are to be congratulated upon the possession of a fine organ, and upon the efficient musical services it is their gain to listen to. The following is the specification :—

GREAT ORGAN. CC TO G.

1. Double Diapason	16 ft.	6. Harmonic Flute	4 ft.
2. Open Diapason	8 „	7. Mixture (2 ranks)	
3. Hohl Flöte	8 „	8. Mixture (3 ranks)	
4. Gamba	8 „	9. Trumpet	8 „
5. Principal	4 „		

SWELL ORGAN. CC TO G.

10. Lieblich Bourdon	16 ft.	14. Salicet	4 ft.
11. Violin Diapason	8 „	15. Mixture (3 ranks)	
12. Voix Celestes	8 „	16. Oboe	8 „
13. Vox Angelica.	8 „	17. Cornopean	8 „

CHOIR ORGAN. CC TO G.

18. Salcional	8 ft.	21. Lieblich Flöte	4 ft.
19. Dulciana	8 „	22. Clarionet	8 „
20. Lieblich Gedact	8 „		

PEDAL ORGAN. CCC TO F.

23. Major Bass	16 ft.	25. Principal Bass	8 ft.
24. Sub Bass	16 „	26. Flute Bass	8 „

COUPLERS.

27. Swell to Great.	30. Great Sub-octave.
28. Swell to Pedal.	31. Swell to Choir.
29. Great to Pedal.	32. Choir to Pedal.

Three Composition Pedals to Great and two to Swell.

HINCKLEY.

The following pieces were played by Mr. Chas. W. King, on Sunday evening, the 4th inst., in the Parish Church :—

Adagio in D (IN MEMORIAM.—Mendelssohn, 1847.)	Mendelssohn.
Funeral March, in A minor	Calkin.
Hommage à Mendelssohn	Silas.
Elegy	Mendelssohn.
Allegretto from Symphony ("Lobgesang")	
Sonata in C minor, No. 2	„

DUNDEE.

The second of the present series of monthly recitals in St. Mark's Parish Church, was given on Monday, November 5th, to a large and appreciative audience. Mrs. Bruce and Miss Winton were the vocalists. Mr M. T. Orton, organist of the church, as usual presided at the organ. The following programme was performed :—

Adagio, Allegro, ma non presto, from an Organ Concerto	Handel
Grand Fantasia in E minor, "The Storm"	Lemmens.
"Holsworthy Church Bells"	Wesley.
Postlude in D major	Hudson.

BURTON-ON-TRENT.

An organ recital was given at St. Paul's Institute, on Monday, November 5th, by Mr. A. B. Plant, Mus.Bac., Oxon. The programme included :—

Overture, "Stradella"	Flotow.
Bell Rondo	Morandi.
Allegretto (with Chorale)	Plant.
Larghetto, from Symphony No. 2	Beethoven.
Elevation	Guilmant.
Nazareth	Gounod.
Allegretto in B flat	Lemmens.
Festal March	Smart.

The Royal Amateur Orchestral Society will give an orchestral concert on Monday next, Nov. 13th, at the Bow and Bromley Institute, under the conductorship of Mr. George Mount.

LONDON : SATURDAY, NOVEMBER 10 1883

A FORM QUESTION.

THE question raised by that astute and courageous thinker Mr. F. Praeger, regarding the abolition of repeats in classical musical forms is one concerning the progress of the art in a not unimportant direction. It is clear that either the active growth of the intelligence of listeners, or their feverish reluctance to listen with old-fashioned patience, will in future somewhat change the position of composer in the matter of setting forth his ideas. The signs in this direction have before now been pointed out; as in the case of curtailments of the older song forms and in the habitual omission of the repeats marked by the masters of the symphonic school extending from HAYDN to SCHUMANN. Of course there was something to be said in favour of the retention of repeats and repetitions, as better fixing composers ideas upon the minds of listeners, and in the case of the repeat of the first part of the structure, as helping to balance the length of different relative portions of a musical structure. Note the case of the Allegro form, when the second portion is prolonged by the intersected development section ; and from the "Figaro" overture by Mozart onwards, the general custom in that preludial form of omitting the development has also resulted in the banishment of the never common repeat and a condensation of the form with advantage. However, it is important to bear in mind that the analogy offered by Mr. Praeger between the supposed repetition of portions of a poem and repetitions of musical themes is not quite an exact one. The composer's themes are his characters rather than his disconnected detailed thoughts ; and the poet does draw together, for their final dramatic reward, his chief characters, just as the musician resumes his leading themes. These processes are indeed identical. The processes of presentation, development, and recapitulation, have been previously shown to be identical, in the arts appealing to the mind through the ear, as poetry, music, literature, and oratory, by slow degrees. For all these arts demand the creation of an artificial memory in order to convey to a listener or reader a full conception of their complete forms and purposes. Again, it must be borne in mind, that music, by the very nature of its fleeting sounds, which receive no strengthening from external impressions as does the constantly used verbal language, is the one art which must ever be the most difficult of mental realisation. As the architect would not dream of a structure which in length, breadth, or height, would pass beyond the scope of the eye, so the musician is in a corresponding way limited in his tone structures to the power and scope of the sense of hearing, which again in music has less of the function of logical continuity than it possesses in dealing with exposition made in the familiar verbal language. This case will call for further present attention.

E. H. Turpin.

A FEW WORDS TO "THE BRITISH PUBLIC."

It is the business of this and other periodicals to deal exclusively with artists and executants, to criticise their performances, to report their successes or shortcomings, to be, in short, a "medium"—not spiritual but spirituel—between the platform and the public. To-day, the pen shall be dipped in lemon juice for the benefit of the so-called "British Public," as Sir Walter Scott sings, "a many-headed, monster thing," it might be added without a fair allowance of brains within the hard numbskull. John Bull has his merits, but he requires an occasional rap over the knuckles for his egotism, self-conceit, and ignorance of any other country beyond the boundaries of England ; for "the travelling fools" of Cowper learn no more than the Bourbons of old from their journeys to Rome, or visits to the now fashionable "Dolomite" formation on the farther side of the Alps.

John Bull, still more Mistress Bull, his too substantial and saucy wife, must be told in the "good "set terms" of melancholy Jacques, to mend their manners in public. What they do at home, whether they gossip over poisonous and nerve-shaking make-believe "Souchong," or play the fool at croquet or lawn-tennis, matters little to the outsider of the press. But the journalist must not only wear his knout, like Mr. Potts at the "fancy dress" déjeuner of Mrs. Leo Hunter, but use it, without sparing, in case of need. No mystery lurks under these prefatory remarks. There is no "adder to crawl into daylight"—to quote Claverhouse's sarcastic sneer at the fanatical Scottish Covenanters, but a valiant lion in the path, ready to roar and to devour ! One misbehaviour of the "genteel" British mob—sufficient for the day be its evil—is the notorious noise and garrulity complained of in concert-rooms, at the Opera, and in public places generally. The nuisance, if slightly abated by authority, exists still, and must be put down by the ghost of poor Sir Peter Laurie, if nobody else will interfere. The suicides, whom our old friend the Alderman and Caledonian saddler wanted to "put " down," tried at least to make away with themselves, and rid the world of their presence. The talkers and tatlers of the company thrust an unwelcome presence upon their intellectual superiors, and if rebuked, often shew their "cheek" without humbly "turning it to " the smiter," as the gospel enjoins.

The Directors of the Crystal Palace have done their best to prevent the annoyance, and they deserve many thanks. An edict is nailed to the walls of the concert-room at Sydenham to prohibit the entrance of any visitor during the performance of a piece, but the edict is not always respected. Late comers open the door, and what is worse, stand in front of the gallery so as to obstruct the view of critics and others not critics, but with equal right to see and be seen. The talkers, it must be allowed, have been less annoying of late, but it should be explained that, hitherto (this season), the gallery has not been overcrowded. The tardy arrivals take precious good care to prove that they wear boots and shoes. Poor Jumbo of the "Zoo," could not stamp, or as servant girls say emphatically, "stomp," with heavier tread.

At the "Popular" concerts, at the "Richter" réunions, and the Philharmonic, the British Public are only partially "put down." Mr. Charles Halle requests his (special) audiences to be in their seats ten minutes before the time, but a schoolboy would irreverently "take a sight" at this modest desire, if only to signify the familiar phrase, "don't you wish," &c., &c. True that at these classical concerts, very late comers are usually made to stand in the corner, and are not guided to their seats until the piece or movement closes ; but these people, alas, meanwhile stand in your light, and "their fathers," again to quote school slang, "were not glaziers !" But during the first quarter-of-an-hour, woe to the wights that sit in the gangways or in the recesses. A process of clothes-brushing and boot-cleaning, rough and ready, but not very "nice," begins at the expense of the punctual, and endeth not soon ! The men give you plenty of kicks and no half-crowns ; the women—no ladies—try to infect you with a cold by the draught from their ample dresses, some of which, with those monstrous queues or "trains," often, en révanche, get trodden upon and torn from the "gussets." You must wait for peace and quietness at least half an hour. Towards the end of the concert, the evil is exaggerated. Selfish old dowagers, anxious to gain their carriages, renew the promenade along the gangway, and do much to stifle the sweet sounds from the orchestra.

The talking may sometimes be stopped or checked by a few angry hushes. On Monday night the writer had the misfortune to sit before two women, one a silly girl, the other *une femme d'un certain âge*, fat, like the majority of stupid people, and of decided anti-Platonic views. The pair of parrots tried to talk aloud and then to whisper. They wanted to *encore* Miss SANTLEY, and said that they should buy her songs (by Mr. F. COWEN), the next day ; but they had not one word for CHOPIN or M. de PACHMANN, so far as the ear attested. These women "thought aloud."

And now for the effectual remedy, or rather prevention of the nuisance complained of. Barring out in the first place, and stern demonstrations from the audience, with aid from authoritative officials in the next. Social offenders, like criminals, have no moral courage; they are easily suppressed and made to look foolish. In some places abroad, the talkers would be turned out without ceremony. Even musical auditors and professors are open to accusation ; they *will* express their views in a shower of gushy platitudes. Why not wait until they reach home and sit down to the unavoidable infusion of sloppy sloe juice, or write to the *Morning Post* or the *Court Journal*? Every dog has his day and may bark at proper times.

A. M.

A NEGLECTED CHURCH FESTIVAL.

THAT comparatively little notice is taken of " All " Saints' Day " may indeed seem strange, especially in these days when there is a yearning on all sides for greater unity in the Church. The Services of that day would lend themselves admirably for purposes of united worship. The festival was first celebrated on May 1st, but altered to Nov. 1st, by one of the Popes, as interfering on May 1st with the services of the Roman Church in honour of the VIRGIN MARY. The first of May was truly an appropriate day, when in the sweet Spring Nature herself in reviving beauty and happiness preaches the doctrine of the resurrection of the Just. It would again certainly be brighter and pleasanter on May Day than it can be on November 1st; and had the original date been adhered to it might have furnished, happily enough, the occasion of a united religious festival, say in "St. Paul's" Cathedral, by way of opening the season of religious meetings in the metropolis. However, it is needless or useless to speculate in this direction. The Church, "though quick and strong in " faith, is slow and feeble as regards any real appre- " hension of her great mission and privileges here on " earth." It is a pity some movement could not be inaugurated for a closer drawing together of the members of the various Christian bodies on "All " Saints' Day." The Services on that day in our leading Churches this year have not generally been characterised by any very distinct effort. It may be mentioned that ten years ago, Dr. JOHN NAYLOR, the new organist at York Minster, but then at Scarborough, composed for a local festival on "All " Saints' Day," an effective and scholarly cantata entitled "The Communion of Saints." This admirable work might fittingly be brought forward upon another recurrence of the feast.

E. H. TURPIN.

Academical Intelligence.

COLLEGE OF ORGANISTS.

The first lecture of the session was given on Tuesday last by Mr. E. Breakspeare, who considered the "Natural Laws of Expression in Musical Exposition and Practical Delivery, and their Systematical Application." Mr. Breakspeare is well-known as an expositor of what may be called the "æsthetics" of music. His lecture, as was expected, was a thoughtful and admirable consideration of a delicate and difficult subject. It will be shortly laid before the reader in full. Mr. Jas. Higgs was the chairman. He addressed the meeting at the close with some valuable words, dealing chiefly with the subject of expression as judiciously applied to contrapuntal music and to the harpsichord music of Bach and Handel, which has no original marks of expression. Mr. E. H. Turpin also spoke, touching upon the analogy between expressions natural to speech and to music. He pointed out too something of the effect of habit of thought and the desire to be mutually intelligible which regulates methods of expression. He also referred to Beethoven's use of inverted climaxes ; and offered testimony to Mr. Breakspeare's valuable thoughts and words. Mr. Higgs proposed a vote of thanks to the able lecturer ; and a corresponding vote of thanks to the chairman closed the meeting.

<hr>

The Edinburgh Choral Union announce their Tenth Series of Concerts, to be given in the Music Hall, George-street, at 8 o'clock evening, on the following dates :—Dec. 10th, Dec. 11th, Dec. 17th, Dec. 26th, Jan. 2nd, Jan. 9th, Jan. 14th, Jan. 16th, Jan. 21st, Jan. 28th, and Feb. 4th; eleven in all, of which the subscription will only include ten; the concert on Wednesday, 2nd Jan., 1884, being given as a Special and Extra Concert. Three choral works will be performed—Haydn's Oratorio of "The Seasons" on Tuesday, 11th Dec., 1883, and Handel's "Ode to St. Cecilia," with Mr. A. C. Mackenzie's "Jason," on Wednesday, 16th Jan., 1884. The orchestral programmes contain works both new and old, of much interest and value, which have been selected and arranged by Mr. Manns with a view to maintain, and even to extend, the reputation and influence already attached to these concerts. The orchestra has again been largely increased, and will now consist of about eighty performers. The principal artists engaged are Miss Hilda Coward; Miss Mary Davies, Miss Carlotta Elliot, Mrs. Hutchinson, Miss Santley, Miss Thudichum, Mdlle. Elly Warnots, Miss Marian Mackenzie, Mdme. Patey, Mr. Edward Lloyd, Mr. Joseph Maas, Mr. John Bridson, and Mr. Santley. Solo pianoforte, Mdme. Montigny-Rémaury, Mdlle. Janotha, M. Vladimir De Pachmann ; solo violin, Herr Hugo Heermann, Signor Papini ; solo violoncello, Signor Piatti. Leader of the orchestra, M. Victor Buziau. Chorus, the Edinburgh Choral Union. Organist and accompanist, Mr. Charles Bradley. The conductor for the choral concerts will be Mr. T. H. Collinson, Mus.Bac. Oxon., and for the orchestral concerts, Mr. August Manns.

Mr. Henry Fincham, of 150 Euston-road, is shortly to open an organ studio for lessons and practice, the instrument being built in accordance with the regulations of the College of Organists' Conference. The same builder has completed an organ lately for St. Mary's Church, Willesboro', near Ashford, Kent ; and has another instrument in the Ecclesiastical Exhibition at the Agricultural Hall.

Foreign Musical Intelligence.

Schumann's "Genoveva" has been successful at Carlsruhe.

"Le Roi de Carreau," M. Lajarte's new operetta has been successful in Paris.

"Les Curiosités de l'Opéra" is a new and entertaining work by M. Th. de Lajarte, published in Paris.

Signor Palminteri's opera, "Amazilia," produced at Milan lately, was pronounced to be wanting in power and variety.

Signor G. Masutti's work, on the Italian "Maestri di Musica" of the 19th century, has had a large sale, it is said.

"Luther at Erfurt," Herr Bernard Schik's cantata, has been performed in Germany in connection with the Luther fêtes.

Herr Jules de Swert, the violoncellist, has had his opera, "Der Graf von Hammerstein" accepted in several German cities.

Three "Intermezzi" pianoforte duets by Hofman, have recently been published in Germany and find favour. The opus number is 66.

The *Neue Zeitschrift für Musik* reports that Hermann Ritter, the viola virtuoso, has been engaged for a number of concerts in Scotland.

Mendelssohn's Scotch Symphony, excellently played, proved at a recent Pasdeloup concert, a "véritable succès d'enthousiasme," says *Le Ménestrel*.

The first performance of Herr K. Kleinmichel's opera, "Schloss de l'Orme," which took place at Hamburg on Oct. 8th, proved to be a great success.

Berlioz's "Te Deum," first heard at St. Eustache, Paris, in 1855, will be given in the Cathedral of Bordeaux, on the 5th of next month by a band and chorus of 1000.

The death on Oct. 30th, of Robert Volkmann at Budapest, deprives the world of a composer of considerable power and individuality. He was born on April 6th, 1815, at Lommatsch, in Saxony. His best works are a Trio, two Quartets in G and in A minor, and two Symphonies, one in D minor being the best known of the two.

The receipts of the Opera Comique in Paris during the past years have been considerably augmented, but the returns of income at the Grand Opéra show a serious falling off during the same period. This is partly to be attributed to the costly mounting of certain works, and to the often second-rate performances given of works lacking the flavour of novelty.

A grand performance of Gounod's "Redemption" took place at Vienna, on the 4th inst., for the benefit of the "Pensions Institut" of the Royal Opera House. All the principal singers, as well as the chorus and orchestra, of that celebrated theatre took part in the performance, the whole being under the conductorship of Herr N. Fuchs.

The *Monthly Musical Record* says:—That M. Hippeau, the editor of *La Renaissance*, has taken the initiative in the formation of an international society of composers, ten of them French and six foreign, for the purpose of giving in the spring some grand performances of instrumental and choral works, at the Trocadéro. M. Ernest Reyer has accepted the presidency of this Society.

Admirers of Mozart had a great and unexpected treat a short time since in Vienna, when the orchestra under the direction of Hellmesberger performed a Mass in C minor by the immortal composer, which, previously unknown, was lately discovered by the energetic conductor among the dusty archives of the Imperial Opera-house. The work was written in 1771, that is, when the composer was fifteen, and gives promise of his future greatness. The first three parts, the "Kyrie," "Gloria," and "Credo," are, contrary to his subsequent practice, carried out at great length, while the other parts are treated much more briefly. The "Crucifixus" is especially impressive. An unusual feature of the instrumentation is the employment of four trumpets and three trombones—a little bit of youthful exuberance.—*Musical World.*

Recently at the Ricardi Theatre, Bergamo, a new opera, "Adello," by Luigi Logheder, and at Piacenza, a new opera, "Donna Innes," by Luigi Ricci, were heard, and it is said, received with applause.

L'Indépendante of Trieste (Oct. 18th), has the following reference to a new opera by Mr. George Carter, of London, entitled "Il Nerone" ("Nero"):—"Il M. Giorgio Carter di Londra, autore di altri Spartiti musicali, e di pregievolissime e dotte composizioni sacre e profane, ha terminato una sua opera nuova, 'Il Nerone.' Rinomati maestri Italiani ai quali venne fatto sentire il nuovo lavoro del M. Carter, dichiarono bellissima quella musica, piena d'ispirazione melodica; e di Sapienti e leggiadre combinazioni armoniche." A contributor, on whose judgment reliance may be placed, reports very favourably of another (English) opera from the prolific pen of Mr. George Carter, "Fair Rosamond," of which the overture, march, and ballet, are in the hands of Mr. Manns, of the Crystal Palace concerts. The performance of the music by this renowned band, an *orchestre d'élite*, is likely to add another laurel to the wreath which Mr. Manns has won for our English composers.

Reviews.

Three Blind Mice. With music and words from an early edition. Illustrated by C. A. Doyle. *Robin! Robin!* Words and music by A. Scott Gatty, and illustrated. (G. Waterston & Sons, Edinburgh and London).—Charming children's books, illustrated with true humour, delicate in fancy without exaggeration, and in every way artistic. The same good taste characterises both words and music. Mr. A. Scott Gatty has done good service in his many clever and tasty contributions to this class of children's books, and our young people ought to be thankful for the many skilful efforts which are constantly being made to instruct them without weariness, and to amuse them with such winning grace and genuine playfulness.

Ray of Sunshine, Carl le Duc; *La Prière d'une Vierge*, T. Badanzewska; *Écoutez Moi*, J. Funke; *Gipsy Rondo*, Haydn; *Carnival of Venice*, J. Asten; *The Merry Peasant*, Schumann; *Slumber Song*, Schumann; *Melody in A*, Rubinstein; *El Dorado*, Oesten; *Les Cloches du Monastère*, Lefebure Wély; *Air de Louis XIII.*, Henry Ghys; *The Battle of Prague*, F. Kotzwara; *True Love*, Gavotte, Johann Resch; *Stéphanie*, Gavotte, A. Czibulka; *Home, Sweet Home*, S. Thalberg. (All Paternoster Row editions, edited and fingered by A. H. Brown.) (F. Pitman, Paternoster Row). *Zweite Barcarole*, Op. 23. Gustav Wolff (W. Dietrich, Leipzig). A goodly number of these pieces are old favourites, played industriously enough five-and-twenty years ago. "The Ray of Sunshine," a more recent production, is taking, and is neatly written in the mazurka style. "The Carnival of Venice" is here printed in A flat. The writer, without being able to say which is the original key, remembers a version in A natural, which was certainly more playable, as many of the passages in that key lie better for the hands. A new edition of Schumann's standard pieces and Rubinstein's effective Melody will be welcome. Gustav Lange's "Edelweiss" is a pretty showy piece in triple measure in E flat. The "Air de Louis XIII." is a popular gavotte. "The Battle of Prague," dear to our great-grandmothers, was the precursor of that class of shamelessly realistic programme music, with unblushing imitations of cannons roaring and trumpets blowing. It is in this edition dignified, as of old, by the wrongly applied title of Sonata. The music shows talent enough, in its way; but its unfortunate composer is said to have been found dead, hanging, the story goes, in a public-house. Certainly he might have had a brighter career had he made better use of his abilities and kept better company. "True Love" is an effective gavotte in a showy style, having piquant and sprightly figures. "Home, sweet home" again reprinted; has been a fortune to the music publishers, for the composer never took any steps to protect his copyright, and allowed everybody apparently to print the piece without payment, making it popular during his lifetime by his own unique performance. Such an obliging genius must have been greatly admired by the publishers, who are said to delight in music they have nobody to pay for the use of. These pianoforte solos are well and carefully edited and fingered. The Barcarolle by Gustav Wolff is fanciful, delicate, and musicianly. Without being servilely planned for the display of cheap playing attainments, it is an effective concert or drawing-room solo, and its performance will reward the artistic player in search of an elegant, light little piece.

Andante in G (Batiste) as Pianoforte Solo and Duet. Boyton Smith. (Weekes & Co., Hanover Street.)—A conscientious and effective arrangement of one of the most popular of the lighter kind of French organ music.

Magnificat and Nunc Dimittis in D by C. E. Miller. (Novello and Co.)—This was composed for the London Church Choir Association Festival in St. Paul's on Nov. 8th. The "Magnificat" is dignified and musicianly; and the composer has taken most commendable pains in his endeavours to duly express the varying character of the words whilst preserving a decorous and church-like style throughout. There is, too, as in the "Gloria," an effective use of unison singing; a style so strangely neglected by the earlier Church composers. The misjudged rise of the bass of a major seventh in the close of this movement is one of few points the critic could speak of save with cordial approval. The "Nunc Dimittis" receives a pastoral treatment in six-four measure; changing emphatically into common time at the words, "And to be the glory." The "Gloria" is interesting and effective. The Service deserves to be well known.

Correspondence.

HENRY SMART'S "JACOB."

TO THE EDITOR OF THE "MUSICAL STANDARD."

SIR,—An error touching the above oratorio in a reply from "S. S. S." occurs in your last number. "Jacob" is not published by Cramer & Co., but by Joseph Williams, Berners Street.　　Yours faithfully,

EDWIN M. LOTT.

270, Cornwall Road, Notting Hill, W.　Nov. 5th, 1883.

FESTIVAL CHAMBER CONCERT IN HONOUR OF SPOHR, on July 2nd, 1843.

TO THE EDITOR OF THE "MUSICAL STANDARD."

SIR,—In the "Reminiscences of an Old Reporter," which appeared in your issue of to-day, there is a description of the curious Chamber Concert with déjeuner à la fourchette, which was given by Mr. Alsager, co-editor of *Times*, in honour of Louis Spohr. In speaking about this princely entertainment, the writer says, "that notwithstanding he had forgotten the selection of music performed at the concert, "*you may rely on my words that no grinding ballads or 'royalty' songs found a place in the schema.*" As a proof of the veracity of the writer's words, I may perhaps be permitted, through the medium of this paper, to have the honour to supply the "Old Reporter" with the following copy of the programme of music, performed on that "Golden Sunday":—

QUEEN SQUARE SELECT SOCIETY.

Musical Festival in honour of the arrival of Spohr in London, Sunday, July 2nd, 1843.

ACT 1

Double Quartet, No. 1	Spohr.
Quintette (Pianoforte, Flute, Clarionet, Horn and Bassoon)	"
Double Quartet, No. 2	"
Nonetto	"

Dejeuner a la Fourchette.

ACT 2.

Quintet	Spohr.
Ottetto	"
Double Quartet, No. 3	"

To commence at 2 o'clock. Dejeuner at 5 o'clock. Second act to commence at 7 o'clock."

The eminent violinist, Spohr, must have felt highly gratified, not only with the magnificent "Festival," but also to see how a company of fifty persons would listen until late in the evening with wrapt attention to his music without evincing the least sign of weariness.　　Yours very truly,

HILDEGARD WERNER. R.A.M. of Stockholm.

Newcastle-on-Tyne, Nov. 3rd, 1883.

SCALE-COLOUR.

TO THE EDITOR OF THE "MUSICAL STANDARD."

SIR,—As Mr. Matthey asks for information, I must try to give it to him so far as I am able, but I cannot help thinking both himself and Mr. Foxall to be, at least, premature in characterising the very notion of a physical correlation between musical notes and colours as an absurdity. For my part, I have never propounded such a notion, the correlation being to my mind rather psychological than physical. I should, however, be no more inclined to deny the physical correlation than to deny the existence of living beings in the planet Mars, since, as yet, so far as I have been able to discover, there is nothing like a proof to be found either for assertion or denial. If Mr. Matthey or Mr. Foxall can give any proof of their negative, it will be interesting to read it.

As to the psychological correlation which I believe to exist, the question is a very difficult one, but may be put thus: Supposing that I characterise light sky-blue as a gaudy, flaring colour, and, on the other hand, maintain that bright scarlet is soft and sweet, would that indicate any defect in my power of mental appreciation? Of course it would, so much so as to destroy all confidence in my judgment of character. These are extreme examples, but the difference between this pair of colours and any other is one only of degree, not of kind; and if there are definite characters attaching to these colours, other colours also must each have their character, though it may not be so clearly marked.

As to the notes of music, the first question to be asked is whether they also have each a separate character. This, I think, must be answered in the affirmative, otherwise we should not be able to distinguish them. I once had the pleasure of conversing with an Oxford Doctor of Music, who maintained stoutly that we could only reckon by the intervals, until I asked him whether it would be impossible to tell if a piece of music were being executed in C or in G, when he was obliged to admit that there would be a great difference. The difference, however, is only of degree, and just as there are many men who could easily distinguish between mauve and orange, but would scarcely see the difference between azure and blue, so there are probably many first-rate musicians who cannot tell whether a piece is being played in C or in C sharp.

It by no means follows, however, that because both colours and musical notes have each a separate character by which they may be distinguished, therefore those characters must agree. This is the point at issue, and it is here we may find the utility of translating music into colour, to see whether the characters do agree. As far as I have gone hitherto, the sameness of character to be found in the musical originals, and the translations which I have made from them, has been very striking, and I am in hopes, now that I have pointed out the separate colours to be used for the purpose, of seeing others engaged upon the same work. It might be taken up, I think, as a new and almost the highest branch of decorative art, so to use colours with a meaning and purpose in place of the meaningless repetitions of some equally meaningless harmony, which now do duty for decoration in England. I say "almost the highest," because it is certainly a higher branch of the same art, when a painter of human forms, instead of translating from the works of musicians, makes his music for himself, and expresses it in colour. Such music in colour is very rare, now-a-days, at the Royal Academy. It may, however, be found in abundance in the works of Italian painters of the time of Raffaelle, and it might soon be developed in England if the training of art-students included a course of translations from music. Meanwhile, the question of the agreement in character between the musical notes and the colours which I have pointed out as correlative, is one which I submit to the good judgment of artists and musicians, and which is only to be determined by repeated experiments, although colour-music-will be, in itself, equally valuable, as a system of finding harmonies, whether the chords of colour have, or have not, a right to the musical names which I give them. If I observe a sunset exhibiting certain colours, which I call D F sharp A C, I may be quite wrong, and in giving to the colours that name, or any other musical name; but still the combination will always have the character of a chord of the minor seventh. And to show the use which may be made of the characters thus inherent in the various chords, perhaps you will allow a brief illustration. Taking a sketch of Mr. Long's "Egyptian Feast," I coloured it in the key of C, using the dominant chord, C B D, or azure, purple and blue, for the cycle of guests, and the tonic, C E G, for the mummy and its attendant priest. Then instead of taking F A C, the subdominant, which would be the ordinary harmony for a background, I used D F A C, blue, yellow, red and mauve for the background and the slaves in front on the left, thereby getting a peculiar accent of sadness on the F, brown, pink, which I used for the dusky Ethiopians. I afterwards satisfied myself, by transposing the harmony (for another picture) into the key of F, which gave me scarlet instead of yellow for the third of the minor chord, that the effect was due to the nature of the chord and not to any peculiarity of the colour, brown pink. This is only one out of hundreds of ways in which the musical chords might be turned to advantage by artists.

I am, Sir, your obedient servant,

A. P. BETHELL.

Passing Events.

Mr. Maas is likely to be the next accession to the Carl Rosa Company.

The Carl Rosa Company are successfully performing in leading Scotch towns.

Miss Alice Aloof gives her second concert at the Brixton Hall, on Nov. 13th.

Mr. H. Holmes has arranged for a series of Chamber Concerts at the Steinway Hall.

There is a probability of German Opera in London next season under Herr Richter.

"Madme. Boniface," a new opera by M. Lecome, was produced recently at the Bouffes Parisiens.

On Oct. 30th Mr. E. Spark gave a concert at the Public Hall, Worcester, with an excellent touring party.

The Maritzburg Philharmonic Society lately performed Aspa's "The Gipsies," and Cowen's "Rose Maiden."

One of Mr. J. Baillie Hamilton's improved vocalions has been introduced into Leeds Parish Church for use with or without the organ.

It is understood that Liszt's "Pianoforte School," to which he has devoted the study of many years, is now to be published in three large volumes.

The committee of the Liverpool National Eisteddfod propose £20 instead of £50 for the best cantata, and £210 for the chief choral competition prize.

The twenty-first anniversary arrangements of the Church of England Temperance Society include a Festival Service in Westminster Abbey, on Nov. 19th.

The Society for the Promotion of Christian Knowledge offer a new book called "The Rehearsal, and other Stories of Musicians and Singers" adapted from the German.

The new comic opera "Falka" at the Comedy Theatre, by Chassaigne, has many pretty catching melodies, and the young composer has done fairly well in this doubtless early work.

It is said that owing to the interest taken in the repetition of Dr. Stainer's "Mary Magdalen" at the Bow and Bromley Institute to-night, all the tickets have been sold in advance.

A society for male voices, the "West London Choral Society," has been formed, and is under the direction of Mr. F. Scarsbrook. The place of meeting is 98, Ledbury Road, Bayswater.

On Monday last, the Abbé Franz Liszt celebrated his seventy-second birthday at Jena, where his oratorio, "Saint Elizabeth," was performed at the Court Theatre, in honour of the day.

The Signal has it that two new pianoforte compositions by Rubinstein are in the press : a trio in C minor and an "unplayable" Concert-Etude for the young English pianist, Eugene d'Albert.

At the Chelsea Congregational Church, Markham-square, King's-road, a performance of Mendelssohn's "Elijah," was given on Nov. 1st, in aid of the fund for the completion of the organ.

An exhibition of ten guineas per annum has been presented for competition amongst pianoforte students of the Guildhall School of Music by Messrs. John Brinsmead and Sons, of Wigmore-street.

The Alhambra will be inaugurated on the 10th, when Mr. F. Clay's "Golden Ring" is to be produced. A large and efficient orchestra has been got together and placed under the direction of M. Riviere.

The Nineteenth Century Art Society, exhibiting British and Foreign modern pictures, held a private press view at the Conduit Street Galleries, on Nov. 3rd. The society is likely to prove a useful body, and to assist greatly the artistic world.

Mr. Walter Lucas, of Douglas, Isle of Man, gave a concert recently. His pianoforte solos were a Fantasia by Weber, Rubinstein's well-known melody, and Handel's "Harmonious Blacksmith." The concert scheme included some well known vocal pieces.

We understand that Mr. Barnby's setting of the 97th Psalm ("The Lord is King,") written for and produced with so much success at the recent Leeds Festival, has already been selected for performance again at Leeds, by the Choral Society, and at Wolverhampton, Stafford, and Eton College.

The Islington Musical Society (conductor Mr. Wm. L. Frost), meet on Mondays in the Lecture Hall, at the rear of Claremont Chapel, Pentonville Road (close to the Angel), for the practice of high-class music. The Hon. Sec. is Mr. Percy Collins, 22, Milner Square, N. An orchestra is in formation. Gentlemen willing to take part are invited to come forward.

The Leeds Band of Hope League gave a concert in the Leeds Town Hall on Saturday evening. The programme was made up of songs, duets, glees and choruses, taken from well-known temperance and other sources. Miss Briscoe and Miss Nicholson were the principal vocalists, and Dr. Spark presided at the organ. The choir consisted of about 500 voices from various Bands of Hope in the Union.

Says L'Independente (Trieste), of Thursday, Oct. 18th, 1883 :—New opera : Mr. George Carter, of London, the author of various sacred works, and of esteemed and clever compositions, both sacred and secular, has finished his new opera, "Nerone." Renowned Italian musicians who have seen the work, speak of the music as being beautiful, full of melodious inspiration and learned and pleasing orchestration.

The Athenaum says : "The Argentina Theatre at Rome is to be shortly opened for a season of opera. 'Mignon' is the first work to be given ; and among other operas which it is intended to produce are Delibes's 'Lakmé,' Bizet's 'Carmen' (a novelty at Rome), Halévey's 'La Reine de Chypre,' Giovannini's 'Tito Vezio,' and a new opera, 'Il Conte di Gleichen,' by Signor Auteri."

The competition for the Mendelssohn Scholarship now vacant is announced to take place early in the approaching year. The scholarship, the value of which, is at least £80 per annum, is conferred with the intention of enabling the scholar either to go abroad to finish his (or her) education at a foreign conservatoire or to attain that object at home with increased facilities under the direction and at the choice of the committee. Sir A. Sullivan was the first Mendelssohn scholar, and Mr. D'Albert, who is now appearing as a successful pianist in Germany, was the last. The scholarship is regarded as a great honour as well as a valuable prize, among musical students.

The Querist.

REPLY.

DR. MAURICE GREEN.—Dr. Maurice Green was buried in the Church of St. Olave, Old Jewry, London (where his father was formerly vicar), on December 10th, 1755 ; but the exact spot has, for many years, been lost sight of.—J. S. BUMPUS.

Service Lists.

London.

ST. PAUL'S CATHEDRAL.—Morn.: Service, Te Deum and Benedictus, Martin in C ; Introit, O Saviour of the world (Goss) ; Holy Communion, Wesley in E, and Barnby in E. Even. : Service, Magnificat and Nunc Dimittis, Steggall in C ; Anthem, Hear, O my flock, Israel, and The Lord hath in Egypt " Sion " (Gade).

TEMPLE CHURCH.—Morn.: Service, Te Deum Laudamus and Jubilate Deo, Cooke in G ; Apostles' Creed, Harmonised Monotone ; Anthem, O Lord, Thou hast searched me out (Croft). Even. : Service, Magnificat and Nunc Dimittis, Cooke in G ; Apostles' Creed, Harmonized Monotone ; Anthem, O God I have mercy (Mendelssohn).

FOUNDLING CHAPEL. — Morn.: Service, Te Deum, and Jubilate, Calkin in G; Anthem, O rest in the Lord (Mendelssohn). Aft.: Children Service.

LINCOLN'S INN CHAPEL.—Morn.: Service, Smart in F; Kyrie, D'Alquen; Anthem, I beheld, and lo, a great multitude (Blow). Even: Service, Tours in F; Anthem, Hear my prayer, O God (Greene).

ALL SAINTS, MARGARET STREET.—Morn.: Service, Te Deum, and Benedictus (Stainer); Holy Communion, Silas in C; Offertory Anthem, As the hart pants (Mendelssohn). Even.: Service, Tours in D; Anthem, My song shall be alway ye nations (Mendelssohn).

CHRIST CHURCH, CLAPHAM.—Morn.: Service, Te Deum, Plain-song; Kyrie and Credo, Mozart in B flat, No. 7; Offertory Anthem, Blest [are the departed (Spohr); Sanctus, Benedictus, Agnus Dei, and Gloria in excelsis (Mozart). Even.: Service, Magnificat and Nunc Dimittis, Goss in A; Anthem, Fear not, O land (Goss).

HOLY TRINITY, TULSE HILL. — Morn.: Service, Chants. Even.: Service, Magnificat and Nunc Dimittis, Stainer in E flat; Anthem, I will extol Thee, and Hosanna (Costa).

ST. JAMES'S PRIVATE EPISCOPAL CHAPEL, SOUTHWARK, —Morn.: Service, Introit, Jesu, Word of God incarnate (Gounod); Communion Service, Gounod in G, No. 1. Even.: Service, Smart in B flat; Anthem, Thou earth, waft sweet incense (Spohr).

ST. MARGARET PATTENS, ROOD LANE, FENCHURCH STREET.—Morn.: Service, Te Deum, and Benedictus, Smart in F; Communion Service, Offertory Anthem, Blessed are the men (Mendelssohn); Kyrie, Credo, Sanctus, Benedictus, Agnus Dei, and Gloria, Hummell in B flat. Even.: Service, Magnificat and Nunc Dimittis, Hopkins in F; Anthem, I will mention (Sullivan).

ST. MARY BOLTONS, WEST BROMPTON, S.W.—Morn.: Service, Te Deum, and Benedictus, Goss in C; Holy Communion, Kyrie, Credo, Sanctus, and Gloria in excelsis, Smart in F; Benedictus, and Agnus Dei, Redhead in F; Offertory (Barnby). Even.: Service, Magnificat and Nunc Dimittis, Hopkins in F; Anthem, Like as a Father pitieth (Hatton).

ST. MAGNUS, LONDON BRIDGE.—Morn.: Service, Opening Anthem, To the Lord our God (Calkin); Te Deum and Jubilate, Attwood in F; Kyrie (Wesley). Even.: Service, Magnificat and Nunc Dimittis, Attwood in F; Anthem, Thy word is a lantern (Purcell).

ST. PAUL'S, AVENUE ROAD, SOUTH HAMPSTEAD.—Morn.: Service, Te Deum, Hopkins in G; Benedictus (Barnby); Kyrie, Monk in C. Even.: Service, Magnificat and Nunc Dimittis, Bridge in C; Anthem, The wilderness (Goss).

ST. PAUL'S, BOW COMMON, E.—Morn.: Service, Te Deum and Benedictus, Stainer in B flat. Even.: Service, Magnificat and Nunc Dimittis, Tours in F; Anthem, O come, let us worship (Mendelssohn).

ST. PETER'S, VERE STREET, W.—Even.: Service, Magnificat and Nunc Dimittis, Gadsby in C; Anthem, Thy word is a lantern (Purcell).

ST. AUGUSTINE AND ST. FAITH, WATLING STREET.— Morn.: Service, Garrett in D throughout. Even.: Service, Stainer in E flat; Anthem, I have surely built Thee (Boyce).

ST. SEPULCHRE'S, HOLBORN. — Morn.: Service, Te Deum Jubilate, and Kyrie, Nares in F; Anthem, Lord of all power (Mason). Even.: Service, Magnificat and Nunc Dimittis, Nares in F; Anthem, Fear not, O Land (Goss).

Country.

ST. ASAPH CATHEDRAL. — Morn.: Service, Goss in F; Anthem, O Lord, Rebuke me not (Browne). Even.: Service, Jones in F; Anthem, I did call upon the Lord (Pattison).

ASHBURNE CHURCH, DERBYSHIRE. — Morn.: Service, throughout, Smart in F. Even.: Service, Walmisley in D minor; Anthem, O give thanks (Purcell).

BEDDINGTON CHURCH, SURREY.—Morn.: Service, Smart in F; Introit, Jesus calls us; Communion Service. Garrett in F. Even.: Service (Stainer); Anthems, O rest in the Lord, and He shall endure (Mendelssohn).

BIRMINGHAM (S. ALBAN THE MARTYR).—Morn.: Service, Te Deum, and Benedictus, Dykes, in F; Holy Communion, Kyrie, Credo, Sanctus and Gloria, Dykes in F; Agnus Dei and Benedictus (Redman). Evensong: Magnificat and Nunc Dimittis, Baraby in D.

BIRMINGHAM (ST. CYPRIAN'S, HAY MILLS).—Morn.: Service, Nares in C; Anthem, In that day (Elvey). Even.: Service, Ebdon in C; Anthem, My soul truly waiteth (Kent).

BIRMINGHAM (ST. MICHAEL'S, HAWORTH).—Morn.: Service, Te Deum and Benedictus; Communion (Dykes). Even.: Service, Magnificat and Nunc Dimittis; Anthem, O come let us worship (Mendelssohn).

BIRMINGHAM (S. PHILIP'S CHURCH). -- Morn.: Service, Stainer in A; Anthem, If ye love me (Heap). Evensong Service, Stainer in A; Anthem, The Lord, even the most mighty God (Greene).

BRISTOL CATHEDRAL.— Morn.: Service, Attwood in D; Even.: Service, Attwood in D; Anthem, Praise the Lord (Mozart).

CARLISLE CATHEDRAL.—Morn.: Service, Gadsby in C: Introit, The Lord is in His holy Temple (Thorne); Kyrie and Creed, Smart in G. Even.: Service, Gadsby in C; Anthem, O give thanks (Purcell).

DONCASTER (PARISH CHURCH).—Morn.: Service, Boyce in C. Even.: Service, Stainer in E flat; Anthem, The Lord gave the word, How beautiful are their feet, Their sound is gone out.

DUBLIN, ST. PATRICK'S (NATIONAL) CATHEDRAL.—Morn.: Service, Te Deum, and Jubilate, Stainer in E flat; Holy Communion, Kyrie, Creed and Sanctus, Stainer in E flat; Anthem, God is love, Part 1 (Mrs. J. Robinson). Even.: Service, Magnificat and Nunc Dimittis, Stainer in E flat; Anthem, God is love, Parts 2, 3, and 4 (Mrs. J. Robinson).

EDINBURGH (ST. JOHN'S).—Aft.: Service, Anthem, Praise His awful name, "Last Judgment" (Spohr). Even.: Service, Anthem, O taste and see (Goss).

ELY CATHEDRAL.—Morn.: Service, Smart in F; Kyrie and Credo, Smart in F; Gloria, Monk in A; Anthem, Blessed is he (Nares). Even.: Service, Smart in F; Anthem, Praise the Lord (Goss).

HARROGATE (ST. PETER'S CHURCH).—Morn.: Service, Te Deum, and Benedictus, Chants; Anthem, The Lord is my strength (Monk). Even.: Service, Magnificat, Peregine Tone, Harmony by Bach; Nunc Dimittis, Haynes in G; Anthem, As pants the hart (Spohr).

LLANDAFF CATHEDRAL.—Morn.: Service, Te Deum and Jubilate, Barnby in E. Even.: Service, Magnificat and Nunc Dimittis, Barnby in E; Anthem, O where shall wisdom be found (Boyce).

LEATHERHEAD (ST. JOHN'S FOUNDATION SCHOOL).—Morn.: Service, Te Deum, Dykes in F; Kyrie, Elvey in B flat; Creed, Goss in D. Even.: Service, Chants; Anthem, O Lord how manifold (Barnby).

LEEDS PARISH CHURCH.—Morn.: Service, Hatton in E; Anthem, And lo, a throne (Spohr); Introit, Kyrie and Credo (Wesley in E). Even.: Service, Hatton in E; Anthem, Wherewithal shall a young man (Elvey).

LINLITHGOW ABBEY, N.B.—Morn.: Service, Te Deum, Hopkins in B flat; Anthem, Comfort the soul (Crotch); Hymn, How bright these glorious spirits shine (Barnby). Even.: Service, Anthem, How lovely are Thy dwellings fair (Spohr); Hymn, Abide with me (Cornwall).

LIVERPOOL CATHEDRAL.—Aft.: Service, Cantate and Deus, Bayley in F; Anthem, O Lord, have mercy upon me, (Pergolesi).

MANCHESTER CATHEDRAL. — Morn.: Service, Te Deum, Jubilate, Kyrie, Creed, Sanctus, and Gloria, Barnby in C; Anthem, This is the day (Oakeley). Aft.: Service, Barnby in E; Anthem, Be dumb, ye sinners (Spohr).

MANCHESTER (ST. BENEDICT'S).—Morn.: Service, Kyrie, Sanctus, Benedictus, and Agnus Dei, Monk in C; Credo and Gloria in excelsis, Williams in D. Even.: Service, Magnificat and Nunc Dimittis, Wesley in F.

MANCHESTER (ST. JOHN BAPTIST, HULME).—Morn.: Service, Te Deum and Benedictus "Gregorian" Kyrie, Credo, Sanctus, Agnus Dei and Gloria in excelsis, Aguiter in B flat. Even.: Service, Magnificat and Nunc Dimittis, Bunnett in F.

ROCHESTER CATHEDRAL. — Morn.: Service, Smart in G; Anthem, O rest in the Lord (Mendelssohn). Even.: Service, Smart in G; Anthem, Blessed is the man (Goss).

SALISBURY CATHEDRAL.—Morn.: Service, Stainer in E flat; Offertory (Stainer). Aft.: Service, Stainer in E flat; Anthem, Not unto us (Mendelssohn).

SHEFFIELD PARISH CHURCH. — Morn.: Service, Kyrie, (Mendelssohn). Even.: Service, Cantate Domine and Deus Misereatur, Trimnell in E major; Anthem, Blessed are the merciful (Hiles).

SHERBORNE ABBEY.—Morn.: Service, Te Deum, Ouseley in D. Even.: Service, Chants; Anthem, I beheld and lo (Lyle).

WELLS CATHEDRAL.—Morn.: Service, Pyne in C; Introit, He cometh forth (Macfarren); Kyrie, Child in F. Even.: Service, Barrow in F; Anthem, Ascribe unto the Lord (Wesley).

WINCHESTER CATHEDRAL. — Morn.: Service (Wesley). Even.: Service, Colborne in D; Anthem, Blessing and glory (Bach).

WOLVERHAMPTON (ST. PETER'S COLLEGIATE CHURCH).— Morn.: Service, Te Deum, Smart in F; Benedictus, Hopkins in G; Anthem, Behold, how good and joyful (Whitfield). Even.: Service, Magnificat, Worgan, in E flat; Nunc Dimittis, Barnby in E; Anthem, As the hart pants (Mendelssohn).

WORCESTER CATHEDRAL. — Morn.: Service, Chipp in A; Anthem, O taste and see (Sullivan). Even.: Service, Chipp in A; Anthem, Blessing and glory (Bach).

APPOINTMENTS.

Mr. ARTHUR T. ROBINSON has been appointed Organist of Gibraltar Cathedral.

Mr. CHARLES SMALL has been appointed Organist and Choirmaster of St. Saviour's, Denmark Park.

ERRATUM.—In our notice of "Music at St. George's Hall," last week, page 273, second column, line 6 from end of report, for W. G. Goss, read Mr. George Gear.

Now ready, price 2d.

NINE LESSONS, WITH CAROLS. Festal Service for Christmas Eve, as used in Truro Cathedral.—A. R. Mowbray & Co., 116, S. Aldates, Oxford; and at 65, Farringdon Street, London, E.C.

Advent Anthem.

"IF WE BELIEVE," Anthem, price 4d. By E. H. TURPIN. (Published by kind permission of C. Mackeson, Esq.). WEEKES & CO., 14, Hanover Street, W.

ART of MODULATION: Handbook, showing at a glance the Modulations from one Key to any other in the Octave, for Organists and Musical Directors. 2s. 6d., paper; 4s., cloth.

FACTS about FIDDLES.—Violins Old and New by JOHN BROADHOUSE. Price 6d.; by post, 6½d. W. REEVES, 185, Fleet-street, London, E.C.

"THE LIFE BOAT." Song, with Pianoforte Accompaniment. Published at 2s., sent post free for 2½d., in stamps.—J. A. Hooper, 268, Gray's Inn Road, King's Cross.

FOR SALE.—ONE SET ONLY.

HANDEL'S WORKS, in Full Score. Edited by Dr. ARNOLD. Fine Original Set, on Large Paper, perfectly clean and unused, in 40 volumes folio, half calf, marbled edges, £10:—Messiah, Israel in Egypt, Occ. Oratorio, Saul, Joseph, Jephtha, Theodora, Athalia, Hercules, Samson, Joshua, Belshazzar, Solomon, Susanna, Esther, Deborah, Alexander Balus, Judas Maccabaeus, Acis and Galatea, Semele, Triumph of Time and Truth, La Resurrezione, Choice of Hercules, Alexander's Feast, Ode for St. Cecilia's Day, Birthday Ode, L'Allegro, Il Penseroso ed Il Moderato; Masque, 12 Chandos Anthems, Wedding, Funeral, Dettingen Anthems, 4 Coronation Anthems, Dettingen Te Deum, Chandos Te Deum, Utrecht Te Deum and Jubilate, Short Te Deum in D, Agrippina, Giulio Cesare, Teseo, Sosarme, Alcades, 2 Trios and 4 Cantatas, 13 Chamber Duets and 12 Cantatas, 12 Grand Concertos, 15 Organ Concertos, 6 Oboe Concertos, Concertante, Harpsichord Lessons (1st, 2nd, and 3rd Sets), 13 Sonatas or Trios, 12 Solos with Thorough Basses, Water Music, Fireworks Music, 6 Fugues for the Organ, Alchymist Music. W. REEVES, 185, Fleet Street, E.C.

THE THROAT IN ITS RELATION TO SINGING. By WHITFIELD WARD. Illustrated, post 8vo, boards, 2s. 6d.—Advice to Singers on every point of interest in reference to the Vocal Organs. W. REEVES: 185, Fleet Street, E.C.

"SISERA."

New Cantata for Treble Voices, composed by

ISIDORE de SOLLA.

Octavo, paper cover, 1s. 6d.

This dramatic and melodious Cantata is well adapted to Ladies' Vocal Societies, Schools, etc.

"The music is admirably suggestive, and lends itself readily to the pathetic portion of the poem."—Stage.

"Interesting and melodious; set to music with decided ability."—Sunday Times.

"A charming poem, by Marmaduke E. Browne, enables the composer to tell a very pathetic story, and to display all the resources of his art."— Illustrated Sporting and Dramatic News.

WEEKES & CO., 14, Hanover Street, Regent Street, W.

THE STUDENT'S HELMHOLTZ.

MUSICAL ACOUSTICS,

OR

THE PHENOMENA OF SOUND AS CONNECTED WITH MUSIC,

With Examination Questions and over 100 Illustrations,

BY JOHN BROADHOUSE.

Price 7s. 6d. net.

London: WILLIAM REEVES, 185, Fleet-street.

PLAYING FROM SCORE.—The Celebrated Treatise on Playing from Score (a Clear Introduction to the Art of making Arrangements for the Organ, Pianoforte, &c.), translated into English, is now appearing in the Orchestra. Monthly, price 3d.; Annual Subscription, 3s. 6d.

W. REEVES 185, Fleet Street, London, E.C.

In Paper Wrapper, 1s. In Cloth Gilt, 2s.

Musical History and Biography.

With Especial Reference to English Music and Musicians.

BY

FREDERIC J. CROWEST.

Author of "The Great Tone Poets," "Phases of Musical England," "A Book of Musical Anecdotes," &c., post 8vo (168 pages), including a Copious Index.

W. REEVES: 185, Fleet Street, E.C.

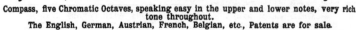
Printed for the Proprietor by BOWDEN, HUDSON & Co., at 23, Red Lion Street, Holborn, London, W.C. ; and Published by WILLIAM REEVES, at the Office, 185, Fleet Street, E.C. West End Agents :—WEEKES & CO., 14, Hanover Street, Regent Street, W. Subscriptions and Advertisements are received either by the Publisher or West End Agents.—*Communications for the* EDITOR *are to be forwarded to his private address, 6, Argyle Square, W.C.*
SATURDAY, NOVEMBER 10, 1883.—*Entered at the General Post Office as a Newspaper.*

MUSICAL STANDARD

A NEWSPAPER FOR MUSICIANS PROFESSIONAL AND AMATEUR

No. 1,007. VOL. XXV. FOURTH SERIES. SATURDAY, NOVEMBER 17, 1883. WEEKLY: PRICE 3D.

IMPROVISATION.

To improvise well upon the piano or organ requires mental power of no ordinary calibre. It is one of the highest and most enjoyable gifts given to musicians. The extempore player is more than a composer : he *invents* the theme, and then proceeds to *develop* it without any preparation. He must have an active imagination—the ground soil and source of all true art; and he must also have a productive imagination to paint in vivid or sombre tone colours. Tone is a very thorough medium for expressing sentiments, and the various keys (major and minor) will be found to express nearly every phase of human feeling. There are bright keys and there are dull keys, light and heavy, grave and gay, and the improvisor should bear in mind a few of these, in order to give more effect to his melodies by introducing them, as it were, in the right key. He who searches for keys will surely forget his ideas the while! The hands must be under the control of the mind and must readily and quickly follow all its dictates.

As the orator, so the improvisor. The one thinks and speaks, and his tongue gives utterance to his thoughts with ready fluency. And so the other. The mind must be ahead of the utterance. So should the improvisor play. He must also be possessed of a certain amount of *quick* discrimination, or discerning at once whether to accept or reject thoughts or ideas as they present themselves in rapid succession. And, further, he must not forget to play with expression, or let the working out mentally interfere, in the slightest degree, with the execution mechanically, lest the performance be deficient in spite of the excellent ideas. When I speak of improvisation, I do not include the after-dinner-playing-by-ear style, which is sometimes unfortunately heard : the subject, for obvious reasons, is better left untouched. Let it, however, be said that only those should extemporise in public who can do so in an artistic manner. Memory plays an exceedingly important part to the extempore player : he must be able to retain the ideas he has chosen, and work in, with ease, the original principal subject after the various episodes and modulations. This comes by practice. He must know the rules of harmony, and chords, their constructions, relations, and resolutions, so as to enable him properly to put his ideas together.

All the great tone poets were improvisors.

Bach, at the age of eighteen, when organist of the Church at Arnstadt, excited much attention both far and near with his wonderful powers of extemporising. The impression he made on Reinken made the veteran, embracing him, exclaim, "I thought this art had died out; now that I see it still lives, I can depart in peace."

Handel, when playing publicly, used to give himself to the workings of his inexhaustible genius.

Of Mozart it was written by Clementi, "I never had thus far heard any one play with so much spirit and grace. Especially was I surprised at his adagios and extemporaneous variations, to which the Emperor gave the theme." From his concert programmes we gather that he also improvised much in public, and from his biographers that he was always eminently successful in his playing.

Rider, who died in 1857, an aged man of eighty years, said : "Even now, an aged man as I am, I hear the heavenly, never-to-be-forgotten harmonies, and I shall go to my grave convinced of this one fact—that there was but one Mozart."

Beethoven was even still greater at this great art. The fire of his imagination, his modulations, and his wonderful treatment of any given theme, were the subject of the admiration of all who were fortunate enough to hear him. It is said that the power of his improvisations far surpassed that of his playing written compositions. Mendelssohn, Chopin, and Liszt, too, were all extempore players. But, alas! this great power is no longer cultivated as it was. We never hear a modern pianist improvise.

Musicians should try their powers, and endeavour to cultivate this grand old long-forgotten art.

ERNEST BIRCH.

THE SONGS OF SCHUBERT.

The following letter has been addressed to the editor of the *Times* :—Sir,—I am anxious to obtain the help of your readers in reference to a new critical edition of the Songs of Schubert, now in progress in Germany. During the fifty-five years that have passed since Schubert's early death, so many alterations have crept into the songs that the original text of the music is in many cases widely departed from. The task of rectifying the published editions by the autographs, or by early copies, has been undertaken by Mr. Max Friedlander, a musician and singer well known in London, whose judgment, accuracy, and enthusiasm alike fit him for the work. The labour involved is great, owing to the wide distances over which the manuscripts are scattered. Mr. Friedländer is at present in Vienna, where the rich collections of the Gesellschaft der Musikfreunde, Messrs. N. Dumba, Bauernfeld (Schubert's friend), Brahms and Franz Lachner (the composers), have been thrown open to him without reserve. He has received similar aid from Mdme. Schumann, Mr. Stockhausen, Mr. Karl Meinert, Count Victor Wimpffen, Geheimrath von Löper, and other possessors of Schubert autographs. Our own Professor Max Müller, son of the Wilhelm Müller who wrote the touching poems of the Schöne Müllerin and the Wintereise, two of Schubert's most noted sets of songs, has contributed a preface, which cannot fail to add to the value of the edition.

My object in writing is to bespeak the help of all possessors of autographs of Schubert's songs in this country. It will be a great favour, and much assistance to an important work, if all such will have the great kindness to communicate on the subject at their early convenience with me, or with Messrs. Peters, of Leipsic, the publishers of the edition.—Your obedient servant, GEORGE GROVE, Royal College of Music, Kensington Gore, W.

OUTTINGS FROM FERDINAND PRAEGER'S RHYMES FOR YOUNG AND OLD CHILDREN.

When notes were without stems forsooth,
And much in music yet uncouth,
They were called *points :* and Counterpoint
When *nota contra notum* joined
And tune 'pon tune by laws' decree
Of their fixed grammar did agree.
But if the added tune had more
Of smaller notes, say two, three, four,
Then *Florid Counterpoint* became
Of this extended form the name.
Should your first subject then admit
That as a bass it could be fit
To underlie the second theme,
Then Double Counterpoint this scheme
Was termed, and looked upon
As grand achievement nobly won.

The Walworth Choral Society gave a capital performance of Haydn's "Creation," on Monday last, at the Surrey Masonic Hall. The soloists were Madame Worrell, Mr. John Cornwall (tenor), and Mr. Frank May (bass), who admirably acquitted themselves in the parts allotted to them. Too much praise cannot be given to Mr. E. Curtis, for his untiring efforts in connection with this society, both as choirmaster and conductor. The choruses on this occasion were, as at other times, extremely well sung.

Musical Intelligence.

CRYSTAL PALACE CONCERTS.

PROGRAMME.

Overture, "Tragic" (Op. 81)	Brahms.
Concerto for strings	Bach.
Air, " In Native Worth " (" Creation ")	Haydn.
Mr. Maas.	
Melody and " A L'Espagnole "	Cowen.
(First time at these concerts).	
Symphony No. 7, in A............................	Beethoven.
Walther's Prize Song, "Die Meistersinger "	Wagner.
Mr. Maas.	
Ballet, "The Dance of the Houris" ("La Gioconda")	Ponchielli.
Conductor . - AUGUST MANNS.	

Why the Crystal Palace people should again alter the
time of their concert from 3.10 to 3 o'clock, I cannot
imagine. A long train, full of people, arrived at the Low
Level station on Saturday last, some minutes behind time
—2.50. This is no unusual occurrence; and even if the train
is punctual, it is quite impossible to be in the gallery of
the concert-room until some minutes after 3. The consequence is, that a great many miss the first number in the
programme, and cause a great commotion at the early
part of the concert, much to the annoyance of those who
are able to be quite in time. This unfortunate arrangement must deter not a few from attending these delightful
concerts.

As Brahms's overture was noticed not very long ago in
the *Musical Standard*, nothing need be said of it on this
occasion beyond the fact of its producing a great impression. Of the concerto of Sebastian Bach, it is a real
pleasure to speak. It is the third of a set of six which
were first published in 1850, and some of them are
remarkable as being amongst the earliest attempts to
combine wind and stringed instruments. The one now
before us is for strings only. The charm of the work consists not only in its constantly clever and brilliant ideas,
but the ever varying, continuous, changeful flow of melody
renders it still more delightful. It hardly need be said
how superbly the ideas are worked out.

Mr. Cowen's contribution was quite worthy of his well-
known ability as an orchestral writer. His scoring is
redundant with the most fascinating combinations and
contrivances. The *violini sordini* with harp; the unison
of reeds and 'celli, with *pizzicato* for contra bassi, with
nice touches for the horns, and judicious use of the trombones, &c.; give to the work a colour and character which
is very taking. The audience, indeed, were so taken with
the Spanish melody as to demand its repetition. Beethoven's symphony was of course greatly enjoyed.

Mr. Maas sang his two songs—chosen perhaps by way
of contrast—in a superb manner.   R. S.

BEETHOVEN'S SYMPHONY IN A.

Only think of two hearings of this immense work—the
writer's special favourite—in one day! I am sorry to notice
an apparent defiance on the part of two great powers last
Saturday, but that is not my business. To avoid odious
and invidious comparisons, I may at once extol Mr.
Manns's performance of the symphony as surpassingly
excellent, a fully developed whole, with the nicest attention to details ; for at the Crystal Palace *individual* artists
not only know their *métier*, but are always "going together," like the steeds of Phœbus Apollo. I hardly know
which particular feature to select for praise. The wail of
the violins at the end of the "dactyl and spondee" movement touched the inmost soul. The horns came out well
in the *scherzo*, and Mr. Manns, active and energetic, without bustle or fussy demonstrations, fully evolved that
delicate modulation from the Trio in D major back to the
Scherzo in F. The elephantine jump in the *finale*, on the
second accent of the bar, where the quaint theme in C
sharp minor occurs, was truly exciting. Mr. Manns got
through his weighty work in 41 minutes ; Herr Richter,
the same evening, in 45.

Herr Richter, loving Beethoven, of course left no
stone unturned to bring out this noble "No. 7" into
boldest relief, and the process may be reported as
stupendous. The masterful swing of the *bâton* elicited
the responsive action, as it were, of one man from a
host of eighty, and on dissection of the score, the nicest
points were all clearly discernible, as the separate features
on the face of Venus Victrix might be studied apart from
that noble *contour* of unsurpassable beauty.

    A. M.

RICHTER CONCERTS.

These splendid performances reached the end of their
autumn season last Saturday with the following programme :—

Overture, "Leonora," No. 3....................	Beethoven.
Orchestral Suite in D	Bach.
Vorspiel, "Die Meistersinger "	Wagner.
Symphony No. 7, in A	Beethoven.

The pleasant, old-fashioned suite was fully appreciated,
and by no means out of place among its more modern
brethren ; for all that is good and true is eternal.

The only Wagner number on the programme called
forth, as is usual at these concerts, the greatest amount
of enthusiasm. Ere it subsided, an evergreen wreath was
presented to Herr Richter, which was the signal for renewed cheers. Richter, with an innate gracefulness
which is the secret of much of his power, placed the
wreath on the desk of the leader, pointed it out to the
orchestra, and repeated the " Meistersinger " overture :
thus unmistakably transferring the honour to its wondrous
author in the first place, and after him to his grand interpreters. Two of the second violins who had left their
seats during the applause, feeling sure the first part of
the concert was over, slid back rather like culprits when
the entirely unexpected "encore" reached their astonished
ears.

And now, before the spring concerts begin, will some
musician of understanding find out for us and define
what " programme music" is ; that our analytical programmes may be clearer and more logical ?

Goethe has somewhere said that there is perhaps no
word which presents exactly the same idea to any two
minds : undoubtedly the term " programme music"
awakens very different currents of thought in the minds
of different musicians. The time has now surely arrived
when the terms, if used at all, should be made to mean
something—something that all musicians alike will accept
as a definition of some particular form of art, honourable
or otherwise. At present " programme music" is usually
considered a term of opprobrium—it signifies, in a vague
sort of way, a production without form or internal life ; a
weak, rambling imitation of the sounds we hear, without
reaching their spiritual meaning. It is true that Sir G.
Grove (whose analysis of Beethoven's symphonies are
reprinted, as occasion requires, in the Richter books)
does not countenance this interpretation ; for, analysing
the " Pastoral " Symphony, he writes :—"Programme
music is music in which the endeavour is made to represent a given scene or occurrence by the aid of instruments
only, without the help of voices." But this talented and
enthusiastic writer cannot have made his interpretation
clear, even to his own mind ; for he has elsewhere called
some airs with variations, as absolute as any by Herz,
" programme music," because the author has chosen to
give them a title. (*Vide* analysis in Crystal Palace book
of Goldmark's " Country Wedding " Symphony.) Are
we, then, to look upon Handel's " Harmonious Blacksmith " as " programme music"? By this rule we shall
have to call some of the most absolute music "programme"; and some which is anything but absolute,
having an evident, though unexpressed, poetical basis,
will be classed as absolute. What is it, then, that constitutes " programme music"? Is it the fact of having a
title, though the form be strictly classical and symphonic,
such as Beethoven's " Pastoral"? If so, why is not the
C minor also "programme music"? Beethoven had a
distinct poetical idea attached to both ; wherein lies the
difference? Haydn—one of the most absolute of musicians—almost invariably wrote from some fixed idea ; he
had some story in his mind as he wrote his symphonies
and chamber music : if he had attached the stories to his
scores, would these most absolute compositions in the
world have been thereby suddenly converted into "programme music"? Schumann's "Rhenish" Symphony is
probably (according to Sir G. Grove) "programme
music"; but if he had called it simply "Symphony No.
3, in E flat," it would be as absolute as is No. 1, in B flat.
" Programme music" is then, as it appears at present,
a fearful and wonderful thing. Who will tear away
its veil of mystery, and reveal to us whether it is really an
honourable art-work, another name for "poetical music,"
and including such works as Berlioz's "Harold," Liszt's
Symphonic Poems and Raff's Symphonies, or merely the
lowest form of sensuous imitation of the baldest and most
unpoetical coarseness, boasting nothing nobler than
Hiller's " Sentinel," another writer's " Turkish Patrol,"

"The Battle of Prague" and Pridham's more modern "Delhi March," wherein the exact moment is announced when the sun rises, the enemy approaches, the wounded groan, &c., &c.

Till we are agreed as to where "programme music" begins and ends, let us, by all means, avoid the use of the term. Let a distinct place be found for it on our list of art-appellations, and may it, in future years, be more faithfully defined than the term "sonata" is in one of our English dictionaries, where it stands revealed to the astonished artist as "a tune for an instrument only."

B. F. WYATT-SMITH.

SATURDAY POPULAR CONCERTS.

These concerts were resumed last week with their usual conservative programme, and (it would appear from the crowded attendance), more than their usual popularity.

PROGRAMME.

Quintet in D major, for two violins, two violas, and
    violoncello .... Mozart.
    Madame Norman-Néruda, MM. L. Ries, Hollander, Zerbini,
       and Piatti.
Songs, "I'm Rhein," and "Ich grolle nicht " .... Schumann.
    Mr. Santley.
Rondeau Brillant in E flat major (Op. 62) .... Weber.
Nocturne in F major, Op. 15, No. 1, and Mazurka in A
    flat major, (Op. 39), No. 2 .... Chopin.
       (For pianoforte alone.)
    M. Vladimir de Pachmann.
Sonata in D major (Op. 5), No. 1, for violin, with piano-
    forte accompaniment .... Corelli.
    Madame Norman-Néruda.
Cantique, "Le Nom de Marie " .... Gounod.
    Mr. Santley.
Quintet in E flat (Op. 44), for pianoforte, two violins,
    viola, and violoncello .... Schumann.
    M. Vladimir de Pachmann, Madame Norman-Néruda, MM. L. Ries,
       Hollander, and Piatti.
Accompanist   ..   ..   Mr. ZERBINI.

When three artists so popular as M. de Pachmann, Mdme. Norman-Néruda, and Mr. Santley take leading parts in a concert, it is no wonder that enthusiasm should be the order of the day—only, unhappily, our enthusiasm is not tempered with discretion; neither are the praises of our great ones sung "with understanding." The good-will of, for instance, such people as applaud M. de Pachmann and Mdme. Néruda's solos, but who walk out unceremoniously in the middle of a movement of Schumann's glorious Quintet, is rather an insult than a glory to a true artist. Those who remained till the end did even worse, by applauding in the noisiest manner and making a rush for their coats and hats just before the coda of the *finale*, when we were neither on the key-note, nor anywhere near it. The quintet has been heard twenty-seven times at these concerts alone, and yet we do not know that its conclusion is not reached till the first subject of the opening movement has reappeared. We may be a musical people, as we often hear we are—*from ourselves*—nevertheless, it must be conceded that we need an immense deal of education. But apart from what we know or do not know, we should on all occasions look to the performers to ascertain *when they allow us to applaud.* We should never forget that they are the greater, we the lesser; and the moment when they are listening to the final vibrations of the harmonies they have produced is not the moment for us to disturb the air with noisy delight. "Where would the artist be without our favour?" is a question often heard from English lips—a question that may well raise a blush of shame. Without pausing to answer it from the lives of many poets who lived and died without our "favour," we may ask in return, "Where should we be without the artist?" Can even the lowest of us, who thinks at all on such matters, bear to think how low we should be if art influence could be taken out of our lives? Let us then, endeavour to honour our artists with an honour more worthy of them and more honourable to ourselves.

M. de Pachmann was heard at his best in the Mazurka, where he appeared as the most sympathetic interpreter of the most polished music in the world. A different accent, a few notes given with unusual prominence, placed the whole piece in a new light, giving it a refinement and nobleness undreamt of before. This was a performance, calculated to make the musician reflect what slight differences divide the commonplace from the most exquisite refinement. Being recalled, M. de Pachmann played the favourite little Valse in D flat.

Mr. Santley, who is entitled to be looked upon as the interpreter of Gounod *par excellence*, sang a simple French romance after "Le Nom de Marie," was it a MS. of his own?

Mdme. Norman-Néruda performed her solo with her usual success. The performance of the Mozart quintet left nothing, and the Schumann quintet but little, to be desired.   B. F. WYATT-SMITH.

MONDAY POPULAR CONCERTS.

At the third concert of the season on Monday evening (November 12th), the Director presented the annexed programme :—

PART 1.

Quartet in E minor (Op. 44), No. 2, for two violins,
    viola, and violoncello .... Mendelssohn.
    Madame Norman-Néruda, MM. L. Ries, Hollander, and Piatti.
Preislied, " Die Meistersinger " .... Wagner.
    Mr. Edward Lloyd.
Fantasia in C minor (dedicated to Madame Mozart) ... Mozart.
Impromptu in A flat (Op. 90), No. 4 .... Schubert.
       (First time.)
    M. Vladimir de Pachmann.

PART 2.

Trio in G minor (Op. 8), for pianoforte, violin, and
    violoncello .... Chopin.
    M. Vladimir de Pachmann, Madame Norman-Néruda, and
       Signor Piatti.
Evening Song, "Good night, beloved " .... Blumenthal.
    Mr. Edward Lloyd.
Sonata in A major (No. 17 of Hallé's edition), for
    pianoforte and violin .... Mozart.
    M. Vladimir de Pachmann, and Madame Norman-Néruda.
Accompanist   ..   ..   Signor ROMILI.

The String Quartet in E minor has only been played fourteen times since April, 1859; the one in E flat comes forward much more frequently. Yet the work is surpassingly fine, and full of features indicative of supreme genius. The *solidità*—here an apt word—of the first allegro is testified by the ingenious interweaving of themes. The thoroughly original and piquant scherzo in the tonic major makes a golden bridge to the andante in G, compared by Sir G. A. Macfarren to a sigh in the air over undulating waters; and lastly, the final *presto agitato*, with its second subject on a pedal-bass and the brilliant coda where viola and violin play in octaves, "caps the bell," as they say in Yorkshire. Mendelssohn thought highly of this quartet, especially the *andante*.

M. Vladimir De Pachmann (engaged for a fourth "Popular," if not more), had his hands quite full on Monday night, and again evoked genuine enthusiasm. The choice of pieces, on the whole, cannot be considered the happiest. Mozart's fantasia, said to bear date A.D. 1782, strikes the hearer as the skeleton, or the *torso*, of a sonata. Well adapted, however, for practice and the display of *technique*, are its numerous flights of "grace" notes, in arpeggios, and the decomposition of the rhythm into demisemiquavers and semi-demisemiquavers. Schubert's Impromptu in A flat, now done to death by school-girls, is very inferior to others of the seven, notably the one in B flat; pupils not well versed in scales and "signatures" would be startled by that transition from the dominant (inverted) of D flat to C sharp major. An *encore* produced a well-known mazurka of Chopin.

The Polish pianist came to the front in Part II., but his piece here failed to please the *connoisseurs*. The Trio in G minor, confessedly an early work, must be denounced as an unfavourable specimen of the master. Dull, overlong, and rambling, as if in pursuit of will-o'-the-wisp ideas, the composition was felt to be a trial of patience. A musician who sat behind remarked that the pianoforte part " was beautifully played, but not worth the trouble!" The odour of the lamp, and the lack of invention, are disclosed in all the four movements : the Adagio in E flat is a mere round of self-asserting recitatives for the pianoforte, with obsequiously acquiescent answers from the strings. Mozart's duet sonata came as a gratifying relief after the trio, and was charmingly played by both artists. This work bears the date of A.D. 1787, and appears in the same catalogue as "Don Giovanni." M. De Pachmann's delicacy of touch, *finesse* of style, and clear enunciation of the florid passages, commanded general admiration. The "Preislied" of Wagner has been sung three times within as many weeks (last Saturday at Sydenham). A weekly contemporary complains that the song is being hackneyed, but who can object to the repetition of so delicious a melody? M. De Pachmann intends to hold two special recitals on Dec. 10th and 17th.   A. M.

Saint-Saëns's "The Lyre and the Harp," produced in Birmingham, has been given in Brussels.

BOW AND BROMLEY INSTITUTE.

The very interesting and in many respects admirable performance of Dr. Stainer's "St. Mary Magdalen" on Oct. 30th, proved that the choir of the Institute is destined to be a power in the list of our London musical institutions. Although the middle parts are somewhat too weak at present and wanting in pure tone, the external parts are of the very best : bright, clear, decided soprani, and solid voiced, full toned and prompt in attack bassi. The general effect of the whole is often most admirable. The choir performed Dr. Stainer's music with a loving enthusiasm delightful to think of. The defects of the performance were, notwithstanding the presence of many of our leading instrumentalists, in the orchestral department. These same defects may be attributed to that want of understanding between conductor and band which can only be completely established by frequent, or at least sufficient, rehearsals ; and, it must be added, that a work which deserves an orchestral rendering imperatively demands and calls for thoroughly efficient rehearsal. Perhaps the spirited committee at Bow will ultimately see their way to the formation of a standing orchestra in connection with their splendidly managed Institute. Such a scheme would enable them to do a service to the locality and the musical world which will in artistic usefulness transcend all the good things they have already done—that is, to familiarise the people's ears with the orchestral masterpieces of the great composers, properly and efficiently rendered. The solos were, upon this same memorable occasion—the first performance in London of Dr. Stainer's hitherto most dramatic and powerful work—sung to perfection by Miss Mary Davies, Miss Hilda Wilson, Mr. Lloyd, and Mr. F. King. The whole performance was a triumph for the Institute. Dr. Stainer's work gains ground upon examination. It is dramatic and yet never weak ; it is dramatic, yet never too realistic or inconsistent. Mr. McNaught must be congratulated upon the obvious pains he has taken in the production of the cantata. Last Saturday, Dr. Stainer's "Mary Magdalen" was repeated. The soloists were ; Misses Ambler and Ada South, Messrs. Kenningham and Brereton. The fine choir of the Institute fully sustained their reputation under the able conductorship of Mr. McNaught. Mr. Willie Hedge was the accompanying organist, and his artistic playing and admirable tact claim for him very high credit indeed. The whole performance was another event to congratulate the committee upon.

On Monday the Royal Amateur Orchestral Society gave a concert. Vocalists : Miss Minnie Gwynne, Miss Frances Hipwell, and Mr. Edward Levetus ; solo violin, Mr. H. Sternburg ; solo pianoforte, Miss Clara Asher ; accompanist, Mr. G. F. Bambridge ; conductor, Mr. George Mount. The concert proved a great treat to the members and friends. The band played excellently ; the only fault to be noticed, perhaps, was a slight want of steadiness in the andante of the "Italian" Symphony. The programme included Beethoven's overture, "Egmont," part of Mendelssohn's "Italian" Symphony, Weber's "Der Freischütz" overture, the popular "Turkish March" (Michaelis) encored, and Suppé's overture, "Pique Dame." Mr. Mount's gifted and very juvenile pupil, Miss Clara Asher, played Andante and Polonaise (Chopin), with much skill, and shows high promise for the future. Mr. Sternburg played in admirable style a polonaise for violin of his own. To-night, Mr. J. W. Phillips, an excellent and exceptionally gifted young organist, of Sheffield, will be the soloist. Miss A. Larkcom will be the vocalist, Mr. Lazarus the solo clarionet, and Mr. Fountain Meen the accompanist.

WESTERN MADRIGAL SOCIETY.

On Wednesday, 14th November, the following selection of music was sung under the direction of Dr. Bridge :—

Madrigal,	"I follow, lo ! the footing "	Morley.
"	"When all alone "	Converso.
"	"Have I found her "	Bateson.
"	"So gracious is thy sweet self "	Ferretti.
Anthem,	"Almighty God "	Ford.
Madrigal,	"Now ev'ry tree "	Weelkes.
Chorus,	"In these delightful pleasant groves "	Purcell.
Madrigal,	"All creatures now "	Bennet.
Madrigal,	"Hark ! how the cheerful birds "	Prendergast.
"	"Down in a valley "	Wilbye.
"	"Ye nightingales "	Lasso.
Anthem,	"O Lord, grant the King "	Child.
Madrigal,	"In going to my lonely bed "	Edwards.
"	"So saith my fair "	Marenzio.
"	{"Stay, Corydon "	Wilbye.
"	{"In pride of May "	Weelkes.

MR. J. B. BONAWITZ'S "HISTORICAL RECITALS."

The second Recital by Mr. J. B. Bonawitz was held at the Blüthner Rooms, Bayswater, on Wednesday evening, Nov. 7th, and proved quite as successful as the first, already reported at length. The scheme was again divided between deceased and living composers for the queen of instruments, if the modern pianoforte may be so termed. An old Latin exercise book laid down a law that "the whale, or as some say the herring, is king among fishes," but alas, the whale is no fish at all !

To return to Mr. Bonawitz. He won the greatest applause for the Sonata Appassionata, Haydn's Sonata, Chopin's Polonaise, Vogel's piece, and his own duet for two pianofortes, where Miss Cecilie Brousil rendered valuable assistance. The two "Lieder" of Mendelssohn were No. 1, from Book V in G major, and No. 5 from the same book, in A major. Beethoven's sonata was played with great vigour, the left hand powerful in the extreme. Mr. Bonawitz's scherzo is thought to be too weighty for its title, a left-handed compliment, perhaps, but a compliment nevertheless. Schubert's Marches (duet) were exceedingly effective. The next recital is on Nov. 21st. The list of numbers is subjoined, viz. : Toccata in D minor (Frohberger), (1637-1701) ; Canon in G minor (Thomas Ford), (1600- ....) ; Fugue in G minor (Bach), (1685-1750) ; Air and variations in D minor (Handel), (1685-1759) ; Sonata in E flat major (Haydn), (1732-1809) ; Sonata Appassionata (Beethoven), (1770-1827) ; Marches in G minor and C major (duet) (Schubert), (1797-1828) ; Nocturne, No. 4 (Field), (1782-1837) ; Two Songs without Words (Mendelssohn), (1809-1847) ; Novellette, Op. 21, No. 8 (Schumann), (1810-1856) ; Polonaise, in A flat major (Chopin), (1809 1849) ; Introduction and Scherzo (Bonawitz) ; Chant sans Paroles (Tschaikowsky) ; Nordische Tanze (Grieg) ; Humoreske (Bernhardt Vogel) ; Duet for two pianofortes (Bonawitz), and March from "Tannhäuser" (Wagner-Liszt).

CHELSEA.

The Right-Hon. Sir Charles Dilke, M.P., presided last night at a public meeting held at the school-room of the Markham-square Congregational Church, to promote the establishment of an orchestral society for the district. Sir Charles, in the course of his opening address, said the movement had his most hearty sympathy, although he was present without any peculiar fitness and appeared before them as an example of failure in music. He was a musical student for a great many years of his life, and rather a hard student, both at the pianoforte and at harmony. But he altogether failed to become a musician, and could only acknowledge himself a humble example of failure. At the same time, his experience led him to the conclusion that the results of the study of music were not comparable to the successes. Music was extremely valuable as a training to all those who took part in it, and he did not think people made a mistake in giving up a good deal of time to the acquisition of a good knowledge of music, even if such knowledge did not result in success from a popular point of view. He thought it needless to say much on the general sympathy of the English public for good music, for they all knew that the great appreciation of the art was recorded in many familiar and apt quotations. In conclusion Sir Charles expressed his hope that the project would be successful, and stated that he should have much pleasure in acceding to the request of the executive to become a vice-president of the society. A hearty vote of thanks was accorded to the right hon. baronet for his attendance.

CHELTENHAM.

The first concert for the season of Mr. J. A. Matthew's Choral and Orchestral Society took place on Oct. 6th, at the Assembly Rooms, before a fairly large audience. The programme was devoted to selections from the Handel oratorios, as performed at the Handel Festival at the Crystal Palace in June last, and it was an undertaking on Mr. Matthews's part in reproducing that which doubtless many of his audience heard so recently, if not to perfection, at any rate at the nearest point thereto. The vocalists on this occasion were Miss Julia Jones, soprano ; Mdme. Florence Winn, contralto ; Mr. Alfred Kenningham, tenor ; and Mr. Fredk. Bevan, bass ; assisted by a band and chorus, numbering in all some 150 performers. The chorus and band performed their share in the programme in a highly creditable manner, the chorus in one instance only being lacking in precision, in the chorus from "Joshua," "Glory to God," in which, however, the effect of the finale fully made up for the want of smartness at starting. The highest praise is due to Mr. J. A. Matthews, who conducted, for his efforts, and one is pleased to say that the fourteenth season of the society under his auspices has commenced in a most satisfactory manner with this the opening concert.

LIVERPOOL.

(From our own Correspondent.)

Nov. 13th.

Really there is nothing very stirring in any way in Liverpool, and certainly not in music, if I except the Promenade concerts started at the Bijou Opera House last week, under the conductorship of Mr. Karl Meyder. The concerts are given every evening, and on Saturdays a *matinée* takes place in addition to the evening performances. So far the audiences have been very good, as far as report goes, but before I can give any reliable information as to the band, the style of the performances, and the number and character of the audiences, a personal visit will be advisable, so that I will reserve further remarks till later on.

Mr. Hallé's second orchestral concert takes place this evening, the chief item being Beethoven's second symphony.

The National Eisteddfod of 1884 is to be held in Liverpool; and on Saturday, under very adverse circumstances as regards the weather, the Gorsedd (an ancient custom preceding and apparently giving the necessary sanction to the Eisteddfod itself), was held in Kensington Fields. A concert was given in the evening at Hope Hall, Madme. Edith Wynne being the principal vocalist.

To-morrow (Wednesday) evening, Mr. G. A. Audsley is to give the first of two musical lectures. The subject for to-morrow evening is Bach, his times and music. Mr. Audsley, who is a cultured and enthusiastic amateur, is to have the valuable assistance of Mr. H. A. Branscombe, who will give illustrations from the works of the old Leipsic contrapuntist.

Mr. Martin Schneider is continuing his organ recitals at Moseley Hill Church. The programme of last Saturday will be found in the proper column.

The *Musical and Dramatic World*, a musical paper lately published in Liverpool, and edited by a Liverpool amateur, has ceased to exist. For a local paper of its class it had a long existence.

Madme. Florence St. John has just completed a successful engagement at the Court Theatre, having appeared in two or three comic operas during the time.

All the Harvest festivals are now over, and so far as I can learn, there has not been a single one anywhere about here where the music has been particularly attractive in regard to novelty. A church festival of this kind gives plenty of opportunity and scope for new musical works, but advantage never seems to be taken of such a rare chance.

J. J. M.

BEDFORD.

Bedford is a musical town and has good Institutes. Several excellent schools flourish there; the advantage of æsthetical culture can never be overlooked, and ought not to be neglected when artists from London make considerable sacrifices with a view to promote the interests of art. At the "Working Men's Institute," Mr. Bond Andrews and Herr Polonaski have projected, for this autumn a series of three monthly classical concerts. The first was to take place last (Friday) night, when a fine sonata of Niels Gade for pianoforte and violin in D minor and major headed the scheme. The music deserves to be heard, and often, in London. Brahms, Liszt, Rubinstein, and Wagner were duly recognised. Mr. Bond Andrews and Herr Polonaski have an extensive *répertoire*, and they are always acting conjointly. The grand "Ascherberg" pianoforte used on these occasions is a splendid instrument and greatly increases the effect of a fine performance.

LEEDS.

The recital on the Town Hall organ on Saturday evening had special reference to the Luther Commemoration, and a large audience assembled to do justice to the memory of the great reformer. Luther's Hymns, "Ein Feste Burg" ("Rejoice to-day with one accord") and the well-known advent hymn, "Great God, what do I see and hear," were sung by the audience with much heartiness. Dr. Spark also played in masterly style some organ solos, including Schellenberg's Fantasia on "Ein Feste Burg," an air and chorus from the *Messiah*, and Dr. Spark's own "Carillon Piece in F major," including chimes in a Cathedral, Nunc Dimittis, Magnificat, and Distant Bells. The latter piece so delighted the audience that it had to be repeated. The last item in the programme was the organ solo, Reminiscences of the Opera, "Les Huguenots," Meyerbeer), including part of the overture, the choral or hymn tune," Ein Feste Burg," the carousal chorus, the cavatina, "Nobil Signor," and the stirring finale that accompanies the massacre of St. Bartholmew's Day, the whole ably played by Dr. Spark. The same programme was repeated on Tuesday afternoon. The Piper of Hamelin," music by V. E. Nesler, was performed for the first time in Leeds at the Grand Theatre, on Monday evening. The principal artists were Madame Blanche Cole, Miss Lucy Franklein, Miss Clara Leslie; Messrs. Jas. Sauvage, and Albert McGuckin. The opera was well received.

German opera under Herr Richter, will, it seems, be really a welcome feature of the musical arrangements in London for next spring.

BLACKBURN.

On Nov. 7th, a somewhat unusual service was held at St. Peter's Church, when an oratorio entitled "Philippi," composed by Dr. Gladstone, was rendered by an augmented choir, consisting of, in addition to the choir of the church, ladies and gentlemen of local musical standing in the town. It remains now only to state that the work was performed to the satisfaction of the congregation assembled. Dr. Gladstone conducted, and Mr. George Mellor, the organist of the church, presided at the organ. After short evensong, the vicar, the Rev. Mr. Hignett, introduced the oratorio, and gave a most succinct and practical analysis of the work, concluding with the words that if the matter was received in a proper light it would be more beneficial than any sermon he or any minister could preach to them. Dr. Gladstone remarked at the conclusion of the service, that the performance had given him great satisfaction, and particularised the choruses, "In that was manifested" and "Now unto God," the former as showing pathetic rendering and the latter as a well and firmly executed chorus, and has since by letter thanked both organist and choir for their able rendering of the work.

On Nov. 5th, the Blackburn Choral and Orchestral Union performed W. Sterndale Bennett's "May Queen" and Rossini's "Stabat Mater," in the Exchange Hall, before a large and appreciative audience. The principal vocalists were Miss Annie Marriott, Madme. Enriques, Mr. Redfern Hollins, and Mr. Iredson. Herr Karl Meyder was the leader of the band, which was chiefly composed of local musicians, Mr. T. S. Hayward accompanist, and Mr. George Mellor, conductor. The band and chorus, numbering upwards of 200 performers, went through their part of "May Queen," with the exception of one or two little hitches, very creditably. The chorus showed throughout a readiness of "attack," Mr. Mellor having them, as usual, well in hand, and they sang for the most part with precision and vigour. In Mr. Hollins' first song it was evident that he was suffering from hoarseness, but the following duet with Miss Marriott elicited deserved applause. Mr. Bridson was successful in the song "'Tis jolly to hunt," which, it need hardly be said, was well received. Madme. Enriques had little to do in this part of the programme, but what she did was done exceedingly well. The "Stabat Mater" formed the second part of the programme. For the fine rendering of "Cujus animam" Mr. Hollins was loudly applauded. A *furore* was created by the duet "Quis est homo," by Miss Marriott and Madme. Enriques. It was the great success of the evening. Mr. Bridson was also enthusiastically applauded for his "Pro peccatis." The recitative and chorus, "Eia, mater," was not, however, sung without accompaniment, as, according to the programme it should have been. Madme. Enriques's "Fac ut portem," and Miss Marriott's "Inflammatus," were sung in first-class style, and were duly appreciated by the audience. The last chorus was a trying ordeal for both band and chorus, but they proved themselves equal to it in every respect. Mr. Mellor as conductor has an aptitude for work of this kind; his energy is inspiring, and he has a most skilful co-worker in Mr. T. S. Hayward as accompanist. The Blackburn Choral and Orchestral Society more than justifies its claim to support by such a performance as that of Monday night.

MUSIC IN DUBLIN.

The Dublin Chamber Music Union inaugurated its ninth season on the 10th inst. with its customary concert at "The Antients." The hall was well filled with an eager and attentive audience, who at the conclusion of the entertainment went away quite satisfied with the fare which had been provided for them. Could they consistently have been otherwise, I ask, with such a programme as the following, and such veteran executants as Mons. A. Billet (piano), Herr Lauer (violin), and Herr Elsner (violoncello)?—

Trio in C, Op. 87 (first time), Pianoforte, Violin, and Violoncello	...	Brahms.
Allegro—Andante con moto—Scherzo, presto—Finale: Allegro giocoso.		
Variations in D, Op. 17, Pianoforte and Violoncello		Mendelssohn.
"Il Trillo del Diavolo," Violin, with Pianoforte accompaniment		Tartini.
Prelude and Fugue, A♭, Tarantella, Pianoforte alone		Bach.
Trio C minor, Op. 1, No. 3. Pianoforte, Violin, and Violoncello		Beethoven.
Menuetto, quasi Allegro—Finale: prestissimo.		

The opening trio (by Brahms) was new to a Dublin audience, this being the first time it has been performed here in public. At the hands of the distinguished artists named it received a most scholarly interpretation, and was very warmly applauded. The variations in D, Op. 17, for piano and 'cello (by Mendelssohn), were faultlessly given. To Herr Lauer's execution of the third item in the programme I must give unqualified praise. Mons. Billet got through the very difficult piano piece (by Bach) with his accustomed ease and gracefulness, and afforded each pleasure to his audience. The trio (by Beethoven) which brought the concert to a conclusion, was admirably played throughout. The next concert of the society is arranged for the 24th inst.

The St. Patrick Oratorio Society opens this season on the 16th inst., with "The Messiah."

T. J. R.

NEWCASTLE-ON-TYNE.

Our present musical season could not be better inaugurated than with the first of Mr. Charles Hallé's orchestral concerts, which took place in the Town Hall, on Nov. 12th, before an enthusiastic audience. There cannot be two opinions about the real service these concerts have done, and will do in the future, in strengthening the refined musical taste in our midst ; by the excellency of the band, the magnificent pianoforte playing of the eminent conductor, and the finished and artistic rendering of the pieces, they have been hitherto unsurpassed in their way by any musical entertainment in our city. We have had many excellent concerts, so far as choral singing, but the want of orchestral concerts of late, at which important works of great composers would be performed, has been much felt, and when Messrs. Alderson and Brentnall, the energetic promoters of the Hallé concerts, announced their new scheme last year, the music-loving public in Newcastle and its neighbourhood hastened to give the enterprising gentlemen such liberal support that they have apparently been able to make these orchestral concerts a permanent institution in Newcastle—a matter of congratulation to every lover of the musical art.

The following formed the programme of the first concert :—

Overture, " Euryanthe "	Weber.
Aria, " Nasce al Bosco " (" Ezio ")	Handel.
Serenade and Allegro Giojoso (for pianoforte and orchestra)	Mendelssohn.
Air, " Ah che Querti Aventurieri "	Mozart.
Symphony Pastorale, No. 6	Beethoven.
Rhapsodie Norwegienne, No. 3, in C	Svendsen.
Air, " A l ou mein holder Abenstern "	Wagner.
Pianoforte solo, " Menuetto Grazioso "and "Tamborin "	Gluck.
Orchestral Pieces { " Entr'acte " (" King Manfred ") { " Liebeslied "	Reinecke. Taubert.
Air " On bruit des loards Marteaux "	Gounod.
Overture, " Mireille "	"

The orchestra led by Herr Straus, played their parts not only with great spirit and power, but at the same time with a delicacy and due observance of light and shade. At the close of the splendid rendering of the "Pastoral" Symphony, the hall rang with applause from the delighted audience. Mr. Charles Hallé, who received quite an ovation when he first entered the hall to lead his band, played with his usual taste, first, Mendelssohn's Serenade and Allegro Glojoso (Op. 43), played by the composer for the first time in public in the spring of 1838, at Madme. Botgorcheck's concert in Leipsig ; and afterwards, the two pieces by Gluck. He was loudly encored, and as the audience would not take a refusal after his last solo, he gave as a substitute, Schubert's lovely Impromptu in A flat.

One of the novelties at this concert was the " Rhapsodie Norwegienne " (No. 3, in C), by the Norwegian composer, Johan S. Swensden (a scholar of Hauptmann and Reineeke, in Leipsig). This rhapsodie opens with a few fragmentary phrases, interrupted by the rude rusticity of some bare fifths (the latter a peculiarity belonging to the national Norwegian dances), before the composer introduces, as the motives, two characteristic "Spring dances," from Hallingdal ; the two reels are charmingly treated, constantly intermingling with each other, until a lovely andante, a simple, tender folk-song (in G minor) interrupts these joyous strains. The work, which concludes with a finale of a graceful and sprightly character, gives a good idea of the songs and dances of the descendants of the hardy Norsemen.

Mr. Santley, the vocalist, a great favourite here, created quite a furore by his splendid singing, and on being encored in Wagner's aria, he repeated a part of it.

Next week there is in store for us, Mendelssohn's oratorio, " St. Paul," which will be performed at Mr. Rea's first subscription concert, on Nov. 21st,

H. W.

DARTFORD.—Mr. Musgrove Tufnall (Medallist) Roy. Academy of Music, gave his first benefit concert on Wednesday, November 7th, at the Victoria Rooms. A large audience assembled, and thoroughly enjoyed an excellent programme of music, well performed by Mr. Tufnail and fellow students of the academy. A MS. trio, from " The Bride of Cambus " (W. G. Wood), was extremely well sung by Mdme. Wilson-Osman, Miss Rees, and Mr. Tufnail. Mr. Dyved Lewis, in a charming song, by Pinsuti, " Queen of the earth," gained great applause by his artistic singing. Mr. Tufnail was most successful in his songs, " Does my love know " (Ed, Hutton), and the celebrated " Torreador's song," from Bizet's " Carmen." Miss Rees and Miss Jones rendered efficient aid. Mr. Alfred Izard and Mr. Wiggins were able accompanists.

Says the Athenæum, Dr. C. Villiers Stanford's opera " Savonarola " is announced to be produced in January next at the Hamburg Opera, under the direction of Herr Sucher. The same composer's Serenade, written for last year's Birmingham Festival, is to be played in December and January at the Crystal Palace, Glasgow, and Edinburgh ; also at the Vienna Philharmonic concerts under Herr Richter ; at Berlin under Herr Joachim ; and at New York under Theodore Thomas,

LEAMINGTON.

Rev. E. Husband on " Musical Development."

A festival of choirs was recently held at the Parish Church. The choirs taking part were those of the Parish Church, Holy Trinity, and St. John's, Leamington ; St. Mary's and St. Nicholas', Warwick ; Whitnash, Milverton, and King's Middle School, Warwick ; together with the members of the Leamington and Warwick Musical Societies, the choirs numbering altogether about 220 voices. Mr. Frank Spinney presided at the organ with his usual ability. The choirs were led by cornets, which raised the effect considerably. " Praise the Lord, O my soul " (Psalm ciii. 1-4, 13), by F. Spinney, was the anthem, and was most expressively sung. Master Whymack, a member of the Parish Church choir, took the treble solo, " Yea, like as a father pitieth his own children," very nicely, and the anthem was concluded with the Doxology in unison, sung slowly, with beautiful effect. An able and appropriate sermon was preached by the Rev. E. Husband, " On Musical Development," from the text, " Let us go up unto perfection " (Heb. vi., 1). The Preacher said :—

These words enshrine a great principle of divine truth. They are but one of the many voices speaking from the Bible, telling us the method of God's dealing with the world. From out these words comes the solemn, stately music of Creation's processional hymn, marching ever onward along a scale of development, from lower to higher things, and from a state of imperfection to that great future of perfection, which our Poet Laureate calls " The Golden Year," when " all men's good " shall be " each man's rule." I think that if there is one truth before another manifestly plain in the world, it is this, that growth and development are the order of God's creations. Every created thing that is divine, seems engaged in a stately, solemn procession, moving on " unto perfection." As to the divine art of music, it is a long way to go back across the by-gone train of grey centuries, to the time before the Flood, when as we read in the 4th chapter of Genesis, " Jubal was the father of all such as handle the harp and the organ." It is beside my purpose to-night, even if I had the time, to enter into any argument as to what kind of musical instruments Jubal's " harp and organ " may have been. All I want to show to-night is, that whatever they may have been, they were doubtless very rough, and as we should term them, unmusical instruments. One of these beautiful melodies that Handel ever wrote he has set to the words which run thus :— " Oh ! had I Jubal's lyre, to sounds like his I would aspire." I love the music of that song, but I cannot say I agree to the words. I think that if Jubal's music could be reproduced in these educated days, we should judge it as hardly fit for anything but a Salvation Army band. But Jubal's music was not unbeauteous in his almost barbaric age. I have no doubt that his mother Adah said, how beautiful it was, it " struck her into amazement. O wonderful son, that can so astonish a mother ! " We live by comparisons and by the education of the times in which our lot is cast, and what would be but jarring, boisterous sounds of discord to us, were harmonies most sweet to an uneducated world before the days of the Deluge. They say that Palestine is the only land where there is no such thing as progress ; where everything is at a standstill ; no improvements, no growth with the spirit of the times ; and if you have listened, as I have done, to the chanting at one of the Greek services in the Church of the Holy Sepulchre at Jerusalem, it must indeed strike us at once how terrible and unmusical the so-called music of by-gone ages must have been. It would be impossible to find words to describe the horrible sounds which the people at the Church of the Holy Sepulchre dare to call by the divine name of music. I don't suppose for one moment that to our modern ears in these cultivated days, the music used in Solomon's Temple would be called beautiful. I know that in the second Book of the Chronicles we read of the trumpeters and singers, the cymbals and other instruments of music ; and I have not the least doubt but that the great congregation bowing before the altar were thrilled at what they felt to be the beauty and the dignity of the music. But could the old Temple choir be reproduced in our temple to-day, I think its chief effect would be to thin the congregation. It was grand music for Solomon's day, but the world has been developing in knowledge, and education, and beauty since then, and the little child, so to speak, has grown up to become the strong man. Art needs time for education, just like a child at school. Age brings cultivation. For example, America is, comparatively speaking, a newly-discovered country, and as yet she has produced no musical composer who can take rank as a " master " in the company of great composers. And why is this ? She is too young a nation in the civilized world to be able as yet to produce that which the development of age alone can bring. Now pass on for a moment to another stage in our argument. Pass on to the fourth century, when St. Ambrose, one of the great fathers of the Western Church, lived. You all know that St. Ambrose, in his day, was a musical light in the darkness. A species of choral music was introduced by St. Ambrose, and we are all familiar with the Ambrosian chant. And these Ambrosian modes of the fourth century developed (I think I may rightly say) into the Gregorian chant of the sixth century, I suppose an improvement which Gregory the Great made on the work of St. Ambrose. I can imagine how thankful the men of Gregory's or St. Ambrose's day must have been for these great developments in music. I think St. Ambrose or St. Gregory must have been to the men of those days what Handel and Beethoven are to us now. In those early days of the fourth or sixth century of the world, imperfect in its education, could not produce anything in music better than a Gregorian Tone. How is it that those early centuries have never produced a Handel, or a Mendelssohn; a Mozart, or a Beethoven? Simply because the world had not sufficiently advanced in its progress of development to make it possible to produce such as these. Had such as one of these appeared, he would have been living out of his time. He would not have been appreciated. He would have been beyond the men of his day, and would have been above their comprehension. But the crude simplicity of the Gregorian Tones were what the men of those days could appreciate. To them it was an advance in the scale of musical development, and they welcomed them with delight. I frankly confess that in these far off days I am no admirer of Gregorian music, much less of that modern custom in vogue with some of "Anglicanising" Gregorian chants, the melody being Gregorian, but the harmony, often in four parts, being Anglican, entirely antagonistic to the unison rendering of pure Gregorian music. And it is a mystery to me how musical persons can say they admire the crude tones of Gregorian music. Of course I can admire such melodious exceptions as the "Tonus Peregrinus," which you have sung this evening, especially when sung so well, and by such a body of fine voices as those to-night. But I am speaking of the rule, not the exception, and it always seems to me as if Gregorian music, as a whole, was—to use an illustration —as if I wished to substitute for the improved harp of our own age, beautiful in tone, in construction, and in compass, the rough and clumsy "harp," or *kinnor* of Jubal's day. But of the Gregorian Tones, especially to the unmusical, I admit their vitality, for they are cherished by many, even in this far off nineteenth century. But I am sure it is their antiquity that is the real secret that enlists sympathy for them, and their connection with the ancient Church which makes them attractive to a certain section of earnest Churchmen. I know the emotion. It comes across me whenever I stand gazing upon some romantic ruin, the scene of some great historic event of bygone days. And now the world was getting ripe for some of those great musicians whose work in the realm of art will last for all time. I only speak to-night of those who have left us, not of those who are still with us, and enriching the music with their music still. But I have mentioned names enough to show that in these later days a great development has taken place. So sublime are some of these composers' works that it seems at first hard to imagine that music could higher go. Is it possible that musical development is still going on—going on unto perfection? I noticed that, so far as I could ascertain, the late talented organist of St. Paul's Cathedral never published a musical setting to the Communion service. There are many services of his to Matins and Evensong, but not for the higher service of Holy Communion. I suppose it was because there was no demand for them. But you will see that his successor, the present gifted organist, never publishes a morning service without including the music for the office of Holy Communion. The development of time has brought the demand, and of course the demand has been met. And so we move on and on. And, to speak for a moment of this Church, you, by your beautiful service to-night, which you have kindly given me the opportunity of enjoying, are helping forward the progress of music. First you render this service for the glory of God, but, by it, you are also helping to extend the divine art and appreciation of music. To do this is to do God's will, and to extend His truth; for music often preaches a more powerful sermon than you hear from the pulpit; I have never yet heard a sermon, speaking for myself, that has risen so high in eloquence, or in heart-melting appeal, as Handel's "Messiah," or Bach's music of the "Passion." And you, by your beautiful service to-night, have taken your part in the endeavour to improve Church music, I have been briefly, and in a fragmentary way, endeavouring to-night to trace the solemn, onward march of music in the history of development. I have referred to a goal of perfection which, as I believe, lies before the Art of Music, towards which she is moving, and to which it is her hope to attain. Where is that goal of perfection; when will it be reached? With all the light that shines upon this world, with its deeds of harmonious kindness and relations love, still it is as yet an imperfect world, and we cannot hope to find the goal of perfection at present. I think for that perfection we must look up—along

> The world's great altar stairs,
>   That slope through darkness up to God—

up to that bright home in Heaven, where the voice is "as the voice of many waters," singing the "new song before the Throne," and where is heard "the voice of harpers harping with their harps."

Throughout the country, in America, and abroad in certain parts, the increase in the number of organ recitals is very striking from year to year; and the present season shows equal, if not greater activity in this same direction.

PRINCIPAL CONTENTS OF THIS NUMBER.

LONDON: SATURDAY, NOVEMBER 17, 1883.

A LUTHERAN TUNE.

THE separate publication of the favourite hymn with its traditional tune, "Ein' feste Burg ist unser Gott", at the time of the LUTHER commemoration was natural, but it might have been hoped that some pains would have been expended upon the securing of the most original form of the melody, if that were possible. MEYERBEER, who notably employed what has been called the "war cry of Protestantism", in his "Huguenots," Prof. ELLA says had met with about ten different versions in different parts of Germany; and he appears to have been unable to arrive at any historical decision as to the precedence of these differing copies of the tune, accepting merely that version he liked best and found to be most popular. When charged by a well-known critic with tampering with the original,

Meyerbeer, Prof. Ella tells, sent the several versions to the critic, aforesaid, asking him to say which was the original one, but the critic was unable to answer the knotty question. The rendering chosen by no less an authority than MENDELSSOHN, and accepted for use in his so-called "Reformation" Symphony, has the characteristic absence of certain passing notes, as in the initial strain. It is well, though, to bear in mind that the absence of connecting notes, and the presence of disjunct intervals in what might be thought to be the simpler and consequently truer version of a traditional tune, by no means point to a safe conclusion that such a version was the original one. The practice in plain-song just prior to LUTHER's day, and the use in the plain-chant he must have been familiar with, at least in his younger days, of numerous connecting notes partly employed to secure conjunct intervals, suggesting also, that melodic types, would rather induce the idea of the presence of what we in harmonic days call passing notes in any original melody LUTHER may have accepted. Two processes have been in action in this matter. When note against note harmony began to characterise the setting of chorals and hymn-tunes, melodies, as was the case to a large extent in the Roman Church—were denuded of what was thought to be superfluous melodic activity, as interfering with the more solid, newly acquired progressions in strong, simple harmony. When the strong contrapuntal impulse in Italy and Germany at the close of the seventeenth and beginning of the eighteenth century which culminated in the works of the greatest of contrapuntists J. S. BACH, came about, the fashion of harmonising upon contrapuntal lines was to a large extent recovered, and the growing taste for simpler and severer methods of harmonising congregational tunes asserted itself. So in the seventeenth Century more or stale or flowing parts became the fashion—especially in England, where the traditional connection between hymns and tunes had developed rigorously maintained—to an extent which led, as an abuse, ending in the constant use of out of place and needless ornamentation in Church Psalmody. This tendency led to some extent to the restoration of, and in some cases the re-adornment of, melodic figures as in use in the later and ornate days of plain song. The fluctuations which have taken place in these diverse directions make it almost impossible to decide as to original tune forms, save on the strength of a comparison of copies and the securing of reliable data in the possession of books of the earliest available printed dates. Dr. E. J. HOPKINS assigns the date of the tune of "Ein' feste Burg" to the year 1529. The date given by the painstaking musical editor should perhaps be a few years earlier. LUTHER first published in 1527 eight of his hymns; in 1527 he enlarged his collection to sixty-three; and in 1543 he had increased it to 125. The real origin of this, as of many other traditional tunes, may perhaps never be safely fixed. Although the odium theologicum reigned in its bitterest forms in LUTHER's day, music was to a large extent a beneficent common possession; and LUTHER himself was an ardent admirer of the great composers of the Roman Church of his own and preceding times. So

it may be the tune in question dates back into the days when Latin hymns with their accepted plain-song melodies prevailed. On the other hand, the determined independence of the Reformers even struck at the too general acceptance of melodies handed down through the Roman Church, and a strong impulse to the composition of a new school of specially composed Protestant music was given to the musicians in Germany, France, and England. And it may readily be conceived that so notable a hymn as "Ein' feste Burg," proved to be, would not only command an original tune, but that no melodies bearing Roman traditions and associations would have been found acceptable to the fiercely-in-earnest band of Reformers. It would be most unlikely that any tune of secular origin should ever have been associated with any of the Lutheran hymns, as was said to be the case in the first thirty or so of the metrical Psalms of CLEMENT MAROT, who, according to good authority, seized upon certain fashionable secular tunes for the purpose of helping to popularise his version of the Psalms. The German Reformers were of a sterner sort than CLEMENT MAROT. Dr. BURNEY and other authorities plainly assert that LUTHER wrote the hymn, set it to music, and sang it, as he entered Worms in 1521. It is not improbable, however, that the musician HENRY, of Göttingen, who rendered LUTHER much good service in arranging and composing music for his hymns and liturgical offices, had a hand in composing or adapting the famous tune now being considered, which BURNEY gives without the passing notes in the first strain and repetitions, just as it is employed by MENDELSSOHN in his "Reformation" Symphony, and, just indeed as it was printed in LUTHER's own time in copies still preserved. Another composer who might very probably be concerned in the formation of this tune, was JOHANN WALTHER, a man highly esteemed by LUTHER. It has been asserted positively that LUTHER composed the tune of "Ein fest Burg," one chief evidence for this assertion being that LUTHER left a copy in his own handwriting of the date 1530 when at Coburg. The fact of making a copy says little or nothing, however, and there are instances, numerous enough of compositions being assigned to prominent men, not the real composers, who have become identified with such pieces in some way or other. It is a pity for musical reasons that the various versions of the famous old tune were not collected and then printed together upon the occasion of the present commemoration.

E. H. TURPIN.

MUSIC AT CITY DINNERS.

THE LORD MAYOR OF LONDON's annual feast on the 9th November suggests a timely reference to civic banquets in general, on the musical, not the gastronomical, side of the question. It would be ungracious not to acknowledge the pleasure derivable from entertainments at the splendid halls of the Goldsmiths, the Fishmongers, and the Merchant Taylors. The City Companies always provide vocal music after their dinners, and eminent artists are often engaged to sing. That genial companion, THOMAS

FRANCIS, Vicar Choral of St. Paul's Cathedral, used to "lead" a goodly company at the old London Tavern, or rather to take the alto parts, whilst he directed as general Superintendent. At the City Companies' banquets, money is no object, so that vocalists of standing, like FRANCIS, and eminent members of Musical Societies, always found a footing and were welcomed like the rest of the gentlemen guests. FRANCIS would tolerate no liberties; he once stopped his choir, in full career, because a rude waiter crossed the path during the particular quartet. The example might be followed at St. James's Hall and the Crystal Palace, where, by the way, the edict to prohibit entrance during the performance has just been repealed.

The recent programmes of two City Companies, the CLOTHWORKERS and the SADDLERS, lie on the table. The first contains a short, but interesting account of the "Loving Cup" and its origin. For the after-dinner music: the "Grace" is an English version of the "Laudi Spirituali," A.D. 1545; a Part-song in F, with some bold harmonic progressions; the National Anthem follows. The miscellaneous music includes part-songs by KUCKEN, REICHHARDT, and Sir HENRY BISHOP; the last of these, the pretty sestet, "Stay, prythee, stay," from "The Miller and his "Men," last heard by the writer at old Covent Garden Theatre in April, 1835, with Mr. BRINDAL, a "walking gentleman" as Count Friburg, and Drinkwater Meadows—as Karl. The famous Round, "When "the wind blows" heralded BISHOP's fame over the continent. To return to our schemes: Miss ALICE FAIRMAN, deservedly a favourite contralto in the chamber, sang "The Minstrel Boy," and Molloy's "London Bridge." ALICE MARY SMITH's "Maying" duet, was sung by Mrs. WORRELL and Mr. PLATTER.

At the SADDLERS' dinner (on Oct. 23rd), may be noticed, out of the medley, Sir H. BISHOP's air, "Tell me, my heart" CHARLES HORN's pretty cavatina, "Thro' the wood," where three verses are written in the tonic, the dominant, and the relative minor, and PURDAY's old song (by request), "The "fine old English Gentleman." Miss ALICE FAIRMAN agreeably varied the scheme with an Italian air, "Il segreto," of DONIZETTI, and also sang an English piece by Mr. RANDEGGER.

These programmes might be much improved. Not one of the fine old glees or madrigals adorns the list. The modern "Part-Songs," good enough in their way, are crowding out the old sterling stuff. Who ever hears now-a-days, at public dinners, the madrigal, "When first I saw thy face," or that exquisite Italian one, "My pretty love was playing." JOHN BARNETT's Trio in G, "This magic-wove scarf" comes out occasionally, like a glowworm in July, to disappear for a season. "Catches," again, so clever and comical, are rarely heard now, such as "Mr. Speaker, though "tis late," "How Sophia," and the like. And here I am reminded of the great benefit that the body, as well as the mind, may derive from a performance of light orchestral music, as in the QUEEN's palaces, *during the repast.* This is done at St. James's Hall, where the band play overtures, waltzes, and pretty dance music in a gallery over the large dining-room.

I lately stood in the corridor, on the first "Popular"

Concert night, to hear a favourite overture of AUBER, to his opera, "Haydée" (1848), where a delicious nautical chorus in triple time is introduced as a second subject, and spiced with the saucy skip of a *diminished* fifth in descent, from G to C sharp, in the key of C major.
                                                                    A. M.

TIMELY ACTION.

THOUGH it may be true that "La vérité n'est pas toujours bonne à dire," there are certainly times when plain outspoken words must be said. Such an opportunity comes to hand in the statement that the "General Convention of the Protestant Episcopal "Church in America has completed its revision of "the Prayer Book; and that the new rubrics, so "revised, provide for a very large discretion on the "part of officiating ministers, in regard both to the "selection of alternative canticles, prayers, and "lessons, and to the abbreviation of the several "Services."

It was natural that this timely action should first take place away from these shores, but there are many signs that the time is at hand when the serious attention of all concerned must here be devoted to the same subject. At present, the prevailing hurry through the Service and Service music, is simply disgraceful; and the natural irreverence is intensified by the knowledge that such indecent haste is encouraged in order that more time may be secured for the generally out of place lecture-sermon. When shall we hear our Services, after being duly put in order and revised, rendered with becoming gravity and consequent earnestness? When shall we have our ostentatious and indecently prolonged sermons properly limited, both as regards the topics treated upon and time occupied in sermon delivery? When again, shall we have in public worship a full supply of food with time to digest it in, and a proper administering of medicine? because pulpit rhetoric should be infinitesimal in its doses; praise and prayer are spiritual food in their way, and preaching is ecclesiastical medicine; necessary at times but hurtful when of untimely use. When we have had the honesty and courage to set about these much called for reforms, then a better development of public worship will truly begin in earnest. Then there will be real hope of the full development of Christian art, and Church music will take her real place in our midst. Music as the purest of the arts, and above all as an ordained means of praise, stands in the scheme of Christian arts in a position corresponding with that occupied by Charity in the list of Christian virtues. Just as faith will be swallowed up in realisation, and hope be lost in enjoyment, and love will still remain, so also preaching will be lost when the Church shall reach her home, and ministerial offices done away in the gloriously completed work of redemption, and music will still live on in everlasting praise. Let us, therefore, strive to place Church music in its true high place even here on earth. And to this end and to the general strengthening of the Church, it is high time to revise, adorn, abbreviate where necessary, and in every way to improve our Church Service, forms, and acts of public worship.
                                                        E. H. TURPIN.

Organ News.

ST. MARGARET'S CHURCH, WESTMINSTER.

On the occasion of the opening of a fine new organ, Dr. Bridge's oratorio, "Mount Moriah," was performed on Wednesday evening, November 14th, with orchestral accompaniment, and a large body of voices. The work itself is now so well known that it will suffice to say that the whole was excellently rendered, the solo parts being sustained by the choristers of the Abbey, and Mr. Robert Hilton, and Mr. Edward Dalzell. Dr. Bridge himself presided at the organ, and after the Service played Handel's second organ concerto, also with orchestral accompaniment. This novelty appeared to attract much attention from the very large congregation assembled.

Messrs. Hill and Son were entrusted with the entire rebuilding and enlargement of the organ in the above-named Church. A fine new case of oak has also been fitted to it, in the style of the fifteenth century gothic, and of somewhat foreign treatment. It was designed by Mr. Arthur G. Hill, M.A., F.S.A. The large front, with sixteen-feet spotted metal pipes (some of which are embossed after the mediæval fashion), faces W. down the N. aisle, and the smaller front looks into the Choir through the easternmost arch. Subjoined is the specification :—

GREAT ORGAN. CC TO G.

1. Double Open Diap.	16 ft.		8. Twelfth		3 ft.
2. Open Diapason	8 ,,		9. Fifteenth		2 ,,
3. Open Diapason	8 ,,		10. Sesquialtera (3 ranks)		
4. Gamba	8 ,,		11. Mixture (2 ranks)		
5. Stopped Diapason	8 ,,		12. Posaune		8 ,,
6. Principal	4 ,,		13. Clarion		4 ,,
7. Harmonic Flute	4 ,,				

CHOIR ORGAN. CC TO G.

14. Dulciana	8 ft.		19. Flute		4 ,,
15. Gamba	8 ,,		20. Flautina		2 ,,
16. Gedact	8 ,,		21. Contra Fagotto		16 ,,
17. Stopped Diapason	8 ,,		22. Clarionet		8 ,,
18. Gemshorn	4 ,,				

SWELL ORGAN. CC TO G.

23. Bourdon	16 ft.		30. Sesquialtera (3 ranks)		ft.
24. Open Diapason	8 ,,		31. Double Trumpet		16 ,,
25. Salicional	8 ,,		32. Horn		8 ,,
26. Vox Angelica	8 ,,		33. Oboe		8 ,,
27. Rohr Flute	8 ,,		34. Clarion		4 ,,
28. Principal	4 ,,		35. Vox Humana		8 ,,
29. Fifteenth	2 ,,				

PEDAL ORGAN. CCC TO F.

36. Open Diapason	16 ft.		39. Quint		10 ft.
37. Bourdon	16 ,,		40. Trombone		16 ,,
38. Violoncello	8 ,,				

COUPLERS.

41. Great to Pedal.	44. Swell to Great.
42. Swell to Pedal.	45. Choir to Great.
43. Choir to Pedal.	46. Choir to Swell.

Seven combination pedals, Pneumatic action to Great organ.

OLDHAM.

An organ recital was given in the Fine Art Exhibition, on Thursday, November 8th, by Mr. C. T. Sutcliffe, F.C.O. The programme included :—

Postlude in F	Calkin.
Marche Romaine	Gounod.
Offertoire in A	Clarke.
Gavotte in B flat	Handel.
Marche on a Theme of Handel	Guilmant.
Prelude and Fugue in C minor	Bach.
Marche "Heroique"	Schubert.
Overture to Alexander's Feast	Handel.

SOUTHBOROUGH, TUNBRIDGE WELLS.

At the re-opening of the Parish Church, on Saturday, 10th inst., Mr. W. de M. Sergison, of St. Peter's, Eaton Square, performed the following programme upon the new organ (two manuals and pedal) by Bishop and Sons :—

Sonata No. 1, in G minor	Handel.
Air, "O rest in the Lord," and Sonata No. 6	Mendelssohn.
Cantilene Pastorale and "Marche Nuptiale "	Guilmant.
Toccata and Fugue in D minor	Bach.
Andante No. 2, in F sharp minor	Wesley.
"Evening Prayer "	Smart.
Offertoire No. 4	Wely.

WATERLOO ROAD, S.E.

An organ recital was given on Tuesday, November 13th, in the Church of St. John the Evangelist, by Mr. James Higgs, Mus.Bac. The following was the programme :—

Sonata No. 3	Mendelssohn.
Con moto Maestoso—Andante tranquillo.	
Andante from Symphony	Mozart.
Pastorale	Merkel.
Prelude and Fugue in C minor	Bach.
Allegro Moderato, from Quartet	Spohr.
Andante in F sharp minor	Wesley.
Concerto, No. 3	Handel.
Adagio—Allegro—Adagio—Allegro.	
Intermezzo	Reinecke.
March, "Efl "	Costa.

BILSTON.

The new organ, at the old Parish Church, has been built by Messrs. Nicholson and Lord, of Walsall. It contains thirty-one stops, and has three Manuals and Pedal. The instrument was opened by Mr. Sidney Dean, on October 21st, and a recital was given by Dr. A. H. Mann, on October 26th. The programme included :—

Fantasia	Stewart.
Andante in C	Bunnett.
Sonata, No. 6	Mendelssohn.
Concerto in D	Handel.
Sonata in D minor	Merkel.

READING.

An organ recital was given in the Town Hall, on Tuesday, October 30th, by Mr. J. C. B. Tirbutt, on the occasion of a banquet, given to the Marquis of Salisbury, K.G. The following was the programme :—

Grand Offertoire in D	Batiste.
Entr'act, " Rosamunde "	Schubert.
Wedding March	Mendelssohn.
Selection, " Der Freischütz "	Weber.
Entr'acte—Gavotte, " Mignon "	Thomas.
Fanfare	Lemmens.
Overture in F minor	Morandi.

BRECHIN, N.B.

The new organ in the City Road United Presbyterian Church, built by Mr. Wadsworth, of Manchester, was opened on November 2nd, by Mr. C. J. Smith. The Brechin Amateur Musical Society rendered the vocal music in excellent style. The programme included :—

" Cantique de Noël "	Adam.
" Austrian Hymn," with variations	Haydn.
" Improvisation "	
Gavotte	Pieracenni.
Adagio in F (Symphony No. 1, "Salaman ")	Haydn.
" March of the Crusaders "	Sibley.
Fugue	Hewlett.

MOSELEY HILL.

An organ recital was given in the Church of St. Matthew and St. James, Moseley Hill, on Saturday, October 20th, by Mr. Martin Schneider. The programme included :—

L'Heure de la Priere	Wely.
Fourth Organ Concerto	Handel.
Allegro moderato—Andante Maestoso—Adagio—Allegro.	
Barcarolle	Spohr.
Fugue in G minor	Bach.
Allegretto in A flat	Schneider.
Marche de la 1re Suite (Lachner)	Luz.

And on Saturday, November 10th :—

Wedding March	Mendelssohn.
Andantino, " Rosamunde "	Schubert.
Fifth Organ Concerto	Handel.
Larghetto—Allegro—Alla Siciliana—Presto.	
Die Sprache die Liebe	Thalberg.
Romance	Chauvet.
Fugue in G	Krebs.
Priere	Schneider.
March	Wely.

NORWICH.

An organ recital was given in the St. Andrew's Hall, by Dr. Bunnett, F.C.O., on Saturday, November 10th, the anniversary of Luther's birth. The following was the programme :—

Concert-Fantasia, on Luther's Choral, " Ein feste Burg ist unser Gott"	
Allegretto Pastorale in A	Jordan.
Canzonetta del Salvator Rosa	Last.
Selection from " The Redemption "	Gounod.
Organ Concerto in D	Handel.
Allegro—Andante un moto—Fuga.	
Air, " God shall wipe away all tears "	Sullivan.
Sonata in C	Mozart.
Larghetto in A, from Symphony in D	Beethoven.
Overture, " Les Huguenots"	Meyerbeer.

PRESTON.

On Saturday evening, Mr. Tomlinson (organist to the Corporation), gave a recital on the grand organ in the New Public Hall, The programme was as follows :—

Con moto in B flat	Smart.
Adagio, Minuetto, Presto (Symphony in C)	Mozart.
Andante from Sonata in D minor	Mailly.
Overture to "La Gazza Ladra"	Rossini.
Pizzicati, "Sylvia"	Delibes.
Fantasia on English Airs	MS.

The "Andante" (Mailly), was rendered in a very pleasing manner. The overture to "La Gazza Ladra," was received with loud applause. The "Pizzicati," and the "Fantasia on English Airs" were rendered with great spirit. The evening being wet, the attendance was not so good as usual.

BRISTOL.

An organ recital was given in the Colston Hall on Saturday, November 10th, by Mr. George Riseley. The following was the programme :—

March in F major	Guilmant.
Andante from 4th Symphony	Mendelssohn.
Fantasia in F minor	Mozart.
Allegro—Andante—Allegro.	
Andante in G major	Batiste.
Organ Sonata, No. 1, in F minor	Mendelssohn.
Air, with variations	Haydn.
Overture, "Les Huguenots"	Meyerbeer.

LEWISHAM HIGH ROAD CONGREGATIONAL CHURCH.

A large congregation attended at the above Church on Thursday last, on the occasion of the re-opening of the organ, after extensive alterations, by Messrs. Hill and Son, involving an outlay of some £300. The organ has three manuals and pedal. General satisfaction was expressed at the appearance and tone of the fine instrument, also at the good selection of music played by the organist, Mr. Byrom, consisting of Bach's "St. Ann's Fugue," overture in C (Mendelssohn); two andantes by Smart and Batiste, and an adagio and finale from a quartet by Spohr. Specially to be noticed was the admirable rendering of the fine fugue and overture (played from memory), The church is to be congratulated on having the valuable aid of so experienced and able an organist. The choir (under the direction of Mr. E. Miles), sang Hopkins' "Te Deum in G," Stainer's "Ye shall dwell in the land" (the effect was marred, however, by the sole being sung "tutti," contrary to the composer's directions), the first chorus, from the "Lobgesang," and Handel's "Hallelujah"; the two latter choruses were excellently rendered. Miss Jessie Griffin contributed "Hear, ye Israel," Costa's "I will extol Thee," and Handel's "O had I Jubal's lyre." The young lady's performance gave much pleasure, the last song, however, suiting her best.

The organ exhibited by Henry Jones and Sons, of Fulham Road, in the International Fisheries Exhibition, which has been much admired during the past season, has been sold to the Roman Catholic Cathedral, at Portsmouth. The same firm, it is stated, have received a commission from the Royal College of Music to erect a second organ in the Royal Albert Hall, for the use of the pupils.

Academical Intelligence.

ROYAL COLLEGE OF MUSIC.

A lecture on the "History and Construction of the Pianoforte" by Mr. A. J. Hipkins was delivered to the pupils of the Royal College of Music on Nov. 6th, in the west theatre of the Royal Albert Hall. The lecture was illustrated by large diagrams and by specimens of the clavichord, spinet, harpsichord, early square piano (1780), and short iron grand piano of the present day, contributed by Messrs. Broadwood, Mr. Herbert Bowman, Mr. Hughes, Mr. Dale, and Mr. Hipkins. It was full of interest and instruction, and was evidently enjoyed by the students. As the progressive forms of the instrument came under consideration, Mr. Hipkins illustrated his statements by performance on each. Mr. Hipkins is not only a master of his subject, but he knows how to fully engage his listeners' attention in a history which is of rare interest, and contains not a little of the romance of the art.

Foreign Musical Intelligence.

Mr. A. Goring Thomas's opera "Esmeralda" was produced in Cologne on Wednesday, last, and met with an enthusiastic reception, the composer being called forward twice at the end of each act. The work was admirably performed and mounted. Mr. Thomas cordially thanked the conductor, Herr Muehldorfer, the singers and players, for their excellent rendering.

There is to be a grand concert on the 18th at Lille, in honour of Delibes.

Organ recitals are to be given shortly in Brussels by MM. Mailly and Wiegand.

Marschner's "The Templar and the Jewess" has been proposed for revival at Vienna.

An excellent orchestral concert was given at Basle on Nov. 4th, including music by Mendelssohn, Wagner, Volkmann, &c.

M. Franz Servaise has completed the score of his dramatic work "L'Apollonide." Presently it will be given at a Brussels concert.

Tito Ricordi, the well-known Italian music-publisher, was 73 years of age on the 29th ult.

At a recent concert given by the Liederkranz, Heidelberg, the principal item in the programme was Wagner's biblical scene, "Das Liebesmahl der Apostel."

M. Jacques Léopold Heugel, the able and learned editor of Le Ménestrel, died, much regretted by a large circle of friends, on Nov. 12th, at the age of 68.

The Choral Society, Auckland, New Zealand, recently gave a performance of Schumann's "Paradies und Peri." For their next concert they announce Haydn's "Creation."

A symphonic poem by Steinbach ("The Birth of Venus") and a so-called "Gothic Symphony" by B. Godard, is said to have been given at Mainz, under Dr. von Bulow's direction.

The Russian author, Ivan Tourgeneff, who died in the house of Mdme. Viardot, has left all his property to that lady by the following will :—"I make Mdme. Pauline Viardot my universal legatee.—IVAN TOURGENEFF."

Le Ménestrel states that Herr Pollini has offered Anton Rubinstein the sum of 500,000 marks (£25,000) for a tour of one hundred concerts in America, and adds that the popular pianist has not yet given his decision.

The Parisian organist Arthur James Leavy, for some time of the church of Saint Germain-en-Laye, died on Oct. 31st, aged 38. He was a pupil of Clapisson and composed some effective Church and organ music.

The revival of Johann Adolf Hasse's one-act opera "Hercules am Scheidewege" at Dresden is a curious proposal not without interest, the work finding favour a hundred and twenty years ago.

Lately "Carmen" has been revived at the Opéra Comique, Paris. The part of the heroine has been pronounced as one of the most remarkable impersonations of Mdme. Galli-Marié.

The popular Théâtre du Château d'Eau, Paris, opened recently for the season, under the direction of M. de Lagrené. Mermet's opera "Roland à Roncevaux," first produced at Paris in 1864, was revived upon this occasion.

The death of the able Belgian composer, François-Marie Demol, occurred at Ostend, on Nov. 3rd. Demol was born at Brussels, on March 3rd, 1844, and was under 40 therefore. His opera, "Le Chanteur de Médine," was successfully brought out two years and a half ago. He was a good organist, able conductor, and skilful all-round musician.

The 4th of Nov. being the anniversary of the death of Mendelssohn, a performance of much interest was given in the theatre, Leipzig, consisting of a selection of the works of the composer, and including, the "Son and Stranger," the "First Walpurgis Night," placed on the stage as a dramatic work, and the splendid finale to "Loreley."

Sir G. A. Macfarren's Oratorio, "King David," had its first hearing in London last night, Nov. 16th, under the auspices of the Sacred Harmonic Society. Sir A. S. Sullivan conducted upon this occasion. A notice will be given next week.

Correspondence.

THE MEMORIAL TO SIR JOHN GOSS.

A SUGGESTION.

TO THE EDITOR OF THE "MUSICAL STANDARD."

SIR,—It is gratifying to find so much zeal and kindly feeling existing amongst professional musicians, who are now anxious to do honour to the memory of the late organist of St. Paul's Cathedral.

It appears to be the custom in these days to reserve or preserve all our kindly feelings and our homage until the subject of our admiration is buried and out of sight—where they cease to be moved by what the world might say or do.

Sir John Goss had, no doubt, during life, many genial friends and admirers, but I very much question that any one ever thought of speaking or writing so glowingly to his honour as they do now, now that he is removed from us. How gratified the dear old man would have felt in his declining years, how the colour would have risen to his pallid cheeks with pleasurable emotion, could he have imagined that his efforts would or could have been so much appreciated.

I should be sorry to say anything at all calculated to damp the ardour or discourage the efforts of those who are wishful to contribute to the proposed memorial. Yet, I do consider that our kindly feelings and our homage should be given unreservedly to those who distinguish themselves and yet are spared to us, so that they may see, hear, and feel the full force of the hearty approval in which they are held.

The authorities of St. Paul's—indeed, all our cathedrals and clergy—should combine (unsolicited) to erect a memorial to the memory of one who served them so faithfully for thirty-four years. Sir John Goss (like all other Church composers) was not enriched by dedicating his talents as a composer to its services. No; but the Church has been greatly enriched by his efforts—therefore, it is only right and seemly that the Church who have been so faithfully served should, to show to posterity their gratitude and appreciation, erect, without delay, a monument worthy of the man we venerate.

I am, yours truly,
THOS. HOPKINSON.
4, Prince-street, Hull.
Nov. 12th, 1883.

MENDELSSOHN AND MOSCHELES.

TO THE EDITOR OF THE "MUSICAL STANDARD."

SIR,—I have been much interested in reading "An Old Reporter's Reminiscences" in the Musical Standard and the story of "Mendelssohn keeping the Band waiting."

When a student at the Leipzig Conservatorium in 1857, I well recollect spending one very delightful evening at the house of my dear old master Moscheles, in the Dresdener Strasse, and meeting there, with others, the celebrated violinist Laub, who played during the evening with Moscheles magnificently several of Beethoven's pianoforte and violin sonatas, I, having the honour to act, by request, as "turnover."

Moscheles had in his possession many remarkable musical curiosities, and showed us several funny scrap-books, MSS. letters of Mendelssohn and others, and among other anecdotes told, I remember Moscheles relating—to illustrate the amiable disposition of Mendelssohn—how they were once together in Cramer's music-shop in Regent Street, when Mendelssohn became so interested in something as to forget the rehearsal which he had to direct until reminded of the time by Moscheles. Their arrival was late, and a member of the band pertly enquired, "if the Conductor's watch went backwards." Mendelssohn was hurt, and the Directors, according to custom, wished to dismiss the offending musician, but Mendelssohn would not hear of or consent to this, and at his earnest request the indiscretion was passed over and the offender retained his position in the orchestra.

In haste, yours &c.,
EDWARD LAWRANCE.
2, Courtland Terrace, Merthyr-Tydfil.
Nov. 8th, 1883.

The South London Musical Club gave an enjoyable private musical evening on Nov. 13th, under the direction of Mr. Charles Stevens.

The Birmingham Post hears from a trustworthy source that M. Gounod has made great progress with his oratorio "Mors et Vita," which he is writing for the next Birmingham Festival. A recent visitor, who has had the privilege of hearing some portions of the work, is of opinion that it will be placed at the head of M. Gounod's compositions, and the composer himself is convinced that it will take rank in advance even of "The Redemption." The work will doubtless be awaited with enthusiastic expectation.

Passing Events.

The second of a series of smoking concerts at the Horns, Kennington, will be given under the direction of Mr. G. F. Grover, on the 21st.

"The Reminiscences of an Old Reporter" will be resumed next week. The "Musical Union" will probably be the subject of the article.

It will be seen in our advertisement columns that Mr. Walter Parratt is to give an organ recital at the City Temple on the 22nd inst. Admission free.

Mr. A. Tamplin has been lecturing at the May Street Schools, West Kensington, on the "History, Construction, and Technicalities of the Pianoforte."

At the next members' meeting of the Central Music Studio, Herbert Street, N., on Nov. 22nd, the Principal (Mr. J. Bailey) will give a recital, "Stephen Heller: his Life and Works." Admission free by ticket, which may be had upon application to the Secretary.

Messrs. Sims Reeves and Santley have again appeared at the Covent Garden Promenade Concerts. Haydn's Symphony in B flat, No. 6, and Beethoven's "Fidelio" Overture were included in the classical selection the other week.

The Liverpool Cathedral Choir, assisted by voices from the principal Church choirs of that city, will give a rendering of Spohr's oratorio, "The Last Judgment," at a special Service to be held in the Cathedral on the evening of the first Thursday in Advent, the 6th of December.

It is stated that a contract has been entered into between Mr. Ernest Gye and Herr Angelo Neumann, by which a series of twenty representations of German opera will be given at Covent Garden next spring. Mesdames Albani and Lucca will appear, and the cast will comprise the best German talent available.

It is announced that Mr. F. Pitman has considerably extended his premises by the addition of No. 21, Paternoster Row, which has been specially fitted up for the better accommodation of professional and retail customers; also by the addition of No. 4½ Ivy Lane, to be used as a stock room.

It is announced that the Boston (U.S.) Symphony Orchestra, under the direction of Mr. George Henschel, commenced its present series of concerts on the 13th ult. Rubinstein's "Ocean" Symphony was the chief item in the programme. Miss Hope Glenn was the vocalist, and made a most favourable impression.

There is something in the protest, endorsed by letters in the Evening Standard and Church Bells, against disturbing tunes firmly associated with given hymns. In France and elsewhere within the pale of the Roman Church, the people find certain tunes touchingly engraved upon their hearts by, one may say, centuries of undisturbed and endeared associations.

The announcement that the Dean and Chapter of Bristol have decided to discontinue the elaborate nave Services in their Cathedral, as the collections do not cover the expenses, gives rise to the natural question, Why do not our rich Cathedral bodies do more for the people without collections? There can be no excuse for cathedral meanness in England, surely.

Mr. W. C. Greaves, 6, Dyer's Buildings, Holborn, will be grateful for votes for Charles Alfred Buddock, for the December election at the Commercial Traveller's Schools, Pinner. The father of the child was an obliging non-professional organist, and composer of several hymn tunes, etc. He died in India a year ago, leaving a widow and six children unprovided for. The case is one deserving kind and prompt support.

The Blackheath chamber concerts given by Mr. Alfred Burnett and Mr. Ridley Prentice will consist of four subscription concerts at the Alexandra Hall, Blackheath, on the same model as before, each programme to include three concerted works. The concerts will take place on Tuesday evenings :—Nov. 20th and Dec. 4th, 1883; Feb. 12th and March 4th, 1884. The artists engaged are of the first rank, and good music is promised.

A new Society has been formed, the "Brixton Philharmonic Society." The post of conductor will be occupied by Mr. Frederick Walker, and Mr. Alfred Izard will be the accompanist. This Society has a chorus of 100 voices, and includes many of the members of the Brixton Choral Society now out of harness through the much regretted illness of Mr. W. Lemare.

Under the auspices of the Lewisham Bicycle Club, a concert was given at Alexandra Hall, Blackheath, on Nov. 14th. The vocalists were: Miss Grace Woodward, Miss Margaret Hoare, R.A.M., Miss Beeman Hughes, Mr. John Henry, Mr. Arthur Thomas, and Mr. R. E. Miles; violin, Miss Marie Schumann; pianoforte, Miss Marian Pope, R.A.M., Miss Robinson, Mr. Hy. R. A. Robinson, accompanist, Mr. Hy. R. A. Robinson.

The Festival of the London Church Choir Association took place in St. Paul's Cathedral on the 8th instant. Mr. C. E. Miller's new Evening Service (Magnificat and Nunc Dimittis, in D) and Dr. Stainer's new Anthem, "And all the people saw the thunderings," both written for the festival, were sung in their respective places, and after the sermon the "Hallelujah" Chorus was given. Mr. Bird of Kensington Parish Church was the organist, and Mr. J. Murray was the conductor as usual.

The Querist.

QUERY.

ORGAN DUETS.—Can you or any of your readers kindly inform me of the names of some good pianoforte and harmonium, or American organ duets; also the names of publishers, if convenient.—J. H. R.

Service Lists.

TWENTY-SIXTH SUNDAY AFTER TRINITY.

NOVEMBER 18th.

London.

ST. PAUL'S CATHEDRAL. — Morn.: Service, Te Deum, Hopkins in A; Benedictus, Selby in A; Introit, From the rising of the sun, No. 531 (Ouseley); Holy Communion, Thorne in E flat. Even.: Service, Magnificat and Nunc Dimittis, Prout in D; Anthem, And all the people saw the thunderings and the lightnings (Stainer).

TEMPLE CHURCH.—Morn.: Service, Te Deum Laudamus and Jubilate Deo, Smart in F; Apostles' Creed, Harmonised Monotone; Anthem, I was glad (Purcell). Even.: Service, Magnificat and Nunc Dimittis, Smart in F; Apostles' Creed, Harmonized Monotone; Anthem, O how amiable (Greene).

LINCOLN'S INN CHAPEL.—Morn.: Service, Boyce in A; Kyrie (Steggall); Anthem, Judge me, O God (Mendelssohn). Even.: Service, Arnold in A; Anthem, Ye people, rend your hearts (Mendelssohn).

ALL SAINTS, MARGARET STREET.—Morn.: Service, Te Deum, Elliot in F; Benedictus, Monk in F; Holy Communion, Guilmant in E flat; Offertory, Anthem, Judge me, O God (Mendelssohn). Even.: Service, Stainer in B flat; Anthem, All they that trust in Thee, O Lord (Hiller).

HOLY TRINITY, GRAY'S INN ROAD. — Morn.: Service, Te Deum (Jackson); Jubilate, Chanted; Kyrie (Goss); Nicene Creed (Percival); Offertory Sentences (Grainger). Even.: Service, Magnificat and Nunc Dimittis, Chanted; Anthem, Solo, His salvation is nigh them (Bennett); Chorus, The Lord is loving unto every man (Garrett).

HOLY TRINITY, TULSE HILL. — Morn.: Service, Chants. Even.: Service, Cantate and Deus Misereatour, Attwood in D; Anthem, O be joyful in God (Monk).

ST. JAMES'S PRIVATE EPISCOPAL CHAPEL, SOUTHWARK. —Morn.: Service, Introit, Blessed be he that cometh (Neukomm); Communion Service, Farmer in B flat. Even.: Service, Martin in B flat; Anthem, O where shall wisdom (Boyce).

ST. MARGARET PATTENS, ROOD LANE, FENCHURCH STREET.—Morn.: Service, Te Deum and Benedictus, Smart in F; Communion Service, Offertory Anthem, Come unto

him (Handel); Kyrie, Credo, Sanctus, Benedictus, Agnus Dei, and Gloria, Weber in E flat. Even.: Service, Magnificat and Nunc Dimittis, Tankerman in F; Anthem, As pants the hart (Spohr).

STS MARY BOLTONS, WEST BROMPTON, S.W.—Morn.: Service, Te Deum, and Benedictus, Chants; Holy Communion, Kyrie, Credo, Sanctus, and Gloria in excelsis, Smart in F; Benedictus, and Agnus Dei (Redhead); Offertory (Barnby). Even.: Service, Magnificat and Nunc Dimittis, Stainer's 3rd Series of Tones; Anthem, Sing to the Lord (Smart).

ST. MAGNUS, LONDON BRIDGE.—Morn.: Service, Opening Anthem, To the Lord our God (Calkin); Te Deum and Jubilate, Attwood in F; Kyrie (Wesley). Even.: Service, Magnificat and Nunc Dimittis, Attwood in F; Anthem, Praise the Lord (Goss).

ST. PAUL'S, AVENUE ROAD, SOUTH HAMPSTEAD.—Morn.: Service, Te Deum, Boyce in A; Benedictus (Goss); Kyrie, Stainer in E flat; Offertory (Stainer); Credo, Sanctus, and Gloria in excelsis, Stainer in E flat. Even.: Service, Magnificat and Nunc Dimittis, Calkin in B flat; Anthem, Blessed are they (Tours).

ST. PAUL'S, BOW COMMON, E.—Morn.: Service, Te Deum and Benedictus, Chants; Holy Communion, Kyrie, Credo, Offertory, Sanctus, Benedictus and Gloria in excelsis, Garrett in D; Agnus Dei (Monk). Even.: Service, Magnificat and Nunc Dimittis, Barnby in E flat; Anthem, He in tears that soweth, and Praise ye the Lord (Hiller).

ST. PETER'S, VERE STREET, W.—Even.: Service, Magnificat and Nunc Dimittis, Gadsby in C; Anthem, O love the Lord (Sullivan).

ST. AUGUSTINE AND ST. FAITH, WATLING STREET.—Morn.: Service, Calkin in B flat; Introit, Behold, O God (South); Communion Service, Hoyte in D. Even.: Service, Walmisley in D minor; Anthem, Whoso dwelleth (Martin).

ST. SAVIOUR'S, HOXTON. — Morn.: Service, Te Deum, Hopkins in G; Holy Communion; Kyrie, Credo, Sursum Corda, Sanctus, and Gloria in excelsis, Armes in A. Even.: Service, Magnificat and Nunc Dimittis, Parry in D; Anthem, If ye love me (Heap).

ST. SEPULCHRE'S, HOLBORN. — Morn.: Service, Te Deum, and Jubilate, Boyce in A; Kyrie and Credo, Agutter in B flat; Anthem, Comfort the soul (Crotch). Even.: Service, Magnificat and Nunc Dimittis, Porter in D; Anthem, We will rejoice (Croft).

Country.

ST. ASAPH CATHEDRAL. — Morn.: Service, Clark in G; Anthem, Come unto me (Couldrey). Even.: Service, The Litany; Anthem, O clap your hands (Trimnell).

ASHBURNE CHURCH, DERBYSHIRE. — Morn.: Service, Field in D. Kyrie, Credo and Gloria, Garrett in D. Even. Service, Garrett in E flat (Cantate); Anthem, As pants the hart (Spohr).

BEDDINGTON CHURCH, SURREY.—Morn.: Service, Te Deum, Boyce in A; Benedictus, Barry in F; Communion Service (Marbeck). Even.: Service, Bunnett in F; Anthem, Sing ye praises, and He counteth all your sorrows (Mendelssohn).

BIRMINGHAM (S. ALBAN THE MARTYR).—Morn.: Service, Te Deum, and Benedictus, Dykes in F; Holy Communion, Kyrie, Credo, Sanctus and Gloria, Dykes in F; Agnus Dei and Benedictus (Redman). Evensong: Magnificat and Nunc Dimittis, Barnby in D.

BIRMINGHAM (ST. CYPRIAN'S, HAY MILLS).—Morn.: Service, Nares in C; Anthem, Hear my prayer (Kent). Even.: Service, Ebdon in C; Anthem, O clap your hands (Stainer).

BIRMINGHAM (ST. MICHAEL'S, HAWORTH).—Morn.: Service, Te Deum and Benedictus; Communion (Tuckerman). Even.: Service, Magnificat and Nunc Dimittis; Anthem, The Lord hath done great things (Smart).

BIRMINGHAM (S. PHILIP'S CHURCH). — Morn.: Service, Chipp in A; Holy Communion, Barnby in E. Evensong Services, Barnby in E; Anthem, Awake, Awake (Stainer).

BELFAST (ST. GEORGE'S). — Morn.: Service, Te Deum, and Jubilate, Woodward in E flat; Apostles' Creed, Harmonised Monotone; Litany (Helmore); Offertory (Barnby). Even.: Service, Magnificat and Nunc Dimittis, Barnby in E; Apostles' Creed, Harmonized Monotone; Anthem, I will magnify Thee, and O God, my king (Calkin).

BRISTOL CATHEDRAL. — Morn.: Service, Smart in F. Even.: Service, Smart in F; Anthem, How lovely (Brahms).

CHESTER (ST. MARY'S CHURCH).—Morn.: Service, Boyce in C; Communion, Nares in F. Even.: Service, Tearne in A; Anthem, In the beginning was the word (Thorne).

CANTERBURY CATHEDRAL.—Morn.: Service, Smart in F; Anthem, O tarry thou the Lord's leisure (Jarratt); Communion, Smart in F. Even.: Service, Smart in F; Anthem, I have set God (Blake).

CARLISLE CATHEDRAL.—Morn.: Service, Walmisley in F; Introit, Remember God (Verrinder); Kyrie, Garrett in D; Nicene Creed, Goss in D. Even.: Service, Parry in D; Anthem, Sing we merrily (Mozart).

DONCASTER (PARISH CHURCH).—Morn.: Service, Boyce in C; Introit, O Lord my God (Wesley). Even.: Service, Stainer in E flat; Anthem, The Wilderness (Goss).

DUBLIN, ST. PATRICK'S (NATIONAL) CATHEDRAL.—Morn.: Service, Te Deum and Jubilate, Tours in F; Holy Communion, Kyrie, Creed and Sanctus, Tours in F; Anthem, I am well pleased (Stevenson). Even.: Service, Magnificat and Nunc Dimittis, Calwick in A; Anthem, Not unto us (Robinson), and O where shall wisdom (Boyce).

EDINBURGH (ST. JOHN'S).—Aft.: Service, Anthem, Praise the Lord (Goss). Even.: Service, Anthem, Great is the Lord (Hayes).

ELY CATHEDRAL.—Morn.: Service, Hopkins in F; Kyrie, Hopkins in F; Credo, Stainer in G; Gloria, Cambridge in C; Anthem, Christ being raised (Elvey). Even.: Service, Hopkins in F; Anthem, O clap your hands (Stainer).

LLANDAFF CATHEDRAL.—Morn.: Service, Te Deum and Jubilate, Smart in G; Introit, Jesus said to His disciples (Stainer); Holy Communion, Smart in G; Offertory Sentences (Stainer). Even.: Service, The Litany; Anthem, Sing praises unto the Lord (Gounod).

LEEDS PARISH CHURCH.—Morn.: Service, Smart in F; Anthem, And every creature (Spohr); Introit, Kyrie and Creed, Smart in F. Even.: Service, Walmisley in D minor; Anthem, Glory, honour (Mozart).

LICHFIELD CATHEDRAL. — Morn.: Service, Dykes in Communion Service, Rogers in D; Anthem, Jesu, word of God (Mozart). Even.: Service, Dykes in F; Anthem, The wilderness (Goss).

LINLITHGOW ABBEY, N.B. — Morn.: Service, Anthem, Sing a song of praise (Stainer). Even.: Service, Anthem, I will lift up mine eyes (Barnby).

LIVERPOOL CATHEDRAL. — Aft.: Service, Magnificat and Nunc Dimittis, Burstall in D; Anthem, O that men would praise the Lord (Bartholomew).

MANCHESTER CATHEDRAL. — Morn.: Service, Hopkins in F; Anthem, Why rage (Mendelssohn). Aft.: Service, Hopkins in F; Anthem, Blessed be Thou, Lord, God of Israel (Kent).

MANCHESTER (ST. BENEDICT'S).—Morn.: Service, Kyrie, Credo, Sanctus, and Gloria in excelsis, Stainer in A; Benedictus, and Agnus Dei, Woodward in E flat. Even.: Service, Magnificat and Nunc Dimittis, Bunnett in F.

MANCHESTER (ST. JOHN BAPTIST, HULME).—Morn.: Service, Te Deum and Benedictus "Gregorian"; Kyrie, Credo, Sanctus, Benedictus, Agnus Dei and Gloria in excelsis, Osborne in E flat. Even.: Service, Magnificat and Nunc Dimittis, Simper in F.

MUSSELBURGH (LORETTO SCHOOL).—Morn.: Service, Introit, O praise the Lord (Goss); Service, Smart in F; Anthem, Plead Thou my cause (Mozart). Even.: Service, Anthem, Lord we pray Thee; and Turn Thee unto us, "1st Mass" (Mozart).

ROCHESTER CATHEDRAL. — Morn.: Service, Elvey in A; Anthem, O Lord, my God (Milan). Even.: Service, Elvey in A; Anthem, God, the all terrible "Hymn for Peace."

SALISBURY CATHEDRAL.—Morn.: Service, Calkin in B flat; Offertory (Barnby). Aft.: Service, Calkin in B flat; Anthem, Praise the Lord (Mozart).

SHERBORNE ABBEY.—Morn.: Service, Chants; Kyrie, Goss in G; Offertories (Barnby). Even.: Service, Anthem, Sing and rejoice (Barnby).

SOUTHAMPTON (ST. MARY'S CHURCH).—Morn.: Service, Te Deum and Benedictus, Woodward in D; Holy Communion, Introit, They that put their trust (Macfarren); Service, Monk in C; Offertory (Barnby); Paternoster (Field). Even.: Service, Magnificat and Nunc Dimittis, Field in D; Apostles' Creed, Harmonized Monotone.

WELLS CATHEDRAL.—Morn.: Service, Russell in A; Introit, Drop down, ye heavens (Macfarren); Kyrie, King in A. Even.: Service, Elvey in A; Anthem, Blessed be Thou (Kent).

WINCHESTER CATHEDRAL. — Morn.: Service, Skelton in D; Creed; Cooper in F. Even.: Service, Attwood in C; Anthem, O praise the Lord of heaven (Goss).

NEWSPAPERS sent should have *distinct marks* opposite to the matter to which attention is required.

₊ *Post-cards must be sent to the Editor, 6, Argyle Square, W.C., by Wednesday. Lists are frequently assisted in consequence of not being received in time.*

THE MUSICAL STANDARD is published every Saturday, price 3d., by post, 3½d.; and may be had of any bookseller or newsagent by ordering its regular supply.

SUBSCRIPTION.—The Musical Standard is posted to subscribers at 15s. a year; half a year, 7s. 6d., payable in advance. The rate is the same to France, Belgium, Germany, Italy, United States, and Canada.

Post Office Orders to be made payable to the Publisher, William Reeves, 185, Fleet Street, London, or to the West-end Agents, Messrs. Weekes & Co., 14, Hanover Street, Regent Street, W.

ADVERTISEMENTS.—The charge for ordinary advertisements in The Musical Standard is 2s. 6d. for three lines or less; and 6d. for each line (10 words) in addition. "Organist wanted," 3s. 6d. for 3 lines or less. A reduction is made for a series.

FRONT PAGE.—Concert and auction advertisements, &c., are inserted in the front page of The Musical Standard, and charged one-third in addition to the ordinary rates. Other advertisements will be inserted on the front page, or in the leader page, if desired, at the same terms.

The MUSICAL STANDARD

A NEWSPAPER FOR MUSICIANS PROFESSIONAL AND AMATEUR

No. 1,008. VOL. XXV: FOURTH SERIES.   SATURDAY, NOVEMBER 24, 1883.   WEEKLY: PRICE 3D.

THE VOICE
MUSICALLY AND MEDICALLY CONSIDERED.
BY
ARMAND SEMPLE, B.A., M.B., Cantab., M.R.C.P., Lond.

Physician to the Royal Society of Musicians.

(*Continued from page 286.*)

ARTICULATION, OR "STROKE" OF THE GLOTTIS.

Preparation having been made, as already indicated, the breath should be drawn in slowly, and the sound emitted with a neat and firm articulation or "stroke" of the glottis upon the broad Italian A. (I shall have more to say concerning the incessant use of this vowel in succeeding pages.) If this movement is performed properly, a sound and bright tone will be produced. The note should not be slurred up to or felt for, but pitched upon or struck at once.

This stroke of the glottis must not be confounded with that of the chest, which is similar to the act of coughing, or clearing the throat, and which act, viz., coughing out the notes of the chest, costs much loss of breath, and produces an uncertain, aspirated, and stifled tone. It has been shown in earlier pages that the glottis is prepared for articulation by closing it, thus producing below it a momentary accumulation of air; and it is then opened by a sudden and vigorous stroke. Some teachers recommend the use of the syllables, Pa, La, Ma, and an old friend and former teacher of mine, Mr. Edwin West, used to advise the employment of the syllable Gla, in order to acquire precision in the striking of notes. Signor Garcia is opposed to this measure, since he is of opinion that thus the lips, tongue, and other organs, not concerned in the emission of the voice, are set in motion, and that it merely disguises the faulty articulation of the glottis, and has no power of correcting it; but I would respectfully submit, that many aspiring vocalists find (I did at one time myself) the greatest difficulty in keeping the tongue down in the mouth, and the syllable La, as I remember an Italian Master, a Signor Farini, always used, ensured the tongue being placed in its proper position before striking the note. Again, the syllable Gla not only places the tongue down, but favours the graceful recession of the mouth, so important in producing perfect vocal tone. Of course it is not necessary that the study should always be continued in this perhaps artificial manner; but I only venture to think that it acts as a good corrective under certain circumstances.

Extreme looseness of the lower jaw is of great importance, for the easy movement of the organs beneath it greatly depends upon the facility with which it moves, or falls, by its own weight, and according to the ease with which the structure moves so is the sound rendered mellow and elastic.

CULTIVATION OF THE FEMALE VOICE.
The Chest Register.

In females the notes which should be first attempted, and which are in most cases the easiest to produce, are those of the chest. They are the following: viz., La (A) flat, La (A), Si (B) flat, Si (B), and Do (C).

If these are well managed, they will come out pure and ringing. They should be repeated several times successively, *not held long*. Ascent may then be made by semitones to Fa (F)

and the descent by semitones as low as the voice allows. Starting from Re (D)

the higher the sounds rise, the more opened must the bottom of the throat be. The Italian A must be enunciated with the utmost clearness, taking care not to stretch the mouth too wide, by which means the sound will be made guttural. In some cases difficulty is found in producing the notes of the chest register on the Italian A; it is then a good plan to try the Italian I (Anglice E), since thus the lips of the glottis are more closely approximated. So important does my friend, Mr. Henry Parker, a well-known pianist, composer and teacher of singing, think the employment of the Italian I, that in his work of the "Voice" he recommends the pupil to commence on this vowel, and gradually draw the A into it. If some sopranos would bear this advice in mind, they would probably lose much of the harsh quality that they possess in the higher notes. The lips of the glottis may be more nearly brought together, and the emission of the chest notes facilitated, by a vigorous slur from a sound already acquired to the one which presented a difficulty. Deep sounds should not be made too forcibly.

The foregoing statements concerning the chest register are applicable to all registers and to every variety of vocalisation.

(*To be continued.*)

"A SONG FOR OCTOBER."
By the late J. H. CHAMBERLAIN.

Fade not so soon, fair leaves,
Fall not so soon;
What though the autumn spider weaves
Her fairy webs, and the large hollow moon
No longer shines upon the yellow sheaves?
Fade not so soon!

Fade not so soon! the calm untroubled sky
Is fair with colour and is glad with light
Still is the stubble golden, and the flight
Full of the summer's perfume. Why
Should ye that are so fair make haste to die?
Winter will linger yet,
Fade not so soon!

Linger a little, oh! remembrance! Time
Oh! player could stay, or entreaty bled,
What worship would the blind . . .

THE RUSSIAN NATIONAL HYMN.

General Alexis Lvow, in his yet unpublished "Memoirs," thus relates the history of the Russian National Hymn, "God protect the Czar," first publicly performed fifty years ago on the 11th December, at the Grand Theatre, Moscow:—

"In 1833, I accompanied the Emperor Nicholas to Prussia and Austria. On our return to Russia, I was informed of a fact that had no National Hymn, and that of the English "God Save the King," the French hymn, the Austrian Hymn . . .

. . . On the 23rd November, 1833, came, accompanied by the Emperors and the Grand Duke Michael, to the Chapel of the Imperial Choristers; I had summoned the whole body of the latter, and backed them up with two full bands. The Emperor and the hymn repeated several times, then sung without accompaniment; and then performed by all the regiments complete. He said to me in French, 'It is superb.' And then afterwards ordered Count de Benkendorff to inform the Minister of War that the hymn was adopted for the whole army." The decree was promulgated on the 4th December, 1833, and the hymn was publicly for the first time on the 11th December, 1833, at the Grand Theatre, Moscow. It seemed as if the audience wanted to see how the Moscow public liked my work. On the 25th December the hymn was heard as the Winter Palace at the ceremony of blessing the standards. The Emperor was pleased to present me with a gold snuff-box set with diamonds as a testimony of his satisfaction, and ordered, furthermore, that the words, 'God protect the Czar,' should be introduced in the armorial bearings of the Lvow family.—*Musical World.*

Musical Intelligence.

"KING DAVID."

"ORATORIO BY SIR GEORGE A. MACFARREN."

The Sacred Harmonic Society exhibited commendable judgment in selecting this noble work as the subject of their opening concert of the new season, on Friday last, the 16th inst., at St. James's Hall. It may be interesting to give an outline of the action, which is as follows :—

The overture is descriptive of the shepherd life of David, the summons to battle, his singing before Saul, the king's envy and death. The first part of the oratorio treats of the rejoicings of the Israelites at the bringing in of the ark ; David's sin with the wife of Uriah the Hittite; the prophet Nathan's denunciation, and David's repentance. The second part relates the murder of Amnon by his brother Absalom's command, the return of the latter and his rebellion against David, the young man's subsequent death, and the restoration of the kingdom.

The following account is a summary of the whole work :—The action starts with the death of Saul and proceeds not so much as a continuous recital, but as a succession of detached numbers; the words being taken from various books of Holy Writ such as the Psalms, Chronicles, Samuel, Isaiah, the Hebrews, Job, St. Matthew, and St. Luke. Thus at the commencement we have a chorus of the twelve tribes swearing allegiance to David with the words, " Behold, David, we are thy bone and thy flesh," and " Behold how good and joyful a thing it is." Then a recitative and song for King David (baritone), " None ought to carry the ark of God but the Levites," and " I will not suffer mine eyes to sleep." Then the Psalm for the bringing in of the ark. Then soprano solo " The faith of the just is as a shining light," and " Let our light so shine." Then the prophecy of Nathan (tenor) " Thus saith the Lord, I took thee from the sheepcote," leading to a chorus " His throne shall be for everlasting." Then song by David, "Who am I, O Lord God, that thou hast brought me hitherto." Then chorus "The seed of David is great." At this point follows a narration by the contralto descriptive of David's sin with Uriah's wife, followed by a chorus "Remember not, Lord, our offences." Now the parable by Nathan of the rich man taking the poor man's ewe lamb, followed by a duet for bass and tenor in which Nathan tells David he is the rich robber. Then a contralto solo " What is a man profited if he gain the whole world and lose his own soul," the first part terminating with a chorus " Vengeance belongeth to the Lord."

The second part opens with a narration by contralto describing the death of Amnon by the command of Absalom, the grief of King David, the flight of Absalom, and the device of the woman of Tekoah, leading to a duet for soprano and baritone, in which the woman of Tekoah induces the king to restore Absalom. Here follows the rebellion of Absalom and a chorus " Absalom prepareth chariots and horses," and a recitative and song for tenor (Absalom), " O that I were judged in the land," and " My judgment shall be as a robe and a diadem." Then chorus of the spies of Absalom, " Give ear, all ye tribes of Israel, as soon as ye hear the sound of the trumpet then shall ye say, Absalom reigneth in Hebron." Then song for contralto, " Woe unto them that call evil good and good evil," followed by a chorus of the faithful to David beseeching him to fly and make good his escape, and narration by contralto describing the retreat of David's army across the Jordan. Then a chorus by the faithful, " Thou O king shalt not go forth to battle," and recitative and song for David " What seemeth you best I will do, but O ye hundreds and thousands, deal gently for my sake with the young man, even with Absalom," and " Lord, where are Thy loving kindnesses." Here follows duet for soprano and contralto, " Like as a father pitieth his own children," and " How high the heaven is in comparison to the earth." Then dialogue by David seated between the two gates, and chorus of female voices descriptive of the events of the battle, terminating with a chorus of male voices announcing the victory and Absalom's death. Then song by David expressive of his grief, " Oh, Absalom, my son, my son, Absalom ! would God I had died for thee." Then chorus with solo (baritone), " Behold, the king weepeth and mourneth for Absalom." Then song by soprano, " Despise not thou the chastening of the Lord," and chorus of people rejoicing for the delivery of Israel from the Philistines. Then a song by David, " Have mercy upon me, O God." Then chorus " Joy is in

Heaven over one sinner that repenteth," and quartet " There shall be joy in the presence of the angels of God over one sinner that repenteth." The whole terminating with the Doxology.

The first part is shorter than the second, and hardly enlists the interest so much as the latter, since it embraces more ground and is in consequence somewhat fragmentary, the second part being confined entirely to the movements of the king and Absalom. The pathetic scene in which the father's racking anxiety for his son is depicted, is a masterpiece of dramatic realism, all thought of the civil war being lost in the cry, " Is the young man Absalom safe ?" All that follows from this point is certainly superfluous and somewhat tiring, although the musical scoring is quite equal to what has preceded, and it would seem a wise proceeding to terminate the work here, bearing in mind that last Friday the work occupied close upon three hours and a half, including the interval between the parts. Sir G. A. Mafarren must be congratulated upon having given to British musical art a work which is throughout impressive, vigorous, admirably scored, endowed with great musical charm, and of thoroughly English tone.

The vocalists were the same as at the Leeds Festival, with the exception of Miss Anna Williams (in the place of Madme. Valleria, who undertook the part at a short notice. This lady sang the part as if she had been long familiar with it, and was specially successful in her rendering of "The path of the just." Madme. Patey sang delightfully throughout, and made a deep impression with "What is a man profited." Mr. Lloyd rendered his numbers with his usual care and refinement, his chief effort being "My judgment shall be as a robe." Mr. Santley invested the part of the king with great dignity, and sang the grief passages with the most exquisite tenderness. His impersonation of this character may well rank with his rendering of Elijah. The duet for the two ladies "Like as a father" was much appreciated. The chorus obtained a good share of applause, an encore for the fugal chorus with organ prelude " The seed of David is great," being so unanimous that it was repeated. The chorus " Remember not, Lord, our offences," and the "Vengeance Chorus" which closes the first part, also demand special notice. The overture was splendidly rendered, and throughout, save for an occasional slip and uncertainty of attack, the orchestra was all that could be desired. Sir Arthur Sullivan conducted with his usual ability, and Mr. Fountain Meen presided at the organ. At the end of the performance, the composer was summoned to the platform and greeted with unanimous and prolonged applause. The National Anthem, as usual, preceded the concert, which was given to a crowded audience. ARMAND SEMPLE.

LONDON LITERARY AND ARTISTIC SOCIETY.

The inauguration of the third season of this society was held at St. James's Banquetting Hall on Tuesday evening, Nov. 6th, The proceedings opened at 8.30, with a concert (promenade), under the direction of Herr Liebich, of which the following is the programme :—

Piano Duet, "Rip Van Winkle"	...	Liebich
Baritone solo, "If Doughty Deeds"	Miss Ada Sellings and Herr Immanuel Liebich	Sullivan
Contralto solo, " The Silver Rhine "	Mr. G. M. Farmer	Murchison
	Miss Pattie Michie	
Violin solo, "Rêverie "	Miss Louise Fowell	Danclas
Soprano solo, "No hand but thine "	Madame Washington Walker	O. Barri
Piano solo, "Invitation à la Valse "	Madame Sophie Tucski	Weber
Mezzo-soprano solo, "The Green Trees whispered "	Miss Minnie Grisdaine	Balfe
Baritone solo, " Out on the Deep "	Mr. G. Farmer	Lohr
Violin solo, "Air de Ballet "	Miss Louise Fowell	Beriot

Of the above, the violin playing of Miss Louise Fowell, and the singing of Miss Pattie Michie, call for special mention. The arrangement of " Rip Van Winkle " (pianoforte duet) is clever and well harmonized. After the concert a lecture was given by E. L. Selioni, Esq., F.L.S., F.S.A., on " Art-Aspects of Modern Drama," followed by an animated discussion, in which several gentlemen joined. At eleven o'clock there was a grand ball, with orchestra. This society affords a centre where ladies and gentlemen of literary, musical, scientific, or artistic tastes, may meet for social intercourse. One cordially sympathises with the objects it has in view, and wishes it every success. ARMAND SEMPLE.

CRYSTAL PALACE CONCERTS.

PROGRAMME.

Overture, "Mountain, Lake, and Moorland" .... Thomas
Airs de Ballet (" Orphée et Eurydice ") .... Gluck
Ophelia's Scena, from " Hamlet " (" Air du Livre ") ...... Thomas
     Miss Griswold.
Concerto for Pianoforte and Orchestra, No. 2, in F minor .... Chopin
     M. Vladimir de Pachmann.
Symphony No. 1, in B flat .... Schumann
Song, " She wandered down the mountain side " ...... Clay.
     Miss Griswold.
Solos for Pianoforte   "Novelette" (Op. 21), No. 7 .. Schumann
     "Wiegenlied" .... Henselt.
     "Toccatina" ....
     M. Vladimir de Pachmann.
Overture, "The Flying Dutchman " .... Wagner.

     Conductor   -   -   AUGUST MANNS.

Again I have to record a decided success on the part of an English composer. The concert-overture by Mr. Harold Thomas afforded the greatest pleasure, both to the critics who were present, as well as to the general audience. Although it had never before been heard at Sydenham, in 1880 it was performed at the Philharmonic concert and subsequently by the Liverpool Philharmonic Society, the Hackney Choral Association, and at the Covent Garden Theatre concerts, &c., and—contrary to the adage—the more familiar it becomes, the better it will be liked. Many beautiful touches in it, remind one of Sir Sterndale Bennet's writings, and as Mr. Harold Thomas had the benefit of his instruction this is perfectly natural. A better school—if I may use the expression—or a better master, it would be impossible for him to follow. Like Sir Sterndale Bennett's overtures, it possesses much poetical beauty and forcible expression, whilst its construction is extremely artistic and shows its author to be possessed of that common sense in art, the influence of which in the direction of sobriety of judgment and self-restraint is altogether wholesome. No phase of art that lacks sobriety and self-restraint will seriously or permanently affect men's minds or the growth of culture.

The grand old Gluck, "the regenerator of the opera," was listened to with profound respect, in the selection from his classical and dramatic opera. His music afforded pleasure both to the student, as well as to others who may be unconscious that the burning desire of infusing into the modern opera a more poetical spirit and a more intense dramatic expression, is only another attempt to do what he—at least in his day—so admirably succeeded in doing.

It is universally acknowledged that no pianoforte player has ever excelled, and but few equalled, M. Vladimir de Pachmann in interpreting the refined music of Chopin. Many qualifications are required for this : a very delicate touch and exceedingly refined style, the most rapid and accurate use of the pedals, with a clear comprehension of the beautiful harmonies and modulations, and an unfailing accuracy of finger in the frequent embellishments. All these qualifications are eminently combined in M. de Pachmann, as was proved beyond doubt—if indeed proof were needed—on Saturday last, in Chopin's well-known concerto.

Miss Griswold, the lady vocalist, was very successful. She has a voice of surprising compass and good quality, with very powerful expression.

Schumann's symphony, and last of all Wagner's overture to the "Flying Dutchman," completed an interesting and successful concert.   R. S.

Another reporter writes :—

I must express my thanks for the capital concert of Nov. 17th. Schumann's early symphony is full of interesting themes, if faulty in other respects ; and Wagner's overture, a glorious marine painting of amplest canvas, certainly stirred up Mr. Manns and his masterful "crew"—not to break the metaphor—to a magnificent voyage of discovery. You might almost hear the winds whistle through the cordage, and sniff as well as see the briny wave. Herr de Pachmann quite enraptured his audience and won, a bis.. He repeated the "Toccatina?" The concerto of Chopin suits him to the very letter. Miss Griswold, from New York, and recently very successful at the Grand Opéra of Paris, has received due and deserved acknowledgment from the daily and weekly press. She has a clear, powerful and penetrating soprano voice of extensive compass and ringing head notes. The lower part of the register is the only weak part of the organ ; and Miss Griswold, whilst taking every advantage of French elegances, in respect of pronunciation and delivery, would do well to

avoid any tendency to the *criard* school. The absence of the vile *vibrato*, the vice of the age, is acknowledged and commended by our daily contemporaries. I agree with the pundit of the *Times* about the English song, quite unfit for a Crystal Palace concert; however passable in the drawing-room and elsewhere. Nor can I say much more for the French *scena*, really a long laboured recitative, and nothing more. Miss Griswold's phrasing and execution give evidence of the best training.   A. M.

SATURDAY POPULAR CONCERTS.

PROGRAMME.

Quartet in C minor (Op. 18), No. 4, for two violins,   Beethoven.
    viola, and violoncello.
    Madame Norman-Néruda, MM. L. Ries, Hollander, and Piatti.
Song, " Dalla sua pace " .... Mozart.
     Mr. Joseph Maas.
Sonata in E minor (Op. 90), for pianoforte alone ...... Beethoven.
     Mr. Charles Hallé.
Adagio in E major, from Concerto in A minor, for   Viotti.
    violin, with pianoforte accompaniment.
     Madame Norman-Néruda.
Air, " Il mio tesoro " .... Mozart.
     Mr. Joseph Maas.
Quartet in A major (Op. 26), for pianoforte, violin,   Brahms.
    viola and violoncello.
   Mr. Charles Hallé, Madame Norman-Néruda, MM. Hollander,
     and Piatti.
    Accompanist   Mr. ZERBINI.

The above programme was announced last Saturday, but a printed apology for Mr. Maas, who was suffering from severe sore throat, was circulated in the hall. Mr. Abercrombie sang in his stead, substituting Handel's "Where'er you walk" and Berthold Tours. The Angel at the Window, for the songs chosen by Mr. Maas, who is advertised to appear at to-day's concert. Mr. Abercrombie is gifted by nature with a really beautiful tenor voice, and there is also something else in his favour, his entire and very apparent self-possession. His "art," however, cannot be so cordially commended. Tours' charming little song calls for the most simple and unaffected rendering ; Mr. Abercrombie's strained expression and undue holding-out of certain notes took from it all its simple grace. With greater experience, he may possibly acquire a purer style.

What possessed Mr. Hallé to take the final movement of the sonata at such a fearfully slow pace? The very character of the melody, its two-four time, with sometimes only one note of melody in a bar (a minim), the accompaniment being absolutely uninteresting, demands a moderate speed—for each separate note holds a meaning the composer intends ; the listener who would keep awake requires note to follow note at a greater rate than 60 to the minute. "Sehr singbar" should not be translated "very drawling," and "nicht zu geschwind" is a negative expression, which should not be rendered positively, "slowly and drearily. With one exception (passing then cursorily in mental review, this assertion is, I believe, correct). Beethoven concludes his pianoforte sonatas with a quick or very quick movement: the "nicht zu geschwind," therefore, probably only means "not so fast as most finales." Mr. Hallé being twice recalled for his truly striking—though not agreeably so—performance, added a Schubert impromptu to the programme; and Mdme. Norman-Néruda, after her graceful rendering, to Mr. Hallé's accompaniment, of her solo, satisfied unreasonable demands with a Bach gavotte.

Brahms' noble quartet was played before a fast-thinning audience. Even in the usually steadfast orchestra, ugly, bald places appeared, and other parts of the hall fared proportionally worse. This is much to be regretted, being calculated to encourage the directors in excluding modern works more severely than heretofore from their scheme. It therefore becomes the duty of those who may be thus persuaded, to declare that the indifference arose, not from the natural conservatism of the audience, nor from any want of merit in a work which, with the same writer's Op. 25, stands at the very head of the list of chamber music by living composers; but from an uninspired and unsympathetic rendering. Brahms makes great demands on his interpreters as well as his audience —a rugged energy, fiery impetuosity, great intellectual vigour, and a most absolute sympathy between the performers. If all these conditions are not fulfilled, the hearers will also fail to prove intelligent and sympathetic recipients of the good things provided, and will rudely and ungratefully leave their seats, perhaps declaring "Brahms is dry, harsh, and ugly," never reflecting that his discords may be " harmony not understood."

     BASIL SMITH.

MONDAY POPULAR CONCERTS.

Many of the *connoisseurs* were absent on Monday night, to hear Audran's opera at the Royalty Theatre, but those who attended this concert did far better, as will be seen from a report elsewhere. Spohr's Quartet in E minor ought not to be little known in England; the director of the "Popular," first produced it in 1862, during the 4th season. The tonality of the movements is peculiar; the larghetto moves in C major, and the minuet in G, with a wink, however, at the original key by writing the "trio" in the relative (E) minor. The applause that ensued at the end may be described as boisterous, considering the select quality of the audience. Beethoven's pianoforte trio needs no comment; the *largo assai* in the tonic minor has, in a complimentary sense, every "mark of the beast." How Herr de Pachmann interprets his favourite master's "Funeral March," ought to be known by this time to the *habitués* an additional treat after his fine performance on the previous Saturday at Sydenham. An *encore* fructified in a well-known Berceuse of Chopin, the one lady mistaken for a "*nocturne*"! as 'if not known,' alas! Signor Piatti's solo, which opened Part II, is an adaptation of an air from a Sonata by Germiniani, (written for violin or violoncello); an antique and old-fashioned style of Clarionet, a sort of "Lied ohne worte." The title "Folia" seems to require explanation, for the air is dignified gravity itself. A Variation ensues, where the melody is arranged to the third string, with a *staccato* accompaniment for the pianoforte; an episode in F further varies the subject, and an excursion is made to A minor and back to D minor; by the simple service of sharpening the mediant (C) of the new key. The clever accompanist rather overbore the interpreter. Signor Piatti, of course, evoked a *furore*. Miss Santley made a better choice of pieces in the second than in the first part. Rubinstein's songs are truly charming. His loveliest of pianoforte trios (in B flat, Op. ......) is set down for next Monday night, with Miss Agnes Zimmermann as pianist. I regret to notice her choice of that very dry solo, Schumann's "Etudes Symphoniques," ...... The very ......

COMIC OPERA AT THE ROYALTY THEATRE.

Miss Kate Santley opened this pretty theatre on Monday night with M. Audran's comic opera (operetta?), entitled "Gillette," adapted from the French, by a very clever *littérateur*, Mr. H. Savile Clarke. The story is a very awkward affair in the original, if that word may be used, when the *delicate incidents*, are converted from one of Boccaccio's "moral tales," ...... I have read the whole of the Decamerone, in a choice Italian. Mr. Savile Clarke, however, has extracted the poison, and left some of the honey. His libretto might, perhaps, be smarter and more highly favoured with *modern wit*, but it is generally approved as the work of an experienced and accomplished dramatic writer. ......

LEEDS.

The Church of England Sunday Schools gave their annual concert last week; in the Town Hall, before an audience which filled the building to every part. The choir consisted of 700 voices, selected from Church schools in Leeds and district. The principal vocalists were Mrs. C. Clark and Messrs. Harrison and Westerman. The first part of the programme consisted of sacred, and the second of secular music. The concert opened with the National Anthem, and the first part included, Dr. Wesley's fine anthem, "Blessed be the God and Father," in which the solo passages were efficiently sung by Mrs. Clark. The chorus, "The Heavens are telling" (Haydn), helped to bring out the careful training of the juvenile choir, the trio being impressively sung by the principals. A carol by Joseph Barnby, and a couple of hymn-tunes, were included in the first part of the programme. The second part comprised a number of glees and part-songs, to which full justice was done by the juvenile choir. Dr. Creser presided at the organ, and played a couple of organ solos: Variations on a Theme, by Handel, and Guilmant's Grand Choir, his efforts being loudly applauded. Mr. J. W. Young, of Wakefield, made an efficient conductor, and succeeded in keeping ......

PEOPLE'S ENTERTAINMENT SOCIETY.

On Saturday the 17th inst., the above Society, which is in its sixth season, gave the third weekly concert of its present session, in the Lammas Hall, Battersea, to a crowded audience. Before I venture my remarks about the programme and the way it was carried out, a few words concerning the scheme of the People's Entertainment Society would not I think be amiss. The object of this excellent Society is to give concerts of good and sound music from time to time to the lower class, entirely free of charge. As I stood in the Hall and watched the much-abused labourer and the hard-working man, take their seats in the most orderly manner possible, until the place was all but crowded to excess; as I watched their eager faces, anxious for the programme to commence, a feeling of great satisfaction came over me, to think that this enormous body of men (who, as the outside world imagine, spend their Saturday nights in drunkenness and rioting) should meet together as quiet and peaceable citizens, for the purpose of enjoying really good music. They were orderly throughout, talking only between the pieces, and from beginning to end bestowing attention and applause in a manner that called forth the highest praise. This admirable Society is under the immediate patronage of Lord and Lady Folkestone, both of whom were present, Lady Folkestone taking a leading part in the programme, of which I shall presently speak. By showing such untiring interest, by giving such unflagging energy in helping forward the work of this truly benevolent object, Lord and Lady Folkestone have fully, fully earned, and eminently deserve, the most hearty thanks and congratulations from us all, by which scheme, let it be said, Art is not lowered, but rather let me say, that its dignity is sustained, and its mighty influence spread broadcast. It would of course be impracticable to have given a Symphony of Beethoven's with the full resources of a large orchestra, but had it been given, I verily believe, from what I heard and saw of Saturday's affair, that these men would have appreciated it as much as persons more initiated, they themselves deserving more than ordinary woeful enthusiasts who, after hearing one of Beethoven's marvellous orchestral works, could only just vent to their artistic feelings, by yawning out, "very pretty." The way that these poor men enjoyed the music, well done, proves to me that education is not the only key by which the door of our musical appreciation can be unlocked. Mr. R. T. Pitt opened the programme with an American organ solo, at which instrument he presided during the evening. "The madrigal, "In going to my lonely bed," was admirably rendered by a well-trained choir, under the able conductorship of Mr. Leslie, who deserves great praise from the promoters of the People's Entertainment Society for his painstaking in bringing the choir to such a successful issue. These were three or four other pieces for the choir, all well performed and appreciated. The programme (continued Miss .....)'s beautiful ...... "Hear my prayer," Lady Folkestone sustaining the well-known solo part. Of her singing I cannot speak too highly, the purity of expression, and the careful production combined, find, for her, a place among genuine singers. Miss Campbell sang prettily. Mr. Henry Yates requires more study, Master Pitt bids fair to hold a good position as a violinist, while Mr. James Budd, who is well known at these concerts, received an ovation. Lord Folkestone, after an admirable speech, requested all present to join in singing the National Anthem, and thus a most enjoyable and pleasing entertainment concluded.

— GEO. F. GROVER.

the juvenile choir thoroughly under control. The new opera, "Victorian," by Mr. Julian Edwards, conductor of the Royal English Opera Company, was performed with great success at the Grand Theatre last week. The principal artists were Mdme. Julia Gaylord, Miss Lucy Franklin, Messrs. Packard, Jas. Sauvage, and A. McGuckin. The other operas produced during the week were, "The Piper of Hamelin," "Maritana," (in which Mr. J. W. Turner appeared), "Faust," and "Lily of Killarney." The performances were in every respect satisfactory.

BIRMINGHAM.

The first half of the concert given by the musical section of the Midland Institute, on the 3rd inst., was chosen "In Memoriam" of the late Mr. J. H. Chamberlain, the eminent architect, whose sudden death in the previous week cast such gloom over the whole town. Mr. Chamberlain's last lecture—on "Exotic Art"—was delivered in the same room in which these concerts are held; and only a proper feeling it was which suggested the introduction of the opening items, with their mournful associations. At the same time it will be seen how difficult it is to deal critically with music, of a funeral character, performed in memoriam, and not produced on artistic grounds alone—if, indeed, criticism is not altogether out of place. Miss Blain performed Mendelssohn's Lied ohne Worte, No. 3 of Book 5, followed by Chopin's Funeral March, from the Sonata Op. 35. I have never before heard this gifted lady (whose talent as a pianist deserves to be much more widely known) play with greater success; devoid of showy display, yet with all the requisite "feeling" and refinement of artistic delivery, her performance, of the Chopin piece particularly, was a truly classic one. Mr. Chamberlain had no mean gifts as a poet, in addition to the many other faculties through which his genius displayed itself. A poem from his pen, set to music by Mr. T. Anderton (with viola obbligato) was performed on this occasion. The words, as the reader will judge for himself—if the Editor be good enough to find space for the copy I send—are certainly above the amateur average. As to the musical setting, those who are acquainted with Mr. Anderton's work will know that a "melodious, refined treatment of the poetical idea was only to be expected. The song is of the arioso type, but melodious in the ordinary sense of the word, without sacrificing consistency of expression with the somewhat sombre tone of the poetry, the latter being more reflective than emotional in character; I am not aware whether Mr. Anderton's music is yet published. Mr. Eleanor Farnol, whose fine powers of musical declamation I have before had occasion to remark upon, did her very best with the song. In the second part of the programme she sang also a very effective composition of Mr. Frank L. Moir "My Crown"—not, however, of such refined, poetical interest as Mr. Anderton's; and Mendelssohn's vocal lieder, "The Charmer," and "Zuleika," which latter, beyond their simple musical interest, did well to display the fair artist's voice. Herr Pettersen, with Mrs. Hale, gave a very fine rendering of Grieg's Sonata for piano and violin, Op. 13. Beethoven's early quintet in E flat, for strings, and Mendelssohn's youthful sextet (published posthumously as Op. 110), were rather wanting in "go." Herr Pettersen, however, was a kindly substitute for Mr. Ward, who was unable to appear at the last moment. Some allowance, no doubt, must be made under these circumstances.

I was, unfortunately, prevented from attending; being away from Birmingham at the time, Mr. Stockley's first orchestral concert of the season, which took place in the Town Hall, on the 8th inst. I can do little more, therefore, than give the bare outline of the programme. The band performances included Mendelssohn's "Scotch" symphony, Mackenzie's "Rhapsodie Ecossaise," the ballet music, "The Dance of the Hours," from Ponchielli's opera, "La Gioconda;" and the overtures to "Mignon" (Thomas), and "Egmont" (Beethoven). At this concert Madame Lemmens-Sherrington, always a favourite with the Birmingham public, made her farewell appearance. The worthy conductor himself informed me that her singing that evening was in every respect equal to any of her past efforts; that her performance of Beethoven's magnificent scena, "Ah l perfido," was a remarkably fine one. In addition to the mentioned piece, she sang the recitative and air—"With verdure clad," from the "Creation," and "Let the bright seraphim," from Handel's "Samson"—pieces well chosen to display the singer's familiar voice and style, only respectfully for the last time. Mr. Edward Lloyd, though a trifle nervous, I am told, was very successful in the splendid Wagnerian excerpt, "Almighty Father" ("Rienzi"), as also in the fine recitative and air of Gounod's "Lend me your aid," which by this time has become the well-ridden "Cheval de bataille" of concert tenors. He made less impression with the air, "Some village Hampden," generally pronounced the best hit in Mr. Collier's musical medley to the words of Gray's "Elegy." Messrs. Ward and Abbott gave still another duo concertante of Spohr's for two violins (No. 8, Opus 67). Candidly, I did not regret missing this; but the violinist's tribute to the manes of that fascinating writer—though paid so often in public as to become a somewhat tiresome instance—was, it seems, well rendered on this occasion by the artist, and well approved by the audience. At the next concert, to take place Dec. 13th, I hope to be present, and to furnish a better report. The "Eroica" Symphony is to be performed, and

Miss Agnes Miller, who has well established her reputation here, will take part in the same capacity. Piano Concerto in C minor. Madame Clara Samuell and Sig. Foli are engaged as vocalists.

The second of the series of six concerts given this season by Mr. Stratton took place on the 13th inst. in the Masonic Hall. On all previous occasions I have had to remark on the presentation of certain novelties; but the programme of last night had all its predecessors in this respect; since every one of the pieces in the following list, if not in each instance, a first performance, were more or less new to Birmingham audiences:—"Morceau de Concert" (MS.) for pianoforte, two violins viola, violoncello, and contra-basso (F. E. Bache); Hebrew melody, for viola (Joachim); Variations, Op. 34, pianoforte (Beethoven); Sonata in F major, Op. 8, piano and violin (Grieg); quartet in A minor, Op. 29, strings (Schubert).

At Mr. Stratton's concerts the pianist generally receives the lion's share of the work, and the concert of last evening formed no exception to the rule. It will be remembered that last season Miss Constance Bache was incapacitated by an accident from taking part in the concert at which she was previously announced to appear. It was, therefore, all the more welcome a reception which awaited her this time. The first item in which she took part is one of the many posthumous works of her brother, the lamented F. E. Bache. Mr. Stratton has already enabled me to form a good idea of the work of our late townsman, and the little work produced last evening is very similar in character to those which have been previously introduced at these concerts. The same melodiousness, spirit, and fluent writing which characterised those works I have before commented upon are also present in this composition. The title alone of the work would disarm criticism on classic lines. Those only could find any fault with the piece for whom lively melody and graceful harmonisation have no charm. The piano certainly is the instrument most engaged throughout, the string instruments seeming much too secondary; but altogether the work is a delightful specimen of purely idiomatic English art. The next item in respect to novelty (since, although not unfamiliar to Birmingham amateurs, it has not been performed here for some years), was the Schubert quartet. This work, ranking next in its class to the quartet in D minor, is one demanding unexceptionable performances. If it cannot be said that the performance of last evening attained to that standard, it was yet a very worthy attempt. Miss Bache chose for her solo performance the variations on a theme in F major, the earliest of Beethoven's works of this class with opus number—locked with other works being distinguished in other ways. The work is one that makes no great demands upon the intellectual capacities of the listener, nor upon more than the ordinary executive abilities of the pianist. Miss Bache's style is in every way that of the true artist; it is a little reserved, perhaps, but certainly the piece is not one calling for much fire and passion. Her touch is beautifully clear and distinct; and the phrasing most artistic. Miss Bache's playing, in short, is studied and deliberate, rather than giving the impression of spontaneity. In the duo sonata with Mr. Abbott, Miss Bache helped no better to familiarise us with a composer who has already gained our ears. In Grieg's music, however, it is often forgotten how much the interest is largely owing to that element in the work for which the composer can hardly have more than the credit of skilfully presenting,—the Northern folks, melodies so natural. The same allowance in the way of adapting national melodies would hardly be made, I fear, in the case of an English writer. Much in Grieg's music is dependent upon the poetical associations of the said melodies. The bizarre contrasts, the awkward technicalities, the "hurdy-gurdy" strains—despite all this, the romantic charm of the work is incontestable. All great art is, however, cosmopolitan; Grieg's art is but local. Whether Scandinavian music is or not but a passing fashionable cultivation, such a performance as the excellent one on this occasion cannot but have proved enjoyable to all, as, indeed, was sufficiently manifested. Of Mr. Ward's performance I can only say that it was a conscientious artistic fulfilment of a thankless task. S. J. Quin, Br.

BEDFORD.—The first serial concert of Herr Polonaski and Mr. Bond-Andrews was held on Friday evening, Nov. 16th, at the Working Men's Institute, before a large audience. Niels Gade's fine, but most intricate, sonata in D major and minor stood first on the list, and received a poetical rendering from the two exponents on the violin and pianoforte. Of Mr. Bond-Andrew's solos may be named, as particularly perfect, Chopin's Berceuse, the polonaise in C sharp, and Liszt's 2nd "Hungarian Rhapsody," which was encored, and replaced by the player's own pretty piece "Return from the Maypole." Herr Polonaski regaled his audience with his own "Pensée Fugitive" and extra of Bach, Gounod, Hauser, and Vieuxtemps. At the "Ave Verum" by Leonard, the clever fingering of four strings on the violin was sufficiently displayed. Mdme. Polonaski sang airs of Rubinstein and Brahms. The success of this concert will, possibly, ensure the establishment of these meetings as a local institution.

DORCHESTER.—A concert in aid of the Abbey Church Restoration Fund, was given on the 13th inst., in the Girls' School. The artists were: Miss Amy Florence (soprano), Miss Evelyn Dickens (contralto), Mr. D'Arcy Ferris (tenor), Mr. Cattermole (baritone), Mr. B. Carrodus (violinist), Signor Colicoff (pianist).

BRIGHTON AQUARIUM ORCHESTRAL CONCERTS.

The second of these attractive concerts took place on Nov. 17th, the room being, as before, crowded. The orchestra, increased to 50 performers, acquitted themselves in a manner it would be impossible to praise too highly. The opening number, Rossini's overture to "Guillaume Tell," was superbly played. This was followed by the beautiful andante "con moto," (from Symphony No. 4 (Mendelssohn), played with great effect, which elicited hearty applause. Special mention is due to Mr. Dobell for his admirable oboe solo. Mr. Kuhe appeared at his best in Weber's Concert-stück, the opening melody, with its staccato accompaniment, being played with delicious crispness; the Con moto agitazione was finely given, the crescendo being worked up to a masterly manner to the Presto assai, which was taken at a tremendous pace, and brilliantly kept up to the end. The work was played without book, and Mr. Kuhe was rapturously encored. Miss Damian, who has a remarkably fine contralto voice, met with a very flattering reception, her songs, "The Spirit Song" (Haydn), "The Last Dream" (Cowen), and a new song "Go and Forget," by Stephen Adams, being rendered in a very artistic manner. She has a faultless intonation, and sings with great feeling. A work for orchestra, a concert overture, "A dream of happiness," by Charles E. Stephens (a delightful work, abounding in melody), was capitally played. Considering that it was known in the orchestra that the gifted composer was among the audience one can quite understand that the instrumentalists did their very best accordingly. The other orchestral works were Scherzo from Symphony No. 9, (Beethoven), Ballet Music Nos. 3 and 4 "Sylvia," (Delibes) (the latter a charming little Danse, found great favour with the audience and was encored), grand selection, "Cinq Mars" (Gounod), and Grand March No. 4, "Aux Flambeaux" (Meyerbeer), introducing the National Anthem. One must not forget the pianoforte solo to the second part, Mendelssohn's "Auf Flugeln," arranged by Liszt, and Valse in A flat (Chopin), played in Mr. Kuhe's finished style. Mr. Jacques Greebe was as usual everything that could be desired as a conductor, and Mr. Greebe, senr., acted in his capacity as leader with great skill. Madame Klauwell (vocalist), and Mr. Howard Reynolds (solo cornet) are announced for the next concert.—Local paper.

A MUSICAL VISIT TO MANCHESTER.

Pleasure is sometimes said to be another word for novelty. Certainly Herr Richter's concert on Nov. 7th was a keen pleasure for the musical elect of Manchester, and perhaps it owed some of its zest to its novelty. If we had been accustomed to the sight of the German leader's commanding figure, with no doubt or music-stand, to impede his personal influence—if this had been as familiar a sight to us for a score, or even a couple of years then, who knows?—it might have seemed tame and ordinary. As it was, when novelty was associated with power, the applause and bravos of the audience testified to their appreciation of it. That audience consisted of such of the citizens of Manchester as delight in music, and take any favourable opportunity of hearing it; as well as the body of professionals, whose faces were all known to us all. But these two sections of society are not large enough to fill the large Free Trade Hall, and one is sorry to learn that the concert was a heavy loss to the originators of it. Perhaps Herr Richter does not understand the constitution of certain concert-going Philistines, whose numbers are necessary for financial success. The programme was made up entirely, with the exception of Beethoven's Eroica symphony, of numbers from Wagner's operas. Herr Richter is known to be a distinguished exponent of Wagner's music. I certainly never heard the beauties of what is called music of the future more expressively wrought out than by the orchestra under his lead. Wagner is spiritual, if nothing else; with him everything resolves itself into an endeavour after an adequate and searching interpretation of emotion. This is his aim, whether or not we may agree that it is a high one; and in comparison with this he reckons as nothing musical science, rules of form, or any other machinery of his art. In this way, he often offends the fastidious in taste; but that he some-times gains very beautiful and singular effects, is undeniable. Some of his themes stand forth on a rich and formless background of orchestral sound, like a picture glowing in mosaic. The constitution of the Wagnerian orchestra is also objected to by many. Certainly, when it is employed in its full force, when several blatant trombones are necessary to enforce the theme in the midst of a very Babel of instrumental noises, then, though the effect may be electrifying, it is also trying to ears educated on classical diet. One cannot see that the motive theory is at all necessary to the appreciation of Wagner's music. As heard under Herr Richter's direction it is beautiful enough in itself to require no explanation. The poetical side of it is then so exquisitely developed—the whimsical, the felling side of it, as exemplified in the "Walküren-ritt"—[the writer has heard it well delivered by a Manchester leader]—that the listener who fails to feel an answering thrill in the complex consciousness of his inner life, need not go to the opera-house to learn to admire Wagner.

Perhaps it is impossible that the pathos, the heart-searchingness of the music to "Tristan and Isolde," for instance, can appear so utterly beautiful to those who have not seen the opera on the stage,—who have not watched the solemn dying of Tristan on the sea-shore, and his weary waiting for the coming of Isolde, while the careless shepherd blows his pipe, and his faithful follower scans the face of the heedless ocean for signs of the expected ship. The music must be doubly beautiful to those who have seen these things. But again I say that this added appreciation does not come from an intimate acquaintance with the leading motive; nor does the recollection burden itself always with the labelling of certain strains; it is only that the general fitness of the music to the sentiment is recognised, and that a greater knowledge of it makes its beauties more apparent. The music is unlocked, is accessible, so to speak, to all the first hearing only turned the key. For it is certain, that the hearing of music is not like the reading of a book; the second and third times being more enjoyment than the first. That this statement may prove true also of the next Richter concert, which is promised for the spring, I hope and trust; and to those who wish to hear Wagner at his best, I would emphatically say, "go and hear Hans Richter's interpretation of him."

M. L. A.

MUSIC IN DUBLIN.

The St. Patrick's Oratorio Society inaugurated its season on 16th inst. with an excellent performance of the "Messiah," at the Cathedral. If I mistake not, the society has opened each season since its formation with the "Messiah," as per arrangement of the committee, I understand. Truly one never tires of the marvellous work; equally true it is that no other in the long list of oratorios can command such an audience, yet I very much question on looking over the numerous works there are suitable for performance in cathedrals, whether it would not be wiser to rehearse a different work for each performance.

I cannot speak too highly of how the work was performed on 16th inst. Soloists and chorus seemed alike desirous of placing the event on record as a highly creditable rendering of the work, and they may well rest content with their laurels. The solo parts for male voices were sustained, as usual, by the members of the Cathedral choir, which is sufficient guarantee for the excellence of the manner in which their work was got through. The soprano music was sung by Miss Russell with very happy effect. The choruses were admirably rendered by a nicely balanced choir of one hundred voices who sang throughout in excellent time. The conductor, Mr. Marchant, presided at the organ with his usual ability. For their next performance (Feb. 24), they intend producing "Te Deum," by Sullivan, and Mendelssohn's "Hymn of Praise." The Dublin Musical Society are busily engaged in rehearsing the "Elijah," which they propose producing on 26th inst.; principal artistes, Mrs. Hutchinson, Mrs. Scott, Fennell, Mr. Henry Guy, and Mr. Santley.

J. T. B.

NORWOOD.—A grand evening concert was given in the Hall, Weston Street, Upper Norwood, on Monday evening, Nov. 19th, by Miss Harriett Morgan, assisted by Miss Lottie West, Mdlle. Keighley, Miss May Petit-Jean (pianist), Mr. Stanley Moore, Mr. Burton Bouquet, Mr. William Dubber, and Mr. F. E. A. Cavell (reciter); the chief honours being won by Miss Lottie West. There was not quite so numerous an audience as could have been desired for the fair bénéficiare.

PRESTON.—On Thursday evening, Nov. 15th, Mr. James Tomlinson (organist to the Corporation) gave a recital on the grand organ in the New Public Hall. The programme was: Concerto in B flat (Handel), overture to "Zanetta" (Auber), "Marche Cortège" (Gounod), overture to "Othello" (Rossini). The concert, followed with great taste, was well received. There was a very large attendance.—The Preston Church Choir Association held their first festival on Monday evening, Nov. 19th, in the Parish Church. The choirs who took part in the service were Holy Trinity, St. George's Parish Church, Emmanuel, St. Luke's, St. Paul's, All Saint's, St. Saviour's, &c. Mr. Galloway (organist St. George's) ably conducted, and Mr. J. Greaves (organist of the Parish Church) presided at the organ, with great ability. The music was as follows: Processional hymn (by Sir G. A. Macfarren); Psalms (E. J. Hopkins and J. Stainer); Magnificat (Goss); Nunc Dimittis (J. Barnby); Anthem, "Sing to the Lord" (Mendelssohn); processional hymn (J. W. Elliott). The anthem was rendered in a pleasing manner. The church was well filled.—The Preston Orchestral Society gave their first concert for this season on Monday, Nov. 5th, in aid of Longton New Church. The programme included: Overture "Caliph of Bagdad" (Boïeldieu); "Cinquanti Lancets," Gavotte, "Elegant" (Williams); overture, "Chevalier de Breton" (Hermann); galop, "Feu de Joie" (Flause); and the songs rendered during the evening were "True till death," "Tit for Tat," "Ehren on the Rhine," etc. The vocalists and instrumentalists were all amateurs. The society has made great improvements since last season. Mr. J. Hogg wielded the bâton, and Mrs. Pye presided at the pianoforte.

Foreign Musical Intelligence.

Herr Scheletterer, of Berlin, has the first volume of his "History of French Music" in the press,

It is stated that an International Guitar Club has been started at Leipsic, and an *International Guitar Journal* has now been started.

At Copenhagen, a new opera, "The Spanish Students," by a Danish composer, Lange-Müller, has appeared. The work is said to be excellent.

It is intended to perform "Tristan and Isolde," at the Dresden Opera next spring, with Fräulein Malten and Herr Gudehus in the principal parts.

The legend of "Loreley" is again to be set this time by a composer of the name of Mehul. Even many where (this is not a name) will set the unfading story.

There can be no doubt about the artistic vitality of Mozart's best operas, the four hundredth performance of "Zauberflöte" at Berlin took place on Nov. 2nd.

The success of Herr Goetz' opera "Esmeralda" at Gotha will, it seems, secure the performance of the work at Berlin, and possibly in other places in Germany.

The prize recently offered by the Belgian Academy of Science for the best essay on the "Life and Works of Gretry" has been announced, awarded to M. Michel Brenet, of Paris. As all music must be set forth.

Méhul's Mass, given in Paris on October's Day, Nov. 22nd, was previously revived on Easter Day at Toulouse, in 1882, then exciting much interest. It will be sung there next Easter also.

Dorothea "Attila," daughter of Richard Wagner's youngest sister, is said to die in New York, almost destitute of the means of living. With her are four children and her crippled husband, once a captain in the Austrian army.

The funeral of the lamented M. Hegel, in connection with Minstrel, etc., took place in Paris on the 13th. The music at St. Roch included movements by Gounod, Verdi, etc., and M. Gigout played the Dead March in "Saul." Several renowned artists assisted, and a large number of notabilities were present.

The amicable and important lectures and meetings of the Society of Arts have commenced their sessions.

A new "Biographical Dictionary of Musicians" with a Bibliography of English Writings on Music," compiled and edited by James D. Brown, an experienced writer and assistant librarian, Mitchell Library, Glasgow, will present an enterprise. The author proposes to give more consideration to the claims of contemporary musicians than has yet been given in any similar work. The compiler adds in his prospectus: "All composers of standing have been adequately noticed; more comprehensively in many respects than formerly; while complete lists of their works, with dates, are given in each case. The almost unworked field of American musical biography has also been carefully noticed; and in every department, whether British, European, or American, numerous original articles will be found. What will serve to give the work a further and higher value in the eyes of persons interested in music, is the fact that nearly the whole of the articles on living musicians are based on information furnished directly by themselves, and which is consequently thoroughly authentic. The total number of articles will be between 8,000 and 10,000. A great feature in connection with the work is a 'Bibliography of English Writings on Music,' which forms an Appendix to the Dictionary. It is designed to display under appropriate headings the English Literature of every subject, as Acoustics, Æsthetics, Composition, Counterpoint, Notation, Organ, Psalmody, Singing, &c.

On the 28th inst., a performance will take place at the Gaiety Theatre for the benefit of Mr. Nordblom, the tenor singer, on which occasion, the first two acts of "Auber's now rarely heard "Fra Diavolo" will be given, with Messrs. Nordblom, Charles Lyell, Richard Temple, Aynsley Cooke, and Fletcher Leigh, and Miss Rose Herbee in the cast. Mr. Joseph Maas will also appear in the course of the performance, and the entertainment will include, among other items, a scene from "Patience."

LONDON: SATURDAY, NOVEMBER 24, 1883.

PURITANISM AND MUSIC.

THE lines of demarcation which for ages have divided the Church from the Sects, have in these later times become, as far as mere service is concerned, almost obliterated. The Church no longer tolerates the monopoly of bells, stained glass windows, gothic architecture, polychrome decoration, or organs. The Dissenting community has at length found out that good music is a most valuable adjunct to divine worship. The typical Nonconformist, so admirably depicted in "Hudibras," who considered that he best served his Maker by hating "steeple-houses," and droning interminable psalms through his nose, is now extinct—though it is just possible that faint reflections may linger in Welsh valleys. Excellent organs are to be found in the best Dissenting chapels, and they are frequently presided at by skilled players, thoroughly...

competent to discharge the important duties committed to them. The anthems, services, hymn-tunes, and chants of our foremost Church composers are performed with us much zeal and intelligence as the best served of churches can display. It must indeed be a matter of congratulation to all who seek for unity, at least in non-essentials, to observe that so far as music is concerned, the old sharp lines which once separated Church from Chapel have well-nigh disappeared. In the Service of Praise in which the divine art necessarily plays so important a part, we can now all meet in harmony on a common platform.

But this uniformity does not entirely obtain. There are at least two quarters where the devotional value of music is not thoroughly recognised. Prejudices have still to be fought, and a considerable educational process has yet to be gone through, ere narrow-mindedness and bigotry can be effectually conquered. It seems useless to point out to the average Scotch mind that the worship music of Biblical times was so elaborate that a large and complete orchestra was required for its proper rendering. The Scots care neither for this, nor the certainty that some such scheme will form part of the hereafter worship. That fearful instrument of torture, the bagpipes, has more charms for northern ears than the religious tones of the majestic organ. It may be that the "bawbee" is at the bottom of the opposition to the king of instruments in Scotland. Organs cost much money, and it is the nature of the canny Scot to think carefully over all unproductive outgoings. The long-winded discussion that has lately been in progress in Scottish Assemblies as to whether it is lawful to employ "artificial instrumental aid to worship"—as it is put—has again been decided in the negative. One might ask these dramas of Tay and Tweed whether any of their saints will happen to be provided with a set of lungs to move such an amount of worship through their mouths, during the service of praise and ... the use of such unnatural dental organs is clearly in violation of their dearly loved, but illogical, precept. Such an amusing exhibition as certain Scotch ministers have lately afforded the world shows that civilisation has yet much work to do before extreme Puritanism is vanquished. However, neither that display, nor the abuse lavished on the "kist o' whistles," nor the suggestion that the "accursed thing was the invention of the Evil One," and his "players are true sons of Belial, will prevent the gradual introduction of the instrument into Scotland. When one reads that an unfortunate farmer in the land o' cakes was lately solemnly debarred from Church privileges because he allowed a harmless dance to be given in his barn, it is patent that what we are told is the greatest of the divine Christian virtues, lacks as yet active appreciation in that part of the United Kingdom. The Presbyterians have probably forgotten that dancing once was an important feature of early ceremonial worship. They are doubtless profoundly ignorant that it still forms a part of the public service existing in at least two branches of the church of to-day, viz., the Coptic and Abyssinian.

The second example of existing Puritanism to which attention may be called is exhibited in a book just issued by the Society of Friends. In the new "Rules for Christian Discipline," which the Quakers have put forth, the omission of the Rule which has hitherto discountenanced music is significant. It shows the change of opinion as to lawfulness and unlawfulness which has taken place in the midst of the members of the sect since their ancestors sternly denounced music as a "foolish and wicked pastime." But it is necessary for them to advance further on the educational road, and quite remove the fetters with which their ruling powers yet deem it necessary to enchain music. Condemnation is still extended to those, "musical exhibitions in which an attempt is made to combine "religion with a certain amount of amusement." For the benefit of Quakers and Quakeresses who are able to appreciate and profit by the hearing of Oratorios, it may be pointed out that there is a delightful amount of elastic obscurity in this dictum. What is a "musical exhibition," and what constitutes "amusement"? According to the Biblical and Church interpretation, exhibition simply means "a setting forth." As all music must be set forth in order to be heard, no heresy can clearly lurk under this quaint expression. "Amusement" is probably from the Italian root, musare, to muse or meditate upon. According to Johnson, "to amuse," means "to entertain with tranquillity; to fill with thoughts that engage the mind without distracting it." Surely, no better definition can be found of the spirit in which the oratorios of the great masters should be heard. This is just the temper in which we should listen to Handel's immortal "setting forth" of the tale of the "Messiah," whether the locale be a concert-room, or still better, a church. If the hearing of this work "amuses" us with tranquil thoughts that engage the mind, its intended illustrative purpose has been completely fulfilled.

It will thus be seen that there remains a way open for Quakers innocently to recreate themselves in music, without breaking this Puritanically framed law. The thought just crosses one's mind whether in view of the performance of the blasphemous "Parsifal," with which London is threatened, the alarmed Quaker authorities have not framed the regulation with the occult object of protecting their members from "a musical exhibition, in which an attempt is made to combine religion with a certain amount of amusement."—In that case their forethought over Wagner's production is decidedly commendable.

T. L. Southgate.

A VETERAN ARTIST.

Truth has an interesting account of the career of John Ella in the number for Nov. 1st, including anecdotes of the worthy Professor's long connection with all the notables in the musical world for a space extending over sixty years. And what an experience this must have been during the advance of music here! Prof. Ella joined the opera band in 1821, when it consisted of 48 players. Under Costa's development chiefly, this same orchestra, when Ella retired from it in 1848 had been increased to a staff of 82 first-rate executants. There are two directions in which the labours of the shrewd painstaking founder of the Musical Union, will ever secure distinction for his name—the practical development if not the planting in the public sense in England of high class chamber music; and the introduction of the Analytical Programme, an invention which has done much for the intelligent growth of the English people in matters musical. JOHN ELLA has ever pursued a liberal policy as regards the introduction of new music of merit; and it is to be regretted that the Musical Union is not still in existence now there are distinct signs of an English school of chamber music. The writer in *Truth*, whose hand is pretty clearly to be traced in his words, tells that JOHN ELLA was once asked his opinion of WAGNER'S operas. His answer was "History tells us that EURIPIDES presented SOCRATES with the writings of HERACLITUS which were characterised by obscurity and involution. EURIPIDES afterwards asked for SOCRATES' opinion of the works in question. 'What I understand,' SOCRATES is said to have replied, 'I find to be excellent, therefore I assume that to be of equal value which I do not understand.' Well," said ELLA in 1859, "under the shelter of SOCRATES I reserve my opinion of WAGNER'S declamatory treatment of the lyric drama." ELLA's operatic experience certainly entitled him to speak on this question, even before WAGNER'S position was an accepted fact, and the writer of the notice rightly says, "It would be a good thing if other people practised now and then a similar reservation." After an unusual career which brought him into contact with a legion of great men of all types and professions, the old musician, now blind, alas! sits quietly at home, still doing kind things for his brother artists, still engaging his friends in delightful recollections of many musicians, and much notable music, and still the good friend of many, who rejoice in his friendship. Long may he be spared to enjoy the calm repose which so happily comes to those who have earned, and are blessed with a quiet old age.

E. H. TURPIN.

PROFESSIONAL EAGERNESS.

A DISTINGUISHED Conservative writer, and a man by no means willing to have existing institutions disturbed, tells us that he only realised what rest and peace meant upon going one Sunday into a village Church, and finding a clergyman able to forego the temptation to indulge in oratorical display, and so the very anti-type of the model London preacher of power, who is bent upon preaching himself either into a bishopric or into magazine popularity. It may be that the writer is somewhat caustic and severe in these words, but it is only fair to allow that living in the London regions of respectability, he has probably had to suffer much. Now this professional eagerness is not peculiar to the sacred profession of the Church's ministry; nay, rather it is so common as even to invade the pulpit, the last place in which indeed it ought to be found. The musical profession is, alas! not free from undue professional eagerness; and the presence of this objectional spirit in

the musical world is not unnatural; for those who follow music as a profession, generally find themselves greatly tried by the severe competition of a much overcrowded calling and by the comparative want of prominent opportunities for the advantageous employment of their artistic powers. The distinction between hunting after popularity and establishing artistic reputation, is one which calls for the earliest attention of all artists. The old Scotch proverb which runs something like—"Spare speaking, spare speeding" seems to counsel, like the saying of a shrewd lawyer, that a man is valued in accordance with his own estimate of himself, a certain amount of self-praise and self-announcement; but the artist should seriously ask himself if any personal attempt in discount public favour is either a dignified proceeding or a safe course. One of the greatest of modern English painters observed that there was a distinct danger to the artist in the possession of a reputation which was empirical in the sense of being, through personal or friendly effort, greater than his real claims to distinction could justify. This danger is twofold; for not only exposes an artist to the liability of being generally mistrusted when he comes to be fairly assessed by critical opinion, but it involves so much anxiety and exertion to be wasted in the maintenance of a blatant popularity, that the misguided artist loses something of that calm, innate self-trust which is a necessary possession of the truly earnest worker; not to add that he encounters a newly equally serious loss of valuable time. Never advance a step you may have to recede from, is therefore sure advice to the artist. Feverish empiricism shows itself in many ways; as in the taking of personal steps to get all one's performances and movements duly chronicled in the papers, in too eagerly seeking for opportunities for the display of one's own acquirements, and in being too anxious to be identified with every scheme which seems to promise publicity. To all who practise such forms of self-seeking advancement, time usually brings a sharp revenge. The grocer may indignantly say, "Try our best tea, it is the best in the world," but the artist must wait to be understood and appreciated. As a rule, too, the true artist will be known by his combined power of "working and waiting." To no class of worker—even in these pushing, showing, and not over scrupulous times—can the grandly patient words, "Cast thy Bread upon the waters and thou shalt find it, after many days," have a truer application, than when applied to the case of the true artist; whose gifts indeed are tenfold the stronger for the possession of faith, self-sacrifice, and patience.

E. H. TURPIN.

Dr. Stainer's "St. Mary Magdalen" and a miscellaneous selection of sacred music were given on the 22nd inst. (St. Cecilia's Day), at St. Alban's, Holborn. The soloists were vocal, Master H. Tebbutt; Messrs. Powell, Knott, Hall, and H. Proffit; organ, Master Gerald Walenn; organ, Mr. Purchartha Walenn, the organist of the church.

Mr. George Carter has just received a very flattering report on his Italian opera "Nerone" from a high musical authority in Trieste. The opera has been found, after a severe trial, to be rich in beauty, truly splendid, and abounding in ingenious, contrapuntal artifices; the orchestration is thought to be greatly developed, in contrast with the thin and flimsy scores of the old school. "Nerone" will presently be produced in Trieste.

REMINISCENCES OF AN OLD REPORTER.

THE MUSICAL UNION.

The genteel mob of mixed people, musicians, amateurs, loungers, fashionable folks that shew themselves off by ordering their carriages *before*, and arriving *after*, the time at concerts, may be reminded that the taste for classical chamber music was not only cultivated, but inspired by the founder of an institution entitled the "Musical Union," Mr. Ella, has been so eloquently eulogized by an accomplished writer in *Truth* (I suspect the Rev. Mr. Haweis, of St. James's, Marylebone), that I shall do little more with regard to the personal matter than say, "ditto to Mr. Burke" and pass on to safer generalities. I use the adjective (safer) because Prof. Ella happens to be rather particular and cares little for compliments.

Half a century ago, only a "happy few," fewer than the British combatants at Agincourt in the reign of Harry the Fifth, could stand the severe test of what is called "chamber" music, or in other words, compositions for four-string instruments and a pianoforte. The ordinary listeners go in for singers of trumpery "royalty" ditties, or require a full band at an enormous expense, not that they can appreciate complicated orchestral combinations, but that they insist on broad and striking effects of some kind or other. But the schoolmaster has been abroad. The "Popular Concerts" prove so much; but of these famous educational entertainments be it ever remembered that the "Musical Union" was the precursor. Inventors and projectors who have been benefactors to the world rarely reap the fruits of their skill and industry. Sir Hugh Middleton's New River left him high and dry in a financial sense, and the enormous profits of the concern fall into the lap of commonplace shareholders. Posterity devours the feasts that wise men have made.

Mr. Ella founded the "Musical Union," in 1845, and it flourished until the year 1880, when the age and infirmities of the venerable director compelled him to retire. To speak more correctly, the Director made a transfer of his interest in 1880, and the result, for reasons that need not be stated, was not satisfactory. Professor Ella continued to act, if one may use the phrase, as master of the ceremonies—none could do the work so well—and his successor in the direction played in the quartet. Musicians, however eminent, may not be men of business. The "Musical Union" ended at the end of the season in 1881, signalised by the appearance of Rubinstein, who came over from St. Petersburg not only to conduct his own opera "Le Démon" at the Royal Italian Opera, but to play at the Musical Union for Professor Ella, to whom he had recently dedicated a quartet (played on this occasion). Rubinstein would have travelled from Kamtschatka to serve his friend Ella, and I know that he felt sorely vexed, not to say angry, when he found that the Musical Union was falling to pieces merely for want of the previous generalship, perfect, in its way as Napoleon's, yet without the alloy of arbitrary discipline or the sledge-hammer sort of domineering that disfigured the military career of the "little corporal."

The writer in *Truth* has graphically described the stances of the Musical Union. The season always began on the Tuesday *after* Easter Tuesday, and continued until the end of June, or at latest until the first week in July. Once a fortnight was the rule, and once a week (at the tag end of the season), the exception. The members met like a family party, for outsiders were not wanted; the "strangers" mainly consisted of notable composers and artists from the continent, only to name Mendelssohn, Hector Berlioz, and Meyerbeer. The orchestra stood in the centre of the room, not at the far end; the audience thus commanded a good view wherever seated. Mr. Ella always recommended the galleries and the (grand) orchestra as the best places, because, "sound ascends." The scheme, printed and distributed on the Saturday *before* the concert, and concise as the texts of Tacitus, gave you the pith of the various compositions, and did not distract the mind with long and tedious quotations from the score. Three concerted works and a few pianoforte solos occupied the minds of the *habitués*, from half-past three o'clock until about a quarter-past five. On the "Grand Matinée," when the two Septets of Beethoven and Hummel were always *pièces de résistance*, the concert began at three. Mr. Ella allowed no *vocal* numbers. One or two, tolerated for a time, on the Grand Matinées, were subsequently discontinued.

I have been and am still complaining of the *talking* at musical performances. Woe, thrice woe, to the visitor who thus offended at the Musical Union! Professor Ella, at half-past three, uttered one significant "hush," and a golden silence prevailed. Any ignorant and uninitiated stranger that presumed to raise his or her voice above a whisper would have been made to look rather more foolish than that proverbial dog at the "Derby" race, always in the way at the wrong time. As a rule, however, ill-bred people at the Musical Union were *rara aves*. They could not obtain admission. The audience, apart from the aristocratic Committee—many of the noblemen accomplished amateurs—consisted of the *élite* of musical London; composers, professors, critics and *connoisseurs*. The motto of the director might have been, *Odi profanum vulgus, et arceo!*

I shall revert to the Musical Union before Christmas. Mr. Ella enlisted all the great artists of Europe: for violinists, sufficient to name Ernst, Joachim, Vieuxtemps, Auer, and Papini; for pianists: Rubinstein, (*facile princeps*), poor Lübeck, Madme. Schumann, Dr. Von Bülow, and Jaell of Paris, whose premature death makes me lachrymose as I write—a thoroughly good, genial fellow, with a *touch* to charm Diogenes, in or out of tub.

Anecdotes hereafter. For the present, one or two. Lubeck, in 1869, once lost his presence of mind and missed his point in the "Sonata Appassionata." According to Mr. Ella, he had looked round and saw Rubinstein enter the stall; this unnerved him. Rubinstein, unhappily affected with partial blindness, has his mental vision—the eyes of his mind—wide open and always open. Hating any approach to egotism, let me mention one little circumstance as an encouragement to attentive students of the art. As a matter of business, and for my own private improvement, I always take copious notes, at the opera or the concert, and am not afraid to ask technical questions. Knowledge ought to be its own reward, but a recognition from any distinguished personage cannot but be flattering unction to the soul. Well, Rubinstein, at a special concert of the Musical Union in 1877, had played his piece and was sitting on one of the audience benches. He beckoned to your unworthy servant and bade me sit by him. "I have observed," said the great man and velvet-fingered pianist, "that you always listen to the music attentively and take so many notes." I like to see it. In 1881, the *maestro* always recognised me in the corridors after the concert and offered his hand.

The author of the article in *Truth* (already referred to) forcibly contrasts the *receptions*, or musical and artistic *réunions* on the continent with the meetings in England. Referring to the weekly parties held by Mdme. Erard at the Château de la Muette, Passy, Paris, the writer pithily remarks: "When shall we look in *England* for such a centre of art and music? In London, such *cultes* degenerate into *cliques*, full of insufferable affectation and narrow conceit. We have good musicians and great painters, but the level of popular appreciation and artistic feeling is still very low, and there is nothing large, Catholic, or genial about our musical or artistic circles. With us, musicians are asked to great houses to amuse the company! At their own gatherings they congregate to extol their own talents; but where do they meet, as they used to meet at Ella's, or as they meet at Mr. Erard's, *to forget themselves* and worship at the shrine of art?"

On Wednesday evening, Nov. 14th, the third of the series of "Entertainments for the People" was given at Bethnal Green Road Congregational Church, by the Bethnal Green Choral Society, and an efficient band. Farmer's oratorio, "Christ and his Soldiers," was excellently rendered. The soloists were Mdme. Clara West, Miss Lottie West, Mr. C. J. Murton, and Mr. H. Prenton. Miss West received a hearty encore for the solo, "By Jesus' Grave," as did also Mr. Murton for "When I survey"; Mdme. West and Mr. Prenton were warmly applauded. The conductor was Mr. R. A. Slater; pianist, Mr. W. West; organist, Mr. E. T. Temple. The audience numbered between 700 and 800.

A sale is announced by Messrs. Puttick and Simpson, to take place on the 26th inst., of a large collection of musical property, including pianofortes, American organs, harps, a small chancel organ, real Chinese cymbals, Italian and other violins, tenors and violoncellos, etc.

Organ News.

MONTON.

An organ recital was given in Monton Church, on Friday, November 23rd, by Mr. W. T. Best, organist of St. George's Hall, Liverpool, on the occasion of the opening of the new organ. The following was the programme :—

Organ Sonata, No. 5, in D major .... Mendelssohn.
    Chorale—Andante—Allegro con brio.
Benediction Nuptiale (" Pièce d'Orgue ") .... Saint-Saëns.
Prelude and Fugue in E major .... Bach.
Andante in G major .... Smart.
Ronde de Campanelli (Bell-Rondo) .... Morandi.
Introduction and Fugue on a Trumpet Fanfare .... Best.
Adagio in E major .... Merkel.
Scherzo-Symphonique .... Guilmant.

The following is the specification of the organ, erected by Messrs. Forster and Andrews, of Hull :—

GREAT ORGAN. CC to G.

1. Open Diapason	8 ft.	5. Harmonic Flute	4	
2. Gamba	8	6. Twelfth	2⅔	
3. Hohl Flöte	8	7. Fifteenth	2	
4. Principal	4	8. Trumpet	8	

CHOIR ORGAN. CC to G.

9. Dulciana	8 ft.	12. Flautino	2 ft.	
10. Gedact	8	13. Clarinet	8	
11. Flauto Traverso	4			

SWELL ORGAN. CC to G.

14. Lieblich Gedact	16 ft.	19. Harmonic Piccolo	2	
15. Open Diapason	8	20. Cornopean	8	
16. Salicional	8	21. Oboe	8	
17. Voix Celestes	8	22. Clarion	4	
18. Gemshorn	4			

PEDAL ORGAN. CCC to F.

23. Open Diapason	16 ft.	25. Violoncello	8 ft.	
24. Bourdon	16			

COUPLERS.

26. Swell to Great.	29. Swell to Choir.
27. Swell Octave.	30. Great to Pedals.
28. Swell to Pedals.	31. Choir to Pedals.

Three composition pedals to great, and three to swell. The organ contains 25 sounding stops, and 1,398 pipes.

NORWICH.

An organ recital was given in the St. Andrew's Hall, by Dr. J. Bunnett, F.C.O., on Saturday, November 17th. The following was the programme :—

Offertoire in G minor .... Batiste
Andante Grazioso in C .... Hummel.
Sources, from Sonata .... Bach.
Offertoire in G minor .... Wely.
Adagio from the Sonata, " Maid of Orleans " .... Bunnett.
Concert Fantasia .... Spark.
Verdi Pout (" Aida ") .... Smith.
Gavotte in G .... Smith.
March (" Camp of Silesia ") .... Meyerbeer.

OLD STREET, E.C.

An organ recital was given in St. Luke's Parish Church, by Mr. Charles Joseph Frost, Mus.Doc., Cantab., on Wednesday, November 14th. The following was the programme :—

Fugue in G .... Wesley.
Andante in G .... Macfarren.
Concert Piece .... Degenhardt.
Adagio in D .... Silas.
Allegretto in B .... Coupe.
Religious March .... Macfarren.
Andante .... Dubois.
Allegro con brio in D .... Milily.

WATFORD.

An organ recital was given on November 21st, by Mr. James Turpin, Mus.Bac., Cam., at St. Andrew's Church. The following was the programme :—

Occasional (" Occasional Oratorio ") .... Handel.
Tema con Variazioni .... Beethoven.
Prelude and Fugue in D .... Bach.
Andante con moto, " Italian Symphony " .... Mendelssohn.
March, " Tannhäuser " .... Wagner.
Andante No. 1 in A .... Smart.
Chorale with variations, from 9th Organ Sonata ...... Mendelssohn.
Fantasia, " Carillons de Dunkerque " .... E. H. Turpin.
Overture, " Harmonie Musik " (Op. 24) .... Mendelssohn.

The organ of St. Matthew's, Brixton, has been enlarged. It will be re-opened on Tuesday next, the 27th at eight o'clock by Mr. W. T. Best, of Liverpool.

BOW AND BROMLEY INSTITUTE.

On Saturday last a new comer to London was introduced in the performances of Mr. J. W. Phillips, a talented Sheffield organist. His first solo was " Grand Chœur " (Salomé). Next Kullak's " Pastorale," as arranged by Mr. Best, received much applause. Mozart's " Fantasia " in F minor was well rendered and duly applauded. Next came a " Cantabile," by Lemmens, and a favourite Fugue in G major, by Krebs, admirably played and greatly applauded. The final organ solo was Nicolai's overture, " The Merry Wives of Windsor." Mr. Phillips is a player of real promise and power; his style is decisive and brilliant. Mr. H. Lazarus displayed his fine tone and wonderful command over the clarionet technicalities in solos by Weber and Mohr, being in both cases most warmly greeted and having to bow his acknowledgments, wisely declining the encore compliment. Miss A. Larkcom sang charmingly; including as her first song Gounod's beautiful " Ave Maria." She was encored in Diehl's " Going to Market," and gave another song in response, Marzials' " When my Jim comes home," was also sung. Mr. Fountain Meen accompanied. To-night Mr. E. H. Turpin will be the organist; Signor Erba, violin; vocalist, Miss Clara Myers. On Saturday, December 1st, M. Alex. Guilmant will appear, that gentleman, to our artistic gain, availing himself of the comparative freedom of the organists of the Roman Church from duty in Advent and Lent, to pay periodical visits to England. On December 10th, Mendelssohn's " Hymn of Praise," and Haydn's " Spring," will be performed under Mr. McNaught's direction, by band and chorus of about 150 performers.

MIRFIELD.

The following is the synopsis of the organ belonging to Mr. S. Wilkinson Pilling, of Mirfield and Bolton, now being entirely reconstructed by Messrs. Brindley and Foster, of Sheffield. The instrument, which contained three manuals and pedal organ, was built in 1872, by Mr. Halmshaw of Birmingham, and has been added to, or altered by, one or two provincial firms—more recently by the London builders, Messrs. T. C. Lewis and Co. Prior to its erection in the new music room at " Fir Cottage," Mirfield, Mr. Pilling has decided, upon the following specification, which will doubtless prove to be one of the most complete and finest chamber organs in the North of England.

GREAT ORGAN. CC to C.

1. Lieblich Bourdon	16 ft.	5. Harmonic Flute	4	
2. Open Diapason	8	6. Mixture (3 ranks)		
3. Hohl Flöte	8	7. Trumpet	8	
4. Octave	4			

SWELL ORGAN. CC to C.

8. Violin Diapason	8 ft.	14. Mixture (3 ranks)		
9. Lieblich Gedact	8	15. Contra Oboe	16	
10. Gamba	8	16. Oboe	8	
11. Voix Celestes	8	17. Cornopean	8	
12. Lieblich Flöte	4	18. Tremulant	8	
13. Gemshorn				

SOLO ORGAN. CC to C.

19. Dulciana	8 ft.	23. Harmonic Piccolo	2	
20. Unda Maris	8	24. Clarinet	8	
21. Concert Flute	8	25. Vox Humana	8	
22. Flauto Traverso	4	26. Tremulant		

PEDAL ORGAN. CCC to F.

27. Violone	16 ft.	30. Flute Bass	8 ft.	
28. Sub Bass	16	31. Octave		
29. Violoncello	8			

COUPLERS.

32. Swell to Great.	37. Great Super-Octave.
33. Swell to Great.	38. Solo Super-Octave.
34. Swell to Solo.	39. Solo to Great.
35. Swell to Pedal.	40. Great to Pedal.
36. Swell Super-Octave.	41. Solo to Pedal.

Two composition Pedals to the great organ.
Three   " to the swell organ.

The stops numbered 33, 36, 37, 38 and 40 are acted upon by Pedals, in addition to drawstop. The coupler stops are placed over the swell keyboard in front. The drawstop jambs, book desks, and fittings are of ebonised wood, and are fixed at an angle, the drawstops being of solid ivory of neat design. Three independent reservoirs are placed in different parts of the instrument, so as to ensure an ample and steady supply of wind.

A pneumatic lever is applied to the swell organ and its couplers. The louvres to both swell and solo organs are placed vertically, and the pedals communicating with them "poised on an axis," that they (the louvres) will remain stationary at any point. The organ is blown by one of Bailey's engines, placed with separate feeders and reservoir in a room underneath the organ. The case, which is artistic in design, is carried out in American walnut, with burnished spotted metal front pipes.

TUNBRIDGE WELLS.

Two organ recitals were given in the Church of St. James, Tunbridge Wells, by Mr. E. Bunnett, Mus.Doc. Cantab., F.C.O., on Thursday, November 15th, on the occasion of the opening and dedication of the organ. The following were the programmes :—

AFTERNOON.

Overture (Occasional)	Handel.
Barcarolle, from Concerto	Bennett.
Allegretto Grazioso in G	Smart.
Prelude and Fuga in A minor	Bach.
Larghetto in A minor	Mozart.
Organ Sonata, No. 2	Mendelssohn.
Grave—Adagio—Allegro maestoso e vivace—Fuga	
Ave Maria	Bunnett.
Larghetto in A from Symphony in D	Beethoven.
Study in F sharp minor	Chopin.
Andante con moto in G	Bolly.
Offertoire in C	

EVENING.

Overture in B minor	Morandi.
Russian Air, with variations	
Organ Concerto in B flat, No. 6	Handel.
Cantone in A minor	Guilmant.
Fantasia in G	Batiste.
Chapel by the Sea	Bennett.
Schiller March	Meyerbeer.

The following is the specification of the organ, as rebuilt and enlarged by Messrs. J. W. Walker and Sons, London, 1883. The instrument has three complete manuals, and an independent pedal organ.

GREAT ORGAN. CC TO G. 56 NOTES.

1. Open Diapason	8 ft.		5. Harmonic Flute	4 ft.
2. Stopped Diapason	8		6. Twelfth	
3. Salicional	8		7. Mixture (3 ranks)	
4. Principal	4		8. Posaune	8

SWELL ORGAN. CC TO G. 56 NOTES.

9. Bourdon	16 ft.		15. Flute	4 ft.
10. Open Diapason	8		16. Harmonic Piccolo	2
11. Stopped Diapason	8		17. Mixture (3 ranks)	
12. Echo Gamba	8		18. Cornopean	8
13. Vox Angelica	8		19. Oboe	8
14. Principal	4		20. Vox Humana	8

CHOIR ORGAN. CC TO G. 56 NOTES.

22. Open Diapason	8 ft.		25. Lieblich Flute	4 ft.
23. Rohr Flöte	8		26. Piccolo	2
24. Dulciana	8		27. Clarionet	8

PEDAL ORGAN. CCC TO F. 30 NOTES.

28. Open Diapason	16 ft.		31. Violoncello	8 ft.
29. Bourdon	16		32. Quint	10⅔
30. Principal	8			

COUPLERS.

33. Swell to Great		37. Great to Pedal
34. Great to Pedal		38. Choir to Pedal
35. Swell to Choir		39. Pedal Octave
36. Swell to Pedal		

Three composition Pedals to great.
Three to swell.
Tremulant to swell.

The bass of the open diapason great organ forms the chancel front, and the violoncello the west front, both of best spotted metal.

BOLTON.

An organ recital was given in the Albert Hall, by Mr. W. Mullineux, F.C.O., on Saturday, November 17th. The following was the programme :—

Chorus, "From the censer curling rise" ("Solomon")	Handel.
Adagio for the Organ in E major	Merkel.
Prelude and Fugue in A minor	Bach.
Minuetto Romantico	Smith.
Air, "Nazareth"	Gounod.
Prayer, from the opera "Der Freischütz"	Weber.

And on Monday, November 19th :—

Sonata in D minor, No. 3	Mendelssohn.
Chorale with variations—Fuga—Andante	
Serenade, "L'enfance du Christ"	Berlioz.
Prelude and Fugue in G minor	Bach.
Elevation in A flat	Guilmant.
Variations on the hymn tune, "O Sanctissima"	Lux.
Organ Concerto in F major	Handel.
Adagio—Allegro—Allegretto con moto—Fuga	
Adagio for the organ in B major	Merkel.
Grand Processional March in E flat	Lefébure Wely.

HUDDERSFIELD.

Mr. J. R. Brooke, organist to the Earl of Carlisle, Castle Howard, gave an organ recital at the Fine Art Exhibition, on the 13th inst., when he performed the following programme in a very able manner :—

Overture, "Samson"	Handel.
Festal March	Clark.
Air, "If with all your hearts" ("Elijah")	Mendelssohn.
Offertoire No. 3	Wely.
Prelude and Fugue in G	Bach.
Air, "But Thou didst not leave" ("Messiah")	Handel.
Chorus, "Let us break their bonds asunder" ("Messiah")	Handel.
Andante	Silas.
Prelude and Fugue on the name of BACH	Rinck.
Air, "Total Eclipse" ("Samson")	Handel.
Chorus, "Hallelujah, Amen"	Judas.

Mr. Joel Hurst was the vocalist, and he gave his songs with great taste and judgment.

The following is the programme of the organ, and is by J. W. Walker & Sons, London.

GLASGOW.

A recital of organ and sacred music was given in Maxwell Parish Church, by Mr. James Rattinson, Mus. Bac., Cantab., on the 15th inst. The programme included :—

Concerto in F	Handel.
Andante maestoso—Adagio—Allegro.	
Andante in D	Silas.
Fugue in B minor	Bach.
Minuetto and Trio	Bennett.
Santa Maria o Marie Religioso	
Andante in B flat	Smart.
Con Moto Moderato in D	Smart.

BRIGHTON.

An organ recital was given in the Aquarium, on Saturday, the 17th inst., by Mr. James Hall. The following was the programme :—

Andante from the Septuor	Beethoven.
Sonata No. 6	Mendelssohn.
Allegro Moderato (Quartet in G minor)	Mozart.
Offertoire in G, No. 4	Wely.
Concerto No. 4	Handel.
Fugue in D major	Bach.
Air, with variations in A	Handel.

PRESENTATION TO THE ORGANIST OF SALISBURY CATHE-DRAL.—An elegant testimonial has just been presented to Mr. C. South, the late organist of St. Augustine and St. Faith, Watling Street, City, by the Rector, Churchwardens, and congregation thereof. It will be remembered that Mr. South was recently appointed to the important position of organist and choirmaster of the great Cathedral of Salisbury, which possesses one of the largest and finest organs in England, after his having for some years filled a similar post at the pretty little church placed under the shadow of our own St. Paul's. The presentation was made at the residence of the Rev. W. H. Milman, M.A., rector, and took the form of a silver teapot, cream ewer, sugar basin, and salver, around the inner part of which latter runs an inscription in Latin, setting forth and bearing testimony to the high qualifies —not only musical, but personal likewise—of the recipient; it may be added that prior to Mr. South's original departure from London for his new and enlarged sphere of usefulness, he received a handsome marble timepiece bearing a plate with the following inscription:—" Presented to C. F. South, Esq., for 15 years Organist and Choirmaster of St. Augustine and St. Faith, London, as a tribute from the gentlemen of the Choir to his many excellences, both as a musician and a friend.—July 2, 1883."

EXETER.—The recital on Nov. 17th proved one of the most enjoyable of the present series. Both the organist (Mr. D. J. Wood, Mus.Bac.) and the vocalist (Miss Grace Godolphin) received numerous marks of approval. Miss Godolphin was called, and bowed her acknowledgments after singing "Happy art thou, Magdalena," from Stainer's "St. Mary Magdalene," her appreciative rendering of Wellings's "Golden Love" elicited so pronounced an outburst of applause that the audience would not desist until she began to repeat the second stanza; while the mingled playfulness and sympathy that marked her vocalisation in Molloy's ever-welcome "Kerry Dance" earned a similarly enthusiastic compliment. Mr. Wood's selections were much admired. The accomplished organist had intended to play the "Andante con moto" in E flat, dedicated to him by M. Guilmant, but as the eminent Frenchman had included the composition for the 5th prox., Mr. Wood with the assent of his listeners, substituted one of Field's nocturnes. Mr. Wood was encored after playing Rossini's overture to "Il Tancredi" and Benedict's Fantasia in Welsh airs. The Handel Concerto in F, with the cuckoo and nightingale duet, were exceedingly liked, and so were Mendelssohn's chorus, "Heaven, and earth display," Beethoven's slow movement (pianoforte concerto in C), and Frog's March in B flat, with which the performance terminated.

Correspondence.

IMPROVISATION.

TO THE EDITOR OF THE "MUSICAL STANDARD."

SIR,—In an article on "Improvisation," published in your last week's paper, I find an omission *too important* not to require correction. One of the greatest of improvisers of all times was *J. N. Hummel*, pupil of Mozart, and to the last an intimate friend of Beethoven, who held Hummel's opinion in such high esteem, that be asked him, when on his deathbed, "Is it not true my dear Hummel that I have had talent"? ("Nicht wahr mein lieber Hummel ich habe talent gehabt"?) Hummel's improvising in public—which I have the good fortune to remember as some of the most powerful impressions of my youth—had left a similar effect on such men as Spohr, Aloys-Schmidt, Lindpaintner, &c., with all of whom I was on terms of intimacy, and have had many conversations about the subject of improvisation, on all occasions of which Hummel, in their opinion, came to the fore !

I am also of opinion that in the *highest* kind of improvisation there is a power at work, infinitely above the "certain amount of quick discrimination or discernment in accepting or rejecting thoughts or ideas as they present themselves," which your correspondent names as conditions.

I deem it to be a state of mental ecstasy which is closely allied to second sight; it is self-acting, and not only does *not* require watchful thinking, but really seems to *exclude* it as a drag on the flow of imagination. That highest kind of improvisation is *heaven-born genius* !

That one can develop the art of extemporising by tuition up to a considerable height, even in minds not gifted with it spontaneously by nature,—admits of no doubt, and I in my long career as teacher, have invariably made it a special labour of love to do it systematically, but I repeat, one can only " go thus far and no farther " with training.

I cannot conclude my letter without, in justice, referring to one *amongst us* who possesses a most remarkable gift of improvising fugues. I allude to the well-known composer Silas ; he will extemporise in the strictest style on several subjects given him, and jocularly add himself, a *popular tune*—working them with masterly skill together, in a manner to surprise anyone who understands the extreme difficulty of such a procedure. Mr. Silas certainly should be induced to give the public at large, as well as his private friends, the advantage of his extraordinary talent.   Yours truly,

FERDINAND PRAEGER.

A RIGHT OF PERFORMANCE QUESTION.

TO THE EDITOR OF THE "MUSICAL STANDARD."

SIR,—I see by your issue of yesterday (Nov. 17th) that you say (speaking of "Music at City Dinners ") John Barnett's Trio in G, "This magic wove scarf," comes out occasionally like a glowworm, etc. Will you please inform me whether this Trio may be sung in public without *payment of a fee* ? A reply in your next issue will oblige,

Yours faithfully,

A. W. H. H.

Passing Events.

Mr. C. Duval's entertainment at St. James's Hall, has reached its 100th presentation this evening.

The programme of an organ recital to hand this week from the North has the ingenious and suggestive sentence " Collection in Silver," printed in capital letters,

The Kyrle Society performed Handel's " Samson " at St. Jude's, St. Peter's Park, on Nov. 21st, under the beat of Mr. M. L. Lawson ; Mr. E. H. Turpin being the organist.

Mr. W. Beattie-Kingston is reported to be engaged upon the English version of the " Bettelstudent " for Mr. Carl Rosa. No better or more experienced translator could be found for the task.

The numerous friends of Mr. J. W. Davison will regret to learn that he has been suffering from severe illness at Margate. It is gratifying to be able to add that he is now much better, and shortly returns to town.

At the Stepney Meeting House a performance of Handel's " Samson," was given by the Kyrle Choir, on Nov. 14th. The soloists were Miss Agnes Allen, Mrs. Oram, Mr. Reginald Groome, Mr. Albert Orme, Mr. A. Herbert ; conductor, Mr. Malcolm Lawson ; organist, Mr. E. H. Turpin.

The announcement is made that Mr. Alfred J. Caldicott, the composer of the oratorio, " The Widow of Nain," " Treasure Trove," and some popular humorous glees, has been appointed one of the professors at the Royal College of Music.

Mr. A. H. Day's weekly organ recital at the Parish Church, Seaford, Sussex, on the 18th, consisted of a selection from the " Messiah," which was listened to by a large congregation. Next Sunday the programme will be a miscellaneous one, as usual.

Local papers call attention to the successful performance of a " Triumphal March " for orchestra and military band, by a young composer, Mr. H. J. Edwards, Mus.Bac., of Barnstaple, at the Covent Garden concerts, and note that other compositions of the same writer have had success.

Mdme. Ronniger gave her first recital at Kensington Town Hall, to a numerous and appreciative audience, but unfortunately the amateur element was too prominent in the programme. The professional vocalists were, Miss Gwynne, and Messrs. Gray, Warwick, and Ria, and a Captain Acklom ; Mdme. Ronniger and Miss Goad gave some most interesting recitations. Mr. Charles Marshall carried out the duties of accompanist and conductor very ably.

The many admirers of Purcell will be glad to know that it is proposed to perform his anthem, " O praise God in his Holiness," with the original string parts, at the church of St. Luke, Chelsea, on the evening of Sunday next, under the direction of Mr. F. E. W. Hulton, Mus.Bac., organist and choirmaster of the church. It is said this will be the first performance, probably, of the work in its complete form since the death of the great composer. Service commences at 7 p.m.

The *Athenæum* announces that Mr. Dannreuther proposes to give a series of four musical evenings, to take place on Thursdays, Nov. 22nd and 29th, and Dec. 6th and 13th. The programmes are highly interesting from the number of important novelties promised. These include Tschaikowski's Pianoforte Trio in A minor ; a Quartet in C by Mr. Henry Holmes ; a Sonata in A minor for piano and violoncello, by Grieg, Op. 36 ; and a Sonata in A for piano and violin, by H. von Herzogenberg. Among the other works promised are Mr. Hubert Parry's Trio in E minor and his newly published Pianoforte Quartet in A flat, and Sgambati's Quintet in F minor, Op. 4.

Service Lists.

TWENTY-SEVENTH SUNDAY AFTER TRINITY.

NOVEMBER 25th.

London.

ST. PAUL'S CATHEDRAL. — Morn.: Service, Te Deum, and Benedictus, Calkin in B flat ; Introit, O send out Thy light (Calkin) ; Holy Communion, Calkin in B flat. Even.: Service, Magnificat and Nunc Dimittis, Calkin in B flat ; Anthem, Yet merciful and tender is the Lord (Gadsby).

FOUNDLING CHAPEL. — Morn.: Service, Te Deum, and Benedictus, Smart in F ; Anthem, The Wilderness (Goss). Aft.: Children Service.

TEMPLE CHURCH.—Morn.: Service, Te Deum Laudamus and Jubilate Deo, Attwood in F ; Apostles' Creed, Harmonised Monotone ; Anthem, Glory, honour, praise and power (Mozart). Even.: Service, Cantate Domino and Deus Misereatur, Attwood in D ; Apostles' Creed, Harmonised Monotone ; Anthem, Sing unto the Lord (Croft).

LINCOLN'S INN CHAPEL.—Morn.: Service, Steggall in G ; Kyrie (Steggall) ; Anthem, Praise the Lord, O my soul (Goss). Even: Service, Steggall in G ; Anthem, Sing unto the Lord, praise His name (Croft).

ALL SAINTS, MARGARET STREET.—Morn.: Service, Te Deum (Stainer) ; Benedictus (Stainer) ; Holy Communion, Schubert in B flat ; Offertory, Anthem, God is a Spirit (Bennett). Even.: Service, Gounod in D ; Anthem, Sing to the Lord " 98th Psalm " (Mendelssohn).

CHRIST CHURCH, CLAPHAM.—Morn.: Service, Te Deum, Plain-song ; Kyrie and Credo, Weber in E flat, Offertory Anthem, How beautiful are the feet (Handel) ; Sanctus, Benedictus, Agnus Dei, and Gloria in excelsis (Weber). Even.: Service, Magnificat and Nunc Dimittis, Martin in A ; Anthem, Praise the Lord, O my soul (Goss).

HOLY TRINITY, GRAY'S INN ROAD. — Morn.: Service, Te Deum, Chanted; Jubilate, Boyce in A; Litany (Mercer). Even.: Service, Magnificat (Chanted); and Nunc Dimittis, Tours in F; Anthem, Sing and rejoice (Barnby).

HOLY TRINITY, HAVERSTOCK HILL.—Morn.: Service Te Deum and Jubilate, Smart in F; Apostles' Creed, Harmonized Monotone; Kyrie, Smart in F; Offertory Sentences (Martin); Anthem, I was glad (Elvey). Even.: Service, Magnificat and Nunc Dimittis, Stainer in B flat; Anthem, O clap your hands (Stainer), and Hallelujah to the Father (Beethoven).

HOLY TRINITY, TULSE HILL. — Morn.: Service, Chants. Even.: Service, Magnificat and Nunc Dimittis, Agutter in D; Anthem, Praise the Lord, O my soul (Stark).

ST. JAMES'S PRIVATE EPISCOPAL CHAPEL, SOUTHWARK. —Morn.: Service, Introit, To Thee, great Lord (Rossini); Communion Service, Hummel in D. Even.: Service, Travers in F; Anthem, Through the darkness, when Thou comest (Rossini).

ST. MARGARET PATTENS, ROOD LANE, FENCHURCH STREET. — Morn.: Service, Te Deum, Tuckerman in F; Benedictus, Smart in F; Communion Service, Offertory Anthem, Cast thy burden (Mendelssohn); Kyrie, Credo, Sanctus, Benedictus, Agnus Dei, and Gloria, Weber in E flat. Even.: Service, Magnificat and Nunc Dimittis, Tuckermann in F; Anthem, I waited for the Lord (Mendelssohn).

ST. MARY BOLTONS, WEST BROMPTON, S.W.—Morn.: Service, Te Deum, and Benedictus, Dykes in F; Holy Communion, Kyrie, Credo, Sanctus, and Gloria in excelsis, Smart in F; Benedictus, and Agnus Dei (Redhead); Offertory (Barnby). Even.: Service, Magnificat and Nunc Dimittis, Dykes in F; Anthem, Here by Babylon's wave (Gounod).

ST. MAGNUS, LONDON BRIDGE.—Morn.: Service, Opening Anthem, To the Lord our God (Chikin); Te Deum and Jubilate, Smart in F; Kyrie (Wesley). Even.: Service, Magnificat and Nunc Dimittis, Attwood in F.; Anthem, I will sing (Goemm).

ST. PAUL'S, AVENUE ROAD, SOUTH HAMPSTEAD.—Morn.: Service, Te Deum, Tilleard in F; Benedictus (Tuzle); Kyrie, Arnold in A. Even.: Service, Magnificat and Nunc Dimittis, Arnold in A; Anthem, Remember now thy Creator (Steggall).

ST. PAUL'S, BOW COMMON, E.—Morn.: Service, Te Deum and Benedictus, Stainer in B flat; Even.; Service, Magnificat and Nunc Dimittis, Tours in D; Anthem, By the waters of Babylon (Boyce).

ST. PETER'S, VERE STREET, W.—Even.: Service, Magnificat and Nunc Dimittis, Tuckermann in F; Anthem, The Lord is my Shepherd (Macfarren).

ST. AUGUSTINE AND ST. FAITH, WATLING STREET.— Morn.: Service, Garrett in F; Introit, He fed them (South); Communion Service, Schubert in G. Even.: Service, Garrett in F; Anthem, The Lord great wonders for us hath wrought (Hiller); After the Sermon, Spohr's, God, Thou art great.

ST. SAVIOUR'S, HOXTON. — Morn.: Service, Te Deum, Hopkins in G; Holy Communion; Kyrie, Credo, Sursum Corda, Sanctus, and Gloria in excelsis, James in A. Even.: Service, Magnificat and Nunc Dimittis (Best); Anthem, O taste and see (Goss).

ST. SEPULCHRE'S, HOLBORN. — Morn.: Service, Te Deum and Jubilate, Smart in F; Kyrie and Credo, Lott in F; Anthem, Call to remembrance (Farrant). Even.: Service, Magnificat and Nunc Dimittis, Cooke in G; Anthem, Praise His awful name (Spohr).

Country.

ST. ASAPH CATHEDRAL. — Morn.: Service, Lewis in C; Anthem, I will greatly rejoice (Haydn Keeton). Even.: Service, Frost in D; Anthem, It shall come to pass (Garrett).

ASHBURNE CHURCH, DERBYSHIRE. — Morn.: Service, throughout, Stanford in B flat.; Even. Service, Stanford in B flat; Anthem, Awake (Stainer).

BEDDINGTON CHURCH, SURREY.—Morn.: Service, Garrett in E; Communion Service, Garrett in F. Even.: Service, Garrett in F; Anthem, But the Lord is mindful, of His own (Mendelssohn).

BIRMINGHAM (S. ALBAN THE MARTYR).—Morn.: Service, Te Deum, and Benedictus, Goss in A; Holy Communion, Woodward in E flat, Evensong: Magnificat and Nunc Dimittis, Bunnett in F.

BIRMINGHAM (ST. CYPRIAN'S, HAY MILLS).—Morn.: Service, Nares in C; Anthem, O sing unto God (Blow). Even.: Service, Ebdon in C; Anthem, O Lord, have mercy (Pergolesi).

BIRMINGHAM (ST. MICHAEL's, HAWORTH).—Morn.: Service, Te Deum and Benedictus; Communion (Thorne). Even.: Service, Magnificat and Nunc Dimittis; Anthem, Come unto me (Gounod).

BIRMINGHAM (S. PHILIP'S CHURCH).— Morn.: Service, Barnby in E; Anthem, O give thanks (Rea). Evensong Service, Stainer in A; Anthem, When the Son of Man (Kent).

BELFAST (ST. GEORGE'S). — Morn.: Service, Te Deum, and Jubilate, Garrett in F; Communion Service, Parry in D; Offertory (Stainer). Even.: Service, Magnificat and Nunc Dimittis, Goss in A; Anthem, Send out Thy light (Gounod).

CANTERBURY CATHEDRAL. — Morn.: Service, Richardson in F; Anthem, Come, my people (Wintle); Communion, Richardson in F. Even.: Service, Richardson in F; Anthem, How lovely are Thy dwellings fair (Spohr).

CARLISLE CATHEDRAL. — Morn.: Service, Chipp in A; Introit, I will love Thee (Macfarren; Kyrie, and Creed Lloyd in E flat. Even.: Service, Garrett in F; Anthem, O sing unto the Lord (Purcell).

DONCASTER (PARISH CHURCH).—Morn.: Service, Wesley in F. Even.: Service, Stainer in B flat; Anthem, I am Alpha and Omega (Stainer).

DUBLIN, ST. PATRICK'S (NATIONAL) CATHEDRAL.—Morn.: Service, Te Deum and Jubilate, Stanford in B flat; Holy Communion, Kyrie, Creed and Sanctus, Stanford in B flat; Anthem, Sing O heavens (Sullivan). Even.: Service, Cantate and Miserator, Stevenson in D; Anthem, Hallelujah (Beethoven); and The Wilderness (Wesley).

EDINBURGH (ST. JOHN'S).—Aft.: Service, Anthem, I was in the Spirit (Blow). Even.: Service, Anthem, O praise God (Weldon).

ELY CATHEDRAL. — Morn.: Service, Stainer in E flat; Kyrie and Credo, Stainer in E flat; Gloria, Chipp in A flat; Anthem, Jesus said, I am the bread of life (Stainer). Even.: Service, Stainer in E flat; Anthem, The wilderness (Wesley).

LEATHERHEAD (ST. JOHN'S FOUNDATION SCHOOL) —Morn.: Service, Te Deum, and Jubilate, Goss in A; Kyrie (Faning); Creed, Goss in D. Even.: Service, Anthem, What are these (Stainer).

LEEDS PARISH CHURCH—Morn.: Service, PrinceConsort in A; Anthem, I saw the Lord (Stainer); Introit, O taste and see (Goss); Kyrie and Creed, Walmisley in F. Even.: Service, Bridge in G; Anthem, Not unto us (Mendelssohn).

LICHFIELD CATHEDRAL. — Morn.: Service, Cooke in G; Anthem, Judge me, O God (Mendelssohn). Even.: Service, Cooke in G; Anthem, Wherewithal shall a young man (Elvey).

LINLITHGOW ABBEY, N.B. — Morn.: Service, Anthem, Come, Holy Ghost (Elvey). Even.: Service, Anthem, Doth not wisdom cry (Haking).

LIVERPOOL CATHEDRAL. — Aft.: Service, Magnificat and Nunc Dimittis, Oakeley in E flat; Anthem, Unto Thee, O Lord (Yates).

MANCHESTER CATHEDRAL. — Morn.: Service, Te Deum, Jubilate, Kyrie, Creed, Sanctus, and Gloria, Chipp in A; Anthem, Lift up your heads (Handel). Aft.: Service, Chipp in A; Anthem, I saw the Lord (Stainer).

MANCHESTER (St. BENEDICT's).—Morn.: Service, Kyrie, Credo, Sanctus, and Gloria in excelsis, Steggall in G; Benedictus and Agnus Dei, Guilmant in E flat (No. 3). Even.: Service, Magnificat and Nunc Dimittis, Bunnett in F.

MANCHESTER (ST. JOHN BAPTIST, HULME).—Morn.: Service, Te Deum and Benedictus " Gregorian "; Kyrie, Credo, Sanctus, Benedictus, Agnus Dei and Gloria in excelsis, (De la Hache). Even.: Service, Magnificat and Nunc Dimittis, Bunnett in F.

MUSSELBURGH (LORETTO SCHOOL).—Morn.: Service, Introit, O praise the Lord (Goss); Service, Smart in F; Anthem, In splendour bright, and the heavens are telling, " Creation " (Haydn). Even.: Service, Anthem, O Lord have mercy (Pergolesi).

SHEFFIELD PARISH CHURCH. —Even.: Service, Trimnell in D; Anthem, O taste and see (Sullivan).

SHERBORNE ABBEY. — Morn.: Service, Te Deum and Jubilate, Lyle in D. Even.: Service, Chants; Anthem, Behold the days come (Lyle).

SOUTHAMPTON (ST. MARY'S CHURCH).—Morn.: Service, Te Deum and Benedictus, Woodward in E flat; Holy Communion, Introit, Father of Heaven; Service, Woodward in E flat; Offertory, Not every one (Barnby); Paternoster (Field). Even.: Service, Magnificat and Nunc Dimittis, Walmisley in D minor; Apostles' Creed, Harmonized Monotone; Anthem, Blessed be Thou (Kent).

WELLS, CATHEDRAL—Morn.: Service, Turle in D, throughout. Even.: Service, Heathcott in B flat; Anthem, Rejoice in the Lord (Purcell).

WORCESTER CATHEDRAL.—Morn.: Service, Croft in A; Anthem, Incline thine ear (Himmel). Even.: Service, Elvey in A; Anthem, Remember now thy Creator (Steggall).

APPOINTMENTS.

Mr. WILLIAM EDGAR WOOD, late organist of Bathford Church, near Bath, has been appointed Organist and Choirmaster of Laura Episcopal Chapel, Bath.

Mr. T. BARROW DOWLING has been appointed Organist and Choirmaster to St. Matthew's Church, Sydenham Hill.

Printed for the Proprietor by BOWDEN, HUDSON & Co., at 23, Red Lion Street, Holborn, London, W.C.; and Published by WILLIAM REEVES, at
the Office, 185, Fleet Street, E.C. West End Agents:—WEEKES & CO., 14, Hanover Street, Regent Street, W. Subscriptions and Advertisements are
received either by the Publisher or West End Agents.—Communications for the EDITOR are to be forwarded to his private address, 6, Argyle Square, W.C.
SATURDAY, NOVEMBER 24, 1883.—Entered at the General Post Office as a Newspaper.

The MUSICAL STANDARD

A NEWSPAPER FOR MUSICIANS PROFESSIONAL AND AMATEUR

No. 1,009. VOL. XXV, FOURTH SERIES. SATURDAY, DECEMBER 1, 1883. WEEKLY: PRICE 3D.

Musical Intelligence.

CRYSTAL PALACE CONCERTS.

PROGRAMME.

Overture, " Der Freischütz " .... Weber.
Concerto for violin and orchestra in D (Op. 82)....... Raiuecke.
      Mons. A. Fischer.
    (His first appearance at the Crystal Palace).
Song, " Bells in the valley " (" Euryanthe ").......... Weber.
    Miss Mary Davies.
Symphony No. 8, in B minor .... Schubert.
Solos for violoncello :— " Nocturne " .... Chopin.
    " Tarantella in A minor " ..... Fischer.
Songs, " Absence," and " If love were what the rose is " Cowen.
    Miss Mary Davies.
Ballad Airs, " La Colomba " .... Mackenzie.
    (First time at these Concerts).

Conductor - - AUGUST MANNS.

It has been well said—the same by the way could be equally well said of almost every other good and familiar work—that the overture to " Der Freischütz " is so well known and so truly appreciated by all lovers of orchestral music, that any eulogy or criticism upon it would be more than superfluous. Nevertheless, it may be well to call to mind that as it was by the music of this opera that Weber first made his mark in the world, we therefore owe to it—with its overture—the possession of " Euryanthe," " Oberon," and a host of other compositions, everything being made easy to him by its great success. Beethoven was as much taken with it as anyone, and said, " I should never have expected it of that quiet fellow. And now he must write operas, one after another, straight ahead, without beating about the bush." That it was splendidly played last Saturday, *va sans dire*.

Reinecke is chiefly known in England as an excellent pianoforte player and composer for that instrument, but his vocal works include masses, an oratorio, cantatas, &c., and his orchestral compositions are very numerous—two or three symphonies, concertos, quartets, quintets, overtures, &c. He occupies a very high position in his native country, being at the present time director of the famous Gewandhaus Concerts at Leipzig. In the concerto in D for violoncello, his orchestration is bold, clear, and masterly, and the solo performer has full scope for producing effects of a charming kind. In the hands of M. Fischer, the composer found a true and conscientious interpreter. The performance was well received, but scarcely so well as it deserved. In Chopin's Nocturne and in M. Fischer's own Tarantelle, he was more heartily applauded.

Schubert's unfinished Symphony was decidedly the gem of the concert ! Although never wanting in individuality, an able writer says, " We find in his later works reminiscences of Beethoven, but compared to Beethoven Schubert is a feminine character, more talkative, gentler, tenderer. True, he has powerful movements, nor is he wanting in breadth and vigour, but as a gentle entreating woman beside a masculine character—though only in comparison to Beethoven. Compared to others, he is masculine enough, for he is the most vigorous and original of modern writers." Happily on this occasion we had nothing tacked on as a *finale* to the two completed movements.

Miss Mary Davies sang in a chaste and refined manner, as she always does, and the concert was brought to a close by the beautiful ballet airs from Mr. Mackenzie's " Colomba." R.S.

WESTERN MADRIGAL SOCIETY.

On Wednesday, 28th November, the following selection of music was sung, under the direction of Dr. Bridge :—

Madrigal, " O hear me love " .... Nanino.
  " Come let us sing " .... Byrd.
  " Hope of my heart " .... Ward.
  " Draw on, sweet night " .... Wilbye.
Motet, " Kyrie Eleison " .... Palestrina.
Madrigal, " Fye, thou silly shepherd " .... Arcadelt.
  " Phillida, come tell " .... Vecchi.
  " Lady, your words " .... Wilbye.
Chorale and Fugue, " Glory to God " .... Graun.
Madrigal, " Phillis, go take thy pleasure " ...... Weelkes.
  " Love wakes and weeps " .... Read.
  " Lo, where with flow'ry head " .... Morley.
  " Now peep, bo peep " .... Pilkington.
  " A garden is my lady's face " .... Alison.
  " Lady, when I behold " .... Wilbye.
  " Now is the month of may " .... Morley.

A stained glass window has been placed in the north aisle of Westminster Abbey in memory of the late organist, Mr. Turle, and his wife.

SATURDAY POPULAR CONCERTS.

PROGRAMME.
Quintet in C major, No. 3, for two violins, two violas,
  and violoncello......................... Mozart.
Madame Norman-Néruda, MM. L. Ries, Hollander, Zerbini,
    and Piatti.
Recit. " Deeper and deeper still " }
Air, " Waft her, angels "   } .... Handel.
    Mr. Joseph Maas.
Humoreske (Op. 20), No. 2, for pianoforte alone ...... Schumann.
    Mr. Charles Hallé.
Quartet in E minor (Op. 21), for pianoforte, violin,
  viola and violoncello .... Fibich.
    (First time).
Mr. Charles Hallé, Madame Norman-Néruda, MM. Hollander,
    and Piatti.
Song, " Dalla sua pace " .... Mozart.
    Mr. Joseph Maas.
Trio in C major, No. 7, for pianoforte, violin, and
  violoncello .... Mozart.
    (First time).
Mr. Charles Hallé, Madame Norman-Néruda, and Signor Piatti.

Accompanist   -   Mr. ZERBINI.

A new work, by an author unknown even by name to most musicians in this country, is a rare and most interesting appearance at these concerts. It is, therefore, the more pleasant to be able to record that the Quartet by Fibich met with a decidedly favourable reception—an honour to which its merits thoroughly entitle it.

Mdenhe Fibich is introduced to the readers of the programmes as a Bohemian, whose musical education was conducted at Prague and afterwards at Leipzic. He has now nearly completed his 33rd year, and, it appears, holds the post in Prague of conductor of the National Theatre and Chorus Director of the Russian Church. He has written much, and judging by the quartet before us, his works are of a character to attain speedy popularity. Of the school of Scharwenka and Tschaikowsky —a school which has sprung from the new spirit which was infused into our Art by Chopin, though we are often told Chopin founded no school—his writings will have a particular fascination for those who are attracted by, what the programme calls, " The Bohemian style of quartet-writing." This " Bohemian style," be it observed, is strictly classical in form ; its chief distinctiveness apparently arises from the somewhat vague, dreamy, long-drawn out nature of its subjects. In this respect Fibich's work stood out in strange contrast to the final Trio (which, by the way, nearly half the audience did not stay to hear, as the concert was prolonged far beyond the usual limits), the subjects of which are, more than is customary even in Mozart, simple, downright, and child-like. The Quartet is in three movements, the first and last in the usual form, and a slow movement—an air with variations. Many of the effects are striking ; the opening, with the long-held dominant of the key at once arrests attention, which the succeeding melodies well sustain. May this, and other works by the same writer, have frequent opportunities of appealing to English musicians !

Mr. Maas's artistic performances were duly appreciated, and Mr. Hallé's reading of the Humoreske was interesting and satisfactory; though the work itself is perhaps calculated to impress a small circle of sympathising listeners, rather than a large and mixed assembly, who look for a well-prepared, logically-arranged oration, rather than gentle, lovely, confidential speeches.

An unusual distraction occurred after the slow movement of the opening quintet. A lady in the orchestra had fainted during its course, and a lengthy pause ensued before the finale, to enable her, with much difficulty, to be carried out.

B. F. WYATT-SMITH.

Mr. E. Aguilar will resume his excellent recitals of pianoforte music the week before Christmas.

In connection with German opera in London, another statement has appeared that Mr. Ernest Gye, director of the Royal Italian Opera Company, has entered into an agreement with Herr Angelo Neumann for twenty performances of German operas at the Covent Garden establishment, to be given next year, during the usual season of Italian Opera performances, and in alternation therewith. The German *répertoire* will, it is said, comprise Wagner's " Der Fliegende Holländer," " Tannhäuser," " Lohengrin," " Die Meistersinger," and " Tristan und Isolde " ; besides which, Gluck's " Orféo " and " Armide," Nicolai's " Die lustigen Weiber von Windsor," and Goldmark's " Die Königin von Saba," are named for performance. It is said that Mdme. Albani and Mdme. Pauline Lucca will be associated with the German company in some of the performances.

MONDAY POPULAR CONCERTS.

Last Monday evening the director arranged the annexed programme:—

Programme.—Part 1.

Quartet in A major, No. 5, for two violins, viola, and violoncello .... Mozart.
Madame Norman-Néruda, MM. L. Ries Hollander, and Piatti.
Song, "Hearken, ye children of men" .... Borton.
Miss Carlotta Elliot.
Etudes Symphoniques (for pianoforte alone) .... Schumann.
Miss Agnes Zimmermann.

Part 2.

Songs :—"My heart and lute" .... Kjerulf.
"Chanson de Florian" .... Godard.
Miss Carlotta Elliot.
Trio in B flat (Op. 52), for pianoforte, violin and violoncello .... Rubinstein.
Miss Agnes Zimmermann, Madame Norman-Néruda, and Signor Piatti.
Accompanist .. Mr. H. DEACON.

M. Vladimir Pachmann, lately the lion both of the afternoon and evening concerts, has given place, for the time being, to Mr. Charles Hallé and Miss Agnes Zimmermann. Of Mr. Hallé's doings a good account is given elsewhere. Miss Zimmermann, a German by birth, happens to be a distinguished prize pupil of our own Royal Academy, which is proud to have her name on the list of its students. The young lady has studied in the best schools here and abroad; she has given to the world, as often before stated, some admirable compositions for the chamber, and the Director of the Popular Concerts has made her one of his half-dozen *pianistes d'élite*. Miss Zimmermann may be styled a strictly objective player, intent on a severely accurate interpretation of the text "according to copy," without pretension to enforce the reading by any intrusive suggestions of her own individual ideas. In a word, to borrow the terminology of her own country's transcendental metaphysics, Miss Zimmermann looks to the "Ding an sich," and, as Fichte would say, maintains the *passività t* (passivity) of the *ego*. Scholastic execution, however, is one thing, choice of pieces another. Schumann's "Symphonic Studies" in C sharp minor, like other and more important forms of the "variation" type that might be mentioned— a notable "32" to wit—fail to excite the soul of the listener, and, to speak in a stage whisper, they are felt by many to be positively dry and tedious. The persistent minor mode, only relieved by a change (before the final march) to G sharp minor, tends to aggravate the monotony. Miss Zimmermann more especially excelled in Variation VI., played with exquisite delicacy and finish, and in Variation IX. (G sharp minor), where the audience listened with rapt attention. A "furious" encore (not reported in the *Times*), induced a charming little gem, suspected to be Miss Zimmermann's own.
Mozart's string quartet, fifth of the famous "Haydn" set, was led by Madme. Norman-Néruda. Careful auditors were particularly delighted with the precise extension of the minuet and the *finale*, where Mozart writes contrapuntally and with extra elaboration. Rubinstein's pianoforte trio must be repeated before Easter 1884 "by desire." Teeming with melodic brilliants, of purest ray serene, the adagio in D minor and the presto (scherzo) in F, with its rapid scale passages in descent, must always stimulate and arrest attention. The reading of the adagio was perfect, the second theme proper, in B flat, decidedly grand. Miss C. Elliot chose songs to suit her voice and won recalls.
Miss Zimmermann, on Monday next, is to play in a new pianoforte quartet in A flat by Mr. C. Hubert Parry. She chooses a Fugue of J. S. Bach for her solo—why not a sonata?   A. M.

ROYAL ALBERT HALL.

Gounod's "The Redemption," first heard at Birmingham in 1882, was performed for the third time at the Albert Hall on Wednesday evening, by the "Royal Albert Hall Choral Society," with Mdme. Albani as principal soprano. Mr. Barnby the conductor was the first to produce the work of Gounod in London, and Mr. Manns followed suit. Judgment has already been delivered by competent authority; next week, perhaps, at a review of the performance, the question of merit and value may again be raised, not with any intention to reverse previous expressions of opinion, but in a broad and comprehensive way.

Mr. F. Penna's Benefit Concert is announced for Dec. 10th, at the Steinway Hall.

MR. J. B. BONAWITZ'S "HISTORICAL RECITALS."

Mr. J. B. Bonawitz held his third recital on Wednesday evening, Nov. 21st, when he played (as will be seen) a long list of pianoforte pieces by the old masters. The living composers were represented by St. Saëns, Reinecke, W. Macfarren, and Liszt. This recital was the most decidedly successful of the three already held; a large audience listened to the music as if in a church, and remained until the end of the evening. The event of the *soirée* was a splendid performance of Beethoven's grand sonata in B flat, Op. 106, a monster work, never heard (in England) until Madme. Arabella Goddard introduced it with so much *éclat*. Mr. Joseph Bennett has written a clever analysis of the sonata, the 29th in order of composition, and written at Mödling in the summer of 1818. He notes the same power, the same solemnity, the same largeness of treatment, and the same difficulties as in the 9th (Choral) symphony. Mr. Bennett also points out to admirers the "brief fantastic" *presto* that intrudes upon the *scherzo*, the "astonishing and far extending *adagio*, too big for words"; the short indecisive *largo*, and the final fugue "with some licenses," called by Lenz "a nightmare"! Dr. Hans von Bülow's reading of this sonata at St. James's Hall, some years ago, will not be forgotten, but Mr. Bonawitz has every reason to be proud of his achievement. Other pieces were much applauded, particularly the Fantasie of Mozart, one of Schumann's, Op. 17 (first movement), and Chopin's Fantasia in F minor. M. Saint-Saëns was well represented by an "Etude de Rhythme," and Liszt humbly appeared as a "transcriber"; Wagner's "Festspiel und Brautlied" (Festival Play and Bridal Song) from "Lohengrin." Weber's Rondo in E flat is a remarkably pretty and sprightly piece, by schoolgirls often assassinated. The selections from Couperin, Rameau, Scarlatti, and old Sebastian were *bonnes bouches* for the *connoisseurs* and musical antiquaries. The fourth and last recital is fixed for Dec. 5th. The scheme of Nov. 21st is subjoined: Andante in A minor (Frohberger), (1637-1701); "Le Reveil-Matin" (Couperin), (1668-1733); "Le Tambourin" (Rameau), (1683-1764); "Tempo di Ballo" (Scarlatti), (1683-1757); Fugue in C minor (Bach), (1685-1750); Allemande in F minor (Handel), (1685-1759); Fantasie (from Fantasia and Sonata in C minor) (Mozart), (1756-1791); Sonata, Op. 106, in B flat (Beethoven), (1770-1827); Rondo in E flat major (Weber), (1786-1826); "Momens musicaux" (Schubert), (1797-1828); Scherzo a Capriccio (Mendelssohn), (1809-1847); Fantasia, Op. 17 (first movement in C major (Schumann), (1810-1856); and Fantasia in F minor (Chopin), (1809-1849). The works of living composers were as follows: "Etude de Rhythme" (St. Saëns); Jagstück (Reinecke); Toccata in G minor (Walter Macfarren); "Festpiel und Brautlied" from "Lohengrin" (Wagner-Liszt).

HIGH WYCOMBE.

On Monday evening, the 19th ult., the Choral Association gave their first concert of the season in the Town Hall to a large audience, many being unable to gain admission. The following excellent scheme formed the programme:—

Overture, "Rosamunde" .... Schubert.
Song, "The distant shore" .... Sullivan.
Concerto in D minor (Pianoforte and Orchestra).... Mendelssohn.
Song, "Bid me discourse" .... Bishop.
Part-song, "Good night, thou glorious sun" ..... Smart.
Sinfonia Cantata, "The Hymn of Praise" .... Mendelssohn.
Conductor - - - MR. J. G. WRIGLEY, Mus. Bac., Oxon.

Mendelssohn's glorious cantata was, of course, the chief attraction; of the work itself I need not write, but will simply content myself with recording an admirable performance. The soloists, Miss Fenna and Mr. Kenningham were in splendid form, and did full justice to their share of the work. The duet, "My song shall be always thy mercy," deserves, however, special mention, both voices blending perfectly. With the exception of one or two slight slips, the small but excellent orchestra did the work well, the long and trying symphony being played with great spirit and much taste. The chorus, however, carried off the honours of the evening; their singing throughout was worthy of the very highest praise. In "Ye nations" the fire and enthusiasm thrown by all into this finale was a feature not soon to be forgotten. The short selection calls for very few words. Mr. J. G. Wrigley gave a brilliant performance of the Concerto, and was warmly applauded at the close. Both vocalists were recalled after the songs. Mr. W. A. Wrigley, Mus. Bac., Oxon., was at the piano, and conducted the band for the concerto in a quiet but steady manner. The next concert is announced for February 25th, 1884, when Mozart's "Requiem" will be given for the first time here.

WEST LONDON TABERNACLE.

A meeting was held on Nov. 23rd at the West London Tabernacle, St. James's Square, Notting Hill, for the purpose of hearing the first of a new organ which has just been added to the edifice.

The Right Hon. Sir CHARLES DILKE, who presided, after congratulating the congregation on the possession of the instrument, spoke as follows : I think we may be proud in England of the general progress which has been made in Church music in modern times. We have not in the past, of whatever else we may be used to boast, been given to boasting of ourselves as a musical nation. Perhaps we have rather hidden our light under a bushel in this regard, for I doubt whether English music has not been always better than its European reputation. As regards Church music this has been the case, and in this particular branch of Church music, viz., organ music, we stand altogether before the rest of the known world. I have heard a good deal of ecclesiastical music in various portions of the civilised world, and have often attended religious services in places where the music is supposed to be before that which we can offer in this country. Now I will undertake to say that the music, generally speaking, of the Roman Catholic Church, of which so much is said, is better probably in this country than it is in other portions of Europe. The music of the Greek and Russian branches of the Eastern Church is often supposed to be better than any of the other ecclesiastical music which can be found in the world. It is very difficult, and that difficulty which separates it from the ecclesiastical music of the rest of Europe has in itself a certain charm. In the music of the Eastern Church there is, as a rule, all through the empire of Russia, a complete absence of all instrumental music ; they trust entirely to the human voice, more especially to bass male voices, and that singing of the old 5th century chants by bass voices alone in the Greek and Russian Churches is a very striking feature of the worship of the Eastern Church. It is extremely beautiful, but I don't think that musicians would place it on a level with the ecclesiastical music of Western Europe. If we can stand our own here in this country, as against the ecclesiastical music which is offered to us by other churches in this country, we are not in fear of comparison even with the Eastern Church. I will undertake to say that the English composers of church music of the last 200 years have stood second to no composers of ecclesiastical music in the world, as seen in modern times. By the popularisation of Church music in this country, by oratorios, and by the labours of the Sacred Harmonic Society and the other societies which have followed in its steps, we can fairly claim to have done as much for Church music as can be claimed by any country in the world. Our own colonies and the United States have followed close behind us in the popularisation of ecclesiastical music, but I think they will still admit that we stand in front of them in the matter. I hope I have established the claim that we in England stand, as far as ecclesiastical music is concerned, altogether in the front rank. Sir Charles Dilke concluded by appealing for subscriptions towards the expenses consequent on the erection of the organ. During the evening Mr. E. H. Turpin gave a recital on the new instrument, and various anthems were rendered by the church choir. On leaving, Sir Charles received a, hearty vote of thanks, which was moved by the Rev. W. T. Moore, the pastor.

Sir Charles Dilke certainly deserves to be congratulated upon his bold, manly, and just standing-up for English music ; and it is to be hoped his attitude in this regard will be followed by other speakers of eminence. The organ, built by Mr. H. Wedlake, of Berkley Road, Regent's Park, has two manuals and pedal. The instrument is of good tone, admirably voiced ; the wind chests are fitted with Wedlake's improved light touch valves, which yield a pleasant elastic touch, to judge from the instrument now noticed. The diapason work of the instrument was found to be even and solid, and the instrument was in every way highly satisfactory.

GLASGOW.

The Carl Rosa Opera Company has just concluded a fortnight's engagement at the Royalty Theatre. The only novelties produced were Mackenzie's "Colomba" and Thomas's "Esmeralda." The latter obtained by far the most popularity, both by reason of its more interesting story and lighter music. The scholarly and powerful work of Mr. Mackenzie was hailed by musicians with every feeling of pleasure, and the event of its production is regarded as an honour to Scotland's music. Musical and other journals are quite wrong in stating that "Colomba" is the first opera ever written by a Scotchman. John Thomson, at one time Professor of Music in Edinburgh University, produced an opera entitled "Hermann, or the Broken Spear," and W. Vincent-Wallace was more Scotch than Irish. Both Thomson and Mackenzie have been hampered by poor librettos.

The first concert of the Choral Union takes place on Dec. 4th, the programme consisting of works by Cherubini, Cowen, Mendelssohn, Berlioz, Wagner, and Delibes. Miss Robertson is the vocalist.

Mr. A. L. Grigor, organist and choirmaster, Glasgow, has prepared a work entitled "Hints and Maxims for Players on

Keyed Instruments," which will shortly be published by Messrs. Porteous Brothers, 43, Renfield Street. The book will include, in addition, to the practical instructions, musical sketches of Carlisle, Dunblane, and Lucerne Cathedrals; other original articles and anecdotes, and hints on Scotch music and how to play it. The book is particularly adapted for performers on the pianoforte, harmonium, American organ, etc., and, will be illustrated by musical examples, and an engraving of St. Cecilia at the organ.

J. B.

MUSIC IN DUBLIN.

It is ever a genuine pleasure to write about the University Choral Society, whose opening concert for the session took place on 24th November in the Examination Hall of Trinity College at 2 o'clock, long before which time every available space in the building was completely occupied. It does not frequently happen thus in concert rooms ; but I would remark, in connection with the University Choral Concerts (and it reflects very creditably on the good taste of the audience), that they enjoy a singular immunity from the annoyance invariably caused at concerts by that unscrupulous class of people who insist on a polite choice to arrive late, or leave early, or perhaps both.

The performance on this occasion was of a most miscellaneous character, and included some very pretty and first-rate numbers. A special interest was attached to this organisation of two instrumental artists, one a pianist (Miss Orr), who delighted the audience with two piano solos—Sonata Appassionata, Op. 57 (Beethoven) and a Berceuse & Polonaise (Chopin). Miss Orr, on entering the hall, was very warmly received, and at the end of each piece was greeted with well-merited applause, for truly the performance was everything that could be desired. The playing of the Sonata was in every respect a scholarly performance, rendered in excellent time, and with a very marked regard for the lights and shades of the composition. The second solo was equally successful, both of which, it may be remarked, Miss Orr played from memory. Our second Miss Mitchell, the vocalist, is gifted with high vocal abilities, combined with that easy cultivation and style, which characterise the real artist. Her voice is a rich, mezzo-soprano, of great power and flexibility, but of which qualities were fairly tested by Mendelssohn's "Infelice." A "Recitative and Aria," by Mercadante, was an excellent piece of vocalism, and was very warmly applauded. Two songs, "Question" and "Answer," written by Sir Robert Stewart, for Madame Roze, were also given by Miss Mitchell, and in such a manner as to reflect great credit upon both herself and composer, who played her a most graceful accompaniment. Her other selection was "Tried and True," composed especially for her by William Gollmick. The society also secured the services of Mr. Bapty, who contributed in no small degree to the enjoyment of the concert. Two Irish melodies, words by Thomas Moore, have been arranged by the Rev. J. P. Mahaffy, and were sung by Mr. Bapty with that grace and finish which distinguishes all his vocalism. The composer, who played the accompaniment, seemed much pleased with the rendering. "Entreatment," by Franz Abt, was admirably rendered by Mr. Bapty, and the same may be said of his singing in the duet with Miss Mitchell, of Rossini's "Mira la bianca." Mr. Carte, a member of the Society, gave a very good rendering of an "Italian boat song," by Tito Mattei. Another member contributed, in a very agreeable manner, "Best of all," a song by F. V. L. Moss. A ballad was also given a very good character interpretation of the "road," a Scotch signor, a satire, from "The Huguenots." The last-but-by-no means-the-least, I have to notice, was those three-part songs, a madrigal, and a chorus, all of which were admirably given by the chorus. I would select as specially worthy of notice, the singing of the part songs by Sir George Macfarren, "The Miller," sung in low and soft subdued tone.

The society announces, for their next concert (in February) Handel's oratorio, "Jephtha," which will be an additional treat, perhaps, be of interest to mention that the University Choral Society was founded in 1837, and since that date have boasted of a long list of members, about ninety works of the different musical societies of which were never previously heard in Dublin. Truly it is to have a most creditable record for a society like the "University Choral," and must afford much gratification to all the authorities of "Trinity." To the respected conductor, Sir Robert Stewart, all praise is due for the ability, energy, and judgment he has over displayed in its advancement.

R. J. H.

READING.—The first of two private subscription concerts of instrumental music, was given on Wednesday evening at Messrs. Binfield and Wellings' Concert Room, Reading, under the direction of Mr. T. J. Read, Mus.Bac., with Mr. Alfred Gibson as first violin, Mr. E. F. Johns, second violin, Mr. H. M. Dowsett, viola, Mr. C. Ould, violoncello, and Mr. T. J. Read, pianoforte. The following was the programme :—Quartet in C minor, No. 4, Op. 18, for two violins, viola, and violoncello (Beethoven) ; solo violoncello ; Quintet in B flat, for pianoforte, two violins, viola, and violoncello (Op. 44), (Schumann) ; solo violin ; Quartet in G major, Op. 54, No. 1, for two violins, viola, and violoncello (Haydn).

WOLVERHAMPTON FESTIVAL CHORAL SOCIETY.

On Monday, Nov. 19th, the above society opened their present season with a highly praiseworthy performance of Gounod's sacred trilogy, "The Redemption." The large and influential audience which was brought together by this, the second, performance of the above work, fully justified the committee in their experiment of a repetition of this work at so short a period of time. The band and chorus, as usual, numbered fully 300, and Dr. Heap, who so highly distinguished himself during the late festival, conducted. The artists engaged for the occasion were Miss Agnes Larkcom, Miss Emilie Lloyd, Mr. Redfern Hollins, and Mrs. Santley. Miss Larkcom, who was in good voice, sang when little music fell to her share with much taste and expression; the solo, "From thy love, as a father," which is associated with a chorus, being very good. Miss Lloyd, a native of Wolverhampton—who received a reception which must have been very gratifying to her—was in splendid voice; indeed, it is doubtful if she has ever been heard with much better effect in her native town, then, on this occasion, her efforts being marked by a breadth of tone that left little to be desired; she was most effective in the concerted items. Mr. Redfern Hollins seemed to be under the influence of a cold, but he struggled bravely on, and, as the evening advanced, sang in a manner that greatly pleased his audience. Mrs. Santley's singing in this work has been so fully written upon in a previous issue that it will be found that her delivery of the "Last Words from the Cross," being marked by all the solemnity and pathos the occasion demanded. Of the singing and playing of the band and chorus, upon whom the lion's share of the work falls, praise is due; the choruses, "Unfold ye portals," and, "The wind is flesh become," being almost perfect models of chorus singing. The band was most effective throughout, but they especially distinguished themselves in the "earthquake" and the "darkness" portions. Mdme. Priscilla Frost was harpist on the occasion, and rendered valuable aid. Dr. Heap was, as usual, a splendid conductor, and much of the success of the concert is due to his untiring efforts for the advancement of the society. As showing the advance the society has made, 100 members have been invited to take part in a performance of "The Redemption" in Birmingham next month.

HORNS ASSEMBLY ROOMS.—On Wednesday evening, Nov. 14th, Miss Haldée Lockhart gave her annual concert at the above rooms. The programme, which was rather long, included some attractive performances, among which may be mentioned a pianoforte selection, admirably played by Miss Lockhart, and two harp solos by Miss Adelaide Arnold, R.A.M. Songs were given by Miss Annie Williams, Mr. A. T. Layton, Mr. Geo. F. Grover, and others.—The second of a series of six smoking concerts, under the direction of Mr. Geo. F. Grover, was given here on Wednesday evening, Nov. 21st, to a crowded audience, which seemed thoroughly to enjoy and appreciate the programme provided. Mr. Geo. E. Fairchild, the well known reciter, met with a hearty reception, while many well known vocalists sang, and in most cases their efforts were successful. Messrs. R. G. Pitt and Geo. F. Grover presided at the piano during the evening.

LYNE, CHERTSEY.—Mr. Fred. Monk, organist of Lyne, and choirmaster of Christ Church, Long Cross, gave an evening concert in the school on Friday, Nov. 16, when he was assisted by Mr. Richard Blagrove, of H.M. private band, &c., and by his sons, Masters Stanley and Arthur Blagrove, Mr. Dyved Lewis, silver medallist of the Royal Academy of Music, also took part; and several lady amateurs resident in the neighbourhood. The first movements from Beethoven's Trio in B flat, Op. 11, and of Mozart's Quartet in G minor, together with Blagrove's "Les Oiseaux," and two of Molique's "Flying Leaves," &c., concertino, finely played by Mr. Blagrove; Handel's Sonata in A for violin, contributed by Master Stanley Blagrove; and Mendelssohn's Romance for 'cello, by Master Arthur Blagrove; the beneficiaire taking pianoforte part in trio and quartet, in addition to several of the accompaniments, during the evening; and playing by desire, an old English ballad. Mr. Dyved Lewis gave, in admirable style, Balfe's "Come into the garden, Maud." Mrs. Monk sang Spohr's song, "The Bird and Maiden," with concertina obligato by Mr. Blagrove, and of the other items of the programme, Mrs. Berner in some German songs by Curschmann, and an effective song, "Hearken, O children of men," by Alice Boston; Miss Ritchie in Smart's "Lady of the Lea," and a ballad by Wellings; and Mrs. Berner's and Mrs. Bramwell in Bendall's duet, "A little bird on a tree?"—much deserved the reception accorded by the crowded audience.

Some curious mistakes have arisen from the simultaneous announcements of two series of German operas. The Covent Garden season will be conducted by Herr Anton Seidl, not by Herr Richter, as stated by some journals. The last-named conductor will direct Herr Franke's enterprise, for which it is hoped "Her Majesty's Theatre will be secured.

THE MANDOLINE.

In the "City of Flowers" there exists one of the quaintest orchestras known to the musical world. It consists almost exclusively of stringed instruments played upon with the plectrum, and is the outcome of a social movement for the revivification of the moribund mandoline. This movement was set on foot two or three years ago by a small number of Florentine gentlemen, *fanatici per la musica*, who had made up their minds that the mandoline was the national instrument of Italy, and, as such, must be, "revived," cultivated, and popularised. The notion found favour in Tuscan society, and soon an association was formed of nearly a hundred members—mostly executants—under the title of "Il Circolo Margherita di Mandolinisti." An excellent local musician, Professor Graziani-Walter, was induced to undertake the training of the members in *ensemble* playing and to direct their concerted performances; numerous attractive *morceaux* were arranged for the Circolo's special class of instruments and assiduously practised; finally, a full orchestra (from the mandolinist point of view) of over fifty performers was got together and untiringly manipulated by its accomplished leader until it attained a remarkably high degree of efficiency. The Margherita Association has now a large repertoire, including several classical works as well as many effective operatic selections and *pièces d'occasion*, specially composed for it by Tuscan *maestri*. It has, moreover, acquired so tremendous a local reputation that, fired by ambition, it aspires to make itself known in the flesh abroad, and, more particularly, to visit these shores. *Pourparlers*, we believe, have already been exchanged between London and Florence with a view to bringing about the appearance of the mandoline orchestra on the platform of a metropolitan concert-room early in the musical season of 1884. Should these negotiations lead to the desired result, we shall hear the Florentine mandolinists next spring. Meanwhile, it may interest readers to learn how the stringed band of the Circolo Margherita is composed. Mandolines and instrumenta *ejusdem generis* form the staple of the orchestra, constituting a stringed quartet of first and second *mandoliné*, corresponding to the violins of an ordinary composite band, and *mandole* of *alto* and high tenor pitches, nearly covering between them the compass of the viola. The lower viola compass is represented by guitars—that of the violoncello by lutes of rich and powerful tone. A harp supplies the deeper bass sounds, and lends variety of tone-colour to the *ensemble*. For absolutely indispensable wind effects, a harmonium is used, and a pair of drums completes the tale of extraneous instrumental elements admitted to the orchestra of the Circolo Margherita, four-fifths of which (taking its average strength at fifty executants) are composed of strings played upon with plectra. The mandola, or mandoline, resembles the half of a huge pear much more closely than the almond, from which it is said to derive its name. All its strings are in pairs. In the smaller or so-called Neapolitan mandolines, there are four pairs; in the larger, or Milanese variety, there are five, tuned in fourths and sixths, instead of in fifths like the former. The lutes of the Circolo are thirteen stringed instruments, for the most part yielding broad and mellow sounds, and in some cases exhibiting on their portly backs veritable *chefs-d'œuvre* of marqueterie, being richly and fancifully inlaid with ivory, precious woods, mother-of-pearl, and silver. Indeed, all the instruments administered to with the plectrum—a slip of tortoiseshell or whalebone when affected to the mandola, while that used with the lute is an eagle or ostrich-quill—are remarkably decorative. Not uncommonly their sounding boards are adorned with paintings of great artistic merit, and the pecuniary value of ancient lutes by celebrated hands (such as Lucas Maler, of Bologna), is scarcely less considerable than that of a Cremona violin.—*The Lute.*

At the funeral service of the late Sir W. Siemens in Westminster Abbey, on the 26th, the music included Dr. Bridge's anthem, "Happy is the man that findeth wisdom," composed originally for Charles Darwin's funeral, the hymn "Now the labourer's task is o'er," and the "Dead March" in "Saul."

A concert was given at the Boys' School Room, Gloucester Street, Queen Square, W.C., on Nov. 27th, under the direction of Mr. A. W. Constantine, in aid of the St. George the Martyr Organ Improvement Fund. The artists included Miss Reymond, Miss Gillington, Miss Mabel Scanlan, Mr. A. Hawkes, Mr. Robert Bell, Mr. J. A. Doyle, Mr. F. Northcott, Mr. Walter Hann, and the choir of St. George the Martyr. The programme was a well selected miscellaneous one, and it is to be hoped the proceeds of the concert amounted to a solid sum. The musical portions of the services at St. George the Martyr are so well rendered, and the choir so carefully trained by the much esteemed organist, Mr. A. W. Constantine, that those who attend the church and those who take an interest in the advance of church music everywhere, will be doing good by contributing to the fund for the improvement of the organ.

THE VOICE
MUSICALLY AND MEDICALLY CONSIDERED.
BY

ARMAND SEMPLE, B.A., M.B., Cantab., M.R.C.P., Lond.

Physician to the Royal Society of Musicians.

(*Continued from page 318.*)

The pupil during study should never go beyond, in the chest register, the notes Mi (E), Fa (F)

no matter how high her voice is capable of ascending in that register.

The Falsetto and Head Registers.

The notes from Re (D) to La (A)

are occasionally difficult to fix, from their excessive feebleness. Under these circumstances, it is useful to find some easier sound of the same register, necessarily a higher one, and then to make the voice descend with a well marked slur to the note at which the difficulty was encountered. If the sounds referred to are notably weak and veiled, Signor Garcia recommends, as the best method to brighten them, to attack *each* in succession on the Italian vowels A, E, I, O, U,* by a short and energetic articulation of the glottis, thus—

A   E   I   O   U   *Simile.*

When the sounds are thin and child-like in quality, which often happens, this fault may be obviated by arching the soft palate, *i.e.*, by employing the closed timbre with the Italian vowel A, half O, or Aw.

This arching must sometimes be extended to the highest notes of the falsetto register, Do (C) sharp and Re (D)

for when not rounded, too great a contrast is apparent between them and the first notes of the head, viz.: Mi (E) flat, Mi (E), and Fa (F)

which are clear and round. The arched position of the pharynx, and the contraction of the glottis is productive of this full and pure character, which may be communicated to all the preceding notes by the employment of similar means. The falsetto and head registers may be rendered equal by exactly the same method. All sounds of the head register below Re (D)

are useless, since by this register the breath is rapidly exhausted. The great attribute of the head voice is roundness. This register is sometimes thin, either from the youth of the singer, or from want of skill; in the first case, age alone will remedy the defect; in the latter case it may be remedied by directing the voice towards the top of the pharynx; but no note above Sol (G)

should ever be attempted. Nothing ruins a voice so rapidly as the injudicious employment of high sounds.

* Anglicè Ah, A, E, O, and the U, as in "cool."

One of the greatest errors is to imagine that high sounds are lost for want of practice. In every case, no matter how high the pitch of the individual voice, the high notes should be treasured and economised with the greatest care, and never until the throat has attained considerable flexibility, should the limits above indicated be exceeded; again, the more firm sustaining power is acquired in the middle notes of the voice, so are the high notes strengthened in a corresponding degree. It is not by sustained notes that a trial should be made, but by vocal passages. Each note mastered should have sufficient time given it to become firm before attempting the next. During this process, the formation of the throat, of necessity, undergoes certain alterations or modifications, and it cannot until firm and capable of sustaining sounds.

(*To be continued.*)

Organ News.

LIVERPOOL.

Two organ recitals were given in St. George's Hall, on Saturday, November 24th, by Mr. W. T. Best. The following were the programmes:—

AFTERNOON.

Fantasia in E flat major (Op. 54)	Bossi
Andante from the 4th Symphony	Gade
Prelude and Fugue in E major	Bach
Hymn, "Il Sol, la Luna, e le Stelle"	Bellini
Scherzo for the organ in B major	Stolje
Overture, "Si J'étais Roi"	Adam

EVENING.

Overture, "Preciosa"	Weber
Duet, "Quis est homo" ("Stabat Mater")	Rossini
Introduction and Fugue in D major	Mozart
Andante Religioso, and Chorale Symphonique	Lemmens
Trio for Flutes and Harp ("L'Enfance du Christ")	Berlioz
Finale, Allegro Vivace in A minor	Lefébure-Wely

BRIXTON.

An organ recital was given on Tuesday, November 27th, in St. Matthew's Church, by Mr. Best, on the opening of the organ. The following was the programme:—

Anthem, "O taste and see"	Goss
Grand Concerto in D minor	Handel
Andante—Aria—Fuga.	
Trio for Flutes and Harp	Berlioz
Organ Sonata, No. 3, in A major	Mendelssohn
Con moto maestoso—Andante Tranquillo	
"By the waters of Babylon" ("From Judah's Captivity")	Shinn
Siciliana and Fugue	Bach
Christmas Pastorale	Merkel
Hymn	
Rondo de Campanelli (Bell Rondo)	Morandi
Festal March	Smart

The organ, by Lewis, is a fine and effective instrument.

BOW AND BROMLEY INSTITUTE.

Mr. E. H. Turpin was the organist on November 24th, when the hall was filled, as is happily the usual experience upon these occasions. The organ solos were, overture, "Jessonda" (Spohr); Andante (Wagner), and Gavotte (Salieri); Fantasia (J. S. Bach), and Prelude and Fugue (J. E. Eberlin); Fantasia on a Theme by Weber (E. H. Turpin), and Hungarian March, "Faust" (Berlioz). Miss Clara Myers made a satisfactory first appearance at these recitals. Her first song, "Little Wanderers," by E. Philp, was excellently sung, and the young lady, who has a sympathetic contralto voice and a dramatic style, was recalled. There is an effective organ obbligato part to this song. Miss Myers sang songs, by Marzials and M. Wellings, with success. Signor Erba played with much taste and skill the violin solos, Reverie (Vieuxtemps), "Les Abeilles" (Bazzini), in which he was encored, and Sarasate's "Zigeunerweisen," loudly applauded. To-night, M. Guilmant is the soloist, with a very interesting programme; and Miss Edith Rees is the vocalist. Mr. Henry Rose will be the organist on December 8th. On December 15th, Dr. Bridge will introduce two of Handel's concertos, with the original string parts; a very interesting programme may, therefore, be expected. Very satisfactory progress has been made with the arrangements for the rendering of Mendelssohn's "Hymn of Praise," on December 20th, under Mr. McNaught's direction. It is said, Mozart's "Requiem," and Mendelssohn's "First Walpurgis Night," will be given presently.

ACCRINGTON.

An organ recital was given by Mr. W. T. Best at the Church of the Sacred Heart, on the occasion of the opening of the new organ, on Wednesday, November 28th. The following was the programme :—

Organ Concerto in A major	Handel.
Largo—Allegro—Larghetto—Fuga	
Christmas Pastorale	Mérkel.
Organ Sonata, No. 4, in B flat major	Mendelssohn.
Allegro con brio—Andante Religioso—Allegro maestoso.	
Air with variations, in A major	Haydn.
Prelude and Fugue in D major	Bach.
Trio for Flutes and Harp	Best.
Andante, with variations and finale	Best.
March from the "Ruins of Athens"	Mendelssohn.

CRYSTAL PALACE.

Mr. A. J. Eyre's performances on Monday, November 12th, included the following :—

Chorus, "Sing unto God"	Handel.
Adagio from the Nonetto	Spohr.
Minuet and Trio	Bridge.
Adagio and Allegro	Handel.
Canzonet, "My mother bids me bind my hair"	Haydn.
Fantasia in F minor	Hesse.
Organ Sonata in F minor (1st movement)	Mendelssohn.
Andante in A	Smart.
Romance, "Rose softly blooming"	Spohr.
Gavotte	Silas.

Postlude in E flat, on Sunday, November 18th.

And after the presentation of prizes to the London Rifle Brigade by the Lady Mayoress, Mr. Eyre gave the following programme :—

Air, "My heart ever faithful"	Bach.
Chorus, "Let the celestial concerts"	Handel.
Adagio for the organ in E	Merkel.
Communion in A minor	Wely.
Pastoral Movement from an organ Sonata	Rheinberger.
Selection, "The Holy City"	Gaul.

WEST CROYDON.

An organ recital was given in the Congregational Church, Campbell Road, Broad Green, on November 27th, by Mr. W. J. Winbolt, whose playing was excellent and duly admired. The programme included :—

Andante in A	Smart.
Prelude and Fugue in G	Mendelssohn.
Toccata, 2nd Organ Sonata	Smart.
Pastorale by Kullak, arranged by Best.	
Andante from the 3rd Symphony	Haydn.
Grand Chœur in A	Salomé.

Vocal performances were given by Miss Evelyn Bawtree, Mrs. Dalgliesh (both ladies sang effectively), Messrs. S. S. Scott, Savage, and Underwood.

LIVERPOOL.

The sixth series of organ recitals were given in the Church of St. Margaret, Prince's Road, by H. A. Branscombe, on Saturday, November 3rd. The programme of the seventh recital included :—

Concerto in F	Bach.
Largo—Allegro—Andante—Fuga	
Conductus Guilmant.	
Allegro—Canto Fermo	Best.
Overture	Beethoven.

And on Saturday, November 10th, the programme of the eighth recital included :—

Pastorale	Merkel.
Prelude in A minor	Kullak.
Prelude and Fugue in D major	Bach.
Sonata in F	Mozart.
Largo—Allegro.	
Suite de Pieces	Corelli.
Largo—Allegro più moderato—Gavotte.	
March in B flat	Boyce.
Aria	Purcell.
Triumphal March	Best.

CHRIST CHURCH, FOLKESTONE.

A recital was recently given in the above Church, by the organist, Miss Theresa Benfey, F.C.O. The following was the programme :—

Offertoire in D minor	Batiste.
Sonata, No. 2	Mendelssohn.
"Three Sketches" (pedal piano)	Schumann.
Fugue in G minor	Bach.
Aria, "Then shall the righteous"	Mendelssohn.
"La Serenata"	Braga.
Fantasia	Lemmens.
Festive March	Smart.

A collection was made on behalf of the fund for effecting improvements in the position of the organ and choir.

BOLTON.

An organ recital was given in the Albert Hall, by Mr. W. Mullineux, F.C.O., on Saturday, November 24th. The following was the programme :—

Overture, "Der Freischütz"	Weber.
Serenade, "L'enfance du Christ"	Berlioz.
Marche Funebre et Chant Seraphique	Guilmant.
Fantasia in F major	Best.
Gavotte in F	Blakeley.
Romance, "Rose softly blooming"	Spohr.

SEAFORD.

An organ recital was given at St. Leonard's Church, on Sunday, November 25th, by Mr. A. H. Day. The following was the programme :—

Grand March	Mendelssohn.
Symphony ("Militaire")	Haydn.
Capricue ("The Monastery")	Kullak.
March	Deane.
"The Storm"	Lemmens.

READING.

Mr. I. C. B. Tirbuff gave an organ recital at the Town Hall, on Thursday afternoon, November 22nd, in connection with a Chrysanthemum Show, held in the adjoining Hall. The following was the programme :—

Offertoire	Morandi.
Air in the 3rd Serenade	Handel.
Marche Solennelle	Guimod.
Hymn of Praise	Wely.
Marche Héroïque	Schubert.

PRESTON.

Two organ recitals were given on Thursday and Saturday evenings, November 22nd and 24th, by Mr. James Tomlinson, organist of the Corporation, in the New Public Hall. The following were the programmes :—

THURSDAY, NOVEMBER 22nd.

Andante in F	Smart.
Introduction and Chaconne	Handel.
Airs, with variations	Hiles.
Overture to "Le Pré aux Clercs"	Hérold.
Communion	Grison.
Triumphal March	Liszt.

SATURDAY, NOVEMBER 24th.

Second Concerto	Bach.
Allegro—Adagio—Allegro.	
Adagio from the Sextet for wind instruments	Beethoven.
Allegro Vivace, from Symphony in F minor	Widor.
Overture to "Zanetta"	Auber.
Serenade, "Berceuse"	Gounod.
March (Sonata in D)	Lemmens.

The Andante in F (Smart), and Adagio (Beethoven), were rendered with great taste. Mr. Tomlinson secured a well-merited encore for the pleasing manner in which he rendered Gounod's "Serenade Berceuse." There were moderate attendances at both recitals.

DARLINGTON.

The organ at Holy Trinity Church, has been thoroughly repaired and cleaned; new action, and two new stops put in, and was re-opened on Thursday, 22nd November, by Mr. Fred. Tovey, the organist, when he gave the following programme in a very able manner :—

Andante in G	Smart.
Air and Fugue	Bach.
Nuptial March	Wely.
The arm of the Lord	Haydn.
Sonata in A minor	Morandi.
Andante in D	Mendelssohn.
First Organ Concerto	Handel.
March	Ouseley.

The organ has three manuals and pedal, and some thirty-eight stops. The whole of the work has been carefully done by Messrs. Peter Conacher and Co., of Huddersfield.

WOODBERRY DOWN, N.

An organ recital was given by Mr. Fountain Meen, at Woodbury Down Chapel, Seven Sisters' Road, on Tuesday evening, November 20th. The programme included :—

Postlude in D	Smart.
Cantilène	Guilmant.
Fugue in G	Krebs.
Pastorale	Clarke.
Andante con moto	Bodly.
Barcarolle	Bennett.
Triumphal March	Guilmant.

At the organ recital at Holy Trinity Church, Gray's Inn Road, on Sunday evening next, the organist, Mr. Stretton Swann, will be assisted by the members of the Orpheus Amateur Orchestral Society.

EDINBURGH.

The following is the programme of an organ recital given on Wednesday last, at St. Mary's Cathedral, by Mr. Thos. H. Collinson, Mus. Bac., the organist :—

Concerto in F, No. 4	Handel.
Larghetto from Clarinet Quintet	Mozart.
Toccata and Fugue in G minor	Eberlin.
Chorus, " Fixed in His Everlasting Seat "	Handel.
Air, " I know that my Redeemer liveth "	Bach.
Fantasie and Fugue in G minor	Mendelssohn.
" War March of Priests " (" Athalie ")	

The organ at Great Stanmore, Herts, has been rebuilt by Mr. Hedgeland, of Wrotham Road, Camden Town, the cost, £400, having been defrayed by a friend of the organist (Mr. A. Collum). The instrument has two manuals, pedal, and twenty-eight stops.

A RUIN AND A MONUMENT.

Our " Old Reporter," discourses at large on the " MUSICAL UNION," directed, for nearly forty years, by Professor John Ella. The tribute of praise awarded to this venerable musician would not be grudged by the veriest gradgrind. Mr. Ella, in founding his " MUSICAL UNION," prepared and made ready the way, so to speak, for such institutions as the " Monday Popular Concerts " and classical chamber music in general, once discarded as dry, but now almost hunted after by all intellectual and highly educated members of society. Mr. Ella not only inspired the very backward " British public " with a taste for the quartets and sonatas of Mozart, Beethoven, and Mendelssohn, but was the happy " medium " of introducing the most eminent celebrities of the continent, Vieuxtemps, Ernst, Auer, Joachim, Rubinstein, Lübeck, Von Bülow, Jaell, Mdme. Schumann —in a word, " all the talent " of the wide world.

The " Old Reporter " has described the interesting re-unions of the MUSICAL UNION, which were held, for a time, at Willis's Rooms, but latterly in St. James's Hall. Why, it will be impatiently asked, is the " MUSICAL UNION " no more ? I could give an answer, but would rather be reticent. Mr. Ella might have carried on the concern prosperously as before, had not age and infirmities compelled his retirement from the office of director. He unfortunately failed to find an equally efficient successor, and a collapse was inevitable. To take up the baton of Professor Ella was something like undertaking to lead the Imperial Guard onwards to victory after the fall of Napoleon. The termination of a glorious career, from A.D. 1845 to A.D. 1881, is not the less to be mourned.

This article is penned whilst the passing bell tolls the departure of Lord Overstone. The " King of City " business, and with little thought beyond money-making and the art of getting rich, makes no mention of Lord Overstone's well-known devotion to music. The " Old Reporter " knows better. Year after year, this great banker and sound financier was to be seen in regular attendance not only at the meetings of the " MUSICAL UNION," but also at the Monday Popular Concerts, and the afternoon recitals of Mr. Charles Hallé.

Of late years, Lord Overstone was carried into the hall on an easy chair, and safely seated on a front bench. What a lesson for millionaires ! Other old men, after money-grubbing and gambling all day in Capel Court or Mincing Lane, go home to their gross " feeds " and after-dinner sleep. Here was to be found a great banker, a nonagenarian, doing his duty in the City, drawing up valuable financial statements, giving literally sterling advice to possible Chancellors of the Exchequer, and then airing his mind, in higher and Empyrean regions by listening to the divine inspirations of the great German masters !   A. M.

Mr. Vladimir de Pachmann announces two pianoforte recitals for Dec. 10th and 19th. Mdme. Montigny-Rémaury, the pet pianist of the Parisians, and always a lionne at the Musical Union of London, holds out her magnetic hands to the public with a pressing invitation to the Prince's Hall, on Wednesday afternoon, Dec. 12th.

It is to be hoped that " La Messe des Morts " of Berlioz, will be repeated at the Crystal Palace after Christmas, and also performed by Mr. Barnby at the Albert Hall. Mr. Manns has fixed a rather unfortunate day for the second performance at Sydenham—so late in the year, when Londoners find the journey most inconvenient, the railway train service is not the most efficient.

LONDON : SATURDAY, DECEMBER 1, 1883.

THE PROMENADE CONCERTS.

NOW that the Annual Promenade Concerts have become a recognised institution of the London off-season, it is not out of place to consider the position and possibilities of what must be regarded as the only means of orchestral exposition, so to speak, the mass of the people can lay claim to. Like most English institutions, the Promenade Concert is liable to be built up too long upon the lines which formed the basis of its first success. Perhaps in some respects there has been even a backward tendency, as in the development of the " lounge " idea, the increase of refreshment appliances, and the persistent employment of the military band as an exciting adjunct to the civil or legitimate orchestra. Of course it is perfectly clear that when large capital is employed, popular support will be eagerly sought for. All the same it is time to ask the plain questions, are the intelligent lovers of music in the minority still ? are the requirements of the thoughtless loungers to be ever paramount ? or is it not high time to assert more definitely the claims and power of a high class orchestral music. The questions may be considered, without overlooking in any way the good work already achieved by the management in the best interests of the art. There are, it may be contended, distinct signs of the largely increased strength of those who love good sound music, and the enthusiastic applause bestowed upon the various performances of the established orchestra under Mr. A. C. Crowe's beat, ought to be taken as sure evidence of solid growth in public taste. On the other hand, budding as it is, erroneously known as popular taste is liable, by being taken, for a disposition to play into the hands of the loungers, to increase a tendency to rowdyism more or less unmanageable, and to incline, oftener, quiet admirers of sterling music, to withhold their support. It is but logical to conclude that a fine orchestra can only properly be employed upon the performance of high class works, and therefore the more frequent rendering of such works should be the constantly increasing desire of all interested in the welfare of these concerts. It is further a logical conclusion to suppose that a majority of those who have taste and discrimination enough to desire to listen to a good orchestra, would further desire to hear such a body of capable performers employed to the best possible advantage. Then a profound mistake is made as regards the provision made by good composers for the exercise of the different emotions of the human mind. Just as we know that no humour exceeds in pungency that of Chas. Dickens, that no wit can excel that of Shakespeare, so we know that the London Journal cannot ... by our great ... in music the ... his ... with grace and ... found one ... sohn's scherzo movements. Nay, just as ordinary witticisms are more or less ponderous and dreary as compared with the sparkle of a real diamond in words from a master mind, so the vapid, jerky, rhythmical monotony of a vulgar dance tune, even when its accents are emphasized by the deafening clang of a military band, falls far short of real life and blackness when heard, in proximity to, a brilliant Allegro from the hand of a great Symphony writer. The moral of these observations is, the hope, that the Promenade Concert management will be able to offer more good music and to place more and more faith in the better and growing artistic impulses of their audiences and to check the noisy, rowdy, vulgar calls for the common place music by unthinking loungers; by declining to pander to their tastes and requirements. The management may also remember that to strive to improve the class of one's customers is a sound common sense business axiom. The direction of the concerts have all the requisite experience and machinery for placing their performances upon the highest artistic basis. Their doing this will now secure a large and solid support and save them probably much trouble in learning the difficult science of how to manage with the expression of such hopes as these, coupled with the grateful acknowledgment of music so good already done by the excellent performances during the last and previous seasons.

For the hymn it ...

TOUCH IN PIANOFORTE PLAYING.

Few of us perhaps think much of that truly wonderful act, the conveyance of every shade of feeling through wood and various mechanisms by the sense of touch to the strings of the pianoforte. The exercise of touch in this way is so familiar that, like many other wonderful yet familiar processes, neither player or listener ... "touch" provided by the skilled manipulation and the highly trained sensitive finger actions of the performer. ... greatly enlarged ...

PROSPECTS OF THE NEXT OPERA SEASON.

... as it were of getting rich beyond dreams of ... and his well-known devotion to music. The "old ... it is a recognized fact that the question, whether ... to have it in 1883-4 ... a audience of ... may be replied, with respect to opera ... a crisis has occurred; a peaceful and bloodless revolution ...

spring, before the beginning of the regular *Italian* season. Good news for musicians pure and simple! The fashionable *dilettanti* who engage boxes as a matter of worldly business, because it is the "proper" thing, will have their innings after Easter ; meanwhile the German *troupe* are to occupy the field and to make hay whilst the sun shines. We may expect a goodly *répertoire* of sterling, standard, classical operas, supported, as at Her Majesty's Theatre in 1882, by an efficient *corps*, that is to say, a galaxy of glittering orbs, without individually prominent "stars." Above all, the public may here enjoy a feast of good music without the payment of monstrous fancy prices. In Germany itself, the finest works of the great masters are to be heard, as at Dresden, Munich, Leipsic, and other large towns every night in the year, at the cost of a few shillings, and at comparatively early hours. It need hardly be added that the works of WAGNER are likely to be made much of at Covent Garden.

Herr FRANKE, director of the Richter concerts, also comes forward with a promising scheme of opera, on the non-exclusive, or cosmopolitan, principle. The financial failure of the splendid undertaking at Drury Lane in 1882, when "Die Meistersinger" first rejoiced the hearts of the realistic Londoners, has not discouraged the enterprising manager. The *locus in quo* remains to be found, for it is reported that the theatre so well used by Herr RICHTER and his company nearly two years ago, will not be available for the purpose of Herr FRANKE. Means, however, are never wanting when a good man has resolved upon a sensible step. A palace of Aladdin would be raised for Herr FRANKE by money magic, one might hope, rather than allow so excellent a project to fall through from merely mechanical difficulties.

Mr. CARL ROSA has already gained his footing throughout the country, and intends to keep it. All lovers of genuine opera regret that he can only arrange to visit London for so short a time in the year. Last spring, the season at Drury Lane only lasted a month ; The two new English operas, by A. GORING THOMAS and Mr. A. C. MACKENZIE, unquestionably deserved their success. Let room be made for all ; but the world wills, with all the "heart, mind, and soul" of a SCHOPENHAUER, to cultivate a still closer acquaintance with "Tannhäuser," "Lohengrin," "Der Fliegende Holländer," and even "Rienzi." "Die Meistersinger" "Tristan "und Isolde" have not yet been mounted by Mr. CARL ROSA in London. Mdme. MARIA ROZE, the (foreign) *prima donna* of the company, has lately achieved a series of triumphs in the provinces, and will be heard with all sympathy and admiration at Drury Lane. The excellent representative of "Co- "lomba," too, is a second tower of strength and a great favourite.

So much, then, for the season of the Bissextile year of grace, 1884. Three courses of opera, opera foreign, and "opera in English ;" the old Italian Opera, nine Richter concerts, and the six Philharmonics, with capital Crystal Palace entertainments up to June, should satisfy even the most exacting lover of music. The popular concerts of Mr. ARTHUR CHAPPELL are permanent performances, and stand apart.

A. M.

Academical Intelligence.

UNIVERSITY OF OXFORD.

FIRST EXAMINATION FOR THE DEGREE OF BACHELOR IN MUSIC.

This examination will commence on Tuesday, Feb. 5, 1884, at ten o'clock, in the Schools.

Attention is directed to the following clause of the statute (Statt. Univ. Tit. V. (VI.), sect iii. § 1) relating to this examination :—" Nemini sese examinandum sistere liceat, nisi qui aut Magistris Scholarum, aut Examinatoribus in prævia quam vocant examinatione in Universitate Cantabrigiensi satisfecerit, aut testimonium a Delegatis, secundum Statutum Tit. XI. ... acceperit, aut examinatoribus seniorum candidatorum qui non sunt de corpore Universitatis in literis Anglicis, in Mathematica, in lingua Latina et vel in lingua Græca vel in una saltem lingua moderna (videlicet Gallica vel Germanica vel Itallica) satisfecerit cujus rei testimonium exhibeatur Professori Musicæ."

The names of gentlemen who intend to present themselves will be received by Mr. Geo. Parker, the Clerk of the schools, on or before Saturday, Feb. 2, 1884, on payment of the statutable fee of £2. Candidates who are not already members of the University must matriculate before the day of examination.

Subjects of Examination :—Harmony and Counterpoint, in not more than four parts. Text-books—Ouseley's "Treatise on Harmony" and his "Treatise on Counterpoint, Canon, and Fugue."

FREDERICK A. GORE OUSELEY,
Professor of Music.

Oxford, Nov. 20, 1883.

TRINITY COLLEGE, LONDON.

A "Student's Invitation Concert" was given on Tuesday, the 27th ult. These pleasant entertainments afford the students opportunities of displaying their abilities and progress they are not slow to take advantage of.

The following was the programme:—

PROGRAMME.

Duets, "Greeting," and "I would that my love" ...... Mendelssohn.
    Miss J. D. Johnson, and Miss A. Hunt.
Andante and Variations in F, for two pianofortes ... Schumann.
    Miss Sunderland and Miss Marie Brooke.
Song, " The Distant Shore " .... Spohr.
    Mr. C. Koch.
Prelude and Fugue for pianoforte in E minor ...... Mendelssohn.
    Mr. Arthur L'Estrange.
Song, " Sei mir gegrüsst " .... Schubert.
    Mr. C. Koch.
Symphony in Dattu's " Elohim Canticada," for soprano and Alto voices, two pianofortes and organ—part ......
    Pianoforte ...... Mrs. Bourne and Miss Fuggr.
    Organ ...... Mr. Francis Pigeon.
    Conductor ...... The Baron Bodog Orczy.

The pianoforte accompaniments were played by Mr. F. G. Cole, L.Mus., T.C.L.

The following medals were distributed to the successful students ; Tallis Gold Medal, Harry Edgar Hyatt, L.Mus. ; Silver Medal for diligence and regularity, Emily Hagger, A.Mus. ; Bronze Medal for diligence and regularity, Beatrice Allen and Bessie E. Walker.

A correspondent, temporarily sojourning at Whitby, North Yorkshire, reports the Æolian harp performances, such as they are, of the railway telegraph wires on the cliff. On Monday afternoon, he heard the notes of a natural, A natural, and E flat, distinctly enunciated ; and on Sunday G. The tension of the wires, according to the state of the atmosphere and the pressure of the wind, no doubt, causes a frequent semi-tonic variation in the notes of the scale, but C natural seemed to be the favourite sound.

Mr. John Boosey's London Ballad Concerts commenced on the 21st ult. The vocalists were Miss Mary Davies, Mdme. Carlotta Patti, Mdme. Sterling, Miss Damian, Mr. Vernon Rigby (in place of Mr. Edward Lloyd), Mr. Maybrick, and Mr. Santley. Only one new song was included in the programme, a little ditty entitled "Swinging," composed by Miss Cecile Hartog, and sung by Miss Davies. Mr. Venables' choir contributed some part music. It may be taken as a sign of the times that ballads occupied little more than half of the programme. Mdme. Néruda played violin solos by Bach, Ries, and Wieniawski, and M. de Pachmann gave pieces by Schumann, Chopin, and Hensel.

MR. GEORGE CARTER'S NEW CANTATA.

The following account of Mr. George Carter's new cantata, "The Golden Legend," will be read with interest :—

"The Golden Legend," a new cantata by Mr. George Carter, is constructed and considerably abridged from Longfellow's picturesque poem. It consists of twenty numbers, the principal solo parts being—soprano (Elsie); tenor (Prince Henry); baritone (Walter, a Minnesinger); and basso (Lucifer); there are also minor parts for alto and a second bass. The dramatic form of the work is somewhat altered, to avoid the necessity of so many personages, and "The Angel" is represented by the chorus as "The Spirit of Good," in contradistinction to the influence of Lucifer.

The numerous personages of the original, some twenty-five without counting the Miracle play (here entirely omitted), and the various "voices," "monks," etc, is here reduced to five and a chorus; this at once giving the work a totally different character, by maintaining a special interest in the movements of all concerned. The overture, far from being a "potpourri" of the airs of the work, is designed to represent the general features of the work and introduces the "motives" afterwards, developed more fully in some instances, while in others they appear here in full form. This may lay claim to a position in that class of music now usually designated "programme," requiring as it does for its perfect appreciation a knowledge of the composer's intentions. That the work has been intended to afford material for choral societies is evident from the important part the chorus has to perform. The first chorus has some unaccompanied music to the words "It is but the rest of the five," as well as a sheet and not by any means difficult fugue to the words "With danceth laughter." They also have the third verse of the Evening Hymn, an elaborate development of the two previous verses, which are in quartet form, for solo voices. Then an anthem for Easter Day, to the words, "This is the day when from the dead our Lord arose," quite suitable for Church purposes, and having accompaniment for organ as well as orchestra, and ending with the words, "Hosanna in the highest," the only addition is the difference of the choir's treatment, to the exact text of Longfellow, in the whole work. The chorus then appear in quite a different class of music, an unaccompanied part-song. There is also another part-song for men's voices, and the work ends with a choral fugue on the motive of Prince Henry's protestations of love and constancy, the grand climax being the harmonized form of the motive of religious fervour in "Elsie's Prayer."

THE MUSICAL NEEDS OF DERBYSHIRE.

Under the heading of "The Needs of Derbyshire," in the Derby Mercury, article No. V. deals with the musical needs of the county, and is from the pen of Mr. John H. Gower, Mus. Doc., Oxon. Dr. Gower's observations are of general application. In the course of the article are the following words :—

With respect to the more pressing and immediate musical needs of the country, the most important of these is an efficient orchestra. What is lost by the lack of this is not easily calculated. The great symphonies of Beethoven, Mozart, Schubert, Schumann, Mendelssohn, Brahms, Rubinstein, &c., are works known to the local societies by name only, except to the few who are fortunate enough to hear them performed elsewhere. Orchestral players are very scarce. Why will everybody learn the pianoforte, a few perhaps, may choose the violin or other instrument, and execute pieces of a showy character fairly well; but they are quite unfit for a desk in the orchestra on account of their ignorance of the rudiments of musical theory.

Again, a concert of classical chamber music is an event of rare occurrence. In the catalogue of such music may be found works no less important than Beethoven's quintets, quartets, and trios, sonatas for pianoforte, sonatas for pianoforte and violin, sonatas for pianoforte and violoncello, and numberless similar and dissimilar compositions by great masters. All the above works may be described as "miniature symphonies"—symphonies written for one, two, three, four, or five instruments. Now, there are no such obstacles in the way of the production of this class of music as those connected with orchestral, and I consider the want of concerts of classical chamber music a slur (musically speaking) which is simply inexcusable.

The Glee is essentially English, and, although imitated by foreign writers, has never in their hands reached that standard of excellence with which our own composers have endowed it. The musical world can but seldom this accompanied choral works of great or high masters are performed with so much success, and not so genuinely led to the neglect of the glee, and practically to the disuse of one of the most delightful and beautiful forms of vocal music. We have a rich library of this speciality; yet we are passively consenting to have it literally shelved.

Music, it is said, is the handmaid of religion, and England can claim to have given birth to, cultivated, and brought to maturity a still more sublime form of the combination of tone and language—I mean the Anthem. And, associated as this is with that which is held to be most sacred and dear by each one of us, it has a higher claim upon our sympathies than any other. And I say, without reserve, that in the range of cathedral music may be found well-nigh numberless works which stand out as ornaments of the most priceless value to the true world of art. The "King of Instruments," which we are unanimous in agreeing is the grandest and most suitable for the sacred purpose it is called upon to serve, may be found in most churches. Doubtless, it is no easy matter to get a good church choir, partly because surplices necessitate boy trebles and boy altos; and really competent singers fail to see any pleasure in adding the tenor and bass parts to the painfully harsh and unmusical sounds usually to be heard proceeding from the front rows of the choir-stalls of our parish churches. The weekly choir-practice, which the national schoolboy is with difficulty induced to attend, is insufficient to ensure that standard of excellence, that mellifluousness of tone, that refinement of pronunciation, so inseparably associated with effective vocalisation.

What I would suggest is that some well-trained society should give annually one concert of anthems and one concert of glees, madrigals, and part-songs. That these would be most interesting, instructive, and enjoyable is beyond all doubt; and the beautiful anthems of our English composers would stand a chance of doing the good in Derby that they have already done in so many cathedral cities. I believe if Derby would take the lead, and bestow the time and trouble requisite for the success of such concerts, other towns would speedily follow the example; and the result would be of incalculable service to the best interests of art.

With regard to the possibilities of organ music, the preludes, toccatas, and fugues of Bach, the concertos of Handel, the sonatas of Mendelssohn and Rheinberger, &c., the works of Rinck and Smart, may possibly be heard occasionally, perhaps on an indifferent organ, and probably during the bustle of a congregation leaving a church. This is a most unsatisfactory state of things. A great and important want is the establishment of regular organ recitals. In many towns there is a borough organist, appointed and paid by the Corporation, whose duty is to give recitals weekly on some public organ, and those entertainments are largely attended and much enjoyed. In London, Liverpool, Manchester, Birmingham, Bristol, Leeds, Preston, and Bolton, lovers of organ music can have their taste gratified, English organs and English organists have long borne the reputation of being amongst the best in Europe.

I have already shown that owing to a marked want of appreciation on the part of the inhabitants, really first-class concerts are the exception rather than the rule. It is, therefore, by the "ordinary concert" that the musical tastes of the people are either improved, elevated, and prepared for better things, or the reverse. And I think the "second class" concerts (if I may be allowed so to designate them in order to distinguish them from those in which all the performers are artists of eminence), are capable of doing great things in musical culture and education; for the great drawback in this respect in "first-class" concerts, viz.: centreing the attention on performers and not on things performed, is, in our ought to be, removed, to a great extent. The amateur element naturally predominates at these concerts, which afford an admirable opportunity for the young and inexperienced to make their first appearances, and for old and well-tried hands to keep the rust off. The charitable object to which the funds or proceeds are to be devoted is easily settled, but not so the programme. Here much difficulty is experienced. "Who will sing in the early part of the programme before the audience has settled down to encores?" "And who cares to appear towards the end, when everyone is longing to go home?" These important questions having been decided after much discussion, each performer selects a piece or song which is most likely to "take," not considering the merits of the composition at all, and frequently the result is a selection from the countless and worthless productions which are now flooding the market; to the extreme detriment of the art. This ear-tickling trash is, therefore, advertised and propagated, whilst the sound and good compositions are lying on the top shelves year by year unknown, unopened, unasked for. Thus what would be the good effect of a concert, if nullified by the harm done in popularising compositions which in a musical country ought never to find a publisher.

In arranging a programme, the following essentials for a good concert should be remembered :—1. That eight pieces of average length in each part is sufficient; "enough is as good as a feast." 2. That musical qualifications take precedence of social. 3. That the advice of some competent professional gentlemen should be taken as to the genuineness of the music selected, and also as to the fitness of any untried performers for the public platform. 4. That the feelings of the 300 or more people constituting the audience be respected equally with those of the single individual whose proffered services it is considered advisable to decline—it is a kindness alike to performers and audience to prevent the possibility of a fiasco. 5. That the audience should be instructed, as well as entertained. 6. That the names of the gross impostors, whose miserable effusions are now being forced upon the public by many musicsellers throughout the country, be never allowed to disgrace the pages of the programme. 7. That the services of a really first-class accompanist should be invariably secured.

It may be a good plan, in conclusion, to draw up a form of the musical wants which appear to me to be the more urgent, and they are here presented:—1. An efficient orchestra. 2. More professionals and amateurs to assist the above for the sake of their art, and 3. The town to support it. 4. Symphony concerts. 5. Concerts of classical chamber music, by first rate artists. 6. The Derby and Derbyshire public to patronise them. 7. Good glee and madrigal societies. 8. A concert of anthems, and a concert of glees, madrigals, part songs, &c., 9. A chance of hearing the best English masters in the place of some inferior foreign composers. 10. More attention given to quality than to quantity in the less pretentious concerts. 11. Organ recitals.

Foreign Musical Intelligence.

Liszt does not propose wintering in Rome, according to his usual custom.

Herr G. A. Heinze, of Amsterdam, has completed a new oratorio, "Saint Vincent de Paul."

Franz Servais has completed the orchestration of his new dramatic work, "Appolonide."

A performance of Gaston Salvayre's opera, "Richard III." is in prospect at St. Petersburg.

Anton Rubinstein will give a series of concerts at the Salle Erard, Paris, during the month of February.

The new Court Theatre at Stuttgart was opened on the 16th ult., with a performance of "Zauberflöte."

There are tidings of a young tenor at Copenhagen with an extraordinary voice. The singer is named Torsler.

Xaver Scharwenka was announced to conduct his symphony performed by the Copenhagen Concert Society on Dec. 1st.

Eugene Ysaye, a talented violinist and favourite pupil of Vieuxtemps, has just completed a successful concert tour in Switzerland.

Beethoven's C minor Symphony, the "Vorspiel" to "Tristan," and Reyer's overture "Sigurd," were played at a recent Pasdeloup concert in Paris.

A new national theatre was opened at Prague on Nov. 18th. An opera called "Libussa," written for the occasion by M. Smetana, formed the programme.

The 70th birthday of Verdi was celebrated at San Francisco by a performance of selections from his works, under the direction of Signor Domenico Speranza.

Mr. Theodore Thomas is said to have secured, during his recent visit to Germany, the services of Winkelmann and Scaria, of Vienna, and of Fräulein Merten, of Dresden, for a tour of the United States next spring.

Verdi's revised "Simon Boccanegra" was produced in Paris on Nov. 27th, before a notable audience, including M. Grévy. The critics present, however, do not appear to have been greatly impressed by the music.

The Madrid papers are enthusiastic in their praise of Arrietta's new opera, "San Franco da Siena." The *Correspondencia Musica* insists that the work (produced on Oct. 27th), marks a new epoch in the annals of the Spanish lyric drama.

M. Vaucorbeil, director of the Paris Opera, announces for 1884, Gounod's "Sapho," the first time of performance for twenty-five years, and to which the composer has added a new act and a new ballet. These interpolations are highly spoken of, and the choruses are being actively rehearsed. "Tabarin," a work in two acts by M. Emile Pessard, is also promised.

"Heil dir im Siegerkanz."—Mr. E. von Kornatzki writes to the *Daily News* from 4, Beresford-road, Highbury New-park, N.:—The news from Madrid stating that on the arrival of the German Crown Prince the band played, not the German march, but "God Save the Queen," as a mark of special attention to him, is liable to give rise to misapprehension to most people, unless it be pointed out at the same time that the Prussians have, since the time of Frederick William III., adopted the English anthem as their own. The German words commencing as above are a free rendering of the English text.

Correspondence.

PURITANISM AND MUSIC.

TO THE EDITOR OF THE "MUSICAL STANDARD."

Sir,—In your .... Mr. Southgate conveys an impression of .... when he speaks of a small body of Dissenters as representing the average Scotch mind. He also leaves any of his intelligent readers ignorant that the only objection—as a class—to the use of instrumental music in public worship is the so-called Free Kirk, a denomination quite distinct from the State or Church of Scotland, which with the .... strongly advocates the use of .... organs. Moreover, any one who knows many Free Churchmen is aware that the majority of their laity, and quite a .... per cent. of their clergy are strongly in favour of using organs, while many more are neutral. Only recently I had the pleasure of establishing some *Episcopal choral service* by request of a leading Free Church elder at his castle in the Highlands. In fact what Mr. Southgate, I regret to see, speaks of as "an unseemly ambition" of intolerance, was really the work of .... but as death has lately removed the leader, Dr. .... this body of Dissenters will shortly fall in with the .... of events. Again, organ builders will tell us that the introduction of organs into Scotland has been anything but "gradual" of late. When I went to .... there was hardly a Presbyterian Church which possessed an instrument; when I left last year there was hardly one save the Free Kirk which did not. The High Kirk, St. Giles' Cathedral, ... a very large four manual organ, but also in .... anthems and services most admirably rendered in the .... Cathedrals in Glasgow, Dundee, &c., choirs meet in the Scotch Churches are now the rule rather than the exception, and the objection to its use, though .... and daily diminishing .... Southgate is quite right about money being often a stumbling block; Dr. .... once confessed that organs and musicians were expensive, and would cause reduction in "the pleasures" salaries. I can, however, speak from experience, that while organ recitals were and are immensely popular, the bag-pipes are seldom heard in Scotch towns. He who would listen to a "skirl" must go to the Highlands, and if he does so he will learn that the "pibroch" of Donald Dhu .... the freshmost air, ... immensely effective. .... and have spent much .... in banishing .... to combat the .... of intolerance which was formerly shown in Scotland, but I think that a church which has now made, in five years, such marvellous musical progress as does our kindly encouragement; and should not the enfeebled, with a body of Dissenters who have to blush to represent the Scotch Church, which, by the way, plays tunes, raise far higher salaries to organists than does the Church of England. ....

I am, your obedient, Yours ....

GEO. ERNEST CLAKE.

TO THE EDITOR OF THE "MUSICAL STANDARD."

Sir,—In a leading article last week, Mr. T. L. Southgate says:—"The long-winded discussion that has lately been in progress in Scottish Assemblies as to whether it is lawful to employ Artificial instruments aid to worship—as it is in .... been again decided in the negative." Happily such is not now the case. At the last Assembly of the Free Church in Scotland, it was decided by a very large majority to allow the use of instrumental music in churches, and, in the Established Church, organs have been in use for more than twenty years; infact it is the exception and not the rule to find an Established Church without an organ; and, as £1200 or £1500 is not an unusual price to give for an organ, the "bawbee" (to again quote Mr. Southgate) can hardly be said to be "at all times at the bottom of the opposition (if such existed) to the king of instruments in people ......

I am, &c., JAMES FINLAY.

[*The article in question was not intended to convey the impression that throughout Scotland organs, as aids to congregational worship, were entirely eschewed. It was rather desired to show that in certain quarters, despite modern enlightenment, extreme Puritanism yet flourished; there a considerable prejudice still existing against this instrument still in country so compared with the universal welcome extended to it in England. The writer is glad to learn from so good an authority as Mr. Lake that bigotry is rapidly waning; and the value of instrumental music in becoming more widely recognised. It should be pointed out that, while there is but one Church to speak of for England, Scotland has Assemblies and Assemblies. That which one of these gatherings may decide another may repudiate, instanced by the Calvinistic and naïve, only conditions summing up of the "de'il." The *Musical Standard* is not the space in which to discuss the bewildering question of "Which is the True Church in Scotland"? No Southern mind, even if trained on the ....

admirable logical systems of Dugald Stewart and Sir William Hamilton, can succeed in discovering to which body this appellation justly belongs, and which should rank as schismatic. The singular divided condition of the Church in North Britain, and the fierce contentions arising therefrom, are beyond both the comprehension and interest of average English people. There are the Free Kirk, the State Church, the United Presbyterian, the Episcopalian, and numerous sects of Dissenters. Ecclesiastical matters seem much mixed. The question which of these associations possess genuine cathedrals, and which those that can but be classed as *soi-disant*, is a burning one whereon strong differences of opinion obtain. Mr. Lake assumes that the Assembly alluded to in the article was not justified in speaking for the Churches generally; he is probably right. His remarks as to the "noisy objectors" and "spirit of intolerance" which organs in Scotland are still subjected to affords valuable testimony as to the temper existing there. It is a proof that the Puritanism commented on in the article, though happily dying out, is not extinct. His candid admission, that "money is often a stumbling-block," completely disposes of Mr. Finlay's assertion that "bawbee-worship" has nothing to do with the introduction of the instrument. It would be useless to dispute with Highlanders on the charm of a "skirl on the pibroch of Donald Dhu." The question is one of nationality, not of artistic merit, of inherited clannishness rather than of cultured taste.—T. L. S.]

"IMPROVISATION."

TO THE EDITOR OF THE "MUSICAL STANDARD."

SIR,—I have perused with much interest the article entitled "Improvisation," and Mr. Ferdinand Praeger's observations thereon. To my mind the aptitude requisite for a display of this description resembles in a marked degree the faculties essential to the impromptu speaker. He, too, after a preliminary observation or so—which may be likened to the prelude in music—sets off with some leading theme to which he must from time to time revert if he would impart to his oration the semblance of logical sequence and cohesion. But it is not merely by means of the skilful manipulation of words, born of long habit and experience, nor by the repetition of well worn phrases, however appropriate they may be to the occasion, that he can succeed in captivating his hearers. To win the applause of a discriminating audience, he must bring to his task a more uncommon talent. He must be gifted with *identity*; and in like manner it is necessary for the musical improviser, who would lay claim to the same of artist, that he should be endowed with the self-same faculty. It is also unquestionably true, though few may be aware of it, that just as the mechanical part of speech-making may be acquired by practice, so, too, the mere reproduction and elaboration of a given musical phrase can be completely mastered. In proof of this assertion I may instance a fact which Mr. Praeger's natural reticence deterred him from mentioning, viz., that by means of his method of tuition his pupils are enabled to arrive at a surprising degree of perfection in this branch of art.

Mr. Praeger's tribute to Mr. Silas's extraordinary power of extemporising is well merited; and having had the privilege of hearing both of these gentlemen many times, I may perhaps be allowed to express the opinion that whilst the latter excels in the fugal development of themes, the performances of the former are characterised by a loftiness of conception combined with poetical sensibility which are, as far as my experience goes, unique.

I am, Sir, yours obediently,

B. L. MOSELY.

TO THE EDITOR OF THE "MUSICAL STANDARD."

SIR,—In your issue of last Saturday, I observed a letter from Mr. Ferdinand Praeger on the subject of "Improvisation" initiated by Mr. Birch, which I read with particular interest, as it has often been my good fortune to listen to Mr. Praeger's actual exposition of his own meaning therein explained.

It is a subject on which Mr. Praeger had a special right to be heard, as he himself possesses the gift in a remarkable degree.

It will be remembered that Shelley, in his "Ode to the Skylark," says:—

"Bird thou never wert;
That from heaven, or near it, pourest thy full heart
In profuse strains of unpremeditated art."

This is real improvisation; and when controlled by the ready mind of a master well stored with the knowledge of his craft, improvisation of the highest order must ensue.

It is Mr. Praeger's possession of this rare faculty, and the justice of stating what is due to him—who with his habitual modesty has effaced himself and praised others—that impels me to write you on the subject.

On the platform Mr. Praeger has been singularly happy in his extemporary illustrations. Their appropriateness and spontaneity have surprised all, and the hope is earnestly expressed that he may be seen more in public.

Yours obediently,

Nov. 27th, 1883. HENRY J. EDWARDS.

Passing Events.

The rehearsals of Mr. Gilbert and Sir A. Sullivan's new opera are now commencing, it is said.

A taking, light, comic operetta has been produced in Madrid, entitled "Politica e tauromachia." The music is by the composers Rubio and Espino.

The Accrington Vocal Union recently gave its first concert of the season, performing Gaul's "Holy City" and Birch's "Robin Hood." Mr. Tattersall conducted with care and skill.

"A concert overture" by Mr. van Heddegham, was played at the Promenade Concerts, Covent Garden, for the first time on Nov. 23rd. The work is interesting, musicianly, and well scored.

Lectures on Bach and Mendelssohn, with copious musical illustrations, have been given recently by Messrs. G. Ashdown Audsley, and H. A. Branscombe, at the St. Margaret's Institute, Liverpool.

At a special Chapter held in Canterbury Cathedral on Nov. 27th, the appointment of precentor with minor canonry, vacant by the resignation of the Rev. R. Hake, was conferred upon the Rev. Frederick Helmore.

At Mr. Hallé's concert on Thursday, Nov. 22nd, at the Free Trade Hall, Manchester, the programme included Brahms's Symphony in D, Mozart's Concerto in C (No. 16), and the overtures to "Leonora" (No. 2) and "La Gazza Ladra."

Isidore di Solla's new cantata, "Sisera," will be performed for the first time on Dec. 5th, at the Student's Concert of the Guildhall School of Music by a ladies' choir of seventy voices, under the conductorship of the principal, Mr. H. Weist Hill.

"Lieutenant Hélène" is a new comic opera by Ernest Catenhusen, lately produced in New York. The music is said to be pretty, but wanting in character and dramatic power. The title is explained by the heroine appearing attired as a dashing young officer.

The Preston Choral Society announce that they will give their first concert of the season on Dec. 10th, when Mendelssohn's oratorio, "Elijah," will be rendered with a full band and chorus of 240 voices. Mr. Santley has been engaged for the occasion. Mr. James Tomlinson will preside at the organ, and Signor Risegari will conduct.

At the first concert of the Philharmonic Society in New York, Bach's Toccata for Organ in F, was played as an orchestral work with striking effect; though pedal tone was found to be lacking. Mr. Mackenzie's "La Belle Dame sans Merci" was also given. The Symphony was Beethoven's No. 4. Mr. Theodore Thomas conducted as usual.

It is announced that Herr Carl Armbruster, the musical conductor, has undertaken to give, on the 17th Dec., at the London Institution, a lecture on "Richard Wagner and his Dramatic Works." The lecture will be musically illustrated by the lecturer himself, vocally assisted by Misses Friedländer and Damian, and Messrs. Ritter and Thorndike.

The extensive and valuable library of music of the late Stephen N. Barber, Esq., of Denmark Hill, including a large selection of organ music, oratorios, masses, etc., in score, instrumental works, a few curious old MSS. works of the History and Theory of Music, and a quantity of miscellaneous music were sold by auction, by Messrs. Puttick and Simpson at their gallery, on Tuesday Nov. 27th.

The "Birds" of Aristophanes, found a first hearing at Cambridge on the 27th. Mr. Hubert Parry, Mus.Doc., wrote the overture, entr'actes, and choral passages, scoring, it is reported, for strings and wood wind only; and Mr. Villiers Stanford, Mus.Doc., conducted. The music is spoken of as bright, melodious and graceful, and so admirably suited to the character of the play.

Says the *Athenæum*:—The various reports from Cologne relative to the production of Mr. Goring Thomas's "Esmeralda" agree as to the genuine and decisive success of the opera. It has already been accepted by Herr Pollini for performance in Hamburg. The new ballet music in the second act and the new *finale* to the fourth act are said to be great improvements.

A Welsh Eisteddfod, under the presidency of Sir Watkin Williams, will be held at the Westminster Town Hall, Caxton-street, S.W., on Tuesday evening, Dec. 4th. There will be a choral competition at 7 by some half-dozen different choral bodies. The musical adjudicators are Mr. E. H. Turpin, assisted by Mr. H. A. Evans, and Mr. Thomas Davies. The accompanist will be Mr. T. West.

Mr. Fountain Meen set a notable example at his concert of Nov. 21st by confining his selection of music to the works of living English composers. The programme included two movements from Mr. Ebenezer Prout's Pianoforte Quartet in C, Op. 2, three movements from a Pianoforte Quartet by Mr. Henry R. Rose, and pianoforte solos by Mr. A. C. Mackenzie, played by Mr. Fountain Meen himself.

Signor Agostmo Giuliano Susini, aged 60 years, an Italian by birth, and formerly an operatic singer, was crossing Westminster Road, near the bridge, on the 17th inst., when a hansom cab came up and knocked him down, the wheel passing over him. He was taken to St. Thomas's Hospital, where his injuries were attended to, and was subsequently conveyed home, but he gradually sank, and expired on the 24th.

Messrs. Ridley Prentice and Alfred Burnett's first chamber concert was given at the Alexandra Hall, Blackheath, on Tuesday evening, the 20th ult. The programme included Beethoven's String Trio in C minor, Op. 9; Mendelssohn's Variations, Op. 17, for piano and violoncello; Schubert's Rondo in B minor, for piano and violin; and E. Prout's Piano Quartet in F, Op. 18; the last work being given for the first time in public.

In Spohr's memoirs is the following:—"At the rehearsals of my Oratorio my little girl of eight years attended. She remained quiet until the final number, which was a fugue; then her eyes grew bright and she listened with sustained attention. We concluded that she had a penchant for music of a severe character, and asking her about it, she replied: 'Oh! no, papa, but I know when that piece is finished, we go directly home for dinner!'"

The Highbury Philharmonic Society gave their first, and a successful concert on Nov. 26th, under the able direction of Dr. Bridge. The programme included Mendelssohn's "Athalie," and a miscellaneous selection. The artists were Miss Mary Davies, Miss Evelyn Gibson, and Miss Marian McKenzie, and the illustrative verses of "Athalie" were read by the Rev. Gordon Calthrop, M.A. The band and chorus of this flourishing society now number 200 performers.

Italian Opera is now all the rage in New York. "Lohengrin" (Italian version) "Faust" and "La Traviata" have been recently performed at the Metropolitan Opera House. "Linda di Chamounix," "Rigoletto," "La Gazza Ladra," "Martha," "Lucia," and "Il Trovatore," have been heard at the Academy of Music. The fashionable people in New York appear to support the performances enthusiastically, though the critics have much to find fault with at both houses.

In honour of St. Cecilia, Patroness of the Little Oratory, Brompton, some choice music was given on Sunday, Nov. 25th. The instrumentalists were: pianoforte, Mr. T. Wingham; oboe, Mr. Malsh; clarinet, Mr. Lazarus; horn, Mr. T. Mann; bassoon, Mr. Wotton. The vocalists were Master Albert Hannagan, Messrs. Russon, Pearson, and Tabb (of the Oratory choir); organ, Mr. Pitts. The music included, Quintet in E flat (Mozart), for piano, oboe, clarionet, horn, and bassoon; Quartet "Blest are the departed" (Spohr) for the wind instruments; and Quartet "Quando Corpus" ("Stabat Mater") (Rossini), sung by Master Hannagan, Messrs. Russon, Pearson, and Tabb.

The following statement is made: "Mr. F. H. Fowler has now delivered the seat plans and elevations of the new National Opera House which Mr. J. H. Mapleson hopes to build on the Victoria Embankment. According to these plans there will be 460 orchestral and 449 balcony stalls, 90 private boxes on three tiers, 500 amphitheatre stalls, and 860 amphitheatre seats. Bouquet and music counters are provided on the stall level, and on the first tier there will be a ladies' boudoir, and a smoking-room. The practical character of this announcement will not convince all the sceptical, who lacking faith in the scheme, seem to have accepted the homely proverb "seeing is believing" with regard to the National Opera House.

The Querist.

QUERY.

"IONE."—I shall be glad if you, or some of your correspondents, could give me any information about an opera, called "Ione," or the Last Days of Pompeii (composer unknown), as to where the music can be obtained, &c.—E. A. SUTTON.

ORGANISTS IN LONDON CHURCHES.—Would some of the readers of the Musical Standard kindly give a list of the present Organists in the London Churches? It would greatly interest provincials, and be a useful guide to them in visiting the metropolis?—HARMONIC FLUTE.

J. H. R. will find "L'Harmonium Concertant," by Vilboe, a most interesting and well-arranged collection of pieces, for pianoforte and harmonium. It is published by Litolff (Vol. 299), at 2s. 6d. nett. Hammond and Co. also publish a set of arrangements for ditto, entitled "Les Beautés Dramatiques."—F. N. BAXTER.

Service Lists.

FIRST SUNDAY IN ADVENT.

DECEMBER 2nd.

London.

ST. PAUL'S CATHEDRAL.—Morn.: Service, Benedicite (Martin); Benedictus, Garrett in F; Introit, Our soul on God with patience waits (Garrett); Holy Communion, Garrett in F. Even.: Service, Magnificat and Nunc Dimittis, Garrett in F; Anthem, The sorrows of death (Mendelssohn).

FOUNDLING CHAPEL. — Morn.: Service, Te Deum, Dykes in F; Jubilate, Attwood in F; Anthem, Comfort ye, and And the glory (Handel). Aft.: Children's Service.

TEMPLE CHURCH.—Morn.: Service, Te Deum Laudamus, and Jubilate Deo, King in C; Apostles' Creed, Harmonised Monotone; Anthem, Comfort ye (Handel). Even.: Service, Magnificat and Nunc Dimittis, King in C; Apostles' Creed, Harmonized Monotone; Anthem, Awake, awake, put on thy strength (Wise).

ALL SAINTS, MARGARET STREET.—Morn.: Service, Benedicite (Stainer); Benedictus, Boyton Smith; Holy Communion, Hoyte in D. Even.: Service, Lasso in C; Anthem, Lo, the children (Gounod); Dies Irae (Hoyte).

CHRIST CHURCH, CLAPHAM.—Morn.: Service, Benedicite, Stainer, &c.; Kyrie and Credo, Dykes in F; Offertory, Anthem, The night is far spent (Smith); Sanctus (Dykes); Benedictus, and Agnus Dei, Eyre, in A flat, t. Gloria in excelsis (Dykes). Even.: Service, Magnificat and Nunc Dimittis, Bennett in F; Anthem, Psalm 137 (Gounod); Dies Irae (Dykes).

HOLY TRINITY, GRAY'S INN ROAD. — Morn.: Service, Te Deum, Dykes in F; Jubilate, Chantel; Nicene Creed (Merbecke). Even.: Service, Magnificat and Nunc Dimittis, Bennett in F; Anthem, Let all men praise the Lord (Mendelssohn).

ST. JAMES'S PRIVATE EPISCOPAL CHAPEL, SOUTHWARK. —Morn.: Service, Introit, Hosanna (Gibbons); Communion Service, Hummel in B flat. Even.: Service, Gibbons in F; Anthem, The sorrows of death (Mendelssohn).

ST. MARGARET PATTENS, ROOD LANE, FENCHURCH STREET.—Morn.: Service, Benedicite and Benedictus, "Gregorian"; Offertory Anthem, The earth is my possession (Gounod); Kyrie, and Credo, Missa de Angelis; Gloria, Sanctus, Benedictus, and Agnus Dei (Bordese). Evensong, Magnificat and Nunc Dimittis, "Gregorian"; Anthem, Comfort ye, and And the glory (Handel).

ST. MARY BOLTONS, WEST BROMPTON, S.W.—Morn.: Service, Benedicite, Stainer, Winn and Walker; Benedictus, Chant; Anthem, Sleepers, wake (Mendelssohn). Even.: Service, Magnificat and Nunc Dimittis, Stainer's 3rd Series of Tones; Anthem, Hosanna in the highest (Stainer).

ST. MATTHEW'S, NEW KENT ROAD.—Anthem, Praise His awful name "Last Judgment" (Spohr).

ST. MAGNUS, LONDON BRIDGE.—Morn.: Service, Opening Anthem, To the Lord our God (Calkin); Te Deum and Jubilate, Smart in F; Kyrie (Wesley). Even.: Service, Magnificat and Nunc Dimittis, Attwood in F; Anthem, Comfort ye; Chorus, And the glory (Handel).

ST. PAUL'S, AVENUE ROAD, SOUTH HAMPSTEAD.—Morn.: Service, Te Deum, 8th Tone, and ending; Benedictus (Barnby); Kyrie, Monk in C; Offertory Sentences (Barnby). Even.: Service, Magnificat and Nunc Dimittis, Monk in G; Anthem, Hosanna in the highest (Stainer); After Service, Dies Irae (Dykes).

ST. PAUL'S, BOW COMMON, E.—Morn: Service, Benedicite, Stainer, Turle and Field; Mendicita, Chant; Holy Communion, Kyrie, Credo, Sanctus, and Gloria in excelsis, Calkin in B flat; Benedictus and Agnus Dei (Redhead); Offertory (Calkin). Even.: Service, Magnificat and Nunc Dimittis, Dykes in F; Anthem, The sorrows of death (Mendelssohn).

ST. PETER'S, VERE STREET, W.—Even.: Service, Magnificat, and Nunc Dimittis, Goss in A; Anthem, The wrath is my possession (Gounod).

ST. AUGUSTINE AND ST. FAITH, OLD CHANGE.—Morn: Service, Benedicite (Best); Benedictus (Gounod), Introit, Drop down ye heavens (Smith); Holy Communion, Steggall in G. Even.: Service, Garrett in D; Anthem, Prepare ye the way (Garrett).

ST. BARNABAS, MARYLEBONE.—Morn.: Service, Benedicite, Hoyte in D; Benedictus, Dykes in F; Anthem, Comfort ye, Every valley; and And the glory (Handel); Kyrie and Nicene Creed (Marbecke). Even.: Service, Magnificat and Nunc Dimittis; Anthem, The Grace of God (Hoyte); Dies irae (Hoyte).

ST. SAVIOUR'S, HOXTON.—Morn.: Service, Te Deum, Hopkins in G; Holy Communion, Kyrie, Credo, Sursum Corda, Sanctus, and Gloria in excelsis, Dykes in F. Even.: Service, Magnificat and Nunc Dimittis (Best); Anthem, It is high time to awake (Barnby).

ST. SEPULCHRE'S, HOLBORN.— Morn: Service, Benedicite, Best in C; Benedictus, Dykes in F; Kyrie and Credo, Agutter in B flat; Anthem, Sleepers, wake (Mendelssohn). Even.: Service, Magnificat and Nunc Dimittis, King in F; Anthem, Comfort ye, and And the glory (Handel).

ST. ASAPH CATHEDRAL.— Morn: Service, Dykes in F; Anthem, Hosanna (Stainer). Even: Service, The Litany; Anthem, Comfort ye (Handel).

ARDINGLY COLLEGE, SUSSEX.—Even.: Service, Walmisley in D minor; Anthem, Hosanna to the Son of David (Macfarren).

ASHBOURNE CHURCH, DERBYSHIRE.— Morn.: Service, Steggall in G; Kyrie, Credo, and Gloria, Garrett in E flat. Even. Service, Garrett in E flat; Anthem, Blow ye the trumpet (Leslie).

BEDDINGTON CHURCH, SURREY.—Morn.; Service, Garrett in D; Introit, Sleepers, wake, a voice is sounding (Mendelssohn). Even.: Service, Garrett in D; Anthem, Awake put on thy strength, O Zion (Stainer).

BIRMINGHAM (S. ALBAN THE MARTYR).—Morn.; Service, Te Deum, and Benedictus, Goss in A; Holy Communion, Woodward in E flat. Evensong : Magnificat and Nunc Dimittis, Russell in F.

BIRMINGHAM (ST. CYPRIAN'S, HAY MILLS).—Morn.: Service, Tours in F; Anthem, Comfort ye, And the glory of the Lord (Handel). Even.: Service, Tours in F; Anthem, Who is this that cometh (Arnold).

BIRMINGHAM (ST. MICHAEL'S, HAWORTH).—Morn.: Service, Benedicite (Best); Benedictus (Stainer); Litany (Tallis); Introit, Sleepers, wake (Mendelssohn). Even.: Service, Magnificat and Nunc Dimittis (Stainer); Anthem, Comfort ye my people, And the glory (Handel).

BIRMINGHAM (S. PHILIP'S CHURCH).— Morn.: Service, Chipp in A; Holy Communion, Best in G. Evening: Service, Barnby in E; Anthem, Hear my prayer (Mendelssohn).

BELFAST (ST. GEORGE'S).— Morn.: Service, Benedicite, Best in C; Benedictus, Chipp in D; Anthem, Send out thy light (Gounod); Communion Service, Parry in D; Offertory (Stainer). Even.: Service, Magnificat and Nunc Dimittis, Walmisley in D minor; Anthem, Comfort ye, and And the glory ("Messiah," Handel).

CANTERBURY CATHEDRAL.— Morn.: Service, Walmisley in D; Anthem, Blow ye the trumpet (Leslie); Communion. Even.: Service, Walmisley in D; Anthem, Comfort ye my people (Handel).

CARLISLE CATHEDRAL. — Morn.: Service, Best in D; Kyrie, Garrett in D; Nicene Creed, Harmonised Monotone. Even.: Service, Garrett in E flat (Cantate); Anthem, Comfort ye, my people, And the glory of the Lord (Handel).

CHESTER (ST. MARY'S CHURCH).—Morn.: Service, Cooke in G; Communion Service, Tours in G. Even.: Service, Barnby in E; Anthem, Comfort ye, Every valley, And the glory of the Lord ("Messiah," Handel).

DONCASTER (PARISH CHURCH).—Morn.: Service, Wesley in F. Even.: Service, Stainer in B flat; Anthem, Comfort ye, Every valley, And the glory (Handel).

EDINBURGH (CHRIST CHURCH, MORNINGSIDE).—Morn.: Service, Benedicite, Benedictus, Chants. Even.: Service, Magnificat and Nunc Dimittis, Kyte in E flat; Anthem, The wilderness (Goss).

EDINBURGH (ST. JOHN'S).—Aft.: Service, Anthem, Thus saith the Lord, But who may abide, And he shall purify ("Messiah" Handel). Even.: Service, Sleepers, wake ("St. Paul" Mendelssohn).

ELY, CATHEDRAL.—Morn.: Service, Te Deum, Barnby in E; Benedictus, Plain-song; Kyrie, Credo, and Gloria, Jackman in D; Anthem, It is high time to awake (Barnby). Even.: Service, Barnby in E; Anthem, Comfort ye my people (Handel).

EXETER CATHEDRAL.—Morn.: Service, Boyce in C; Communion, Aldrich in G; Introit, Sleepers, wake (Mendelssohn). Even.: Service, Attwood in C; Anthem, Comfort ye my people (Handel).

LLANDAFF CATHEDRAL.—Morn.: Service, Te Deum and Jubilate, Stanford in B flat; Introit, Sleepers, wake (Mendelssohn); Holy Communion, Dykes in F. Even.: Service, The Litany; Anthem, Comfort ye, Ev'ry valley, And the glory (Handel).

LICHFIELD CATHEDRAL. — Morn.: Service, Garrett in F; Anthem, Prepare ye the way of the Lord (Wise). Even.: Service, Garrett in F; Anthem, Comfort ye, Ev'ry valley, And The glory (Handel).

LINLITHGOW ABBEY, N.B. — Morn.: Service, Anthem, Sleepers, wake (Mendelssohn). Even.: Service, Anthem, Lead kindly light (Stainer).

LIVERPOOL CATHEDRAL.— Aft.: Service, Magnificat and Nunc Dimittis, Fitzgerald in E flat; Anthem, Blow ye the trumpet in Zion (Leslie).

MANCHESTER CATHEDRAL.—Morn.: Service, Te Deum, Jubilate, Kyrie, Creed, Sanctus, and Gloria, Smart in F; Anthem, The voice of one crying (Garrett). Aft.: Service, Comfort ye my people (Handel).

MANCHESTER (ST. BENEDICT'S).—Morn.: Service, Kyrie and Credo, Nares in F; Sanctus, Benedictus and Agnus Dei, Gloria in excelsis, Casciolini in A minor. Even.: Service, Magnificat and Nunc Dimittis (Jordan).

MITCHAM PARISH CHURCH.—Morn.: Service, Te Deum, Sullivan in D; Anthem, Prepare ye the way of the Lord (Wise); Kyrie and Creed (Marbecke). Even.: Service, Magnificat and Nunc Dimittis, Thorne in E flat; Anthem, O Lord my God (Nares).

PETERBOROUGH CATHEDRAL. — Morn.: Service, Ross in G; Anthem, Sleepers, wake (Mendelssohn); Communion Service, Thorne in E flat. Even.: Service, Litany; Anthem, 1st part of Spohr's "Last Judgment."

SALISBURY CATHEDRAL.—Morn.: Service, Stainer in A; Offertory (Stainer). Aft.: Service, Stainer in A; Anthem, The sorrows of death (Mendelssohn).

SHEFFIELD PARISH CHURCH.—Morn.: Service, Schubert in F. Even.: Service, Magnificat and Nunc Dimittis, Stainer in D; Anthem, The Prologue, "Redemption" (Gounod).

SHERBORNE ABBEY. — Morn.: Service, Te Deum and Jubilate, Lyle in D. Even.: Service, Chants; Anthem, Behold the days come (Lyle).

SOUTHAMPTON (ST. MARY'S CHURCH).—Morn.: Service, Te Deum and Benedictus, Calkin in B flat; Holy Communion, Introit, O how amiable (Macfarren); Service, Agutter in B flat; Offertory, Zaccheus stood forth (Barnby); Paternoster (Hoyte). Even.: Service, Magnificat and Nunc Dimittis, King in F; Apostles' Creed, Harmonized Monotone; Litany Tallis (Ferial).

SOUTHWELL MINSTER, NOTTS.—Morn.: Service, Nares in C; It is high time (Barnby); Kyrie and. Creed, Marriott in F. Even.: Service, Stainer in B flat; Anthem, Comfort ye, And the glory (Handel).

WELLS CATHEDRAL.—Morn: Service, Nares in F, throughout. Even.: Service, Nares in F; Anthem, Comfort ye, Every valley, and And the glory (Handel).

WIMBORNE MINSTER.—Morn.: Service, Boyce in C; Offertory Sentences (Barnby); Anthem, Comfort ye (Solo); Chorus, And the glory (Handel). Even.: Service, King in F.

WINCHESTER CATHEDRAL. — Morn.: Service, Arnold in C; Creed, Walmisley in D. Even.: Service, Russell in A; Anthem, Comfort ye (Handel).

WORCESTER CATHEDRAL.—Morn.: Service, Garrett in D; Anthem, Blow ye the trumpet (Leslie). Even.: Service, Garrett in E flat; Anthem, Comfort ye (Handel).

NEWSPAPERS sent should have distinct marks opposite to the matter to which attention is required.

ERRATUM.—The programme announced last week as played by Mr. Mullineux, at Bolton, should have been given as at St. James's Church, Daisy Hill, Westhoughton.

NOTICE TO CORRESPONDENTS.—J. J. F., and E. E. L., next week.

Printed for the Proprietor by BOWDEN, HUDSON & Co., at 97, Red Lion Street, Holborn, London, W.C.; and Published by WILLIAM REEVES, at
the Office, 185, Fleet Street, E.C. West End Agents:—WEEKES & CO., 14, Hanover Street, Regent Street, W. Subscriptions and Advertisements are
received either by the Publisher or West End Agents.—Communications for the EDITOR are to be forwarded to his private address, 6, Argyle Square, W.C.
SATURDAY, DECEMBER 1, 1883.—Entered at the General Post Office as a Newspaper.

THE MUSICAL STANDARD

A NEWSPAPER FOR MUSICIANS PROFESSIONAL AND AMATEUR

NO. 1,010. VOL. XXV. FOURTH SERIES. SATURDAY, DECEMBER 8, 1883. WEEKLY: PRICE 3D.

Musical Intelligence.

CRYSTAL PALACE CONCERTS.

PROGRAMME.

"Grand Messe des Morts" (Op. 5) .... Berlioz.
(Second performance in England.)
The work is Choral throughout.

Requiem and Kyrie, Introit.	Lachrymosa.
Dies Iræ. Prose.	Domine Jesu Christ, Offertorium.
Tuba Mirum.	Hostias et Preces.
Quid sum Miser.	Sanctus (Tenor Solo and Chorus).
Rex Tremendæ.	Solo .. Mr. Harper Kearton.
Quærens Me (unaccomp. chorus).	Agnus Del.

Conductor - - AUGUST MANNS.

For the second time in England, Berlioz's "Grande Messe des Morts" was performed on Saturday last. It was first brought out last spring at the Crystal Palace, and although the choral part was at that time indifferently done, the general impression produced, and the interest aroused in the work were so great, that another and more perfect performance became necessary. It was suggested at that time by a leading critic that Mr. Baraby's choir and orchestra at the Albert Hall should at once take it in hand, but this was a little ungracious, seeing that Mr. Manns had first of all had the courage and enterprise to make it known to the English people. Besides, things are now looking up at the Crystal Palace as regards choral singing; the orchestra, so indispensable in all Berlioz's works, always was, and still is, the most perfect in London.

It soon became evident on Saturday that the choir was well up to its work. Careful and untiring rehearsals, with the advantage of a professional semi-chorus—which added greatly to the effect in certain portions of the work, and afforded rest and relief to the general chorus, in enabling them to take up the points with vigour and accuracy—produced a highly satisfactory result. No number was transposed, as was given out by some who were sitting near me, and the tenor part, which is so trying, was admirably sung; in short the entire performance of both choir and orchestra, merits high commendation. Absolute perfection in so great and difficult a work could only be expected by the hypercritical. Mr. Harper Kearton again won golden opinions in the solo part of the "Sanctus," and Mr. Eyre presided most ably at the organ.

As I before gave a detailed description of the work, I need only now remark that after a second hearing, I am still more favourably impressed with it. Opinions of course vary respecting its value. Some contend that it is "a mere grand display," but when the subject demands it, Berlioz is not wanting in stern masculine simplicity and strength. So far as Sydenham is concerned, public opinion has already pronounced in its favour, and anon other places will doubtless join in the verdict there given. Controversy on the subject is useless. *Per troppo dibatter la verita si perde.* R. S.

SATURDAY POPULAR CONCERTS.

PROGRAMME.

Sextet in B flat (Op. 18), No. 1, for two violins, two
violas, and two violoncellos .... Brahms.
Madame Norman-Néruda, MM. L. Ries, Holländer, Zerbin
Pezze, and Piatti.
Song, "Wanderlied" .... Schumann.
Mr Santley.
Sonata in B minor (Op. 58), for pianoforte alone ...... Chopin.
M. Vladimir de Pachmann.
Song, "Medjé" .... Gounod.
Mr. Santley.
Quartet in G minor, for pianoforte, violin, and
violoncello .... Mozart.
M. Vladimir de Pachmann, Madame Norman-Néruda,
Herr Holländer, and Signor Piatti.
Accompanist .. .. .. Mr. ZERBINI.

There is an altogether unusual pleasure in being able to speak with genuine enthusiasm of a work by Brahms. It is unfortunately true that the earlier is the opus number attached to one of his compositions, the more chance there is of its proving enjoyable. His two sextets for strings afford proof of this, if proof be wanted. The lafer of these works (Op. 36 in G major), was presented by the same artists as are named in the above programme, with the exception of Herr Straus in place of Herr Holländer, last season, and was received in a manner little short of apathetic: the earlier, (Op. 18) was given, as will be seen, last Saturday, and was received with expressions of the keenest delight, the Scherzo being

unanimously encored. This Sextet is one of Brahms's happiest inspirations, or it would perhaps be more correct to say, it is one of his *inspirations*, not one of his cold, laboured, disagreeable studies. Few works are more unpleasant to listen to than his Sextet, Op. 36; few more entirely delightful than his Sextet, Op. 18. The melodies are simple and lovely, the distribution of the parts generally judicious, though in the first movement the melody is occasionally hampered by unsatisfactory accompaniments, and in the air with variations the effects are not always entirely agreeable; but, judging the work broadly, it is conspicuous for the very merits that are rarely found in Brahms: grace, spontaneousness, simplicity, tenderness, and geniality. The scherzo is gracefulness itself, and seldom does one meet with a melody so sweetly simple as the subject of the final Rondo. The work was played by each performer with the most sympathetic appreciativeness, which resulted in an interpretation seldom equalled for delicacy and finish—seldom equalled even by these accomplished artists.

M. de Pachmann's rendering of the sonata left nothing to be desired: his poetical phrasing and exquisite touch are ever more and more appreciated. In response to the perhaps too-natural encore, he played one of Chopin's valses.

Mr. Santley's welcome always awaits him. After his undoubtedly favourite "Medjé," he sang the same composer's "Maid of Athens."

Mozart's Quartet was *not* in its place after so much modern music: it is cold and stiff even amid more old-fashioned surroundings, and does not appear to be of those works (of which Mozart has written many) which, because the youngest generation still loves them, "will never grow old"; for Bulwer Lytton's aphorism, "We are ever young while the young can love us," applies to the inner life of a work of art as well as of an individual human being.

B. F. WYATT-SMITH.

MONDAY POPULAR CONCERTS.

On the evening of Monday, Dec. 3rd., a new work by an English composer headed the programme.

PART I.

Quartet in A flat, for pianoforte and strings .... Parry.
(First time.)
Miss Agnes Zimmermann, Madame Norman-Néruda, MM. Straus
and Piatti.
Song, "Pénitence" ("Bass-Lied ") .... Beethoven.
Prelude and Fugue in G minor, for pianoforte alone .... Bach.
Miss Agnes Zimmermann.

PART II.

Quartet in B flat (Op. 17), No. 6, for two violins,
viola and violoncello .... Haydn.
Madame Norman-Néruda, MM. L. Ries, Straus, and Piatti.
Song, "Zuleika" .... Mendelssohn.
Trio for pianoforte, violin, and violoncello .... Mozart.
Miss Agnes Zimmermann, Madame Norman-Néruda, and Signor
Piatti.
Accompanist .. .. .. Mr. ZERBINI.

The production of Mr. Parry's new work naturally interested the subscribers, but the audience—rare occurrence at these concerts—was not so numerous as might have been expected. Mr. Hubert Parry, said to be the "proselyte" of a particular school, so far establishes his footing that he relies on learning and technical devices of art rather than inspiration, although the divine *afflatus* may not be wanting on occasions. The first allegro, bold and effective, sounds slightly common-place; the annotator of the programme notices the "utter disregard of *form*," and the "peripatetic" style of the construction, hardly on a par with the philosophy of the famous Stagyrite whose school gave meaning to the word. Contrapuntal writing is here introduced as a matter of course, and a canon on the octave, happily brief, dragged into service. This canon is the opening theme, here written in F major. This work is well laid out between the string instruments and the pianoforte. The Scherzo in F minor, quaint and lively, depends for its point on long skips, but there are several efflorescences, with a remarkable episode in C major, where the measure also is changed from 6.8 to 3-4 time. The andante in D flat, and triple measure, made a very favourable impression; but must be heard again for full appreciation. The *finale*, spirited, but again tending to *banalité*, adopts the now rather conventional and so far tiresome custom of re-introducing the chief theme of the first movement (already canonized): it here occurs in B flat. This quartet will not derogate from Mr. Parry's already recognized reputation. Uproarious applause broke forth at the end, from a section of the audience, but the unmeaning *encore* was very properly declined.

"Papa" Haydn's string quartet, one of about twelve in the same key, was admirably played, and fully appreciated. Mozart's delicious pianoforte trio, introduced at these concerts for the first time—(*credat Judæus*)—bears date A.D. 1783. All three movements might be stamped and labelled "Salzburg," so saturated are they with the master's own inimitable characteristics. Sir Henry Bishop may have formed the opening phrase of his hackneyed vocal trio, "Blow, gentle gales," from the theme of the Allegro in F major. How obviously and elegantly Mozartean is the creeping up to this phrase by chromatic intervals; the sharpening of the tonic and the supertonic; as in other instances, to be found in Mozart's scores *passim*. The *andantino*, a Minuet in G major, also suggests the first phrase of Bishop's glee. In the *finale* (6-8 time), so pert and vivacious, good memories might recall the air of, "Life let us cherish," a pleasing theme, borrowed by Woelfl in his impudently entitled sonata, "Ne plus ultra," gone beyond, and *far* beyond, by Dussek.

Miss Agnes Zimmermann, who played in Mr. Parry's quartet and this last trio, plays Bach's piece without a book; the arrangement for pianoforte is by the Abbé Liszt. Accuracy and clearness distinguished the elegant reading. Thanks to the lucidity of the evolution, the theme of the Fugue was not once lost sight of, amidst all its intricate surroundings. Beethoven's "Buss-Lied," a very dolorous piece, suitable for penitential Lent, and perhaps to the "preparatory" season of Advent, won a recall for Miss Ambler, the vocalist of the evening.

M. Vladimir de Pachmann is to play again on Monday night (three pieces of Chopin.) He has enough on his hands for Dec. 10th, when the first recital of the gifted Polish pianist will be held in St. James's Hall at half-past 3 o'clock.　　　　　　　　　　　　　　　　A. M.

"FALKA" AT THE ROYAL COMEDY THEATRE.

This last production at the above theatre is an opera comique in three acts, after MM. Leterrier and Vanloo, the libretto by H. B. Farnie, and the music composed by F. Chassaigne. The scene is laid in Hungary, and the plot turns upon the finding of a 'nephew, Tancred, as collateral heir to a military governor named Folbach, who is himself childless. The nephew on his way to his uncle is, however, waylaid by robbers, but rescued by Edwige, (sister of the robber chief Boleslas), who falls in love with his voice, as she cannot see him through the intensity of the darkness. In the meanwhile, Falka, the niece of the governor, who has been sent to a convent, appears on the scene, having escaped with a young lover named Arthur. Tancred follows, but dares not reveal his identity from fear of the robber chief who has pursued him; and the niece, to escape being taken back by Pelican, the porter of the convent, assumes a hussar's dress and declares herself Tancred. Upon this change of characters the whole comic *embroglio* of the piece turns.

The music of this work is in many instances decidedly tuneful, and of the kind often described as "ear tickling," but it can scarcely lay claim to much originality, and is in this respect far behind its predecessor, "Rip Van Winkle." The most attractive numbers are the opening patrol chorus "While all the town is sleeping," the trio, "'Tis the Captain Boleslas," the air Tzigane, "Cradled upon the heather," with its chorus "To the greenwood" and Bohemian dance, and the Romance, "At eventide." Mr. Harry Paulton (Folbach), displayed his well-known quaint comicalities. Mr. Hamilton (Boleslas), has a good stage presence, and is the possessor of a fine bass voice, and if he would only adopt the closed *timbre* a little more often in some of his upper notes, his singing would be all that could be desired. He was especially successful in the air with refrain, "I am the Captain Boleslas"; and in the trio, "Cradled upon the Heather," the latter in my opinion the cleverest number in the opera. Miss Violet Cameron (Falka), played and sang in her accustomed manner, and her efforts in the song, "At Eventide," were duly appreciated. Miss Wadman (Edwige) in appearance, acting, and singing, was charming throughout. Mr. Kelleher (Arthur) rendered his part, as he always does, in a highly satisfactory manner. Mr. Penley (lay-brother Pelican), provoked considerable merriment. Mr. Ashley

made the most of and was irresistibly funny in the somewhat silly part of Tancred. The choruses have evidently been very carefully trained, and the whole opera went very steadily under the able conductorship of M. Van Biene. The scenery and dresses are alike beautiful, and considering its amusing character, the piece should have a long run.　　　　　　　　　　　　　ARMAND SEMPLE.

THE "REDEMPTION" OF GOUNOD.

The performance of Gounod's grand oratorio attracted to the Albert Hall on the night of November 28th, the largest audience, perhaps, on record since the opening.

The "principal" vocalists were Mdme. Albani, Miss M. Fenna, Miss Hilda Wilson, Mr. Joseph Maas, Mr. R. Hilton, and Mr. Santley. Mr. Barnby waved the *bâton*, and Dr. Stainer made his organ "a thing of life and soul."

The performance of the band was almost perfect throughout, except that, more than once, in the early part of the oratorio, the flutes, though very prominent, failed in respect of precise intonation, and the horns were sometimes slightly flat. The "Prologue" was delivered with great effect, and the "typical" melody fully asserted its beauty. The Chorus struck attentive auditors as an unusually excellent *corps*; they certainly maintained the pitch, or, in other words, sang in tune. The entire scenery of the Crucifixion was solemn and thrilling; in parts, very pathetic. Salient points were Mary's solo, "While my watch I am keeping"; the "Darkness"; the "Earthquake," and the chorales. Once more to speak of Gounod's work as a composition, the First Part appears, after three or four hearings, to be superior to the other two, because more powerful and positive. The gem solo, "From Thy love as a Father," exquisitely rendered by Mme. Albani, won an *encore*, happily the only *bis* of the evening. Happily, it may be said, because the effect of a repetition in these sacred works seems equivalent to the second reading of a Prayer or Collect in the Liturgy. The audience further displayed their good taste and forbearance, so unusual in England, by refraining from applause, so as not to interrupt the performance. Mr. Santley sang very impressively, and the other solos were all well rendered. The scene of "The Holy Women at the Sepulchre," again sounded rather trivial; indeed, some of the music unavoidably recalls the composer of "Faust" in certain hints of the Garden Scene and Mephistopheles.

Much as "The Redemption" may be admired by pious persons and lovers of the eccentric style of writing, the fact remains obstinately and stubbornly fixed—that many musicians, connoisseurs of theoretical and practical authority, decline to accept this oratorio as a sterling specimen of its kind. Some details of their criticism have been given on previous occasions. The work never ascends to the celestial dignity of Milton's "high argument." It is admitted by ardent admirers, that the *vis dramatica* gradually declines, so as to produce the uncanonical effect of anti-climax. Few of the themes, "leading" or "subordinate," sound as if animated by the *afflatus Minervæ*. Above all, the vague, restless, and erratic character of the incessant tonal changes seem to denote a limitation of spontaneous thought to be covered and concealed by a meteoric shower of sharps and flats.

Mr. Barnby has been loudly called upon to perform "La Messe des Morts," of Hector Berlioz. Let him accept the flattering invitation by all means, next Lent or before.

ST. PAUL'S CATHEDRAL.

The annual Advent Service was held on Dec. 4th, the chief musical portion of which was derived from Spohr's "Last Judgment" ("Die Letzten Dinge.") If occasionally the musical treatment is somewhat secular in tone, this is felt as less antagonistic amid the surroundings of our metropolitan cathedral than would be the case in an ancient Gothic temple, where a severer style is perhaps more appropriate. The performance was given without orchestral accompaniments, the want of which detracts somewhat from the effect of music in which the instrumentation is so essential a feature, Spohr having been one of the greatest masters of orchestral colouring. The want was supplied by the Cathedral organ, the extensive resources of which were most skilfully and artistically used by Dr. Stainer. The choruses were excellently sung by the Cathedral choir, with bright, fresh quality of tone, true intonation, and excellent execution. Several movements produced a great effect, especially the opening chorus, "Praise His awful name," the Sanctus, "All glory to the Lamb," "Blessing, honour, glory, and power," and the final jubilant, "Great and wonderful"—the quartet and chorus, "Blest are the departed" having been particularly impressive. Among the pieces for solo voices the duet, "Forsake me not" was, as usual, a special feature. This was very well sung by Master Burry and and Mr. A. Kenningham, as were other portions of the music by these vocalists, and Masters Richardson and Birch, Mr. Hansom, and Mr. Kempton.

GUILDHALL SCHOOL OF MUSIC.

A Students' Concert was held on Wednesday evening (5th inst.) at the City of London School, Victoria Embankment, under the conductorship of Mr. H. Weist Hill. The proceedings commenced with the Cantique " Nazareth," Gounod, sung by Mr. A. S. Tucker and the ladies' choir ; and this was followed by " Sisera," a cantata for treble voices, in which the solos were taken by Miss Edith Umpleby, Miss Florentia Bernani, Miss Clara Field, Miss H. Newman, Miss Clara Wolleston, and Miss Crux, and it was well received, the singing of Miss Umpleby being especially applauded. Miss Elizabeth Arthur, a pupil of Signor Li Calsi, gave a pianoforte solo, Prelude and Étude, (Golinelli), in a very creditable manner. The next number on the programme was, Trio in G major, Adagio, Rondo Hongroise, (Haydn) ; pianoforte, Miss Rosalie Kaufmann, pupil of Mr. O'Leary ; violin, Miss Adela Duckham, Corporation Exhibitioner and pupil of Mr. G. Palmer ; violoncello, Miss Lilian Watson ; and the large audience were much astonished when these students came on the platform to find they were small children. The way in which each of them performed their parts was wonderful, and they were twice recalled, encores not being permitted at these concerts. The youngest of the three was the violinist, Miss Adela Duckham, who is nearly nine years of age ; she was last year awarded a Corporation Exhibition of six guineas per annum, at the Guildhall School, where she is studying both the violin and pianoforte, the last-mentioned being under Mr. Lindsay Sloper. Last April she won a first prize for pianoforte solo playing, and a first-class certificate for pianoforte sight-playing at the Stratford Musical Festival. A selection was given from John Barnett's opera, "The Mountain Sylph," in which Miss May Hallam, Miss Newman, Miss Nelly McEwen, and Messrs. Richardson, Henderson, Pierpoint, Jones and Lister, took part, and their efforts were much appreciated, and there were several recalls. A very successful concert was brought to a close by the glee, " Mynheer van Dunck," by the members of the sight-singing class. Mr. J. Henry Leipold was the accompanist.

THE LOMBARD AMATEUR MUSICAL SOCIETY.

This society gave their first smoking concert for the season 1883-4, in the large hall of the Cannon Street Hotel, on Wednesday evening, Nov. 28th, conducted by Mr. Arthur H. D. Prendergast. The society (established in 1872) consists of twenty-five singing members (altos, tenors, and basses), and of some 250 subscribers for admission to the smoking concerts, of which four are usually given during the season. The programmes consist chiefly of unaccompanied madrigals and part-songs, interspersed with a few vocal and instrumental solos. The following was the programme for last week's concert :—

Madrigal, " Come, let us join "	Beale.
Glee, " The Angler's Glee "	Netherclift.
Violin solo, " Two Spanish Dances "	Sarasate.
Violin, Mr. H. C. Esthoven.	
Part-song, " Tell me where is fancy bred "	Pinsuti.
" The Arrow and the Song "	Macfarren.
Gloria 'in excelsis, " Messe des Orpheonistes," in C minor	Gounod.
Song; " The wreck of the Hesperus "	Hatton.
Mr. Frank Connery.	
Violin Solo, " Rêverie "	Vieuxtemps.
Mr. H. Enthoven.	
Part-song, " Shall o'er my heart "	Winter.
" " Go speed thy flight "	Otto.
" " " Daybreak "	Cusins.
" " " A garden is my lady's face "	Prendergast.
Pianoforte solo, " Two Polish dances "	Scharwenka.
Mr. F. Peachey, junr., honorary pianist to the Society.	
Song, " The Bugler "	Pinsuti.
Mr. T. H. Lloyd.	
Part-song, " The long day closes "	Sullivan.
Ballad Madrigal, " Shoot, false love "	Pearsall.

The remaining three smoking concerts will be on January 16th, March 13th, and May 1st, followed by a " Ladies' Night " fixed for May 7th.

PEOPLE'S ENTERTAINMENT SOCIETY.

On Saturday evening, December 1st, to an audience of nearly 2,000 people, the above Society gave another of their series of free concerts, at the new [Town Hall, Bermondsey. The programme, which was an attractive one, consisted of a sacred and secular part. The Concert started with a good rendering, by the Bermondsey Band of the Metropolitan Choral Union, of Handel's " For unto us." The Choir also gave the " Hallelujah Chorus," which concluded the first part, A certain steadiness, which was somewhat lacking in " For unto us," was fully maintained in the " Hallelujah Chorus." Mr. James Budd gained an encore for his rendering of "Thou'rt passing hen.e " (Sullivan). Miss Mordaunt sang " O rest in the Lord," which neither suited her nor the audience. Mr. Henry Yates gave a fair rendering of " Come ye Children,"—" Recit and aria," from Sullivan's "Prodigal Son." Viscountess Folkestone followed on with a careful and artistic interpretation of Gounod's beautiful sacred song " There is a green hill far away " ; and for a well earned encore, gave " The Children's Home."

The second part opened with a good rendering by the choir of Edwards's Madrigal " In going to my lonely bed." I was

pleased to hear this vociferously cheered. The choir also gave a part-song, entitled " The Pilgrims," by Henry Leslie, which was also re-demanded. The readings of Mr. E. Stidolph were not impressive. I pass on to something more worthy of notice and praise,—the violin playing of Mr. J. J. White. Seldom have I heard a better violinist, a man at once original in style and execution, whose abilities are not merely technical, but purely artistic. His first solo was from his own pen, entitled, " Delires de Sappho." I cannot, however, speak so highly of his composition ; it was, in parts, clever, but never pleasing. He met with a hearty reception, which was well deserved. Mr. James Budd, with his two " Royalty " songs, pleased all present. Miss Mordaunt was more successful in her secular effort. While an admirable rendering of a song by Viscountess Folkstone, entitled " Last Night we sailed," was fully appreciated. Mr. Edward Morton was an efficient accompanist,—and Mr. W. H. Leslie must be congratulated for his careful conducting. I must in conclusion remark, that I sincerely trust, such an admirable scheme as this will flourish as it deserves, and meet with whatever assistance it may at any time be in need of.

GEO. F. GROVER.

ST. ANDREW'S DAY AT THE ALBERT HALL.

On the evening of Friday, Nov. 30 (St. Andrew's Day), Mr. William Carter held a " grand Scotch Festival " at the Royal Albert Hall. The choir sang several part-songs in good time and with much spirit ; one of these, Mr. Carter's own arrangement of " The Blue Bells of Scotland," evoked loudest applause. The " principal " artists were Mdme. Lemmens-Sherrington, Mrs. Antoinette Sterling, Mr. Joseph Maas, Mr. Barrington Foote, Mr. Foli, and Miss Pauline Winter ; many of them won encores for popular Scottish ditties. Mrs. Antoinette Sterling introduced a new song, the composition of Mr. W. Carter, entitled " The Child's Way to Heaven," inspired by words of the orthodox " goody " type, quite on a level, for inanity and silliness, with the ordinary run of juvenile magazines and Sunday-school books. An encore was declined by the vocalist. Mr. Foli sang another piece of Mr. W. Carter's (composed for him), " Brave and Fair," the old story of a " red rose on a woman's breast," well rendered and much applauded. The band of the Scots Guards played Scottish tunes. Mr. W. Carter and Mr. Bending played their stock duet for pianoforte and organ, the adagio in D minor from the " Scottish " symphony of Mendelssohn. Mr. J. B. Poznanski, as before, greatly pleased the people with his Scottish violin solos, clever adaptations of popular themes, and really very lucid developments of the genius of the instrument. Mr. W. Carter projects another Scottish concert on the " Burns Anniversary," Friday, Jan. 25, 1884.

EALING CHORAL ASSOCIATION.

The first concert of the season was given on Monday last in the Lyric Hall before a crowded audience, and many well-known musicians. The programme included the " Requiem for Mignon" (Schumann), the " Ray Blas" overture, the Scena " Infelice," and Rondo in E flat for piano and orchestra of Mendelssohn, and Sir Arthur Sullivan's Cantata, " On Shore and Sea." These, together with the Scherzo in B flat minor of Chopin, and two choruses, " Daybreak," and the " Rose and Lily Bell," by Mr. Eaton Faning and Mr. Ernest Ford respectively (the latter being re-demanded), complete the list. The band was composed mainly of well-established favourites, among whom were Mr. F. Ralph (leader), Messrs. Sautzmanowski, G. Horton, C. Harper, and Woolhouse, whilst the chorus consisted of about 100 voices. The soloists were Miss Thudichum, Mr. Fulkerson, and Mr. H. R. Russell, with Mr. T. A. Matthay as pianist. Concerning the performance, it may be said to have been a complete success, and to have quite justified the attempt of the committee to raise the association to a pitch of more than local importance. Miss Thudichum was in splendid voice, and sang the Scena superbly, the band playing with admirable precision and delicacy. Mr. Matthay won an encore for his rendering of the Chopin Scherzo, and then gave two of the same master's studies in a manner such as to call forth prolonged applause from the audience. Mr. Fulkerson and Mr. Russell performed the parts allotted to them satisfactorily. Mr. Ernest Ford conducted.

WARE.

An excellent concert of vocal and instrumental music was given by the Ware Musical Society on Tuesday evening in the Town Hall. There was a good attendance, and the audience thoroughly enjoyed the performances, which were altogether of a high order of merit. Mr. James L. Gregory, F.C.O., was conductor. The solo vocalists were Miss Florence Norman, Mr. Trelawny Cobham, and the Rev. S. W. P. Webb. The instrumentalists were Mr. J. E. Hilton (Nottingham), 1st violin ; Mr. G. Hannell (Derby), 2nd violin ; Mr. R. Read (Derby), viola ; Mr. J. A. Adcock (Leicester), violoncello ; Mr. Livesey Carroll, pianoforte ; and Mr. G. H. Gregory, Mus. B. Oxon., harmonium. The programme was divided into two parts, the first being devoted to " Spring," Part 1 of Haydn's oratorio, " The Seasons;" and the second to Macfarren's cantata, " May Day," selections from Donizetti, Gounod, Rubinstein, Pinsuti, and other composers coming between.

CHELTENHAM.

The certificates gained for musical knowledge in connection with the Trinity College examinations were distributed at the Assembly Rooms on Tuesday evening, Nov. 27th. The chair was occupied by the Rev. E. Cornford, and he was supported by Mr. J. A. Matthews, the local secretary of the College, Mr. Humphrey J. Stark, Mus.Bac., who attended as Registrar of Trinity College. There was a good attendance. Mr. Matthews announced letters of apology from the Mayor, the Baron de Ferrieres, M.P., the Revs. A. Scott and R. Chamney, &c. The Warden of Trinity College (the Rev. H. G. Bonavia Hunt) wrote regretting his inability to be present. He paid a warm compliment to Mr. Matthews, who for several years had worked so well and so patiently in the cause of musical education in the town, and congratulated him on the result numerically and educationally, of the Cheltenham examinations, which were as usual "highly satisfactory, and compared most favourably with those of other centres of similar size and importance in the United Kingdom." The Warden further showed the value of the Trinity College examinations, remarking that they tested the capabilities of those who were really worth the honour of so great a distinction as that of sound and successful tuition. Mr. Matthews gave a short sketch of the present position of the examinations in this town. They had made very satisfactory progress at the examination held this week. There were 118 entries this year, an excess of nine over last year. Since the examinations were commenced in the year 1876, no less than 700 had entered at this centre, the majority of whom had passed, for the most part with honours; 75 entered this year for the examination in theoretical music, of whom 55 passed, and 34 obtained honours. Mr. Stark, in distributing the certificates, remarked that over 5,000 local candidates were examined by Trinity College, London, during last year.

BERKHAMPSTED.

The fifth annual concert of the Philharmonic Society was given at King Edward Sixth's Grammar School on Nov. 28th, before a crowded audience. Bennett's "May Queen," and a miscellaneous selection, were capitally given. Mr. J. Turpin, Mus.Bac., conducted. The Rev. C. J. Langley played a sonata by Tartini for violin in an admirable and artistic style, which elicited much admiration. Miss Ward Field, an excellent young soprano, gave great satisfaction. The entire performance formed an enjoyable evening's entertainment. Mr. J. Turpin and Rev. C. J. Langley played the accompaniments on the pianoforte and harmonium.

WEYMOUTH.

The Weymouth Oratorio Society gave their first concert of the season at the Royal Hotel Assembly Rooms on Thursday evening, Nov. 29th. Dr. Stainer's "Daughter of Jairus" was performed with much success. The solo vocalists were Madame Eva Scorey, of Southampton, from the Brussels Conservatoire. Mr. John Hayden, principal tenor of Salisbury Cathedral, and Mr. Hopkins, R.A.M., from Bridport; bass, all of whom were highly successful and much appreciated by the audience. The second part was miscellaneous, the principal items, of which were two choruses by the Society, "The Heavens are telling" (Creation), and "Coronation Anthem" (Handel); solo, Mr. Hayden, "Be thou faithful unto death" (St. Paul); violoncello obbligato, Mr. W. Alcock, of Weymouth; solo, "Let the bright Seraphim" (Samson); Madame Eva Scorey; trumpet obbligato, Mr. Watts, of Weymouth; trio (piano, violin, and violoncello); Allegro, Adagio, Scherzo, and Finale (Reissiger) by Messrs. G. Thorne, conductor of the Society, Mr. W. Stone, leader of the local orchestra, and Mr. W. Alcock, of Weymouth. The conductor and leader might well be congratulated on the success of the concert, and their choice of soloists. Madame Scorey, in her solos, held her audience spell-bound, and received great applause.

UPTON CHORAL SOCIETY.

On Monday, the 3rd inst., the Upton Choral Society gave its third concert in the Town Hall, Stratford, the audience filling every part of the hall a long time before the performance was due to commence. Spohr's cantata, "God, Thou art great," formed the chief part of the programme, the principal vocalists being Miss Helen D'Alton, Miss F. Jones, and Mr. Arthur Thompson, all of whom sang with distinguished success ; the duet, "Children, pray this love to cherish," was most effectively rendered. The choruses also were good throughout, Mendelssohn's 43rd Psalm, "Judge me, O God," being, perhaps, the best of the evening. The entertainment included some songs and part songs, besides a selection of instrumental music. Of the former, "The sands o' Dee" was exquisitely rendered by Mr. Arthur Thompson, while the honours of the instrumental part of the performance were heartily given to Herr Emil Mahr for his skilful execution of some beautiful and difficult music on the violin. Messrs. Kitson and Gilbert accompanied with pianoforte and harmonium respectively, with recognized ability, and Mr. Joseph Proudman conducted with his usual care and good judgment.

YARMOUTH.

The first concert of the present season, of the Yarmouth Musical Society, took place at the Aquarium on November 29th, and was in every respect successful. The Hall of this handsome building is admirably adapted for musical entertainments, while there is ample accommodation both for performers and the public. There was a large attendance. The general performance was praiseworthy. The execution of the choruses was good ; indeed certain numbers, such as "Yet doth the Lord see it not," with its pendant chorale "For He, the Lord our God," and the most glorious of all songs of gratitude, "Thanks be to God," were given with great power and majesty. To relate all the successes of the choir, however, would be to catalogue all the choruses in the work. The playing of the small, but select, band throughout was admirable. The principal singers were Miss Anna Williams, Madame Fassett ; Messrs. Redfern Hollins and Bridson.

Taken altogether the concert was one of the best that has been given by the Society, and credit is due not only to the leader, Mr. Cooke ; Mr. Lane, who skillfully presided at the harmonium ; and the band and choir, but to the indefatigable conductor, Mr. Stonex, under whose experienced guidance the inhabitants of this town were provided with a performance which has been seldom equalled here, and certainly not excelled.

NORTHAMPTON.

The first concert of the season of the local Choral Society took place on Nov. 27th. The programme consisted of Mendelssohn's "Hymn of Praise," and his equally exquisite "Hear my prayer," and also of popular songs and ballads. The "Hymn of Praise" constituted the first part of the concert, and was excellently rendered, professional artists, band, and chorus, all triumphing over every exigency, and evidencing thorough appreciation of the music performed. The professional vocalists were Miss Marian Fenna (soprano), Miss Jeanie Rosse (contralto), and Mr. Edward Lloyd (tenor). The band, though weak in some departments, worked well and effectively. The choruses were throughout well rendered. The second part included certain popular songs, etc. Mr. J. H. Twinn, in the violin solos, "Cavatina" (Raff), "Gavotte" (Stephanie Ozihulka), played with a delicacy, phrasing power, and crispness of touch that delighted the audience, and called forth the praise of cultured music-lovers. Mr. Brook Sampson discharged the double duty of conductor and accompanist in a style thoroughly worthy of his reputation. Mr. A. W. Warren was leader of the band, and Mr. R. W. Strickland organist.

LIVERPOOL.

The fifth concert of the Liverpool Philharmonic Society takes place this evening, the principal attraction, vocally, being Mr. Bridson. The Andante and Scherzo from Huthmel's septet in D minor is to be performed, and the so-called "grand symphony," is to be Goldmark's "Rustic Wedding."

The overtures will be Cherubini's "Lodoiska," Bennett's "The Naiades," and Gounod's "Mireille." A noteworthy fact in connection with this society is the advertisement offering gallery stalls for sale, a thing which has, I believe, never been done before. This is significant !   J. J. M.

WORCESTER.

Mr. Spark's second concert was given on Nov. 27th at the Public Hall, to a large audience. The soloists were Miss Annie Marriott, Mdme. Enriquez, Mr. Redfern Hollins, and Mr. Bridson, names sufficiently well known in the musical world to justify every agreeable expectation, and the interest was increased by the announcement of the part to be taken by the Worcester Amateur Vocal Union, for the first time in connection with these concerts. The vocal solos included sundry of the favourite songs, etc. These, with a trio and quartet; and Mr. Cliffe's pianoforte solos, which were well appreciated, one being encored, made up the programme, apart from the performances of the Worcester Amateur Vocal Union. It has at different times been suggested to Mr. Spark that the members of the Union might, without sacrifice of modesty, take part in one of his concerts, which are attended by many persons who have not had other opportunities of hearing them. The Union has now had an existence of a little more than ten years, having been established in March, 1873, and of the twelve members who sang on this occasion just a moiety joined it at that date. They performed three selections —the part-song, "Vineta" (Abt), which was given with praiseworthy delicacy of expression ; "The Wanderers' Song," by the same composer, which was sung with excellent crispness, and was loudly encored ; and the serenade, "The Image of the Rose" (Reichardt), in which Mr. C. Fleet sang the solo with marked taste. The members of the Union are to be congratulated, with Mr. Spark, on their exhibition of the results of careful practice and experienced conductorship. It should be added that Mr. Stanley James played on one of the Ithica American organs, for which Mr. Spark is agent.

MUSIC IN DUBLIN.

The Dublin Musical Society's opening performance for the present season took place on the 26th of November, in the large concert hall of the Royal University Buildings, the accommodating capacities of which were tested far beyond their resources, as the hall in some parts was uncomfortably crowded. Support has ever been held out to this society, and truly, it well deserves it. It has been labouring unremittingly for a number of years past in bringing before the public a large number of the works of the masters, and can therefore lay claim to having done much towards educating and developing the taste for classical music. The work selected for this concert was Mendelssohn's "Elijah"; and amongst the artists were Mrs. Hutchinson, Mrs. Scott Fennel, Mr. Henry Guy, and Mr. Santley. The society is indeed to be congratulated on the manner in which the work was got through, and the conductor, Mr. Joseph Robinson, to be complimented on the high degree of perfection which marked the choral parts; nor must I omit to mention the completeness of the orchestra, and the very effective manner in which they performed their work. Mrs. Hutchinson rendered her music with great taste and judgment; but it must be remarked that, at times, her singing had all the appearance of over-strain. Mrs. Scott Fennel acquitted herself in her usual graceful and artistic manner. To say that Mr. Santley gave a successful rendering of the music of the prophet is what everyone expects. Mr. Santley is well known to a Dublin audience; and those who had the pleasure of hearing him on the 26th of November may well say they enjoyed a treat. His vocalisation was simply perfect, full of feeling and sympathy. Mr. Henry Guy sustained the tenor part very creditably, and has created a very favourable impression in Dublin.

The second performance of the Dublin Chamber Music Union, for this its ninth season, took place on the 28th of November. The programme was as follows:—

Third Trio, in G minor (Op. 110) for pianoforte, violin,
    and violoncello .... Schumann.
    Con moto ma non troppo—Un poco Adagio—Presto—Finale—
        Allegro giocoso.
Pavane, and Gavotte and Musette, from "Suite de
    Pieces," for pianoforte and violin (Op. 210) ...... Raff.
Ballade, No. 1 in G minor (Op. 23), for pianoforte alone   Chopin.
Largo and Rondo Giocoso (violoncello, with pianoforte
    accompaniment) .... Boccherini.
Trio in E minor (Op. 119), for pianoforte, violin and
    violoncello .... Spohr.
    Moderato—Larghetto—Scherzo—Finale vivace.

Too high praise cannot be accorded to the gifted artists Mons. Billet, piano, Herr Lauer, violin, and Herr Elsner, 'cello, who preside at these concerts. Where all is excellence, or so near approach thereto, it is a delicate task to make invidious distinctions; and I will therefore content myself on this occasion by saying that the performance throughout was of the highest order of merit, and afforded very great pleasure to a large, attentive, and most appreciative audience. For myself, I must say, that I do not remember any concert of the Society which afforded me such unqualified enjoyment as that under notice.   T. J. B.

CORK.

A reaction, after the dulness consequent on the closing of the Exhibition has begun to set in, and the various musical societies are busy preparing for the coming season.

There have been several amateur concerts held in various places, but they call for no special comment. The programmes consisted of miscellaneous items, principally ballads.

Amongst the works to be produced here shortly by the Cork Musical Society, I see with pleasure, that Gounod's "Redemption," and Gaul's "Holy City" are down, the former being in rehearsal at present.

Miss Santley's Comic Opera Company are at the Theatre this week, with Audran's "La Mascotte," and Clay's "Merry Duchess." I went to hear the former on Tuesday, and cannot say I was greatly edified; the author (query, adapter) seeming to think that Comic Opera and Burlesque mean pretty much the same thing. The soloists were fairly good; the chorus, however, was not so good, though I have heard many a worse, trying to make in quantity what they lacked in quality. Several times also during the evening the orchestra and chorus seemed to be at loggerheads; and in one of his choruses Mr. Bolini (Pipps) had to stop, as the orchestra were playing faster than he could possibly sing. I may especially mention Miss Crofton (Bettina) and Mr. J. Pierpoint (Prince Fritellini); the latter, although having only one song, sang it in such a manner as to obtain an encore.   F. St. John Lacy.

ENFIELD.—A large and fine hall has just been opened. During the winter, concerts and entertainments will be given at the new "Athenæum." The concerts will be under the direction and management of Mr. Harold E. Stidolph, of Ealing, who has had much experience in giving high-class concerts. The increase of public halls, and the spread of good concerts, will do much to bring down the selfish, foolishly perpetuated concert monopolies, which do so much harm to art in London in the way of restricting the number of accepted performers, and by practically ignoring the claims of young artists of merit.

BATH.

Recently a vocal and instrumental concert for the benefit of a Bath citizen, Mr. J. C. Mather, was given at the Assembly Rooms. During his brief career in English opera Mr. Mather attained very gratifying successes, and the numerous friends who rallied round him, both as audience and performers, testified by their presence to his well-merited popularity. Mr. Mather was in excellent voice, and sang with a dramatic intensity that drew from the audience the warmest plaudits. His success was pronounced in the "Toreador song," from "Carmen," and in Gatty's fine song, "True till death." The latter seemed specially suited to display the wide range and power of his voice, and was enthusiastically encored. Verdi's quartet, "Un di se ben" (Rigoletto), Sir Michael Costa's "Ecco quel fiero" (quartet), and "This magic wove scarf" (Barnett), were very acceptable items of the programme, the vocalists being successively Miss Edwards, Miss Ada Curtis, Miss F. Edwards, Mr. Atwell, Mr. Clark, and Mr. Mather. Mr. H. T. Sims, who combined the duties of accompanist and conductor, played Beethoven's "Andante in F," and Mr. Broom, in a flute solo, "American fantasia," displayed the art of difficult manipulation with effect. An efficient band contributed an overture and a march. Mr. Mather and his friends may be congratulated on having produced an entertainment so thoroughly enjoyed by a crowded house, though the evening was unduly prolonged by the frequency of the encores.

NEWBURY.

The Newbury Amateur Orchestral Union gave two concerts, in aid of the Marsh Improvement Fund, on Nov. 27th. The soloists were Miss Agnes Larkcom, Mdme. Mudie Bolingbroke, and solo violin Mr. T. E. Gatehouse. There was a very well balanced orchestra of 35 performers, the conductor being Mr. W. D. Eatwell. The accompanist was Mr. A. Walton, Mus.Bac. F.C.O. The afternoon concert was thinly attended. The programme included Reverie (Schumann), Symphony Movement by Haydn, and De Beriot's 1st Violin Concerto, played well by Mr. Gatehouse. The evening performance was largely attended, the hall being quite full. The programme included: Auber's lively "Fra Diavolo" overture, a noisy repetition of De Beriot's Concerto; fantasia, "The Forge in the Forest" (Michaelis), with an absurd anvil part, too barbarous surely for a concert room. This piece was given at both performances. The several dance tunes and marches were felt to be errors of selection, and the society will do well to select higher class for study and performance. The solo singers pleased greatly in their English songs. As a whole the performances were good, and thoroughly creditable to the society.

LEAMINGTON.—Mr. F. Spinney's second chamber concert, recently given, was in every way a success. A large audience testified to their admiration of the brilliant pianoforte solos by Madame Mary Meyer, an artist of whom Leamington may indeed be proud. The Valse Brilliante, and that in minuet time being greatly appreciated, and receiving the only recall during the performance. Our readers will doubtless remember Madame Meyer formerly playing in public as Miss Mary Mander. She is the daughter of a respected townsman, Mr. H. Mander, of the Parade. Since that time she has been studying in Germany with excellent results. The vocalist was Miss Minnie Gwynne, a distinguished pupil of Mr. Alberti Visetti. This lady gave the beautiful song, "Piano, piano cantopiù," from Der Freischütz, with great effect; and two charming songs, "Si tu, Mamma," and "Embarrassment," in a most finished style. It is unnecessary to do more than allude to the "strings." Where all was good it seems invidious to particularise, but Mr. J. Ward's admirably performed violin solo should not pass unnoticed. Mr. Spinney certainly deserves general support for these delightful concerts.

MIRFIELD.—The Battyeford Amateur Musical Society, assisted by the Manningham Vocal Union, gave the opening concert of their session on Nov. 29th, in the Town Hall, Mirfield, before a large and fashionable audience. The works selected were "The Building of the Ship," for the first part; and Mendelssohn's Psalm, "Hear my Prayer," with a miscellaneous second part. This was the first time that Barnett's cantata, "The Building of the Ship," has been performed in this neighbourhood since it was brought out, three years ago, at the Leeds Musical Festival. Many listeners were quite unprepared for such an excellent rendering of this difficult work; and those who are acquainted with the cantata will know what credit is due to the chorus, for the way in which some of the more exacting passages were sung. The solos were taken by Miss Norton, Mrs. Clarke, Messrs. Peacock and Riley. A well-selected band, led by Mr. Dawson, supported, in a satisfactory manner, the efforts of the chorus. Besides the very effective rendering of Mendelssohn's "Hear my Prayer," in the second part, Handel's "Angels ever bright and fair," was beautifully sung by Miss Norton; while Gounod's "Nazareth," was given with great success by Mr. Riley. This is the second concert which has been given under the training of Mr. J. H. Rooks, of Bradford, and the society must be congratulated upon having for their conductor a man of such energy and ability.

SALISBURY.—The Members of the Salisbury Vocal Union gave an excellent concert, on the 28th of November, to one of the largest audiences ever seen in the Hamilton Hall, many persons being unable to obtain admission. The first part of the programme was devoted to Dr. Stainer's Cantata, "The Daughter of Jairus." The soloists were Miss Julia Jones, Mr. J. A. Acott, and Mr. Arthur Crick. The Cantata was exceedingly well rendered, and gave great satisfaction. In the second part a miscellaneous selection was given. The soloists were Miss Julia Jones, Messrs. Marr, Hayden, Crick and Kelsey, of the Cathedral choir, all of whom received encores for their songs. Miss Harwood and Mr. Alfred Foley very ably presided at the pianoforte and organ respectively. Mr. John M. Hayden as usual conducted.

PRESTON.—On Saturday evening, December 1st, the first of a series of Cheap Concerts for the People, given by Mr. Sam. Lee, took place in the New Public Hall. The band of the Preston Rifles occupied the orchestra, and during the evening rendered in a pleasing manner, selection "Patience" (Sullivan); Cavatina La Rossignol (Reynolds); Chorus, "The Heavens are telling" (Haydn); selection, "Il Guiramento" (Mercadante); Fantasia "Field of the Cloth of Gold" (Victor Boat); and chorus, "Hallelujah" (Handel). Miss Marsh sang sweetly "Going to Market,"—"No Sir,"—"Killarney,"—"The Bailiff's Daughter of Islington." Mr. McMahon sang "The Death of Nelson,"—"The Pilgrim of Love,"—"Love's Request." Mr. J. Thompson sang "The Little Hero,"—"The Flying Dutchman." The concert was a great success, the building being well filled. The prices of admission were the same as those charged at the organ recitals, viz., 6d. and 3d. Mr. T. Hogg rendered the accompaniments in a tasteful manner.

MAIDENHEAD.—On Tuesday evening, the 20th ult., the Philharmonic Society gave their first concert of the season in the Town Hall, to a large audience. The first part of the programme was devoted to a selection from Sir Arthur Sullivan's oratorio, "The Light of the World." The principal artists were Miss Fenna, Miss Eliza Thomas, Mr. Kenningham, and Mr. Musgrove Tufnail. Of their singing it would be difficult to speak in too high terms; their rendering of the exquisite quartet, "Yea, though I walk through the valley of the shadow of death," was perfect, and not soon to be forgotten. The chorus singing was very good, the final fugue, "Now is come salvation and strength," being exceedingly well sung. A miscellaneous selection of songs, etc., formed the second part of the programme. Mr. W. A. Wrigley, Mus.Bac., Oxon., presided at the harmonium, and Mr. J. G. Wrigley, F.C.O., Mus.Bac., at the pianoforte. Mendelssohn's "Lauda Sion" is announced for the second concert.

ENNISKILLEN, IRELAND.—Mr. Arnold's benefit concert was given in the Town Hall, before a crowded house, on Wednesday, the 28th November. The church choir, augmented for the occasion, sang with considerable effect the following glees :—"Dawn of day" (S. Reay), "The Chough and Crow" (Bishop), the "Carnovale" (Rossini), "Glory and love to the men of old" (Gounod) ; the two latter were accompanied by the band of the 13th Somersetshire Light Infantry. Solos and duets were performed respectively by Miss C. McTiernan (violin), Miss M. Cooney (piano), and the Misses McTierhan, McKeague, Weaver, Benson, E. Graham ; Messrs. Mercer and Veevers. The selections by band included overture, "Giovanna di Arco" (Verdi), "Polacco di Concert" (La Thière), Mrs. Valentine presided at the piano; Bandmaster Veevers conducted. A purse of gold has also been recently presented to Mr. Arnold, whose services as organist and choirmaster are thus practically appreciated.

BOW AND BROMLEY INSTITUTE.

M. Alex. Guilmant gave the recital on Saturday last at the Bow and Bromley Institute to a crowded audience, who gave the accomplished organist a very cordial welcome. His first solo was "Fantasia and Fugue in F" (Emile Bernard), an interesting work, received with loud applause. M. Guilmant's second sonata in D major finely played, was also loudly applauded. A "Prayer in G flat" (E. Lemaigre) and Lemmens's "Pastorale in F," came next. This graceful movement was charmingly played, encored and repeated. An improvisation on Weber's "Last Waltz," really a composition of Reissiger's it is authoritively stated, was worked out with sound musicianship, and much applauded. The player's own "Bridal Chorus" was the final solo. Miss Eleanor Rees, a talented and promising young vocalist, and worthy student of the R.A.M., sang in a highly creditable style. She was encored in F. Clay's "She wandered down the mountain side," substituting another song. To-night the soloists are Mr. H. Rose and Miss Clara Samuell. On Dec. 10th (not 20th, as announced by mistake), Mendelssohn's "Hymn of Praise" will be given. Mr. J. F. Bridge, Mus.Doc., has a highly interesting programme on Dec. 15th, including two of Handel's concertos with accompaniment of strings.

Organ News.

LIVERPOOL.

An organ recital was given on Thursday, November 29th, in St. George's Hall, on Saturday, November 24th, by Mr. W. T. Best. The following was the programme :—

Prelude and Fugue in G major	Bach.
Andante Espressivo in A minor	Smart.
Concerto for Stringed and Wind Instruments	Handel.
Offertoire Funèbre	Wely.
Selection from "Le Prophète"	
Introduction and Pastorale Chorus }	Meyerbeer.
Hymn, sung in the Cathedral }	
Finale in E major from an Orchestral Suite (Op. 52)	Schumann.

And on Saturday, December 1st :—

Organ Concerto in D minor	Handel.
Adagio from a Symphony in G major	Haydn.
Composed in London, 1793, for Saloman's Concerts.	
Organ Sonata, No. 3, in A minor	Van Eyken.
Air, "Domine Deus, rex cœlestis"	Rossini.
Overture for the Organ	Smart.

BROWNSWOOD PARK, N.

A special service and organ recital was given on November 29th, at St. John the Evangelist Church, on the occasion of the opening of the new organ. The instrument was built by Messrs. W. Hill and Son, at a cost of £1,000. The recital was played by Mr. J. Frederick Bridge, Mus.Doc., Oxon., organist of Westminster Abbey, who rendered in masterly style the following programme :—

"Three Sketches"	Schumann.
Adagio from Septet	Beethoven.
Prelude and Fugue on the Name of Bach	Bach.
Schubert	Schubert.
Andante from Symphony	Haydn.
"Pilgrims' Chorus" ("Tannhäuser ")	Wagner.
Air, varied	Lemmens.
Sonata in D minor	Bridge.
Allegro moderato—Andante—Introduction and Fugue.	
March	Silas.

Another recital was given on December 5th, by Mr C. F. Jekyll, organist of the Chapel Royal. Other recitals will also be given on December 12th, by Mr. C. Warwick Jordan, Mus Bac., organist of St. Stephens, Lewisham, and on December 19th, by Mr. W. S. Hoyte, organist, All Saints, Margaret Street, W. The organ has three manuals and pedal, with some thirty-seven draw-stops, and six combination pedals.

NORWICH.

An organ recital was given by Dr. Bunnett, F.C.O., in the St. Andrew's Hall, on Saturday, December 1st. The following was the programme :—

Offertoire à la flat	Vincent.
Andante con moto	Smith.
Larghetto in F	Bunnett.
Concert-Stuck for the Organ	Spark.
Cavatina	Raff.
The Sylphs, from "Faust "	Berlioz.
Organ Concerto in F	Handel.
Allegro—Andante maestoso—Adagio and Allegro.	
Air," Le Chemin en Paradis "	Blumenthal.
Romance Sans Paroles	Gounod.
Overture to the Opera, "Tolomeo"	Handel.

STRANGEWAYS.

Programme of an organ recital given in Salem Chapel, by Wm. Mullineux, F.C.O., on Wednesday, December 5th. Vocalist, Miss Fanny Bristowe. The following was the programme :—

Organ Concerto in F major	Handel.
Serenade, "L' Enfance du Christ "	Berlioz.
Minuetto Romantique in E flat	Smith.
Grand Organ Sonata in D minor, No. 1	Guilmant.
Fantasia for the Organ, "Thy will be done "	Mullineux.
Grand Prelude and Fugue in D major	Bach.
Communion for the Organ in F major	Grison.
Processional March in E flat	Wely.

CRYSTAL PALACE.

Mr. A. J. Eyre's performances on Saturday, December 1st, included the following :—

Overture, "The Last Judgment "	Spohr.
Andante in G	Smart.
Selection from "St Paul "	Mendelssohn.
Grand Prelude in D minor	
Fugue, "Wir Glauben all' au einen Gott "	Bach.
Thanksgiving March	Lambert.
Air composed for Holsworthy Church Bells	Wesley.
Motet, "Judge me, O God "	Mendelssohn.
Song, "The Lost Chord "	Sullivan.

On December 5th, Mr. E. H. Turpin gave an organ recital at Maldon, Essex, upon the organ, rebuilt by Mr. A. Kirkland, of Wakefield. The vocalist was Mr. A. L. Freyer, of St. Paul's Cathedral, whose artistic singing was duly appreciated.

EDINBURGH UNIVERSITY.

"Sir Herbert Oakeley gave last week his first recital this session to a crowded audience. There was a large attendance of students, by whom the Professor was warmly welcomed. These recitals are not confined to the Professor's own class, but are open to all matriculated students; and must prove an invaluable means of musical culture to those who avail themselves of the opportunity of hearing selections from the great masters played on the finest organ in Scotland. The fortnightly organ recitals will this session generally alternate with fortnightly lectures on Thursdays, which are also to be open to matriculated students—another instance of Sir Herbert Oakeley's desire to disseminate musical knowledge. The programme commenced with Martin Luther's grand chorale, "Ein' feste Burg," in evident allusion to the fourth centenary of the great Reformer. In Handel's air for soprano, an adaptation from one of the operas, the stops used appeared to be a combination of oboes, clarinets, and horns, which absolutely "sang" the melody. In the fugue for organ, which followed, the fine counterpoint of the "Saxon Giant," was listened to with special satisfaction by true lovers of organ music; although Haydn's far more obvious and more comprehensible air and chorus were, as might be expected, more acceptable to so mixed an audience. Mozart's highly-impressioned andante, was redemanded, but not repeated; the protracted applause, however, after Beethoven's exquisite *mercata* (Op. 14) seemed to indicate that the audience would brook no denial, and the *encore* was complied with. The staccato, contrasted to the legato effects seemed to be especially appreciated. The movement from a quartet by Spohr, so effective and so elaborately developed, was again more acceptable to those of the more musical portion of listeners; but Hummel's "Melody," or air for variations in his Septuor, seemed to suit all tastes. Gluck's Gavotte caused quite *a furore*, and on the bye please including the Professor played another of those popular movements by Handel. The recital concluded with one of the most effective pieces sung at the concerts of the University Musical Society—Bishop's admirable setting of Sir Walter Scott's lines in "The Lady of the Lake," in which all contrasts of light and shade, fortissimo, and its dying echoes, were introduced on the magnificent organ. Perhaps no recital in the music classroom has ever given more general satisfaction.

F. H. Turpin.

BRISTOL.

An organ recital was given by Mr. George Riseley in the Colston Hall, Bristol, on Saturday, November 24th. The following was the programme :—

Overture, "Occasional" .... Handel
Andante—Allegro—Adagio—March.
Andante from the Symphony in C minor ...... Beethoven
Organ Sonata, No. 4, in B flat .... Mendelssohn
Allegro—Andante Religioso—Allegretto—Allegro Maestoso.
Sonata No. 3, in A .... Corelli
"Ave Maria Dolente" .... Cherubini
Overture, "William Tell" .... Rossini

And on Saturday, December 1st :—

Overture in D major .... Handel
Andante from the 3rd Symphony .... Beethoven
Organ Sonata, No. 1, in F .... Mendelssohn
Allegro with Choral in Pedal—Andante.
Grand March in C, Caractacus .... Gounod
Air and Gavotte in E minor .... Gluck
"Olivia" ....
"Don Pasquale" ....

BIRMINGHAM.

Mr. C. J. B. Meacham, Mus. Bac., Oxon., organist of St. Philip's Church, Birmingham, gave an organ recital in Holy Trinity Church, Birchfields, on November 29th. The following was the programme :—

Overture, "Samson" .... Handel
Adagio (1st Symphony) .... Haydn
Grand Andante .... Rossini
Slow Movement, "Maid of Orleans" .... Moscheles
Adagio Nixon .... Morandi
Adagio (Scotch Symphony) .... Mendelssohn
Cavatina de Dunkerque .... Batiste
Corporation, "March" .... Meyerbeer

Mr. Samuel ... read a paper before the College of Organists on Tuesday last; particulars of which will be given next week.

THE SATURDAY POPULAR ORGAN RECITALS at the BOW and BROMLEY INSTITUTE.—The Recital TO-NIGHT, Dec. 8th, at eight o'clock, will be given by Mr. HENRY R. EYES (Professor), Royal Academy of Music, and Organist to St. Pancras Church. Vocalist, Miss CLARA SAMUELL, Accompanist, Mr. FOUNTAIN MEEN. North Limited Railway Station, Bow, E.

PRINCIPAL CONTENTS OF THIS NUMBER.

LONDON: SATURDAY, DECEMBER 8, 1883.

THE LOGIC OF COUNTERPOINT.

Third Series.

XV.

So far from such progressions being difficult,

TO the student who has honestly and carefully prepared himself for the work of part-writing by practising the various contrapuntal types in 4, 5 and 6 parts, there is but little to say with regard to the construction of counterpoint in 5, 6, 7, and 8 parts. In truth, the obvious and necessary relaxation of the rules increases in proportion with the number of parts employed; and such relaxation of the laws governing part action is productive of no bad effect, inasmuch as the ear loses the power of tracing out the progress of the parts when more than four are used. However great the results may seem to be in increased richness and dignity from a score having more than four parts, it is questionable whether the employment of such a score does not involve as a rule a more than counterbalancing loss of perspicuity and well defined tone outlines. The greatest masters in their works for 6 and 8 parts have practically endorsed this view by a frequent division of the parts for antiphonal use, and by rarely writing for a large number of parts with that degree of strictness which justifies the technical expression—"Counterpoint in 6, 7, or 8 real parts." The effect of a large number of parts moving independently may be aptly compared with the corresponding appeal to the brain which would be made through the eye, by the undue exertions involved in watching the course of a large number of independent objects or things. Just as the eye resents such a strain upon its powers and in self-defence, as it were, groups the different objects of its view in a small number of general masses, so the ear declines to follow excessive part activity, and merely accepts the general, richly combined effects of the harmony. So it is needless to spend too much time on a species of contrapuntal activity, which for most practical purposes may be fairly called superfluous. All the same, the student will do well to essay some practice in the conduct of counterpoint employing 6, 7, and 8 parts; and such practice will not only be found useful in occasional choral effects, but it will have an undoubted use in the art of scoring for an orchestra, in which clearness of contrapuntal vision not only helps the composer to write with rapidity and perspicuity, but enables him to realise with advantage the best distribution of the elements of widely spread harmonies. The chief directions in which the laws are relaxed in favour of the composer in scoring for a large number of parts are naturally with regard to the more nearly allowed proximity of consecutive perfect concords, and it may be added greater license in the treatment of discords, in the way especially of joining with some impunity to transfer those to other parts lying close at hand. The first important concession with regard to the progress of perfect concords is the permission to not external, to proceed in contrary [...] in octaves, as here in ascent and descent [...]

$$C/G \backslash D/A$$
$$C\backslash G/D\backslash A$$

THE LOGIC OF COUNTERPOINT.

$$E\backslash A/D\backslash G$$
$$E/A\backslash D/G.$$

So far from such progression having in [...] occasionally frequently in 7 or 8 parts a bad effect they [...] this the harmony with gain, and strengthen, by a species of allowable doubling, a sequential figure to which strength and prominence may be rightfully and effectually given.

E. H. TURPIN.

ON THE ORIGIN OF THE WORD "MASS."

To Church musicians of all branches of the Church the origin of the word at the head of this leaderette is a matter of some interest, especially as furnishing the familiar title of the Communion Service of the Roman branch of the Church, the musical setting of which supplies probably the richest departmental treasure of Church music the world has yet known and which has been contributed to by all the greatest continental musicians with the exception of HANDEL and MENDELSSOHN. A recent consideration of the question prompts the present words. Authorities of the Roman Church have, without speaking ex cathedrá, traced the word to the dismissal at the end of the Service pronounced by the officiating priest in the words—"Ite "missa est," and sung to plain song notes at High Mass liberally adorned by graceful Pneuma figures. This sentence is answered by the words, "Deo "gratias," doubtless an expression of thankfulness for the privileges vouchsafed in the greatest of sacrifices, of which the Communion Service—accepted by Christians of all shades of belief as a Divine ordinance—furnishes a commemorative type. The word "Missa," or "Mass" as familiarly rendered in English in the sentence alluded to, is of course a verbal use of the word, forming the root of our words "mission" (Latin missio), missionary, etc. So it is possible that its employment as the designation of the Communion Office of the Roman Church had originally a wider application than the explanation already quoted seems to offer; that is, it might be intended as expressive of the act of spreading "the glad "tidings" to be preached to all the nations by means of the central idea of religious faith, "sacrifice." It is possible, however, that the name "Mass" might have an inferential application from the English language itself, to the Roman Communion Office, having reference to the doctrine of transubstantiation or "real presence." The word "Mass" as used in England for many centuries would seem however to be only a corruption of the Latin missa, and as such possesses little or no etymological interest. The word "mass" in its ordinary meaning is derived it may be from the corresponding Latin massa, and has no connection with the word as used in a religious sense. The Anglican Church has therefore done wisely in adopting the words "Holy Communion" as the simple, expressive designation of the sacred office.

E. H. TURPIN.

THE MUSICAL ASSOCIATION.

On Monday last, at a meeting of the Musical Association, Mr. W. H. Cummings in the chair, Mr. E. Behnke threw on a screen by means of the oxy-hydrogen light, some marvellous photographs of his own vocal cords and soft palate in the act of singing, which had been taken under the joint direction of himself and Mr. Lennox Browne, and he read a paper descriptive of the photographic process, and of the lessons taught by these photographs. Mr. Behnke said that one objection which had been urged against the use of the laryngoscope in vocal art, was proved to be groundless, viz., that by it the vocal organs were distorted, since his photographs showed that he was able to keep his tongue flat in his mouth, thereby preventing the disturbance of the vocal organs. The lecturer also claimed to have proved by these photographs that the false vocal cords have nothing whatever to do with tone-production. He pointed out the influence exerted over the pitch and quality of tone by the soft palate, particularly showing how nasal tone was caused, and how it might be prevented. At the conclusion of a highly instructive paper, Mr. Behnke gave a laryngoscopic demonstration of the various points mentioned in his lecture. Signór Garcia, Signór Randegger, and many other members of the association availed themselves of the opportunity of verifying the photographs in the throat of the lecturer, who, at Signor Randegger's special request, sang, in different registers and on different vowels. Mr. Behnke also proved that his explanation of the enormous influence of the soft palate upon the voice is perfectly correct, and he concluded his intensely interesting demonstration by vocalising, with the laryngeal mirror at the back of the throat. There was a spirited discussion, and the usual votes of thanks to the lecturer and to the chairman brought the proceedings to a close.

CHURCH CHOIRS.

At the recent "Church Workers' Festival" at Canterbury, Dr. LONGHURST read an excellent paper on the burning questions concerning Church choirs, in the course of which he observed :—

" What is understood now-a-days by church choirs? Some will answer, "A very tiresome lot of people, very difficult to deal with, especially when possessed of the little knowledge that is dangerous." (Laughter.) Others will say, " An egotistical body of amateur musicians, associated together for the purpose, not so much of assisting at Divine worship, as for the mere selfish gratification of being known as the professed and acknowledged leaders of the congregation." (Renewed laughter.) And this remark, "leaders of the congregation," induces me to say that I consider that to be their legitimate function, and as such should be felt by them as an important privilege. (Hear, hear.) The chief points we ought to touch upon are these :—1. The efficiency of church choirs ; 2. The *esprit de corps* with which they should be animated ; 3. The mode of rehearsals ; 4. How individual members can aid and help forward the movement. As to efficiency, a justifiable emulation is, I think, quite excusable if in the right direction; not as in some choirs, where you meet with a man whose object is to make himself heard above all the others, but the emulation which prompts the desire to try and do all to the praise and glory of God. Much good may be accomplished and the true *esprit-de-corps* maintained, if the organist or choir-master throw himself into the work as heartily as the choir, and if at the rehearsals, he, as well as they, be actuated by one and the same feeling. No desire of novelty should induce them to be continually craving for fresh music, but rather a wish to perform that which is allotted to them in as perfect and devotional a manner as possible. (Hear, hear.) We all know how difficult a thing it is to persuade choirmen and boys out of the notion that because they know (as they consider) a certain chant, hymn, or anthem that there is no need of rehearsal. (Hear, hear.) This is one of the many stumbling-blocks which beset choir training; but it should not be allowed to impede the improvements which a regular course of practices by all parties concerned would eventually bring about. In some parishes it is customary to hold all the rehearsals in the church, in others in the school-room. I do not think either a good plan. If the first be adopted, the practice should be conducted with great care, the proper reverence for sacred things being imperilled. I do not think it a good plan to hold all the rehearsals in the church, especially when new music has to be learnt. If the harmonium or pianoforte be available in the school-room, by all means let that be the place for practice, and then, when all the parts are fairly correct, another rehearsal in the church might render all more satisfactory and more devotional. (Hear, hear.) Of the choice of music, too, it will be expected that I should say something. It is generally known that most Cathedral men are averse to what is called Gregorian music, which is, at least to my mind, music without music—for where music is intended as a help to devotion, I fail to see of allow that that help can possibly be rendered by the music people call Gregorian. (Hear, hear, and No.) We might as well hold up Chaucer as the most elegant of all writers, and expect all our modern poets to imitate him. (Laughter.) I think too that much of the Anglican music, if of too florid a character, is open to objection. (Hear, hear.) The recent improvement in congregational singing is mainly due to the excellent and careful manner in which the various hymn-books are now printed ; taking first the most popular, "Hymns Ancient and Modern," Barnby's "Hymdiary," Sullivan's "Church Hymns," and many others. There is now no excuse for having bad tunes, or good tunes tortured by bad harmony, for all possible care has been bestowed on these and other similar works. Speaking somewhat critically, I should say that in the later edition of "Hymns Ancient and Modern," the editors have gone too far (if possible) in the expression marks. What village organist, with a small one-manual organ, could possibly make all the changes of tone indicated by the numerous p's and f's (to say nothing of the crescendos and diminuendos), which abound in the last verse of No. 222, and Nos. 91 and 256. In No. 223, the first tune does not require nearly so many as the 2nd, although the same words are used. That danger to the general effect is imminent may be clearly proved ; for if the organist attempts to make the changes thus indicated, he loses much tone by repeatedly leaving the manuals to shift his stops; and if he does not do so, the choir, after having been drilled to observe these marks by some perhaps over-fastidious choir-master, either lose confidence in their organist, or sing with an utter disregard to effect. Let me not be misunderstood in this matter. I am not advocating a system of disregarding these excellent marks of expression (which are, if properly rendered, great helps to devotion), but rather giving my opinion that if a less number of marks had been used, greater attention to them would have been paid. Much has been said and written for and against the introduction of female singers into the choir ; it is now often thought that boys are the only trebles and altos we ought to have. If good singers can be so obtained I think it may be considered better, and in such churches where a surpliced choir is established it is often necessary, but even in such choirs the female part of the congre-gation should be invited to attend the rehearsals regularly, and in the services these valuable adjuncts would materially help the congregation in joining them to sound forth the glory and praise of God.

After quoting scriptural and musical authority for the judicious employment of female singers, Dr. Longhurst observed :—

We have then the prototype of such grand services which we have had in our glorious cathedral of Canterbury during the last few years, when the finest oratorios by the greatest composers have drawn together such large congregations (quite thousands) that have never—as far as we have record—been equalled. And on these special occasions where would our small choristers' voices have been heard had they not been supported (and strongly supported) by female voices? Where should our altos weak voices have been heard had they not been equally supported by female voices? Among the hopeful signs of better things are the occasional festivals in our cathedrals and parish churches. Several I could mention, not only in town, emulated by the noble example set by our metropolitan cathedral, St. Paul's; but also in the country, and frequently in Canterbury, where we have had, as on the occasion of the recent enthronement, a special service of praise (Mendelssohn's "Lobgesang") with a mixed choir, instruments, and organ ; and thus drawing together an immense congregation of worshippers. These signs of better things point, let us hope, to the ultimate restoration of the oratorio to its true home—the church—and this grand movement must depend in its onward progress to no small extent upon the judicious employment of female voices, not to the exclusion of boys' voices, but to the beautifying and rounding off the mass of vocal tones. (Hear, hear.) It is rather to be regretted that certain High Church authorities will recognize no high pitched voices save those of rough country lads, who may have had, during several weeks, no other mode of practising their vocal organs, than that obtained by screaming in the cornfields and orchards as living scarecrows. (Laughter.) By an infusion of female voices that rough tone of these country lads would be greatly ameliorated, and the congregation most grateful for such a real blessing, saving them all the ear-splitting, which is, in some of the rural districts, truly distressing. (Hear, hear.) What I have advanced has not been the result of a passing impression, but that of mature judgment ; for, without egotism, I may safely assert that very few men have had more, or even as much, experience in training choir boys than I have had. Commencing (when a mere boy myself) in 1836 as an assistant to my late esteemed friend, Mr. Jones, I have ever since that period had the charge of the cathedral choristers, and although here, as elsewhere, the inevitable weakness which occasionally pervades all choristers in cathedral or parish choirs will present itself when a number of big boys either leave for some better appointment or lose their voices by age (as at the present time when all my boys are, as some say, mere bables), still, I think most of those whom I have now the honour of addressing will acknowledge that the Canterbury Cathedral choristers have held, and I trust will yet again hold their own by the side of other boys who have not greater advantages of birth or education than we have in our choir. Unfortunately for me, our boys are far worse off in this respect than any other. In conclusion, I may perhaps be allowed to offer a few suggestions on what I consider to be the proper management of church choirs. Keep the choirmen in good temper if possible. I say this in all sincerity, for musicians are, most unfortunately, proverbially cranky (if such a word be admissible) ; take particular care that the music selected for service, be it chant, hymn-tune, or anthem, be suitable to the psalm, hymn, or season. Let the choirmen have a sufficient quantity of new music for practice to keep down that egotistic feeling (to which allusion has been made in this paper) of being able to sing anything at sight ; so few amateurs possess this gift. Let the rehearsals be regular and in every sense good practices, and so a real pleasure to those who take part in them. Make it a *sine qua non* that every member of the choir (unless prevented by illness, or some other cogent reason) should be present at least at three-fourths of the rehearsals, and those members who cannot so attend advise to retire from the choir. Rest assured these are most important things in the working of church choirs, and I trust these hints may be received in the same spirit of toleration by which they are prompted. (Applause.)

Unhappily, in accordance with the general clerical belief that, whether they understand the subject under consideration or not, the clergy are born to do all the talking in the world and perhaps anxious to stifle all artistic development in the Church, several of the clergy present having little or nothing to say of value (probably in their hearts dreading the growth of Church music) indulged in the customary inane observations and feeble efforts to provoke a smile, and chirped generally in much too characteristic a vein of clerical drivel anent musical matters.

The Rev. T. HIRST (rector of Bishopsbourne) remarked that he preferred Anglican music, but he thought they must allow Gregorian music fair play and toleration. (Hear, hear.) It was evident that parish choirs stood in need of improvement. He read in the *Standard* on the previous Monday that the Archbishop of Canterbury was about to move in the Lower House of Convocation for the appointment of a committee to consider what could be done to raise the tone of parish choirs. This showed that the question was rapidly becoming a "burning" one. (Hear, hear.) The great points to be aimed at were reverence in church, regularity in practice, and devotion in the lives of the choir men and boys themselves. The services should be made as congregational as possible ; and anyone who aimed at anything lower than that made a great and fatal mistake. (Hear, hear.)

So far so good ; and had the reverend gentleman sat down at this point, his opening sensible remarks would not have suffered by a too close proximity to the following sublime twaddle, which was only relieved by a proper recognition of a 'sense of duty, in the statement regarding his worthy to be followed example of constantly attending choir practices. The speaker

Understood that Dr. Longhurst approved of ladies singing in parish choirs ; but he (Mr. Hirst) must confess that he did not approve of it. He did not think the place for ladies was in the parish chancel. (Hear, hear.) He liked to hear their sweet voices in the congregation, but he did not, he confessed, care to have ladies in the choir of the parish church, especially if two or three of them happened, as they did in his case, to be rather good looking. (Laughter.) After a short residence at Bishopsbourne he determined to speedily get rid of these young ladies. He called them together. He invited them to tea (laughter), and told them there was to be a surpliced choir. The girls retired, but they had always been good friends. He gave each of them a little present at parting (laughter), and the whole matter was amicably arranged. Having got rid of the young ladies, the thing was to supply their places. There were numbers of boys who, at the age of eight or nine, could, after a little training, be placed in the choir as chorister boys ; and he endeavoured to select as choirmen men of moral lives, fairly well educated, and with a small knowledge of music. In his parish, with a population of 320, he had a choir of twelve men and twelve boys (applause) ; and he thought every clergyman might obtain a fair choir so far as numbers were concerned. If the incumbent did not attend the practices regularly, depend upon it the choir would become irregular. He had been connected with church choirs for thirty years, and during that period he had never, except in cases of illness or absence on his annual holiday, left his choir practices unattended. (Applause.) The best hymnal was the Ancient and Modern one, but when they had gone through it he did not think they would find more than thirty really good tunes. (Oh.) Whenever they heard of a good tune they should get it, and adapt it to their own hymns. It might be a good thing to have an anthem in a parish church, but he objected to anthems strongly as an inducement to the choir to persevere in its practice. He also objected very much to solos and duets. Every choir, he thought, should have an annual outing ; if a clergyman did not give his choir a treat once a year he was a very jolly fellow. (Hear, hear, and laughter.)

The BISHOP OF DOVER mentioned that in one church in the diocese the lady singers were placed behind a lattice, and it could not be seen whether they had the features of Venus or of Medusa.

Surely these gentlemen, who thought fit thus to twaddle about the attractions of pretty faces and air their nonsensical leanings towards mediæval monasticism with regard to the presence of women in church, did not desire it to be supposed they were personally liable to the distractions which, arising from the near presence of pretty faces, create sentiment in the mundane minds of overgrown school boys? If these observations were intended for other people, such remarks were still in the worst possible taste. Alas ! that an opportunity for the serious consideration of a vital topic should have been swamped by such time-wasting trifling as this ! However, it is to be devoutly hoped that the organist of Canterbury Cathedral and others who *are* in earnest with regard to this very important subject, will not rest, but will again and again press for a full examination of the constitution and requirements of the Church choir. It is a pleasure to note that Mr. W. de Manby Sergison will presently read a paper bearing upon the subject before the members of the College of Organists. May such efforts for the consideration and opportunities for the discussion of the highest and purest thing we have as the production of men's hearts and minds, Church music, multiply and bear good fruit from day to day. This will be the earnest wish of every Christian thinker and large-minded Churchman who is climbing Zion's hill, with the motto "Excelsior" upon the banner of faith and hope.   E. H. T.

There is to be, it is reported, English opera in London in January next.

THE SOCIETY OF PROFESSIONAL MUSICIANS.

On December 1st, the Society of Professional Musicians held their meeting in the Mayor's Parlour, Town Hall, Southport. The chairman was Mr. Henry Watson, Mus. Bac., of Manchester ; and amongst the members present were Dr. G. Marsden, Dr. Henry Hiles, Mr. J. Wrigley, R.A.M., Mr. J. Marsden, and Mr. C. B. Grundy, all of Manchester ; Dr. H. Fisher, of Blackpool ; Mr. W. D. Hall and Mr. James J. Monk, of Liverpool ; Mr. James Dawber, Mus. Bac. (honorary secretary), Wigan ; Mr. J. M. Field, of Bolton ; Mr. George Clafton, of Oldham ; and Messrs. Hiacheriffe and H. Hawkins, of Southport.

The minutes of the previous meeting, held at Manchester, were confirmed.

The SECRETARY reported that the Revisional Committee appointed at the last meeting to revise the examination scheme, had met. It was at first thought that it would take more than one meeting to get through the work, but it turned out that the members had been working privately, and when they came together they found the road pretty clear, and in a little over three hours went through the whole book, largely augmenting the lists of pieces by which candidates might be examined, and adding several compositions of well-known members. Other branches came in for a considerable share of alteration. They were now at work on the final proof, and the work was expected to appear in a saleable form shortly. The Committee decided, after a long discussion, that books should be published at half-a-crown, as the previous price was reckoned too high.

On the motion of Dr. HILES, seconded by Dr. MARSDEN, a cordial vote of thanks was given to Senior Risegari, and Mr. H. Smith, of Manchester, for their valuable assistance in the preparation of a scheme for instruction in violin and violoncello playing.

On the motion of Dr. MARSDEN, seconded by Mr. J. J. MONK, "The best thanks of the meeting were given to the Revisional Committee for their services, in completing the examination scheme."

Mr. FIELD moved that members be allowed to vote by proxy. He said his object in proposing that, was to give outside, professional musicians some inducement to join the Society, and thus extend its usefulness.

Mr. GRUNDY seconded the motion.

Dr. FISHER thought if that resolution were passed it would be unfair to those who were in the habit of attending the meetings ; if members were allowed to vote by proxy they would probably never attend. If a restriction were put upon the application of the rule, it would perhaps serve a better purpose, for instance, if voting by proxy were only allowed when the member who did so was more than thirty or forty miles from the place of meeting.

Dr. HILES believed that that plan was not the proper way to give members an interest in the Society. He thought a system of branch societies would answer the purpose better.

Mr. J. WRIGLEY thought that the great charm which the Society had for him was because by attending its councils he was enabled to meet so many gentlemen of his profession ; and he did not see that it could in any way be useful to members who did not go to its meetings, because they could, not then profit by any of the debates, and thus would lose almost altogether the benefits to be derived from membership.

After further discussion, Mr. FIELD withdrew his motion.

It was moved by Mr. MONK, seconded by Mr. HALL, and agreed that the Secretary be requested to arrange for a meeting of professional musicians, either at Leicester, or Nottingham, or Birmingham, during the Christmas holidays, with a view of, by inducing professional men to join, extending the usefulness of the Society ; and that members of the Society in this part of the country be invited to attend the meeting, for the purpose of co-operating with the Secretary for that object.

It was decided that all subjects for discussion, and any proposed resolution, should be stated in the circular convening each meeting ; and that no vote be taken upon any other subject.

The next general meeting of the Society was arranged to take place in Liverpool in February next, and Dr. Fisher was appointed chairman.

On the motion of Dr. HILES, seconded by Dr. FISHER, the best thanks of the meeting were given to the Mayor for his kindness in permitting the Society to hold their council in his parlour.

The Church Oratorio Society sang Spohr's "Last Judgment" at Oxley Church, Bushey, on Dec. 3rd. Mr. J. Turpin, Mus.Bac., conducted, and the organist was Mr. E. H. Turpin. The music was attentively listened to by a congregation which filled the church.

"Spohr's "Last Judgment" will be performed in its entirety with organ accompaniment only at St. Paul's, Bow Common, on Friday evening, Dec. 14th, at 8 p.m., by the choir of the church alone, under the direction of Mr. Horace Buttery. On Christmas Eve the usual Christmas selection from the "Messiah" of Handel will be rendered in the same way.

Reviews

Glees: The Three Topers. By M. L. Gordon. (H. Davies, 19, Treherne-road, Brixton).—This is not, as its title would seem to suggest, a roaring Bacchanalian piece. But it concerns the praise of good wine in a seemly and graceful verbal and musical fashion. The piece is written for alto, two tenors, and bass. It is accompanied obbligato. The different voices have solos and the pieces have several distinct movements. The writing is fluent, bold, effective, and interesting, and the piece will be duly valued by our many choirs of men's voices as a spirited transcription to the store of glees of the more modern type.

The Praise of Flowers, Jubilee cantata. By Weber; English version by F. W. Rosier. (Goodwin and Tabb, 71, Great Queen-street, W.C., Lamborn Cock, 23, Hollis Street ; J. Curwen, & Warwick Lane).—A new edition of this characteristic and effective work clearly and handsomely printed for 1s 6d, with a well-arranged pianoforte accompaniment, having the orchestration marked thereon. A Tonic Sol-fa edition is printed ; and the orchestral parts may be had of the obliging music librarians, Messrs. Goodwin and Tabb, whose address has just been given.

Christmas Hymns and *Carols.* Edwin Lemare (Weekes and Co.).—A dozen settings of Mrs. Gaskell's works printed together or separately as required. Both melodies and harmonies are good, while being in a natural and not servile style. Some, as "Lullaby," "Christ is born," and "Hosannah," are excellent specimens of the carol type.

Foreign Musical Intelligence.

Max Josef Beer is writing new comic opera entitled "Der Pfeifeskönig."

A new opera, "L'Antiquario," music by Dessy, has been produced at Cagliari.

Grammann's opera, "Das Andreasfest," has been very successfully given in Augsburg.

Rubinstein's receipts at his three recent concerts in Berlin, are said to have been enormous.

Delibes' "Lakmé," was performed at Frankfort-on-Main, on Dec. 3rd, with a German translation by Herr Gumbert.

A bust of Peter Benoit has been presented to the Duke of Campofelice by the Belgian composer's friends and admirers.

Mackenzie's "Colomba" has been accepted by the direction of the Vienna Opera House, Mdme. Pauline Lucca being engaged for the title rôle.

There are now four weekly orchestral Sunday concerts in Paris, with orchestras of 70 or 80 players each. These performances are continued over seven months of the year.

A new comic opera in three acts, "Una Congiura," by A. Biagi, professor of the piano at the local Instituto Musicale, has been produced at the Teatro Niccolini, Florence.

Ludwig Meinardus' oratorio, "Luther in Worms," gave so much satisfaction, on the 7th and 9th November, in Elberfeld, that the managing committee presented him with job marks.

The Musical Society of Rotterdam announce a forthcoming performance of Handel's "Saul," with additional accompaniments by the well known composer, F. Gernsheim, the conductor of the Society.

A new comic opera called "Spanish Students," by a Danish composer, named Langemüller, has been played several times at Copenhagen, with extraordinary success. The work is said to be after the style of "Carmen."

M. Georges Auvray, at the head of an excellent orchestra, is taking a provincial tour with a *répertoire* of new works by Delibes, Massenet, Wider, and other rising French composers. Rouen, Havre, Caen, Orléans, Chartres, Amiens, and other towns, will have the benefit of this admirable undertaking.

Herr Max Friedländer, the baritone, has discovered some valuable Schubert manuscripts, amongst others, a part of the music to "Rosamunde." The newly found pieces are soon to be performed by the Vienna Philharmonic Society.

ANCIENT ORGAN IN THE DUOMO OF COMO

Berlioz's great Te Deum, produced at the Church of St. Eustache, Paris, in 1855, under the direction of its composer, and not heard since, was performed in the Cathedral of Bordeaux recently, with a band and chorus numbering 1,000.

From Zwambeck is announced the death of the famous dance music composer, Josef Gungl, aged 73. This report has been seemingly corrected by the statement that the deceased composer was Johann Gungl, a relation of the more famous Josef Gungl.

Robert Volckman, who died last October, has left a parcel of manuscripts labelled "Unpublished Compositions," which contains, with other smaller works, two sonatas for piano, a duo for piano and violin, a string quartet, and the music to a dramatic fairy tale entitled "Midas."

The death is announced of Ludwig Erk, a popular Berlin composer, whose part-songs and vocal music for schools are in much repute in Germany. He was in receipt of a life-pension of £150 from the municipality of Berlin in consideration of his services rendered to the art in the national schools.

The announcements are made that Mr. Max Pauer, son of the well-known and esteemed London professor, E. Pauer, recently played with great success at Frankfort; and he was invited to play Chopin's E minor concerto at Heidelberg on the 15th ult. He is also announced to appear at Mainz, Darmstadt, Mannheim, and in other places.

The oldest living German musician is Herr Hill, a former member of the town band at the watering-place of Elsier, who celebrated last month his 100th birthday. In company with his sons and grandsons, who would seem to have inherited his talent for music, he may still occasionally be seen taking part in the town band performances.

Herr Pollini, director of the Hamburg Theatre, has offered Anton Rubinstein the sum of £15,000 for 100 concerts, to be given during a tour of five months in the United States. The composer has not as yet, however, accepted this munificent offer. Joachim, Sarasate, and a great many other well-known artists will go over with him to the "land of dollars."

Says *The Monthly Musical Record:* The Commission de l'Opéra-Populaire, appointed by the Municipal Council of Paris, has unanimously decided that a subvention of 300,000 francs should be given to M. Taffanel, the director of the Théâtre du Château d'Eau, if the Council ratifies the decision of the Commission. A long-discussed question will at last be settled, the improvement of an existing establishment being resorted to, instead of the foundation of a new one. The subvention is granted only for the year 1883-4, and under the condition that six first *sujets* approved of by the Council will be engaged before the 1st of January. When shall we hear of similar actions by our municipal authorities? The object of the Paris Municipal Council is, of course, to ensure good operatic entertainments for the people at reasonable prices.

No more earnest worker for the poor can be found than Mrs. W. H. Monk (wife of Dr. W. H. Monk, of King's College), who earnestly pleads for the Cottage Mission in East London, to help feed hundreds who are so wretched and hungry. The only dinner in any week that they ever have is the "Irish Stew Dinner," prepared for a swarming crowd of nearly naked, starving children, by Mr. Austin and his ready helpers. Funds are urgently needed to prevent the recurrence of the heartrending calamity of last winter, when upon one occasion there was nothing in hand to provide material, and the poor, despairing, famishing children could not be made to believe that they *must go away unfed*. Ever one penny will be thankfully received by the founder of these Irish Stew Dinners, Mr. Walter Austin, of 44, Finsbury Pavement, E.C. Musical people, who stand brightly forth as among the best servers of charity, will surely help in a cause so good, in some way or other.

Correspondence.

ANCIENT ORGAN IN THE DUOMO OF ORVIETO, TUSCANY.

To the Editor of "THE MUSICAL STANDARD."

Sir,—When travelling in Italy during the winter of last year (Venice), among other small towns of the interior, I visited the decayed old city of Orvieto, distant within two hours' journey from Rome. The grand old cathedral, with its magnificent stalls, altar-piece and screens, and its noble frescoes by Signorelli, contains, in addition to these and other works of art, a fine organ of great size, placed in a gallery in the north transept, and reaching nearly to the vaulting. Having at that time almost completed my large work on organ-cases and the art-archæology of the instrument generally, and being thoroughly enthusiastic on the subject of old organs, I persuaded the sacristan to admit me and my friend to the organ-loft, reached by a spiral staircase from the sacristy. Like nearly all Italian organ-cases, this one presented a flat front, the space between the side pilasters and the top entablature being divided up into compartments, containing pipes of various sizes, from two or three feet to 40 feet in length, the group of the 32 feet metal diapasons standing majestically in the centre. The total height of the case was about 70 feet, and from the details of the architecture I judged the work to date from c. 1570 or 1580, and from what I saw of the internal mechanism, I have little doubt that the greater part of it belongs to the same period.

The bellows are, as usual in old organs, placed away from the instrument; and, in this case, were situated in the triforium passage, but being out of order and detached from the trunks, I was unable to play, as I wished. ... In there is but one row of keys; CC to G, 56 notes, of which the upper few have, doubtless, been added in modern times; and 18 octaves of pedals, of which the upper half octave is minus sharps. The stops are drawn by means of levers, placed in double rows on either side of the manual, and move from right to left, and not up and down as in other old examples I have seen. The following is the list of stops, as indicated by labels placed under the levers:—

On the left-hand side:—

1. Tromba di 16 piedi bassi.	8. Cornetto soprani.
2. Tromba di 16 piedi sopra.	9. Ottavino soprani.
3. Tomba di 8 piedi bassi.	10. Corni dolci soprani.
4. Clarinetto soprani.	11. Flauti in 8 bassi.
5. Clarone bassi.	12. Flauti in 8 soprani.
6. Trombe soprani.	13. Flauti traverso soprani.
7. Violino soprani.	14. Voce umana soprani.

PEDALIERA.

15. Gran 16 piedi.	19. Bombardone.
16. Gran 8 piedi.	20. Bombardo.
17. Quintadona.	21. Timballi.
18. Ottava al pieno.	

On the right-hand side:—

32. 16 piedi bassi.
33. 16 piedi soprani.
34. 16 bassi.
35. 12 e 15.
36. 15 e 19.
37. 12 e 26.
38. 19 e 33.
39. 29, 33, e 36.
40. Radoppio di 4 pieni.
41. Radoppio di 2 pieni.
42. Unionetti Pedale.
43. 8 secondo bassi.

As it was unable to play the organ, I cannot say which of the above belonged to the pedal; and which to the manual, but am inclined to think that all, with the exception of the first fourteen, belong to the pedal!

As the duomo, like so many other churches throughout Europe (England, certainly not excepted), is suffering severely from the modern craze of "restoration," it is likely that this old organ will not long survive the renovating powers, or will, at any rate, be rebuilt internally, so I think the above description will be worth recording, and be of interest to your readers.

I found but few fine organ-cases in Italy, and none that can be compared with some of the magnificent works I have seen in Germany and France; but there are three or four very beautiful examples at Siena, the work of Baldassare Peruzzi, in the Ospedale della Scala, the Palazzo Publico, and the Duomo. These date from the beginning of the 16th century, and have made drawings of them. Faithfully yours,

         ARTHUR G. HILL, F.S.A.

Oxford and Cambridge Club, Nov. 26, 1883.

At the recent festivities at Sandringham, in honour of the birthday of H. R. H. the Princess of Wales, the Duke of Albany's new valse was played by the band of the Norfolk Artillery.

Passing Events.

"King David" is to be given at the first concert of Mr. Willing's choir.

Mr. E. H. Morris is giving a series of popular concerts in the Victoria Hall, Plymouth.

Rossini's "Moses in Egypt" was performed at St. George's Hall, Bradford, last week.

The Royal Academy of Music has now some 190 students, with a very large yearly revenue. ... the club valued for its many ...

"The Golden Ring" was successfully produced at the re-opening of the Alhambra on Monday last.

Spohr's "Last Judgment" was to be sung in the Leeds Parish Church, on Friday evening, Dec. 7th, the choir to be augmented for the occasion.

At St. Margaret's Pattens, Rood Lane, Eastcheap Street, Spohr's "Last Judgment," will be sung on Friday next the 14th inst., after 7.30, under the direction of Mr. Stedman.

Mr. Packmann kindly gave a recital at the Royal Academy of Music the other day. He was assisted by an English lady pianist, of whom it is said we shall hear more presently.

A new and spirited paper, called *The London Musical Critic*, for December, not only includes interesting letterpress matter, but an effective "Festal March" by Mr. G. W. Pearce, Mus. Bac. ...

The subject of David has engaged the attention of three English composers, Charles Horsley, Dr. W. H. Longhurst (1871), whose work has not yet been printed ... and Mr. C. H. Warren (1883).

At a recent meeting of the governors of Heriot's Hospital, Edinburgh, it was unanimously resolved "That instruction in the theory and practice of music in the outdoor schools should, in future, be made continuous and systematic."

A chief element in the success of Berlioz's "Requiem" at the Crystal Palace on Saturday last, was the employment of a chorus of students from the R.A.M. This was a notable gain. We sadly need the development of professional choruses in England.

St. Cecilia Magazine for Dec., has an interesting and appreciative account of the life and works of the English composer, Dr. Samuel Arnold, (1739—1802); who wrote some excellent music, and whose oratorio "The Prodigal Son," at least, deserves revival.

Readers will learn with sympathetic regret that Mr. Frederic Clay was on Tuesday night seized with paralysis whilst walking in Bow Street, from the Alhambra theatre, with his colleague in the production of "The Golden Ring," Mr. G. Sims. It is ... to add that the esteemed composer is improving.

At a meeting of the Committee acting in reference to the National Eisteddfod meetings held in Cardiff in August last, a final balance-sheet, which had been looked forward to with much interest, was presented. A large expenditure had been incurred in prizes offered in the different competitions; but, over and above the aggregate expenses, a credit balance of £140 was announced.

A. M. it seems was wrong in describing Lord Overstone as an attendant at the Musical Union Matinées. Lady Overstone and her daughter did attend, but Lord Overstone was never present, it is confidently asserted. The person mistaken for Lord Overstone by A. M. was the Rev. M. Goddard, a member of the Musical Union Committee, who was carried into the room when it confirmed invalid.

A small but no less sure sign of the times, is the meeting of a number of clergymen of moderate doctrinal views in mid-London to discuss the vital question, Church music; and it is gratifying to add, *mirabile dictu*, the presence of a practical musician was thought to be not undesirable. It is earnestly to be hoped that such meetings will multiply, and that the clergy, who are beginning to open their eyes to the fact that Church music must be improved and advanced, will seriously add their great and legitimate influence in guiding and furthering the movement.

At the Royal Pavilion, Brighton, on Dec. 8th, Miss Augusta M. Draper was to give her fourth annual Matinée Musicale, with the assistance of her pupils, Miss Maude Ballard, Miss Fanny Coke, Miss Rosie Ballard, and the following artists :—vocalist, Mdme. Osborne Williams ; solo clarionet, Mr. Lazarus ; solo violoncello, Mr. William C. Haan, R.A.M. ; solo pianoforte, Miss Augusta M. Draper, and Miss Emily Slade. Accompanist, Mr. R. Taylor. The programme includes a Weber Duet (Op. 48), for clarionet and pianoforte, and a Beethoven Trio for clarionet, violoncello, and pianoforte.

At St. George's Hall, Langham-place, an interesting amateur vocal and dramatic performance was given on the afternoon of Dec. 3rd, when Balfe's cantata " Mazeppa," which has recently created much interest, formed the first part of the programme, the remaining portion of which was appropriated to a new operetta, entitled " The Ferry Girl," the libretto of which is adapted from the French by the Dowager Marchioness of Downshire, the music being the composition of Lady Arthur Hill. The performances were given in aid of the funds of the parish church of Easthampstead (Berkshire).

Lady Brabazon gave a concert at the Brompton Hospital on Nov. 27th, in the handsome large hall, which was crowded with the patients. Mr. Cb. Bishenden gained encores for both his songs, " John Olden " was especially encored ; Mrs. Bishenden uses her sweet and sympathetic voice to great advantage in the duets she sings with her husband. The songs of Miss Burdett always please ; Miss Warburton sang in an artistic manner. Mr. Owens sang two of Sims Reeves' favourite songs, and Mr. Hubert Smith played two solos on the Broadwood grand in a highly-finished style. A vote of thanks to the performers was received with the greatest enthusiasm.

A glance at the advertisement columns in the last number of the *Musical Standard* will inform the reader that Mr. Charles E. Stephens' new Sonata for flute and pianoforte is to be introduced at the next meeting of the Musical Artists' Society on Dec. 15th. Mr. Stephens has treated wood-wind instruments in a remarkably original and effective manner—no facile feat. A sonata for the same instruments by the late Henry Westrop is extant, but such compositions seem to be rare. Mr. Stephens's overture, " A Dream of Happiness," has been recently played at Brighton with great éclat. More than a " dream," the overture is a reality.

A special matinée was given on Nov. 28th, at the Gaiety Theatre by Mr. Henry Nordblom, the well-known tenor of English opera companies. The first two acts of " Fra Diavolo " were given, Mr. Nordblom himself appearing as the principal character of the robber chief, in which he was supported by the singing of Miss Rose Hersee, Mr. Aynsley Cook, Mr. R. Temple, and Mr. Faulkner Leigh. The performance however did not by any means go smoothly, owing to an evident insufficiency of the rehearsal, and also to the ineffectual efforts of the lady who appeared as Lady Allcash to sing the difficult music allotted to that part. Mr. Joseph Maas sang in his own admirable way " Come into the garden, Maud," between the acts, and also, in response to an encore, " When other lips." Mr. Charles Warner gave a recitation, and there were some other miscellaneous items.

The critic of the *Times* says of Mr. Parry's new pianoforte quartet :—" It is a composition of high aim and serious import, free from any concession to the taste of the vulgar. Mr. Parry's motto is *odi profanum vulgus ;* he is a composer for *composers*, and his works frequently appeal to the mind rather than the heart, even as do those of his favourite master and model, Brahms. By adding that, of the 4 movements, the Andante in D flat appears to be the most successful, we imply a high opinion of the composer's powers. It is in a slow movement that a musician's talent is put to the severest and most conclusive test. Mere learning or fanciful imagery avail little or nothing. Mr. Parry is further praised for his continuity, possessed by him in a rare degree, and this atones for a certain want of spontaneous utterance. If no single melodic phrase strikes the ear by its innate beauty, there is no flagging of inspiration from the opening notes to the fine climax to which the piece gradually rises ; the first movement is said to be remarkable for its elaborate contrapuntal writing ; the *scherzo* strikes the critic as fresh and lively, and the finale, with a resemblance to the item of the first allegro, as effective."

The Querist.

QUERIES.

ZIEGLER.—Could any of your readers kindly inform me if there are pianoforte manufacturers by the name of " Ziegler." I have seen pianos bearing that name, and I believe they are manufactured in Paris.—C. B.

A correspondent writes in reference to a march, from Weber's opera, " Sylvana," arranged as a pianoforte duet, and published by Lamborn Cock. The key is A major. Can any one give the date and other particulars of this opera ; the title is not familiar ?—A. M.

REPLIES.

LONDON ORGANISTS.—For a list of the organists of the London Churches, I beg to refer " Harmonic Flute" to Mackeson's " Guide to the Churches of London and its Suburbs," published by Metzler and Co., 35, Great Marlborough Street and Parker and Co., 6, Southampton Street, Strand, price 1s. 6d. Besides the names of the organists and dates of appointment, there will be found in the guide much concise and useful information about the organ, choir, music, etc., at the various churches.—J. S. BUMPUS.

A. W. H. H. may not use Barnett's trio, " The Magic Wove Scarf," in public, without payment of a certain taking sum to purchaser of the copyright, whose name I forget. The musical copyright runs for thirty years after the composer's death, and I hope that John Barnett is still alive.—A. M.

" IONE."—This opera, was composed by Petrelli. If E. A. Sutton will communicate direct with me I shall be most happy to give him every information I can. The opera is not, I believe, in print, but I have a copy that is available. —FREDK. W. COOKE, Graveley Hill, Birmingham.

Service Lists.

SECOND SUNDAY IN ADVENT.

DECEMBER 9th.

London.

ST. PAUL'S CATHEDRAL. — Morn.: Service, Benedicite (Best) ; Benedictus, Stainer in F flat ; Introit, Lo, He comes ! with clouds descending ; Holy Communion, Stainer in E flat. Even.: Service, Magnificat and Nunc Dimittis, Stainer in E flat ; Anthem, Day of anger (Mozart).

FOUNDLING CHAPEL. — Morn.: Service, Garrett in D ; Anthem, Blessed be the God and Father (Wesley). Aft.: Children's Service.

LINCOLN'S INN CHAPEL—Morn.: Service, Boyce in A ; Kyrie (Steggall) ; Anthem, Thy word is a lantern (Purcell). Even.: Service, Arnold in A ; Anthem, O! how amiable are thy words (Steggall).

TEMPLE CHURCH.—Morn.: Service, Te Deum Laudamus, and Jubilate Deo, Aldrich in G ; Apostles' Creed, Harmonized Monotone ; Anthem, The Wilderness (Wesley). Even.: Service, Magnificat and Nunc Dimittis, Stainer in A ; Apostles' Creed Harmonized Monotone ; Anthem, Sing, O heavens (Sullivan).

ALL SAINTS, MARGARET STREET.—Morn.: Service, Benedicite, Hoyte in D ; Benedictus, Monk in F ; Holy Communion, Stainer in A ; Offertory Anthem, Sleepers wake (Mendelssohn). Even.: Service, Wesley in F ; Anthem, The sorrows of death, The night is departing (Mendelssohn) ; Dies Iræ (Hayes).

CHRIST CHURCH, CLAPHAM.—Morn.: Service, Benedicite, Stainer, etc. ; Kyrie and Credo, Monk in C ; Offertory Anthem, Sleepers, wake (Mendelssohn) ; Sanctus, Benedictus, Agnus Dei, and Gloria in excelsis (Monk). Even.: Service, Magnificat and Nunc Dimittis, Arnold in A ; Anthem, Comfort ye, Ev'ry valley, And the glory of the Lord (Handel).

HOLY TRINITY, GRAY'S INN ROAD. — Morn.: Service, Te Chanted ; Jubilate, Goss in A ; Litany (Merbecke). Even.: Service, Magnificat, Parry in D ; Nunc Dimittis, Chanted ; Anthem, Like as the hart (Novello).

ST. JAMES'S PRIVATE EPISCOPAL CHAPEL, SOUTHWARK. —Morn.: Service, Introit, Prologue to the " Redemption " (Gounod) ; Communion Service (Marbecke). Even.: Service, Dykes in F ; Anthem, Rejoice greatly, Ev'ry valley, And the glory (Handel).

ST. MARY BOLTONS, WEST BROMPTON, S.W.—Morn.: Service, Benedicite, Stainer, Winn and Walker ; Benedictus, Chant ; Holy Communion, Kyrie, Credo, Sanctus, and Gloria in excelsis, Dykes in F ; Benedictus and Agnus Dei (Redhead) ; Offertory (Barnby). Even.: Service, Magnificat and Nunc Dimittis, Stainer's 3rd Series of Tones ; Anthem, Prepare ye the way (Crament).

ST. MATTHEW'S, NEW KENT ROAD.—Anthem, Recit. And lo, a mighty host; Chorus, Lord God of heaven and earth ("Last Judgment" Spohr).

ST. MAGNUS, LONDON BRIDGE.—Morn.: Service, Opening Anthem, If we say (Reynolds); Te Deum and Jubilate, Cooke in G; Kyrie (Wesley). Even.: Service, Magnificat and Nunc Dimittis, Cooke in G.; Anthem, Now we are ambassadors (Mendelssohn).

ST. MARGARET PATTENS, ROOD LANE, FENCHURCH STREET.—Morn.; Service, Benedicite and Benedictus, "Gregorian"; Kyrie, Credo, and Gloria in excelsis, Miss de Angelis'; Sanctus, Benedictus, and Agnus Dei (Bordese). Offertory Anthem, Sleepers, wake (Mendelssohn). Evensong; Magnificat and Nunc Dimittis, "Gregorian"; Anthem, He counteth all your sorrows.

ST. PAUL'S, AVENUE ROAD, SOUTH HAMPSTEAD.—Morn.: Service, Benedicite, 5th Tone; Benedictus (Goss); Kyrie, Mendelssohn in G. Even.; Service, Magnificat and Nunc Dimittis, "Parisian Tone" (Stainer); Anthem, Sleepers, wake ("St. Paul," Mendelssohn). Afternoon Service, Litany of "Four last things", (Monk).

ST. PAUL'S, BOW COMMON, E.—Morn.; Service, Benedicite, Best in C; Benedictus, Dykes in F. Even.; Service, Magnificat and Nunc Dimittis, King in F; Anthem, Day of anger (Mozart).

ST. PETER'S (EATON SQUARE).—Morn.: Service, Benedicite, Keeton in E flat. Even.; Service, Stainer in E flat; Anthem, Remorseful and bitter sorrow (Haydn).

ST. AUGUSTINE AND ST. FAITH, OLD CHANGE.—Morn.: Service, Benedicite (Martin); Benedictus, Barnby in E; Communion Service, Hoyte in D. Even.: Service, Stainer in B flat; Anthem, Day of anger (Mozart).

ST. BARNABAS, MARYLEBONE.—Morn.: Service, Benedicite, Hoyte in E flat; Benedictus, Dykes in F; Anthem, Sleepers wake (Mendelssohn); The Litany. Even.; Service, Magnificat and Nunc Dimittis, Wesley in F; Anthem, And the glory of the Lord (Handel).

ST. PETER'S, VERE STREET, W.—Even.; Service, Magnificat and Nunc Dimittis, Garrett in F; Anthem, Comfort Ye, And the glory of the Lord (Handel).

ST. SAVIOUR'S, HOXTON. — Morn.: Service, Te Deum, Hopkins in G; Holy Communion; Kyrie, Credo, Sursum Corda, Sanctus, and Gloria in excelsis, Dykes in F. Even.: Service, Magnificat and Nunc Dimittis (Best); Anthem, Hosanna (Macfarren).

ST. SEPULCHRE'S, HOLBORN.—Morn.: Service, Benedicite, Best in C; Benedictus, Dykes in F; Kyrie and Credo, Nares in F; Anthem, Comfort the soul (Crotch). Even.: Service, Magnificat and Nunc Dimittis, Arnold in A; Anthem, It is high time (Barnby).

Country.

ST. ASAPH CATHEDRAL.—Morn.: Service, Tuckermann in F; Ho! everyone that thirsteth (Martin). Even.: Service, Tuckermann in F; Anthem, Thy word is a lantern (Purcell).

ARDINGLY COLLEGE, SUSSEX.—Even.: Service, Calkin in B flat; Anthem, I wrestle and pray (Bach).

ASHBURNE CHURCH, DERBYSHIRE.—Morn.: Service throughout, Dykes in F. Even.: Service, Walmisley in D minor; Anthem, It is high time (Barnby).

BEDDINGTON CHURCH, SURREY.—Morn.: Service, Te Deum, Boyce in A; Benedictus, Burry in F; Introit, Lord, her watch Thy church is keeping. Even.: Service, Calkin in D; Anthem, Forsake me not, and If with all your hearts (Spohr).

BIRMINGHAM (S. ALBAN THE MARTYR).—Morn.: Service, Te Deum, and Benedictus, Goss in A; Holy Communion, Woodward in E flat. Evensong: Magnificat and Nunc Dimittis, Bunnett in F.

BIRMINGHAM (ST. CYPRIAN'S, HAY MILLS).—Morn.: Service, Tours in F; Anthem, The trumpet shall sound, and But thanks (Handel). Even.; Service, Tours in F; Anthem, Thy word is a lantern (Purcell).

BIRMINGHAM (ST. MICHAEL'S, HAWORTH).—Morn.: Service, Benedicite (Best); Benedictus (Stainer); Communion (Tours); Introit, Sleepers, wake (Mendelssohn). Even.: Service, Magnificat and Nunc Dimittis (Stainer); Anthem, Hearken unto me (Sullivan).

BIRMINGHAM (S. PHILIP'S CHURCH).— Morn.: Service, Chant (Best); Anthem, Sleepers, wake (Mendelssohn). Even.: Service, Chipp in A; Anthem, Comfort ye (Handel).

BRISTOL CATHEDRAL.—Morn.: Service, Mendelssohn in A; Even.: Service, Garrett in E flat; Anthem, Thus saith the Lord (Handel).

CANTERBURY CATHEDRAL. — Morn.: Service, Garrett in D; Anthem, Let our hearts be joyful (Mendelssohn); Communion, Garrett in D. Even.: Service, Garrett in D; Anthem, Behold, He cometh with clouds (Gilbert).

CARLISLE CATHEDRAL. — Morn.: Service, Turle in D; Introit, Drop down, ye heavens (Macfarren); Kyrie and Nicene Creed, Turle in D. Even.: Service, Turle in D; Anthem, Awake, awake (Stainer).

CHESTER (ST. MARY'S CHURCH).—Morn.: Service, Garret in F; Communion Service, Nares in F. Even.: Service, Turle in D; Anthem, But the Lord is mindful of His own, and Sleepers wake ("St. Paul," Mendelssohn).

DONCASTER (PARISH CHURCH).—Morn.: Service, Tours in F. Even.: Service, Tours in F; Anthem, I know that my Redeemer liveth (Handel).

DUBLIN, ST. PATRICK'S (NATIONAL) CATHEDRAL.—Morn.: Service, Te Deum and Jubilate, Aldrich in G; Holy Communion, Kyrie, and Creed and Sanctus, Aldrich in G; Anthem, Sleepers, wake, and O God, have mercy (Mendelssohn). Even.: Service, Magnificat and Nunc Dimittis King in D; Anthem, God is a Spirit (Bennett), and As pants the hart (Mendelssohn).

EDINBURGH (ST. JOHN'S).—Aft.: Children's Service. Even.: Service, Anthem, And lo, a mighty host ("Last Judgment," Spohr).

ELY CATHEDRAL. — Morn.: Service, Benedicite, Chants; Benedictus, Plain-song; Kyrie, and Credo, Armes in A; Gloria, Armes in B flat; Anthem, Listen, O isles (Allen). Even.: Service, Garrett in E flat; Anthem, Day of anger (Mozart).

EXETER CATHEDRAL.—Morn.: Service, Boyce in A; Communion, Smart in F. Even.: Service, Elvey in A; Anthem, Let God arise (Greene).

LEEDS PARISH CHURCH.—Morn.: Service, Boyce in A; Anthem, Saviour of sinners (Mendelssohn); Kyrie and Creed, Best in F. Even.: Service, Turle in D; Anthem, Lord, God of heaven (Spohr).

LLANDAFF CATHEDRAL.—Morn.: Service, Benedicite, Brooksbank in F; Jubilate, Goss in A. Even.: Service, Magnificat and Nunc Dimittis, Walmisley in D minor; Anthem, Prepare ye the way (Garrett).

LICHFIELD CATHEDRAL. — Morn.: Service, Wesley in F; Anthem, Lead kindly light (Stainer). Even.: Service, Turle in D; Anthem, In that day (Elvey).

LIVERPOOL CATHEDRAL.—Morn.: Service, Wesley in F; Anthem, Lord, let me know my end (Greene). Even.: Service, Anthem, Thou judge of quick and dead (Wesley); Dies Iræ (Stainer).

LIVERPOOL CATHEDRAL.—Aft.: Service, Magnificat and Nunc Dimittis, Chipp in A; Anthem, Hear my prayer (Mendelssohn).

MANCHESTER CATHEDRAL. — Morn.: Service, Te Deum, Jubilate, Boyce in A; Kyrie, Creed, Sanctus, and Gloria, Cobb in G; Anthem, Blessed is he (Gounod). Aft.: Service, Arnold in A; Anthem, Thus saith the Lord (Handel).

MANCHESTER (ST. BENEDICT'S).—Morn.: Service, Kyrie and Credo, Nares in F; Sanctus, Benedictus, Agnus Dei and Gloria in excelsis, Caecilian in A minor. Even.: Service, Magnificat and Nunc Dimittis (Jordan).

MANCHESTER (ST. JOHN BAPTIST, HULME).—Morn.: Service, Benedicite (Marbecke); Kyrie, Credo, Sanctus, Benedictus, Agnus Dei and Gloria in excelsis, "Missa de Angelis." Even.: Service, Magnificat and Nunc Dimittis, "Gregorian"; Dies Iræ (Dykes).

MUSSELBURGH (LORETTO SCHOOL).—Morn.: Service, Introit, Sleepers, wake ("St. Paul," Mendelssohn); Service, Smart in F; Anthem, He was despised, and Surely He hath borne our griefs ("Messiah," Handel). Even.: Service, Anthem, O Lord have mercy (Pergolesi).

ROCHESTER CATHEDRAL.—Morn.: Service, Richardson in F; Anthem, Prepare ye the way (Wise). Even.: Service, Richardson in F; Anthem, Wherewithal shall a young man (Elvey).

SALISBURY CATHEDRAL.—Morn.: Service, Barnby in E; Offertory (Barnby). Aft.: Service, Barnby in E; Anthem, Day of Anger (Mozart).

SHEFFIELD PARISH CHURCH. — Morn.: Service, Kyrie, Lilies in G. Even.: Service, Cantate Domine and Deus, Misereatur, Chants; Anthem, The sorrows of death, and Sleepers, wake (Mendelssohn).

SHERBORNE ABBEY. — Morn.: Service, Te Deum, Stainer in B flat. Even.: Service, Chants; Anthem, Awake, put on thy strength (Smallwood).

WELLS CATHEDRAL.—Morn: Service, Elvey in F; Introit, Remember me, O Lord (Macfarren); Kyrie, King in B flat. Even.: Service, Turle in D; Anthem, Thus saith the Lord (Handel).

WIMBORNE MINSTER.—Morn.: Service, Sullivan in D; Offertory Sentences (Field). Even.: Service, Taylor in F; Anthem, O thou that tellest, solo and chorus.

WINCHESTER CATHEDRAL.—Morn.: Service, Ouseley in D; Creed, Porter in D. Even.: Service, Garrett in F; Anthem, Thus saith the Lord (Handel).

WOLVERHAMPTON (ST. PETER'S COLLEGIATE CHURCH).—Morn.: Service, Te Deum, Smart in F; Benedictus, Barnby in D (Chant); Litany, "Ferial" (Barnby). Even.: Service, Magnificat, Hopkins in G (Chant); Nunc Dimittis, Gilbert in G; Anthem, God be merciful (Wesley).

APPOINTMENT.

Mr. E. A. SYDENHAM has been appointed Organist and Director of the Choir at All Saints, Scarborough, vacant by the appointment of Dr. Naylor to York Minster.

The MUSICAL STANDARD

A NEWSPAPER for MUSICIANS
PROFESSIONAL AND AMATEUR

No. 1,011, Vol. XXV. FOURTH SERIES.   SATURDAY, DECEMBER 15, 1883.   WEEKLY: PRICE 3D.

THE
NATURAL LAWS OF "EXPRESSION" IN MUSICAL EXPOSITION AND PRACTICAL DELIVERY, AND THEIR SYSTEMATICAL APPLICATION.*

BY EUSTACE J. BREAKESPEARE.

I.

In a paper which, a short time ago, I had the honour of reading before the Musical Association, on the subject of "Musical Æsthetics," I made passing reference to a work on Musical Expression, by the French writer Lussy,—"Traité de l'expression musicale." This I did in order to illustrate my argument that the philosophic side of music was not without its practical bearings. A very clever exposition of the Frenchman's views had been made some time before by Mr. J. S. Curwen. Mr. Curwen's paper, which was devoted entirely to M. Lussy and his treatise, hardly succeeded in gaining unqualified support to the theories of the latter. I was rather inclined, in making reference to Mr. Curwen in my paper, to find fault with the discussionists for misapprehending the writer's argument. After better reflection upon this subject, I began to see that, after all, the French author did not deserve such unbounded admiration and support as I myself at first was disposed to grant; although as a unique appearance in musical literature, I feel it is worthy of most careful consideration. What are the faulty points therein I hope to show. At the same time, although the subject of my present discourse obliges me at least to mention this book of Lussy, I wish it not to appear that I am concerned chiefly in making a new exposition of its doctrines. As far as is possible within the limits of a "paper," Mr. Curwen has already performed this exegetical task to perfection. Apart from the fact that to show ignorance or profess indifference to what is at present the best review of the most important, if not the only work on the subject I treat upon, would be unpardonable; reference to it (insomuch as I may perhaps presume upon a certain acquaintance with the "Traité") will help me better to express what I have to say upon my own responsibility. At the same time, then, that I guard against the possibility of my argument being bound up with Lussy's theories, I escape the charge of presumptuousness in going over Mr. Curwen's track again, which might fitly be laid against me if my paper were simply an *exegesis* of Lussy's work.

Without making much presumption upon previous acquaintance with this work, it may be remembered that the aim of the writer is to establish rules by which the expressive qualities of accent, rhythm, force, etc., in playing may be practically acquired; the grand objection being that any such regulation of musical expression would induce a mechanical delivery, quite opposed to all *natural* expression.

There is no doubt that such law-giving may be too arbitrary. Lussy observes that such and such observances in performance are common to players in general, and he tabulates them accordingly. Naturally it is demurred that like passages may be performed by different players, or by the same player at different times, in quite opposite ways.

To instance a few of his rules. He finds that single notes when occurring at weak parts of the bar, when carrying on the rhythm (i. e., when the other parts are stationary), are nevertheless accentuated. [This, by the way, is what is sometimes loosely termed syncopation; though properly syncopation is the union of notes belonging to different sections of the measure, the combined force of the two notes coming at the weak point of the measure; to be distinguished from

simple *displaced accent* where the beats of the measure go on as ordinarily]. That in passages of slurred notes in couples, where the first note of the new couplet is a repetition of the final note of the preceding couplet, the accent is placed upon the repeated note. That a note preceded by a "silence" is strong. Then with respect to *pathetic* accent, as he terms it in distinction to *metrical* accent, he finds repeated notes are duly emphasized, and demand a *crescendo*. That chromatic chords require enforcement. That enharmonic changes also call for enforced tone. That appoggiaturas are always accented. That dissonances always require greater vigour of attack. That a *rallentando* is made with any change in the sentiment of a piece from joyful to sad. That with a repeated figure, or sequence, the bass moving stepwise up or down, an *accelerando* is required.

From this alone it will be perceived what Lussy's teaching is like. What opens these rules to objection is the same which affects all inductive methods: that the rule may be established upon insufficient data; and, again, admitting the correctness of the observation, it may be questioned whether any performance in simple obedience to the rule, as such, can be tolerated—whether, in short, any law-giving is at all possible, since all "expression" is supposed to be the direct outcome of the inward feeling, any obedience to outward prompting resulting only in a stereotyped form of delivery quite opposed to the spontaneity of true natural expression. With respect to the first objection, certainly no rule can obtain in which the exceptions are so obvious as, e.g., to prescribe that all ascending passages are to be accompanied with a *crescendo;* or where the author has not derived his rule from the study of the music itself, but from some incorrect or slovenly indications of the composer. Lussy has been unwittingly betrayed in this way. He says when we come upon unexpected triplets these are to be accented, and points out a vocal passage by Bellini, where certainly the triplet notes are each marked with an accent; but although there is nothing false about this, there is no obvious reason why all such unexpected triplets demand similar treatment, or even why this passage in itself demanded the same. He has mistaken a composer's arbitrary indication for the necessary expression of the music. Some composers are less careful about their indications than others—despite the tendency of the present time to minutely prescribe every nuance; and many instances there are, especially in operatic music, where the passages being perhaps of a florid kind, written simply with a view to display of the singer's voice, though the signs may not altogether run counter to the meaning, which yet seem to admit, with equal justice to natural truthfulness of expression, of being executed in a variety of ways.

The ambiguity of the word "expression" as employed in these rules will perhaps not have escaped you. It shifts from the simple metrical distinctions to those having emotional significance. The meaning of the word "expression," as employed by Lussy, is, I fear, not a very elevated one. The prime object of the work was to afford a guide for musical learners; and I judge the author (in his capacity as teacher of the pianoforte) would have been sufficiently satisfied of the correctness of the pupil's "expression," had the latter simply followed after the rules laid down in his book. The work is, in short, a codification of the rhythmic, dynamic, and other nuances as they ordinarily exhibit themselves. But it is one thing to make observations of this kind; another to formulate "rules." The natural laws of expression lead to some agreement in the forms; but it is a question whether, reversely, from the close imitation of the form you reproduce the original impulse. It is the way in which such *data* are utilised that makes all the difference. If a pupil puts a stress in a certain place, because M. Lussy tells him that stresses invariably occur here—admitting the correctness of the observation, the naturalness with which this originally comes about, and the unanimity of all executants in this observance—one need not be a musician to see that the result will be valueless. And even if M. Lussy were to deny that the teaching of his book were such as I have made it appear, he has certainly not sufficiently guarded against this interpretation as to make such objections (which, as I have remarked, have already been raised elsewhere) seem so surprisingly unjust as I admit they did to me at first.

The fact that no hard-and-fast rules are possible does not, of course, affect the value of the *data* in themselves. We must not do a thing because it has been ascertained that the generality of performers do in this manner; but, nevertheless, to have insured this unanimity on the part of players, there must be some underlying principle; and the solution of the matter would be to show the rules as far as possible in the light of these. How far is it possible to arrive at these underlying principles? It is true Lussy attempts this to some extent; but his explanations are sometimes vague, fanciful illustrations—as, *e. g.*, in connection with his rule that on leaping to a high note and descending through a series of notes we glide to the high note but detach the descending notes; he illustrates this by the reboundings (smaller by degrees as they go on) of an india-rubber ball upon the floor. But, of course, however apt this illustration, it is no explanation of the *reason* of notes invariably occurring (taking Lussy's observation as correct and holding good in all instances of this kind) in this way. The fact also of a rule, instituted on some faulty theory, being found not to obtain generally, as when ascending passages are found not to be invariably accompanied with a crescendo, or a descending passage with a diminuendo, this rule, founded on some fanciful analogy with actual height and depth and the difficulties attending ascents, might not of necessity cause all explanation to appear hopeless. It might simply be that whenever the same sort of passage appears admitting of opposite manners of rendering, there are counter-ruling principles at work at different times. But not to let it seem that I am occupied throughout in book-criticism, for the present I will dismiss M. Lussy and the "Traité de l'expression musicale."

(To be continued.)

Spohr's "Last Judgment," will be given at St. John's, Edinburgh, on Saturday Dec. 22nd by the choir, under the direction of the organist, Mr. F. Bates, Mus.Bac., and on Christmas Eve the first part of the "Messiah."

"A. M." can only say that Lord Overstone's name was on the list of the Committee of the Musical Union, and that he probably attended some of the *matinées*. Very unlikely that such a musician never "put in an appearance." "A. M." knew the Rev. Mr. Goddard by sight, and his face must have been quite changed if he was the gentleman carried in a chair. Mr. Ella will be referred to to decide the matter of fact. It is never safe to make positive assertions.

The Upton Choral Society gave a concert at the Stratford Town Hall, on Dec. 3rd. The soloists were, Miss Helen D'Alton, Mr. Arthur Thompson; violin, Herr Emil Mahr; conductor, Mr. Joseph Proudman. Accompanists, pianoforte, Mr. F. C. Kitson; harmonium, Mr. G. B. Gilbert. The programme included, "God, Thou art Great!" (Spohr); "Judge me, O God" (Mendelssohn"), and a miscellaneous selection of sacred and secular music.

Musical Intelligence.

CRYSTAL PALACE CONCERTS.

PROGRAMME.

Overture, "Genoveva "	Schumann.
Air, "O Araby" ("Oberon ")	Weber.
Miss Alexandra Ehrenberg.	
(Her first appearance at the Crystal Palace).	
Concerto for pianoforte and orchestra, No. 3, in C minor	Beethoven.
Mme. Montigny-Rémaury.	
Recit. and Air, "Shall I in Mamre's fertile plain"	
("Joshua ")	Handel.
Signor Foli.	
Serenade for orchestra in D	Stanford.
(First time at the Crystal Palace.)	
New song, "Night and Love"	Bennett.
Miss Alexandra Ehrenberg.	
Solo for pianoforte, Serenade and Minuet, "Don Juan"	Thalberg.
Mdme. Montigny-Rémaury.	
Song, "I am a roamer" ("Son and Stranger ")	Mendelssohn.
Signor Foli.	
Selection from the Incidental Music to " The Birds of Aristophanes "	Parry.
(First time of performance)	

Conductor of this Concert, Mr. C. VILLIERS STANFORD.

"Genoveva" is the title of Schumann's only opera. The story is that of a knight who was compelled to leave his lady-love for the Holy War, and came back to find her apparently unfaithful. Many tragical incidents are bound up in the libretto, and the overture depicts the intense suffering and passion of the unhappy pair. A more interesting story, by the way, was told me, when in Germany, many years ago, respecting a worthy knight, who took part in the so-called "Holy" Wars, and the wonder is that no operatic genius has, as yet, set it to music. Those of your readers who have climbed the far-famed Drachenfels, will remember the little Island of Nonnenwerth at its foot; and on the other side of the Rhine the grand old ruins of Rolandseck. Roland was the knight, the island long ago contained a nunnery, which is now turned into an unpicturesque hotel. The story is, that while Roland was away, the news came that he was slain in battle. His faithful lady was so inconsolable that she forthwith discarded the world and took the veil. Of course the news she received was false! Roland came back safe and sound, but the lady, alas! was beyond recovery. Roland's only consolation was in building a castle, from whose tower he could catch sight of her figure as she walked in the nunnery garden. Whether she was at last rescued or no I cannot remember, but the story might be made a very effective one for music. Schumann's overture to "Genoveva " was superbly played and greatly enjoyed.

Mdme. Montigny-Rémaury is a great favourite at these concerts, and deservedly; her playing of the C minor concerto was eminently successful. The *cadenza*, written by Rubinstein, is as may be imagined, no trifling matter, and was executed by her with perfect ease and splendid effect.

Dr. Stanford, who conducted on this occasion—Mr. Manns having gone to Glasgow—favoured us with his own Serenade for orchestra. It was first brought out with success at the last Birmingham Festival, and its merits fully set forth in the *Musical Standard*. It was much appreciated at the Crystal Palace, the *intermezzo* especially making a marked impression.

As a rule here, the last number in the programme fares but badly, owing to so many having to leave for particular trains; and on Saturday last comparatively few Londoners could remain to hear Mr. Hubert Parry's graceful incidental music to "The Birds of Aristophanes." It is more simple than most of his other compositions, but it is none the less acceptable on this account. The Entr'acte in F, the gathering of the birds, and the nuptial processional march were the only three numbers performed out of the twenty contained in the Incidental Music, a larger selection from which would have been listened to with pleasure.

Miss Ehrenberg, the lady vocalist, gave much pleasure in Weber's "Araby " and in Mr. G. F. Bennett's new and pretty song "Night and Love," and Signor Foli sang as usual with great effect.

R. S.

The Archbp. of Canterbury has conferred the degree of Mus.Doc. on Mr. Langdon Colborne, organist of Hereford Cathedral. Mr. Colborne was recommended for the degree by Sir F. Ouseley, Sir Arthur Sullivan, and Sir George Elvey.

SATURDAY POPULAR CONCERTS.

Quintet in G minor, for two violins, two violas,
　and violoncello .... Mozart.
　Mdme. Norman-Néruda, MM. L. Ries, Holländer, Zerbini,
　　and Piatti.
Song, "Lusinghe più care" ("Allessandro") .... Handel.
　　Miss Thudichum.
Rhapsodie in G minor, Intermezzo in A flat (Op. 76),
　No. 3, and Hungarian Dance in D flat, No. 6, for
　pianoforte alone .... Brahms.
　　Miss Agnes Zimmermann.
Serenade, trio, in D major, for violin, viola and violon-
　cello .... Beethoven.
　Mdme. Norman-Néruda, MM. Holländer and Piatti.
Song, "Im Herbst" .... Franz.
　　Miss Thudichum.
Pensées Fugitives, for pianoforte and violin .... Heller-Ernst.
　Miss Agnes Zimmermann, and Mdme. Norman-Néruda.

Accompanist　-　-　-　-　-　Mr. Zerbini.

A comparatively small audience listened to the above
programme, a strong argument against the opinion that
well-known works are most generally acceptable, for a
more familiar selection could scarcely have been made.
The two works for strings were beautifully rendered,
Beethoven's light and pleasant serenade trio should have
the sub-title of "suite," or it runs the risk of being looked
upon as informal (which it is not). It is legitimately one
of the few links of that period uniting the old suites of
Bach and Handel to the modern writers of suites, among
whom Raff stands foremost. Does it strike any listener
how the variations in this trio foreshadow those in the
septet? The resemblance is most striking in the second
variation. Beethoven, with all his affection for the variation form, rarely got beyond the goal aimed at by his
predecessors—to deck his subject in a variety of ribbons,
laces, and frillings; it was left to a later master, Schumann, to reveal in variation form the higher power
alluded to by Goethe, in speaking of another art, of "so
awakening our imagination that all we here see concreted
shall again become fluid without losing its character."
By the way, it is difficult to understand why the short
allegro, built upon the theme of the andante should not
be considered as another (the 5th) variation instead of
being treated in our programmes as an independent
movement.

Miss Zimmermann responded to the encore that her
solos called forth. In her accompaniment of the favourite
Heller-Ernst pieces she was occasionally hard and unsympathetic, but every pianist knows the difficulty of
playing the by-no-means unimportant pianist's part of
these real little treasures just as it should be played.
The numbers chosen were the Lied No. 4, the Intermezzo
No. 11, and "Abschied," No. 6.

Miss Thudichum does not appear to me to have made
any striking progress in her art since last season, but
now, as then, she promises well.

　　　　　　　　　B. F. WYATT-SMITH.

MONDAY POPULAR CONCERTS.

Last Monday evening, the 11th concert, and last but
one before Christmas, the programme comprised :—

　　　　　　PART 1.
Sextet in G major (Op. 36), for two violins, two violas,
　and two violoncellos .... Brahms.
　Mdme. Norman-Néruda, MM. L. Ries, Holländer, Zerbini,
　　Ries and Piatti.
Song, "Creation's Hymn" .... Beethoven.
　　Miss Hilda Wilson.
Fantasie in F minor (Op. 49), Berceuse (Op. 57), Valse
　in D flat (Op. 64), for pianoforte alone .... Chopin.
　　M. Vladimir de Pachmann.

　　　　　　PART 2.
Adagio in E major, from Concerto in A minor, for
　violin, with pianoforte accompaniment .... Viotti.
　　Mdme. Norman-Néruda.
Song, "The golden thread" .... Gounod.
　　Miss Hilda Wilson.
Quartet in D minor (Op. 42), for two violins, viola, and
　violoncello .... Haydn.
　Mdme. Norman-Néruda, MM. L. Ries, Holländer and Piatti.
Accompanist　-　-　-　-　Mr. Zerbini.

Brahms's first string Sextet, in B flat was performed, and
duly noticed at the Saturday afternoon concert of Dec. 1.
It will be observed that M. de Pachmann appeared on
Monday at 8 o'clock to play the pieces of his favourite
composer, after a laborious recital of nearly two hours the
same afternoon (elsewhere recorded). Miss Hilda Wilson,
a protégé of Mrs. Ellicott, wife of the Bishop of Gloucester, made the vocal numbers notable by choosing good
pieces and rendering them well.

M. de Pachmann merely repeated his successes of the
afternoon; how he plays these fugitive pieces of Chopin
is matter of musical history. The usual recalls ensued ;

---

as regards encores, it were to be wished that none were
reported, for the sake of the artists themselves ; but the
"public" would not thereby be cured of their selfishness.
The Sestet of Brahms, a work of riper age, was first performed at the instance of Madame Norman-Néruda, in
February, 1879, and will never be repeated without satisfaction to the subscribers. The details of the text are
very interesting—such as the inner pedal of the leading
viola, which serves as a bourdonnement ; the collision of
the keys E flat and G, the lively style of the scherzo, and
the peculiar treatment of the poco adagio in E minor, with
its several divisions. The finale, in 9-8 time, starting
with a figure of semi-quavers for violin and violoncello
only, which leads to a pretty pastoral subject, is full of
animation and stirring subjects.

The adagio of Viotti in E was excellently rendered by
the fair leader of the strings, and Haydn's quartet, played
for the fifth time, is so concise as to leave no excuse for
the rushing out, as usual, before the presto finale. The last
Monday concert will be followed by one on Saturday,
Dec. 22.

M. DE PACHMANN'S RECITALS.

M. Vladimir de Pachmann held his first Pianoforte Recital
on Monday afternoon. The following is a copy of the programme :—

Sonata in G major, No. 4 .... Bach.
"Le Carnaval" (Op. 9) in A flat .... Schumann.
Barcarolle in G major .... Rubinstein.
Caprice (Op. 30) No. 4, Valse (Op. 34) No. 2 .... Chopin.
Nocturne .... Leschetitzky.
"Frühlingslied" (Op. 19), and Toccatina (Op. 36) ... Heller.
Ballade in G minor (Op. 23), Mazurka (Op. 59) No. 2,
　and Valses .... Chopin.
Toccata (Op. 7) ....

This scheme speaks for itself. The Sonata of Philip Emmanuel Bach was read with great "objective" exactness ; and
the Chopin selection, of course, evoked rapturous plaudits. The
third Valse was played separately from the rest ; the favourite
one, in D flat, made its usual mark. The Nocturne of Leschetitzky
(inscribed to M. De Pachmann), is a graceful and elegant
effusion, if bearing a family likeness to many pieces in other
genre. The Toccatina of Henselt has been heard, this autumn,
both at the Popular and the Crystal Palace concerts. The
Barcarolle of Rubinstein won a bis, and deserved the honour.
M. De Pachmann's version of "Le Carnaval" could to have
satisfied the most exacting, and probably did so ; if not quite
the same as Rubinstein's, which may be thought unrivalled and
unattainable. The second Recital is fixed for Wednesday next,
Dec. 19.　　　　　　　　　　　　　　　　　　A. M.

MR. J. B. BONAWITZ'S "HISTORICAL" PIANOFORTE RECITALS.

The fourth and last recital on the evening of, Wednesday,
Dec. 5th, attracted so large an audience at the Bluthner Room,
that it was found necessary to place carpets on the staircase in
order to seat the visitors, for room inside could not be found.
The scheme is as follows :—

Allegro in G minor .... Scarlatti, 1683–1757.
Gavotte in D minor .... Bach, 1685–1750.
Fugue in B flat .... Porpora, 1685–1767.
Fantasia in D minor .... Mozart, 1756–1791.
Sonata (Op. 2), in C .... Beethoven, 1770–1827.
Rondo in E flat major .... Hummel, 1778–1837.
Impromtu No. 4 .... Schubert, 1797–1828.
Fantasia (Op. 17) and movement .... Schumann, 1810–1856.
Nocturnes in A and D flat, Mazurka in B
　flat minor, and Valse in D flat major .... Chopin, 1809–1849.
"Les Huguenots" ("Fantaisie de Concert") .... Thalberg, 1810–1871.

The works of living composers included :—

"Liebeslieder Walzer" (Duet) .... Brahms.
Tanz (Op. 106) (Duet) .... Hiller.
Bilder aus Schiller's, "William Tell" .... Zapff.
Gavotte .... Scambati.
Five Dances (Op. 3) (Duet) .... Bonawitz.
Galop Chromatique .... Liszt.

Mr. Bonawitz laboured under indisposition, but played ad-
mirably, nevertheless, and the audience applauded vociferously.
The numbers that seemed to please the most were Porpora's
Fugue, the last Sonata of Beethoven in C minor and major,
Schumann's Fantasia, and the Chopin pieces. Mr. Bonawitz
played the valse of Chopin (D flat) in octaves, and some of the
audience appeared to be taken by surprise. Miss Cecile
Brousil assisted Mr. Bonawitz in the duets.　　　A. M.

Mr. F. F. Rogers, of Malvern, has, it is announced,
completed the setting of his cantata entitled, "Deborah,"
upon which he has been occupied for some considerable
time.

GUILDHALL SCHOOL OF MUSIC.

The Guildhall School of Music gave a choral concert at the Mansion House on Dec. 8th, when Mendelssohn's "Walpurgis Night" music, with pianoforte accompaniment, served to manifest the good singing of the choristers, which was afterwards also effectively displayed in several part-songs. The vocal solos in Mendelssohn's work were well rendered by Miss A. Haale, and Messrs. D. Henderson, A. Lister, and S. H. Beckley. The programme comprised various items, from among which may be specified the eleven solo vocal performances of Misses J. Bowman, M. Hallam, E. Aloof, N. McEwen, and J. Turner; and the violin playing of Miss L. R. Dixon. This City musical institution, under the energetic direction of Mr. Weist Hill, is doing good service. It might have been wished (one critic says) that the capital orchestra associated therewith had co-operated in Saturday's concert.

MR. WILLING'S CHOIR.

Macfarren's "King David" was given by Mr. Willing's choir on Tuesday evening, Dec. 11th, at St. James's Hall. The soloists originally engaged were Miss Anna Williams, Miss Hilda Wilson, Mr. Vernon Rigby, and Mr. Frederick King. Mr. Rigby was, however, suffering from a severe cold, and his place was supplied, at a short notice, by Mr. William Shakespeare, who proved a very efficient substitute. The performance was in every respect a fine one, and the orchestra entitled to special mention.　　　　　　　　　　　　　　　A. S.

MR. FREDERICK PENNA'S CONCERT.

The benefit concert of this well-known and excellent artist took place at the Steinway Hall, on Monday evening, Dec. 10th, in the presence of a numerous and highly appreciative audience.

PROGRAMME.—PART 1.

Trio, "Queen of the Night" .... Smart.
　　Mdme. Catherine Penna, Miss Isabel Chatterton, and
　　　　　Mr. J. D. Perrott.
Aria, "It is enough" ("Elijah") .... Mendelssohn.
　　　　　Mr. J. D. Perrott.
Song, "Only a Rose" .... Boyton Smith.
　　　　　Miss Isabel Chatterton.
Violin solo, "Elegie" .... Ernst.
　　　　　Herr Pollitzer.
Song, "Sweet, have the roses" .... Salaman.
　　　　　Mdme. Catherine Penna.
Song, "Queen of the Earth" .... Pinsuti.
　　　　　Mr. Frederic Penna.
Pianoforte solo, "L'Elegante," and "Waltz-Galop" .... Mattei.
　　　　　Signor Tito Mattei.
Song, "Adelaide" .... Beethoven.
　　　　　Signor Odoardo Barri.
Harp solo, "Clouds and Sunshine" .... Oberthür.
　　　　　Herr C. Oberthür.
Melodia, "La Rimembranza" .... d'Alessio.
　　　　　Signor Ria.

PART 2.

Recitation (Dramatic Scene), "Henry V." .... Shakespeare.
　　　　　Mr. Frederic Penna.
Song, "Nella calma" .... Gounod.
　　　　　Mdme. Catherine Penna.
Song, "Dans delle memorie" .... Caracciolo.
　　　　　Signor Ria.
Violin solo, "Légende," "Mazurka" .... Wieniawski.
　　　　　Herr Pollitzer.
Duet, "Maying" .... Smith.
　　　　　Mdme. Catherine Penna, and Signor O. Barri.
Song, "The right way to go" .... Penna.
　　　　　Mr. Frederic Penna.
Duet, "Quando di sangue tinto" .... Donizetti.
　　　　　Signor Ria, and F. Penna.

Conductor　-　-　Mr. Wilhelm Ganz.
Accompanist　-　-　Herr Lehmeyer.

It is always a pleasure to have nought to give but unqualified praise, and in this instance such praise can be conscientiously accorded to all concerned. Mr. Penna's recitations were admirable, and the performances of Herr Pollitzer (violin), Herr Oberthür (harp), and Signor Tito Mattei (pianoforte), were little short of perfection. Signor Odoardo Barri whose name appears in the programme, failed to put in an appearance. Mr. Penna's lecture on the "Art of Singing" is replete with interest, and worthy of careful perusal by all lovers of music.　　　A. S.

TOTTENHAM.—On December 7th, a concert was given by the Tottenham Musical Society, in the large new Hall in Bruce Grove. The principal vocalists were Mdme. Clara West, Miss Alice Woodruffe, Miss Marian Johnson, Miss L. Lyle, Mr. T. Moncrieff, Mr. S. H. Hagon, and Mr. W. H. Webb. Solo cornet, Mr. J. W. Grieves; solo clarionet, Mr. J. G. Brookes. Band and chorus of 100 performers. Accompanist, Mr. E. A. Crushla; organist, Mr. H. J. Belchambers; conductor, Mr. Fred S. Oram. The audience (which was highly appreciative) numbered at least a thousand persons; and the concert was altogether a distinct success.

The death of Signor Mario is announced as taking place at Rome on Dec. 11th.

WINDSOR.

Princess Christian of Schleswig-Holstein assisted, on Dec. 8th, at a concert given by the Windsor and Eton Amateur Madrigal Society at St. Mark's School, Windsor, upon the occasion of the presentation of a testimonial to Sir George Elvey. There was a large audience. During the interval between the parts, Princess Christian, in the name of the subscribers, presented Sir G. J. Elvey with a portrait of himself (a capital likeness), painted by Mr. Val Prinsep, A.R.A., a gift which was duly acknowledged by the talented musician. Princess Christian (piano) and Miss Spinner (violin) subsequently played Schumann's "Phantasiestück;" a romance for ladies' voices, "Die Nonne" (Brahms); a song, "Genesung" (R. Franz), very clearly and musically enunciated by Mr. Donaldson, and the part-song, "The larks aloft, the wind blows soft" (Garrett), bringing the entertainment to a close.

HARROW.

The Harrow School Musical Society recently gave a recital of "Cinderella," a fairy opera in four acts, composed by Mr. John Farmer, the well-known musical professor at that school, to words written by the late H. S. Leigh. It was given in the Speech-room of the school; the choir, band, and singers, including present and late Harrovians and members of the Royal Academy of Music. Signor Randegger conducted the affair with his usual excellence and sympathy. The great hall was quickly filled in very orderly fashion by the boys of the school, leaving only space for certain musical professors, critics, the masters and their families, and friends. The work, which Mr. Farmer calls a "little opera for big children," or a "big opera for little children," is natural, graceful, and full of rhythmical life, without rhythmical vulgarities, and is sure to be very popular when presented to the public. I hear it is to be performed in Liverpool in January next by the Carl Rosa Company, and subsequently in London. Much of the music of this opera can hardly be reproduced on the piano. There are songs in it to suit all voices and all tastes, and delightful dances, too; a minuet and gavotte which are most taking. There is a children's ballet in which the tough "singing quadrilles" written by Mr. Farmer some time ago are reproduced. The nursery rhymes are given most brightly, and will be a great feature of the performance, when scenery and costumes are introduced.

HORNS ASSEMBLY ROOMS.

On Wednesday evening, Dec. 12th, Messrs. R. J. Pitt and G. F. Grover gave their second evening concert at the Horns Assembly Rooms, Kennington Park, before a large and appreciative audience. The principal artists were Mesdames Vincent and Clark, Misses Bocquet and Kissel, Messrs. Murton, Reynolds, Budd, and Pitt, and Master J. H. Pitt, violinist. Amid much that was excellent, we should fail to do justice to a good concert, if we omitted to draw attention to the very effective and artistic singing of Miss Alice Bocquet, who possesses all the elements of a fine contralto, and to the admirable rendering of Sir H. R. Bishop's "Pretty Mocking Bird," by Mrs. Clark. Mr. Budd in a popular song, met with a very cordial reception. The most interesting feature, however, was the violin playing of Master Pitt, whose accurate tune and time spoke eloquently for his careful training, whilst his fulness of tone and delicacy of expression were remarkable in one so young. Messrs. Pitt and Grover are to be congratulated on the success of their musical work in South London. The arduous labours of Mr. Grover especially, in this direction, are most praiseworthy, and are doubtless destined to bear a good harvest.

THE LONDON TRICYCLE CLUB.

The annual dinner of the above club was held at the Cannon Street Hotel, on Thursday, Dec. 6th, Dr. B. W. Richardson M.A., LL.D., F.R.S., being the chairman. During the evening, a selection of pieces was given by Miss Medora Collins, Miss Lapworth, Dr. Armand Semple, and Dr. Broughton Stirling, with Mr. E. J. Williams as accompanist. The efforts of all were duly appreciated, but the violin performances of Mr. Viotti Collins and Dr. Stirling, and the concertina playing of Miss Medora Collins, were the chief features of the entertainment.

PUDSEY.—The sixth annual concert of the Choral Union Concert was given on December 3, in the Public Room, when Mendelssohn's "Elijah" was given, with a band and chorus of 120 performers. The Principals were:—Miss Cockroft, Miss Cragg, Mr. Blagbro, and Mr. Jackson: Mr. H. Heap being leader of the band; Mr. P. A. Strickland, A.C.O., organist of the Parish Church, conducted the whole. The audience numbered 600 persons, and included a large portion of the élite of the district. The oratorio, on the whole, was very carefully and creditably given, while certain portions were admirably rendered. Great credit is due to all who took part in the performance for contributing to the very successful result in so difficult a work—a result that evidently took many people by surprise.

LEICESTER.

The first of the second series of Mr. Harvey Löhr's chamber concerts, in this town, was given on Nov. 29th, in the lecture-room of the Museum. The programme comprised selections from the classic school of instrumental music, which were interpreted by a number of musicians of the highest efficiency. With the recollection of what was experienced last year, the attendance was an indication that these intellectual and instructive evenings are increasing in popularity among our music-loving townspeople; and that the enterprise exhibited in their arrangement is being worthily recognised. The lecture-room was filled; and the hearty applause bestowed by an audience—which was nothing if not critical—was sufficient testimony to the general merit of the work. The programme opened with Beethoven's Quartet in C minor, Op. 18 (No. 4), for two violins, viola, and violoncello; the performers being Mr. W. Frye Parker, Mr. W. Easton, Mr. W. V. Waud, and Mr. W. Buels. The same gentlemen also played Haydn's Quartet in G major, Op. 17 (No. 5), which is even more sparkling and melodious than Beethoven's composition, and was listened to with the deepest pleasure throughout. Mr. Harvey Löhr gave a pianoforte selection—Prelude and Fugue in E minor, Op. 31 (No. 1) (Mendelssohn). The selection was well chosen; and the performance was perfect. Mr. W. Frye Parker played Beethoven's Romance in F Op. 50, for violin, with pianoforte accompaniment, which afforded ample opportunity for the display of his great ability as an executant. The tone produced was remarkable for purity. Another treat was the Introduction and Polonaise, in C major, Op. 3, for pianoforte and violoncello (Chopin), by Mr. Harvey Löhr and Mr. Buels. This is one of the most taking and melodious compositions Chopin ever wrote, out of the vast number which he wrote. The vocalist was Miss Ambler, who thus, we believe, formed her first acquaintance with a Leicester audience. She sang with considerable energy and feeling. She undertook no mean task in submitting Liszt's ballad "Loreley," a melody by Gounod, and the German "Der Herrlichste" (Schumann). But in each effort she was very successful, the enunciation being clear, and the music interpreted with due expression and feeling.

BATH.

On Dec. 4th, at the Assembly Rooms, the Bath Choral Union gave its first concert for the session. The Messrs. Hazel Sonderbraun on past concerts induced some of the members of the Choral Union to make such arrangements as would relieve the conductor of all pecuniary anxieties. A committee was formed, Mr. R. S. Blaine kindly consenting to become president, and subscriptions were invited for three concerts to be given through the season. The result was, a very general response. The first part of the concert consisted of Mendelssohn's "Hymn of Praise." Of course, to give this work with any approach to completeness, a good band was required; and to obtain this, the conductor secured the services of Herr Van Praag as leader, and selected competent performers from Birmingham, Bristol, and Gloucester, to supplement our local musicians. The result was, a band of thirty-eight, with the defects which are almost inseparable from an orchestra so constructed. Solidity and refinement, of the highest character can only be obtained by the performers constantly playing together; and it cannot, and should not, be expected that thirty-eight musicians, who occasionally meet, should play with the same amount of evenness and smoothness as those who are always working together. The "reeds," were a little coarse, and the "brass" too powerful. The choral part of the oratorio generally, was very well done. Mrs. Hutchinson, to whom was entrusted the soprano solos, started a little out of tune, but she soon rectified the difficulty, and gave the music with much taste and devotional feeling. The duet "I waited for the Lord," in which she was joined by Miss Ellen Shackell, of this city, was sweetly sung by both; and so was the duet "My song shall be alway," by Mrs. Hutchinson and Mr. E. Lloyd. The second part was of a miscellaneous character. Here Mrs. Hutchinson again distinguished herself, and won a hearty encore for her pleasing singing of "Deh vieni non tardar." Mr. Lloyd was again and again recalled after his fine rendering of "Walther's Preislied," from Wagner's "Die Meistersinger." One must give a word of praise to Mr. Brownell for his part in Handel's "Largo;" and also to Miss Mendum for her harp accompaniment. Wagner's "Tannhäuser" march closed an excellent concert.

Thanks to Messrs. Simms and Son, the local public had the opportunity of hearing M. Pachmann at the Assembly Rooms, on Dec. 6th. The programme was well calculated to enable the audience to judge of his style and method of interpretation. It embraced five selections from Chopin, three from Henselt, two from Schumann, and one each from J. S. Bach, Beethoven, Brahms and Rubinstein, all of which were played from memory, and with exquisite finish. The great merit of the artist is his thorough conscientiousness. He loves his art apparently too well to sacrifice it to mere meretricious displays. There was no lack of power, but it was used with discretion; and the result was, that the recital was characterised by rare taste and refinement, which repeated plaudits showed how thoroughly the audience appreciated the music.

MANCHESTER.

Prior to last week I have had nothing worthy of communication to you, the only novelty we have lately had being a visit from Richter—without his orchestra—which has already been noticed in your columns. Last week, however, Mr. Hallé produced for the first time here Rossini's "Mosè," in concert garb. The cast of principals comprised Mesdames Albani, Trudichum, and Hilda Wilson, and Messrs. Lloyd, Kearton, Newth, Hilton, Bridson, and Foli—a goodly roll! In every sense the performance was a great success, and the most unstinted praise is due to Mr. Hallé in regard to it. Although the performance lasted three hours, one almost begrudged the omission of the ballet music, which, I suppose, however, is absolutely necessary for the due appreciation by the English public of an "oratorio." All the principals were excellent, and band and chorus alike good. The printer's devil made one of our local critics say next day that "the little Miss Hilda Wilson was highly satisfactory." She certainly was the latter, but I rather demur to the qualifying adjective.   J. H.

LEEDS.

The Leeds Philharmonic Society gave an excellent concert in the Town Hall on Wednesday evening, Dec. 5. The programme included Bach's Magnificat, Beethoven's "Mount of Olives," and Gade's "Psyche,"—rather too much; it was thought, to get through in one evening. "Psyche" was performed for the first time in Leeds, and was very well received; though it scarcely received full justice, coming as it did at the close of a long programme. The principals were Miss Marian Fenna, Miss F. Sellers, Mdme. Isabel Fassett, Mr. Piercy, Mr. Wood Higgins, and Mr. Oswald; and principals and chorus all did their work in a satisfactory manner. The band was led by Mr. Otto Bernhardt; Mr. James Broughton made a thoroughly efficient conductor; and Mr. Alfred Broughton ably presided at the organ.

On Friday evening, Dec. 7, Spohr's "Last Judgment" was sung at Leeds Parish Church before a large congregation. The choir was increased to 100 voices, including about thirty females. The principals were—Miss E. Norton (soprano), Master Bramham, of Leeds Parish Church choir (contralto), Mr. C. Stagbro (tenor), and Mr. Morton (bass). It would be unfair to criticise a sacred performance of this sort; but special mention must be made of Miss Norton's exquisite rendering of the recitative—"I saw a new heaven and a new earth," also of her share in the duet with Mr. Blagbro, "Forsake me not." The lovely quartets, "Yes, every tear," and "Blest are the Departed," were given with much feeling; while the chorus, "Lord God of Heaven and Earth," as well as the other choral numbers with which the work abounds, were rendered in a manner that left nothing to be desired. The performance as a whole was admirable, and evidently produced a great impression. Dr. Creser gave valuable assistance at the organ.   J. D. T.

WORCESTER.

There was a meeting on Dec. 1st at the Guildhall, Worcester, of the stewards of the next Festival of the Three Choirs, the Mayor (Mr. W. B. Williamson) in the chair, when the first steps were taken towards arranging for the Worcester Festival of 1884. Beginning, as at the last Worcester meeting on Sunday, there will be an opening service at the Cathedral, with band and chorus, on Sunday, September 7. Monday (8th) will be devoted to rehearsal, and there will be oratorios on each succeeding morning of the week at the Cathedral, viz., Tuesday, Gounod's "Redemption;" Wednesday, a miscellaneous collection of Masses and Cantatas; Thursday, Dvorak's "Stabat Mater," and Part 2 of Mendelssohn's "St. Paul;" and Friday, Handel's "Messiah." Mendelssohn's "Elijah" will be given on Wednesday evening, and there will be secular concerts on Tuesday and Thursday evenings; the week's music ending on Friday evening with cathedral music with band and chorus. On the whole, this is a good selection, and it is satisfactory to find Mendelssohn well represented. The large services, with orchestra, are commendable features, and will help on the good work of again putting the divine art in a rightful and exalted position as an ordained expression of praise and worship.

TAUNTON.—It is to be hoped that the Philharmonic concert was as great a success financially as it was musically. Taunton, as well as the Society, has to thank Mr. Dudeney, the conductor, for the treat of December 6th; because, though we often enjoy selections from the "Messiah," this is the first time for many years that Handel's grandest oratorio has been performed in toto in Taunton. The soprano parts, taken by Miss Florence Rowe, were admirably rendered. The contralto parts were well given by Mdme. Rose Bailey, and her solos, "Oh, Thou that tellest," and "He was despised," were much appreciated. Mr. W. Clinch's voice and style were excellent. Mr. Edwin Welsh's knowledge of the music, and firmness of tone, was very marked in the recitative "Thus saith the Lord," and also in the air "Why do the nations rage." Altogether, the Society may well be congratulated on the success of this their last concert of the season.

NEWCASTLE-ON-TYNE.

Such a remarkable occurrence as the production in our town of two new English compositions, viz., Mr. Mackenzie's "Colomba," and Mr. Goring Thomas's "Esmeralda," which have been performed by the Carl Rosa Opera Company at the Tyne Theatre, has created quite a stir among all who have faith in native talents and hopes of a National Opera in England. Never before have the visits here of this talented company excited such enthusiasm as the present series of representations called forth, for every space of the splendid Tyne Opera House has been nightly crowded to excess—in fact, many persons were unable to gain admittance.

The present season opened on Nov. 26th with Donizetti's "Lucrezia Borgia," when we had the good fortune of hearing the Parisian *prima donna*, Mdme. Marie Roze, as the heroine, a *rôle* in which this charming singer displayed not only great histrionic power, but also a marvelous vocalization. Miss M. Burton as Orsini, and Mr. Ludwig as the Duke, and Mr. B. Davies as Gennaro, were also successful in their parts.

The first performance on November 27th of Mr. Goring Thomas's "Esmeralda," was such a decided success that it had (by desire) to be produced again on Saturday, Dec. 1st, when it drew an equally large and enthusiastic audience as at the first representation. The principal parts were artistically sustained by Mdme. Georgina Burns (Esmeralda), Miss C. Perry (Fleur-de-Lys), Mr. B. McGuckin (Phœbus), Mr. L. Crotty and Mr. Ludwig (Quasimodo and Frollo), Mr. Snazelle (Clopin), and Mr. B. Davies (Gringoire). The chorus did their work well and the band played satisfactorily under the skilful conductorship of Mr. Goossen. Mdme. Burns's magnificent singing of the brilliant air, "Oh, fickle, light-hearted swallow," in the first act, and the beautiful quintet with chorus in the second act, were enthusiastically *encored*. The same compliment was paid to Mr. McGuckin for his rendering of "O vision entrancing," and to Mr. Crotty for his fine singing of "What would I do for my queen." "Esmeralda" is a clever and pretty opera, containing much bright and pleasing music, which, if not always strictly original, is skilful and well scored for the orchestra. Unlike the music of Mr. Mackenzie's "Colomba," which appeals more to the thoughtful listener and the educated musician, the melodious music in "Esmeralda" accords more with the present taste of an ordinary English audience. It seems that people have yet to learn to submit to a little training before they can appreciate an English opera based upon the Wagner theories, like "Colomba." That such, at least, was the case in Newcastle, cannot be denied. The first performance of "Colomba" on Friday, Nov. 30th, did not succeed in creating a very favourable impression upon the vast audience assembled. It is to be regretted, for in no other English opera performed here has so much true, ingenious, and fine workmanship been displayed as in Mackenzie's "Colomba." Notwithstanding, the parts were well sustained by Mdme. Marie Roze, Miss Perry, Miss Annie Albu, and Mr. McGuckin, Mr. Ludwig, Mr. H. Pope, and Mr. Snazelle. All the performers, including the chorus and the orchestra, seemed more or less over-weighted by the music—the latter were also inadequate in tonal power and quality to give a fair hearing of the work. The beautiful ballad, "So he thought of his Love" (with its strong flavour of a popular Scandinavian Folk-song), won the only *encore*; it was sung most effectively by Miss Perry.

On Wednesday evening, "Carmen," a favourite here, was excellently performed by the artists engaged. Mdme. Marie Roze—a fascinating Carmen—was repeatedly recalled, and bouquets were freely thrown down after the fall of the curtain. Miss Annie Albu (Michael) evoked much applause for her fine singing in the third act; Mr. Crotty (Escamillo) sang magnificently, and Mr. B. Davies made his mark as José. The band and chorus played and sang admirably.

Balfe's popular opera, "The Bohemian Girl," did not attract quite so large an audience on Thursday as the others had done, nor was it put on the stage in the best form. One reason was because at the last moment Mr. Pope had to be substituted for Mr. Crotty (who was suffering from hoarseness) in the character of Count Arnheim. Mr. W. Mockridge (Thaddeus), was encored in the song "When other lips," Miss Annie Albu (Arline) received well deserved applause, and Mr. Snazelle (Devilshoof), as usual, excited great hilarity by his comic fun.

The operas have been splendidly mounted, and the acoustic properties of the large Tyne Opera House proved to be most satisfactory; in fact Mr. Younge, the manager of this popular theatre, may be congratulated on the success he has achieved in every way.　　　　　　　　　　　　　　H. W.

His Royal Highness the Duke of Edinburgh visited the Royal College of Music on Dec. 1st during the weekly *ensemble* class, and listened to portions of the Quartetts in D by Haydn, and of Mozart in E flat. The class was conducted by Mr. Henry Holmes, professor of the violin, and the following students performed :—Sutcliffe, Bent, McCunn, Squire, Miss Holiday, Dolmetch, Kreuz, and Werge.

BRIDPORT.

The members of the Bridport Choral Society opened their winter concert season at the Drill Hall under very encouraging circumstances. It was the first concert of the season, and although the programme was of a somewhat different character to that which is usually presented, it was of a varied and pleasing description. There was a satisfactory attendance, the reserved seats being nearly all occupied, whilst the other seats were fairly filled. Mr. Hopkins, the conductor, and the promoters of the concert, were fortunate in securing the services as vocalists of Miss F. M. Gill, of Blandford, who has previously appeared before a Bridport audience under the auspices of this society, and of Mr. W. Clinch, from Wells Cathedral. The first part of the programme consisted of a pastoral cantata by Louis N. Parker, A.R.A.M., called "Silvia," in which the scene was laid on the borders of a wood, and the characters represented being these :—Silvin (Miss Gill), Sybil (Mrs. J. T. Stephens), the Poet (Mr. Clinch), the Huntsman (Mr. Hopkins), and a chorus. The cantata was one of the most pleasing productions which the society has placed before the public since its resuscitation, and the audience evidently appreciated it. The music is very taking and was sustained in such an efficient manner that there was no lack of interest. The accompaniments were played in a careful manner by Mrs. Benham (pianoforte), and Miss Champ (harmonium). The heartiest applause greeted the conclusion of cantata, which lasted for about an hour and a half, during the whole of which time the interest and pleasure of the audience was well maintained. The second part of the programme consisted of a miscellaneous selection.

GREENOCK.

The members of the Greenock Philosophical Society were entertained, on Nov. 30th, by a musical lecture, given by Mr. W. Spark, Mus. Doc., of Leeds. The vocalists were—Madame Pauline Evison, Miss Emmeline Kennedy, Mr. Jackson, and Mr. T. Dodds, and their individual and combined efforts proved them to be worthy of the flattering reception accorded by a numerous and critical audience. The subject of Dr. Spark's lecture was, "Bach to Gounod, or Music, Ancient and Modern." In his opening remarks he said, it was his privilege that evening to draw their attention to the works of some of the great musical composers—the great thinkers and workers of the divine art. The Doctor dwelt upon the eminent musicians of the past 150 years, their difference of style, form, and effect, their greatness of originality ; and intimated that in drawing up his programme he had not chosen the most elaborate or effective of musical compositions, but simply such as were brief, yet which were strikingly characteristic as possible. The lecture and illustrations were of a most enjoyable nature, both from a literary and musical point of view. Dr. Spark handled his subject effectively, dwelling upon the history, the development of the talents, the peculiarities of the genius, and the characteristics of the great creators of living music ; and an occasional dash of humour seasoned the intellectual repast.

BRIXTON.—An excellent concert was given by Miss Mary Mackway at the Brixton Hall, on Thursday evening, the 6th inst. Miss Mackway was assisted by a numerous array of vocalists and instrumentalists. The following were amongst the most successful items in the programme :—"With verdure clad," very artistically sung by the *beneficiare* ; "Ave Maria," composed by Walter Mackway, and sung by Mdme. Worrell, with violoncello obbligato by Mr. W. Hann ; this was vociferously encored and repeated ; "When the Moon is brightly shining" (Molique), Mr. Arthur Thompson ; and the "Toreador's Song" ("Carmen"), Mr. Musgrove Tufnell. Mention should also be made of the two MS. songs—"Peacefully slumber," by C. S. Macpherson ; and "The Rainy Day," by W. Mackway ; both being sound compositions above the ordinary type of song. Mr. W. Hann and Mr. Mackway respectively contributed violoncello and pianoforte solos ; and Messrs. A. Izard, Kiver, Macpherson, and Mr. Frederick Walker conducted.

BURTON-ON-TRENT.—The members of the St. Paul's Institute Choral Society gave the opening concert for the season, in the large hall of St. Paul's Institute on a recent evening, when there was a very fair attendance. The programme opened with the overture from "Samson" (Handel), very efficiently performed by the band, assisted by Mr. Geo. Barnes at the organ. This was followed by the eight-part motet, "Judge me, O God," (Mendelssohn), sung by the chorus. The chief feature of the evening was the performance of Stainer's cantata "S. Mary Magdalen," in which the chorus was assisted by Miss Blanthorne, Miss Emily Harris, Mr. R. Clarke, and Mr. Geo. Harris. The chorus may be fairly congratulated (together with the conductor, Mr. A. B. Plant, F.C.O., Mus. Bac.) for the efficient manner in which they interpreted the music. The rapid transitions from one key to another make it a work of no small difficulty, but they proved themselves fully adequate to the task, and did credit to themselves and their leader. Mr. Plant conducted and Mr. Geo. Barnes efficiently presided at the organ. The society will put in practice Gounod's "Redemption," it is said.

MUSIC IN PARIS.

THE LOST ART OF COUNTERPOINT

(From our own Correspondent.)

PARIS, Nov. 30th, 1883.

The great and overshadowing musical event of the month has been, of course, the re-opening of the Theatre-Italien. When the Salle Ventadour, after passing from one unlucky management to another, was finally closed and converted into a bank, it was generally thought that we had seen the last of Italian opera in Paris,—no one certainly expected that it would be resuscitated in our generation. The sudden taste for Wagner, and jealousy of all rivals of the native composers who were following in the footsteps of the German prophet, combined, or seemed to combine to make the public indifferent to the light and stereotyped art of Bellini, Donizetti, and their contemporaries, which ten years earlier had delighted it. The critics, headed by M. Jonciéres, joyfully sung a requiem over the Italians, and a golden age seem opening for all the ambitious "Prix de Rome," who had so long been clamouring for an opportunity of producing their masterpieces. And yet here we find Italian Opera, or at all events an Italian Opera house, not only open again in Paris, but so fashionable that it bids fair to prove a serious danger to MM. Vaucorbeil and Carvalho. How is a fact so singular to be explained?

Well, the most natural explanation is perhaps afforded by the presence of the many strangers and foreigners in Paris. It is tolerably safe to say that there is a population of at least ten thousand wealthy foreigners here, hungry for amusement, and glad to have a rendezvous in which to display their charms and riches. The Opéra House, that is the open-house of M. Vaucorbeil, only very partially satisfies their requirements; for it is the rendezvous of French fashion, and contains but a limited number of seats. The Conservatoire is still more inaccessible. The Cirque is vulgar. It is not astonishing, therefore, that when M. Maurel announced his intention of reviving the Ventadour at the Theâtre des Nations, his idea was welcomed with enthusiasm. There is another reason, too, for his success. M. Vaucorbeil cannot, or will not, give his subscribers the variety that he had fallaciously promised them when he was angling for the post of M. Halanzier. "The "Huguenots," and "Faust," and "Sylvia," and "L'Africaine," will pall upon the most patient ear, if they are given month after month, and week after week; and especially if given with inferior casts. Lastly, M. Maurel was clever enough to include French composers in his programme. He will not perform Italian Opera exclusively, but will find room in his scheme for German and French Opera, who in Italian.

The work chosen for the inauguration-night was Verdi's "Simon Boccanegra," sung by Maurel, Ed. de Reszké, Nouvelli, and by Mme. Fides-Devriès, who, after a long and more regretted absence from the Paris stage, has issued from her retirement and returned to the boards. After being the "Star" of the French Opéra House, she bids fair to be a still more brilliant "Star" as an interpreter of the Italian répertoire!

"Simon Boccanegra" is not, as is constantly asserted, a youthful composition of the maestro. It was written after "Trovatore" and "Rigoletto," and belongs to the transitional period which preceded the composition of "Don Carlos," "La Forza del Destino," and "Aïda." As you are aware, Verdi lately re-wrote portions of the work; but despite this, or possibly to some extent on account of this, it is very inferior to his best operas, and lacks interest. The orchestration is either commonplace or pretentious—often both; the melodic inspiration is imperfectly sustained; and the form is undecided. There is an unpleasant savour in parts of the libretto, too, and the story told is neither very clear, nor very fascinating. Yet so, fine was the interpretation that, in a sense, "Simon Boccanegra," may be said to have succeeded. That it will have a long life in Paris I do not believe, but it will fill the house in attendant the production of "Erodiade" and "Mefistofele."

The Concerts are as well-attended as ever this year. M. Lamoureux seems to be rapidly gaining the public favour, and the Theâtre du Chateau d'Eau is now more crowded than the Cirque every Sunday. Amongst the novelties which are to be given by M. Lamoureux this season is a performance of Bach's little-known work "Le Déà de Phœbus et de Pan,"—which has not yet been heard in Paris. En attendant, he has treated us to two magnificent executions of "The Italian" Symphony. M. Lamoureux gives quite a new reading of the work, taking the tempi throughout much faster than customary here, and yet managing to bring out a number of delicate lights and shades which, too often, are slurred over and not understood.

M. Colonne holds his ground at the Chatelet. For Sunday we are promised Meyerbeer's "Struensee" music, Félicien David's "Désert," and some fragments of Saint-Saëns's "Henri VIII."

On the same day M. Pasdeloup will give us Beethoven's Symphonie en la, an Andante and Rondo by Chaussier, Peter Benoit's "Ouverture de Charlotte Corday," Haydn's "Serenade," a Concerto of Mozart, and Massenet's "Fête Bohême."

C. H. M.

Bizet's "La Jolie Fille de Perth" was recently given with great success at the Argentina Theatre, Rome.

LONDON: SATURDAY, DECEMBER 15, 1883.

THE PROPORTIONATE STRENGTH OF BAND AND CHORUS.

THE recent performance of Berlioz's "Requiem" Mass at the Crystal Palace, the admirable effect of a small chorus of really reliable, because trained and responsible artists, opened up in a practical fashion the consideration of the topic forming the title of this article. We are justly proud of our hosts of amateur chorus singers, and all musicians gratefully recognise the good work they have done and are still doing for the Art. Yet there are compositions requiring a choral performance of a character it is unreasonable to expect from non-professional singers, and it is artistically unjust to the composers of such works to assign the choral department to amateur singers. I am here using the word amateur as distinguishing non-paid and to some extent irresponsible and not strictly trained performers. The very nature of some elaborately orchestrated scores demands a choral strength which is not unwieldy, but which is sharp and prompt in attack, courageous, vigorous, instantaneously under control at all times, passionate and nervous in utterance, and consisting of well picked voices carefully balanced, and built up of such reasonable numbers as will secure an incisive and well concentrated vocal army. Chosen troops and not straggling hosts of inert, ill-prepared irregulars are wanted for the elucidation of the scores of BER-LIOZ and other modern writers. It is high time to consider the questions bearing upon vocal and instrumental tone balance. Eminent musicians have long set their faces against monster choruses swamping with their sluggish, indecisive harmonies all the sharply-cut outlines, and delicate effects of modern elaborate instrumentation. A distinguished foreign musician hearing once a performance of "Elijah" at the Albert Hall under such conditions, left the room after the earlier portion of the oratorio, with the remark that he had no pleasure in a performance in which the texture of the orchestration was so outrageously submerged by an overwhelming, yet indefinite chorus. Sir MICHAEL COSTA is said to have estimated the balance of tone suitable for the Albert Hall as only to be justly realised by a band of 500, with a chorus also of 360. One may not be inclined altogether to endorse this dictum, for monster bands are usually as inartistic in their performances, however imposing in array, as are monster choruses. Still, only to think of a chorus, to count from 300, 400, or 500, up to 800 with a band of about 80, performing works of a modern type with a dominant orchestration, is, if one may make such a comparison, to picture a feast with a bill of fare nearly limited to bread and potatoes. Without in any way checking or interfering with the amateur choruses, it is now time at the least of earnest musical culture to take steps with regard to the better balancing of our vocal and instrumental forces; and if, for frequent employment we ought for special occasions to build up possible professional choruses. The time is past for chorus singers who at the best read music indifferently, who consequently lack fire and certainty, and who singing merely for the pleasure of singing, to be identified with exciting public occasions, or to get free tickets for themselves and their friends. Art must, to be sound and true, be practised upon a basis of undeniable earnestness, and served by artists nurtured by careful technical preparation. When we come to hear modern choral works, performed by such artists, whether professional or amateur, balanced in about the proportion of 90 instruments, to 100 singers, then we shall really begin to know what perfect music may be like. A good basis of proportion may be obtained by a comparison of the mass of strings employed with the number of chorus singers engaged, accepting the wind instruments and percussion as at a fixed standard. Thus, if the strings number 50 (with complete phalanx of wind in addition) the chorus, of well picked singers, should number about 100, or represent twice the strength of the combined strings.

E. H. TURPIN.

THE LOGIC OF COUNTERPOINT.

THIRD SERIES.

XVI.

THERE are, it is true, no special rules for the conduct of counterpoint in more than four parts, seeing that the enlarged score not only necessitates the relaxation of the leading laws affecting contrapuntal activity, but by the preservation of a thickened tone texture releases both composer and listener from obligations naturally more stringent in the clearly to be traced outlines of more limited scores. Still there are points upon which the student may be advised with advantage concerning the writing of counterpoint in more than four parts. In order to obtain moving power in handling parts lying close together, as is the case in counterpoint having 6 or more parts in action, the student may, with decided gain, take some preliminary practice in the conduct of counterpoint of all species in three high, in three low, then in four high and in four low parts. Such practice in writing for, say, separate choirs of female and male voices, will tend to secure a clear vision in laying out closely fitting harmonic strata, and will consequently help to give readiness of resource and speed in writing for a large score. Then, in the actual practice of counterpoint in 6 or more parts, it is well, in order to avoid massing the parts too much together, and producing stiffness in the texture of the harmony, to adopt in a general sense the following suggestions:—Do not permit, save exceptionally, more than three voices in six parts, or more than four in, seven or eight parts, to move in the same direction at the same time; and when the three or four parts do move in the same direction, as must constantly be the case in large contrapuntal scores, endeavour to break up the mass of voices proceeding thus, by intermingling layers of parts moving in opposite directions; so that, for example, if even four parts move at once in a given course, the voices thus proceeding shall not be those nearest to each other, but shall be mixed up with intervening voices having a different kind of movement.

E. H. TURPIN.

At the New Town Hall, Westminster, Mr. S. V. Balfour's concert was given on Dec. 3rd, 1884. The vocalists were Miss Elise Worth, Miss Florence Rachelle, Miss Alice Kean, Signor Oddardo Barri, and Mr. F. G. Caldicott. Instrumentalists; solo pianoforte, Herr Georg Asch; solo flute and piccolo, Miss Cora Cardigan; Solo piccolo, Mr. O. Booth. There was an orchestra of 40 performers. The programme included, overture, "Bronze Horse" (Auber); descriptive fantasia, "Smithy in the Wood" (T. Michaelis), encored; descriptive march, "La Caravanne" (George Asch), conducted by the composer and encored; overture, "Poet and Peasant" (Suppé); pizzicato, "Mandolina" (for string instruments) (O. Langey); and gavotte "Mignon" (A. Thomas).

At the West End Eisteddfod, held at the Town Hall Westminster, under the presidency of Sir Watkin Williams on Dec. 4th, some good solo singing was to be heard in the musical competitions, though defective voice production was the chief complaint to be made in most cases. Two of the choirs in the choral competition sang "But as for His people" (Handel), with such evenly balanced excellences, that the adjudicator (Mr. E. H. Turpin) divided the prize between the two choirs; a decision which was received by a crowded and enthusiastic audience with such loud applause as betokened general approval.

EDINBURGH UNIVERSITY MUSICAL SOCIETY.

The thirteenth annual meeting was held on Nov. 22nd ("St. Cecilia's Day"), in the music class room. There were present —Sir Herbert Oakeley, President of the Society; Vice-Presidents—Sir Alexander Grant, Professors Flint, Butcher, Rutherford, and Muirhead; Dr. Woodhead, Dr. Sydney Marsden, Mr. G. Gordon, Mr. Small, and others.

The chair was taken, as usual, by Professor Sir HERBERT OAKELEY, President, who said :—"Sir Alexander, Professors, and Members of our Musical Society,—In welcoming the Society here for the thirteenth year since its re-organisation, my first duty is to explain to novices the main objects of this annual meeting, which are, to hear the Chairman and Honorary Treasurer's reports, to elect office-bearers for the session, and to re-animate members—or embers which, after the brilliant success of last March, must still remain aglow, and which, let us hope, will be fanned into flame during a year in which the occurrence of the Tercentenary will draw increased attention to this University, and will attract here many *savants* in science and art. These illustrious guests will require, amongst other festal greetings, some serenading by our Choral Society. To new-comers here, some reference to the aim and history of that excellent institution, which I hope they are about to join, seems necessary, and although older members may find such details wearisome, it cannot do them harm to be once a year reminded of regulations, responsibilities, privileges, and achievements. Of the latter, echoes have been heard in other lands, and our example here has been successfully followed by students of the other universities of Scotland."

The Society's rules having been read, Sir HERBERT continued—

"As to responsibilities, the chief one is regularity in coming here once a week to practise. And in the way of privileges—well, they are so great and so many that if I attempted to enumerate half of them we should be here a long time. In respect to shortcomings, too, or rather hindrances, I might give a tolerably long recital, but it is pleasanter to recite some achievements, and to touch on some salient points in our history. The first public hint towards the formation in Scotland of such an association as ours seems to have been dropped in an inaugural address delivered in this class-room in 1866, in which it was said, in allusion to the practical working of this Chair,—'Premising that all attempts as regards a difficult question must necessarily be experimental. . . . I think that a choral class might be formed. When I was an undergraduate at Oxford, an association existed among the students under the title of the "University Amateur Musical Society," and enabled us to give, with professional instrumental help, terminal concerts ; . . . it would afford opportunity of introducing excellent glees and choruses for men's voices.' And the germ of our Society may be traced to a concert given, a few months after that address, by the Committee of the Athletic Club, which was announced simply as ' University Amateur Concert, in which the performers will consist chiefly of members of the University.' In 1873 the good work effected by the Association was recognised by Royalty, in my receiving the assent of H.R.H. the Duke of Edinburgh to become our Patron. And as such patronage is carefully and exceptionally granted, the favour should be duly appreciated. By this time our concerts had become popular in Edinburgh, and heard of abroad. The best known German musical paper, *Die Signale*, published at Leipzig, at once the biblical and musical centre of Germany, gave a favourable mention of our programme of 1874—a fact worth recording.

"Each year I affirm that our last concert was our best. But, as I tell you the truth, it is a matter of much congratulation, that in the face of difficulties which, I may safely say, are experienced by no other musical society existing, we should be able, year by year, to keep up the gradual *crescendo* which commenced so *pianissimo* some seventeen years ago. There is no doubt that the performance of the chorus last March was better than any previously attained. Not very many years ago it was seldom indeed that so rare a male bird as an amateur male instrumentalist was to be seen, or rather heard, in these latitudes, and his appearance was not a wholly welcome phenomenon, being sometimes supposed to have something supernatural or uncanny about it. In these more enlightened and less superstitious days the apparition is so frequent as to be divested of any mystery or peculiarity. The proportion of men among the audience at a concert is about 20 to 1 to what it was twenty years ago ; and as to amateur male performers on some instrument, or those who can take part in a chorus or part-song, the increase is about as great. Indeed, among students of this University not only has some insight into choral music been attained, but recently some promising attempts have been made towards the formation of an amateur orchestra, which I hear of with great satisfaction, and wish the movement every possible success. Here, however, the difficulties are far greater than those of forming an amateur student chorus. Every one has a voice of some sort, and a great authority on vocal music asserts that any one can learn to sing, but to play even tolerably well on an instrument requires far more and far earlier study and practice than to take a part in choral music. An excellent musician, in giving some hints to amateur violinists, closes with two practical remarks :—(1) 'Do not take up the violin unless you mean to work hard at it.' (2)

'It is almost hopeless to attempt to master the violin after the age of ten.' The whole family of stringed instruments require long and arduous study, and some of the wind instruments, such as the oboe or horn, are scarcely ever successfully manipulated by amateurs. In fact, the musical training and artistic competency necessary for orchestral players are generally much underrated, especially if high class compositions are attempted.

"Assuring students instrumentally inclined of all sympathy, I now return to the affairs of our Choral Society.

"As it grows older, its work and its influence bear fruit, and its name and its doings are wafted far away by its many members who travel or who settle in foreign lands."

Mr. JAMES H. MACDONALD, addressing the meeting, said that he had passed last winter at Leipzig, and had been enrolled a member of the "Paulus Männerchor Verein," which was founded by Mendelssohn, with a view to form a bond of union with his Conservatorium (Music School) and the University, and had become the most efficient and famed student-chorus in Germany. Professor Langer, director of this Society, on hearing that he (Mr. Macdonald) hailed from Edinburgh University, inquired with much interest about our Choral Society, saying that he knew the President by repute, and would propose to send him from the " Paulus Verein " a sympathetic and friendly greeting, in the shape of the Mütze, or cap worn by that Society as a badge of membership. This proposal having been seconded by the Leipzig students, Mr. Macdonald was commissioned to present the blue Mütze, and in doing so at this meeting explained that it was hoped that when any of our members were in Germany and saw wearers of this cap it would be remembered that it was a bond of union and of friendly intercourse between the two Societies. The cap having been presented amidst applause, Sir Herbert Oakeley expressed his thanks and that of his Society for the honour thus paid, assuring Mr. Macdonald that " the cap would be carefully preserved and placed in view for members, that a German letter should be sent to Professor Langer, expressing appreciation of the gift ; and that he hoped that members might recognise the ' blue bonnet ' when at Leipzig, and that in all cases the cap might fit."

Mr. JOHN SMALL, honorary treasurer, read the financial statement for the past year. Total income resulting from accumulated subscriptions or donations, and from concert receipts, £387 11s., and expenditure, £185 19s. 2d., leaving a balance in hand of £201 11s. 11d.

Principal Sir ALEXANDER GRANT moved the adoption of the report and the financial statement. In the course of his remarks he congratulated the Society on its continued prosperity and advance in choral singing, and on the President's interesting account of the Society, to which he had listened with much pleasure. At the Tercentenary celebration the University would be anxious to exhibit all its treasures and resources to the strangers and illustrious foreigners who might come to visit them on that occasion, and he would say they should have great pride and pleasure in bringing forward the Choral Society, because it was a Society which would do the University honour and credit.

Professor FLINT moved the election of the office-bearers for the year, including H.R.H. the Duke of Edinburgh as Patron ; Professor Sir Herbert Oakeley, *ex officio* President, and Conductor.

Dr. R. SYDNEY MARSDEN intimated that at the last meeting of the committee, last session, a sum of £40 was placed in the hands of the committee to commemorate in some way, in connection with their Musical Society, the Tercentenary of the University. The result of their deliberations was a resolution to purchase a bust of their President, Sir Herbert Oakeley, which would be presented to the University, and placed in the class-room.

Professor RUTHERFORD, rising in response to repeated cheers, said that the lateness of the hour forbade more than a few words of congratulation on the condition of the Society.

Sir HERBERT OAKELEY, after expressing his thanks to Dr. Marsden for the very kind proposal to which he had alluded, and which would receive more adequate acknowledgment later, requested a vote of thanks to the Principal and Professors who had honoured the meeting with their presence, thereby shewing that no fears were entertained on their part that severer studies could be interfered with by the practice of choral music.

The members of the St. George's Glee Union, under the direction of Mr. Joseph Monday, gave their usual monthly concert at the Pimlico Rooms on the 7th inst. The programme was miscellaneous, and included songs by Miss Clara Denison, Miss Clara Myers, Miss Louise Augarde, Mr. Hirwen Jones, and Mr. Thurley Beale ; also several part-songs, amongst which were " Here in cool grot and mossy cell " (Mornington), " Tis silent eve " (Watson), " You stole my love " (W. Macfarren), " The Soldier's Chorus " from " Faust " (Gounod), etc. Pianoforte solos were contributed by Miss Denison, Miss Matilda Crimp, and Mr. F. R. Kinkee, the latter also supplying the pianoforte accompaniments.

Organ News.

NORWICH.

An organ recital was given by Dr. Bunnett, F.C.O., in the St. Andrew's Hall, on Saturday, December 8th. The following was the programme:—

Marche Solennelle	Gounod.
Organ Sketch	Chipp.
Andante in A major	Smart.
Organ Sonata in C	Mozart.
Largo in D, from Symphony	Haydn.
Tema con Variazioni, from Septet	Beethoven.
Pastoral Symphony	Bach.
Finale to 6th Concerto	Handel.
Offertoire in F	Batiste.
Overture ("Athalie")	Mendelssohn.

LIVERPOOL.

Mr. H. A. Branscombe's series of organ recitals, given in St. Margaret's, Church, Prince's Road, was resumed on Saturday, the 1st inst. The following are the programmes up to Date:—

Saturday, December 1st:—

PROGRAMME.

Overture, "Alcina"	Handel.
Pomposo—Musette—Minuet.	
Romance in B minor	Rubinstein.
Sonata, No. 4	Mendelssohn.
Allegro con brio—Andante Religioso—Allegretto—Allegro Maestoso.	
Largo, "Serse"	Handel.
Prelude and Fugue in E flat major	Bach.
Il Lamento	Henselt.
Minuet	Grieg
Gavotte in D	Rameau.

Saturday, December 8th:—

PROGRAMME.

Fantasia in F minor	Fryer.
Larghetto in D	Mozart.
Air, with variations in A, with Finale Fugato	Smart.
Souvenir in F and Minuet in F	Silas.
Prelude and Fugue in B minor	Bach.
Gavotte	Rea.
March "Prophète"	Meyerbeer.

Saturday, December 15th:—

PROGRAMME.

Concerto, No. 6	Handel.
Andante maestoso—Allegro—Allegro ma non presto.	
Cavatina	Raff.
Prelude and Fugue	Silas.
Andante (Violin Concerto)	Mendelssohn.
Fantasia in E minor, "The Storm"	Lemmens.
Adantino	Heller.
Gavotte	Elvey.
March Cortège ("Irene")	Gounod.

WARE.

An organ recital was given on Thursday, November 29th, in the Parish Church, by Mr. James L. Gregory, F.C.O., assisted by Mr. Alfred E. Gregory, A.Mus. T.C.L., who kindly consented to sing on this occasion. The following was the programme:—

Sonata in D minor (Op. 65), No. 6	Mendelssohn.
Chorale with variations—Fugue—Finale.	
Recit., "Thus saith the Lord," and Air, "But who may abide" ("Messiah")	Handel.
Andante from an Organ Sonata (Op. 1)	Mailly.
Vocal, "It is enough" ("Elijah")	Mendelssohn.
Minuet and Trio from Symphony in C minor	Bennett.
Sacred Song, "Nazareth"	Gounod.
Jubilant March	Stig....

BOLTON.

An organ recital was given in the Albert Hall, on Saturday, December 1st, by the borough organist, Mr. Wm. Mullineux, F.C.O. The following was the programme:—

Overture, "Zampa"	Hérold.
Communion in F major	Jules-Grison.
Fantasia for the Organ on the favourite hymn tune, "Thy will be done"	Mullineux.
Welsh Air, "Bells of Aberdovey"	
Grand Fantasia in E minor, "The Storm"	Lemmens.
Selection from the Opera, "Patience"	Sullivan.
Processional March in E flat	Wely.

And on Saturday, December 8th:—

Introduction, Offertoire and Fugue	Hewlett.
Duet, "Quis est homo" ("Stabat Mater")	Rossini.
Grand Fantasia in E major, "The Storm"	Lemmens.
Organ Sonata in D minor, No. 1	Guilmant.
Andante in F major	Wely
March and Chorus, "Gloria Patri"	Barnby.

On Dec. 5th Mr. E. H. Turpin gave an organ recital at the Congregational Chapel, Maldon. Mr. A. L. Fryer gave much pleasure by his artistic singing; his rendering of Gounod's "There is a green hill faraway" being repeated by desire.

BOW AND BROMLEY INSTITUTE.

True to the liberal policy of the committee, the engagement of Mr. Henry R. Rose at the recital on Dec. 8th, added another artist of eminence to the list of those who appeared at the famous recitals. Mr. Rose's talents and skill were already widely recognised; so his marked success was a gratifying result looked for by many far in advance. His opening piece was Sir R. P. Stewart's fine Fantasia in D minor, one of the most notable and effective organ pieces written in these days. A Trio for two claviers and pedal by Bach, and a Fugue on Bach's name by Schumann, came next and were received with loud applause. An Andante Grazioso by Smart, and Guilmant's Funeral March and Chant Séraphique, finely played and admirably registered for, received an encore and was in part repeated. Bennett's "Barcarolle" as excellently arranged by Dr. Steggall, and "O ruddier" (Handel) neatly played on the pedals found much applause. Morandi's E minor Overture was the last organ piece. The organist made a decided impression by his manifest talents and skill, and the committee are to be congratulated upon his introduction to a Bow audience. Miss Clara Samuell sang very charmingly, being encored in two songs and recalled for another. After Sullivan's "My dearest heart," she returned and sang "Robin Adair," and Cowen's "Spinning" was similarly followed by the "Little Maid of Arcadie." Mr. Fountain Meen ably accompanied. On the 10th Mendelssohn's "Hymn of Praise" was given without the Symphony by a small band of some fourteen players, the organ (Mr. Alfred Carder), and the choir of the institute. The vocal soloists were Miss Larkcom, Messrs. Sidney Town and Brereton. Mr. McNaught conducted with his usual success. The choir admirably sustained the high credit already secured. Haydn's "Spring" formed the second part of the concert. To-night Dr. Bridge will play an interesting programme, including Handel's Concerto No. 2, set 1, and No. 9, set 2. The accompaniments will be rendered by a body of instrumentalists, conducted by Dr. F. E. Gladstone, mostly members of the Highbury Philharmonic Society. So excellent a programme with such artists promises a marked success.

CRYSTAL PALACE.

Mr. A. J. Eyre's performances on Saturday, December 1st, included the following:—

Postlude in D	Smart.
Adagio from a Quartet	Spohr.
Short Prelude and Fugue in E minor	Bach.
Allegretto for the Organ	Bennett.
Final Chorus, "The Holy City"	Gaul.
Double Chorus, "The Horse and his Rider"	Handel.
Andante, "Evening Prayer"	Smart.
Air, "Love in her eyes is playing" ("Acis")	Handel.
Allegretto from Symphony No. 4 ("Lobgesang")	Mendelssohn.
Bourrée and Variations in B minor	Bach.
Chorus, "The Seed of David" ("King David")	Macfarren.

PERTH, N.B.

Mr. R. Woodthorpe Browne gave the fifth monthly organ recital in Kinnoul Church, on the 10th ult. The programme consisted of the following:—

Marcia di Processione	Morandi.
Adagio Cantabile	Haydn.
Prelude and Fugue in C minor	Bach.
Andante (varied)	Westbrook.
Sonata in B flat, No. 4	Mendelssohn.
Two Sketches, Andante con moto in F sharp minor, and Canzonet	Chipp.
Concert Fantasia	Stewart.

MOSSLEY HILL.

An organ recital was given in the Church of St. Matthew and St. James, Mossley Hill, on Saturday, December 1st, by Mr. Martin Schneider. The following was the programme:—

March	Spohr.
Largo	Handel.
Sonata No. 3	Mendelssohn.
Con moto maestoso—Andante tranquillo.	
Repos d'Amour	Henselt.
Bourrée	Handel.
Fugue in E minor	Bach.
Andante	Schneider.
Offertoire	Wely.

M. Guilmant is giving a number of organ recitals in the provinces just now. The other evening he gave a fine performance at the Albert Hall, Nottingham, on the large organ built by Messrs. Brindley and Foster.

ST. MICHAEL'S, FOLKESTONE.

On Tuesday evening last the Rev. E. Husband, Incumbent, gave the last organ recital on the present instrument, the organ being unsuitable in shape for the new organ gallery now being built at this church. The music is always a special feature at St. Michael's, and a "Cathedral" Service is performed daily, The music is "Anglican" throughout, and on Sundays is executed by a choir of about 50 voices, and on week days by a choir of about 30 boys. A peculiarity about this Church is, that Mr. Husband is his own organist, and on this account the key-board has been placed beside the Vicar's stall. The present organ has been in use about nine years, and on this instrument Mr. Husband has himself given 85 recitals. The new organ is being built by Messrs. Jones and Sons, and, it is hoped, will be in its place in the course of the next few weeks. The Church is at the present time being enlarged at a cost of about £7,000, and the great east window has just been filled with painted glass. When completed, St. Michael's will be one of the most imposing churches in Kent.

BURTON-ON-TRENT.

An organ recital was given on Thursday, December 6th, in the Presbyterian Church of England, Cross Street, by Mr. A. B. Plant, Mus.Bac., Oxon., F.C.O., assisted (vocally) by Miss Georgina Wragge, and Mr. W. B. Dunbar. The following was the programme:—

Toccata and Fugue	Bach.
Air, " Holyworthy Church Bells "	Wesley.
Allegretto in E	Plent.
Chorale Song and Fugue	Wesley.
Andante	Batiste.
Allegretto in B minor	Guilmant.
Adagio, from Sextet	Beethoven.
Rondo	Morandi.
"Occasional" Overture	Handel.

CASTLE HOWARD.

An organ recital was given on Sunday the 2nd ult., in the private chapel, Castle Howard, by the organist, Mr. J. R. Brooke. The following was the programme:—

Overture, "Messiah"	Handel.
Kyrie Eleison, and Gloria, from 12th Mass	Mozart.
Weihnacht's Pastorale (Op. 56)	Merkel.
Marche Heroique in D (Op. 27)	Guilmant.
Qui Tollis" from 12th Mass	Mozart.
Offertoire in C	Wely.
Air, "Return, O God of hosts" ("Samson")	Handel.
Dona nobis pacem	Mozart.

SEAFORD.

An organ recital was given in St. Leonard's Church, on Sunday, December 2nd, by Mr. A. H. Day. The following was the programme:—

Organ Concerto, No. 2	Handel.
"Ave Maria"	Cherubini.
"Coronation March"	Meyerbeer.
Air, "Total Eclipse"	Handel.
Prelude and Fugue	Hesse.
Pastorale	Zipoli.
"Zubel" Overture	Weber.

WEST HARTLEPOOL.

An organ recital was given by Dr. Spark, in the New Connection Chapel, on Monday, December 3rd. The following was the programme:—

Concerto in G minor	Handel.
Andante in A flat	Spark.
"Two Andantes, "Angelic Voices"	Batiste.
Coronation March, "Le Prophete"	Meyerbeer.
Motet, "Splendente Te Deus"	Mozart.
Air, varied, in G major	Haydn.
Selections from "Eli"	Costa.

KINGSTON-ON-THAMES.

An organ recital was given at All Saints' Church on Thursday, December 6th, by Mr. W. J. Lancaster, A.C.O. The following was the programme:—

"The night is departing " ("Hymn of Praise")	Mendelssohn.
Fugue in B minor	Bach.
Andante in G major	Smart.
Grand Chœur	Guilmant.
Maidensong	Reinecke.
Air from "Rosamunde"	Schubert.
Andante in A flat	Guilmant.
Marche Réligieuse	Gounod.
Organ Sonata, Pastorale in G	Rheinberger.

The second of a series of organ recitals upon the new instrument, by Brindley and Foster, at St. Andrew's, Watford, was given on Dec. 11th by Mr. E. H. Turpin.

EDINBURGH.

An organ recital was given in St. John's Episcopal Church, on Monday, December 3rd, by Mr. Frank Bates, Mus.Bac. The following was the programme:—

Overture, "The Last Judgment"	Spohr.
Graduale "Evening Prayer"	Smart.
Fantasia in E minor	Merkel.
Prelude and Fugue in G	Mendelssohn.
"Processional March"	Morandi.
"If with all your heart" ("Elijah")	Mendelssohn.
Prelude and Fugue in G major	Bach.
Cantilene, "Grand Chœur "	Salome.

LEEDS.

A recital on the grand organ was given in the Town Hall, on Tuesday, November 27th, by Dr. Spark, organist to the Corporation. The following was the programme:—

Festival March, "Ebenezum"	Spark.
Romanza in G minor	Bennett.
The Dead March in "Saul"	Handel.
Air, "In Memoriam," Sacred Cross Eve, 1865	Handel.
Theme in A major	Handel.
Offertoire in B minor	Batiste.
Reminiscences of the Romantic Opera, "Der Freyschütz"	Weber.

And on Tuesday, December 4th:—

Overture for the Organ in F minor	Morandi.
Largo con gran expressione, in C major	Beethoven.
Theme in F major	Bach.
Grand Toccata in F major	Bach.
Selection from "Carmen"	Bizet.

And on Saturday, December 8th:—

Andante in C major, from the 2nd Symphony, "The Surprise"	Haydn.
Gavotte in D major	Bach.
Andante Espressivo in A flat	Spark.
Allegro Brillante in F	
Two Andantes, "Angelic Voices"	Batiste.

OXFORD.

Mr. T. W. Dodds, the organist of Queen's gave a recital on the chapel organ, on Thursday, November 29th. There was a good attendance, and the programme, which included a Sonata, from Bach, in E major, for violin and organ, the former being taken by Mr. W. Garnett Smith, was listened to with interest.

WICK.

An organ recital was given in the Parish Church, on November 22th, by Mr. A. S. Round, A.C.O. The following was the programme:—

Sonata No 1	Mendelssohn.
Barcarolle from 4th Concerto	Bennett.
Andante in G	Batiste.
Elegy" in B flat minor	Silas.
Musette	Turpin.
Chorus, "Fixed in His Everlasting Seat"	Handel.
"Schiller" March	Meyerbeer.

KEIGHLEY, YORKSHIRE.

On November 17th, an organ recital was given in the Wesleyan Chapel, New Road Side, Keighley, by Mr. J. H. Rooks, organist of St. Paul's, Manningham, and late private organist to the Earl of Zetland. The organ has been presented by Mr. H. I. Butterfield, of Cliffe Castle, and should have been opened a few months since, but unfortunately the builders were unable to have it finished on the date fixed. The chapel was filled by an appreciative audience. The programme was of a high-class character, including selections from J. S. Bach, Guilmant, Mozart, Widor, Batiste, and Sir M. Costa. Mr. Rooks played in his usual masterly manner. The vocal movements were taken from Sir Michael Costa's "Eli," Mendelssohn's "St. Paul," and Handel's "Messiah," and were sustained by Miss Cockroft, of Allerton, and Mr. W. H. Emsley, of Bradford, in a very pleasant and satisfactory way.

GREENOCK.

An organ recital was given by Dr. Spark, of Leeds, at the Episcopal Church of St. John's on November 29th, when the programme included:—

Andante Expressivo in A flat	Spark.
Allegro Brillante in F major	
Extemporaneous Introduction and Grand Fugue on Tune "St. Ann's"	Bach.

The music gave much satisfaction to the congregation assembled.

At a special service on Nov. 30th (St. Andrew's Day), a new organ was opened at Holy Trinity Church, West Brighton. The organ was opened by Mr. J. Crapps, F.C.O., the organist of St. Andrew's Church, Waterloo Street, who played the Introductory Voluntary, and accompanied the whole of the service in his usual faultless style. An organ recital was commenced after service; the varied programme selected by Mr. Crapps, fully developed the power, sweetness, and quality of tone of the instrument. Smart's Andante in F was played with great taste and neatness. Bach's Prelude and Fugue in C minor was well performed. The remaining items were also well and effectively played. The organ stands in the chapel on the north side of the chancel and is built by Messrs. Harper Bros., Brighton, at their factory in King-street, and is said to be the largest organ that has yet been constructed in the town. It consists of two complete manuals, CC to G, 56 Notes, and independent Pedal organ, CCC to F, 30 Notes, pedals concave and parallel. Recitals will be given upon this instrument on the Sunday evenings in Advent (after the usual service) by well-known organists.

Foreign Musical Intelligence.

Bach's B minor Mass was performed at Frankfort-on-Maine on Nov. 26th.

Gobatti is engaged, it is said, upon the composition of a new opera, "Janko."

Dominique Rubini, of Russia, vocal teacher, died lately at Reuil, aged 77.

Maurizio Borella, a bass singer of note, died at Milan last week, aged 64.

The first performance of Suppé's "Voyage en Afrique," conducted by the composer, was very successful in Hanover.

Herr Josef Gungl is in the best of health living in Cassel at the house of his daughter, Frau Naumann-Gungl. It is his nephew, Johann Gungl, who is dead.

It is said that Arrieta's new opera, "San Franco de Sena," will presently be performed at the Teatro San Carlo, Lisbon.

The members of the Riedel Verein, Leipsig, recently gave a performance of Kiel's oratorio, "Christus," in the musically historical St. Thomas's Church.

It is announced by the *Gazetta Teatrale*, Rome, that Arriga Boito is writing the words and music of a new opera, to be entitled "Pier Luigi Farnese."

The report is that Signor Lucilla has withdrawn his new opera, "Il Conte Rosso," from the Teatro Regio, Turin, and it will be produced at the Teatro Carlo Felice, Genoa.

The Wagnerian opera series began in Vienna on Nov. 30th. All the composer's works are to be given with the exception of "Parsifal," of which Bayreuth keeps the monopoly.

Herr Gramman's new opera, "Das Andreasfest," produced with success a short time since at the Stadttheater, Augsburg, is now accepted for performance at the Imperial Opera House, Vienna.

Another English pianist has appeared on the musical stage. Miss Maggie Okey, once a student of the Royal Academy of Music and now under the tuition of M. de Pachmann, has played with a measure of success as a pianist at Vienna.

It is said of the performances at Bayreuth next year, that King Ludwig of Bavaria will guarantee all the expenses, and ten performances of "Parsifal," with the Munich performers will take place between July 20th and August 8th. Afterwards some performances will be given of the "Nibelung's Ring."

The management of the Stadttheater, Leipsig, produce next March a new opera, "Hellantus," by Adalbert von Goldschmidt, composer of the oratorio, "Die sieben Todsünden." Several notable musicians, including Franz Liszt, it is said, speak highly of the new work, and prognosticate for it a marked success.

Passing Events.

Sir A. Sullivan contributes a Christmas carol to this month's *Lute*, it is said.

The Strolling Players' Amateur Orchestral Society gave a concert on Dec. 13th, at St. Andrew's Hall.

The new opera on the subject of "Marie Stuart" by Sir Arthur Sullivan, is in progress, and the first act was completed recently.

It is, we hear, not improbable that a daughter of the eminent tenor, Mr. Sims Reeves, will shortly make her début on the stage.

Mr. C. E. Stephens's duet sonata for flute and pianoforte will be played to-night (Saturday) at a concert of the British Artists' Society.

A new operetta by Mr. A. J. Caldicott "A Moss Rose Rent," will be produced at Mr. and Mrs. German Reed's entertainment on Dec. 17th.

Mdlle. Nevada, or rather Miss Wixom, late of Her Majesty's, and now of the Paris Opéra Comique, has been secured for the Norwich Festival next year.

"The Quack Composer," is the title of No. 10 of Musical Sketches" in the *Musical World*, by H. E. D. The article is severely just and very timely.

Mr. Audran's comic opera "Gillette" was withdrawn on Saturday night, and Miss Kate Santley has, it is understood, relinquished the direction of the theatre.

It is announced that a cantata on the subject of "Hero and Leander," by Mr. Harford Lloyd, has been accepted for performance at the Worcester Festival of next year.

The committee of the "Earl of Wilton" Memorial to be placed in St. Margaret's Church, Holyrood, Prestwich, near Manchester, have decided upon a stained glass window, to be executed by the firm of Ward and Hughes, of Soho, London.

One sign of the return of the oratorio to its true home, the church, is the increased seasonable use of given appropriate works; thus "Spohr's Last Judgment" has been frequently given in church already during the present Advent.

Mr. Nelson Varley, a well known tenor and *protégé* of M. Lemmens, died at Cardiff on Dec. 1st. For the last four years he has been a chorister in Mr. D'Oyly Carte's provincial troupe, joining the "Iolanthe" company some ten weeks ago.

The College of Preceptors, holding important examinations including music as a subject, are about to build a large college in a central position. It is said the candidates entered for the Christmas examination number a good many over 8000.

A special service will be held in Canterbury Cathedral at 8.15, on Christmas Eve, when the Christmas music in the "Messiah" will be sung with band and auxiliary choir of ladies and gentlemen. Dr. Longhurst will conduct, and Mr. Maxted will play the organ.

At the next members' meeting of the Central Music Studio, Herbert Street, N., on Dec. 20th, the principal (Mr. W. J. Batley), will give a lecture—"Stephen Heller; his Life and Works." Admission free by ticket, which may be had upon application to the secretary.

Mr. von Zastrow has begun his Drawing Room concerts at the Glendower Mansions, South Kensington; and due notice will be taken of them next week. His pianist and violinist, Mr. Bond Andrews and Herr Polonaski, are both fine artists. An aristocratic assembly attended the first *séance* on Saturday afternoon, Dec. 1st.

Mdme. Montigny-Rémaury's pianoforte recital on Monday afternoon agreeably entertained a select audience; but a report must be reserved till next week. The scheme was slightly varied, and sundry "extras" were played by the fair Parisian, who is to visit Glasgow and other towns in the north before her return to Paris.

The Costa testimonial has, is is said, been given up. Although it may be right to duly recognize artistic merits and labour, there is truth in the pointed words of a contemporary that with the heavy burden of our poor at our doors, this is not the time to be making large money offerings to foreign musicians who have already been handsomely dealt with.

Miss Florence St. John has, it is said, been retained to "create" the part of "Nell Gwynne" in M. Planquette's forthcoming opera, which, however, will not be produced at the Avenue till after Jan. 15th, or late.

The centennial of the birthday of the celebrated painter Peter. von Cornelius was celebrated by the Academy of Arts, Berlin, on Dec. 11th. The proceedings opened with a performance of Beethoven's festival overture, followed by a commemoration address, delivered by Dr. Jordan, director of the National Galleries, and closed with Mendelssohn's Cornelius march.

Admirers of one of the greatest, if not the *the* greatest of song composers, will be glad to read that Herr Friedländer, of Frankfort, is preparing a complete and critical edition of Schubert's "Lieder," to be published by Peters of Leipzig. It is said that the numerous errors of previous editions will here be carefully eliminated. The work is to have a preface by Herr Max Müller.

Miss E. Madeline Kelley gave an evening concert at the Athenæum, Shepherd's Bush, on Dec. 11th, and was assisted by the following artists—Mrs. Irene Ware, Mdme. Szilárdka Dumtsa, and Miss Amy Carter; Mr. John Probert, Mr. Benjamin Nickels, jun., and Mr. J. Clifford Mill. Solo violoncello, Mr. J. A. Brousil; pianoforte, Mdme. Harry Brett.

Mr. Barnby, conductor of the Royal Albert Hall Choral Society gave a capital performance of "Elijah" on Wednesday night, with Mdme. Albani as his principal soprano; and Miss Hilda Wilson, Mr. E. Lloyd, and Mr. Santley as her coadjutors. Mdme. Albani sang deliciously. The audience attempted to encore several pieces, but the conductor was inflexible. More details next week.

The analytical programme of a pianoforte recital given by the Rev. J. H. Davis, in aid of the fund for supplying a hydraulic engine for the organ at West Derby Church, Liverpool, where Mr. Best is the organist, affords the local paper the *Porcupine*, an occasion for the humorous dissection of a remarkable specimen of its kind. Analytical programmes need not be written when the writer has not the justifiable technical and historical knowledge.

Mr. Banner's Liverpool Choir, which, since leaving St. Cuthbert's Church, have been actively engaged in the rehearsal of Spohr's "Last Judgment," produced that impressive work on Wednesday, 5th inst., at Mr. Banner's house, with organ and pianoforte accompaniment. On Wednesday next they are announced to sing the same oratorio in St. Bridget's Church, Wavertree, near Liverpool, when they will be supported by a body of string instruments. The wind parts will be arranged for organ from the full score. Mr. J. W. Collinson will be leader, and Mr. S. Claude Ridley, who has trained the choir, will conduct.

The first stage rehearsal of Messrs. Gilbert and Sullivan's new opera founded upon Mr. Tennyson's "Princess," took place at the Savoy Theatre last Monday. The leading part of the Princess Ida will be played by Miss Lilian Russell, the young American mezzo-soprano. The King Gama will be Mr. George Grossmith, while Mr. Rutland Barrington will represent King Hildebrand. Mr. Bracy, the tenor—a new comer— Mr. Lely, and Mr. Riley play the Three Princes, and Mr. Temple one of the Princess's sturdy brothers. The other performers are Mr. Warwick Grey, Miss Brandram, Miss Jessie Bond, and Miss Leonora Braham. The opera is in a prologue and two acts—a departure from the usual form of the author and composer.

The Querist.

QUERIES.

MUSIC.—I have an Amateur Orchestral Society. Many of the members are very fair players of their respective instruments, but, living in the Provinces, I am at a loss to get suitable music for them. Would any of your readers kindly give me a list of some good music, or tell me the best publishers to apply to for catalogues, &c.?—D.C.M.

SACRED PART SONGS.—Will any of your numerous readers kindly inform me if there any good *sacred* part-songs to be obtained, after the style of Sullivan's "Say, watchman, what of the night"?—AN OLD SUBSCRIBER.

Service Lists.

THIRD SUNDAY IN ADVENT.

DECEMBER 16th.

London.

ST. PAUL'S CATHEDRAL. — Morn.: Service, Benedicite (Martin); Benedictus, Barnby in E; Introit, O come, O come, Emmanuel; Holy Communion, Barnby in E. Even.: Service, Magnificat and Nunc Dimittis, Barnby in E; Anthem, Think, good Jesu (Mozart).

FOUNDLING CHAPEL. — Morn.: Service, Barnby in E; Jubilate, Foster in A; Anthem, How beautiful are the feet (Handel). Aft.: Children's Service.

LINCOLN'S INN CHAPEL.—Morn.: Service, King in F; Kyrie (Nares); Anthem, How beautiful are the feet, The Lord gave the word (Handel). Even: Service, King in F; Anthem, Awake, awake, put on thy strength, O Zion (Wise).

TEMPLE CHURCH.—Morn.: Service, Te Deum Landamus, and Jubilate Deo, Hopkins in A; Apostles' Creed, Harmonized Monotone; Anthem, O Lord, my God (Wesley). Even.: Service, Cantate Deo and Deus Miseratur, Hopkins in A; Apostles' Creed, Harmonized Monotone; Anthem, In the beginning (Kent).

ALL SAINTS, MARGARET STREET.—Morn.: Service, Benedicite (South); Benedictus (Stainer); Holy Communion, Barnby in E; Offertory Anthem, The night is departing. Even.: Service, Lasso in G minor; Anthem, How lovely (Mendelssohn); Dies Iræ (Hoyte).

CHRIST CHURCH, CLAPHAM.—Morn.: Service, Benedicite, Stainer, etc.; Kyrie Credo, and Sanctus, Smart in F; Benedictus, and Agnus Dei, Eyre in A flat; Communion, Hail, Thou living bread (Foster); Gloria in excelsis (Smart). Even.: Service, Magnificat and Nunc Dimittis, Tuckerman in F; Anthem, Send out Thy light (Gounod); Dies Iræ (Dykes).

HOLY TRINITY, GRAY'S INN ROAD. — Morn.: Service, Te Deum, Goss in A; Jubilate, Chanted; Nicene Creed, Percival in C; Offertory Sentences (Grainger). Even.: Service, Magnificat, Chanted; Nunc Dimittis, Tours in F; Anthem, How lovely are the messengers (Mendelssohn).

ST. JAMES'S PRIVATE EPISCOPAL CHAPEL, SOUTHWARK. —Morn.: Service, Introit, The grace of God (Barnby); Communion Service, Second Mass (Gounod). Even.: Service, Barnby in E; Anthem, Rise up, arise, and Sleepers, wake (Mendelssohn).

ST. MARY BOLTONS, WEST BROMPTON, S.W.—Morn.: Service, Benedicite, Turle in D; Benedictus (Turle); Holy Communion, Kyrie, Credo, Sanctus, and Gloria in excelsis, Dykes in F; Benedictus and Agnus Dei (Redhead); Offertory (Barnby). Even.: Service, Magnificat and Nunc Dimittis, Stainer's 3rd Series of Tones; Anthem, The sorrows of death (Mendelssohn).

ST. MATTHEW'S, NEW KENT ROAD.—Anthem, Recit., Comfort ye my people; Solo, Every valley shall be exalted; Chorus, And the glory of the Lord ("Messiah," Handel).

ST. MAGNUS, LONDON BRIDGE.—Morn.: Service, Opening Anthem, To the Lord our God (Reynolds); Te Deum and Jubilate, Cooke in G; Kyrie (Wesley). Even.: Service, Magnificat and Nunc Dimittis, Cooke in G; Anthem, Solo and Chorus, O Thou that tellest (Handel).

ST. MARGARET PATTENS, ROOD LANE, FENCHURCH STREET.—Morn.: Service, Benedicite and Benedictus, "Gregorian"; Offertory Anthem, Incline Thine ear (Hummel); Kyrie, Credo and Gloria in excelsis, Missa di Angelis; Sanctus, Benedictus, and Agnus Dei (Bordese). Evensong.: Service, Magnificat and Nunc Dimittis, "Gregorian"; Anthem, The sorrows of death (Mendelssohn).

ST. MICHAEL'S, CORNHILL. — Morn.: Service, Te Deum and Benedictus Dykes in F; Anthem, Awake, awake (Wise); Kyrie and Creed, Wesley in E. Even.: Service, Magnificat and Nunc Dimittis, Walmisley in D minor; Anthem, Prepare ye the way (Wise).

ST. PAUL'S, AVENUE ROAD, SOUTH HAMPSTEAD.—Morn.: Service, Bededicite, 8th Tone; Benedictus (Goss); Kyrie (Merbecke); Offertory Sentences (Barnby); Credo, Sanctus, and Gloria in excelsis (Merbecke). Even.: Service, Magnificat and Nunc Dimittis (Helmore); Anthems, Now we are ambassadors, and How lovely are the messengers ("St. Paul," Mendelssohn). After Service, "Dies Iræ" (Dykes).

ST. PAUL'S, BOW COMMON, E.—Morn.: Service, Benedicite Stainer, Winn and Walker; Benedictus (Walker); Holy Communion, Kyrie, Credo, Sanctus, and Gloria in excelsis, Dykes in F; Benedictus (Redhead); Offertory (Stainer). Even.: Service, Magnificat and Nunc Dimittis, Dykes in F; Anthem, O that I knew where I might find Him (Bennett).

ST. AUGUSTINE AND ST. FAITH, OLD CHANGE.—Morn.: Service, Benedicite (Best); Benedictus, Tours in F; Offertory Anthem, Enter not into judgment (Attwood); Communion Service, Tours in F. Even.: Service, Rogers in D; Anthem, The sorrows of death (Mendelssohn).

ST. BARNABAS, MARYLEBONE.—Morn.: Service, Benedicite, Hoyte in D; Benedictus, Dykes in F; Anthem, Sleepers wake (Mendelssohn); Kyrie and Creed, Wesley in F. Even.: Service, Magnificat and Nunc Dimittis, Wesley in F; Anthem, The grace of God (Barnby); Die Iræ (Hoyte).

ST. PETER'S (EATON SQUARE).—Morn.: Service, Benedicite, Best in C. Even.: Service, Clarke-Whitfeld in B; Anthem, As pants the hart (Spohr).

ST. PETER'S, LEIGHAM COURT ROAD, STREATHAM, S.W.—Morn.: Service, Gregorian, throughout; Holy Eucharist, Asperges (Novello); Introit and Gradual (Chantwise); Mass, Kyrie, Credo and Sanctus, Arnold in B minor; Benedictus and Agnus Dei (Carnall in B minor); Offertory, Communion and Post Communion. [Even.: Service, Magnificat on 6th Tone (Sheppard); Nunc Dimittis, Comfort ye (Handel).

ST. PETER'S, VERE STREET, W.—Even.: Service, Magnificat and Nunc Dimittis, Garrett in F; Anthem, The Lord is my lamp (Benedict).

ST. SAVIOUR'S, HOXTON. — Morn.: Service, Te Deum, Hopkins in G; Holy Communion; Kyrie, Credo, Sursum Corda, Sanctus, and Gloria in excelsis, Dykes in F. Even.: Service, Magnificat and Nunc Dimittis (Best); Anthem, The night is far spent (Smith).

ST. SEPULCHRE'S, HOLBORN. — Morn.: Service, Benedicite, Best in C; Jubilate, Sullivan in D; Kyrie and Credo, Lott in F. Anthem, The Lord gave the word (Handel). Even.: Service, Magnificat and Nunc Dimittis, Cooke in G; Anthem, The wilderness (Goss).

Country.

ST. ASAPH CATHEDRAL.—Morn.: Service, Goss in A; Anthem, Sing of judgment (Mendelssohn). Even.: Service, The Litany; Anthem, Prepare ye the way (Garrett).

ASHBURNE CHURCH, DERBYSHIRE. — Morn.: Service, Boyce in C; Kyrie, Credo, and Gloria, Martin in C. Even.: Service, Goss in E; Anthem, Send out Thy light (Gounod).

BELFAST (ST. GEORGE'S). — Morn.: Service, Benedicite Best in C; Benedictus, Woodward in E flat; Anthem, Comfort ye, And the glory ("Messiah," Handel); Dies Iræ (Dykes); Offertory (Monk). Even.: Service, Magnificat and Nunc Dimittis, Arnold in A; Anthem, Now we are ambassadors, and How lovely are the messengers ("St. Paul," Mendelssohn).

BIRMINGHAM (S. ALBAN THE MARTYR).—Morn.: Service Te Deum, and Benedictus, Goss in A; Holy Communion Woodward in E flat. Evensong: Magnificat and Nunc Dimittis, Bunnett in F.

BIRMINGHAM (ST. MICHAEL'S, HAWORTH).—Morn.: Service, Benedicite (Best); Benedictus (Stainer); Communion (Garrett); Introit, Sleepers, wake (Mendelssohn). Even.: Service, Magnificat and Nunc Dimittis (Stainer); Anthem, O thou that tellest (Handel).

CANTERBURY CATHEDRAL. — Morn.: Service, Rogers in D.; Anthem, Our conversation is in heaven (Gilbert); Communion, Rogers in D. Even.: Service, Goss in E; Anthem, O where shall wisdom be found (Boyce).

CARLISLE CATHEDRAL.—Morn.: Service, Benedicite (Best); Introit, Blessed is the man (Stainer); Kyrie and Nicene Creed, Best in G. Even.: Service Prout in D; Anthem, The voice of one crying (Garrett).

CHESTER (ST. MARY'S CHURCH).—Morn.: Service, Oakeley in E flat; Communion Service, Tuckerman in F. Even.: Service, Cooke in G; Anthem, If with all your hearts, Lord God of Abraham, Isaac and Israel, and He that shall endure to the end ("Elijah" Mendelssohn).

DONCASTER (PARISH CHURCH).—Morn.: Service, Tours in F; Introit, Sleepers, wake (Mendelssohn). Even.: Service, Tours in F; Anthem, In that day (Elvey).

DUBLIN, ST. PATRICK'S (NATIONAL) CATHEDRAL.—Morn.: Service, Te Deum and Jubilate, Boyce in C; Holy Communion, Kyrie, and Creed and Sanctus, King in C; Anthem, Thus saith the Lord ("Messiah" Handel). Even.: Service, Magnificat and Nunc Dimittis, Smart in B flat; Anthem, Hosanna to the Son of David (Gibbons); and Rejoice in the Lord ("The Bell Anthem" Purcell).

EDINBURGH (ST. JOHN'S).—Aft.: Service, Anthem, O rest in the Lord, and He that shall endure (Mendelssohn). Even.: Service, Anthem, Rejoice in the Lord (Purcell).

EDINBURGH (ST. MARY'S CATHEDRAL).—Morn.: Service, Chants. Aft.: Service, Goss in E; Anthem, This is the record (Gibbons). Even.: Service, Chants; Anthem, From the rising of the sun (Ouseley).

ELY CATHEDRAL. — Morn.: Service, Benedicite, Chants; Jubilate, Plain-song; Kyrie, and Credo, Roberts in D; Gloria, Monk in A; Anthem, Sleepers, wake (Mendelssohn). Even.: Service, Roberts in D; Anthem, The voice of one crying, Prepare ye (Garrett).

EXETER CATHEDRAL.—Morn.: Service, Ouseley in B minor; Communion, Ouseley in B minor. Even.: Service, Ouseley in B minor; Anthem, Praise His awful name (Spohr).

FOLKESTONE (ST. MICHAEL'S). — Morn.: Service, Kyrie, Credo, Sanctus and Gloria in excelsis (Bordèse). Even.: Service, Magnificat and Nunc Dimittis, Attwood in C; Anthem, They that go down to the sea in ships (Attwood).

LEEDS PARISH CHURCH—Morn.: Service, Mendelssohn in A; Anthem, How beautiful (Handel); Introit, Sleepers, wake (Mendelssohn); Kyrie and Creed, Turle in D; Even.: Service, Attwood in A; Anthem, The sorrows of death (Mendelssohn).

LLANDAFF CATHEDRAL.—Morn.: Service, Benedicite, Brooksbank in F; Jubilate, Smart in A; Introit. It is high time to awake (Barnby); Holy Communion, Prout in F. Even.: Service, The Litany; Anthem, Hosanna (Stainer).

LICHFIELD CATHEDRAL. — Morn.: Service, Walmisley in F; Communion Service, Walmisley in F; Anthem, O how amiable are Thy dwellings (Barnby). Even.: Service, Attwood in F; Anthem, He shall feed His flock, and All we like sheep (Handel).

LIVERPOOL CATHEDRAL. — Aft.: Service, Magnificat and Nunc Dimittis, Garrett in D; Anthem, Prepare ye the way of the Lord (Wise).

MANCHESTER CATHEDRAL.—Morn.: Service, Te Deum and Jubilate, Pyne in D; Kyrie, Creed, Sanctus, and Gloria Pyne in A flat; Anthem, He that shall endure (Mendelssohn). Aft.: Service, Behold a virgin (Handel).

MANCHESTER (ST. BENEDICT'S).—Morn.: Service, Kyrie and Credo, Nares in F; Sanctus, Benedictus, and Agnus Dei "Æterna Christi Munera" (Palestrina). Even.: Service, Magnificat and Nunc Dimittis, "Gregorian."

MANCHESTER (ST. JOHN BAPTIST, HULME).—Morn.: Service, Benedicite (Marbecke); Kyrie, Credo, Sanctus, Benedictus, Agnus Dei and Gloria in excelsis, Cobb. Even.: Service, Magnificat and Nunc Dimittis, "Gregorian"; Dies Iræ (Dykes).

PETERBOROUGH CATHEDRAL.—Morn.: Service, Hopkins in A; Anthem, Listen, O Isles (Allen); Communion Service, Barnby in E. Even.: Service, Litany; Anthem, Lauda Sion (Mendelssohn).

SALISBURY CATHEDRAL—Morn.: Service, Walmisley in D; Offertory (Stainer). Aft.: Service, Walmisley in D; Anthem, Comfort ye (Handel).

SHEFFIELD PARISH CHURCH. — Morn.: Service, Kyrie Hiles in G. Even.: Service, Cantate Domine and Deus, Misereatur, Chants; Anthem, When the son of man (Kent).

SHERBORNE ABBEY. — Morn.: Service, Chants; Kyrie, Smart in G; Offertories (Barnby). Even.: Service, Chants; Anthem, Prepare ye the way (Garrett).

SOUTHAMPTON (ST. MARY'S CHURCH).—Morn.: Service, Te Deum, Whitfeld in E; Benedictus (Chant); Holy Communion, Introit, Drop down ye heavens (Macfarren); Service, Custard in E flat; Offertory, Let him (Barnby); Paternoster (Field). Even.: Service, Magnificat and Nunc Dimittis, Russell in A; Apostles' Creed, Harmonized Monotone; Anthem, O rest in the Lord, and He that shall endure (Mendelssohn).

WELLS CATHEDRAL—Morn.: Service, Hodges in C; Introit, The Lord is my light (Macfarren); Kyrie, Browne in G. Even.: Service, Rogers in G; Anthem, It shall come to pass (Gilbert).

WIMBORNE MINSTER. — Morn.: Service, Garrett in F; Anthem, Now we are ambassadors, and How lovely are the messengers; Offertory Sentences (Monk). Even.: Service, Kent in D.

WINCHESTER CATHEDRAL.—Morn.: Service, Smart in F; Creed, Arnold in B minor. Even.: Service, Smart in F; Anthem, Behold, a virgin (Handel).

WORCESTER CATHEDRAL.—Morn.: Service, Lloyd in E flat; Anthem, Listen, O isles (Allen). Even.: Service, Hopkins in A; Anthem, Thus saith the Lord (Handel).

NOTICE.—All communications intended for the Editor are to be sent to his private address. Business communications to be addressed to 185, Fleet Street, E.C.

NOTICE TO CORRESPONDENTS.—J. J. F., and J. S. McArthur received. The article was built upon corresponding statements in the Times. I fear it is not possible to continue the controversy as it has drifted away from musical matters. However, I will consider the position fully.—ED. Mus. Stand.

APPOINTMENT.

Mr. J. HERBERT OLDING, A.C.O., has been appointed Organist to St. Stephen's Church, Grove Road, Clapham Park, S.W.

Printed for the Proprietor by BOWDEN, HUDSON & Co., at 23, Red Lion Street, Holborn, London, W.C.; and Published by WILLIAM REEVES, at
the Office, 185, Fleet Street, E.C. West End Agents :—WEEKES & CO., 14, Hanover Street, Regent Street, W. Subscriptions and Advertisements are
received either by the Publisher or West End Agents.—Communications for the EDITOR are to be forwarded to his private address, 6, Argyle Square, W.C.
SATURDAY, DECEMBER 15, 1883.—Entered at the General Post Office as a Newspaper.

The MUSICAL STANDARD

A NEWSPAPER FOR MUSICIANS PROFESSIONAL AND AMATEUR

No. 1,012, VOL. XXV. FOURTH SERIES. SATURDAY, DECEMBER 22, 1883. WEEKLY: PRICE 3D.

THE LATE SIGNOR MARIO.

Giuseppe Mario Marchese di Candia, who died at Rome after a short illness on Tuesday evening, December 11th, was born according to some accounts at Turin in 1808 or 1810, and to other accounts at Genoa in 1812 or 1814, but according to his own account at Cagliari in 1810. His father was a general in the Piedmontese army and afterwards governor of Nice. The young Italian commenced his military career by joining the Sardinian Chasseurs de la Garde, then garrisoned at Genoa, and having been detained at Cagliari on suspicion of some political intrigue he resigned his commission; but upon his resignation being refused, he escaped and made his way to Paris in 1836. As a youth he had studied music at the Turin Royal Academy, and his success as an amateur had been superb, but at this stage of events being offered an engagement by M. Daponchel, then manager of the Paris Opéra at 1,500 francs a month, he determined to try his fortune as a dramatic singer. He therefore underwent a course of study with Professor Bordogni for singing, and Ponchard for French pronunciation. He then assumed the *nom de théâtre* of Mario. He appeared first in 1838 as Rambaldo in Meyerbeer's "Robert le Diable," and although his refinement of manner, elegant appearance, and charm of voice were conspicuous qualities, yet with these were associated little or no stage experience, a certain *nonchalance*, and a total absence of dramatic power, and his French pronunciation was marked by his native Italian accent.

Théophile Gautier describes his voice as a genuine tenor of considerable extent, reaching to the B and C of the chest, attacking the notes freely and holding them well; his passages from one register to another were executed with facility, only that at points where power is required the high chest notes became deficient in fulness and slightly guttural. Mario soon realised the fact that he was not in his proper element in French opera; and therefore he joined the company of the Théâtre des Italiens, in which he at once made his mark in the midst of a magnificent assemblage of singers, including Tamburini, Lablache, Malibran, Sontag, Persiani, and Grisi. He made his *début* at this theatre as Nemorino in Donizetti's "L'Elisire D'Amore," in which opera he was supported by Persiani as Adina, Tamburini as Belcore, and Lablache as Dottore Dulcamara. In London he appeared for the first time in 1840 as Gennaro in Donizetti's "Lucrezia Borgia," and it is written of him that his acting did not at that time go beyond that of a Southern man with a strong feeling for the stage.

From 1840 onwards for many years Mario sang alternately at the Théâtre des Italiens at Paris and Her Majesty's Theatre in London, forming after the retirement of Rubini and Sontag, a member of that celebrated quartet which consisted of himself, Grisi, Tamburini, and Lablache, and for which Donizetti expressly wrote the "Don Pasquale." It is worthy of note that his first success was made in 1842 at the Theatre Royal, Dublin, where he sang with Grisi and Lablache; the latter was at the time co-director with Tamburini of the Théâtre des Italiens at Paris. Rubini was making most extravagant demands for the renewal of his engagement, and after Mario's first night in Dublin, Lablache despatched a special messenger to Paris authorising Tamburini to refuse Rubini's extortionate terms, as a tenor had been found to take his place. He remained at Her Majesty's Theatre until 1846, at which period occurred the rupture with Mr. Lumley and the secession from his management, to which circumstance the Royal Italian Opera owes its establishment. At the last mentioned house Mario resumed the dramatic parts or those of the grand opera, and it was here that his dramatic genius developed itself,

instances of which may be remembered in the Raoul of "Gli Ugonotti," and the Giovanni di Leyden, of "Il Profeta" of Meyerbeer. Fernando in Donizetti's "La Favorita" was another of his splendid creations.

In 1848 he sang in the "Stabat Mater" in company with Grisi and Alboni, and his rendering of the "Cujus Animam" must be green in the memory of many opera-goers.

In the season of 1850 the minor part of Rambaldo in "Roberto il Diavolo" was invested by him with unwonted importance; and although associated with an unparalleled cast, namely, Tamberlik as Roberto, Grisi as Alice, Castellan as Isabella, and Formes as Bertramo, it is said that his part was the gem of the opera. In 1851 the *rôle* of "Don Giovanni" transposed for him into a higher key proved a comparative failure.

During the opera season he occasionally appeared at concerts, and he has been heard in English ballads, as "Good-bye, sweetheart," and "I strive to forget thee." He also sang the tenor solos in the "Elijah" at the Birmingham (1849) and Hereford (1855) Festivals.

As an actor Mario was always the accomplished gentleman, his Almaviva, even when acting the roysterer, being never vulgar. At first the great tenor was merely a young nobleman with a "vox et praeterea nihil," but he possessed to the full a capacity for taking pains, which as Carlyle has said is the "essential element of genius"; his bearing was gallant, his presence handsome, his voice exquisite and under the most perfect control, his mezza-voce delightful, and he was possessed of a fine artistic instinct. On the stage he was always *picturesque*; whether as the peasant Nemorino, the fisherman Masaniello, or the gorgeously apparelled prophet-king, he delighted the artistic eye. He undoubtedly excelled in certain characters, such as Faust, Raoul, Fernando, and Romeo. His voice could hardly be called a tenore robusto, but rather a tenore con grazia of the quality termed *argentine*, having extreme power of modulation and with sufficient vigour upon emergency; but its greatest charm consisted in delicate passages, of which the "Ah! dillo ancor tu m'ami," of the grand duet in the "Huguenots," with its beautiful ascent to the high C flat is a typical instance. He was clearly the best opera-lover ever seen. His articulation was most distinct, his phrasing full of meaning, and the beauty and smoothness of his melodies unsurpassed. He represented to the present generation the traditions of an historic era in the development of the lyric stage, and he was the sole survivor of a group of artists probably never to be approached in excellence.

During the time Mario occupied the operatic boards he stood alone. Great singers of the other sex have appeared in succession: Grisi, Jenny Lind, Viardot, Bosio, Piccolomini, Lucca, Patti, Titiens, Nilsson; but no tenor with the single exception of Giuglini (who was far behind him as an actor), in the union of dramatic and lyrical qualities, could claim to be his rival.

His association with the famous prima donna, Giulia Grisi, had unquestionably a direct and potent influence in the development of his dramatic powers. Courteous, affable, good-natured, and generous to a fault, he was beloved by all, from the humblest employé at the theatre to those of the highest rank. The public not only recognised in him the artist, they went still further, and delighted to call themselves his friends, and numbers who never shook his hand or exchanged with him a single word, have received the news of his death with more than a passing sorrow.

His name and reputation will remain in the history of the opera for all time.

Mario retired from the stage on July 19th, 1871,

choosing the character of Fernando for his farewell representation. Inspired by the occasion, he recovered much of his old fire, and his impersonation was manly and pathetic in the highest degree. At the end of 1871 the Marchese di Candia went to Rome, accepting the curatorship of a museum, a post congenial to his tastes since he delighted in pictures and all artistic work, and his last years were occupied in philological and archæological pursuits.

Although it has been stated that during his career Mario must have received large sums of money, yet from his lordly ways and extreme generosity he left the stage in comparatively straitened circumstances. Two subscriptions were raised for him since his retirement, and a concert was given for his benefit at St. James's Hall, in May, 1878, in which Nilsson, Trebelli, and Santley took part, and which proved a brilliant success.

The house in which this celebrated artist breathed his last was in the Via Ripetta, having in its front a terrace hung with flowers and overlooking the Tiber. He was buried on Dec. 13th, and it is stated that his remains will be eventually laid in the ancestral vault at Cagliari. His funeral was attended by Signor Mancini, the Marchese di Villamarina, Prince Odescalchi, the President of the Artists' Club, and numerous other notabilities. Mr. W. G. Cusins, Master of the Music to the Queen, was also present as Her Majesty's representative, and in her name placed a wreath of flowers upon the coffin, upon which among a number of other wreaths was one from the English visitors at Rome. ARMAND SEMPLE.

Musical Intelligence.

CRYSTAL PALACE CONCERTS.

PROGRAMME.

Symphony in D, No. 2 of the Salomon Series	Haydn.
Recit. and Air, " Softly sighs " (" Der Freischütz ") ..	Weber.
Miss Thudichum.	
Concerto for pianoforte and orchestra in F minor (Op. 49)	Dupont.
(First time of performance in England.)	
Mdme. Frickenhaus.	
Liebeslied, " Winterstürme wichen den Wonnemond "	Wagner
(" Die Walküre ")	
Herr Georg Ritter.	
Two Orchestral Sketches, " The Ebbing Tide," and	Barnett.
Elfland "	
Songs, " Better far," and " There is dew for the	Cowen.
flow'ret "	
Miss Thudichum.	
Capriccio in F sharp minor (Op. 5)	Mendelssohn.
Mdme. Frickenhaus.	
Song, " The Erl King "	Schubert.
Herr Georg Ritter.	
Overture, " Leonore," No. 3	Beethoven.
Conductor - - - AUGUST MANNS.	

All musicians know how infinitely indebted we stand to " Papa " Haydn for changing the monotonous contrapuntal style of orchestral music into what is called the melodic thematic, pursuing one thought or theme through all the shades and intricacies of which it is susceptible, and causing it to represent every possible alternation of feeling. " Secondary subjects " are also derived from it, and unity of design and constant variety are exchanged for pedagogic display and pedantic ostentation. The above symphony, though numbered second, was really the first of the Salomon set, and was performed in London on March 11th, 1791, conducted by Haydn himself. Although the orchestra has been greatly developed since his day, there is still a charm about his writings which makes them as welcome as the flowers of May, and Mr. Manns does well in reminding us that *dramatic* music can occasionally be dispensed with.

Dupont was educated at the Conservatoire at Liège—the birthplace of Grétry—and is now professor of the pianoforte at Brussels. His concerto in F minor is a remarkably clever work, and made a favourable impression, but the themes are overcrowded and individual development to any extent becomes impossible. The orchestra, as is usual with the new school, is the most important part and the piano is at times heard bravely struggling against a gorgeous mist of dramatic effect. The slow movement is an exception. Here the horns and the pianoforte are heard discoursing in a very lovely manner. It is a work that should not be passed over with a few words only, but a second hearing is necessary before giving a decided opinion upon it, and judging by the hearty applause that followed each movement, another opportunity will probably be afforded of treating it more in detail. Too much praise cannot be given to Mdme. Frickenhaus for the part she took in it.

Mr. J. F. Barnett's two sketches are very descriptive of the "Ebbing Tide" and "Elfland." Mr. Barnett sometimes makes excursions beyond his own province, as he did a short time since in "finishing" Schubert's barely sketched symphony, but on this occasion he has had the good sense to undertake a much easier task, and the hand of the master is clearly visible even in these unpretending pieces. The second was re-demanded.

Miss Thudichum was heard to great advantage in Weber's air, and Herr Ritter was especially good in the "Erl King."

Beethoven's grand overture " Leonore No. 3," fittingly closed the Saturday concerts for 1883. The *connoisseurs* who waited to the end for this, were amply rewarded. The next concert of this series will not take place till Saturday, Feb. 16th, 1884. R. S.

Another contributor writes:—

I must speak in guarded and qualified terms of the new pianoforte concerto. "Extension," the usual fault of the modern school, is certainly to be noticed in this case. The first movement, an adagio in D flat, struck me as weak, vague, rambling, and rather dreary, although well "laid out " for the pianoforte and the orchestral score. The *finale*, brisk and rhythmical, affords amplest scope for energetic execution on the part of the soloist, but it is after all but a series of national dance tunes. All the three movements are in common time. M. Dupont is a Belgian of mature age, 55 years. His interpreter, an Englishwoman, well known at the "Popular concerts," played with great power and decision of purpose. I did not wait for the solo—no favourite of mine—in F sharp minor. The beautiful air from " Die Walküre," not very effectively rendered, made no apparent impression upon the common herd of auditors, to whom it was probably *caviare*. The gallery was rather thinly occupied ; only two critics sat near me, and one of these soon disappeared. The second "sketch" of Mr. J. F. Barnett won an *encore*. Haydn's symphony was a great treat to musicians of catholic mind who still think that *order* is " heaven's first law," however warmly they may admire the erratic excursions of fiery geniuses that move in orbits of very eccentric ellipse. A. M.

SATURDAY POPULAR CONCERTS.

PROGRAMME.

Quartet in C major (Op. 59), No. 3, for two violins,	Beethoven.
viola, and violoncello	
Mdme. Norman-Néruda, MM. L. Ries, Straus and Piatti.	
Air, " Adelaide "	Beethoven.
Mr. Edward Lloyd.	
Novellette in B major (Op. 21), No. 7, Novellette in	Schumann.
A major (Op. 21), No. 6, and Traumeswirren, for	
pianoforte alone	
Miss Agnes Zimmermann.	
Follia, for violoncello, with pianoforte accompaniment	Piatti.
Signor Piatti.	
Air, " When the orb of day " (" Euryanthe ")..	Weber.
Mr. Edward Lloyd.	
Trio in B flat (Op. 99), for pianoforte, violin and	Schubert.
violoncello	
Miss Agnes Zimmermann, Mdme. Norman-Néruda, and	
Signor Piatti.	
Accompanist - - Signor Romili.	

When the first part of the opening Allegro in the above Quartet had about half run its course at last week's concert, things came to a sudden standstill, owing to the breaking of a string on Herr Straus's instrument. Some considerable time elapsed before the artist reappeared, having repaired the mischief. The allegro was then begun again from the beginning, the introduction being omitted ; and this time all went well.

Signor Piatti's invaluable services are so thoroughly recognised, that when he comes forward as soloist the audience never fails to express its gratitude by loading him with honour. His "Follia."—a re-arrangement of an air by Geminiani—was introduced at a recent Monday concert. As an encore, he played a delightful arrangement of one of Mendelssohn's (posthumous) "Songs without Words," with great tenderness and expression. Signor Romili, who was for the first time accompanist at a Saturday concert, though he is not a stranger to the Monday audience, showed much tact in his accompaniment of the "Lied." If not quite an ideal accompanist, he is at least thoroughly at home in his seat at the piano, and has both discretion and animation to recommend him.

Mr. Lloyd's rendering of "Adelaida," gave universal satisfaction. The last verse of the sweet, purely-melodious song from "Euryanthe," was repeated, as an encore.

Miss Zimmermann played the two novelettes with both intellectual and physical grasp of her subject: the "Phantasiestück (Traumes-wirren)," was not so well suited to her style and capabilities; one missed the exquisite lightness of touch, giving an airy nothingness to the "dream," the slight, scarcely perceptible ritenute at the eighth bar, and other points that Mdme. Schumann has taught us to look for and appreciate in this graceful and spontaneous little composition.

Schubert's noble trio was interpreted in an entirely satisfactory manner. May we be allowed a hearing of its companion in E flat before the season is over.

B. F. WYATT-SMITH.

___

THE MUSICAL ARTISTS' SOCIETY.

The 30th performance of new compositions by the Musical Artists' Society, took place last Saturday evening (Dec. 15th), at Aberdeen House, Argyll Street.

PROGRAMME.

Quartet in C major, for two violins, viola, and
  violoncello .... Adler.
      Herr J. Rosenthal, Mr. E. Halfpenny, Mr. W. H. Hann,
          ; and Mr. Edmund Woolhouse.
Scena, "Medea in Corinto" .... Gear.
      (The orchestral accompaniment arranged for pianoforte).
                  Miss Edith Ruthven.
Sonata Piacevole (Op. 25), for flute and pianoforte ... Stephens.
  Herr Oluf Svendsen, and Mr. Charles E. Stephens.
Songs, "The rainy day," and "Stay, stay at home, my
  heart, and rest" .... Bailey.
                  Miss Kate Heath.
Quintet (MS.), in E flat, for pianoforte, two violins,
  viola, and violoncello, with vocal quartet ..... Gilbert.
    Mr. Alfred Gilbert, Herr J. Rosenthal, Mr. E. Halfpenny,
      Mr. W. H. Hann, and Mr. Edmund Woolhouse.
    Vocalists :—Miss Josephine Pulham, Miss Eames, Mr.
          Henry Brine, and Mr. Stanley Smith.
Sacred Cantata, "By the Waters of Babylon" .... Cole.
  Conductor   -   -   -   Mr. J. PARRY COLE.

The first work on the list, a string quartet in C, by F. Adler (alias Mrs. Swinburne) has the usual fault of essayists at this difficult style of composition, namely, want of concentration, and incoherence in the development of themes. A vocal scena, "Medea in Corinto," by Mr. George Gear, sung by Miss E. Ruthven, is a very effective piece; the orchestral accompaniment has been "arranged" for the pianoforte. A pianoforte quintet by Mr. Alfred Gilbert was omitted, for reasons unknown to the writer. Mr. J. Parry Cole's sacred cantata, "By the Waters of Babylon," pleased some connoisseurs, but struck others as a réchauffé of old ideas, already "used up." The cantata includes solos, quartets, choruses, and double choruses. The vocalists were Misses J. Pulham, K. Brooks, and Eames, Mrs. Susanna Cole, Messrs. E. Levetus, H. Brine, Lansmere, and Stanley Smith. A select band of strings and pianoforte accompanied the vocal score. Mr. Parry Cole conducted.

The signal success of the soirée was achieved by Mr. Charles E. Stephens, treasurer of the Philharmonic Society, who introduced a new "Sonata Piacevole" for flute and pianoforte, in F major. Mr. H. W. Carte, anxious to display the qualities and capabilities of the modern flute, which (as he shows) has changed in a short time from a very imperfect, to a perfect orchestral wind instrument, invites several eminent composers to write flute sonatas, and Mr. C. E. Stephens comes forward the first. This sonata comprises three movements, an allegro grazioso in F ; a Romanza (andante con moto) in B flat, and a molto vivo (alla Tarantella) in F. The sonata is sprightly, melodious, and strictly orthodox in form, whilst the spécialité of introducing in the finale repetitions of the first theme of the opening movement. The rhythm of this subject is slightly changed when repeated, and thus the composer verges on "metamorphosis of theme." The Romance in B flat is exquisitely melodious and graceful. The whole work, bright and genial as the composer's own soul—always "dreaming of happiness"—has the pleasantly exhilarating effects of an excursion through charming and picturesque country on a slightly breezy day. The performance was perfect. Mr. Stephens played the pianoforte part with animation and brilliancy, whilst Mr. Oluf Svendsen fully sustained his well-earned reputation. In the last movement occur most ingenious combinations of the first and second subjects; also of the "Tarantella" theme with the first subject of the opening movement.

Another contributor, of high authority, eulogises Mr. Stephens's sonata as "an enjoyable, elegiac, refined and scholarly work, well written for the wood-wind instrument, and giving it as much to do as the thing is capable of." The writer adds that the sonata was "charmingly played."

Hector Berlioz, in his invaluable book on orchestration, defends the flute from the charge of an alleged inferiority as regards its power of expression; admitting, of course, its impotence to equal the "artless gaiety" of the hautboy or the "noble tenderness" of the clarionet. Berlioz boldly asserts that the flute has an unrivalled aptitude for rendering certain sentiments, as, for example, in an air written to express the accent of devotion, modified by humility and resignation. He cites a movement in D minor from the "Elysian Fields" scena in Gluck's "Orfeo," where the hautboy would have been too puerile, the corno inglese too low, and the clarionet rather too powerful. The flute, in Gluck's score, moves (in D minor) mainly above the lines, and holds high A natural ; the range is from A to F in alt. Beautiful examples of two flutes playing in the medium register successions of thirds in A flat or in E flat can be found in the operas "Œdipus" and the "Vestale." Gluck, and also Weber, have shown what may be done with the low sounds of the flute. Thus, in Agatha's scena from "Der Freischütz" two flutes move in thirds from low D to A, when the girl is contemplating the beauty of the night.

A. M.

___

MONDAY POPULAR CONCERTS.

The 13th concert of the season on Monday evening was the last before Christmas.

PROGRAMME.

Part I.

Quartet in A minor, Op. 29, for two violins, viola,
  and violoncello .... Schubert.
    Mdme. Norman-Néruda, MM. L. Ries, Straus, and Piatti.
Songs, "Du bist wie eine Blume," and "Ich grolle
  nicht" .... Schumann.
                  Mr. Santley.
Sonata in G minor, Op. 22, for pianoforte alone .... Schumann.
              M. Vladimir de Pachmann.

Part II.

Song, "Noel" .... Gounod.
                  Mr. Santley.
          Violin obbligato, Mdme. Norman-Néruda.
Trio in C minor, Op. 9, No. 3, for violin, viola, and
  violoncello .... Beethoven.
    Mdme. Norman-Néruda, Herr Straus, and Signor Piatti.
          Accompanist   -   -   Signor Romilo.

Schubert's quartet, first played by Joachim in 1859, has long served as a stock piece, and requires no further notice, beyond a bow of respectful recognition. Mdme. Norman-Néruda was at her best and afterwards signalized herself in the obbligato accompaniment to Gounod's very appropriate song. The fourth trio of Beethoven for strings, thought to be his best, detained most of the audience. Harmonists, controversially disposed or not, may notice the use, at the very outset, of a chord of the 6-5 on the subdominant (F minor), the root whereof has given rise to some dry discussions. The "added" sixth on the subdominant in the major mode, has been considered a derived discord of the seventh, with a minor third to the root ; as, in C major, the root of F (the subdominant) would be D, and the seventh, C natural. In this, the minor mode, not only is the third minor, but the fifth imperfect. How Beethoven shocked the pedants and perruques of his day by opening the sonata in E flat, Op. 31, with a 6-5 on the major sub-dominant (A flat) may be remembered with a sardonic smile.

M. de Pachmann excited a furore in the solo sonata, one of Schumann's early "period," and by no means a superior specimen of his genius. The prevalence of the minor mode (nearly all movements were minor last Monday) increases the pervading gloom of the work. The second theme of the first presto (rasch) movement, and the episode in the finale (both in B flat major), are as gleams of sunshine that break out between dark nimbus clouds. In the slow getragen (andantino) theme, delicious was the humouring of the cantabile by the exponent, who produced the most delicate pianos, and, in particular passages, made each separate note, so to speak, tell its own little tale without detriment to the integral idea. A recall ensued, which ended in an encore. M. De Pachmann hereupon chose a peculiar piece, unknown

to many of the *connoisseurs* present in force. This is a
"study" in G by the once famous composer and pianist
Ignace Moscheles, an effective piece of music, *as music*,
and supplying good work for both hands, inasmuch as
strength and decision are required with the left, and a velvet
gossamer touch with the right, for proper execution of the
light fairy runs in the upper register of the instrument.
The double notes were marvellously executed. A second
storm of applause sounded like a demand of the "insa-
tiables" for another piece. Mr. Santley won a *bis* for
"Ich grolle nicht."

On Monday, January 7th, 1884, the concerts will be
resumed, when Mdme. Frickenhaus is to play Beethoven's
Sonata in D minor, and conduct Schumann's pianoforte Quartet in E flat.

MADAME MONTIGNY-REMAURY'S RECITAL.

Madame Montigny-Rémaury's Recital, at Prince's Hall, Piccadilly, on Wednesday, Dec. 12th, drew a select audience. The
scheme (subjoined) was not strictly adhered to, as the lady
suffered from slight indisposition :—

PROGRAMME.

Sonata (Op. 31)	Beethoven.
Sarabande	Bach.
Pièce en Sol	Scarlatti.
Novellette	Schumann.
Preludes, Mazurka and Valse	Chopin.
Passacaille	Handel.
Romance	Rubinstein.
Impromptu Valse	Liszt.
Serenade et Minuet de Don Juan	Thalberg.

Rubinstein and other great pianists are not wont, strictly, to
specify their numbers ; and Madame Montigny-Rémaury allowed
her publisher to print "Sonata, Op. 31," as, if only *one* Sonata
were intended under that title, whereas there are three. As
anticipated, the Sonata in D minor proved to be the selection,
and, admirably was it read throughout, with power and emphasis, grace, *finesse*, and nicest observance of *nuances*, such as
the subscribers to the Musical Union were long accustomed
to note. The "Preludes" of Chopin, and the "Valse," were
well chosen, and charmingly played. Thalberg's piece was
omitted ; but no person of taste would go into mourning on that
account ;—or for Liszt either. Madame Montigny-Rémaury
interpolated the "Lied Ohne Worte" of Mendelssohn in A
minor, called the "Volks Lied ;" and the pretty "Gavotte" in
A, from "Mignon." Many of the auditors, ignorant of pianoforte literature, remained in the hall after the pianist's final
retirement, as if, like Oliver Twist, expecting more ! A grand
"Erard" was used. Mr. Stanley Lucas ably officiated as
manager.

M. DE PACHMANN'S RECITALS.

M. Vladimir de Pachmann held his second Pianoforte Recital
on Wednesday afternoon, when the following programme was
performed :—

Sonata (Op. 27)	Beethoven.
Rondo in A minor (Op. 71)	Mozart.
Aus der Kreisleriana (Op. 16), Nos. 4, 5, and 6, and	
Novellette (Op. 21), No. 7	Schumann.
"Wiegenlied" (by desire)	Henselt.
Rhapsodie, No. 1, (Op. 79)	Brahms.
"Benediction de Dieu"	Liszt.
Valse de Concert	Lamberg.
(Dedicated to M. Pachmann.)	
Nocturne (Op. 37), No. 2 ; Fantasie in F minor (Op. 49) ;	
Etudes, and Tarantella (Op. 43)	Chopin.

The "Sonata" was rendered in a style the most exquisitely
poetical, and occupied about fourteen minutes. The excerpts
from the "Kreisleriana," were in G minor and B flat. "Cradle
Song" of Henselt, in G flat (substituted for Rubinstein's
"Mélancolie,") entranced the assembly—a very large one—and
ought to have won a *bis*. Liszt's fine religious piece, in F sharp
major 'gains' by every repetition. Lamberg's "Valse," in B
minor, sounds rather dull, vague, and undetermined, for the
style of the piece. The "Studies" of Chopin were charmingly
played ; and the second, "a familiar friend," in G flat, was
repeated by desire. The "Tarantelle" wound up the audience
to a pitch of ecstasy. The hall and the orchestra were
crowded. M. De Pachmann will repeat Schumann's "Le
Carnaval" to-day (Dec. 22) at a "Saturday Popular." A. M.

The paralytic seizure which came upon Mr. Frederic
Clay with such awful suddenness, resulted in complete
loss of speech and the use of the limbs on one side. In
these respects no improvement is to be expected for some
little time it is feared ; but as the mischief has not spread,
Sir William Jenner is now confident of the ultimate recovery of his patient ; and it is gratifying to learn there
are signs of improvement, which everyone will rejoice to
hear go to justify this good hope.

THE ROYAL SOCIETY OF MUSICIANS.

The annual performance of the "Messiah" took place on Dec.
14th, at St. James' Hall. The soloists included such excellent
artists as Miss Santley, Miss A. Williams, Miss Hilda Wilson,
Madame Isabel Fassett, Mr. W. H. Cummings, Mr. Brereton,
Mr. H. Jones, and Mr. Lucas Williams. Miss Santley sang very
sweetly, "Rejoice greatly," and "Come unto Him." Miss Hilda
Wilson's contralto voice was very effective in "He was despised,"
and Mr. W. H. Cummings delivered the air, "Behold and see,"
and "But thou didst not leave," with exquisite pathos. Miss A.
Williams and Mr. Cummings sang the soprano and tenor airs of
Part II., and Mr. W. H. Brereton undertook "Why do the nations," etc. Madame Isabel Fassett succeeded admirably in the
air, "He shall feed His flock." The soprani in the choruses were
rather shrill, and the basses made a peculiar "entry" in "For
unto us a child is born," once or twice. Excess of *staccato* must
be noted with disapproval in many of the choruses. Not one
good *piano* can be recorded, but the choir, as a rule, sang in
tune. The first part, which ended with the chorus, "Lift up your
heads," was not over until after ten o'clock. The chorus contained some good material, and the band was made up of well-
known artists. Mr. E. J. Hopkins, Mus.-Doc., presided carefully
and skilfully at the organ, and the conductor was Signor Rai-
degger. Why a foreign musician should have been selected to
conduct the performance of a work Englishmen best know the
traditions of, for a professedly national society, is one of the
mysteries of the art in England, by which the alien is being constantly exalted and benefited to the neglect and loss of the
native professor. Without knowing who are the members of the
Royal Society of Musicians, the writer does know that no large
body of English musicians can exist without counting a dozen or
twenty, or perhaps more native artists who could conduct the
"Messiah" quite as well, doubtless, as the esteemed foreign
teacher who was chosen for this duty the other evening. However, it may be assumed that the committee do not run out
of their way to find aliens to accept pensions, intended,
it may be presumed, for British artists. The soloists did
their work admirably, and it is needless to say how artistically they went through their familiar part, and several parts
chorally ; but speaking generally of the broad effects, the music
was not so happily rendered. In "Let us break their bonds
asunder," for instance, the chorus seemed to be anxious to attach
a practical meaning, not intended by the Scriptural text, to the
words, by trying to escape from the grip of the conductor, and
accompanying instrumentalists. Want of rehearsal may perhaps
be urged, but no important performance should have the excuse
of want of due preparation. Some of the achieved effects were
excellent, however, notwithstanding the too obvious blemishes.
The Royal Society of Musicians is one of those solid, well sustained and carefully nurtured benevolent institutions which do so
much good in our midst, and of which we may so well be proud
of, in keeping with the importance of the institution, a large
and influential audience attended the performance now noticed.

WESTERN MADRIGAL SOCIETY.

On Wednesday, December 12th, the following selection
of music was sung, under the direction of Dr. Bridge :—

Madrigal,	"Sister, awake "	Bateson.
"	"Cynthia, thy song "	Croce.
"	"Fair Shepherd's Queen "	Mossenloll.
Motet,	"Fair is the morn "	Taylor.
Madrigal,	"Hear my prayer "	Haydn.
"	"Oft have I vowed "	Wilbye.
Motet,	"Smile not, fair Amarillis "	Pierson.
"	"Let me careless "	Linley.
Madrigal,	"Hallelujah, hark those voices "	Elvey.
"	"Amarillis, fair as lilies "	Vecchi.
"	"Draw on, sweet night "	Wilbye.
"	"Love wakes and weeps "	Read.
"	"My lady fair doth fly me "	Ferretti.
"	"A Shepherd with his bonny "	Pilkington.
"	"Flow, O my tears "	Bennet.
"	"My bonny Lass "	Morley.

STROLLING PLAYERS' ORCHESTRAL SOCIETY.

The Strolling Players' Amateur Orchestral Society opened
their second season with a concert on Dec. 13th, at St. Andrew's
Hall, Newman Street. The programme was chiefly made up of
orchestral music, for the performance of which the society is
particularly strong, numbering as it does no fewer than 92
players. Vocal music was not neglected, the "Ave Maria," of
Gounod, and other songs by Marzials and Marriott, and a recitative and cavatina from "Ernani," being included in the programme. The vocalists were Miss Annie Marriott, Miss Edith
Millar, and Mr. Hirwen Jones. The orchestra performed with
much precision, generally good attack, and excellent style, Mendelssohn's "Italian" Symphony, besides which the instrumental
portion of the entertainment comprised Handel's Largo in G,
the overture from "William Tell," the ballet music from Gounod's "Faust," and a new grand march, called the "Festmarsch,"
composed expressly for the Society by Herr Otto Standke.
There was a large audience, and it was felt that the society has
a future of much promise.

OXFORD.

On Thursday evening, Dec. 13th, the Oxford Musical Society gave an excellent performance of Handel's "Judas Maccabæus." In the Town Hall. The principal soprano part was taken by Madame Clara West, who had repeatedly to bow in response to the heartiest applause. The other solo parts were well sustained, mostly by local talent ; and the band and chorus acquitted themselves admirably, under their conductor, Mr. R. Horsley. There was a very good attendance.

BRIGHTON.

The following pieces were included in the programme as undertaken by eight of Mr. E. Aguilar's young lady pupils at the Pavilion, Brighton, on Dec. 15th, viz.:—Preamble, Bach ; Prelude and Fugue in E minor, Mendelssohn ; Fantaisie Impromptu, Chopin ; Warum, Schumann ; Aufschwung, Schumann ; Prelude and Fugue in F, Bach ; Sonata quasi Fantasia in C sharp minor, "The Moonlight," Beethoven ; Polish Dance, Scharwenka ; Ballade in A flat, Chopin ; "Invitation pour la Danse, Weber ; Rhapsody (No 1), Brahms ; Marche de Nuit, Gottschalk ; Nocturne in B, Chopin ; Auf Flügeln des Gesanges, Mendelssohn and Liszt ; Rhapsodie Hongroise (No. 2), Liszt ; Etude in A, Thalberg. Mr. Aguilar played the first and last pieces. Mr. Aguilar prefaced the performance by remarking that these essays of pianoforte playing were to be regarded as specimens of ordinary school, or school-room work, as no special preparation had been made. A large audience quite filled the "King's Room," and the performances were all highly creditable. Mr. Aguilar, whose "school" of teaching the instrument is unique and original, may be fairly congratulated on the refined style and excellent command of the keyboard displayed by the pupils. In some cases were noticed a grandeur of style and decision of touch truly remarkable in the case of players so juvenile. The auditors loudly applauded Mr. Aguilar's reading of Bach's "Preamble," and Thalberg's "Study" in A. His recital on Thursday (Dec. 30th), will be noticed next week.

SALISBURY.

The Sarum Choral Society gave their second concert of the season, in the Assembly Rooms, on Tuesday evening, the 15th. Gaul's Sacred Cantata, "The Holy City," was given with full band and chorus. The solo vocalists were—Mrs. Wells, Mrs. Sly, Miss Lily Mullings, Mr. John M. Haydon, and Mr. W. Thomas. The work was very successfully rendered by all concerned, and well received. In the second part, Haydn's Symphony (No 11), in D, was very finely played ; and Mr. Haydon met with much success in the Air " In Native Worth ; " as did also Mr. Thomas, in Pinsuti's "Bedouin Love Song." The concert closed with the overture to "Le Nozze di Figaro." Miss Aylward presided at the pianoforte ; Mr. Wiltshire at the harmonium ; Mr. Gamblin led the orchestra ; and Mr. Aylward again conducted with much ability.

The St. Martin's Choral Society gave a successful concert in the Boys' School-room, on the 13th inst., to a large audience. The first part of the programme was devoted to Mendelssohn's "42nd Psalm," which was well rendered. The second part was a miscellaneous selection of songs and part-songs ; all of which gave much satisfaction. The soloists were Mrs. Nersling, Miss Fowle, Miss Cothen, and Messrs. Bush and Percy Smith. Mr. Alfred Foley was leader of the orchestra, and the Rev. S. E. Davis conducted.

MUSIC IN DUBLIN.

The pupils of the Royal Irish Academy of Music selected for their performance, on the 30th ult., a recital of the music of "La Sonnambula," by Bellini, which was fairly got through ; although at times, it was apparent that the venture was rather too much, especially in the solo parts.—The third concert for this season of the Amateur Orchestral Union took place on the 4th inst. The pieces included overture "Pique Dame," by Suppé ; Suite de Ballet, "Reine de Saba," Gounod ; the Andante movement from Haydn's Symphony in D, and a March "Habt Acht " (Gung'l). Two piano solos, "Gavotte " and "Musette," by Raff, and an "Impromptu," Chopin, were given by Miss Irwin, whose sister, if I mistake not, gave two violin solos, " Spinnerlied," by Drodet, and Mendelssohn's famous violin concerto. Some vocal pieces were also introduced into the programme. The orchestral items were under the guidance of the respected conductor, Mr. W. H. Telford, Mus.Bac.—The Dublin Chamber Music Union gave its third concert for this season on the 8th inst. The artists were the same as on previous occasions ; and amongst the items on the programme were Mendelssohn's Quartet in B minor (the viola part was sustained by Mr. Griffiths, piano solos by Mons. Billet) ; "A theme with variations," (Rubinstein) ; "A la Valse," (St. Saëns) ; concluding with Beethoven's delightful Serenade, in seven movements. The performance in every way, I am informed, quite sustained the high reputation which the Society has gained for the perfect production of select chamber music.

MANCHESTER.

I have to record the first appearance in England—at Mr. Hallé's concert, last week—of Mr. W. J. Winch, the leading American tenor. Mr. Winch, I understand, contemplates remaining some time in England ; and, judging by his reception here, his success is assured. His singing is thoroughly artistic, and his mezza voce especially remarkable.

Signor Patti played a dry and wearisome Concerto of Rubinstein's. The only other item of interest in the programme was one of Dvorak's Rhapsodies.

The Concert Hall is not to collapse. Active friends have come forward and—with a little new blood in the management —a return to the old days of prosperity may be looked for.

C. J. H.

MUSIC AT EDINBURGH.

The Edinburgh Choral Union opened its season this week under most auspicious circumstances. Two excellent concerts were given on Monday and Tuesday evenings, the 10th and 11th inst., in the Music Hall ; the first being orchestral, the second choral. On Monday evening the programme ran as follows :—

PROGRAMME—PART 1.

Overture to "Anacreon"	Cherubini.
Suite in D for strings, " In the Olden Time "	Cowen.
Recitative and air, " Waft her, Angels " ("Jephtha ")	Handel.
Mr. Joseph Maas.	
Symphony in A (" Italian ")	Mendelssohn.

PART 2.

Overture, "King Lear"	Berlioz.
Walther's prize Song, " Die Meistersinger "	Wagner.
Mr. Joseph Maas.	
Introduction to Act III... "Meistersinger"	"
Song, " The Anchor's Weighed "	Braham.
Mr. Joseph Maas.	
Ballad Airs, from " Coppélia "	Délibes.
Conductor	MR. AUGUST MANNS.

It will be seen that several novelties were included. The band, composed, for the most part, of members of the Saturday Crystal Palace orchestra, played magnificently under Mr. Manns' bâton. The evergreen Italian Symphony went splendidly, especially the first movement. Mr. Joseph Maas was the vocalist, and created quite a furore by his singing of "The Anchor's weighed ;" nor was he less successful in "Waft her Angels." On Tuesday, Haydn's "Seasons" was given, and was a great success. Mr. Collinson, the talented organist of St. Mary's Cathedral, who has succeeded Mr. Adam Hamilton as conductor of the Choral Union, assumed the bâton for the first time, and conducted with great care, keeping his forces well in hand. Great credit is due to him for the way in which the choruses were given, the freshness of the voices, and solidity of attack being particularly noticeable. The soloists were—Miss Mary Danes, Mr. Maas, and Mr. Bridson ; and it would have been difficult to have selected three artists who would have rendered the various soli with better taste. Miss Danes' singing was, as usual, most pleasing and painstaking. Mr. Bradley gave good service at the organ, such as it is. It is certainly high time that the Music Hall was provided with a better one.

The third concert took place on Monday evening, the 17th inst., when the following programme was performed :—

PART I.

Overture, " Euryanthe "	Weber.
Serenade for Orchestra (composed for the Birmingham Festival, 1882)	Stanford.
(Conducted by the Composer.)	
Concerto for Pianoforte and Orchestra, No. 1 in C	Beethoven.

PART II.

Symphony in G minor, Op. 43	Bennett.
Solos for Pianoforte—Passacaille, Romance, and Serenade and Minuet, "Don Juan "	Thalberg.
Mdme. Montigny-Rémaury.	
Ballet, "The Dance of the Hours (" La Gioconda")	Ponchielli.

It will be seen that Dr. Villiers Stanford's Serenade in G, for orchestra, written for the Birmingham Festival of last year, was one of the items performed. That this work will greatly add to the reputation of Dr. Stanford, there can be little doubt. It bears the musician's hand throughout, being full of skilful orchestration. The "Scherzo" is very piquant. The composer conducted his own work, and was loudly applauded at the close of it. Madame Montigny-Rémaury made her first appearance in Edinburgh, and met with a most flattering reception. Her rendering of Beethoven's 1st Concerto in C major, was most brilliant ; her touch and execution being alike admirable. She played two or three solos in the second part of the programme. The Romance, by Rubinstein, being very good. Sterndale Bennett's Symphony in G minor, opened the second part of the concert. It was splendidly played ; all the delicate points being brought out with great clearness and finish. We must especially notice the rendering of the charming trio, written for the brass instruments ; it was capitally played. Miss Carlotta Elliot was the vocalist, who was, however, somewhat over-weighted in Handel's song. The " Swallow Song,"—from "Esmeralda,"— was well rendered. Two songs by Cowen call for no comment. Mr. Manns conducted with his usual skill. C. E.

PRESTON.

On Friday evening the Preston Choral Society gave a grand performance of Mendelssohn's "Elijah" in the New Public Hall, before a large and fashionable audience. The vocalists were : Miss Annie Marriott (soprano), Madame Mudie-Bolingbroke (contralto), Mr. Hy. Guy (tenor), Mr. Santley (bass). The chorus consisted of 260 voices ; and the orchestra was occupied by distinguished members of Mr. Charles Hallé's band. Mr. James Tomlinson (organist to the Society) presided at the organ, with great ability, and Signor Risegari ably conducted. Miss Marriott gave the airs and recitatives allotted to her with admirable skill ; her sweet voice, of remarkable compass, being heard to the best advantage. Her best effort of the evening was the air "Hear ye Israel." Madame Bolingbroke fully sustained the high character she has earned as a singer, by the careful rendering of her part. In the air "O Rest in the Lord," her fine contralto voice was heard to perfection, and she secured a well merited encore. Mr. Guy ably rendered the tenor airs. Mr. Santley's singing was beyond all praise, and he was frequently encored. The quartets were given with fine effect, and the choruses left nothing to be desired. The concert was a decided success.—On Friday, Dec. 7th, an organ recital and Sacred Concert were given in Lune Street Chapel. The vocalists were Miss Bessie Holt (of Manchester), and Mr. R. Hilton (principal bass at Westminster Abbey). Mr. T. Hogg presided at the organ, in the absence of Mr. J. Dawber, Mus.Bac., Cantab. Miss Holt sang in a pleasing manner " Let the bright Seraphim " (Handel), and " I know that my Redeemer liveth " (Handel). Mr. Robert Hilton sang "Nazareth" (Gounod), " Arm, arm, ye brave " ("Judas Maccabæus" ; Handel), and sang with Miss Holt the duet, "Graceful consort" ("Creation,"; Haydn). Mr. Hogg rendered, Offertoire in A minor (Batiste), "Fugue in G minor " (Bach), "Sicilian Mariner's Hymn " (Lux) Andante (Dussek), Minuet (Calkin), Communion (Grison), March for the Organ (Dawber). The concert was given in aid of the Wesleyan bazaar, to take place early next year.

BLACKBURN.

The first concert of the ninth season of the Blackburn St. Cecilia Society was given in the Exchange Hall on Monday evening, the 10th inst., and proved to be one of the most successful yet given by the Society.

The programme was a very attractive one, including Dr. Stainer's Cantata, "The Daughter of Jairus," and Sir Arthur Sullivan's "On Shore and Sea,"—together with a miscellaneous selection of songs and orchestral music. The principal vocalists were—Miss Fanny Bristowe (soprano) ; Mr. Seymour Jackson (tenor), and Mr. Higginson (bass) ; and they, without exception, sang the music thoroughly well, while the members of the Society sang the choruses in the Cantatas with great breadth of tone and expression ; the choruses "Awake, thou that sleepest," "The Wailing Chorus," and the final choruses in both cantatas, evincing the greatest care on the part of the choir and conductor to give a correct reading of the music. Henry Leslie's part-song, "Lullaby of Life," was sung with such delicacy and correctness of phrasing, as to gain an unanimous encore,—a most unusual occurrence at these concerts. The band was selected from Charles Hallé's and De Jong's orchestras, and was, therefore, fully au fait with the somewhat trying accompaniments of Sullivan's work ; and the selection in the second part of the concert, Boüillon's " Overture," and the " Love Song " of Taubert, were beautifully rendered. Miss Bristowe received an encore for her singing of Bevignani's "La Floria ;" and Mr. Higginson sang Gounod's "Nazareth" in a very satisfactory manner. Mr. James H. Rooks (of Bradford), the Society's conductor, deserves the highest praise, for the able manner in which he fulfilled his onerous duties ; much of the success of the concert being due to his untiring energy and tact. The attendance was large and brilliant.

BROMPTON.—At the Trevor Congregational Church, Trevor Square, Brompton, a performance of sacred music in aid of the repairs fund took place on Dec. 6th. The selections were taken from the two oratorios of Mendelssohn's "Elijah" and Handel's "Messiah." The principal vocalists by whom they were sustained were as follows :—Miss Annie E. Taylor, R.A.M. ; Mrs. Joseph Somes, Miss Annie Layton, the Rev. J. J. Goundry, Mus.Bac., A Montague Shepherd, R.A.M. ; Mr. Edward Layton, and Mr. Alfred J. Layton. Mr. A. J. Layton, Fell. Coll. Org., accompanied throughout on the church organ, and Mr. Henry A. Evans ably conducted, a strong choir, about sixty in number, comprising the choir of Markham Square Church, and many members of the larger musical societies. The favourite airs and choruses of these well-known oratorios were very creditably rendered throughout, more especially those of the "Messiah," which were given with the greater precision and strength. Mrs. Somes has an excellent soprano voice. Miss Annie Layton made a marked impression. She has a clear contralto voice, and a good enunciation. Mrs. Layton played the organ in a very artistic manner. Her only solo, the pastoral symphony in the "Messiah," was admirably played. Messrs. Edward Layton and Alfred J. Layton, with Mr. A. Montague Shepperd, effectively divided much of the work between them. There was a large and appreciative audience.

BANBURY.

The first concert of the season by the Banbury New Philharmonic Society was given on Dec. 4th at the Exchange Hall, when there was gathered together the largest audience that has yet patronised the society. The programme on this occasion consisted of Mendelssohn's "42nd Psalm," Costa's serenata, "The Dream," and a miscellaneous selection. The society had again given preference to local talent, and had engaged Miss Ferrari as the leading soloist. Her performance on the last occasion was all that could be wished, and it was therefore only right that her ability should be recognised. The only other outside element was that imported by Mr. John Probert, tenor, of the London Ballad Concerts, and who possesses a pleasing voice of much capacity. The quintet, "The Lord hath commanded," was sung by Miss Ferrari and Messrs. P. S. Edmunds, F. P. Edmunds, W. Thompson, and W. Walkley. Mr. M. J. Monk wielded the bâton, and is to be complimented on the success of the concert. The accompaniments were played by Miss Lewis (pianoforte) and Mr. Walter Clough (organ), assisted during a portion of the concert by Miss Fortescue on the harp. The choruses were rendered by a choir of about a hundred voices.

WANDSWORTH TOWN HALL.—Miss Rosel Ayers' evening concert was given on Tuesday evening in the Town Hall. Praise is due to Miss Hipwell for her rendering of "Daddy" (Behrend), and for the song, "I cannot tell you why " (Bartl). Mr. Edward Lewetus gave "Only once more," and Pinsuti's "Queen of the Earth," both of which were fairly done. Air Varié (Vieuxtemps) was performed on the violin by Mr. Sternberg with good effect. An encore was demanded of Miss Edith Blair for "The Children of the City." A capital duet on "Don Juan" was rendered by Miss Rosel Ayers and Mr. Bambridge. The conductors of the entertainment were Mr. Stafford Trego, Mus.Bac., Oxon., and Mr. E. M. Flavell, R.A.M. There was a large attendance.

OLDHAM.—On Thursday evening, Dec. 13th, a concert was given by the Oldham Vocal Society, in the Town Hall. The first part opened with the Cantata, " The Ancient Mariner," by J. F. Barnett. The conductor and accompanist was Mr. Joseph Clafton. The performance of the Cantata reflected much credit upon the conductor and the Society, by the manner of its performance. The audience was both critical and appreciative, but was exceedingly select.

READING.—The annual popular concert of the United Band of Hope and Temperance Choir was given on Dec. 4th. There was a large attendance. A varied programme was presented, and the solo vocalists were Miss Susie Fenn, R.A.M., and Mr. C. Abercrombie, gentleman of Her Majesty's Chapel Royal ; a further noteworthy attraction being provided in the presence of Miss Marie Schumann, of the Guildhall School of Music, whose accomplished mastery of the violin was already well known to the people of Reading. A source of sympathetic disappointment was the enforced absence of the respected conductor of the choir, Mr. Waite, through sudden indisposition ; but his place was ably filled by Mr. Marsh. Mr. F. J. Read, Mus. Bac., Oxon., undertook the tasks of solo organist and accompanist, in both of which he acquitted himself with his usual ability. The choir numbered 250 voices, and, speaking generally, they have not been heard to greater advantage. The chorus "O Father, whose Almighty Power" was a good performance, and other pieces were also effectively rendered ; the whole testifying to the perfect training which the choir have undergone, and the wide range of composition which they have successfully traversed. Miss Fenn was, in each of her songs, rewarded with hearty plaudits. Mr. Abercrombie fully merited the appreciative expressions which followed his various performances. His excellent voice found full scope in the air from Handel, "Where'er you walk," which he sang with great pathos ; and his singing was much enjoyed in the two other pieces. Unquestionably the great feature of the evening was the violin playing of Miss Schumann. The talent this youthful artist displayed from the first, in the treatment of the violin, has much matured under the skilled direction of the Guildhall School professors ; and there can be little doubt that her early promise will be realised in a very distinguished career. She took a liberal share in the programme, contributing three solos, and responding once to what appeared to be, the too exacting demands of the audience. The success of the concert was largely due to the able way in which Mr. Read presided at the organ and piano, and not less for his solo on the organ, Batiste's Offertoire in F minor.

BABBACOMBE.—Disappointment has been expressed by the congregation of All Saints' Church, Babbacombe, at the resignation of their respected and talented organist, Mr. Claude R. Fowles. That gentleman was originally appointed in March, 1878 ; but four years afterwards he was compelled, in consequence [of] ill-health, to relinquish the duties. Later on Mr. Fowles was requested to resume his connection with the church, and has held office up to the present time. Mr. Fowles produced the masses of Schubert, Gounod, Mozart, and other composers, which were on several occasions rendered by a full string band, in addition to the ordinary choir and organ. He has the esteem of the clergy and members of the congregation, and his resignation has been received with universal regret.

Foreign Musical Intelligence.

Early this month Dr. Hans von Bülow played a Raff programme at Wiesbaden.

A new choral society has been formed in Rome under the title of "Società Royale Palestrina."

Wagner's "Ring des Nibelungen" is to be given presently at St. Petersburg and Moscow.

A new alto clarionet has been invented by M. Roze, a member of one of the Paris orchestras.

A new opera, "Antonius und Cleopatra," by E. F. Wittgenstein, has been successfully played in Graz.

Felix Weingartner's opera, "Sakuntala," will probably receive its first hearing in Weimar, next February.

Sophie Menter has been giving pianoforte recitals to enthusiastic audiences in Odessa.

Maurice Dengremont, the young violinist, gave no less than thirty-eight concerts in Germany from October 15th to November 21st inclusive.

The Parisian paper L'Art Musical, founded by the late M. Escudier, and afterwards the property of the publisher Girod, has been acquired by the publishing house of Leduc.

Anton Rubinstein has begun a concert tour through Germany. His two first appearances at Dresden and Leipsic were the cause of much enthusiasm.

A new opera, "Helianthus," by Herr Adalbert Goldschmidt, who has written his own libretto, is to be produced at Leipzig shortly.

The announcement is made that a complete edition of Schubert's works, on the model of the editions of Mozart and Beethoven, published by Messrs. Breitkopf and Härtel, will be issued.

After an artistic tour through Germany, Sarasate has proceeded to Russia. In March he is expected in Paris, and the following month will visit London.

A sensation was created at one of M. Lamoureux's recent concerts at the Château d'Eau, Paris, when Bach's dramatic cantata, "Der Streit zwischen Phœbus und Pan," was performed.

Herr Brahms's new symphony is said to have produced a marked effect on its recent first performance by the Philharmonic Society of Vienna. The introduction and finale are described as especially fine.

Ambroise Thomas had a very flattering reception lately at the hands of the Antwerp public. The occasion was a concert given in his honour by the Société Royale d'Harmonie, when the programme was exclusively formed of the French composer's works.

A new manuscript work called "Sainte Cécile," curiously styled an oratorio melodrama, by R. P. de Doss was recently heard in Liège, and appears to have made a favourable impression.

A point of law has recently been decided at Paris. Herr Angelo Neumann brought an action against M. Lamoureux for performing the first act of "Lohengrin" at one of his concerts at Paris. The verdict of the court is that a rendering of the music without scenery, dresses, or acting, is not a performance in the sense assumed by Herr Neumann, who has to pay M. Lamoureux 500 francs damages, besides the costs incurred by the trial.

The papers of Milan speak of a new opera entitled "Nerone," written by an English musician, Mr. George Carter, well known in his own country for other excellent compositions. Among other things, it is stated that musicians of note having seen the score of "Nerone," judge it as being very skilful, replete with melody and clear orchestral effects. Unfortunately in Italy professors have much difficulty in coming to the front, and it seldom happens that they are in a position to place the efforts of their genius on the stage. But if the music of Mr. Carter is as beautiful as is reported in Milan, why does not "blonde Albion" open the way of honour to one of her gifted sons? Why do they not place on the stage this "Nerone"? Is the proverb also true in England : "No one is a prophet in his own country." So writes L'Artes of Trieste, on Nov. 30th.

PRINCIPAL CONTENTS OF THIS NUMBER.

LONDON : SATURDAY, DECEMBER 22, 1883.

THE PHILHARMONIC SOCIETY.

THE circular announcing the seventy-second season of the Philharmonic Society, has just been issued. A series of six concerts is to be given next year, commencing in February. Before this time arrives, and during the recess in concert-giving which obtains at Christmas-tide, it will be well to reflect on what this society has done for the art of music, and to take into consideration its aims and present position.

In the limited space that can here be allotted to an article, it would be impossible to do more than glance at the history of the Society, and recount in the briefest possible way its past achievements. There is indeed little necessity to do this in detail. The account of the Philharmonic Society written by its old Secretary, G. HOGARTH, and the excellent article concerning it in Sir GEORGE GROVE's Dictionary, to which the name of Mr. STANLEY LUCAS is appended, supply sufficient general information. As, however, these books are not available to all who are interested in the Society, a few remarks may be permitted on the past career of the institution, before coming to the special purpose to which attention is desired to be called.

When the annals of English music come to be written by some pen at once equal to the difficult task, and in full sympathy with the theme to be illustrated, surely the history of the society quietly founded by CRAMER, CORRI, and DANCE in 1813, will form a chapter of the deepest interest—an interest, it may be pointed out, by no means confined to the art in this country, but radiating far and wide over the whole civilised world that recognises the dignity and rejoices in the delights of sweet sounds. Musicians are indebted to the Philharmonic Society of London for many a work since become immortal that it has commissioned and first brought forward. From the year which succeeded its birth, when £200 was accorded to CHERUBINI for a new symphony and overture, some music being also commissioned from BEETHOVEN, down to 1867, when Sir ARTHUR SULLIVAN's classical "Marmion" overture was written by request, what a long list of new and valuable music produced under its ægis is entered on the roll of the old Society! To catalogue no more than SPOHR's No. 2, BEETHOVEN's colossal Choral, and MENDELSSOHN's Italian Symphonies, and the "Infelice" scena, is to recall to mind works of genius that must ever rank as masterpieces of the art. Again and again has the Philharmonic supplied us with fresh compositions that occupy an important place among the classics of music. So long ago as forty-two years, BERLIOZ's "Benvenuto Cellini" overture was heard there for the first time in England; and to show that despite its green old age the Society is still undecayed in vigour, it was but two seasons ago that the same composer's neglected, but wondrous "Romeo and Juliet" music, was first completely revealed to the astonished and somewhat sceptical musicians of London, under the painstaking direction of Mr. CUSINS. All MENDELSSOHN's symphonies, save the posthumous "Reformation," as well as his poetical violin concerto, "Athalie," music, and "Ruy Blas" overture were first brought to a hearing under its auspices, the composer himself wielding the *bâton*; similar services were rendered to most of BEETHOVEN's symphonies, his pianoforte concertos, grand Mass in D, and music to "Egmont;" SCHUMANN's B flat, Symphony, "Genoveva" overture, and his cantata "Paradise and the Peri," WAGNER's magnificent prelude to "Tannhäuser," and the "Rienzi" overture, together with a selection from his "Lohengrin"; RUBINSTEIN's pianoforte concerto in G, "Paradise Lost," and Dramatic Symphony; GADE's A minor symphony, and overture to "Ossian." To this brief epitome, space will only permit to be added the honoured names of the following composers, as among those who have enjoyed the distinction of having had some of their important contributions to music first introduced at the Philharmonic Society's concerts:—MOSCHELES, MOLIQUE, HILLER, GOUNOD, SILAS, MACFARREN, MAX BRUCH, STERNDALE BENNETT, BARNETT, COWEN, RAFF, and BRAHMS; all names entitled to honour in the realm of music.

The services rendered by the Philharmonic have not been confined merely to the production and presentation of music to English audiences. Nearly all the great players have made their *début* at the Society's concerts. The artistic recognition there accorded confers world-wide celebrity, for the *cachet* of the Philharmonic is respected far and wide. LISZT, still living and working, made his first appearance there in a concerto of HUMMEL's, so long ago as fifty-six years, and just seventeen years after, in 1844, the prince of violinists, JOACHIM, first came before a London audience, playing BEETHOVEN's violin concerto. MENDELSSOHN played again and again, ever meeting with that hearty appreciation to which his genius entitled him. It would occupy more than a column to catalogue merely the names of the distinguished artists who have assisted at the six hundred concerts the Society has given since its foundation. It is sufficient to say that from ROMBERG, who appeared in 1814, down to Herr de PACHMANN, who played last season, nearly every artist and composer of note has been afforded the opportunity of playing or singing there. Among the honoured names of those who have conducted its concerts, are to be found those of CLEMENTI, CHERUBINI, SPOHR, WEBER, MENDELSSOHN, HILLER, WAGNER, GOUNOD, MOSCHELES, HUMMEL, Sir HENRY BISHOP, Sir GEORGE SMART, Sir STERNDALE BENNETT, Sir MICHAEL COSTA, and Mr. W. G. CUSINS.

It would require a lengthy essay to trace out, and comment on, the value of the work done by the Philharmonic Society. As becomes the foremost musical institution of our land, it has ever been the encourager and exponent of the highest and best forms of music. For many years past it has held aloft the sacred lamp of pure art, and its banner is proudly emblazoned with triumphs such as no other musical institution can boast of. May the time be far distant when that banner comes to be suspended in the Temple of Art, as a relic of the past. Through the energy and sound judgment with which the affairs of the Society have been directed, it has gained a firm hold on the sympathies of the public. If its Directors will only adhere to the same high standard, and—bearing in mind that art is progressive and acknowledges no finality—accord a place on their programmes to composers of the day, whose works exhibit distinct merit, then the support granted to the institution in the past, is not likely to become lessened in the future.

One can hardly help indulging in the remembrance of an episode in the history of the Society, showing that it is something more than a mere concert-giving institution. Amidst the treasures in the library of the Philharmonic, there is perhaps none more highly valued than the touching letter written by BEETHOVEN but eight days before his death. In this, the mighty tone poet expresses heartfelt thanks for the receipt of the £100 which the Society, in answer to his appeal, had despatched to the sorrowing and suffering musician. It is indeed something to move the heart and stir the pulse of us English musicians, to know that it was to our land that BEETHOVEN turned when distress seemed upon him, rather than to his German friends. We are proud to remember that the Philharmonic Society did not flinch from the duty devolving upon it from its prominent position, granting an immediate response to the expressed wants of the dying musician. To say that the Directors of the day did their duty, is to accord the highest praise that can be given. BEET-HOVEN'S own words were :—"Should Heaven only be "pleased to restore me again to health, I will prove "to the noble English how much I value their sym-"pathy in my melancholy fate."

There now remains one question connected with the Philharmonic to which the attention of the readers of this paper is especially requested. That is, the very important matter of support. The concerts of the Society must necessarily be expensive. Mingled with much pecuniary success, the institution has had its times of difficulty and trouble. Its most disastrous season was that of 1855, when the fortunes of the Society under the direction of WAGNER fell to a low ebb. Happily, STERNDALE BENNETT, who took office in the following year, rescued it from the dilemma that it had been left it in ; his reign as conductor was successful financially, as well as artistically. In the year 1875, losses again occurred, necessitating further sales of its monies funded in more prosperous times. In 1881, the stock became exhausted, and a guarantee fund was formed among the subscribers and supporters of the Society. This answered very well the purpose for which it was intended ; as the season did not result in a profit, a trifling *pro rata* call was made on the guarantors, and the Directors of the year were relieved from an anxious responsibility. Neither the profession nor the public seem thoroughly to recognize the devotion to their onerous duties, and the zeal for the interests of the Society that its Directors have ever displayed. They freely give up much valuable time in occupying themselves with its affairs, and, moreover, assume a serious pecuniary responsibility as to its finances. Such devotion should do more than excite our gratitude, it ought to enlist our help. In two ways can this help be accorded. First, by attending and subscribing to the concerts of the Society, and secondly, by wellwishers to the Philharmonic inscribing their names among the guarantors for the coming season. The first list (just published) shows a promise of nearly £1,300. It may be, that not a penny of this will be called for. The last season was so successful that not only was none of the guarantee wanted, but a profit was made on the concerts, and some money again funded. The risk, therefore, seems a distant one ; in any case it can hardly amount to more than a few shillings in the pound. The Guarantee Form runs as follows :—

"In the event of the seventy-second season of the Philhar-"monic Society being attended with pecuniary loss, I hereby "guarantee to pay you the sum of £   , or any proportion of "that amount which I may become liable to pay, *pro rata*, with "other guarantors of the said season of 1884."

The various reforms that from time to time have been introduced into the composition of the Society have invigorated its constitution ; they give a healthy augury for the future, in spite of its having to compete with powerful rivals, and contend with various concert speculators for public favour. English music is rapidly coming to the fore, and our composers are daily better able to hold their own against all comers. One is glad to perceive that of late, the policy of the Directors has been to accord a hearing to native writers, while not neglecting foreign composers of dis-

tinction. Here is a feature, on the score of which our support can fairly be claimed. Every one, and every institution has at certain periods to strike a balance between successes and failures ; no one is wise at all times—as the Latin grammar of by-gone days used to teach us. And so, the Society at times has made mistakes, and laid itself open to criticism. Fair criticism is never to be feared, but that differs very much from the prescient self-satisfaction of those, who, on imperfect knowledge, condemn in advance every arrangement that does not conform to their nostrums, or run just on the lines they think should be followed. Such dogmatists ostentatiously invite the world to display a perfect confidence in their ability to advise, quite touching as to its sympathy, and amusing for the assurance exhibited. Others discourse over the past, and perform the interesting feat of being wise after the event. Just now, in certain quarters, there obtains a worship of conductors, together with an extravagance of language respecting their supposed qualifications, that betrays considerable ignorance, and want of sound judgment. In the old times, it is quite true that there were few good conductors. But with modern training, widened experience, and general culture, the matter has been entirely altered, and now we can boast of having a dozen and more capable conductors. Give a good painstaking conductor a reliable and experienced band, and in all probability you will get a satisfactory rendering of any work.

The section of the British public frequenting high class concerts is daily becoming more educated. Musical people are now better able to judge the value of the utterances of some of the specialists, who set up their wisdom to confound the opinions of others, presumably less perfectly instructed. These remarks are suggested by the attacks that have already appeared on the novel arrangement that has been made as to each concert of the coming season being directed by a different conductor. But Messrs. BARNETT, COWEN, MOUNT, and VILLIERS STANFORD, together with Sir ARTHUR SULLIVAN, who will conduct his "In Memoriam" overture, are no novices. With the excellent band placed at their disposal, it will be strange indeed if they do not give us good performances. Herr EDWARD GRIEG, Dr. FERDINAND VON HILLER, and Herr ANTONIN DVORAK, who are also to conduct and will produce new works, are musicians of continental reputation, quite equal to the task assigned to them.

There remains but another sentence to say. That is, the urging of those friends of the Philharmonic Society who may read these lines, not to dismiss the matter now brought before them, relegating the duty of support to others. If they have at heart the welfare of the institution, let them apply to CHARLES E. STEPHENS, Esq., of 37, Howley Place, W., the Hon. Treasurer, or to HENRY HERSEE, Esq., the Hon. Sec., St. James's Hall, for a Guarantee Form to fill in, and add their names to the list of supporters. The individual guarantees already announced, range from sums of £100 to £5, and afford a satisfactory proof of the estimation and confidence with which the arrangements of the Directors for the coming season are regarded by the friends of the institution.

T. L. SOUTHGATE

THE LOGIC OF COUNTERPOINT.

THIRD SERIES.

XVII.

IN remarking that the austerity of the rules lessen as the employed number of parts increases, CHERUBINI observes that "Unisons (or rather notes of the same "name of different octaves) are tolerated in a large "number of parts, as well as are two fifths by con-"trary motion, even between the two extreme parts." As already shown, this increased liberty is a rightful freedom; but it may be pointed out that the extension of the license regarding successions of perfect concords between external parts by contrary motion, ought to be a matter of rarity. Such progressions even the fullest harmony are apt to be suggestive of weakness, and are best avoided. In all contrapuntal combinations of any number of parts, it is well as far as possible, to treat the outside voices as two-part counterpoint, on the ground of their extreme prominence as outlining the mass of harmony in action. The licenses to employ "two fifths by direct move-"ment when one is perfect and the other imperfect," to quote CHERUBINI, in a large number of parts, and to use leaps of a major sixth (this may surely be done at all times and in any number of parts), are matters so natural and sensible as to call for no further comment. By the way, in Mrs. COWDEN CLARKE'S valuable translation of CHERUBINI, published by NOVELLO & Co., this passage is somewhat confused, unless altered in a recent edition, by the license to take leaps of major sixths being connected as a sub-sentence with the words just previously allowing the immediate proximity of a "perfect and a diminished or "imperfect fifth." However, the passage is doubtless clear enough to all students, and it is correctly rendered in J. A. HAMILTON'S early translation printed by COCKS & Co. in 1837. CHERUBINI observes that "in florid counterpoint having from five to eight "parts, when two, three, or four parts only are pro-"ceeding at the same time, the same strict precepts "which were laid down in the rules for two-part, "three-part, and four-part counterpoint, hold good; "and it is only when five, six, seven, or eight parts "proceed together, that any abatement of the severity "of the rules may be fairly claimed." This is logical, seeing that the thinning of the score to a small or average number of parts for a time, restores to the listener a larger and usual power of perceptivity with regard to the tracing out of contrapuntal action. The Florentine theorist alludes to the two methods of writing in eight parts, by placing the two parts of each kind under each other as first and second throughout, the score, which is thus piled up with all the parts in their real position in the harmonic *strata;* or by writing for two choirs, each body of voices having its own score so to speak. He further points out that the ancient masters took care to render the harmony of each choir complete as far as possible, when employing the double choir scheme. They imposed this condition upon themselves on account of the distance frequently intervening between the choral bodies in order that complete harmony should be heard by all listeners, whether near one choir or the other;

at the same time, adds CHERUBINI, this condition is not indispensable. It may be remarked indeed that many striking effects may be obtained by departing from such a rule as in the use of sustained doubled pedal notes in one choir and the employment of moving parts in the other, and as in the enunciation by one choir of perfect concords, and by the presence of successions of imperfect concords in the harmony of the other. CHERUBINI judiciously recommends the student to advance in the use of a large number of parts, by first using two trebles, then two contraltos, then two tenors, and lastly two basses. For six voices he advises the student to similarly double alternately any two of the distinct and representative parts; and to proceed in a corresponding manner to advance in the practice of scoring for seven and eight parts, when at last all the representative parts are doubled.

The student is not likely in these days to venture to write as TALLIS did in forty parts, or as has been done for six choirs, or by way of a crowning perplexity for twenty-four choirs (ninety-six voices); a needless feat of which MARPURG furnishes an example in the shape of an overgrown canon. Indeed, eight part writing is rarely useful or effective, especially when accompanied by all the tonal ramifications of an orchestral score. It must be added that, however imposing in theory, in real practice double choir music, when the choirs are placed close to each other as in a concert-room and accompanied by a large orchestra, does not furnish those striking antiphonal effects the imagination of the listener or the examiner of a score might anticipate. This is in part to be accounted for by the limited hearing powers of even the best trained listeners in fully realising the ingenious overplus of musical riches provided by the lavish composer, and a want of distance between the two choirs to give picturesque power to the antiphonal enunciations. If two choirs are employed in the orchestra the wind instruments should be sparely used. HANDEL'S "Israel "in Egypt" is probably never so effective chorally as when accompanied according to the original scheme, by the strings, with only oboes, trumpets, and drums to occasionally brighten and lighten up the choral masses. CHERUBINI points out that considerable latitude is allowable in seven or eight parts, in the way of permitting double suspensions of a free character and in allowing the sixth to be struck against the seventh, the octave against the ninth, etc., providing the parts move clearly and boldly on their several courses, and providing the dissonant sounds are not as a rule too close together, as would be the case with seconds, and granting that the parts move conjunctly. In full masses of harmony, excellent effects may indeed be obtained by the bold and courageous employment of progressions which would not be tolerable in a thin score of the four customary parts.

E. H. TURPIN.

The *Society of Arts' Journal* has a good portrait of the late Sir W. Siemens. The new chairman of the Society's council will be Sir Frederick Abel.

From Rome we hear that Mr. W. G. Cusins, who is just now recruiting his health in Italy, has been elected an honorary member of the Academy of St. Cecilia.

Reviews.

Trio for Pianoforte, Violin, and Violoncello, by C. Gurlitt (Augener and Co.)—This composer enjoys in Germany a reputation for writing refined and graceful pieces, free from the harshness that characterizes so much modern original music. The trio, a pleasing example of his style, is expressly labelled "easy" (*In leichten style*). It consists of three movements—an allegro, andantino, and finale vivace. The correct and classical construction of the work may well serve as a model to young writers ; but it is not necessary to bestow praise on its form. This should rather be accorded to the poetical feeling that so deftly clothes the main scaffolding. Some of the variations are ingenious, and the finale is a reflex—though an independent one—of the gaiety and *brio* to be found in the delightful works of this character, written by Papa Haydn.

May Joy come to Greet Thee, by G. A. Osborne (Metzler and Co.)—A long life of ceaseless activity has not diminished Mr. Osborne's ardour for the art of which he is still a conspicuous ornament. It is a common remark that when musicians have long been engaged in the daily round of teaching, they gradually lose artistic sensibility, and become mechanical exponents rather than sympathetic disciples. The remark is in many cases but too true, but there are plenty of exceptions to the contrary. Such an one is old Kalkbrenner's favourite pupil, and the whilom friend of Chopin, Berlioz, Mendelssohn, Meyerbeer, and other famous dead musicians. Those who enjoy the privilege of hearing Mr. Osborne play, whether it be a sonata of Beethoven, a fugue by Bach, a piece by Liszt or Rubinstein, or one of the nocturnes of his idol Chopin, can testify that the soul which gives life to music, and the fingers under delicate control that do their perfect illustrative duty, are still to be found united in him ; his true artist playing satisfies and touches one, as it must have done our fathers many years ago. Though George Osborne thoroughly enjoys his well-earned leisure, he still favours us with some of his thoughts ; and whether it is a paper he reads before the members of the Musical Association, or such a trifle as a song, his productions are always marked by a freshness of thought, which compels attention and ensures approval. In the song under notice, he has supplied to Miss Marion Chappell's sensible and tasteful words, a most appropriate setting. Specially notable is a little octave figure in the accompaniment, which occurring again and again in major and minor mode, haunts the ear by its quaintness.

Chant du Gondolier, pour le Piano. Six Morceaux de Piano, by J. B. Wekerlin (W. Czerny).—Mr. Wekerlin is an original thinker, and his music always possesses a charm of its own. Though his pieces are slight, the diction is by no means common, and the sentiments reflected appeal with success to those possessing cultivated taste. All the pieces here noticed may be commended. The "Gondola song" is a suave melody in F, with an interlude in D flat, the return to the initial key being cleverly managed. Of the serial pieces, No. 1, "Rose de Noël," is an elegant Romance ; 2, a "Madrigal," a quaint thought, the syncopated accent of a secondary theme being striking and uncommon ; 3 is an Allemande, somewhat in the form of the old German Ländler ; 4 is a simple Passacaile ; 5, an elegant little sonnet ; and 6, a minuet which presents several points of novel interest.

A Christmas Carol, Words by Frank Silvester, Music by G. Gaffe, F.C.O. (Weekes and Co., 14, Hanover Street). —Words and music are alike excellent. A good effect is obtained in some sentences by the soprano and tenor taking the theme in octaves, while the alto and bass support the harmony in the refrain "Gloria in excelsis." The compact verbal sentences are tunefully set in the traditional pastoral manner, and the carol deserves popular favour.

A Christmas Carol, Words by W. E Lloyd Trevor, Music by A. C. White (J. Masters, Bond Street).—Set in March form with a well-marked melody, closely harmonised (though the bass is carried too low in the episodical passage), and preluded by the familiar ring of a peal of bells. The little piece will be found effective in performance.

Liszt's "Christus" was given lately by the Hamburg Bach Society.

Organ News.

LIVERPOOL.

An organ recital was given in St. George's Hall, by Mr. W. T. Best, on Thursday, December 13th. The following was the programme :—

Overture, " Die Letzen Dinge "	Spohr
Andante, " Priere "	Benoit.
Fugue in E flat major	Albrechtsberger.
Air, " Sombre Forêt "	Rossini.
Canzonetta from the First Quartet	Mendelssohn.
Andante (six Concert Pieces, No. 5)	Best.
Triumphal March, " Sardanapalus "	Hatton.

And on Saturday, December 15th :—

Overture, " Sosarme "	Handel.
Chorus, " La Carità "	Rossini.
Organ Sonata No. 4, in B flat major	Mendelssohn.
Marche Solennelle in E flat minor	Schubert.
Scherzo for the Organ	Best.

An organ recital was given on Wednesday, December 19th, in Great Homer Street Wesleyan Chapel, by Mr. Henry Grimshaw. The following was the programme :—

Overture for the Organ in E	Morandi.
Air with variations in F major	Wely.
Fantasia and Fugue in C minor	Bach.
First Overture on Christmas Carols	Guilmant.
March, with " Hymn of Priests "	Chauvet.
Elevation in F major	Batiste.
Choruses, " Worthy is the Lamb," and " Amen " (" Messiah ")	Handel.

NORWICH.

The last afternoon organ recital before Christmas was given by Dr. Bunnett, F.C.O., in the St. Andrew's Hall, on Saturday, December 15th. The following was the programme :—

Fanfare	Lemmens.
Pastorale (For Christmas-tide)	Corelli.
The " Cuckoo and Nightingale" Concerto	Handel.
Adagio and Allegro.	
Barcarolle	Bennett.
Air, " Waft her, Angela"	Handel.
" Nazareth "	Gounod.
Organ Sketch	Bennett.
Andante Graz'oso in G	Smart.
Fugue in A minor	Bach.
Adagio in A flat	Mendelssohn.
"Schiller" March	Meyerbeer.

BOLTON.

An organ recital was given in the Albert Hall, on Saturday, December 15th, by the borough organist, Mr. Wm. Mullineux, F.C.O. The following was the programme :—

Processional March in C major	Van-Eyken.
Communion for the Organ in E flat	Batiste.
Grand Offertoire in G major (No. 4)	Wely.
Cantilène Pastorale	Guilmant.
Serenade, " Good night I beloved "	Balfe.
Overture from the Incidental Music to " Henry VIII."	Sullivan.

An organ recital was given by Mr. Charles J. Whittington, on Dec. 14th, at the Argyle Square Church, W.C. Vocal selections were introduced by the church choir.

At the Lay Wesleyan College, Cambridge, a small effective two-manual organ, built by Mr. A. Kirkland, of Wakefield, was recently opened by Mr. F. O. Carr, Mus.Bac., whose playing is pronounced to be exellent.

An organ recital was given by Mr. E. H. Turpin, at the Trinity Congregational Chapel, Poplar, on Dec. 19th. The vocalists were Miss H. Akroyd, Mrs. Harrison, and Miss Maud Vivian. Mr. E. Blandford was the accompanist.

On Dec. 20th, the annual Advent Service, including Handel's "Messiah," was given at St. John's, Ealing Dean. The Rev. Julius Summerhayes, the vicar, conducted, and Mr. E. H. Turpin was the organist. The music was effectively sung, and a large congregation attended the service.

The addition of another organ studio, with an organ with two Manuals and Pedal at Mr. Fincham's, 150, Euston Road, in a conveniently accessible position will be a welcome item of news to the numerous and increasing class of organ students. The possibility of getting regular practice must add to the popularity of the organ, as a more available instrument and another organ studio in a central position are a distinct gain.

BOW AND BROMLEY INSTITUTE.

Last Saturday the organist was Dr. Bridge, who introduced a novelty in the shape of stringed accompaniments, to a couple of Handel's concertos. The band consisted of about 20 strings, selected from the Highbury Philharmonic Society, and Dr. Gladstone conducted. The concertos were very admirably performed, and received with great applause, and gave evident pleasure to the crowded audience, who were delighted with the innovation, which can only be regarded as a step in the right direction. Dr. Bridge played with his usual skill, and received a hearty welcome. The vocalist, a Madame Cecilia Grey, an American lady, received a recall for "Softly sighs;" but in her other selections appeared to be suffering from the nervousness incidental to a first appearance. It must be allowed that she sings in German better than she sings in English. It should be noted that Dr. Bridge introduced into the concerto, No. 2, set 2, a cadenza of his own. The concerto No. 1, set 2, though less known, is quite as enjoyable as the popular No. 2, set 1. The organ solos included "Andante," from a symphony in E flat; Haydn, "Serenade" (Schubert); "Introduction and Double Fugue (Silas); "Air varied" (Lemmens); and Fugue on the name of Bach (J. S. Bach). To-night Dr. Pringuer will be the organist, and the choir of his church will sing a selection of Christmas music. After to-night these notable Recitals will stop until Jan. 26th. The work done so far this season, and the consequent success, are matters for sincere congratulations, and show there is no falling off in these, the most famous organ recitals in the world.

Correspondence.

THE ROYAL COLLEGE OF MUSIC.

TO THE EDITOR OF THE "MUSICAL STANDARD."

SIR,—In the last issue of your journal appears a paragraph respecting the above institution, suggestive of a matter that has for some time been discussed in private circles, and to which an official answer might now well be given. The paragraph in question states, that on the occasion of H.R.H. the Duke of Edinburgh recently visiting the school, portions of quartets were performed by students of Mr. H. Holmes' *ensemble* class. Among the names of the performers are to be found those of Dolmetch, Kreuz, and Werge. These names are unquestionably German. Will Sir George Grove, the courteous Director of the institution, inform us whether these lads are English born? and if they were British subjects at the date of their admission to our new national school? A rumour to the contrary has long obtained, and indeed it is asserted that one youth did us the honour to come direct from Cologne to the Royal College, innocent of the language of his new adopted country. It may be that rumour is entirely wrong in supposing that foreigners, who have plenty of conservatoires of music of their own, would elect to come over here, and be educated at the expense of the British public, rather than study under their own distinguished countrymen. As public subscriptions have been collected for the Royal College, and are still solicited, the question is clearly a public one, and should be answered. A line from Sir George Grove would at once set this matter right, and possibly enlist support to his school from a section of our people, who at present object to tax themselves for the benefit of strangers.

Yours, &c.,
S. M. EAGLETON.

Passing Events.

In the pantomime for Her Majesty's Theatre, "Red Riding Hood," some choruses for children's voices by Mr. W. C. Levey are to be introduced in a market place scene.

Miss A. Presscott's valuable pamphlet on "Form or Design in Music" has been reprinted from the columns of the *Musical World* by Messrs. Duncan Davison and Co.

It seems that a poll of the congregation of St. Stephen's, Westminster, on the question of vesting the choir in surplices, has resulted in a vote of 514 in favour, with only 60 against.

Mdme. Essipoff has accepted an engagement to play at the Philharmonic concerts next spring: she will appear, it is understood, at two *soirées*. All admirers of the pianoforte will rejoice to hear this good news.

The announcement is made that the performances of the English Opera Company, under the direction of Mr. T. H. Friend, will commence early in January, with Victor Nesler's romantic opera, "The Piper of Hamelin."

As a sign of our increased love of music in England, it may be noted that it is supposed that in no pre-Christmas winter season have so many concerts been given, or so much musical activity been displayed as during the past few weeks.

Our readers will regret to hear that, on leaving the Savage Club, the other evening, Mr. Barrett, the eminent flute player, was set upon by some miscreants, robbed of a presentation watch recently given him, and very seriously injured.

A choral competition on a large scale, and a great Tonic Sol-fa festival is to be held at the Crystal Palace, on June 14th. The adjudicators are Messrs. J. Stainer, M.A., Mus.Doc., Henry Leslie, and E. H. Turpin.

Mr. W. G. Cusins announces a Christmas performance of the "Messiah" on the 24th at St. James' Hall. Handel's *chef-d'œuvre* is, it is true, a safe thing to give, but it is time Bach's Christmas Oratorio and other seasonable works are remembered.

Mendelssohn's "Hymn of Praise" was well rendered, say the local papers, in St. John's Cathedral, Denver, Colorado, U.S., lately, at a Thanksgiving Service, under the direction of the organist, Mr. W. E. Hall, F.C.O. Brass instruments were employed with the organ.

Mr. Weist Hill, principal of the Guildhall School of Music, directed a concert of the students at the Mansion House on Dec. 8th. The principal feature of the programme was Mendelssohn's "Walpurgis Night." The Guildhall Choir, an excellent choral force, sang the choruses in the "Walpurgis Night," Mr. Faning's "The Vikings," etc., with due effect.

The congregation of Christ Church, Claughton, Birkenhead, have recognised Mr. E. T. Driffield's arduous labours as honorary organist and choir-master during the last three years by a birthday gift of a magnificent silver tea service and tray and beautiful gilt clock and ornaments, valued at one hundred guineas. The choir added their quota in the form of an elegant china tea and coffee service.

On Dec. 10th, the Borough of Hackney Choral Association gave its second subscription concert at Shoreditch Town Hall, when Rossini's "Stabat Mater," Mozart's "Prague" Symphony (in D), and a selection from Weber's "Oberon," were the chief works performed. This excellent society is doing honest and good work in the best interests of the art.

The papers have the following:—A new singer is expected to create a sensation at the opera this season. His story is slightly romantic. When Patti was down at her château in South Wales she heard a great deal of a miner who had a lovely voice. She not only heard of him, but she heard him, and the result of the performance was that the miner left the scene of his industrial labours, and cultivated such musical capacity as he combined with his rich voice, and will come out this season—if all be well—a great baritone.

Votes for the May election will be duly appreciated for the Infant Orphan Asylum, Wanstead, on behalf of Lionel George Craxford. The boy's father was blind and friendless. He became a clever and industrious pupil of Dr. W. H. Monk, and was appointed organist of the Parish Church of Heydour, in Lincolnshire, where for fourteen years he was highly esteemed. In November, 1881, he died suddenly of paralysis of the brain, leaving a sorrowful widow and five very young children with no provision whatever. Proxies will be gratefully accepted by Mrs W. H. Monk, Glebe Field, Stoke Newington, N.

Mr. Carl Armbruster delivered a lecture at the London Institute, on Dec. 17th, on "Richard Wagner and his Works," with vocal and instrumental illustrations. The audience was large, and the close attention with which the lecturer was followed, broken only by frequent applause, showed how deep was the interest taken in the subject of the lecture. Mr. Armbruster played, with exceptional ability, several excerpts from Wagner's works on the piano, and had the valuable co-operation of Miss Friedlander, Mr. Ritter, and Mr. Thorndike in the rendering of the vocal illustrations.

The Morning Post of Dec. 18th has a long account of Mr. J. Brinsmead and Son's recent improvements in pianoforte building, in the direction of better action, increased strength, and consequent greater power of keeping in tune, and improved internal arrangements by which increased length of string and larger sonority are obtained.

The Horley Choral Society appear to have been successful in their application to the Brighton Railway Company for the stopping of a late train for the convenience of Redhill members. The society gave their sixth concert, under the direction of their conductor, Mr. W. E. Bartlett, on Dec. 18th, when Mendelssohn's 42nd Psalm, and Spohr's "God, Thou art great," were performed.

A good local concert in aid of the funds of the Royal United Hospital was given at 3, Lansdown Crescent, Bath, on Dec. 18th. Miss Agnes Ellaby, Miss Ada Morris, Miss E. Fowkes, Miss C. Evans, Signor Pieraccini, Mr. Harris, Herr Ehnke, and others took part in the performance, and gave proof that Bath is rich in the possession of good executive artists.

On Tuesday, Dec. 18th, a number of valuable musical instruments including pianofortes, harmoniums, Cremona violins, violas, and violoncellos, including a very choice violin by Stradiuarius, purchased by Viotti for his friend, Mr. Hankey, together with wind instruments, a few valuable copyrights, and a quantity of miscellaneous music, were sold by Messrs. Puttick and Simpson.

The music halls intend to bid vigorously for holiday custom. Says a contemporary :—Mr. Jennings has issued an interesting and gigantic programme for the due celebration of the Christmas holidays at the Oxford Music Hall ; while Mr. Purkess promises the *début* of a real live Princess at the Royal, in the person of Princess Pignatelli who has created quite a sensation at La Scala, Paris. This noble lady, with three little children, has been cruelly deserted by her husband, and though her sisters are fabulously rich, she has been compelled to sing for her living.

On Dec. 13th, Mdme. Sainton-Dolby gave an excellent concert, sustained chiefly by the pupils of her vocal academy, at Steinway Hall. Several of the young lady students proved by their performances the value of the instruction at the institution under the charge of the distinguished lady artist and teacher. A select chorus of female voices and some clever violin playing by Miss W. Robinson (of the Royal Academy of Music), formed good contrasts to the performances of the solo vocalists. M. Sainton conducted, and Mr. H. Leipold presided at the pianoforte.

At a reception held by Dr. and Mrs. Harper, at their residence in Addison Road, last Saturday afternoon, some good music was heard by the guests. Mdme. Viard-Louis played classical pieces in her usual style of excellence, and a violinist, M. Henkel, introduced a solo by Henri Wieniawski. Mr. F. Quatremayne scored a point by singing what is now an interesting piece, namely, the introductory romance from Verdi's early opera "Simon Boccanegra" in F sharp minor, "Il lacerato spirito," recently restored by the composer, with extra parts for performance at the new Italian Opéra in Paris. Mr. Quatremayne took low F sharp at the close and quite excited his audience. An amateur, Miss Johnston, well read in the texts of Schubert, Schumann, and Brahms, accompanied the vocal numbers, and herself played with *éclat.*

Says *Figaro* anent the score of Berlioz's "Requiem":— To analyse or criticise so extraordinary a score would be impossible in a newspaper, and indeed it was found impracticable in the ordinary Crystal Palace programmebook. Otherwise a pertinent enquiry might be allowed why the call to the Resurrection, the prayer for pity to the tremendous King of Majesty, and the pathetic " Lachrymósa " should be accompanied by the hideous noise of trombones and ophicleides, of ten able-bodied men thwacking at kettle-drums, of tubas and cornets, of double drums, cymbals, and tam-tams. The tam-tam is not usually considered a celestial instrument, and the din, which caused music lovers with delicate oral apparatus to close their ears on Saturday, could not well have been greater if Berlioz had been trying to describe the casting out of that old serpent which deceiveth the whole world, and if the ancient reptile were energetically protesting against his punishment. In truth it may be added, Berlioz had realised the dramatic rather than the religious character of the words.

WEBER'S "SYLVANA."—This was the sixth of his dramatic works, and, after many disappointments, was produced at Frankfort, September 16th, 1810. An interesting account may be found in the first volume of the "Life of Weber," by his son, Baron Max von Weber (English translation by J. Palgrave Simpson, Chapman and Hall).—S.S.S.

MUSIC FOR CHOIR.—"An Old Subscriber" may perhaps find something to suit him in the "Sunday Part-Songs" of W. H. Cummings, published in *The Choir,* by Metzler and Co. I think that Boosey and Co., published some sacred part-songs, by F. H. Cowen, and the *Musical Times* contains many pieces fairly corresponding to that description.—S. S. S.

Service Lists.

FOURTH SUNDAY IN ADVENT.

DECEMBER 23rd.

London.

ST. PAUL'S CATHEDRAL. — Morn.: Service, Holy Communion, Smart in F. Even.: Service, Magnificat and Nunc Dimittis, Smart in F ; Comfort ye, my people (Handel).

FOUNDLING CHAPEL. — Morn.: Service, Te Deum, Goss in F ; Jubilate, Nares in F ; Anthem, Rejoice in the Lord (Purcell). Aft.: Children's Service.

LINCOLN'S INN CHAPEL.—Morn.: Service, Steggall in G ; Kyrie (Steggall): Anthem, Comfort ye, my people, And the glory of the Lord (Handel). Even: Service, Steggall in G ; Anthem, I will meet the loving kindness of the Lord (Steggall).

TEMPLE CHURCH.—Morn.: Service, Te Deum Laudamus, and Jubilate Deo, Attwood in A ; Apostles' Creed, Harmonised Monotone ; Anthem, Behold a virgin shall conceive . (Handel). Even.: Service, Cantate Domino and Deus Misereatur, Hayes in E flat ; Apostles' Creed, Harmonized Monotone ; Anthem, Rejoice in the Lord (Purcell).

ALL SAINTS, MARGARET STREET.—Morn.: Service, Benedicite (Irons) ; Benedictus (Simcox) ; Holy Communion, Stanford in B flat ; Offertory Anthem, The night is departing (Mendelssohn) ; Benedictus (Gounod) ; Agnus Dei (Mozart). Even.: Service, Hoyte in G ; Anthem, Comfort ye, And the glory (Handel) ; Dies Iræ (Hoyte).

CHRIST CHURCH, CLAPHAM.—Morn.: Service, Benedicite, Stainer, etc. ; Kyrie, Credo, and Sanctus, Tours in F ; Offertory Anthem, The Lord is my Shepherd (Macfarren) ; Sanctus (Tours) ; Benedictus and Agnus Dei, Monk in C ; Gloria in excelsis (Tours). Even.: Service, Magnificat and Nunc Dimittis, Stainer in A ; Anthem, O Zion, that bringest good tidings (Stainer) ; Dies Iræ (Dykes).

HOLY TRINITY, GRAY'S INN ROAD. — Morn.: Service, Te Deum, chanted ; Jubilate, Goss in A. Even.: Service, Cantate, Bunnett in F ; Deus Misereatur, chanted ; Anthem, Behold, I bring you (Goss) ; Selection of Carols.

ST. JAMES'S PRIVATE EPISCOPAL CHAPEL, SOUTHWARK. —Morn.: Service, Introit, O come, O come, Emmanuel ; Communion Service, Schubert in F. Even.: Service, Aldrich in G ; Anthem, O Thou that tellest, He shall feed, His yoke (Handel).

ST.MARY BOLTONS, WEST BROMPTON, S.W.—Morn. : Service, Benedicite, Stainer, Winn, and Walker; Benedictus, chant ; Holy Communion, Kyrie, Credo, Sanctus, Benedictus, Agnus Dei and Gloria in excelsis, Monk in C. Even.: Service, Magnificat and Nunc Dimittis, Wesley in F ; Anthem, And the glory of the Lord (Handel).

ST. MAGNUS, LONDON BRIDGE.—Morn.: Service, opening Anthem, If we say (Reynolds) ; Te Deum and Jubilate, Cooke in G ; Kyrie (Wesley). Even.: Service, Magnificat and Nunc Dimittis, Cooke in G ; Anthem, Recit. There were Shepherds ; Chorus, Glory to God (Handel).

ST. MARGARET PATTENS, ROOD LANE, FENCHURCH STREET.—Morn.: Service, Benedicite and Benedictus, Gregorian ; Offertory Anthem, The earth is my possession (Gounod); Kyrie, Credo, Sanctus, Benedictus, Agnus Dei and Gloria, Missa de Angelis, and Bordese. Even. : Service, Magnificat and Nunc Dimittis, Gregorian ; Anthem, The sorrows of death (Mendelssohn).

ST. MICHAEL'S, CORNHILL. — Morn.: Service, Te Deum and Benedictus, Stainer in E flat ; Anthem, Sing, O daughter of Zion (Naylor) ; Kyrie and Creed, Wesley in E. Even.: Service, Magnificat and Nunc Dimittis, Nares in F ; Anthem, Rejoice in the Lord (Purcell).

ST. PAUL'S, AVENUE ROAD, SOUTH HAMPSTEAD.—Morn.: Service, Benedicite, 5th Tone; Benedictus (Turle); Kyrie' Arnold in A. Even.: Service, Magnificat and Nunc Dimittis, (Helmore); Anthem, It is high time (Barnby); after Service, Litany of the "Four Last Things" (Monk).

ST. PAUL'S, BOW COMMON, E.—Morn.: Service, Benedicite, Stainer, Turle, and Tours; Benedictus (chants). Even.: Service, Magnificat and Nunc Dimittis, Rogers in D; Anthem, Rejoice in the Lord (Purcell).

ST. AUGUSTINE AND ST. FAITH, OLD CHANGE.—Morn.: Service, Benedicite, Stainer, Winn, &c.; Benedictus, Garrett in F; Offertory, Sleepers, wake (Mendelssohn); Communion Service, Garrett in F. Even.: Service, Gadsby in C; Anthem, Sweet is Thy mercy (Barnby).

ST. BARNABAS, MARYLEBONE.—Morn.: Service, Benedicite Hoyte in E flat; Benedictus, and Jubilate, Dykes in F; Anthem, Rejoice in the Lord (Purcell). Even.: Service, Magnificat and Nunc Dimittis, Wesley in F; Anthem, Sleepers, wake (Mendelssohn); Dies Iræ (Hoyte).

ST. PETER'S (EATON SQUARE).—Morn.: Service, Benedicite' Best in C. Even.: Service, Bridge in G; Anthem, The sorrows of death (Mendelssohn).

ST. SAVIOUR'S, HOXTON. — Morn.: Service, Te Deum, Hopkins; Holy Communion; Kyrie, Credo, Sursum Corda, Sanctus, and Gloria in excelsis, Dykes in F. Even.: Service, Magnificat and Nunc Dimittis (Best); Anthem, Hearken unto me, my people (Sullivan).

ST. SEPULCHRE'S, HOLBORN. — Morn.: Service, Benedicite Best in C; Jubilate, Kyrie and Credo, Nares in F; Anthem, Sing, O heavens (Lucas). Even.: Service, Magnificat and Nunc Dimittis, King in F; Anthem, O Thou that tellest (Handel).

Country.

ASHBURNE CHURCH, DERBYSHIRE. — Morn.: Service, Kyrie and Credo, Field in D. Even.: Service, Anthem, Prepare ye the way (Garrett).

ST. ASAPH CATHEDRAL.—Morn.: Service, Ordination; Veni Creator (Palestrina). Even.: Service, Turle in D; Anthem, Behold, a virgin (Handel).

BELFAST (ST. GEORGE'S). — Morn.: Service, Benedicite, Best in C; Benedictus, Chipp in D; Litany (Helmore); Communion Service, Parry in D; Offertory (Monk). Even.: Service, Magnificat and Nunc Dimittis, Barnby in E; Anthem, Hosanna to the son of David (Macfarren).

BIRMINGHAM (S. ALBAN THE MARTYR).—Morn.: Service, Te Deum, and Benedictus, Goss in A; Holy Communion, Woodward in E flat. Evensong: Magnificat and Nunc Dimittis, Bunnett in F.

BIRMINGHAM (ST. CYPRIAN'S, HAY MILLS).—Morn.: Service, Tours in F; Anthem, O Lord, my God (Nares). Even.: Service, Tours in F; Anthem, Rejoice in the Lord alway (Purcell).

BIRMINGHAM (ST. MICHAEL'S, HAWORTH).—Morn.: Service, Benedicite (Best); Benedictus (Stainer); Communion (Stainer); Introit, "Nazareth" (Gounod). Even.: Service, Magnificat and Nunc Dimittis (Stainer); Anthem, There were Shepherds, Glory to God (Handel).

BEDDINGTON CHURCH, SURREY.—Morn.: Service, Benedicite (South); Benedictus (Garrett); Introit, O quickly come; Communion Service (Marbecke). Even.: Service, Calkin in D; Anthem, It is high time to awake (Barnby); Dies Iræ.

CANTERBURY CATHEDRAL. — Morn.: Service, Gibbons in F; Anthem, Why standest Thou so far (Ouseley); Communion, Gibbons in F. Even.: Service, Gibbons in F; Anthem, God is our hope and strength (Greene).

CARLISLE CATHEDRAL.— Morn.: Service, Wesley in E; Introit, Hosanna (Macfarren); Kyrie and Nicene Creed, Dykes in F. Even.: Service, Macfarren in E flat; Anthem, Behold, a virgin, and O Thou that tellest (Handel).

CHESTER (ST. MARY'S CHURCH).—Morn.: Service, Goss in C; Communion Service, Lee in G; Even.: Service, Goss in E; Anthem, For behold darkness, The people that walked in darkness, and For unto us a child is born ("Messiah," Handel).

DONCASTER (PARISH CHURCH).—Morn.: Service, Calkin in B flat. Even.: Service, Calkin in B flat; Anthem, The sorrows of death (Mendelssohn).

DUBLIN, ST. PATRICK'S (NATIONAL) CATHEDRAL.—Morn.: Service, Te Deum and Jubilate, Smart in F; Holy Communion, Kyrie, and Creed and Sanctus, Smart in F; Anthem, Heaven and earth display, "Athalie" (Mendelssohn). Even.: Service, Cantate and Deus Misereatur, Stevenson in E; Anthem, In the Lord put I my trust (Stewart), and Behold a virgin (Handel).

DUBLIN (ST. STEPHEN'S CHURCH).—Morn.: Service, Te Deum, Stainer in A; Jubilate, Garrett in F; Anthem, Sing and rejoice (Barnby); Introit (Hoyte); Kyrie (Mendelssohn); Anthem, For behold darkness, For unto us (Handel); Carols.

DURHAM CATHEDRAL. — Morn.: Service, Goss in D; Anthem, Rejoice in the Lord (Purcell); Introit, To God on high (Mendelssohn); Communion, Hatton in E. Even.: Service, Stanford in A; Anthem, And when the Lord had spoken "St. John the Evangelist" (Armes).

EDINBURGH (ST. JOHN'S).—Aft.: Service, Anthem, Comfort ye, Ev'ry valley, And the Glory (Handel). Even.: Service, Anthem, O Thou that tellest; solo and chorus (Handel).

ELY CATHEDRAL.—Morn.: Service, Plain-song; Introit, Kyrie, and Credo, Calkin in B flat; Veni Creator (Jackman); Gloria (Richardson). Even.: Service, Calkin in B flat; Anthem, Awake, awake (Stainer).

EXETER CATHEDRAL.—Morn.: Service, Aldrich in F; Communion, Hopkins in F; Anthem, The Lord gave the word. Even.: Service, Aldrich in G; Anthem, How lovely are the messengers (Mendelssohn).

FOLKESTONE (ST. MICHAEL'S). — Morn.: Service, Kyrie, Credo, Sanctus and Gloria in excelsis (Bordèse). Even.: Service, Magnificat and Nunc Dimittis, Attwood in C; Anthem, They that go down to the sea in ships (Attwood).

LEEDS PARISH CHURCH.—Morn.: Service, Garrett in F; Anthem. Rejoice in the Lord (Purcell); Kyrie and Creed, Dykes in F. Even.: Service, Garrett in F; Anthem, Forsake me not (Spohr).

LINLITHGOW ABBEY, N.B. — Even.: Service, Anthem, Lead, kindly light (Stainer).

MANCHESTER CATHEDRAL.—Morn.: Service, Te Deum, Benedictus, and Creed, Goss in D; Kyrie, Smith in D; Gloria, Hopkins in D; Anthem, Hosanna (Gibbons). Aft.: Service, Goss in E; Anthem, For behold darkness (Handel).

MANCHESTER (ST. BENEDICT'S).—Morn.: Service, Kyrie and Credo, Nares in F; Sanctus, Benedictus, and Agnus Dei "Æterna Christi Munera" (Palestrina). Even.: Service, Magnificat and Nunc Dimittis, Gregorian.

MANCHESTER (ST. JOHN BAPTIST, HULME).—Morn.: Service, Benedicite (Marbeck); Kyrie, Credo, Sanctus, Benedictus, Agnus Dei and Gloria in excelsis (Marbeck). Even.: Service, Magnificat and Nunc Dimittis, Gregorian; Dies Iræ, (Dykes).

ROCHESTER CATHEDRAL. — Morn.: Service, King in F; Anthem, O most merciful (Hullah). Even.: Service, Cooke in G; Anthem, Comfort ye, Ev'ry valley, And the glory (Handel).

SALISBURY CATHEDRAL.—Morn.: Service, Te Deum and Jubilate, Aldrich in G; Communion Service, Armes in A; Offertory (Barnby). Aft.: Service, Martin in B flat; Anthem, The sorrows of death (Mendelssohn).

SHEFFIELD PARISH CHURCH. — Morn.: Service, Kyrie Hiles in G. Even.: Service, Cantate Domine and Deus, Misereatur, Chants; Anthem, When the son of man (Kent).

SHERBORNE ABBEY.—Morn.: Service, Te Deum, Lyle in F. Even.: Service, Chants; Anthem, Rejoice in the Lord (Purcell).

SOUTHAMPTON (ST. MARY'S CHURCH).—Morn.: Service, Te Deum, and Benedictus, Stainer in E flat; Holy Communion, Introit, I am the bread of life (Stainer); Service, Stainer in E flat; Offertory, Not every one (Stainer); Paternoster (Hoyte). Even.: Service, Magnificat and Nunc Dimittis, Stainer in E flat; Apostles' Creed, Harmonized Monotone.

WELLS CATHEDRAL.—Morn.: Service, Boyce in C; Anthem, Cast thy burden (Mendelssohn); Introit, Let us not be weary (Macfarren); Come Holy Ghost (Attwood); Kyrie, Clarke in E. Even.: Service, Heathcote in B flat; Anthem, Behold, a virgin (Handel).

WIMBORNE MINSTER. — Morn.: Service, Boyce in A; Sanctus, and Kyrie, Aldrich in G. Even.: Service, Bunnett in F; Anthem, Thus saith the Lord (Handel); and But who may abide, Sleepers, wake (Mendelssohn).

WINCHESTER CATHEDRAL.—Morn.: Service, Skelton in D; Creed, Walmisley in F. Even.: Service, Attwood in F; Anthem, Then shall the eyes (Handel).

WORCESTER CATHEDRAL.—Morn.: Service, Hall in F; Anthem, It is high time (Barnby). Even.: Service, Hopkins in A; Anthem, Rejoice in the Lord (Purcell).

NOTICE.—All communications intended for the Editor are to be sent to his private address. Business communications are to be addressed to 185, Fleet Street, E.C.

⁂ Post-cards must be sent to the Editor, 6, Argyle Square, W.C., by Wednesday. Lists are frequently omitted in consequence of not being received in time.

NEWSPAPERS sent should have distinct marks opposite to the matter to which attention is required.

Printed for the Proprietor by BOWDEN, HUDSON & CO., at 23, Red Lion Street, Holborn, London, W.C.; and Published by WILLIAM REEVES, at the Offices, 185, Fleet Street, E.C. West End Agents:—WEEKES & CO., 14, Hanover Street, Regent Street, W. Subscriptions and Advertisements are received either by the Publisher or West End Agents.—Communications for the Editor are to be forwarded to his private address, 6, Argyle Square, W.C.
SATURDAY, DECEMBER 22, 1883.—Entered at the General Post Office as a Newspaper.

THE MUSICAL STANDARD

A NEWSPAPER FOR MUSICIANS PROFESSIONAL AND AMATEUR

No. 1,013. VOL. XXV. FOURTH SERIES. SATURDAY, DECEMBER 29, 1883. WEEKLY: PRICE 3D.

THE
NATURAL LAWS OF "EXPRESSION" IN MUSICAL EXPOSITION AND PRACTICAL DELIVERY, AND THEIR SYSTEMATICAL APPLICATION.*

By Eustace J. Breakespeare.

(*Continued from page* 367.)

II.

It is well understood that in all debated questions settlement is hopeless, unless there is a perfect agreement upon the exact application of the leading terms employed. From a confusion of ideas brought about by misapplication or imprecision of terms, many wrong-headed notions (as I account them) are still clinging to educated musicians (not to speak of amateurs), which might possibly be dissipated if it could be made apparent that the quarrel after all attaches to a word, rather than to a High-Art principle. Such a ground for dispute is opened by the assertion, so very frequently made, that where the proper feeling is resident, the expression is certain to be easy, natural, and good. Does it occur to those who make so much use of the word "expression"—its indispensability to truly musical performance and so on—that the word is not so definite in its meaning as ought to be one so commonly used ; that what A means by " expression " in his playing is something which B would refuse to admit as that quality? To tell anyone to sing or play with expression—assuming ability in the performer to produce the thing required at simple will—is none the less absurd for its being such a familiar ordinance. It is forgotten the immense distance between emotional susceptibility, "feeling" (or whatever we may please to term it), and artistic exposition. The want of distinction between what I will term *naïve* expression and *artistic* expression is the great source of misunderstanding upon this subject. By "*naïve* expression"—to make my own terms as clear as I possibly can,—I mean that untutored, simple, artless delivery, without any recognition of the fictive element in the expositional part of Art. You meet with those not only holding that this is the most to be admired, but who would denounce any other expression as artificial, formal, and false. If these were correct, then that expression would logically be the best in which the performer was most under the sway or dominancy of some determinate passion or sentiment. But we know as a matter of fact that no singer is, actually impelled or dominated by feelings of jealousy, hatred, despair. However much his subject takes hold upon him; the artist always preserves his consciousness of the fictional character of the emotion expressed, so long as he is an artist. Even if it were otherwise (apart from the question whether the reality of his emotion could in any way insure the correctness of his expression), such a thing would simply not be Art, whatever it were.

The amateur's feeling is no doubt perfectly genuine ; but the question is, not so much as to the truth or importance of the feeling in itself, as to whether its *naïve* expression is sufficient to it. Then we have to consider the expression as it is brought to bear upon the reproduction of others' creations. It is a different thing altogether with the direct unburdening of our own emotions, and the representation of feelings already expressed in some form by others. It is a question how far—even with respect to the simple delivery of a ballad tune—the performance, in so far as it is *reproduction*, can be said to be perfectly *naïve ;* but not to make too many nice distinctions of this sort, and assuming the player or singer delivers the work

as if it were actually his own spontaneous production, how far does this expression accord with that intended by the first originator? It may differ entirely from the latter ; some super-addition (*hineinlegen,* as the Germans term it) of the representant's subjectivity (especially with works of a certain "plastic" character) may distort the composer's meaning entirely. Thus, we have not only to consider how far the possession of the requisite emotional nature also finds its adequate means of expressing itself, but also to distinguish between the *naïve* expression of actual sentiment and the *naïve* expression, as far as may be, of already-fashioned productions.

On the other hand, by artistic expression, we are not necessarily to understand an artificial one devoid of all natural impulse ; but properly one where the artist is fully self-conscious, and able to regulate the utterance of his sentiment by a clear appreciation of all the *media* of expression. Music is a language in which the nature of the ideas expressed cannot be explained by words, but where the medium of expression permits of being viewed and studied separately. The forms through which the "Inhalt" or subject-matter of music is expressed, are not, like the latter, of such mysterious nature, not allowing of analysis. Just as in language, the elocutionary part is distinct from the ideas expressed. I have heard it said that if a man knows his own mind, or has a clear idea therein, his expression, however rude his oratory, will yet be good. This is, of course, corresponding to what I have been saying with respect to *naïve* musical expression. I am not so much concerned with the question of its goodness, as with making clear the distinction that it is in this *expository, rhetorical, or elocutionary part* that the *artistry* of the performance resides ; and just what the rude orator misses (apart from the question of the genuineness of his sentiments or the simple adequacy of their expression) is alike what is wanting to the *naïve* performer in music.

Let it not be thought that I am advocating some artificial overlay upon the natural feeling. I wish only to make understood that the artistic element consists largely in the clear recognition and deliberate adaptation of the various means of expression to their end ; and that this artistic part is much more than is generally recognised—I suspect from some fear of possibly lowering the ideal dignity of Art—much more under the ruling of the purely intellectual faculties. This view does not, I need perhaps hardly say, open itself to any inference that the mere elocutionary or rhetorical qualities would alone be sufficient to a musical performance. The objection raised by Mr. Stephens, on the reading of Mr. Curwen's paper, that you might observe every mark in a piece of music and yet not be said to play with expression (the word used in a particular sense), will not run counter to what I have said. In Lussy's sense, you might be said to play with expression if your playing, in its recognition of *nuances,* followed ordinary usages. To any such interpretation as this of the word "expression," Mr. Stephens's objection would, I consider, be fatal. While maintaining that *naïve* expression is uncertain and variable, to say the least (not to consider the point I have raised as to the player's subjectivity interfering with the composer—if not false to its own nature, it may not be that intended by the author of the work), there is need to adopt the opposite extreme of artificiality. But very often, what some take to be "expression," is this artificiality. If, as I have remarked before, a teacher calls upon his pupil to play "with expression" the result is some ridiculous, nauseating, vulgar, "make-believe"—some imitation of forms of delivery which conventionally is understood as "expression." We have all made the acquaintance of the sentimental vocalist. But

---

* A Paper read before the College of Organists, on Nov. 6th, 1883.

then, again, if this is not the expression, neither is it the artistry I mean. To say that all good musicians obey the natural laws of expression, by virtue of their musical faculty, does not do away with the desirability for some inquiry into this province of musical art. You may say, why should a thing naturally done be any the better for reflection thereupon? Apart from the fact that if this doubt obtained, all literary—not necessarily philosophic—concernment with art could have no *raison d'être*; it is not so certain that minds, even those specifically musical, are able by virtue of their feeling to command all the media of art. It is the same with poetical sentiment. We may have ever so much understanding of, and sympathy with, a Shakespearean character, but should we thereby think ourselves justified in engaging to represent the character upon the stage or even to recite the part? Just as in the actor's business, the expository element in music demands separate education. Owing to some misunderstanding of this kind, it has been feared that any such education was intended as a substitute for the musicianly nature itself. I will not say how far Lussy's method would help to confirm this error. The theory of the self-unconsciousness of the musician, I am aware, obtains very widely—of his singing "wie der Vogel singt, der in den Zweigen wohnet"; and if it is clearly shown that that performance is best in which the artist has least reviewed his materials, I must, of course, give in. A similar opinion is that which holds that the best music after all is the people's music—the best songs, the simple old ballads. This is a very favourite theorem with amateurs. Art takes root in the life-giving emotion, but to say that its genius is impaired when it becomes self-reflective or when the expressional *media* are deliberated, is to have no understanding of the distinction between Art and Nature, and to take away its position among the intellectual forces. The expression, as I understand it, is the *form* which the feeling takes; if one is never taught to reflect upon the means of expression at their command, they cannot strictly be said to deliver themselves expressively. I claim that any views I advance are the results of practical conversance with the art, and not formulated like the German philosopher's camel. At the same time I have remarked that the theories of many musicians are curiously at variance with their practice. Some time ago I was reminded of the fact, that the general tendency is *not* to return upon the sources of our pleasures. But no truth is affected by any reference to things as they commonly exist; else it would be reasonless to attempt to institute such a thing as moral law, since we know very well most men's actions are determined without reference to ethics. Beyond the direct pleasures of Art, there is a new element of pleasure afforded in the conscious observation and control of our feelings, and the careful estimation and control of the effects required in practical Art. To say that the possession of this faculty is not general does not argue against its desirability or even necessity. It is at any rate the mark of distinction between the artist (properly so called) and the *naïve* amateur.

(*To be continued.*)

The lectures founded by Sir Thomas Gresham will be read to the public on the following days at 6 o'clock, p.m., in the theatre of Gresham College, Basinghall Street, in the following order:—Divinity (Dean Burgon), January 8, 9, 10, and 11; Rhetoric (Mr. Nixon), January 15, 16, 17, and 18; Geometry (Dean Cowie), January 22, 23, 24, and 25; Law (Dr. Abdy), January 29, 30, and 31, and February 1; Astronomy (Rev. E. Lenger), February 5, 6, 7, and 8; Physic (Dr. Symes Thompson), February 12, 13, 14, and 15; and *Music* (*Dr. Henry Wylde*), *February* 19, 20, 21, *and* 22.

THE VOICE

MUSICALLY AND MEDICALLY CONSIDERED.

BY

ARMAND SEMPLE, B.A., M.B., Cantab., M.R.C.P., Lond.

Physician to the Royal Society of Musicians.

(*Continued from page* 338.)

CULTIVATION OF THE MALE VOICE.

The preceding remarks are equally applicable to male and female voices, but in the former the following points must, in addition, be borne in mind.

The CHEST VOICE of the Bass should be attacked about Si (B) or Do (C)

That of the Tenor at Re (D), or Mi (E) flat

In Basses the tones Fa (F), Fa (F) sharp, Sol (G), Sol (G) sharp, and La (A)

and in Tenors, the tones Sol (G), Sol (G) sharp, La (A), and La (A) sharp

present a peculiar and interesting phenomenon. Without great care, these sounds are very difficult to produce with a clear ringing quality, since the larynx always has a tendency to render them muffled and sombre, and thus they are a source of annoyance to the singer. To overcome this tendency, and render the voice firm, the only method is to emit the Italian A, E or I (Anglicé Ah, A, E) in the clear timbre, with more and more openness. The Bass singer at La (A) flat

and the Tenor at Si (B), or Do (C)

should begin gently to "*round*" or "cover" the voice; for at these points in the respective voices the actual clear quality would be too thin. The word "rounding," not closing, is here used advisedly: closing the voice is accomplished by the employment of the Italian I, but rounding is performed by slightly arching the soft palate. This proceeding applies to the sounds Si (B), Do (C), and Do (C) sharp

or

at and from the Re (D), following, the two qualities agree. In this part of the vocal scale the bright timbre is the most difficult to attain, and it should therefore be thoroughly overcome at this point by careful practice before the closed timbre is employed in these sounds, otherwise the voice may become permanently muffled or veiled.

(*To be continued.*)

"Hero and Leander" is the title of the new cantata composed by Mr. Harford Lloyd, and accepted by the Worcester Festival Committee for next year's performance.

Musical Intelligence.

SATURDAY POPULAR CONCERTS.

PROGRAMME.

Septet in F. flat (Op. 20, for violin, viola, clarionet,
　　horn, bassoon, violoncello, and double bass) .... Beethoven.
　　Mdme. Norman-Néruda, MM. Hollländer, Lazarus, Weadsland,
　　　　Wotton, Reynolds, and Piatti.
Irish Lullaby .... Stanford.
　　　　　　　　Miss Santley.
"Carnaval (Op. 9), for pianoforte alone .... Schumann.
　　　　　　M. Vladimir de Pachmann.
Sarabande and Tambourin, for violin, with pianoforte
　　accompaniment .... Leclair.
　　　　　　Mdme. Norman-Néruda.
Songs { "Mary Morison" .... White.
　　　　 "O let the solid ground" .... Borton.
　　　　　　　Miss Santley.
Fragments of Quartet for two violins, viola, and
　　violoncello........................... Mendelssohn.
　　Mdme. Norman-Néruda, MM. L. Ries, Hollländer, and Piatti.
　　Accompanist · · · Signor Romili.

Beethoven's Septet invariably attracts a larger and more appreciative audience than any other work of his, or perhaps than any work of any writer. By an odd coincidence, the same andante with variations and scherzo, fragments of Mendelssohn's unfinished quartet, were included in the programme last season when the septet was given. The performance of both works left nothing to be desired.

As was to be expected, neither of the solo instrumentalists escaped the customary encore. Miss Santley's selection was very interesting. Dr. Stanford's lullaby calls for the most subdued and careful accompaniment; an ordinary, monotonous reading of the peculiar discordant harmonies would be fatal. Signor Romili, however, again proved beyond question his perfect appreciation of what is fittest. The two songs by English ladies are of far more than average merit. In both the spirit of the poems (by Burns and Tennyson respectively) has been happily caught, and no higher praise than this could be given.

Those who are thoroughly acquainted with M. de Pachmann's playing and with Schumann's Carnival scenes, will probably be unanimous of opinion that the favourite pianist was not at his best on Saturday last. At his recital a fortnight earlier, the rendering of these "Scènes Mignonnes" were, with a Chopin ballade, what dwelt on the mind of the hearer as having been most unconventional, most perfect, most inspired. But the performance on Saturday was far from perfect; several inaccuracies occurred, most noticeably in "Coquette," and the "Promenade," but a machine alone is always alike satisfactory, and there is nothing mechanical about M. de Pachmann. At his second recital, three days before, he was not in his most perfect and genial form, and he seemed in haste to bring the performance to a close. His cutting short, on that occasion, of Liszt's "Bénédiction de Dieu" (playing only the first movement), must have been a great disappointment to all those anxious to compare his reading with that of our own pianist and Liszt-interpreter, Mr. Walter Bache.

A peculiarity, however, in his reading of Arlequin in the "Carnaval" was conspicuous at both performances—a peculiarity that involves a scarcely warrantable liberty on the part of any pianist, as it is nothing less than changing the time, accent, and phrasing of the entire movement. He played it without on both occasions in 4-4 instead of 3-4 time, making two bars into one, and playing the first two notes of the 2nd, 4th, and every alternate bar as quavers instead of crotchets. In the middle portion of the movement he was obliged to shorten his dotted crotchet and quaver by one half in each bar and play two bars as one in order to keep up his 4-4 time. It is a question if such changes are within the rights of even the most splendid and accomplished of executants.

Our programme writer is not usually happy in his remarks on Schumann's music. I have before called attention to the absurd observation that the "'Carnaval' was begun in 1834 and finished in 1835, whereas Beethoven or Mendelssohn would have done with it in a couple of days," as if we had proof that Schumann was working away at it assiduously the whole time, instead of having, quite accidentally, direct proof to the contrary. Besides this remarkable criticism as to the time it took to compose, we have equally remarkable contradictions as to its essence. First we read, "A brief citation from *each of the many themes* of which it is made up will answer all purposes," and immediately after the "citations," the puzzled student is told that "the 'Carnaval' is *neither more* or less than a theme with variations in different measures. Which is it? It cannot be both, any more than it could have taken Schumann a year of actual work to compose.

B. F. WYATT-SMITH.

SACRED HARMONIC SOCIETY.

The second concert of this venerable society on Wednesday, Dec. 19, was appropriately devoted to "The Messiah." St. James's Hall was filled with an attentive and appreciative audience, and Mr. Chas. Hallé conducted the performance. The solo principals were Miss Anna Williams, Mdme. Enriquez, Mr. Harper Kearton, and Mr. F. King. The grand "Christmas" Chorus in G evoked tremendous applause, but no encores were accepted. Miss Williams sang very well. The reading of the air in E flat, "He was despised," by Mdme. Enriquez, was thought to be wanting in pathos, and in one passage an introduced ("extra") note hardly improved Handel's text! Mr. Harper Kearton excelled in the tenor airs, and Mr. F. King, in "Why do the nations," scored a good point. This bass air, which Henry Phillips so nobly sang some 40 years ago, always makes one deep impression in the "Messiah." A. M.

ROYAL NORMAL COLLEGE FOR THE BLIND.

During the Christmas-tree festival of this institution, which was held on the 21st, at the College, Westow Street, Upper Norwood, there was a display of the musical talent of the pupils; and the concert, including as it did, Bach's Chorai in A minor, Madrigals from Gibbons and Morley; a chorus from Sir G. Macfarren's "King David," and the sacred cantata by Berlioz, "The Flight into Egypt," reflected the highest credit on the training of the pupils. Viscountess Folkestone had kindly promised to sing for the pupils; but, to their disappointment and sympathetic sorrow, her ladyship was prevented from attending by a domestic bereavement. By special request Miss Cousin, one of the pupils, and the choir, sang, in lieu of one of Lady Folkestone's songs, "Weel may the keel row," the last verse of which had to be repeated in response to a hearty return. After Mrs. Richardson-Gardner had unveiled the Christmas-tree, Dr. Campbell, the Principal of the College, expressed to her the thanks of the pupils, and intimated that in pursuance of a suggestion by Mr. Richardson-Gardner, M.P., a provincial tour would be undertaken by some of the scholars next year, when it was hoped that the work of the institution would thus become better known throughout the kingdom.

MR. F. VON ZASTROW'S DRAWING-ROOM CONCERTS.

At the first concert, early in December, Gade's Duet Sonata for pianoforte and violin, was well played by Messrs. Bond-Andrews and Polonaski; Mr. Bond-Andrews produced some of his own pretty pieces for the keyed instrument.—At the matinée of Dec. 15, Mr. Hargrave played pianoforte solos by Rheinberger, Chopin, Raff; and Mr. Bond-Andrews the "Spinning Song." Mr. Faulkner (tenor), and Mr. Grime (bass), sang effectively. Mdme. Florence Grant and Miss Lilian Curtis also appeared.

TIVERTON.

The first concert of the tenth season of the Musical Society, which took place on Dec. 13th, at Heathcote Hall, has shown that the taste for high-class music amongst the inhabitants of Tiverton and the district is in no way on the wane. During the Society's existence many of the great works of well-known composers have been placed before the public with success. At the concert on Thursday evening, the programme was made up of Mozart's "Requiem" Mass, and Mendelssohn's "Hymn of Praise." In former seasons, one such work was considered sufficient to tax the powers of the members; but, advancing years has evidently increased the confidence of the leaders in the efficiency of the choir and orchestra under their charge. Notwithstanding the inclement weather, the hall was well filled, nearly all the reserved seats, 200, being occupied by the leading families of the neighbourhood. The chorus consisted of 60 voices, and was aided as soloists by Madame Bellamy, Mrs. Rogers Bate, Miss Melbuish, Mr. Ferris Tozer, Mr. J. Hutchings. The band consisted of some 35 players; and, on the whole, did their work satisfactorily. The chorus was also good; the sopranos giving their high notes with much point and clearness. Of the two works, the "Hymn of Praise" was the best performed, all things considered. The symphony of this work was really excellently rendered. Great credit is due to the conductor, Mr. T. Russe, for his successful labours as a leader of the Society.

SPOHR'S "LAST JUDGMENT" AT ST. MARGARET PATTENS, E.C.

This Advent three City churches have given a performance of this oratorio, so admirably suited in its sentiment to illustrate one of the chief lessons of the season. Those who heard the oratorio were most favourably impressed, especially as the church possesses the perfection of an auditorium, both in respect of form and resonant qualities. St. Margaret's has an excellent choir, under the training and direction of Mr. Stedman. This was strengthened to a chorus of about fifty, the only addition to the leading voices of the church being Mr. Fryer, of St. Paul's Cathedral, as principal tenor, with whom was associated Mr. Price, Mr. Hutchinson taking the bass solos; Masters Townsend and Hull, the treble; and Master Walenn the alto. Mr. Stedman, of course, conducted, thus supplementing with excellent command and precision his labour in preparation. He was well and successfully aided by Mr. W. Stark, who had no light task, with a trying accompaniment, on an organ, which, though sweet in tone, was by no means planned as a substitute for an orchestra. All the numbers of the work were carefully given, the body and quality of tone being remarkably good, as were the precision of attack in the choruses, and the attention to light and shade. The most impressive effect, perhaps, was produced by the duet, "Forsake me not," and the quartet and chorus, "Blest are the departed." It is intended to perform a new oratorio next Lent.

BIRMINGHAM.

The concert given at the Midland Institute, on the 1st inst., was more than usually interesting. The choir, formed a little time ago, under Mr. Stockley's direction, for the study and practice of the old English madrigals and part songs, made its first public appearance. The pieces selected were, John Wilbye's madrigal, "Flora gave me fairest floweth"; Thos. Morley's so-called *ballet*, "Now is the month of maying"; John Dowland's "Awake, sweet love"; Festa's "Down in a flow'ry vale"; Weelkes's madrigal, "In pride of may"; and Benedict's partsong, "The Wreath." Mr. Stockley has had good material to work with, (his choir numbering many of the very best amateur voca lists of the town), and it goes without saying that, under his *bâton*, every attention was given to the light and shade, making up so much of the charm of these historical little gems. It is strange that little or nothing has for years and years been done toward the cultivation, in the town, of this interesting and most neglected class of English art. We have really only one glee party, and that with a limited *repertoire*, and whose members are, in their several ways, "not what they once were." Breaking the succession of the choral items came two pianoforte solos, rendered by Miss Agnes Miller,—Schumann's "Faschangschwank," and a selection from the harpsichord works of Scarlatti. In both performances Miss Miller was highly successful. Scarlatti's glittering passages, (how modern they seem, 1601) are well adapted to display the crisp touch and faultless precision of Miss Miller's playing. In Schumann's work the pianist seemed to flag a little toward the close; the hurly-burly of the final scene of the Carnival requiring a masculine vigour and an untired wrist.

At Mr. Stockley's orchestral concert, on the 18th of the month, the following was the programme offered:—

Overture, "Stradella"	Flotow.
"Creation's Hymn"	Beethoven.
"Voi che sapete"	Mozart.
Intermezzo Moresque	Elgar.
"O d'amour messagiers" ("Mireille")	Gounod.
Pianoforte Concerto in C minor	Beethoven.
Symphony, "The Eroica"	
"Sleep, my love, sleep"	Sullivan.
Pianoforte Polonaise in E sharp minor	Chopin.
"Spinning"	Cowen.
"Beware"	Molloy.
Overture, "Semiramide"	Rossini.

The "Eroica" Symphony was performed in splendid style. Mr. Stockley's orchestra is now fully able to assert its claims to a position among the finest provincial societies of its kind, few as they are. Of London I had better not speak. The technical slips in the performance of Beethoven's grand martial epic were few and unimportant; the "reading" of the work was absolutely faultless. No higher treat has been for very long afforded us than that given in this most worthy performance. The "Eroica" has not been heard in its entirety for many years, in Birmingham. The piano concerto was a grand achievement of Miss Miller's; every note of the work seemed to have been most carefully studied, in the higher æsthetical as well as the practical sense. In Chopin, however, I cannot but think she is a little out of her element. Not that it was anything but a fine, musicianly performance; but the fair pianist's style is somewhat too reserved, I may say a little cold; as a representative of works belonging to the grand classic school she is undoubtedly without reproach; in those of the romantic school there is something a little wanting yet. The Intermezzo Moresque is by one of the members of Mr. Stockley's band, a young violinist of Worcester. It is rather inaptly styled, there being nothing Moorish about it, a few *ad captandum* effects with cymbals, being excepted and excused. The piece is constructed of some very pleasing and graceful, if not very original themes, and the instrumentation is decidedly ingenious. Mr. Elgar may well be congratulated on

the success of his first essay. Miss Samuell seems to improve with every song she sings. In Mozart's charming, never-to-be-hackneyed aria she was very fine; the over-loudness of the accompaniment (orchestral), alone prevents me saying that the song "was heard to perfection." This is the only defect still to remedy in the orchestra. In Cowen's song (with Dr. Winn's judicious help at the piano) she was again highly successful. The other songs were well rendered by Miss Helen d'Alton (a substitute, and a worthy one, for Signor Foli, who disappointed Mr. Stockley at the last moment). Although I say it with fear and trembling, I do not greatly admire "Creation's Hymn"; still less in its transposed form. In Sullivan's and Moulton's well-known strains she pleased much better. At the next concert (Feb. 7th), Schumann's Symphony in B flat is to be produced, along with Svendsen's Norwegian Rhapsody.

Mr. Stratton's Chamber Concert, given on the 11th, abounded as usual, in novelties. The director himself came forward as pianist, with some agreeable little specimens by a new Italian writer, who seems to be making his mark—Giovanni Rinaldi. Like a good deal of the modern Italian music, Rinaldi's style seems to have been very much influenced by German models—Schumann in particular. Still, in Rinaldi there is much originality, and the true Italian character of melody, Mr. Stratton selected three pieces from a collection published by Breitkopf, ("Reflets et Paysages")—"Nel Giardino," "Lungo il viale," and "Al Torneo." [Why works written by an Italian and published by a German house, should bear a French title, is more than I can say.] Beethoven's magnificent quartet, Op. 59, No. 3—one of the three "Rasoumowski" quartets—was performed here, under Mr. Ward's leadership, in a very worthy manner. Field's "Quintet," so called—properly a *nocturne*, was rendered remarkably well; it is one of Field's characteristically sweet things, just a little bit too much spun-out for some tastes. A MS. sonata, for piano and 'cello by Mr. Praeger was produced by way of novelty. Without making assumption to any higher insight than possessed by any other critic present, I certainly found much to admire in the work. The themes are interesting, indeed beautiful; and the way in which piano and 'cello are occupied in dialogue, so to speak, is remarkably ingenious. Mr. Praeger seems to have followed out the Wagnerian principles of the *leit-motif*—a certain theme, running throughout the entire work, as a connecting link between the different movements. This is also a feature of the work to be admired; and I look upon the sonata as a forerunner of what will be possible in a future development of instrumental forms, as far as possible upon the Wagnerian principles of vocal melody. A performance followed of Raff's Octet in C (for strings), one of the most genial works of this writer. The style of the last movement is, perhaps, a little too boisterous, but throughout the work there is a continuous stream of beautiful ideas, both harmonic and melodic. This work was performed excellently and received enthusiastically.

I can only mention in a line the performance of Mr. Cowen's "St. Ursula," which was given by the Festival Choral Society, on the 29th ult. Even if I had more space at command I regret to say I was unable to be present, so my comments could only be made at secondhand. The performance, I am told, was a very good one; the work fully sustaining Mr. Cowen's reputation, though rather unequal in interest, some parts being comparatively tame, others reaching a high dramatic pitch—the music throughout highly pleasing and effective. Mr. Cowen seems to have satisfied these ordinary expectations, if he has done nothing beyond.

A very interesting amateur concert (under Mr. Dutton's direction) given for the benefit of the Birmingham Dental Hospital, took place at the Midland Institute last week. Gounod's "Messe Solennelle," a movement of Beethoven's B flat Symphony, the overtures to Molique's "Abraham" and Auber's "Haydée," and a pleasing selection of songs, made up the programme. Considered as an amateur affair the performances of band (in which several ladies took part), chorus, and soloists were surprisingly good.

A few remarks I have to make respecting the musical doings at the "Clef Club" I must withhold till next time.

A new musical society is in process of formation, with a constitution and aims similar to those of the Musical Association (London). Some time ago it was suggested that this society should institute provincial branches: but no practical steps were taken. In certain societies already existing the lay element is too largely felt. It is time the musical profession in Birmingham had a Musical Association of its own. B.

The death is announced of M. Auguste Offenbach, son of the late well-known composer. M. Offenbach, who died at Nice, whither he had gone for the benefit of his health, inherited a considerable share of his father's talent.

Mr. John C. Ward, on the occasion of his retirement from the organistship of Quebec Chapel, has been presented with a testimonial, consisting of a handsome silver "Queen Anne" kettle and a purse of money. The kettle bears the following inscription:—"Presented to John C. Ward Esq., in grateful remembrance of fifteen years' faithful and kindly work in connection with Quebec Chapel and district, and the Hampden Gurney Schools,"

EDINBURGH.

The fifth annual "Social," under the auspices of the Students' Club, was held in the Waterloo Rooms on Dec. 18th—Professor Sir Herbert Oakeley presiding. The large hall was crowded. The chairman opened the proceedings with an address, making special reference to the Students' Orchestra, which has been organised. This orchestra, numbering about thirty performers, began the programme with the overture "La Dame Blanche," by Boïeldieu, showing wonderful efficiency. Their subsequent pieces were Haydn's symphony (No. 2), and Mozart's overture "Le Nozze di Figaro;" while several solo pieces were also creditably played by individual members. The part-song choir, too, sang, very tastefully, such pieces as "The Arrow and the Song," and "The Norse Queen's Gift," both by Walter Hay; and "The Red Cross Knight," by Callcott. Several of the young gentlemen made quite a mark as vocalists—Mr. George de B. Watson, who possesses a fine tenor voice, gaining a deserved *encore* for Sir Herbert Oakeley's song, "Tyrant Love," the composer playing the pianoforte accompaniment. Mr. Reginald E. Horsley gave a highly dramatic delivery of the interesting classical story, "Clytemnestra." Mr. Dambmann was conductor of the music.

The formation of orchestras in connection with our colleges is a noteworthy movement; and Sir H. Oakeley is entitled to much praise for his labour in this direction. If our college students devoted themselves more to artistic studies and less to athletic sports, the world would gain; for our Universities would not only produce more intelligent—because more generally cultivated—scholars, but more real gentlemen; many parents, too, would be saved from the misery of having to support misguided youths who have grossly squandered away much time and money; and an influential class of intelligent art patrons would be formed.

LEEDS.

As soon as it was announced that the Committee of the Leeds Musical Festival, held last October, had declined the services of Madame Albani, Mr. Archibald Ramsden—with his usual enterprise—entered into an engagement with that lady to appear at his annual performance of the "Messiah;" an event which came off with the greatest success on Tuesday evening, Dec. 18. Lovers of music in Leeds have, indeed, reason to be grateful to Mr. Ramsden, for the rich treat afforded them on this occasion; and, judging from the crowded state of the Town Hall, the concert was as great a success, financially, as it was artistically. Madame Albani met with a reception which must have been most flattering; and nothing could be more delightful or impressive than the manner in which she rendered the beautiful soprano music of the oratorio. Her singing of the recit. "There were Shepherds," and following airs, will not soon be forgotten by those present. And the chaste and devotional manner in which she gave the lovely air—" I know that my Redeemer liveth,"—was much admired. The contralto music was entrusted to Miss Hilda Wilson, who sang throughout with much feeling and expression. Mr. Barton McGuckin's fine voice was heard to advantage in the opening recit.—" Comfort ye,"— as well as in the whole of the tenor music. Mr. Bridson was very successful in his share of the oratorio music, his rendering of the airs "Behold, I tell you a mystery," and "The trumpet shall sound," being particularly fine. The choruses were taken in a manner that was highly satisfactory, and the members of the band did their work well. Mr. R. S. Burton made a thoroughly efficient conductor; and Mr. J. P. Bowling Atby presided at the organ.   J. D. T.

SALISBURY.

On Dec. 20th, Spohr's sacred oratorio, "The Last Judgment," was given at the Cathedral. The music was excellently rendered, the first chorus, "Praise His awful name," and the quartet and chorus, "Blest are the Departed" being most effective. Mr. Hayden gave "And, lo! a throne was set in Heaven" with much expression and power. Mr. Marr and Mr. Crick efficiently took the alto and bass parts, and Salter did well in the treble. The Cathedral was well filled and the congregation showed the greatest reverence and attention, so that one may hope that the Dean will soon arrange for a repetition of what has proved a musical treat of a high order. Mr. South's playing was greatly admired. It is gratifying to note, indeed, that Mr. South who went to Salisbury an amateur organist without professional reputation, has already won the admiration of all by his artistic playing and by the manifest improvements he has brought about in the Cathedral music.

A "Saturday Evening Entertainment" at the "Welcome," with a good miscellaneous programme, arranged by Miss Harriette Morgan, was given on December 15 in aid of the Norwood Cottage Hospital.

It seems now unlikely that German opera will be given in London next season,

CIRENCESTER.

On Thursday evening, Dec. 6th, the parish church was filled by an immense congregation, the occasion being the holding of a special Advent service, the principal characteristic of which was the singing of Spohr's beautiful oratorio of "The Last Judgment," with full orchestral accompaniment. The project has been under consideration for some time, and it was not without much thoughtful deliberation that the Ven. Archdeacon Hayward decided on taking advantage of the magnificent proportions of the church, and the facilities afforded by the existence and attainments of the Cirencester Choral Society to hold a service specially appropriate to the season, and to introduce into it as its chief feature the performance of an oratorio so eloquent, both in its words and music, of teaching suitable to Advent-tide. During the interval before the service opened, Mr. Ralph Norris, organist of Holy Trinity Church, skilfully played a number of voluntaries. The service opened with the well-known Advent hymn, "Lo! He comes in clouds descending," sung to the tune Helmsley, with orchestral accompaniment by the band.

The Ven. Archdeacon Hayward delivered an address from Psalm lxxxv. 8, "I will hearken what the Lord God will say concerning me, for He shall speak peace unto His people and to His saints, that they turn not again." The Archdeacon said: The question is often raised whether the music in our churches ought to be purely congregational—only of such a kind and character that the assembled worshipers can join in it, or whether it is legitimate and desirable that some of it should be performed for them, so that they may be edified by simply listening to it. Looking at the strides which music has made, we shall not be far wrong in saying that, like its elder sister arts of Architecture and Painting, it is emphatically a product of Christianity. The point from which all music starts is within us. Its progress is the development of a gift originally planted within us. Christianity has stirred this gift directly and indirectly. It has excited the imagination and kindled the enthusiasm, and may not we say the inspiration, of gifted men known to us as our great composers. Their works move and stir those feelings which colour our lives, inspire our words, and nerve us for all our actions. We believe that these oratorios with which Christ's Church is now enriched are one out of God's many voices to us; one of the many ways he would have employed to bring home to us His eternal truths. We believe that these splendid compositions—the offspring of so many prayers—of so many hours of rapt meditation (it is said of Haydn that when he began to write one of his oratorios he wrote on the top of his first sheet of paper before he put a note upon it, "Glory to God," and when he concluded it he put at the end of the manuscript, "Thanks be to God") come to us laden with a divine message to our souls, as true, if not as universally telling, as the message of the preacher. No doubt there are dangers attending their performance. They may captivate the fancy and not reach the mind—they may please the taste and not touch the conscience. But what good thing is there that may not be abused? We have done all we can do in pointing to the dangers. We have tried to guard you from it by prefacing this oratorio with a special service of prayer. "The rest is in your hands—all I would say in deep earnestness is—"He that hath ears to hear let him hear." The words of the oratorio speak for themselves. You have them now before you."

At the conclusion of the address, the oratorio was sung. The principals were Miss Mary Beare, Miss Lizzie Hellis, Mr. John Probert, and Mr. Thomas Brandon. The whole was under the able *bâton* of Mr. Edward Brind, choirmaster and organist of the parish church and conductor of the Choral Society, and on whom the manner in which the oratorio was rendered reflects the highest credit. The work was interpreted most admirably throughout, with the greatest taste and feeling, and the style of its performance evidenced much painstaking study in its preparation. The choruses were most satisfactorily sustained, being sung with marked precision. The band accompaniments were most successful, and the beautiful orchestral effects, for instance, in the quartet and chorus, "Lord God of heaven and earth," were exceedingly well illustrated. While the offertory was taken, Luther's hymn, "Great God, what do I see and hear," was sung with band accompaniment, which was introduced with remarkable success, the trombones taking up the last verse in unison with fine effect. The orchestral parts for the hymns were arranged by Mr. Brind.

CAMBERWELL.—The Christmas Entertainment of the Mary Datchelor School, Camberwell, was given on the 20th. Dramatic selections from Classical English and French plays were given. The musical performances were as follow:—Pianoforte solos by Misses May Barnes, Lizzie Laud, Kate Keeble, Clara Goodlatte, Grace Henshaw, Hannah Easton, Lillie Lloyd, and Jane Calder; a pianoforte concerto, Miss Fitch, R.A.M. superintendent of music, accompanied by Miss Llewellyn, L.R.A.M.; a violin solo, Miss Marie Schumann; and a song, ".There is a green hill far away," The Mary Datchelor School and at the Guildhall School of Music. There were also several part-songs, sung by a choir selected from pupils of the school. Miss Kimpton was the accompanist.

CORK.

The opening concert for this season of the Cork Musical Society was held in the Assembly Rooms on Wednesday evening, the 12th inst. The first part of the concert was entirely devoted to "The Holy City," by A. R. Gaul, Mus.Bac., the first time of its production in Ireland. Of its merits, as a composition, I shall not speak here; it was duly commented on in the *Musical Standard* at the time of its production at the late Birmingham Festival. Suffice it for me to say, that the choruses form the best portion of the work; the solos, with the exception of the first bass solo in the second part, being very tame. The instrumental prelude, though bringing to mind the introduction to "Lohengrin," is one of the best numbers, the instrumentation, though simple, adding greatly to the effect. In the performance, the sopranos were exceedingly good, their intonation and attack being remarkable; but they were too strong for the other voices. The basses and tenors were not alone weak, but bad; they sang the music fairly, but that was all. The chorus, "They that sow in tears," was about the best rendered. The solo singers calling for notice were—Miss Davidson (contralto), and Mr. Sullivan (bass); both singing their parts with great taste and expression. Miss Day and Mrs. Layfield also are deserving of some notice, but the others were very bad; some of them could not possibly be worse. The orchestra was very fair. The second part of the concert was opened with S. Clark's Grand March, "Flambeaux," interesting on account of the addition of five ladies to the strings of the orchestra. This is worth noticing on account of the change in public opinion: some time ago no lady would possibly countenance the appearance of ladies in the orchestra; but now, it appears to be becoming a fashion. The audience, being by this time in thoroughly good humour, encored nearly everything from this to the end of the programme that would admit of an encore. Now followed a recitative and song. "Oh, would I were a village girl,"—from Ramdegger's "Rival Beauties,"—sung with great effect by Miss Davidson, who possesses, in addition to natural musical ability, a splendid contralto voice, especially in the lower register. Liszt's "Rhapsodie Hongroise," No. 9 (Pesther Carnival), was played in very good style by Miss Annie Atkins. The startling gradations of *piano* and *forte* which abound in Liszt's music being rendered *con amore*. Mr. Longfield next sang "It was a thorn," by the Viscountess Folkstone. Gounod's "Nazareth," (with instrumental accompaniment and chorus), sung by Mr. J. Sullivan, was decidedly the gem of the concert. "The Lark now leaves his watery nest" (Hatton) was sung, with much expression, by Dr. Burke. The chorus next gave Pinsuti's "The Sea hath its pearls," which was followed by a quartet and chorus, by the same composer, "Where wavelets rippled gently," the same being a choral setting of the "Blue Bells of Scotland." The less said about the singing of the soloists in this number the better. The concert concluded with "The Wine Cup is circling," for the entire body of voices.

F. ST. JOHN LACEY.

TAUNTON.

Recently a successful concert was given at the Independent College by the students, assisted by friends. The programme was carried out in a manner which reflected the highest credit upon the musical trainer of the students—Mr. T. J. Dudeney—who occupied the post of conductor. The Rev. F. W. Aveling, M.A., B.Sc., addressed a few words to the students before the commencement of the concert. The opening piece, the overture, "Chevy Chase," a notable composition by G. A. Macfarren, was given in a very spirited manner by the orchestra. Mr. T. R. Glanvill, who was suffering from a bad cold, sang with expression the somewhat difficult song, "Estelle," by Henry Smart. This was followed by a pianoforte solo by A. Clements, who selected Macfarren's Sonata in A, one of the finest specimens of its class. The choristers sang "The Sea King," a part-song by Henry Smart, with great energy and a careful observance of light and shade. In the duet, "There be dreams which fade and perish," (Macfarren), the voices of T. R. Glanvill and R. Sommerville blended admirably, and the first part of the concert concluded with the beautiful part-song, "O Mistress Mine," by the same composer.

The second part commenced with the overture, "The May Queen," by W. Sterndale Bennett; and gave extreme pleasure. The part-song, "Hark, hark, the lark," another of Macfarren's compositions, is difficult, requiring great promptitude of attack and a close observance of light and shade to make it thoroughly effective. The rendering of it was, on the whole, satisfactory. A piece of considerable local interest was the old English ditty of "Near the Town of Taunton Dean," arranged by Mr. T. J. Dudeney. The melody is ancient, and the harmony by Mr. Dudeney is excellent. It was well sung. This was followed by the trios for soprano, tenor, and bass, "The Hawthorn in the Glade," from Sterndale Bennett's beautiful cantata, "The May Queen." A Mozart Symphony proved one of the most successful pieces of the evening, the concert concluding with "England," a part-song of a national character, by J. L. Hatton.

LIVERPOOL.

Spohr's oratorio the "Last Judgment" was rendered, on Dec. 19th, in St. Bridget's, Wavertree, by the body of vocalists which has become known as the "Banner" Choir. The church was crowded to its utmost capacity long before the service commenced, hundreds of applications for tickets having been refused. The many beauties of the work seemed to create a deep feeling, and by means of the string orchestra employed a splendid effect was obtained. Mr. W. A. Roberts most effectively interpreted the wind parts on the organ, especially in the stately overture and symphony, the latter of which foreshadows several of the subjects treated in the second part. Regarding the choir, the boys may be said to have carried off first honours for purity and power of tone. The soloists all acquitted themselves creditably. The majestic choruses "Praise His awful name," "Blessing and honour," and the dramatic "Destroyed is Babylon," were excellently sung. The recitatives were the least satisfactory features in the performance; and, in this particular, considerable difference existed between the full score and the band parts. Mr. S. Claude Ridley, who conducted, is to be congratulated, after weeks of careful training, upon the success which crowned his efforts.

BEDFORD.

The first series of "Musical Evenings" at Bedford came to an end on Friday, Dec. 14. The first *soirée* has been already noticed. The second was opened by Beethoven's Sonata in F, Op. 23. Mr. Bond-Andrews, the pianist, played, for solos, a prelude and fugue of J. S. Bach; Handel's Air and variations in E major; two from a set of his own, "Village Scenes," and Chopin's Polonaise in E flat. Herr Polonaski played several violin solos, to wit, a barcarolle of Spohr, Bach's Adagio on the G string; a fantasie of De Beriot; a ballade and polonaise of Vieuxtemps. The artist, as before, fully enlisted the sympathies of the audience. Mdme. Polonaski contributed vocal pieces, including her own setting of "How like a flower." At the 3rd concert, Grieg's sonata, called the "divine" (*Gottliche*) was finely interpreted by MM. Bond-Andrews and Polonaski. The former gentleman's treatment of Beethoven's funeral march, Sonata in A flat, attracted much attention as a careful and well-studied performance. A second series of concerts is projected next autumn.

CROYDON.—A first-rate concert was given by the Literary and Scientific Institution Vocal Union, under the directions of Mr. Frederick Cambridge, on Dec. 13th, in the Public Hall, when there was a very good attendance. The first piece performed was Mr. J. Barnby's sacred cantata "Rebekah," the solo parts of which were, taken by Mrs. Baker, Mr. T. L. Warner, and Mr. F. Bevan (Her Majesty's Chapel Royal). Unfortunately Mr. Warner was suffering from a severe cold, and so was not heard to advantage; but Mr. Bevan, who possesses a fine bass voice, gained considerable applause for his singing, both in this and the following piece. The second piece performed was Hofmann's "Melusina," and the solo parts were taken as follows:—"Melusina," Mrs. Mauser; "Clotilda," Miss Kate Hoyand; "Count Raymond," Mr. F. Bevan; "Sintram," Mr. F. J. Thrift; and "The King of the Water Spirits," Mr. F. G. White. The choruses in both pieces were exceedingly well rendered, and reflected great credit on their conductor, Mr. Frederick Cambridge. Mr. Walmsley Little (Mus.Bac.) ably presided at the harmonium; and Mr. C. J. Wood admirably performed the duties of pianist.

HALSTEAD, ESSEX.—On Dec. 11th a concert was given in the Town Hall, in aid of the funds of the Cottage Hospital. The concert had been arranged by the Halstead String Band, who were assisted by friends from Haverhill, Sudbury, Ipswich, Ardleigh, Colne Engaine, and Braintree, the orchestra comprising some thirty performers, among whom were a number of lady violinists. Mr. George Leska, A.C.O., wielded the *bâton*. There was a fairly large audience. The performance commenced with the overture, "Tancredi" (Rossini), which was played in excellent style. The band pieces also included the overture, "Zampa" (Hérold), and overture, "Semiramide" (Rossini), the last mentioned being undoubtedly the piece of the evening. The vocalists were Miss B. Horner, Mr. J. R. Vaizey, and Mr. L. Andrews. Mr. Pratt, of Ipswich, gave a violin solo in the first part, entitled "Reverie" (Vieuxtemps), and one in the second part, which was much more appreciated, a Fantasia on "Faust" (Alard). The flute solo, "Canzona" (Raff), was given by Mr. V. W. Taylor, and the encore which was awarded that gentleman, was well deserved. He responded by playing "Gigue" (Handel), and was equally successful. Mr. G. Leake was encored for an air with variations (Beethoven), and replied by playing "Lieder ohne Worte," No. 1.

An American paper has discovered that it requires some piano-forte-tude to hear some players practise a pianoforte etude two or three hours a day.

EUGENE D'ALBERT.

It may be of interest to give some particulars of the training and early career of this gifted young English musician, whose recent playing abroad has met with signal success. Eugene d'Albert is the youngest son of Mr. Charles d'Albert, an Englishman (of French extraction) residing at Newcastle-on-Tyne. In his youth, Mr. C. d'Albert was a dancer at the Italian Opera in London. There he probably imbibed a love of dance music, and appreciation for its marked rhythms, developing in later years into a happy facility for writing and arranging melodious music of this type, that has charmed a generation of the votaries of Terpsichore. Eugene was born at Newcastle, in the year 1863, Mr. T. Chappell, the well known London publisher, who issued most of his father's music, standing godfather to him. The boy's talent for the art was soon manifested, and to Mr. G. A. Osborne, among others, he was indebted for some early tuition.

In the year 1876 "The National Training School for Music," the pioneer of the now established Royal College of Music, was opened, the President being H.R.H. the Duke of Edinburgh. Among the pupils who commenced their career there, was young d'Albert. He was at that time but 13 years of age, and was elected to a free scholarship at the school, after a local competitive examination. The boy commenced his studies under the following eminent musicians :—Sir (then Mr.) Arthur Sullivan, the Principal of the new school, for Composition and Instrumentation ; Harmony and Counterpoint, under Dr. J. Stainer ; Pianoforte, Mr. E. Pauer ; and, later on, Orchestration under Mr. E. Prout. The boy was most assiduous in his studies—once writing and scoring a complete Mass as a holiday task ; his progress was so satisfactory, that, after a competitive examination among the pupils, he was elected to the "Queen's Scholarship," founded by Her Majesty. He enjoyed the advantages of this until he left the school in 1881. He was then, on the recommendation of Sir Arthur Sullivan, nominated to the "Mendelssohn Scholarship." This, the most valuable prize in the United Kingdom, was founded in London in the year 1848, by way of commemorating the great musician, whose death the world of music was then lamenting. Its object is to enable native musicians who have shown decided talent to continue their musical studies, either in England or abroad, forwarding to the Trustees, from time to time, fresh compositions. There is a stipend of about £90 per annum paid to the scholar. Young d'Albert held this post for some time. During the period of his studentship, he appeared in public at the grand concert given before the Prince and Princess of Wales in St. James's Hall, by the pupils of the National Training School, an overture by the youth for full orchestra being performed. Subsequently, he played at the Philharmonic Society's and Crystal Palace Saturday Concerts. On these occasions his marked abilities, both as composer and performer, were heartily recognized by the most highly cultured audiences that can be found ; his clever pianoforte concerto, written, amongst other pieces, while in statu pupillari, meeting with deserved success.

After playing at the Richter Concerts, the well known conductor took Mr. d'Albert to Vienna, rather more than a year ago. Since that time, he has doubtless been increasing his knowledge and powers by contact with foreign musicians of eminence, from the sage of Weimar to the exponents of the newest school to be found in Berlin. One is glad to learn that the concerts he has given in the chief towns of Austria, Germany, and in St. Petersburgh have been uniformly successful, both artistically and financially ; his reception by brother artists and able foreign critics having been cordial and appreciative. Mr. Eugene d'Albert is now but twenty years of age, and can hardly yet be said to have perfected his studies. There seems every prospect of his future career being bright, and one likely to afford conspicuous testimony as to the painstaking care with which his natural gifts were educed, and trained by his able masters at our National Training School for Music.

There is, say some American authorities, just a possibility that Herr Hans Richter will spend the next autumn and winter conducting concerts in Boston, U.S.

Mr. Hamilton Clarke's music to the "Merchant of Venice" used for Mr. Irving's representation of that play in New York has pleased American critics well able to recognise talent.

LONDON : SATURDAY, DECEMBER 29, 1883.

WORDS RETROSPECTIVE AND PROSPECTIVE.

ALTHOUGH an eminent writer has poetically striven to point out that time as measured out by man's own mechanical contrivances has been made into a means of self-torture, whereby man by turns often needlessly recalls and anticipates events which for the most part give rise to thoughts of pain and sadness; it is useless to deny that time measurements and especially the great yearly divisions afford valuable means of watching our human progress, forming new resolutions, alas ! for the most part to be speedily broken, and gathering *data* for the formation of experience by experience. So the editor, as he finds the old year waning away in the brief, dark wintry days and the new year about to peep out of the midnight gloom, bethinks himself of giving some account of his stewardship and offering some promises as to the future. With regard to the past nothing can here be done beyond the expression of personal gratitude for the esteemed and faithful labours of the contributors and staff of the paper, whereby my own task has been made so much the lighter. With regard to the future, without feeling it wise or necessary to enter into a string of promises, I do nevertheless desire to assure the readers of the *Musical Standard* that the peculiarly independent position of the paper, with the assistance of a staff of able contributors accustomed to the advantage of the free, invigorating atmosphere of a journal which has no publishing or other musical interest to protect or forward, but which is devoted solely to the best and highest interests of the art and its followers, will be fully maintained and devoted as heretofore to the advancement of sound, good music, and to the use of all earnest artists both professional and amateur. In view of the earnest attitude I claim for the *Musical Standard*, a series of papers upon practical musical subjects will be presented, for the reader's consideration from week to week. The concert criticisms and reviews of new music, etc., will continue to be based upon the same ground of practical investigation and independence from self interests of any kind whatever. The musical world, like all the other departments of life, has its tendencies to crystallisation into sets and cliques ; a process resulting as elsewhere, in the creation of that elaborate form of selfishness known as class interest, and a process which may be and often is developed into a standing danger to the best interests of our national life and a weakness to the very society from which such faction interests themselves emanate. The articles devoted to the social and professional interests of our musical artists will be written, therefore, in the interests of all and not to the gain of the few. The development of church and organ music the elevation of both these high departments of art, will still receive earnest attention in the columns of this paper. The advancement of orchestral music—without which no national musical life can be sound and healthy—will be unceasingly advocated. Our great educational institutions and other societies devoted to the art, will still command in the *Musical Standard* a full and fair consideration. In all matters discussed the best interests of the art and the social and professional gain of its followers —whether writers, executants, or teachers—will be duly borne in mind. And while fair criticism will be independently maintained, the maxim "Let those who "claim to be artists first learn to be gentlemen," will be kept well in sight, and all personalities or biassed opinions will still be rigorously excluded. It seems unnecessary to say so much as to one's future proposals; but I desire to inform my readers of my convictions, which arising from only a brief editorial experience of three years, are nevertheless firmly fixed upon my mind, that an art journal, like the artist himself, must to be useful be both earnest and practical. I can say no more ; and now claim the privilege of heartily wishing my kind and indulgent readers a very seasonable joy, and a Happy New Year.

　　　　　　　　　　　　　　　E. H. TURPIN.

THE LOGIC OF COUNTERPOINT.

THIRD SERIES.

XVIII.

THERE are two points in writing for more than four parts which call for the consideration of the student, both tending indeed to one end—the building up of harmony according to the natural harmonic scheme, whereby the harmonic *strata* stand more closely together in the upper than in the lower section of the score. In choosing voices for a score of five voices, therefore, the most favourable plan is that of having two trebles, and one of each of the other parts. When six parts are employed, then, two trebles, two altos, one tenor, and one bass form the most effective score. Similarly in writing for seven voices, it is well to employ two representations of each of the three upper parts, and one bass only. Of course there are times when the dramatic exigencies of a work or the peculiar formation of a choir may compel different and less advantageous groupings of the voices ; but departures from the plans just recommended are apt to be more or less unsatisfactory in effect and difficult to write for with good results. In conducting Counterpoint in more than four, and even in eight parts, it is important to arrange the chords with the closest harmonic elements in the higher parts, and to further copy the natural scheme by taking care not to double the thirds needlessly. A good rule to lay down is to say that while in an eight part vocal score it is possible to simultaneously double in three octaves the foundation note or fifth of any chord, it is only possible to double the third in two octaves with due regard to cleanness and properly balanced sonority. To sum up the principles of the contrapuntal science by which harmonic richness is secured in combination with melodic clearness, independence, and strength, it may be said that the chief tasks of the writer are the avoidance of such forms of consecution of perfect concords as result in palpable weakness or in prominences damaging to the harmonic effects, and in the proper and complete control and absorption of discordant elements. ST. PAUL tells us that the laws are for the wrong-doers and not for the righteous ; so the rules of Counterpoint are merely for dangerous consecutives and unruly discords, and properly distributed concords are elements free from restraint. Then, to get a general view of the main conditions of contrapuntal writing, the questions anent style must be borne in mind. These concern the purity of the melodies employed in musical facework, so to speak ; in the homogeneity of the materials used ; in the appropriateness of the sentences to the vocal or instrumental mediums of their exposition, and in their suitability to the thoughts embodied in the composition at large ; and, in the well-proportioned distribution of the contrapuntal activity in use. Good music has been forcibly spoken of as common-sense in sound ; and let the composer duly remember that the use of that disciplined judgment ordinarily spoken of, as common-sense, but really that uncommon form of practical wisdom which chiefly goes to make up the careers of good and useful people, is not only far more important than the exercise of technical knowledge, which is pedantic when it is wrongfully or ostentatiously applied, but this common-sense is the very essence itself of all the best learning and experience a life-time of earnest study can produce. The laws as mere verbal forms may indeed for the most part be forgotten with safety when the spirit they embody becomes a part of the composer's nature, when he writes not without the rays of light which the lamp of wisdom diffuses to those, who having mental gifts strengthen them by the exercise of good sense, earnestness, patience, and humility. With regret I lay the pen down with regard to the subject of these articles, which have, alas! for my readers' patience extended over so many pages, for I feel how unworthily I have dealt with a great subject. If I may tell the whole truth, I find some consolation in the thought that I may presently extend these observations to the kindred subjects of Double Counterpoint and Fugue; in which case I may again venture to make large claims upon the already well-tried and kindly extended patience of my readers.   E. H. TURPIN.

MR. CHARLES E. STEPHENS'S SONATA PIACEVOLE.

A new work from the pen of this most popular and genial English musician is a most welcome appearance. The sonata, for flute and piano, was introduced by the composer and Herr Oluf Svendsen the other evening at the Musical Artists' Society's thirtieth performance of new compositions. Flautists possess anything but an abundance of duet sonatas; those, therefore, who are fortunate enough to be acquainted with a pianist able to render the elaborate and effective pianoforte part, may hail this addition to their store with peculiar satisfaction. Seldom has Mr. Stephens written in so happy a vein. The melodies bear the unmistakable stamp of spontaneity and genial simplicity; there is nothing forced or affected from the first bar to the last, and the pleasurable feeling of brightness and sunshine aroused by the opening subject continues in full force to the end.

Written strictly in orthodox form, with the modern device of reintroducing the first subject towards the end of the finale, the sonata aims at nothing higher (or lower) than it attains—the happy expression of happy thoughts. It is in three movements—an allegro grazioso, a romanza, and finale alla tarantella. Perhaps the first movement contains the writing most interesting to a musician: the return of the first subject after the "free fantasia" (to mention only one point), most cleverly and charmingly brought about. On the other hand, the romance is more likely to be popular; this movement might be introduced at a non-classical concert, and it would not fail to give pleasure to all listeners. Those musicians who are troubled with a mania for hunting out resemblances—it is a disease, like punning—may accuse the principal melody of this movement of having a likeness to "Robin Adair"; the chance resemblance does not, however, take from the merit or the beauty of the work. Judged as a whole, it not only far surpasses the few flute and piano sonatas one is familiar with (not forgetting the graceful specimens by Reissiger), but is worthy of an abiding and honourable place in the larger repertory of universal chamber music.

B. F. WYATT-SMITH.

On Dec. 20th, the nineteenth annual soirée and distribution of prizes in connection with the South London High Schools, took place in the great hall of the Cannon Street Hotel. The hall was very much overcrowded. The proceedings of the evening, however, passed off satisfactorily, and included an entertainment, consisting of a selection from the opera of "La Traviata" and a representation of the Opera Comique, "Rip Van Winkle," both performances being very creditable to the juvenile actors.

A goodly array of artists gave a concert at St. James' Hall on the 21st, in aid of the Christmas Dinner Fund of the Lodging House Mission.

Reviews.

Æsop's Fables, Versified and arranged for the pianoforte, by L. Williams (B. Williams).—An appropriate gift-book for children at this season of the year. The author has ingeniously versified some of these immortal fables, and set them to well-known tunes, for the most part, old favourites. The book is nicely illustrated, well got up, and moderate in price.

Dance Album. (B. Williams).—This last contribution to our store of dance-music is acceptable just now. It contains waltzes, quadrilles, polkas, a schottische, galop, and gavotte, the dancing of which stately measure is coming into vogue again. It suffices to say that the music is written by some of the best known composers, and is good; as the price of the nine pieces collectively amounts to one shilling, the volume will doubtless not lack purchasers.

The Ebbing Tide. Elf Land. For the pianoforte, by J. F. Barnett (Patey & Willis).—These two clever and tastefully written tone-pictures, as the author terms them, were composed for orchestral use, and are now transcribed for the pianoforte. They are excellent specimens of Mr. Barnett's melodious and musicianly work, and must please all cultured players. The melody of "The Ebbing Tide" lies chiefly in the alto part, a delicate arpeggio figure above supplying an interesting accompaniment against soft chords in the bass. "Elf Land" was written for the strings of the orchestra alone, *pizzicato*. It is a delicious little fresh thought, skilfully and ingeniously laid out. Both pieces were recently played at one of the Crystal Palace Saturday concerts, and gained much applause; "Elf Land" being awarded an encore.

Fugue, composed by F. Westlake (Stanley, Lucas Weber and Co.)—This piece is really an octave study, in the fugal form. Though written in two parts only, it is effective, and well adapted for the purpose of giving elasticity and freedom to the wrists.

Menuet Impromptu, pour Piano, par Walter Macfarren (Stanley, Lucas, Weber and Co.)—One of the best pieces Mr. W. Macfarren has written. Its boldly marked subject is cleverly treated throughout the work, and the episodical theme in the major affords a capital and grateful contrast to the vigour of the main portion of the work, with its solid and effective full harmonies.

Ah! Fading Joy, Madrigal for five voices, composed by Charles Lucas (Stanley Lucas, Weber and Co.)—A reprint of an excellent madrigal, by the late Principal of the R.A.M. It deserves to be still more widely known and sung by our madrigal and choral societies.

Gigue in G major, for the pianoforte, and *Gavotte in D major*, for the pianoforte, by Lillie Albrecht (Duncan Davison, and Co., Regent Street)—Both these pieces have been played with great success by the gifted young composer at her recitals in Lowndes Square, Belgravia; where the reviewer had the pleasure to hear them. Mr. Duncan Davison has found some effective music in Miss Albrecht's numerous pieces, whereof he has published a tempting list for Christmas; many of the numbers are new editions, demanded by an eager public. The Gigue is in 6-8 time. The Gavotte begins, according to rule, on the second half of the bar. Miss Albrecht writes for her instrument with a loving regard for its genius, and never puts pen to paper, except to record worthy ideas.

La Caravane (March) and *Sweet Dreams* (Valse)—Mr. George Asch, a prolific writer of march and dance music, publishes, through the medium of J. B. Cramer and Co., and Duff and Stewart, his Oriental March in C, "La Caravane," and a pretty Valse in B flat, "Sweet Dreams." These pieces have been played with great success at the Crystal Palace and the Covent Garden Promenade Concerts, and won frequent encores, also at the Fisheries' Exhibition.

The fact that the theatre bands in New York, although limited, are, as a rule, well balanced, and served by artists of often more than merely respectable skill, affords one of many proofs that our cousins across the Atlantic possess a real and intelligent interest in the art.

Academical Intelligence.

ROYAL ACADEMY OF MUSIC.

The Westmorland Scholarship was competed for the other day. There were 15 candidates, and the Scholarship was awarded to Eleanor Rees.

Our musical institutions holding examinations and granting diplomas—the Royal Academy of Music, the College of Organists, and Trinity College, London—will all be busy with examination work during the week beginning with Jan. 7th.

Foreign Musical Intelligence.

Boïto has finished a new opera, "Pierluigi Farnese."

Signor N. Coccon, of Venice, has written a new Mass for Christmastide.

Petrella's new operetta, the "Promesi Sposi," has been heard at Genoa.

A musical festival begins at Cincinnati on the very threshold of the new year.

Mr. F. H. Cowen's American friends seem to hope that his visit to New York will come off in the spring.

M. Saint-Saëns has been conducting two concerts of his own works, given in his honour by the people of Angers.

Madame Helen Hopekirk made her appearance in America at Boston on Dec. 8th, at one of the symphony concerts.

Before leaving Antwerp, M. Ambroise Thomas was made a citizen of that town, as a mark of appreciation of his musical services.

Herr Ludwig Christian Erk, well known as a composer and conductor, died on Nov. 25th in Berlin. He was born on Jan. 6th, 1807.

Liszt's new pianoforte method, to be issued shortly, it is said, in Leipzig, in three volumes, is reported to be a work of importance and value.

During the absence of Rubinstein, Leopold Auer, the violinist, is conducting the concerts given by the St. Petersburg Society of Music.

Signorina Luisa Cognetti, described as a pianist of singular merit and fine technical powers, has been playing with success in Florence.

There is a proposal, it is said, for a choir of 100 Welsh singers to come over from America to compete at the Liverpool Eisteddfod next year.

A symphony, called "Pologne," by Madame Augusta Holmès, created a marked impression at one of M. Pasdeloup's concerts in Paris recently.

The chief of the French Opera claque died the other day at the mature age of 90. It would be well now to do away with the claque altogether.

M. Massenet's new opera, "Manon," is now in full rehearsal at the Italian Theatre, Paris, and will probably be produced by the middle of January.

The festival at Boston, U.S., beginning on April 24th. will have a good presentation of Wagner's music, under the direction of Mr. Theodore Thomas.

Under the title of "Note di un Pianista," M. Gottschalk contributes to La Gazetta Musicale di Milano some of his artistic experiences in foreign lands.

A "Church Choir Society" has been formed in New York, consisting of choristers and others interested in the cause for the advancement and popularization of church music.

Flotow's opera "Marta" was performed at the Italian Opéra in Paris, last week. Ravelli the tenor, and Reszki the baritone, won the honours of the evening.

Mr. Mapleson is now announced as the purchaser of the partly-built Opera House on the Thames Embankment, and he proposes, it is said, to now finish the structure.

Mr. Villiers Stanford's new opera on the capital subject of the "Canterbury Pilgrims" will, it is hoped, be heard early in the Carl Rosa opera season of next year in London.

Herr Gustavus Hoelz died recently, aged 70. He has been called the Austrian Béranger, and was the author and composer of many popular Austrian songs.

"Estrella," a comic opera by Mr. Luscombe Sarelle, was announced by Messrs. Brooks and Dickson for production, for the first time in America, on Dec. 10th.

Madame Patti created a new success in New York in Verdi's "Aïda." Signor Nicolini has largely gained in artistic reputation during the New York opera season.

There are signs that even rich and liberal New York cannot support two Italian opera houses. The Mapleson party have left the coast clear by a tour to Philadelphia and Boston, but propose to return to New York in January.

Selections from Wagner's operas will be given during a tour in the United States of Mr. Theodore Thomas, with Frau Friedrich Materna and Herren Winkelman and Scaria, together with a complete and competent orchestra.

Last Friday, at the Grand Opéra, Paris, a pretty ballet by Dubois, called "Farandole," was produced with success. The libretto is from the pen of M. Mortier, a theatrical critic. Mdlle. Rosita Mauri, a most graceful artist, was twice encored.

Popular concerts are greatly in vogue at Turin. They are given in the Victor-Emmanuel Theatre, a large building capable of holding several thousand people. The orchestra, 90 strong, is conducted by Signor Fasso, and the programmes are arranged to suit all tastes.

"Don Giovanni," "Rigoletto," "Lohengrin," "Lucia," "Aïda," "I Puritani," "La Traviata," and "Faust," have recently delighted the people of New York, who, though presumably smitten with Wagnerism, find Italian opera delightfully pleasant, notwithstanding its artificialities. Tune, "pure and simple," is something.

At the second concert of the New York Symphony Society, on Dec. 8th, the programme included Tschaikowsky's symphony in C, Beethoven's grand Quatuor in C sharp minor, scored for orchestra by Carl Mueller-Berghaas, and three pieces for string orchestra by J. S. Bach. Mendelssohn's music to "Midsummer Night's Dream" was also given.

Paolo Fodale has been criticising a new method with regard to the employment of the chromatic genus on the pianoforte, and a new system of writing music by Bartolemeo Grassi-Landi. The critic goes minutely into the proposed reform of the chromatic methods, and the substitution of a new system in place of the scales as now used. He states the new system to be based upon a chromatic scale formed in harmony with the diatonic system, and evidently believes the proposed new scale plan will offer more scope in the musical art for the creation of new effects, and present a clearer definition of the tone affinities.

As an instance of the sound artistic feeling of the late tenor, Mario, it may be related that he once objected to the somewhat heavy accompaniments of the "Cujus animam" of Rossini's "Stabat Mater" being unduly subdued on his account; pointing out that the accompanying forces had to realise on their part an artistic and powerful effect, and that if his voice was no longer equal to the full enunciation of his part, that was not their business, they had their own duties to fulfil. Though one may not care for too noisy an accompaniment, the spirit of the great artist's words forms a striking rebuke to our many vain singers, "a feeble folk," who have an unrighteous horror of any, often necessary and often artistic, climax power in their accompaniments.

The Arpa of Bologna gives an account of the present condition of the Liceo Musicale in that city. The institution has 233 students, and is clearly in a prosperous condition. A very notable feature of its work is the large percentage of students of orchestral instruments numbering some 92 scholars. Would that our English institutions showed less singers and pianists on their student lists, and more orchestral players. The singing students of Bologna number only about 49, the pianoforte, less cultivated in Italy than in some musical countries, has some 46 aspirants; the organ, 15. The students of composition are: harmony, 11; counterpoint, the goodly number of 25, a creditable fact in modern Italy; and the general principles of composition, as form, are being studied by three scholars. The professonal staff is an efficient one.

Organ News.

DUNDEE.

At St. Mark's Church, another of the present series of recitals was given, on Monday, December 10th. Mr. Martin T. Horton, organist of the Church, presided at the organ. The vocalists on this occasion were Miss Steel and Mr. Stephens. The audience was large and appreciative. The programme included :—

Introduction and Concert upon the Russian National Air	Fryer.
Minuetto from String Quintet	Boccherini.
Organ solo, " The Flute Concerto "	Rink.
Offertoire in G major, No. 30	Batiste.

PRESTON.

On Saturday evening, Mr. James Tomlinson (organist to the Corporation) gave his usual weekly recital on the grand organ in the New Public Hall. The programme was as follows :—

Marche Religieuse	Perelli.
Adagio for violin and organ	Merkel.
Third Grand Concerto	Handel.
Overture to " Fra Diavolo "	Auber.
" Liebesfrühling "	Voger.
Military March	Pauer.

The Third Concerto (Handel) and the Adagio for violin and organ (Merkel) were rendered with great taste. The overture to " Fra Diavolo," and the " Military March " (Pauer) were played with great spirit. There was a moderate attendance.

ACCRINGTON.

An organ recital was given in the Congregational Church, Albert Street, Oswaldtwistle, on Monday, December 10th, by Mr. Wm. Tattershall, organist of the Parish Church. The vocalist was Mr. John Whittaker. The programme included :—

Organ Concerto in B flat	Handel.
Variations on Pleyel's Hymn Tune	Westbrook.
Christmas Offertoire	Wely.
Barcarolle, from 4th Concerto	Bennett.
Fantasia Pastorale, " The Storm "	Wely.

ST. JOHN'S, BROWNSWOOD PARK, N.

On December 19th an organ recital was given, after the special service, by Mr. W. S. Hoyte. The programme ran thus :—

Symphony to " Hymn of Praise "	Mendelssohn.
Scherzo	Best.
Andante con moto	Silas.
Fugue in G major (Book 9)	Bach.
Allegretto from " Reformation " Symphony	Mendelssohn.
" Ave Maria "	Henselt.
Grand Chorus Dialogue	Gigout.

BURNLEY.

An organ recital was given on Thursday, November 15th, in Wesley Chapel, Hargreaves Street, by Mr. John Ashworth. The following was the programme :—

Prelude and Air, with variations, from the Suite des Pièces	Handel.
Andante in E flat	Morandi.
Organ Study on Pleyel's Hymn Tune	Calkin.
Festival March	
Fantasia Pastorale in G major	Wely.
Marche Religieuse	Adam.
Berceuse, " Serenade "	Gounod.
Scherzo (Finale)	Lemmens.

And on Thursday, December 20th :—

Organ Sonata, No. 3	Mendelssohn.
Adagio in F, from a quartet	Haydn.
March in E flat	Wely.
Minuet de Boccherini	E. H. Turpin.
Offertoire sur Deux Noëls	Guilmant.
Overture to " Œlius "	Handel.
Pastorale for Christmas-tide, from Cordelli's Concerto	E. H. Turpin.
Grand Chœur	Lemaigre.

KINGSTON-ON-THAMES.

An organ recital was given in All Saints' Church, on Thursday, December 20th, by Mr. Lancaster, A.C.O. The following was the programme :—

" Christmas " Offertoire	Lemmens.
Barcarolle from 4th Concerto	Bennett.
Organ Sonata, No. 6	Mendelssohn.
Andante in A	Smart.
March, " Cornelius "	Mendelssohn.
Cantilène in A minor, and Melodie in C	Salome.
Toccata and Fugue in F	Bach.
" Nazareth "	Gounod.

MORNINGSIDE, N.B.

A recital of organ and sacred music was given on December 18th by Mr. W. H. Hopkinson, in Morningside Church. The programme included :—

Organ Sonata No. 2	Mendelssohn.
Grave—Adagio—Allegro maestoso, and Fugue.	
Andante in E minor, and Andante in A major	Smart.
Fugue on " St. Ann's Tune "	Bach.
Theme with variations, from the " Septuor "	Beethoven.

There were given, also, several movements from Mr. Gaul's " Holy City."

A recital was also given in the United Presbyterian Church, on Friday, December 21st, by Mr. William Blakeley. The programmes was as follows :—

Overture in D major	Smart.
Berceuse in E flat	Gounod.
Sketch, " The Lake "	Spark.
Prelude and Fugue in C minor	Mendelssohn.
Larghetto from Quintet	Mozart.
Cavatina	Raff.
Gavotte in A major	Gluck.
Christmas Fantasy	Best.

GLASGOW.

A recital was given in the United Presbyterian Church, Berkeley Street, on Thursday, December 13th, by Dr. A. L. Peace, on the occasion of the inauguration of the new organ. The programme included :—

Organ Concerto in D minor and major	Handel.
Adagio from Symphony in C	Haydn.
Andante in G major, and Grand Solemn March in E flat	Smart.
Berceuse and " Marche aux Flambeaux "	Guilmant.
Overture for a Church Festival	Moradi.

The organ, which was built by Messrs. Forster and Andrews, Hall, has two Manual Claviers, from CC to G, and one Pedal from CCC to F.

A recital, the second of the series, was given in Maxwell Parish Church, by Mr. James Pattinson, Mus.Bac., Cantab., on Thursday, December 20th, with a programme including :—

Concerto in B flat	Handel.
Andante maestoso—Allegro.	
Pastoral Symphony (" Messiah ")	Handel.
Offertoire sur Deux Noëls	Guilmant.
Christmas Fantasy on Old English Carols	Best.
Christmas Pastorale	Merkel.
Offertoire in G	Wely.

PORTSMOUTH.

An organ recital was given in St. Mark's Church, on Thursday, November 29th, by Mr. A. Blissett. The programme included :—

Sonata in A	Mendelssohn.
Flute Concerto	Rink.
Overture in E	Weber.
Andante in D	Haydn.
" O Sanctissma "	Eaz.
Finale Volontary, " Scherzo "	Best.

GALASHIELS.

The fifth organ recital and service of sacred music, was given by Mr. J. W. Oxley, L.Mus., T.C.L. and the members of the church choir, on Wednesday evening, December 19th, in St. Paul's Church. The programme included :—

Grand March	Meyerbeer.
" Carillons de Dunkerque "	Wely.
Song, " Consider the Lilies "	Topliff.
Andante from the Symphony in C major	Beethoven.
Larghetto from the Quartet in B flat	Mozart.
Chorus, " Hallelujah " (" Mount of Olives ")	Beethoven.

Mr. Oxley's playing is highly spoken of, and gave much satisfaction.

WAVERTREE.

An organ recital was given in St. Bridget's Church, after evening service, on Sunday, December 23rd, by Mr. S. Claude Ridley. The programme included :—

" Christmas Hymn," with variations	Wely.
Fantasia, " The Storm "	Lemmens.
Prelude and Fugue in B flat	Bach.
" Christmas " March	Merkel.

PERTH, N.B.

The sixth monthly organ recital, was given in Kinnoull Church, by Mr. R. Woodthorpe Browne, to a large and interested audience. The programme was as follows :—

Adagio and Finale, from the Quartet in C (Op. 4)	Spohr.
Sonata in D	Mendelssohn.
Chorus, Andante non moto—Allegro Maestoso.	
Andante in G	Batiste.
Offertoire in G	Wely.
Adagio, from the 6th Quartet (Op. 18)	Beethoven.
" Coronation " March	Meyerbeer.
" Wedding March "	Gounod.

BOSTON (U.S.) EXHIBITION.

Music and musical instruments are well represented at the Foreign Exhibition, now being held in Boston. England, it will be observed, is only represented by one firm.

In the Italian Department there are various works on Music, from Giusto Dacci, director of the Royal School of Music, Parma. These works include treatises on Vocalization, Harmony, etc. Santucci (Verona) contributes musical instruments.

Germany sends a concert piano with harmonium attachment, exhibited by Phillippi (Forst, Deutschland) ; piano, from Schnabe (Berlin) ; concert piano, complete iron frame, case carved Renaissance style ; accordeons, harmonicas, etc., from Bufe (Gera Unterhaus) ; zither, Tiefenbrunner (Munich).

Holland : Thirty volumes of Music for piano, guitar, etc., Buhrmann (Amsterdam).

France : Musical instruments, harmonichords, Lauvet (Paris) ; musical works, with and without illustrations, Hennuyer (Paris) ; opera glasses, Avizard (Paris) ; musical instruments, Courtois (Paris).

England : Works on Music, Trübner (London).

Canada : Organs, Bell (Guelph).

East Indies : Indian musical instruments ; drawing-room instruments played upon with a steel plectrum ; *Kachua Satar*, owing its name to the shape of the gourd, which is flat, like the back of a tortoise, the instrument being a classical one ; class B includes instruments played upon with a wooden plectrum ; class C, those played with two small sticks ; D, played upon with the bow ; and E, played with the tips of the fingers. In this exhibit there are also wind instruments, percussion instruments made of metals, pulsatile instruments covered with skin, etc. In all, there are 50 instruments. Among them is the *Nyastaranga*. It is believed that an instrument of this description is scarcely to be met with in any other part of the world than India. It is known in Sanscrit as the *Upanga*, and is extensively used by Hindu musicians in the North-Western Provinces, particularly at Mathura and Brindaban. The East Indian exhibit also includes works on music by Tagore and others.

Japan : Piano, from Kuaisha (Tokio).

Austria : Harmonicas, Bornbauer (Vienna) ; musical instruments and strings, Lutz (Vienna) ; instruments, Riedl (Graslitz) ; harmonicas, Thie (Vienna).

Sweden : Violins, Amati model, Leonardson (Orebo).

Spain : Musical instrument strings, Marti (Barcelona).

THE NATIONAL OPERA HOUSE.

The recently issued report of the architect, Mr. Fowler, upon the proposed completion of the National Opera House on the Embankment, the first stone of which was laid by the Prince of Wales eight years ago, gives particulars regarding the structure of the building and the objects to which it is to be dedicated, in the event of the projected completion being accomplished. Fifty thousand pounds have already been expended upon it, but the owners have agreed to grant a lease of the building as it stands, and so much of the site as is required for it, for £15,000, to be paid on completion in boxes or stalls. The estimated cost of completion is £55,000, but it is now proposed that the building shall be on a less elaborate scale than was intended, both as regards the interior and exterior, though it is to have the same spacious internal accommodation. It will be larger even than "La Scala," but very similar in design. Altogether, it will provide comfortable accommodation for about 3,000 persons, a larger number than can be accommodated in the Grand Opéra in Paris. Of these one thousand persons will be in the gallery. It is calculated that this great accommodation will permit the lessee to give opera at half the present Italian opera prices. The structure will be fire-proof, and will comprise a promenade, refreshment rooms, and smoking divan on a grand scale. It is contemplated that access shall be given from the District Railway by a covered way. It is said to be Mr. Mapleson's intention to give Italian, French, or German opera during the summer season. During the spring and autumn it will be devoted to English opera, while at Christmas it will pass into the hands of " an English theatrical manager, under whose care the national drama is to be cultivated."

A very pleasant evening was spent on Saturday at the Freemasons' Tavern by the members of the Council of the Artists' Annuity Fund, and their guests. The form of entertainment was that of a " smoking concert," at which a number of excellent soloists and the St. Paul's choir assisted. Some very good recitations were also delivered. The walls of the room were hung with pictures, including some original sketches by the Queen and the members of the Royal Family.

"Die Pomposaner," a new opera by Max Leythœuser, editor of the *Würzburger Presse*, was well received on its first performance in Wurzburg recently.

Correspondence.

THE ROYAL SOCIETY OF MUSICIANS.

TO THE EDITOR OF THE " MUSICAL STANDARD."

SIR,—Your current number has a kindly written notice of this Society, for which we are grateful ; but the following paragraphs call for some remarks and explanation.

" The conductor was Signor Randegger. Why a foreign " musician should have been selected to conduct the performance " of a work Englishmen best know the traditions of, for a pro- " fessedly national Society, is one of the mysteries of art in " England by which the alien is being constantly exalted and " benefited to the neglect and loss of the native professor. " Without knowing who are the members of the Royal Society " of Musicians, the writer does know that no large body of " English musicians can exist without counting a dozen or " twenty, or perhaps more, natives who could conduct the " 'Messiah' quite as well, doubtless, as the esteemed foreign " 'teacher' who was chosen for this duty the other evening. " However, it may be assumed that the Committee do not run " out of their way to find aliens to accept pensions, intended, it " may be presumed for British artists."

We scarcely regard *Mr.* (not Signor) Randegger as a foreigner, for he has been domiciled in England many years, and his long been a good friend to the Royal Society of Musicians, as is proved by the annual subscription list. The Society was founded by natives and foreigners (40 of the latter were included in the first roll of members), for the benefit of both ; the condition, that the claim for the bounty of the Society should be founded on membership and actual need. A section of the 1st Law declares, that " A Candidate (for membership) being a foreigner, must have practised music for a maintenance *in Great Britain*, at least seven years immediately preceding " his nomination.

Our history tells us that the first recipients of aid from the Society's funds were the orphan children of Kytch, the oboe player, a German.

The Society is greatly indebted to foreigners for handsome donations ; for example : Storace (1793), £100 ; Signora Storace (1820), £1,000 ; Mazzinghi (1844), £100 ; Begrez (1864), £1,000 ; Schultz (1877), £1,000 ; with the exception of two, all members of the Society. We also gratefully record a donation (1862) of £441 18s. 2d. from Mdme. Jenny Lind Goldschmidt, and M. Otto Goldschmidt.

With every sympathy for nationality, and a desire to see Englishmen " always to the fore," I should be sorry if a wrong impression respecting the un-selfish benevolence of the Founders, and present members of the Royal Society of Musicians, were to get abroad.

If our talented English musicians, on attaining the age of 21,* would make it their pride and their duty to become members of the Society, they would spare themselves, and those dear to them, many an anxious hour ; and would do something to aid in comforting the orphan and the widow in the time of need and affliction.

Yours faithfully,

WILLIAM H. CUMMINGS,
Hon. Treasurer, Royal Soc. of Mus.

Dec. 22, 1883.

CURIOSITIES OF MUSICAL CRITICISM.

TO THE EDITOR OF THE " MUSICAL STANDARD."

SIR,—In your issue of the *Musical Standard* for Dec. 15th, I find the following with reference to M. de Pachmann's playing of Schumann's " Carnaval " :—" M. de Pachman's version of the ' Carnaval ', ought to have satisfied the most exacting, and probably did so." In the *Athenæum* of the same date, the critic, a well-known and able authority, says : " M. de Pach- man's worst performance was that of the ' Carnaval.' Not only was his reading of this work eccentric to an extraordinary degree, but it was persistently inaccurate in a technical sense, while the wilful alterations of the composer's text were altogether without justification. Judged by this alone, the player would be unworthy of serious criticism." The *Academy* of the same date says : " We did not expect to hear of a *travesty* of 'The Car- naval ;' technically, intellectually and poetically, the performance was unsatisfactory."

Yours,
A. R. A. M.

Dec. 18, 1883.

P.S.—I may add that I entirely coincide with the views of the two critics above quoted.

A pleasant feature of the Christmas music arrangements will be the singing of carols on the 29th (to-day), at Westminster Abbey by the fine choir after the three o'clock service.

* Candidates for membership must be over 21 and under 45 years of age.

Passing Events.

Dr. John Hullah, though not quite recovered from his recent illness, is somewhat better.

Mr. W. Ganz gave a *matinée musicale* at his residence on the 19th inst., his pupils being the performers.

The London Tonic Sol-fa *soirée* will be held at 6 p.m. on Jan. 5th, at the Falcon Square Chapel, Aldersgate Street, E.C.

The deaths of Dr. C. W. Corfe (formerly organist of Oxford Cathedral), and of Mr. Henry Corri (a well-known English bass singer) at Philadelphia, are announced with regret.

In the December number of the Boston, U.S. *Musical Record* Mr. Hamilton C. Macdougall, of Providence, U.S., gives an animated and pleasant account of his successful experience of an English Examination at the College of Organists.

It is pleasant to read, that at the performances of "As you like it," at Dulwich College, Dr. Arne's "Under the greenwood tree," and Stevens' glee, "Blow, blow," were sung by the performers, and the orchestra, under the direction of Mr. J. Brabham, played a selection of music in the interval.

The Keynote is the title of a new American journal, apparently succeeding the New York *Music and Drama*. It is well got up, with an effective front page; and, what is still more to the point, it contains practical and spirited articles and criticisms. Mr. Frederick Archer, the eminent organist, is the editor. No. 3 contains Mr. E. Prout's valuable article on Handel's Chandos Anthems.

The music for the cantata, which will form an important feature of the ceremonial upon the opening day of the forthcoming International Exhibition at the Crystal Palace, which is fixed for St. George's Day, April 23, will be composed by Sir George Alexander Macfarren. The display of foreign exhibits will be large and varied, and there is every probability of most of the principal countries of Europe and Asia being well represented. Negotiations are on foot to secure collections of Belgian, French, German, Spanish, and Swedish pictures; and it is hoped that there will be a goodly representation of the works of British artists. And it may be further hoped that an important collection of musical instruments will be exhibited.

On Dec. 19th, Prof. J. Ella reached the age of 81, his birthday being duly honoured by many artistic and notable friends. He is the only survivor of the Italian Opera band of 1821. The late Sir John Goss and Prof. Ella, both pupils of Attwood, were elected together in 1824 members of the Royal Society of Musicians, and since the death of Sir John Goss, Mr. Ella is now the senior member of that excellent institution; also since the death of the late Dr. Stebbing, the veteran artist is the only survivor of the staff of the *Athenæum* newspaper of some sixty years ago. Of the distinguished artists who appeared at the first season of the Musical Union in 1845, the following are still living, viz., Sivori, Sainton, Lazarus, Osborne, and Sir Julius Benedict. Within the present week has died one of the most zealous members of the Musical Union, Lady Mary Christopher Nisbet Hamilton, at the age of 82, who with her only daughter, now living, seldom failed to be present at the *matinées*.

The Christmas music has not presented any marked novelties this year. In London, Paris, and other great cities, carol singing on Christmas eve, midnight Masses, and celebrations, have taken place, to be followed by New Year's Eve midnight services. Sensible people of all religious bodies protest that man is not the slave of time but the servant of the ever-living God; and that the watching of the clock at midnight savours either of superstitious observance or of that love of excitement which better characterises the Salvation Army than a body of sensible Christians who build up their faith upon the free gifts promised by the scriptures. This year carol singing has been heard in London, and will be heard at the Abbey to-day after the three o'clock service, truly a sensible hour. In Paris carols were sung, notably at St. Eustache and of a more modern type, some written by Adolphe Adam, says report, at the Madaleine and Trinity Church. That common-sense will in time teach us to dispense with public religious services held when the body is fatigued and the mind unduly excited, is a result devoutly to be hoped for, surely.

M. Henri Logé, an admirable pianist, gave a recital the other day at St. George's Hall, Langham Place, playing a good programme, including some of his own pieces.

The story of Mdme. Patti being vain enough to wear some £50,000 worth of diamonds in "La Traviata," and her being attended by four detectives, is going the round of the papers.

During the season at the Royal Institution, Professor Ernst Pauer will give six lectures on "The History and Development of the Music for the Pianoforte and its Predecessors, the Clavecin, Harpsichord, &c."

On Friday, Dec. 21st, a special evening service was held at Sherborne Abbey, at which the choir, strengthened for the occasion, sang most of the first or Christmas part of the "Messiah," concluding with the "Hallelujah" Chorus.

An annual Christmas performance of the "Messiah" was given by the South London Choral Association on Dec. 21st. The soloists were Miss Edith Phillips, Miss Sneddon, Mr. Harper Kearton, and Mr. James Budd; the band and chorus numbered about 220. The performance was under the able conductorship of Mr. Leonard C. Venables.

Many theatre-goers will be inclined to agree with the abolition of out of place music between the acts of a drama. The question has been raised by Liszt. The Comédie Française, Paris, still follows the old custom of the playhouse of Molière, according to old tradition, with no music between the acts. Perhaps, however, if proper care were taken to always select music appropriate to the closing sentiments of the preceding act, and to secure its adequate rendition, the musical entr'acte might still survive as an institution, not without value.

The concert given at the Royal Hospital, City Road, on Wednesday, Dec. 19th, by Lady Brabazon, was a great treat to the audience. It was a well-arranged programme and amongst the most successful songs were the "Mermaid," "John Olden," and "Bonnie Dundee," all sung by Mr. Bishenden, the spirited chorus of the last named song being especially well received. Mr. Smith, a tenor with a well trained voice, distinguished himself in "I'm waiting." Miss Grey and Miss Chure also sang, and Mr. Thornell gave recitations in a highly finished manner. Altogether the concert gave great satisfaction.

The authorities at Durham have not, it appears, satisfied the people with regard to a new arrangement of the Sunday morning services at the Cathedral, in view of lightening what even very orthodox people of the city call a "long, wearisome service." The cry is now at Durham, "We want shorter sermons." Every one knows that the three services in one on Sunday morning, to which is tacked on the Puritanical lecture-sermon, is a matter calling for division or revision; and any movement which will secure a better arrangement, and compel, by force of public opinion, shorter sermons, will be a distinct gain to the Church. The musical services in Durham Cathedral are served by a choir of exceptionally fine voices.

The Querist.

QUERY.

ORGAN MUSIC.—Will anyone kindly inform me who are the publishers of the organ music of Sir R. P. Stewart, Mus.Doc., and Morandi.—A. SUBSCRIBER.

[Sir R. P. Stewart's organ music (alas! that so little of it is in print) may be obtained at Novello's for the most part. Some of it appears in "The Organist's Quarterly Journal," and in "English Organ Music." Morandi's organ works are published by Ricordi (Regent Street)].—ED. *Mus. Stand.*

OCARINA.—Can you, or any of your readers inform me if the ocarina is a moderately easy instrument to learn; for one who understands music, how long would it take? also, if there are different kinds and which kind and tone are the best.—A. H. F.

[The ocarina is not a difficult instrument to learn, but it would be well to remember that instruments of easy mastery are of poor resources; and of single-toned instruments, those employed in the orchestra are not only the most perfect, but their study best advances the art. The larger sized ocarinas are, probably, the best. Keith, Prowse and Co., 48, Cheapside, would probably give all particulars].—ED. *Mus. Stand.*

Service Lists.

FIRST SUNDAY AFTER CHRISTMAS.

DECEMBER 30th.

London.

ST. PAUL'S CATHEDRAL. — Morn.: Service, Te Deum and Benedictus, Walmisley in D; Introit, While shepherds watched their flocks, Hymn 62; Holy Communion, Mozart in B flat. Even.: Service, Magnificat and Nunc Dimittis, Martin in B flat; The morning stars sang together (Stainer); Carol, 'Twas in the winter cold (Barnby).

FOUNDLING CHAPEL. — Morn.: Service, Te Deum, Dykes in F; Benedictus, Smart in F; Anthem, Arise, shine (Elvey). Aft.: Children's Service.

LINCOLN'S INN CHAPEL.—Morn.: Service. Smart in F; Kyrie (Gibbs); Anthem, Sing unto God, O ye kingdoms (Croft). Even: Service, Tours in F; Anthem, Lord, let me know mine end (Greene).

TEMPLE CHURCH.—Morn.: Service, Te Deum Laudamus and Jubilate Deo, Nares in F; Apostles' Creed, Harmonized Monotone; Anthem, Sing, O heavens (Kent). Even.: Service, Magnificat and Nunc Dimittis, Nares in F; Apostles' Creed, Harmonized Monotone; Anthem, O sing unto the Lord (Purcell).

CHRIST CHURCH, CLAPHAM.—Morn.: Service, Te Deum, Plain-song; Kyrie, and Credo, Weber in G; Offertory Anthem, Let us now go even unto Bethlehem (Hopkins); Sanctus, Benedictus, Agnus Dei, and Gloria in excelsis (Weber); Post Communion, Bethlehem (Gounod). 'Even.: Service, Magnificat and Nunc Dimittis, Martin in B flat; Anthems, Arise, shine (Elvey); Nazareth (Gounod); For unto us (Handel); When I view the mother holding (Barnby); The word is flesh become "Redemption" (Gounod); Solemn Te Deum, Smart in F, Carols after the Service.

HOLY TRINITY, GRAY'S INN ROAD. — Morn.: Service, Te Deum (Hopkins); Jubilate, Goss in A; Kyrie (Mendelssohn); Credo (Merbecke). Even.: Service, Magnificat, Tours in F; Nunc Dimittis, Chanted; Anthem, Sing and rejoice (Barnby).

ST. JAMES'S PRIVATE EPISCOPAL CHAPEL, SOUTHWARK. —Morn.: Service, Introit, Behold, I bring you (Vittoria); Communion Service, Bach in B minor. Even.: Service, Field in D; Anthem, The word is flesh become (Gounod). After Service, Carols.

ST. MAGNUS, LONDON BRIDGE.—Morn.: Service, Opening Anthem, If we say (Reynolds); Te Deum and Jubilate, Cooke in G; Kyrie (Wesley). Even.: Service, Magnificat and Nunc Dimittis, Cooke in G; Anthem, solo, O Lord, have mercy; chorus, Sleepers, wake (Mendelssohn).

ST. MICHAEL'S, CORNHILL. — Morn.: Service, Te Deum and Jubilate, Wesley in F; Anthem, Behold I bring you glad tidings (Purcell); Kyrie and Creed, Thorne in E flat. Even.: Service, Magnificat and Nunc Dimittis, Garrett in F; Anthem, In the beginning was the word (Thorne).

ST. PAUL'S, AVENUE ROAD, SOUTH HAMPSTEAD.—Morn.: Service, Smart in F; Benedictus Calkin in B flat; Kyrie, Monk in C. Even.: Service, Magnificat and Nunc Dimittis, Stainer in A; Anthem, And the glory of the Lord (Handel). Hallelujah Chorus (Handel), and Bethlehem (Gounod). After Service, Carols; Processional, Now thank we all our God (Mendelssohn).

ST. PAUL'S, BOW COMMON, E.—Morn.: Service, Stainer in B flat; Te Deum and Benedictus; Holy Communion, Kyrie, Credo, Sanctus, Benedictus, Agnus Dei, and Gloria in excelsis, Mozart in C, No. 4; Offertory (Stainer); Paternoster (Stainer). Even.: Service, Magnificat and Nunc Dimittis, Barnby in E flat; Anthem, The morning stars (Stainer).

ST. AUGUSTINE AND ST. FAITH, OLD CHANGE.—Morn.: Service, Smart in F; Introit, For unto us a child (South); Communion Service, Schubert in G. Even.: Service; Stanford in A; Anthem, The morning stars (Stainer). Carols after the Service.

ST. BARNABAS, MARYLEBONE.—Morn.: Service, Te Deum, and Benedictus, Calkin in B flat; Kyrie and Nicene Creed, Dykes in F; Anthem, The people that walked, For unto us (Handel). Even.: Service, Magnificat and Nunc Dimittis, Calkin in B flat; Anthem, Bethlehem (Gounod).

ST. PETER'S (EATON SQUARE).—Morn.: Service, Te Deum, Boyce in A. Even.: Service, Barnby in E flat; Anthem, Blessing, glory (Bach).

ST. SAVIOUR'S, HOXTON. — Morn.: Service, Te Deum, Smart in F; Holy Communion; Kyrie, Credo, Sursum Corda, Sanctus, and Gloria in excelsis, Smart in F. Even.: Service, Magnificat and Nunc Dimittis Smart in G; Anthem, For unto us a child is born (Handel). After Service, Carols.

ST. SEPULCHRE'S, HOLBORN.—Morn.: Service, Te Deum Jubilate and Kyrie, Sullivan in D; Credo, Agutter in B flat; Anthem, Arise, shine (Elvey). Even.: Service, Magnificat and Nunc Dimittis, Arnold in A; Anthem, The morning stars (Stainer).

Country.

ASHBURNE CHURCH, DERBYSHIRE. — Morn.: Service, Laurence in D, throughout. Even.: Service, Lloyd in E flat; Anthem, There were shepherds (Handel).

ST. ASAPH CATHEDRAL.—Morn.: Service, Hopkins in F; Anthem, Sing, O heavens (Tours). Even.: Service, The Litany; Anthem, The morning stars (Stainer).

BIRMINGHAM (S. ALBAN THE MARTYR).—Morn.: Service, Te Deum, and Benedictus, Goss in A; Holy Communion, Woodward in E flat. Evensong: Magnificat and Nunc Dimittis, Bunnett in F.

BIRMINGHAM (ST. CYPRIAN'S, HAY MILLS).—Morn.: Service, Tours in F; Anthem, Sing and rejoice (Barnby). Even.: Service, Clarke-Whitfeld in D; Anthem, O Thou that tellest (Handel).

BIRMINGHAM (ST. MICHAEL's, HAWORTH).—Morn.: Service, Te Deum and Jubilate; Communion (Parry). Even.: Service, Magnificat and Nunc Dimittis; Anthem, Sing, O heavens (Stevens).

CHESTER (ST. MARY'S CHURCH).—Morn.: Service, Boyce in C; Communion Service, Tearne in G. Aft.: Service, Selection of Carols. Even.: Service, Barnby in E; Anthem, Pastoral Symphony, There were shepherds, Glory to God, and Hallelujah Chorus (" Messiah " Handel).

DUBLIN (ST. PATRICK'S (NATIONAL) CATHEDRAL.—Morn.: Service, Te Deum and Jubilate, Stewart in E flat; Holy Communion, Kyrie, Creed and Sanctus, Stainer in E flat! Anthem, There were shepherds (Handel). Even.: Service, Cantate and Deus Misereatur, Smith in B flat; Anthem, Hallelujah (Beethoven), and There were shepherds (Handel).

EDINBURGH (CHRIST CHURCH, MORNINGSIDE).—Morn.: Service, Te Deum and Jubilate, Smart in F. Even.: Service, Magnificat and Nunc Dimittis, Smart in F; Anthem, Arise shine (Elvey).

EDINBURGH (ST. JOHN'S).—Aft.: Service, Anthem, For behold darkness, The people that walked in darkness, For unto us a child is born (Handel). Even.: Service, Anthem, There were shepherds, And the angel, And suddenly, Glory to God (Handel).

ELY CATHEDRAL.—Morn.: Service, Garrett in E; Kyrie, Credo, and Gloria, Richardson in F; Anthem, The year, Hymn 72. · Even. : Service, Garrett in D; Anthem, Lord, Thou hast been our refuge (Hayes).

LIVERPOOL CATHEDRAL. — Aft.: Service, Magnificat and Nunc Dimittis, Oakeley in E flat; Anthem, Behold, a virgin, and O Thou that tellest (Handel).

MANCHESTER CATHEDRAL.—Morn.: Service, Te Deum, Jubilate, Kyrie, Creed, Sanctus, and Gloria, Tours in F; Anthem, Magnificat. Aft.: Service, Tours in F; Anthem, Drop down ye heavens (Barnby).

MANCHESTER (ST. BENEDICT's).—Morn.: Service, Credo, and Gloria in excelsis, Steggall in G; Kyrie, Sanctus, Benedictus, and Agnus Dei, Messe Solennelle (Gounod). Even.: Service Magnificat and Nunc Dimittis, Bunnett in F.

MANCHESTER (ST. JOHN BAPTIST, HULME).—Morn.: Service, Kyrie, Credo, Sanctus, Benedictus, and Agnus Dei (Gounod); Gloria in excelsis, Tours in F; Offertory, Bethlehem (Gounod). Even.: Service, Magnificat and Nunc Dimittis, Tours in F; Anthem, Let us now go even unto Bethlehem (Hopkins). Carols.

SALISBURY CATHEDRAL.—Morn.: Service, Garrett in D; Offertory (Redhead). Aft.: Service, Garrett in D; Anthem, The morning stars (Stainer).

SHERBORNE ABBEY.—Morn.: Service, Te Deum, Lyle in B flat. Even.: Service, Chants; Anthem, I will consider the days of old (Lyle).

SOUTHAMPTON (ST. MARY'S CHURCH).—Morn.: Service, Te Deum, and Benedictus, Field in D; Holy Communion, Introit, Labour not (Field); Service, Field in D; Offertory (Field); Paternoster (Field). Even.: Service, Magnificat and Nunc Dimittis, Field in D; Apostles' Creed, Harmonized Monotone; Anthem, The grace of God, that bringeth salvation (Barnby).

WELLS CATHEDRAL.—Morn.: Service, Arnold in D; Introit, Behold, to' obey (Macfarren); Kyrie, Marshall in E flat. Even.: Service, Ebdon in C; Anthem, Praise the Lord (Mozart).

WESTON-SUPER-MARE (ALL SAINTS CHURCH).—Morn.: Te Deum, Garrett in F; Anthem, Behold I bring you (Goss). Even.: Service, Litany of the Incarnate Word; Preces and Responses (Tallis).

WORCESTER CATHEDRAL.—Morn.: Service, Barnby in E; Anthem, Let us now go (Hopkins). Even.: Service, Barnby in E; Anthem, The morning stars (Stainer).

APPOINTMENTS.

MR. EDWIN H. LEMARE, A.C.O., has been appointed Organist of St. John the Evangelist, Brownswood Park, N.

Mr. J. R. BROOKE, organist to the Earl of Carlisle, Castle Howard, has been appointed organist to Ladhope Parish Church, Galashiels.

NOTICE.—*All communications intended for the Editor are to be sent to his private address. Business communications to be addressed to* 185, *Fleet Street, E.C.*

ERRATUM.—In the report of the Edinburgh Choral Union, which appeared last week, on page 386, for Miss Mary Danes, read, Miss Mary Davies.

NEWSPAPERS sent should have *distinct marks* opposite to the matter to which attention is required.

Printed for the Proprietor by BOWDEN, HUDSON & Co., at 23, Red Lion Street, Holborn, London, W.C.; and Published by WILLIAM REEVES, at the Office, 185, Fleet Street, E.C. West End Agents :—WEEKES & CO., 14, Hanover Street, Regent Street, W. Subscriptions and Advertisements received either by the Publisher or West End Agents.—*Communications for the* EDITOR *are to be forwarded to his private address,* 6, Argyle Square, W.C.
SATURDAY, DECEMBER 29, 1883.—*Entered at the General Post Office as a Newspaper.*

Lightning Source UK Ltd.
Milton Keynes UK
UKHW010424231118
332756UK00007B/350/P